WISDEN

CRICKETERS' ALMANACK

2016

EDITED BY LAWRENCE BOOTH

WISDEN

CRICKETERS' ALMANACK

2016

153rd EDITION

John Wisden & Co

An imprint of Bloomsbury Publishing Plc

John Wisden & Co Ltd
An imprint of Bloomsbury Publishing Plc

50 Bedford Square
London
WC1B 3DP
UK

1385 Broadway
New York
NY 10018
USA

www.bloomsbury.com

WISDEN and the wood-engraving device are trademarks of John Wisden & Company Ltd,
a subsidiary of Bloomsbury Publishing Plc

WISDEN CRICKETERS' ALMANACK

Editor **Lawrence Booth**
Co-editor **Hugh Chevallier**
Deputy editors **Steven Lynch** and **Harriet Monkhouse**
Assistant editors **James Coyne** and **James McCall**
Contributing editor **Richard Whitehead**
Production co-ordinator **Peter Bather**
Chief statistician **Philip Bailey**
Proofreader **Charles Barr**
Database and typesetting **Stephen Cubitt**
Publisher **Charlotte Atyeo**
Consultant publisher **Christopher Lane**

Reader feedback: almanack@wisden.com

www.wisden.com

www.wisdenrecords.com

Follow Wisden on Twitter @WisdenAlmanack

and on Facebook at Wisden Sports

British Library Cataloguing-in-Publication Data
A catalogue record for this book is available from the British Library.

Hardback 978-1-4729-2454-4   £50
Soft cover 978-1-4729-2457-5   £50
Large format 978-1-4729-2456-8   £65
Leatherbound 978-1-4729-2455-1   £280
The Shorter Wisden (eBook) 978-1-4729-3522-9   £8.99

2 4 6 8 10 9 7 5 3 1

Typeset in Times New Roman and Univers by David Lewis XML Associates, Bungay NR35 1JB
Printed and bound in Great Britain by CPI Group (UK) Ltd, Croydon CR0 4YY

To find out more about our authors and books, visit www.wisden.com. Here you will find extracts,
author interviews, details of forthcoming events and the option to sign up for our newsletters.

A Taste of Wisden 2016

A few even cheered, which some thought rather poor form, until it was pointed out that the opposition were Australia, and the usual conventions did not apply.
Drink up! Drink up! And miss the game, page 27

* * *

You bought his wares without even realising they were for sale; as with the best salesmen, the transaction left you feeling enriched.
Richie Benaud 1930–2015, page 49

* * *

When he was 100% fit he was as slippery as anyone. I would bowl with the wind and he'd bowl into it – that's where he lost most of his hair, I think.
Obituaries, page 238

* * *

On an island famed for nutmeg, the game was proceeding with a distinct lack of spice.
West Indies v England, 2014-15, Second Test, page 292

* * *

Not since S. F. Barnes at Johannesburg's Old Wanderers in December 1913 had an England bowler pilfered five before lunch on the first day. Broad, needing only 39 minutes, had done it before the mid-morning drinks.
England v Australia 2015, Fourth Test, page 358

* * *

Scottish taunts of "Your captain's Irish" were irrefutable.
England v Scotland, World Cup, page 878

* * *

A feverish Haris Sohail was unnerved by what he said was a supernatural presence shaking his bed at a Christchurch hotel.
New Zealand v Pakistan, 2014-15, page 1033

* * *

He prodded at Kaushal, offering a genial handshake, but the ball was leaning in for the kiss on both cheeks.
Sri Lanka v Pakistan in 2015-16, Second Test, page 1110

LIST OF CONTRIBUTORS

Timothy Abraham
Ujjwal Acharya
Andrew Alderson
Dean Allen
Chris Aspin
Mike Atherton
Philip August
Philip Barker
Charles Barr
Greg Baum
Will Beaudouin
Benedict Bermange
Scyld Berry
Edward Bevan
Paul Bird
Paul Bolton
Stephen Brenkley
Daniel Brettig
Liam Brickhill
Simon Briggs
Gideon Brooks
Tim Brooks
Colin Bryden
Andy Bull
Ian Callender
Brian Carpenter
Stephen Chalke
Adam Collins
Patrick Collins
Philip Collins
Tom Collomosse
Tony Cozier
John Crace
Jon Culley
John Curtis
Martin Davies
Geoffrey Dean
Ralph Dellor
William Dick
George Dobell
Paul Edwards

Vithushan Ehantharajah
Mark Eklid
Matthew Engel
Peter English
John Etheridge
Paul Farbrace
Melinda Farrell
Andrew Fernando
Warwick Franks
Alan Gardner
Mark Geenty
Haydn Gill
Nagraj Gollapudi
Gideon Haigh
Duncan Hamilton
Kevin Hand
David Hardy
Douglas Henderson
Andrew Hignell
Paul Hiscock
Richard Hobson
Jesse Hogan
Tristan Holme
Nick Hoult
Steve James
Paul Jones
Nishant Joshi
Austin Karonga
R. Kaushik
Abid Ali Kazi
Jarrod Kimber
Stephen Lamb
Richard Latham
Geoff Lemon
Jonathan Liew
Andrew McGlashan
Will Macpherson
Neil Manthorp
Ali Martin
Andrew Miller
Mohammad Isam

R. Mohan
Firdose Moonda
Benj Moorehead
Paul Newman
Raf Nicholson
Mark Pennell
Dileep Premachandran
Andrew Radd
Paul Radley
Alvin Sallay
Osman Samiuddin
Jared Savage
Neville Scott
Mike Selvey
Shahid Hashmi
Utpal Shuvro
Mehluli Sibanda
Rob Smyth
Saurabh Somani
Richard Spiller
Fraser Stewart
Andy Stockhausen
Chris Stocks
Pat Symes
Bruce Talbot
Sa'adi Thawfeeq
Tunku Varadarajan
Anand Vasu
Telford Vice
Phil Walker
Mike Walters
John Ward
David Warner
Tim Wellock
John Westerby
Tim Wigmore
Simon Wilde
Marcus Williams
Dean Wilson
Robert Winder
John Woodcock

Photographers are credited as appropriate. Special thanks to Graham Morris and Philip Brown. **Cartoons** by Nick Newman. Contributors to **Round the World** section are listed after their articles.

The editor also acknowledges with gratitude assistance from the following: Robin Abrahams, Dave Allen, Derek Barnard, Hywel Barrett, Mike Bechley, John Bolloten, Derek Carlaw, Adam Chadwick, Liam Cromar, Brian Croudy, Prakash Dahatonde, Nigel Davies, Christopher Douglas, Sandeep Dwivedi, Gulu Ezekiel, M. L. Fernando, Ric Finlay, Alan Fordham, David Frith, Victoria Groves, Gulfraz Riaz, Clive Hitchcock, Julia and John Hunt, David Kendix, Edward Liddle, Nirav Malavi, Errol Manners, Mahendra Mapagunaratne, Colin Maynard, Clayton Murzello, Michael Owen-Smith, Francis Payne, Mick Pope, Qamar Ahmed, Andrew Samson, Angela Singer, Clare Skinner, Steven Stern, Jeremy Tagg, Tushar Trivedi, Chris Walmsley, Charlie Wat, Jean and Chris Whipps, Alan Williams, Yajurvindra Singh.

The production of *Wisden* would not be possible without the support and co-operation of many other cricket officials, county scorers, writers and lovers of the game. To them all, many thanks.

PREFACE

As recently as 2003, *Wisden* would pull up the drawbridge at the end of the English summer. Anything that happened after the county champions were crowned in September did not appear in print until 18 months later, which gave England fans enough time to come to terms with their team's latest overseas disaster, before they finally got to read about it.

Now, though, the Almanack is about as up to date as an annual can be, this year's edition more than ever: it includes reports on 55 England games, played on 112 days, right up to February 21, when England lost the second Twenty20 at Johannesburg. The cricketers looked exhausted by the end of it all; our editorial staff can empathise.

Some old friends are no longer with us. Richie Benaud wrote regularly for *Wisden*, including the profile of his fellow 1962 Cricketer of the Year Alan Davidson, and four of the five profiles in 1973, when John Snow was the only non-Australian to make the cut. Benaud's old mate Jack Bannister was our Warwickshire correspondent for 18 years until 2001. And Ghulam Mustafa Khan, the kind of conscientious statistician who keeps our cogs oiled, contributed to every Almanack since 1959. The obituaries of Bannister and Khan will appear in *Wisden 2017*.

Briefly, two items of housekeeping: Twenty20 scorecards now include the number of dot balls in a bowler's analysis (in brackets at the end of the figures); and Mohammad Aamer, the prodigal son of Pakistan cricket, has become Mohammad Amir, which is how most of the world spell his name.

My thanks go, as ever, to a tireless team, not least Hugh Chevallier, the co-editor. Both deputy editors have recently raised their bats: in October, Steven Lynch brought up 30 years of work for various Wisden publications; and in November, Harriet Monkhouse racked up 25. I'm simply the latest editor to benefit from their diligence and vast expertise. Thanks, too, to our assistant editors, James Coyne and James McCall, and to our consultant publisher, Christopher Lane, whose input remains indispensable. Contributing editor Richard Whitehead handled a frantic year with his usual aplomb.

Another anniversary is celebrated by our production co-ordinator Peter Bather, who this year put his 40th Almanack to bed with customary good humour. Charlotte Atyeo at Bloomsbury was especially supportive, and I'm grateful for the typesetting of Stephen Cubitt and Mike Hatt, the statistical acumen of Philip Bailey, and the proofreading of Charles Barr. I'd also like to thank Lee Clayton, sports editor of the *Daily Mail*, for continuing to allow me the time for *Wisden*.

To Anjali Doshi, my wife, go my love and gratitude for her affection and understanding. We moved house last year, and it will be intriguing to spend my waking hours in a room other than the study.

LAWRENCE BOOTH
Barnes, February 2016

CONTENTS

Part One – Comment

Part Two – The Wisden Review

Part Three – English International Cricket

Part Four – English Domestic Cricket

STATISTICS

LV= COUNTY CHAMPIONSHIP

ONE-DAY COUNTY COMPETITIONS

OTHER ENGLISH CRICKET

EUROPEAN CRICKET

Part Five – Overseas Cricket

Part Eight – The Almanack

SYMBOLS AND ABBREVIATIONS

*	In full scorecards and lists of tour parties signifies the captain. In short scorecards, averages and records signifies not out.
†	In full scorecards signifies the designated wicketkeeper. In averages signifies a left-handed batsman.
‡	In short scorecards signifies the team who won the toss.
MoM/PoM	In short scorecards signifies the Man/Player of the Match.
MoS/PoS	In short scorecards signifies the Man/Player of the Series.
D/L	Signifies where a result has been decided under the Duckworth/Lewis method for curtailed matches.

Other uses of symbols are explained in notes where they appear.

FIRST-CLASS MATCHES

Men's matches of three or more days' duration are first-class unless otherwise stated. All other matches are not first-class, including one-day and Twenty20 internationals.

SCORECARDS

Where full scorecards are not provided in this book, they can be found at Cricket Archive (www.cricketarchive.co.uk) or ESPNcricinfo (www.cricinfo.com). Full scorecards from matches played overseas can also be found in the relevant *ACS Overseas First-Class Annuals*.

In Twenty20 scorecards, a number in brackets after a bowler's analysis indicates how many dot balls he or she delivered.

RECORDS

The entire Records section (pages 1255–1389 can now be found at www.wisdenrecords.com. The online Records database is regularly updated and, in many instances, more detailed than in *Wisden 2016*. Further information on past winners of tournaments covered in this book can be found at www.wisden.com/almanacklinks.

PART ONE

Comment

Wisden Honours

THE LEADING CRICKETERS IN THE WORLD

Kane Williamson (page 96)
Suzie Bates (page 1217)

The Leading Cricketers in the World are chosen by the editor of *Wisden* in consultation with some of the world's most experienced writers and commentators. Selection is based on a player's class and form shown in all cricket during the calendar year, and is merely guided by statistics rather than governed by them. There is no limit to how many times a player may be chosen. A list of past winners can be found on page 96. A list of notional past winners, backdated to 1900, appeared on page 35 of *Wisden 2007*.

FIVE CRICKETERS OF THE YEAR

Jonny Bairstow (page 97)
Brendon McCullum (page 99)
Steve Smith (page 101)
Ben Stokes (page 103)
Kane Williamson (page 105)

The Five Cricketers of the Year are chosen by the editor of *Wisden*, and represent a tradition that dates back to 1889, making this the oldest individual award in cricket. Excellence in and/or influence on the previous English summer are the major criteria for inclusion. No one can be chosen more than once. A list of past winners can be found on page 1482.

WISDEN SCHOOLS CRICKETER OF THE YEAR

Ben Waring (page 801)

The Schools Cricketer of the Year, based on first-team performances during the previous English summer, is chosen by *Wisden's* schools correspondent in consultation with the editor and other experienced observers. The winner's school must be in the UK, play cricket to a standard approved by *Wisden* and provide reports to this Almanack. A list of past winners can be found on page 803.

WISDEN BOOK OF THE YEAR

The Test by Simon Jones and Jon Hotten (page 143)

The Book of the Year is selected by *Wisden's* guest reviewer; all cricket books published in the previous calendar year and submitted to *Wisden* for possible review are eligible. A list of past winners can be found on page 145.

WISDEN–MCC CRICKET PHOTOGRAPH OF THE YEAR

was won by Robert Cianflone (whose entry appears opposite page 64)

The Wisden–MCC Cricket Photograph of the Year is chosen by a panel of independent experts; all images on a cricket theme photographed in the previous calendar year are eligible.

WISDEN'S WRITING COMPETITION

was won by Will Beaudouin (page 117)

Wisden's Writing Competition is open to anyone (other than previous winners) who has not been commissioned to write for, or has a working relationship with, the Almanack. Full details appear on page 118.

Full details of past winners of all these honours can be found at www.wisden.com

NOTES BY THE EDITOR

At faraway Hobart, in long-ago January 2015, Ben Stokes played an innings that had English cricket quietly sobbing at the perversity of it all. The squad for the World Cup was already picked, and Stokes – after enough ducks to fill a pond – had been left out. Now, wearing the liberating Big Bash colours of Melbourne Renegades, he smashed 77 off 37 balls. Gleeful Aussies had their fun: the Poms couldn't even pick the right blokes! And they had a point: a few weeks later, England messed up their sixth World Cup in a row.

By January 2016, Stokes was making his countrymen cheer, not weep, his 258 off 198 balls at Cape Town the most sustained act of wanton violence by an England batsman in any format. Under a fiery sun, by Table Mountain's giant anvil, he was forging his team's future. As for the immediate past, the year between his two innings had been one of the most significant in the history of English cricket.

The transformation began in earnest in May, when a timid defeat in Barbados was followed by a tumultuous victory over New Zealand at Lord's – and England instantly became a side you wanted to tell your friends about. There would be rapids down river, but the players were now approaching them head on, not paddling round the edge, quoting the percentage chance of falling in. Like Shakespeare's King John, they were discovering that their "soul hath elbow room". To watch them was to share their sense of release.

Records fell like confetti. England passed 400 for the first time in a one-day international, and knocked off 350 in another. They made their highest one-day score overseas, in Dubai (355 for five), then smashed it a few weeks later, in Bloemfontein (399 for nine). Jos Buttler scored a hundred off 66 balls, – as if unsated – off 46. Stuart Broad took eight for 15 as Australia were demolished for 60 in the Trent Bridge Test, then six for 17 to skittle South Africa for 83 at Johannesburg. Joe Root passed 50 on 21 occasions in 2015 alone, leaving England's previous best (16 by Marcus Trescothick in 2003) in his wake. The two most resonant national records fell one after the other: in Antigua, Jimmy Anderson overtook Ian Botham's number of Test wickets, and went on past 400; at Leeds, Alastair Cook surpassed Graham Gooch's number of Test runs, and approached 10,000. Wherever you looked, pulses raced. Even in quieter moments, England were rewriting history: Cook's innings of 263 in Abu Dhabi was Test cricket's third-longest.

None of this guaranteed success, and the one-day defeat in South Africa in February, after England had led 2–0, underlined the importance of brain as well as brawn. But better this than what had come before. And the change in mood was hard to miss: after the sobs and the scowls, England were cracking a smile.

The joy made the preceding year all the more exasperating. Leading the charge sheet was the drearily predictable World Cup – a car crash that took place in slow motion while everyone pleaded for fifth gear. When Paul Downton, the managing director, returned from the tournament, he unwittingly confirmed the problem: 50-over cricket, he announced – as if letting us in on a secret – was now being played at Twenty20 speed. Forget leather on willow: the sound of the English game in early 2015 was palm on forehead.

Downton's inevitable sacking in April was soon followed by the botched dismissal of coach Peter Moores, announced moments after Andrew Strauss had been confirmed as Downton's replacement. When Strauss made it clear there was no way back for Kevin Pietersen – just as he was blitzing a triple-century – one wondered what awkwardness was next. But subsequent events suggested Strauss was right. In a delightful turn-up for the form guide, the ECB – having spent the previous year losing touch with reality – were making some smart decisions.

Just as when he was captain, Strauss wanted cricketers who could think for themselves. Confirmed as the man who would continue to dictate the direction of the limited-overs sides, Eoin Morgan was reborn. It caught on: from June until the end of the South Africa series, no team could match England's one-day run-rate of 6.27. Back in March, at the World Cup, a batsman had been berated for getting out as he attempted to go over the top; three months later, against New Zealand at Edgbaston, England did nothing else, turning 202 for six into an era-defining 408 for nine. Five days after that, batting first at the Rose Bowl, they were bowled out for 302 with 28 balls unused. Careless? On the contrary, said Morgan: it was all part of the new philosophy.

Strauss also took his time over the appointment of Moores's long-term successor, which allowed the genial assistant coach Paul Farbrace to seep into the team's core. And it meant Strauss could work on persuading Trevor Bayliss to join the fold, having recognised a man who, like himself, was comfortable in his own skin – and who, in Sri Lanka, had already worked well with Farbrace. In an age of obsessive measurability, there were moments when Bayliss felt like the anti-coach, an endearingly scruffy retort to the audit culture. He had come to the attention of his future boss during a ten-minute timeout at the 2014 IPL final, when Bayliss was in charge of Kolkata Knight Riders. Milling around, hands in pockets, he was – noted Strauss – "calming his batsmen down, rather than geeing them up". It was a wonderful irony that England played their most electrifying cricket for years after choosing an expert at lowering the volume.

The English game had begun 2015 apparently clinging to G. K. Chesterton's definition of hope as "the power of being cheerful in circumstances that we know to be desperate". Victory at the Wanderers in January 2016, to knock South Africa off the top of the Test rankings, confirmed that a different kind of hope had taken hold. It was the most uplifting story in international cricket all year, the more so for being utterly unexpected.

Captain Cook changes tack

Cook's soul found elbow room too. A few months after being sacked as one-day captain, he cited the World Cup debacle as evidence that the selectors had got it wrong: famously stubborn, he was still in denial. But, as the summer progressed, he was both given space to breathe, and encouraged to listen to others – a balancing act delicately handled by Bayliss and Farbrace.

During that Lord's Test against New Zealand, his second-innings 162 allowed Root and Stokes to be themselves, establishing a model in which the captain's safety valve at one end usually gave rise to just the right amount of combustion at the other. As Cook's confidence grew, his ears opened, ending an era in which those outside the bubble were regarded with suspicion, and sometimes worse. By the Ashes, with the dressing-room well and truly his, he was out-captaining Michael Clarke. In South Africa, he looked more at ease than either Hashim Amla, who resigned after two Tests, or A. B. de Villiers, who *sounded* resigned after only one: "I almost feel like all hope is gone."

Yet both series threw up an unforeseen problem: England used to be slow starters; but Cook's team were actually winning too early. Defeats in the dead Tests at The Oval and Centurion were a reminder that talk of returning to No. 1 in the rankings was premature. Indeed, England had now lost seven out of eight concluding Tests of a series, and had needed the Trent Bridge tour de force to end a sequence of seven alternate wins and defeats, which had made them the most reliably inconsistent Test team ever.

Gaps needed plugging. At the end of the South Africa series, five of England's top seven had a career average under 35; the second opener's slot looked like a curse; and the lack of a world-class spinner – so evident during the 2–0 defeat by Pakistan in the United Arab Emirates – had been glossed over. The excitement was tempered by the work that remained.

Nor had everyone been convinced by the quality of the Ashes. Yet, at a time when bat has too often held sway over ball, it was curious to nitpick about events at Edgbaston and Trent Bridge, even if Australia's pair of first innings seemed intent on proving the *Annie Hall* theory that life is divided into the horrible and the miserable. Wickets threatened to lose their value, and the only over-my-dead-body batting of the series came from Cook, in losing causes at Lord's and The Oval. It made his character transplant as captain all the more notable.

The land of the long white cordon

There were patronising ruffles of the hair for the New Zealanders, who had allegedly helped rid England of their stiff upper lip, as if their main function was to loosen Cook's men up ahead of the Ashes. But the first telling partnership of the new era – 161 at five an over between Root and Stokes on the first day at Lord's – came about not because England were trying to match the New Zealanders' *joie de vivre* (they hadn't batted yet), but because Brendon McCullum's aggressive fields left them with little option. Spaces opened up, runs flowed.

Did he over-attack? Probably. But, with apologies to the American wit James Thurber, "you might as well fall flat on your face as lean over too far backward". McCullum deserves every cricket-lover's thanks for treating it like a game, not a war by other means. For the first time, few English fans wanted the pre-Ashes appetiser to end.

It says something about cricket's standing in New Zealand right now that both McCullum and Kane Williamson are among our Five – the first Kiwi double in their 86-year Test history (dare we point out that a third member of this year's selection, Ben Stokes, was born in Christchurch?) In late February, in his final game at international level, McCullum bade farewell *in excelsis*, with a Test-record 54-ball hundred off Australia. Williamson is also the first from his country to be named *Wisden's* Leading Cricketer in the World, while Suzie Bates wins the women's equivalent. For so long, the black cap denoted underdoggedness. This summer, like never before, county cricket will be full of disarmingly modest, talented New Zealanders, and barely a grim forward defensive between them.

Out of the darkness

It was to the cricket media's embarrassment that *Death of a Gentleman*, a documentary by Sam Collins and Jarrod Kimber, was one of the few attempts to tackle the sport's maladministration. Yet the film attracted a strange gripe: it apparently lacked a smoking gun – beloved of those who have read too much Agatha Christie, or possibly of journalists who prefer others to do the work for them.

Not only did the grumble betray the low standards to which sporting executives are held (heck, wasn't cricket governance the exemplar next to football, cycling, athletics, tennis and the rest?) It also overlooked the fact that the gun had been smouldering since early 2014, when the Big Three effected their heist, splitting cricket into the haves and the have-sod-alls, then telling us with a straight face that it was for the good of the game. If *DoaG* was a howl at the loss of a sport's innocence, then events either side of its London premiere in July confirmed it was not vanishing into the void.

One by one, willingly or otherwise, the masterminds behind the ICC takeover left the positions that had allowed them such unaccountable power in the first place. Dean Kino, Cricket Australia's head of legal affairs, had departed in September 2014. Then, in May 2015, ECB chairman Giles Clarke bumped himself upstairs into the attic of the presidency. A few months later, CA chairman Wally Edwards stepped down, full of praise for India's N. Srinivasan, who was doing "a fantastic job". The Indian Supreme Court thought otherwise. Embroiled in a seemingly interminable corruption scandal, Srinivasan had already lost the BCCI presidency, and in November was finally forced out of his cushy ICC chairmanship. Sundar Raman, Srinivasan's right-hand man and previously head of the IPL, jumped before he was pushed. And then there were none; cricket breathed a little more freely.

All along, a small but dependable group of apologists argued that England and Australia had been obliged to join forces with India, because the alternative meant the Indians going it alone, presumably in some eternal dystopia of DLF Maximums. This was ludicrous: India's fans would never stand for a world in which their country couldn't be champions, or the next Sachin Tendulkar couldn't score all his hundreds.

The excuse sounded even feebler when Shashank Manohar, having replaced Srinivasan at the head of the BCCI and the ICC, gave an interview to *The Hindu* in which he regretted "the three major countries bullying the ICC", condemned India's 22% share of global cricket's pie ("you cannot make the poor poorer and the rich richer only because you have the clout"), and stressed the importance of competitive bilateral series. Surprise, surprise: the takeover, it turned out, had been a matter of urgency only for those who urgently wanted more money.

The iniquities of the power grab, which left Big Three representatives in charge of all the major ICC departments, hardly needed spelling out, but Manohar was on hand to help: "You should have the best man, whether he comes from Zimbabwe or West Indies, or even from an Associate or Affiliate, to work on a committee, who will promote the interests of the ICC." Lord Woolf had made a similar point in a 2012 report considered so damaging to the status quo that it was lowered, nostrils pinched, into the bin.

But Manohar seemed to have accepted the idea, mooted in these pages and elsewhere in recent years, that the BCCI have a wider duty to the game. Crucially, Indian cricket's very own glasnost belied the suggestion that resistance is futile, that *DoaG* was farting against thunder. When Justice Lodha delivered a list of recommendations for the Indian game – including the appointments of an ethics officer and an independent auditor – he was speaking the language of reconciliation, not the *de haut en bas* discourse that had filmgoers booing Clarke when he appeared on screen during an early showing in Sheffield.

Then, in February this year, came a breakthrough that would never have happened if a few – though far too few – journalists hadn't continued to rattle the gilded cage: the ICC chair could no longer be filled by a current office-holder at a national governing body, which was bad news for Clarke. And the Big Three's reforms would be reviewed in full. There was talk of banning the term "Big Three" altogether (two syllables had rarely sounded so toxic). There was even talk of India giving back some of the money.

So there are reasons to be cheerful. They are fragile, it's true, and a reversal of the heist would simply mean a return from the fire to the frying pan that so troubled Lord Woolf. But the age of the Big YouKnowWhat, as murky an episode as any in the annals of cricket administration, may be over before it has properly begun. With any luck, *DoaG* will not need a sequel.

No time to stand and stare

Cricket, though, is not in a position to be complacent. One afternoon in late September, two days after the end of the County Championship, it ought to have shifted uneasily in its still-grassy whites. Nearly 90,000 spectators had arrived at Wembley to watch a game of rugby between Ireland and Romania. One of the teams could barely claim home advantage, the other was ranked 17th in the world. It was like packing out the MCG for a one-day international between New Zealand and Papua New Guinea.

Two months later, a match between Australia and New Zealand that might normally have elicited a groan about Test cricket's irrelevance instead drew a gasp, as 123,000 poured into Adelaide Oval over three days of low-scoring tension. The first day/night Test worked a treat, though it left an unsettling thought: national boards had spent years nodding solemnly at the idea of Test cricket's primacy, yet the pink-ball initiative had been the work of MCC.

Then, on January 2, in another awkward moment for those who believe cricket's charm lies in its immutability, over 80,000 turned up in Melbourne to cheer on the two local Twenty20 franchises, only 7,500 fewer than the combined home four-day Championship attendances in 2015 of Yorkshire and Lancashire. Until late 2011, the Stars and the Renegades had been nothing more than a twinkle in the marketing executive's eye, yet the Big Bash has already moved into ninth place in the list of the world's most-watched sporting leagues, not far behind Spanish football's long-established La Liga.

There are lessons here, and they will determine cricket's future. If that sounds like a familiar warning, then the truth is that the sport is changing more quickly than ever – so quickly that it has little time to work out where it's going, let alone how to get there. Cricket is "here today, in next week tomorrow", to quote Mr Toad. Keeping up is half the trick.

The ICC appear to have few doubts, since they want their sport to become "the world's favourite" (which may come as a surprise to football). Yet they have equivocated over cricket's presence at the Olympics, and contracted the World Cup. Rugby, by contrast, will appear at the Rio Games in the seven-a-side format, and reaped the rewards of its broader horizons when Japan beat South Africa at their own World Cup in September – a story that resonated beyond the back pages.

Even the pink-ball Test was approached with caution, the build-up characterised by the kind of anguish – the ball may misbehave, the statistics shouldn't count, lunch *cannot* be taken at tea – that too often passes as concern for the game's integrity. In the event, one of cricket's most traditional venues witnessed an arresting blend of old and new: pink and green, whites and floodlights, a technicolour sunset that didn't require photoshop. And it all happened at a time of day/night when families were free to attend. The limited-overs formats realised this a while back, and it was hammered home repeatedly during the winter, when a flick of the TV remote revealed full houses for all manner of domestic 20-over games, and empty seats at too many Tests. It was like trading a rave for a library.

To which the defiant response may well be: "What's wrong with that?" But the era of taking pride in Test cricket's exclusivity is over. These days crowds gather for Test matches only on special occasions. Otherwise, they stay away. The risk is that more players will start to emulate their West Indian colleagues and stay away too. Even de Villiers, speaking before the match in January which marked his long-awaited ascent to South Africa's Test captaincy, already seemed to be looking forward to a breather – though not from the IPL, where he is thought to earn about ten times as much as he does from his central contract.

Day/night Test cricket must be given a chance, even in countries where we're continually told it can't work. If English crowds can sit through chilly floodlit one-days in September, why can't they cope in June, July and August? The ECB chairman Colin Graves is open to the idea, and so are the Test-match counties. And if it takes off everywhere, boards can use the extra revenue to prove to their stars that they needn't become soulless freelancers, forever scouring the globe for their next fix.

The relevance is all

Quiz question: how many international games in 2015 counted for nothing beyond pride? If the definition is games which couldn't affect the outcome of a bilateral series, the answer is 18, of which five occurred in the 11 Test series (of at least three games) that either finished or started in the calendar year. And the new year began as the old ended, with Australia taking a 3–0 lead over India in their five-match one-day series, and India retaliating with a 2–0 lead in the three-match Twenty20 series.

Walkovers happen, but cricket would benefit if they didn't happen in a vacuum. A former *Wisden* editor, Matthew Engel, devised an easy-to-grasp Test championship, which gave rise to the ICC's own version, based on a well-meaning formula no one can understand. Yet last summer's women's Ashes provided a glimpse of a solution, already suggested elsewhere for the good reason that it makes sense: hand out points for every win on a bilateral tour (say, six for a Test, three for a one-day international and two for a Twenty20), tot them up, then award three to the overall winner, or one each in case of a draw. England against Australia (the men's version) would have resulted in a 26-21 home win, with England taking their three points into a league table in which every Full Member play every other over four years, home and away, to determine an overall world champion. And the second Twenty20 between South Africa and England at Johannesburg on February 21, the final game of the tour, would have determined its outcome. South Africa won the game, which under this system would have earned them a 19–18 victory. Rather than fade away, England might have kept going until the end.

The system could operate within the formats as well, so that Associate teams who have official status in one of the limited-overs versions, but can't play Test cricket, can challenge for their leagues. This wouldn't eliminate dead games altogether, but it might make the difference between losing a Test series 3–0 or 2–1 significant enough to focus minds: 18–0 compared with 12–6. The lure of corruption would also be reduced. Cricket is crying out for a wider context that appeals to the floating fan. This could be a start.

Now or never

No one seemed sure quite how offended to be when not a single member of England's Ashes-winning team made the 12-strong shortlist for the BBC's Sports Personality of the Year award. One thing was clear: the four cricketers to have won the gong – Jim Laker (1956), David Steele (1975), Ian Botham

(1981) and Andrew Flintoff (2005) – all attested to the fact that, when Australia are in town, cricket invades the national psyche. Not this time. Perhaps the public has got used to England beating them. But when Root's batting or Broad's bowling can't make the top dozen, something is amiss.

Since England's home internationals will be hidden away on satellite TV until 2019 and almost certainly beyond, it's time for a terrestrial channel to step in and offer to cover the domestic game. And since that domestic game has to grab the attention of a generation who have never – if their parents don't own Sky – experienced the thrill of stumbling across the cricket on an idle afternoon, this means a franchise Twenty20 tournament.

Most of the counties don't want it, of course, just as many of them didn't want Twenty20 when it was narrowly voted through more than a decade ago. Neither did they welcome the franchise proposal mooted by MCC and Surrey in 2008. Had they done so, they might not now be watching Australia's Big Bash with such envy – or wondering why every other nation has developed a domestic Twenty20 tournament that packs a more powerful punch than their own.

The ECB are rightly concerned by the counties' grip on the game. The fear is that cricket will fade into obscurity if something isn't done to court new fans. Given the talent on show in the England team at the moment, that would be a scandal. But the ECB can help too. When Surrey asked if they could digitally broadcast home matches not on Sky, the ECB said no. Similarly, the free online coverage of Nottinghamshire's home Championship matches has to stop when Sky are televising another domestic game. This is monopolism gone mad. But if counties continue to pander to their mainly traditionalist members – Twenty20, remember, was never about preaching to the converted – the very last chance for a franchise competition to help bankroll the four-day stuff may disappear for good.

Fleshing out the problem

A chat with one of the very few female journalists in the Lord's media centre last summer was interrupted when a former Test star passed behind her, pinched her bottom, and disappeared without a word. Was she OK? A shrug. "It's just the way he is." During England's limited-overs series in the UAE in November, play kept stopping because people were walking in front of the sightscreen. After the third instance in quick succession, TV identified the miscreant, a young blonde cheerleader. The commentator considered how best to exploit this gift, then drooled: "I think she'll be forgiven." And whenever there was female flesh to be found among the spectators during England's tour of South Africa, the camera found it. Ladies, if your thigh or cleavage was not broadcast from the grassy banks of Kingsmead or Newlands in 2015-16, you probably weren't there.

So when Chris Gayle asked Channel Ten's Mel McLaughlin out for a drink during the Big Bash while she was trying to interview him live on air, the line he was crossing probably didn't feel like a line at all. Gayle even had the good manners ("Don't blush, baby") to check she wasn't making a spectacle of herself. Back in 2014 at the Caribbean Premier League, he had been asked by a female journalist how the pitch felt, an innocuous question replete in the Gayle mind with possibilities. "Well, I haven't touched yours yet," he replied, "so I don't know how it feels." A CPL spokesman helpfully clarified what he had really meant: "Chris is excited for the tournament and was having a laugh with a journalist, who had a laugh back; there was no malice intended."

The absence of malice seems to be the yardstick by which cricket gauges its treatment of women, yet the reaction to Gayle's belittling of McLaughlin suggested all is not lost. Not everyone on Twitter got it (one respondent pointed out that it wasn't as if he had given her cancer). But Melbourne Renegades fined Gayle, and Andrew Flintoff said he had made himself look "a bit of a chop", which is quite an insult in Preston.

In one sense, Gayle was right to be taken aback by the outrage: he was merely fulfilling a role ascribed to him by domestic Twenty20 tournaments everywhere, hamming it up and trowelling on the charm. As he himself put it, with typical self-effacement: "I build leagues around the world." But even if cricket's problem is also society's, McLaughlin's discomfort ought to be cricket's. As another female journalist explained, two useful skills in male-dominated press boxes are "evade" and "deflect". It needn't be like this. And, no, mate: it really isn't just banter.

Good night, everyone

Banter was not for Richie Benaud. Instead, there were two measures of his unique place in cricket commentary. The first was the number of colleagues who, following his death, said how often they tried to bear in mind his dictum about speaking only when you can add to the picture. The second was the number of colleagues who actually managed to put his dictum into practice. For it was easier said – or, in Benaud's case, not said – than done.

This is where cricket will miss him. Not because he always made for great TV: viewers often longed to know what he really thought, and his perennial irritation about the front-foot no-ball law proved he could do trenchant opinion. It will miss him because his pithiness balanced out the tactic of talking more and more about less and less until everything has been said about nothing. Benaud has gone now, and with him his pact with the cricket-watching public, who are a lot brighter than most commentators evidently imagine.

The phantom fifty

Wisden called it "the most heroic nine not out in history". When Alec Stewart was left unbeaten after the abandonment of the 1997-98 Kingston Test because of a dangerous pitch, there was no question he had earned his runs and red ink. Mike Atherton, Mark Butcher and Nasser Hussain – with three runs between them that morning – may not have shared his pride. But it would have been an insult to everyone to have pretended the game never happened.

The same went for the abandoned Test at North Sound, Antigua, in 2008-09, when Andrew Strauss was grateful for his unbeaten six, and Cook for his one not out. Then there was the strange case last October of the New Zealanders' tour game at Sydney's Blacktown International Sportspark being halted after the Cricket Australia XI's openers had put on 503, again because of an unsafe pitch (imagine what they might have scored on a belter).

So the decision by the ECB's Cricket Discipline Commission to expunge from the records the 50-over game between Glamorgan and Hampshire at Cardiff in August because of threat to life and limb was not just nonsensical – it was without precedent. *Wisden* feels obliged to respect the ruling; the alternative would be statistical anarchy. But it does so with apologies to Glamorgan's Colin Ingram, who could have sworn he had made a painstaking 86-ball 51, and must now wonder why he bothered.

What's yours?

Collectors of cricket press releases may have been taken aback to read of the resignation of the "Castle Lager Proteas" Test captain in January. Had the ICC relented, and allowed another nation to join the fold? No: this was what the South African national side call themselves these days. Still, they may be thankful they are not Western Australia, who now rejoice in the name "Alcohol. Think Again Western Warriors". That full stop is crucial: it gives you all the time you need to break out into a cold sweat – and reach for a restorative beer.

FIVE DAYS AT THE ASHES

Drink up! Drink up! And miss the game

Patrick Collins

The tout stood in Cathedral Road, a small middle-aged man in a rumpled suit. He was waving a wad of paper and pleading with the passing crowd: "Tickets for the cricket! 'Oo wants tickets for the cricket?" One or two nodded politely, but walked on. It was 10.30, half an hour before the start of play, and the tout was becoming anxious. "Come on!" he yelled. "Tickets for the cricket!" Then it started to drizzle, and he shuffled off to shelter beneath a tree. He seemed resentful. Here we were, on the first morning of an Ashes series, and he couldn't find a customer. If this were rugby, they'd be biting his hands off. But, when it came to cricket, the Welsh didn't seem bothered. It was going to be a difficult summer.

Drizzle turned to downpour and, inside Sophia Gardens, wretched groups huddled under umbrellas. Several wore sun hats, in perverse disregard of the conditions. Stoically they sat and stared at three platoons of soldiers performing pointlessly intricate manoeuvres across the soggy outfield.

The morning headlines had spoken boldly of "England's New Era", and the early-summer matches with New Zealand had carried hints of promise. But the Ashes demanded something more. An elderly philosopher at the Taff End described it as "hoping for the best, but fearing the worst – rather like going to the dentist". Yet he was smiling as he spoke. And, as you looked around, you became aware that most people seemed to be smiling. For suddenly the sun was shining, the crowd was swelling, and Alastair Cook was winning the toss. "First blood to us," remarked the Taff End sage, chuckling at his own frivolity. At lunch, England were three down, and normal service was being resumed, yet the public mood remained buoyant, their pleasure almost tangible.

On the first day of each Ashes Test, every venue assumed a character of its own. Lord's was self-assured, Edgbaston rowdy, Trent Bridge intelligently absorbed, The Oval relaxed. But Cardiff was characterised by its sheer niceness, with the hosts going out of their way to welcome their visitors. Surprisingly, the drinking was a shade less obvious than at other grounds. Pleasingly, most seemed to have come for the cricket.

Despite England's travails, the morning passed in tranquil fashion. This was partly due to the merciful absence of most of the Barmy Army. Once or twice, the trumpeter piped up, adding "Bread of Heaven" to his limited repertoire. But few joined in, most preferring to watch the Test match. "Can't get them to sing," complained a Barmy camp follower, which is not a remark one often hears in Wales.

In the grandstand, Andrew Strauss was obliging with a series of selfies. "Who's that, dad?" asked a small boy. "Kevin Pietersen," replied his father.

Do not adjust your set: a bevy of air stewardesses settle in for the long haul.

Then, coyly: "Only joking!" By now, the sun was beaming. High in the stand, a straw-hatted young man turned to his stunning companion. "Who's batting?" he asked. The lady stared, quizzically. "England," she said. "Just testing, darling," he replied. "Well done." She looked as if she might kill him.

But, overall, the mood was benign, as Joe Root dug England out of their turbulent first hour. Drink was widely taken at lunchtime and, by mid-afternoon, the songs were louder, the abuse more forthright. Mitchell Johnson was on the receiving end, but he was not obviously bothered. "You're a shit bowler and a shit fielder, Johnson," bellowed one brave soul. "And you can't catch!" Johnson picked up a plastic bottle on the boundary edge. "There you go, mate," he called. "Catch that!" And he lobbed the bottle with an evil grin. The drunk fumbled, and the crowd cheered. Johnson had actually noticed them. He was their hero for the day.

By tea, a good many watchers seemed befuddled. The stadium bars featured groups of middle-aged men shouting at each other: one bunch telling jokes, another repeating them. At times, it grew surreal. A troop of porky gentlemen in lederhosen and feathered trilbies were discovered lurking behind the grandstand – an oompah band, no less, awaiting the call to the pitch. "Right, lads!" barked the leader. "Let's give it some welly!" And on they marched, feet stomping, horns blaring, to mighty applause.

By close of play, England had scored 343 for seven, with Root contributing 134. The series had taken encouraging shape, and a tout in a rumpled suit was reassessing business opportunities for the summer.

* * *

Before the week was through, England had taken the First Test, the circus had moved 150 miles east to Lord's, and the nation at large was hugely enthused. The usually slumbrous Long Room raised its voice as England took the field that Thursday morning. A few even cheered, which some thought rather poor form, until it was pointed out that the opposition were Australia, and the usual conventions did not apply.

As the ground filled, the *Test Match Special* team attempted to define the Lord's noise. "Is it a buzz or a hum?" asked Phil Tufnell. "It's a hum," decided Jonathan Agnew. "A contented hum, I'd say." One of the delights of attending a Test in England is to watch the cricket unfold to the comforting hum, or buzz, of *TMS*. This being Lord's, of course, a good many patrons had precious little intention of actually watching cricket.

Lord's has long since joined Royal Ascot and Henley as part of the English summer pageant – a place less concerned with seeing than being seen. For a sizeable slice of the crowd, it is an extension of school sports day, at which old friends are encountered and elderly anecdotes exhumed. The drinking started early in the Harris Garden behind the Pavilion. Darren Lehmann, the Australian coach, came hurrying past the fringe of the crowd, returning from last-minute nets at the Nursery End. "Fancy a drink, Boof?" drawled an impertinent young chancer. Lehmann strode on without a glance.

An hour after the start, the crowd in the Harris Garden numbered around 300. A large screen had been set up on the edge of the lawn, but only three people were watching. The rest were gossiping, posing, supping; tall young men, for the most part, fresh from broking house or merchant bank, in beautifully cut, dark blue, lightweight suits, their hair impeccably groomed, likewise their accents. The uniform of a caste. Few women were present, even fewer than at Cardiff, and those who came along conformed, by and large, to the prevailing stereotype.

Their hair was impeccably groomed, likewise their accents – the uniform of a caste

Down at the Nursery End, the clientele was far earthier. There were beer and burritos, and stalls called Chicken Hut and Fish 'n' Chips. There was an even larger screen available, and many more eyes were following the cricket. One man, stout and pallid, wore khaki shorts and a grubby white T-shirt bearing the slogan "England's Barmy Army… Down Under 2010/11… You All Live In A Convict Colony". For almost five years he had carried on his chest the same dire joke. You imagined him chortling as he pulled it over his head that morning.

At lunch, the crowds choked the bars at both ends of the ground, and there, for the most part, they stayed. When play resumed, Lord's was ringed with swathes of empty white seats, save for the cluster of yellow-capped Aussies in the Edrich Stand. The Australian batsmen were piling up

the runs, and their followers were resolved not to miss a ball of the revival
Come tea, there were one or two casualties in the Harris Garden as the
Chardonnay took its toll. At the Nursery End, the carousers grew louder
with small groups of men shouting jokes at each other and repeating the
punchlines. Lord's is unique in lots of ways, but its drinkers have much in
common with every other Test ground in the land.

* * *

As Test followed Test, the drinking gathered pace. A significant section of
fans saw the Ashes as an extended pub crawl, with a little cricket between
pints. And yet, with Australia having levelled the series, public interest had
intensified. Thus, on a gloomy Wednesday morning, the touts were out in force
on Edgbaston's Pershore Road, diligently exploiting the renewed public
appetite for "tickets for the cricket".

The Australians had been told to expect an aggressive crowd, yet the reality
was surely beyond their expectations. If Lord's had been Royal Ascot, then
Edgbaston was Aintree. The noise was dramatic, a sustained assault on the
senses. The singing was stolen
straight from the football terraces, so
that Anderson, J. M. (Lancashire and
England) instantly became: "Oh
Jimmy Jimmy! Jimmy Jimmy Jimmy
Jimmy An-der-son!" And the old
chap seemed to revel in the adulation
as he squeezed every last crumb
of assistance from a helpful pitch.
Wickets fell at a comforting rate, each
greeted with thunderous acclaim.
The fact that rain imposed three
interruptions on Australia's brief first
innings merely offered opportunities
for refuelling, and the chances were
gladly taken.

John Walton, PA Photos

Refuelling: vital supplies are ferried to those
in need.

The Hollies Stand accommodates
6,000. During the rainbreaks, only
a handful remained: the rest were
clustered beneath the stand, queuing
for the gents or buying cold lager at
£4.20 a pint from young men bearing

large containers on their backs. Many wore fancy dress: suits of armour,
cowboy outfits, Spiderman costumes. And there was something else which
revived the Aintree comparison. At every Grand National meeting, newspapers
publish wickedly mocking pictures of plump, painted ladies in micro-skirts,
towering stilettos and plunging necklines. And here they were, transported en
masse to Edgbaston: same drinks, same make-up, same dress sense. Only their
gender had changed.

Attempting to understand this communal appetite for cross-dressing,
I approached one vision in purple beneath the Wyatt Stand. He was wearing

ustrous black wig, a cocktail dress in purple chiffon, and a preposterously inflated bosom. He said his name was Derek, from Moseley: "But today I'm Kim Kardashian." Asked why he had dressed in this way, he seemed puzzled. It's a Test match, innit?" Kim/Derek was puffing a cigarette, and he was not alone. Unlike the other Test grounds, it seemed that most at Edgbaston were smoking, dragging desperately at the declining stub when the announcer informed them that the umpires were out and play would resume. They hurried back to their seats to watch England send the Aussies packing for 136, with Oh Jimmy Jimmy taking six for 47. How they cheered! How they cackled! And how they then scampered, fast as their heels would carry them, back to the bars and tents for yet more drink.

The consumption was staggering, and so, come teatime, were many of the spectators. As at Aintree, there were a good many fallers, yet the lager kept coming. "I won't have another drink," said one brave young man. "I fancy a coffee." "Poof!" bawled his companions. Moeen Ali strode past, padded up, on his way to the indoor nets. He seemed bemused by the chaos.

Yet, for all the boozing, the crowd had become an authentic factor in the match. England were lifted by the ceaseless din, while the Australians were clearly affected – none more than the chief target, Johnson. In the field he was relentlessly barracked, so much so that his throwing became frenzied and wayward. More importantly, he began to lose control of his bowling action. Towards the end of the game, he ran through the crease without releasing the ball, then delivered one from 24 yards. The England fans hugged themselves. Time and again, they screamed their daft ditty: "He bowls to the left, he bowls to the right…" Shortly after, Johnson was rested, to save him from further punishment, and the roars rolled around the ground.

Back to day one and, while the home side were ahead, there was much work to be done. But a curious coalition of cowboys, cross-dressers and bawling Brummies had helped England secure a significant advantage. That evening, in his suburban lounge in Moseley, Derek would tug off his wig, slip out of his heels and toast a triumphant day.

* * *

If you're just switching on in Australia, turn the radio off and go out and do some gardening." Jim Maxwell's memorable advice to his countrymen was delivered with the Fourth Test only 12.4 overs old. Stuart Broad was dancing a demented jig, Mitchell Starc was slouching back to the dressing-room, and the scoreboard was telling the world that Australia were 46 for eight.

The Nottingham crowd were almost subdued. Naturally, they had celebrated the fall of each wicket, but the atmosphere was a world away from the perpetual cacophony of Edgbaston. Instead, there was an air of disbelief, as if reality had been suspended, and replaced by some farcical fantasy. It had been this way since the opening over, when Broad took his first two wickets. Many spectators reached for their plastic earpieces, the ones which receive *TMS*, as if they needed an independent witness to confirm what they were watching. At 19 for four, they heard Phil Tufnell chuckle "'Appy days!" so they knew it must be true.

Beefeater beer-drinkers: being traditional is thirsty work at Trent Bridge.

A glance around the ground suggested that all 15,000 spectators had stayed in their seats, as if afraid to break the spell. A swift check outside confirmed the impression. The bars and stands, where long queues usually form, seemed lonely. "What are they all watching in there?" asked the girl on the Gluten Free Curry stall. "We were told we'd be really busy." I apologised for taking her time. "Nice to find someone to talk to," she replied.

When the Australians reached 50, nine wickets down, their followers gave them a standing ovation. They were cheered in turn by the England fans, who by now were in magnanimous mood. And any lingering disbelief was replaced by rapturous delight when Broad dismissed Nathan Lyon, and Australia were done and dusted for 60. In 18.3 overs and 94 minutes, England had effectively ensured the return of the urn. The entire ground paused for a few moments to hear the stadium announcer drool out the details of this gloriously improbable morning, then cast off their restraint and made for the bars. Which was where I met Gareth.

Now Trent Bridge does not actively encourage exhibitionists and, on this first morning, they were relatively few in number. But Gareth stood out, since he was dressed as a banana. A Londoner, he had come to the cricket with three Australian friends, all dressed as bananas. "We're a bunch. Geddit?" When did they decide to dress up? "A few weeks back," he said. "It just came to us. Inspiration, I suppose. No, I don't feel a bit silly. Why did I do it? I wanted to be on telly, simple as that. I wonder why I've never done it before. This is what cricket is all about." Gareth, a "theatrical producer", then prepared himself for an afternoon of waving and gurning in the hope of being caught by the kindly eye of a Sky cameraman.

Those who chose to watch the cricket saw England's batsmen start to compose the kind of innings which would remove all doubts about the outcome of the match and the series. Strong drink worked its wonders late on, as a brilliant young Yorkshire batsman reached his hundred and was greeted – to the tune of "Hey Jude" – by choruses of: "La, la, la, la-la-la-laaah… Joe Rooooot!" At the close, England led by 214. 'Appy days indeed.

* * *

With the Ashes secure, The Oval offered England's players and fans a relaxing experience. But, if the match was free from stress, the cost to the watchers was as steep as ever. The most expensive tickets were priced at £110 on days one to four, while the lowest came in at £25. Yet demand remained high, hence the presence of those ubiquitous touts, snuffling around Oval Tube station.

The match itself contained little of the eccentric flamboyance we had come to expect from the series. Instead, the opening day offered old-fashioned Test cricket, with Australian batsmen batting soberly, patiently. The crowd, or most of them, seemed to relish it, since this was the game they recognised, the game they remembered before the onset of this manic summer.

Once again, a minority seized the chance to attack the booze. The noise from the hospitality boxes grew louder with the day, while by mid-morning there was a queue of 23 at the Gin and Tonic Bar, which boasted three kinds of gin and, intriguingly, five kinds of tonic, including elderflower. One optimistic soul edged through the crowds with a tray of green paper cups. He was offering samples of Yorkshire Tea, a series sponsor. His wares were not widely taken up.

At lunch, the Oval alleyways were thronged with enormous crowds, jovial and pleased to be at a Test match. It is a ground devoid of pretension, a place where the game is appreciated more than the trappings which surround it. On the first day, there was little or no fancy dress, since The Oval caters for grown-ups. Whereas Lord's has its champagne garden, The Oval has a small champagne stall, and trade was not flourishing. When the players came out after lunch, the alleyways swiftly emptied. As at Cardiff and Trent Bridge, you felt they had come to watch the cricket.

Australia batted on, methodically compiling a total which would win them the game. Nobody seemed to mind. For England, this had been less a Test match, more a protracted lap of honour, and the fans appeared to understand. In the long queue for the Tube, two elderly Surrey members attempted to apply historical perspective. "Not a vintage series," said one. "Not like '05 or '53. Two pretty ordinary teams, I'd say." His friend agreed: it had been less than vintage, certainly. And yet, he added: "Everyone seemed to enjoy it, didn't they."

Indeed they did. They always do. The game may face all manner of challenges and problems, but any time the Aussies arrive in England, with reputations to make and the Ashes at stake, we shall always want our tickets for the cricket.

For 33 years Patrick Collins was the chief sports writer for the Mail on Sunday. *He is the winner of five Sports Journalist of the Year awards.*

THE BRITISH-ASIAN QUESTION

Winds of change blow ever stronger

Andrew Miller

At Sharjah in November, English cricket's most ethnically representative team of the 21st century took the field. Since the ECB themselves acknowledge that British Asians make up almost 40% of recreational cricketers in England and Wales, the historic selection of Moeen Ali, Adil Rashid and Samit Patel for the Third Test against Pakistan was not before time.

It should have been the culmination of a concerted and inclusive campaign to tap into the talents of a vast and under-represented community. Instead, the trio existed as an anomaly on the team sheet. Their simultaneous selection owed more to a separate, equally unresolved, English cricket crisis: an alarming dearth of Test-quality spinners. That's not to say the selections were not on merit, nor to play down their significance. But their route to recognition had been circuitous: Patel and Rashid had both made their England debuts in the previous decade, yet remained on the fringes, while Ali had been ignored until the age of 27, and owed his selection to the weaker of his two suits.

Yet, by England's next Test, at Durban on Boxing Day, only Ali remained. It was a case of as you were: the path for Asian cricketers to England's Test team – such as it exists at all – is as underdeveloped as the inner-city parks on which so many of their communities play.

Take Springfield Park, a publicly owned cricket field on the banks of the River Lea in Stamford Hill. It is a picturesque part of one of London's more diverse neighbourhoods, but the facilities are spartan. Teams get changed on a pile of logs by the northern end of the pitch, or under the trees at cow corner, where Orthodox Jews and canal-boat-dwelling refuseniks form the bulk of the passing spectators.

It is not the sort of place you would expect to encounter a No. 1-ranked international batsman. However, Zubair Ghardiwala, the star player for GI Strikers – winners of the North East London League – is a talented and hard-hitting opener whose final act of the 2015 season was to score 55 of the 58 needed to beat the Camel pub team, and secure a nine-wicket win in the space of six overs. Zubair's claim to fame lies in the Last Man Stands format – an eight-a-side competition endorsed by the ECB and now played in 11 countries by more than 40,000 cricketers. His highest score in the 20-over format is 15 not out, while his ranking stems from a career strike-rate that is a shade under three a ball. On the back of his exploits, North London Muslim CC – GI Strikers' parent club – were last summer crowned regional LMS champions. Yet no one expects anything to come of Zubair's exploits. "We've made a few enquiries, but no one has approached him," says Haroon Ali, NLM's club manager. "To be honest, he's a bit old now, 27 or 28."

Step in the right direction: England's three spinners – Moeen Ali, Samit Patel and Adil Rashid – take the field at Sharjah, November 2015.

Since their foundation in the 1980s, NLM have been a fertile source of British-Asian talent, despite a hiatus in the early 2000s, when their ground was compulsorily purchased to make way for the Olympic Park, and the club was temporarily disbanded. In 2009, Maaz Haffeji, then 22, captained his side in the inaugural Wisden City Cup, and weeks later was bowling in the nets to the Australians before the Lord's Test.

But, with no obvious pathway from park cricket to the professional game, Haffeji – like so many other British Asians – was always playing on borrowed time. "He went over to Twickenham and played Premier Division for a while," says Haroon. "But he soon realised his time was over, so he left cricket. We've produced three or four guys with real talent, guys who have captained London schools, but we've always known the probability of any of them going on and progressing is tough."

These tales are echoed up and down the country. For 40 years, Asian cricket in England has been as marginalised as it has been ubiquitous. Enthusiasm alone has allowed its league structures to thrive as a subculture, in spite of the indifference of the mainstream – a situation diametrically opposite to the crisis besetting the English club scene.

It took a devastating player survey in November 2014 to ram home the concerns that every club cricketer in the land had been feeling for years. Traditional clubs were going out of business at a rate to rival traditional pubs. A year-on-year fall of 64,000 players went hand in hand with the fact that 5% of matches were conceded because one or both sides were unable to raise a team. Society, we are told, is time-poor, and the ECB know urgent action is required to arrest the seepage of interest.

On the fringes: scorers at Great Horton Church CC in the Bradford Mutual Sunday School League.

"We recognise that the landscape has changed," says Gordon Hollins, the board's chief operating officer. "It used to be a captive market: you were told what your sports were, and got on with them. Now there are some 35 different sporting options available for kids aged seven to 17, not to mention laptops and other distractions." Hollins has around him a team of like-minded progressive thinkers, including a director of participation and growth, the Australian Matt Dwyer, whose championing of the Big Bash helped reinvigorate spectator interest in his native country. However, the most obvious solution to the participation crisis has been staring the sport in the face since the earliest stirrings of the Asian league structure in the 1970s.

Asian cricket, wrote Mike Marqusee in 1998, "represents an immense potential resource for English cricket, provided that English cricket is prepared to redefine its notions about what constitutes 'Englishness'". Back then, the sport – still a year away from admitting women to the Long Room at Lord's, let alone immigrants to the inner sanctum – clearly wasn't ready. That year, academic study by Ian McDonald and Sharda Ugra posited that mainstream leagues "hid behind league regulations and cultural stereotypes… to prevent the admission of black and Asian clubs into the official leagues".

In theory, the creation of the ECB in 1997 as a single unified body for all levels of cricket in England and Wales ought to have been the first step towards tackling that disconnect. And yet those cultural differences have been allowed to calcify, leaving a legacy of mistrust that cannot be resolved simply with a change of attitude at the top.

As recently as November 2015, Ali Cricket Club in Merton, south London, were expelled from the Surrey League, only weeks after being presented with the League Championship Cup for the second year running. Their crime was to have been awarded zero points for sportsmanship by the other nine teams. Separately, the ECB have been threatened with legal action by an east London team owner who accused them of racism following the barring of his club from the National Club Championship. The lack of a home ground for his wandering side, who wish to remain anonymous, meant they failed to attain the ECB Clubmark accreditation required to continue in the competition.

Such threats exist as a legacy of previous decisions, but Hollins is phlegmatic about the game's current direction. "Are we doing the right thing?" he asks. "If we are, and a lawsuit still comes in, then we will deal with it. I'd be much more worried if we weren't trying."

Nevertheless, the issue of ground ownership is arguably the single biggest stumbling block for the acceptance of Asian teams into the mainstream. It is especially galling given how many village teams with pavilions and grounds to maintain are struggling to fulfil their fixtures. Some administrators, however, believe the sport is in the process of catching up with its needs.

"Communities become communities because they are comfortable in their surroundings," says Gulfraz Riaz, the development manager of the Club Cricket Conference. "It is a fact that traditional Sunday cricket is declining and grounds are becoming available. So, if you have a South-Asian community on your doorstep who are willing to pay the going rate to play on a grass wicket and leave it as they found it, surely that represents a fantastic integration opportunity."

> Reports of senior management trying out turbans

Riaz is the driving force behind the National Asian Cricket Council, the nascent organisation that is seeking to present a unified front to a governing body who are finally ready to listen. His efforts began in the summer of 2012, when he toured the M25 to gauge interest among the many, disparate Asian leagues. It takes a rare cause to persuade all of South Asia's competing cultures to speak with one voice, and the urgency of his work reflects the recognition that the credibility of cricket is at stake.

In 2014, Riaz arranged a one-day seminar at Edgbaston, attended by representatives of 65 Asian clubs from all creeds, cultures and corners of the country. Within five hours, the majority of attendees were agreeing in principle to the NACC's formation. At the Asian Cricket Awards in October 2015, Hollins made a solemn but significant pledge about the partnership the ECB were ready to forge.

There have been hiccups and headaches, with frustrations on both sides about what might constitute – as Hollins puts it – the "low-hanging fruit" that would enable a greater mutual understanding. There has been cynicism, too, about some of the ECB's attempts to fast-track a culture of inclusivity – among them eyebrow-raising reports of senior management trying out turbans for size in a quest for better cultural insight.

Sadi Khan, the founder of Khan Noble, the cultural and religious consultants to whom the ECB have turned, defends the board's efforts. "Inclusion is about people, and if you don't understand the people who make up the second-largest population in the country, how are you going to get them to buy into what you are doing?" she says. "We all learn French at school, but how many of us know how to say good morning to our Bangladeshi neighbours, or even which culture they belong to in the first place?"

Hollins asks: "Would we, in hindsight, have started this process ten years ago? Of course we would. But good things start with rhetoric. Before you can take action, you have to get people to believe you are serious. Only then can we see results."

Money, inevitably, was crucial in confirming the shift in the ECB's attitude. In the wake of the London Olympics, Sport England provided cricket with a grant of £20m (with a further £7.5m going to the Chance to Shine charity), largely with a view to "harnessing the inherent appeal of the game within South-Asian communities". The challenge was clear: it would no longer suffice for the ECB to pay lip service to the notion that they represented all cricket in all communities. A proper strategy was needed, and that has manifested itself in the selection of five target cities – London, Birmingham, Bradford, Leicester and Leeds – with high Asian populations that have already benefited from Sport England's four-year investment. Among the most notable projects is the £5.5m refurbishment of Yorkshire's Bradford Park Avenue ground, primarily as a community hub for the city's burgeoning league scene, but also with a view to regaining its first-class status in time for the 2019 season.

Even so, with the next round of funding in 2017, the onus is on the ECB to demonstrate a return on that investment. For that reason, some at the NACC have argued that "the ECB need us more than we need them" – though the relationship is changing, and Hollins readily admits that a board in need of good PR have to earn the trust of those they wish to represent.

But there is an acceptance within the Asian communities that some of the fault of the past 40 years lies in their own intransigence. Riaz is adamant that, if they now miss their chance to embed themselves in the mainstream culture, there is no guarantee of another. "It's too easy to blame the ECB for all of Asian cricket's problems. There's no doubt they shoulder a lot of the blame but, equally, there are some guys who have been in charge of their leagues for 25 years. What have they done for their young players in that time? Have they ever picked up the phone to the counties, or found out when the trials are? It's a two-way thing, and they have a duty of care."

He sees alarming parallels with the fate of Caribbean cricket in the UK, a demographic which had a big head start on its Asian counterpart, not to mention the gift of a once-in-a-generation Test team to inspire new recruits. In 2016, that culture is all but extinct. African-Caribbean kids play football, rather than cricket (the name Walcott is synonymous with an Arsenal and England forward, not a great West Indies batsman), and Riaz warns that the same could happen to the Asian communities. "If you fail to invest in your junior set-ups, you basically have 50 years before that community disappears. The Caribbean elders admit it to this day: they held the game too tightly, and their kids went off to play football, athletics and basketball.

"It is only a matter of time before we get the first British-born Asian football star," he adds, citing the emergence of Aston Villa's Easah Suliman, captain of England Under-17, and a player who has already taken advice from Moeen

Generation game: experience and youth help cricket flourish at Girlington CC in Bradford.

Ali. "When that happens, think of the parents, the taxi drivers and restaurant workers. Will they encourage their sons to play football, with low overheads and massive prospects, or cricket, which needs expensive equipment and offers limited prospects? It will be a no-brainer."

The question of cricket's prospects is arguably the biggest obstacle to the ECB's ambitions. It stems once again from the rootlessness of many Asian leagues, but manifests itself in the county coaching structures that have been conditioned to know what they like, and like what they know. County cricket's current bias, for instance, is towards the 6% of the population privately educated; the proliferation of South African-born cricketers on the circuit is another factor. Yet the volume of Asians in the recreational game means more than a handful ought by now to be finding their way through the system.

Inevitably, mutterings of institutional racism are rarely far from the surface. One Asian hopeful reportedly turned up to a county trial to be told by the director of cricket: "You've got six balls to impress me, son." It cannot help, either, that many of the coaches who decide on the year-group squads also provide extra tuition to those kids whose parents have sufficiently deep pockets.

But Mohammad Arif, an ECB coach-education tutor who also works as an Under-14 assistant coach at Warwickshire, says the race card should be used with care. "Some Asian parents believe their kids are a lot more talented than they actually are," he says. "The managing of expectations is crucial." Warwickshire, who recently added two more South-Asian coaches – Mo Sheikh and Kadeer Ali – to their roster of full-time staff, have also introduced a feedback form to help triallists who don't make the grade. "Rejection is rejection, whether you are South Asian or not," says Arif. "But constructive criticism is most important when you fail."

Ultimately, the future of English recreational cricket will depend on the cultural alignment between the old ways and the new. But if, as the ECB and NACC both acknowledge, the long-term aim is for such Asian-focused initiatives to become redundant, then the experience of one club in Oxfordshire provides a ray of hope. Ten years ago, Checkendon CC – a traditional village team on the outskirts of Henley – had been staring into the abyss. "We were failing to draw new members and to attract youth in a rich area of south Oxfordshire, where a good handful of equal-level teams were all vying for a diminishing pool of cricketers," says Stewart Manning, their captain.

The answer to Checkendon's prayers lay in the burgeoning IT industry of nearby Reading, where a wave of first-generation Indian immigrants were starting new lives in an otherwise alien culture, and regarded cricket as a means of embedding themselves. And they encountered a culture that was delighted, not to mention desperate, to embrace them.

A decade down the line, the needs of both parties have been handsomely met. The pool of available cricketers is now a harmonious 50–50 split of white and Asian players, one of whom, Vikas Chib, is the first-team captain; his young family have made the club the focus of their new lives.

"These guys grew up playing with tennis balls on dustbowls," says Manning. "They love the fact that they now belong to a lowly grassroots village club, and they love the associated traditions. They soak up the English culture, then give it back in terms of club days, when their families produce vats and vats of various curries, and laugh at how little chilli we can cope with."

Chib confirms the benefits cut both ways. "If it wasn't for the club I'm not sure we'd have taken the decision to make our home in England," he says. "We love the social life that cricket gives us. It has really bound us to the culture, and it has opened so many doors."

Such tales are a reminder of the difference that sport in general, and cricket in particular, can make to British society. "No other recreational pastime can compete with cricket in that regard," says Hollins. The responsibility on the ECB's shoulders is as vast as the opportunity that awaits them – as long as they can work the common ground that has been lying uncultivated for so long.

Andrew Miller is UK Editor of ESPNcricinfo.

STUART BROAD TAKES EIGHT FOR 15

Just a perfect day

SCYLD BERRY

The most remarkable figures by an England pace bowler could not have been recorded at a more valuable moment. England were 2–1 up with two to play, but James Anderson had broken down, and Australia would retain the Ashes if the series finished all square. So Stuart Broad did not sleep much the night before the Fourth Test at Trent Bridge. "It's always that feeling of not knowing what the next day holds," he says. "The toss of a coin decides if I go and make a cup of tea, or have the pressure of leading the attack."

After the Edgbaston Test, Anderson and Ben Stokes had stayed with Broad, rather than go home. They had eaten in and out, including a barbecue cooked by Broad's former Nottinghamshire team-mate Charlie Shreck. "He was the most nervous chef you've ever seen. All he could think of was poisoning three of England's Ashes players." Yet, even after several days of mentally adjusting to his new role, the thought was still making Broad more nervous than usual. Anderson had always been there – and Broad had not bowled the first over of a Test for four years.

"Trevor [Bayliss] and Cooky's talk was: the first hour is everything, we performed so well at Edgbaston, make sure we stamp our authority on the game. Whether you've got the ball or the bat in your hand, it's up to the opening partnership to set the tone. I took that to heart."

The pressure increased when Alastair Cook decided England should bowl. "The whole day started with me thinking we should bat," says Broad. "But when I was marking my run-up, Shane Warne walked past and said: 'What do you reckon?' I said: 'I like batting first at Trent Bridge, but there's a bit more grass on this pitch than normal.' And he said: 'Even I might consider bowling today.' When he said that, I thought, well, he's the biggest bat-first man ever, isn't he? More than Swanny, probably. It made me believe bowling first was the right call."

A shower delayed the start until 11.05. "It gave me extra time to compose myself, but actually it was the Clive Rice applause that probably settled me the most." Rice had died during the Edgbaston Test, and Nottinghamshire arranged for the tribute. "He was my dad's captain at Trent Bridge, and my mum was close to him and his wife. I was sad for a Nottingham legend, but when it got announced you could tell what passion the members had for him. We were standing by the members' entrance, and it really took my nerves away. My mindset was: it's a game of cricket at the end of the day – and also just being out there at Trent Bridge and realising I've bowled loads of overs at this ground. And there's nothing to be too scared about."

Another duty Broad had already inherited from Anderson was to pick a new ball from the two boxes of six brought to the dressing-room by the fourth

The procession begins: Stuart Broad celebrates the dismissal of Chris Rogers, his 300th Test victim, from the third ball of the Nottingham Test.

umpire. Anderson had passed on the job to Broad in the Caribbean in the spring; on the only subsequent occasion Anderson had chosen it, for the Second Test at Lord's, Australia had scored 566 for eight. Broad picked the ball which felt smallest and smoothest in his hand. He had to choose two new balls, as customary, but the second would not be needed; and the first, as it turned out, received barely a scratch on the Dukes gold markings.

"All I tried to focus on was not being driven first ball, and not wanting to set the tone with a boundary. I didn't want to float one up there and have Rogers hit me through the covers and we get off to a shocking start. All I was thinking was back of a length. If he wants to pull me out of the ground first ball, then fair play, but he's not getting an easy drive."

A few months after his feat, Broad is watching a video of it for the first time. "So you can see, I slammed it into the wicket. I actually slipped a little – that gave me some encouragement, because it showed a bit of moisture in the pitch." As another first, Broad had started from round the wicket. The second ball went for four leg-byes, but then the plan worked. "Ottis Gibson and I chatted before the game in the nets and said, why don't we start from round the wicket and try to pitch it on off stump. If it leaves him, he could nick it." Third ball, Rogers did precisely that.

"As it was in the air, I never considered Cooky dropping it. As soon as he caught it, my first thought was, I hope that's not a no-ball, because they always check it now, don't they? It was only when Rooty came over to shake my hand that I realised it was my 300th in Tests. And Rogers's first-ever nought, wasn't it? Now Rogers is gone, all you're thinking about is the plan to Steve Smith – set the field we're going to have. You celebrate the wicket for ten seconds, then your mindset completely changes." Especially after Smith hit his first ball for two, and his second for four.

"He crunched me through cover point, but it gave me a huge amount of encouragement, because it's a full-blooded drive on a wicket that is just offering a bit. And I could tell his beans were going. He wanted to feel bat on ball. So I knew if I got my length bang on, and it seamed, that's a very dangerous shot." Sure enough, Smith stabbed – and was caught at third slip. After one over, Australia were ten for two.

Graciously, Broad says the wicket of David Warner, caught behind off an inside edge in the next over, Mark Wood's first, was "the biggest of the lot. Jos [Buttler] said: 'What's happening here, lads? Feels like we're going to get a wicket every ball.' This was the moment we started to believe something could happen for us. The other changing-room's in turmoil. We had no plan to go round the wicket at all to Shaun Marsh. But I just said to Cooky, if I bowl the ball I bowled to Rogers, any left-hander's going to nick that. And it was very tough for Marsh: he'd not played for, what, probably eight weeks? He's going to want to feel bat on ball too, and fortunately he edged one."

> Look at his face – he looks like a three-year-old, doesn't he?

Australia, after 2.4 overs of a Test match, not a Twenty20, were 15 for four. Watching his first ball to Adam Voges, Broad says: "It was very greedy. I'm trying to do a big inswinging half-volley." It went for four leg-byes. "That made me think, I don't need to get too fancy here, I don't need to try inswing, outswing. If I hold the seam straight and hit off stump, and if it does anything either way, I'm in the game.

"That sounds so simple, but sometimes in conditions that really suit fast bowlers we overcomplicate, and think we have to make a batsman try a new thing every ball. It was that poor ball that went for four leg-byes that made me think: 'Let's make the batsmen play as many balls as possible, whether it goes in or out from fourth stump.'"

Broad runs in, Voges thrusts hard, and there is a blur as Stokes leaps to his right at fifth slip. "That was the moment of the series for me. It was like the Strauss moment in '05 [when, at the same ground, he leapt to catch Adam Gilchrist off Andrew Flintoff]. I never thought he was going to catch it. It shocked everyone. Look at his face – he looks like a three-year-old, doesn't he?

"I thought it was four. As a bowler, you have an instinct straightaway from what shot the batsman lines up or where the ball's gone. I had that sinking feeling that it had beaten him. Lythy had turned and was running down to third man. And then he dived that far and caught it behind him. It's certainly the best catch I've seen live. To witness it from 12 yards away was very special: he just had no right to catch it. He does that sort of thing in training, but in an Ashes-deciding Test match?

"Did you see him take down Jonny Bairstow at short leg? Look at Stokesy. You know his mum and dad play rugby league? Watch him. He absolutely bulldozes Jonny." Trying to celebrate with Stokes, Bairstow is sent flying like an Australian batsman. After 4.1 overs, it is 21 for five.

On the edge: Ian Bell catches Shaun Marsh at second slip to give Stuart Broad his third wicket – and Australia teeter at 15 for four.

"The economy-rate is far too high," adds Broad with a smile. "Jimmy would be very grumpy about that."

He is far from finished. "That Clarke dismissal is interesting. We had plans to try to make him think we would bounce him, but we actually bounced him quite rarely. So I just moved fine leg ten yards to the right. Trevor is into his cricket theatre, as he calls it. Put a fielder somewhere so the batsman thinks: 'Why is he there? What plan have they got?'

"So we created this theatre – that I was going to bowl a bouncer, but my plan was to try to swing it away outside off stump to bring a straight-bat edge. And this is the worst ball I bowled: it's so far away from where I wanted it to be. It's a wide, but Clarke was probably thinking: 'I need to get runs as quickly as possible while I'm out here.' Cooky took a brilliant catch. I didn't realise I'd got a five-for until they'd chucked me the ball, because everything happened so fast."

Two days before the match, the bowling unit had dinner with Bob Willis, at the instigation of Andrew Strauss. All his career, Broad had been told to aim for the top of off stump, but Willis told them to aim – on grounds like Trent Bridge and Headingley, where the ball tends to move more – an inch or two lower: in other words, to bowl a touch fuller and get the batsman driving. Steven Finn produced a beauty that castled Peter Nevill (33 for seven). "That's the length Bob had been talking about," says Broad.

Only Australia's tail were left. But the lower order had helped shape the Ashes of 2013-14. "We had a mindset that you should bowl a lot shorter at the tail, but in Spain [during England's pre-Ashes camp] we sat down as a group and said: 'Why don't we pitch it up?' Because if David Warner's nicking balls from the top of off stump, then tailenders will."

Duly the tailenders were wrapped up in the shortest of all opening innings in Tests, in just 18.3 overs. The ball beat the bat only a couple of times; otherwise it took the edge, normally a thick one, as is the case when the ball is seaming (swing tends to take thinner edges). Broad had dismissed four right-handers and four left-handers – and only Devon Malcolm, with nine for 57 against South Africa at The Oval in 1994, had produced a better analysis among England's pace bowlers than his 9.3–5–15–8.

"It was probably only now that I could enjoy the moment, job done – let's get batting. But I was saying to myself, look for my mum in the crowd. This is one of those moments I should soak in, look round the ground, take in my team-mates' congratulations. It's the most fun I've had in an hour on a cricket field, that's for sure – an absolute dream on my own ground to walk off after bowling Australia out before lunch. I've never bowled better.

"It's amazing how sport moves on, though. We got in the changing-rooms and had handshakes, well done, and then we had 15 minutes to bat before lunch. And all of our talk was that it's a very important 15 minutes, lads. Don't let them back in the game.

"What made it special after bowling Australia out for 60 was to make 274 for four by the close. If we had only got 120, people would have said it was just a green seamer. But Rooty got a hundred, and Jonny got a great 70. It was one of those days that just couldn't have been more perfect."

Scyld Berry is the cricket correspondent of the Daily Telegraph.

RICHIE BENAUD, 1930–2015

The sound of silence

Gideon Haigh

It turns out that the last occasion on which the cricket public heard Richie Benaud was the 30-second tribute he delivered in honour of the late Phillip Hughes, played at Adelaide Oval before the First Test between Australia and India in December 2014. Benaud summed Hughes up in a few, well-chosen words, with a paternally warm concluding sentiment: "Rest in peace, son."

This somehow reflected his relationship with cricket. When you heard it from Benaud, it felt official, credible, true – even in the ghastliest circumstances. He had been there and he had seen it, but the sun would rise on cricket tomorrow, and the game would go on. Had a politician been able to achieve such trustworthiness, there would have been no need for elections, or even opinion polls. Benaud's was the blue-chip stock in every portfolio, the household brand in every home.

He was being marketed before he was even aware of it. He was born Richard, his father's middle name, but this was too formal for down-dressing Australia, where Jack was as good as his master partly because he preferred it to John. There was a threat he might be "Dick", until mother Rene subtly imposed her will by a quiet campaign for something a little less curt.

So Richie he became. One of the very few organs to lean towards formal address was this one, Harry Gee's Cricketer of the Year profile in the 1962 edition beginning: "If one player, more than any other, has deserved well of cricket for lifting the game out of the doldrums, that man is Richard Benaud." And Rene was right: he was *never* a Dick.

Did he market himself? Benaud was too intelligent a man not to understand the impression he made, and its usefulness. After all, he was a professional presenter: meeting audiences was his business. But he could not have succeeded had Richieness simply been a guise he adopted when the cameras rolled. No, like a stick of rock, he was Richie through and through, which fascinated those he met, such as Michael Clarke at an awards evening in 2005: "I remember talking to Richie on stage and marvelling at the fact that he sounded in the flesh exactly as he sounded on television. I have no idea why I was so surprised. Maybe it was the fact that he had been parodied so often, but somehow I had it in my head that the television voice was just that, and he would probably be different face to face."

When Benaud died, on April 10, 2015, there were a great many such tributes. No fewer than four books have followed, anthologising extracted writing about and by him. Not bad for someone who had played his last cricket more than half a century earlier; not bad for someone whom most knew only as a disembodied voice, economical in expression, cool in tone; *so* not bad that such an astonishing consistency of appeal cries out for explanation.

The voice of summer: Richie Benaud at The Oval, August 1998.

Benaud's media career must be described in terms of two related broadcasting revolutions in which he was intimately involved: the rise of the ex-player expert; and the precipitous rise in the commercial value of television rights. Both lay well in the future when Benaud was playing, even if in hindsight he seems always to have been a media performer in the making – an enterprising all-rounder who became an imaginative captain and a gifted communicator, a colourful figure in an austere period. It was thought extremely unusual when 26-year-old Benaud organised with the BBC's head of light entertainment, Tom Sloan, to spend three weeks after the 1956 Ashes tour watching the corporation at work in a medium – television – that was shortly to arrive in Australia.

As he often reflected, Benaud shadowed the racing commentator Peter O'Sullevan at work at Newbury; he watched the Wimbledon final, called by Dan Maskell; he followed the Open golf, with Henry Longhurst. Each was a master of the "pyramid" technique espoused by Seymour de Lotbinière, the BBC's pioneer of outside broadcasts: start with the core facts of the score, then broaden to discussion of weather, venue and other material. The cardinal principle was often condensed thus: "Don't speak unless you can add to the picture." Its influence on Benaud was obvious.

The irony is that, at the time, this approach had only limited application to cricket. Like the other sports, it was also the preserve of professional broadcasters: television's voices of cricket were the ebullient Brian Johnston and the mandarin E. W. Swanton. But here pyramidal principles were not felt so binding: as John Arlott said, de Lotbinière had "no particular liking for the game, and little knowledge of its finer points".

The picture in televised cricket was not yet so good that it often spoke for itself, so commentators talked quite a lot, sometimes irritatingly so. On the occasion of Benaud's last Test in England, at The Oval in 1961, Johnston and his Australian summariser Jack Fingleton caused considerable annoyance by whiling away the closing stages of a draw with rambling stories unrelated to the play, and chatting with statistician Roy Webber about his glamorous wife.

In the second half of his playing career, meanwhile, Benaud dabbled in a variety of media, but not television. On Sydney's tabloid *Sun* he learned the basic principles of daily reporting as a junior police roundsman, and of opinion-making as a regular sports columnist. With the assistance of a literary agent George Greenfield, he published three cricket books; Greenfield also arranged his first media engagements in England, with the *News of the World* and BBC radio in 1960. He appeared on television in 1963, initially only as a summariser – the first of 84 consecutive summers on either side of the globe.

For Benaud had retired from cricket at precisely the right time. Instrumental to his rise was Bryan Cowgill, a no-nonsense northerner who had just become the BBC's head of sport. Forever associated with *Grandstand* and *Match of the Day*, Cowgill argued that the era of the genial waffler was done. For one thing, television pictures were improving: the coming of colour and the 625-line screen finally made it sensible to apply to cricket the principle of the picture's predominance. For another, the public wanted to hear from former players, preferably those with a bit of stardust.

As Benaud, Jim Laker, Ted Dexter and Denis Compton took up their television microphones in the 1960s, so Swanton and Johnston moved to radio. Johnston with a tart comment or two in *It Never Rains* about the new ways not being his "cup of tea". "Cricket includes so many other things besides what goes on in the middle," he complained. "It is a game full of character and fun and there is always laughter not far away. But not if you have a producer shouting down your ear: 'Steady – no jokes – stick to the cricket!'"

Fidelity to what goes on in the middle had other implications. Television was a compelling medium, immediate and potentially intimate. But its limit tended to be the edge of the screen. It was far less interested in issues requiring deep analysis, as Benaud himself was to find when he followed Australia's 1964-65 tour of the West Indies for the *Sun*, also commentating for local radio and television.

It was expected to be an exciting trip, as the first rematch of the contestants for the 1960-61 Frank Worrell Trophy; it was also bound to be controversial, featuring as it did Charlie Griffith, the fastest bowler in the world, with the most-discussed action. Benaud was typically well prepared, having undertaken training in photography from Harry Martin, of the *Sydney Morning Herald*, the *Sun's* broadsheet sister, and brought a Minolta SR7 with a Tamron lens and a hundred rolls of film. And, after due consideration of the photographic evidence he collected during the First Test at Sabina Park, Benaud labelled Griffith a thrower in the *Sun* and the *Jamaica Gleaner*.

In doing so, he courted considerable unpopularity: "I was to find out that not only was the press not keen to publish the photos but that radio and television, which I was serving, were very keen that nothing of a disquieting note should e mentioned on either medium, and I was effectively gagged the following day at Sabina Park." In a radio talk on the BBC, he scolded administrators for their inaction. "I believed that Griffith threw in this game and I was prepared to say so. The alternative was to burn the photographs and shut up about it, but the time for wishy-washy diplomacy in this matter is long past." But when the BBC covered the visit of West Indies to England in 1966, Benaud and his commentary-box colleagues said nothing about Griffith's action, even though it was extensively debated in print.

So emerged a characteristic of televised cricket, a kind of tacit restraint: while it might dwell on moments of telegenic conflict, it has tended, at least in England and Australia, to shrink from controversy towards… well, wishy-washy diplomacy. As Jack Williams notes in *Cricket and Broadcasting*: "Televised cricket has not followed the example of televised football and rugby in replaying in detail foul play and making this an important aspect of recorded highlights… Radio and TV have not gone out of their way to uncover instances of poor sportsmanship."

Benaud fulfilled all the early expectations of Cowgill and his BBC producers Nick Hunter and David Kenning. No commentator was more respectful of the nostrum about speaking only when necessary, on which he developed his own variations: "If you can add to the pictures, do so"; "No one ever complained about silence"; "Silence can be your greatest weapon." Benaud liked the last so much that he believed in it not only for broadcasting but for "my general organisation, working in the office and in business".

Silence didn't express only the superfluity of comment. After that early brush with trenchancy in the Griffith affair, Benaud seemed to agree that television was not a place for debate or contention. In *Richie: The Man Behind The Legend*, the golf commentator Jack Newton remembers Benaud counselling him that, in the event of an on-air colleague airing a debatable sentiment,

Mastering the art: Benaud, then Test captain rehearses for commentary duties, October 1962.

the best response was none: "If it happens you don't agree, don't say anything." Newton followed the commandment to the letter, "essentially doing what I was taught by Richie".

Benaud was also ever wary of the commentary of the first person, where it involved mention of his own career or era. Once, Doug Walters recalls in *Richie*, he attempted to draw his colleague on the subject of the turning pitch with a cheerful jest: "Gee, Richie, I bet you would love to be bowling on this sort of wicket." He got no answer. He repeated himself. He got no answer again. At last came the ad break and a gentle reprimand: "I don't answer hypothetical questions."

Why such self-denying ordinances? Why not a bit of disputation or contradiction? Why not a telling anecdote from personal experience? Might they not have "added to the picture"? Not, thought Benaud, if they were a distraction. From outright criticism of players, especially that which might involve in-my-day comparison, he recoiled. And the breadth of his appeal while observing such tenets of commentary suggest an acute understanding of the preferences of his audience.

So did the boldest step of Benaud's broadcasting career: his involvement in Kerry Packer's World Series Cricket, to whose success he was among the most fundamental ingredients. Cricket was a primly shockable game in 1977. Benaud imparted a patina of respectability to WSC. If it was a circus, at least it had an undeniably competent ringmaster.

Television coverage of cricket in Australia had traditionally lagged behind England, the Australian Broadcasting Corporation a pale shadow of the BBC. WSC changed all that: Australian coverage became the standard, in technical proficiency and narrative verve, and viewers embraced it – more of them indeed, than before.

At the same time, while Nine's modus operandi is often interpreted as a profound break with the past, with its lavish array of cameras and compelling use of replays, Benaud was never other than himself. All the novelty was presented with the moderating influence of a man who believed commentators should behave as a guest in the viewer's home. His less-is-more habit withstood even Packer's injunctions. In *Richie*, Benaud's old confrère Bill Lawry recalls their boss's telephoned complaints during an early WSC fixture:

> He informed us in very clear terms that this was not the BBC, most of the people watching didn't have a clue about cricket, and we were supposed to be telling them what was going on. Richie wasn't going to change or in any way dilute the commentary lessons he lived by: you only spoke if you could add to the pictures. So the next over was again virtually word-free. After that, I thought keeping Kerry on side was a bit more important, so I started rattling on. The pattern sort of stuck.

Indeed it did. If such an audit were possible, a study of Benaud commentaries down the years would reveal a word ratio growing in favour of the garrulous colleagues with whom he shared a microphone.

In fact, Benaud's natural vein made him the perfect commentator for the new order. Under the Nine regime, commentators had less time: commercial breaks deprived them of 25 seconds every over, and the previous convention of the 40-minute stint was shortened to half an hour. The subtly smaller canvas played to Benaud's strengths. Nine also gradually relieved commentators of mundanities such as repeating the score or reciting statistics by presenting these on-screen. Benaud could confine his scrupulously rationed remarks to what mattered, which probably no commentator has done so well.

The great change that WSC presaged, of course, was economic. It hastened the end of a world in which cricket was covered by national broadcasters as kind of public trust. It ushered in a present day when the game is funded by the sale of the rights to televise it.

In some ways, that involved a continuation of television's tendency to exclude matters outside the screen, which was now about commerce. The modern commentator became not simply a critic, but a promoter too. With his natural moderation and understatement, Benaud balanced these roles as effectively as anyone in history. You bought his wares without even realising they were for sale; as with the best salesmen, the transaction left you feeling enriched. Because he always looked for the best in cricket, he entitled one to optimism. Because he never mentioned his own career, he remained startlingly contemporary. His presence was a stamp of quality. When cricket at last left the BBC, Benaud's ongoing presence assuaged all concerns, even those of the former corporation pillar

> While Benaud was at the microphone, progress was generally benign

Swanton. "I don't despair of Channel 4 at all," he said. "After all, they've got Richie Benaud, the great arbiter."

There was a degree of artificiality about this great arbitration. From the 1980s on, cricket seemed to lurch from one crisis to the next: rebel tours, match-fixing, illegal actions, ball-tampering, aggression that trembled on the brink of cheating, commercial chicanery that skirted the bounds of legality, rock-bottom standards of governance. Yet none of this intruded on a Benaud commentary stint, the super-smooth succinctness of "super shot" and "marvellous" interrupted only every so often by an oracular comment or an inscrutable silence that might, or might not, convey displeasure. Indeed, it may have enhanced his appeal: while Benaud was at the microphone, externalities were always suspended, and progress was generally benign.

It's tempting when a great figure is lost to opine about the qualities the next generation would do well to emulate. Yet while Benaud was extraordinarily adept at accommodating change, he was *sui generis*. Cricket's biggest audiences are now young, Indian, well informed and social-media savvy, brought up on short-form cricket and shouty current-affairs television. What to them is the commentator dispensing terse advice between silences from an Olympian remove? The televised cricket of the future will be geared to their values, their expectations.

Benaud, one suspects, would not have been uncomfortable with that. In *Richie*, Nine's head of sport Steve Crawley recalls the circumstances of his last on-air words, and of presenting Benaud with a script that ended "God bless you, son." Benaud amended it to "rest in peace" with a polite but firm: "I don't do God." Good thing too.

Gideon Haigh is a journalist.

Accuracy, cunning and a glass of something white

JOHN WOODCOCK

When, as chairman of selectors, Sir Donald Bradman invited Richie Benaud to captain Australia, he must have known he had found a cricketer after his own heart, and one of a similarly calculating disposition. Benaud was never to play a part in the administration of the game, as the Don did, but he became, for one reason or another, scarcely less celebrated. They both valued their privacy, and neither ever did or said anything without weighing and reweighing the consequences, whether on or off the field.

Although in the forefront of all-rounders, as a fine, free-hitting batsman and one of the best wrist-spinners of his time, it was as a captain that Benaud truly excelled. Bradman's Invincibles after the Second World War had nothing much to beat. As Australia's captain in Australia in 1958-59, on the other hand, Benaud came straight up against an England side containing as many illustrious names as any to tour under the aegis of MCC.

Had Neil Harvey beaten Benaud to the captaincy, as he was expected to do, the story of the Ashes might well have been very different. It is certainly unlikely that Peter May's side, hot favourites to retain them, would have been humbled as they were in Australia, or put out of their stride again in England two years later. For a start, I expect, knowing that they would find him significantly more at ease than the more reticent May, Benaud introduced press conferences at the end of each day's play, always taken by the captains. These were a new departure and duly worked to Benaud's advantage. As we were to see later, in his commentating days, his facility was not so much with words as with the way he never wasted them.

There can be no doubt about his finest hour as a player. The blend of experience, attitude, skill and grit with which, almost single-handedly, he stole the Fourth Test, and the Ashes with it, from under England's very noses at Old Trafford in 1961, must be ingrained in the memories of all who were there. Set 256 to win, England were coasting at 150 for one, with Ted Dexter at his imperious best, Raman Subba Row his pertinacious partner. Throughout the tour, already three and a half months old, Benaud had been suffering with a shoulder injury, causing him to miss the Lord's Test. He couldn't give the ball a real tweak without a lot of pain.

In England's four previous innings of that 1961 series he had, in fact, taken two for 255 runs in 100 overs, including nought for 80 in their first innings at Old Trafford. In view of this, over a drink on the penultimate evening, he and Ray Lindwall, discussed the possibility of Richie going round the wicket, more as a last resort than a regular ploy. If nothing else, the bowlers' footmarks should supply their own supplement of spin. In the event it was this that turned the tide. As soon as he tried it, he had Dexter caught at the wicket and bowled May round his legs, second ball. England were no more immune to collapse in those days than they are now, the disappointment no less acute, let alone with

"I do": Richie Benaud and Daphne Surfleet on their wedding day in Westminster, July 26, 1967.

the Ashes in the balance. The panache, not to say hint of hauteur, with which Richie finished England off, only added to the misery.

As a gamesman, albeit a scrupulously fair one, Richie had nothing to learn. Sledging in any depraved form had yet to come in and would anyway have been anathema to him, as would the incessant hollering that is looked upon today as an obligatory means of mutual encouragement. Richie ran a tight ship. He would have stood no nonsense from Kevin Pietersen, nor, I believe, have had any truck with Steve Waugh's so-called "mental disintegration".

That I came to know him as well as I did was partly because he was courting his future wife, Daphne Surfleet (the inimitable "Daphers"), then personal assistant to my opposite number on the *Daily Telegraph*, Jim Swanton. Just as importantly, players and press mingled in a way that led to many a friendship but which, I gather, has not always been the case since.

In his retirement, and during his annual visits to England to take his place in the commentary box, Richie regularly came to stay with me at Longparish in Hampshire, turning out for my side on the village ground, convivially and never with any suggestion of condescension. He would never offer advice but, if asked, would gladly give it. Nowhere else, I imagine, would he have found himself, at different times, in the same XI as Denis Compton, Colin Cowdrey, Len Hutton and Frank Tyson. He took enthusiastically, too, to fishing for trout on the Test. Casting a fly over a fish wagging its tail at the head of a piece of weed called for the same accuracy and cunning as bowling to Dexter or May in a Test match, with a touch of the same tension but none of the frenzy, he would say. He was happy to do it all day long and, being the *bon vivant* he was, to eat what he had caught for supper, with a glass of something white.

Then came Kerry Packer's World Series Cricket and its reciprocal ruptures. After initial misgivings, Richie opted in; and, having done so, gave it not only

an invaluable token of respectability but his unremitting loyalty. WSC and the haste with which the no-ball law was changed from the back foot to the front were the only things I know of about which Bradman and Richie did not see eye to eye. Being as vehemently opposed as I, too, was to Mr Packer meant a break in Richie's Longparish visits, of his volition not mine. By the time he came again, with our differences long buried, he was past bowling or wading the river.

One last story. During the MCC tour to Australia in 1965-66, I was editing in memory of Ron Roberts, an especially popular and prolific freelance cricket writer and pioneer of worldwide multiracial cricket

Test appearance: Richie Benaud fishes for trout near Longparish.

tours. Such was the regard in which he was held that on one of these he had in his side three current Test captains – Richie, Dexter and John Reid of New Zealand. In August 1965, when still in his thirties, Ron died, hence the book. The following winter, as we boarded an evening flight from Adelaide to Melbourne, Richie handed me his own contribution – 1,500 warm-hearted, well-chosen words.

Having read it, I put it in the pocket of my seat and, fool that I am, left it there. After frantic, unavailing calls to the airport, the news had to be broken to Richie. I thought he was fairly sure to have a carbon copy – we were in the days of the typewriter – but he didn't. The equanimity with which he accepted what had happened, and the speed and readiness with which he wrote another 1,500 words, saying he preferred them to his original piece, no doubt owed much to his affection for Roberts. But it was typical of one of the sporting world's genuinely outstanding people.

John Woodcock, cricket correspondent of The Times *for 33 years, edited* Wisden *between 1981 and 1986.*

WHEN ENGLAND WON TWO WORLD CUPS

Rimet and Rothmans

PHILIP BARKER

It is 50 years since Bobby Moore lifted the Jules Rimet Trophy at Wembley – and you can forgive English sporting fans for thinking it was the only World Cup triumph that summer. But, seven weeks later, and about six miles away at Lord's, a far smaller gathering saw Colin Cowdrey raise a slightly precarious piece of silverware made up of a cricket ball balanced on three criss-crossed stumps. This was the Rothmans World Cup, a tournament long forgotten – even by those who took part.

FIFA had scheduled *their* 1966 World Cup for July, and – in an early example of football's encroachment on cricket's territory – there was a four-week gap between the Third and the Fourth Tests against West Indies. Six days after Charlie Griffith was knocking over John Snow's stumps at Trent Bridge to wrap up a 139-run win for the tourists, England and Uruguay were fighting out a 0–0 draw at Wembley. Neither result looked especially promising.

Rothmans claimed that their own World Cup, added to the fixture list as late as March, was "the most ambitious exercise cricket had ever known". Even its launch was overshadowed by football: that week, the Jules Rimet Trophy was stolen from a display in London only to be found soon after by Pickles the dog. England, West Indies and a Rest of the World XI would contest three

Before they ruled the world: England footballers visit Lord's for the Middlesex v Essex game, July 18. Among them are Geoff Hurst (second left), Jimmy Greaves (with pipe, obscuring Bobby Moore), and Bobby Charlton (seated, fourth from right).

50-over matches over four days at Lord's in mid-September – more than four years before Australia and England contested the first official one-day international in Melbourne, and three decades before 50 overs became the format's standard length.

The games were brokered by sports agent Bagenal Harvey, who had made his name representing Denis Compton (the first deal he signed for his client involved Compton applying Brylcreem – and Harvey collecting his 10%). A year earlier, he had set up the all-star Rothmans Cavaliers, who played televised limited-overs matches before Sundays huge crowds; venues ranged from Trent Bridge to Hampshire's Tichborne Park, the home of Sir Anthony Doughty-Tichborne. Harvey was nothing if not entrepreneurial.

Australia's Bobby Simpson was to captain the World XI, and – long before viewers were voting for cricketers in spangled shirts on *Strictly Come Dancing* – the BBC set up a *Radio Times* readers' poll to choose the other ten from shortlists in five categories (opening batsmen, batsmen, wicketkeepers, fast bowlers, spinners). Compton solemnly told them: "You must bear in mind that some of the famous names may well be better suited than others to this particular form of cricket." Coupons were "published early so that schoolboys home on holiday can have a chance to take part". Of schoolgirls, there was no mention.

At Lord's, September 10, 1966. **England XI won by 82 runs.** ‡**England XI 201-7** (50 overs) (E. R. Dexter 32, J. M. Parks 42, B. L. D'Oliveira 49; R. G. Nadkarni 3-31); **Rest of the World XI 119** (36.3 overs) (R. B. Simpson 38; K. Higgs 5-34, B. R. Knight 3-19).

At Lord's, September 12, 1966. **West Indies XI won by 18 runs. West Indies XI 254-7** (50 overs) (C. C. Hunte 57, S. M. Nurse 88); ‡**Rest of the World XI 236-8** (50 overs) (Hanif Mohammad 63, R. G. Pollock 65; W. W. Hall 4-40).

At Lord's, September 13, 1966. **England XI won by 67 runs. England XI 217-7** (50 overs) (J. H. Edrich 33, J. M. Parks 33; P. D. Lashley 3-46); ‡**West Indies XI 150** (40.4 overs) (S. M. Nurse 58; K. Higgs 4-50).

With Simpson an automatic choice, there was only one other opening slot: Hanif Mohammad was selected ahead of Eddie Barlow and Bill Lawry. Doug Walters had to withdraw to complete his military service. Despite that, the electorate had settled on a handy side: Simpson (Australia), Hanif (Pakistan), Grahame Thomas (Australia), Graeme Pollock, Colin Bland (both South Africa), the Nawab of Pataudi (India), Mushtaq Mohammad (Pakistan), Deryck Murray (West Indies), Bapu Nadkarni (India), Peter Pollock (South Africa) and Graham McKenzie (Australia).

Football was everywhere, yet Alf Ramsey's squad sought relaxation at Lord's ahead of the final. Bobby Moore and Martin Peters were keen cricketers, and Geoff Hurst had once played a first-class game for Essex, against Lancashire at Aigburth in 1962, making nought not out from No. 10 and nought from No. 8; he didn't get a bowl, but did take a catch off Jim Laker. Four years later, as Hurst's hat-trick beat the West Germans at Wembley, Jim Parks – who would make 42 and 33 in the England XI's two Rothmans

They think it's all over. England's other world champions: Barry Knight, Fred Titmus, Basil D'Oliveira, John Edrich, Peter Parfitt, Jim Parks, Ted Dexter (partly obscured by trophy), John Murray (in cap), Colin Cowdrey, John Snow and Ken Higgs. On the extreme left, wearing a suit, is Rohan Kanhai.

World Cup matches – was leading Sussex against Gloucestershire at Hove, and saw the goals only on the television highlights. "We had the same agent, so I got to know the three West Ham players very well and would often watch them play. I've been a fan ever since."

English cricketers had played the one-day game since the Gillette Cup began in 1963, but the majority of the World XI had little experience. Even so, they won their only limited-overs warm-up match, against the Cavaliers at Ascott Park, by 46 runs. The cricket World Cup, however, was not officially recognised: at a meeting at Lord's, the minutes recorded that, though MCC "had agreed to send out the invitations, it should be made clear that the teams were not selected by [them]".

England wicketkeeper John Murray confirmed the underwhelming mood: "It wasn't taken that seriously, but it was quite a decent couple of days." In the first match, England easily defended a modest 201 for seven against the Rest. "It was clear that much of the great talent lay dormant because of lack of match practice," said *Wisden*. The World XI were skittled for 119, with Ken Higgs taking five for 34.

The closest a batsman came to a century in the tournament was Seymour Nurse, with 88 as West Indies also beat the World XI. In the third match – in effect the final – Garry Sobers inserted England, who recovered from a slow start to reach 217. Cowdrey left the field with a muscle injury, so Ted Dexter directed affairs. *Wisden* recorded: "He brought to bear the considerable knowledge gained in leading Sussex successfully in the Gillette Cup." In what passed back then for one-day tactics, Dexter told his bowlers to "aim at the stumps, pitch it up and, if someone starts whacking it, pitch it up a bit further".

There were no powerplays or fielding restrictions, and the ball came on more slowly off an uncovered wicket. "Ted had it all worked out," said Parks. "He kept the field defensive all the time to put the pressure on." England easily contained the West Indian batting to win by 67 runs, with Higgs picking up four more. Cowdrey hobbled out to lift the trophy.

Only 13,036 turned up over the three days. "One would have thought West Indian supporters would have flocked to Lord's," lamented the television commentator, Peter West. "But the Caribbean contingent was pretty thin on the ground. One wonders whether it was fully aware of the matches."

In the tournament's official programme, Crawford White had written optimistically of "an exploratory rocket in space for far more ambitious world level tournaments". Though the Rothmans Cavaliers continued to flourish, their World Cup was repeated only in 1967, with a World XI captained by Garry Sobers seeing off England and Pakistan. Again, crowds were disappointing, and MCC reported "extreme difficulty in finding suitable pitches at that stage of the season". The trophy itself has since vanished (like the Jules Rimet, stolen again in 1983).

Many advocated a football-style World Cup for cricket, but the authorities remained wary. Meanwhile, major changes in domestic cricket were afoot, including a new Sunday League in 1969. Harvey attended a stormy meeting with MCC, and discovered Rothmans were not part of the new order: players were discouraged from taking part in Cavaliers cricket once the League began. MCC denied they had imposed a ban, but it was clear many officials remained suspicious of anything outside their control.

"If we are in a rebel situation it is not by choice," said an angry Harvey. "Cricket will be the loser." To add to the fire, the League was sponsored by Rothmans' cigarette rivals John Player. The Cavaliers continued to play on Sundays, but no longer attracted TV coverage. After 1970, they disappeared from the scene.

The first official men's World Cup did not take place until 1975 (although the women beat them to it by two years). Even then, the organisers insisted on calling it "International Championship Cricket". Those in power seemed astonished that the tournament, won by Clive Lloyd's West Indies, was such a success. England still await their first one-day World Cup. Fifty years of hurt is not merely the preserve of the footballers.

Philip Barker is a freelance broadcaster, writer and author of Lord's Firsts, *a bicentenary history of the ground.*

KUMAR SANGAKKARA RETIRES

In perspective – even the obsession

PAUL FARBRACE

"What do you think? How's it looking?" It was another practice session at the Premadasa Stadium in Colombo, and Kumar Sangakkara was as inquisitive and conscientious as ever. And very precise. He wanted his back foot to move from middle and leg to middle and off. Not forward or back – just a fraction across, which allowed his shoulders and hips to align when facing right-arm seamers.

I was in the first of two coaching stints with Sri Lanka, as an assistant to Trevor Bayliss (a few years later I would return as head coach), and was doing my best to keep on top of the session. But I could see Sanga was hitting the ball nicely. "Brilliant," I told him. "No problems whatsoever."

He was unimpressed with my forensic analysis. "The first ten balls I faced, I moved my back foot in four or five different ways," he said. "If I ever ask you again, tell me the truth or don't tell me anything." It was a big lesson for me as a coach. And it told me plenty about Kumar Sangakkara.

When I first arrived in the Sri Lankan dressing-room, in July 2007, he wasn't yet the main man, although he had just taken a pair of unbeaten double-hundreds off Bangladesh. Instead, he was one of the Big Five, along with Sanath Jayasuriya, Muttiah Muralitharan, Chaminda Vaas and Mahela Jayawardene. You could see his qualities, and you knew he was going to be a driving force. His strength was enhanced by his great friendship with Mahela, and the team benefited from their different qualities. Mahela was instinctive, competitive, a real winner. Sanga was more organised and methodical, and would watch endless videos. But they were both patriots who felt they were representing the country, not just their team-mates.

One of Sanga's first deeds after I arrived was to make 192 at Hobart after Australia had set us 507. We made 410, and Sanga was given out by Rudi Koertzen, caught at slip off shoulder and helmet: a stinker. That night we were in the hotel bar when the umpires walked in. There was a pause, then Sanga stepped forward: "Rudi! What can I get you to drink?"

If that was typical of him, so was the way in which he used that innings to get even better. Over a year later – by which stage he already had more than 6,000 Test runs – we were in the indoor school at Colombo's SSC. Sanga couldn't quite get his movements right, so he asked our analyst to access footage of the Hobart innings. He wanted to check the movement of his left foot in relation to Brett Lee's delivery stride. Once he'd absorbed the information he needed, he was ready to bat again.

Nothing distracted him from his practice. There were times when, frankly, this made him a pain in the backside. Net sessions had to be just so. You'd think they were over, then he'd march back in for a few more throwdowns. They could last anything from 20 minutes to an hour. When he was wearing

Insatiable: Kumar Sangakkara hones his technique, here against Muttiah Muralitharan in 2007.

his game head, there was a selfishness about him. But no one minded, because that selfishness was usually for the greater good.

Every coach who worked with him knew you ended up needing reconstructive shoulder surgery. And your throwdowns had to be accurate. I was giving him a few at Sydney, and in the previous game he'd missed a couple of square-drives, so I thought I'd throw one or two a little wider. He left the first alone, and just looked at me. When I did the same again a few balls later, he stared back, then walked straight past me and into the dressing-room. We never mentioned it again, but I got the message.

People usually think of his amazing Test record, but it's easy to forget what a top-class limited-overs player he became. When I returned to the Sri Lankan set-up at the end of 2013, his one-day game had gone to another level – not that he was exactly struggling. Back in 2008, there was a debate about where he should bat in the Asia Cup in Pakistan. Trevor wanted him to open, because the new ball wasn't going to do much, but others were worried about him nicking off early. Trevor won: Sanga opened and made three hundreds, and Sri Lanka lifted the trophy.

He soon established his niche at No. 3, and the hundred he made against England at Wellington in the 2015 World Cup was probably the best one-day innings I saw him play. Though I had moved to the England team by then, I told him so as he came off the field. Once he got to 20, I just slumped back in my chair. Unless he was going to run himself out, I couldn't see how he was going to lose his wicket.

Because he was such a structured, thoughtful player, there was sometimes a perception that one-day cricket didn't suit him. It's true that he didn't have the flair of Jayasuriya or Jayawardene, or the improvisational skills of Tillekeratne Dilshan. But he showed you could bat normally and still score big hundreds. He was never very good at slogging, yet the way he came down the track to spin, and hit over straight extra cover or straight midwicket – there weren't many in the world who could do that.

Across the formats, I'd say the greatest innings he played during my time with Sri Lanka came in the final of the World Twenty20 against India in 2014. Sanga hadn't scored many runs leading up to it, and felt he owed the team. No one needed to tell him that. There was a short discussion about whether he should play or not, but I was adamant I wanted him in.

Both he and Mahela had ruffled a few feathers at Sri Lanka Cricket by announcing they would be retiring from Twenty20s at the end of the tournament, and we played on the news a bit: do it for Sanga and Mahela, that kind of thing. In our team meeting before the final against India, our analyst asked if he could play a video he'd put together. It was a corny montage of the two of them smiling, laughing, walking off the field arm in arm, all put to music. At the end of it, I turned to our manager Michael de Zoysa to ask if he wanted to say his customary few words, and he just made this sniffing

> I looked around and all the players were drying their eyes

noise. I looked around and all the players were drying their eyes. No one said another word. All you could hear was the scraping of chairs as they all got up and quietly embraced Sanga and Mahela.

He then went out and made an unbeaten 52 off 35 balls to take us home with a couple of overs to spare. It wasn't a pretty innings, but it was effective, and the emotion at the end of it was something else. The most impressive part was that, though he was out of nick, he found a way. Given the significance of the game, and all the finals Sri Lanka had lost in previous years, it was a terrific display of temperament.

Despite being an outsider, I was always made to feel welcome. The number of dinners he and Mahela paid for got a bit embarrassing, but that's the Sri Lankan way. I remember how well they looked after some of the Yorkshire lads when they were on a training camp in Sri Lanka. His wife, Yehali, cooked dinner one night and a few of us were invited over. He and Andrew Gale, whom he'd never met before, spent two hours talking about being left-handers – how to hit over the top, how to deal with the rough and the swinging ball and different angles of attack. At one point, they disappeared down the corridor, swapping tips about when to pick your hands up when you come down the wicket. Sanga won't thank me for saying this, but he's a proper cricket badger.

He put his considerable brain to good use, though it was better if you weren't on the receiving end. If he was ever in danger of losing an argument (which I believe is yet to happen), he would adopt one of two tactics: speak more loudly, or use words you'd never heard of. He would dazzle you into submission. No wonder he once trained to be a lawyer.

SHIVNARINE CHANDERPAUL RETIRES

West Indies' defiant defender

TONY COZIER

West Indies have never possessed a batsman quite like Shivnarine Chanderpaul. And the influence of Twenty20 means they almost certainly will never possess another. Tests were ideal for his temperament and his distinctive, no-frills method of accumulating runs, a contrast to the electrifying strokeplay on which the reputation of West Indian batting had traditionally been based. Nothing gave him more satisfaction than defying bowlers for hour after hour, occasionally day after day, in the cause of a team that grew ever weaker throughout his 21-year career.

His fighting qualities – he was nicknamed "Tiger" – were most evident after a Brett Lee bouncer struck him on the helmet at Kingston in May 2008. He hit the deck, and there was concern he could not go on – but the prospect of a hundred, soon ticked off, was enough to revive him.

He was not out in 49 of his 280 Test innings, which encouraged the accusation of selfishness. But that ignored how much worse off West Indies would have been without him. When they tottered after he was gone, no new Chanderpaul emerged to guide a Test innings into calmer waters. He relished such challenges. He could, it's true, carry self-indulgence to extremes: in a bore draw against India in Antigua in May 2002, his unbeaten 136 occupied 510 deliveries and over 11 hours. But he had an occasionally destructive streak too, blasting his way to a 69-ball hundred against Australia in Georgetown less than a year later. In the final Test of that series, in a more familiar guise, his century – and one for Ramnaresh Sarwan – helped West Indies to 418 for seven in Antigua, still the Test record for a successful fourth-innings chase.

One-day internationals offered him scope to indulge his aggressive side – and brought him 11 centuries – but the frivolity of Twenty20 offended his senses: he felt batsmen didn't care about getting out. For its searching examination of stamina and commitment, Test cricket would "always be the ultimate". Ironically, his first port of call after his exit was Dubai, and the new Twenty20 Masters Champions League.

For all the indignation over the disagreeable manner of his departure, it arrived at an opportune time. There were signs that, at 41, the powers which had kept him going for more Tests, over a longer period, than any other West Indian were waning. After Clive Lloyd told him the selection panel had "decided to move on with younger players", Chanderpaul continued to play for Guyana. He could not abandon the game that had been his life since his father, Khemraj, with help from family and friends, prepared his six-year-old son for the future on makeshift pitches in the fishing village of Unity, on the banks of the Demerara. Now, his son Tagenarine also plays for Guyana.

In 1993, Shivnarine toured England with West Indies Under-19, and an unbeaten 203 at Trent Bridge drew a prophetic observation from Robin Marlar in *The Sunday Times*: "He has all the footwork of a mature player. His judgment was impressive too. As best he could, he left alone anything that threatened his outside edge, playing the leave-alone stroke as a positive event, like all the finest left-handed run-makers. Furthermore, when he was bowled a bad ball, he put it away with certainty and wide of the field."

The assessment held true throughout his stay as West Indies' defiant defender; the only necessary addition would be the profound change in his stance, from side on to front on, a rotation of almost 90 degrees. It was mocked as crab-like; Chanderpaul didn't care, spending days in the nets honing a shift that, he noted, improved his balance.

He had been chosen for the first of his 164 Tests in March 1994, against England at his home ground of Bourda following an outstanding Red Stripe Cup season in which he had topped Guyana's batting averages – and their bowling, with his long-forgotten, flattish leg-spin. He made 62. Then, in his fourth Test, he provided Brian Lara with company during his 375. By the time his career ended, on May 3, 2014, with a duck against England at Bridgetown, Chanderpaul had 11,867 Test runs, only 45 short of Lara's West Indies record (though Lara also made 41 for the World XI). He had scored 30 Test centuries, and averaged over 51, yet still ended up on the losing side 77 times, comfortably a world record. That his departure denied him the chance to pass Lara infuriated those who agreed with Lara himself that he had "earned the right to say goodbye in an acceptable way".

Chanderpaul, whose forefathers had arrived from India as indentured labour after the abolition of slavery, credited his Hindu religion for the concentration needed to build scores. One of *Wisden's* Cricketers of the Year in 2008, he told his former team-mate Ian Bishop, the writer of his profile, that his faith was "a divine gift bestowed on him by Lord Shiva".

Even so, the humble, softly spoken Chanderpaul was twice enraged by incidents, exposing a feisty side. In 2005, he was appointed captain after Lara withdrew over a contracts dispute. His first innings in charge was an unbeaten 203 against South Africa at Bourda; a year later he quit, after Lara and the leading players returned for a tour of Australia following a strike. Chanderpaul complained he got no support from management, the coach or some players, and was unable to concentrate on his batting.

Then, when he, Sarwan and Chris Gayle were dropped from the one-day team after the 2011 World Cup, he became embroiled in a heated exchange with the board, who had linked him to charges of indiscipline and lack of commitment. The Guyanese public rallied round, and the president, Bharrat Jagdeo, paraded around Georgetown's new Providence Stadium during a match against Pakistan with a placard proclaiming "The WICB is a disgrace". Chanderpaul did not play another one-dayer.

While there were three more years of Test cricket, an average of 16 over his final six Tests – in South Africa and at home against England – suggested that his long career had reached its inevitable conclusion. With his departure ends an era.

His best one-day innings? Sangakkara scores freely against England in the 2015 World Cup.

His best sledge was aimed at Nasser Hussain in Sri Lanka in 2003-04, when England were playing in Kandy. Nasser had called Murali – the hometown hero – various names, so the locals weren't best pleased. And it's fair to say Nasser was a bit grumpy with his own team-mates too. When he came in to bat, Sanga piped up with: "What's it like to be hated by both teams?" It wasn't abusive, but he knew how to get under your skin. I cracked a few times, and he had this way of talking about me in the team bus, especially to Murali, who shared his sarcastic sense of humour. "Hey, Murali," he'd say. "Our fat coach – do you think he's got any fatter?"

When I left Sri Lanka to join England in 2014, I wasn't very comfortable about the fact that my first series was against my old team. A few people had accused me of leaving for the money, which was never the case, but Sanga broke the ice ahead of the opening international of the tour, a Twenty20 match at The Oval. As I was walking up the steps to the pavilion, he was at the top. There were quite a few journalists waiting around, and he shouted down: "Traitor! Traitor's here. Don't talk to him, boys." All the way through the series, we would shake hands after every game, and he would pull me in and, with a twinkle in his eye, say: "Traitor." He made it easy for me.

Maybe the best thing about him is that he had life in perspective. Nothing was too much trouble, and he always stayed humble. One afternoon, after he'd kindly driven me to a local hospital because of an ear infection, we stopped off to pick up his dad, then drove to a nearby ground. For 20 minutes, his dad threw some balls at him on a concrete strip, just to make sure all the basics were working correctly. Sanga obviously held him in high regard.

And I'll never forget how he helped keep spirits up after the terrorist attack in Lahore in 2009. He and I were among the four who were at the front of the bus on the left and got hit by shrapnel, and we all spent a few days together in hospital back in Colombo. One afternoon, we had some important visitors – the leaders of the opposition in parliament. I could hear Sanga coming down the corridor shouting: "Fat coach, fat coach! Where are you?" Then he entered the room, saw who was there, and suddenly changed tack: "Ah, sir, very good to see you! Thank you for coming!"

That was Sanga to a T: he was mischievous, quick-witted and charming, and everyone loved him for it. Sri Lankan cricket will miss him like mad.

Paul Farbrace, England's assistant coach, was assistant coach of Sri Lanka between July 2007 and July 2009, and head coach between December 2013 and April 2014. He was talking to Lawrence Booth.

THE WISDEN–MCC CRICKET PHOTOGRAPH OF 2015   Robert Cianflone wins the award for his image of Craig Simmons, of Adelaide Strikers, suffering an equipment malfunction during the Big Bash semi-final. The photograph was taken in Adelaide on January 24.

Robert Cianflone

The sixth Wisden–MCC Cricket Photograph of the Year, in association with J.P. Morgan, attracted almost 350 entries. Any image with a cricket theme taken during 2015 was eligible. The independent judging panel, chaired by former *Sunday Times* chief photographer Chris Smith, comprised award-winning photographers Patrick Eagar, Bob Thomas and Nigel Davies, and Kevin Cummins, and the former art director of *The Cricketer*. For more details, go to www.lords.org/photooftheyear

THE WISDEN–MCC CRICKET PHOTOGRAPH OF 2015 Darrian Traynor is one of two runners-up for this image of Dale Dhamarrandji and two of his Miwatj Dolphins team-mates playing by a dry river in Arnhem Land, Northern Territory, in February. They were preparing for the 2015 Imparja Cup, a tournament for Indigenous Australians.

Darrian Traynor

THE WISDEN–MCC CRICKET PHOTOGRAPH OF 2015   The other runner-up is Vishnur V. Nair, who captures the never-say-dry attitude of cricketers in Dadar, central Mumbai, playing through monsoon rain in June..

Vishnur V. Nair

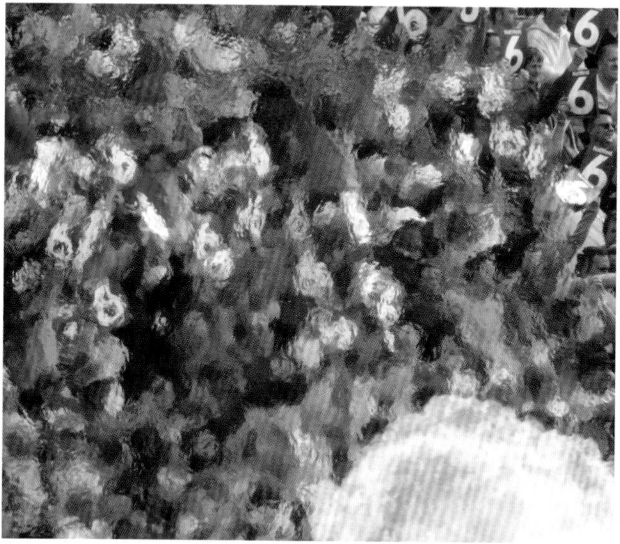

FIRE, WALK WITH ME   Pyrotechnics at Cardiff turn the crowd at a Twenty20 international into a painterly shimmer. At Melbourne in December, Chris Gayle and Aaron Finch brave a blazing welcome to a Big Bash match.

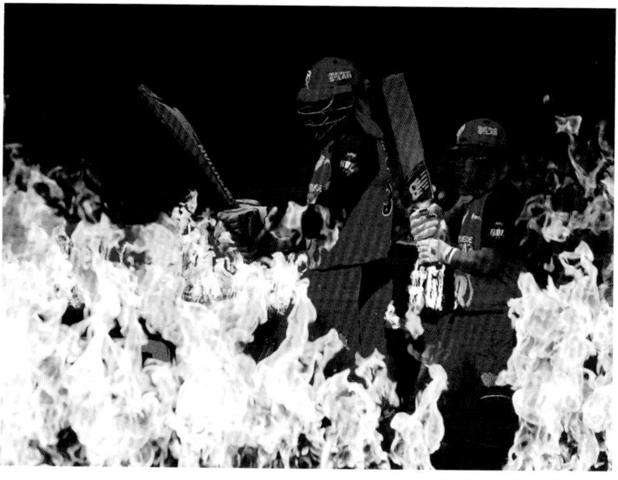

Scott Barbour, Getty Images

ONE-WAY TRAFFIC   Boys beside the Eastern Freeway in Mumbai find their pitch plays rather like a road; at The Oval, Australia crush England to gain a consolation win.

THERE IN SPIRIT The owner of the ghostly bat is Lancashire's Alex Davies, who lost his grip during the Twenty20 Blast semi-final at Edgbaston. In the New Year Test at Sydney, a group of Richie Benauds pay tribute to their inspiration, who died in 2015.

Dan Mullan, Getty Images

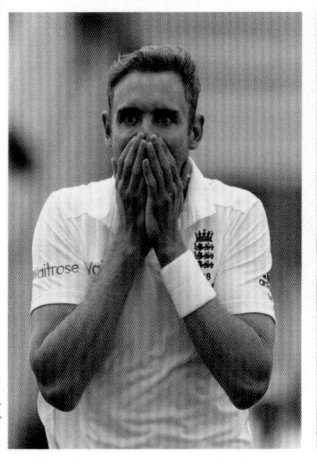

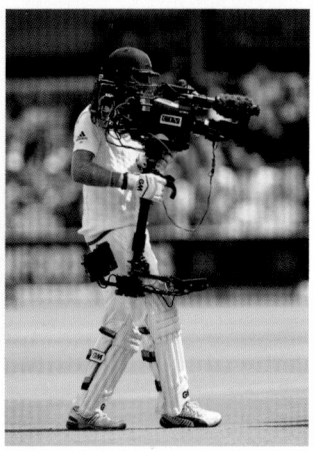

SEEING IS BELIEVING? Stuart Broad is flabbergasted at Ben Stokes's catch to dismiss Adam Voges at Trent Bridge, while at Lord's Joe Root flirts with a change of profession. In Adelaide in October, England's Sarah Taylor becomes the first woman to take part in a men's two-day grade match.

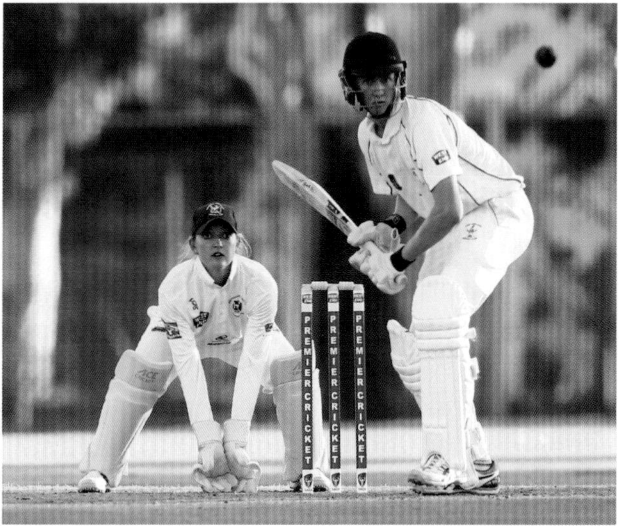

THE LEADING WOMAN CRICKETER IN THE WORLD   Suzie Bates.

FIRST-CLASS CRICKET BEFORE THE WAR

Last men in

ROBERT WINDER

Most days, John Manners strides out of his house in Hungerford, splashes a drop of water over his tomatoes and crosses the road to buy *The Times*. Occasionally, he marches up the High Street for a pint of milk or something from the butcher. Anyone watching might think he is doing well for a man his age, for there is a crispness in his stride. But few would guess that he made his debut for Hampshire in 1936, and celebrated his 100th birthday on September 25, 2014. He is the oldest living member of MCC, and very probably the oldest first-class cricketer in the world today.

Leo Harrison is not far behind. And, following the death last year of Northamptonshire's Ian Philips, he and Manners are the only two men alive to have played first-class cricket in England before the Second World War. Born in Mudeford on the south coast in June 1922, Harrison made his first-class debut, also for Hampshire, as a 17-year-old in the summer of 1939, as the storm clouds were massing over Europe. Today he still lives only a mile or two from the Bournemouth ground where he made that debut, in a house he and his father built with their own hands, using the £3,000 he netted from his benefit season in 1957.

Manners and Harrison came at the game from different angles. Manners was an amateur who played only 21 first-class matches before he retired in 1953, Harrison a solid professional who enjoyed a busy career in the days before wicketkeepers were expected to score big runs. He managed 8,854 of them in 396 games at an average of 17, held 578 catches and made 103 stumpings. In 1952 he scored 153 against Nottinghamshire and, in 1966, as a member of the coaching staff, he pulled on his gloves one last time in first-class cricket, got rid of John Edrich and Micky Stewart, and scored 23. He was famed for his lightning-fast leg-side stumpings off Derek Shackleton's strangulating seam.

Though they played for the same county, they did so only once, against Essex at Colchester in July 1948. And they opposed each other too: at Aldershot a month earlier, Harrison turned out for Hampshire, Manners for Combined Services. Harrison, batting at No. 11, made 15; Manners nought and, with his team following on, six. But, late in life, they were a unique partnership: cricket veterans with rare memories of a lost time.

For modern players, a county debut is usually the climax of a major commitment to the game over many years. It was not always like that. When Manners played his first match for Hampshire, against Gloucestershire at Portsmouth's United Services Ground, he had literally stepped off a yacht. He took a deep breath, and buckled on his pads. He remembers it vividly. "Quite a few of us amateurs would come in during August in those days – schoolmasters, university men, people like that. I was serving on the Royal

Family service: John Manners stands between his father, Sir Errol Manners, and his sister Angela; on the left is John's brother Sherard, who also played for the Royal Navy.

Yacht in Portsmouth, and since the King didn't want to go to Cowes that year we had nothing to do. Someone said: 'Hampshire have a game – you must play.' Some poor fellow was asked to stand down for me, and that was that."

Such is the tenacious grip exerted by cricket memories. "It rained a bit on the first day, but I was still there at lunch on the second. Then the captain said we had to get a move on. I cracked a ball hard into my foot, and it trickled slowly back on to the stumps." Manners had scored 81, and the bowler was off-spinner Reg Sinfield (who two years later, in his only Test appearance, removed Don Bradman). An 80-year-old dismissal can still rankle.

Manners made a strong enough impression to be selected three more times that year, making 39 against the Maharajkumar of Vizianagram's Indians, 48 against a Surrey side including Andy Sandham and Alf Gover, and 38 against a powerful Yorkshire. He was soon off to sea again (the America and West Indies Station). And then the world turned upside down. He played whenever he happened to be back in English waters. But his maiden first-class ton, for Hampshire against Kent, came in 1947. He can still see it today. "Doug Wright bowled a full toss, and I was in two minds whether to pull or drive. I drove, and we ran three. Only just got there."

Harrison has a looser sense of such details, perhaps because his Hampshire career was so long. His first-class debut, against Worcestershire, at Bournemouth's Dean Park, was followed immediately by the visit of Yorkshire. "Got about 13, I think [he made nought and 16]. No idea how I was out. I expect I was big-headed enough to think I could win the match on my own. The ground was packed. It was the end of the season, festival week, and the whole of Yorkshire was down on holiday. I couldn't say who I faced… We lost by an innings."

Not many would forget the day they faced Bill Bowes and Hedley Verity, but Harrison is not one to dwell on such things. As a player he was famous for his genial chit-chat: "Hard luck, mate. It ain't half a bloody game, is it?" He has the same throwaway manner today: "Yes, I got hit a few times. Knocked a bit of sense out of me – or into me, more likely." His father kept scrapbooks and, though he cannot read the columns himself (his eyesight has faded almost to nothing), he still chuckles to hear the way the papers reported his early doings: "Fighting innings by Harrison… Junior makes his mark… Magnificent batting at a critical time."

The grandest thing that came out of these early days was a lifelong friendship with John Arlott. "I was a teenager, and Arlott was the local policeman. Every day he would walk to the ground and watch us in the nets. That's how I got to know him. We became best friends." They holidayed together, drank wine and talked cricket – all in the same mellow Hampshire accents. In Harrison's benefit year, Arlott wrote a privately published monograph on him which now sells (as part of a signed limited edition) for anything up to £360. Every now and then they went fishing, though Arlott was by no means a natural. "One time we were after sea trout right here in Christchurch, and John flicked his rod and somehow sent his hook through someone's window. We had to crawl up and ask for the spinner back. First time I ever saw someone catch a bungalow."

Cricket before the war exists, in many a mind's eye, as a black and white scene from another time. But Manners can still remember fielding on his

Natural keeper: Leo Harrison behind the stumps (and Tom Clark in front), as Hampshire play Surrey at Guildford in 1958.

Hampshire debut, against Gloucestershire in 1936, when Wally Hammond came out to bat: "He was out twice in the day, and everyone could see he'd been on the tiles and was three sheets to the wind." Manners also faced Verity that summer at Bournemouth, recalling him as "accurate but not particularly penetrative". This may be a touch unkind: Verity claimed nine for 90 in that match off 46 overs. But, true, he didn't dismiss Manners, who fell cheaply to Bowes in the first innings, and scored 38 in the second before he was caught and bowled by a whippersnapper named Len Hutton, two years his junior.

It was a different world, a different game. The stumps had polished brass ferrules, lending them a military air, and the boundary was little more than spectators' toes. Equipment was built to last. "I only ever had one pair of pads," says Manners. "That did me, my whole career." Harrison reckons he had only three bats in his life, all of them 2lb 2oz. "We'd scrub 'em with glass at the beginning of the season to clean 'em up. These days they get through a couple an innings, far as I can tell." And, of course, there were no helmets (after the war, Harrison wore glasses). Following Bodyline, bouncers were not cricket at all, dear me no.

The uncovered wickets were "unplayable, some days", which meant plenty of dreary afternoons hanging about in pavilions waiting for the pitch to dry.

Young driver: Leo Harrison, early in his Hampshire career.

Things that would raise an eyebrow now were less surprising back then. "At Hampshire we had a medium-pacer called Creese," says Manners. "The first thing he did when he came on to bowl was bend down and rub the ball in the dirt."

Harrison relishes the story of a colleague who finally broke his vow of abstinence by paying for the team's wine, and was rewarded next day with a century against Surrey. And Manners, playing for Incogniti, once watched John Badcock edge a ball on to his wicket, only to see it trickle between the stumps – a splendid joke! Fielding was a side issue. "There were many more older players back then," says Manners. "Look at Rhodes. And Hobbs was 42 when he got all those centuries in a season. They were pretty sluggish in the field, some of these fellows. Even the younger ones stopped the ball with their foot sometimes. You don't see that now."

The four Championship innings Manners played in 1936 put him top of the Hampshire averages. The following summer, MCC waived their usual qualification rule to admit him, recognising that it was hard to turn out in Bristol when you were stationed in Madras. It never occurred to him to play as a full-time professional: there was no need. It was easy for talented amateurs to have it all: a distinguished public life and lashings of top-class cricket. A young naval officer such as Manners, fresh out of Dartmouth, could play for MCC, Hampshire and Combined Services, while also enjoying country-house cricket for society XIs.

"It's easy to smile now, but it was marvellous. Two-day games in these wonderful places – like Stansted Park, near Chichester – with great players, a black-tie dinner in the middle, bands playing… You played for fun. Fun and friendliness."

Manners came from what he calls "a family of empire builders" (his father, Sir Errol, was an admiral and a theologian), and by the time he notched that 81 in Portsmouth he had already served on *HMS Hood*. But, when war came, it was still a shock. He was in Singapore, aware that "things were beginning to hot up", and faced a long voyage home. Soon he was on destroyers off Malta, before heading north to escort Arctic convoys out of Scapa Flow – one of the bitterest duties in the war. On one trip, his 43-ship convoy ran into a line of German submarines and a sky full of Luftwaffe bombers: 13 were sunk. "The sky was black with planes," he recalls. "Heinkels and Junkers, about 50 of them, their wingtips almost touching."

It wasn't his only close shave. When he took a day's leave to get married (in St John's Wood church, next to Lord's), his hotel on Hyde Park was hit by a bomb that failed to explode. "We would have been in its crater if it had gone off." By 1943 he was back in the Mediterranean for the invasion of Sicily, launched by the cricket-loving Field Marshal Montgomery with a characteristic speech about "hitting the Germans for six". Manners himself never knew, until the autumn of 2015, that Verity himself perished as a result of wounds sustained in that assault.

> **Manners packed the brandy in a presentation box and sent it to Churchill**

Manners ended the war in command of a destroyer – *HMS Viceroy*. In April 1945, with the Allies closing in on Germany, he was guarding a convoy in the North Sea when sonar picked up an echo; then the *SS Athelduke* was hit. He released his depth charges, jumped when his own ship "leapt a foot or two into the air", and watched as debris from a German submarine came bobbing to the surface. There was a cylinder in the icy waves carrying 72 bottles of brandy, and Manners packed one of them in a presentation box and sent it as a gift to Winston Churchill. His own prize was a Distinguished Service Cross, awarded for "gallantry, determination and skill".

Harrison's war was quieter: he never left Britain. And, though he immediately joined the RAF, he failed the pilot's eyesight test ("I always had trouble with my eyes") and was sent to Slough to train as an engineer. He spent the rest of the war making instruments for Bomber Command. "My shift was 8pm until 8am, which wasn't much good for the eyes either." It is sobering to realise that his endlessly poor sight, though not bad enough to stop his wicketkeeping, probably saved his life.

If he did not see action himself, his work on airbases in East Anglia and Yorkshire brought him achingly close to those who did. "It was awful, awful.

In command: John Manners sails towards a hundred for the Navy at Lord's in 1951. Keeping wicket for a strong Army side – Brian Close hit a century – is the future Test player Keith Andrew.

You see, the air crew were just marvellous. They'd always invite us to their parties and give us their sweet ration – because they were given extra, the flyers. But what could you say? You knew that half of them wouldn't come back, and so did they."

Few modern cricketers can claim to have sunk a submarine or helped build a Lancaster. But the perspective of war work allowed this rare sporting generation to accept the amateur–professional divide with a grace that seems odd now. Hardly anyone could afford to play without being paid, so the status of the amateur was maintained only through a charade of fake jobs and expenses. But no one wanted another fight. "What could you do?" shrugs Harrison. "In the holidays the amateurs would come in and we professionals would have to make way. We didn't like it, but there it was." Manners echoes him: "You look back at the players with their different entrances and changing-rooms, separate travel arrangements and so on, and it seems extraordinary now. But we didn't question it: it was just the way things were."

Arlott regarded Manners as a vivid advert for the role of the amateur, even in the modern game. In the 1990 county yearbook he wrote: "No player in Hampshire's history is more intriguing… not only was he potentially prolific, but his strokeplay was brilliant." He appeared for both the Navy and the Combined Services (scoring 147 against Gloucestershire in 1948), but as a serving officer he was never more than an occasional performer. Fortunately, amateur cricket was still prestigious and serious: thanks to national service, the armed forces were full of top players. "The RAF took the best," he recalls, "so they'd get a shock when they turned up expecting an easy game and ran into Peter May."

As a full-time professional, locked into a game in which only amateurs were felt to have the leadership qualities necessary to captain a side, Harrison could not pick and choose. His father's scrapbook contains a telegram from Lord's in 1955, one of many, which sounds like a military order: "MCC committee invite Harrison replace Evans in Players side Wednesday." The reply, scribbled on the cable sheet, was concise: "Harrison available and honoured play Wednesday." Professionals were expected to jump to it when they were bid.

In Mudeford today, Harrison winces at the thought of that match. "Alec Bedser was bowling and, well, I'd never kept to him before. The first ball swung down the leg side and went for four byes; so did the second. That damned inswinger. I wasn't too popular after that." Of all the world-class batsmen he played against, the one he most admired was May. "He never seemed to get less than a hundred against us. I remember that all right. Sometimes two hundred."

In his final game for Combined Services, in 1953, Manners, a naval officer in his late thirties, was caught by Tom Graveney for 45; barely a week later, representing Free Foresters in the Parks, he came up against another youngster, Colin Cowdrey. Who could have wished for more? He still follows the game on television, marvelling at the quicksilver fielding and lush outfields ("they always seemed to be brown in my day"). But he doesn't wish things had been otherwise: he has had, as the saying goes, a pretty good innings. MCC threw a lunch in honour of his 100th birthday, and his only cricketing regret is that he never came up against Bradman.

Nor did Harrison. "I was supposed to play him at Southampton in 1948. But Desmond Eagar dropped me. They brought in Jack Andrews instead." He still shakes his head at the memory. But, as it turned out, Bradman missed the game too. It is rather a pity the two never met, but pleasant to imagine the affable Harrison whispering to the Don, after yet another hundred before lunch, "It ain't half a bloody game, is it?" – then inviting him to nip over to Mudeford for fish and chips and a pint.

Robert Winder's most recent book is Half-Time: The Glorious Summer of 1939.

REGINA v CAIRNS

The road to hell – paved with scorched reputations

JARED SAVAGE

On a grey, windy morning in late November, Chris Cairns walked out of Southwark Crown Court a free man. Eight weeks after he uttered the words "Not guilty", the foreman of the jury did the same. Cairns had entered court that morning carrying a backpack, just in case he needed to head straight to prison. Now he could take his gear home to his wife, Mel, and their two children in Australia.

Twenty minutes earlier, the significance of those two words had overwhelmed him, though not immediately: the foreman spoke so quietly that Cairns had to rely on the reaction of his friend and co-defendant, Andrew Fitch-Holland, to learn his fate. He patted Fitch-Holland, emotional at his own acquittal, on the back, then sat, briefly, stunned in the dock.

Waiting outside were the press pack. For nearly two months, photographers had captured his lonely arrival at Southwark's drab brick fortress, even his lunch run to Pret A Manger. Now journalists wanted to hear from the man who – for the second time, following a libel case against Lalit Modi more than three years earlier – had emerged victorious from a bruising saga that stretched back to January 2010, when Modi tweeted that Cairns had been involved in corrupt activities during the 2008 Indian Cricket League. "You have to be careful because it's not a victory as such," said Cairns, sensibly avoiding triumphalism. "In a case like this, I really don't think there are any winners. It's been hell for everyone involved."

There were no bitter words for former New Zealand team-mates who had given evidence against him, not even for Lou Vincent or Brendon McCullum, his protégé. Asked what he would say to McCullum, there was a long pause, then a simple "Why?" And with that Cairns was done. As photographers trailed him for one final image, he walked away, smiling. "I'm off for a beer."

At his peak, there was real excitement when Chris Cairns strode to the wicket or was thrown the ball – even if the prosecution's contention that he was "the golden boy… whom every cricketer wanted to emulate" was over-egging it. But when he first entered court on October 5, to defend himself against charges of perjury and perverting the course of justice, the old desire to win must have tugged at him more urgently than ever.

Cairns, the prosecution suggested, was "an arrogant individual and very aware of the power he held over people around him". Yet he was unfailingly polite. He would pause every morning to let the cameramen get their shot, nod to reporters, and hold the door open as a matter of course. But, it was true: he wasn't without ego. With every major news organisation in New Zealand sending someone to cover the case, the trial was a big story back home. Early

Leon Neal, AFP/Getty Images

The accused: Chris Cairns and Andrew Fitch-Holland.

on, Cairns indicated he wasn't following the coverage but, after an article suggested he had "appeared to lose sight of the ball" during a typically testy exchange with Sasha Wass, QC, Cairns joked with the journalist that he would never lose sight of the ball (unless it was pink, since he is colour-blind).

Waiting for him inside Court 1 was the dock – a stark, sterile rectangular glass box – the bubble in which Cairns and Fitch-Holland sat listening, staring, scribbling, sighing. Around them, the arcane machinery of a criminal trial cranked into gear.

The jury of five men and seven women could be forgiven for wondering why they were there: a cricketer from New Zealand answering charges relating to an unofficial tournament in India that had taken place seven years earlier, all being litigated in a windowless bunker by the Thames. Opening the Crown's case, Wass – who in 2014 had successfully prosecuted the entertainer Rolf Harris on charges of indecently assaulting young girls – explained rudimentary elements of the game. It was "played by two teams of 11 players each"; the stumps were "three sticks" at each end of the pitch, with "two small pieces of wood balanced on top called 'bales'" [as the court's official transcription had it]. It was anyone's guess what the jurors were thinking when Vincent and Cairns debated whether a boundary Vincent had scored during an ICL game had come from a thick edge or a late cut.

At times, the language of cricket was used as a comforting metaphor. When Vincent, the Crown's first witness, arrived hand in hand with his wife, Susie, he quipped: "First in to bat. Hope it's a green one." Instead of being dismissed early, however, he was subjected to three days of questioning, during which his life was dissected for the world to see. He claimed Cairns had lured him into the murky world of match-fixing during the ICL. Lies, said Cairns, who countered that Vincent had given the authorities a "big name" simply to escape punishment when he himself had been caught.

The Vincent sideshow was as sad as it was compelling. Fourteen years earlier, he had begun his Test career as one of four centuries in New Zealand's first innings at the WACA. In 2005, he scored 172 from 120 balls against Zimbabwe, breaking Glenn Turner's 30-year-old record for the highest one-day innings by a New Zealander. But, by the end of 2007, his international career was over. For every high, there was a low, his fluctuating form linked to his battles with mental illness. "When everything was good, his cricket was amazing," testified Andre Adams, a close friend and former team-mate. "He was funny, happy and consistent. When things went badly, his cricket went badly. He got into a vicious circle and needed time to get rid of the demons."

Now, Vincent cannot coach even schoolchildren. He was banned for life by the ECB after he admitted fixing county games at Sussex. But he was never investigated by UK police, let alone charged, despite receiving around £120,000 for underperforming. This was a key part of Cairns's defence. Vincent was torturously cross-examined by Orlando Pownall, QC – not just about his match-fixing, but about lying to investigators and having sex in an Indian hotel with a woman provided by a bookmaker as a "gift".

"I was," said Vincent, "a disgraceful human being." On one occasion he left the witness stand in tears, and looked comfortable only when talking about cricket. He explained that the "art of underperforming" was not as easy as it sounded. In fixed games, he claimed his task was to score 10–15 runs off 20 balls, and described his efforts in the final of the ICL World Series in April 2008, when he tried to get out stumped on 17. The plan did not go well. Facing left-arm spinner Ali Murtaza, Vincent charged down the pitch, "but the ball did something funny". He smashed it back over the bowler's head for six. Vincent told the jury: "My heart just raced, how did this happen?" He tried to miss the next ball in the hope of getting bowled; instead, he edged it for four. "I was supposed to get out, I've just hit ten runs, this is a disaster." He ended up scoring 28.

But Pownall suggested the six was a "beaut" ("You bring the bat back and you deliberately smite it"), and the four a classic late cut. Vincent said his "footwork was horrendous". When Pownall disputed this, Vincent drew laughs from the public gallery: "I disagree with your cricket opinion."

Later, Cairns – understandably keen to suggest Vincent had not been involved in any kind of scam – took issue with his assessment of the six as a "fluke". Television footage was played to the jury, and Cairns commentated from the witness box, sometimes unprompted, leaving his lawyer no choice but to cut him off. "I think he came down and gave himself room, did nothing but follow through with the shot," he said of the six. "It was a good shot timed very, very well." The disputed late cut was, said Cairns, "a tough shot which came off the face of the bat". The differing opinions merely illustrated the difficulty the jury faced in deciding whether a player was deliberately underperforming.

Like Vincent, Cairns was most at ease when the subject was cricket. But there were no easy deliveries from Wass, and her first question was a bouncer. Did he agree he was a "most unfortunate individual" to have former team-mates and acquaintances accuse him of match-fixing? When Cairns failed

The witness and the defence: Brendon McCullum and Orlando Pownall.

to answer, she leaned in over the folders stacked at her table and pressed her point. "Because, if you're telling the truth, you've been accused of match-fixing not once, not twice, but on three separate occasions. Do you think it's unlucky to be accused on three separate occasions of something you haven't done?"

Cairns said he was not in the witness box to give his opinion, but to provide evidence and answer questions. "Well, perhaps you'll answer this one," Wass shot back. She pointed out that "perfectly reasonable, sane people" do not make up false allegations without a motive, repeating the question several times, and adding: "Perhaps if you answer the questions rather than think about where they're going."

Their exchanges were feisty: they even sparred over whether the video link, used by some overseas-based witnesses, was of sufficient quality. As theatre, it was gripping. Eventually, Mr Justice Sweeney – a legal heavyweight who had presided over the trials of former MP Chris Huhne and entertainer Rolf Harris – rebuked both: Wass, who successfully prosecuted Harris, should stop dressing up comments as questions, Cairns should answer them. Later, she pushed Cairns about his conversations with McCullum. "Are you referring to his first, second or third statement?" Cairns replied confidently, alluding to discrepancies in the three accounts, spread over three years, that McCullum had given to the ICC's Anti-Corruption Unit and police. Why would McCullum stitch him up? "Brendon is doing what is best for Brendon," said Cairns.

If Vincent was vulnerable, McCullum was not: cricket was the only thing the Crown's two key witnesses had in common. McCullum and Cairns, on the other hand, were almost kindred spirits – aggressive cricketers, forever on the front foot. It was Baz v Cairnsy, and New Zealand fans in flip-flops and All Black jerseys queued up to enjoy the show.

NO WINNERS: TIMELINE OF A TRIAL

Oct 5   Mr Justice Sweeney outlines the case against Chris Cairns and his former legal advisor Andrew Fitch-Holland. Cairns is charged on two counts. The first, perjury, is that he "wilfully made a statement… which he knew to be false, namely that he has 'never, ever cheated at cricket and nor would he ever contemplate such a thing'" during his libel action against Lalit Modi, the former IPL chairman, in 2012. The second, perverting the course of justice – of which Finch-Holland is also accused – is that both men tried to persuade Lou Vincent, the former New Zealand batsman and a confessed match-fixer, to provide false witness statements during the Modi trial.

Oct 12   Vincent testifies that, in 2008, Cairns offered him $US50,000 to underperform while they were team-mates with Chandigarh Lions in the Indian Cricket League. Vincent describes how his depression, specifically the "meltdown" he suffered after being dropped by New Zealand in 2007, made him vulnerable to match-fixing approaches.

Oct 14   According to Vincent, former New Zealand captain Stephen Fleming approached him in a bar and accused him and Cairns of being "dirty".

Oct 15   New Zealand captain Brendon McCullum alleges Cairns asked him to participate in match-fixing on three occasions in 2008: twice in Kolkata, once in Worcester. McCullum did not report the approaches to the ICC until 2011 because he "did not want it to be true". The defence suggest McCullum's three statements (two to the ICC, one to police) had been inconsistent, and that he was trying to protect "Brand McCullum". Asked why he had not come forward with evidence during the Modi trial, McCullum claims it was "not my responsibility".

Oct 16   The court hears evidence via video link from Andre Adams and Kyle Mills, two former New Zealand players. Adams claims Cairns told him corruption in the ICL could not be investigated properly because the tournament had not been sanctioned by the ICC. Mills says McCullum told him in 2009 about Cairns's alleged approaches to him.

Oct 19   Eleanor Riley, Vincent's ex-wife, claims Cairns told her at a bar in Manchester in 2008 that he was "very confident" he could get away with match-fixing as "everyone was doing it in India". Riley stresses her acrimonious divorce from Vincent means she has no motive to lie on his behalf. The defence suggest her testimony is unreliable as she had been drinking heavily at the time of the conversation.

Oct 20   Former Australian captain Ricky Ponting describes how he overheard a phone conversation between McCullum and Cairns during which they discussed a "business proposition".

Oct 21   Sir Ronnie Flanagan, chairman of the ICC's Anti-Corruption Unit, denies the organisation are determined to prosecute a famous player.

Oct 22   Former New Zealand captain Daniel Vettori tells the court he is aware McCullum was approached by Cairns, which he advised McCullum to report. Vettori describes an incident in which he asked Cairns to buy him a $15,000 diamond ring, payment for appearing in an Indian toothpaste commercial, as "fairly innocuous".

Oct 26   Chris Harris, a former New Zealand all-rounder, claims Cairns "almost seemed like he was not pleased" when Chandigarh Lions beat Mumbai Champs in a 2008 ICL game containing "a number of strange incidents".

Oct 28	The jury are played statements made by Cairns to the Metropolitan Police in April and May 2014, in which he reacts angrily to allegations of corruption: "Seriously? These are the accusations in regard to this? I've been fucked over."
Oct 29	Representatives from the Crown Prosecution Service are asked by the defence why criminal charges have not yet been brought against Vincent. Detective chief superintendent Michael Duthie says the police are primarily concerned with investigating the allegations against Cairns; match-fixing issues, he says, are the responsibility of the ECB and the ICC.
Nov 3	Cairns takes the stand, frequently responding with one word when asked if he has ever contemplated or been involved with match-fixing: "No."
Nov 4	The judge warns Cairns to stop "making speeches". He is asked to explain why he received a $250,000 retainer to work for Indian diamond firm Vijay Dimon; Cairns insists his business dealings are legitimate. Asked why the owners of the firm, Vijay and Vishal Shah, had not come forward to testify on his behalf, Cairns says: "I've become rather toxic because of everything that has gone on. I understand why they would not want to come here and be with me."
Nov 5	Via video link, Mel Cairns – Cairns's wife – denies discussing match-fixing with Riley in 2008: "I would never lie to help my husband in court."
Nov 10	Fitch-Holland denies that a recorded Skype conversation between him and Vincent proves he tried to procure a false witness statement at the 2012 libel trial.
Nov 12	The prosecution close their case by calling Cairns the "Lance Armstrong" of cricket. Sasha Wass, QC, claims the defence have failed to establish a credible motive for the willingness of prosecution witnesses to fabricate their statements. There was no reason, she adds, for the ICC to pursue an innocent man, and calls the evidence laid against Cairns "unanswerable."
Nov 16	Defence counsel Orlando Pownall, QC, claims that four prosecution witnesses – McCullum, Vincent, Vettori and Riley – all lied. He argues that Vincent's primary motivation for inventing testimony was to allow him to create publicity for an upcoming book: "We submit the title won't be *The Truth, The Whole Truth, and Nothing But the Truth*." Pownall says cricket's hierarchy decided to target Cairns because they needed "a big scalp".
Nov 17	Pownall says the case against Cairns is built on nothing "beyond rumour" and "self-motivated lies". He highlights apparent inconsistencies in McCullum's testimony, and theorises that McCullum and Vettori could have lied in order to support Modi, supposedly helping them retain their lucrative IPL contracts.
Nov 18	Jonathan Laidlaw, QC, finishes his defence of Fitch-Holland by claiming the prosecution were so focused on Cairns that his client's case has become "a sideshow". The jury, says Laidlaw, are being asked to trust the word of Vincent, a man who had "lied and lied and has literally escaped scot-free".
Nov 20	Mr Justice Sweeney begins his summing up by warning the jury of the "potential danger" of believing the testimony of Vincent, who "might have his own interests to serve in giving evidence".
Nov 23	The jury retire after the judge describes Riley's evidence as "the most important" in the trial, as it emanated directly from an alleged conversation with Cairns.
Nov 30	After 10 hours 17 minutes of deliberation, the jury find Cairns and Fitch-Holland not guilty on all charges.

Compiled by James McCall

"When I grew up watching New Zealand cricket, Chris Cairns was very much a superstar of that team and certainly one of my idols," said McCullum. Normally an assured speaker, he gave evidence which those in the public gallery strained to hear. He was subdued, and never bristled when challenged. He regretted the three-year delay in reporting Cairns's alleged approaches to him in 2008, prompting Pownall to suggest he waited so long because he was unsure what had happened: an innocent conversation was misconstrued and evolved over time, said Pownall, so that McCullum could escape a ban.

"I'm very certain about what happened on those two occasions: Chris Cairns asked me to spot-fix," McCullum replied. "I was scared to come forward to say a guy I looked up to… had asked me to fix a match. There's no reason for me to be here other than to tell the truth. There's no benefit." One final question: Wass asked McCullum whether it had been easy to accuse his former friend. "No." With that, the biggest test of his career was over. McCullum walked out as he came in – looking straight ahead – with Cairns's gaze following him.

For eight weeks, Cairns and Fitch-Holland – who stood accused of trying to persuade Vincent to provide false testimony on Cairns's behalf against Modi – had sat side by side. Cairns's tie came off after the first day, only to return when McCullum and Daniel Vettori gave evidence. That felt significant: the only other time Fitch-Holland claimed he had seen him wearing a tie was in a photograph of the New Zealand team meeting the Queen.

One witness described Fitch-Holland, a 50-year-old barrister, as a "cricket groupie", which irked him. He admitted he had been star-struck when he met Cairns while managing the Lashings exhibition team. But over time they had forged a genuine friendship. Fitch-Holland was a loyal supporter during the 2012 libel case, managing media requests and acting as a go-between in the legal team. This was an unpaid role for "countless hours" of work, although there was an understanding Cairns would reimburse Fitch-Holland's expenses if he won. Despite being awarded £90,000 in damages, Cairns did not repay the £400 Fitch-Holland spent catching the train to London each day for the trial. He wrote an email, with mutual friends copied in, to "shame" him into honouring his promise.

The jury were told they were still friends, but the trial threw up moments of profound awkwardness, not least when Fitch-Holland described Mel Cairns during a police interview played to the court as "a girl who liked bright, shiny things". And Fitch-Holland claimed that a drunken comment ("Oh, he's guilty, Cairnsy's guilty") to Chris Harris, another former New Zealand international who gave evidence, was a reference to his personal life, not match-fixing. "I would have said the only thing Chris Cairns is guilty of is not keeping his trousers zipped up."

The trial did little for the reputation of the ICC's Anti-Corruption Unit, whose chairman, Sir Ronnie Flanagan, grabbed headlines when he compared the grooming tactics of match-fixers to paedophiles. But another key plank of Cairns's defence was an attack on the ACU's reaction when McCullum reported him in February 2011. This was "potentially momentous", said Pownall when questioning John Rhodes, the head of the ACU's Australasian branch. Yet nothing happened. Rhodes, who said he had lost his diary which chronicled the period around McCullum's statement, said his job was to collect information; his bosses then decided what to do. The ICL, he said, was an unsanctioned tournament, outside the ICC's jurisdiction.

Without the powers and tools of police officers, such as wiretaps or search warrants, the ACU investigators rely on players breaking the dressing-room *omertà*. But what potential whistle-blower will now want to step forward, knowing their integrity might be called into question by a QC? And words alone are unlikely to be enough to convince a jury, especially when the evidence is contradictory. One unnamed umpire who had suspicions about Cairns's final ICL game – and was listed as a witness, but never called – gave a sworn statement in which he said Cairns had bowled terribly and been stumped after rushing up the pitch, while Chandigarh team-mate Dinesh Mongia offered up a "silly catch".

The reality, as the defence pointed out after going to the trouble of checking the scorecards, was that Cairns did not bowl during the game in question because of an ankle injury, and was not stumped during the entire tournament; as for Mongia, he had top-scored. The umpire was not lying, said Pownall, but his statement was an illustration of "confirmation bias", in which evidence is embraced without scrutiny. "A mistake has been made," said Pownall. "A telling one. What he saw, never happened."

But while such details bolstered the defence's case, a steer from the judge might have settled matters. In order to convict Cairns of perjury, he said, the jury had to be certain about the evidence of two of the three key Crown witnesses: McCullum, Vincent and his ex-wife Ellie Riley, who had claimed Cairns had told her that "everyone" was match-fixing in India. They were unconvinced.

Outside on the steps, Cairns said he had been "through the mill" and come out the other side, though with his reputation "completely scorched". In a grubby few weeks for cricket, even the victor felt slightly defeated.

Jared Savage is a senior journalist for the New Zealand Herald, *and the only reporter to sit through every day of the trial.*

A HISTORY OF CELEBRATIONS

Champagne moments

JOHN CRACE

It was the image of the summer: Stuart Broad wide-eyed and open-mouthed as Ben Stokes somehow caught Adam Voges at fifth slip on the first morning at Trent Bridge. And it was a celebration like no other.

When a fast bowler takes a wicket these days, the default response is to run joyously into the arms of the keeper and slips, with the option of firing off a few sledges at the departing batsman. But, for a split second, Broad seemed to stop in his tracks, the amazement undisguised; along with everyone else, he had assumed the ball was heading to third man. Professional cricketers like to make out they've seen it all before, that genius is to be taken for granted. But the mask slipped – and Broad became almost childlike.

Most cricket celebrations are lost: there is no visual record of how W. G. Grace acknowledged a century, and such first-hand written accounts as do exist are refracted by the stiltedness of the time. The emphasis is on the effect WG has on the crowd (match reports contain plenty of "cheering"), rather than the man himself.

It makes the odd exception all the more delightful. So when WG scored his 100th hundred in May 1895, his brother EM arrived in the middle with a bottle of champagne. WG was evidently unsated: two hours later, EM returned with another bottle to celebrate the double-hundred. Fortunately for Bristol's champagne supplies, he eventually fell for 288. But, at a time when sportswriters could still describe the action and the atmosphere safe in the knowledge that the story would not be common currency by the time their reports appeared, the very modern impulse to get inside players' minds was all but absent.

With decorum the cricketers' watchword, it was the crowds who continued to express the emotion of the moment. The Bodyline tour of 1932-33 was one of the first for which newsreel footage exists. Watch the highlights, however, and you might struggle to realise this was one of the most ill-tempered series in history. Nor would you have guessed that England's 4–1 victory was the result of Douglas Jardine's meticulous planning. Australian wickets are greeted with nothing more than a gentle stroll towards the bowler, and the occasional gentlemanly shake of the hand. The only hint of menace comes from beyond the boundary.

A revealing loss of self-restraint comes at Lord's in 1948, when Australia won by 409 runs. Each of England's second-innings wickets is greeted by stony faces. But, when the last falls, the veneer cracks. It emerges that the Australians haven't spent their time working out how to dismiss England (like so many over the years, the England batsmen have worked that out for themselves). No, they have been ensuring they are handily placed for the

The spoils of war? "The usual scramble for the stumps and bails... marked the close," said *Wisden* of the final moments of the 1948 Ashes at The Oval. Bill Johnston, who has just had Eric Hollies caught by Arthur Morris, has two, while even the not-out batsman, Jack Young, has one.

memorabilia. When Doug Wright is caught by Ray Lindwall off Ernie Toshack, there is the briefest of pauses to mark the fall of an old enemy – before the Australians make an unholy dash for a souvenir. While four players engage in a scrap for the stumps at one end, a fifth wrestles one out of the umpire's arms at the other.

That followed farcical scenes at Trent Bridge, where Australia's Sid Barnes had nearly reached the pavilion, stump in hand, having made what he thought was the winning run. In fact, the scores were level. When the *coup de grâce* was applied moments later by his partner, Lindsay Hassett, *Wisden* recorded that "another scramble for souvenirs took place; and in this Barnes was unlucky". The authorities soon made sure that such indecorous scenes became a thing of the past.

Even so, the modern fan might be shocked by the lack of emotion at Old Trafford in 1956, when Jim Laker's tenth wicket of Australia's second innings – and 19th of the match – was greeted with something close to sheepishness. As he explained nearly three decades later in *Cricket Contrasts*: "There were no leaps in the air, no embraces, no punching the sky, just a dozen polite handshakes as I slung my sweater over one shoulder and jogged quietly up the pavilion steps." That's how men were back then.

On his way home that evening, Laker stopped in a pub in Lichfield, and bought "a couple of very stale cheese sandwiches" and a beer. He sat quietly at the end of the bar, watching highlights of the day's play on a black and white TV, "listening in fascination to the comments of the other customers". No one congratulated him because no one recognised him. Fast-forward nearly 50 years to the Trafalgar Square celebrations for England's 2005 Ashes winners, and there was no such issue.

It's hard to pick a turning point. Some believe it was the final over of the tied Test between Australia and West Indies at Brisbane in 1960-61. When Richie Benaud was eighth out, caught behind off the second ball of the final over, only wicketkeeper Gerry Alexander looked at all pleased. And when, with Wally Grout pushing for a third run that would have brought Australia victory, Conrad Hunte ran him out, the West Indians made little fuss: Wes Hall returned to his mark as if it was another day at the office. It was only when Joey Solomon ran out Ian Meckiff that bedlam ensured.

It was as if cricket needed a cliffhanger to get the blood pumping. When Fred Trueman became the first bowler to 300 Test wickets, at The Oval in 1964, by having Neil Hawke caught at slip by Colin Cowdrey, the fielder appeared as relieved as the bowler. Trueman was nearing the end of his career, wickets were getting harder to come by, and there would have been hell to pay had he dropped it. As it was, Trueman barely broke stride as he shook the outstretched hand of the outgoing batsman. Truly, another era.

By 1967, when I attended my first Test – against Pakistan at The Oval – celebrations were still on the quiet side of muted. My only memory is of training dad's binoculars on Saeed Ahmed, as his middle stump was sent cartwheeling by Geoff Arnold. I seemed to find the event infinitely more thrilling than Arnold did: I celebrated more extravagantly in my own back garden when I yorked my mother. Maybe it was because I watched more sport on TV than the average professional cricketer. I had seen England win the World Cup at Wembley in 1966, when the near-toothless Nobby Stiles danced his jig. I had seen George Best run to the fans, arms aloft, after scoring wondergoals on *Match of the Day*. This was more my kind of sport, red in tooth and claw. I longed for cricket to catch up.

Too much man-love is too non-cricket, especially in 1970s Australia

It took a while. Cricket, more than most games, is defined by its codes and conventions. No one wanted to break ranks and give full expression to their delight. It was as if some of the freer spirits were secretly hoping a colleague would go wild, so they could follow suit.

Even some of the greatest mavericks of the 1970s kept a lid on it, including Dennis Lillee and Jeff Thomson during their demolition of England. Thomson lazily puts one arm – sometimes two – in the air and walks diffidently towards the slips. Only Rod Marsh looks excited, tucking his knees into his ample stomach as he jumps in the air. Too much man-love is too non-cricket, especially in 1970s Australia.

Nor were the great West Indian pacemen much more expressive. Michael Holding would merely turn to check the umpire had given the correct decision before jogging towards his slip fielders. Joel Garner seldom got round to raising an arm. Perhaps wickets came too easily. The cricket may have been terrifying, but the celebrations were low-key. Pundits liked to call it a sign of respect for opponents, but that was a misguided distortion. You can still respect your opponents and embrace the excitement of the moment: there is no contradiction.

Unusually close encounter: a tired Fred Trueman embraces Colin Cowdrey, at The Oval, 1964.

Central Press/Getty Images

If anything, batsmen were even coyer: a landmark would be greeted with a tip of the cap or, in extremis – such as Geoff Boycott scoring his 100th hundred at Leeds in 1977 – with both arms held aloft. The closest to genuine personality had been Derek Randall doing a cartwheel after taking the winning catch in the same game. "It is something I had been coaxing him to do at some opportune moment throughout the series," said his captain Mike Brearley. "He had been afraid of both the selectors' and the public's opinion but now, at the most opportune time, he had done it." But then over-the-top celebrations can always look premature if you are out shortly afterwards. Far better to keep things understated. And, for years, batsmen had seen themselves as the officer class. It wouldn't do to let oneself go before the bowlers.

Memory is invariably selective and culturally specific: everyone will have their own image of the moment cricket finally gave in to the thrill of the thrill. For me, it was the 1981 Ashes: Bob Willis running round in a – by his standards – delirious little circle after bowling Ray Bright to win at Headingley, and Ian Botham racing down the wicket and pulling out a stump after bowling Terry Alderman to win at Edgbaston. For Indians, the key memory may be when their team beat West Indies to win the 1983 World Cup. Certainly it was in the early 1980s that the dams broke. By now cricket had become a global game, with television highlights available almost anywhere. Celebrations could be seen all over the world as they happened – and copied.

Since then, they've become ever more elaborate. We've had batsmen kissing the turf or the badge on their helmet or the crest on their shirt – although the Australian Doug Bollinger once mistakenly kissed the sponsors' beer logo instead. We've had bowlers submerged in joyous huddles of fist-pumps and high-fives (except South African leg-spinner Imran Tahir, who heads off on a lap of honour). We've had Monty Panesar's ingenuous skips and leaps, and Indian seamer Sreesanth twirling his bat round his head like a cowboy with a lasso after hitting South Africa's Andre Nel for a straight six. And we've even had anti-celebrations, such as Nasser Hussain gesticulating grumpily to the No. 3 on his back in the direction of the Lord's media centre after reaching a

one-day century against India in 2002 (England still lost, so perhaps his critics, who said he was batting too high, were right all along). Cricket is the better for all of them.

The only celebration that feels wrong is the one that seems unnatural. Glenn McGrath's attempt to claw back some credit for the bowlers by holding the ball aloft after taking a five-for felt awkwardly self-conscious. Which is why Broad's reaction was so memorable. Where some victory dances look scripted, his was entirely spontaneous and unrepeatable, an act of accidental creativity that defined a series.

My turn: Glenn McGrath takes a five-for at Brisbane, November 2006.

In the end, though, it's a matter of taste. My own favourite is the sight of the Bermudian Dwayne Leverock catching India's Robin Uthappa during the 2007 World Cup in the West Indies. Leverock was about 20 stone, mostly made up of fat. He was almost certainly fielding at slip only because he would have been a liability anywhere else. Early in the innings, Uthappa got a thick edge, and Leverock dived horizontally to his right to pull off a remarkable airborne catch. He didn't know what to do with himself, running first towards fine leg, then third man, before coming to a halt, presumably exhausted. This was the victory of the common man, for all those of us who are the wrong shape and a bit useless yet still turn out every week for club sides. It was the celebration that fulfilled cricket's ultimate promise, that every dog can have his day.

John Crace is the parliamentary sketchwriter for The Guardian *and author of the Digested Read column. He is a regular contributor to* The Nightwatchman.

DEATHS IN CRICKET

More dangerous than we knew

ANDY BULL

Around 3pm on Tuesday, November 25, 2014, Dr Peter Brukner left a meeting in downtown Melbourne. He checked his phone, which had been set to silent. A message from his son in New York: "What's happened to Phil Hughes? Doesn't sound good." Alarmed, Brukner flicked over to Twitter and thumbed through his timeline. One phrase leapt out at him from the many he saw: "Mouth-to-mouth resuscitation". Brukner swore to himself. Then he drove to the airport. On the way he called his employers, Cricket Australia, and asked them to book him on the next flight to Sydney. A little over two hours later, he arrived at St Vincent's Hospital in Darlinghurst, where Hughes was in the operating theatre, undergoing emergency surgery to relieve the swelling on his brain.

Brukner has worked in Aussie Rules, and with Australian national teams in athletics, swimming, hockey and football, and been head of sports medicine at Liverpool FC. In all that time, in all those sports, he had never lost an athlete or player to an on-field injury – but at lunchtime the next day, the hospital staff told him there was nothing more they could do. Brukner's training helped him push his shock aside. When Hughes's team-mates started to arrive, he organised their trips to his bedside, two-by-two. Hughes was unconscious, covered in tubes, wires, and bandages. Brukner saw how hard it hit the players. "A lot of them had never been in the intensive unit of a hospital before, had never seen anyone dying, or brain dead, let alone their own mate."

On Thursday afternoon, Brukner took part in CA's press conference. He was keen to talk. He wanted to explain what had happened, in layman's terms. The ball had hit Hughes's vertebral artery, which had split, flooding his brain with blood, and causing a subarachnoid haemorrhage. The specialists at St Vincent's had known similar wounds to be caused by car crashes and street fights, but never by a blow on a cricket field. And this was the point Brukner wanted to make to the watching world. "I wanted to emphasise how freakish it was, because I was worried people would be too terrified to play cricket. I wanted to reassure everyone that they, their sons and daughters were not at risk of dying the next time they picked up a bat and ball. I felt that was really important."

After the press conference, Brukner's memories get blurry. Everyone went to the SCG, where the bar was opened. "All the cricket family were there having a drink." One of the Australian Test players told him: "Doc, look, you've got to keep telling us this is rare, that it's not going to happen to us, otherwise we can't go out there." As team doctor, Brukner's duty now was to the other players, to try to help them cope. And so this became his message, repeated over and over in the next few days. Even then, he could see how they

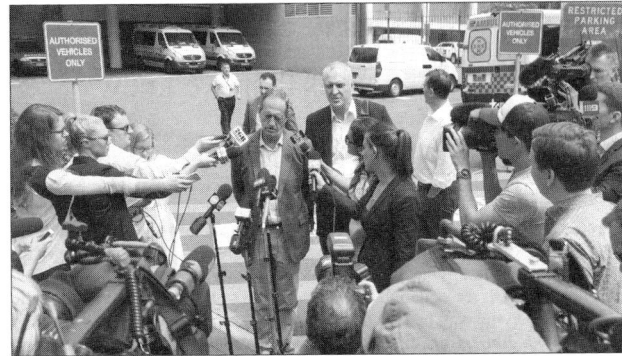

Dr Peter Brukner gives an update on the condition of Phillip Hughes, outside St Vincent's Hospital in Sydney, November 26, 2014.

struggled in the run-up to the First Test against India, which had been postponed until December 9 in Adelaide. In the nets, "some of them went in for three balls and walked out again. They just couldn't face it, couldn't do it, it was just so raw." Brukner thought there was no way they would be ready for the Test.

It was only later, once the game was over and Australia had won, that Brukner began to think again about what had happened. "Maybe cricket lost its innocence," he says. "I suppose we're better able to cope with [Aussie Rules] footballers dying in collisions and things like that, but cricketers, they're not supposed to die." But they do. Two days after Hughes's death there was another, when Hillel Awasker, an umpire, was struck on the jaw by a ball during a league match in Israel, and died of a suspected heart attack. Around the world, there have been at least a dozen deaths from injuries sustained while playing cricket in the last decade, and most likely more. It is impossible to be sure: while cricket keeps assiduous records of all manner of trivial statistics, there is no list of fatalities.

The records are piecemeal, and have to be pulled together from internet searches, newspaper archives and reference books. Even so, a pattern quickly emerges. In 1967, Patrick Turpie, 17, died in Sydney after being hit on the heart while batting. The coroner said it was "a million-to-one chance". In 1975, Martin Bedkober, 22, died in Brisbane in similar circumstances; the doctor called it a "freak accident". In 1991, Daniel Brown, 13, was killed in Norfolk by a short ball that hit him on the neck. This time the coroner said it was "a million-to-one fluke".

Given how many games are played each day, in gardens, streets, fields, grounds and stadia around the world, deaths obviously are rare. But how many times can they be described as "a million to one" before we question whether those odds are wrong? If we don't know exactly how many deaths there have been, how can we quantify the risk? And, if we don't know what caused them, how can we try to stop them from happening again?

Brukner decided to put together a database recording the fatalities – a simple idea, which, it soon became apparent, would be complicated to realise. Brukner worked with Tom Gara, an amateur cricketer, professional historian and expert researcher. Gara started by combing through local newspaper archives in England and Australia. A major problem was that – for complex copyright reasons – there are few digital newspaper archives for periods *later* than the mid-1950s, oddly making it easier to collect information for the first half of the 20th century than the second. Nor did Gara have access to equivalent archives in other countries, such as India, Pakistan, Bangladesh and Sri Lanka. Brukner, whose work is being supported by Cricket Australia, is still investigating deaths since 1950, and is also hoping to find research partners in other countries.

Still, thanks to Gara's hard work, Brukner was able to compile a list of deaths that had occurred in England, Australia and New Zealand between 1850 and 1950. The headline finding is that cricket is – or certainly was – a more dangerous game than many believe. In that 100-year period, there were at least 358 cricket-related deaths in Great Britain and Ireland, 131 in Australia, and 17 in New Zealand. That's a total of 506, and an average of around five a year, though the frequency has ebbed and flowed. There is a noticeable spike in the mid-1930s, for instance, possibly because bowlers were trying their hand at Bodyline: there were 18 deaths in England in 1933–35, eight of them firmly identified as being caused by batsmen being hit on the head or heart by short balls.

Many of the 358 known deaths in Britain and Ireland, it should be said, came about in ways which needn't cause so much concern today. A large number were from sepsis or tetanus, as wounds and cuts suffered while playing became infected and went untreated. A smaller number died in less conventional circumstances. In 1921, two gunmen attacked a match between the Gentlemen of Ireland and the Military of Ireland at Trinity College in Dublin. The men, IRA members, fired shots through the railings on Nassau Street. While the players, "realising what was happening, threw themselves flat on the field", the spectators were not so quick to duck. Kathleen Wright, 21, was hit in the back, and died on the way to hospital.

In 1943 nine boys were killed during a match at Downside School in Somerset, when a Hawker Hurricane fighter making a low pass over the ground clipped a tree and nosedived into the outfield. The debris flew into the crowd on a grass embankment. A year earlier, a corporal in the Royal Army Medical Corps, C. J. Harris, was killed when nine German aeroplanes made a surprise attack on a match between the local police and an Army XI on the south-east coast. Harris was apparently "killed while fielding the ball", as he "ran straight into the path of a falling bomb, which hit the ground only a few yards from the pitch".

Bombs and bullets aside, there are a surprising variety of hazards at your average ground. At least seven children were killed in accidents involving pitch rollers. At least six men were struck by lightning. Four were killed trying

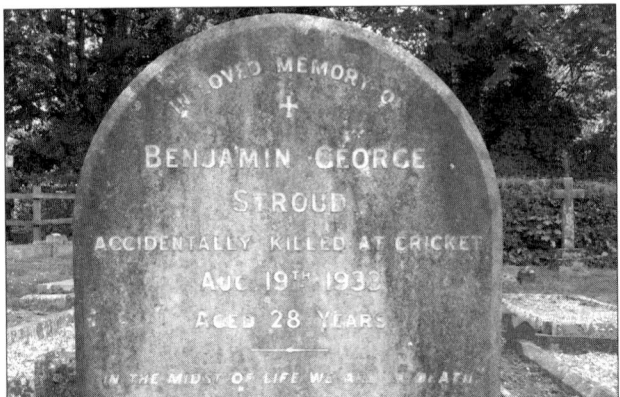

A grave in Weston Patrick, Hampshire, records that 28-year-old Benjamin Stroud was "accidentally killed at cricket". Playing for nearby Upton Grey in August 1933, he was hit on the neck after his partner middled a straight-drive, and pronounced dead 45 minutes later.

to retrieve balls, three climbing high fences, the other hit by a train as he ran across the tracks. Two died fighting fellow players, who hit them with their bats. In both cases, the assailants were tried for manslaughter – and acquitted. And, in 1881, a spectator named Clements died after a replacement stump was thrown on to the field and pierced his skull. Gara and Brukner decided not to include the case of an umpire who, in 1904, died after he tripped down a staircase while sneaking into the cellar beneath the pavilion to fetch a beer at lunch.

The vast majority of deaths were caused by balls bowled, thrown, or struck, in a match or at practice, the victims a mix of batsmen, bowlers, fielders, umpires, spectators, and passers-by. From Albert Judd (1894), hit on the back of the neck after a fielder threw the ball up in celebration of a catch; through Seward Biffen (1914), struck on the head while stooping to tie his shoelaces during batting practice; to George Dodman (1919), who was hit on the chest while keeping wicket, went home sick, then returned to take part in a 500-yard walking race. He collapsed and died at the finish line.

As diverse as the circumstances were, the causes of death tended to be one of three: a blow to the head, causing delayed death in the hours or days after the match; a blow to the neck, causing a brain haemorrhage; or a blow to the heart, triggering a condition known as *commotio cordis*.

This last seems almost impossible to guard against. "It is all about being hit over the heart at a particular moment in the cycle of the heartbeat," Brukner explains. "If you get hit in that thousandth of a second, you can go into cardiac arrest." Research done in baseball has shown that chest protection doesn't necessarily prevent it. Brukner estimates that "it probably happens once a year around the world somewhere in cricket". The data concerning deaths from 1950 onwards is incomplete, but Brukner says: "Before the introduction of helmets the vast majority were from head injuries. After helmets, head injuries became relatively rare, and there were probably more deaths from vertebral artery injuries than we realised. Now you would probably argue that the hit over the heart is the most common cause of death."

Of the 358 deaths in Britain and Ireland between 1850 and 1950, around 20 are likely to have been caused by vertebral artery dissection, the injury which killed Hughes. There have certainly been more cases in the years since, though it's unclear exactly how many. Brukner hopes and believes these deaths will become rarer in the future, now that helmet manufacturers have started providing stem guards to protect the back of the neck. "It amazes me that everyone isn't using them already," he says.

The former Australian opener Chris Rogers was one of the first players to make the transition. Then, in the Lord's Test last summer, he was hit by a short ball from Jimmy Anderson. He turned and ducked, and was caught just behind his right ear – flush on the stem guard. "He was one of the few players at the time wearing it," Brukner says, "and we both said to each other afterwards, if he hadn't been wearing it, who knows what would have happened?"

What we do now know is that the risks involved in cricket are greater than we imagined, and have tended to be underplayed. In 2015, there were more fatalities. Bavalan Pathmanathan, 24, died after being struck on the heart while batting in a club match in Surrey. Vamshi Krishna, aged only six, died after being hit on the chest while fielding close in during a playground game in Hyderabad. Soon after, also in Hyderabad, 31-year-old Saba Tasleem was killed by a ball that hit her on the temple as she was drying clothes at her home near a gully game. Surprise no longer seems the appropriate emotion. Better, instead, to follow Brukner's lead, and start figuring what more can be done.

Andy Bull is a senior sportswriter at The Guardian.

TWENTY YEARS OF THE ECB

A whole new board game

SIMON BRIGGS

Lord's had never heard anything like it. Neither had the residents of St John's Wood. On June 29, 2000, windows around the ground rattled to the beat of a Jamaican reggae band named Third World, who had set up stage to provide lunchtime entertainment on the first day of the Second Test against West Indies. The noise sent a group of MCC traditionalists retreating into their private box, where they were quickly startled a second time: Lord MacLaurin, the most powerful man in the English game, was banging on the window. "Gentlemen! You have just closed the door on the future of English cricket!"

Change was afoot. The previous year, Channel 4's giant billboards had proclaimed: "Cricket just got better." The counties were embarking on the first summer of a two-division Championship, and England's players on their first central contracts. Construction would soon be under way on the National Academy at Loughborough University, there was a new focus on participation for women and the disabled, and in 2001 marketing man Stuart Robertson launched an expensive survey of consumer habits that would lead to the creation of Twenty20.

Cricket – that most cobwebby and cautious of sports – was finally beginning to modernise. And if Channel 4's arrival as host broadcaster provided a more youthful and dynamic face, the roots of change could be traced back to a more traditional milieu: a committee room in the Lord's Pavilion. It was here, in 1994, after MCC had gathered the great and the good to consider cricket's governance, that the England and Wales Cricket Board was conceived.

Judging from their report, the 12 members of the Griffiths Working Party felt misgivings about the beast they were about to unleash: the untrammelled force of sporting capitalism. (The report expresses concern at the prospect of "some vast and ever-growing central bureaucracy".) Yet this was unquestionably the time for change, with the imminent arrival of the National Lottery promising direct funding for grassroots sport. The old division of cricket's governance into the professional body (the Test and County Cricket Board) and the amateur one (the National Cricket Association) could no be sustained.

MCC's jury recommended a new overarching governing body: the BCBC or British Cricket Board of Control. After a three-year gestation period, we ended up instead with the ECB. Despite the best efforts of Glamorgan chairman David Morgan, instrumental in setting up the new board, "W" never made it into the abbreviation. The official birthday was January 1, 1997, and the original management team were led by chief executive Tim Lamb – a former Middlesex and Northamptonshire seamer who had gone on to work for the TCCB – and chairman Ian MacLaurin, the man credited with turning Tesco

Window dresser: Lord MacLaurin introduces MCC to the brave new world of marketing.

into a high-street giant. So, as the 20th anniversary approaches, it is time for cricket to paraphrase *Monty Python*: "What have the ECB ever done for us?"

It would be wrong to portray the TCCB as sleepy old duffers, even if they were a cottage industry with barely more than a dozen employees. After all, they brought in some far-reaching changes of their own: the first Sky deal, Sunday play in Tests, and cheap Kwik Cricket sets for primary schools. Yet MacLaurin's recollection of what he encountered in 1997 is a damning "no money and a shambles". He was especially horrified by the England team, described by one former captain as "a bunch of raggy-arsed rangers". The players would drive to a home Test on Tuesday night, put in a weary net session on Wednesday, and take the field on Thursday in an assorted mismatch of kit. As Lamb wryly points out: "Ian was very hot on getting the shop window right, which meant the dressing of the grounds, the corporate branding, the whole look and feel of the game."

MacLaurin says now: "The national team were ranked eighth in the world. It was Tetley Bitter hats, and white and pink helmets – no discipline at all. It was quite sad in some ways, but we ditched the MCC colours and the hat with St George and the dragon – a tradition for many years – and replaced everything with three lions and a coronet. It caused a few ruffles with MCC."

What struck the players was the immediate improvement in their living conditions, in particular the end of another tradition: room-sharing on tour. "MacLaurin came in from more of a business angle," says Nasser Hussain, who became England captain in 1999. "His stance was: 'Would you ask two businessmen on a foreign assignment to share a room?' It was give and take: he expected us to be clean-shaven and look smart. But he was very good with the families, booked everyone business-class travel, and treated us like grown-ups."

Not everything clicked. England got worse before they got better, slipping to last in the new Wisden Test rankings after losing at home to New Zealand in 1999. And the World Cup organised by the ECB that same summer was handicapped by a risible opening ceremony and a rumbling pay dispute between the board and the players that contributed to England's hapless exit at the pool stage.

POWER PEOPLE

The men in charge of the ECB since its inception:

Chairman		*Chief executive*	
1997–2002	Lord MacLaurin	1997–2004	Tim Lamb
2003–07	David Morgan	2005–14	David Collier
2007–15	Giles Clarke*	2014	Brian Havill†
2015–	Colin Graves	2015–	Tom Harrison

*   *Clarke took up the new post of president in 2015.*
†   *Interim chief executive.*

But Hussain's fiery attitude – complemented by Duncan Fletcher's coolly analytical coaching – provided a rallying point. And central contracts were a game-changer. "Before they came in, I felt like an Essex player called up for England," says Hussain. "Afterwards, the priorities were reversed. Bowlers of the mid-1990s like Devon Malcolm and Angus Fraser would have played twice as many Tests if they had come along just that little bit later."

If England's performances picked up, however, peaking with the glory of the 2005 Ashes, a significant opportunity was missed behind the scenes. In 2002, MacLaurin visited the 18 county chairmen to explain that he would happily serve another three years. There was a caveat: they had to welcome several non-executive directors from outside cricket on to the ECB's cumbersome 15-man board. He received two letters of support: MacLaurin walked.

This classic piece of sporting parochialism attracted some caustic comment. In hindsight, it looks even worse. Here was the ECB's chance to move closer to the enlightened model set up by New Zealand in the mid-1990s – a board equipped with five business brains and two former Test cricketers, so that self-interest would not be the guiding principle. But the counties protected their own, and set the tone for a more inward-looking ECB, in which balancing the books often seemed to take priority over the sport's public projection.

The five years Morgan spent as ECB chairman were hardly uneventful, despite his emollient style. He fought an interminable battle over Zimbabwe, rooted in the Labour government's distaste for Robert Mugabe, which played havoc with the 2003 World Cup. Yet there was one moment, early in Morgan's reign, that is now remembered above all else. The deal to give all England's

Head honchos: Giles Clarke and David Collier, June 2013.

live TV rights to Sky, struck in 2004, is often placed at the door of Giles Clarke, who led the negotiations as chair of the ECB's marketing committee. Yet, despite the subsequent bellyaching, it is hard to see what else Clarke could have done. The BBC's daytime schedules had closed over since Channel 4 poached Test cricket in 1999, with *Cash in the Attic* earning bigger audiences than Test matches ever had. And Channel 4's bid of £54m for four years was only £2m higher than their offer for the same timespan in 1998. Sky went in with £220m.

The hidden costs were harder to judge. Channel 4 usually drew a little over a million viewers to their live coverage, and – on average – twice that for the 2005 Ashes. Sky's audiences were around 250,000. The radical solution would have been for the game to swallow the financial hit and reform itself in a leaner model, with fewer first-class counties. But business realpolitik held sway and, after the glorious Oval Test of 2005, the paywall fell on English cricket.

Some would argue it has never been the same since. "It's definitely sad," says MacLaurin. "If I'd been there, I would have taken a lot of persuading. We've got what we've got." Lamb, meanwhile, concedes there had been some form of gentleman's agreement with culture secretary Chris Smith not to take cricket off terrestrial TV, but says it would have been unfair to bind their successors to it. "Come 2004," he added, "the world was a very different place. Channel 4 made it clear there was not another penny on the table. But critics said we reneged on our promise."

In September 2007, the Clarke era got under way in earnest, when he replaced Morgan. Here was a character who could have been created by Dickens, with his penchant for outlandish suits and habit of dismissing challengers with a sneer. Not everyone warmed to him. In a powerful column in the *Daily Telegraph* last year, Simon Heffer wrote that Clarke displayed "the arrogant, patronising, utter lack of self-awareness one normally associates with the unpleasantly stupid: yet he is an Oxford man and a successful businessman, so has clearly had to work at cultivating this persona".

Together with his trusted chief executive David Collier (who succeeded Lamb in 2005), Clarke governed with one and a half eyes on his electorate – the first-class counties, especially the smaller ones – and seemed to have little concern for views beyond the parish boundaries. Even his opponents, and there were plenty, admit he was devilishly good at it. "Giles always got the conclusion he wanted and managed to make it seem consensual," said one former county chief executive. "His agenda was all about financial imperatives, keeping the counties alive. He was very clever at making sure he kept at least ten of the 18 onside, and was re-elected twice on that platform. Plus, some people became too scared to vote against him. They feared he wouldn't give them a winter cash-flow loan or an international match."

Almost everything in Clarke's eight-year reign can be traced back to this logic. He recoiled instinctively from the Indian Premier League (because it threatened to steal marquee names away from the start of the home summer), and did his best to smother suggestions that a franchise-based Twenty20 competition might work in England (this would have antagonised the smaller counties). Then, in an attempt to mollify the England players who had missed out on the Indian gold rush, he signed up for the ill-fated Stanford Super Series.

The bad smell of that shocking misjudgment lingered

Clarke never fully recovered from the day the Texan fraudster Allen Stanford landed a helicopter at Lord's and unloaded a giant Perspex box of fake cash, though he brazened his way through the ensuing humiliation of Stanford's collapsed Ponzi scheme. But the bad smell of that shocking misjudgment lingered. When England imploded during the 2013-14 Ashes, prompting the sacking of Kevin Pietersen, it felt like a tipping point. The word "toxic" began to attach itself to the ECB.

Yet, while Clarke's chairmanship ended in May 2015, he did not go away. A new position – ECB president – was created so he could continue to patrol the corridors of the International Cricket Council's headquarters in Dubai. And he has always had his supporters among the counties. "In terms of value, income, profitability, he has transformed the ECB," said the former Essex chairman, Nigel Hilliard. "England also went to No. 1 in the world in both Test and limited-overs formats. Over seven years he has faced one problem after another, and not always handled them well. He can be a bull in a china shop. But after the Stanford affair, Rod Bransgrove [the Hampshire chairman] was the only one calling for his demise. Who wants to do the job? It's an unpaid position."

Hilliard is not quite right: Leicestershire chairman Neil Davidson was even more outspoken than Bransgrove. "In any normal organisation," Davidson said, "the chairman's position would be untenable in these circumstances." But then the ECB are not a normal organisation, equipped as they are with a constitution that demands a two-thirds majority for any structural change. Should we be surprised that the dynamism of the early 2000s has slipped back into something more ambiguous.

Since January 1, 1997, the ECB's chairmen have largely been go-getting sharp-eyed business types. Together, they brought a slickness to the presentation of elite cricket, and an expertise at milking it for revenue. Yet a large part of the original intention had been to better the circumstances of local clubs and everyday players. On that front, it is difficult to discern any radical impact. It is true that the finance department can boast a turnover of around £150m – five times what MacLaurin and Lamb inherited in 1997. What, though, has happened to the soul of the game? Where is the connection with the public? Participation levels stood at a record low in the last national survey. Many would argue that the new body's early promise, so vigorously expressed in that reggae concert at Lord's, has been squandered in the headlong pursuit of cash.

Since May 2015, the ECB have reverted to a familiar-looking combination: Colin Graves is a chairman who once ran a major supermarket (Costcutter), and Tom Harrison a chief executive who once played professional cricket. Can this combination of business acumen and sporting experience, not seen since MacLaurin and Lamb, restore some of the lost faith?

The early signals have been encouraging. County chairmen report a more consensual style of government, despite familiar misgivings in late 2015 about ECB proposals to limit the number of county representatives on their executive board to just one. Meanwhile Matt Dwyer – the new director of participation and growth – has launched what reporter David Hopps called the "most coherent, ambitious, self-aware proposals I have seen in more than 30 years covering English cricket," including a greater focus on juniors, and an insistence that matches be played earlier in the day.

Bransgrove is among those who believe the ECB are entering a brave new era – even if the next five years are unlikely to prove as eventful as MacLaurin's tenure. "I read somewhere that every organisation and corporation will start to assume the characteristics of the man at the top," he said. "Kevin Pietersen spoke of a culture of bullying within the England team and perhaps that trickled all the way down. But I feel the game is in a better state now, and I am excited about the new administration. There is a lot of healing to be done."

Simon Briggs writes on cricket and tennis for the Daily Telegraph.

THE LEADING CRICKETER IN THE WORLD IN 2015

Kane Williamson

Kane Williamson ended the Test year as he began it – with a century at home against Sri Lanka. In between his 242 at Wellington in January and his 108 at Hamilton in December, both unbeaten, he confirmed himself as one of the talents of his generation, a No. 3 who combined an aesthete's technique with a glutton's appetite. The sight of Williamson modestly raising his bat to acknowledge another landmark became uncannily familiar.

Others hit the ball harder (David Warner) or in more places (A. B. de Villiers) or even in stranger places (Steve Smith); others shone in marquee series (Joe Root) or bloody-mindedly proved points (Alastair Cook and Younis Khan). But Williamson floated serenely along, an advert for elegant under-statement in a New Zealand team who could hardly believe their luck.

By Christmas, Brendon McCullum – who watched his national record for most Test runs in a year (1,164 in 2014) fall to his young team-mate – had made up his mind. "He's a genius," he said. "He's going to hate me saying it, but he's No. 1 in the world. He's a consummate professional, he's a champion fella and he's only 25. He's going to be one of the best players the game has ever seen." When McCullum announced he would be calling it a day in early 2016, the captaincy for the World Twenty20 passed inevitably to Williamson.

Only four men finished 2015 with more Test runs than his 1,172 at 90, but all four – Smith, Root, Cook and Warner – enjoyed at least eight more innings. And only team-mate Martin Guptill scored more one-day international runs than his 1,376 at 57. Williamson, however, was alone in reaching four figures in both formats, and his overall international tally was an eye-watering 2,692 – a full 323 ahead of second-placed Smith, and the third-highest annual total of all time. No matter how tightly opposition captains packed the off side, Williamson seemed to find a way through.

There were eight hundreds, 14 fifties, 309 fours and – as if to surprise those who might have been blinded by his orthodoxy – 14 sixes. If there was room for improvement – he was out five times in the nineties – then it merely underlined how prolific he had become.

THE LEADING CRICKETER IN THE WORLD 2003–15

2003	R. T. Ponting (Australia)	2010	S. R. Tendulkar (India)
2004	S. K. Warne (Australia)	2011	K. C. Sangakkara (Sri Lanka)
2005	A. Flintoff (England)	2012	M. J. Clarke (Australia)
2006	M. Muralitharan (Sri Lanka)	2013	D. W. Steyn (South Africa)
2007	J. H. Kallis (South Africa)	2014	K. C. Sangakkara (Sri Lanka)
2008	V. Sehwag (India)	**2015**	**K. S. Williamson (New Zealand)**
2009	V. Sehwag (India)		

A list of notional past winners from 1900 appeared in Wisden 2007, *page 32.*

FIVE CRICKETERS OF THE YEAR, AND THE LEADING CRICKETER IN THE WORLD   Kane Williamson.

FIVE CRICKETERS OF THE YEAR   Jonny Bairstow.

FIVE CRICKETERS OF THE YEAR   Brendon McCullum.

FIVE CRICKETERS OF THE YEAR   Steve Smith.

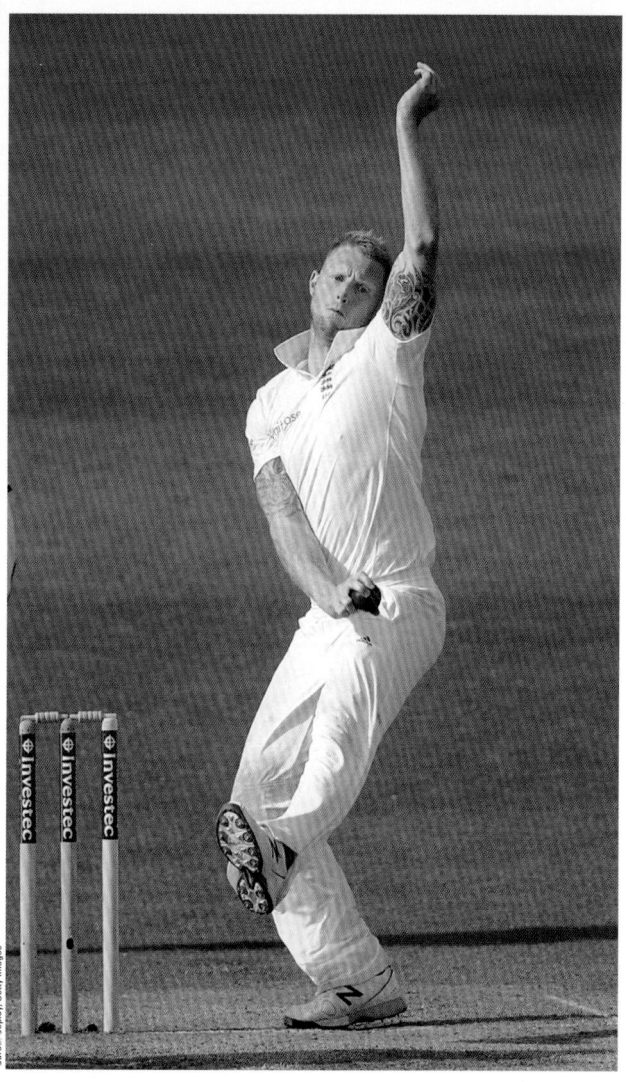

FIVE CRICKETERS OF THE YEAR   Ben Stokes.

Gareth Copley, Getty Images

Julian Finney, Getty Images

THE LONG AND THE SHORT OF IT   In Abu Dhabi, Pakistan's Mohammad Irfan dwarfs England's James Taylor; in Cape Town, Chris Morris towers over Temba Bavuma. Meanwhile, at Derby, Kent's Daniel Bell-Drummond makes his ground by the skin of his teeth.

David O Man

COME AGAIN ANOTHER DAY... Workington CC's ground was one of several in the North-West to be flooded in December. When Napoleon was exiled to St Helena, he complained about the climate; cricketers at Francis Plain may be about to share his view.

ASHES TO ASHES, DUST TO DUST   England celebrate victory at Trent Bridge in August. Outside Calais, a team of refugees line up for a game against a side visiting from across the Channel, who also brought aid and supplies.

FIVE CRICKETERS OF THE YEAR

The Five Cricketers of the Year represent a tradition that dates back in Wisden *to 1889, making this the oldest individual award in cricket. The Five are picked by the editor, and the selection is based, primarily but not exclusively, on the players' influence on the previous English season. No one can be chosen more than once. A list of all Cricketers of the Year appears on page 1482.*

Jonny Bairstow

Simon Wilde

Jonny Bairstow was a good man for a crisis in 2015. All five of his Championship centuries for title-winners Yorkshire were carved from adversity after he strutted out, gimlet-eyed, at No. 5. So was his bristling unbeaten 83 off 60 balls to carry England over the line in the deciding one-day international against New Zealand in Durham, after he had arrived late the previous night as a replacement for the injured Jos Buttler. The strife on that occasion had been particularly deep: 40 for four when he reached the crease soon became 45 for five, at which point the requirement was 147 off 107 balls. England got home with an over to spare. The sight of Bairstow throwing his arms aloft in celebration was one of the images of the summer.

Three weeks later, his 74 in the Ashes-clinching Fourth Test at Nottingham had a different context. With Australia out before lunch for 60, England were hardly in difficulty at 96 for three when Bairstow joined fellow Yorkshireman Joe Root. But someone had to show batting was possible on a Trent Bridge greentop, and Bairstow needed to justify his recent return to the Test side after an absence of more than 18 months. In the previous match, at Edgbaston, his comeback had been nipped in the bud by a Mitchell Johnson ripsnorter. By the time he fell to Josh Hazlewood in Nottingham, he and Root had added 173 – and the Ashes were as good as England's.

JONATHAN MARC BAIRSTOW, born in Bradford on September 26, 1989, is never happier than in the midst of the action. At St Peter's, York, he juggled Yorkshire age-group cricket with county rugby and hockey, as well as football at Leeds United's Academy. And, in 2007, he was *Wisden's* inaugural Schools Cricketer of the Year, after averaging 218 (not to mention captaining the side, keeping wicket and bowling a bit of off-spin). "Fly-half in rugby, centre-mid in hockey, right-back in football, keeping wicket – you've got to be in the thick of it," he says. "I like those pressure situations. It has helped me develop into an all-round athlete, and led to the position I'm in now."

His first appearances for county and country were typical. Summoned as a teenager for a Championship match against Somerset in 2009, he gave Yorkshire a chance of victory with an unbeaten second-innings 82 before running out of partners; he then took four catches as stand-in keeper. Bairstow took the gloves in the next three games, until Gerard Brophy recovered from injury, and played the rest of the season as a batsman. Two years later, on his England debut in a one-day international against India, he slog-swept his fifth ball for six, hit two more out of Sophia Gardens, and turned a stiff chase into a stroll in the park.

Bairstow sometimes found squad selection as reserve keeper and spare batsman easier than getting into the England team and staying there. His first 21 Test caps spanned ten series – "It's been very disjointed" – and he spent much of the build-up to the 2013 Ashes carrying drinks at the Champions Trophy. That winter, he had little meaningful preparation before being thrust in as keeper for the final two Tests of a chaotic tour of Australia. Last May, he joined Yorkshire after four weeks with England in the Caribbean where he did little besides netting. But he hit the ground running – and kept running. If he felt frustration, he channelled it well.

By the end of the summer, Bairstow had scored 1,108 Championship runs at 92, with a strike-rate of 76. Six men scored more heavily in Division One, but from roughly twice as many innings as Bairstow's 15. An unbeaten 219 at Chester-le-Street – where he added an English-record 366 for the seventh wicket with Tim Bresnan – was especially brutal. But his undefeated 125 out of 229 against Middlesex at Headingley, and 108 out of 213 against Warwickshire at Edgbaston underlined his importance to Yorkshire's cause. All his five hundreds for them led to victories.

It was not that England had ignored his talent. His innings of 95 and 54 against a potent South Africa pace attack at Lord's in 2012, when he replaced the suspended Kevin Pietersen, ought to have been a defining moment. It certainly scotched suspicions from earlier in the summer that Kemar Roach of West Indies had exposed a flaw against the short ball. "I was more gutted to get out in the second innings than the first," he said of England's spirited pursuit of 346 against the South Africans, "because I thought I had a chance of chasing down the runs. I don't go looking to counter-attack, but if you stay positive you'll get balls to hit." Come the next Test, in Ahmedabad, however, he was jettisoned to accommodate an extra spinner.

Yorkshire have viewed him as their first-choice wicketkeeper across all formats since 2012, but England seemed unsure how to use him. "Keeping wicket is something I love doing and have worked ridiculously hard on," he says. "People keep asking if I want to do it. It feels like an insult. Of course I do. I wouldn't have invested so many hours, and put myself through so much pain, if I didn't." Inevitably his ability came into question when stumping chances went begging at Sharjah (expensively) and Durban (less so), but few Test keepers can claim perfection in their early outings.

Then, after 36 Test innings without a hundred – a sequence that he admits made him fret "a little" – he hit a sparkling unbeaten 150 from just 191 balls in January 2016 at Cape Town, sharing a world-record sixth-wicket stand of 399 with Ben Stokes. The emotion on show as he reached three figures with an off-side carve for four off Stiaan van Zyl had been bubbling under for too many years.

Bairstow was only eight when he found his father, David, hanging at their family home, a suicide brought on by financial worries and depression. His mother, Janet, herself seriously ill at the time, packed him and his sister Becky off to school next day. Life had to go on. "It was not the best time," he says. "It's something that develops you into the people you are. Massive credit has to go to the family – mum, grandma, grandpa and uncle Andrew [Jonny's elder half-brother, who kept wicket briefly for Derbyshire]. We're only a small family, and would like to think a pretty tough one."

His time with David was brief, but the inspiration lasting. "I remember dad teaching me how to hold a bat and sawing down one of his broken bats for me to use. I've still got it. I've got a lot of his bats and patched-up gloves." David Bairstow would have been proud as Punch that Jonny emulated him in keeping wicket for England, the first father and son combination to do so.

Brendon McCullum

LAWRENCE BOOTH

Two vignettes from New Zealand's early-season tour of England offered telling glimpses of their captain. With his team 1–0 down in the Tests, and in trouble on the first day at Leeds, Brendon McCullum drove his first delivery, from Stuart Broad, high and handsome over cover for six. Then, at Chester-le-Street, moments after England had clinched a raucous one-day series win, McCullum could be seen chatting amiably with Eoin Morgan – two captains united by the thrill of the game, the victor indistinguishable from the vanquished.

Of the first-ball six, McCullum says with an engaging frankness: "I don't know what was going on inside my head. We hadn't really had time to recalibrate our defensive game for the Tests, so I decided to play almost as if it was Twenty20: watch the ball, react to it, and see what happens." And the bonhomie? "Both sides played the whole tour in the right spirit. It was one of the most enjoyable series I've been part of. Some good relationships were struck up. That's how cricket should be played – win, lose or draw."

In the event, New Zealand lost more games (five across the three formats) than they won (three). But what lingered was an enviable combination of bravado and goodwill – embodied by McCullum and embraced by his teammates. England supporters were left wondering whether the two Tests allocated to New Zealand, and the five to Australia, were the wrong way round.

As a batsman, McCullum was hardly prolific: he did reach 35 in six of his ten international innings during the tour, but did not go past the 55 he made in the second innings at Leeds. But he was never dull, failing to hit at least one six in only three of those innings. And he led by example: at Headingley, New Zealand racked up more than 800 runs at nearly five an over. An English summer has rarely witnessed a more popular touring captain.

For BRENDON BARRIE McCULLUM, born in Dunedin on September 27, 1981, it was always going to be sport. He and brother Nathan, less than 13 months his senior and a future international team-mate, would hang around the dressing-room of the local Albion club, where dad Stuart – an Otago batsman himself – was a prominent figure.

He could have been pinched by rugby. McCullum was once picked as fly-half for South Island's secondary school side ahead of Dan Carter, who went on to become rugby union's leading international points-scorer. And, after being selected for New Zealand's one-day side at the age of 20, McCullum remembers a phone call from Richard Hadlee the day after a training session with the Southern rugby team. Hadlee advised him against a repeat. "Yeah," said McCullum. "He was a bit grumpy."

If cricket claimed him, then he was far from an instant hit. McCullum was dismissed in single figures in 14 of his first 21 innings for New Zealand, starting in 2002, and did not make an international century against a top-eight nation until India visited Napier for a Test match in March 2009. Some felt he was cocky; others, sniffily noting the tattoos that cover his arms, wondered if he was brash. That he had rustled up a dream entrée for the Indian Premier League, creaming an unbeaten 158 on the tournament's opening night in 2008, merely confirmed the stereotype.

But when Ross Taylor was controversially sacked as Test captain at the end of 2012, it was to McCullum that an embattled board turned. He began with a nightmare: 45 all out at Cape Town in January 2013, when a team that had always lived in a giant All Black shadow was in danger of disappearing from the national consciousness altogether. The only way, McCullum decided, was up.

"We were bottoming out," he says. "We had no other options. We had to look at our performances and the way the public viewed us. It was pretty obvious we had to make some shifts, both on and off the field. We needed a group of guys who were ready to give it a crack. "We've got criticised at times for being over-aggressive, and when you play like that you will get beaten occasionally. But you will also get better results, more consistently, against bigger teams than you did in the past."

Later in 2013, his team embarked on a golden two years, going unbeaten in seven successive Test series, the longest run in New Zealand's history. It included a heady few days in February 2014 against India: McCullum made 224 at Auckland, quickly followed by a nation-stopping 302 at Wellington – the country's first Test triple.

They also reached the 2015 World Cup final playing a style of cricket that failed them only at the last: by his own wry admission, McCullum forgot to watch the delivery from Mitchell Starc that bowled him for a third-ball duck. But his tournament strike-rate of 188, including 77 off 25 deliveries against England at Wellington and 50 off 24 against Australia at Auckland, had been among the highlights. The captain caught the mood, referring after the last-over semi-final win against South Africa to "the time of our lives".

Then came the trip to England, where New Zealand's sledge-free, smiling approach felt like the enactment of a philosophy, not a PR stunt. "We probably won some fans around the world because of the way we carried ourselves," says McCullum. "That kind of thing can be hard to quantify."

By the time he returned to London to testify in the Chris Cairns perjury trial in October, it was in the knowledge that his reputation would be able to withstand cross-examination. And, in December, he could announce his plans to quit the international game after a home Test series against Australia in February 2016 armed with the comforting realisation that "I had played on for a year longer than I thought I would." Typically, he signed off with a 54-ball century, the fastest in Test history.

There is one slight problem. He loves nothing more than a quiet beer at the bar, yet the new IPL franchise that signed him up for the 2016 tournament is based in Rajkot, in the dry state of Gujarat. "Could be interesting," he laughs. With McCullum, it has rarely been anything else.

Steve Smith

DANIEL BRETTIG

Oh, how they laughed. When Steve Smith first appeared in an Ashes series, in 2010-11, he told the press it was his job to "be fun". The media's mirth was merely heightened when he proved neither technically nor mentally ready, in a series England won 3–1.

Smith disappeared from the Test side, but re-emerged two years later as a cricketer who had embraced his strengths and shaved off some rough edges. His evolution into a high-class batsman coincided with the last days of a dramatic era in Australian cricket. Smith found himself moving up the order – not only of batsmen, but of leaders. And, by the time he arrived in England last summer, he was anything but a laughing matter.

The 2015 Ashes twice showed Smith at his very best, as he followed a coruscating double-century at Lord's with a match-shaping 143 at The Oval. It also revealed how reliant on him Australia had become: when, in between, he failed twice at both Edgbaston and Trent Bridge, the team failed with him. He ended the series nursing plenty of pain, but with more runs (508) than anyone on either side, and cradling a fresh commission as Australia's Test captain.

STEVEN PETER DEVEREUX SMITH was born on June 2, 1989, in Sydney, the son of Peter and Gillian. He grew up in the south-west of the city, first playing cricket at the age of five, when he was the youngest member of his Under-8 team. His heroes were Mark Waugh and Michael Slater, who inspired him to adopt the brand of aggressive, fleet-footed batting that would later become a trademark. To Smith's young eyes, Waugh "made everything look so easy".

Peter, a biochemist, worked from home, affording him extra time to help his son's game develop. "That was handy," says Steve. "Pretty much every day after school he used to take me up to the nets and bowl at me. Each year he'd go over the crease a little bit further. So he'd bowl a no-ball by about a foot when I was 12, and then when I was 14 he was probably two foot over the line. That helped with my hand–eye co-ordination, and with facing faster bowling. I reckon the last time he bowled to me, when I was 15 or 16, he was about two metres over."

Like Michael Clarke, Smith was playing grade cricket at 16, and handed his baggy blue New South Wales cap at 18. He had already learned to hold his own. When an older opponent spent hours sledging him, Smith eventually asked: "Mate, how old are you?" Thirty, came the reply. "And you're still in second grade?" From then on Smith batted in relative peace.

His mother is from Kent, and Smith was always attracted to the idea of summers on the other side of the world. An NSW Under-19 tour gave him an early sight of the English game, and in 2007 he returned for a stint of club cricket that evolved into a few appearances for Kent and Surrey Second XIs, and a tantalising county contract offer. But he was never in any doubt about his allegiance.

Smith earned a Test debut, aged 21, against Pakistan in England in 2010, as a leg-spinning all-rounder at No. 8. He knows now he wasn't ready, but he learned plenty. Older and wiser, he returned to England in 2013, initially as vice-captain of the Australia A side that was shadowing the Champions Trophy team in the last, fretful days of Mickey Arthur's coaching tenure. A hundred on a seaming pitch in Belfast earned Smith the final place in the Ashes squad, in a selection meeting that occurred minutes before Arthur's sacking. Against England his fortunes oscillated, but he reached his first Test hundred with a clumping six off Jonathan Trott at The Oval.

Of batting in England, he says: "It's about playing the ball late, and making sure you're not out in front of yourself. In Australia you can play out in front a little bit more because the ball doesn't quite as much. When you're under pressure and your heart's pumping, you almost go back to what you know. So it's making sure you stay in the bubble of the way you want to play, and not revert to the way of playing in Australia."

Smith arrived last summer as the world's top-ranked batsman, having recently been promoted to No. 3 in the order. He squandered a pair of starts at Cardiff, but then found a willing ally at Lord's in Chris Rogers, who provided a sturdy counterpoint to the swash in Smith's buckle. Their first-day partnership dictated the course of a match he will always remember fondly. "We played extremely well," says Smith. "It was a place I'd never had much success, so I was pretty keen to turn that around. To get my name up on the board with 215 is pretty special."

But heavy defeats on seaming pitches in Birmingham and Nottingham gave Smith a sobering reminder that he was not as in control of his game as he thought. With the Ashes gone, it would have been easy to coast through the final Test at The Oval. But he was desperate to learn from his mistakes. "There were a few things I was doing with my technique that had crept in. My prelim movement was going a little bit too far, which squared me up a couple of times, so I played at balls I probably didn't have to play at."

Smith's century helped set up an innings win to give Clarke and Rogers a suitably triumphant farewell, and offered a glimpse of what might be achieved when he next returns to England as an Ashes tourist.

Ben Stokes

ALI MARTIN

During a summer in which the Ashes were regained, the limited-overs teams rebooted and an audience re-energised, few embodied England's unshackled cricket as vividly as Ben Stokes. Having been dropped from both the Test and World Cup squads over the previous 12 months, he set about starring in a series of match-changing interventions and incidents. Consistency was not the point: his contribution was about more than numbers.

Flame-haired, sporting tattoos and straining every sinew, Stokes felt at times more rock star than cricketer – especially during the First Test against New Zealand, where a virtuoso performance turned the Lord's crowd up to 11 on the amplifier and lacked only a guitar-smashing finale. A dashing 92 from 94 balls on the first day to help dig England out of a 30-for-four-shaped hole was just a taster for an 85-ball century on the fourth – a Test record at Lord's, with Alastair Cook compiling a nine-hour 162 at the other end. "Cooky wasn't telling me to stop, so that was a good sign," says Stokes.

As Joe Root led the celebrations from the balcony with a military salute, Stokes's hundred felt cathartic – not just for him, but for an England side emerging from 18 months of acrimony. As with the incident Root was mimicking – Stokes's send-off from Marlon Samuels in the Caribbean a month earlier – the pictures went viral. By way of an encore, and thanks to the time bought by his own batting, Stokes then claimed three wickets, including Kane Williamson and Brendon McCullum with successive balls. It was a victory charge watched by supporters who – on a Monday in May, no less – had queued down Wellington Road to get in.

Such batting feats proved tough to sustain, and his season became one of cameos, though a watchful 87 in the Second Ashes Test at Lord's hinted at a growing maturity. Not until Cape Town in January 2016, when he made a sensational 258 from 198 balls, the highest score by a Test No. 6, did everything come together. It was rated by many as the most destructive innings ever played by an England batsman.

In the field, Stokes was a prowling presence at backward point or fifth slip, where he held the catch of the summer, a diving one-hander to remove Adam Voges and prompt *that* reaction from Stuart Broad during Australia's first-morning meltdown at Trent Bridge. It stuck, Stokes claims, only because three operations had left his right index finger permanently crooked.

His fast-medium was muscular and fiery, even though it didn't always bring a cascade of wickets. At least not until the second innings in Nottingham, where he marshalled late swing to pick up six for 36 and, in tandem with Durham team-mate Mark Wood, help secure the urn. In white-ball cricket, Stokes remained a talent with which to persevere, rather than an established force. But his bowling improved, and he masterfully closed out the Twenty20 against Australia in Cardiff.

Even his mishaps got everyone talking. The less said about his failure to ground his bat when he was run out for a second-innings duck against Australia at Lord's, the better. A few weeks later, against the same opposition at the same venue, he became the first Englishman given out obstructing the field in a one-day international, when in an apparent act of self-defence he palmed away the bowler Mitchell Starc's attempted run-out. "I knew it would be news all over the world as soon as it happened. I'm still amazed it got given. I wasn't even looking at the ball, and I've watched it back so many times since."

BENJAMIN ANDREW STOKES was born in Christchurch, New Zealand, on June 4, 1991, and moved to the UK aged 12 when his father Ged, a former rugby league forward with one cap for the Kiwis, became coach of Workington Town in Cumbria. Stokes played both rugby codes and cricket – the sport of his mother, Deborah – at Cockermouth School and local clubs. And sport took precedence over academia. "I even played football once," he recalls, "but that was to get out of a detention."

Spotted by Durham when playing for Cumbria age-groups, he joined their Academy in 2006, aged 15, with his parents committing to a twice-weekly, five-hour round trip across the Pennines. "I didn't realise what they were doing for me, taking me to something that would end up being my job." He watched Durham secure back-to-back Championships in 2008 and 2009, making a List A debut in the second of those two gilded seasons – and claiming Mark Ramprakash at The Oval as his first senior scalp. England's Under-19 World Cup campaign in New Zealand that winter brought him a round 100 against India at Lincoln, before a first-class debut against MCC in Abu Dhabi kick-started a breakthrough season. Stokes made 740 Championship runs, topped the Durham averages, and was picked by the Lions. The following summer he was playing in a one-day international in Dublin.

Progress has not always been smooth. His Lions tour to Australia in 2012-13 ended early when he and Kent's Matt Coles were sent home after one night out too many. The presence of Andy Flower, the England team director, made it bad timing. "A few things he said did take me aback, and I said a few things in return," says Stokes. "But coming home set my mind as to how I wanted to do things. It helped get me where I am."

Durham were first to benefit, securing a third Championship title in 2013, with Stokes contributing 615 runs and 42 wickets. It earned him an Ashes tour, from which he would emerge as England's one shining light, scoring a maiden international hundred in his second Test, at Perth, then claiming six for 99 at Sydney.

Briefly, Stokes stalled. He missed the 2014 World Twenty20 in Bangladesh after breaking his wrist with an open-handed slap on a dressing-room locker during a 20-over international in Barbados. And his return to the Test side that summer ended after three ducks against India. But a brutal 164 off 113 balls against Nottinghamshire in the Royal London One-Day Cup semi-final was a reminder of his gifts. When he was left out of the 2015 World Cup, rival teams expressed disbelief, which stemmed from the knowledge that Stokes had the talent to produce moments of wonder. He has since proved them right.

Kane Williamson

ANDREW ALDERSON

In a sport prone to narcissism and neurosis, Kane Williamson is an antidote. He appears as balanced in life as he is at the crease. A cricket tragic? Yes. An unbridled egotist? No. "Would you like a glass of water before we chat?" he asks, with an old-fashioned charm. He may be becoming a doyen of the game, but he is no diva.

Williamson appears destined to break most of New Zealand's batting records. Before the 2015 World Cup, Martin Crowe suggested we were "seeing the dawn of probably our greatest-ever batsman". It was quite a tribute from the incumbent. Soon after, Williamson made a classy 132 at Lord's, joining Don Bradman, Neil Harvey, Garry Sobers, Sachin Tendulkar and Graeme Smith in scoring ten Test centuries before the age of 25.

His preparation, fresh from a largely redundant spell at the IPL, was revelatory. Drawing on his English experience – he had spent two seasons each with Gloucestershire and Yorkshire – he camped in his batting armour at the Nursery End nets and absorbed everything the New Zealand bowlers could offer. Once they had gone, he faced throwdowns, checking his alignment after each delivery, engaging in the odd discussion to see he was meeting expectations, never forcing a shot.

Order and structure are important: he doesn't seem the sort of room-mate for whom you'd duct-tape a demarcation line. Williamson strokes rather than slogs; is altruistic but not puritanical; prefers the company of a private circle of family and friends to social-media sycophants. Statistics hold little sway. His sole barometer is the team ethos.

He demonstrated this during the one-day leg of the England tour, when he showed scant regard for pursuing hundreds after reaching the nineties, though he made 118 at Southampton. Instead he went for his shots – as long as the team had already laid a platform. Employing orthodox strokes, he averaged 79 from five innings, with a strike-rate of 104. In 26 ODI innings in 2015, he made three centuries and was out five times in the nineties. Williamson was unfazed; imperturbability is his modus operandi.

And, when he wasn't contributing with the bat, he could chip in with the ball. On the last day of the Headingley Test, his three for 15 in seven overs – including the wicket of Alastair Cook – hastened England's demise. Having been banned for five months in 2014 for throwing, Williamson was also demonstrating his versatility: a dart-like action had been replaced by something more upright.

But it was his neurosurgeon's hands, apparently gifting him an ability to bat with precision for hours or to seize the moment, which stole the headlines – as when he lofted himself into national folklore with a sangfroid six to beat Australia by one wicket at Eden Park during the World Cup. "I felt a silence after I hit it, then the crowd erupted," he says. "To see people so engaged in the game was pretty cool."

Despite New Zealand's improvement, the opposition sense vulnerability if Williamson goes cheaply, yet no bowler appears capable of riling him. His appetite to improve meant he sought advice from No. 3 specialists such as Hashim Amla, Rahul Dravid and Kumar Sangakkara. "I enjoy talking to players I grew up watching, and working out how they achieved success," he says. "Being a professional provides a challenging environment, with a lot of distractions. I like the way those players were calm. They took everything in their stride." The English county scene also played its part: "The volume of cricket helps, regardless of how well you're going. It allows you to be philosophical about the game's ups and downs, without getting too intense."

KANE STUART WILLIAMSON, born in Tauranga on August 8, 1990, was a cricketing prodigy. His home town, on the coast of the North Island's Bay of Plenty – a destination for holidaymakers, young families and retirees – provided an idyllic childhood. He grew up with parents Brett and Sandra, older sisters Kylie, Anna and Sophie, and twin brother Logan. His phenomenal work ethic was fostered here.

"My parents said I was about two when I first picked up a bat. My dad had a cricketing background, and every day I was at him, wanting to practise. At Pillans Point School, dad organised the building of artificial nets. A bunch of parents raised the money and added a centre wicket. Our place backed on to the field, which was handy. Dad was big on back-foot play and using footwork to spin. He'd lob balls up, and I'd run down to hit them."

Another mentor was David Johnston, the former Bay of Plenty Cricket general manager. He recalls Williamson's character as much as his skill. At a primary-school tournament in Gisborne, the coach – Williamson's dad – swapped the batting line-up around to give others a chance after they had won their first two games. The top order collapsed, and Williamson, batting at No. 7, reached a hundred off the game's penultimate ball with his side nine down. "Without prompting, he stood before the boundary rope and clapped his partner off, to demonstrate it was more than a one-man show," said Johnston. "He had more centuries by the time he got to Tauranga Boys' College than most cricketers score in their lives. But he has always been a balanced young man."

That attitude extended into the international ranks. Former New Zealand batsman Glenn Turner noted Williamson's demure celebrations when, barely out of his teens, he became his country's second-youngest Test centurion, at Ahmedabad (less than a month earlier, in Mirpur, he had become their youngest one-day centurion). "It indicated he felt the job wasn't done," said Turner. "If you let yourself go too much emotionally, it's hard to get yourself back. I remember doing some work with the Under-19s, when Kane was a bit younger than the rest of the group. He stood out, not only because of natural talent but because he was one of the few who asked questions."

New Zealand are grateful he has provided so many answers.

FRANK TYSON AND BRIAN CLOSE

Fast and unflinching

JOHN WOODCOCK

The deaths of Frank Tyson and Brian Close within a fortnight of each other last September divested the game of two of its legends. Although never a national treasure in the way Close was, there were certainly weeks in the winter of 1954-55 when Tyson was a national hero for the part he played in first unnerving, then putting to flight, a strong and buoyant Australian side.

Two decades later, having just watched Clive Lloyd's West Indies being demoralised and routed by Jeff Thomson and Dennis Lillee, much as England had been the previous winter in 1974-75, I had the pleasure of being driven back to my Adelaide hotel by Sir Donald Bradman. "There's no disgrace in not being able to cope with those two," he said. It was Lloyd's sufferings on that tour which prompted him, on his return to the Caribbean, to assemble a battery of fast bowlers – not two or three of them, but five or six – to quell the cricket world. "And who's the fastest you've seen?" I asked the Don, thinking he would probably say Harold Larwood, for the havoc he had caused on the Bodyline tour. Instead, without a second thought, he replied: "Oh, Frank Tyson."

Lloyd's initiative had yet to come up with Malcolm Marshall, Wayne Daniel, Sylvester Clarke and Patrick Patterson, all terrifyingly fast, or Joel Garner and Courtney Walsh, both toweringly awesome. But nothing testifies to Frank's pace on that 1954-55 tour more graphically than something said to me by Arthur Morris, one of Australia's opening batsmen at the time, and one of the best of them all (who himself died the month before Close and Tyson). It needs to be understood that Brian Statham, Frank's indispensable and indefatigable new-ball partner, was himself very quick – quicker, if anything, than James Anderson, who so resembles him, and capable of over 90mph. Yet Morris put the difference between facing Tyson at one end and Statham at the other as being comparable with facing Statham and Trevor Bailey, and Bailey's pace was no more than medium-fast or fast-medium, whichever is meant to be the faster.

There were, I think, two reasons why Frank was only sporadically the same bowler after that: for one, his rhythm (every sportsman's holy grail) became elusive, and on top of that he was never so fiercely fit again. In South Africa in 1956-57, and when he went back to Australia in 1958-59, he was injury-prone, his figures in Australia being three wickets in two Tests at 64, as against 28 at 20 four years earlier. Once in a while, when it did all come together, slips and wicketkeeper took two or three paces back, and anything could happen. Playing for E. W. Swanton's XI, for example, against Barbados at Bridgetown in March 1956, for example, Frank bowled Clyde Walcott for two and nought in successive matches, beating him for pace. This was only a year after Walcott had scored five centuries in a series against Australia.

On the charge: Frank Tyson steams in at Adelaide during the Fourth Test of the 1954-55 Ashes.

If there was one over on which that 1954-55 series turned, it was Frank's first on the last day of the Second Test, which England claimed by 38 rapidly diminishing runs. Australia had won at Brisbane at a canter, by an innings and 154, so turning us all into apostles of gloom, and they began the day needing only 151 to win again, with eight second-innings wickets in hand and nothing much the matter with the pitch. Never was hope more frail; the Ashes seemed as good as lost.

Unlike most genuine quicks, Frank used the bouncer sparingly. He'd say the yorker might be harder to bowl – but had more chance of a wicket, and it was yorkers that dismissed Jimmy Burke and Graeme Hole, his third and seventh balls of that memorable day. By cutting yards off his run-up over the course of the tour, he had lost nothing in pace while gaining crucially in accuracy, a transformation every aspiring fast bowler would do well to heed. Len Hutton, Frank's captain and an unshakeable believer in the virtue of speed as the likeliest means of victory, had pricked up his ears on hearing from Bill Edrich, during the summer of 1954, of the ball – a bouncer, as it happens – with which Frank had sent him to hospital during the Championship match between Middlesex and Northamptonshire at Lord's. Hutton already wanted Edrich in his side for Australia; from then on, he wanted Tyson too. Frank became the bowler he did, not through natural ability – Fred Trueman and Statham both had appreciably more of that – but by strength (particularly through his shoulders) and application.

Brian Close, on the other hand – Alan Gibson's "Old Bald Blighter" – had as much pure cricketing talent as almost any Englishman you care to mention. Although there were only eight months between them, their careers never converged. Frank's was probably only ever intended to provide him with a livelihood before he became a schoolmaster; Brian's, once he had abandoned the idea of going to university, something of which his headmaster thought him well capable, was always going to be his life's work. On their respective voyages to Australia, I recall Brian reading up on his maths, science and physics, while Frank buried himself in Wordsworth.

Spread over an extraordinary 28 years, Brian's first-class career was one of the longest and most uncompromising of all. Can any other cricketer have left his mark as arrestingly as he did on two such great counties as his native Yorkshire and adopted Somerset? Those who knew him only as a confident, affectionately parodied and perpetually combative character must find it surprising that his only major tour – to Australia in 1950-51 at the age of 19 – was by his own admission an unhappy one, especially when it started so encouragingly with an unbeaten century against Western Australia. No one comes out with any credit, including Brian himself for his seeming impenitence, and Freddie Brown, his bluff, genial and plain-speaking captain, whose tolerance of what he saw as youthful bravado had not been enhanced by years as a prisoner of war.

Had the tour been England's next one to Australia – Frank's first, that is – George Duckworth, the scorer-cum-baggage-master, but much more of a father figure, would have seen to it that Brian, something of a loner though he was, was embraced by his fellow players. Now there is no one left from the original party of 18 players, the manager (Geoffrey Howard), Duckworth and 19 journalists who sailed out on the *Orsova* – other, I suppose, than myself – who knows just what a vital part Duckworth played in holding things together in 1954-55 after that crushing defeat at Brisbane and with Hutton near the end of his tether. George was an institution and venerated as such, not least among the Australian rugby league fraternity through his lifelong link with Warrington.

Brian's cricket could veer from delight to despair to derring-do – sometimes it involved all three. The one certainty was that he would never flinch. The delight might come from a succession of right-royal strokes. As for despair, two ill-fated sweeps come to mind, both against Australia, 11 years apart: the first at Melbourne in the Christmas Test of 1950, the other at Old Trafford in the Fourth Test in 1961, the first on the point of lunch, the second just before tea. For all the awful tension of such occasions, and all the wiles of Jack Iverson and Richie Benaud respectively, Brian had the game and the guts to have won a Test match against Australia, though it was never to happen.

Then there was the derring-do, seen by some as foolhardiness or folly, whether it took the form of fielding suicidally close to the bat, or giving Wes Hall and Charlie Griffith the charge during his one outstanding Test innings, 70 against West Indies at Lord's in 1963. No greater compliment could have been paid to his courage than to be asked, at the age of 45, to open the batting against West Indies, at Old Trafford in 1976, "to set an example to the younger players", as Tony Greig, the England captain, put it. Enough has been written

Ringmaster: Brian Close and Trevor Bailey play quoits on the deck of the *SS Stratheden,* at the start of their 1950 voyage to Australia.

about the virulence with which West Indies were allowed, and opted, to bowl against Brian and John Edrich for the last 80 minutes of the third day of that match, though Brian, being who he was, took it in good part. The innings of Edrich – who was 39 – was no less indomitable.

As a captain, whether of England, Yorkshire or Somerset, Brian never doubted himself or let a game stagnate, always preferring the enterprising option. His own players, no less than the opposition, didn't know what to expect next. Having already played nearly 70 Tests, Ken Barrington said that when Brian became captain he would find himself being moved not three yards or even three feet this way or that, but three inches, and not once but twice an over! Brian would not admit it, but he had only himself to blame for losing the England captaincy in 1967, in spite of having won six of his seven Tests in the job.

I saw the time-wasting incident in the Championship match at Edgbaston in August that year, which was the catalyst for his sacking, and for which there was really no defence. Yorkshire bowled 24 overs in 100 minutes (slow by the standards of the day), and only two in the last 15. The only good thing to come out of it was that it led directly to the regulation requiring a set minimum number of overs in the last hour. But nothing would persuade Brian to give an undertaking that he would not do the same again in a similar situation on the pending and potentially turbulent tour of the West Indies. I am not saying there was a hint of prejudice in MCC's decision to sack him, or that there wasn't. It was just a pity it happened, for Brian was a fine sportsman and the most inveterate lover of the game.

Not that long ago I came across a photograph I had taken of him playing deck quoits against Cecil Pepper on the ship coming home from Australia in 1951, and sent it to him. The handwritten letter I had in acknowledgment could just as easily have come from Colonel D. de B. Close of Tunbridge Wells. It ended: "When you think of all the great batsmen and bowlers we had in those days, compared with the present!!" Should Brian ever run into Freddie Brown in the celestial Long Room, it will be Freddie who is on the back foot, not that he will mind that.

John Woodcock covered the 1950-51 and 1954-55 Ashes tours for The Times. *He was editor of* Wisden *from 1981 to 1986.*

ON RETIREMENT

If not now, when?

MIKE ATHERTON

The retirement of Virender Sehwag in October was nothing if not postmodern. On parade in Dubai at the launch of the golden oldies Twenty20 Masters Champions League, whose rules precluded any current internationals, Sehwag was forced to announce the end of his career summarily, on Twitter – though not before journalists attending the launch had beaten him to it. His words, like his batting, were to the point: "I hereby retire from all forms of international cricket and from the Indian Premier League. A statement will follow."

What actually followed was an outpouring which betrayed Sehwag's sense of frustration at the underwhelming manner of his departure – unlike that of Sachin Tendulkar, his team-mate of many years, who had been feted gloriously in Mumbai two years earlier. Like the actor dragged off-stage with the spotlight still aglow and the audience in full-throated roar, Sehwag – whose last game for India had been back in March 2013 – felt he had not received the encore he was due. Later he asked, plaintively: "Should not a player who has played 12 to 13 years for his country deserve a farewell match?"

It is a good question – and the modern cricketer has answered it in the affirmative. The grand goodbye is a relatively recent phenomenon: Don Bradman received three cheers from the opposition (and even that was considered boisterous). There was no extended au revoir across the grounds of England, no guard of honour, and certainly not one off the mark.

Contrast that with the series-long homage paid to Steve Waugh, who – perhaps more than any other cricketer – gave rise to the right of farewell. Keen to dampen speculation, he had confirmed that the Australia v India series of 2003-04 would be his last Test, inadvertently turning the Border–Gavaskar Trophy into a circus, the focus on one man and his going, rather than on the contest and the result. A Sydney newspaper even offered readers a replica of Waugh's famous red rag, to be waved whenever he walked to and from the crease, thus commercialising an event that, not many years before, would hardly have qualified as an event in the first place. Not that his greatness could mould the cricket completely to his will: in his first innings of the series, at Brisbane, he trod on his stumps before he had scored. At times, wrote one Australian writer, it was like watching the final performance of a great singer who had suddenly caught a frog in his throat.

A leaked letter from coach John Buchanan to his team gave voice to a wider concern. "In the lead-up to this game," he wrote before the Second Test, "the issues that have dominated conversations, priorities and by definition your attention have been deal-making, sponsors and Tug's [Waugh's] farewell to Adelaide." Such is the danger of trying to pre-empt the moment or shape it to your desires. The game, after all, is about the many, as well as the individual.

Allsport/Getty Images

And quiet goes the Don: at The Oval in 1948, Bradman's last Test innings consisted of three cheers, two balls – and a duck.

But, as with much of what Waugh brought to cricket, the episode set a template, so that the manner of a player's departure now reflects his stature: the more emotional and fervent it is, the more power and lustre are added to the brand.

In 2015, a cynic might have concluded that Waugh's most recently retired successor, Michael Clarke, awarded himself not one farewell, but two. The first was at the World Cup final, which he announced would be his last one-day international and so guaranteed an emotional send-off; the second came after the Fourth Ashes Test at Trent Bridge, when he ensured something grand at The Oval. England duly fell in line, granting Clarke a guard of honour before his final innings. His team-mate Chris Rogers, on the other hand, left the stage quietly. When Clarke announced in January 2016 that he was planning to play franchise Twenty20 cricket, he seemed to capture the spirit of the age: careers rarely come to an abrupt halt these days.

Like Clarke and Sehwag, Shivnarine Chanderpaul – another modern batting giant – felt he merited proper acknowledgment after a long and decorated career. Leaked email conversations before West Indies' home series against Australia in June – first between Chanderpaul and chief selector Clive Lloyd, then between Chanderpaul and head coach Phil Simmons – revealed the possibilities for friction. A player's feelings of entitlement do not always dovetail with the selectors' responsibility of choosing the best team. After being informed by Lloyd that he would be omitted for reasons of form, Chanderpaul reportedly wrote: "My request to finish up with the Australian series is not asking too much. It gives me a chance to acknowledge my supporters at home and the possibility of the WICB properly honouring me for my contribution to West Indies cricket. I should not be pushed into retirement." It was a plea for the kind of send-off granted to Waugh – or at least for the kind belatedly craved by Sehwag.

Simmons's response was sympathetic, if firm, and emphasised not so much Chanderpaul's needs as his own duty as a selector. Simmons paid tribute to his long service and indicated he would be properly recognised by the West Indian board, but reiterated that neither longevity nor public opinion was a basis for being picked. Were it so, he said, Chanderpaul could hope to play until he was 50. Simmons said the selectors were trying to "dignify" the situation by giving him the chance to go gracefully, rather than be dropped. The Guyana Cricket Board backed their man, accusing WICB of "gross disrespect".

Despite my admiration for Chanderpaul as a player, and my disappointment that he did not get the finale his career deserved, my sympathies lie with the selectors. Whether they were right or wrong in their judgment that Chanderpaul, then 40, no longer merited his place was immaterial. But, once they had made it, they were duty-bound not to pick him, because sport is nothing if not a meritocracy, one of the few areas in life where status, breeding or ability to schmooze should not matter. The next-generation Chanderpaul, who might have worked tirelessly to become the best he can be, deserves the same opportunity to play as Chanderpaul himself was given at the old Bourda ground in Georgetown, as a whip-thin teenager, back in March 1994.

Is this a touch unsympathetic? Possibly. And what about the supporters? It would have been wonderful if they had seen off Chanderpaul in style: only the hardest of hearts does not warm to these occasions. But only if he warranted his place. Supporters deserve to know that any team is picked on merit, not reputation. In January 2016, he bowed to the inevitable – and signed up for the Masters Champions League.

The light seemed to have gone from his eyes

In any case, players are not necessarily the best judges of the right time to go. Sportsmen, they say, die not once but twice, the first death bringing an end to a career, the second to life itself. And, because of the uncertainties of a post-sporting existence, the first death can be more difficult to handle. Now, with financial temptations greater than ever, it has become even harder. Asked why he was retiring, England's great pre-war batsman Patsy Hendren replied that it was precisely because he was being asked "why now?" rather than "why not now?" These days, the well-remunerated cricketer may invert the question: why not play on just a little longer?

Last summer, I sat with a fellow journalist at Clarke's pre-Ashes press conference in Cardiff. After it, we looked at each other and articulated the same thought: the light seemed to have gone from his eyes. Normally such a sparky communicator, and despite being on the verge of the most-hyped series in cricket, he looked and sounded distracted, bored even. Given that this was the third Ashes series in two years, who could blame him? But, later, when he cited a loss of love for the game, the sentiment rang truer than anything he had uttered to the contrary during the series.

Hamish Blair, Getty Images

Quitting at the top: Steve Waugh is carried shoulder-high after his last Test, at Sydney in 2004.

As it unfolded, and Clarke's batting and leadership difficulties became obvious, the thought persisted that this was a tour too far. The desire to finish on a high was stronger than the mind or, in his case, the body would allow. There were echoes of the struggles of his predecessor, Ricky Ponting, who in his autobiography wrote rather well about the nagging voice on a sportsman's shoulder during the dying days of his first life: "It's a negative voice, one that says you're no good, that you can't win, that it's not worth it, that you should give up… I couldn't get rid of the little bastard at the end."

Ponting might not have been able to get rid of it but, like all sportsmen, he did his best to convince himself he could. Bluff is one of a batsman's most potent weapons against poor form, low confidence, a stronger opponent or Father Time. Not for nothing does a Test batsman puff out his chest and stride to the wicket trying to look invincible, even while, deep down, he is feeling as vulnerable as a Sunday-league hacker. Not for nothing did Clarke, only one match before he announced his retirement, write in an Australian newspaper: "People are talking about how I am going to retire after this series. Well, they don't know me. I'm 34, not 37, and I want to keep playing."

If sportsmen are masters of self-deception, then this is strengthened by the dressing-room, often a place of glib reinforcement rather than honest assessment. It is a place where confidence, false or not, is fostered; a place of positive messages and massaged egos. Come on, skipper, you can do it! It is not a place for self-doubt or negativity. And off the field? For wives, partners, children and hangers-on, the modern tour is a very nice place to be, thank you. Not much chance of honest evaluation there. Keep the gravy train rolling.

Timing a retirement, then, is problematic: the desire to keep going and finish fittingly is often at odds with the realities of professional sport, which creep up quickly and unexpectedly. It is why, perhaps, there has been a rise of mid-match retirements: Shoaib Malik in Sharjah, Mitchell Johnson in Perth. The realisation hits home that it is time to go, but the player would still like a decent send-off. Johnson was given a guard of honour, and carried off on his team-mates' shoulders.

Even those who do not demand an ego-soothing exit can get it wrong. Graeme Swann retired abruptly in the middle of the 2013-14 Ashes when, given England's implosion, it might have been better for him and the team had he sat quietly and supportively until the end – as Australia's wicketkeeper Brad Haddin did during the return leg in 2015. Unavailable (for family reasons) at Lord's, and ignored controversially thereafter, he later admitted he had "lost the hunger". But he kept his counsel, waited until the series was over, then retired in dignified, low-key fashion.

Possibly, the manner of retirement reflects a cricketer's character above all. My own favourite of recent times was studded with a little mystery. As a complete surprise to his team-mates, and despite the next match being on his home ground at the WACA, Damien Martyn retired abruptly after the Adelaide Test of the 2006-07 Ashes. Puff, gone, with a simple two-line acknowledgment. It spoke of humility and an awareness that the game moves on, that every player, no matter how good, is just a speck in an ever-growing cloud of dust.

Mike Atherton played 115 Tests for England. He announced his retirement the day after the final Test of the 2001 Ashes.

WISDEN WRITING COMPETITION WINNER IN 2015

From Baltimore to Colwyn Bay

WILL BEAUDOUIN

Strangely enough, on most of my summer days, lunch comes before breakfast. I don't have much say in the matter. It's not as if some subsistence-related idiosyncrasy begets the disjointed chronology of my meals. Rather, it's a side effect of following the English County Championship from a not-so-English place – Washington DC. As many of my friends and co-workers rise from their beds, I'm already up, chewing on a biscuit, mulling over Lancashire's fortunes in the first session of play.

It's a cursed existence, really.

If there's anything rarer than an American who loves cricket, it's an American who loves county cricket. I can say this with a degree of certainty for – as a native Baltimorean – I often feel as if I'm a sort of unthinkable mutation, a sporting two-headed frog. Or, as Hunter S. Thompson once wrote, someone "never even considered for mass production. Too weird to live, and too rare to die." In other words, it's a solitary hobby.

This is not to say that the United States as a whole is devoid of an interest in cricket. By some measures, there are more than 25,000 active cricketers here – the overwhelming majority rooted in the expat community. This diversity should be celebrated and is, perhaps, the strongest facet of the beleaguered US cricketing infrastructure that does exist. But, if I were to mention Ashwell Prince's magical 261-run innings against Glamorgan at Colwyn Bay in the company of Americans even semi-literate in cricket, I'd be met with silence. After they asked why I was getting misty-eyed, that is. (I've yet to recover from Prince's retirement.)

Beyond the strange hours and the lonely nature of following county cricket, my geographic predicament presents another hurdle. I'm unable to visit a game at my leisure and, due to the lack of televised matches, there's no video-based alternative. Instead, I'm reliant on the marriage of the radio and the internet, of technology old and new.

The BBC's radio streams represent a lifeline – my only tangible connection to the matches as they're played. However, much like any form of oral storytelling, the commentators' narratives exist in a liminal space between factual account and imagination. The eyes are documentarians; they leave very little to incertitude. But the spoken word not only permits interpretation – it requires it.

Through the interplay of their nouns, verbs and adjectives, the broadcasters provide the building blocks that allow me to construct a mental image of the match. Yet, skilled as they are – and imaginative as I try to be – my personal vision of county cricket will always be a reverie, ephemeral, and somehow less than real. It is a singular creation – one all my own.

Perhaps that's the allure, and why it provides my preferred form of escapism. As far away as the County Championship is geographically and culturally, it also feels out of step with reality: a quiet, solitary place where the commotion of the world is washed away, and I can sit back, listen, and dream.

Will Beaudouin is an editor living in Washington DC. He is one half of the cricket blog "From Hyderabad to Hove", where he writes as Dilscoop.

THE COMPETITION

Wisden received 89 entries for its fourth writing competition. As always, they arrived from all corners of the globe, all ages, and both genders. (Will Beaudouin is the first winner not to live within the British Isles.) The standard remained high, and the business of judging as exacting as ever. The prize is publication, adulation, and an invitation to the launch dinner, held in April.

The rules are unchanged from 2015. Anyone who has never been commissioned for *Wisden* can take part. Entries, which should not have been submitted before (and are restricted to a maximum of two per person), must be:

- the entrant's own work
- unpublished in any medium
- received by the end of 30 November, 2016
- between 480 and 520 words (excluding the title)
- neither libellous nor offensive
- related to cricket, but not a match report.

Articles should be emailed to almanack@wisden.com, with "Writing Competition 2016" as the subject line. (Those without access to email may post their entry to Writing Competition 2016, John Wisden & Co, 13 Old Aylesfield, Golden Pot, Alton, Hampshire GU34 4BY, though email is preferred.) Please provide your name, address and telephone number. All entries will be acknowledged by the end of 2016, and the winner informed by the end of January 2017. Bloomsbury staff and those who in the editor's opinion have a working relationship with *Wisden* are ineligible. The editor's decision is final. Once again, we much look forward to receiving your contributions.

THE 2015 ENTRANTS

Nick Alford, Christopher Ashman, Azfar Alam, David Battersby, Mike Battrum, Will Beaudouin, Jon Boaden, Leslie Bone, Simon Burrowes, Harry Bywaters, Nick Campion, Ed Capes, Francis Carty, Paul Caswell, Vince Cross, David Cuffley, George Davies, Ed Davis, Simon Day, Philip Fisher, David Fraser, Mark Gannaway, Allan Garley, Nick Gormack, Ian Gray, Steve Green, Hannan Hussain, Adam Hill, Adam Hopkins, Peter Horne, Wayne Hunter, Alexis Isaacs, Michael Jones, Reece Lane, Ross Lawson, Bob Lethaby, Huw Lloyd, Michael Marr, Greg McKie, Duncan McLeish, Paul McLeod, Tim Mickleburgh, Anthony Morrissey, Robert Niederer, Colin Norton, Hugh Oxlade, Lev Parikian, Greg Philp, David Potter, Roland Potts, Santosh Pradhan, Geoff Price, Rajiv Radhakrishnan, Harry Reardon, Richard Reardon, Dave Redford, Andy Reeves, Miles Reucroft, John Rigg, Ian Rose, Tim Sanders, Mark Sanderson, Abhijato Sensarma, Paul Severn, Christopher Sharp, Simon Skinner, Jane Smillie, Peter Stone, Brian Tyers, Ned Vessey, Steve Vickery, David Walsh, Stephen Ward, Graham Willard, Derek Wood.

WINNERS

2012	Brian Carpenter	2014	Peter Casterton
2013	Liam Cromar	**2015**	**Will Beaudouin**

CRICKET'S FIRST FOUR-FIGURE INNINGS

Instant immortality – or utter mismatch?

Nagraj Gollapudi

On January 5, 2016, around noon, Pranav Dhanawade dragged himself into the K. C. Gandhi English School changing-room and told his coach, Harish Sharma: "Sir, I'm really very tired. Can we declare?" It was the second day of a two-day Under-16 match against Arya Gurukul at the Union Cricket Academy ground on the outskirts of Mumbai. The 15-year-old Dhanawade was unbeaten on 980, and K. C. Gandhi were 1,337 for three. "I told him as soon as he crossed 1,000 I would declare," says Sharma.

Dhanawade soon hit three consecutive sixes to gallop from 982 to four figures. Sharma was dealing with a media scrum and, by the time he had extricated himself and signalled the declaration, 1,000 had become 1,009 – the highest individual score in any cricket. In fact, the record had already fallen the previous evening, when Dhanawade finished on 652, eclipsing A. E. J. Collins's 628 not out for Clark's House against North Town in a junior house match at Clifton College, Bristol, in June 1899. Gandhi's eventual 1,465 for

Man of the thousand runs: Pranav Dhanawade celebrates one of a string of milestones.

Unbowed: Arya Gurukul bowlers Ayush Dubey, Sarth Salunke, Mayank Gupta and Pratik Bedekar.

three was another record, for the highest total in all cricket, beating Victoria's 1,107 against New South Wales at Melbourne in December 1926.

Dhanawade's mind-boggling innings lasted 396 minutes, and took just 327 deliveries. He hit 59 sixes, 130 fours (one of them all run), four threes, 24 twos and 75 singles; there were 26 dot balls, and nine deliveries went in the extras basket. He used two bats. The first had been an old favourite, but it was worn out and splintered, and broke when he was on 200. He then picked one of the spares from the school kit bag – and carried on. The onslaught had started at 11.14 on January 4, when K. C. Gandhi began their reply to Arya Gurukul's first-innings 31. At lunch, he had 60 from 22 balls; at tea, 355 from 116; at stumps, 652 from 199. His feat quickly went viral.

Huge scores have become a familiar part of Mumbai schools cricket. The much-chronicled unbroken 664-run stand between Sachin Tendulkar (then 14) and Vinod Kambli came in the Lord Harris Shield in February 1988 at the famous Azad Maidan. In November 2013, at the same ground, Prithvi Shaw made 546, going past Arman Jaffer's pair of quadruples (498 in December 2010 and 473 in February 2013). Dhanawade's innings came a month after Rahul Dravid, delivering the M. A. K. Pataudi Memorial lecture, had spoken about the pointlessness of scoring big hundreds while other kids, some taking a day off school, look on, vainly awaiting their chance. But logic does not always come into it – and Dhanawade had an enthusiastic coach.

Sharma had long resented the fact that cricketers from suburbs such as Dhanawade's Kalyan were ignored by the Mumbai Cricket Association and mainstream media. Sharma, a club-standard left-arm spinner in the late 1980s, recollects how he and his friends would be treated as *gaonwallahs* (from the villages) by the coaches, other clubs, players and the MCA. So when

Dhanawade left the field on the first evening, Sharma sowed in his mind the thought of 1,000. "Yes, 652 was indeed a big score," he says. "But I wanted him to score a record that for 100 years no one – importantly, no *Mumbaiwallah* – could break. I wanted to open everyone's eyes, including MCA."

A leafy borough, Kalyan is about 25 miles by road from downtown Mumbai; even a fast local train takes about an hour to get there. Mumbaikars consider Kalyan a separate city, and the feeling is mutual. The cricketing infrastructure is modest, and reports of Dhanawade's achievement drew attention to the size of the ground. The pitch was a standard 22 yards, with the straighter boundaries pulled in – though still long enough for schoolkids. It was the square boundaries that were unusually short; one newspaper measured them at just 32 yards. But Sharma insists he asked Dhanawade not to hit square, encouraging him to score in the V. "Of the 59 sixes, hardly ten to 12 might have been over the square boundaries," he says. "Otherwise he hit all straight boundaries."

Dhanawade looks his age: 5ft 5in, with a lean body and a pencil-thin moustache. "Because of his power, people felt the opposite team is weak," says Mobin Shaikh, his coach at Modern CC. "He is only 15. He has not done any age-fudging." Dhanawade had not played schools cricket for three years – and had been used by Shaikh as a tailender – until Sharma asked him to open. He made 80 in his first game; this was his seventh.

Even as he was shattering records, he was asked by the Arya Gurukul bowlers why there was no declaration. One of them, Ayush Dubey – ten years old and 4ft 4in – told the *Indian Express*. "I said: *Bas kar na. Aur kitna marega?* (How many more will you hit?). But he asked me to go back, and said: *Ja, ja bowling kar. Aur bahut maarna hai* (Go and bowl. I have to hit a lot more)." Dubey returned his side's best figures: two for 350 from 23 overs; Sarth Salunke had 20–0–284–0. Neither would have been playing had school rules not prevented older students from taking part, so they could focus on

Field of dreams: the Union Cricket Academy ground in Kalyan.

their studies in the run-up to exams. For Dubey and Salunke, both used to bowling with smaller balls, holding a normal-sized ball was not easy.

Was it, as Arya Gurukul's coach Yogesh Jagtap argues, a mismatch? Sharma disagrees. "The same team which had those four or five senior players they said were missing against us, lost their first match of the quarter-final league phase against S. V. Joshi School very badly. So how can you say if the boys who were missing would have made a difference?" Against K. C. Gandhi, Arya Gurukul went down by an innings and 1,382 runs.

For Dhanawade and his lower-middle-class family, life changed overnight. Praise flooded in, including from M. S. Dhoni, who said his effort should not be rubbished; Sachin Tendulkar sent a signed bat, the MCA awarded him a monthly stipend to fund his education for the next five years, and numerous kit sponsors provided equipment. Dhanawade wants to play for Mumbai Under-19 in 2016-17. As for the record, he is confident no one can break it. "If anyone does it, it should be an Indian," he says with a smile.

Nagraj Gollapudi is assistant editor at ESPNcricinfo.

Close of play: first day, K. C. Gandhi English School 956-1 (Dhanawade 652, S. Patil 100).

Arya Gurukul CBSE

*†S. Deshmukh b Kamath	0	– (3) c S. Patil b Kamath	0
S. Salunke b Shetty	13	– not out	20
R. Pathak c Jagtap b Sandesh Shinde	4	– (1) b Kamath	0
A. Kasare b Shetty	0	– absent hurt	
K. Ghansolkar b C. Patil	1	– (4) c Dhanawade b Kamath	0
A. Solanki c Shubham Shinde b C. Patil	0	– (5) b Kamath	0
P. Bedekar c and b C. Patil	0	– (6) c and b Kamath	0
A. Dubey lbw b C. Patil	0	– (7) b Kamath	0
M. Gupta c S. Patil b Shetty	0	– (8) run out	0
T. Misar b C. Patil	1	– (9) b Kamath	16
H. Jadhav not out	0	– (10) b Kamath	0
B 8, l-b 1, w 3	12	B 10, w 6	16

1/0 (1) 2/10 (3) 3/15 (4) (17 overs) 31 1/0 (1) 2/4 (3) (14.5 overs) 52
4/19 (5) 5/23 (6) 6/23 (7) 3/4 (4) 4/9 (5) 5/9 (6)
7/23 (8) 8/28 (9) 9/29 (10) 10/31 (2) 6/9 (7) 7/10 (8) 8/52 (9) 9/52 (10)

Kamath 4–3–4–1; Sandesh Shinde 5–4–1–1; Shetty 5–1–14–3; C. Patil 3–2–3–5. *Second innings*— Kamath 7.5–5–16–8; Sandesh Shinde 3–1–5–0; C. Patil 2–2–0–0; Shetty 2–0–21–0.

K. C. Gandhi English School

Aakash Singh b Jadhav	173
†P. P. Dhanawade not out	1,009
S. Patil lbw b Dubey	137
S. Jagtap b Dubey	58
A. Yadav not out	36
B 14, l-b 3, w 32, n-b 3	52

1/546 (1) (3 wkts dec, 94 overs) 1,465
2/1,077 (3) 3/1,331 (4)

*A. Kamath, Sandesh Shinde, S. Nair, Shubham Shinde, C. Patil and S. Shetty did not bat.

Salunke 20–0–284–0; Bedekar 18–0–241–0; Dubey 23–0–350–2; Misar 6–0–142–0; Jadhav 18–0–281–1; Gupta 2–0–37–0; Deshmukh 5–0–80–0; Solanki 2–0–33–0.

Umpires: S. Landage and S. Sen.

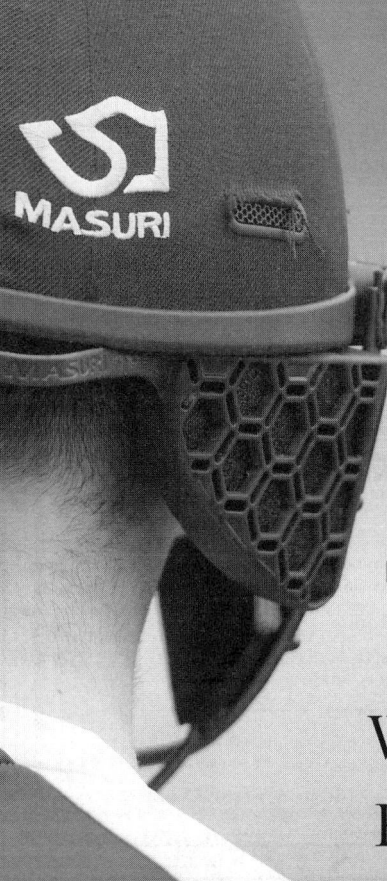

PART TWO

The
Wisden
Review

CRICKET BOOKS IN 2015

An unsolvable riddle

DUNCAN HAMILTON

To endure life, rather than enjoy it, is a tragedy for anyone. But that, it appears, is what happened to Peter Roebuck. Contentment seems to have been a fleeting companion. That's because wrapped around Roebuck's considerable talent – first as a cricketer, then as a writer – was the labyrinthine nature of his personality. He emerges from **Chasing Shadows** as a Chinese box of a man; a box, moreover, that was armour-plated to ward off intruders. Written by Tim Lane and Elliot Cartledge, it is the saddest cricket story I have ever read. Indeed, there were times – a lot of them – when I wished I wasn't reading it at all. The book is disturbing, but grimly gripping. I never met Roebuck. Something in me regrets that very much. Something else is relieved.

The title is plucked from a piece of advice his mother offers the authors: "You'll never know Peter until you look back. You'll be chasing shadows." The subtitle – *The Life and Death of Peter Roebuck* – reinforces the point. Lane and Cartledge think only the former can explain what led to the latter: his fall, aged 55, from the sixth floor of Cape Town's Southern Sun hotel, where police had gone to arrest him in November 2011 following a claim of sexual assault on a 26-year-old Zimbabwean man. Roebuck's death was declared as suicide. The book investigates whether that verdict was accurate, whether the procedures to determine it were correctly carried out, and whether alternative possibilities have credence.

Reopening his case means re-examining his character. The authors – Lane worked alongside Roebuck at the Australian Broadcasting Corporation – call him a "cerebral loner" who was an "eccentric [and] sometimes shambolic figure". He is described as "strangely detached from life's normal polite transactions". This is putting it kindly. Depression, which could descend on him like a shelf cloud, doesn't completely explain behaviour that, over several decades, was extremely odd and often troubling. After one game, for Somerset at Sussex, he stopped his car at traffic lights, tossed the keys to a travelling companion and declared that he was going to walk from Worthing to Taunton; he spent that night at a B&B in Salisbury. During another match, as captain of Devon, he bowled three balls, then sat on the pitch yelling: "What's the point of life?" (Within an hour he'd taken nine for 12.) In a restaurant he knocked a carafe of red wine over a fellow diner, oblivious to both her distress and the chaos around him.

Without apparently realising it, Roebuck could be spectacularly rude or emotionally cold, unable to empathise either with friends or press-box acquaintances. He had only a loose relationship with personal hygiene, and was ignorant of how others became aware of it, especially in confined spaces and on hot days.

Lane and Cartledge ponder the perceived "darkness" in Roebuck. He led some friends to believe that his mother was dead, and became paranoid about Ian Botham, considering him a Mephistopheles, forever masterminding devilish setbacks in retribution for the infamous "Somerset Affair". His conviction for the reprehensible caning of three teenage South African cricketers, lodging at his home in Taunton, provoked more resentment in him than remorse. The judge concluded that Roebuck did it to "satisfy some need, whatever that may have been" – he'd asked afterwards to inspect the welts on his victims' buttocks. Spared jail after pleading guilty to common assault, he claimed not to know the consequences of doing so. Then, amid the hiss of public opprobrium, he blamed everyone but himself.

Some regard Roebuck as a repressed homosexual, who created a home for Zimbabwean men to sexually exploit them; some as a repressed heterosexual (an ex-girlfriend speaks tenderly about their relationship); some as asexual. Such wildly conflicting assessments make you appreciate why Vic Marks, his friend and Somerset colleague, told of the authors' search for the "real" Roebuck, replied: "Good luck on an impossible task."

In a triumph of perseverance Lane and Cartledge diligently pile up testimonies and opinions. But this is a book without an ending, a 283-page riddle never solved. On the matter of his sexuality, and much else besides, Roebuck eludes them. The epilogue, carrying Lane's byline alone, offers a psychoanalytical interpretation, suggesting Roebuck could have suffered from schizoid personality disorder. From the first chapter until the last, I wondered whether the diagnosis was high-functioning autism. Maybe. Maybe not.

The authors pick through conspiracies surrounding his death without sounding convinced by any of them. What does come across, unequivocally and mournfully, is that so many who came into his orbit saw Roebuck as a doomed soul. When the manner of his death became clear, they assumed it was suicide.

Chasing Shadows is as comprehensive as it can be in the circumstances, except in one crucial aspect. It lacks a lyrical appreciation of the books and journalism that defined Roebuck for readers who knew little of his unfathomable nature. There are scores of things we don't know about him. What we do know is this: he was one of the best cricket correspondents of his and most other generations, a prose stylist with the writerly sensibilities of a poet. Someone needs to stitch together an anthology of his work before we forget.

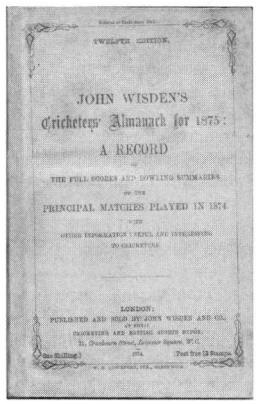

YouTube has a 22-minute masterclass from Abdul Qadir prosaically called "A Compilation of his Best Bowling". The ball fizzes through the air or takes flight in a slow, elegant loop, as if he's releasing a butterfly from his hand. The clip is my antidote to day upon day of watching medium-pacers dominate county matches. Now I have an alternative: Justin Parkinson's **The Strange Death of English Leg Spin**. He nabs his title from George Dangerfield's seminal political work, *The Strange Death of Liberal England*. It is a misnomer. When Dangerfield joined the dots, he found they revealed nothing strange at all about the collapse of liberalism after the Great War. In truth there is nothing strange about the death of English leg-spin either. A combination of factors sent it to the embalmer: climate, pitches, the change in the lbw law, prejudice, impatience and the bone-weary slog of becoming even half-proficient at the job.

That doesn't diminish an immensely enjoyable book. Whether Parkinson is raking over the development of leg-spin, or tracking the characters who dominated it – such as Bosanquet, "Father" Marriott and Freeman – he does so with brio. He's good on Ian Peebles and the suicide of his mentor, Aubrey Faulkner. He's good on the naysayers of leg-spin: Archie MacLaren despised the googly, thinking preposterously that it killed the "beauty of high-class batting". He is good, too, on the tribulations of the modern-day leggie (though anyone contemplating a career in the trade should skip the pages on Ian Salisbury, Andy Clarke and Chris Schofield; you'll feel their pain while reading about it).

Parkinson thinks England "developed a national inferiority complex about leg-spin" after Shane Warne showed us how it should be done. (Others think it goes much further back, perhaps to before the war.) He also thinks youngsters ought to be encouraged to play twisti-twosti, a table-top game beloved of Bosanquet, which necessitates contortions of the wrist to spin a ball. I think youngsters are more likely to dress in doublet and hose on a Friday night out – unless twisti-twosti becomes available as an iPad app. Yet Parkinson lives in hope of a revival, and dedicates his book in part to Richie Benaud. Who knows? Perhaps an English Benaud was recently born. If your child's first words this summer are "Morning, everyone", take him or her to the nets as soon as possible.

We all miss him, especially when a commentator goes into blabbering rapture to describe something Benaud would have summed up in a sentence short enough to fit on a first-class stamp. "The art of commentary is sometimes to let what happened speak for itself," writes Michael Parkinson, using Benaud-like concision to capture his gift in **Remembering Richie**, a collection of his writing for Hodder & Stoughton, a Darby and Joan publishing marriage that lasted more than 55 years. It is one book in an honour guard of titles. **Benaud in Wisden**, edited by Rob Smyth, contains some lovely lines, perfectly weighted, from Dileep Premachandran: "Benaud never made the commentary about him. He could have if he wanted to. After all, he had been one of the great all-rounders of his era… But he wore that greatness as lightly as a cream linen suit." Paul Connolly's **Richie Benaud 1930–2015, Those Summers of Cricket** is heavily illustrated. My favourite photograph shows Benaud leaning back on a padded bench, one booted foot resting on a rail, as he talks to Don

Bradman during the tied Test at Brisbane in 1960-61. Bradman wears a dark suit, inappropriately pale socks and a pair of sunglasses. With his hair swept slickly back, he's the spit of Tony Soprano's Uncle Junior, about to condemn someone to a concrete overcoat and eternity with the fishes.

The cure for admiring Ted McDonald was surely to have met him. He was a duplicitous rake. Even R. C. Robertson-Glasgow, who saw the best in everyone, conceded that McDonald "fell into ways… that somehow foreshadowed tragedy". Nick Richardson's **The Silk Express**, a compelling book about a complicated figure, articulates what Robertson-Glasgow was too polite to say explicitly. McDonald's achievements in the 1920s coincided with the end of Jack Gregory's career and the bloom of Harold Larwood's. He appeared in only 11 Tests for Australia, preferring to play in England, where he eventually became Nelson's pro in the Lancashire League. History has consequently marginalised him, even though he took almost 1,400 first-class wickets. He claimed 205 of them for Lancashire in 1925, the prelude to their four Championship wins in five high summers. For almost a decade, McDonald's scary pace, achieved with a supremely gorgeous action, made him the highest-paid cricketer on God's earth. Nelson lured him with wages and perks that are the equivalent of a lottery win today: £500 per season, plus talent money and free accommodation. But successes were constantly interrupted by calamities, usually self-inflicted, which make both his life and his career seem like a string of comebacks. He liked to get drunk with society's underbelly. This was a minor vice compared with his chief one – crazy gambling. If two flies were buzzing around a room, McDonald would put a wad on which of them flew out of the window first. When he died at the age of 46, following a freak road accident in 1937, his estate was worth a mere £300. He embodied that ancient Greek belief about a man's character determining his fate.

There is widespread admiration for Scyld Berry's *Cricket Wallah*, his impressions from England's tour to India in 1981-82. That's because how Boycott got out in Bombay or the number of wickets Willis took in Kanpur was never the story. The matches were Berry's salaried reason for being there, but his purpose was to tell us about the country through its people, past as well as present. Less lauded, probably because cricket makes only a cameo appearance, is *Train to Julia Creek*, his railway journey across Australia. The jacket blurb compares it with Paul Theroux's *Great Railway Bazaar* and Geoffrey Moorhouse's *To the Frontier*. I liked it the most until the postman delivered **Cricket, The Game of Life**. The publishers should have cut the superfluous subtitle – Every reason to celebrate. Of course Berry, a former editor of this parish, regards cricket as something to celebrate. And cricket has shaped his life to the extent that he can date events – including the early death of his dearly loved mother – from its fixtures, a poignant example of the power of involuntary memory. He remembers Yorkshire at Bramall Lane, where his mother took him, and writes of Sheffield's sights – soot-black walls and factory chimneys, shops advertising Craven "A" and Tizer – and also the "yeasty smell" from Ward's brewery when the wind blew in the wrong direction. "Bramall Lane is where I am most alive," he declares of his youth.

The Game of Life is Berry's attempt to explain why cricket entrances others as much as it entrances him. Around that short question, demanding a long answer, he builds a book that defies categorisation. It is memoir, polemic, investigation – social, political and historical – and also gossip, reportage and travelogue. In this respect Berry most closely resembles neither Theroux nor Moorhouse, but Bruce Chatwin, whose work is liable to dart off into recondite asides. So is *The Game of Life*, which includes charts, timelines, diagrams, blocks of other writers' prose, and footnotes. These are as entertaining as

the main text. Berry asks Tiger O'Reilly: "Would you take Ray Bright on the tour of England?" O'Reilly replies: "I wouldn't take him on a trip to Manly." He watches Australia's Peter Sleep "as helpless as a tethered goat" against Imran Khan. He remembers Mike Brearley coming to the press tent in Bahawalpur with a list of the 50 greatest batsmen to have played for England, which his team have just compiled to offset boredom (imagine that happening today). Berry also finds himself in Hyderabad, where England have no one to bowl wrist-spin in the nets, except him (ditto).

The charm of *The Game of Life* is its quirkiness: a study of the Babylonian numeral system, which would render the nervous nineties redundant; the way the language of cricket settled into common usage; how much the growth of the game owed to the growth of railways. Berry is an explorer too. He sleeps in a bedroom once occupied by Ivo Bligh. He wanders around Ranji's palace. He treks to Lascelles Hall, formerly the home of England's premier team, and bowls an imaginary ball at sheep grazing on the moor. The book hooked me in slowly, and then wouldn't let go because Berry evokes so beautifully the sun's rise and fall over seasons past.

To launch its bicentenary in 1985, *The Times* published a commemorative brochure. It contained a studio portrait of John Woodcock perched on a stool. He's holding a pair of huge binoculars; a softback copy of *Wisden,* the spine slightly bent, rests at his feet. Like one of Holbein's oils of the nobility, it conveys authority and gravitas. **The Times on the Ashes** confirms everything the photograph says about him.

Woodcock's main broadsheet competition during most of his three decades as cricket correspondent was E. W. Swanton, whose match reports in the *Daily Telegraph* could put a reader to sleep faster than any hospital anaesthetist. Woodcock possessed what his contemporary didn't, a sparky line in simile and metaphor. A portly Colin Cowdrey running a single is "like a ship in full sail".

The stonewaller "Slasher" Mackay and the consummate stylist Neil Harvey evoke "the difference between the parsimonious days of war and the extravagant days of peace".

A depressing number of anthologies are cut-and-paste travesties. Those worth buying are a damn hard slog to produce. You have to throw out a lot of very good stuff simply to squeeze in the best. This can feel like chopping down a forest to make a box of pencils. The selections of Richard Whitehead, *Wisden*'s contributing editor, are first-rate. What you get is what matters. There's Alan Lee's description of a gung-ho Allan Border, who looks "like a man intent on going off the high board to find out if there is any water in the pool". There's Michael Henderson's put-down of Geraint Jones, wearing wicketkeeping gloves "that might have been forged in a Black Country foundry". There's the welcome appearance of the underrated Dudley Carew, who says of Denis Compton that he "looked an artist, and the instincts of the great cricketers who played in the days when the war meant the Boer War moved in his strokes".

The book underlines how the job of reporting the greatest rivalry has changed too. Woodcock was among the last tourists to travel to Australia by boat. There was no tweeting on the high seas. He filed a short dispatch from Tilbury Docks, another during a stopover in Ceylon, and a third after docking at Fremantle. As L. P. Hartley almost wrote, the past is a foreign country: they do things differently without super-fast broadband.

On a scorching day at Scarborough, during a summer when Twenty20 was still in its mewling infancy, I came across a gut-heavy man who seemed to have fallen out of one of Donald McGill's saucy postcards. He was sitting on the bleachers, which slope gently towards the pavilion at North Marine Road. He'd folded the bottoms of his black trousers to his calf, as if about to go paddling, and the sleeves of his white shirt were rolled to his biceps. He was shouting into a mobile phone, his accent as thick as the limestone karst of the Dales. "Reyt. Gerr thissen daahn 'ere," he urged a stay-away friend. "This is propa crikkit – nun o' that summat abaht nowt nunsense." I suppose he'd have been brought up on fatherly reminiscences of Holmes and Sutcliffe, and come into adulthood when Yorkshire, under Brian Close, considered the County Championship to be the family silver. No wonder his heart belonged to propa crikkit.

I thought about him as I read Stephen Chalke's **Summer's Crown**, which members of The Cricket Society – propa crikkit's high church – will reread until the pages drop out. Sumptuously produced and written in window-clear prose, Chalke's history of the 125-year-old Championship makes you wish the world's physicists weren't dawdling over the invention of a time machine, enabling us to pop back and see for ourselves what he describes.

You can't help thinking Chalke's previous books were always pulling him towards this one, the ideal match of author to anniversary. He pours his accumulated knowledge into it. The only thing missing is a set of Championship tables, an omission future editions ought to correct. You forgive their absence because Chalke, whose radar for choice dialogue is infallible, abides by Kipling's instruction to write about the factory worker rather than the factory.

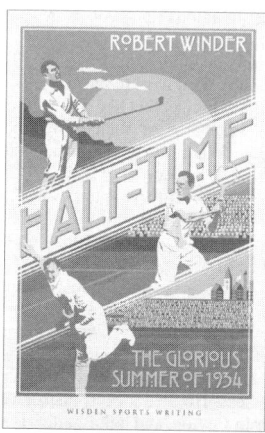

The standard nuts and bolts – the Championship's awkward birth and repeated tinkering with the points system – never obscure the characters, each spotlighted through quotation, anecdote and portraiture.

Two of the best are locked together to illustrate what Chalke calls the "no-nonsense hardness" of the post-war era. Warwickshire's Tom Dollery fought in Africa. On his return, hearing a team-mate complain of thirst and asking for a drinks break, he is aghast: "Drinks? What do you want drinks for? In the desert we had two pints of water a day – and that was for you *and* your vehicle." George Emmett, of Gloucestershire, bore a passing resemblance to Prince Philip and could be just as cantankerous. Anyone applauding a catch too loudly was quickly rebuked: "There's enough exhibitionism in cricket without your adding to it." A third vignette has Derek Randall answering the door in his pads during a snowy January. "I'm breaking them in for the summer," he explains to his bemused caller, before escorting him into the lounge, where Mrs Randall is breaking in a second pair.

Chalke devotes a spread to Gloucestershire against Middlesex at Cheltenham in 1947. The seesaw drama of the title decider is less significant than one statistic. Of day two, he says: "There were 15,000 in the ground – more, incredibly, than had been fitted in on Saturday." That summer, attendances reached nearly 2.3m. You'll find last year's total elsewhere in this edition of *Wisden*. The ECB are apparently quite chuffed with the figure, but I'd still advise anyone of a nervous disposition to knock back three fingers of Scotch before looking.

Simply by showing how grand the Championship used to be, Chalke also shows what a parlous state it is in now. It gives *Summer's Crown*, essentially about what is lost and cannot be regained, a plangent air. It's like reading an elegy on a tombstone. Never mind. The book will allow us to remember the past from whatever future the Championship has left.

George Bernard Shaw's loathing of the game – he considered players and spectators alike to be fools – shouldn't obscure the minuscule debt it owes him. Shaw unintentionally summed up in a sentence what batsmen have known since "Silver Billy". That sentence is: "It is easy – terribly easy – to shake a man's faith in himself." Simon Hughes's **Who Wants to be a Batsman?** proves Shaw was spot on. Calling himself "a jobbing county cricketer", Hughes, a former bowler, is self-deprecating about his own batsmanship. This is just as well: in a 13-year first-class career, he made 33 ducks. Mike Gatting dismissed his efforts as "fannying about". But if critics were permitted to express opinions only about things they could actually do, there'd be half a dozen blank pages in every newspaper, and publishers would go broke.

Hughes has watched cricket microscopically since his playing days, absorbing himself in the minutiae that modern technology allows him to see in super-slow motion. He's become one of the best television analysts of any sport. He interprets what he sees with clarity, rather than bombast, and doesn't patronise the armchair spectator. As it is on screen, so it is in print.

He draws on personal experience and friendships to frame arguments and discuss the corrosive effect of those twin hobgoblins, stress and pressure. He turns a lively phrase. Batting against Curtly Ambrose is "like facing someone letting the ball go from an upstairs window". A contest against Shane Warne was a "slow death", from which "there was rarely any escape". Hughes illuminates two other scenes you may want to expunge from your memory. The first is of Wayne Daniel, clad only in a white towel, chatting to a woman on the dressing-room telephone while fondling his genitals. The second is of a "former colleague" who develops "a strange compulsion for pleasuring himself before going out to bat".

"The key to batting is fearlessness," says Hughes, who supplies an instance when he lacked it. After much kerfuffle, he gives himself out against Malcolm Marshall, despite not being sure whether he's nicked it and the umpire saying not out. "I didn't really feel I *belonged* out there," he admits. A team-mate tells the dressing-room of a different conclusion: "I fink his arsehole fell out." The overriding message in *Who Wants to be a Batsman?* is that possessing a cover-drive like Wally Hammond won't save you when you get the yips. Hughes quotes Michael Vaughan: "When you're in form you're thinking about nothing. When you're out of form you're thinking about everything." Hughes's verdict is that "batting can be a head-fuck". Neville Cardus may have chosen a more felicitous phrase, but without adding anything to its truth.

Hughes didn't score a century (though he reckons he gave a few away). Steve James did, and had a first-class average above 40. He can write too, which is proof that some guys really do get all the luck. I saved a piece James did a couple of years back for the *Daily Telegraph* in which he made a passing reference to his England career during a period when the dressing-room had a revolving door. It spun at such a rate that NASA could have trained astronauts in it before shooting them to the moon. He compared England caps to blown-around leaves, remarking with mouse-modesty that "a couple even landed in my garden". The same tone permeates **The Art of Centuries**. James generally plays down his own abilities and achievements while buffing to a shine everyone else's.

Comparisons with *Who Wants to be a Batsman?* are inevitable. James says batting "frazzles the mind", that a "constant" and "exhausting" battle goes on within it to score runs. He makes the startling confession that, as Glamorgan captain and opening batsman, he once bowled someone he thought unlikely to take a wicket near the end of a day so he could avoid going in himself that evening. James accepted how fickle "Lady Luck" can be – either "beautiful, kind, generous" or "a horrible, cruel bitch" – and created superstitions to combat her. These sound certifiable. His fear of scoring nought prevented him from eating duck, and his daughter wasn't allowed to play with plastic ducks in the bath. As a boy, he telephones his father in an awful fret after forgetting his grey marl socks, convinced no substitute is acceptable. The father brings his lad those socks and watches him make his first hundred. James says he was "always batting for my dad" because "I wanted to make him proud". He is the hero of *The Art of Centuries*. He died before James completed the book, but is alive again here. No son can do more for his father.

Simon Lister waits until the last page of **Fire in Babylon** before quoting C. L. R. James's most resonant line: "What do they know of cricket…?" He should have planted it on the first page because he answers the question just as

comprehensively as James did, and also gives it a modern relevance. Books usually inspire films. In flipping that process, Lister's important work does much more than merely complement Stevan Riley's 2010 documentary, which explained how West Indies, unleashing fast bowlers like some nuclear attack, pummelled everyone into submission from the mid-1970s. The staging posts of that process are familiar. But what Lister does in print, with Jamesian scholarship, is something Riley couldn't have done on screen without making his film longer than *Apocalypse Now*. He adds depth and breadth, and places the story in the wider context of social history, genealogy and race. He explains why cricket in the 1970s was so welded to identity and status in the disparate Caribbean islands, and also why the thunderous success of the team mattered to first- and second-generation West Indians in Britain (especially during the racial tensions of the early 1980s).

Lister's dignified central character is Clive Lloyd, the subject of his earlier biography, *Supercat*. "Those who say Lloyd was a limited captain… understand little of cricket, less of leadership and nothing of the West Indies," snorts Lister with a peppery brusqueness. Lloyd made a splintered dressing-room whole again through judicious man-management, and rid it of the "detested" sobriquet "calypso cricketers", a euphemism for sparkly entertainers lacking substance. Lister is even-handed. He gives a fair shout to critics who complained about intimidatory tactics. Geoffrey Boycott is then summoned to the witness box to point out the bleeding obvious: "Any human being who tries to tell me he wouldn't have played four fast bowlers because they were winning Test matches is a liar," he says. "We'd all have done it." I finished *Fire in Babylon* certain that C. L. R. James would have greatly admired it.

The second essay in Samir Chopra's **Eye on Cricket** has the off-putting title "Of Cricket Bats and Economic Divisions", which sounds like a stodgy academic discourse on the production of willow. What Chopra actually produces is a bittersweet moment from his boyhood in Delhi. His friend is given a Duncan Fearnley DF Jumbo, the bat Chopra has seen Viv Richards use destructively on television. He discovers it cost 1,000 rupees. His own bat was bought for 50 rupees from the local market. Chopra is suddenly aware of the "difference in our families' stations", which had barely occurred to him before because the culture of cricket had bound him to his friend so solidly. In summoning memories of his cricketing childhood, Chopra compels you to think of your own. Halfway through, I was linseed-oiling my first bat again. A professor of philosophy and a blogger living in America, Chopra hasn't been institutionalised in press boxes, making *Eye on Cricket* agreeably eccentric. He highlights the Dewey Decimal System classification of cricket books; the "little starts of recognition" figures can generate; and also how cricket explained the world's time zones to him. His pieces are discursive without being dreamy, and serious without being po-faced. I loved them.

The difficulty of writing about the 19th century becomes apparent as soon as you start the research: there are so few writers of substance to crib from. Back then, reporters went everywhere, but what the copy boy took to the telegraph office was usually as informative as a lighthouse-keeper's log. There was no Atherton or Haigh to describe the way a place looked, the trigger movements of a batsman, or how a bowler hitched up his strides. Hardly anyone chased a headline quote. So largely what's left, apart from statistics as dry as Neolithic bones, are black holes of ignorance. Even so, John Lazenby's **The Strangers Who Came Home: The First Australian Cricket Tour of England** and Scott Reeves's **The Champion Band: The First English Cricket Tour** do a spirited job of digging up the long-dead and making them dance.

Reeves follows George Parr's team on the steamship to Canada and the United States in 1859. The expedition was a heroic mess. The journey out was bad enough. There were gales and extreme seasickness, and the ship's captain sounds more like Pugwash than Columbus. (The journey back was even worse: an anchor crushed a deckhand to death.) In Manhattan, its buildings barely taller than the factory chimneys of a Lancashire mill town, Surrey's Julius Caesar supped too much beer and quarrelled with a local, who pointed a gun at his head. After that, the matches seem incidental. Reeves relies heavily on John Lillywhite's brother, Fred, who packed a printing press to crank out scorecards, and afterwards produced his own book of reminiscences. Lazenby is indebted to the cricketer Tom Horan, writing as "Felix" for *The Australasian*. He's referenced 124 times in the index, almost enough to qualify for co-authorship.

Conceit and snobbery led the hosts to dismiss the 1878 Australian tourists as an inept bunch of no-hopers – "a joke", as *Lillywhite's Cricketers' Annual* admitted, retrospectively expressing its embarrassment at the slur. The English were so ignorant of these strangers, who regarded the old country as home, that crowds choking the platform at one station expected to see an Aboriginal team. By demolishing MCC at Lord's, the Australians "whetted the appetite for international competition and propelled the game into the modern era," says Lazenby, establishing himself as one of our foremost historians. But *The*

Strangers Who Came Home does highlight another problem for anyone delving into the period. We read a lot about "The Demon" Spofforth. In print he's a terrifying prospect, as though Lillee and Thomson were bowling to you at the same time. In photographs, taken when he was 51, Spofforth looks like your grandad, wheezing to the wicket with a gyppy shoulder. Oh, what the Victorians would have given for the digital camera.

I confess prejudice towards W. G. Grace. The more I read about his shenanigans, the less I like him. In **Wisden on Grace**, edited by Jonathan Rice, Geoffrey Moorhouse's opinion of his character chimes with my own. "He has

never been a hero of mine," writes Moorhouse, recalling the moment he discovered Grace was "sometimes a shameless cheat" and not a "particularly attractive" personality. Not much he wasn't. He was violently bad-tempered, dictatorial, vindictive, thin-skinned, snobby and colossally arrogant. As a cricketer, he was stellar; as a human being, he was not. Nowadays the shamateur would hardly be a candidate for MCC's Spirit of Cricket Lecture at Lord's – he might not even be allowed through his own gates.

Richard Tomlinson's **Amazing Grace**, marking the centenary of WG's death, runs into some speculative cul-de-sacs. Even someone as mega-famous as Grace left mysteries behind, which means observations often have to be prefaced with "possibly" or "probably". There's a further quandary for Tomlinson: how many anecdotes were wishful thinking, misremembrances or deliberate fabrications designed to enhance the reputation of the teller? As Tomlinson points out, MCC's *Memorial Biography* was sanitised to satisfy Mrs Grace's desire to immortalise her husband as "bluff, genial and boyish". Grace's memoirs are as unreliable as some of the eyewitness testimony, and Tomlinson also says that bandwagon-jumpers "exaggerated their familiarity" with him. Chief among them was that terrible fraud Pelham Warner who, while never a member of Grace's inner circle, imagined enough "personal reminiscences" to con the BBC into making a programme about them.

Tomlinson's brief afterword, going into detail about his research, ought really to be read first, because you learn how Grace's public persona was initially shaped and subsequently preserved. In it you glimpse what *Amazing Grace* could have been if Tomlinson had freed himself from the corset of conventional biography. The best bits aren't descriptions of events or the regurgitation of established facts – recorded in a yard of other books – but his interpretation of them. His WG is an innovator in tactics and technique. He portrays Grace as a relatively impecunious and socially inferior chap whose stupendous talent enabled him to soar above the hypocrisies of the class system. Tomlinson thinks his grab for money – Grace was a financial incompetent, soon parted from what he earned – stemmed from the nagging fear of being without it. This wasn't the most darkly troubling of his psychological burdens. Food and drink were consumed gluttonously, first for solace, then as a dependency, finally as a compulsive disorder. Despite his swagger, Grace was as vulnerable and insecure as anyone. I still didn't warm to him. I did, however, warm to Tomlinson, a good and insightful writer.

David Frith has spent almost half a century chasing WG's contemporary, A. E. Stoddart, which makes Boswell's shadowing of Dr Johnson seem like a recreational pursuit. **Stoddy: England's Finest Sportsman** is the product of a magnificent obsession. It is his third book about him, each surpassing the last. Stoddart tears through the pages like a fictional character in an improbable yarn. He was born in South Shields and spoke with the "faintest" Geordie accent, but looked like a Home Counties gent. He behaved like one, too, even when shooting himself in 1915. The reasons for his suicide were manifold: money worries, bad mental and physical health, a lacklustre marriage. Incompetence, stupidity or malice had also led MCC to refuse an application to reactivate his lapsed membership. Frith is incandescent that nothing publicly – such as an English Heritage blue plaque – commemorates Stoddart's feats. He shouldn't worry. With words, he builds his monument high.

A book about snow-covered cricket grounds? It sounds like one of those ideas you'd regard as spiffing late at night – after a large nightcap – and preposterous next morning. But Graham Coster's **Snow Stopped Play** is a small, polished pearl. I declare an interest: I am name-checked near the end. Even if I weren't, I'd describe it in the same way. The photographs are like arty Christmas cards. Lord's is caught in low drifts whiter than a doctor's coat. The Canterbury lime is bare and spindly against an Atkinson Grimshaw sky. The Oval is shown as the birds see it, sitting like a spaceship that has landed from a distant nebula. Coster's words are as good as the pictures, if not better. He likens one pavilion to "the dacha of a Russian police chief", and compares the first two days of a Championship game to reading the first few hundred pages of a George Eliot novel: "You know getting to the point where it will have been hugely worth it is going to require a ton of patience." Coster is writing extended picture captions only, but he gets them just right, packing a lot into a little space. He really ought to tackle a full-length book.

> ## Like a spaceship that has landed from a distant nebula

The vast proportion of ghosted autobiographies are bland, self-justifying and bereft of insight or wit. As a rule, you'll find more literary merit in the *Argos Catalogue*. Here are three exceptions. The fabulous opening chapter of David Lloyd's **Last in the Tin Bath** is a bit like Tony Capstick's "They Dunt Know They're Born Today". Anyone under 40 won't recognise the boyhood Lloyd describes. Anyone under 20 will assume he once shook hands with Queen Victoria. But anyone of roughly the same generation, from a working-class background, will see their past unspool in front of them: the rows of terraced housing without central heating; the outside lavatory; the extended family everywhere in the town; the stumps chalked roughly on walls. It offers a new definition of earthy Northern Soul.

Andrew Flintoff's **Second Innings** reminds us that the best of men – even superheroes are only men at best. It separates the Flintoff we know from the Flintoff we don't. Developing a split personality, a mask for his fame, macho "Fred", the ultra-confident showman, coexists with Andrew, the timid introvert. Flintoff likens his career peak to "being in a soap opera and gradually turning into the character you're acting". He is frank about the bouts of depression that grew from it, which will help a lot of people suffering in silence.

Simon Jones's **The Test** is exceptional. Along with Marcus Trescothick's revelatory *Coming Back to Me*, published in 2008, it has succeeded in renewing my faith in the genre. Jones weaves his life story around the 2005 Ashes. Making the series freshly relevant is a feat in itself. We couldn't start the last Ashes without first celebrating the tenth anniversary of that belting summer, the scenes from which ran on a perpetual loop. It was nostalgia overkill, suggesting we were taking refuge in old memories because we didn't fancy our chances of matching them. But everything about 2005 had been said or seen so often that, soon, nothing about it carried any emotional charge.

Jones restores it by personalising the journey from Lord's to The Oval. The best sports books are never about sport alone, but the human condition. Jones shares his fears, failings and fallibilities. He discusses his hell-bent ambition and the business of bowling brutally fast, likening it to the possession of a "superpower". None of this would have been possible without Jon Hotten, his literary ventriloquist, who helps give him such a distinctive voice. The style and rhythm of the early chapters are reminiscent of a mud-and-grit David Peace novel in which the first-person narrator becomes luminously aware of being caught up in something much bigger than himself.

The Jones–Hotten partnership makes you feel as though you're watching from the non-striker's end. As in all fine writing, the minor details matter. Take the description of the first morning of the First Test at Lord's. Jones, then a tender 24, remembers "a day already warm" under low grey clouds. He recalls the way "time seems to stand still and then accelerate" towards the hour when he is walking through the Long Room, "studs clacking". He tells you about the new Dukes, held in the well of his hand, which is "so rich and dark it's almost brown... an English ball for an English day". Even the accounts of the matches themselves – Hotten must have gone goggle-eyed rewatching DVDs – retain the snap of tension.

Jones reveals all – or at least all that is fit to print – and isn't afraid of making himself look a chump. He is trapped in a kiss-and-tell tabloid story, saying to his girlfriend (who doesn't stay his girlfriend for much longer): "Nothing happened. You can believe me, or you can believe that paper, but this is the most important summer of my life, and I can't have anything distracting me." He spills a skyer on the last morning at Edgbaston, believing "in that fraction of a second... I've just lost us the match, and in all probability the series". He discusses Duncan Fletcher's gaze, cold enough to crack ice. And he explains the medical consequences of being a quick in the modern game. You're pain-free for only 5% of your career. You swallow a couple of ibuprofen and two paracetamol with your breakfast tea. You have cortisone injections when those tablets fail you.

There is some prodigious drinking; the muse of fast bowling is always thirsty. The night before his England debut Jones downs six or seven pints of Stella: "I felt great. And then in the morning I didn't." His head is "zinging" when Nasser Hussain hands him his cap: "There you go, Sheepshagger." In Australia he binges until 4am, missing the bus to the Gabba. As for 2005… well, there's 12 cans of lager as he goes home from Lord's. There's the long night after Edgbaston when he's "steaming drunk" in the Walkabout bar. There's an early morning sandwiched between the Old Trafford and Trent Bridge Tests when he has "more than a few" and ends up playing cricket in the street with his mates at 2am. And there's the open-top bus parade after The Oval. Nursing a colossal hangover, Jones is aware one remedy alone will ensure he stays upright: he must drink even more than he did the night before.

The Test is about a personal tragedy within a team triumph, and knowing from the beginning how it will end only accentuates the misery. How dearly you want the outcome to be different. There's no self-pity, no sorrowful ifs or buts or what-might-have-beens. Apart from firing a couple of barrels of buckshot at his county – on this evidence, Glamorgan were far from benevolent employers – Jones is without resentment. Referring obliquely to the injuries that took him out of the series early and stole his career, he reflects: "Sometimes I'd think about my success… and wonder what I'd done wrong, who I'd offended." He takes comfort from a conversation with Ricky Ponting, who tells him: "I used to have nightmares about facing you." That tribute says much about the bowler Jones had once been, but a lot more about the bowler he would undoubtedly have become. *The Test* is our consolation for being denied that pleasure. In the closing paragraphs Jones says: "I still dream about cricket… and in my dreams I'm bowling really fast, like I used to, but this time in a big final somewhere. The game is still in my subconscious, and there bowling fast is pain-free and exhilarating, like it used to be. And I wake up and think back to those days when it felt like flying."

If you've read the previous 243 pages and aren't viscerally moved by that passage, then I suggest you check your pulse: you probably died ten minutes ago. *The Test* by Simon Jones and Jon Hotten is *Wisden's* Book of the Year.

Duncan Hamilton is a journalist who lives in the Yorkshire Dales. He has twice won the William Hill Sports Book of the Year award.

> " The match coincided with the 800th anniversary of the sealing of the Magna Carta between King John, who is buried in Worcester Cathedral, and a group of rebel barons. It was marked by four hours of bell-ringing from noon on the first day."
> Worcestershire v Warwickshire, page 698

WISDEN BOOK OF THE YEAR

Since 2003, *Wisden's* reviewer has selected a Book of the Year. The winners have been:

2003 *Bodyline Autopsy* by David Frith
2004 *No Coward Soul* by Stephen Chalke and Derek Hodgson
2005 *On and Off the Field* by Ed Smith
2006 *Ashes 2005* by Gideon Haigh
2007 *Brim Full of Passion* by Wasim Khan
2008 *Tom Cartwright: The Flame Still Burns* by Stephen Chalke
2009 *Sweet Summers: The Classic Cricket Writing of JM Kilburn* edited by Duncan Hamilton
2010 *Harold Larwood: The authorized biography of the world's fastest bowler* by Duncan Hamilton
2011 *The Cricketer's Progress: Meadowland to Mumbai* by Eric Midwinter
2012 *Fred Trueman: The Authorised Biography* by Chris Waters
2013 *Bookie Gambler Fixer Spy: A Journey to the Heart of Cricket's Underworld* by Ed Hawkins
2014 *Driving Ambition* by Andrew Strauss
2015 *Wounded Tiger: A History of Cricket in Pakistan* by Peter Oborne
2016 *The Test: My Life, and the Inside Story of the Greatest Ashes Series* by Simon Jones

OTHER AWARDS

The Cricket Society Literary Award has been presented since 1970 to the author of the cricket book judged best of the year. The 2015 award, made by the Cricket Society in association with MCC, was won in May by Dan Waddell for **Field of Shadows: The Remarkable True Story of the English Cricket Tour of Nazi Germany 1937** (Bantam); he received £3,000. A month later, Peter Oborne won the cricket category at the British Sports Book Awards with **Wounded Tiger: A History of Cricket in Pakistan** (Simon & Schuster).

BOOKS RECEIVED IN 2015

GENERAL

Beaumont, David **From Third Man to Third Base** Richard Daft's Tour to Canada and USA in 1879 (privately published, paperback, £9.99; details from dj.beaumont1@btinternet.com)

Berry, Scyld **Cricket: The Game of Life** Every reason to celebrate (Hodder & Stoughton, £25)

Bird, Jeffrey and Woolley, Malcolm **1840 and all that** History and Reflections of Cowbridge Cricket Club (privately published, paperback, £10 + £1.50 p&p; more information from jrb@rsbird.com)

Carroll-Smith, Adam **The Pictures are Better on the Radio** A fan's love affair with sport on the wireless (Pitch, paperback, £12.99)

Chalke, Stephen **Summer's Crown** The Story of Cricket's County Championship (Fairfield Books, £20)

Chopra, Samir **Eye on Cricket** Reflections on the Great Game   Foreword by Gideon Haigh (Harper Sport, paperback, Rs399)

Coward, Mike **The Bradman Museum's World of Cricket** (Allen & Unwin, $A49.99)

Dawson, Marc **Inside Edge** Another Eclectic Collection of Cricketing Facts, Feats & Figures   Foreword by Tom Moody (Pitch, £12.99)

Diaper, Dr Dan **Watching Cricket on the Radio** (New Generation, paperback, £9.98 inc p&p)

Gower, David **David Gower's 50 Greatest Cricketers of All Time** (Icon Books, £12.99)

Hounsome, Keir **A Game Well Played** A History of Cricket in Norfolk (privately published, paperback, £14 inc p&p; details from the author at 27 The Avenues, Norwich NR2 3PH)

Hughes, Simon **Who Wants to be a Batsman?** The Analyst unveils the secrets of batting (Simon & Schuster, £18.99)

James, Steve **The Art of Centuries** (Bantam, £20)

Lazenby, John **The Strangers Who Came Home** The First Australian Cricket Tour of England (Bloomsbury, £18.99)

Lezard, Tim, ed. **Never say die** A celebration of Gloucestershire CCC winning the 2015 Royal London One-Day Cup   Foreword by Jonathan Agnew (One Out, All Out, paperback, £14.99)

Lister, Simon **Fire in Babylon** How the West Indies cricket team brought a people to its feet (Yellow Jersey Press, £18.99)

McCrery, Nigel **Final Wicket** Test & First Class Cricketers Killed in the Great War (Pen & Sword Military, £30)

Parkinson, Justin **The Strange Death of English Leg Spin** How Cricket's Finest Art Was Given Away (Pitch, paperback, £12.99)

Piesse, Ken **Favourite Cricket Yarns** From Laughs & Legends to Sledges & Stuff-Ups Foreword by Ricky Ponting (The Five Mile Press, $A39.95)

Pietersen, Kevin, with Harris, Daniel **On Cricket** (Sphere, £20)

Quelch, Tim **Stumps & Runs & Rock 'n' Roll** Sixty Years Spent Beyond a Boundary (Pitch, £17.99)

Reeves, Scott **The Champion Band** The First English Cricket Tour: The fascinating story of George Parr's XI in Canada and the United States in 1859 (Chequered Flag, paperback, £11.99)

Robinson, Neil **Long Shot Summer** The Year of the Four England Captains 1988 (Amberley, paperback, £14.99)

Samiuddin, Osman **The Unquiet Ones** A History of Pakistan Cricket (HarperCollins India, Rs799)

Simpson, Peter **The History of Whalley Range Cricket & Lawn Tennis Club** Volume 1 1845–1945 (from Whalley Range C&LTC, Kingsbrook Road, M16 8NR, £10 inc p&p)

Smyth, Rob **Gentlemen and Sledgers** A History of the Ashes in 100 Quotations and Confrontations (Head of Zeus, £16.99)

Stephen, Duncan D. **South Northumberland** 150 Not Out 1864–2014 (South Northumberland Cricket Club, paperback, £20 + £5 p&p; more information from ddstephen@dsas.freeserve.co.uk)

Sweetman, Simon **Dimming of the Day** The Cricket Season of 1914 Foreword by Eric Midwinter (ACS, paperback, £14)

Thomas, Andrew **Pears 150** The life and times of Worcestershire County Cricket Club 1865–2014 (privately published, paperback, £28 – more details from the author on pears80wyverns@gmail.com)

Tossell, David **Sex & Drugs & Rebel Tours** The England Cricket Team in the 1980s (Pitch, £18.99)

White, Simon **Quick Singles** The Cricket Paper columns Foreword by David Emery (The White Words, paperback, £14.99)

Wigmore, Tim and Miller, Peter **Second XI** Cricket in its Outposts Foreword by Gideon Haigh (Pitch, paperback, £12.99)

Winder, Robert **Half-Time** The Glorious Summer of 1934 (Bloomsbury, £18.99)

Woolley, Trevor **Unnatural Selection** 50 Years of England Test Teams (Von Krumm, £15)

ILLUSTRATED

Coster, Graham **Snow Stopped Play** The Mysterious World of the Cricket Ground in Winter (Safe Haven, £14.99)

Lockyer, Alain, with Walsh, Richard **Somerset County Cricket Club** The Return to Glory 2001–2007 (Halsgrove, £19.99)

BIOGRAPHY

Allen, Dean **Empire, War & Cricket in South Africa** Logan of Matjiesfontein (Zebra Press, £18.99)

Bonnell, Max **Lucky** The Life of H. L. "Bert" Collins: cricketer, soldier, gambler (CricketBooks.com.au, $A50)

Burns, Michael **A Flick of the Fingers** The Chequered Life and Career of Jack Crawford (Pitch, £17.99)

Connelly, Charlie **Gilbert** The Last Years of W. G. Grace (John Wisden, £10.99)

Connolly, Paul, ed. **Richie Benaud** 1930–2015 Those Summers of Cricket (Hardie Grant, £20)

Dolman, Steve **Edwin Smith** A Life in Derbyshire Cricket (ACS, paperback, £14)

Frith, David **Stoddy** England's Finest Sportsman (Von Krumm, £17)

Holder, James **Sport's Great All-Rounders** A Biographical Dictionary (AuthorHouse, £19.99)

Howe, Martin **Norman Yardley** Yorkshire's Gentleman Cricketer (ACS, paperback, £14)

Jones, Tim **Don Kenyon** His Own Man (Amberley, paperback, £17)

Lane, Tim and Cartledge, Elliot **Chasing Shadows** The Life & Death of Peter Roebuck (Hardie Grant, paperback, £12.99)

McLeish, Duncan **Alec Watson** Chucker? (ACS, paperback, £13)

Meredith, Anthony **W. G. Grace** In the Steps of a Legend (Amberley, £18.99)

Murtagh, Andrew **Sundial in the Shade** The Story of Barry Richards: The Genius Lost to Test Cricket (Pitch, £18.99)

Rendell, Brian **Frank and George Mann** Brewing, Batting and Captaincy (ACS, paperback, £14)

Richardson, Nick **The Silk Express** The Story of E. A. "Ted" McDonald (CricketBooks.com.au, $A50)

Shindler, Colin **Bob Barber** The Professional Amateur (Max Books, £16)

Tomlinson, Richard **Amazing Grace** The Man who was W.G. (Little, Brown, £25)

AUTOBIOGRAPHY

Adams, Chris, with Talbot, Bruce **Grizzly** My Life and Times in Cricket (Pitch, £18.99)

Ambrose, Curtly and Sydenham, Richard **Time to Talk** Forewords by Richie Benaud and Steve Waugh (Aurum, £18.99)

Broad, Stuart, with Peters, Sam **Broadside** How We Regained the Ashes (Simon & Schuster, £20)

Flintoff, Andrew, with Smith, Ed **Second Innings** My Sporting Life (Hodder & Stoughton, £20)

Harris, Ryan, with Gray, Stephen and Phelan, Jason **Rhino** (Hardie Grant, £20)

Jones, Simon, and Hotten, Jon **The Test** My Life, and the Inside Story of the Greatest Ashes Series (Yellow Jersey, £18.99)

Lloyd, David **Last in the Tin Bath** The Autobiography (Simon & Schuster, £20)

Root, Joe, with Gibson, Richard **Bringing Home The Ashes** (Hodder & Stoughton, £20)

Tufnell, Phil **Where Am I?** My Autobiography (Headline, £20)

ANTHOLOGY

Benaud, Richie & friends **Remembering Richie** Foreword by Michael Parkinson (Hodder & Stoughton, £20)

Rice, Jonathan, ed. **Wisden on Grace** An Anthology (John Wisden, £20)

Smyth, Rob, ed. **Benaud in Wisden** Foreword by Alan Davidson (John Wisden, £10.99)

Whitehead, Richard, ed. **The Times on the Ashes** Covering Sport's Greatest Rivalry from 1877 to the Present Day Foreword by Mike Atherton (The History Press, £20)

FICTION

Aspin, Chris **Out of this World** Cricket as you've never known it (Royd House, paperback, £4.95. Available from the author: 21 Westbourne, Helmshore Road, Haslingden, Rossendale, Lancashire BB4 4QD)

Cattell, Bob **First XI** Eleven Stories of the World of Cricket (Charlcombe Books, paperback, £7.99)

STATISTICAL

Bailey, Philip comp. **First-Class Cricket Matches 1950** and **1951** (ACS Sales, Ivymead, Castle Road, Pevensey, East Sussex BN24 5LG, email: sales@acscricket.com, paperback, £27 and £30 respectively)

Lawton Smith, Julian, ed. **The Minor Counties Championship 1909** and **1910** (ACS, paperback, £16 each)

Lynch, Steven, ed. **The Wisden Book of Test Cricket 2009–2014** (John Wisden, £25)

Percival, Tony **Wiltshire Cricketers 1858–1914** (ACS, paperback, £12)

HANDBOOKS AND ANNUALS

Bailey, Philip, ed. **ACS International Cricket Year Book 2015** (ACS, paperback, £30)

Bryant, John, ed. **ACS Overseas First-Class Annual 2015** (ACS, paperback, £65)
Full scorecards for first-class matches outside England in 2014-15.

Bryden, Colin, ed. **South African Cricket Annual 2015** (CSA, www.sacricketshop.co.za, R200 + p&p)

Clayton, Howard, ed. **First-Class Counties Second Eleven Annual 2015** (ACS, paperback, £12)

Colliver, Lawrie, ed. **Australian Cricket Digest 2015-16** (paperback, $A25 + p&p; more information from lawrie.colliver@gmail.com)

Harman, Jo, ed. **The Cricketers' Who's Who 2015** Foreword by Moeen Ali (PCA/All Out Cricket, £19.99)

Marshall, Ian, ed. **Playfair Cricket Annual 2015** (Headline, paperback, £8.99)

Payne, Francis and Smith, Ian, ed. **2015 New Zealand Cricket Almanack** (Upstart Press, \$NZ55)

REPRINTS AND UPDATES

Booth, Keith **The Father of Modern Sport** The Life and Times of Charles W. Alcock   Foreword by Sir John Major (Chequered Flag, paperback, £11.99)

Lynch, Steven, ed. **Wisden on the Ashes** The Authoritative Story of Cricket's Greatest Rivalry (new edition includes the 2015 series; John Wisden, £50)

Ponting, Ricky **Ponting** At the Close of Play (HarperSport, paperback, £9.99)

PERIODICALS

All Out Cricket ed. Phil Walker (PCA Management/TriNorth, £4.25; £39.99 for 12 print issues, £29.99 digital. Subscriptions: alloutcricket.subscribeonline.co.uk)

The Cricketer (monthly) ed. Simon Hughes (The Cricketer Publishing, £4.50; £44.99 for 12 print issues, £24.99 digital, £49.99 print & digital. Subscriptions: www.thecricketer.com or ring 0844 815 0864)

The Cricket Paper (weekly) ed. David Emery (Greenways Publishing, £1.50; £20 for ten issues inc. p&p. From www.thecricketpaper.com)

The Cricket Statistician (quarterly) ed. Simon Sweetman (ACS, £3 to non-members)

The Journal of the Cricket Society (twice yearly) (from D. Seymour, 13 Ewhurst Road, Crofton Park, London, SE4 1AG, £5 to non-members)

CRICKET IN THE MEDIA IN 2015

Me mum and a stick o' rhubarb

PHILIP COLLINS

The truism about news in an age when spectrum is no longer scarce is that there is more of it. With series from India, the West Indies and South Africa, as well as the visits to England of New Zealand and Australia, all taken in by your correspondent in 2015 for more love than money, there is certainly more cricket to watch. The veteran of the radio-under-the-bedclothes, after-the-lights-have-gone-off commentary from Tests in Australia might think there is a beauty in scarcity. Yet it is likely that, somewhere in Britain, a small boy or girl will be nurturing a love for the game, under the covers, watching furtively on an iPad. The nagging question, however, remains. There is a lot to see and read, but is more and more reaching fewer and fewer?

Viewers with subscriptions have a cornucopia every time they turn on the TV. It is a rare day when the latest 20-over smash-and-grab from a domestic cash-cow league is not playing out somewhere. All of it is loud, and none of it memorable. The coverage of Australia's Big Bash featured Adam Gilchrist, Ricky Ponting and Mark Waugh trying to outshout each other for 40 overs of instantly forgettable cricket.

But, to forget it, you have to have watched it in the first place, and the biggest concern is that Test cricket in England is not reaching enough people (even when you factor in the nightly highlights package on Channel 5). When England secured victory on the Saturday of the First Test against Australia, it was in front of a television audience of 467,000. During the 2001 Ashes, Channel 4 pulled in an average of 1.1m a day; in 2005, that had risen to 2.5m, with an amazing 8.4m watching the climax of the Fourth Test at Trent Bridge. The move to Sky was lucrative, and £65m a year is not to be sniffed at. But an audience has been lost.

Meanwhile, there are still the hardy perennials. *Test Match Special* is rather like George Orwell's photograph on the mantelpiece. What do you have in common with that picture of yourself as a five-year-old, he asks, before responding: "Nothing, except that you happen to be the same person." But the danger of longevity is of toppling into self-parody. At its worst, *TMS* sounds like a bunch of boys acting out what it must be like to be on *TMS*. Graeme Swann and Phil Tufnell have things to say, but they need to be careful not to be tempted into tomfoolery. Also, just as shots minted in one-day cricket are appearing in Tests, so the breathless pace of Twenty20 is turning up on *TMS*. Every day is a new story for Michael Vaughan, who – unlike his batting – struggles with Test cricket's rhythmic ebbs and flows.

That said, *TMS* still provides moments of magic. Geoffrey Boycott can too easily slide into caricature but, on a car journey during the Third Ashes Test, I witnessed him, in concert with the best broadcaster of the lot, hooking in a

Keeping up appearances: former New Zealand gloveman Ian Smith gains some last-minute attention before his next television stint.

new pair of fans from the next generation. As Boycott embarked on one of his funny-the-first-time tirades about his mum and a stick o' rhubarb, the estimable Jonathan Agnew intervened with a gently mocking "Yes, Geoffrey." The humour also contained some wisdom: hidden in Boycott's imprecation was a truth about Ian Bell and soft dismissals, which Bell, to his credit, acknowledged next day with a half-century. It is largely due to Agnew, the BBC's cricket correspondent, and the calm help of Australia's Jim Maxwell, that *TMS* spent most of the summer on the right side of caricature.

Over at Sky, there is a palpable need for a refresh. Nowhere is the limitation of preferring the former Test player over the professional journalist more evident. As I write, one of David Gower's multi-clause questions is still winding its way towards a banal statement which leaves the respondent with nothing to say. Sir Ian Botham sounds, by turns, bored and weary, becoming animated only to demand that the batting team declare. David Lloyd plays the joker with charm; his enthusiasm is welcome, though he does not often bring insight.

The two exceptions are Michael Atherton and Nasser Hussain, both of whom add more than the viewer can see – surely the point of television commentary. On radio, the listener needs a picture painted. On TV, we can see for ourselves where the ball pitched and how the batsman played it. When Peter Siddle belatedly returned to the Australian team, at The Oval, Hussain provided an informed lament about bowlers who offer a captain no control, which served to underline Siddle's value.

Atherton's on-screen analysis of Michael Clarke's last day in the field had all the sympathy you would expect from another Test captain with a bad back. The commentary made you feel you knew the player better – and not many can do it. Michael Holding, for example, is mellifluous but doesn't say much. Room should be made for more guests. Ian Smith was sparky and intelligent during the New Zealand series, and Ponting had his moments during the Ashes.

There is plenty of good analysis before and after the actual cricket. The sessions in the nets, hosted by Ian Ward, are unlikely to feature in montages of great TV, but for the aficionado there is treasure. Both Shane Warne and Ponting were able to describe how they did what they did in tones that were compelling and not patronising to cricketers who will never reach their level.

After the day's play, Sky's *The Verdict* draws the threads. Unobtrusively chaired by Charles Colvile, it allows three pundits time for reflection. Jeremy Coney and Tom Moody were impartial and incisive representatives of the two touring countries. Despite the regrettable attempt to turn him into a character, Bob Willis is sparing with his praise, which is therefore more meaningful when it comes. *The Verdict* is also making a broadcasting star of Mark Butcher, who is articulate and forthright, and ought to be used more widely. One cannot help think that his Test career wasn't quite stellar enough (Gower, Botham, Vaughan) and his comic value isn't quite high enough (Lloyd, Boycott, Blofeld) to warrant a place at the top table.

> The newspapers have not been entirely colonised by old pros

If the supply of cricket broadcasting is abundant to a shrunken audience, the newspapers are cutting their cloth accordingly. Declining circulation leads to falling revenue, which plays havoc with county cricket reports. The days when a reader could settle down to 700 finely wrought words on the second day at Hove are long gone. Even in the broadsheets, reports are compressed into a column or two, and sometimes scorecards are elusive. The lover of county cricket is now better served by the fine range of cricket magazines and websites.

There is still some excellent writing around, though. Vic Marks and Mike Selvey in *The Observer* and *The Guardian*, and Atherton in *The Times* all show that the divide between playing the game and writing on it can be straddled. The newspapers have not been entirely colonised by old pros: Scyld Berry remains an elegant presence in the *Daily Telegraph*. In the tabloids, cricket feels as if it is hanging on under assault from a football season that goes on ever longer and starts ever earlier, but laurels are due to Paul Newman of the *Daily Mail*, who is continuing a tradition of sports writing in a newspaper that has a claim to be bettered by none.

As is traditional, the early part of the summer was dominated by a Kevin Pietersen saga; his continued absence from the international scene was drily noted by Marks: "Outside England, they think we are all mad. Even Kumar Sangakkara, the sagest of cricketing sages, thinks we are mad." The issue largely disappeared once the cricket started, when it was a pleasure to welcome Gideon Haigh to the British pages. There was no better guide to a series that broke an Australian side in half. On the retirement of Clarke, Haigh was

Laurence Griffiths, Getty Images

Broad-minded: a spectator at Trent Bridge reads about the first day's play of the Fourth Test, which put cricket on front and back pages.

typically waspish and vivid: "Clarke's dedication could not be faulted. But, then, nor could an anchorite's. And it is possible that Clarke's personal austerity this summer shaded his own team's ambitions. Certainly while England players have been talking of expressing themselves and showing off their talents, their counterparts have fallen back on those joyless clichés about 'work rate' and 'work ethic', as though toiling in a coal mine."

The oddity of an Ashes in which England had two shocking games in London yet won handsomely in the provinces was reflected in less than exuberant prose. In *The Guardian*, Selvey deftly rose to the occasion when the Ashes were won, while subtly acknowledging that the occasion was flatter than it might have been: "'If it were done when 'tis done, then 'twere well it were done quickly,' spoke Macbeth. At Trent Bridge, the end was indeed swift, the assassination of an Australian team that had arrived full of bluster and proved to be a lot of hot air… There was no real resistance."

Among the good material there was one lacuna in 2015, and one excess. The mostly missing element was the game's politics. In a time when the sport's central question is where the money is flowing and how, cricket journalists have rarely broken new ground. That complacency is best illustrated by the insufficient attention paid to the documentary *Death of a Gentleman*, made by Sam Collins and Jarrod Kimber.

DoaG was an accusation that administrators are greedy and amateur, and that too much money leads inevitably to corruption. In the shadow of a spate of match-fixing accusations, it was a cogent critique of the ICC and cricket's myopic politics, and an examination of three influential men: Giles Clarke of the ECB, Narayanaswami Srinivasan, then the chairman of the ICC, and Lalit Modi, the founder of the Indian Premier League. This story is not as easy to write about as Steve Smith's strange technique, but it matters more.

The excess was the Ashes hype. A wonderful series against New Zealand was written up as little more than a prelude, the tourists patted on the head for being so entertaining. Even in Berry's appreciative look back in the *Daily Telegraph*, there is a hint that their function was to warm England up for the Ashes: "It was not only the best of the early-season tours of England since they were inaugurated in 2000. New Zealand's visit was one of the happiest, most stimulating and most memorable of all international cricket tours to England… By playing so enterprisingly, New Zealand brought England out of themselves."

The journalistic pack seemed to take the Ashes at the estimation of the marketing people. As a rule, things that are special do not need their specialness pointed out. Ironically, perhaps, the best advert for what was to follow came from the supreme over-sellers at Sky. Set to Billy Joel's "We Didn't Start The Fire", with quick excerpts from pundits, it managed to make the impending series both funny and engrossing. Cricket coverage has to be wary of self-parody and excessive solemnity. This clever advert got the tone right.

It was, however, preaching to the converted. Cricket, like all other media pursuits, is being winnowed down into a niche: a subscription audience on television and tighter column inches in the newspapers. For the committed fan, these are days of glory. The worry is that there will never be any passing observers to stumble on the game, to have there imagination caught by the wonder of it all. Cricket in the media is a good example of everything else in the media, slowly being driven into avenues populated only by the cognoscenti. It is no longer the radio under the bedclothes, but it can be just as exciting. We need to get the message out.

Philip Collins is a columnist on The Times.

CRICKET AND BLOGS IN 2015

Nostalgia: a retrospective

Brian Carpenter

It would be all too easy to get the impression that cricket is in decline. After all, it always has been. Glance idly at an old *Wisden*, and the editor's Notes will probably be tinged with anxiety at the game's shifting sands. This is an established part of cricket's emotional narrative, as confirmed by one of Giles Clarke's many memorable contributions to the *Death of a Gentleman* documentary film. At one point, he responds with customary irritation to a line of questioning from producer Sam Collins by telling him that his concerns about the game's future are "straight out of *Wisden 1909*".

Blogging may be rather younger, but it too conveys a sense that things aren't quite what they used to be. That one of the original siren voices of cricket's blogosphere, Jarrod Kimber, is now an established voice on ESPNcricinfo and collaborated on *DoaG*, shows how the blogosphere's foundations are moving. Writers such as Kimber and the peerless Jon Hotten increasingly appear in places that guarantee a wider readership. Others, meanwhile, find it hard to weave writing into crowded lives.

Yet cricket's amateur scribes still produce many finely crafted views on the game's past, present and future. They reflect their authors' knowledge, dedication, intelligence and humour. Until recently, they might not have found an audience at all.

One essential element of cricket's internal dialogue is nostalgia, which in the writing of Peter Hoare (mylifeincricketscorecards.blogspot.com) is for the sights, sounds and experiences of a 1970s upbringing in Kent infused with county cricket. Hoare's fine portfolio includes an often sublime appreciation of Derek Underwood on his 70th birthday: "Swiss-clock accurate" and feeding on the New Zealand batting "like a whale at a plankton convention". And he recalls the day in 1975 when Kent beat the Australians. You were not there – you barely remember the players – but, reading Hoare's description of Colin Cowdrey hooking Dennis Lillee, you feel like the boy on the St Lawrence Ground boundary.

Elsewhere, Hoare writes about how his adopted country embraced cricket during the 2015 World Cup: "New Zealand's two World Cup games at the Cake Tin have been two of the best days I have ever spent at the cricket. Years hence I shall remember them if I can't recall my own name. The nation has become consumed with cricket. You hear people talking about it as you walk down the street. I have always wanted to live in such a place." Hoare encompasses the longings and desires of those of us who love the game and want others to love it too. In New Zealand, March 2015 was cricket's time in the sun.

Inevitably, nostalgia greeted the death of Richie Benaud. This was the end not just of a great cricketing life, but of a central part of the consciousness

of virtually anyone who followed the game in the late 20th century. With his customary sureness of touch, the tireless Gary Naylor, at 99.94 (**nestaquin.wordpress.com**), writes about what Benaud meant to him. With feeling and understated lyricism, Naylor later reflects on the ways in which his love affair with cricket has developed, including his reading about it, and how he has come to appreciate the architecture of the game's grounds.

But the blogosphere has far more to offer than nostalgia, and continues to provide pungent contemporary comment. As in 2014, the fortunes of someone who, it soon became apparent, still had no future in the international game, occupied the thoughts of many writers. Christian Drury (**adomesticghost.wordpress.com**) was in typically descriptive mood while marking the tantalising return of Kevin Pietersen for Surrey at Oxford's Parks in April: "He scooped a delivery from a medium-pacer for four, like a man shovelling dirt over his shoulder." The indefatigable Dmitri Old, latterly at **beingoutsidecricket.com**, and Maxie Allen at **thefulltoss.com** made sure KP's virtues could not be forgotten, even as his career at the highest level, for good or ill, faded into the past. Neither, is a one-trick pony: along with Peter Casterton ("Tregaskis") at **dropinpitch.com**, they fight to keep the mainstream cricket media honest. Allen appeared to have reached the end of the road in the autumn. But then we thought that about Old last year.

At Declaration Game (**chrispscricket.wordpress.com**), Chris Smith interweaves a range of themes, including personal memories, the game's vocabulary and statistics, and youth cricket in England's North-West. His high points were two vivid similes in one post in July. Allan Border's walk to the crease, richly familiar to those of a certain age, was "like a meerkat

CRICKET AND TWITTER IN 2015

Better luck next year

Nishant Joshi

According to the former ECB managing director Hugh Morris, allowing cricketers on Twitter was "like giving a machine gun to a monkey". But, in 2015, it seemed the monkeys had learned – after a great deal of introspection – that a machine gun is a dangerous object and must be used with discretion. After several years of reliable tragicomedy, in which you could set your watch by a cricketer tweeting abuse at a sneering fan or an unappreciative selector, we have reached an uneasy stalemate. Players are so scarred by previous excursions that they will not be trolled. They are playing for the draw, dead-batting the long-hops.

The glory days of Kevin Pietersen questioning Nick Knight's commentary credentials – and earning a fine of £2,500 from the ECB – seem to be over. And so we move ever closer to an anaesthetised, self-censored version of Twitter. Cricketers receive training in social media and, in many cases, their agents post tweets on their behalf. Some boards encourage their players to avoid even looking at tweets from fans, let alone replying. After all, an inoffensive half-joke could be misinterpreted, which could result in negative publicity… and who knows what other horrors.

Many tweets are now photos of cricketers showcasing the latest freebies from their sponsors, or photos of their dog, or photos of their dog wearing freebies from their sponsors. That's not to say there's no controversy. "Look out for the bouncers at the @Qantas lounges," tweeted Shaun Tait (@shaun_tait32). "Refused entry for inappropriate footwear. Getting all a bit serious aren't we." In a year dominated by the plight of Syrian refugees and the scourge of Isis, it was a reminder that we must never take for granted the inconvenience that accompanies wearing flip-flops. Only one hashtag felt appropriate in the circumstances: #PrayforTait.

Of course, the odd delivery can slip through even the tightest of defences, as Kumar Sangakkara (@KumarSanga2) and well over 500,000 followers discovered in September, when a photo of an erect penis was tweeted from his account during a game between Surrey and Derbyshire. Deletion was as swift as his apology: "Guys my Twitter account has been hacked. I need to reset my account. It's unbelievable. Apologies. In the middle of a county game… Thank god we walked in for lunch." Ian Botham had suffered a similar indignity the previous year, which makes you wonder which legend these hackers have lined up for 2016.

New Zealand's Jimmy Neesham (@JimmyNeesh), meanwhile, had an encouraging year in international cricket, but his future as its foremost tweeter is just as bright. Acerbic and witty, with a mixed bag of original jokes, live commentary and judicious use of memes, Neesham stole the show with tweets such as: "First ever erectile dysfunction ad during a day-night Test. Historic."

Neesham was unafraid to venture into contentious waters: "You don't do a public vote to decide how to build a bridge or run an airport, and the flag referendum shows why," he tweeted as New Zealanders pondered whether to cut ties with the Union flag. "People are dumb."

He also offered candid insight into his domestic life, far beyond what other cricketers were prepared to share: "I'm playing monopoly with my girlfriend. The trust levels are such that she's just taken the bank to the toilet with her." @JimmyNeesh, you are our beacon of hope.

Nishant Joshi tweets @AltCricket.

looking out for airborne predators". And Jonny Bairstow "works his limbs like someone unfamiliar with cross-country skis trying to escape a polar bear over snow".

Even in a sphere of activity where anyone can write anything and have it read anywhere, William le Breton (**downatthirdman.wordpress.com**) remains an outlier. He can be oblique, but his considerable strengths lie in his understanding of the game and in his willingness to kick against cosy consensus. During the Ashes he was one of the few to raise doubts about the way in which pitches were prepared to suit England. He also highlighted the influence of a brief shower shortly before the start of the Fourth Test at Trent Bridge which, coupled with what he saw as inadequate covering, left the track compromised on the first morning. Everyone knows what happened next.

As the year closed, le Breton's tribute to the retiring Mitchell Johnson was written in characteristic style: Johnson's "physique and deportment were those of an Olympic athlete. His approach… delivered him to the crease like a piston-driven engine, and then there was that curvy flick of a drag from the trailing leg that appropriately each ball wrote a question mark in the air an inch above the bowling crease."

It is tempting to see the relationship between blogging and Twitter as that of Test cricket and Twenty20. In an age of shortening attention spans, Test cricket feels vulnerable to Twenty20's more superficial attractions. But there is enough depth of regard for its qualities, laid down over countless decades, and enough new talent replacing the old, to make it feel as though it will be around long into the future.

Instinctively, this feels less true of blogging – and yet the blogosphere's strength is that it represents so many things to so many people. For some, it is a valuable repository for individual memories and an aid to solitary reflection; for others, it acts as a collective focus for hopes, fears and antagonisms. In cricket, things are never quite what they used to be, but the game, with all its glorious contradictions, will endure. The strong suspicion is that blogging will do the same.

Brian Carpenter has been reading and writing about cricket for many years. In 2013 he was the inaugural winner of Wisden's *writing competition.*

RETIREMENTS IN 2015

Putting the gloves away

STEVE JAMES

It was not a good year for wicketkeepers, as **Matt Prior**, Craig Kieswetter and Geraint Jones took their leave. All were born abroad, but all represented England with distinction. The best was undoubtedly Prior, who will be remembered as one of England's finest Test batsmen-keepers: only Alan Knott snaffled more than his 256 dismissals, and he was ninth on the all-time Test list when he called it a day.

If that was just reward for much hard work with the gloves after an indifferent beginning, Prior's class with the bat was never in doubt. The first of his seven Test hundreds, on debut against West Indies at Lord's in 2007, was his fastest, from just 105 balls, and two of his three other quickest centuries also came at Lord's: against Sri Lanka (107 balls) and India (120), both in 2011. But he could rein it in, too, saving the Auckland Test – and the series – in March 2013 with an unbeaten 110 in four and a half hours.

Born in South Africa, but arriving in England aged 11, Prior was an aggressive batsman who favoured the off side with his clean inside-out hitting. That allowed him to exploit the untenanted boundaries in Test cricket, but in one-day internationals, with the field more widely spread, he was more easily restrained. His one-day average of 24 was 16 fewer than his Test figure.

His career was ended prematurely by an Achilles injury, and he didn't play any first-class cricket in 2015, when he devoted plenty of time to a new passion, cycling. But he was involved in three Ashes victories, and his energy, especially between the wickets at the end of every over, made him the heartbeat of the side who reached the top of the Test rankings in 2011.

Graham Morris

Geraint Jones

Craig Kieswetter also helped England to the pinnacle, in his case the World Twenty20 title in the Caribbean in 2010 when, opening the innings in the final against Australia, he won the match award for his swift 63. Born, like Prior, in Johannesburg, Kieswetter played for South Africa Under-19 before attending Millfield School. I witnessed his Somerset senior debut in 2007, when he made a startling 69 not out off 58 balls from No. 8 against Glamorgan in a one-day match. He also took a catch, to dismiss Alex Wharf, that his director of cricket, Brian Rose, correctly called "world-class".

Blessed with the quickest of hands, Kieswetter whacked the ball as far as any of his England colleagues, both in the range-hitting practices that became the norm, and in his 46 ODIs and 25 T20Is. Sadly, in 2014, he was hit in the face by a bouncer from Northamptonshire's David Willey, resulting in a broken nose and significant damage to his right eye. He attempted to play again, but his eyesight was impaired, and in June he retired, aged just 27.

Geraint Jones will be for ever remembered for his contribution to the 2005 Ashes, especially his catch down the leg side at Edgbaston to dismiss Michael Kasprowicz and secure England's heart-stopping two-run victory. He was always a controversial choice by coach Duncan Fletcher ahead of the more classical keeping qualities of Chris Read, but he brought many valuable runs, as well as a significant voice behind the stumps, in his 34 Tests.

Jones, part of Kent's proud wicketkeeping lineage, was born in Papua New Guinea to Welsh parents. His first club in England was my own, at Lydney in Gloucestershire, where he made such an impression as an affable youngster that my father, the club president, felt moved to write to his parents to compliment them on their son's character. He played in two one-day internationals for PNG against Hong Kong in 2014, and ended his career on a high at Gloucestershire, top-scoring in the final of the Royal London One-Day Cup at Lord's to help pip Surrey.

Also part of England's World Twenty20 success in 2010 was **Michael Yardy**, whose darting not-so-slow left-armers formed a useful alliance with Graeme Swann's off-spin. But it was as an unorthodox left-handed batsman – with an exaggerated pre-delivery movement across his crease – that Yardy forged a successful county career with Sussex. He made 23 first-class centuries, and helped Sussex win seven trophies, including three Championships; he was captain for two one-day titles. All this came despite a constant battle with depression that forced him to return early from the 2011 World Cup in India. He was hugely respected on the county circuit, as a cricketer and a man.

Whereas Yardy made the most of his talents, **Chris Tremlett**, who seemed to have everything, could not. He stood 6ft 7in and possessed a strong-looking physique, yet robustness failed him: injuries became a recurring and debilitating theme. He played 12 Tests for England, claiming 17 wickets in three of them in Australia in 2010-11. That was as good as it got. Maybe he was just too genial for a fast bowler, often giving the impression he did not begrudge a batsman's occupation of the crease. Son of Tim and grandson of Maurice, he began his career at Hampshire before moving to Surrey.

Vikram Solanki, too, ended up at Surrey, but he played his best cricket at Worcestershire, where his supple elegance (and extraordinarily high pick-up) helped him to 34 first-class centuries. He appeared in 51 ODIs – an England record for a non-Test cricketer – scoring two hundreds. **Stephen Peters** became a very reliable county batsman, recovering from the expectation of being touted as a future England player after his century guided England to the 1998 Under-19 World Cup. He was most consistent at his third county, Northamptonshire, having previously been at Essex and Worcestershire.

Paul Franks played in one ODI, in 2000, but had to settle for a long and productive career at Nottinghamshire, as an energetic seamer and useful left-handed batsman. **Kabir Ali**, of Worcestershire, Hampshire and Lancashire, won a single Test cap, in 2003, against South Africa at Headingley, and appeared in 14 ODIs. With a slingy, low arm, he could swing the ball at a decent pace, but his fitness was not always dependable.

A fine left-arm spinner, **Gary Keedy** was unfortunate never to have played Test cricket. He took 696 first-class wickets, turning out for Lancashire for 18 years, before

Graham Morris

Paul Franks

flirting with Surrey and Nottinghamshire. **Ashwell Prince** finished at Lancashire, having played 66 Tests for South Africa, the last in December 2011. He had intended to retire at the end of the 2014 season, but was persuaded to stay on, and helped Lancashire to promotion. At Colwyn Bay in July, he put on 501 with compatriot Alviro Petersen.

Rory Hamilton-Brown was a gifted strokemaker, who captained Surrey at the age of just 22, but he retired at 27 during his second spell at Sussex, because of a wrist injury. He was greatly affected by the death of his close friend, Tom Maynard, in 2012. New Zealander **Andre Adams** called a halt to his 17-year career after a brief spell at Hampshire, but he enjoyed eight prosperous seasons at Nottinghamshire where he took 344 first-class wickets at 24, prompting flattering comparisons with Richard Hadlee.

CAREER FIGURES
Players not expected to appear in county cricket in 2016
(minimum 50 first-class appearances)

BATTING

	M	I	NO	R	HS	100	Avge	1,000r/ season
A. R. Adams	173	237	24	4,540	124	3	21.31	–
A. P. Agathangelou	53	96	6	2,774	158	5	30.82	0+1
G. M. Andrew	90	136	17	2,909	180*	1	24.44	–
D. J. Balcombe . . .	67	83	20	958	73	0	15.20	–
M. D. Bates	52	69	10	1,177	103	1	19.94	–
M. A. Chambers . .	64	86	24	410	58	0	6.61	–
J. L. Clare	57	82	9	1,725	130	2	23.63	–
P. J. Franks	215	313	56	7,185	123*	4	27.95	–
G. O. Jones	203	309	29	9,087	178	15	32.45	2
G. Keedy	227	262	128	1,448	64	0	10.80	–
C. Kieswetter.	115	171	25	5,728	164	11	39.23	1
T. E. Linley	64	89	20	569	42	0	8.24	–
S. D. Peters	260	440	32	14,231	222	31	34.87	4
K. P. Pietersen . . .	217	358	26	16,522	355*	50	49.76	3
A. G. Prince	288	465	49	18,484	261	45	44.43	4+1
M. J. Prior	249	381	44	13,228	201*	28	39.25	3
R. M. Pyrah	51	61	8	1,621	134*	3	30.58	–
D. J. Redfern	85	145	9	3,905	133	2	28.71	–
G. M. Smith	124	202	18	5,635	177	7	30.62	–
V. S. Solanki	325	546	33	18,359	270	34	35.78	6
A. C. Thomas	164	228	49	4,130	119*	2	23.07	–
C. T. Tremlett . . .	146	183	45	2,462	90	0	17.84	–
B. J. Wright	89	146	10	3,684	172	6	27.08	–
M. H. Yardy	193	320	27	10,693	257	23	36.49	2

1+1 indicates one season in England and one overseas.

BOWLING

	R	W	BB	Avge	5I	10M	Ct/St
A. R. Adams	16,581	692	7-32	23.96	32	6	115
A. P. Agathangelou	469	10	2-18	46.90	–	–	85
G. M. Andrew. . . .	7,793	231	5-40	33.73	6	–	30
D. J. Balcombe	6,436	196	8-71	32.83	9	2	14
M. D. Bates	–	–	–	–	–	–	149/7
M. A. Chambers . . .	5,383	155	6-68	34.72	3	1	19
J. L. Clare	4,268	154	7-74	27.71	6	1	28
P. J. Franks	17,322	524	7-56	33.05	11	–	69
G. O. Jones	26	0	–	–	–	–	599/36
G. Keedy	21,851	696	7-68	31.39	35	7	57
C. Kieswetter	–	–	–	–	–	–	331/12
T. E. Linley	5,519	200	6-57	27.59	6	1	21
S. D. Peters	31	1	1-19	31.00	–	–	192
K. P. Pietersen . . .	3,760	73	4-31	51.50	–	–	152
A. G. Prince	179	4	2-11	44.75	–	–	221
M. J. Prior	–	–	–	–	–	–	642/41
R. M. Pyrah	2,527	55	5-58	45.94	1	–	22
D. J. Redfern	815	21	3-33	38.80	–	–	41
G. M. Smith	6,502	184	5-42	35.33	4	–	43
V. S. Solanki	4,230	90	5-40	47.00	4	1	350
A. C. Thomas	14,412	547	7-54	26.34	25	4	42
C. M. Tremlett . . .	13,158	459	8-96	28.66	13	–	38
B. J. Wright	174	2	1-14	87.00	–	–	47
M. H. Yardy	2,192	29	5-83	75.58	1	–	184

CRICKETANA IN 2015

Magnificent shot selection

MARCUS WILLIAMS

It may be a little premature to call it a trend. But for the second edition running this article leads with the lesser-known sibling of a famous name. Where last year the spotlight fell on Roger Hancock (brother of Tony), whose cricket library sold for over £450,000, it shone now on E. M. Grace, older brother of perhaps the most fabled cricketer of all time. His collection of memorabilia, including many unique items, was offered on behalf of his great-grandson at a Knights Sporting auction in Leicester, and achieved some spectacular results.

Edward Mills Grace established a reputation as a prolific all-rounder before falling, like all other contemporary cricketers, under the shadow of WG, seven years his junior. However, EM continued playing on into his late sixties, longer even than his brother. There is no doubt he enjoyed his cricket, and the numbers associated with his career are prodigious. He is estimated to have hit 76,760 runs and taken 12,078 wickets; he also married four times and fathered 18 children. And, as the contents of the sale showed, he wrote many thousands of words in his diaries and letters.

Appropriately enough, a bid of £76,000 secured the prime lot: the original manuscript of *The Cricketer's Trip to Australia [and New Zealand] 1863 & 1864 by Edward Mills Grace*, which ran to 224 large handwritten pages and described in great detail the tour by George Parr's team:

> For the cricketer I have attempted as good an account as I could give of the different matches, for the lovers of scenery, for the lovers of wild adventure, for the observer of the customs which obtain in new countries, for those who enquire as to the elements of Australia's future greatness, for the philosopher, for the intending emigrant, for the bulk of English people who feel drawn to the distant land because many of their friends are there, for each and all I have attempted to do my best.

The account was intended for publication on his return from the eight-month expedition – but it never found a publisher. The pre-sale estimate was £18,000–25,000, yet was far exceeded: once buyer's premium was added (the inclusive figure is used for the rest of this article) the successful bidder paid £93,328.

Other items also attracted fierce competition. At Canterbury in 1862, Grace, a late call-up for MCC, took all ten wickets "with my slow underhand" – having already hit 192 not out – against Gentlemen of Kent. The ball, complete with a circular silver plaque, fetched £29,472; a colourful crocheted belt, with clasp inscribed to him by "a few lady friends of Redcliff Cricket Club" and worn throughout the 1863-64 trip, realised £15,964; and a leatherbound diary from the tour, devoted to the sea travel to Australia and New Zealand, and the early matches played in Melbourne, £42,980.

Where Waterloo was won? An album containing an 1860s photograph of the playing fields of Eton fetched over £5,000.

All told, the 135 lots made £321,010. "I knew it would be a very good sale," said the auctioneer, Tim Knight, "as the majority of the items were unique and so very early, but it exceeded all my expectations. The collection came direct from the family, having been passed down through the generations."

At a later Knights sale there was vigorous bidding for another rare Victorian tour lot, comprising a 28-page booklet and an album of 17 photographs from the visit to India of Lord Hawke's team in 1892-93. It is believed these items – belonging to Henry Wright – were printed solely for members of the touring party. Again, they were put up for sale by his descendants. Despite the booklet missing its front cover and the album being slightly distressed, they fetched £20,876.

The collection of a more recent cricketer who also wrote many thousands of words went under the hammer in a sale organised by the Sussex Cricket Museum, who benefited from 25% of the proceeds of more than £180,000. It was assembled by Robin Marlar, a major figure in the history of the club. Captain from 1955 to 1959, he had served as their chairman and president, as well as president of MCC; for 26 years he was a forthright cricket correspondent of *The Sunday Times*. Marlar had attended cricket sales in the 1970s and 1980s, a time of high inflation, and aimed to buy artefacts that would preserve their value, but with an "approach that was haphazard, woolly, and often downright romantic. Like my bowling, in fact – often all over the place!"

The collection included some rare books. *Indian Cricket Chronology*, one of the scarcest of Ashley-Cooper publications, was sold for £1,680; R. D. Beeston's *St Ivo and The Ashes* (1882-83) £3,360, despite a taped spine; and a complete bound set of *Cricket: A Weekly Record of The Game* (1882–1913), £4,256. Yet it was the paintings that caught the eye.

The most spectacular bidding was for an unsigned oil of *Kent v Sussex at Malling* in the 1770s, which sold for £38,080, as compared to an estimate of £2,000–3,000. It had strong Sussex associations, having hung behind the desk of Colonel G. S. Grimston, the county secretary from 1950 to 1964, and had been bought by Marlar from the club in 1980. Also exceeding their estimates were a watercolour, believed to be by William Burgess, of *Kent v All England at Canterbury* in around 1855, which realised £10,080 (despite a prediction of £800–1,000) and a small oil from around 30 years later. This painting was of an unspecified cricket ground – until professional cleaning showed it to be Trent Bridge, with Nottinghamshire's initials on the pavilion flag. Also valued at between £800 and 1,000, it fetched £11,200.

A different image attracted interest in the national media when Dominic Winter Auctioneers, of Cirencester, offered for sale a photograph of cricket at Eton College, taken in the early 1860s. In excellent condition, it showed an apparently informal game in the shadow of the college buildings, with several players wearing dark trousers and waistcoats. It had been discovered by the auctioneers in an album that had belonged to three generations of one family who went to the school. Chris Albury, the senior valuer, said: "Some photographs in the album were familiar, but this cricketing one stood out, and was luckily signed on the mount by the photographer, Victor Albert Prout." The album, containing 11 prints, sold for almost £5,400. "We are ecstatic about the price – and the owner even more so," Albury added.

At the time of the April sale, the Eton scene was the second-oldest cricket photograph; only the match recorded by Roger Fenton at Hunsdonbury in 1857 was known to be older. But in the autumn/winter edition of the *MCC Magazine*, Paul Smith reported the discovery, in Portland, Oregon, of a picture of cricket at Lord's dating from 1859.

This photograph is in an album compiled by the wife of Albert Ricardo, a financier, cricket-lover and active member of the I Zingari CC. It shows a scene – posed because of the long exposure required by the camera, and captioned *IZ Lords 1859* – taken during their match against the Household Brigade on June 9. The famous slope is visible, but otherwise the ground is unrecognisable. There was nothing on what is now the Grand Stand side, apart from the low wall, fence and trees dividing it from the adjacent houses. There are three more

Remembrance of things past: the match between A. E. Stoddart's XI and New South Wales contained twin hundreds for Archie MacLaren in a convincing English victory.

shots of players near the old pavilion. These four photos are two decades older
than any other photographic record of players on the field at Lord's.

So how did the album end up in Portland? Long after the Ricardos died, it
fell into the hands of a photographic historian, who in 1972 emigrated to the
United States, where his library was later bought by an Oregon book dealer. A
chance meeting in Horsham steered Smith's researches across the Atlantic –
and the result is a fine piece of detective work.

At Lord's itself, MCC's formidable archive was extended by a wealth of
material belonging to the late statistician Bill Frindall. At the heart of the
collection are his ball-by-ball scoresheets covering England home Tests
between 1966 and 2008, and home one-day internationals from 1972 to 2005.

And, at a sale in Sydney, a couple of late 19th-century scorebooks emerged
that had been part of the collection of the Australian statistician Ian Moir.
Rather than the meticulously compiled single sheets favoured by Frindall,
these are rare illustrated souvenir books that cover two games: *Stoddart's
English Eleven versus Combined Queensland and N. S. W. Team* in 1895, and
the *English Eleven v N. S. Wales* match in 1897. The first ran to 56 pages and
realised around £500; the second had 98 pages and made £1,200.

CRICKET AND THE WEATHER IN 2015

The South–North divide

Andrew Hignell

Overall, slightly less time was lost to rain and bad light in Championship matches than in 2014. The total fell from 445 hours to 433.75, though both years were well below the average of 587 (based on the 1998–2014 period). The most marked feature, however, was an unusual north–south split: Durham and Yorkshire suffered least disruption to their Championship programme, both at home and in total. (A word of warning: sides with more outright results – Durham drew just one of their 16 games – have less scope for weather interruptions simply because their matches finish sooner.)

In fact, the standard textbooks for precipitation patterns across the UK show a marked west–east division. Eastern areas tend to be drier because they are shielded from rain-bearing fronts blown in off the Atlantic on the prevailing south-westerly winds. As the fronts meet the windward hills, they lose much of their moisture on their ascent and on the upland areas, before warming as they descend the leeward slopes.

But, in 2015, there was no discernible distinction. In the east, Essex lost as much time as Durham and Yorkshire combined. And in the west, Worcestershire lost 11.5 hours in their home games, less than a third of the total endured at Edgbaston by neighbouring Warwickshire. In terms of hours lost, Northampton had been the driest of county headquarters in 2014, but in 2015 it was the wettest.

TIME LOST TO THE WEATHER IN THE 2015 CHAMPIONSHIP

| | Hours lost | | 2015 | 2014 | |
	Home	Away	total	total	Difference
Derbyshire.	30.00	16.75	46.75	49.00	−2.25
Durham.	15.00	**10.00**	**25.00**	60.00	**−35.00**
Essex.	24.00	34.00	58.00	51.25	6.75
Glamorgan	29.75	32.00	61.75	48.50	13.25
Gloucestershire	20.00	**43.50**	63.50	62.00	1.50
Hampshire.	20.25	14.00	34.25	**64.00**	−29.75
Kent.	35.25	23.75	59.00	45.00	14.00
Lancashire	22.50	29.75	52.25	57.00	−4.75
Leicestershire	31.50	18.25	49.75	36.75	13.00
Middlesex	19.25	24.50	43.75	58.75	−15.00
Northamptonshire	**49.00**	23.00	**72.00**	30.50	41.50
Nottinghamshire	13.25	28.50	41.75	42.50	−0.75
Somerset	21.75	20.50	42.25	50.75	−8.50
Surrey	25.00	27.50	52.50	63.50	−11.00
Sussex	21.00	16.00	37.00	56.75	−19.75
Warwickshire	35.25	18.75	54.00	33.00	21.00
Worcestershire	11.50	29.50	41.00	47.75	−6.75
Yorkshire	**9.50**	23.50	33.00	33.00	0.00
Total	433.75	433.75	867.50	890.00	−22.50

CRICKET PEOPLE IN 2015

One small step

ALI MARTIN

When Queensland played a Cricket Australia XI in the one-day Matador Cup on October 19, **Claire Polosak** made history as the first female third umpire during a men's List A match in Australia. She became nervous only when former Test captain Mark Taylor mentioned the fact on commentary. The 27-year-old Polosak – who had won a Cricket Australia contract for the development of young umpires – turned the sound down so she could concentrate on the events in front of her. And, in a match broadcast on Gem, Channel Nine's free-to-air sister station, she was called upon to make four decisions.

"My first was a bump ball/disputed catch," she says. "I took a breath, went through the replays and got the decision right. From there, I had two very close run-outs, and one that wasn't, so it was a straightforward game and a good introduction." So it's a simple job, then? "No. One of the senior umpires told me you used to bring a newspaper into the box, but that is certainly not the case now. It's not just decisions: you look after over-rates and substitutions, liaise between the director and the on-field umpires for advert breaks, and all the while you're keeping track of the score."

Originally from Goulburn in New South Wales, Polosak did not play cricket growing up, but followed the sport, and – aged 15 – was encouraged by a friend's father to sign up for an umpiring course. "I actually failed the first couple of exams," she says. "I'd never played, so there were scenarios I couldn't picture in my head. But I got better and better, and eventually passed."

While studying at Sydney's Macquarie University, Polosak continued officiating at weekends. As part of the CA contract, she stood in grade cricket and has now become one of five umpires below the 12-strong (all-male) national panel. Polosak, who is a full-time science and agriculture teacher at Pittwater High School in Sydney, has had international recognition too, as one of four female umpires at the ICC Women's World Twenty20 Qualifier in Thailand at the end of 2015. In February 2016, she went a step further, appointed – along with New Zealand's Kathy Cross – to stand at the women's World Twenty20 in India.

"There have been more female astronauts than Test umpires, and the guys at the top are doing a great job," she says. "It's up to us below to create pressure on the guys in the national panel, and then on the Test-level umpires."

Warwickshire's former captain **Jim Troughton** says he has always been a doodler by nature, especially while in meetings or on the phone, but in 2015 his habit helped him become a published illustrator for the second time. Troughton, who joined the back-room set-up at Edgbaston as fielding coach after retiring from playing in 2014, was approached before the start of last season by local author Rachael Wong to provide the artwork for a children's book she was writing to raise money for the Warwickshire Cricket Board.

The result of their two-month collaboration was *The Legend of Morvidus: The Bear, the Bat and the Ragged Staff*, with a foreword by Ian Bell. It tells the tale of a young cricketer conquering his nerves ahead of his first match. "Rachael, whose daughter is in the girls' team, has driven the whole thing," says Troughton.

Troughton, who played six one-day internationals for England in 2003, was inspired to start drawing when visiting his aunt, the children's illustrator Joanna Troughton, and went on to study art at A-level. "I used to love going up to her room to play with the light box, the pens and the pencils. The sketching came from there." His first caricature was former Warwickshire coach Bob Woolmer while on twelfth-man duty, with colleagues at the club becoming his preferred muses. In 2008, as he recovered from a back injury, sketching his team-mates proved a good way of channelling his energies.

The results were turned into a booklet, *The Push for Promotion*, which chronicled the club's Division Two title that summer, with profits donated to the Bunbury charity. "I wouldn't call myself an artist like Jack Russell," says Troughton. "It's just a habit I've developed."

Kathleen Galligan, a 30-year-old American, had barely heard of the sport when she first met her cricket-mad husband, Subash Jayaraman (founder of the cricket couch website), in an Irish pub in Pennsylvania in 2007. Seven years later, they both gave up full-time jobs to embark on a nine-month trip around the world dedicated to his passion. Starting at the Caribbean Premier League in July 2014, the voyage took them to England, Ireland, India, the United Arab Emirates, Sri Lanka, Bangladesh and South Africa, before finishing off at the World Cup in Australia and New Zealand. Galligan documented her conversion from cricket novice to globe-trotting supporter in a popular diary for the Wisden India website.

As well as taking in international games, she immersed herself in all levels of the sport, from the beaches of Trinidad to the streets of the subcontinent. Among her favourite experiences was making a ball using a bicycle tube, newspaper and rocks, as her husband had done growing up near Chennai. "It brought me an insight into his childhood that was very special," she explains.

"We spent about 200 of our 270 nights away staying for free with people, many of whom we had never met, but who opened their lives to us. A lot was done by social media, and one person actually heard us on the radio in South Africa and invited us to stay with them in Cape Town, sight unseen."

They returned to their home in the USA with just $400 to their name, but Galligan says the shared experience has brought them even closer together. "I probably can't claim to be a huge fan now, compared to many, but I still like to know what's going on, and can appreciate a good moment in a game enough to yell at the television. By the World Cup, I was even going to matches alone."

CRICKET IN THE COURTS IN 2015

The Mote in thy brother's eye

FROM A CELL TO WORLD CUP TRIUMPH

Bangladeshi fast bowler Rubel Hossain spent three days in jail before the 2015 World Cup after a former girlfriend accused him of rape. He was released "in the national interest" on January 11 to allow him to play in the tournament. After he had taken four for 53 against England at Adelaide to put Bangladesh into the quarter-finals, the complainant – 19-year-old actor Naznin Akter Happy – announced she had forgiven Rubel and was withdrawing the charge.

THE DECISION IS FINAL

Two former Test umpires, Peter Willey and George Sharp, lost an appeal to stay on the English first-class list beyond the age of 65. They took the ECB to an employment tribunal under UK age-discrimination legislation which bars employers from enforcing a standard retirement age without justification.

The ECB accepted there was no issue with either man's fitness, eyesight or competence, but said they wanted to maintain the 65-limit to ensure succession planning and to give younger ex-players the chance to join the list. Chris Kelly, the board's umpiring manager, also argued it was right for both to retire with "dignity" rather than face the axe when their performance began to decline. On March 13, the tribunal rejected this argument, but agreed the first point was legitimate.

The board said in a statement they would maintain the rule "in the interests of intergenerational fairness and in order to ensure that umpiring remains a viable career option for professional cricketers who are nearing the end of their playing careers".

RICH MAN, POOR MAN, CRICKET FAN, THIEF

A serial thief toured Britain for nearly 20 years stealing money from amateur cricket and rugby dressing-rooms. Travelling by bus and staying in cheap guest houses, he often wore an official-looking blazer, and players assumed he was a representative of the opposing team.

Lewes Crown Court was told Alan Philip, 62, was "talkative and pleasant", and fitted in so well he even helped during drinks breaks. He always arrived early and sometimes collected valuables for "safe keeping" before vanishing; on other occasions he simply stole money and phones from the dressing-rooms. Philip (aka Anthony Tye) was caught in January 2015 after he carelessly took a photo with a phone stolen in a raid on Hove rugby club. This was uploaded to the victim's computer and gave away his location. He was jailed for five years.

COUNTY PLAYER IN £100m CON

Michael Foster, 43, an all-rounder for Yorkshire, Northamptonshire and Durham in the 1990s, was sent to prison for his part in a property swindle that cost lenders £112m. Foster was sentenced to three years and nine months at Teesside Crown Court on October 16, after being described as the "right-hand man" of the scheme's mastermind, David Purdie.

Purdie borrowed heavily to build his property empire, buying homes cheaply from people struggling with their repayments, but many of his mortgage applications were fraudulent, and the firm collapsed in the 2008 crash.

LAWYER IMPERSONATES DEAD CLIENT

A Sydney criminal lawyer used the identity of a long-dead client to gain access to the members' reserve at the Melbourne Cricket Ground. Denis Anderson went to the MCG's most popular occasion, the AFL Grand Final, for at least eight successive years in the guise of Michael Alfred Starkey, who had died in 1998. Anderson, 79, told a professional tribunal that Starkey had left him his membership in his will, though passes are not transferable. The waiting list to join Melbourne Cricket Club is of a similar length to their Marylebone counterparts, but has traditionally been less well managed. Anderson was fined $A10,000 on June 6 and reprimanded; he was not struck off the legal roll, after undertaking not to practise again.

EX-COUNTY CAPTAIN JAILED

Former Somerset captain Andy Hayhurst was jailed for two years after pleading guilty to stealing £107,000 from the Lancashire Cricket Board, money that was earmarked for coaching young players. Between 2006 and 2013, Hayhurst – a full-time director of the board – submitted a series of fake invoices that were thought to be intended for facilities at Worsley CC. The club received just £7,000. Hayhurst – who also played for his native Lancashire, and Derbyshire – pleaded guilty to fraud, theft, obtaining property by deception, false accounting and concealing criminal property. Sentencing him at Manchester Crown Court on June 12, Judge James Potter said his actions were "selfish and inspired by greed".

CRICKET AUTHOR JAILED, AGAIN

Ashley Mote, a former winner of the Cricket Society literary award, was sentenced to five years' imprisonment, at Southwark Crown Court on July 13. He had claimed nearly £500,000 in fake expenses while a member of the European Parliament between 2004 and 2010. He used some of the money to fund his defence in 2007, when he was sentenced to nine months for false benefit claims. (See *Wisden 2008*, page 1637.)

Mr Justice Stuart-Smith told Mote: "Your greed and dishonesty were matched only by your hypocrisy, because while this was going on you carried out a high-profile campaign condemning corruption and the improper use of public money in the very institution from which you were leeching it."

Mote, 79, was originally elected for the UK Independence Party, but was later expelled. He had been allowed to remain an MEP during his previous sentence, as it was for less than a year. His history of the Hambledon club, *The Glory Days of Cricket*, was published in 1997.

CHARLTON KINGS CASE FINALLY SETTLED

The lengthy saga involving Charlton Kings CC, near Cheltenham, who were in dispute with a woman claiming ownership of part of the outfield (see *Wisden 2015*, page 167), was finally resolved in favour of the club on March 31, when the Supreme Court refused permission to appeal. "We can all breathe a sigh of relief," said a club official.

A MERE RIFLE

West Indies batsman Andre Fletcher was fined $EC2,000 (a little over £500) in June after customs officials confiscated a package of live ammunition at Douglas Charles Airport in Dominica. Fletcher said he thought the bullets were in fact pellets, which he had bought for his air rifle, and had not inspected them closely enough. Lockhart Sebastian, the manager of Windward Islands, his domestic side, said: "It could happen to anybody."

For coverage of the trial of Chris Cairns and Andrew Fitch-Holland, see page 72.

CRICKET AND THE LAWS IN 2015

Sin bin on the cards?

Fraser Stewart

During the one-day international between England and Australia at Lord's in September, Ben Stokes was dismissed obstructing the field after he blocked a throw from the bowler, Mitchell Starc. Australia's appeal was immediately referred to the third umpire, who gave Stokes out – but opinion was split over whether it was the correct decision.

Those who felt it was harsh said that – for Stokes – the incident looked worse in slow motion; they claimed he was trying to protect himself rather than deliberately block the ball. Law 37.1 states that "either batsman is out obstructing the field if he *wilfully* [our emphasis] attempts to obstruct or distract the fielding side by word or action". A caveat is provided if the obstruction was in self-defence: the umpires must decide if it was wilful.

Despite a debate that overshadowed the result of the match, only Stokes knows if his actions were borne of instinctive self-defence, or an attempt to prevent a run-out. He claimed self-defence, as it is natural to put your hand up when a ball is being hurled at you from 15 yards. The Australians argued with equal vehemence that, quite simply, he had blocked the path of the ball, which would not have hit his body, and might have gone on to hit the stumps. Such decisions remain the prerogative of the officials.

Another dismissal occurred in a first-class match between Karnataka and Bengal in October. As with the Stokes incident, the bowler, Vinay Kumar, threw the ball back towards the batsman, Shreevats Goswami, who unfussily turned round and grounded his bat. But the ball hit it, knocking it upwards, then ricocheted on to the stumps; the bat was now in the air and Goswami himself still out of his ground. The third umpire correctly gave him out, although some felt Kumar, the Karnataka captain, should have withdrawn the appeal. MCC are scrutinising this area of the Law, particularly in relation to bats which bounce up, often when the batsman has dived to make his ground.

A change to the Law governing movement by fielders, as mooted in these pages last year, came into force in October. The alterations to Laws 40.4 and 41.7 allow a fielder or wicketkeeper to move significantly before the ball has reached the batsman, provided it is in response to a stroke he is playing, or one which his actions suggest he is intending to play. Previously, the fielder was prevented from significantly altering his position until the ball had reached the batsman. Close fielders were allowed only minor adjustments to stance or position, whereas outfielders were permitted to walk in towards the batsman or his wicket; anything other than slight movement off line, or away from the batsman, was not allowed.

The intention of the redraft was to retain the thrust of the previous Law, and also to allow fielders to pre-empt the batsman's intentions. In particular, if he positions himself for a switch-hit or reverse sweep before the bowler has released the ball, the fielding side may move in response – but only from the moment the batsman has moved in preparation for the stroke. However, any movement intended to distract or deceive the batsman will not be allowed – such as mid-on moving back towards long-on as the bowler is running in.

It was felt that the new Law should not override the restriction of no more than two fielders, other than the wicketkeeper, behind the popping crease on the leg side at the instant of delivery (Law 41.5). Otherwise the fielding side might try to move fielders into close-catching positions for bouncers, potentially leading to short balls being bowled more frequently. After the ball has been released, however, a fielder may move to this position if it is in reaction to the batsman's intended shot.

Following a global consultation carried out in 2015 on all aspects of the Laws, there has been a strong response in relation to improving player behaviour, which tends to be worse in the amateur game. Last summer in England, at least five matches were abandoned because of violence. Meanwhile, in Bermuda, wicketkeeper Jason Anderson was banned for life after an on-field fight in which he hit an opposition batsman on the head. Footage of the incident was widely shared on social media, and it even attracted censure in parliament. "What was to be a family and community event has instead been marred by a repugnant incident of violence, lawlessness and unsportsmanlike conduct," said Bermuda's shadow sports minister, Michael Weeks.

Cricket is one of the few sports where disciplinary action can be taken only after the game. A captain can ask one of his players to leave the field, but an umpire has no such right. So the perpetrator can still take part in the match, possibly winning it for his team. MCC have been reluctant to introduce a sin bin or card system, as they have always relied on captains to control the players. The question is whether such a deterrent would help improve declining standards. Trials in New Zealand strongly suggest it would. Some umpires have called for the Laws to give them more authority during a match, rather than reporting incidents afterwards. While no decision has yet been taken, MCC have started to draft possible options. It is hoped that, over the coming year, certain leagues or competitions will trial some of these suggestions.

A further five Laws animations, narrated by Stephen Fry and translated into Urdu and Hindi, were released in 2015, and help explain the Laws in an easy, light-hearted way. One of the earlier animations concerned the issue of catches near the boundary, which continue to cause confusion. Australia's Glenn Maxwell took a wonderful catch to dismiss England's Liam Plunkett in a one-day international at Headingley, after throwing the ball back into play while he was airborne on the wrong side of the rope, then catching it. This was perfectly legal, since he had taken off from within the boundary, but Maxwell later criticised the Law for being too lenient towards the fielding side. MCC are content with the current wording, which they feel has allowed fielders to pull off some breathtaking catches.

Fraser Stewart is Laws Manager at MCC. The Laws appear on the MCC website (www.lords.org/laws).

CRICKET EQUIPMENT IN 2015

Making helmets safer

TIM WIGMORE

The death of Phillip Hughes in November 2014 was a terrible reminder of the dangers intrinsic to cricket. While helmet technology will never eradicate them, it can lessen the chances of a serious accident. In 2011, the ICC had commissioned a study into improving the protection helmets offered, and in 2013 the British Standard was updated for the first time in 15 years. In June last year, this new standard was adopted by all ICC members, though it failed to address the need to give greater protection to the back of the neck, focusing instead on the face – which research had shown was the most vulnerable part of the head.

Hughes's death did, however, prompt action from a range of manufacturers. Within weeks, Masuri – whose helmet Hughes was wearing – began work on a new stem guard, a separate element attached to the back of the helmet. But it wasn't simply a case of giving the wearer greater safety: the design, according to Sam Miller, managing director of Masuri Cricket Helmets, "would be worthless if it were uncomfortable".

The roll-out of the new helmets was sluggish, and Masuri did not produce the stem guard attachments until the 2015 season was over. Gunn & Moore and Shrey have also brought out their own. "We're getting there slowly – you might argue too slowly – but it's not through lack of effort," said Angus Porter, who was chief executive of the Professional Cricketers' Association until September 2015. By summer 2016, he expected all first-class cricketers in England to wear helmets that comply with the 2013 safety standards; Masuri believe around 80% of batsmen will be using stem guards. The new designs were "significantly safer" for batsmen, Miller asserted, but helmet technology does not stand still: "We have more to learn, and more development to do, to continue to improve safety."

Porter welcomed the innovation. But, while all ICC members have agreed the new helmet standard, he was concerned that the ICC had not made their use mandatory. "I would hate to be in a position where in the future we have different standards in different parts of the world," said Porter. "That would be wrong for all sorts of reasons." Tony Irish, the executive chairman of the Federation of International Cricketers' Associations, shared these concerns. "We say [mandatory use of the new standard] should be centralised, while the ICC say it should be left up to each board member."

No one believes the new designs will prevent all accidents. "There will still be injuries, and a ball travelling at the speeds now seen in international cricket may still force its way between the peak and the grille," said Porter. "We're just trying to do our best to mitigate the risks."

CRICKET AND FILM IN 2015

Not so trivial pursuits

CHARLES BARR

"No one is going to buy a newspaper or turn on a television programme to watch a news story about administration in sport. People aren't interested, and why should they be?"

Those are the words of Giles Clarke, then chair (now president) of the ECB, speaking impatiently to his interviewers in the film *Death of a Gentleman*. Wishful thinking indeed: people have proved extremely interested in stories about the administration of cycling, football, athletics and the Olympics, as one scandal after another is laid bare in the press and on TV. Cricket has made fewer headlines, but Sam Collins and Jarrod Kimber set out in *DoaG* to expose "one of the biggest scandals in sport". The international game, they argue, has been taken over by – and in the interests of – the Big Three: England, Australia and the new centre of power, India.

The issues have already been discussed within these pages (see *Wisden 2014*, where Clarke himself and Gideon Haigh rehearsed the case for and against). *DoaG* is different, as film always is: weak on intellectual analysis, strong on image and emotion. Its genre is that of the hard-hitting investigative feature-documentary, as popularised by the flamboyant American film-maker Michael Moore. His breakthrough was *Bowling for Columbine*, an Oscar winner in 2003, which tackled head-on the madness of American gun culture. The climax was Moore's visit to the veteran Hollywood star Charlton Heston, president of the National Rifle Association. He was taken aback by Moore's hostile questioning, and walked out. This is echoed in *DoaG's* pursuit of Clarke, who also becomes uncomfortable and brings the interview to a grumpy end, but not before being stung into a revealing statement. Making cricket an Olympic sport might, as widely claimed, boost the game in non-Test countries and attract extra funding from their governments, but it would intrude for a few weeks every four years into the English summer, and is therefore to be opposed: "I have every right to put my board's interests first."

This moment alone justifies the film. There is no doubt it is the protracted Clarke interview that – as with Heston – sticks in the memory. Of the other Big Three representatives on the ICC, Australia's Wally Edwards simply refused to talk, while India's N. Srinivasan surprised the film-makers by *not* refusing, though he gives little away. Less evasive and more eloquent are the critics, experts bruised by their experience: Lord Woolf, whose report on governance was bluntly rejected; David Becker, head of legal at the ICC, who resigned and turned whistle-blower; Tim May, the players' representative who was replaced in a palace coup by a Srinivasan client.

The film was put together between 2011 and 2014, and matters have moved on since. Shashank Manohar has succeeded Srinivasan at both the BCCI and

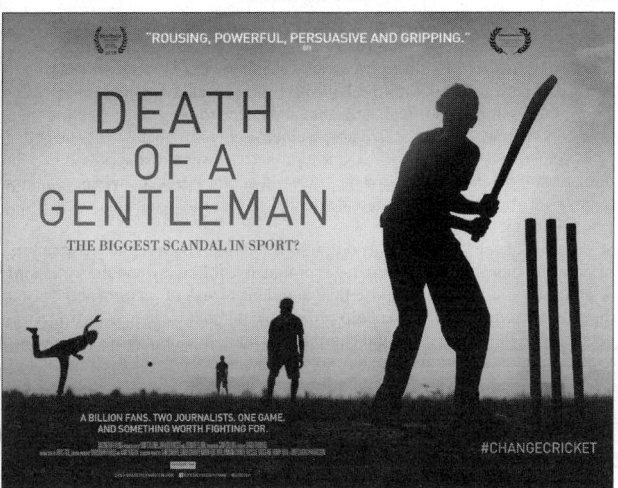

ICC, and there are signs he will be a less divisive figure. But *DoaG* maintains its value as a record of the longer-term problems and pressures that the game has to tackle, in and beyond boardrooms. There is far more to it than talking heads. We go back and forth between footage of Twenty20 and Test matches, as the makers lament the decline of the longer format, and fear for its future. Indeed Test cricket is the gentleman of the title, whose health – until the power games at the ICC – was intended to be the film's major theme. This accounts for another thread, concerning Australian batsman Ed Cowan, a Test specialist whose rise and painful fall we follow closely. It no longer quite fits with the main agenda, yet it is part of the charm of a very personal film that its two engagingly amateur creators get the chance to bowl in the nets to a real Test batsman.

Equally personal is the year's other feature-documentary on cricket, *Warriors*, though its director, another debutant, does not put himself on screen. Barney Douglas's film operates at a level well below ICC radar, celebrating a team of Masai tribesmen, who are new to the game, as they travel from Kenya to England and then back home. Neither film could have been commissioned through normal TV or film-company channels. Instead, they were financed independently with the help of the modern system of crowd-funding: a mass of people chip in small amounts, not expecting any control, but keen to help get the film completed and to see the result – and receive an acknowledgment in small print in the end credits. Famous names are visible in each list, as well as on screen, and England's James Anderson has an associate producer credit on *Warriors*.

It is important that such films do not go straight to DVD. Cinema release helps generate publicity and promote audience interaction. I saw both in the course of a round of English provincial screenings. For *DoaG*, Cinema City in Norwich had linked up with the Norfolk Cricket Society, who publicised the show successfully and leafleted the audience coming out, gaining new members. For *Warriors*, the Broadway cinema in Nottingham went one better, following the screening with a question-and-answer session involving the director and others. As it turned out, many in another packed audience wanted to talk, not about cricket, but female genital mutilation, which is central to the whole concept of the film.

The tribal society we meet is dominated by elders wedded to the practices of polygamy and early-teen marriage for females, following compulsory FGM. A group of younger men oppose this, and their means of gaining authority of their own is cricket. With the help of benefactors that include a British Army detachment, they get a pitch and equipment, and before long are off to England to join the international amateur eight-a-side tournament Last Man Stands, where they acquit themselves vividly and honourably. Back in Kenya, they use their enhanced confidence and prestige to persuade the elders to renounce FGM and to countenance women's education.

The cricket element of the film, without a trace of scoreboards or league tables, is not especially easy to follow; nor are there any hard facts to document the process of change back home. But it succeeds as an inspirational fairy tale, a poetic, feel-good film, full of powerful images ranging from Masai country to Lord's, which the team visit in full tribal costume.

In their different ways, *Warriors* and *Death of a Gentleman* communicate a passion for the game, for its pleasures and its therapeutic powers. Both are available on DVD, and should be part of any cricket-lover's collection.

Charles Barr is Emeritus professor of film history at the University of East Anglia.

OBITUARIES

AFZAAL AHMED RIZVI, SYED, who died on April 23, aged 66, was a batsman from Karachi who played 91 first-class matches for various sides in Pakistan; his six centuries included an undefeated 155 for National Bank against PIA at Faisalabad in 1981-82. He had a season in the Lancashire League as Colne's professional, and later became an umpire, standing in a one-day international in 1994-95, and acting as the TV official in other games.

AMINUL HAQUE MONI, who died on May 31, aged 66, was general secretary of the Bangladesh Cricket Board from 1991 to 1996, and later served on their board of directors. At his suggestion, all Dhaka Premier League matches in 1996-97 were contested on artificial pitches as preparation for the 1997 ICC Trophy in Malaysia. Bangladesh won the tournament, and qualified for their first World Cup, in England in 1999.

AMM, PHILIP GEOFFREY, who died on September 10, aged 51, was a consistent opening batsman who made a dozen first-class centuries in South Africa. The best was an 11-hour 214 against Transvaal to set up Eastern Province's maiden Currie Cup title in the 1988-89 final. "He wasn't Herschelle Gibbs in terms of talent," remembered Jimmy Cook, who played for Transvaal in that match. "But he was gutsy." Amm, whose older brother Peter also played first-class cricket, was unfortunate that his best years coincided with South Africa's exile. But he was still on the fringe of selection when they returned in 1991-92, and was a useful one-day performer, finishing with five hundreds. He suffered with alcohol-related problems in later life.

APPLEYARD, ROBERT, MBE, died on March 17, aged 90. Even on its own, Bob Appleyard's cricket career was remarkable. Throw in his backstory, and it becomes one of the most extraordinary in the history of the game. Appleyard was approaching his 27th birthday when, in 1951, he became an established member of the Yorkshire team – and took 200 wickets at 14, the most productive first full season of any bowler. He seemed on course for greatness, but little in his life ran according to plan. Early the following summer, he was struck down by tuberculosis and had part of a lung removed. It should have meant the end of his professional career, but he returned two years later after a gruelling rehabilitation to make his Test debut and play a significant role in England's 1954-55 Ashes triumph.

In all, his career amounted to little more than six seasons, but he retired with 708 wickets at 15.48; since the First World War only Hedley Verity has boasted a lower average. Bill Bowes, Verity's Yorkshire and England team-mate, believed Appleyard deserved to be mentioned in the same breath as Sydney Barnes and Bill O'Reilly, two others who defied easy categorisation.

Serious illness was only one of the setbacks Appleyard endured. His mother Maud left home when he was seven, and his sister Margaret died of diphtheria when he was 13; his father John remarried and started a new family but, horrified by the declaration of war in 1939, gassed himself, his wife and their two young daughters, having first sent his son off to his grandmother. Appleyard discovered the bodies on returning home. Later, he had to bear the deaths of his own son, Ian, and grandson, Peter – both from leukaemia.

He had a successful career outside the game, and was a senior executive for the British Printing Corporation when it was taken over. The new owner, the publishing tycoon Robert Maxwell, dismissed him on fabricated grounds. But Appleyard refused to buckle and fought a long and successful battle for compensation. He was an indefatigable fundraiser for the Yorkshire Academy at Bradford, work which earned him an MBE. Appleyard internalised much of his trauma until he was persuaded to tell his story to Stephen Chalke and Derek Hodgson in 2003. *No Coward Soul* – a phrase from Emily Brontë's last poem before her death from TB – was *Wisden's* second Book of the Year.

No coward souls: an indomitable Yorkshire quartet – Bob Appleyard, Brian Close, Johnny Wardle and Fred Trueman – chew the fat on the Headingley balcony, 1955.

Appleyard's bowling displayed unusual versatility. He could open the attack with Fred Trueman, deploying conventional seam and swing. When the shine disappeared, or if the pitch was helpful, he would bowl off-spin, still at a lively pace. "He was a very, very fine bowler," said Yorkshire team-mate Ray Illingworth. "He was a tall bloke and in his pomp he had a very high arm, which meant he got a lot of bounce." Appleyard changed styles without altering his 16-pace run-up or his action, which he believed was a key element in deceiving batsmen. "Sometimes he was like Alec Bedser, sometimes like Jim Laker," said Johnny Wardle.

He also drew eagerly on the accumulated wisdom of several greats. As a boy at the Headingley nets, he was tutored in the rudiments of swing by George Hirst. Later, he was coached by Emmott Robinson: "Tha' knows tha' has to bowl five good balls an over. And the sixth hasn't to be a bad 'un." Early in his Yorkshire career, he spent precious minutes in conversation with Barnes during a game against Staffordshire; at Scarborough, he would seek out Wilfred Rhodes. Appleyard experimented regularly with new grips, always carrying a ball in his coat pocket, and studied yoga, believing it helped him reach a peak of concentration as he approached the wicket.

Appleyard's Bradford school was a ten-minute dash from Park Avenue and, by the age of seven, he knew his calling. His first invitation to Yorkshire nets came in 1938, but the war intervened, and he joined the Navy. Back home he resumed cricket as a professional with Bowling Old Lane, but had to wait until 1950 before Yorkshire took an interest. It was only after he began to dabble in spin that he was recognised as first-team material. He travelled to Edinburgh to take on Scotland, claiming match figures of five for 41 in 26 overs, then played Surrey at The Oval, which he regarded as his real debut. He had been allocated a room with the combustible Alec Coxon who, as Appleyard slept fitfully, burst in at 1am and began trying to fix a cigarette lighter for a woman he had met that evening. Next morning, the room-mates shared the new ball, and Appleyard took four for 47. *The Times* praised his "high and virile action".

His triumphal progress through the summer of 1951 began with four for 26 in the Parks, and six for 38 (five of them bowled) against the South Africans at Bradford. With Coxon sacked and Brian Close on national service, Yorkshire were in need of two bowlers; instead they discovered that one man could replace both. Nevertheless, much of his success could be attributed to a happy accident during the winter. Norman Yardley, the Yorkshire captain, was keen for him to develop his off-breaks, but he soon developed a blister on his spinning finger. Unwilling to stop bowling, Appleyard tried spinning the ball off his middle finger. "I found I could bowl it much quicker than the normal off-break," he recalled. The Yorkshire coach Arthur Mitchell was summoned to his net: "If you can bowl like that you can bowl any bugger out."

Laid low by TB, he missed a couple of matches in July but, fighting fatigue, had reached 189 wickets by the start of the season's final game, against MCC at Scarborough. He took eight in the first innings, but in the second bowled unchanged for hour after hour, once pleading with Yardley to take him off when he felt that pursuit of the 200th wicket was "spoiling the game". Finally, Roy Tattersall hit the penultimate ball of his 46th over into the hands of Trueman at mid-on. Appleyard had got through 1,323.2 overs that summer, and was named a Wisden Cricketer of the Year.

He spent the winter months trying to improve his stamina, yet could not shake off his exhaustion. Suffering from a cough and a soaring temperature, he was sent home from Yorkshire's first Championship match in 1952, against Somerset. Four days later he was in hospital, beginning a five-month period of preparation for surgery to remove the top of his left lung. He was fortunate to be in the hands of the eminent surgeon Geoffrey Wooler, who assured him: "You will play again, Mr Appleyard. In fact I shall come to Headingley to watch you bowl." His wife smuggled a cricket ball into the hospital, and he worked on it for hours under the bedcover, determined to maintain strength in his hands. The operation was successful but the recovery arduous: his muscles wasted by months in bed, Appleyard first had to learn to walk. By the winter of 1953-54, he was well enough to bowl again, and Yorkshire sent him to a Swiss resort for a month before the start of the season.

Appleyard always rated his achievements in 1954 – when he took 143 wickets at 14 while bowling more than 1,000 overs – more highly than his record-breaking summer three years earlier. His return seemed complete when he was called up for the Second Test against Pakistan at Trent Bridge: he dismissed Hanif Mohammad with his second ball, and ended his first day in Test cricket with five for 51. It was enough to earn him selection ahead of Laker in Len Hutton's star-studded squad for the Ashes. He found Australian pitches unresponsive but – ever thoughtful – used flight and variations in pace. He was chosen for the Second Test at Sydney, and ended the series with 11 wickets at 20, all of them frontline batsmen, before playing in the two Tests that followed in New Zealand. But Appleyard won only two more caps in the next two summers and, despite passing 100 wickets in 1956, found his effectiveness reduced by injuries, especially a trapped nerve in the shoulder that meant he played just one match in the 1955 series against South Africa. He was never quite as formidable as he had been before his illness. In 1958, he announced his retirement.

Appleyard could be a difficult man. "He had strong views and he did not mind making enemies," said Chalke. Illingworth added: "I'm not saying he was my best friend, because he wasn't; he was an awkward bugger." But it was his cussedness that gave him the resolve to take on Maxwell. "I know that Appleyard," he said. "He's a bloody-minded Yorkshireman. He'll take me all the way." Maxwell settled just before the case reached the High Court.

Of Appleyard's greatness as a bowler there was no question. "We'll never see the like again," said Trueman. Illingworth rated him higher than Laker: "He had a bigger heart than Jim. Bob always wanted to bowl, whatever the pitch was like."

ATKINSON, GRAHAM, who died on November 12, aged 77, was a heavy scorer who was close to England selection in the early 1960s. Born in Yorkshire, but recommended to Somerset by the Taunton favourite and renowned coach Johnny Lawrence, Atkinson made his debut aged 16 in 1954, although it was five seasons before he became a county regular, partly because of two years' national service. While on leave from the RAF in July 1958 he made 164 against Warwickshire at Taunton, and was promptly capped; the following summer – fully available again – he amassed 1,727 runs.

"He was very strong on the on side," said his long-time opening partner Roy Virgin. "He always had so much time to play the quick bowlers – never looked ruffled. And

he could really dig in on bad wickets." In 1960, Atkinson compiled a career-best 190 against Glamorgan at Bath, a fortnight after being involved in a unique feat against Cambridge University at Taunton. Atkinson and Virgin put on 172 in the first innings and 112 in the second, while Roger Prideaux and Tony Lewis started with 198 and 137 for the students: it remains the only first-class match to contain four century opening stands. "We were good as a pair," said Virgin, "because I was all off side – at first, anyway."

Atkinson just missed out on 2,000 runs that year, but got there in 1961 (at 23, the youngest Somerset player to do so) and 1962. The selectors took note: he became a regular in MCC's annual matches against the county champions and the tourists, and took 176 off his native Yorkshire at Lord's in April 1963. But, with Geoff Boycott and John Edrich about to start long Test careers, Atkinson never quite made the step up, perhaps not helped by his average fielding. He remained a heavy scorer with Somerset until, miffed at being offered only a one-

"The best captain Somerset never had" was Roy Virgin's assessment of Graham Atkinson.

year contract extension for 1967, he upped sticks for Old Trafford. "He was a man of great integrity – probably the best captain Somerset never had," said Virgin. "The rest of us had been offered two-year deals, but his was only for one, supposedly because of his fielding – although I always thought it was quite good!"

Another 1,300 runs – and a second county cap – followed in Atkinson's first season for Lancashire, but his fortunes declined as Jack Bond's side focused more on one-day cricket. After averaging only 24 in 1968 and 1969 he was released, and was lost to the first-class game at 31. He was secretary of Salford rugby league club for a dozen years, then managed Manchester University's sports grounds.

After his death, Atkinson's son Richard asked ESPNcricinfo for a copy of their photograph of him. "He always loved it," he said, "because it showed him smashing one over mid-on in an era where opening batsmen did that once a season rather than once an over. Most of his old mates insist it must have been photoshopped."

AUSTIN, RICHARD ARKWRIGHT, died on February 7, aged 60. His death completed a distressing story that had begun with optimism for a bright cricketing future, and ended with years of debilitating cocaine addiction that reduced him to a bedraggled vagrant on the streets of Kingston, dependent on handouts from those who recalled his time as one of Jamaica's finest sportsmen. In his more coherent moments, Austin would chat intelligently about the state of West Indies cricket and his experiences as a fine all-rounder not just for

Jamaica but for several West Indian sides. These comprised two Tests, World Series Cricket, and two rebel teams that toured apartheid South Africa in the early 1980s. In his youthful heyday, he was also a noted footballer, and might have played for Jamaica but for cricket.

An opening batsman and versatile bowler capable of taking the new ball or switching to off-spin, Austin forced his way into the West Indies side when Australia toured early in 1978. He was almost impossible to ignore: he started the home season with 74 against the Combined Islands and 127 against a Guyana attack including Colin Croft, then scored 88 and 56, and took four for 45 and eight for 71, against Trinidad. Austin played in the first two Tests, but signed for WSC's second season before the Third and was promptly dropped, along with two other Packer players, triggering a mass withdrawal of all the rebels, led by captain Clive Lloyd.

When WSC ended, Austin could not break back into the Test team, and started looking for other opportunities. The South Africa tours offered lucrative pay, as well as competitive cricket in another land; like several others, he underestimated the depth of feeling against the apartheid regime, particularly in Jamaica, where the government were fiercely opposed to any contact, let alone by a team of black West Indians. On their return, Austin and the other Jamaicans – the captain Lawrence Rowe, Herbert Chang, Everton Mattis and Ray Wynter – were treated as pariahs, forsaken by their countrymen and, most hurtfully, by previous team-mates.

Patrick Eagar

Better days: Richard Austin in his second Test, against Australia at Bridgetown in 1977-78.

Rowe moved to Miami, where he started a successful new life. Mattis and Wynter also emigrated to the States to avoid the public anger. Unable to follow, Austin and Chang were left broken, at first condemned by society, then forgotten. Chang, a Jamaican of Chinese descent who won a solitary Test cap in India in 1978-79, became a recluse. Austin turned to drugs, surfacing occasionally as "Danny Germs" in sorrowful interviews.

AZMAT RANA, who died on May 30, aged 63, played one Test for Pakistan against Australia in his native Lahore in 1979-80, scoring 49 in his only innings of a high-scoring draw. A left-hander who cut and drove well, he had already played two one-day internationals, against India, but never appeared again, despite amassing over 6,000 runs in first-class cricket, with 16 centuries – the highest 206 not out for Punjab Greens against North West Frontier Province at Peshawar in 1977-78. He had also toured England, in 1971 – but was unable to shrug off malaria – and New Zealand in 1972-73, without much success. Azmat was a member of a prominent cricketing family: his brother Shafqat Rana and two nephews also represented Pakistan, while the umpire Shakoor Rana was another brother.

BANNON, Dr JOHN CHARLES, AO, who died on December 13, aged 72, was a reforming Labor Party Premier of South Australia from 1982 to 1992. Bannon was forced to resign after taking the blame for the collapse of the state bank, and retired to study for a doctorate in Australian history and watch cricket quietly – before Ian McLachlan, the president of the South Australian Cricket Association and a political opponent, recruited him to join the SACA board. Bannon's skills and contacts were crucial in securing the redevelopment of Adelaide Oval; he also became a member of the Cricket Australia board, taking special responsibility for both the indigenous game and speechmaking (at which he excelled). He was a charming, modest, gifted and honourable man who genuinely loved cricket; but for the cancer that bedevilled his last decade, he might have brought these qualities to global administration.

BARBER, RICHARD TREVOR, died on August 7, aged 90. A hard-hitting batsman for Wellington, Trevor Barber played one Test for New Zealand, at home on the Basin Reserve against West Indies in 1955-56, in the absence of the injured Bert Sutcliffe. Barber pulled off a fine gully catch to dismiss Garry Sobers – although Barber was lucky to still be on the field. "I was at silly short leg, the bowler bowled a short one, Sobers hooked it and it went past my right ear, just touched right there, and went for six. Had it been a little bit closer, I would have been gone." When he batted, Barber was out cheaply twice, trying to sweep Sonny Ramadhin, and was dropped for good. He turned down the chance to be twelfth man in the next match, as he had to work – and missed New Zealand's inaugural Test victory after 26 years of trying. More consistent runs might have earned him a recall, but he always liked to attack: the *Dominion Post* was not alone in wondering "how much greater Barber would have been with more patience". He made only one first-class century, 117 at Wellington in 1953-54, which just failed to secure victory over Otago. Barber had been New Zealand's oldest surviving Test player, and succeeded by John Reid.

BARRABLE, PETER RITCHIE, who died on September 17, aged 72, played 16 first-class matches for Northern Transvaal over a decade from 1964-65. He made 73 after opening against Orange Free State in Pretoria in 1974-75. By then he was Northern Transvaal's captain and, in an unusual double, their president. "He had the skills and knowledge to lead in the boardroom and on the field," said Jacques Faul, the current association's chief executive.

BARUAH, HEMANGA, who died of liver failure on November 14, aged 49, was a medium-pacer who took 50 wickets in 20 Ranji Trophy matches for Assam, with a best of five for 38 against Tripura at Guwahati in 1991-92. In March 1985 he played an Under-19 Test at Patna, sharing the new ball with Jaspal Singh (see below) and dismissing Tom Moody and the Australian captain Dean Reynolds.

BENAUD, RICHARD, OBE, died on April 10, aged 84. The career of the man known across the cricketing world simply as "Richie" is almost impossible to sum up succinctly. He was one of the game's finest all-rounders, developed into an outstanding and innovative captain, and then – for 50 of the 70 years in which cricket has been televised – acquired an unrivalled reputation as its leading TV broadcaster. Perhaps Benaud's most significant contribution, however, was his most contentious. In 1977 he broke with the game's establishment and joined Kerry Packer's World Series Cricket as chief commentator and spiritual father. He gave the venture a credibility and respectability that was essential to its triumph, and the transformation that ensued.

At the root of all he did was a sense of determination and integrity that went beyond fierce and bordered on the intimidating. He was successful at almost everything he attempted because he left as little as possible to chance, even when he was betting on horses. It was an attitude he acquired early. Richie's father, Lou, was an accomplished grade leg-spinner – he once took all 20 wickets in a two-innings game – who sacrificed his hopes of a first-class career because he was a schoolteacher in New South Wales, a state in which teachers were expected to go where they were sent. Despatched in the thick of the Depression to be the sole teacher in Jugiong, 200 miles from Sydney, Lou gave up his cricketing ambitions to support his wife and, at the time, his only child. (Brother John, who also became a Test cricketer, was born when Richie was 13.) Lou cleared a small room to teach Richie how to play properly, defensive shots first. The leg-spin came later.

By the time the family returned to the city, it was too late for the father but perfectly timed for the son. At 16 he was playing first-grade for Cumberland; at 18, on New Year's Eve 1948, he made his debut for New South Wales, alongside four of the newly returned Invincibles. In a rain-affected match, he scored two and was not asked to bowl.

Benaud's progress was far from serene. A week later he went to Melbourne for a state Second XI match against Victoria. Sent in as nightwatchman, he progressed to 13 comfortably enough, but next morning misjudged a hook and shattered a bone in his forehead – early confirmation of a penchant for on-field accidents. For nearly a year after that he had to concentrate on his job as a clerk in an accountancy firm, and the next chapter in his autobiography was headed "Promising much but delivering little".

He promised enough, however, and in December 1951 delivered a maiden first-class century, earning him an unexpected debut in the final Test of the 1951-52 series against West Indies, which Australia had already won. His major achievement was to run out Frank Worrell, his future opponent and comrade-in-arms, yet he did not look overawed. In those post-Bradman summers, with Australia now far from invincible, the selectors were searching for agile youth, especially the next season against the fleet-footed South Africans. Benaud can hardly have been worth a place on his figures either as batsman or bowler. But fielding was high on the list of virtues instilled by Lou. And, along with the prodigy Ian Craig, Richie seemed to embody the new spirit the selectors wanted.

He tried their patience, though, as South Africa held the mortified Australians to a 2–2 draw. Benaud appeared in the last four Tests, played a decent yet ultimately futile rearguard at the MCG, and bowled manfully at Adelaide; but he achieved neither a fifty nor a five-for. He was even less successful in 1953, when England regained the Ashes after 19 years, and was omitted from the Third and Fifth Tests. He continued to get injured in strange ways; the seam was ripping his fingers to shreds; and there was a sense that he concentrated too hard and thought too much.

But he was steadfast around the counties and, at Scarborough in September, got something out of his system, smashing 135 against T. N. Pearce's XI, England players all, including 11 sixes, equalling the world record. Something even more important happened in Scarborough. The previous night, Benaud – who never believed you could learn too much – had dinner with Bill O'Reilly, the sage of leg-spin. "Bill talked, and I listened." He did more than listen; he made notes, and referred to them again and again, later adapting them to give masterclasses of his own.

Back home, in the wholly domestic summer of 1953-54, he was New South Wales's leading batsman – he hit a ferocious 158 against Queensland – and, at 23, was appointed Cumberland's captain. When England successfully defended the Ashes in 1954-55, Benaud was ever-present but again largely irrelevant: after that series, he had played 13 Tests, averaging 14 with the bat and 37 with the ball. However, almost immediately afterwards Australia travelled to the Caribbean, and here he finally began to make an impact: three wickets in four balls at Georgetown, and a 78-minute hundred in the final Test at Kingston. These were soft successes: the not-quite-hat-trick involved tailenders, and his century was the fifth in an innings that reached 758 for eight. But Australia won the series well against a mighty batting team, and there was no need for scapegoats.

And so he came back to England in 1956. It was no kind of summer for Australia – except, as was the 20th-century custom, at Lord's: Benaud took a brilliant gully catch to dismiss Colin Cowdrey, and hit a decisive 97, the Australians' highest score of the series (he fell trying to smash Fred Trueman for four). Mostly, though, in journalist Malcolm Knox's words, he was being picked as "an investment that had gone too far to wind back". On the way home, the team faced four Tests in the subcontinent. Benaud was still working on his bowling, this time shortening his run, which produced a startling seven for 72 in Madras. But he contracted dengue fever, and his fingers were a perpetual bloody, painful mess. The answer to that came a few months later, on a non-Test tour of New Zealand, when he walked into a chemist's shop and met an affable pharmacist called Ivan James. "I think I've tried everything," said Benaud despairingly. James suggested a combination of

Perfectly executed: Richie Benaud bowls round the wicket at Old Trafford, 1961. Fred Trueman is the non-striker; John Langridge the umpire.

oily calamine lotion and boracic-acid powder. "The word genius is much overused in our society," Benaud wrote later. "Mr Ivan James turned out to be a genius."

In South Africa in 1957-58 he had a further weapon, a flipper, perfected in the nets at the Wanderers on hot afternoons when his team-mates were having fun. In the opening game against a Northern Rhodesia XI it brought him nine for 16: seven batsmen lbw or bowled playing back to his new trick, deliberately pitched short to barrel through low. He made 122 in the opening Test of the ensuing series; in the middle three, his flipper and Ivan James's magic formula helped him to 23 wickets in five innings. There was no more underachievement, and a year later he was captain. It had, however, been no smooth ascent. Craig, the anointed one, contracted hepatitis; Neil Harvey had antagonised the Australian board – he complained about the pathetic pay (£375 for a full Ashes series plus £50 expenses), moved from Melbourne to Sydney to accept a job, and led an Australian XI to a disastrous pre-series defeat against MCC in which the England captain Peter May scored two lordly centuries. Don Bradman, influential as ever, pushed for Benaud and prevailed.

England, expecting their fourth successive Ashes win, in 1958-59, were hardly perturbed. The cricket grapevine worked slowly in those days, and they still thought Benaud was the indifferent bowler they had seen in 1956; instead he took 31 wickets. And May certainly never foresaw the flair he would bring to leadership in a series when his own captaincy was "stereotyped", while his opponent was, according to *Wisden*, "inspiring", "fearless" and a "driving force". Benaud was backed up by total loyalty from Harvey, two big centuries from Colin McDonald, and an attack featuring Ian Meckiff, who – it has to be said – chucked. Australia won 4–0.

In 1959-60 Benaud captained the team to Pakistan and India and won both series, taking 47 wickets in eight Tests. His apotheosis came a year later when Worrell, belatedly appointed West Indies captain, arrived in Australia with a side willing and able to play in a manner that moved Test cricket forward from the dull defensiveness of the 1950s. The glorious freak of the tied Test at Brisbane brought forth an enchanting series, the tone set by the two captains. But it seemed characteristically Benaudish that, for all the gambling and attacking, it was Australia who narrowly prevailed. The same would happen again a few months later in England, where another tight series was settled by Benaud in just 20 minutes before tea at Old Trafford. England were 150 for one and coasting towards a target of 256. Benaud tried the then-novel tactic of bowling round the wicket into the footmarks: he took five for 12 in 25 balls, one of the most decisive spells in Test history, and six for 70 in all. It was widely described as a last throw of the dice; as ever with Benaud there was more to it than that. It was a bet on an outsider, but a shrewdly placed bet. He had talked the idea through the previous night with Ray Lindwall, who approved, while warning that it would have to be perfectly executed – which it was. He was one of the Five Cricketers of the Year in *Wisden 1962*, completing a unique double by also contributing the essay on one of the others, his mate Alan Davidson.

By now Benaud was recognised not just as an outstanding captain, but as a standard-bearer for the game: he had come to England promising no dawdling, no ill feeling, no arguments; he had kept his word. With his good looks, his openness and his informality – an extra shirt button usually undone – he seemed to fit with the emerging global cult of youth. But he no longer felt so young himself. He had missed Australia's win at Lord's because his right shoulder was in a terrible state, and the Old Trafford win was made possible only by intensive physio.

But he was not done: he led NSW to their ninth successive Sheffield Shield in 1961-62, and retained the Ashes in 1962-63 after a 1–1 draw with Ted Dexter's team, ensuring he never lost any of his six series as captain; *Wisden* noted that his leadership did seem a little more cautious. He planned to fade out after the home series against South Africa a year later; in the opening Test at the Gabba he became the first player to reach 2,000 runs and 200 wickets in Tests. The following weekend, playing for Cumberland, he went for a slip catch and broke his poor old spinning finger in three places. Calamine could not save him this time. He missed the Second Test and, though he would return for the last three, ceded the captaincy to Bob Simpson. He retired at Sydney, after his 63rd Test, still only 33. He had, however, been planning for this moment. He was not going to be an accounts clerk.

Benaud had long since moved from his first dreary job to the finance department of the Sydney *Sun*, under a kindly cricket-loving boss. But, in 1956, already in the Australian team yet far from secure, he had asked for a transfer to the editorial department. Sure, said the editor, who offered him a sports column and, if he liked, a ghostwriter to do the actual work. No, said Benaud: he wanted to learn the trade the hard way. The competition between Sydney's evening papers in the 1950s made old-time Chicago look soft, and Benaud asked to be assigned to the police round, the toughest, most competitive area of all. It was not unhelpful being a celebrity, but he did the hard yards. That same year, with TV just starting in Australia, Benaud organised a special three-week BBC training stint in the gap between the team's English and subcontinental tours. He was allowed to shadow the racing commentator Peter O'Sullevan (who died nearly four months after Benaud), and observe his meticulous preparation; and he watched, listened and learned. These experiences also helped develop a sense of the embryonic art of PR that served him well as captain. And, in 1960, he came to Britain again to work for the Sydney *Sun*, the BBC and the *News of the World*, beginning a connection with Britain's top-selling newspaper that lasted more than half a century until it predeceased him, in 2011. Three years later, in the brilliant summer when Worrell's team toured England, the BBC invited him to join the TV commentary team, starting the career that would make him more famous than ever.

This would also last half a century, and long before the end his commentaries were regarded by the public – even his colleagues – with a quasi-religious reverence ("But Richie said…"). Unlike Bradman, he never became an official administrator, but the power of TV gave him arguably greater influence. It was, for instance, Benaud's verdict of "disgraceful" which ensured that Trevor Chappell's underarm ball in 1980-81 would be a one-off aberration.

He was not an instinctive genius with words, as John Arlott was; people did not habitually switch on because Richie might be commentating. Indeed, a minority found his style rather chilly. The crucial element of Benaud's commentary was absence: the absence of prattle, the absence of errors. Behind this was the meticulousness he learned from his father, O'Reilly and O'Sullevan. He would scan the ground with binoculars while on air, looking for detail on the field and off. And he could rush between stints on the BBC (or, later, Channel 4) and Packer's Channel Nine, switching as required between the understated English style and the more talkative Australian one, always remembering to give the score the right way round: 50 for one for the Poms; one for 50 for the Aussies. The attention to detail never wavered, even when he left the box for the day: he would always, a colleague noted, carry two bags so he could reasonably refuse to sign autographs until he reached his car. Once there, though, he obliged happily.

Probably his greatest influence on cricket emerged from a private meeting in 1977, when he met Packer and agreed to lend his name and voice to World Series Cricket.

Second home: Richie Benaud in 1998.

Graham Morris

Characteristically, he said yes before even discussing his fee. He had no loyalty to Australian cricket's existing broadcaster, the ABC, which had apparently never asked him to commentate for them. And he had long been contemptuous of many of the arrogant and petty-minded old-line Australian administrators. He genuinely believed the players deserved more money and so, front and centre of Packer's Pirates, alongside the more contentious figures of Packer himself and Tony Greig, there was Peter Pan. Without Benaud to legitimise it, the venture might never have survived its difficult early months. Afterwards, some of his relationships would never be quite the same again, with Bradman most of all. But it made him one of the fathers of modern cricket, and for the quarter-century that followed he would be the most distinctive, most respected and most recognised sight and sound ("Morning, everyone") in both cricketing hemispheres.

He remained ferociously energetic. In England, he continued to write his own column for the otherwise disreputable *News of the World*, which, like Packer, employed Benaud to give them a veil of holiness (it took columns from a former Archbishop of Canterbury on the same basis). Before a full day's work at provincial Tests in England he would habitually play, not a gentlemanly nine, but a full 18 holes of golf. His golf was in character: every shot carefully considered. Playing with Michael Parkinson in Sydney, Benaud advised his partner that the 18th green was ferociously fast and that he should on no account overshoot the hole. Parky disobeyed and turned a possible three into a seven. "I know what you're thinking," he said ruefully as they walked off. "You don't," said Benaud. "Because you're still here."

Confronted with foolishness, Benaud could always be withering, and he appeared unapproachable. But, among friends, he was a famously genial dinner companion; and anyone who came up to him politely was granted politeness back, and sound advice if requested. He did seem to be good at almost everything. Even his punting was all of a piece. For 30 years, until the week he died, he had a private tipping competition with the shrewd Jack Bannister: one notional bet on English racing every Saturday, loser every six months to buy dinner for four. "Much of the time I was at home, and he would pick horses studying the form-book from Australia," said Bannister. "And he would still stuff me out of sight more often than not."

Richie's original marriage, in 1953, was his biggest failure; his first wife, Marcia, offered a lone dissenting voice amid the funerary tributes, and his relationship with his two sons was fraught. However, Richie's partnership – in life and business – with Daphne, his second wife, was successful and lasting, and their regime of perpetual summer, flitting between their homes in Sydney, London and France, seemed utterly enviable. Some thought driving was not his greatest skill. And when he crashed his beloved Sunbeam Alpine in Sydney in 2013, that and skin cancer – maybe the result of his bare-headed playing days – combined to end his commentary career and hasten his final decline.

Perhaps nothing summed him up better than the last of the several pieces he wrote for *Wisden*: a tribute to his friend and hero Keith Miller in 2005. The editor muttered apologetically about the feebleness of the fee. No, he said, he didn't want a fee. This was a duty, an obligation, the right thing to do.

BILBIE, ANTHONY ROBIN, died on August 29, aged 73. An attacking batsman, Robin Bilbie played 14 matches for Nottinghamshire without improving on his debut 39 against Hampshire at Trent Bridge in 1960. He did make a hundred for the Second XI in 1962, but was released at the end of the following season.

BISHOP, JAMIE, was found dead at his home on May 1, after an apparent heart attack. He was 44. A wicketkeeper who scored heavily for the Pontarddulais club, and also represented the Wales national team, Bishop played one first-class match for Glamorgan – against Oxford University in the Parks in 1992 – and made 51 not out in his only innings. The previous year he had scored 50 for Wales against the West Indian tourists at Brecon.

BLAKE, DAVID EUSTACE, who died on May 21, aged 90, was an attractive left-hand batsman and wicketkeeper who made 50 appearances for Hampshire. On his debut, against Combined Services in 1949, he made 47 and 54 after stumping Peter May. Blake scored 100 in a Championship victory over Somerset at Bournemouth in 1954, and five years later another round 100, for Free Foresters against Oxford University in the Parks. He had opened at Aldenham School with John Dewes (see below), a future England batsman, and in 1960, playing for MCC against Ireland in Dublin, went in first with Len Hutton, who made 89 in his final first-class innings. Blake fitted cricket in around his work as a dentist in Portsmouth. His older brother John – an Oxford Blue who also played for Hampshire – was killed in action in Yugoslavia in 1944.

BOWYER, WILLIAM, RA, who died on March 1, aged 88, was a distinguished landscape and portrait artist, whose love of cricket inspired one of his best-known works – the vivid depiction of Viv Richards playing a characteristically aggressive pull, now in the National Portrait Gallery. Bowyer was born in the Midlands, and as a young man played for Leek in the North Staffordshire League. He spent some of the Second World War working underground in the Staffordshire coalfield as a Bevin Boy. But, when his cricketing prowess became known to the colliery management, he was swiftly transferred to a job in the offices so he could play for the pit team. Bowyer became a fast bowler and frontline batsman for Chiswick CC, and always said he would not paint a batsman playing a stroke he could not execute himself. Other subjects included Mike Gatting, Ian Botham and Bob Willis, and in 1987 he was commissioned by MCC to paint the bicentenary match at Lord's.

BRAILSFORD, FRANK COLLISS, died on June 19, aged 81. A regular in Derbyshire's Second XI in the 1950s, "Jim" Brailsford played only three first-team games, all in August 1958 – but they were eventful ones. On his debut, against Sussex at Derby, he had Ted Dexter caught from his first ball in first-class cricket, while his second match – against Hampshire at the old Ind Coope ground in Burton-on-Trent – saw 39 wickets go down on the second day (Derbyshire had made eight for one on the rain-affected first). Hampshire were skittled for 23 and 55 in a match containing only one bowling change;

Brushstrokes: Bowyer's depiction of the 1987 bicentenary match at Lord's.

Brailsford's 14 after opening in the second innings remained his highest score. He was associated with the Chesterfield club for more than 70 years, although he was Undercliffe's professional when they won the Bradford League in 1970 and 1971. Later Brailsford joined the Derbyshire committee, and was their vice-chairman for a time.

BRIND, HENRY THOMAS, MBE, who died on August 31, aged 85, was the best-known groundsman in cricket, and the leading authority on pitch preparation. Brind, always "Harry", made his reputation at The Oval where, as Surrey's head groundsman from 1975 to 1994, he transformed the nature of the square and made the pitches a byword for pace and bounce; batsmen were in his debt as much as fast bowlers. It was fitting that, in the year of his retirement, Devon Malcolm bowled with lightning speed to record his fabled nine for 57 against South Africa. "The surface shone," said Brind. "It was the best pitch I ever prepared." His success was such that he was appointed the ECB's pitch inspector in 2000, and his formula repeated on surfaces around the country.

Brind was born in Hammersmith, just a few miles from the ground where he made his name, but his early ambitions centred on football: he was good enough to be recruited by Chelsea, who won the League under Ted Drake in 1955, but a knee injury ended his chances of becoming one of Drake's Ducklings, as Fleet Street dubbed the club's youth-team graduates. He first worked as a groundsman at a school in Putney, before moving to Barkingside and, when Trevor Bailey begged a loan from Warwickshire to secure Essex's first permanent ground at Chelmsford in 1965, Brind was hired. He had a minuscule budget and no assistance. "We had no proper covers – only trestles with sheets draped over them."

Nevertheless he created an excellent square, and his work came to the attention of administrators at Test venues. Surrey, keen to lose their reputation for slow, lifeless pitches, took him on, but Brind soon realised he had his work cut out: "If you dropped a ball from a 16-foot pole, it should bounce two or three feet, but when I arrived at The Oval, it was bouncing three inches." Brind persuaded Surrey that the square needed relaying after his initial excavations revealed compressed loam to a depth of around a foot; underneath that was nothing but shale. He knew that the construction of the M11 in Essex

Groundwork: Harry Brind on the heavy roller, The Oval, 1980.

meant there was a surfeit of Ongar loam, and tons were brought to The Oval, where Brind mixed it with Surrey loam. It was his magic formula.

The transformation did not happen overnight, though the first time a relaid pitch was used in a Test – for the final match of the 1981 Ashes – it drew praise from the captains, Mike Brearley and Kim Hughes. Brind also insisted on better equipment, and argued that groundstaff should concentrate on their main tasks, not clearing rubbish from the stands at the close of play. He had a testimonial season in 1993, and was succeeded at The Oval by his son Paul. His work with the board saw him advise on pitch preparation around Britain, as well as in Australia, Sri Lanka and Pakistan. He also laid the square at Sir Paul Getty's ground at Wormsley.

On his death, the Surrey flag flew at half-mast over the pavilion. "Harry produced some of the best pitches I ever played on, with terrific pace and bounce," said Alec Stewart. "He was one of the most forward-thinking groundsmen in the world." In retirement Brind moved back to Essex, and in later life was forced to accept the role of supervisor while his wife Pat mowed their immaculate grass. "We have the finest lawn in Chelmsford," he said.

BROWN, WILFRED MARTIN, died in a fire which destroyed his home in the southern Queensland town of Warwick on April 25. He was 85. He played two unsuccessful matches for Queensland, yet his unwavering patience and defensive skills made him a thorn in the side of a succession of touring teams for Country XIs, his best effort 78 against MCC at Rockhampton in 1954-55.

BULBULIA, AHMED SAMED, died on July 10, aged 82. Sam Bulbulia, a member of a prominent Johannesburg cricketing family, was a fine batsman who represented Transvaal's non-white side for many years, including some of the later games (from 1971-72) which are now considered first-class. He played for the South African non-white team, led by Basil D'Oliveira, in representative matches against the touring Kenyans in 1956-57. Soon after that, his family were ordered to leave their home in the Johannesburg suburb of Fietas and move 20 miles away to the non-white township of Lenasia, in accordance with the apartheid government's Group Areas Act – but the Bulbulias defiantly stayed put, and were still there in 2015. Sam remained active in cricket, and in 2014 was one of the inaugural recipients of Cricket South Africa's Heritage Blazers, which recognise prominent players and administrators from the apartheid era. His brother, Mahmood "Koeka" Bulbulia – a swing bowler – died eight days later, aged 80.

BURROWS, ALFRED, who died on August 16, aged 61, had a peculiar career in India domestic cricket, scoring 193 – his fourth first-class century – in what turned out to be hi final match, for Railways against Vidarbha in December 1985. A stylish batsman, born into an Anglo-Indian family in Madras, Burrows had twice been selected for Central Zone including against the 1983-84 West Indian tourists; he made 31 against an attack spearheaded by Michael Holding and Wayne Daniel. He later took up coaching and umpiring, and stood in the first two seasons of the unauthorised Indian Cricket League Four years before his death he emigrated to Western Australia.

BYFIELD, ARNOLD STANLEY, OAM, died on July 4, aged 91. "Bud" Byfield was an outstanding Western Australian country cricketer whose uncomplicated batting and medium-pace earned him six state matches in the early 1950s. In 1993, he was given the Medal of the Order of Australia for his extensive involvement in Aussie Rules as player, umpire and administrator. His sister, Joan, is the mother of the former Test batsman Geo Marsh, and grandmother of current internationals Shaun and Mitchell.

CAMACHO, GEORGE STEPHEN, died on October 2, aged 69. Steve Camacho was the longest-serving chief executive of the West Indies Cricket Board, and the last Test cricketer

West Indies servant: Steve Camacho in 1973.

to hold the position. Appointed the firs executive secretary in 1982, he operated virtually on his own from a small office a Kensington Oval in Bridgetown. He wa upgraded to CEO when the board moved their headquarters to Antigua, but stood down in 2000 after the first signs of the cancer that eventually killed him. During his 18 years in charge he also served a manager, assistant manager and selector o West Indies teams, and was a valued member of the ICC's chief executives committee. A Guyanese of Portuguese descent, he was one of their last whit Test players.

A patient, technically correct opene who batted in glasses, Camacho played 1 Tests for West Indies and 35 times for hi native Guyana between 1964-65 and 1978-79. His modest averages – 29 in Test and 34 in first-class cricket – did littl justice to his talent, which was first evident in an innings of 157 for Guyana Colt against the Australian tourists in 1964-6 at Bourda, where he had developed hi

passion for the game. He was then 19. A year later, he made the first of his seven first-class centuries: 106 for Guyana against Trinidad at Queen's Park Oval. He was part of a phenomenally powerful batting side, which included his dashing left-handed opening partner Roy Fredericks, Rohan Kanhai, Basil Butcher, Joe Solomon and Clive Lloyd, and later Alvin Kallicharran.

Camacho's 87 against England at Port-of-Spain in his debut series in 1967-68 remained his highest Test score: "He played hitherto unrevealed strokes all round the wicket, reported *Wisden*. He struggled in Australia in 1968-69, but retained his place for the tour of England that followed, where he topped the Test averages with 46. But an unremarkable home series against India in 1970-71 proved his last: an unexpected opportunity to revive his Test career in England in 1973 was cut short by a crushing blow to the face from Andy Roberts in the tour game against Hampshire. He continued playing for Guyana, latterly as captain, until he turned to administration in 1979.

During the years when West Indies dominated, he was uncompromising in his attention to detail, and managed the board under the presidencies of Jeffrey Stollmeyer, Allan Rae, Sir Clyde Walcott and Peter Short, who predeceased him by two months (see below). An affable personality, Camacho would speak passionately, humorously and precisely about his days in the game and the vast number of friends he made.

His grandfather, G. C. Learmond, represented British Guiana (as Guyana was known), Trinidad and Barbados in the intercolonial tournaments at the turn of the 20th century, and toured England with the West Indian teams of 1900 and 1906, before they achieved Test status. His father, George Camacho, a left-handed batsman, played 15 matches for British Guiana, three as captain.

CAMPBELL, IAN PARRY, who died on May 31, aged 87, was a prolific wicketkeeper-batsman at Canford School in Dorset, passing 1,000 runs in 1945 and 1946, when he was called up to play for Kent against Middlesex at Lord's; he had little chance to shine after Les Todd, Jack Davies and Les Ames all made hundreds. That was his only Championship appearance, although he was an Oxford Blue in 1949 and 1950; his highest score, 60 not out, came against Leicestershire the following year, when he missed the Varsity Match. In all he played 22 first-class games, his 41 dismissals including 16 stumpings (he once made five in an innings in a school match). A fine all-round sportsman, Campbell played hockey for England and rugby for Kent. He later lived in New Zealand.

CLAYTON, RHEINHALT EDWARD, died on October 8, aged 80. "Rene" Clayton never got beyond twelfth man in two seasons on the Glamorgan groundstaff, but became a legendary figure in club cricket in North Wales: a batsman who bowled teasing leg-spin, he did the 1,000-run/100-wicket double for Colwyn Bay in 1976 and 1977, after nine years as Llandudno's professional. Part of the first national team selected by the new Welsh Cricket Association in 1969, Clayton was also Colwyn Bay's groundsman.

CLOSE, DENNIS BRIAN, CBE, who died on September 14, aged 84, was one of the most colourful and enduring characters in English cricket. His fame extended to featuring in an Eric Morecambe one-liner, yet he achieved recognition without coming near to fulfilling the potential that in 1949 had made him, aged 18, England's youngest player. Close played in 22 Tests over 27 years (and four decades) with only modest results – but he was proof that some cricketers are far more than the sum of their statistics.

At times his ability as an all-rounder, his outstanding record as a captain, and the store of anecdotes he inspired, were lost amid awestruck admiration for his courage against fast bowling or in the field, close to the bat. It was his reckless bravery that inspired Morecambe's joke about the return of summer being signalled by "the sound of leather on Brian Close". When he died, the wince-inducing footage of his encounter with the West Indies pace attack at Old Trafford in 1976 was shown so frequently it was easy to overlook the fact that he led Yorkshire to four County Championships, had a successful spell as England captain, and enjoyed a late-career renaissance at Somerset as a growling mentor to Ian Botham and Viv Richards.

Close had the bravado to walk down the pitch to Wes Hall and Charlie Griffith at Lord's in 1963 but, while these exploits burnished his reputation, they disguised a sensitive man who was wounded by his setbacks. His friend Ray Illingworth believed his callous treatment by senior pros on the 1950-51 Ashes tour left scars that took years to heal. Likewise, the recollection of his brutal sacking as Yorkshire captain in 1970 could bring him to the point of tears nearly 40 years later. And he always maintained that his removal from the England captaincy in 1967 was part of an Establishment plot to get rid of an outspoken northerner. As Yorkshire team-mate Richard Hutton said: "He had difficulty at times keeping quiet. He did not do himself many favours."

Close was born in Rawdon, near Leeds, and was in the local club's first team at the age of 11. He was a bright schoolboy with a gift for maths, but his sporting talent led him towards football with Leeds United – and cricket. In 1949 he made his Yorkshire debut, along with Fred Trueman and Frank Lowson, at Fenner's (*Wisden* referred to Trueman as

"a spin bowler"). The Championship was shared with Middlesex that summer, and Close – a hard-hitting left-hander in the middle order and a swing or off-spin bowler – became the youngest player to complete the double. He was called up for a Test debut against New Zealand and, although he made an inauspicious start, his potential was such that sensible notions of letting him mature in county cricket were ignored. National service meant he missed most of the following season, but Signalman Close was granted extended leave of absence after he was selected to go to Australia in 1950-51.

By his own admission, Close was "a naive young lad", and the experienced players who might have harnessed his teenage exuberance were aloof and unhelpful. "Some thought Close a trifle swollen-headed," wrote E. M. Wellings in his tour book *No Ashes for England*. He started with a century and four wickets against Western Australia at the WACA, but was troubled by injuries. Captain

Likely lad: Brian Close bowls on his Test debut, against New Zealand at Manchester, July 1949.

Freddie Brown persuaded him to play in the Second Test at Melbourne but, with a groin heavily strapped, he scored nought and one, having returned to dressing-room silence after a rash shot in the first innings. The Australians noted his distress, and Ian Johnson urged Brown to offer him some help. "Let the bugger stew," said Brown, who even confiscated his golf clubs.

"He came back from that tour a very different person, and that went on for a long time," said Illingworth, who noted the lack of swagger in his batting. "Before then, he always wanted to bat. It was always, 'I'll murder this bowler when I get in.'" Close completed his national service and did the double again in 1952, but missed most of the following summer because of a serious knee injury sustained while turning out for Bradford City (he did not make the first team at Leeds nor, subsequently, Arsenal). It ended his football career, but proved a blessing for cricket. In 1955, he was playing well enough to be called up for the Fifth Test against South Africa at The Oval, where he opened the batting.

By the late 1950s, Close had become the senior professional at Yorkshire and regained much of his youthful ebullience. They were champions three times in four years and, when Vic Wilson retired as captain in 1962, Close took over. He proved an instant success, handling players shrewdly, leading aggressively and forming an unmatched tactical alliance with Illingworth. "Closey was a great man-manager," said the fast bowler Mel Ryan (who died two months after Close). "He was a dominant character. Even Fred Trueman was frightened of him, and he got the best out of people." And part of that was his willingness to field at short leg even when captain.

But his Test career remained a thing of fits and starts, and looked to have been dealt a mortal blow on the climactic afternoon of the Old Trafford Ashes Test in 1961, when England's run-chase subsided as Richie Benaud began to bowl round the wicket into the rough. Close came in at 150 for three and, characteristically, felt their best chance lay in continuing to pursue a target of 256. He also reckoned that, as a left-hander, he was better equipped to take on Benaud. But, after driving him for six, he was caught playing a big sweep. The press excoriated him, John Woodcock writing in *The Times* that "he swung wildly at his first ball and continued to play as if out of his cricketing senses".

He returned against West Indies two years later, playing his only full five-match series and making 315 runs at 31. Amid the drama of the final afternoon in the Second Test at Lord's, he struck a belligerent 70, his highest – and best – Test innings. He frequently walked down the pitch, and he was struck several times. Next day, photographs of his bruised torso decorated back pages. With Yorkshire winning the Championship, it was the high point of his career, and he was named a Wisden Cricketer of the Year.

A hat-trick of Championships followed from 1966, and the Gillette Cup was won in 1965 and 1969. Close led by unselfish example, moving up and down the order, or switching between off-spin and his now gentle seamers to suit the situation. "He did not have great personal ambition," said Hutton. "He would say that everything he was doing was for Yorkshire." In the field his exploits became legendary, and his brooding presence, intimidatingly close at short leg, induced anxiety in batsmen. Close explained: "I used to get down with my legs half-bent, my upper body always horizontal and my head stuck out in front. The only places they could hit me point blank were my legs, my shoulders and my head." And he was hit often, but was only interested in whether a team-mate had caught the rebound. The one time his colleagues recalled him admitting to pain was when he came in contact with a boiled kettle while walking naked around the dressing-room.

Getting it off his chest: Brian Close is hit by Michael Holding at Manchester in 1976.

In August 1966, with England 3–0 down against West Indies, the 35-year-old Close was summoned to replace Colin Cowdrey as captain for the final Test, at The Oval. Time had not dimmed his self-belief. Doug Insole, the chairman of selectors, recalled: "The first selection meeting after he became captain was in Leicester on a Sunday. We quickly picked nine players and I said, 'Let's stop for a minute and see what we've got and where the gaps are. What about openers?' Closey said, 'Well, at Yorkshire we have Boycott and Ken Taylor, but if we need quick runs I go in first because I can see the ball better than either of them.' I said, 'OK. Do we need a second spinner?' Closey said, 'Well, we have Don Wilson and Ray Illingworth, but if the ball is really turning I go on because I turn it more than those two.' I said, 'OK then, what about seam bowlers?' Closey said, 'At Yorkshire we have Fred and Tony Nicholson, but if it's really swinging I bowl because I can swing it more than either of them.' So I said, 'Well then, doesn't look like we need to bother with the other two players.'"

England won by an innings, and Close enhanced his reputation for innovative thinking by instructing John Snow to bowl Garry Sobers a first-ball bouncer in West Indies' second innings, calculating that he would not be able to resist the hook. Sobers's mistimed stroke lobbed into the hands of a jubilant Close, still upright at short leg. The following summer, England went undefeated against India and Pakistan, but Close had a sense of foreboding when Crawford White of the *Daily Express* warned him to stay out of trouble because MCC were "looking for any excuse" not to select him as captain for the tour of the Caribbean.

Instead, Close walked into a full-blown row when, on the final afternoon of a Championship match at Edgbaston, he was accused of adopting time-wasting tactics to stop Warwickshire winning. The fate of the England captain became front-page news, and Close faced an MCC disciplinary panel on the day before the final Test against Pakistan. The decision was delayed until after the match, but MCC ruled he would not be asked to lead the team in the West Indies. Insole recalled: "I said to him, 'Closey, all you have to do is say sorry and you can carry on as captain,' but before the panel he said he had done it to prevent Yorkshire losing the game and would do so again. One of the panel said, 'If he does that in the West Indies we will have a riot.'"

At Yorkshire, the departure of Illingworth and retirement of Trueman made the team less formidable. The committee were keen to introduce new blood, but the captain did not share their enthusiasm for the club's emerging players. "Brian's great quality was that he was very loyal to the players who were tried and tested, but this brought about his downfall," said Hutton. In November 1970 he was summoned to a meeting with Brian Sellers, chairman of the cricket committee, and given the option of resigning or being sacked. Deep in shock, Close was sick by the side of the road as he drove away from Headingley. Initially he chose to resign, but quickly changed his mind. He was devastated. At Harrogate several years later, he encountered Sellers, who told him: "I can honestly say that sacking you was the biggest mistake of my life."

He chose Taunton over higher-profile destinations and made five centuries – including one when Yorkshire came visiting – in his first season with Somerset. He had no captaincy ambitions, but was persuaded to take over from Brian Langford in 1972. At the end of the summer, with Illingworth injured, Close was asked to lead England against Australia in the post-Ashes one-day matches, the first on English soil, winning 2–1. At Somerset, an exciting generation was emerging – Vic Marks, Brian Rose and Peter Roebuck, as well as Botham and Richards – and Close and the veteran seamer Tom Cartwright proved the perfect mentors. He was, said Marks, "selfless, generous, hilariously funny (although he did not always appreciate why), a wee bit mad and awesomely brave".

There were as many stories about his driving as his cricket. He would study form in *Sporting Life* in the fast lane of a motorway, or ask his passenger to lean over and take over the steering while he poured a mug of tea. Cartwright recalled going into Taunton one morning to see Close's car perched on top of a hedge; he had been leaning across to grab a portable radio while negotiating a bend.

His career had one more improbable twist. In 1976, Tony Greig was looking to stiffen England's spine for the series against West Indies and, aged 45, Close was recalled. "It's the first year I haven't put the Test dates in my diary," he said. He did well in the middle order at Trent Bridge and Lord's, but at Old Trafford was asked to open with John Edrich, aged 39. On the Saturday evening they were caught in one of Test cricket's most notorious passages of play, as Andy Roberts, Wayne Daniel and Michael Holding bowled with unrelenting hostility on a cracked pitch. Close took several blows on the body, buckled at least once, but refused to show any pain. Richards, his Somerset protégé, was fielding close to the bat. "Are you OK, skipper?" he asked, only to be told to "fuck off". Somehow the pair survived for 80 minutes. Close was one not out.

He did not play for England again, and retired at the end of the following season. Only Wilfred Rhodes had a longer Test career span than his 27 years, and in first-class cricket his total of 813 catches is bettered by just four men. Yet a wistfulness lingered. "Of all the players who were around at that time, his career was the most disappointing," said Insole, who had captained Cambridge on Close's Yorkshire debut. "He had more ability in every aspect of the game."

CLOUGH, BRIAN, who died on January 28, aged 82, was one of the finest batsmen to appear in the Bradford League, scoring more than 10,000 runs, often choosing between his "hookin' bat" and one for "drivin'". He made his league debut for Spen Victoria's second team when he was 11, and played for the firsts at 14 – but was mainly associated with Bowling Old Lane, helping to keep the inner-city club going during tough times in the 1990s. His son, David, is the Press Association's England cricket reporter.

CORBETT, PETER LLEWELLYN, who died on May 23, aged 74, extended his maiden first-class hundred – against Transvaal B at the Wanderers in January 1963 – to a lofty 237. That remained the record for North Eastern Transvaal until Martin van Jaarsveld made an unbeaten 238 in November 1999 (when the team were known as Northerns). Corbett added 132 in his next match, against Griqualand West, and scored 560 runs in just six matches in 1962-63 – but managed only one more century, three years later. He had played for South African Schools in 1958-59, alongside Ali Bacher and Peter Pollock. His brother, John, also played for North Eastern Transvaal.

DALMIYA, JAGMOHAN, who died on September 20, aged 75, turned an Anglocentric sport into an Indocentric one, converting India's enormous passion for the game into a worldwide marketing tool – to much national joy and international apprehension.

Dalmiya was president of the Board of Control for Cricket in India from 2001 to 2004, after stints as secretary in the 1990s. The BCCI had a deficit of 8.5m rupees when he took over; the national broadcaster Doordarshan demanded 500,000 to show each Test, based on an obscure 1885 Act of Parliament. "There is money in cricket," said Dalmiya, "but none of it is coming to the BCCI." And so he set about changing all that. The TV battle came to a head in 1993 when, following a Supreme Court ruling, the BCCI were able to sell the rights for the home series against England for $US40,000. A little more than a decade later, the rights fetched $612m over four years.

With his impeccable safari suit and brushed-back hair, "Jaggu-da," as he was affectionately known, was the picture of a successful businessman. His ambitions as a player had ended when his father died and, aged 19, he had to focus on the family business, the M. L. Dalmiya Construction Company, which built the Birla Planetarium in Calcutta. Until then he had been an enthusiastic opening batsman and wicketkeeper for the Rajasthan club in the Calcutta League.

It took him less than a decade to transform the world game. Along with the BCCI president, I. S. Bindra, Dalmiya ensured that the veto enjoyed by England and Australia, the ICC's founder members, was removed. And, at a time when England was seen as the natural home for the World Cup, Dalmiya helped make it a global tournament in both form and content, taking it to the subcontinent in 1987 and 1996.

When he became the ICC's first Asian president in 1997, they had only a few thousand pounds in the bank. On Dalmiya's watch, that swelled to more than $17m. His tactics were a mix of politics, diplomacy, blackmail and charm. First he courted the non-Test countries, each of whom had a single vote to the Full Members' two; guaranteed their support, he took on the rest. His method may have lacked universal appeal, his motives often put down to colonial resentment, but there was no denying his influence. What Tiger Pataudi did on the field, Dalmiya did in the boardroom, forcing respect from countries long used to looking down on Indian cricket.

Now that India's position as the engine that drives world cricket is a cliché, it is difficult to understand the opposition he had to face from the traditionalists. Malcolm Speed, a former ICC chief executive, once spoke of Dalmiya's "manic determination to make India a world cricketing power", and described him as "the most resolute, able, difficult, prickly and unpredictable man" he had ever met.

Unusually for an administrator, Dalmiya was also a players' man, putting in place central contracts during his time at the BCCI. The former Test captain Anil Kumble called him a "players' president", always keeping the door open for dialogue. "My generation was very comfortable dealing with the board," said Kumble, "because Mr Dalmiya was always receptive." Ian Chappell characterised him as "a man I didn't want to have as an enemy", but added that he did "a hell of a lot for the game". Another ex-captain, Sourav

The picture of a businessman: Jagmohan Dalmiya, Trent Bridge, 1997.

Ganguly, succeeded him as president of the Cricket Association of Bengal. "These are big shoes to fill," he said. "I began playing cricket when he was the president. He was a companion through my career."

The fall came in 2006, when Dalmiya was expelled by the BCCI for alleged misappropriation of funds. He claimed the accusations were unfounded: he didn't need the money. In July the following year, the Calcutta High Court dismissed the charges and, in 2013, when Narayanaswami Srinivasan was forced to stand aside by the Supreme Court, Dalmiya returned as interim president. In March 2015 he was voted back to power but, his faculties in decline, he was a mere figurehead.

Asked once what drove him, Dalmiya replied: "In a corner of our hearts, isn't there a desire for recognition, for having more contacts and friends, being on television and in newspapers?" Simple ambitions from a simple man – but ambitions that changed cricket.

DAULTREY, STUART GEORGE, died on December 14, aged 68. A geography lecturer, Stu Daultrey became one of Ireland's leading umpires, after losing an arm in a motorcycle accident. He stood in two first-class matches, including Ireland's game against Australia A in 1998. After being forced to give up umpiring through ill health, he wrote thought-provoking articles for cricket websites.

DAVIDSON, REV. WILLIAM WATKINS, died on May 26, aged 95. Bill Davidson kept wicket for Oxford University in 1947 and 1948, and made four Championship appearances for Sussex; he had been their oldest surviving player. A modest batsman, he reached double figures only three times in 23 first-class innings. Davidson enlisted in the Army during the Second World War, seeing action in Burma and Malaya, even though, as a theological student, he was exempt from military service. He became a chaplain in the Royal Navy, and later a vicar in Surrey and Westminster. On retirement from the church he took up sailing, once being dismasted in a storm in the Bay of Biscay.

DAVIS, ALEXANDER EDWARD, died on August 14, aged 91. A former quantity surveyor, Alex Davis was Warwickshire's scorer for ten years from 1988, and did the job for England in the West Indies in 1993-94 and Australia the following winter. He was therefore in charge of the scorebook for Brian Lara's then-record 375 in the Antigua Test in April 1994, and his 501 not out – still the first-class best – for Warwickshire against Durham at Edgbaston a few weeks later. Davis is the only person known to have seen every ball of both. "The two innings were very different," he reflected in *Wisden 1995*, "because the first I was doing manually in a scorebook, whereas the second I was doing on the computer and a manual scoresheet, so I was working twice as hard. And the second one was scored at such a rate, we kept having to answer the phone to the press to give the details of each of the fifties. At one time the pressman said: 'Shall I stay on for the next fifty?'"

DE SILVA, PIYAL BANDULA, who died on February 17, aged about 80, was the secretary of the Board of Control for Cricket in Sri Lanka for two years from 1978. The board had no central office at the time, and meetings were held in de Silva's house in Colombo; his home telephone served as the board's contact number, and he paid for all their international calls. He later founded *Score*, a cricket magazine, and received an ICC medal for his services to the game.

DEWES, JOHN GORDON, died on May 12, aged 88. It may have been an act of optimism induced by the mood of euphoria, or possibly a gamble forced by a lack of alternatives, but the team for the Third Victory Test against the Australian Services at Lord's in July 1945 included three teenage batsmen. They were "the best schoolboy cricketers of 1944", according to the Press Association: John Dewes and Luke White, freshmen at Cambridge, and Donald Carr, training to become an army officer in Kent. Dewes was not overawed. "I was in form: I thought I was going to make it," he remembered. "Little did I realise what a big jump I was making."

All three were on their first-class debuts, and Dewes enjoyed the most success, scoring 27 at No. 3 in the first innings, despite receiving some sharp blows from Keith Miller, who eventually sent his off stump flying. Promoted to open in the second, he was bowled by Miller for a duck. "I had no idea bowling could be that fast," Dewes told the author Stephen Chalke. "After that match, I always had Keith Miller in the back of my mind."

He later made five appearances in official Tests and – when teaching duties allowed – played for Middlesex until 1956. He was an obdurate left-handed opener, determined rather than stylish. "He was a practical player," said his former Cambridge team-mate Hubert Doggart. "He had a good eye and he was a very strong cutter, hooker and puller."

The highlights of Dewes's career were three huge partnerships, all for Cambridge. In May 1949, he and Doggart put on an unbroken 429 in a day against Essex at Fenner's, an English domestic record for the second wicket that lasted until 1974; Dewes made 204. But Doug Insole declared overnight, denying them the chance to pass the world record of 455, set five months earlier by K. V. Bhandarkar and B. B. Nimbalkar for Maharashtra against Kathiawar at Poona. It was suggested that Insole's decision disappointed the players, as well as the fresh posse of pressmen, but Doggart insisted: "We had talked about declaring at tea on the first day. We were quite happy about it – we wanted to win the match."

The following summer Dewes (183) and his great friend David Sheppard put on 343 for the first wicket against the West Indians, again at Fenner's, leaving Alf Valentine and Sonny Ramadhin wicketless. A month later they managed 349 (Dewes 212) at Hove. It was the most productive season of his career: 2,432 runs at 59 left him fifth in the averages. No other batsman matched his nine hundreds, one of which came for Middlesex at Headingley in Len Hutton's benefit match.

Dewes was born in North Latchford, Cheshire, and educated at Aldenham, where he was captain in 1944. That summer he made 107 for The Rest against Lord's Schools, earning selection alongside Carr and White for Public Schools against a Lord's XI, a match interrupted when a V1 flying bomb was seen heading their way over Baker Street. It cut out overhead, landing just outside the ground, but left a coating of dust on the wicket. Play swiftly resumed, and spectators emerged from under their seats to applaud the boys' courage. "It was very frightening," said Dewes.

Great deeds writ large: Hubert Doggart and John Dewes at Fenner's, scene of their 1949 triumph.

He made his Test debut at The Oval in 1948, scoring one (bowled Miller) and ten in England's innings defeat. His encounter with Miller three years earlier had left lasting memories: when the Australians visited Fenner's, Jack Fingleton was amused by the amount of improvised padding Dewes had stuffed into his trousers. He played twice against West Indies in 1950, and a second-innings 67 at Trent Bridge was enough to earn him a place in Freddie Brown's squad for the Ashes tour. He played in the first two Tests but did not get into double figures and was dismissed twice by Miller. Later, he was fond of telling stressed pupils or parents that their anxieties were nothing compared with facing Miller at the MCG.

There were no more Test opportunities, and Dewes moved into teaching full-time, appearing for Middlesex in the holidays. In 1955 he was still good enough to score 67 runs at 48 in eight matches, including a century against a Surrey attack including Ale

Bedser, Jim Laker and Tony Lock. He taught at Tonbridge and Rugby, before moving to Australia to become head of Barker College in the Sydney suburbs, where one of Richie Benaud's sons was a pupil. He returned to England in the early 1960s, and became a housemaster and careers teacher at Dulwich. One pupil was Nigel Farage, later to become leader of UKIP; Dewes told him he would make an excellent auctioneer.

He visited Aldenham in 2010 for the first annual match between a John Dewes XI and the school. The connection between the cricketing families of Doggart and Dewes has endured. His son Jim Dewes, a Cambridge Blue in 1978, played for Free Foresters alongside Simon Doggart, Hubert's son. More recently, John and Hubert both had two grandsons at Wellington College, where Jim teaches. In a house match in 2009, James Doggart scored a hundred and Adam Dewes a half-century, almost 60 years to the day after their grandfathers' partnership against Essex.

DIMMOCK, PETER HAROLD, CBE, CVO, died on November 20, aged 94. As a producer and presenter, Peter Dimmock was one of the most influential figures in the history of British television. He made his reputation by overseeing the landmark coverage of the Coronation in 1953, after convincing sceptical Establishment figures that the public deserved to see the event in as much detail as possible. He was always a sports enthusiast – he had been racing correspondent of the Press Association before joining the BBC – and became a pioneer of the corporation's outside broadcasts, including their sports coverage; he also became well known in front of the camera, presenting *Sportsview* and later *Grandstand*. Dimmock produced the BBC's first live Test coverage from outside London – West Indies' ten-wicket victory over England at Trent Bridge in 1950. Much of his skill lay in negotiating with administrators. He once attended a meeting with senior MCC figures at Lord's, after they had hesitated over signing a new contract for Test coverage. He told them £100,000 was the BBC's "one and final offer". After waiting outside during their deliberations, he returned to be informed the offer was not high enough. "Although

Race meeting: Peter O'Sullevan and Peter Dimmock in November 1950. O'Sullevan had helped Richie Benaud at the start of his broadcasting career. All three died in 2015.

it's only of academic interest," the chairman said, "the lowest price we could have accepted would have been £120,000." Dimmock smacked his hand down on the table: "Done!"

DINDAR, NAZIER, who died of cancer on July 6, aged 49, was an all-rounder who played several games now considered first-class for Transvaal's non-white side, and three for other Transvaal teams in 1991-92, the first season of integration between the various boards. He scored 132 not out against Western Province in a Howa Bowl match in 1988-89, sharing a substantial partnership with Haroon Lorgat, now Cricket South Africa's chief executive, who said: "He was one of the many talented cricketers who were regrettably denied opportunity when in the prime of their lives." Dindar later emigrated to England, although he was working in Saudi Arabia at the time of his death.

DRUMMER, FRANCOIS THEODORE MAX, died on August 3, aged 76. Frankie Drummer was a fast bowler for South Africa's Western Province in the 1960s, and later moved to Transvaal. He was quite quick but, in the days of little or no coaching, rarely swung the ball until a selector noticed he was holding it across the seam. Drummer's eight for 28 (and 11 for 69 in the match) demolished Border for 68 at East London in 1966-67; in his next game, against the touring Australians at Newlands, he dismissed Ian Redpath and Grahame Thomas, then compiled a four-hour 48 as nightwatchman. His brother Desmond also played for Western Province.

DUCKMANTON, ALBERT GEORGE, died on February 1, aged 81. Alby Duckmanton was a handy off-spinning all-rounder who played 17 matches for Canterbury spread over ten years from his debut in 1951-52. On January 19, 1961, he took a career-best five for 29 against Northern Districts at Hamilton, and exactly a year later – in what turned out to be his final game – made his highest score of 69 against Central Districts at Nelson. He then had a long career in cricket administration, becoming Canterbury's chairman and president. Duckmanton served on the New Zealand Cricket Council from 1981 to 1988 when he occasionally managed the national team at home. A talented badminton player and a rugby referee, he was awarded the Queen's Service Medal in 2013 for his contributions to sport.

DUFFY, GERARD ANTHONY ANDREW, died on June 15, aged 84. A hard-hitting batsman who also mixed innocuous-looking leg-rollers with seam-up, Gerry Duffy played for Ireland for 20 years, and at club level for 43, mainly with Leinster. He scored more than 10,000 runs for them, with a highest of 264, and amassed over 900 wickets; they won a dozen league and cup titles during his time. In all he made 55 appearances for Ireland, scoring 79 and 92 against MCC at Clontarf in 1970; the previous year he was part of the side which skittled the West Indian tourists for 25 at Sion Mills. In 1961, his six for 29 against the Australians included the wicket of a rather more distinguished leg-spinner, Richie Benaud – who said during an 80th-birthday tribute, Duffy was the best all-rounder never to have played Test cricket. After finally retiring, he turned to coaching, his star pupils being the Joyce family, five of whom have played for Ireland.

ELLIS, REGINALD SIDNEY, died on June 21, aged 97. Reg Ellis was the last survivor of the famous wartime Australian Services team which toured England, then went to India, and finally entertained around Australia. He was a key member of their attack, able to vary his orthodox left-arm spin with the more exotic, back-of-the-hand variety. He was, as the Perth historian Ed Jaggard had it, "tirelessly effective": 70% of his victims in the five Victory Tests in England in 1945 came from the top six. His best performance was against H. D. G. Leveson Gower's XI at Scarborough, where he bowled the Services to victory with five wickets in each innings. The ensuing slog through the subcontinent and back home in Australia took its toll, but did produce career-best figures of six for 144 in a New South Wales total of 551 for seven.

Ellis had volunteered for the Royal Australian Air Force, his training revealing skills which led him to become a flight instructor in the UK. From 1944 he flew ten missions with the Lancasters of No. 463 RAAF Squadron. Back in Australia, he found work as a

Normal service resumed: Reg Ellis bowls to Wally Hammond in the Second Victory Test, at Bramall Lane, Sheffield, in 1945.

flying instructor with the Royal Aero club of South Australia; the job often required weekend work, and he played only one further state match, against Victoria in March 1946. Working hard again, he took five for 210.

In 2011, Ellis was a guest of honour at Sachin Tendulkar's Bradman Oration at the Australian War Memorial in Canberra. On the flights to and from Adelaide, he amused himself by rating the skill of the take-offs and landings.

ERICKSON, BERT, who died on May 28, aged 83, was a tireless administrator in South African non-white cricket, chiefly with Avendale in Cape Town, which – helped by the England batsman and future international coach Bob Woolmer – he helped develop into a club capable of holding their own in the highest division of the local league. Erickson had represented the South African Coloured Cricket Association team during his playing days, and in 2014 was one of the inaugural recipients of Cricket South Africa's Heritage Blazers.

FAWCETT, GEORGE WALTER, died on December 10, aged 86. Walter Fawcett was a wicketkeeper, primarily associated with the strong Waringstown club in County Down. A schoolteacher, he played a dozen times for Ireland in the late 1950s, and became an umpire.

FEATHER, ROBERT LEIGH, died on July 28, aged 82. A successful Bradford wool merchant, "Robin" Feather captained Yorkshire's Second XI for four years from 1962, starting with youngsters such as Geoff Boycott and John Hampshire under his command. In one early game, against Durham, he sent someone in to run Boycott out, "because he was making no effort to score" in pursuit of a small target. "This was the first real indication I had of just how selfish a player he was," said Feather. Around this time he was mooted as a possible successor to the retiring Vic Wilson as county captain, but the job went to Brian Close. Feather had led Harrow to victory over Eton at Lord's in 1952, top-scoring with 38; he played his first game for Yorkshire Seconds in 1958, when they won the Minor Counties Championship. He served on committees at Headingley for 17 years from 1967, standing down after Boycott was reinstated as a player.

FENNER, Group Captain MAURICE DAVID, who died on April 5, aged 86, had the unenviable task of deputising for Godfrey Evans as Kent wicketkeeper in 14 matches between 1951 and 1954. After a successful trial at the end of the war he had been offered a chance to sign for Kent on a full-time basis, but opted to continue his education before joining the RAF. The other 19 of his 33 first-class games were for Combined Services, including one against the 1953 Australians at Kingston, where he allowed just seven byes in a first-innings total of 592 for four. Fred Trueman, David Allen and Fred Titmus were among the bowlers he kept to while they were on national service. He was secretary of Kent from 1977 until 1982. His father, George, also played for Kent.

FERNANDES, ANTHONY LONGINUS, died on December 19, aged 70. Tony Fernandes was a tall, nippy swing bowler who took exactly 100 first-class wickets, mainly for Baroda, with a best of six for 41 against Maharashtra in 1968-69. And he was a handy batsman, who hit ten first-class fifties. Fernandes also represented West Zone, appearing in three Duleep Trophy finals and against the 1969-70 Australian tourists, when he dismissed Ian Chappell. His brother Leslie, a wicketkeeper, also played for Baroda; they combined to have Sunil Gavaskar caught behind in a Ranji Trophy match in 1972-73.

FLANAGAN, Sir MAURICE, KBE, who died on May 7, aged 86, was the brains behind the rise of Emirates Airlines. He was appointed in the mid-1980s by the ruling Maktoum family in Dubai to launch the airline, which grew from two planes to a fleet of over 230. Flanagan was a Lancastrian with a passion for sport – he once had a trial for Blackburn Rovers – and believed its value as a marketing tool far exceeded advertising. Australia wore the Emirates logo on their shirts while winning the 1999 World Cup, and he later expanded its involvement in cricket to sponsorship of international umpires and acquiring the naming rights of Old Trafford and Chester-le-Street's Riverside. Flanagan also backed the UAE's own team, as opener Arshad Ali recalled: "Whenever I played a good knock, he would either be present on the ground, or the next day he would telephone and congratulate me."

FLETCHER, DAVID GEORGE WILLIAM, died on April 27, aged 90. While Denis Compton was scoring centuries for fun in the run-soaked summer of 1947, Surrey's Dave Fletcher was quietly acquiring a record of his own: 1,857 runs remains the most by anyone in their first full season of county cricket, beating Herbert Sutcliffe's 1,839 in 1919. In only his second Championship match, Fletcher hit 194 – which remained a career-best – as Surrey piled up 706 for four against Nottinghamshire at Trent Bridge. He was promptly capped, and the runs continued to flow: he carried his bat for 127 against Yorkshire at Bradford, and two weeks later made 77 for the Players in the annual Lord's match against the Gentlemen. In September he was called up late to play for the North, who were a man short for a festival game at Kingston against the South – and hit 168.

Great things were forecast for this tidy, correct opener with a full range of strokes, but they never quite happened. Second-season syndrome (824 runs at 25) extended over three further summers, not helped by indifferent health, before a renaissance in 1952 under the vibrant new captain Stuart Surridge brought 1,960 runs, with five centuries. That was the first of Surrey's seven successive Championships, and Fletcher contributed to them all, often opening with Eric Bedser. Surridge felt he was a little too correct, and encouraged him to play his shots. "We were told to get on with it," recalled Fletcher. "He said he wasn't interested in sitting in the pavilion for too long watching us bat." He remained an admirer of Surridge, who was in charge for the first five years of that famous run before handing over to Peter May: "I would say the difference was that Stuart won it for us for five years, and we won it for Peter for two."

Even after the glory days, Fletcher made 1,371 runs in 1960, when he was 36. But he retired the following season after breaking a finger, and became a respected coach, particularly associated with Surrey Young Cricketers. Latterly he lived in Cheam, near the playing fields of his old school, Sutton Grammar, and could occasionally be spotted doing the gardening in his old boys' blazer. He was Surrey's oldest surviving player when he died.

FOORD, CHARLES WILLIAM, died on July 9, aged 91. Bill Foord was a bespectacled schoolteacher – and an enthusiastic fast bowler who enjoyed some success for Yorkshire, taking 126 wickets in 51 matches over six years from 1947. He often shared the new ball with Fred Trueman, who was wary of this academic interloper – rated more highly by the Yorkshire hierarchy, Trueman suspected, because of his accuracy. His mood was not improved when, sent to Grimsby as twelfth man for the Second XI against Lincolnshire in 1951, he was told off for falling asleep in a deckchair, while Foord took seven for 35. In 1953, with Trueman largely absent on national service, Foord collected 62 wickets, including a career-best six for 63 to set up an innings victory over Hampshire at Bournemouth in August. A fortnight earlier he had taken five for 61 against Surrey at Headingley – the top five in the eventual champions' batting order. That was Foord's best season; but he retired at the end of it, and returned to full-time teaching, although he continued to play and coach at the Scarborough club, ending up with over 1,000 wickets for them in more than 30 years. "Many players said there was no finer sight than Bill Foord bounding in from the Tea Room End at North Marine Road," said David Byas, a later Scarborough favourite. Foord produced a good-natured book of verse, *Cricket Rhymeniscing*, in 2010.

FRASER, JOHN MALCOLM, AC, CH, died on March 20, aged 84. Malcolm Fraser was prime minister of Australia from 1975 until 1983 and, like many who have held his country's highest office, a cricket-lover. He was following the World Cup closely at the time of his death, having tweeted his congratulations to Sri Lanka for their valiant performance against Australia at the SCG on March 8. Fraser was a staunch supporter of racial equality and an outspoken opponent of apartheid. He visited Nelson Mandela in prison, and recalled that, among the first questions Mandela asked, was whether Don Bradman was still alive. When Mandela became president years later, Fraser took him a bat inscribed: "To Nelson Mandela, in recognition of a great unfinished innings, Donald Bradman."

FURLONGE, CARL DOMINIQUE, who died on December 18, aged 83, was the oldest of three brothers to represent Trinidad: the middle one, Hammond, won four Test caps in the mid-1950s. Carl's son, David, also played for Trinidad, and is now the coach at the Queen's Park club in Port-of-Spain. A left-hander, Carl made 99 for North Trinidad against the South in the annual Beaumont Cup match in 1959, when it had first-class status; his highest score for the full Trinidad side was just 32. But he is remembered for his exceptional fielding, especially close in on the leg side. His three quicksilver catches at leg slip against the 1954-55 Australian tourists are said to have helped the bowler, Lennox "Bunny" Butler, into the side for the next Test. Without Furlonge's help there, Butler took two for 151 and never played again.

GARDENER, BRIAN EDWARD FRANCIS, who died on January 19, aged 73, invested £2m of his own fortune in a magnificent new ground on the Isle of Wight. He did not live to see his dream of returning first-class cricket to the island for the first time since 1962, but the Newclose ground received many plaudits. Gardener, owner of one of the leading local hotels, had once lived near Sir Paul Getty's ground at Wormsley, and loved to tell the story of being mistaken for the groundsman by Brian Johnston during one of his strolls around the perimeter. Wormsley proved his inspiration, and Newclose shared many of its attributes, not least the rural setting. Its extensive pavilion cost £900,000, and boasts a large electronic scoreboard and benches modelled on those in the Lord's Pavilion. Newclose hosts home matches for Ventnor in the Southern Electric Premier League, and representative games.

GOVINDAN, I. VELAYUDHAN, who died on March 18, aged about 80, was a medium-paced all-rounder who played 15 Ranji Trophy matches for Kerala from 1957-58. After sporadic early success he was ignored for five seasons after 1960-61 but, recalled in November 1966, made an undefeated 102 from No. 9 against Andhra at Vijayawada. However, in the next two games he fell for ducks to two Test bowlers – Syed Abid Ali and Bhagwat Chandrasekhar – and was dropped again, this time for good.

GRAVENEY, JOHN KENNETH RICHARD, who died on October 25, aged 90, was a fast-medium swing bowler who mixed great skill with wholehearted commitment, until his career was curtailed by a back injury. Older brother of Tom, and father of David,

Ken was the founder of Gloucestershire's Graveney dynasty, and served the county as captain, chairman and president, sometimes in fractious times.

The brothers' talent was not spotted until the family moved to Bristol from their native Northumberland via Lancashire in the late 1930s. At Bristol Grammar, Ken was the star batsman, although the two-and-a-half-year age difference meant he and Tom played together only once for the school. Graveney saw active service with the Royal Marines – he took part in the Normandy landings – but, after being demobbed, struggled to adapt to civilian life, and was thinking of re-enlisting when he was offered a week's trial by Gloucestershire. He did enough to earn a contract, making his debut against Worcestershire at Gloucester in July 1947.

His potential was underlined early in 1949, when he took six for 65 against Surrey at The Oval. But even that was put in the shade at Chesterfield in early August, when he took all ten for 66 in Derbyshire's

And all that... The highlight of Ken Graveney's career was ten for 66 at Chesterfield in 1949.

second innings, on what was expected to be a last-day spinners' pitch. While Tom Goddard toiled fruitlessly, Graveney took wickets each time he was recalled to the attack – though when the last pair, Bill Copson and Les Jackson, proved hard to shift, Gloucestershire captain Basil Allen warned him he was in danger of being taken off. If it was a motivational trick, it worked: Copson was soon caught by George Emmett at extra cover. That summer Graveney took 59 wickets at 28, and passed 500 runs.

But he was seldom free from back trouble. He had suffered injuries during his wartime service, and reckoned he had made things worse by bowling flat out during his Gloucester trial. He never gave less than his all, but sometimes had to be helped from the field at the close. At the end of the 1951 season he bowed to the inevitable and retired; Tom wrote that it "nearly broke his heart". There was one more bravura performance: on the last afternoon at Taunton in May, with the match ambling towards a draw, he took five quick wickets, held three catches in the gully off Sam Cook and, promoted up the order, hit a rapid 25 as Gloucestershire sneaked home.

By the late 1950s he was able to play club cricket again, and in 1962 captained Gloucestershire Second XI. But it was still an astonishing development when, in 1963, after 11 years out of the first-class game and at the age of 38, he was asked to take over from Tom Pugh as Gloucestershire's captain. It was the summer in which the distinction between amateur and professionals was abolished, but the club committee remained wedded to the idea of amateur captains, not least because they were cheap. Graveney had forged a successful career in the catering business, and his employers were willing to give him the summer off – but he contributed little as a player, and failed to inspire as a leader. After Gloucestershire finished bottom of the Championship in 1964, he returned to his business career. His final haul was 172 wickets at 28.

But it was not the end of his involvement with Gloucestershire cricket, and he became vice-chairman, then chairman. In 1982, after David had assumed the captaincy, he wondered whether it was ethical to continue but, after deciding to stand again, he was voted out at the AGM. He later served as president, and was Gloucestershire golf captain in 1968. Perhaps his greatest service to the county, however, had come in August 1947 when, in the midst of a hectic season, they were struggling to field 11 players for a Sunday benefit match. He introduced a potential new recruit. "This is my brother," he said. "I can't get the ball past his bat."

GRAVENEY, THOMAS WILLIAM, OBE, died on November 3, aged 88, nine days after his brother Ken. When it came to earning marks for artistic impression, or inspiring lines of poetic enchantment, few England batsmen have ranked higher than Tom Graveney. Not everyone was keen to rhapsodise: many of cricket's more pragmatic minds – Len Hutton and Peter May among them – remained immune to his charms, and doubted his temperament for Test cricket. Like David Gower, Graveney became the subject of anguished national debate.

Perhaps only in England could a player of such natural talent have been treated with suspicion: Richie Benaud, Ian Johnson and Frank Worrell insisted he would have been an automatic selection in their sides. It was hard to argue with his weight of runs: in a career lasting more than 20 years, he scored nearly 48,000 at almost 45, including 122 centuries. Of English players since the war, only Geoff Boycott has been more prolific. And, in a fragmented Test career that began in 1951 and ended in 1969, he scored almost 5,000 at 44, with 11 hundreds. These were hardly the figures of a dilettante.

What was not up for debate was his easy grace. He had a long reach and a high backlift, and his off-side play was a study in elegance. Through leg he was less orthodox, hooking off the front foot, but he was never flustered. If cricket were destroyed and only Graveney survived, wrote Neville Cardus, it could be reconstructed "from his way of batting, from the man himself". He relied on his top hand, allowing the bat to swing through the stroke like a pendulum. But, while he might have conveyed the impression that he was naturally gifted, he trained assiduously, always arriving first at the ground. "He would not miss his morning practice for anything," said Ron Headley, a future team-mate at Worcestershire. "He liked to have a bat in his hand every day." Graveney approached nets like an innings, batting defensively at first, then easing into a more attacking mode. His talent extended to his fielding, and he was a magnificent golfer.

His public persona was of an affable West Countryman who took top-flight sport in his stride. The reality was different. Born in Northumberland, he retained a propensity for plain speaking. "He was his own man and would tell you exactly what he thought," said his Gloucestershire team-mate Frank McHugh. His single-mindedness shone through in two major controversies. In 1960, when he lost the Gloucestershire captaincy, he left immediately and spent a year playing Second XI and club cricket while qualifying for Worcestershire. And, nine years later, his international career was cut short when he appeared in a benefit match during a Test, and was suspended.

Graveney was only six when his father died, but a love of sport had already been instilled by visits to see Durham face touring teams at Ashbrooke in Sunderland. His mother remarried and in 1938 the family moved to Bristol, where his stepfather was employed as an accountant in the docks. At Bristol Grammar, Graveney showed promise at rugby, and at cricket shone more as a bowler. He left school at 17 and joined the Army early in 1945. The war was over before he could see active service, but he was posted to Egypt, where he found an agreeable role supervising sport for the troops, and his batting developed on the matting wickets used for service matches.

Off again: Tom Graveney on his way to 96 against West Indies at Lord's in June 1966.

Graveney had every intention of remaining in uniform but, while on leave in the summer of 1947, he went to watch his brother Ken – now at Gloucestershire – in a benefit match for Charlie Barnett. They were short, and Tom ended up playing: although he made only 30-odd, his class and poise were obvious. As he unbuckled his pads, Barnett approached him with the offer of an alternative to life in khaki – a professional contract with Gloucestershire. It meant a pay cut, but Graveney accepted, and arrived for pre-season nets at Bristol in 1948. His potential was clear, but the runs did not immediately flow: he made nought on debut against Oxford University, and was dropped after a pair against Derbyshire. Salvation came when George Emmett was called up by England. Graveney got another chance and, while scoring 47 against Hampshire, something clicked. He finished the season with almost 1,000 runs, and his first century.

That winter he spent hours in Gloucestershire's indoor nets learning to play more comfortably off the back foot. It did the trick: in 1949 he scored nearly 1,800 runs. "His elegant strokeplay stamped him as one of the best young batsmen in the country," said *Wisden*. A first England call-up came against South Africa at Old Trafford in 1951. He was afflicted by nerves and his technique was tested on a damp pitch; but though he made only 15, he created a good impression. "Full of cultured promise," said John Arlott on the radio. Graveney scored more than 2,000 runs at 48 that summer to earn a place in an understrength England team to tour the subcontinent. In the Second Test at Bombay he compiled 175 in eight hours, one of six centuries on a productive trip.

He played in all four Tests against India at home in 1952, but with a best of only 73. In county cricket, however, he was in imperious form. "Undoubtedly no brighter star has appeared in the Gloucestershire cricket firmament since the early days of Hammond himself," said *Wisden*, who made him a Cricketer of the Year.

By his own admission, he was fortunate to keep his place throughout the 1953 Ashes, his one significant contribution a first-innings 78 at Lord's. He and Hutton were in command against a tiring attack on the second evening when, an hour from the close, the captain ordered: "Right, that's it for tonight." Graveney retreated into his shell, and was bowled by Ray Lindwall next morning without addition. In the Caribbean that winter, Graveney hit two fours in an over on a day of funereal scoring. "We don't want any of that," said Hutton. "We've got to grind it out." Graveney was convinced Hutton did not entirely trust any player with rosy cheeks.

His Test record gave his critics ammunition: too often he did not convert promising starts, and in Australia in 1954-55 he was dropped after the Second Test at Sydney. He was a spectator as Hutton's team won the Ashes, and was unsure if he would play in the final match, again at Sydney, after being named in the 13. It rained for three days, and the batting order had still not been confirmed when Australia put England in: Hutton returned to the dressing-room and told Graveney he was opening. Don Bradman had remarked to Hutton that Graveney had the technique for the job, and he proved the shrewdness of that observation with his only century against Australia, passing three figures in scintillating style with four fours in an over off Keith Miller.

He bought his first car – a Ford Anglia – with his tour bonus, but endured a barren summer against the South Africans in 1955 (he kept wicket at Old Trafford when Godfrey Evans was injured) and was dropped after failing twice against Australia the following year. Recalled for the Fourth Test at Old Trafford, he withdrew with an injured hand, to the undisguised chagrin of chairman of selectors Gubby Allen, who thought Graveney was shying away from another failure before the squad was chosen for South Africa; according to one story, when May offered a sympathetic handshake, Graveney did not wince. In county cricket that summer he was unstoppable, leading the run-charts with 2,397 runs at nearly 50. But, when the tour party was named, he was not included. Graveney felt his mistake had been to beat Allen on the golf course.

Against that background the 1957 home series against West Indies might have represented his last chance. He made a duck at Lord's, but in the Third Test at Trent Bridge he survived an early scare, glancing perilously close to Garry Sobers at leg slip, to make a glorious 258. He did not rate it his best Test innings, but it was probably the most important. He followed it with 164 at The Oval.

At Gloucestershire, he became captain in 1959, and led them to second place. They slipped back to eighth in 1960, and Graveney was asked to resign in favour of Tom Pugh, an Old Etonian who fulfilled the committee's desire for an amateur captain. Graveney felt results had been reasonable, and that he was hardly responsible for the county's worsening financial position. He stepped down just before Christmas, but matters turned ugly when Gloucestershire went back on a verbal agreement to allow him to join another county, and MCC rules prevented him from playing Championship cricket for a year.

There was much media interest when he arrived for pre-season nets at Worcestershire alongside fellow recruits Bob Carter, from Durham, and Yorkshire's Duncan Fearnley. "We both had to qualify and it was good news for me because I played with him a lot," said Fearnley. "He treated those Second XI and Birmingham League games as seriously as a Test match." Graveney was allowed to play against the Australians and in the university matches, but it was not until 1962 that he would embark on a happy and fruitful second half of his career. His exile had also sharpened his appetite for Test cricket, and he averaged 100 against Pakistan.

But he struggled again on his third Ashes tour, in 1962-63, and there was a widespread assumption that, at 35, his Test career was over. Compensation came in the stately surroundings of New Road, where his game found fresh resolve; seamer Len Coldwell said Graveney had played for Gloucestershire but worked for Worcestershire. In 1964 and 1965 the club were county champions. When a supporter thanked Coldwell and new-ball partner Jack Flavell, Coldwell pointed at Graveney: "No, he won the Championship for us." He was ever-helpful to fellow batsmen, and an inspirational figure to young bowlers. "Every ball I bowled, I would be looking to him for approval," said Carter. He never departed from the rituals of the morning net, nor from putting his chewing-gum on his bat handle if he was not out overnight. "He did not watch the game until he was the next man in," said Fearnley. "Then he would watch every ball intently."

Despite his habitual modesty, Graveney felt he was the best batsman in the country during his years out of the Test arena. Eventually the clamour for a return could not be

Winding down: Tom Graveney in 1970, his last year in county cricket; Alan Knott keeps wicket.

ignored. In 1966, surfing waves of goodwill, he made 96 on his comeback, against West Indies at Lord's, followed by centuries at Trent Bridge and The Oval, where his brilliant counter-attacking partnership of 217 with John Murray turned the match. He scored heavily again the next summer, against India and Pakistan, and rated his 151 against Bedi, Prasanna and Chandrasekhar on a turning Lord's pitch as his finest Test innings. In the 1968 Ashes, he stood in as emergency captain in Colin Cowdrey's absence during the drawn Fourth Test at Headingley. His final Test century came against Pakistan in Karachi in 1968-69, more than 17 years after his first.

Graveney had been vindicated in his second coming as a Test batsman, but he knew it could not last. His benefit year was in 1969, and a businessman offered him £1,000 to play in a Sunday charity match at Luton – on the rest day of the First Test against West Indies at Old Trafford. What happened next was for ever disputed. Graveney insisted he called Alec Bedser, the chairman of selectors, explaining the situation; when he was refused permission to play in the benefit game, he asked to be left out of the Test squad. When his name was included, he assumed Bedser had agreed to his absence. It was only as he soaked in the bath on 56 not out at the end of the first day in Manchester that he was told the ban remained. Determined to collect his fee, Graveney took a desultory part in the match at Luton, but retribution was swift: next day, while he was in the field, the Old Trafford PA announced he had been summoned to a disciplinary hearing at Lord's later that week. It was his 42nd birthday; he knew his international career was over. He was officially banned from the next three Tests, and never chosen again.

He stayed on at Worcester, where he had assumed the captaincy, until the end of the 1970 season, and was then briefly player-coach of Queensland. He was for many years the landlord of a pub near Cheltenham racecourse, and spent more than a decade as a BBC commentator, rekindling his love of the game. His job as an ICC match referee ended when he was appointed in 1992 to a West Indies–Pakistan series, and the Pakistan Cricket Board excavated some injudicious remarks he had made in the wake of the Shakoor Rana affair: "They've been cheating us for 37 years." His greatest honour came in 2004, when he was the first former professional cricketer to be named president of MCC.

Perhaps the most famous of the many tributes to the fragile grace of Graveney's batting, of which the cover-drive remained his signature shot, was by Alan Ross, who discerned "a player of yacht-like character, beautiful in calm seas, yet at the mercy of every change of weather". Following the deaths of Bob Appleyard and Frank Tyson earlier in the year, he had been the last survivor of the stellar squad that brought home the Ashes in 1954-55. It was the end of a glorious era in English cricket.

GRIFFITHS, SHIRLEY SPENCER, who died on February 3, aged 84, was a fast bowler from Barbados who moved to Birmingham and had three seasons on the Warwickshire staff. Amateur batsmen found his pace hot, but the pros were more capable: of his 74 first-class wickets, only 41 came in the Championship. Still, in 1958 he claimed seven for 62 against Kent, then five for 37 – four bowled and one lbw – as Middlesex were skittled for 77, also at Edgbaston. But five more Championship matches that season produced only seven more wickets and, with Warwickshire having several other seamers, he was released. He continued to terrorise club players on spicier pitches: one batsman, who had trials with Warwickshire, remembered being "conscious of backing away when I saw him start his run-up".

GRIFFITHS, LORD (William Hugh), PC, MC, who died on May 30, aged 91, was decorated for bravery in the Second World War, became one of the most distinguished figures in the British judiciary and, uniquely, president of both MCC and the Royal & Ancient Golf Club. But alongside those considerable achievements he never forgot his excellent record in first-class cricket, nor his experience at the wicket.

Griffiths burst on to the cricket scene in 1946, taking six for 129 on debut for Cambridge University against Lancashire. His five for 85 in the Varsity Match could not prevent an Oxford victory; he did bowl Martin Donnelly, but only after he had made 142. Griffiths took 28 wickets at 22 in eight matches that summer, his victims including Vijay Merchant, Bill Edrich, Bob Wyatt and Les Ames. He was seriously quick, once forcing Denis Compton to retire hurt after hitting him in the face. "Hugh really was a tearaway," recalled his Cambridge team-mate Hubert Doggart. "He ran up and let it go." In all, he made 38 first-class appearances, mainly for Cambridge, for whom he won a Blue in each of his three years at St John's College. He also played six times for Glamorgan, four of them in 1948, when he contributed eight wickets to the county's first Championship title.

Patrick Eagar

Lord's lord: Hugh Griffiths.

That summer he also appeared against Don Bradman's Invincibles at Fenner's. Unwisely, given he was no batsman, he taunted the Australians' stand-in captain Lindsay Hassett about the quality of his pace attack. Hassett instructed Keith Miller and Ray Lindwall to "condition the lad a bit". Griffiths' reward was a dented box, courtesy of Miller, who dismissed him twice. But he considered it a privilege to have faced two greats in their pomp. When Tony Lewis suggested he was the eternal No. 11, Griffiths replied: "I never got partners skilful enough to stay with me."

With his luxuriant eyebrows, Griffiths was an unmistakable figure in both the legal and sporting worlds. He became a High Court judge in 1971 and a Law Lord in 1985. He was involved in a number of high-profile cases, including the obscenity trial against the editors of *Oz* magazine, and the unmasking of the Foreign Office mole Sarah Tisdall. He became MCC president in 1990, and was well placed to advise on a legal dispute over the delayed completion of the Compton and Edrich Stands; he also had to deal with the publicity when Tim Rice proposed Rachael Heyhoe Flint for membership. Griffiths said members had to decide the issue and, while he privately supported women's membership, it was no surprise when a majority voted against. In 1993 he chaired an MCC working party that proposed the amalgamation of the TCCB with the National Cricket Association. In the course of the review, Griffiths – conscious that the Laws of cricket alone could not govern the behaviour of players – composed a Preamble to the Laws. It was based on the understanding that, in his words, "cricket is a game that owes much of its unique appeal to the fact that it should be played not only within its Laws, but also within the spirit of the game".

HARRIS, NORMAN HILLIER, who collapsed and died in a London street on November 20, aged 75, was perhaps the most original cricket journalist of his generation. He was also well known as an athletics writer and founding father of the fun run sponsored by his then newspaper, *The Sunday Times*, which was a major event in the early days of the keep-fit craze. He may even deserve the credit for rescuing the word "jogging" from disuse before would-be joggers felt obliged either to run properly or stay on the sofa. But he was also fond of cricket, and as a teenager in his native New Zealand was manning the Hamilton scoreboard in 1958-59 when MCC came to town and Colin Cowdrey was out for a duck. He joined *The Sunday Times* in 1969, and one of his earliest exclusives was an explanation for a plague of misshapen balls in that summer's county matches: Harris tracked the fault down to a production error by an assistant in the ball factory. It was a classic Harris story, of the kind he would keep giving the paper for the next 20 years. "He had a curiosity for the bits of cricket nobody else was interested in," said its former deputy sports editor, Nick Mason. "Long before bowlers' speeds were regularly clocked, he was trying to look at old film to work it out. He once got a bee in his bonnet about what percentage of left-handed batsmen were actually left-handed. I think he rang up every left-hander then playing to ask. That was the way his mind worked." Harris also wrote with great zest about village cricket. Later he went to live in Northumberland, and covered Durham's home matches for *The Times*, but he still brought his quirky interest in bats, balls and other paraphernalia to the Cricket Equipment column in *Wisden*, which he wrote from its inception in 1993 until 2011.

HASAN JAMIL ALVI, who died on October 7, aged 63, was a left-handed all-rounder who played six one-day internationals for Pakistan, all at home. He took three for 18 at Sahiwal to set up victory over India in October 1978, which helped win a place in the squad for the 1979 World Cup – but he did not appear in any of the matches in England. He was a consistent performer over a 15-year career in domestic cricket, scoring four first-class hundreds – the highest 172 for PIA against Dawood Industries in 1975-76 – and also taking 204 wickets, with a best of five for 38 for Pakistan Universities against Railways in 1973-74.

HAYWARD, SIR JACK ARNOLD, OBE, who died on January 13, aged 91, was a businessman who made his fortune from the development of Freeport in the Bahamas, and used much of his wealth in acts of idiosyncratic philanthropy. He became known as "Union Jack"; the *Daily Telegraph* called him "a British patriot to the point of eccentricity". Hayward was always keen on sport, and poured millions into an unavailing attempt to restore Wolverhampton Wanderers to their former greatness. His patronage of cricket was less well known, but he was a key benefactor of the women's game, sponsoring two England teams on tours of the Caribbean in the early 1970s. His interest went beyond flourishing his chequebook, however. Rachael Heyhoe Flint, the England captain, recalled: "He threw himself into whatever project he got involved in, and often came to watch us play." Hayward financed the first women's World Cup in 1973 – two years ahead of the men – and was rewarded with an England victory over Australia in the decisive game at Edgbaston. After an approach by E. W. Swanton, he also provided capital for the building of the first indoor school at Lord's in 1978; the net space was named Hayward Hall.

HEATHCOTE, PHILIP, who died in the terrorist attack on Sousse, Tunisia, on June 26, aged 52, was a familiar member of the cricket community in and around Felixstowe. He moved to Suffolk from his native Manchester in the early 1990s, and joined the Felixstowe Corinthians as a fast-medium bowler. "Philip was a good and loyal cricketer," said their president Bob Wilson. "He was a bit fiery. He wanted to win games all the time." On retiring from playing, Heathcote became a coach of the club's junior players, and an umpire. He and his wife Allison (the club secretary) had flown to Tunisia to celebrate their 30th wedding anniversary. She was hit by five bullets, but survived.

HILTON, COLIN, who died on October 30, aged 78, was for a few short summers in the late 1950s and early '60s one of the most feared fast bowlers on the county circuit. He joined Lancashire in 1957 via Atherton, his home club, and Ribblesdale Wanderers, and was identified as the long-term successor to Brian Statham. But, as the new decade wore on and Statham showed few signs of decline, Hilton became a victim of the competition for places created by the presence of Ken Higgs and Peter Lever.

He was no more than average height, but broad across the shoulders, and muscular. While his run-up was not especially long, his formidable strength and athleticism generated real pace. A book about his career was called *The White Flash: the story of the fastest English bowler of his time*, yet he had more than just speed. On a helpful pitch he found seam movement and, blessed with long fingers, mastered the subtleties of cutting the ball. He was, however, prone to nerves. The Lancashire captain Bob Barber recalled a match at Trent Bridge against Nottinghamshire, who included Reg Simpson, then in his forties. "He bowled a couple of beamers at Reg, who just moved out of the way as they went whistling past. I said: 'What's going on?' Colin replied: 'Sweaty fingers.' He showed me his hands and they were sweaty. His nervousness was genuine."

therogermanncollection.com

More than just fast: Colin Hilton.

In 1961, Hilton took 75 wickets at 24, and the following season 94 at 26. But his efforts were overshadowed by the internal strife at Lancashire, who were under the captaincy of Joe Blackledge, a 34-year-old amateur with no first-class experience. They finished second from bottom. Against Nottinghamshire at Liverpool that dismal summer, Hilton took 11 for 127 – and still finished on the losing side. A knee injury meant he hardly featured in 1963, and was released. He had taken 263 wickets at 36 in 91 appearances for Lancashire, but the feeling lingered of potential unfulfilled. "He really was quick, and the batters knew it," said Barber. "If he had concentrated and had discipline he would have gone further."

Hilton moved to Essex in 1964, but endured a traumatic time, *Wisden* calling him "rather more of a liability than an asset". Unable to cope with the new front-foot no-ball law, he was called 230 times. Hilton moved back to the sanctuary of the leagues, where he prospered again. He was the professional at Oldham, before joining Morecambe in 1968, when he claimed 113 wickets, still the Northern League record. The following season he took all ten wickets against Lancaster on the Saturday, and nine against Kendal on the Sunday.

For a time he lived in a caravan on an isolated part of the Welsh coast near Cardigan, but moved back to Atherton, where he ran the Conservative club with his partner, and coached and umpired at his first club. Hilton's earthy humour made him a popular and rumbustious presence at Lancashire former players' lunches.

HODGSON, PHILIP, who died on March 30, aged 79, was a 6ft 8in opening bowler who played 13 matches for Yorkshire between 1954 and 1956. In his first season, Hodgson (five for 41) combined with Fred Trueman (five for 40) to knock Sussex over for 117 at Hove. A schoolteacher, Hodgson played most of his club cricket for Sheffield United, although he also represented Len Hutton's old team Pudsey St Lawrence. Later, while serving in the RAF, he had four first-class matches for Combined Services.

HOWE, LORD (Richard Edward Geoffrey), CH, QC, PC, died on October 9, aged 88. No politician can ever have used the language of cricket to such seismic effect as the former Conservative Foreign Secretary Geoffrey Howe, in the House of Commons on November 13, 1990. Enraged by Prime Minister Margaret Thatcher's continued hostility to the European Union, he described her impact on the work of businessmen, financiers and, especially, the Chancellor, John Major, and the Governor of the Bank of England, Robin Leigh-Pemberton. "Mr Speaker, I believe that both the Chancellor and the Governor are cricketing enthusiasts, so I hope there is no monopoly on cricketing metaphors," said Howe, before adding the words that entered political folklore and put in motion a chain of events that led to Thatcher's downfall. "It is rather like sending your opening batsmen to the crease, only for them to find, the moment the first balls are bowled, that their bats have been broken before the game by the team captain." Howe always denied that his wife, Elspeth, who had captained her school team at Wycombe Abbey, had provided the analogy.

HURN, BRIAN MORGAN, OAM, died on October 18, aged 76. "Bunger" Hurn spent a decade as a useful all-rounder for South Australia without ever securing a permanent position. He was an aggressive left-hander, but adaptable enough to take three hours over his highest score of 77, against Queensland in 1964-65. He also claimed five for 62 against the 1958-59 MCC tourists, including Colin Cowdrey, Ted Dexter and Tom Graveney in quick succession. Hurn was a stalwart of Kensington, Don Bradman's former club, for 18 seasons. He also had a long and successful career in country Australian Rules football; his grandson, Shannon, captained the West Coast Eagles in the 2015 AFL Grand Final. Part of a pioneer family from the Angaston district in South Australia's Barossa Valley, Hurn farmed sheep and cattle, and grew grapes for wine.

HUTCHISON, PAUL JAMES, died of cancer on February 26, aged 47. A peripatetic professional cricketer who bowled at a fair pace from a small frame, Hutchison plied his trade in Queensland before moving to Darwin, then went south to Adelaide, where he took five for 87 on first-class debut, for South Australia against Tasmania in 1991-92. He soon moved to Tasmania, playing three times for them, before returning to Brisbane club cricket, where he was a mentor to the young Shane Watson. Hutchison also had spells with Burnley, Rawtenstall and Walsden in the Lancashire leagues in the 1990s.

IQBAL HUSSAIN SHEIKH died on January 9, aged 80. Iqbal Sheikh was a Karachi doctor who fitted in 22 first-class matches in Pakistan around his medical duties. A batsman and occasional leg-spinner, he scored 91 for Hyderabad against Khairpur in the Ayub Trophy in 1965-66.

JADEJA, LALUBHA RAMSINHJI, who died on July 19, aged 93, played 31 matches in India, mainly for Saurashtra, over a long career that stretched until 1962-63. A medium-pacer, he took seven for 61 (and 11 for 137 in the match) against Maharashtra at Rajkot in

1958-59. Three seasons later, by now 39, he claimed successive five-fors against Maharashtra and Baroda. His early matches were for Nawanagar, though he was not a member of their princely Jadeja family, which included Ranjitsinhji and Duleepsinhji.

JASPAL SINGH BANSAL, who died of cancer on November 12, aged 47, was a brisk opening bowler who started with Delhi in the Ranji Trophy, but had more success with Punjab, taking six for 87 against Jammu & Kashmir in November 1989. He was also a handy batsman, spanking 78 against Haryana in the next match. When West Indies toured in 1987-88, Jaspal played for India Under-25 at Chandigarh, and encountered an in-form Viv Richards: "My captain Sanjay Manjrekar asked me not to pitch the ball on the leg side after I had been hit for a couple of boundaries through midwicket – but I was actually bowling outside off stump!" Richards escaped him (he retired after making 138), but Jaspal dismissed Richie Richardson and Roger Harper, and later scored 70. In 2000 he moved to Australia, where he turned out for Dubbo. His older brother, Gursharan Singh, played one Test for India in 1989-90.

JONES, BENEDICT MARK RHYDDERCH, died on April 20, aged 67. Mark Jones was head of the BBC Sound Archives for 15 years, and a studious and dedicated historian of the Corporation's recorded legacy. He was also an enthusiastic member of the Bushmen, the cricket team based at the World Service, after being recruited because he always seemed glued to the Test match. He played in flared whites, and captained the side to a record eight wins in 1982. Jones's match reports were much enjoyed and, at the end of that summer, he caught the post-Falklands mood: "Arguments rage as to how to celebrate the year of victory. One faction favours a march past Bush House in full cricketing kit; the Bushmen doves talk feebly of an interdenominational thanksgiving service for the sportsmanship of the defeated teams."

JONES, PETER LANGLEY, died on July 10, aged 85. As the indefatigable editor of *Record Mirror*, Peter Jones was at the epicentre of London's 1960s pop music boom. He wrote one of the first books on the Beatles, but perhaps his most significant contribution was to point the ambitious publicist Andrew Loog Oldham in the direction of a young rhythm and blues band he had seen performing in Richmond. Oldham quickly became manager of the group, then still called The Rollin' Stones. At school Jones was a talented cricketer and footballer, and had covered both sports for the *Sunday Dispatch*; he had a lifelong passion for Essex and Chelsea. Jones died at home while watching the First Test of last summer's Ashes. His cricket library has been donated to Essex.

KANITKAR, HEMANT SHAMSUNDER, who died on June 9, aged 72, was a compact batsman, noted for the late cut and an inside-out lofted drive. "He could hit a six over extra cover on demand," remembered Milind Gunjal, a former team-mate. He was also a serviceable wicketkeeper. Kanitkar piled up more than 3,500 Ranji Trophy runs for Maharashtra, beginning with 151 not out on debut, against Saurashtra at Poona in 1963-64. His dozen centuries for Maharashtra included 250 against Rajasthan in 1970-71; the following season he made 168 for the Rest against an Indian XI. A belated call to national colours came in 1974-75, when he was nearly 32, for the First Test against West Indies at Bangalore. He started by top-scoring with 65, but three failures followed, and he was jettisoned for good. Kanitkar later turned to coaching, and was a state selector. "He had an astute cricketing brain," said his state colleague Yajurvindra Singh. "He was a fabulous captain to play under, and never ruffled. He had an expressionless demeanour that stood him well, especially when we played cards." His son, Hrishikesh, also played two Tests for India, in Australia in 1999-2000.

KARIA, PANKIL DHIRAJILAL, died on March 29, aged 48, of a presumed heart attack while watching the World Cup final on television. A bowler who won two Under-19 one-day caps for India against Australia in 1984-85, Karia also played twice for Saurashtra.

KENNEDY, GEORGE MICHAEL SINCLAIR, CBE, died on December 31, 2014, aged 88. Michael Kennedy was a distinguished journalist on the *Daily Telegraph*, and the author of several notable books on music, including biographies of Vaughan Williams and Elgar. His love of cricket was sealed when he saw Walter Hammond score 160 at Horsham in 1937. At Old Trafford in 1948, he was no less enthralled by Denis Compton's undefeated century against Australia after a blow on the head from Ray Lindwall; Compton and Ian Botham remained his favourite players. During post-war service in the Royal Navy, Kennedy was posted to Australia, where he met Neville Cardus: they began a long friendship based on their shared passions for cricket and music. A collection of their correspondence is held in the Old Trafford library. Kennedy first joined the *Telegraph* as a copy boy in their Manchester office in 1940, and rose to become northern editor for 26 years. During Old Trafford Tests, he would take the paper's cricket correspondent, E. W. Swanton, out to dinner in Manchester – recoiling at Swanton's occasional rudeness to restaurant staff.

KESHRI, ANKIT RAJ, died on April 20, three days after colliding with a team-mate during a league game for East Bengal in Kolkata. He was 20. Keshri, who was part of Bengal's Under-23 squad, dashed in for a catch from deep cover – but the bowler ran for it too, and hit Keshri in the head with his knee. He was treated immediately, and reached hospital in 15 minutes, but failed to recover.

KISSELL, RONALD KEITH, died on June 26, aged 86. Ron Kissell was a stocky left-hander who made an enterprising 80 not out for New South Wales against the 1946-47 MCC tourists, when he was just 18. He could not score consistently enough to secure a permanent place in a strong NSW side, but made over 9,000 runs in more than two decades of Sydney grade cricket, chiefly for Glebe.

KLINE, LINDSAY FRANCIS, who died on October 2, aged 81, faced the last delivery of one of the most famous of all matches – the tied Test between Australia and West Indies at Brisbane in December 1960. With the scores level, last man Kline nudged the ball, from Wes Hall, towards square leg, and set off for the winning run – but his partner, Ian Meckiff, was run out when Joe Solomon hit the stumps from side-on.

In the famous photograph of that frenzied finale (see *Wisden 2015*, page 238), Kline is running to the safety of the bowler's end, looking over his shoulder to see whether Meckiff has made it. In the heat of the moment, the batsmen were confused: "There was me running for a win," said Kline, "and him running for a tie." Meckiff thought Australia had lost, and was inconsolable until Kline assured him they hadn't.

Although he missed the next two matches, Kline's part in an exciting seesaw series wasn't quite over. He was recalled for the Fourth Test at Adelaide, where West Indies seemed set to take a 2–1 lead when Australia's ninth wicket fell with nearly two hours remaining. A left-arm wrist-spinner with few pretensions to batting, Kline had prepared by having a net against Australia's part-time bowlers, who confounded him repeatedly. A female spectator lamented that it was hardly worth sending him out to the middle, and Kline was forced to agree. But somehow he survived everything the West Indians could muster for 109 minutes, and an unlikely draw was secured when Ken "Slasher" Mackay chested away Hall's final thunderbolt.

Kline's unbeaten 15 was his highest score, but that was the last of his 13 Tests, after 34 wickets at 22, around five runs cheaper than his overall first-class average. He did tour England later in 1961, but there were few opportunities for another slow bowler in a side captained by leg-spinner Richie Benaud. Kline nonetheless took 54 wickets in the county games, including five for 16 against Nottinghamshire. He retired from first-class cricket after one more season at home.

Born in 1934 in Camberwell, east Melbourne, Kline was playing for the prestigious Melbourne Cricket Club by 1952-53. A tall man, with a kangaroo-like hop just before delivery, he was unusually accurate for a bowler of his type. He did not turn his stock ball prodigiously, but had a well-disguised variant – the left-arm wrist-spinner's googly.

Hop to it: Lindsay Kline practises at Lord's at the start of the Australians' 1961 tour.

He made his Sheffield Shield debut for Victoria in 1955-56, and the following season took six for 57 in the final innings of the then-traditional Christmas clash with New South Wales. With Meckiff claiming the other four, it too ended in a tie.

Early in 1957, Australia's recently retired Test captain Ian Johnson wrote that Kline's wrong'un was "fast becoming the most dangerous and successful ball in Australian cricket", and he was selected to tour South Africa. After going wicketless on debut, he wrapped up the Second Test at Cape Town with a hat-trick – the last to date in any Test in South Africa (since then, there have been 28 elsewhere). Kline had Eddie Fuller caught at short leg, trapped Hugh Tayfield lbw – "It must have been close," said Kline, "because they were South African umpires!" – then had last man Neil Adcock well caught by Bob Simpson at slip.

Kline took 15 wickets in the series, but was overshadowed by Benaud, who reaped 106 wickets in all on the tour, and never looked back. Next season he took over as Australia's captain, which meant Kline – an inferior batsman and fielder – was likely to play only on spin-friendly pitches. On one, at Lahore in November 1959, he claimed a career-best seven for 75 as Australia completed their first series victory in Pakistan.

In the previous match, on a matting wicket in Dacca (now Dhaka), Kline had an important role, even though he wasn't actually playing. He was deputed to travel to the ground early each morning, to ensure the groundstaff stretched out the coir mat as taut as possible before nailing it down. "Those of us on the tour," wrote Benaud, "will never forget stepping off the bus and hearing the ringing cries of 'Pull, you bastards, pull!' floating across the ground. Not politically correct, but effective!"

KRISHNA, T. VAMSHI, died after being hit by a cork ball on a school playground in Vanasthalipuram, near Hyderabad in India, on April 24. Although aged only six, he was fielding close in, and was struck on the chest by a powerful shot from a 12-year-old.

LA FRANTZ, ERROLD CAMPBELL, MBE, who died on February 20, aged 95, played only once for Queensland – in the final match before the Second World War closed down first-class cricket in Australia – but became such a significant presence in the game that he was awarded an MBE in 1977 for services to cricket. A Queensland selector for a decade from 1954-55, he was also an authoritative commentator on both national radio and Brisbane television. In 1973 La Frantz helped fix Jeff Thomson's well-paid move north to Brisbane from Sydney by securing him a radio job. He was a member of Toombul CC in Brisbane for 83 years.

LARKINS, WARWICK NORWOOD, who died on May 16, aged 68, was a stalwart of the Albion club in Dunedin, who have produced more than two dozen New Zealand cricketers since their foundation in 1862. An avid collector of cricket books, he was New Zealand's scorer on their tour of England in 1978, and played for them against the Netherlands at the end of the trip, although his leg-breaks were kept under wraps.

LEE, ALAN PETER, who died suddenly on December 19, aged 61, was cricket correspondent of *The Times* from 1988 to 1999. Among his colleagues, he was perhaps the most respected sports journalist of his generation. Sports desks loved the fact that, when they asked for however many words at whenever o'clock, Lee would deliver precisely. His fellow writers were fearful that, whatever was going on behind the scenes, Lee probably had more information than they did.

He was a born journalist, writing football reports as a nine-year-old, joining the *Watford Observer* at 16 and moving on to the boot camp of Hayter's sports agency, where tyros had to work fast and furiously. Still only 24, he went to Australia to report the Kerry Packer-led breakaway and produced a remarkably mature book, *A Pitch in Both Camps*. He later freelanced before becoming cricket correspondent of the *Mail on Sunday*, then edged out Christopher Martin-Jenkins to succeed John Woodcock at *The Times*. All the while, he would produce biographies, ghosted autobiographies and other books at a matchless pace (Greig, Gower, Gooch, Dexter, Willis, etc.), without ever neglecting the day job. Surrounded by press-box chaos, he was always orderly and focused. "Eff-all's happened and they still want 800 words," wailed Martin Johnson of *The Independent* one rained-off day. "I've written three stories already," replied Lee.

Though he would be tap-tapping away during the lunch interval, he was unperturbed if interrupted with a plaintive "Leapy, what *is* going on?" and was generous with his knowledge. He was already a racing enthusiast (and owner) when a new editor who did want CMJ invited him to become racing correspondent instead. This was a big ask, the horsey press being wary of outsiders. His professionalism won them over, and blew them away – two years later he was named Sports Journalist of the Year.

Lee's great strength was his mobility, social and actual. He cultivated administrators and gained their trust, sometimes at the cost of being over-respectful. But he put himself about, driving miles to outgrounds or gaff tracks and talking to everyone; in racing, he far preferred the roughness of the jump season to the glitz of the flat. He was a good companion, and for many years took delight in his annual cricket match in Sussex, in which his XI would play a racing team led by the trainer Josh Gifford. No colleague could recall him having a day's illness until he was rushed to hospital last summer for a major coronary operation, and he was on the brink of returning to work when he had a heart attack. Divorced, he had a long-term relationship with the former England cricketer Sarah Potter.

LEESON, RAYMOND JOHN, OAM, died on June 26, aged 90. During the Second World War, Ray Leeson was the only survivor when a Wellington bomber crashed during a snowstorm near Leicester. The upshot was that, in order to spare himself movement, he took up wicketkeeping at home in Goulburn, on the southern tablelands of New South Wales, where he played until he was 53; he might well have been chosen for the state side had he moved to Sydney. As it was, he captained the Southern NSW team that stretched the 1960-61 West Indian tourists. He was a close friend of Trevor Bayliss, his fellow townsman, who is now England's coach. Leeson edited the *Goulburn Evening Post* for 36 years, writing about 9,000 editorials, and frequently updating his own obituary.

LEQUAY, DR ALLOY REMIGUS, who died on March 15, aged 90, was a long-serving politician and sports administrator who had a profound influence on cricket in his native Trinidad, and the wider West Indies. For 70 years, the island's cricket was under the control of the Queen's Park CC in Port-of-Spain, the owners of the largest and best appointed of the Caribbean Test grounds. Lequay felt it was inappropriate for the national sport to be managed by a private club, especially when the country was emerging from its colonial past into political independence – and, in the face of powerful opposition, undertook a personal campaign to end the arrangement. He was to the fore in the establishment in 1956 of the Trinidad Cricket Council, and became their president in 1978. Lequay was the Trinidad & Tobago board's chairman until his retirement in 2002, adding the role of chief executive officer in 1994 after completing another of his ambitions in developing the National Cricket Centre in the central Trinidad town of Balmain – it contains the organisation's offices, a first-class ground, and an academy named after Frank Worrell. A Trinidadian of Chinese descent, Lequay devoted much of his life to national politics, and was elected to parliament in 1966.

LESTER, EDWARD IBSON, died on March 23, aged 92. Ted Lester served Yorkshire with quiet dedication in three contrasting roles for 45 years. He began immediately after the war as a hard-hitting middle-order batsman, moved on to become an influential Second XI captain, then spent three decades as the club's impeccable scorer. He managed to remain above the factionalism that so often dominated cricket in the county, and took great pride in sharing with Percy Holmes the distinction of being the only Yorkshire batsmen to score a century in each innings of a Roses match.

He was born in a house overlooking the ground at North Marine Road, Scarborough, and lived in the town all his life. Enraptured early, Lester went to games from the age of six, and recalled seeing Wilfred Rhodes and Harold Larwood. He soon graduated to playing: and made the Scarborough first team while still at school. But the war put his career on hold: flat feet kept him out of the armed services, where he felt he would have played a better class of cricket than in the denuded Yorkshire leagues.

He was not stalled for long. Lester made his debut for Yorkshire – opening with Len Hutton – against the RAF at Scarborough in 1945, Herbert Sutcliffe's last first-class match. Near the end of the 1946 season he was summoned by telegram to play in the final three Championship games, all away. But Lester was working in the treasurer's office of the local authority in Scarborough, and could not quickly arrange leave. And, with clothes rationing in force, he lacked enough kit for three games. As a compromise he appeared only in the final match, against Nottinghamshire, and was surprised by his first meeting with the martinet Brian Sellers – a fatherly chat in the captain's room before play on the first day. On the second, when Yorkshire were fielding, he found that Sellers's reputation

Top scorer: Ted Lester swapped a bat (here in 1954) for a pencil.

was well deserved. "I went down to third man and he was in the gully," Lester recalled. "When a wicket fell he beckoned me up and gave me the biggest mouthful I had ever heard. The problem was that I was wearing my cap at an angle."

In 1947 Lester was allowed time off to play in seven Championship matches, and made three successive centuries: against Derbyshire at Scarborough and one in each innings at Northampton. But his form did not spare him another dressing-down from Sellers, who barred his way when he attempted to board the team coach without a tie. In that celebrated summer Lester scored 657 runs at 73, and finished third in the averages behind Denis Compton and Bill Edrich. The following year he left the borough treasurer's office behind for good, and was a fixture in the Yorkshire side for the next seven summers, passing 1,000 runs six times. Having been schooled on fast Scarborough pitches, he had a good eye and quick reflexes, and was particularly strong on the leg side. He was also a superb cutter. His best season was 1949, when Yorkshire shared the title and he contributed 1,801 runs at 37.

By the mid-1950s, Lester's feet had begun to trouble him again, and he made fewer Championship appearances. He was asked to take over as Second XI captain, and regarded his four years in charge as some of his happiest. His brief was to develop the county's emerging talent. "He had a very shrewd cricket brain and he was highly respected," said John Hampshire, one of his youngsters. "We knew the rudiments but he taught us the finer points." Another young charge was Geoff Boycott, of whom Lester remained a staunch supporter through some turbulent years.

Lester continued to spend his winters in accountancy, and the Yorkshire committee decided his talent for numbers would make him an ideal candidate for the vacant role of scorer in the early 1960s, though he had never done the job before. He made an unimpressive start: unable to locate the ladder to the scorebox in the Grand Stand at Lord's, he missed the first three balls of the match. He was seldom caught out again, and became one of the best-known scorers on the circuit, introducing to county boxes the linear system favoured by the BBC. He made a brief playing comeback in a Gillette Cup tie against Middlesex at Lord's in 1964, when Hampshire was taken ill after the team had travelled with only 11 men. In borrowed kit, he relished the fielding but was bowled second ball by John Price as Yorkshire were dismissed for 90.

At the close of play, Lester would deliver the day's statistics to the dressing-room, but Hampshire noted that he kept a discreet distance from the players. Nevertheless he remained a confidant of Boycott and David Bairstow during their captaincies, and was regarded as a sage on pitch and weather conditions at Scarborough. He did not enjoy the political infighting at Yorkshire in the 1980s, and felt three-day cricket on covered pitches had become dull and formulaic. Lester was a highly regarded companion for the Yorkshire press corps. "He knew as much about cricket as anybody I have known," said *Wisden's* Yorkshire correspondent David Warner. Always a prodigious walker, he thought nothing of covering a couple of miles in pursuit of "the right pint at the right price".

LUCAS, FREDERICK CHARLES, died on September 11, aged 81. Fred Lucas was one of those cricketers whose career was killed off by the years lost to national service. When he was called up, Lucas had been progressing nicely in the Kent Second XI as an off-spinner and useful batsman. But the services offered him little cricket of a good standard, and his bowling was not as effective on his return to Kent in 1954 – though he was still given two Championship games that summer, at Ilford and Chesterfield. At school he had been an outstanding all-round sportsman, but his career in football was rather more successful: a wing-half, he made 185 appearances for Charlton Athletic between 1956 and 1964. He played in the famous match at The Valley in December 1957, when Charlton recovered from 5–1 down to beat Huddersfield Town 7–6. Remarkably, there were four first-class cricketers playing – Lucas, Derek Ufton and Stuart Leary (all of Kent) for the home team, and Yorkshire's Ken Taylor for Huddersfield.

MARQUSEE, MICHAEL JOHN, died on January 13, a fortnight short of his 62nd birthday. Mike Marqusee was a cricketing exotic: an American Marxist who moved to Britain, became obsessed with its most distinctive game, and started writing about it. One of his books, *Anyone But England*, was his answer to the question "Who do you support in Test cricket?" His zeal was not that of the average convert, as he admitted when he was naturalised: "Becoming British was for me a process laden with irony and the odd embarrassment." Perhaps his best work was *War Minus the Shooting*, a perceptive and original travel book written during the 1996 World Cup. It was one of the first to place Indian cricket squarely in its social context, and drew comparisons with C. L. R. James. However, *Anyone But England*, published two years earlier, typified the weaknesses of the Marqusee approach, in which the facts always had to be filtered through his political preconceptions; his unyieldingness reduced his influence. He also wrote a cricket-themed novel, *Slow Turn*, and books on Bob Dylan and Muhammad Ali.

MARRON, PETER, who died on May 4, aged 59, was for 25 years the head groundsman at Old Trafford, where he established an enviable reputation for fast and bouncy pitches that made for compelling cricket. Whatever his secret – and he played his cards close to his chest – his work was appreciated by generations of domestic and international cricketers. Marron liked to joke that he made Shane Warne's reputation by producing the turning surface on which he bowled Mike Gatting in 1993.

One of the best demonstrations of Marron's skill came in the Test against Pakistan in 2006, when the contrasting skills of Steve Harmison and Monty Panesar were both able to prosper on a typically hard, true pitch: they shared 19 wickets. Pakistan's coach Bob Woolmer had invested in a granite slab that he used in the nets to help his batsmen cope with Old Trafford's extra bounce, but it was to no avail.

Marron was not overly concerned by how his pitches looked – "What do you want to do, kiss 'em?" he once asked Mike Atherton – but how they played. Paul Allott recalled a Championship match against Worcestershire in 1989, when he bowled alongside Patrick Patterson and Phil DeFreitas, while the visitors' new-ball attack was Graham Dilley and Neal Radford: "It was one of the best games you could wish to see."

Marron was a friendly, welcoming figure with a quick sense of humour. But he could be stubborn if the Lancashire committee tried to influence him. "He was very protective of his domain," said Allott. The ECB once tried to recruit him to produce pitches of Old

Packing the covers: Peter Marron and an occupational hazard of being Old Trafford groundsman.

GREAT WAR OBITUARY – 100 YEARS ON

A power in the land

MARSHAL, ALAN, who died of typhoid fever on July 23, 1915, aged 32, was one of the shining stars of Edwardian county cricket. He struck the ball with immense power – *Wisden* editor Sydney Pardon did not shy away from comparisons with Gilbert Jessop – and his seam bowling regularly contributed vital wickets; as a fielder, he had few rivals in England. But, when he left Surrey in 1910, a year after being named a Wisden Cricketer of the Year, following an unexplained falling-out with the committee, there was a sense of a talent not quite fulfilled. He returned to his native Queensland, and later enlisted with the Australian Imperial Forces. He died in a military hospital in Malta after being involved in the fighting at Gallipoli.

George Beldam, Popperfoto/Getty Images

Alan Marshal, 1905.

The son of an émigré from Lincolnshire, Marshal was a prodigy in Brisbane schools cricket, and gave credit for his early development to watching Test pioneers Harry Boyle, Percy McDonnell and Sammy Jones. He played three first-class matches for Queensland and some club cricket for Paddington in Sydney (in one of those games, Victor Trumper scored a triple-century), before coming to England. In his first match, for the Gentlemen of England against Oxford University in the Parks in May 1905, he took five wickets and made 94 in an opening stand of 168 with W. G. Grace.

Marshal agreed to undertake the two-year residency period to qualify for Surrey – who coveted his signature sufficiently to pay him a winter allowance – and in the meantime played for London County. He was plainly too good for most opposition, scoring more than 6,000 runs and taking more than 300 wickets in two years. In 1907, his first season for Surrey, he just passed 1,000 runs, but the following summer he became a power in the land with a little under 2,000 at 40, including five centuries; he also took 56 wickets at 18. At Worcester in May he scored 176 in 200 minutes; earlier in the month he had taken seven for 41 against Derbyshire at The Oval, including five in 13 balls without conceding a run. Sam Apted, the Surrey groundsman, had predicted that, when Marshal found his best form, the ground would "not be big enough for him". At times, the prophecy did not look far-fetched.

But he failed to match that performance in 1909, and at one point during the summer was suspended by Surrey. After six games of the following season, his contract was terminated and he returned to Australia – though not before scoring 259 for Whitcomb Wanderers against W. Jones's XI at Acton the day before his departure.

Wisden first published an obituary for Marshal in 1916. For the next three years, an updated appreciation of a player killed in the Great War will appear 100 years after the original obituary.

Trafford standard around the country. Marron would not divulge his formula, though one acknowledged innovation was his use of glue to bind cracks. He left Lancashire in 2008 to become head groundsman at the multi-sports Bowdon Club near Altrincham. "One thing I won't miss is everyone telling me how to grow grass," he said. He was a passionate critic of the failure of local authorities to provide proper sports pitches, and of private schools for not offering their facilities to local communities. And he was clear on the best advice for aspiring groundsmen: "Go into golf."

MARTIN, ERIC JAMES, who died on September 30, aged 90, hit three centuries for Nottinghamshire – all at Trent Bridge – in a ten-year career from 1949. His best season was 1954, when he was awarded his county cap after making 977 runs, including a hundred against a Yorkshire attack comprising six Test bowlers. Although Martin did well for the Second XI, consistent first-team runs proved elusive, and he was released after the 1959 season, despite making his highest score – a rapid unbeaten 133 – to pilot Nottinghamshire to a four-wicket victory over Leicestershire after they were set 240 in 140 minutes. Martin became a heavy scorer for Steetley in the Bassetlaw League for almost 30 years, captaining the league's representative team from 1969 to 1981.

MENDIS, LIONEL, who died on October 9, aged 80, was a celebrated coach in Sri Lanka. He supervised the strong Ananda College team for many years, bringing on the future national captain Arjuna Ranatunga, and had run a coaching school at Colombo's Nondescripts CC since 1986. Mahela Jayawardene, one of his charges there, called him "the best teacher I had". In 2000, Mendis wrote *Cricket Huruwa*, the first coaching manual in the Sinhala language.

MEYER, BARRIE JOHN, who died on September 13, aged 83, was a genial, quietly authoritative figure who became one of the world's leading umpires. He stood in the World Cup finals of 1979 and 1983, and in the fabled Headingley Test of 1981. "He had just the right temperament for the job," said his colleague David Constant. Meyer, known as BJ, was never above offering a discreet word of advice or congratulation to a player. When Ian Botham began his match-turning Headingley innings of 149 in skittish fashion, Meyer suggested England might have a better chance of saving the game if he had a look at the bowling first. "But BJ," Botham replied, "that's exactly what I've just done."

Meyer was reprimanded by the TCCB for apologising to Viv Richards after giving him out leg-before in the Lord's Test of 1984, but he maintained he had done the honourable thing, and was backed by a *Daily Mail* leading article which compared his actions favourably with those of politicians. There were more column inches when he gave Graham Gooch not out in a one-day international against Australia in 1989. "Chumpire", read *The Sun* headline.

He fell into cricket almost by accident. Meyer came from a staunch football family in Bournemouth and, although he was good enough to captain his school team, he regarded cricket as "what you played in the summer when it was too hot to play football". He joined Bristol Rovers, where he became a quick and effective forward,

Making a difference: Barrie Meyer, 1993.

Patrick Eagar

who was nevertheless profligate in front of goal. "He used to joke that his nickname was 'Curly Toes' because he shot over the bar so often," said Constant. Even so, he scored the second goal when Rovers, then in the second division, thrashed Manchester United 4–0 in the third round of the FA Cup in 1956.

It was common for Rovers players to spend the summer months doing odd jobs at Gloucestershire's County Ground, while playing occasional matches for the club and ground team. Meyer kept wicket in some of these games and, although his only previous experience had been while on national service, his potential was noted: he quickly became the Second XI wicketkeeper. He progressed to a Championship debut against Essex at Romford in 1957, and the following summer became first choice, after Peter Rochford was sacked and Bobby Etheridge was forced to prioritise his football career with Bristol City.

Meyer never looked back. He became a highly competent keeper, and displayed particular expertise to off-spinners John Mortimore and David Allen on dusty Bristol pitches. "For Barrie there was never the need for showmanship," wrote Jim Parks. "His work behind the stumps was done with the quiet efficiency of a man who knows what true professionalism is all about." He was less competent as a batsman, but was called upon to open the innings against the Indians at Cheltenham in 1959 and made a career-best 63.

He continued as Gloucestershire's first-choice keeper until 1971, playing in 259 successive Championship matches and making 406 appearances overall. He took 707 catches and made 119 stumpings, third on the county's all-time list. These were largely unsuccessful and sometimes turbulent years for Gloucestershire, but Meyer became the embodiment of the uncomplaining club man who did much for dressing-room morale.

He joined the first-class umpires list in 1973, and stood in his first Test in 1978 after a one-dayer between England and Australia the previous year. In all he umpired 26 Tests and 23 ODIs until 1993. In 1983, he officiated with Constant in the Second Test against New Zealand at Headingley, after England had won a thumping victory in the first match. The umpires used the same facilities as the New Zealanders and, as they celebrated a first Test victory in England, Constant recalled: "When we went in there they were all still in the showers, singing to the tune of "Bread of Heaven": Barrie Meyer, Barrie Meyer – what a difference you have made!"

MHONDORO, PADDINGTON, died in a road accident in Zimbabwe on March 13, while returning home from watching a Logan Cup match in Kwekwe. He was 28. Mhondoro had captained the Chegutu club in central Mashonaland, and played one List A match against Southern Rocks in December 2013, taking two wickets but later becoming one of five Mid West Rhinos players out for ducks as they were skittled for 55.

MINNAAR, NORMAN PHILIP, died on March 15, aged 57, while visiting his son's school in Grahamstown. Minnaar played 22 matches for South Africa's Border province over five seasons from 1982-83, scoring 82 against Natal B in East London on New Year's Day, 1984. He worked as sponsorship manager for South African Breweries, who underwrote the 1981-82 rebel England tour.

MOIR, IAN MALCOLM, who died on September 5, 2013, aged 79, was the general manager of Time Inc., Australia for 20 years. He collected a trove of cricket books and memorabilia, including a complete run of *Wisden*, mostly originals. His son, Malcolm, said the collection provided his father with the raw material to feed his passion for cricket statistics: "It was the numbers which told the story more than the tears or the heartbreak." The collection, unusual for Australia in its breadth and depth, attracted spirited bidding when it was put up for auction in August 2015.

MORRIS, ARTHUR ROBERT, MBE, died on August 22, aged 93. In the decade immediately following the Second World War, left-hander Arthur Morris vied with Len Hutton for the title of Test cricket's best opening batsman. Strong on the back foot, he was the leading scorer for Don Bradman's 1948 Invincibles – when his 696 Test runs trumped even the Don (508). By the end of the series Morris's average was 74 and, if that tailed off a little, he remained a heavy scorer – and an immensely popular team-mate and opponent.

By nature he was an artistic batsman, although he could also be destructive. Jack McHarg's biography was subtitled *An Elegant Genius*, but the English journalist Denzil Batchelor wrote: "Strange that one so essentially pink and cherubic should wield a bat with so richly a basso voice. Arthur Morris should, from the look of him, be a caresser of leg-glides, a fingerer of porcelain-fine late cuts; instead he is the author of weighty pulls worthy of a whole fleet of Volga boatmen, and a driver of proconsular imperiousness." Batchelor's purple prose might have been describing Morris's onslaught on the Queensland attack to finish a match at Sydney in January 1949 when, instead of a leisurely stroll to a target of 143, he blazed an unbeaten 108 in 82 minutes.

Sport & General/PA Photos

A big hand: Don Bradman congratulates Arthur Morris on his hundred, as Australia move towards 404 to win the Headingley Test in 1948.

Morris the player and Morris the man were inseparable: John Arlott wrote that he was "one of the best-liked cricketers of all time – charming, philosophical and relaxed", while Gideon Haigh referred to him as "the acme of elegance and the epitome of sportsmanship". In conversation, Morris was generous to his fellow players – self-deprecating, but obviously delighted by the satisfaction cricket had afforded him, even if its material legacy was, in his own word, "poverty".

One of his favourite accounts was of the Oval Test of 1948, when Bradman's duck overshadowed all else. Eyes twinkling, Morris would tell of enlightening a questioner that, yes, he had indeed been at The Oval that Saturday afternoon. And, yes, he had actually been batting at the other end when Eric Hollies did for the Don. When pressed, he would confess to having scored 196. Around this time, such was Morris's dominance that Bradman might have echoed W. G. Grace – an admirer of Arthur Shrewsbury – by saying "Give me Arthur" as a measure of his value. Although Bradman tempered the praise with a reminder that "he wasn't always straight in defence", he immediately qualified it with "but this was merely a sign of his genius".

Morris was born in the Sydney seaside suburb of Bondi in January 1922, but his family soon moved to the small country town of Dungog, near Newcastle, following the transfer north of his father, a teacher. His English-born mother left the marriage, so Morris had the unusual experience for that time of growing up mainly in the care of a single father. When they returned to Sydney, he was educated at Canterbury Boys' High School, which later produced a cricket-loving Australian prime minister in John Howard, and the cricket historian David Frith. At school, Morris's prime strength appeared to be as a dispenser of left-arm unorthodox spin, with tennis and rugby union completing a trio of sporting accomplishments.

He turned out for the St George first-grade side at the age of 14. Their legendary leg-spinner, the bluff Bill O'Reilly, directed him to forget the childish baubles of spin – despite a recent haul of 55 wickets at five apiece in an Under-16 competition – and concentrate on becoming an opening batsman. Morris followed this advice so well that, in his first match for New South Wales, in December 1940, aged 18, he scored 148 and 111 against Queensland at Sydney, to become the first to make twin centuries on first-class

Men of letters: Arthur Morris and Richie Benaud before the 1953 Ashes.

debut. When "Doc" Evatt, later president of the United Nations General Assembly and leader of the Australian Labor Party, heard that Morris had made his runs using a borrowed bat, he sent him to Stan McCabe's shop in Sydney to choose a new one.

After three years' service in Papua and New Guinea with the Australian army, Morris returned to first-class cricket in 1946-47. He started in rich touch, scoring runs for fun, except in his first two Tests, against England: he made two and five, then 21 in the first innings of the Third Test at Melbourne. But, in the second, he removed any question marks with six hours of concentration and care, putting the match virtually beyond the reach of Wally Hammond's side with 155. Morris added a century in each innings of the next Test, in stifling heat on a country road of a pitch in Adelaide.

The Ashes tour of 1948 found Morris at his best. He amassed 1,922 runs at 71, and Australia won 4–0. *Wisden* selected him as one of the Five Cricketers, praising an "air of complete composure", and adding that "he combines unusual defensive qualities with the ability to decide early in the ball's flight what his stroke shall be". At Headingley, it was Morris who propelled the last-day chase of 404, protecting Bradman when Denis Compton's tweakers were causing him anxiety, and hitting him out of the attack. His 182 took only 291 minutes, while his partnership with Bradman produced 301 for the second wicket in only 217. His long Oval innings was a more sedate affair, lasting 406 minutes – but it ensured England would pay dearly for collapsing for 52 in their first innings. Morris's 196 set up an innings victory, which also meant Bradman did not have another chance to lift his average back into three figures.

After a fruitful series in South Africa in 1949-50, Morris's seasons of plenty grew fewer, his favourite opening partner Sid Barnes having fallen foul of the selectors. During the 1950-51 Ashes, the perception of Morris as the bunny of his close friend Alec Bedser was reinforced. After Morris fell to him four times in his first five innings, Bedser handed over a copy of Lindsay Hassett's *Better Cricket*, with the sections on batting underlined in red. Morris scored 206 in the next match at Adelaide – the highest of his dozen Test centuries – and returned the book with the sections on bowling similarly highlighted. It is true that, in 21 Tests against each other, Bedser dismissed him 18 times – but, Morris would politely point out, he averaged more than 50 against England overall.

He struggled for consistency throughout the 1952-53 series against Jack Cheetham's South Africans, until the final Test, at Melbourne, where hesitancy was replaced by the old model. He dominated the bowling until he reached 99, only to sacrifice his wicket in a mix-up over a single with the in-form Neil Harvey, who went on to make 205.

Morris was never Australia's permanent captain, although he did the job twice as a stand-in – both defeats, by West Indies at Adelaide in 1951-52 (the first Test to feature play on Christmas Day), and by England in the Second Ashes Test of 1954-55 at the SCG. Still, he was named in the national Team of the Century in 2000, and the following year inducted into the Australian Cricket Hall of Fame.

IT'S THAT MAN AGAIN

Batsmen dismissed most often by the same bowler in Tests:

Dismissals	Batsman	Bowler	Tests	Ducks
19	M. A. Atherton (E)	G. D. McGrath (A)	17	3
18	**A. R. Morris (A)**	**A. V. Bedser (E)**	**21**	**2**
17	M. A. Atherton (E)	C. E. L. Ambrose (WI)	26	4
17	M. A. Atherton (E)	C. A. Walsh (WI)	27	1
16	G. A. Gooch (E)	M. D. Marshall (WI)	21	2
15	T. W. Hayward (E)	H. Trumble (A)	22	4
15	M. E. Waugh (A)	C. E. L. Ambrose (WI)	22	3
15	B. C. Lara (WI/World)	G. D. McGrath (A)	24	2
15	I. A. Healy (A)	C. A. Walsh (WI)	28	5

During the 1953 Ashes tour, Morris had gone backstage at the Victoria Palace Theatre, where he met Valerie Hudson, a member of the chorus. Despite his shyness, their relationship developed to the point where he sponsored her migration to Sydney, and they were married in September 1954. She was taken ill with cancer while he was touring the West Indies the following year, but did not tell him until his return to Australia, when he announced his retirement. Financial assistance from Vivian Van Damm, the owner of London's Windmill Theatre, enabled them to travel back to England to see her family; Morris covered the 1956 Ashes for the *Daily Express*. Valerie died, only 33, in January 1957. Morris married Judith Menmuir in 1968, a long and happy union.

He spent a long period in the motor trade, then played a significant part in the introduction of tenpin bowling to Australia, before finishing in PR. He remained an honoured guest at cricket grounds everywhere, his dignity never puffing up into pomposity, thanks to an acute sense of the ironic and the whimsical. He was appointed MBE in 1974, and was a member of the Sydney Cricket and Sports Ground Trust for 22 years. Three days before he died, the Arthur Morris Gates were unveiled as a tribute to his long association with the SCG. When his wife asked why he had four gates named after him, he shot back that it was "because I was an opener".

Morris was the oldest surviving Australian Test player, a distinction that passed to the former wicketkeeper Len Maddocks – although Harvey, Morris's friend and team-mate in 35 Tests, was the last surviving Invincible. "You wouldn't find a nicer bloke in the world," he said. "A great sense of humour, a great team man."

NASIM HASAN SHAH, who died on February 3, aged 85, was president of the Pakistan Cricket Board from 1992 to 1994. A tiny (4ft 8in) lawyer, he was a member of the Supreme Court bench which in 1979 upheld the death sentence handed down to Pakistan's former prime minister Zulfiqar Ali Bhutto.

NAYSMITH, ANNE, who died on February 10, aged 77, was for many years a familiar and well-liked presence at games held at Chiswick House's cricket ground. Her dishevelled appearance made her an unlikely figure in such grand surroundings, but Naysmith – or the "car lady of Chiswick", as the press called her – was something of a celebrity in the west

London suburb. She had lived in the area during her promising career as a concert pianist in the 1960s, and remained there after she turned her back on music and was evicted from her home. She was simply Anne Smith, but added the "Nay" in later life, some thought as a reference to her unmarried status after the end of a relationship with a choral singer. She spent 26 years living in an ever more dilapidated Ford Consul, before it was towed away in 2002 and she was forced to move to a patch of ground near Stamford Brook Tube station. She regularly watched Old Meadonians at Chiswick House and would score using a stub of old pencil. No one understood her method and she did not know the names of the players or their opponents, but she still sometimes pointed out mistakes – and was usually found to be correct. At the start of each season she would push a note under the dressing-room door wishing the team luck, and enclose a dozen postage stamps as a donation. Graham Hall, vice-president of Chiswick and Whitton, successors to Old Meadonians, recalled: "One afternoon, when she was sitting in her usual place at the foot of a tree, she was struck on the forehead by the ball, which split her open, with much blood. While she allowed us to help a little to stem the flow, she was absolutely adamant that she would not go to hospital or let us call an ambulance – part of her total mistrust of the State in all of its forms."

NEETHLING, JOHN JAMES, died on June 10, aged 82. "Coetie" Neethling followed Basil D'Oliveira, another star performer in South African non-white cricket, to the Lancashire leagues. Neethling toured East Africa under D'Oliveira in 1958-59 and, after D'Oliveira's success for Middleton, was signed up by Colne for 1962. A lively medium-pacer and a handy batsman, he collected 150 wickets over two seasons, once scoring 50 not out against an Accrington side spearheaded by the West Indian fast bowler Wes Hall, before taking seven for 39 himself. In the 1970s he played 13 matches now considered first-class for Western Province's non-white team, despite being in his forties, and took five for 51 against Natal in Cape Town.

NOBBS, DAVID GORDON, who died on August 8, aged 80, was a novelist and scriptwriter most associated with the 1970s sitcom *The Fall and Rise of Reginald Perrin*. Nobbs's passion for cricket began when The City of London School, where his father was a teacher, was evacuated to Marlborough College. It was cemented by the friendship he struck up with Peter Tinniswood, future author of several humorous cricket books, when both were trainee reporters on the *Sheffield Star*. Nobbs, who went on to write about contemporary cricket matters on his blog, loved introducing it into his writing: in the first Perrin novel, Reggie rediscovers an old scorebook from his matches of dice cricket. In one fixture, England take on My Girls, an XI made up of "all the girls I'd got a crush on". Scorecard entries include: Jill Ogleby c Leyland b Larwood 2, and Angela Borrowdale c and b Verity 0. The Tall Girl on the 8.21 made a match-winning 92 not out.

PANDIT, BAL JAGANNATH, who died on September 17, aged 86, was a popular cricket commentator in India for more than 40 years, usually on All India Radio's Marathi service. His lively delivery, which included several cricket terms of his own invention, was credited with popularising the game in Maharashtra. He also wrote several books, and translated Sunil Gavaskar's early autobiography *Sunny Days* into Marathi. Bal Pandit played one Ranji Trophy match in 1959-60, going in first against Gujarat and scoring 25, and was later secretary of the Maharashtra Cricket Association.

PATHMANATHAN, BAVALAN, died on July 7, two days after being struck on the chest while batting in a club game in Long Ditton in Surrey. He was 24. Playing for Hersham's Manipay Parish in the British Tamil League, Pathmanathan collapsed at the crease after being hit by a rising delivery. He was taken to Kingston Hospital by air ambulance, but never recovered.

PAYNE, IAN ATTWOOD, who died on September 13, aged 65, was an opener who played 19 matches for Western Province, mainly for their B team. He had a purple patch in 1976, hitting 132 against Border, 52 and 77 not out against Orange Free State, and 97

Obituaries

and 65 against Northern Transvaal in successive innings. Payne added another century, against Griqualand West in January 1977, but his highest score for the A side was 20. He later worked as director of sport at Herzlia High School, on the slopes of Table Mountain.

PETHERICK, PETER JAMES, who died on June 7, aged 72, was the first New Zealander to take a Test hat-trick – in his first match, at the age of 34, less than a year after being hoicked out of the garage where he worked in Alexandra to make his first-class debut for Otago. At Lahore in 1976-77, off-spinner Petherick had Javed Miandad caught at square leg off a top edge, before Wasim Raja drove back his first ball uppishly. "Amazingly, he caught it," said Warren Lees, the wicketkeeper. "He couldn't even catch it when I threw it back to him, so this was quite a surprise." Then Intikhab Alam flicked one straight to Geoff Howarth at bat–pad: Petherick had completed a hat-trick – only James Franklin has since done so for New Zealand in Tests – although Pakistan already had 336 by then, and the 19-year-old Miandad, also on debut, 163. They won easily. "Most of his bowling was flight and guile, and he had a wee bit of outswing with his slower arm-ball," said Lees. "There was minimal effort in his run-up: it was a three-metre shuffle."

But, as the *Otago Daily Times* noted, "Petherick could make the ball turn square on any pitch which gave him help." That ability brought a record 42 wickets in his belated first season for Otago, including nine for 93 against Northern Districts and six for 36 in his next match, against the Indian tourists, both at Dunedin. When Hedley Howarth, New Zealand's incumbent spinner, was unavailable for the tour of Pakistan and India the following year, Petherick was called up: including the hat-trick, he collected 16 wickets in five Tests. Early in 1977 he took seven for 65 against the Australian tourists, and played the Auckland Test that soon followed – but he failed to strike there, and was never chosen again, despite breaking his own Otago record with 45 wickets in 1977-78. Petherick then moved to Wellington, and signed off in 1980-81, aged 38, by dismissing Stephen Boock with his final delivery in first-class cricket. He became an accomplished player of lawn bowls, reaching the national pairs final in 2006, and later joined his son in Australia.

PHILIPS, STANLEY IAN, died on October 27, aged 95. Not long after leaving Brighton College, 18-year-old Ian Philips played twice for Northamptonshire in 1938; he made four more appearances the following year. His death brought the number of surviving pre-war first-class players to two (see page 65). He hit a highest score of 22, but exceeded that in his only other first-class match, in the Bombay Pentangular tournament. Philips scored 26 and 42 for the Europeans, who were up against it after the Parsees had amassed 532 at the Brabourne Stadium in December 1941. The previous year he had made 178 for Oxford University against a British Empire XI, and played a few trial games on returning to Oxford after the war, without making the first team. He followed his father as headmaster of Eaglehurst College, a private school in Northampton, then taught nearby when Eaglehurst closed in 1972.

RALPH, LOUIS HENRY ROY, died in April, aged 95. Roy Ralph was a latecomer to county cricket. A heavy wicket-taker for Ilford, he made his first-class debut for Essex against a Commonwealth XI at Romford in 1953, when he was already 33, and dismissed Everton Weekes and Frank Worrell with his deceptive swingers. The following season Ralph fitted in a few more games around work at the family's East End tailoring business; he collected 36 wickets, and asked if he could join the staff full-time. He soon became an important and popular member of the Essex attack: in 1956 he took seven for 77 against Worcestershire and a career-best seven for 42 in an innings victory over Gloucestershire, both within a week at Romford. "He bowled awayswingers at a steady medium-pace, but he swung the ball significantly," remembered his captain, Doug Insole. Indeed, Ralph's big outswinger occasionally provoked jovial shouts of "Ripe bananas!" from the slips.

In 1957 he took 102 wickets, demolishing Somerset at Colchester with six for 33. He also claimed six for 56 against the 1958 New Zealanders, and five for 33 against the 1959 Indians, both at his old club ground at Ilford. Ralph was an enthusiastic tailender whose runs, said Insole, "included a high proportion of boundaries". His highest score was 73, with four sixes, as nightwatchman against Northamptonshire at Leyton in 1960. He played on until he was 41, and was still good enough to take five for 23 against Worcestershire in 1961, his final season. After leaving Essex he had a spell as a professional in the North Staffordshire League, before returning to Ilford.

RAMPRASAD, KALADEVANHALLI MURUDEVAGOWDA, who died on November 22, aged 82, was president of the Karnataka State Cricket Association from 1998 to 2007, and had also been a vice-president of the BCCI. He played four games for the state (then known as Mysore) as a medium-pacer, including the 1959-60 Ranji Trophy final defeat by Bombay; against Kerala in October 1961 he took six for 26. He managed the Indian team at the Champions Trophy in Sri Lanka in 2002.

RASDIEN, HASHIM, died on March 7, aged 80. "Rosie" Rasdien was a talented all-round sportsman who played representative cricket, rugby and soccer for the South African Malays and for Transvaal's non-white teams. A hard-hitting batsman, useful seam bowler and superb fielder, Rasdien made 112 against Eastern Province in the Dadabhay Trophy in Johannesburg in 1961-62. In 2014 he was one of the inaugural recipients of Cricket South Africa's Heritage Blazers.

REYNOLDS, BRIAN LEONARD, who died on February 7, aged 82, was at the heart of Northamptonshire cricket throughout his life – as player, coach, cricket development officer and elder statesman. He was staunch in his belief in the sport's verities and in his affection for his home county. As John Arlott wrote in his benefit brochure: "In his own mind he is not only a cricketer, he is a Northamptonshire cricketer." Born and rooted in Kettering, Reynolds joined the club in 1950. Over the next 20 years he made 426 first-class appearances, becoming a fixture at the top of the order, and occasionally keeping wicket. "He was very correct, good on the drive and determined," said his team-mate Peter Arnold. "He got runs when you needed them and he made himself into a very good county cricketer." Reynolds was particularly prolific in the early 1960s, when he passed 1,500 runs five years running. Occasionally, he surprised even himself, hitting 141 in three hours off Lancashire's Brian Statham, Ken Higgs and Sonny Ramadhin at Old Trafford in 1964. He was always immensely fit and, as a coach, expected to see his charges match his own national service-honed standards, which was not always appreciated by later generations. He loved the game – but hated the reverse sweep, players who failed to remove their headgear to acknowledge applause, and Twenty20. He liked it when those games were played inside a few weeks: it was the ideal time to take his wife on holiday.

RICE, CLIVE EDWARD BUTLER, died on July 28, five days after his 66th birthday. Of all the great South African cricketers confined to the margins during more than 20 years of sporting isolation, few felt the pain more acutely than Clive Rice. His bristling frustration was especially visible during the 1980s, when Ian Botham, Richard Hadlee, Kapil Dev and Imran Khan fought a running battle to be considered the world's leading all-rounder. Rice knew he had the talent to be part of the scrap.

Instead he channelled his skills as a superb middle-order batsman, combative fast bowler and inspiring captain into domestic cricket – and became a serial winner. In England he joined forces with Hadlee to turn Nottinghamshire from also-rans into county champions in 1981 and 1987, while in his homeland he led Transvaal to five Currie Cup victories. He was a feisty, unyielding figure who led by example rather than tactical inspiration. According to Derek Randall, "You would have followed him through a brick wall."

His yearning to play Test cricket was never realised, but he had the distinction of leading the first South African team after readmission in 1991. A hastily arranged one-day series in India was as much a PR exercise as a cricketing one, and the 42-year-old Rice handled it with aplomb. He was photographed with Mother Teresa in Kolkata, and gave an appropriate sound bite before the first match, at Eden Gardens: "Now I know how Neil Armstrong felt when he stood on the moon." Rice returned home and began to plan for the World Cup in Australia early the next year, but the selectors chose Kepler Wessels to lead the team instead. It was a bitter blow and, many felt, unjust. "He should have been our captain in the 1992 World Cup," said Graeme Pollock. "The guys who had kept cricket going in South Africa for 20 years should have been involved more when we came back."

Rice's squabbles with his country's administrators lasted until his death. He became an outspoken opponent of what he called the "inverted racism" of the quota system, believing that selection should only ever be on merit, and he was angered by Cricket South Africa's treatment of players from the apartheid era. His stance was regarded by some as unacceptably blinkered. Rice was also unflinching in claiming foul play in the deaths of Hansie Cronje and Bob Woolmer. He returned to Nottinghamshire as cricket manager between 1999 and 2002, when he imported a young Kevin Pietersen.

Rice, whose grandfather Philip Bower had played for Oxford University in 1919, was born in Johannesburg and made his debut in the B section of the Currie Cup in 1969-70. By the following season he was in Trans-vaal's first team. His progress was such that he was named in the South Africa squad to go to Australia in 1971-72, but the tour was called off and his Test aspirations were stalled for ever. He came to England to play for Ramsbottom in the Lancashire League in 1973, and two years later was given the task of replacing Garry Sobers as overseas player at Trent Bridge. *Wisden* introduced him as Pat Rice, perhaps thinking Nottinghamshire had acquired the Arsenal full-back, but the unfamiliarity did not last long. In his first season he passed 1,000 Championship runs and led their bowling averages, and in 1976 and 1977 he topped both the batting and the bowling. But the county still finished bottom in 1977, and he was appointed captain in the hope that his competitiveness would rub off.

Awards time: Clive Rice and a young Derek Pringle, 1977 winners of the Cricket Society's awards for the leading all-rounder in the first-class game, and in schools cricket.

The plan went awry when Rice signed for Kerry Packer during the winter, which left Nottinghamshire – staunch critics of World Series Cricket – with little choice but to sack him. However, the threat of legal action forced his reinstatement as a player, and he responded with 1,727 runs at 61, and 41 wickets at 20. The row had another serendipitous benefit: before Rice's return, Nottinghamshire had recruited Hadlee to replace him. That summer, the pair bowled in tandem for the first time.

Rice's innate edge was perfectly suited to the intensity of WSC, although he suffered broken ribs, courtesy of Dennis Lillee, during an exhibition match in Auckland. He discovered a mentor in Tony Greig, Packer's chief recruiting officer. "Greig had told him, 'Look, you are a good player but you have to be more aggressive and demanding,'" said Pollock. "He was always a good cricketer but that added something." When Packer signed his peace treaty with the Australian authorities, the South African players felt the end of WSC most keenly. Rice broke down in front of his wife. "It was as if someone had taken my right arm," he said. "I never knew the truth of 'it is better to have loved and lost than never to have loved at all'. But I believe it now."

In July 1979, back at Trent Bridge, he took over the captaincy from Mike Smedley, whom he did not rate, and set about shaping the team in his own image; he banished any notion that it was good enough simply to finish above Derbyshire. "He was tough, and he expected high standards and he always played hard," remembered Hadlee. "He played the

Lighting up a modest stage: ten years before his international debut, Rice competes against John Emburey, Mike Gatting and wicketkeeper Paul Downton at Uxbridge in 1981.

game to win – he would take high-risk options." Rice was an early proponent of improved fitness and, when the players returned in the spring of 1980, they were put through their training runs; Rice made sure he was always home first. They came third in the Championship, and his five unbeaten centuries included one in each innings against Somerset. He was a *Wisden* Cricketer of the Year, but it was just a warm-up for 1981, when the Championship returned to Trent Bridge for the first time since 1929. Nine wins in the last 11 games carried them irresistibly to the title, and Rice understood the significance of the achievement when county stalwart Reg Simpson wept in the dressing-room. Rice and Hadlee made a formidable pair, especially on the greentops prepared by Ron Allsopp, and played in every game that summer. They shared 170 wickets (not to mention 2,200 runs) and became as synonymous with Nottinghamshire's new-ball threat as Larwood and Voce.

Rice was not blessed with Hadlee's subtleties, but he moved the ball off the seam and could generate considerable pace. He had a nasty bouncer and put every ounce of effort into every ball. "His hand would hit the pitch on his follow-through," said Randall. "You would often see he had bruised fingers." Hadlee added: "When he was 100% fit he was as slippery as anyone. I would bowl with the wind and he'd bowl into it – that's where he lost most of his hair, I think."

As a batsman, Rice was adaptable and technically correct. "He would have got into the top six of a Test batting order even without his bowling," said Pollock. Deprived of Test cricket, Rice relished the chance to compete against many of the world's leading players in the Championship. "That's how I measured how good he was," said Hadlee. He was also highly motivated for the single-wicket competitions involving the world's best all-rounders held between 1984 and 1987, winning three of them.

Rice and Hadlee enjoyed a memorable swansong with Nottinghamshire in 1987, winning the Championship again and adding the NatWest Trophy, their first knockout success. The captaincy had switched to Tim Robinson, but Rice took the reins for the last two matches of the campaign. In 13 seasons at Trent Bridge he never failed to pass 1,000 runs, and in all scored 17,053 first-class runs for Nottinghamshire at 44, and took 476 wickets at 23. He was captain of Transvaal for a hat-trick of Currie Cup and Nissan Shield doubles between 1982-83 and 1984-85, two accompanied by victories in the Benson and Hedges one-day competition. His team's relentless approach earned the nickname the "Mean Machine". He also led South Africa against rebel touring sides, again relishing the scent of international combat, but a row with chairman of selectors Peter van der Merwe about the make-up of the one-day squad against the Australians had far-reaching consequences: van der Merwe was still in charge when Rice was left out of the 1992 World Cup.

He had two final seasons at Natal, eventually under the captaincy of Malcolm Marshall, in the early 1990s before retiring, and did not go quietly, scoring a one-day century against Transvaal at the age of 44. Rice remained a prominent figure in South African cricket, and once made unusual headlines when he posed naked, save for a strategically placed Jumbo bat, to advertise a sports-goods company. "People still remember me for doing that ad rather than for the runs I scored," he said. The ill health of his later years – chiefly an invasive brain tumour – did not dim his passion for fast cars or his candour when discussing the state of South African cricket. He died a little over a week before the Fourth Ashes Test at Trent Bridge, where there was a minute's applause in his memory before the first day's play. Pietersen, to whom he became a mentor in his early days in England, said: "He was such a tough character on the field, but such a caring person off it, a gentleman."

RIDGWAY, FREDERICK, died on September 26, aged 92. Fred Ridgway carried the Kent new-ball attack on his muscular shoulders from immediately after the Second World War until the early 1960s. He was not one of the tallest fast bowlers on the circuit – he was about 5ft 9in – but he could be one of the quickest and, summer after summer, charged in for his adopted county. In an era when the selectors could call on Bedser, Trueman, Statham, Tyson, Bailey and Loader, international opportunities were scarce, but Ridgway toured India with an understrength England team in 1951-52. He played in all five Tests, taking only seven wickets on painfully unhelpful pitches. "Sheer bloody hard work," was his verdict.

In a 16-year career for Kent, Ridgway took 955 wickets – second only to Derek Underwood since the war, and eighth on the county's all-time list. He accepted his prodigious workload uncomplainingly, even though it hampered his ability to bowl flat out. He was seen to best effect at the start of the day or an innings. "All the openers around the country would try to keep away from Fred," said his team-mate Derek Ufton. "His opening overs were devastating."

Ridgway was born in Stockport, and at school discovered his aptitude for fast bowling almost by accident, having initially kept wicket. He served in the Royal Marines

Short but sweet: Fred Ridgway in 1959.

at Deal during the war, and after marrying a Kent woman, stayed put. In May 1946, he attended Kent's first post-war trial. "There was this fellow who seemed to knock down the stumps every time he bowled," said Ufton. "He wasn't tall but he had a beautiful run-up and a long final stride. By lunchtime he had a contract." Ridgway made his debut against Lancashire at Maidstone, and in his third match took six for 59 against Hampshire.

With Norman Harding claiming four at the other end, it looked as if Kent had chanced upon a potent new-ball pairing. But Harding died in the 1947 polio epidemic, and Ridgway was left to toil with a succession of medium-paced partners. His pace came from that lengthy, rhythmical approach and delivery stride, and he moved the ball late, mainly away. "Fred would have challenged Trueman and Statham if he had been six inches taller," said team-mate Bob Wilson. "He was as accurate as Statham, but because of his height he did not get the bounce. His consistency and his pace were as good as either."

On the subcontinent, Ridgway operated alongside Statham and Derek Shackleton, and in five months bowled more than 400 overs, taking 41 wickets at 26. Recalling the tour with Andy Bull of *The Guardian* in 2012, Ridgway tapped the top of a table to demonstrate the consistency of the pitches. "The pitches were like this – brown, no grass, no movement at all. The longer you bowled, the slower it'd go. And the sweat. I bowled one over in Bombay and thought 'Oh crikey,' the ground was wobbling under my feet. So I said to Nigel Howard [the captain], 'I can't bowl on this, mate, it's too hot.' But someone had to. So I cut my run down and bowled for another hour."

It was perhaps the memory of his fruitless endeavour that provoked a rare show of temper when the Indians played at Canterbury in 1952. Unable to disturb Polly Umrigar's serene progress towards a double-century, Ridgway blatantly threw a short-pitched delivery at him (Umrigar calmly collected another four). The incident went virtually unreported, but he was summoned by the Kent committee that evening. Another batsman whose constant aggression could disturb his equilibrium was Dickie Dodds of Essex. "One year," said Wilson, "Fred refused to bowl at him any more."

Ridgway passed 100 wickets once, in 1949, while his best season for Kent was 1958, his benefit year, with 98 at 14. He took eight for 39 against Nottinghamshire at Dover in 1950, and the following summer four wickets in four deliveries against Derbyshire at Folkestone after being reluctantly persuaded to take the second new ball.

RIGG, HERBERT WILLIAM HARDY, died on March 16, aged 91. A member of a prominent sporting family, Bert Rigg had to wait over a decade from his first appearance for Western Australia – against the 1946-47 MCC tourists – to play his only full season of state cricket. A steady middle-order batsman, he scored 76 against Queensland at Perth. Rigg later had a long career as an administrator, chairing the WACA executive for eight years and spending a decade as his state's representative on the Australian Cricket Board.

ROSENDORFF, NEIL, who died on September 12, aged 70, had a long career with Orange Free State, scoring nearly 5,000 runs in 67 matches spread over 16 seasons from 1962-63. The highest of his 11 centuries, 178, came against North Eastern Transvaal – who had two Test opening bowlers – in Pretoria in 1964-65, when he was 19. A graceful left-hander, Rosendorff might have improved his chances of Test selection if he had moved to a bigger team, but he stayed put in Bloemfontein. The 1968-69 and 1969-70 seasons both brought him more than 500 runs, and he was named as one of the *South African Cricket Annual's* cricketers of the year in 1969. But this was a golden age for South African batting, and the call never came; he was still only 25 when the country's cricketing isolation began. Rosendorff was also a handy change bowler, recording figures of 29.1–19–16–6 against Griqualand West at Kimberley in 1971-72. He had been less economical against the Australian tourists two seasons previously, Ian Redpath clobbered him for 32 in an over (666644). Rosendorff's son, Craig, also played first-class cricket.

RYAN, MELVILLE, who died on November 16, aged 82, was a tall, physically imposing seamer who won four County Championship titles with the formidable Yorkshire team of the late 1950s and '60s – a useful strike-rate for a player who made just 150 first-class appearances. Ryan, usually known as Mel, made his debut in 1954, but had to wait seven years to become a regular.

Born in Huddersfield, he showed early promise at football and cricket. He had little interest in schoolwork, knowing he would eventually run the family newsagency business if he did not realise his sporting ambitions. He was first invited to Yorkshire nets – as a batsman – aged 14, and played league cricket in his home town for Bradley Mills – before joining Eccleshill in the Bradford League. On his Yorkshire debut, against Combined Services at Harrogate in 1954, he had the pleasure of watching a Len Hutton century. His appearances were sporadic, but against Warwickshire at Edgbaston in 1958 he took a career-best seven for 45.

He had, in the words of team-mate Bob Platt, a "busy and effective run-up", and bowled at a lively pace. "He did not bowl bouncers. His main thing was line and length." In 1959, when Yorkshire won the Championship under Ronnie Burnet, he took 21 wickets in five appearances. He was a more regular presence in later title-winning sides, taking 37 wickets in 1960, then 73 in 1962 and 57 in 1963. Ryan's final season was 1965, and he retired with 413 wickets at just under 23. "He was a great bowler, straight-talking, and a kindly and generous man," said team-mate Ken Taylor.

Ryan loved opening the bowling with Fred Trueman, but recalled: "He had the best end. It was uphill and against the wind for the rest of us. The only time it would change was if we were getting wickets and he wasn't. I would say 390 of my wickets were batsmen one to six. I would probably have taken another 100 if I'd been able to bowl at nine, ten and eleven, and from the right end. And no question, I would have been more successful if Fred hadn't been at the other."

SALIWA, MARIO NGQIUYOMIZI, died on May 31, a few days after being stabbed in an incident in Mdantsane, the major township on the outskirts of East London in South Africa. He was 31. Saliwa was a fast bowler, once likened to Makhaya Ntini; he took 65 first-class wickets, most of them for Free State, including five for 56 against Griqualand West at Bloemfontein in October 2007. "He was one of the most feared bowlers of his generation," said Lions coach Geoffrey Toyana, who recalled Saliwa's "bounce and unbelievable pace". He had a successful spell with Kidderminster in the Birmingham League, and spent a season as Walsden's professional in the Central Lancashire League.

SCOTT, DEREK, who died on July 20, aged 86, was a tireless historian of cricket in Ireland, and served the Irish Cricket Union for more than half a century as assistant secretary, secretary, and president. During his time Ireland developed from a cricketing outpost into a thriving Associate Member of the ICC. A genial man with a twinkling smile, Scott painstakingly researched all their fixtures back to 1855, after discovering the official records went only as far as 1933. He wrote about Irish cricket in *The Cricketer* for 20 years, and in *Wisden* for 50: "It was a delight to have him as a contributor – a lovely man," said the former Almanack editor Matthew Engel. Scott had been a modest player, a source of irritation being that he never managed a fifty in senior cricket, but his leadership skills were clear when he led Railway Union to the Leinster Senior League title in 1960.

SHORT, CAPTAIN PETER DESMOND BOWEN, who died on August 4, aged 89, was intimately involved in West Indian cricket administration for 32 years, with the Barbados Cricket Association and the West Indies Cricket Board of Control. Both teams have never been stronger, before or since. West Indies' subsequent decline began when "Control" was erased from the board's title.

Born in Trinidad, Short spent most of his life in Barbados, where he was educated and was vice-captain of The Lodge. On leaving school, Short joined the British Army, and served in Malaya. Twice mentioned in despatches, he rose to the rank of captain, a title by which he was respectfully addressed for the rest of his life. In 1950, he hit 56 for the Royal Artillery against the Royal Engineers at Lord's. Back in Barbados, he was a reliable middle-order batsman for Wanderers, the island's oldest club; he captained them to the first of a hat-trick of championships in 1959, with four former or future Test players in the team. Short was also a commentator on local radio, which led to his name being included in the title of the media centre at Kensington Oval, and he received Barbados's Silver Crown of Merit award in 1989.

During his time as head of the West Indian board he persuaded Brian Lara to return after walking out during the 1995 England tour. He was criticised for encouraging Lara to believe he was greater than the game; Short saw it as saving Lara from himself.

At a time of marked changes in all aspects of West Indian life, a white Barbadian with an enormous handlebar moustache who had served in the British Army was regarded by some as an anachronism. It was a misleading stereotype. "Peter Short, I believe, was misunderstood," wrote Sir Hilary Beckles, now vice-chancellor of the University of the West Indies, in *The Development of West Indies Cricket* in 1992. "He was part of the respected nationalist network of civic society that believed in cricket as a cultural activity for gentlemen, part of the infrastructure of high moral values and social contact."

SHRIMPTON, MICHAEL JOHN FROUD, died on June 13, aged 74. Mike Shrimpton had a tough task in his first Test, against England at Wellington in 1962-63: he entered at 40 for four, after a lively spell from Fred Trueman, but applied himself for a tenacious 28. He had been selected on the back of a career-best 150 for Central Districts against Canterbury, and continued to do well at domestic level, but could never nail down a Test place; his highest score, in ten games spread over 11 years, was 46, against England at Auckland in 1970-71. An attractive batsman and a handy leg-spinner – he bamboozled Otago with six for 40 at Dunedin in January 1970 – "Shrimpo" played on to 1979-80, latterly as Central Districts' captain. He then won arguably greater fame as a coach, his most notable achievement coming when New Zealand's women's won the World Cup at home in 2000-01. Haidee Tiffen, one of the side that edged out Australia by four runs in the final in Lincoln, remembered "a wonderful coach and mentor. Mike made cricket fun for everyone. He had a really dry sense of humour and made people laugh." He was also a (men's) Test selector for a while, coached the New Zealand A team, and worked at schools at home and in England.

SHUKLA, ANAND, who died on February 2, aged 74, scored more than 4,000 runs and took nearly 400 wickets in Indian domestic cricket with his leg-breaks, chiefly for Bihar and neighbouring Uttar Pradesh. His career started in 1959-60, and ended with the Ranji Trophy final in April 1978. Shukla was unlucky to be plying his trade in the golden era of Indian slow bowling: one giant obstacle to Test selection was Bhagwat Chandrasekhar. Shukla took seven for 91 in his third match, for Uttar Pradesh against Vidarbha in January 1960, and the following season allied ten wickets in the match against Rajasthan to an undefeated 168. In 1969-70 he took 42 wickets at 16, including a career-best eight for 50 in the Moin-ud-Dowlah Cup. Although he could be devastating against the weaker teams – he took 71 Ranji Trophy wickets against Assam, and 69 against Orissa, both at under 11 apiece – he was less of a force against stronger opposition, and in the Duleep Trophy zonal tournament his wickets cost around 35. And so a national call never came, even though Shukla was a much better batsman than his rivals. He hit nine first-class centuries, the highest 242 not out for Bihar against Orissa at Cuttack in December 1967, after taking five for 68 in the first innings. His younger brother Rakesh Shukla, another leg-spinner, played one Test for India in 1982-83.

SINGH, CHARRAN KAMKARAN, who died on November 19, eight days short of his 80th birthday, was a left-arm spinner from Trinidad whose Test debut – against England at Port-of-Spain in 1959-60 – was marred by the first serious crowd disturbance at a match in the West Indies. England had made 382, and West Indies had struggled to 98 for seven in reply before Singh was run out for a duck. Angered mainly by the batting failure, many of the estimated 30,000 crowd – the largest for any sporting event in the Caribbean at the time – started throwing bottles, then streamed on to the ground. The riot squad and the fire brigade were summoned, and play was abandoned for the day. Cricket resumed next morning, and England rolled on to win by 256 runs, the only outright result of the series.

Singh's fleeting Test career ended after his second match, at Georgetown; his five wickets overall included Colin Cowdrey, Ted Dexter and Peter May. He had been selected after five-fors in his first two matches for Trinidad, against Jamaica in October 1959 and the England tourists the following January. "A 21-year-old messenger on the Aranguez Estates, Singh bowled 34 overs on a perfect batting pitch to take five for 57," wrote Alan Ross of that second game. "He has a gently curving flight with some late dip, though no evident sharpness of spin."

Singh's first-class career was brief: he appeared in only 11 matches, in which he took 48 wickets, including seven for 38 against Barbados at Port-of-Spain in 1960-61. He played Second XI cricket for Leicestershire and Northamptonshire in 1962, and later had several seasons in the leagues in Scotland, where he lived for 34 years before returning to Trinidad.

SMALES, KENNETH, died on March 10, aged 87. Of all Nottinghamshire's distinguished bowlers, only Ken Smales managed ten wickets in an innings. It happened over two days against Gloucestershire, in the first Championship match at the Erinoid Ground, Stroud, in June 1956, a month before Jim Laker's feat against the Australians at Old Trafford. Smales took four for 12 on the first evening, then returned on Monday morning to finish with ten for 66; *Wisden* put it down to "accuracy and judicious use of spin and change of pace". Smales was an off-spinner who sometimes had to switch to medium-pace and open the bowling when Nottinghamshire's resources were stretched. He arrived at Trent Bridge in 1951 after 13 appearances for Yorkshire, including five for 44 against the 1950 West Indians at Bradford. He played for Nottinghamshire for the next eight summers, and finished his career with 389 wickets at almost 31. His hat-trick against Lancashire at Trent Bridge in 1955 was the first for the county since the war.

At the end of the 1958 season he accepted an offer to become assistant secretary of Nottingham Forest, taking over as secretary three years later and becoming one of football's most respected administrators. He worked closely with manager Brian Clough during Forest's extraordinary run of success in the late 1970s; it was a partnership cemented by a shared love of cricket. Duncan Hamilton, who covered Forest for the *Nottingham Evening Post*, said: "You would go down to the City Ground in the summer, and find BC and Ken in the office watching the Test match on television together." The pair would sneak over to Trent Bridge whenever possible. Smales's signature was on football's first £1m transfer, when Forest signed Trevor Francis from Birmingham City in

Gripping yarns: Ken Smales learns the art of off-spin from Yorkshire's Ellis Robinson in 1949.

1979. He played club cricket for Bulwell and meticulously compiled their records, bringing the same attention to detail to a published complete record of Forest.

His heroics at Stroud had not been enough to earn victory after Gloucestershire fast bowler Frank McHugh took six wickets in Nottinghamshire's second innings. "I remember when we congratulated Ken on taking all ten wickets," recalled McHugh. "He surprised us by saying that it was only seven. When I queried this, he replied, 'Yes, seven batsmen and three rabbits, one of them a king rabbit.' Bomber Wells asked who this was, and Ken, with a smile on his face, pointed at me."

SMART, LAWRENCE MAXWELL, AM, died on October 13, aged 87. A seam-bowling all-rounder (and a state baseball pitcher) Lawrie Smart played five matches for South Australia in the 1950s, split by a seven-year absence in Britain doing postgraduate studies in dentistry. He became a Member of the Order of Australia in January 2015 for "significant service to dentistry in the field of clinical orthodontics".

SMITH, DONALD JAMES, who died on April 7, aged 81, was a low-slung but nippy seamer who took 73 wickets for Cambridge University, all but two of them in 1955 and 1956, when he won Blues. That included seven for 55 against Gloucestershire at Bristol in his first year, and match figures of eight for 72 against Warwickshire at Fenner's in 1956. By the time he went up to study law at Cambridge he had already been capped for Cheshire, and continued to play for them in the Minor Counties Championship throughout the 1960s, after rejecting offers from first-class sides. Smith took eight for 26 (and 13 for 78 in the match) against Staffordshire at Neston in 1960.

SMITH, VIVIAN IAN, died on August 25, aged 90. Ian Smith played nine Tests for South Africa, with diminishing success after his big-turning leg-breaks and dipping top-spinners claimed seven wickets on his debut, at Trent Bridge in 1947. His victims included Bill Edrich – twice bowled soon after reaching fifty – and Godfrey Evans in both innings. England escaped with a draw after following on, then won the next three Tests as Edrich and Denis Compton hit their stride in their record-breaking season. Smith was a fresh-faced 22-year-old at the time: John Arlott called him "almost delightfully the boy of the party, with the perfect rebellious schoolboy's forelock". He was hamstrung by the lack of a serviceable googly, but could be devastating on helpful pitches: he took seven for 65 at Derby, then ripped out six for one – including a hat-trick – in the second innings as Derbyshire folded for 32. That helped him top the tour averages with 58 wickets at 23. But, after that Test debut, eight further matches produced only five wickets, and on his second England tour in 1955 he was a back number behind off-spinner Hugh Tayfield. Smith had come to prominence in 1946-47, when 33 wickets in his first full season for Natal included nine for 88 against Border at Pietermaritzburg. He played on to 1957-58, and made his last Test appearance that season, dismissing Australia's Colin McDonald in both innings at Johannesburg.

STAPLETON, HAROLD VINCENT, who died on September 16, aged 100, was a left-handed all-rounder who played one first-class match for New South Wales, against South Australia at Adelaide in February 1941. Also skilled at tennis and table tennis, he was the oldest Australian first-class player at the time of his death, a position that passed to the Western Australia leg-spinner Dave Watt.

STEYN, GODFREY EDWARD, who died on June 14, aged 80, was a slow left-armer called into the South African squad after only three first-class matches in his debut season of 1957-58. He was named in the XII for the Second Test against Australia at Cape Town, a few days after taking seven for 32 there for Western Province against Border. "He does not spin the ball a great deal, but relies on an accurate length," wrote the South African batsman Roy McLean, who also noted "a strange hesitation at the top of his action when delivering his arm-ball." Steyn was summoned partly because Clive van Ryneveld, South Africa's captain and a leg-spinner, was recovering from a hand injury. But van Ryneveld passed himself fit, and Steyn was told he would be twelfth man – by whom, it is not clear.

McLean thought the selectors seemed aggrieved that Steyn had been informed already, as if they had intended to choose him in the XI. He never did play a Test, even though he took another seven-for in his next match, against Eastern Province. Steyn played on at provincial level for various teams until 1963-64, finishing with 92 wickets at less than 20.

THWAITES, Dr IAN GUY, who died on September 30, aged 72, played for Cambridge University in 1963 and 1964 under the captaincy of Mike Brearley. He won a Blue in his second year, during which he made his highest score, 61, against MCC at Lord's. He later played for Sussex's Second XI. After a spell as a flying doctor in Rhodesia, Thwaites worked as a GP in Horsham from 1970 to 1990, before concentrating on sports medicine; his patients included Christopher Martin-Jenkins.

TORRENS, WARWICK WILLIAM, who died on August 18, aged 80, was an indefatigable researcher into the history of Queensland cricket, particularly its early years. He produced several books and pamphlets, of which his *Queensland Cricket and Cricketers 1862–1981* is arguably the most important.

TOWNLEY, DAVID CHARLES, who died on June 29, aged 63, was a hard-working advocate for blind cricket during years of great change. Born in Hereford, where he played mainstream club cricket, Townley moved to London for art college, and worked in several fields until his eyesight began to fail him in his mid-forties, eventually leaving him with light perception only. But he continued to paint and take photographs, and taught art to visually impaired children. He discovered blind cricket with London Metro; his 46 against Essex at Edgbaston in 2009 remains the highest score by a B1 (totally blind) player in the final of the domestic 40-over competition. And, in the inaugural Blind Ashes of 2004, Townley's 40 not out in the fourth match was crucial to England winning the series 3–2. He helped set up Blind Cricket England & Wales as a dedicated charity to run the game and, as chairman from 2007, was quick to embrace the ECB's increased support for disability cricket, realising the greater opportunities it could give the elite players. In later years, Townley – clad in trademark black shirt and Panama hat – made several trips to the West Indies with Cricket for Change, and was the first Englishman appointed president of the World Blind Cricket Council; some felt other countries did not give him the support he deserved. After his death, a round of league fixtures was postponed, and the Twenty20 competition renamed in his honour.

TURNER, FRANCIS MICHAEL, MBE, died on July 21, aged 80. Mike Turner's title at Leicestershire changed over time – from secretary to secretary/manager to chief executive – but for 33 years there was never much doubt who was in charge at Grace Road. He exercised such control that he would sometimes forget even the pretence of collectivity, and refer to the club as "I". He got away with it because he was a brilliant administrator who improved every aspect of Leicestershire: their cricket, finances, facilities and reputation.

Turner was a Leicester boy who tried to make his way at the club as a leg-spinning all-rounder. He played ten first-class games in six years, but was about to give up when he was invited upstairs to help out in the office. Within two years he had studied enough about business on day release to beat off 86 outside applicants and be chosen, at 25, as the county game's youngest-ever secretary. And just two years later, in 1962, he invited three other Midland counties to join in an experimental mini-knockout cup, a success which persuaded Lord's to initiate the Gillette Cup the following season.

Success on the field took a little longer, but in 1966 Turner appointed Tony Lock captain after a few games the previous year, a role he fulfilled with such laughing, snarling exuberance that in 1967 Leicestershire finished joint-second, at that stage their best position. After Lock came Ray Illingworth and a host of other retreads and discards, ready to be refurbished and given a new lease of life. For the rest of his time the club were almost always competitive: in the mid-1970s they won four one-day trophies in six seasons and, in 1975, their first Championship. "He was a talented guy who knew his stuff and he made good signings," recalled Martin Johnson, who covered almost half the Turner era for the *Leicester Mercury*. "And he had his hands on everything. If the flush broke in the ladies' toilets, he had to know. He would bollock people for planting the tulips the wrong way." Turner was also very skilful at making sure he could declare an annual profit, even if it was tiny.

He was often seen as half of a double act with his namesake and counterpart at Northamptonshire, Ken Turner, who adopted similar techniques to keep a small club afloat. But whereas Ken was gruff and did not worry about tulips, Mike was normally urbane and had a better sense of public relations. But his power started to grate on a new generation of committee men. In 1990 he was obliged to bring in a cricket manager: Bob Simpson was chosen after Illingworth turned him down. This did not arrest the team's decline, or halt the outflow of talent now leaving Leicestershire. Internal relations grew more strained, and Turner was forced out in 1993. He remained active in cricket, and specialised in helping clubs large and small get access to Lottery and other funds. The indoor school at Grace Road bears his name.

TYSON, FRANK HOLMES, died on September 27, aged 85. Long before the name Tyson became associated with heavyweight boxing, it struck terror into the heart of Australians. Frank Tyson reached his fast-bowling peak for just two Tests in the space of three weeks over Christmas and New Year 1954-55. But what a peak it was: 19 wickets to give England come-from-behind wins at Sydney and Melbourne, and set up Len Hutton's team for one of the most resonant of all Ashes victories. And, though his descent was unexpectedly rapid and his subsequent career anticlimactic, his place in the pantheon was never disputed. Everyone who saw him on that tour, and in flashes of ferocity before and after, recognised him as one of the quickest of all time.

Tyson came from Middleton outside Manchester and learned to play on rough wasteland near his home. Lancashire rejected him after an ill-starred trial in which he turned up late because of a rail strike, then pulled a muscle. In any case he was distracted by national service and making his way from grammar school to Durham University. However, Northamptonshire's Australian import, Jock Livingston, happened to play against him in a game in Staffordshire, made a not-exactly-legal approach, and reeled him in. Obliged to sit out the Championship for two years, Tyson bowled his opening first-class over against the 1952 Indians: the first ball swung so much it was taken by first slip; the next four were breathtakingly fast; the sixth had Pankaj Roy caught behind. He took no more wickets in the game, and did not reappear for nearly a year. But word was out, and it got louder the second time, because the opponents were the Australians and the Saturday crowd was around 14,000, the biggest in Northamptonshire's history. Running in almost from the sightscreen, and with the wicketkeeper, Keith Andrew, standing almost as far back, Tyson had two wickets in his first over: Colin McDonald hobbled off lbw, having been hit inside the pad; Graeme Hole was bowled with his bat still in mid-air. The moment passed – Australia won in two days – but again the memory lingered.

Tyson was available for the Championship after that, and continued to unnerve top batsmen in short bursts. In 1954, he was mentioned as a possible for the winter Ashes, despite concerns he lacked stamina and control. The matter appears to have been settled when Northamptonshire played Middlesex at Lord's, and Tyson sent Bill Edrich to hospital with a blow on the head. Tyson helped him into the Pavilion but, when Edrich returned next morning, swollen and bandaged, he was greeted with another short one which hit him above the heart. When this story reached the unsqueamish Hutton, it is said to have made him think this was precisely the sort of bowler he wanted. A week later the squad for Australia was named, with two surprises: Tyson, who edged out Fred Trueman, and Andrew, his county team-mate.

The announcement was made before the Oval Test against Pakistan, when England complacently fielded a weakened team, and lost. But Tyson made a good impression with four for 35 on the opening day. He and Andrew went off to Australia, armed with their cine cameras like wide-eyed schoolboys. They both suffered with the others when England

Start of the journey: Frank Tyson waits at Northampton before catching the train to join the 1954-55 England tour party.

were mashed at Brisbane. Andrew, who had deputised for a sickly Godfrey Evans, would not be given another Test for nearly nine years; but Tyson was not blamed and, when he took six for 68 against Victoria, Hutton had renewed confidence that he possessed a lethal weapon. He used him only in brief spells; Tyson, with help from Alf Gover, who was covering the tour as a journalist, cut down his run and concentrated on yorkers not bouncers, which was his inclination anyway.

Come the Sydney Test, there was a bonus: Tyson got cross. No mug with the bat, and in at No. 7 ahead of the out-of-form Evans, he was hit by a bouncer from Ray Lindwall and rendered briefly unconscious. At 72 for two on the fourth evening, chasing 223, Australia were on top. But Andrew always said his mate bowled better when angry. In his second over next morning, Tyson yorked Jim Burke and Graeme Hole; later he held on – just – to a swirling catch to get Richie Benaud off Bob Appleyard, and soon the score was 145 for nine, with the last man Bill Johnston joining Neil Harvey, who was in majestic form. Harvey nursed the strike, and both Tyson and his partner Brian Statham were fading. The score crept upwards until, at last, Tyson had Johnston facing at the start of an over. There was a leg-side glance to Evans: England by 38 runs, the series all-square, Tyson six for 85 and ten for 130 in the match. A star was born: "Typhoon" Tyson. Two days later he made a Christmas Eve pilgrimage to Harold Larwood's house in the suburbs. "When you've got 50,000 Aussies shouting at you," his great predecessor told him, "you know you've got 'em worried."

The Melbourne Test began on New Year's Eve. The pitch was difficult but England, 40 behind on first innings, set a target of 240. Again Australia started the final morning hopefully, at 75 for two. But this time there was less tension, and Tyson was even more irresistible: seven for 27, victims of pace, control and, when necessary, cunning. He was a vital, if less spectacular, contributor in Adelaide, where England clinched the series, and was later far too hot for New Zealand to handle (11 for 90 in the two Tests). But, the world being a bigger place in those days, he was largely insulated from the response back home. "You think you've bowled reasonably well," he reflected from retirement. "When, three months later, you get off an aircraft and there are 50 pressmen to meet you, you think 'What *have* I done?'"

And for a while the wickets kept coming at the same rate: seven for 44 against Worcestershire on his hero's return to Northampton in May 1955; and six for 28 in the second innings of the opening Test against South Africa, including a final blast of five for five. He was one of *Wisden's* Five Cricketers of the Year. But, despite a handful of triumphs, the rest of his career lacked the earlier drama.

Tyson believed (as Hutton did) that he was ruined by the Northampton pitches, prepared to suit their array of spinners. But he also became susceptible to injuries. He was chosen for the 1956-57 tour of South Africa, and for the disastrous return to Australia in 1958-59, but was applauded from a Test match field only once more, when he took six for 40 at Port Elizabeth, on a shocking pitch and in a losing cause. He still had his moments in county cricket too, notably when he destroyed Glamorgan with seven for 25 at the Arms Park in 1957 – backing up Andrew's theory about making him angry: someone had snipped his tie in half as a prank. That was the only year he took 100 wickets.

Before the storm: Frank Tyson is helped from the SCG. Next day he bowled England to victory.

Having a degree in English literature, Tyson was, for his era, a most unusual professional. And he had other ambitions. He retired in 1960 and taught for a while in Northampton before taking the Larwood route to Australia, along with his Aussie wife Ursula. Unlike Larwood, he had no animosity to overcome: he had never attracted controversy. And he was a thoughtful, affable and kindly man. He taught at Carey Grammar School in Melbourne, nurturing scholars in English, French and history, as well as cricketers like Graham Yallop. In 1975 he became Victoria's first coaching director, staying for 12 years before retiring to the Gold Coast. Between whiles, he was a skilful and sympathetic cricket broadcaster. He wrote well, producing a succession of books including, in 2004, the charming diary he had quietly written 50 years earlier during the time of his life. In retirement, he took up oil painting.

Tyson was not a big drinker, but he was one of those men on whom a little had a remarkable effect. In 1978 the teenage Jonathan Agnew was sent to Australia on a fast-bowling scholarship and billeted with the Tysons. After barely a sniff of beer, Agnew recalled, the amiability would suddenly vanish. "You think yer a fast bowler, do yer?" he would roar and rush out into the garden. "He'd roll up his sleeves and be racing round the garden, bowling the ball into the hedgerows and goodness knows where else, like a man possessed."

VAN SCHOOR, RAYMOND, died on November 20, aged 25, five days after collapsing during Namibia's match against Free State at Windhoek in the South African one-day competition. Namibia were 16 short of their eventual victory when, on 15 not out, van Schoor fell into the arms of his batting partner, Nicolaas Scholtz, and was rushed to hospital. He had suffered a stroke. A batsman who often kept wicket, van Schoor had played a record 265 matches for Namibia in all formats since his debut at 17 in 2007, appearing five times alongside his father, Melt. "He was a sensational fielder and could basically do anything," said the former national coach Doug Watson. "If you asked him to play wicky, he'd probably be the best wicketkeeper in Namibia. He was just as brilliant in the slips as he was at backward point." Van Schoor was the player of the tournament in the World Twenty20 Qualifier early in 2012, scoring 323 runs as Namibia won all seven of their group games. He also hit five first-class centuries, including 157 – during an opening stand of 348 with Ewald Steenkamp – against Bermuda in the ICC Intercontinental Shield at Windhoek in April 2010.

WEBB, ALVIN BERNARD, died on January 25, aged 79. Al Webb was an American journalist who was decorated for bravery during the Vietnam War, after being injured by shrapnel while trying to help a wounded marine. Later assignments included Guyana, where he reported the Jonestown Massacre in 1978: "The exact number [of dead] turned out to be 913," he said later. "It's a number I've never forgotten." Webb had first spied cricket during a posting to London, and eventually returned there to live. He rekindled his fascination for the game, becoming a member of MCC and qualifying as an umpire. "It became his passion," said his wife Elizabeth. "He went to all the big matches".

WELD, WILFRID JOSEPH, JP, DL, who died while on holiday in Tahiti on December 3, aged 81, was a long-time supporter of Hampshire, joining their committee in 1973, serving as president in 1990 and, from 2002, as patron. The head of the Lulworth Estate in Dorset, which had been in his family since 1641, Weld was hugely influential in Hampshire's move from Northlands Road to the Rose Bowl in 2001. "I have never known Hampshire cricket without Wilfrid," said county chairman Rod Bransgrove. "I will miss his enthusiasm, ebullience and good humour."

WESTAWAY, COLIN EDWARD, died on October 15, aged 79. A leg-spinner who took six for 88 against New South Wales at the Gabba in 1960-61 – his victims included Brian Booth, Neil Harvey and Grahame Thomas – Col Westaway was poorly treated by Queensland's selectors, who cast him aside for good two years later. He was a member of a cricket-playing family who owned a pineapple farm at Moggill, near Brisbane.

WHITCOMBE, PHILIP ARTHUR, who died on August 11, aged 92, was a 6ft 6in seamer briefly mentioned as an England possible during the fast-bowling drought of the immediate post-war years. His name came to wider attention when, playing for Middlesex at Lord's in 1948, he dismissed Don Bradman for six; in his previous match, for Oxford University against Yorkshire, Whitcombe had twice bowled Len Hutton. "He took full advantage of his great height, and used the wicket most intelligently," wrote Bradman. "Whilst there was any moisture and greenness in it he made the ball move towards slips and to the leg side. One of the latter deliveries found the inside edge of my bat." But the ever-shrewd Don also spotted a potential problem: "Sometimes these extremely tall athletes find the strain of bowling too severe."

And so it proved: bothered by injuries to ankle and shoulder, Whitcombe played only one more county game, later that season. He did return to Oxford to win a third Blue in 1949, and finished with 80 wickets for them at 19. In 1948, not long after outfoxing Bradman, he had cranked up his inswinger to good effect for a career-best seven for 51 – including future Test players Trevor Bailey, Hubert Doggart and Doug Insole – as Oxford won the Varsity Match by an innings. In the 1950s, though, constrained by those injuries and the need to work for a living – first as a shipping agent, then as a Surrey sheep farmer – Whitcombe confined his first-class appearances to MCC and the Free Foresters, for whom he claimed five top-order wickets for 62 against Cambridge in 1954. Cricket had long been part of his life: his father, a major-general who played briefly for Essex, had taught him to bowl as a boy, aiming at a handkerchief placed on a good length on the lawn at home. Whitcombe married the daughter of Lord Clydesmuir, the last Governor of Bombay.

WIGHT, PETER BERNARD, who died on December 31, aged 85, was one of the most attractive batsmen in English county cricket in the late 1950s and early '60s, his runs a vital part of a Somerset revival that followed four successive years at the foot of the Championship table.

With Scottish and Portuguese ancestry, he was part of a large sporting family in Georgetown, British Guiana. His cousin Vibart was vice-captain of the West Indies team that toured England in 1928; his brother Leslie played one Test, at Georgetown in 1952-53; and other family members represented British Guiana (now Guyana) at cricket, hockey, tennis and football.

In March 1951, the 20-year-old Wight made his debut, against Jamaica, scoring 39 before being given caught behind, to his annoyance. It was his only match in the West Indies: within days he was on a cargo boat to England, linking up with fellow countryman Bruce Pairaudeau at Burnley. He planned to become an engineer, but England did not impress him – the cold, the rationing, the outside toilets – and his employer refused to give him time off for his night-school exams. However, his cricket prospered in the Lancashire League, and he met his future wife Joyce.

"Why don't you play for Somerset?" his sister's husband suggested when he visited them in Bridgwater in 1953. "They've got no players." Next day they were on the bus to

Lovely ring: Peter Wight in 1958.

Sport & General/PA Photos

Taunton, and soon enough he was making his debut against the touring Australians. Out for a duck, and feeling low during a skittles evening, he was consoled by Richie Benaud: "Don't worry, you'll get a century in the second innings." And he did.

A waif-like figure, Wight gained a reputation for hypochondria. "I kept fit running down the chemist for him," one twelfth man recalled. But, with a bat in his hands, he was no weakling. "His perfect timing," wrote John Arlott, "invests his most delicate strokes with a power remarkable for one so slightly built." His team-mate Graham Atkinson recalled: "There was always a lovely ring to his bat. I used to stand at the other end and drool."

His way of playing the quicks – backing away and freeing up his arms – gained him an unwarranted reputation for being vulnerable against pace. Yet at Blackpool in 1959 he made a fine 106 against Brian Statham; and, at The Oval in 1956, when Peter Loader skittled Somerset for 159 and 196, he hit 62 and 128, both unbeaten. Only Fred Trueman consistently got the better of him. When, in 1962 the Yorkshire captain Vic Wilson dropped Trueman for

arriving late at Taunton, Wight celebrated with the second double-century of his career. In all, he hit 16,965 first-class runs for Somerset, a total exceeded only by Harold Gimblett. He also enjoyed occasional success as an off-spinner, most notably at Chesterfield in 1957 when, on as fifth change, he won the match with six for 29.

After his retirement he set up a cricket school in Bath, where he spent his winters coaching, and became an umpire, standing for 30 summers until 1995, but never in an international; in fact he never saw an international day's cricket in his life. His total of first-class appearances in England (328 as player, 567 as umpire) is a post-war record. Never losing his high-pitched Caribbean accent, he was not one for the coarser aspects of

English cricket – the drinking and the swearing – and perhaps as a result his contribution has been undervalued. "He's done so much for cricket," Somerset's Brian Langford once said. "He doesn't get the recognition he deserves."

WILLIAMS, ALVADON BASIL, died on October 25, aged 65. Known as "Shotgun" for his approach to opening the batting for Jamaica and West Indies, Basil Williams played seven Tests in the absence of those signed up by Kerry Packer for World Series Cricket. He started superbly, with a rapid 100 in the second innings of his debut, against Australia at Georgetown in April 1978. He added a more sedate 111 against India at Calcutta in December, and averaged 39 overall – but had to make way on the return of Gordon Greenidge and Desmond Haynes when WSC was disbanded the following year.

That 118-ball 100 at Bourda typified his attitude. "A fascinating duel between [Jeff] Thomson and Williams held the crowd's attention," reported the *West Indies Cricket Annual*. "Although beaten several times for pace, Williams kept on going for his shots, cutting and driving with relish and having 11 fours in 60 when stumps were drawn on the second day." He collected eight more boundaries within an hour on the third morning to reach his hundred, then hooked the next ball, from Wayne Clark, straight to fine leg.

Strong off the back foot, and an especially ferocious cutter, Williams made five first-class centuries, the highest 126 not out against Karnataka on the 1978-79 Indian tour. After retirement he became a Jamaican selector, board member and team manager. One of his sons, Germaine, became an entertainer in a different sphere in the United States, as the popular rap artist Canibus.

WILLIAMS, KENNETH MARK, died on June 4, aged 70. Mark Williams was a cricket-loving naval-officer-turned-diplomat who became chief executive of the Lord's Taverners and an MCC committee member. His diplomatic tasks included persuading prime ministers John Major and Bob Hawke to open the batting together in a match against schoolboys during a Commonwealth summit in Zimbabwe. He also wrote about Zimbabwe for *Wisden 1993*. Williams ran the Taverners between 1999 and 2007, ensuring cricket remained at the heart of the charity. "He was very efficient, very committed," said the former chairman Neil Durden-Smith. "He ate, drank and slept the Taverners." Later he became an equally passionate opponent of the MCC establishment in the complex long-running argument about the land above the railway tunnels at the Nursery End. In 2015 he failed to regain his place on the committee when the club resurrected an old system of putting stars on the ballot paper beside their four preferred candidates; this was interpreted as a move to keep Williams out. However, his supporters believe the resulting furore helped bring about a change of tack, even though he did not live to see it.

WOOD, MARTIN JOHN, who died on February 10, aged 66, was one of the first specialist sellers of cricket books, turning a youthful passion for collecting into a business, which started when he sold duplicate copies of *Wisden*. By 1970 he had filled the basement of his parents' home in Sevenoaks with cricket paraphernalia, and became a familiar figure at county grounds, often lugging books around for signature by the authors to increase their value. He was also a diverting presence at book sales, occasionally surprising suave auctioneers by barking out a bid for an unexpected amount: "He could be very animated in the auction-room," remembered David Frith.

Wood's distinctive shuffling gait was the result of a polio-like disease which afflicted him from the age of eight, but was never satisfactorily diagnosed. It left him with left-side paralysis; but to visit his book-lined basement and watch him expertly wrap a parcel using one good arm and one good leg was spellbinding. He was a shrewd negotiator, once crossing swords with Robert Maxwell about the price of a complete set of *Wisden*: Wood never blinked, and Maxwell paid up in full. After the death of his father, he moved to a nearby bungalow, where the garage was fitted with shelves and filled with books. But he never mastered the internet, which changed the habits of buyers, and ill health began to intrude. Still, as his brother Andrew said: "He never complained about his lot, and his bravery was inspirational."

WOODCOCK, ROY GORDON, who died on August 15, aged 81, was a left-arm spinner who won Blues at Oxford in 1957 and 1958. Forced to operate on what were in the main good batting tracks, Woodcock kept the runs down, but was not a prolific wicket-taker. He never took five wickets in an innings, although he did manage four lots of four, his best return including three past and future Test players – Bill Edrich, Eric Russell and John Murray – against Middlesex in the Parks in 1957. Woodcock was also a useful lower-order batsman, who made 57 against the New Zealand tourists the following summer. He never appeared in county cricket, although he did play a few matches for Worcestershire's Second XI. He taught geography at his old school, Worcester Royal Grammar, and wrote several walking guides, including one to the nearby Malvern Hills.

WYATT, JOHN LEONARD, died on January 29, aged 95. Len Wyatt was part of the first Northern Districts side to compete in New Zealand's Plunket Shield, in 1956-57, and was their oldest surviving player. His four matches all came that season, which he rounded off with 54, opening against a Wellington side containing several Test players. Wyatt played club cricket until he was 59, and claimed to have scored 42,175 runs, with 128 centuries, and taken 1,165 wickets. His brother, Ivan, played first-class cricket for Auckland.

YAWAR SAEED, who died on October 21, aged 80, was the manager of Pakistan's troubled tour of England in 2010, which was tarnished by the spot-fixing controversy, in which Mohammad Asif and Mohammad Amir, under the instruction of their captain Salman Butt, bowled deliberate no-balls in the Lord's Test. Yawar saw the tour out, but stepped down shortly afterwards, ending a career in cricket administration which had featured long stints as a board member and selector, and managing overseas tours, including the only Pakistan team to win the annual triangular one-day series in Australia, in 1996-97. Yawar's father, Mian Mohammad Saeed, had been the first captain of independent Pakistan, skippering them in unofficial Tests – but he was sidelined by the autocratic Abdul Hafeez Kardar, who may have stymied Yawar's international career too.

A handy medium-pacer, he had two seasons with Somerset. According to Peter Roebuck's county history, "Yawar was apt to ask colleagues, 'Don't you think I'm quick?' but wisely he rarely waited for the answer." He took 76 wickets for them, including a career-best five for 61 against the 1955 South African tourists. The previous year he had played against the Pakistan team on their first Test tour of England. He took five wickets in the match at Taunton, but was upset his compatriots did not speak to him, apparently under orders from Kardar, their captain. It might not have helped that Pakistan's star bowler Fazal Mahmood, with whom Kardar had an uneasy relationship, was his brother-in-law. Yawar played only nine first-class matches at home in Pakistan, although he did claim five for 133 for Punjab against the 1955-56 MCC A team, and five for 89 the following season to help Punjab beat Karachi Whites in the Quaid-e-Azam Trophy final.

ZAFAR ALTAF, who died on December 5, aged 74, was secretary of the Board of Control for Cricket in Pakistan between 1972 and 1975, and later the board's chairman and a national selector. He was assistant manager of Pakistan's tour of England in 1974, and manager in 1999, when they reached the World Cup final. He had also been a fine batsman, scoring 99 in his third match and 111 in the fourth, in 1958-59; two years later he toured India under Fazal Mahmood's captaincy, but did not play a Test. For Lahore Greens against Bahawalpur in the Ayub Trophy in 1965-66, Zafar scored 268, and shared a stand of 346 with Majid Khan, who made 241. An economist, he joined Pakistan's civil service, and was the Federal Secretary for Agriculture for ten years.

ZEESHAN MOHAMMED, who was 18, died after he was struck by the ball in a club game in Pakistan on January 25. "He was hit in the chest by a fast bowler while batting and collapsed on the pitch," said a doctor at the Orangi Town hospital near Karachi.

The obituaries section includes those who died, or whose deaths were noted, in 2015. Wisden always welcomes information about those who might be included: please send details to almanack@wisden.com, or to John Wisden & Co, 13 Old Aylesfield, Golden Pot, Alton, Hampshire GU34 4BY.

BRIEFLY NOTED

The following, whose deaths were noted during 2015, played or umpired in a small number of first-class (fc) matches.

	Died	Age	Main team
AHMED, Kadir	20.5.2015	82	Madhya Pradesh

Slow left-armer who played three Ranji Trophy matches, but failed to take a wicket.

| **ARLOW**, William Beattie, BEM | 7.5.2015 | 72 | Umpire |

Official who stood in two fc matches in Ireland, and at the 1998 Commonwealth Games.

| **BHATNAGAR**, Kant Swarup | 28.6.2015 | 89 | Holkar |

Although a bowler, made 63 in ninth-wicket stand of 157 on debut against Bihar in 1948-49.

| **BOSE**, Sujit | 25.4.2015 | 80 | Bengal |

All-rounder who played 11 fc matches in late 1950s: 50 against Rajasthan in 1958-59.

| **CAPRANI**, Joseph Desmond | 16.7.2015 | 95 | Ireland |

First to 10,000 runs for Leinster: five fc matches, HS 44 v Scotland in 1955. Later coached in Dublin.

| **CHAMBERS**, Thomas William | 8.6.2015 | 83 | Eastern Province |

Left-hand batsman who played one fc match in 1956-57, scoring three and seven against Border.

| **DANIEL**, Desmond Ashley | 2.3.2015 | 72 | Orange Free State |

Nine fc matches in 1960s: 55 v Natal B in 1966-67; killed on bicycle in Sharjah, where he worked.

| **DRAKE**, Alan | 2.7.2015 | 76 | Umpire |

Sydney umpire who stood in eight Sheffield Shield matches in the late 1970s.

| **DURING**, Daniel Nicholas | 29.4.2015 | 83 | Border |

Medium-paced all-rounder: eight fc matches in the 1950s; 51 against Griqualand West in 1954-55.

| **GRAHAM**, Peter Colin | 17.4.2015 | 60 | Northumberland |

Fast bowler: 9-37 against Suffolk at Ipswich in 1991. One fc match for Minor Counties in 1994.

| **GRIFFIN**, Neville Featherstone | 17.12.2014 | 89 | Surrey |

Prolific batsman for South Hampstead CC; 83 in only fc match, for Surrey v Oxford U. in 1963.*

| **HOLTEN**, Charles Valentine | 14.1.2015 | 87 | Victoria |

Successful club batsman who played five fc games in early 1950s; 59 v Queensland in 1952-53.*

| **KESHAVAMURTHY**, M. S. | 5.7.2015 | c81 | Umpire |

Stood in 11 Ranji Trophy matches in India from 1979-80 to 1987-88.

| **KRISHNAPRASAD**, Venkataraman | 27.11.2015 | 69 | Mysore |

One fc match in 1969-70, captained by his brother, V. Subramanya, who played nine Tests for India.

| **LAKAY**, Neville Matthew | 2.11.2015 | 77 | Western Province |

Prominent non-white batsman who played one match now considered first-class, in 1971-72.

| **LINDLEY-JONES**, Hugh Mawdesley | 10.8.2015 | 95 | Europeans |

One fc match in India in 1942-43; a member of the Bromley club in Kent for 76 years.

| **O'REILLY**, Ronald | 27.1.2015 | 75 | Umpire |

Irish official: stood in match against the South African tourists at Clontarf in 2003.

| **PRABHAKARAN**, K. K. | 8.5.2015 | c75 | Kerala |

Medium-pacer who played one fc match, against Madras in 1960-61.

| **ROBERTS**, Allen Christian | 6.9.2015 | 92 | Auckland |

Medium-pacer whose two fc matches included one for New Zealand Services in England in 1945.

| **SADER**, Ismail ("Chota") | 23.1.2015 | 71 | Transvaal |

Wicketkeeper-batsman who played three fc matches for Transvaal's non-white team in 1972-73.

| **SATHE**, Mukund Sripath | 27.11.2015 | 78 | Maharashtra |

Medium-pacer who failed to take a wicket in only fc match, against Gujarat in 1958-59.

| **SHARMA**, Surendra Kumar | 17.4.2015 | 62 | Umpire |

Mumbai official who stood in 16 fc matches from 1981-82; son of Test umpire H. P. Sharma.

| **TURNER**, Brian | 27.12.2015 | 77 | Yorkshire |

Medium-pacer: two fc matches in 1960–61. Son of Cyril (200 matches for Yorkshire 1925–46).

	Died	Age	Main team
VENKOBA RAO, V. R.	19.6.2015	89	Mysore

Played two Ranji Trophy matches in late 1940s, scoring 1, 1, 13 and 0.

WHITE, Peter	15.2.2015	70	Umpire

Irish official: ten internationals, including Ireland's victory over West Indies at Stormont in 2004.

WOOD, Russell Brown ("Rusty")	1.7.2015	85	Gloucestershire

Wicketkeeper: eight fc matches in 1951-52, scoring 48 on debut against Cambridge University.

WYLIE, Robert Norman	8.9.2015	67	Central Districts

All-rounder who played five fc matches in 1973-74: scored 55* v Otago.

A LIFE IN NUMBERS

	Runs	Avge	Wkts	Avge		Runs	Avge	Wkts	Avge
Afzaal Ahmed	4,010	30.61	33	25.90	**Kanitkar**, H. S.	5,006	42.78	1	54.00
Amm, P. G.	6,860	35.00	–	–	Karia, P. D.	9	9.00	0	–
Appleyard, R.	776	8.52	708	15.48	Kissell, R. K.	372	31.00	–	–
Atkinson, G.	17,654	31.13	5	52.00	**Kline**, L. F.	559	8.60	276	27.39
Austin, R. A.	2,097	33.82	73	31.21	La Frantz, E. C.	13	6.50	0	–
Azmat Rana	6,001	47.62	1	134.00	Lester, E. I.	10,912	34.20	3	53.33
Barber, R. T.	2,002	23.01	0	–	Lucas, F. C.	62	15.50	0	–
Barrable, P. R.	626	22.35	3	40.33	Martin, E. J.	4,086	22.82	–	–
Baruah. H.	289	20.64	50	26.94	Meyer, B. J.	5,367	14.19	0	–
Benaud, R.	11,719	36.50	945	24.73	Minnaar, N. P.	771	19.76	2	32.00
Bilbie, A. R.	291	11.19	–	–	**Morris**, A. R.	12,614	53.67	12	49.33
Bishop, J.	51	–	–	–	Neethling, J. J.	266	19.00	19	27.26
Blake, D. E.	2,909	24.24	–	–	Pandit, B. J.	25	25.00	–	–
Brailsford, F. C.	41	8.20	1	2.00	Payne, I. A.	1,152	37.16	–	–
Brown, W. M.	10	3.33	0	–	**Petherick**, P. J.	200	5.88	189	24.47
Bulbulia, A. S.	63	12.60	–	–	Philips, S. I.	156	14.18	0	–
Burrows, A.	1,269	37.32	4	14.75	Ralph, L. H. R.	3,763	16.87	460	24.02
Byfield, A. S.	251	27.88	2	21.50	Ramprasad, K. M.	23	5.75	11	16.45
Camacho, G. S.	4,079	34.86	8	27.00	Reynolds, B. L.	18,824	28.01	4	71.00
Campbell, I. P.	482	15.06	–	–	Rice, C. E. B.	26,331	40.95	930	22.49
Close, D. B.	34,994	33.26	1,171	26.42	**Ridgway**, F.	4,081	11.00	1,069	23.74
Corbett, P. L.	2,232	32.82	1	121.00	Rigg, H. W. H.	431	23.94	2	56.50
Davidson, W. W.	118	6.94	–	–	Rosendorff, N.	5,014	42.49	68	37.82
Dewes, J. G.	8,564	41.77	2	35.50	Ryan, M.	682	7.49	413	22.92
Dindar, N.	970	20.20	64	20.34	Saliwa, M. N.	169	8.89	67	36.25
Drummer, F. T.	684	25.33	121	25.24	**Shrimpton**, M. J. F.	5,812	29.80	81	29.45
Duckmanton, A. G.	387	14.88	32	23.75	Shukla, L.	4,312	33.68	386	21.00
Duffy, G. A. A.	317	15.09	15	28.40	**Singh**, C. K.	102	8.50	48	23.93
Ellis, R. S.	47	2.93	78	26.53	Smales, K.	2,512	14.43	389	30.70
Fawcett, G. W.	56	8.00	–	–	Smart, L. M.	156	19.50	3	44.66
Fenner, M. D.	708	14.75	1	1.00	Smith, D. J.	128	8.00	73	31.46
Fletcher, D. G. W.	14,461	30.25	0	–	**Smith**, V. I.	547	10.32	365	22.55
Foord, C. W.	125	6.25	128	27.10	Stapleton, H. V.	1	1.00	0	–
Furlonge, C. D.	551	22.95	0	–	Steyn, G. E.	529	18.24	92	19.71
Govindan, I. V.	331	18.38	18	30.11	Thwaites, I. G.	769	22.61	4	31.75
Graveney, J. K. R.	2,034	14.42	173	27.85	Turner, F. M.	196	17.81	3	74.33
Graveney, T. W.	47,793	44.91	80	37.96	**Tyson**, F. H.	4,103	17.09	767	20.89
Griffiths, S. S.	76	5.42	74	24.68	van Schoor, R.	4,303	27.40	28	46.85
Griffiths, W. H.	137	3.91	102	31.47	Westaway, C. E.	207	13.80	52	32.75
Hasan Jamil	4,230	29.58	204	30.77	Whitcombe, P. A.	956	18.74	112	22.22
Hilton, C.	665	7.47	321	28.15	**Wight**, P. B.	17,773	33.09	68	33.26
Hodgson, P.	65	9.28	39	24.25	**Williams**, A. B.	2,702	36.02	0	–
Hurn, B. M.	842	21.05	56	37.91	Woodcock, R. G.	779	18.11	53	33.83
Hutchison, P. J.	80	8.00	20	41.10	Wyatt, J. L.	163	23.28	–	–
Iqbal Sheikh	816	21.47	3	38.66	Yawar Saeed	1,547	15.47	106	34.05
Jadeja, L. R.	378	9.45	74	31.06	Zafar Altaf	2,448	32.21	8	37.87
Jaspal Singh	450	32.14	33	39.66					

Test players are in bold; their career figures can be found on page 1390.

Bishop made four catches and no stumpings; Blake 91 and 30; Campbell 25 and 16; Davidson 34 and six; Fawcett eight and four; Fenner 47 and 13; Kanitkar 70 and 20; Meyer 707 and 119; van Schoor 161 and six.

PART THREE

English
International
Cricket

THE ENGLAND TEAM IN 2015

A Dickens of a time

George Dobell

Consistently inconsistent and reliably unreliable. Charles Dickens might not have had England's cricketers in mind when he wrote his line about the best of times and the worst of times. But, before their dramatic triumph at Johannesburg in January 2016 threatened to change the narrative, it neatly described their fortunes in 2015. No year that includes an Ashes victory can be all bad, though a fifth series win against Australia since 2005 meant the novelty was in danger of wearing off; certainly, the days when it masked other faults were gone. But, over the year, England won six Tests, lost six more, and emerged victorious from only one of the four completed series they contested. The success in South Africa, who were knocked off their No. 1 perch, at least meant they would approach the new summer with a spring in their step.

But the inconsistencies of 2015 could not be easily dismissed, beginning with their failure in the World Cup. While that was hardly new – since reaching

ENGLAND IN 2015

	Played	Won	Lost	Drawn/No result
Tests	14	6	6	2
One-day internationals	26	12	13	1
Twenty20 internationals	5	5	–	–

JANUARY FEBRUARY	Triangular ODI tournament (in Australia) v Australia and India	(page 273)
MARCH	ICC World Cup (in Australia and New Zealand)	(page 860)
APRIL MAY	3 Tests (a) v West Indies 1 ODI (a) v Ireland	(page 283) (page 299)
JUNE	2 Tests, 5 ODIs and 1 T20I (h) v New Zealand	(page 300)
JULY AUGUST SEPTEMBER	5 Tests, 5 ODIs and 1 T20I (h) v Australia	(page 327)
OCTOBER NOVEMBER	3 Tests, 4 ODIs and 3 T20Is (a) v Pakistan (in UAE)	(page 375)
DECEMBER JANUARY FEBRUARY	4 Tests, 5 ODIs and 2 T20Is (a) v South Africa	(page 403)

the final in 1992, England have won only five matches in six tournaments against top-eight Test teams – this felt worse. England had been extended every advantage: the Ashes schedule had been moved to allow them plenty of preparation, and they had played only white-ball cricket since late August. Yet the margins of defeat were embarrassing, especially at Wellington, where New Zealand galloped to victory with nearly 38 overs to spare.

While there was shock at the loss to Bangladesh that sentenced England to exit the event at the same stage as Scotland, the UAE, Afghanistan, Ireland and Zimbabwe, the fact that it was their third defeat in four one-day internationals against the Bangladeshis (after 12 wins out of 12) suggested it was no aberration. England were, quite simply, way off the pace.

Yet the World Cup may come to be viewed as a watershed moment. The pain of the humiliation jolted the ECB into action: Paul Downton, the George Lazenby of sporting administrators, was sacked after an indifferent 14-month spell as managing director of England cricket, and a review launched into the effectiveness of the county game. Peter Moores, the coach, survived to oversee the Test tour of the Caribbean. But, though England won in Grenada, defeat in Barbados allowed a West Indies side unhelpfully dubbed "mediocre" by Colin Graves, the board's chairman-elect, to square the series – and sealed Moores's fate. Underlining the suspicion that the ECB were not fully in control, his impending sacking was reported before he himself had been informed. That was during a one-day international in Ireland, which – absurdly, and typically of a fixture list bursting at the seams – took place just three days after the scheduled finish in Barbados.

Perhaps Moores was unfortunate. A decent man caught up in the mud-slinging of the Kevin Pietersen saga, he was never able to shake off his baggage. His main fault may have been to care too much and try too hard. Andrew Strauss, confirmed as Downton's replacement two days before Pietersen had thrashed a triple-century for Surrey, admitted his decision to sack Moores related, in part, to the need for a fresh start. Every game, said Strauss, had become a referendum on the coach. (Pietersen remained on the outer because of what Strauss called "trust issues", despite Pietersen's claim that Graves had offered him a way back.) It was telling that Alastair Cook and Joe Root credited Moores after the Ashes success. Some of the seeds of their revival may have been sown during his tenure, but his success as a coaching consultant with Nottinghamshire seemed to support the view he was better suited to the domestic game.

The performance of several senior players at the World Cup – notably Ian Bell, James Anderson, Stuart Broad and Eoin Morgan – did Moores few favours. The team talked a good game, pledging aggressive cricket, but the reality was timid and outdated. Bell, whose half-centuries against Scotland, Bangladesh and Afghanistan inflated his average above its true impact, was later dropped from the one-day side – along with Anderson and, until early 2016, Broad – and announced his retirement from the format.

But, amid the rubble of defeats and sackings, something fresh and exciting began to emerge. A young team who had developed in the age of Twenty20 played fearless cricket, and appeared to relish the job of re-engaging a public

Laid back: Trevor Bayliss, Alastair Cook and Paul Farbrace before the Cardiff Test.

wearied by infighting, an elitist hierarchy and an attritional style of play. With every request for a selfie accepted and every autograph signed, 2015 was the year in which the smile returned to the face of English cricket.

Trevor Bayliss, the Australian coach with an outstanding record in white-ball cricket in particular, won many plaudits for the resurgence. With his quiet authority, simplicity and desire to see players take responsibility for their own games, he deserved some credit for the side's uncompromisingly belligerent approach in limited-overs cricket. He also had the confidence to allow other coaches – such as Mahela Jayawardene and Paul Collingwood – to spend time with the squad in consultancy roles.

But the changes had started before Bayliss's arrival. The avuncular Paul Farbrace – his assistant during their time with Sri Lanka, and Moores's assistant until his sacking – had overseen the team for the games against New Zealand. Reasoning that his priority was a happy, united squad, he reintroduced football as a warm-up routine – it had been banned because of concerns over injuries – and subtly changed the dressing-room terminology. Gone was talk of "scrapping" and "fighting"; in came "having fun" and "showing off skills." Dour England were replaced by dynamic England.

The transformation in the limited-overs side was dramatic. Cagey, percentage cricket was replaced by new faces, heroes and results. In the space of nine glorious days against New Zealand in June, England thrashed three of their (then) five highest one-day totals – including 408 for nine at Edgbaston, and a record chase of 350 for three, with six overs to spare, at Trent Bridge. They not only beat the team that had humiliated them at the World Cup, they convinced supporters they were finally worth watching.

Australia, won a well-contested 50-over series 3–2, but Morgan's new-look white-ball side went on to win the one-dayers against Pakistan in the UAE, with Jos Buttler putting aside a disappointing year in Tests to contribute the quickest century by an England player, from 46 balls. They also won all five of their Twenty20 matches in 2015. The progress from the World Cup debacle was undeniable.

Blessed by the presence of two all-rounders – Ben Stokes and Moeen Ali – their Test team had greater depth than for some years: a batting line-up with international centuries down to No. 9, and an attack spreading the load

LIFE AFTER STRAUSS

How England's openers have fared in the 43 Tests since Andrew Strauss's retirement in 2012:

	Series	*T*	*I*	*NO*	*Runs*	*HS*	*100*	*50*	*Avge*
A. N. Cook		43	80	3	3,409	263	8	18	44.24
N. R. D. Compton .	*v Ind and NZ 2012-13, NZ 2013*	9	17	2	479	117	2	1	31.93
J. E. Root.	*v Australia 2013*	5	10	1	339	180	1	1	37.66
M. A. Carberry . . .	*v Australia 2013-14*	5	10	0	281	60	0	1	28.10
S. D. Robson	*v SL and India 2014*	7	11	0	336	127	1	1	30.54
I. J. L. Trott	*v West Indies 2014-15*	3	6	0	72	59	0	1	12.00
A. Lyth	*v NZ and Aus 2015*	7	13	0	265	107	1	0	20.38
M. M. Ali	*v Pakistan 2015-16*	3	6	0	84	35	0	0	14.00
J. C. Buttler	*v Pakistan 2015-16†*	1	1	0	4	4	0	0	4.00
A. D. Hales	*v South Africa 2015-16*	4	8	0	136	60	0	1	17.00
The rest.		43†	82	3	1,996	180	5	6	25.26

†   *Buttler opened instead of Cook in the second innings of the First Test at Abu Dhabi.*

between four seamers and a spinner. There were days when they were irresistible. In archetypal English conditions, notably at Edgbaston and Trent Bridge, the bowlers maintained an immaculate length and gained lethal lateral movement. Broad, in particular, was hugely impressive during the Ashes, embracing the responsibility thrust on him by the mid-series injury to Anderson, and bowling a fuller, more probing length than has sometimes been the case. It culminated in a spell of eight for 15 on a memorable morning in Nottingham, which he almost matched with six for 17 at the Wanderers five months later – a performance that took him top of the world rankings. Anderson passed Ian Botham's England record for most Test wickets, and went beyond the 400 barrier, while Steven Finn put some miserable times behind him with an irrepressible return at Edgbaston; Durham's Mark Wood showed promise, and made people smile, though ankle surgery took the gloss off his year.

Joe Root led the way with the bat. No England player had scored so many international runs in a year as his 2,228, nor passed 50 in Tests as many times – though he converted only three of those 13 half-centuries into hundreds. Meanwhile, in the Lord's Test against New Zealand, Stokes – ignored for the World Cup – reacted to adversity by thrashing 92, and followed it with the quickest Test century the ground had seen, from 85 balls. He also produced a spell of swing bowling of which Anderson would have been proud, before repeating the trick against Australia at Trent Bridge. When he began 2016 with an innings of 258 in 198 balls at Cape Town, anything seemed possible.

Cook's captaincy – once so conservative – also improved. He was granted more options by a deeper bowling attack, and infused with confidence by a return to form with the bat that had begun in the Caribbean and soon took him past Graham Gooch's England-record 8,900 Test runs. His field-placings grew more imaginative, his tactics more aggressive; even Shane Warne, previously a staunch critic, took note.

But there were moments his side's inexperience told. Six times England thought they had taken a wicket, only for replays to reveal a no-ball; in Abu Dhabi, where Broad was deprived of Shoaib Malik's scalp only 40 runs into his eventual 245, it may have cost them the series. Top-order collapses also became wearily familiar. Fifteen times in 27 Test innings in 2015, England lost their third wicket for 74 or fewer.

While the excellence of Root and the depth of their batting masked the problem – Ali, at No. 8, and Broad, at No. 9, repeatedly punished tired Australian bowlers – England went from wonderful (Grenada and Cardiff) to wretched (Barbados and Lord's) with remarkable haste. Had Root been caught on nought at Cardiff by Brad Haddin, Australia might still have the Ashes. The inconsistency infuriated Cook.

By the time they reached South Africa, Alex Hales had become his eighth opening partner since Andrew Strauss, with Jonathan Trott, Adam Lyth and Ali all tried and discarded (or demoted) in 2015 alone. Gary Ballance, despite being named the previous year's ICC Emerging Player, was also dropped from the Test team, as were Buttler and Bell. Buttler's chances of a recall were on hold after his replacement, Jonny Bairstow, hit an unbeaten 150 at Cape Town. For Bell, it felt like the final chapter in an illustrious international career.

Debate over the spin-bowling position continued. It is true that, in a different era, England may have had many more assured options than Ali. But, at a time when county cricket – with its green pitches and plethora of medium-pacers – is offering so few chances to develop spinners, his all-round skills were probably the best option. While there were days, notably in Barbados, when he struggled, he also enjoyed better times, and ended the year with a Man of the Match performance at Durban.

By then, though, England's spin issues had come back to haunt them in the UAE. Despite Cook's admirable batting, they had succumbed to a slightly unflattering 2–0 loss, with Ali and Adil Rashid (and, in the Third Test, Samit Patel) unable to replicate the potency of Yasir Shah, and England's batsmen the mastery of Misbah-ul-Haq. A decision to experiment with the regulations concerning the toss in county cricket was designed, primarily, to produce conditions that provided more encouragement to spinners.

From the depths of the World Cup, though, this was a year of improvement. It was not always smooth: with a young team and a new approach, that was never likely. Yet, with several talented players able to look forward to many more years in the international game, and a team playing vibrant, attractive cricket, England were moving in the right direction.

ENGLAND PLAYERS IN 2015

Lawrence Booth

The following 33 players (there were 33 in 2014 and 34 in 2013) appeared in 2015, when England played 14 Tests, 26 one-day internationals and five twenty20 internationals. Statistics refer to the full year, not the 2015 season.

MOEEN ALI — Worcestershire

Ali deserved top marks for versatility. Whether he was launching late counter-attacks during the Ashes, thrashing 72 from 46 balls from No. 3 during the Cardiff Twenty20 against Australia, or surprising South Africa with his off-breaks at Durban, he did it with a serenity and a selflessness treasured by the dressing-room. Not every ploy was a success: his one-day runs dried up when he moved from opener to No. 7, so too his Test runs when he moved in the UAE from No. 8 to opener. But six Ashes scores of 30-plus kept giving England timely boosts, and he finished 2015 among the world's top ten Test wicket-takers. Stats, though, never seemed to mean as much to him as the simple thrill of being involved.

13 Tests: 563 runs @ 24.47; 39 wickets @ 39.94.
19 ODI: 376 runs @ 25.06, SR 91.70; 23 wickets @ 33.39, ER 4.72.
3 T20I: 72 runs @ 36.00, SR 135.84; 3 wickets @ 18.33, ER 6.11.

JAMES ANDERSON — Lancashire

Each landmark confirmed Anderson's ascent towards greatness. He began in the Caribbean, passing Ian Botham's England Test record of 383 wickets, then one by one – hauled in a star-studded cast: Ntini, Steyn, Ambrose, Wasim Akram, Harbhajan Singh, Pollock and Hadlee. By the end of the South Africa series in early 2016, he sat on 433, only one behind sixth-placed Kapil Dev. At times, he bowled more skilfully than ever. He won the Grenada Test almost by himself, expertly unpicked Australia at Edgbaston, and located a near-perfect length in the UAE, where Pakistan concluded there was little point trying to score off him. At 33, his body was starting to creak, and the selectors sensibly took him out of the white-ball firing-line. But, chillingly for batsmen, the suggestion of winding-down merely elicited a dry chuckle.

11 Tests: 78 runs @ 6.50; 46 wickets @ 22.65.
10 ODI: 14 runs @ 7.00, SR 82.35; 12 wickets @ 31.75, ER 4.56.

JONNY BAIRSTOW — Yorkshire

When his chances came, he generally took them – with the bat, at least. His international year didn't start properly until June, when an unbeaten 83 off 60 balls powered England to a one-day series win over New Zealand at Chester-le-Street; and it gathered momentum in August at Trent Bridge, where his first-day alliance with Root sealed Australia's fate. All the while, he was a giant at Yorkshire. Runs came less easily against Pakistan's spinners, but – having grabbed the Test gloves off Buttler – he hit an emotional unbeaten 150 in Cape Town. If his keeping was fallible, his gumption was unquestionable.

7 Tests: 372 runs @ 31.00; 7 catches and 1 stumping in 2 games as wicketkeeper.
5 ODI: 141 runs @ 47.00, SR 117.50; 7 catches, 1 stumping.
1 T20I: 1 run @ 1.00, SR 50.00; 2 catches.

GARY BALLANCE   Yorkshire

A year of three thirds ended all too soon, as if 2014 had been a mirage. A late inclusion in the World Cup squad, Ballance looked hopelessly miscast, scoring a trio of stodgy tens from No. 3. The Test series in the Caribbean was more like it: slow pitches and undemanding bowling played to his strength, which was temperament rather than technique, and he averaged 66. But a tendency to hang back, compounded by a failure to transfer his weight into his strokes, proved damaging back home against better seamers and on livelier tracks. Against New Zealand and Australia, Ballance was bowled or leg-before in five innings out of eight, which brought a lone half-century – though a crucial one in the first innings of the First Ashes Test at Cardiff – and just 134 runs. He was soon dropped, only to make the South Africa tour as a spare batsman.

7 Tests: 465 runs @ 35.76.
4 ODI: 36 runs @ 9.00, SR 50.70.

IAN BELL   Warwickshire

Bell's stasis was summed up in Sharjah, where at one point during the Third Test against Pakistan he managed 16 runs in a session. The selectors decided not to take him to South Africa, so ending a six-year run in the side that had embraced his elegant best and infuriating worst. After a polished 143 in Antigua in April, he averaged just 20 in 23 Test innings, briefly bucking the trend with a pair of half-centuries at Edgbaston, having been promoted to No. 3. But the duck that rounded off his year in the UAE was his ninth Test score of one or nought in 2015, prompting some to conclude that he ought to have called it a day – as Bell himself had pondered – after taking part in his fifth Ashes win. His most fluent batting of the year became a distant memory: a brilliant 141 off 125 balls as one-day opener against Australia at Hobart in January. When, to little fanfare, he retired from the format, he had quietly become England's leading 50-over run-maker, with 5,416. Otherwise, Bell batted as if so much experience counted for so little.

13 Tests: 571 runs @ 25.95.
11 ODI: 509 runs @ 56.55, SR 88.06.

Gareth Copley, Getty Images

SAM BILLINGS   Kent

Ribbed for being the team's posh kid, Billings provided a touch of new-boy's class. He showed off his 360-degree skill during a 16-ball 34 against New Zealand at the Rose Bowl, then aided and abetted Bairstow in the chase at Chester-le-Street. It was eye-catching stuff from a player hidden away at No. 7. A half-century from

24 balls in the first Twenty20 at Dubai in November, when he was also given the gloves, confirmed a rare talent.

    5 ODI: 90 runs @ 22.50, SR 132.35.
    5 T20I: 94 runs @ 18.80, SR 156.66; 2 catches, 1 stumping in 1 game as wicketkeeper.

RAVI BOPARA   Essex

Bopara was limited to a few fitful appearances in the start-of-year triangular in Australia, and the consolation prize of a World Cup dead rubber against Afghanistan. But the sacking of Peter Moores left him without an obvious advocate, and meant a mainly unfulfilling summer on the county circuit. At 30, time was running out.

    6 ODI: 57 runs @ 14.25, SR 57.57; 2 wickets @ 27.50, ER 5.00.

STUART BROAD   Nottinghamshire

The scariest bit for opposition batsmen was that Broad, not yet 30, was getting better. As 2015 wore on, he added Glenn McGrath-style attrition to his penchant for hot streaks: his instantly historic eight for 15 at Trent Bridge felt like the work of an athlete approaching his prime, not a flash in the pan. By the end of the year, he was the leading seam-bowling wicket-taker in Test cricket, having sent down more overs (450.3) than anyone; six for 17 at the Wanderers in January 2016 confirmed his class. His batting, meanwhile, picked up as the memory of being hit in the face against India in 2014 faded: starting with a restorative 46 against New Zealand at Headingley, he reached 20 nine times in Tests. But, with the ball, Broad was now indisputably a world force to be reckoned with.

    14 Tests: 353 runs @ 19.61; 56 wickets @ 23.82.
    11 ODI: 40 runs @ 10.00, SR 85.10; 9 wickets @ 56.44, ER 5.63.

JOS BUTTLER   Lancashire

When Buttler trusted himself, the bowlers muttered a quiet prayer. While his Test batting foundered on the rocks of self-doubt, his one-day game rode the crest of a tsunami. Before the end of the year, he was out of the Test side *and* the owner of the three fastest one-day hundreds in England's history. Significantly, his 52-ball 116 not out in Dubai came after he had been dropped from the Test team – and Buttler was honest enough to admit his axing had come as a relief. His Ashes form betrayed a nervous self-consciousness and an overly dominant bottom hand, both easily exploited. But 50-over cricket produced no such introspection, and his 129 off 77 balls against New Zealand at Edgbaston embodied the team's new-found chutzpah. His keeping improved, and his quiet determination was so respected by colleagues that he assumed the captaincy for the second of the two Twenty20 games in Dubai.

    12 Tests: 430 runs @ 23.88; 38 catches.
    21 ODI: 642 runs @ 42.80, SR 118.88; 29 catches, 2 stumpings.
    3 T20I: 46 runs @ 15.33, SR 158.62; 1 catch, 2 stumpings.

ALASTAIR COOK   Essex

It was as if the previous two years had never happened. When Cook made 105 at Bridgetown in May, he did so with a stoicism that some feared had vanished altogether. England lost that game, yet drew comfort from familiarity. Against New Zealand at Lord's, where he compiled 162 in nine hours, he was more Mt Cook than Captain Cook; in Abu Dhabi, Pakistan needed an unnoticed no-ball to end his 263, chiselled out in four minutes short of 14 hours. Having belatedly accepted his dropping from the one-day team, he reacquainted himself with the feel of bat on fresh air, leaving outside off stump and persuading exasperated bowlers to feed his strengths. And, in the middle of it all, as he finally cocked an ear to advice from beyond the dressing-room, he managed to out-captain Michael Clarke to claim a second Ashes success in three summers and defer thoughts of quitting. If his batting faltered in South Africa, then another series win sugared the pill – and he was closing in on 10,000 Test runs.

14 Tests: 1,364 runs @ 54.56.

STEVEN FINN   Middlesex

His return to Test cricket was patchy but glorious. Two years after losing his captain's faith at Trent Bridge (and with every feature article still obliged to

reference his "unselectable" 2013-14 Ashes tour), Finn took Edgbaston by storm – and eight Australian wickets, including Steve Smith cheaply twice. An injury to his left foot ruled him out of the Pakistan series, but in late December he was dismantling South Africa's second innings in Durban. His white-ball form had mirrored England's. A five-for against India in Brisbane helped them to the final of the Tri-Series. But, at the World Cup, he followed the most forgotten hat-trick in England history, against Australia, with two overs for 49 during the humiliation by New Zealand. So it was to Finn's credit that he dismissed his tormentor, Brendon McCullum, in the first over of the New Zealanders' reply at Edgbaston in June.

4 Tests: 21 runs @ 21.00; 18 wickets @ 20.05.
18 ODI: 25 runs @ 4.16, SR 31.64; 31 wickets @ 27.67, ER 5.75.
2 T20I: did not bat; 1 wicket @ 68.00, ER 8.50.

ALEX HALES   Nottinghamshire

Hales felt like New England. Used at the World Cup only as an afterthought, he was a natural fit in the summer, when a change of management meant a change of tempo. A 38-ball 67 against New Zealand set up England's record chase at Trent Bridge and, though he struggled against the pace of Australia's Pat Cummins, a maiden ODI hundred – at Abu Dhabi in November – and five successive scores of 50-plus in South Africa restored the upward curve. The decision to back Hales for what he could do, rather than fret over what he couldn't, eventually fed into Test selection: at Durban on Boxing Day, he became the umpteenth cab off the opener's rank. Questions remained over his technique, but at least he was being given a chance to answer them.

    1 Test: 36 runs @ 18.00.
    17 ODI: 453 runs @ 28.31, SR 93.01.
    4 T20I: 49 runs @ 12.25, SR 98.00.

CHRIS JORDAN   Sussex

Two highlights weren't quite enough to quell the sense that Jordan remained more outer-ring than bullseye. His slip catching during the Tests in the West Indies, especially off the spinners, belonged in the all-time-great category, while six yorkers in Sharjah set up England's super-over win against Pakistan. But he lacked incision with the red ball, and – Sharjah apart – precision with the white.

    3 Tests: 55 runs @ 13.75; 6 wickets @ 42.66.
    5 ODI: 22 runs @ 7.33, SR 78.57; 7 wickets @ 33.57, ER 6.43.
    2 T20I: no runs without being dismissed; no wicket for 76, ER 9.50.

ADAM LYTH   Yorkshire

A composed century on home turf at Headingley in his second Test, against New Zealand, promised much, but in the Ashes Lyth simply looked out of his depth. A tendency to flirt outside off produced a string of edges: in all, ten of his 13 innings resulted in a catch for the cordon, often before he had played himself in (six times he reached double figures without passing 20). Left-armers troubled him, especially Trent Boult and Mitchell Starc. His Facebook columns maintained their air of wide-eyed enjoyment but, come autumn, Lyth's reputation as a good team man was not enough to save him.

    7 Tests: 265 runs @ 20.38; no wicket for 0.

EOIN MORGAN   Middlesex

As Morgan buoyantly clutched an outsized Twenty20 trophy in Sharjah at the end of November, it was hard to reconcile his smile with his po-faced helplessness during England's dismal World Cup. But the departure of Moores freed him to implement his own white-ball philosophy. Having followed an innings of 121 at Sydney in January with 92 runs in eight innings, including four ducks, he treated the start of the summer like the start of the rest of his career. His next 14 one-day internationals yielded 754 runs at 58, with a strike-rate of 101, including 88 off 47 balls at The Oval and 113 off 82 at Trent Bridge, both against New Zealand. Just as devastating was a T20 innings of 74 off 39 against Australia at Cardiff. Morgan, who took a month out of county cricket in August to refresh body and soul, finished the year with 967 one-day runs – 244 clear of Root, England's next-best – and 30 sixes, behind only A. B. de Villiers, Martin Guptill and Brendon McCullum. He did not look out of place.

    25 ODI: 967 runs @ 43.95, SR 93.79.
    4 T20I: 138 runs @ 46.00, SR 142.26.

LIAM PLUNKETT   Yorkshire

Rarely can a player have seemed so ubiquitous yet so peripheral. The sum total of Plunkett's many squad selections was seven limited-overs matches, in which his batting often outshone his bowling. His 44 off 30 deliveries gave England an unlikely sniff against New Zealand at The Oval, while a ten-ball 17 eased nerves against Australia at Leeds. Even when he was picking up two Twenty20 three-fors in Dubai, it felt like a sop after missing out on the Test tour of South Africa.

5 ODI: 99 runs @ 24.75, SR 176.78; 6 wickets @ 42.83, ER 6.42.

2 T20I: 1 run @ 1.00, SR 50.00; 6 wickets @ 9.00, ER 6.75.

ADIL RASHID   Yorkshire

English cricket's fraught relationship with leg-spin played out across eight months in which Rashid eased himself into the limited-overs teams, yet took an age to win his first Test cap. When it arrived, there were more downs than

Martin Rickett, PA Photos

ups. Five late wickets in Abu Dhabi almost set up a remarkable win, while his four-hour 61 in Dubai almost clinched an unlikely draw. But his three other Pakistani Test scalps cost 164 each, and he conceded four an over. In white-ball cricket, with batsmen obliged to attack his good balls (including a tidy googly) as well as his bad, he was encouraged to place strike-rate over economy-rate. Rashid was also at the heart of England's first 50-over score over 400, putting on a thrilling 177 with Buttler against New Zealand at Edgbaston. There

were, though, concerns over his temperament – whispers emerged about his reluctance to make that Test debut against Australia at Lord's – and the absence of an extra 5mph. But no one said leg-spin was easy, either to master or, in England, to appreciate.

3 Tests: 103 runs @ 20.60; 8 wickets @ 69.50.

15 ODI: 171 runs @ 28.50, SR 104.26; 19 wickets @ 41.10, ER 6.10.

5 T20I: 10 runs without being dismissed, SR 200.00; 4 wickets @ 28.00, ER 7.46.

JOE ROOT   Yorkshire

This was the stuff of the big league. Only Kane Williamson and Steve Smith scored more than Root's 2,228 international runs in 2015, and he was 864 ahead of Cook, England's second-best. He was a man for all formats, without ever sacrificing the class that made his back-foot force through the covers one of the year's signature shots. It was typical of him to hit ten more Test sixes than any of his team-mates, without the trend being noticed. If there was a weakness, it was almost a strength: he fell between 71 and 98 seven times in Tests, though it meant a world-record 13 scores of 50-plus in a calendar year. And his 134 against Australia at Cardiff may have been England's most tone-setting hundred in the first Test of an Ashes since Ian Botham at Brisbane in 1986-87.

14 Tests: 1,385 runs @ 60.21; 8 wickets @ 40.25.

20 ODI: 723 runs @ 42.52, SR 91.98; 1 wicket @ 119.00, ER 5.95.

3 T20I: 120 runs @ 40.00, SR 142.85.

JASON ROY **Surrey**

England's limited-overs revolution had begun unpromisingly at Edgbaston in
June, when Roy squeezed his first ball in one-day internationals to backward
point. The only way was up. After impressing the coaches by placing the team
imperative above personal stats, Roy outshone Hales, his opening partner, in
the 50-over games against Australia, then chalked off his first hundred, against
Pakistan in Dubai. Though there was a touch of Kevin Pietersen about his
wristy flourish through the covers, concerns about a slapdash technique came
to the fore in South Africa.

15 ODI: 462 runs @ 33.00, SR 98.29.
5 T20I: 72 runs @ 14.40, SR 124.13.

BEN STOKES **Durham**

Numbers be damned. It was Stokes's ability to grab a game, to enthuse those
on the field and in the stands, that lingered. No doubt he would have preferred
more than one Test fifty in 13 innings after an uncharacteristically patient 87
against Australia at Lord's. But he would always have his own highlights
package: scores of 92 and 101, plus the wickets of Kane Williamson and
Brendon McCullum in successive balls, to turn the Lord's Test against New
Zealand into a symbol of England's regeneration; that catch to send back
Adam Voges at Trent Bridge; lavish swing the following day to take six for
36; then, best of all, a murderous 258 at Cape Town in early 2016. And he
collected flashpoints as if on a loyalty scheme: a sarcastic send-off from
Marlon Samuels, a mindless Ashes run-out at Lord's, a dismissal for obstructing
the field. Through it all, he balanced the Test side – and kept people talking
about the cricket.

14 Tests: 719 runs @ 28.76; 24 wickets @ 47.79.
10 ODI: 262 runs @ 29.11, SR 101.15; 12 wickets @ 31.91, ER 6.27.
2 T20I: 25 runs without being dismissed, SR 178.57; 3 wickets @ 17.66, ER 7.57.

JAMES TAYLOR **Nottinghamshire**

His one-day form confirmed the suspicion that Taylor was a middle-order
banker in the making, not least during a high-class century on a turning pitch
at Manchester against Australia. It parked the disappointment of his unbeaten
98 during the World Cup at Melbourne, where he was diddled by the umpires,
and persuaded the selectors to name him in the Test squad for the UAE. When
he got a chance, in Sharjah, he sparkled in his first Test for more than three
years; Durban proved it was no fluke, even if he struggled on South Africa's
bouncier tracks thereafter. But some impishly electric fielding at short leg
helped even up the ledger, and Taylor never lost his apparently inbuilt awareness of the greater good.

2 Tests: 190 runs @ 47.50.
21 ODI: 691 runs @ 46.06, SR 82.06.

REECE TOPLEY **Essex/Hampshire**

Aged only 21, Topley quickly earned the approval of Morgan. His first
international wicket came as he outwitted Mitchell Marsh with a slower ball in
Cardiff, and by his second game – the decisive one-dayer against Australia at

Old Trafford – he was opening the bowling. In Abu Dhabi, he singlehandedly reduced Pakistan to 41 for three. Tall, rangy and tattooed, he was hard to miss.
 5 ODI: 6 runs @ 6.00, SR 19.35; 6 wickets @ 31.83, ER 4.63.
 2 T20I: did not bat; 4 wickets @ 14.75, ER 7.37.

JONATHAN TROTT — Warwickshire

Trott's England return, nearly 18 months after leaving the 2013-14 Ashes tour because of stress, became a wistful coda to a gutsy career. Invited to open in the Caribbean, he was dismissed for single figures in five of his six innings, including a trio of third-ball ducks. A susceptibility to the short one was especially telling, and only a dogged 59 in Grenada summoned the glue of old. A day after shedding tears on the outfield at Bridgetown, a relieved Trott announced his retirement from international cricket, taking gratitude and good wishes with him.
 3 Tests: 72 runs @ 12.00; no wicket for 2 runs.

DAVID WILLEY — Northamptonshire/Yorkshire

Willey's left-armers added a welcome dimension to England's white-ball attack, especially against right-handers when there was swing in the air. He could be expensive – New Zealand hit him for 89 at Trent Bridge – but he had a knack of removing good batsmen, and his new-ball burst set up the 50-over win over Australia at Leeds. Bowlers, though, learned not to indulge his favoured diet of length and width, leaving a sense of batting promise unfulfilled.
 10 ODI: 40 runs @ 10.00, SR 75.47; 18 wickets @ 24.22, ER 5.51.
 4 T20I: 13 runs @ 6.50, SR 130.00; 8 wickets @ 16.87, SR 9.41.

CHRIS WOAKES — Warwickshire

Unfussy and dependable, Woakes became part of the limited-overs furniture, chipping in with some deceptively destructive innings, and claiming a pair of four-fors to seal England's 50-over fightback in the UAE. It was to his credit that the selectors felt he was central to their white-ball attack after they moved on without Anderson, though work remained at Test level.
 1 Test: 23 runs @ 11.50; 1 wicket @ 53.00.
 17 ODI: 155 runs @ 17.22, SR 81.15; 21 wickets @ 37.04, ER 5.67.
 2 T20I: 52 runs @ 52.00, SR 167.74; 3 wickets @ 22.00, ER 8.25.

MARK WOOD — Durham

Wood claimed the summer's first wicket by an England bowler – on debut in soggy Dublin – and, three months later, the one that secured the Ashes. In between, he quickly established himself as that rarest of gems: a go-to seamer, and thus the captain's friend. Eight innings hauls of two or three in eight Tests showed he was more consistent than his explosive approach to the crease, reminiscent of Simon Jones, suggested. And, at Dubai, in his final Test of the year before his fragile left ankle persuaded medics to wrap him in cotton wool, he added accuracy to his CV, conceding only 83 runs from 33.5 overs (and taking five wickets). His fielding could be iffy, but he added verve to the lower order and earned himself the nightwatchman's gig. If others enjoyed his imaginary horse, then Wood clearly enjoyed the ride.

8 Tests: 185 runs @ 20.55; 25 wickets @ 34.40.
7 ODI: 26 runs @ 26.00, SR 96.29; 5 wickets @ 68.80, ER 5.83.
1 T20I: did not bat; 3 wickets @ 8.66, ER 8.66.

AND THE REST…

James Tredwell (Kent; 1 Test, 1 ODI) earned a second Test cap, in Antigua, five years after his first, but couldn't back up first-innings figures of four for 47 with any penetration in the second. After a three-year absence, **Samit Patel** (Nottinghamshire; 1 Test) did a reasonable job as a horse for Sharjah's course. Another returnee, **Nick Compton** (Middlesex; 1 Test), showed off his patience and desire while making 85 and 49 in Durban, the city of his birth. **James Vince** (Hampshire; 1 ODI, 3 T20I) claimed the Man of the Series award after his first three T20 games produced 41, 38 and 46 in the UAE. **Stephen Parry** (Lancashire; 2 T20I) marked his comeback after a 20-month absence with some loopy slow left-arm in Dubai, removing Shahid Afridi for a second-ball duck. **Tim Bresnan** (Yorkshire; 1 ODI) had to settle for a new-ball burst at rainy Malahide, but post-Moores England simply weren't interested. **Zafar Ansari** (Surrey; 1 ODI) made his debut in that game, then dislocated a thumb on the day he was chosen for the UAE.

ENGLAND TEST AVERAGES
IN CALENDAR YEAR 2015

BATTING AND FIELDING

	T	I	NO	R	HS	100	50	Avge	SR	Ct/St
N. R. D. Compton	1	2	0	134	85	0	1	67.00	38.06	0
J. E. Root	14	26	3	1,385	182*	3	10	60.21	63.70	24
†A. N. Cook	14	26	1	1,364	263	3	8	54.56	43.67	16
J. W. A. Taylor	2	4	0	190	76	0	2	47.50	47.02	2
†G. S. Ballance	7	14	1	465	122	1	3	35.76	43.66	7
J. M. Bairstow	7	12	0	372	79	0	2	31.00	55.27	11/1
†B. A. Stokes	14	25	0	719	101	1	5	28.76	67.76	11
I. R. Bell	13	24	2	571	143	1	4	25.95	43.85	12
†M. M. Ali	13	23	0	563	77	0	4	24.47	54.13	8
J. C. Buttler	12	21	3	430	73	0	3	23.88	53.28	38
S. R. Patel	1	2	0	42	42	0	0	21.00	51.85	1
S. T. Finn	4	6	5	21	12	0	0	21.00	31.81	0
A. U. Rashid	3	5	0	103	61	0	1	20.60	30.83	0
M. A. Wood	8	14	5	185	32*	0	0	20.55	54.73	2
†A. Lyth	7	13	0	265	107	1	0	20.38	50.09	8
†S. C. J. Broad	14	23	5	353	46	0	0	19.61	69.48	4
A. D. Hales	1	2	0	36	26	0	0	18.00	33.96	0
C. J. Jordan	3	5	1	55	21*	0	0	13.75	52.88	6
I. J. L. Trott	3	6	0	72	59	0	1	12.00	38.09	0
C. R. Woakes	1	2	0	23	23	0	0	11.50	58.97	1
†J. C. Tredwell	1	1	0	8	8	0	0	8.00	33.33	1
†J. M. Anderson	11	18	6	78	20	0	0	6.50	43.09	14

BOWLING

	Style	O	M	R	W	BB	5I	Avge	SR
S. T. Finn	RFM	108.5	22	361	18	6-79	1	20.05	36.2
J. M. Anderson	RFM	393.3	114	1,042	46	6-42	2	22.65	51.3
S. C. J. Broad	RFM	450.3	111	1,334	56	8-15	2	23.82	48.2
J. C. Tredwell	OB	66	26	140	5	4-47	0	28.00	79.2
M. A. Wood	RFM	254.3	59	860	25	3-39	0	34.40	61.0
M. M. Ali	OB	403.2	57	1,558	39	4-69	0	39.94	62.0
J. E. Root	OB	97.3	24	322	8	2-22	0	40.25	73.1
C. J. Jordan	RFM	104	32	256	6	2-65	0	42.66	104.0
B. A. Stokes	RFM	315.1	65	1,147	24	6-36	1	47.79	78.7
C. R. Woakes	RFM	24	6	53	1	1-25	0	53.00	144.0
S. R. Patel	SLA	42	4	164	3	2-85	0	54.66	84.0
A. U. Rashid	LBG	136.5	9	556	8	5-64	1	69.50	102.6
A. Lyth	RM	1	1	0	0	0-0	0	–	–
I. J. L. Trott	RM	1	0	2	0	0-2	0	–	–

> " Ronchi was also the first Luke to play Test cricket, completing all four gospels
> – as if Yorkshiremen needed convincing this was hallowed turf."
> England v New Zealand, 2015, Second Test, page 313

ENGLAND ONE-DAY INTERNATIONAL AVERAGES IN CALENDAR YEAR 2015

BATTING AND FIELDING

	M	I	NO	R	HS	100	50	Avge	SR	Ct/St
I. R. Bell	11	11	2	509	141	1	4	56.55	88.06	6
J. M. Bairstow	5	4	1	141	83*	0	1	47.00	117.50	7/1
J. W. A. Taylor	21	20	5	691	101	1	5	46.06	82.06	6
E. J. G. Morgan	25	23	1	967	121	2	7	43.95	93.79	9
J. C. Buttler	21	18	3	642	129	2	2	42.80	118.88	29/2
J. E. Root	20	18	1	723	121	3	4	42.52	91.98	15
J. J. Roy	15	14	0	462	102	1	3	33.00	98.29	5
B. A. Stokes	10	10	1	262	68	0	1	29.11	101.15	7
A. U. Rashid	15	9	3	171	69	0	1	28.50	104.26	6
A. D. Hales	17	16	0	453	109	1	2	28.31	93.01	3
M. A. Wood	7	3	2	26	13	0	0	26.00	96.29	1
M. M. Ali	19	18	3	376	128	1	0	25.06	91.70	4
L. E. Plunkett	5	5	1	99	44	0	0	24.75	176.78	3
S. W. Billings	5	4	0	90	41	0	0	22.50	132.35	1
C. R. Woakes	17	13	4	155	42*	0	0	17.22	81.15	8
R. S. Bopara	6	4	0	57	33	0	0	14.25	57.57	1
S. C. J. Broad	11	8	4	40	24	0	0	10.00	85.10	2
D. J. Willey	10	5	1	40	13	0	0	10.00	75.47	4
G. S. Ballance	4	4	0	36	10	0	0	9.00	50.70	1
C. J. Jordan	5	4	1	22	17	0	0	7.33	78.57	5
J. M. Anderson	10	4	2	14	8	0	0	7.00	82.35	1
R. J. W. Topley	5	2	1	6	6	0	0	6.00	19.35	0
S. T. Finn	18	10	4	25	10	0	0	4.16	31.64	3
Z. S. Ansari	1	–	–	–	–	–	–	–	–	0
T. T. Bresnan	1	–	–	–	–	–	–	–	–	0
J. C. Tredwell	1	–	–	–	–	–	–	–	–	1
J. M. Vince	1	–	–	–	–	–	–	–	–	1

BOWLING

	Style	O	M	R	W	BB	4I	Avge	SR	ER
T. T. Bresnan	RFM	6	2	11	1	1-11	0	11.00	36.00	1.83
D. J. Willey	LFM	79	5	436	18	3-25	0	24.22	26.33	5.51
J. C. Tredwell	OB	7	0	25	1	1-25	0	25.00	42.00	3.57
R. S. Bopara	RM	11	1	55	2	2-31	0	27.50	33.00	5.00
S. T. Finn	RFM	149	10	858	31	5-33	3	27.67	28.83	5.75
J. M. Anderson	RFM	83.3	6	381	12	4-18	1	31.75	41.75	4.56
R. J. W. Topley	LFM	41.1	3	191	6	3-26	0	31.83	41.16	4.63
B. A. Stokes	RFM	61	0	383	12	3-52	0	31.91	30.50	6.27
M. M. Ali	OB	162.4	2	768	23	3-32	0	33.39	42.43	4.72
C. J. Jordan	RFM	36.3	2	235	7	2-13	0	33.57	31.28	6.43
C. R. Woakes	RFM	137.1	5	778	21	4-33	0	37.04	39.19	5.67
A. U. Rashid	LBG	128	2	781	19	4-55	2	41.10	40.42	6.10
L. E. Plunkett	RFM	40	0	257	6	3-60	0	42.83	40.00	6.42
S. C. J. Broad	RFM	90.1	4	508	9	3-55	0	56.44	60.11	5.63
M. A. Wood	RFM	59	1	344	5	1-25	0	68.80	70.80	5.83
J. E. Root	OB	20	0	119	1	1-27	0	119.00	120.00	5.95

ENGLAND TWENTY20 INTERNATIONAL AVERAGES IN CALENDAR YEAR 2015

BATTING AND FIELDING

	M	I	NO	R	HS	50	Avge	SR	4	6	Ct/St
A. U. Rashid.	5	2	2	10	7*	0	–	200.00	1	0	2
†B. A. Stokes	2	2	2	25	24*	0	–	178.57	4	0	1
C. R. Woakes	2	2	1	52	37	0	52.00	167.74	3	3	0
J. C. Buttler	3	3	0	46	33	0	15.33	158.62	2	4	1/2
S. W. Billings	5	5	0	94	53	1	18.80	156.66	8	4	5/1
J. E. Root	3	3	0	120	68	1	40.00	142.85	13	3	0
†E. J. G. Morgan	4	4	1	138	74	1	46.00	142.26	6	9	2
†M. M. Ali	3	3	1	72	72*	1	36.00	135.84	6	3	1
†D. J. Willey	4	3	1	13	6	0	6.50	130.00	0	1	2
J. J. Roy	5	5	0	72	29	0	14.40	124.13	4	4	1
J. M. Vince	3	3	0	125	46	0	41.66	119.04	12	4	0
A. D. Hales	4	4	0	49	27	0	12.25	98.00	4	1	0
J. M. Bairstow	1	1	0	1	1	0	1.00	50.00	0	0	2
L. E. Plunkett	2	1	0	1	1	0	1.00	50.00	0	0	0
C. J. Jordan	2	1	1	0	0*	0	–	–	0	0	1
S. T. Finn	2	–	–	–	–	–	–	–	0	0	2
S. D. Parry	2	–	–	–	–	–	–	–	0	0	0
R. J. W. Topley	2	–	–	–	–	–	–	–	0	0	1
M. A. Wood	1	–	–	–	–	–	–	–	0	0	0

BOWLING

	Style	O	M	R	W	BB	4I	Avge	SR	ER
M. M. Ali	OB	9	0	55	3	1-3	0	18.33	18.00	6.11
L. E. Plunkett	RFM	8	0	54	6	3-21	0	9.00	8.00	6.75
R. J. W. Topley	LFM	8	0	59	4	3-24	0	14.75	12.00	7.37
A. U. Rashid.	LBG	15	0	112	4	2-18	0	28.00	22.50	7.46
B. A. Stokes	RFM	7	0	53	3	2-24	0	17.66	14.00	7.57
S. D. Parry	SLA	8	0	66	3	2-33	0	22.00	16.00	8.25
C. R. Woakes	RFM	8	0	66	3	2-40	0	22.00	16.00	8.25
S. T. Finn	RFM	8	0	68	1	1-39	0	68.00	48.00	8.50
M. A. Wood	RFM	3	0	26	3	3-26	0	8.66	6.00	8.66
D. J. Willey	LFM	14.2	0	135	8	3-22	0	16.87	10.75	9.41
C. J. Jordan	RFM	8	0	76	0	0-37	0	–	–	9.50

> **"** The resulting bedlam would normally have led to a noise-control call-out in this suburb of Mount Eden, but no New Zealander begrudged the decibel levels."
> New Zealand v Australia, World Cup, page 882

CARLTON MID TRI-SERIES IN 2014-15

DEAN WILSON

1 Australia   2 England   3 India

On one level, this triangular series between world cricket's Big Three was a reminder of their increasing mutual reliance. But, for the players themselves, it was useful preparation for the World Cup a fortnight later, of which the Australian games would be played on the same grounds, under the same conditions. The exception was the absence here of DRS, which India objected to because it was "not 100% accurate", despite the fact that they and everyone else were about to use it in the World Cup.

Australia's focus had switched from reclaiming the Border–Gavaskar Trophy to reclaiming the World Cup, but they remained uncertain about the identity of their captain. Michael Clarke had suffered another hamstring injury during the Test series against India, and his one-day deputy, George Bailey, was battling form and the perception that he was fortunate to be in the 15-man squad at all. Clarke sat out the tri-series to rebuild his fitness, while Bailey and the young pretender Steve Smith led Australia on an unbeaten run to the trophy, culminating in a straightforward victory over England in the final at Perth.

The format provided ample opportunities for Australia to rest and rotate first-choice players such as Mitchell Johnson and David Warner, and find out more about those on the fringes. That allowed Mitchell Starc to establish himself as perhaps the world's most devastating white-ball practitioner, demolishing England and India in the first two games; Glenn Maxwell blossomed to the extent that Australia eventually felt confident enough to use him as their sole spinner. They were by far the most powerful of the teams, and the selection of three left-arm seamers in the final (Johnson, Starc and James Faulkner) provided a taster of their successful tactics at the World Cup.

Not that England took much notice, arriving with a squad of six right-arm seamers and three off-spinners. They did not look especially confident setting a score. But a pair of successful run-chases against India gave them something to cling to following a difficult series in Sri Lanka before Christmas, which had triggered the dismissal of captain Alastair Cook. Eoin Morgan, his replacement, made 121 in the first game, against Australia at Sydney, but just two more runs in his next three innings. (Morgan also had to deal with a failed extortion attempt by an ex-lover's former boyfriend, who emailed the ECB threatening to release explicit images unless they coughed up £35,000.)

Ian Bell, entrusted with Cook's old opening slot ahead of the inconsistent but potentially destructive Alex Hales, crashed 141 off 125 balls against Australia in Hobart, and finished as the competition's leading run-scorer, with 247. James Taylor chipped in from No. 3 with two hefty scores against India, and Chris Woakes bowled fast with the new ball, creating the impression that

Gareth Copley, Getty Images

Left reeling: England found Mitchell Starc a handful.

England had settled on their World Cup formula – only for Taylor and Woakes to be shifted from their roles when the tournament began.

India's seam bowling improved from their 2–0 Test defeat by Australia, but they were unusually sketchy about their batting plans, holding Virat Kohli back from No. 3 if an early wicket fell. Two months into their tour, they ended the competition without a win in eight games. "What is important right now is a break," said captain M. S. Dhoni. "Lock the kitbag [away]. Keep it somewhere you don't even want to see it, and completely switch off from cricket." When India did start winning during the World Cup, their team director Ravi Shastri was scathing about the relevance of this tournament: "Frankly speaking, I believe this tri-series was a sheer waste of time and energy."

Ultimately, Australia were too good for the cricket to be earth-shattering. There was just one truly close game among the seven, at Hobart, where England failed to beat what was essentially a second-string Australian team sprinkled with a few senior pros. It was a supremacy Australia would ram home over the next few weeks.

NATIONAL SQUADS

Australia *G. J. Bailey, P. J. Cummins, X. J. Doherty, J. P. Faulkner, A. J. Finch, B. J. Haddin, J. R. Hazlewood, M. C. Henriques, M. G. Johnson, M. R. Marsh, S. E. Marsh, G. J. Maxwell, K. W. Richardson, G. S. Sandhu, S. P. D. Smith, M. A. Starc, D. A. Warner, S. R. Watson, C. L. White. *Coach:* D. S. Lehmann.

M. J. Clarke was named as captain for this series and the World Cup, but did not feature as he recovered from a torn hamstring; Bailey captained the side when available. Richardson and Sandhu provided early cover for Johnson and M. R. Marsh (who both had hamstring injuries). Watson suffered a hamstring injury in the second game, and was replaced by Henriques.

England *E. J. G. Morgan, M. M. Ali, J. M. Anderson, G. S. Ballance, I. R. Bell, R. S. Bopara, S. C. J. Broad, J. C. Buttler, S. T. Finn, A. D. Hales, C. J. Jordan, J. E. Root, J. W. A. Taylor, J. C. Tredwell, C. R. Woakes. *Coach:* P. Moores.

India *M. S. Dhoni, R. Ashwin, Bhuvneshwar Kumar, S. T. R. Binny, S. Dhawan, R. A. Jadeja, V. Kohli, D. S. Kulkarni, Mohammed Shami, A. R. Patel, A. M. Rahane, S. K. Raina, A. T. Rayudu, I. Sharma, M. Sharma, R. G. Sharma, U. T. Yadav. *Coach:* D. A. G. Fletcher.

For reports of the Australia–India Tests that preceded this series, see Wisden 2015, *page 840.*

At Canberra, January 12, 2015. **England XI won by 216 runs.** ‡**England XI 364-6** (50 overs) (I. R. Bell 51, M. M. Ali 50, J. W. A. Taylor 55, J. E. Root 56, R. S. Bopara 56*); **Australian Capital Territory Invitational XI 148** (32.4 overs) (J. C. Tredwell 3-11). *The ACT XI chose men from 15 players, and England 13. Eoin Morgan took charge of England's one-day team on a permanent basis, and was the only member of the top six not to reach 50 (he made 32) as they eased into Australian conditions against a young side. Ravi Bopara struck five sixes in 27 balls; James Tredwell picked up three wickets in nine.*

At Canberra, January 14, 2015 (day/night). **England XI won by 60 runs.** ‡**England XI 391-6** (50 overs) (I. R. Bell 187, M. M. Ali 71, J. W. A. Taylor 71; J. P. Behrendorff 4-79); **Prime Minister's XI 331** (48.1 overs) (G. J. Maxwell 136; S. C. J. Broad 4-40). *MoM: I. R. Bell. Ian Bell's 187 was the highest score for England in 50-over cricket, although the match did not carry List A status. Bell, who had made just three hundreds in 150 one-day internationals, batted until the penultimate ball. Glenn Maxwell freewheeled to 136 from 89 deliveries before the Prime Minister's XI's challenge dissipated. Chris Woakes, running in from deep square leg, fumbled a skied hook from the Papua New Guinea batsman Lega Siaka, but kicked the ball up with his right boot and plucked a one-handed catch.*

AUSTRALIA v ENGLAND

At Sydney, January 16, 2015 (day/night). Australia won by three wickets. Australia 5pts. Toss: England.

Australia were in front from the start, as Starc used the brief window of swing offered by the white Kookaburra on a dazzlingly sunny day to pin Bell and Taylor in the first three balls. Starc's eventual four for 42 earned him the match award; he suggested Australia had "reopened a few scars" from the 2013-14 Ashes. There was, though, a welcome return to form for Morgan, England's newly installed captain. After a single fifty in one-day internationals in the previous 12 months, he made 121, the first hundred by an England one-day captain in Australia. But so tamely did his side give away their wickets in the middle overs – no one else reached 30 – that Morgan accounted for more than half their runs. Warner clumped a typically pugnacious 127 in reply – his first one-day international hundred in almost three years – and a calm 37 from Steve Smith put the game beyond doubt. Australia's rush to reach their target inside 40 overs, and earn a bonus point, produced a late flurry of wickets. Woakes finished with four, but it was the 61 unused balls, rather than the three untaken wickets, that reflected the gulf between the sides.

Man of the Match: M. A. Starc. *Attendance:* 26,045.

England

I. R. Bell lbw b Starc	0	S. C. J. Broad not out	0
M. M. Ali c Maxwell b Faulkner	22	S. T. Finn b Starc	0
J. W. A. Taylor lbw b Starc	0		
J. E. Root c Watson b Cummins	5	B 2, l-b 3, w 14, n-b 1	20
*E. J. G. Morgan c Maxwell b Starc	121		
R. S. Bopara c Maxwell b Doherty	13	1/0 (1) 2/0 (3) 3/12 (4) (47.5 overs)	234
†J. C. Buttler c Warner b Faulkner	28	4/33 (2) 5/69 (6) 6/136 (7)	
C. R. Woakes c Smith b Maxwell	8	7/168 (8) 8/224 (9) 9/234 (5)	
C. J. Jordan c Maxwell b Faulkner	17	10/234 (11) 10 overs: 39-4	

Starc 8.5–0–42–4; Cummins 9–1–42–1; Watson 4–0–23–0; Faulkner 10–1–47–3; Maxwell 6–0–37–1; Doherty 10–0–38–1.

Australia

D. A. Warner c Bell b Woakes	127	J. P. Faulkner not out	6
A. J. Finch b Woakes	15	M. A. Starc not out	0
S. R. Watson c Woakes b Jordan	16	L-b 7, w 1	8
S. P. D. Smith b Ali	37		
*G. J. Bailey c Buttler b Woakes	10	1/33 (2) 2/71 (3) (7 wkts, 39.5 overs)	235
G. J. Maxwell c Buttler b Woakes	7	3/158 (4) 4/199 (5)	
†B. J. Haddin run out	16	5/200 (6) 6/227 (1) 7/233 (7) 10 overs: 55-1	

P. J. Cummins and X. J. Doherty did not bat.

Woakes 8–1–40–4; Finn 8–1–48–0; Broad 6.5–0–49–0; Jordan 6–0–33–1; Ali 9–0–45–1; Bopara 2–0–13–0.

Umpires: H. D. P. K. Dharmasena and S. D. Fry.   Third umpire: J. D. Ward.
Referee: A. J. Pycroft.

AUSTRALIA v INDIA

At Melbourne, January 18, 2015 (day/night). Australia won by four wickets. Australia 4pts. Toss: India. One-day international debut: G. S. Sandhu.

Following a fractious Test series, Warner courted more controversy in front of a large Indian expat contingent with an outburst at Rohit Sharma, in which he repeatedly shouted at him to "speak English!" Warner felt Sharma had pinched a single in the 23rd over after a shy at the stumps cannoned off his pads; in fact, the throw missed everything. Told to "stop looking for trouble" by Cricket Australia chief executive James Sutherland, and rested for the next game, Warner was also fined 50% of his fee; Bailey was suspended for a match for a second over-rate penalty in 12 months. Sharma's innings of 138 was as good as any by an Indian against the white ball in Australia. He and Raina put on 126 for the fourth wicket, before Starc's yorkers swept through the middle and lower order. He finished with six for 43, removing Greg Chappell's improbable record for the best figures in a home one-day international for Australia (five for 15 against India at Sydney in 1980-81). Gurinder Sandhu, born in Sydney's western suburbs to parents who had emigrated from the Punjab, had Rahane caught behind with his eighth ball in international cricket. Finch kept the reply under control with a measured 96, then Haddin and Faulkner hurried things to a conclusion.

Man of the Match: M. A. Starc.   *Attendance:* 34,253.

India

R. G. Sharma c Maxwell b Starc	138
S. Dhawan c Finch b Starc	2
A. M. Rahane c Haddin b Sandhu	12
V. Kohli c Bailey b Faulkner	9
S. K. Raina c Maxwell b Starc	51
*†M. S. Dhoni b Starc	19
A. R. Patel lbw b Starc	0
R. Ashwin not out	14

Bhuvneshwar Kumar b Starc	0
Mohammed Shami not out	2
B 1, l-b 3, w 15, n-b 1	20
	—
1/3 (2) 2/33 (3) (8 wkts, 50 overs) 267	
3/59 (4) 4/185 (5)	
5/237 (6) 6/237 (7)	
7/262 (1) 8/262 (9)	
	10 overs: 45-2

U. T. Yadav did not bat.

Starc 10–2–43–6; Cummins 10–0–52–0; Sandhu 10–0–58–1; Faulkner 10–0–63–1; Watson 8–0–33–0; Maxwell 2–0–14–0.

Australia

A. J. Finch c Dhoni b Yadav	96
D. A. Warner c Raina b Yadav	24
S. R. Watson b Patel	41
S. P. D. Smith c Ashwin	
b Mohammed Shami	47
G. J. Maxwell c and b Bhuvneshwar Kumar	20
*G. J. Bailey c Dhoni b Ashwin	5

†B. J. Haddin not out	13
J. P. Faulkner not out	9
L-b 3, w 11	14
	—
1/51 (2) 2/115 (3) (6 wkts, 49 overs) 269	
3/216 (4) 4/219 (1)	
5/230 (6) 6/248 (5)	
	10 overs: 56-1

M. A. Starc, P. J. Cummins and G. S. Sandhu did not bat.

Bhuvneshwar Kumar 9.5–0–44–1; Yadav 10–1–55–2; Mohammed Shami 8.1–0–44–1; Patel 10–0–45–1; Ashwin 9–0–54–1; Raina 2–0–24–0.

Umpires: H. D. P. K. Dharmasena and J. D. Ward.   Third umpire: M. D. Martell.
Referee: A. J. Pycroft.

ENGLAND v INDIA

At Brisbane, January 20, 2015 (day/night). England won by nine wickets. England 5pts. Toss: India.

Both sides might have been relieved not to be playing Australia again. But the first one-day international meeting between these teams in Australia since the 1992 World Cup emphatically went the way of England, who cruised to just their second nine-wicket victory over India; never before had they beaten one of the top eight nations with as many as 22.3 overs unused. In the city where he had been branded "unselectable" a year earlier, Finn enjoyed a degree of redemption with a one-day best five for 33, without ever approaching express pace. He helped reduce India

ENGLAND'S MOST EMPHATIC OVERSEAS RUN-CHASES

Balls unused	Winning total		
135	156-1	v India (153) at Brisbane...	**2014-15**
112	121-3	v South Africa (119) at Port Elizabeth.........................	2009-10
97	179-3	v New Zealand (178-7) at Auckland	1991-92
94	102-3	v Australia (101) at Melbourne	1978-79
76	226-1	v Pakistan (222) at Dubai...	2011-12
75	186-5	v New Zealand (185) at Auckland	2012-13

This table excludes matches against Bangladesh, Zimbabwe and Associates.

from 57 for one to 67 for five, then returned to claim Dhoni – one of five dismissals for Buttler – and Akshar Patel with successive balls as they stumbled to 153, their lowest all-out total against England. At the other end, Anderson – in his first one-day international since September – quietly claimed four for 18. England were able to knock off 41 in six overs before the dinner-break: Bell continued his sparkling form from the warm-up matches with a fluent 88 not out, adding an unbroken 131 with Taylor. Even before night descended on Brisbane, England had claimed the bonus point.

Man of the Match: S. T. Finn. *Attendance:* 8,078.

India

A. M. Rahane c Taylor b Finn...........	33	Mohammed Shami c Ali b Anderson	1
S. Dhawan c Buttler b Anderson.........	1	U. T. Yadav not out...................	0
A. T. Rayudu c Buttler b Finn...........	23		
V. Kohli c Buttler b Finn...............	4	L-b 3, w 3, n-b 1	7
S. K. Raina st Buttler b Ali	1		
*M. S. Dhoni c Buttler b Finn	34	1/1 (2) 2/57 (1) 3/64 (4) (39.3 overs)	153
S. T. R. Binny c Morgan b Anderson	44	4/65 (5) 5/67 (3) 6/137 (6)	
A. R. Patel b Finn	0	7/137 (8) 8/143 (9) 9/153 (7)	
Bhuvneshwar Kumar b Anderson	5	10/153 (10) 10 overs: 36-1	

Anderson 8.3–2–18–4; Woakes 7–0–35–0; Broad 7–0–33–0; Finn 8–0–33–5; Ali 9–0–31–1.

England

I. R. Bell not out	88
M. M. Ali c Kohli b Binny	8
J. W. A. Taylor not out	56
W 3, n-b 1	4

1/25 (2)   (1 wkt, 27.3 overs) **156**
                         10 overs: 67-1

J. E. Root, *E. J. G. Morgan, R. S. Bopara, †J. C. Buttler, C. R. Woakes, S. C. J. Broad, S. T. Finn and J. M. Anderson did not bat.

Binny 7–0–34–1; Bhuvneshwar Kumar 2–0–18–0; Yadav 6–0–42–0; Mohammed Shami 4–0–23–0; Patel 7.3–0–32–0; Raina 1–0–7–0.

Umpires: H. D. P. K. Dharmasena and M. D. Martell.　　Third umpire: S. D. Fry.

Referee: A. J. Pycroft.

AUSTRALIA v ENGLAND

At Hobart, January 23, 2015 (day/night). Australia won by three wickets. Australia 4pts. Toss: Australia.

England had arrived in Hobart with a spring in their step, while Australia were missing first-choice players through injury, suspension or rest. Steve Smith was elevated to the captaincy because of George Bailey's ban, and opportunities were given to Shaun Marsh, White (his first one-day international in nearly four years), Henriques and Sandhu, none of whom was in the World Cup squad. It made little difference, and Australia secured their place in the final with two group games to go. This should have been Bell's day after he became the second England player to reach 5,000 ODI runs, then passed Paul Collingwood's national record of 5,092 (though he was only 65th on the overall list). He pressed on to his fourth hundred and highest score, but only Ali – who had helped Bell put on England's first century opening partnership for 48 innings – and Root, with 69 off 70 balls, offered more than paper-thin support. Morgan fell first ball, nibbling behind off Sandhu, but refused to blame a blackmail plot by the boyfriend of an ex-lover. Australia produced exceptional death bowling to claim six for 59 in the final ten overs, including three wickets off the last three balls, two of them underarm run-outs by Haddin. A total of 303 for eight looked on the light side, and Finch and Marsh began destructively. Finn found reverse swing in the 17th over to claim two wickets in three balls, but Smith stole the show, becoming the first man to score hundreds on captaincy debut in both Tests and one-day internationals, and adding a crucial 81 for the sixth wicket in ten overs with the aggressive Haddin. Starc carved Woakes over cover for the winning run with a ball to spare. Anderson was making his 304th international appearance, breaking Alec Stewart's England record.

Man of the Match: S. P. D. Smith.　　*Attendance:* 10,784.

England

M. M. Ali c sub (X. J. Doherty) b Faulkner	46		S. C. J. Broad not out	0
I. R. Bell c Starc b Sandhu	141			
J. W. A. Taylor c Faulkner b Henriques	5		B 1, l-b 4, w 5	10
J. E. Root c Finch b Cummins	69			
*E. J. G. Morgan c Haddin b Sandhu	0		1/113 (1) 2/132 (3)	(8 wkts, 50 overs) 303
†J. C. Buttler run out	25		3/253 (2) 4/254 (5)	
R. S. Bopara b Starc	7		5/275 (4) 6/303 (7)	
C. R. Woakes run out	0		7/303 (6) 8/303 (8)	10 overs: 69-0

S. T. Finn and J. M. Anderson did not bat.

Starc 10–0–60–1; Cummins 10–0–74–1; Sandhu 10–0–49–2; Maxwell 3–0–22–0; Faulkner 10–0–59–1; Henriques 7–0–34–1.

Australia

A. J. Finch b Ali	32		M. C. Henriques run out	4
S. E. Marsh c Bell b Finn	45		M. A. Starc not out	1
*S. P. D. Smith not out	102		L-b 3, w 3	6
C. L. White lbw b Finn	0			
G. J. Maxwell c Root b Ali	37		1/76 (1) 2/92 (2)	(7 wkts, 49.5 overs) 304
J. P. Faulkner c Bell b Woakes	35		3/92 (4) 4/161 (5)	
†B. J. Haddin c Bell b Woakes	42		5/216 (6) 6/297 (7) 7/302 (8)	10 overs: 67-0

P. J. Cummins and G. S. Sandhu did not bat.

Woakes 9.5–0–58–2; Anderson 10–0–56–0; Broad 9–0–61–0; Ali 10–0–50–2; Finn 10–0–65–2; Bopara 1–0–11–0.

Umpires: M. Erasmus and S. D. Fry.　　Third umpire: J. D. Ward.

Referee: A. J. Pycroft.

AUSTRALIA v INDIA

At Sydney, January 26, 2015 (day/night). No result. Australia 2pts, India 2pts. Toss: Australia.

By moving the traditional Australia Day fixture from Adelaide to Sydney – with its more cosmopolitan catchment area – Cricket Australia hoped to capitalise on the presence of India, on what was also their Republic Day. But rain brought a premature conclusion after 16 overs, during which Dhawan again dabbed uncertainly outside off stump. The two points awarded to each team meant India could still qualify for the final with victory over England four days later.

Attendance: 22,692.

India

A. M. Rahane not out	....	28
S. Dhawan c Finch b Starc	....	8
A. T. Rayudu c Warner b Marsh	....	23
V. Kohli not out	....	3
W 7	....	7

1/24 (2) 2/62 (3)   (2 wkts, 16 overs) 69
                              9 overs: 41-1

S. K. Raina, *†M. S. Dhoni, S. T. R. Binny, R. A. Jadeja, A. R. Patel, Mohammed Shami and I. Sharma did not bat.

Starc 4–0–11–1; Hazlewood 5–0–25–0; Marsh 3–0–21–1; Doherty 3–0–10–0; Faulkner 1–0–2–0.

Australia

A. J. Finch, D. A. Warner, S. P. D. Smith, *G. J. Bailey, G. J. Maxwell, M. R. Marsh, †B. J. Haddin, J. P. Faulkner, M. A. Starc, J. R. Hazlewood, X. J. Doherty.

Umpires: M. Erasmus and P. Wilson.   Third umpire: M. D. Martell.
Referee: A. J. Pycroft.

ENGLAND v INDIA

At Perth, January 30, 2015. England won by three wickets. England 4pts. Toss: England.

England won what was in effect a semi-final, leaving India still searching for their first victory of the tour. A pitch of unpredictable bounce made life tough for batsmen: left-arm spinner Patel got one to rear off a length, while Dhoni was struck on the helmet by Anderson, then given out lbw in the same over, hit below the knee-roll by a delivery pitching on a similar length. India had established a solid opening foundation of 83 in 20 overs, their best start in 12 international innings on this trip; Dhawan struck his first boundary since December 27. But things quickly unravelled at the start of Woakes's second spell. Buttler took a good catch to remove Dhawan for 38, and Rahane was the only batsman to cope with the pace and bounce of the England seamers as India rolled over for 200; all ten had fallen for 117. England, though, had batting fragilities of their own, and Binny's gentle pace was enough to expose them. His three-wicket burst upended the middle order and left England reeling on 66 for five. Taylor and the fluent Buttler applied a low-risk approach to put on 125 in 23.2 overs, until each threw their wickets away. Woakes and Broad finished the task with 19 balls to spare.

Man of the Match: J. W. A. Taylor.   *Attendance:* 7,653.

India

A. M. Rahane c Buttler b Finn	73	M. Sharma not out	7
S. Dhawan c Buttler b Woakes	38	Mohammed Shami c Buttler b Woakes	25
V. Kohli c Root b Ali	8		
S. K. Raina c Woakes b Ali	1	L-b 2, w 4	6
A. T. Rayudu c Buttler b Broad	12		
*†M. S. Dhoni lbw b Anderson	17	1/83 (2) 2/103 (3)	(48.1 overs) 200
S. T. R. Binny c Bell b Broad	7	3/107 (4) 4/134 (5) 5/136 (1)	
R. A. Jadeja c Finn b Broad	5	6/152 (7) 7/164 (6) 8/164 (8)	
A. R. Patel c Bell b Finn	1	9/165 (9) 10/200 (11)	10 overs: 34-0

Anderson 9–1–24–1; Woakes 9.1–1–47–2; Broad 10–1–56–2; Finn 10–0–36–3; Ali 10–0–35–2.

England

I. R. Bell lbw b Sharma	10	C. R. Woakes not out	4
M. M. Ali c Rayudu b Patel	17	S. C. J. Broad not out	3
J. W. A. Taylor c Binny b Sharma	82	W 7, n-b 2	9
J. E. Root c and b Binny	3		
*E. J. G. Morgan c Dhawan b Binny	2	1/14 (1) 2/40 (2)	(7 wkts, 46.5 overs) 201
R. S. Bopara c Jadeja b Binny	4	3/44 (4) 4/54 (5)	
†J. C. Buttler c Rayudu b Mohammed Shami	67	5/66 (6) 6/191 (3) 7/193 (7)	10 overs: 35-1

S. T. Finn and J. M. Anderson did not bat.

Binny 8–0–33–3; Sharma 10–1–36–2; Mohammed Shami 9–0–31–1; Patel 10–1–39–1; Jadeja 9.5–0–62–0.

Umpires: M. Erasmus and J. D. Ward.   Third umpire: S. D. Fry.
Referee: A. J. Pycroft.

FINAL TABLE

	Played	Won	Lost	No result	Bonus points	Points	Net run-rate
AUSTRALIA	4	3	0	1	1	15	0.46
ENGLAND	4	2	2	0	1	9	0.42
India	4	0	3	1	0	2	–0.94

Win = 4pts. One bonus point was awarded for achieving victory with a run-rate 1.25 times that of the opposition.

FINAL

AUSTRALIA v ENGLAND

At Perth, February 1, 2015. Australia won by 112 runs. Toss: England.

The return of Mitchell Johnson after a month's rest lent the final an extra frisson – and he disappointed nobody, ripping out England's top order with three for five in ten balls to condemn this to a rout. It had not looked that way early on, as England's confident bowlers made inroads into a powerful Australian batting line-up still missing Shane Watson and Michael Clarke. The top four could muster only 54 between them, with Bailey, continuing his lean spell, bounced out by Broad. That was Broad's 500th international wicket – making him the third England bowler to reach the mark, after Ian Botham and James Anderson. But England still had the all-rounders to deal with, and they hit a brick wall as Maxwell and Marsh added 141. Maxwell had already taken a destructive hundred off England for the Prime Minister's XI, and he seemed set for another until he swung once too often at Broad and edged behind for 95. Marsh followed for 60, but Faulkner thundered the third fifty of the innings, from just 24 balls, to put up a strong total. Bell was superbly caught by Haddin low to his right off Hazlewood, and Johnson came on to bowl the seventh over. By the end of the 11th, he had all but ended the contest: he had Taylor caught on the drive at backward point, got one to rear at Ali, then castled Morgan, playing no shot, for his second golden duck of the series. It was devastating. Maxwell mopped up four wickets, after Faulkner limped off with a side strain in his third over. Australia's margin of victory was emphatic, and the problems England had encountered with Johnson a year before showed no signs of abating.

Man of the Match: G. J. Maxwell. *Attendance:* 12,508.

Man of the Series: M. A. Starc.

Australia

A. J. Finch c Root b Anderson	0	M. G. Johnson c Morgan b Finn 3
D. A. Warner c Taylor b Anderson	12	M. A. Starc not out 0
S. P. D. Smith st Buttler b Ali	40	B 1, l-b 3, w 3 7
*G. J. Bailey c Taylor b Broad	2	
G. J. Maxwell c Buttler b Broad	95	1/0 (1) 2/33 (2) (8 wkts, 50 overs) 278
M. R. Marsh run out	60	3/46 (4) 4/60 (3)
†B. J. Haddin c Taylor b Broad	9	5/201 (5) 6/217 (6)
J. P. Faulkner not out	50	7/224 (7) 8/269 (9) 10 overs: 42-2

J. R. Hazlewood did not bat.

Anderson 10–2–38–2; Woakes 10–0–89–0; Broad 10–1–55–3; Finn 10–0–53–1; Ali 10–0–39–1.

England

M. M. Ali c Finch b Johnson	26	S. T. Finn b Hazlewood 6
I. R. Bell c Haddin b Hazlewood	8	J. M. Anderson not out 5
J. W. A. Taylor c Maxwell b Johnson	4	
J. E. Root lbw b Faulkner	25	L-b 8, w 10 18
*E. J. G. Morgan b Johnson	0	
R. S. Bopara c Bailey b Maxwell	33	1/18 (2) 2/35 (3) (39.1 overs) 166
†J. C. Buttler c sub (P. J. Cummins) b Maxwell	17	3/46 (1) 4/46 (5)
C. R. Woakes c and b Maxwell	0	5/71 (4) 6/98 (7)
S. C. J. Broad c sub (P. J. Cummins) b Maxwell	24	7/98 (8) 8/130 (9)
		9/160 (6) 10/166 (10) 10 overs: 46-2

Starc 7–0–40–0; Hazlewood 6.1–2–13–2; Johnson 7–2–27–3; Marsh 7–0–18–0; Maxwell 9–0–46–4; Faulkner 2.3–1–11–1; Finch 0.3–0–3–0.

Umpires: M. Erasmus and S. D. Fry. Third umpire: J. D. Ward.
Referee: A. J. Pycroft.

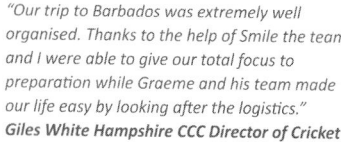

WEST INDIES v ENGLAND IN 2014-15

Review By Mike Selvey

Test matches (3): West Indies 1, England 1

It is rare that the England wagon runs entirely smoothly. But, from preamble to postscript, this Caribbean tour had it lurching over cobblestones and rutted tracks, the players almost incidental to dramas in the background. The series was honourably shared, though there was dishonour in England's capitulation in the final Test at Bridgetown, following a draw in Antigua which they had dominated, and a hard-earned victory in Grenada, inspired by Jimmy Anderson. But, for West Indies – largely shorn of their IPL fortune-seekers, and with a new coach, Phil Simmons, who had already made his mark with Ireland – there were signs of genuine promise.

Yet, while the players zigzagged from island to island, subplots dictated the agenda. In March, following England's ignominious exit from the World Cup, ECB chairman-elect Colin Graves suggested – in a parody of the comedian Harry Enfield's blunt Yorkshireman "saying what I like, and liking what I say" – that there would be "inquiries" if the Test team could not beat a "mediocre" West Indies. Without having the same undertones as Tony Greig's infamous "grovel" remark in 1976, it nonetheless resonated in the Caribbean, and was pinned up in the West Indies dressing-room to serve as a motivational tool. After they took the final Test by five wickets, captain Denesh Ramdin might have been "Yeah Graves, Talk Nah", an echo of his message to Viv Richards at Edgbaston in 2012. Graves later said he stood by his words, claiming he was happy to be proved wrong.

Be that as it may, Graves's remarks were only a precursor. Five days before the First Test Paul Downton was sacked, only 14 months into his role as managing director – even as he was preparing to fly to the West Indies. It was part of a restructuring process, led by the ECB's new chief executive Tom Harrison, that would result in the appointment of the former captain Andrew Strauss to a more specific position as director of the England team. This, in turn, would result in the sacking of head coach Peter Moores, which had something to do with the defeat in Barbados, but rather more to do with the World Cup. Some felt Moores might have been saved had England been bolder in selection for the final Test, where Adam Lyth, Adil Rashid – two of six Yorkshiremen in the squad – and Mark Wood were denied debuts. But the decision had long been made: as Strauss was to point out, each match had become a referendum on the coach, which was not fair on anyone.

Concerns remained about the make-up of the team. Reasons to be encouraged in the longer term were tempered by other, more immediate, issues – the identity of Alastair Cook's opening partner, an effective third seamer, and the quality of the spin bowling. An attempt to resurrect the career of Jonathan Trott – who had not played for England since being laid low by stress in Brisbane in November 2013 – by converting him into an opener was fraught with risk.

Calamitous comeback: Jonathan Trott chops on to Shannon Gabriel at Grenada – one of his five single-figure dismissals.

Perhaps Trott felt he had something to prove, which was not the case. He had a horrible time against the new ball, a specially developed Dukes suitable for more abrasive overseas pitches, and used brilliantly by Jerome Taylor. Trott selflessly offered to stand down before the final Test, and the manner of his first-innings dismissal there, bounced out in uncompromising fashion by Shannon Gabriel, was the sad clincher. One half-century in six innings – and three ducks – did not reflect his service to the side since his Test debut in 2009. He announced his retirement from international cricket the day after the series ended, but the advancement of Lyth had been delayed by three matches.

The late arrival of Moeen Ali, recovering from a side strain picked up at the World Cup, meant James Tredwell was England's spinner in the First Test, where he acquitted himself better in the first innings than the second. Hindsight says Ali needed to bowl more before returning for the last two games in which Joe Root looked the most threatening. There had been a clamour for the inclusion of leg-spinner Rashid after a successful season with Yorkshire, but his performances in South Africa with the Lions, and during one of the warm-up matches in St Kitts, were not encouraging. He was thought to lack the capacity to bowl at a pace appropriate to Tests.

FIVE STATS YOU MAY HAVE MISSED

BENEDICT BERMANGE

- In Antigua, Jason Holder made his maiden Test century, after a previous first-class best of just 52. Only two men have had a lower career-best at the time of their first Test hundred:

Previous HS

40	J. E. Taylor	106, West Indies v New Zealand at Dunedin	2008-09
49	†B. R. Taylor	105, New Zealand v India at Calcutta	1964-65
52	**J. O. Holder**	**103*, West Indies v England at North Sound** . . .	**2014-15**
52*	H. G. Owen-Smith	129, South Africa v England at Leeds	1929

† *On Test debut.*

- Before Alastair Cook and Jonathan Trott put on 125 in Grenada, England had gone 40 innings without a three-figure opening partnership, breaking their record of 36, between January 1954 (Len Hutton and Willie Watson 130 against West Indies at Kingston) and June 1956 (Colin Cowdrey and Peter Richardson 151 against Australia at Nottingham).

- James Tredwell had missed 55 matches since his previous Test, but took four for 47 in the first innings in Antigua. Only three men had missed more Tests before returning with at least four wickets in their first innings back:

Missed

86	P. I. Pocock	4-121, England v West Indies at Manchester	1984
78	R. J. Sidebottom	4-42, England v West Indies at Leeds	2007
58	M. R. Whitney	4-92, Australia v New Zealand at Melbourne	1987-88
55	**J. C. Tredwell**	**4-47, England v West Indies at North Sound**	**2014-15**
49	P. P. Chawla	4-69, India v England at Nagpur	2012-13
45	C. D. Collymore	5-66, West Indies v Sri Lanka at Gros Islet	2003
42	P. R. Sleep	4-132, Australia v England at Adelaide	1986-87
42	D. R. Tuffey	4-64, New Zealand v Pakistan at Wellington	2009-10

- Joe Root was involved in three run-outs during his 182* in Grenada, only the second instance for England after Bill Athey, in his 14* against Pakistan at Birmingham in 1987.

- Before his century in Barbados, Cook had gone 35 innings without one, the second-longest spell for any England opener:

Inns				*Inns*			
41	J. M. Brearley . .		1976 to 1981	30	M. A. Butcher . .	1998-99 to 2003-04	
35	**A. N. Cook**		**2013 to 2014-15**	28	P. E. Richardson	1958 to 1963	
33	T. W. Hayward .		1901-02 to 1909	28	G. Boycott	1964-65 to 1966	

These figures exclude innings not as an opener. Butcher scored six hundreds from No. 3 between these dates, but Brearley never made a Test century from any position.

Benedict Bermange is the cricket statistician for Sky Sports.

The third seamer's spot was filled by Chris Jordan, a diligent cricketer and a stunning slip fielder, especially off the spinners. His bowling progressed significantly, with a smoother run-up more in keeping with his natural athleticism, and a high action, but he still lacked a cutting edge.

The pace attack was held together by the brilliance of Anderson: in Antigua he overtook Ian Botham's England-record 383 Test wickets, and contributed a match-winning spell in Grenada; 17 wickets at 18 apiece earned him his third successive Man of the Series award. Stuart Broad, though, was patchy, too frequently down on speed. It was hard to tell whether he was deliberately holding something back on slow pitches, or simply out of kilter. Only one spell, in Grenada, bucked the trend, and Broad was as guilty as any in failing to polish off West Indies' lower order on the last afternoon in Antigua.

There, Jason Holder announced himself as a Test cricketer of serious worth, saving the match with an unbeaten maiden century, to follow Jermaine Blackwood's in the first innings. Those hundreds, combined with one apiece for Kraigg Brathwaite and Marlon Samuels, plus 11 wickets at 18 for the nippy Taylor, kept West Indies competitive. For the 40-year-old Shivnarine Chanderpaul, a haul of 92 runs at 15 cost him his place in the two-Test series at home to Australia; after 21 years at the highest level, the end seemed nigh.

England's batting was a mixed bag, too, with centuries from Ian Bell and Gary Ballance in Antigua, Root in Grenada, and Cook in Barbados, but with old-school collapses thrown in – most damagingly when they slipped to 39 for five on the second evening of the Barbados Test. Bell's hundred was followed by 12 runs in four innings, concluding with a pair. But Root continued his wonderful form since being dropped at Sydney at the start of 2014, scoring 358 runs at almost 90, while Ballance's solidity brought him 331 at 66. There was promise of better things to come from Jos Buttler and Ben Stokes, who ought to have learned plenty after being wound up to breaking point by Marlon Samuels; the mock salute with which Samuels greeted his demise in Grenada was a rare example of a genuinely funny send-off.

There were signs that Cook had started to regain the synchronicity of movement that had been lacking over the previous two years, and he was able to concentrate fully on the bowling rather than his technique. If his pre-World Cup sacking as one-day captain was controversial, it allowed him to focus once more on what he did best. The benefit was evident as he overcame a double failure in Antigua to make 244 runs in Grenada and Barbados, where he ended the long spell without a Test hundred. His alignment improved through opening his stance a little, and he rediscovered his immaculate judgment outside off stump. The century was both timely and cathartic, a return to his best, although his uncharacteristic dismissal in the final over of the opening day destabilised the innings. Harsh though it sounds, it was a factor in the collapse the following morning – and England's ultimate defeat.

ENGLAND TOURING PARTY

*A. N. Cook (Essex), M. M. Ali (Worcestershire), J. M. Anderson (Lancashire), J. M. Bairstow (Yorkshire), G. S. Ballance (Yorkshire), I. R. Bell (Warwickshire), S. C. J. Broad (Nottinghamshire), J. C. Buttler (Lancashire), C. J. Jordan (Sussex), A. Lyth (Yorkshire), L. E. Plunkett (Yorkshire), A. U. Rashid (Yorkshire), J. E. Root (Yorkshire), B. A. Stokes (Durham), J. C. Tredwell (Kent), I. J. L. Trott (Warwickshire), M. A. Wood (Durham).

Ali joined the squad after the First Test, having recovered from a side strain.

Coach: P. Moores. *Assistant coach:* P. Farbrace. *Batting coach:* M. R. Ramprakash. *Fast-bowling coach:* O. D. Gibson. *Fielding coach:* C. G. Taylor. *Strength and conditioning coach:* P. C. F. Scott. *Team operations manager:* P. A. Neale. *Physiotherapist:* C. A. de Weymarn. *Team doctor:* N. S. Peirce. *Analyst:* R. J. Lewis. *Massage therapist:* M. E. S. Saxby. *Psychologist:* C. K. Marshall. *Security manager:* T. Minish. *Media relations manager:* R. C. Evans.

TEST MATCH AVERAGES

WEST INDIES – BATTING AND FIELDING

	T	I	NO	R	HS	100	50	Avge	Ct/St
J. Blackwood	3	6	2	311	112*	1	1	77.75	4
†D. M. Bravo	3	6	0	237	82	0	2	39.50	6
M. N. Samuels	3	6	0	225	103	1	0	37.50	0
J. O. Holder	3	5	1	148	103*	1	0	37.00	3
K. C. Brathwaite	3	6	0	186	116	1	0	31.00	1
D. Ramdin	3	6	1	138	57	0	1	27.60	6/2
†D. S. Smith	2	4	0	93	65	0	1	23.25	1
†S. T. Gabriel	2	3	2	20	20*	0	0	20.00	0
†S. Chanderpaul	3	6	0	92	46	0	0	15.33	1
K. A. J. Roach	2	4	1	31	15*	0	0	10.33	0

Played in two Tests: J. E. Taylor 0, 15. Played in one Test: †S. J. Benn 2 (1 ct); †D. Bishoo 30, 15*; S. D. Hope 5, 9 (1 ct); V. Permaul 18 (1 ct).

BOWLING

	Style	O	M	R	W	BB	5I	Avge
J. E. Taylor	RFM	63.4	18	201	11	3-33	0	18.27
S. T. Gabriel	RFM	51	13	150	6	2-47	0	25.00
J. O. Holder	RFM	89.5	29	249	8	3-15	0	31.12
V. Permaul	SLA	31	4	129	4	3-43	0	32.25
D. Bishoo	LBG	59	10	209	4	4-177	0	52.25
K. A. J. Roach	RFM	78	12	265	5	4-94	0	53.00
M. N. Samuels	OB	90.1	11	259	3	1-38	0	86.33

Also bowled: S. J. Benn (SLA) 52–6–200–2; J. Blackwood (OB) 1–0–14–0; K. C. Brathwaite (OB) 5–1–9–0.

ENGLAND – BATTING AND FIELDING

	T	I	NO	R	HS	100	50	Avge	Ct
J. E. Root	3	5	1	358	182*	1	2	89.50	4
†G. S. Ballance	3	6	1	331	122	1	2	66.20	2
J. C. Buttler	3	5	3	110	59*	0	1	55.00	13
†A. N. Cook	3	6	1	268	105	1	2	53.60	4
†B. A. Stokes	3	5	0	176	79	0	1	35.20	1
I. R. Bell	3	5	0	155	143	1	0	31.00	1
†M. M. Ali	2	3	0	66	58	0	1	22.00	2
C. J. Jordan	3	5	1	55	21*	0	0	13.75	6
I. J. L. Trott	3	6	0	72	59	0	1	12.00	1
†J. M. Anderson	3	4	0	24	20	0	0	6.00	2
†S. C. J. Broad	3	4	0	10	10	0	0	2.50	1

Played in one Test: †J. C. Tredwell 8 (1 ct).

BOWLING

	Style	O	M	R	W	BB	5I	Avge
J. M. Anderson	RFM	119.2	38	306	17	6-42	1	18.00
J. C. Tredwell	OB	66	26	140	5	4-47	0	28.00
S. C. J. Broad	RFM	111	26	320	10	4-61	0	32.00
J. E. Root	OB	46	18	101	3	2-22	0	33.66
M. M. Ali	OB	60.2	13	208	6	3-51	0	34.66
C. J. Jordan	RFM	104	32	256	6	2-65	0	42.66
B. A. Stokes	RFM	64	10	256	3	1-17	0	85.33

Also bowled: I. J. L. Trott (RM) 1–0–2–0.

At Basseterre, St Kitts, April 6–7, 2015 (not first-class). **Drawn. ‡St Kitts Invitational XI 59** (26.3 overs) (B. A. Stokes 3-10) **and 76-7** (35 overs) (J. C. Tredwell 3-35); **England XI 379-6 dec** (115.2 overs) (A. N. Cook 101, I. J. L. Trott 72, I. R. Bell 59, J. E. Root 64. *Each side chose from 14 players. After a local side lamentably weak in batting was bundled out in around two hours, England applied themselves to practice: Alastair Cook, having began by putting on 158 with Jonathan Trott, retired out after reaching a 257-minute century, and Ian Bell also retired, after 212 minutes at the crease and a stand of 118 with Joe Root. A declaration left the Invitational XI 35 overs to survive, which they managed – just.*

At Basseterre, St Kitts, April 8–9, 2015 (not first-class). **Drawn. St Kitts Invitational XI 303-9 dec** (90 overs) (J. M. Bairstow 98, A. Saunders 50, J. E. Root 87*; B. A. Stokes 3-32); **‡England XI 222** (78.1 overs). *Each side chose from 17 players, and it was agreed that each would bat for a day of 90 overs. The Invitational XI was bolstered by the inclusion of several of the tourists. Trott, opening for St Kitts, was dismissed by Jimmy Anderson for a three-ball duck, and Gary Ballance also fell cheaply. Jonny Bairstow and local man Akeem Saunders put on 135, then Root batted out the first day. Trott went in again for the England XI on the second morning, and was caught behind by Bairstow for two; Ballance also swapped sides, and retired out for 23.*

WEST INDIES v ENGLAND

First Test Match

Chris Stocks

At North Sound, Antigua, April 13–17, 2015. Drawn. Toss: West Indies.

Anderson's pair of two-wicket hauls would normally have been a footnote to a nailbiting draw which pleased West Indies more than England. But they took him – in his 100th Test, and with his family in attendance – to 384 overall, one more than Ian Botham's national record. And they offered some consolation for England's failure to finish off the game.

The record fell at 3.52 on the final afternoon when Ramdin, the West Indies captain, fended to a diving Cook, his England counterpart, at first slip. Anderson's guttural roar as he ran, arms outstretched, to his team-mates was a release of the pressure that had built up as England prepared for their first Test in eight months since defeating India at The Oval. There was a more immediate context, too. Ramdin's dismissal broke a seventh-wicket partnership of 105 with Holder, and gave England renewed hope of victory. With three wickets needed in 18.4 overs, that was plausible, even on a benign pitch that offered the seamers little.

But Holder was in no mood to acquiesce. In only his fourth Test, he scored a magnificent, belligerent maiden hundred to earn his team a draw that had looked beyond them when they started their second innings the previous afternoon, chasing 438 – or, more realistically, needing to bat 130 overs. That England fell short, extending their winless record on Antigua's two grounds to nine matches – including the Test abandoned six years previously after ten balls because of a sandlogged outfield – was not only down to Holder's skill or the unhelpful surface. The bowlers were also culpable, failing to strike when West Indies were most vulnerable.

Broad, Jordan and Stokes could manage only two for 159 between them and, despite a tidy first-innings performance, Tredwell – playing his second Test, more than five years after his debut, in Mirpur – was unable to exploit the turn on offer on the final day. Root's part-time off-breaks offered the greater threat. Yet, with just 35 deliveries remaining, Tredwell almost benefited when Holder, on 87, drove the ball into Ballance's ankle at silly point; it deflected towards Tredwell, but dropped tantalisingly short.

Much water had flowed under various bridges since The Oval. Any goodwill had evaporated during a painful winter of one-day cricket, culminating in England's

Long-playing record: Jimmy Anderson overtakes Ian Botham as Denesh Ramdin nicks to slip.

group-stage exit at the World Cup. Peter Moores, the head coach, found himself under intense scrutiny, which increased when Paul Downton, who had appointed him a year earlier, was sacked as ECB managing director back in London during the second of England's warm-up matches. Neither the low-grade opposition nor the political upheaval was ideal preparation for the Tests.

So it was no surprise when England made a sluggish start, collapsing to 34 for three inside 17 overs after being inserted. Trott was back, but as an opener, rather than at his accustomed No. 3 – Cook's fifth partner since the retirement of Andrew Strauss in 2012. But he was out to the fifth delivery of the match, edging a probing outswinger from Taylor to first slip. Cook had troubles of his own: sacked as England's one-day captain in December, he was without a Test hundred since May 2013. His barren run continued when he allowed a delivery from Roach to sneak between bat and pad. Ballance, who averaged 60 in his first year of Test cricket, had endured a tough World Cup, and spent 77 minutes accumulating ten runs before a tentative prod at Holder flew to slip. Those breakthroughs were just rewards for the West Indians, who swung the ball far more than their England counterparts. It was also the perfect start for new coach Phil Simmons, in his first match in charge after eight years with Ireland.

Yet early local optimism, buoyed by a public holiday that encouraged a large turnout, was punctured by a 177-run fourth-wicket partnership between Bell and the lively Root. Bell then put on 130 with Stokes, revelling in the responsibility of the No. 6 slot in the absence of the injured Moeen Ali. Bell finished with 143 – his first overseas hundred since December 2012 at Nagpur, and his 22nd in all Tests, drawing him level with Wally Hammond, Colin Cowdrey and Geoff Boycott. He departed in the penultimate over of the day to Roach, edging the second new ball, but this was one of the most satisfying innings of his career: it was in Antigua, six years earlier, where he had been dropped, following

ENGLAND'S LEADING WICKET-TAKER

How the record has progressed since Johnny Briggs reached 100 wickets in 1894-95:

Eventual wickets		Broke record	Eventual wickets		Broke record
112	G. A. Lohmann	1895-96	307	F. S. Trueman	1962-63
118	J. Briggs	1897-98	325	R. G. D. Willis	1983-84
189	S. F. Barnes.	1912	383	I. T. Botham	1985
236	A. V. Bedser	1953	**433***	**J. M. Anderson**	**2014-15**
242	J. B. Statham	1962-63			

* *As at January 31, 2016.*

Barnes held the record for almost 41 years, Botham for nearly 30, and Statham for 49 days.

the 51-all-out defeat in Jamaica. His was the first of five wickets to fall for 20 – four of them on the second morning – and England needed a last-ditch stand of 38 between Jordan and Anderson to reach 399.

Wickets for Anderson bookended the West Indian reply, which was dominated by a maiden century for Jermaine Blackwood, a 23-year-old Jamaican playing only his sixth Test. He rode his luck: on the second evening, Stokes had him caught in the slips off a no-ball on 21; on the third morning, it was Stokes again who had him dropped in the gully by Tredwell on 43. Having arrived with West Indies in trouble at 99 for four, Blackwood was never short on courage. He drove his second ball, from Tredwell, for six, and took 40 runs off the luckless Stokes alone. By the end of an innings in which the next-best score was Chanderpaul's 46, Blackwood was unbeaten on 112. England led by 104.

They stumbled at the start of their second innings, but wrested back control thanks to a fine century – his fourth in nine Tests – from a revitalised Ballance. The skittish Trott fell for four when he was caught behind wandering up the pitch to Taylor, who then exposed Cook's frailties outside off stump. When Bell was carelessly run out, England were 52 for three, and in danger of wasting their advantage. But Ballance added 114 with Root, who made an impressive half-century before being bowled by Holder, and restored calm to an innings that concluded with an inventive 47-ball half-century from Buttler. It allowed Cook to declare with 40 overs of the fourth day remaining.

England bargained for more than two wickets before stumps, especially after Broad had Brathwaite fending a bouncer to short leg in the second over. Yet the late dismissal of Darren Bravo – Jordan taking a sensational slip catch off Root – kept them in the ascendancy. Two more wickets in the first hour next morning raised their hopes: Tredwell had Devon Smith caught at mid-on, and Anderson extracted a hint of reverse to find Samuels's edge and draw level with Botham. By lunch, Root had added the prized scalp of Chanderpaul to reduce West Indies to 155 for five.

A rush of blood from Blackwood, edging Jordan after a reckless charge an over before the second new ball was available, brought Holder to the crease. England needed four wickets in 51 overs, but he was unperturbed. First he joined forces with Ramdin to eat up 32 of them. Then, after Anderson had removed Ramdin, Roach helped Holder blunt England for a further 18. By the time Holder reached his century in the penultimate over, lofting Tredwell over long-off for four, West Indies had done enough to clinch a deserved draw. Only once before, when they made 408 for five in 164.3 overs against England during a timeless Test in Jamaica in April 1930, had they batted longer to save a game. More importantly, Holder had helped restore some cheer to the Caribbean game.

Man of the Match: J. O. Holder.

Close of play: first day, England 341-5 (Stokes 71, Tredwell 0); second day, West Indies 155-4 (Chanderpaul 29, Blackwood 30); third day, England 116-3 (Ballance 44, Root 32); fourth day, West Indies 98-2 (Smith 59, Samuels 2).

England

*A. N. Cook b Roach	11	– c Benn b Taylor	13
I. J. L. Trott c Bravo b Taylor	0	– c Ramdin b Taylor	4
G. S. Ballance c Bravo b Holder	10	– c Blackwood b Benn	122
I. R. Bell c Ramdin b Roach	143	– run out	11
J. E. Root b Taylor	83	– b Holder	59
B. A. Stokes c Holder b Taylor	79	– st Ramdin b Benn	35
J. C. Tredwell c Bravo b Holder	8		
†J. C. Buttler c Ramdin b Roach	0	– (7) not out	59
C. J. Jordan not out	21	– (8) c Bravo b Roach	13
S. C. J. Broad c Blackwood b Roach	0		
J. M. Anderson c Holder b Samuels	20		
B 7, l-b 3, w 8, n-b 6	24	B 1, l-b 6, w 5, n-b 5	17

1/1 (2) 2/22 (1) 3/34 (3) (110.4 overs) 399   1/15 (2) (7 wkts dec, 86 overs) 333
4/211 (5) 5/341 (4) 6/357 (6)   2/20 (1) 3/52 (4)
7/357 (7) 8/361 (8) 9/361 (10) 10/399 (11)   4/166 (5) 5/226 (6) 6/281 (3) 7/333 (8)

Taylor 20–4–90–3; Roach 29–6–94–4; Holder 25–11–69–2; Benn 26–3–85–0; Samuels 10.4–0–51–1. *Second innings*—Taylor 14–5–42–2; Roach 14–1–53–1; Holder 17–5–63–1; Benn 26–3–115–2; Samuels 15–0–53–0.

West Indies

K. C. Brathwaite c Jordan b Tredwell	39	– c Root b Broad	5
D. S. Smith c Buttler b Anderson	11	– c Ballance b Tredwell	65
D. M. Bravo c Buttler b Jordan	10	– c Jordan b Root	32
M. N. Samuels c Buttler b Broad	33	– c Tredwell b Anderson	23
S. Chanderpaul c Stokes b Tredwell	46	– lbw b Root	13
J. Blackwood not out	112	– c Buttler b Jordan	31
*†D. Ramdin c Buttler b Broad	9	– c Cook b Anderson	57
J. O. Holder c Ballance b Tredwell	16	– not out	103
K. A. J. Roach c Buttler b Tredwell	5	– not out	15
J. E. Taylor run out	0		
S. J. Benn c Root b Anderson	2		
L-b 4, w 6, n-b 2	12	B 2, l-b 2, n-b 2	6

1/19 (2) 2/42 (3) 3/89 (4) (113 overs) 295   1/7 (1) (7 wkts, 129.4 overs) 350
4/99 (1) 5/192 (5) 6/227 (7)   2/90 (3) 3/119 (2)
7/276 (8) 8/292 (9) 9/292 (10) 10/295 (11)   4/127 (4) 5/155 (5) 6/189 (6) 7/294 (7)

Anderson 23–9–67–2; Broad 22–2–67–2; Jordan 23–8–46–1; Stokes 19–3–64–0; Tredwell 26–12–44–4. *Second innings*—Anderson 24.4–3–72–2; Broad 21–5–61–1; Tredwell 40–14–93–1; Jordan 18–6–48–1; Stokes 13–0–50–0; Root 13–6–22–2.

Umpires: B. F. Bowden and S. J. Davis.   Third umpire: B. N. J. Oxenford.
Referee: A. J. Pycroft.

WEST INDIES v ENGLAND

Second Test Match

Paul Newman

At St George's, Grenada, April 21–25, 2015. England won by nine wickets. Toss: England.
Two hours of unexpectedly sumptuous Test cricket produced a display to rank with anything Jimmy Anderson had achieved in a tireless career. Having overtaken Ian Botham's record in the First Test, he now conjured up a performance of which Botham himself would have been proud.

The script heading into the final day appeared to have been written in advance: this would be the second draw of an attritional series played out on the kind of slow, lifeless pitch that had become a blight on the Caribbean game – though this was only the third Test here. On an island famed for nutmeg, it was proceeding with a distinct lack of spice. Yet, in one of those passages of play that keeps Test cricket relevant in a fast-moving world, a slow burner exploded into life. Not long after, England had completed the most satisfying victory of Peter Moores's second spell as coach; though he didn't know it at the time, it would also be his last.

Anderson's journey towards Botham's tally had become a protracted affair, as nerves – and perhaps fatigue – threatened to slow him. Now, in a manner reminiscent of the final day against Australia at Trent Bridge in 2013, he sewed up a Test almost on his own. He was involved in all six West Indian wickets to fall on the last morning, leaving England just 143 for victory. They cruised home, with Cook and Ballance both contributing their second half-centuries of the game. Almost from nowhere, England led 1–0.

Ben Stokes is basically battling himself

Those six wickets had come in all shapes and sizes. It was hardly unusual for Anderson to take three with the new ball: Brathwaite, having completed his fourth Test hundred, fell to a beauty that reared at him; Chanderpaul was caught at first slip by Cook, twisting, turning and juggling to collect a rebound from Bell at second; and Samuels, caught behind off the toe-end as he tried to withdraw his bat. But Anderson, who claimed that trio for one run in 23 balls, also held two catches and – the cherry on the cake – ran out Holder with a direct hit from mid-off after Ballance had fumbled at cover. From the apparent security of 224 for two – a lead of 59 – West Indies had plummeted to 282 for eight, including the first of three wickets at a cost of three runs for Ali's off-breaks, and, after four days and two sessions of hard toil, an English victory was in sight.

Even before West Indies' last-day collapse, there was still plenty of incident for the spectators to absorb. Not for the first time against England, much of it involved Samuels. During West Indies' visit to England in 2012, he had clashed with Graham Onions at Edgbaston; this time, his target was Stokes. He had been at the centre of the action on the first day after Cook won an important toss. The pitch started damp but, in humid conditions, Anderson – despite striking early to bowl Brathwaite with a perfect inswinger – was below his best, and Broad off-key. Stokes, who had bowled 32 wicketless overs in Antigua raised fears of a serious injury when he slipped on the greasy outfield, but recovered to strike with his second ball, as Chanderpaul squirted low to point. England, though, missed a chance to skittle West Indies when Cook dropped Samuels at slip on 32 off Jordan. By the end of a first day shortened by rain to 70 overs, Samuels had made exactly half his side's 188 for five.

In the meantime, Stokes had evidently concluded it was a good idea to test him out with some sledging. Initially, at least, the policy backfired: Samuels enjoyed the sight of Stokes conceding an overthrow with a wild run-out attempt. And, at the close-of-play press conference, Samuels scored a few more points. "Ben Stokes is basically battling himself," he said, "because he has just come into cricket, while I've been around for a while. I keep telling him that, but tomorrow I might have to tell him something different, because he's not listening. He keeps talking to me, and when you talk to me it motivates me to keep batting. It's obvious the English boys don't learn. Let's see what they say when I'm 150."

Samuels did reach three figures next day, but he had overplayed his hand, falling in the 13th over for 103 as he drove Anderson to Bell at second slip, the bowler earning a rebuke from umpire Bruce Oxenford for roaring in Samuels's face. It was the cue for Broad, who had bowled at barely 80mph for much of the first day, to produce one of the potent spells that have defined his career. Suddenly clocking closer to 90mph, an improvement he put down to a technical adjustment, he took three for six in 20 balls, before a last-wicket stand

Ricardo Mazalan, AP/PA

Mark of disrespect: Marlon Samuels riles Ben Stokes with his sarcastic send-off.

of 52 between Bishoo and Gabriel – who had replaced Suliemann Benn and the injured Jerome Taylor – helped West Indies to 299.

Cook went about regaining the initiative, putting on 125 with Trott – the first three-figure stand by England's openers since March 2013, when Cook and Nick Compton made 231 at Dunedin. In this innings he overtook Alec Stewart to become his country's second-highest Test run-scorer behind Graham Gooch; his first run in the second innings broke Wally Hammond's England record of 4,245 Test runs overseas. Yet England's reply belonged to the two Yorkshire batsmen who, Cook said afterwards, would go on to break plenty of records themselves.

The undoubted star was Root, who lifted his side to 464 – and a decisive lead of 165. He was sublime, immediately upping the scoring-rate, and dominating a fourth-wicket stand of 165 with his county colleague Ballance. On the way to his sixth Test hundred, Root equalled the England record of six scores of 50 or more in succession.

Not that Samuels and Stokes could be kept out of the picture. After Stokes had carelessly pulled the leg-spin of Bishoo to deep midwicket, Samuels found a novel way of celebrating the dismissal, standing alongside him and saluting, poker-faced and military-style. His gesture became an instant internet hit, though Stokes did not see the funny side.

Root – who hit four sixes, all off Bishoo – would surely have reached his second double-century if Anderson, after helping him add 33 for the final wicket, had not run himself out, failing to ground his bat while seemingly unaware that Holder had collected the ball by the stumps. Root walked off shaking his head.

But Anderson had been forgiven his carelessness by lunch on the last day, and West Indies' eventual dismissal for 307 – extending their collapse either side of the interval to eight for 83 – left England's batsmen with little to do. Trott dragged Gabriel on to his stumps in the second over to depart for a duck. But Cook and Ballance, who completed 1,000 Test runs in only his tenth game, wrapped up their first win abroad for 11 Tests, stretching back to December 2012 in Kolkata, to retain the Wisden Trophy.

Man of the Match: J. E. Root.

Close of play: first day, West Indies 188-5 (Samuels 94, Ramdin 6); second day, England 74-0 (Cook 37, Trott 32); third day, England 373-6 (Root 118, Buttler 4); fourth day, West Indies 202-2 (Brathwaite 101, Samuels 22).

West Indies

K. C. Brathwaite b Anderson	1	– c Root b Anderson	116
D. S. Smith c Buttler b Jordan	15	– b Anderson	2
D. M. Bravo c Cook b Broad	35	– c Buttler b Broad	69
M. N. Samuels c Bell b Anderson	103	– c Buttler b Anderson	37
S. Chanderpaul b Ali b Stokes	1	– c Cook b Anderson	7
J. Blackwood lbw b Jordan	26	– c Anderson b Jordan	10
*†D. Ramdin c Buttler b Broad	31	– lbw b Ali	28
J. O. Holder c Buttler b Broad	22	– run out	2
K. A. J. Roach c Root b Broad	1	– c Anderson b Ali	10
D. Bishoo lbw b Ali	30	– not out	15
S. T. Gabriel not out	20	– lbw b Ali	0
B 5, l-b 6, w 1, n-b 2	14	B 8, l-b 2, n-b 1	11

1/2 (1) 2/28 (2) 3/65 (3) (104.4 overs) 299   1/3 (2) 2/145 (3) (112 overs) 307
4/74 (5) 5/129 (6) 6/223 (4)   3/224 (1) 4/238 (5)
7/233 (7) 8/246 (8) 9/247 (9) 10/299 (10)   5/239 (4) 6/257 (6) 7/260 (8)
8/282 (9) 9/307 (7) 10/307 (11)

Anderson 24–10–47–2; Broad 24–9–61–4; Jordan 25–4–65–2; Ali 13.4–1–47–1; Stokes 17–7–66–1; Trott 1–0–2–0. *Second innings*—Anderson 22.7–7–43–4; Broad 21–2–71–1; Ali 24–9–51–3; Jordan 21–6–69–1; Stokes 8–0–34–0; Root 16–7–29–0.

England

*A. N. Cook b Gabriel	76	– not out	59
I. J. L. Trott c Blackwood b Bishoo	59	– b Gabriel	0
G. S. Ballance b Samuels	77	– not out	81
I. R. Bell b Gabriel	1		
J. E. Root not out	182		
M. M. Ali run out	0		
B. A. Stokes c Blackwood b Bishoo	8		
†J. C. Buttler st Ramdin b Bishoo	13		
C. J. Jordan run out	16		
S. C. J. Broad c Smith b Bishoo	0		
J. M. Anderson run out	2		
B 9, l-b 2, w 1, n-b 18	30	W 1, n-b 3	4

1/125 (2) 2/159 (1) 3/164 (4) (144.1 overs) 464   1/2 (2) (1 wkt, 41.1 overs) 144
4/329 (5) 5/335 (6) 6/364 (7)
7/387 (8) 8/426 (9) 9/431 (10) 10/464 (11)

Roach 28–4–100–0; Gabriel 22–3–67–2; Holder 21.1–6–57–0; Bishoo 51–10–177–4; Samuels 21–4–38–1; Blackwood 1–0–14–0. *Second innings*—Roach 7–1–18–0; Gabriel 7–3–20–1; Holder 1.4–0–11–0; Samuels 12.3–1–54–0; Bishoo 8–0–32–0; Brathwaite 5–1–9–0.

Umpires: S. J. Davis and B. N. J. Oxenford.   Third umpire: B. F. Bowden.
Referee: A. J. Pycroft.

> " Their fielding had been mercurial throughout the series but, as befits this unusually daring impression of an England side, when they were good they were damn well irresistible."
> South Africa v England in 2015-16, Third Test, page 420

WEST INDIES v ENGLAND

Third Test Match

GIDEON BROOKS

At Bridgetown, Barbados. May 1–3, 2015. West Indies won by five wickets. Toss: England. Test debut: S. D. Hope.

Sport's capacity to send victors and vanquished on opposing trajectories had rarely felt more pointed than at the post-match presentation. For West Indies, there were waves to family and friends, and vocal support from the stands, following a win which provided the perfect riposte to incoming ECB chairman Colin Graves's pre-series assessment that they were "mediocre", and hopes of renewal for Caribbean cricket. For England, there was much contemplation of bootlaces, the only smiles were nervous ones, and a familiar feeling descended: English cricket was about to enter yet another period of introspection and blood-letting.

At least Cook had cause for some cheer, having shaken a monkey from his back: his 26th Test century arrived on the first evening, 704 days, 20 Tests and 36 innings after the 25th, against New Zealand at Headingley in May 2013. He finished the series with 268 runs at 53, and looked more secure than he had done for some time.

Yet other concerns crowded in. From a position of authority, England had frittered away a first-innings lead of 68 and, on a wearing pitch, failed to take hold of the chances West Indies offered on the third, and final, afternoon. Cook, coach Peter Moores and the other three England selectors were also turning out empty pockets, after a risky gamble to reinvent Trott as the captain's latest opening partner proved a comprehensive failure. The upshot was West Indies' first Test win over England in 12 attempts, since skittling them for 51 in Jamaica in February 2009, and only their second in 29 since winning at Edgbaston in June 2000. It also meant a share of the series, the first they hadn't lost against a side other than New Zealand, Bangladesh or Zimbabwe since drawing at home with Pakistan in May 2011.

MOST DUCKS IN A SERIES BY AN OPENING BATSMAN

Ducks	T					Ducks	T				
5	4	P. Roy	I v E	1952		3	4	M. A. Atherton . .	E v A	1998-99
3	3	A. C. Bannerman .	A v E	1888		3	4	M. T. G. Elliott . .	A v WI	1998-99
4	4	V. T. Trumper . . .	A v E	1907-08		3	5	G. Kirsten	SA v WI	2000-01
5	5	P. Holmes	E v SA	1927-28		3	3	C. H. Gayle	WI v SL	2001-02
5	5	V. Mankad	I v A	1947-48		3	3	Taufeeq Umar . . .	P v A	2002-03
5	5	D. L. Amiss	E v A	1974-75		3	3	M. D. Bell	NZ v E	2007-08
3	3	G. M. Wood	A v NZ	1980-81		3	3	K. C. Brathwaite .	WI v A	2011-12
3	3	Mudassar Nazar . .	P v E	1982		**3**	**3**	**I. J. L. Trott . . . .**	**E v WI**	**2014-15**

Despite a bone-dry pitch, England chose not to go with an extra spinner, leaving Adil Rashid and James Tredwell to whirl away in the nets. But they were able to name an unchanged side only after Stokes overcame a back injury sustained in training the day before the match. West Indies made three changes: they brought in slow left-armer Permaul (their third spinner in three Tests, after Devendra Bishoo injured a finger); recalled Taylor after he had missed Grenada with a shoulder injury, and handed a debut to 21-year-old opener Shai Hope, who received his cap on his home ground from Clive Lloyd.

Cook's decision to bat looked a potentially significant advantage, yet within nine balls Trott – still preferred to Adam Lyth – had been unpicked again. It was the first time an

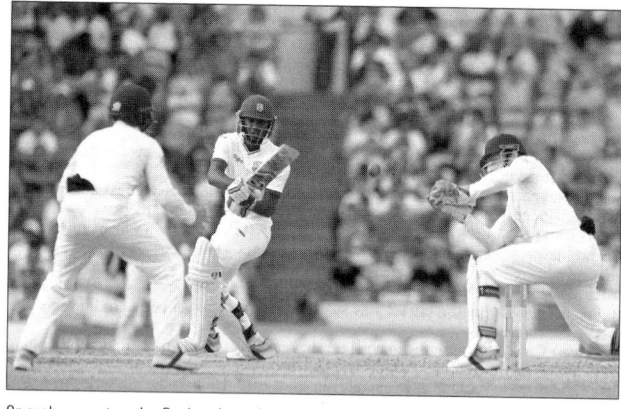

On such moments... Jos Buttler misses the chance to stump Jermaine Blackwood, with West Indies more than 100 adrift of victory.

England opener had recorded three ducks in a series of three Tests or fewer. But it was the manner of his dismissal, as much as the unwanted statistic, that hurt most. Ramdin had spoken during the build-up about Trott's perceived weakness against the short ball. And, when Gabriel banged a rising delivery at his ribs, Trott turned his head towards point and fended tamely to Permaul at square leg.

By contrast, Cook left judiciously – a mark of his returning form – though his march to a century was punctuated with good fortune: on 22 he dabbed Permaul to Blackwood at short leg, only for TV umpire Steve Davis to rule the ball had brushed the turf; on 33 he flashed an inside edge off Taylor past leg stump; and on 40 a top-edge off Permaul fell to safety.

His hundred arrived with a flick off his legs off Gabriel. It had taken 259 balls and prompted, by his standards, an effusive celebration – helmet off and arms aloft, before embracing his partner, Buttler. His luck ran out, however, in the last over of the day, when he under-edged one of Samuels's largely unthreatening off-breaks. It left West Indies buoyant. But, with the exception of Cook and Ali, who contributed a careful half-century in a fifth-wicket stand of 98 with his captain, England's batsmen had played indifferently. A score of 240 for seven was a poor return after winning the toss, yet the events of day two were to make it look like a small fortune.

England added just 17 runs for the final three wickets next morning, as Buttler failed to shepherd the tail. That early rush presaged some car-crash cricket: 18 wickets fell in all, the most in a day's cricket in the 231 Tests played in the West Indies. By the close, England had staggered to 39 for five, a precarious lead of 107. It meant their contribution to the day had been 56 runs for eight wickets. Such carelessness would cost them a series victory.

West Indies, bowled out in between for 189 in less than 50 overs, were thankful for a stubborn effort from Blackwood, who added 85 to his unbeaten century in Antigua. Without him, they would have been dead and buried: no one else passed 25. Anderson was once again the architect of their demise, producing two irresistible spells, one with the new ball (6–4–4–3) and one with the old, immediately after tea (3.4–0–29–3), to leave ʰ him six for 42, the 17th five-for of his career, and 396 Test wickets. His ability to ᵉʳ responsibility when nothing was happening for anyone else, allied with Jordan's hands – he took two more blinders at slip off the spinners – put England back in control. Yet, before stumps, West Indies had wrestled them back to the canvas.

Trott's second failure in the match, pinned by Taylor in the fifth over, prompted a brief discussion with his captain about a possible review. As if symbolically, Cook suggested his time was up. Trott walked off to a standing ovation from the travelling support – a carriage clock of sorts – as he departed with his familiar rolling gait. Two days later, he announced his retirement from international cricket. Cook followed in the next over, nicking to slip and, as in the first innings, Bell's liberal application of sun cream proved a waste of effort: nailed lbw by Taylor, he registered his first pair in Tests since the 2005 Ashes finale at The Oval. As England ground to a halt, Root edged Holder to first slip, before Ali dragged Permaul on to his stumps. In 15 overs of sheer timidity, they had lost five for 28 – and the initiative.

It was an understandably grumpy Anderson who suggested that, from the position England had been in, a lead of 400 would have been acceptable; he added that 200 might prove tricky to chase. Next morning, England fell short even of those expectations, despite thirties from Stokes and Buttler, who this time cajoled 25 out of the last wicket from Anderson. West Indies needed 192, and had history on their side: they had never been bowled out chasing a target of less than 214.

For 35 overs, it was nip and tuck. Aggressive at first, West Indies became bogged down at 70 for three. More aggression preceded the loss of Chanderpaul, who finished the Test – which turned out to be his last – with a duck, and only 45 short of Brian Lara's record 11,912 runs for West Indies. That left them wondering whether to stick or twist, but England helped make up their minds. At 87 for four, Blackwood – unable to release the handbrake – skipped down the wicket, attempted to heave Root over long-on, and misjudged the line. Unfortunately for England, so did Buttler, who fluffed the gather to his left – and the stumping. It proved the turning point, as Blackwood, on four at the time, and Bravo steadily rebuilt. Cook tried all his combinations, to no avail.

With the match threatening to go into a fourth day, a message arrived from the dressing-room under the pretext of a fresh pair of gloves. The batsmen immediately accelerated, and the last 50 came off 34 balls, as Ali – who had let the pressure of being England's only spinner get to him, and strove too hard for wickets – absorbed the bulk of the bruising. Bravo fell with four still needed, but Blackwood hit the winning runs to spark celebrations, and recriminations.

Man of the Match: J. Blackwood.   *Man of the Series:* J. M. Anderson.

Close of play: first day, England 240-7 (Buttler 0); second day, England 39-5 (Ballance 12, Stokes 0).

England

*A. N. Cook c Ramdin b Samuels	105	c Brathwaite b Gabriel	4
I. J. L. Trott c Permaul b Gabriel	0	lbw b Taylor	9
G. S. Ballance b Holder	18	c Bravo b Permaul	23
I. R. Bell c and b Holder	0	lbw b Taylor	0
J. E. Root c Ramdin b Permaul	33	c Bravo b Holder	1
M. M. Ali run out	58	b Permaul	8
B. A. Stokes c Hope b Gabriel	22	c Chanderpaul b Permaul	32
†J. C. Buttler not out	3	not out	35
C. J. Jordan c Ramdin b Taylor	3	lbw b Holder	2
S. C. J. Broad b Taylor	10	b Holder	0
J. M. Anderson b Taylor	0	lbw b Taylor	2
L-b 1, w 1, n-b 3	5	B 4, l-b 2, n-b 1	7

1/0 (2) 2/38 (3) 3/38 (4) (96.3 overs) 257
4/91 (5) 5/189 (6) 6/233 (7)
7/240 (1) 8/247 (9) 9/257 (10) 10/257 (11)

1/11 (2) 2/13 (1) (42.1 overs) 123
3/18 (4) 4/28 (5)
5/39 (6) 6/62 (3) 7/95 (7)
8/98 (9) 9/98 (10) 10/123 (11)

Taylor 18.3–8–36–3; Gabriel 15–3–47–2; Holder 16–4–34–2; Samuels 27–5–53–1; Permaul 20–1–86–1. *Second innings*—Taylor 11.1–1–33–3; Gabriel 7–4–16–1; Holder 9–3–15–3; Permaul 11–3–43–3; Samuels 4–1–10–0.

West Indies

K. C. Brathwaite c Jordan b Anderson	0	– c Jordan b Ali	25
S. D. Hope c Cook b Anderson	5	– lbw b Jordan	9
D. M. Bravo c Jordan b Ali	9	– c Broad b Stokes	82
M. N. Samuels lbw b Anderson	9	– b Broad	20
S. Chanderpaul c Jordan b Root	25	– b Anderson	0
J. Blackwood c Ali b Anderson	85	– not out	47
*†D. Ramdin c Buttler b Broad	13	– not out	0
J. O. Holder c Buttler b Stokes	5		
V. Permaul c sub (A. Lyth) b Anderson	18		
J. E. Taylor b Anderson	15		
S. T. Gabriel not out	0		
B 4, l-b 1	5	B 5, l-b 6	11

1/0 (1) 2/5 (2) 3/21 (4)   (49.4 overs) 189   1/35 (2)   (5 wkts, 62.4 overs) 194
4/37 (3) 5/82 (5) 6/107 (7)   2/35 (1) 3/70 (4)
7/124 (8) 8/162 (9) 9/178 (10) 10/189 (6)   4/80 (5) 5/188 (3)

Anderson 12.4–5–42–6; Broad 10–3–31–1; Ali 10–2–56–1; Root 9–1–34–1; Jordan 6–3–4–0; Stokes 2–0–17–1. *Second innings*—Anderson 13–4–35–1; Broad 13–5–29–1; Jordan 11–5–24–1; Ali 12.4–1–54–1; Root 8–4–16–0; Stokes 5–0–25–1.

Umpires: B. F. Bowden and B. N. J. Oxenford.   Third umpire: S. J. Davis.
Referee: A. J. Pycroft.

IRELAND v ENGLAND

One-Day International

MIKE WALTERS

At Malahide, May 8, 2015. No result. Toss: England. One-day international debuts: Z. S. Ansari, J. J. Roy, J. M. Vince, D. J. Willey, M. A. Wood.

Lurking beneath the surface of soggy anticlimax, as persistent rain restricted play to 78 minutes, a darker subplot emerged, spelling the end of Peter Moores's second reign as England coach. That he was among the last to know, discovering his fate amid more leaks in the media than in the slate-grey skies above Dublin, reflected little credit on the ECB. Moores had travelled straight to Ireland upon his return from England's Test series in the Caribbean to support inexperienced captain James Taylor and a young side containing five debutants – one short of the England record – and no one who played in the West Indies. Only once had they blooded more new players in a one-day international (six against West Indies at Headingley in 1973), apart from the very first one in 1970-71; they also included five new caps against Pakistan at Old Trafford in 1996. On a green pitch, Taylor's attack made promising inroads in the 18 overs possible, with maiden wickets for Wood, the slippery Durham fast bowler, and Northamptonshire all-rounder Willey. But the real drama was unfolding beyond the boundary. Tom Harrison, the ECB's chief executive, had flown to Ireland with no intention of humiliating Moores by sacking him on foreign soil. But he was armed with the open secret that Andrew Strauss would be the new director of cricket – and it was known that Strauss did not regard Moores as the long-term solution to England's problems. By the time play was called off at 3pm, news of Moores's demise had been around for three hours – though the dressing-room remained in the dark. Precisely 24 hours later, successive edicts from Lord's confirmed what everyone already knew: Strauss was the new kingmaker, and his first act in office was to dismiss Moores.

Ireland

*W. T. S. Porterfield b Wood	7	†G. C. Wilson not out	3
P. R. Stirling run out	2	L-b 2, w 3, n-b 1	6
E. C. Joyce not out	23		
N. J. O'Brien c Vince b Bresnan	10	1/6 (2) 2/23 (1)	(4 wkts, 18 overs) 56
A. Balbirnie c Roy b Willey	5	3/44 (4) 4/53 (5)	10 overs: 37-2

K. J. O'Brien, J. F. Mooney, G. H. Dockrell, A. R. Cusack and C. A. Young did not bat.

Wood 5–0–25–1; Bresnan 6–2–11–1; Willey 4–1–17–1; Finn 3–2–1–0.

England

A. D. Hales, J. J. Roy, J. M. Vince, *J. W. A. Taylor, †J. M. Bairstow, Z. S. Ansari, A. U. Rashid, T. T. Bresnan, D. J. Willey, M. A. Wood and S. T. Finn.

Umpires: M. Hawthorne and I. N. Ramage.　Referee: D. T. Jukes.

ENGLAND v NEW ZEALAND IN 2015

Review by Simon Wilde

Test matches (2): England 1, New Zealand 1
One-day internationals (5): England 3, New Zealand 2
Twenty20 international (1): England 1, New Zealand 0

Back in 1999, England's home defeat by New Zealand left them languishing at the foot of the Wisden World Championship, the precursor to the ICC's official rankings. It was a humiliation that gave Duncan Fletcher and Nasser Hussain, the new coach and captain, a mandate for change, and the revival of the Test team was launched. Sixteen years on, New Zealand again acted as a catalyst, but of a different kind: confronted by a team playing in the cavalier image of their captain, Brendon McCullum, England felt emboldened, not to say obliged, to up the tempo themselves. Before the tour had ended seven weeks later, New Zealand – who had contributed to England's winter of crisis by handing out a World Cup hammering in Wellington in February – were feeling the backlash.

The early signs, though, had not been encouraging. Over the weekend of New Zealand's arrival at the start of May, England were crashing to defeat in the final Test in the West Indies; and, as the tourists began their first warm-up game in Taunton, reports were emerging of Peter Moores's sacking as head coach during the one-day trip to Dublin. With Andrew Strauss, the ECB's new director of England cricket, handed the task of rebooting their one-day game, and the clock running down to the Ashes, the matches with New Zealand acquired immense significance.

English cricket was on trial, all the more so because Strauss had ruled out a return for Kevin Pietersen just after he had apparently bolstered his case with a triple-century for Surrey. As McCullum – whose New Zealand side appeared as settled and confident as England looked fragile and uncertain – was committed to his ultra-positive style, both teams were set on risking all. The confluence proved glorious, producing arguably the most memorable cricket seen in the first half of an English summer since the twin-tour schedule was expanded in 2000.

If the style of play was one joy, and the good spirit between the teams another, the public's positive response was an additional boon. Having spent 18 months being ridiculed for mismanagement off the field and wild inconsistency on it, England were finally back in favour – not necessarily because they were winning (though, overall, they claimed five victories to New Zealand's three), but because they were playing with a smile and sense of adventure. As England turned things round on the fourth and fifth days of the Lord's Test, and later raised the heat in the opening one-day international at Edgbaston, the overriding sentiment among onlookers was incredulity. Entertainment evidently counted for as much as results, at least against opponents who inspired little of the antipathy usually reserved for Australia.

It's catching: Moeen Ali celebrates a hugely popular win for England at Lord's.

Several key New Zealanders, including McCullum, joined the tour late from the IPL. But, with the nature of Tests and limited-overs matches fast converging, this seemed increasingly irrelevant. A lack of conventional preparation – the IPL players took red Dukes balls to India for net practice – hardly affected New Zealand at Lord's, where they were on top until the fourth morning. Indeed, England had used one-day methodology to extract themselves from a precarious situation on the first day, when Joe Root and Ben Stokes – doing what came naturally to them – went on a rampaging counter-attack during a stand of 161. In the second innings, with the contest again in the balance, Stokes struck the fastest Test hundred seen at Lord's. Credit went to Paul Farbrace, England's acting-coach, for promoting him back to No. 6 and encouraging the players to express themselves, regardless of the consequences. Stokes's second-innings runs also contributed to a large crowd on the last day, previously unheard of in May. Again he gave them plenty to cheer about, removing Kane Williamson and McCullum with successive balls. Marlon Samuels's mock salute in the Caribbean had given way to salutes of admiration from Root.

New Zealand then won the Headingley Test in stunning fashion – a huge collective effort typified by superior fielding and a scoring-rate of 4.92, unequalled by any side topping 750 runs in a Test. Their haste was such that losing the equivalent of a day to rain did not matter. It was the first two-match series to breach 3,000 runs.

But the frenzy had only just started. The England selectors, with some long-distance input from Trevor Bayliss – who was preparing to take over as head coach in time for the Ashes – threw caution to the wind and retained only seven of the one-day squad that had exited the World Cup at the group stage.

As Farbrace said, playing against New Zealand was perfect for England as they strove to forge a new philosophy: McCullum's attacking fields meant they had no alternative but to attack. Absolved of blame if things went wrong, the players followed the instruction to the letter. The transformation was astonishing, quickly burying the bad news of Headingley.

The charge was led by the unshackled World Cup survivors. Eoin Morgan (shrewdly retained as captain by Strauss), Jos Buttler and Root hit three of England's six fastest one-day hundreds, and played prominent parts in their highest total (408 for nine at Edgbaston), their highest total batting second

---

VALUE FOR MONEY

Most runs in Test matches in which all 40 wickets fell:

Runs per over		
1,753	Australia (354 and 582) beat England (447 and 370) at Adelaide	1920-21
1,646	South Africa (482 and 360) beat Australia (465 and 339) at Adelaide	1910-11
1,619	Australia (600 and 250) beat England (479 and 290) at Melbourne	1924-25
1,611	Australia (450 and 452) beat England (298 and 411) at Sydney.	1924-25
1,610	**England (389 and 478) beat New Zealand (523 and 220) at Lord's**	**2015**
1,553	England (515 and 345) beat Pakistan (538 and 155) at Leeds	2006
1,514	Australia (586 and 166) lost to England (325 and 437) at Sydney	1894-95
1,475	Australia (505 and 256) beat India (269 and 445) at Adelaide	1977-78
1,474	West Indies (453 and 284) tied with Australia (505 and 232) at Brisbane	1960-61
1,467	Australia (489 and 250) beat England (365 and 363) at Adelaide	1924-25

Six of the above, including the top four, were in timeless matches (all Tests in Australia between 1882-83 and 1936-37 were played to a finish).

(365 for nine at The Oval, in 46 overs), and their highest successful chase (350 for three at Trent Bridge, in just 44).

Less established members of the squad joined in the fun, too. Openers Jason Roy and Alex Hales laid the groundwork for the chase in Nottingham with 100 in 10.4 overs, while Sam Billings produced attractive cameos at Southampton and Chester-le-Street, full of thoroughly 21st-century strokeplay. Adil Rashid justified his selection with bat and ball: encouraged to take wickets and forget about conceding runs, he put himself into the frame for the Ashes. So did Mark Wood, who across the three formats bowled more overs for England than anyone; his 50-over economy-rate of 5.23 was the best on either side. With his infectious fooling around, he epitomised England's new laissez-faire attitude. Jonny Bairstow, summoned at short notice to keep wicket in the deciding one-day international in Durham, following an injury to Buttler, swiftly caught the mood, winning the game from the unlikeliest of positions with an unbeaten 83 from 60 balls. Many wondered why none of this had happened under Moores.

The upshot was that New Zealand, one of the world's strongest and most seasoned one-day sides, were outgunned and – after taking a 2–1 lead – beaten 3–2. Even so, their own batsmen were no slouches: Williamson (396 runs from No. 3) and Ross Taylor (375 from No. 4) were powerful presences, always contributing at least 42 each, while Williamson added another half-century in the one-off Twenty20 game in Manchester, though England won again.

McCullum the batsman had a relatively quiet tour. He occasionally showed the attacking spirit for which his side had become famous, never more so than when hitting the first delivery he faced during the Headingley Test over cover for six. But he fared best when adopting a more orthodox approach. His only half-century in ten international innings came at Headingley, where he helped put the game beyond England's reach. It was a measure of Wood's potential that his bustling pace accounted for McCullum five times in all formats. David Willey, the Northamptonshire all-rounder, displayed a similar knack for dismissing good players, claiming Martin Guptill, Williamson and Taylor twice each with the white ball.

In mitigation, New Zealand lost Trent Boult, their most dangerous bowler, to injury mid-tour, just as they had in 2013; his nine wickets represented the best haul by a left-arm fast bowler in a Lord's Test. Tim Southee looked less potent without him after the second one-dayer, and failed to build on his sensational return of seven for 33 against England during the World Cup. New Zealand were also still coming to terms with the retirement of Daniel Vettori, although all-rounder Mitchell Santner's left-arm spin came in handy. With McCullum declining to confirm his future in 50-over cricket, there was a sense that England might have caught a New Zealand one-day side coming down the other side of the hill.

The statistics confirmed the extraordinary nature of the one-day games, with records set in a five-match series for most runs (3,151) and sixes (76), and highest run-rate (7.15). On July 5, less than a fortnight after the tour had ended with a Twenty20 match at Old Trafford, the ICC's amended regulations governing ODIs came into force, scrapping the batting powerplay, and allowing a fifth fielder outside the ring in the final ten overs. But, for exhausted bowlers in both sides, change had come too late.

Both teams emerged with some satisfaction, and a drawn Test series meant neither suffered the injustice of dropping to seventh in the rankings. At Leeds, New Zealand had recorded their first Test victory in England since 1999, in the process extending their unbeaten run to seven series, which began after their defeat here in 2013. On this evidence, they deserved better than to provide the warm-up act in an English summer. England, meanwhile, had beaten New Zealand at home in a one-day series for the first time since 1994.

The fortunes of the captains formed a major subplot. McCullum was feted for his enterprising captaincy, but his eagerness to attack sometimes proved detrimental to New Zealand's cause (as it had in the World Cup final). When, for example, Stokes cut loose on the fourth day at Lord's, Southee was suckered into trying to bounce him out, and simply fed a strength. The next day, with 345 needed to win and 77 overs left, New Zealand's front-foot approach continued even after the loss of both openers for ducks. Even after McCullum was out first ball, Corey Anderson struck a breezy fifty. When Boult was last to go, upper-cutting to third man, only 57 balls remained. Had they been less carefree, New Zealand might have saved the game, and left Cook facing questions about why he had not declared.

Cook's own 162 in England's second innings confirmed that his runs in the West Indies were no fluke. At Headingley, he overtook his mentor Graham

FIVE STATS YOU MAY HAVE MISSED

BENEDICT BERMANGE

- In England's first innings at Lord's, Nos 5 to 8 all made fifties, for just the fourth time in Tests:

C. D. McMillan (84), A. C. Parore (50), C. L. Cairns (126), D. J. Nash (63)		
	New Zealand v India at Hamilton	1998-99
J. D. Ryder (201), J. E. C. Franklin (52), B. B. McCullum (115), D. L. Vettori (55)		
	New Zealand v India at Napier	2008-09
I. R. Bell (52), E. J. G. Morgan (79), M. J. Prior (126), S. C. J. Broad (54)		
	England v Sri Lanka at Lord's	2011
J. E. Root (98), B. A. Stokes (92), J. C. Buttler (67), M. M. Ali (58)		
	England v New Zealand at Lord's	**2015**

- New Zealand's total of 523 at Lord's was their highest in defeat. Their previous highest was 451, in the fourth innings against England at Christchurch in 2001-02, when they lost by 98 runs.

- Ben Stokes became the sixth England player to hit a century against the country of his birth:

M. C. Cowdrey v India	160 at Leeds	1959
born in Ootacamund	107 at Calcutta	1963-64
	151 at Delhi	1963-64
N. Hussain v India	128 at Birmingham	1996
born in Madras	107* at Nottingham	1996
	155 at Lord's	2002
	110 at Leeds	2002
G. A. Hick v Zimbabwe	101 at Lord's	2000
born in Salisbury		
A. J. Strauss v South Africa	126 at Port Elizabeth	2004-05
born in Johannesburg	136 at Durban	2004-05
	147 at Johannesburg	2004-05
K. P. Pietersen v South Africa	152 at Lord's	2008
born in Pietermaritzburg	100 at The Oval	2008
	149 at Leeds	2012
B. A. Stokes v New Zealand	**101 at Lord's**	**2015**
born in Christchurch		

- Luke Ronchi's 70-ball 88 at Leeds was the second-fastest innings of 50-plus on Test debut:

SR			
192.50	T. G. Southee (77*)	New Zealand v England at Napier	2007-08
125.71	**L. Ronchi (88)**	**New Zealand v England at Leeds**	**2015**
120.00	Yuvraj of Patiala (60)	India v England at Madras	1933-34
109.61	A. W. White (57*)	West Indies v Australia at Kingston	1964-65
107.47	S. Dhawan (187)	India v Australia at Mohali	2012-13
102.40	J. C. Buttler (85)	England v India at Southampton	2014

The number of balls faced is not known for many early Test matches. Ronchi's fifty was brought up in 37 balls, the second-fastest on debut; Southee's came from 29.

- Jimmy Anderson reached 1,000 Test runs at Headingley, in his 104th match. The previous slowest was Muttiah Muralitharan's 95 for Sri Lanka.

Played, lad: Alastair Cook goes beyond Graham Gooch's record at Headingley.

Gooch as England's leading Test run-scorer, then became the youngest man to reach 9,000. He conceded that his remedial work in the nets with Gooch and Gary Palmer, the former Somerset all-rounder, following his omission from the World Cup, had done him a lot of good. No longer needing to manufacture runs outside off stump, as he had been obliged to do in the one-day game, he reaccustomed himself to leaving the ball, forcing New Zealand's attack to come to him instead.

His revival was mirrored by Morgan's, who rediscovered his best touch. Seemingly weighed down with worry at the World Cup, he now went for his shots like an ex-drinker who had fallen off the wagon. His tally of 16 sixes was an England record for a one-day series or tournament. In private, Cook and Morgan might both have conceded that the change of coaching regime had benefited them.

Nothing encapsulated the good spirit of the tour better than the warmth between the opposing captains. McCullum said he had texted Cook during his troubles in 2014 to wish him well, while he and Morgan had developed a close friendship at the IPL. They knew each other's games – McCullum set fields that almost parodied Morgan's favourite scoring areas, such as four men square on the off side – and chatted amiably at the end of the final one-dayer.

New Zealand left with reasons to be cheerful. Williamson's masterly century at Lord's confirmed his reputation as his country's next great batsman, and possibly their finest ever. Martin Guptill (whose Test scores were 70, 0, 0, 70) justified his recall after a two-year absence. A knee injury to B-J. Watling at Lord's led to a hugely successful double change at Leeds: playing purely as a batsman, he scored his side's first century in eight Tests there, while Luke Ronchi, who took over the gloves, treated his debut like a one-dayer and smashed 88 off 70 balls.

Off-spinner Mark Craig recovered from a poor match at Lord's to show that England did not possess a monopoly in useful lower-order all-rounders, scoring 41 and 58, both unbeaten, taking three catches at second slip and returning match figures of 57.5–24–121–5. His tidy spell on the second afternoon at Headingley was one of the few moments of the tour when the batsmen did not have it all their own way.

NEW ZEALAND TOURING PARTY

*B. B. McCullum (T/50/20), C. J. Anderson (T), T. A. Boult (T/50), D. A. J. Bracewell (T), M. D. Craig (T), G. D. Elliott (50/20), M. J. Guptill (T/50/20), M. J. Henry (T/50/20), T. W. M. Latham (T/50/20), M. J. McClenaghan (50/20), N. L. McCullum (50/20), A. W. Mathieson (50/20), C. Munro (50/20), L. Ronchi (T/50/20), H. D. Rutherford (T), M. J. Santner (50/20), T. G. Southee (T/50/20), L. R. P. L. Taylor (T/50/20), N. Wagner (T), B-J. Watling (T), B. M. Wheeler (50), K. S. Williamson (T/50/20).

IPL commitments meant that Anderson and Henry missed the first warm-up, and Boult, B. B. McCullum, Southee and Williamson arrived two days before the First Test. Their places were covered by J. A. Duffy, Santner and Wheeler. Anderson was originally selected in all formats, but withdrew after a back injury in the First Test. A. F. Milne was originally selected in the two limited-overs formats, but failed to recover from a heel injury. Boult injured his back during the one-day series, and was replaced by Munro.

Coach: M. J. Hesson. *Batting coach:* C. D. McMillan. *Bowling coach:* A. D. Mascarenhas. *Manager:* M. Sandle. *Physiotherapist:* J. Montgomery. *Strength and conditioning coach:* C. Donaldson. *Massage therapist:* J. Bland. *Analyst:* P. Warren. *Tour liaison:* W. Bentley. *Security manager:* S. T. Dickason. *Media relations manager:* P. B. Thornton. *Videographer:* C. Elder.

SOMERSET v NEW ZEALANDERS

At Taunton, May 8–11. New Zealanders won by 66 runs. Toss: Somerset. County debut: J. H. Davey.

Watling, captaining a New Zealand side shorn of six IPL players, produced a solid half-century to turn around an unpromising position of 133 for six on the opening day. The damage was inflicted by Groenewald and debutant Josh Davey, a medium-pacer known to the New Zealanders after his three wickets for Scotland unsettled them during the World Cup in February. A fragile Somerset, defeated in their first three Championship games, trailed on first innings after left-arm seamer Ben Wheeler, one of three young replacements for the missing seniors, carved through the top order in an aggressive opening spell of 7–5–6–4. Santner was out six short of a century as the New Zealanders stretched their advantage to 343, despite Groenewald completing career-best match figures of nine for 136. Although Hildreth, their one truly in-form batsman, made a sparkling hundred, Somerset crashed to 142 for seven, before Overton and Groenewald put up a bit more of a fight. Craig exploited the first real turn of the match to pick up five wickets, profiting when Overton trod on his stumps attempting a pull.

Close of play: first day, New Zealanders 202-7 (Watling 52, Wagner 9); second day, New Zealanders 149-3 (Santner 70); third day, Somerset 142-6 (Hildreth 62, Davey 5).

New Zealanders

	First innings		Second innings	
T. W. M. Latham	c Barrow b Davey	6	lbw b Allenby	57
H. D. Rutherford	c Allenby b Davey	37	c Abell b Groenewald	11
M. J. Santner	c and b Groenewald	27	c Trego b Overton	94
L. R. P. L. Taylor	c Barrow b Allenby	32	(5) c Barrow b Allenby	10
L. Ronchi	c Abell b Groenewald	8	(6) c Barrow b Allenby	7
†B-J. Watling	c Cooper b Groenewald	65	(7) c Barrow b Groenewald	46
M. D. Craig	lbw b Allenby	7	(8) c Barrow b Overton	20
D. A. J. Bracewell	c Barrow b Groenewald	20	(9) lbw b Groenewald	16
N. Wagner	b Overton	29	(4) c Allenby b Groenewald	4
B. M. Wheeler	not out	2	c Allenby b Groenewald	33
J. A. Duffy	b Overton	0	not out	1
	L-b 3, n-b 1	4	B 9, l-b 2	11
		237		**310**

1/31 (1) 2/44 (2) 3/99 (3)   (71.1 overs) 237
4/109 (5) 5/119 (4) 6/133 (7)
7/190 (8) 8/235 (6) 9/237 (9) 10/237 (11)

1/20 (2) 2/144 (1)   (87.5 overs) 310
3/149 (4) 4/168 (5)
5/180 (6) 6/206 (5) 7/240 (7)
8/270 (9) 9/281 (5) 10/310 (10)

Trego 7–1–22–0; Groenewald 22–4–71–4; Davey 18–5–54–2; Overton 15.1–4–50–2; Allenby 8–1–33–2; Abdur Rehman 1–0–4–0. *Second innings*—Trego 13–4–53–0; Groenewald 18.5–3–65–5; Davey 14–3–63–0; Overton 16–3–39–2; Abdur Rehman 12–1–43–0; Allenby 14–4–36–3.

Somerset

	First innings		Second innings	
T. B. Abell	c Craig b Duffy	1	c Ronchi b Craig	43
J. G. Myburgh	lbw b Wheeler	3	lbw b Wheeler	4
T. L. W. Cooper	b Wheeler	0	b Wagner	9
J. C. Hildreth	b Wheeler	13	c Watling b Craig	115
J. Allenby	c Ronchi b Wheeler	28	c Bracewell b Craig	4
*A. W. R. Barrow	lbw b Craig	32	c Taylor b Bracewell	5
*P. D. Trego	c Santner b Wagner	40	c Ronchi b Bracewell	2
J. H. Davey	b Wheeler	15	lbw b Bracewell	5
C. Overton	c Taylor b Bracewell	24	hit wkt b Craig	25
T. D. Groenewald	not out	3	c Craig	47
Abdur Rehman	c Ronchi b Wagner	19	not out	5
	B 3, l-b 8, n-b 4	26	B 3, l-b 5, w 1, n-b 4	13
		204		**277**

1/4 (2) 2/4 (1) 3/9 (3)   (46.5 overs) 204
4/43 (4) 5/54 (5) 6/110 (7)
7/139 (8) 8/165 (6) 9/182 (9) 10/204 (11)

1/21 (2) 2/37 (3)   (66.5 overs) 277
3/104 (1) 4/108 (5)
5/117 (6) 6/123 (7) 7/142 (8)
8/214 (9) 9/236 (4) 10/277 (10)

Duffy 10–2–36–1; Wheeler 11–6–18–5; Bracewell 13–3–67–1; Wagner 7.5–0–41–2; Craig 5–0–31–1. *Second innings*—Duffy 9–2–39–0; Wheeler 15–3–74–1; Bracewell 16–4–62–3; Wagner 14–4–60–1; Craig 11.5–3–34–5; Santner 1–1–0–0.

Umpires: N. L. Bainton and S. J. O'Shaughnessy.

At Worcester, May 14–17 (not first-class). **New Zealanders won by 15 runs. ‡New Zealanders 261-9 dec** (71.4 overs) (H. D. Rutherford 75) **and 275-9 dec** (72 overs) (M. J. Guptill 150; S. H. Choudhry 5-78); **Worcestershire 291-7 dec** (94 overs) (R. A. Whiteley 103*) **and 230** (47.2 overs) (T. Köhler-Cadmore 55; M. J. Henry 3-58, M. D. Craig 4-56). County debut: E. G. Barnard. *Worcestershire chose from 15 players, and the New Zealanders 14. Worcestershire, needing 55 with seven wickets and 16 overs in hand, collapsed to hand victory to a shape-shifting New Zealand team. After they had set Worcestershire 246 in 50 overs, their well-drilled bowling and close catching came to the fore. Perhaps the result would have been different had Moeen Ali not departed on the third evening to join up with England at Lord's. After a first-day washout, Hamish Rutherford, propped up the tourists' batting, and it took a stand of 70 for the ninth wicket between Doug Bracewell and Neil Wagner to steer them past 250. But their seamers soon had Worcestershire 130-6, before No. 7 Ross Whiteley countered with his first century for the county. Corey Anderson* *was able to get a few overs under his belt on the third day, having waited to receive clearance to play from Mumbai Indians, his IPL franchise. Martin Guptill, who missed the game at Taunton owing to a side strain picked up with Derbyshire, dominated the second innings with 150 from 210 balls – enough to secure a Test recall ahead of Rutherford.*

ENGLAND v NEW ZEALAND

First Investec Test Match

STEVEN LYNCH

At Lord's, May 21–25. England won by 124 runs. Toss: New Zealand. Test debuts: A. Lyth, M. A. Wood; M. J. Henry.

A classic match lasting the full five days featured several comebacks, more runs than any Test at Lord's, and its fastest hundred. The highlights were a Bothamesque performance from Stokes, and stirring batting from Cook and Root. New Zealand played their part in their 400th Test, and 100th against England. More than that, a large crowd – culminating in a walk-up final-day attendance of 21,052 – were engaged throughout. After a period of exasperation, including a disastrous World Cup and the clumsy handling of the Kevin Pietersen affair, the queue for tickets extending round the ground on a Bank Holiday Monday suggested cricket was finally reconnecting with the British public.

A lot had happened since the defeat in Barbados. In the intervening 17 days – the shortest time between home and away Tests for England – the ECB had acquired a new director of cricket, Andrew Strauss, who sacked coach Peter Moores, then informed Pietersen, hours after his maiden triple-century, that he would not be considered for selection.

And when England dipped to 30 for four after being put in, you could sense KP's cheerleaders flexing their Twitter-fingers: a confident New Zealand, containing eight of their World Cup final XI, were on the march. But the counter-attack came straight out of the McCullum manual: Root and Stokes scorched to a fifty stand in 46 balls, and in all put on 161 at five an over. Restored to No. 6 by Paul Farbrace, despite ducks in his three previous Test innings in England, Stokes took on the seamers in memorable style, clattering two fours and a six in four balls from the debutant Matt Henry.

England, meanwhile, had two newcomers: Yorkshire opener Adam Lyth accepted the dubious honour of shirt No. 666, while the Durham fast bowler Mark Wood showed signs of pacy promise and a welcome sense of humour, celebrating his first Test catch by riding an imaginary horse.

Ten overs before tea, Stokes allowed Craig's arm-ball to crash into his stumps, and departed for 92 from 94 deliveries. Buttler kept the momentum going, and Ali chimed in after Root, on 98, under-edged Henry and was caught behind by Latham; he was deputising ably for Watling, who was resting an injured knee (he had also been forced to hand over the gloves at Lord's in 2013). The last ball of the day accounted for Buttler, but England's 354 for seven was quite a recovery, and their eventual 389 the highest in a Test innings in which a team had been 30 for four or worse.

Guptill and Latham responded with a stand of 148, although they might have been parted much earlier: when 24, Guptill was well held at slip by Cook, but Wood's delight at his first Test wicket was cut short when replays showed a marginal no-ball. Wood had to wait nearly a day before he could celebrate properly. Guptill caught the eye, swinging Jimmy Anderson for a one-bounce four. Both openers eventually departed in three balls on the second afternoon, but the third-wicket pair lifted New Zealand close to parity with a stand of 189. Williamson often played the ball impossibly late, and purred to his tenth Test century, the innings after hitting 242 not out against Sri Lanka at Wellington.

Taylor made a subdued 62, before Buttler took an acrobatic leg-side catch, but that only brought in McCullum. He took his side level – only three wickets down – with a controlled

The only way is up: Ben Stokes helps launch England's revival on the first day.

cut over the slips, then heaved Stokes into the Grand Stand. But in the next over he gave Wood his belated maiden wicket, spiralling a catch to deep third man.

Williamson rolled on, passing Taylor's New Zealand record for Test runs between dismissals (362) before bat-padding Ali to short leg; Craig survived a confident lbw appeal first ball, but perished to the second, a mite straighter. Watling, seemingly unworried by his injury, took New Zealand past 500, a total swelled by 67 extras, the most in any Test innings in England. Only nine higher totals had led to defeat.

Trailing by 134, England made another shaky start: Lyth, poking tentatively, was well caught low at third slip by Southee, who then trimmed Ballance's off bail with his best delivery of an otherwise indifferent match. Bell fell to him in the first over of the fourth day, snicking a widish one with England still 60 behind, but Cook and Root settled in to wipe off the deficit. Cook left the ball well, and tucked in to his trademark pulls and cuts with more certainty than for a year or two. And, although Root again fell within sight of a century, Cook made no mistake, reaching his 27th in Tests by straight-driving Henry for three. He survived a marginal lbw shout in the next over, from Craig, and buckled down again.

England were now more than 100 in front, and Stokes set about doubling that, with Cook an admiring spectator. An airy drive off Henry flew wide of third slip, but the next two balls produced more authentic fours. After tea Southee also went for three fours in an over; then, trying to bounce Stokes, he saw eight successive deliveries swatted for 30. Henry received similar treatment: a superb straight-drive took Stokes to 99, and two balls later a single gave him the fastest hundred in a Lord's Test, from 85 deliveries. India's Mohammad Azharuddin got there in 87 in 1990; the only known faster hundred for England was Gilbert Jessop's famous onslaught in the 1902 Ashes Test at The Oval.

Craig snared Stokes shortly afterwards, but Cook continued. By the close England's lead was 295 and, on the final morning, as the queues snaked down the road to St John's Wood station, one worry was that they might bat on too long. Instead, Cook's nine-hour vigil (and his highest Test score since December 2012 in Kolkata) ended when he tickled Boult to the keeper – a deflection missed by umpire Ravi but confirmed by Hot Spot – and the last three wickets used up less than five overs. The incisive Boult finished with a five-for, and New Zealand needed 345 in 77 – implausible but, given the breakneck rate of the match, not impossible.

A HUNDRED AND A NINETY IN THE SAME TEST FOR ENGLAND

P. A. Gibb†	93 and 106	v South Africa at Johannesburg	1938-39
M. C. Cowdrey	114 and 97	v West Indies at Kingston.	1959-60
K. F. Barrington	101 and 94	v Australia at Sydney	1962-63
A. P. E. Knott	101 and 96	v New Zealand at Auckland	1970-71
G. Boycott	99 and 112	v West Indies at Port-of-Spain	1973-74
M. A. Atherton	94* and 118	v New Zealand at Christchurch	1996-97
A. J. Strauss	126 and 94*	v South Africa at Port Elizabeth	2004-05
A. N. Cook	94 and 139*	v West Indies at Bridgetown	2008-09
A. N. Cook	96 and 106	v Sri Lanka at Lord's	2011
B. A. Stokes	**92 and 101**	**v New Zealand at Lord's**	**2015**

† *On debut.*

Overall there have been 48 instances of a batsman scoring a century and a ninety in the same Test; Cook and S. Chanderpaul (West Indies) are the only men to do it twice.

Research: Charlie Wat

After seven balls, though, it had become just about impossible, as both openers departed for ducks. Guptill edged the second delivery into the slips, where Ballance clasped a good low catch to give Anderson his 399th Test wicket. The first ball of the second over, from Broad, trapped Latham in front, and it would have been six for three had Root held Taylor at third slip. Taylor did not make the most of the let-off, pinned so obviously in front that Broad hardly bothered checking the umpire's decision.

Watling entered at No. 5, instead of McCullum, who had stretched a hamstring in the field but also wanted to give the more adhesive man a chance to settle in. Watling and Williamson survived past lunch but, just as they seemed to have weathered the storm, England's man of the moment struck. Stokes unsettled Williamson with one that reared at him, then another that whistled past the edge. Williamson was not quite over the next ball, which flew low to Root in the gully. The crowd went wild – and wilder still when Stokes immediately cramped McCullum with an inducker which crashed into the stumps via bat handle and thigh pad.

Stokes had 3–3–0–2, but New Zealand weren't finished. Showing little sign of the back strain that had forced him off the field (and would keep him out of the Second Test), Corey Anderson dented those figures by carting two fours and a six in Stokes's next over, and skeetered to a 44-ball half-century. Nine overs after tea it was 168 for five, a draw the likeliest result with 27 overs left. But Watling feathered Wood to Buttler after 192 minutes of defiance, and three overs later Root's flattish off-break trapped Anderson. Stokes returned to clean up Craig, and Southee drove the next ball loosely back at Ali. A review against Boult, the No. 11, proved unsuccessful; England grew anxious as the weather became gloomier, and the final pair survived into the last hour.

With ten overs left, Broad went round the wicket and dug the ball in. Boult pushed a two past short leg, then stepped back to upper-cut him. Earlier, with runs immaterial, Cook

FASTEST TEST HUNDREDS FOR ENGLAND

Balls

76	G. L. Jessop (104)	v Australia at The Oval	1902
85	**B. A. Stokes (101)**	**v New Zealand at Lord's**.	**2015**
86	I. T. Botham (118)	v Australia at Manchester	1981
87	I. T. Botham (149*)	v Australia at Leeds.	1981
88	K. P. Pietersen (102)	v West Indies at Port-of-Spain.	2008-09
99	I. T. Botham (103)	v New Zealand at Nottingham.	1983

The number of balls faced is not known for many early hundreds, but there are not thought to be any additions to this list.

Beginning of the end: Brendon McCullum is bowled first ball by Ben Stokes on a dramatic final day.

had been castigated by the commentators for having a third man. But now it seemed inspired: Ali moved smartly to his left and caught the ball over his shoulder as he tumbled in front of the pavilion. To the delight of the crowd, England had won a breathless game, which produced 1,610 runs, seven more than any other Lord's Test (England–India in 1990 was the previous highest). It was also the most for a time-limited Test in which all 40 wickets fell, beating 1,553 between England and Pakistan at Headingley in 2006.

All that was missing was Old Father Time, who had been blown off his perch beside the Tavern Stand a few weeks previously, and was still under repair. English cricket, it seemed, was also on the mend.

Man of the Match: B. A. Stokes. *Attendance:* 128,734.

Close of play: first day, England 354-7 (Ali 49); second day, New Zealand 303-2 (Williamson 92, Taylor 47); third day, England 74-2 (Cook 32, Bell 29); fourth day, England 429-6 (Cook 153, Ali 19).

England

A. Lyth c Watling b Southee	7	– c Southee b Boult	12
*A. N. Cook c Watling b Henry	16	– c Latham b Boult	162
G. S. Ballance c Southee b Boult	1	– b Southee	0
I. R. Bell b Henry	1	– c Latham b Southee	29
J. E. Root c Latham b Henry	98	– c Boult b Henry	84
B. A. Stokes b Craig	92	– c Taylor b Craig	101
†J. C. Buttler lbw b Boult	67	– c Latham b Henry	14
M. M. Ali c Latham b Boult	58	– lbw b Boult	43
S. C. J. Broad c Latham b Boult	3	– b Boult	10
M. A. Wood not out	8	– not out	4
J. M. Anderson c and b Henry	11	– b Boult	0
B 16, l-b 6, w 2, n-b 3	27	B 2, l-b 12, w 5	19

1/17 (1) 2/25 (3) 3/25 (2)   (100.5 overs) 389
4/30 (4) 5/191 (6) 6/251 (5)
7/354 (7) 8/363 (8) 9/368 (9) 10/389 (11)

1/14 (1) 2/25 (3)   (129 overs) 478
3/74 (4) 4/232 (5)
5/364 (6) 6/389 (7) 7/455 (2)
8/467 (9) 9/478 (8) 10/478 (11)

Boult 29–6–79–4; Southee 24–1–104–1; Henry 24.5–3–93–4; Craig 18–2–77–1; Anderson 5–1–14–0. *Second innings*—Boult 34–8–85–5; Southee 34–4–162–2; Henry 29–3–106–2; Craig 28–3–96–1; Anderson 3–0–13–0; Williamson 1–0–2–0.

New Zealand

M. J. Guptill c Ballance b Broad	70	– c Ballance b Anderson 0
T. W. M. Latham lbw b Ali	59	– lbw b Broad 0
K. S. Williamson c Ballance b Ali.............	132	– c Root b Stokes 27
L. R. P. L. Taylor c Buttler b Broad...........	62	– lbw b Broad 8
*B. B. McCullum c Root b Wood	42	– (6) b Stokes 0
C. J. Anderson c Buttler b Wood	9	– (7) lbw b Root 67
†B-J. Watling not out	61	– (5) c Buttler b Wood 59
M. D. Craig lbw b Ali	0	– b Stokes 4
T. G. Southee c Wood b Anderson	11	– c and b Ali 20
M. J. Henry c Root b Wood	10	– not out 10
T. A. Boult c Anderson b Broad	0	– c Ali b Broad 10
B 26, l-b 34, w 6, n-b 1	67	B 5, l-b 7, w 2, n-b 1 15

1/148 (2) 2/148 (1) 3/337 (4)   (131.2 overs) 523   1/0 (1) 2/0 (2)   (67.3 overs) 220
4/403 (5) 5/420 (6) 6/470 (3)   3/12 (4) 4/61 (3)
7/470 (8) 8/493 (9) 9/515 (10) 10/523 (11)   5/61 (6) 6/168 (5) 7/174 (7)
                                                           8/198 (8) 9/198 (9) 10/220 (11)

Anderson 29–7–88–1; Broad 26.2–4–77–3; Wood 27–2–93–3; Stokes 21–2–105–0; Ali 26–4–94–3; Root 2–0–6–0. *Second innings*—Anderson 14–5–31–1; Broad 16.3–3–50–3; Wood 13–3–47–1; Stokes 11–3–38–1; Ali 8–3–35–1; Root 5–3–7–1.

Umpires: M. Erasmus and S. Ravi.   Third umpire: R. J. Tucker.
Referee: D. C. Boon.

ENGLAND v NEW ZEALAND

Second Investec Test Match

James Coyne

At Leeds, May 29–June 2. New Zealand won by 199 runs. Toss: England. Test debut: L. Ronchi.

If a victory by the touring team had ever raised more smiles, then it must have taken place during a more generous age. It was typical of Brendon McCullum's New Zealand to respond to defeat at Lord's – and a few accusations of recklessness – by squeezing the throttle. McCullum said he did not view his country's fifth and most emphatic Test win in England as "vindication" for going flat out. But, if it meant the ECB mandarins would stop treating New Zealand as just a pre-Ashes stocking filler, so much the better.

No side batting more than 150 overs in a Test had scored more quickly than New Zealand. Remarkably, they did so from two for two in the first innings, and 23 for two in the second. It translated into some beautifully absurd moments: McCullum leaned into his first ball and crashed it for six over cover, then leaned back to the first after tea, and skewed to a grateful mid-off. New Zealand's method of combating the second new ball was apparently to flay as many runs as possible before it became available.

But not all their tactics were so revolutionary. Best of all, their seamers swung the ball on a good length, even when they were being hit to the boundary, knowing their captain would keep backing them with a fully stocked cordon. When Boult and Southee induced a series of prods on the second evening and third morning, New Zealand's catching approached majestic levels.

Cook, for his part, spent uncomfortably long periods standing alone at slip, after Broad had shoved most of his catchers out on the hook. Among those unimpressed was Jason

HIGHEST RUN-RATE BY ONE TEAM IN A TEST

R/O	Overs			
4.92	**163.1**	**New Zealand (350 and 454-8 dec)**	**beat England at Leeds**	**2015**
4.60	177.2	Australia (550 and 267-8 dec)	drew with South Africa at Adelaide . .	2012-13
4.50	198.2	England (568 and 325-5 dec)	beat West Indies at Lord's	2004
4.47	160	Australia (382 and 334-6)	beat South Africa at Cape Town	2001-02
4.44	163.3	India (726-9 dec)	beat Sri Lanka at Mumbai (Brabourne)	2009-10
4.40	159	India (566-6 dec and 135-7)	drew with Sri Lanka at Madras	1982-83
4.39	154.2	South Africa (600-3 dec and 79-1)	beat Zimbabwe at Harare	2001-02
4.34	153.4	Pakistan (539-6 dec and 128-2)	beat India at Lahore	1978-79
4.30	165.3	Sri Lanka (713-3 dec)	beat Zimbabwe at Bulawayo	2003-04

Qualification: 150 overs.

Gillespie, the Yorkshire head coach who had just lost out on the England job to Trevor Bayliss. "You're just taking out possible modes of dismissal," he said. "If you see some intent from a lower-order player, and then scatter the field, you're not backing your own abilities."

Ballance and Bell had a similarly torrid match, and were responsible for three missed slip catches between them. It didn't need a Headingley regular to point out that Lyth's hands at second slip had been crucial in Yorkshire's 2014 County Championship title. Instead, he found himself in the ring or at short leg, presumably because this was his second Test.

England's new slimline knitwear – which had tickled London's fashion columnists – proved inadequate for the bracing south-westerly that swept frequent bands of rain across Headingley and prevented the toss until 1pm. During the World Cup quarter-final, Guptill had clattered West Indies' Andre Russell on to the lid of Wellington's Cake Tin. But that was of little use against Jimmy Anderson, armed with the shiny red Dukes under heavy cloud. Guptill groped at two outswingers before feathering a third, giving Anderson his 400th Test wicket; as a congratulatory message flashed up on the big screen, another shower had the players scurrying off. To the second delivery after the resumption, Williamson followed in near-identical fashion. Latham, though, showed all the nous of a top-drawer left-handed opener, timing the ball sweetly off his pads or when offered width, and stealing quick singles. Wood and Stokes, who burned so brightly at Lord's, struggled to settle into the fabled Leeds line and length, and were routinely picked off.

The injuries to Watling and Corey Anderson in the opening Test had left New Zealand struggling for balance. They retained Watling as a specialist No. 6, and gave the gloves to Luke Ronchi, meaning they had as many Test wicketkeepers in the team as genuine bowlers. At 34, Ronchi was their oldest Test debutant for nearly half a century, through a circuitous route of seven limited-overs caps for Australia and 57 for New Zealand. He was also the first Luke to play Test cricket, completing all four gospels – as if Yorkshiremen needed convincing this was hallowed turf. Ronchi was determined not to forsake his game:

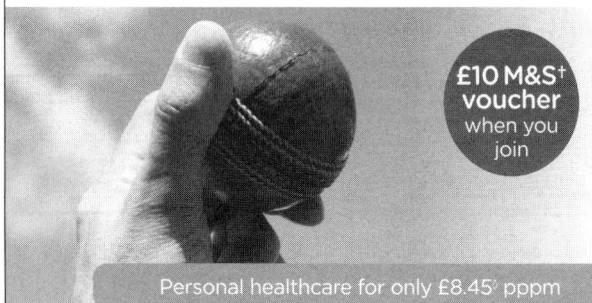

Slipping up: Gary Ballance misses Ross Taylor – one of four drops by England in the match.

he flashed his first ball over the slips, and hummed along as if playing a one-dayer, catching Latham up on 72 in the 49th over.

It was then that England's fielding fell apart. Latham was dropped three times in eight balls: off Ali at square leg and leg slip, then in Broad's next over when Bell, at second slip, declined to go for a chance high to his right which Cook, diving behind him, could only fingertip away. Latham was eventually held at first – but not before he and Ronchi had put on New Zealand's fifth hundred partnership for the sixth wicket since the start of 2014. Their score of 297 for eight at stumps was the most in a day's Test cricket in which an entire session had been lost.

Broad's aversion to being driven had been telegraphed when he began digging the ball in from round the wicket, and duped Ronchi into picking out fine leg. It seemed hasty to resume the strategy on the second morning, though a 40-run stand for the last wicket seemed minor by England's recent standards.

By contrast, Cook and Lyth emitted an old-world assurance as they settled in for England's first century opening stand at home since 2011. On 29, Cook square-drove Southee for four to pass Graham Gooch's Test aggregate of 8,900 runs; for the first time since Jack Hobbs and S. F. Barnes in February 1914, England had both their leading run-scorer and wicket-taker in the same side. The openers took the total to 177 – an

LEAST ECONOMICAL TEST FIVE-WICKET HAULS

ER			
6.34	**S. C. J. Broad (17.1–0–109–5)**	**England v New Zealand at Leeds**	**2015**
6.22	D. W. Steyn (13.1–1–82–5)	South Africa v Sri Lanka at Colombo (PSO)	2006
5.92	J. R. Thomson (13–1–77–6)	Australia v West Indies at Bridgetown	1977-78
5.73	J. N. Gillespie (15.2–2–88–5)	Australia v England at Perth	1998-99
5.72	Rubel Hossain (29–1–166–5)	Bangladesh v New Zealand at Hamilton	2009-10
5.68	Kapil Dev (38.4–3–220–7)	India v Pakistan at Faisalabad	1982-83
5.52	G. D. McGrath (20.5–1–115–5)	Australia v England at Manchester	2005

England record for the first wicket at Headingley – at which point Cook missed a sweep and was given out on review, the second time an lbw verdict from umpire Ravi had been overturned by DRS.

Lyth's only indiscretions came in the nineties: a chip towards mid-on wrong-footed the substitute fielder Neil Wagner, and another delivery had rolled back on to his leg stump without dislodging the bail; Lyth's fresh-air kick at the ball confirmed, on FA Cup final day, that this one-time Manchester City triallist had chosen the right sport.

But England's hopes of a big lead were soon up in smoke. Ballance did for Lyth while attempting a suicidal single and, as the last hour began, with the new ball imminent, the skies darkened and Yorkshire sparked up their new rose-shaped floodlights. Boult and Southee licked their lips, and England's lengthy middle order, from Ballance to Ali, was gutted for 29 runs. Broad, showing signs of a return to confidence with the bat, was able to slap a further 83 alongside the last two, which hoisted England up to 350 – the eighth instance of first-innings parity in a Test.

New Zealand's next task was to shed a tag of third-innings vulnerability. When Broad nipped out Latham and Williamson, their second wicket had mustered nought, nought, nought and eight across the series. But, in the next over, Ballance missed another chance at slip; somehow Anderson, who had just been spoken to for running on the pitch, did not blow a gasket. Guptill and Taylor embarked on their version of a repair job, stroking 99 at almost seven an over, before McCullum reined himself in to add a precious 121 with the sturdy Watling, whose sore knee proved no impediment to a fifth Test hundred.

Most obliging: Kane Williamson moves to leg slip, and Ian Bell guides the next ball straight to him.

With New Zealand 338 ahead and two days remaining, England were up against it. Their bowling coach Ottis Gibson acknowledged they should have plugged away on a good length, so it was telling when Cook favoured Wood to start next morning, and again with the second new ball. When Broad was brought on, a few lusty blows from Southee soon had him banging it in, with no change in fortunes. After a final avalanche of 77 runs in seven overs, New Zealand declared on 454 for eight. For the first time in a Test innings, eight different batsmen had struck a six.

Cook and Lyth began steadily, but rain arrived after lunch, and filled in for the day. That ought to have boosted England's survival chances, but it also meant New Zealand's three seamers could return fresh on the last day, when the weather was set fair. Root's overnight promise that England would go for the runs regardless was either impressive self-belief or an attempt to lure out the Yorkshire public. But this was a working day in term-time: fewer than 17,000 attended across the last three days, despite virtual giveaways on the Monday and Tuesday.

Any hopes of a late stampede were scotched by lunch: the dismissals of Ballance, bowled for the third time in the series, and Bell, turning Craig round the corner into the hands of Williamson, who had just been moved to leg slip, were especially anaemic. With the exception of a fleet-footed riposte from Buttler, Craig wheeled away unchallenged into the footmarks at the Rugby Stand End; Williamson's remodelled off-spin swept up three partnership-breaking wickets. Just before five o'clock, England slumped to their fourth defeat in six Tests at Headingley.

McCullum had now won a greater percentage of his Tests than any New Zealand captain. But his appeal was best captured by the small details. In the hour before play on the fourth day, usually a time for pep-talks, drills and protocol, he had sidled up to David Boon, the ICC match referee, who was perched on the light roller by the edge of the square. For about 20 minutes they were just two cricket men shooting the breeze. A year earlier, it had been Boon's job to wade through the muck of the Anderson–Jadeja dispute at Trent Bridge, as world cricket's two richest boards indulged in pointless litigation. Watching New Zealand was some kind of therapy.

Man of the Match: B-J. Watling. *Attendance:* 43,971.

Men of the Series: England – A. N. Cook; New Zealand – T. A. Boult.

Close of play: first day, New Zealand 297-8 (Craig 16, Henry 14); second day, England 253-5 (Bell 12, Buttler 6); third day, New Zealand 338-6 (Watling 100, Craig 15); fourth day, England 44-0 (Lyth 24, Cook 18).

New Zealand

M. J. Guptill c Bell b Anderson	0	– (2) c Root b Wood	70
T. W. M. Latham c Root b Broad	84	– (1) c Buttler b Broad	3
K. S. Williamson c Buttler b Anderson	0	– c Buttler b Broad	6
L. R. P. L. Taylor lbw b Broad	20	– c Stokes b Wood	48
B. B. McCullum c Wood b Stokes	41	– lbw b Wood	55
B-J. Watling b Wood	14	– c Root b Anderson	120
L. Ronchi c Anderson b Broad	88	– c Buttler b Anderson	31
M. D. Craig not out	41	– not out	58
T. G. Southee c Lyth b Wood	1	– c Anderson b Ali	40
M. J. Henry c Buttler b Broad	27	– not out	12
T. A. Boult c Lyth b Broad	15		
B 4, l-b 14, n-b 1	19	B 4, l-b 6, w 1	11

1/2 (1) 2/2 (3) 3/68 (4) (72.1 overs) 350   1/15 (1) (8 wkts dec, 91 overs) 454
4/123 (5) 5/144 (6) 6/264 (2)   2/23 (3) 3/122 (4)
7/265 (7) 8/281 (9) 9/310 (10) 10/350 (11)   4/141 (2) 5/262 (5)
6/315 (7) 7/368 (6) 8/435 (9)

Anderson 13–3–43–2; Broad 17.1–0–109–5; Wood 14–4–62–2; Stokes 17–4–70–1; Ali 11–3–48–0. *Second innings*—Anderson 23–4–96–2; Broad 16–1–94–2; Wood 19–2–97–3; Stokes 12–1–61–0; Ali 16–0–73–1; Root 5–0–23–0.

England

A. Lyth run out	107	– c Ronchi b Boult	24
*A. N. Cook lbw b Craig	75	– lbw b Williamson	56
G. S. Ballance b Boult	29	– b Boult	6
I. R. Bell c Craig b Southee	12	– c Williamson b Craig	1
J. E. Root c Ronchi b Southee	1	– c Latham b Craig	0
B. A. Stokes c Craig b Boult	6	– c Ronchi b Williamson	29
†J. C. Buttler c Taylor b Southee	10	– lbw b Craig	73
M. M. Ali c Guptill b Southee	1	– b Henry	2
S. C. J. Broad b Henry	46	– b Williamson	23
M. A. Wood c Ronchi b Craig	19	– c Craig b Southee	17
J. M. Anderson not out	10	– not out	8
B 19, l-b 5, w 5, n-b 5	34	B 12, l-b 2, w 2	16

1/177 (2) 2/215 (1) 3/238 (3)   (108.2 overs) 350
4/239 (5) 5/247 (6) 6/257 (4)
7/266 (7) 8/267 (8) 9/318 (10) 10/350 (9)

1/47 (1) 2/61 (3)   (91.5 overs) 255
3/62 (4) 4/62 (5)
5/102 (6) 6/141 (2) 7/153 (8)
8/188 (9) 9/230 (10) 10/255 (7)

Boult 30–7–98–2; Southee 30–5–83–4; Henry 20.2–4–92–1; Craig 26–12–48–2; Williamson 2–1–5–0. *Second innings*—Boult 23–4–61–2; Southee 18–7–43–1; Craig 31.5–12–73–3; Henry 12–2–49–1; Williamson 7–1–15–3.

Umpires: S. Ravi and R. J. Tucker.   Third umpire: M. Erasmus.
Referee: D. C. Boon.

At Leicester, June 6. **New Zealanders won by 198 runs. ‡New Zealanders 373-5** (50 overs) (L. R. P. L. Taylor 77, G. D. Elliott 106*, L. Ronchi 106*; A. Sheikh 3-49); **Leicestershire 175** (42.3 overs) (A. J. Robson 67; M. J. McClenaghan 4-31). *Grant Elliott's century was well received at Grace Road, where he had recently been one of Leicestershire's Twenty20 overseas players. Elliott and Luke Ronchi each struck 106* (from 79 and 76 balls respectively), as they added 221* for the sixth wicket. Atif Sheikh, one of three List A debutants – along with Aadil Ali and Rob Sayer – bowled with gusto in an opening spell of 5–0–18–2, but the New Zealanders were assisted by some sloppy fielding. With Trent Boult and Tim Southee rested, Mitchell McClenaghan led a new-look New Zealand attack.*

LIMITED-OVERS INTERNATIONAL REPORTS BY ANDREW ALDERSON

ENGLAND v NEW ZEALAND

First Royal London One-Day International

At Birmingham, June 9 (day/night). England won by 210 runs. Toss: New Zealand. One-day international debuts: S. W. Billings; M. J. Santner.

The series opener spectacularly confounded its tag line as World Cup finalists versus World Cup flops. England's 408 for nine, including 38 fours and a record 14 sixes, was both their highest total (beating 391 for four against Bangladesh at Trent Bridge in 2005) and the highest conceded by New Zealand (beating India's 392 for four at Christchurch in 2008-09). By bowling the New Zealanders out for 198 – with almost 19 overs to spare – England also achieved their largest win by runs. After Roy had fallen to the first delivery of the match, slicing Boult to backward point, Root's 104 off 78 balls and Buttler's incendiary 129 off 77 produced Roman-candle wagon wheels. It was the first time two players had made centuries in a one-day international innings without batting together. Root's high-class, unflustered century, from 71 deliveries, was England's third fastest – but only for as long as it took Buttler to get there in 66, second only to his own 61-ball hundred against Sri Lanka at Lord's the previous summer. Four wickets had fallen for 31 to leave the innings at a crossroads on 202 for six after 30 overs, but Rashid, who went on to his maiden international fifty, helped Buttler in a raucous world-record seventh-wicket stand of 177 inside 18 overs. Only Boult had any impact.

Needing to score at more than eight an over to scale the Himalayas, New Zealand never reached base camp. McCullum went in the first over, charging at Finn, and Taylor alone reached 50. With Rashid making clever use of his googly to add career-best figures with the ball – and the best by an England leg-spinner – the last six wickets fell for 13. A kitchen fire at Edgbaston the day before the game, reportedly caused by burning peppers, had led to the evacuation of the England dressing-room, and several staff were treated for smoke inhalation.

Man of the Match: J. C. Buttler.   *Attendance:* 19,700.

England

J. J. Roy c Guptill b Boult	0	L. E. Plunkett not out		13
A. D. Hales c Henry b Boult	20	S. T. Finn not out		0
J. E. Root c Ronchi b Boult	104			
E. J. G. Morgan lbw b McClenaghan	50	W 8		8
B. A. Stokes b Boult	10			—
J. C. Buttler c Henry b McClenaghan	129	1/0 (1) 2/50 (2)	(9 wkts, 50 overs)	408
S. W. Billings lbw b Santner	3	3/171 (4) 4/180 (3)		
A. U. Rashid c Guptill b Elliott	69	5/195 (5) 6/202 (7) 7/379 (6)		
C. J. Jordan c Boult b Elliott	2	8/394 (9) 9/394 (8)	10 overs: 68-2	

Boult 10–0–55–4; Henry 10–0–73–0; N. L. McCullum 7–0–66–0; McClenaghan 10–0–93–2; Elliott 5–0–57–2; Santner 8–0–64–1.

New Zealand

M. J. Guptill c Buttler b Finn	22	M. J. McClenaghan c Hales b Jordan		2
B. B. McCullum b Finn	10	T. A. Boult not out		0
K. S. Williamson c Root b Rashid	45			
L. R. P. L. Taylor lbw b Finn	57	L-b 10, w 8		18
G. D. Elliott run out	24			—
M. J. Santner c Jordan b Rashid	15	1/11 (2) 2/52 (1) 3/94 (3)	(31.1 overs)	198
L. Ronchi b Rashid	0	4/160 (5) 5/185 (6) 6/185 (7)		
N. L. McCullum c Jordan b Finn	5	7/190 (4) 8/195 (9) 9/198 (8)		
M. J. Henry lbw b Rashid	0	10/198 (10)	10 overs: 70-2	

Finn 7–1–35–4; Jordan 5.1–0–33–1; Plunkett 5–0–37–0; Rashid 10–0–55–4; Stokes 4–0–28–0.

Umpires: M. A. Gough and B. N. J. Oxenford.   Third umpire: S. J. Davis.
Referee: J. Srinath.

ENGLAND v NEW ZEALAND

Second Royal London One-Day International

At The Oval, June 12 (day/night). New Zealand won by 13 runs (D/L). Toss: New Zealand.
New Zealand levelled the series thanks to another mammoth first-innings total, but they were grateful for a little meteorological help. Rain struck with England on 345 for seven, needing 54 runs from 37 balls, and an enterprising stand between Rashid and Plunkett already worth 70. But when play resumed the equation became an even more testing 34 from 13. Both batsmen fell in the same over, bowled by Nathan McCullum – a remarkable relay catch between Southee and Boult to dismiss Rashid on the long-on boundary sealed the game. England's highest total batting second (despite facing only 46 overs) was little consolation. New Zealand's top seven had all contributed to a daunting 398 on a pitch that offered all the seam movement of a tennis ball on tarmac. The upshot was 40 fours, 13 sixes and their second-highest one-day total, behind 402 for two against Ireland at Aberdeen in 2008. Williamson, with 93 from 88 balls, and Taylor, who made an unbeaten 119 from 96 after being dropped by Roy at backward point on seven, stood out. England chased competitively after Roy and Hales began with 85 inside 13 overs and, at 259 for four after 32, might even have been favourites. But Buttler was caught behind off Boult, later ruled out of the tour with a back injury. Then Morgan – who looked set for England's fastest one-day century – scythed McClenaghan

Unshackled: Eoin Morgan throws off his inhibitions (and his helmet) at The Oval.

to deep point to depart for a swashbuckling 88 from 47 balls. Billings followed quickly, before Rashid and Plunkett threatened to turn the game. New Zealand closed it out for their 300th ODI win; it had taken 684 matches, more than the seven other sides to have reached the mark.

Man of the Match: L. R. P. L. Taylor. *Attendance:* 21,723.

New Zealand

M. J. Guptill c Jordan b Stokes	50	M. J. Santner not out	15
*B. B. McCullum c Stokes b Plunkett	39	L-b 3, w 12, n-b 2	17
K. S. Williamson c Plunkett b Stokes	93		
L. R. P. L. Taylor not out	119	1/61 (2) 2/114 (1)	(5 wkts, 50 overs) 398
G. D. Elliott lbw b Jordan	32	3/235 (3) 4/307 (5)	
†L. Ronchi c Buttler b Finn	33	5/352 (6)	10 overs: 77-1

N. L. McCullum, T. G. Southee, M. J. McClenaghan and T. A. Boult did not bat.

Finn 10–1–69–1; Jordan 9–0–97–1; Plunkett 9–0–71–1; Rashid 10–0–72–0; Stokes 9–0–66–2; Root 3–0–20–0.

England

J. J. Roy c Taylor b N. L. McCullum	39	C. J. Jordan not out	3
A. D. Hales c Boult b Santner	54	S. T. Finn not out	6
J. E. Root c N. L. McCullum b Santner	6		
*E. J. G. Morgan c Elliott b McClenaghan	88	B 1, l-b 2, w 7	10
B. A. Stokes c Ronchi b McClenaghan	28		
†J. C. Buttler c Ronchi b Boult	41	1/85 (1) 2/100 (3)	(9 wkts, 46 overs) 365
S. W. Billings c Guptill b Boult	12	3/100 (2) 4/163 (5)	
A. U. Rashid c Boult b N. L. McCullum	34	5/259 (6) 6/274 (4)	
L. E. Plunkett c B. B. McCullum		7/275 (7) 8/351 (9)	
b N. L. McCullum	44	9/355 (8)	10 overs: 65-0

Southee 9–0–68–0; Boult 10–1–53–2; McClenaghan 9–0–61–2; N. L. McCullum 9–0–86–3; Santner 7–0–73–2; Guptill 1–0–12–0; Elliott 1–0–9–0.

Umpires: S. J. Davis and R. T. Robinson. Third umpire: B. N. J. Oxenford.
Referee: J. Srinath.

ENGLAND v NEW ZEALAND

Third Royal London One-Day International

At Southampton, June 14. New Zealand won by three wickets. Toss: England. One-day international debut: B. M. Wheeler.

New Zealand's successful chase of 303 – small fry for this series – felt like an open-wicket practice. This was especially so while the inevitable pair of Williamson and Taylor, who both made centuries, were adding 206. It was the highest for New Zealand's third wicket, surpassing 180 by Adam Parore and Ken Rutherford against India at Baroda in 1994-95, and for any New Zealand wicket against England, beating an unbroken 165 between openers Brendon McCullum and Jesse Ryder at Hamilton in 2007-08. But they were helped by a spate of dropped catches. Taylor was missed on 67 by Buttler and on 72 by Stokes at short midwicket, both off Wood, who spilled a simple chance at mid-off to reprieve Williamson on 109. New Zealand's late wobble brought those errors into sharper perspective. England had been careless with the bat, too. From 288 for five, they subsided to 302 all out, with 28 deliveries unused, as the debutant left-arm seamer Ben Wheeler finished with three wickets. But there was entertainment to be had, not least from Stokes, who smashed 68 from 47, and landed one six – a whopper, presumably – in the Gourmet Burgers caravan. Billings made an inventive 34 from 16, but Morgan was left to defend England's gung-ho approach, which seemed even more wasteful when their fielding disintegrated later.

Man of the Match: K. S. Williamson. *Attendance:* 16,752.

England

J. J. Roy b Southee	9	M. A. Wood not out		3
A. D. Hales c Southee b Wheeler	23	S. T. Finn b Southee		0
J. E. Root b Santner	54			
*E. J. G. Morgan b Williamson	71	L-b 5, w 14		19
B. A. Stokes b Wheeler	68			
†J. C. Buttler c Ronchi b Southee	13	1/34 (2) 2/34 (1)	(45.2 overs)	302
S. W. Billings c McClenaghan b Wheeler	34	3/139 (3) 4/194 (4) 5/227 (6)		
A. U. Rashid c Guptill b Henry	0	6/288 (7) 7/290 (8) 8/298 (5)		
D. J. Willey c McCullum b Henry	8	9/300 (9) 10/302 (11)	10 overs: 41-2	

Southee 8.2–1–44–3; Wheeler 10–0–63–3; Henry 10–0–64–2; McClenaghan 8–0–67–0; Santner 5–0–30–1; Elliott 2–0–17–0; Williamson 2–0–12–1.

New Zealand

M. J. Guptill lbw b Willey	2	B. M. Wheeler not out		3
*B. B. McCullum lbw b Wood	11	T. G. Southee not out		5
K. S. Williamson c Wood b Willey	118	L-b 6, w 12		18
L. R. P. L. Taylor b Willey	110			
G. D. Elliott c Root b Rashid	5	1/4 (1) 2/36 (2)	(7 wkts, 49 overs)	306
M. J. Santner c Root b Stokes	21	3/242 (3) 4/249 (5)		
†L. Ronchi c Roy b Stokes	13	5/284 (6) 6/290 (4) 7/300 (7)	10 overs: 64-2	

M. J. Henry and M. J. McClenaghan did not bat.

Finn 10–0–55–0; Willey 10–1–69–3; Wood 10–0–48–1; Rashid 10–0–72–1; Stokes 6–0–35–2; Root 3–0–21–0.

Umpires: B. N. J. Oxenford and R. T. Robinson.   Third umpire: S. J. Davis.
Referee: J. Srinath.

ENGLAND v NEW ZEALAND

Fourth Royal London One-Day International

At Nottingham, June 17 (day/night). England won by seven wickets. Toss: New Zealand.

England squared the series in emphatic fashion, recording their highest successful one-day chase, eclipsing 306 for five at Karachi in 2000-01. They also passed 300 for the fourth game in succession, having never previously done so more than twice in a row. The day belonged to their top four, who

SHATTERED RECORDS: THE ONE-DAY SERIES IN STATS

3,151 Runs scored overall, the most in any five-match bilateral one-day series, beating 2,963 by Pakistan and India in 2003-04.

763 Runs scored at The Oval (from 96 overs), the most in an ODI in England, and the third-highest overall. Nottingham produced 699 runs, also beating the old record, which was 651 by England and India at Lord's in 2002.

408-9 England's total at Birmingham was the 16th of 400-plus in ODIs, but the first in or by England.

398-5 New Zealand's total at The Oval was the highest England had conceded in ODIs, beating 387-5 by India at Rajkot in 2008-09.

365-9 England's reply at The Oval was their highest total batting second in ODIs. Their 350-3 at Nottingham also broke the old record – 338-8 in the tie with India at Bangalore during the 2011 World Cup – and was the first time they had successfully chased 300-plus at home.

210 England's margin of victory at Birmingham was their highest by runs in ODIs, beating 202 against India at Lord's during the 1975 World Cup.

97 Runs conceded by Chris Jordan at The Oval, equalling the England record established by Steve Harmison, against Sri Lanka at Leeds in 2006 (Harmison bowled ten overs, to Jordan's nine).

27 Sixes at The Oval, a record for an ODI in England, and the fourth-highest overall. The 21 sixes at Nottingham, and 15 at Birmingham, also beat the old mark of 14, by New Zealand (13) and the United States (one) at The Oval in the 2004 Champions Trophy.

7.15 Average runs per over throughout, a record for any series of more than one match, beating 6.64 by India and Australia in 2013-14.

Research: Steven Lynch

tore into New Zealand's pace quartet as if afraid of missing last orders at the Larwood & Voce. Set 350, England were sent on their way by an opening stand of 100 in 10.4 overs between Roy and Hales, before Root and Morgan thrashed 198 in 26.2. The in-form Morgan hit his eighth one-day international hundred, in all facing 82 balls and launching five sixes, while Root's unbeaten 106 – his sixth – came from 97. Their partnership was England's best for any wicket against New Zealand whose bowlers seemed powerless to intervene. Victory came with a resounding six overs to spare; until now, no side had made more than India's 326, at Lord's in 2002, to win a one-day international in England. New Zealand had looked in command with the bat, and the only stumble en route to 349 came during some miserly bowling in the second powerplay from Finn and Wood. But Willey went for 89, and Rashid 75 off eight overs, including 28 from the 48th as Santner connected with four sixes over midwicket. It was brave of Morgan to give his leg-spinner the 50th over too: he responded with the wicket of Southee and conceded only four off the bat. Williamson had again been in sublime touch, easing his way to 90 from 70 balls, but England's pursuit left him in the shade. Injuries to Chris Jordan and Liam Plunkett had led to the call-up of Craig and Jamie Overton, the two Somerset quick bowlers – briefly raising the possibility of England fielding twins in the same match for the first time. Neither was selected.

Man of the Match: E. J. G. Morgan.   *Attendance:* 16,726.

New Zealand

M. J. Guptill c Finn b Stokes	53		T. G. Southee c Stokes b Rashid	1
*B. B. McCullum c Buttler b Wood	35		B. M. Wheeler not out	3
K. S. Williamson c Rashid b Willey	90		L-b 2, w 13, n-b 3	18
L. R. P. L. Taylor lbw b Finn	42			
G. D. Elliott not out	55		1/88 (2) 2/116 (1) (7 wkts, 50 overs)	349
†L. Ronchi c Stokes b Willey	8		3/217 (4) 4/250 (3)	
M. J. Santner c Billings b Stokes	44		5/271 (6) 6/342 (7) 7/344 (8) 10 overs: 64-0	

M. J. Henry and M. J. McClenaghan did not bat.

Willey 10–0–89–2; Finn 10–1–51–1; Wood 10–0–49–1; Stokes 10–0–73–2; Rashid 8–0–75–1;
Root 2–0–10–0.

England

J. J. Roy c Williamson b Henry	38
A. D. Hales b Henry	67
J. E. Root not out	106
*E. J. G. Morgan c Henry b Southee	113
B. A. Stokes not out	19
L-b 4, w 3	7

1/100 (2) 2/111 (1) (3 wkts, 44 overs) 350
3/309 (4) 10 overs: 97-0

†J. C. Buttler, S. W. Billings, A. U. Rashid, D. J. Willey, M. A. Wood and S. T. Finn did not bat.

Wheeler 8–1–75–0; Southee 10–0–70–1; McClenaghan 8–0–64–0; Henry 10–0–77–2; Williamson
4–0–28–0; Santner 4–0–32–0.

Umpires: R. J. Bailey and S. J. Davis.   Third umpire: B. N. J. Oxenford.
Referee: J. Srinath.

ENGLAND v NEW ZEALAND

Fifth Royal London One-Day International

At Chester-le-Street, June 20. England won by three wickets (D/L). Toss: England. One-day
international debut: A. W. Mathieson.

Bairstow's first international innings since the Sydney Test of January 2014 produced an
exhilarating format-best 83 not out from 60 balls as England fought back to claim a rain-affected
decider. Recalled after Jos Buttler split the webbing between his left thumb and forefinger in training,
Bairstow marshalled their pursuit of a revised 192 in 26 overs after they had slipped to 45 for five.
First he added 80 with the lively Billings, then – after Willey went cheaply – an unbroken 54 in 29
deliveries with Yorkshire team-mate Rashid. Had Santner caught an easy chance at third man when
Bairstow had 56, New Zealand might have won. His glovework left its mark too: when he caught
Taylor, the scorebook recorded "c Bairstow b Willey" for the first time since December 1979, when
their fathers – David, another wicketkeeper, and Peter – combined to dismiss Rod Marsh in a one-
day international at Melbourne. Earlier, the biggest surprise was that New Zealand failed to add to a
series tally of seven 300-plus totals – second only to the nine managed by India and Australia in late
2013. Rashid produced his tightest spell of the series, but Wheeler hit the last three balls of the
innings, from Finn, for 16 to lift New Zealand's spirits. Rain held up play for more than two and a
half hours and, when England finally batted, they almost unravelled against the left-arm spin of
Santner, opening with Southee. He struck three times in his first eight deliveries, including Morgan,

PARTNERS IN CRIME

Most runs in a one-day international series from one batting partnership (bilateral series only):

	I	R	Avge p'ship	100 p'ships		
Yasir Hameed/ Imran Farhat (P)	5	590	118.00	4	(h) v NZ	2003-04
R. G. Sharma/ S. Dhawan (I)	6	533	106.60	3	(h) v A	2013-14
H. M. Amla/ R. R. Rossouw (SA)	4	526	131.50	2	(h) v WI	2014-15
S. C. Ganguly/ S. R. Tendulkar (I)	7	472	67.42	3	(a) v E	2007
K. S. Williamson/ L. R. P. L. Taylor (NZ)	**4**	**470**	**117.50**	**3**	**(a) v E**	**2015**
K. S. Williamson/ L. R. P. L. Taylor (NZ)	4	463	115.75	3	(h) v I	2013-14
J. E. Root/ E. J. G. Morgan (E)	**3**	**424**	**141.33**	**3**	**(h) v NZ**	**2015**

caught at deep midwicket as he slog-swept his first ball. When seamer Andrew Mathieson's first delivery for New Zealand induced a toe-ended miscue from Roy, England were sinking fast. But Bairstow changed the momentum of the day, and they were soon celebrating their first one-day series win at home in six attempts.

Man of the Match: J. M. Bairstow. *Attendance:* 13,788.

Man of the Series: K. S. Williamson.

New Zealand

M. J. Guptill c Bairstow b Stokes 67	M. J. Henry c Stokes b Finn 12
*B. B. McCullum b Finn 6	A. W. Mathieson not out 0
K. S. Williamson b Stokes 50	
L. R. P. L. Taylor c Bairstow b Willey 47	L-b 3, w 2 5
M. J. Santner b Rashid 2	
G. D. Elliott st Bairstow b Rashid 35	1/7 (2) 2/101 (3) (9 wkts, 50 overs) 283
†L. Ronchi c Morgan b Willey 2	3/150 (1) 4/155 (5)
B. M. Wheeler not out 39	5/210 (6) 6/212 (4) 7/219 (7)
T. G. Southee b Stokes 18	8/244 (9) 9/267 (10) 10 overs: 59-1

Finn 10–0–73–2; Willey 10–0–50–2; Wood 10–0–60–0; Stokes 10–0–52–3; Rashid 10–0–45–2.

England

J. J. Roy c Guptill b Mathieson 12	D. J. Willey c Santner b Wheeler 7
A. D. Hales c Williamson b Santner 1	A. U. Rashid not out 12
J. E. Root st Ronchi b Santner 4	B 1, l-b 6, w 8 15
*E. J. G. Morgan c Guptill b Santner 0	
B. A. Stokes c McCullum b Wheeler 17	1/8 (2) 2/20 (3) (7 wkts, 25 overs) 192
†J. M. Bairstow not out 83	3/20 (4) 4/40 (5)
S. W. Billings c Taylor b Henry 41	5/45 (1) 6/125 (7) 7/138 (8) 5 overs: 23-3

M. A. Wood and S. T. Finn did not bat.

Southee 4–0–28–0; Santner 6–0–31–3; Wheeler 5–0–33–2; Mathieson 4–0–40–1; Henry 5–0–37–1; Elliott 1–0–16–0.

Umpires: M. A. Gough and B. N. J. Oxenford.   Third umpire: S. J. Davis.
Referee: J. Srinath.

ENGLAND v NEW ZEALAND

NatWest Twenty20 International

At Manchester, June 23 (floodlit). England won by 56 runs. Toss: England. Twenty20 international debuts: S. W. Billings, D. J. Willey, M. A. Wood; M. J. Santner.

New Zealand collapsed from 89 for two in the ninth over as England's revival crossed over into the shortest format. The last five wickets fell in 12 balls, and the decisive blow came when Williamson, having reached 50 for the sixth time in ten international innings on the tour, was superbly run out by Root after an initial flurry from Roy. England's own innings had been organised impeccably by Root, before late hitting from Billings and Stokes helped them to 191. Santner was the pick of the New Zealand attack, removing Bairstow – England's hero at Riverside three days earlier – with a beauty that hit the top of middle. Willey bowled Guptill with the third ball of the New Zealand chase, but Brendon McCullum was in pugnacious mood, hitting four sixes from his first 12 deliveries. Wood and Willey chipped away, however, and New Zealand's highly entertaining trip ended in anticlimax.

Man of the Match: J. E. Root. *Attendance:* 16,046.

England

		B	4/6
1 J. J. Roy *run out*	23	13	1/2
2 A. D. Hales *c 2 b 7*	27	23	2/1
3 J. E. Root *c 1 b 11*	68	46	8/1
4 †J. M. Bairstow *b 7*	1	2	0
5 *E. J. G. Morgan *c 4 b 10*	4	6	0
6 S. W. Billings *c 6 b 11*	21	11	2/1
7 B. A. Stokes *not out*	24	13	4
8 D. J. Willey *c 7 b 9*	6	3	0/1
9 A. U. Rashid *not out*	7	3	1
B 1, l-b 2, w 7	10		

6 overs: 60-1 (20 overs) **191-7**

1/25 2/76 3/79 4/101 5/144 6/157 7/169

10 M. A. Wood and 11 S. T. Finn did not bat.

Santner 4-0-28-2 (9); McClenaghan 4-0-37-2 (11); Southee 4-0-45-1 (4); N. L. McCullum 4-0-46-0 (2); Henry 4-0-32-1 (7).

New Zealand

		B	4/6
1 M. J. Guptill *b 8*	6	3	1
2 *B. B. McCullum *b 10*	35	15	2/4
3 K. S. Williamson *run out*	57	37	8
4 L. R. P. L. Taylor *c 8 b 9*	17	13	2
5 C. Munro *b 7*	1	2	0
6 †L. Ronchi *c 4 b 7*	5	4	1
7 M. J. Santner *b 10*	9	13	0
8 N. L. McCullum *c 11 b 8*	3	9	0
9 T. G. Southee *c 5 b 10*	0	1	0
10 M. J. Henry *not out*	0	0	0
11 M. J. McClenaghan *c 4 b 8*	0	1	0
L-b 1, w 1	2		

6 overs: 73-2 (16.2 overs) **135**

1/6 2/48 3/89 4/95 5/101 6/131 7/131 8/131 9/135

Willey 2.2-0-22-3 (6); Finn 4-0-29-0 (9); Wood 3-0-26-3 (6); Rashid 4-0-33-1 (5); Stokes 3-0-24-2 (9).

Umpires: R. J. Bailey and R. T. Robinson. Third umpire: M. A. Gough.
Referee: J. Srinath.

ENGLAND v AUSTRALIA IN 2015

Review by Jonathan Liew

Test matches (5): England 3, Australia 2
Twenty20 international (1): England 1, Australia 0
One-day internationals (5): England 2, Australia 3

BSE, or mad cow disease, emerged in the 1980s. Essentially, it was caused by greed and cannibalism. To save money, cattle were fed meat and bone meal produced from the remains of sheep or cows, disregarding the fact that for thousands of years they had quite happily been vegetarian. Mutation spread through the food chain like a nasty rumour. By the time the disease was under control, almost four and a half million cattle had been slaughtered – and the entire British beef industry was close to ruin. About 180 people in the UK have died of variant CJD, the human form of the disease.

The 2015 Ashes series killed no humans and no cows. Its effect on the cricket industry, however, was harder to ascertain. More simply put, this third Ashes encounter in the space of two years was the point at which the long and venerable rivalry between England and Australia started to cannibalise itself, mutate, and go thoroughly mad as a result.

It was a series that defied predictions, statistics, narrative, and at times appeared to defy even gravity. England took an emphatic lead at Cardiff, surrendered it just as emphatically at Lord's, lurched back with resounding victories at Edgbaston and Trent Bridge inside three days, then collapsed horribly in the dead rubber at The Oval. Australia took more wickets, scored more runs, made more centuries – and lost.

There were contradictions: it was a close series that was never really very close, all five matches being won by thumping margins; and it was a series short on quality, yet brimming with entertainment. The 3–2 scoreline was also misleading. In truth, England's fingers were clasped on the urn from the first morning at Trent Bridge, when Australia were bowled out for 60 in a melee of swinging balls and groping bats.

OVER IN A FLASH

The shortest opening innings in Test matches:

Balls

111	**Australia (60) v England at Nottingham**	**2015**
113	Australia (53) v England at Lord's	1896
116	New Zealand (45) v South Africa at Cape Town	2012-13
120	India (76) v South Africa at Ahmedabad	2007-08
140	South Africa (36) v Australia at Melbourne	1931-32
143	England (45) v Australia at Sydney	1886-87
152	Bangladesh (62) v Sri Lanka at Colombo (PSO)	2007
157	South Africa (58) v England at Lord's	1912
161	Pakistan (104) v New Zealand at Hamilton	2000-01
162	India (83) v New Zealand at Mohali	1999-2000

Stand and deliver: whenever Stuart Broad and Moeen Ali shared a fifty partnership, England won.

None of the matches required a fifth day, unique since Ashes Tests were fixed at their current extent in 1948. Indeed, it was only the second Ashes series in England since 1896 not to feature a draw. The whole thing was over in 7,920 balls, equivalent to less than 15 full days' play, the sixth-shortest five-match series in Test history. The inability of both teams to alter the course of a match once it had been set was so fundamental that, in every game bar the first, the result could safely be predicted by stumps on day two.

All of which, admittedly, obscures the sheer drama. And drama, rather than suspense or mystery, is the operative word. You may have seen dozens of James Bond films, you may know exactly how they are going to end, but there remains a thrill in watching each unfold. So it was here. Australia's capitulation in Nottingham must take its place as one of the most stunning passages of play the sport has seen. One by one the Australian batsmen strode out; one by one they strode back, coaxed to perdition by the spell of Stuart Broad's life (eight for 15), and the catch of Ben Stokes's, diving full length to his right at fifth slip to pluck Adam Voges' thick edge out of thin air. The look on Broad's face – eyes wide as satellite dishes, hands over mouth in shock – was one of the defining emblems of a series that frequently made no sense whatsoever. Oscar-winning stuff? Perhaps not. But box-office dynamite it certainly was.

Nor should the series' essential silliness detract from what was an impressive triumph by England. Bookmakers had them at about 4-1, which felt about right. For all the vim and jollity of the New Zealand visit, this was still a team unaccustomed to winning: they had prevailed in just one of their previous five series and, since ascending to the top of the world rankings in 2011, had lost as many Tests (16) as they had won. Throw in a new coach in Trevor Bayliss, and a new director of cricket in Andrew Strauss, and most observers reckoned the Ashes had come a little too soon for this new-model England. Indeed, the

BEST TEST FIGURES FOR ENGLAND

10-53	J. C. Laker	v Australia at Manchester (*second innings*)	1956
9-28	G. A. Lohmann	v South Africa at Johannesburg	1895-96
9-37	J. C. Laker	v Australia at Manchester (*first innings*)	1956
9-57	D. E. Malcolm	v South Africa at The Oval.	1994
9-103	S. F. Barnes	v South Africa at Johannesburg	1913-14
8-7	G. A. Lohmann	v South Africa at Port Elizabeth	1895-96
8-11	J. Briggs	v South Africa at Cape Town	1888-89
8-15	**S. C. J. Broad**	**v Australia at Nottingham**	**2015**
8-29	S. F. Barnes	v South Africa at The Oval.	1912
8-31	F. S. Trueman	v India at Manchester	1952

ECB's stated objective on giving Strauss the job was to win back the Ashes in 2019 – suggesting that 2015 was, if not a write-off, then at least a free swing.

Perhaps all this emboldened the Australians, still flush with happy memories of the whitewash in 2013-14, more than was wise. Steve Smith had betrayed their mood in an interview in April. "If we continue the same way we've played over the last 12–18 months," he said, "I don't think they'll come close to us, to be honest."

And, by the end of the summer, Australia had lost more than the Ashes. They had lost a strike bowler in Ryan Harris, whose injury-forced retirement just before the First Test unsettled Australia more than was apparent at the time. They had lost a wicketkeeper and senior counsel in Brad Haddin, a stalwart all-rounder in Shane Watson, a selfless opening batsman in Chris Rogers. They had lost a little of the irresistible aura of Mitchell Johnson, who began the tour as Australia's most feared weapon, and finished it with an average of almost 35 and the jeers of partisan crowds ringing in his ears again.

Most significantly of all, they had lost their leader. During his time in charge, Michael Clarke had conquered chronic injury, press intrusion, public ridicule, personal grief and ignominious defeat. But, for a captain who had always sought to lead by example, his alarming lack of runs could be ignored no longer. Having failed to play his way back into form in almost ideal circumstances at Lord's – coming in on a belting pitch against a weary attack at 362 for two – Clarke ended up looking more liability than asset, a walking wicket with only the most cursory awareness of his off stump. "They've got 11, and we've only got ten," he said with brutal frankness after Australia's defeat at Edgbaston.

Surrender of the Ashes at Trent Bridge gave way to the inevitable. Clarke announced that the Oval Test would be his last before retiring. There, England's players granted him a guard of honour, and a capacity crowd offered a fittingly warm reception. Clarke drank in the applause, before folding into the embrace of his tearful wife. He looked proud, exhausted, relieved, distraught – all at the same time. The things sport does to a man.

Just as surprising as Clarke's decline and fall was the renaissance of his opposite number. Alastair Cook entered the summer a tarnished brand: his one-day international career extinguished, his captaincy derided, his reputation on the line. He left it as one of only three Englishmen – along with W. G. Grace and Mike Brearley – to have skippered more than one home

Tall story: Steven Finn leads England off at Edgbaston after taking six wickets.

Ashes-winning team (and the last time England had beaten Australia four times in a row at home was in the 19th century). Not only had he been a better batsman than Clarke, he had been a better captain. It was a remarkable transformation for a player who a year earlier had considered giving up the job, only to be talked round by his wife.

How had Cook done it? Batting is a function of practice and talent; captaincy, on the other hand, is largely a function of personality. There is no such thing as a leadership net session. The very stubbornness that made Cook a wonderful batsman had been hampering him as a leader. There was a certain coldness with the media, a resistance to advice, an innate conservatism that cost England Test victories. And yet it was to Cook's great credit that he not only identified these flaws, but changed his approach. The Cook of old would never have installed Joe Root under the helmet as an unconventional short third slip, as he did at Cardiff; nor would he have cheekily declared at 391 for nine, as he did at Trent Bridge. This was the summer when Cook discovered his sense of fun, and at times it was a joy to watch.

Root, his first lieutenant, had a defining series. His century at Trent Bridge lifted him – briefly – to No. 1 in the world rankings. No other England batsman reached three figures; Root did it twice, becoming the first Englishman to score three Ashes centuries before the age of 25. His skill was in quickening the match to his tempo, making bowlers play to his tune, punching through the off side with impeccable timing, gliding through leg with faultless footwork. In the field he was effervescent and ever-present, and his off-breaks chipped in with four wickets.

Root's were an increasingly safe pair of hands, whatever they were doing. He held eight catches in the series – among fielders he was second only to his captain's nine, including three in the first innings at Trent Bridge. That was where England's close fielding, honed during a four-day pre-Ashes trip to Spain – reached its apogee. The now-familiar cries of "Rooooooot", which had taken on the hue of a populace acclaiming their new king, were heard throughout the summer.

Shamelessly mining their home advantage, Cook and a number of England players used media interviews to remind groundsmen of their responsibility to prepare "traditional English wickets". In practice, this meant slow, seaming surfaces: slow enough to absorb the missiles of Johnson and Mitchell Starc, probably the two fastest bowlers in the series, but with enough lateral movement to reward England's battery of technical seamers.

It worked a treat at Cardiff, where Root's flamboyant, insouciant 134 paved the way for a big total and a big victory, banishing any lingering hangover from 2013-14. Conversely, Lord's – where you suspect the groundsman Mick Hunt would rather water his pitch with human tears than let somebody tell him how to prepare it – was more benign. After Smith's brilliant double-century had ground England into the dirt, Johnson's stiletto finished them off.

Now it was England's turn to moan about the pitch, a grumble that would become a motif. Clarke even devoted a portion of his retirement press conference to complaining about the standard of the surfaces, which he blamed for the string of early finishes: "Fans of the game deserve to see a really good contest for five days."

He was right, but he should probably have started by pointing the finger at his batsmen. At Edgbaston and Trent Bridge, Australia displayed an inadequacy against the moving ball, essentially losing the Ashes in those two first innings. The top three all had decent series – Smith, Rogers and David Warner were among its four highest scorers – but too often the middle order were ripped out. Smith's summer proved symptomatic: on fire in London, where he averaged 138, he was extinguished elsewhere, averaging 15. Voges, one of the most experienced Australians in English conditions, struggled in his second Test series, and was lucky to see it out.

These were not the Australian selectors' finest few months. On purely cricketing grounds, there was a strong case for replacing the fading Haddin with another New South Wales keeper-batsman, Peter Nevill. Haddin was 37. His form was going south. He had kept poorly at Cardiff, where his second-ball drop of Root proved critical. But the ham-fisted management of what was essentially the termination of a man's international career had the effect of splitting and distracting the team, at the very moment they needed to be focused and united.

Haddin had asked to be excused from the Second Test at Lord's to attend to his daughter, Mia, who was in a London hospital. That was fine, and Nevill made a strong debut. The trouble started at Edgbaston, where Nevill was retained, but the handling of Haddin's demise caused resentment among his many allies. Ricky Ponting wrote an angry column in *The Australian*, describing him as the "heart and soul of the cricket team", and claiming he had been penalised for putting his family first, a line the board claimed to support.

Dropping Watson was an easier decision. A long-standing leg-before candidate with a reputation for wasting reviews, Watson scarcely helped his

Head scratching… Australia coach Darren Lehmann looks on as his side fall apart at Trent Bridge.

cause by falling twice in precisely that fashion at Cardiff. A ready-made, in-form replacement was available in all-rounder Mitchell Marsh, who proved surprisingly potent with the ball on pitches that rewarded discipline more than raw speed. Yet, after just two matches, he was misguidedly discarded in favour of his brother Shaun, before being reinstated at The Oval. It no longer looked as if Australia knew what they were doing.

By contrast, England benefited from continuity of selection. They made only three changes over the course of the series – two of them enforced, after Mark Wood exacerbated an ankle injury at Lord's, and James Anderson strained his side at Edgbaston. It allowed them to hone their bowling plans and develop rhythm. There were echoes of 2005 as a five-pronged attack – including two genuine all-rounders in Stokes and Moeen Ali – hunted as a pack. Stokes was hit and miss, starting well with the bat before scoring just 20 runs, including three ducks, in his last five innings, and taking more than half his wickets in a single innings at Nottingham. Ali, conversely, found the cartoon-slugfest tenor of the cricket to his liking, gleefully counter-punching from No. 8 and winkling out valuable wickets, including Warner four times.

Broad, with whom Ali added at least 50 in each of England's three wins, enjoyed another sparkling Ashes. His remarkable Trent Bridge haul was the centrepiece of a series in which he claimed 21 wickets at just under 21, and made a legitimate grab for greatness. At Edgbaston, Steven Finn returned after two years in the Test wilderness, removed Smith in his first over, and claimed six in the second innings – part of an unprecedented sequence, starting with Anderson at Edgbaston and ending with Stokes at Trent Bridge, in which four different England seamers picked up a six-for or better. Wood looked convincing rather than impressive, while Jonny Bairstow – replacing the struggling Gary Ballance at Birmingham, the only unenforced change – looked impressive rather than convincing.

FIVE STATS YOU MAY HAVE MISSED

BENEDICT BERMANGE

- When Steve Smith reached his Test double-century, at Lord's, he became only the second player to make a maiden Test double after falling twice in the 190s. Smith had previously struck 192 and 199; Pakistan's Mohammad Hafeez followed scores of 196 and 197 with 224.

- In Australia's first innings at Trent Bridge, Extras top-scored, with 14, for the first time in Ashes history.

- Joe Root was the first player to reach a century on the opening day of an Ashes Test in the *second* innings of the match. His 124* was the second-highest in the second innings by anyone on the first day of a Test:

151	M. E. Trescothick	England v Bangladesh at Chester-le-Street	2005
124*	**J. E. Root**	**England v Australia at Nottingham**	**2015**
123*	E. D. Weekes	West Indies v New Zealand at Dunedin	1955-56
122*	G. C. Smith	South Africa v West Indies at Durban	2007-08
121	G. C. Smith	South Africa v Zimbabwe at Cape Town	2004-05

- When Ben Stokes delivered the second ball of the 16th over of Australia's second innings at Nottingham, it was the 1,000,000th legal delivery in Tests in Britain. David Warner hit it for four.

- Australia's win at The Oval was just the second instance in Ashes history of teams trading innings victories in successive Tests in the same series. In 1965-66, England won by an innings and 93 at Sydney, only for Australia to claim the next, at Adelaide, by an innings and nine.

Adam Lyth, meanwhile, neither impressed nor convinced anyone as Cook's sixth opening partner since the retirement of Andrew Strauss less than three years earlier. While he made double figures six times – more than Smith – he appeared to lack a cogent innings-building strategy. Not since Graham Gooch in 1981 had an England opener batting at least seven times averaged lower than Lyth's 12.77. Jos Buttler was England's other major failure, looking in white a pale shadow of the assassin he had so often been in blue, and four times falling cheaply to the off-breaks of Nathan Lyon.

By the time the circus reached The Oval, the fate of the urn already decided, ennui had set in. The subplots had been exhausted, the audience sated, and the protagonists were now weary of each other. Even the Johnson taunts felt stale. Australia rolled over a half-interested England by an innings. It was time for a break. Everyone agreed that the next Ashes series, in 2017-18, seemed pleasantly distant.

Such was the anticlimax to the Test series, in fact, that the subsequent one-day matches felt almost lustrous by comparison. In the event, they followed a similarly madcap pattern. Australia imploded in a pulsating Twenty20 match at Cardiff, losing six wickets in the final seven overs, before coasting to a 2–0 lead in the one-day series, largely on the back of a resurgent Pat Cummins. England gaily counter-attacked in Manchester and Leeds to set up a decider, whereupon they crumbled. And so Australia, finally, were able to leave these shores with something more than bad memories and dirty laundry.

Tim Ireland, AP/PA

Sinister pair: left-armers Mitchell Johnson and Mitchell Starc shared 33 wickets, though neither proved a consistent threat.

You might describe it as a series of its time – cricket for the attention-deprived, 140-character age. And yet there was something queerly retro about it all. Three-day Tests? Pitifully low totals? England v Australia playing each other every few months to the exclusion of almost everything else? Never mind 2015: this could have been 1895.

Plus ça change, plus c'est la même chose. And, in a summer defined by flux and craziness, that may well have been the maddest notion of the lot.

AUSTRALIAN TOURING PARTY

*M. J. Clarke (T), A. C. Agar (50/20), G. J. Bailey (50/20), C. J. Boyce (20), J. A. Burns (50/20), N. M. Coulter-Nile (50/20), P. J. Cummins (T/50/20), Fawad Ahmed (T), A. J. Finch (50), B. J. Haddin (T), P. S. P. Handscomb (50), R. J. Harris (T), J. W. Hastings (50), J. R. Hazlewood (T), M. G. Johnson (T), N. M. Lyon (T), M. R. Marsh (T/50/20), S. E. Marsh (T), G. J. Maxwell (50/20), P. M. Nevill (T), J. L. Pattinson (50/20), C. J. L. Rogers (T), P. M. Siddle (T), S. P. D. Smith (T/50/20), M. A. Starc (T/50/20), M. P. Stoinis (50/20), A. C. Voges (T), M. S. Wade (50/20), D. A. Warner (T/50/20), S. R. Watson (T/50/20).

A chronic injury to his right knee forced Harris to retire from all cricket before the First Test; Cummins was called up. During the one-day series, Warner broke his left thumb, Coulter-Nile injured his right hamstring, and Watson strained his right calf. They were replaced by Finch, Hastings and Handscomb. Smith captained in the shorter formats.

Coach: D. S. Lehmann. *Batting coach:* M. J. Di Venuto. *Manager:* G. Dovey. *Bowling coaches:* C. J. McDermott (T); T. J. Cooley (50/20). *Fielding coach:* G. S. Blewett. *Analyst:* D. F. Hills. *Physiotherapists:* A. Kountouris (T); D. Beakley (50/20). *Doctors:* P. Brukner (T); J. Orchard (50/20). *Strength and conditioning coaches:* D. Mednis (T); A. Weller (50/20). *Logistics/Massage therapist:* G. Baldwin. *Security manager:* F. A. Dimasi. *Media managers:* K. Hutchison (T); B. H. Murgatroyd (50/20).

TEST MATCH AVERAGES

ENGLAND – BATTING AND FIELDING

	T	I	NO	R	HS	100	50	Avge	Ct
J. E. Root	5	9	1	460	134	2	2	57.50	8
°A. N. Cook	5	9	0	330	96	0	2	36.66	9
†M. M. Ali	5	8	0	293	77	0	2	36.62	2
J. M. Bairstow	3	4	0	118	74	0	1	29.50	0
I. R. Bell	5	9	1	215	65*	0	3	26.87	7
M. A. Wood	4	7	3	103	32*	0	0	25.75	0
†B. A. Stokes	5	8	0	201	87	0	2	25.12	6
°G. S. Ballance	2	4	0	98	61	0	1	24.50	2
°S. C. J. Broad	5	8	1	134	31	0	0	19.14	1
J. C. Buttler	5	8	0	122	42	0	0	15.25	12
°A. Lyth	5	9	0	115	37	0	0	12.77	6
†J. M. Anderson	3	5	1	11	6*	0	0	2.75	3
S. T. Finn	3	4	4	9	9*	0	0	–	0

BOWLING

	Style	O	M	R	W	BB	5I	Avge
S. C. J. Broad	RFM	143.3	34	439	21	8-15	1	20.90
S. T. Finn	RFM	78.1	15	270	12	6-79	1	22.50
J. M. Anderson	RFM	87	20	275	10	6-47	0	27.50
B. A. Stokes	RFM	105	26	368	11	6-36	1	33.45
J. E. Root	OB	28.3	1	135	4	2-28	0	33.75
M. A. Wood	RFM	118.4	31	391	10	3-69	0	39.10
M. M. Ali	OB	123.4	13	546	12	3-59	0	45.50

Also bowled: A. Lyth (OB) 1–1–0–0.

AUSTRALIA – BATTING AND FIELDING

	T	I	NO	R	HS	100	50	Avge	Ct
°C. J. L. Rogers	5	9	1	480	173	1	3	60.00	1
S. P. D. Smith	5	9	0	508	215	2	1	56.44	1
°D. A. Warner	5	9	0	418	85	0	5	46.44	3
A. C. Voges	5	8	1	201	76	0	2	28.71	7
P. M. Nevill	4	6	0	143	59	0	1	23.83	17
°M. A. Starc	5	8	1	157	58	0	2	22.42	4
°M. G. Johnson	5	8	0	141	77	0	1	17.62	1
M. J. Clarke	5	9	1	132	38	0	0	16.50	4
†J. R. Hazlewood	4	6	3	45	14*	0	0	15.00	1
†M. R. Marsh	3	5	1	48	27*	0	0	12.00	1
N. M. Lyon	5	7	3	47	12*	0	0	11.75	2

Played in one Test: B. J. Haddin 22, 7 (5 ct); †S. E. Marsh 0, 2; P. M. Siddle 1; S. R. Watson 30, 19 (2 ct).

BOWLING

	Style	O	M	R	W	BB	5I	Avge
P. M. Siddle	RFM	37.4	17	67	6	4-35	0	11.16
M. R. Marsh	RFM	44.1	13	149	8	3-30	0	18.62
J. R. Hazlewood	RFM	112	18	412	16	3-68	0	25.75
N. M. Lyon	OB	137.1	25	452	16	4-75	0	28.25
M. A. Starc	LF	142.2	23	549	18	6-111	2	30.50
M. G. Johnson	LF	140.1	29	524	15	3-21	0	34.93

Also bowled: S. P. D. Smith (LBG) 3–0–16–1; D. A. Warner (LBG) 5–0–27–0; S. R. Watson (RFM) 13–0–47–0.

KENT v AUSTRALIANS

At Canterbury, June 25–28. Australians won by 255 runs. Toss: Kent.

The Australians claimed a convincing victory, though not before Hunn's maiden five-for and a stunning 92-ball century from Bell-Drummond had given the crowd, which totalled more than 13,000 over four days, something to shout about. Shaun Marsh and Steve Smith hit carefree hundreds in Australia's 507 for eight, while Rogers and Clarke joined in. The total might have been even higher but for Hunn's five for 99. Johnson then had a useful workout: his four wickets helped restrict Kent's reply to 280, as Key top-scored with 87. "I was happy I could still see a ball bowled at that sort of pace," he said. Despite a lead of 227, Australia batted again, allowing Watson – promoted to No. 3 – and Mitchell Marsh, with a 93-ball hundred, to fill their boots. Clarke's second declaration set Kent 550. After a duck on day two, Bell-Drummond made amends with a magnificent 127, denting leg-spinner Fawad Ahmed's figures, and admitting: "I really don't know how I did that." Harris opened the bowling in both Kent innings, but a chronic knee injury meant this was his final first-class game; his retirement was not announced until the last day of the next match, against Essex.

Close of play: first day, Australians 348-3 (Smith 71, Watson 8); second day, Kent 203-5 (Billings 24, Ball 21); third day, Australians 322-4 (Haddin 11, Johnson 27).

Australians

C. J. L. Rogers lbw b Hunn	84	– c sub (S. D. Weller) b Riley	45
S. E. Marsh c Bell-Drummond b Hunn	114		
S. P. D. Smith retired out	111		
*M. J. Clarke c Billings b Hunn	56	– (2) c Harmison b Riley	47
S. R. Watson c Denly b Hunn	21	– (3) c sub (S. D. Weller) b Riley	81
M. R. Marsh b Hunn	30	– (4) retired out	101
†B. J. Haddin c Ball b Riley	35	– (5) not out	11
M. G. Johnson not out	32	– (6) not out	27
R. J. Harris c Billings b Ball	9		
L-b 10, w 2, n-b 3	15	B 9, l-b 1	10

1/181 (1) 2/242 (2) (8 wkts dec, 124.4 overs) 507   1/91 (1) (4 wkts dec, 62 overs) 322
3/337 (4) 4/398 (3)   2/110 (2) 3/263 (4)
5/419 (5) 6/438 (6) 7/498 (7) 8/507 (9)   4/290 (3)

P. M. Siddle and Fawad Ahmed did not bat.

Thomas 26–2–104–0; Claydon 29–6–111–0; Hunn 27–3–99–5; Ball 16.4–0–87–1; Riley 26–3–96–1. *Second innings*—Claydon 8–2–25–0; Hunn 9–1–50–0; Thomas 15–2–64–0; Riley 19–2–114–3; Ball 5–0–39–0; Denly 6–2–20–0.

Kent

D. J. Bell-Drummond lbw b Johnson	0	– lbw b Harris	127
J. L. Denly c Haddin b Siddle	36	– b Siddle	22
R. W. T. Key c S. E. Marsh b Fawad Ahmed	87	– c Johnson b Fawad Ahmed	14
*S. A. Northeast c Haddin b Johnson	25	– c Haddin b M. R. Marsh	11
B. W. Harmison b Johnson	5	– c Harris b Smith	31
†S. W. Billings c Haddin b Harris	24	– c S. E. Marsh b Harris	3
A. J. Ball c Siddle b Harris	45	– c Siddle b Smith	1
M. E. Claydon c and b M. R. Marsh	10	– c Rogers b Fawad Ahmed	53
A. E. N. Riley b Johnson	9	– c Watson b Johnson	0
M. D. Hunn not out	18	– not out	15
I. A. A. Thomas c Johnson b Fawad Ahmed	13	– c S. E. Marsh b Smith	0
B 1, l-b 2, n-b 5	8	B 8, l-b 8, n-b 1	17

1/0 (1) 2/81 (2) 3/140 (4) (80.2 overs) 280   1/55 (2) 2/84 (3) (58.4 overs) 294
4/152 (3) 5/168 (5) 6/205 (6)   3/100 (4) 4/193 (1)
7/234 (7) 8/237 (8) 9/255 (9) 10/280 (11)   5/203 (6) 6/220 (7) 7/232 (5)
   8/233 (9) 9/284 (8) 10/294 (11)

Johnson 18–4–56–4; Harris 16–2–51–2; Siddle 15–3–46–1; Fawad Ahmed 17.2–2–82–2; M. R. Marsh 11–3–35–1; Smith 3–0–7–0. *Second innings*—Harris 14–4–59–2; Johnson 12–4–29–1; Siddle 12–4–34–1; Fawad Ahmed 9–0–74–2; M. R. Marsh 6–1–28–1; Smith 5.4–0–54–3.

Umpires: B. J. Debenham and N. J. Llong.

ESSEX v AUSTRALIANS

At Chelmsford, July 1–4. Australians won by 169 runs. Toss: Essex.

The Australians shuffled their pack, bringing in pace bowlers Starc and Hazlewood, and off-spinner Lyon. As they had a week earlier, they inflicted a heavy defeat on second division opponents who nevertheless put on a good show – despite losing two batsmen to injury (Browne dislocated his right index finger, while bruised ribs prevented Westley from adding to his stylish first-innings century). An understrength Essex attack were meat and drink to Warner, eventually dismissed in sight of a hundred by Porter. Clarke departed first ball, but Mitchell Marsh bolstered his case for Test selection with sound technique and a bold approach. Essex's reply to a daunting 562 began well: Westley, underlining his potential, added 213 for the second wicket in 49 overs with Bopara, who reminded England of his trademark drives and flicks. Starc's career-best six for 51 confirmed he could be a handful in the Tests, but Lyon, expensive and unthreatening, suggested otherwise. The county bowlers were more incisive second time around – though Clarke fared better. A target of 370 was unrealistic for a depleted batting line-up. Starc and Hazlewood – much sharper in the second innings – bowled the Australians to victory under blue skies.

Close of play: first day, Australians 440-6 (Marsh 136); second day, Essex 299-3 (Bopara 86); third day, Australians 212-8 (Hazlewood 9, Siddle 13).

Australians

C. J. L. Rogers c Foster b Moore	21	– c Foster b Salisbury	32
D. A. Warner c Bopara b Porter	94	– b Porter	4
M. J. Clarke c ten Doeschate b Moore	0	– b Nijjar	77
A. C. Voges run out	49	– lbw b Nijjar	1
S. R. Watson b ten Doeschate	52	– lbw b ten Doeschate	6
M. R. Marsh b Salisbury	169	– b Salisbury	37
P. M. Nevill c sub (S. M. Imtiaz) b Ryder	78	– c Ryder b Bopara	12
M. A. Starc c Browne b Porter	7	– c Nijjar b Moore	13
J. R. Hazlewood c ten Doeschate b Porter	0	– not out	12
P. M. Siddle not out	37	– b Porter	19
N. M. Lyon c sub (A. P. Beard) b ten Doeschate	41	– c ten Doeschate b Porter	0
B 5, l-b 7, n-b 2	14	B 6, n-b 2	8

1/60 (1) 2/60 (3) 3/132 (2)   (111 overs) 562   1/17 (2) 2/58 (1)   (72.4 overs) 221
4/204 (5) 5/252 (4) 6/440 (7)   3/65 (4) 4/76 (5)
7/449 (8) 8/463 (9) 9/489 (6) 10/562 (11)   5/138 (6) 6/169 (3) 7/182 (7)
                                          8/190 (8) 9/221 (10) 10/221 (11)

Porter 22–1–97–3; Ryder 12–1–56–1; Salisbury 19–2–102–1; Moore 18–2–74–2; Westley 11–1–63–0; ten Doeschate 14–0–78–2; Nijjar 14–0–77–0; Browne 1–0–3–0. *Second innings*—Porter 15.4–1–42–3; Moore 8–3–18–1; Salisbury 13–3–29–2; ten Doeschate 6–0–27–1; Nijjar 24–2–80–2; Bopara 6–1–19–1.

Essex

T. Westley b Starc	144	– absent hurt	
J. C. Mickleburgh b Siddle	29	– (1) lbw b Hazlewood	4
*R. S. Bopara c Clarke b Marsh	107	– lbw b Starc	42
J. A. Porter b Starc	0	– (8) lbw b Hazlewood	0
J. D. Ryder c Lyon b Marsh	10	– (2) b Starc	37
R. N. ten Doeschate c Nevill b Starc	36	– (4) lbw b Hazlewood	61
†J. S. Foster c Warner b Starc	23	– (5) c Clarke b Starc	0
M. E. T. Salisbury b Starc	0	– (6) c Nevill b Hazlewood	8
A. S. S. Nijjar not out	11	– (7) c Rogers b Lyon	15
T. C. Moore b Starc	0	– (9) not out	16
N. L. J. Browne absent hurt		– absent hurt	
B 31, l-b 13, w 2, n-b 8	54	B 6, l-b 7, w 1, n-b 3	17

1/78 (2) 2/291 (1) 3/299 (4)   (91.2 overs) 414   1/42 (1) 2/43 (2)   (48.4 overs) 200
4/325 (5) 5/332 (3) 6/399 (6)   3/140 (3) 4/152 (5)
7/399 (8) 8/408 (7) 9/414 (10)   5/165 (6) 6/174 (4) 7/174 (8) 8/200 (7)

Starc 20.2–5–51–6; Hazlewood 21–6–73–0; Marsh 8–0–47–2; Siddle 13–4–37–1; Watson 6–1–17–0; Lyon 22–0–136–0; Voges 1–0–9–0. *Second innings*—Starc 8–2–26–3; Hazlewood 8–3–42–4; Siddle 8–4–15–0; Watson 6–3–15–0; Lyon 12.4–2–64–1; Marsh 6–1–25–0.

Umpires: M. J. D. Bodenham and G. D. Lloyd.

ENGLAND v AUSTRALIA

First Investec Test Match

HUGH CHEVALLIER

At Cardiff, July 8–11. England won by 169 runs. Toss: England.

Root is late on the ball; he jams his bat down and the edge flies to Haddin, who flings himself in front of first slip and holds an airborne one-handed catch. Root is late on the ball; he jams his bat down and the edge flies to Haddin, who flings himself in front of first slip and spills an airborne one-handed chance. This is no Pullmanesque tale of parallel universes, but moments from successive Ashes series.

The shots, at Perth and Cardiff around 18 months apart, were identical. The contrast, however, wasn't simply where the ball fetched up. In Australia, as deliveries whistled through at extreme pace, Haddin stood back; in Wales, where they did not, he was much nearer the stumps. Cardiff is anti-Perth, the pitch snoozier than Alice's dormouse, and yet – thanks to four days of decent weather – it conspired to create a fizzing spectacle of compelling cricket that England won handsomely, for two main reasons: the failure of the Australians to adapt to alien conditions, and the 134 runs Root scored after his second-ball reprieve.

Haddin's fumble also drew attention to the fallibility of age. At 37, he was one of six Australians longer in the tooth than Bell, England's oldest. (Indeed, Jason Gillespie, Yorkshire's Australian coach, had labelled Clarke's squad "Dad's Army" – and with friends like that…) It hadn't helped that Ryan Harris, the leading wicket-taker across the previous two Ashes but now a rickety 35-year-old, was forced into retirement four days before the Test. England, meanwhile, were unchanged for the third match in a row.

After their 5–0 humiliation in 2013-14, they and new coach Trevor Bayliss – another Australian – cried out for a decent start. So did the crowd after being subjected to a handful of sparklers, a puff or two of blue smoke, some corny choreography involving three outsize flags, and four interminable anthems. Despite laughable ECB claims of "tradition" it added up to neither an opening ceremony nor a row of beans. Even the weather seemed embarrassed, further dampening the dampest of squibs with a shower that delayed the palaver – and therefore the cricket – by 15 minutes.

Taking shape: Joe Root, dropped second ball, revives England from a precarious 43 for three.

England won the toss, Australia the first hour: one Ashes debutant gave a leading edge off another when Lyth was squared up by the disciplined Hazlewood; Cook paid the price for premeditated attack when he cut a ball from Lyon that was too close to him; and Bell's sorry run was now 56 in nine innings. Root, though, said arriving at such a juncture could be a boon: "You get opportunities to score because they have aggressive fields." But could England have recovered from 43 for four?

Ballance, in a rut almost as grim as Bell's, scrapped his way out with a doggedness more mongrel than pedigree. Root's batting, meanwhile, had the precision of a miniaturist, and runs came at a lick. The pair made hay as the sun shone, adding 153 in the afternoon. Helped by the lack of bounce and Clarke's unwillingness to temper his attacking instinct, Root reached an ebullient hundred from 118 balls, the fastest in the first innings of an Ashes series. When he eventually fell, he had squirrelled away 1,452 runs at 85 since being left out at Sydney in January 2014. And, with Stokes larruping a playful half-century, England closed on 343 for seven. Next morning, Ali stroked his second-highest Test score to coax England to 430, five adrift of the total they made here in 2009 (when Australia countered with 674 for six).

Johnson, whose bite on this track was more a gentle peck, was out of luck. When he did find enough nip to zero one in on Broad's chin, Voges claimed the catch at short leg, only for reviews to show the ball had touched grass. As the Barmy Army whooped at Johnson's misfortune, or rose in mock admiration as he reached three figures – none for 111 was his worst Test return – he had the presence of mind to doff his cap or give a wry smile. Starc, struggling with an ankle injury that had him hobbling after each delivery, gained occasional swing, and a curate's-egg five for 114.

Australia sat down to lunch unscathed but, at 52, Warner edged Anderson. The ball seemed to have shot past the slips when Cook held a blinding catch. After Smith had crashed three of his first four balls from Ali for four – both teams tried to target the spinner – he again shimmied up the wicket. Ali saw his intent and speared the ball down the leg side. Desperate to avoid being stumped, Smith got in a tangle and popped the ball to short mid-on. It was intelligent captaincy from Cook, who had persisted with Ali – and stationed himself for the miscue.

Rogers was in a rut too, if a happier one than Ballance or Bell, since his problem was not scoring runs, but reaching three figures. His polished innings ended on 95 when he nibbled at one angled across him by the inventive Wood, making Rogers the first to hit seven successive Test fifties without converting any into a hundred. At 180 for three or 207 for four, neither side held an advantage. But late on the second evening Stokes nudged England ahead when Voges chased a widish one that stalled a little. At the close, Australia were five down for 264.

Next day, England quelled all doubt over who was bossing this Test. Much depended on Watson, but – in a form of words that has appeared in many a match report – he played in front of his pads, was given out lbw, and squandered a review trying to overturn the

---

SEVEN CONSECUTIVE SCORES OF 50-PLUS IN TESTS

E. D. Weekes (WI)	141 v E; 128, 194, 162, 101, 90, 56 v I	1947-48–1948-49
A. Flower (Z)	65 v NZ; 183*, 70, 55, 232* v I; 79 v NZ; 73 v B. . . .	2000-01
S. Chanderpaul (WI)	69 v P; 74, 50, 116*, 136*, 70 v E; 104 v SA	2006-07–2007-08
K. C. Sangakkara (SL)	75, 319, 105 v B; 147, 61, 79, 55 v E.	2013-14–2014
C. J. L. Rogers (A)	**55, 55, 57, 69, 95, 56 v I; 95 v E**	**2014-15–2015**

---

decision. Six years earlier, Australia had cornered the market with four centuries here. Now they hoarded a feebler commodity: never in Tests had Nos 3–6 all been dismissed in the thirties. In 75 minutes of immaculate bowling on the third morning, England sliced through Australia's last five wickets for 44, ensuring a handy lead of 122.

Not that everything flowed their way. Cook, persisting with his aggressive approach, fell before lunch and then, in a torrid spell after the resumption, Hazlewood removed Ballance for a duck, undone by one that reared. Bell knew he would get a working over, but the longer he survived, the more his old elegance returned. In one 20-ball sequence, he and Lyth added 41. At tea, with seven sessions left in the game, England led by 271 for the loss of three, Root again hinting that an army of fielders would not stop him gathering runs, so exquisite was his placement.

The scoring-rate over the first two days had been above four, and the third day zipped merrily along too. For a sell-out crowd soaking up warm summer sun and cool Welsh beer, it was perfect entertainment. And in a fit of bonhomie they even applauded Johnson when – having racked up 160 runs for no reward – he seamed one into Bell's off stump. Meanwhile the good ship Root sailed serenely on: for the third time in his last six Tests, he shot past 50 in both innings.

Given a gloomy last-day forecast, Cook must have worried about the timing of a declaration. However, a positive approach took the decision out of his hands. Swinging bats brought runs and wickets at a faster pace than the surface suggested, though from a position of dominance – 358 ahead and only five down – England lost three for nine. Enter Wood, who thumped the lead past 400. When Anderson was last out, the target had swelled to 412 in six sessions – maybe three if the rain arrived as predicted.

Would Australia's batsmen be as meek again? Would England's bowlers and fielders be as lion-hearted? The answer to the second question seemed to be no when Root, in almost his only false move all match, spurned a tough but catchable chance at third slip. It was England's sole drop, but they had reprieved a man in record form. Rogers, though, fell soon afterwards as Broad found swing, variable bounce and a dangerous length. He might have taken half a dozen wickets but, at 97 for one and with Warner and Smith on the attack, Australia were sowing doubt in English minds. Ali's two overs had gone for 22, so when Cook brought him back for the last over of the morning it was essentially for him to regain confidence.

He found that in spades when Warner abandoned his natural aggression, played for lunch – and non-existent spin – and fell lbw. It proved the catalyst for a pell-mell

It's behind you! Alastair Cook parries a swipe from Brad Haddin – before somehow holding on.

procession, some the architects of their own downfall, others undone by inspired bowling or catching. England's captain had not always had Velcro hands, but – to mix proverbs – it now became impossible to have too many Cooks, since all he touched turned to gold. Haddin middled an ordinary ball from Ali, only for Cook at short midwicket to spring to his right, palm the ball upwards and cling on as he fell back to earth. Then Wood became the seventh and, it transpired, last England seamer to land a fatal blow on Watson's front pad. As in the first innings, Watson demanded corroboration; as in the first innings, the review was futile. It felt like a forlorn finale to an unfulfilled career, and in early September – having played no further part in the series – he announced his retirement from Tests.

At 151 for seven just before tea, Australia's only hope was to survive until stumps and look to the heavens, but if that's rarely their way, it's never Johnson's. He crashed, banged and walloped a chirpy half-century, until more golden-touch captaincy hastened the end. Cook brought on Root, himself something of a Midas, if not an off-spinner to strike fear into the soul. He had Starc and Johnson held at slip and, with 20 overs left, confirmed a thumping four-day victory by taking the final catch, at long-off.

PADDED OUT

Test batsmen with the greatest percentage of lbws per innings:

%		M	I	NO	Runs	lbws
29.06	D. Ganga (WI)	48	86	2	2,160	25
28.08	R. S. Mahanama (SL)	52	89	1	2,576	25
26.60	**S. R. Watson (A)**	**59**	**109**	**3**	**3,731**	**29**
26.37	C. D. McMillan (NZ)	55	91	10	3,116	24
26.25	Javed Omar (B)	40	80	2	1,720	21
25.00	Khaled Mashud (B)	44	84	10	1,409	21
24.09	Taufeeq Umar (P)	44	83	5	2,963	20
23.58	**Misbah-ul-Haq (P)**	**61**	**106**	**17**	**4,352**	**25**
23.25	G. A. Gooch (E)	118	215	6	8,900	50
23.15	**H. M. R. K. B. Herath (SL)**	**65**	**95**	**22**	**1,024**	**22**
23.00	G. Gambhir (I)	56	100	5	4,046	23

Minimum 80 innings.

CARDIFF NOTES AND QUOTES

Instead of a boot camp in Bavaria (as before the 2010-11 Ashes) or tracking fake criminals in Staffordshire (2013-14), England undertook a more conventional training camp, at the Desert Springs Golf Resort in Almería, Spain. The emphasis was on fielding drills, but England also played golf, cycled 14km to the beach, and staged a quiz night. The three quizmasters donned fancy dress: Joe Root was a matador, Ben Stokes a Brit abroad, and fielding coach Chris Taylor the Spanish golf legend Seve Ballesteros.

Hostilities began with a curious turn of phrase from Alastair Cook, who said the weather in Cardiff had become cooler over the previous "64 hours". Was this a ploy to confuse Australians still suffering from jet lag?

Few sportsmen do bullish predictions quite like Australian cricketers. A journalist, spotting former captain Ricky Ponting at practice, approached him for his forecast. "Three–nil!" he barked, feeling no need to specify to whom.

Ignoring the convention of picking young bucks, Glamorgan chose 37-year-old left-arm spinner Dean Cosker as one of England's substitute fielders. Cosker said it was "a nice touch", but admitted he would rather have been playing in the county's Championship game at Chesterfield: he was just three wickets away from his 600th in first-class cricket (and was still on 597 by the end of the summer).

When Cook invited the Australians into the England dressing-room for a post-match beer – a tradition revived against New Zealand – he was told that such an offer would be accepted only at the end of the series.

All Notes and Quotes compiled by Tom Collomosse

England had arrived as underdogs. They left Sophia Gardens with their chests puffed out and the belief they had the ability – and the captain – to wrench back the Ashes. And puddles deepened by the snoozy pitch.

Man of the Match: J. E. Root. *Attendance:* 59,358.
Close of play: first day, England 343-7 (Ali 26, Broad 0); second day, Australia 264-5 (Watson 29, Lyon 6); third day, England 289.

England

A. Lyth c Warner b Hazlewood	6	– c Clarke b Lyon	37
*A. N. Cook c Haddin b Lyon	20	– c Lyon b Starc	12
G. S. Ballance lbw b Hazlewood	61	– b Hazlewood	0
I. R. Bell lbw b Starc	1	– b Johnson	60
J. E. Root c Watson b Starc	134	– c Hazlewood	60
B. A. Stokes b Starc	52	– b Starc	42
†J. C. Buttler c Johnson b Hazlewood	27	– c Haddin b Lyon	7
M. M. Ali c Watson b Starc	77	– c Haddin b Johnson	15
S. C. J. Broad c Haddin b Lyon	18	– c Hazlewood b Lyon	4
M. A. Wood not out	7	– not out	32
J. M. Anderson b Starc	1	– b Lyon	1
B 17, l-b 3, w 5, n-b 1	26	B 7, l-b 6, w 6	19

1/7 (1) 2/42 (2) 3/43 (4)   (102.1 overs) 430
4/196 (3) 5/280 (5) 6/293 (6)
7/343 (7) 8/395 (9) 9/419 (8) 10/430 (11)

1/17 (2) 2/22 (3)   (70.1 overs) 289
3/73 (1) 4/170 (4)
5/207 (5) 6/236 (7) 7/240 (6)
8/245 (9) 9/288 (8) 10/289 (11)

Starc 24.1–4–114–5; Hazlewood 23–8–83–3; Johnson 25-3–111–0; Lyon 20–4–69–2; Watson 8–0–24–0; Warner 2–0–9–0. *Second innings*—Johnson 16–2–69–2; Hazlewood 13-2–49–2; Starc 16–4–60–2; Lyon 20.1–4–75–4; Watson 5–0–23–0.

Australia

C. J. L. Rogers c Buttler b Wood	95	– c Bell b Broad	10
D. A. Warner c Cook b Anderson	17	– lbw b Ali	52
S. P. D. Smith c Cook b Ali	33	– c Bell b Broad	33
*M. J. Clarke c and b Ali	38	– c Stokes b Broad	4
A. C. Voges c Anderson b Stokes	31	– c Buttler b Wood	1
S. R. Watson lbw b Broad	30	– c Lyth b Wood	19
N. M. Lyon lbw b Wood	6	– (11) not out	0
†B. J. Haddin c Buttler b Anderson	22	– (7) c Cook b Ali	7
M. G. Johnson c Ballance b Broad	14	– (8) c Lyth b Root	77
M. A. Starc c Root b Anderson	0	– (9) c Lyth b Root	17
J. R. Hazlewood not out	2	– (10) c Root b Ali	14
B 6, l-b 11, w 3	20	B 4, l-b 3, n-b 1	8

1/52 (2) 2/129 (3) 3/180 (1)   (84.5 overs) 308   1/19 (1) 2/97 (2)   (70.3 overs) 242
4/207 (4) 5/258 (5) 6/265 (6)   3/101 (3) 4/106 (4)
7/265 (7) 8/304 (8) 9/306 (9) 10/308 (10)   5/106 (5) 6/122 (7) 7/151 (6)
8/223 (9) 9/242 (8) 10/242 (10)

Anderson 18.5–5–43–3; Broad 17–4–60–2; Wood 20–5–66–2; Ali 15–1–71–2; Stokes 14–5–51–1. *Second innings*—Anderson 12–3–33–0; Broad 14–3–39–3; Ali 16.3–4–59–3; Stokes 8–2–23–0; Wood 14–4–53–2; Root 6–1–28–2.

Umpires: H. D. P. K. Dharmasena and M. Erasmus.   Third umpire: C. B. Gaffaney.
Referee: R. S. Madugalle.

ENGLAND v AUSTRALIA

Second Investec Test Match

Geoff Lemon

At Lord's, July 16–19. Australia won by 405 runs. Toss: Australia. Test debut: P. M. Nevill.

It was inevitable, really. At some stage, England were going to get Smithed. Anyone who has visited a replica historical town knows this generally involves being left among burning coals, then hammered flat. England endured both – and the only red-hot form emerging from the forge belonged to Australia's captain-in-waiting.

No player was more stung by Cardiff than Steve Smith. He had publicly castigated himself for a pair of 33s that, for some, would not have constituted a bad day at the office. But, since his maiden century – at The Oval in 2013 – he had answered to stricter criteria. By the second day here, those two years had produced ten hundreds in 35 innings, a rate not quite up with Bradman, but close enough to stir his name; all ten had come in his team's first innings, none in a losing cause, and his average across the period was 80.

What Buttler saw (a lot of): Steve Smith en route to a double-century.

Following a recent pair of 190s, he now completed his first Test double-century – only Australia's third at Lord's – leading them to 566.

To build such scores requires a partner. Australia's march really began with Rogers, ordained in the Church of the Latter-Day Bloom, a 37-year-old opener in the final series of an unexpected Test career. Clarke had won the toss and, on a pure batting track prepared to quell English fears of Johnson, cheerfully gave Rogers first use. With half his previous 72 first-class centuries made in England, he had been key to Australia's planning. Yet things could have gone differently had the third ball of the match been edged a little lower. Instead, Rogers cleared Root in the cordon. Two balls later he unspooled a cover-drive like a roll of silk.

For the first hour Rogers surfed adrenaline. At one stage he had 23 runs to Warner's six, but his partner soon joined in and, despite a fine spell from Broad, Australia's openers added 78. Their stand ended when Warner gave the final ball of Ali's first over, the 15th

HIGHEST ASHES PARTNERSHIPS AT LORD'S

284 (2nd wkt)	**C. J. L. Rogers and S. P. D. Smith (Australia)**	**2015**
260 (1st)	M. A. Taylor and M. J. Slater (Australia)	1993
231 (2nd)†	W. M. Woodfull and D. G. Bradman (Australia)	1930
222 (4th)†	W. R. Hammond and E. Paynter (England)	1938
221 (4th)	G. H. S. Trott and S. E. Gregory (Australia)	1896
216 (5th)	A. R. Border and G. M. Ritchie (Australia)	1985
196 (1st)	A. J. Strauss and A. N. Cook (England)	2009
192 (3rd)†	D. G. Bradman and A. F. Kippax (Australia)	1930
186 (6th)†	W. R. Hammond and L. E. G. Ames (England)	1938
185 (6th)	M. J. Clarke and B. J. Haddin (Australia)	2009

†   *The same innings.*

LORD'S NOTES AND QUOTES

Jimmy Anderson let slip that the Australians had rejected a beer at Cardiff. But Peter Siddle said Australia had done nothing out of the ordinary. "It's my fifth Ashes series," he said, "and it's the first time anyone has ever gone to have a drink after one Test. It's an interesting story, especially from Jimmy, considering the last time we had a drink, at The Oval [in 2013], he said he didn't know why we did this and that he couldn't stand it."

A Cricket Australia feature on opening partners David Warner and Chris Rogers left many viewers with the impression they did not particularly like each other. Warner admitted they were different characters, but denied any outright hostility: "He reads a lot of books; I wouldn't read a book. He is on his Kindle, but I'm on my iPhone looking at news."

In June, Rogers had been forced to apologise after he was involved in the unsanctioned resale of tickets for the Lord's Test. He and former Middlesex team-mate Tom Scollay had set up a company, Inside Edge Experience, offering hospitality packages at up to £2,910. But Middlesex said the pair did not have permission to sell tickets on a corporate website, or use the club logo, and had failed to go through the proper ECB channels. Middlesex chief executive Vinny Codrington put the issue down to a "misunderstanding" and "too much enthusiasm and naivety" on Rogers's part. But MCC launched an investigation. "There was no intent to deceive," said Rogers. "I thought I was open and honest with everything I did. No one I spoke to suggested we did it any other way. [The business] was something I was hoping to develop after I finished playing. The concussion and now this… it's not how I saw my last tour." Codrington resigned a few days later, after 18 years at Lord's, but denied the saga had influenced his decision.

Steve Smith could not resist a dig at England's tactics at the end of the first day. "I was a little surprised Trevor Bayliss allowed Alastair Cook to have a deep point for as long as he did," he said. "It was a good pitch to bat on, but they got defensive quite quickly." Told of Smith's comment, Bayliss – who had worked with him at New South Wales – replied: "Cheeky little bugger!"

Police said a home-made bomb found next to Brad Haddin's house in Sydney was not thought to be targeted at him or his family. A neighbour found the device, believed to have been made from two butane canisters, on July 17; there had apparently been an attempt to light it.

of the morning, an ugly slap that settled with Anderson at mid-off: a team compulsion to attack England's off-spinner had failed again.

As if Warner were an intoxicant leaving his system after a wild night, Rogers blinked and asked himself what on earth he had been doing. The ground was immaculate, the sun shining, and the sober Smith prepared to guide him through temptation. They added 26 in 12 overs to lunch, and 87 in the session after, the only excitement coming when Bell dropped Smith low down at slip on 50. The hurt that would inflict was not yet clear.

As the day wound on, Rogers assumed a persona familiar to Middlesex fans. Slinking from end to end was the old fox of 46 Lord's fixtures. Time and again he played between keeper and point – late cuts, square-drives and dabs, targeting the downhill run. It was local knowledge at its best.

The partnership swelled after tea, each batsman registering a century, before Australia closed on 337 for one. Local opinion frothed about the pitch, and the groundsman frothed about ignorance of sporting horticulture. First ball next day, Rogers took an Anderson bouncer on the head. He played on to Broad five overs later for a career-defining 173, the

HIGHEST TEST SCORES AT LORD'S

333	G. A. Gooch	England v India	1990
259	G. C. Smith	South Africa v England	2003
254	D. G. Bradman	Australia v England	1930
240	W. R. Hammond	England v Australia	1938
226	I. J. L. Trott	England v Bangladesh	2010
221	R. W. T. Key	England v West Indies	2004
215	**S. P. D. Smith**	**Australia v England**	**2015**
214*	C. G. Greenidge	West Indies v England	1984
211	J. B. Hobbs	England v South Africa	1924
208	D. C. S. Compton	England v South Africa	1947

partnership of 284 Australia's highest at the ground for any wicket. "I've scored a hundred at the MCG and one at the SCG," said Rogers. "So for me to get one at Lord's was the trifecta."

Clarke's bad back was evident as he pulled Wood to square leg for seven, Voges nibbled behind for 25, and Broad added a third when Mitchell Marsh, an all-round replacement for the out-of-favour Shane Watson, played on for 12. But wicketkeeper Peter Nevill, playing in Brad Haddin's absence for family reasons, stuck around to help put on 91 with Smith; Nevill later held seven catches.

Party time arrived when Smith passed 200, and it took the fiesta to distract him, falling for 215 to a reverse sweep at a Root off-break. Nevill went for 45, and Clarke called off the show eight wickets down. Broad's four for 83 was exemplary in the circumstances: his three seam-bowling colleagues managed one for 268 between them, while Anderson would finish the match without a wicket for the first time in his 18 Lord's Tests. Australia had batted 149 overs.

Cook is their man for such times. A radio wit called him "The Crowbar", one of the great levers. His stubbornness was displayed in a fight across two days and 79 overs. If only something similar had happened at the other end. Australia had faced one over after tea before declaring and, if that was meant to unsettle England, it worked. Lyth went

Look away now: Chris Rogers is clonked on the helmet by James Anderson.

Gareth Copley, Getty Images

THE DEVIL'S NUMBER?

Unlucky for some

STEVEN LYNCH

Lovers of cricket's more arcane statistics purred with delight after Ben Stokes provided the 87th instance of a Test batsman falling for 87. It's supposed to be Australia's unlucky number, though only 15 Aussies had succumbed to it, compared with 22 Englishmen (and 15 Indians, nine South Africans, seven Pakistanis and West Indians, six New Zealanders, four Sri Lankans, a Bangladeshi and a Zimbabwean).

Six have been dismissed for 87 twice: Mohammad Azharuddin, Sourav Ganguly, Richard Hadlee, Clem Hill, Alec Stewart and Younis Khan. Hill's first came at the end of the 1901-02 Ashes, in which he'd already scored 99, 98 and 97 in successive innings. But the Stewart family are the biggest sufferers: Alec's father Micky made 87 – his highest Test score – against West Indies at Old Trafford in 1963.

Received wisdom has it that 87 is unlucky because it's 13 short of a hundred. But Keith Miller, the great Australian all-rounder, had another explanation. He told the historian David Frith that, as a ten-year-old in Melbourne, he watched Don Bradman bat in a Sheffield Shield match in December 1929. Miller looked up at the MCG scoreboard, which showed the Don on 87 – whereupon he was bowled by the Victorian quick, "Bull" Alexander. "That score stuck in my mind," said Miller. "Every weekend I'd look through the club scores searching for more 87s. It became a sort of fixation. When I began to play myself, I was still conscious of this 87 thing – I always tried to avoid it when I was batting. Later, Richie Benaud and Alan Davidson and some of those blokes picked it up."

Eventually Miller checked the record books, to confirm his memory. And there it was: D. G. Bradman b H. H. Alexander... 89. "The big old MCG scoreboard used to be a bit slow sometimes," he said, "and it must have been slow again that day!"

second ball, fiddling unnecessarily at Starc. Then, after eight overs, it was time for Johnson. He can impose himself so hard on matches you feel the structure shudder, as if he's running into the wall of a flimsy holiday home. Watch from behind the batsman and you see a shifting block of muscle, broader than seems possible in profile. Take in the litheness of his movement, the prowl of his run, the explosion of his action, and it's no surprise he can get inside 11 heads.

Even with only three wickets for the innings, he did for England, generating pace and bounce from a pitch derided as a batsman's paradise. The immobile Ballance was hypnotised, and his stumps detonated; Root followed a short ball outside off as if entranced by a swinging pendulum. In between, Hazlewood trimmed Bell's stumps with a beauty that straightened: 30 for four.

Not that the next pair gave it away. The word to describe Stokes is "bottle", poorly defined and quickly understood. Through 44 overs he alternately counter-attacked and toughed it out, until near lunch on day three. Then it became Marsh's moment. To bowling that was once popgun he had added speed and swing. Stokes drove without gauging either, dragging on for 87; deep in the second session, Cook, on 96, did the same, still short of a home Ashes hundred.

Ali and Broad carted a few, but when Broad was last out, edging Johnson to slip, 312 was still miles adrift. With almost seven sessions to play, Clarke declined the follow-on, before Rogers and Warner – dropped by Lyth at gully on nought – put on 108 before stumps. But, again, the morning brought drama, when dizziness overtook Rogers, thought

to be a delayed response to that hit on the head. He retired one short of a ninth score of 50-plus in ten innings. Warner holed out for 83, Smith slapped 58, which fractionally decreased his career average – but meant he became the first Australian since Bradman at The Oval in 1934 to score a double-hundred and a half-century in the same Ashes Test – while Marsh scattered the members in the Pavilion. Clarke left England 509 to win, or five sessions to draw.

They survived the three overs to lunch, but hope soon collapsed. It was no surprise to see Lyth nick Starc for the second time in the match, but it was to see Cook's flat-footed whack at a Johnson delivery so wide he almost had to write it a letter. The captain was clearly exhausted. Marsh's first ball snorted Ballance, and Bell edged to short leg. Then came the match's iconic moment: Root clipped Marsh to midwicket, where Johnson produced a raptor swoop and in a miracle of fluid motion smashed the stumps at the striker's end. Stokes had run 23 yards, but had somehow levitated over his crease like Yogi Bear after a picnic basket, both feet suspended mid-air.

When your pace spearhead is producing direct-hit run-outs, you know the force is with you: Flintoff at The Oval in 2009, Johnson at the MCG in 2013, now this – the energy, the charisma, smashing stumps even when he's not bowling, surging, swarming the opposition, carrying team-mates along. Johnson resumed after tea: a nick from Buttler first ball, a panic-catch skewed from Ali's throat with the fifth. England were crushed in 37 overs for 103, the margin of 405 Australia's third-biggest Ashes win in terms of runs. Johnson finished with 299 Test wickets.

The wreckage was notable for many things. For Johnson, a vanquishing of his Lord's demons. For Rogers, conviction at last that he belonged. For Smith, the next level. For Australia, back in the series, a reclaiming of the citadel at which they had lost once in 113 years before 2009. But there was significance too for England, stung as Australia had been at Cardiff, and suddenly questioning their tremulous focus on neutralising Johnson. Outside the team, a clamour arose to abandon defensive pitches, to change English thinking and back English bowling. Inside, it began to have an effect. Somewhere out there in the darkness was a green beast, its hour come round at last, slouching towards Birmingham to be born.

Man of the Match: S. P. D. Smith. *Attendance:* 114,955.

Close of play: first day, Australia 337-1 (Rogers 158, Smith 129); second day, England 85-4 (Cook 21, Stokes 38); third day, Australia 108-0 (Rogers 44, Warner 60).

Australia

C. J. L. Rogers b Broad	173	– retired hurt		49
D. A. Warner c Anderson b Ali	38	– c Cook b Ali		83
S. P. D. Smith lbw b Root	215	– b Ali		58
*M. J. Clarke c Ballance b Wood	7	– not out		32
A. C. Voges c Buttler b Broad	25			
M. R. Marsh b Broad	12	– (5) not out		27
†P. M. Nevill c Ali b Root	45			
M. G. Johnson c Anderson b Broad	15			
M. A. Starc not out	12			
B 8, l-b 14, w 1, n-b 1	24	L-b 5		5

1/78 (2) 2/362 (1) (8 wkts dec, 149 overs) 566 1/165 (2) (2 wkts dec, 49 overs) 254
3/383 (4) 4/426 (5) 2/210 (3)
5/442 (6) 6/533 (3) 7/536 (7) 8/566 (8)

J. R. Hazlewood and N. M. Lyon did not bat.

In the second innings Rogers retired hurt at 114-0.

Anderson 26–4–99–0; Broad 27–5–83–4; Wood 28–7–92–1; Ali 36–4–138–1; Stokes 19–2–77–0; Root 12–0–55–2; Lyth 1–1–0–0. *Second innings*—Anderson 7–0–38–0; Broad 8–2–42–0; Ali 16–0–78–2; Wood 10–3–39–0; Stokes 3–0–20–0; Root 5–0–32–0.

England

A. Lyth c Nevill b Starc	0	– c Nevill b Starc	7
*A. N. Cook b Marsh	96	– c Nevill b Johnson	11
G. S. Ballance b Johnson	23	– c Nevill b Marsh	14
I. R. Bell b Hazlewood	1	– c sub (S. E. Marsh) b Lyon	11
J. E. Root c Nevill b Johnson	1	– b Hazlewood	11
B. A. Stokes b Marsh	87	– run out	0
†J. C. Buttler c Nevill b Lyon	13	– c Nevill b Johnson	11
M. M. Ali lbw b Hazlewood	39	– c sub (S. E. Marsh) b Johnson	0
S. C. J. Broad c sub (S. E. Marsh) b Johnson	21	– c Voges b Lyon	25
M. A. Wood b Hazlewood	4	– not out	2
J. M. Anderson not out	6	– b Hazlewood	0
B 12, l-b 8, (3)	21	B 4, l-b 1	5

1/0 (1) 2/28 (3) 3/29 (4) (90.1 overs) 312
4/30 (5) 5/175 (6) 6/210 (7)
7/266 (2) 8/294 (8) 9/306 (10) 10/312 (9)

1/12 (1) 2/23 (2) (37 overs) 103
3/42 (3) 4/48 (4)
5/52 (6) 6/64 (7) 7/64 (8)
8/101 (9) 9/101 (5) 10/103 (11)

Starc 22–1–86–1; Hazlewood 22–2–68–3; Johnson 20.1–8–53–3; Lyon 16–1–53–1; Marsh 8–3–23–2; Smith 2–0–9–0. *Second innings*—Starc 7–3–16–1; Hazlewood 8–2–20–2; Johnson 10–3–27–3; Marsh 3–2–8–1; Lyon 9–3–27–2.

Umpires: H. D. P. K. Dharmasena and M. Erasmus.   Third umpire: C. B. Gaffaney.
Referee: R. S. Madugalle.

DERBYSHIRE v AUSTRALIANS

At Derby, July 23–25. Drawn. Toss: Australians. First-class debuts: W. S. Davis, H. J. White.
  Warner made his first century of the tour, while Shaun Marsh gave a reminder of his credentials in case Chris Rogers – still troubled by inner-ear problems after his dizziness at Lord's – did not recover. Both openers retired after reaching 101, though none of the later batsmen made a compelling case for inclusion in the Third Test. Clarke, not in fear of losing his place but in need of runs, had made 16 when he became a memorable maiden first-class victim for 19-year-old seamer Will Davis, who finished with three for 63. Both teams rested left-arm spearheads: the Australians left out two Mitchells, Johnson and Starc (as well as the right-armer, Josh Hazlewood), while at England's request Derbyshire omitted the incisive Mark Footitt. Cummins, called up when injury forced Ryan Harris into retirement, claimed a wicket two years after his last first-class match, though Mitchell Marsh grabbed four. In what turned out to be his last first-class game, Haddin relinquished the gloves to Nevill. After two sessions of the second day were lost to rain, Derbyshire slipped to 129 for seven on the last, but were rescued by Palladino's belligerent 82. There was time for Clarke to tiptoe towards fluency.
  Close of play: first day, Australians 413-9 (Cummins 21, Fawad Ahmed 4); second day, Derbyshire 81-2 (Madsen 14, Elstone 13).

Australians

D. A. Warner retired out	101		
S. E. Marsh retired out	101	– (1) retired out	30
*M. J. Clarke c Knight b Davis	16	– (2) not out	44
A. C. Voges lbw b Davis	1	– (3) not out	16
M. R. Marsh c Hosein b White	53		
†P. M. Nevill c Elstone b Davis	1		
S. R. Watson c Hosein b White	61		
B. J. Haddin b Palladino	32		
P. M. Siddle run out	2		
P. J. Cummins not out	21		
Fawad Ahmed not out	4		
B 4, l-b 4, w 1, n-b 11	20	L-b 1, n-b 4	5

1/154 (1) 2/195 (3) (9 wkts dec, 90 overs) 413
3/197 (4) 4/275 (2) 5/280 (6)
6/302 (5) 7/368 (7) 8/385 (8) 9/391 (9)

1/51 (1) (1 wkt dec, 24.1 overs) 95

Palladino 21–4–83–1; White 19–3–85–2; Clare 17–0–64–0; Davis 15–2–63–3; Elstone 6–0–35–0; Wainwright 10–1–54–0; Knight 2–0–21–0. *Second innings*—Palladino 5–1–20–0; White 5–0–31–0; Davis 7–2–18–0; Clare 4–1–14–0; Wainwright 2.1–0–3–0; Slater 1–0–8–0.

Derbyshire

B. T. Slater c Voges b Watson	20	W. S. Davis not out	8
H. D. Rutherford c Nevill b Cummins	14	H. J. White b Fawad Ahmed	3
*W. L. Madsen lbw b M. R. Marsh	18		
S. L. Elstone c Warner b M. R. Marsh	19	B 4, l-b 18, w 6, n-b 5	33
†H. R. Hosein c Watson b Siddle	17		
T. C. Knight c Voges b M. R. Marsh	3	1/49 (2) 2/55 (1) (82.3 overs) 259	
J. L. Clare b Fawad Ahmed	4	3/93 (4) 4/95 (3)	
D. J. Wainwright c Clarke b M. R. Marsh	38	5/104 (6) 6/116 (7)	
A. P. Palladino c sub (N. M. Lyon)		7/129 (5) 8/234 (8)	
b Fawad Ahmed	82	9/248 (9) 10/259 (11)	

Siddle 15–6–35–1; Cummins 17–3–56–1; M. R. Marsh 15–3–41–4; Watson 14–5–30–1; Fawad Ahmed 20.3–4–68–3; Warner 1–0–7–0.

Umpires: C. B. Gaffaney and T. Lungley.

ENGLAND v AUSTRALIA

Third Investec Test Match

STEPHEN BRENKLEY

At Birmingham, July 29–31. England won by eight wickets. Toss: Australia.

Early on the third afternoon, Australia's dramatic downturn was embodied in a fateful lapse. England had made most of the running in a frenetic match, largely thanks to two outstanding bowling performances – first by Anderson, then by the returning Finn – but had been left with a potentially ticklish chase of 121.

With the score on 35, and one wicket already down, Bell – in full attacking mode – guided the ball into the hands of Clarke at second slip. It was a regulation offering. But it went to ground, continuing a wretched tour for Australia's captain. Although a second wicket did fall soon after, that was the crucial moment. It might have instilled doubt and uncertainty in England's batsmen. Bell, promoted to No. 3 for this Test, went on to his second half-century of the game, and was still there at the end when Root hit the winning boundary. It not only restored England's lead, but extended to seven their unprecedented sequence of results, which – beginning with the Grenada Test in April – now read: win, lose, win, lose, win, lose, win, win.

Throughout its eight sessions, this match was played at a fever pitch of excitement. Rarely, if ever, can a Test crowd in the UK have lent such fervent support. They were rewarded with an energetic, enterprising display from England, who put behind them their limp performance at Lord's ten days earlier. This was also the first time since Headingley in 1981 that they had won the Third Test in an Ashes series. That they did so was largely because of bowling conditions, which their attack adeptly exploited.

The anodyne surface at Lord's had been replaced by a pitch that had some grass left on, offered pace and bounce and, in the early stages at least, was accompanied by cloud cover,

Graham Morris

Pointing the way: Ben Stokes clings on, Mitchell Johnson departs, and Australia are 94 for seven.

which also encouraged movement. If, considering all this, Clarke was tempted to bowl, then he resisted, perhaps for two reasons: he backed batsmen who had been in resplendent form in the previous Test, and was keen to avoid comparisons with 2005, when Ricky Ponting asked England to bat, only to see them plunder 407 on the first day.

England recalled Finn for his first Test in two years in place of Mark Wood, who rested a sore ankle, while Bairstow, not selected for 18 months, came in for Gary Ballance, which itself led to a reshuffled batting order. It all meant Stokes was the only member of the team born overseas (in New Zealand). And it was the first time in 140 Tests since April 2004 in Antigua that England had not featured a player born in southern Africa.

It quickly became clear that questions would be asked quite unlike those at Cardiff and Lord's. Whether this was by accident or design, it seemed – for England at least – to make sense. These were traditional English conditions, in which their skilful swing and seam bowlers might prosper, and their batsmen might cope through familiarity and application.

Australia were exposed. The first ball of the match, from Anderson, jagged away to suggest something might be afoot; the second brought a close call, with Warner having to dive to make his ground; and the 14th produced the first wicket as Anderson pinned Warner. Finn's return could hardly have started more sweetly: with the last ball of his first over in Tests since the Ashes opener at Trent Bridge in July 2013, he found late away movement – and the man of the moment, Smith, edged to first slip. And he was soon producing a swinging yorker to knock over Clarke.

After lunch, Anderson was at his most potent, moving the ball both ways at will, and persuading Australia to play when they might have been wiser to leave. Voges half-heartedly withdrew his bat, but too late, and Marsh essayed a needless drive: both were caught behind. Nevill then *did* ignore one – which was a mistake, since Anderson was bringing it back in. Johnson pushed at one going away and was held at gully. If it was defective batting – only Rogers passed 16, before Broad trapped him for 52 from round the wicket – it was also a faultless exhibition of swing bowling and seam control. Anderson finished with six for 47, his best figures in 26 Ashes Tests. When he went down with a side strain later in the match, it seemed England's chances for the rest of the summer might suffer accordingly.

The circumstances suggested a lead of 150 or so would make England difficult to beat. They were well on the way by the end of the first day, despite the early loss of Lyth, flashing outside off stump, and the later departure of Cook, the victim of a freak catch at short leg when his full-blooded pull somehow stuck in Voges' stomach. Then, with rain imminent and the close looming, Bell, who had been at his handsome best, had a rush of blood, miscuing as he tried to hit Lyon into the stratosphere.

EDGBASTON NOTES AND QUOTES

After weeks of steady rain, the playing surface was prepared with the help of cannabis lamps, which Edgbaston groundstaff had been using since 2014. They were donated by West Midlands Police, after being confiscated from local cannabis cultivators. Head groundsman Gary Barwell had seen them employed during his time at Notts County FC, where they helped treat troublesome patches on the pitch.

Warwickshire, having gambled on a result pitch, were relieved when the Test stretched into three days. Had it ended on the second evening, they would have lost up to £400,000 in hospitality takings alone.

Instead of recalling wicketkeeper Brad Haddin, the Australian selectors retained Peter Nevill – a decision criticised by Matthew Hayden, Ricky Ponting and Shane Warne. However, Darren Lehmann claimed Haddin's batting had deteriorated. "That would be the hardest decision I've had to make," he said. "Brad has been a brilliant cricketer for Australia. The cold, hard facts are he's played the last 12 Test matches and made 250 runs at 15, with 16 bowleds out of 21 [innings]. So it comes down to performance." (In fact, it was eight bowleds out of 17 dismissals.) But Chris Rogers's reaction suggested it was an open sore among the players. "That's something for the selection panel," he said. "Maybe at the end of the series I can think about that, but at the moment I don't really want to."

The folly of this was compounded on the second morning: with England only six ahead, Johnson produced two brutal bouncers in quick succession to account for Bairstow – his 300th Test wicket – and Stokes, both blameless for offering catches behind with neither time nor room for evasive action. It seemed England's lead would be curtailed. For reasons he could not fully explain later, Johnson then tempered his use of the short ball, and England gradually revived. Root went on to a pleasant half-century, while a significant partnership formed between Ali and Broad, who enjoyed themselves hugely in the afternoon: Ali drove beautifully, Broad carved effectively. Their stand of 87 might have been the most important of the series, and England led by 145.

When Australia batted again, it was Finn's turn to demonstrate their fallibility against the moving ball. Only Warner – chancing his arm, and seemingly playing a different game from his colleagues – supplied much resistance, equalling Graham Yallop's record for the fastest Ashes fifty when he cover-drove his 35th ball for three. By the time he was sixth out at 111, Finn had run through the middle order, finding a rhythm and accuracy that had been elusive for much of the preceding two years.

He removed Smith, top-edging an ill-advised pull, and Clarke, wonderfully caught by a swooping Lyth at fourth slip – both for the second time in the match. When Voges edged his first ball to second slip, the Edgbaston crowd were at their most boisterous. For a few weeks in 2014, Finn's very career had seemed in doubt. Sent home from the ill-fated tour of Australia because his action had broken down, he had painstakingly rebuilt it from scratch. This was the reward for his labours. When Anderson returned to dismiss Warner, making a mess of a lazy flick-pull, it seemed Australia might plunge to their first two-day defeat since 1890. But Anderson left the arena shortly afterwards, and the lower order found some gumption.

On the third morning, which Australia began, in effect, on 23 for seven, Nevill and Starc made fighting half-centuries as English hearts started to beat a little faster. Nevill had been dropped down the leg side by Buttler off Broad on 35 the previous evening, and now seemed to have been caught on 53 in similar fashion off the same bowler – seeking his 300th Test wicket – only for umpire Gaffaney to rule him not out. Replays showed he had gloved the ball, but England had wasted both reviews.

Philip Brown

Michael Steele, Getty Images

Danse macabre: Ben Stokes and Jonny Bairstow are undone by vicious short balls from Mitchell Johnson.

Poor reviews were becoming a feature. Of 25 referrals in the series by the end of this Test, only one had been upheld, though whether that said more for the proficiency of the umpiring or the margins of error built into the system was a moot point. Finally, on 59, Nevill's third leg-side flick proved fatal, giving Finn a highly popular career-best. For the first time since Botham and Willis at Headingley in 1981, two England bowlers had claimed at least six in an innings in the same Ashes Test. Hazlewood fell to a stunning slip catch by Root, before Ali prised out the obdurate Starc.

Australia's last four wickets had added 154, setting England 121. Only once, in the Oval Test of 1882 that spawned the Ashes, had they been left fewer in the fourth innings and lost. But when Cook went early, bowled by a beauty from Starc that curved away, a

TWO SIX-FORS FOR ENGLAND IN AN ASHES TEST

W. Bates (7-28 and 7-74) at Melbourne	1882-83
E. Peate (6-85) and G. Ulyett (7-36) at Lord's	1884
F. Martin (6-50 and 6-52) at The Oval	1890
J. Briggs (6-49 and 6-87) at Adelaide	1891-92
T. Richardson (7-168 and 6-76) at Manchester	1896
J. T. Hearne (6-41) and R. Peel (6-23) at The Oval	1896
S. F. Barnes (6-42 and 7-121) at Melbourne	1901-02
W. Rhodes (7-56 and 8-68) at Melbourne	1903-04
H. Verity (7-61 and 8-43) at Lord's	1934
A. V. Bedser (7-55 and 7-44) at Nottingham	1953
J. C. Laker (9-37 and 10-53) at Manchester	1956
I. T. Botham (6-95) and R. G. D. Willis (8-43) at Leeds	1981
J. M. Anderson (6-47) and S. T. Finn (6-79) at Birmingham	**2015**
S. C. J. Broad (8-15) and B. A. Stokes (6-36) at Nottingham	**2015**

All matches won by England, except 1896 (Manchester), 1901-02 (both lost) and 1953 (drawn).

rare silence hung over the ground. Bell unfurled five fours from his first nine balls to calm nerves and, after Clarke dropped him, Hazlewood trapped Lyth. There followed a steady and inexorable procession to victory. Bell took his foot off the gas a touch, Root was reassuring, and their unbroken stand of 73 finished amid a cacophony of pantomime jeers aimed at Johnson. England led 2–1, an advantage they had squandered only once in Ashes history, back in 1936-37. If ticket holders for the fourth day had reason to feel short-changed, the mood around English cricket was about getting the job done. Nottingham could not come soon enough.

Man of the Match: S. T. Finn. *Attendance:* 73,668.

Close of play: first day, England 133-3 (Root 30, Bairstow 1); second day, Australia 168-7 (Nevill 37, Starc 7).

Australia

C. J. L. Rogers lbw b Broad	52	– lbw b Broad	6
D. A. Warner lbw b Anderson	2	– c Lyth b Anderson	77
S. P. D. Smith c Cook b Finn	7	– c Buttler b Finn	8
*M. J. Clarke b Finn	10	– c Lyth b Finn	3
A. C. Voges c Buttler b Anderson	16	– c Bell b Finn	0
M. R. Marsh c Buttler b Anderson	0	– b Finn	6
†P. M. Nevill b Anderson	2	– c Buttler b Finn	59
M. G. Johnson c Stokes b Anderson	3	– c Stokes b Finn	14
M. A. Starc c Buttler b Broad	11	– c sub (J. E. Poysden) b Ali	58
J. R. Hazlewood not out	14	– c Root b Stokes	11
N. M. Lyon b Anderson	11	– not out	12
L-b 7, n-b 1	8	B 2, l-b 9	11

1/7 (2) 2/18 (3) 3/34 (4)   (36.4 overs) 136
4/77 (5) 5/82 (6) 6/86 (7)
7/94 (8) 8/110 (5) 9/119 (9) 10/136 (11)

1/17 (1) 2/62 (3)   (79.1 overs) 265
3/76 (4) 4/76 (5)
5/92 (6) 6/111 (2) 7/153 (8)
8/217 (9) 9/245 (10) 10/265 (9)

Anderson 14.4–2–47–6; Broad 12–2–44–2; Finn 10–1–38–2. *Second innings*—Anderson 8.3–5–15–1; Broad 20–4–61–1; Finn 21–3–79–6; Ali 16.1–3–64–1; Stokes 11–3–28–1; Root 2.3–0–7–0.

England

A. Lyth c Voges b Hazlewood	10	– lbw b Hazlewood	12
*A. N. Cook c Voges b Lyon	34	– b Starc	7
I. R. Bell c Warner b Lyon	53	– not out	65
J. E. Root c Voges b Starc	63	– not out	38
J. M. Bairstow c Nevill b Johnson	5		
B. A. Stokes c Nevill b Johnson	0		
†J. C. Buttler lbw b Lyon	9		
M. M. Ali c Warner b Hazlewood	59		
S. C. J. Broad c Marsh b Hazlewood	31		
S. T. Finn not out	0		
J. M. Anderson c Nevill b Starc	3		
B 6, l-b 4, w 4	14	W 2	2

1/19 (1) 2/76 (2) 3/132 (3)   (67.1 overs) 281
4/142 (5) 5/142 (6) 6/182 (4)
7/190 (7) 8/277 (9) 9/278 (8) 10/281 (11)

1/11 (2)   (2 wkts, 32.1 overs) 124
2/51 (1)

Starc 16.1–1–71–2; Hazlewood 15–0–74–3; Johnson 16–2–66–2; Marsh 7–2–24–0; Lyon 13–2–36–3. *Second innings*—Starc 6–1–33–1; Hazlewood 7–0–21–1; Lyon 11–1–52–0; Johnson 7–3–10–0; Marsh 1.1–0–8–0.

Umpires: Aleem Dar and C. B. Gaffaney.   Third umpire: M. Erasmus.
Referee: R. S. Madugalle.

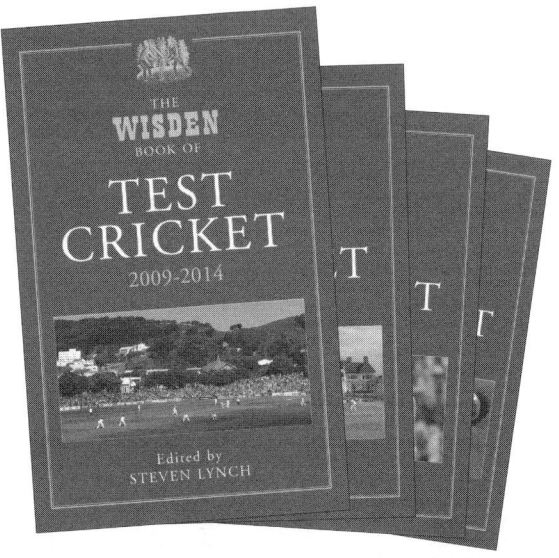

ENGLAND v AUSTRALIA

Fourth Investec Test Match

LAWRENCE BOOTH

At Nottingham, August 6–8. England won by an innings and 78 runs. Toss: England.

Before this Test, a local hotel offered a free stay to anyone called Alastair Cook. A year earlier, with the captain fighting for his credibility, the stunt would have looked like a spoof. But the PR people had gauged English cricket's temperature. Forty minutes into the third morning of another indecently hasty Test, Cook joined W. G. Grace and Mike Brearley as the only England captains to have won at least two home series against Australia. Since there are an estimated 43 Alastair Cooks on the British electoral register, this was unlikely to cause queues at Nottingham's Premier Inn. But everyone could agree it had been a good few days to be called Alastair Cook.

The early finish might have jarred with spectators, but a capacity Saturday morning crowd were in a forgiving mood – and, for a couple of hours on the first day of the new football season, cricket had the headlines. As England's players did their lap of honour, pausing for autographs, selfies and a quick trot for Wood's imaginary horse, the (Australian) hairs on the back of Trevor Bayliss's neck were, he said later, standing on end.

Emotion was in the air. Clarke had to collect himself as he announced he would be retiring after The Oval; moments later Cook wavered too, gently chiding his opposite number for setting him off, and allowing the ups and – mainly – downs of the previous 18 months to wash over him. Kim Hughes was once defined by his tears, but Clarke and Cook are post-Diana Test captains, and no one else batted an eyelid. With the Ashes usually climaxing in south London, Nottingham had rarely had such fun. Well, not for 48 hours, anyway.

The first day had dawned damp and grey, lending a malevolent tinge to the pitch's light coating of green. At a venue that had become a shrine to Jimmy Anderson's swing, English observers wondered what mischief he might have inflicted had he not been injured at Edgbaston. That allowed Wood to return from an ankle niggle, and – after Cook won a crucial toss – Broad to bowl the opening over for the first time in four years. Anderson could not have done better: after six deliveries, Australia were ten for two. Trent Bridge settled down for something special.

What followed was not so much a batting collapse as the repudiation of a philosophy. For so long a term of praise, "the Australian way" now amounted to little more than the two-minute walk from pavilion to pitch and back again. In 18.3 overs – or 111 balls – the shortest completed opening innings in all 2,175 Tests – Australia subsided to 60. It was their lowest Ashes total since Brisbane in 1936-37, and their joint-sixth-lowest (all out) anywhere. Broad, meanwhile, finished with eight for 15, England's best since Devon Malcolm's nine for 57 against South Africa at The Oval in 1994, as well as the best Ashes figures by a seamer, and Test cricket's cheapest eight-for since 1896. His disbelieving expression – hands clasped in front of mouth, eyes agog – when Stokes dived to his right at fifth slip to pouch an edge from Voges which seemed to have gone behind him, earned that highest of contemporary compliments: it went viral.

At his home ground, Broad had stressed to team-mates the importance of nailing a Nottingham length: full enough to give the ball a chance to swing, not so full that batsmen felt emboldened to drive. The cordon soon twigged they were in business. Rogers registered his first duck in 46 Test innings when he poked the game's third delivery to first slip, making Broad the fifth England bowler to reach 300 wickets in Tests; three balls later, Smith – after a fierce drive through point – was squared up and edged to third.

Wood immediately took care of Warner with one that nipped back to kiss the inside edge, which meant both Australian openers had made nought in the same Ashes innings for the first time since Jack Moroney and Arthur Morris at Brisbane in 1950-51. From ten

Stretching belief: Ben Stokes grabs a ball that seemed halfway to the third-man boundary to dismiss Adam Voges.

for three, things actually got worse. Shaun Marsh, a curious replacement for his younger brother Mitchell – since he weakened the bowling without strengthening the batting – prodded Broad to second slip, before Stokes pulled off his instant candidate for catch of the season: 21 for five.

A more raucous ground might have been dancing in the aisles. Instead, the crowd sat in rapt fascination. With the first ball of his fourth over, Broad had the out-of-sorts Clarke flashing a wider one high to Cook at first slip, to leave Australia 29 for six and the bowler brandishing a still pristine ball in acknowledgement of a five-for. At 19 deliveries, it was the quickest from the start of a Test; not since S. F. Barnes at Johannesburg's Old Wanderers in December 1913 had an England bowler pilfered five before lunch on the first day. Broad, needing only 39 minutes, had done it before the mid-morning drinks.

Finn bowled Nevill with a beauty that threatened to shape away before jagging in, and Broad had 7–3–11–7 when, in three balls, Starc and Johnson fended to Root at third slip. Six overs later, Lyon became the ninth to fall in the cordon, which took Broad level with Fred Trueman, on 307. If there was a freakishness to the collapse – every fend produced an edge, every edge a catch – then it also told of two cultures separated by a common sport: the swing and seam of England versus Australia's hard hands and thrusting bats.

BIGGEST LEADS AT THE END OF THE FIRST DAY OF A TEST

Lead

286	South Africa (340-3) v Zimbabwe (54) at Cape Town	2004-05
233	England (286-8) v Australia (53) at Lord's	1896
214	**England (274-4) v Australia (60) at Nottingham**	**2015**
207	South Africa (252-3) v New Zealand (45) at Cape Town	2012-13
165	England (269-3) v Bangladesh (104) at Chester-le-Street	2005
160	West Indies (234-3) v New Zealand (74) at Dunedin	1955-56
156	Sri Lanka (246-1) v Bangladesh (90) at Colombo (SSC)	2001-02
147	South Africa (223-4) India (76) at Ahmedabad	2007-08
138	Sri Lanka (227-3) v Bangladesh (89) at Colombo (SSC)	2007
132	Australia (191-4) v Pakistan (59) at Sharjah	2002-03

TRENT BRIDGE NOTES AND QUOTES

After years of England adopting all methods Antipodean, Australia's batting woes led Ricky Ponting to advocate a very English staple for the Sheffield Shield. "One thing I am going to recommend as soon as I get home is that we change the balls we use," he told ESPNcricinfo. "I think we should be using Dukes now. It will be a good start, because even when the wicket hasn't seamed here the ball's still swung. And it's been swing as much as anything that's got our players out." Australia have used Kookaburra balls since the Second World War.

Former wicketkeeper Ian Healy suggested Australia players were preoccupied by the presence of wives and girlfriends. "All their partners are here, and some of the most respected cricketers I played with hated that distraction," he said. "They weren't allowed on tour until after the series had been won. Cricket is a sport that requires complete concentration." Michael Clarke's response, via Triple M radio, was forthright: "What a load of shit."

High on victory, Joe Root donned a mask of a white-haired man for a dressing-room interview with Ian Ward, and unveiled a passable impersonation of Ward's Sky Sports colleague Bob Willis. "I'm very flattered, Joe, that you likened me to Albert Einstein," Willis responded. "A good impression of Brian Clough, I thought."

Darren Lehmann felt the full force of Twitter when he raised the possibility of acquiring tickets for a Premier League game shortly after his side had surrendered the Ashes: "Would like to go to Stoke v Liverpool with a couple of people anyone help? @stokecity or @LFC can you please retweet." A barrage of criticism later, he tweeted: "Thanks so much for the abuse was asking a question that people might help. Don't bother now! Thanks again people for being so abusive."

"04W24W0W04100000W40000110W020000401000W00000000101000011W00 11200010040040000W1W30000000000000400000000000001004W: Aus innings in one tweet." This went viral on Twitter soon after the event it describes, though @rameshsrivats neglected to take account of two instances of a batsman running a single from a no-ball, meaning the numbers add up to 58, not 60.

Their entire innings, ball by ball, fitted into a tweet, with room to spare for weeping emoticons. By 12.40, the heavy roller was in use.

Australia needed a miracle, but had to settle for Starc's early removal of Lyth and Bell, who was trapped by an inswinging yorker, before Cook played round another full-length delivery just before tea. But, from 96 for three, Root and Bairstow took advantage as the sun emerged, scoring the bulk of the 175 runs that came in a final session of 36 overs. Bairstow was the more obviously busy, urging himself forward and meeting the bowlers head on; Root hung back and cut late, toying with an attack that strained in vain to replicate Broad. Not long after Root had reached the most complete of his eight Test hundreds, and shortly before the close, Bairstow clipped Hazlewood to square leg on 74. Still, after a single day's play, England led by 214, and had a hand on the urn.

Starc struck back on the second morning, only for Ali and Broad to notch up their third half-century stand of the series. That prompted a declaration from Cook 20 minutes before lunch – the earliest by an England captain armed with a lead and batting second. That lead was 331 and, for the second Test in a row, talk turned to a two-day finish (for which Nottinghamshire, unlike Warwickshire, were insured). As if distracted by the prospect, England began making errors. Cook dropped Warner at first slip on ten, and so did Bell, at second, on 42; when Root held Rogers at third, replays revealed a Wood no-ball. Australia's openers were past 100; the ground had gone quiet.

Laurence Griffiths, Getty Images

High and mighty: Alastair Cook leaps to catch Michael Clarke, as Stuart Broad has Australia
spiralling towards perdition.

Stokes, however, was making it swing like never before in his England career. In
successive overs, he removed Rogers, Warner – reprising his careless flick-pull from
Edgbaston – and Marsh, taking his wicket tally for the series to five. And when Smith
lacerated Broad towards a shortish cover point, it was Stokes who made the catch look
easy. Tea was taken at 138 for four. Australia were disintegrating once more.

England's quicks again took turns. Wood had Clarke fiddling to Cook in the slips,
where he juggled the chance, then – falling backwards – finger-tipped the ball towards
Bell. After a superb spell of 10–2–22–3, Stokes had given way to Finn, whose first three
overs had cost 30. But his next nine yielded just 12, and would have brought him a wicket
had he not overstepped when Nevill edged him on two. He soon shouldered arms to
Stokes, who had recovered from cramp and then had Johnson fending to slip. The lights
were on, but gloom was descending, scotching the possibility of an extra half-hour.
Australia were seven down, still 90 behind.

The third and final morning was a formality. Stokes picked up Starc in the fourth over –
he would finish with a career-best six for 36 – and Wood yorked Hazlewood in the seventh,
both for ducks. When Wood bowled Lyon off the edge four overs later, Trent Bridge
erupted. It had been 599 days since England surrendered the Ashes on a mercilessly hot
day in Perth. Now, under the gentler blue skies of Nottingham, a man called Alastair Cook
was claiming them back.

Man of the Match: S. C. J. Broad.   *Attendance:* 51,021.

BEST TEST FIGURES AT TRENT BRIDGE

8-15	**S. C. J. Broad, England v Australia**	**2015**
8-70	M. Muralitharan, Sri Lanka v England	2006
8-107	B. J. T. Bosanquet, England v Australia	1905
7-43	J. M. Anderson, England v New Zealand	2008
7-44	A. V. Bedser, England v Australia (*second innings*)	1953
7-54	W. J. O'Reilly, Australia v England	1934
7-55	A. V. Bedser, England v Australia (*first innings*)	1953
7-64	F. J. Laver, Australia v England	1905

Close of play: first day, England 274-4 (Root 124, Wood 2); second day, Australia 241-7 (Voges 48, Starc 0).

Australia

C. J. L. Rogers c Cook b Broad	0	– c Root b Stokes	52
D. A. Warner c Butler b Wood	0	– c Broad b Stokes	64
S. P. D. Smith c Root b Broad	6	– c Stokes b Broad	5
S. E. Marsh c Bell b Broad	0	– c Root b Stokes	2
*M. J. Clarke c Cook b Broad	10	– c Bell b Wood	13
A. C. Voges c Stokes b Broad	1	– not out	51
†P. M. Nevill b Finn	2	– lbw b Stokes	17
M. G. Johnson c Root b Broad	13	– c Cook b Stokes	5
M. A. Starc c Root b Broad	1	– c Bell b Stokes	0
J. R. Hazlewood not out	4	– b Wood	0
N. M. Lyon c Stokes b Broad	9	– b Wood	4
L-b 11, n-b 3	14	B 20, l-b 16, w 1, n-b 3	40

1/4 (1) 2/10 (3) 3/10 (2)   (18.3 overs)   60   1/113 (1) 2/130 (2)   (72.4 overs) 253
4/15 (4) 5/21 (6) 6/29 (5)   3/136 (4) 4/136 (3)
7/33 (7) 8/46 (9) 9/47 (8) 10/60 (11)   5/174 (5) 6/224 (7) 7/236 (8)
                                       8/242 (9) 9/243 (10) 10/253 (11)

Broad 9.3–5–15–8; Wood 3–0–13–1; Finn 6–0–21–1. *Second innings*—Broad 16–5–36–1; Wood 17.4–3–69–3; Finn 12–4–42–0; Stokes 21–8–36–6; Ali 6–0–34–0.

England

A. Lyth c Nevill b Starc	14	S. C. J. Broad not out	24
*A. N. Cook lbw b Starc	43	S. T. Finn not out	0
I. R. Bell lbw b Starc	1		
J. E. Root c Nevill b Starc	130	B 14, l-b 2, w 2, n-b 4	22
J. M. Bairstow c Rogers b Hazlewood	74		
M. A. Wood b Starc	28	1/32 (1) (9 wkts dec, 85.2 overs) 391	
B. A. Stokes c Nevill b Hazlewood	5	2/34 (3) 3/96 (2)	
†J. C. Buttler b Starc	12	4/269 (5) 5/297 (4) 6/306 (6)	
M. M. Ali c Smith b Johnson	38	7/320 (8) 8/332 (7) 9/390 (9)	

Starc 27–2–111–6; Hazlewood 24–4–97–2; Johnson 21.2–2–102–1; Lyon 10–1–47–0; Warner 3–0–18–0.

Umpires: Aleem Dar and S. Ravi.   Third umpire: M. Erasmus.
Referee: R. S. Madugalle.

NORTHAMPTONSHIRE v AUSTRALIANS

At Northampton, August 14–16. Drawn. Toss: Australians. First-class debuts: R. J. Gleeson, H. G. Munsey.

With the Ashes gone – and rain wiping out the first day – the Australians struggled to rouse themselves against a second-string Northamptonshire side including two first-class debutants (Richard Gleeson, a 27-year-old seamer, and George Munsey, a 22-year-old Scotland international). As it transpired, the main honours went to an Australian playing for the home team. After Coetzer laid the foundations for a useful total, the Adelaide-born Crook hit 24 fours and four sixes in a career-best unbeaten 142 from 96 balls; Northamptonshire's last three wickets added 123 in 17 overs. Crook earned a standing ovation and grabbed attention in his native and adoptive lands. He rounded off the day with a catch at third slip to remove Warner. Next morning, the Australians slid to 87 for five; Steve Smith, captaining in place of Michael Clarke, who was resting, made a six-ball duck. But they avoided the ignominy of being asked to follow on, thanks to Cummins's first fifty in senior cricket, and Lyon's 41. Even so, it was a fixture to forget for the Australians – bar one.

Close of play: first day, no play; second day, Australians 13-1 (S. E. Marsh 7).

Northamptonshire

†D. Murphy c S. E. Marsh b Lyon	20	B. W. Sanderson c Smith b M. R. Marsh	3
B. M. Duckett lbw b M. R. Marsh	50	M. A. Chambers b Cummins	0
K. J. Coetzer b Lyon	86	R. J. Gleeson lbw b Cummins	6
R. I. Keogh b M. R. Marsh	17	B 12, l-b 11, w 1	24
*J. J. Cobb c Voges b M. R. Marsh	0		
S. A. Zaib c Smith b Lyon	21	1/68 (2) 2/109 (1) 3/162 (4) (90.4 overs)	396
S. P. Crook not out	142	4/162 (5) 5/199 (6) 6/212 (3)	
H. G. Munsey c Lyon b Cummins	27	7/273 (8) 8/337 (9) 9/344 (10) 10/396 (11)	

Siddle 17–6–58–0; Cummins 20.4–6–64–3; Watson 14–2–54–0; Lyon 19–3–93–3; M. R. Marsh 14–1–56–4; Fawad Ahmed 6–0–48–0.

Australians

S. E. Marsh c Keogh b Gleeson	24	N. M. Lyon st Murphy b Keogh	41
D. A. Warner c Crook b Chambers	6	Fawad Ahmed not out	4
*S. P. D. Smith c Murphy b Chambers	0		
A. C. Voges c Duckett b Crook	21	L-b 6, w 6	12
M. R. Marsh b Gleeson	68		
S. R. Watson lbw b Sanderson	20	1/13 (2) 2/13 (3) (9 wkts dec, 89 overs)	312
†P. M. Nevill b Crook	25	3/49 (1) 4/54 (4)	
P. M. Siddle c Sanderson b Crook	9	5/87 (6) 6/156 (7)	
P. J. Cummins not out	82	7/174 (5) 8/180 (4) 9/278 (10)	

Chambers 20–5–75–2; Gleeson 20–4–70–2; Sanderson 13–7–21–1; Crook 12–3–38–3; Keogh 14–2–50–1; Zaib 10–0–52–0.

Umpires: J. H. Evans and C. M. Watts.

ENGLAND v AUSTRALIA

Fifth Investec Test Match

MIKE ATHERTON

At The Oval, August 20–23. Australia won by an innings and 46 runs. Toss: England.

"Shame on you, Alastair Cook. Deer do not want to die." It was a puzzling start to the final Test of a puzzling series. Outside The Oval, in the hour before the game began, two demonstrations were taking place: one protesting at the incompetence of the game's administrators; the other at an old image of the England captain, a man of the countryside, posing with a shotgun and his spoils.

Inside The Oval, events proved no less perplexing. This was the last match in a three-series Ashes extravaganza compressed into two years. The score stood at 6–6: England had gained three home wins in 2013 and again in this series, matched by Australia's 5–0 whitewash in between, plus their victory at Lord's a month earlier; there had been only two draws, both rain-affected. If that suggested equality, it was of an unequal kind: of the 14 matches, only the Trent Bridge Test of 2013 had been remotely close. Now, this game went according to type: Australia won by a thumping margin.

Whether this reversal from the previous two Tests occurred because the Ashes had already been decided was a moot point. After all, the hosts didn't seem complacent: keen to heap further humiliation on Australia, and hoping to lead the first England team to win four times in a home Ashes, Cook had rung his players in the build-up to demand renewed effort and focus. But for some – notably Root and Stokes – it looked a game too far. And

Anthony Devlin, PA Photos

Oval and out: Michael Clarke leaves the field after his final Test innings.

that put Cook's remarkable second-innings performance, when he batted for five and a half hours, into context.

For Australia's players, with Clarke about to retire, there was the future to play for – and a captain-elect, Steve Smith, to impress. Selection had been a troubling feature throughout the series, with players coming and going amid a whiff of panic. The return of the 22-year-old Pat Cummins for what would have been his second Test, almost four years after his first, was widely expected. But, in an apparently late change of heart from the selectors – and one made against Clarke's wishes – Siddle was brought back instead.

He fully justified his inclusion. Match figures of 37.4–17–67–6 highlighted how badly he had been missed in the Midlands – both for his control and his ability to present an upright seam and allow the ball to respond from helpful surfaces. Smith won the match award for his hundred, but it could equally have gone to Siddle.

Australia had made one further tweak, reversing that of the previous Test, as one Marsh (Mitchell) replaced another (Shaun); England were unchanged. At the toss, Clarke's rueful smile when the coin landed in Cook's favour told its own story. He had already said he expected the match to be over swiftly because of a thick matting of grass. That, allied to the heavy overhead conditions, meant he would have made the same mistake as Cook, and bowled – a mistake, that is, in hindsight. Few disagreed at the time with the decision, even if it was only the 13th time in 98 Oval Tests that a captain had chosen to bowl.

The tourists' batting had been their Achilles heel all summer, with Clarke horribly out of touch, and a lower-middle order full of poor form and inexperience. They remained reliant on a top three of Rogers, Warner and Smith, who now found conditions easier than in the last two Tests. The openers put on 110 in a wise show of restraint – it was 88 balls until they found the boundary – and built a platform that enabled Smith to flourish for the second time in the capital, following his double-century at Lord's.

Rogers, also heading into retirement, had proved a redoubtable opponent on pitches that were, in the main, bowler-friendly, relying on a homespun technique developed in England as much as in Australia. He played the ball noticeably later and more softly than his colleagues, and so looked the least inconvenienced by movement off the seam. To Rogers

THE OVAL NOTES AND QUOTES

England football manager Roy Hodgson, a friend of Australia team doctor Peter Brukner from their time together at Liverpool, watched pre-Test training. Hodgson and his assistant, Ray Lewington, chatted with England coaches Trevor Bayliss and Paul Farbrace while the players warmed up with a game of football. Hodgson's quip that there was "a place or two available" for the upcoming European Championship qualifier, "because we're playing San Marino", did not go down well everywhere. San Marino coach Pierangelo Manzaroli thought "that comment was a bit too much. We are much smaller than England, but we deserve respect."

The *North Somerset Times*, local newspaper of ECB president Giles Clarke, printed a mock obituary for the death of Test cricket on the eve of the game. The advert, placed by the #changecricket campaign and funded by clothing manufacturer SKINS, mimicked the original 1882 Ashes obituary. It criticised the role of "Giles Clark [sic]… and Cricket Australia Chairman Wally 'The Wally' Edwards" for their role in the Big Three takeover of the ICC. It also called on cricket-lovers to join #changecricket – launched by Sam Collins and Jarrod Kimber, producer-directors of the documentary film *Death of a Gentleman* – at a protest outside the Hobbs Gate before the first morning's play. Around 100 showed up, including Damian Collins, Conservative MP for Folkestone and Hythe, who had suggested Clarke should appear in front of the Culture, Media and Sport select committee to explain his actions.

Shane Warne, commentating on TV, attacked the Australian selectors for preferring Peter Siddle to Pat Cummins. Warne claimed Darren Lehmann and Michael Clarke – no longer a selector – were overruled by chairman of selectors Rod Marsh. "For me they've got the selection wrong again, and Rod Marsh has to be accountable," said Warne. Lehmann responded: "Shane Warne doesn't know what goes on behind the scenes." Siddle took six wickets.

Usually cautious with the media, Michael Clarke was a little bolder after his final Test. Discussing the pitches, he said: "I don't know what influence the ECB had. I've got a feeling the groundsmen haven't been able to do as they wanted to do."

Kevin Pietersen's capacity to offend fellow cricketers had not dimmed as sharply as his prospects of a recall. Tweeting about Adam Lyth's series total (115 runs at 12), Pietersen boasted he would have "averaged more than 10 batting left handed without pads!" He said Lyth was "out of his depth!" and should be replaced by Alex Hales.

---

fell the honour of leading the team out on the final day, and he later received Australia's Man of the Series award, nominated by the England coach, Trevor Bayliss. Over the three Ashes series, he scored more runs (1,310) than anyone, a testament to his adaptability and staying power.

Rogers made 43, before edging Wood to slip. Warner hit 85 – his fifth half-century of the series, though his first in the first innings – then fell to Ali for the fourth time. And Smith was finally dismissed on the second afternoon, eighth out for a composed 143, though he had been caught behind off a Finn no-ball on 92, with the bowler still on 99 Test wickets. It was his 11th Test hundred. What turned out to be Clarke's last Test innings began with a guard of honour and a handshake from Cook, and ended with a faint edge off Stokes (and a futile review). As if it needed confirming, his batting had lost its spark. Voges made 76, underlining the good impression he made during his career-saving half-century at Nottingham. But Broad, unable to scale the heights of Trent Bridge, went wicketless, and England rued the continued absence of the convalescing Jimmy Anderson, who was spotted only during the intervals, sprinting from cone to cone. At least Finn finally reached his 100th Test wicket when Marsh sparred to second slip.

Back in the fold: Peter Siddle, unwanted until the Ashes were lost, removes Ian Bell for ten.

Australia's resurgence had put a dampener on what was supposed to be a coronation for England's Ashes winners. A packed house roused themselves in the mornings with the usual renditions of "Jerusalem", but the atmosphere grew subdued. Occasionally, a cheer of "Stand up if you're 3–1 up!" rang around The Oval, while a sign hung from the window of a flat beyond the Peter May Stand: "Don't panic, we've won them back!" But, with Starc's 58 cancelling out the two wickets Ali claimed in the last over before lunch on day two, it was clear England supporters would have to search hard for any good news to finish the series.

In reply to Australia's 481 – the highest score here by a team being put in, beating South Africa's 476 in 1935 – England batted abjectly, declining for no apparent reason from 46 for one to 92 for eight. Nobody passed Ali's 30; that his alliances with Broad had produced more runs in the series than any other England partnership summed up its curious nature. The wickets were shared around, though there were none for Starc. Certainly, with Siddle and Lyon applying constant pressure, and Mitchell Marsh an impactful fifth bowler, Australia's attack looked more balanced, and allowed Johnson to revisit his role as shock, rather than stock, bowler. Even so, England were dire.

They didn't improve much on the third morning, when – for the first time, having declined four previous opportunities – Clarke enforced the follow-on. It was a move determined by a 332-run lead, the relative freshness of his bowlers, and a forecast suggesting rain. Lyth concluded a poor series – and Bell an inconsistent one – by nicking to Clarke at second slip, while Root and Stokes fell to sloppy, weary shots. Root, England's Man of the Series, would be rested from the limited-overs matches.

Cook battled gamely, and looked set for his third century in three follow-ons, after Galle in 2007-08 and Ahmedabad in 2012-13. But he was deceived by Smith's leg-spin two overs before the third-day close – Clarke's final rabbit-from-the-hat flourish. Buttler, who had been keeping wicket better than at any stage in England colours, finally found some form and rhythm with the bat, until he scooped to mid-off on the fourth morning. Rain held Australia up for nearly three hours, before Broad was bowled and Ali caught behind, both off the persevering Siddle.

For Clarke it was a fitting send-off. A player and captain of his calibre deserved to go out on a winning note, and he received a warm ovation. But an Ashes defeat was fitting, too, since this was his fifth in seven series (though the match tally was 15 wins and 13 defeats). Coming after the great Australian teams either side of the millennium, his was an era in which England had, for the most part, been in the ascendant. And so, amid the familiar pomp and circumstance, the urn was returned to their keeping. While they celebrated after an innings defeat, Australia bade farewell to nearly half a team, having played some of their best cricket of the summer. With or without dead deer, it was a puzzling series.

Man of the Match: S. P. D. Smith.   Attendance: 89,137.

Men of the Series: England – J. E. Root; Australia – C. J. L. Rogers.

Compton–Miller medal: J. E. Root.

Close of play: first day, Australia 287-3 (Smith 78, Voges 47); second day, England 107-8 (Ali 8, Wood 8); third day, England 203-6 (Buttler 33, Wood 0).

Australia

C. J. L. Rogers c Cook b Wood	43	P. M. Siddle c Lyth b Finn		1
D. A. Warner c Lyth b Ali	85	N. M. Lyon not out		5
S. P. D. Smith b Finn	143			
*M. J. Clarke c Buttler b Stokes	15	B 1, l-b 24, w 6, n-b 3		34
A. C. Voges lbw b Stokes	76			
M. R. Marsh c Bell b Finn	3	1/110 (1) 2/161 (2)	(125.1 overs)	481
†P. M. Nevill c Buttler b Ali	18	3/186 (4) 4/332 (5)		
M. G. Johnson b Ali	0	5/343 (6) 6/376 (7) 7/376 (8)		
M. A. Starc lbw b Stokes	58	8/467 (3) 9/475 (9) 10/481 (10)		

Broad 20–4–59–0; Wood 26–9–59–1; Stokes 29–6–133–3; Finn 29.1–7–90–3; Ali 18–1–102–3; Root 3–0–13–0.

England

A. Lyth c Starc b Siddle	19	– c Clarke b Siddle	10
*A. N. Cook b Lyon	22	– c Voges b Smith	85
I. R. Bell b Siddle	10	– c Clarke b Marsh	13
J. E. Root c Nevill b Marsh	6	– c Starc b Johnson	11
J. M. Bairstow c Lyon b Johnson	13	– c Voges b Lyon	26
B. A. Stokes c Nevill b Marsh	15	– c Clarke b Lyon	0
†J. C. Buttler b Lyon	1	– c Starc b Marsh	42
M. M. Ali c Nevill b Johnson	30	– (9) c Nevill b Siddle	35
S. C. J. Broad c Voges b Marsh	0	– (10) b Siddle	11
M. A. Wood c Starc b Johnson	24	– lbw b Siddle	6
S. T. Finn not out	0	– not out	9
B 1, l-b 7, n-b 1	9	B 12, l-b 18, w 7, n-b 1	38

1/30 (2) 2/46 (1) 3/60 (3)   (48.4 overs) 149
4/64 (4) 5/83 (5) 6/84 (7)
7/92 (6) 8/92 (9) 9/149 (10) 10/149 (8)

1/19 (1) 2/62 (3)   (101.4 overs) 286
3/99 (4) 4/140 (5)
5/140 (6) 6/199 (2) 7/221 (8)
8/223 (7) 9/263 (10) 10/286 (9)

Starc 8–3–18–0; Johnson 8.4–4–21–3; Lyon 10–2–40–2; Siddle 13–5–32–2; Marsh 9–2–30–3. *Second innings*—Johnson 16–2–65–1; Starc 16–4–40–0; Lyon 28–7–53–2; Siddle 24.4–12–35–4; Marsh 16–4–56–2; Smith 1–0–7–1.

Umpires: Aleem Dar and H. D. P. K. Dharmasena.   Third umpire: S. Ravi.
Referee: J. J. Crowe.

At Belfast, August 27. AUSTRALIA beat IRELAND by 23 runs (D/L) (see Cricket in Ireland, page 839).

MICHAEL CLARKE RETIRES

Australia's first Gen-Y captain

ADAM COLLINS

"It's complicated." Perhaps it's appropriate to define Michael Clarke, and Australia's relationship with him, through the lens of the Facebook idiom. It was always likely that such a prodigy would join the hundred-club club. Six for nine with the ball a couple of Tests later, and he was Australia's golden boy.

Too golden, maybe. An unflattering 2005 Ashes, some failures back home, and he was booted. Tears weren't shed – harvesting tall poppies is an Australian tradition. He prospered again; his talent demanded it. Clarke's 2006-07 Ashes centuries sat in deference to more feted performances from Shane Warne and Adam Gilchrist, but were no less integral. By 2009, his ascent appeared undeniable: now vice-captain, his career average was hovering around 50.

But, within a year, he nearly missed a Test after flying home from New Zealand to break up with his celebrity fiancée. Australia cringed; his form plummeted. In the 20 innings between that episode and taking the captaincy, Clarke averaged 31. When he stood in for Ricky Ponting in the final Test of the calamitous 2010-11 Ashes at Sydney, sections of his home crowd booed him. And, when Cricket Australia considered Ponting's full-time replacement soon after, alternative candidates were pitched, even though none truly existed. The anyone-but-Clarke squad were as active in the boardroom as they were at the bar.

His response could not have been more impressive. A pattern emerged: Australia would be three for a pittance; Clarke would save the day. He innovated in the field, and gambled with daring declarations and shrewd bowling changes. It was welcome, fun, and usually effective. With the bat, a patch commenced where the purple was at its deepest. After 12 centuries in his first 30 Tests as full-time skipper of a developing team, with three doubles and a triple, the detractors lost their ammunition.

When, two years on, the Ashes were captured 5–0, seemingly from nowhere, suddenly we were all Clarke people. Yet his most meaningful work was to follow. First, an unbeaten 161 at Cape Town in March 2014, in defiance of a rampaging Morne Morkel, when he was floored brutally and repeatedly, but never relinquished his composure. The boundary that brought his century – a drive full of balance, pronounced footwork and precise timing – defied the nature of the ordeal.

Following the death of his best mate Phillip Hughes in November 2014, his grief was expressed with dignity at a time of unprecedented public mourning. Clarke became the spokesman for a shattered nation, as much as for himself. With a creaking back and shredded hamstrings, he demanded to play at Adelaide in tribute. He retired hurt, spent a sleepless night on the physio's table – quite literally – then returned to raise his most improbable and inspirational century.

Should that have been it? If he had his time over, maybe it would – even accounting for the World Cup win that followed. The numbers were as ominous as his weary limbs; the magic looked sapped. By his final tour, the public savaging gathered pace as if it had never stopped, even his own team briefing they wanted him gone. With the Ashes ceded, Clarke was finished, four weeks short of four years in the gig.

Hostility towards the unknown is a regrettable part of human nature. Clarke wasn't just a cricketer, he was a brand: Australia's first Gen-Y captain, the binary opposite of the grizzled familiarity of Border, Waugh and Ponting. No matter how many runs he scored, wins he earned, or innings he salvaged, the last chapter reinforced the suspicion that the confused agitation towards him never abated.

Michael Clarke: object of awe, subject of derision, everything in between.

L IMITED -OVERS I NTERNATIONAL R EPORTS BY N ICK H OULT

ENGLAND v AUSTRALIA

NatWest Twenty20 International

At Cardiff, August 31. England won by five runs. Toss: Australia. Twenty20 international debuts: R. J. W. Topley; M. P. Stoinis.

Finally these sides produced a close contest, with England winning in the last over thanks to composed bowling from Stokes. He ensured they did not waste the work of Morgan, who had smashed 74 from 39 balls on his return from a self-imposed, month-long break from the professional game. Morgan's stand of 135 in 12 overs with the equally fluent Ali, who made his first fifty in Twenty20 internationals, was a thrill to watch. Willey removed Warner in the first over of Australia's chase, then Watson was bowled by Finn in the second, trying in vain to kick the ball away after playing a forward defensive. But Smith, leading Australia for the first time in the format, looked to be delivering victory during a high-class 90 – only for Stokes to shift the match England's way with a brilliant diving catch at long-on to dismiss Maxwell, who had put on 112 with his captain. Reece Topley, on his international debut, bowled Mitchell Marsh. The penultimate over, from Willey, turned the screw: with 20 still needed, Australia managed eight and lost Smith, caught at deep midwicket aiming for his fifth six. Stokes then bowled full and straight. Wade was run out off the first ball after a mix-up with debutant Marcus Stoinis, and Coulter-Nile's heave ended up at short third man. Cummins, whose pace had done for England's openers, was also run out, as Australia lost five for 16 in their last 15 balls.

Man of the Match: M. M. Ali. *Attendance:* 15,029.

England

		B	4/6
1 J. J. Roy *c 8 b 9*	11	16	1
2 A. D. Hales *b 9*	3	7	0
3 M. M. Ali *not out*	72	46	6/3
4 *E. J. G. Morgan *c 2 b 8*	74	39	3/7
5 †J. C. Buttler *c 9 b 10*	11	4	1/1
6 S. W. Billings *run out*	2	7	0
7 B. A. Stokes *not out*	1	1	0
L-b 3, w 5	8		

6 overs: 27-2   (20 overs) 182-5

1/17 2/18 3/153 4/168 5/180

8 A. U. Rashid, 9 D. J. Willey, 10 S. T. Finn and 11 R. J. W. Topley did not bat.

Starc 4–0–32–1 (12); Coulter-Nile 4–0–24–1 (10); Cummins 4–0–25–2 (12); Marsh 2–0–21–0 (5); Maxwell 2–0–12–0 (2); Stoinis 1–0–13–0 (1); Watson 2–0–33–0 (3); Boyce 1–0–19–0 (0).

Australia

		B	4/6
1 D. A. Warner *c 10 b 9*	4	6	0
2 S. R. Watson *b 10*	8	5	2
3 *S. P. D. Smith *c 6 b 9*	90	53	7/4
4 G. J. Maxwell *c 7 b 3*	44	32	6/1
5 M. R. Marsh *b 11*	13	13	1
6 M. P. Stoinis *not out*	10	8	1
7 †M. S. Wade *run out*	2	2	0
8 N. M. Coulter-Nile *c 8 b 7*	0	1	0
9 P. J. Cummins *run out*	0	0	0
10 M. A. Starc *not out*	0	0	0
L-b 5, w 1	6		

6 overs: 45-2   (20 overs) 177-8

1/4 2/12 3/124 4/161 5/165 6/172 7/174 8/175

11 C. J. Boyce did not bat.

Willey 4–0–34–2 (9); Finn 4–0–39–1 (10); Topley 4–0–35–1 (7); Rashid 3–0–32–0 (2); Stokes 4–0–29–1 (9); Ali 1–0–3–1 (3).

Umpires: M. A. Gough and R. T. Robinson.   Third umpire: R. J. Bailey.
Referee: J. J. Crowe.

ENGLAND v AUSTRALIA

First Royal London One-Day International

At Southampton, September 3 (day/night). Australia won by 59 runs. Toss: Australia.

England's run-making exploits against New Zealand had so raised expectations that even 306 felt gettable. But a late-summer pitch did not aid flamboyant strokeplay, and the skill of Australia's quicks underlined how much England missed the rested Joe Root. Australia, fielding only five members of their World Cup final side, were weakened too, but Wade filled the gap left by Brad

Haddin. He had begun shakily, running out Watson from the last ball of Rashid's tenth over (his four for 59 were the best one-day figures on this ground by a spinner). That left Australia – at one stage 133 for one – on 193 for six with 13 overs left. The error spurred Wade on to the innings of the match, an unbeaten 71 off 50 balls, as Australia took 93 from the final ten overs – in which, for the first time in England since the introduction of new fielding regulations, five men were allowed outside the ring. His unbroken stand of 112 with Mitchell Marsh was the highest for the seventh wicket between the teams. Roy, with his first one-day international half-century, and Taylor gave hope to England supporters wrapped up against the biting cold. But Roy cut a gentle off-break from Maxwell to point, and Taylor had a rush of blood against Watson. Morgan's dismissal, gloving an attempted pull, sparked a collapse of three for none in four balls as England faded to a fifth successive one-day defeat in Southampton.

Man of the Match: M. S. Wade.   *Attendance:* 21,500.

Australia

J. A. Burns c and b Rashid	44	M. R. Marsh not out	40
D. A. Warner c Woakes b Rashid	59		
*S. P. D. Smith c Stokes b Rashid	44	L-b 2, w 1	3
G. J. Bailey lbw b Rashid	23		
G. J. Maxwell c Buttler b Wood	15	1/76 (1) 2/133 (2) (6 wkts, 50 overs) 305
S. R. Watson run out	6	3/164 (3) 4/178 (4)	
†M. S. Wade not out	71	5/192 (5) 6/193 (6) 10 overs: 54-0

M. A. Starc, N. M. Coulter-Nile and P. J. Cummins did not bat.

Finn 7–0–41–0; Wood 10–0–72–1; Woakes 9–0–57–0; Rashid 10–0–59–4; Ali 8–0–37–0; Stokes 6–0–38–0.

England

J. J. Roy c Warner b Maxwell	67	M. A. Wood not out	10
A. D. Hales c Watson b Marsh	22	S. T. Finn b Cummins	10
J. W. A. Taylor b Watson	49		
*E. J. G. Morgan c Wade b Watson	38	L-b 1, w 4	5
B. A. Stokes c Burns b Starc	13		
†J. C. Buttler c Marsh b Coulter-Nile	4	1/70 (2) 2/112 (1) (45.3 overs) 246
M. M. Ali c Marsh b Cummins	17	3/152 (3) 4/172 (5) 5/194 (4)	
C. R. Woakes c Wade b Coulter-Nile	0	6/194 (6) 7/194 (8) 8/220 (9)	
A. U. Rashid c Wade b Starc	11	9/232 (7) 10/246 (11) 10 overs: 61-0

Starc 10–0–55–2; Coulter-Nile 8–1–39–2; Cummins 9.3–1–48–2; Marsh 4–1–35–1; Watson 8–0–39–2; Maxwell 6–0–29–1.

Umpires: M. A. Gough and J. S. Wilson.   Third umpire: H. D. P. K. Dharmasena.
Referee: J. J. Crowe.

ENGLAND v AUSTRALIA

Second Royal London One-Day International

At Lord's, September 5. Australia won by 64 runs. Toss: England.

Australia eased into a 2–0 lead, but were jeered after the controversial dismissal of Stokes proved the flashpoint of the summer. He became only the seventh international player to be given out obstructing the field, after his outstretched left hand blocked a shy at the stumps from Starc, the bowler. Australia appealed, believing he was defending his wicket, while Stokes – who was trying to regain his ground – claimed he had acted instinctively, out of self-defence. Law 37 states that a

OUT OBSTRUCTING THE FIELD IN ONE-DAY INTERNATIONALS

Ramiz Raja (99)	Pakistan v England at Karachi	1987-88
M. Amarnath (28)	India v Sri Lanka at Ahmedabad	1989-90
Inzamam-ul-Haq (16)	Pakistan v India at Peshawar	2005-06
Mohammad Hafeez (0)	Pakistan v South Africa at Durban	2012-13
Anwar Ali (7)	Pakistan v South Africa at Port Elizabeth	2013-14
B. A. Stokes (10)	**England v Australia at Lord's**	**2015**

L. Hutton, playing for England against South Africa at The Oval in 1951, is the only batsman to be out obstructing the field in Test cricket.

batsman is out if he "wilfully strikes the ball with a hand not holding the bat, unless this is in order to avoid injury". The on-field officials, Kumar Dharmasena and Tim Robinson, told Stokes they thought he was not out, yet still referred the incident to the third umpire, Joel Wilson. Focusing on the slow-motion pictures, which made Stokes's action look more deliberate than the real-time replay, Wilson gave him out. The decision incensed Morgan, batting at the other end, who later claimed England would have withdrawn the appeal. That, in turn, infuriated Smith, who insisted: "If you wilfully put your hand out in front of the ball, then you're given out, and that's the way it went." The incident soured a match that had started an hour late, but in dramatic fashion, when Finn's second ball broke Warner's left thumb, ending his tour. However, Australia recovered as Smith continued his love of London: all his four innings in the capital on this tour had produced scores above 50. Marsh then ensured another target of over 300 with a thumping 64 off 31 balls. England were not too far behind, until the dismissal of Stokes made it 141 for four in the 26th over, which soon became 187 for eight. All that was left was for Morgan, in partnership with Plunkett, to take out his frustration on the bowlers. But the row could not disguise Australia's dominance.

Man of the Match: M. R. Marsh.   *Attendance:* 27,311.

Australia

J. A. Burns b Finn	22	†M. S. Wade c and b Stokes	1
D. A. Warner retired hurt	1	N. M. Coulter-Nile not out	0
*S. P. D. Smith c Taylor b Rashid	70	L-b 3, w 5, n-b 1	9
G. J. Bailey b Ali	54		
G. J. Maxwell lbw b Finn	49	1/42 (1) 2/141 (4) (7 wkts, 49 overs) 309	
S. R. Watson c Plunkett b Stokes	39	3/171 (3) 4/218 (5)	
M. R. Marsh c Buttler b Stokes	64	5/281 (6) 6/295 (8) 7/309 (7) 10 overs: 46-1	

M. A. Starc and P. J. Cummins did not bat.

Warner retired hurt at 2-0.

Finn 9–0–55–2; Woakes 8–1–37–0; Plunkett 8–0–42–0; Stokes 9–0–60–3; Rashid 7–0–44–1; Ali 8–1–68–1.

England

J. J. Roy c Wade b Cummins	31	L. E. Plunkett b Starc	24
A. D. Hales c Smith b Coulter-Nile	18	S. T. Finn not out	1
J. W. A. Taylor c Wade b Marsh	43		
*E. J. G. Morgan c Maxwell b Cummins . . .	85	L-b 9, w 6, n-b 2	17
B. A. Stokes obstructing the field	10		
†J. C. Buttler lbw b Maxwell	0	1/37 (2) 2/68 (1) (42.3 overs) 245	
M. M. Ali c Marsh b Maxwell	8	3/119 (3) 4/141 (5) 5/142 (6)	
C. R. Woakes c Wade b Cummins	6	6/171 (7) 7/183 (8) 8/187 (9)	
A. U. Rashid c Coulter-Nile b Cummins . . .	2	9/242 (10) 10/245 (4) 10 overs: 57-1	

Starc 7–0–35–1; Coulter-Nile 8–1–50–1; Marsh 9–0–51–1; Cummins 8.3–0–56–4; Maxwell 10–0–44–2.

Umpires: H. D. P. K. Dharmasena and R. T. Robinson.   Third umpire: J. S. Wilson.
Referee: J. J. Crowe.

ENGLAND v AUSTRALIA

Third Royal London One-Day International

At Manchester, September 8 (day/night). England won by 93 runs. Toss: England. One-day international debut: A. C. Agar.

England won an important toss, allowing their spinners to operate second on a dry pitch, and capitalise on Taylor's maiden international century. The upshot was their first victory against Australia in eight one-dayers, and Australia's first defeat by anyone in ten. For Taylor, promoted to vice-captain after an exhausted Jos Buttler was rested for the remainder of the series, it put a gloss on a frustrating year. Having been denied a hundred against the Australians during the World Cup by an umpiring error, he had begun the summer captaining England in a one-off game in Ireland, only to lose his place against New Zealand. Rarely expansive but always busy, he reached three figures from 112 balls. The pitch precluded grand gestures: Taylor hit only five fours, happily scurried 47 singles and 11 twos, and dealt well with Cummins, who clocked speeds of 96mph. He unsettled Morgan, who still managed 62 off 56 deliveries, and Hales, again eclipsed by his opening partner. Roy's fluency brought 63 off 45, including four fours in five balls from Starc, who leaked a career-worst 79. Australia pegged England back, but a target of 301 was always tough on a turning pitch: Ali and Rashid claimed five for 73 from 20 overs. Smith was brilliantly – and unexpectedly – caught by a diving Finn at short midwicket off Rashid, who then had the dangerous Finch caught at long-on. Ali changed his pace to great effect, removing Maxwell, aiming a third successive reverse sweep, en route to his best one-day figures. It was left to Wade to avert the threat of Australia's heaviest defeat by England.

Man of the Match: J. W. A. Taylor. *Attendance:* 18,002.

England

J. J. Roy c Maxwell b Agar	63	C. R. Woakes not out		14
A. D. Hales c Marsh b Cummins	9	A. U. Rashid not out		1
J. W. A. Taylor c Agar b Starc	101	B 1, l-b 5, w 11		17
*E. J. G. Morgan c Starc b Maxwell	62			—
B. A. Stokes c Finch b Maxwell	14	1/52 (2) 2/86 (1)	(8 wkts, 50 overs)	300
†J. M. Bairstow run out	17	3/205 (4) 4/231 (5)		
M. M. Ali c Pattinson b Cummins	1	5/271 (6) 6/273 (7)		
L. E. Plunkett run out	1	7/279 (8) 8/291 (3)	10 overs: 57-1	

S. T. Finn did not bat.

Starc 10–0–79–1; Pattinson 6–1–36–0; Agar 9–0–45–1; Cummins 10–1–50–2; Maxwell 10–0–56–2; Marsh 5–0–28–0.

Australia

J. A. Burns c Morgan b Finn	9	P. J. Cummins c Roy b Plunkett		5
A. J. Finch c Woakes b Rashid	53	J. L. Pattinson not out		2
*S. P. D. Smith c Finn b Rashid	25			
G. J. Bailey c Stokes b Ali	25	L-b 3, w 7		10
G. J. Maxwell c Bairstow b Ali	17			
M. R. Marsh c Woakes b Plunkett	13	1/33 (1) 2/75 (3)	(44 overs)	207
†M. S. Wade b Finn	42	3/106 (2) 4/128 (5) 5/141 (4)		
A. C. Agar c Roy b Plunkett	5	6/154 (6) 7/165 (8) 8/167 (9)		
M. A. Starc c Bairstow b Ali	1	9/172 (10) 10/207 (7)	10 overs: 51-1	

Finn 8–1–43–2; Woakes 4–0–22–0; Plunkett 10–0–60–3; Rashid 10–1–41–2; Ali 10–1–32–3; Stokes 2–0–6–0.

Umpires: R. J. Bailey and J. S. Wilson. Third umpire: H. D. P. K. Dharmasena.
Referee: J. J. Crowe.

ENGLAND v AUSTRALIA

Fourth Royal London One-Day International

At Leeds, September 11. England won by three wickets. Toss: Australia. One-day international debut: M. P. Stoinis.

Morgan overtook Graham Gooch to become England's leading one-day run-scorer against Australia, delivering another captain's performance to level the series. His run-a-ball 92 inspired only their fourth successful chase of 300 or more – but their second of the summer. Despite lofting Hastings on to the roof at the Football Stand End, Morgan offered more than showy strokeplay. He had consolidated after the dismissal of Taylor left England 89 for three, sharing partnerships of 91 with Stokes and 58 with Bairstow, and looked set for a century until Maxwell clung on to a brilliant one-handed take at backward point. It would be the catch of the game for less than six overs. Plunkett, promoted to No. 8, had slotted 17 off nine balls when he tried to hit Cummins into the West Stand, only for Maxwell to perform a piece of magic at deep midwicket. Holding on high to his left, but falling over the rope, he tossed the ball up, then caught it with an outstretched left hand as he regained his balance and jumped back into play – a perfectly legal manoeuvre, even if Maxwell later criticised the law that allowed it. Home fans chorused "Yorkshire, Yorkshire" in honour of one of their overseas players, but the coda belonged to England, as Willey helped Ali – badly dropped on 11 by Wade off Cummins – knock off the 18 required. Earlier, Willey had swung his way to three quick wickets as Australia struggled after winning the toss. Bailey rebuilt in a stand of 137 with Maxwell, who dazzled in a 64-ball 85. Then, following the loss of three wickets for five runs, Wade smashed 50 from 26 balls, in the company of Hastings, to lift Australia to a total that, not so long ago, would have proved well beyond England.

Man of the Match: E. J. G. Morgan.   *Attendance:* 15,931.

Australia

J. A. Burns b Willey		2
A. J. Finch c Bairstow b Willey		15
*S. P. D. Smith lbw b Willey		5
G. J. Bailey c and b Plunkett		75
G. J. Maxwell b Ali		85
M. R. Marsh b Willey b Plunkett		17
†M. S. Wade not out		50

M. P. Stoinis c Rashid b Ali		4
J. W. Hastings not out		34
L-b 8, w 3, n-b 1		12
1/14 (1) 2/25 (3) (7 wkts, 50 overs)		299
3/30 (2) 4/167 (5)		
5/210 (6) 6/210 (4) 7/215 (8) 10 overs: 39-3		

P. J. Cummins and J. L. Pattinson did not bat.

Willey 8–0–51–3; Wood 9–0–65–0; Plunkett 8–0–47–2; Stokes 5–0–25–0; Rashid 10–0–63–0; Ali 10–0–40–2.

England

J. J. Roy c Finch b Cummins		36
A. D. Hales lbw b Cummins		0
J. W. A. Taylor c Wade b Marsh		41
*E. J. G. Morgan c Maxwell b Cummins		92
B. A. Stokes b Marsh		41
†J. M. Bairstow c Wade b Maxwell		31
M. M. Ali not out		21

L. E. Plunkett c Maxwell b Cummins		17
D. J. Willey not out		12
L-b 3, w 8, n-b 2		13
1/1 (2) 2/73 (1) (7 wkts, 48.2 overs)		304
3/89 (3) 4/180 (5)		
5/238 (4) 6/261 (6) 7/282 (8) 10 overs: 73-1		

A. U. Rashid and M. A. Wood did not bat.

Pattinson 9–0–73–0; Cummins 10–0–49–4; Hastings 6.2–0–56–0; Marsh 9–0–52–2; Maxwell 10–0–54–1; Stoinis 4–0–17–0.

Umpires: H. D. P. K. Dharmasena and M. A. Gough.   Third umpire: J. S. Wilson.
Referee: J. J. Crowe.

ENGLAND v AUSTRALIA

Fifth Royal London One-Day International

At Manchester, September 13. Australia won by eight wickets. Toss: England. One-day international debut: R. J. W. Topley.

The series decider descended into anticlimax, as Australia cruised to victory with more than half their overs unused. England crashed to 22 for three, then lost Morgan, whose brilliant summer ended with a nasty blow on the side of the helmet from Starc, causing concussion; Smith said it brought back memories of the death of Phillip Hughes. Starc, the only member of this Australia side to have played in the match which led to Hughes's death, immediately called for help after Morgan turned his head away from a bouncer. He eventually left the field flanked by medical staff, and did not return, leaving Taylor to captain the side. The match had started with Roy being given out lbw in the first over, a decision that would have been overturned had he or Hales, his partner, asked for a review: technology showed Starc's full toss was comfortably missing leg. Hastings, who owed his mid-series call-up to injury and fatigue in the Australian ranks, had spent the summer with Durham, and his familiarity with English conditions proved crucial as he bowled tightly, and with enough movement, to take three for 21; of his 60 deliveries, 49 were dot balls. Marsh claimed three lbws – and a caught behind – with a wicket-to-wicket line, and England's total of 138 was their lowest at home after choosing to bat, undercutting 176 against Australia at The Oval in 2001. England opened with Willey and ODI debutant Topley, their first all-left-arm new-ball attack in any format since 1933 – E. W. Clark and James Langridge in the second innings against West Indies at Manchester. Willey quickly had Burns chasing a wide one, and Smith was caught behind off Wood to leave Australia 31 for two. But Finch and Bailey ensured no further slip-ups, as a pulsating summer came to a tame conclusion.

Man of the Match: M. R. Marsh.   *Attendance:* 21,678.

Man of the Series: M. R. Marsh.

England

J. J. Roy lbw b Starc	4	A. U. Rashid not out		35
A. D. Hales c Maxwell b Hastings	4	M. A. Wood c Agar b Hastings		13
J. W. A. Taylor c Wade b Hastings	12	R. J. W. Topley lbw b Agar		6
*E. J. G. Morgan retired hurt	1	L-b 1, w 5		6
B. A. Stokes lbw b Marsh	42			
†J. M. Bairstow lbw b Marsh	10	1/4 (1) 2/13 (2) 3/22 (3)	(33 overs)	138
M. M. Ali c Wade b Marsh	5	4/56 (6) 5/72 (7) 6/72 (8)		
D. J. Willey lbw b Marsh	0	7/85 (5) 8/106 (10) 9/138 (11)	10 overs: 40-3	

Morgan retired hurt at 22-3.

Starc 9–1–44–1; Hastings 10–2–21–3; Cummins 6–0–33–0; Marsh 6–0–27–4; Agar 2–0–12–1.

Australia

J. A. Burns c Bairstow b Willey	0
A. J. Finch not out	70
*S. P. D. Smith c Bairstow b Wood	12
G. J. Bailey not out	41
L-b 10, w 6, n-b 1	17

1/2 (1) 2/31 (3)   (2 wkts, 24.2 overs) 140

10 overs: 36-2

G. J. Maxwell, M. R. Marsh, †M. S. Wade, A. C. Agar, J. W. Hastings, M. A. Starc and P. J. Cummins did not bat.

Willey 6–3–13–1; Topley 5.2–1–33–0; Wood 5–1–25–1; Rashid 4–0–34–0; Ali 4–0–25–0.

Umpires: R. J. Bailey and J. S. Wilson.   Third umpire: H. D. P. K. Dharmasena.

Referee: J. J. Crowe.

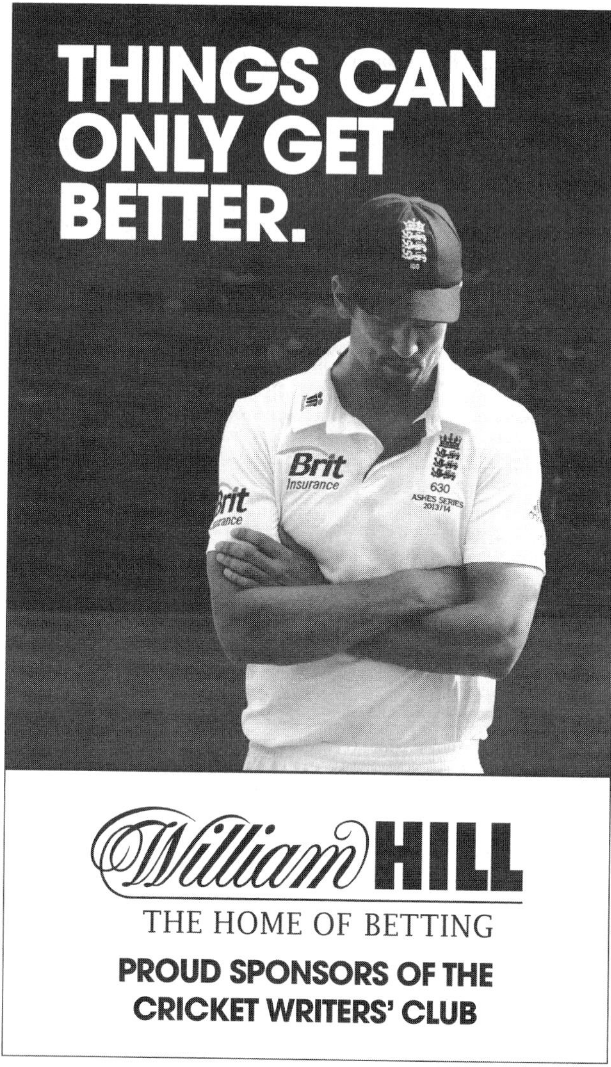
THINGS CAN
ONLY GET
BETTER.
Brit
Insurance
630
ASHES SERIES
2013/14
William HILL
THE HOME OF BETTING
PROUD SPONSORS OF THE
CRICKET WRITERS' CLUB

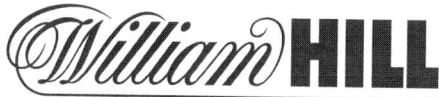

PAKISTAN v ENGLAND IN THE UAE IN 2015-16

REVIEW BY JOHN ETHERIDGE

Test matches (3): Pakistan 2, England 0
One-day internationals (4): Pakistan 1, England 3
Twenty20 internationals (3): Pakistan 0, England 3

Defeat in the Tests was followed by limited-overs dominance, making England's second visit to the United Arab Emirates to play Pakistan truly a tour of two halves. Familiar issues with spin – bowling it and batting against it – characterised their 2–0 Test loss, before a new-found confidence in the shorter formats illuminated six wins out of seven, the last of them, a Twenty20 game in Sharjah, courtesy of their first super over.

The Test scoreline probably flattered Pakistan. England were competitive – certainly more so than during their 3–0 defeat in the UAE in early 2012 – and each of the three matches went deep into a fifth day. The often attritional nature of the cricket contrasted starkly with England's high-octane Ashes victory three months previously. Indeed, Alastair Cook's monumental 263 in the First Test in Abu Dhabi lasted 836 minutes, longer than the entire Trent Bridge Test against Australia.

England would have won the Abu Dhabi game had the light allowed another few overs; they were 39 balls from saving the Second Test in Dubai after an astonishing rearguard; and they gained a first-innings lead of 72 in Sharjah. The truth, however, was that once leg-spinner Yasir Shah – the most dangerous bowler on either side – was fit (he had missed the First Test after injuring his back the day before the game) Pakistan were much the stronger. By the end, they were still to lose a Test series in the UAE since it became their home in 2010-11. England, meanwhile, had won only one away Test in 15 since winning in Kolkata three winters earlier.

Yasir bowled with a pace and potency that England's spinners could not equal. The failure of Adil Rashid in particular, and to a lesser extent Moeen Ali and Samit Patel, to trouble the Pakistan batsmen caused much hand-wringing about the lack of slow bowlers in English cricket. Within weeks the ECB had decided to allow the away team in County Championship matches the choice of bowling first, without the need for a toss, mainly in the hope that groundsmen wouldn't simply produce greentops to favour the home seamers.

Rashid started the series with 34–0–163–0, the worst innings analysis by any Test debutant. He did take five wickets in the second innings, but his series haul was eight at nearly 70, while conceding 4.06 an over. He was struck for 12 sixes, of which Misbah-ul-Haq hit eight; Ali also went for more than four an over. The Pakistan batsmen's plan, with Misbah its most ruthless exponent, was clear: block the seamers, attack the spinners. In fact, they had only to wait for the bad ball, which usually arrived at least once an over. And, with Rashid operating at below 50mph, the batsmen had time to punish it properly.

Casting a long shadow: Yasir Shah was unfit for the drawn First Test but, once he recovered, Pakistan won twice.

Not even a visit from Shane Warne helped much. He spent 90 minutes offering Rashid advice on the eve of the Third Test, encouraging him to straighten his run-up and drive through his action, and discussed field-settings with Cook, an indication that their relationship – strained by Warne's criticism on TV – was now more cordial. He also had a session with Yasir and, though he praised Rashid, it was clear Warne believed Yasir the superior bowler. A total of 15 wickets in two Tests – taking him to 76 in his first 12 – made it easy to see why. When Yasir failed a drugs test in December, it felt like a blow to the world game.

It was left to James Anderson to offer an end-of-series warning to Rashid and the other spinners: "They will take a lot from this tour, but you have to learn fast in international cricket. If you don't, then you don't stick around."

The task of containment fell instead to England's seamers. Anderson took 13 wickets at 15, and conceded a miserly 1.87 runs an over. On dry, unhelpful pitches, and with little conventional swing, he produced a string of masterclasses, featuring a mixture of reverse swing, slower balls, cutters, bouncers and even spinners, dismissing Misbah in the Second Test with a genuine off-break. Opener Shan Masood found Anderson especially unplayable, falling to him four times in 17 balls before being dropped for Sharjah. Stuart Broad took only seven wickets, but was hardly less economical, costing just above two an over; neither had enjoyed a thriftier Test series. When Pakistan were bowled out for 234 in the first innings at Sharjah, their combined figures read 28.1–15–30–6.

England's cause was not helped by Cook losing all three tosses, though he did his best to make up for it by scoring 450 runs, taking his tally in 2015 to 1,357, already his most prolific year. His 263 was the third-longest Test innings of all time, and his 33rd century in all international formats, taking

Worth a try: England experimented with unorthodox fields, as at Abu Dhabi, where what at first glance resembles a slip cordon is in fact two short straight mid-ons, the bowler and the non-striker.

him past Kevin Pietersen's England record; he also completed a Test hundred in all nine countries in which he has played (ten if you separate England and Wales). Even Cook, a famous non-sweater, had some beads on his forehead when he removed his helmet. But not losing as much fluid as other players allowed him to bat for more than two days in the ferocious heat without cramping.

When England arrived at the end of September, the temperature was around 45°C: the players used ice towels and drank rehydration fluids to replace salt and minerals. As late summer in the Gulf moved towards autumn, the temperature dropped around two degrees a week. But, whatever the reading, head coach Trevor Bayliss – or Trevor Bliss, as one local paper had it – wore long sleeves, tracksuit trousers and a floppy hat; an Australian, he knew about the dangers of the sun. Bayliss's understated manner and economy of words surprised some players: he preferred to observe and offer the occasional nugget. And he would have noted during the Tests that England were in effect a four-man team – Anderson, Broad, Cook and Joe Root, who passed 70 three times but did not record a century.

Ian Bell endured a difficult tour, showing little of the authority one might expect from a player of his experience. When he batted with James Taylor in Sharjah, it was the busy, confident Taylor who looked like the veteran of 118 Tests, and the apprehensive Bell the three-match novice. His final innings, when he missed a straight ball delivered from round the wicket by Shoaib Malik, brought him a duck – his ninth Test dismissal for either nought or one in 2015, the most in a year by any specialist batsman. He had also spilled two costly slip catches on the opening day of the series. Bell was subsequently omitted from the tour of South Africa, having managed just 428 runs in his previous 23 Test innings.

FIVE STATS YOU MAY HAVE MISSED

BENEDICT BERMANGE

- The last England leg-spinner before Adil Rashid to take a five-wicket haul on Test debut was Charles "Father" Marriott, with five for 37 and six for 59 against West Indies at The Oval in 1933 – in what turned out to be his only Test appearance.

- Only four men have hit hundreds on their return after missing more Tests than Shoaib Malik:

Tests missed		From	Return
53	A. M. J. Hilditch (Australia).....................	1979-80	1984-85
49	J. M. Parks (England)...........................	1954	1959-60
47	Ijaz Faqih (Pakistan)...........................	1981-82	1986-87
44	M. D. Bell (New Zealand).......................	2001-02	2007-08
42	**Shoaib Malik (Pakistan)**.......................	**2010**	**2015-16**

- Shoaib's innings of 245 was the highest to be paired with a duck in the same Test, beating Ricky Ponting's 242 and 0 for Australia against India at Adelaide in 2003-04.

- In Dubai, Misbah-ul-Haq became only the third batsman to be out twice in the same Test without adding to his overnight score:

C. P. H. Ramanayake (13 and 11)	Sri Lanka v New Zealand at Hamilton.....	1990-91
D. Ramnarine (2 and 11)	West Indies v South Africa at Port-of-Spain.	2000-01
Misbah-ul-Haq (102 and 87)	**Pakistan v England at Dubai**..........	**2015-16**

- In England's second innings at Sharjah, Alastair Cook and Stuart Broad batted together for the first time in 87 Tests in which they had both played. The record is held by Sanath Jayasuriya and Muttiah Muralitharan, who appeared in the same Sri Lankan team on 90 occasions in Tests, but never batted together.

Jos Buttler lost his place for the Third Test after scoring only 156 in seven matches stretching back to the start of the Ashes. He had struggled to find a method and tempo in five-day cricket, despite being urged to play his natural game; slogs and switch hits, however, are not necessarily recommended when trying to stave off defeat. But he found few such problems in one-day cricket, and finished the 50-over series with an astonishing 46-ball century, easily beating his own record as the fastest for England. And, with the selectors looking to cover all bases ahead of the World Twenty20, he also captained them for the first time, in the second T20 game.

In order to allow an extra bowler, Ali had become Cook's seventh opening partner since the retirement of Andrew Strauss in 2012 and, in Abu Dhabi, the first England player to open in the first innings of a Test without having previously done the job in first-class cricket. No one was terribly surprised when his technique appeared too loose to face the new ball, and England forfeited his dynamic contributions at No. 8 during the Ashes. Opening the batting may also have affected his bowling.

Ben Stokes showed signs of learning the virtue of patience with the ball, and scored a half-century in the First Test, though little else. In the Third, he hurt his right collarbone as he attempted a spectacular catch, and went home with his arm in a sling (though he would have been rested from the limited-overs matches anyway). His was not the only injury. Steven Finn had bowled

He's behind you! At Dubai in the first Twenty20 international, Pakistan's pantomime running had Umar Akmal and Sohaib Maqsood hurtling towards the same end.

well in one of the practice matches in Sharjah, but missed the rest of the tour when he was diagnosed with a bone stress injury in his left foot. Mark Wood, after some encouraging performances in the first two Tests, missed the Third and returned home for surgery on his left ankle.

Pakistan's batting was far more consistent. Five players scored centuries and, in Dubai, Misbah became the oldest since Bob Simpson in 1977-78 to do so in a Test, at the age of 41 years 147 days. His calm character was one of the reasons for the absence of the sort of ball-tampering, match-fixing and illegal-action stories that have marred previous Test series between Pakistan and England. When Root complained that Wahab Riaz, who bowled some ferocious spells in the desert sun, had deliberately trodden on the ball in Dubai, it was about as fractious as things got.

There were mutterings about the third one-day international, in Sharjah, where Pakistan's batsmen perished to a series of run-outs and brainless strokes, but anti-corruption officials were satisfied that in-play betting patterns, in both regulated and unregulated markets, provided no cause for alarm. Even so, some of the cricket was curious. In two of the Twenty20 games, two Pakistanis found themselves at the same end, and on each occasion the third umpire had to decide not if a batsman was out, but which. Mohammad Hafeez was involved in five run-outs during the tour though, without his high-class 151 in Sharjah, England might have squared the Test series. Shoaib scored 245 in Abu Dhabi, then announced his retirement from Test cricket mid-game at Sharjah. Younis Khan was persuaded to continue in one-day cricket but, bizarrely, then announced that the first game would be his last.

The lack of Hot Spot and Snicko – the host broadcaster, Ten Sports – would not fork out the necessary £125,000 – meant some decisions were a lottery, which might have caused friction under less phlegmatic captains than Cook and Misbah. England were frustrated at being denied victory by bad light in the First Test, though Cook took the decision in his stride. He understood that the light-meter readings had been set earlier in the match, and queried only gently whether the players were actually in danger.

England grew in confidence with the white ball, and won the final six matches of the tour, which would have pleased Strauss, the team's new supremo, who wanted to give one-day cricket equal footing with Tests. He had hired the former Sri Lanka captain Mahela Jayawardene as a batting consultant in the early weeks of the Test tour, and Paul Collingwood to work with the one-day team.

Alex Hales and Jason Roy made their first one-day international centuries, and James Vince was top scorer in the T20 series. England were rarely at their best, but kept winning, which was a good sign for an emerging team. Captain Eoin Morgan said there were only two perfect performances – Buttler's marauding century, and Chris Jordan's six balls in the final match's super over, when he nailed his yorkers so successfully that he conceded only three runs. It summed up a tour on which England's white-ball evolution was in danger of leaving their Test cricket in the shade.

ENGLAND TOURING PARTY

*A. N. Cook (Essex; T); M. M. Ali (Worcestershire; T/50/20), J. M. Anderson (Lancashire; T); J. M. Bairstow (Yorkshire; T/50); I. R. Bell (Warwickshire; T), S. W. Billings (Kent; 50/20), S. C. J. Broad (Nottinghamshire; T), J. C. Buttler (Lancashire; T/50/20), S. T. Finn (Middlesex; T), A. D. Hales (Nottinghamshire; T/50/20), C. J. Jordan (Sussex; T/50/20), E. J. G. Morgan (Middlesex; 50/20), S. D. Parry (Lancashire; 20), S. R. Patel (Nottinghamshire; T), L. E. Plunkett (Yorkshire; T/50/20), A. U. Rashid (Yorkshire; T/50/20), J. E. Root (Yorkshire; T/50/20), J. J. Roy (Surrey; 50/20), B. A. Stokes (Durham; T), J. W. A. Taylor (Nottinghamshire; T/50), R. J. W. Topley (Essex; 50/20), J. M. Vince (Hampshire; 20), D. J. Willey (Northamptonshire; 50/20), C. R. Woakes (Warwickshire; 50/20), M. A. Wood (Durham; T).

Morgan captained in the limited-overs matches. Z. S. Ansari (Surrey) was originally selected for the Test squad, but dislocated his thumb; Patel replaced him. Finn suffered a stress fracture to the foot and returned home, to be replaced in the Test and 50-over squads by Jordan, originally chosen only for the Twenty20s. Wood, selected for all formats, aggravated an ankle problem and flew home for surgery after the Tests; he was replaced for the limited-overs matches by Plunkett, originally chosen only for the Tests.

Coach: T. H. Bayliss (T/50/20). *Assistant coach:* P. Farbrace (T/50/20). *Batting coach:* M. R. Ramprakash (T), P. D. Collingwood (50/20). *Fast-bowling coach:* O. D. Gibson (T/50/20). *Consultant coaches:* B. N. French (T/50), D. P. M. D. Jayawardene (T). *Strength and conditioning coach:* P. C. F. Scott (T/50/20). *Operations manager:* P. A. Neale (T/50/20). *Team analyst:* R. J. Lewis (T), N. A. Leamon (50/20). *Team doctor:* R. H. J. Young (T), M. G. Wotherspoon (50/20). *Physiotherapist:* C. A. de Weymarn (T), B. T. Langley (50/20). *Massage therapist:* M. E. S. Saxby (T), J. Alty (50/20). *Security manager:* R. C. Dickason (T/50/20). *Media manager:* R. C. Evans (T/50/20).

> **"** When he was 100% fit he was as slippery as anyone. I would bowl with the wind and he'd bowl into it – that's where he lost most of his hair, I think."
> Obituaries, page 238

TEST MATCH AVERAGES

PAKISTAN – BATTING AND FIELDING

	T	I	NO	R	HS	100	50	Avge	Ct/St
Mohammad Hafeez	3	6	0	380	151	1	2	63.33	4
Misbah-ul-Haq	3	6	0	352	102	1	3	58.66	1
Asad Shafiq	3	6	0	326	107	1	2	54.33	1
Younis Khan	3	6	0	302	118	1	1	50.33	7
Shoaib Malik	3	6	0	292	245	1	0	48.66	2
Sarfraz Ahmed	3	6	1	139	39	0	0	27.80	9/4
†Shan Masood	2	4	0	58	54	0	1	14.50	2
Yasir Shah	2	3	0	27	16	0	0	9.00	1
Wahab Riaz	3	5	1	30	21	0	0	7.50	1
Zulfiqar Babar	3	5	2	10	6*	0	0	3.33	1
Rahat Ali	2	3	1	4	4	0	0	2.00	0

Played in two Tests: Imran Khan, sen. 0, 0*. Played in one Test: Azhar Ali 0, 34 (2 ct).

BOWLING

	Style	O	M	R	W	BB	5I	Avge
Shoaib Malik	OB	77.5	14	228	11	4-33	0	20.72
Yasir Shah	LBG	124	24	323	15	4-44	0	21.53
Imran Khan, sen.	RFM	54.2	15	148	6	2-33	0	24.66
Rahat Ali	LFM	55	14	157	4	2-48	0	39.25
Wahab Riaz	LF	108	17	347	8	4-66	0	43.37
Zulfiqar Babar	SLA	189	53	409	9	3-53	0	45.44

Also bowled: Asad Shafiq (LBG) 7–0–19–0; Azhar Ali (LBG) 2–0–7–0.

ENGLAND – BATTING AND FIELDING

	T	I	NO	R	HS	100	50	Avge	Ct
†A. N. Cook	3	5	0	450	263	1	2	90.00	2
J. E. Root	3	6	1	287	88	0	3	57.40	4
†S. C. J. Broad	3	5	3	95	30	0	0	47.50	2
I. R. Bell	3	6	1	158	63	0	1	31.60	3
J. M. Bairstow	3	6	0	134	46	0	0	22.33	7
A. U. Rashid	3	5	0	103	61	0	1	20.60	0
†B. A. Stokes	3	6	0	88	57	0	1	14.66	2
†M. M. Ali	3	6	0	84	35	0	0	14.00	2
M. A. Wood	2	3	0	34	29	0	0	11.33	0
J. C. Buttler	2	4	0	34	23	0	0	8.50	5
†J. M. Anderson	3	5	3	14	7	0	0	7.00	6

Played in one Test: S. R. Patel 42, 0 (1 ct); J. W. A. Taylor 76, 2.

BOWLING

	Style	O	M	R	W	BB	5I	Avge
J. M. Anderson	RFM	108.1	37	203	13	4-17	0	15.61
S. C. J. Broad	RFM	92	32	191	7	3-44	0	27.28
M. A. Wood	RFM	62.5	17	170	6	3-39	0	28.33
B. A. Stokes	RFM/OB	69.1	17	198	5	4-57	0	39.60
M. M. Ali	OB	107.2	9	438	9	3-108	0	48.66
S. R. Patel	SLA	42	4	164	3	2-85	0	54.66
A. U. Rashid	LBG	136.5	9	556	8	5-64	1	69.50

Also bowled: J. E. Root (OB) 8–1–39–0.

At Sharjah, October 5–6, 2015. **Drawn. ‡England XI 286-5 dec** (90 overs) (A. N. Cook 53, J. E. Root 59, J. M. Bairstow 66*, A. U. Rashid 51*; Zafar Gohar 3-72); **Pakistan A 216-5** (90 overs) (Fawad Alam 55, Iftikhar Ahmed 92*; M. M. Ali 3-41). *Both sides chose from 15 players, and batted for a day apiece by agreement. Joe Root retired after 62 overs, whereupon England lost two quick wickets to be 183-5 – but the Yorkshire pair of Jonny Bairstow and Adil Rashid shared a stand of 103*. Pakistan A dipped to 32-3 on the second morning, before Fawad Alam and the uncapped Iftikhar Ahmed added 112 in 44 overs. Moeen Ali took three wickets, but Rashid failed to strike in 20 overs, finishing with 0-55.*

At Sharjah, October 8–9, 2015. **Drawn. Pakistan A 192-12 dec** (87.5 overs) (Adnan Akmal 74*; S. T. Finn 4-16, A. U. Rashid 3-53); **‡England XI 198-11** (78 overs) (I. R. Bell 53, J. W. A. Taylor 61; Mir Hamza 4-34). *Both sides chose from 15 players. Khurram Manzoor, Ali Asad and Usman Salahuddin batted twice for Pakistan A – Asad bagged an unusual pair. There were five ducks in all, and from 73-6 the innings was rescued by Umar Amin (39) and wicketkeeper Adnan Akmal, who added 83. Finn claimed 4-16 from 15 overs in what turned out to be his only bowl of the tour. England batted indifferently, with the exception of Ian Bell and James Taylor, whose stand of 102 took the score to 118-2 before they both retired (Taylor resumed later). England then lost 6-20 to make it 142-8. Only Jos Buttler (32* in 85 minutes) survived for long after that, although it was his second innings of the day. Ali, slated to open in the First Test, also went in twice, and was out for seven and 12.*

PAKISTAN v ENGLAND

First Test Match

Richard Hobson

At Abu Dhabi, October 13–17, 2015. Drawn. Toss: Pakistan. Test debut: A. U. Rashid.

Talk of moral victories and PR defeats followed a largely turgid battle that was flattered by the final afternoon. As the clock ticked and the light faded, England's dash for runs resembled a blitz finish to a cagey game of chess. And, when dusk brought their unexpected chase to a close, the statisticians alone – swamped by facts, figures and curiosities – could feel satisfied. Paradise for them was a graveyard for bowlers, and only the flurry of late wickets, as fatigue and irresponsibility hit Pakistan, spared match referee Andy Pycroft from having to decide whether the pitch deserved to be marked "poor".

Two monumental innings dominated the scorecard. Shoaib Malik, in his first Test for more than five years, hit 245 – a unique score in Tests – in 639 minutes, and was put on a drip in the dressing-room to rehydrate. He was trumped by Cook, whose minor medical condition allowed him to retain liquid where others sweated profusely. He knuckled down to play the longest Test innings by an England batsman, and the third-longest by anyone. For 836 minutes – four short of 14 hours – he exercised supreme skill and concentration to make 263, the second-highest of his career and, like Shoaib, an unprecedented Test score. It left only 229, 238 and 252 unclaimed among scores below 264. Cook forced just 18 out of 528 balls to the boundary.

This feat of endurance almost set up the most unlikely success. After England had declared with a first-innings lead of 75, Anderson made inroads with an exacting new-ball spell, before a direct hit by Stokes ran out the dilly-dallying Mohammad Hafeez to leave Pakistan 47 for three. Then, after tea, panic spread through their ranks. Only 10 wickets had fallen on the first four days; now they were all falling at once. With Pakistan's lead 38, Younis Khan gifted Rashid a first Test wicket with a loose drive to cover, before Asad Shafiq edged a wide one to give him a second, and Misbah-ul-Haq inexplicably tried to hit Ali over the top when his task was to bat out time. Pakistan lost their last seven wickets for 60 in 16.5 overs to the turning ball. Having suffered the most expensive wicketless

Double double – part one: Shoaib Malik advances towards a career-best 245.

innings figures by any debutant, Rashid now claimed the first international five-for by an England wrist-spinner since Tommy Greenhough against India at Lord's in 1959. It was also the first five-wicket haul by an England leggie in Asia. The story of Lazarus seemed even-keeled by comparison.

And so, from contemplating early handshakes, England needed 99 to win from a theoretical 19 overs – though they knew the light would allow little more than an hour, and Pakistan would slow things down. England promoted the hitters, while Pakistan relied on the spin of Shoaib and Zulfiqar Babar to take pace off the ball. Watched by a crowd that was not officially counted, but could not have been more than 2,000, Buttler, Ali and Stokes departed to aggressive shots in the first six overs, from which England made 35. But, while they gave it a good go, they were always behind the rate. It felt appropriate that, when Bairstow smashed Wahab Riaz over deep midwicket for six, time was lost in retrieving the ball from an empty stand.

The floodlights were switched on around 5.20, but made only a brief impact before Paul Reiffel and Bruce Oxenford called time at 5.46. Pakistan had bowled 11 overs in 58 minutes, and England were 25 runs short. The umpires had blamelessly followed their brief, using a previous light-meter reading as their guide: play had actually gone on for ten

LONGEST TEST INNINGS

Mins			
970	Hanif Mohammad (337)	Pakistan v West Indies at Bridgetown	1957-58
878	G. Kirsten (275)	South Africa v England at Durban	1999-2000
836	**A. N. Cook (263)**	**England v Pakistan at Abu Dhabi**	**2015-16**
799	S. T. Jayasuriya (340)	Sri Lanka v India at Colombo (RPS)	1997-98
797	L. Hutton (364)	England v Australia at The Oval	1938
790	H. M. Amla (311*)	South Africa v England at The Oval	2012
778	B. C. Lara (400*)	West Indies v England at St John's	2003-04
777	D. S. B. P. Kuruppu (201*)†	Sri Lanka v New Zealand at Colombo (CCC)	1986-87
775	B. B. McCullum (302)	New Zealand v India at Wellington	2013-14
773	A. N. Cook (294)	England v India at Birmingham	2011

† *On debut.*

minutes longer than the day before. But, to casual followers unaware of rules, regulations and the properties of a red ball in twilight, the conclusion – or lack of one – must have seemed ridiculous. After four and a half days of tedium, a positive finish had been denied, despite beaming floodlights and batsmen sensing glory rather than danger. And people wonder why cricket has never taken off in America.

Cook said he felt disappointed rather than angry. Perhaps he would have settled for a draw at the start of the contest, given meagre preparation of two uncompetitive two-day

games, and a lost toss at a venue where Pakistan had never been beaten. Yet things had already begun to go wrong for the hosts on the eve of the game, when Yasir Shah, their leg-spinner and most important bowler, suffered a back spasm in practice. They now scrambled to engineer a return to the UAE for left-arm spinner Zafar Gohar, the best of the Pakistan A slow bowlers against England in those warm-ups. But visa complications meant he stayed put in Pakistan: it was harder for players from the so-called home side to enter the country than it was for England's. A disgruntled Misbah described the situation as "mismanagement".

Pakistan had recalled Shoaib, citing outstanding one-day form, and the withdrawal of Azhar Ali (because of a foot infection reportedly picked up during a pilgrimage to Mecca) prompted his inclusion at No. 3. Fate smiled, and Shoaib reached stumps on 124, not bad for a player whose most recent first-class appearance had been for Zarai Taraqiati Bank against Water and Power Development Authority ten months earlier.

But his hundred was only part of the first day's tale. Critically, England missed three clear opportunities: Bell, at second slip, dropped Hafeez on twice low to his left, then – an easier catch – Shafiq shortly before the close on ten, both off Anderson. In between, Broad had Shoaib caught off a no-ball on 40. Those three incidents were

Philip Brown

Double double – part two: Alastair Cook resists the temptation to handle the ball, and goes on to 263.

to cost 393 runs: Hafeez advanced to 98, while Shoaib and Shafiq were still together at tea the next day. Wood held his hands to the sky when he finally broke their stand of 248, though not before Shafiq had made his eighth Test hundred, all at No. 6 – from where only Garry Sobers had scored as many.

Shoaib, whose last Test century had come more than six years previously in Colombo, played especially well through the leg side on a slow surface, before eventually clipping his 420th ball to Bell at midwicket, after collecting 24 fours and four sixes. Younis, meanwhile, overtook Javed Miandad as Pakistan's leading Test run-scorer when he moved to 21 in the first innings with a six over long-on off Ali, only to fall soon after to the straightest of three close fielders in an arc around short midwicket.

Three strikes in eight balls after tea on the second day gave Stokes respectable figures, but spin took a pounding in a total of 523 for eight. The 302 conceded by Rashid, Ali, Root and – in a single, desperate over of off-breaks – Stokes, was the most in a Test

WORST INNINGS FIGURES ON TEST DEBUT...

34–0–163–0	**A. U. Rashid**	**England v Pakistan at Abu Dhabi**.............	**2015-16**
18–2–149–0	†B. E. McGain	Australia v South Africa at Cape Town............	2008-09
37–8–146–0	Pankaj Singh	India v England at Southampton	2014
36–4–142–0	J. J. Warr	England v Australia at Sydney...................	1950-51
34–1–136–0	†T. Mupariwa	Zimbabwe v Sri Lanka at Bulawayo	2003-04
54–13–132–0	R. G. Nadkarni	India v New Zealand at Delhi...................	1955-56
21–2–131–0	Sohail Khan	Pakistan v Sri Lanka at Karachi	2008-09
40–6–120–0	S. J. Benn	West Indies v Sri Lanka at Providence...........	2007-08
34–7–115–0	G. O. B. Allen	England v Australia at Lord's...................	1930

† *Only Test.*

...BEST INNINGS FIGURES BY ENGLAND SPINNERS ON DEBUT

17–4–56–7	J. Langridge (SLA)	v West Indies at Manchester	1933
37–9–103–7	J. C. Laker (OB)	v West Indies at Bridgetown	1947-48
16–3–43–6	G. H. T. Simpson-Hayward (OB‡)	v South Africa at Johannesburg ...	1909-10
29.2–6–59–6	†C. S. Marriott (LBG)	v West Indies at The Oval *(2nd inns)*	1933
33.3–9–67–6	P. M. Such (OB)	v Australia at Manchester........	1993
20–7–28–5	P. H. Edmonds (SLA)	v Australia at Leeds	1975
26–11–35–5	N. G. B. Cook (SLA)	v New Zealand at Lord's	1983
11.5–2–37–5	†C. S. Marriott (LBG)	v West Indies at The Oval *(1st inns)*	1933
40.1–15–51–5	R. Peel (SLA)	v Australia at Adelaide..........	1884-85
28.4–8–61–5	L. C. Braund (LBG)	v Australia at Sydney	1901-02
31.5–13–63–5	R. Berry (SLA)	v West Indies at Manchester	1950
18.5–3–64–5	**A. U. Rashid (LBG)**	**v Pakistan at Abu Dhabi**	**2015-16**
34–2–146–5	†D. W. Carr (LBG)	v Australia at The Oval	1909

† *Only Test.*   ‡ *Bowled underarm.*

innings by a wicketless set of slow bowlers, beating the 275 leaked by Sri Lanka's spinners in Wellington in 1990-91. At this point, Pakistan seemed the only plausible winners, not least because England had been in the field for five draining sessions. But their own bowlers were unable to coax anything more from the lifeless track.

Cook showed second ball that he was on his mettle. A defensive shot against Rahat Ali ricocheted backwards, then looped towards his stumps. Instinct prompted Cook to put out a hand, but he backed away just in time to avoid being dismissed handled the ball; it fell just wide. He barely wavered after that, and a small split in the webbing of his right little finger sustained in the field proved no handicap. Cook survived a tight review for leg-before when 101, and was dropped at 147 and 173. Yet he swept confidently, and drove with rare assurance. He never became bogged down. Afterwards he said he had reached "a blissful state" at the crease. And, when he was eventually dismissed, to a top-edged sweep, replays showed Shoaib had no-balled, sliding his foot back in his delivery stride as if performing Michael Jackson's moonwalk.

Cook's 28th Test hundred was his eighth in Asia, matching Jacques Kallis's record for a non-subcontinental batsman. He enjoyed good support. Ali saw off the new ball in a stand of 116, and Bell overcame a nervous start to help add 165, taking 134 deliveries over his fifty. Root and Stokes were more fluent. Spin finally secured a wicket with its 1,021st ball of the game, when Shoaib turned one past the advancing Stokes. Too tired and, perhaps, fed up to celebrate, he sat down and rested while the new batsman came in. Not since 1979-80, against Australia at Faisalabad, had Pakistan bowled more than 206 overs in an innings. And Shoaib was forced to toil a little longer as Cook delayed a declaration until the final morning, scarcely imagining how close his team would come to success.

Man of the Match: A. N. Cook.

Close of play: first day, Pakistan 286-4 (Shoaib Malik 124, Asad Shafiq 11); second day, England 56-0 (Cook 39, Ali 15); third day, England 290-3 (Cook 168, Root 3); fourth day, England 569-8 (Rashid 6, Broad 0).

Pakistan

Mohammad Hafeez lbw b Stokes	98	– run out	34
Shan Masood b Anderson	2	– b Anderson	1
Shoaib Malik c Bell b Stokes	245	– c Bairstow b Anderson	0
Younis Khan c Cook b Broad	38	– c Stokes b Rashid	45
*Misbah-ul-Haq c Buttler b Anderson	3	– b Ali	51
Asad Shafiq lbw b Wood	107	– c Buttler b Rashid	6
†Sarfraz Ahmed c Bell b Stokes	2	– c Anderson b Rashid	27
Wahab Riaz not out	2	– c Bairstow b Ali	1
Zulfiqar Babar c Anderson b Stokes	0	– c Anderson b Ali	1
Rahat Ali (did not bat)		– not out	0
Imran Khan, sen. (did not bat)		– c Anderson b Rashid	0
B 4, l-b 21, n-b 1	26	B 3, l-b 2, n-b 2	7

1/5 (2) 2/173 (1) (8 wkts dec, 151.1 overs) 523   1/3 (2) 2/3 (3) (57.5 overs) 173
3/247 (5)   3/47 (1) 4/113 (4)
5/499 (6) 6/514 (7) 7/521 (3) 8/523 (9)   5/139 (6) 6/159 (5) 7/165 (8)
   8/168 (4) 9/173 (7) 10/173 (11)

Anderson 22–7–42–2; Broad 21–8–44–1; Stokes 17.1–3–57–4; Wood 22–5–58–1; Rashid 34–0–163–0; Ali 30–2–121–0; Root 5–1–13–0. *Second innings*—Anderson 10–3–30–2; Broad 8–5–8–0; Wood 7–2–29–0; Rashid 18.5–3–64–5; Stokes 7–4–9–0; Ali 7–0–28–2.

England

*A. N. Cook c Shan Masood b Shoaib Malik	263		
M. M. Ali c Sarfraz Ahmed b Imran Khan	35	– (1) c Shoaib Malik b Zulfiqar Babar	11
I. R. Bell c Mohammad Hafeez b Wahab Riaz	63	– (6) not out	5
M. A. Wood b Wahab Riaz	4		
J. E. Root c Sarfraz Ahmed b Rahat Ali	85	– (3) not out	33
J. M. Bairstow lbw b Wahab Riaz	8	– (5) st Sarfraz Ahmed b Zulfiqar Babar	15
B. A. Stokes b Shoaib Malik	57	– (4) c Mohammad Hafeez b Shoaib Malik	2
†J. C. Buttler c Asad Shafiq b Zulfiqar Babar	23	– (2) lbw b Shoaib Malik	4
A. U. Rashid b Imran Khan	12		
S. C. J. Broad not out	17		
J. M. Anderson not out	3		
B 7, l-b 7, w 3, n-b 11	28	L-b 2, w 2	4

1/116 (2) 2/281 (3) (9 wkts dec, 206 overs) 598   1/13 (2) (4 wkts, 11 overs) 74
3/285 (4) 4/426 (5) 5/443 (6)   2/29 (1) 3/35 (4)
6/534 (7) 7/549 (1) 8/563 (8) 9/590 (9)   4/66 (5)

Rahat Ali 28–1–86–1; Imran Khan 27–7–74–2; Zulfiqar Babar 72–17–183–1; Wahab Riaz 37–3–125–3; Asad Shafiq 7–0–19–0; Shoaib Malik 35–4–97–2. *Second innings*—Zulfiqar Babar 5–0–27–2; Shoaib Malik 4–0–25–2; Wahab Riaz 2–0–20–0.

Umpires: B. N. J. Oxenford and P. R. Reiffel.   Third umpire: S. Ravi.
Referee: A. J. Pycroft.

> "He prodded at Kaushal, offering a genial handshake, but the ball was leaning in for the kiss on both cheeks."
> Sri Lanka v Pakistan in 2015-16, Second Test, page 1110

PAKISTAN v ENGLAND

Second Test Match

OSMAN SAMIUDDIN

At Dubai, October 22–26, 2015. Pakistan won by 178 runs. Toss: Pakistan.

Perhaps even more than they realise, Pakistan have increasingly operated to the rhythms of the batting of Misbah-ul-Haq, their captain. Long periods of waiting and waiting – then, when no one expects it, striking for the kill. It could be argued that this is how they have always worked. In so many of their finest Test triumphs, they have meandered for hours, even days. And, before anyone has cottoned on to what's happening, they've won. No team has proved so often that the meaning of five days can actually become clear in an hour or so.

It happened here on the third morning. England began it upright and calm, and ended horizontal and frazzled, having lost their last seven wickets for 36 in 18 overs – and their best chance of claiming the series. That they ultimately came so close to recovering from this kick in the guts, almost saving the Test on a delicious slow-burner of a final day, was proof of their progress and potential. Rashid so nearly became a national hero. But they had simply left themselves too much to do.

By numbers, their first-innings collapse was familiar; indeed, a comprehensive history of the Pakistan–England rivalry could be based on collapses alone. The causes were familiar, too: extreme pace at one end, quality leg-spin at the other, inevitably casting minds back to Wasim Akram and Mushtaq Ahmed in the 1992 World Cup final. The only thing missing was aural: as Wahab Riaz and Yasir Shah took six of those seven wickets, there was no sound of stumps being clattered, nor fielders screeching around the bat.

Wahab took the lead role in an unbroken nine-over spell that was as remarkable for its duration as for the pace he maintained – an average of nearly 88mph. If it was one of the cooler mornings of the series then, at just under 30°C, the relief was relative: bowling that long, with such force, was superhuman. His reward was three wickets, all caught behind by Sarfraz Ahmed, all reversing away. The big one was Root, who had guided England to 206 for three in reply to Pakistan's 378, but chased a widish one after Wahab had worked away

Gareth Copley, Getty Images

Sharp shooter: Wahab Riaz, the fastest bowler in the series, took four key wickets in England's first innings.

with discipline outside off stump. Then he really cranked it up, attacking Stokes and Buttler with a fierceness recognised by those who have tracked his development since his return to the Test side in August 2014.

Pakistan's coach Waqar Younis had been instrumental in that growth, insisting that Wahab needed to become the leader of the attack and worry about nothing other than bowling fast. And it was a bit of timely Waqar tinkering that helped Wahab reap the benefits. He had bowled an electric spell in Abu Dhabi, but without the same results.

OLDEST BATSMEN TO SCORE A TEST CENTURY

Yrs	Days			
46	82	J. B. Hobbs (142)	England v Australia at Melbourne	1928-29
45	151	E. H. Hendren (132)	England v Australia at Manchester...........	1934
43	201	W. Bardsley (193*)	Australia v England at Lord's...............	1926
42	295	A. W. Nourse (111)	South Africa v Australia at Johannesburg......	1921-22
42	61	F. E. Woolley (154)	England v South Africa at Manchester........	1929
42	6	E. A. B. Rowan (236)	South Africa v England at Leeds	1951
41	360	R. B. Simpson (100)	Australia v India at Adelaide	1977-78
41	268	W. W. Armstrong (123*)	Australia v England at Melbourne	1920-21
41	264	T. W. Graveney (105)	England v Pakistan at Karachi	1968-69
41	242	H. W. Taylor (117)	South Africa v England at Cape Town	1930-31
41	**147**	**Misbah-ul-Haq (102)**	**Pakistan v England at Dubai**	**2015-16**
41	109	B. Sutcliffe (151*)	New Zealand v India at Calcutta.............	1964-65
41	64	G. Boycott (105)	England v India at Delhi...................	1981-82

Only the last hundred for each batsman is shown. Hobbs made eight centuries after the age of 40; this was Misbah's fourth. Armstrong, Boycott, Graveney, Hendren and C. G. Macartney (Australia) all scored three. Nourse's century was his first, in his 34th Test, 19 years after his debut.

Unimpressed by the lack of wickets, Waqar worked on getting his wrist more upright at release. The impact was immediate and, though he did not target the stumps in Dubai as he had in Abu Dhabi, there was greater control. The spell consigned England to a wholly inadequate total. Round these parts, once a team concede a lead as big as 136, it is almost impossible to plot a way back.

Until then, they might have harboured visions of going further than the near-victory of Abu Dhabi. Just as in the First Test, England fought back – in this case from a first day that had ended with Pakistan in control. It belonged to Misbah, who made his seventh Test century as captain, equalling the Pakistan record of Inzamam, the other great and equanimous ul-Haq. Misbah's innings was also as characteristic as it could possibly be. When he arrived to face the second ball after lunch, Pakistan – having won another toss – were 85 for three. The surface was livelier than Abu Dhabi's, but three wickets at that stage looked too many to have lost.

For the umpteenth time, Misbah settled down with Younis Khan and, like sensible parents, they guided Pakistan away from trouble. Their approach, as it proved all series, was straightforward: fasting against the seamers, feasting off the spinners. Misbah scored 26 runs from 125 balls of pace, but 76 off 72 from Ali and Rashid; Younis managed 20 from 28 bowled by the spinners, and a more sedate 36 off 87 from the seamers. So assured was Misbah, so dismissive of spin, that in the last over of the day he had no qualms in hitting Ali for two sixes and attempting two reverse sweeps, moving from 87 to 102. Pakistan closed at 282 for four, with Asad Shafiq providing the support.

But it was Misbah's dismissal by the fifth ball of a superb, tone-setting over by Broad on the second morning that began England's surge. Wood, deservedly, and Ali, a little more fortuitously, reaped the spoils as Pakistan lost their last five for 44. Ali and Bell fell cheaply, but England knew a total of 378 was less imposing than it might have been. Much of that confidence lay in the form of Cook and the undoubted quality of Root, his heir apparent. They put on 113 largely untroubled runs – although Cook, on 27, almost played on against Zulfiqar Babar, only for the bails to remain unmoved as the ball rolled on to the stumps. They also handled their first brush with Yasir impeccably, until Cook was caught at leg slip following sharp captaincy from Misbah, who set the trap and instructed Yasir to change his line.

Root was exemplary and his footwork immaculate, especially against Yasir and Zulfiqar; his unobtrusive but urgent style helped him glide along. The signs that he was one of the world's finest young batsmen were unmissable: fewer tics than Steve Smith, as economically efficient as Kane Williamson, and with the presence of Virat Kohli. No

Hammering home the advantage: Misbah-ul-Haq strikes a six on the third evening.

wonder England stuttered when he fell on that third morning. That it was the fifth time he had fallen between 83 and 98 in 2015 seemed indicative of nothing but a statistical quirk.

Once England's prize pair had been dismissed, the Test began to slip into the pattern of Pakistan's wins against Australia the previous year. Time was their only serious opponent. Younis worked his way to his 31st hundred in Tests, his tenth in 24 matches in the UAE, and an innings he had been threatening to play all series. He was inevitably partnered by Misbah, who became only the second batsman, after Andrew Flintoff against Australia at Edgbaston in 2005, to hit at least four sixes in both innings of a Test. Pakistan declared half an hour after lunch on the fourth day, leaving England to bat out just under five sessions or 144 overs, rather than entertain thoughts of chasing down 491. In recent years, they had pulled off some great escapes – and been involved in some great near misses – but this would surely have been the greatest. Astonishingly, they got to within six and a half overs of redemption.

Twice on the final day, a Pakistan triumph looked a formality: first when Root, having passed 3,000 Test runs, fell after another accomplished fifty (his 12th in 2015, the most by an England player in a calendar year, beating Keith Fletcher in 1973); then, after Broad was eighth out, bowled by Wahab, with 41 overs left. Yet, in cahoots with Wood, Rashid got his head down. On a fifth-day pitch, they batted for 29.2 overs, a Test record for the ninth wicket in the fourth innings. Rashid's was a dual-purpose effort, designed to save a Test and atone for his horror swipe against Yasir two days earlier.

The surface had not crumbled as Pakistan hoped, and Rashid read the spinners with ease, playing them with firmness of intent and great restraint. So it was a surprise when, with 39 deliveries left, the sun setting and a close circle of fielders lying in wait, he drove at Yasir. Who knows why he chose that of all options, but he hit it straight to Zulfiqar at cover, one of two men in the outfield. Thus ended four hours of resistance, in which England's last four had faced 322 balls, another fourth-innings Test record. Even so, Cook – still stung by his side's first-innings surrender – admitted they probably hadn't deserved "to get out of jail".

As Pakistan celebrated their largest Test win over England in terms of runs, Yasir wheeled away and belly flopped, football-style. It was his eighth wicket of the Test. But, as the destination of the match award suggested, the three Wahab had taken on the third morning were the wickets that turned the game.

Man of the Match: Wahab Riaz.

Close of play: first day, Pakistan 282-4 (Misbah-ul-Haq 102, Asad Shafiq 46); second day, England 182-3 (Root 76, Bairstow 27); third day, Pakistan 222-3 (Younis Khan 71, Misbah-ul-Haq 87); fourth day, England 130-3 (Root 59, Bairstow 6).

Pakistan

Mohammad Hafeez c Bairstow b Ali	19	– c Root b Wood	51
Shan Masood c Buttler b Anderson	54	– c Buttler b Anderson	1
Shoaib Malik c Bairstow b Stokes	2	– b Wood	7
Younis Khan c Buttler b Wood	56	– c Ali b Rashid	118
*Misbah-ul-Haq lbw b Broad	102	– c Cook b Anderson	87
Asad Shafiq c Root b Wood	83	– lbw b Ali	79
†Sarfraz Ahmed c Anderson b Ali	32	– not out	3
Wahab Riaz c Anderson b Ali	6		
Yasir Shah c Stokes b Rashid	16		
Zulfiqar Babar lbw b Wood	3		
Imran Khan, sen. not out	0		
L-b 4, w 1	5	B 6, l-b 1, n-b 1	8

1/51 (1) 2/58 (3) 3/85 (2)   (118.5 overs) 378   1/1 (2)   (6 wkts dec, 95 overs) 354
4/178 (4) 5/282 (5) 6/334 (7)   2/16 (3) 3/83 (1)
7/342 (8) 8/370 (9) 9/377 (10) 10/378 (6)   4/224 (5) 5/337 (4) 6/354 (6)

Anderson 20–5–40–1; Broad 17–4–48–1; Ali 25–3–108–3; Wood 19.5–7–39–3; Stokes 17–3–55–1; Rashid 20–1–84–1. *Second innings*—Anderson 15–7–22–2; Broad 10–1–34–0; Wood 14–3–44–2; Ali 11–0–60–1; Stokes 17–3–54–0; Rashid 25–1–107–1; Root 3–0–26–0.

England

*A. N. Cook c sub (Ahmed Shehzad) b Yasir Shah	65	– c Wahab Riaz b Yasir Shah	10
M. M. Ali c Shan Masood b Wahab Riaz	1	– c Younis Khan b Imran Khan	1
I. R. Bell c Sarfraz Ahmed b Imran Khan	4	– c Younis Khan b Zulfiqar Babar	46
J. E. Root c Sarfraz Ahmed b Wahab Riaz	88	– c Younis Khan b Zulfiqar Babar	71
J. M. Bairstow lbw b Yasir Shah	46	– b Yasir Shah	22
B. A. Stokes c Sarfraz Ahmed b Wahab Riaz	4	– c Misbah-ul-Haq b Imran Khan	13
†J. C. Buttler c Sarfraz Ahmed b Wahab Riaz	0	– c Younis Khan b Yasir Shah	7
A. U. Rashid c Mohammad Hafeez b Yasir Shah	0	– c Zulfiqar Babar b Yasir Shah	61
S. C. J. Broad not out	15	– b Wahab Riaz	30
M. A. Wood c Younis Khan b Yasir Shah	1	– c Mohammad Hafeez b Zulfiqar Babar	29
J. M. Anderson c Sarfraz Ahmed b Imran Khan	4	– not out	0
B 4, l-b 1, w 5, n-b 4	14	B 12, l-b 4, w 1, n-b 5	22

1/5 (2) 2/14 (3) 3/127 (1)   (75.2 overs) 242   1/9 (2) 2/19 (1)   (137.3 overs) 312
4/206 (4) 5/212 (6) 6/216 (7)   3/121 (3) 4/157 (4)
7/218 (8) 8/223 (5) 9/233 (10) 10/242 (11)   5/163 (5) 6/178 (7) 7/193 (6)
                                         8/253 (9) 9/308 (10) 10/312 (8)

Imran Khan 13.2–4–33–2; Wahab Riaz 19.5–5–66–4; Zulfiqar Babar 10–2–35–0; Yasir Shah 29–4–93–4; Shoaib Malik 4–1–10–0. *Second innings*—Imran Khan 14–4–41–2; Wahab Riaz 25–4–78–1; Yasir Shah 41.3–15–87–4; Shoaib Malik 10–2–37–0; Zulfiqar Babar 47–23–53–3.

Umpires: B. N. J. Oxenford and P. R. Reiffel.   Third umpire: C. B. Gaffaney.
Referee: A. J. Pycroft.

PAKISTAN v ENGLAND

Third Test Match

Lawrence Booth

At Sharjah, November 1–5, 2015. Pakistan won by 127 runs. Toss: Pakistan.

    A half-hour cab ride from Dubai to Sharjah feels like a trip from one world to another. Glamorous high-rises give way to modest flats, bright lights to pink neon, and expat hangouts to subcontinental bustle. England had never played a Test here, but instead of being inspired, they found themselves retelling a hoary tale.

They were in touch with Pakistan until the fourth afternoon, but disintegrated as if in homage to their previous tour of the UAE, in 2011-12, when their batsmen could scarcely leave their hotel rooms without wondering whether the corridors would take spin. Now, as Pakistan celebrated a 2–0 triumph and briefly climbed to second in the Test rankings, Cook's team reflected on a series that had continually tantalised them but ultimately reinforced stereotypes about western batsmen in Asia.

Though they refused to feel sorry for themselves, their hard-luck narrative – deprived of victory in Abu Dhabi and of a draw in Dubai – took further sustenance from a series-clinching century by Mohammad Hafeez. Early in Pakistan's second innings, he was given out caught behind off Anderson for two, only to be saved by a review. If the unsatisfactory absence of Hot Spot and Snicko meant the overrule by TV umpire Paul Reiffel was less than clear-cut, then the effect on the game was clarity itself. Hafeez went on to an accomplished 151, before England folded with *fin de série* decadence.

As during the first two Tests, it was the difference between the teams' spinners that took its toll. While Yasir Shah, Zulfiqar Babar and Shoaib Malik managed 17 wickets for 313 and conceded only 2.34 runs an over between them, the English trio lagged behind in every respect: Moeen Ali, Rashid and Patel took seven for 423 and leaked 3.66. Most galling for England was the manner in which their batsmen allowed Shoaib, with only 25 wickets from 34 Tests, to harvest career-best match figures of seven for 59. As if his first-innings figures of four for 33, also a personal-best, had scratched some significant itch, he announced his Test retirement that evening.

English hopes of squaring the series had taken an early nosedive when Misbah-ul-Haq won his third toss in a row and offered a half-apologetic hand to an unamused Cook. Selection had been geared towards batting first: Mark Wood was rested because of his fragile left ankle, so Patel came in for his first Test in nearly three years to provide some left-arm spin and batting depth; Jos Buttler's miserable form meant the gloves passed to Bairstow, while James Taylor returned to Tests for the first time since his disparagement by Kevin Pietersen in 2012.

But it was the seamers who gave England a chance. Anderson drew level with Shaun Pollock on 421 Test wickets – joint-eighth in the all-time list – when he had Azhar Ali caught behind, and would finish a triumphant first day with 15.1–7–17–4. Thirteen overs from Broad, who at one stage sent down 48 successive dot balls, yielded an equally miserly two for 13. Pre-Test warnings that the pitch would offer less seam movement than the pitiless Sheikh Zayed Road that connects Abu Dhabi and Sharjah via Dubai were forgotten.

Moeen Ali induced miscues from Hafeez and Sarfraz Ahmed, but Patel's two wickets – bounce to undo Asad Shafiq, turn to bowl Wahab Riaz – provided a different kind of warning: England would be batting last. Without Misbah's typically quirky 71 (of which 62 came from the spinners), Pakistan would not have scraped even 234, though a slow outfield disguised the total's true worth.

England's response contained more grunt than panache, yet their hopes of a decisive lead needed a combination of both. Cook made a gritty 49 to take his Test tally in 2015 to 1,294, surpassing Graham Gooch (1,264 in 1990) as the most by an England captain in a calendar year, but fell for the third time in a row to Yasir. Bell seemed stifled by responsibility, scoring only 16 during a painful session between lunch and tea, and finishing with one of a quartet of neither-here-nor-there forties. It needed Taylor, as alert as a pickpocket in a souk, and Bairstow (rarely at ease on a pitch that had turned on the first day) to shepherd the total to a promising 222 for four at stumps.

Since Stokes was uncertain to bat – but certain not to bowl – after injuring his right shoulder attempting a typically wholehearted catch on the first afternoon, day three loomed as pivotal to England's chances. But Taylor could add only two to his overnight 74 before poking at Rahat Ali, back in the side after Imran Khan split the webbing in his bowling hand two days before the game; and Bairstow, who himself had added only six, cut a delivery from Zulfiqar that hurried on. Patel batted pleasantly for 42, but Yasir bowled him with a delivery that recalled Warne to Gatting in 1993, and encouraged similar apprehension in the England dressing-room. Stokes's plucky emergence at No. 11 could

Out of reach: Mohammad Hafeez bypasses James Taylor at short leg, as Pakistan fight back.

extend the lead only to 72. It was no more than a basis for negotiation. The suspicion was that Anderson and Broad would have to perform like a pair of Atlases once more.

After Hafeez's early escape, Pakistan's openers settled down to contribute their first meaningful stand of the series, though with Azhar in place of the misfiring Shan Masood. By the time he fell victim to one of Hafeez's head-in-the-clouds calls for a single, Pakistan were 29 in front. Anderson, immaculate once more, found some reverse to snare Shoaib, and Broad repeated the trick against Younis Khan shortly before stumps. Early on the fourth morning, when England wore black armbands following the death of Tom Graveney, Anderson bowled nightwatchman Rahat. Pakistan were, in effect, 80 for four. The series was salvageable.

Hafeez, so often outshone by Younis and Misbah, moved front and centre. Having survived a stumping chance on 97 in the day's first over (neither he nor Bairstow managed to pick Rashid's googly), he dominated a fifth-wicket stand of 93 with his captain, and had made 151 out of 257 by the time he launched Moeen Ali to long-on. Again, England had a glimmer: 185 behind, four wickets to take. But Pakistan knew how to stay ahead: the diligent Shafiq and the energetic Sarfraz ensured the final reckoning would be 284 in 112 overs, 75 more than England had ever made in the fourth innings to win a Test in Asia. Anderson and Broad deserved better for a combined match analysis of 77.1–29–126–11.

Moeen Ali's experimental stint as an opener came to a tame end when – having been clattered on the back of the helmet by Wahab – he didn't get forward to one from Shoaib that kept low. Shoaib then bowled Bell from round the wicket with a ball that behaved perfectly but still exposed Bell's timidity. Cook and Root were in occupation at the start of the final day, but England required a further 238.

Hope evaporated under the morning sun. Root played back to Yasir and was hit in line with leg, Taylor edged Zulfiqar to slip, Bairstow misjudged a sweep, and Patel was pinned in front: four for 11 in 31 balls, or – taking in the evening before – six for 25. The eight runs contributed by Nos 3–7 equalled England's worst such effort, at Sydney in 1886-87. On that occasion, a team led by Arthur Shrewsbury were bowled out for 45 – and won.

But Sharjah was in no mood for a miracle. Cook and Rashid restored some decorum with a stand of 49, but the end came soon after lunch. Cook was close to becoming the first Englishman to carry his bat for 19 years, before he was stumped off Shoaib. Close, but – in a region that prefers the hookah – no cigar. And, for England, that summed up the series.

Man of the Match: Mohammad Hafeez.   *Man of the Series:* Yasir Shah.

Close of play: first day, England 4-0 (Cook 0, Ali 4); second day, England 222-4 (Taylor 74, Bairstow 37); third day, Pakistan 146-3 (Mohammad Hafeez 97, Rahat Ali 0); fourth day, England 46-2 (Cook 17, Root 6).

Pakistan

Mohammad Hafeez c Broad b Ali	27	– c Bell b Ali 151
Azhar Ali c Bairstow b Anderson	0	– run out 34
Shoaib Malik c Bairstow b Broad	38	– lbw b Anderson 37
Younis Khan lbw b Anderson	31	– lbw b Broad 14
Misbah-ul-Haq c Root b Anderson	71	– (6) lbw b Broad 38
Asad Shafiq c Bairstow b Patel	5	– (7) b Broad 46
Sarfraz Ahmed c Root b Ali	39	– (8) b Patel 36
Wahab Riaz b Patel	0	– (10) run out 21
Yasir Shah c Patel b Broad	7	– c Broad b Rashid 4
Zulfiqar Babar not out	6	– (11) not out 0
Rahat Ali c Ali b Anderson	4	– (5) b Anderson 0
B 1, l-b 5	6	B 6, l-b 5 11

1/5 (2) 2/49 (1) 3/88 (3) (85.1 overs) 234   1/101 (2) 2/105 (3) (118.2 overs) 355
4/103 (4) 5/116 (6) 6/196 (7)   3/146 (4) 4/152 (5)
7/196 (8) 8/224 (9) 9/224 (5) 10/234 (11)   5/245 (6) 6/257 (1) 7/312 (8)
   8/319 (9) 9/354 (7) 10/355 (10)

Anderson 15.1–7–17–4; Broad 13–8–13–2; Stokes 11–4–23–0; Patel 23.3–5–85–2; Ali 13.3–3–49–2; Rashid 10–1–41–0. *Second innings*—Anderson 26–8–52–2; Broad 23–6–44–3; Patel 19–1–79–1; Ali 21.2–1–72–1; Rashid 29–3–97–1.

England

*A. N. Cook c Azhar Ali b Yasir Shah	49	– (2) st Sarfraz Ahmed b Shoaib Malik 63
M. M. Ali c Younis Khan b Shoaib Malik	14	– (1) lbw b Shoaib Malik 22
I. R. Bell st Sarfraz Ahmed b Yasir Shah	40	– b Shoaib Malik 0
J. E. Root c Sarfraz Ahmed b Rahat Ali	4	– lbw b Yasir Shah 6
J. W. A. Taylor c Sarfraz Ahmed b Rahat Ali	76	– c Younis Khan b Zulfiqar Babar 2
‡J. M. Bairstow b Zulfiqar Babar	43	– lbw b Yasir Shah 0
S. R. Patel b Yasir Shah	42	– lbw b Zulfiqar Babar 0
A. U. Rashid c Azhar Ali b Shoaib Malik	8	– b Rahat Ali 22
S. C. J. Broad not out	13	– c Shoaib Malik b Yasir Shah 20
J. M. Anderson b Shoaib Malik	7	– (11) not out 0
B. A. Stokes b Shoaib Malik	0	– (10) st Sarfraz Ahmed b Yasir Shah . 12
L-b 6, n-b 4	10	B 7, w 1, n-b 1 9

1/19 (2) 2/90 (1) 3/97 (4) (126.5 overs) 306   1/34 (1) 2/34 (3) (60.3 overs) 156
4/139 (3) 5/228 (5) 6/245 (6)   3/48 (4) 4/57 (5)
7/285 (8) 8/287 (7) 9/296 (10) 10/306 (11)   5/58 (6) 6/59 (7) 7/108 (8)
   8/138 (9) 9/150 (2) 10/156 (10)

Rahat Ali 22–12–48–2; Yasir Shah 36–3–99–3; Wahab Riaz 20.5–5–33–0; Zulfiqar Babar 37–6–80–1; Shoaib Malik 9.5–3–33–4; Azhar Ali 2–0–7–0. *Second innings*—Rahat Ali 5–1–23–1; Wahab Riaz 5–0–25–0; Zulfiqar Babar 18.5–5–31–2; Shoaib Malik 15–4–26–3; Yasir Shah 17.3–2–44–4.

Umpires: C. B. Gaffaney and B. N. J. Oxenford.   Third umpire: P. R. Reiffel.
Referee: A. J. Pycroft.

At Abu Dhabi (Nursery 1), November 8, 2015. **England XI won by 161 runs. ‡England XI 342-8** (50 overs) (A. D. Hales 67, M. M. Ali 76); **Hong Kong 181** (43 overs) (Babar Hayat 78; D. J. Willey 4-43). *Both sides chose from 13 players. The ECB came in for some criticism when it was decided not to elevate this game to official ODI status. But Hong Kong had been a late replacement for a UAE XI, and said they did not expect the English authorities to fund the match costs required for an official game, thought to be around £50,000. Jason Roy (42) and Alex Hales gave England a good* *start, and later Ali smashed 76 from 36 balls, with five sixes and six fours. Hong Kong's batsmen struggled, apart from Babar Hayat, who hit eight fours; he added 81 with 18-year-old wicketkeeper Chris Carter, who made 34.*

LIMITED-OVERS INTERNATIONAL REPORTS BY JOHN WESTERBY

PAKISTAN v ENGLAND

First One-Day International

At Abu Dhabi, November 11, 2015 (day/night). Pakistan won by six wickets. Toss: England.

England's recently revamped side began this series eager to maintain the white-ball momentum they had gained during the summer, but were perhaps a little over-eager at first. After being undone by spin in the Tests, they found themselves surprised by Pakistan's seamers, and never fully recovered from losing three wickets in the first 19 deliveries. Roy was bowled pushing half-forward to the second ball of the game, Mohammad Irfan curling an inswinger between bat and pad. Root fell leg-before when Anwar Ali nipped one back, then Hales departed to a juggling catch at slip by Younis Khan, who had been recalled after a poor World Cup, only to announce on the morning of the game that this would be his final one-day international; Shaharyar Khan, the chairman of the Pakistan Cricket Board, criticised the timing of the decision. From 14 for three, Morgan and Taylor forged a restorative stand of 133. But both fell in a second cluster of wickets, this time four in 32 balls, including a poor call from Taylor that led to the run-out of Buttler. Topley, in his second one-day international, gave England brief hope, swinging the new ball to take three early wickets, including Younis for nine. But Mohammad Hafeez, continuing his form from the Tests, went on to reach his 11th ODI hundred – and first against England – while Babar Azam confirmed his promise with a sparky unbeaten half-century. An ultimately straightforward win came with more than six overs to spare.

Man of the Match: Mohammad Hafeez.

England

J. J. Roy b Mohammad Irfan	0	
A. D. Hales c Younis Khan b Anwar Ali	10	
J. E. Root lbw b Anwar Ali	0	
*E. J. G. Morgan c Sarfraz Ahmed b Shoaib Malik	76	
J. W. A. Taylor c Azhar Ali b Shoaib Malik	60	
†J. C. Buttler run out	1	
M. M. Ali c Babar Azam b Yasir Shah	7	
C. R. Woakes run out	33	
A. U. Rashid c sub (Zafar Gohar) b Mohammad Irfan	7	
D. J. Willey b Mohammad Irfan	13	
R. J. W. Topley not out	0	

L-b 5, w 4 9

1/0 (1) 2/7 (3)   (49.4 overs) 216
3/14 (2) 4/147 (4)
5/148 (6) 6/157 (5)
7/161 (7) 8/180 (9)
9/213 (10) 10/216 (8)   10 overs: 46-3

Mohammad Irfan 10–2–35–3; Anwar Ali 6–0–32–2; Shoaib Malik 10–0–45–2; Yasir Shah 10–0–38–1; Wahab Riaz 9.4–1–29–0; Bilal Asif 4–0–32–0.

Pakistan

*Azhar Ali lbw b Topley	8	
Bilal Asif lbw b Topley	2	
Mohammad Hafeez not out	102	
Younis Khan c Rashid b Topley	9	
Shoaib Malik c Roy b Ali	26	
Babar Azam not out	62	

B 2, l-b 2, w 4 8

1/12 (1) 2/15 (2)   (4 wkts, 43.4 overs) 217
3/41 (4) 4/111 (5)   10 overs: 41-3

†Sarfraz Ahmed, Anwar Ali, Wahab Riaz, Yasir Shah and Mohammad Irfan did not bat.

Willey 7–0–43–0; Topley 9–1–26–3; Woakes 8.4–0–40–0; Rashid 9–0–60–0; Ali 7–0–32–1; Root 3–0–12–0.

Umpires: Ahsan Raza and J. D. Cloete.   Third umpire: C. B. Gaffaney.
Referee: R. S. Madugalle.

PAKISTAN v ENGLAND

Second One-Day International

At Abu Dhabi, November 13, 2015 (day/night). England won by 95 runs. Toss: England. One-day international debut: Iftikhar Ahmed.

Hales made his first one-day international hundred to help England square the series. They had clearly heeded the lessons from the first game, as the batsmen permitted themselves more time to calibrate their strokeplay to the demands of another slow pitch. Hales began as the junior partner in a measured opening stand of 102 inside 18 overs with Roy, then put on 114 with Root. By the time he brought up his century, from 111 balls – ending a drought in which he had not passed 27 in nine international innings – England looked primed for a big score. It did not quite happen. Hales was stumped as he swept at the debutant Iftikhar Ahmed's off-spin, then Root and Morgan grew frustrated in their attempts to accelerate – partly because of the pitch, partly because of some excellent death bowling from Wahab Riaz and Mohammad Irfan. Only 56 runs came from the last ten overs, raising hopes among Pakistanis in a Friday crowd of about 10,000. They were soon disappointed: Willey swung one back into Babar Azam, and pushed another across Mohammad Hafeez. Pakistan's middle order then subsided, a slump typified by Shoaib Malik's careless pull to short midwicket. That was one of four scalps for Woakes, who had gone wicketless in his previous six ODIs, stretching back to the World Cup.

Man of the Match: A. D. Hales.

England

J. J. Roy c Shoaib Malik b Wahab Riaz	54	J. W. A. Taylor not out		9
A. D. Hales st Sarfraz Ahmed		M. M. Ali not out		2
b Iftikhar Ahmed	109	L-b 3, w 3		6
J. E. Root b Wahab Riaz	63			
E. J. G. Morgan c Babar Azam		1/102 (1) 2/216 (2)	(5 wkts, 50 overs)	283
b Mohammad Irfan	29	3/256 (3) 4/270 (5)		
J. C. Buttler b Wahab Riaz	11	5/274 (4)	10 overs: 51-0	

C. R. Woakes, A. U. Rashid, D. J. Willey and R. J. W. Topley did not bat.

Mohammad Irfan 10–0–46–1; Anwar Ali 9–0–48–0; Yasir Shah 9–0–70–0; Wahab Riaz 10–0–43–3; Shoaib Malik 6–0–42–0; Iftikhar Ahmed 6–0–31–1.

Pakistan

Azhar Ali b Woakes	22	Yasir Shah not out		16
Babar Azam lbw b Willey	4	Mohammad Irfan b Topley		0
Mohammad Hafeez c Buttler b Willey	0			
Iftikhar Ahmed c Willey b Woakes	5	B 7, l-b 8, w 4		19
Shoaib Malik c Taylor b Woakes	13			
Mohammad Rizwan b Rashid	17	1/5 (2) 2/10 (3) 3/24 (4)	(45.5 overs)	188
Sarfraz Ahmed c Buttler b Woakes	64	4/46 (5) 5/50 (1) 6/80 (6)		
Anwar Ali c Woakes b Ali	23	7/145 (8) 8/163 (9) 9/181 (7)		
Wahab Riaz c Buttler b Willey	5	10/188 (11)	10 overs: 19-2	

Willey 8–0–25–3; Topley 9.5–1–33–1; Woakes 8–0–33–4; Rashid 10–0–32–1; Ali 10–0–50–1.

Umpires: C. B. Gaffaney and Shozab Raza.   Third umpire: J. D. Cloete.
Referee: R. S. Madugalle.

> " Dhoni said the Associate nations deserved more opportunities against Full Members, before adding: 'Not against India.'"
> India v UAE, World Cup, page 905

PAKISTAN v ENGLAND

Third One-Day International

At Sharjah, November 17, 2015 (day/night). England won by six wickets. Toss: Pakistan. One-day international debut: Zafar Gohar.

Taylor's skill against spin was once again in evidence as England claimed a 2–1 lead on a turning pitch. He and Buttler, who returned to form in an unbroken fifth-wicket stand of 117, rescued them from a perilous 93 for four to overcome Pakistan's 208 with all of nine overs to spare. Using his feet nimbly and sweeping decisively, Taylor finished with 67 from 69 balls, and Buttler on 49 from 50, his first innings of substance for England for more than five months. Mohammad Irfan had bowled a hostile opening spell to account for Roy, and Taylor and Buttler came together when Shoaib Malik and Zafar Gohar, the debutant left-arm spinner, were turning the ball sharply. But Sarfraz Ahmed missed a stumping off Shoaib before Buttler had scored; Pakistan would not get another opportunity. Their own innings had featured an extraordinary collapse from 132 for two. Three of the top six fell to absurd run-outs, and five others provided catches on the boundary. Woakes finished with another haul of four as the last eight wickets tumbled for 76. It was a capitulation of such baffling incompetence that the former England captain Michael Vaughan tweeted: "I hate the fact we watch cricket with so much suspicion. It shouldn't be that way." Some late blows from Wahab Riaz gave Pakistan's total a veneer of respectability, but their efforts had been pitiful.

Man of the Match: J. W. A. Taylor.

Pakistan

*Azhar Ali run out	36	Zafar Gohar c Buttler b Woakes	15	
Babar Azam c Rashid b Woakes	22	Mohammad Irfan b Woakes	0	
Mohammad Hafeez c Root b Willey	45			
†Sarfraz Ahmed c sub (C. J. Jordan) b Ali	26	L-b 1, w 3	4	
Shoaib Malik run out	16			
Mohammad Rizwan run out	1	1/45 (2) 2/92 (1) 3/132 (3) (49.5 overs) 208		
Iftikhar Ahmed c Root b Woakes	3	4/135 (4) 5/138 (6) 6/145 (7)		
Anwar Ali c Ali b Topley	7	7/156 (8) 8/161 (5) 9/187 (10)		
Wahab Riaz not out	33	10/208 (11) 10 overs: 43-0		

Willey 10–0–45–1; Topley 10–0–41–1; Woakes 9.5–0–40–4; Rashid 10–1–51–0; Ali 10–0–30–1.

England

J. J. Roy c Shoaib Malik b Mohammad Irfan	7	†J. C. Buttler not out	49
A. D. Hales c Mohammad Rizwan b Zafar Gohar	30	B 2, l-b 3, w 6	11
J. E. Root c Iftikhar Ahmed b Zafar Gohar	11		
*E. J. G. Morgan b Shoaib Malik	35	1/12 (1) 2/27 (3) (4 wkts, 41 overs) 210	
J. W. A. Taylor not out	67	3/87 (2) 4/93 (4) 10 overs: 41-2	

M. M. Ali, C. R. Woakes, A. U. Rashid, D. J. Willey and R. J. W. Topley did not bat.

Mohammad Irfan 7–0–29–1; Anwar Ali 3–0–17–0; Zafar Gohar 10–0–54–2; Wahab Riaz 6–0–23–0; Iftikhar Ahmed 4–0–18–0; Shoaib Malik 9–0–56–1; Azhar Ali 2–0–8–0.

Umpires: J. D. Cloete and Shozab Raza. Third umpire: C. B. Gaffaney.
Referee: R. S. Madugalle.

PAKISTAN v ENGLAND

Fourth One-Day International

At Dubai, November 20, 2015 (day/night). England won by 84 runs. Toss: England.

The fickleness of form had seldom been more starkly illustrated than in Jos Buttler's fortunes on this tour. Dropped from the Test team a couple of weeks earlier, he rediscovered his touch in spectacular fashion, paving the way for England's 3–1 series win with an imperious 46-ball

The late show: despite not reaching the crease until the 36th over, Jos Buttler finds time to make a savage hundred.

century. He sliced a full 15 deliveries off his own record for the fastest one-day hundred for England, set against Sri Lanka at Lord's 18 months earlier, having also scored the next-quickest, off 66 balls, against New Zealand at Edgbaston in June. Roy hit a century too, his first in international cricket, and a total of 355 for five was England's highest overseas, surpassing 340 for six against New Zealand at Napier in 2007-08. Buttler's final tally of 116 not out from 52 balls included eight sixes, the most by an England batsman in a one-day innings (Andrew Flintoff hit seven against West Indies at Lord's in 2004). But even the statistics did scant justice to his strokeplay. He seemed to make use of all 360 degrees, with powerful drives back over the bowler's head, ramps over his own, and sweeps of every description. Having zipped to 50 from 30 balls, he needed only 16 more to reach his hundred, with a six – his third in four deliveries – over midwicket off Anwar Ali. Buttler had come in with England already well placed, on 194 for two, after Roy had demonstrated there was more to his game than quick starts, and a sparkling run-a-ball 71 from Root. The last ten overs yielded 129. Pakistan raced off in reply and, while Shoaib Malik was compiling a 31-ball half-century, an unlikely pursuit remained alive.

But a superb diving catch from Hales, running in from midwicket, ended his flurry, and the spinners did the rest.

Man of the Match: J. C. Buttler.   *Man of the Series:* J. C. Buttler.

England

J. J. Roy c Babar Azam b Yasir Shah 102	M. M. Ali not out	4
A. D. Hales c Shoaib Malik		
b Mohammad Irfan . 22		
J. E. Root st Sarfraz Ahmed b Azhar Ali . . . 71		
†J. C. Buttler not out 116	L-b 4, w 8, n-b 1	13
*E. J. G. Morgan st Sarfraz Ahmed		
b Azhar Ali . 14	1/54 (2) 2/194 (1) (5 wkts, 50 overs) 355	
J. W. A. Taylor c Ahmed Shehzad	3/201 (3) 4/227 (5)	
b Mohammad Irfan . 13	5/306 (6) 10 overs: 51-0	

C. R. Woakes, A. U. Rashid, D. J. Willey and R. J. W. Topley did not bat.

Mohammad Irfan 10–0–64–2; Anwar Ali 9–0–75–0; Wahab Riaz 9–0–70–0; Yasir Shah 10–0–57–1; Shoaib Malik 7–0–59–0; Azhar Ali 5–0–26–2.

Pakistan

*Azhar Ali c and b Willey 44	Yasir Shah c Woakes b Ali	5
Ahmed Shehzad c Ali b Willey 13	Mohammad Irfan not out	0
Mohammad Hafeez run out 37		
Babar Azam c Hales b Rashid 51	L-b 2, w 7	9
Shoaib Malik c Hales b Topley 52		
Mohammad Rizwan c Buttler b Rashid. . . . 11	1/45 (2) 2/64 (1) 3/129 (3) (40.4 overs) 271	
†Sarfraz Ahmed c Willey b Rashid 24	4/176 (4) 5/194 (6) 6/228 (5)	
Anwar Ali c Rashid b Ali 24	7/249 (7) 8/259 (9) 9/271 (10)	
Wahab Riaz c and b Ali 1	10/271 (8) 10 overs: 71-2	

Willey 6–0–34–2; Topley 7–0–58–1; Woakes 8–1–46–0; Ali 9.4–0–53–3; Rashid 10–0–78–3.

Umpires: Ahsan Raza and C. B. Gaffaney.   Third umpire: J. D. Cloete.
Referee: R. S. Madugalle.

At Abu Dhabi, November 23, 2015 (floodlit). **England XI won by 79 runs. England XI 174-6** (20 overs) (J. J. Roy 59, A. D. Hales 40); ‡United Arab Emirates 95-9 (20 overs) (M. M. Ali 4-11). *England chose from 15 players and the UAE from 17. England already had 92 on the board when Roy was out in the seventh over, after hitting 59 from 29 balls, with 48 in boundaries. The UAE struggled to 43-5, and Ali mopped up.*

PAKISTAN v ENGLAND

First Twenty20 International

At Dubai, November 26, 2015 (floodlit). England won by 14 runs. Toss: England. Twenty20 international debuts: Rafatullah Mohmand; J. M. Vince.

With one eye on the forthcoming World Twenty20, England adopted a rotation policy for this series, and Sam Billings was the fringe candidates who most advanced his case. They had slipped to 19 for three, but – in the absence of the rested Jos Buttler and Joe Root – were rescued by a stand of 76 in ten overs between Vince and Morgan. Vince hit a composed 41 on his Twenty20 international debut, then left centre stage to Billings. Employing strong wrists to good effect, he flicked Sohail Tanvir through midwicket and scooped Wahab Riaz over fine leg for six, reaching his maiden international fifty from 24 balls. Pakistan also included untested players: Rafatullah Mohmand, a

39-year-old opening batsman, and Imran Khan, a left-arm medium-pacer (not the Imran Khan who had featured in the first two Tests; this one had played two previous T20 internationals in Zimbabwe). But Rafatullah was one of two early wickets for Plunkett, who bowled rapidly in his first meaningful game of a long tour, and Pakistan soon slumped to 75 for seven. Their collapse included a comical run-out, with Umar Akmal and Sohaib Maqsood racing each other to the bowler's end; Maqsood's longer reach prevailed. Topley then nipped Wahab's late fightback in the bud.

Man of the Match: S. W. Billings.

England

		B	4/6
1 J. J. Roy *c 11 b 9*	9	6	1
2 A. D. Hales *c 7 b 8*	8	9	1
3 J. M. Vince *b 10*	41	36	6/1
4 M. M. Ali *c 6 b 9*	0	6	0
5 *E. J. G. Morgan *not out*	45	38	3/1
6 †S. W. Billings *run out*	53	25	5/2
L-b 2, w 2	4		

6 overs: 40-3   (20 overs) 160-5

1/16 2/18 3/19 4/95 5/160

7 A. U. Rashid, 8 C. J. Jordan, 9 S. D. Parry, 10 L. E. Plunkett and 11 R. J. W. Topley did not bat.

Anwar Ali 4–0–19–1 (12); Sohail Tanvir 4–1–31–2 (10); Wahab Riaz 4–0–33–1 (10); Shahid Afridi 4–0–33–0 (9); Imran Khan 4–0–42–0 (4).

Pakistan

		B	4/6
1 Rafatullah Mohmand *c 6 b 10*	16	20	1
2 †Sarfraz Ahmed *c 10 b 11*	1	2	0
3 Mohammad Hafeez *c 11 b 10*	7	7	1
4 Mohammad Rizwan *b 9*	6	9	1
5 Sohaib Maqsood *st 6 b 4*	24	16	1/1
6 Umar Akmal *run out*	19	14	1/1
7 *Shahid Afridi *c 1 b 9*	0	2	0
8 Anwar Ali *c 5 b 10*	20	14	0/2
9 Sohail Tanvir *not out*	25	22	2/1
10 Wahab Riaz *c 4 b 11*	21	13	4
11 Imran Khan, jun. *c 6 b 11*	0	1	0
L-b 1, w 6	7		

6 overs: 32-3   (20 overs) 146

1/8 2/20 3/25 4/42 5/74 6/74 7/75 8/100 9/145

Jordan 4–0–37–0 (10); Topley 4–0–24–3 (13); Plunkett 4–0–21–3 (13); Ali 4–0–30–1 (9); Parry 4–0–33–2 (10).

Umpires: Ahsan Raza and Shozab Raza.   Third umpire: Ahmed Shahab.
Referee: R. S. Madugalle.

PAKISTAN v ENGLAND

Second Twenty20 International

At Dubai, November 27, 2015 (floodlit). England won by three runs. Toss: England.

England clinched the series when Woakes held his nerve with the last ball, which Anwar Ali needed to hit for four. But he failed to connect with a yorker outside off stump, ensuring that Pakistan's late surge, inspired by Shahid Afridi, proved in vain. The frantic final stages were a test for Buttler, captaining England – and indeed any senior side – for the first time while Eoin Morgan sat out; Buttler reclaimed the gloves from Billings. When Afridi came in, Pakistan were 120 for six following a tidy spell from Rashid, and still required 53 from 20 balls. But, in front of an adoring full house, he blasted Woakes for three sixes in five deliveries – the third of them a no-ball on height – during the 18th over, only to fall to the sixth, slicing to short third man. Pakistan wanted 11 from the last over, and though Sohail Tanvir swung the second ball through square leg for four, Woakes proved equal to the task. Vince had top-scored for England with a fluent 38 from 24 balls, before becoming one of three victims for Afridi. But Buttler hit three sixes to propel them to a total that, in the end, was just enough.

Man of the Match: L. E. Plunkett.

England

		B	4/6
1 J. J. Roy c 7 b 8	29	22	1/2
2 A. D. Hales *lbw* b 8	11	11	1
3 J. M. Vince c 9 b 8...........	38	24	3/2
4 J. E. Root c 8 b 4	20	16	1/1
5 *‡J. C. Buttler c 7 b 10	33	22	1/3
6 S. W. Billings c 6 b 11	11	9	0/1
7 D. J. Willey c 5 b 9	4	5	0
8 L. E. Plunkett c 7 b 9	1	2	0
9 C. R. Woakes *not out*........	15	7	2
10 A. U. Rashid *not out*	3	2	0
L-b 1, w 6	7		

6 overs: 45-1   (20 overs) 172-8

1/32 2/47 3/74 4/109 5/136 6/150 7/151 8/154

11 S. D. Parry did not bat.

Anwar Ali 4–0–27–2 (7); Sohail Tanvir 4–0–43–1 (8); Wahab Riaz 4–0–44–1 (5); Shahid Afridi 4–0–15–3 (13); Ahmed Shehzad 1–0–10–0 (0); Shoaib Malik 3–0–32–1 (4).

Pakistan

		B	4/6
1 Ahmed Shehzad *st 5 b 11*	28	18	2/2
2 Rafatullah Mohmand *st 5 b 10* .	23	24	3
3 Mohammad Hafeez c 7 b 8	25	20	3/1
4 Shoaib Malik c 6 b 8	26	21	1/1
5 Sohaib Maqsood *b 10*	2	6	0
6 Umar Akmal c 5 b 8	3	5	0
7 ‡Sarfraz Ahmed *b 9*..........	19	13	1/1
8 *Shahid Afridi c 8 b 9	24	8	1/3
9 Anwar Ali *not out*	3	4	0
10 Sohail Tanvir *not out*	6	3	1
L-b 2, w 6, n-b 2	10		

6 overs: 54-1   (20 overs) 169-8

1/51 2/60 3/90 4/93 5/107 6/120 7/148 8/162

11 Wahab Riaz did not bat.

Willey 4–0–43–0 (5); Woakes 4–0–40–2 (12); Plunkett 4–0–33–3 (8); Parry 4–0–33–1 (9); Rashid 4–0–18–2 (12).

Umpires: Ahmed Shahab and Shozab Raza.   Third umpire: Ahsan Raza.
Referee: R. S. Madugalle.

PAKISTAN v ENGLAND

Third Twenty20 International

At Sharjah, November 30, 2015 (floodlit). England won after an eliminator over, following a tie. Toss: England. Twenty20 international debut: Aamer Yamin.

Neither Chris Jordan nor England had been involved in a super over before, yet the response to Twenty20's tie-breaker was magnificent. Jordan delivered six precise yorkers, restricting Shahid Afridi and Umar Akmal to two leg-byes and a single. It meant Morgan and Buttler could almost pace themselves against Afridi's leg-spin, leaving England with their first Twenty20 wins out of five in 2015. That the scores had finished level after 20 overs apiece was thanks to another skilful piece of death bowling by Woakes, who limited Pakistan to two runs from the last four balls. That included the wicket of Shoaib Malik, who departed for an enterprising 75 from 54 deliveries when he drove the penultimate ball hard to long-on. Earlier, Aamer Yamin, a bustling seamer, had produced a sharp nip-backer to remove Roy with his first ball in Twenty20 internationals. Root sparkled briefly, and Vince – starved of the strike – played an anchor role before he fell to the penultimate delivery of the innings. But Woakes hit a valuable 37 from 24, then intervened with the ball as England finished their tour on an optimistic note.

Man of the Match: Shoaib Malik. *Man of the Series:* J. M. Vince.

England

		B	4/6
1 J. J. Roy *lbw b 10*	0	1	0
2 J. M. Vince *c 6 b 8*	46	45	3/1
3 J. E. Root *b 7*	32	22	4/1
4 M. M. Ali *c and b 7*	0	1	0
5 *E. J. G. Morgan *b 4*	15	14	0/1
6 †J. C. Buttler *run out*	2	3	0
7 S. W. Billings *c 6 b 9*	7	8	1
8 C. R. Woakes *c 6 b 8*	37	24	1/3
9 D. J. Willey *not out*	3	2	0
10 C. J. Jordan *not out*	0	0	0
L-b 4, w 8	12		

6 overs: 48-3   (20 overs) 154-8

1/0 2/48 3/48 4/68 5/75 6/86 7/146 8/152

11 A. U. Rashid did not bat.

Aamer Yamin 2-0-12-1 (7); Sohail Tanvir 4-0-36-2 (8); Mohammad Irfan 4-0-40-0 (9); Shahid Afridi 4-0-19-2 (7); Anwar Ali 4-0-35-1 (11); Shoaib Malik 2-0-8-1 (6).

Pakistan

		B	4/6
1 Ahmed Shehzad *b 9*	4	5	1
2 Rafatullah Mohmand *lbw b 9*	0	1	0
3 Mohammad Hafeez *run out*	1	1	0
4 Shoaib Malik *c 7 b 8*	75	54	8/2
5 †Mohammad Rizwan *c and b 11*	24	23	4
6 Umar Akmal *c 10 b 4*	4	9	0
7 *Shahid Afridi *b 9*	29	20	0/3
8 Sohail Tanvir *not out*	10	7	0/1
9 Anwar Ali *not out*	0	0	0
B 1, l-b 1, w 5	7		

6 overs: 40-3   (20 overs) 154-7

1/5 2/9 3/11 4/50 5/65 6/128 7/153

10 Aamer Yamin and 11 Mohammad Irfan did not bat.

Willey 4-0-36-3 (9); Woakes 4-0-26-1 (11); Jordan 4-0-39-0 (5); Rashid 4-0-29-1 (9); Ali 4-0-22-1 (13).

Eliminator over: **Pakistan 3-1** (1 over) (Shahid Afridi 0*, Umar Akmal 1, Extras 2; Jordan 1-0-1-1 (5)); **England 4-0** (0.5 over) (Morgan 3*, Buttler 1*; Shahid Afridi 0.5-0-4-0 (2)).

Umpires: Ahmed Shahab and Ahsan Raza. Third umpire: Shozab Raza.
Referee: R. S. Madugalle.

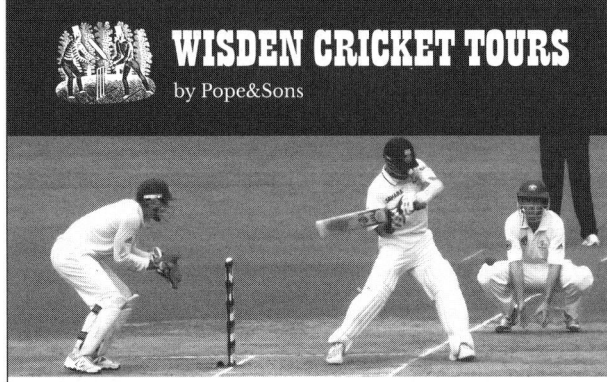

SOUTH AFRICA v ENGLAND IN 2015-16

Review by Stephen Brenkley

Test matches (4): South Africa 1, England 2
One-day internationals (5): South Africa 3, England 2
Twenty20 internationals (2): South Africa 2, England 0

Few Test series have everything, but the four matches between South Africa and England came mighty close. They contained imperishable, sometimes record-breaking, individual performances, a dramatic resignation, the emergence of two black players who may yet change the course of the game in their country, and an unexpected 2–1 triumph for the tourists.

South Africa had the leading run-scorer in Hashim Amla – revitalised, even freed, by his decision to give up the captaincy halfway through the series – the leading wicket-taker in Kagiso Rabada, and the leading outfield catcher in Dean Elgar. They had more centuries (six to three) and five-wicket hauls (four to one). Yet England, despite some obvious weaknesses – especially in their batting and catching – thoroughly deserved victory, which removed their opponents from the No. 1 spot in the rankings. Only a late meltdown in the limited-overs matches robbed the tour of some of its gloss.

Alastair Cook's team secured the Test series with overwhelming wins in the first game at Durban, by 241 runs, and the third at Johannesburg, by seven wickets. If the initial victory was a collective effort, the next yielded scintillating exhibitions from Joe Root and Stuart Broad, whose burst of five for one in 31 balls was among the greatest spells by an England bowler. The Second Test at Cape Town was drawn, but produced a litany of memorable displays, most spectacularly from Ben Stokes, who scored England's fastest double-hundred, and shared a Test-record sixth-wicket stand of 399 with Jonny Bairstow.

The fourth match at Centurion, a dead rubber, went resoundingly to South Africa. Although it was difficult to dispel the feeling that England played as a team who had already completed their mission, this should not diminish the redemptive nature of their hosts' win. Nor did it detract from the contributions of Rabada, who took 13 wickets – to give him 22 in the series at 21 apiece – and Temba Bavuma, who embellished his charming maiden hundred, at Cape Town, the first by a black South African, with another vivid innings. They represented the hope that cricket in their country could be truly inclusive.

But it was Stokes who was Man of the Series. Consistently dazzling with the bat – his strike-rate was a one-day-like 109 – he was increasingly impressive with the ball. He was the first to score 400 runs and take ten wickets in a series for England since Andrew Flintoff during the 2005 Ashes. These seven weeks may come to be seen as Stokes's coming of age as an all-rounder of the highest calibre. But too many of the rest were less productive, leaving England with unresolved issues that included at least three places in the batting order and, that old chestnut, the requirements of the modern-day wicketkeeper. Of equal

Fast forward: Kagiso Rabada's pace troubled England throughout.

concern was the manner in which they gave up a 2–0 lead in the one-day series, then disintegrated in the final Twenty20 match.

If England began as underdogs, South Africa had their own difficulties, having recently returned from a 3–0 mauling in India, where their concerns were many and varied. They started at the top – with the widespread opinion that the understated Amla was the wrong captain – but embraced the balance of the side in all respects. Almost a quarter of a century after readmission, the quota system was still causing angst. But that was compounded by the simpler issue of how many bowlers and batsmen should be in the team. The injuries to the new-ball partners Dale Steyn, who played only the first game, and Vernon Philander, unfit throughout, exacerbated the selectoral muddle. The impression was of constant bewilderment, with players added match by match, and 17 used in all – four of them only once, and four twice. England, by contrast, needed only 12, with Chris Woakes's presence in the first and last games prompted by injuries.

There could hardly have been a falser portent than when Steyn removed both their openers inside seven overs on the first day in Durban. England went on to record their first victory in the opening Test of an overseas series – Bangladesh excepted – since defeating the same opponents in Port Elizabeth 11 years earlier. But their diligent recovery was itself an unreliable guide to subsequent events.

It was marshalled by Nick Compton and James Taylor, the chief beneficiaries of a restructured batting order. Compton had not played Test cricket since May 2013, when he was dropped, partly because of form, and partly – it was widely inferred – because his face did not fit. But, at Durban, he offered a minor

THE ARREST OF WALTER READ

Expense account

DEAN ALLEN

The journey home for England's cricketers from South Africa has not always been as uneventful as it was in late February 2016. Almost 125 years earlier, they arrived in the country for a tour which would finish with the arrest of their captain, Walter Read, as the team boarded the ship, following a pay dispute with the trip's organiser, James Logan.

A Scotsman born in 1857 in Reston, a working-class Berwickshire village, Logan had arrived in Cape Town in 1877, when British imperial intentions were focused upon achieving control of the region. Having acquired great wealth through insider trading and shady diamond deals, he made a name for himself by setting up a model village, with all the latest trappings of Victorian Britain, in Matjiesfontein, over 130 miles north-east of Cape Town, where locals quickly christened him the "Laird". His support of first-class cricket was part of his overall strategy of personal advancement.

The first tour with which he was associated was Read's, in 1891-92 – the second by England to South Africa, following C. Aubrey Smith's side three years earlier. At the time, W. G. Grace was busy leading another England team, to Australia, and it was thought there would be little interest among the South African public. This proved the case – and a year later Logan was in court contesting repayment of his investment.

The dispute revolved around the sum of £750, lent by Logan to Read, a Surrey amateur, and Edwin Ash, the team secretary. Ash claimed the loan was to be paid back only from tour profits. Logan, however, had allegedly told him that "he did not make money out of sport, but only wanted his money back with reasonable interest" – and before the team left for England. Fearing he would not be repaid, Logan had Read and Ash arrested moments before their departure for England on March 23, 1892. They were released on giving security, pending an action, and were eventually allowed – along with the rest of the embarrassed England team – to sail home.

If ever proof were needed of the financial motives behind these early tours in the supposedly golden age of amateurism, this case provides it. The essence of Logan's complaint was that his money had been spent dishonourably on the "so-called amateurs", while Read and Ash accused him of profiteering. There was little evidence of this, however, and in a unanimous decision in June 1893 the case was awarded to Logan with full costs.

Not only had he exploited a moral repugnance of shamateurism to his advantage in court, but Read, Billy Murdoch and the other gentleman players suspected of receiving payment were pilloried in the South African press. The *Cape Times* alleged that Read had originally demanded £850 (around £75,000 today) to appear on the tour, and that Murdoch had been paid over £350.

"Everyone knows that the curse of sport at the present day… is the group of evils spoken of familiarly as professionalism," declared the *Cape Argus* the day after Logan's victory. The *Cape Times* added: "The colony will at least be wary of men calling themselves 'amateur' cricketers – men who bargain for payment of up to £850, over and above all first-class touring expenses, before they consent to come out to a young and comparatively poor sporting country like South Africa for a few months' tour, while the acknowledged 'professionals' are only paid a hundred or so apiece."

Dean Allen is the author of Empire, War & Cricket in South Africa: Logan of Matjiesfontein.

masterclass in the craft of batting in unpromising circumstances, leaving the
ball again and again, and playing shots only on his terms. Yet, as the series
wore on, he seemed to neglect this principle, which was so essential to his
style. He was lured into something alien, playing at balls he would have been
wiser to ignore. There was conjecture he had been influenced by remarks made
by England's coach, Trevor Bayliss, about wanting two attacking batsmen in
the top three. Bayliss was not being prescriptive, but the Compton of the last
two Tests was not quite the Compton of the first two.

Taylor, too, never looked as determinedly solid as he did in the First, and
didn't pass 27 in the last three. Instead, it was in another capacity that he left
an impression, taking three stunning catches at short leg, two of them in quick

---

... 'TWERE WELL IT WERE DONE QUICKLY

Highest-known batting strike-rates in a Test series:

SR		Runs	Balls		
121.32	Shahid Afridi	330	272	Pakistan v India	2005-06
119.23	B. B. McCullum	217	182	New Zealand v Sri Lanka	2014-15
114.14	**D. A. Warner**	**226**	**198**	**Australia v West Indies**	**2015-16**
109.01	**B. A. Stokes**	**411**	**377**	**England in South Africa**	**2015-16**
108.62	Shahid Afridi	214	197	Pakistan in West Indies	2004-05
108.14	V. Sehwag	491	454	India v Sri Lanka	2009-10
107.35	Kapil Dev	292	272	India in England	1982
103.28	N. J. Astle	314	304	New Zealand v England	2001-02
102.76	V. Sehwag	372	362	India v South Africa	2007-08
102.69	A. C. Gilchrist	343	334	Australia in New Zealand	2004-05
102.47	I. V. A. Richards	331	323	West Indies v England	1985-86
102.46	A. C. Gilchrist	333	325	Australia v England	2002-03
101.77	A. C. Gilchrist	229	225	Australia v England	2006-07

*Qualification: 200 runs. D. P. M. D. Jayawardene (SL) scored 230 runs in 218 balls (SR 105.50) in
the Asian Test Championship in 2001-02. Full information is not known for many early series.*

---

succession during the march to victory at Johannesburg. In an age when every
ball is analysed, and data processed to the nth degree, short leg has seemed
like an unturned stone. But Taylor reminded us it is a specialist position
demanding specialist skills, as well as bravery.

One other incident in England's victory at Kingsmead provided a motif for
the series. When Amla edged behind early in his first innings, Bairstow –
moving slightly late to his right – muffed the chance. It was the first of seven
lapses behind the stumps – six catches and a missed stumping – which revived
the argument about the basis on which Test wicketkeepers are selected. Sound
judges insisted there was plenty to work on, and Bairstow seemed eager to
learn. And, despite his shortcomings, his 20 victims were a record for England
in a four-match series.

His batting, however, was almost beyond approach. He was at his finest
during the astonishing partnership with Stokes at Newlands. While Stokes
embarked on a blaze of unfettered strokeplay – he later confirmed he wanted
to hit every ball for four or six – Bairstow was an admirable foil. England were

History man: Temba Bavuma became the first black South African to hit a Test century.

left holding the Test partnership records for the sixth, eighth and tenth wickets, all established in the previous six years.

Few nailed-on draws – and England's second-innings wobble barely altered that perception – can have supplied such a welter of drama. Not the least of it came as Bavuma and Rabada, playing together in a Test for the first time, gave a nation hope for the future. Despite concentrated efforts – sometimes frantic, sometimes misguided – in the past 24 years, cricket has not always been a sport of choice among the black population. Stars can change that: Rabada and Bavuma already have. At one hotel on the final morning of the series, the (mostly black) reception staff were excited about impending victory: "We're gonna win today, we're gonna win!" That would not have happened even ten years ago. There were no more exciting words spoken all series.

And it helped soften the blow of Amla's resignation. The timing was odd: he had just returned to form with a double-hundred to ensure England would not go 2–0 up. But he had never seemed comfortable with the captaincy. He had made his mind up, it appeared, before the series started, and the manner of his exit was characteristically dignified – though it could be asked why he was appointed in the first place. The job went to A. B. de Villiers, temporarily at first, then permanently once the Tests were over. A more vocal presence, he delivered occasionally conflicting messages. He wanted the job – and to manage his playing schedule more constructively. As captain of South Africa's one-day team, and one of the most sought-after players in Twenty20 franchise cricket, he faces a constant struggle in an overcrowded programme. While de Villiers never quite confirmed how he might resolve it, his acceptance of the role was an indication of his intentions – despite the discovery that captaincy can brutally affect a player's form: he finished the series with three successive ducks, and rarely looked comfortable against Broad.

FIVE STATS YOU MAY HAVE MISSED

BENEDICT BERMANGE

- Ben Stokes scored 130 runs before lunch on the second day of the Second Test at Cape Town, breaking the 80-year-old record for any day's play:

130	**B. A. Stokes (258)**	**England v South Africa at Cape Town**	**2015-16**
123	L. E. G. Ames (148*)	England v South Africa at The Oval	1935
119	A. B. de Villiers (129)	South Africa v India at Centurion	2010-11
118	W. Bardsley (164)	Australia v South Africa at Lord's	1912
116	C. Hill (142)	Australia v South Africa at Johannesburg	1902-03
114	B. C. Lara (191)	West Indies v Zimbabwe at Bulawayo	2003-04
113	†K. S. Ranjitsinhji (154*)	England v Australia at Manchester	1896
112	C. G. Macartney (151)	Australia v England at Leeds	1926
111	W. R. Hammond (336*)	England v New Zealand at Auckland	1932-33
109	C. P. Mead (182*)	England v Australia at The Oval	1921

† *On Test debut.*

- Only five Test batsmen before Stokes had reached 100 and 200 in the same session:

C. A. Roach (209)	West Indies v England at Georgetown	1929-30
D. G. Bradman (201)	Australia v India at Adelaide	1947-48
D. C. S. Compton (278)	England v Pakistan at Nottingham	1954
N. J. Astle (222)	New Zealand v England at Christchurch	2001-02
M. S. Dhoni (224)	India v Australia at Chennai	2012-13
B. A. Stokes (258)	**England v South Africa at Cape Town**	**2015-16**

- During the Third Test at Johannesburg, Hardus Viljoen became only the second player to hit his first ball in Test cricket for four *and* take a wicket with his first delivery, following Matt Henderson in New Zealand's maiden Test, against England at Christchurch in 1929-30.

- At Johannesburg, all 11 South Africans scored fewer runs in the second innings than in the first. This had occurred only once before in Tests, by Bangladesh in their inaugural match, against India at Dhaka in 2000-01.

- South Africa's 475 in the Fourth Test at Centurion was the lowest all-out total to include three individual centuries, beating 494 by Australia (Bill Woodfull 141, Charles Macartney 151, Arthur Richardson 100) against England at Leeds in 1926.

The first of those ducks came at the Wanderers, where Broad swept aside the entire South African top order, having already made light of the absence of the injured Jimmy Anderson at Durban. In the three matches Steven Finn played before injury struck him down again, he did enough to suggest he was fully restored as a Test fast bowler, claiming 11 wickets at 26. Moeen Ali still took important wickets, including seven at Durban, but at 48 apiece (which more or less cancelled out the contribution of South Africa's own off-spinner, Dane Piedt, who collected ten at 45).

Root bestrode the rest of England's batting like a colossus. He was in too early too often, as at the Wanderers, where his 110 was exemplary. It followed another failure for the opening pair of Cook and Alex Hales; six of their partnerships did not go beyond 22. Hales, Cook's eighth opening partner since Andrew Strauss, played fitfully – and uncertainly enough to suggest there would need to be a ninth.

But England were hardly alone in having a defective top order. South Africa's confused thinking was further reflected by the selection of Stiaan van Zyl, a non-specialist opener, for the first three matches. When they eventually turned to the 33-year-old Stephen Cook, a lifelong opener, they were rewarded with a craftsman's century – and a solid partner for the reliable Elgar.

By then England had run out of steam, and were duly steamrollered. For all the apologies offered, and their assurance that Test cricket remained the acme, they could not disguise the feeling that their work had already been done. For the first time since Michael Vaughan's England lifted the new Basil D'Oliveira Trophy in 2004-05, a visiting team other than Australia had won a Test series in South Africa.

South Africa won both the limited-overs series which followed. If this put into perspective the progress England had made in both formats in recent months, they could – and perhaps should – have won the one-day series.

Victories in the first two matches, with the sort of uninhibited strokeplay which had marked their renaissance, suggested a team full of conviction. Hales, Root and Buttler were at the top of their game. Freed from the confused approach which plagued his batting in the Tests, Hales looked as if he knew once more what he was supposed to do. He finished the 50-over series with a century and four fifties, including 99 to anchor the chase at Port Elizabeth.

England's strategy appeared plain and simple: make big totals at a rapid lick to ease the burden on the bowlers. And in the series opener at Bloemfontein, they reached 399, comfortably their highest score overseas, with Buttler butchering a 73-ball hundred. The trouble occurred when it started to go awry. When Plan A was not working, there was no Plan B, and it cost them dear, as South Africa rediscovered their own reserves of self-belief.

Eoin Morgan's team had one golden chance to take an unassailable lead in the ODI series. At 2–1 ahead, they reduced South Africa to 211 for eight in the fourth match at the Wanderers, still requiring 52 when Rashid put down a steepling catch in the deep off Morris. England lost the plot a little thereafter. South Africa's batsmen, not least de Villiers, found their range.

But England kept contriving to lose quick middle-order wickets, and in the first Twenty20 game missed the chance to force a super over when Topley fumbled Root's over-the-stumps return. The limitations of their bowling were also exposed, with the new ball and at the death, and the tour ended in a humbling defeat at the Wanderers – a few weeks earlier the scene of one of their most memorable Test victories. It was a tour which, ultimately, couldn't quite settle on a storyline.

ENGLAND TOURING PARTY

*A. N. Cook (Essex; T), M. M. Ali (Worcestershire; T/50/20), J. M. Anderson (Lancashire; T), J. M. Bairstow (Yorkshire; T/50), G. S. Ballance (Yorkshire; T), S. W. Billings (Kent; 20), S. C. J. Broad (Nottinghamshire; T/50), J. C. Buttler (Lancashire; T/50/20), N. R. D. Compton (Middlesex; T), S. T. Finn (Middlesex; T), M. H. A. Footitt (Surrey; T), A. D. Hales (Nottinghamshire; T/50/20), C. J. Jordan (Sussex; T/50/20), E. J. G. Morgan (Middlesex; 50/20), S. R. Patel (Nottinghamshire; T), A. U. Rashid (Yorkshire; 50/20), J. E. Root (Yorkshire; T/50/20), J. J. Roy (Surrey; 50/20), B. A. Stokes (Durham; T/50/20), J. W. A. Taylor (Nottinghamshire; T/50), R. J. W. Topley (Hampshire; 50/20), J. M. Vince (Hampshire; 20), D. J. Willey (Yorkshire; 50/20), C. R. Woakes (Warwickshire; T/50/20).

Morgan captained in the limited-overs matches. Finn was originally selected for the whole tour, but strained his side during the Third Test and withdrew from the limited-overs matches; L. E. Plunkett (Yorkshire) was announced as his replacement, but injured his thigh while playing for England Lions, and Broad stayed on instead.

Coach: T. H. Bayliss (T/50/20). *Assistant coach:* P. Farbrace (T/50/20). *Batting coach:* M. R. Ramprakash (T), G. P. Thorpe (50/20). *Fast-bowling coach:* O. D. Gibson (T/50/20). *Spin-bowling coach:* R. D. B. Croft (50). *Consultant coach – wicketkeeping:* B. N. French (T). *Strength and conditioning coach:* P. C. F. Scott (T/50/20). *Operations manager:* P. A. Neale (T), G. A. M. Jackson (50/20). *Team analyst:* N. A. Leamon (T), R. J. Lewis (50/20). *Team doctor:* R. H. J. Young (T), M. G. Wotherspoon (50/20). *Physiotherapist:* C. A. de Weymarn (T/50/20). *Massage therapist:* M. E. S. Saxby (T/50/20). *Security manager:* R. C. Dickason (T/50/20). *Media manager:* R. C. Evans (T/50/20).

TEST MATCH AVERAGES

SOUTH AFRICA – BATTING AND FIELDING

	T	I	NO	R	HS	100	50	Avge	Ct/St
†Q. de Kock	2	3	2	143	129*	1	0	143.00	11
H. M. Amla	4	7	0	470	201	2	1	67.14	1
T. Bavuma	4	7	2	248	102*	1	1	49.60	3
†D. Elgar	4	7	1	284	118*	1	0	47.33	6
C. H. Morris	2	3	0	98	69	0	1	32.66	2
A. B. de Villiers	4	7	0	210	88	0	1	30.00	9/1
F. du Plessis	3	5	0	127	86	0	1	25.40	1
†J-P. Duminy	2	4	1	73	29	0	0	24.33	3
†K. Rabada	3	4	1	42	24	0	0	14.00	0
†S. van Zyl	3	5	0	69	33	0	0	13.80	2
D. L. Piedt	3	3	0	20	19	0	0	6.66	2
†M. Morkel	4	5	1	24	12	0	0	6.00	4
K. J. Abbott	2	3	0	18	16	0	0	6.00	1

Played in one Test: S. C. Cook 115, 25 (2 ct); D. W. Steyn 17, 2; D. J. Vilas 26, 8 (5 ct); G. C. Viljoen 20*, 6.

BOWLING

	Style	O	M	R	W	BB	5I	Avge
D. W. Steyn	RF	29	5	80	4	4-70	0	20.00
K. Rabada	RF	109.4	17	482	22	7-112	3	21.90
S. van Zyl	RM	25.1	4	69	3	3-20	0	23.00
M. Morkel	RF	151.5	34	446	15	4-76	0	29.73
D. L. Piedt	OB	126	25	455	10	5-153	1	45.50
C. H. Morris	RFM	61	10	253	4	1-8	0	63.25

Also bowled: K. J. Abbott (RFM) 66.4–16–174–2; J-P. Duminy (OB) 7–0–28–1; D. Elgar (SLA) 35.4–6–112–2; G. C. Viljoen (RFM) 19–2–94–1.

ENGLAND – BATTING AND FIELDING

	T	I	NO	R	HS	100	50	Avge	Ct/St
J. M. Bairstow	4	7	2	359	150*	1	1	71.80	19/1
†B. A. Stokes	4	7	0	411	258	1	1	58.71	3
J. E. Root	4	8	1	386	110	1	3	55.14	4
N. R. D. Compton	4	8	0	245	85	0	1	30.62	1
†M. M. Ali	4	7	3	116	61	0	1	29.00	1
J. W. A. Taylor	4	8	1	186	70	0	1	26.57	5
†A. N. Cook	4	8	0	184	76	0	1	23.00	2
A. D. Hales	4	8	0	136	60	0	1	17.00	1
C. R. Woakes	2	4	0	54	26	0	0	13.50	1
†S. C. J. Broad	4	5	1	51	32*	0	0	12.75	1
S. T. Finn	3	3	1	12	12	0	0	6.00	0
†J. M. Anderson	3	3	2	5	5*	0	0	5.00	1

BOWLING

	Style	O	M	R	W	BB	5I	Avge
S. C. J. Broad	RFM	139.1	38	371	18	6-17	1	20.61
S. T. Finn	RFM	90.4	16	287	11	4-42	0	26.09
B. A. Stokes	RFM	113.1	15	350	12	4-86	0	29.16
J. M. Anderson	RFM	118.2	29	301	7	3-47	0	43.00
M. M. Ali	OB	161	38	485	10	4-69	0	48.50

Also bowled: A. D. Hales (RM) 3–1–2–0; J. E. Root (OB) 27–5–77–0; C. R. Woakes (RFM) 59.2–9–197–2.

At Potchefstroom, December 15–17, 2015 (not first-class). **Drawn. ‡England XI 470-7 dec** (88 overs) (N. R. D. Compton 58, J. W. A. Taylor 114, B. A. Stokes 158; T. Mnyaka 3-66) **and 190** (52.4 overs) (C. J. Dala 5-34, A. L. Phehlukwayo 3-36); **South African Invitation XI 188** (57.1 overs) (S. C. J. Broad 3-18) **and 5-0** (2 overs). *Both sides chose from 13 players. England made a slow start, losing openers Alastair Cook and Alex Hales for single figures. But Nick Compton settled in, then James Taylor made 114 in four hours. He shared a fifth-wicket stand of 195 with Ben Stokes, who gave a hint of things to come by belting 23 fours and five sixes in 158 from 131 balls. Stuart Broad struck with his fourth delivery of the tour, and the Invitation XI were bowled out nearly 300 behind. England built on their lead, but any hopes of victory were dashed by a thunderstorm, which washed out the last two sessions.*

At Pietermaritzburg, December 20–22, 2015. **England XI won by an innings and 91 runs. South Africa A 136** (56 overs) (S. C. Cook 53*; B. A. Stokes 3-25, S. T. Finn 4-34) **and 187** (42.5 overs) (Q. de Kock 53; M. M. Ali 6-77); **‡England XI 414-6 dec** (97.5 overs) (A. N. Cook 126, A. D. Hales 56, J. E. Root 117, B. A. Stokes 66; K. A. Maharaj 4-129). *England produced a fine performance to despatch a strong South Africa A side, containing four men who would feature in the Test series (and two other Test players). Steven Finn demolished the middle order on the first afternoon with three wickets in nine balls, though Stephen Cook carried his bat, before Alastair Cook and Joe Root constructed a big lead. On the third morning Moeen Ali put a sobering time against Pakistan behind him, finishing with his best figures since taking 6-67 against India at the Rose Bowl in 2014. Finn removed Khaya Zondo for a pair.*

SOUTH AFRICA v ENGLAND

First Test Match

TELFORD VICE

At Durban, December 26–30, 2015. England won by 241 runs. Toss: South Africa. Test debut: A. D. Hales.

Perhaps the South Africans thought they were still in India, where they had been thumped 3–0 only three weeks earlier. Perhaps England thought they were still in the United Arab Emirates, where they had reeled off six victories in seven matches in the shorter formats after losing the Test series. Perhaps that 2–0 defeat by Pakistan was why, the day before the game, Amla said: "Both teams are looking to start the resurgence. Both teams are probably searching for a bit of hope."

A match robbed of its sharpest arrows – a shoulder strain limited Steyn to 29 overs, while James Anderson was ruled out altogether with a calf problem – changed the perceptions and perspectives of those still standing. In England's case, it allowed Woakes to earn his fifth cap, and gave Broad the choice of ends. For South Africa, unsettlingly, it was déjà vu: Steyn had not bowled after the first innings of the First Test in India because of a groin injury. "India was a wake-up call for a lot of us," he said as Kingsmead's Christmas cracker loomed. "We found we're probably not as good as we thought. The boys have hurt. We're going to go back to being a basic cricket team."

Julian Finney, Getty Images

Special delivery: Moeen Ali bowls England to victory, their first in an overseas Test – other than against Bangladesh – since 2004-05.

Anderson would have enjoyed a pitch apparently made for bowls rather than bowling. Indeed, Amla's insertion of England after he won the toss for only the third time in 13 Tests was less a decision than a concession to indecision. But the surface suited the bloody-mindedness of both Elgar, who scored his fourth century, an innings made up of equal parts steadiness and scrapping, and Compton, who – in the city of his birth – made 85 and 49 on his return to Test cricket after a two-and-a-half-year absence. His father, Richard, watched from the Old Fort Road End, and his uncle, Patrick, reported for his newspaper at the Umgeni End. "I don't want to talk to no Compton," joked South Africa's coach, Russell Domingo, when Patrick asked him a press conference question. The understated off-spin of Ali, meanwhile, claimed seven for 116 – which proved enough to trump Compton, and earn him his first match award in Tests.

By stumps on an opening day which lost most of the final session to unseasonal rain, England had overcome the shock of losing Cook, Hales – their latest opener – and Root on just 49 on the board. They were righted by a stand of 125 between Compton and Taylor, which was ended shortly before the close when Taylor was caught behind off a pumped-up Steyn. But Compton was still there, having faced 179 balls for his unbeaten 63. Next day he would smother, ignore, or occasionally think about taking a run out, another 57 deliveries (and, almost always, change his mind). When he finally bottom-edged a pull off Morkel through to de Villiers – who had been asked nicely to keep wicket again, even while rumours swirled about his future – it was as if all South African supporters had been put out of their misery.

Passions boiled over around the tea urn in the commentators' lounge. "Nick Compton is batting too slowly," mused Herschelle Gibbs, once an entertaining opener for South Africa. "You need to score at least three runs an over." That stirred Geoffrey Boycott: "Herschelle bloody Gibbs! I loved you as a player, but you have about as much brains as a bloody squashed tomato!"

Something else must have stirred the South Africans, who took England's last seven wickets for 129 in a total of 303. For the first time since they beat West Indies at home in January 2015, they looked like a team with places to go and things to do – none more than Steyn and Morkel, who claimed eight between them. But, by the close on the second day,

CARRYING BAT FOR SOUTH AFRICA IN A TEST

A. B. Tancred	26*	(47)	v England at Cape Town	1888-89
J. W. Zulch	43*	(103)	v England at Cape Town	1909-10
T. L. Goddard	56*	(99)	v Australia at Cape Town	1957-58
D. J. McGlew	127*	(292)	v New Zealand at Durban	1961-62
G. Kirsten	100*	(239)	v Pakistan at Faisalabad	1997-98
D. Elgar	**118***	**(214)**	**v England at Durban**	**2015-16**

Tancred was the first to achieve the feat in Test cricket.

they had reverted to recent type, and shambled to 137 for four. Broad did most of the wrecking, with superb control of line and length. He bowled van Zyl, who offered no stroke, with the second ball of the innings, and quickly added Amla, who had been dropped by Bairstow off Woakes on two. Broad later claimed the prize scalp of de Villiers, for the eighth time in Tests.

Du Plessis charged fatally at Ali, but Elgar resumed on 67, went to his century an hour into the third morning, and carried his bat for 118. He contributed 55% of his side's total, the most for South Africa since readmission, passing Gibbs's 54% against India at Port Elizabeth in 2001-02. "India didn't give us a lot of confidence, but personally it did me the world of good," he said. "Sometimes you need that kick up the backside." But South Africa had been dismissed, 89 behind. While Broad had bulldozed four at the top, Ali bamboozled four lower down. Finn took the last two in the same over.

Piedt's off-spin, introduced in the eighth over, removed Cook and Hales, before that man Compton and Root threatened to build England's lead out of sight. But, an hour

MOST TEST RUNS IN A CALENDAR YEAR FOR ENGLAND

Runs	Year		T	I	NO	HS	100	50	Avge
1,481	2002	M. P. Vaughan	14	26	2	197	6	2	61.70
1,385	**2015**	**J. E. Root**	**14**	**26**	**3**	**182***	**3**	**10**	**60.21**
1,379	1974	D. L. Amiss	13	22	2	262*	5	3	68.95
1,364	**2015**	**A. N. Cook**	**14**	**26**	**1**	**263**	**3**	**8**	**54.56**
1,343	2006	K. P. Pietersen	14	26	1	158	4	6	53.72
1,325	2010	I. J. L. Trott	14	24	4	226	4	4	66.25
1,323	2005	M. E. Trescothick	13	24	0	194	4	4	55.12
1,287	2010	A. N. Cook	14	24	2	235*	5	4	58.50
1,264	1990	G. A. Gooch	9	17	1	333	4	5	79.00
1,249	2012	A. N. Cook	15	29	3	190	4	3	48.03

before the close, Morkel excised Compton by way of an edge down the leg side. Still, England resumed on the fourth day with a lead already 261 runs large. They also knew they would no longer have to deal with Steyn, who had sent down just 23 balls in their second innings before his shoulder forced him off for good. And they knew South Africa's confidence in their fielding would have been shaken by the three catches they dropped, two of them by the stellar de Villiers.

Taylor helped Root add 73 for the fourth wicket, as Root passed 50 for the 13th time in Tests in 2015 to equal the world record. But it was Bairstow's purposeful 79 off 76 balls that lifted England to their eventual lead of 415. Piedt's five for 153, a labour of something like love, made him the first South African off-spinner to take five or more in a Test innings at Kingsmead since Hugh Tayfield managed eight for 69 against Peter May's England in 1956-57.

South Africa rushed to 53 without loss in the 11th over, only to limp to the close on 136 for four. When Elgar was third out, edging Finn to Root at second slip after tea, he stood for a moment, before perhaps realising he could finally take a break: until then, he had been on the field for all 1,406 minutes of the match. The bristling, bustling Finn also dealt with Amla and du Plessis, which meant only de Villiers could save South Africa on the last day.

But, with the third ball of the morning, Ali – coming round the wicket – pitched a delivery on leg. It stayed low and rapped de Villiers, playing fatally back, on the pads. Aleem Dar gave him out and, after the inevitable review, technology suggested the ball had pitched in line and would have dealt leg stump a glancing blow. Duminy excepted, the rest collapsed in a heap, extending South Africa's slump from the previous evening to seven for 38 inside 25 overs as England surged to a comprehensive victory, with four for Finn and three for Ali, including Bavuma for a duck – England's first Test stumping for three years. It was their sixth win in 16 Tests in Durban, to go with a lone defeat, way back in 1927-28.

The start of the Second Test at Cape Town was just three days away, but Cook – having drawn level with Mike Brearley on 18 victories as captain – couldn't make out Table Mountain for the glow of victory. "You see the guys training, from one to 17 in this squad, and think: 'There are good times ahead.'"

Man of the Match: M. M. Ali.

Close of play: first day, England 179-4 (Compton 63, Stokes 5); second day, South Africa 137-4 (Elgar 67, Bavuma 10); third day, England 172-3 (Root 60, Taylor 24); fourth day, South Africa 136-4 (de Villiers 37, Steyn 0).

England

*A. N. Cook c Elgar b Steyn	0 – lbw b Piedt	7
A. D. Hales c de Villiers b Steyn	10 – c Abbott b Piedt	26
N. R. D. Compton c de Villiers b Morkel	85 – c de Villiers b Morkel	49
J. E. Root lbw b Piedt	24 – c van Zyl b Abbott	73
J. W. A. Taylor c de Villiers b Steyn	70 – st de Villiers b Piedt	42
B. A. Stokes c Duminy b Morkel	21 – c Elgar b Piedt	5
†J. M. Bairstow c Elgar b Abbott	41 – c Duminy b van Zyl	79
M. M. Ali c de Villiers b Morkel	0 – lbw b Piedt	16
C. R. Woakes lbw b Morkel	0 – c Duminy b van Zyl	23
S. C. J. Broad not out	32 – c de Villiers b van Zyl	0
S. T. Finn lbw b Steyn	12 – not out	0
B 1, l-b 3, w 1, n-b 3	8	B 3, l-b 3	6

1/3 (1) 2/12 (2) 3/49 (4)   (100.1 overs) 303   1/13 (1) 2/48 (2)   (102.1 overs) 326
4/174 (6) 5/196 (6) 6/247 (3)   3/119 (3) 4/192 (4)
7/253 (8) 8/253 (9) 9/267 (7) 10/303 (11)   5/197 (6) 6/224 (5) 7/272 (8)
                                       8/315 (9) 9/315 (10) 10/326 (7)

Steyn 25.1–5–70–4; Abbott 24–4–66–1; Morkel 26–5–76–4; Piedt 16–2–63–1; van Zyl 2–1–2–0; Elgar 7–2–22–0. *Second innings*—Steyn 3.5–0–10–0; Morkel 20.3–5–38–1; Abbott 21.4–3–62–1; Piedt 36–4–153–5; Elgar 9–0–32–0; van Zyl 10.1–3–20–3; Duminy 1–0–5–0.

South Africa

S. van Zyl b Broad	0 – (2) b Stokes	33
D. Elgar not out	118 – (1) c Root b Finn	40
*H. M. Amla c Bairstow b Broad	7 – c Bairstow b Finn	12
†A. B. de Villiers c Bairstow b Broad	49 – lbw b Ali	37
F. du Plessis b Ali	2 – c Cook b Finn	9
T. Bavuma b Broad	10 – (7) st Bairstow b Ali	0
J-P. Duminy c Stokes b Ali	2 – (8) not out	26
K. J. Abbott c Taylor b Finn	0 – (9) lbw b Ali	2
D. W. Steyn c Woakes b Ali	17 – (6) b Finn	2
D. L. Piedt c Bairstow b Finn	1 – c Taylor b Woakes	0
M. Morkel c Root b Finn	0 – lbw b Broad	8
B 4, l-b 3, w 1	8	B 2, l-b 3	5

1/0 (1) 2/14 (3) 3/100 (4)   (81.4 overs) 214   1/53 (2) 2/85 (3)   (71 overs) 174
4/113 (5) 5/137 (6) 6/150 (7)   3/88 (1) 4/136 (5)
7/156 (8) 8/210 (9) 9/214 (10) 10/214 (11)   5/136 (4) 6/136 (7) 7/138 (6)
                                       8/143 (9) 9/155 (10) 10/174 (11)

Broad 15–6–25–4; Woakes 14–1–28–0; Ali 25–3–69–4; Finn 15.4–1–49–2; Stokes 9–1–25–0; Root 3–1–11–0. *Second innings*—Broad 13.5–5–29–1; Woakes 10–5–25–1; Finn 15–6–42–4; Stokes 7–1–26–1; Ali 26–9–47–3.

Umpires: Aleem Dar and R. J. Tucker.   Third umpire: B. N. J. Oxenford.
Referee: R. S. Madugalle.

Innings of a lifetime: Ben Stokes blasts his way to 258.

SOUTH AFRICA v ENGLAND

Second Test Match

SIMON WILDE

At Cape Town, January 2–6, 2016. Drawn. Toss: England. Test debut: C. H. Morris.

There were only a few periods when an outright result looked even remotely on the cards – most distinctly on the final day, when England stumbled as they sought to bat out time. But this was a Test that will burn brightly in the memory of anyone who witnessed it. It produced four hundreds, of which two were doubles, and one, by Temba Bavuma –

STOKED!

How Ben Stokes's numbers stacked up:

399 The partnership between Stokes and Jonny Bairstow was the highest for the sixth wicket in all Tests, beating 365* by Kane Williamson and B-J. Watling for New Zealand v Sri Lanka at Wellington in 2014-15. England's previous best was 281, by Graham Thorpe and Andrew Flintoff against New Zealand at Christchurch in 2001-02. Their only higher stand for any wicket was 411, for the fourth, by Peter May and Colin Cowdrey against West Indies at Birmingham in 1957.

258 Stokes's score was the highest in Tests by a No. 6, beating 250 by Doug Walters for Australia v New Zealand at Christchurch in 1976-77. England's previous best was 178, by Graeme Hick against India at Mumbai (Wankhede) in 1992-93.

196 Balls required for Stokes's 250 – the fastest in all Tests, beating 207 by Virender Sehwag during his 293 for India v Sri Lanka at Mumbai (Brabourne) in 2009-10.

196 Runs added by Stokes and Bairstow on the second morning – the second-highest in the first session of any day's play in a Test, behind 225 by South Africa on the third day against India at Centurion in 2010-11, when they went from 366-2 to 591-3.

163 Balls for Stokes's double-century – the only faster one in Tests was reached in 153 balls by Nathan Astle (222), for New Zealand v England at Christchurch in 2001-02. England's previous fastest was 220 balls, by Ian Botham (208) v India at The Oval in 1982.

46.4 Overs required for Stokes and Bairstow's 300 partnership, the fastest in all Tests; Virender Sehwag and Rahul Dravid needed 57.1 for India v Pakistan at Lahore in 2005-06.

11 Sixes hit by Stokes, the most in an innings for England, beating ten by Wally Hammond against New Zealand at Auckland in 1932-33. Wasim Akram holds the Test record with 12, for Pakistan v Zimbabwe at Sheikhupura in 1996-97; there are four other instances of 11, two by Brendon McCullum, and one each by Astle and Matthew Hayden.

---

the first for South Africa by a member of the majority black African population in 127 years of Test cricket – resonated beyond the context of the match itself.

No sooner had the game been called off with 31 overs remaining after a halt for rain, than Cricket South Africa announced Amla was stepping down as Test captain, and handing the reins to de Villiers. As Amla had just batted 11 and three-quarter hours for 201 to keep his side in the contest, it could hardly be said the job was affecting his form in this match, even if this was his first score over 43 in 12 Test innings. But it was clearly a role he found uncomfortable. He felt someone else could do better. The timing may have been a surprise; the sentiment was not.

To what extent Amla's mind had been made up by the innings Stokes played on the first two days, in scorching heat, is unclear. But his murderous assault on South Africa's bowlers, which eventually brought him 258 runs from 198 balls, including 30 fours and 11 sixes, would have driven many captains to distraction. Even seasoned observers were left scratching their heads.

If Amla had a plan for either Stokes or Bairstow, who assisted him in a Test-record sixth-wicket partnership of 399 in 346 balls, the fastest above 200 in Tests, it was not altogether divinable. Five or six men were pinned to the boundary, apparently more in hope than expectation of doing anything useful, while an inexperienced attack, missing the injured Dale Steyn and Kyle Abbott, ploughed on into a storm of unprecedented severity. By moving from 74 to 204 on the second morning, Stokes scored more runs in a pre-lunch Test session than anyone; his double-century, from 163 balls, was the second-fastest in Tests, and his 250, from 196, the fastest. His 258, more than twice his previous best, was the highest for England against South Africa (beating 243 by Eddie Paynter at Durban in 1938-39), and also the highest by a Test No. 6.

Ups and downs: Hashim Amla acknowledges his double-hundred, before resigning as captain.

If Stokes ultimately battered South Africa into submission, it was only after a tooth-and-claw battle for supremacy on the first evening, when England were in danger of squandering a golden opportunity to bat them out of the game. Cook, having usefully won his first toss in five, fell to a blinding catch by the newcomer Chris Morris at third slip, while Hales, after applying himself well for a maiden Test fifty, also edged into the slips on a pitch with decent bounce. The potential killer was losing the adhesive Compton, then Taylor, to successive deliveries from the waspish Rabada either side of tea. Stokes survived the hat-trick ball, and also a referral for caught behind on 11. But, when Root was out straight after reaching a typically accomplished half-century, to give Morris a maiden wicket, much work remained.

Step forward England's two redheads. Stokes and Bairstow not only held firm, but forged on against a flagging four-man attack. The first five overs of the second new ball yielded 46, with Morris – curiously tried ahead of Morkel – conceding seven fours in 13 deliveries, six of them hit by Stokes. By stumps England were 317 for five and on top. It was a position speedily strengthened next morning when, despite Morkel's restoration as pack leader, another 60 were plundered off the first six overs – Stokes hitting nine fours, and Bairstow two. Then, after a brief lull, another violent wave brought 93 runs in nine: Morkel was picked off at the end of his first spell of the day, before Rabada – having leaked 20 runs in three overs in *his* first – was put to the sword in his second. Piedt, the off-spinner, was savaged from the outset, conceding 42 in four overs to Stokes alone, including five sixes. Stokes took eight balls to move from 197 to his double-century, yet a session of 25 overs had brought him 130, and England 196. At lunch on the second day, they were a scarcely plausible 513 for five.

Bairstow reached the break on 95, level with his best in 36 previous Test innings. He spent 22 balls picking off the remaining five runs but, after he cut van Zyl for four, the emotion and relief poured out, a look to the skies conjuring thoughts of his late father, David, and his grandfather, who had died in the summer; his mother, Janet, and sister, Becky, were in the crowd. A cricketer sometimes too tense to give his best for England had never batted so serenely, remarkable given the carnage Stokes was inflicting.

The pair went into overdrive again: 80 came off what proved to be the last five overs and five balls of the innings. Stokes, too hot to run, was now trying to hit everything for six, which – facing Rabada – was how he perished: six, six, out, though only after de Villiers shelled a simple catch off a miscue, then hit the stumps as Stokes, assuming the worst, did indeed not run. Two balls later Bairstow reached 150, and Cook called an end to the mayhem at 629 for six. England had made their biggest score under his captaincy.

By scoring so fast, they had created plenty of time to dismiss South Africa twice. As they were to discover, they had also created time for their own position to become vulnerable – although, had they taken their chances, South Africa would probably have been batting on the final day.

In this regard, the self-inflicted early run-out of van Zyl was misleading, as was Compton's smart catch to remove Elgar off a looping edge induced by the omnipresent Stokes. Instead, Root's failure to hold a routine chance at gully from de Villiers, on five, was a sign of things to come. Enjoying several narrow escapes, de Villiers, who passed 8,000 runs in his 104th Test, was unconvincing but, by surviving 69 overs and putting on 183 with Amla, he did much to thwart England's charge.

The third day could not have been more different from the second, as South Africa painstakingly strove for safety. They added only 212 in 87 overs, but lost just one wicket,

HIGHEST TEST SCORES BY A NO. 6

258	B. A. Stokes	England v South Africa at Cape Town	2015-16
250	K. D. Walters	Australia v New Zealand at Christchurch	1976-77
234	D. G. Bradman	Australia v England at Sydney	1946-47
224	M. S. Dhoni	India v Australia at Chennai	2012-13
217*	A. B. de Villiers	South Africa v India at Ahmedabad	2007-08
214	G. S. Blewett	Australia v South Africa at Johannesburg	1996-97
204*	H. P. Tillekeratne	Sri Lanka v West Indies at Colombo (SSC)	2001-02
203*	Hanif Mohammad	Pakistan v New Zealand at Lahore	1964-65
201	S. E. Gregory	Australia v England at Sydney	1894-95
200	Mushfiqur Rahim	Bangladesh v Sri Lanka at Galle	2012-13

though it could have been more. Anderson, at slip, repaid Root for dropping de Villiers by missing Amla, on 76, off Root's bowling. Amla was then missed off Finn on 120 by Compton, who seemed late sighting the ball at point. England's think tank, running near empty, briefly threw the ball to Hales. The Amla–de Villiers stand was South Africa's first century partnership since 2014, but another came along immediately, as Amla and du Plessis put on 171, batting into the fourth afternoon. Three wickets in five overs for Broad and Anderson with the third new ball revived England, who still led by 180 when Broad bounced out de Kock, who had returned to take the gloves from de Villiers. But, in his first Test innings, Morris – hit on the helmet third ball by Broad – rallied to help Bavuma restore equanimity in the home dressing-room.

Despite being under pressure after his failures at Durban, the diminutive Bavuma batted beautifully: organised, yet adventurous when the chance arose, he struck 11 fours in his first 50, and – after surviving a chance on 77 to Bairstow off Broad – 16 in a hundred that detained him only 141 balls. Stokes directed a few choice words at him, but was among the first to congratulate Bavuma as multicultural South Africa savoured a special moment. Broad's frustration at Bairstow's drop, meanwhile, had led to him kicking the ground and being fined 30% of his fee for exchanging words with umpire Aleem Dar. He soon had more to ruck about as Morris, who had already survived a return chance to Finn on 22, was put down by Root on 57.

When Amla imaginatively declared, two runs behind, shortly before stumps on the fourth day, South Africa had recorded their biggest home score against England, beating 572 for seven, another famous rearguard, at Durban in 1999-2000; England, meanwhile, had not spent so many overs in the field in one innings since 1987, against Pakistan at The Oval. For only the fifth time, both sides had reached 600 in their first innings.

Cook and Hales negotiated six overs but, when both went early in successive overs next morning – Cook strangled down the leg side, Hales to another superb slip catch by Morris – England were the only side who could lose. Compton reacted to the pressure by going into his shell, Root and Stokes by scoring at around a run a ball. Taylor, caught at short leg after almost two hours of resistance, gave Piedt his third wicket to leave a nervy England six down. But Bairstow – who narrowly escaped a stumping off Elgar, with the lead 149 and a potential 41 overs remaining – and Ali were looking comfortable before the rain came.

Man of the Match: B. A. Stokes.

Close of play: first day, England 317-5 (Stokes 74, Bairstow 39); second day, South Africa 141-2 (Amla 64, de Villiers 25); third day, South Africa 353-3 (Amla 157, du Plessis 51); fourth day, England 16-0 (Cook 8, Hales 5).

England

*A. N. Cook c Morris b Rabada	27	– c de Kock b Rabada	8
A. D. Hales c de Villiers b Morkel	60	– c Morris b Morkel	5
N. R. D. Compton c Bavuma b Rabada	45	– c du Plessis b Piedt	15
J. E. Root c de Kock b Morris	50	– b Morris	29
J. W. A. Taylor c de Kock b Rabada	0	– c Bavuma b Piedt	27
B. A. Stokes run out	258	– c Morkel b Piedt	26
†J. M. Bairstow not out	150	– not out	30
M. M. Ali not out	0	– not out	10
B 12, l-b 6, w 13, n-b 8	39	L-b 4, n-b 5	9

1/55 (1) 2/129 (2) (6 wkts dec, 125.5 overs) 629 1/17 (1) (6 wkts, 65 overs) 159
3/167 (3) 4/167 (5)   2/19 (2) 3/55 (4)
5/223 (4) 6/622 (6)   4/85 (3) 5/115 (6) 6/116 (5)

S. C. J. Broad, S. T. Finn and J. M. Anderson did not bat.

Morkel 29–5–114–1; Morris 28–3–150–1; Rabada 29.5–2–175–3; Piedt 25–5–112–0; van Zyl 10–0–43–0; Elgar 4–0–17–0. *Second innings*—Morkel 16–7–26–1; Rabada 13–2–57–1; Morris 12–4–24–1; Piedt 18–8–38–3; Elgar 6–2–10–0.

South Africa

D. Elgar c Compton b Stokes	44	C. H. Morris c Root b Finn	69
S. van Zyl run out	4	K. Rabada not out	2
*H. M. Amla b Broad	201	B 4, l-b 9, w 13	26
A. B. de Villiers c Anderson b Finn	88		
F. du Plessis c Stokes b Anderson	86	1/7 (2) 2/85 (1) (7 wkts dec, 211 overs) 627
T. Bavuma not out	102	3/268 (4) 4/439 (3)
†Q. de Kock c Anderson b Broad	5	5/439 (5) 6/449 (7) 7/616 (8)

D. L. Piedt and M. Morkel did not bat.

Anderson 35–12–77–1; Broad 34–8–94–2; Ali 52–14–155–0; Finn 39–5–132–2; Root 20–4–54–0; Stokes 28–4–100–1; Hales 3–1–2–0.

Umpires: Aleem Dar and B. N. J. Oxenford. Third umpire: R. J. Tucker.
Referee: R. S. Madugalle.

> " The only English player around for the concluding fortnight was Kevin Pietersen, basking in reflected inglory, as a commentator."
> The World Cup, 2014-15, page 865

SOUTH AFRICA v ENGLAND

Third Test Match

PHIL WALKER

At Johannesburg, January 14–16, 2016. England won by seven wickets. Toss: South Africa. Test debut: G. C. Viljoen.

On a riotous third afternoon at the Wanderers, South Africa were torn apart by England's seam attack in front of a local crowd that turned from raucous to stunned across 33 overs of unchecked mayhem. The passage sealed England's first overseas series win since December 2012. And, as so often, it was Broad who flicked the switch, claiming five or more wickets in a single Test spell for the seventh time, and passing Bob Willis's tally of 325 to become England's third-highest wicket-taker.

But, just as it had been at Trent Bridge against Australia the previous August, this was emphatically a team effort: Broad's brilliance was buttressed by insistent fast bowling at the other end, and inspired close catching. Their fielding had been mercurial throughout the series but, as befits this unusually daring impression of an England side, when they were good, they were damn well irresistible.

If identifying clutch moments, and being able to turn it on accordingly, was a sign of a team's class, then this one, in the words of Trevor Bayliss, had it in them to become "something special". Indeed it was England's routinely taciturn head coach who chose the lunch break on the third day to administer what Cook called a "kick up the arse". The game was on a knife-edge: South Africa were six runs ahead, with all ten second-innings wickets in hand; by tea, they were 71 for eight.

Broad's innate sense of theatre has arguably made him England's most potent match-winner of the last decade. First he discerns the moment, then he dictates the rhythm. His

On the charge: Stuart Broad removes Hashim Amla, courtesy of a magnificent catch at short leg by James Taylor.

six wickets here, including a spell of five for one in 31 balls – and four successive wicket maidens – left South Africa in tatters after they had progressed to 23 without loss. Even the one run was a struggle: van Zyl was almost caught by a diving Anderson at second slip, the ball ricocheting away for a single. In all, Broad – who at one point had figures of 3.4–1–13–0 – claimed six for four in 51 deliveries. The home fans had turned up in good numbers and were in even better voice, the din bouncing around the amphitheatre all the way up to the gods. Through the morning session they had danced for Rabada, whose maiden five-for heralded the arrival of a beautiful new talent. But by dusk they had traipsed away, their day ruined by Broad, who smiled, mid-carnage, at their insistence that he resemble a banker, or something similar.

South Africa's main chance of setting any kind of target lay with Amla. His successor as captain, de Villiers, had just gone for nought, feathering an inside edge to the keeper to make it 31 for three. Now Amla whipped the ball meatily off his pads but, by the time he

---

BROAD'S BURSTS OF BRILLIANCE

This match provided the seventh instance of Stuart Broad taking five or more wickets in a spell. One was interrupted by a tea interval when he had four, but otherwise he took at least five in one spell in a single session:

Wicket to wicket	Match (final figures)	
7.5–1–19–5	v Australia at The Oval (12–1–37–5)	2009
2.4–2–0–5	v India at Nottingham (24.1–8–46–6)	2011
6.1–1–29–5†	v South Africa at Leeds (16.4–2–69–5)	2012
10.4–0–44–7‡	v New Zealand at Lord's (11–0–44–7)	2013
6.4–1–20–5	v Australia at Chester-le-Street (18.3–3–50–6)	2013
9.1–5–15–8	**v Australia at Nottingham (9.3–5–15–8)**	**2015**
5.1–3–1–5	v South Africa at Johannesburg (12.1–6–17–6)	**2015-16**

† *Spell broken by tea (at which point he had 4.3–1–12–4).*
‡ *Spell interrupted by lunch (5.2–0–22–5).*
England won all the matches except Leeds 2012, which was drawn.

Research by Harriet Monkhouse

---

had completed his shot, a miniature white blur was already scampering across the pitch into the arms of his team-mates. From connection to catch, which Taylor – standing slightly deeper at short leg because of the extra bounce – took down by his bootlaces, just 0.41 seconds had elapsed. It was freakish, and Taylor somehow repeated the trick six overs later, springing to his right to take a one-handed catch and see off Vilas.

It was one of those crazed passages of play that have come to define this England side. Edges were sought and found, chances sniffed and snaffled, the series settled in 167 minutes. Appropriately it was Broad who finished things off, diving full-length to take a one-hander after du Plessis had edged a heave into his pads, and the ball ballooned back towards the bowler. South Africa were all out for 83, their second-lowest total since readmission, behind 79 against India at Nagpur seven weeks earlier.

A hapless scene echoed the chaos which had engulfed their preparations. On the eve of the match, their young keeper-batsman Quinton de Kock had twisted his knee walking his Jack Russells, necessitating a call-up for Vilas; he arrived halfway through the opening session. And so, as the players geared up for fielding practice, and the captains assessed conditions on the first morning, Vilas was on the 8.40 flight from Port Elizabeth to Johannesburg, hoping to arrive in time for his first home Test.

Other, more sinister stories were doing the rounds. It's impossible to say whether the rumours surfacing about match-fixing in South Africa's domestic Ram Slam T20 Challenge affected the Test team's state of mind, but a sense of self-inflicted collapse was in the air: first in the media box, where murmurs would crystallise into an official statement, confirming that Gulam Bodi – who had played three limited-overs internationals for South

Julian Finney, Getty Images

DIY: Stuart Broad catches Faf du Plessis off his own bowling to dismiss South Africa for 83.

Africa in 2007 – had been charged with "contriving to fix, or otherwise improperly influence" aspects of the tournament; then on the pitch, where five of the seven wickets to fall on the first day were down to batsman error. There were two boundary catches, a run-out, a toe-ended hook and, in the case of de Villiers, who had raced to 36 from 39 balls, a feathered flap at a Stokes bouncer. It was skittish, tetchy and – for the world's top-ranked team – deeply unflattering.

When their innings concluded on the second morning, South Africa's total of 313 was the first in Test history to contain 11 double-figure scores (12, if you include extras) but no half-century. The sense of a missed opportunity may have been acute, yet when England lurched to 91 for four under heavy skies that afternoon, the home side, led by Rabada's preternatural brilliance, scented blood. Perhaps it was little wonder: the most red-blooded cricketer on the planet was walking to the middle.

It was becoming a theme: Stokes joins Root with their team in strife, which they treat as if they're still mucking about for North of England Under-15. In less than 16 overs of oddly inevitable bedlam, they added 111. As well as the natural rhythms, the shared past and the pleasure of seeing the other make the fiendishly difficult look easy, a sense of fun bound them together. Root, famously and vocally, "just loves it". Stokes – less hammy, less impish – simply swatted his fifth ball, a sharp bouncer from Rabada, into the stands and looked down at his sleeve.

He would eventually perish for 58 from 54, an innings that was as valuable in its own way as his Cape Town epic (if precisely 200 runs fewer). Root, having started a little stodgily, moved through the gears with almost bashful imperiousness. A Root century is fully equipped with all mod cons. There was a cut and a short-arm pull to get himself going, and a lovely cover-drive off Morkel. A rare loose one from Rabada allowed him the luxury of a straight-drive; an upper-cut dropped inches inside the rope, and an Athertonian flick raced off his legs. There were nine fours in his 77-ball fifty, giving way to a run-a-ball canter to three figures, crowned with another of those immaculate drives through the covers. This was his ninth hundred in his 38th Test, and his finest yet.

In the relative normality of that third morning, before Broad blew in across the high veld, Rabada had kicked off proceedings by removing Root, and careered to his five-wicket haul. It was the least he deserved, having performed like a seasoned veteran with the first new ball. Fast bowlers, more than any other cricketing species, can seemingly emerge fully formed. South Africa had found one.

With the hosts only ten behind on first innings, observers craving a rare nip-and-tuck Test keenly awaited their second. Here were two reasonably well-matched teams tied in a one-innings match. The narrative was set – but Broad improvised to steal the show. After that, it was just a merry procession, the game suddenly done. England needed only 74, and Cook and Hales knocked off 64, before three fell for seven – including Compton, trying to slog his second delivery for a match-winning six. That was a gentle reminder of the unfinished articles that lurked within the team. But at the Wanderers there was simply joy, imbued with a healthy dose of defiance. England had gone into the Ashes as second favourites, and won. Now 2–0 up with one to play, they had done the same here. "Yeah," said Stokes. "We proved them wrong again."

Man of the Match: S. C. J. Broad.

Close of play: first day, South Africa 267-7 (Morris 26, Rabada 20); second day, England 238-5 (Root 106, Bairstow 4).

South Africa

D. Elgar c Bairstow b Ali	46	c Bairstow b Broad	15
S. van Zyl c Bairstow b Stokes	21	c Bairstow b Broad	11
H. M. Amla c Bairstow b Finn	40	c Taylor b Broad	5
*A. B. de Villiers c Bairstow b Stokes	36	c Bairstow b Broad	0
F. du Plessis c Hales b Finn	16	c and b Broad	14
T. Bavuma run out	23	b Broad	0
†D. J. Vilas c Ali b Broad	26	c Taylor b Finn	8
C. H. Morris c Bairstow b Broad	28	b Stokes	1
K. Rabada c Bairstow b Anderson	24	c Bairstow b Stokes	16
G. C. Viljoen not out	20	lbw b Anderson	6
M. Morkel c Cook b Stokes	12	not out	4
B 9, l-b 9, w 1, n-b 2	21	L-b 2, n-b 1	3
(99.3 overs)	313	(33.1 overs)	83

1/44 (2) 2/117 (1) 3/127 (3) (99.3 overs) 313
4/161 (4) 5/185 (5) 6/212 (6)
7/225 (7) 8/281 (8) 9/281 (9) 10/313 (11)

1/23 (1) 2/28 (2) (33.1 overs) 83
3/30 (4) 4/31 (3)
5/35 (6) 6/45 (7) 7/46 (8)
8/67 (9) 9/77 (10) 10/83 (5)

Anderson 25.2–5–60–1; Broad 22–5–82–2; Finn 18–4–50–2; Ali 16–4–50–1; Stokes 18.1–1–53–3. *Second innings*—Anderson 10–1–26–1; Broad 12.1–6–17–6; Stokes 8–1–24–2; Finn 3–0–14–1.

England

*A. N. Cook c Vilas b Viljoen	18	c Vilas b Morris	43
A. D. Hales c de Villiers b Rabada	1	lbw b Elgar	18
N. R. D. Compton c Elgar b Rabada	26	c Morkel b Elgar	0
J. E. Root c Vilas b Rabada	110	not out	4
J. W. A. Taylor c Bavuma b Morkel	7	not out	2
B. A. Stokes c and b Morkel	58		
†J. M. Bairstow c van Zyl b Rabada	45		
M. M. Ali c Vilas b Morris	19		
S. C. J. Broad b Rabada	12		
S. T. Finn c Vilas b Morkel	0		
J. M. Anderson not out	0		
B 1, l-b 14, w 9, n-b 3	27	B 4, l-b 2, w 1	7
(76.1 overs)	323	(3 wkts, 22.4 overs)	74

1/10 (2) 2/22 (1) 3/74 (3) (76.1 overs) 323
4/91 (5) 5/202 (6) 6/242 (4)
7/279 (8) 8/309 (9) 9/311 (10) 10/323 (7)

1/64 (2) (3 wkts, 22.4 overs) 74
2/68 (3) 3/71 (1)

Morris 15–1–71–1; Rabada 23.1–5–78–5; Morkel 20–1–76–3; Viljoen 15–0–79–1; van Zyl 3–0–4–0. *Second innings*—Morkel 5–2–7–0; Rabada 4–0–28–0; Viljoen 4–2–15–0; Morris 6–2–8–1; Elgar 3.4–1–10–2.

Umpires: Aleem Dar and R. J. Tucker.   Third umpire: C. B. Gaffaney.
Referee: R. S. Madugalle.

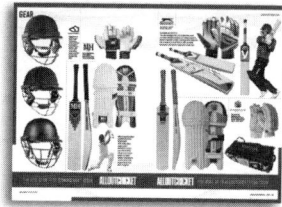

SOUTH AFRICA v ENGLAND

Fourth Test Match

Neil Manthorp

At Centurion, January 22–26, 2016. South Africa won by 280 runs. Toss: South Africa. Test debut: S. C. Cook.

Kagiso Rabada placed a broad and much-needed smile on the face of South African cricket with a remarkable match haul of 13 for 144 to gloss over their series defeat. It served as a consolation which had seemed impossible in the days before the match, and prompted Alastair Cook to predict "a very bright future". England were made to pay for a dreadful bowling performance in the first two sessions, and an embarrassing capitulation on the final morning, when they lost seven for 43 in 65 deliveries after Cook promised they would "show some fight". Following events at The Oval five months earlier, it seemed dead games were not for them.

Just as England had done throughout the first three Tests, South Africa won the decisive moments, capitalising on the tourists' poor start, adding 139 for their final three wickets, then dismissing Cook and Root for 76 apiece when both looked set to minimise the lead. A first-innings advantage of 133 was always likely to be crucial on a surface full of character, which cracked and deteriorated at the perfect rate. Amla narrowly missed the

chance to emulate Jacques Kallis's feat of twice scoring two centuries in a Test, but the contrasting natures of his 109 – his 25th Test hundred – and 96 perfectly illustrated the change in conditions. Silky, entertaining and fluent on day one, with cover-drives and pulls aplenty, he was hit on the body and hands half a dozen times three days later, when grit and courage replaced panache and flair.

Despite Amla's artistry, it was the 33-year-old Stephen Cook who had dominated the initial exchanges. Son of the prolific Jimmy – whose own Test debut in November 1992, at the age of 39, had been delayed for different reasons, but produced a diamond duck – Stephen warmed the hearts of his many admirers, and all those to whom the "past it" label has been unfairly attached, with an emotional century. At least, it was emotional for everyone else; for Cook, it looked like just another day at the office.

A heavy scorer at domestic level, he succeeded where so many international debutants fail: he played his own game. His demeanour commanded Test member-

Natural born opener: Stephen Cook heads towards a hundred on Test debut.

ship from the start, when he left the ball expertly, through to the time he spent in the nineties, unfazed by England's tactics. He could wait – and did, acknowledging the moment with no more than a quiet removal of the helmet and a smile. "That's his nature," said Jimmy, who had cancelled an overseas coaching trip to be at Centurion. "It means the world to him, but he'll never show it."

THE YOUNG ONES

The youngest to take five wickets in a Test innings for South Africa:

Years	Days			
19	253	†M. G. Melle (5-113)	v Australia at Jo'burg (Ellis Park)	1949-50
19	271	†C. N. McCarthy (6-43)	v England at Durban	1948-49
19	324	P. R. Adams (6-55)	v India at Kanpur	1996-97
19	327	C. N. McCarthy (5-114)	v England at Jo'burg (Ellis Park).	1948-49
20	165	†P. M. Pollock (6-38)	v New Zealand at Durban	1961-62
20	**236**	**K. Rabada (5-78)**	**v England at Jo'burg (Wanderers).**	**2015-16**
20	**244**	**K. Rabada (7-112)**	**v England at Centurion** (*1st inns*)	**2015-16**
20	**250**	**K. Rabada (6-32)**	**v England at Centurion** (*2nd inns*)	**2015-16**
20	356	H. J. Tayfield (7-23)	v Australia at Durban	1949-50
20	361	E. P. Nupen (5-53)	v England at Jo'burg (Old Wanderers) . . .	1922-23
20	363	J. M. Blanckenberg (5-83)	v England at Jo'burg (Old Wanderers) . . .	1913-14

† *On debut.*

Cook's precision clips and tucks, checked drives and low-risk singles to cover were classic fare for an opening batsman. That was in stark contrast to de Kock, who had recovered from his dog-walking injury to replace Dane Vilas behind the stumps, and arrived with South Africa – having stumbled from 237 for one to 273 for five – in danger of wasting a dominant start. De Kock was one of five changes they had made after their humiliation at the Wanderers, with Stiaan van Zyl, Faf du Plessis, Chris Morris and Hardus Viljoen joining Vilas in exile; Cook's debut, plus recalls for Duminy, Abbott and Piedt completed the set. England made only one change, bringing back Woakes after Steven Finn had picked up a side strain.

De Kock was positive from the outset. He looked to score from every ball, despite defensive fields and negative bowling, and often jumped outside off stump to take advantage of the spaces on the leg side. More than happy to hook with a deep square leg in place, he displayed the fighting confidence South Africa had lacked. His maiden Test century came from just 104 deliveries, and convinced many seasoned observers there were more to come. He put on 82 for the ninth wicket with Piedt, though he was helped by a blundering performance in the field, not least when he edged Woakes between the motionless Bairstow and Cook on 80.

England's two highlights, other than four wickets for the persevering Stokes, were tellingly fleeting. The first was another extraordinary catch at short leg by Taylor, in the game's 11th over. Following his two logic-defying grabs in Johannesburg, he now produced an equally jaw-dropping snaffle following a firm clip by the left-handed Elgar. By maintaining his position, Taylor was aware of the ball's whereabouts, but unable to react in conventional fashion with his hands. Instead, he enveloped it with his body, trapping it between his thighs, before rolling over and retrieving it from behind, as if he had laid an egg. Luck or brilliance? Most agreed a bit of both, with the emphasis on brilliance. The second highlight was Broad's dismissal of de Villiers, taken in the slips second ball after sparring at a stunning leg-cutter. It was the tenth time in Tests Broad had dismissed him, four more than any other bowler.

But England's reply to South Africa's 475 never delivered on its promise. Hales drove tamely to cover, and Compton received a shooter from Rabada. At 177 for two, though, with their two biggest names at the crease, there was hope of parity. But Alastair Cook's assured innings (and his only score above 43 in the series) was ended by a vicious delivery from Morkel, and Root ten overs later by movement at extreme pace from Rabada. Taylor played a shot a ball in a curiously hyper innings, Bairstow couldn't get his glove out of the way. England, had lost three for three, and staggered into lunch at 211 for six. Stokes briefly threatened to take over after the break, before Rabada struck again, eventually finishing with seven for 112. Without Ali's assured 61, the deficit would have been worse than 133.

Anderson finally made an impact, removing South Africa's first three with only 49 on the board – including de Villiers, trapped by an inswinger for a four-ball pair. Having endured just four ducks in his first 173 innings, he had now made three in a row. For Anderson, the moment was sweet: before the game de Villiers had suggested some of England's bowlers had "lost pace", a comment widely interpreted as a dig at Anderson, who now had 433 Test wickets, seventh on the all-time list.

But Bavuma removed any doubts about South Africa's superiority with an unbeaten 78 which showed a level of courage and skill not required during his ground-breaking century at Newlands. Sceptics who felt he had benefited there from a flat pitch and a flatter attack were put in their place by an innings of real character.

An hour's rain after tea on the fourth afternoon hastened the declaration, leaving England 21 overs and a day to make 382. It was never on the cards. Hales was lbw to a searing Rabada off-cutter, before Cook gave a one-handed return catch to Morkel, when a delivery held up on one of the many cracks, leaving him just 36 runs adrift of becoming the first Englishman to reach 10,000 in Tests. Compton edged Rabada to the keeper, and bizarrely wasted a review, but Root and Taylor survived with determination until the close. Possessing almost unprecedented batting depth, England clearly believed they could bat out the final day from 52 for three.

Their heart, though, wasn't in it. Next morning, Taylor gloved the final ball of the third over, from Morkel – an act of self-defence rather than a cricket shot – and the rest of the innings played out like a highlights package. De Villiers, curiously, did not introduce Rabada into the attack for the first 20 minutes, even though he had nine wickets in the bag. But, after Root edged off-spinner Piedt to slip, Rabada was held back no longer. He soon had Bairstow caught by de Villiers at second slip – only for the third umpire to confirm he had overstepped. The horror lasted as long as it took Bairstow to edge the very next delivery to de Kock.

Stokes had just been painfully felled by a Morkel delivery which crashed into his hip, and soon heaved the same bowler to deep square leg, before Rabada obliterated the tail. That completed South Africa's first win in ten Tests, and a performance which will live long in the memory. The only bowler younger than Rabada to take at least 13 wickets in a Test was Indian leg-spinner Narendra Hirwani, who was 19 years 89 days when he claimed 16 for 136 on debut against West Indies at Madras in 1987-88. More importantly, Rabada's heroics could play a crucial role as South Africa continue to grapple with the need for role models in an unapologetic agenda of what CSA's chief executive Haroon Lorgat has called "aggressive transformation".

Man of the Match: K. Rabada. *Man of the Series:* B. A. Stokes.

Close of play: first day, South Africa 329-5 (Bavuma 32, de Kock 25); second day, England 138-2 (Cook 67, Root 31); third day, South Africa 42-1 (Cook 23, Amla 16); fourth day, England 52-3 (Root 19, Taylor 19).

South Africa

S. C. Cook b Woakes	115	– c Bairstow b Anderson	25
D. Elgar c Taylor b Ali	20	– c Bairstow b Anderson	1
H. M. Amla b Stokes	109	– c Bairstow b Broad	96
*A. B. de Villiers c Root b Broad	0	– lbw b Anderson	0
J-P. Duminy lbw b Ali	16	– c Bairstow b Stokes	29
T. Bavuma c Bairstow b Broad	35	– not out	78
†Q. de Kock not out	129	– not out	9
K. Rabada lbw b Anderson	0		
K. J. Abbott lbw b Stokes	16		
D. L. Piedt c Bairstow b Stokes	19		
M. Morkel lbw b Stokes	0		
L-b 12, w 4	16	B 2, l-b 5, w 3	10

1/35 (2) 2/237 (3) 3/238 (4)   (132 overs) 475
4/271 (1) 5/273 (5) 6/335 (6)
7/336 (8) 8/386 (9) 9/468 (10) 10/475 (11)

1/5 (2)   (5 wkts dec, 83.2 overs) 248
2/49 (1) 3/49 (4)
4/106 (5) 5/223 (3)

Anderson 30–6–91–1; Broad 28–4–91–2; Ali 25–5–104–2; Woakes 22–3–91–1; Stokes 27–3–86–4. *Second innings*—Anderson 18–5–47–3; Broad 15–4–33–1; Stokes 16–4–36–1; Woakes 13.2–0–53–0; Ali 17–3–60–0; Root 4–0–12–0.

England

*A. N. Cook c de Kock b Morkel	76	– c and b Morkel	5
A. D. Hales c Piedt b Rabada	15	– lbw b Rabada	1
N. R. D. Compton lbw b Rabada	19	– c de Kock b Rabada	6
J. E. Root c de Kock b Rabada	76	– b Elgar b Piedt	20
J. W. A. Taylor c de Kock b Rabada	14	– c de Kock b Morkel	24
B. A. Stokes c Amla b Rabada	33	– c Cook b Morkel	10
†J. M. Bairstow c de Kock b Rabada	0	– c de Kock b Rabada	14
M. M. Ali c Piedt b Morkel	61	– not out	10
C. R. Woakes c Elgar b Duminy	26	– c Cook b Rabada	5
S. C. J. Broad c Cook b Rabada	5	– c de Villiers b Rabada	2
J. M. Anderson not out	5	– lbw b Rabada	0
B 2, l-b 7, w 3	12	L-b 2, w 1, n-b 1	4

1/22 (2) 2/78 (3) 3/177 (1)   (104.2 overs) 342
4/208 (4) 5/211 (5) 6/211 (7)
7/252 (6) 8/295 (9) 9/320 (10) 10/342 (8)

1/2 (2) 2/8 (1)   (34.4 overs) 101
3/18 (3) 4/58 (5)
5/58 (4) 6/83 (7) 7/83 (6)
8/91 (9) 9/101 (10) 10/101 (11)

Abbott 19–9–36–0; Rabada 29–6–112–7; Piedt 24–4–78–0; Morkel 23.2–4–73–2; Elgar 4–0–13–0; Duminy 5–0–21–1. *Second innings*—Morkel 12–5–36–3; Rabada 10.4–2–32–6; Abbott 2–0–10–0; Piedt 7–2–11–1; Elgar 2–1–8–0; Duminy 1–0–2–0.

Umpires: H. D. P. K. Dharmasena and C. B. Gaffaney.   Third umpire: R. J. Tucker.
Referee: R. S. Madugalle.

At Kimberley, January 30, 2016 (day/night). **England XI won by 163 runs. ‡England XI 368-7** (50 overs) (J. W. A. Taylor 116, J. M. Bairstow 58); **South Africa A 205** (30.5 overs) (T. B. de Bruyn 73*; R. J. W. Topley 3-38, A. U. Rashid 3-55, C. J. Jordan 3-48). *Taylor's run-a-ball 116 underpinned England's big score – but couldn't get him into the team for the one-day series. He shared three half-century stands: 80 for the third wicket with Eoin Morgan (41), 51 for the fifth in seven overs with Jos Buttler (20), and 78 in nine for the sixth with Bairstow, who thrashed six sixes (but no fours) from 30 balls. South Africa A slipped to 50-4 in the 11th over and, although Theunis de Bruyn put on 73 with Dane Vilas (40), England wrapped up a convincing victory with nearly 20 overs to spare. Chris Jordan held three slip catches to go with his three wickets.*

Limited-Overs International reports by Richard Hobson

SOUTH AFRICA v ENGLAND

First One-Day International

At Bloemfontein, February 3, 2016 (day/night). England won by 39 runs (D/L). Toss: England.
    South Africa needed 150 from 99 balls when heavy rain halted their chase, after England had recorded their highest total overseas (beating 355 for five at Dubai, as recently as November) and their second-highest in all. With de Kock at ease on 138 from just 96 deliveries, de Villiers felt his side had been on course, despite being five down. De Kock's third hundred in four one-day internationals took only 67 balls, six fewer than Buttler had needed a couple of hours earlier. England, though, had scored more consistently, against a depleted attack on a prime batting surface: for the first time in an ODI, the top eight all hit sixes, and the total of 15 was an England record. Buttler joked about the slowest of his four international hundreds, but it was still the joint-seventh-quickest for England, vindicating the decision to promote him to No. 4 after a brisk start. Buttler's first six hit the roof of the ground's operations centre, but Stokes and Ali also dropped jaws with blows over the longer, square boundaries. Behardien almost pulled off a one-handed catch in the

DOUBLE STRIKE

Both wicketkeepers scoring a century in an ODI:

K. C. Sangakkara (138*), M. S. Dhoni (183*)	I v SL at Jaipur	2005-06
A. B. de Villiers (107), T. Taibu (107*)	Z v SA at Harare	2007-08
A. B. de Villiers (125*), K. C. Sangakkara (102)	SA v SL at Johannesburg	2011-12
W. Barresi (137*), I. A. Karim (108)	Neth v Kenya at Lincoln	2013-14
K. C. Sangakkara (112), J. C. Buttler (121)	E v SL at Lord's	2014
J. C. Buttler (105), Q. de Kock (138*)	**SA v E at Bloemfontein**	**2015-16**

deep with Buttler on 68. Instead, the fielding crown went to Stokes, for a running, one-handed, shoulder-high effort at deep midwicket to remove de Villiers. Replays showed part of the rope, near where Stokes held on, had been pushed slightly back, and de Villiers mischievously referenced "rumours and theories" in the South African camp. But Stokes was clearly inside the playing area when the catch was taken. Winds had built by this stage, and Ali profited as three batsmen, including the well-set du Plessis, fell trying to clear the ropes – even in their designated position.

Man of the Match: Q. de Kock.

England

J. J. Roy c Behardien b Morkel	48	D. J. Willey not out	5
A. D. Hales c de Villiers b de Lange	57	R. J. W. Topley not out	0
J. E. Root b Morris	52		
†J. C. Buttler c de Villiers b Behardien	105	L-b 4, w 4, n-b 9	17
*E. J. G. Morgan c Morkel b Imran Tahir	23		—
B. A. Stokes b Morris	57	1/68 (1) 2/130 (2) (9 wkts, 50 overs)	399
M. M. Ali c Morris b Imran Tahir	19	3/227 (3) 4/256 (5)	
C. J. Jordan c Duminy b de Lange	14	5/317 (4) 6/371 (6) 7/376 (7)	
A. U. Rashid b Morris	2	8/379 (9) 9/391 (8) 10 overs: 75-1	

Morris 10–0–74–3; de Lange 10–0–87–2; Morkel 10–0–70–1; Duminy 5–0–48–0; Imran Tahir 10–0–71–2; Behardien 5–0–45–1.

South Africa

†Q. de Kock not out	138	F. Behardien not out	4
H. M. Amla b Willey	6	L-b 5, w 2	7
F. du Plessis c Hales b Ali	55		—
*A. B. de Villiers c Stokes b Ali	8	1/11 (2) 2/121 (3) (5 wkts, 33.3 overs)	250
J-P. Duminy c and b Topley	13	3/151 (4) 4/197 (5)	
R. R. Rossouw c Willey b Ali	19	5/245 (6) 10 overs: 72-1	

C. H. Morris, M. Morkel, M. de Lange and Imran Tahir did not bat.

Willey 5–0–30–1; Topley 6–0–43–1; Jordan 5.3–0–56–0; Rashid 6–0–42–0; Ali 6–0–43–3; Stokes 5–0–31–0.

Umpires: C. B. Gaffaney and S. George.   Third umpire: H. D. P. K. Dharmasena.
Referee: J. Srinath.

SOUTH AFRICA v ENGLAND

Second One-Day International

At Port Elizabeth, February 6, 2016. England won by five wickets. Toss: South Africa.

An old-fashioned game of care, manipulation and even the dreaded dull middle overs ended with a modern flourish from Buttler, whose three successive sixes off Imran Tahir sped England towards a 2–0 lead with 22 balls to spare. Things had moved gently for the most part in a relaxed atmosphere, and South Africa appeared confident when they removed Hales for 99, leaving England five down, with 61 needed from 52 on an ever-slowing pitch. Ultimately, the South Africans were left to rue poor use of the DRS, and a brilliantly judged leg-side catch by Jordan in a strong, swirling wind to remove the dangerous de Villiers. Until then, Rashid and Ali had kept the scoring tight, and only du Plessis batted fluently. The loss of de Villiers and Duminy within four balls early in the final powerplay changed the momentum. Duminy was unluckily adjudged leg-before – Topley's delivery

ONE SHORT

Batsmen scoring 99 in a one-day international for England:

G. Boycott	v Australia at The Oval	1980
A. J. Lamb	v India at The Oval	1982
B. C. Broad	v Pakistan at The Oval	1987
A. Flintoff	v India at The Oval	2004
J. C. Buttler	v West Indies at North Sound	2013-14
A. D. Hales	**v South Africa at Port Elizabeth**	**2015-16**

There have been 31 cases of batsmen being dismissed for 99 in one-day internationals, three of them by S. R. Tendulkar (India). The list includes E. J. G. Morgan, in his first ODI, for Ireland against Scotland at Ayr in 2006. There are a further 13 instances of batsmen stranded on 99*.

was heading down leg – but de Kock had already wasted South Africa's review. Rossouw was then given out caught behind on review, despite marginal evidence. Topley, having caused problems with the new ball, finished with three wickets in his second spell, and Hales and Root gave the reply a strong foundation in a second-wicket stand of 97, with Root overturning an lbw decision in the sixth over. Hales worked hard for his runs and hit only eight fours in his 99, before being caught down the leg side trying to pull his 124th delivery, which looped off his thigh and brushed the back of the bat with the stroke nearly completed. That left Buttler, who faced only 28 balls, to finish the job with the help of Ali, and celebrate his first IPL contract, secured earlier in the day.

Man of the Match: A. D. Hales.

South Africa

H. M. Amla b Topley	4	K. Rabada c Morgan b Topley	12
†Q. de Kock lbw b Stokes	22	K. J. Abbott not out	7
F. du Plessis c Jordan b Rashid	46	L-b 8, w 9	17
*A. B. de Villiers c Jordan b Stokes	73		
J-P. Duminy lbw b Topley	47	1/4 (1) 2/53 (2) (7 wkts, 50 overs) 262	
R. R. Rossouw c Buttler b Topley	11	3/98 (3) 4/205 (4)	
F. Behardien not out	23	5/206 (5) 6/225 (6) 7/245 (8) 10 overs: 52-1	

M. Morkel and Imran Tahir did not bat.

Topley 9–1–50–4; Willey 7–2–33–0; Stokes 9–0–54–2; Rashid 10–0–43–1; Ali 10–1–41–0; Jordan 5–0–33–0.

England

J. J. Roy b Abbott	14	M. M. Ali not out	21
A. D. Hales c de Kock b Abbott	99	L-b 11, w 3	14
J. E. Root b Abbott	38		
*E. J. G. Morgan c de Villiers b Morkel	29	1/20 (1) 2/117 (3) (5 wkts, 46.2 overs) 263	
B. A. Stokes b Morkel	0	3/169 (4) 4/176 (5)	
†J. C. Buttler not out	48	5/202 (2) 10 overs: 39-1	

C. J. Jordan, A. U. Rashid, D. J. Willey and R. J. W. Topley did not bat.

Abbott 9–1–58–3; Rabada 9–0–35–0; Morkel 8.2–0–31–2; Imran Tahir 10–0–66–0; Behardien 6–0–35–0; Duminy 4–0–27–0.

Umpires: J. D. Cloete and H. D. P. K. Dharmasena.   Third umpire: C. B. Gaffaney.
Referee: J. Srinath.

SOUTH AFRICA v ENGLAND

Third One-Day International

At Centurion, February 9, 2016 (day/night). South Africa won by seven wickets. Toss: England.

Hundreds by de Kock and Amla eased their side towards a ground-record chase against a subdued England. Their partnership of 239 was the second-highest for South Africa's first wicket in one-day internationals, and the eighth-highest by any team. As de Villiers had predicted after losing the toss, conditions improved greatly in the second innings: whereas England had encountered deliveries that stopped or kept low, South Africa enjoyed the extra zip under lights. Not that England helped their cause with their worst bowling of the series. They were either too full or short with the new balls, and lacked penetration mid-innings. Forecast thunderstorms failed to materialise, but South Africa remained ahead on Duckworth/Lewis, just in case. De Kock in particular took advantage of a shortish boundary, playing beautifully off his legs and becoming the youngest batsman, at 23 years 54 days, to register ten one-day hundreds, in only his 55th innings – another record, beating his partner Amla's mark of 57. Amla was less destructive, but a quick outfield rewarded his sweet timing. Though it proved way short, England's 318 for eight was their third-highest total against South Africa, and came despite a rare failure from Buttler, who clipped his first ball to leg gully. The enterprising Root hit five sixes in his best one-day score of 125 from 113 deliveries – England's highest against South Africa – while Hales completed his third half-century in a row. But the innings stuttered briefly in the final powerplay, and Root sacrificed himself after a mix-up with Stokes, when the ball ricocheted into the leg side via the bowler's stumps. Stokes went on to a 37-ball 53, before South Africa's openers kept the series alive.

Man of the Match: Q. de Kock.

England

J. J. Roy run out.	20	D. J. Willey not out	13
A. D. Hales c Morkel b Rabada.	65	A. U. Rashid not out	13
J. E. Root run out.	125	B 4, l-b 3, w 8	15
†J. C. Buttler c Duminy b Rabada.	0		
*E. J. G. Morgan c Amla b Wiese.	8	(8 wkts, 50 overs)	318
B. A. Stokes c Behardien b Abbott	53		
M. M. Ali c Amla b Morkel	3		
C. J. Jordan c Duminy b Abbott	3		10 overs: 56-1

1/36 (1) 2/161 (2) (8 wkts, 50 overs) 318
3/162 (4) 4/187 (5)
5/269 (3) 6/284 (7)
7/291 (6) 8/291 (8) 10 overs: 56-1

R. J. W. Topley did not bat.

Abbott 10–0–50–2; Rabada 10–0–65–2; Morkel 10–0–63–1; Wiese 10–0–64–1; Imran Tahir 8–0–56–0; Behardien 2–0–13–0.

South Africa

†Q. de Kock c Root b Rashid	135
H. M. Amla c Buttler b Jordan	127
D. Wiese b Ali.	7
F. du Plessis not out.	33
*A. B. de Villiers not out.	0
L-b 5, w 9, n-b 3	17

1/239 (1) 2/249 (3) (3 wkts, 46.2 overs) 319
3/311 (2) 10 overs: 57-0

J-P. Duminy, F. Behardien, K. Rabada, K. J. Abbott, M. Morkel and Imran Tahir did not bat.

Willey 5–0–40–0; Topley 6–0–46–0; Stokes 8.2–0–54–0; Jordan 7–0–54–1; Ali 10–0–75–1; Rashid 10–0–45–1.

Umpires: J. D. Cloete and C. B. Gaffaney.   Third umpire: H. D. P. K. Dharmasena.
Referee: J. Srinath.

SOUTH AFRICA v ENGLAND

Fourth One-Day International

At Johannesburg, February 12, 2016 (day/night). South Africa won by one wicket. Toss: South Africa.

England looked dazed when Imran Tahir cut his first ball for the winning runs to square the series. By the time it crossed the boundary, many heads were already in hands, minds doubtless reflecting on opportunities lost. South Africa had needed 52 from 50 deliveries, with two wickets remaining, when Morris miscued Topley to deep mid-off, only for Rashid to spill the chance. Morris collected two runs, then proceeded to thrash 46 from his next 22 balls, including four sixes, before falling to Rashid's googly with the scores level. England had also dropped Duminy and de Villiers, missed a chance to stump Behardien, and shied wide of the stumps several times with batsmen struggling to make their ground. A capacity Pink Day crowd – in support of breast-cancer awareness – was stirred by the twists and turns, and roused by a deafening sound system: the Wanderers may be nicknamed the Bull Ring, but it felt more like metal night at the Hammersmith Odeon. Not that England let the game slip in the field alone. They had collapsed from 87 for one in the 18th over, losing five for 21 to Tahir and Abbott, and forcing Root to rebuild. His stand of 95 with Woakes was a seventh-wicket best at the ground, and – having overturned an lbw decision on 95 – he went on to his eighth one-day international hundred, a responsible and skilful affair. The pitch was not quite as flat as predicted, and Broad got rid of Amla with his sixth ball on his first one-day appearance since the World Cup. Outstanding athleticism by Woakes ran out de Villiers in his follow-through, and Topley held an instinctive left-handed return catch to remove Behardien. But such moments merely underlined the errors that meant the series headed to Cape Town for a decider.

Man of the Match: C. H. Morris.

England

J. J. Roy c Abbott b Rabada	6	
A. D. Hales c sub (D. A. Miller)		
b Imran Tahir	50	
J. E. Root c Imran Tahir b Morris	109	
*E. J. G. Morgan c Behardien b Imran Tahir	2	
B. A. Stokes c Amla b Imran Tahir	2	
†J. C. Buttler c and b Abbott	1	
M. M. Ali c Amla b Abbott	4	
C. R. Woakes c de Kock b Rabada	33	

A. U. Rashid c de Villiers b Rabada	39	
S. C. J. Broad c Duminy b Rabada	6	
R. J. W. Topley not out	0	
L-b 4, w 6	10	

1/18 (1) 2/87 (2) 3/95 (4) (47.5 overs) 262
4/97 (5) 5/100 (6) 6/108 (7)
7/203 (8) 8/233 (3) 9/258 (10)
10/262 (9) 10 overs: 39-1

Abbott 9-1-57-2; Rabada 9.5-1-45-4; Morris 9-0-52-1; Wiese 10-0-58-0; Imran Tahir 10-0-46-3.

South Africa

H. M. Amla b Broad	0	
†Q. de Kock b Stokes	27	
F. du Plessis b Woakes	34	
*A. B. de Villiers run out	36	
J-P. Duminy lbw b Rashid	31	
F. Behardien c and b Topley	38	
D. Wiese c Morgan b Stokes	20	
C. H. Morris b Rashid	62	
K. Rabada c Root b Topley	0	

K. J. Abbott not out	3	
Imran Tahir not out	4	
L-b 8, w 3	11	

1/2 (1) 2/63 (2) (9 wkts, 47.2 overs) 266
3/63 (3) 4/121 (4)
5/143 (5) 6/191 (6) 7/207 (7)
8/210 (9) 9/262 (8) 10 overs: 53-1

Broad 7-0-55-1; Topley 8-1-39-2; Woakes 8-1-42-1; Stokes 10-0-45-2; Ali 9-0-39-0; Rashid 5.2-0-38-2.

Umpires: H. D. P. K. Dharmasena and S. George.   Third umpire: C. B. Gaffaney.
Referee: J. Srinath.

SOUTH AFRICA v ENGLAND

Fifth One-Day International

At Cape Town, February 14, 2016. South Africa won by five wickets. Toss: South Africa.

South Africa became the fourth side to recover from 2–0 down to win a one-day series, thanks to a composed unbeaten hundred from de Villiers, which he ranked among his best. His side had collapsed to 22 for three against the swing of Topley, but Amla provided typical stability in a recovery stand of 125 – his 11th three-figure partnership with de Villiers in only 37 innings – before Wiese powered late runs to secure victory with six overs in hand. A below-par target of 237 meant de Villiers, in his 200th one-day international, could eschew risk. But he still reached three figures, for the 24th time, from a deceptively brisk 94 balls. For the third game in a row, an England centurion ended up on the losing side: without Hales's 112 – the higher of his two ODI hundreds – the scorecard would have looked particularly forlorn. He needed some luck after early-morning showers had freshened the pitch, but also played commanding shots, and his fifth successive score of 50-plus took his aggregate to 383, both England records for a five-match series (Root's 351 in this series was second on the list); only Yasir Hameed (for Pakistan at home to New Zealand in 2003-04) and Kane Williamson (for New Zealand at home to India in 2013-14) had previously reached 50 in every innings of a five-match series. Otherwise, too many batsmen fell to over-adventure, not least Morgan, who shimmied at Wiese, and flashed a wide delivery to the keeper; his series return was a measly 64 runs. Imran Tahir threatened in every spell, and was rewarded for imploring de Villiers to review a leg-before decision against Root. South Africa's seamers overdid the short ball, but the loss of Stokes – bowled behind his legs – and Buttler to successive legitimate deliveries from Rabada left England without their biggest hitters too early in the piece. The last seven wickets fell for 81 runs, with five overs unused.

Man of the Match: A. B. de Villiers.   *Man of the Series:* A. D. Hales.

England

J. J. Roy lbw b Imran Tahir	8		S. C. J. Broad c de Villiers b Imran Tahir	13
A. D. Hales c Rossouw b Rabada	112		R. J. W. Topley not out	1
J. E. Root lbw b Imran Tahir	27			
*E. J. G. Morgan c de Kock b Wiese	2		B 4, l-b 8, w 11	23
B. A. Stokes b Rabada	29			
†J. C. Buttler b Rabada	0		1/15 (1) 2/76 (3) 3/85 (4) (45 overs)	236
M. M. Ali c Behardien b Abbott	12		4/155 (5) 5/156 (6) 6/181 (7)	
C. R. Woakes c Abbott b Wiese	0		7/183 (8) 8/192 (9) 9/223 (2)	
A. U. Rashid c Rabada b Wiese	9		10/236 (10) 10 overs: 59-1	

Abbott 9–0–28–1; Rabada 9–1–34–3; Imran Tahir 10–0–53–3; Morris 8–0–59–0; Wiese 9–0–50–3.

South Africa

†Q. de Kock c Buttler b Topley	4		D. Wiese not out	41
H. M. Amla st Buttler b Ali	59		W 14, n-b 1	15
F. du Plessis b Topley	0			
R. R. Rossouw c Hales b Topley	4		1/14 (1) 2/14 (3) (5 wkts, 44 overs)	237
*A. B. de Villiers not out	101		3/22 (4) 4/147 (2)	
F. Behardien c Stokes b Rashid	13		5/166 (6) 10 overs: 32-3	

C. H. Morris, K. Rabada, K. J. Abbott and Imran Tahir did not bat.

Broad 9–1–34–0; Topley 7–1–41–3; Woakes 5–0–32–0; Stokes 5–0–34–0; Rashid 10–0–59–1; Ali 8–1–37–1.

Umpires: J. D. Cloete and C. B. Gaffaney.   Third umpire: H. D. P. K. Dharmasena.
Referee: J. Srinath.

At Paarl, February 17, 2016. **England XI won by 44 runs.** ‡**England XI 202-6** (20 overs) (A. D. Hales 78, E. J. G. Morgan 42; W. D. Parnell 3-26); **South Africa A 158-8** (20 overs) (M. N. van Wyk 32, T. B. de Bruyn 56, J. T. Smuts 30; R. J. W. Topley 3-29). *England completed a hat-trick of thumpings of South Africa A across the formats. Hales led the way, continuing his good streak from the one-dayers with 78 from 52 balls, while Morgan showed signs of a return to form, blasting five sixes in 42 from 13. South Africa A looked on course while Morné van Wyk and Theunis de Bruyn were adding 88 for the second wicket in ten overs, but the innings subsided once they were separated.*

SOUTH AFRICA v ENGLAND

First Twenty20 International

At Cape Town, February 19, 2016 (floodlit). South Africa won by three wickets. Toss: South Africa.
　　England's run of six Twenty20 wins was halted amid a flurry of arms and legs on the final ball. By fumbling Root's throw from wide long-off, Topley failed to run out Abbott at the bowler's end and take the game to a super over. Ill-judged batting had marked a low-scoring encounter on a two-paced pitch. Morris changed that by striking the 14 required from Topley's last five deliveries – this after Topley had misjudged a chance to catch him first ball at third man in the previous over. Chasing a below-par 135, South Africa failed to heed the lessons of the England innings. Batsmen fell trying to drive over the ropes, and they needed 32 from 15 deliveries before Miller hit successive boundaries off Ali. A fine penultimate over by the ice-calm Jordan put England back ahead, only for Morris to reprise his match-winning role of Johannesburg a week earlier; a frustrated Topley smashed off the bails with his hand, earning him a salt-in-the-wound reprimand from the ICC. England had struck 50

Sinking in: Alex Hales looks away, and Reece Topley crouches in despair. Topley fluffed a run-out chance that would have tied the game – and forced a super over.

Gareth Copley, Getty Images

in the powerplay, but stumbled once Hales top-edged Imran Tahir: Duminy and Rabada were fortunate to escape injury when they collided, with Duminy holding on. Tahir continued to deceive, and almost completed a hat-trick with a googly that baffled Jordan but missed the stumps by a fraction. Buttler's unbeaten 32 from 30 balls proved the highest score of a match featuring only five sixes.

Man of the Match: Imran Tahir.

England

		B	4/6
1 J. J. Roy *c 1 b 10*	15	10	1/1
2 A. D. Hales *c 4 b 11*	27	21	5
3 J. E. Root *c 5 b 7*	8	12	1
4 *E. J. G. Morgan *c 7 b 11*	10	12	1
5 B. A. Stokes *st 2 b 11*	11	7	1/1
6 †J. C. Buttler *not out*	32	30	2
7 M. M. Ali *c 3 b 11*	0	1	0
8 C. J. Jordan *c 6 b 9*	15	15	2
9 A. U. Rashid *c 1 b 9*	2	6	0
10 D. J. Willey *not out*	7	6	0
L-b 2, w 5	7		

6 overs: 50-1 (20 overs) 134-8

1/38 2/52 3/53 4/68 5/81 6/81 7/108 8/120

11 R. J. W. Topley did not bat.

Abbott 4–0–31–2 (8); Rabada 4–0–29–1 (10); Morris 4–0–32–0 (8); Imran Tahir 4–0–21–4 (12); Wiese 4–0–19–1 (11).

South Africa

		B	4/6
1 H. M. Amla *c 10 b 5*	22	21	3
2 †A. B. de Villiers *c 2 b 8*	7	10	0
3 *F. du Plessis *c 5 b 7*	25	30	1
4 J-P. Duminy *c 3 b 9*	23	21	2
5 R. R. Rossouw *c 9 b 7*	18	18	0/1
6 D. A. Miller *c 3 b 8*	13	9	1/1
7 D. Wiese *b 8*	2	2	0
8 C. H. Morris *not out*	17	7	1/1
9 K. J. Abbott *not out*	2	2	0
L-b 5, w 1	6		

6 overs: 35-2 (20 overs) 135-7

1/31 2/35 3/76 4/98 5/103 6/114 7/119

10 K. Rabada and 11 Imran Tahir did not bat.

Willey 2–0–15–0 (5); Topley 3–0–27–0 (6); Jordan 4–0–23–3 (6); Stokes 4–1–19–1 (11); Rashid 4–0–24–1 (9); Ali 3–0–22–2 (6).

Umpires: J. D. Cloete and S. George. Third umpire: A. T. Holdstock.
Referee: A. J. Pycroft.

SOUTH AFRICA v ENGLAND

Second Twenty20 International

At Johannesburg, February 21, 2016. South Africa won by nine wickets. Toss: South Africa.

South Africa flattened England to secure the Twenty20 series 2–0, and leave Trevor Bayliss lamenting that it had been "men against boys". From 157 for three in the 17th over, with Buttler and Morgan powering along, England lost their last seven for 14 in 20 balls, then conceded 88 in the six powerplay overs. De Villiers hit South Africa's fastest 20-over half-century, from 21 deliveries, and Amla got there from 27. Eight boundaries alone came from Jordan's first two overs, which cost 41. Morgan lacked alternatives, as England had recalled Billings for David Willey in an attempt to stiffen the batting, and du Plessis hit the winning boundary with 32 balls to spare. Abbott and Rabada had bowled well with the new ball, but Root found some rhythm, while Buttler forced two of his four sixes into the top tiers. Morgan recovered from a scratchy start, and the pair added 96 in 51 balls. However, Buttler drove low to extra cover, and Morgan was run out next ball, when Abbott deflected a push by Stokes on to the non-striker's stumps. From there, a faltering innings comprised swings, misses, edges, scrambles and wickets as bowlers offered little width, and fielders held their chances. South Africa were clinical.

Man of the Match: A. B. de Villiers. *Man of the Series:* Imran Tahir.

England

		B	4/6
1 J. J. Roy *b 10*	9	15	0
2 A. D. Hales *run out*	16	16	0/1
3 J. E. Root *c 6 b 11*	34	17	4/2
4 *E. J. G. Morgan *run out*	38	23	0/4
5 †J. C. Buttler *c 3 b 9*	54	28	4/4
6 B. A. Stokes *c and b 8*	1	3	0
7 S. W. Billings *c 2 b 9*	5	6	1
8 M. M. Ali *c 4 b 8*	1	3	0
9 C. J. Jordan *c 3 b 9*..........	1	2	0
10 A. U. Rashid *b 10*...........	2	3	0
11 R. J. W. Topley *not out*	1	2	0
L-b 3, w 6	9		

6 overs: 47-1   (19.4 overs) 171

1/10 2/60 3/61 4/157 5/157 6/158 7/160 8/166 9/166

Rabada 3.4–0–28–2 (11); Abbott 4–0–26–3 (12); Morris 4–0–33–2 (11); Wiese 3–0–40–0 (5); Imran Tahir 4–0–25–1 (8); Duminy 1–0–16–0 (1).

South Africa

		B	4/6
1 †A. B. de Villiers *c 3 b 10*	71	29	6/6
2 H. M. Amla *not out*	69	38	8/3
3 *F. du Plessis *not out*	22	21	2
B 2, l-b 3, w 5	10		

6 overs: 88-0   (14.4 overs) 172-1

1/125

4 J-P. Duminy, 5 R. R. Rossouw, 6 D. A. Miller, 7 D. Wiese, 8 C. H. Morris, 9 K. J. Abbott, 10 K. Rabada and 11 Imran Tahir did not bat.

Topley 2–0–32–0 (4); Stokes 3–0–32–0 (7); Jordan 2.4–0–48–0 (2); Rashid 4–0–30–1 (9); Ali 3–0–25–0 (2).

Umpires: J. D. Cloete and A. T. Holdstock.   Third umpire: S. George.
Referee: A. J. Pycroft.

PART FOUR

English
Domestic
Cricket

FIRST-CLASS AVERAGES IN 2015

These include MCC v Yorkshire at Abu Dhabi

BATTING AND FIELDING (10 innings)

		M	I	NO	R	HS	100	50	Avge	Ct/St
1	J. M. Bairstow (*Yorks & England*)	13	20	3	1,226	219*	5	6	72.11	33
2	†A. G. Prince (*Lancs*)	16	23	1	1,478	261	5	5	67.18	13
3	J. C. Hildreth (*MCC & Somerset*)	19	32	1	1,758	220*	5	9	56.70	8
4	S. P. D. Smith (*Australians*)	7	11	0	619	215	3	1	56.27	3
5	†C. J. L. Rogers (*Australians*)	7	13	1	662	173	1	4	55.16	3
6	R. N. ten Doeschate (*Essex*)	13	21	4	929	88	0	8	54.64	9
7	S. P. Crook (*Northants*)	10	14	3	597	142*	1	4	54.27	4
8	J. E. Root (*England*)	7	13	1	643	134	2	4	53.58	14
9	†B. M. Duckett (*Northants*)	13	21	2	1,002	154	5	3	52.73	9
10	C. M. W. Read (*Notts*)	14	23	5	937	121	3	6	52.05	37/2
11	B. T. Foakes (*Surrey*)	10	16	4	617	140*	2	2	51.41	20/3
12	J. W. A. Taylor (*Notts*)	13	23	2	1,078	291	2	6	51.33	6
13	†S. M. Davies (*Surrey*)	12	19	3	819	200*	2	2	51.18	4
14	A. D. Hales (*Notts*)	12	20	0	1,021	236	3	5	51.05	2
15	M. R. Marsh (*Australians*)	7	11	1	506	169	2	2	50.60	4
16	†D. J. Malan (*Middx*)	10	17	3	690	182*	2	4	49.28	5
17	†R. J. Sidebottom (*Yorks*)	11	13	11	98	28	0	0	49.00	3
18	†D. J. Willey (*Northants*)	6	10	1	438	104*	1	2	48.66	3
19	†R. J. Burns (*Surrey*)	14	24	3	1,019	158	2	5	48.52	11
20	†D. A. Warner (*Australians*)	8	13	0	623	101	1	6	47.92	5
21	G. C. Wilson (*Surrey*)	13	23	6	811	74*	0	6	47.70	40/1
22	J. J. Roy (*Surrey*)	12	19	2	810	143	2	4	47.64	19
23	W. L. Madsen (*Derbys*)	14	27	5	1,033	172*	1	6	46.95	13
24	L. J. Wright (*Sussex*)	17	29	3	1,220	226*	2	8	46.92	12
25	M. Klinger (*Glos*)	6	11	1	468	103	2	2	46.80	5
26	†K. C. Sangakkara (*Surrey*)	11	19	0	870	149	5	1	45.78	7
27	T. T. Bresnan (*Yorks*)	18	25	5	907	169*	2	4	45.35	15
28	†M. E. Trescothick (*Somerset*)	17	30	1	1,311	210*	3	8	45.20	29
29	K. R. Brown (*Lancs*)	12	17	0	766	132	1	7	45.05	12
30	†S. G. Borthwick (*Durham*)	17	33	2	1,390	104	2	11	44.83	19
31	S. A. Northeast (*Kent*)	17	30	3	1,204	139	1	9	44.59	11
32	†B. A. Godleman (*Derbys*)	14	28	4	1,069	108	3	7	44.54	12
33	†C. D. J. Dent (*Glos*)	17	29	4	1,112	268	3	7	44.48	23
34	R. E. Levi (*Northants*)	11	18	3	663	168	1	5	44.20	5
35	T. Westley (*Essex*)	13	22	1	926	179	2	4	44.09	6
36	†A. Harinath (*Surrey*)	8	13	0	568	120	2	2	43.69	1
37	A. N. Petersen (*Lancs*)	14	21	1	861	286	3	1	43.05	6
38	B. C. Brown (*Sussex*)	17	28	4	1,031	144*	4	4	42.95	46/1
39	†N. L. J. Browne (*Essex*)	17	29	2	1,157	151*	5	3	42.85	17
40	†M. J. Cosgrove (*Leics*)	16	29	1	1,185	156	4	5	42.32	10
41	D. L. Lloyd (*Glam*)	10	20	6	589	92	0	3	42.07	4
42	T. C. Fell (*Worcs*)	17	27	0	1,127	171	3	4	41.74	22
43	†M. A. Carberry (*MCC & Hants*)	18	33	1	1,334	146	1	10	41.68	4
44	S. J. Croft (*Lancs*)	16	23	2	874	122	2	6	41.61	21
45	†J. D. Ryder (*Essex*)	15	26	5	853	124	2	3	40.61	15
46	A. L. Davies (*Lancs*)	14	19	1	730	99	0	7	40.55	46/4
47	P. S. P. Handscomb (*Glos*)	7	13	2	443	76	0	4	40.27	10
48	L. A. Dawson (*Hants & Essex*)	16	28	5	922	140	1	3	40.08	13
49	J. L. Denly (*Kent*)	17	31	4	1,081	161*	2	7	40.03	9
50	R. W. T. Key (*Kent*)	13	24	0	958	158	2	5	39.91	4
51	†M. W. Machan (*Sussex*)	14	24	0	955	192	3	3	39.79	3
52	†Ashar Zaidi (*Sussex*)	7	10	1	354	106	1	1	39.33	3
53	†A. N. Cook (*MCC, England & Essex*)	11	20	0	782	162	1	5	39.10	15

		M	I	NO	R	HS	100	50	Avge	Ct/St
54	M. H. Wessels (*Notts*)	17	30	2	1,093	117	2	7	39.03	19
55	A. C. Voges (*Middx & Australians*)	12	21	2	740	132	1	5	38.94	17
56	†A. W. Gale (*Yorks*)	16	27	0	1,045	164	3	3	38.70	4
57	†M. H. Yardy (*Sussex*)	11	18	0	694	124	2	4	38.55	14
58	†J. A. Rudolph (*Glam*)	15	27	2	962	111	1	7	38.48	13
59	C. B. Cooke (*Glam*)	16	28	5	884	112	2	5	38.43	18
60	J. A. Leaning (*Yorks*)	17	29	3	988	123	3	3	38.00	20
61	N. R. D. Compton (*MCC & Middx*)	18	35	2	1,245	149	2	7	37.72	5
62	A. M. Ali (*Leics*)	7	12	1	412	80	0	3	37.45	2
63	†C. A. Ingram (*Glam*)	16	28	3	931	105*	2	4	37.24	10
64	D. W. Lawrence (*Essex*)	7	12	1	409	161	1	1	37.18	8
65	†Z. S. Ansari (*MCC & Surrey*)	15	24	2	810	106	1	4	36.81	8
66	H. J. H. Marshall (*Glos*)	13	18	2	588	92	0	6	36.75	7
67	N. D. Pinner (*Leics*)	6	12	1	365	165*	1	1	36.50	10
68	G. J. Muchall (*Durham*)	11	21	2	693	145	2	4	36.47	10
69	S. R. Hain (*Warwicks*)	10	17	2	547	106	2	3	36.46	8
70	W. R. Smith (*Hants*)	17	31	5	948	93	0	5	36.46	19
71	†R. A. Whiteley (*Worcs*)	8	13	1	436	101	1	3	36.33	6
72	O. B. Cox (*Worcs*)	17	27	5	793	109	1	5	36.04	48/3
73	P. J. Horton (*Lancs*)	12	18	1	611	168	1	5	35.94	16
74	D. K. H. Mitchell (*MCC & Worcs*)	17	28	3	895	206*	2	3	35.80	21
75	†B. A. Stokes (*England*)	7	12	0	429	101	1	3	35.75	7
76	B. R. M. Taylor (*Notts*)	17	30	0	1,070	152	4	3	35.66	12
76	†I. J. Westwood (*Warwicks*)	14	25	1	856	196	1	6	35.66	6
78	A. U. Rashid (*Yorks*)	8	11	0	389	127	1	2	35.36	4
79	J. M. Clarke (*Worcs*)	11	16	1	530	104*	1	4	35.33	3
80	P. D. Trego (*Somerset*)	18	29	3	913	130*	2	4	35.11	8
81	G. G. Wagg (*Glam*)	17	24	0	842	200	1	6	35.08	6
82	A. G. Wakely (*Northants*)	16	27	2	876	123	2	4	35.04	12
83	A. L. Hughes (*Derbys*)	7	11	3	279	111*	1	0	34.87	2
84	M. J. Richardson (*Durham*)	17	34	5	1,007	96*	0	6	34.72	46/3
85	S. J. Mullaney (*Notts*)	16	27	0	937	118	2	4	34.70	23
86	L. J. Evans (*Warwicks*)	15	27	3	826	213*	1	4	34.41	16
87	A. M. Rossington (*Northants*)	14	24	1	776	116	1	7	33.73	35
88	P. D. Collingwood (*Durham*)	16	29	5	807	127	2	3	33.62	25
89	T. B. Abell (*Somerset*)	15	27	4	770	131	1	5	33.47	7
90	C. D. Nash (*Sussex*)	16	27	1	866	142*	2	3	33.30	15
91	†M. D. Stoneman (*Durham*)	17	34	0	1,131	131	5	3	33.26	7
92	G. H. Roderick (*Glos*)	16	26	2	791	100*	1	6	32.95	55
93	†E. C. Joyce (*Sussex*)	15	26	0	855	100	1	4	32.88	25
94	†M. M. Ali (*Worcs & England*)	11	20	1	624	77	0	5	32.84	5
95	J. M. Vince (*Hants*)	16	29	2	883	144	2	5	32.70	22
96	A. J. Robson (*Leics*)	17	34	1	1,079	120	1	9	32.69	16
97	†C. F. Hughes (*Derbys*)	13	26	1	816	104	2	4	32.64	6
98	†N. J. O'Brien (*Leics*)	13	24	2	718	95	0	5	32.63	54/4
99	†K. K. Jennings (*Durham*)	11	21	1	650	177*	1	3	32.50	6
100	R. S. Bopara (*Essex*)	13	23	1	714	107	1	4	32.45	4
101	†S. M. Ervine (*Hants*)	13	20	4	518	102	1	2	32.37	15
102	W. A. Tavaré (*Glos*)	16	27	2	801	93	0	6	32.04	11
103	A. H. T. Donald (*Glam*)	5	10	1	288	98	0	2	32.00	4
104	†A. Z. Lees (*Yorks*)	18	31	3	885	100	1	6	31.60	20
105	G. O. Jones (*Glos*)	10	16	1	472	88	0	4	31.46	13
106	C. A. J. Meschede (*Glam*)	17	24	3	655	107	2	2	31.19	6
107	†A. S. S. Nijjar (*Essex*)	7	10	5	155	53	0	1	31.00	1
108	K. G. Berg (*Hants*)	17	25	3	674	99	0	5	30.63	11
109	†K. H. D. Barker (*Warwicks*)	13	20	3	516	102*	1	2	30.35	2
110	R. I. Keogh (*Northants*)	18	31	2	876	163*	2	2	30.20	6
111	J. S. Foster (*Essex*)	17	25	2	694	98	0	5	30.17	46/3
112	†L. Wood (*Notts*)	11	16	2	420	100	1	2	30.00	2
112	C. J. C. Wright (*Warwicks*)	11	16	6	300	65	0	2	30.00	2
114	R. I. Newton (*Northants*)	12	21	0	628	107	1	4	29.90	3

		M	I	NO	R	HS	100	50	Avge	Ct/St
115	J. G. Myburgh (*Somerset*)	12	22	3	568	150*	2	3	29.89	6
116	G. J. Batty (*Surrey*)	15	18	5	388	50*	0	2	29.84	5
117	T. R. Ambrose (*Warwicks*)	14	22	0	651	153	2	1	29.59	34/5
118	S. D. Robson (*Middx*)	17	33	2	917	178	1	4	29.58	14
119	J. M. R. Taylor (*Glos*)	11	14	0	414	156	2	0	29.57	4
120	†W. M. H. Rhodes (*Yorks*)	11	18	2	469	79	0	2	29.31	5
121	J. Leach (*Worcs*)	14	19	2	498	95	0	3	29.29	4
122	J. A. Burns (*Middx*)	7	11	0	320	87	0	3	29.09	1
123	I. R. Bell (*England & Warwicks*)	9	16	1	436	111	1	4	29.06	12
124	†J. H. K. Adams (*Hants*)	16	31	1	868	136	1	6	28.93	4
125	D. J. Bell-Drummond (*Kent*)	17	31	0	894	127	3	2	28.83	9
126	†W. D. Bragg (*Glam*)	14	24	1	659	120	2	2	28.65	3
127	M. J. Clarke (*Australians*)	8	15	2	372	77	0	2	28.61	7
128	J. K. Fuller (*Glos*)	11	14	2	343	73	0	2	28.58	6
129	†A. Lyth (*Yorks & England*)	15	27	1	739	113	2	3	28.42	20
130	C. Overton (*Somerset*)	12	16	3	369	55	0	3	28.38	9
131	†G. S. Ballance (*England & Yorks*)	12	21	0	592	165	1	3	28.19	12
132	W. J. Durston (*Derbys*)	11	21	5	451	85	0	2	28.18	12
133	J. Clark (*Lancs*)	12	17	2	419	63	0	1	27.93	3
134	A. J. A. Wheater (*Hants*)	15	24	2	613	111	1	4	27.86	29/2
135	N. J. Dexter (*Middx*)	10	19	2	473	112	1	1	27.82	2
136	†J. E. C. Franklin (*Middx*)	15	27	3	667	135	2	3	27.79	15
137	T. S. Roland-Jones (*Middx*)	13	19	4	416	103*	1	1	27.73	7
138	†R. M. L. Taylor (*Leics*)	8	15	7	221	42	0	0	27.62	4
139	D. I. Stevens (*Kent*)	15	23	0	635	92	0	6	27.60	5
140	†B. T. Slater (*Derbys*)	15	29	0	799	94	0	7	27.55	4
141	J. M. Kettleborough (*Glam*)	9	16	1	413	81	0	3	27.53	4
142	J. J. Cobb (*Northants*)	18	30	5	688	95	0	5	27.52	8
143	V. Chopra (*Warwicks*)	15	25	1	658	119*	2	2	27.41	20
144	†J. A. Simpson (*Middx*)	17	30	7	628	64	0	3	27.30	55/2
145	S. D. Peters (*Northants*)	10	17	0	464	82	0	4	27.29	4
146	M. A. Wood (*Durham & England*)	7	13	5	218	66	0	1	27.25	2
147	P. M. Siddle (*Lancs & Australians*)	9	11	1	272	89	0	1	27.20	3
148	†L. W. P. Wells (*Sussex*)	14	23	0	625	108	1	4	27.17	6
149	B. L. D'Oliveira (*Worcs*)	8	12	1	297	49	0	0	27.00	4
150	A. J. Hodd (*Yorks*)	10	13	2	296	57	0	3	26.90	24/2
151	R. D. Pringle (*Durham*)	9	17	1	427	99	0	3	26.68	3
152	S. W. Billings (*MCC & Kent*)	13	21	2	500	100*	1	1	26.31	36/1
153	†N. R. T. Gubbins (*Leeds/Br MCCU & Middx*)	9	16	0	417	92	0	2	26.06	3
154	P. M. Nevill (*Australians*)	7	10	0	259	78	0	2	25.90	20
155	J. S. Patel (*Warwicks*)	16	23	2	543	98	0	2	25.85	10
156	{ J. E. Burke (*Surrey*)	7	10	1	232	79	0	2	25.77	5
	{ S. P. Terry (*Hants*)	5	10	1	232	62*	0	2	25.77	4
158	†B. W. Harmison (*Kent*)	7	11	0	283	123	1	1	25.72	7
159	B. A. Hutton (*Notts*)	9	13	2	278	72	0	1	25.27	5
160	C. J. McKay (*Leics*)	12	22	4	452	51*	0	1	25.11	2
161	I. J. L. Trott (*Warwicks*)	11	18	0	451	87	0	2	25.05	6
162	†M. G. Johnson (*Australians*)	6	10	2	200	77	0	1	25.00	3
163	E. J. H. Eckersley (*Leics*)	17	33	0	814	147	2	2	24.66	9
164	†C. J. Haggett (*Kent*)	11	16	2	345	80	0	2	24.64	4
165	M. G. Hogan (*Glam*)	14	19	8	271	57	0	1	24.63	11
166	S. T. Finn (*Middx & England*)	11	14	9	123	41*	0	0	24.60	3
167	T. L. W. Cooper (*Somerset*)	14	24	0	590	118	1	2	24.58	7
168	A. P. R. Gidman (*Worcs*)	13	20	2	440	78	0	3	24.44	13
169	S. R. Patel (*Notts*)	17	29	1	681	100	2	2	24.32	9
170	D. P. Sibley (*Surrey*)	6	10	0	242	74	0	1	24.20	6
171	A. G. Salter (*Glam*)	12	19	2	411	73	0	2	24.17	5
172	B. A. C. Howell (*Glos*)	12	17	0	409	102	1	1	24.05	8
173	J. C. Buttler (*England*)	7	12	0	286	73	0	2	23.83	20
174	†M. A. Wallace (*Glam*)	16	24	2	522	92	0	3	23.72	43/3
175	S. A. Patterson (*Yorks*)	17	20	4	379	44*	0	0	23.68	3

		M	I	NO	R	HS	100	50	Avge	Ct/St
176	J. Allenby (*Somerset*)	18	30	2	654	64	0	5	23.35	19
177	D. R. Briggs (*Hants*)	9	14	3	256	48	0	0	23.27	1
178	R. Clarke (*Warwicks*)	16	26	3	535	67	0	2	23.26	22
179	P. Coughlin (*Durham*)	7	11	1	232	64	0	2	23.20	1
180	K. M. Jarvis (*Lancs*)	13	15	9	139	47	0	0	23.16	3
181	A. Shahzad (*Sussex*)	6	10	2	182	45*	0	0	22.75	1
182	G. R. Napier (*Essex*)	13	17	1	363	73	0	2	22.68	5
183	†K. Noema-Barnett (*Glos*)	11	15	3	272	61	0	1	22.66	4
184	†S. C. J. Broad (*England & Notts*)	9	16	1	339	50	0	1	22.60	2
185	C. S. MacLeod (*Durham*)	8	15	3	271	67	0	1	22.58	6
186	†R. K. Oliver (*Worcs*)	13	22	0	494	101	1	1	22.45	8
187	L. J. Hill (*Leics*)	9	18	2	356	126	1	1	22.25	15
188	J. A. R. Harris (*Middx*)	17	26	5	467	73	0	3	22.23	4
189	I. A. Cockbain (*Glos*)	7	12	1	244	66*	0	1	22.18	2
190	S. J. Thakor (*Derbys*)	12	17	1	349	83	0	1	21.81	4
191	R. K. Kleinveldt (*Northants*)	13	21	3	391	56	0	2	21.72	9
192	†M. A. G. Boyce (*Leics*)	6	12	0	260	60	0	2	21.66	4
193	†M. E. Claydon (*Kent*)	7	11	4	151	53	0	1	21.57	0
194	J. C. Mickleburgh (*Essex*)	11	20	0	431	61	0	2	21.55	6
195	S. L. Elstone (*Derbys*)	8	13	1	253	103*	1	0	21.08	3
196	J. Overton (*Somerset*)	9	10	3	146	50	0	0	20.85	0
197	†D. J. Redfern (*Leics*)	6	12	1	229	74	0	1	20.81	2
198	A. P. Agathangelou (*Leics*)	6	12	1	225	54	0	1	20.45	12
199	†B. A. Raine (*Leics*)	17	29	2	546	57	0	2	20.22	4
200	O. E. Robinson (*Sussex*)	11	17	3	282	110	1	0	20.14	3
201	D. A. Payne (*Glos*)	10	10	3	138	23	0	0	19.71	4
202	†M. A. Starc (*Australians*)	6	10	1	177	58	0	2	19.66	4
203	J. W. Hastings (*Durham*)	15	25	0	487	91	0	3	19.48	6
204	†W. R. S. Gidman (*Notts*)	7	12	1	213	57	0	1	19.36	3
205	Azharullah (*Northants*)	15	19	9	189	58*	0	1	18.90	5
206	T. K. Curran (*Surrey*)	16	18	2	297	60	0	1	18.56	5
207	N. M. Lyon (*Australians*)	7	10	3	129	41	0	0	18.42	4
208	A. P. Palladino (*Derbys*)	13	17	3	255	82	0	1	18.21	4
209	†W. T. S. Porterfield (*Warwicks*)	6	11	0	196	61	0	1	17.81	4
210	O. P. Stone (*Northants*)	13	17	4	231	38	0	0	17.76	6
211	†Abdur Rehman (*Somerset*)	9	15	5	177	55*	0	1	17.70	1
212	T. E. Bailey (*Lancs*)	12	16	3	224	34	0	0	17.23	2
213	O. P. Rayner (*Middx*)	14	23	2	360	52	0	1	17.14	30
214	H. R. Hosein (*Derbys*)	12	18	2	273	61	0	1	17.06	32/1
215	P. R. Stirling (*Middx*)	8	16	1	254	41	0	0	16.93	5
216	J. K. H. Naik (*Leics*)	8	14	3	184	73	0	1	16.72	1
217	Saeed Ajmal (*Worcs*)	8	12	2	162	37	0	0	16.20	5
218	Craig Cachopa (*Sussex*)	9	17	0	270	54	0	2	15.88	6
219	C. Rushworth (*MCC & Durham*)	18	29	4	393	43	0	0	15.72	6
220	†W. B. Rankin (*Warwicks*)	13	18	8	155	56*	0	1	15.50	4
221	J. A. Brooks (*Yorks*)	16	18	3	225	50*	0	1	15.00	4
222	†M. T. Coles (*Kent*)	14	22	3	277	66	0	1	14.57	15
223	A. W. R. Barrow (*Somerset*)	8	13	2	157	32	0	0	14.27	21
224	†T. J. Murtagh (*Middx*)	14	19	6	185	24	0	0	14.23	4
225	B. D. Cotton (*Derbys*)	8	12	3	126	43	0	0	14.00	2
226	C. N. Miles (*Glos*)	12	18	1	237	41	0	0	13.94	4
227	J. T. Ball (*Notts*)	14	21	3	244	49*	0	0	13.55	1
228	L. Gregory (*Somerset*)	13	19	1	242	32	0	0	13.44	11
229	T. A. I. Taylor (*Derbys*)	9	13	3	133	49	0	0	13.30	2
230	†P. Mustard (*Durham & Lancs*)	8	11	0	146	43	0	0	13.27	24
231	A. C. Thomas (*Somerset*)	7	10	4	79	32*	0	0	13.16	6
232	T. D. Groenewald (*Somerset*)	10	18	3	192	47	0	0	12.80	5
233	†J. M. Anderson (*England & Lancs*)	7	11	4	88	42	0	0	12.57	11
234	†J. D. Shantry (*Worcs*)	17	22	4	221	41*	0	0	12.27	4
235	D. D. Masters (*Essex*)	7	10	3	85	28	0	0	12.14	3
236	G. Onions (*MCC & Durham*)	17	27	15	142	36*	0	0	11.83	3

		M	I	NO	R	HS	100	50	Avge	Ct/St
237	A. E. N. Riley (*MCC & Kent*)	10	15	5	114	34	0	0	11.40	7
238	T. J. Wells (*Leics*)	6	10	1	102	30*	0	0	11.33	4
239	S. C. Kerrigan (*Lancs*)	14	15	5	110	34*	0	0	11.00	6
240	†S. J. Magoffin (*Sussex*)	17	24	4	208	41	0	0	10.40	7
241	J. Harrison (*Durham*)	5	10	0	99	53	0	1	9.90	0
242	†J. C. Tredwell (*Kent*)	7	11	0	107	53	0	1	9.72	13
243	M. E. Hobden (*Sussex*)	11	17	8	84	65*	0	1	9.33	3
244	G. P. Smith (*Notts & Leics*)	5	10	0	84	20	0	0	8.40	3
245	L. C. Norwell (*Glos*)	15	19	9	83	19	0	0	8.30	5
246	C. A. J. Morris (*Worcs*)	15	21	10	85	24	0	0	7.72	2
247	M. H. A. Footitt (*Derbys*)	16	21	6	110	34	0	0	7.33	3
248	J. M. Bird (*Hants*)	6	10	2	54	12	0	0	6.75	1
249	J. A. Porter (*Essex*)	16	21	5	98	34	0	0	6.12	5
250	†J. A. Tomlinson (*Hants*)	9	13	3	52	17	0	0	5.20	1
251	†M. P. Dunn (*MCC & Surrey*)	10	12	2	46	13	0	0	4.60	1
252	I. A. A. Thomas (*Kent*)	11	18	8	40	13	0	0	4.00	1
253	C. E. Shreck (*Leics*)	14	22	7	41	15	0	0	2.73	5
254	H. F. Gurney (*Notts*)	12	15	8	15	8	0	0	2.14	1

BOWLING (10 wickets in 5 innings)

		Style	O	M	R	W	BB	5I	Avge
1	A. Shahzad (*Sussex*)	RFM	129.2	19	461	26	5-46	1	17.73
2	R. J. Sidebottom (*Yorks*)	LFM	268	71	778	43	6-34	3	18.09
3	M. R. Marsh (*Australians*)	RFM	104.1	22	381	20	4-41	0	19.05
4	C. R. Woakes (*Warwicks*)	RFM	74	20	217	11	3-48	0	19.72
5	B. W. Sanderson (*Northants*)	RFM	78	23	223	11	4-44	0	20.27
6	D. I. Stevens (*Kent*)	RM	419.1	100	1,242	61	5-58	2	20.36
7	C. Rushworth (*MCC & Durham*)	RFM	641.4	154	1,849	90	6-39	7	20.54
8	F. H. Edwards (*Hants*)	RFM	240.5	38	940	45	6-88	3	20.88
9	J. E. Burke (*Surrey*)	RFM	104	19	347	16	4-19	0	21.68
10	J. D. Shantry (*Worcs*)	LFM	546.5	149	1,456	67	5-8	5	21.73
11	C. Overton (*Somerset*)	RFM	313.3	62	1,022	47	6-74	1	21.74
12	J. P. Faulkner (*Lancs*)	LFM	186	44	501	23	5-39	1	21.78
13	J. A. Brooks (*Yorks*)	RFM	465.5	97	1,614	74	5-35	3	21.81
14	W. A. White (*Derbys & Leics*)	RFM	153.5	26	568	26	6-25	3	21.84
15	A. Carter (*Glam & Notts*)	RFM	141.1	25	464	21	4-46	0	22.09
16	S. C. J. Broad (*England & Notts*)	RFM	271	50	970	43	8-15	3	22.55
17	S. J. Magoffin (*Sussex*)	RFM	594	143	1,677	73	6-50	4	22.97
18	L. J. Fletcher (*Notts & Surrey*)	RFM	86.1	20	253	11	4-58	0	23.00
19	T. K. Curran (*Surrey*)	RFM	544.4	129	1,754	76	7-20	5	23.07
20	N. J. Dexter (*Middx*)	RM	163.2	35	485	21	5-64	1	23.09
21	M. A. Starc (*Australians*)	LF	170.4	30	626	27	6-51	3	23.18
22	P. Coughlin (*Durham*)	RFM	134	34	443	19	4-10	0	23.31
23	L. C. Norwell (*Glos*)	RFM	507.3	109	1,592	68	6-33	3	23.41
24	M. T. Coles (*Kent*)	RFM	433	82	1,574	67	6-55	2	23.49
25	M. H. A. Footitt (*Derbys*)	LFM	537.4	113	1,796	76	7-71	5	23.63
26	P. M. Siddle (*Lancs & Australians*)	RFM	257.2	76	662	28	4-35	0	23.64
27	V. D. Philander (*Notts*)	RFM	154.3	40	384	16	4-56	0	24.00
28	C. N. Miles (*Glos*)	RFM	373.4	76	1,224	50	6-63	4	24.48
29	B. A. Hutton (*Notts*)	RM	262.1	51	912	37	5-29	2	24.64
30	O. E. Robinson (*Sussex*)	RFM	320.1	66	1,137	46	6-33	1	24.71
31	H. F. Gurney (*Notts*)	LFM	326.5	63	1,063	43	5-43	2	24.72
32	K. M. Jarvis (*Lancs*)	RFM	450.5	87	1,533	62	5-13	4	24.72
33	O. H. Freckingham (*Leics*)	RFM	131	17	520	21	5-39	1	24.76
34	C. J. McKay (*Leics*)	RFM	480.5	122	1,439	58	6-54	3	24.81
35	S. T. Finn (*Middx & England*)	RFM	353.4	71	1,071	43	6-79	1	24.90
36	R. S. Bopara (*Essex*)	RM	154.2	25	524	21	4-29	0	24.95
37	J. S. Patel (*Warwicks*)	OB	497.5	113	1,466	58	7-38	3	25.27
38	B. A. C. Howell (*Glos*)	RM	180.2	36	582	23	3-28	0	25.30
39	A. C. Thomas (*Somerset*)	RFM	237.4	54	735	29	5-73	1	25.34

		Style	O	M	R	W	BB	5I	Avge
40	S. A. Patterson (*Yorks*)	RFM	476.1	160	1,242	49	5-11	2	25.34
41	J. A. R. Harris (*Middx*)	RFM	489.2	75	1,854	73	9-34	5	25.39
42	M. J. Leach (*Somerset*)	SLA	152.1	41	408	16	7-106	1	25.50
43	R. Clarke (*Warwicks*)	RFM	387.3	83	1,206	47	5-62	1	25.65
44	W. M. H. Rhodes (*Yorks*)	RFM	98.5	23	311	12	3-42	0	25.91
45	J. D. Middlebrook (*Yorks*)	OB	126.3	22	441	17	5-82	1	25.94
46	T. J. Murtagh (*Middx*)	RFM	413.2	91	1,194	46	4-55	0	25.95
47	J. D. Ryder (*Essex*)	RM	345.4	71	1,176	45	6-47	3	26.13
48	S. M. Curran (*Surrey*)	LFM	145.2	21	575	22	5-67	2	26.13
49	G. Onions (*MCC & Durham*)	RFM	495.4	90	1,807	69	7-68	3	26.18
50	W. B. Rankin (*Warwicks*)	RFM	272.3	28	1,127	43	6-55	2	26.20
51	J. R. Hazlewood (*Australians*)	RFM	141	27	527	20	4-42	0	26.35
52	A. U. Rashid (*England*)	LBG	250	35	936	35	4-48	0	26.74
53	M. G. Hogan (*Glam*)	RFM	482.1	126	1,297	48	5-44	2	27.02
54	T. S. Roland-Jones (*Middx*)	RFM	471	112	1,298	48	5-27	1	27.04
55	D. A. Payne (*Glos*)	LFM	290.3	65	921	34	4-50	0	27.08
56	R. K. Kleinveldt (*Northants*)	RFM	407.5	69	1,547	57	5-41	5	27.14
57	J. M. Anderson (*England & Lancs*)	RFM	239.5	56	740	27	7-77	2	27.40
58	M. D. Craig (*New Zealanders*)	OB	120.4	32	359	13	5-34	1	27.61
59	K. H. D. Barker (*Warwicks*)	LFM	424.4	91	1,274	46	5-68	2	27.69
60	J. A. Porter (*Essex*)	RFM	431.3	66	1,557	56	4-28	0	27.80
61	B. A. Raine (*Leics*)	RFM	537.1	127	1,698	61	5-43	2	27.83
62	G. R. Napier (*Essex*)	RFM	281	39	979	35	4-27	0	27.97
63	G. J. Batty (*Surrey*)	OB	400	77	1,127	40	6-51	2	28.17
64	C. J. Haggett (*Kent*)	RM	268	60	792	28	4-43	0	28.28
65	R. D. Pringle (*Durham*)	OB	160.4	37	566	20	5-63	1	28.30
66	G. K. Berg (*Hants*)	RFM	442.1	97	1,218	43	4-64	0	28.32
67	T. D. Groenewald (*Somerset*)	RFM	312.5	54	1,112	39	5-65	1	28.51
68	C. J. Jordan (*Sussex*)	RFM	197.4	28	686	24	5-68	1	28.58
69	S. J. Croft (*Lancs*)	RFM/OB	96.1	13	286	10	4-35	0	28.60
70	E. G. Barnard (*Worcs*)	RFM	100.1	20	345	12	3-63	0	28.75
71	A. M. Lilley (*Lancs*)	OB	234.3	44	751	26	5-23	1	28.88
72	P. D. Collingwood (*Durham*)	RM/OB	93.5	20	320	11	5-57	1	29.09
73	J. T. Ball (*Notts*)	RM	339.3	63	1,210	41	6-49	1	29.51
74	M. A. Chambers (*Northants*)	RFM	114.3	21	415	14	3-44	0	29.64
75	C. E. Shreck (*Kent*)	RFM	512.4	116	1,691	57	5-71	2	29.66
76	Azharullah (*Northants*)	RFM	425.5	97	1,342	45	5-31	2	29.82
77	J. Leach (*Worcs*)	RFM	467	74	1,772	59	6-73	2	30.03
78	L. Wood (*Notts*)	LM	247.2	53	907	30	3-27	0	30.23
79	D. D. Masters (*Essex*)	RFM	224.2	54	606	20	4-45	0	30.30
80	M. G. Johnson (*Australians*)	LF	170.1	37	609	20	4-56	0	30.45
81	M. A. Wood (*Durham & England*)	RFM	219.4	48	764	25	4-39	0	30.56
82	M. D. Hunn (*Kent*)	RFM	199	35	704	23	5-99	1	30.60
83	O. P. Stone (*Northants*)	RFM	350.4	62	1,166	38	5-44	1	30.68
84	T. T. Bresnan (*Yorks*)	RFM	457.5	123	1,482	48	5-85	2	30.87
85	S. J. Mullaney (*Notts*)	RM	129.5	27	464	15	3-44	0	30.93
86	C. A. J. Morris (*Worcs*)	RFM	494	99	1,549	50	5-71	1	30.98
87	A. P. Palladino (*Derbys*)	RFM	382.4	110	993	32	3-19	0	31.03
88	G. M. Andrew (*Worcs*)	RFM	78.1	12	311	10	5-85	1	31.10
89	W. J. Durston (*Derbys*)	OB	203	23	753	24	6-109	2	31.37
90	Z. S. Ansari (*MCC & Surrey*)	SLA	454.4	75	1,445	46	6-30	3	31.41
91	S. R. Patel (*Notts*)	SLA	320.1	88	944	30	4-23	0	31.46
92	J. Allenby (*Somerset*)	RM	288	78	728	23	3-36	0	31.65
93	J. W. Hastings (*Durham*)	RFM	425	88	1,458	46	7-60	2	31.69
94	L. A. Dawson (*Hants & Essex*)	SLA	300.4	58	926	29	5-139	1	31.93
95	S. C. Kerrigan (*Lancs*)	SLA	460.2	100	1,321	41	4-28	0	32.21
96	O. P. Rayner (*Middx*)	OB	273	71	780	24	3-44	0	32.50
97	L. E. Plunkett (*Yorks*)	RFM	115.1	17	459	14	4-61	0	32.78
98	L. Gregory (*Somerset*)	RFM	354.1	53	1,351	41	6-101	3	32.95
99	C. J. C. Wright (*Warwicks*)	RFM	274.2	36	1,033	31	5-40	1	33.32
100	M. S. Crane (*Hants*)	LBG	77	11	336	10	5-35	1	33.60

		Style	O	M	R	W	BB	5I	Avge
101	T. A. I. Taylor (*Derbys*)	RFM	241.2	34	946	28	6-61	1	33.78
102	T. E. Bailey (*Lancs*)	RFM	347.3	64	1,192	35	5-12	1	34.05
103	I. A. A. Thomas (*Kent*)	RFM	289.4	57	923	27	4-48	0	34.18
104	B. L. D'Oliveira (*Worcs*)	LBG	118.5	22	445	13	5-48	1	34.23
105	D. R. Briggs (*Hants*)	SLA	258	66	723	21	4-74	0	34.42
106	K. Noema-Barnett (*Glos*)	RM	190.5	53	598	17	3-28	0	35.17
107	S. P. Crook (*Northants*)	RFM	172.1	23	678	19	3-28	0	35.68
108	J. K. Fuller (*Glos*)	RFM	292.5	58	972	27	4-35	0	36.00
109	M. P. Dunn (*MCC & Surrey*)	RFM	278.5	39	1,086	30	4-72	0	36.20
110	D. J. Willey (*Northants*)	LFM	155	25	547	15	4-72	0	36.46
111	S. G. Borthwick (*Durham*)	LBG	183.2	29	734	20	4-46	0	36.70
112	P. D. Trego (*Somerset*)	RFM	298.3	62	1,037	28	4-73	0	37.03
113	J. Overton (*Somerset*)	RFM	188.5	36	633	17	4-37	0	37.23
114	N. M. Lyon (*Australians*)	OB	190.5	30	745	20	4-75	0	37.25
115	G. G. Wagg (*Glam*)	SLA/LM	467.4	73	1,681	45	5-54	1	37.35
116	C. A. J. Meschede (*Glam*)	RM	438.3	69	1,609	43	4-89	0	37.41
117	L. W. P. Wells (*Sussex*)	LBG	226	27	862	23	3-35	0	37.47
118	R. McLaren (*Hants*)	RFM	128.5	24	419	11	4-60	0	38.09
119	J. K. H. Naik (*Leics*)	OB	182.5	33	690	18	8-179	1	38.33
120	J. A. Tomlinson (*Hants*)	LFM	252	61	778	20	4-37	0	38.90
121	C. J. Liddle (*Sussex*)	LFM	110	15	391	10	3-49	0	39.10
122	J. M. Bird (*Hants*)	RFM	207.2	34	755	19	4-146	0	39.73
123	C. A. Ingram (*Glam*)	LBG	103.3	9	398	10	3-90	0	39.80
124	R. M. L. Taylor (*Leics*)	LM	167.4	24	720	18	3-41	0	40.00
125	J. C. Tredwell (*Kent*)	OB	164.5	45	443	11	3-59	0	40.27
126	A. S. S. Nijjar (*Essex*)	SLA	121.3	12	489	12	2-33	0	40.75
127	M. D. Taylor (*Glos*)	LM	157.1	36	544	13	5-93	1	41.84
128	Ashar Zaidi (*Sussex*)	SLA	188.1	42	461	11	3-55	0	41.90
129	B. A. Stokes (*England*)	RFM	166	36	642	15	6-36	1	42.80
130	J. Harrison (*Durham*)	LFM	115.4	15	436	10	2-42	0	43.60
131	D. L. Lloyd (*Glam*)	RM	215.2	23	942	21	3-68	0	44.85
132	A. G. Salter (*Glam*)	OB	339.1	42	1,150	25	3-5	0	46.00
133	J. Clark (*Lancs*)	RM	244.4	38	880	19	4-101	0	46.31
134	J. M. R. Taylor (*Glos*)	OB	159	29	466	10	3-119	0	46.60
135	A. E. N. Riley (*MCC & Kent*)	OB	188.5	22	752	16	4-47	0	47.00
136	M. E. Hobden (*Sussex*)	RFM	261.3	37	1,114	23	4-48	0	48.43
137	G. Chapple (*Lancs*)	RFM	166	44	489	10	4-62	0	48.90
138	B. D. Cotton (*Derbys*)	RFM	223.1	49	745	15	3-26	0	49.66
139	M. E. Claydon (*Kent*)	RFM	175.5	19	656	13	4-103	0	50.46
140	S. J. Thakor (*Derbys*)	RM	188.4	33	667	13	2-11	0	51.30
141	M. M. Ali (*Worcs & England*)	OB	269.4	29	1,068	20	3-59	0	53.40
142	R. I. Keogh (*Northants*)	OB	310	42	1,069	20	3-35	0	53.45
143	Saeed Ajmal (*Worcs*)	OB	272.3	42	890	16	5-28	1	55.62
144	Abdur Rehman (*Somerset*)	SLA	219.2	35	766	10	2-60	0	76.60

The following bowlers took ten wickets in fewer than five innings:

	Style	O	M	R	W	BB	5I	Avge
M. Carter (*Notts*)	OB	49.4	6	195	10	7-56	1	19.50
T. A. Boult (*New Zealanders*)	LFM	116	25	323	13	5-85	1	24.84

BOWLING STYLES

LBG	Leg-breaks (6)	**OB**	Off-breaks (20)
LF	Left-arm fast (2)	**RFM**	Right-arm fast medium (78)
LFM	Left-arm fast medium (13)	**RM**	Right-arm medium (16)
LM	Left-arm medium (4)	**SLA**	Slow left-arm (10)

The total comes to 149 because P. D. Collingwood, S. J. Croft and G. G. Wagg have two styles of bowling.

INDIVIDUAL SCORES OF 100 AND OVER

There were **244** three-figure innings in 170 first-class matches in 2015, four more than in 2014, when 166 first-class matches were played. Of these, 17 were double-hundreds, compared with 12 in 2014. The list includes 208 hundreds hit in the County Championship, compared with 206 in 2014.

J. M. Bairstow (5)
102 Yorks v Hants, Leeds
125* Yorks v Middx, Leeds
219* Yorks v Durham, Chester-le-Street
108 Yorks v Warwicks, Birmingham
139 Yorks v Worcs, Scarborough

N. L. J. Browne (5)
143 Essex v Surrey, The Oval
105 Essex v Lancs, Manchester
129 Essex v Glam, Chelmsford
114 Essex v Surrey, Colchester
151* Essex v Leics, Leicester

B. M. Duckett (5)
101* Northants v Camb MCCU, Cambridge
134 Northants v Lancs, Manchester
154 Northants v Derbys, Northampton
145 Northants v Kent, Canterbury
120 Northants v Surrey, The Oval

J. C. Hildreth (5)
102 Somerset v Durham MCCU, Taunton Vale
187 Somerset v Middx, Taunton
115 Somerset v New Zealanders, Taunton
220* Somerset v Worcs, Taunton
118 Somerset v Warwicks, Taunton

A. G. Prince (5)
106 Lancs v Kent, Manchester
153 Lancs v Northants, Northampton
230 Lancs v Derbys, Southport
104 Lancs v Leics, Manchester
261 Lancs v Glam, Colwyn Bay

K. C. Sangakkara (5)
149 Surrey v Glam, Cardiff
111 Surrey v Northants, Northampton
110 Surrey v Kent, The Oval
118 Surrey v Lancs, Manchester
101 Surrey v Northants, The Oval

B. C. Brown (4)
144* Sussex v Hants, Southampton
119* Sussex v Warwicks, Birmingham
106* Sussex v Yorks, Hove
103 Sussex v Worcs, Worcester

M. J. Cosgrove (4)
113 Leics v Kent, Canterbury
102 Leics v Derbys, Leicester
110 Leics v Northants, Northampton
156 Leics v Derbys, Derby

B. R. M. Taylor (4)
105 Notts v Lough MCCU, Nottingham
106 Notts v Middx, Lord's
103 Notts v Hants, Southampton
152 Notts v Somerset, Taunton

D. J. Bell-Drummond (3)
103 Kent v Leics, Canterbury
123 Kent v Glam, Canterbury
127 Kent v Australians, Canterbury

C. D. J. Dent (3)
104* Glos v Northants, Northampton
116 Glos v Lancs, Manchester
268 Glos v Glam, Bristol

T. C. Fell (3)
114 Worcs v Yorks, Worcester
143 Worcs v Middx, Uxbridge
171 Worcs v Middx, Worcester

A. W. Gale (3)
148 Yorks v Notts, Leeds
164 Yorks v Worcs, Scarborough
125 Yorks v Hants, Southampton

B. A. Godleman (3)
101 Derbys v Leics, Leicester
108 ⎱ Derbys v Kent, Derby
105*⎰

A. D. Hales (3)
236 Notts v Yorks, Nottingham
141 Notts v Hants, Southampton
189 Notts v Warwicks, Nottingham

J. A. Leaning (3)
116 Yorks v Notts, Nottingham
123 Yorks v Somerset, Taunton
110 Yorks v Notts, Leeds

M. W. Machan (3)
135 Sussex v Worcs, Hove
192 Sussex v Somerset, Taunton
108 Sussex v Notts, Horsham

A. N. Petersen (3)
115 Lancs v Derbys, Derby
113 Lancs v Derbys, Southport
286 Lancs v Glam, Colwyn Bay

C. M. W. Read (3)
101* Notts v Middx, Lord's
108 Notts v Middx, Nottingham
121 Notts v Sussex, Horsham

S. P. D. Smith (3)
111 Australians v Kent, Canterbury
215 Australia v England, Lord's
143 Australia v England, The Oval

M. D. Stoneman (3)
111 Durham v Warwicks, Birmingham
131 Durham v Yorks, Chester-le-Street
112 Durham v Warwicks, Chester-le-Street

M. E. Trescothick (3)
140 Somerset v Middx, Taunton
153 Somerset v Hants, Taunton
210* Somerset v Sussex, Hove

T. R. Ambrose (2)
113 Warwicks v Hants, Birmingham
153 Warwicks v Sussex, Birmingham

S. G. Borthwick (2)
104 Durham v Durham MCCU, Chester-le-St
103 Durham v Worcs, Worcester

W. D. Bragg (2)
120 Glam v Leics, Leicester
104 Glam v Kent, Canterbury

T. T. Bresnan (2)
100* Yorks v Somerset, Taunton
169* Yorks v Durham, Chester-le-Street

R. J. Burns (2)
110* Surrey v Lancs, The Oval
158 Surrey v Essex, Colchester

V. Chopra (2)
119* Warwicks v Hants, Birmingham
107 Warwicks v Worcs, Birmingham

P. D. Collingwood (2)
109* Durham v Somerset, Taunton
127 Durham v Worcs, Worcester

N. R. D. Compton (2)
117 Middx v Hants, Southampton
149 Middx v Yorks, Lord's

C. B. Cooke (2)
112 Glam v Cardiff MCCU, Cardiff
102* Glam v Glos, Bristol

S. J. Croft (2)
102 Lancs v Leics, Leicester
122 Lancs v Essex, Manchester

S. P. Crook (2)
102* Northants v Lancs, Northampton
142* Northants v Australians, Northampton

S. M. Davies (2)
200* Surrey v Glam, Cardiff
115* Surrey v Leics, The Oval

J. L. Denly (2)
117 Kent v Glos, Bristol
161 Kent v Glam, Cardiff

E. J. H. Eckersley (2)
147 Leics v Glam, Leicester
118 Leics v Surrey, The Oval

B. T. Foakes (2)
118 Surrey v Glos, The Oval
140* Surrey v Glos, Bristol

J. E. C. Franklin (2)
115* Middx v Somerset, Taunton
135 Middx v Worcs, Uxbridge

S. R. Hain (2)
106 Warwicks v Yorks, Birmingham
103* Warwicks v Somerset, Birmingham

A. Harinath (2)
120 ⎫
104 ⎭ Surrey v Glam, Guildford

C. F. Hughes (2)
104 Derbys v Northants, Derby
101 Derbys v Leics, Derby

C. A. Ingram (2)
105* Glam v Kent, Cardiff
101* Glam v Glos, Bristol

R. I. Keogh (2)
100 Northants v Lancs, Northampton
163* Northants v Derbys, Derby

R. W. T. Key (2)
113 Kent v Lancs, Canterbury
158 Kent v Glam, Cardiff

M. Klinger (2)
102 Glos v Lancs, Bristol
103 Glos v Essex, Bristol

A. Lyth (2)
113 Yorks v MCC, Abu Dhabi
107 England v New Zealand, Leeds

W. L. Madsen (2)
112 Derbys v Essex, Chelmsford
172* Derbys v Leics, Leicester

D. J. Malan (2)
182* Middx v Notts, Nottingham
120* Middx v Sussex, Lord's

M. R. Marsh (2)
101 Australians v Kent, Canterbury
169 Australians v Essex, Chelmsford

S. E. Marsh (2)
114 Australians v Kent, Canterbury
101 Australians v Derbys, Derby

C. A. J. Meschede (2)
101* Glam v Surrey, Cardiff
107 Glam v Northants, Cardiff

D. K. H. Mitchell (2)
142* Worcs v Hants, Southampton
206* Worcs v Hants, Worcester

G. J. Muchall (2)
115 Durham v Sussex, Arundel
145 Durham v Hants, Southampton

S. J. Mullaney (2)
118 Notts v Lough MCCU, Nottingham
112 Notts v Warwicks, Nottingham

J. G. Myburgh (2)
150* Somerset v Durham MCCU, Taunton Vale
118 Somerset v Durham, Taunton

C. D. Nash (2)
121 Sussex v Warwicks, Birmingham
142* Sussex v Somerset, Taunton

S. R. Patel (2)
100 Notts v Sussex, Nottingham
100 Notts v Durham, Nottingham

M. L. Pettini (2)
134 Essex v Surrey, Colchester
117* Essex v Derbys, Derby

J. E. Root (2)
134 England v Australia, Cardiff
130 England v Australia, Nottingham

J. J. Roy (2)
140 Surrey v Northants, Northampton
143 Surrey v Lancs, The Oval

J. D. Ryder (2)
124 Essex v Northants, Northampton
116 Essex v Lancs, Chelmsford

J. M. R. Taylor (2)
120 Glos v Derbys, Derby
156 Glos v Northants, Cheltenham

J. W. A. Taylor (2)
291 Notts v Sussex, Horsham
164 Notts v Warwicks, Birmingham

P. D. Trego (2)
130* Somerset v Worcs, Taunton
100* Somerset v Sussex, Hove

J. M. Vince (2)
140 Hants v Lough MCCU, Southampton
125* Hants v Warwicks, Southampton

A. G. Wakely (2)
104 Northants v Glos, Cheltenham
123 Northants v Leics, Northampton

M. H. Wessels (2)
117 Notts v Durham, Chester-le-Street
104 Notts v Hants, Nottingham

T. Westley (2)
179 Essex v Northants, Northampton
144 Essex v Australians, Chelmsford

D. J. Willey (2)
104* Northants v Glos, Northampton
103 Northants v Derbys, Derby

L. J. Wright (2)
110 Sussex v Warwicks, Birmingham
226* Sussex v Worcs, Worcester

M. H. Yardy (2)
124 Sussex v Yorks, Hove
104 Sussex v Somerset, Hove

The following each played one three-figure innings:

T. B. Abell, 131, Somerset v Hants, Taunton; J. H. K. Adams, 136, Hants v Somerset, Taunton; Z. S. Ansari, 106, Surrey v Derbys, The Oval; Ashar Zaidi, 106, Sussex v Warwicks, Birmingham. G. S. Ballance, 165, Yorks v Sussex, Hove; K. H. D. Barker, 102*, Warwicks v Durham, Birmingham; I. R. Bell, 111, Warwicks v Worcs, Worcester; S. W. Billings, 100*, Kent v Essex, Tunbridge Wells; A. D. Blofield, 105, Cambridge U v Oxford U, Cambridge; R. S. Bopara, 107, Essex v Australians, Chelmsford; K. R. Brown, 132, Lancs v Glam, Manchester.

M. A. Carberry, 146, Hants v Lough MCCU, Southampton; J. M. Clarke, 104*, Worcs v Sussex, Worcester; A. N. Cook, 162, England v New Zealand, Lord's; T. L. W. Cooper, 118, Somerset v Hants, Taunton; O. B. Cox, 109, Worcs v Somerset, Worcester; M. J. J. Critchley, 137*, Derbys v Northants, Derby.

L. A. Dawson, 140, Hants v Yorks, Southampton; N. J. Dexter, 112, Middx v Durham, Chester-le-Street.

S. L. Elstone, 103*, Derbys v Glam, Cardiff; S. M. Ervine, 102, Hants v Warwicks, Birmingham; L. J. Evans, 213*, Warwicks v Sussex, Birmingham.

J. P. Faulkner, 121, Lancs v Surrey, The Oval.

M. J. Guptill, 227, Derbys v Glos, Bristol.

B. W. Harmison, 123, Kent v Essex, Tunbridge Wells; L. J. Hill, 126, Leics v Surrey, The Oval; P. J. Horton, 168, Lancs v Glos, Manchester; B. A. C. Howell, 102, Glos v Leics, Cheltenham; A. L. Hughes, 111*, Derbys v Northants, Northampton; M. S. T. Hughes, 116, Oxford U v Cambridge U, Cambridge.

K. K. Jennings, 177*, Durham v Durham MCCU, Chester-le-Street; E. C. Joyce, 100, Sussex v Yorks, Hove.

T. Köhler-Cadmore, 130*, Worcs v Middx, Worcester.

D. W. Lawrence, 161, Essex v Surrey, The Oval; A. Z. Lees, 100, Yorks v Notts, Nottingham; R. E. Levi, 168, Northants v Essex, Northampton.

G. J. Maxwell, 140, Yorks v Durham, Scarborough; D. Murphy, 135*, Northants v Surrey, The Oval.

R. I. Newton, 107, Northants v Glam, Cardiff; S. A. Northeast, 139, Kent v Lancs, Canterbury.

R. K. Oliver, 101, Worcs v Sussex, Hove.

K. P. Pietersen, 355*, Surrey v Leics, The Oval; N. D. Pinner, 165*, Leics v Cambridge MCCU, Cambridge; C. A. Pujara, 133*, Yorks v Hants, Leeds.

A. U. Rashid, 127, Yorks v Durham, Scarborough; O. E. Robinson, 110, Sussex v Durham, Chester-le-Street; A. J. Robson, 120, Leics v Essex, Chelmsford; S. D. Robson, 178, Middx v Durham, Lord's; G. H. Roderick, 100*, Glos v Cardiff MCCU, Bristol; C. J. L. Rogers, 173, Australia v England, Lord's; T. S. Roland-Jones, 103*, Middx v Yorks, Lord's; A. M. Rossington, 116, Northants v Surrey, The Oval; J. A. Rudolph, 111, Glam v Leics, Leicester; H. D. Rutherford, 108, Derbys v Glam, Chesterfield.

B. A. Stokes, 101, England v New Zealand, Lord's.

A. C. Voges, 132, Middx v Somerset, Taunton.

G. G. Wagg, 200, Glam v Surrey, Guildford; D. A. Warner, 101, Australians v Derbys, Derby; B-J. Watling, 120, New Zealand v England, Leeds; L. W. P. Wells, 108, Sussex v Durham, Arundel; I. J. Westwood, 196, Warwicks v Yorks, Leeds; A. J. A. Wheater, 111, Hants v Sussex, Hove; R. A. Whiteley, 101, Worcs v Yorks, Scarborough; K. S. Williamson, 132, New Zealand v England, Lord's; L. Wood, 100, Notts v Sussex, Nottingham.

FASTEST HUNDREDS BY BALLS...

Balls	Mins		
57	77	S. M. Davies	Surrey v Leics at The Oval.
70	117	M. W. Machan	Sussex v Worcs at Hove.
76	87	C. M. W. Read	Notts v Middx at Lord's.
77	98	S. P. Crook	Northants v Australians at Northampton.
79	128	D. J. Willey	Northants v Glos at Northampton.
82	132	A. J. A. Wheater	Hants v Sussex at Hove.
84	103	B. C. Brown	Sussex v Yorks at Hove.
85	92	B. A. Stokes	England v New Zealand at Lord's.
86	128	J. M. R. Taylor	Glos v Northants at Cheltenham.
88	111	A. M. Rossington	Northants v Surrey at The Oval.
90	101	S. P. Crook	Northants v Lancs at Northampton.
92	137	D. J. Bell-Drummond	Kent v Australians at Canterbury.
93	100	M. R. Marsh	Australians v Kent at Canterbury.
93	117	J. M. Vince	Hants v Lough MCCU at Southampton.
94	117	B. M. Duckett	Northants v Cambridge MCCU at Cambridge.
95	103	L. Wood	Notts v Sussex at Nottingham.
95	125	C. A. J. Meschede	Glam v Northants at Cardiff.
98	146	D. J. Willey	Northants v Derbys at Derby.
99	126	G. G. Wagg	Glam v Surrey at Guildford.
99	158	M. W. Machan	Sussex v Notts at Horsham.

...AND THE SLOWEST

Balls	Mins		
269	334	V. Chopra	Warwicks v Hants at Birmingham.
265	349	C. D. J. Dent	Glos v Northants at Northampton.
249	265	C. F. Hughes	Derbys v Northants at Derby.
248	299	D. K. H. Mitchell	Worcs v Hants at Southampton.
229	282	H. D. Rutherford	Derbys v Glam at Chesterfield.
229	282	G. J. Muchall	Durham v Hants at Southampton.
223	267	A. Z. Lees	Yorks v Notts at Nottingham.
220	268	C. A. Ingram	Glam v Glos at Bristol.
217	322	K. R. Brown	Lancs v Glam at Manchester.
217	252	A. G. Wakely	Northants v Glos at Cheltenham.
216	275	L. W. P. Wells	Sussex v Durham at Arundel.
215	271	G. J. Muchall	Durham v Sussex at Arundel.

TEN WICKETS IN A MATCH

There were **14** instances of bowlers taking ten or more wickets in a first-class match in 2015, three fewer than in 2014. Thirteen were in the County Championship.

The following each took ten wickets in a match on one occasion:

M. Carter, 10-195, Notts v Somerset, Taunton; M. T. Coles, 10-98, Kent v Leics, Leicester; T. K. Curran, 10-176, Surrey v Northants, The Oval.

F. H. Edwards, 10-145, Hants v Notts, Nottingham.

M. H. A. Footitt, 10-155, Derbys v Leics, Derby.

J. A. R. Harris, 13-103, Middx v Durham, Lord's; B. A. Hutton, 10-106, Notts v Durham, Nottingham.

M. J. Leach, 11-180, Somerset v Warwicks, Taunton.

S. J. Magoffin, 12-159, Sussex v Notts, Nottingham; C. N. Miles, 10-121, Glos v Lancs, Bristol.

L. C. Norwell, 10-65, Glos v Essex, Chelmsford.

J. D. Ryder, 10-100, Essex v Glam, Chelmsford.

J. D. Shantry, 10-26, Worcs v Oxford MCCU, Oxford; R. J. Sidebottom, 11-76, Yorks v Warwicks, Birmingham.

LV= COUNTY CHAMPIONSHIP IN 2015

ALAN GARDNER

Division One 1 Yorkshire 2 Middlesex
Division Two 1 Surrey 2 Lancashire

The uncertainty principle, as laid out by Werner Heisenberg in the first half of the 20th century, is fundamental to our understanding of quantum mechanics and the physics of the universe. Something similar applies to the County Championship, a subject which provokes almost as much head-scratching. Second only in complexity to the structure of the atom, its formulae are annually subject to theory and revision. Establishing a model in which the component particles revolve around each other in perfect harmony is likely to be beyond even a Nobel Prize winner.

Uncertainty is also one of the primary attractions of sport but, while debate about the future of the competition threw up all sorts of possibilities, a sense emerged of the established order. For the first time since the splitting of the Championship in 2000, only one of the counties without a Test ground (Somerset) will play in Division One in 2016, and only one *with* a Test ground (Glamorgan) in Division Two.

COUNTY CHAMPIONSHIP TABLE

	Division One	Matches	Won	Lost	Drawn	Bonus points Batting	Bonus points Bowling	Penalty	Points
1	Yorkshire (**1**)	16	11	1	4	45	45	0	286
2	Middlesex (**7**)	16	7	2	7	29	43	1*	218
3	Nottinghamshire (**4**)	16	6	5	5	45	45	0	211
4	Durham (**5**)	16	7	8	1	26	45	0	188
5	Warwickshire (**2**)	16	5	5	6	31	45	0	186
6	Somerset (**6**)	16	4	6	6	46	43	0	183
7	Hampshire (*1*)	16	4	6	6	31	38	0	163
8	Sussex (*3*)	16	4	8	4	36	41	0	161
9	Worcestershire (*2*)	16	3	10	3	44	44	0	151

	Division Two	Matches	Won	Lost	Drawn	Bonus points Batting	Bonus points Bowling	Penalty	Points
1	Surrey (*5*)	16	8	1	7	56	45	0	264
2	Lancashire (**8**)	16	7	1	8	58	44	0	254
3	Essex (*3*)	16	6	5	5	37	42	0	200
4	Glamorgan (*8*)	16	4	4	8	42	37	0	183
5	Northamptonshire (**9**) . . .	16	3	3	10	38	46	2*	180
6	Gloucestershire (*7*)	16	5	5	6	31	36	0	177
7	Kent (*6*)	16	4	7	5	28	44	0	161
8	Derbyshire (*4*)	16	3	7	6	34	42	1*	153
9	Leicestershire (*9*)	16	2	9	5	36	41	16†	118

2014 positions are shown in brackets: Division One in bold, Division Two in italic.

Win = 16pts; draw = 5pts.

* *Penalties deducted for slow over-rates.* † *Penalties deducted under disciplinary code.*

Concern about the widening gap became more acute as plans emerged for another significant restructuring. Although the ECB's strategic plan was only halfway through a four-year cycle, a new management team – headed by the chairman, Colin Graves, and the chief executive, Tom Harrison – undertook a review of the entire domestic schedule, amid promises of radical reform and a streamlined season; Andrew Strauss, freshly installed as England's director of cricket, was also heavily involved. Appointed in the wake of another feeble World Cup campaign, Strauss had called for an increased focus on limited-overs cricket to aid England's cause at the next two ICC 50-over tournaments – both to be held in the UK – as well as more time in the fixture list for rest and recovery. "Controversially, that probably means playing one or two less first-class matches," said Harrison in mid-August.

It was a statement liable to cause dyspepsia, and not solely among grammarians. If a 14-game Championship was considered the best – or least worst – option, then to retain the integrity of Division One it would need to be reduced to eight teams. What would become of the unwashed down below? An asymmetrical fixture list might be the least of their worries: the possibility of only one team going up each year would mean an even greater scramble for attention and resources. A deeper fear lurked about this being the thin end of a city-based, T20-franchise-branded wedge.

Nevertheless, initial reports suggested that county chairmen were prepared to vote through such proposals, only for the ECB to announce in September that there would be no immediate "substantial change", and that "constructive, collaborative discussions on the future shape of the domestic cricket season will continue". The arguments between traditionalists and modernisers might have been part of a reassuring ritual, but in private Strauss expressed frustration at the lack of progress. Perhaps he could derive comfort from William Hazlitt: "When a thing ceases to be a subject of controversy, it ceases to be a subject of interest." Controversy by no means guaranteed interest, but the fact that so many were engaged by the debate was heartening.

The boardroom tussles may have been more closely fought than the title race, but that was of little concern to followers of **Yorkshire**, as the most successful county in the history of the Championship won their 32nd outright title with embarrassing ease. The celebrations were extended as captain Andrew Gale lifted the trophy three weeks running – at Lord's, the Rose Bowl and, finally, in front of home support at Headingley. Having been denied the opportunity 12 months earlier for disciplinary reasons, Gale was understandably happy to indulge.

This was Yorkshire's first back-to-back triumph since 1968 – when they won the third of three successive titles – and their strength was such that some foresaw a period of dominance comparable to that golden generation. While England called up seven of their players at various times – and also threatened to poach the head coach, Jason Gillespie – the club could tap into deep reserves of talent. They drew three of their opening five matches, offering their rivals a hint of encouragement, before reeling off six victories on the way to a record-breaking final analysis: 11 wins was one better than any team had achieved in the two-tier Championship, and a points tally of 286 smashed the previous

County of the broad smiles: Ryan Sidebottom is mobbed by team-mates after he takes his fifth wicket against Middlesex; later, on a busy first day, Yorkshire are confirmed as champions.

high mark, both in Division One (Sussex's 257 in 2003) and Division Two (Somerset's 266 in 2007).

Because of the staggering of rounds, Yorkshire did not actually take the lead until the midway point of the season but, on the hottest July day recorded in the UK, they roasted Durham by an innings at Chester-le-Street to replace them at the top. The majority of their wins were similarly emphatic, with only two coming by fewer than seven wickets or 100 runs. Yorkshire's lone defeat came after the title had been secured – even then, Middlesex had to overcome a 193-run deficit, their task possibly aided by the number of champagne corks in the visitors' dressing-room.

That result meant **Middlesex** – who had also given Yorkshire a game at Headingley – finished second, but they were never realistically close to challenging them. Two numbers illustrated the gap between t'best and t'rest: Yorkshire's margin of victory was 68 points, while 67 was all that separated the eight teams below. Middlesex were beaten only twice on the way to their highest Championship finish since 1995, but drew as many as they won.

Behind them came **Nottinghamshire**, who had been joint-bottom with Hampshire after eight games. The appointment of Peter Moores as a coaching consultant, after his second sacking by England, coincided with their resurgence – and added to Moores's impressive CV at county level – as they climbed the table with five victories in the second half of season. **Durham**, by contrast, did not win between June and September, and dropped back to fourth, despite having the Championship's leading wicket-taker by some distance in Chris Rushworth. **Warwickshire** also finished with a splutter, having briefly been second, only to lose three and draw two of their last five games.

Once again, it was the matter of relegation, responsible for contrasting emotions on the south coast, that kept fans guessing into the final weeks. **Somerset** captain Marcus Trescothick helped make sure of his side's survival by piling up more than 450 runs in their last three fixtures, belatedly joining team-mate James Hildreth in the top three first division run-scorers, while **Worcestershire's** journey in the opposite direction – their fifth relegation in 12 seasons – was confirmed in the penultimate round. They were left adrift at the bottom, defeated ten times, despite taking a first-innings lead on as many occasions; Saeed Ajmal, so integral to their promotion campaign, returned with the kinks hammered out of his action, along with much of the potency.

Instead it was **Hampshire** who managed to get the afterburners started in time to achieve escape velocity, at the expense of neighbours **Sussex**, who had won convincingly when the teams met in the opening round. Fidel Edwards returned from the Caribbean Premier League with renewed vigour (having spent his initial weeks tweeting about the lack of things to do in Southampton), and took 32 wickets at 17 as Hampshire won three of their last five matches to complete the most unlikely Houdini act since Worcestershire in 2011. Victory at Trent Bridge on the final day helped them make up a 16-point gap as Sussex, whose injury-hit bowling attack had become more of a defence, finally discovered their deckchairs were below the waterline.

The queue to decide which teams Division Two would send as replacements was also disappointingly orderly, although **Surrey**, the eventual champions, and **Lancashire** contested the title until the last. Both promotions were practically assured by late August, as theoretical rivals failed to land a glove on the two grandees, who each lost only once.

Surrey actually drew their opening two games, but Kevin Pietersen – perhaps fuelled by equal parts *amour propre* and patriotism – hammered 355 not out to provide the spark for victory over Leicestershire, achieved by chasing 216 inside 22 overs. They gradually asserted themselves, blending the experience of Kumar Sangakkara and Gareth Batty with young talent such as Zafar Ansari and the Curran brothers. Still, the fact that Lancashire were overhauled was in large part due to their drop-off after victory on T20 Finals Day. A seaside stroll at Colwyn Bay in July – during which Alviro Petersen and Ashwell Prince, the leading run-scorer in either division, put on a Lancashire-record partnership of 501 – seemed to confirm they were operating at a higher level. But that was to be their final win of the season as they coasted to the finish.

The rest filed into place with nary a murmur. **Essex** lived down to expectations by finishing third for the third season running, and sacked Paul Grayson after eight years in charge. **Glamorgan** could be encouraged by percolating up from eighth to fourth, although they won only one more game than in 2014. **Northamptonshire**, under severe financial threat, laboured to ten draws and found greater success in the limited-overs competitions, as did **Gloucestershire** and **Kent**, both rewarded for a willingness (perhaps born of necessity) to put their trust in youth.

At **Leicestershire**, the arrival of new management had stirred hope of a long-overdue revival: Wasim Khan, the chief executive, talked of aiming for promotion. But, despite emotional scenes at Chelmsford, where they ended a

37-game winless streak, they were left in possession of their fifth wooden spoon in seven years. Still, there might have been greater disappointment at **Derbyshire**, who finished next to bottom.

For some, it was all a bit of a slog. Eoin Morgan called the schedule "terrible", during a period in which Middlesex were due to play 12 days out of 14, in locations as far-flung as Southampton, Cardiff and Leeds. He felt it was dangerous, too: "Travelling and playing is a recipe for disaster." Alex Hales described the regular switching between formats as "detrimental to skill level". Bowlers, perhaps reflecting their traditional status, tended not to complain, but it was clear one aspect of the craft remained under threat.

With conditions favouring a preponderance of medium-pace, spinners operated at the margins. One of the Ashes subplots centred on whether the preparation of English pitches was a justified tactic. While green seamers turned out to be exactly what the doctor ordered in England's attempts to beat Australia, it was doubtful that a prescription would promote the long-term health of the game. Only four slow men – Jeetan Patel, Simon Kerrigan, Ansari and Batty – reached 30 Championship wickets, although Adil Rashid would have joined them had he not been a regular among Yorkshire's England contingent. Patel, the most successful by far, questioned whether English spinners practised their art enough, prompting a detailed public response from Middlesex's Ollie Rayner, in which he cited a lack of coaching, as well as the challenges thrown up by the fixture list. Whatever the reasons, the downward trend was as clear as it was dispiriting, with the proportion of wickets taken by spin falling below 17%.

The overriding sense was of an ecosystem in delicate balance and, rather like extreme weather and its possible connection to climate change, the 2015 Championship seemed to contain an unusually high incidence of freak events. There was 17-year-old Dan Lawrence of Essex becoming the third-youngest player to make a Championship hundred; the extraordinary first-class debut of Sussex's Ollie Robinson, in which he scored a run-a-ball century at No. 9 during a last-wicket stand of 164; the match between Middlesex and Durham at Lord's, in which 20 second-innings wickets fell inside 50 overs, including nine for James Harris; a 215-ball double-hundred from Glamorgan's Graham Wagg at No. 8; and Warwickshire's 612 for six in response to Sussex's 601 for six.

What to make of it all? No one quite knew. We were back in the realms of uncertainty, looking for a quantum of solace.

Pre-season betting (best available prices): *Division One* – 3-1 YORKSHIRE; 9-2 Warwickshire; 5-1 Nottinghamshire; 8-1 Durham; 10-1 Somerset and Sussex; 12-1 Hampshire; 16-1 Middlesex; 50-1 Worcestershire. *Division Two* – 3-1 SURREY; 100-30 Lancashire; 5-1 Essex; 8-1 Derbyshire; 9-1 Northamptonshire; 10-1 Kent; 18-1 Glamorgan; 25-1 Gloucestershire; 50-1 Leicestershire.

Prize money

Division One
£532,100 for winners: YORKSHIRE.
£221,020 for runners-up: MIDDLESEX.
£103,022 for third: NOTTINGHAMSHIRE.
£32,121 for fourth: DURHAM.
£24,000 for fifth: WARWICKSHIRE.

Division Two
£111,050 for winners: SURREY.
£51,052 for runners-up: LANCASHIRE.

Leaders: *Division One* – from April 14 Durham; April 22 Sussex; May 5 Middlesex; May 27 Durham; June 3 Middlesex; June 9 Durham; July 1 Yorkshire. Yorkshire became champions on September 9.

Division Two – from April 15 Glamorgan; April 22 Glamorgan and Lancashire; April 29 Lancashire; September 4 Surrey. Surrey became champions on September 25.

Bottom place: *Division One* – from April 22 Somerset; April 29 Somerset and Worcestershire; May 5 Somerset; May 21 Worcestershire and Hampshire; May 27 Hampshire; June 9 Somerset; June 17 Worcestershire; June 24 Hampshire and Nottinghamshire; July 1 Hampshire; September 4 Worcestershire.

Division Two – from April 21 Kent; May 21 Essex and Leicestershire; June 3 Essex; June 16 Kent; July 7 Leicestershire.

Scoring of Points

(*a*) For a win, 16 points plus any points scored in the first innings.

(*b*) In a tie, each side score eight points, plus any points scored in the first innings.

(*c*) In a drawn match, each side score five points, plus any points scored in the first innings.

(*d*) If the scores are equal in a drawn match, the side batting in the fourth innings score eight points, plus any points scored in the first innings, and the opposing side score five points, plus any points scored in the first innings.

(*e*) First-innings points (awarded only for performances in the first 110 overs of each first innings and retained whatever the result of the match):

    (i) A maximum of five batting points to be available: 200 to 249 runs – 1 point; 250 to 299 runs – 2 points; 300 to 349 runs – 3 points; 350 to 399 runs – 4 points; 400 runs or over – 5 points. Penalty runs awarded within the first 110 overs of each first innings count towards the award of bonus points.

    (ii) A maximum of three bowling points to be available: 3 to 5 wickets taken – 1 point; 6 to 8 wickets taken – 2 points; 9 to 10 wickets taken – 3 points.

(*f*) If a match is abandoned without a ball being bowled, each side score five points.

(*g*) The side who have the highest aggregate of points shall be the champion county of their respective division. Should any sides in the Championship table be equal on points, the following tie-breakers will be applied in the order stated: most wins, fewest losses, team achieving most points in head-to-head contests, most wickets taken, most runs scored.

(*h*) The minimum over-rate to be achieved by counties will be 16 overs per hour. Overs will be calculated at the end of the match, and penalties applied on a match-by-match basis. For each over (ignoring fractions) that a side have bowled short of the target number, one point will be deducted from their Championship total.

(*i*) Penalties for poor and unfit pitches are at the discretion of the Cricket Discipline Commission.

Under ECB playing conditions, two extras were scored for every no-ball bowled, whether scored off or not, and one for every wide. Any runs scored off the bat were credited to the batsman, while byes and leg-byes were counted as no-balls or wides, as appropriate, in accordance with Law 24.13, in addition to the initial penalty.

CONSTITUTION OF COUNTY CHAMPIONSHIP

At least four possible dates have been given for the start of county cricket in England. The first, patchy, references began in 1825. The earliest mention in any cricket publication is in 1864, and eight counties have come to be regarded as first-class from that date, including Cambridgeshire, who dropped out after 1871. For many years, the County Championship was considered to have started in 1873, when regulations governing qualification first applied; indeed, a special commemorative stamp was issued by the Post Office in 1973. However, the Championship was not formally organised until 1890, and before its champions were proclaimed by the press; sometimes publications differed in their views and no definitive list of champions can start before that date. Eight teams contested the 1890 competition – Gloucestershire, Kent, Lancashire, Middlesex, Nottinghamshire, Surrey, Sussex and Yorkshire. Somerset joined the following year, and in 1895 the Championship began to acquire something of its modern shape, when Derbyshire, Essex, Hampshire, Leicestershire and Warwickshire were added. At that point MCC officially recognised the competition's existence. Worcestershire, Northamptonshire and Glamorgan were admitted in 1899, 1905 and 1921 respectively, and are regarded as first-class from these dates. An invitation in 1921 to Buckinghamshire to enter the Championship was declined, owing to the lack of necessary playing facilities, and an application by

Devon in 1948 was unsuccessful. Durham were admitted in 1992 and were granted first-class status prior to their pre-season tour of Zimbabwe.

In 2000, the Championship was split for the first time into two divisions, on the basis of counties' standings in the 1999 competition. From 2000 onwards, the bottom three teams in Division One were relegated at the end of the season, and the top three teams in Division Two promoted. From 2006, this was changed to two teams relegated and two promoted.

COUNTY CHAMPIONS

The title of champion county is unreliable before 1890. In 1963, *Wisden* formally accepted the list of champions "most generally selected" by contemporaries, as researched by the late Rowland Bowen (see *Wisden 1959*, pp 91–98). This appears to be the most accurate available list but has no official status. The county champions from 1864 to 1889 were, according to Bowen: 1864 Surrey; 1865 Nottinghamshire; 1866 Middlesex; 1867 Yorkshire; 1868 Nottinghamshire; 1869 Nottinghamshire and Yorkshire; 1870 Yorkshire; 1871 Nottinghamshire; 1872 Nottinghamshire; 1873 Gloucestershire and Nottinghamshire; 1874 Gloucestershire; 1875 Nottinghamshire; 1876 Gloucestershire; 1877 Gloucestershire; 1878 undecided; 1879 Lancashire and Nottinghamshire; 1880 Nottinghamshire; 1881 Lancashire; 1882 Lancashire and Nottinghamshire; 1883 Nottinghamshire; 1884 Nottinghamshire; 1885 Nottinghamshire; 1886 Nottinghamshire; 1887 Surrey; 1888 Surrey; 1889 Lancashire, Nottinghamshire and Surrey.

Year	County	Year	County	Year	County
1890	Surrey	1935	Yorkshire	1979	Essex
1891	Surrey	1936	Derbyshire	1980	Middlesex
1892	Surrey	1937	Yorkshire	1981	Nottinghamshire
1893	Yorkshire	1938	Yorkshire	1982	Middlesex
1894	Surrey	1939	Yorkshire	1983	Essex
1895	Surrey	1946	Yorkshire	1984	Essex
1896	Yorkshire	1947	Middlesex	1985	Middlesex
1897	Lancashire	1948	Glamorgan	1986	Essex
1898	Yorkshire	1949 {	Middlesex / Yorkshire	1987	Nottinghamshire
1899	Surrey			1988	Worcestershire
1900	Yorkshire	1950 {	Lancashire / Surrey	1989	Worcestershire
1901	Yorkshire			1990	Middlesex
1902	Yorkshire	1951	Warwickshire	1991	Essex
1903	Middlesex	1952	Surrey	1992	Essex
1904	Lancashire	1953	Surrey	1993	Middlesex
1905	Yorkshire	1954	Surrey	1994	Warwickshire
1906	Kent	1955	Surrey	1995	Warwickshire
1907	Nottinghamshire	1956	Surrey	1996	Leicestershire
1908	Yorkshire	1957	Surrey	1997	Glamorgan
1909	Kent	1958	Surrey	1998	Leicestershire
1910	Kent	1959	Yorkshire	1999	Surrey
1911	Warwickshire	1960	Yorkshire	2000	Surrey
1912	Yorkshire	1961	Hampshire	2001	Yorkshire
1913	Kent	1962	Yorkshire	2002	Surrey
1914	Surrey	1963	Yorkshire	2003	Sussex
1919	Yorkshire	1964	Worcestershire	2004	Warwickshire
1920	Middlesex	1965	Worcestershire	2005	Nottinghamshire
1921	Middlesex	1966	Yorkshire	2006	Sussex
1922	Yorkshire	1967	Yorkshire	2007	Sussex
1923	Yorkshire	1968	Yorkshire	2008	Durham
1924	Yorkshire	1969	Glamorgan	2009	Durham
1925	Yorkshire	1970	Kent	2010	Nottinghamshire
1926	Lancashire	1971	Surrey	2011	Lancashire
1927	Lancashire	1972	Warwickshire	2012	Warwickshire
1928	Lancashire	1973	Hampshire	2013	Durham
1929	Nottinghamshire	1974	Worcestershire	2014	Yorkshire
1930	Lancashire	1975	Leicestershire	2015	Yorkshire
1931	Yorkshire	1976	Middlesex		
1932	Yorkshire	1977 {	Middlesex / Kent		
1933	Yorkshire				
1934	Lancashire	1978	Kent		

Notes: Since the Championship was constituted in 1890 it has been won outright as follows: Yorkshire 32 times, Surrey 18, Middlesex 10, Lancashire 8, Warwickshire 7, Essex, Kent and Nottinghamshire 6, Worcestershire 5, Durham, Glamorgan, Leicestershire and Sussex 3, Hampshire 2, Derbyshire 1. Gloucestershire, Northamptonshire and Somerset have never won.

The title has been shared three times since 1890, involving Middlesex twice, Kent, Lancashire, Surrey and Yorkshire.

Wooden spoons: Since the major expansion of the Championship from nine teams to 14 in 1895, the counties have finished outright bottom as follows: Derbyshire 15; Leicestershire and Somerset 12; Northamptonshire 11; Glamorgan 10; Gloucestershire 9; Nottinghamshire and Sussex 8; Worcestershire 6; Durham and Hampshire 5; Warwickshire 3; Essex and Kent 2; Yorkshire 1. Lancashire, Middlesex and Surrey have never finished bottom. Leicestershire have also shared bottom place twice, once with Hampshire and once with Somerset.

From 1977 to 1983 the Championship was sponsored by Schweppes, from 1984 to 1998 by Britannic Assurance, from 1999 to 2000 by PPP healthcare, in 2001 by Cricinfo, from 2002 to 2005 by Frizzell, and from 2006 by Liverpool Victoria (LV).

COUNTY CHAMPIONSHIP – FINAL POSITIONS, 1890–2015

	Derbyshire	Durham	Essex	Glamorgan	Gloucestershire	Hampshire	Kent	Lancashire	Leicestershire	Middlesex	Northamptonshire	Nottinghamshire	Somerset	Surrey	Sussex	Warwickshire	Worcestershire	Yorkshire
1890	–	–	–	–	6	–	3	2	–	7	–	5	–	1	8	–	–	3
1891	–	–	–	–	9	–	5	2	–	3	–	4	5	1	7	–	–	8
1892	–	–	–	–	7	–	4	–	–	5	–	2	3	1	9	–	–	6
1893	–	–	–	–	9	–	4	2	–	3	–	6	8	5	7	–	–	1
1894	–	–	–	–	9	–	4	4	–	3	–	7	6	1	8	–	–	2
1895	5	–	9	–	4	10	14	2	12	6	–	12	8	1	11	6	–	3
1896	7	–	5	–	10	8	9	2	13	3	–	6	11	4	14	12	–	1
1897	14	–	3	–	5	9	12	1	13	8	–	10	11	2	6	7	–	1
1898	9	–	5	–	3	12	7	6	13	2	–	8	13	4	9	9	–	1
1899	15	–	6	–	9	10	8	4	13	2	–	10	13	1	5	7	12	3
1900	13	–	10	–	7	15	3	2	14	7	–	5	11	7	3	6	12	1
1901	15	–	10	–	14	7	7	3	12	2	–	9	12	6	4	5	11	1
1902	10	–	13	–	14	15	7	5	11	12	–	3	7	4	2	6	9	1
1903	12	–	8	–	13	14	8	4	14	1	–	5	10	11	2	7	6	3
1904	10	–	14	–	9	15	3	1	7	4	–	5	12	11	6	7	13	2
1905	14	–	12	–	8	16	6	2	5	11	13	10	15	4	3	7	8	1
1906	16	–	7	–	9	8	1	4	15	11	11	5	11	3	10	6	14	2
1907	16	–	7	–	10	12	8	6	11	5	15	1	14	4	13	9	2	2
1908	14	–	11	–	10	9	2	7	13	4	15	8	16	3	5	12	6	1
1909	15	–	14	–	16	8	1	2	13	6	7	10	11	5	4	12	8	3
1910	15	–	11	–	12	6	1	4	10	3	9	5	16	2	7	14	13	8
1911	14	–	6	–	12	11	2	4	15	3	10	8	16	5	13	1	9	7
1912	12	–	15	–	11	6	3	4	13	5	2	8	14	7	10	9	16	1
1913	13	–	15	–	9	10	1	8	14	6	4	5	16	3	7	11	12	2
1914	12	–	8	–	16	5	3	11	13	2	9	10	15	1	6	7	14	4
1919	9	–	14	–	8	7	2	5	9	13	12	3	5	4	11	15	–	1
1920	16	–	9	–	8	11	5	2	13	1	14	7	10	3	6	12	15	4
1921	12	–	15	17	7	6	4	5	11	1	13	8	10	2	9	16	14	3
1922	11	–	8	16	13	6	4	5	14	7	15	2	10	3	9	12	17	1
1923	10	–	13	16	11	7	5	3	14	8	17	2	9	4	6	12	15	1
1924	17	–	15	13	6	12	5	4	11	2	16	6	8	3	10	9	14	1
1925	14	–	7	17	10	9	5	3	12	6	11	4	15	2	13	8	16	1
1926	11	–	9	8	15	7	3	1	13	6	16	4	14	5	10	12	17	2
1927	5	–	8	15	12	13	4	1	7	9	16	2	14	6	10	11	17	3
1928	10	–	16	15	5	12	2	1	9	8	13	3	14	6	7	11	17	4

	Derbyshire	Durham	Essex	Glamorgan	Gloucestershire	Hampshire	Kent	Lancashire	Leicestershire	Middlesex	Northamptonshire	Nottinghamshire	Somerset	Surrey	Sussex	Warwickshire	Worcestershire	Yorkshire
1929	7	–	12	17	4	11	8	2	9	6	13	1	15	10	4	14	16	2
1930	9	–	6	11	2	13	5	1	12	16	17	4	13	8	7	15	10	3
1931	7	–	10	15	2	12	3	6	16	11	17	5	13	8	4	9	14	1
1932	10	–	14	15	13	8	3	6	12	10	16	4	7	5	2	9	17	1
1933	6	–	4	16	10	14	3	5	17	12	13	8	11	9	2	7	15	1
1934	3	–	8	13	7	14	5	1	12	10	17	9	15	11	2	4	16	5
1935	2	–	9	13	15	16	10	4	6	3	17	5	14	11	7	8	12	1
1936	1	–	9	16	4	10	8	11	15	2	17	5	7	6	14	13	12	3
1937	3	–	6	7	4	14	12	9	2	17	10	13	8	5	11	15		1
1938	5	–	6	16	10	14	9	4	15	2	17	12	7	3	8	13	11	1
1939	9	–	4	13	3	15	5	6	17	2	16	12	14	8	10	11	7	1
1946	15	–	8	6	5	10	6	3	11	2	16	13	4	11	17	14	8	1
1947	5	–	11	9	2	16	4	3	14	1	17	11	11	6	9	15	7	7
1948	6	–	13	1	8	9	15	5	11	3	17	14	12	2	16	7	10	4
1949	15	–	9	8	7	16	13	11	17	1	6	11	9	5	13	4	3	1
1950	5	–	17	11	7	12	9	1	16	14	10	15	7	1	13	4	6	3
1951	11	–	8	5	12	9	16	3	15	7	13	17	14	6	10	1	4	2
1952	4	–	10	7	9	12	15	3	6	5	8	16	17	1	13	10	14	2
1953	6	–	12	10	6	14	16	3	3	5	11	8	17	1	2	9	15	12
1954	3	–	15	4	13	14	11	10	16	7	7	5	17	1	9	6	11	2
1955	8	–	14	16	12	3	13	9	6	5	7	11	17	1	4	9	15	2
1956	12	–	11	13	3	6	16	2	17	5	4	8	15	1	9	14	9	7
1957	4	–	5	9	12	13	6	4	17	7	2	15	8	1	9	11	16	3
1958	5	–	6	15	14	2	8	7	12	16	10	11	17	3	1	13	16	9
1959	7	–	9	6	2	8	13	5	16	10	11	17	12	3	15	4	14	1
1960	5	–	6	11	8	12	10	2	17	3	9	16	14	7	4	15	13	1
1961	7	–	6	14	5	1	11	13	9	3	16	17	10	15	8	12	4	2
1962	7	–	9	14	4	10	11	16	17	13	8	15	6	5	12	3	2	1
1963	17	–	12	2	8	10	13	15	16	6	7	9	3	11	4	4	14	1
1964	12	–	10	11	17	12	7	14	16	6	3	15	8	4	9	2	1	5
1965	9	–	15	3	10	12	5	13	14	6	2	17	7	8	16	11	1	4
1966	9	–	16	14	15	11	4	12	8	12	5	17	3	7	10	6	2	1
1967	6	–	15	14	17	12	2	11	2	7	9	15	8	4	13	10	5	1
1968	8	–	14	3	16	5	2	6	9	10	13	4	12	15	17	11	7	1
1969	16	–	6	1	2	5	10	15	14	11	9	8	17	3	7	4	12	13
1970	7	–	12	2	17	10	1	3	15	16	14	11	13	5	9	7	6	4
1971	17	–	10	16	8	9	4	3	5	6	14	12	7	1	11	2	15	13
1972	17	–	5	13	3	9	2	15	6	8	4	14	11	12	16	1	7	10
1973	16	–	8	11	5	1	4	12	9	13	3	17	10	2	15	7	6	14
1974	17	–	12	16	14	2	10	8	4	6	3	15	5	7	13	9	1	11
1975	15	–	7	9	16	3	5	4	1	11	8	13	12	6	17	14	10	2
1976	15	–	6	17	3	12	14	16	4	1	2	13	7	9	10	5	11	8
1977	7	–	6	14	3	11	1	16	5	1	9	17	4	14	8	10	13	12
1978	14	–	2	13	10	8	1	12	6	3	17	7	5	16	9	11	15	4
1979	16	–	1	17	10	12	5	13	6	14	11	9	8	3	4	15	2	7
1980	9	–	8	13	7	17	16	15	10	1	12	3	5	2	4	14	11	6
1981	12	–	5	14	13	7	9	16	8	4	15	1	3	6	2	17	11	10
1982	11	–	7	16	15	3	13	12	2	1	9	4	6	5	8	17	14	10
1983	9	–	1	15	12	3	7	12	4	2	6	14	10	8	11	5	16	17
1984	12	–	1	13	17	15	5	16	4	3	11	2	7	8	6	9	10	14
1985	13	–	4	12	3	2	9	14	16	1	10	8	17	6	7	15	5	11
1986	11	–	1	17	2	6	8	15	7	12	9	4	16	3	14	12	5	10
1987	6	–	12	13	10	5	14	2	3	16	7	1	11	4	17	15	9	8
1988	14	–	3	17	10	15	2	9	8	7	12	5	11	4	16	6	1	13

	Derbyshire	Durham	Essex	Glamorgan	Gloucestershire	Hampshire	Kent	Lancashire	Leicestershire	Middlesex	Northamptonshire	Nottinghamshire	Somerset	Surrey	Sussex	Warwickshire	Worcestershire	Yorkshire
1989	6	–	2	17	9	6	15	4	13	3	5	11	14	12	10	8	1	16
1990	12	–	2	8	13	3	16	6	7	1	11	13	15	9	17	5	4	10
1991	3	–	1	12	13	9	5	2	8	16	15	10	4	17	5	11	6	14
1992	5	18	1	14	10	15	2	12	8	11	3	4	9	13	7	6	17	16
1993	15	18	11	3	17	13	8	13	9	1	4	7	5	6	10	16	2	12
1994	17	16	6	18	12	13	9	10	2	4	5	3	11	7	8	1	15	13
1995	14	17	5	16	6	13	18	4	7	2	3	11	9	12	15	1	10	8
1996	2	18	5	10	13	14	4	15	1	9	16	17	11	3	12	8	7	6
1997	16	17	8	1	7	14	2	11	10	4	15	13	12	8	18	4	3	6
1998	10	14	18	12	4	6	11	2	1	17	15	16	9	5	7	8	13	3
1999	9	8	12	14	18	7	5	2	3	16	13	17	4	1	11	10	15	6
2000	9	8	2	3	4	7	6	2	4	8	1	7	5	1	9	6	5	3
2001	9	8	9	8	4	2	3	6	5	5	7	7	2	4	1	3	6	1
2002	6	9	1	5	8	7	3	4	5	2	7	3	8	1	6	2	4	9
2003	9	6	7	5	3	8	4	2	9	6	2	8	7	3	1	5	1	4
2004	8	9	5	8	6	2	2	8	6	4	9	1	4	3	5	1	7	7
2005	9	2	5	9	8	2	5	1	7	6	4	1	8	7	3	4	6	3
2006	5	7	3	8	7	3	5	2	4	9	6	8	9	1	1	4	2	6
2007	6	2	4	9	7	5	7	3	8	3	5	2	1	4	1	8	9	6
2008	6	1	5	8	9	3	8	5	7	3	4	2	4	9	6	1	2	7
2009	6	1	2	6	4	6	1	4	9	8	3	2	3	7	8	5	9	7
2010	9	5	9	3	5	7	8	4	4	8	6	1	2	7	1	6	2	5
2011	5	3	7	6	4	9	8	1	9	1	3	6	4	2	5	2	7	8
2012	1	6	5	6	9	4	3	8	7	3	8	5	2	7	4	1	9	2
2013	8	1	3	8	6	4	7	1	9	5	2	7	6	9	3	4	5	2
2014	4	5	3	8	7	1	6	8	9	7	9	4	6	3	3	2	2	1
2015	8	4	3	4	6	7	7	2	9	2	5	3	6	1	8	5	9	1

For the 2000–2015 Championships, Division One placings are in bold, Division Two in italic.

MATCH RESULTS, 1864–2015

County	Years of Play	Played	Won	Lost	Drawn	Tied	% Won
Derbyshire	1871–87; 1895–2015	2,531	622	932	976	1	24.57
Durham	1992–2015	394	107	166	121	0	27.15
Essex	1895–2015	2,493	725	724	1,038	6	29.08
Glamorgan	1921–2015	2,024	449	693	882	0	22.18
Gloucestershire	1870–2015	2,766	807	1,019	938	2	29.17
Hampshire	1864–85; 1895–2015	2,602	687	874	1,037	4	26.40
Kent	1864–2015	2,890	1,029	867	989	5	35.60
Lancashire	1865–2015	2,964	1,095	613	1,253	3	36.94
Leicestershire	1895–2015	2,459	549	897	1,012	1	22.32
Middlesex	1864–2015	2,669	971	682	1,011	5	36.38
Northamptonshire	1905–2015	2,228	554	762	909	3	24.86
Nottinghamshire	1864–2015	2,799	850	759	1,189	1	30.36
Somerset	1882–85; 1891–2015	2,501	602	968	928	3	24.07
Surrey	1864–2015	3,044	1,189	677	1,174	4	39.06
Sussex	1864–2015	2,938	837	999	1,096	6	28.48
Warwickshire	1895–2015	2,473	693	701	1,077	2	28.02
Worcestershire	1899–2015	2,412	618	841	951	2	25.62
Yorkshire	1864–2015	3,068	1,330	540	1,196	2	43.35
Cambridgeshire	1864–69; 1871	19	8	8	3	0	42.10
		22,637	13,722	13,722	8,890	25	

Matches abandoned without a ball bowled are wholly excluded.

Counties participated in the years shown, except that there were no matches in 1915–1918 and 1940–1945; Hampshire did not play inter-county matches in 1868–1869, 1871–1874 and 1879; Worcestershire did not take part in the Championship in 1919.

COUNTY CHAMPIONSHIP STATISTICS FOR 2015

County	For Runs	For Wickets	For Avge	Runs scored per 100 balls	Against Runs	Against Wickets	Against Avge
Derbyshire (8)	7,593	254	29.89	55.82	7,949	229	34.71
Durham (4)	8,088	286	28.27	62.25	8,205	284	28.89
Essex (3)	7,928	233	34.02	58.27	6,957	231	30.11
Glamorgan (4)	8,035	238	33.76	60.63	8,923	223	40.01
Gloucestershire (6)	7,006	228	30.72	55.54	7,619	236	32.28
Hampshire (7)	7,737	255	30.34	53.03	7,984	222	35.96
Kent (7)	7,214	244	29.56	57.68	6,646	236	28.16
Lancashire (2)	8,129	207	39.27	59.57	8,504	266	31.96
Leicestershire (9)	7,661	282	27.16	57.63	8,738	257	34.00
Middlesex (2)	7,880	264	29.84	53.40	7,410	261	28.39
Northamptonshire (5)	8,218	257	31.97	64.34	7,914	226	35.01
Nottinghamshire (3)	8,666	260	33.33	60.72	7,276	249	29.22
Somerset (6)	7,653	251	30.49	63.35	8,069	238	33.90
Surrey (1)	9,137	218	41.91	62.08	7,671	257	29.84
Sussex (8)	8,194	261	31.39	62.08	8,444	251	33.64
Warwickshire (5)	7,168	249	28.78	52.23	7,675	260	29.51
Worcestershire (9)	7,191	239	30.08	58.22	8,114	240	33.80
Yorkshire (1)	8,307	219	37.93	57.68	7,707	279	27.62
	141,805	4,445	31.90	58.50	141,805	4,445	31.90

2015 Championship positions are shown in brackets; Division One in bold, Division Two in italic.

ECB PITCHES TABLE OF MERIT IN 2015

	First-class	One-day		First-class	One-day
Derbyshire	5.22	4.83	Sussex	4.11	5.64
Durham	4.50	5.36	Warwickshire	5.10	5.29
Essex	4.40	5.25	Worcestershire	4.78	4.88
Glamorgan	4.00	4.69	Yorkshire	5.60	5.42
Gloucestershire	5.00	5.23			
Hampshire	4.89	5.69			
Kent	5.18	5.09	Cambridge MCCU	5.11	
Lancashire	5.11	4.93	Cardiff MCCU	5.00	
Leicestershire	4.63	5.18	Durham MCCU	5.67	
Middlesex	4.50	5.04	Leeds/Bradford MCCU	4.67	
Northamptonshire	4.89	5.30	Loughborough MCCU	4.50	
Nottinghamshire	4.70	5.46	Oxford MCCU	4.60	
Somerset	5.40	5.90			
Surrey	5.00	5.00			

Each umpire in a match marks the pitch on the following scale: 6 – Very good; 5 – Good; 4 – Above average; 3 – Below average; 2 – Poor; 1 – Unfit.

The tables, provided by the ECB, cover major matches, including Tests, Under-19 internationals, women's internationals and MCCU games, played on grounds under the county's or MCCU's jurisdiction. Middlesex pitches at Lord's are the responsibility of MCC. The "First-class" column includes Under-19 and women's Tests, and inter-MCCU games.

Essex had the highest marks for first-class cricket, and Yorkshire for one-day cricket, though the ECB point out that the tables of merit are not a direct assessment of the groundsmen's ability. Marks may be affected by many factors, including weather, soil conditions and the resources available.

COUNTY CAPS AWARDED IN 2015

Derbyshire	B. A. Godleman.
Essex	N. L. J. Browne, J. A. Porter.
Glamorgan*	W. D. Bragg.
Gloucestershire*. . . .	T. R. G. Hampton, P. S. P. Handscomb, K. Noema-Barnett.
Hampshire	W. R. Smith.
Kent	D. J. Bell-Drummond, S. W. Billings.
Lancashire	K. R. Brown, K. M. Jarvis, S. D. Parry.
Middlesex.	J. E. C. Franklin, J. A. R. Harris, O. P. Rayner.
Northamptonshire. . . .	Azharullah.
Nottinghamshire. . . .	B. W. Hilfenhaus, Imran Tahir, V. D. Philander, B. R. M. Taylor.
Somerset.	L. Gregory.
Surrey	K. C. Sangakkara.
Worcestershire*	E. G. Barnard, J. M. Clarke, S. T. Gabriel, A. P. R. Gidman, C. Munro, S. M. S. M. Senanayake.

* Glamorgan's capping system is now based on a player's number of appearances; Gloucestershire now award caps to all first-class players; Worcestershire have replaced caps with colours awarded to all Championship players. Durham abolished their capping system after 2005.

No caps were awarded by Sussex, Warwickshire or Yorkshire. Leicestershire awarded "gold fox" caps to M. J. Cosgrove, C. J. McKay and Umar Akmal.

COUNTY BENEFITS AWARDED FOR 2016

Durham	P. Mustard.		Warwickshire.	T. R. Ambrose.
Hampshire	S. M. Ervine.		Worcestershire	D. K. H. Mitchell.
Kent	D. I. Stevens.		Yorkshire	A. W. Gale.

None of the other 12 counties awarded a benefit for 2016.

DERBYSHIRE

Life in the slow lane

M ARK E KLID

Finishing second from bottom of the County Championship, and sliding out of both one-day competitions before the knockout stages, are not unusual experiences for Derbyshire. Yet, for the second season running, they had started out with raised expectations. Graeme Welch had now had more than a year to bed in his "elite performance coaching system", the team had finished strongly in 2014, and there were hopes that a promising group of players would make real progress.

Such progress as there was could not be measured in results, which were mostly down on the previous summer. Too often, when maturity and poise were needed, flaws emerged under the strain. Too many opportunities were wasted with victory in sight: when there was a chance to seize the upper hand, Derbyshire seemed likelier to crumble.

A young squad had not yet developed the know-how needed to win on a regular basis: they never managed two victories in a row, either within a competition or across all three. In an attempt to speed up the learning process, three high-profile overseas batsmen were recruited for short shifts: Hashim Amla, South Africa's Test captain; Tillekeratne Dilshan, who had helped Sri Lanka win the World Twenty20 in 2014; and New Zealander Martin Guptill, the leading run-scorer in the 2015 World Cup. But the strategy failed because none was around long enough to make a difference, though Guptill did secure a Championship victory at Bristol with a spectacular 227.

The most successful import was another New Zealander, Test batsman Hamish Rutherford, who stayed for six weeks. Such was his impact that he was offered a contract for the full 2016 season – which also led to the recruitment of his Otago team-mate, one-day international Neil Broom, who was signed on a two-year deal as the holder of a British passport.

Derbyshire's best performers were their established players. Left-arm quick Mark Footitt came close to repeating his formidable haul of 84 first-class wickets in 2014, with 76 (only Durham's Chris Rushworth had more), and earned his first call-up to an England squad, as cover for James Anderson ahead of the Fourth Test against Australia. But he left for Surrey at the end of the season, hoping to further his international ambitions. He signed off with seven for 71 – and ten in the match for the first time – against Leicestershire, and was selected for the tour of South Africa. Though Derbyshire signed Andy Carter from Nottinghamshire and Tom Milnes from Warwickshire, the seam attack face an onerous task filling the gap left by Footitt.

In the season's final session, club captain Wayne Madsen passed 1,000 Championship runs for the third successive year. Wes Durston responded to being handed the captaincy in limited-overs cricket by leading from the front as a batsman, and Tony Palladino was again a dependable bowler in Championship matches. The most welcome improvement came from opener Billy Godleman, in his third season with Derbyshire following spells with Middlesex and Essex. He reached 1,000 runs for the first time, contributed well in the limited-overs formats, and led the side in three Championship matches while Madsen was injured.

Billy Godleman

Chesney Hughes and Ben Slater scored around 800 first-class runs each, and seamer Tom Taylor claimed 28 wickets. Academy products Harvey Hosein, the regular first-class wicketkeeper, and Ben Cotton continued to advance after making their debuts the previous season. Tom Poynton, after missing the whole of the 2014 season following the car accident in which his father was killed and he was badly injured, played only five Championship matches, but was the limited-overs keeper. Matt Critchley, primarily a leg-spinner, who had slipped out of the Lancashire system, marked his second first-class innings by becoming Derbyshire's youngest centurion, at the age of 18 years and 270 days. All had scope to do even better, but their inexperience fed the inconsistency which hampered the whole team.

Derbyshire were without a home Championship win for the first time since 2005, despite winning six out of eight tosses; each time they opted to bowl first in seam-friendly conditions, but only once, against Surrey, did they bowl a team out for under 293. The most damning reflection of their weakness came in their results against the second division's eventual top three, Surrey, Lancashire and Essex. All six fixtures were lost – four by an innings, the other two by more than 220 runs.

In the event, some of Derbyshire's best cricket came in the Royal London One-Day Cup. As in 2014, when they reached the quarter-finals, they collected four wins, but this time that was enough to gain only seventh place in their group. They finished bottom of the pile again in the NatWest T20 Blast, though at least they managed four wins out of 14, compared with the previous year's one. Australian Nathan Rimmington was recruited as a Twenty20 specialist death bowler, but missed the start of the campaign with a broken finger, and could not bring the change of fortune Derbyshire sought.

By the end of the season David Wainwright and Jon Clare, two players who had seemed to be part of a bright future when Derbyshire won Division Two in 2012, had been released; so too Wayne White, who sparkled briefly in his second spell with his native county before rejoining Leicestershire. Their departures added to the feeling that Derbyshire were still in a state of flux, and some way from the stability they had hoped for back in April.

Championship attendance: 12,463.

DERBYSHIRE RESULTS

All first-class matches – Played 17: Won 3, Lost 7, Drawn 7.
County Championship matches – Played 16: Won 3, Lost 7, Drawn 6.

LV= County Championship, 8th in Division 2;
NatWest T20 Blast, 9th in North Group; Royal London One-Day Cup, 7th in Group A.

COUNTY CHAMPIONSHIP AVERAGES, BATTING AND FIELDING

Cap		Birthplace	M	I	NO	R	HS	100	Avge	Ct/St
2012	M. J. Guptill§	Auckland, NZ	2	4	1	290	227	1	96.66	5
2011	W. L. Madsen	Durban, SA	13	26	5	1,015	172*	4	48.33	13
	H. D. Rutherford§	Dunedin, NZ	3	6	0	273	108	1	45.50	1
2015	B. A. Godleman	Islington	14	28	4	1,069	108	3	44.54	12
	M. J. J. Critchley	Preston	6	8	2	246	137*	1	41.00	2
	A. L. Hughes	Wordsley	7	11	3	279	111*	1	34.87	2
	C. F. Hughes	Anguilla	13	26	1	816	104	2	32.64	6
2012	W. J. Durston	Taunton	11	21	5	451	85	0	28.18	12
	B. T. Slater	Chesterfield†	14	28	0	779	94	0	27.82	4
	H. M. Amla§	Durban, SA	2	4	0	101	69	0	25.25	2
	S. J. Thakor	Leicester	12	17	1	349	83	0	21.81	4
	S. L. Elstone	Burton-on-Trent	7	12	1	234	103*	1	21.27	2
	W. A. White	Derby†	3	5	1	71	38*	0	17.75	0
	T. M. Dilshan§	Kalutara, SL	3	6	2	69	27*	0	17.25	1
	H. R. Hosein	Chesterfield†	11	17	2	256	61	0	17.06	30/1
	B. D. Cotton	Stoke-on-Trent	8	12	3	126	43	0	14.00	2
2012	A. P. Palladino	Tower Hamlets	12	16	3	173	35*	0	13.30	4
	T. A. I. Taylor	Stoke-on-Trent	9	13	3	133	49	0	13.30	2
	T. P. Milnes	Stourbridge	2	4	0	37	23	0	9.25	0
2014	M. H. A. Footitt	Nottingham	16	21	6	110	34	0	7.33	3
	T. Poynton	Burton-on-Trent	5	9	0	47	19	0	5.22	11/3

Also batted: T. C. Knight (*Sheffield*) (1 match) 25, 14* (1 ct); D. J. Wainwright (*Pontefract*) (cap 2012) (2 matches) 8*, 5, 10.

† *Born in Derbyshire.*   § *Official overseas player.*

BOWLING

	Style	O	M	R	W	BB	5I	Avge
W. A. White	RFM	79.3	18	279	17	6-25	2	16.41
M. H. A. Footitt	LFM	537.4	113	1,796	76	7-71	5	23.63
A. P. Palladino	RFM	356.4	105	890	31	0		28.70
W. J. Durston	OB	203	23	753	24	6-109	2	31.37
T. A. I. Taylor	RFM	241.2	34	946	28	6-61	1	33.78
B. D. Cotton	RFM	223.1	49	745	15	3-26	0	49.66
S. J. Thakor	RM	188.4	33	667	13	2-11	0	51.30

Also bowled: M. J. J. Critchley (LBG) 76.1–6–363–4; T. M. Dilshan (OB) 17–1–76–1; S. L. Elstone (OB) 50–7–187–4; A. L. Hughes (RM) 81.5–12–281–5; C. F. Hughes (SLA) 41.2–4–200–3; W. L. Madsen (OB) 17.4–2–51–1; T. P. Milnes (RFM) 41–3–182–1; D. J. Wainwright (SLA) 31–0–131–1.

LEADING ROYAL LONDON CUP AVERAGES (100 runs/4 wickets)

Batting

	Runs	HS	Avge	SR	Ct
H. D. Rutherford	181	110	60.33	95.76	1
W. J. Durston	380	129	47.50	103.54	7
W. L. Madsen	315	106*	45.00	89.74	3
S. L. Elstone	109	52	36.33	72.66	5
B. A. Godleman	232	109*	33.14	66.66	4
S. J. Thakor	135	68	27.00	84.90	1

Bowling

	W	BB	Avge	ER
G. T. G. Cork	4	2-17	14.00	6.22
S. J. Thakor	11	3-37	24.00	4.19
B. D. Cotton	11	3-11	26.00	4.84
A. L. Hughes	10	3-31	29.20	4.70
M. H. A. Footitt	10	2-38	32.80	5.85
W. J. Durston	4	2-27	34.25	4.89
M. J. J. Critchley	6	4-48	40.66	5.54

LEADING NATWEST T20 BLAST AVERAGES (100 runs/18 overs)

Batting	Runs	HS	Avge	SR	Ct/St		Bowling	W	BB	Avge	ER
H. D. Rutherford	209	62	29.85	145.13	2		W. J. Durston	9	3-14	28.33	7.72
W. J. Durston	431	88	33.15	138.14	3		A. L. Hughes	6	2-21	41.16	7.75
C. F. Hughes	276	59	21.23	130.18	1		S. J. Thakor	15	3-25	25.66	8.25
T. Poynton	132	27*	18.85	129.41	5/2		W. A. White	11	3-21	27.18	9.01
A. L. Hughes	137	24	19.57	129.24	2		N. J. Rimmington	10	3-24	38.80	9.27
S. L. Elstone	161	37	14.63	123.84	3						
W. L. Madsen	169	51*	18.77	113.42	5						

FIRST-CLASS COUNTY RECORDS

Highest score for	274	G. A. Davidson v Lancashire at Manchester	1896
Highest score against	343*	P. A. Perrin (Essex) at Chesterfield	1904
Leading run-scorer	23,854	K. J. Barnett (avge 41.12)	1979–98
Best bowling for	10-40	W. Bestwick v Glamorgan at Cardiff	1921
Best bowling against	10-45	R. L. Johnson (Middlesex) at Derby	1994
Leading wicket-taker	1,670	H. L. Jackson (avge 17.11)	1947–63
Highest total for	801-8 dec	v Somerset at Taunton	2007
Highest total against	677-7 dec	by Yorkshire at Leeds	2013
Lowest total for	16	v Nottinghamshire at Nottingham	1879
Lowest total against	23	by Hampshire at Burton-upon-Trent	1958

LIST A COUNTY RECORDS

Highest score for	173*	M. J. Di Venuto v Derbys County Board at Derby	2000
Highest score against	158	R. K. Rao (Sussex) at Derby	1997
Leading run-scorer	12,358	K. J. Barnett (avge 36.67)	1979–98
Best bowling for	8-21	A. M. Holding v Sussex at Hove	1988
Best bowling against	8-66	S. R. G. Francis (Somerset) at Derby	2004
Leading wicket-taker	246	A. E. Warner (avge 27.13)	1985–95
Highest total for	366-4	v Combined Universities at Oxford	1991
Highest total against	369-6	by New Zealanders at Derby	1999
Lowest total for	60	v Kent at Canterbury	2008
Lowest total against	42	by Glamorgan at Swansea	1979

TWENTY20 COUNTY RECORDS

Highest score for	111	W. J. Durston v Nottinghamshire at Nottingham	2010
Highest score against	**158***	**B. B. McCullum (Warwicks) at Birmingham**	**2015**
Leading run-scorer	**1,891**	**W. J. Durston (avge 29.09)**	**2010–15**
Best bowling for	5-27	T. Lungley v Leicestershire at Leicester	2009
Best bowling against	5-14	P. D. Collingwood (Durham) at Chester-le-Street	2008
Leading wicket-taker	51	T. D. Groenewald (avge 27.52)	2009–14
Highest total for	222-5	v Yorkshire at Leeds	2010
Highest total against	**242-2**	**by Warwickshire at Birmingham**	**2015**
Lowest total for	72	v Leicestershire at Derby	2013
Lowest total against	84	by West Indians at Derby	2007

ADDRESS

The 3aaa Ground, Nottingham Road, Derby DE21 6DA; 0871 350 1870; info@derbyshireccc.com; www.derbyshireccc.com.

OFFICIALS

Captain W. L. Madsen
    (limited-overs) W. J. Durston
Elite performance director G. Welch
Academy director A. J. Harris
President G. Miller

Chairman C. I. Grant
Chief executive S. Storey
Head groundsman N. Godrich
Scorer J. M. Brown

At Cambridge, April 12–13. DERBYSHIRE beat CAMBRIDGE MCCU by an innings and 264 runs.

DERBYSHIRE v LANCASHIRE

At Derby, April 19–22. Lancashire won by 250 runs. Lancashire 21pts, Derbyshire 4pts (after 1pt penalty). Toss: Derbyshire. County debut: P. M. Siddle.

A contest delicately balanced on the third afternoon, when Taylor removed Prince for a career-best sixth wicket – leaving Lancashire seven down and 233 ahead – tipped spectacularly when Davies cut loose. A cavalier 89, his highest yet, included five sixes, utterly out of context with everything that had passed before. And last man Jarvis tagged on 100, a tenth-wicket record for Lancashire against Derbyshire, and pushed the target up to an unlikely 365. Jarvis – the Zimbabwean who had managed only two Championship wickets in 2014 – went on to tear the heart out of the run-chase with five for ten in 39 balls. On the opening day Petersen, who had recently ended his career

CENTURY ON FIRST-CLASS DEBUT FOR LANCASHIRE

195*	J. Ricketts	v Surrey at The Oval	1867
108	A. C. MacLaren	v Sussex at Hove	1890
131*	R. Whitehead	v Nottinghamshire at Manchester	1908
126	M. B. Loye	v Surrey at The Oval	2003
134	A. Symonds	v Essex at Manchester	2005
102	M. F. Maharoof	v Somerset at Liverpool	2011
115	**A. N. Petersen**	**v Derbyshire at Derby**	**2015**
121	**J. P. Faulkner**	**v Surrey at The Oval**	**2015**

Only the first three were making their overall first-class debut.

with South Africa, became only the seventh batsman to score a century on first-class debut for Lancashire, before Footitt claimed him as his 200th victim. Another overseas recruit, Australia's Siddle, removed Guptill (in his first first-class match for 14 months) and Madsen for ducks. Lancashire's new captain, Tom Smith, made a winning start, but a back problem meant this was his last game of the season.

Close of play: first day, Lancashire 292-8 (Bailey 0); second day, Lancashire 36-3 (Petersen 3, Prince 9); third day, Derbyshire 27-2 (Guptill 9, Taylor 2).

Lancashire

P. J. Horton c Hosein b Palladino	5	– b Footitt	2
L. M. Reece b Footitt	0	– c Hosein b Taylor	8
A. N. Petersen c Guptill b Footitt	115	– (4) lbw b Taylor	9
A. G. Prince b Thakor	21	– (5) c Hosein b Taylor	97
S. J. Croft lbw b Palladino	1	– (6) c Durston b Taylor	70
*T. C. Smith b Hughes	38	– (7) c Hosein b Taylor	1
†A. L. Davies lbw b Thakor	40	– (8) c Thakor b Durston	89
P. M. Siddle c Taylor b Palladino	46	– (3) c Madsen b Taylor	5
T. E. Bailey c Godleman b Taylor	0	– b Durston	14
S. C. Kerrigan b Taylor	0	– c Durston b Palladino	0
K. M. Jarvis not out	1	– not out	17
B 8, l-b 14, n-b 4	26	B 21, l-b 9, w 1, n-b 2	33

1/5 (1) 2/5 (2) 3/54 (4)	(98 overs) 293	1/14 (1) 2/14 (2)	(91.5 overs) 345
4/55 (5) 5/190 (6) 6/206 (3)		3/21 (3) 4/43 (4)	
7/292 (8) 8/292 (7) 9/292 (10) 10/293 (9)		5/203 (6) 6/209 (7) 7/214 (5)	
		8/244 (9) 9/245 (10) 10/345 (8)	

Footitt 24–9–63–2; Palladino 24.5–5–70–3; Taylor 20–4–55–2; Thakor 13–5–28–2; Durston 10–1–39–0; Hughes 7–1–16–1. *Second innings*—Footitt 20–7–53–1; Taylor 21.7–61–6; Durston 20.5–0–94–2; Palladino 17–3–50–1; Thakor 4–0–24–0; Hughes 9–1–33–0.

Derbyshire

B. T. Slater lbw b Bailey		11 – c Davies b Siddle	7
B. A. Godleman c Davies b Jarvis	76	– lbw b Bailey	4
M. J. Guptill c Smith b Siddle	0	– c Davies b Jarvis	32
*W. L. Madsen c Smith b Siddle	0	– (5) lbw b Jarvis	29
W. J. Durston c Prince b Kerrigan	85	– (6) c Kerrigan b Jarvis	3
S. J. Thakor c Horton b Bailey	0	– (7) lbw b Jarvis	4
A. L. Hughes c Reece b Croft	37	– (8) lbw b Bailey	9
†H. R. Hosein c and b Croft	33	– (9) b Bailey	6
A. P. Palladino c Davies b Kerrigan	16	– (10) not out	4
T. A. I. Taylor not out	4	– (4) c Croft b Bailey	2
M. H. A. Footitt c Bailey b Kerrigan	2	– lbw b Kerrigan	0
B 3, l-b 1, n-b 6	10	B 1, l-b 8, w 1, n-b 4	14

1/17 (1) 2/18 (3) 3/26 (4)   (78.5 overs) 274   1/8 (2) 2/19 (1)   (41.2 overs) 114
4/174 (5) 5/175 (6) 6/204 (2)   3/36 (4) 4/77 (3)
7/229 (7) 8/262 (8) 9/272 (9) 10/274 (11)   5/83 (6) 6/88 (5) 7/102 (8)
                                                            8/105 (7) 9/113 (9) 10/114 (11)

Siddle 17–0–60–2; Jarvis 12–0–66–1; Bailey 15–1–60–2; Smith 10–1–54–0; Kerrigan
18.5–7–21–3; Croft 6–2–9–2. *Second innings*—Siddle 10–2–30–1; Bailey 14–3–38–3; Kerrigan
1.2–0–3–1; Smith 7–1–21–0; Jarvis 9–3–13–5.

Umpires: M. R. Benson and M. J. D. Bodenham.

At Bristol, April 26–29. DERBYSHIRE beat GLOUCESTERSHIRE by seven wickets.

At Cardiff, May 3–6. DERBYSHIRE drew with GLAMORGAN.

DERBYSHIRE v NORTHAMPTONSHIRE

At Derby, May 10–13. Drawn. Derbyshire 11pts, Northamptonshire 11pts. Toss: Northamptonshire.
County debut: H. M. Amla.
     In only his second first-class innings, Matt Critchley became the youngest Derbyshire batsman to
score a century, aged 18 years and 270 days. But Northamptonshire denied the home side victory
after being asked to chase 427, which would have been the largest fourth-innings total in their
history. They managed 390 for nine, their third-highest, thanks to missed chances and Keogh's
defiant unbeaten 163, supported by Cobb and Wakely, both forced down the order by damaged
hands. Amla, coming in at No. 11, helped Keogh see out the final 20 overs; he had not batted first
time round after injuring himself dropping Critchley on 20 at slip. (His fellow captain, Madsen,
broke a finger at slip trying to catch Keogh on 114.) Picked for his leg-spin, Critchley beat team-
mate Chesney Hughes's landmark by 220 days, with fearless strokes all around the wicket; his stand
of 162 with Taylor, an eighth-wicket record between the sides, salvaged Derbyshire's first innings.
Cobb and Willey retaliated with 163, Northamptonshire's seventh-wicket best in this fixture, to keep
the deficit to 19. But Hughes and Slater put Derbyshire well ahead in an opening partnership of 205,
Hughes completing his first century for a barren two years.
     Close of play: first day, Northamptonshire 0-0 (Azharullah 0, Peters 0); second day, Derbyshire
76-0 (Slater 27, Hughes 41); third day, Northamptonshire 40-2 (Newton 8, Azharullah 19).

Derbyshire

B. T. Slater c Rossington b Azharullah	37	– c Rossington b Willey	94
C. F. Hughes b Azharullah	40	– lbw b Keogh	104
H. M. Amla lbw b Kleinveldt	1	– b Willey	20
*W. L. Madsen c Rossington b Willey	25	– not out	51
S. L. Elstone lbw b Azharullah	0	– c Rossington b Willey	25
S. J. Thakor c Rossington b Crook	10	– b Crook	28
†H. R. Hosein c Peters b Crook	0	– not out	46
M. J. J. Critchley not out	137		
T. A. I. Taylor c Rossington b Kleinveldt	49		
B. D. Cotton c Crook b Azharullah	19		
M. H. A. Footitt c and b Azharullah	1		
L-b 6, n-b 18	24	B 14, l-b 18, w 3, n-b 4	39

1/65 (1) 2/80 (2) 3/80 (3) (92.5 overs) 343 1/205 (2) (5 wkts dec, 121.5 overs) 407
4/83 (5) 5/103 (6) 6/103 (7) 2/246 (1) 3/255 (3)
7/151 (4) 8/313 (9) 9/341 (10) 10/343 (11) 4/307 (5) 5/339 (6)

Kleinveldt 26–4–101–2; Willey 15–2–71–1; Azharullah 20.5–7–59–5; Cobb 12–3–35–0; Crook 14–3–58–2; Keogh 5–1–13–0. *Second innings*—Kleinveldt 20–6–40–0; Willey 22–4–70–3; Azharullah 20–7–42–0; Crook 18.5–5–83–1; Keogh 41–5–140–1.

Northamptonshire

Azharullah c Critchley b Taylor	0	– (4) c Madsen b Footitt	19
S. D. Peters c Hosein b Footitt	14	– (1) c Elstone b Footitt	0
K. J. Coetzer c Hosein b Footitt	13	– (2) c Hosein b Footitt	11
R. I. Newton c Thakor b Cotton	1	– (3) b Thakor	35
R. I. Keogh c Hughes b Taylor	31	– not out	163
†A. M. Rossington c Hughes b Taylor	14	– c Slater b Elstone	0
J. J. Cobb c Hosein b Thakor	95	– (9) c Hosein b Cotton	43
D. J. Willey c Amla b Thakor	103	– (7) c Madsen b Elstone	4
S. P. Crook c Madsen b Footitt	22	– (8) c Madsen b Elstone	18
R. K. Kleinveldt not out	5	– c Slater b Footitt	35
*A. G. Wakely absent hurt		– not out	36
B 8, l-b 3, w 1, n-b 14	26	B 12, l-b 4, w 2, n-b 8	26

1/3 (1) 2/29 (2) 3/30 (4) (61 overs) 324 1/0 (1) (9 wkts, 104 overs) 390
4/60 (3) 5/76 (6) 6/101 (5) 2/17 (2) 3/41 (4)
7/264 (7) 8/309 (8) 9/324 (9) 4/113 (3) 5/124 (6) 6/146 (7)
7/182 (8) 8/265 (9) 9/340 (10)

Footitt 18–2–91–3; Taylor 16–1–72–3; Cotton 11–1–47–1; Thakor 9–1–47–2; Critchley 7–0–56–0. *Second innings*—Footitt 22–4–94–4; Taylor 21–3–61–0; Elstone 18–3–68–3; Cotton 15–4–53–1; Thakor 10–3–30–1; Critchley 16–2–56–0; Hughes 2–0–12–0.

Umpires: R. T. Robinson and B. V. Taylor.

At Southport, May 24–27. DERBYSHIRE lost to LANCASHIRE by an innings and 15 runs.

DERBYSHIRE v GLOUCESTERSHIRE

At Derby, May 31–June 3. Drawn. Derbyshire 8pts, Gloucestershire 8pts. Toss: Derbyshire.

An exchange of declarations created a compelling end to a weather-ravaged match. Only 119 overs were possible during the first two days, before fierce overnight winds ripped the covers from their fixings and left the bowlers' take-off and landing area at one end sodden, preventing any play on a sunny third day. The captains' deal set Derbyshire 302 in a minimum of 80 overs, but they were soon 63 for four. It took Godleman's resolute performance to ensure the draw. Standing in as captain for the injured Madsen, he batted out time; over both innings, he survived seven and a half hours and saw off 278 dot balls in between 94 unbeaten runs. Jack Taylor's maiden century had been more forceful. He came in when Palladino's 300th first-class wicket reduced Gloucestershire to 159 for six, and added 92 with Klinger by the close. Klinger, making his Championship return on the ground where Footitt broke his arm the previous August, now fell to him on 93, but Taylor accelerated as he almost doubled his highest score.

Close of play: first day, Gloucestershire 251-6 (Klinger 93, Taylor 58); second day, Derbyshire 77-2 (Godleman 30, Dilshan 17); third day, no play.

Gloucestershire

W. A. Tavaré c Godleman b Taylor	20	– (2) not out		26
C. D. J. Dent lbw b Footitt	14	– (1) not out		22
M. Klinger c Hosein b Footitt	93			
†G. H. Roderick c Taylor b Palladino	20			
H. J. H. Marshall lbw b Taylor	2			
*G. O. Jones lbw b Taylor	0			
B. A. C. Howell c and b Palladino	15			
J. M. R. Taylor c sub (R. P. Hemmings) b Taylor	120			
C. N. Miles c Hosein b Footitt	3			
D. A. Payne not out	9			
L. C. Norwell c Hosein b Footitt	0			
B 9, l-b 4, n-b 20	33	L-b 1		1

1/27 (2) 2/49 (1) 3/111 (4)   (86.4 overs) 329   (no wkt dec, 14 overs) 49
4/113 (5) 5/119 (6) 6/159 (7)
7/251 (8) 8/255 (9) 9/329 (10) 10/329 (11)

Footitt 24.4–7–60–4; Palladino 22–4–76–2; Taylor 21–2–89–4; Thakor 11–1–34–0; Critchley 1–0–13–0; Dilshan 7–0–44–0. *Second innings*—Hughes 7–0–22–0; Elstone 4–0–12–0; Critchley 3–0–14–0.

Derbyshire

B. T. Slater c Dent b Norwell	17	– lbw b Payne		0
*B. A. Godleman not out	30	– not out		64
C. F. Hughes c Roderick b Howell	9	– c Marshall b Miles		12
T. M. Dilshan not out	17	– b Payne		6
S. L. Elstone (did not bat)		– c Howell b Payne		16
S. J. Thakor (did not bat)		– lbw b Taylor		43
†H. R. Hosein (did not bat)		– b Norwell		11
M. J. J. Critchley (did not bat)		– b Miles		12
A. P. Palladino (did not bat)		– b Taylor		5
T. A. I. Taylor (did not bat)		– not out		1
B 1, l-b 3	4	B 8, l-b 5, w 2, n-b 4		19

1/47 (1) 2/58 (3)   (2 wkts dec, 32 overs) 77   1/0 (1) 2/22 (3)   (8 wkts, 81 overs) 189
                                                     3/35 (4) 4/63 (5)
                                                     5/132 (6) 6/143 (7) 7/164 (8) 8/184 (9)

M. H. A. Footitt did not bat.

Payne 10–5–19–0; Miles 9–2–26–0; Norwell 7–2–21–1; Howell 6–2–7–1. *Second innings*—Payne 19–6–36–3; Miles 17–3–38–2; Howell 6–1–29–0; Norwell 20–4–49–1; Taylor 16–8–19–2; Dent 3–1–5–0.

Umpires: S. A. Garratt and R. T. Robinson.

At Canterbury, June 7–9. DERBYSHIRE beat KENT by eight wickets.

At Chelmsford, June 14–16. DERBYSHIRE lost to ESSEX by an innings and 31 runs.

DERBYSHIRE v SURREY

At Derby, June 21–23. Surrey won by 222 runs. Surrey 20pts, Derbyshire 4pts. Toss: Derbyshire. County debut: D. Elgar.

After Derbyshire collapsed inside 40 overs on the third evening, chairman Chris Grant used Twitter to apologise to "members, supporters & sponsors". He described the performance as "totally unacceptable batting again" and promised to "address the issues behind it". Derbyshire had set out after tea needing 348, but batted so ineptly that they were 48 for five by the 19th over. Batty claimed the extra half-hour, and took the last four himself. Surrey had lost several regulars to injury, but Wilson and Batty, both dropped off Footitt during a seventh-wicket stand of 80, helped them reach 239 on the opening day, before Fletcher, in his last game on loan from Nottinghamshire, removed Derbyshire's first four wickets. In the second innings, Surrey were six down with the lead 202. But an excellent 73 from Burke, in his second Championship match, tipped the balance away from Derbyshire, who did not help themselves by conceding 61 extras, 22 of them from Footitt no-balls.

Close of play: first day, Derbyshire 64-1 (Slater 21, Rutherford 23); second day, Surrey 77-2 (Sibley 20, Elgar 14).

Surrey

A. Harinath c Poynton b White	35	– b Footitt	6
Z. S. Ansari c Durston b Taylor	13	– b Footitt	19
D. P. Sibley b Taylor	10	– lbw b White	46
D. Elgar c Palladino b Durston	44	– b Palladino	19
B. T. Foakes lbw b Footitt	15	– b Footitt	16
†G. C. Wilson lbw b White	65	– b Footitt	9
J. E. Burke st Poynton b Durston	1	– lbw b Taylor	73
*G. J. Batty c Poynton b White	41	– c Godleman b Durston	37
T. K. Curran c Poynton b Footitt	0	– run out	13
L. J. Fletcher not out	2	– c Durston b Taylor	14
T. E. Linley c Poynton b Footitt	0	– not out	2
B 5, l-b 1, w 1, n-b 6	13	B 12, l-b 20, w 3, n-b 26	61

1/54 (1) 2/56 (2) 3/69 (3) (72.5 overs) 239
4/103 (5) 5/149 (4) 6/155 (7)
7/235 (8) 8/236 (9) 9/238 (6) 10/239 (11)

1/12 (1) 2/50 (2) (90.2 overs) 315
3/84 (4) 4/143 (3)
5/147 (5) 6/170 (6) 7/253 (8)
8/294 (9) 9/294 (7) 10/315 (10)

Footitt 21.5–2–74–3; Palladino 16–4–41–0; White 15–3–43–3; Taylor 7–0–30–2; Durston 11–1–31–2; Hughes 2–0–14–0. *Second innings*—Footitt 26–2–102–4; White 17–6–42–1; Taylor 17.2–3–65–2; Palladino 18–7–30–1; Durston 11–3–38–1; Hughes 1–0–6–0.

Derbyshire

B. T. Slater c Wilson b Fletcher	28	– b Burke	18
B. A. Godleman c Wilson b Fletcher	10	– b Curran	10
H. D. Rutherford c Elgar b Curran	59	– c Sibley b Fletcher	8
*W. L. Madsen c Wilson b Fletcher	4	– c Ansari b Fletcher	0
C. F. Hughes lbw b Fletcher	0	– c Wilson b Burke	9
W. J. Durston c Wilson b Linley	33	– not out	22
W. A. White c Burke b Curran	1	– lbw b Curran	23
†T. Poynton c Sibley b Burke	2	– lbw b Batty	0
A. P. Palladino not out	35	– lbw b Batty	7
T. A. I. Taylor c Elgar b Burke	3	– b Batty	0
M. H. A. Footitt c Wilson b Curran	2	– c Burke b Batty	20
B 13, l-b 6, w 1, n-b 10	30	B 5, l-b 3	8

1/24 (2) 2/88 (1) 3/96 (4) (65 overs) 207
4/110 (5) 5/138 (3) 6/144 (7)
7/166 (8) 8/166 (6) 9/177 (10) 10/207 (11)

1/11 (1) 2/24 (3) (39.5 overs) 125
3/24 (4) 4/45 (5)
5/48 (1) 6/78 (7) 7/81 (8)
8/95 (9) 9/95 (10) 10/125 (11)

Curran 19–6–48–3; Fletcher 20–5–58–4; Burke 10–2–32–2; Linley 16–6–50–1. *Second innings—* Curran 14–6–31–2; Fletcher 9–2–21–2; Burke 5–2–12–2; Linley 4–0–17–0; Batty 6.5–0–32–4; Ansari 1–0–4–0.

Umpires: N. G. B. Cook and P. J. Hartley.

DERBYSHIRE v GLAMORGAN

At Chesterfield, July 6–9. Drawn. Derbyshire 10pts, Glamorgan 13pts. Toss: Derbyshire.

When Derbyshire were 120 for two at lunch on the final day, still 38 behind in the follow-on, Glamorgan were hopeful of securing a fifth successive Championship victory for the first time. But they were denied by a resolute century from the New Zealander Rutherford, his first for Derbyshire. He suppressed his free-scoring instincts for most of the five hours and 18 minutes he batted, apart from a flurry of 23 in 15 balls, including three sixes – the last two, off consecutive deliveries from Ingram over long-on, carrying him to three figures. Though Rutherford's 132-run stand with Madsen salvaged the draw, Glamorgan had dominated a game plagued by showers. They declared just after tea on the second day, at 410 for nine, which took less than 80 overs; two-thirds of their runs came in boundaries. Derbyshire's first innings lasted longer but mustered 158 fewer runs. With four sessions to go – trimmed by a further shower and bad light – Welsh spirits were high, but they faded after Rutherford was granted a couple of lives.

Close of play: first day, Glamorgan 167-3 (Ingram 73, Meschede 34); second day, Derbyshire 122-2 (Godleman 49, Madsen 19); third day, Derbyshire 37-0 (Rutherford 15, Godleman 20).

Glamorgan

*J. A. Rudolph c Palladino	1	A. G. Salter c Godleman b C. F. Hughes	29
W. D. Bragg b Taylor	37	R. A. J. Smith not out	6
B. J. Wright c Hosein b Footitt	0	B 13, l-b 2, n-b 25	40
C. A. Ingram c Palladino b Footitt	89		
†M. A. Wallace c Durston b Footitt	21	1/7 (1) (9 wkts dec, 79.3 overs)	410
C. A. J. Meschede c Godleman b Footitt	70	2/10 (3) 3/73 (2)	
G. G. Wagg b Taylor	62	4/198 (4) 5/238 (6) 6/325 (7)	
D. L. Lloyd b A. L. Hughes	55	7/349 (5) 8/389 (8) 9/410 (9)	

M. G. Hogan did not bat.

Wallace, when 0, retired hurt at 81-3 and resumed at 325-6.

Footitt 25–3–98–4; Palladino 20–3–80–1; Taylor 13–2–63–2; Thakor 7–0–50–0; A. L. Hughes 11–0–71–1; Durston 3–0–29–0; C. F. Hughes 0.3–0–4–1.

Derbyshire

H. D. Rutherford run out	36	– lbw b Lloyd	108
B. A. Godleman b Wagg	53	– lbw b Salter	28
C. F. Hughes lbw b Smith	3	– lbw b Salter	10
*W. L. Madsen c sub (A. H. T. Donald) b Hogan	24	– not out	79
W. J. Durston c Hogan b Wagg	1	– not out	32
A. L. Hughes c Rudolph b Lloyd	28		
S. J. Thakor c Lloyd b Salter	41		
†H. R. Hosein c Ingram b Smith	10		
A. P. Palladino c Hogan b Smith	1		
T. A. I. Taylor b Hogan	30		
M. H. A. Footitt not out	4		
B 8, l-b 7, n-b 6	21	B 5, l-b 12, w 3, n-b 4	24

1/77 (1) 2/83 (3) 3/130 (4) (86 overs) 252
4/132 (2) 5/137 (5) 6/181 (6)
7/210 (8) 8/214 (9) 9/218 (7) 10/252 (10)

1/60 (2) (3 wkts dec, 90.4 overs) 281
2/84 (3) 3/216 (1)

Hogan 21–6–62–2; Meschede 11–1–49–0; Wagg 15–0–50–2; Salter 18–5–33–1; Smith 11–2–23–3; Lloyd 8–1–17–1; Ingram 2–0–3–0. *Second innings*—Wagg 11–4–28–0; Hogan 17–5–39–0; Salter 25–6–51–2; Meschede 9–2–24–0; Smith 7–1–34–0; Ingram 6–1–23–0; Lloyd 10–2–50–1; Bragg 5.4–1–15–0.

Umpires: P. K. Baldwin and M. J. Saggers.

At Northampton, July 18–20. DERBYSHIRE beat NORTHAMPTONSHIRE by seven wickets.

At Derby, July 23–25. DERBYSHIRE drew with AUSTRALIANS (see Australian tour section).

At Leicester, August 7–10. DERBYSHIRE lost to LEICESTERSHIRE by three wickets.

DERBYSHIRE v KENT

At Derby, August 21–24. Drawn. Derbyshire 10pts, Kent 8pts. Toss: Kent. Championship debut: S. R. Dickson.

A finely poised contest was spoiled when rain wiped out the final session. Harmison had just gone, leaving Kent 98 short of a target of 329 with five wickets standing – in all probability four, because wicketkeeper Billings had played no part since dislocating his left ring finger in the game's third over. Derbyshire suffered two injuries of their own: Thakor was concussed in their first innings and Alex Hughes struck on the hand in the second. An otherwise low-scoring match was a triumph for Godleman, who became the 17th player to score twin hundreds for Derbyshire, and the fifth – following Bill Storer, Levi Wright, Peter Kirsten and Kim Barnett – to hit three in successive innings. In between, Footitt reduced Kent to 69 for five on the second morning, which helped Derbyshire take a lead of 94. But Key and Northeast produced a determined response on the final day, before rain intervened for the last time. Bell-Drummond had kept wicket in place of Billings on day one until the afternoon, when Ryan Davies arrived from the England Under-19 series against Australia.

Close of play: first day, Kent 27-0 (Bell-Drummond 8, Key 18); second day, Derbyshire 73-1 (Godleman 42, C. F. Hughes 9); third day, Kent 30-0 (Bell-Drummond 18, Key 11).

Derbyshire

B. T. Slater b Hunn	33	– b Thomas	20
B. A. Godleman c Tredwell b Haggett	108	– not out	105
C. F. Hughes c Tredwell b Haggett	7	– b Tredwell	50
*W. L. Madsen b Hunn	46	– b Thomas	43
A. L. Hughes c Tredwell b Hunn	11	– retired hurt	12
S. J. Thakor retired hurt	0		
†H. R. Hosein c Thomas b Tredwell	10	– (6) not out	0
M. J. J. Critchley c Northeast b Thomas	12		
A. P. Palladino c Harmison b Thomas	0		
M. H. A. Footitt not out	7		
B. D. Cotton c sub (R. C. Davies) b Haggett	15		
L-b 4	4	B 1, l-b 1, w 2	4

1/93 (1) 2/116 (3) 3/178 (2)	(83 overs) 253	1/43 (1) (3 wkts dec, 67 overs) 234
4/207 (4) 5/214 (5) 6/230 (8)		2/157 (3) 3/214 (4)
7/230 (7) 8/230 (9) 9/253 (11)		

In the first innings Thakor retired hurt at 207-4; in the second, A. L. Hughes retired hurt at 232-3.

Hunn 21–7–45–3; Thomas 17–4–71–2; Haggett 20–3–70–3; Tredwell 24–4–57–1; Denly 1–0–6–0. *Second innings*—Hunn 17–3–52–0; Haggett 12–2–44–0; Thomas 17–3–68–2; Tredwell 21–6–68–1.

Kent

D. J. Bell-Drummond lbw b Cotton	19	– b Cotton	19
R. W. T. Key lbw b Footitt	29	– lbw b Palladino	67
J. L. Denly b Footitt	7	– c Hosein b Footitt	1
*S. A. Northeast c Hosein b Palladino	1	– c Hosein b Footitt	76
B. W. Harmison b Footitt	3	– c Madsen b C. F. Hughes	50
S. R. Dickson lbw b Cotton	22	– not out	1
C. J. Haggett c Godleman b Palladino	6		
J. C. Tredwell b Footitt	20		
M. D. Hunn not out	23		
I. A. A. Thomas run out	2		
†S. W. Billings absent hurt			
B 12, l-b 4, w 7, n-b 4	27	B 9, l-b 2, n-b 6	17

1/50 (2) 2/63 (1) 3/64 (4)   (57.5 overs) 159   1/33 (1)   (5 wkts, 66.5 overs) 231
4/68 (3) 5/69 (5) 6/95 (7)   2/34 (3) 3/139 (2)
7/119 (6) 8/144 (8) 9/159 (10)   4/211 (4) 5/231 (5)

Footitt 19.5–5–61–4; Cotton 18–4–45–2; Palladino 16–7–21–2; Critchley 3–1–16–0; A. L. Hughes 1–1–0–0. *Second innings*—Footitt 24–3–64–2; Cotton 19–3–70–1; Palladino 15–5–36–1; Critchley 6–0–31–0; C. F. Hughes 2.5–0–19–1.

Umpires: P. K. Baldwin and J. W. Lloyds.

At The Oval, September 1–4. DERBYSHIRE lost to SURREY by an innings and 98 runs.

DERBYSHIRE v ESSEX

At Derby, September 9–11. Essex won by an innings and 188 runs. Essex 24pts, Derbyshire 2pts. Toss: Derbyshire. First-class debut: J. R. Winslade.

It was a dreadful opening day for Derbyshire. After winning the toss, they bowled wastefully, dropped catches and lost two of their four seamers to injury: Palladino dislocated his shoulder making a sliding stop in the field, while Thakor pulled up with a bad back. Lawrence, whose trip to Derby three weeks earlier had brought him the first of two one-day centuries for England Under-19, prepared the way for Pettini, Foster and ten Doeschate to plunder what remained of the home attack. Essex cruised past 400 next morning, before Derbyshire melted to 94 all out, which would have been 78 had not Thakor, in obvious pain, put in an appearance with a runner. Debutant Jack Winslade – a 20-year-old seamer formerly on Surrey's books – claimed the last four in 19 deliveries, and was invited to share the new ball when Derbyshire, trailing by 370, inevitably followed on. Now down to nine men, they suffered an innings defeat – their second of the season by Essex – by lunch on the third day.

Close of play: first day, Essex 360-6 (Pettini 70, Foster 9); second day, Derbyshire 102-3 (Madsen 1, Cotton 0).

Essex

D. W. Lawrence c Cotton b Durston	87	*†J. S. Foster c Footitt b Madsen	60	
N. L. J. Browne b Footitt	18	B 20, l-b 12, n-b 6	38	
T. Westley lbw b Cotton	21			
R. S. Bopara c Poynton b Thakor	25	1/48 (2)	(7 wkts dec, 119.4 overs)	464
J. D. Ryder c Hughes b Footitt	10	2/97 (3) 3/159 (4)		
R. N. ten Doeschate c Durston b Footitt	88	4/176 (1) 5/199 (5)		
M. L. Pettini not out	117	6/344 (6) 7/464 (8)	110 overs: 408-6	

J. R. Winslade, J. A. Porter and T. C. Moore did not bat.

Footitt 34–6–110–3; Cotton 31–6–104–1; Palladino 17–7–46–0; Thakor 13.5–1–64–1; Durston 11.1–1–44–1; Hughes 2–0–24–0; Elstone 2–0–13–0; Madsen 8.4–1–27–1.

Derbyshire

B. T. Slater c Bopara b Moore	12	– c Foster b Bopara	29
B. A. Godleman c Foster b Porter	22	– c Lawrence b Ryder	23
C. F. Hughes c Pettini b Moore	0	– b Bopara	38
*W. L. Madsen c Pettini b Moore	2	– c Foster b ten Doeschate	38
W. J. Durston lbw b Porter	5	– (6) not out	20
S. L. Elstone c Westley b Winslade	10	– (7) c Westley b ten Doeschate	0
†T. Poynton c Foster b Winslade	10	– (8) lbw b ten Doeschate	0
M. H. A. Footitt c Foster b Winslade	0	– (9) c Pettini b Bopara	4
B. D. Cotton not out	15	– (5) c Ryder b Bopara	13
S. J. Thakor c Foster b Winslade	2	– absent hurt	
A. P. Palladino absent hurt		– absent hurt	
L-b 2, n-b 14	16	B 1, n-b 16	17

1/38 (1) 2/38 (3) 3/38 (2)   (33 overs) 94   1/35 (2) 2/87 (1)   (62.4 overs) 182
4/48 (5) 5/48 (4) 6/71 (6)   3/100 (3) 4/130 (5)
7/73 (8) 8/78 (7) 9/94 (10)   5/171 (4) 6/171 (7) 7/177 (8) 8/182 (9)

Porter 12–3–29–2; Ryder 9–2–29–0; Westley 2–1–2–0; Moore 6–4–12–3; Winslade 4–0–20–4.
Second innings—Porter 12–1–48–0; Winslade 11–2–38–0; Ryder 12–5–30–1; Moore 5–1–14–0; Westley 6–1–7–0; Bopara 12.4–4–29–4; ten Doeschate 4–1–15–3.

Umpires: J. W. Lloyds and N. A. Mallender.

DERBYSHIRE v LEICESTERSHIRE

At Derby, September 22–25. Drawn. Derbyshire 12pts, Leicestershire 11pts. Toss: Derbyshire. First-class debut: Z. J. Chappell.

In the tournament's dying moments, its lowest-placed teams entered the final over with all outcomes possible. Needing 341, which would have been their second-highest successful Championship run-chase, Derbyshire were favourites to win (and overtake Kent in seventh place) when they needed 14 off 15 balls with six wickets in hand. But four succumbed in ten deliveries, and Knight – one of four Toms who batted in the last two overs, alongside Poynton, Milnes and Taylor – saw out the draw. It was a timid end to an absorbing game. On his first day of first-class cricket, 19-year-old Zak Chappell had arrived with Leicestershire 154 for eight and, backed by Freckingham's career-best 34, helped them reach 329. He eclipsed Phillip DeFreitas's 81 against Durham in 2000 as the county record for a No. 10, but fell four short of a century when Footitt claimed seven in an innings for the first time. Madsen also just missed three figures, before a career-best 43 from Cotton, the other No. 10, ensured a narrow home lead. Despite Footitt completing his first ten-wicket haul, and Durston collecting an innings-best six for 109, a dynamic century from Cosgrove, who passed 150 with his third six, built a formidable target. A hundred from Hughes and another fifty from Madsen set up the climax.

Close of play: first day, Derbyshire 54-0 (Slater 19, Godleman 28); second day, Derbyshire 281-9 (Milnes 0, Taylor 0); third day, Leicestershire 307-7 (Cosgrove 126, Taylor 1).

Leicestershire

E. J. H. Eckersley c Hughes b Footitt	50	– b Cotton	8
A. J. Robson b Footitt	8	– c Poynton b Footitt	24
D. J. Redfern b Footitt	0	– c Durston b Footitt	18
*M. J. Cosgrove c Slater b Footitt	3	– st Poynton b Durston	156
A. M. Ali c Poynton b Milnes	37	– lbw b Durston	62
†N. J. O'Brien c Footitt b Cotton	19	– lbw b Footitt	0
L. J. Hill c Godleman b Footitt	5	– c Slater b Durston	28
B. A. Raine c Poynton b Footitt	6	– c Madsen b Durston	27
R. M. L. Taylor c Knight b Durston	37	– lbw b Durston	10
Z. J. Chappell b Footitt	96	– st Poynton b Durston	7
O. H. Freckingham not out	34	– not out	0
B 10, l-b 12, w 6, n-b 6	34	B 13, l-b 2, n-b 8	23

1/42 (2) 2/42 (3) 3/62 (4) (80.1 overs) 329
4/73 (1) 5/117 (6) 6/123 (7)
7/131 (8) 8/154 (5) 9/235 (9) 10/329 (10)

1/13 (1) 2/44 (3) (87.1 overs) 363
3/55 (2) 4/199 (5)
5/201 (6) 6/262 (7) 7/306 (8)
8/320 (9) 9/334 (10) 10/363 (4)

Footitt 20.1–4–71–7; Cotton 13–0–52–1; Milnes 17–1–70–1; Taylor 17–3–62–0; Durston 13–2–52–1. *Second innings*—Footitt 22–4–84–3; Cotton 16–3–62–1; Milnes 9–1–34–0; Taylor 5–0–35–0; Durston 26.1–1–109–6; Madsen 9–1–24–0.

Derbyshire

B. T. Slater c Ali b Chappell	70	– lbw b Chappell	56
B. A. Godleman lbw b Taylor	31	– lbw b Raine	51
C. F. Hughes b Freckingham	14	– b Taylor	101
*W. L. Madsen b Freckingham	95	– c O'Brien b Taylor	66
W. J. Durston lbw b Raine	29	– c Taylor b Freckingham	29
T. C. Knight b Freckingham	25	– not out	14
†T. Poynton lbw b Raine	0	– b Raine	2
T. P. Milnes c O'Brien b Redfern	23	– run out	1
T. A. I. Taylor c O'Brien b Freckingham	3	– run out	0
B. D. Cotton b Taylor	43	– not out	0
M. H. A. Footitt not out	1		
B 11, l-b 5, w 2	18	L-b 7, n-b 4	11

1/59 (2) 2/83 (3) 3/166 (1) (106.4 overs) 352
4/236 (5) 5/262 (4) 6/277 (7)
7/281 (6) 8/285 (9) 9/350 (8) 10/352 (10)

1/103 (2) (8 wkts, 81 overs) 331
2/128 (1) 3/285 (3)
4/292 (4) 5/327 (5)
6/329 (7) 7/330 (8) 8/331 (9)

Raine 30–6–70–2; Chappell 17–0–71–1; Taylor 24.4–5–79–2; Freckingham 24–3–91–4; Redfern 8–5–8–1; Cosgrove 3–0–17–0. *Second innings*—Raine 20–3–96–2; Freckingham 16–1–52–1; Taylor 13–1–68–2; Redfern 22–1–65–0; Chappell 9–1–35–1; Ali 1–0–8–0.

Umpires: M. J. D. Bodenham and N. A. Mallender.

DURHAM

Turning it up to eleven

Tim Wellock

It was a classic tale of two halves: Durham won six of their first eight games, then lost six of the next seven. They finished fourth, but it was only when they won their final match that they were certain of remaining in Division One for a record 11th successive season – no other county has managed more than nine in one stretch. Only the two divisional winners (Yorkshire, with 11, and Surrey, with eight) claimed more than Durham's seven victories, while only the two wooden-spoonists (Worcestershire, with ten, and Leicestershire, with nine) suffered more than their eight defeats. Their second-half decline was accompanied by one-day failure, adding to the impression that the golden era which brought five trophies in eight seasons was over. With the purse strings drawn tight, a lack of depth in the squad was largely to blame, although a spate of dropped catches did not help.

The fragility of the batting was evident by May, when they were all out for 71 at Lord's. Yet Durham kept finding ways to win, often on the back of outstanding bowling by Chris Rushworth. He beat Ottis Gibson's county record of 80 first-class wickets in a season, and was on target for 100 until – having played everything bar four Twenty20 games – he faded and finished with 90 (two of them for MCC against Yorkshire at Abu Dhabi).

His one wicket in the final game did take him to 100 in all competitions, of which 83 came in the Championship, where Graham Onions collected 65 and the Australian John Hastings 45. Mark Stoneman and Scott Borthwick both ticked off 1,000 Championship runs for the third successive season, Michael Richardson edged past 1,000 in first-class cricket, and Paul Collingwood's all-round efforts meant that the seven players who were virtually ever-present each contributed.

Collingwood had enjoyed remarkable form since taking on the captaincy in 2012 and, though he slowed down a little, became the first man to score 10,000 first-class runs for Durham. Having already extended his career beyond his intended retirement, he decided to go on another year, past his 40th birthday; he knew his hand was needed on the tiller during a transitional phase.

The batting frailties prompted a new one-year contract for Gordon Muchall, to whom Calum MacLeod was initially preferred, with little success. Muchall, who had been told in July he was likely to be released, made two Championship hundreds in the south, but continued to struggle on home pitches during a year of learning for new groundsman Vic Demain, formerly deputy to Steve Birks at Trent Bridge.

In his third season as Stoneman's opening partner, Keaton Jennings's Championship average fell to 23, and he was dropped for the last six games. He survived longer than Phil Mustard, who lost his place after five matches and ended up on loan to Lancashire. Mustard was awarded a benefit for 2016, the final year of his contract, but at 33 his career seemed under threat, unless he could resume his swashbuckling ways. As an opener in 50-over cricket, his average of 37 was respectable, but a strike-rate of 77 was below expectation. One-day captain Stoneman averaged 43 with a strike-rate of 101 but, after Durham scrambled through the group stage of the Royal London One-Day Cup, his hopes of retaining the trophy fizzled out in a truncated quarter-final at Trent Bridge.

Mark Stoneman

Mustard's axing from the four-day team meant Richardson took over the gloves, and it created a vacancy at No. 7, eventually filled by Ryan Pringle. He scored 99 at home to Hampshire, and his off-breaks improved, but not enough to remove concerns about the spin department. Borthwick's 15 Championship wickets at 42 did not suggest he would add to his one Test cap, at Sydney in January 2014.

With Mark Wood joining Ben Stokes on England duty, a strong battery of seamers was further weakened by injuries to Paul Coughlin, Usman Arshad and Jamie Harrison. In six games before succumbing to back trouble, Coughlin showed every sign of becoming the established fourth seamer, capable of useful runs at No. 8. Arshad was easily the leading Twenty20 wicket-taker, with 22, but a side injury ruined his prospects of a four-day run, while left-armer Harrison found returning from a knee operation a painful – and short-lived – process.

Four Academy products were blooded. Cumbrian batsman Graham Clark and 18-year-old local lad Jack Burnham were tried as openers, without success, although Burnham did score a debut fifty from No. 6 at Scarborough, and Clark equalled Durham's Twenty20 record with an unbeaten 91 at Headingley. Seam-bowling all-rounders James Weighell, a Teessider, and Irishman Barry McCarthy played two games each; McCarthy fared better. Another Irishman, Peter Chase, who had made his mark in September 2014, was ruled out by back problems. Off-spinner Ryan Buckley was released, his five-wicket haul on debut at The Oval in 2013 a distant memory.

Hastings, otherwise ubiquitous, missed the last two games after being called into Australia's one-day squad. His popularity and wholehearted approach were thought to outweigh the need for a batsman. Durham wanted him back, but IPL commitments, and the possibility of shoulder surgery put that in jeopardy.

Off the field, there was some early-season disruption while permanent floodlights were finally installed, despite 113 letters of objection. They included one from the Lumley Castle Hotel, which benefits from cricket on its doorstep but might lose business if plans for a hotel on the ground ever come to fruition.

Championship attendance: 27,393.

DURHAM RESULTS

All first-class matches – Played 17: Won 8, Lost 8, Drawn 1.
County Championship matches – Played 16: Won 7, Lost 8, Drawn 1.

LV= County Championship, 4th in Division 1;
NatWest T20 Blast, 6th in North Group; Royal London One-Day Cup, quarter-finalists.

COUNTY CHAMPIONSHIP AVERAGES, BATTING AND FIELDING

Cap		Birthplace	M	I	NO	R	HS	100	Avge	Ct/St
	S. G. Borthwick	Sunderland†	16	32	2	1,286	103	1	42.86	18
2005	G. J. Muchall	Newcastle-u-Tyne	11	21	2	693	145	2	36.47	10
	M. J. Richardson	Port Elizabeth, SA	16	32	5	964	96*	0	35.70	45/3
	M. D. Stoneman	Newcastle-u-Tyne	16	32	0	1,090	131	3	34.06	7
1998	P. D. Collingwood	Shotley Bridge†	15	28	4	752	127	2	31.33	24
	U. Arshad	Bradford	3	4	0	111	60	0	27.75	3
	B. J. McCarthy	Dublin, Ireland	2	4	2	55	38*	0	27.50	2
	R. D. Pringle	Sunderland†	9	17	1	427	99	0	26.68	3
	P. Coughlin	Sunderland†	6	10	1	213	64	0	23.66	1
	K. K. Jennings¶	Johannesburg, SA	10	20	0	473	98	0	23.65	4
	J. W. Hastings§	Penrith, Australia	14	24	0	449	91	0	18.70	5
	W. J. Weighell	Middlesbrough	2	4	0	69	25	0	17.25	1
	C. Rushworth	Sunderland†	16	26	4	376	43	0	17.09	6
	C. S. MacLeod	Glasgow	7	13	2	161	44	0	14.63	6
	G. Onions	Gateshead†	15	24	15	131	36*	0	14.55	3
	J. T. A. Burnham	Durham†	4	8	0	115	50	0	14.37	2
	G. Clark	Whitehaven	3	6	0	65	36	0	10.83	2
	J. Harrison	Whiston	5	10	0	99	53	0	9.90	0
	P. Mustard	Sunderland†	5	7	0	51	22	0	7.28	19

Also batted: M. A. Wood‡ (*Ashington*) (1 match) 1, 66.

† *Born in Durham.*   ‡ *ECB contract.*   § *Official overseas player.*
¶ *Other non-England-qualified player.*   *Durham ceased to award caps after 2005.*

BOWLING

	Style	O	M	R	W	BB	5I	Avge
C. Rushworth	RFM	585.4	134	1,711	83	6-39	7	20.61
P. Coughlin	RM	116	27	412	16	4-10	0	25.75
G. Onions	RFM	467.5	83	1,744	65	7-68	3	26.83
R. D. Pringle	OB	160.4	37	566	20	5-63	1	28.30
P. D. Collingwood	RM/OB	93.5	20	320	11	5-57	1	29.09
J. W. Hastings	RFM	401	81	1,397	45	7-60	2	31.04
S. G. Borthwick	LBG	149.1	21	641	15	4-46	0	42.73
J. Harrison	LFM	115.4	15	436	10	2-42	0	43.60

Also bowled: U. Arshad (RFM) 46.2–4–196–5; K. K. Jennings (RM) 12–0–51–0; C. S. MacLeod (RFM) 5–1–16–0; B. J. McCarthy (RM) 39–4–154–4; G. J. Muchall (RM) 2–0–7–0; M. D. Stoneman (OB) 3–0–24–0; W. J. Weighell (RM) 36.3–5–179–1; M. A. Wood (RFM) 28–6–74–6.

LEADING ROYAL LONDON CUP AVERAGES (100 runs/4 wickets)

Batting

	Runs	HS	Avge	SR	Ct/St
G. J. Muchall	183	45	45.75	82.43	2
M. D. Stoneman	349	112	43.62	101.45	2
P. D. Collingwood	213	132	42.60	112.69	1
S. G. Borthwick	266	87	38.00	88.07	7
P. Mustard	301	98	37.62	77.77	13/2
G. Clark	142	42	20.28	92.20	0
R. D. Pringle	122	35	17.42	107.01	4
J. W. Hastings	120	46	17.14	111.11	4

Bowling

	W	BB	Avge	ER
J. W. Hastings	18	5-41	15.44	4.35
P. D. Collingwood	8	3-26	19.87	4.54
S. G. Borthwick	13	5-38	22.30	6.39
C. Rushworth	9	4-41	36.88	5.10
U. Arshad	4	3-80	58.00	7.17

LEADING NATWEST T20 BLAST AVERAGES (100 runs/18 overs)

Batting	Runs	HS	Avge	SR	Ct/St
J. W. Hastings ..	186	43*	23.25	**163.15**	2
M. D. Stoneman	342	89*	28.50	**134.11**	2
C. S. MacLeod..	210	60	21.00	**128.83**	3
G. J. Muchall .	299	42*	49.83	**118.65**	1
P. Mustard	303	51	23.30	**112.22**	5/2
P. D. Collingwood	242	41	18.61	**112.03**	4

Bowling	W	BB	Avge	ER
P. D. Collingwood	5	1-4	54.20	**6.77**
J. W. Hastings...	13	3-10	25.07	**7.01**
U. Arshad	22	3-18	13.27	**7.89**
S. G. Borthwick.	9	2-20	23.77	**7.92**
C. Rushworth....	8	2-13	30.12	**8.03**
R. D. Pringle....	4	1-18	58.75	**8.39**

FIRST-CLASS COUNTY RECORDS

Highest score for	273	M. L. Love v Hampshire at Chester-le-Street ..	2003
Highest score against	501*	B. C. Lara (Warwickshire) at Birmingham	1994
Leading run-scorer	10,049	**P. D. Collingwood** (avge 34.18)	**1996–2015**
Best bowling for	10-47	O. D. Gibson v Hampshire at Chester-le-Street.	2007
Best bowling against	**9-34**	**J. A. R. Harris** (Middlesex) at Lord's	**2015**
Leading wicket-taker	518	S. J. E. Brown (avge 28.30)	1992–2002
Highest total for	648-5 dec	v Nottinghamshire at Chester-le-Street	2009
Highest total against	810-4 dec	by Warwickshire at Birmingham.............	1994
Lowest total for	67	v Middlesex at Lord's	1996
Lowest total against	18	by Durham MCCU at Chester-le-Street........	2012

LIST A COUNTY RECORDS

Highest score for	164	B. A. Stokes v Nottinghamshire at Chester-le-St	2014
Highest score against	151*	M. P. Maynard (Glamorgan) at Darlington	1991
Leading run-scorer	5,596	**P. D. Collingwood** (avge 32.91)	**1995–2015**
Best bowling for	7-32	S. P. Davis v Lancashire at Chester-le-Street..	1983
Best bowling against	6-22	A. Dale (Glamorgan) at Colwyn Bay	1993
Leading wicket-taker	298	N. Killeen (avge 23.96)	1995–2010
Highest total for	353-8	v Nottinghamshire at Chester-le-Street	2014
Highest total against	361-7	by Essex at Chelmsford	1996
Lowest total for	72	v Warwickshire at Birmingham..............	2002
Lowest total against	63	by Hertfordshire at Darlington..............	1964

TWENTY20 COUNTY RECORDS

Highest score for	91*	**G. Clark v Yorkshire at Leeds**...............	**2015**
Highest score against	102*	J. M. Bairstow (Yorkshire) at Chester-le-Street ...	2014
Leading run-scorer	2,917	**P. Mustard** (avge 24.72)	**2003–15**
Best bowling for	5-6	P. D. Collingwood v Northants at Chester-le-St ...	2011
Best bowling against	5-16	R. M. Pyrah (Yorkshire) at Scarborough.......	2011
Leading wicket-taker	93	G. R. Breese (avge 21.56)	2004–14
Highest total for	225-2	v Leicestershire at Chester-le-Street	2010
Highest total against	213-4	by Nottinghamshire at Nottingham...........	2011
Lowest total for	93	v Kent at Canterbury	2009
Lowest total against	47	by Northamptonshire at Chester-le-Street......	2011

ADDRESS

Emirates Durham International Cricket Ground, Riverside, Chester-le-Street, County Durham DH3 3QR; 0191 387 1717; reception@durhamcc.co.uk; www.durhamcc.co.uk.

OFFICIALS

Captain P. D. Collingwood
(limited-overs) M. D. Stoneman
Director of cricket G. Cook
First-team coach J. J. B. Lewis
Academy coach J. B. Windows

Chairman C. W. Leach
Chief operating officer R. Dowson
Chief executive D. Harker
Head groundsman V. Demain
Scorer B. Hunt

DURHAM v DURHAM MCCU

At Chester-le-Street, April 7–9. Durham won by 379 runs. Toss: Durham MCCU. First-class debuts: W. D. B. Phillips, B. P. R. Williams.

In pleasant sunshine, Jennings emerged from his famine in late 2014 with a career-best 177 not out, steadily gaining fluency and climaxing with consecutive sixes off Cameron Steel's leg-spin. He shared century stands with Borthwick, who also reached three figures, MacLeod and Collingwood. The university were coached by Gareth Breese and Callum Thorp because Graeme Fowler was ill; he was later to resign, after 19 years in charge, as MCC proposed to shift the MCCUs' emphasis towards "community hubs", which he feared might dilute their role in developing first-class cricketers. Their limited attack was weakened further when Jack Wood strained a hamstring while batting and played no further part. The only student batsman to catch the eye was Oliver Steele, whose 82 runs took his average against Durham over three seasons to 77. Onions proved his fitness with four wickets in the first innings and, after a reshuffled Durham order lifted their lead to 549, Borthwick added four in the second.

Close of play: first day, Durham MCCU 39-0 (MacDonell 16, Gibson 15); second day, Durham 216-5 (MacLeod 18, Rushworth 2).

Durham

M. D. Stoneman c McInley b Williams	5	– c Ratnayake b Phillips	36
K. K. Jennings not out	177		
S. G. Borthwick c Steel b Ratnayake	104		
M. J. Richardson lbw b Ratnayake	6	– (3) c Ratnayake b Jenkins	37
C. S. MacLeod c McInley b Ratnayake	67	– (6) not out	43
*P. D. Collingwood not out	55		
†P. Mustard (did not bat)		– (2) lbw b Ratnayake	39
P. Coughlin (did not bat)		– (4) c Steele b Jenkins	19
J. W. Hastings (did not bat)		– (5) b Bishnoi	38
C. Rushworth (did not bat)		– (7) c McInley b Phillips	11
G. Onions (did not bat)		– (8) b McInley	10
B 5, l-b 2, w 7, n-b 20	34	B 2, l-b 2, w 5, n-b 18	27

1/18 (1)　2/204 (3)　　　　(4 wkts dec, 92 overs)　448　　　1/80 (2)　　(7 wkts dec, 54.4 overs)　260
3/212 (4)　4/339 (5)　　　　　　　　　　　　　　　　　　　　　2/88 (1)　3/138 (4)
　　　　　　　　　　　　　　　　　　　　　　　　　　　　　　　4/155 (3)　5/209 (5)　6/237 (7)　7/260 (8)

Williams 14–0–66–1; Wood 10–3–36–0; MacDonell 8–2–28–0; McInley 11–0–85–0; Phillips 8–1–40–0; Ratnayake 15–1–72–3; Bishnoi 22–2–82–0; Steel 4–0–32–0. *Second innings*— Williams 3–0–19–0; MacDonell 5–2–21–0; McInley 6.4–0–30–1; Ratnayake 11–0–47–1; Phillips 11–2–53–2; Bishnoi 11–1–38–1; Jenkins 5–0–27–2; Steel 2–0–21–0.

Durham MCCU

C. M. MacDonell c Mustard b Rushworth	19	– lbw b Borthwick	37
R. A. M. Gibson c Mustard b Onions	18	– c Richardson b Coughlin	24
*C. T. Steel b Onions	0	– b Rushworth	21
C. Bishnoi b Onions	27	– b Rushworth	9
W. H. Jenkins b Coughlin	3	– lbw b Borthwick	2
†O. J. Steele not out	48	– c Jennings b Borthwick	34
D. E. M. Ratnayake c Borthwick b Onions	0	– c Jennings b Rushworth	8
W. D. B. Phillips c Hastings b Rushworth	1	– b Borthwick	14
J. M. Wood retired hurt	2	– absent hurt	
H. P. S. McInley b Coughlin	4	– (9) c Collingwood b Hastings	8
B. P. R. Williams b Borthwick	0	– (10) not out	0
B 12, l-b 4, w 5, n-b 16	37	L-b 3, n-b 10	13

1/45 (1)　2/45 (4)　3/50 (3)　　　(66.5 overs)　159　　　1/62 (1)　2/66 (2)　　(64.2 overs)　170
4/53 (5)　5/98 (4)　6/102 (7)　　　　　　　　　　　　　　3/86 (4)　4/93 (3)　5/95 (5)
7/108 (8)　8/148 (10)　9/159 (11)　　　　　　　　　　　　6/144 (6)　7/144 (7)　8/168 (9)　9/170 (8)

In the first innings Wood retired hurt at 121-7.

Onions 15–6–21–4; Rushworth 14–4–25–2; Coughlin 11–3–19–2; Borthwick 10.5–3–32–1; Stoneman 3–0–13–0; Hastings 13–3–33–0. *Second innings*—Onions 9–1–34–0; Rushworth 14–7–32–3; Borthwick 23.2–5–61–4; Hastings 11–4–28–1; Coughlin 7–4–12–1.

Umpires: M. A. Gough and P. R. Pollard.

At Taunton, April 12–14. DURHAM beat SOMERSET by seven wickets.

DURHAM v SUSSEX

At Chester-le-Street, April 26–29. Durham won by six wickets. Durham 22pts, Sussex 6pts. Toss: Durham. First-class debut: O. E. Robinson.

Borthwick and Rushworth helped Durham make it two in two, instead of three in three for Sussex. But the match will be remembered for a last-wicket stand of 164 and a run-a-ball debut century from Ollie Robinson, sacked for disciplinary reasons by Yorkshire the previous season. The 21-year-old stepson of England's acting-coach Paul Farbrace, he was the first Sussex player to score a hundred on first-class debut in the Championship since 1920; their previous tenth-wicket record had been 156 by George Cox and Harry Butt at Cambridge in 1908. He almost doubled the total with Hobden, who more than doubled a career aggregate of 50 in ten innings. Robinson used his height to get forward when batting, and hit the pitch hard when bowling; he rounded off the first day, which started with frost on the outfield but brought 438 runs, by dismissing the Durham openers. He finished with four, but Durham took a narrow first-innings lead – thanks to a 116-run ninth-wicket stand between Hastings and Arshad. Rushworth worked through Sussex's second innings (this time Hobden's partnership with Robinson lasted one ball). On the last day Durham needed 147 with eight wickets left, a potentially awkward target, but Borthwick made light of it with an unbeaten 97.

Close of play: first day, Durham 103-2 (Borthwick 3, Rushworth 0); second day, Sussex 115-3 (Machan 25, Finch 9); third day, Durham 115-2 (Borthwick 26, Richardson 7).

Sussex

C. D. Nash c MacLeod b Onions	0	– (2) c Mustard b Rushworth		24
*E. C. Joyce c Stoneman b Arshad	43	– (1) lbw b Rushworth		30
M. W. Machan lbw b Hastings	41	– lbw b Arshad		80
C. Cachopa c Mustard b Hastings	17	– c Stoneman b Onions		24
L. J. Wright c Arshad b Onions	16	– (6) b Rushworth		39
H. Z. Finch lbw b Rushworth	11	– (5) c Mustard b Arshad		22
†B. C. Brown lbw b Rushworth	18	– c Borthwick b Rushworth		4
A. Shahzad c Collingwood b Rushworth	0	– lbw b Rushworth		17
O. E. Robinson c Borthwick b Arshad	110	– not out		4
S. J. Magoffin c Mustard b Arshad	9	– c Mustard b Hastings		3
M. E. Hobden not out	65	– b Hastings		0
L-b 4, w 1	5	L-b 12, n-b 6		18

1/0 (1) 2/88 (3) 3/88 (2)   (72.2 overs) 335   1/55 (2) 2/62 (1)   (69.4 overs) 265
4/112 (4) 5/121 (5) 6/143 (6)   3/98 (4) 4/160 (5)
7/145 (8) 8/151 (7) 9/171 (10) 10/335 (9)   5/217 (3) 6/223 (7) 7/255 (8)
                                            8/260 (6) 9/265 (10) 10/265 (11)

Onions 14–1–72–2; Rushworth 19–3–78–3; Hastings 19–3–81–2; Arshad 10.2–1–41–3; Borthwick 4–0–21–0; Collingwood 5–0–28–0; Jennings 1–0–10–0. *Second innings*—Onions 15–3–58–1; Rushworth 23–5–81–5; Hastings 19.4–4–57–2; Arshad 10–1–43–2; Borthwick 2–0–14–0.

Durham

M. D. Stoneman c Joyce b Robinson	57	– lbw b Shahzad	41
K. K. Jennings c Joyce b Robinson	35	– c Brown b Shahzad	38
S. G. Borthwick c Brown b Robinson	23	– not out	97
C. Rushworth c Hobden b Robinson	9		
M. J. Richardson lbw b Shahzad	37	– (4) b Shahzad	8
C. S. MacLeod c Brown b Shahzad	22	– (5) c Magoffin b Shahzad	26
*P. D. Collingwood c Finch b Robinson	18	– (6) not out	35
†P. Mustard c Nash b Shahzad	0		
U. Arshad b Shahzad b Magoffin	35		
J. W. Hastings c Robinson b Magoffin	72		
G. Onions not out	0		
L-b 13, w 1, n-b 17	31	B 4, l-b 10, n-b 4	18

1/88 (2) 2/101 (1) 3/119 (4)   (82.2 overs) 339   1/80 (1)   (4 wkts, 69.2 overs) 263
4/165 (3) 5/189 (5) 6/222 (6)   2/91 (2) 3/122 (4)
7/222 (8) 8/222 (7) 9/338 (9) 10/339 (10)   4/205 (5)

Magoffin 23.2–8–56–2; Shahzad 19–3–72–4; Robinson 17–4–71–4; Hobden 16–3–85–0; Nash 7–0–42–0. *Second innings*—Magoffin 20–8–40–0; Shahzad 22–3–86–4; Robinson 14.2–2–76–0; Hobden 13–2–47–0.

Umpires: P. J. Hartley and G. D. Lloyd.

At Lord's, May 2–5. DURHAM lost to MIDDLESEX by 187 runs.

DURHAM v NOTTINGHAMSHIRE

At Chester-le-Street, May 10–12. Durham won by six wickets. Durham 19pts, Nottinghamshire 4pts. Toss: Durham.

In his only Durham appearance of the season – he had toured the Caribbean but played only warm-ups, then made his England debut in Dublin – Mark Wood followed four for 39 with a career-best 66 as nightwatchman. (He had played the same role in the first innings, but fell in the opening day's final over.) Durham's target of 261 had looked a tall order after the second day, when 18 wickets fell on a seaming pitch. But Wood and Jennings batted on to reach lunch on 107 for one, the platform for victory. Nottinghamshire had been 102 for seven on the opening afternoon until Wessels, despite a bruised thumb, showed run-scoring was possible, adding 110 with Philander on his way to a century; he patiently awaited errors in length and clinically punished them. Luke Wood and Brett Hutton, both playing their third first-class game, took three apiece in Durham's first innings. But the home attack's greater experience paid off, even though Onions struggled: the first ten deliveries of his second spell on the second day went for 22 until halted by tea, taken mid-over because the ball had disappeared under seating. The two Woods mirrored each other with spectacular strikes: Luke knocked out two of Onions's stumps, Mark did the same to Read.

Close of play: first day, Durham 69-3 (Borthwick 3, Richardson 0); second day, Durham 15-1 (Jennings 7, Wood 1).

Nottinghamshire

S. J. Mullaney c Mustard b Onions	15	– c Mustard b Rushworth	33
B. R. M. Taylor lbw b Rushworth	0	– lbw b Onions	4
A. D. Hales lbw b Rushworth	6	– b Rushworth	16
J. W. A. Taylor lbw b Hastings	9	– c Mustard b Wood	45
S. R. Patel c Mustard b Wood	16	– c Rushworth b Wood	0
M. H. Wessels c Hastings b Onions	117	– not out	42
*†C. M. W. Read b Rushworth	2	– b Wood	9
B. A. Hutton c Mustard b Wood	3	– b Wood	1
V. D. Philander c Borthwick b Hastings	41	– lbw b Collingwood	12
L. Wood c Mustard b Hastings	4	– lbw b Collingwood	8
H. F. Gurney not out	4	– c Mustard b Collingwood	0
B 3, l-b 8, w 1, n-b 16	28	L-b 2, n-b 6	8

1/4 (2) 2/22 (3) 3/22 (1)   (75.1 overs) 245
4/40 (4) 5/72 (5) 6/91 (7)
7/102 (8) 8/212 (9) 9/226 (10) 10/245 (6)

1/20 (2) 2/40 (1)   (54.1 overs) 178
3/83 (3) 4/86 (5)
5/115 (4) 6/133 (7) 7/135 (8)
8/160 (9) 9/174 (10) 10/178 (11)

Onions 17.1–4–52–2; Rushworth 18–3–52–3; Wood 14–3–35–2; Hastings 18–4–66–3; Collingwood 6–0–20–0; Borthwick 2–0–9–0. *Second innings*—Rushworth 16–3–34–2; Onions 10–1–67–1; Wood 14–3–39–4; Hastings 11–3–29–0; Collingwood 3.1–0–7–3.

Durham

M. D. Stoneman lbw b Hutton	44	– lbw b Philander	7
K. K. Jennings c Read b Gurney	18	– c Mullaney b Wood	61
M. A. Wood lbw b Hutton	1	– b Gurney	66
S. G. Borthwick c J. W. A. Taylor b Wood	18	– lbw b Patel	51
M. J. Richardson lbw b Philander	19	– not out	51
C. S. MacLeod c Read b Philander	0	– not out	20
*P. D. Collingwood c B. R. M. Taylor b Wood	14		
†P. Mustard lbw b Hutton	17		
J. W. Hastings lbw b Philander	15		
C. Rushworth not out	1		
G. Onions b Wood	0		
L-b 7, w 1, n-b 8	16	L-b 5	5

1/65 (1) 2/65 (2) 3/69 (3)   (48.4 overs) 163
4/110 (5) 5/110 (4) 6/110 (6)
7/136 (8) 8/162 (7) 9/162 (9) 10/163 (11)

1/14 (1)   (4 wkts, 63.3 overs) 261
2/130 (3) 3/146 (3)
4/232 (4)

Philander 13–4–27–3; Wood 10.4–2–58–3; Hutton 14–3–44–3; Gurney 11–2–27–1. *Second innings*—Philander 15–3–53–1; Wood 13–6–34–1; Hutton 14–2–58–0; Gurney 10–0–45–1; Mullaney 8–1–32–0; Patel 3.3–0–34–1.

Umpires: R. J. Evans and N. A. Mallender.

At Birmingham, May 17–20. DURHAM lost to WARWICKSHIRE by eight wickets.

At Worcester, May 24–27. DURHAM beat WORCESTERSHIRE by six wickets.

DURHAM v SOMERSET

At Chester-le-Street, June 7–9. Durham won by 120 runs. Durham 19pts, Somerset 4pts. Toss: Durham.

As they had at Worcester, Durham staged a remarkable recovery. For the fourth game running they failed to gain a batting point, yet their fifth win in seven took them back to the top of Division One – and left Somerset bottom. There were suspicious looks at the pitch after 12 wickets in the first 55 overs of the second day, which left Durham 101 for six in their second innings, only 65 ahead. But Collingwood called on his vast experience to bat two and a quarter hours for 58, Coughlin backed him with a run-a-ball fifty, Hastings thrashed 79 off 68 balls, and Rushworth weighed in with 43. Somerset needed 279, and variable bounce on the third day ensured they fell well short. Coughlin continued his all-round form with a career-best four for ten in ten overs, bowling Hildreth with his third ball; Richardson held five catches behind the wicket. The pick of Somerset's five seamers had been Craig Overton, who concentrated on accuracy but exploited steep bounce to take seven wickets in all.

Close of play: first day, Somerset 147-4 (Myburgh 57, Allenby 13); second day, Durham 314.

Durham

M. D. Stoneman lbw b Overton	16	– c Overton b Groenewald	25
K. K. Jennings lbw b Groenewald	49	– b Groenewald	1
S. G. Borthwick c Trego b Groenewald	8	– c Gregory b Overton	14
*P. D. Collingwood lbw b Overton	0	– c Barrow b Overton	58
†M. J. Richardson c Trescothick b Allenby	32	– c Allenby b Overton	4
G. J. Muchall c Trescothick b Overton	24	– lbw b Trego	17
C. S. MacLeod c Myburgh b Allenby	0	– lbw b Gregory	0
P. Coughlin lbw b Groenewald	0	– c Groenewald b Trego	54
J. W. Hastings b Overton	28	– c Trescothick b Groenewald	79
C. Rushworth c Overton b Trego	13	– b Gregory	43
G. Onions not out	1	– not out	3
B 4, l-b 8, w 2, n-b 4	18	B 1, l-b 9, n-b 6	16

1/31 (1) 2/45 (3) 3/46 (4) (49.5 overs) **189**
4/117 (2) 5/119 (5) 6/119 (7)
7/120 (8) 8/172 (9) 9/183 (6) 10/189 (10)

1/4 (2) 2/37 (1) (71.2 overs) **314**
3/53 (3) 4/65 (5)
5/98 (6) 6/101 (7) 7/174 (4)
8/220 (8) 9/292 (9) 10/314 (10)

Gregory 12–1–63–0; Groenewald 14–2–37–3; Overton 11–1–40–4; Trego 5.5–0–25–1; Allenby 7–2–12–2. *Second innings*—Gregory 17.2–0–82–2; Groenewald 22–2–97–3; Overton 14–2–41–3; Allenby 7–2–31–0; Trego 11–1–53–2.

Somerset

*M. E. Trescothick lbw b Rushworth	26	– c MacLeod b Rushworth	35
T. B. Abell c Richardson b Rushworth	4	– lbw b Onions	2
J. G. Myburgh c Richardson b Hastings	61	– c Richardson b Onions	0
J. C. Hildreth c Hastings b Borthwick	35	– b Coughlin	27
T. L. W. Cooper c Muchall b Rushworth	8	– c Richardson b Onions	7
J. Allenby c Collingwood b Rushworth	20	– c Richardson b Hastings	17
P. D. Trego c and b Coughlin	19	– c Richardson b Coughlin	35
L. Gregory c Collingwood b Hastings	10	– c Richardson b Coughlin	18
†A. W. R. Barrow not out	10	– lbw b Rushworth	0
C. Overton c Onions b Coughlin	12	– not out	1
T. D. Groenewald c Hastings b Onions	11	– c Stoneman b Coughlin	4
B 7, l-b 2	9	B 1, l-b 1, n-b 10	12

1/21 (2) 2/34 (1) 3/107 (4) (65.5 overs) **225**
4/118 (5) 5/154 (5) 6/158 (6)
7/188 (7) 8/188 (8) 9/205 (10) 10/225 (11)

1/10 (2) 2/10 (3) (52 overs) **158**
3/63 (4) 4/69 (1)
5/78 (5) 6/104 (6) 7/145 (8)
8/146 (9) 9/154 (7) 10/158 (11)

Rushworth 22–6–54–4; Onions 4.5–1–14–1; Coughlin 12–1–43–2; Hastings 19–4–67–2; Collingwood 5–1–19–0; Borthwick 3–0–19–1. *Second innings*—Rushworth 15–2–46–2; Onions 13–2–73–3; Hastings 14–5–27–1; Coughlin 10–6–10–4.

Umpires: S. C. Gale and S. J. O'Shaughnessy.

At Arundel, June 15–18. DURHAM beat SUSSEX by 178 runs.

DURHAM v YORKSHIRE

At Chester-le-Street, June 28–July 1. Yorkshire won by an innings and 47 runs. Yorkshire 23pts, Durham 3pts. Toss: Durham.

Durham lost top spot to Yorkshire in a match decided by the third-highest seventh-wicket stand in first-class cricket – and the highest in England. Put in, Yorkshire had grafted diligently in seaming conditions but, from 124 for two in the 54th over, they had slipped to 191 for six when Bresnan joined Bairstow. That brought a shift in momentum as Bairstow counter-attacked, punishing anything short. The day's final 16 overs with the new ball yielded 92, as he completed his second fifty in 53 deliveries. Next day, Bairstow and Bresnan went on to career-best scores of 219 and 169, and an

---

HIGHEST SEVENTH-WICKET PARTNERSHIPS IN ENGLAND

366*	**J. M. Bairstow (219*)/ T. T. Bresnan (169*), Yorkshire v Durham at Chester-le-Street**	**2015**
344	K. S. Ranjitsinhji (230)/W. Newham (153), Sussex v Essex at Leyton	1902
340	K. J. Key (281)/H. Philipson (150), Oxford University v Middlesex at Chiswick	1887
336	F. C. W. Newman (101)/C. R. N. Maxwell (268), Sir J. Cahn's XI v Leicestershire at West Bridgford	1935
325	G. Brown (140*)/C. H. Abercrombie (165), Hampshire v Essex at Leyton	1913
315	D. M. Benkenstein (151)/O. D. Gibson (155), Durham v Yorkshire at Leeds	2006
301	C. C. Lewis (247)/B. N. French (123), Notts v Durham at Chester-le-St (Ropery Lane) .	1993

---

unbroken partnership of 366, an all-wicket record at Riverside. Durham tried nine bowlers, including Jennings, whose first ball Bairstow cut for four to reach 200 off 244 deliveries. Eight days earlier, Bairstow had scored a match-winning 83 in a one-day international at the same ground, where he was alone in making a Twenty20 century. A well-balanced, consistent attack made Durham follow on, and only Stoneman's second-innings century – his fourth in his last nine Championship innings against Yorkshire – offered prolonged resistance. The last six wickets fell in 82 minutes on the final morning.

Close of play: first day, Yorkshire 329-6 (Bairstow 102, Bresnan 66); second day, Durham 140-5 (Borthwick 35, Pringle 34); third day, Durham 244-4 (Stoneman 116, Muchall 21).

Yorkshire

A. Z. Lees c Richardson b Onions	40		T. T. Bresnan not out	169
W. M. H. Rhodes b Harrison	24			
J. A. Leaning b Harrison	28		B 2, l-b 13, w 1, n-b 8	24
*A. W. Gale c Collingwood b Hastings	22			—
†J. M. Bairstow not out	219		1/56 (2)	(6 wkts dec, 148 overs) 557
A. J. Finch c Borthwick b Hastings.	10		2/82 (1) 3/124 (3) 4/130 (4)	
A. U. Rashid c Collingwood b Rushworth . .	21		5/152 (6) 6/191 (7)	110 overs: 378-6

S. A. Patterson, J. A. Brooks and R. J. Sidebottom did not bat.

Rushworth 30–10–70–1; Onions 26–5–98–1; Harrison 23–1–77–2; Hastings 31–8–122–2; Collingwood 13–3–36–0; Pringle 8–0–47–0; Borthwick 12–1–65–0; Stoneman 2–0–13–0; Jennings 3–0–14–0.

Durham

M. D. Stoneman b Patterson	25	– lbw b Sidebottom	131
K. K. Jennings c Bresnan b Rashid	12	– c Lees b Rashid	41
S. G. Borthwick c Bairstow b Bresnan	54	– c Bairstow b Patterson	11
*P. D. Collingwood lbw b Patterson	0	– c Bresnan b Rashid	20
†M. J. Richardson lbw b Sidebottom	31	– c Bairstow b Brooks	29
G. J. Muchall b Bresnan	0	– b Patterson	26
R. D. Pringle not out	69	– c sub (R. Gibson) b Brooks	22
J. W. Hastings c Bairstow b Bresnan	0	– lbw b Brooks	7
J. Harrison b Brooks	11	– lbw b Brooks	2
C. Rushworth c Bairstow b Brooks	2	– c Bairstow b Brooks	3
G. Onions lbw b Rashid	0	– not out	0
L-b 2, n-b 2	4	B 2, l-b 6, n-b 2	10

1/37 (2) 2/41 (1) 3/41 (4)   (65.1 overs) 208
4/80 (5) 5/81 (6) 6/169 (3)
7/169 (8) 8/193 (9) 9/195 (10) 10/208 (11)

1/116 (2) 2/129 (3)   (90.4 overs) 302
3/168 (4) 4/213 (5)
5/251 (6) 6/275 (1) 7/289 (8)
8/299 (7) 9/299 (9) 10/302 (10)

Sidebottom 15–4–57–1; Brooks 10–1–59–2; Patterson 12.1–3–30–2; Bresnan 10–2–40–3. *Second innings*—Brooks 18.4–2–66–4; Patterson 14–1–48–2; Rashid 31–2–90–2; Sidebottom 12–1–41–2; Bresnan 12–1–40–0; Rhodes 3–0–9–0.

Umpires: P. K. Baldwin and S. J. O'Shaughnessy.

DURHAM v WARWICKSHIRE

At Chester-le-Street, July 12–15. Warwickshire won by two wickets. Warwickshire 19pts, Durham 6pts. Toss: Durham.

Fighting back from a first-innings deficit of 116, Warwickshire lost their eighth wicket straight after lunch on the fourth day, with 38 required – only for Patel and Milnes to see them home. They were missing three bowlers through injury, and Trott for paternity leave. But Woakes made his first appearance of the season, after a knee problem, and turned the game with a burst of three for three in ten balls to reduce Durham to nine for four in their second innings. It was 55 for seven when Harrison arrived, but the second half-century of his career enabled them to leave a target of 265 in four sessions, with batting conditions at their best on the final morning. The opening day had brought Stoneman's second century in a row, and a second-wicket stand of 153 with Borthwick. Warwickshire replied in gloomy weather and suffered seven lbws as Rushworth passed 50 Championship wickets, but Hain kept them afloat with an assured 57. Collingwood was reprimanded for lingering at the crease when given lbw in the first innings.

Close of play: first day, Warwickshire 10-0 (Chopra 6, Westwood 2); second day, Warwickshire 167-7 (Woakes 12, Patel 4); third day, Warwickshire 125-3 (Evans 52, Hain 5).

Durham

M. D. Stoneman b Milnes	112	– c Ambrose b Woakes	3
K. K. Jennings lbw b Clarke	7	– b Clarke	2
S. G. Borthwick c Evans b Woakes	67	– c Ambrose b Woakes	0
*P. D. Collingwood lbw b Clarke	31	– lbw b Woakes	1
†M. J. Richardson lbw b Clarke	3	– c Evans b Clarke	21
G. J. Muchall c Ambrose b Milnes	11	– c Ambrose b Clarke	13
R. D. Pringle c sub (A. R. I. Umeed) b Clarke	53	– c Ambrose b Milnes	22
J. W. Hastings c Westwood b Patel	1	– c Chopra b Hannon-Dalby	5
J. Harrison b Milnes	14	– b Patel	53
C. Rushworth c Ambrose b Clarke	4	– lbw b Patel	19
G. Onions not out	0	– not out	0
L-b 8, w 1, n-b 2	11	L-b 5, n-b 4	9

1/31 (2) 2/184 (3) 3/199 (1)   (89.2 overs) 314
4/202 (5) 5/219 (6) 6/253 (4)
7/256 (8) 8/296 (9) 9/307 (10) 10/314 (7)

1/5 (1) 2/5 (2) 3/6 (4)   (50.3 overs) 148
4/9 (3) 5/33 (5) 6/50 (6)
7/55 (8) 8/95 (7) 9/143 (10) 10/148 (9)

Clarke 21.2–7–62–5; Hannon-Dalby 18–4–55–0; Woakes 13–2–51–1; Milnes 22–3–96–3; Patel 15–5–42–1. *Second innings*—Clarke 16–6–19–3; Woakes 12–3–52–3; Hannon-Dalby 11–1–38–1; Milnes 8–0–24–1; Patel 3.3–0–10–2.

Warwickshire

*V. Chopra lbw b Rushworth	6	– c Richardson b Onions	11
I. J. Westwood lbw b Hastings	19	– c Richardson b Hastings	36
J. P. Webb lbw b Rushworth	0	– b Rushworth	0
L. J. Evans lbw b Rushworth	0	– c Richardson b Rushworth	70
S. R. Hain c Jennings b Hastings	57	– c Richardson b Onions	13
†T. R. Ambrose lbw b Collingwood	41	– c Collingwood b Harrison	25
R. Clarke lbw b Rushworth	13	– lbw b Onions	28
C. R. Woakes c Borthwick b Rushworth	15	– lbw b Rushworth	14
J. S. Patel c Collingwood b Onions	4	– not out	24
T. P. Milnes not out	12	– not out	14
O. J. Hannon-Dalby lbw b Harrison	4		
B 11, l-b 3, w 1, n-b 12	27	B 6, l-b 12, n-b 12	30

1/10 (1) 2/12 (3) 3/12 (4)   (58.4 overs) 198
4/40 (2) 5/138 (5) 6/142 (6)
7/159 (7) 8/174 (9) 9/176 (8) 10/198 (11)

1/33 (1)   (8 wkts, 67.3 overs) 265
2/38 (3) 3/103 (2) 4/138 (5)
5/158 (4) 6/192 (6) 7/225 (8) 8/227 (7)

Rushworth 20–7–43–5; Harrison 7.4–1–24–1; Onions 16–2–57–1; Hastings 12–1–57–2; Collingwood 3–1–3–1. *Second innings*—Rushworth 23–2–81–3; Onions 21.3–0–79–3; Harrison 8–3–29–1; Hastings 11–0–40–1; Borthwick 2–0–12–0; Pringle 1–1–0–0; Collingwood 1–0–6–0.

Umpires: G. D. Lloyd and D. J. Millns.

At Southampton, July 19–22. DURHAM drew with HAMPSHIRE.

At Scarborough, August 7–9. DURHAM lost to YORKSHIRE by 183 runs.

DURHAM v MIDDLESEX

At Chester-le-Street, August 21–24. Middlesex won by 71 runs. Middlesex 19pts, Durham 3pts. Toss: Durham. First-class debut: W. J. Weighell.

Middlesex secured the double over Durham, in a seamers' match where neither side gained a batting point. Onions claimed seven in the first innings, his best figures for two years, and Rushworth's seventh five-wicket haul of the season later took him past Ottis Gibson's Durham record of 80 first-class victims in 2007. But it was Middlesex's Harris who completed victory, adding eight more wickets to his 13 against Durham at Lord's. After rain wiped out half the first day, 19 fell on the second, which was heavily overcast. None went down in the final hour, however, when Malan survived a first-ball chance to third slip and began a crucial stand of 110 with Dexter. The skies cleared next day, when Malan fell early, but Dexter, driving fluently, took only 65 balls to hurry from his overnight 46 to a century. Durham needed 308 from 136 overs; Borthwick passed 1,000 Championship runs for the third successive season in making 95, but the end came soon after he was caught behind.

Close of play: first day, Middlesex 141-5 (Dexter 23, Simpson 2); second day, Middlesex 118-4 (Malan 56, Dexter 46); third day, Durham 134-5 (Borthwick 68, Pringle 6).

Middlesex

P. R. Stirling c Collingwood b Onions	3	– (2) c Richardson b Rushworth	8
S. D. Robson b Onions	14	– (1) b Rushworth	0
N. R. D. Compton c Richardson b Hastings	71	– lbw b Onions	5
D. J. Malan lbw b Onions	0	– c Richardson b Onions	63
*J. E. C. Franklin c Collingwood b Onions	16	– lbw b Rushworth	3
N. J. Dexter c Pringle b Onions	23	– c Richardson b Pringle	112
†J. A. Simpson not out	11	– lbw b Borthwick	21
O. P. Rayner lbw b Onions	6	– lbw b Borthwick	0
J. A. R. Harris c Collingwood b Rushworth	0	– c Collingwood b Rushworth	41
T. S. Roland-Jones c Muchall b Onions	27	– b Rushworth	23
T. J. Murtagh c Collingwood b Hastings	13	– not out	1
B 1, l-b 4, w 5, n-b 2	12	L-b 1, n-b 2	3

1/15 (1) 2/18 (2) 3/18 (4) (62.5 overs) 196
4/72 (5) 5/138 (3) 6/141 (6)
7/149 (8) 8/150 (9) 9/181 (10) 10/196 (11)

1/0 (1) 2/13 (3) (84.4 overs) 280
3/13 (2) 4/29 (5)
5/139 (4) 6/212 (6) 7/212 (7)
8/213 (8) 9/273 (10) 10/280 (9)

Rushworth 19–5–54–1; Onions 20–3–68–7; Weighell 8–1–38–0; Pringle 3–1–3–0. *Second innings*—Rushworth 19.4–6–49–5; Onions 22–5–86–2; Weighell 10–1–40–0; Hastings 9–0–37–0; Collingwood 2–0–15–0; Pringle 9–3–33–1; Borthwick 13–5–19–2.

Durham

M. D. Stoneman b Roland-Jones	3	– lbw b Murtagh	12
G. Clark b Roland-Jones	0	– c Simpson b Roland-Jones	0
S. G. Borthwick c Simpson b Roland-Jones	13	– c Simpson b Dexter	95
*P. D. Collingwood c Compton b Murtagh	1	– lbw b Harris	20
†M. J. Richardson lbw b Harris	21	– b Murtagh	13
G. J. Muchall c Franklin b Murtagh	64	– lbw b Roland-Jones	13
R. D. Pringle b Harris	0	– b Harris	36
W. J. Weighell b Harris	25	– c Stirling b Harris	24
J. W. Hastings c Stirling b Dexter	16	– c Simpson b Harris	8
C. Rushworth c Roland-Jones b Dexter	6	– c Robson b Harris	5
G. Onions not out	13	– not out	2
L-b 3, n-b 4	7	L-b 5, n-b 4	9

1/3 (1) 2/6 (2) 3/7 (4) (47.3 overs) 169
4/31 (3) 5/51 (5) 6/51 (7)
7/85 (8) 8/115 (9) 9/130 (10) 10/169 (6)

1/6 (2) 2/14 (1) (64.1 overs) 236
3/58 (4) 4/85 (5)
5/113 (6) 6/190 (7) 7/194 (3)
8/211 (9) 9/223 (10) 10/236 (8)

Murtagh 14.3–3–40–2; Roland-Jones 17–1–58–3; Harris 10–0–52–3; Dexter 6–1–16–2. *Second innings*—Murtagh 18–2–60–2; Roland-Jones 19–3–58–2; Harris 15.1–1–71–5; Franklin 4–1–18–0; Rayner 2–1–1–0; Dexter 6–1–23–1.

Umpires: N. A. Mallender and R. T. Robinson.

DURHAM v HAMPSHIRE

At Chester-le-Street, September 1–3. Hampshire won by seven wickets. Hampshire 21pts, Durham 4pts. Toss: Durham. First-class debut: R. A. Stevenson. County debut: R. McLaren.

Hampshire moved off the foot of Division One by making it two wins and a draw since Vince became captain, while Durham slipped to a fourth successive home defeat. Batting first, they were 65 for five when Pringle came in; dropped on 27 by former Durham captain Will Smith, he hit a career-best 99 – two-thirds of the remaining runs. The seaming pitch suited South Africa's Ryan McLaren, who earned seven in the match on his Hampshire debut; Onions was also excellent, removing the visitors' top three on the first evening. But Hampshire gained the lead after newcomer Ryan Stevenson scored a confident 30 from No.10. Stevenson, from Torquay, and James Weighell, an Academy product from Teesside, both claimed maiden first-class victims during the game. But Edwards and McLaren dominated Durham's second innings, when Smith held three catches at gully. Hampshire's eventual target was 163; Vince, in his new role at No. 3, knocked it off with a day to spare.

Close of play: first day, Hampshire 77-3 (Smith 22, Dawson 13); second day, Durham 126-6 (Pringle 10, Weighell 2).

Durham

M. D. Stoneman b Edwards	7	– c Smith b Edwards 14
J. T. A. Burnham c Wheater b McLaren	4	– c Dawson b McLaren 8
S. G. Borthwick c Wheater b Berg	9	– c Smith b McLaren. 5
*P. D. Collingwood c Wheater b McLaren	10	– lbw b McLaren. 37
†M. J. Richardson c Vince b McLaren	20	– b Edwards 8
G. J. Muchall lbw b Berg	23	– c Smith b Edwards 32
R. D. Pringle c Wheater b Edwards	99	– c Wheater b Berg 13
W. J. Weighell b Berg	0	– b Edwards 20
J. W. Hastings c Dawson b Edwards	6	– lbw b Berg 0
C. Rushworth c Smith b McLaren	18	– not out 33
G. Onions not out	0	– c Adams b Stevenson 15
B 2, l-b 3, n-b 12	17	B 8, l-b 7 15

1/15 (2) 2/17 (1) 3/32 (4)   (63.1 overs) 213
4/59 (5) 5/65 (3) 6/134 (6)
7/134 (8) 8/168 (9) 9/211 (7) 10/213 (10)

1/16 (2) 2/22 (1)   (53.5 overs) 200
3/34 (3) 4/56 (5)
5/98 (4) 6/115 (6) 7/134 (7)
8/134 (9) 9/164 (8) 10/200 (11)

McLaren 18.1–2–60–4; Edwards 15–3–57–3; Stevenson 11–1–58–0; Berg 16–7–27–3; Dawson 3–1–6–0. *Second innings*—Edwards 12.2–1–43–4; McLaren 18–5–54–3; Berg 14–4–53–2; Stevenson 8.5–2–33–1; Dawson 0.4–0–2–0.

Hampshire

M. A. Carberry c Muchall b Onions	16	– c Richardson b Onions 39
J. H. K. Adams b Onions	4	– b Rushworth 3
*J. M. Vince c Pringle b Onions	9	– not out 76
W. R. Smith c Rushworth b Hastings	38	– c Richardson b Onions 1
L. A. Dawson c Richardson b Hastings	25	– not out 34
S. M. Ervine b Weighell.	47	
†A. J. A. Wheater lbw b Onions	25	
R. McLaren b Hastings	30	
G. K. Berg c Borthwick b Hastings	1	
R. A. Stevenson c Weighell b Rushworth	30	
F. H. Edwards not out	9	
B 8, l-b 3, n-b 6	17	B 5, l-b 8 13

1/4 (2) 2/36 (3) 3/47 (1)   (82.5 overs) 251
4/105 (5) 5/110 (4) 6/158 (7)
7/205 (8) 8/207 (9) 9/219 (6) 10/251 (10)

1/35 (2)   (3 wkts, 34.3 overs) 166
2/75 (4) 3/84 (4)

Rushworth 22.5–7–44–1; Onions 23–7–61–4; Hastings 20–3–49–4; Weighell 15–2–72–1; Pringle 1–0–9–0; Borthwick 1–0–5–0. *Second innings*—Rushworth 13–3–58–1; Onions 13–5–35–2; Hastings 4–1–20–0; Weighell 3.3–1–29–0; Stoneman 1–0–11–0.

Umpires: R. J. Evans and J. W. Lloyds.

At Nottingham, September 9–11. DURHAM lost to NOTTINGHAMSHIRE by 52 runs.

DURHAM v WORCESTERSHIRE

At Chester-le-Street, September 14–17. Durham won by three wickets. Durham 20pts, Worcestershire 7pts. Toss: Durham. County debut: S. T. Gabriel.

Worcestershire's relegation was confirmed after their hand was forced by a second-day washout. They dominated the game but had to set a target to have a chance of winning – and staying up – and 291 in 71 overs proved too few on a placid pitch. Led by Borthwick and Richardson, Durham completed their season by getting home with 4.2 overs to spare, ending a run of six defeats and a draw. It was tough on Worcestershire's youngsters. Fell had made a high-class 83 before being run out in a mix-up, mistakenly believing the ball had crossed the boundary; Köhler-Cadmore batted strongly twice, and D'Oliveira earned a career-best five wickets with his leg-spin. This was a surprise: expecting a seaming pitch, Worcestershire had brought in the West Indian fast bowler Shannon Gabriel to replace Saeed Ajmal, but he proved less effective than the lively Barnard as Durham trailed by 73. Worcestershire ran up 175 in 25 overs on the last morning, with Whiteley's 21-ball 47 setting up the declaration; Rushworth looked fatigued but did manage his 100th wicket of the season in all competitions. Borthwick's 73 and 99 meant he had passed 50 a dozen times in the Championship campaign; his only century had come at Worcester in May.

Close of play: first day, Worcestershire 223-4 (Köhler-Cadmore 46, Whiteley 16); second day, no play; third day, Worcestershire 42-0 (Mitchell 10, D'Oliveira 32).

Worcestershire

*D. K. H. Mitchell lbw b Pringle	17	– b Rushworth	21
B. L. D'Oliveira lbw b McCarthy	36	– b Onions	49
T. C. Fell run out	83	– c McCarthy b Onions	28
J. M. Clarke c Muchall b Onions	19	– b Onions	0
T. Köhler-Cadmore st Richardson b Borthwick	89	– c McCarthy b Pringle	38
R. A. Whiteley b Pringle	51	– c Borthwick b Pringle	47
†O. B. Cox not out	26	– lbw b Borthwick	6
J. Leach st Richardson b Pringle	5	– c Stoneman b Borthwick	2
E. G. Barnard not out	14	– lbw b Pringle	17
J. D. Shantry (did not bat)		– not out	3
B 4, l-b 6	10	L-b 2, n-b 4	6

1/50 (2) 2/67 (1) (7 wkts dec, 101.4 overs) 350
3/109 (4) 4/194 (3)
5/284 (6) 6/324 (5) 7/329 (8)

1/68 (1) (9 wkts dec, 34 overs) 217
2/72 (2) 3/72 (4)
4/111 (3) 5/180 (5) 6/191 (7)
7/195 (6) 8/204 (8) 9/217 (9)

S. T. Gabriel did not bat.

Rushworth 19–5–36–0; Onions 18–5–61–1; McCarthy 14–2–51–1; Harrison 13–5–39–0; Pringle 25.4–3–94–3; Borthwick 9–0–49–1; Collingwood 3–0–10–0. *Second innings*—Rushworth 10–1–55–1; Onions 12–0–63–3; Pringle 5–0–45–3; Harrison 5–0–33–0; Borthwick 2–0–19–2.

Durham

M. D. Stoneman b Shantry	52	– c D'Oliveira b Shantry	28
J. T. A. Burnham c Köhler-Cadmore b Barnard	21	– lbw b Gabriel	1
S. G. Borthwick b D'Oliveira	73	– lbw b D'Oliveira	99
*P. D. Collingwood c Mitchell b Barnard	2	– c Cox b Gabriel	47
†M. J. Richardson c Mitchell b Leach	13	– not out	65
G. J. Muchall lbw b D'Oliveira	29	– c Cox b Barnard	12
R. D. Pringle b Barnard	21	– c Barnard b Leach	9
J. Harrison b D'Oliveira	13	– lbw b D'Oliveira	1
B. J. McCarthy st Cox b D'Oliveira	3	– not out	12
C. Rushworth not out	20		
G. Onions lbw b D'Oliveira	13		
B 4, l-b 7, n-b 6	17	B 1, l-b 10, n-b 6	17

1/83 (2) 2/83 (1) 3/88 (4) (64 overs) 277
4/121 (5) 5/181 (6) 6/218 (7)
7/241 (8) 8/242 (3) 9/251 (9) 10/277 (11)

1/4 (2) (7 wkts, 66.4 overs) 291
2/79 (1) 3/183 (3)
4/215 (4) 5/243 (6) 6/266 (7) 7/270 (8)

Leach 12–0–57–1; Gabriel 10–0–56–0; Shantry 13–3–42–1; Barnard 14–1–63–3; D'Oliveira 15–3–48–5. *Second innings*—Leach 10–1–61–1; Gabriel 12–0–56–2; Shantry 15–2–44–1; Barnard 8–2–34–1; D'Oliveira 21.4–4–85–2.

Umpires: R. A. Kettleborough and N. J. Llong.

ESSEX

The Third Men

P<small>AUL</small> H<small>ISCOCK</small>

Essex finished third in the second division for the third successive year, but were never really in the running for promotion, finishing 54 points behind second-placed Lancashire. Quarter-final defeats in both limited-overs competitions meant the overall verdict was another mediocre season, the seventh in a row with no trophies. And the atmosphere was not helped by long-running machinations behind the scenes.

Before the summer was over, head coach Paul Grayson decided to quit "by mutual consent", instead of waiting to be sacked. His assistant, the former England fast bowler Chris Silverwood, took over, a position made permanent in December; two months later, Yorkshire's Anthony McGrath was appointed his deputy. Graham Saville also stood down as chairman of the cricket committee, a role he had filled for 27 years, after he was informed that a majority of his colleagues no longer had faith in him. The former Essex captain Ronnie Irani replaced Saville, having spent much of the season griping about Grayson's approach: it was no surprise when he eventually departed.

The Championship campaign produced six victories – but also five defeats, two of them coming after embarrassing performances. Kent won at Tunbridge Wells by an innings and 207 runs, while Leicestershire tasted victory at Chelmsford – their first Championship win for nearly three years, and their first away from home since 2010.

There were two standout performers in four-day cricket, both products of the well-respected Essex Academy. Left-handed opener Nick Browne continued the favourable impression he had left when given an opportunity in mid-2014, and made his first full year one to savour. A batsman who loves to occupy the crease, he scored five centuries and was the first Essex player to reach 1,000 Championship runs since Ravi Bopara in 2008. In November, he became the first Englishman to hit a double-century in Sydney grade cricket, beating Mike Gatting's 194. The 22-year-old seamer Jamie Porter – who had been playing club cricket for Chingford before a run in the first team late in 2014 – became an integral part of the side, taking 50 Championship wickets. Both were capped.

Another to emerge with credit was Tom Westley, who was selected for the England Performance Programme during the winter, and given the Essex vice-captaincy. A sound technique helped him top Essex's overall run-list, with 1,754 in all matches. His off-spin could also develop, if he gets the chance.

Browne's best support in four-day cricket came from Ryan ten Doeschate, with 832 runs, although he failed to convert any of his seven fifties into a century. New Zealander Jesse Ryder, signed as the overseas player in 2014 primarily for his powerful batting, proved an effective all-rounder with his

Jamie McDonald, Getty Images

Nick Browne

seemingly innocuous medium-pace, allying 44 Championship wickets – the same as in 2014, when he topped the bowling averages – to 806 runs. James Foster, still a fine wicketkeeper at 35, did reasonably well with the bat, although 694 first-class runs was his lowest aggregate since 2003. He was relieved of the captaincy in December, and was replaced as club captain by ten Doeschate – who in turn ceded the limited-overs job to Bopara. Foster signed a new two-year contract.

However, Bopara – overlooked by England after the World Cup – failed to sparkle in the Championship, managing only 565 runs with four half-centuries. In the final game, he hit 99, against Lancashire at Chelmsford, where he and Ryder added 186. Worryingly, the new-ball workhorse David Masters was restricted by injury to only seven appearances, in which he claimed 20 wickets. At 37, he was approaching the end, leaving Essex with a disconcerting hole to fill. Graham Napier said the 2016 season would be his last before retiring.

Bopara proved an effective limited-overs all-rounder, with 617 runs and 29 wickets, while Westley and Ryder did well with the bat. Reece Topley was the pick of the white-ball bowlers, taking 36 wickets, and his decision to join Hampshire for 2016 was a blow. Mark Pettini, a former captain, also decided to leave: after a successful return to the Championship side brought him two centuries – and an average over 100 – he was offered a new deal, but preferred to take his chances with Leicestershire. Both will be missed. The lanky left-armer Topley, 21, had been carefully managed after suffering a stress fracture of the back during the winter. He made only two Championship appearances in 2015, although he was a regular member of the limited-overs sides, and made a successful start for England during the summer.

All-rounder Greg Smith was released, as was the former England spinner Monty Panesar, who failed to set the world alight during two full seasons at Chelmsford, and later said he had been suffering from mental-health issues. Left-arm spinner Ashar Zaidi arrived from Sussex. The club also signed Pakistani left-arm quick Wahab Riaz for the first half of the T20 Blast, to be replaced by New Zealand fast-bowler Adam Milne.

Silverwood's task – a daunting one – will be to kick-start a new era for Essex cricket, and banish the underachievement of recent years. One urgent need was for an incisive fast bowler, so his first signing was the 22-year-old New Zealander Matthew Quinn, who has a British passport. However, there is some exciting young talent in the wings, including England Under-19 players Dan Lawrence (who made a superb 161 in the Championship against Surrey before his 18th birthday) and all-rounder Callum Taylor. Aron Nijjar and Kishen Velani, both 21, caught the eye too.

Championship attendance: 23,224.

ESSEX RESULTS

All first-class matches – Played 17: Won 6, Lost 6, Drawn 5.
County Championship matches – Played 16: Won 6, Lost 5, Drawn 5.

LV= County Championship, 3rd in Division 2;
NatWest T20 Blast, quarter-finalists; Royal London One-Day Cup, quarter-finalists.

COUNTY CHAMPIONSHIP AVERAGES, BATTING AND FIELDING

Cap		Birthplace	M	I	NO	R	HS	100	Avge	Ct/St
2006	M. L. Pettini	Brighton	5	7	3	402	134	2	100.50	5
	L. A. Dawson	Swindon	2	4	1	169	99	0	56.33	2
2006	R. N. ten Doeschate¶	Port Elizabeth, SA	12	19	4	832	88	0	55.46	6
2015	N. L. J. Browne	Leytonstone†..	16	29	2	1,157	151*	4	42.85	16
2014	J. D. Ryder§	Masterton, NZ..	14	24	5	806	124	2	42.42	14
2013	T. Westley	Cambridge	12	21	1	782	179	1	39.10	6
	D. W. Lawrence	Whipps Cross† ...	7	12	1	409	161	1	37.18	8
	A. S. S. Nijjar	Goodmayes†	6	8	4	129	53	0	32.25	—
2001	J. S. Foster	Whipps Cross† ...	16	23	2	671	98	0	31.95	44/3
2005	R. S. Bopara	Forest Gate†....	12	21	1	565	99	0	28.25	3
	K. S. Velani	Newham†	4	7	0	190	58	0	27.14	3
2005	A. N. Cook‡	Gloucester	3	5	0	135	80	0	27.00	4
2003	G. R. Napier	Colchester†....	13	17	1	363	73	0	22.68	5
2013	J. C. Mickleburgh	Norwich	10	18	0	398	61	0	22.11	6
	G. M. Smith¶	Johannesburg, SA.	4	5	1	76	50*	0	19.00	3
2008	D. D. Masters	Chatham	7	10	3	85	28	0	12.14	3
	M. E. T. Salisbury	Chelmsford† ...	4	6	0	56	24	0	9.33	2
	Adeel Malik¶	Sialkot, Pakistan .	3	6	0	48	25	0	8.00	1
2015	J. A. Porter	Leytonstone†....	15	19	5	98	34	0	7.00	5

Also batted: T. C. Moore† (*Basildon*) (2 matches) 0* (1 ct); M. S. Panesar (*Luton*) (3 matches) 11, 11*, 2* (1 ct); R. H. Patel (*Harrow*) (1 match) 0*, 0; C. J. Taylor (*Norwich*) (1 match) 26, 22; R. J. W. Topley (*Ipswich*) (cap 2013) (2 matches) 0, 4*, 0 (1 ct). J. R. Winslade (*Epsom*) (2 matches) did not bat.

† *Born in Essex.*   ‡ *ECB contract.*   § *Official overseas player.*
¶ *Other non-England-qualified player.*

BOWLING

	Style	O	M	R	W	BB	5I	Avge
R. S. Bopara	RM	148.2	24	505	20	4-29	0	25.25
J. D. Ryder	RM	333.4	70	1,120	44	6-47	3	25.45
G. R. Napier	RFM	281	39	979	35	4-27	0	27.97
J. A. Porter	RFM	393.5	64	1,418	50	4-28	0	28.36
D. D. Masters	RFM	224.2	54	606	20	4-45	0	30.30
A. S. S. Nijjar	SLA	83.3	10	332	10	2-33	0	33.20

Also bowled: Adeel Malik (LBG) 46.5–5–224–4; N. L. J. Browne (LBG) 2.5–1–7–0; L. A. Dawson (SLA) 27.2–6–73–4; T. C. Moore (RFM) 24–6–95–3; M. S. Panesar (SLA) 75.1–17–270–7; R. H. Patel (SLA) 18–2–92–1; M. E. T. Salisbury (RFM) 32–3–125–1; G. M. Smith (OB/RFM) 33.2–5–110–5; R. N. ten Doeschate (RM) 40–5–144–6; R. J. W. Topley (LFM) 53–10–206–7; T. Westley (OB) 98.4–7–310–6; J. R. Winslade (RFM) 21–2–97–4.

LEADING ROYAL LONDON CUP AVERAGES (100 runs/4 wickets)

Batting	Runs	HS	Avge	SR	Ct
R. S. Bopara	301	101*	75.25	89.58	1
R. N. ten Doeschate	198	52	66.00	92.09	5
T. Westley	315	108	45.00	86.30	2
M. L. Pettini	313	126	44.71	75.97	1
J. D. Ryder	156	81*	31.20	115.55	1
N. L. J. Browne	153	69	25.50	82.70	2

Bowling	W	BB	Avge	ER
R. J. W. Topley	20	4-26	17.95	4.84
R. S. Bopara	10	4-31	31.30	5.04
J. A. Porter	5	3-39	35.80	5.50
G. R. Napier	5	2-37	38.00	5.13
D. D. Masters	6	2-28	43.50	3.67

LEADING NATWEST T20 BLAST AVERAGES (100 runs/18 overs)

Batting	Runs	HS	Avge	SR	Ct/St
G. R. Napier	100	27	12.50	185.18	7
J. D. Ryder	350	107*	29.16	165.87	6
J. S. Foster	168	33	18.66	164.70	4/1
R. N. ten Doeschate	264	68	22.00	141.93	12
M. L. Pettini	281	74	28.10	135.09	3
T. Westley	384	68	38.40	123.87	6

Bowling	W	BB	Avge	ER
R. S. Bopara	19	3-12	16.10	6.62
D. D. Masters	5	2-21	69.00	6.96
T. Westley	5	2-27	32.40	8.10
S. W. Tait	23	3-28	19.34	8.39
R. J. W. Topley	16	3-25	22.93	9.02
G. R. Napier	11	3-30	42.18	9.43

FIRST-CLASS COUNTY RECORDS

Highest score for	343*	P. A. Perrin v Derbyshire at Chesterfield	1904
Highest score against	332	W. H. Ashdown (Kent) at Brentwood	1934
Leading run-scorer	30,701	G. A. Gooch (avge 51.77)	1973–97
Best bowling for	10-32	H. Pickett v Leicestershire at Leyton	1895
Best bowling against	10-40	E. G. Dennett (Gloucestershire) at Bristol	1906
Leading wicket-taker	1,610	T. P. B. Smith (avge 26.68)	1929–51
Highest total for	761-6 dec	v Leicestershire at Chelmsford	1990
Highest total against	803-4 dec	by Kent at Brentwood	1934
Lowest total for	20	v Lancashire at Chelmsford	2013
Lowest total against	14	by Surrey at Chelmsford	1983

LIST A COUNTY RECORDS

Highest score for	201*	R. S. Bopara v Leicestershire at Leicester	2008
Highest score against	158*	M. W. Goodwin (Sussex) at Chelmsford	2006
Leading run-scorer	16,536	G. A. Gooch (avge 40.93)	1973–97
Best bowling for	8-26	K. D. Boyce v Lancashire at Manchester	1971
Best bowling against	7-29	D. A. Payne (Gloucestershire) at Chelmsford	2010
Leading wicket-taker	616	J. K. Lever (avge 19.04)	1968–89
Highest total for	391-5	v Surrey at The Oval	2008
Highest total against	321-5	by Derbyshire at Leek	2013
Lowest total for	57	v Lancashire at Lord's	1996
Lowest total against {	41	by Middlesex at Westcliff-on-Sea	1972
	41	by Shropshire at Wellington	1974

TWENTY20 COUNTY RECORDS

Highest score for	152*	G. R. Napier v Sussex at Chelmsford	2008
Highest score against	153*	L. J. Wright (Sussex) at Chelmsford	2014
Leading run-scorer	2,782	M. L. Pettini (avge 26.75)	2003–15
Best bowling for	6-16	T. G. Southee v Glamorgan at Chelmsford	2011
Best bowling against	5-11	Mushtaq Ahmed (Sussex) at Hove	2005
Leading wicket-taker	101	G. R. Napier (avge 26.48)	2003–15
Highest total for	242-3	v Sussex at Chelmsford	2008
Highest total against	226-3	by Sussex at Chelmsford	2014
Lowest total for	74	v Middlesex at Chelmsford	2013
Lowest total against	82	by Gloucestershire at Chelmsford	2011

ADDRESS

County Ground, New Writtle Street, Chelmsford CM2 0PG; 01245 252420;
administration.essex@ecb.co.uk; www.essexcricket.org.uk.

OFFICIALS

Captain 2015 J. S. Foster
    2016 R. N. ten Doeschate
    2015 (limited-overs) R. N. ten Doeschate
    2016 (limited-overs) R. S. Bopara
First-team coach 2015 A. P. Grayson
Head coach 2016 C. E. W. Silverwood
President D. J. Insole

Chairman 2015 N. R. A. Hilliard
Acting-chairman J. F. Faragher
Chief executive D. W. Bowden
Chairman, cricket committee R. C. Irani
Head groundsman S. G. Kerrison
Scorer A. E. Choat

At Chelmsford, April 12–14 (not first-class). **Drawn.** ‡**Essex 487-7 dec** (102 overs) (T. Westley 108, N. L. J. Browne 100, J. C. Mickleburgh 114, J. D. Ryder 86) **and 324-7 dec** (63 overs) (G. M. Smith 83, J. C. Mickleburgh 69, N. L. J. Browne 104*); **Cardiff MCCU 186** (68.3 overs) (A. S. S. Nijjar 55*, D. E. Lewis-Williams 75; J. A. Porter 3-8, J. D. Ryder 3-46) **and 116-2** (39 overs). *County debut: D. W. Lawrence. Essex gorged on some undemanding bowling on the first day: the top three all completed centuries before retiring out, then Jesse Ryder thumped 86 from 63 balls. Next morning Cardiff crashed to 53-7, but were rescued by a stand of 118 between Aron Nijjar, a product of Essex's Academy, and Dan Lewis-Williams, who hit a dozen fours. Despite leading by 301, Essex opted for more batting practice on a flat pitch. They slipped to 136-6 after tinkering with the order, before a partnership of 127 between Jaik Mickleburgh and Nick Browne, who completed his second century to set up another declaration. Trailing by 625, the students survived 39 overs without much difficulty.*

ESSEX v KENT

At Chelmsford, April 19–21. Essex won by five wickets. Essex 19pts, Kent 3pts. Toss: Essex. First-class debut: D. W. Lawrence.

A green pitch, sporting tufts of grass, encouraged the seamers throughout. The match lasted only seven sessions and nine balls – but it was an absorbing encounter. Sixteen wickets clattered on the first day, which left portions of the crowd confused as Chelmsford's flashy new scoreboard resolutely refused to work, owing to "internet issues". A late shift from the IT department meant all was well next day, when the board had to cope with another 17 wickets. The key innings was played by Foster on the third morning. He entered in the second over at 66 for four, chasing 193, but batted with great authority, hitting ten fours and a six in the highest score of the match. He was helped by Porter, who streakily survived two hours for 14 after going in as nightwatchman for the second day running. Batsmen had struggled from the start. Ryder did the early damage, with his fifth first-class five-for – all in his 13 matches for Essex – and Kent reached 193 thanks only to the veteran Stevens. In turn, Essex declined to 69 for seven, before a forceful 40-ball 57 from Napier reduced the deficit. Northeast dominated Kent's second innings, batting for two and a half hours; no one else could last even one. Essex had the upper hand, and refused to surrender it, going on to their sixth successive Championship win since July.

Close of play: first day, Essex 67-6 (Mickleburgh 20); second day, Essex 66-3 (Porter 4, Lawrence 3).

Kent

D. J. Bell-Drummond c Browne b Masters	30	– c Foster b Masters	4
J. L. Denly c Foster b Porter	3	– c Lawrence b Porter	0
*R. W. T. Key lbw b Ryder	18	– c Foster b Masters	14
S. A. Northeast c Smith b Ryder	6	– lbw b Smith	77
F. K. Cowdrey b Ryder	18	– c Foster b Masters	0
D. I. Stevens lbw b Ryder	50	– c Foster b Ryder	36
†S. W. Billings c Browne b Masters	20	– c Panesar b Smith	6
M. T. Coles c Mickleburgh b Smith	8	– c Porter b Napier	2
M. E. Claydon c Westley b Ryder	7	– c Browne b Smith	14
A. E. N. Riley not out	18	– lbw b Masters	5
I. A. A. Thomas c Lawrence b Porter	0	– not out	0
B 6, l-b 6, w 1, n-b 2	15	L-b 4, w 1	5

1/10 (2) 2/39 (3) 3/49 (4) (68.5 overs) 193
4/72 (1) 5/87 (5) 6/125 (7)
7/142 (8) 8/168 (9) 9/169 (6) 10/193 (11)

1/0 (2) 2/8 (1) (51 overs) 163
3/43 (3) 4/49 (5)
5/111 (6) 6/136 (7) 7/143 (4)
8/144 (8) 9/163 (9) 10/163 (10)

Masters 15-3-39-1; Porter 17.5-6-39-2; Ryder 18-5-43-5; Napier 11-2-34-0; Smith 7-0-26-2. *Second innings*—Masters 13-3-45-4; Porter 10-1-37-1; Ryder 8-2-28-1; Napier 9-0-27-1; Smith 11-3-22-3.

Essex

T. Westley c Denly b Coles	5	– (2) b Thomas 0
N. L. J. Browne b Thomas	11	– (1) c Billings b Claydon 25
J. C. Mickleburgh c Cowdrey b Claydon	46	– c Coles b Claydon 23
D. W. Lawrence lbw b Stevens	10	– (5) c Cowdrey b Claydon 3
*†J. S. Foster c and b Coles	3	– (6) not out 80
J. D. Ryder b Stevens	12	– (7) not out 17
J. A. Porter c Cowdrey b Stevens	3	– (4) b Coles 14
G. M. Smith c Coles b Stevens	0	
G. R. Napier c Northeast b Coles	57	
D. D. Masters not out	1	
M. S. Panesar b Coles	11	
L-b 3, n-b 2	5	B 15, l-b 5, w 3, n-b 8 31

1/18 (1) 2/18 (2) 3/34 (4)   (46.5 overs) 164   1/9 (2)   (5 wkts, 51.3 overs) 193
4/47 (5) 5/60 (6) 6/67 (7)   2/57 (1) 3/60 (3)
7/69 (8) 8/149 (9) 9/153 (3) 10/164 (11)   4/66 (5) 5/132 (4)

Claydon 7–0–30–1; Thomas 13–4–36–1; Coles 13.5–5–48–4; Stevens 13–2–47–4. *Second innings*—Coles 12–2–38–1; Thomas 10.3–3–37–1; Stevens 14–6–43–0; Claydon 14–2–55–3; Riley 1–1–0–0.

Umpires: P. K. Baldwin and N. A. Mallender.

At The Oval, April 26–29. ESSEX drew with SURREY. *Daniel Lawrence, 17, becomes the third-youngest Championship century-maker.*

ESSEX v GLOUCESTERSHIRE

At Chelmsford, May 3–5. Gloucestershire won by nine wickets. Gloucestershire 20pts, Essex 3pts. Toss: Gloucestershire. County debut: Adeel Malik.

Another green pitch, another three-day finish – but this time Essex were on the receiving end. Put in after rain delayed the start for 90 minutes, they survived the first hour, then lost eight for 45 in an inept display, as the pacy Norwell took four for two in 16 balls. Leg-spinner Adeel Malik, the brother of the former Pakistan captain Shoaib, and Masters inched the total past 150, but diligent innings from Dent and Handscomb took Gloucestershire in front. Seamers Porter and Ryder kept Essex in touch, but the eventual lead of 86 proved decisive. They lost four wickets clearing off the deficit, before bad light ended the second day. Next morning only a maiden half-century from 20-year-old Velani ensured a three-figure target; Norwell completed his best innings figures – including a spell of three for two in 11 balls – and his maiden ten-for. Gloucestershire's openers knocked off 106 of the runs required at five an over, before Tavaré fell in sight of victory.

Close of play: first day, Gloucestershire 77-0 (Tavaré 32, Dent 42); second day, Essex 91-4 (Foster 13, Velani 3).

Essex

N. L. J. Browne c Roderick b Miles	19	– c Dent b Norwell 9
J. C. Mickleburgh b Norwell	42	– b Norwell 31
D. W. Lawrence c Dent b Norwell	6	– lbw b Norwell 3
*†J. S. Foster c Dent b Norwell	1	– b Norwell 13
J. D. Ryder c Roderick b Norwell	8	– c Marshall b Taylor 21
K. S. Velani c Dent b Payne	7	– c Handscomb b Payne 58
G. M. Smith c Roderick b Miles	11	– b Payne 12
G. R. Napier c Tavaré b Payne	4	– c Dent b Miles 4
Adeel Malik b Payne	25	– c Handscomb b Payne 13
D. D. Masters lbw b Taylor	26	– not out 11
J. A. Porter not out	3	– b Norwell 7
L-b 1, n-b 6	7	B 4, l-b 11, n-b 2 17

1/61 (1) 2/73 (2) 3/74 (3)   (45.4 overs) 159   1/42 (1) 2/49 (2)   (68.5 overs) 199
4/75 (4) 5/82 (5) 6/94 (6)   3/52 (3) 4/85 (5)
7/98 (8) 8/106 (7) 9/130 (9) 10/159 (10)   5/99 (4) 6/127 (7) 7/153 (8)
                                                     8/180 (9) 9/180 (6) 10/199 (11)

Taylor 8.4–2–26–1; Payne 13–0–64–3; Norwell 12–3–32–4; Miles 9–1–29–2; Noema-Barnett 3–2–7–0. *Second innings*—Taylor 16–5–56–1; Payne 20–5–67–2; Norwell 18.5–5–33–6; Noema-Barnett 1–0–1–0; Miles 13–4–27–1.

Gloucestershire

W. A. Tavaré b Porter	32	– (2) c Lawrence b Porter	57
C. D. J. Dent c Browne b Ryder	57	– (1) not out	52
†G. H. Roderick c Foster b Porter	6	– not out	2
P. S. P. Handscomb lbw b Porter	66		
H. J. H. Marshall lbw b Masters	11		
*G. O. Jones b Ryder	20		
K. Noema-Barnett lbw b Ryder	0		
C. N. Miles c Foster b Napier	9		
D. A. Payne c Smith b Masters	23		
L. C. Norwell c Lawrence b Porter	0		
M. D. Taylor not out	7		
L-b 8, n-b 6	14	L-b 1, n-b 2	3

1/77 (1) 2/83 (3) 3/103 (2)   (72.2 overs) 245   1/106 (2)   (1 wkt, 21.2 overs) 114
4/137 (5) 5/175 (6) 6/179 (7)
7/192 (8) 8/227 (4) 9/235 (10) 10/245 (9)

Masters 21.2–4–51–2; Porter 20–3–59–4; Ryder 16–0–75–3; Napier 12–2–37–1; Adeel Malik 3–0–15–0. *Second innings*—Masters 7–1–16–0; Porter 5.2–0–43–1; Napier 3–0–17–0; Ryder 4–0–21–0; Adeel Malik 2–0–16–0.

Umpires: R. J. Bailey and N. A. Mallender.

At Cardiff, May 18–21. ESSEX lost to GLAMORGAN by 89 runs.

ESSEX v LEICESTERSHIRE

At Chelmsford, May 31–June 3. Leicestershire won by six wickets. Leicestershire 21pts, Essex 3pts. Toss: Leicestershire. First-class debut: A. S. S. Nijjar. County debut: A. P. Agathangelou.

After 37 games and 992 days, Leicestershire finally won a Championship match – their first since beating Gloucestershire at Grace Road on September 14, 2012. It was also their first away win since the last game of 2010, at Northampton. Their advantage was established by Raine, swinging and seaming his way to a maiden five-for on a blustery opening day – as Essex were dismissed for 166 – and cemented by Robson, who batted more than five and a half hours for 120. Napier restricted the damage with three for seven in mid-innings, but Essex lost four wickets clearing the arrears, before Westley and ten Doeschate put on 128. However, Raine trapped Westley just short of his hundred as the last five tumbled for 20; the 37-year-old Shreck finished with his first five-for in three seasons. Any nerves Leicestershire might have felt contemplating a target of 163 were dissipated by an opening stand of 87 in 26 overs. And although Robson departed for 71, a fortnight innings from Agathangelou – selected after making 163 for the Second XI against Afghanistan, who were preparing for an Intercontinental Cup match against Scotland – consigned Essex to their third

MOST CONSECUTIVE CHAMPIONSHIP MATCHES WITHOUT A WIN

P	L	D			
99	60	39	Northamptonshire .	1935–1939	
53	30	23	Worcestershire	1927–1929	
43	7	36	Nottinghamshire . . .	1966–1968	

P	L	D		
40	14	26	Leicestershire	1936–1937
37	**21**	**16**	**Leicestershire . . . .**	**2013–2015**

After 99 matches without a win, Northamptonshire won the 100th – against Leicestershire at Northampton in May 1939 – by an innings and 193 runs.

consecutive defeat. The winning runs came from Lewis Hill, Leicestershire's new wicketkeeper, just before lunch on the final day. He and his team-mates were delighted to have removed the monkey from their backs, but their new Australian coach, Andrew McDonald, was more down to earth: "I've only been here two months, and that's our first win in two months. I've never been too bothered about what happened in the past." Umpire Steve Gale was hit on the hand by a ball during the pre-match warm-ups, and was unable to officiate until the second day; Essex match-day official Danny Saddai stood at square leg for three overs until Ben Debenham arrived.

Close of play: first day, Leicestershire 28-0 (Boyce 15, Robson 8); second day, Essex 43-2 (Westley 18, Bopara 7); third day, Leicestershire 55-0 (Robson 34, Boyce 20).

Essex

N. L. J. Browne c Agathangelou b McKay	2	– c Boyce b McKay	2
J. C. Mickleburgh b Raine	16	– b Raine	7
T. Westley lbw b Raine	27	– lbw b Raine	97
R. S. Bopara c Hill b McKay	4	– lbw b McKay	19
J. D. Ryder c Eckersley b Raine	38	– b Shreck	20
R. N. ten Doeschate c Hill b Raine	0	– c Agathangelou b Shreck	77
*†J. S. Foster lbw b Raine	3	– c Agathangelou b Shreck	22
G. R. Napier c Agathangelou b Shreck	29	– lbw b Raine	3
M. E. T. Salisbury c Wells b Naik	24	– c Hill b Shreck	4
A. S. S. Nijjar not out	9	– not out	1
J. A. Porter lbw b Naik	7	– c and b Shreck	2
L-b 4, w 1, n-b 2	7	B 2, l-b 17, w 1, n-b 2	22

1/2 (1) 2/45 (3) 3/46 (2) (61.3 overs) 166
4/58 (4) 5/59 (6) 6/67 (7)
7/121 (8) 8/125 (5) 9/152 (9) 10/166 (11)

1/12 (1) 2/16 (2) (94.2 overs) 276
3/62 (4) 4/92 (5)
5/220 (6) 6/256 (3) 7/266 (7)
8/272 (8) 9/272 (9) 10/276 (11)

McKay 17–5–42–2; Shreck 10–2–31–1; Raine 18–4–48–5; Wells 8–1–32–0; Naik 8.3–6–9–2. *Second innings*—McKay 21–9–57–2; Raine 27–11–59–3; Shreck 26.2–6–71–5; Wells 9–1–33–0; Naik 11–1–37–0.

Leicestershire

M. A. G. Boyce c Ryder b Porter	21	– (2) c Browne b Ryder	24
A. J. Robson c Browne b Ryder	120	– (1) c Foster b Porter	71
E. J. H. Eckersley b Ryder	18	– b Porter	3
*M. J. Cosgrove lbw b Porter	24	– b Porter	2
A. P. Agathangelou c Ryder b Napier	1	– not out	42
†L. J. Hill c Bopara b Napier	2	– not out	18
B. A. Raine c Browne b Napier	1		
T. J. Wells c Westley b Nijjar	14		
C. J. McKay b Bopara	45		
J. K. H. Naik not out	5		
C. E. Shreck c Foster b Porter	0		
L-b 17, n-b 12	29	B 1, l-b 2	3

1/58 (1) 2/91 (3) 3/130 (4) (84.5 overs) 280
4/156 (5) 5/160 (6) 6/170 (7)
7/200 (8) 8/274 (9) 9/279 (2) 10/280 (11)

1/87 (1) (4 wkts, 44.3 overs) 163
2/96 (3) 3/100 (4)
4/117 (1)

Porter 18.5–3–69–3; Ryder 22–7–42–2; Napier 19–4–62–3; Salisbury 9–1–36–0; Nijjar 8–1–27–1; ten Doeschate 5–0–14–0; Bopara 3–0–13–1. *Second innings*—Ryder 21–5–56–1; Porter 10–0–38–3; Napier 10–1–41–0; Nijjar 3.3–0–25–0.

Umpires: S. C. Gale and N. J. Llong. D. Saddai and B. J. Debenham stood in for Gale on the first day.

At Northampton, June 7–10. ESSEX drew with NORTHAMPTONSHIRE.

ESSEX v DERBYSHIRE

At Chelmsford, June 14–16. Essex won by an innings and 31 runs. Essex 23pts, Derbyshire 2pts. Toss: Essex.

Essex emphatically ended a run of five matches without a win, making Derbyshire pay for a lack of application on the first day. After being put in, they slid to a below-par 148 in the face of some brisk swing from Porter, who recorded career-best figures of four for 28. Cook made good use of his first Championship appearance of the season, grafting to 80 in nearly four hours and sharing an opening stand of 134 with Browne. White persevered for six wickets, but Footitt had trouble with his run-up, and Essex biffed 72 from 91 balls – to stretch the lead to 325. Two quick wickets from Porter jolted Derbyshire, before the aggressive Hughes and the more patient Madsen combined in a stand worth 166. But, after they were parted, Essex's seamers worked their way through the rest. Napier claimed four wickets in 23 overs, and Ryder ended proceedings late on the third day with two in five balls.

Close of play: first day, Essex 108-0 (Browne 47, Cook 50); second day, Essex 449-8 (Foster 51, Nijjar 14).

Derbyshire

B. T. Slater c Ryder b Porter	1	– c Napier b Porter	0
B. A. Godleman b Ryder	0	– c ten Doeschate b Porter.	7
C. F. Hughes b Porter	14	– b Bopara	80
*W. L. Madsen lbw b Ryder	0	– c Cook b Napier	112
W. J. Durston b Foster b Salisbury	18	– b Napier	28
S. L. Elstone b Porter	0	– c Foster b Ryder	24
S. J. Thakor c Cook b Napier	44	– lbw b Napier	15
W. A. White not out	38	– b Ryder	9
†T. Poynton c Napier b Porter	14	– b Napier	0
A. P. Palladino run out	5	– not out	2
M. H. A. Footitt b Napier	0	– c Porter b Ryder	0
B 4, l-b 10	14	B 13, l-b 4	17

1/2 (2) 2/2 (1) 3/11 (4) (35 overs) 148
4/23 (3) 5/25 (6) 6/53 (5)
7/113 (7) 8/134 (9) 9/147 (10) 10/148 (11)

1/0 (1) 2/13 (2) (84 overs) 294
3/179 (3) 4/219 (5)
5/261 (6) 6/273 (4) 7/288 (7)
8/288 (9) 9/294 (8) 10/294 (11)

Porter 10–3–28–4; Ryder 11–1–55–2; Napier 11–1–32–2; Salisbury 3–0–19–1. *Second innings*— Porter 8–2–32–2; Ryder 15–5–26–3; Napier 23–7–64–4; Westley 13–1–42–0; Nijjar 12–0–62–0; Bopara 11–1–44–1; Salisbury 2–0–7–0.

Essex

N. L. J. Browne lbw b White	60	A. S. S. Nijjar lbw b White	16
A. N. Cook b Durston	80	J. A. Porter not out	1
T. Westley b White	43		
R. S. Bopara c Durston b White	57	B 11, l-b 5, n-b 12	28
J. D. Ryder b Hughes	52		
R. N. ten Doeschate b Durston	20	1/134 (1) 2/168 (2) (138.5 overs) 473
*†J. S. Foster c Godleman b White	72	3/230 (3) 4/287 (4) 5/321 (6)
G. R. Napier c Thakor b White	35	6/345 (5) 7/396 (8) 8/427 (9)
M. E. T. Salisbury b Palladino	9	9/452 (10) 10/473 (7) 110 overs: 362-6

Footitt 29–4–90–0; Palladino 29–10–70–1; White 27.5–6–113–6; Thakor 15–1–57–0; Durston 21–5–68–2; Hughes 17–3–59–1.

Umpires: N. G. C. Cowley and J. H. Evans.

At Bristol, June 21–23. ESSEX beat GLOUCESTERSHIRE by five wickets.

At Chelmsford, July 1–4. ESSEX lost to AUSTRALIANS by 169 runs (see Australian tour section).

At Manchester, July 6–9. ESSEX drew with LANCASHIRE.

ESSEX v GLAMORGAN

At Chelmsford, July 12–15. Essex won by 248 runs. Essex 21pts, Glamorgan 3pts. Toss: Essex.

A dominant performance gave Essex their third win in four matches, and closed the gap on third-placed Glamorgan to 20 points. Hogan was a menace at first, but consistent contributions down the order took Essex to 279. Only Ingram showed much conviction as Glamorgan then failed to secure a single batting point. Ryder took the first five wickets with his medium-pace wobblers, on the way to career-best figures, and Essex's openers hammered home the advantage with a stand of 237. Browne – capped at lunch on the fourth day – completed his hundred with the first six of his first-class career, in his 38th innings, while Dawson (going in first as Mickleburgh had suffered a back spasm) provided a return catch on 99. He was playing the second Championship game of what was supposed to be a month-long loan, but was quickly recalled by Hampshire. Set an unlikely 462, Glamorgan batted ineptly again, although Aneurin Donald – only 18 and in his second Championship match – made a spirited 67 before becoming one of five catches for Foster. Ryder completed his second ten-for, both for Essex, as Glamorgan slid to their first defeat of the season. Umpire C. K. Nandan, from India, was standing in his first match in England under an exchange system between the two boards.

Close of play: first day, Glamorgan 40-3 (Rudolph 17); second day, Essex 78-0 (Browne 42, Dawson 30); third day, Glamorgan 110-1 (Rudolph 45, Donald 42).

Essex

N. L. J. Browne lbw b Meschede	12	– c Wallace b Ingram		129
J. C. Mickleburgh c Wallace b Wagg	50			
T. Westley b Hogan	4	– lbw b Ingram		5
R. S. Bopara b Wagg	30	– st Wallace b Salter		11
J. D. Ryder c Wallace b Salter	24	– not out		41
R. N. ten Doeschate lbw b Hogan	48	– not out		40
L. A. Dawson lbw b Hogan	13	– (2) c and b Ingram		99
*†J. S. Foster c Ingram b Meschede	16			
G. R. Napier c Hogan b Ingram	43			
D. D. Masters c and b Hogan	28			
J. A. Porter not out	3			
B 2, l-b 4, n-b 2	8	B 8, l-b 7, w 2, n-b 2		19

1/40 (1) 2/73 (2) 3/73 (3)   (78.3 overs) 279   1/237 (1)   (4 wkts dec, 85 overs) 344
4/111 (5) 5/159 (4) 6/189 (6)   2/247 (3) 3/254 (2)
7/192 (7) 8/230 (8) 9/264 (9) 10/279 (10)   4/270 (4)

Hogan 19.3–9–36–4; Wagg 20–6–69–2; Meschede 15–2–59–2; Lloyd 12–3–40–0; Salter 10–0–52–1; Ingram 2–0–17–1. *Second innings*—Wagg 11–4–29–0; Hogan 18–6–46–0; Meschede 10–3–29–0; Salter 16–0–87–1; Lloyd 13–2–48–0; Ingram 17–0–90–3.

Glamorgan

W. D. Bragg c Foster b Ryder	3	– (2) c ten Doeschate b Dawson	22
*J. A. Rudolph b Ryder	24	– (1) c Foster b Ryder	47
A. H. T. Donald lbw b Ryder	14	– c Foster b Masters	67
A. G. Salter lbw b Ryder	4	– (10) c Foster b Masters	0
C. A. Ingram b Masters	43	– (4) c Foster b Ryder	12
C. B. Cooke c Westley b Ryder	4	– (5) c Mickleburgh b Ryder	0
†M. A. Wallace lbw b Masters	21	– (6) c Foster b Porter	3
C. A. J. Meschede lbw b Ryder	9	– (7) c sub (C. J. Taylor) b Masters	5
G. G. Wagg c Browne b Masters	13	– (8) c Napier b Ryder	28
D. L. Lloyd not out	20	– (9) c and b Dawson	13
M. G. Hogan b Napier	3	– not out	11
L-b 2, n-b 2	4	B 2, l-b 1, n-b 2	5

1/16 (1) 2/34 (3) 3/40 (4)	(40.5 overs)	162
4/53 (2) 5/59 (6) 6/96 (7)		
7/107 (8) 8/138 (9) 9/139 (5) 10/162 (11)		

1/42 (2) 2/112 (1)	(60.3 overs)	213
3/138 (4) 4/146 (5)		
5/153 (6) 6/158 (3) 7/165 (7)		
8/182 (9) 9/183 (10) 10/213 (8)		

Masters 12–3–53–3; Porter 10–3–42–0; Ryder 15–2–47–6; Dawson 1–0–2–0; Napier 2.5–0–16–1. *Second innings*—Masters 10–2–37–3; Porter 12–2–41–1; Ryder 17.3–5–53–4; Dawson 11–3–34–2; Napier 5–0–26–0; Westley 4–0–15–0; Bopara 1–0–4–0.

Umpires: P. J. Hartley and C. K. Nandan.

At Tunbridge Wells, July 19–21. ESSEX lost to KENT by an innings and 207 runs.

ESSEX v SURREY

At Colchester, August 7–10. Surrey won by three wickets. Surrey 22pts, Essex 7pts. Toss: Essex.
Surrey took another step towards promotion with a close-run victory in an absorbing match at Castle Park. Essex seemed to have the upper hand when they amassed 369, mainly thanks to centuries from Browne and Pettini, celebrating his 32nd birthday in his first Championship match for more than a year. But Burns, who unrolled some regal drives, anchored Surrey's reply with a five-hour 158. Porter took four wickets, as did Panesar, back in the team for the first time since April after fellow slow left-armer Ravi Patel was recalled by Middlesex from a loan spell. The highlight was one that jagged in to bowl Davies, shouldering arms. When Essex batted again, countering some incisive spin from Batty and Ansari, who finished with eight wickets between them, Westley, driving and cutting well, made 90 when Essex batted again, countering some incisive spin from Batty and Ansari, who finished with eight wickets between them. On the final day, Surrey needed 313 in what became 82 overs, and tottered after a decent start when Burns and Davies fell in quick succession. But Harinath and Roy steadied the ship, then Wilson settled in. Three more wickets tumbled for 12 towards the end, but Batty completed Surrey's fourth straight win with 17 balls to spare.
Close of play: first day, Essex 323-7 (Pettini 107, Nijjar 14); second day, Surrey 301-7 (Burns 157, T. K. Curran 5); third day, Essex 214-4 (Westley 90, Pettini 15).

Essex

N. L. J. Browne c Roy b Ansari	114	–	b Batty		29
J. C. Mickleburgh b S. M. Curran	2	–	b Batty		30
T. Westley c Burke b Batty	25	–	c Roy b Batty		90
R. S. Bopara c Burns b Batty	4	–	c Roy b Batty		23
*†J. S. Foster c Wilson b Ansari	13	–	b Dernbach		26
M. L. Pettini lbw b T. K. Curran	134	–	lbw b Batty		25
K. S. Velani c Wilson b Burke	34	–	c Dernbach b Ansari		33
M. E. T. Salisbury c Roy b Ansari	4	–	(9) c Roy b Batty		13
A. S. S. Nijjar c Burns b Ansari	20	–	(8) c Burns b Ansari		11
J. A. Porter c and b Ansari	0	–	(11) not out		4
M. S. Panesar not out	11	–	(10) not out		2
B 4, l-b 2, w 2	8		B 2, l-b 1		3

1/12 (2) 2/65 (3) 3/70 (4)   (107.1 overs) 369   1/57 (1)   (9 wkts dec, 99 overs) 289
4/115 (5) 5/202 (1) 6/263 (7)   2/65 (2) 3/119 (4)
7/280 (8) 8/343 (9) 9/347 (10) 10/369 (6)   4/184 (5) 5/215 (3) 6/234 (6)
                                          7/251 (8) 8/282 (9) 9/284 (7)

T. K. Curran 20.1–3–81–1; S. M. Curran 13–1–53–1; Burke 6–0–38–1; Batty 25.3–61–2; Ansari 32–4–108–5. *Second innings*—T. K. Curran 8–1–18–0; S. M. Curran 4–1–14–0; Batty 34–4–102–5; Ansari 43–6–128–3; Dernbach 10–4–24–1.

Surrey

R. J. Burns c Velani b Porter	158	–	c Mickleburgh b Nijjar		71
Z. S. Ansari c Pettini b Porter	6	–	b Nijjar		34
A. Harinath c Porter b Panesar	34	–	lbw b Westley		87
S. M. Davies b Panesar	16	–	c Pettini b Westley		1
J. J. Roy st Foster b Panesar	4	–	c Salisbury b Westley		37
†G. C. Wilson lbw b Porter	37	–	not out		56
J. E. Burke st Foster b Nijjar	17	–	(8) c Foster b Westley		0
*G. J. Batty b Westley	20	–	(9) not out		5
T. K. Curran b Panesar	18				
S. M. Curran not out	30	–	(7) c Porter b Panesar		6
J. W. Dernbach lbw b Porter	1				
B 2, l-b 3	5		B 9, l-b 8		17

1/23 (2) 2/72 (3) 3/106 (4)   (98.1 overs) 346   1/95 (2)   (7 wkts, 79.1 overs) 314
4/112 (5) 5/187 (6) 6/222 (7)   2/132 (1) 3/133 (4)
7/284 (8) 8/305 (1) 9/331 (9) 10/346 (11)   4/205 (5) 5/297 (3) 6/308 (7) 7/309 (8)

Porter 26.1–1–96–4; Salisbury 7–2–18–0; Panesar 37–8–112–4; Westley 11–0–47–1; Nijjar 10–0–48–1; Bopara 7–0–20–0. *Second innings*—Porter 14–4–49–0; Salisbury 1–0–2–0; Panesar 19.1–5–88–1; Nijjar 20–2–83–2; Westley 25–2–75–4.

Umpires: J. H. Evans and P. J. Hartley.

ESSEX v NORTHAMPTONSHIRE

At Chelmsford, September 1–4. Drawn. Essex 12pts, Northamptonshire 9pts. Toss: Northamptonshire.
    Essex were under new management, after the resignation of head coach Paul Grayson was confirmed mid-match; his assistant, Chris Silverwood, took charge. His side made a poor start, dipping to 119 for six on a rain-shortened first day, before Foster – who fell just short of a hundred – put on 146 with Pettini and 74 with the 20-year-old Nijjar, who completed a maiden half-century. Several Northamptonshire batsmen got starts, but only Kleinveldt, down at No. 8, reached 50. When Ryder polished off the innings with three wickets in five balls, Essex led by 85. More rain curtailed the third day, and on the fourth a flurry from ten Doeschate and Pettini, who added 77 in 14 overs,

stretched the lead to 301. Northamptonshire's coaches David Ripley and Kevin Innes were forced to field after Levi broke a knuckle and Murphy injured his thumb (Duckett took over as wicketkeeper, although Murphy was able to open in the second innings). Essex sniffed victory when Nijjar, making the ball turn sharply, claimed the fourth wicket in the 24th over, with a theoretical 25 remaining – but bad light soon intervened.

Close of play: first day, Essex 177-6 (Pettini 29, Foster 25); second day, Northamptonshire 143-3 (Keogh 37, Levi 13); third day, Essex 55-1 (Lawrence 23, Westley 16).

Essex

D. W. Lawrence	c Keogh b Kleinveldt	8	– b Stone	36
N. L. J. Browne	c Kleinveldt b Azharullah	24	– c Keogh b Stone	14
T. Westley	c Murphy b Stone	20	– b Chambers	20
R. S. Bopara	c Duckett b Kleinveldt	19	– lbw b Keogh	25
J. D. Ryder	b Azharullah	1	– c Duckett b Chambers	29
R. N. ten Doeschate	lbw b Azharullah	43	– not out	43
M. L. Pettini	c Murphy b Kleinveldt	68	– not out	37
*†J. S. Foster	c Cobb b Keogh	98		
A. S. S. Nijjar	c Murphy b Stone	53		
J. A. Porter	c Murphy b Azharullah	10		
T. C. Moore	not out	0		
	B 6, l-b 6, n-b 4	16	B 4, l-b 4, n-b 4	12

1/18 (1) 2/48 (2) 3/52 (3)   (113.1 overs) 360   1/22 (2)   (5 wkts dec, 63 overs) 216
4/53 (5) 5/115 (4) 6/119 (6) 7/265 (7)   2/59 (3) 3/83 (1)
8/339 (8) 9/356 (9) 10/360 (10)   110 overs: 354-8   4/121 (4) 5/139 (5)

Kleinveldt 26–3–88–3; Stone 29–3–77–2; Azharullah 30.1–6–74–4; Chambers 17–3–60–0; Keogh 9–0–37–1; Cobb 1–0–2–0; Wakely 1–0–10–0. *Second innings*—Azharullah 11–1–35–0; Kleinveldt 10–3–25–0; Stone 15–5–55–2; Chambers 16–2–47–2; Keogh 11–0–46–1.

Northamptonshire

†D. Murphy	c Lawrence b Porter	8	– b Porter	7
B. M. Duckett	c Foster b Bopara	32	– not out	34
*A. G. Wakely	c Browne b Nijjar	43	– b Porter	19
R. I. Keogh	b Porter	45	– run out	17
R. E. Levi	retired hurt	31		
A. M. Rossington	c Foster b Porter	0	– not out	4
J. J. Cobb	c Moore b Nijjar	26	– (5) b Nijjar	0
R. K. Kleinveldt	not out	52		
O. P. Stone	b Ryder	22		
Azharullah	lbw b Ryder	0		
M. A. Chambers	lbw b Ryder	0		
	B 5, l-b 5, n-b 6	16	B 2, l-b 5, n-b 4	11

1/16 (1) 2/58 (2) 3/115 (3)   (69.1 overs) 275   1/12 (1)   (4 wkts, 27 overs) 92
4/151 (4) 5/151 (6) 6/216 (7)   2/48 (3) 3/82 (4)
7/271 (9) 8/271 (10) 9/275 (11)   4/85 (5)

In the first innings Levi retired hurt at 188-5.

Porter 24–4–93–3; Ryder 18.1–4–53–3; Bopara 7–0–32–1; Moore 10–1–46–0; Nijjar 10–1–41–2. *Second innings*—Porter 11–3–27–2; Ryder 4–1–21–0; Moore 3–0–23–0; Nijjar 6–2–7–1; Westley 3–0–7–0.

Umpires: M. J. D. Bodenham and M. J. Saggers.

At Derby, September 9–11. ESSEX beat DERBYSHIRE by an innings and 188 runs.

At Leicester, September 14–17. ESSEX beat LEICESTERSHIRE by five wickets.

ESSEX v LANCASHIRE

At Chelmsford, September 22–25. Drawn. Essex 12pts, Lancashire 11pts. Toss: Lancashire.

Lancashire, already assured of promotion, were seeking a victory that might have given them the second division title – but an easy-paced pitch and the weather, which chopped off nearly 130 overs (including the entire first day), ensured a draw. Essex had stumbled to 29 for three, losing two wickets to the 41-year-old Chapple, before Ryder put on 186 with Bopara, who fell one short of a century, and 95 with ten Doeschate. Anderson swept through the rest, finishing with seven for 77, his best figures in 14 seasons for Lancashire. Reece then shared useful stands with two players separated by 20 years: Haseeb Hameed (aged 18) hit ten fours in his 63, before Prince scuttled to 51 from 38 balls on the last morning of what he later said would be his final first-class match. But Lancashire lost their last seven for 41, gifting Essex a lead of 84. Porter, capped at lunch the previous day, celebrated by dismissing Reece, his 50th Championship wicket of the season. A draw was certain, although there was time for Cook (like Anderson, making a rare county appearance ahead of England's Test series against Pakistan in the UAE) to fall cheaply for the second time in the match. He faced only 23 balls in all, having been lbw to his Test team-mate for a single in the first innings. "I didn't get a smile at lunch," joked Anderson.

Close of play: first day, no play; second day, Essex 328-7 (Foster 8, Napier 0); third day, Lancashire 131-2 (Reece 25, Prince 2).

Essex

N. L. J. Browne c Anderson b Chapple	27	– c Brown b Anderson	4
A. N. Cook lbw b Anderson	1	– c Anderson b Chapple	6
T. Westley c Mustard b Chapple	0	– lbw b Bailey	34
R. S. Bopara c Mustard b Anderson	99	– not out	52
J. D. Ryder b Bailey	116	– not out	38
R. N. ten Doeschate c Chapple b Anderson	59		
M. L. Pettini b Anderson	8		
*†J. S. Foster c Brown b Anderson	17		
G. R. Napier lbw b Anderson	31		
A. S. S. Nijjar not out	17		
J. A. Porter b Anderson	7		
B 1, l-b 9, n-b 2	12	B 1, l-b 2, w 1	4

1/3 (2)　2/14 (3)　3/29 (1)　　　　(110.5 overs) 394 ⏐ 1/6 (1)　2/10 (2)　(3 wkts, 30 overs) 138
4/215 (5)　5/310 (6)　6/311 (4)　7/322 (7)　　　　　⏐ 3/80 (3)
8/347 (8)　9/374 (9)　10/394 (11)　　110 overs: 394-9

Anderson 31.5–6–77–7; Chapple 33–10–88–2; Bailey 15–1–87–1; Clark 15–3–61–0; Reece 5–0–27–0; Kerrigan 8–0–29–0; Croft 3–0–15–0. *Second innings*—Anderson 6–4–13–1; Chapple 12–3–35–1; Bailey 8–1–48–1; Kerrigan 2–0–14–0; Hameed 1–0–9–0; Brown 1–0–16–0.

Lancashire

K. R. Brown c Foster b Napier	39	G. Chapple c Ryder b Bopara	8
H. Hameed c Cook b Ryder	63	S. C. Kerrigan b Bopara	1
L. M. Reece c Foster b Porter	82	J. M. Anderson not out	6
A. G. Prince c Bopara b Napier	51		
*S. J. Croft c Napier b Bopara	32	B 2, l-b 3, w 1, n-b 4	10
†P. Mustard run out	5		
J. Clark st Foster b Nijjar	8	1/66 (1)　2/122 (2)　3/203 (4)　(88.4 overs) 310
T. E. Bailey b Nijjar	5	4/269 (3)　5/281 (6)　6/289 (5)
		7/289 (7)　8/302 (8)　9/302 (9)　10/310 (10)

Porter 17–4–63–1; Ryder 24–7–77–1; Westley 10–0–43–0; Napier 13–0–49–2; Bopara 15.4–4–40–3; Nijjar 9–2–33–2.

Umpires: M. Burns and N. G. B. Cook.

GLAMORGAN

Problems resurface

EDWARD BEVAN

At the halfway stage of the season, Glamorgan had cause for optimism. Eleven points behind second-placed Surrey in Division Two of the Championship with a game in hand, they were also in contention in the T20 Blast. But, after they failed to beat Derbyshire at Chesterfield – despite making them follow on – the prospect of promotion slowly disappeared. They lost their next three Championship matches, while Gloucestershire scuppered their Twenty20 hopes by snatching the final group game, which rain had reduced to a five-over lottery.

Glamorgan had also made a promising start in the Royal London One-Day Cup, but their progress was abruptly halted when the fourth game, in early August, was abandoned because the umpires decided the Cardiff pitch was too dangerous. Hampshire were awarded the match, while Glamorgan were fined £4,000 and penalised two points, which came on top of a similar deduction carried over from the previous season. They finished next to bottom in the group.

The abandonment had unfortunate ramifications off the field, too. Head groundsman Keith Exton was suspended, and eventually left the club, to be succeeded by his deputy Robin Saxton. It was an embarrassing episode for Glamorgan, especially as a Twenty20 international was due to be played at Sophia Gardens a few weeks later.

There was a significant change in the back-room staff in December. Coach Toby Radford departed a year early, after two seasons in charge, and was replaced by England off-spinner and club stalwart Robert Croft.

It was perhaps not surprising that Glamorgan fell away during the second half of the summer, when a punishing schedule forced them to play on 14 days out of 17 in July. Journeys from Chesterfield to Hove, and from Chelmsford to Colwyn Bay via a Twenty20 game at Tunbridge Wells, took their toll on a squad of only 15 players. However, although they failed to win a Championship game after late June, Glamorgan did show improvement overall, rising four places to fourth in the table, and collecting 30 more points than in 2014.

No one reached 1,000 runs, yet the club gained more batting points (42) than anyone in their division apart from the two promoted teams, Surrey and Lancashire. They also scored three more hundreds than the previous year, the highlight being Graham Wagg's rollicking double-century at Guildford. But the search for a reliable opening pair continued. Neither James Kettleborough nor Will Bragg performed consistently as Jacques Rudolph's partner, which prompted Hugh Morris, the director of cricket, to say at the end of the season that "we need to create more competition at the top of the order". Nick Selman, a 20-year-old from Brisbane with a British passport, was given a contract after doing well for the Second XI.

Stu Foster, Getty Images

Colin Ingram

Colin Ingram, a Kolpak signing from South Africa, took time to adjust to conditions, but then hit three hundreds and a fifty in the Royal London Cup; he also finished as Glamorgan's leading Championship run-scorer, with 931, four more than skipper Rudolph.

But it was often left to the lower order to stage recoveries and build substantial first-innings totals. Wagg in particular had an outstanding season, scoring 838 Championship runs, in five fewer innings than Ingram. During his 200 against Surrey – equalling the highest Championship score by a No. 8 – Wagg struck 11 sixes, a county record.

The South African-born all-rounder Craig Meschede, signed on a season-long loan from Somerset, also made significant contributions down the order, scoring two centuries – then joined on a permanent basis. Mark Wallace's remarkable record of playing in 230 successive Championship matches since 2001 came to an end when he was forced to miss the last game because of a torn calf muscle. Although his glovework was again immaculate, 507 runs was his lowest Championship return since the long sequence began.

Michael Hogan again did a manful job leading the attack and, if his 48 victims were fewer than the two previous seasons, he was a willing workhorse – and still the leading wicket-taker. Wagg and Meschede also reached the 40-wicket mark; in a bid to reduce the load on these three, the club signed Dutch international seamer Timm van der Gugten. Dean Cosker, the experienced slow left-armer, was dropped after five Championship games – and marooned on 597 first-class wickets – in favour of Andrew Salter, the 22-year-old off-spinner. Salter is undoubtedly talented, but his 25 wickets came at a pricey 46, and Cosker proved the better bet in one-day cricket.

The emergence of David Lloyd and Nye Donald – both local products – vindicated Glamorgan's policy of encouraging home-grown youngsters. Lloyd averaged 39, while the 18-year-old Donald, great-nephew of the long-serving Glamorgan batsman Bernard Hedges, made two fifties in five appearances. One came in the last match at Bristol, where he failed by two runs to become Glamorgan's youngest Championship centurion.

The financial position is now more secure after Glamorgan's three primary creditors agreed to a 70% writedown. The original £16m debt could have been crippling, but is now more manageable. The First Ashes Test, won by England, was hugely successful, and financially rewarding; it was followed later in the summer by an England–Australia Twenty20 double-header, featuring the men's and women's teams.

Championship attendance: 17,347

GLAMORGAN RESULTS

All first-class matches – Played 17: Won 4, Lost 4, Drawn 9.
County Championship matches – Played 16: Won 4, Lost 4, Drawn 8.

LV= County Championship, 4th in Division 2;
NatWest T20 Blast, 6th in South Group; Royal London One-Day Cup, 8th in Group B.

COUNTY CHAMPIONSHIP AVERAGES, BATTING AND FIELDING

Cap		Birthplace	M	I	NO	R	HS	100	Avge	Ct/St
2000	D. A. Cosker	Weymouth	5	6	3	146	69	0	48.66	6
	D. L. Lloyd	St Asaph†	12	19	5	547	92	0	39.07	4
2014	J. A. Rudolph§	Springs, SA	14	26	2	927	111	1	38.62	13
	C. A. Ingram¶	Port Elizabeth, SA	16	28	3	931	105*	2	37.24	10
2013	G. G. Wagg	Rugby	16	23	0	838	200	1	36.43	6
	C. B. Cooke	Johannesburg, SA	15	27	5	772	102*	1	35.09	18
	A. H. T. Donald	Swansea†	5	10	1	288	98	0	32.00	4
	C. A. J. Meschede	Johannesburg, SA	16	23	3	635	107	2	31.75	5
2015	W. D. Bragg	Newport†	13	23	1	588	120	2	26.72	3
	J. M. Kettleborough	Huntingdon	8	15	1	364	81	0	26.00	4
2013	M. G. Hogan¶	Newcastle, Australia	14	19	8	271	57	0	24.63	11
	A. G. Salter	Haverfordwest†	12	19	2	411	73	0	24.17	5
2003	M. A. Wallace	Abergavenny†	15	23	2	507	92	0	24.14	42/3
	A. Carter	Lincoln	4	4	2	42	21*	0	21.00	0
2011	B. J. Wright	Preston	4	6	0	115	68	0	19.16	2

Also batted: K. A. Bull (*Haverfordwest†*) (2 matches) 31, 7; J. L. Lawlor (*Cardiff†*) (1 match) 0, 0;
D. Penrhyn Jones (*Wrexham†*) (2 matches) 17, 9* (1 ct); R. A. J. Smith (*Glasgow*) (2 matches) 49*, 6*.

† *Born in Wales.* § *Official overseas player.* ¶ *Other non-England-qualified player.*

BOWLING

	Style	O	M	R	W	BB	5I	Avge
A. Carter	RFM	121.1	23	373	16	4-53	0	23.31
M. G. Hogan	RFM	482.1	126	1,297	48	5-44	2	27.02
G. G. Wagg	SLA/LM	459.4	71	1,656	45	5-54	1	36.80
C. A. J. Meschede	RM	429.3	66	1,591	40	4-89	0	39.77
C. A. Ingram	LBG	103.3	9	398	10	3-90	0	39.80
A. G. Salter	OB	339.1	42	1,150	25	3-5	0	46.00
D. L. Lloyd	RM	206.2	22	912	19	3-68	0	48.00

Also bowled: W. D. Bragg (RM) 23.4–3–86–1; K. A. Bull (OB) 21.5–4–104–0; D. A. Cosker
(SLA) 168–20–637–6; J. L. Lawlor (RM) 4–1–11–0; D. Penrhyn Jones (RFM) 32–1–190–5; J. A.
Rudolph (LBG) 3–0–11–0; R. A. J. Smith (RM) 33–5–134–5.

LEADING NATWEST T20 BLAST AVERAGES (100 runs/18 overs)

Batting	Runs	HS	Avge	SR	Ct/St
C. A. Ingram	376	96	28.92	149.80	5
C. A. J. Meschede	175	35*	15.90	143.44	1
C. B. Cooke	259	46*	28.77	137.76	6
J. A. Rudolph	461	101*	41.90	127.34	9
G. G. Wagg	209	53*	34.83	122.94	4
B. J. Wright	116	63*	19.33	118.36	1
M. A. Wallace	127	37	14.11	99.21	5/2

Bowling	W	BB	Avge	ER
W. D. Parnell	8	2-16	25.87	7.39
M. G. Hogan	15	3-33	24.33	7.87
D. A. Cosker	17	4-25	22.00	7.98
A. G. Salter	7	2-43	33.85	9.48
G. G. Wagg	13	4-27	30.76	9.75
C. A. J. Meschede	8	2-14	37.50	10.00

LEADING ROYAL LONDON CUP AVERAGES (80 runs/3 wickets)

Batting	Runs	HS	Avge	SR	Ct
C. A. Ingram	354	130	88.50	96.72	0
G. G. Wagg	80	62*	80.00	93.02	1
C. B. Cooke	164	94*	54.66	112.32	1
W. D. Bragg.....	111	59	27.75	60.32	1
J. A. Rudolph....	82	58	20.50	50.61	1

Bowling	W	BB	Avge	ER
M. G. Hogan......	5	2-60	24.40	3.93
R. A. J. Smith....	4	2-12	34.50	5.75
D. A. Cosker......	4	2-37	34.75	5.31
C. A. J. Meschede .	3	2-23	52.00	5.37

FIRST-CLASS COUNTY RECORDS

Highest score for	309*	S. P. James v Sussex at Colwyn Bay	2000
Highest score against	322*	M. B. Loye (Northamptonshire) at Northampton	1998
Leading run-scorer	34,056	A. Jones (avge 33.03)	1957–83
Best bowling for	10-51	J. Mercer v Worcestershire at Worcester.....	1936
Best bowling against	10-18	G. Geary (Leicestershire) at Pontypridd	1929
Leading wicket-taker	2,174	D. J. Shepherd (avge 20.95)................	1950–72
Highest total for	718-3 dec	v Sussex at Colwyn Bay	2000
Highest total against	712	by Northamptonshire at Northampton	1998
Lowest total for	22	v Lancashire at Liverpool	1924
Lowest total against	33	by Leicestershire at Ebbw Vale	1965

LIST A COUNTY RECORDS

Highest score for	169*	J. A. Rudolph v Sussex at Hove.............	2014
Highest score against	268	A. D. Brown (Surrey) at The Oval..........	2002
Leading run-scorer	12,278	M. P. Maynard (avge 37.66)	1985–2005
Best bowling for	7-16	S. D. Thomas v Surrey at Swansea	1998
Best bowling against	7-30	M. P. Bicknell (Surrey) at The Oval	1999
Leading wicket-taker	356	R. D. B. Croft (avge 31.96)	1989–2012
Highest total for	429	v Surrey at The Oval	2002
Highest total against	438-5	by Surrey at The Oval	2002
Lowest total for	42	v Derbyshire at Swansea	1979
Lowest total against {	59	by Combined Universities at Cambridge......	1983
	59	by Sussex at Hove	1996

TWENTY20 COUNTY RECORDS

Highest score for	116*	I. J. Thomas v Somerset at Taunton..........	2004
Highest score against	117	M. J. Prior (Sussex) at Hove	2010
Leading run-scorer	1,578	J. Allenby (avge 33.57)	2010–14
Best bowling for	5-14	G. G. Wagg v Worcestershire at Worcester....	2013
Best bowling against	6-5	A. V. Suppiah (Somerset) at Cardiff	2011
Leading wicket-taker	92	D. A. Cosker (avge 31.15)	2003–15
Highest total for	240-3	v Surrey at The Oval	2015
Highest total against	239-5	by Sussex at Hove	2010
Lowest total for	94-9	v Essex at Cardiff	2010
Lowest total against	81	by Gloucestershire at Bristol	2011

ADDRESS

The SSE SWALEC, Sophia Gardens, Cardiff CF11 9XR; 029 2040 9380; info@glamorgancricket. co.uk; www.glamorgancricket.com.

OFFICIALS

Captain J. A. Rudolph	**Chairman** B. J. O'Brien
Head coach 2015 T. A. Radford	**Chief executive and**
2016 R. D. B. Croft	**director of cricket** H. Morris
Head of talent development R. V. Almond	**Head groundsman** R. Saxton
President F. D. Morgan	**Scorer/archivist** A. K. Hignell

GLAMORGAN v CARDIFF MCCU

At Cardiff, April 2–4. Drawn. Toss: Cardiff MCCU. First-class debuts: N. Brand, J. L. Lawlor, D. E. Lewis-Williams, J. R. Murphy, M. J. Norris, T. D. Rouse. County debuts: J. M. Kettleborough, C. A. J. Meschede.

Headed by Cooke, who retired after reaching a fluent century, Glamorgan's batsmen took the chance of some early-season practice in a match severely disrupted by rain: the first day was washed away, and the other two were frequently interrupted. Cardiff MCCU included off-spinner Kieran Bull, who played three Championship matches for Glamorgan in 2014, and left-arm seamer Jack Murphy, also on the county staff; he claimed a distinguished maiden scalp in Rudolph. Another of Cardiff's six debutants, 18-year-old left-hander Neil Brand – who broke Jos Buttler's batting records at King's College, Taunton – played well for 46, but the others made little impression.

Close of play: first day, no play; second day, Glamorgan 316-4 (Cooke 66, Wallace 15).

Glamorgan

J. M. Kettleborough b Westphal	49	C. A. J. Meschede c and b Rouse	20
*J. A. Rudolph c Rouse b Murphy	35	D. A. Cosker not out	2
W. D. Bragg c Murphy b Bull	71		
B. J. Wright c Bracey b Lewis-Williams	63	B 5, l-b 14, w 2	21
C. B. Cooke retired out	112		
†M. A. Wallace c Norris b Murphy	15	1/76 (2) (8 wkts dec, 124 overs) 434
G. G. Wagg run out	4	2/94 (1) 3/203 (4) 4/270 (3)
D. L. Lloyd not out	42	5/320 (6) 6/345 (7) 7/378 (5) 8/430 (9)

R. A. J. Smith did not bat.

Murphy 28–4–90–2; Westphal 22–6–68–1; Lewis-Williams 27–4–98–1; Griffiths 18–3–75–0; Bull 22–4–63–1; Brand 5–0–18–0; Rouse 2–0–3–1.

Cardiff MCCU

*J. George b Meschede	8	†S. N. Bracey not out	0
J. L. Lawlor c Wright b Smith	3	D. E. Lewis-Williams c Meschede b Cosker	0
N. Brand c Wallace b Lloyd	46	L-b 2, w 1, n-b 6	9
T. D. Rouse b Lloyd	6		
M. J. Norris b Meschede	16	1/6 (2) 2/26 (1) (8 wkts dec, 43.5 overs) 110
S. W. Griffiths b Meschede	0	3/40 (4) 4/72 (5)
J. R. Murphy b Cosker	22	5/72 (6) 6/106 (3) 7/110 (7) 8/110 (9)

A. A. Westphal and K. A. Bull did not bat.

Wagg 8*–2–25–0; Smith 9–0–21–1; Meschede 9–3–18–3; Lloyd 9–1–30–2; Cosker 7.5–0–14–2; Bragg 1–1–0–0.

Umpires: J. H. Evans and R. J. Warren.

At Leicester, April 12–15. GLAMORGAN drew with LEICESTERSHIRE.

GLAMORGAN v SURREY

At Cardiff, April 19–22. Drawn. Glamorgan 9pts, Surrey 12pts. Toss: Surrey. County debut: K. C. Sangakkara.

Kevin Pietersen stoked media interest by returning to Championship action for the first time since 2013. But his attempts to win back an England place took a knock when he was caught at first slip off Meschede for 19, after which Sangakkara – making his Surrey debut – stroked a typically elegant hundred. He put on 294, a record for Surrey's fourth wicket against Glamorgan, with Davies, who went on to his maiden double-century. "He never looked rushed, he never looked ruffled," said Sangakkara, one of four wicketkeepers in Surrey's line-up. The scoring-rate remained under four an over as the Glamorgan attack kept their discipline, and Batty eventually declared midway through the second day. Surrey's bowlers also found it hard going, but they stuck at their task and – with Cooke run out by Ansari's 70-yard direct hit from the cover boundary – the follow-on was looming at 293 for eight. Then Meschede cracked a maiden first-class century from No. 9, adding 119 with

Cosker, whose 19 occupied 133 minutes. Meschede completed a memorable match by dismissing Pietersen and Sangakkara. Glamorgan were all out on the stroke of time on the third day, which left little room for manoeuvre on the fourth; Pietersen scored an unbeaten half-century before a declaration, but Glamorgan made no attempt at a target of 352 in 57 overs.

Close of play: first day, Surrey 363-3 (Sangakkara 112, Davies 109); second day, Glamorgan 124-2 (Bragg 19, Ingram 14); third day, Glamorgan 419.

Surrey

R. J. Burns c Wallace b Wagg		50	– c and b Wagg		3
Z. S. Ansari lbw b Carter		48			
K. C. Sangakkara c Bragg b Lloyd		149	– c Cosker b Meschede		40
K. P. Pietersen c Ingram b Meschede		19	– not out		53
S. M. Davies not out		200	– (2) b Wagg		21
J. J. Roy c Wallace b Carter		32	– (5) c Wagg b Cosker		29
†G. C. Wilson lbw b Carter		5	– (6) not out		47
*G. J. Batty b Carter		0			
T. K. Curran not out		23			
B 4, l-b 14, w 5, n-b 14		37	B 5, l-b 7, n-b 2		14

1/104 (1) 2/111 (2)   (7 wkts dec, 146 overs) 563   1/16 (1)   (4 wkts dec, 37 overs) 207
3/150 (4) 4/444 (3)   2/41 (2) 3/78 (3)
5/494 (6) 6/504 (7) 7/510 (8)   110 overs: 434-3   4/121 (5)

J. W. Dernbach and M. P. Dunn did not bat.

Wagg 32–6–108–1; Carter 35–4–110–4; Meschede 27–3–102–1; Lloyd 21–0–96–1; Cosker 31–2–129–0. *Second innings*—Wagg 10–0–46–2; Carter 5–0–36–0; Lloyd 5–0–33–0; Meschede 6–0–31–1; Cosker 11–0–49–1.

Glamorgan

J. M. Kettleborough b Dunn		15	– not out		50
*J. A. Rudolph c Roy b Batty		69	– not out		52
W. D. Bragg b Dunn		37			
C. A. Ingram c Dernbach b Curran		56			
C. B. Cooke run out		20			
†M. A. Wallace c Wilson b Curran		51			
G. G. Wagg b Batty		31			
D. L. Lloyd lbw b Batty		4			
C. A. J. Meschede not out		101			
D. A. Cosker lbw b Roy		19			
A. Carter c Dernbach b Ansari		1			
B 5, l-b 6, w 4		15	B 8, l-b 6		14

1/47 (1) 2/104 (2) 3/160 (3)   (138.2 overs) 419   (no wkt, 37 overs) 116
4/204 (5) 5/206 (4) 6/261 (7)
7/293 (8) 8/293 (6) 9/412 (10)
10/419 (11)   110 overs: 323-8

Dernbach 24–7–62–0; Dunn 28–7–93–2; Curran 28–7–85–2; Batty 43–7–110–3; Ansari 14.2–5–52–1; Roy 1–0–6–1. *Second innings*—Dernbach 6–2–11–0; Dunn 5–2–6–0; Batty 6–1–10–0; Curran 4–0–21–0; Ansari 10–2–36–0; Roy 3–1–10–0; Burns 3–0–8–0.

Umpires: P. J. Hartley and D. J. Millns.

GLAMORGAN v DERBYSHIRE

At Cardiff, May 3–6. Drawn. Glamorgan 8pts, Derbyshire 7pts. Toss: Glamorgan. First-class debut: M. J. J. Critchley.

The main talking point of a match in which more than half the scheduled overs were lost to rain was the objection of Graeme Welch, Derbyshire's elite performance director, to Rudolph's declaration 102 behind after yet another interruption on the third day. Welch thought the closure had come because Glamorgan had a tardy over-rate and faced a points deduction. He also felt it was against the spirit of the game, as it denied Derbyshire the chance of bonus points "which could be massive at the end of the season"; but the ECB took no action. Glamorgan's coach Toby Radford said they had hoped to skittle an inexperienced side – without five injured players and the suspended Billy Godleman – and set up the possibility of an unlikely victory. Glamorgan's seamers, led by Carter, on loan from Nottinghamshire, had dismantled Derbyshire for 205 in between showers over the first two days, but a maiden century from Elstone, who put on an unbroken 177 with Madsen, scotched any notion of a repeat.

Close of play: first day, Derbyshire 47-2 (Slater 25, Elstone 2); second day, Glamorgan 84-2 (Bragg 14, Ingram 2); third day, Glamorgan 103-4 dec.

Derbyshire

B. T. Slater c Wallace b Carter	53	– c Ingram b Cosker	13
C. F. Hughes c Meschede b Wagg	9	– lbw b Hogan	7
*W. L. Madsen lbw b Carter	1	– not out	72
S. L. Elstone c Cooke b Hogan	48	– not out	103
S. J. Thakor c Wagg b Carter	18		
A. L. Hughes c Wallace b Meschede	14		
†H. R. Hosein c Wallace b Carter	1		
D. J. Wainwright not out	8		
M. J. J. Critchley c Wallace b Hogan	8		
B. D. Cotton c Rudolph b Wagg	7		
M. H. A. Footitt c Hogan b Wagg	4		
B 8, l-b 4, w 2, n-b 20	34	B 7, l-b 2, w 1, n-b 4	14

1/26 (2) 2/31 (3) 3/132 (1)   (63.1 overs) 205   1/20 (2)   (2 wkts dec, 55 overs) 209
4/132 (4) 5/172 (5) 6/175 (7)   2/32 (1)
7/177 (6) 8/188 (9) 9/195 (10) 10/205 (11)

Wagg 14.1–2–56–3; Hogan 17–4–43–2; Carter 19–5–53–4; Meschede 11–2–29–1; Cosker 2–0–12–0. *Second innings*—Carter 5–1–16–0; Hogan 10–1–30–1; Cosker 22–2–83–1; Meschede 4–0–14–0; Rudolph 3–0–11–0; Wagg 8–0–34–0; Bragg 3–0–12–0.

Glamorgan

J. M. Kettleborough b Thakor	17	†M. A. Wallace not out	2
*J. A. Rudolph lbw b Thakor	43	L-b 9	9
W. D. Bragg c Hosein b A. L. Hughes	14		
C. A. Ingram c Hosein b Footitt	12	1/62 (2) (4 wkts dec, 36.5 overs) 103	
C. B. Cooke not out	6	2/71 (1) 3/89 (3) 4/95 (4)	

C. A. J. Meschede, G. G. Wagg, D. A. Cosker, M. G. Hogan and A. Carter did not bat.

Footitt 11–4–26–1; Cotton 9–2–33–0; Thakor 7–1–11–2; Critchley 4–1–5–0; A. L. Hughes 5.5–1–19–1.

Umpires: N. G. C. Cowley and A. G. Wharf.

At Canterbury, May 10–13. GLAMORGAN drew with KENT.

GLAMORGAN v ESSEX

At Cardiff, May 18–21. Glamorgan won by 89 runs. Glamorgan 22pts, Essex 4pts. Toss: Essex. First-class debut: C. J. Taylor.

Glamorgan won their first Championship match of the season after four draws, overcoming an Essex side lacking four regulars. They included two 17-year-olds – Daniel Lawrence and the debutant

Callum Taylor – but still ran their hosts close with more pace and bounce than earlier ones at Cardiff. Rudolph's 82 in 285 minutes was the backbone of Glamorgan's first innings, which was swelled by another forthright display from Meschede, whose 52-ball 68 included four sixes, three in one over from Adeel Malik's leg-spin. In reply, all Essex's top seven got to double figures, but no one reached 50 – and, from 201 for four, the last six wickets tumbled for 20, Wagg taking four for seven in 15 balls. Glamorgan led by 93, but subsided to 78 for five. Wallace then put on 98 with the ubiquitous Wagg, and the eventual target was a distant 364. Lawrence made a composed 43, but the loss of Foster and Porter in the space of six balls set Essex back. Ten Doeschate survived for more than three hours, and at tea they needed 110 with three wickets left – but, a few overs into the final session, the last three fell to the new ball for five runs.

Close of play: first day, Glamorgan 187-5 (Rudolph 81, Wagg 17); second day, Essex 183-4 (ten Doeschate 38, Taylor 23); third day, Essex 51-2 (Lawrence 13, Porter 2).

Glamorgan

J. M. Kettleborough lbw b Porter	1	– c Velani b Masters	10
*J. A. Rudolph c Mickleburgh b Porter	82	– c Browne b Porter	7
W. D. Bragg lbw b Napier	17	– lbw b Masters	13
C. A. Ingram c Foster b ten Doeschate	26	– c ten Doeschate b Porter	31
C. B. Cooke lbw b ten Doeschate	20	– lbw b Porter	0
†M. A. Wallace c Browne b Napier	15	– lbw b Adeel Malik	79
G. G. Wagg lbw b Masters	47	– b Napier	43
C. A. J. Meschede c Lawrence b Masters	68	– c Foster b Napier	31
D. L. Lloyd c Mickleburgh b Masters	16	– c and b Adeel Malik	10
A. G. Salter c Foster b Napier	6	– not out	14
M. G. Hogan not out	4	– c Porter b Adeel Malik	20
B 4, l-b 3, w 3, n-b 2	12	B 6, l-b 6	12

1/9 (1) 2/36 (3) 3/77 (4)   (93.3 overs) 314
4/118 (5) 5/151 (6) 6/189 (2)
7/281 (7) 8/304 (8) 9/306 (9) 10/314 (10)

1/16 (2) 2/20 (1)   (55.5 overs) 270
3/33 (3) 4/38 (5)
5/78 (4) 6/176 (7) 7/214 (6)
8/228 (8) 9/240 (9) 10/270 (11)

Masters 29–8–51–3; Porter 23–4–77–2; Napier 20.3–2–84–3; ten Doeschate 8–0–30–2; Adeel Malik 13–1–65–0. *Second innings*—Masters 17–3–77–2; Porter 14–1–49–3; Napier 11–0–75–2; ten Doeschate 4–0–18–0; Adeel Malik 9.5–1–39–3.

Essex

N. L. J. Browne c Wallace b Lloyd	31	– lbw b Wagg	13
J. C. Mickleburgh c Rudolph b Lloyd	19	– st Wallace b Salter	13
D. W. Lawrence c Wallace b Meschede	10	– c Cooke b Salter	43
*†J. S. Foster b Wagg	38	– (5) c and b Salter	9
R. N. ten Doeschate c Wallace b Meschede	49	– not out	74
C. J. Taylor c Hogan b Wagg	26	– (8) c Ingram b Wagg	22
K. S. Velani b Wagg	12	– b Hogan	31
G. R. Napier c Wallace b Wagg	0	– (9) c Wallace b Meschede	8
Adeel Malik c Hogan b Meschede	6	– (10) b Meschede	2
D. D. Masters not out	2	– (11) c Rudolph b Hogan	0
J. A. Porter b Wagg	0	– (4) b Hogan	34
B 5, l-b 6, w 1, n-b 16	28	B 10, l-b 9, n-b 6	25

1/54 (2) 2/59 (1) 3/86 (3)   (61.3 overs) 221
4/140 (4) 5/201 (5) 6/212 (6)
7/212 (8) 8/219 (7) 9/221 (9) 10/221 (11)

1/21 (2) 2/43 (2)   (87.4 overs) 274
3/112 (3) 4/130 (5)
5/130 (4) 6/198 (7) 7/242 (8)
8/269 (6) 9/273 (10) 10/274 (11)

Hogan 21–1–61–0; Meschede 20.4–3–73–3; Lloyd 4.2–0–14–2; Wagg 12.3–2–54–5; Bragg 2–0–7–0; Salter 1–0–1–0. *Second innings*—Hogan 23.4–5–67–3; Wagg 22–2–81–2; Meschede 15–1–53–2; Salter 27–7–54–3.

Umpires: G. D. Lloyd and J. W. Lloyds.

GLAMORGAN v NORTHAMPTONSHIRE

At Cardiff, May 31–June 3. Glamorgan won by ten wickets. Glamorgan 23pts, Northamptonshire 3pts. Toss: Northamptonshire.

Glamorgan won consecutive matches for the first time in four years, hammering Northamptonshire despite the loss of 116 overs to rain. At tea on a truncated first day Glamorgan were 150 for six, but piled on 221 more in 37.3 overs afterwards, with Meschede making his second Championship hundred – he hit Cobb into the River Taff – and Ruaidhri Smith cuffing 49 from 33 deliveries. From 28 for nought, Northamptonshire lost five for five in 36 balls before Cobb and Rossington stopped the rot, but they were still bowled out 214 behind, the last three snapped up by Salter. The total was swelled by five penalty runs after Wallace ran to field the ball, and Ingram collected his return in the keeper's discarded glove. Peters fell to the first delivery of the follow-on, but Newton kept Glamorgan at bay for almost four hours before he played on. There was little resistance after that, apart from Rossington's second half-century of the game. Rudolph's captaincy was inspired: four times a bowler took a wicket in the first over of a new spell.

Close of play: first day, Northamptonshire 0-0 (Azharullah 0, Peters 0); second day, Northamptonshire 79-5 (Cobb 21, Rossington 24); third day, Northamptonshire 163-4 (Newton 89, Rossington 25).

Glamorgan

*J. A. Rudolph lbw b Willey	1	– (2) not out	29
W. D. Bragg lbw b Kleinveldt	4	– (1) not out	26
B. J. Wright lbw b Azharullah	22		
C. A. Ingram lbw b Willey	45		
C. B. Cooke c Kleinveldt b Cobb	73		
†M. A. Wallace c and b Chambers	6		
G. G. Wagg c Kleinveldt b Azharullah	17		
C. A. J. Meschede c Willey b Coetzer	107		
A. G. Salter lbw b Kleinveldt	8		
R. A. J. Smith not out	49		
M. G. Hogan c Willey b Kleinveldt	0		
B 13, l-b 7, n-b 19	39	N-b 2	2

1/9 (1) 2/19 (2) 3/65 (3)   (71.3 overs) 371
4/92 (4) 5/107 (6) 6/150 (7)   (no wkt, 20.5 overs) 57
7/258 (5) 8/304 (9) 9/367 (8) 10/371 (11)

Kleinveldt 19.3–2–91–3; Willey 13–0–71–2; Azharullah 18–6–56–2; Chambers 14–2–88–1; Cobb 5–0–37–1; Coetzer 2–0–8–1. *Second innings*—Kleinveldt 5–0–16–0; Keogh 10–0–25–0; Azharullah 2–0–3–0; Cobb 3.5–0–13–0.

Northamptonshire

Azharullah c Rudolph b Meschede	15	– (10) not out	14
S. D. Peters b Hogan	5	– (1) c Wallace b Wagg	0
K. J. Coetzer c Meschede b Hogan	0	– (2) b Wagg	4
R. I. Newton c Wallace b Meschede	0	– (3) b Meschede	107
R. I. Keogh c Rudolph b Smith	5	– (4) run out	42
J. J. Cobb lbw b Salter	54	– (5) c Meschede b Ingram	1
†A. M. Rossington run out	50	– (6) c Wallace b Salter	55
B. M. Duckett c Wallace b Meschede	0	– (7) c Ingram b Salter	16
*D. J. Willey c Wright b Salter	6	– (8) c Rudolph b Salter	4
R. K. Kleinveldt not out	11	– (9) c Wallace b Smith	8
M. A. Chambers b Salter	0	– c Bragg b Hogan	14
L-b 2, n-b 4, p 5	11	L-b 2, n-b 2	4

1/28 (2) 2/28 (3) 3/28 (1)   (48 overs) 157
4/29 (4) 5/33 (5) 6/124 (7)   (84.2 overs) 269
7/128 (8) 8/136 (9) 9/157 (6) 10/157 (11)   1/0 (1) 2/15 (2)
3/122 (4) 4/129 (5)
5/199 (3) 6/220 (7) 7/228 (8)
8/240 (9) 9/244 (6) 10/269 (11)

Hogan 12–4–36–2; Wagg 11–0–41–0; Meschede 12–2–19–3; Smith 9–0–49–1; Salter 4–2–5–3. *Second innings*—Wagg 18–4–54–2; Hogan 20.2–4–59–1; Salter 21–2–64–3; Meschede 12–1–49–1; Smith 6–2–28–1; Ingram 7–1–13–1.

Umpires: M. Burns and R. K. Illingworth.

At Guildford, June 15–18. GLAMORGAN beat SURREY by seven wickets. *Graham Wagg scores 200 from No. 8.*

GLAMORGAN v LEICESTERSHIRE

At Cardiff, June 22–25. Glamorgan won by 137 runs. Glamorgan 21pts, Leicestershire 5pts. Toss: Glamorgan.

Glamorgan completed their fourth win in a row for the first time since 2010. It kept them third, 11 points behind Surrey (whose first defeat they had inflicted the previous week) with a game in hand. Victory came despite some unconvincing batting: in the first innings they had dipped to 136 for six before being rescued by Cooke and Wagg, who thrashed six sixes in his 94, the week after hitting a double-century at Guildford. Then three wickets in seven balls from Raine, who finished with career-best figures, threatened to derail Glamorgan's second innings after the South Africans Rudolph and Ingram had put on 96. But the other bowlers let them off the hook: Salter struck three sixes in his maiden half-century as the last three wickets added 139, and Leicestershire, who had trailed by only 25 after a consistent first-innings performance, were left 126 overs to make 324. Boyce survived more than three hours for 60, but, of the others only O'Brien resisted for long.

Close of play: first day, Leicestershire 37-1 (Boyce 18, Eckersley 8); second day, Glamorgan 64-2 (Rudolph 14, Ingram 38); third day, Leicestershire 75-3 (Boyce 33, Naik 6).

Glamorgan

*J. A. Rudolph c O'Brien b McKay	1	– b Wells	74
W. D. Bragg run out	17	– c O'Brien b Raine	0
B. J. Wright lbw b Naik	18	– c Robson b McKay	0
C. A. Ingram c Wells b McKay	0	– c O'Brien b Raine	60
C. B. Cooke b Shreck	84	– c O'Brien b Raine	8
C. A. J. Meschede lbw b Raine	24	– lbw b Raine	0
†M. A. Wallace b McKay	14	– b Raine	0
G. G. Wagg c Cosgrove b Raine	94	– b Shreck	32
A. G. Salter c Agathangelou b Wells	10	– not out	54
M. G. Hogan b Shreck	0	– c Cosgrove b Shreck	37
A. Carter not out	10	– c Cosgrove b Shreck	10
B 2, l-b 3, w 1	6	B 11, l-b 6, n-b 6	23

1/5 (1) 2/19 (2) 3/23 (4) (79 overs) 278
4/57 (3) 5/116 (6) 6/136 (7)
7/180 (5) 8/199 (9) 9/200 (10) 10/278 (8)

1/0 (2) 2/1 (3) (87.2 overs) 298
3/97 (4) 4/105 (5)
5/105 (6) 6/105 (7) 7/159 (8)
8/207 (1) 9/277 (10) 10/298 (11)

McKay 16–2–61–3; Raine 19–4–51–2; Shreck 19–2–67–2; Naik 15–6–48–1; Agathangelou 3–0–15–0; Wells 7–1–31–1. *Second innings*—McKay 29–12–81–1; Raine 16–4–43–5; Naik 10–2–41–0; Shreck 25.2–7–76–3; Wells 6–0–39–1; Agathangelou 1–0–1–0.

Leicestershire

A. J. Robson b Hogan	11	– (2) c Wallace b Meschede 8
M. A. G. Boyce lbw b Hogan	50	– (1) c Cooke b Ingram 60
E. J. H. Eckersley b Meschede	10	– b Wagg 9
*M. J. Cosgrove c Wright b Salter	38	– lbw b Hogan................ 14
A. P. Agathangelou b Meschede	42	– (6) c Wallace b Hogan 6
†N. J. O'Brien c Wallace b Carter	39	– (7) c Wallace b Carter 41
T. J. Wells c Rudolph b Wagg	17	– (8) b Wagg 0
B. A. Raine c Meschede b Carter	16	– (9) b Meschede............. 14
C. J. McKay c Cooke b Salter	13	– (10) not out................ 13
J. K. H. Naik b Hogan	2	– (5) b Salter 6
C. E. Shreck not out	0	– lbw b Carter 0
B 4, l-b 5, n-b 6	15	B 6, l-b 2, w 1, n-b 6 15

1/18 (1) 2/40 (3) 3/104 (4)   (86.4 overs) 253   1/20 (2) 2/37 (3)   (73 overs) 186
4/148 (2) 5/181 (5) 6/222 (6)   3/60 (4) 4/75 (5)
7/222 (7) 8/243 (9) 9/253 (10) 10/253 (8)   5/86 (6) 6/140 (1) 7/143 (8)
                                                             8/165 (9) 9/184 (7) 10/186 (11)

Hogan 16–1–54–3; Wagg 10–4–35–1; Carter 15.4–3–29–2; Salter 30–7–64–2; Meschede
10–1–45–2; Ingram 5–0–17–0. *Second innings*—Hogan 13–5–27–2; Meschede 9–2–29–2; Carter
6–2–19–2; Wagg 12–4–15–2; Salter 18–3–45–1; Ingram 15–2–43–1.

Umpires: M. R. Benson and R. J. Evans.

At Chesterfield, July 6–9. GLAMORGAN drew with DERBYSHIRE.

At Chelmsford, July 12–15. GLAMORGAN lost to ESSEX by 248 runs.

GLAMORGAN v LANCASHIRE

At Colwyn Bay, July 19–22. Lancashire won by an innings and 157 runs. Lancashire 24pts,
Glamorgan 3pts. Toss: Lancashire.

This match will be remembered for the colossal partnership by Lancashire's two South Africans
from Port Elizabeth. Petersen and Prince piled up 501 for the third wicket, the highest stand for
Lancashire or against Glamorgan, and only the 13th of 500 or more (and the fourth in Britain) in
first-class cricket; it was the first in which neither batsman reached 300, so Steve James's ground-
best (309 not out against Sussex in 2000) stayed intact. Both men did, however, make their highest
scores; Prince hit seven sixes and Petersen two, in addition to 35 fours apiece (six of Petersen's came
in seven balls off Lloyd). It was the first time a Lancashire innings had included two double-
centuries. Croft's declaration midway through the second day left Glamorgan needing 549 to avoid
the follow-on; with Chapple, aged 41, taking four wickets in his second match of the season, they

HIGHEST PARTNERSHIPS IN THE COUNTY CHAMPIONSHIP

Runs	Wkt			
555	1st	P. Holmes/H. Sutcliffe	Yorkshire v Essex at Leyton	1932
554	1st	J. T. Brown/J. Tunnicliffe	Yorkshire v Derbyshire at Chesterfield	1898
523	3rd	M. A. Carberry/N. D. McKenzie	Hampshire v Yorkshire at Southampton	2011
501	**3rd**	**A. N. Petersen/A. G. Prince**	**Lancashire v Glamorgan at Colwyn Bay** ..	**2015**
490	1st	E. H. Bowley/J. G. Langridge	Sussex v Middlesex at Hove	1933
470	4th	A. I. Kallicharran/G. W. Humpage	Warwickshire v Lancashire at Southport....	1982
465*	2nd	J. A. Jameson/R. B. Kanhai	Warwickshire v Glos at Birmingham	1974
448	4th	R. Abel/T. W. Hayward	Surrey v Yorkshire at The Oval...........	1899
438*	3rd	G. A. Hick/T. M. Moody	Worcestershire v Hampshire at Southampton	1997
425*	4th	A. Dale/I. V. A. Richards	Glamorgan v Middlesex at Cardiff	1993

finished 201 short, despite No. 11 Hogan's career-best. Seven wickets had fallen before Glamorgan collected their first bonus point of the match, which Wagg marked by launching Lilley's off-breaks into the gardens on Penrhyn Avenue three times in the same over. Following on, Glamorgan were five down by the end of the third day, and although rain delayed the start until 1pm on the fourth, the remaining five tumbled for 12 as Lancashire completed a massive victory which took them 32 points clear at the top of the table.

Close of play: first day, Lancashire 425-2 (Petersen 205, Prince 154); second day, Glamorgan 165-6 (Wallace 39, Wagg 7); third day, Glamorgan 146-5 (Cooke 43, Salter 11).

Lancashire

P. J. Horton lbw b Hogan	1
K. R. Brown b Lloyd	54
A. N. Petersen c Hogan b Lloyd	286
A. G. Prince c Salter b Lloyd	261
*S. J. Croft not out	57
J. P. Faulkner c Wagg b Ingram	21
B 2, l-b 6, w 2, n-b 8	18

1/6 (1)   (5 wkts dec, 136.4 overs) 698
2/104 (2) 3/605 (4)
4/625 (3) 5/698 (6)   110 overs: 488-2

†A. L. Davies, A. M. Lilley, K. M. Jarvis, S. C. Kerrigan and G. Chapple did not bat.

Hogan 22–4–75–1; Wagg 24–4–89–0; Meschede 21–3–94–0; Lloyd 23–0–164–3; Cosker 20–0–114–0; Salter 22–0–122–0; Ingram 4.4–0–32–1.

Glamorgan

*J. A. Rudolph b Chapple	32	– c Croft b Jarvis	13
W. D. Bragg lbw b Faulkner	25	– c Davies b Jarvis	14
C. A. Ingram c Davies b Chapple	0	– c Petersen b Kerrigan	7
C. B. Cooke b Chapple	5	– c Horton b Faulkner	56
D. L. Lloyd c Jarvis b Lilley	21	– lbw b Lilley	34
†M. A. Wallace b Chapple	41	– b Kerrigan	2
C. A. J. Meschede c Faulkner b Kerrigan	21	– (8) lbw b Lilley	0
G. G. Wagg c Brown b Lilley	45	– (9) b Lilley	0
A. G. Salter b Jarvis	43	– (7) lbw b Kerrigan	34
D. A. Cosker not out	40	– not out	4
M. G. Hogan c Horton b Lilley	57	– c Jarvis b Kerrigan	6
B 6, l-b 5, w 5, n-b 2	18	B 9, l-b 10, n-b 4	23

1/35 (1) 2/35 (3) 3/60 (4)   (101.2 overs) 348   1/32 (1) 2/33 (2)   (71.4 overs) 193
4/70 (2) 5/124 (5) 6/157 (7)   3/57 (3) 4/109 (5)
7/173 (6) 8/228 (8) 9/273 (9) 10/348 (11)   5/120 (6) 6/181 (4) 7/181 (8)
          8/181 (9) 9/183 (7) 10/193 (11)

Jarvis 22–4–67–1; Chapple 24–8–62–4; Faulkner 15–1–45–1; Kerrigan 20–6–50–1; Lilley 20.2–2–113–3. *Second innings*—Jarvis 15–2–46–2; Chapple 14–5–33–0; Kerrigan 21.4–9–28–4; Faulkner 9–3–29–1; Lilley 12–1–38–3.

Umpires: M. J. D. Bodenham and N. A. Mallender.

> " His big outswinger occasionally provoked jovial shouts of 'Ripe bananas!' from the slips."
> Obituaries, page 235

GLAMORGAN v GLOUCESTERSHIRE

At Swansea, August 6–9. Gloucestershire won by seven wickets. Gloucestershire 23pts, Glamorgan 4pts. Toss: Glamorgan.

Injury-hit Gloucestershire arrived without four senior players – although one of them, Hamish Marshall, was fit enough to be hastily summoned over the Severn Bridge when Craig Miles was hurt in the pre-match warm-up. And Marshall top-scored as Gloucestershire amassed 416, with everyone reaching double figures, to set up their third victory in succession, and their fifth overall. Earlier, Glamorgan had again started indifferently: only Rudolph lasted long, but the tail wagged once more, with Salter improving his career-best for the second time in the summer. He put on 90 for the ninth wicket with Bull, playing his first Championship match of the season – but Gloucestershire's consistency showed up Glamorgan's batting, and the second innings was even worse, when the biggest stand was the last pair's 59. Roderick took five catches, while left-armer Payne, who would have missed out had Miles not broken down, claimed four wickets in each innings. The late resistance stretched the target into three figures and the match into the final day, but Gloucestershire – captained by Tavaré for the first time – strolled home after lunch.

Close of play: first day, Glamorgan 271-8 (Salter 73, Bull 21); second day, Gloucestershire 301-6 (Hammond 17, Taylor 22); third day, Glamorgan 224.

Glamorgan

*J. A. Rudolph c Marshall b Taylor	68	– c Roderick b Payne	14
W. D. Bragg c Taylor b Payne	0	– lbw b Noema-Barnett	6
C. A. Ingram c Tavaré b Norwell	21	– c Roderick b Noema-Barnett	45
A. H. T. Donald c Tavaré b Norwell	0	– c Roderick b Payne	4
C. B. Cooke b Howell	11	– lbw b Norwell	18
G. G. Wagg c Taylor b Payne	15	– c Roderick b Payne	25
C. A. J. Meschede c Howell b Noema-Barnett	16	– c Marshall b Payne	6
†M. A. Wallace c Payne b Norwell	24	– c Roderick b Howell	4
A. G. Salter c Dent b Payne	73	– c Marshall b Noema-Barnett	38
K. A. Bull c Roderick b Payne	31	– lbw b Smith	7
M. G. Hogan not out	18	– not out	37
B 4, l-b 11, w 1, n-b 6	22	B 8, l-b 5, w 1, n-b 6	20

1/1 (2) 2/41 (3) 3/41 (4) (102.4 overs) 299
4/69 (5) 5/106 (6) 6/144 (7)
7/146 (1) 8/186 (8) 9/276 (9) 10/299 (10)

1/27 (2) 2/27 (1) (62.5 overs) 224
3/32 (4) 4/72 (5)
5/103 (3) 6/121 (7) 7/132 (8)
8/132 (6) 9/165 (10) 10/224 (9)

Payne 19.4–2–73–4; Norwell 28–4–89–3; Noema-Barnett 20–9–36–1; Howell 8–2–34–1; Smith 11–1–23–0; Taylor 16–3–29–1. *Second innings*—Norwell 19–2–67–1; Payne 15–6–50–4; Noema-Barnett 10.5–3–28–3; Howell 8–3–24–1; Taylor 5–0–18–0; Smith 5–0–24–1.

Gloucestershire

*W. A. Tavaré c Donald b Salter	47	– (2) c Wallace b Wagg	12
C. D. J. Dent b Meschede	11	– (1) not out	65
†G. H. Roderick c Ingram b Wagg	19	– c Donald b Wagg	7
B. A. C. Howell c Wallace b Meschede	67	– c Ingram b Hogan	7
H. J. H. Marshall lbw b Hogan	70	– not out	10
K. Noema-Barnett c Cooke b Meschede	14		
M. A. H. Hammond c Wallace b Hogan	30		
J. M. R. Taylor b Meschede	44		
T. M. J. Smith not out	37		
D. A. Payne b Salter	12		
L. C. Norwell c Hogan b Salter	19		
B 20, l-b 11, w 3, n-b 12	46	L-b 4, w 1, n-b 2	7

1/31 (2) 2/56 (3) 3/111 (1) (117.1 overs) 416
4/240 (5) 5/245 (4) 6/262 (6)
7/320 (7) 8/347 (8) 9/386 (10)
10/416 (11)
110 overs: 378-8

1/37 (2) (3 wkts, 36.5 overs) 108
2/59 (3) 3/84 (4)

Wagg 16.2–3–67–1; Hogan 29–8–59–2; Meschede 25–5–89–4; Salter 24.1–4–81–3; Bull 11–2–48–0; Ingram 10.4–0–35–0; Bragg 1–0–6–0. *Second innings*—Hogan 14–7–21–1; Meschede 10–3–37–0; Wagg 6–1–8–2; Salter 1–0–14–0; Bragg 5–2–16–0; Bull 0.5–0–8–0.

Umpires: N. L. Bainton and D. J. Millns.

At Manchester, August 21–24. GLAMORGAN drew with LANCASHIRE.

GLAMORGAN v KENT

At Cardiff, September 9–12. Kent won by 316 runs. Kent 22pts, Glamorgan 4pts. Toss: Kent. County debut: J. L. Lawlor.

Glamorgan were blown away by a whopping defeat, set up by a second-wicket stand of 222 between Key and Denly, who passed 1,000 runs for the season during his unbeaten 161. Key, whose hundred was the 54th of his career, had warmed up with 94 in the first innings, in which Kent reached 260 for four but surrendered their last six for 49. That was still more than enough for the lead, as Glamorgan's top order – without their captain, Jacques Rudolph, who was on paternity leave – misfired yet again, before Wagg and Meschede stretched the total to 207. But even the combative Wagg proved toothless as Key and Denly set up a distant target of 554. Ingram's maiden Championship century held Kent up, as did rain, which ended proceedings after tea on the third day, and disrupted the following morning. But once play resumed, Glamorgan lost five for 23, with Stevens taking four wickets in 17 balls. Opener Jeremy Lawlor, whose father Peter played once for Glamorgan in 1981, recorded a ten-ball pair on his Championship debut. The pitch, a good one, was prepared by Cardiff's new groundsman Robin Saxton, previously the assistant to Keith Exton, who had left the club not long after the abandonment of the Royal London Cup game against Hampshire on August 2, when conditions were deemed dangerous.

Close of play: first day, Glamorgan 65-4 (Cooke 20, Salter 0); second day, Kent 256-1 (Key 117, Denly 66); third day, Glamorgan 101-2 (Kettleborough 52, Ingram 42).

Kent

D. J. Bell-Drummond b Hogan	5	– c Ingram b Salter	54
R. W. T. Key c Wallace b Lloyd	94	– c Kettleborough b Wagg	158
S. R. Dickson c Wallace b Lloyd	59		
*S. A. Northeast c Wallace b Hogan	56	– not out	50
J. L. Denly c Donald b Lloyd	11	– (3) not out	161
D. I. Stevens c Salter b Meschede	64		
C. J. Haggett b Hogan	0		
†R. C. Davies c Donald b Hogan	0		
M. T. Coles lbw b Wagg	0		
A. E. N. Riley not out	6		
M. D. Hunn b Wagg	0		
L-b 5, w 3, n-b 6	14	B 4, l-b 4, w 6, n-b 14	28

1/5 (1) 2/127 (3) 3/212 (2)   (78.3 overs) 309
4/230 (5) 5/260 (4) 6/264 (7)
7/275 (8) 8/291 (9) 9/301 (6) 10/309 (11)

1/114 (1)   (2 wkts dec, 102 overs) 451
2/336 (2)

Wagg 18.3–3–58–2; Hogan 20–4–51–4; Lloyd 15–1–80–3; Meschede 15–1–65–1; Salter 5–0–36–0; Ingram 1–0–3–0; Lawlor 4–1–11–0. *Second innings*—Hogan 18–3–78–0; Wagg 21–1–89–1; Meschede 14–1–51–0; Lloyd 5–0–30–0; Salter 25–1–120–1; Ingram 19–2–75–0.

Glamorgan

J. M. Kettleborough lbw b Coles	4	– b Stevens	56
J. L. Lawlor b Hunn	0	– b Coles	0
D. L. Lloyd c Stevens b Riley	16	– c Davies b Coles	4
C. A. Ingram c Davies b Coles	20	– not out	105
C. B. Cooke c Davies b Hunn	31	– lbw b Stevens	0
A. G. Salter b Stevens	0	– (10) c Denly b Coles	31
A. H. T. Donald b Stevens	16	– (6) b Stevens	6
G. G. Wagg c Bell-Drummond b Riley	58	– (7) b Stevens	0
C. A. J. Meschede c Bell-Drummond b Riley	33	– (8) lbw b Coles	3
*†M. A. Wallace b Riley	9	– (9) c Davies b Stevens	10
M. G. Hogan not out	4	– b Hunn	16
B 1, l-b 15	16	B 1, l-b 1, n-b 4	6

1/4 (1) 2/4 (2) 3/35 (4)   (43.5 overs) 207   1/5 (2) 2/23 (3)   (62.3 overs) 237
4/57 (3) 5/65 (6) 6/91 (7)   3/109 (1) 4/117 (5)
7/101 (5) 8/158 (9) 9/184 (10) 10/207 (8)   5/127 (6) 6/127 (7) 7/132 (8)
                                       8/155 (9) 9/209 (10) 10/237 (11)

Coles 14–3–47–2; Hunn 10–1–45–2; Haggett 2–1–9–0; Riley 7.5–0–47–4; Stevens 10–1–43–2. *Second innings*—Coles 19–1–76–4; Stevens 22–4–58–5; Hunn 10.3–0–52–1; Riley 6–1–31–0; Haggett 4–1–16–0; Denly 1–0–2–0.

Umpires: M. J. D. Bodenham and A. G. Wharf.

At Northampton, September 14–17. GLAMORGAN drew with NORTHAMPTONSHIRE.

At Bristol, September 22–25. GLAMORGAN drew with GLOUCESTERSHIRE.

GLOUCESTERSHIRE

Dark horses seize the limelight

A N D Y   S T O C K H A U S E N

After 11 years without a trophy, Gloucestershire rediscovered their one-day nous to vanquish a star-studded Surrey and win the 50-over Royal London Cup in a breathless finish. It was a triumph for the underdogs, built around a resolve to fight until the last ball. And it meant 2015 would go down as the year when talented home-grown players began to shed their inhibitions and express themselves.

Past underachievement had been explained away by claims that the team were supposedly too young to compete against experienced opposition. Shortcomings on the field, some believed, could also be put down to financial pressures off it, and the playing budget, one of the smallest on the circuit, often cited as a handicap. Another reason was that, when the heat was on, lesser lights tended to hide behind key performers such as Michael Klinger. Gloucestershire had become dependent upon a small handful of players: if they failed, so did the team.

Change had come the previous winter, when long-serving director of cricket John Bracewell, a father figure to many, stepped down, and later joined Ireland. New head coach Richard Dawson, parachuted in from Yorkshire for a second stint on the Nevil Road staff, appointed former Gloucestershire one-day hero Ian Harvey as his assistant. Together they urged their charges to take responsibility for their own actions, especially since the influential Gidman brothers, Alex and Will, had left at the end of the 2014 season. The younger players left behind were told to believe their time had come.

A few greybeards remained. As well as Klinger, who led the side in white-ball cricket, Geraint Jones arrived from Kent to captain the four-day team, while Hamish Marshall embarked on his tenth season at Bristol. They all possessed much-needed know-how, and were generous in passing it on to younger team-mates. Perhaps more than any other factor, it was this healthy blend of experience and youth that steered Gloucestershire to one-day success. The stars of an epic Lord's final were the 39-year-old Jones, who compiled a canny fifty, and all-rounder Jack Taylor, aged 23, who walloped quick runs before reining in the Surrey batsmen with his off-spin.

Gloucestershire came fifth in their T20 Blast group, narrowly missing out on a quarter-final after losing several knife-edge games. However, they put those experiences to good use, and devised a winning formula for the 50-over competition. So, in late July and early August, when three successive matches went to the wire, Gloucestershire won the lot. They prevailed twice more to end as runners-up in the group and secure a home quarter-final. Klinger had been the leading scorer in the group stages of the T20 Blast, and he continued his imperious form, especially in the knockout stages of the one-day cup.

He struck 87 against Hampshire and a consummate unbeaten 137 in the semi-final at Leeds. When he failed at Lord's (despite a duck, he was the tournament's top scorer) it felt as though Gloucestershire had blown their chance. Instead, their self-belief shone through, allowing Jones a triumphant end to his career; a run of poor Championship scores had prompted him to give up the captaincy in July, and announce his retirement with a year left on his contract. Ian Cockbain led the side for the next two four-day matches, before Will Tavaré took over.

Michael Klinger

Klinger's decision to decline offers from unnamed first division clubs, and sign a deal that would keep him at Nevil Road for another two years, may have raised eyebrows outside the county, but there were compelling reasons for him to stay. Gloucestershire were midway through a project that had begun with his arrival in 2013, so he believed he had unfinished business with a team he felt should push for promotion in the Championship and challenge for further honours in the white-ball formats.

His decision was also influenced by the impression of a club more generally on the up after years of struggle. Awarded four matches in the 2019 World Cup, Nevil Road was also hoping to host women's World Cup cricket in 2017, while the installation of permanent floodlights is going ahead following a lengthy battle for planning permission. The reappearance of international games in Bristol after a fallow year in 2015 – England play Sri Lanka in an ODI in June – should ensure a return to profitability, and allow Gloucestershire to retain their best young players, as well as having the power to recruit. It was a blow, though, when seamer James Fuller headed for Middlesex after five years on the staff. The gap was filled by left-armer Chris Liddle, released by Sussex, and Australian pace bowler Andrew Tye, signed for 20-over games.

Gloucestershire managed five Championship wins, one more than in 2014, and rose a place to sixth. Even so, they were a country mile behind Surrey and Lancashire, the teams promoted to Division One, and improvement in the four-day format must be a priority. The failure to make competitive first-innings totals was at the heart of the problems facing a side that lost four games and drew two at their Bristol HQ. Chris Dent was alone in passing 1,000 first-class runs, though the seam bowling fared best: Liam Norwell and Craig Miles claimed 118 first-class wickets between them.

In October, chief executive Will Brown revealed the club were exploring the possibility of a change of name – to Bristol – for the T20 Blast, in an attempt to remind locals of their existence.

Championship attendance: 22,369.

GLOUCESTERSHIRE RESULTS

All first-class matches – Played 17: Won 6, Lost 5, Drawn 6.
County Championship matches – Played 16: Won 5, Lost 5, Drawn 6.

LV= County Championship, 6th in Division 2;
NatWest T20 Blast, 5th in South Group; Royal London One-Day Cup, winners.

COUNTY CHAMPIONSHIP AVERAGES, BATTING AND FIELDING

Cap		Birthplace	M	I	NO	R	HS	100	Avge	Ct
2013	M. Klinger§	Kew, Australia	6	11	1	468	103	2	46.80	5
2015	P. S. P. Handscomb¶ .	Melbourne, Australia	6	11	2	401	76	0	44.55	8
2010	C. D. J. Dent	Bristol†	16	28	4	1,062	268	3	44.25	23
2006	H. J. H. Marshall	Warkworth, NZ	13	18	2	588	92	0	36.75	7
2013	T. M. J. Smith	Eastbourne	5	5	2	98	47*	0	32.66	1
2010	J. M. R. Taylor	Banbury	11	14	0	414	156	2	29.57	4
2014	W. A. Tavaré	Bristol†	15	26	2	708	66	0	29.50	9
2013	G. H. Roderick¶	Durban, SA	15	24	1	663	76	0	28.82	48
2014	G. O. Jones	Kundiawa, PNG . . .	9	15	0	400	88	0	26.66	10
2011	J. K. Fuller	Cape Town, SA . . .	10	13	1	300	73	0	25.00	5
2012	B. A. C. Howell	Bordeaux, France . .	11	16	0	395	102	1	24.68	8
2015	K. Noema-Barnett¶ . .	Dunedin, NZ	11	15	3	272	61	0	22.66	4
2011	D. A. Payne	Poole	9	10	3	138	23	0	19.71	4
2011	C. N. Miles	Swindon	11	18	1	237	41	0	13.94	3
2011	I. A. Cockbain	Liverpool	6	10	0	139	28	0	13.90	2
2011	L. C. Norwell	Bournemouth	14	19	9	83	19	0	8.30	5
2013	M. D. Taylor	Banbury	5	8	3	24	8	0	4.80	0

Also batted: M. A. H. Hammond (*Cheltenham†*) (cap 2013) (1 match) 30; T. R. G. Hampton (*Kingston-upon-Thames*) (cap 2015) (2 matches) 0*.

† *Born in Gloucestershire.* 　　§ *Official overseas player.* 　　¶ *Other non-England-qualified player.*

BOWLING

	Style	O	M	R	W	BB	5I	Avge
L. C. Norwell	RFM	480.3	102	1,525	61	6-33	3	25.00
C. N. Miles	RFM	350.4	70	1,155	46	6-63	4	25.10
B. A. C. Howell	RM	163.3	31	538	20	3-28	0	26.90
D. A. Payne	LFM	260.4	60	838	31	4-50	0	27.03
K. Noema-Barnett	RM	190.5	53	598	17	3-28	0	35.17
J. K. Fuller	RFM	265.5	51	918	24	4-35	0	38.25
M. D. Taylor	LM	157.1	36	544	13	5-93	1	41.84
J. M. R. Taylor	OB	159	29	466	10	3-119	0	46.60

Also bowled: C. D. J. Dent (SLA) 40-5-168-2; T. R. G. Hampton (RFM) 33-4-171-1; P. S. P. Handscomb (RM) 2-0-21-0; H. J. H. Marshall (RM) 14-5-31-3; T. M. J. Smith (SLA) 85.4-7-329-3; W. A. Tavaré (RM) 7-0-24-0.

LEADING ROYAL LONDON CUP AVERAGES (100 runs/4 wickets)

Batting	Runs	HS	Avge	SR	Ct/St
M. Klinger	531	137*	106.20	92.02	6
H. J. H. Marshall	105	78*	52.50	84.67	2
G. O. Jones	344	87	43.00	95.02	2
B. A. C. Howell .	300	80	42.85	85.71	4
G. H. Roderick . .	373	104	37.30	76.74	10/2
J. K. Fuller	104	45	26.00	88.88	1
J. M. R. Taylor . .	166	41*	23.71	153.70	9
C. D. J. Dent. . . .	220	49	22.00	82.70	6

Bowling	W	BB	Avge	ER
B. A. C. Howell	15	3-37	28.00	4.94
C. N. Miles . . .	12	4-29	28.41	5.86
J. K. Fuller . . .	18	3-26	29.86	5.12
D. A. Payne . . .	17	5-40	31.58	5.56
T. M. J. Smith .	11	3-45	33.45	4.97
J. M. R. Taylor	9	3-43	36.66	5.10

LEADING NATWEST T20 BLAST AVERAGES (100 runs/18 overs)

Batting	Runs	HS	Avge	SR	Ct/St
H. J. H. Marshall .	322	93	46.00	**160.19**	6
I. A. Cockbain . . .	392	91*	39.20	**149.61**	9
M. Klinger	654	126*	81.75	**142.17**	1
G. O. Jones	217	40	27.12	**136.47**	5/6
B. A. C. Howell . . .	173	57	28.83	**121.83**	10
P. S. P. Handscomb	142	39	14.20	**97.93**	4

Bowling	W	BB	Avge	ER
T. M. J. Smith . .	23	5-39	13.13	**7.02**
B. A. C. Howell	17	3-18	22.17	**7.25**
C. N. Miles	10	3-25	18.90	**7.50**
J. K. Fuller . . .	13	2-19	28.69	**8.10**
J. M. R. Taylor .	5	1-22	66.60	**8.57**
D. A. Payne. . . .	13	5-24	22.15	**9.54**

FIRST-CLASS COUNTY RECORDS

Highest score for	341	C. M. Spearman v Middlesex at Gloucester	2004
Highest score against	319	C. J. L. Rogers (Northants) at Northamptonshire .	2006
Leading run-scorer	33,664	W. R. Hammond (avge 57.05)	1920–51
Best bowling for	10-40	E. G. Dennett v Essex at Bristol	1906
Best bowling against {	10-66	A. A. Mailey (Australians) at Cheltenham	1921
	10-66	K. Smales (Nottinghamshire) at Stroud	1956
Leading wicket-taker	3,170	C. W. L. Parker (avge 19.43)	1903–35
Highest total for	695-9 dec	v Middlesex at Gloucester.	2004
Highest total against	774-7 dec	by Australians at Bristol	1948
Lowest total for	17	v Australians at Cheltenham	1896
Lowest total against	12	by Northamptonshire at Gloucester	1907

LIST A COUNTY RECORDS

Highest score for	177	A. J. Wright v Scotland at Bristol	1997
Highest score against	189*	J. G. E. Benning (Surrey) at Bristol.	2006
Leading run-scorer	7,825	M. W. Alleyne (avge 26.89)	1986–2005
Best bowling for	7-29	D. A. Payne v Essex at Chelmsford.	2010
Best bowling against	6-16	Shoaib Akhtar (Worcestershire) at Worcester. . .	2005
Leading wicket-taker	393	M. W. Alleyne (avge 29.88)	1986–2005
Highest total for	401-7	v Buckinghamshire at Wing	2003
Highest total against	496-4	by Surrey at The Oval	2007
Lowest total for	49	v Middlesex at Bristol	1978
Lowest total against	48	by Middlesex at Lydney	1973

TWENTY20 COUNTY RECORDS

Highest score for	**126***	**M. Klinger v Essex at Bristol**	**2015**
Highest score against	116*	C. L. White (Somerset) at Taunton	2006
Leading run-scorer	**2,335**	**H. J. H. Marshall (avge 28.82)**	**2006–15**
Best bowling for	**5-24**	**D. A. Payne v Middlesex at Richmond**	**2015**
Best bowling against	5-16	R. E. Watkins (Glamorgan) at Cardiff.	2009
Leading wicket-taker	49	J. Lewis (avge 30.89)	2003–11
Highest total for	254-3	v Middlesex at Uxbridge	2011
Highest total against	250-3	by Somerset at Taunton.	2006
Lowest total for	68	v Hampshire at Bristol.	2010
Lowest total against	97	by Surrey at The Oval	2010

ADDRESS

County Ground, Nevil Road, Bristol BS7 9EJ; 0117 910 8000; reception@glosccc.co.uk; www.gloscricket.co.uk.

OFFICIALS

Captain 2015 G. O. Jones
    (limited-overs) M. Klinger
Head coach R. K. J. Dawson
Academy director O. A. Dawkins
President R. J. Body

Chairman R. M. Cooke
Chief executive W. G. Brown
Head groundsman S. P. Williams
Scorer A. J. Bull

GLOUCESTERSHIRE v CARDIFF MCCU

At Bristol, April 7–9. Gloucestershire won by 217 runs. Toss: Cardiff MCCU. First-class debuts: T. N. Cullen, K. S. Leverock. County debut: P. S. P. Handscomb.

Gloucestershire's batsmen took advantage of a docile pitch to play themselves into form for the Championship. The openers made half-centuries in the sun against an attack featuring Bermuda's Kamau Leverock, nephew of the heavyweight slow left-armer Dwayne. Geraint Jones, Gloucestershire's new captain, chipped in too. Fuller and the accurate Norwell scattered the students for 95. Declining to enforce the follow-on, Jones gave another chance to Peter Handscomb, recently arrived from Australia, but he fell to the seam of Andrew Westphal for ten. Roderick, preferred as keeper to Handscomb or Jones, walloped 100 from 135 balls, hastening a second declaration. Set 463, Cardiff fought on into the last evening, with Sean Griffiths again top-scoring. At tea on the second day, the heavy roller became stuck on the outfield, and for the next session the boundary was shortened to exclude it from the playing area.

Close of play: first day, Cardiff MCCU 18-1 (Norris 13, Westphal 0); second day, Cardiff MCCU 59-2 (Brand 1, Rouse 6).

Gloucestershire

W. A. Tavaré b Leverock	93			
C. D. J. Dent b Griffiths	50			
P. S. P. Handscomb c Bull b Rouse	32	– (2) b Westphal	10
†G. H. Roderick c Brand b Bull	28	– (1) not out	100
I. A. Cockbain c Cullen b Griffiths	39	– (3) not out	66
*G. O. Jones not out	72			
B. A. C. Howell c Griffiths b Westphal	14			
J. K. Fuller not out	43			
L-b 6	6	L-b 4	4

1/94 (2) 2/143 (3) (6 wkts dec, 90 overs) 377 1/28 (2) (1 wkt dec, 41.4 overs) 180
3/208 (1) 4/208 (4)
5/277 (5) 6/311 (7)

C. N. Miles, D. A. Payne and L. C. Norwell did not bat.

Murphy 12–1–45–0; Westphal 11–3–47–1; Leverock 16–2–61–1; Griffiths 16–2–63–2; Bull 22–1–83–1; Brand 2–0–19–0; Rouse 11–0–53–1. *Second innings*—Leverock 6–0–31–0; Westphal 7–1–20–1; Griffiths 4–0–22–0; Bull 13.4–0–65–0; Brand 9–0–30–0; Rouse 2–0–8–0.

Cardiff MCCU

*J. George c Tavaré b Fuller	5	– b Norwell	14
M. J. Norris b Fuller	15	– c Roderick b Miles	32
A. A. Westphal c Roderick b Fuller	2	– (10) not out	5
N. Brand c Jones b Payne	16	– (3) c Tavaré b Norwell	32
T. D. Rouse c Roderick b Miles	10	– (4) c and b Miles	22
B. R. M. Scriven c Jones b Norwell	2	– (5) c Roderick b Miles	5
S. W. Griffiths c Handscomb b Norwell	26	– (6) c Handscomb b Howell	34
†T. N. Cullen c Roderick b Norwell	4	– (7) c Roderick b Howell	26
J. R. Murphy lbw b Norwell	0	– (8) c Jones b Norwell	17
K. S. Leverock c Fuller b Howell	9	– (9) c Roderick b Payne	25
K. A. Bull not out	0	– lbw b Payne	0
L-b 1, w 1, n-b 4	6	B 5, l-b 10, w 3, n-b 15	33

1/15 (1) 2/21 (3) 3/34 (2) (39.5 overs) 95 1/48 (2) 2/52 (1) (86.5 overs) 245
4/44 (4) 5/52 (6) 6/53 (5) 3/85 (4) 4/101 (5)
7/76 (8) 8/76 (9) 9/95 (7) 10/95 (10) 5/131 (3) 6/159 (6) 7/192 (8)
8/219 (7) 9/245 (9) 10/245 (11)

Payne 12–2–36–1; Fuller 10–4–14–3; Miles 7–2–18–1; Norwell 8–3–16–4; Howell 2.5–0–10–1. *Second innings*—Payne 17.5–3–47–2; Fuller 17–3–40–0; Norwell 19–4–51–3; Miles 16–4–51–3; Howell 14–5–34–2; Tavaré 2–0–6–0; Cockbain 1–0–1–0.

Umpires: J. W. Lloyds and B. V. Taylor.

At Northampton, April 12–15. GLOUCESTERSHIRE drew with NORTHAMPTONSHIRE.

GLOUCESTERSHIRE v DERBYSHIRE

At Bristol, April 26–29. Derbyshire won by seven wickets. Derbyshire 24pts, Gloucestershire 4pts. Toss: Derbyshire.

A spellbinding display of clean hitting by Martin Guptill proved the difference. Dropped on 57 and 101, he struck a Derbyshire-record 11 sixes in a career-best 227 occupying just 176 balls; he needed 101 to make three figures, and another 64 to reach his double. (A month earlier, he had plundered 237, also with 11 sixes, during New Zealand's defeat of West Indies in the World Cup quarter-final.) Gloucestershire were hampered by insufficient first-innings runs – they slipped from 200 for three to 275 all out – several dropped catches, and wayward bowling that haemorrhaged 241 in a session on the second evening. Their attempts to save the game were undermined by the ubiquitous Guptill, who held four second-innings catches, three of them blinders, and Footitt, whose left-arm pace claimed nine wickets in the match. Roderick's fifth successive score of fifty or more, as well as runs down the order (and 56 extras), delayed Derbyshire, though not long enough to set them a demanding target. There was an unpleasant episode on the third day when Gloucestershire ran a quick single. Godleman hurled the ball towards the keeper, and hit Handscomb, who was incensed, and the umpires intervened. As Godleman had been reprimanded for an altercation the previous September, he was given a two-match ban.

Close of play: first day, Derbyshire 24-0 (Slater 14, Godleman 7); second day, Derbyshire 511-8 (Hosein 43, Taylor 1); third day, Gloucestershire 253-6 (Marshall 48).

Gloucestershire

W. A. Tavaré c Madsen b Thakor	48	– (2) lbw b Palladino		45
C. D. J. Dent c Hosein b Palladino	22	– (1) c Hosein b Footitt		2
†G. H. Roderick c Hughes b Footitt	76	– b Taylor		75
P. S. P. Handscomb b Taylor	17	– c Hosein b Palladino		14
H. J. H. Marshall lbw b Hughes	41	– c Guptill b Footitt		79
*G. O. Jones b Taylor	14	– c Guptill b Footitt		10
K. Noema-Barnett c Durston b Footitt	21	– c Guptill b Footitt		31
J. K. Fuller lbw b Hughes	6	– b Footitt		51
C. N. Miles c Madsen b Palladino	6	– not out		31
L. C. Norwell b Footitt	0	– c Hosein b Footitt		17
M. D. Taylor not out	2	– c Guptill b Thakor		0
B 1, l-b 5, n-b 16	22	B 13, l-b 8, w 1, n-b 34		56

1/30 (2) 2/98 (1) 3/139 (4)   (87.4 overs) 275
4/200 (3) 5/227 (6) 6/249 (5)
7/265 (8) 8/271 (7) 9/271 (10) 10/275 (9)

1/6 (1) 2/121 (2)   (123.5 overs) 411
3/145 (4) 4/147 (3)
5/171 (6) 6/253 (7) 7/347 (8)
8/360 (5) 9/406 (10) 10/411 (11)

Footitt 18–2–72–3; Palladino 20.4–3–41–2; Taylor 17–3–70–2; Thakor 14–4–44–1; Hughes 13–3–34–2; Durston 5–2–8–0. *Second innings*—Footitt 34–6–94–6; Palladino 28–8–59–2; Taylor 20–3–85–1; Thakor 11.5–2–45–1; Hughes 23–5–71–0; Durston 7–0–36–0.

Derbyshire

B. T. Slater c Dent b Norwell	56	– c Tavaré b Fuller	25
B. A. Godleman c Roderick b Norwell	44	– c Dent b Taylor	51
M. J. Guptill c Handscomb b Taylor	227	– not out	31
*W. L. Madsen b Taylor	2	– c Dent b Fuller	20
W. J. Durston b Jones b Taylor	1	– not out	6
S. J. Thakor c Roderick b Taylor	83		
A. L. Hughes lbw b Taylor	0		
†H. R. Hosein c Roderick b Norwell	61		
A. P. Palladino c Norwell b Miles	20		
T. A. I. Taylor not out	17		
B 5, l-b 11, w 4, n-b 14	34	L-b 3, n-b 6	9

1/88 (2) 2/162 (1)   (9 wkts dec, 113 overs) 545   1/81 (1)   (3 wkts, 33.5 overs) 142
3/181 (4) 4/191 (5)   2/81 (2) 3/133 (4)
5/381 (6) 6/381 (7) 7/457 (3)
8/486 (9) 9/545 (8)   110 overs: 533-8

M. H. A. Footitt did not bat.

Fuller 17–4–77–0; Taylor 28–7–93–5; Noema-Barnett 12–1–73–0; Norwell 27–6–137–3; Miles 21–1–111–1; Dent 5–1–16–0; Handscomb 2–0–21–0; Tavaré 1–0–1–0. *Second innings*—Taylor 11–1–42–1; Fuller 9–0–51–2; Miles 6.5–0–37–0; Norwell 7–3–9–0.

Umpires: R. J. Bailey and M. J. Saggers.

At Chelmsford, May 3–5. GLOUCESTERSHIRE beat ESSEX by nine wickets. *Gloucestershire secure their first Championship win at Chelmsford since 1930.*

At Manchester, May 10–13. GLOUCESTERSHIRE beat LANCASHIRE by 91 runs.

GLOUCESTERSHIRE v KENT

At Bristol, May 18–21. Kent won by eight wickets. Kent 20pts, Gloucestershire 3pts. Toss: Kent.
    After rain had stolen the first session, Gloucestershire careered from 97 for two just after tea to 193 all out by the close. Handscomb fared best in bowler-friendly conditions, as Coles and Stevens claimed three victims each. Next day, again interrupted by the weather, the wickets continued to clatter: with Norwell and Payne reducing Kent to 98 for seven, Gloucestershire eyed a handy lead, only to be thwarted by a stubborn stand of 119 between Haggett and Coles. Haggett reached his maiden first-class fifty from 149 balls as Kent established an advantage of 42. Gloucestershire made a better fist of their second innings – Marshall and Jones hit half-centuries – before another uncertain display from the tail. With the pitch flattening out, a target of 241 was unlikely to be enough. Denly, who struck his first Championship century in three years, and Northeast batted with growing fluency in an unbroken third-wicket partnership of 208, and Kent coasted to their first win of the season.
    Close of play: first day, Gloucestershire 193; second day, Kent 223-9 (Riley 0, Thomas 0); third day, Gloucestershire 282-9 (Norwell 14, Taylor 7).

Gloucestershire

†G. H. Roderick c Billings b Stevens	28	– (2) c Stevens b Thomas	47
C. D. J. Dent c Coles b Haggett	11	– (1) b Stevens	22
I. A. Cockbain b Coles	24	– c Billings b Stevens	3
P. S. P. Handscomb c Billings b Coles	69	– c Billings b Thomas	5
H. J. H. Marshall c and b Coles	0	– c Cowdrey b Coles	83
*G. O. Jones b Haggett	13	– lbw b Thomas	55
K. Noema-Barnett lbw b Stevens	8	– c Haggett b Coles	0
C. N. Miles c Denly b Stevens	4	– c Riley b Stevens	22
D. A. Payne not out	20	– c Northeast b Haggett	15
L. C. Norwell c Billings b Thomas	4	– not out	14
M. D. Taylor c Riley b Thomas	0	– c Bell-Drummond b Thomas	7
B 1, l-b 11	12	L-b 7, n-b 2	9

1/36 (2) 2/61 (1) 3/91 (3)   (64.4 overs) 193
4/93 (5) 5/129 (6) 6/164 (7)
7/164 (4) 8/176 (8) 9/193 (10) 10/193 (11)

1/59 (1) 2/67 (3)   (86.1 overs) 282
3/74 (4) 4/81 (2)
5/215 (6) 6/221 (7) 7/221 (6)
8/257 (9) 9/261 (8) 10/282 (11)

Coles 19–7–49–3; Thomas 12.4–2–22–2; Haggett 15–2–53–2; Stevens 17–3–50–3; Riley 1–0–7–0. *Second innings*—Coles 21–3–77–2; Thomas 19.1–5–53–4; Haggett 19–5–57–1; Stevens 22–4–67–3; Riley 5–0–21–0.

Kent

D. J. Bell-Drummond b Norwell	26	– c Dent b Miles	3
J. L. Denly c Roderick b Payne	4	– not out	117
B. P. Nash c Dent b Norwell	12	– c Roderick b Norwell	25
*S. A. Northeast b Norwell	21	– not out	88
F. K. Cowdrey lbw b Noema-Barnett	6		
D. I. Stevens b Miles	4		
†S. W. Billings c Roderick b Payne	16		
C. J. Haggett c Roderick b Payne	54		
M. T. Coles c and b Dent	66		
A. E. N. Riley c Roderick b Norwell	4		
I. A. A. Thomas not out	7		
B 6, l-b 5, n-b 4	15	L-b 6, n-b 4	10

1/7 (2) 2/40 (3) 3/47 (1)   (84 overs) 235
4/67 (5) 5/76 (6) 6/80 (4)
7/98 (8) 8/217 (9) 9/223 (8) 10/235 (10)

1/3 (1)   (2 wkts, 64.4 overs) 243
2/35 (3)

Payne 18–4–41–3; Miles 19–2–73–1; Norwell 24–8–44–4; Taylor 9–2–38–0; Noema-Barnett 10–3–24–1; Dent 4–2–4–1. *Second innings*—Payne 11–2–34–0; Miles 14–3–49–1; Taylor 10.4–2–51–0; Norwell 14–2–57–1; Noema-Barnett 10–3–29–0; Dent 5–0–17–0.

Umpires: R. J. Evans and R. A. Kettleborough.

At Derby, May 31–June 3. GLOUCESTERSHIRE drew with DERBYSHIRE.

GLOUCESTERSHIRE v LANCASHIRE

At Bristol, June 7–10. Lancashire won by 91 runs. Lancashire 21pts, Gloucestershire 5pts. Toss: Gloucestershire.

Gloucestershire matched their opponents in every department – until a dramatic final-day collapse. The loss of Dent proved the turning point: chasing 252, they crashed from 113 for two to 160 all out in the face of some incisive seam bowling from Jarvis. Defeat was tough on Miles, whose maiden ten-wicket haul had kept Gloucestershire in contention: he took five for 61 as Lancashire were dismissed for 275 on the first day, then five for 60 to set up an intriguing finale. For Lancashire, who went 31 points clear at the top of the table, Brown hit a pair of fifties. On the second day, Klinger, the former Gloucestershire captain, and Jones, his successor, had shared a sixth-wicket stand of 167 as they recovered from 72 for five. Klinger played beautifully in crafting 102, while the forthright Jones hit 88, and a meaningful lead seemed on the cards until – in a familiar failing – five wickets vanished for 38. Roderick fractured a thumb on the first day before completing a pair; Jones, and later Cameron Herring, the substitute, took the gloves.

Close of play: first day, Gloucestershire 15-2 (Miles 9, Klinger 0); second day, Lancashire 14-0 (Horton 6, Brown 3); third day, Gloucestershire 26-1 (Dent 10, Klinger 15).

Lancashire

P. J. Horton c Howell b Miles	4	– lbw b Miles	6
K. R. Brown b Miles	57	– c sub (C. L. Herring) b Howell	56
A. N. Petersen lbw b M. D. Taylor	20	– c Cockbain b Miles	6
A. G. Prince b Miles	1	– run out	43
*S. J. Croft lbw b Miles	65	– lbw b Miles	0
†A. L. Davies lbw b M. D. Taylor	11	– c Tavaré b Howell	28
J. P. Faulkner c Jones b Miles	9	– c Howell b M. D. Taylor	4
J. Clark c Jones b Howell	35	– c Dent b Norwell	48
T. E. Bailey b M. D. Taylor	30	– not out	27
K. M. Jarvis c Cockbain b Howell	0	– c sub (C. L. Herring) b Miles	0
G. Chapple not out	29	– (10) c J. M. R. Taylor b Miles	6
B 3, l-b 9, w 2	14	B 9, l-b 12, n-b 8	29

1/10 (1) 2/55 (3) 3/56 (4)   (83.5 overs) 275
4/106 (2) 5/147 (6) 6/158 (7)
7/190 (5) 8/239 (8) 9/239 (10) 10/275 (9)

1/18 (1) 2/40 (3)   (89 overs) 253
3/117 (4) 4/117 (5)
5/138 (2) 6/147 (7) 7/200 (6)
8/235 (8) 9/252 (10) 10/253 (11)

Miles 20–5–61–5; M. D. Taylor 21.5–5–67–3; Norwell 18–4–63–0; Howell 17–3–53–2; J. M. R. Taylor 7–2–19–0. *Second innings*—Miles 24–7–60–5; M. D. Taylor 18–5–33–1; Norwell 26–7–61–1; Howell 14–1–53–2; J. M. R. Taylor 7–0–25–0.

Gloucestershire

W. A. Tavaré lbw b Bailey	4	– (2) b Jarvis	0
C. D. J. Dent c Davies b Jarvis	2	– (1) c Prince b Jarvis	54
C. N. Miles b Jarvis	12	– (3) c Faulkner b Clark	17
M. Klinger c Petersen b Croft	102	– (3) c Davies b Faulkner	42
†G. H. Roderick c Horton b Bailey	0	– b Miles	0
I. A. Cockbain b Chapple	28	– (4) lbw b Jarvis	15
*G. O. Jones b Bailey	88	– (6) c Davies b Faulkner	14
B. A. C. Howell c sub (S. C. Kerrigan) b Jarvis	19	– (7) lbw b Jarvis	0
J. M. R. Taylor c Prince b Bailey	1	– (8) b Jarvis	0
M. D. Taylor c Brown b Jarvis	8	– c Davies b Faulkner	0
L. C. Norwell not out	4	– not out	3
L-b 5, w 2, n-b 2	9	B 2, l-b 9, n-b 4	15

1/4 (2) 2/8 (1) 3/22 (3)   (91.3 overs) 277
4/27 (5) 5/72 (6) 6/239 (4)
7/246 (7) 8/257 (9) 9/266 (8) 10/277 (10)

1/0 (2) 2/68 (3)   (69 overs) 160
3/113 (1) 4/118 (4)
5/118 (5) 6/119 (7) 7/119 (8)
8/154 (6) 9/156 (10) 10/160 (9)

Bailey 21–8–52–4; Jarvis 23.3–5–67–4; Faulkner 13–5–40–0; Chapple 12–2–39–1; Clark 14–2–47–0; Croft 8–1–27–1. *Second innings*—Bailey 21.5–5–47–1; Jarvis 21–8–39–5; Chapple 12–5–40–0; Faulkner 12–7–18–3; Croft 1–0–1–0; Clark 2–1–4–1.

Umpires: B. J. Debenham and P. J. Hartley.

GLOUCESTERSHIRE v ESSEX

At Bristol, June 21–23. Essex won by five wickets. Essex 22pts, Gloucestershire 3pts. Toss: Essex.

Gloucestershire paid the price for an abysmal first-innings batting display, and plummeted to a fourth successive home defeat. On the opening day, all the Essex top order made contributions, Cook hitting 48 in his last match before the Ashes. Having squandered the new ball in the morning, the

Gloucestershire attack reduced Essex to 169 for five, before a stand of 115 between ten Doeschate and Foster shored things up. A late collapse left them 319 all out at the close, and the wickets clattered again next morning. Roderick and Howell offered brief resistance, until Napier's late swing rounded off the Gloucestershire shemozzle with three wickets in five balls. Armed with a lead of 203, Foster enforced the follow-on. Klinger battled more than four hours, but the game looked over when he departed for a painstaking 103. Eventually set 114 after a useful ninth-wicket stand between Norwell and Miles, Essex made a meal of the chase, losing Cook first ball and slipping to 26 for four. But a polished unbeaten 65 from Westley steered them home inside three days.

Close of play: first day, Essex 319; second day, Gloucestershire 126-3 (Klinger 62, Cockbain 25).

Essex

N. L. J. Browne c Taylor b Norwell	36	– c Jones b Fuller		6
A. N. Cook lbw b Howell	48	– c Dent b Fuller		0
T. Westley c Jones b Norwell	33	– not out		65
R. S. Bopara lbw b Fuller	30	– c Jones b Miles		5
J. D. Ryder c Jones b Norwell	17	– (7) not out		20
R. N. ten Doeschate c Jones b Miles	73	– (5) lbw b Norwell		1
*†J. S. Foster c and b Howell	63	– (6) lbw b Fuller		14
G. R. Napier lbw b Howell	1			
M. E. T. Salisbury c Jones b Fuller	2			
A. S. S. Nijjar not out	2			
J. A. Porter b Fuller	0			
L-b 12, n-b 2	14	L-b 3, w 1, n-b 2		6

1/58 (1) 2/112 (2) 3/121 (3)   (96 overs) 319
4/163 (5) 5/169 (4) 6/284 (7)
7/292 (8) 8/302 (9) 9/318 (6) 10/319 (11)

1/2 (2)   (5 wkts, 29 overs) 117
2/16 (1) 3/25 (4)
4/26 (5) 5/73 (6)

Miles 19–2–73–1; Fuller 22–3–85–3; Norwell 23–6–75–3; Howell 21–5–50–3; Taylor 11–2–24–0. *Second innings*—Miles 9–2–30–1; Fuller 9–1–32–3; Norwell 9–3–43–1; Howell 2–0–9–0.

Gloucestershire

W. A. Tavaré c Cook b Porter	6	– (2) c Foster b Porter		4
C. D. J. Dent lbw b Ryder	12	– (1) lbw b Napier		0
M. Klinger c Ryder b Porter	4	– c Foster b ten Doeschate		103
G. H. Roderick c Foster b Bopara	28	– c Foster b Ryder		24
I. A. Cockbain lbw b Napier	10	– b Porter		25
*†G. O. Jones c Ryder b Bopara	1	– c Napier b Nijjar		37
B. A. C. Howell b Napier	29	– c Browne b Porter		48
J. M. R. Taylor c Ryder b Porter	1	– lbw b Napier		5
J. K. Fuller b Napier	9	– c Foster b Napier		3
C. N. Miles b Napier	0	– c Salisbury b Ryder		37
L. C. Norwell not out	0	– not out		0
L-b 8, n-b 8	16	B 8, l-b 11, w 1, n-b 10		30

1/8 (1) 2/18 (3) 3/32 (2)   (39.5 overs) 116
4/59 (4) 5/61 (6) 6/88 (5)
7/89 (8) 8/115 (7) 9/115 (10) 10/116 (9)

1/0 (1) 2/10 (2)   (101.4 overs) 316
3/65 (4) 4/126 (5)
5/195 (3) 6/221 (6) 7/227 (8)
8/231 (9) 9/302 (10) 10/316 (7)

Porter 10–2–30–3; Ryder 9–1–24–1; Napier 9.5–3–27–4; Salisbury 4–0–8–0; Bopara 7–2–19–2. *Second innings*—Napier 23–6–53–3; Porter 20.4–4–66–3; Ryder 19.5–5–78–2; Bopara 14–2–39–0; Nijjar 5–2–6–1; Salisbury 6–0–35–0; ten Doeschate 12–4–19–1; Westley 1–0–1–0; Browne 1–1–0–0.

Umpires: S. C. Gale and J. W. Lloyds.

At The Oval, June 27–29. GLOUCESTERSHIRE lost to SURREY by an innings and 180 runs.

GLOUCESTERSHIRE v NORTHAMPTONSHIRE

At Cheltenham, July 8–9. Gloucestershire won by nine wickets. Gloucestershire 23pts, Northamptonshire 4pts. Toss: Gloucestershire.

A brilliant counter-attacking innings from Jack Taylor turned this high-speed contest upside down, and inspired Gloucestershire to a remarkable two-day victory, following four successive defeats at Bristol. Taylor came in on the second morning at 108 for six, with his team in danger of conceding a sizeable first-innings deficit. But once he had smashed a career-best 156 from 125 balls – dominating stands of 113 with Howell and 104 with Miles – the lead was a healthy 126. It drew the wind from Northamptonshire's sails: they lurched to five for three, then 38 for five, before Levi oversaw a modest recovery. Even so, they were shot out for 160 in 37 overs, their destroyer-in-chief was Miles, the naggingly accurate Miles, who claimed five for 28. There was time for Gloucestershire to zip past their target in six overs. The stars of the first day had been Wakely, who struck a measured hundred, and Norwell, who collected six wickets. Gloucestershire were led by Cockbain, after Geraint Jones relinquished the captaincy on the first morning; he announced he would retire at the end of the season.

Close of play: first day, Gloucestershire 82-4 (Marshall 25, Cockbain 6).

Northamptonshire

S. D. Peters c Roderick b Miles	0	– b Miles	0
B. M. Duckett c Howell b Norwell	53	– c Tavaré b Miles	5
*A. G. Wakely c Klinger b Fuller	104	– c Roderick b Fuller	0
R. I. Keogh c Dent b Norwell	2	– lbw b Fuller	1
R. E. Levi c Roderick b Norwell	14	– c Dent b Miles	64
†A. M. Rossington c Klinger b Norwell	0	– c Fuller b Norwell	10
J. J. Cobb b Norwell	1	– lbw b Howell	16
S. P. Crook c Howell b Taylor	27	– c Roderick b Norwell	13
R. K. Kleinveldt c Miles b Norwell	13	– b Miles	37
G. G. White b Marshall b Howell	24	– c Roderick b Miles	0
O. P. Stone not out	0	– not out	10
L-b 2, n-b 6	8	L-b 1, w 1, n-b 2	4

1/0 (1) 2/90 (2) 3/92 (4)   (69.3 overs) 246
4/116 (5) 5/118 (6) 6/122 (7)
7/191 (8) 8/215 (3) 9/246 (10) 10/246 (9)

1/0 (1) 2/5 (2)   (37.1 overs) 160
3/5 (3) 4/18 (4)
5/38 (6) 6/77 (7) 7/97 (8)
8/145 (9) 9/145 (10) 10/160 (5)

Miles 15–2–55–1; Fuller 18–2–54–1; Norwell 13.3–2–41–6; Howell 12–1–36–1; Taylor 11–1–58–1. *Second innings*—Miles 10.1–4–28–5; Fuller 9–1–36–2; Norwell 9–0–40–2; Howell 6–0–45–1; Taylor 3–0–10–0.

Gloucestershire

W. A. Tavaré lbw b Kleinveldt	10	– (2) not out	13
C. D. J. Dent c Kleinveldt b Stone	0	– (1) b Stone	6
M. Klinger c Rossington b Kleinveldt	10	– not out	12
H. J. H. Marshall c Wakely b Stone	34		
†G. H. Roderick lbw b Crook	23		
*I. A. Cockbain c Wakely b Stone	11		
B. A. C. Howell c Wakely b Stone	36		
J. M. R. Taylor c Rossington b Kleinveldt	156		
J. K. Fuller c White b Kleinveldt	13		
C. N. Miles c Kleinveldt b White	41		
L. C. Norwell not out	0		
L-b 10, n-b 28	38	B 2, l-b 1, n-b 4	7

1/2 (2) 2/12 (1) 3/35 (3)   (75.5 overs) 372
4/76 (5) 5/93 (4) 6/108 (6)
7/221 (7) 8/258 (9) 9/362 (10) 10/372 (8)

1/6 (1)   (1 wkt, 6 overs) 38

Kleinveldt 24.5–2–129–4; Stone 22–4–91–4; Crook 9.2–0–50–1; Keogh 9–0–40–0; White 10.4–1–52–1. *Second innings*—Stone 3–0–18–1; Kleinveldt 2–0–13–0; Wakely 1–0–4–0.

Umpires: J. H. Evans and P. R. Pollard.

GLOUCESTERSHIRE v LEICESTERSHIRE

At Cheltenham, July 15–18. Gloucestershire won by 155 runs. Gloucestershire 20pts, Leicestershire 4pts. Toss: Leicestershire.

It was quite a week for Benny Howell: marriage on Monday; starring role in a Twenty20 defeat of Hampshire on Tuesday; maiden first-class hundred on Friday; Championship victory on Saturday. After the teams traded blows for two days on a slow pitch, Leicestershire cracked first. When Gloucestershire reached 131 for four in their second innings, with Klinger dismissed for a patient half-century, it looked as if a familiar pattern would ensue. (They were not helped when Cockbain, the new captain, broke his wrist in the nets before the second day.) But a crucial fifth-wicket stand of 139 in 35 overs transformed their fortunes: Howell, having shown great restraint to reach a gritty fifty from 156 balls, opened out as the pitch eased, and strode to his hundred from the next 46; Noema-Barnett, eventually one of five wickets for the persevering Shreck, hit a county-best 61 to help set a target of 325 in just over a day. Leicestershire, their confidence sapped by four successive defeats, were shot out for 169 before tea. In challenging first-day conditions well exploited by seamer McKay, Gloucestershire had been indebted to Roderick's 61; next day, Leicestershire were kept afloat by Cosgrove.

Close of play: first day, Leicestershire 56-3 (Cosgrove 26, Naik 1); second day, Gloucestershire 54-2 (Klinger 11, Roderick 11); third day, Leicestershire 11-0 (Boyce 2, Robson 5).

Gloucestershire

W. A. Tavaré c Hill b McKay	15	– (2) b Shreck	8
C. D. J. Dent lbw b McKay	5	– (1) lbw b Shreck	23
M. Klinger c Hill b Shreck	24	– c Hill b Shreck	60
†G. H. Roderick c and b Shreck	61	– c Hill b McKay	19
*I. A. Cockbain c Robson b Raine	5	– absent hurt	
B. A. C. Howell c Hill b McKay	1	– (5) lbw b McKay	102
K. Noema-Barnett lbw b Cosgrove	5	– (6) c Smith b Shreck	61
J. M. R. Taylor b Boyce b Shreck	28	– (7) b McKay	11
J. K. Fuller c Boyce b McKay	41	– (8) not out	17
C. N. Miles c Eckersley b McKay	8	– (9) c Cosgrove b Shreck	9
L. C. Norwell not out	0	– (10) c Hill b Raine	5
B 10, l-b 11, w 2, n-b 2	25	L-b 4, n-b 2	6

1/9 (2) 2/30 (1) 3/62 (3) (72.2 overs) 218
4/97 (5) 5/102 (6) 6/114 (7)
7/159 (4) 8/170 (8) 9/218 (9) 10/218 (10)

1/27 (2) 2/32 (1) (112.4 overs) 321
3/93 (4) 4/131 (3)
5/270 (6) 6/284 (5) 7/295 (7)
8/306 (9) 9/321 (10)

McKay 21.2–6–59–5; Raine 20–9–41–1; Shreck 19–7–58–3; Naik 9–2–34–0; Cosgrove 3–0–5–1. *Second innings*—McKay 34–10–93–3; Raine 23.4–8–65–1; Shreck 34–11–82–5; Naik 10–0–44–0; Cosgrove 11–4–33–0.

Leicestershire

A. J. Robson c Tavaré b Fuller	8	– (2) b Miles	6
M. A. G. Boyce lbw b Howell	18	– (1) lbw b Noema-Barnett	22
E. J. H. Eckersley b Fuller	2	– c Klinger b Miles	0
*M. J. Cosgrove c Roderick b Noema-Barnett	74	– lbw b Howell	24
J. K. H. Naik c Dent b Howell	10	– (10) c sub (M. A. H. Hammond) b Taylor	0
G. P. Smith c and b Noema-Barnett	20	– (5) c Dent b Fuller	4
A. M. Ali b Fuller	40	– (6) c Fuller b Taylor	41
†L. J. Hill b Norwell	18	– (7) c sub (M. A. H. Hammond) b Miles	10
B. A. Raine c and b Miles	7	– (8) run out	21
C. J. McKay c Miles b Fuller	13	– (9) c Roderick b Norwell	18
C. E. Shreck not out	0	– not out	4
L-b 5	5	L-b 19	19

1/15 (1) 2/19 (3) 3/49 (2)   (87.2 overs) 215
4/89 (5) 5/120 (6) 6/149 (4)
7/187 (8) 8/202 (9) 9/202 (7) 10/215 (10)

1/20 (2) 2/20 (3)   (65.2 overs) 169
3/61 (1) 4/65 (4)
5/73 (5) 6/87 (7) 7/141 (8)
8/147 (6) 9/147 (10) 10/169 (9)

Miles 20–4–61–1; Fuller 15.2–4–35–4; Norwell 20–3–42–1; Howell 14–4–28–2; Taylor 6–3–6–0; Noema-Barnett 15–6–38–2. *Second innings*—Miles 15.7–27–3; Fuller 13–8–18–1; Norwell 13.2–6–26–1; Noema-Barnett 11–3–45–1; Howell 4–1–9–1; Taylor 9–3–25–2.

Umpires: J. W. Lloyds and M. J. Saggers.

At Swansea, August 6–9. GLOUCESTERSHIRE beat GLAMORGAN by seven wickets.

GLOUCESTERSHIRE v SURREY

At Bristol, August 21–24. Drawn. Gloucestershire 8pts, Surrey 11pts. Toss: Surrey.

After three straight wins had pushed them up to fourth, Gloucestershire splashed back to earth at a damp Bristol, where they had lost all four Championship games in 2015. Rain washed away the last two days, probably preventing Surrey from making it five. Exploiting early moisture and movement off the pitch, the Curran brothers sliced through the home batting. Roderick was the only one of Gloucestershire's top seven to pass 12 and, when he went for a resourceful 71, the innings was in a shambles at 111 for seven. The last three wickets more than doubled the score, suggesting the pitch held few demons, though Tom Curran, who passed 50 wickets for the season, posed questions throughout. Surrey's reply was the inverse of the Gloucestershire innings, with only one of the top seven *not* reaching 12. Foakes hoped to increase his career-best unbeaten – and chanceless – 140, and Surrey to build on a lead already worth 116, but they were frustrated by the rain.

Close of play: first day, Surrey 74-2 (S. M. Curran 5, Foakes 4); second day, Surrey 349-6 (Foakes 140, Burke 11); third day, no play.

Gloucestershire

*W. A. Tavaré lbw b S. M. Curran	0	J. K. Fuller b T. K. Curran	48
C. D. J. Dent b S. M. Curran	12	D. A. Payne c Burns b T. K. Curran	21
†G. H. Roderick c Wilson b T. K. Curran	71	L. C. Norwell b Batty	5
H. J. H. Marshall b T. K. Curran	0	L-b 6, n-b 12	18
B. A. C. Howell c Roy b T. K. Curran	3		
K. Noema-Barnett c Wilson b Dernbach	6	1/1 (1) 2/32 (2) 3/41 (4) (71.2 overs) 233
J. M. R. Taylor c Wilson b T. K. Curran	2	4/63 (5) 5/103 (6) 6/106 (7)
T. M. J. Smith not out	47	7/111 (3) 8/168 (9) 9/224 (10) 10/233 (11)

T. K. Curran 25–8–61–6; S. M. Curran 10–3–47–2; Burke 12–1–49–0; Dernbach 17–5–41–1; Batty 7.2–1–29–1.

Surrey

R. J. Burns c Fuller b Howell	24	J. E. Burke not out	11
A. Harinath c Roderick b Norwell	39		
S. M. Curran c Payne b Noema-Barnett	49	B 5, l-b 1, n-b 10	16
B. T. Foakes not out	140		
S. M. Davies b Taylor	23	1/64 (2) 2/66 (1) (6 wkts, 98.2 overs)	349
J. J. Roy lbw b Noema-Barnett	39	3/179 (3) 4/235 (5)	
†G. C. Wilson c Noema-Barnett b Norwell	8	5/292 (6) 6/313 (7)	

*G. J. Batty, T. K. Curran and J. W. Dernbach did not bat.

Fuller 24–2–64–0; Payne 16–2–72–0; Norwell 23–2–97–2; Howell 7–1–22–1; Noema-Barnett 15–5–35–2; Smith 5.2–0–23–0; Taylor 8–0–30–1.

Umpires: R. J. Evans and G. D. Lloyd.

At Leicester, September 1–4. GLOUCESTERSHIRE drew with LEICESTERSHIRE.

At Canterbury, September 14–17. GLOUCESTERSHIRE drew with KENT.

GLOUCESTERSHIRE v GLAMORGAN

At Bristol, September 22–25. Drawn. Gloucestershire 13pts, Glamorgan 12pts. Toss: Glamorgan.

Chris Dent made a magnificent career-best 268, the 11th-highest score for Gloucestershire, as the batsmen finally came good on a greenish but true Nevil Road pitch. First-innings underachievement had been a feature of their five Championship matches at headquarters during the summer, but now – with little at stake – they piled on the runs. Dent and Fuller came together at 334 for seven, still 99 adrift of Glamorgan. But, when Fuller departed for a personal-best 73 just 31 overs later, they had added 168, an eighth-wicket record for this fixture. Dent was last out, on the third evening, having

HIGHEST SCORES AT NEVIL ROAD

310*	M. E. K. Hussey	Northamptonshire v Gloucestershire	2002
302*	W. R. Hammond	Gloucestershire v Glamorgan	1934
301	W. G. Grace	Gloucestershire v Sussex	1896
290	A. R. Morris	Australians v Gloucestershire	1948
288	W. G. Grace	Gloucestershire v Somerset	1895
271	W. R. Hammond	Gloucestershire v Lancashire	1938
268	**C. D. J. Dent**	**Gloucestershire v Glamorgan**	**2015**
264	W. R. Hammond	Gloucestershire v West Indians	1933
264	A. P. R. Gidman	Gloucestershire v Leicestershire	2014
257	D. Brookes	Northamptonshire v Gloucestershire	1949
250	A. O. Jones	Nottinghamshire v Gloucestershire	1899

faced 347 balls and hit 34 fours and two sixes. On the first day, which began an hour late, Kettleborough had struck 81 – another career-best – while next morning, Aneurin Donald, aged 18 years and 277 days, fell two runs short of eclipsing Matthew Maynard as Glamorgan's youngest Championship centurion. Any prospects of a result were snuffed out when, on an instantly forgettable last day, Ingram and Cooke added an unbroken 180 for the fourth wicket. On the first evening, Roderick had injured his hand, so the gloves passed – with Glamorgan's permission – to 18-year-old Academy player James Bracey, who made a stumping and held a catch.

Close of play: first day, Glamorgan 338-4 (Donald 91, Lloyd 29); second day, Gloucestershire 243-3 (Dent 102, Howell 40); third day, Glamorgan 88-0 (Rudolph 56, Kettleborough 31).

Glamorgan

*J. A. Rudolph lbw b Payne	17	–	lbw b Payne	69
J. M. Kettleborough c Roderick b Payne	81	–	lbw b Smith	34
C. A. Ingram c Roderick b Fuller	30	–	not out	101
A. H. T. Donald c Dent b Fuller	98	–	run out	35
†C. B. Cooke c Payne b Fuller	65	–	not out	102
D. L. Lloyd b Fuller	47			
G. G. Wagg lbw b Hampton	24			
C. A. J. Meschede st sub (J. R. Bracey) b Howell	28			
A. G. Salter c Smith b Howell	1			
D. Penrhyn Jones not out	9			
M. G. Hogan c sub (J. R. Bracey) b Howell	4			
B 5, l-b 14, n-b 10	29		B 8, l-b 8, w 6, n-b 2	24

1/38 (1) 2/109 (3) 3/165 (2)   (99.3 overs) 433   1/99 (2)   (3 wkts dec, 102 overs) 365
4/266 (5) 5/363 (4) 6/364 (6)   2/124 (1) 3/185 (4)
7/414 (7) 8/416 (8) 9/417 (9) 10/433 (11)

Payne 24–5–106–2; Fuller 21–5–59–4; Noema-Barnett 11–0–54–0; Hampton 19–3–109–1; Howell 8.3–3–28–3; Smith 10–1–31–0; Taylor 5–0–26–0; Marshall 1–0–1–0. *Second innings*—Payne 16–6–32–1; Fuller 16–1–64–0; Taylor 16–1–58–0; Hampton 11–1–42–0; Smith 22–3–79–1; Howell 14–2–43–0; Tavaré 4–0–11–0; Dent 3–0–20–0.

Gloucestershire

*W. A. Tavaré c Cooke b Meschede	8		D. A. Payne b Salter	7
C. D. J. Dent c Wagg b Meschede	268		T. R. G. Hampton not out	0
†G. H. Roderick b Hogan	9			
H. J. H. Marshall c Cooke b Hogan	58		B 10, l-b 7, w 5, n-b 30	52
B. A. C. Howell b Hogan	40			
K. Noema-Barnett c Salter b Meschede	5		1/21 (1) 2/32 (3) (121.5 overs) 558	
J. M. R. Taylor c Cooke b Penrhyn Jones	35		3/169 (4) 4/251 (5) 5/262 (6)	
T. M. J. Smith c Cooke b Penrhyn Jones	3		6/315 (7) 7/334 (8) 8/502 (9)	
J. K. Fuller c Penrhyn Jones b Salter	73		9/542 (10) 10/558 (2) 110 overs: 504-8	

Hogan 29–8–82–3; Meschede 27.5–3–152–3; Penrhyn Jones 22–0–135–2; Wagg 19–1–86–0; Salter 21–2–64–2; Ingram 3–0–22–0.

Umpires: P. K. Baldwin and N. G. C. Cowley.

HAMPSHIRE

The great escape

PAT SYMES

Hampshire supporters will remember 2015 for a sixth successive appearance at Twenty20 finals day, followed less than a month later by the club's remarkable last-ditch survival in Division One of the County Championship. Throw in a Royal London One-Day Cup quarter-final and, at first glance, it was not a bad year.

But those achievements masked a dismal first half of the season, when little went right. After one win in ten Championlship matches, Hampshire were bottom, with 76 points, seemingly destined for relegation the year after promotion. And, having lost six of their first 12 games in the NatWest T20 Blast, they were in danger of failing to qualify for the knockout stages. An experienced batting line-up was not functioning, and Jimmy Adams had stood down as captain of the four-day side. It was hard to foresee a recovery. But recover they did.

If there was a catalyst for the dramatic change, it came at the Rose Bowl on July 22, when Hampshire's novice last-wicket pair of Lewis McManus and Mason Crane held out for 32 balls against Durham. It gave everyone a huge psychological boost, and they began to repair the damage. With James Vince now in charge in all formats, they won three of their last five Championship matches, gleaning a further 77 points, to send Sussex, who began the last round 16 clear, down instead.

Going into that last round, Hampshire had needed to beat Nottinghamshire at Trent Bridge, and hope Sussex folded at Headingley. West Indian fast bowler Fidel Edwards took ten wickets in a match for only the second time in his career, and Hampshire won by eight wickets; Sussex did their part by losing to Yorkshire.

After being fifth in the T20 Blast's South Division with two matches remaining, Hampshire beat Sussex by four runs, and – the day after the Durham escape – Somerset by six, to nip into the quarter-finals. There, Vince hit an unbeaten 107 to see off Worcestershire, only for a calamitous batting performance on finals day to hand an easy victory to Lancashire.

In the 50-over competition, Hampshire had required some luck to progress. They won only three times, but were awarded two points at Cardiff when the pitch was deemed unsafe, and escaped from Trent Bridge with a point after rain interrupted Nottinghamshire at 256 for three from 39 overs. Once through to the last eight, though, they were comfortably beaten by Gloucestershire.

Gareth Berg was a popular choice as Player of the Year for his 42 Championship wickets and 672 runs, which included a match-turning 99 from No. 9 at Hove. After an injury-ruined spell at Middlesex, culminating in a shoulder operation and the sack, he was a revelation.

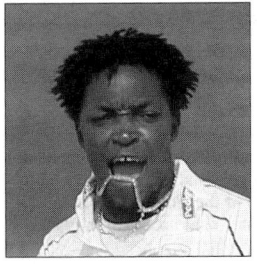

John Walton, PA Photos

Fidel Edwards

But, if one man encapsulated the spirit of Hampshire's revival, it was Edwards. He could produce fearsome pace from the most docile of surfaces, and claimed 45 wickets at 20 in eight Championship matches, cutting a swathe through county ranks just as Malcolm Marshall, his fellow Barbadian, had done for the county a generation earlier. Edwards arrived having played only three first-class games since November 2012 (his most recent appearance for West Indies), but brought an edge not seen in Southampton for years. He signed up again for 2016, while South African all-rounder Ryan McLaren will return as the official overseas player.

Edwards picked up three five-fors, and spinners Crane and Liam Dawson one each, but there were no others; only Edwards and Berg managed more than 22 Championship wickets. And such underwhelming statistics spread to the batting: just five centuries were scored in the Championship, a malaise typified by Michael Carberry (who managed ten half-centuries without converting any) and Will Smith (six). Carberry, though, was alone in reaching 1,000 runs.

There was also disappointment when left-arm spinner Danny Briggs, an Academy product who has represented England in both limited-overs formats, chose to leave with a year of his contract remaining; he joined Sussex in a bid to prevent his career stalling. Briggs had become marginalised, and his appearances increasingly confined to the T20 Blast.

Another item on the agenda when the club conducted their post-season inquest was the strange decision to take a chance on the fitness of 39-year-old New Zealander Andre Adams; a hero at Nottinghamshire, he lasted three matches. Nor was the choice of Australian seamer Jackson Bird as overseas player a great success. He arrived with a shoulder injury, and mustered only 19 wickets in six games. Joe Gatting and Sean Terry were both released.

The future looks rosier: Crane, nurtured at Lancing College by former Hampshire slow left-armer Raj Maru, is a leg-spinner of promise, and he picked up a five-wicket haul in only his second first-class match, against Warwickshire. Off-spinner Brad Taylor captained England Under-19 in a tri-series in Sri Lanka ahead of the 2016 World Cup, while the highly rated left-arm pace bowler Reece Topley arrived from Essex.

The Rose Bowl – whose hotel was now fully functional – staged one-day internationals with New Zealand and Australia, and will host Sri Lanka and Pakistan in 2016. It will be a season when Hampshire's players have to be on their best behaviour. In June, the club were fined £4,000 by the ECB and given a suspended points deduction, for five separate offences in the previous year.

Championship attendance: 21,469.

HAMPSHIRE RESULTS

All first-class matches – Played 17: Won 4, Lost 6, Drawn 7.
County Championship matches – Played 16: Won 4, Lost 6, Drawn 6.

LV= County Championship, 7th in Division 1;
NatWest T20 Blast, semi-finalists; Royal London One-Day Cup, quarter-finalists.

COUNTY CHAMPIONSHIP AVERAGES, BATTING AND FIELDING

Cap		Birthplace	M	I	NO	R	HS	100	Avge	Ct/St
	J. S. Gatting	Brighton	4	8	2	280	64*	0	46.66	1
	L. D. McManus	Poole	2	4	1	120	53*	0	40.00	4
2006	M. A. Carberry	Croydon	16	30	1	1,129	97	0	38.93	4
2013	L. A. Dawson	Swindon	13	23	3	695	140	1	34.75	11
2015	W. R. Smith	Luton	16	30	5	859	93	0	34.36	19
2005	S. M. Ervine	Harare, Zimbabwe.	12	19	4	508	102	1	33.86	14
	G. K. Berg	Cape Town, SA	16	24	3	672	99	0	32.00	11
	R. McLaren§	Kimberley, SA	4	4	0	123	52	0	30.75	1
2013	J. M. Vince	Cuckfield	15	28	2	743	125*	1	28.57	22
2006	J. H. K. Adams	Winchester†	15	29	1	760	136	1	27.14	4
	A. J. A. Wheater	Leytonstone	14	22	1	563	111	1	26.80	26/2
	S. P. Terry	Southampton†	5	10	1	232	62*	0	25.77	4
2012	D. R. Briggs	Newport, IoW†	8	13	2	231	48	0	21.00	1
	A. R. Adams¶	Auckland, NZ.	3	5	1	58	31	0	14.50	3
	F. H. Edwards¶	Gays, Barbados.	8	8	5	32	17*	0	10.66	1
	M. S. Crane	Shoreham-by-Sea	3	4	2	18	13	0	9.00	1
	J. M. Bird§	Paddington, Aust.	6	10	2	54	12	0	6.75	1
2008	J. A. Tomlinson	Winchester†	8	13	3	52	17	0	5.20	1
	B. T. J. Wheal¶	Durban, SA	4	6	1	17	10	0	3.40	1

Also batted: R. A. Stevenson (*Torquay*) (3 matches) 30, 4, 0; C. P. Wood (*Basingstoke†*) (1 match) 48, 30.

† *Born in Hampshire.*   § *Official overseas player.*   ¶ *Other non-England-qualified player.*

BOWLING

	Style	O	M	R	W	BB	5I	Avge
F. H. Edwards	RFM	240.5	38	940	45	6-88	3	20.88
G. K. Berg	RFM	429.1	94	1,181	42	4-64	0	28.11
M. S. Crane	LBG	77	11	336	10	5-35	1	33.60
D. R. Briggs	SLA	251.3	64	711	19	4-74	0	37.42
R. McLaren	RFM	128.5	24	419	11	4-60	0	38.09
L. A. Dawson	SLA	271.2	52	850	22	5-139	1	38.63
J. M. Bird	RFM	207.2	34	755	19	4-146	0	39.73
J. A. Tomlinson	LFM	241	57	754	18	4-37	0	41.88

Also bowled: A. R. Adams (RFM) 120–26–359–9; M. A. Carberry (OB) 7.4–4–22–0; S. M. Ervine (RFM) 125.2–31–443–8; J. S. Gatting (OB) 3–1–7–0; W. R. Smith (OB) 46.4–13–111–3; R. A. Stevenson (RFM) 56.5–9–215–3; J. M. Vince (RM) 19–2–74–1; B. T. J. Wheal (RFM) 94–10–393–8; C. P. Wood (LFM) 29–5–101–2.

LEADING ROYAL LONDON CUP AVERAGES (100 runs/4 wickets)

Batting	Runs	HS	Avge	SR	Ct/St	Bowling		W	BB	Avge	ER
L. A. Dawson ..	324	85	64.80	86.40	1	L. A. Dawson ...		12	6-47	26.33	5.01
J. H. K. Adams .	348	97	58.00	84.87	3	C. P. Wood		9	2-43	30.33	5.25
W. R. Smith ...	183	65	45.75	105.78	2	M. S. Crane		9	4-30	31.33	6.17
M. A. Carberry .	180	66*	30.00	105.88	1	F. H. Edwards ...		8	3-32	31.75	5.40
A. J. A. Wheater	172	111	28.66	89.58	3/3	Yasir Arafat.....		5	3-56	44.00	5.94
J. M. Vince	162	103	27.00	90.50	2						

LEADING NATWEST T20 BLAST AVERAGES (100 runs/18 overs)

Batting	Runs	HS	Avge	SR	Ct/St
S. M. Ervine ..	200	49	25.00	**166.66**	3
A. J. A. Wheater	314	78	28.54	**138.32**	11/5
M. A. Carberry .	456	72*	30.40	**135.71**	1
J. M. Vince	710	107*	59.16	**134.46**	8
J. H. K. Adams .	152	55*	16.88	**132.17**	3
O. A. Shah	402	64	26.80	**129.26**	2

Bowling	W	BB	Avge	ER
D. R. Briggs.....	18	3-21	23.00	**7.01**
W. R. Smith.....	14	3-24	27.21	**7.32**
F. H. Edwards ...	5	2-41	39.60	**7.61**
Yasir Arafat.....	17	4-37	28.64	**8.88**
C. P. Wood	18	4-16	26.33	**8.97**

FIRST-CLASS COUNTY RECORDS

Highest score for	316	R. H. Moore v Warwickshire at Bournemouth .	1937
Highest score against	303*	G. A. Hick (Worcestershire) at Southampton ..	1997
Leading run-scorer	48,892	C. P. Mead (avge 48.84)	1905–36
Best bowling for	9-25	R. M. H. Cottam v Lancashire at Manchester ..	1965
Best bowling against	10-46	W. Hickton (Lancashire) at Manchester	1870
Leading wicket-taker	2,669	D. Shackleton (avge 18.23)	1948–69
Highest total for	714-5 dec	v Nottinghamshire at Southampton	2005
Highest total against	742	by Surrey at The Oval	1909
Lowest total for	15	v Warwickshire at Birmingham	1922
Lowest total against	23	by Yorkshire at Middlesbrough	1965

LIST A COUNTY RECORDS

Highest score for	177	C. G. Greenidge v Glamorgan at Southampton .	1975
Highest score against	203	A. D. Brown (Surrey) at Guildford	1997
Leading run-scorer	12,034	R. A. Smith (avge 42.97)	1983–2003
Best bowling for	7-30	P. J. Sainsbury v Norfolk at Southampton.....	1965
Best bowling against	7-22	J. R. Thomson (Middlesex) at Lord's	1981
Leading wicket-taker	411	C. A. Connor (avge 25.07).	1984–98
Highest total for	371-4	v Glamorgan at Southampton	1975
Highest total against	358-6	by Surrey at The Oval	2005
Lowest total for	43	v Essex at Basingstoke.	1972
Lowest total against	{ 61	by Somerset at Bath	1973
	61	by Derbyshire at Portsmouth	1990

TWENTY20 COUNTY RECORDS

Highest score for	124*	M. J. Lumb v Essex v Southampton	2009
Highest score against	116*	L. J. Wright (Sussex) at Southampton	2014
Leading run-scorer	2,688	M. A. Carberry (avge 31.62)	2006–15
Best bowling for	5-14	A. D. Mascarenhas v Sussex at Hove	2004
Best bowling against	5-21	A. J. Hollioake (Surrey) at Southampton......	2003
Leading wicket-taker	119	D. R. Briggs (avge 19.40)	2010–15
Highest total for	225-2	v Middlesex at Southampton	2006
Highest total against	220-4	by Somerset at Taunton	2010
Lowest total for	85	v Sussex at Southampton	2008
Lowest total against	67	by Sussex at Hove	2004

ADDRESS

The Ageas Bowl, Botley Road, West End, Southampton SO30 3XH; 023 8047 2002; enquiries@ageasbowl.com; www.ageasbowl.com.

OFFICIALS

Captain 2015 J. H. K. Adams
2016 J. M. Vince
Cricket operations manager T. M. Tremlett
Director of cricket G. W. White
First-team coach D. M. Benkenstein
Academy director C. R. M. Freeston

President N. E. J. Pocock
Chairman R. G. Bransgrove
Chief executive D. Mann
Chairman, members committee T. P. Crump
Head groundsman K. McDermott
Scorer K. R. Baker

HAMPSHIRE v LOUGHBOROUGH MCCU

At Southampton, April 2–4. Drawn. Toss: Loughborough MCCU. First-class debuts: R. N. Gamble, Hasan Azad, G. K. R. McKinley, I. Prowse, R. G. White, S. G. Whittingham. County debut: G. K. Berg.

A Loughborough team containing six first-class debutants could not contain Hampshire. Carberry lofted the match's second ball for six, from Basil Akram, and the runs flowed: Akram, on Hampshire's books, and new-ball partner Stuart Whittingham endured combined figures of one for 196 from 29 overs. Carberry reached a century from 104 deliveries, Vince from 93. Hampshire declared on their overnight 474, but rain allowed just 25 overs on the second day, which ended with the students three down for 88. They had reached 131 for five when spinners Dawson and Briggs grabbed five for 18, including four tail-end ducks, leaving Michael Burgess marooned on 34 not out. Adams, the sole failure of Hampshire's first innings, was in sight of a first century against his old university when Nitish Kumar had him lbw. Loughborough's opening pair suffered again.

Close of play: first day, Hampshire 474-4 (Dawson 58, Wheater 5); second day, Loughborough MCCU 88-3 (Kumar 20, Prowse 4).

Hampshire

M. A. Carberry b Gamble	146		
*J. H. K. Adams c White b Whittingham	10	– (1) lbw b Kumar	98
W. R. Smith run out	89		
J. M. Vince c Gamble b Kumar	140		
L. A. Dawson not out	58		
†A. J. A. Wheater not out	5	– (2) lbw b McKinley	45
S. M. Ervine (did not bat)		– (3) lbw b Gamble	10
G. K. Berg (did not bat)		– (4) b Prowse	2
C. P. Wood (did not bat)		– (5) not out	52
D. R. Briggs (did not bat)		– (6) not out	25
B 3, l-b 2, w 3, n-b 18	26	B 1, w 3	4

1/48 (2) 2/248 (1)   (4 wkts dec, 81 overs) 474   1/117 (2)   (4 wkts dec, 51 overs) 236
3/281 (3) 4/463 (4)   2/132 (3) 3/143 (4)
4/179 (1)

J. A. Tomlinson did not bat.

Akram 17–1–119–0; Whittingham 12–0–77–1; McKinley 12–0–63–0; Gamble 23–3–113–1; Prowse 12–1–59–0; Kumar 5–0–38–1. *Second innings*—Akram 4–0–35–0; Whittingham 6–0–32–0; Gamble 19–8–41–1; McKinley 7–0–42–1; Prowse 10–1–50–1; Kumar 5–0–35–1.

Loughborough MCCU

*A. K. Patel c Wheater b Wood	16		G. K. R. McKinley lbw b Dawson	0
M. T. Best b Ervine	23		R. N. Gamble lbw b Dawson	0
Hasan Azad c Wheater b Berg	21		S. G. Whittingham c Ervine b Briggs	0
N. R. Kumar lbw b Tomlinson	28		N-b	8
I. Prowse c Wheater b Tomlinson	15			
M. G. K. Burgess not out	34			149
†R. G. White b Briggs	4		1/24 (1) 2/62 (2) 3/76 (3) (47.3 overs)	149
B. M. R. Akram lbw b Dawson	0		4/107 (4) 5/108 (5) 6/131 (7)	
			7/140 (8) 8/146 (9) 9/148 (10) 10/149 (11)	

Wood 9–1–44–1; Tomlinson 11–4–24–2; Berg 13–3–37–1; Ervine 6–1–29–1; Briggs 6.3–2–12–2; Dawson 2–0–3–3.

Umpires: B. J. Debenham and M. J. Saggers.

HAMPSHIRE v SUSSEX

At Southampton, April 12–15. Sussex won by 92 runs. Sussex 22pts, Hampshire 3pts. Toss: Sussex.

At the close of the third day it looked as if Sussex might have miscalculated. On a wicket showing few signs of deterioration, Joyce had waived the follow-on, and Hampshire – who trailed by 213 on first innings – were 181 for four, needing another 197 for a stirring victory on their return to Division

One. Spearheaded by Carberry's belligerence, they had shown no inclination to block out a draw. Much depended on Smith and Wheater making a sound start next morning, but Hobden removed both early on – and Hampshire lost their last six wickets before lunch. Brown's first-innings hundred had led Sussex's recovery from 128 for five, and Wright's twin half-centuries seemed to put them in control. Just as important was their new pace attack: Shahzad and Mills had joined Magoffin and Hobden over the winter. Hampshire had been 95 for seven on the second day, but secured a batting point thanks to an eighth-wicket stand of 109 between Ervine and Wood.

Close of play: first day, Sussex 300-6 (Brown 85, Shahzad 12); second day, Hampshire 220-9 (Ervine 57); third day, Hampshire 181-4 (Smith 22, Wheater 11).

Sussex

C. D. Nash b Berg	11	– (2) lbw b Wood	21
L. W. P. Wells b Tomlinson	0	– (1) c Vince b Tomlinson	14
M. H. Yardy c Wheater b Berg	6	– c Wheater b Tomlinson	0
*E. C. Joyce c Ervine b Briggs	42	– c Briggs b Berg	14
C. Cachopa b Smith b Wood	41	– c Wheater b Tomlinson	4
L. J. Wright c Dawson b Tomlinson	96	– c Wheater b Briggs	61
†B. C. Brown not out	144	– c Dawson b Tomlinson	0
A. Shahzad b Berg	35	– c Smith b Briggs	28
S. J. Magoffin c Berg b Briggs	41	– b Briggs	7
T. S. Mills b Briggs	1	– b Dawson	4
M. E. Hobden b Briggs	12	– not out	0
B 9, l-b 6	15	L-b 11	11

1/7 (2) 2/17 (1) 3/22 (3)   (142.4 overs) 444   1/24 (1) 2/24 (3)   (53 overs) 164
4/92 (4) 5/128 (5) 6/274 (6)   3/47 (4) 4/55 (5)
7/347 (8) 8/420 (9) 9/422 (10)   5/67 (5) 6/71 (7) 7/144 (8)
10/444 (11)   110 overs: 343-6   8/153 (6) 9/164 (10) 10/164 (9)

Tomlinson 27–5–95–2; Ervine 21–5–65–0; Berg 28–5–73–3; Wood 20–3–71–1; Briggs 32.4–9–74–4; Dawson 10–2–28–0; Vince 3–0–19–0; Carberry 1–0–4–0. *Second innings*— Tomlinson 12–3–37–4; Ervine 4–1–17–0; Berg 11–2–25–1; Wood 9–2–30–1; Briggs 11–2–27–3; Dawson 6–1–17–1.

Hampshire

M. A. Carberry lbw b Shahzad	25	– c Joyce b Yardy	79
L. A. Dawson lbw b Hobden	22	– (5) b Shahzad	30
W. R. Smith c Yardy b Shahzad	0	– c Brown b Hobden	23
J. M. Vince c Brown b Magoffin	37	– c Joyce b Shahzad	9
†A. J. A. Wheater c Joyce b Hobden	0	– (6) b Hobden	12
*J. H. K. Adams c Brown b Shahzad	4	– (2) b Mills	24
S. M. Ervine not out	66	– c Cachopa b Wells	42
G. K. Berg b Magoffin	0	– c Wright b Shahzad	14
C. P. Wood c Wright b Mills	48	– c Brown b Magoffin	30
D. R. Briggs c Joyce b Mills	4	– not out	10
J. A. Tomlinson run out	1	– b Wells	6
B 14, l-b 2, w 6, n-b 2	24	B 15, l-b 8, n-b 10	33

1/47 (1) 2/47 (3) 3/57 (3)   (50 overs) 231   1/76 (2) 2/145 (1)   (65.3 overs) 285
4/58 (5) 5/63 (6) 6/95 (4)   3/154 (4) 4/158 (5)
7/95 (8) 8/204 (9) 9/220 (10) 10/231 (11)   5/182 (3) 6/191 (6) 7/234 (8)
                                                              8/244 (7) 9/270 (9) 10/285 (11)

Magoffin 14–3–53–2; Shahzad 12–1–54–3; Hobden 9–1–55–2; Mills 9–2–28–2; Nash 6–0–25–0. *Second innings*—Magoffin 18–1–67–1; Shahzad 16–2–63–3; Hobden 11–2–54–2; Mills 11–1–37–1; Yardy 5–1–17–1; Wells 4.3–1–24–2.

Umpires: R. J. Evans and A. G. Wharf.

At Birmingham, April 19–22. HAMPSHIRE drew with WARWICKSHIRE.

HAMPSHIRE v NOTTINGHAMSHIRE

At Southampton, April 26–29. Drawn. Hampshire 10pts, Nottinghamshire 11pts. Toss: Hampshire.

Nottinghamshire had the better of the first three days but, with rain allowing less than ten overs on the last, they could not press home their advantage. Despite Hampshire's winter signings Berg and Andre Adams, against his former county, sharing six wickets in the first innings, Hales hit a century; he later added 94 before a leading edge denied him a third hundred in April, and now had 639 from eight first-class innings. Hampshire, who had chosen to bowl, trailed by 95 at the halfway stage, after Nottinghamshire's teenage left-arm pace bowler Luke Wood picked up three wickets in his second Championship appearance. Runs then came at five an over as the visitors looked to strengthen their position: Hales and Brendan Taylor added 164 for the second wicket in 31. In theory, Nottinghamshire's overnight declaration gave them at least 96 overs on a benign pitch to bowl out Hampshire, who needed 392. But the weather had the last word.

Close of play: first day, Nottinghamshire 301-6 (Hales 136, Gidman 22); second day, Hampshire 167-4 (Smith 25, Wheater 5); third day, Nottinghamshire 296-4 (J. W. A. Taylor 53, Wessels 9).

Nottinghamshire

S. J. Mullaney c Wheater b Ervine	66	– lbw b Berg	23
B. R. M. Taylor b Briggs	24	– lbw b Dawson	103
A. D. Hales b A. R. Adams	141	– c and b Dawson	94
J. W. A. Taylor c Ervine b Dawson	10	– not out	53
S. R. Patel c Dawson b A. R. Adams	4	– c Berg b Briggs	8
M. H. Wessels c Dawson b Berg	17	– not out	9
*†C. M. W. Read c A. R. Adams b Berg	4		
W. R. S. Gidman c Wheater b A. R. Adams	34		
V. D. Philander c Dawson b Berg	1		
L. Wood not out	26		
J. T. Ball b Dawson	26		
B 8, l-b 6, n-b 4	18	B 4, l-b 2	6

1/61 (2) 2/145 (1) 3/186 (4) (120.4 overs) 371 1/35 (1) (4 wkts dec, 59 overs) 296
4/205 (5) 5/251 (6) 6/261 (7) 2/199 (2) 3/254 (3)
7/311 (3) 8/312 (9) 9/324 (8) 4/269 (5)
10/371 (11) 110 overs: 337-9

Tomlinson 25–8–69–0; Berg 27–5–88–3; Ervine 10–2–29–1; A. R. Adams 30–6–93–3; Briggs 22–8–53–1; Dawson 6.4–1–25–2. *Second innings*—Tomlinson 7–1–41–0; Berg 10–2–29–1; Ervine 7–1–32–0; A. R. Adams 11–1–51–0; Briggs 12–0–70–1; Dawson 12–0–67–2.

Hampshire

*J. H. K. Adams c Read b Wood	61	– not out	10
L. A. Dawson b Philander	4	– not out	19
M. A. Carberry c Patel b Wood	30		
J. M. Vince run out	32		
W. R. Smith b Wood	35		
†A. J. A. Wheater lbw b Gidman	14		
S. M. Ervine c Mullaney b Patel	31		
G. K. Berg c Read b Mullaney	1		
D. R. Briggs c Mullaney b Philander	18		
A. R. Adams b Ball	31		
J. A. Tomlinson not out	0		
L-b 5, n-b 14	19		

1/5 (2) 2/71 (3) 3/129 (1) (95.1 overs) 276 (no wkt, 9.4 overs) 29
4/142 (4) 5/176 (6) 6/196 (5)
7/197 (8) 8/229 (9) 9/276 (7) 10/276 (10)

Philander 23–2–58–2; Wood 22–6–68–3; Gidman 21–5–46–1; Ball 5–1–26–1; Mullaney 10.1–2–41–1; Patel 14–4–32–1. *Second innings*—Wood 5–1–17–0; Philander 4.4–1–12–0.

Umpires: N. G. C. Cowley and S. J. O'Shaughnessy.

At Leeds, May 10–13. HAMPSHIRE lost to YORKSHIRE by 305 runs.

HAMPSHIRE v MIDDLESEX

At Southampton, May 17–20. Drawn. Hampshire 11pts, Middlesex 10pts. Toss: Middlesex. First-class debut: B. Wheal.

Come the end of this match, another marred by rain, Middlesex were sitting on top of Division One, and Hampshire, without a win in five, had gone bottom. Yet once Franklin – captaining Middlesex because Adam Voges had joined the Australians in the Caribbean – had chosen to field, Hampshire enjoyed the better of the contest. Adams, Carberry and Will Smith all passed 60 on a greenish wicket, before Berg – released by Middlesex in 2014 – made a breezy half-century. Dexter claimed the third five-for of his career. Middlesex stumbled to 152 for five, with Brad Wheal, an 18-year-old from Durban on a British passport, bowling Robson with a beauty in his third over, but having no more success. They needed another 112 to prevent the follow-on, but Compton came to the rescue with his first century since returning from Somerset during the winter. He batted almost six hours before being seventh out at 269, the task of making Hampshire bat again safely achieved. Roland-Jones and Finn added 75 for the last wicket, limiting the deficit to 51. With barely more than two innings completed over three days, Hampshire batted out the fourth.

Close of play: first day, Hampshire 295-5 (Smith 52, Ervine 7); second day, Middlesex 102-3 (Compton 32); third day, Hampshire 4-0 (Adams 0, Dawson 4).

Hampshire

*J. H. K. Adams b Harris	61	– c Simpson b Harris	37
L. A. Dawson c Simpson b Dexter	36	– c Simpson b Dexter	19
M. A. Carberry c Franklin b Harris	67	– c sub (N. A. Sowter) b Franklin	57
J. M. Vince c Dexter b Harris	27	– c Franklin b Rayner	32
†A. J. A. Wheater lbw b Finn	7	– c Simpson b Robson	13
S. M. Ervine b Roland-Jones	8	– not out	1
G. K. Berg c Gubbins b Dexter	50		
F. H. Edwards c Finn b Dexter	1		
B. Wheal not out	3		
J. A. Tomlinson c Roland-Jones b Dexter	17		
W. R. Smith c Simpson b Dexter	93	– not out	15
B 14, l-b 6, w 9, n-b 14	43	L-b 1, n-b 10	11

1/85 (2) 2/160 (1) 3/209 (4)   (130.2 overs) 413   1/34 (2)   (5 wkts dec, 79 overs) 185
4/235 (3) 5/270 (6) 6/297 (7)   2/74 (1) 3/133 (3)
7/388 (8) 8/392 (5) 9/393 (9)   4/159 (4) 5/184 (6)
10/413 (11)   110 overs: 336-6

Finn 29–8–84–1; Roland-Jones 28–9–66–1; Harris 22–4–91–2; Dexter 27.2–7–64–5; Rayner 20–4–72–1; Franklin 4–0–16–0. *Second innings*—Finn 11–3–27–0; Roland-Jones 13–2–38–0; Harris 14–4–35–1; Dexter 8–0–17–1; Rayner 15–5–14–1; Franklin 7–0–21–1; Burns 5–0–14–0; Gubbins 3–1–10–0; Robson 3–0–8–1.

Middlesex

S. D. Robson b Wheal	10	T. S. Roland-Jones c Wheal b Ervine	61
N. R. T. Gubbins lbw b Edwards	16	S. T. Finn not out	18
N. R. D. Compton lbw b Dawson	117		
J. A. Burns c Wheater b Ervine	38	B 11, l-b 3	14
*J. E. C. Franklin lbw b Edwards	8		
N. J. Dexter lbw b Berg	14	1/17 (1) 2/33 (2) (118.2 overs) 362
†J. A. Simpson c Carberry b Ervine	36	3/102 (4) 4/117 (5) 5/152 (6)
O. P. Rayner c Wheater b Edwards	29	6/211 (7) 7/269 (3) 8/270 (9)
J. A. R. Harris c Vince b Edwards	1	9/287 (8) 10/362 (10) 110 overs: 331-9

Tomlinson 20–7–35–0; Wheal 20–2–97–1; Berg 20–8–34–1; Edwards 22–1–100–4; Ervine 16.2–7–37–3; Dawson 20–4–45–1.

Umpires: R. J. Bailey and I. J. Gould.

HAMPSHIRE v WORCESTERSHIRE

At Southampton, May 31–June 3. Drawn. Hampshire 7pts, Worcestershire 13pts. Toss: Worcestershire. First-class debuts: E. G. Barnard, J. M. Clarke. Championship debut: C. Munro.

Trailing by 181 on first innings, Hampshire had to see out the last day to avoid defeat. At 173 for six, it looked as if Worcestershire might translate dominance into victory, only for Will Smith, nursing a hand injury, and Berg to bat 21 overs to reach safety. In fact, Worcestershire had been denied as much by rain as by their opponents: swathes of the first and third days were lost. Leach continued his good form by taking five Hampshire wickets in the first innings and four in the second to finish with career-best figures of nine for 152, while debutant Ed Barnard – whose father Andy is in charge of cricket at Shrewsbury School – claimed three for 88. Also making his debut, and also born (though not educated) in Shrewsbury, was Barnard's England Under-19 colleague Joe Clarke. Hampshire had struggled after being put in on a wicket that helped the quicks. Mitchell hit his first century since the previous July, but to little avail. Hampshire's coach, Dale Benkenstein, said his team's performance was the worst since he took over at the start of the 2014 season.

Close of play: first day, Hampshire 119-4 (Vince 2); second day, Worcestershire 221-3 (Mitchell 80, Munro 4); third day, Hampshire 1-0 (Adams 1, Dawson 0).

Hampshire

*J. H. K. Adams lbw b Leach	48	– lbw b Leach	47
L. A. Dawson c Mitchell b Barnard	39	– c Cox b Leach	7
M. A. Carberry c Cox b Shantry	14	– c Oliver b Shantry	6
J. A. Tomlinson lbw b Leach	5		
J. M. Vince b Leach	8	– (4) lbw b Barnard	12
W. R. Smith b Munro	40	– (5) not out	64
†A. J. A. Wheater c Cox b Morris	15	– (6) b Leach	52
S. M. Ervine c Cox b Barnard	17	– (7) c Fell b Leach	8
G. K. Berg not out	10	– (8) not out	32
D. R. Briggs c Gidman b Leach	7		
B. Wheal c Cox b Leach	0		
B 5, l-b 5, n-b 9	19	B 8, l-b 9	17

1/88 (2) 2/112 (3) 3/114 (1)   (79 overs) 222   1/10 (2)   (6 wkts, 90 overs) 245
4/119 (4) 5/134 (5) 6/170 (7)   2/30 (3) 3/83 (4)
7/201 (6) 8/205 (8) 9/222 (10) 10/222 (11)   4/83 (1) 5/151 (6) 6/173 (7)

Morris 18–5–43–1; Leach 22–4–63–5; Shantry 19–6–46–1; Barnard 17–5–50–2; Munro 3–0–10–1. *Second innings*—Morris 23–6–40–0; Leach 28–6–89–4; Shantry 20–6–40–1; Barnard 13–3–38–1; Munro 5–2–19–0; Mitchell 1–0–2–0.

Worcestershire

*D. K. H. Mitchell not out	142	†O. B. Cox not out	69
R. K. Oliver c Smith b Berg	33	B 14, l-b 12, n-b 16	42
T. C. Fell c Dawson b Berg	48		
A. P. R. Gidman c Vince b Wheal	29	1/62 (2) (5 wkts dec, 96 overs) 403
C. Munro c sub (L. D. McManus) b Briggs	34	2/156 (3) 3/214 (4)
J. M. Clarke c sub (L. D. McManus) b Briggs	6	4/267 (5) 5/289 (6)

J. Leach, E. G. Barnard, J. D. Shantry and C. A. J. Morris did not bat.

Tomlinson 22–2–77–0; Wheal 14–3–76–1; Berg 22–5–66–2; Ervine 16–3–89–0; Briggs 21–7–67–2; Dawson 1–0–2–0.

Umpires: M. R. Benson and M. A. Gough.

At Hove, June 7–9. HAMPSHIRE beat SUSSEX by six wickets.

HAMPSHIRE v SOMERSET

At Southampton, June 21–23. Somerset won by nine wickets. Somerset 22pts, Hampshire 3pts. Toss: Somerset.

Somerset's decisive three-day victory was the more remarkable given the loss of the second morning to rain. The pitch, though, was at its most awkward when play resumed that afternoon and, of the 16 wickets which fell in 65 overs, 12 were Hampshire's. Some were undone by uneven bounce or lateral movement, others by a combination of the two. Somerset's Craig Overton, the most adept at exploiting the conditions, claimed four in each innings. Life for the Somerset batsmen had been a fraction easier on the opening day, when Trescothick chose to bat, and they reached stumps at 310 for six. (One of the overnight batsmen was Michael Bates, the highly rated wicketkeeper released by Hampshire in 2014; he was given a generous reception, and later held five catches.) Next afternoon came the rash of wickets, first for Berg, then Thomas – who took three in his first five overs – and later Overton. Hampshire were dealt with in 43 overs. Armed with a lead of 199, Trescothick enforced the follow-on. By the close, Hampshire were two down and still 158 in arrears. Wheater and Berg offered some resistance on the third day, and Ervine, batting at No. 11 with a broken finger, survived ten balls. But Somerset sped home in little more than an hour.

Close of play: first day, Somerset 310-6 (Gregory 5, Bates 8); second day, Hampshire 41-2 (Carberry 16, Tomlinson 0).

Somerset

*M. E. Trescothick b Berg	53	– lbw b Briggs	35
T. B. Abell b Dawson	88	– not out	21
J. G. Myburgh c Berg b Bird	23	– not out	6
J. C. Hildreth lbw b Tomlinson	76		
J. Allenby c Terry b Dawson	9		
P. D. Trego b Ervine	21		
L. Gregory c Ervine b Berg	17		
†M. D. Bates b Bird	14		
C. Overton c Carberry b Berg	17		
Abdur Rehman c Dawson b Berg	0		
A. C. Thomas not out	1		
B 16, l-b 5, n-b 6	27	N-b 2	2

1/92 (1) 2/142 (3) 3/202 (2)   (105.1 overs) 346   1/57 (1)   (1 wkt, 17 overs) 64
4/214 (5) 5/286 (6) 6/294 (4)
7/328 (7) 8/328 (8) 9/345 (10) 10/346 (9)

Tomlinson 14–2–63–1; Bird 27–8–75–2; Berg 24.1–5–64–4; Ervine 9–4–25–1; Briggs 13–4–39–0; Dawson 18–3–59–2. *Second innings*—Tomlinson 6–1–26–0; Bird 6–1–27–0; Dawson 3–1–8–0; Briggs 2–1–3–1.

Hampshire

*J. H. K. Adams c Abell b Thomas	1	– b Thomas	5
S. P. Terry lbw b Thomas	8	– b Trego	19
M. A. Carberry c Bates b Thomas	6	– c Gregory b Trego	28
L. A. Dawson c Abdur Rehman b Overton	25	– (5) lbw b Trego	4
W. R. Smith c Gregory b Overton	4	– (6) c Overton b Abdur Rehman	37
†A. J. A. Wheater b Gregory	13	– (7) b Overton	49
S. M. Ervine b Allenby	23	– (11) not out	3
G. K. Berg c Trego b Overton	38	– c Bates b Overton	86
D. R. Briggs c Hildreth b Overton	8	– c Bates b Overton	15
J. M. Bird b Gregory	11	– c Bates b Allenby	0
J. A. Tomlinson not out	0	– (4) c Bates b Overton	5
B 3, l-b 6, w 1	10	B 5, l-b 4, n-b 2	11

1/6 (1) 2/18 (3) 3/21 (2)   (43.2 overs) 147   1/11 (1) 2/39 (2)   (79.3 overs) 262
4/36 (5) 5/65 (4) 6/65 (6)   3/64 (4) 4/64 (3)
7/105 (7) 8/131 (8) 9/147 (9) 10/147 (10)   5/69 (5) 6/144 (7) 7/180 (6)
                                            8/241 (9) 9/244 (10) 10/262 (8)

Thomas 13–3–38–3; Gregory 11.2–2–54–2; Overton 9–4–24–4; Allenby 7–3–14–1; Abdur Rehman 3–1–8–0. *Second innings*—Gregory 17–2–62–0; Thomas 11–2–28–1; Overton 18.3–5–57–4; Trego 13–2–49–3; Allenby 5–0–16–1; Abdur Rehman 15–3–41–1.

Umpires: N. L. Bainton and M. J. Saggers.

At Lord's, June 28–July 1. HAMPSHIRE lost to MIDDLESEX by nine wickets.

At Worcester, July 6–9. HAMPSHIRE lost to WORCESTERSHIRE by an innings and 33 runs.

HAMPSHIRE v DURHAM

At Southampton, July 19–22. Drawn. Hampshire 10pts, Durham 11pts. Toss: Durham. First-class debuts: M. S. Crane; G. Clark.

The last-wicket pair of Lewis McManus and Mason Crane, with just one previous appearance between them, prevented a fourth successive defeat for Hampshire. McManus, aged 20, and Crane, an 18-year-old leg-spinner from Lancing College who claimed five wickets on debut, came together at 167 for nine, and frustrated Durham for 32 deliveries. It wasn't just the batsmen who hindered them: after Durham had reduced Hampshire to 39 for five, rain cut nine overs from the final afternoon. Collingwood, though, did drop Crane in the slips, before McManus confidently hit Rushworth for four to reach a maiden fifty from the last ball of the match, his 166th. Durham's early domination had been built around a century from Muchall, and they led by 114 once Hampshire succumbed to Rushworth, who achieved an unusual hat-trick, spread across two days and three overs. On the third afternoon, he dismissed Tomlinson with the last ball of the 109th over, polished off the first innings with the first of the 111th, and then on the final morning removed Carberry with the first ball of the second innings. Rushworth was unaware of his feat until his father told him during the fourth-day lunch break. Hampshire were captained by Vince, after Adams chose to concentrate on his batting – but made only five and 12.

Close of play: first day, Durham 278-6 (Muchall 85, Arshad 19); second day, Hampshire 119-3 (Carberry 57, Smith 27); third day, Durham 61-1 (Stoneman 39, Borthwick 4).

Durham

M. D. Stoneman lbw b Bird	0	– b Crane		88
G. Clark lbw b Tomlinson	8	– c Dawson b Crane		15
S. G. Borthwick lbw b Dawson	49	– b Crane		39
*P. D. Collingwood c Adams b Tomlinson	8	– (5) not out		29
†M. J. Richardson lbw b Bird	91	– (6) not out		5
G. J. Muchall c Smith b Dawson	145			
R. D. Pringle c Vince b Bird	0			
U. Arshad c Vince b Berg	60			
J. W. Hastings c Crane	22	– (4) c Smith b Crane		7
C. Rushworth not out	12			
G. Onions c Bird b Dawson	0			
B 12, l-b 14	26	B 7		7

1/0 (1) 2/14 (2) 3/59 (4) 4/91 (3) (131.5 overs) 421
5/233 (5) 6/233 (7) 7/361 (8)
8/409 (9) 9/409 (6) 10/421 (11) 110 overs: 327-6

1/49 (2) (4 wkts dec, 44 overs) 190
2/120 (3) 3/132 (4)
4/184 (1)

Bird 29–7–105–3; Tomlinson 25–8–71–2; Berg 22–5–61–1; Dawson 28.5–6–70–3; Crane 24–4–75–1; Carberry 2–1–5–0; Smith 1–0–8–0. *Second innings*—Bird 13–1–56–0; Tomlinson 2–0–12–0; Dawson 13–3–43–0; Crane 16–3–72–4.

Hampshire

M. A. Carberry c Collingwood b Pringle	73	– c Richardson b Rushworth	0
J. H. K. Adams lbw b Rushworth	5	– c Richardson b Rushworth	12
L. A. Dawson c Arshad b Hastings	9	– lbw b Rushworth	20
*J. M. Vince c Collingwood b Pringle	19	– lbw b Pringle	0
W. R. Smith lbw b Borthwick	85	– c Collingwood b Pringle	0
J. S. Gatting c Collingwood b Rushworth	43	– lbw b Pringle	32
†L. D. McManus c Muchall b Rushworth	29	– not out	53
G. K. Berg c Hastings b Rushworth	31	– b Borthwick	36
J. M. Bird lbw b Rushworth	2	– lbw b Pringle	12
J. A. Tomlinson b Rushworth	0	– lbw b Pringle	0
M. S. Crane not out	0	– not out	5
B 1, l-b 8, n-b 2	11	B 4, l-b 3, n-b 2	9

1/17 (2) 2/47 (3) 3/68 (4)		(110.1 overs) 307	1/0 (1) 2/32 (3) (9 wkts, 66 overs) 179
4/151 (1) 5/216 (6) 6/266 (5)			3/33 (4) 4/35 (2)
7/292 (8) 8/306 (9) 9/306 (10)			5/39 (5) 6/82 (6) 7/135 (8)
10/307 (8)		110 overs: 307-9	8/153 (9) 9/167 (10)

Rushworth 22.1–8–39–6; Onions 15–4–53–0; Hastings 17–6–30–1; Pringle 27–9–79–2; Arshad 7–1–21–0; Borthwick 22–3–76–1. *Second innings*—Rushworth 13–3–39–3; Onions 3–1–11–0; Hastings 8–1–22–0; Pringle 26–8–63–5; Borthwick 16–5–37–1.

Umpires: N. G. B. Cook and C. K. Nandan.

HAMPSHIRE v WARWICKSHIRE

At Southampton, August 7–10. Hampshire won by 216 runs. Toss: Hampshire. Hampshire 21pts, Warwickshire 3pts.

Hampshire's only home victory of the season came thanks to the hostility of the experienced Edwards and the guile of youthful wrist-spinner Crane. After Hampshire had recovered from 102 for five to reach a steady 285, Edwards consistently coaxed life from an unblemished surface to hep scupper Warwickshire's reply while Crane removed five of their top six. They were 78 for one before Crane bowled Chopra, and from there the innings became a procession, the next nine wickets adding just 47. Buttressed by a lead of 160, Hampshire hastened towards a declaration: Carberry and Vince put on 180 for the second wicket, before Gatting helped Vince, who made his sole hundred in the 2015 Championship, add 79 in under ten overs. Facing a target of 444, Warwickshire showed slightly more application. But Edwards snatched another four wickets to claim match figures of nine for 87. Hampshire remained bottom, though only five points behind Worcestershire, in seventh; Warwickshire's Championship hopes were fading fast.

Close of play: first day, Hampshire 255-8 (Berg 42, Crane 12); second day, Hampshire 82-1 (Carberry 34, Vince 34); third day, Warwickshire 161-6 (Clarke 53, Woakes 4).

YOUNGEST HAMPSHIRE PLAYERS TO TAKE A FIRST-CLASS FIVE-FOR

Yrs	Days		
17	173	A. S. Kennedy (6-41) v Gentlemen of Philadelphia at Southampton	1908
18	**171**	**M. S. Crane (5-35) v Warwickshire at Southampton**	**2015**
18	190	T. Sutherland (6-111) v Warwickshire at Southampton	1898
18	191	A. S. Kennedy (6-45) v Sussex at Hove	1909
18	233	R. M. H. Cottam (5-74) v Middlesex at Lord's	1963
18	248	R. M. H. Cottam (6-55) v Essex at Ilford	1963
18	279	T. A. Dean (5-58) v Yorkshire at Bournemouth	1939
18	299	Aaqib Javed (6-91) v Nottinghamshire at Nottingham	1991
18	307	R. M. H. Cottam (6-10) v Leicestershire at Portsmouth	1963
18	310	A. D. Mascarenhas (6-88) v Glamorgan at Southampton	1996
18	320	Aaqib Javed (5-49) v Northamptonshire at Northampton	1991

Hampshire

M. A. Carberry c Ambrose b Rankin	36	– c Ambrose b Rankin 91
J. H. K. Adams lbw b Woakes	0	– c Westwood b Woakes 6
*J. M. Vince c Chopra b Woakes	1	– not out 125
W. R. Smith c Patel b Rankin	43	– c Ambrose b Rankin 2
J. S. Gatting c Chopra b Patel	43	– not out 31
L. A. Dawson lbw b Clarke	7	
†A. J. A. Wheater c Evans b Rankin	57	
G. K. Berg c Rankin b Clarke	54	
J. M. Bird c Ambrose b Barker	3	
M. S. Crane c Trott b Clarke	13	
F. H. Edwards not out	17	
B 8, l-b 3	11	B 11, l-b 12, w 5 28

1/2 (2) 2/4 (3) 3/78 (1) (108 overs) 285
4/85 (4) 5/102 (6) 6/194 (5)
7/198 (7) 8/214 (9) 9/267 (8) 10/285 (10)

1/14 (2) (3 wkts dec, 66 overs) 283
2/194 (1) 3/204 (4)

Barker 22–7–50–1; Woakes 13–6–19–2; Rankin 23–6–55–3; Clarke 26–8–66–3; Patel 24–4–84–1. *Second innings*—Barker 12–2–41–0; Woakes 11–3–29–1; Clarke 9–0–44–0; Patel 23–0–100–0; Rankin 10–0–46–2; Trott 1–1–0–0.

Warwickshire

*V. Chopra b Crane	37	– lbw b Berg 11
I. J. Westwood c Berg b Edwards	12	– c Smith b Dawson 53
L. J. Evans c Carberry b Crane	35	– b Bird 0
I. J. L. Trott c Vince b Crane	0	– lbw b Dawson 5
S. R. Hain c Wheater b Crane	5	– lbw b Edwards 11
†T. R. Ambrose lbw b Crane	0	– c Vince b Edwards 16
R. Clarke lbw b Edwards	12	– c Gatting b Bird 55
C. R. Woakes c Wheater b Edwards	4	– c Crane b Smith 42
K. H. D. Barker b Edwards	0	– lbw b Edwards 0
J. S. Patel b Edwards	12	– c Smith b Edwards 10
W. B. Rankin not out	6	– not out 16
L-b 2	2	B 8 8

1/16 (2) 2/78 (1) 3/78 (4) (54 overs) 125
4/86 (5) 5/86 (6) 6/99 (7)
7/105 (8) 8/105 (9) 9/115 (3) 10/125 (10)

1/34 (1) 2/47 (3) (74 overs) 227
3/56 (4) 4/71 (5)
5/91 (2) 6/155 (6) 7/163 (7)
8/168 (9) 9/186 (10) 10/227 (8)

Bird 15–3–34–0; Edwards 14–2–32–5; Berg 9–3–11–0; Dawson 6–2–11–0; Crane 10–2–35–5. *Second innings*—Bird 15–2–50–2; Edwards 19–5–55–4; Berg 4–0–16–1; Dawson 20–5–43–2; Crane 10–2–46–0; Carberry 2–1–1–0; Smith 4–1–8–1.

Umpires: M. Burns and I. J. Gould.

At Chester-le-Street, September 1–3. HAMPSHIRE beat DURHAM by seven wickets.

At Taunton, September 9–12. HAMPSHIRE drew with SOMERSET.

HAMPSHIRE v YORKSHIRE

At Southampton, September 14–17. Yorkshire won by five wickets. Yorkshire 19pts, Hampshire 6pts. Toss: Hampshire.

Hampshire were eighth, 11 points below the two counties tied above them, and Yorkshire were champions, which explains why Vince threw down a gauntlet on the last day, and Gale was happy to pick it up. Vince forfeited Hampshire's second innings and set a target of 304 in 96 overs rather than settle for a rain-ruined draw. The bold move looked as if it might pay off when Yorkshire were 37 for three, but Gale – who made the most of being dropped in the slips on 35 to reach his third hundred of the summer – and Leaning added 190, and victory came with plenty to spare. Yorkshire, who perhaps through Championship celebrations had just lost heavily at Lord's, were not their dominant selves: they allowed Hampshire to run up full batting points for the only time all season, thanks mainly to Dawson's first hundred since 2013. But rain washed away more than 130 overs during the first three days, and ensured either a draw or a contrivance. Defeat meant Hampshire's situation was bleak: 16 points from safety with one game to go.

Close of play: first day, Hampshire 219-4 (Dawson 47, Ervine 26); second day, Yorkshire 82-4 (Lees 31, Bresnan 4); third day, Yorkshire 97-4 (Lees 37, Bresnan 12).

Hampshire

M. A. Carberry c Hodd b Brooks 28	G. K. Berg not out 27
J. H. K. Adams c Lees b Patterson 52	R. A. Stevenson c Hodd b Fisher 4
*J. M. Vince b Bresnan 3	B 8, l-b 9, n-b 10 27
W. R. Smith c Hodd b Brooks. 46	
L. A. Dawson c Hodd b Middlebrook 140	1/74 (1) (9 wkts dec, 108.5 overs) 400
S. M. Ervine st Hodd b Middlebrook 43	2/77 (3) 3/109 (2)
†A. J. A. Wheater c Gale b Brooks 7	4/181 (4) 5/305 (6) 6/320 (7)
R. McLaren c Leaning b Fisher. 23	7/368 (8) 8/374 (5) 9/400 (10)

F. H. Edwards did not bat.

Brooks 22–4–97–3; Fisher 23.5–10–61–2; Patterson 24–8–68–1; Bresnan 22–7–69–1; Middlebrook 16–1–77–2; Lyth 1–0–11–0.

Hampshire forfeited their second innings.

Yorkshire

A. Lyth c Vince b Edwards	0	– run out	12
A. Z. Lees not out	37	– b Edwards.	5
G. S. Ballance c Berg b Stevenson.	30	– c Wheater b Berg	17
*A. W. Gale c Wheater b McLaren	3	– c Adams b Edwards	125
J. A. Leaning c Ervine b McLaren	3	– c Wheater b Edwards	76
T. T. Bresnan not out	12	– not out	35
†A. J. Hodd (did not bat)	–	– not out	17
L-b 3, w 5, n-b 4.	12	L-b 8, w 1, n-b 9.	18

1/0 (1) 2/51 (3) (4 wkts dec, 41.4 overs)	97	1/13 (2) (5 wkts, 91.2 overs)	305
3/58 (4) 4/62 (5)		2/18 (1) 3/37 (3)	
		4/227 (5) 5/264 (4)	

J. D. Middlebrook, S. A. Patterson, J. A. Brooks and M. D. Fisher did not bat.

Edwards 13–3–26–1; McLaren 14.4–3–33–2; Berg 7–2–15–0; Stevenson 7–0–20–1. *Second innings*—Edwards 20–1–74–3; McLaren 21–0–81–0; Berg 10–0–41–1; Stevenson 10–3–26–0; Dawson 25.2–7–63–0; Smith 5–2–12–0.

Umpires: P. J. Hartley and R. T. Robinson. Third umpire: N. G. C. Cowley.

At Nottingham, September 22–25. HAMPSHIRE beat NOTTINGHAMSHIRE by eight wickets. *Hampshire escape relegation when Sussex lose at Leeds.*

KENT

Coles keeps the home fires burning

MARK PENNELL

Kent might have been the only county to spurn the services of a bona fide overseas player in 2015, but the return of Matt Coles felt like the next-best thing. He rejoined the club less than two years after moving to Hampshire and, back among friends, was named Player of the Season.

Coles missed only four matches all summer, and claimed 67 Championship wickets at 23 apiece with his bustling pace. Across the formats, he finished with 100 scalps, which was testament to his work ethic, stamina and – having been sent home for indiscipline from an England Lions tour in Australia along with Ben Stokes in February 2013 – his growing maturity.

Described by Sam Northeast, Kent's new captain, as a "wrecking ball who would run through brick walls for us", Coles briefly wrought destruction with the bat too. On an otherwise disappointing day at The Oval, where Kent lost their Royal London One-Day Cup quarter-final, he smashed Surrey for a 71-ball hundred – his first in List A cricket – including nine sixes.

In the Championship, Coles received useful seam-bowling support from the evergreen Darren Stevens, who sent down more than 400 overs while taking 61 wickets, though to the detriment of his batting; for his unstinting efforts, he was awarded a benefit for 2016. Matt Hunn and Ivan Thomas, and budding all-rounder Calum Haggett – a trio with youth on their side – all chipped in. Preferred for the shorter formats, Mitch Claydon was used only sparingly in four-day cricket; firebrand David Griffiths missed most of the season and underwent back surgery, while left-arm seamer Adam Ball struggled for form.

But, if blame has to be apportioned for Kent's inability to dismiss sides twice – they did so only five times – then the spinners should shoulder much of it. Slow bowlers James Tredwell and Adam Riley took 19 Championship wickets between them. Tredwell, though hugely experienced and effective in the limited-overs formats, lacked any threat in the four-day games, where his 11 wickets cost 40 each; Riley, meanwhile, spent much of the summer trying to regain his action after it was remodelled on the England Performance Programme in Sri Lanka. Joe Denly's leg-spin was underused, while Fabian Cowdrey's round-arm lefties were ignored altogether. There is also Imran Qayyum, a 22-year-old slow left-armer untried in the first-class game, but it is a department Kent needed to strengthen if they were to succeed in their ambition of playing First Division cricket, something they had not done since 2010.

At least their batting had one shining example after a below-par season in which 28 bonus points represented the fewest in Division Two: Northeast's one-day form was a revelation, and was chiefly responsible for the club's pair of white-ball quarter-finals. And, in scoring his only four-day century of the

Dan Mullan, Getty Images

Matt Coles

summer, against Lancashire, he reached 1,000 first-class runs for the first time. The fortunes of Rob Key improved once he relinquished the leadership again – having previously done so after the 2012 season – and he might also have reached four figures had he not missed the final Championship game, against Gloucestershire.

Like Coles, Denly returned from exile, after three seasons at Middlesex. His conversion rate needed work, but he passed 1,000 Championship runs at a respectable average. His opening partner, Daniel Bell-Drummond, hit centuries in the season's first two games at Canterbury, and a stunning 92-ball hundred against the Australians. But Cowdrey, Ben Harmison and Brendan Nash were disappointing. Nash left in August, while Harmison was released. The signing in February of New Zealand opener Tom Latham to play in all formats helped fill the gaps.

Sam Billings kept tidily but, perhaps distracted by international selection, managed only 474 first-class runs, although that did include a maiden Championship century, against Essex at Tunbridge Wells. His understudy, Ryan Davies, opted to join Somerset on a three-year deal. Former England Under-19 keeper Adam Rouse was given a two-year contract. After a stunning run of scores in the Second XI, South African-born Sean Dickson earned a contract, and made a half-century in his second game, at Cardiff. Zak Crawley, a 17-year-old batsman from Bromley and a product of the Academy, and Hugh Bernard, an England Under-19 seamer, won contracts, emphasising Kent's determination to play fearless one-day cricket, and their willingness to give home-grown talent a chance.

In the shorter formats, Kent were usually dangerous. They comfortably topped the NatWest T20 Blast South Group and, but for a last-ball straight-drive that deflected off the stumps and enabled Lancashire to scramble a second, they would have reached finals day for the fourth time. Kent finished fourth in Group B of the Royal London Cup, but Coles's heroics were not enough at The Oval. After troubling England over the winter, Kagiso Rabada, the South African fast bowler, signed up for the first half of the T20 Blast.

The club's once-parlous financial state continued to revive, as they declared pre-tax profits of £1,250,655 for the year ending October 31, 2014. A further boost came in the unlikely shape of a Madness concert at the St Lawrence Ground in September 2015, watched by a crowd of over 12,500. Kent also won a planning appeal for consent to build a complex of retirement flats on the Old Dover Road side of the ground – the third and final stage of Canterbury's redevelopment programme. The ground at Worsley Bridge Road in Beckenham, along with its satellite academy and training facilities for metropolitan Kent, were also upgraded.

Championship attendance: 26,529.

KENT RESULTS

All first-class matches – Played 17: Won 4, Lost 8, Drawn 5.
County Championship matches – Played 16: Won 4, Lost 7, Drawn 5.

LV= County Championship, 7th in Division 2;
NatWest T20 Blast, quarter-finalists; Royal London One-Day Cup, quarter-finalists.

COUNTY CHAMPIONSHIP AVERAGES, BATTING AND FIELDING

Cap		Birthplace	M	I	NO	R	HS	100	Avge	Ct/St
	S. R. Dickson¶	Johannesburg, SA	3	4	2	113	59	0	56.50	0
2012	S. A. Northeast	Ashford†	16	28	3	1,168	139	1	46.72	11
2008	J. L. Denly	Canterbury†	16	29	4	1,023	161*	2	40.92	8
2001	R. W. T. Key	East Dulwich	12	22	0	857	158	2	38.95	1
2015	S. W. Billings	Pembury†	11	17	2	447	100*	1	29.80	31/1
2013	B. P. Nash¶	Attadale, Australia	4	8	0	229	49	0	28.62	0
2005	D. I. Stevens	Leicester	15	23	0	635	92	0	27.60	5
	B. W. Harmison	Ashington	6	9	0	247	123	1	27.44	6
2015	D. J. Bell-Drummond	Lewisham†	16	29	0	767	123	2	26.44	8
	C. J. Haggett	Taunton	11	16	2	345	80	0	24.64	4
	F. K. Cowdrey	Canterbury†	5	9	0	169	54	0	18.77	4
	M. E. Claydon	Fairfield, Australia	6	9	4	88	24	0	17.60	0
2012	M. T. Coles	Maidstone†	14	22	3	277	66	0	14.57	15
	A. E. N. Riley	Sidcup†	8	11	4	97	34	0	13.85	7
	M. D. Hunn	Colchester	7	6	4	26	23*	0	13.00	3
	A. J. Ball	Greenwich†	3	5	0	53	32	0	10.60	4
2007	J. C. Tredwell‡	Ashford†	7	11	0	107	53	0	9.72	13
	R. C. Davies	Thanet†	5	6	0	35	17	0	5.83	9
	I. A. A. Thomas	Greenwich†	10	16	8	27	7*	0	3.37	1

A. J. Blake (*Farnborough*†) (1 match) did not bat.

† *Born in Kent.*   ‡ *ECB contract.*   ¶ *Non-England-qualified player.*

BOWLING

	Style	O	M	R	W	BB	5I	Avge
D. I. Stevens	RM	419.1	100	1,242	61	5-58	2	20.36
M. T. Coles	RFM	433	82	1,574	67	6-55	2	23.49
I. A. A. Thomas	RFM	248.4	53	755	27	4-48	0	27.96
C. J. Haggett	RFM	268	60	792	28	4-43	0	28.28
M. D. Hunn	RFM	163	31	555	18	4-47	0	30.83
M. E. Claydon	RFM	138.5	11	520	13	4-103	0	40.00
J. C. Tredwell	OB	164.5	45	443	11	3-59	0	40.27

Also bowled: A. J. Ball (LFM) 4–0–13–0; J. L. Denly (LBG) 17–2–50–1; A. E. N. Riley (OB) 108.5–13–424–8.

LEADING ROYAL LONDON CUP AVERAGES (100 runs/4 wickets)

Batting	Runs	HS	Avge	SR	Ct/St	**Bowling**	W	BB	Avge	ER
D. J. Bell-Drummond	272	80*	54.40	72.72	5	M. T. Coles	16	4-34	19.00	4.99
S. W. Billings	271	118*	54.20	103.04	8/1	M. E. Claydon	15	4-66	24.26	6.24
A. J. Blake	203	89	50.75	123.78	6	D. I. Stevens	11	4-29	27.72	4.62
M. T. Coles	113	100	37.66	115.30	4	F. K. Cowdrey	5	3-32	35.60	5.08
D. I. Stevens	193	110	32.16	107.22	5	M. D. Hunn	5	2-31	38.20	5.78
S. A. Northeast	198	74	28.28	68.27	4	J. C. Tredwell	6	3-47	54.83	4.76
J. L. Denly	182	78	26.00	92.85	1					
F. K. Cowdrey	102	51	17.00	90.26	6					

LEADING NATWEST T20 BLAST AVERAGES (100 runs/18 overs)

Batting	Runs	HS	Avge	SR	Ct/St
A. J. Blake	304	71*	38.00	167.03	6
S. A. Northeast. . . .	644	114	49.30	152.98	2
D. I. Stevens.	206	90	17.16	151.47	4
J. L. Denly	281	70	23.41	147.89	6
S. W. Billings.	228	46	25.33	133.33	7/3
D. J. Bell-Drummond	338	77	24.14	131.51	4
F. K. Cowdrey	184	42	14.15	127.77	5

Bowling	W	BB	Avge	ER
J. C. Tredwell	7	2-21	34.71	6.94
M. E. Claydon. . .	20	3-16	20.30	7.63
D. I. Stevens	15	4-39	27.53	8.42
F. K. Cowdrey. . .	8	2-15	31.87	8.79
M. T. Coles	17	3-22	25.35	9.36
C. J. Haggett	6	2-12	36.66	10.47

FIRST-CLASS COUNTY RECORDS

Highest score for	332	W. H. Ashdown v Essex at Brentwood	1934
Highest score against	344	W. G. Grace (MCC) at Canterbury	1876
Leading run-scorer	47,868	F. E. Woolley (avge 41.77)	1906–38
Best bowling for	10-30	C. Blythe v Northamptonshire at Northampton .	1907
Best bowling against	10-48	C. H. G. Bland (Sussex) at Tonbridge	1899
Leading wicket-taker	3,340	A. P. Freeman (avge 17.64)	1914–36
Highest total for	803-4 dec	v Essex at Brentwood.	1934
Highest total against	676	by Australians at Canterbury	1921
Lowest total for	18	v Sussex at Gravesend	1867
Lowest total against	16	by Warwickshire at Tonbridge.	1913

LIST A COUNTY RECORDS

Highest score for	146	A. Symonds v Lancashire at Tunbridge Wells .	2004
Highest score against	167*	P. Johnson (Nottinghamshire) at Nottingham . .	1993
Leading run-scorer	7,814	M. R. Benson (avge 31.89)	1980–95
Best bowling for	8-31	D. L. Underwood v Scotland at Edinburgh . . .	1987
Best bowling against	6-5	A. G. Wharf (Glamorgan) at Cardiff	2004
Leading wicket-taker	530	D. L. Underwood (avge 18.93)	1963–87
Highest total for	384-6	v Berkshire at Finchampstead	1994
Highest total against	371-8	by Somerset at Taunton	2014
Lowest total for	60	v Somerset at Taunton	1979
Lowest total against	60	by Derbyshire at Canterbury	2008

TWENTY20 COUNTY RECORDS

Highest score for	114	S. A. Northeast v Somerset at Taunton	2015
Highest score against	151*	C. H. Gayle (Somerset) at Taunton	2015
Leading run-scorer	2,847	D. I. Stevens (avge 30.61).	2005–15
Best bowling for	5-17	Wahab Riaz v Gloucestershire at Beckenham . .	2011
Best bowling against	5-17	G. M. Smith (Essex) at Chelmsford.	2012
Leading wicket-taker	107	J. C. Tredwell (avge 25.76)	2003–15
Highest total for	231-7	v Surrey at The Oval	2015
Highest total against	224-7	by Somerset at Taunton.	2015
Lowest total for	72	v Hampshire at Southampton	2011
Lowest total against	82	by Somerset at Taunton	2010

ADDRESS

St Lawrence Ground, Old Dover Road, Canterbury CT1 3NZ; 01227 456886; kent@ecb.co.uk; www.kentcricket.co.uk.

OFFICIALS

Captain 2015 R. W. T. Key
    2016 S. A. Northeast
Head coach J. C. Adams
High-performance director S. C. Willis
President Lady Kingsdown

Chairman G. M. Kennedy
Chief executive J. A. S. Clifford
Chairman, cricket committee G. W. Johnson
Head groundsman S. Williamson
Scorer L. A. R. Hart

At Canterbury, April 12–14 (not first-class). **Drawn. ‡Kent 394-7 dec** (82.2 overs) (D. J. Bell-Drummond 134, F. K. Cowdrey 51, S. W. Billings 102) **and 364-8 dec** (74 overs) (R. W. T. Key 92, F. K. Cowdrey 78, D. I. Stevens 100; S. G. Whittingham 4-86); **Loughborough MCCU 409-9 dec** (113 overs) (N. R. Kumar 119, M. G. K. Burgess 116, R. N. Gamble 53*; I. A. A. Thomas 3-59, J. L. Denly 3-76). *Bell-Drummond hit a circumspect 134 on an easy-paced pitch, before Billings lit up an otherwise humdrum encounter by reaching three figures from 76 balls. They were matched by Canadian international Nitish Kumar, who hit an elegant, chanceless hundred from 96 deliveries, and Michael Burgess who together steered Loughborough towards a modest lead. Despite scant encouragement for the bowlers, Thomas, a seamer, and part-time leg-spinner Denly (back after three seasons with Middlesex) shared six wickets. On the final day Stevens, who retired out, and Key bullied the student attack.*

At Chelmsford, April 19–21. KENT lost to ESSEX by five wickets.

At Manchester, April 26–29. KENT lost to LANCASHIRE by nine wickets.

KENT v LEICESTERSHIRE

At Canterbury, May 3–6. Drawn. Kent 10pts, Leicestershire 12pts. Toss: Kent. First-class debut: L. J. Hill.

A hard-fought contest ran out of time with both sides eyeing victory. Cosgrove's feisty century, his first since joining Leicestershire as captain, had called into doubt Key's decision to bowl: the lightweight Kent attack conceded 300 in the two sessions possible on the first day, though five for 28 by Stevens next morning limited the damage to 386. Kent relied on eighties from Denly and Northeast, who added 139 for the fourth wicket, before seven fell for 53 as McKay bagged six. Leicestershire, 118 to the good, then stumbled to 86 for seven before being bailed out by the tail. Rain, which snaffled 20 overs on the last day, left Kent with what became 71 overs to make 315. This time they depended on Bell-Drummond, who recorded their first Championship century of the season. McKay pitched in with another couple of wickets, Shreck with four, and the asking-rate proved too steep once Stevens had fallen to a disputed catch at the wicket. In the end, Kent were 42 runs short of victory – and Leicestershire three wickets. In a fiery match, there were 14 lbw dismissals, while Key, after a spat with umpire O'Shaughnessy, was handed three penalty points under the ECB's disciplinary code. He later passed the captaincy to Northeast, and asked not to be considered for the next Championship game.

Close of play: first day, Leicestershire 300-5 (Hill 13, Raine 11); second day, Kent 155-3 (Denly 56, Northeast 38); third day, Leicestershire 189-8 (Taylor 33, Naik 23).

Leicestershire

A. J. Robson c Northeast b Coles	0	– (2) b Stevens		30
M. A. G. Boyce lbw b Coles	17	– (1) lbw b Thomas		4
E. J. H. Eckersley lbw b Coles	67	– b Thomas		4
*M. J. Cosgrove c sub (M. D. Hunn) b Riley	113	– lbw b Claydon		29
N. D. Pinner c Billings b Coles	68	– c Riley b Stevens		1
†L. J. Hill b Stevens	57	– lbw b Coles		3
B. A. Raine lbw b Stevens	12	– lbw b Thomas		7
C. J. McKay c Bell-Drummond b Stevens	6	– b Stevens		43
R. M. L. Taylor not out	33	– c Coles b Thomas		34
J. K. H. Naik b Stevens	1	– not out		28
C. E. Shreck c Northeast b Stevens	0	– b Coles		1
B 6, l-b 4, n-b 2	12	B 5, l-b 6, w 1		12

1/0 (1) 2/31 (2) 3/149 (3)   (91.5 overs) 386   1/13 (1) 2/21 (3)   (62.3 overs) 196
4/264 (4) 5/287 (5) 6/304 (7)   3/71 (4) 4/71 (2)
7/312 (8) 8/378 (6) 9/380 (10) 10/386 (11)   5/74 (5) 6/86 (7) 7/86 (6)
                                          8/148 (8) 9/193 (9) 10/196 (11)

Coles 24–2–87–4; Thomas 14–3–61–0; Claydon 24–1–103–0; Stevens 22.5–4–88–5; Riley 7–0–37–1. *Second innings*—Coles 14.3–3–42–2; Thomas 17–2–48–4; Claydon 12–1–39–1; Stevens 14–2–45–3; Riley 5–1–11–0.

Kent

D. J. Bell-Drummond c Taylor b McKay	14	– c Raine b McKay ... 103
J. L. Denly lbw b Raine	87	– b Shreck ... 9
*R. W. T. Key lbw b McKay	8	– lbw b Shreck ... 7
B. P. Nash c Hill b Taylor	21	– lbw b Taylor ... 49
S. A. Northeast lbw b Shreck	84	– lbw b McKay ... 37
D. I. Stevens c Hill b McKay	23	– c Hill b Shreck ... 34
†S. W. Billings lbw b Shreck	0	– not out ... 12
M. T. Coles c Pinner b McKay	4	– lbw b Shreck ... 2
M. E. Claydon not out	4	– not out ... 2
A. E. N. Riley c Robson b McKay	1	
I. A. A. Thomas b McKay	0	
B 2, l-b 16, n-b 4	22	B 7, l-b 9, n-b 2 ... 18

1/24 (1) 2/40 (3) 3/76 (4)   (90.5 overs) 268   1/20 (2)   (7 wkts, 71 overs) 273
4/215 (2) 5/257 (5) 6/257 (6)   2/40 (3) 3/145 (4)
7/261 (8) 8/261 (7) 9/268 (10) 10/268 (11)   4/202 (5) 5/250 (1) 6/253 (6) 7/267 (8)

McKay 23.5–6–54–6; Shreck 22–6–67–2; Raine 17–5–51–1; Taylor 17–4–50–1; Naik 11–1–28–0. *Second innings*—McKay 20–5–65–2; Shreck 23–3–75–4; Naik 9–3–22–0; Raine 13–0–60–0; Taylor 6–0–35–1.

Umpires: D. J. Millns and S. J. O'Shaughnessy.

KENT v GLAMORGAN

At Canterbury, May 10–13. Drawn. Kent 12pts, Glamorgan 10pts. Toss: Kent.

A second successive Championship century for Bell-Drummond was the highlight of a tense draw that, to Kent, felt more like defeat. He faced 249 balls and, aided by Stevens and 39 extras, guided the total to 357, even though Hogan found generous seam movement – after head groundsman Simon Williamson had left a little extra grass on the pitch. At 182 for seven, Glamorgan were in danger of following on, but the stubborn Bragg limited the arrears to 76. Hogan, who took nine in the match, proved a handful in Kent's second innings too, removing Bell-Drummond and nightwatchman Tredwell, though not until he had scored his first half-century for Kent in almost three years. Denly and Cowdrey – contributing his maiden Championship fifty – joined in, and the lead stretched past 400. Coles soon plucked out Rudolph's leg stump (it had been his off stump first time round), leaving Kent to take nine wickets on the final day. Six down by tea, Glamorgan seemed bound for defeat as Haggett, who ended with a career-best four for 61, made inroads. The ninth wicket fell with more than half an hour to go, but Stevens spilled a slip catch in the next over, and the last pair hung on for Glamorgan's fourth consecutive draw.

Close of play: first day, Kent 330-8 (Coles 2); second day, Kent 1-0 (Tredwell 1, Bell-Drummond 0); third day, Glamorgan 32-1 (Kettleborough 16, Cosker 1).

Kent

D. J. Bell-Drummond lbw b Hogan	123	– (2) lbw b Hogan ... 1
J. L. Denly c Rudolph b Hogan	30	– (3) b Wagg ... 66
B. P. Nash c Wallace b Hogan	34	– (4) c Wallace b Meschede ... 45
*S. A. Northeast lbw b Meschede	8	– (5) b Hogan ... 0
F. K. Cowdrey c Wallace b Lloyd	14	– (6) c Kettleborough b Lloyd ... 54
D. I. Stevens c Rudolph b Wagg	50	– (7) c Wallace b Wagg ... 10
†S. W. Billings c Cooke b Meschede	26	– (8) c Hogan b Cosker ... 37
C. J. Haggett c Rudolph b Hogan	4	– (9) b Hogan ... 16
M. T. Coles b Hogan	25	– (10) c Kettleborough b Cosker ... 6
J. C. Tredwell c Wallace b Meschede	0	– (1) c Cooke b Hogan ... 53
I. A. A. Thomas not out	0	– not out ... 5
B 1, l-b 4, w 3, n-b 31	39	B 14, l-b 13, w 3, n-b 4 ... 34

1/68 (2) 2/134 (3) 3/145 (4)   (102 overs) 357   1/10 (2) 2/124 (3)   (83.4 overs) 327
4/190 (5) 5/277 (6) 6/289 (6)   3/175 (1) 4/175 (5)
7/325 (7) 8/330 (8) 9/331 (10) 10/357 (9)   5/197 (4) 6/236 (7) 7/284 (6)
                                      8/297 (8) 9/309 (10) 10/327 (9)

Hogan 28–11–71–5; Wagg 22–3–95–1; Meschede 25–3–100–3; Lloyd 16–3–47–1; Cosker 10–2–33–0; Bragg 1–0–6–0. *Second innings*—Hogan 19.4–4–65–4; Meschede 14–4–43–1; Wagg 15–1–64–2; Cosker 23–2–81–2; Lloyd 12–0–47–1.

Glamorgan

J. M. Kettleborough lbw b Thomas	23	– lbw b Stevens	20
*J. A. Rudolph b Coles	6	– b Coles	14
W. D. Bragg b Thomas	104	– (4) lbw b Coles	0
C. A. Ingram c Stevens b Coles	0	– (5) c Tredwell b Thomas	51
C. B. Cooke c Denly b Stevens	19	– (6) c Northeast b Haggett	11
†M. A. Wallace c Billings b Thomas	17	– (7) lbw b Coles	29
G. G. Wagg c Tredwell b Stevens	7	– (8) lbw b Haggett	51
C. A. J. Meschede c Tredwell b Haggett	14	– (9) b Haggett	1
D. L. Lloyd c Bell-Drummond b Coles	45	– (10) not out	43
D. A. Cosker not out	14	– (3) lbw b Haggett	69
M. G. Hogan b Stevens	19	– not out	9
B 1, l-b 12	13	L-b 6, w 5	11

1/29 (1) 2/35 (2) 3/41 (4)   (84 overs) 281   1/25 (2)   (9 wkts, 107 overs) 309
4/108 (5) 5/142 (6) 6/166 (7)   2/45 (1) 3/50 (4)
7/182 (8) 8/246 (9) 9/259 (3) 10/281 (11)   4/137 (5) 5/158 (6) 6/173 (3)
                                                    7/230 (7) 8/243 (9) 9/277 (8)

Coles 20–4–84–3; Thomas 17–2–40–3; Stevens 15–1–47–3; Haggett 15–4–47–1; Tredwell 17–3–50–0. *Second innings*—Coles 31–7–101–3; Thomas 19–5–55–1; Stevens 23–7–42–1; Haggett 23–7–61–4; Tredwell 11–1–44–0.

Umpires: R. J. Bailey and N. G. B. Cook.

At Bristol, May 18–21. KENT beat GLOUCESTERSHIRE by eight wickets.

KENT v SURREY

At Beckenham, May 24–27. Surrey won by three wickets. Surrey 21pts, Kent 5pts. Toss: Kent.

Key, who grew up in Beckenham, returned to the Kent side for their first Championship match at the newly refurbished Worsley Bridge Road ground in six years, though Northeast retained the captaincy. The pair added 133 for the third wicket until Key fell to a contentious lbw decision. His departure, coupled with a plethora of rash shots, sparked a mid-afternoon collapse that ultimately saw Kent dismissed for an unsatisfactory 282. Despite a chilly crosswind, Surrey scored consistently down the order, if not heavily, as Coles, bowling with gusto, and Stevens kept the lead to ten. With Fletcher suffering back spasms, Surrey found a hero in left-arm spinner Ansari who, after Kent had reached a promising 97 for two, ripped the heart out of the middle order, including three victims in four balls. Batty claimed another three with his off-breaks as more poor strokeplay meant the target was a gettable 195. Mirroring Kent's penchant for soft dismissals, Surrey tottered to 108 for five, before Roy – reaching their only half-century of the game, from just 41 balls – took control.

Close of play: first day, Surrey 17-1 (Burns 8, Dunn 1); second day, Surrey 250-8 (Batty 36, Curran 8); third day, Surrey 44-1 (Burns 29, Dunn 1).

Kent

D. J. Bell-Drummond lbw b Ansari	20	– lbw b Dunn	9
J. L. Denly lbw b Fletcher	0	– b Batty	66
R. W. T. Key lbw b Ansari	89	– c Wilson b Dunn	26
*S. A. Northeast c Roy b Curran	73	– c Davies b Ansari	26
F. K. Cowdrey lbw b Dunn	39	– st Wilson b Ansari	9
D. I. Stevens c Ansari b Dunn	0	– c Roy b Ansari	1
†S. W. Billings c Wilson b Curran	35	– c Sibley b Ansari	0
C. J. Haggett c Sangakkara b Curran	0	– c Sibley b Batty	24
M. T. Coles c and b Roy	21	– c Davies b Batty	29
A. E. N. Riley not out	2	– not out	4
I. A. A. Thomas b Dunn	2	– c Wilson b Dunn	0
L-b 1	1	B 2, l-b 8	10

1/0 (2) 2/49 (1) 3/182 (3) (85.3 overs) 282   1/16 (1) 2/56 (3) (65.4 overs) 204
4/182 (4) 5/189 (6) 6/235 (7)   3/97 (4) 4/113 (5)
7/237 (8) 8/270 (9) 9/278 (5) 10/282 (11)   5/115 (6) 6/115 (7) 7/159 (2)
                                           8/188 (8) 9/201 (9) 10/204 (11)

Dunn 20.3–4–65–3; Fletcher 6–1–9–1; Curran 22–4–64–3; Ansari 27–3–97–2; Batty 8–0–39–0; Roy 2–1–7–1. *Second innings*—Dunn 13.4–1–61–3; Curran 14–5–35–0; Ansari 21–5–58–4; Batty 17–5–40–3.

Surrey

R. J. Burns c Billings b Coles	18	– b Stevens	37
Z. S. Ansari lbw b Coles	3	– lbw b Stevens	10
M. P. Dunn b Thomas	10	– c Key b Stevens	13
K. C. Sangakkara c Haggett b Stevens	10	– lbw b Coles	8
D. P. Sibley c Riley b Stevens	41	– c Stevens b Thomas	17
S. M. Davies c Haggett b Riley	45	– c Coles b Riley	35
J. J. Roy c Bell-Drummond b Stevens	16	– not out	60
†G. C. Wilson c Billings b Coles	42	– c Billings b Coles	5
*G. J. Batty lbw b Coles	37	– not out	1
T. K. Curran not out	26		
L. J. Fletcher lbw b Stevens	23		
B 4, l-b 9, w 6, n-b 2	21	L-b 8, n-b 2	10

1/11 (2) 2/32 (1) 3/52 (3) (100.1 overs) 292   1/41 (2) (7 wkts, 50.1 overs) 196
4/52 (4) 5/128 (6) 6/155 (7)   2/60 (1) 3/75 (4)
7/170 (5) 8/225 (8) 9/256 (9) 10/292 (11)   4/75 (3) 5/108 (5) 6/162 (6) 7/177 (8)

Coles 26–7–81–4; Haggett 18–5–50–0; Stevens 19.1–4–48–4; Thomas 16–5–41–1; Riley 20–5–52–1; Denly 1–0–7–0. *Second innings*—Coles 17.1–1–75–2; Thomas 7–1–15–1; Riley 16–1–69–1; Stevens 10–2–29–3.

Umpires: P. J. Hartley and P. R. Pollard.

KENT v DERBYSHIRE

At Canterbury, June 7–9. Derbyshire won by eight wickets. Derbyshire 19pts, Kent 4pts. Toss: Kent. First-class debut: R. C. Davies.

A schedule requiring teams to play a Championship match barely 36 hours after a Twenty20 game was cited as mitigation after 31 wickets cascaded in the first five sessions of a contest that limped into the third day. On a blameless pitch, batsman after batsman found that an airy leg-side flick against a hard, red, new ball often ended in dismissal. Footitt, with five for 45, and the wily Palladino, whose 18 overs brought three for 19, gave nothing away during Kent's first innings, when only Northeast suggested permanence. Coles then snapped up three wickets before a run had been scored, and at one stage had 6–5–8–5. Durston fought back but, with Derbyshire skittled for 86 in 32 overs, Kent were building on their 119-run advantage soon after 11.30 on the second morning. They looked impregnable when, one down, they led by 182. But White, off-colour and wayward on day one, switched ends – and the course of the game – to record a career-best six for 25, as Kent's last nine toppled for 49. Derbyshire's second-wicket pair of Godleman and Hughes made light of a target of 232. All told, the game contained 21 single-figure dismissals, including a pair on debut by Ryan Davies, Kent's 18-year-old keeper, standing in for Sam Billings, who was on England duty.

Close of play: first day, Derbyshire 67-7 (Poynton 19, Palladino 11); second day, Derbyshire 169-1 (Godleman 61, Hughes 82).

Kent

D. J. Bell-Drummond lbw b Footitt	2	– run out	45
J. L. Denly b White	30	– lbw b Palladino	6
R. W. T. Key lbw b Footitt	0	– b White	18
*S. A. Northeast b Palladino	85	– c Dilshan b White	29
F. K. Cowdrey b Palladino	22	– b White	7
D. I. Stevens c Poynton b Footitt	1	– lbw b White	0
†R. C. Davies b Footitt	0	– b White	0
C. J. Haggett not out	20	– b Footitt	1
M. T. Coles c Durston b Palladino	5	– lbw b Footitt	6
A. E. N. Riley c Poynton b Footitt	34	– c Poynton b White	0
I. A. A. Thomas run out	0	– not out	0
B 1, w 1, n-b 4	6		

1/2 (1) 2/2 (3) 3/98 (2) (66.2 overs) 205
4/135 (4) 5/146 (6) 6/146 (5)
7/146 (7) 8/151 (9) 9/204 (10) 10/205 (11)

1/17 (2) 2/63 (3) (36.4 overs) 112
3/73 (1) 4/89 (5)
5/89 (6) 6/95 (7) 7/98 (8)
8/104 (9) 9/105 (10) 10/112 (4)

Footitt 17–6–45–5; *Palladino* 18–10–19–3; *Taylor* 11–2–56–0; *White* 10–1–56–1; *Hughes* 3–1–13–0; *Durston* 7.2–2–15–0. *Second innings*—*Footitt* 11–5–24–2; *Taylor* 8–0–29–0; *Palladino* 8–1–34–1; *White* 9.4–2–25–6.

Derbyshire

B. T. Slater b Coles	0	– lbw b Coles	2
*B. A. Godleman c Northeast b Coles	2	– not out	82
C. F. Hughes lbw b Coles	0	– b Coles	94
T. M. Dilshan c Riley b Coles	0	– not out	27
W. J. Durston lbw b Stevens	35		
S. L. Elstone lbw b Coles	0		
W. A. White lbw b Stevens	0		
†T. Poynton c Bell-Drummond b Thomas	19		
A. P. Palladino c Davies b Thomas	27		
T. A. I. Taylor c Riley b Thomas	1		
M. H. A. Footitt not out	2		
		B 10, l-b 5, w 5, n-b 7	27

1/0 (1) 2/0 (3) 3/0 (4) (32 overs) 86
4/15 (2) 5/23 (6) 6/37 (5)
7/40 (7) 8/67 (8) 9/73 (10) 10/86 (9)

1/6 (1) (2 wkts, 63.2 overs) 232
2/192 (3)

Coles 12–6–24–5; *Thomas* 9–2–31–3; *Stevens* 7–2–16–2; *Haggett* 4–1–15–0. *Second innings*—*Coles* 19–4–75–2; *Thomas* 13.2–3–31–0; *Stevens* 14.2–1–62–0; *Haggett* 8.4–3–16–0; *Riley* 8–0–33–0.

Umpires: R. J. Evans and D. J. Millns.

At Northampton, June 20–22. KENT lost to NORTHAMPTONSHIRE by eight wickets.

At Canterbury, June 25–28. KENT lost to AUSTRALIANS by 255 runs (see Australian tour section).

At Leicester, July 5–7. KENT beat LEICESTERSHIRE by eight wickets.

At The Oval, July 13–16. KENT lost to SURREY by six wickets.

KENT v ESSEX

At Tunbridge Wells, July 19–21. Kent won by an innings and 207 runs. Kent 24pts, Essex 3pts.
Toss: Essex. County debut: R. H. Patel.

Kent cantered to an innings victory inside three days, gathering maximum points for the only time
in 2015. Foster had chosen to bat, a decision that looked healthier at 204 for four than at 260 all out.
Stevens, the wind at his back, proved nigh unplayable, bowling 12 maidens en route to figures of
four for 37. Bell-Drummond and Key rushed to 68 by the close, and next day brought up Kent's first

HIGHEST TOTALS BY KENT

803-4 dec	v Essex at Brentwood.	1934
652-7 dec	v Middlesex at Uxbridge	2009
633-8 dec	**v Essex at Tunbridge Wells**.	**2015**
621-6 dec	v Essex at Tonbridge	1922
620-7 dec	v Surrey at The Oval	2009
616-6 dec	v Oxford University at Oxford.	1982
616-7 dec	v Somerset at Canterbury.	1996
615	v Derbyshire at Derby	1908
615	v Lancashire at Tunbridge Wells	2004
610	v Hampshire at Bournemouth	1906

three-figure opening stand in over a year. All the batsmen joined in: never before had six of their top
seven reached 50 (and the one who didn't, Northeast, still made 43). The upshot was 633 for eight
declared, a county record on home soil. There were hundreds from Harmison – his only one of a lean
season – and Billings, who shook a monkey from his back with a maiden Championship century, off
113 balls. Kent then reduced Essex to 68 for five within 19 overs, and seamers Hunn and Haggett
hastened a thumping win, finishing with four wickets each.

Close of play: first day, Kent 68-0 (Bell-Drummond 46, Key 19); second day, Kent 420-4
(Harmison 63, Stevens 69).

Essex

N. L. J. Browne lbw b Haggett.	30	– c Denly b Hunn	1
J. C. Mickleburgh c Billings b Hunn	3	– c Northeast b Haggett	9
T. Westley c and b Hunn	77	– c Billings b Haggett	22
R. S. Bopara c Northeast b Stevens	42	– c Northeast b Haggett.	5
J. D. Ryder c Denly b Claydon	24	– c Hunn b Tredwell	29
R. N. ten Doeschate c Billings b Stevens	54	– lbw b Stevens	27
*†J. S. Foster c Billings b Stevens	6	– c Tredwell b Hunn	24
G. R. Napier c and b Haggett.	11	– not out	35
D. D. Masters c Billings b Haggett	5	– c sub (P. F. B. Richardson) b Hunn . . .	8
J. A. Porter c Billings b Stevens.	0	– lbw b Haggett.	1
R. H. Patel not out	0	– c Harmison b Haggett	0
L-b 4, w 2, n-b 2.	8	L-b 5.	5

1/16 (2) 2/38 (1) 3/149 (3)	(81.5 overs) 260	1/1 (1) 2/10 (2)	(44.1 overs) 166
4/163 (4) 5/204 (5) 6/240 (7)		3/31 (4) 4/66 (5)	
7/253 (6) 8/260 (9) 9/260 (8) 10/260 (10)		5/68 (3) 6/104 (6) 7/133 (7)	
		8/153 (9) 9/156 (10) 10/166 (11)	

Claydon 20–0–68–1; Hunn 19–3–78–2; Haggett 16–4–54–3; Stevens 23.5–12–37–4; Tredwell
3–0–19–0. *Second innings*—Claydon 9–1–30–0; Hunn 11–2–47–4; Haggett 13.1–2–43–4; Stevens
10–3–36–1; Tredwell 1–0–5–1.

Kent

D. J. Bell-Drummond b Ryder	81	J. C. Tredwell c Foster b Bopara	1
R. W. T. Key c Browne b Napier	71	M. E. Claydon not out	7
J. L. Denly b Patel	69	L-b 10, w 2, n-b 22	34
*S. A. Northeast b Porter	43		
B. W. Harmison c Masters b Bopara	123	1/127 (1) (8 wkts dec, 143.5 overs)	633
D. I. Stevens c Foster b Porter	76	2/200 (2) 3/271 (4)	
†S. W. Billings not out	100	4/303 (3) 5/437 (6) 6/536 (5)	
C. J. Haggett c ten Doeschate b Bopara	28	7/609 (8) 8/616 (9) 110 overs: 444-5	

M. D. Hunn did not bat.

Masters 32–8–85–0; Porter 23–1–123–2; Ryder 19–1–96–1; Patel 18–2–92–1; Napier 20–1–77–1; Bopara 20–3–89–3; Westley 6.5–0–28–0; ten Doeschate 5–0–33–0.

Umpires: M. Burns and J. H. Evans.

KENT v NORTHAMPTONSHIRE

At Canterbury, August 4–6. Northamptonshire won by an innings and 23 runs. Northamptonshire 23pts, Kent 3pts. Toss: Kent. First-class debut: S. A. Zaib.

After the zenith of their Championship summer – the crushing victory at Tunbridge Wells – Kent plummeted to the nadir, themselves flattened inside three days. Awash with runs against Essex, they could find few in a decent Canterbury Week pitch. The match had begun at noon because Northamptonshire's late one-day finish the night before, but it was Kent – in the face of some fiery bowling from Stone – who looked the wearier, capitulating for 167 inside two sessions. By the first-day close, a weakened Northamptonshire had already edged ahead, only two down. Next morning, the left-handed Duckett reached his fifth first-class hundred, from 115 balls, though the biggest cheer of the day greeted Azharullah's maiden senior fifty in any format, in his 148th innings. Armed with a lead of 231, Northamptonshire quickly set about dismantling Kent for a second time, as the seamers shared the wickets. Wakely described it as "the best collective effort" under his captaincy. It was an uneventful debut for 17-year-old all-rounder Saif Zaib: dismissed for a duck and given just one over of left-arm spin.

Close of play: first day, Northamptonshire 172-2 (Duckett 94, Keogh 11); second day, Kent 81-1 (Key 22, Denly 27).

Kent

D. J. Bell-Drummond c Levi b Stone	0	– b Sanderson	26
R. W. T. Key c Murphy b Chambers	16	– c Azharullah b Sanderson	42
J. L. Denly lbw b Stone	50	– c Cobb b Azharullah	33
*S. A. Northeast b Chambers	0	– lbw b Azharullah	6
B. W. Harmison b Azharullah	1	– lbw b Sanderson	3
D. I. Stevens c Keogh b Sanderson	34	– lbw b Stone	15
†S. W. Billings lbw b Stone	0	– c Murphy b Sanderson	43
C. J. Haggett c Levi b Stone	49	– b Stone	0
J. C. Tredwell c Murphy b Sanderson	1	– c Cobb b Azharullah	7
M. T. Coles c Sanderson b Azharullah	5	– not out	20
M. D. Hunn not out	3	– b Chambers	0
L-b 6, n-b 2	8	L-b 7, w 1, p 5	13

1/0 (1) 2/40 (2) 3/40 (4)	(51.2 overs)	167
4/41 (5) 5/83 (3) 6/87 (7)		
7/117 (6) 8/119 (9) 9/133 (10) 10/167 (8)		

1/36 (1) 2/90 (3)	(78 overs)	208
3/104 (4) 4/114 (5)		
5/121 (2) 6/150 (6) 7/150 (8)		
8/172 (9) 9/201 (7) 10/208 (11)		

Stone 16.2–3–59–4; Azharullah 13–4–42–2; Chambers 10–3–21–2; Sanderson 10–2–34–2; Keogh 2–1–5–0. *Second innings*—Stone 26–8–51–2; Azharullah 27–9–68–3; Sanderson 12–4–44–4; Chambers 11–2–27–1; Keogh 1–0–2–0; Zaib 1–0–4–0.

Northamptonshire

†D. Murphy c Harrison b Tredwell	42	B. W. Sanderson c Harrison b Haggett	42
B. M. Duckett lbw b Tredwell	145	M. A. Chambers c Harrison b Tredwell	2
*A. G. Wakely c Billings b Hunn	19		
R. I. Keogh c and b Coles	11	B 4, l-b 14, n-b 6	24
R. E. Levi run out	25		
J. J. Cobb c Billings b Stevens	30	1/105 (1) 2/142 (3) (107.4 overs) 398
S. A. Zaib lbw b Coles	0	3/172 (4) 4/234 (5)
O. P. Stone c Billings b Coles	0	5/261 (2) 6/272 (7) 7/272 (8)
Azharullah not out	58	8/305 (6) 9/387 (10) 10/398 (11)

Coles 25–3–118–3; Hunn 20–4–81–1; Stevens 14–2–64–1; Haggett 17–1–58–1; Tredwell 31.4–11–59–3.

Umpires: R. J. Evans and S. J. O'Shaughnessy.

At Derby, August 21–24. KENT drew with DERBYSHIRE.

KENT v LANCASHIRE

At Canterbury, September 1–4. Drawn. Kent 12pts, Lancashire 8pts. Toss: Lancashire.

Kent enforced the follow-on against the division leaders, but on the final day could take only two of the eight wickets they needed. Lancashire slipped to second, yet still secured promotion. Key reached his first hundred of the summer to brighten an opening day shortened by rain and bad light, before Northeast, his successor as captain, followed suit on the second, passing 1,000 for the season for the first time. With a brisk 92 coming from Stevens, Northeast declared that evening at 570 for eight. Brown and Croft passed 50, and Clark contributed a dogged 44, but a nagging line from Kent's efficient and hard-working attack meant Lancashire were batting again, 311 behind, an hour or so before the third-day close. They lost two by stumps, including Petersen, whose hare-brained waft gifted Tredwell a wicket in the last over. Croft had batted more than four hours in the first innings, and he did so again, adding an unbroken 120 in 50 overs with Alex Davies – the wicketkeepers shared a surname – as Lancashire dead-batted their way to safety.

Close of play: first day, Kent 235-3 (Tredwell 3, Northeast 7); second day, Lancashire 25-0 (Brown 16, Hameed 6); third day, Lancashire 47-2 (Hameed 17).

Kent

D. J. Bell-Drummond lbw b Bailey	37	†R. C. Davies c Lester b Croft	17
R. W. T. Key c Brown b Clark	113	M. T. Coles not out	3
J. L. Denly lbw b Clark	65	B 10, l-b 13, w 3, n-b 12	38
J. C. Tredwell c Hameed b Clark	11		
*S. A. Northeast st Davies b Kerrigan	139	1/72 (1) (8 wkts dec, 147 overs) 570
B. W. Harmison c Lester b Bailey	19	2/221 (3) 3/224 (2)
D. I. Stevens c Hameed b Kerrigan	92	4/257 (4) 5/315 (6) 6/498 (7)
C. J. Haggett not out	36	7/511 (5) 8/548 (9) 110 overs: 374-5

M. D. Hunn did not bat.

Chapple 33–5–126–0; Lester 23–3–99–0; Bailey 28–4–89–2; Clark 30–6–87–3; Kerrigan 19–1–95–2; Croft 14–0–51–1.

Lancashire

K. R. Brown c Harmison b Coles	53	– lbw b Coles	0
H. Hameed c Tredwell b Stevens	14	– b Haggett	44
A. N. Petersen lbw b Stevens	0	– b Tredwell	28
A. G. Prince c Davies b Hunn	17	– lbw b Stevens	39
*S. J. Croft lbw b Coles	85	– not out	72
†A. L. Davies b Coles	4	– not out	58
J. Clark c Tredwell b Haggett	44		
T. E. Bailey b Tredwell	18		
G. Chapple c Hunn b Haggett	8		
S. C. Kerrigan c Davies b Hunn	2		
T. J. Lester not out	0		
B 4, l-b 4, w 2, n-b 4	14	B 5, l-b 7, w 3, n-b 2	17

1/42 (2) 2/46 (3) 3/76 (4)   (87.1 overs) 259
4/97 (1) 5/101 (6) 6/192 (7)
7/227 (8) 8/242 (9) 9/259 (10) 10/259 (5)

1/0 (1)   (4 wkts, 102 overs) 258
2/47 (3) 3/109 (4)
4/138 (2)

Coles 22.1–4–75–3; Hunn 22–8–47–2; Stevens 17–4–51–2; Haggett 15–1–44–2; Tredwell 11–3–34–1. *Second innings*—Coles 23–7–67–1; Hunn 17–2–57–0; Stevens 19–4–57–1; Haggett 18–5–41–1; Tredwell 20–12–17–1; Denly 5–2–7–0.

Umpires: N. L. Bainton and G. D. Lloyd.

At Cardiff, September 9–12. KENT beat GLAMORGAN by 316 runs.

KENT v GLOUCESTERSHIRE

At Canterbury, September 14–17. Drawn. Kent 5pts, Gloucestershire 5pts. Toss: Gloucestershire. County debut: T. R. G. Hampton.

Kent's season ended in damp anticlimax when this game was almost completely swallowed up by rain and bad light. In the hour that escaped the weather on the first day, Sean Dickson, a South African-born right-hander, caught the eye.

Close of play: first day, Kent 67-1 (Dickson 31, Denly 9); second day, no play; third day, no play.

Kent

D. J. Bell-Drummond lbw b Payne	22
S. R. Dickson not out	31
J. L. Denly not out	9
W 1, n-b 4	5

1/24 (1)   (1 wkt, 15 overs) 67

*S. A. Northeast, D. I. Stevens, A. J. Blake, †R. C. Davies, M. T. Coles, M. E. Claydon, A. E. N. Riley and M. D. Hunn did not bat.

Payne 5–2–22–1; Fuller 5–2–14–0; Howell 2–0–11–0; Hampton 3–0–20–0.

Gloucestershire

*W. A. Tavaré, C. D. J. Dent, †G. H. Roderick, H. J. H. Marshall, B. A. C. Howell, K. Noema-Barnett, J. M. R. Taylor, T. M. J. Smith, J. K. Fuller, D. A. Payne, T. R. G. Hampton.

Umpires: P. K. Baldwin and D. J. Millns.

LANCASHIRE

Princely spoils

PAUL EDWARDS

When Lancashire drew their match with Kent on September 4, Steven Croft's players celebrated the completion of one task, well aware that their reward would be a more difficult job in the year ahead. The eight points gained at Canterbury secured immediate promotion, the fourth successive season to end with Lancashire changing divisions.

Relegation in 2014 had led to the appointment of Ashley Giles as director of cricket; his next priority was to stop his team remaining one of English cricket's yo-yo counties. The following match, a visit from Surrey, suggested that might not be straightforward. They had ensured promotion on the same day as Lancashire, simultaneously overtaking them as leaders of Division Two. But, at Old Trafford, they outplayed their hosts and looked fully equipped for the challenges of the top tier. The fact that Lancashire conceded huge first-innings deficits against both them and Kent showed how much work remained to complete Giles's longer-term project – the club's restoration to the summit of domestic cricket.

Yet 2015 was a fine season. Lancashire won six of their first nine matches in the Championship, and headed Division Two for all but the last three weeks. They finished 54 points ahead of third-placed Essex, highlighting the gap between the two promoted sides and the rest. Such success, however, was expected by supporters at Old Trafford.

What few imagined was that Lancashire would shrug off failure at five previous finals days and win the NatWest T20 Blast. The most joyful moment of the season came as the players performed their team song in front of delighted fans in Edgbaston's Raglan Stand. A few of those cricketers were little known outside the county, but their inexperience was outweighed by the confidence of youth and an ability to perform under pressure. After winning only seven of their 14 group matches, they had qualified on net run-rate for the quarter-finals, where they beat Kent by losing fewer wickets in a tie. (Some of the gloss was removed when the players become involved in a pub brawl in Ashford, during which Liam Livingstone was glassed in the face, and needed around 20 stitches.) On finals day, the form guide was confounded by the chutzpah of Arron Lilley and Alex Davies. Their daring, complemented by the international quality of Ashwell Prince and James Faulkner, brought Lancashire their first limited-overs trophy since 1999. In the Royal London One-Day Cup, however, a combination of rain and inconsistency meant it was their turn to be squeezed out of the quarter-finals on net run-rate.

Prince was an even more pivotal figure in the Championship: having been persuaded to carry on for one more season before retirement, aged 38, he scored 1,478 runs and five centuries, including a career-best 261. He was instrumental in most of Lancashire's victories, and he scored 600 more than any of his team-mates. Unsurprisingly, Prince was named Player of the Year, although Croft and Kyle Jarvis ensured the accolade was not a formality.

Dave Thompson, Getty Images

Ashwell Prince

Jarvis was almost unrecognisable from the seamer who had struggled to find any rhythm or accuracy in 2014. Bowling with a fine, high action and good pace, he demanded respect from all Division Two batsmen, and claimed 55 wickets in the first nine matches. He had taken that to 62 before a broken hand prevented him playing in the T20 finals or the last three Championship games. By then, though, Jarvis had made Glen Chapple's gradual move into coaching (aged 41, he played five times) easier to bear, and offered evidence that he would test techniques in Division One. Lancashire also fielded two Australian seamers: Peter Siddle ended an early four-match stint with 18 wickets and was followed by Faulkner, who claimed 23 in seven games before dislocating a finger in the T20 final (he was also fined £10,000 in August after pleading guilty to drink-driving). New Zealand seamer Neil Wagner was signed for 2016. Tom Bailey enjoyed a breakthrough season, with 35 victims. Simon Kerrigan's 41 made him the leading slow bowler. He was partnered impressively in six games by the off-spinning all-rounder Lilley, who dismissed 26 batsmen and was unfortunate not to be selected for the England Performance Programme (though one-day specialist Stephen Parry was).

Prince dominated the batting, but there were other reasons for encouragement. His fellow South African Kolpak, Alviro Petersen, scored 861 runs in his first season with Lancashire, 514 of them in three innings; his stand of 501 with Prince at Colwyn Bay was the highest in the county's history. Karl Brown was unexpectedly promoted to open after Luis Reece broke his hand, and returned to form with 766 runs, while Davies's aggregate of 730 confirmed his status as one of Lancashire's grittiest competitors. The end of the season saw the keenly awaited debut of 18-year-old opener Haseeb Hameed, who made two half-centuries and displayed uncoachable calmness. Hameed's emergence made the decision not to offer Paul Horton another contract more explicable, despite his proven success in Division One.

If the season's saddest feature was the back injury which forced out new club captain Tom Smith after one Championship game, one of the most heartening was the accomplished performance of his deputy, Croft, who excelled in every discipline. In November, Smith officially stepped down, handing the job to Croft on a full-time basis. Only Prince scored more than his 874 runs in the Championship, and no one could better his Twenty20 haul of 478. In addition, he took useful wickets when they were most needed, fielded brilliantly and led the team shrewdly.

Championship attendance: 29,370.

LANCASHIRE RESULTS

All first-class matches – Played 16: Won 7, Lost 1, Drawn 8.
County Championship matches – Played 16: Won 7, Lost 1, Drawn 8.

LV= County Championship, 2nd in Division 2;
NatWest T20 Blast, winners; Royal London One-Day Cup, 5th in Group B.

COUNTY CHAMPIONSHIP AVERAGES, BATTING AND FIELDING

Cap		Birthplace	M	I	NO	R	HS	100	Avge	Ct/St
2010	A. G. Prince¶	Port Elizabeth, SA .	16	23	1	1,478	261	5	67.18	13
2015	K. R. Brown	Bolton†	12	17	0	766	132	1	45.05	12
	A. N. Petersen¶	Port Elizabeth, SA .	14	21	1	861	286	3	43.05	6
	H. Hameed	Bolton†	4	6	0	257	91	0	42.83	2
2010	S. J. Croft	Blackpool†	16	23	2	874	122	2	41.61	21
	A. L. Davies	Darwen†	14	19	1	730	99	0	40.55	46/4
	A. M. Lilley	Tameside†	7	8	2	230	63	0	38.33	3
2007	P. J. Horton	Sydney, Australia .	12	18	1	611	168	1	35.94	16
	J. P. Faulkner§	Launceston, Aust. .	7	9	0	310	121	1	34.44	3
	P. M. Siddle§	Traralgon, Aust. . .	4	6	0	204	89	0	34.00	1
	J. Clark	Whitehaven	12	17	2	419	63	0	27.93	3
2015	K. M. Jarvis¶	Harare, Zimbabwe	13	15	9	139	47	0	23.16	3
	L. M. Reece	Taunton	5	8	0	142	82	0	17.75	1
	T. E. Bailey	Preston†	12	16	3	224	34	0	17.23	2
1994	G. Chapple	Skipton	5	5	1	51	29*	0	12.75	2
2013	S. C. Kerrigan	Preston†	14	15	5	110	34*	0	11.00	6

Also batted: J. M. Anderson‡ (*Burnley*†) (cap 2003) (2 matches) 42, 6* (5 ct); N. L. Buck (*Leicester*)
(2 matches) 4, 17, 25 (1 ct); T. J. Lester (*Blackpool*†) (2 matches) 0* (2 ct); P. Mustard (*Sunderland*)
(2 matches) 43, 8, 5 (3 ct); T. C. Smith (*Liverpool*†) (cap 2010) (1 match) 38, 1 (2 ct).

† *Born in Lancashire.*   ‡ *ECB contract.*   § *Official overseas player.*
¶ *Other non-England-qualified player.*

BOWLING

	Style	O	M	R	W	BB	5I	Avge
J. M. Anderson	RFM	73.5	17	207	11	7-77	1	18.81
P. M. Siddle	RFM	139.4	32	370	18	4-39	0	20.55
J. P. Faulkner	LFM	186	44	501	23	5-39	1	21.78
K. M. Jarvis	RFM	450.5	87	1,533	62	5-13	0	24.72
S. J. Croft	RFM/OB	96.1	13	286	10	4-35	0	28.60
A. M. Lilley	OB	234.3	44	751	26	5-23	1	28.88
S. C. Kerrigan	SLA	460.2	100	1,321	41	4-28	0	32.21
T. E. Bailey	RFM	347.3	64	1,192	35	5-12	1	34.05
J. Clark	RM	244.4	38	880	19	4-101	0	46.31
G. Chapple	RFM	166	44	489	10	4-62	0	48.90

Also bowled: K. R. Brown (RM) 1–0–16–0; N. L. Buck (RFM) 45.3–3–210–6; H. Hameed (LBG)
1–0–9–0; P. J. Horton (RM) 2–0–7–0; T. J. Lester (LFM) 44–8–172–3; A. N. Petersen (RM/OB)
4–2–9–0; L. M. Reece (LM) 17–0–97–0; T. C. Smith (RFM) 17–2–75–0.

LEADING ROYAL LONDON CUP AVERAGES (100 runs/4 wickets)

Batting

	Runs	HS	Avge	SR	Ct/St
A. L. Davies	209	73*	52.25	112.36	4/2
A. G. Prince	236	102	39.33	92.18	6
K. R. Brown	211	77	35.16	69.18	3
A. N. Petersen . . .	178	82	29.66	69.53	2
S. J. Croft	126	55	21.00	63.95	4

Bowling

	W	BB	Avge	ER
S. D. Parry	10	3-60	21.60	4.33
K. M. Jarvis	7	3-46	26.28	4.36
J. Clark	4	2-27	29.25	4.33
J. P. Faulkner	8	2-27	30.12	4.75
G. T. Griffiths	4	3-41	34.75	4.68

LEADING NATWEST T20 BLAST AVERAGES (100 runs/18 overs)

Batting	Runs	HS	Avge	SR	Ct/St	Bowling	W	BB	Avge	ER
J. C. Buttler	161	71*	53.66	**165.97**	5	J. P. Faulkner	25	3-19	12.64	**6.25**
A. L. Davies	235	47	18.07	**143.29**	14/3	A. M. Lilley	16	3-31	19.81	**6.46**
J. P. Faulkner	302	73	37.75	**141.12**	3	S. D. Parry	25	4-16	15.68	**6.87**
S. J. Croft	478	94*	43.45	**127.80**	14	S. J. Croft	12	2-16	27.91	**7.28**
A. G. Prince	455	78	30.33	**127.45**	12	G. A. Edwards	11	4-20	14.72	**7.96**
K. R. Brown	362	69	24.13	**121.47**	6	K. M. Jarvis	9	3-24	22.00	**8.25**
L. S. Livingstone	137	27	12.45	**114.16**	3	J. Clark	12	3-41	20.75	**9.27**
P. J. Horton	136	63	22.66	**107.93**	2	T. E. Bailey	7	2-24	35.14	**10.69**

FIRST-CLASS COUNTY RECORDS

Highest score for	424	A. C. MacLaren v Somerset at Taunton	1895
Highest score against	315*	T. W. Hayward (Surrey) at The Oval	1898
Leading run-scorer	34,222	E. Tyldesley (avge 45.20)	1909–36
Best bowling for	10-46	W. Hickton v Hampshire at Manchester	1870
Best bowling against	10-40	G. O. B. Allen (Middlesex) at Lord's	1929
Leading wicket-taker	1,816	J. B. Statham (avge 15.12)	1950–68
Highest total for	863	v Surrey at The Oval	1990
Highest total against	707-9 dec	by Surrey at The Oval	1990
Lowest total for	25	v Derbyshire at Manchester	1871
Lowest total against	20	by Essex at Chelmsford	2013

LIST A COUNTY RECORDS

Highest score for	162*	A. R. Crook v Buckinghamshire at Wormsley	2005
Highest score against	186*	C. G. Greenidge (West Indians) at Liverpool	1984
Leading run-scorer	11,969	N. H. Fairbrother (avge 41.84)	1982–2002
Best bowling for	6-10	C. E. H. Croft v Scotland at Manchester	1982
Best bowling against	8-26	K. D. Boyce (Essex) at Manchester	1971
Leading wicket-taker	480	J. Simmons (avge 25.75)	1969–89
Highest total for	381-3	v Hertfordshire at Radlett	1999
Highest total against	360-9	by Hampshire at Manchester	2014
Lowest total for	59	v Worcestershire at Worcester	1963
Lowest total against	52	by Minor Counties at Lakenham	1998

TWENTY20 COUNTY RECORDS

Highest score for	102*	L. Vincent v Derbyshire at Manchester	2008
Highest score against	108*	I. J. Harvey (Yorkshire) at Leeds	2004
Leading run-scorer	**2,709**	**S. J. Croft** (avge 31.13)	**2006–15**
Best bowling for	5-29	M. J. McClenaghan v Notts at Manchester	2013
Best bowling against	5-21	J. Allenby (Leicestershire) at Manchester	2008
Leading wicket-taker	**96**	**S. D. Parry** (avge 22.73)	**2009–15**
Highest total for	231-4	**v Yorkshire at Manchester**	**2015**
Highest total against {	202-3	by Hampshire at Southampton	2013
	202-8	**by Yorkshire at Manchester**	**2015**
Lowest total for	91	v Derbyshire at Manchester	2003
Lowest total against	81-8	by Derbyshire at Manchester	2011

ADDRESS

Emirates Old Trafford, Talbot Road, Manchester M16 0PX; 0161 282 4000; enquiries@lccc.co.uk; www.lccc.co.uk.

OFFICIALS

Captain 2015 T. C. Smith
2016 S. J. Croft
Cricket director/Head coach A. F. Giles
President Sir Howard Bernstein

Chairman M. A. Cairns
Chief executive D. Gidney
Head groundsman M. Merchant
Scorer D. M. White

At Manchester, April 12–14 (not first-class). **Drawn.** ‡**Lancashire 482** (113.4 overs) (P. J. Horton 83, L. M. Reece 81, A. N. Petersen 82, A. G. Prince 74; W. T. Root 4-49); **Leeds/Bradford MCCU 278** (90.2 overs) (S. F. G. Bullen 97; S. C. Kerrigan 5-52). *County debuts:* N. L. Buck, A. N. Petersen. *Paul Horton hit 83 in 89 balls out of 120 for the first wicket before lunch on the opening day, when Liam Watkinson, son of Lancashire's former cricket director Mike, shared the new ball. The next two sessions were washed out. On the second day, after ice had been removed from the covers, Luis Reece and Alviro Petersen also passed 80 before retiring out; Billy Root, Joe's brother, claimed four late-order wickets. For the students, Steve Bullen batted nearly four hours, falling for 97 to become one of five victims for Simon Kerrigan.*

At Derby, April 19–22. LANCASHIRE beat DERBYSHIRE by 250 runs.

LANCASHIRE v KENT

At Manchester, April 26–29. Lancashire won by nine wickets. Lancashire 23pts, Kent 4pts. Toss: Lancashire. First-class debut: J. Clark.

Lancashire needed 104 off 21 overs on the final evening to begin their Championship campaign with two wins. Hailstorms seemed a greater threat than Kent's bowling, but they got home with 14 balls to spare. Key criticised his batsmen's inability to convert starts: their carelessness in the first innings had been especially culpable, forcing them to follow on. Second time around, Denly stood firm for three hours, and Northeast again batted responsibly, but no one could match the application of Prince during his first-day century (extending his record against Kent to four hundreds and two fifties in six innings), or of Davies, who fell one short of a maiden century a week after his 89 at Derby. Jarvis followed his Championship-best there with four wickets in each innings, six of them from the top five, suggesting he would test batsmen far more sternly than he had in Division One in 2014; Siddle supported him well. Jordan Clark made his first-class debut nearly five years into his Lancashire career, following 20 one-day games and 25 Twenty20s.

Close of play: first day, Lancashire 317-5 (Davies 47, Clark 16); second day, Kent 214-7 (Northeast 48); third day, Kent 148-3 (Nash 18, Northeast 11).

Lancashire

P. J. Horton c Billings b Riley	71	– not out	67
L. M. Reece c Stevens b Coles	18	– c Northeast b Claydon	16
A. N. Petersen c Billings b Coles	0	– not out	22
A. G. Prince c sub (C. F. Hartley) b Claydon	106		
*S. J. Croft c Riley b Coles	37		
†A. L. Davies c Coles b Claydon	99		
J. Clark c Billings b Stevens	16		
P. M. Siddle c Billings b Thomas	12		
T. E. Bailey c Billings b Claydon	21		
S. C. Kerrigan c Billings b Claydon	10		
K. M. Jarvis not out	26		
B 5, l-b 13, n-b 10	28	B 1, l-b 1	2

1/38 (2) 2/38 (3) 3/136 (1) (127.1 overs) 444   1/47 (2) (1 wkt, 18.4 overs) 107
4/211 (5) 5/286 (4) 6/317 (7)
7/344 (8) 8/399 (6) 9/412 (9)
10/444 (10)   110 overs: 367-7

Claydon 30.1–6–103–4; Thomas 27–9–75–1; Coles 19–2–79–3; Stevens 19–6–55–1; Riley 29–4–102–1; Denly 3–0–12–0. *Second innings*—Claydon 6.4–0–30–1; Thomas 1–0–8–0; Coles 5–0–30–0; Stevens 3–0–23–0; Riley 3–0–14–0.

Kent

D. J. Bell-Drummond c Croft b Jarvis	28	– c Davies b Clark	18
J. L. Denly c Horton b Jarvis	28	– lbw b Jarvis	60
*R. W. T. Key c Davies b Jarvis	5	– b Siddle	34
B. P. Nash c Davies b Clark	16	– c Prince b Jarvis	27
S. A. Northeast c Siddle b Jarvis	55	– b Siddle	43
D. I. Stevens lbw b Siddle	15	– lbw b Siddle	16
†S. W. Billings run out	28	– c Davies b Jarvis	11
M. T. Coles b Kerrigan	19	– (10) c Croft b Kerrigan	28
M. E. Claydon c Prince b Siddle	21	– (10) st Davies b Kerrigan	24
A. E. N. Riley c Horton b Kerrigan	6	– (9) lbw b Jarvis	17
I. A. A. Thomas not out	4	– not out	4
B 4, l-b 11, n-b 12	27	B 1, l-b 4, w 2, n-b 6	13
	252		**295**

1/62 (1) 2/70 (3) 3/85 (2)   (71.2 overs) 252
4/93 (4) 5/148 (6) 6/190 (7)
7/214 (8) 8/240 (9) 9/242 (5) 10/252 (10)

1/39 (1) 2/111 (3)   (123.4 overs) 295
3/128 (2) 4/161 (4)
5/187 (6) 6/216 (7) 7/216 (5)
8/265 (8) 9/283 (9) 10/295 (10)

Siddle 19–5–57–2; Bailey 13–1–53–0; Jarvis 18–5–50–4; Clark 9–1–43–1; Kerrigan 10.2–3–27–2; Croft 2–0–7–0. *Second innings*—Siddle 20–5–36–3; Bailey 13–1–50–0; Clark 20–5–54–1; Jarvis 28–8–67–4; Croft 8–4–7–0; Reece 4–0–26–0; Kerrigan 30.4–11–50–2.

Umpires: J. H. Evans and R. T. Robinson.

At Northampton, May 3–6. LANCASHIRE drew with NORTHAMPTONSHIRE.

LANCASHIRE v GLOUCESTERSHIRE

At Manchester, May 10–13. Gloucestershire won by 91 runs. Gloucestershire 22pts, Lancashire 7pts. Toss: Gloucestershire.

Gloucestershire outplayed the Division Two leaders to record only their ninth win in 90 first-class games in Lancashire. Jones's final-morning declaration set a target of 300 in 70 overs; Payne and Miles removed both openers by lunch, and reduced Lancashire to 22 for four soon after. Petersen and Davies put on 118 to revive hopes of a win, but their dismissals either side of tea allowed Norwell and Miles to complete Gloucestershire's second successive victory, which lifted them to second. Their resilience had been apparent in Dent's accomplished century on the opening day, though he eventually became the first of Siddle's seven victims in his last match before joining Australia. Horton responded with a fine 168, but Handscomb and Marshall extended Gloucestershire's slender lead, adding 130 on the third evening. Lancashire's gloom thickened with the news that opener Reece had broken his left hand. Returning to the dressing-room after falling lbw for two on the fourth day – taking his Championship aggregate to 60 in seven innings – he punched a locker in frustration.

Close of play: first day, Gloucestershire 322-7 (Noema-Barnett 8); second day, Lancashire 276-6 (Horton 134, Siddle 6); third day, Gloucestershire 206-3 (Handscomb 74, Marshall 71).

Gloucestershire

W. A. Tavaré c Davies b Clark	53	– (2) b Buck		34
C. D. J. Dent c Davies b Siddle	116	– (1) b Siddle		9
†G. H. Roderick lbw b Kerrigan	31	– lbw b Siddle		4
P. S. P. Handscomb c Prince b Kerrigan	22	– run out		76
H. J. H. Marshall c Davies b Jarvis	58	– b Jarvis		92
*G. O. Jones b Jarvis	8	– c Petersen b Kerrigan		6
K. Noema-Barnett c Buck b Jarvis	33	– not out		21
T. M. J. Smith lbw b Siddle	7	– lbw b Kerrigan		4
C. N. Miles lbw b Siddle	16	– c sub (A. M. Lilley) b Siddle		12
D. A. Payne c and b Jarvis	18	– b Siddle		3
L. C. Norwell not out	4			
B 4, l-b 9, w 1, n-b 8	22	B 1, l-b 4, w 1, n-b 8		14

1/81 (1) 2/159 (3) 3/217 (4) (109 overs) 388　　1/12 (1) (9 wkts dec, 86.4 overs) 275
4/298 (2) 5/298 (5) 6/313 (6)　　　　　　　　2/30 (3) 3/76 (2)
7/322 (8) 8/346 (9) 9/375 (10) 10/388 (7)　　4/210 (4) 5/218 (6) 6/237 (5)
　　　　　　　　　　　　　　　　　　　　　7/252 (8) 8/271 (9) 9/275 (10)

Siddle 27–8–55–3; Jarvis 31–5–121–4; Buck 16–1–83–0; Reece 3–0–9–0;
Kerrigan 17–4–55–2; Croft 2–0–7–0. *Second innings*—Siddle 18.4–5–39–4; Jarvis 18–2–58–1;
Clark 11–0–36–0; Buck 7–1–41–1; Kerrigan 26–4–78–2; Croft 6–0–18–0.

Lancashire

P. J. Horton c Roderick b Norwell	168	– c Roderick b Miles		9
L. M. Reece c Roderick b Norwell	16	– lbw b Payne		2
A. N. Petersen b Miles	7	– c Handscomb b Payne		63
A. G. Prince c Roderick b Miles	57	– c Roderick b Miles		2
*S. J. Croft lbw b Noema-Barnett	20	– c Roderick b Payne		1
†A. L. Davies run out	0	– c Marshall b Noema-Barnett		58
J. Clark lbw b Norwell	7	– lbw b Miles		34
P. M. Siddle lbw b Norwell	40	– c Roderick b Norwell		12
N. L. Buck c Dent b Miles	4	– c Roderick b Norwell		17
S. C. Kerrigan not out	6	– b Miles		0
K. M. Jarvis c Norwell b Smith	6	– not out		5
L-b 20, w 1, n-b 12	33	L-b 3, n-b 2		5

1/27 (2) 2/73 (3) 3/207 (4) (116.2 overs) 364　　1/11 (2) 2/11 (1) (56.5 overs) 208
4/247 (5) 5/247 (6) 6/265 (7)　　　　　　　　3/13 (4) 4/22 (5)
7/347 (8) 8/350 (1) 9/357 (9)　　　　　　　　5/140 (6) 6/148 (3) 7/165 (8)
10/364 (11)　　　　　　　　　　　　　　　　8/203 (9) 9/203 (7) 10/208 (10)
　　　　　　　　　　　　　110 overs: 353-8

Payne 23–6–54–0; Miles 27–4–71–3; Norwell 29–6–95–4; Noema-Barnett 13–3–46–1; Smith
24.2–2–78–1. *Second innings*—Payne 15–2–31–3; Miles 14.5–3–58–4; Norwell 13–5–27–2; Smith
8–0–71–0; Noema-Barnett 6–1–18–1.

Umpires: M. A. Gough and G. D. Lloyd.

At Leicester, May 17–20. LANCASHIRE beat LEICESTERSHIRE by 244 runs.

LANCASHIRE v DERBYSHIRE

At Southport, May 24–27. Lancashire won by an innings and 15 runs. Lancashire 24pts, Derbyshire
6pts. Toss: Derbyshire.

　　An innings defeat with two sessions to spare was hard on a young Derbyshire team, led for the
first time by Godleman after Wayne Madsen had broken his finger. Godleman and Slater batted past
lunch on the opening day to raise 141, and a total of 370 appeared perfectly respectable – until
Petersen and Prince piled up 258, a third-wicket record at Southport and between these counties.
Taylor was the pick of the attack, and 18-year-old Hosein kept well in difficult circumstances, but
Prince went on to his third double-century, and Lancashire to 551, another ground record.

Derbyshire's attempt to save the game was going well at 119 for one on the third evening, just 62 behind, until Slater and Hughes were both caught at forward short leg by Croft in the last two overs. Next morning, no one – not even Amla – could make anything of Lilley's off-spin and Kerrigan's slow left-armers on a pitch renowned for taking turn later on. Lilley's 63 and five for 23 were career-bests. The game was a splendid advertisement for the charm of outground cricket.

Close of play: first day, Derbyshire 335-9 (Critchley 13, Footitt 0); second day, Lancashire 348-4 (Prince 156, Davies 28); third day, Derbyshire 123-3 (Taylor 0, Amla 0).

Derbyshire

B. T. Slater c Horton b Bailey	69	– c Croft b Lilley	58
*B. A. Godleman c Brown b Jarvis	75	– c Croft b Bailey	7
C. F. Hughes c Davies b Bailey	37	– c Croft b Kerrigan	41
H. M. Amla b Jarvis	69	– (5) b Kerrigan	11
S. L. Elstone lbw b Kerrigan	8	– (6) c Prince b Lilley	0
S. J. Thakor lbw b Kerrigan	0	– (7) c Petersen b Kerrigan	2
†H. R. Hosein c Clark b Jarvis	18	– (8) b Kerrigan	5
D. J. Wainwright b Bailey	5	– (9) c Davies b Lilley	10
M. J. J. Critchley c Brown b Jarvis	41	– (10) not out	0
T. A. I. Taylor c Croft b Clark	21	– b Lilley	2
M. H. A. Footitt not out	6	– b Lilley	5
B 2, l-b 5, n-b 14	21	B 11, l-b 6, n-b 8	25

1/141 (1) 2/155 (2) 3/238 (3) (106.3 overs) 370
4/257 (5) 5/257 (6) 6/294 (7)
7/301 (8) 8/301 (4) 9/335 (10) 10/370 (9)

1/21 (1) 2/119 (1) (83.1 overs) 166
3/119 (3) 4/133 (4)
5/137 (6) 6/141 (5) 7/150 (7)
8/161 (2) 9/161 (8) 10/166 (11)

Bailey 23–6–73–3; Jarvis 27.3–1–132–4; Clark 14–1–61–1; Lilley 20–1–52–0; Kerrigan 22–2–45–2. *Second innings—*Bailey 10–6–20–1; Jarvis 11–5–26–0; Kerrigan 36–15–80–4; Lilley 26.1–16–23–5.

Lancashire

P. J. Horton c Hughes b Footitt	4	S. C. Kerrigan c Hosein b Critchley	1
K. R. Brown c Hosein b Taylor	6	K. M. Jarvis not out	0
A. N. Petersen c Hosein b Taylor	113		
A. G. Prince c Elstone b Critchley	230	B 21, l-b 1, w 8, n-b 6	36
*S. J. Croft lbw b Taylor	22		
†A. L. Davies c Hughes b Taylor	37	1/12 (1) 2/18 (2) (130.1 overs) 551
J. Clark lbw b Wainwright	39	3/276 (3) 4/304 (5) 5/364 (6)
A. M. Lilley c Amla b Elstone	63	6/442 (7) 7/523 (4) 8/533 (9)
T. E. Bailey b Critchley	0	9/551 (8) 10/551 (10) 110 overs: 473-6

Footitt 21–3–82–1; Taylor 27–1–113–4; Thakor 14–1–59–0; Wainwright 31–0–131–1; Elstone 26–4–94–1; Critchley 11.1–1–50–3.

Umpires: R. J. Bailey and N. G. B. Cook.

At The Oval, May 31–June 3. LANCASHIRE drew with SURREY.

At Bristol, June 7–10. LANCASHIRE beat GLOUCESTERSHIRE by 91 runs.

LANCASHIRE v LEICESTERSHIRE

At Manchester, June 14–16. Lancashire won by an innings and 157 runs. Lancashire 23pts, Leicestershire 2pts. Toss: Leicestershire. Championship debut: Umar Akmal.

In an attempt to attract spectators at the end of the working day, this game was scheduled to run from 12.30 to 7.30. With the match beginning on a Sunday, the initiative's modest success could be judged only on the second day's evidence, when an attendance of 1,195 was at least 25% up on previous fixtures; 53 tickets were sold after 4pm. Poor weather had limited the first day to 50 overs under floodlights, and a confident Lancashire wrapped up an overwhelming victory by 6.45 on Tuesday. For the second time in a month, their attack proved far too strong for Leicestershire, whose two innings occupied a mere 98.4 overs. Cosgrove had won the toss on the truncated first day, when they were bowled out shortly after "supper"; lunch had become "tea". Faulkner became the first Lancashire player to take a first-class hat-trick (split between overs) since James Anderson in 2003, and Jarvis the first bowler to claim 50 wickets in the English season, in his ninth match (all in the Championship). In Lancashire's formidable reply, Brown fell just short of only the second century in his 109 first-class innings, while Prince completed his fourth of the season, which made him the leading scorer in the country. He was eventually one of Naik's career-best eight victims – three of them stumped by O'Brien – but Jarvis and Lilley swept Leicestershire aside on the third evening.

Close of play: first day, Leicestershire 207; second day, Lancashire 314-4 (Prince 74, Davies 7).

Leicestershire

A. J. Robson c Davies b Jarvis	23	– b Jarvis		27
†N. J. O'Brien c Davies b Jarvis	14	– lbw b Jarvis		10
E. J. H. Eckersley c Horton b Bailey	2	– c Horton b Lilley		27
*M. J. Cosgrove lbw b Bailey	26	– c Lilley b Faulkner		4
Umar Akmal c Davies b Bailey	13	– c Davies b Lilley		20
A. P. Agathangelou c Davies b Bailey	54	– c Davies b Lilley		18
B. A. Raine c Kerrigan b Faulkner	26	– c Prince b Lilley		0
J. K. H. Naik lbw b Faulkner	9	– lbw b Jarvis		3
R. M. L. Taylor not out	20	– b Jarvis		0
C. E. Shreck lbw b Faulkner	0	– lbw b Jarvis		0
A. Sheikh c Davies b Jarvis	5	– not out		0
B 5, l-b 2, n-b 8	15	B 6, l-b 4		10

1/26 (2) 2/31 (3) 3/47 (1)   (50 overs) 207
4/75 (5) 5/78 (4) 6/165 (6)
7/179 (7) 8/182 (8) 9/182 (10) 10/207 (11)

1/24 (2) 2/47 (1)   (48.4 overs) 119
3/58 (4) 4/85 (5)
5/90 (3) 6/90 (7) 7/107 (8)
8/107 (9) 9/115 (6) 10/119 (10)

Bailey 20–2–69–4; Jarvis 14–0–72–3; Faulkner 15–2–53–3; Kerrigan 1–0–6–0. *Second innings*— Bailey 10–1–25–0; Jarvis 15.4–4–44–5; Faulkner 7–2–11–1; Lilley 15–5–28–4; Kerrigan 1–0–1–0.

Lancashire

P. J. Horton c Agathangelou b Taylor	54	K. M. Jarvis b Naik		0
K. R. Brown lbw b Raine	96	S. C. Kerrigan not out		7
A. N. Petersen lbw b Naik	46			
A. G. Prince st O'Brien b Naik	104	B 10, l-b 13, w 6, n-b 2		31
*S. J. Croft c Sheikh b Naik	22			
†A. L. Davies b Shreck b Naik	29	1/91 (1) 2/174 (3) (124.3 overs) 483
J. P. Faulkner c Agathangelou b Naik	8	3/248 (2) 4/303 (5) 5/355 (6)
A. M. Lilley st O'Brien b Naik	59	6/371 (7) 7/428 (4) 8/474 (9)
T. E. Bailey st O'Brien b Naik	27	9/474 (10) 10/483 (8) 110 overs: 371-5

Sheikh 16–4–64–0; Raine 20–2–53–1; Naik 44.3–7–179–8; Shreck 29–7–82–0; Taylor 14–5–77–1; Agathangelou 1–0–5–0.

Umpires: S. C. Gale and M. J. Saggers.

LANCASHIRE v NORTHAMPTONSHIRE

At Manchester, June 29–July 2. Drawn. Lancashire 11pts, Northamptonshire 13pts. Toss: Northamptonshire.

"We got away with that one," said Lancashire coach Ashley Giles, after rain denied Northamptonshire a deserved third Championship victory. Wakely had challenged the Division Two leaders to score 414 in 102 overs, which would have been a county fourth-innings record to win. Horton and Brown, with his fifth successive fifty, opened with 130 in 36, but the bowlers fought back on the final afternoon, when Stone claimed three for six in 24 deliveries; Lancashire were seven down with at least 35.4 overs left when the weather closed in. Northamptonshire's dominance had been established on the first day, when 20-year-old Duckett's 134 in 151 balls laid the foundations for a solid total. Lancashire appeared set to match it, with Brown again in sight of a century before falling cruelly short, and Prince the first to reach 1,000 runs in the English season. But they lost their last eight for 82, and in sweltering heat Duckett nearly made a second hundred as Northamptonshire built on their 130-run lead. After a hat-trick in the previous game, Faulkner took two wickets in two balls in both innings here.

Close of play: first day, Northamptonshire 388-6 (Rossington 79, Crook 15); second day, Lancashire 257-4 (Croft 13, Faulkner 5); third day, Lancashire 19-0 (Horton 5, Brown 12).

Northamptonshire

K. J. Coetzer lbw b Jarvis	1	– c Davies b Bailey	5
B. M. Duckett lbw b Kerrigan	134	– c Prince b Lilley	88
*A. G. Wakely b Faulkner	56	– c Kerrigan	9
R. I. Keogh c Croft b Kerrigan	19	– lbw b Faulkner	20
R. E. Levi c Davies b Faulkner	57	– lbw b Faulkner	0
†A. M. Rossington lbw b Jarvis	89	– c Croft b Lilley	15
J. J. Cobb c Croft b Faulkner	0	– not out	52
S. P. Crook c Clark b Bailey	34	– lbw b Lilley	37
G. G. White c Horton b Faulkner	0	– c Lilley b Kerrigan	8
O. P. Stone c Horton b Jarvis	8	– c Horton b Kerrigan	35
Azharullah not out	12		
B 12, l-b 7, w 1, n-b 8	28	B 4, l-b 7, w 1, n-b 2	14

1/1 (1) 2/171 (3) 3/227 (2)   (110.3 overs) 438   1/6 (1)   (9 wkts dec, 66.5 overs) 283
4/228 (4) 5/370 (5) 6/370 (7)   2/36 (3) 3/91 (4)
7/406 (6) 8/407 (9) 9/422 (10)   4/91 (5) 5/110 (6) 6/155 (2)
10/438 (8)   110 overs: 438-9   7/225 (8) 8/236 (9) 9/283 (10)

Bailey 18.3–3–61–1; Jarvis 26–3–122–3; Faulkner 28–5–63–4; Clark 10–1–40–0; Lilley 13–1–63–0; Kerrigan 15–0–70–2. *Second innings*—Bailey 3–0–14–1; Jarvis 12–2–36–0; Kerrigan 21.5–2–94–3; Faulkner 7–1–31–2; Lilley 23–3–97–3.

Lancashire

P. J. Horton b Stone	0	– b Stone	65
K. R. Brown b Stone b White	97	– c Rossington b Crook	82
†A. L. Davies c Rossington b Keogh	51	– lbw b Stone	1
A. G. Prince b Stone b Keogh	83	– c Rossington b Stone	7
*S. J. Croft b Crook	25	– lbw b Keogh	0
J. P. Faulkner c Wakely b Azharullah	7	– lbw b Keogh	9
J. Clark b Crook	18	– not out	4
A. M. Lilley c Rossington b Stone	1	– lbw b White	13
T. E. Bailey b Crook	7	– not out	4
K. M. Jarvis not out	3		
S. C. Kerrigan c Cobb b Azharullah	2		
B 1, l-b 11, n-b 2	14	B 18, l-b 3	21

1/1 (1) 2/110 (3) 3/226 (2)   (97.3 overs) 308   1/130 (1)   (7 wkts dec, 66.2 overs) 206
4/246 (4) 5/262 (6) 6/279 (5)   2/132 (3) 3/146 (4)
7/280 (8) 8/298 (7) 9/303 (9) 10/308 (11)   4/147 (5) 5/179 (2)
                             6/185 (6) 7/202 (8)

Azharullah 19.3–4–57–2; Stone 19–2–49–2; White 19–7–46–1; Keogh 27–2–93–2; Crook 9–2–28–3; Cobb 3–0–19–0; Coetzer 1–0–4–0. *Second innings*—Stone 14–2–26–3; Azharullah 6–0–33–0; Keogh 25–5–69–2; Crook 9–1–21–1; White 12.2–3–36–1.

Umpires: R. J. Evans and B. V. Taylor.

LANCASHIRE v ESSEX

At Manchester, July 6–9. Drawn. Lancashire 13pts, Essex 8pts. Toss: Lancashire. County debuts: T. J. Lester; L. A. Dawson.

Nearly 140 overs were lost to rain and bad light, most of them on the first two days, but Lancashire earned maximum bonus points and even threatened to pull off an unexpected win. Croft displayed an excellent temperament during a century which spread across the first three days, and was well supported by Davies and Faulkner. Then Lilley and Jarvis clinched a fifth batting point by scoring 55 in seven overs to hasten the declaration. Toby Lester, a 22-year-old left-arm seamer from Blackpool who was Lancashire's 666th first-class player, struck twice in his opening spell, and his joy was heart-warming. Browne stood firm for Essex, despite dislocating a right index finger playing the Australians a few days earlier, reaching his century on the fourth morning, but could not prevent them following on by lunch. He added a second fifty before being dismissed again by Lilley, who claimed three wickets on a pitch taking some turn, to offer home supporters faint hope of a dramatic victory. But Dawson, playing his first match on loan from Hampshire, and Ryder blocked for nearly an hour.

Close of play: first day, Lancashire 96-4 (Croft 9, Davies 4); second day, Lancashire 257-5 (Croft 85, Faulkner 37); third day, Essex 139-5 (Browne 78, Foster 13).

Lancashire

P. J. Horton c Ryder b Porter	25	A. M. Lilley not out	40
K. R. Brown c Dawson b Porter	18	K. M. Jarvis not out	15
A. N. Petersen lbw b Dawson	14	B 1, l-b 11, n-b 14	26
A. G. Prince b Dawson	21		
*S. J. Croft c Mickleburgh b Topley	122	(8 wkts dec, 100.2 overs)	402
†A. L. Davies lbw b Bopara	38		
J. P. Faulkner c Foster b Topley	68		
J. Clark lbw b Topley	15		

1/48 (1) 2/49 (2) 3/73 (3) 4/92 (4) 5/171 (6) 6/315 (5) 7/346 (7) 8/347 (8)

T. J. Lester did not bat.

Porter 20–4–81–2; Topley 24–6–90–3; Ryder 7–0–30–0; Napier 15–2–54–0; Dawson 15.2–3–37–2; Smith 9–0–49–0; Bopara 10–0–49–1.

Essex

N. L. J. Browne c Davies b Lilley	105	– c Prince b Lilley	50
J. C. Mickleburgh b Lester	1	– c Croft b Lilley	37
L. A. Dawson b Lester	17	– not out	40
R. S. Bopara c Davies b Faulkner	6	– c Brown b Lilley	22
J. D. Ryder c Lilley b Faulkner	4	– not out	9
R. N. ten Doeschate lbw b Faulkner	0		
*†J. S. Foster lbw b Faulkner	14		
G. M. Smith b Faulkner	3		
G. R. Napier c Davies b Lester	23		
J. A. Porter not out	0		
R. J. W. Topley b Lilley	0		
B 9, l-b 2, w 1, n-b 18	30	B 4, l-b 6	10

1/12 (2) 2/50 (3) 3/73 (4) (71 overs) 203   1/86 (2) (3 wkts, 59 overs) 168
4/81 (5) 5/81 (6) 6/160 (7)   2/87 (1) 3/127 (4)
7/164 (8) 8/197 (9) 9/203 (1) 10/203 (11)

Jarvis 19–4–54–0; Lester 16–5–50–3; Faulkner 17–5–39–5; Clark 6–2–19–0; Lilley 13–1–30–2. *Second innings*—Lester 5–0–23–0; Lilley 24–5–63–3; Jarvis 8–2–30–0; Faulkner 11–1–30–0; Clark 4–3–1–0; Croft 7–2–11–0.

Umpires: R. A. Kettleborough and D. J. Millns.

At Colwyn Bay, July 19–22. LANCASHIRE beat GLAMORGAN by an innings and 157 runs. *Alviro Petersen and Ashwell Prince add 501 for the third wicket, an all-wicket record for Lancashire.*

LANCASHIRE v GLAMORGAN

At Manchester, August 21–24. Drawn. Lancashire 11pts, Glamorgan 7pts. Toss: Lancashire. First-class debut: H. Hameed.

When Glamorgan followed on early on the final day, Lancashire hoped to sew up promotion with a month to go. But Rudolph's four-hour vigil and Cooke's resilience prevented their eighth win, and left them five points short. The much-anticipated debut of 18-year-old Haseeb Hameed, and only the second hundred of a nine-year career for Brown, his fellow Boltonian, were the highlights of a rain-affected draw. News of Paul Horton's release had broken the day before the game; Hameed took over the opener's role, batting patiently for 150 minutes with Brown, who closed on 80. "Don't bottle it this time," he was ordered by Stan, the Old Trafford gateman, as he drove in next morning – Brown had perished in the nineties twice in his previous five innings – but he soon banished such fears. A flurry from Davies secured three batting points with two balls to spare; he added 128 in 23 overs with Faulkner before again missing out on a maiden century. Glamorgan batted poorly in their first innings – nightwatchman Salter top-scored – and Kerrigan profited to claim their last three in 25 deliveries, with Bull absent because of a bad back.

Close of play: first day, Lancashire 161-3 (Brown 80, Croft 9); second day, Glamorgan 48-1 (Rudolph 18, Salter 3); third day, Glamorgan 182-6 (Wallace 20, Wagg 0).

Lancashire

K. R. Brown c Cooke b Lloyd	132	K. M. Jarvis c Wallace b Meschede		5
H. Hameed lbw b Wagg	28	S. C. Kerrigan not out		1
A. N. Petersen c Cooke b Lloyd	29			
A. G. Prince c Bragg b Wagg	4	B 2, l-b 7, w 5, n-b 8		22
*S. J. Croft c Wallace b Meschede	67			
†A. L. Davies c Wagg b Ingram	95	1/76 (2) 2/125 (3)	(140.1 overs)	462
J. P. Faulkner c Lloyd b Meschede	63	3/142 (4) 4/274 (1) 5/307 (5)		
A. M. Lilley st Wallace b Ingram	16	6/435 (7) 7/444 (6) 8/450 (9)		
G. Chapple c Lloyd b Meschede	0	9/460 (10) 10/462 (8)	110 overs: 301-4	

Wagg 30–8–83–2; Hogan 30–10–75–0; Lloyd 26–9–86–2; Meschede 24–3–101–4; Salter 17–2–51–0; Bull 10–2–48–0; Ingram 3.1–0–9–2.

Glamorgan

*J. A. Rudolph c Davies b Chapple	22	– lbw b Croft	63
W. D. Bragg lbw b Lilley	27	– c Brown b Jarvis	8
A. G. Salter st Davies b Kerrigan	45		
C. A. Ingram b Faulkner	17	– (3) c Davies b Faulkner	18
C. B. Cooke lbw b Faulkner	31	– (4) not out	41
D. L. Lloyd b Chapple	15	– (5) not out	20
†M. A. Wallace b Kerrigan	22		
G. G. Wagg st Davies b Kerrigan	20		
C. A. J. Meschede not out	7		
M. G. Hogan c Chapple b Kerrigan	2		
K. A. Bull absent hurt			
L-b 3, n-b 2	5	B 4, l-b 1, n-b 4	9

1/40 (2) 2/57 (1) 3/96 (4)	(79.4 overs)	213	1/16 (2) (3 wkts, 82 overs) 159
4/122 (3) 5/149 (6) 6/182 (5)			2/45 (3) 3/136 (1)
7/188 (7) 8/211 (8) 9/213 (10)			

Jarvis 10–1–37–0; Chapple 17–4–41–2; Kerrigan 24.4–5–60–4; Lilley 13–2–36–1; Faulkner 15–4–36–2. *Second innings*—Chapple 9–2–25–0; Jarvis 11–2–27–1; Kerrigan 31–16–42–0; Lilley 17–5–39–0; Faulkner 8–4–18–1; Croft 6–3–3–1.

Umpires: R. J. Bailey and R. K. Illingworth.

At Canterbury, September 1–4. LANCASHIRE drew with KENT. *Lancashire ensure promotion.*

LANCASHIRE v SURREY

At Manchester, September 14–17. Drawn. Lancashire 9pts, Surrey 12pts. Toss: Surrey. County debut: P. Mustard.

Both teams were already promoted, and Surrey might have clinched the title but for Batty's absurdly late declaration and two stoppages for bad light on the final afternoon – as well as a brief pause when an aeroplane, apparently struggling after a bird strike, flew low over the ground. On the first day, Ansari's 99 displayed the diligence that earned him an England call-up to the Test squad against Pakistan announced the following morning. That afternoon, however, he parried a ferocious cover-drive from Prince, dislocating his left thumb; a week later, he was ruled out of the tour. Having steered Surrey past 400, the Curran brothers shared eight wickets to secure a lead of 208, which would have been more but for a county-best 42 from Anderson, returning for his first county game of the season after the side strain he suffered during the Ashes. Batty's decision not to enforce the follow-on allowed Sangakkara to score a superb century, but setting Lancashire 492 in just over a day was cautious in the extreme. Hameed batted nearly five and a half hours for a composed 91, and was dismissed a few minutes before bad light ended play with nine overs left and three wickets standing. Anderson had taken his 700th first-class wicket on the second day – caught by Phil Mustard, on loan from Durham because Alex Davies had hurt his knee.

Close of play: first day, Surrey 262-4 (Davies 32, Roy 15); second day, Lancashire 141-5 (Prince 38, Clark 9); third day, Lancashire 22-0 (Brown 12, Hameed 10).

Surrey

R. J. Burns b Bailey	50	– c Anderson b Kerrigan		44
Z. S. Ansari c Anderson b Croft	99			
K. C. Sangakkara c Croft b Anderson	9	– c and b Croft		118
†B. T. Foakes c Petersen b Lilley	45	– (2) lbw b Bailey		14
S. M. Davies b Brown b Anderson	35	– (4) c Kerrigan b Croft		21
J. J. Roy b Kerrigan	66	– (5) b Lilley		6
G. C. Wilson c Brown b Kerrigan	51	– not out		30
S. M. Curran c Prince b Kerrigan	29	– (6) c Anderson b Croft		0
T. K. Curran c Mustard b Anderson	23	– (8) b Croft		19
*G. J. Batty not out	50			
M. P. Dunn c Prince b Kerrigan	3			
L-b 16, w 2, n-b 2	20	B 20, l-b 9, n-b 2		31

1/89 (1) 2/108 (3) 3/175 (4)   (138 overs) 480   1/42 (2)   (7 wkts dec, 54.1 overs) 283
4/244 (2) 5/268 (5) 6/363 (6) 7/384 (7)   2/150 (1) 3/210 (4)
8/421 (9) 9/423 (8) 10/480 (11)   110 overs: 389-7   4/217 (5) 5/218 (6) 6/243 (3) 7/283 (8)

Anderson 30–6–85–3; Bailey 26–6–78–1; Clark 18–1–79–0; Lilley 19–2–87–1; Kerrigan 43–7–128–4; Croft 2–0–7–1. *Second innings*—Anderson 6–1–32–0; Bailey 7–0–33–1; Lilley 19–0–82–1; Kerrigan 15–0–72–1; Croft 7.1–0–35–4.

Lancashire

K. R. Brown lbw b S. M. Curran	27	– lbw b T. K. Curran		16
H. Hameed lbw b S. M. Curran	17	– c T. K. Curran b S. M. Curran		91
A. N. Petersen lbw b T. K. Curran	9	– c Burns b Dunn		13
A. G. Prince c Sangakkara b T. K. Curran	45	– c Sangakkara b Dunn		11
*S. J. Croft c Foakes b S. M. Curran	5	– c Foakes b T. K. Curran		40
†P. Mustard st Foakes b Batty	43	– c Sangakkara b Dunn		8
J. Clark lbw b S. M. Curran	29	– c Foakes b T. K. Curran		3
A. M. Lilley c Dunn b Batty	33	– not out		5
T. E. Bailey b S. M. Curran	0	– not out		1
S. C. Kerrigan not out	23			
J. M. Anderson b T. K. Curran	42			
L-b 3, n-b 4	7	B 2, l-b 5		7

1/28 (2) 2/33 (3) 3/47 (1)   (71.3 overs) 272   1/32 (1)   (7 wkts, 84.3 overs) 195
4/57 (5) 5/120 (6) 6/153 (4)   2/53 (3) 3/71 (4)
7/201 (7) 8/201 (9) 9/207 (8) 10/272 (11)   4/162 (5) 5/171 (6) 6/182 (7) 7/194 (2)

T. K. Curran 23.3–6–54–3; S. M. Curran 19–2–67–5; Dunn 10–0–62–0; Batty 19–1–86–2. *Second innings*—T. K. Curran 29.3–16–46–3; S. M. Curran 18–3–68–1; Dunn 17–3–46–3; Batty 17–8–24–0; Burns 3–1–4–0.

Umpires: R. J. Evans and J. H. Evans.

At Chelmsford, September 22–25. LANCASHIRE drew with ESSEX.

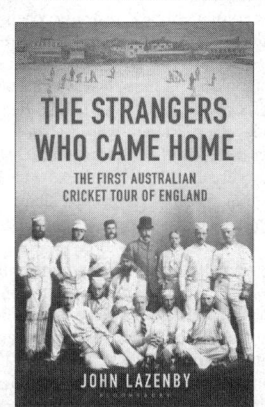

LEICESTERSHIRE

Baggy Green shoots of recovery

PAUL JONES

Achievement is relative: a season consisting of a third consecutive Championship wooden spoon, failure to qualify for the knockout phase of the NatWest T20 Blast, and a solitary point in the Royal London One-Day Cup would not be considered successful by most counties.

But when Leicestershire beat Essex by six wickets at Chelmsford in June, they ended a wretched run in which they had failed to win a Championship game since September 2012 (it was also their first away win since 2010). The players admitted to celebrating as if they had won the title, and Richard Rae – commentating on BBC Radio Leicester – sounded distinctly emotional as Lewis Hill struck the winning run. The season ended amid talk of developing Grace Road: plans were announced to install Twenty20-friendly floodlights and a new stand on the Milligan Road side of the ground. It would be difficult to deny that Leicestershire had finished the summer in better shape than they had done 12 months earlier.

On-field improvements, which included two Championship wins and a rain-affected near miss against Northamptonshire, reflected the managerial changes made at the end of the previous season. Chief executive Wasim Khan and Australian head coach Andrew McDonald formed an effective partnership, and McDonald – whom Khan believes good enough to be "Australia coach in six or seven years" – was rewarded with a new contract that will keep him at Leicestershire until 2017.

Australian seamer Clint McKay was a hit, taking 58 first-class wickets and earning himself another season as the club's overseas player. He also had a positive influence on emerging all-rounder Ben Raine, who finished as Leicestershire's highest first-class wicket-taker, with 61 (his value was underlined by 546 runs, too). Add in the veteran Charlie Shreck, who in September re-signed for 2016 after claiming 57 wickets at less than 30, and Leicestershire boast a penetrative seam attack – as long as this trio stay injury-free.

Beyond them, the cupboard looked rather emptier: Rob Taylor, a medium-paced left-armer who played for Scotland at the World Cup, was next on the list of Championship wicket-takers, with 18 at 40. Spin must be a concern. Off-spinner Jigar Naik played seven matches with moderate success, but Leicestershire often opted not to field a frontline slow bowler.

In a new back-room set-up for 2016, Shreck became bowling development coach on top of his playing duties, while the former Hampshire wicketkeeper Nic Pothas took charge of the Academy, and another ex-keeper, Leicester-born Keith Piper, was appointed elite development coach. Moving in the other direction were Lloyd Tennant and club stalwart, Ben Smith, after a combined 45 years at Leicestershire as players and coaches.

Another Australian, Mark Cosgrove – in his first season as player and captain – finished the year strongly to score over 1,000 first-class runs; it is vital he shows the same consistency in 2016. He will need to improve discipline: Leicestershire can ill afford to lose 16 points, as they did in 2015 for breaching the ECB code of conduct on five occasions.

Angus Robson also went past 1,000 first-class runs, but urgently requires a steady partner at the top of the order; the signing of the experienced Paul Horton from Lancashire in September could be the

Chris Ison, PA Photos

Ben Raine

answer. Extra nous was added to the middle order with the arrival of Mark Pettini from Essex and Neil Dexter from Middlesex, both former captains. They will increase competition for places, and may yet spur Ned Eckersley on to regain the form that saw him amass 1,302 runs in 2013. He was an ever-present in 2015, though his average was half the 50 he managed two years earlier. He signed a two-year contract in September, and was reappointed vice-captain.

Aadil Ali, a local batsman who turned 21 in December, emerged from their Academy programme to play seven Championship matches, scoring 412 runs at a healthy average of 37. He caught the eye with his calm, composed manner, while his ability to leave anything wide of off stump confirmed the calculating nature of his game. The short Leicestershire careers of Dan Redfern and Andrea Agathangelou came to an end when both were released.

The club were disappointing in the two white-ball tournaments. They never got going in the Royal London One-Day Cup, and it was a blessing when the group stages came to an end. They had been better in the T20 Blast, and Pakistani hitter Umar Akmal, who replaced Grant Elliott after he was selected to play for New Zealand, became a cult hero following blistering innings to win games against Nottinghamshire and Warwickshire. Leicestershire fell away towards the end of the competition after Ireland pair Kevin and Niall O'Brien were called up for international duty. Kevin was re-signed for both competitions in 2016, while Akmal was retained for the Blast.

From the bottom of Division Two, some members and supporters might feel Leicestershire are light years away from being able to challenge for promotion and one-day silverware. They aren't. There is little to choose between the bulk of the teams in the second division, and drafting in the right player here and there can help to bring about a quick transformation. The atmosphere around the club is one of optimism, on both the playing and commercial sides. That feeling must now be translated into solid results.

Championship attendance: 12,517.

LEICESTERSHIRE RESULTS

All first-class matches – Played 17: Won 3, Lost 9, Drawn 5.
County Championship matches – Played 16: Won 2, Lost 9, Drawn 5.

LV= County Championship, 9th in Division 2;
NatWest T20 Blast, 7th in North Group; Royal London One-Day Cup, 9th in Group A.

COUNTY CHAMPIONSHIP AVERAGES, BATTING AND FIELDING

Cap		Birthplace	M	I	NO	R	HS	100	Avge	Ct/St
	M. J. Cosgrove¶	Elizabeth, Aust.	15	28	1	1,093	156	4	40.48	8
	A. M. Ali	Leicester†	7	12	1	412	80	0	37.45	2
	N. J. O'Brien	Dublin, Ireland	12	22	2	693	95	0	34.65	51/4
	A. J. Robson	Darlinghurst, Aust.	16	32	1	967	120	1	31.19	13
	R. M. L. Taylor	Northampton	8	15	7	221	42	0	27.62	4
2013	E. J. H. Eckersley	Oxford	16	31	0	798	147	2	25.74	9
	C. J. McKay§	Melbourne, Aust.	12	22	4	452	51*	0	25.11	2
	D. J. Redfern	Shrewsbury	5	10	1	226	74	0	25.11	1
	L. J. Hill	Leicester†	9	18	2	356	126	1	22.25	15
2013	M. A. G. Boyce	Cheltenham	6	12	0	260	60	0	21.66	4
	O. H. Freckingham	Oakham	4	7	4	65	34*	0	21.66	0
2012	W. A. White	Derby	3	4	0	84	43	0	21.00	0
	A. P. Agathangelou¶	Rustenberg, SA	6	12	1	225	54	0	20.45	12
	B. A. Raine	Sunderland	16	28	2	502	57	0	19.30	3
	N. D. Pinner	Stourbridge	5	10	1	168	68	0	18.66	7
2013	J. K. H. Naik	Leicester†	7	13	3	111	30	0	11.10	1
	T. J. Wells	Grantham	5	8	0	71	18	0	8.87	3
	G. P. Smith	Leicester†	2	4	0	24	20	0	6.00	1
	C. E. Shreck	Truro	14	22	7	41	15	0	2.73	5

Also batted: Z. J. Chappell (*Grantham*) 96, 7; R. J. Sayer (*Huntingdon*) (4 matches) 23, 1, 34 (1 ct); A. Sheikh (*Nottingham*) (2 matches) 1, 5, 0* (1 ct); Umar Akmal§ (*Lahore, Pakistan*) (1 match) 13, 20.

† *Born in Leicestershire.*   § *Official overseas player.*
¶ *Other non-England-qualified player.*

BOWLING

	Style	O	M	R	W	BB	5I	Avge
C. J. McKay	RFM	480.5	122	1,439	58	6-54	3	24.81
B. A. Raine	RFM	521.1	121	1,673	59	5-43	2	28.35
C. E. Shreck	RFM	512.4	116	1,691	57	5-71	2	29.66
O. H. Freckingham	RFM	113	13	458	14	4-91	0	32.71
R. M. L. Taylor	LM	167.4	24	720	18	3-41	0	40.00
J. K. H. Naik	OB	173	33	661	16	8-179	1	41.31

Also bowled: A. P. Agathangelou (LBG/OB) 9–1–33–1; A. M. Ali (OB) 4–0–19–0; Z. J. Chappell (RFM) 26–1–106–2; M. J. Cosgrove (RM) 60.2–14–192–3; L. J. Hill (RM) 2–0–6–0; D. J. Redfern (OB) 38.1–8–100–2; R. J. Sayer (OB) 86–7–352–4; A. Sheikh (LFM) 38.1–6–186–3; T. J. Wells (RFM) 85.5–12–369–7; W. A. White (RFM) 74.2–8–289–9.

LEADING NATWEST T20 BLAST AVERAGES (100 runs/16 overs)

Batting

	Runs	HS	Avge	SR	Ct/St
T. J. Wells	166	64*	41.50	159.61	13
Umar Akmal	133	76*	133.00	143.01	2
K. J. O'Brien	160	48*	26.66	139.13	0
M. J. Cosgrove	299	74	27.18	131.71	3
B. A. Raine	111	32*	18.50	129.06	0
G. D. Elliott	225	56	32.14	120.96	5
N. J. O'Brien	169	47*	42.25	114.96	8/2
E. J. H. Eckersley	174	39	13.38	106.09	3

Bowling

	W	BB	Avge	ER
C. J. McKay	14	4-24	23.71	7.29
J. K. H. Naik	11	3-23	25.36	7.34
B. A. Raine	14	3-23	27.00	8.46
A. Sheikh	4	2-13	35.25	8.81
R. M. L. Taylor	4	2-32	37.50	8.82

LEADING ROYAL LONDON CUP AVERAGES (100 runs/3 wickets)

Batting	Runs	HS	Avge	SR	Ct/St
R. M. L. Taylor . .	148	42*	37.00	88.09	0
L. J. Hill	103	86	34.33	87.28	0
M. G. K. Burgess	101	49	25.25	90.99	1
E. J. H. Eckersley	159	71	22.71	56.98	0
A. J. Robson	158	90	22.57	72.47	2
A. M. Ali	151	84	21.57	71.22	5
N. J. O'Brien	143	50	20.42	72.22	3/1

Bowling	W	BB	Avge	ER
C. J. McKay	9	3-36	19.66	4.02
R. M. L. Taylor . .	7	2-19	31.57	5.81
T. J. Wells	3	2-45	34.66	6.93
B. A. Raine	5	2-48	39.80	5.52
A. Sheikh	3	1-43	69.33	5.80
R. J. Sayer	3	1-46	81.00	6.23

FIRST-CLASS COUNTY RECORDS

Highest score for	309*	H. D. Ackerman v Glamorgan at Cardiff	2006
Highest score against	**355***	**K. P. Pietersen (Surrey) at The Oval**	**2015**
Leading run-scorer	30,143	L. G. Berry (avge 30.32)	1924–51
Best bowling for	10-18	G. Geary v Glamorgan at Pontypridd	1929
Best bowling against	10-32	H. Pickett (Essex) at Leyton	1895
Leading wicket-taker	2,131	W. E. Astill (avge 23.18).	1906–39
Highest total for	701-4 dec	v Worcestershire at Worcester	1906
Highest total against	761-6 dec	by Essex at Chelmsford	1990
Lowest total for	25	v Kent at Leicester.	1912
Lowest total against {	24	by Glamorgan at Leicester	1971
	24	by Oxford University at Oxford	1985

LIST A COUNTY RECORDS

Highest score for	201	V. J. Wells v Berkshire at Leicester	1996
Highest score against	201*	R. S. Bopara (Essex) at Leicester	2008
Leading run-scorer	8,216	N. E. Briers (avge 27.66).	1975–95
Best bowling for	6-16	C. M. Willoughby v Somerset at Leicester	2005
Best bowling against	6-21	S. M. Pollock (Warwickshire) at Birmingham	1996
Leading wicket-taker	308	K. Higgs (avge 18.80)	1972–82
Highest total for	406-5	v Berkshire at Leicester	1996
Highest total against	**373-5**	**by New Zealanders at Leicester**	**2015**
Lowest total for	36	v Sussex at Leicester	1973
Lowest total against {	62	by Northamptonshire at Leicester	1974
	62	by Middlesex at Leicester	1998

TWENTY20 COUNTY RECORDS

Highest score for	111	D. L. Maddy v Yorkshire at Leeds	2004
Highest score against	95	D. J. Willey (Northamptonshire) at Northampton . .	2014
Leading run-scorer	1,455	P. A. Nixon (avge 21.71).	2003–11
Best bowling for	5-13	A. B. McDonald v Nottinghamshire at Nottingham .	2010
Best bowling against	5-21	J. A. Brooks (Yorkshire) at Leeds	2013
Leading wicket-taker	69	C. W. Henderson (avge 26.95)	2004–12
Highest total for	221-3	v Yorkshire at Leeds	2004
Highest total against	225-2	by Durham at Chester-le-Street	2010
Lowest total for	90	v Nottinghamshire at Nottingham	2014
Lowest total against	72	by Derbyshire at Derby	2013

ADDRESS

County Ground, Grace Road, Leicester LE2 8AD; 0116 283 2128; enquiries@leicestershireccc.co.uk; www.leicestershireccc.co.uk.

OFFICIALS

Captain M. J. Cosgrove
2016 (limited-overs) M. L. Pettini
Elite performance director A. B. McDonald
First-team coach 2015 B. F. Smith
Elite development coach 2016 K. J. Piper
Academy director N. Pothas

President D. W. Wilson
Chairman P. R. Haywood
Chief executive W. G. Khan
Operations manager P. Atkinson
Head groundsman A. Ward
Scorer P. J. Rogers

At Cambridge, April 7–9. LEICESTERSHIRE beat CAMBRIDGE MCCU by 344 runs.

LEICESTERSHIRE v GLAMORGAN

At Leicester, April 12–15. Drawn. Leicestershire 11pts, Glamorgan 12pts. Toss: Glamorgan. County debuts: A. Carter, C. A. Ingram.

Leicestershire began the season with a new chief executive, head coach, captain and overseas player – although Australian seamer Clint McKay did not arrive in time to lead the attack in the Championship opener. Glamorgan took little note of all that and, after winning the toss, built a huge total in buffeting winds that taxed the bowlers; the 44 conceded by Leicestershire in no-balls, mainly by Sheikh, certainly helped. Rudolph, missed on nought by Eckersley above his head at third slip, and Bragg, with a career-best 120, both struck centuries and put on 227 for the second wicket. Eckersley responded in kind, equalling his career-best 147 as Leicestershire made an encouraging 435. With Andy Carter drafted in on loan from Nottinghamshire to replace the injured Michael Hogan, Rudolph erred on the side of caution in his first Championship match as Glamorgan captain, eventually setting Leicestershire 306 in 50 overs. They lost two early wickets, but an unbeaten fifty from Cosgrove, a former Glamorgan player, steered his new side to safety. Wallace became the first Glamorgan specialist wicketkeeper – and their 24th player – to pass 10,000 first-class runs, while his Leicestershire counterpart held nine catches.

Close of play: first day, Glamorgan 294-2 (Bragg 113, Ingram 14); second day, Leicestershire 202-1 (Robson 82, Eckersley 81); third day, Glamorgan 47-3 (Ingram 2, Cooke 0).

Glamorgan

J. M. Kettleborough c O'Brien b Sheikh	10	– c O'Brien b Shreck 13
*J. A. Rudolph c O'Brien b Sheikh	111	– c O'Brien b Wells 15
W. D. Bragg lbw b Sheikh	120	– lbw b Shreck 6
C. A. Ingram b Shreck	38	– c O'Brien b Freckingham ... 17
C. B. Cooke c Eckersley b Freckingham	48	– c Shreck b Raine 81
†M. A. Wallace lbw b Freckingham	10	– c O'Brien b Raine 8
G. G. Wagg lbw b Raine	5	– c O'Brien b Freckingham .. 21
D. L. Lloyd not out	59	– not out 15
C. A. J. Meschede c O'Brien b Shreck	30	– not out 33
D. A. Cosker c O'Brien b Freckingham	0	
A. Carter not out	21	
B 1, l-b 11, w 5, n-b 44	61	B 3, l-b 2, w 1, n-b 12 ... 18

1/27 (1)　2/254 (2)　　　　(9 wkts dec, 120 overs) 513　　1/35 (1)　　(7 wkts dec, 63.5 overs) 227
3/315 (3)　4/354 (4)　　　　　　　　　　　　　　　　　　2/45 (2)　3/47 (3)
5/373 (6)　6/396 (7)　7/396 (5)　　　　　　　　　　　　　4/83 (4)　5/104 (6)　6/179 (5)　7/179 (7)
8/464 (9)　9/476 (10)
110 overs: 451-7

Sheikh 18–1–108–3; Raine 27–6–101–1; Shreck 35–10–138–2; Freckingham 25–3–111–3; Wells 8–2–26–0; Redfern 5–2–13–0; Cosgrove 2–0–4–0. *Second innings*—Sheikh 4.1–1–14–0; Raine 14–4–50–2; Shreck 20.5–3–59–2; Wells 10.5–2–52–1; Freckingham 14–3–47–2.

Leicestershire

D. J. Redfern c Cooke b Wagg	24	– c Cosker b Wagg 0
A. J. Robson b Meschede	83	– b Cosker 18
E. J. H. Eckersley c Cosker b Meschede	147	– c Cosker b Meschede 1
*M. J. Cosgrove b Lloyd	33	– not out 59
N. D. Pinner b Cosker	4	– not out 42
†N. J. O'Brien not out	70	
T. J. Wells c Cosker b Meschede	0	
B. A. Raine b Carter	24	
O. H. Freckingham c Cosker b Carter	0	
C. E. Shreck b Carter	4	
A. Sheikh b Carter	1	
B 21, l-b 13, w 7, n-b 4	45	B 12, l-b 1, n-b 8 21

1/33 (1)　2/204 (2)　3/290 (4)　　　(120.3 overs) 435　　1/0 (1)　2/1 (3)　(3 wkts, 38 overs) 141
4/297 (5)　5/356 (3)　6/356 (7)　7/411 (8)　　　　　　　3/42 (2)
8/417 (9)　9/425 (10)　10/435 (11)
110 overs: 392-6

Carter 26.3–4–95–4; Wagg 21–2–94–1; Meschede 22–3–68–3; Cosker 40–11–100–1; Lloyd 10–1–39–1; Bragg 1–0–5–0. *Second innings*—Wagg 6–0–17–1; Meschede 11–3–43–1; Carter 9–4–15–0; Cosker 9–1–36–1; Lloyd 2–0–12–0; Bragg 1–0–5–0.

Umpires: S. A. Garratt and M. J. Saggers.

LEICESTERSHIRE v NORTHAMPTONSHIRE

At Leicester, April 26–29. Northamptonshire won by 92 runs. Northamptonshire 19pts (after 2pt penalty), Leicestershire 6pts. Toss: Leicestershire. County debut: C. J. McKay.

On the third morning, Leicestershire could scent a long-awaited Championship victory. Northamptonshire, meanwhile, looked likely to extend their own winless streak to 21 matches: at 142 for five, with McKay nipping out two quick wickets on an impressive debut, they were just 88 ahead. But Cobb, on his return to Grace Road after heading down the M1 during the winter, was dropped on nought by Pinner in the slips, diving to his left in front of Cosgrove. He set in train a recovery, before Willey and Kleinveldt blasted 97 inside 12 overs, knocking the stuffing out of Leicestershire, who were left to chase 376 in 113 overs. Kleinveldt got into his stride with the ball and, despite donating 50 extras, Northamptonshire ended up comfortable winners. It was their first Championship victory since beating Glamorgan at home in August 2013, during their promotion season. Some of their joy, though, was tempered by the loss of two points for a slow over-rate. Leicestershire had enjoyed the better of the first two days, with the fiery Raine twice finding himself on a hat-trick, then making a useful 47 down the order. But it counted for little.

Close of play: first day, Leicestershire 102-1 (Robson 52, Eckersley 10); second day, Northamptonshire 105-2 (Wakely 28, Newton 2); third day, Leicestershire 44-1 (Robson 25, Eckersley 6).

Northamptonshire

S. D. Peters c Pinner b Raine	40	– c Robson b Shreck	50
R. E. Levi c Cosgrove b McKay	22	– c Pinner b Raine	20
*A. G. Wakely c Pinner b Shreck	10	– c Shreck b Freckingham	40
R. I. Newton lbw b Raine	71	– b Raine	58
R. I. Keogh b Raine	0	– b McKay	1
†A. M. Rossington c Cosgrove b Shreck	22	– c O'Brien b McKay	7
J. J. Cobb b McKay	13	– c O'Brien b Shreck	54
D. J. Willey c Eckersley b Wells	36	– c Wells b McKay	88
R. K. Kleinveldt lbw b Raine	0	– c Wells b McKay	56
O. P. Stone b Redfern	19	– b Shreck	28
Azharullah not out	2	– not out	4
B 1, l-b 15	16	B 12, l-b 7, w 2, n-b 2	23

1/47 (2) 2/73 (3) 3/93 (1) (72.1 overs) 251
4/93 (5) 5/122 (6) 6/155 (7)
7/220 (4) 8/220 (9) 9/224 (8) 10/251 (10)

1/49 (2) 2/88 (1) (114.1 overs) 429
3/129 (3) 4/134 (5)
5/142 (6) 6/220 (4) 7/272 (7)
8/369 (9) 9/418 (10) 10/429 (8)

McKay 17–3–75–2; Shreck 21–7–41–2; Freckingham 11–1–47–0; Raine 16–4–55–4; Wells 7–2–17–1; Redfern 0.1–0–0–1. *Second innings*—McKay 34–6–95–3; Shreck 28.1–8–91–4; Raine 20–4–82–2; Wells 11–2–51–0; Cosgrove 3–2–10–0; Redfern 3–0–14–0; Freckingham 15–1–67–1.

Leicestershire

A. J. Robson c Peters b Willey	75	– b Azharullah	32
D. J. Redfern c Wakely b Azharullah	40	– c Cobb b Willey	6
E. J. H. Eckersley c Wakely b Stone	28	– lbw b Kleinveldt	37
*M. J. Cosgrove b Stone	11	– lbw b Stone	2
N. D. Pinner b Willey	0	– lbw b Azharullah	12
†N. J. O'Brien c Rossington b Azharullah	9	– b Kleinveldt	58
T. J. Wells c Rossington b Stone	18	– lbw b Kleinveldt	13
B. A. Raine b Azharullah	47	– c Rossington b Azharullah	4
C. J. McKay c Willey b Cobb	47	– c Newton b Stone	30
O. H. Freckingham not out	4	– not out	26
C. E. Shreck c Levi b Kleinveldt	0	– c Rossington b Kleinveldt	13
B 12, l-b 12, n-b 2	26	B 22, l-b 17, w 1, n-b 10	50

1/83 (2) 2/139 (1) 3/147 (3)   (80.5 overs) 305
4/158 (5) 5/162 (4) 6/176 (6)
7/201 (7) 8/288 (9) 9/302 (8) 10/305 (11)

1/16 (2) 2/58 (1)   (75.5 overs) 283
3/67 (4) 4/93 (5)
5/152 (3) 6/186 (7) 7/199 (6)
8/224 (8) 9/261 (9) 10/283 (11)

Kleinveldt 19.5–7–53–1; Willey 18–6–46–2; Stone 18–3–68–3; Azharullah 21–4–94–3; Cobb 4–1–20–1. *Second innings*—Kleinveldt 23.5–4–87–4; Willey 15–4–48–1; Azharullah 19–1–77–3; Stone 18–6–32–2.

Umpires: N. L. Bainton and M. A. Gough.

At Canterbury, May 3–6. LEICESTERSHIRE drew with KENT.

At The Oval, May 10–13. LEICESTERSHIRE lost to SURREY by seven wickets.

LEICESTERSHIRE v LANCASHIRE

At Leicester, May 17–20. Lancashire won by 244 runs. Lancashire 23pts, Leicestershire 4pts. Toss: Leicestershire.

The second division leaders had far too much in all departments for a woeful Leicestershire, who capitulated horribly on the final day. When Croft declared after lunch, 322 in front, they were tasked with seeing out the last 59 overs. But Lancashire's seamers dismantled the home batting, if not always with magic deliveries: Cosgrove and Pinner were both caught attempting to hook Jarvis. By the 15th over, Leicestershire were 29 for seven, and they eventually keeled over for 78 – the fifth time in six seasons they had been dismissed for under 100. Bailey claimed a maiden five-for. Leicestershire had let Lancashire off the hook on the opening day, too: Cosgrove banished himself to the covers after dropping Horton on 20 at first slip, only for Taylor to put down Prince twice in the same position; Raine was the bowler on all three occasions. Croft rammed home the advantage with a century, before Jarvis, in a single 48-over session, exploited a pitch that had spent much of the day under covers; Robson disputed his dismissal at short leg, and was reprimanded by the ECB. Just 24 overs were bowled on the third day, but Prince and Davies added 107 at almost a run a ball on the last to set up a victory all too easily earned. It was Leicestershire's 21st defeat in 37 Championship games.

Close of play: first day, Lancashire 356-9 (Croft 98); second day, Leicestershire 195-6 (Cosgrove 65, Wells 3); third day, Lancashire 39-2 (Petersen 15, Prince 5).

Lancashire

P. J. Horton c O'Brien b Wells	70	– run out	7
K. R. Brown c O'Brien b McKay	21	– c O'Brien b Shreck	8
A. N. Petersen c O'Brien b Wells	8	– lbw b Raine	34
A. G. Prince lbw b Shreck	29	– not out	76
*S. J. Croft c Taylor b Raine	102	– lbw b McKay	1
†A. L. Davies c O'Brien b Shreck	0	– c Cosgrove b McKay	54
J. Clark c O'Brien b Wells	44	– not out	12
T. E. Bailey b Taylor	2		
N. L. Buck c Robson b McKay	25		
S. C. Kerrigan c Eckersley b Shreck	2		
K. M. Jarvis not out	8		
B 21, l-b 24, n-b 12	57	B 4, l-b 6, w 1	11

1/41 (2) 2/63 (3) 3/156 (1)   (98.4 overs) 368   1/19 (1)   (5 wkts dec, 45 overs) 203
4/156 (4) 5/156 (6) 6/229 (7)   2/22 (2) 3/71 (3)
7/254 (8) 8/331 (9) 9/356 (10) 10/368 (5)   4/72 (5) 5/179 (6)

McKay 23–6–62–2; Shreck 27–8–100–3; Raine 20.4–5–42–1; Wells 15–1–68–3; Cosgrove 3–0–13–0; Taylor 10–0–38–1. *Second innings*—McKay 15–3–54–2; Shreck 13–1–56–1; Raine 10–0–37–1; Taylor 3–0–26–0; Wells 4–0–20–0.

Leicestershire

A. J. Robson c Brown b Jarvis	5	– (2) c Croft b Bailey	4
L. J. Hill c Davies b Clark	25	– (1) c Horton b Bailey	10
E. J. H. Eckersley b Bailey	13	– b Bailey	0
*M. J. Cosgrove lbw b Buck	79	– c Davies b Jarvis	1
N. D. Pinner c Croft b Buck	0	– c Kerrigan b Jarvis	0
†N. J. O'Brien c Davies b Jarvis	22	– c Croft b Bailey	3
B. A. Raine b Buck	15	– b Bailey	0
T. J. Wells lbw b Jarvis	7	– b Clark	2
C. J. McKay c Davies b Jarvis	26	– c Davies b Buck	24
R. M. L. Taylor not out	2	– not out	17
C. E. Shreck lbw b Jarvis	2	– c Prince b Buck	0
B 6, l-b 11, w-b 16, n-b 20	53	B 9, l-b 6, n-b 2	17

1/5 (1) 2/44 (3) 3/68 (2)   (56.1 overs) 249   1/20 (1) 2/20 (3)   (30.3 overs) 78
4/78 (5) 5/137 (6) 6/188 (7)   3/21 (4) 4/25 (5)
7/203 (8) 8/245 (4) 9/245 (9) 10/249 (11)   5/26 (2) 6/26 (7) 7/29 (6)
                                            8/41 (8) 9/65 (9) 10/78 (11)

Bailey 9–0–53–1; Jarvis 19.1–2–69–5; Clark 11–3–44–1; Buck 16–1–64–3; Kerrigan 1–0–2–0. *Second innings*—Bailey 9–5–12–5; Jarvis 9–5–10–2; Buck 6.3–0–22–2; Clark 6–2–19–1.

Umpires: M. J. D. Bodenham and S. J. O'Shaughnessy.

At Chelmsford, May 31–June 3. LEICESTERSHIRE beat ESSEX by six wickets. *Leicestershire win a Championship match for the first time since September 2012.*

At Leicester, June 6. LEICESTERSHIRE lost to NEW ZEALANDERS by 198 runs (see New Zealand tour section).

LEICESTERSHIRE v SURREY

At Leicester, June 7–9. Surrey won by 178 runs. Surrey 21pts, Leicestershire 3pts. Toss: Leicestershire. Championship debut: J. E. Burke.

Leicestershire tackled promotion favourites Surrey with their enthusiasm rekindled, having ended a 992-day wait for a Championship win in the previous round. But there was no end in sight for long-suffering home supporters, as their batsmen failed to deal with movement in the air and off the pitch. Curran's maiden first-class half-century was crucial, helping the obdurate Sibley post a competitive 261 after Surrey were put in and reduced to 139 for seven. His pace bowling, though, proved even more decisive: Curran finished with nine wickets in the match. His first four came as Leicestershire collapsed from 100 without loss to 190 all out, after 24-year-old James Burke – replacing captain Gareth Batty in the side, as Surrey played Ansari as the lone spinner – split the opening stand with his first ball in the Championship, gloved down the leg side by Boyce. Surrey took the game away from Leicestershire on the second evening, and a target of 356 proved well beyond them. Boyce was lbw to Dunn's opening delivery, and Curran blew away the middle order. Only O'Brien put up much resistance.

Close of play: first day, Leicestershire 35-0 (Robson 19, Boyce 8); second day, Surrey 217-6 (Burke 19, Davies 20).

Surrey

R. J. Burns lbw b Taylor	38	– c Agathangelou b McKay	14
Z. S. Ansari lbw b Shreck	39	– lbw b Shreck	25
K. C. Sangakkara c Agathangelou b McKay	21	– c O'Brien b Taylor	20
D. P. Sibley c O'Brien b Raine	74	– lbw b Shreck	6
S. M. Davies lbw b Raine	0	– (8) not out	47
B. T. Foakes c O'Brien b Raine	4	– (5) b Raine	46
*†G. C. Wilson lbw b McKay	3	– (6) c Raine b Taylor	42
J. E. Burke c O'Brien b Shreck	0	– (7) lbw b Shreck	27
T. K. Curran c O'Brien b Naik	60	– c Naik b Shreck	1
C. T. Tremlett b Agathangelou	6	– b Raine	19
M. P. Dunn not out	1	– c O'Brien b Raine	9
B 1, l-b 13, w 1	15	B 4, l-b 20, w 2, n-b 2	28

1/82 (1) 2/82 (2) 3/122 (3) (85.1 overs) 261
4/131 (5) 5/135 (6) 6/138 (7)
7/139 (8) 8/221 (9) 9/245 (10) 10/261 (4)

1/29 (1) 2/68 (2) (72 overs) 284
3/76 (3) 4/90 (4)
5/163 (6) 6/190 (5) 7/228 (7)
8/230 (9) 9/257 (10) 10/284 (11)

McKay 19–6–57–2; Shreck 25–8–66–2; Raine 14.1–5–33–3; Naik 12–1–47–1; Taylor 13–4–37–1; Agathangelou 2–1–7–1. *Second innings*—Raine 20–4–74–3; McKay 17–1–72–1; Taylor 11–1–43–2; Shreck 23–3–67–4; Naik 1–0–4–0.

Leicestershire

A. J. Robson b Burke	68	– (2) b Tremlett	14
M. A. G. Boyce c Wilson b Burke	27	– (1) lbw b Dunn	0
E. J. H. Eckersley b Burke	34	– b Curran	32
*M. J. Cosgrove lbw b Dunn	4	– c Foakes b Curran	5
A. P. Agathangelou c Burns b Tremlett	7	– lbw b Curran	0
†N. J. O'Brien c Sibley b Curran	7	– c Wilson b Ansari	54
B. A. Raine c Wilson b Curran	5	– lbw b Burke	28
R. M. L. Taylor c Wilson b Curran	0	– c Wilson b Curran	0
C. J. McKay not out	0	– c Tremlett b Curran	6
J. K. H. Naik lbw b Burke	2	– not out	14
C. E. Shreck lbw b Curran	0	– lbw b Burke	0
B 18, l-b 2, w 2, n-b 8	30	B 9, l-b 7, n-b 8	24

1/100 (2) 2/121 (1) 3/126 (3) (47.5 overs) 190
4/150 (5) 5/167 (6) 6/179 (7)
7/179 (8) 8/187 (3) 9/189 (10) 10/190 (11)

1/0 (1) 2/28 (2) (48 overs) 177
3/33 (4) 4/33 (5)
5/78 (3) 6/150 (6) 7/151 (8)
8/161 (9) 9/177 (7) 10/177 (11)

Dunn 9–0–43–1; Tremlett 15–1–69–1; Curran 17.5–3–39–4; Burke 6–1–19–4. *Second innings*—Dunn 8–2–34–1; Tremlett 11–3–27–1; Curran 16–4–53–5; Burke 7–0–35–2; Ansari 6–3–12–1.

Umpires: G. D. Lloyd and N. A. Mallender.

At Manchester, June 14–16. LEICESTERSHIRE lost to LANCASHIRE by an innings and 157 runs.

At Cardiff, June 22–25. LEICESTERSHIRE lost to GLAMORGAN by 137 runs.

LEICESTERSHIRE v KENT

At Leicester, July 5–7. Kent won by eight wickets. Kent 20pts, Leicestershire 3pts. Toss: Kent. First-class debut: A. M. Ali.

Northeast called for the ECB to crack down on Division Two result pitches despite Kent completing their second victory of the season in the equivalent of barely six sessions. "We seem to be going from place to place and playing on this type of wicket," he said. "I don't think it's great for producing England players, or for cricket in general." Nonetheless, Kent climbed off the bottom at the expense of Leicestershire, who had now lost four in a row after the euphoria of Chelmsford. Kent could afford three dropped catches and the loss of Thomas to a side strain, yet still dismissed Leicestershire – without captain Mark Cosgrove, who was attending the birth of his first child – inside 52 overs. The wicket was not impossible, but offered unusual sideways movement and indifferent bounce. Stevens, who has often enjoyed his return to Grace Road, raced to a 47-ball fifty, and in all hit 12 fours – plus a six on to the newly painted Meet roof. He went on to take three wickets, while Coles claimed the second ten-wicket match haul of his career, reaching 50 for the season when he completed a pair for Greg Smith, back at his old county for a month's loan from Nottinghamshire. Despite heavy overnight rain, play resumed on time, and Kent brought up victory shortly after lunch.

Close of play: first day, Kent 44-2 (Key 2, Northeast 10); second day, Leicestershire 110-9 (Raine 30, Shreck 0).

Leicestershire

A. J. Robson c Billings b Coles	29	– (2) lbw b Haggett	21
M. A. G. Boyce c Ball b Coles	12	– (1) lbw b Coles	5
*E. J. H. Eckersley b Coles	41	– lbw b Stevens	14
G. P. Smith c Coles b Haggett	0	– c Ball b Coles	0
A. P. Agathangelou c Ball b Stevens	11	– lbw b Stevens	8
A. M. Ali c Coles b Stevens	13	– c Billings b Haggett	8
†L. J. Hill c Northeast b Coles	8	– c Billings b Stevens	0
B. A. Raine b Coles	16	– not out	41
C. J. McKay c Denly b Coles	4	– b Coles	1
O. H. Freckingham c Bell-Drummond b Haggett	1	– lbw b Haggett	0
C. E. Shreck not out	1	– b Coles	1
L-b 17, n-b 6	23	B 8, l-b 10, w 6	24

1/29 (2) 2/87 (1) 3/88 (4)   (51.1 overs) 159
4/94 (5) 5/122 (5) 6/123 (6)
7/140 (7) 8/148 (9) 9/155 (8) 10/159 (10)

1/28 (1) 2/32 (2)   (48.2 overs) 123
3/33 (4) 4/47 (5)
5/66 (3) 6/66 (7) 7/66 (6)
8/97 (9) 9/99 (10) 10/123 (11)

Coles 15–3–55–6; Thomas 3–0–18–0; Stevens 16–7–36–2; Haggett 13.1–4–20–2; Ball 4–0–13–0. *Second innings*—Coles 17.2–3–43–4; Haggett 17–7–35–3; Stevens 14–4–27–3.

Kent

D. J. Bell-Drummond lbw b McKay	7	– c Robson b Raine	5
J. L. Denly c Boyce b Raine	16	– not out	37
R. W. T. Key lbw b Raine	8	– c Eckersley b Raine	4
*S. A. Northeast lbw b McKay	19	– not out	28
B. W. Harmison lbw b Shreck	7		
D. I. Stevens c Hill b Freckingham	63		
†S. W. Billings c Eckersley b Freckingham	13		
A. J. Ball c Ali b Freckingham	32		
C. J. Haggett b Shreck	20		
M. T. Coles not out	4		
I. A. A. Thomas c McKay b Shreck	0		
B 12, l-b 5, n-b 4	21		

1/28 (2) 2/28 (1) 3/58 (3)   (54.4 overs) 210   1/13 (1)   (2 wkts, 15.2 overs)   74
4/60 (4) 5/94 (5) 6/145 (7)   2/35 (3)
7/146 (6) 8/206 (8) 9/210 (9) 10/210 (11)

McKay 17–3–54–2; Raine 20–5–57–2; Shreck 11.4–2–50–3; Freckingham 6–1–32–3. *Second innings*—McKay 6–1–29–0; Raine 7.2–0–34–2; Freckingham 2–0–11–0.

Umpires: S. C. Gale and N. A. Mallender.

At Cheltenham, July 15–18. LEICESTERSHIRE lost to GLOUCESTERSHIRE by 155 runs.

LEICESTERSHIRE v DERBYSHIRE

At Leicester, August 7–10. Leicestershire won by three wickets. Leicestershire 22pts, Derbyshire 6pts. Toss: Leicestershire. First-class debut: R. J. Sayer.

Leicestershire showed fighting spirit to conjure their second Championship win of the season, and first in 22 matches at home since the final game of 2012. But their delight was tempered four days later, when the ECB docked them 16 points, and fined them £5,000, for persistent disciplinary breaches. Chasing 273, they had been reduced to 50 for four – all lbw – as the ball began to creep through on the third evening. But a fifth-wicket stand of 118 between O'Brien, showing just enough aggression to keep the scoreboard ticking, and the fast-developing Aadil Ali, who ground out 42 in more than four hours, turned the game Leicestershire's way. The umpires delayed tea for the permitted 15 minutes, only to take the players off with just five needed; Raine completed the job two balls after the resumption. Madsen did not deserve to finish on the losing side after his obstinate unbeaten 172 dominated Derbyshire's first innings, though he was lucky to survive on 54, when he cut Cosgrove's first ball to gully, only to be reprieved because the bowler had knocked off a bail in his delivery stride. Footitt followed a career-best 34 with a five-wicket haul. Madsen briefly removed him from the attack following a second warning for running on the pitch. Although Cosgrove held Leicestershire together with his first home century, and Godleman put Derbyshire firmly on top, until they lost their last seven wickets for 68, succumbing to McKay's clever seam movement.

Close of play: first day, Derbyshire 320-8 (Madsen 164, Footitt 21); second day, Leicestershire 304-8 (Sayer 14, McKay 17); third day, Leicestershire 56-4 (Ali 4, O'Brien 3).

Derbyshire

B. T. Slater b Shreck	11	– b Shreck	17
B. A. Godleman lbw b Raine	1	– c O'Brien b Raine	101
*W. L. Madsen not out	172	– b Raine	22
T. M. Dilshan c Robson b Shreck	4	– c Robson b Sayer	15
A. L. Hughes c O'Brien b McKay	23	– c Cosgrove b Sayer	28
W. J. Durston c O'Brien b Shreck	8	– (9) c O'Brien b McKay	1
S. J. Thakor lbw b Sayer	41	– (6) c O'Brien b Raine	10
†H. R. Hosein c Agathangelou b McKay	12	– (7) lbw b McKay	9
A. P. Palladino lbw b Raine	7	– (8) c Agathangelou b McKay	0
M. H. A. Footitt b Shreck	34	– not out	3
B. D. Cotton b McKay	4	– c Agathangelou b McKay	5
B 4, l-b 19, w 1, n-b 4	28	B 12, l-b 16, n-b 2	30

1/2 (2) 2/30 (1) 3/38 (4) (103 overs) 345
4/96 (5) 5/118 (6) 6/189 (7)
7/249 (8) 8/285 (9) 9/340 (10) 10/345 (11)

1/57 (1) 2/93 (3) (66.3 overs) 241
3/117 (4) 4/173 (5)
5/190 (6) 6/212 (7) 7/212 (8)
8/220 (9) 9/230 (2) 10/241 (11)

McKay 27–8–51–3; Raine 22–6–71–2; Shreck 25.5–8–84–4; Cosgrove 11–1–50–0; Sayer 16–1–61–1; Agathangelou 2–0–5–0. *Second innings*—McKay 14.3–5–39–4; Raine 15–3–53–3; Shreck 13–0–51–1; Sayer 21–2–59–2; Ali 3–0–11–0.

Leicestershire

A. J. Robson c Hosein b Footitt	53	– (2) lbw b Cotton	4
L. J. Hill c Durston b Footitt	5	– (1) lbw b Palladino	21
E. J. H. Eckersley run out	0	– lbw b Thakor	13
*M. J. Cosgrove c Madsen b Footitt	102	– lbw b Palladino	9
A. M. Ali lbw b Palladino	10	– b Cotton	42
†N. J. O'Brien lbw b Thakor	60	– lbw b Footitt	87
A. P. Agathangelou b Palladino	4	– lbw b Palladino	32
B. A. Raine c Hughes b Footitt	3	– not out	31
R. J. Sayer c Madsen b Dilshan	23		
C. J. McKay b Footitt	18	– (9) not out	14
C. E. Shreck not out	0		
B 20, l-b 12, n-b 4	36	B 3, l-b 9, w 2, n-b 6	20

1/11 (2) 2/15 (3) 3/72 (1) (90.2 overs) 314
4/110 (5) 5/207 (4) 6/221 (7)
7/254 (8) 8/278 (6) 9/314 (9) 10/314 (10)

1/8 (2) (7 wkts, 88.2 overs) 273
2/36 (3) 3/45 (4)
4/50 (1) 5/168 (6) 6/222 (7) 7/238 (5)

Footitt 22.2–10–53–5; Palladino 18–8–43–2; Cotton 20–7–75–0; Thakor 16–2–54–1; Hughes 7–0–26–0; Durston 4–0–22–0; Dilshan 3–0–9–1. *Second innings*—Footitt 22.2–4–87–1; Cotton 21–5–57–2; Thakor 21–5–62–1; Palladino 17–5–32–3; Dilshan 7–1–23–0.

Umpires: P. K. Baldwin and G. D. Lloyd.

At Northampton, August 21–24. LEICESTERSHIRE drew with NORTHAMPTONSHIRE.

LEICESTERSHIRE v GLOUCESTERSHIRE

At Leicester, September 1–4. Drawn. Leicestershire 11pts, Gloucestershire 9pts. Toss: Gloucestershire.

Bad weather stymied the captains' attempt to engineer a result. After a rain-halved opening day, Leicestershire laid a solid platform, thanks in large part to another mature innings from Ali. Gloucestershire were affected by a sickness bug, which kept Jack Taylor off the field for the second day, and pressed assistant coach Ian Harvey into action as a substitute. With McKay claiming his 200th first-class wicket, they were then reduced to 249 for eight by the time bad light ended play on the third evening, still 17 away from avoiding the follow-on. But they went past the mark without further mishap, prompting a declaration from Tavaré, captain in place of Michael Klinger, who had flown home to Australia in between the Royal London One-Day Cup quarters and semis. That put the ball back in Leicestershire's court: Redfern responded with a polished 74, before a clatter of wickets and a declaration from Cosgrove left Gloucestershire 56 overs to pursue 302. They made a solid start, reaching 162 for two in the 34th. Leicestershire hit back with three quick wickets, but were forced to take off their pace bowlers in fading light, and the chase was abandoned.

Close of play: first day, Leicestershire 127-2 (Redfern 29, Sayer 2); second day, Gloucestershire 22-0 (Tavaré 12, Dent 7); third day, Gloucestershire 249-8 (Noema-Barnett 27, Payne 5).

Leicestershire

E. J. H. Eckersley c Noema-Barnett b Norwell	23	– c Howell b Norwell	6
A. J. Robson c Roderick b Norwell	61	– c Roderick b Norwell	4
D. J. Redfern c Handscomb b Payne	49	– c Roderick b Fuller	74
R. J. Sayer lbw b Marshall	34		
*M. J. Cosgrove c Tavaré b Payne	12	– (4) lbw b Howell	21
A. M. Ali c Norwell b Marshall	80	– (5) c and b Noema-Barnett	12
†N. J. O'Brien c Roderick b Payne	4	– (6) c and b Payne	2
W. A. White c Roderick b Norwell	38	– (7) b Norwell	1
C. J. McKay c Dent b Norwell	29	– b Payne	0
B. A. Raine c Handscomb b Marshall	51	– (8) run out	6
R. M. L. Taylor not out	2	– (10) not out	17
B 10, l-b 12, w 2, n-b 8	32	B 4, l-b 4, n-b 4	12

1/59 (1) 2/118 (2) 3/177 (3) (119 overs) 415
4/197 (4) 5/197 (5) 6/201 (7)
7/257 (8) 8/314 (9) 9/399 (6)
10/415 (10)

1/9 (1) (9 wkts dec, 31.3 overs) 155
2/15 (2) 3/55 (4)
4/84 (5) 5/96 (6) 6/103 (7)
7/115 (8) 8/115 (9) 9/155 (3)

110 overs: 362-8

Fuller 28–5–90–0; Payne 26–7–94–3; Norwell 30–5–97–4; Noema-Barnett 20–6–62–0; Marshall 13–5–30–3; Dent 2–0–20–0. *Second innings*—Payne 10–0–43–2; Norwell 10–1–48–3; Fuller 4.3–0–28–1; Howell 4–0–21–1; Noema-Barnett 3–0–7–1.

Gloucestershire

*W. A. Tavaré c O'Brien b Raine	37	– (2) c O'Brien b Raine	52
C. D. J. Dent lbw b Taylor	73	– (1) c and b Taylor	52
†G. H. Roderick b White	1	– lbw b Taylor	4
P. S. P. Handscomb c Sayer b Taylor	53	– not out	39
H. J. H. Marshall lbw b Taylor	5	– lbw b White	0
B. A. C. Howell c O'Brien b McKay	11	– c O'Brien b Raine	7
K. Noema-Barnett not out	37	– not out	22
J. M. R. Taylor c Redfern b McKay	10		
J. K. Fuller b Raine	1		
D. A. Payne not out	10		
B 4, l-b 17, w 2, n-b 8	31	B 25, l-b 6, w 1, n-b 4	36

1/51 (1) 2/52 (3) (8 wkts dec, 90.3 overs) 269
3/172 (4) 4/179 (2)
5/186 (5) 6/202 (6) 7/233 (8) 8/234 (9)

1/108 (1) (5 wkts, 47.2 overs) 212
2/128 (3) 3/162 (1)
4/163 (5) 5/172 (6)

L. C. Norwell did not bat.

McKay 26.3–6–83–2; Raine 21–7–41–2; White 16–2–41–1; Taylor 13–1–41–3; Cosgrove 5–2–10–0; Sayer 9–1–32–0. *Second innings*—Raine 10–4–22–2; McKay 9–0–33–0; White 12–1–44–1; Taylor 8–1–37–2; Sayer 8–2–43–0; Cosgrove 0.2–0–2–0.

Umpires: N. G. B. Cook and N. G. C. Cowley.

LEICESTERSHIRE v ESSEX

At Leicester, September 14–17. Essex won by five wickets. Essex 18pts, Leicestershire 2pts. Toss: Essex.

Essex knocked off a contrived target with 13 balls to spare, condemning Leicestershire to the wooden spoon for the fifth year out of seven. But both sides could be praised for making something of a match which lost seven sessions to heavy rain and bad light. After two blank days, Robson and Cosgrove each ticked off 1,000 first-class runs for the season, and Ryder picked up his third five-for. Three declarations were required on the final morning to set Essex 307 in what became 62 overs, on what was effectively a day-two pitch under clear skies. They were further assisted by the absence of the rested Clint McKay, while Shreck had to leave the field with a leg injury after bowling just five overs, and Raine battled cramp. Browne delivered victory with a measured unbeaten 151, and became the first Essex player to achieve 1,000 Championship runs since Bopara in 2008. This time Bopara weighed in with 69 in a pivotal partnership of 157 for the third wicket.

Close of play: first day, no play; second day, no play; third day, Leicestershire 222-5 (Ali 33, White 2).

Leicestershire

E. J. H. Eckersley c Foster b Ryder	13	– c Ryder b Westley	30
A. J. Robson c Lawrence b Bopara	50	– not out	26
D. J. Redfern c Foster b Ryder	0	– not out	15
*M. J. Cosgrove c Westley b Ryder	94		
A. M. Ali not out	53		
†N. J. O'Brien c Foster b Ryder	0		
W. A. White c Foster b Ryder	2		
B. A. Raine c Foster b Porter	4		
R. M. L. Taylor not out	4		
B 4, l-b 6, w 1, n-b 20	31	L-b 2	2

1/21 (1) 2/27 (3)	(7 wkts dec, 69 overs) 251
3/121 (2) 4/220 (4)	
5/220 (6) 6/226 (7) 7/235 (8)	

1/44 (1)	(1 wkt dec, 14 overs) 73

R. J. Sayer and C. E. Shreck did not bat.

Porter 18–5–59–1; Ryder 25–5–89–5; Winslade 4–0–25–0; Napier 6–2–20–0; Bopara 16–4–48–1. *Second innings*—Porter 3–0–28–0; Winslade 2–0–14–0; Bopara 5–0–18–0; Westley 4–0–11–1.

Essex

D. W. Lawrence not out	14	– c Robson b Raine	28
N. L. J. Browne not out	4	– not out	151
T. Westley (did not bat)		– c sub (L. J. Hill) b White	1
R. S. Bopara (did not bat)		– c O'Brien b Raine	69
R. N. ten Doeschate (did not bat)		– c Robson b White	28
J. D. Ryder (did not bat)		– c O'Brien b Taylor	8
M. L. Pettini (did not bat)		– not out	13
		L-b 3, w 2, n-b 4	9

(no wkt dec, 5 overs) 18	1/36 (1) (5 wkts, 59.5 overs) 307
	2/56 (3) 3/213 (4)
	4/247 (5) 5/274 (6)

*†J. S. Foster, G. R. Napier, J. R. Winslade and J. A. Porter did not bat.

Raine 3–0–13–0; Shreck 2–1–5–0. *Second innings*—Raine 16.3–3–73–2; Shreck 5–0–23–0; White 13.2–0–69–2; Sayer 11–0–60–0; Taylor 10–0–61–1; Cosgrove 4–0–18–0.

Umpires: S. A. Garratt and G. D. Lloyd.

At Derby, September 22–25. LEICESTERSHIRE drew with DERBYSHIRE.

MIDDLESEX

Best of the rest

KEVIN HAND

Second place in the Championship was an outstanding recovery from the tribulations of 2014, when Middlesex narrowly escaped relegation – although the gap to Yorkshire (68 points, and four victories) was more like a chasm.

Still, for the second year running Middlesex were the only county to beat the champions, thanks to a stunning comeback after Ryan Sidebottom kicked off the match at Lord's with a triple-wicket maiden – even if Yorkshire possibly lost focus once it was confirmed they had retained their title.

The sides' previous meeting, at Headingley, was arguably the decisive match of the season: set 213, Yorkshire sneaked home by four wickets. It was a shame such an important fixture was sandwiched between a raft of Twenty20 games: Middlesex had played under lights in Southampton on the Thursday, and Cardiff on the Friday, and stayed overnight in Leicester en route to Leeds for the match on Sunday. Unsurprisingly, it was a low-scoring game, marked by poor shot selection.

The bowling highlight had come even earlier. Seamer James Harris, largely a disappointment since a high-profile move, was in the last season of a three-year deal; he had even briefly returned to Glamorgan on loan. But he roared back with nine for 34 against Durham, the second-best innings analysis for Middlesex since the Second World War, after Richard Johnson's ten for 45 against Derbyshire in 1994. The delighted Johnson, now Middlesex's bowling coach, teased Harris that "only very good bowlers can take all ten".

That set Harris on the way to 69 Championship wickets – having managed 12 from seven appearances in 2014. His improvement made up for a subdued season from 34-year-old Tim Murtagh, who failed to reach 50 wickets for the first time in five years. Toby Roland-Jones helped pick up the slack, with 48, and hit a maiden century during the Lord's fightback against Yorkshire.

The batting was led by Nick Compton, who amassed 1,123 runs in the Championship – Sam Robson was next with 891 – and successfully reclaimed the England place he had been unlucky to lose in 2013. Dawid Malan suffered a broken finger early on, but returned in fine form in the one-day game.

Angus Fraser, the amiable director of cricket, had bad luck with his overseas choices. Knowing Chris Rogers would miss half the season, he signed up Adam Voges as an experienced replacement – only for Voges to make a belated Test debut, in the Caribbean in June, then play in the Ashes as well. He managed just four Championship appearances, although that did include a superb 132 as Middlesex chased down 402 to beat Somerset. He will captain in 2016 at the start and end of the season.

One more call Down Under whistled up Joe Burns, who fitted in seven matches before being summoned by Australia A, but he found English pitches hard going: he made only three half-centuries, including two against

Worcestershire after being pushed down the order to accommodate the 21-year-old left-hander Nick Gubbins. Towards the end of the season, Middlesex did without an official overseas player, which contributed to a measly two batting points from the last five games.

James Harris

A better example of Fraser's shrewd eye came in the shape of the former New Zealand Test all-rounder James Franklin, who had an Irish passport. He scored a century at Taunton and – having stood in for Voges as captain – added 135 and 91 not out against Worcestershire. That match was at Uxbridge, where a typically slow surface made the atmosphere more funeral than festival: Middlesex's lack of control over their home pitches continued to hamper their chances. However, the wicket at Merchant Taylors' School did prove lively, though a probable double over Somerset was stymied by the weather. For 2016, Franklin will lead the 50-over side and Malan in Twenty20.

A pre-season trip to Abu Dhabi was supposed to tune the players up for limited-overs cricket after a poor showing in 2014. But, when the desert sun was replaced by a dank evening for the opening T20 Blast game, in Bristol, Middlesex lost again. They won only four of their 13 completed matches, and finished bottom of the South Group; since winning the trophy in 2008, they have failed to reach the knockouts.

The Royal London One-Day Cup was almost as bad – seventh out of nine, although one extra win would have brought a quarter-final place. The itinerary was brutal, forcing madcap dashes from one venue to the next, while 10.30 starts meant the toss was often crucial. After beating Kent, for example, Middlesex had to travel from Radlett to Southampton, which entailed an exciting evening on the M25. Next morning there was no way back from 22 for five, though a mysterious decision to bat first did not help.

Fraser's frustration with the white-ball performances was shown when he recruited Gloucestershire seamer James Fuller. Then, in December, Brendon McCullum signed for most of the limited-overs season. Fraser was understandably thrilled: "When he walks out to bat, everybody stops to watch." His fellow New Zealander, left-arm fast bowler Mitchell McClenaghan returns for another stint.

There were departures, too. Neil Dexter joined Leicestershire, while left-arm paceman Gurjit Sandhu was released. Middlesex's popular chief executive Vinny Codrington stood down after 18 years, comforted by the best Championship performance in his time. He had overseen the restructuring of the committee, and created an executive board in 2009, the year Fraser started as director of cricket. Richard Goatley, who had worked at Lord's since 2005, was named as the new chief executive in October.

Championship attendance: 49, 947.

MIDDLESEX RESULTS

All first-class matches – Played 17: Won 8, Lost 2, Drawn 7.
County Championship matches – Played 16: Won 7, Lost 2, Drawn 7.

LV= County Championship, 2nd in Division 1;
NatWest T20 Blast, 9th in South Group; Royal London One-Day Cup, 7th in Group B.

COUNTY CHAMPIONSHIP AVERAGES, BATTING AND FIELDING

Cap		Birthplace	M	I	NO	R	HS	100	Avge	Ct/St
	A. C. Voges§	Perth, Australia . . .	4	8	0	451	132	1	56.37	7
2010	D. J. Malan	Roehampton	9	15	2	629	182*	2	48.38	3
2006	N. R. D. Compton . . .	Durban, SA	16	31	2	1,123	149	2	38.72	5
2013	S. D. Robson	Paddington, Aust. . .	16	31	2	891	178	1	30.72	12
	J. A. Burns§	Herston, Australia . .	7	11	0	320	87	0	29.09	1
2011	J. A. Simpson	Bury	16	29	7	619	64	0	28.13	50/2
2010	N. J. Dexter	Johannesburg, SA . .	10	19	2	473	112	1	27.82	2
2015	J. E. C. Franklin¶ . . .	Wellington	15	27	3	667	135	2	27.79	15
2012	T. S. Roland-Jones . . .	Ashford†	13	19	4	416	103*	1	27.73	7
	N. R. T. Gubbins	Richmond	7	13	0	354	92	0	27.23	2
2015	J. A. R. Harris	Morriston	16	25	5	462	73	0	23.10	4
2015	O. P. Rayner	Fallingbostel, Ger.	14	23	2	360	52	0	17.14	30
	P. R. Stirling	Belfast, N. Ireland .	7	14	0	224	41	0	16.00	3
2008	T. J. Murtagh	Lambeth	13	18	6	180	24	0	15.00	4
2009	S. T. Finn‡	Watford	7	9	4	73	21*	0	14.60	3
2008	E. J. G. Morgan‡	Dublin, Ireland . . .	4	6	0	61	44	0	10.16	1

Also batted: S. S. Eskinazi¶ (*Johannesburg, SA*) (1 match) 4, 22 (1 ct); T. G. Helm (*Stoke Mandeville*) (1 match) 0, 5; R. H. Patel (*Harrow†*) (1 match) 6*, 3.

† *Born in Middlesex.*   ‡ *ECB contract.*   § *Official overseas player.*
¶ *Other non-England-qualified player.*

BOWLING

	Style	O	M	R	W	BB	5I	Avge
N. J. Dexter	RM	163.2	35	485	21	5-64	1	23.09
J. A. R. Harris	RFM	460.2	66	1,776	69	9-34	3	25.73
T. S. Roland-Jones	RFM	471	112	1,298	48	5-27	1	27.04
S. T. Finn	RFM	252.3	49	752	27	4-41	0	27.85
T. J. Murtagh	RFM	385.2	85	1,127	40	4-55	0	28.17
O. P. Rayner	OB	273	71	780	24	3-44	0	32.50

Also bowled: J. A. Burns (RM) 5–0–14–0; N. R. D. Compton (OB) 1–0–4–0; J. E. C. Franklin (LFM) 104–12–381–7; N. R. T. Gubbins (LBG) 3–0–13–0; T. G. Helm (RFM) 28–4–101–3; D. J. Malan (LBG) 8–0–25–1; R. H. Patel (SLA) 28–10–84–5; S. D. Robson (LBG) 5–0–26–1; P. R. Stirling (OB) 33–5–127–3; A. C. Voges (SLA) 30–3–132–6.

LEADING ROYAL LONDON CUP AVERAGES (100 runs/4 wickets)

Batting	Runs	HS	Avge	SR	Ct
D. J. Malan	406	156*	67.66	102.01	3
N. R. T. Gubbins . . .	339	141	56.50	104.30	0
S. D. Robson . . .	185	88	30.83	61.87	2
J. A. Simpson . . .	134	50	26.80	93.05	7
J. E. C. Franklin .	149	63	24.83	77.60	3

Bowling	W	BB	Avge	ER
N. J. Dexter	7	3-46	19.42	5.91
J. A. R. Harris	9	4-38	24.22	4.80
O. P. Rayner	11	4-35	25.27	4.96
T. S. Roland-Jones . .	7	2-26	26.14	4.57
G. S. Sandhu	4	3-64	30.50	7.10
Junaid Khan	6	3-32	57.66	5.58

LEADING NATWEST T20 BLAST AVERAGES (100 runs/18 overs)

Batting	Runs	HS	Avge	SR	Ct/St	Bowling	W	BB	Avge	ER
P. R. Stirling . . .	343	90	42.87	**175.00**	0	S. T. Finn	12	4-28	11.83	**6.17**
J. A. Simpson . .	367	84*	45.87	**141.69**	5/2	N. J. Dexter	7	3-12	19.85	**6.61**
D. J. Malan	299	115*	37.37	**139.71**	6	O. P. Rayner	3	1-29	72.33	**7.75**
J. E. C. Franklin	221	41	36.83	**134.75**	1	K. J. Abbott	7	5-14	26.14	**8.71**
N. R. T. Gubbins	121	46	20.16	**134.44**	4	J. E. C. Franklin	12	5-21	19.33	**8.92**
N. R. D. Compton	127	78	15.87	**123.30**	2	J. A. R. Harris . . .	6	3-39	31.33	**8.95**
E. J. G. Morgan	237	54	26.33	**112.32**	9	R. H. Patel	0	0-22	–	**9.36**

FIRST-CLASS COUNTY RECORDS

Highest score for	331*	J. D. B. Robertson v Worcestershire at Worcester	1949
Highest score against	341	C. M. Spearman (Gloucestershire) at Gloucester	2004
Leading run-scorer	40,302	E. H. Hendren (avge 48.81)	1907–37
Best bowling for	10-40	G. O. B. Allen v Lancashire at Lord's	1929
Best bowling against	9-38	R. C. Robertson-Glasgow (Somerset) at Lord's	1924
Leading wicket-taker	2,361	F. J. Titmus (avge 21.27)	1949–82
Highest total for	642-3 dec	v Hampshire at Southampton	1923
Highest total against	850-7 dec	by Somerset at Taunton	2007
Lowest total for	20	v MCC at Lord's	1864
Lowest total against {	31	by Gloucestershire at Bristol	1924
	31	by Glamorgan at Cardiff	1997

LIST A COUNTY RECORDS

Highest score for	163	A. J. Strauss v Surrey at The Oval	2008
Highest score against	163	C. J. Adams (Sussex) at Arundel	1999
Leading run-scorer	12,029	M. W. Gatting (avge 34.96)	1975–98
Best bowling for	7-12	W. W. Daniel v Minor Counties East at Ipswich	1978
Best bowling against	6-27	J. C. Tredwell (Kent) at Southgate	2009
Leading wicket-taker	491	J. E. Emburey (avge 24.68)	1975–95
Highest total for	**367-6**	**v Sussex at Hove**	**2015**
Highest total against	368-2	by Nottinghamshire at Lord's	2014
Lowest total for	23	v Yorkshire at Leeds	1974
Lowest total against	41	by Northamptonshire at Northampton	1972

TWENTY20 COUNTY RECORDS

Highest score for	129	D. T. Christian v Kent at Canterbury	2014
Highest score against	119	K. J. O'Brien (Gloucestershire) at Uxbridge . . .	2011
Leading run-scorer	**2,260**	**D. J. Malan (avge 33.73)**	**2006–15**
Best bowling for	5-13	M. Kartik v Essex at Lord's	2007
Best bowling against	6-24	T. J. Murtagh (Surrey) at Lord's	2005
Leading wicket-taker	**54**	**N. J. Dexter (avge 25.25)**	**2008–15**
Highest total for	**221-2**	**v Sussex at Hove**	**2015**
Highest total against	254-3	by Gloucestershire at Uxbridge	2011
Lowest total for	92	v Surrey at Lord's	2013
Lowest total against	74	by Essex at Chelmsford	2013

ADDRESS

Lord's Cricket Ground, London NW8 8QN; 020 7289 1300; enquiries@middlesexccc.com; www.middlesexccc.com.

OFFICIALS

Captain A. C. Voges
    2016 (50-over) J. E. C. Franklin
    2016 (Twenty20) D. J. Malan
Managing director of cricket A. R. C. Fraser
Head coach R. J. Scott
Academy director A. J. Coleman

President A. H. Latchman
Chairman 2015 I. N. Lovett
    2016 M. O'Farrell
Secretary/chief executive R. J. Goatley
Head groundsman M. J. Hunt
Scorer D. K. Shelley

At Oxford, April 7–9. MIDDLESEX beat OXFORD MCCU by seven wickets.

MIDDLESEX v NOTTINGHAMSHIRE

At Lord's, April 12–15. Drawn. Middlesex 8pts, Nottinghamshire 10pts. Toss: Nottinghamshire. County debut: V. D. Philander. Championship debut: B. R. M. Taylor.

Middlesex started the new season as they had ended the old – by holding out for a defiant draw. In his first Championship match back after five seasons with Somerset, Compton batted more than four hours, and Gubbins three and a half; finally, the eighth-wicket pair survived for 19 overs. Middlesex – without Malan, who had broken his hand attempting a slip catch – were always struggling after an inadequate reply to Nottinghamshire's 298, which might have been more but for a mid-innings burst of four wickets in 11 balls from Harris. Either side of that, the former Zimbabwe captain Brendan Taylor drove crisply to a chanceless hundred in his maiden appearance at Lord's – just a month after his last international appearance – and Read made the first of two punchy contributions; Taylor, who had just hit 105 against Loughborough MCCU, was the first to score centuries in his opening two matches for Nottinghamshire. Middlesex floundered against some disciplined bowling, then had to watch their opponents build on a lead of 117. Read's hundred came from just 76 balls, including 22 off one over from Stirling, then his declaration set Middlesex 519 in 119 overs.

Close of play: first day, Nottinghamshire 298-9 (Read 62, Gurney 8); second day, Nottinghamshire 101-2 (Hales 14, Gidman 5); third day, Middlesex 57-1 (Gubbins 13, Compton 37).

Nottinghamshire

S. J. Mullaney b Helm	22	– b Helm	44
B. R. M. Taylor lbw b Harris	106	– c Finn b Murtagh	34
A. D. Hales run out	0	– c Simpson b Murtagh	37
J. W. A. Taylor c Gubbins b Harris	36	– (5) lbw b Stirling	61
S. R. Patel lbw b Harris	0	– (6) c Harris b Voges	33
M. H. Wessels lbw b Harris	1	– (7) lbw b Murtagh	38
*†C. M. W. Read not out	62	– (8) not out	101
W. R. S. Gidman c Simpson b Helm	9	– (4) c Robson b Voges	18
V. D. Philander st Simpson b Voges	17	– c Robson b Harris	14
J. T. Ball c Stirling b Finn	16	– not out	8
H. F. Gurney c sub (R. F. Higgins) b Finn	8		
B 1, l-b 14, n-b 6	21	B 5, l-b 8	13

1/70 (1)   2/72 (3)   3/180 (4)   (93.2 overs) 298   1/77 (1)   (8 wkts dec, 96 overs) 401
4/180 (5)   5/182 (6)   6/183 (2)   2/85 (2)   3/136 (4)
7/203 (8)   8/224 (9)   9/264 (10)   10/298 (11)   4/140 (3)   5/209 (6)
                                                        6/258 (5)   7/304 (7)   8/388 (9)

Murtagh 21–3–51–0; Finn 23.2–2–55–2; Harris 23–6–75–4; Helm 18–3–70–2; Voges 5–1–19–1; Stirling 3–0–13–0. *Second innings*—Murtagh 24–3–69–3; Finn 17–6–41–0; Harris 20–1–116–1; Helm 10–1–31–1; Stirling 11–1–66–1; Voges 14–1–65–2.

Middlesex

S. D. Robson b Ball	35	– (2) lbw b Ball	0
N. R. T. Gubbins b Gurney	23	– (1) c Wessels b Patel	37
N. R. D. Compton b Philander	3	– c Wessels b Gurney	85
*A. C. Voges lbw b Gurney	29	– b Gurney	72
P. R. Stirling c Patel b Ball	11	– c Patel b Gurney	0
†J. A. Simpson c Wessels b Gurney	35	– b Ball	11
J. A. R. Harris lbw b Patel	16	– not out	36
T. G. Helm lbw b Patel	0	– lbw b Patel	5
T. J. Murtagh c B. R. M. Taylor b Patel	19	– not out	18
S. T. Finn not out	5		
D. J. Malan absent hurt			
B 1, n-b 4	5	B 4, l-b 21, w 1, n-b 10	36

1/51 (2) 2/59 (3) 3/71 (1)   (66 overs) 181   1/0 (2)   (7 wkts, 118.5 overs) 300
4/103 (4) 5/107 (5) 6/147 (7)   2/132 (1) 3/174 (3)
7/147 (8) 8/167 (6) 9/181 (9)   4/174 (5) 5/231 (6) 6/253 (4) 7/264 (8)

Philander 14–5–25–1; Ball 14–3–38–2; Gurney 15–3–50–3; Gidman 13–5–29–0; Patel 6–0–30–3; Mullaney 4–2–8–0. *Second innings*—Philander 23.5–6–55–0; Ball 23–9–55–2; Gurney 24–6–69–3; Gidman 11–4–26–0; Patel 31–9–67–2; Mullaney 6–4–3–0.

Umpires: N. G. B. Cook and M. A. Gough.

At Taunton, April 26–29. MIDDLESEX beat SOMERSET by five wickets. *Middlesex overhaul 402.*

MIDDLESEX v DURHAM

At Lord's, May 2–5. Middlesex won by 187 runs. Middlesex 23pts, Durham 4pts. Toss: Durham.
When Middlesex crashed to 50 for nine in their second innings, with Rushworth and Hastings running riot, it looked as if a hard-earned first-innings lead of 169 would go to waste. But, after a last-ditch stand stretched the target to 259, Harris – a disappointment since signing from Glamorgan in 2013 – bowled superbly from the Nursery End, despite operating into a strong wind. "It didn't swing too much and it just did a little bit off the surface," he said. "I was on a bit of a roll and thankfully it kept happening." Pitching the ball up, he finished with nine for 34, the second-best

BEST CHAMPIONSHIP BOWLING FIGURES AT LORD'S

10-40	G. O. B. Allen	Middlesex v Lancashire	1929
9-34	**J. A. R. Harris**	**Middlesex v Durham**	**2015**
9-38	R. C. Robertson-Glasgow	Somerset v Middlesex	1924
9-48	C. L. Townsend	Gloucestershire v Middlesex	1898
9-57	F. J. Titmus	Middlesex v Lancashire	1964
9-59	F. A. Tarrant	Middlesex v Nottinghamshire	1907
9-65	J. J. Warr	Middlesex v Kent	1956
9-71	M. W. Tate	Sussex v Middlesex	1926
9-82	J. W. Hearne	Middlesex v Surrey	1911
9-97	C. Blythe	Kent v Surrey†	1914
9-111	R. A. Sinfield	Gloucestershire v Middlesex	1936

† *Surrey's game against Kent in August 1914 – Jack Hobbs's benefit match – was played at Lord's as The Oval had been requisitioned for military purposes.*

Championship figures at Lord's, and bowled unchanged with Finn, who spoiled a possible ten-for by removing Arshad, the eighth wicket to fall. Durham narrowly passed their lowest first-class total (67, also at Lord's, in 1996; Collingwood made a duck in that one, too) but still lost heavily. From 30 for two, they surrendered their last eight for 41. It was quite a turnaround from the opening day when, under sunny skies, Robson batted over six hours for a superb 178, his first first-class century since the Headingley Test against Sri Lanka the previous June. In reply, Jennings resisted more than five hours for 98 against an attack shorn of the injured Murtagh; Harris claimed four wickets as a prelude to his final-day heroics.

Close of play: first day, Middlesex 329-4 (Franklin 14, Harris 2); second day, Durham 157-4 (Jennings 61, Rushworth 0); third day, Durham 24-2 (Borthwick 8, Richardson 5).

Middlesex

S. D. Robson c Borthwick b Coughlin	178	– (2) lbw b Rushworth	17
N. R. T. Gubbins c Borthwick b Coughlin	23	– (1) lbw b Rushworth	8
N. R. D. Compton b Borthwick	50	– c MacLeod b Rushworth	5
*A. C. Voges lbw b Rushworth	57	– b Rushworth	4
J. E. C. Franklin b Hastings	18	– c Mustard b Hastings	1
J. A. R. Harris c Mustard b Hastings	9	– (9) c MacLeod b Rushworth	6
N. J. Dexter c Arshad b Hastings	33	– c Collingwood b Hastings	6
†J. A. Simpson c Rushworth b Hastings	58	– (7) c Richardson b Hastings	0
O. P. Rayner b Rushworth	16	– b Hastings	0
T. J. Murtagh b Borthwick	11	– (11) not out	22
S. T. Finn not out	0	– (10) lbw b Hastings	15
B 2, l-b 6, n-b 2	10	L-b 1, n-b 4	5

1/66 (2) 2/179 (3) 3/306 (4)   (137 overs) 463
4/326 (1) 5/334 (5) 6/341 (6)
7/399 (7) 8/440 (9) 9/455 (10)
10/463 (8)   110 overs: 361-6

1/12 (1) 2/22 (3)   (24.2 overs) 89
3/26 (4) 4/35 (2)
5/35 (5) 6/37 (7) 7/37 (8)
8/50 (6) 9/54 (9) 10/89 (10)

Rushworth 31–6–96–2; Arshad 19–1–91–0; Hastings 33–8–87–4; Coughlin 20–4–71–2; Collingwood 13–7–26–0; Borthwick 9–0–46–2; Jennings 8–0–27–0; MacLeod 4–1–11–0. *Second innings*—Rushworth 12–2–38–5; Coughlin 3–0–22–0; Hastings 8.2–2–24–5; Borthwick 1–0–4–0.

Durham

M. D. Stoneman c Rayner b Harris	21	– c Voges b Harris	11
K. K. Jennings c Simpson b Voges	98	– c sub (A. Balbirnie) b Harris	0
S. G. Borthwick c Simpson b Franklin	26	– c Voges b Harris	14
M. J. Richardson c Simpson b Harris	26	– b Harris	10
C. S. MacLeod b Finn	13	– lbw b Harris	0
C. Rushworth lbw b Rayner	40	– (11) c Simpson b Harris	11
*P. D. Collingwood not out	38	– (6) b Harris	0
†P. Mustard b Voges	1	– (7) c Franklin b Harris	3
U. Arshad c sub (A. Balbirnie) b Harris	9	– (8) c Robson b Finn	7
J. W. Hastings c Rayner b Finn	2	– (9) lbw b Harris	0
P. Coughlin c Simpson b Harris	4	– (10) not out	13
B 4, l-b 11, w 1	16	L-b 2	2

1/46 (1) 2/90 (3) 3/132 (4)   (92.5 overs) 294
4/156 (5) 5/229 (6) 6/239 (2)
7/243 (8) 8/270 (9) 9/289 (10) 10/294 (11)

1/5 (2) 2/14 (1)   (24.1 overs) 71
3/30 (4) 4/34 (5)
5/34 (6) 6/38 (7) 7/39 (3)
8/47 (8) 9/53 (9) 10/71 (11)

Murtagh 0.2–0–0–0; Harris 22.3–2–69–4; Finn 24–4–69–2; Rayner 22–7–51–1; Dexter 12–1–34–0; Franklin 8–0–36–1; Voges 4–1–20–2. *Second innings*—Harris 12.1–2–34–9; Finn 12–4–35–1.

Umpires: N. L. Bainton and P. J. Hartley.

At Hove, May 10–12. MIDDLESEX beat SUSSEX by 79 runs.

At Southampton, May 17–20. MIDDLESEX drew with HAMPSHIRE.

MIDDLESEX v WARWICKSHIRE

At Lord's, May 31–June 3. Drawn. Middlesex 10pts, Warwickshire 11pts. Toss: Middlesex. Championship debut: J. P. Webb.

A rain-spattered match, which lost almost 100 overs, crackled into life on the final morning, when Warwickshire lost four for two in 19 balls. But the last three wickets occupied more than an hour, and Middlesex were eventually set 270 in 54 overs. It looked possible at 80 without loss after 26, but two wickets apiece for Clarke and Rankin changed the mood. Burns weathered the storm, surviving nearly 50 overs until he fell to Patel shortly before the end. It might have been a different story if, on an unusually green first-day pitch, the scoreless Evans had not been dropped by Morgan at leg slip in the final over of Finn's incisive new-ball spell. Evans ground his way to 98 in 271 minutes before Finn had his revenge next day, but solid contributions down the order pushed Warwickshire to 342. Middlesex struggled to match that: only Compton and Dexter lasted long, though Morgan made 44 in his first Championship innings since returning from the IPL.

Close of play: first day, Warwickshire 148-3 (Trott 44, Evans 41); second day, Middlesex 39-1 (Robson 26, Compton 5); third day, Warwickshire 58-2 (Chopra 31, Trott 12).

Warwickshire

*V. Chopra c Rayner b Finn	14	– lbw b Harris	73
A. Javid c Robson b Finn	18	– c Franklin b Roland-Jones	8
J. P. Webb c Robson b Finn	14	– b Harris	4
I. J. L. Trott c Simpson b Roland-Jones	45	– run out	29
L. J. Evans b Finn	98	– lbw b Harris	7
†T. R. Ambrose c Rayner b Dexter	20	– c Roland-Jones b Finn	16
R. Clarke run out	15	– lbw b Roland-Jones	1
K. H. D. Barker b Roland-Jones	37	– c Burns b Roland-Jones	0
J. S. Patel lbw b Rayner	37	– b Roland-Jones	27
C. J. C. Wright not out	9	– lbw b Finn	9
W. B. Rankin b Rayner	2	– not out	8
B 11, l-b 4, w 5, n-b 8, p 5	33	L-b 3, n-b 2	5

1/37 (1) 2/53 (3) 3/56 (2)   (105.1 overs) 342   1/26 (2) 2/33 (3)   (64.2 overs) 187
4/152 (4) 5/200 (6) 6/233 (7)   3/105 (4) 4/125 (1)
7/253 (5) 8/325 (9) 9/331 (8) 10/342 (11)   5/126 (5) 6/127 (7) 7/127 (8)
                                           8/170 (9) 9/170 (6) 10/187 (10)

Finn 28–9–84–4; Roland-Jones 31–9–73–2; Harris 22–7–75–0; Dexter 13–3–40–1; Franklin 6–0–19–0; Rayner 5.1–1–31–2. *Second innings*—Finn 19.2–1–61–2; Roland-Jones 23–6–51–4; Harris 17–2–49–3; Dexter 4–1–18–0; Franklin 1–0–5–0.

Middlesex

S. D. Robson c Chopra b Wright	30	– (2) c Ambrose b Clarke	29
J. A. Burns lbw b Wright	4	– (1) st Ambrose b Patel	72
N. R. D. Compton c Trott b Rankin	74	– c Chopra b Clarke	0
E. J. G. Morgan c Javid b Barker	44	– b Rankin	2
*J. E. C. Franklin b Clarke	0	– b Rankin	9
N. J. Dexter not out	47	– not out	17
†J. A. Simpson c Evans b Patel	1	– not out	0
O. P. Rayner c and b Clarke	3		
J. A. R. Harris c Patel b Clarke	0		
T. S. Roland-Jones c Webb b Rankin	32		
S. T. Finn lbw b Rankin	1		
B 8, n-b 16	24	B 4, l-b 8, w 1, n-b 10	23

1/8 (2) 2/52 (1) 3/122 (4)   (72.2 overs) 260   1/80 (2)   (5 wkts, 50 overs) 152
4/123 (5) 5/192 (3) 6/195 (7)   2/80 (3) 3/91 (4)
7/202 (8) 8/206 (9) 9/253 (10) 10/260 (11)   4/105 (5) 5/150 (1)

Barker 20–7–80–1; Wright 19–0–65–2; Clarke 14–2–42–3; Rankin 10.2–1–52–3; Patel 9–2–13–1. *Second innings*—Barker 10–1–24–0; Wright 12–1–43–0; Rankin 13–1–40–2; Clarke 11–2–32–2; Patel 4–3–1–1.

Umpires: M. J. D. Bodenham and S. J. O'Shaughnessy.

At Leeds, June 7–9. MIDDLESEX lost to YORKSHIRE by four wickets.

MIDDLESEX v WORCESTERSHIRE

At Uxbridge, June 21–24. Drawn. Middlesex 10pts, Worcestershire 12pts. Toss: Middlesex.

More grass than usual was left on the notoriously docile Uxbridge pitch, but – for the 16th game in a row here, stretching back to 1996 – Middlesex failed to force victory. They had lurched to 51 for four after opting to bat, although that might have owed more to a break for Twenty20 than the surface. Robson fell to the first delivery of the match, then Compton clumped a full toss straight to midwicket, and departed suggesting the ball had bounced before it reached Oliver (who was later given out caught behind, convinced he had not touched it). Shantry bowled well, but Middlesex recovered through Burns and Franklin, who made his highest score in England. In reply, Mitchell took 33 balls to get off the mark, and used up two hours in scoring 18. But Fell made 143 – a career-best, until the return game with Middlesex in September – as Worcestershire ground out a lead of 76. Robson completed a three-ball pair, before Burns and Franklin again prospered, and Harris made his first half-century for Middlesex. There was, though, never much likelihood of a result, and Franklin declared – denying himself a possible second century – to allow Middlesex to massage their flagging over-rate on what he called "a tough pitch to play cricket on".

Close of play: first day, Middlesex 289-7 (Rayner 8); second day, Worcestershire 195-3 (Fell 75, Gidman 30); third day, Middlesex 140-3 (Burns 29, Stirling 39).

Middlesex

S. D. Robson c Fell b Morris	0	– (2) c Cox b Morris 0
N. R. T. Gubbins c Saeed Ajmal b Shantry	21	– (1) b Saeed Ajmal 23
N. R. D. Compton c Oliver b Leach	3	– b Gidman b Shantry 47
J. A. Burns c Fell b Shantry	57	– c Leach b Shantry 87
P. R. Stirling lbw b Shantry	4	– b Ali 39
*J. E. C. Franklin c Fell b Shantry	135	– not out 91
†J. A. Simpson c Mitchell b Morris	41	– b Leach 5
O. P. Rayner lbw b Leach	25	– lbw b Leach 0
J. A. R. Harris lbw b Leach	1	– not out 59
T. S. Roland-Jones c Gidman b Leach	0	
T. J. Murtagh not out	1	
B 6, l-b 14, w 1	21	B 1, l-b 5, w 1, n-b 4 11

1/0 (1) 2/5 (3) 3/45 (2) (103 overs) 309   1/3 (2) (7 wkts dec, 118 overs) 362
4/51 (5) 5/102 (4) 6/272 (7)   2/63 (1) 3/73 (3)
7/289 (6) 8/298 (9) 9/298 (10) 10/309 (8)   4/147 (5) 5/250 (4) 6/257 (7) 7/259 (8)

Morris 22–3–64–2; Leach 25–3–81–4; Shantry 26–7–66–4; Saeed Ajmal 18–4–41–0; Ali 12–1–37–0. *Second innings*—Morris 22–6–55–1; Leach 20–5–64–2; Ali 27–3–82–1; Shantry 17–5–37–2; Saeed Ajmal 30–1–106–1; Mitchell 1–0–5–0; Fell 1–0–7–0.

Worcestershire

*D. K. H. Mitchell c Rayner b Roland-Jones	18	– not out 11
R. K. Oliver c Simpson b Harris	6	– c Compton b Rayner 6
M. M. Ali c Roland-Jones b Franklin	54	– not out 21
T. C. Fell c Robson b Roland-Jones	143	
A. P. R. Gidman b Murtagh	30	
J. M. Clarke lbw b Murtagh	17	
†O. B. Cox c Rayner b Harris	6	
J. Leach b Harris	19	
J. D. Shantry not out	41	
Saeed Ajmal b Murtagh	20	
C. A. J. Morris b Murtagh	0	
B 18, l-b 11, n-b 2	31	B 1 1

1/8 (2) 2/52 (1) 3/112 (3) (116.5 overs) 385   1/10 (2) (1 wkt, 11 overs) 39
4/195 (5) 5/227 (6) 6/258 (7) 7/308 (8)
8/332 (4) 9/385 (10) 10/385 (11)   110 overs: 352-8

Murtagh 30.5–10–76–4; Roland-Jones 30–10–97–2; Harris 32–8–103–3; Franklin 11–3–41–1; Rayner 13–6–39–0. *Second innings*—Stirling 4–0–9–0; Rayner 4–2–7–1; Robson 2–0–18–0; Compton 1–0–4–0.

Umpires: M. J. D. Bodenham and A. G. Wharf.

MIDDLESEX v HAMPSHIRE

At Lord's, June 28–July 1. Middlesex won by nine wickets. Middlesex 22pts, Hampshire 2pts. Toss: Middlesex.

Middlesex kept their Championship hopes alive with a fourth win of the season, though their first for nearly two months. Hampshire were undone on the opening day by the seamers, with four wickets apiece for Roland-Jones and Harris, who was capped at tea. The main resistance on the first day came from a familiar name at Lord's: Joe Gatting, nephew of Mike, made 64 in his first Championship match of the summer. Middlesex started indifferently, dipping to 113 for five, but Compton and Simpson both settled in, then Rayner pushed the lead to 154. Hampshire's top order struggled again, with only Terry passing 50. Then, after Smith and Wheater put up some resistance, Rayner removed both in successive balls, and quickly added Gatting with what he jokingly claimed was his doosra. Harris finished with four more wickets to move to 53 in the season, and Middlesex completed victory before a delayed lunch on the final day.

Close of play: first day, Middlesex 59-0 (Stirling 36, Robson 17); second day, Middlesex 298-8 (Rayner 34, Roland-Jones 1); third day, Hampshire 195-7 (Berg 18, Briggs 5).

Hampshire

*J. H. K. Adams c Simpson b Murtagh	0	– c Simpson b Harris	28
S. P. Terry c Simpson b Roland-Jones	23	– lbw b Murtagh	52
M. A. Carberry lbw b Roland-Jones	15	– c Simpson b Harris	1
J. M. Vince b Harris	13	– b Harris	3
W. R. Smith lbw b Roland-Jones	18	– c Murtagh b Rayner	30
†A. J. A. Wheater b Murtagh	17	– lbw b Rayner	50
J. S. Gatting not out	64	– b Rayner	4
G. K. Berg c Compton b Roland-Jones	10	– lbw b Murtagh	25
D. R. Briggs c Simpson b Harris	8	– c Rayner b Roland-Jones	19
B. Wheal b Harris	3	– lbw b Harris	1
J. M. Bird c Rayner b Harris	1	– not out	9
B 1, l-b 3	4	L-b 2, w 3	5

1/0 (1) 2/28 (2) 3/41 (3)   (62.3 overs) 176   1/44 (1) 2/52 (3)   (97 overs) 227
4/55 (4) 5/83 (6) 6/97 (5)   3/56 (4) 4/106 (2)
7/129 (8) 8/150 (9) 9/170 (10) 10/176 (11)   5/164 (5) 6/167 (6) 7/178 (7)
                                         8/214 (9) 9/216 (8) 10/227 (10)

Murtagh 19–4–49–2; Roland-Jones 20–7–60–4; Harris 15.3–3–48–4; Franklin 6–0–11–0; Rayner 2–0–4–0. *Second innings*—Murtagh 23–6–41–2; Roland-Jones 23–5–57–1; Harris 23–3–80–4; Rayner 25–14–44–3; Franklin 3–0–3–0.

Middlesex

P. R. Stirling c Vince b Bird	38	– (2) b Berg		16
S. D. Robson lbw b Berg	17	– (1) not out		36
N. R. D. Compton c Vince b Briggs	87	– not out		16
J. A. Burns b Wheal	13			
E. J. G. Morgan c Smith b Wheal	0			
*J. E. C. Franklin c Wheater b Berg	5			
†J. A. Simpson c Wheater b Bird	64			
O. P. Rayner b Wheal	52			
J. A. R. Harris b Wheal	15			
T. S. Roland-Jones b Bird	14			
T. J. Murtagh not out	1			
L-b 7, w 1, n-b 16	24	B 4, l-b 3, n-b 2		9

1/60 (2) 2/62 (1) 3/100 (4)   (119 overs) 330   1/38 (2)   (1 wkt, 17.4 overs) 77
4/100 (5) 5/113 (6) 6/224 (3) 7/260 (7)
8/297 (9) 9/318 (10) 10/330 (8)   110 overs: 301-8

Bird 30–4–88–3; Wheal 27–1–101–4; Berg 24–4–47–2; Briggs 22–7–44–1; Vince 10–1–33–0; Smith 6–1–10–0. *Second innings*—Bird 7–1–33–0; Wheal 5–1–20–0; Berg 5–0–13–1; Smith 0.4–0–4–0.

Umpires: N. G. B. Cook and P. J. Hartley.

At Nottingham, July 5–8. MIDDLESEX drew with NOTTINGHAMSHIRE.

MIDDLESEX v SOMERSET

At Merchant Taylors' School, Northwood, July 11–14. Drawn. Middlesex 10pts, Somerset 8pts. Toss: Middlesex.

A draw looked certain after the third day was lost to rain, only for the match to come alive when Franklin's enterprising declaration set Somerset 219 in 40 overs. They looked on course at 126 for three in the 28th, but ended up grateful for a draw once four wickets had tumbled for 19. The absence of Finn – who joined the England squad for the Second Ashes Test after taking four for 41 in the first innings – might have made a difference for Middlesex, although his replacement Harris did take two late wickets. It was the first Championship action at the Sandy Lodge ground: the inaugural game there, against Sussex in 2014, had been washed out. And the pitch was lively, at least to begin with: three batsmen were hit on the helmet on the opening day, including Compton, who had to retire after being struck by Overton. Morgan was out for the first half of a pair, but Malan's four-hour 69 guided Middlesex towards 283. Somerset then declined against Finn and Murtagh after a decent start on a truncated second day, though Trescothick made the first of two important half-centuries. Middlesex hit out on the fourth day, but were not helped by more rain, which cost another 75 minutes around lunchtime.

Close of play: first day, Middlesex 283; second day, Somerset 185-8 (Bates 2, Groenewald 4); third day, no play.

Middlesex

S. D. Robson c Myburgh b Groenewald	67	– c Bates b Groenewald	18
J. A. Burns c Bates b Gregory	10	– c Trescothick b Trego	10
N. R. D. Compton lbw b Gregory	32	– c Trescothick b Overton	30
D. J. Malan lbw b Trego	69	– b Overton	16
E. J. G. Morgan c Allenby b Groenewald	0	– c Gregory b Trego	0
*J. E. C. Franklin lbw b Gregory	17	– c Allenby b Gregory	32
†J. A. Simpson c Bates b Groenewald	24	– not out	17
O. P. Rayner lbw b Groenewald	31	– not out	4
T. S. Roland-Jones not out	20		
T. J. Murtagh c Trescothick b Gregory	0		
S. T. Finn b Gregory	0		
B 6, l-b 3, n-b 4	13	L-b 5	5

1/23 (2) 2/124 (1) 3/128 (5)   (93.1 overs) 283   1/23 (1)   (6 wkts dec, 29 overs) 132
4/154 (6) 5/192 (7) 6/248 (4)   2/33 (2) 3/66 (4)
7/256 (8) 8/283 (3) 9/283 (10) 10/283 (11)   4/79 (3) 5/83 (5) 6/128 (6)

J. A. R. Harris replaced Finn, who left to join England's Test squad.

In the first innings Compton, when 18, retired hurt at 69-1 and resumed at 256-7.

Gregory 15.1–2–58–5; Groenewald 23–7–55–4; Trego 13–2–38–1; Overton 15–3–44–0; Allenby 12–3–27–0; Abdur Rehman 13–1–45–0; Myburgh 2–1–7–0. *Second innings*—Gregory 6–0–33–1; Groenewald 7–2–27–1; Trego 9–2–39–2; Overton 7–1–28–2.

Somerset

*M. E. Trescothick lbw b Roland-Jones	52	– c Franklin b Roland-Jones	50
T. B. Abell c Simpson b Finn	26	– lbw b Murtagh	21
J. G. Myburgh c Simpson b Murtagh	1	– c Franklin b Murtagh	14
J. C. Hildreth b Finn	4	– c Simpson b Roland-Jones	25
J. Allenby c Rayner b Finn	43	– c Morgan b Harris	23
P. D. Trego lbw b Rayner	15	– (7) c Robson b Murtagh	4
L. Gregory c Simpson b Finn	11		
†M. D. Bates run out	8	– (9) not out	0
Abdur Rehman c Robson b Murtagh	2		
T. D. Groenewald c Compton b Murtagh	4	– (8) not out	2
J. Overton not out	6	– (6) c and b Harris	5
B 8, l-b 17	25	L-b 3	3

1/76 (2) 2/77 (3) 3/86 (4)   (75 overs) 197   1/39 (2)   (7 wkts, 39.4 overs) 147
4/117 (1) 5/152 (6) 6/167 (7)   2/57 (3) 3/99 (4)
7/178 (5) 8/181 (9) 9/185 (10) 10/197 (8)   4/126 (1) 5/135 (6) 6/141 (5) 7/145 (7)

Murtagh 22–6–60–3; Finn 21–3–41–4; Roland-Jones 14–3–26–1; Franklin 7–0–22–0; Rayner 9–2–20–1; Harris 2–1–3–0. *Second innings*—Murtagh 12–5–43–3; Roland-Jones 16–4–45–2; Harris 10.4–0–49–2; Rayner 1–0–7–0.

Umpires: S. C. Gale and N. A. Mallender.

MIDDLESEX v SUSSEX

At Lord's, August 7–10. Middlesex won by 20 runs. Middlesex 19pts (after 1pt penalty), Sussex 6pts. Toss: Middlesex.

An exciting match was staged on the pitch used for the previous day's 50-overs game against Nottinghamshire. That had turned, so Middlesex recalled Patel from a loan spell at Essex, and opted to bat – though it was the seamers who held their nerve on a tense final day. Middlesex's narrow win took them second in the table. The in-form Malan had kept things together on the opening day with a spirited 93, a second-wicket stand of 134 between Wells and the aggressive Machan put Sussex on top. At 199 for three a big lead looked on the cards, but Patel and Roland-Jones kept the advantage down to 66, despite Yardy's 70. Robson provided a platform with a fluent 77, then Malan again took the eye: his unbeaten 120 – his third century of the season against Sussex, to accompany 115 not out in the T20 Blast and 131 in the Royal London One-Day Cup – ensured a competitive target. Magoffin's five-for included his 500th first-class wicket (Franklin), while Robinson switched to off-spin and took three. Set 266, Sussex were five down for 103, before Nash and Brown added 60 on a surface not yielding the expected tun. Three strikes from Roland-Jones regained the initiative for Middlesex, but there was time for a final twist, as the last pair – needing 51 – put on 30, before Murtagh winkled out Brown.

Close of play: first day, Sussex 33-1 (Wells 17, Machan 3); second day, Middlesex 47-0 (Gubbins 23, Robson 41); third day, Middlesex 326-8 (Malan 118).

Middlesex

S. D. Robson c Wright b Magoffin	6	– (2) c Brown b Ashar Zaidi	77
N. R. T. Gubbins c Joyce b Liddle	17	– (1) c Brown b Magoffin	10
N. R. D. Compton c Nash b Magoffin	39	– b Ashar Zaidi	21
D. J. Malan c Brown b Robinson	93	– not out	120
*J. E. C. Franklin c Yardy b Robinson	1	– c Joyce b Magoffin	5
†J. A. Simpson b Brown b Liddle	1	– c Joyce b Robinson	29
J. A. R. Harris c Wells b Liddle	0	– c Nash b Robinson	17
O. P. Rayner c Ashar Zaidi b Magoffin	28	– lbw b Magoffin	17
T. S. Roland-Jones b Robinson	16	– lbw b Robinson	36
T. J. Murtagh c Wright b Magoffin	13	– c Liddle b Magoffin	0
R. H. Patel not out	6	– c Yardy b Magoffin	3
B 10, l-b 2, n-b 2	14	B 3, l-b 10	13

1/16 (1) 2/24 (2) 3/114 (3)   (77.4 overs) 234
4/119 (5) 5/121 (6) 6/123 (7)
7/178 (8) 8/211 (4) 9/216 (9) 10/234 (10)

1/61 (1) 2/109 (2)   (113.1 overs) 331
3/125 (3) 4/137 (5)
5/215 (6) 6/215 (5) 7/249 (8)
8/326 (9) 9/327 (10) 10/331 (11)

Magoffin 21.4–5–48–4; Robinson 23–9–64–3; Liddle 16–4–49–3; Ashar Zaidi 10–0–35–0; Wells 7–2–26–0. *Second innings*—Magoffin 27.1–7–73–5; Robinson 24–2–88–3; Liddle 22–5–62–0; Wells 18–3–50–0; Ashar Zaidi 20–2–39–2; Nash 2–0–6–0.

Sussex

*E. C. Joyce lbw b Roland-Jones	12	– (2) lbw b Harris	22
L. W. P. Wells c Franklin b Patel	61	– (1) c Simpson b Harris	16
M. W. Machan b Patel	81	– c Franklin b Harris	5
C. D. Nash c Roland-Jones b Patel	22	– c Rayner b Roland-Jones	66
M. H. Yardy b Harris	70	– b Patel	11
L. J. Wright b Murtagh	1	– c Rayner b Murtagh	20
†B. C. Brown c Rayner b Patel	4	– c Franklin b Murtagh	68
Ashar Zaidi c Simpson b Roland-Jones	16	– c Simpson b Roland-Jones	16
O. E. Robinson lbw b Roland-Jones	26	– c Rayner b Roland-Jones	10
S. J. Magoffin not out	0	– b Harris	1
C. J. Liddle b Harris	4	– not out	4
L-b 3	3	L-b 4, w 2	6

1/21 (1) 2/155 (3) 3/160 (2)   (94.4 overs) 300
4/199 (4) 5/205 (6) 6/216 (7)
7/254 (8) 8/294 (9) 9/296 (5) 10/300 (11)

1/36 (1) 2/43 (2)   (69.4 overs) 245
3/44 (3) 4/70 (5)
5/103 (4) 6/163 (4) 7/197 (8)
8/207 (9) 9/215 (10) 10/245 (7)

Murtagh 26–11–73–1; Roland-Jones 26–5–88–3; Harris 13.4–0–55–2; Rayner 10–3–34–0; Patel 17–7–42–4; Franklin 2–0–5–0. *Second innings*—Murtagh 13.4–2–40–2; Roland-Jones 23–3–78–3; Harris 16–3–57–4; Patel 11–3–42–1; Rayner 6–1–24–0.

Umpires: M. J. D. Bodenham and M. J. Saggers.

At Chester-le-Street, August 21–24. MIDDLESEX beat DURHAM by 71 runs.

At Birmingham, September 1–4. MIDDLESEX drew with WARWICKSHIRE.

MIDDLESEX v YORKSHIRE

At Lord's, September 9–12. Middlesex won by 246 runs. Middlesex 19pts, Yorkshire 5pts. Toss: Yorkshire. First-class debut: S. S. Eskinazi.

Yorkshire retained the County Championship on a manic opening day, then slipped to a defeat which looked implausible after Sidebottom had begun the match with a triple-wicket maiden, starting with his 700th first-class victim. Middlesex were skittled for 106 but, with Compton making 149 in the second innings and Roland-Jones blasting a century, the tables were turned so dramatically that Yorkshire never sniffed a target of 381. They possibly lost focus after Nottinghamshire's failure to take more than one batting point against Durham at Trent Bridge confirmed the fate of the title: Gale, Yorkshire's captain, was at the crease when the news filtered through just after 3pm, but was

THE COMEBACK KINGS

Winning a first-class match after being nought for three in the first innings:

Sussex (169 and 78) beat Nottinghamshire (144 and 80) at Nottingham	1837
South† (83 and 179-2) beat North (107 and 154) at Canterbury	1869
Oxford University† (123) beat Middlesex (61 and 47) at Chelsea	1874
Gents of Philadelphia† (157 and 79-2) beat Players of USA (114 and 121) at Philadelphia	1893
Kent† (134 and 78-0) beat Surrey (148 and 60) at Beckenham	1905
Derbyshire† (83 and 193-8) beat Glamorgan (168 and 106) at Cardiff	1921
Hampshire† (15 and 521) beat Warwickshire (223 and 158) at Birmingham	1922
Pakistan (245 and 599-7 dec) beat India (238 and 265) at Karachi	2005-06
Jamaica (165 and 188) beat Barbados (162 and 128) at Bridgetown	2012-13
Derbyshire† (86 and 232-2) beat Kent (205 and 112) at Canterbury	**2015**
Middlesex (106 and 573-8 dec) beat Yorkshire (299 and 134) at Lord's	**2015**

† *Batted second.*

Research: Philip Bailey

eventually out after hitting 18 fours in his 98, one of 19 wickets to tumble on the first day. Brooks's maiden fifty for Yorkshire propelled them to a lead of 193 next morning, and a routine victory looked inevitable as Middlesex declined to 143 for five. But Compton buckled down, putting on 150 with Franklin, and Simpson proved similarly adhesive. When he was trapped in front by Lyth's occasional medium-pace, Middlesex led by 234 with two second-innings wickets in hand – adequate, but far from conclusive. Enter Roland-Jones, who sprinted to a 119-ball maiden century – the first by a Middlesex No. 10 since Jim Smith in 1939 – dominating an unbroken ninth-wicket stand of 146 with Harris, a county record against Yorkshire. Franklin declared before the final morning – Middlesex's total was their highest against Yorkshire, surpassing 527 at Huddersfield in 1887 – then watched Roland-Jones maintain the magic with five for 27 from 21 overs. As in 2014, the champions' only defeat had come at Lord's.

Close of play: first day, Yorkshire 238-9 (Brooks 12, Sidebottom 9); second day, Middlesex 274-5 (Compton 86, Franklin 60); third day, Middlesex 573-8 (Harris 67, Roland-Jones 103).

Middlesex

P. R. Stirling lbw b Sidebottom	0	– (2) b Middlebrook	34
S. D. Robson c Lees b Bresnan	26	– (1) b Bresnan	53
N. R. D. Compton c Hodd b Sidebottom	0	– lbw b Middlebrook	149
D. J. Malan b Sidebottom	0	– lbw b Middlebrook	0
S. S. Eskinazi c Lyth b Sidebottom	4	– b Patterson	29
N. J. Dexter c Hodd b Bresnan	18	– c and b Brooks	13
*J. E. C. Franklin c Leaning b Bresnan	12	– lbw b Sidebottom	63
†J. A. Simpson c Hodd b Middlebrook	28	– lbw b Lyth	47
J. A. R. Harris not out	9	– not out	67
T. S. Roland-Jones lbw b Bresnan	0	– not out	103
T. J. Murtagh b Sidebottom	3		
L-b 4, n-b 2	6	B 6, l-b 8, n-b 8	22

1/0 (1) 2/0 (3) 3/0 (4)   (33 overs) 106   1/87 (1)   (8 wkts dec, 175 overs) 573
4/14 (5) 5/44 (6) 6/55 (2)   2/87 (2) 3/87 (4)
7/92 (8) 8/95 (7) 9/95 (10) 10/106 (11)   4/128 (5) 5/143 (6)
                                              6/293 (7) 7/380 (3) 8/427 (8)

Sidebottom 12–5–18–5; Brooks 6–0–39–0; Patterson 6–2–11–0; Bresnan 8–1–30–4; Middlebrook 1–0–4–1. *Second innings*—Sidebottom 28–7–70–1; Brooks 27–3–122–1; Patterson 33–8–96–1; Bresnan 37–13–108–1; Middlebrook 40–7–130–3; Lyth 8–0–19–1; Leaning 2–0–14–0.

Yorkshire

A. Lyth lbw b Roland-Jones	25	– c Simpson b Harris	14
A. Z. Lees lbw b Stirling	39	– c Malan b Roland-Jones	62
G. S. Ballance lbw b Roland-Jones	0	– c Simpson b Harris	0
*A. W. Gale c Robson b Dexter	98	– lbw b Dexter	17
J. A. Leaning lbw b Dexter	9	– c Robson b Roland-Jones	4
T. T. Bresnan lbw b Dexter	11	– c Simpson b Harris	9
†A. J. Hodd b Murtagh	20	– c Simpson b Roland-Jones	0
J. D. Middlebrook c Simpson b Roland-Jones	4	– c Malan b Roland-Jones	0
S. A. Patterson c Simpson b Murtagh	0	– b Murtagh	9
J. A. Brooks not out	50	– c Eskinazi b Roland-Jones	2
R. J. Sidebottom c and b Murtagh	28	– not out	6
B 2, l-b 1, w 2, n-b 10	15	L-b 7, n-b 4	11

1/45 (1) 2/51 (3) 3/129 (2)   (72 overs) 299   1/28 (1) 2/28 (3)   (58 overs) 134
4/163 (5) 5/187 (6) 6/198 (4)   3/92 (4) 4/106 (2)
7/217 (7) 8/217 (9) 9/221 (8) 10/299 (11)   5/111 (5) 6/111 (7) 7/115 (6)
                                              8/115 (8) 9/117 (10) 10/134 (9)

Murtagh 18–1–81–3; Roland-Jones 25–5–93–3; Harris 12–0–67–0; Franklin 5–1–18–0; Stirling 4–1–13–1; Dexter 8–2–24–3. *Second innings*—Murtagh 7–3–18–1; Roland-Jones 21–10–27–5; Harris 14–6–37–3; Franklin 4–2–7–0; Stirling 4–2–7–0; Dexter 8–2–31–1.

Umpires: S. J. O'Shaughnessy and R. T. Robinson.

At Worcester, September 22–24. MIDDLESEX lost to WORCESTERSHIRE by an innings and 128 runs.

NORTHAMPTONSHIRE

Staying alive

ANDREW RADD

With a precariously small playing staff – just 17 professionals at the start of the season – and against a background of continuing financial anxiety, Northamptonshire could be quietly satisfied with their summer's work. Focusing, understandably, on the more lucrative white-ball competitions, they finished runners-up in the T20 Blast and were denied the chance of a Royal London One-Day Cup quarter-final when their last group match, against Yorkshire, was rained off. The Championship campaign blended the good, the bad and the indifferent: fifth place in Division Two, with three wins and three defeats (no other county clocked up as many as ten draws), was probably a fair outcome.

South African warhorse Rory Kleinveldt and wicketkeeper-batsman Ben Duckett, a product of the county's youth system, shared the principal honours at the end-of-season presentations. But, in terms of column inches, all-rounder David Willey eclipsed both. In May, he became only the eighth Northamptonshire-born cricketer to play for England, and proved his worth in the shorter formats. This fuelled speculation about a move to a bigger club, and in August he signed a three-year deal with Yorkshire, a week after securing Northamptonshire a place at T20 finals day with one of the summer's most destructive innings. Willey's 40-ball 100, including 34 runs off a Michael Yardy over, sank Sussex in the quarter-finals and earned him the Walter Lawrence Trophy for the fastest century of the season.

Willey called it "a tough decision", while head coach David Ripley insisted the club harboured "no bitterness". A repeat of his 2013 trophy-winning performance at Edgbaston would have been an appropriate send-off. It wasn't to be but, in the eyes of most supporters, Willey will always remain a local lad.

Northamptonshire benefited from the return of Alex Wakely, who captained in all competitions after missing 2014 through injury. A thoughtful and unselfish leader, he contributed useful runs – including Championship centuries against Gloucestershire and Leicestershire – and, crucially, worked hard to keep the players focused amid boardroom uncertainty.

The management had set down an early marker by omitting the 20-year-old Duckett from the pre-season tour to Barbados after he failed to meet fitness targets. In July, the club expressed disappointment at his "huge mistake", following a conviction for drink-driving. He did, however, excel on the field: the only Northamptonshire batsman to pass 1,000 first-class runs, he was capable of breathtaking improvisation in the limited-overs formats. Duckett was named the club's Young Player of the Year.

Rob Keogh, another promising young batsman, began the season well, and made an impressive 163 not out in nearly six hours to save the match at Derby.

David Rogers, Getty Images

Ben Duckett

He lost his touch towards the middle of the season, but it was a relief when he and Duckett agreed new contracts to keep them at Northamptonshire until the end of 2017.

Fortunately, the farcical overseas player situation of 2014 was not repeated. Kleinveldt, who had faced questions about his ability to withstand the rigours of a full English season, was an ever-present in the white-ball competitions, missed only three Championship games and was named Player of the Season. He was set to return for 2016. Kleinveldt, Azharullah and the improving Olly Stone shared 139 Championship wickets, giving Northamptonshire a more than adequate seam attack.

In contrast, slow bowling was in short supply, a state of affairs given added piquancy by off-spinner James Middlebrook's born-again appearances for champions Yorkshire following his release in 2014. Slow left-armer Graeme White missed the start of the season through injury, and barely featured in the longer game, leaving the likes of Keogh and Josh Cobb – a positive presence in his first year at the club – to fill in as best they could. It made the development of 17-year-old Saif Zaib, a left-arm-spinning all-rounder who made his first-class debut in August, even more important.

Northamptonshire's determination to make progress in the T20 Blast prompted the surprise signing of Pakistan's Shahid Afridi, initially for six group matches. The local interest he generated undoubtedly justified the outlay. Following a stint in the Caribbean Premier League and an international series in Sri Lanka, he returned for finals day, making a mark in both matches. South African Kolpak player Richard Levi again demonstrated his explosive short-form hitting and, less predictably, scored ugly runs in the Championship, selflessly reining in his natural exuberance. He signed a two-year deal.

The retirement of Stephen Peters ended a distinguished first-class career that stretched back to 1996 and yielded over 14,000 runs for Essex, Worcestershire and – in his last ten seasons – Northamptonshire. A model professional who led the county to Championship promotion in 2013, he paid tribute to a small club "with a big heart". Seamer Maurice Chambers and Scotland international Kyle Coetzer were released.

In August, Northamptonshire approached the ECB for additional funding, but denied claims they could be dissolved or forced to leave Wantage Road for a new ground at Sixfields. Two months later, the club agreed a loan of up to £250,000 from Northampton Borough Council, to be repaid within five years. Much of the club's history has been a battle for survival; the faithful will always maintain that, like old age, struggle is preferable to the alternative.

Championship attendance: 12,432.

NORTHAMPTONSHIRE RESULTS

All first-class matches – Played 18: Won 3, Lost 3, Drawn 12.
County Championship matches – Played 16: Won 3, Lost 3, Drawn 10.

LV= County Championship, 5th in Division 2;
NatWest T20 Blast, finalists; Royal London One-Day Cup, 5th in Group A.

COUNTY CHAMPIONSHIP AVERAGES, BATTING AND FIELDING

Cap		Birthplace	M	I	NO	R	HS	100	Avge	Ct
	D. Murphy	Welwyn Garden City.	5	8	2	324	135*	1	54.00	15
2013	D. J. Willey	Northampton†	5	9	1	407	104*	2	50.87	3
	B. M. Duckett	Farnborough, Kent	11	19	1	851	154	4	47.27	8
	R. E. Levi¶	Johannesburg, SA	11	18	3	663	168	1	44.20	8
2013	S. P. Crook	Modbury, Australia	8	12	1	445	102*	1	40.45	3
2012	A. G. Wakely	Hammersmith	15	26	2	853	123	1	35.54	12
	A. M. Rossington	Edgware	13	23	1	738	116	1	33.54	34
	R. I. Keogh	Dunstable	16	29	2	850	163*	2	31.48	5
	J. J. Cobb	Leicester	16	28	5	678	95	0	29.47	8
2007	S. D. Peters	Harold Wood	9	16	0	440	82	0	27.50	4
	R. I. Newton	Taunton	11	20	0	534	107	1	26.70	3
	R. K. Kleinveldt§	Cape Town, SA	13	21	3	391	56	0	21.72	9
2015	Azharullah	Burewala, Pakistan	14	19	9	189	58*	0	18.90	5
	O. P. Stone	Norwich	12	17	4	231	38	0	17.76	6
	B. W. Sanderson	Sheffield	3	5	2	48	42	0	16.00	1
	G. G. White	Milton Keynes	3	6	0	43	24	0	7.16	1
2013	K. J. Coetzer	Aberdeen	4	7	0	37	13	0	5.28	0
	M. A. Chambers	Port Antonio, Jam.	5	8	0	22	14	0	2.75	1

Also batted: R. J. Gleeson (*Blackpool*) (1 match) 2 (2 ct); S. A. Zaib (*High Wycombe*) (1 match) 0.

† *Born in Northamptonshire.*　　§ *Official overseas player.*
¶ *Other non-England-qualified player.*

BOWLING

	Style	O	M	R	W	BB	5I	Avge
B. W. Sanderson	RFM	65	16	202	10	4-44	0	20.20
R. K. Kleinveldt	RFM	407.5	69	1,547	57	5-41	5	27.14
M. A. Chambers	RFM	94.3	16	340	12	3-44	0	28.33
Azharullah	RFM	419.5	95	1,329	44	5-31	2	30.20
O. P. Stone	RFM	344.4	60	1,148	38	5-44	1	30.21
D. J. Willey	LFM	148.1	24	511	14	4-72	0	36.50
S. P. Crook	RFM	154.1	19	630	15	3-28	0	42.00
R. I. Keogh	OB	296	40	1,019	19	3-35	0	53.63

Also bowled: J. J. Cobb (OB) 103.5–12–363–4; K. J. Coetzer (RM) 3–0–12–1; R. J. Gleeson (RM) 12–0–67–2; R. I. Newton (LBG) 1–0–6–0; A. M. Rossington (RM) 1–0–6–0; A. G. Wakely (RM) 4–0–17–0; G. G. White (SLA) 67.4–13–240–8; S. A. Zaib (SLA) 1–0–4–0.

LEADING ROYAL LONDON CUP AVERAGES (90 runs/4 wickets)

Batting	Runs	HS	Avge	SR	Ct/St
J. J. Cobb	318	104	45.42	70.35	4
B. M. Duckett	252	69	36.00	88.73	15/2
R. E. Levi	176	87	25.14	82.62	4
D. J. Willey	175	91	25.00	87.93	2
R. I. Keogh	90	50	12.85	68.18	1

Bowling	W	BB	Avge	ER
G. G. White	9	4-37	18.66	4.25
S. P. Crook	8	4-37	23.25	5.02
O. P. Stone	9	3-34	28.00	4.58
Azharullah	9	4-22	28.44	5.77
R. K. Kleinveldt	7	2-20	37.42	4.44
D. J. Willey	5	2-36	47.60	5.40

LEADING NATWEST T20 BLAST AVERAGES (100 runs/18 overs)

Batting	Runs	HS	Avge	SR	Ct
D. J. Willey	288	100	28.80	**174.54**	3
Shahid Afridi	138	34	34.50	**151.64**	0
R. E. Levi	485	67*	34.64	**143.49**	7
J. J. Cobb	431	84	30.78	**133.43**	7
B. M. Duckett	224	40*	28.00	**128.73**	9
S. P. Crook	190	56*	31.66	**127.51**	4
A. G. Wakely	235	51*	29.37	**107.79**	4

Bowling	W	BB	Avge	ER
Shahid Afridi	10	3-14	17.40	**6.44**
D. J. Willey	15	3-27	17.00	**7.08**
R. K. Kleinveldt	15	2-16	25.40	**7.25**
J. J. Cobb	6	2-30	38.33	**8.51**
Azharullah	15	3-28	25.53	**8.87**
G. G. White	7	2-27	34.71	**9.00**
S. P. Crook	9	3-30	38.11	**9.02**
O. P. Stone	4	1-11	68.00	**9.37**

FIRST-CLASS COUNTY RECORDS

Highest score for	331*	M. E. K. Hussey v Somerset at Taunton	2003
Highest score against	333	K. S. Duleepsinhji (Sussex) at Hove	1930
Leading run-scorer	28,980	D. Brookes (avge 36.13)	1934–59
Best bowling for	10-127	V. W. C. Jupp v Kent at Tunbridge Wells	1932
Best bowling against	10-30	C. Blythe (Kent) at Northampton	1907
Leading wicket-taker	1,102	E. W. Clark (avge 21.26)	1922–47
Highest total for	781-7 dec	v Nottinghamshire at Northampton	1995
Highest total against	673-8 dec	by Yorkshire at Leeds	2003
Lowest total for	12	v Gloucestershire at Gloucester	1907
Lowest total against	33	by Lancashire at Northampton	1977

LIST A COUNTY RECORDS

Highest score for	172*	W. Larkins v Warwickshire at Luton	1983
Highest score against	175*	I. T. Botham (Somerset) at Wellingborough	1986
Leading run-scorer	11,010	R. J. Bailey (avge 39.46)	1983–99
Best bowling for	7-10	C. Pietersen v Denmark at Brøndby	2005
Best bowling against	7-35	D. E. Malcolm (Derbyshire) at Derby	1997
Leading wicket-taker	251	A. L. Penberthy (avge 30.45)	1989–2003
Highest total for	360-2	v Staffordshire at Northampton	1990
Highest total against	424-7	by New Zealand A at Northampton	2014
Lowest total for	41	v Middlesex at Northampton	1972
Lowest total against	56	by Leicestershire at Leicester	1964
	56	by Denmark at Brøndby	2005

TWENTY20 COUNTY RECORDS

Highest score for	111*	L. Klusener v Worcestershire at Kidderminster	2007
Highest score against	116*	G. A. Hick (Worcestershire) at Luton	2004
Leading run-scorer	**1,482**	**A. G. Wakely** (avge 26.00)	**2009–15**
Best bowling for	6-21	A. J. Hall v Worcestershire at Northampton	2008
Best bowling against	5-6	P. D. Collingwood (Durham) at Chester-le-Street	2011
Leading wicket-taker	**73**	**D. J. Willey** (avge 19.45)	**2009–15**
Highest total for	224-5	v Gloucestershire at Milton Keynes	2005
Highest total against	227-6	by Worcestershire at Kidderminster	2007
Lowest total for	47	v Durham at Chester-le-Street	2011
Lowest total against	86	by Worcestershire at Worcester	2006

ADDRESS

County Ground, Abington Avenue, Northampton NN1 4PR; 01604 514455; reception@nccc.co.uk; www.northantscricket.com.

OFFICIALS

Captain A. G. Wakely
Head coach D. Ripley
Academy coach P. Rowe
President Lord Naseby

Chairman G. Warren
Chief executive R. Payne
Head groundsman P. Marshall
Scorer A. C. Kingston

At Cambridge, April 2–4. NORTHAMPTONSHIRE drew with CAMBRIDGE MCCU.

NORTHAMPTONSHIRE v GLOUCESTERSHIRE

At Northampton, April 12–15. Drawn. Northamptonshire 11pts, Gloucestershire 10pts. Toss: Gloucestershire. County debuts: R. K. Kleinveldt; K. Noema-Barnett. Championship debut: P. S. P. Handscomb.

Willey enhanced his reputation as Northamptonshire reacclimatised quickly to life in the second tier. But the gulf between the divisions was betrayed by the number of catches and run-out chances Gloucestershire missed – as many as 30, in new head coach Richard Dawson's estimate – and Willey's all-round heroics were still not enough to bring victory on a bland surface in blustery conditions. Northamptonshire left out Ben Duckett, who had missed their pre-season tour on fitness grounds, despite a century against Cambridge MCCU. From 162 for six on the opening day, Willey joined Rossington in a spirited counter-attack that produced 127 inside 19 overs, before Miles tidied up for a career-best six for 63. He was aided by Roderick's six catches behind the stumps, which equalled the Gloucestershire record. Then, despite Geraint Jones's battling 80, Willey secured a first-innings lead by dismissing Fuller, Miles and Norwell in four deliveries with the second new ball as Gloucestershire lost their last four wickets on 296. Northamptonshire toiled to press home the advantage until Willey blazed his way to a maiden first-class hundred off just 79 balls, hitting four of his six sixes in the space of seven deliveries. Gloucestershire were left with an hour and a day to survive, and achieved the task with ease, thanks largely to the patience of Dent, who survived two near misses on 99 to bat through to the final handshakes.

Close of play: first day, Gloucestershire 18-0 (Tavaré 12, Dent 5); second day, Northamptonshire 68-2 (Wakely 21, Newton 10); third day, Gloucestershire 35-0 (Dent 22, Tavaré 13).

Northamptonshire

S. D. Peters c Roderick b Fuller	27	– b Miles 16
R. E. Levi c Roderick b Miles	29	– c Roderick b Miles 13
*A. G. Wakely b Miles	31	– c and b Norwell 43
R. I. Newton c Roderick b Miles	1	– c Handscomb b Fuller 19
R. I. Keogh c Dent b Noema-Barnett	46	– lbw b Dent 81
†A. M. Rossington c Roderick b Miles	95	– c Handscomb b Norwell 4
J. J. Cobb c Roderick b Miles	0	– c Fuller b Noema-Barnett 58
D. J. Willey c Roderick b Noema-Barnett	62	– not out 104
R. K. Kleinveldt c Fuller b Noema-Barnett	19	– b Taylor 48
O. P. Stone not out	3	– not out 9
Azharullah c Norwell b Miles	8	
B 4, l-b 2, n-b 6	12	B 2, l-b 9, n-b 10 21

1/59 (2) 2/61 (1) 3/64 (4)   (83.5 overs) 333   1/29 (2)   (8 wkts dec, 97 overs) 416
4/132 (5) 5/162 (3) 6/162 (7)   2/34 (1) 3/83 (4)
7/289 (8) 8/319 (6) 9/321 (9) 10/333 (11)   4/104 (5) 5/110 (6)
          6/211 (7) 7/281 (5) 8/396 (9)

Fuller 16–1–66–1; Taylor 17–3–77–0; Norwell 16–2–73–0; Miles 19.5–3–63–6; Noema-Barnett 15–4–48–3. *Second innings*—Fuller 19–3–114–1; Taylor 17–4–61–1; Miles 19–4–74–2; Norwell 16–4–47–2; Noema-Barnett 15–4–47–1; Dent 9–0–50–1; Tavaré 2–0–12–0.

Gloucestershire

W. A. Tavaré lbw b Azharullah	34	– (2) b Azharullah	66
C. D. J. Dent c Rossington b Azharullah	40	– (1) not out	104
†G. H. Roderick b Azharullah	56	– lbw b Keogh	52
P. S. P. Handscomb b Stone	15	– not out	25
H. J. H. Marshall lbw b Willey	0		
*G. O. Jones b Kleinveldt	80		
K. Noema-Barnett c Wakely b Stone	8		
J. K. Fuller lbw b Willey	35		
C. N. Miles c Kleinveldt b Willey	0		
L. C. Norwell b Willey	0		
M. D. Taylor not out	0		
B 15, l-b 3, n-b 10	28	B 4, l-b 3, w 5, n-b 8	20

1/85 (2) 2/102 (1) 3/138 (4)　　　　(82.2 overs) 296　　1/137 (2)　　　(2 wkts, 95 overs) 267
4/139 (5) 5/185 (3) 6/214 (7)　　　　　　　　　　　　2/218 (3)
7/296 (8) 8/296 (9) 9/296 (10) 10/296 (6)

Kleinveldt 19.2–6–74–1; Willey 18–2–72–4; Stone 19–4–57–2; Azharullah 16–4–44–3; Cobb 9–1–23–0; Keogh 1–0–8–0. *Second innings*—Kleinveldt 15–4–60–0; Willey 18–3–48–0; Azharullah 21–4–44–1; Stone 13–1–53–0; Cobb 13–4–28–0; Keogh 15–5–27–1.

Umpires: P. J. Hartley and S. J. O'Shaughnessy.

At Leicester, April 26–29. NORTHAMPTONSHIRE beat LEICESTERSHIRE by 92 runs. *Northamptonshire's first Championship win in 21 matches.*

NORTHAMPTONSHIRE v LANCASHIRE

At Northampton, May 3–6. Drawn. Northamptonshire 12pts, Lancashire 13pts. Toss: Lancashire.

Lancashire, chasing a fifth straight Championship victory over Northamptonshire, were able to claim only three wickets on the final day. An unbeaten century by Crook capped an excellent match with the bat against his former county, having been called into the side to replace Willey, who was set to make his England debut in Dublin. An interrupted opening day ended controversially with Keogh and Cobb dismissed by successive balls from Jarvis shortly before the umpires halted play for bad light; Wakely felt they should have come off earlier. But Crook and Stone batted purposefully next morning, and Lancashire were rocked by two early strikes from Kleinveldt – only for Prince, driving fluently and supported by Siddle in a century stand for the seventh wicket, to retrieve the situation during a five-hour stay. In the end, forcing a win proved as impossible as remaining vertical in the gale-force winds that plagued the match: Kleinveldt wore a beanie hat under his cap for much of the third day, the bails were dispensed with altogether, spectators sought shelter, and bowlers chose their ends with greater care than usual. Levi was unable to bat a second time because of a dislocated finger, but Peters passed 14,000 first-class runs with his third consecutive fifty, and Keogh made his fourth first-class hundred.

Close of play: first day, Northamptonshire 198-6 (Rossington 33, Crook 0); second day, Lancashire 216-4 (Prince 104, Davies 33); third day, Northamptonshire 42-2 (Peters 19, Keogh 14).

Northamptonshire

S. D. Peters c Croft b Clark	56	– c Kerrigan b Clark	81
R. E. Levi c Croft b Siddle	7		
*A. G. Wakely c Davies b Siddle	59	– c Davies b Siddle	2
R. I. Newton c Davies b Clark	8	– (2) c Petersen b Jarvis	0
R. I. Keogh c Davies b Jarvis	21	– (4) c Bailey b Clark	100
†A. M. Rossington lbw b Clark	57	– (5) c Croft b Kerrigan	23
J. J. Cobb c Davies b Jarvis	0	– (6) not out	46
S. P. Crook lbw b Jarvis	91	– (7) not out	102
R. K. Kleinveldt lbw b Kerrigan	4		
O. P. Stone c and b Clark	38		
Azharullah not out	15		
B 14, l-b 7, n-b 8	29	B 2, l-b 12, w 7, n-b 16	37

1/15 (2) 2/120 (1) 3/136 (4)   (92.4 overs) 385
4/150 (3) 5/197 (5) 6/197 (7)
7/277 (6) 8/298 (9) 9/333 (8) 10/385 (10)

1/0 (2) 2/13 (3)   (5 wkts, 92 overs) 391
3/138 (1) 4/191 (5)
5/235 (4)

Siddle 16–5–56–2; Bailey 15–1–62–0; Jarvis 23–5–79–3; Clark 22.4–3–101–4; Kerrigan 16–1–66–1. *Second innings*—Siddle 12–2–37–1; Jarvis 15–2–53–1; Bailey 12–1–53–0; Kerrigan 25–3–95–1; Croft 8–0–37–0; Clark 13–0–58–2; Reece 5–0–35–0; Petersen 2–0–9–0.

Lancashire

P. J. Horton lbw b Azharullah	49	T. E. Bailey b Cobb	34
L. M. Reece c Rossington b Kleinveldt	0	S. C. Kerrigan c Rossington b Azharullah	21
A. N. Petersen lbw b Kleinveldt	1	K. M. Jarvis not out	6
A. G. Prince c sub (D. Murphy) b Crook	153	B 10, l-b 8, w 5, n-b 16	39
*S. J. Croft lbw b Azharullah	7		
†A. L. Davies c Crook b Kleinveldt	37	1/1 (2) 2/3 (3) 3/115 (1) (107.2 overs) 436	
J. Clark c Rossington b Kleinveldt	0	4/143 (5) 5/221 (6) 6/221 (7)	
P. M. Siddle lbw b Kleinveldt	89	7/321 (4) 8/398 (9) 9/427 (10) 10/436 (8)	

Kleinveldt 27.2–4–99–5; Stone 21–4–85–0; Crook 19–0–89–1; Azharullah 27–3–104–3; Cobb 13–1–41–1.

Umpires: P. K. Baldwin and M. J. Saggers.

At Derby, May 10–13. NORTHAMPTONSHIRE drew with DERBYSHIRE.

NORTHAMPTONSHIRE v SURREY

At Northampton, May 18–21. Drawn. Northamptonshire 10pts, Surrey 13pts. Toss: Surrey. County debut: L. J. Fletcher.

Rain washed out the first day, and only 28 overs were possible on the second before a violent hailstorm left Wantage Road with a wintry coating. Both sides then focused on the pursuit of bonus points – and, in Northamptonshire's case, avoiding a second over-rate penalty of the season. But the crowd were at least treated to a last-day batting tutorial from Sangakkara: he added 170 inside 36 overs with Roy, who stroked a career-best 140 from 145 balls. Northamptonshire's innings had subsided rapidly – the last five wickets fell for 21 – after Tom Curran prospered on his maiden first-class appearance at the ground graced by his late father, Kevin, during the 1990s. Fletcher, signed by Surrey on loan from Nottinghamshire after a spate of injuries, dismissed Coetzer in the fourth over of his opening spell.

Close of play: first day, no play; second day, Northamptonshire 107-2 (Peters 64, Newton 28); third day, Surrey 155-3 (Sangakkara 28, Davies 30).

Northamptonshire

S. D. Peters c Wilson b Curran	82	S. P. Crook c Davies b Batty		0
K. J. Coetzer lbw b Fletcher	3	O. P. Stone b Batty		7
*A. G. Wakely c Roy b Curran	8	Azharullah not out		0
R. I. Newton c Wilson b Curran	95	B 2, l-b 6, w 1		9
R. I. Keogh b Curran	29			
†A. M. Rossington c and b Ansari	58	1/7 (2) 2/51 (3) 3/148 (1) (84.4 overs)		309
J. J. Cobb c Batty b Ansari	18	4/213 (5) 5/238 (4) 6/288 (7)		
D. J. Willey b Ansari	0	7/288 (8) 8/289 (9) 9/303 (10) 10/309 (6)		

Fletcher 19–2–67–1; Curran 23–3–89–4; Meaker 16–1–73–0; Ansari 17.4–4–50–3; Roy 3–0–12–0; Batty 6–2–10–2.

Surrey

R. J. Burns lbw b Azharullah	34	*G. J. Batty not out		19
Z. S. Ansari c Rossington b Azharullah	39			
K. C. Sangakkara c Rossington b Crook	111	B 5, l-b 21, w 9		35
D. P. Sibley c Rossington b Willey	3			
S. M. Davies c Azharullah b Crook	44	1/89 (2) (6 wkts dec, 118 overs)		499
J. J. Roy c Crook b Keogh	140	2/95 (1) 3/108 (4) 4/202 (5)		
†G. C. Wilson not out	74	5/372 (3) 6/449 (6) 110 overs: 473-6		

T. K. Curran, S. C. Meaker and L. J. Fletcher did not bat.

Willey 29.1–3–85–1; Stone 16.5–2–79–0; Crook 16–2–77–2; Azharullah 21–1–75–2; Keogh 19–0–91–1; Cobb 13–1–57–0; Wakely 2–0–3–0; Newton 1–0–6–0.

Umpires: N. L. Bainton and M. A. Gough.

At Cardiff, May 31–June 3. NORTHAMPTONSHIRE lost to GLAMORGAN by ten wickets.

NORTHAMPTONSHIRE v ESSEX

At Northampton, June 7–10. Drawn. Northamptonshire 13pts, Essex 9pts. Toss: Essex.

Wakely admitted the pitch was "not ideally what we were looking for" as Essex, responding to a substantial deficit, got out of jail with their highest second-innings total since 2002. It made for the fourth consecutive Championship draw of the season at Northampton. But Essex, after three defeats on seaming pitches at Chelmsford and Cardiff, were surely grateful for such a docile surface – especially when, shortly after lunch on the third day, they found themselves three down in the second innings, still 84 behind. Westley, who hit 29 fours, and Ryder rode to the rescue, adding 258 in 63 overs and exposing Northamptonshire's lack of a front-rank spinner; Keogh had enjoyed some success on the first day with his off-breaks, claiming more than a single wicket in a Championship innings for the first time. Northamptonshire had taken charge thanks to their Kolpak signing Levi – recalled to the four-day side, but down the order – whose ferocious career-best 168 from 231 balls was his first century in first-class cricket since February 2013. Browne, the ninth bowler used, dropped out of the attack with an injured finger after one ball, which Crook hit for four. But the surface deteriorated only slowly, Foster and ten Doeschate were both missed, and Essex were able to set a hypothetical 339 in 42 overs before the match fizzled out.

Close of play: first day, Northamptonshire 43-0 (Peters 15, Newton 21); second day, Northamptonshire 397-6 (Levi 157, Crook 38); third day, Essex 300-3 (Westley 164, Ryder 90).

Essex

N. L. J. Browne c Duckett b Kleinveldt	58	– c Duckett b Kleinveldt	30
J. C. Mickleburgh lbw b Crook	8	– lbw b Kleinveldt	0
T. Westley run out	14	– c Duckett b Kleinveldt	179
R. S. Bopara c Wakely b Azharullah	17	– b Kleinveldt	1
J. D. Ryder c Peters b Crook	87	– c Peters b Stone	124
R. N. ten Doeschate c Duckett b Keogh	32	– not out	76
*†J. S. Foster not out	21	– c Duckett b Crook	35
G. R. Napier b Keogh	5	– c Duckett b Crook	1
Adeel Malik b Keogh	0	– lbw b Keogh	2
D. D. Masters lbw b Kleinveldt	4	– c Stone b Kleinveldt	0
R. J. W. Topley b Kleinveldt	0	– not out	4
B 21, l-b 2, w 1, n-b 6	30	B 22, l-b 14, n-b 18	54

1/48 (2) 2/90 (3) 3/109 (1) (82 overs) 276
4/147 (4) 5/237 (5) 6/243 (6)
7/265 (8) 8/271 (9) 9/276 (10) 10/276 (11)

1/5 (2) (9 wkts dec, 136 overs) 506
2/82 (1) 3/84 (4)
4/342 (3) 5/385 (5) 6/467 (7)
7/477 (8) 8/480 (9) 9/484 (10)

Kleinveldt 15–1–59–3; Azharullah 19–3–60–1; Crook 16–2–48–2; Stone 14–4–46–0; Keogh 16–4–35–3; Cobb 2–0–5–0. *Second innings*—Kleinveldt 31–1–138–5; Azharullah 21–5–64–0; Crook 22–3–74–2; Keogh 32–5–108–1; Stone 19–0–61–1; Cobb 11–0–25–0.

Northamptonshire

S. D. Peters c Ryder b Bopara	44		
R. I. Newton c Topley b Masters	27	– lbw b Bopara	33
*A. G. Wakely b Bopara	11	– (1) c Masters b Topley	13
R. I. Keogh b Topley	36	– (3) c Browne b Napier	3
R. E. Levi c Foster b Napier	168	– (4) not out	53
J. J. Cobb c Browne b Adeel Malik	40	– (5) not out	11
†B. M. Duckett lbw b Topley	20		
S. P. Crook c ten Doeschate b Napier	39		
R. K. Kleinveldt c ten Doeschate b Topley	14		
O. P. Stone c Masters b Napier	10		
Azharullah not out	9		
B 4, l-b 14, w 2, n-b 6	26	B 1, l-b 1	2

1/55 (2) 2/84 (3) 3/95 (1) 4/158 (4) (120 overs) 444
5/249 (6) 6/315 (7) 7/404 (8)
8/424 (5) 9/424 (9) 10/444 (10)   110 overs: 409-7

1/31 (1) (3 wkts, 33 overs) 115
2/34 (3) 3/56 (2)

Masters 26–10–47–1; Topley 24–3–102–3; Ryder 13–2–62–0; Adeel Malik 13–0–54–1; Napier 23–2–85–3; Bopara 14–2–44–2; Westley 4.5–2–13–0; ten Doeschate 2–0–15–0; Browne 0.1–0–4–0. *Second innings*—Masters 4–1–13–0; Topley 5–1–14–1; Napier 5–0–15–1; Bopara 5–2–17–1; Westley 8–0–19–0; Adeel Malik 6–0–35–0.

Umpires: R. J. Bailey and M. R. Benson.

NORTHAMPTONSHIRE v KENT

At Northampton, June 20–22. Northamptonshire won by eight wickets. Northamptonshire 20pts, Kent 3pts. Toss: Northamptonshire.

Kent succumbed inside six sessions on a surface which – though much greener than anything previously served up at Northampton over the summer – did not make batting impossible. Steady drizzle washed out the first day, and Kent made a solid enough start until Kleinveldt and Azharullah shared four wickets in four overs immediately before lunch. The last four batsmen followed in 21 balls, and Northamptonshire pressed home their advantage through a careful 70-run stand between

Keogh and Wakely. Coles kept his side in the match with three strikes in 16 deliveries late in the day – continuing the pattern of wickets falling in clusters – but a restrained half-century from Levi carried the lead past 100. Denly offered some resistance second time around, but was out hooking the lively Stone, who – in a spell described as "phenomenal" by Wakely – took five wickets in six overs, capturing career-best figures. Northamptonshire knocked off just 46 for their first Championship win at home since August 2013.

　　Close of play: first day, no play; second day, Northamptonshire 193-7 (Levi 20).

Kent

D. J. Bell-Drummond	c Rossington b Kleinveldt	12	– lbw b Kleinveldt	10
J. L. Denly	c Newton b Azharullah	8	– c Levi b Stone	39
R. W. T. Key	b Azharullah	35	– lbw b Azharullah	1
*S. A. Northeast	c Rossington b Kleinveldt	36	– b Kleinveldt	4
D. I. Stevens	lbw b Kleinveldt	0	– c Wakely b Stone	28
A. J. Ball	b Azharullah	5	– lbw b Stone	7
J. C. Tredwell	b Azharullah	0	– lbw b Stone	9
†R. C. Davies	lbw b Kleinveldt	12	– c Keogh b Azharullah	6
M. T. Coles	c Rossington b Kleinveldt	12	– c Wakely b Stone	2
M. E. Claydon	b Azharullah	1	– not out	8
I. A. A. Thomas	not out	0	– c Rossington b Kleinveldt	3
	B 8, l-b 3, n-b 8	19	B 14, l-b 14, n-b 6	34

1/20 (1) 2/24 (2) 3/93 (4)　　　　(36.2 overs) 140
4/93 (5) 5/93 (3) 6/97 (7)
7/122 (8) 8/122 (6) 9/126 (10) 10/140 (9)

1/20 (1) 2/25 (3)　　　　(38.5 overs) 151
3/58 (4) 4/100 (5)
5/112 (6) 6/123 (2) 7/128 (7)
8/130 (9) 9/144 (8) 10/151 (11)

Kleinveldt 13.2–4–41–5; Azharullah 13–7–31–5; Stone 5–0–25–0; Crook 5–1–32–0. *Second innings*—Kleinveldt 9.5–0–44–3; Azharullah 10–3–16–2; Stone 10–2–44–5; Crook 9–0–19–0.

Northamptonshire

R. I. Newton	lbw b Coles	14	– c Davies b Thomas	27
B. M. Duckett	run out	19	– c Coles b Stevens	1
*A. G. Wakely	b Stevens	50	– not out	13
R. I. Keogh	c Tredwell b Coles	68	– not out	1
R. E. Levi	b Claydon	50		
†A. M. Rossington	c Davies b Coles	4		
O. P. Stone	b Coles	0		
J. J. Cobb	c Coles b Claydon	10		
S. P. Crook	lbw b Stevens	22		
R. K. Kleinveldt	c Tredwell b Stevens	0		
Azharullah	not out	0		
	B 2, l-b 6, w 1	9	L-b 4	4

1/14 (1) 2/63 (2) 3/133 (3)　　　　(71 overs) 246
4/168 (4) 5/174 (6) 6/182 (7)
7/193 (8) 8/231 (9) 9/231 (10) 10/246 (5)

1/32 (1) 2/32 (2)　　(2 wkts, 9 overs) 46

Coles 24–4–83–4; Thomas 13–0–37–0; Claydon 16–0–62–2; Stevens 18–4–56–3. *Second innings*—Coles 2–0–13–0; Stevens 4–1–21–1; Thomas 3–0–8–1.

　　　　　　Umpires: S. A. Garratt and N. A. Mallender.

At Manchester, June 29–July 2. NORTHAMPTONSHIRE drew with LANCASHIRE.

At Cheltenham, July 8–9. NORTHAMPTONSHIRE lost to GLOUCESTERSHIRE by nine wickets.

NORTHAMPTONSHIRE v DERBYSHIRE

At Northampton, July 18–20. Derbyshire won by seven wickets. Derbyshire 23pts, Northamptonshire 3pts. Toss: Derbyshire. County debut: B. W. Sanderson.

A high-quality innings for each side – from Alex Hughes to lay the foundations for Derbyshire's first victory at Wantage Road in 13 seasons, from Duckett in a vain attempt to prevent it – lifted this match above the humdrum. Hughes completed his maiden first-class hundred, with No. 11 Cotton for company, as Derbyshire's last four wickets added 165; Extras totalled 50. Northamptonshire's bowlers failed to exploit swinging conditions, but Footitt showed what was possible, and Derbyshire were able to enforce the follow-on with a lead of 245. Duckett, out first ball to Footitt in the first innings, survived a chance to Rutherford at cover on 26, and kept Derbyshire at bay for five and a quarter hours, coming through a nervy period on 99, when play was held up so Rossington could receive treatment on his hamstring. He drew Northamptonshire level with six wickets down at the end of the third day, and he was still there 18 overs into the third morning, when he reached a career-best 154. But Durston broke through, and Derbyshire knocked off their small target after lunch. Chesney Hughes retired hurt at the interval, following a blow to the helmet from Kleinveldt.

Close of play: first day, Northamptonshire 6-1 (Peters 4, Stone 0); second day, Northamptonshire 245-6 (Duckett 132, Cobb 3).

Derbyshire

H. D. Rutherford c Stone b Sanderson	60	– c Cobb b Kleinveldt		2
B. A. Godleman c Rossington b Kleinveldt	25	– c Kleinveldt b Sanderson		14
C. F. Hughes c Stone b Keogh	32	– retired hurt		4
*W. L. Madsen lbw b Chambers	16	– run out		11
W. J. Durston c Rossington b Kleinveldt	20	– not out		12
A. L. Hughes not out	111	– not out		6
S. J. Thakor c Rossington b Kleinveldt	8			
†H. R. Hosein c Rossington b Stone	23			
A. P. Palladino lbw b Sanderson	11			
M. H. A. Footitt c Wakely b Kleinveldt	0			
B. D. Cotton c Rossington b Chambers	5			
B 17, l-b 19, n-b 14	50	L-b 9, n-b 14		23

1/47 (2) 2/123 (1) 3/123 (3) (91.4 overs) 361 1/2 (1) (3 wkts, 14.2 overs) 72
4/148 (4) 5/176 (5) 6/196 (7) 2/38 (4) 3/61 (2)
7/272 (8) 8/307 (9) 9/314 (10) 10/361 (11)

In the second innings C. F. Hughes retired hurt at 11-1.

Kleinveldt 21–0–99–4; Stone 19–2–84–1; Chambers 13.4–2–40–2; Sanderson 20–7–49–2; Keogh 18–3–53–1. *Second innings*—Kleinveldt 7–1–37–1; Stone 5–1–15–0; Sanderson 2–1–7–1; Chambers 0.2–0–4–0.

Northamptonshire

S. D. Peters b Palladino	13	– c Thakor b Footitt		12
B. M. Duckett c Godleman b Footitt	0	– c Godleman b Durston		154
O. P. Stone c and b Footitt	19	– (7) b Palladino		3
*A. G. Wakely b Footitt	8	– (3) c Palladino b Cotton		5
R. I. Keogh c Hosein b Cotton	9	– (4) b Palladino		11
R. E. Levi b Thakor	34	– (5) lbw b Cotton		22
†A. M. Rossington lbw b Cotton	17	– (6) lbw b Palladino		39
J. J. Cobb not out	7	– c Madsen b Durston		35
R. K. Kleinveldt c Rutherford b Footitt	0	– c Cotton b Durston		6
M. A. Chambers b Footitt	1	– b Footitt		5
B. W. Sanderson c Godleman b Cotton	2	– not out		0
B 4, n-b 2	6	B 10, l-b 5, w 1, n-b 8		24

1/3 (2) 2/21 (1) 3/46 (4) (38.1 overs) 116 1/14 (1) 2/54 (3) (80.3 overs) 316
4/51 (3) 5/74 (5) 6/104 (6) 3/100 (4) 4/133 (5)
7/106 (7) 8/106 (9) 9/108 (10) 10/116 (11) 5/231 (6) 6/237 (7) 7/291 (2)
8/303 (9) 9/312 (8) 10/316 (10)

Footitt 12–4–41–5; Palladino 10–4–25–1; Cotton 7.1–1–26–3; Thakor 9–4–20–1. *Second innings*—Footitt 15.3–1–73–2; Palladino 21–4–62–3; Cotton 16–4–62–2; Thakor 13–2–38–0; Durston 10–0–55–3; A. L. Hughes 5–0–11–0.

Umpires: P. J. Hartley and G. D. Lloyd.

At Canterbury, August 4–6. NORTHAMPTONSHIRE beat KENT by an innings and 23 runs.

At Northampton, August 14–16. NORTHAMPTONSHIRE drew with AUSTRALIANS (see Australia tour section).

NORTHAMPTONSHIRE v LEICESTERSHIRE

At Northampton, August 21–24. Drawn. Northamptonshire 11pts, Leicestershire 12pts. Toss: Leicestershire.

Leicestershire, within reach of back-to-back Championship victories for the first time in almost five years, were denied by rain, which scrubbed out the afternoon session on the third day and allowed just 45 minutes' play on the fourth. Both captains distinguished themselves with the bat: Wakely rescued Northamptonshire from a desperate start against the skilful McKay with crisp and assertive strokeplay; then Cosgrove followed suit to repair early damage caused by Kleinveldt and earn Leicestershire an unexpected lead. O'Brien relished the battle against his former county, and missed a hundred because of a superb diving catch by David Willey, one of eight substitute fielders used by Northamptonshire following injuries to Crook (ankle), Newton (thumb), and Levi (finger). Leicestershire themselves ended up with a two-man pace attack after Raine (thigh) and Shreck (hamstring) pulled up, but they still took charge through White – who had recently rejoined from Derbyshire – and might have won in three days but for rain and Levi's out-of-character three-hour fifty. McKay polished off the innings with the second ball of the last day but, needing only 116, Leicestershire could barely start the job before the weather closed in.

Close of play: first day, Leicestershire 30-3 (Sayer 1, Cosgrove 5); second day, Leicestershire 372; third day, Northamptonshire 162-8 (Levi 54, Sanderson 1).

Northamptonshire

R. I. Newton c Raine b McKay	9	– (8) lbw b Cosgrove	9
B. M. Duckett lbw b McKay	1	– c O'Brien b McKay	5
*A. G. Wakely c O'Brien b Shreck	123	– b McKay	2
R. I. Keogh b McKay	14	– c O'Brien b White	36
R. E. Levi b McKay	0	– not out	54
J. J. Cobb c O'Brien b Shreck	30	– c O'Brien b White	3
S. P. Crook st O'Brien b Sayer	40	– absent hurt	
†D. Murphy c sub (A. P. Agathangelou) b Cosgrove	38	– (1) b White	35
R. K. Kleinveldt c O'Brien b Shreck	43	– (7) c sub (A. P. Agathangelou) b White	4
Azharullah c O'Brien b McKay	10	– (9) c Eckersley b White	2
B. W. Sanderson not out	3	– (10) lbw b McKay	1
L-b 8, n-b 6	14	L-b 11	11

1/5 (2) 2/14 (1) 3/38 (4)   (78.2 overs) 325   1/9 (2) 2/23 (3)   (67.2 overs) 162
4/42 (5) 5/113 (6) 6/191 (7)   3/74 (1) 4/89 (4)
7/260 (8) 8/298 (3) 9/317 (9) 10/325 (10)   5/105 (6) 6/111 (7)
    7/136 (8) 8/151 (9) 9/162 (10)

McKay 19.2–4–54–5; Raine 9–1–42–0; Shreck 22–6–60–3; White 11–0–84–0; Cosgrove 6–2–9–1; Sayer 9–0–62–1; Hill 2–0–6–0. *Second innings*—McKay 21.2–9–35–3; Shreck 6.2–1–18–0; White 22–5–51–5; Cosgrove 5.4–2–12–1; Sayer 12–1–35–0.

Leicestershire

A. J. Robson c Murphy b Kleinveldt	13	– (2) lbw b Kleinveldt	10
L. J. Hill c Murphy b Kleinveldt	9	– (1) not out	11
E. J. H. Eckersley b Kleinveldt	0		
R. J. Sayer c Murphy b Kleinveldt	1		
*M. J. Cosgrove lbw b Kleinveldt	110		
A. M. Ali c Murphy b Sanderson	14		
†N. J. O'Brien c sub (D. J. Willey) b Keogh	95	– (3) not out	5
W. A. White c Wakely b Keogh	43		
C. J. McKay not out	51		
B. A. Raine c Murphy b Keogh	0		
C. E. Shreck c Levi b Azharullah	15		
B 4, l-b 7, w 4, n-b 6	21	L-b 4	4

1/10 (2) 2/18 (3) 3/23 (1)   (110.2 overs) 372   1/23 (2)   (1 wkt, 6.4 overs) 30
4/34 (4) 5/105 (6) 6/221 (7) 7/295 (5)
8/325 (8) 9/325 (10) 10/372 (11)   110 overs: 372-9

Kleinveldt 25–12–68–5; Azharullah 26.2–6–91–1; Sanderson 21–2–68–1; Crook 7–0–51–0; Keogh 23–4–61–3; Cobb 8–1–22–0. *Second innings*—Kleinveldt 3.4–0–14–1; Azharullah 3–0–12–0.

Umpires: M. Burns and A. G. Wharf.

At Chelmsford, September 1–4. NORTHAMPTONSHIRE drew with ESSEX.

NORTHAMPTONSHIRE v GLAMORGAN

At Northampton, September 14–17. Drawn. Northamptonshire 10pts, Glamorgan 9pts. Toss: Northamptonshire. First-class debut: D. Penrhyn Jones. Championship debut: R. J. Gleeson.

Persistent showers ruined the match, but Lloyd, who came close to a maiden first-class hundred, and debutant seamer Dewi Penrhyn Jones gave Glamorgan some satisfaction. On the other hand, Wallace tore his calf setting off for a single – "a bit of an old man's injury... not a great day for me

MOST CONSECUTIVE CHAMPIONSHIP APPEARANCES

423	K. G. Suttle (Sussex)	1954–1969	276	R. B. Nicholls (Glos)	1962–1972
412	J. G. Binks (Yorks)	1955–1969	272	J. T. Hearne (Middx)	1890–1906
399	J. Vine (Sussex)	1899–1914	266	L. T. A. Bates (Warwicks)	1924–1934
344	E. H. Killick (Sussex)	1898–1912	262	A. E. Dipper (Glos)	1921–1930
326	C. N. Woolley (Northants)	1913–1931	259	B. J. Meyer (Glos)	1958–1967
305	A. H. Dyson (Glam)	1930–1947	231	W. G. Quaife (Warwicks)	1895–1907
301	B. Taylor (Essex)	1961–1972	**230**	**M. A. Wallace (Glam)**	**2001–2015**
287	H. H. I. H. Gibbons (Worcs)	1927–1937	227	G. L. Berry (Leics)	1933–1948
287	G. O. Dawkes (Derbys)	1950–1961	222	H. Elliott (Derbys)	1929–1937
282	H. G. Davies (Glam)	1947–1957	219	B. A. Langford (Somerset)	1957–1964

after a heavy blow in the box" – which forced him out of the next game, ending his sequence of Championship appearances since the middle of 2001. Only 35 balls were bowled on the first day, and the second was disjointed because of lengthy stoppages. But Lloyd managed to keep his concentration until holing out to Lancastrian seamer Richard Gleeson in the deep on 92. The 21-year-old Penrhyn Jones took three wickets – two caught behind by stand-in wicketkeeper Cooke – as Northamptonshire opened a small lead. But the inability of Wakely and Wagg – deputising as captain for Rudolph – to agree on a run-chase meant the game dribbled to a close. Stone pulled up with a side injury, the day after being named in the England Performance Programme fast-bowling camp.

Close of play: first day, Glamorgan 23-1 (Wallace 7, Ingram 0); second day, Glamorgan 166-6 (Lloyd 64, Salter 0); third day, Northamptonshire 128-5 (Rossington 25, Murphy 7).

Glamorgan

J. M. Kettleborough c Murphy b Kleinveldt	16	– c Murphy b Gleeson	14
*†M. A. Wallace retired hurt	27		
C. A. Ingram c Stone b Kleinveldt	5	– lbw b Gleeson	14
A. H. T. Donald b Kleinveldt	8	– not out	40
C. B. Cooke lbw b Kleinveldt	7	– not out	22
D. L. Lloyd c Gleeson b Stone	92		
G. G. Wagg c Cobb b Kleinveldt	0		
C. A. J. Meschede c Kleinveldt b Stone	17		
A. G. Salter c Gleeson b Stone	11	– (2) c Kleinveldt b Azharullah	4
D. Penrhyn Jones c Newton b Stone	17		
M. G. Hogan not out	0		
B 1, l-b 18, n-b 14	33	B 2, l-b 1, n-b 2	5

1/22 (1) 2/36 (3) 3/54 (4)   (52.2 overs) 233   1/20 (2)   (3 wkts dec, 26 overs) 99
4/84 (5) 5/84 (7) 6/166 (8)   2/32 (1) 3/39 (3)
7/194 (9) 8/232 (10) 9/233 (6)

In the first innings Wallace retired hurt at 66-3.

Kleinveldt 20–1–83–5; Stone 21.2–3–73–4; Azharullah 6–1–26–0; Gleeson 5–0–32–0. *Second innings*—Stone 1.1–1–0–0; Azharullah 6–2–11–1; Kleinveldt 3.5–1–15–0; Gleeson 7–0–35–2; Keogh 5–1–22–0; Cobb 2–0–7–0; Rossington 1–0–6–0.

Northamptonshire

R. I. Newton c Hogan b Meschede	0	O. P. Stone c sub (J. L. Lawlor) b Salter	20
B. M. Duckett c Cooke b Penrhyn Jones	20	Azharullah c Cooke b Wagg	20
*A. G. Wakely c Cooke b Penrhyn Jones	40	R. J. Gleeson c Kettleborough b Wagg	2
R. I. Keogh c Cooke b Wagg	32	B 16, l-b 4	20
J. J. Cobb b Wagg	0		
A. M. Rossington c Lloyd b Penrhyn Jones	59	1/0 (1) 2/52 (2) 3/81 (3) (64.4 overs) 278
†D. Murphy not out	58	4/90 (5) 5/103 (4) 6/179 (6)
R. K. Kleinveldt b Hogan	7	7/200 (8) 8/237 (9) 9/266 (10) 10/278 (11)

Meschede 13–3–46–1; Hogan 14–3–46–1; Wagg 18.4–2–77–4; Penrhyn Jones 10–1–55–3; Salter 9–0–34–1.

Umpires: N. L. Bainton and S. C. Gale.

At The Oval, September 22–25. NORTHAMPTONSHIRE drew with SURREY.

NOTTINGHAMSHIRE

Moores helps dispel midsummer blues

JON CULLEY

Halfway through the season, Nottinghamshire were in free fall. Bottom of the Championship's first division after an innings defeat at Headingley on June 24, they suffered a Twenty20 thrashing at Derby two days later, leaving them on the brink of elimination from a competition in which they had been highly fancied. After a crisis summit at Trent Bridge, it was announced that Peter Moores, the former England coach, was to join in a consultancy role. Director of cricket Mick Newell, who had spent 13 years at the helm, admitted the need for fresh ideas, and Moores – based near Loughborough, with his son Tom on a Nottinghamshire Academy contract – was the obvious man to ask.

Fortunes improved immediately. Even before Moores had officially started, Nottinghamshire beat Worcestershire, launching a run of five wins in six Championship matches. Far from facing relegation, they would eventually finish third. A similar upturn in the NatWest T20 Blast brought four wins in five, though they were squeezed out of the quarter-finals on net run-rate when their last group game was washed away. In the Royal London One-Day Cup, five wins in five completed matches clinched a place in the knockout with two rounds to spare; they defeated Durham convincingly in the quarter-final, and only a brilliant 166 from Surrey's Kumar Sangakkara denied them a trip to Lord's.

It was impossible to say how much could be credited to Moores, whose brief was not to help with selection or tactics, merely to work with players. Yet clearly there was an effect. Initially hired for the remaining three months of the season, he signed a two-year contract in October.

Among the other factors behind Nottinghamshire's recovery, the most encouraging was the emergence of a clutch of home-grown bowlers. Jake Ball, from Mansfield, and Brett Hutton and Luke Wood, both from the Worksop area, shared half the seam-bowling workload in the Championship, collecting 106 wickets between them. The pacy Ball, a late developer at 24, reaped the benefits of a winter of strength and fitness training, earning an England Lions call-up after picking up 67 victims in all formats, including a career-best six for 49 against Sussex. Hutton, a 22-year-old all-rounder, took 37 first-class wickets, including ten in the victory over Durham in September. Left-armer Wood, who turned 20 in August, collected 30, and hit a remarkable maiden century – in 95 balls, from No. 9 – against Sussex. Matthew Carter, a tall off-spinner, claimed seven for 56, and ten in the match, on debut at Taunton, but a hip injury meant that was his only appearance.

Then there was Chris Read, whose captaincy, glovework and ability to rescue a sorry scoreboard were never more valued than when they were absent. He was out for a month mid-season with a strained hamstring, and it was no coincidence that the county's darkest moments came during his lay-off. Read

Mike Egerton, PA Photos

Chris Read

still scored 873 Championship runs at 51 and headed the averages. In his 18th season, he passed 15,000 first-class runs, but that was eclipsed by the moment in September when Paul Collingwood nicked a delivery from Hutton, giving Read the 1,000th dismissal of his first-class career. In July, he had passed 300 in one-day games for Nottinghamshire, a county record. There were no dissenters when, at the age of 37, he was named Player of the Season.

Alex Hales and James Taylor each produced outstanding innings: Hales hit 236 in gloomy April conditions against Yorkshire, Taylor 291 – Nottinghamshire's fourth-highest score – at Horsham in July. Hales also smashed six consecutive sixes against Warwickshire in the opening Twenty20 match, plus a 61-ball century against them at Sookholme in the 50-over competition. Both averaged 49 in the Championship, in which the consistent Riki Wessels alone reached 1,000 runs. Brendan Taylor, the former Zimbabwe captain who joined as a Kolpak, matched Read and Hales in making three hundreds. Michael Lumb, absent until June with a torn tendon in his left arm, had a disappointing year, and Samit Patel underperformed with the bat – only to be called up to England's Test squad for the UAE after injury to Surrey's Zafar Ansari. Steven Mullaney enjoyed a productive run after dropping from opener to No. 3, but new signings Will Gidman and Greg Smith made little impact, until Smith announced himself with a century in the losing run-chase in the Royal London semi-final.

Injuries hampered left-arm seamer Harry Gurney, although he bowled with real pace at times, and no one bettered his 41 Championship wickets. But Luke Fletcher, who also had fitness issues, spent time on loan to Surrey. Andy Carter, Matthew's older brother, bowled heroically with a side strain to help beat Worcestershire in his one first-class appearance, but left for Derbyshire. All-rounder Paul Franks announced his retirement as a first-team player, as did 40-year-old left-arm spinner Gary Keedy, though he had a swansong with five wickets at Horsham, the first Championship victory he had taken part in since Lancashire clinched the 2011 title at Taunton.

Of five official overseas players, Dan Christian made the most meaningful contribution, in the 50-over competition, and was signed for the Twenty20 for 2016. His fellow Australian Ben Hilfenhaus, who was to have played the last four months of the season, lasted only one before flying home with a bad hip. He was replaced by their compatriot, Peter Siddle, who returned to Trent Bridge on a two-year deal.

Trent Bridge set Twenty20 attendance records for the largest single crowd (13,582 against Derbyshire in July) and highest aggregate (71,203). Membership also reached an all-time high, at 8,354.

Championship attendance: 37,290.

NOTTINGHAMSHIRE RESULTS

All first-class matches – Played 17: Won 6, Lost 5, Drawn 6.
County Championship matches – Played 16: Won 6, Lost 5, Drawn 5.

LV= County Championship, 3rd in Division 1;
NatWest T20 Blast, 5th in North Group; Royal London One-Day Cup, semi-finalists.

COUNTY CHAMPIONSHIP AVERAGES, BATTING AND FIELDING

Cap		Birthplace	M	I	NO	R	HS	100	Avge	Ct/St
1999	C. M. W. Read....	Paignton..........	13	21	4	873	121	3	51.35	36/1
2011	A. D. Hales‡	Hillingdon........	11	18	0	892	236	3	49.55	2
2012	J. W. A. Taylor‡..	Nottingham†......	12	21	0	991	291	2	49.55	6
2014	M. H. Wessels....	Marogudoore, Aust..	16	28	2	1,033	117	2	39.73	18
2015	B. W. Hilfenhaus§.	Ulverstone, Aust..	3	6	4	76	28*	0	38.00	1
2015	B. R. M. Taylor¶..	Harare, Zimbabwe..	16	28	0	956	152	3	34.14	12
2013	S. J. Mullaney....	Warrington.......	15	26	0	819	112	1	31.50	22
2008	S. C. J. Broad‡....	Nottingham†......	2	4	0	123	50	0	30.75	1
	L. Wood........	Sheffield.........	11	16	2	420	100	1	30.00	2
2015	V. D. Philander§..	Bellville, SA.....	5	9	2	177	41	0	25.28	0
	B. A. Hutton	Doncaster........	9	13	2	278	72	0	25.27	5
2008	S. R. Patel	Leicester........	16	28	1	650	100	2	24.07	8
2012	M. J. Lumb	Johannesburg, SA..	5	9	0	195	73	0	21.66	3
	W. R. S. Gidman..	High Wycombe	6	11	0	185	57	0	16.81	3
	J. T. Ball	Mansfield†.......	13	20	3	235	49*	0	13.82	1
	G. P. Smith	Leicester........	3	6	0	60	14	0	10.00	2
	J. D. Libby	Plymouth........	3	4	0	37	34	0	9.25	0
2014	H. F. Gurney.....	Nottingham†......	11	14	8	15	8	0	2.50	1

Also batted: A. Carter (*Lincoln*) (1 match) 24*, 17* (1 ct); M. Carter (*Lincoln*) (1 match) 0, 11 (1 ct); L. J. Fletcher (*Nottingham†*) (cap 2014) (2 matches) 5, 7, 24*; Imran Tahir§ (*Lahore, Pakistan*) (cap 2015) (1 match) 2; W. T. Root (*Sheffield*) (1 match) 37, 15. G. Keedy (*Sandal*) (1 match) did not bat (1 ct).

† *Born in Nottinghamshire.* ‡ *ECB contract.* § *Official overseas player.*
¶ *Other non-England-qualified player.*

BOWLING

	Style	O	M	R	W	BB	5I	Avge
M. Carter.........................	OB	49.4	6	195	10	7-56	1	19.50
V. D. Philander...................	RFM	154.3	40	384	16	4-56	0	24.00
H. F. Gurney......................	LFM	305.5	58	1,000	41	5-43	2	24.39
B. A. Hutton	RM	262.1	51	912	37	5-29	2	24.64
J. T. Ball.........................	RM	314.3	59	1,121	39	6-49	1	28.74
L. Wood..........................	LM	247.2	53	907	30	3-27	0	30.23
S. R. Patel.......................	SLA	302.1	83	891	26	4-23	0	34.26
S. J. Mullaney....................	RM	120.3	25	436	12	3-44	0	36.33

Also bowled: S. C. J. Broad (RFM) 51.3–8–201–9; A. Carter (RFM) 20–2–91–5; L. J. Fletcher (RFM) 12–2–42–2; W. R. S. Gidman (RFM) 92–26–259–4; B. W. Hilfenhaus (RFM) 97–22–294–7; Imran Tahir (LBG) 36–5–145–4; G. Keedy (SLA) 40–12–107–5; W. T. Root (OB) 5–2–6–0; B. R. M. Taylor (OB) 3–0–12–0.

LEADING ROYAL LONDON CUP AVERAGES (100 runs/4 wickets)

Batting

	Runs	HS	Avge	SR	Ct
G. P. Smith.....	124	124	124.00	92.53	1
J. W. A. Taylor.	401	109	66.83	91.76	4
D. T. Christian.	251	72	62.75	135.67	2
S. R. Patel.....	284	124*	47.33	81.60	1
S. J. Mullaney.	141	51	47.00	98.60	1
A. D. Hales.....	401	103	44.55	114.24	5
M. H. Wessels .	396	132	44.00	88.59	8
B. R. M. Taylor.	149	62	24.83	79.25	4

Bowling

	W	BB	Avge	ER
D. T. Christian ...	9	5-40	19.77	5.93
Imran Tahir	6	3-38	21.00	4.34
S. R. Patel	13	4-11	22.07	5.21
J. T. Ball	13	4-47	25.15	4.84
B. A. Hutton	6	3-72	32.83	5.62
S. J. Mullaney ...	8	3-32	38.62	5.51

LEADING NATWEST T20 BLAST AVERAGES (100 runs/18 overs)

Batting	Runs	HS	Avge	SR	Ct/St	Bowling	W	BB	Avge	ER
M. H. Wessels . .	439	97	33.76	150.34	8	S. J. Mullaney	12	2-27	23.66	6.92
A. D. Hales	283	86*	31.44	140.79	4	S. R. Patel	8	3-17	35.75	7.52
S. J. Mullaney . .	131	38	13.10	131.00	5	H. F. Gurney	9	3-25	42.33	8.37
S. R. Patel	386	90*	38.60	129.53	6	D. T. Christian . . .	4	2-34	53.25	8.87
J. W. A. Taylor .	253	38*	31.62	123.41	7	J. T. Ball	13	3-36	26.07	8.92
M. J. Lumb.	120	45	17.14	122.44	1	L. J. Fletcher	10	3-24	21.40	9.51
B. R. M. Taylor .	113	47	16.14	117.70	1/1					

FIRST-CLASS COUNTY RECORDS

Highest score for	312*	W. W. Keeton v Middlesex at The Oval	1939
Highest score against	345	C. G. Macartney (Australians) at Nottingham . .	1921
Leading run-scorer	31,592	G. Gunn (avge 35.69)	1902–32
Best bowling for	10-66	K. Smales v Gloucestershire at Stroud.	1956
Best bowling against	10-10	H. Verity (Yorkshire) at Leeds	1932
Leading wicket-taker	1,653	T. G. Wass (avge 20.34)	1896–1920
Highest total for	791	v Essex at Chelmsford.	2007
Highest total against	781-7 dec	by Northamptonshire at Northampton	1995
Lowest total for	13	v Yorkshire at Nottingham.	1901
Lowest total against {	16	by Derbyshire at Nottingham.	1879
	16	by Surrey at The Oval	1880

LIST A COUNTY RECORDS

Highest score for	167*	P. Johnson v Kent at Nottingham	1993
Highest score against	191	D. S. Lehmann (Yorkshire) at Scarborough. . . .	2001
Leading run-scorer	11,237	R. T. Robinson (avge 35.33)	1978–99
Best bowling for	6-10	K. P. Evans v Northumberland at Jesmond	1994
Best bowling against	7-41	A. N. Jones (Sussex) at Nottingham	1986
Leading wicket-taker	291	C. E. B. Rice (avge 22.60).	1975–87
Highest total for	368-2	v Middlesex at Lord's	2014
Highest total against	361-8	by Surrey at The Oval	2001
Lowest total for	57	v Gloucestershire at Nottingham	2009
Lowest total against	43	by Northamptonshire at Northampton	1977

TWENTY20 COUNTY RECORDS

Highest score for	97	M. H. Wessels v Durham at Chester-le-Street	2015
Highest score against	111	W. J. Durston (Derbyshire) at Nottingham	2010
Leading run-scorer	2,689	S. R. Patel (avge 28.01)	2003–15
Best bowling for	5-22	G. G. White v Lancashire at Nottingham	2013
Best bowling against	5-13	A. B. McDonald (Leicestershire) at Nottingham	2010
Leading wicket-taker	108	S. R. Patel (avge 25.23)	2003–15
Highest total for	220-4	v Leicestershire at Leicester.	2014
Highest total against	209-4	by Yorkshire at Leeds	2015
Lowest total for	91	v Lancashire at Manchester	2006
Lowest total against	90	by Leicestershire at Nottingham	2014

ADDRESS

County Cricket Ground, Trent Bridge, Nottingham NG2 6AG; 0115 982 3000;
administration@nottsccc.co.uk; www.nottsccc.co.uk.

OFFICIALS

Captain (Championship) C. M. W. Read
(limited-overs) J. W. A. Taylor
Director of cricket M. Newell
Coaching consultant P. Moores
Academy director C. M. Tolley
President T. I. Hepburn

Chairman P. G. Wright
Chief executive L. J. Pursehouse
Chairman, cricket committee W. Taylor
Head groundsman S. Birks
Scorer R. Marshall

NOTTINGHAMSHIRE v LOUGHBOROUGH MCCU

At Nottingham, April 7–9. Drawn. Toss: Nottinghamshire. First-class debut: T. M. Nugent. County debuts: W. R. S. Gidman, B. R. M. Taylor.

The students matched the county run for run in the first innings, but Nottinghamshire pulled away in their second, when they settled for batting practice on a flat wicket in dry spring weather. On the opening day, Mullaney made his first century in red-ball cricket since September 2013; on the last, Brendan Taylor – the Zimbabwean captain who had retired from international cricket after the World Cup – became the 12th player to score a hundred on debut for Nottinghamshire. Irish seamer Robert McKinley had claimed three wickets as the county's last eight fell for 97 in their first innings, and next day opener Anish Patel and Hasan Azad, a 21-year-old left-hander who had played for Nottinghamshire Second XI, both came close to maiden hundred.

Close of play: first day, Loughborough MCCU 36-1 (Patel 25, Hasan Azad 6); second day, Nottinghamshire 104-0 (B. R. M. Taylor 49, Wessels 55).

Nottinghamshire

S. J. Mullaney b McKinley	118			
B. R. M. Taylor lbw b Gamble	9	– (1) c Burgess b Nugent	105	
A. D. Hales b Nugent	46	– b Kumar	83	
J. W. A. Taylor c Burgess b Nugent	25	– not out	62	
S. R. Patel run out	31			
M. H. Wessels run out	0	– (2) lbw b Gamble	60	
*†C. M. W. Read c Hasan Azad b Kumar	18	– (5) not out	46	
W. R. S. Gidman not out	28			
L. J. Fletcher c Nugent b Prowse	3			
J. T. Ball c Burgess b McKinley	9			
H. F. Gurney b McKinley	0			
B 15, l-b 4, n-b 2	21	L-b 2, w 3	5	

1/33 (2) 2/111 (3) 3/211 (1)   (79 overs) 308
4/213 (4) 5/215 (6) 6/246 (7)
7/271 (5) 8/283 (9) 9/308 (10) 10/308 (11)

1/115 (2)   (3 wkts dec, 65 overs) 361
2/212 (1) 3/292 (3)

Gamble 20–4–73–1; Grant 15–1–80–0; McKinley 17–1–67–3; Nugent 14–5–32–2; Kumar 5–0–25–1; Prowse 8–4–12–1. *Second innings*—Gamble 24–6–100–1; Grant 12–0–58–0; Nugent 11–0–75–1; Kumar 14–0–97–1; McKinley 3–0–29–0; Prowse 1–1–0–0.

Loughborough MCCU

*A. K. Patel lbw b Patel	83	– b Gurney	5	
M. T. Best b Gurney	4	– c Wessels b Mullaney	42	
Hasan Azad c Read b Ball	99	– not out	29	
N. R. Kumar c Patel b Mullaney	6	– not out	5	
I. Prowse lbw b Mullaney	8			
M. G. K. Burgess st Read b Patel	43			
†R. G. White b Patel	0			
S. E. Grant c Mullaney b Patel	0			
G. K. R. McKinley b Ball	39			
R. N. Gamble b Fletcher	5			
T. M. Nugent not out	4			
L-b 2, w 5, n-b 10	17	B 4, l-b 1	5	

1/24 (2) 2/137 (1) 3/150 (4)   (91.1 overs) 308
4/170 (5) 5/229 (6) 6/229 (7)
7/235 (8) 8/295 (9) 9/304 (3) 10/308 (10)

1/5 (1)   (2 wkts, 24.2 overs) 86
2/79 (2)

Ball 21–3–72–2; Fletcher 15.1–5–50–1; Gurney 16–4–45–1; Gidman 17–0–66–0; Patel 16–4–51–4; Mullaney 6–1–22–2. *Second innings*—Ball 4–1–17–0; Gurney 5–1–18–1; Fletcher 5–3–6–0; Gidman 5–0–32–0; Mullaney 3.2–1–6–1; Patel 2–1–2–0.

Umpires: R. J. Evans and S. A. Garratt.

At Lord's, April 12–15. NOTTINGHAMSHIRE drew with MIDDLESEX.

NOTTINGHAMSHIRE v YORKSHIRE

At Nottingham, April 19–22. Drawn. Nottinghamshire 11pts, Yorkshire 11pts. Toss: Yorkshire. First-class debut: M. D. Fisher.

Yorkshire conceded 393 on the opening day after putting Nottinghamshire in, yet glimpsed a possible victory before lunch on the fourth, when they reduced them to 134 for five, only 121 ahead. Patel and Read saw off the crisis, however, and Yorkshire claimed only two more wickets. Matthew Fisher, a seamer who became their sixth-youngest Championship debutant at 17 years 161 days, dismissed Brendan Taylor with his seventh delivery on the first morning. But none of the seven bowlers used by Gale, resuming the captaincy after his four-match suspension, could contain Hales. In a show of his credentials to play Test cricket as well as the shorter formats, he scored his first double-hundred, advancing to a formidable six-hour 236. On a flat pitch, Yorkshire responded with two centuries of their own: Lees, just past his 22nd birthday, had two lives on the way, before becoming Will Gidman's first wicket for his new county, then Leaning, six months younger, batted more fluently for a maiden hundred. Nottinghamshire trailed by 13, and lost three wickets on the third evening to offer that hint of a result.

Close of play: first day, Nottinghamshire 393-7 (Hales 222); second day, Yorkshire 226-3 (Gale 13, Leaning 3); third day, Nottinghamshire 74-3 (J. W. A. Taylor 7, Gidman 7).

Nottinghamshire

S. J. Mullaney lbw b Patterson	27	– lbw b Fisher	20
B. R. M. Taylor c Lees b Fisher	27	– b Brooks	32
A. D. Hales b Patterson	236	– c Hodd b Bresnan	2
J. W. A. Taylor lbw b Brooks	59	– c sub (M. A. Ashraf) b Rhodes	35
S. R. Patel c Lees b Brooks	4	– (6) c Hodd b Rhodes	76
M. H. Wessels c Leaning b Rhodes	18	– (7) c Hodd b Leaning	43
*†C. M. W. Read lbw b Bresnan	7	– (8) not out	83
W. R. S. Gidman c Lees b Patterson	8	– (5) c Hodd b Patterson	13
V. D. Philander c Leaning b Brooks	7	– not out	38
J. T. Ball b Bresnan	14		
H. F. Gurney not out	0		
B 9, l-b 7, w 1, n-b 4	21	B 2, l-b 6, n-b 4	12

1/37 (1) 2/77 (2) 3/248 (4)   (108.2 overs) 428
4/252 (5) 5/324 (6) 6/344 (7)
7/393 (8) 8/414 (9) 9/414 (3) 10/428 (10)

1/46 (1)   (7 wkts dec, 105 overs) 354
2/52 (3) 3/58 (2)
4/92 (5) 5/134 (4) 6/213 (6) 7/245 (7)

Bresnan 21.2–4–85–2; Brooks 27–5–99–3; Patterson 29–10–78–3; Fisher 15–3–68–1; Pyrah 7–0–26–0; Rhodes 6–0–28–1; Leaning 3–0–28–0. *Second innings*—Bresnan 21–6–77–1; Brooks 21–5–67–1; Fisher 16–3–34–1; Patterson 15–4–32–1; Rhodes 15–4–42–2; Leaning 14–2–82–1; Lees 3–0–12–0.

Yorkshire

A. Z. Lees c Read b Gidman	100	J. A. Brooks c Gidman b Gurney	5
W. M. H. Rhodes c Patel b Gurney	41	M. D. Fisher lbw b Patel	0
C. A. Pujara c sub (B. M. Kitt) b Patel	57		
*A. W. Gale c Wessels b Gurney	13	B 3, l-b 12, w 5	20
J. A. Leaning st Read b Patel	116		
R. M. Pyrah c Mullaney b Philander	37	1/66 (2) 2/182 (3) (147.5 overs) 441
†A. J. Hodd b Philander	6	3/215 (1) 4/235 (4) 5/346 (6)
T. T. Bresnan c Mullaney b Patel	34	6/353 (5) 7/422 (8) 8/427 (5)
S. A. Patterson not out	12	9/438 (10) 10/441 (11) 110 overs: 320-4

Philander 26–9–51–2; Ball 24–6–66–0; Gurney 28.4–7–90–3; Gidman 25–8–75–1; Mullaney 11.2–1–42–0; Patel 32.5–9–102–4.

Umpires: R. J. Bailey and R. J. Evans.

At Southampton, April 26–29. NOTTINGHAMSHIRE drew with HAMPSHIRE.

At Chester-le-Street, May 10–12. NOTTINGHAMSHIRE lost to DURHAM by six wickets.

NOTTINGHAMSHIRE v SOMERSET

At Nottingham, May 17–19. Somerset won by 133 runs. Somerset 22pts, Nottinghamshire 4pts. Toss: Nottinghamshire.

Somerset completed their first victory in 2015, after defeats in three Championship matches plus one by the New Zealanders. On a vividly green pitch, Nottinghamshire had reduced them to 101 for five in the opening session – but the next five wickets took 40 overs and added 211, a key passage in a low-scoring contest. Craig Overton's 31-ball 55 was crucial to the recovery; so were his four wickets as Nottinghamshire subsided from 121 for three to 226 all out. With 52 overs wiped out on the second day, their first innings stretched into the third, when 22 wickets fell on a capricious surface under heavy cloud. Philander again bowled Trescothick in his first over – inflicting only the second pair of his career – and added Myburgh, also for a duck, in his next. Somerset were soon 86 for seven, but once more Nottinghamshire gave away late runs, this time 75 for the last three wickets. Needing 248 for a win, they never got close: Somerset had them seven down for 81, and claimed the extra half-hour to finish the job.

Close of play: first day, Nottinghamshire 57-2 (B. R. M. Taylor 11, J. W. A. Taylor 3); second day, Nottinghamshire 195-8 (Patel 35, Ball 2).

Somerset

*M. E. Trescothick b Philander	0	– b Philander	0
T. B. Abell c Read b Philander	10	– lbw b Wood	11
J. G. Myburgh b Mullaney	49	– c Mullaney b Philander	0
J. C. Hildreth b Philander	32	– lbw b Mullaney	23
T. L. W. Cooper c J. W. A. Taylor b Mullaney	1	– lbw b Wood	2
J. Allenby c B. R. M. Taylor b Philander	64	– b Ball	14
P. D. Trego b Mullaney	41	– lbw b Ball	24
L. Gregory b Wood	17	– not out	26
†A. W. R. Barrow not out	23	– c Mullaney b Gurney	25
C. Overton b Gurney	55	– lbw b Philander	2
T. D. Groenewald b Wood	0	– c Gurney b Mullaney	21
B 8, l-b 10, n-b 2	20	B 8, l-b 3, n-b 2	13

1/0 (1) 2/21 (2) 3/99 (3) (69.4 overs) 312
4/101 (4) 5/101 (5) 6/186 (7)
7/229 (8) 8/241 (6) 9/311 (10) 10/312 (11)

1/0 (1) 2/4 (3) (44 overs) 161
3/12 (2) 4/26 (5)
5/45 (4) 6/59 (6) 7/86 (7)
8/125 (9) 9/136 (10) 10/161 (11)

Philander 19–6–56–4; Wood 13.4–2–61–2; Gurney 15–1–65–1; Ball 11–1–68–0; Mullaney 11–2–44–3. *Second innings*—Philander 16–4–47–3; Wood 9–2–34–2; Mullaney 9–2–34–2; Ball 6–1–18–2; Gurney 4–0–17–1.

Nottinghamshire

S. J. Mullaney lbw b Gregory	19	– c Abell b Groenewald	7
B. R. M. Taylor lbw b Gregory	22	– lbw b Gregory	8
G. P. Smith lbw b Groenewald	8	– c Trescothick b Overton	4
J. W. A. Taylor b Groenewald	45	– lbw b Allenby	8
M. H. Wessels c Trescothick b Allenby	8	– c Trescothick b Gregory	30
S. R. Patel c Hildreth b Overton	56	– c Trescothick b Overton	1
*†C. M. W. Read c and b Overton	8	– c Abell b Allenby	1
V. D. Philander b Overton	12	– not out	35
L. Wood c and b Overton	0	– c Barrow b Groenewald	0
J. T. Ball c Myburgh b Allenby	9	– c Myburgh b Groenewald	9
H. F. Gurney not out	1	– b Groenewald	0
B 9, l-b 16, w 7, n-b 6	38	B 1, l-b 3, w 5, n-b 2	11

1/36 (1) 2/48 (3) 3/88 (2) (76.4 overs) 226
4/121 (5) 5/137 (4) 6/152 (7)
7/189 (8) 8/189 (9) 9/206 (10) 10/226 (6)

1/7 (1) 2/24 (2) (35.2 overs) 114
3/28 (3) 4/57 (4)
5/58 (6) 6/59 (7) 7/81 (5)
8/82 (9) 9/110 (10) 10/114 (11)

Gregory 17–3–57–2; Groenewald 16–6–42–2; Trego 11–4–32–0; Overton 16.4–6–40–4; Allenby 16–6–30–2. *Second innings*—Gregory 11–3–27–2; Groenewald 11.2–2–41–4; Overton 8–0–29–2; Allenby 5–1–13–2.

Umpires: N. G. B. Cook and R. T. Robinson.

NOTTINGHAMSHIRE v SUSSEX

At Nottingham, June 1–3. Nottinghamshire won by 159 runs. Nottinghamshire 21pts, Sussex 3pts. Toss: Sussex.

A remarkable performance from 19-year-old Luke Wood, in his fifth first-class match, set up Nottinghamshire's first victory of the season, despite Magoffin grabbing six in each innings. A left-arm seamer who had never reached three figures even in club cricket, Wood hit a 95-ball hundred, took three wickets to help secure a 66-run lead, bolstered that with another fifty, then added two more wickets as Sussex collapsed again. Arriving with Nottinghamshire a dismal 98 for seven on a green-tinged pitch – including Brendan Taylor for a sixth consecutive lbw – he targeted a short boundary on the New Stand side to hit six sixes. On 72 when the ninth wicket fell, he completed his century in a further 27 deliveries, without last man Gurney facing a single one. It was the first by a Nottinghamshire No. 9 since 1982, when Eddie Hemmings scored 127 against Yorkshire at Worksop, Wood's home town. Ball, another local product, claimed six wickets – double his previous best – before Wood took part in a second rescue act as Magoffin threatened to run through Nottinghamshire again, joining Patel at 108 for seven to add 133. Set 310, Sussex subsided tamely; Gurney, though not at his best, collected a career-best five for 43.

Close of play: first day, Sussex 39-3 (Nash 2, Wright 0); second day, Nottinghamshire 228-7 (Patel 88, Wood 52).

Nottinghamshire

S. J. Mullaney c and b Jordan	11	– c Jordan b Robinson	20
B. R. M. Taylor lbw b Magoffin	9	– b Magoffin	7
A. D. Hales b Jordan	6	– c Brown b Magoffin	5
*J. W. A. Taylor lbw b Robinson	0	– lbw b Robinson	5
†M. H. Wessels c Brown b Magoffin	7	– c Wright b Jordan	26
S. R. Patel c Jordan b Magoffin	17	– c Cachopa b Magoffin	100
G. P. Smith b Robinson	14	– c Brown b Magoffin	11
W. R. S. Gidman c Jordan b Magoffin	57	– b Magoffin	0
L. Wood c Brown b Wells	100	– c Nash b Robinson	53
J. T. Ball c Wells b Magoffin	15	– c Brown b Magoffin	1
H. F. Gurney not out	0	– not out	0
B 6, l-b 5, n-b 8	19	B 5, l-b 8, n-b 2	15

1/13 (2) 2/21 (1) 3/22 (4)   (55.3 overs) 255
4/30 (3) 5/38 (5) 6/55 (6)
7/98 (7) 8/173 (8) 9/219 (10) 10/255 (9)

1/28 (2) 2/32 (1)   (63.2 overs) 243
3/38 (3) 4/48 (4)
5/76 (5) 6/108 (7) 7/108 (8)
8/241 (9) 9/243 (6) 10/243 (10)

Magoffin 22–2–109–6; Jordan 18–2–69–2; Robinson 8–1–37–1; Hobden 7–2–27–0; Wells 0.3–0–2–1. *Second innings*—Magoffin 18.2–4–50–6; Jordan 14–3–49–1; Robinson 17–2–81–3; Hobden 7–1–30–0; Wells 7–0–20–0.

Sussex

L. W. P. Wells lbw b Ball	10	– (2) c B. R. M. Taylor b Wood	16
M. H. Yardy c B. R. M. Taylor b Wood	2	– (1) lbw b Ball	0
M. W. Machan c Gidman b Wood	20	– lbw b Ball	0
*C. D. Nash lbw b Ball	15	– c Smith b Wood	7
L. J. Wright b Ball	15	– b Gurney	39
C. Cachopa b Ball	54	– c Wessels b Gurney	0
†B. C. Brown c Wessels b Ball	0	– not out	27
C. J. Jordan b Wood	39	– c Wessels b Gurney	8
O. E. Robinson c Gidman b Mullaney	13	– c Smith b Gurney	0
S. J. Magoffin not out	1	– b Gurney	35
M. E. Hobden lbw b Ball	3	– c Wessels b Ball	0
B 4, l-b 13	17	B 8, l-b 10	18

1/16 (1) 2/16 (2) 3/39 (3)   (43 overs) 189
4/61 (4) 5/84 (5) 6/84 (7)
7/153 (8) 8/181 (9) 9/185 (6) 10/189 (11)

1/12 (1) 2/16 (3)   (32 overs) 150
3/24 (4) 4/49 (4)
5/66 (6) 6/79 (5) 7/97 (8)
8/97 (9) 9/149 (10) 10/150 (11)

Ball 17–6–49–6; Wood 12–1–61–3; Gurney 7–1–25–0; Gidman 4–1–26–0; Mullaney 3–0–11–1. *Second innings*—Ball 8–4–18–3; Wood 10–1–35–2; Gurney 9–0–43–5; Mullaney 5–0–36–0.

Umpires: R. J. Bailey and N. L. Bainton.

At Taunton, June 14–17. NOTTINGHAMSHIRE lost to SOMERSET by two wickets.

At Leeds, June 22–24. NOTTINGHAMSHIRE lost to YORKSHIRE by an innings and eight runs.

NOTTINGHAMSHIRE v WORCESTERSHIRE

At Nottingham, June 29–July 2. Nottinghamshire won by 113 runs. Nottinghamshire 20pts, Worcestershire 5pts. Toss: Worcestershire.

After a dismal first day, on which their batsmen struggled and two of their bowlers broke down, bottom-placed Nottinghamshire announced that former England coach Peter Moores would join as a consultant for the rest of the season. Spirits seemed to rise, leading to their second Championship win. The match turned soon after lunch on day two: once Gidman, struck on the helmet by a

Hilfenhaus bouncer, retired with concussion, Worcestershire slumped from 204 for three to 283 all out. In sweltering heat, and despite a deficit of 43, Nottinghamshire built a commanding lead: James Taylor, using a runner because of a pulled hamstring, added 105 with Wessels, before Read marked his return from injury with 73. But, even without Gidman, a target of 324 looked attainable on a benign pitch against a depleted attack. Worcestershire entered the final session on 189 for three, before Mitchell's dismissal triggered a collapse of six for 17, three of them to Carter, heroically bowling with heavy strapping on an abdominal tear (Fletcher was absent with a hamstring strain). The result was tough on Worcestershire's youthful seamers: Ed Barnard had shown control in his second first-class match, and Morris claimed three wickets in 12 deliveries on the first afternoon.

Close of play: first day, Worcestershire 89-2 (Oliver 52); second day, Nottinghamshire 115-3 (J. W. A. Taylor 20, Wessels 25); third day, Worcestershire 13-0 (Mitchell 2, Oliver 11).

Nottinghamshire

B. R. M. Taylor c Barnard b Shantry	69	– lbw b Barnard	32
M. J. Lumb c Clarke b Shantry	26	– c Clarke b Morris	12
A. D. Hales b Leach	15	– c Morris b Leach	24
J. W. A. Taylor lbw b Leach	8	– run out	56
M. H. Wessels c Fell b Saeed Ajmal	65	– c Clarke b Shantry	55
S. R. Patel c Fell b Morris	10	– lbw b Saeed Ajmal	31
*†C. M. W. Read c Cox b Morris	5	– b Shantry	73
B. A. Hutton c Cox b Morris	0	– b Shantry	34
B. W. Hilfenhaus c Gidman b Barnard	0	– c sub (T. Köhler-Cadmore) b Shantry	9
L. J. Fletcher run out	5	– b Shantry	7
A. Carter not out	24	– not out	17
B 6, l-b 4, w 1, n-b 2	13	B 4, l-b 12	16

1/74 (2) 2/98 (3) 3/108 (4)   (66.3 overs) 240
4/140 (1) 5/159 (6) 6/169 (7)
7/169 (8) 8/170 (9) 9/190 (10) 10/240 (5)

1/29 (2) 2/44 (1)   (126.4 overs) 366
3/69 (3) 4/174 (5)
5/201 (6) 6/234 (6) 7/327 (8)
8/332 (7) 9/341 (9) 10/366 (10)

Morris 14–3–70–3; Leach 18–3–79–2; Barnard 16–4–33–1; Shantry 17–4–39–2; Saeed Ajmal 1.3–0–9–1. *Second innings*—Morris 21–6–55–1; Leach 20–2–97–1; Shantry 35.4–13–48–5; Barnard 15–1–67–1; Saeed Ajmal 35–6–83–1.

Worcestershire

*D. K. H. Mitchell lbw b Hilfenhaus	25	– c Carter b Patel	76
R. K. Oliver c Read b Patel	99	– b Hilfenhaus	11
C. A. J. Morris b Hilfenhaus	1	– (10) c Lumb b Carter	0
T. C. Fell c Read b Hutton	72	– (3) lbw b Hutton	58
A. P. R. Gidman retired hurt	13	– absent hurt	
J. M. Clarke lbw b Hilfenhaus	0	– (4) b Carter	29
†O. B. Cox b Hutton	9	– (5) c sub (S. J. Mullaney) b Hutton	19
E. G. Barnard lbw b Hutton	4	– (6) b Patel	0
J. Leach not out	24	– (7) c Wessels b Carter	2
J. D. Shantry lbw b Hilfenhaus	9	– (8) not out	4
Saeed Ajmal lbw b Carter	7	– (9) lbw b Carter	0
B 1, l-b 10, w 1, n-b 8	20	L-b 4, n-b 6	10

1/83 (1) 2/89 (3) 3/160 (2)   (86.3 overs) 283
4/207 (6) 5/233 (7) 6/239 (8)
7/240 (4) 8/264 (10) 9/283 (11)

1/17 (2) 2/129 (3)   (82.4 overs) 210
3/175 (4) 4/193 (1)
5/201 (5) 6/203 (7) 7/205 (6)
8/206 (9) 9/210 (10)

In the first innings Gidman retired hurt at 204-3.

Hilfenhaus 25–7–67–4; Fletcher 3–1–2–0; Hutton 24–7–85–3; Carter 7.2–0–45–1; Patel 27.1–6–73–1. *Second innings*—Hilfenhaus 16–2–53–1; Hutton 24–4–71–2; Carter 12.4–2–46–4; Patel 30–16–36–2.

Umpires: J. W. Lloyds and M. J. Saggers.

NOTTINGHAMSHIRE v MIDDLESEX

At Nottingham, July 5–8. Drawn. Nottinghamshire 11pts, Middlesex 11pts. Toss: Nottinghamshire.

Rain and bad light ruled out a positive result, with just 45 overs on the final day. Injuries compelled Nottinghamshire to make four changes from the previous week, but their revamped attack reduced Middlesex to 165 for seven, before Malan and Harris shared a partnership of 175 – seven short of the county eighth-wicket record, by Mordaunt Doll and Joe Murrell in 1913. Dropped at point on 29, the left-handed Malan advanced to a career-best 182 not out, scoring heavily square or behind square on the off side. It was only his second Championship match since he broke a bone in his right hand in the season opener, against these opponents. That match had featured a hundred by Read, and he followed up with a second here after surviving a chance on 54. He guided his side into the lead as the pitch eased during a seventh-wicket stand of 157 with Hutton, who notched up a maiden half-century in his fifth first-class match. Early wickets on the final morning might have offered Nottinghamshire a glimmer, but only six overs were bowled before lunch.

Close of play: first day, Middlesex 312-7 (Malan 159, Harris 68); second day, Nottinghamshire 180-4 (Mullaney 56, Patel 12); third day, Middlesex 7-0 (Harris 3, Robson 4).

Middlesex

S. D. Robson lbw b Ball	15	– (2) not out	77
J. A. Burns b Wood	5		
N. R. D. Compton c Read b Hutton	19	– not out	36
D. J. Malan not out	182		
E. J. G. Morgan c Read b Wood	15		
*J. E. C. Franklin lbw b Gurney	4		
†J. A. Simpson c Hutton b Gurney	2		
O. P. Rayner c Taylor b Mullaney	5		
J. A. R. Harris b Hutton	73	– (1) lbw b Gurney	44
T. S. Roland-Jones lbw b Hutton	14		
T. J. Murtagh lbw b Gurney	12		
B 4, l-b 10, n-b 14	28	B 2, l-b 3	5

1/7 (2) 2/25 (1) 3/63 (3)　　　　(108 overs) 374　　1/83 (1)　　　　(1 wkt, 47 overs) 162
4/105 (5) 5/122 (6) 6/132 (7)
7/165 (8) 8/340 (9) 9/356 (10) 10/374 (11)

Wood 23-2-83-2; Ball 22-2-93-1; Gurney 22-5-68-3; Hutton 30-9-81-3; Mullaney 7-0-24-1; Patel 4-1-11-0. *Second innings*—Wood 7-4-17-0; Ball 8-1-31-0; Hutton 5-0-30-0; Gurney 7-1-17-1; Patel 13-4-39-0; Taylor 3-0-12-0; Mullaney 4-1-11-0.

Nottinghamshire

B. R. M. Taylor b Franklin	77	L. Wood c Franklin b Malan	14
A. D. Hales b Harris	18	J. T. Ball not out	6
M. J. Lumb c Simpson b Franklin	9	B 7, l-b 16, n-b 2	25
S. J. Mullaney c Murtagh b Rayner	76		
M. H. Wessels c and b Franklin	0	1/40 (2)　　(9 wkts dec, 136.3 overs) 419
S. R. Patel b Murtagh	14	2/74 (3) 3/145 (1) 4/145 (5)
*†C. M. W. Read b Roland-Jones	108	5/184 (6) 6/229 (4) 7/386 (7)
B. A. Hutton lbw b Rayner	72	8/411 (9) 9/419 (8)　　110 overs: 315-6

H. F. Gurney did not bat.

Murtagh 33-6-88-1; Roland-Jones 34-7-86-1; Harris 29-4-113-1; Franklin 15-3-41-3; Rayner 18.3-4-47-2; Malan 7-0-21-1.

Umpires: B. J. Debenham and R. J. Evans.

At Horsham, July 19–21. NOTTINGHAMSHIRE beat SUSSEX by an innings and 103 runs.

At Worcester, August 7–10. NOTTINGHAMSHIRE beat WORCESTERSHIRE by five wickets.

NOTTINGHAMSHIRE v WARWICKSHIRE

At Nottingham, August 21–24. Nottinghamshire won by an innings and 123 runs. Nottinghamshire 24pts, Warwickshire 4pts. Toss: Warwickshire.

Nottinghamshire's fourth win in five games lifted them to third. Their ascent from the bottom had coincided with Moores's arrival, although Read also praised "the other back-room staff and the work ethic of the players, which has improved greatly". The light on the final evening was so poor the umpires would not allow Nottinghamshire to use their quicker bowlers to hunt down the four wickets still needed at tea, which seemed a significant handicap: Ball and Hutton, the brightest of an emerging crop of seamers, had shared ten in the match and made Warwickshire follow on. But the combination of Mullaney's off-cutters and Samit Patel's left-arm spin, which earned his best figures for four years, proved enough. Victory had been set up by an invigorating 189 from 216 balls from Hales – raising his aggregate against Warwickshire to 883 at 98 – after Nottinghamshire were put in. He added 257 at nearly five an over with Mullaney, a second-wicket record between these counties. Read passed 50 for the fifth time in five completed innings, and Ball smashed a career-best 49 in 20 deliveries.

Close of play: first day, Nottinghamshire 404-5 (Patel 20, Wood 4); second day, Warwickshire 100-4 (Evans 39, Ambrose 18); third day, Warwickshire 42-0 (Porterfield 23, Westwood 18).

Nottinghamshire

B. R. M. Taylor c Ambrose b Rankin	22	
A. D. Hales b Wright	189	
S. J. Mullaney c Patel b Barker	112	
J. W. A. Taylor c Ambrose b Rankin	29	
M. H. Wessels c Porterfield b Clarke	15	
S. R. Patel b Wright	46	
L. Wood c Evans b Clarke	12	
*†C. M. W. Read c Trott b Rankin	69	
B. A. Hutton c Evans b Patel	37	
J. T. Ball not out	49	
H. F. Gurney b Wright	0	

B 4, l-b 7, w 1, n-b 8 20

1/61 (1) 2/318 (3)   (140.3 overs) 600
3/351 (2) 4/372 (4) 5/400 (5)
6/416 (7) 7/453 (6) 8/544 (9)
9/560 (8) 10/600 (11)   110 overs: 453-6

Barker 30–2–117–1; Wright 25.3–4–97–3; Clarke 29–7–90–2; Rankin 19–2–104–3; Patel 33–2–155–1; Trott 4–0–26–0.

Warwickshire

*W. T. S. Porterfield c Read b Ball		1 – b Patel	61
I. J. Westwood c Read b Wood		1 – c Read b Ball	19
L. J. Evans b Ball	41	– c Read b Ball	12
I. J. L. Trott lbw b Ball	8	– lbw b Hutton	22
S. R. Hain c Mullaney b Gurney	25	– c Wood b Hutton	7
†T. R. Ambrose c Read b Hutton	46	– lbw b Patel	12
R. Clarke c B. R. M. Taylor b Hutton	5	– not out	30
K. H. D. Barker c Mullaney b Patel	71	– c Wessels b Mullaney	8
J. S. Patel c Hutton b Gurney	12	– c J. W. A. Taylor b Mullaney	28
C. J. C. Wright c Mullaney b Hutton	22	– lbw b Patel	0
W. B. Rankin not out	14	– c J. W. A. Taylor b Patel	4

L-b 14 14   B 4, l-b 6, w 2, n-b 2 14

1/2 (2) 2/2 (1) 3/10 (4)   (80.5 overs) 260   1/45 (2) 2/59 (3)   (95.1 overs) 217
4/41 (5) 5/111 (3) 6/129 (7)   3/101 (4) 4/111 (5)
7/154 (6) 8/171 (9) 9/236 (8) 10/260 (10)   5/142 (6) 6/143 (1) 7/172 (8)
                                        8/208 (9) 9/209 (10) 10/217 (11)

Ball 19–7–35–3; Wood 15–6–32–1; Gurney 18–7–45–2; Hutton 18.5–2–73–3; Mullaney 1–0–4–0; Patel 9–1–57–1. *Second innings*—Ball 18–4–48–2; Wood 14–4–35–0; Hutton 14–3–32–2; Gurney 15–6–34–0; Patel 22.1–15–23–4; Mullaney 12–6–35–2.

Umpires: S. C. Gale and S. J. O'Shaughnessy.

NOTTINGHAMSHIRE v DURHAM

At Nottingham, September 9–11. Nottinghamshire won by 52 runs. Nottinghamshire 20pts, Durham 7pts. Toss: Durham. First-class debut: B. J. McCarthy.

Nottinghamshire conceded a first-innings lead of 168, yet emerged with a fourth consecutive Championship win – Durham's fourth successive defeat. Adding to captain Chris Read's triumph was his 1,000th first-class dismissal (and 950th catch). He received a personal message from Jack Russell, who had reached 1,000 in September 1997, a week after Read's one senior appearance for Gloucestershire, deputising for Russell in a one-day game. Since then, only Steve Rhodes had achieved the feat. Read's landmark victim was Collingwood, who had just become the first man to score 10,000 runs for Durham, but departed as the match swung Nottinghamshire's way. Chasing 215, Durham collapsed from 58 to nine for six: Gurney removed Borthwick and Stoneman in four balls, before Hutton collected Richardson, Collingwood and Pringle in 15. Former Ireland Under-19 seamer Barry McCarthy top-scored on first-class debut as Durham subsided for 162. Hutton twice improved his career-best figures and finished with his first ten in a match. Onions had taken five on the opening day, his 33rd birthday, when Nottinghamshire sank to 73 for seven; Richardson's unbeaten 96 steered Durham to 372 before Patel and Wessels began the fightback.

Close of play: first day, Durham 174-2 (Borthwick 56, Collingwood 16); second day, Nottinghamshire 138-4 (Wessels 16, Patel 21).

Nottinghamshire

B. R. M. Taylor c Burnham b Onions	1	– b Harrison	33
J. D. Libby c Muchall b Rushworth	0	– c Borthwick b Onions	34
S. J. Mullaney lbw b McCarthy	63	– b Onions	11
M. J. Lumb c Richardson b Onions	1	– c Rushworth b Onions	14
M. H. Wessels c Richardson b McCarthy	13	– c Collingwood b McCarthy	85
S. R. Patel c Richardson b Rushworth	1	– c Onions b Rushworth	100
*†C. M. W. Read c Richardson b Harrison	19	– c Rushworth b Pringle	15
B. A. Hutton lbw b Onions	1	– b Pringle	27
L. Wood not out	65	– c Collingwood b Borthwick	35
J. T. Ball b Onions	15	– b Pringle	6
H. F. Gurney b Onions	0	– not out	0
B 9, l-b 12, n-b 4	25	B 4, l-b 4, n-b 14	22

1/1 (2) 2/1 (1) 3/7 (4) (54 overs) 204 1/53 (1) 2/69 (3) (101.1 overs) 382
4/36 (5) 5/37 (6) 6/70 (7) 3/98 (2) 4/99 (4)
7/73 (8) 8/165 (3) 9/204 (10) 10/204 (11) 5/252 (6) 6/278 (7) 7/309 (6)
8/362 (8) 9/376 (10) 10/382 (9)

Rushworth 16–7–15–2; Onions 15–3–56–5; McCarthy 10–1–51–2; Harrison 10–0–41–1; Borthwick 3–0–20–0. *Second innings*—Rushworth 24–2–81–1; Onions 24–4–86–3; McCarthy 15–1–52–1; Harrison 16–2–48–1; Pringle 17–0–93–3; Borthwick 5.1–0–14–1.

Durham

M. D. Stoneman c Mullaney b Ball	62	– b Gurney	31
J. T. A. Burnham run out	31	– b Ball	0
S. G. Borthwick b Wood	63	– b Gurney	25
*P. D. Collingwood b Hutton	40	– c Read b Hutton	6
†M. J. Richardson not out	96	– b Hutton	5
G. J. Muchall c Lumb b Patel	32	– lbw b Ball	36
R. D. Pringle c Wessels b Hutton	19	– lbw b Hutton	0
J. Harrison b Hutton	0	– c Wessels b Ball	5
B. J. McCarthy b Wood	2	– not out	38
C. Rushworth c Wessels b Hutton	14	– c Lumb b Hutton	10
G. Onions c Read b Hutton	0	– b Hutton	1
L-b 3, w 2, n-b 8	13	L-b 1, n-b 4	5

1/78 (2) 2/131 (1) 3/188 (3) (88.2 overs) 372 1/1 (2) 2/58 (3) (40.4 overs) 162
4/224 (4) 5/281 (6) 6/324 (7) 3/59 (1) 4/64 (5)
7/334 (8) 8/343 (9) 9/368 (10) 10/372 (11) 5/69 (4) 6/71 (7) 7/105 (8)
8/136 (6) 9/158 (10) 10/162 (11)

Ball 16–0–80–1; Wood 15–1–78–2; Gurney 15–3–48–0; Mullaney 10–1–42–0; Hutton 22.2–4–77–5; Patel 10–1–44–1. *Second innings*—Ball 10–1–63–3; Wood 4–0–25–0; Hutton 10.4–3–29–5; Gurney 9–1–29–2; Patel 7–3–15–0.

Umpires: M. Burns and D. J. Millns.

At Birmingham, September 14–17. NOTTINGHAMSHIRE drew with WARWICKSHIRE.

NOTTINGHAMSHIRE v HAMPSHIRE

At Nottingham, September 22–25. Hampshire won by eight wickets. Hampshire 22pts, Nottinghamshire 6pts. Toss: Hampshire. County debut: W. T. Root.

In the end, the momentum that had propelled Nottinghamshire to third place could not match Hampshire's improbable escape from relegation. Starting 16 points behind seventh-placed Sussex, they conjured their third win in five games just before lunch on the final day – then had to wait two hours and 45 minutes for Sussex's defeat at Headingley to confirm their survival. Carberry organised the run-chase with 84 not out, but the architect of their victory was West Indian pace bowler Fidel Edwards, who claimed ten wickets. His second-innings burst of three in seven deliveries, reverse-swinging a ball that was 50 overs old to remove Read, Billy Root and Broad soon after Brendan Taylor had perished ten short of a century, shaved perhaps 100 off Hampshire's target. Edwards also took six on the opening day, when Wessels scored a well-constructed hundred. At 203 for eight, Hampshire looked likely to concede a substantial first-innings lead, before McLaren and Berg added 123 to cut the deficit to 14. An encouraging debut for Root – younger brother of England's Joe – was some consolation for Nottinghamshire.

Close of play: first day, Hampshire 0-1 (Adams 0); second day, Hampshire 298-8 (McLaren 44, Berg 52); third day, Hampshire 89-0 (Carberry 37, Adams 46).

Nottinghamshire

B. R. M. Taylor c Berg b Edwards	2	– c Vince b Dawson	90
J. D. Libby lbw b Edwards	1	– b Edwards	2
S. J. Mullaney b Dawson	58	– lbw b Stevenson	19
S. R. Patel c Wheater b Edwards	19	– b Berg	25
M. H. Wessels c Berg b Ervine	104	– b McLaren	9
W. T. Root c Ervine b Berg	37	– c Vince b Edwards	15
*†C. M. W. Read b Edwards	9	– lbw b Edwards	5
B. A. Hutton c Vince b Berg	46	– not out	5
S. C. J. Broad c McLaren b Edwards	37	– c Wheater b Edwards	2
J. T. Ball b Edwards	6	– b McLaren	7
H. F. Gurney not out	0	– b McLaren	0
L-b 15, n-b 6	21	L-b 6	6

1/2 (1) 2/11 (2) 3/39 (4)   (92.3 overs) 340   1/11 (2) 2/49 (3)   (62 overs) 185
4/154 (3) 5/236 (6) 6/241 (5)   3/127 (4) 4/151 (5)
7/247 (7) 8/321 (9) 9/330 (10) 10/340 (8)   5/157 (1) 6/171 (7) 7/176 (6)
                                                         8/178 (9) 9/185 (10) 10/185 (11)

Edwards 21–3–88–6; McLaren 22–2–74–0; Berg 19.3–3–51–2; Stevenson 14–1–63–0; Dawson 10–1–38–1; Ervine 6–2–11–1. *Second innings*—Edwards 17–4–57–4; McLaren 12–6–22–2; Berg 10–3–28–2; Stevenson 6–2–15–1; Dawson 17–4–57–1.

Hampshire

R. A. Stevenson c Read b Broad	0		
J. H. K. Adams c Read b Gurney	19	– b Ball	70
M. A. Carberry lbw b Hutton	11	– (1) not out	84
*J. M. Vince b Gurney	42	– (3) b Ball	0
W. R. Smith c Read b Gurney	3	– (4) not out	34
L. A. Dawson lbw b Mullaney	69		
S. M. Ervine c Broad b Patel	32		
†A. J. A. Wheater c Read b Hutton	16		
R. McLaren b Gurney	52		
G. K. Berg c Read b Broad	72		
F. H. Edwards not out	0		
L-b 4, n-b 6	10	B 5, l-b 5, n-b 2	12

1/0 (1) 2/29 (2) 3/51 (3) (89.5 overs) 326 1/129 (2) (2 wkts, 53.3 overs) 200
4/68 (5) 5/89 (4) 6/159 (7) 2/129 (3)
7/193 (8) 8/203 (6) 9/326 (9) 10/326 (10)

Broad 15.5–1–73–2; Ball 18–3–61–0; Gurney 19–4–70–4; Hutton 15–4–44–2; Patel 13–3–46–1; Mullaney 5–1–22–1; Root 4–1–6–0. *Second innings*—Broad 9–2–44–0; Gurney 12–2–34–0; Hutton 10–2–41–0; Patel 8.3–3–35–0; Ball 10–3–30–2; Root 1–1–0–0; Mullaney 3–0–6–0.

Umpires: J. W. Lloyds and S. J. O'Shaughnessy.

SOMERSET

The confidence of youth

RICHARD LATHAM

Somerset suffered a severe bout of déjà vu as they finished sixth in the Championship for the third successive season, and for the second year running failed to reach the knockout stages of the limited-overs competitions. The year was nearly disastrous, as well as repetitive, with relegation avoided only in the final round of matches. Matthew Maynard ended his first season as director of cricket with a sigh – of relief rather than satisfaction.

A fragile batting line-up was at fault for a poor start in which Somerset lost four of their first six matches. They failed to pass 300 in 16 of their first 22 innings, or hit a century in nine of the opening 11 games. The Royal London One-Day Cup proved the turning point. Following five successive defeats in a dismal T20 Blast campaign, Maynard opted to build his 50-over side around a nucleus of young talent. The 20-over team beaten by Kent at Canterbury in July had an average age of nearly 32; by the start of the Royal London Cup 16 days later, that had become 27. The likes of Adam Hose, Tom Abell and Alex Barrow took a while to get going, but Somerset finished the tournament strongly with three wins, including Yorkshire and finalists Surrey.

Supporters responded positively to the influx of less experienced players, and the confidence gained from the final 50-over games was taken into the last five Championship fixtures. Scoring more consistently, they claimed maximum batting points in four of their last five matches, which brought them 63 in all – and saved the season.

The most reliable batsman throughout the summer was James Hildreth. He notched 1,758 first-class runs – more than anyone in the country – and five centuries, with a top score of 220 not out against Worcestershire. A former England Lions captain, he showed that – now past 30 – he was maturing like a fine Cheddar. Hildreth's best seasons may be ahead of him, if his role model is anything to go by: in his 40th year, Marcus Trescothick hit 1,311 first-class runs, including 153 against Hampshire and 210 not out at Hove, both crucial matches in the fight to avoid relegation. He also had the satisfaction of completing the club's pre-season trip to Spain, the first time he had finished an overseas tour since a stress-related illness forced him to leave England's visit to India in 2005-06. Even so, time was catching up with him: Trescothick required glasses to field and, after a poor T20 Blast, took a break from the white-ball game. In January, he quit as captain after six years; former Australian opener Chris Rogers arrived at his fifth county to lead the four-day team, with Jim Allenby given the limited-overs job.

Peter Trego, in his benefit year, averaged 35 with the bat, claimed 28 wickets, and was another player who saved his best performances for the second half of the season. The 21-year-old Abell, playing regular Championship cricket for the first time, could feel satisfied with 770 first-class runs at 33, including a maiden century, against Hampshire. In contrast, one-day captain Jim Allenby was effective only in the shorter formats, finishing his first summer at Taunton with a top score of 64 in 30 first-class innings.

Craig Overton was the county's leading first-class wicket-taker, with 47, despite being suspended for the final two games of the season after picking up nine penalty points for indiscipline. The ban was enforced in part due to an ugly incident

Tom Shaw, Getty Images

James Hildreth

against Sussex, in which he told the Karachi-born Ashar Zaidi to "go back to your own fucking country". Many, not least Yorkshire – whose captain Andrew Gale had received a longer ban for a similar incident in 2014 – felt he had escaped lightly. His twin Jamie finished with only 16 wickets, but bowled with genuine pace and hostility, and both Overtons were called up to England's one-day squad against New Zealand.

The other seamers performed respectably: Lewis Gregory finished with 41 first-class wickets and Tim Groenewald 39. But the spinners struggled. Pakistani slow left-armer Abdur Rehman was nothing like the force he had been in 2012, and leg-spinner Max Waller was again confined to limited-overs cricket. Ireland's George Dockrell failed to make a single first-team appearance, and was released in September. The one bright spot came after another left-arm spinner, Jack Leach, returned from a bizarre injury and finished the season with 11 for 180 against Warwickshire. He had suffered concussion and a double skull fracture after fainting in his bathroom in the middle of the night. "The physio was worried I might be scared of the ball when batting," he said. "But if anything, I'm more scared going for a wee at night."

The signing of Chris Gayle for the T20 Blast caused major excitement and he lived up to the hype, scoring 328 runs in three innings while being dismissed only once, and walloping 29 sixes. His power hitting helped win two games, but Somerset fell short at home to Kent despite his thrashing 151 not out from 62 balls, and they eventually exited the competition having won only four of their 14 group matches. Gayle will return for six more games in 2016.

Maynard spoke of a lack of backbone when opponents were on top, and responded by signing not just Rogers, but South African Roelof van der Merwe (on a Dutch passport) after a spell at Taunton as a T20 player in 2011. The teenage wicketkeeper Ryan Davies was signed from Kent to fill the void left by Craig Kieswetter's enforced retirement in June, the result of a serious eye injury sustained the previous summer. The most notable departure was Alfonso Thomas, who took more than 550 wickets in all competitions in eight seasons at Somerset.

Championship attendance: 46,654.

SOMERSET RESULTS

All first-class matches – Played 18: Won 4, Lost 7, Drawn 7.
County Championship matches – Played 16: Won 4, Lost 6, Drawn 6.

LV= County Championship, 6th in Division 1;
NatWest T20 Blast, 8th in South Group; Royal London One-Day Cup, 6th in Group A.

COUNTY CHAMPIONSHIP AVERAGES, BATTING AND FIELDING

Cap		Birthplace	M	I	NO	R	HS	100	Avge	Ct/St
2007	J. C. Hildreth	Milton Keynes . . .	16	27	1	1,390	220*	3	53.46	7
1999	M. E. Trescothick . . .	Keynsham†	16	29	1	1,284	210*	3	45.85	28
	T. B. Abell	Taunton†	13	24	4	726	131	1	36.30	5
2007	P. D. Trego	Weston-super-Mare†	16	27	3	871	130*	2	36.29	7
	C. Overton	Barnstaple	11	14	3	320	55	0	29.09	9
	T. L. W. Cooper¶ . . .	Wollongong, Aust. .	13	22	0	581	118	1	26.40	6
	L. Ronchi§	Dannevirke, NZ . . .	4	5	0	121	51	0	24.20	14/3
	J. G. Myburgh¶	Pretoria, SA	10	19	2	411	118	1	24.17	6
	J. Allenby	Perth, Australia . . .	16	27	1	568	64	0	21.84	15
	J. Overton	Barnstaple	8	10	3	146	50	0	20.85	0
	Abdur Rehman§	Sialkot, Pakistan . .	8	13	4	153	55*	0	17.00	1
	M. J. Leach	Taunton†	5	5	2	43	21*	0	14.33	1
2015	L. Gregory	Plymouth	12	19	1	242	32	0	13.44	11
	A. W. R. Barrow	Bath†	6	11	2	120	28	0	13.33	12
2008	A. C. Thomas	Cape Town, SA . . .	7	10	4	79	32*	0	13.16	6
	T. D. Groenewald . . .	Pietermaritzburg, SA	9	16	2	142	34	0	10.14	4
	M. D. Bates	Frimley	6	9	3	53	16	0	8.83	13

† *Born in Somerset.*   § *Official overseas player.*   ¶ *Other non-England-qualified player.*

BOWLING

	Style	O	M	R	W	BB	5I	Avge
C. Overton	RFM	282.2	55	933	43	6-74	1	21.69
A. C. Thomas	RFM	237.4	54	735	29	5-73	1	25.34
M. J. Leach	SLA	145.1	37	391	15	7-106	1	26.06
T. D. Groenewald	RFM	272	47	976	30	4-41	0	32.53
L. Gregory	RFM	341.1	47	1,314	38	6-101	3	34.57
P. D. Trego	RFM	268.3	52	946	26	4-41	0	36.38
J. Allenby	RM	261	70	657	18	3-54	0	36.50
J. Overton	RFM	179.5	32	612	16	4-37	0	38.25
Abdur Rehman	SLA	206.2	34	719	10	2-60	0	71.90

Also bowled: T. B. Abell (RM) 4.4–0–11–1; T. L. W. Cooper (OB) 65–6–226–6; J. G. Myburgh (OB) 55–13–162–3.

LEADING ROYAL LONDON CUP AVERAGES (100 runs/4 wickets)

Batting	Runs	HS	Avge	SR	Ct
T. L. W. Cooper . . .	359	104	59.83	100.56	1
J. C. Hildreth	217	85*	43.40	78.33	3
T. B. Abell	202	80	33.66	65.37	2
P. D. Trego	234	71*	33.42	129.28	2
J. Allenby	139	53*	27.80	75.13	8
C. Overton	100	49	25.00	140.84	1
A. J. Hose	168	46	21.00	75.33	4

Bowling	W	BB	Avge	ER
J. H. Davey	4	2-22	14.75	3.68
C. Overton	12	3-37	20.83	4.95
M. T. C. Waller . . .	5	2-11	22.00	4.45
L. Gregory	9	3-26	22.55	5.38
P. D. Trego	10	4-29	23.60	5.59
M. J. Leach	9	3-52	31.33	4.70
J. Overton	4	3-52	41.25	6.14
T. D. Groenewald .	5	3-53	42.00	4.77

LEADING NATWEST T20 BLAST AVERAGES (100 runs/20 overs)

Batting	Runs	HS	Avge	SR	Ct
C. H. Gayle	328	151*	328.00	**192.94**	1
T. L. W. Cooper	242	84*	26.88	**143.19**	6
J. Allenby	295	89*	29.50	**137.20**	1
J. G. Myburgh ..	207	63	29.57	**124.69**	0
P. D. Trego	222	51	20.18	**122.65**	6
J. C. Hildreth ...	226	51	25.11	**108.65**	3

Bowling	W	BB	Avge	ER
J. Allenby.......	8	3-10	27.37	**7.55**
M. T. C. Waller ..	9	3-17	31.11	**7.56**
Sohail Tanvir	7	2-38	25.42	**8.09**
J. Overton.......	7	2-33	49.85	**9.69**
A. C. Thomas	15	4-37	26.00	**10.17**

FIRST-CLASS COUNTY RECORDS

Highest score for	342	J. L. Langer v Surrey at Guildford	2006
Highest score against	424	A. C. MacLaren (Lancashire) at Taunton	1895
Leading run-scorer	21,142	H. Gimblett (avge 36.96)	1935–54
Best bowling for	10-49	E. J. Tyler v Surrey at Taunton	1895
Best bowling against	10-35	A. Drake (Yorkshire) at Weston-super-Mare	1914
Leading wicket-taker	2,165	J. C. White (avge 18.03)	1909–37
Highest total for	850-7 dec	v Middlesex at Taunton.	2007
Highest total against	811	by Surrey at The Oval	1899
Lowest total for	25	v Gloucestershire at Bristol.	1947
Lowest total against	22	by Gloucestershire at Bristol.	1920

LIST A COUNTY RECORDS

Highest score for	184	M. E. Trescothick v Gloucestershire at Taunton .	2008
Highest score against	167*	A. J. Stewart (Surrey) at The Oval	1994
Leading run-scorer	7,374	M. E. Trescothick (avge 36.87).	1993–2014
Best bowling for	8-66	S. R. G. Francis v Derbyshire at Derby.	2004
Best bowling against	7-39	A. Hodgson (Northamptonshire) at Northampton .	1976
Leading wicket-taker	309	H. R. Moseley (avge 20.03)	1971–82
Highest total for	413-4	v Devon at Torquay.	1990
Highest total against	383-7	by Kent at Taunton	2014
Lowest total for	58	v Essex at Chelmsford.	1977
	58	v Middlesex at Southgate	2000
Lowest total against	60	by Kent at Taunton	1979

TWENTY20 COUNTY RECORDS

Highest score for	**151***	**C. H. Gayle v Kent at Taunton**	**2015**
Highest score against	**122***	**J. J. Roy (Surrey) at The Oval**..............	**2015**
Leading run-scorer	**2,604**	**J. C. Hildreth (avge 23.67)**	**2004–15**
Best bowling for	6-5	A. V. Suppiah v Glamorgan at Cardiff	2011
Best bowling against	5-18	O. P. Rayner (Sussex) at Hove	2011
Leading wicket-taker	**137**	**A. C. Thomas (avge 20.17)**	**2008–15**
Highest total for	250-3	v Gloucestershire at Taunton	2006
Highest total against	227-4	by Gloucestershire at Bristol.	2006
	227-7	**by Kent at Taunton**	**2015**
Lowest total for	82	v Kent at Taunton	2010
Lowest total against	73	by Warwickshire at Taunton	2013

ADDRESS

County Ground, St James's Street, Taunton TA1 1JT; 0845 337 1875;
enquiries@somersetcountycc.co.uk; www.somersetcountycc.co.uk.

OFFICIALS

Captain 2015 M. E. Trescothick
2016 C. J. L. Rogers
(limited-overs) J. Allenby
Director of cricket M. P. Maynard
Assistant coach J. I. D. Kerr
Academy director S. D. Snell

President R. Parsons
Chairman A. J. Nash
Chief executive G. W. Lavender
Chairman, cricket committee V. J. Marks
Head groundsman S. Lee
Scorer G. A. Stickley

SOMERSET v DURHAM MCCU

At Taunton Vale, April 2–4. Drawn. Toss: Somerset. First-class debuts: R. A. M. Gibson, C. M. MacDonell, H. P. S. McInley, E. J. Pollock, D. R. Williams, J. M. Wood. County debut: J. Allenby.

Myburgh's first century for Somerset, a brisk hundred from Hildreth, and an unbeaten fifty on debut by Allenby allowed the county to dominate a game destined for a draw after only 11 overs were bowled on the first day. Myburgh, who went to the crease in the second over, batted on all three days as bad weather intervened again before the declaration. Cameron Steel responded with a nuggety 80, but much of the Durham MCCU line-up was blown away before the end.

Close of play: first day, Somerset 49-1 (Trescothick 21, Myburgh 22); second day, Somerset 264-3 (Myburgh 115, Allenby 2).

Somerset

*M. E. Trescothick b Wood	27
T. B. Abell c Steele b Wood	0
J. G. Myburgh not out	150
J. C. Hildreth c Williams b Bishnoi	102
J. Allenby not out	54
L-b 3, n-b 18	21

1/2 (2) 2/90 (1) (3 wkts dec, 70.5 overs) 354
3/262 (4)

†A. W. R. Barrow, P. D. Trego, L. Gregory, A. J. Dibble, J. Overton and M. J. Leach did not bat.

Jenkins 9–0–61–0; Wood 10–3–32–2; MacDonell 12–1–71–0; McInley 11–3–38–0; Bishnoi 13.5–2–55–1; Williams 12–0–83–0; Ratnayake 3–0–11–0.

Durham MCCU

C. M. MacDonell c Trescothick b Gregory	0	D. E. M. Ratnayake not out	0
R. A. M. Gibson c Leach b Trego	5	J. M. Wood not out	0
*C. T. Steel c Barrow b Leach	80	B 4, l-b 8, n-b 2	14
C. Bishnoi c Allenby b Gregory	1		
W. H. Jenkins c Leach b Gregory	12	1/0 (1) 2/8 (2) (7 wkts dec, 51 overs) 129
†O. J. Steele b Overton	2	3/9 (4) 4/52 (5)
E. J. Pollock c Barrow b Trego	15	5/76 (6) 6/129 (3) 7/129 (7)

H. P. S. McInley and D. R. Williams did not bat.

Gregory 13–6–37–3; Trego 10–5–16–2; Overton 9–4–21–1; Dibble 5–1–21–0; Allenby 5–3–2–0; Leach 7–4–17–1; Myburgh 2–1–3–0.

Umpires: I. D. Blackwell and A. G. Wharf.

SOMERSET v DURHAM

At Taunton, April 12–14. Durham won by seven wickets. Durham 23pts, Somerset 5pts. Toss: Somerset. County debut: T. L. W. Cooper.

A three-day defeat was hardly the outcome Matthew Maynard was looking for in his first competitive match as Somerset's director of cricket. Collingwood was "more surprised than anyone" to play a leading role with ball, as well as bat – tipping the contest with only his second first-class five-wicket haul, after Somerset had reached 224 for two on the opening day. Myburgh struck the first century of the new Championship season but, after a partnership of 93 with Tom Cooper – the Australian-born Netherlands international – Somerset were flummoxed as Collingwood wobbled the old ball about, and slumped to 299 all out. Borthwick and Collingwood, with his 20th first-class hundred for Durham, then pressed home the advantage, guiding them to a useful first-innings lead of 81. Although Coughlin pulled up with a side strain, Rushworth – who took his 200th first-class wicket – and Onions gave the home bowlers a lesson in line and length. Somerset's partial recovery from 96 for eight, thanks to a defiant 99-run stand between Trego and Abdur Rehman, was insufficient to stretch Durham. Borthwick knocked off the target with his second half-century of the game.

Close of play: first day, Durham 98-2 (Borthwick 52, Richardson 35); second day, Somerset 54-4 (Allenby 4, Barrow 28).

Somerset

*M. E. Trescothick c Collingwood b Onions	11	– b Rushworth	0
J. G. Myburgh c Richardson b Collingwood	118	– lbw b Rushworth	9
T. L. W. Cooper lbw b Coughlin	47	– c Mustard b Onions	5
J. C. Hildreth lbw b Collingwood	53	– c Borthwick b Rushworth	8
J. Allenby c Stoneman b Collingwood	8	– lbw b Rushworth	9
†A. W. R. Barrow b Collingwood	4	– b Rushworth	28
P. D. Trego lbw b Collingwood	0	– c and b Onions	79
L. Gregory c Mustard b Onions	13	– c Borthwick b Rushworth	0
T. D. Groenewald c Richardson b Onions	9	– c MacLeod b Hastings	9
Abdur Rehman c Borthwick b Onions	16	– not out	55
J. Overton not out	8	– b Collingwood	14
L-b 2, n-b 10	12	B 9, l-b 3, n-b 2	14

1/30 (1) 2/123 (3) 3/224 (2) (75 overs) 299
4/245 (4) 5/249 (6) 6/249 (7)
7/266 (5) 8/270 (8) 9/280 (9) 10/299 (10)

1/3 (1) 2/10 (2) (59.4 overs) 230
3/18 (3) 4/26 (4)
5/54 (6) 6/71 (5) 7/71 (8)
8/96 (9) 9/195 (7) 10/230 (11)

Onions 19-4-59-4; Rushworth 15-2-52-0; Coughlin 13-5-41-1; Hastings 12-2-58-0; Collingwood 12-0-57-5; Borthwick 4-0-30-0. *Second innings*—Onions 20.1-7-54-2; Rushworth 22-5-92-6; Borthwick 1-0-6-0; Coughlin 5.5-1-24-0; Collingwood 2.4-0-20-1; Hastings 8-0-22-1.

Durham

M. D. Stoneman c Hildreth b Gregory	4	– c Hildreth b Overton	26
K. K. Jennings c Barrow b Gregory	0	– c Allenby b Abdur Rehman	26
S. G. Borthwick lbw b Overton	94	– not out	51
M. J. Richardson c Barrow b Gregory	59	– c Allenby b Groenewald	28
C. S. MacLeod lbw b Groenewald	44	– not out	14
*P. D. Collingwood not out	109		
†P. Mustard c Barrow b Trego	22		
P. Coughlin c Trego b Gregory	18		
J. W. Hastings c and b Groenewald	1		
C. Rushworth c Hildreth b Gregory	7		
G. Onions b Trego	1		
B 16, l-b 3, n-b 2	21	L-b 3, n-b 2	5

1/4 (2) 2/13 (1) 3/157 (4) (92.5 overs) 380
4/190 (3) 5/238 (5) 6/280 (7)
7/347 (8) 8/348 (9) 9/373 (10) 10/380 (11)

1/53 (2) (3 wkts, 32.3 overs) 150
2/53 (1) 3/106 (4)

Trego 14.5-1-58-2; Gregory 21-0-99-5; Groenewald 20-4-84-2; Overton 13-1-48-1; Abdur Rehman 14-2-45-0; Allenby 10-2-27-0. *Second innings*—Trego 3-1-9-0; Gregory 7-0-38-0; Groenewald 6-1-30-1; Overton 6-0-27-1; Abdur Rehman 10.3-2-43-1.

Umpires: M. R. Benson and N. G. C. Cowley.

SOMERSET v MIDDLESEX

At Taunton, April 26–29. Middlesex won by five wickets. Middlesex 22pts, Somerset 8pts. Toss: Middlesex. County debut: J. E. C. Franklin.

For the second time in a row, Somerset contrived to lose from a formidable first-innings position, as Voges and Franklin inspired Middlesex to the third-highest successful run-chase at Taunton. After Voges had been seduced into bowling first on a deceptively green surface, Trescothick bludgeoned 16 fours and a six before lunch, as he and Hildreth took advantage of a short boundary towards the retirement flats, galloping to big centuries at five an over. But, from 377 for three, Somerset surrendered their last seven wickets for 31 either side of the new ball, with the rejuvenated Harris sweeping up four for seven in 18 deliveries. In all, five batsmen made ducks. Gubbins and Voges replied with a third-wicket stand of 139, but a lengthy break for rain and bad light on the second afternoon played into Somerset's hands: Gregory and a fired-up Jamie Overton shared five wickets in the evening session. With a back spasm removing Murtagh from the action, Somerset were able to set a target of 402 from 103 overs. But Overton limped off with a heel injury in his second over, and was unable to play any part on the last day, when the other Somerset bowlers lacked bite. Voges put on 92 with Gubbins, then a pivotal 200 in 56 overs with Franklin, the former New Zealand all-rounder making his Middlesex debut on an Irish passport. Simpson struck the winning runs with seven balls to spare – a year and a day after Middlesex had chased down 472 to beat Yorkshire at Lord's.

Close of play: first day, Middlesex 10-0 (Robson 5, Gubbins 5); second day, Middlesex 306-7 (Franklin 41, Harris 5); third day, Middlesex 31-0 (Gubbins 8, Robson 15).

Somerset

*M. E. Trescothick c Harris b Voges	140	– b Rayner		76
T. B. Abell b Murtagh	16	– b Harris		13
T. L. W. Cooper lbw b Harris	0	– b Rayner		42
J. C. Hildreth c Franklin b Harris	187	– c Voges b Finn		86
J. Allenby c Simpson b Harris	23	– lbw b Harris		28
†A. W. R. Barrow c Rayner b Harris	0	– c Rayner b Harris		4
P. D. Trego c Voges b Harris	0	– b Finn		25
L. Gregory c Finn b Murtagh	5	– c sub (N. A. Sowter) b Rayner		12
T. D. Groenewald c Voges b Finn	0	– run out		5
Abdur Rehman c Compton b Finn	0	– not out		1
J. Overton not out	4	– b Finn		6
B 14, l-b 11, w 2, n-b 6	33	B 8, n-b 4		12

1/50 (2) 2/51 (3) 3/312 (1) (89.2 overs) 408   1/26 (2) 2/108 (3) (80.3 overs) 310
4/377 (5) 5/391 (6) 6/397 (7)   3/159 (1) 4/196 (5)
7/400 (4) 8/404 (9) 9/404 (8) 10/408 (10)   5/206 (6) 6/254 (7) 7/289 (8)
   8/297 (9) 9/304 (10) 10/310 (11)

Murtagh 17–4–62–2; Finn 21.2–3–82–2; Harris 18–1–83–5; Dexter 6–1–31–0; Franklin 6–0–45–0; Rayner 16–1–61–0; Voges 5–0–19–1. *Second innings*—Finn 17.3–3–66–3; Harris 18–2–64–3; Dexter 11–2–48–0; Rayner 28–3–90–3; Franklin 4–0–25–0; Voges 2–0–9–0.

Middlesex

S. D. Robson c Trescothick b Gregory	5	– (2) c Trescothick b Gregory		15
N. R. T. Gubbins c Trescothick b Overton	92	– (1) b Abdur Rehman		78
N. R. D. Compton c Barrow b Gregory	28	– b Gregory		4
*A. C. Voges lbw b Gregory	98	– c Barrow b Groenewald		132
J. E. C. Franklin lbw b Gregory	46	– not out		115
N. J. Dexter c and b Gregory	7	– b Abdur Rehman		11
†J. A. Simpson b Overton	13	– not out		18
O. P. Rayner b Overton	0			
J. A. R. Harris not out	7			
S. T. Finn lbw b Gregory	4			
T. J. Murtagh absent hurt				
B 10, l-b 7	17	B 13, l-b 14, w 5		32

1/10 (1) 2/60 (3) 3/199 (2) (87 overs) 317   1/37 (2) (5 wkts, 101.5 overs) 405
4/246 (4) 5/256 (6) 6/297 (7)   2/45 (3) 3/137 (1)
7/297 (8) 8/313 (5) 9/317 (10)

Gregory 23–1–101–6; Groenewald 18–2–64–0; Abdur Rehman 13–1–39–0; Trego 9–1–25–0; Overton 13–1–45–3; Allenby 9–2–20–0; Cooper 2–0–6–0. *Second innings*—Gregory 27–2–100–2; Overton 1.1–0–1–0; Groenewald 19.5–5–78–1; Trego 10–0–55–0; Abdur Rehman 29.5–4–100–2; Allenby 8–0–25–0; Cooper 6–0–19–0.

Umpires: R. A. Kettleborough and A. G. Wharf.

At Worcester, May 3–5. SOMERSET lost to WORCESTERSHIRE by an innings and 62 runs.

At Taunton, May 8–11. SOMERSET lost to NEW ZEALANDERS by 66 runs (see New Zealand tour section).

At Nottingham, May 17–19. SOMERSET beat NOTTINGHAMSHIRE by 133 runs.

SOMERSET v YORKSHIRE

At Taunton, May 24–27. Drawn. Somerset 12pts, Yorkshire 13pts. Toss: Somerset.

A trying week for Jason Gillespie – who learned on the second morning that Trevor Bayliss had beaten him to the post of England's new head coach – ended in relief when Yorkshire strung together a last-day rearguard to preserve their unbeaten Championship record. Not for the first time, a true Taunton surface had the final say. Yorkshire had put aside the England hubbub to make a good start, with Leaning scoring a responsible career-best hundred, and Bairstow and Bresnan tearing into an all-seam attack. (Somerset had been required to de-register the Pakistani spinner Abdur Rehman, in order to name Chris Gayle and Sohail Tanvir as their two overseas players in the Twenty20 competition two days later, yet still omitted the eligible George Dockrell.) One blow by Bresnan over midwicket struck Mel Pillar, a spectator from Cardiff, on the head; he required four stitches, but returned bandaged next day, when Bresnan presented him with the signed ball. Except for Patterson, Yorkshire bowled loosely, and the Overton twins thrashed 76 from six overs for the last wicket, with Jamie's 18-ball half-century the fastest by a No. 11 in the Championship since 1983 (when balls replaced minutes as the measure for quick scoring). Their efforts, after Cooper had been strangled down the leg side on 99, put Somerset in front. Craig Overton then found reverse to take three wickets in 19 balls, leaving Yorkshire effectively 70 for five after tea on the third day. But Bairstow and Rashid, who also fell for 99, doubled the score from 117, and solid contributions down the order made sure of Yorkshire's survival.

Close of play: first day, Yorkshire 345-8 (Bresnan 56); second day, Somerset 309-4 (Cooper 55, Thomas 4); third day, Yorkshire 171-5 (Bairstow 33, Rashid 23).

Yorkshire

A. Z. Lees lbw b Trego	34	– c Barrow b Trego	1
W. M. H. Rhodes c Cooper b J. Overton	28	– c Allenby b Myburgh	40
J. A. Leaning b Trego	123	– c Hildreth b C. Overton	52
*A. W. Gale c Allenby b Trego	22	– c Trescothick b C. Overton	12
†J. M. Bairstow c Trescothick b C. Overton	50	– c Barrow b Thomas	66
G. J. Maxwell c Abell b C. Overton	4	– b C. Overton	2
A. U. Rashid b Thomas	9	– c Thomas b Myburgh	99
T. T. Bresnan not out	100	– lbw b Myburgh	29
L. E. Plunkett lbw b Thomas	0	– run out	21
S. A. Patterson c Barrow b Trego	42	– not out	44
J. A. Brooks c Barrow b C. Overton	0	– c Barrow b Abell	24
B 10, l-b 18, n-b 2	30	B 10, l-b 12, w 1, n-b 6	29

1/55 (1) 2/79 (2) 3/118 (4)   (114.2 overs) 438
4/211 (5) 5/211 (6) 6/225 (7)
7/344 (3) 8/345 (9) 9/437 (10)
10/438 (11)

1/5 (1) 2/82 (2)   (146.4 overs) 419
3/108 (3) 4/109 (4)
5/117 (6) 6/234 (5) 7/323 (8)
8/331 (7) 9/355 (9) 10/419 (11)

110 overs: 412-8

Thomas 26–7–90–2; J. Overton 18–4–78–1; Trego 19–6–73–4; C. Overton 22.2–4–74–3; Allenby 22–5–61–0; Myburgh 3–0–18–0; Cooper 4–0–16–0. *Second innings*—Thomas 18–3–57–1; Trego 19–3–57–1; C. Overton 24–3–73–3; J. Overton 21–4–60–0; Allenby 19–6–36–0; Myburgh 28–10–57–3; Cooper 13–1–46–0; Abell 4.4–0–11–1.

Somerset

*M. E. Trescothick c Bairstow b Patterson	56	– c Plunkett b Maxwell	4
T. B. Abell c Bresnan b Rashid	62	– not out	1
J. G. Myburgh lbw b Patterson	41	– not out	1
J. C. Hildreth c and b Rashid	82		
T. L. W. Cooper c Bairstow b Plunkett	99		
A. C. Thomas b Plunkett	4		
J. Allenby b Patterson	31		
P. D. Trego b Patterson	10		
†A. W. R. Barrow c Bairstow b Patterson	0		
C. Overton not out	31		
J. Overton c Bresnan b Rashid	50		
B 4, l-b 2, w 1, n-b 12	19		

1/84 (1) 2/163 (2) 3/165 (3)   (102.4 overs) 485   1/5 (1)   (1 wkt, 2 overs)   6
4/294 (4) 5/311 (6) 6/369 (7)
7/387 (8) 8/389 (9) 9/409 (5) 10/485 (11)

Bresnan 11–1–69–0; Brooks 19–4–88–0; Plunkett 23–4–101–2; Patterson 23–10–70–5; Rashid 20.4–0–121–3; Rhodes 4–1–13–0; Maxwell 2–0–17–0. *Second innings*—Bresnan 1–0–4–0; Maxwell 1–0–2–1.

Umpires: P. K. Baldwin and D. J. Millns.

At Chester-le-Street, June 7–9. SOMERSET lost to DURHAM by 120 runs.

SOMERSET v NOTTINGHAMSHIRE

At Taunton, June 14–17. Somerset won by two wickets. Somerset 20pts, Nottinghamshire 8pts. Toss: Nottinghamshire. First-class debut: M. Carter. County debut: M. D. Bates. Championship debut: B. W. Hilfenhaus.

For the second time in two months, a Taunton pitch proved conducive to a large run-chase, as Nottinghamshire passed up the chance to win here for the first time in 30 years. Their top order had prospered, with Brendan Taylor making a near-faultless 152, ended by a superlative slip catch from

BEST BOWLING FIGURES ON CHAMPIONSHIP DEBUT SINCE 1918

8-187	H. H. Jarrett	Warwickshire v Leicestershire at Hinckley	1932
7-32	J. A. Bailey	Essex v Nottinghamshire at Southend	1953
7-36	K. Higgs	Lancashire v Hampshire at Manchester	1958
7-46	J. E. Walsh	Leicestershire v Northamptonshire at Leicester	1938
7-50	P. M. Hutchison	Yorkshire v Hampshire at Portsmouth	1997
7-50	S. P. Kirby	Yorkshire v Kent at Leeds	2001
7-56	**M. Carter**	**Nottinghamshire v Somerset at Taunton**	**2015**
7-60	J. E. C. Franklin	Gloucestershire v Lancashire at Cheltenham	2004
7-63	A. J. G. Pearson	Somerset v Worcestershire at Bristol	1961
7-88	M. F. Malone	Lancashire v Nottinghamshire at Blackpool	1979

J. E. B. B. P. Q. C. Dwyer holds the all-time record: 9-35 for Sussex v Derbyshire at Hove in 1906.

Trescothick, who grabbed the ball low to his left when it was slightly past him. The 19-year-old Matt Carter then found surprising turn and bounce for his off-spin from the River End, wreaking havoc with 16–2–56–7, the second-best figures on Championship debut for Nottinghamshire, after Richard Hardstaff in 1894. Stand-in captain Wessels, expecting the wicket to turn even more on the last day, declined to enforce the follow-on with a lead of 210, and Nottinghamshire slipped to 95 for six before Patel and the lower order lifted the target to 401. That required Somerset to achieve their second-highest chase at Taunton, after their own 476 to beat Yorkshire in 2009 (Middlesex had scored 405 here in April). They were not fazed: Trescothick and Abell began with a stand of 129, Allenby and Trego added 116 for the sixth wicket, and Somerset were left needing 20 from the last two partnerships. Bates, the former Hampshire wicketkeeper replacing the out-of-form Alex Barrow, held up an end, and Abdur Rehman struck Carter for three fours in four balls to finish the job.

Close of play: first day, Nottinghamshire 391-6 (Wessels 59, Wood 11); second day, Nottinghamshire 89-4 (Wessels 28, Wood 0); third day, Somerset 274-5 (Allenby 32, Trego 26).

Nottinghamshire

S. J. Mullaney b Abdur Rehman	42	– c Cooper b Abdur Rehman	34
B. R. M. Taylor c Trescothick b Thomas	152	– lbw b Groenewald	7
G. P. Smith b Thomas	11	– b Allenby	12
M. J. Lumb c Allenby b Abdur Rehman	73	– lbw b Allenby	6
*†M. H. Wessels c Thomas b Groenewald	63	– lbw b Groenewald	28
S. R. Patel lbw b Thomas	0	– (7) c Thomas b Abdur Rehman	46
W. R. S. Gidman c Trescothick b Thomas	20	– (8) c and b Groenewald	22
L. Wood c Myburgh b Groenewald	16	– (6) b Thomas	1
B. W. Hilfenhaus not out	0	– not out	12
M. Carter b Thomas	0	– run out	11
J. T. Ball b Groenewald	0	– b Thomas	4
B 12, l-b 9, n-b 2	23	L-b 2, w 1, n-b 4	7

1/82 (1) 2/109 (3) 3/266 (4)   (104.4 overs) 410   1/12 (2) 2/34 (3)   (52.2 overs) 190
4/300 (2) 5/300 (6) 6/370 (7)   3/53 (4) 4/87 (1)
7/399 (8) 8/402 (5) 9/409 (10) 10/410 (11)   5/89 (5) 6/95 (6) 7/143 (8)
                                             8/163 (7) 9/186 (10) 10/190 (11)

Thomas 24–4–73–5; Groenewald 22.4–5–92–3; Trego 8–2–37–0; Abdur Rehman 28–2–129–2; Myburgh 11–1–34–0; Allenby 11–5–24–0. *Second innings*—Thomas 12.2–3–43–2; Groenewald 13–1–65–3; Allenby 8–3–13–2; Abdur Rehman 16–4–60–2; Trego 2–0–6–0; Cooper 1–0–1–0.

Somerset

*M. E. Trescothick c Taylor b Wood	16	– c and b Patel	65
T. B. Abell not out	76	– c Mullaney b Gidman	72
J. G. Myburgh b Wood	0	– c Mullaney b Carter	56
J. C. Hildreth c Wessels b Carter	41	– c Carter b Gidman	4
T. L. W. Cooper c Hilfenhaus b Carter	8	– c Patel b Carter	0
J. Allenby b Carter	0	– lbw b Patel	62
P. D. Trego b Ball	0	– c Mullaney b Carter	79
†M. D. Bates c Patel b Carter	1	– (9) not out	14
A. C. Thomas c Taylor b Carter	8		
Abdur Rehman c Ball b Carter	25	– not out	15
T. D. Groenewald c Wood b Carter	14	– (8) lbw b Patel	13
B 4, l-b 3, n-b 4	11	B 6, l-b 10, n-b 6	22

1/24 (1) 2/24 (3) 3/112 (4)   (53 overs) 200   1/129 (1)   (8 wkts, 107.4 overs) 402
4/132 (5) 5/135 (6) 6/142 (7)   2/197 (2) 3/201 (4)
7/143 (8) 8/153 (9) 9/183 (10) 10/200 (11)   4/210 (5) 5/243 (3)
                                             6/359 (6) 7/365 (7) 8/381 (8)

Wood 10–0–44–2; Hilfenhaus 14–4–42–0; Ball 10–1–32–1; Carter 16–2–56–7; Patel 3–0–19–0. *Second innings*—Wood 10–0–50–0; Hilfenhaus 19–4–57–0; Carter 33.4–4–139–3; Ball 14–2–54–0; Patel 20–2–57–3; Gidman 11–2–29–2.

Umpires: M. R. Benson and S. A. Garratt.

At Southampton, June 21–23. SOMERSET beat HAMPSHIRE by nine wickets.

SOMERSET v SUSSEX

At Taunton, July 5–8. Drawn. Somerset 10pts, Sussex 9pts. Toss: Somerset.

A third-wicket partnership of 290 between Machan and Nash in Sussex's second innings turned this game on its head. Machan's 192 from 237 deliveries was a career-best and Nash's unbeaten 142 ensured it was Somerset feeling the heat in the closing stages. The home bowlers had exploited a green and variable pitch on a rain-affected first day, with Thomas and Gregory sharing seven wickets as Sussex were restricted to a single batting point. Somerset teetered to 36 for four, before Hildreth and Trego – irked by sledging – counter-attacked in characteristic fashion, each striking ten fours and a six in a stand of 163. Craig Overton's 53 off 44 balls – during which he suffered concussion after ducking into a bouncer from Hobden, keeping him out of the next Championship game – earned Somerset a useful first-innings lead. But Joyce responded with 66, and the excellence of Machan and Nash, rounded off by five sixes in a 12-ball thrash from Wright, left them facing an impossible 425 in what became 68 overs. At 84 for five, they appeared to be slipping to defeat, until Trego defied his instincts to put on a patient 120 with Gregory, and shepherd them to safety.

Close of play: first day, Sussex 145-6 (Wright 9, Magoffin 0); second day, Somerset 176-4 (Hildreth 63, Trego 71); third day, Sussex 311-2 (Machan 137, Nash 76).

Sussex

*E. C. Joyce c Bates b Gregory	28	– (2) c Thomas b Trego	66
L. W. P. Wells lbw b Trego	54	– (1) c Allenby b Thomas	9
M. W. Machan c Allenby b Gregory	0	– b Abdur Rehman	192
C. D. Nash b Overton	35	– not out	142
C. Cachopa c Allenby b Trego	8	– lbw b Abdur Rehman	6
L. J. Wright c Thomas b Gregory	51	– not out	39
†B. C. Brown c Trescothick b Thomas	9		
S. J. Magoffin c Trescothick b Thomas	5		
Ashar Zaidi c Bates b Thomas	14		
O. E. Robinson not out	1		
M. E. Hobden c Bates b Thomas	0		
L-b 1, n-b 2	3	B 13, l-b 4, w 3, n-b 16	36

1/56 (1) 2/56 (3) 3/113 (4)   (84.2 overs) 208   1/28 (1)   (4 wkts dec, 98 overs) 490
4/122 (5) 5/129 (6) 6/138 (7)   2/150 (4) 3/440 (3)
7/154 (8) 8/202 (9) 9/208 (6) 10/208 (11)   4/448 (5)

Thomas 24.2–10–46–4; Gregory 19–3–58–3; Overton 18–5–55–1; Allenby 8–2–16–0; Trego 15–6–32–2. *Second innings*—Thomas 19–0–70–1; Gregory 19–0–101–0; Overton 7–2–32–0; Abdur Rehman 26–3–121–2; Trego 11–1–75–1; Myburgh 11–1–46–0; Allenby 5–0–28–0.

Somerset

*M. E. Trescothick c Nash b Magoffin	8	– b Wells	33
T. B. Abell c Brown b Robinson	16	– c Nash b Wells	36
J. G. Myburgh lbw b Hobden	9	– c Machan b Wells	6
J. C. Hildreth c Joyce b Robinson	82	– c and b Ashar Zaidi	1
J. Allenby c Brown b Robinson	0	– c Joyce b Ashar Zaidi	4
P. D. Trego b Robinson	81	– not out	95
L. Gregory c Wright b Magoffin	0	– c Wright b Robinson	32
†M. D. Bates c Nash b Magoffin	0	– not out	0
C. Overton not out	53		
Abdur Rehman c Wells b Hobden	11		
A. C. Thomas st Brown b Wells	4		
B 1, l-b 7, n-b 2	10	B 1	1

1/12 (1) 2/33 (2) 3/33 (3)   (73.5 overs) 274   1/69 (1)   (6 wkts, 67.3 overs) 208
4/36 (5) 5/199 (6) 6/200 (7)   2/75 (3) 3/76 (4)
7/200 (8) 8/232 (4) 9/259 (10) 10/274 (11)   4/80 (2) 5/84 (5) 6/204 (7)

Magoffin 20–3–61–3; Robinson 22–5–79–4; Hobden 14–1–71–2; Ashar Zaidi 10–2–29–0; Wells 7.5–1–26–1. *Second innings*—Magoffin 11–4–32–0; Robinson 12–1–39–1; Hobden 8–0–35–0; Nash 7–0–29–0; Wells 18.3–3–56–3; Ashar Zaidi 11–7–16–2.

Umpires: S. A. Garratt and S. J. O'Shaughnessy.

At Merchant Taylors' School, Northwood, July 11–14. SOMERSET drew with MIDDLESEX.

At Birmingham, July 18–21. SOMERSET lost to WARWICKSHIRE by seven wickets.

SOMERSET v WORCESTERSHIRE

At Taunton, August 21–24. Drawn. Somerset 11pts, Worcestershire 6pts. Toss: Worcestershire.
Somerset were the happier of these two relegation-threatened sides, though bad weather blighted the last three days. Trescothick had lost the toss but in helpful bowling conditions, produced a masterclass to see off the new ball alongside Cooper, and clear the way for the middle-order strokemakers. Hildreth's glorious double-century, crowned by an unbroken stand of 221 with Trego in 44 overs, confirmed this was one of the best seasons of his life. Worcestershire lurched to 33 for four when Jack Leach – replacing overseas spinner Abdur Rehman, who had been let go early from his contract – removed Mitchell with his first ball of the Championship season. Somerset's players rushed to congratulate him, but the mood changed when Jamie Overton hobbled away from a celebratory pile-up with a leg injury, and had go off for treatment. Shortly afterwards, a storm wiped out the evening session. Overton returned to bowl the following day, when Whiteley and Cox took their stand to 139 in the 22 overs possible. But more rain set in overnight, denying Worcestershire the chance to chalk up any batting points.
Close of play: first day, Somerset 349-5 (Hildreth 133, Trego 4); second day, Worcestershire 44-4 (Whiteley 8, Cox 8); third day, Worcestershire 172-4 (Whiteley 78, Cox 52).

Somerset

*M. E. Trescothick b D'Oliveira	85		P. D. Trego not out		130
J. G. Myburgh lbw b Shantry	0		B 4, l-b 11, w 1, n-b 2		18
T. L. W. Cooper c Gidman b Leach	57				
J. C. Hildreth not out	220		1/8 (2)	(5 wkts dec, 138.4 overs)	565
J. Allenby c Cox b Shantry	50		2/116 (3) 3/209 (1)		
M. J. Leach b Leach	5		4/331 (5) 5/344 (6)	110 overs: 416-5	

L. Gregory, †M. D. Bates, C. Overton and J. Overton did not bat.

Leach 25–4–111–2; Shantry 27.4–8–84–2; Morris 26–4–83–0; Saeed Ajmal 29–3–112–0; Whiteley 13–1–79–0; D'Oliveira 18–2–81–1.

Worcestershire

*D. K. H. Mitchell c Bates b Leach	13		†O. B. Cox not out		52
B. L. D'Oliveira c Trescothick b C. Overton	0		B 8, l-b 2, n-b 8		18
T. C. Fell c Allenby b Gregory	11				
A. P. R. Gidman b Gregory	0		1/0 (2) 2/15 (3)	(4 wkts, 41 overs)	172
R. A. Whiteley not out	78		3/15 (4) 4/33 (1)		

J. M. Clarke, J. Leach, J. D. Shantry, Saeed Ajmal and C. A. J. Morris did not bat.

Gregory 16–5–61–2; C. Overton 12–2–59–1; J. Overton 10–3–35–0; Leach 2–0–5–1; Trego 1–0–2–0.

Umpires: M. J. D. Bodenham and J. H. Evans.

At Leeds, September 1–3. SOMERSET lost to YORKSHIRE by an innings and 126 runs.

SOMERSET v HAMPSHIRE

At Taunton, September 9–12. Drawn. Somerset 13pts, Hampshire 7pts. Toss: Somerset.
Hampshire went into the match buoyant after back-to-back wins, but quickly found themselves battling to stay in touch. They were bowled out for 240 by tea, with New Zealand wicketkeeper Luke Ronchi, on home Championship debut, equalling Rob Turner's Somerset record for most dismissals in an innings with seven catches. Jamie Overton's pace – and his direct hit from the deep to run out Adams as he ambled a third – proved Hampshire's undoing. Somerset raced to 147 without loss by the close, and next morning Trescothick celebrated his decision to stay on for a 24th season with another century, while chivvying 21-year-old Abell along to his first, celebrated raucously;

Trescothick passed 1,000 first-class runs in a season for the seventh time. Cooper added a maiden Championship hundred as Somerset cruised to 551 for three, before a late flurry of wickets included Edwards's 300th first-class scalp. But, armed with a first-innings lead of 390, Somerset came up against the familiar problem of bowling visitors out a second time on a prime Taunton strip, despite having more than five sessions at their disposal. Adams scored his first hundred of a difficult benefit season – helped by a bad miss from Allenby at slip when 94 – and dug in for more than six and a half hours. The rest of the top six followed his example as Hampshire, second-bottom in the table, comfortably batted out a draw, but now trailed Somerset and Sussex by 11 points with two rounds to go.

Close of play: first day, Somerset 147-0 (Trescothick 67, Abell 70); second day, Somerset 569-5 (Allenby 39, Ronchi 11); third day, Hampshire 258-1 (Adams 117, Vince 69).

Hampshire

M. A. Carberry c Ronchi b J. Overton	59	– lbw b Leach	56
J. H. K. Adams run out	7	– c Ronchi b Trego	136
*J. M. Vince c Allenby b Gregory	60	– c Abell b C. Overton	77
W. R. Smith c Ronchi b Allenby	21	– c sub (C. G. Harrison) b Cooper	50
L. A. Dawson b J. Overton	48	– not out	44
S. M. Ervine c Ronchi b Allenby	4	– not out	13
†A. J. A. Wheater c Ronchi b Allenby	0		
R. McLaren c Ronchi b C. Overton	18		
G. K. Berg c Ronchi b J. Overton	8		
M. S. Crane c Ronchi b J. Overton	0		
F. H. Edwards not out	0		
B 9, l-b 6	15	B 28, l-b 5, n-b 2	35

1/49 (2) 2/117 (1) 3/146 (3)	(62.4 overs) 240	1/143 (1)	(4 wkts, 159 overs) 411
4/172 (4) 5/176 (6) 6/176 (7)		2/271 (4) 3/314 (2)	
7/203 (8) 8/227 (9) 9/227 (10) 10/240 (5)		4/386 (4)	

Gregory 13–3–41–1; C. Overton 11–2–60–1; Trego 12–3–27–0; J. Overton 10.4–2–37–4; Allenby 14–3–54–3; Leach 2–0–6–0. *Second innings*—Gregory 22–8–56–0; C. Overton 24–3–95–1; J. Overton 19–8–23–0; Leach 51–19–116–1; Allenby 14–7–15–0; Cooper 21–1–62–1; Trego 8–5–11–1.

Somerset

*M. E. Trescothick b Edwards	153	C. Overton c Dawson	24
T. B. Abell lbw b Berg	131	J. Overton b Dawson	4
T. L. W. Cooper c Ervine b Dawson	118	B 5, l-b 14, w 7, n-b 26	52
J. C. Hildreth b Dawson	71		
J. Allenby not out	56	1/272 (2)	(9 wkts dec, 136.5 overs) 630
P. D. Trego c Smith b Dawson	2	2/341 (1) 3/483 (3)	
†L. Ronchi lbw b Edwards	19	4/551 (4) 5/557 (6) 6/578 (7) 7/579 (8)	
L. Gregory c Ervine b Berg	0	8/612 (9) 9/630 (10)	110 overs: 483-3

M. J. Leach did not bat.

Edwards 26–2–123–2; McLaren 23–6–95–0; Berg 23–4–94–2; Ervine 10–2–44–0; Dawson 34.5–1–139–5; Crane 17–0–108–0; Smith 3–0–8–0.

Umpires: J. H. Evans and G. D. Lloyd.

At Hove, September 14–17. SOMERSET drew with SUSSEX.

SOMERSET v WARWICKSHIRE

At Taunton, September 22–25. Somerset won by 17 runs. Somerset 24pts, Warwickshire 6pts. Toss: Somerset. First-class debut: M. R. Adair. Championship debut: F. R. J. Coleman.

After a minute's silence in memory of Brian Close, once a Somerset captain, Trescothick won one of the more important tosses of his career. With Somerset needing seven points to guarantee survival, it meant Warwickshire would have to bat last on a dry pitch which, unusally for Taunton, offered so much assistance to the spinners on the last two days that three of them picked up career-best figures. Hildreth completed the fifth hundred of a prolific summer, while Leach and Jamie Overton secured maximum batting points as they thrashed 61 for the last wicket. And, when Leach dismissed Clarke during a remarkable spell of four wickets for no runs in 13 balls, during which Warwickshire lost five with the score on 105, Somerset clinched their seventh point. Patel led a strong fightback with 98 – smacking four sixes – followed by seven for 38 as a demob-happy Somerset plunged to 110 all out in their second innings, leaving Warwickshire 225 to win and sew up fourth spot. But Leach and Cooper, who claimed five wickets with his occasional off-spin, bowled Somerset to their first victory in eight games, despite Bell's fighting half-century. Leach's match figures of 11 for 180 were comfortably his best in 17 first-class appearances.

Close of play: first day, Somerset 360-5 (Hildreth 118, Ronchi 38); second day, Warwickshire 180-7 (Evans 23, Patel 37); third day, Warwickshire 20-0 (Chopra 13, Westwood 6).

Somerset

*M. E. Trescothick c Ambrose b Adair	87	– c Chopra b Barker	6
T. B. Abell c Ambrose b Hannon-Dalby	4	– b Barker	1
T. L. W. Cooper b Clarke	43	– b Patel	26
J. C. Hildreth lbw b Barker	118	– lbw b Barker	0
J. Allenby c Ambrose b Barker	29	– c Coleman b Patel	10
P. D. Trego c Coleman b Barker	24	– lbw b Patel	4
†L. Ronchi c Clarke b Barker	51	– lbw b Patel	4
L. Gregory c Bell b Clarke	0	– c Evans b Patel	11
A. C. Thomas c Bell b Clarke	4	– not out	13
M. J. Leach not out	21	– (11) c Chopra b Patel	15
J. Overton lbw b Patel	40	– (10) c Clarke b Patel	9
B 5, l-b 3, n-b 4, p 5	17	B 10, l-b 1	11

1/30 (2) 2/98 (3) 3/199 (1)   (100.1 overs) 438
4/254 (5) 5/284 (6) 6/360 (4)
7/365 (8) 8/373 (7) 9/377 (9) 10/438 (11)

1/8 (1) 2/9 (2) 3/9 (4)   (34 overs) 110
4/30 (5) 5/34 (6) 6/44 (7)
7/68 (8) 8/73 (3) 9/83 (10) 10/110 (11)

Barker 24-3-94-4; Hannon-Dalby 19-2-91-1; Patel 23.1-3-88-1; Clarke 19-1-91-3; Adair 15-3-61-1. *Second innings*—Barker 11-2-37-3; Hannon-Dalby 3-2-2-0; Patel 14-3-38-7; Clarke 6-2-22-0.

Warwickshire

*V. Chopra c Allenby b Leach	54	– b Cooper	33
I. J. Westwood b Leach	34	– c Ronchi b Thomas	17
I. R. Bell lbw b Thomas	12	– b Cooper	55
L. J. Evans b Leach	73	– c Ronchi b Cooper	4
F. R. J. Coleman c Gregory b Leach	0	– st Ronchi b Cooper	0
†T. R. Ambrose b Leach	0	– c Gregory b Cooper	0
R. Clarke lbw b Leach	0	– c Trego b Leach	5
K. H. D. Barker c Ronchi b Overton	9	– st Ronchi b Leach	46
J. S. Patel st Ronchi b Leach	98	– c and b Leach	27
M. R. Adair not out	24	– not out	10
O. J. Hannon-Dalby lbw b Allenby	7	– c Cooper b Leach	0
B 5, l-b 6, n-b 2	13	B 8, l-b 2	10

1/88 (2) 2/105 (3) 3/105 (1)   (110.3 overs) 324
4/105 (5) 5/105 (6) 6/105 (7)
7/120 (8) 8/286 (4) 9/295 (9)
10/324 (11)   110 overs: 324-9

1/43 (2) 2/79 (1)   (64.1 overs) 207
3/83 (4) 4/87 (5)
5/89 (6) 6/104 (7) 7/144 (3)
8/170 (8) 9/197 (9) 10/207 (11)

Thomas 21-7-54-1; Overton 17-0-47-1; Leach 40-11-106-7; Trego 11-2-32-0; Gregory 15-3-52-0; Allenby 6.3-0-22-1. *Second innings*—Thomas 11-4-30-1; Leach 31.1-12-74-4; Overton 4-0-17-0; Cooper 18-4-76-5.

Umpires: R. J. Bailey and A. G. Wharf.

SURREY

Swept along by the Currans

RICHARD SPILLER

Promotion was Surrey's goal at the start of the season, and they clinched it with two matches to spare, before sewing up the second division title in the last round. They also reached the Royal London One-Day Cup final, where the disappointment of losing to Gloucestershire reflected heightened expectations at a club for whom undershooting targets had become a worrying habit.

Surrey's return to the elite after two years was hardly a shock, though the manner of it was surprising. A season which started with fanfare for the arrival of Kumar Sangakkara and – briefly – the return of Kevin Pietersen, who stole the headlines in May with a quite brilliant 355 not out against Leicestershire, was instead characterised by youngsters maturing rapidly. Surrey won three of their first eight Championship matches, but the sole defeat was followed by a run of four victories, which all but assured promotion.

They owed a huge debt to Tom Curran, forced by a chronic injury crisis among the fast bowlers to shoulder an enormous workload for a 20-year-old. He alone was ever-present in the Championship, and his 76 wickets at 23 was Surrey's best return for 21 years; he missed only one competitive match all season, and claimed 105 wickets in total. Brisk pace, an economic run-up and the ability to locate any assistance meant he was rarely collared in almost 550 overs – a dream for his captain, Gareth Batty. Curran sometimes looked close to exhaustion, yet stayed fit while the rest were dropping.

It was just as well Curran kept going. Tim Linley (knee) retired before the end of the season, as did Chris Tremlett (back), who failed to finish three of his four matches. Jade Dernbach suffered a side injury in April, then tweaked a calf muscle was never fully fit, even when claiming six wickets – and a hat-trick – in the Lord's final. Matt Dunn missed eight weeks with a side strain, yet bowled with pace and hostility when available. But Stuart Meaker, struggling with a shoulder injury, was nowhere near his best, while David Balcombe – signed from Hampshire – seemed to lose all confidence. Even Luke Fletcher, borrowed from Nottinghamshire, suffered back spasms. Surrey showed they meant business in the first division by snapping up the left-arm quick Mark Footitt, from Derbyshire.

But the extended sick list opened the door for the remarkable arrival of Curran's brother Sam who, at 17, was Surrey's youngest debutant since Tony Lock in 1946. He was immediately opening the bowling alongside his brother – and with the assurance of a veteran. Sam's skiddy left-arm pace and swing brought an extra element to the attack, while his batting – regarded as his stronger suit by Academy coaches – helped pick up valuable bonus points, and nearly secured the Royal London final.

Surrey's injury problems were at their worst in mid-season, especially in the T20 Blast, where they failed to reach the quarter-finals, not helped by three abandonments. One of these followed a horrifying incident at Arundel, where the Australian Moises Henriques had his jaw broken in three places and needed dental implants after a collision in the field with Rory Burns, who was also knocked unconscious and suffered facial cuts.

Adam Davy, PA Photos

Tom Curran

Given the problems in the pace attack, a key factor was Batty's spin partnership with slow left-armer Zafar Ansari, who – often given first opportunity by his unselfish senior colleague – developed a cunning change of pace and almost doubled his first-class wicket tally. The extra burden did affect his batting, and his only century came after he dropped down the order. Ansari deserved the call for England's series against Pakistan, but dislocated his thumb the same day, and had to withdraw.

Batty bowled as well as ever, securing promotion with a hat-trick to finish off Derbyshire. Tactically he was cautious, but the presence of just one captain for the whole season, for the first time in four years, provided invaluable stability. It was a shame when, in January, head coach Graham Ford took the Sri Lanka job.

Burns was the only batsman to reach 1,000 Championship runs, but there was depth to the line-up, and seven other players also scored centuries. Sangakkara's five in 11 Championship matches, plus a match-winning 166 in the Royal London semi-final, showed his enduring quality – and inspired Steven Davies, who had started in a blaze of form until a broken hand put him out for six weeks. Gary Wilson, the first-choice wicketkeeper when free from Ireland duty, was not among the centurions, but did pass 800 runs. With Sangakkara due at the Caribbean Premier League, Australian Aaron Finch has been signed as cover. West Indies all-rounder Dwayne Bravo will fly in for a handful of T20 matches.

Without achieving the heights of a year earlier, Jason Roy also reached 800, and looked increasingly at home in England's short-form sides. Ben Foakes did well with both bat and gloves, while Arun Harinath's centuries at Guildford – and a superb innings at Colchester on a turning track – suggested a burgeoning talent. All-rounder James Burke took his opportunities and, when Sangakkara was away and Henriques injured, the South African Dean Elgar stepped in with a precious 98 against Gloucestershire.

But they were all dwarfed by Pietersen's heroics against Leicestershire. During his innings – the second-highest in Surrey's history – he heard there would be no England recall, the latest instalment of a saga that, by the end of the summer, seemed from another age. He appeared in just one more Championship game, and a single Twenty20 match, before heading off to the Caribbean Premier League. Vikram Solanki, 39, also departed, after three seasons in which his helpful influence had more impact than his runs.

Championship attendance: 34,491.

SURREY RESULTS

All first-class matches – Played 16: Won 8, Lost 1, Drawn 7.
County Championship matches – Played 16: Won 8, Lost 1, Drawn 7.

LV= County Championship, winners of Division 2;
NatWest T20 Blast, 7th in South Group; Royal London One-Day Cup, finalists.

COUNTY CHAMPIONSHIP AVERAGES, BATTING AND FIELDING

Cap		Birthplace	M	I	NO	R	HS	100	Avge	Ct/St
	K. P. Pietersen	*Pietermaritzburg, SA*	4	6	3	469	355*	1	156.33	1
	B. T. Foakes	*Colchester*	10	16	4	617	140*	2	51.41	20/3
2011	S. M. Davies	*Bromsgrove*	12	19	3	819	200*	2	51.18	4
2014	R. J. Burns	*Epsom†*	14	24	3	1,019	158	2	48.52	11
	S. M. Curran	*Northampton*	6	8	3	239	61*	0	47.80	1
2014	G. C. Wilson	*Dundonald, N. Ire.*	14	23	6	811	74*	0	47.70	40/1
2014	J. J. Roy	*Durban, SA*	12	19	2	810	143	2	47.64	19
2015	K. C. Sangakkara§	*Matale, SL*	11	19	0	870	149	5	45.78	7
	A. Harinath	*Sutton†*	8	13	0	568	120	2	43.69	1
2014	Z. S. Ansari	*Ascot*	14	22	1	771	106	1	36.71	8
2011	G. J. Batty	*Bradford*	15	18	5	388	50*	0	29.84	5
	J. E. Burke	*Plymouth*	7	10	1	232	79	0	25.77	5
	D. P. Sibley	*Epsom†*	6	10	0	242	74	0	24.20	6
2014	C. T. Tremlett	*Southampton*	3	5	1	85	30	0	21.25	1
	T. K. Curran¶	*Cape Town, SA*	16	18	2	297	60	0	18.56	5
	M. P. Dunn	*Egham†*	9	10	2	45	13	0	5.62	1

Also batted: J. W. Dernbach (*Johannesburg, SA*) (cap 2011) (4 matches) 0*, 1 (3 ct); D. Elgar§ (*Welkom, SA*) (2 matches) 44, 19, 98 (2 ct); L. J. Fletcher (*Nottingham*) (3 matches) 23, 2*, 14; A. Kapil (*Wolverhampton*) (1 match) 21, 0; T. E. Linley (*Leeds*) (1 match) 0, 2*; S. C. Meaker (*Pietermaritzburg, SA*) (cap 2012) (3 matches) 13, 0, 0; V. S. Solanki (*Udaipur, India*) (cap 2014) (1 match) 1, 33 (2 ct).

† *Born in Surrey.*　　　§ *Official overseas player.*　　　¶ *Other non-England-qualified player.*

BOWLING

	Style	O	M	R	W	BB	5I	Avge
J. E. Burke	RFM	104	19	347	16	4-19	0	21.68
T. K. Curran	RFM	544.4	129	1,754	76	7-20	5	23.07
S. M. Curran	LFM	145.2	21	575	22	5-67	2	26.13
G. J. Batty	OB	400	77	1,127	40	6-51	2	28.17
Z. S. Ansari	SLA	425.3	71	1,363	44	6-30	3	30.97
M. P. Dunn	RFM	253.4	37	984	28	4-72	0	35.14

Also bowled: R. J. Burns (RM) 6–1–12–0; J. W. Dernbach (RFM) 80.2–27–204–2; L. J. Fletcher (RFM) 54–10–155–8; A. Harinath (OB) 25.1–3–85–1; A. Kapil (RFM) 12–1–68–2; T. E. Linley (RFM) 20–6–67–1; S. C. Meaker (RF) 61.2–8–281–5; K. P. Pietersen (OB) 2–0–8–0; J. J. Roy (RM) 24.4–2–115–3; C. T. Tremlett (RFM) 68–14–219–6.

LEADING ROYAL LONDON CUP AVERAGES (100 runs/4 wickets)

Batting	Runs	HS	Avge	SR	Ct/St
K. C. Sangakkara	489	166	61.12	94.03	3
S. M. Davies	509	115	56.55	93.05	2
Z. S. Ansari	216	66*	54.00	94.32	3
R. J. Burns	364	95	52.00	91.91	3
J. J. Roy	411	112	45.66	102.75	6
G. C. Wilson	233	59	25.88	82.91	17/2
T. K. Curran	124	44	24.80	134.78	1
B. T. Foakes	147	44	21.00	62.82	7/1

Bowling	W	BB	Avge	ER
J. E. Burke	16	5-28	20.06	6.00
J. W. Dernbach	19	6-35	22.26	5.10
Z. S. Ansari	13	3-58	25.30	6.17
S. M. Curran	15	4-32	30.80	5.37
T. K. Curran	15	4-65	31.26	5.62
G. J. Batty	11	2-35	36.36	5.00

LEADING NATWEST T20 BLAST AVERAGES (100 runs/18 overs)

Batting	Runs	HS	Avge	SR	Ct		Bowling	W	BB	Avge	ER
S. M. Davies	117	58	23.40	172.05	1		Azhar Mahmood ..	9	3-14	26.22	7.53
Z. S. Ansari	201	67*	40.20	164.75	6		G. J. Batty	5	2-19	52.60	7.73
J. J. Roy	273	122*	30.33	150.00	5		S. M. Curran	7	3-17	23.28	8.15
K. C. Sangakkara	332	58	41.50	149.54	4		Z. S. Ansari	8	3-17	26.50	8.48
Azhar Mahmood .	104	34	20.80	136.84	1		T. K. Curran	14	4-35	28.71	9.20
G. C. Wilson	173	55	24.71	106.79	7		J. E. Burke	9	3-23	22.11	9.25
							M. P. Dunn.......	9	3-34	23.77	9.30

FIRST-CLASS COUNTY RECORDS

Highest score for	357*	R. Abel v Somerset at The Oval	1899
Highest score against	366	N. H. Fairbrother (Lancashire) at The Oval....	1990
Leading run-scorer	43,554	J. B. Hobbs (avge 49.72)	1905–34
Best bowling for	10-43	T. Rushby v Somerset at Taunton	1921
Best bowling against	10-28	W. P. Howell (Australians) at The Oval	1899
Leading wicket-taker	1,775	T. Richardson (avge 17.87)	1892–1904
Highest total for	811	v Somerset at The Oval	1899
Highest total against	863	by Lancashire at The Oval..................	1990
Lowest total for	14	v Essex at Chelmsford	1983
Lowest total against	16	by MCC at Lord's	1872

LIST A COUNTY RECORDS

Highest score for	268	A. D. Brown v Glamorgan at The Oval	2002
Highest score against	180*	T. M. Moody (Worcestershire) at The Oval ...	1994
Leading run-scorer	10,358	A. D. Brown (avge 32.16)	1990–2008
Best bowling for	7-30	M. P. Bicknell v Glamorgan at The Oval	1999
Best bowling against	7-15	A. L. Dixon (Kent) at The Oval.............	1967
Leading wicket-taker	409	M. P. Bicknell (avge 25.21).................	1986–2005
Highest total for	496-4	v Gloucestershire at The Oval	2007
Highest total against	429	by Glamorgan at The Oval..................	2002
Lowest total for	64	v Worcestershire at Worcester	1978
Lowest total against	44	by Glamorgan at The Oval..................	1999

TWENTY20 COUNTY RECORDS

Highest score for	**122***	**J. J. Roy** v Somerset at The Oval	**2015**
Highest score against	106*	S. B. Styris (Essex) at Chelmsford...........	2010
Leading run-scorer	**1,969**	**J. J. Roy** (avge 28.95)...................	**2008–15**
Best bowling for	6-24	T. J. Murtagh v Middlesex at Lord's	2005
Best bowling against	4-9	D. J. Willey (Northamptonshire) at Birmingham	2013
Leading wicket-taker	**75**	Azhar Mahmood (avge 23.86)...............	**2003–15**
Highest total for	224-5	v Gloucestershire at Bristol	2006
Highest total against	**240-3**	**by Glamorgan** at The Oval...............	**2015**
Lowest total for	88	v Kent at The Oval........................	2012
Lowest total against	68	by Sussex at Hove	2007

ADDRESS

The Oval, Kennington, London SE11 5SS; 0844 375 1845; enquiries@surreycricket.com; www.surreycricket.com.

OFFICIALS

Captain G. J. Batty	**President** P. I. Pocock
Director of cricket A. J. Stewart	**Chairman** R. W. Thompson
Head coach 2015 G. X. Ford	**Chief executive** R. A. Gould
2016 M. J. Di Venuto	**Head groundsman** L. E. Fortis
Assistant head coach S. N. Barnes	**Scorer** K. R. Booth
Academy director G. T. J. Townsend	

At Oxford, April 12–14. SURREY drew with OXFORD MCCU.

At Cardiff, April 19–22. SURREY drew with GLAMORGAN.

SURREY v ESSEX

At The Oval, April 26–29. Drawn. Surrey 9pts, Essex 12pts. Toss: Essex.

Surrey started well, but ended up grateful for the rain which washed out the final day. Pietersen's first scoring shot took him to 1,000 for Surrey in 17 first-class innings – one quicker than Mark Ramprakash and Zander de Bruyn – then Davies's sublime timing lit up the rest of the opening day. But the match changed course early on the second, as the last four wickets tumbled for no runs in 13 balls. Helped by Batty's reluctance to post a third man, Browne and Daniel Lawrence – both products of Essex's Academy – wore down an attack lacking Dernbach with a side strain. In his second match,

YOUNGEST CENTURIONS IN ENGLISH FIRST-CLASS CRICKET

Yrs	Days			
16	263	Mushfiqur Rahim (115*)	Bangladeshis v Northamptonshire at Northampton...	2005
17	180	S. J. Thakor (134)	Leicestershire v Loughborough MCCU at Leicester .	2011
17	112	S. R. Tendulkar (119*)	India v England at Manchester	1990
17	194	S. D. Peters (110)	Essex v Cambridge University at Cambridge	1996
17	215	D. N. Patel (100*)	Worcestershire v Oxford University at Oxford	1976
17	272	G. J. Bryan (124)	Kent v Nottinghamshire at Nottingham...........	1920
17	**290**	**D. W. Lawrence (161)**	**Essex v Surrey at The Oval**...............	**2015**
17	296	A. T. Rayudu (101*)	India A v Surrey at The Oval..................	2003
18	5	J. J. Cobb (148*)	Leicestershire v Middlesex at Lord's	2008
18	12	W. G. Grace (224*)	England v Surrey at The Oval	1866
18	21	D. P. Sibley (242)	Surrey v Yorkshire at The Oval.................	2013

Tendulkar scored another hundred 17 days after his first one. Patel made another (107 v Surrey at Worcester) 55 days after his first; only he and Bryan have scored centuries in the County Championship when younger than Lawrence.

the 17-year-old Lawrence became the Championship's third-youngest century-maker, wasting few opportunities on a pitch progressively less friendly to the bowlers, and in all batted four and a half hours for a superb 161; later Greg Smith and Napier plundered 116 from 20 overs. Foster declared 270 ahead, then Lawrence at cover ran out Ansari in the first over. Burns and Pietersen – who survived being bowled by Masters when he pulled away after being distracted by a low-flying bird – were still there at the end of the third day, but were spared an awkward examination by the weather.

Close of play: first day, Surrey 293-5 (Davies 69, Wilson 23); second day, Essex 266-2 (Lawrence 48, Porter 0); third day, Surrey 95-2 (Burns 41, Pietersen 8).

Surrey

R. J. Burns c Smith b Panesar	78	– not out 41
Z. S. Ansari lbw b Porter	18	– run out 0
K. C. Sangakkara lbw b Ryder.............	52	– c Browne b Napier 43
K. P. Pietersen lbw b Ryder..............	32	– not out 8
S. M. Davies c Ryder b Masters.............	81	
J. J. Roy lbw b Ryder...................	0	
†G. C. Wilson lbw b Napier................	46	
*G. J. Batty c Velani b Panesar	10	
T. K. Curran c Ryder b Napier.............	0	
J. W. Dernbach not out	0	
M. P. Dunn b Napier	0	
B 4, l-b 9, n-b 10	23	L-b 3 3

1/61 (2) 2/140 (1) 3/175 (3) (112.5 overs) 340 | 1/1 (2) 2/77 (3) (2 wkts, 32 overs) 95
4/243 (4) 5/243 (6) 6/311 (5)
7/340 (7) 8/340 (8) 9/340 (9)
10/340 (11)

110 overs: 340-6

Masters 29–7–66–1; Porter 19–0–53–1; Ryder 23–3–78–3; Napier 21.5–3–63–3; Panesar 12–3–51–2; Smith 6.2–2–13–0; Browne 1.4–0–3–0. *Second innings*—Masters 9–1–26–0; Porter 5–0–19–0; Napier 7–1–21–1; Ryder 4–2–7–0; Panesar 7–1–19–0.

Essex

N. L. J. Browne c Wilson b Dunn	143	G. R. Napier c Davies b Roy 73
J. C. Mickleburgh lbw b Batty	61	
D. W. Lawrence c Wilson b Ansari	161	B 8, l-b 11, w 2, n-b 4 25
J. A. Porter lbw b Ansari	2	
*†J. S. Foster c Batty b Curran	23	1/155 (2) (8 wkts dec, 140.4 overs) 610
J. D. Ryder lbw b Ansari	57	2/264 (1) 3/271 (4)
K. S. Velani b Ansari	15	4/339 (5) 5/460 (6) 6/469 (3)
G. M. Smith not out	50	7/494 (7) 8/610 (9) 110 overs: 431-4

D. D. Masters and M. S. Panesar did not bat.

Dernbach 12.2–4–44–0; Dunn 30–3–131–1; Curran 32.4–3–159–1; Roy 10.4–0–51–1; Batty 18–5–49–1; Ansari 35–4–149–4; Pietersen 2–0–8–0.

Umpires: M. J. D. Bodenham and N. G. B. Cook.

SURREY v LEICESTERSHIRE

At The Oval, May 10–13. Surrey won by seven wickets. Surrey 24pts, Leicestershire 5pts. Toss: Leicestershire.

Pietersen's monumental 355 not out – two short of Bobby Abel's 116-year-old county record – was the centrepiece of Surrey's victory, although Davies's scintillating 57-ball hundred was equally important as they sprinted home at ten an over on the final evening. Pietersen batted for seven and a half hours, faced 396 balls, and hit 36 fours and 15 sixes in his highest first-class score; next best was Sangakkara's 36. It was an easy-paced pitch, with a short boundary on one side, and he was dropped five times – but it was still a superb effort. Pietersen's characteristic crunching drives, whips and flicks were all in evidence, as well as the fist-clenched celebrations of landmarks on the ground where, ten years earlier, his 158 had secured the Ashes. For at least half his innings, he was battling to keep his side afloat, after Lewis Hill's century in his second Championship game had taken Leicestershire close to 300. Pietersen ended the second day unbeaten on 326, and – on the eve of Andrew Strauss's unveiling as England's new director of cricket – declared: "They say that timing is everything." His optimism lasted a couple of hours, until Strauss and ECB chief executive Tom Harrison told him during a meeting at a London hotel that there was no chance of an international return before the end of the summer. After penning an angry column in *The Daily Telegraph*, in which he said he felt "deeply misled" by the ECB, Pietersen carried on next morning, taking the tenth-wicket stand to 139, of which last man Dunn made five; Tremlett had also helped add 101 for the ninth. In that short time, Pietersen also picked up a calf injury, which meant he had to cancel his imminent spell with Sunrisers Hyderabad at the IPL. Facing a deficit of 265, Leicestershire applied themselves well. Both Eckersley and O'Brien survived for around three hours and, with Tremlett

IS ANYONE ELSE THERE?

Biggest difference between the top two scorers in a first-class innings:

Highest score	*Second-highest*		
396 Hanif Mohammad (499)	W. Mathias (103)	Karachi v B'walpur at Karachi...	1958-59
385 B. C. Lara (501*)	K. J. Piper (116*)	Warwicks v Durham at B'ham...	1994
356 B. Sutcliffe (385*)	A. W. Gilbertson (29)	Otago v C'bury at Christchurch...	1952-53
349 G. A. Hick (405*)	S. J. Rhodes (56)	Worcs v Somerset at Taunton....	1988
337 D. G. Bradman (452*)	A. F. Kippax (115)	NSW v Queensland at Sydney...	1929-30
319 K. P. Pietersen (355*)	K. C. Sangakkara (36)	**Surrey v Leics at The Oval**....	**2015**
308 W. H. Ponsford (437)	H. S. T. L. Hendry (129)	Victoria v Qld at Melbourne...	1927-28
301 Naved Latif (394)	Misbah-ul-Haq (93)	Sargodha v Gujranwala at G'wala	2000-01
300 B. C. Lara (375)	S. Chanderpaul (75*)	W. Indies v Eng at St John's	1993-94

tweaking a hamstring, the last three wickets used up 40 overs in adding 93. When Ansari, claiming a career-best six for 152, finished the resistance shortly after tea, Surrey had only 24 overs to score 216. But Roy tonked 67 from 39 balls, and the dazzling Davies made sure Pietersen didn't have to bat again.

Close of play: first day, Surrey 105-2 (Sangakkara 35, Pietersen 35); second day, Surrey 528-9 (Pietersen 326, Dunn 5); third day, Leicestershire 310-5 (O'Brien 38, Raine 21).

Leicestershire

A. J. Robson b Dunn	6	– (2) lbw b Ansari	55
L. J. Hill b Dunn	126	– (1) lbw b Dunn	0
E. J. H. Eckersley c Roy b Curran	48	– c Roy b Ansari	118
*M. J. Cosgrove c Wilson b Dunn	0	– c Burns b Batty	44
N. D. Pinner c Sangakkara b Curran	17	– lbw b Ansari	24
†N. J. O'Brien c Sangakkara b Curran	16	– c Burns b Curran	78
B. A. Raine c Wilson b Tremlett	57	– lbw b Ansari	33
C. J. McKay lbw b Batty	4	– lbw b Ansari	41
R. M. L. Taylor c Wilson b Dunn	3	– c Wilson b Ansari	42
J. K. H. Naik c Roy b Tremlett	1	– c Roy b Batty	30
C. E. Shreck not out	0	– not out	0
B 2, l-b 4, n-b 8	14	B 9, l-b 2, n-b 4	15

1/12 (1) 2/103 (3) 3/104 (4)   (66 overs) 292
4/127 (5) 5/155 (6) 6/275 (2)
7/280 (8) 8/291 (9) 9/291 (7) 10/292 (10)

1/0 (1) 2/161 (2)   (161.1 overs) 480
3/194 (3) 4/236 (4)
5/260 (5) 6/336 (7) 7/387 (6)
8/418 (8) 9/480 (10) 10/480 (9)

Dunn 18–2–72–4; Tremlett 16–5–38–2; Ansari 10–0–57–0; Curran 12–1–74–3; Batty 8–0–32–1; Roy 2–0–13–0. *Second innings*—Dunn 27–1–104–1; Tremlett 7–2–15–0; Curran 29–3–92–1; Ansari 51.1–12–152–6; Batty 46–13–100–2; Roy 1–0–6–0.

Surrey

R. J. Burns b Raine	15	– (5) not out	2
Z. S. Ansari c O'Brien b Raine	15		
K. C. Sangakkara c Pinner b McKay	36	– c Robson b Naik	12
K. P. Pietersen not out	355		
S. M. Davies c Pinner b Raine	6	– (2) not out	115
J. J. Roy c O'Brien b Shreck	27	– (1) c Robson b Taylor	67
†G. C. Wilson c McKay b Naik	18	– (4) c Robson b Naik	10
*G. J. Batty c Eckersley b Naik	15		
T. K. Curran c O'Brien b McKay	18		
C. T. Tremlett b McKay	30		
M. P. Dunn b Hill b Raine	5		
B 1, l-b 4, n-b 12	17	L-b 2, w 2, n-b 8	12

1/24 (2) 2/51 (1) 3/106 (3)   (130.5 overs) 557
4/119 (5) 5/164 (6) 6/241 (7)
7/283 (8) 8/317 (9) 9/418 (10)
10/557 (11)   110 overs: 448-9

1/145 (1)   (3 wkts, 21.2 overs) 218
2/177 (3) 3/204 (4)

McKay 27–6–78–3; Shreck 25–2–139–1; Raine 29.5–4–124–4; Taylor 20–2–93–0; Naik 26–4–114–2; Cosgrove 3–1–4–0. *Second innings*—McKay 6–0–56–0; Raine 2–0–32–0; Naik 6–0–54–2; Shreck 2–0–34–0; Taylor 5–0–35–1; Cosgrove 0.2–0–5–0.

Umpires: P. K. Baldwin and N. G. C. Cowley.

At Northampton, May 18–21. SURREY drew with NORTHAMPTONSHIRE.

At Beckenham, May 24–27. SURREY beat KENT by three wickets.

SURREY v LANCASHIRE

At The Oval, May 31–June 3. Drawn. Surrey 13pts, Lancashire 12pts. Toss: Lancashire. County debut: B. T. Foakes. Championship debut: J. P. Faulkner.

Bad weather, and the bat's dominance over the ball – except when it was new – ensured a stalemate between the top two teams. With Bailey and Jarvis achieving early movement, Surrey were soon 74 for four, including Pietersen, out for two from three balls in what turned out to be his last innings before decamping to the Caribbean Premier League. But they later took control as the skies cleared. Roy was impossible to contain on the second morning, giving Kerrigan a harsh reminder of his painful Test debut on this ground two years earlier; Roy needed only nine deliveries from him (and three from the Australian all-rounder Faulkner, which brought just a single) to hurtle from 77 to 103, and completed Surrey's first hundred before lunch since Ian Greig in the same fixture 25 years earlier. Ben Foakes, replacing Gary Wilson (playing for Ireland) behind the stumps for Surrey, added a sprightly half-century, and later made five dismissals. Lancashire were rescued by Faulkner, who had also made his debut in that 2013 Oval Test. He took advantage of a tiring attack, in company with the solid Clark, to avert the follow-on. Faulkner's maiden first-class century made him the eighth to score one on debut for Lancashire (earlier in the season, Petersen had been the seventh). That effectively killed the match; Burns and Ansari enjoyed an extended net on the final day.

Close of play: first day, Surrey 145-4 (Davies 41, Roy 21); second day, Surrey 435-8 (Foakes 60, Meaker 13); third day, Lancashire 342-8 (Bailey 21, Jarvis 13).

Surrey

R. J. Burns c Davies b Bailey	12	– not out	110
Z. S. Ansari c Horton b Jarvis	37	– not out	66
K. C. Sangakkara c Faulkner b Clark	10		
K. P. Pietersen c Horton b Jarvis	2		
S. M. Davies c Horton b Bailey	86		
J. J. Roy c Prince b Jarvis	143		
†B. T. Foakes not out	63		
*G. J. Batty lbw b Clark	36		
T. K. Curran c Davies b Clark	6		
S. C. Meaker b Jarvis	13		
M. P. Dunn c Davies b Bailey	4		
B 18, l-b 6, n-b 12	36	B 6, l-b 4	10

1/26 (1) 2/46 (3) 3/51 (4) 4/74 (2) (117 overs) 448
5/310 (6) 6/318 (5) 7/396 (8)
8/408 (9) 9/435 (10) 10/448 (11)   110 overs: 421-8

(no wkt dec, 61 overs) 186

Bailey 30–5–101–3; Jarvis 26–4–118–4; Faulkner 24–4–65–0; Clark 21–0–74–3; Kerrigan 12–1–52–0; Croft 4–0–14–0. *Second innings*—Bailey 7–3–14–0; Jarvis 7–1–30–0; Kerrigan 21–2–58–0; Faulkner 5–0–23–0; Clark 5–2–7–0; Croft 12–1–37–0; Petersen 2–2–0–0; Horton 2–0–7–0.

Lancashire

P. J. Horton c Foakes b Dunn	4	K. M. Jarvis c Foakes b Meaker	47
K. R. Brown c Roy b Curran	4	S. C. Kerrigan not out	34
A. N. Petersen c Foakes b Meaker	46		
A. G. Prince lbw b Curran	20	B 8, l-b 11, w 5, n-b 10	34
*S. J. Croft c Pietersen b Ansari	21		
†A. L. Davies c Foakes b Meaker	1	1/8 (2) 2/9 (1) 3/55 (4) (112 overs) 429
J. P. Faulkner b Dunn	121	4/91 (5) 5/102 (3) 6/108 (6)
J. Clark b Dunn	63	7/291 (8) 8/312 (7) 9/377 (9)
T. E. Bailey st Foakes b Batty	34	10/429 (10) 110 overs: 421-9

Dunn 20–4–76–3; Curran 22–7–81–2; Meaker 23–5–92–3; Ansari 28–1–91–1; Batty 17–3–60–1; Roy 2–0–10–0.

Umpires: B. V. Taylor and A. G. Wharf.

At Leicester, June 7–9. SURREY beat LEICESTERSHIRE by 178 runs.

SURREY v GLAMORGAN

At Guildford, June 15–18. Glamorgan won by seven wickets. Glamorgan 23pts, Surrey 6pts. Toss: Surrey.

A blistering assault from Wagg tilted the match irrevocably Glamorgan's way. Surrey had expected a sizeable lead as Glamorgan dipped to 106 for six on the second afternoon. But, after helping Wallace retrieve the situation in a counter-attacking stand of 152, Wagg blasted the bowling all round the ground as 114 were added in 64 chaotic minutes next morning (and three balls were lost on Woodbridge Road). He belted the unfortunate Curran for five of his 11 sixes – there were also 21 fours – and Glamorgan looted 66 from his last four overs. It was only the second Championship double-century by a No. 8, after Dominic Cork's 200 not out for Derbyshire against Durham at Derby in 2000. Harinath then took his chance on his first appearance of the season, having replaced Rory Burns, who was recovering from a horrifying on-field collision with Moises Henriques in the previous day's Twenty20 game at Arundel. He became the first to make twin centuries here, and the first for Surrey in any match since Mark Ramprakash in 2010. However, in both innings Surrey's depleted line-up lost the initiative against probing seam from Wagg and the lofty Hogan. Second time round their last five fell for just four runs, and Glamorgan never looked stretched in chasing 247.

Close of play: first day, Surrey 289-6 (Ansari 91); second day, Glamorgan 323-8 (Wagg 116, Salter 4); third day, Surrey 276-8 (Solanki 33, Tremlett 0).

Surrey

A. Harinath c Salter b Hogan	120	– lbw b Salter	104
Z. S. Ansari lbw b Hogan	91	– c Wallace b Hogan	29
D. P. Sibley c Rudolph b Lloyd	21	– lbw b Bragg	13
B. T. Foakes c Wallace b Lloyd	2	– c Wallace b Hogan	33
V. S. Solanki c Wallace b Meschede	1	– b Wagg	33
A. Kapil lbw b Wagg	21	– lbw b Hogan	0
S. C. Meaker lbw b Wagg	0	– (11) b Wagg	0
†G. C. Wilson not out	38	– (7) c Wallace b Hogan	54
*G. J. Batty lbw b Wagg	2	– (8) c Wallace b Hogan	0
T. K. Curran c Rudolph b Lloyd	45	– (9) lbw b Ingram	0
C. T. Tremlett c Meschede b Wagg	29	– (10) not out	1
B 7, l-b 17, w 8, n-b 4	36	B 8, n-b 2	10

1/208 (1) 2/241 (3) 3/243 (4) (121.4 overs) 406 1/56 (2) 2/103 (3) (80.5 overs) 277
4/244 (5) 5/287 (6) 6/289 (7) 3/167 (4) 4/189 (1)
7/291 (2) 8/294 (9) 9/359 (10) 5/192 (6) 6/273 (7) 7/273 (8)
10/406 (11) 110 overs: 343-8 8/274 (9) 9/277 (5) 10/277 (11)

Hogan 29–6–70–2; Wagg 24.4–3–89–4; Salter 25–1–97–0; Meschede 24–7–46–1; Lloyd 16–0–68–3; Ingram 3–0–12–0. *Second innings*—Hogan 21–7–44–5; Meschede 12–1–51–0; Wagg 10.5–1–40–2; Salter 20–0–75–1; Lloyd 8–0–41–0; Bragg 4–0–14–1; Ingram 5–3–4–1.

Glamorgan

*J. A. Rudolph b Curran	13	– c Harinath b Batty	40
W. D. Bragg c Wilson b Curran	5	– c Wilson b Kapil	83
B. J. Wright c Solanki b Tremlett	7	– run out	68
C. A. Ingram c Solanki b Kapil	43	– not out	25
C. B. Cooke b Tremlett	4	– not out	5
C. A. J. Meschede c Wilson b Meaker	11		
†M. A. Wallace lbw b Curran	92		
G. G. Wagg c Batty b Meaker	200		
D. L. Lloyd c sub (S. J. Erwee) b Harinath	18		
A. G. Salter c Wilson b Curran	6		
M. G. Hogan not out	24		
B 8, l-b 3, w 1, n-b 2	14	B 16, l-b 9, w 1	26

1/14 (2) 2/25 (3) 3/25 (1) (83.2 overs) 437 1/77 (1) (3 wkts, 63.1 overs) 247
4/30 (5) 5/54 (6) 6/106 (4) 2/205 (3) 3/230 (2)
7/258 (7) 8/310 (9) 9/332 (10) 10/437 (8)

Tremlett 14–1–50–2; Curran 24–1–153–4; Meaker 12.2–1–78–2; Kapil 10–1–55–1; Batty 4–0–23–0; Ansari 9-2-49–0; Harinath 10-3-18-1. *Second innings*—Tremlett 5–2–20–0; Curran 10–0–34–0; Meaker 10–1–38–0; Batty 17–4–41–1; Ansari 16–1–67–0; Harinath 3.1–0–9–0; Kapil 2–0–13–1.

Umpires: P. K. Baldwin and S. J. O'Shaughnessy.

At Derby, June 21–23. SURREY beat DERBYSHIRE by 222 runs.

SURREY v GLOUCESTERSHIRE

At The Oval, June 27–29. Surrey won by an innings and 180 runs. Surrey 22pts, Gloucestershire 1pt. Toss: Surrey.

Surrey's determination to bat long in the first innings, on a pitch green in the middle but shaved at the ends, paid off handsomely. Ansari boosted the profits of the ground's beer festival by resisting grimly until he fell in the over before tea, while Elgar (in the second of his two Championship matches as Kumar Sangakkara's overseas locum) just missed a hundred. But Foakes made no mistake, completing his first for Surrey; he was last out, batting more than five hours until tea on the second day. Tom Curran then picked up five for 17 as seven wickets tumbled in the final session. He mopped up on the final morning to finish with a career-best seven for 20, including four men out for ducks. Gloucestershire folded with worrying ease again in the follow-on. The damage this time was done by Ansari, whose flight and well-disguised slower ball brought him six for 30 – another personal best – including top scorer Tavaré.

Close of play: first day, Surrey 279-5 (Foakes 57, Wilson 8); second day, Gloucestershire 102-7 (Marshall 30).

Surrey

R. J. Burns c Jones b Norwell	21	T. K. Curran b Taylor		4
Z. S. Ansari lbw b Taylor	64	M. P. Dunn not out		0
A. Harinath c Klinger b Miles	1			
D. Elgar c Klinger b Taylor	98	B 6, l-b 4, w 5, n-b 8		23
B. T. Foakes c sub (T. M. J. Smith) b Norwell	118			
J. J. Roy b Norwell	14	1/42 (1) 2/43 (3)	(144.5 overs)	448
†G. C. Wilson c Tavaré b Norwell	37	3/174 (2) 4/211 (4) 5/234 (6)		
J. E. Burke lbw b Fuller	18	6/317 (7) 7/363 (8) 8/443 (9)		
*G. J. Batty c sub (T. M. J. Smith) b Norwell	50	9/448 (10) 10/448 (5)	110 overs: 309-5	

Miles 29–7–104–1; Fuller 20–9–31–1; Norwell 34.5–7–112–5; Howell 13–2–36–0; Taylor 39–6–119–3; Dent 9–1–36–0.

Gloucestershire

W. A. Tavaré b Curran	19	– (2) c Roy b Ansari		58
C. D. J. Dent c Wilson b Curran	0	– (1) lbw b Dunn		8
M. Klinger b Curran	6	– c Foakes b Ansari		12
H. J. H. Marshall not out	34	– c Wilson b Curran		11
I. A. Cockbain c Batty b Curran	1	– lbw b Ansari		17
B. A. C. Howell c and b Burke	7	– (7) lbw b Ansari		3
*†G. O. Jones b Burke	30	– (6) c and b Burke		24
J. M. R. Taylor b Curran	0	– c Foakes b Burke		1
C. N. Miles c Wilson b Curran	0	– c Burns b Ansari		10
L. C. Norwell b Curran	0	– not out		8
J. K. Fuller b Dunn	3	– lbw b Ansari		0
B 12, l-b 1	13	B 1, l-b 2		3

1/0 (2) 2/29 (1) 3/34 (3)	(44.3 overs) 113	1/10 (1) 2/41 (3)	(72.2 overs) 155
4/36 (5) 5/50 (6) 6/97 (7)		3/59 (4) 4/101 (5)	
7/102 (8) 8/102 (9) 9/104 (10) 10/113 (11)		5/110 (2) 6/120 (7) 7/131 (8)	
		8/143 (6) 9/151 (9) 10/155 (11)	

Dunn 8.3–1–39–1; Curran 15–7–20–7; Ansari 10–1–27–0; Burke 11–5–14–2. *Second innings*—Dunn 12–3–31–1; Curran 14–3–37–2; Ansari 21.2–3–30–6; Burke 8–0–19–1; Batty 17–4–35–0.

Umpires: N. L. Bainton and M. Burns.

SURREY v KENT

At The Oval, July 13–16. Surrey won by six wickets. Surrey 22pts, Kent 6pts. Toss: Surrey. First-class debut: S. M. Curran.

Surrey completed the double over Kent, assisted by a notable first Championship appearance from Sam Curran. At 17 years 40 days, he was their second-youngest debutant, after Tony Lock (32 days younger) against the same opponents on the same ground, 69 years earlier. Sam and Tom Curran became only the third pair of brothers to open the bowling in a Championship innings since the war, following Tony and Mike Buss for Sussex against Somerset in 1967, and Alec and Eric Bedser for Surrey at Worcester in 1956; two months later, Craig and Jamie Overton became the fourth, at Hove. If Sam was overawed it did not show: he struck with his fourth delivery on a rain-hit first day. The solid Haggett put on 151 (a seventh-wicket record for Kent against Surrey) with Billings, who fell to Sam Curran one short of a maiden Championship hundred, as the second new ball did its job on a pitch grassy enough to justify Batty's decision to bowl. Harinath briefly outshone Sangakkara with some fluid strokeplay on the second evening, but it was Sangakkara who kept Surrey in the match next day with his third century of the season. Sam Curran earned an extra bonus point with a flurry of fours, then grabbed three wickets in five overs to begin Kent's slide to 99, in which Ansari and Batty enjoyed the turn from the scrubbed ends. A potentially tense final morning was controlled by Burns and Foakes.

Close of play: first day, Kent 132-4 (Harmison 11, Stevens 6); second day, Surrey 144-1 (Harinath 76, Sangakkara 34); third day, Surrey 4-1 (Burns 4).

Kent

D. J. Bell-Drummond lbw b Ansari	39	– lbw b S. M. Curran	5
J. L. Denly b S. M. Curran	1	– c and b S. M. Curran	10
A. J. Ball c Ansari b T. K. Curran	9	– c Sibley b S. M. Curran	0
*S. A. Northeast c Foakes b T. K. Curran	45	– c Roy b Ansari	33
B. W. Harmison lbw b S. M. Curran	17	– c Foakes b Batty	24
D. I. Stevens c Foakes b Burke	9	– (7) st Foakes b Batty	14
†S. W. Billings lbw b S. M. Curran	99	– (6) c and b Ansari	1
C. J. Haggett c Sangakkara b S. M. Curran	80	– c Foakes b Batty	3
J. C. Tredwell b T. K. Curran	3	– b T. K. Curran	2
M. T. Coles c Foakes b S. M. Curran	8	– c Foakes b Batty	2
M. D. Hunn not out	0	– not out	0
B 1, l-b 17, n-b 8	26	B 5	5

1/2 (2) 2/27 (3) 3/88 (1)   (92.2 overs) 336   1/5 (1) 2/9 (3)   (41.1 overs) 99
4/114 (4) 5/137 (6) 6/154 (5)   3/22 (2) 4/54 (4)
7/305 (7) 8/308 (9) 9/331 (10) 10/336 (8)   5/56 (6) 6/86 (5) 7/90 (8)
                                          8/91 (7) 9/99 (9) 10/99 (10)

T. K. Curran 32–9–75–3; S. M. Curran 22.2–2–101–5; Burke 13–4–38–1; Ansari 18–1–78–1; Batty 7–0–26–0. *Second innings*—T. K. Curran 11–5–25–1; S. M. Curran 9–2–19–3; Ansari 10–2–19–2; Burke 3–0–19–0; Batty 8.1–2–12–4.

Surrey

R. J. Burns c Ball b Coles	31	– b Tredwell	46
A. Harinath c Coles b Stevens	76	– (5) c Tredwell b Denly	14
K. C. Sangakkara b Hunn	110	– st Billings b Tredwell	1
Z. S. Ansari c Coles b Stevens	10	– (2) b Tredwell	0
J. J. Roy c Billings b Haggett	17	– (6) not out	4
D. P. Sibley lbw b Coles	11		
†B. T. Foakes lbw b Stevens	5	– (4) not out	57
J. E. Burke c Billings b Stevens	6		
*G. J. Batty c Tredwell b Hunn	3		
T. K. Curran c Denly b Hunn	4		
S. M. Curran not out	18		
L-b 16, w 4	20	B 6	6

1/80 (1) 2/145 (2) 3/171 (4) (82.3 overs) 311 1/4 (2) (4 wkts, 38.1 overs) 128
4/204 (5) 5/234 (6) 6/250 (7) 2/26 (3) 3/81 (1)
7/264 (8) 8/275 (9) 9/288 (3) 10/311 (10) 4/115 (5)

Coles 16–1–92–2; Stevens 28–5–76–4; Haggett 15–2–47–1; Tredwell 8–2–29–0; Hunn 15.3–1–51–3. *Second innings*—Stevens 10–5–18–0; Tredwell 17.1–3–61–3; Coles 2–0–15–0; Haggett 3–0–12–0; Denly 6–0–16–1.

Umpires: B. J. Debenham and S. A. Garratt.

At Colchester, August 7–10. SURREY beat ESSEX by three wickets.

At Bristol, August 21–24. SURREY drew with GLOUCESTERSHIRE.

SURREY v DERBYSHIRE

At The Oval, September 1–4. Surrey won by an innings and 98 runs. Surrey 23pts, Derbyshire 5pts. Toss: Derbyshire. County debut: T. P. Milnes.

The victory which confirmed Surrey's promotion – and took them top, ahead of Lancashire – was secured in spectacular fashion: skipper Batty had Palladino scooped up by Foakes (keeping wicket in place of the injured Wilson), before bowling Footitt and Cotton to complete a hat-trick. Batty and his team-mates – and a small but appreciative crowd – could barely take in the sudden achievement of their goal. They had the final day to bowl out Derbyshire, only for Madsen and Durston to settle in. But Batty, who finished with his best figures of the season, broke through shortly after lunch, and the floodgates opened. "My only other hat-trick came for Yorkshire Under-11s against Lancashire back in the late 1980s," he said. "I think Freddie Flintoff may have been one of my victims." On another rain-hit first day, during which five catches were dropped, Derbyshire had failed to take advantage of first use of a slow pitch which turned increasingly, if never violently. When Surrey batted, everyone reached double figures. Burns again looked good, but it was Ansari's five-hour hundred which hurt a tiring attack the most, as the last five wickets piled on 388. Durston achieved career-best figures, while Burke made his highest score.

Close of play: first day, Derbyshire 209-5 (Hughes 85, Milnes 3); second day, Surrey 227-5 (Ansari 21, Wilson 36); third day, Surrey 560.

Derbyshire

B. T. Slater lbw b Ansari	42	– lbw b T. K. Curran	0
B. A. Godleman b Ansari	45	– c Foakes b S. M. Curran	0
C. F. Hughes c Ansari b T. K. Curran	96	– run out	5
*W. L. Madsen c and b Ansari	9	– not out	76
W. J. Durston lbw b Ansari	6	– lbw b Batty	57
†H. R. Hosein lbw b T. K. Curran	11	– c Burns b Batty	0
T. P. Milnes b Burke	10	– c Burns b Batty	3
M. J. J. Critchley c and b T. K. Curran	31	– lbw b Ansari	5
A. P. Palladino lbw b T. K. Curran	31	– c Foakes b Batty	2
M. H. A. Footitt c Burke b T. K. Curran	15	– b Batty	0
B. D. Cotton not out	0	– b Batty	0
B 5, l-b 6, n-b 6	17	L-b 1	1

1/79 (2) 2/128 (1) 3/152 (4)   (102.1 overs) 313   1/0 (2) 2/0 (1)   (57.4 overs) 149
4/162 (5) 5/206 (6) 6/228 (7)   3/9 (3) 4/95 (5)
7/239 (3) 8/289 (9) 9/306 (8) 10/313 (10)   5/95 (6) 6/107 (7) 7/144 (8)
                                       8/149 (9) 9/149 (10) 10/149 (11)

T. K. Curran 24.1–8–71–5; S. M. Curran 12–1–59–0; Burke 19–3–59–1; Ansari 27–7–61–4; Batty 20–4–52–0. *Second innings*—T. K. Curran 11–3–32–1; S. M. Curran 8–3–14–1; Burke 4–1–13–0; Ansari 18.5–5–38–1; Batty 16.4–2–51–6.

Surrey

R. J. Burns c Critchley b Durston	92	T. K. Curran st Hosein b Durston	24
A. Harinath c Durston b Palladino	14	*G. J. Batty not out	35
K. C. Sangakkara c Hosein b Palladino	10		
B. T. Foakes c Godleman b Durston	31	B 12, l-b 10, w 1, n-b 6	29
S. M. Davies b Critchley	22		
Z. S. Ansari lbw b Durston	106		
†G. C. Wilson c Hosein b Footitt	72		
J. E. Burke c Hosein b Durston	79		
S. M. Curran c Madsen b Durston	46		

1/32 (2) 2/48 (3)   (158.3 overs) 560
3/131 (4) 4/150 (1) 5/172 (5)
6/281 (7) 7/429 (6) 8/460 (8)
9/499 (9) 10/560 (10)   110 overs: 365-6

Footitt 23–6–84–1; Cotton 27–9–59–0; Palladino 22–7–55–2; Milnes 15–1–78–0; Critchley 25–1–122–1; Durston 42.3–6–113–6; Hughes 4–0–27–0.

Umpires: M. Burns and J. H. Evans.

At Manchester, September 14–17. SURREY drew with LANCASHIRE.

SURREY v NORTHAMPTONSHIRE

At The Oval, September 22–25. Drawn. Surrey 13pts, Northamptonshire 8pts. Toss: Surrey.

Surrey secured the second division title, collecting enough points to keep Lancashire behind them, despite the loss of the first day and the transformation of Northamptonshire's batting from famine to feast. A beautifully constructed century from Sangakkara, his fifth of the season, put Surrey in command; he celebrated by raising the county cap he had just been awarded. Sam Curran gave more notice of his prodigious talent with a maiden fifty to help secure maximum batting points, but then played second fiddle to brother Tom, who found bite in the pitch and movement through the air as Northamptonshire subsided for 110. The Currans became the first siblings to share all ten wickets in a Championship innings since Jack and Charlie Oakes for Sussex against Somerset at Taunton in 1950. The follow-on started in similar fashion, with Tom removing Newton in the first over on the way to his first ten-wicket haul. But then things got harder. Duckett's timing was especially sweet during a stand of 227 with Wakely. And, after three more wickets for the Currans against their late father Kevin's former county, Northamptonshire regrouped with centuries from Rossington and Murphy, who extended his maiden ton to an undefeated 135. Surrey were left to score 215 in 33 overs, though their title was confirmed after eight once Lancashire had drawn with Essex. Roy celebrated by smashing three sixes in Keogh's next over, and hit eight in all from just 35 balls. Surrey, already in celebratory mode, abandoned the chase a few overs after he was caught at long-off.

Close of play: first day, no play; second day, Surrey 378-8 (S. M. Curran 52, Batty 5); third day, Northamptonshire 223-1 (Duckett 116, Wakely 93).

Surrey

R. J. Burns c Azharullah b Chambers	30	– (4) b White	0
A. Harinath c Murphy b Chambers	26	– (5) b Cobb	12
K. C. Sangakkara c Rossington b Keogh	101	– c Azharullah b Chambers	9
B. T. Foakes b White	16	– (7) not out	12
S. M. Davies c Rossington b Keogh	21	– (2) b Azharullah	0
J. J. Roy lbw b White	32	– (1) c Cobb b White	77
†G. C. Wilson c Keogh b Kleinveldt	49	– (6) not out	13
S. M. Curran not out	61		
T. K. Curran b Kleinveldt	13		
*G. J. Batty lbw b Chambers	27		
M. P. Dunn b White	0		
B 8, l-b 10, n-b 16	34	L-b 1, w 1	2

1/44 (2) 2/60 (1) 3/108 (4)   (95.5 overs) 410   1/1 (2)   (5 wkts, 15.5 overs) 125
4/172 (5) 5/224 (6) 6/266 (3)   2/22 (3) 3/38 (4)
7/337 (7) 8/353 (9) 9/409 (10) 10/410 (11)   4/99 (5) 5/106 (1)

Kleinveldt 19.3-3-73-2; Azharullah 19-6-69-0; Chambers 10.3-2-44-3; Keogh 25-4-115-2; White 19.5-1-81-3; Cobb 2-0-9-1. *Second innings*—Azharullah 4-1-42-1; Chambers 2-0-9-1; White 5.5-1-25-2; Keogh 2-0-29-0; Cobb 2-0-19-1.

Northamptonshire

R. I. Newton b S. M. Curran	20	– c Wilson b T. K. Curran	0
B. M. Duckett c Wilson b T. K. Curran	4	– lbw b T. K. Curran	120
*A. G. Wakely lbw b T. K. Curran	16	– lbw b T. K. Curran	93
R. I. Keogh c Roy b T. K. Curran	6	– c Foakes b S. M. Curran	0
J. J. Cobb not out	29	– c Foakes b Batty	6
A. M. Rossington lbw b T. K. Curran	0	– c Wilson b Dunn	116
†D. Murphy c Wilson b S. M. Curran	1	– not out	135
G. G. White b T. K. Curran	11	– c T. K. Curran b Dunn	0
Azharullah b T. K. Curran	0	– c T. K. Curran b Dunn	1
M. A. Chambers lbw b S. M. Curran	0	– b Dunn	0
R. K. Kleinveldt c Wilson b T. K. Curran	9	– c and b Batty	20
B 10, l-b 2, n-b 2	14	B 10, l-b 11, n-b 2	23

1/11 (2) 2/37 (3) 3/54 (1)   (29.5 overs) 110   1/0 (1) 2/227 (2)   (115 overs) 514
4/66 (4) 5/66 (6) 6/75 (7)   3/228 (4) 4/228 (3)
7/90 (8) 8/90 (9) 9/101 (10) 10/110 (11)   5/279 (5) 6/441 (6) 7/441 (8)
                                          8/443 (9) 9/443 (10) 10/514 (11)

T. K. Curran 13.5-4-35-7; S. M. Curran 12-2-46-3; Dunn 4-0-17-0. *Second innings*—T. K. Curran 30-3-141-3; S. M. Curran 18-1-87-1; Dunn 23-4-104-4; Harinath 12-0-58-0; Batty 32-8-103-2.

Umpires: S. A. Garratt and N. J. Llong.

SUSSEX

Tragedy brings perspective

B R U C E   T A L B O T

January 2016 brought terrible news. Fast bowler Matt Hobden, regarded as a potential England player, had died, aged just 22. For new head coach Mark Davis, a Sussex player when Umer Rashid drowned in Grenada in 2002, it brought back painful memories. A few weeks before Hobden fell to his death while celebrating New Year with friends in Scotland, Davis had awarded him a new three-year contract, and he had been due to spend time with the England Performance Programme in South Africa. Hobden had taken 23 Championship wickets in 2015, his breakthrough season. His raw pace evoked John Snow as he pounded in down the Hove slope, and he was popular among his team-mates. "He was a gentle giant, and a terrific prospect," said Davis.

Sussex will miss him as they try to haul themselves back into Division One. They had become used to their top-flight status, but, after finishing third for the past two seasons, they were relegated for only the second time since 2000. When they edged a one-wicket victory over Warwickshire in late May, they were briefly second; but one more win in 11 games saw them sent down by Hampshire's win at Trent Bridge on the last day of the season.

To no one's great surprise, Ed Joyce stood down after three years as captain. Although it was never likely he would match the eight first-class hundreds he hit in 2014, leadership and Ireland commitments seemed to grind him down. His deputy, Chris Nash, was considered, but the captaincy went to Luke Wright, who – until running into a David Willey-inspired Northamptonshire – had led the side confidently in the NatWest T20 Blast.

In November, coach Mark Robinson was appointed to run the England Women's set-up, and was replaced by Davis, his assistant. He and Wright will have a smaller squad at their command: the chairman, Jim May, confirmed there was little spare cash for recruitment, and a second division county can be less of a draw. Former Sussex batsman Keith Greenfield was named the club's first director of cricket, while Carl Hopkinson took charge of the Academy. It was, though, a boost when slow left-armer Danny Briggs joined from Hampshire, and New Zealand batsman Ross Taylor agreed to play for the first half of 2016. Ashar Zaidi, Steffan Piolet and Chris Liddle were all released.

Robinson refused to put all the blame on a long injury list, but they clearly had an impact. At various stages Sussex had six seamers out. Ajmal Shahzad and Tymal Mills, expensively recruited to ease the workload on Steve Magoffin, bowled less than 150 Championship overs between them. James Anyon missed the season, Lewis Hatchett didn't return until August, and Chris Jordan spent two months nursing a rib injury. The loss of Jordan's full England contract was another burden on the hard-pressed finances.

In total, 22 players were used in the Championship; in 2003, when Sussex won their first title, it was 15. With little faith in the left-arm spin of Zaidi, who left for Essex, they brought in George Dockrell on loan and Peter Burgoyne, though they claimed one wicket for 395. Tim Linley's brief return from Surrey was more successful (though he later retired), but leg-spinner Will Beer was ignored in red-ball cricket – in part because Luke Wells had worked hard on his own leg-spin, and ended with 23 at 37.

The big positive of the summer was the strapping seamer, Ollie Robinson. Released in 2014 by Yorkshire on disciplinary grounds, he hit a hundred from No. 9, on debut against Durham, putting on 164 for

Charlie Crowhurst/Getty Images

Ollie Robinson

the last wicket with Hobden to break a Sussex record set in 1908. Robinson, the stepson of England assistant coach Paul Farbrace, didn't recapture those heights with the bat, but he was soon sharing the new ball. Despite missing three games through wear and tear, he managed 46 wickets at 24. Magoffin – who has applied for a British passport – was not quite the force of previous years, but still led the attack superbly and, to everyone's relief, stayed fit. He claimed 69 at 24.

When fitness allowed, the seamers relished Hove's spicy relaid wickets, even if the balance sometimes tilted too much in their favour. Top-order damage often had to be repaired by the reliable pair of Wright and Ben Brown, whose four hundreds enhanced his reputation as one of the best wicketkeeper-batsmen on the circuit. They were alone in passing 1,000 runs. Matt Machan came close, but the suspicion remained he was not a natural No. 3.

The summer saw the departure of the last two links to the 2003 side. Matt Prior, unable to return after Achilles surgery, announced his retirement in June: then Mike Yardy was given a rapturous ovation in his final game at Hove. He marked it with a hundred, underlining how much he will be missed, though he was made coach of the Under-17 side. Another who never fully recovered from surgery, on his wrist, was Rory Hamilton-Brown, once tipped for an international career. He retired in March 2015.

Sussex's one-day performances were mixed. They were second in the South Group of the T20 Blast, but outplayed by Northamptonshire in the quarter-final. It was an embarrassment not to manage a single win in the Royal London Cup, especially as crowds remained healthy.

Off the field, the merger between the club and the Sussex Cricket Board – to form Sussex Cricket Ltd – was agreed, a move that should make the sport in the county stronger at every level. However, poor attendance led Sussex to abandon their long-standing Horsham Festival.

Championship attendance: 31,851.

SUSSEX RESULTS

All first-class matches – Played 17: Won 4, Lost 8, Drawn 5.
County Championship matches – Played 16: Won 4, Lost 8, Drawn 4.

LV= County Championship, 8th in Division 1;
NatWest T20 Blast, quarter-finalists; Royal London One-Day Cup, 9th in Group B.

COUNTY CHAMPIONSHIP AVERAGES, BATTING AND FIELDING

Cap		Birthplace	M	I	NO	R	HS	100	Avge	Ct/St
2007	L. J. Wright	Grantham	16	28	2	1,210	226*	2	46.53	11
2014	B. C. Brown	Crawley†	16	27	4	1,031	144*	4	44.82	45/1
	M. W. Machan	Brighton†	14	24	0	955	192	3	39.79	3
	Ashar Zaidi	Karachi, Pakistan	7	10	1	354	106	1	39.33	3
2005	M. H. Yardy	Pembury	10	17	0	606	124	2	35.64	14
2008	C. D. Nash	Cuckfield†	15	26	1	833	142*	1	33.32	15
2009	E. C. Joyce	Dublin, Ireland	14	25	0	786	100	1	31.44	22
2014	C. J. Jordan‡	Lowlands, Barbados	6	8	2	177	56*	0	29.50	18
	L. W. P. Wells	Eastbourne†	13	22	0	615	108	1	27.95	6
	A. Shahzad	Huddersfield	5	10	2	182	45*	0	22.75	1
	O. E. Robinson	Margate	11	17	3	282	110	1	20.14	3
	Craig Cachopa¶	Welkom, SA	8	16	0	220	54	0	13.75	5
	H. Z. Finch	Hastings†	4	6	2	46	22	0	11.50	3
2013	S. J. Magoffin§	Corinda, Australia	16	24	4	208	41	0	10.40	2
	M. E. Hobden	Eastbourne†	10	17	8	84	65*	0	9.33	3
	C. J. Liddle	Middlesbrough	4	4	2	18	10*	0	9.00	1
	T. S. Mills	Dewsbury	2	4	0	18	8	0	4.50	0

Also batted: P. I. Burgoyne (*Nottingham*) (2 matches) 13, 13; G. H. Dockrell (*Dublin, Ireland*) (1 match) 37*, 0; L. J. Hatchett (*Shoreham-by-Sea*†) (2 matches) 2*, 25, 8* (1 ct); F. J. Hudson-Prentice (*Haywards Heath*†) (1 match) 15, 0; T. E. Linley (*Leeds*) (1 match) 10, 21*.

† *Born in Sussex.*   ‡ *ECB contract.*   § *Official overseas player.*
¶ *Other non-England-qualified player.*

BOWLING

	Style	O	M	R	W	BB	5I	Avge
A. Shahzad	RFM	111.2	17	411	22	5-46	1	18.68
S. J. Magoffin	RFM	582	140	1,660	69	6-50	4	24.05
O. E. Robinson	RFM	320.1	66	1,137	46	6-33	1	24.71
C. J. Jordan	RFM	197.4	28	686	24	5-68	1	28.58
L. W. P. Wells	LBG	226	27	862	23	3-35	0	37.47
C. J. Liddle	LFM	110	15	391	10	3-49	0	39.10
Ashar Zaidi	SLA	188.1	42	461	11	3-55	0	41.90
M. E. Hobden	RFM	252.3	36	1,088	23	4-48	0	47.30

Also bowled: B. C. Brown 8–0–31–0 (RM); P. I. Burgoyne (OB) 52–5–215–1; G. H. Dockrell (SLA) 44–2–180–0; L. J. Hatchett (LFM) 58–9–206–4; F. J. Hudson-Prentice (RFM) 8–0–51–0; E. C. Joyce (RM) 4–0–8–0; T. E. Linley (RFM) 41.4–8–156–8; M. W. Machan (OB) 6–0–28–0; T. S. Mills (LF) 38.3–7–135–3; C. D. Nash (OB) 64–3–282–0; L. J. Wright (RFM) 9–0–39–0; M. H. Yardy (LM/SLA) 8–1–41–1.

LEADING ROYAL LONDON CUP AVERAGES (100 runs/3 wickets)

Batting

	Runs	HS	Avge	SR	Ct
G. J. Bailey	264	112	52.80	96.00	2
L. J. Wright	226	72	45.20	111.33	1
M. W. Machan	179	93	29.83	82.11	1
C. D. Nash	100	49	25.00	107.52	3
E. C. Joyce	123	48	24.60	65.07	1

Bowling

	W	BB	Avge	ER
C. J. Jordan	3	3-39	13.00	4.87
L. W. P. Wells	3	2-44	35.66	5.35
M. H. Yardy	3	2-68	46.00	6.84
T. S. Mills	3	2-76	46.00	8.11
O. E. Robinson	3	2-61	47.33	6.45
C. J. Liddle	4	2-45	61.25	5.25
A. C. Thomas	3	1-29	77.66	5.97

LEADING NATWEST T20 BLAST AVERAGES (100 runs/18 overs)

Batting	Runs	HS	Avge	SR	Ct
L. J. Wright......	564	111*	51.27	171.95	6
Craig Cachopa...	291	89*	41.57	143.34	9
D. P. M. D.					
Jayawardene ..	273	53	34.12	140.72	0
C. D. Nash......	444	88	37.00	133.33	2
M. W. Machan ..	198	52*	24.75	117.15	2

Bowling	W	BB	Avge	ER
W. A. T. Beer.....	11	3-23	29.18	7.29
T. S. Mills	19	4-22	18.84	7.95
O. E. Robinson ...	14	3-16	24.07	8.79
M. H. Yardy......	9	2-25	42.11	8.81
C. J. Liddle.......	9	2-17	35.66	9.00

FIRST-CLASS COUNTY RECORDS

Highest score for	344*	M. W. Goodwin v Somerset at Taunton	2009
Highest score against	322	E. Paynter (Lancashire) at Hove	1937
Leading run-scorer	34,150	J. G. Langridge (avge 37.69)	1928–55
Best bowling for	10-48	C. H. G. Bland v Kent at Tonbridge	1899
Best bowling against	9-11	A. P. Freeman (Kent) at Hove	1922
Leading wicket-taker	2,211	M. W. Tate (avge 17.41)	1912–37
Highest total for	742-5 dec	v Somerset at Taunton	2009
Highest total against	726	by Nottinghamshire at Nottingham	1895
Lowest total for {	19	v Surrey at Godalming	1830
	19	v Nottinghamshire at Hove	1873
Lowest total against	18	by Kent at Gravesend....................	1867

LIST A COUNTY RECORDS

Highest score for	163	C. J. Adams v Middlesex at Arundel.........	1999
Highest score against	198*	G. A. Gooch (Essex) at Hove..............	1982
Leading run-scorer	7,969	A. P. Wells (avge 31.62)	1981–96
Best bowling for	7-41	A. N. Jones v Nottinghamshire at Nottingham .	1986
Best bowling against	8-21	M. A. Holding (Derbyshire) at Hove.........	1988
Leading wicket-taker	370	R. J. Kirtley (avge 22.35).	1995–2010
Highest total for	399-4	v Worcestershire at Horsham	2011
Highest total against	377-9	by Somerset at Hove....................	2003
Lowest total for	49	v Derbyshire at Chesterfield..............	1969
Lowest total against	36	by Leicestershire at Leicester..............	1973

TWENTY20 COUNTY RECORDS

Highest score for	153*	L. J. Wright v Essex at Chelmsford..........	2014
Highest score against	152*	G. R. Napier (Essex) at Chelmsford..........	2008
Leading run-scorer	2,746	L. J. Wright (avge 33.08).................	2004–15
Best bowling for	5-11	Mushtaq Ahmed v Essex at Hove	2005
Best bowling against	5-14	A. D. Mascarenhas (Hampshire) at Hove	2004
Leading wicket-taker {	77	C. J. Liddle (avge 22.68)	2008–15
	77	M. H. Yardy (avge 28.02)	2004–15
Highest total for	239-5	v Glamorgan at Hove....................	2010
Highest total against	242-3	by Essex at Chelmsford	2008
Lowest total for	67	v Hampshire at Hove....................	2004
Lowest total against	85	by Hampshire at Southampton.............	2008

ADDRESS

County Ground, Eaton Road, Hove BN3 3AN; 0844 264 0202; info@sussexcricket.co.uk; www.sussexcricket.co.uk.

OFFICIALS

Captain 2015 E. C. Joyce
     2016 L. J. Wright
Cricket manager 2015 M. A. Robinson
Director of cricket 2016 K. Greenfield
Head coach 2016 M. J. G. Davis
President D. B. R. Bowden

Chairman J. R. May
Chief executive Z. Toumazi
Chairman, cricket committee J. R. T. Barclay
Head groundsman A. Mackay
Scorer M. J. Charman

SUSSEX v LEEDS/BRADFORD MCCU

At Hove, April 2–4. Drawn. Toss: Sussex. First-class debuts: J. S. E. Ellis-Grewal, D. T. P. Pratt, W. T. Root, G. F. B. Scott, C. F. Wakefield, L. Watkinson, L. P. Weston. County debuts: T. S. Mills, A. Shahzad.

This was one of the few occasions in a season of injuries when Sussex could field their strongest side, yet none of their batsmen truly mastered accurate bowling on a slow, seaming pitch in bone-numbing cold. Yardy, at least, appeared to relish the attritional conditions: his 88 took up more than four hours. The students survived 14 overs on the first evening unscathed but, after rain washed out the second day, Magoffin's probing length made him virtually unplayable on the last morning. Sussex paraded two new bowlers: Shahzad, from Nottinghamshire, who found consistent seam movement, and Mills, recruited from Essex, who worked up a decent pace. Liam Watkinson hit a well-organised 35 – and was unlucky not to have taken a wicket with his seamers. Another of the seven first-class debutants was Billy Root, younger brother of Joe.

Close of play: first day, Leeds/Bradford MCCU 27-0 (Thompson 12, Gubbins 14); second day, no play.

Sussex

C. D. Nash b Pratt	33	†B. C. Brown b Ellis-Grewal	0	
L. W. P. Wells c Wakefield b Lilley	10	B 2, l-b 7, n-b 14	23	
M. H. Yardy c Weston b Scott	88			
*E. C. Joyce c Lilley b Pratt	69	(6 wkts dec, 75.2 overs)	283	
C. Cachopa c Watkinson b Scott	50	1/31 (2)		
L. J. Wright not out	10	2/50 (1) 3/163 (4)		
		4/261 (3) 5/282 (5) 6/283 (7)		

A. Shahzad, S. J. Magoffin, T. S. Mills and M. E. Hobden did not bat.

Lilley 16–1–49–1; Watkinson 14–0–53–0; Pratt 20–1–64–2; Ellis-Grewal 11.2–1–41–1; Scott 14–0–67–2.

Leeds/Bradford MCCU

H. L. Thompson c Brown b Shahzad	15	J. S. E. Ellis-Grewal c Joyce b Magoffin	2	
N. R. T. Gubbins c Joyce b Magoffin	14	D. T. P. Pratt not out	0	
W. T. Root c Cachopa b Magoffin	4			
*C. A. L. Davis c Joyce b Nash	59	B 9, l-b 13, w 2, n-b 6	30	
L. P. Weston c Wright b Magoffin	0			
G. F. B. Scott b Shahzad	4	(9 wkts, 60 overs)	176	
†C. F. Wakefield b Shahzad	0	1/27 (2) 2/37 (1)		
L. Watkinson b Shahzad	35	3/39 (3) 4/39 (5)		
A. E. Lilley not out	13	5/44 (6) 6/44 (7)		
		7/137 (8) 8/169 (4) 9/176 (10)		

Magoffin 12–3–17–4; Shahzad 18–2–50–4; Mills 10–4–22–0; Hobden 9–1–26–0; Yardy 6–0–32–0; Nash 5–2–7–1.

Umpires: M. R. Benson and B. V. Taylor.

At Southampton, April 12–15. SUSSEX beat HAMPSHIRE by 92 runs.

SUSSEX v WORCESTERSHIRE

At Hove, April 19–22. Sussex won by 61 runs. Sussex 22pts, Worcestershire 7pts. Toss: Sussex.

Shahzad, now at his fourth county, shrugged off food poisoning to take a career-best five for 46 and wreck Worcestershire's assault on a gettable 247. They struggled to combat a potent mix of conventional and reverse swing, plus the occasional yorker – a fine effort considering Shahzad had spent most of the first two days recovering from his upset stomach. Even so, Worcestershire emerged with plenty of credit. Oliver had made the most of three reprieves – one of them when the ball rolled on to his stumps without dislodging a bail – to score a characterful century, while Kervezee, with only two wickets in his previous 88 first-class games, snared three top-order batsmen with nicely flighted off-breaks. The difference, though, was a spectacular first-day innings by Machan, Sussex's pugnacious left-hander. On a pitch of unreliable bounce, he leathered a hundred from 70 deliveries – his first seven scoring shots were boundaries – and had made a career-best 135 when he fell to his 100th ball. His less fluent team-mates contributed a combined 194 from 374. Mills was bothered by an injury throughout, and was later rested from the Championship side because of a back condition.

Close of play: first day, Worcestershire 45-0 (Mitchell 18, Oliver 21); second day, Sussex 8-0 (Wells 2, Joyce 6); third day, Worcestershire 47-0 (Mitchell 16, Oliver 23).

Sussex

*E. C. Joyce c Gidman b Shantry	49	– (2) c Köhler-Cadmore b Kervezee	82
L. W. P. Wells c Köhler-Cadmore b Morris	9	– (1) c Gidman b Morris	4
M. W. Machan c Oliver b Shantry	135	– lbw b Kervezee	55
C. Cachopa c Mitchell b Morris	8	– lbw b Morris	0
L. J. Wright c Senanayake b Gidman	51	– c Oliver b Kervezee	21
†B. C. Brown c sub (J. Leach) b Andrew	19	– b Shantry	44
Ashar Zaidi c Fell b Senanayake	7	– c Fell b Senanayake	16
A. Shahzad not out	45	– b Senanayake	35
S. J. Magoffin lbw b Senanayake	0	– c Mitchell b Senanayake	9
T. S. Mills b Andrew	5	– c Fell b Senanayake	8
M. E. Hobden c Fell b Andrew	1	– not out	0
B 7, l-b 9	16	B 8, l-b 8	16

1/16 (2) 2/161 (1) 3/192 (4) (79 overs) 345
4/231 (3) 5/270 (6) 6/286 (5)
7/306 (7) 8/306 (9) 9/337 (10) 10/345 (11)

1/10 (1) 2/129 (3) (87 overs) 290
3/132 (4) 4/157 (5)
5/194 (2) 6/233 (6) 7/235 (7)
8/257 (9) 9/269 (10) 10/290 (8)

Andrew 17–1–73–3; Morris 20–0–79–2; Shantry 13–2–86–2; Senanayake 25–1–79–2; Mitchell 1–0–1–0; Gidman 3–1–11–1. *Second innings*—Morris 16–2–67–2; Shantry 16–2–48–1; Andrew 8–0–37–0; Senanayake 27–8–50–4; Kervezee 20–1–72–3.

Worcestershire

*D. K. H. Mitchell b Hobden	26	– lbw b Magoffin	21
R. K. Oliver c Wright b Wells	101	– b Shahzad	27
T. C. Fell c Brown b Hobden	3	– lbw b Ashar Zaidi	21
A. P. R. Gidman lbw b Magoffin	29	– lbw b Shahzad	7
T. Köhler-Cadmore c sub (H. Z. Finch) b Magoffin	9	– c Brown b Shahzad	0
A. N. Kervezee c Joyce b Shahzad	93	– lbw b Hobden	7
†O. B. Cox lbw b Wells	0	– not out	48
G. M. Andrew b Hobden	70	– b Shahzad	7
J. D. Shantry c Joyce b Magoffin	3	– lbw b Magoffin	1
S. M. S. M. Senanayake b Ashar Zaidi	32	– c Brown b Shahzad	1
C. A. J. Morris not out	0	– c Joyce b Wells	24
B 7, l-b 5, w 3, n-b 8	23	B 7, l-b 2, w 2, n-b 10	21

1/56 (1) 2/60 (3) 3/137 (4) (105.1 overs) 389
4/153 (5) 5/227 (2) 6/227 (7)
7/315 (6) 8/332 (9) 9/389 (8) 10/389 (10)

1/57 (1) 2/59 (2) (59.3 overs) 185
3/69 (4) 4/69 (5)
5/91 (6) 6/99 (3) 7/116 (8)
8/127 (9) 9/134 (10) 10/185 (11)

Magoffin 26–6–69–3; Shahzad 13–2–44–1; Hobden 26.5–7–86–3; Mills 16.3–3–63–0; Ashar Zaidi 12.1–1–48–1; Wells 10.4–1–67–2. *Second innings*—Magoffin 16–2–46–2; Hobden 12–2–39–1; Shahzad 16–4–46–5; Ashar Zaidi 12–3–33–1; Mills 2–1–7–0; Wells 1.3–0–5–1.

Umpires: N. L. Bainton and S. J. O'Shaughnessy.

At Chester-le-Street, April 26–29. SUSSEX lost to DURHAM by six wickets. *Ollie Robinson hits a century from No. 9 on first-class debut.*

SUSSEX v MIDDLESEX

At Hove, May 10–12. Middlesex won by 79 runs. Middlesex 21pts, Sussex 3pts. Toss: Sussex.

This low-quality encounter was marked by poor shot selection on a pitch of erratic bounce and excessive sideways movement. The game's only half-century, from Yardy (who also held six catches), did not arrive until the fourth innings, when Sussex were in pursuit of 287. It would have been fewer had they not donated 84 extras – twice as many as the more disciplined Middlesex. Perhaps the crucial contribution came from Dexter: his gentle seamers broke the back of Sussex's chase after they had reached a promising 92 for one. He and Finn, seemingly at his best once more, shared eight wickets to bring Middlesex a third successive victory. A chest injury had forced Shahzad from the attack on the first day, and Sussex badly missed him on the third morning, when the last three partnerships cobbled together 66. More encouragingly for the home side, Robinson took eight wickets on his home debut, and Hobden, despite a rash of overstepping and only two expensive wickets, showed glimpses of his raw talent.

Close of play: first day, Sussex 66-3 (Joyce 3, Magoffin 3); second day, Middlesex 126-6 (Simpson 0, Rayner 19).

Middlesex

S. D. Robson c Brown b Magoffin	8	– (2) b Magoffin	15
N. R. T. Gubbins c Hobden b Shahzad	0	– (1) c Yardy b Robinson	6
N. R. D. Compton c Yardy b Robinson	30	– run out	33
*A. C. Voges c Hobden b Robinson	38	– c Yardy b Robinson	21
J. E. C. Franklin c Yardy b Shahzad	0	– c Yardy b Magoffin	5
N. J. Dexter c Joyce b Magoffin	34	– c Brown b Robinson	16
†J. A. Simpson lbw b Magoffin	16	– b Magoffin	34
O. P. Rayner lbw b Hobden	17	– c Yardy b Robinson	23
J. A. R. Harris c Brown b Robinson	9	– c Brown b Hobden	28
T. S. Roland-Jones c Cachopa b Robinson	34	– not out	2
S. T. Finn not out	21	– c Cachopa b Magoffin	9
B 9, l-b 22, w 1, n-b 30	62	B 5, l-b 7, n-b 10	22
	269		**209**

1/10 (1) 2/10 (2) 3/69 (4) (77.5 overs) 269
4/76 (5) 5/121 (3) 6/169 (7)
7/174 (6) 8/203 (9) 9/231 (8) 10/269 (10)

1/7 (1) 2/56 (2) (55.4 overs) 209
3/68 (3) 4/68 (5)
5/102 (6) 6/103 (4) 7/143 (8)
8/188 (7) 9/192 (9) 10/209 (11)

Magoffin 23–8–61–3; Shahzad 9.2–2–28–2; Hobden 16.4–3–82–1; Robinson 20.5–6–46–4; Nash 8–1–21–0. *Second innings*—Magoffin 20.4–7–49–4; Robinson 17–1–62–4; Hobden 16–2–80–1; Nash 2–0–6–0.

Sussex

C. D. Nash b Harris	23	– (2) c Rayner b Roland-Jones	22
M. H. Yardy lbw b Roland-Jones	9	– (1) c Simpson b Dexter	52
M. W. Machan c Rayner b Finn	13	– c Roland-Jones b Dexter	29
*E. C. Joyce c Dexter b Harris	8	– c Simpson b Dexter	0
S. J. Magoffin c Roland-Jones b Harris	25	– (9) c Voges b Rayner	10
C. Cachopa c Simpson b Roland-Jones	1	– (5) b Finn	18
L. J. Wright c Rayner b Finn	26	– (6) b Dexter	12
†B. C. Brown c Simpson b Rayner	46	– (7) c Rayner b Finn	29
O. E. Robinson b Rayner	2	– (8) c Voges b Finn	25
A. Shahzad not out	5	– c Simpson b Finn	0
M. E. Hobden run out	0	– not out	2
B 10, l-b 6, w 6, n-b 12	34	B 1, l-b 3, n-b 4	8
	192		**207**

1/32 (1) 2/45 (3) 3/59 (2) (49.1 overs) 192
4/71 (4) 5/76 (6) 6/110 (7)
7/151 (5) 8/161 (9) 9/192 (8) 10/192 (11)

1/46 (2) 2/92 (3) (52.5 overs) 207
3/94 (4) 4/123 (5)
5/138 (6) 6/147 (1) 7/185 (7)
8/205 (8) 9/205 (9) 10/207 (10)

Harris 16–1–79–3; Finn 13.1–1–56–2; Roland-Jones 10–5–6–2; Dexter 5–1–20–0; Franklin 1–0–10–0; Rayner 4–1–5–2. *Second innings*—Finn 15.5–2–51–4; Roland-Jones 10–0–44–1; Harris 11–1–52–0; Rayner 4–1–15–1; Dexter 12–3–41–4.

Umpires: S. A. Garratt and J. W. Lloyds.

SUSSEX v WARWICKSHIRE

At Hove, May 24–26. Sussex won by one wicket. Sussex 19pts, Warwickshire 3pts. Toss: Warwickshire.

Jordan, unwanted by England, led Sussex to a tense victory. The relief was all the greater once the ECB had decided not to punish them for a pitch, marked as poor by the umpires, that again offered uneven bounce and, occasionally, alarming lateral movement. Three players needed treatment after being hit; according to Warwickshire's Ambrose, batting was "nigh on impossible". However, Wells, the Sussex opener, had shown what could be achieved with care: he was ninth out for 92, having steered his side towards a small but useful lead. No one passed 35 for Warwickshire in either innings, but another dollop of extras – 63 all told – meant Sussex needed a tricky 190. At 45 for five and with Chris Wright rampant, they looked dead in the water. Brown gave them hope, but Rankin snatched three wickets in ten balls, leaving Sussex 15 from their target and the last pair at the crease. Jordan, dropped on 44 by Barker, was unfazed, reaching his half-century from 33 deliveries, before walloping Rankin back over his head for the winning six. On the first day, Robinson had dismantled the Warwickshire batting, taking the first six wickets to fall.

Close of play: first day, Sussex 140-5 (Wells 73, Brown 8); second day, Warwickshire 180-7 (Clarke 32, Patel 11).

Warwickshire

*V. Chopra c Jordan b Robinson	16	– lbw b Magoffin	6
I. J. Westwood c Magoffin b Robinson	13	– (10) b Magoffin	2
A. Javid c Brown b Robinson	2	– (2) c Nash b Robinson	27
I. J. L. Trott b Jordan	35	– c Jordan b Hobden	16
L. J. Evans c Brown b Robinson	6	– b Hobden	9
†T. R. Ambrose lbw b Robinson	0	– c Brown b Hobden	32
R. Clarke c Finch b Robinson	11	– c Finch b Jordan	34
K. H. D. Barker c Cachopa b Magoffin	24	– b Magoffin	0
J. S. Patel c Brown b Magoffin	16	– not out	27
C. J. C. Wright not out	13	– (3) c Jordan b Hobden	22
W. B. Rankin b Magoffin	6	– b Jordan	0
L-b 8, l-b 1, n-b 14	38	B 4, l-b 13, n-b 8	25

1/35 (2) 2/35 (1) 3/54 (3)   (49 overs) 180   1/6 (1) 2/49 (3)   (53.4 overs) 200
4/76 (5) 5/76 (6) 6/100 (7)   3/87 (4) 4/91 (2)
7/100 (4) 8/159 (9) 9/168 (8) 10/180 (11)   5/126 (6) 6/129 (5) 7/134 (8)
                                       8/192 (7) 9/199 (10) 10/200 (11)

Magoffin 14–1–45–3; Jordan 15–1–48–1; Robinson 13–4–33–6; Hobden 7–1–30–0. *Second innings*—Magoffin 19–3–55–3; Jordan 15.4–3–38–2; Hobden 11–1–48–4; Robinson 8–1–42–1.

Sussex

C. D. Nash c Chopra b Clarke	17	– (2) c sub (Sukhjit Singh) b Wright	2
L. W. P. Wells b Patel	92	– (1) c Javid b Wright	19
*E. C. Joyce c Ambrose b Barker	9	– lbw b Clarke	13
H. Z. Finch b Patel	12	– b Wright	1
L. J. Wright st Ambrose b Patel	0	– c Patel b Clarke	7
C. Cachopa c Clarke b Patel	2	– c Evans b Patel	20
†B. C. Brown c Patel b Clarke	18	– c Patel b Rankin	53
C. J. Jordan c Ambrose b Clarke	2	– not out	56
O. E. Robinson lbw b Barker	1	– c Ambrose b Rankin	8
S. J. Magoffin not out	15	– b Rankin	0
M. E. Hobden lbw b Wright	1	– not out	0
L-b 7, w 1, n-b 14	22	B 4, l-b 1, n-b 6	11

1/46 (1) 2/75 (3) 3/115 (4)   (59.3 overs) 191
4/125 (5) 5/129 (6) 6/156 (7)
7/160 (8) 8/161 (9) 9/186 (2) 10/191 (11)

1/14 (2)   (9 wkts, 46.1 overs) 190
2/31 (1) 3/35 (4)
4/38 (3) 5/45 (5) 6/98 (6)
7/153 (7) 8/173 (9) 9/175 (10)

Barker 18–6–38–2; Wright 12.3–3–55–1; Clarke 16–3–45–3; Rankin 2–0–16–0; Patel 10–3–24–4; Trott 1–0–6–0. *Second innings*—Barker 15–4–49–0; Wright 13–2–54–3; Patel 6–1–15–1; Clarke 7–1–35–2; Rankin 5.1–0–32–3.

Umpires: R. J. Evans and M. A. Gough.

At Nottingham, June 1–3. SUSSEX lost to NOTTINGHAMSHIRE by 159 runs.

SUSSEX v HAMPSHIRE

At Hove, June 7–9. Hampshire won by six wickets. Hampshire 23pts, Sussex 5pts. Toss: Sussex. First-class debut: F. J. Hudson-Prentice. Championship debut: J. M. Bird.

    Hampshire gained their first win since promotion, despite another difficult pitch. The game was turned their way by Wheater's whirlwind century, Berg's all-round excellence and, in Sussex's second innings, the quickest spell seen at Hove for years. Wheater, with a string of improvised shots, and Berg took advantage of a weakened attack to plunder 165, an eighth-wicket record for Hampshire against Sussex; the innings ended when Berg was run out on 99 by Hobden's direct hit. When Sussex batted again, 141 behind, Edwards tore in down the slope for his first five-for since 2012, even having what amounted to a long-stop after Wright upper-cut him over the slips; largely, though, he reaped the rewards of a fuller length, and Sussex led by just one when their sixth wicket fell. Wright and Brown went on the counter-attack, until Brown ran out his partner looking for a non-existent single. In the ensuing collapse, Sussex lost their last four for four, and Terry saw Hampshire home with more than a day to spare.

    Close of play: first day, Hampshire 116-4 (Vince 52, Briggs 0); second day, Sussex 142-5 (Wright 28, Magoffin 0).

Sussex

M. H. Yardy c Smith b Berg	41	– (2) lbw b Edwards 15
L. W. P. Wells c Vince b Berg	16	– (1) c Smith b Edwards 0
M. W. Machan lbw b Bird	13	– b Edwards 1
*E. C. Joyce c Vince b Berg	9	– c Vince b Berg 36
C. D. Nash c Terry b Vince	48	– lbw b Edwards 50
L. J. Wright c Ervine b Briggs	59	– run out 84
†B. C. Brown c Ervine b Edwards	6	– (8) c Ervine b Bird 52
O. E. Robinson c Ervine b Berg	6	– (9) c Berg b Bird 1
F. J. Hudson-Prentice c Berg b Bird	15	– (10) c Terry b Briggs 0
S. J. Magoffin c Vince b Bird	11	– (7) c Vince b Edwards 0
M. E. Hobden not out	0	– not out 0
B 8, l-b 6, n-b 12	26	B 3, l-b 11, w 3, n-b 10 27

1/47 (2) 2/72 (3) 3/86 (1)   (61.2 overs) 251
4/87 (4) 5/202 (5) 6/202 (6)
7/211 (8) 8/227 (7) 9/240 (9) 10/251 (10)

1/12 (1) 2/16 (3)   (79.5 overs) 266
3/23 (2) 4/94 (4)
5/134 (5) 6/142 (7) 7/262 (6)
8/263 (8) 9/264 (9) 10/266 (10)

Bird 14.2–4–69–3; Edwards 12–1–54–1; Berg 22–8–67–4; Briggs 11–2–40–1; Vince 2–1–7–1.
Second innings—Edwards 17–5–58–5; Bird 16–1–72–2; Berg 16–4–41–1; Briggs 30.5–7–81–1.

Hampshire

*J. H. K. Adams run out	11	– c Yardy b Wells 30
S. P. Terry c Nash b Robinson	30	– not out 62
M. A. Carberry c Brown b Magoffin	14	– c Brown b Hobden 6
J. M. Vince c Joyce b Hobden	76	– c Joyce b Wells 10
W. R. Smith lbw b Robinson	7	– c Wells b Hobden 6
D. R. Briggs c Brown b Robinson	12	
†A. J. A. Wheater c Joyce b Wells	111	– (6) not out 5
S. M. Ervine lbw b Hobden	15	
G. K. Berg run out	99	
F. H. Edwards c Wright b Wells	2	
J. M. Bird not out	6	
B 5, l-b 1, w 1, n-b 2	9	L-b 5, w 2 7

1/28 (1) 2/44 (2) 3/81 (3)   (85.3 overs) 392
4/99 (5) 5/139 (6) 6/171 (4)
7/197 (8) 8/362 (7) 9/366 (10) 10/392 (9)

1/51 (1)   (4 wkts, 29.5 overs) 126
2/78 (3) 3/101 (4)
4/120 (5)

Magoffin 22.3–6–59–1; Robinson 23–3–101–3; Hobden 19–2–88–2; Hudson-Prentice 8–0–51–0;
Wells 8–0–48–2; Nash 2–0–15–0; Yardy 3–0–24–0. *Second innings*—Magoffin 8–3–21–0;
Robinson 4–0–22–0; Wells 10.5–0–53–2; Hobden 7–0–25–2.

Umpires: N. G. C. Cowley and S. A. Garratt.

SUSSEX v DURHAM

At Arundel, June 15–18. Durham won by 178 runs. Durham 22pts, Sussex 4pts. Toss: Sussex.
County debut: G. H. Dockrell.

Sussex had requested an easy surface to help their batsmen regain confidence, but only on the last
two days did it flatten out – by which time Championship leaders Durham were heading for their
sixth win. Joyce might have got wind of conditions when he chose to bowl, but Shahzad lasted just

four overs on his comeback from injury. Linley, though, in the only game of his loan spell from Surrey, took up the slack with three wickets in 15 balls, and later completed his first five-for since 2012 (he had also appeared for Sussex in 2006, against the Sri Lankans). Another borrowed bowler, slow left-armer Dockrell, finished with none for 180 on arrival from Somerset, but did take Sussex to a batting point after they were shredded by Rushworth. Armed with a lead of 100, Durham lurched to 13 for four thanks to a devastating burst of four for two by Magoffin, also in 15 balls. Then Muchall, who had made an unbeaten 81 in the first innings, led the fightback: Sussex, notionally chasing 514, had four and a half sessions to survive. That they took it to tea on the final day owed much to a first hundred of the summer by Wells, whose improving leg-spin had accounted for five wickets.

Close of play: first day, Sussex 44-2 (Machan 11, Joyce 0); second day, Durham 168-6 (Muchall 66, Coughlin 5); third day, Sussex 114-2 (Wells 53, Joyce 5).

Durham

M. D. Stoneman c Joyce b Linley	51	– c Wright b Magoffin	0
K. K. Jennings b Magoffin	5	– c Brown b Magoffin	0
S. G. Borthwick c Yardy b Linley	24	– b Wells	74
*P. D. Collingwood lbw b Linley	9	– b Magoffin	2
†M. J. Richardson c Nash b Magoffin	46	– b Magoffin	115
G. J. Muchall not out	81	– lbw b Wells	115
R. D. Pringle b Linley	5	– b Linley	15
P. Coughlin c Yardy b Linley	0	– c Joyce b Magoffin	64
J. W. Hastings c Machan b Wells	23	– b Linley	91
C. Rushworth c sub (C. J. Liddle) b Wells	39	– c Wells b Linley	19
G. Onions c Nash b Wells	1	– not out	15
B 4, l-b 10, w 1, n-b 2	17	B 3, l-b 9, w 6	18

1/11 (2) 2/80 (3) 3/87 (1) (77.1 overs) 301   1/0 (1) 2/1 (2) (101.4 overs) 413
4/96 (4) 5/179 (5) 6/197 (7)   3/11 (4) 4/13 (5)
7/197 (8) 8/233 (9) 9/296 (10) 10/301 (11)   5/131 (3) 6/155 (7) 7/271 (6)
   8/334 (8) 9/382 (10) 10/413 (9)

Magoffin 19–3–84–2; Shahzad 4–0–18–0; Linley 19–6–63–5; Nash 1–0–5–0; Dockrell 20–0–66–0; Wright 3–0–16–0; Wells 11.1–3–35–3. *Second innings*—Magoffin 30–8–89–5; Linley 22.4–2–93–3; Wright 5–0–21–0; Dockrell 24–2–114–0; Wells 20–1–84–2.

Sussex

M. H. Yardy b Rushworth	20	– (2) c Richardson b Coughlin	28
L. W. P. Wells b Rushworth	13	– (1) c Collingwood b Pringle	108
M. W. Machan c Jennings b Onions	21	– c Richardson b Hastings	24
*E. C. Joyce c Jennings b Hastings	23	– c Richardson b Hastings	12
L. J. Wright c Richardson b Rushworth	5	– (6) c and b Borthwick	49
†B. C. Brown c Richardson b Coughlin	15	– (7) lbw b Borthwick	60
C. D. Nash b Rushworth	16	– (5) c Rushworth b Onions	13
A. Shahzad b Rushworth	15	– st Richardson b Borthwick	2
G. H. Dockrell not out	37	– c Richardson b Borthwick	0
S. J. Magoffin c Collingwood b Rushworth	14	– c Muchall b Onions	0
T. E. Linley c sub (G. Clark) b Onions	10	– not out	21
B 1, l-b 5, n-b 6	12	B 4, l-b 4, w 6, n-b 4	18

1/28 (1) 2/33 (2) 3/57 (3) (58.5 overs) 201   1/60 (2) 2/97 (3) (116 overs) 335
4/64 (5) 5/91 (6) 6/103 (4)   3/125 (4) 4/150 (5)
7/126 (7) 8/135 (8) 9/161 (10) 10/201 (11)   5/242 (1) 6/242 (6) 7/254 (8)
   8/256 (9) 9/271 (10) 10/335 (7)

Rushworth 21–5–49–6; Onions 15.5–3–60–2; Hastings 15–2–64–1; Coughlin 5–1–14–1; Borthwick 2–0–8–0. *Second innings*—Rushworth 19–3–70–0; Onions 18–3–71–2; Pringle 28–10–54–1; Hastings 21–6–58–2; Coughlin 8–3–19–1; Collingwood 3–1–9–0; Borthwick 19–7–46–4.

Umpires: J. W. Lloyds and A. G. Wharf.

At Birmingham, June 28–July 1. SUSSEX drew with WARWICKSHIRE. *Four Sussex batsmen hit hundreds, for only the third time in their history.*

At Taunton, July 5–8. SUSSEX drew with SOMERSET.

SUSSEX v NOTTINGHAMSHIRE

At Horsham, July 19–21. Nottinghamshire won by an innings and 103 runs. Nottinghamshire 24pts, Sussex 2pts. Toss: Nottinghamshire.

Nottinghamshire continued the revival that had coincided with the appointment of former England coach Peter Moores as a consultant at the end of June. An innings victory, their first outside Trent Bridge since 2008, was set up by James Taylor's magnificent career-best 291; he batted for more than eight hours and gave not a single chance, confirming the docility of the pitch. It was the highest

HIGHEST SCORES FOR NOTTINGHAMSHIRE

312*	W. W. Keeton	v Middlesex at The Oval	1939
296	A. O. Jones	v Gloucestershire at Nottingham	1903
294	J. R. Gunn	v Leicestershire at Nottingham	1903
291	**J. W. A. Taylor**	**v Sussex at Horsham**	**2015**
275	D. J. Hussey	v Essex at Nottingham	2007
274	A. O. Jones	v Essex at Leyton	1905
273	W. Gunn	v Derbyshire at Derby	1901
272	†J. Iremonger	v Kent at Nottingham	1904
268*	J. A. Dixon	v Sussex at Nottingham	1897
267	A. Shrewsbury	v Middlesex at Nottingham	1887
267	A. Shrewsbury	v Sussex at Nottingham	1890

† *The innings mentioned by James Joyce in* Ulysses: *". . . the exploits of King Willow, Iremonger having made a hundred and something second wicket not out for Notts . . ."*

score for Nottinghamshire since 1939, Taylor's third above 150 against Sussex – since leaving Leicestershire at the end of 2011 he averaged 117 against them – and a ground record. He credited sessions with Moores for his return to form, not that it gave Moores much pleasure to see his old county so out of sorts. The Sussex attack, with at least four seamers missing through injury, toiled away as Taylor and Read took their sixth-wicket stand to 365. Three weeks earlier, four Sussex batsmen had struck centuries in the same innings; now four bowlers racked up hundreds. Even so, it was their batsmen who let them down: 16 Sussex wickets fell on the third day. In a team bereft of confidence only Machan and Wright offered resistance. Whispers of relegation spread round the boundary edge.

Close of play: first day, Nottinghamshire 358-5 (J. W. A. Taylor 163, Read 54); second day, Sussex 157-4 (Wright 21, Cachopa 13).

Nottinghamshire

B. R. M. Taylor lbw b Hobden	7	B. A. Hutton not out	12
A. D. Hales c Nash b Robinson	3	B 1, l-b 4, n-b 13	18
S. J. Mullaney c Brown b Robinson	15		
J. W. A. Taylor c Nash b Magoffin	291		
M. H. Wessels c Wells b Robinson	94	1/8 (2)	(7 wkts dec, 136.1 overs) 570
S. R. Patel c and b Robinson	9	2/14 (1) 3/30 (3)	
*†C. M. W. Read c Brown b Hobden	121	4/174 (5) 5/186 (6)	
		6/551 (7) 7/570 (4)	110 overs: 416-5

L. Wood, G. Keedy and H. F. Gurney did not bat.

Magoffin 31.1–13–53–1; Robinson 31–7–112–4; Hobden 26–3–143–2; Wells 26–2–120–0; Burgoyne 15–0–102–0; Nash 7–0–35–0.

Sussex

*E. C. Joyce c Hutton b Gurney	40	– (2) c Hales b Gurney		32
L. W. P. Wells c Read b Gurney	40	– (1) c Mullaney b Wood		0
M. W. Machan c Read b Gurney	20	– c Mullaney b Gurney		108
C. D. Nash c Mullaney b Keedy	11	– lbw b Hutton		15
L. J. Wright c Mullaney b Gurney	50	– c Read b Keedy		67
C. Cachopa lbw b Hutton	13	– c Keedy b Patel		4
†B. C. Brown c Read b Gurney	5	– c J. W. A. Taylor b Gurney		0
O. E. Robinson c Read b Keedy	0	– c Read b Wood		8
P. I. Burgoyne b Wood	13	– lbw b Wood		13
S. J. Magoffin not out	6	– c Wessels b Keedy		0
M. E. Hobden c Read b Keedy	0	– not out		0
L-b 5, n-b 10	15	B 3, l-b 1, w 1, n-b 2		7

1/79 (1) 2/84 (2) 3/119 (4)   (69 overs) 213
4/123 (3) 5/162 (6) 6/187 (7)
7/194 (5) 8/198 (8) 9/212 (9) 10/213 (11)

1/0 (1) 2/92 (2)   (61 overs) 254
3/124 (4) 4/183 (3)
5/192 (6) 6/192 (7) 7/222 (8)
8/250 (5) 9/254 (10) 10/254 (9)

Wood 12–6–30–1; Hutton 9–0–35–1; Gurney 19–4–75–5; Keedy 23–11–45–3; Patel 6–2–23–0. *Second innings*—Wood 10–4–27–3; Hutton 11–1–68–1; Gurney 16–2–56–3; Keedy 17–1–62–2; Patel 7–0–37–1.

Umpires: S. C. Gale and B. V. Taylor.

At Lord's, August 7–10. SUSSEX lost to MIDDLESEX by 20 runs.

SUSSEX v YORKSHIRE

At Hove, August 21–24. Drawn. Sussex 12pts, Yorkshire 11pts. Toss: Yorkshire.

After serving up spicy Hove pitches for much of the season, Sussex now produced the blandest of surfaces. The idea was to negate Yorkshire's heavyweight seam attack, and give their own batsmen the chance to find some form. It worked on both counts: even before the final day was washed out there was little chance of a positive result. Sussex hit three centuries and, for the first time in 2015, claimed maximum batting points. Yardy, with his first century for 15 months, and Brown put on 135 for the seventh wicket as Yorkshire's bowlers were rendered anodyne. Earlier, though, their batsmen had also filled their boots: in an innings of immense quality, Ballance added 197 with Bresnan – a seventh-wicket record between these counties – and completed his first hundred since the Antigua Test in April. Eighteen years after being locked in the umpires' room at Hove for a couple of hours, Yorkshire president Dickie Bird suffered another trauma when he lost his cap.

Close of play: first day, Yorkshire 346-6 (Ballance 98, Bresnan 44); second day, Sussex 175-4 (Yardy 7, Robinson 0); third day, Sussex 493-7 (Brown 106, Jordan 9).

Yorkshire

†A. J. Hodd c Jordan b Robinson	11	S. A. Patterson c Brown b Liddle	0
A. Z. Lees b Robinson	69	R. J. Sidebottom not out	17
J. A. Leaning c and b Jordan	0		
*A. W. Gale lbw b Jordan	39	B 8, l-b 12, w 4, n-b 13	37
G. S. Ballance b Liddle	165		
G. J. Maxwell c Jordan b Robinson	43	(136.3 overs) 494	
A. U. Rashid c Brown b Jordan	7		
T. T. Bresnan run out	78		
L. E. Plunkett run out	28		

1/21 (1) 2/22 (3)   (136.3 overs) 494
3/110 (4) 4/134 (2) 5/203 (6)
6/252 (7) 7/449 (5) 8/454 (8)
9/459 (10) 10/494 (9)   110 overs: 393-6

Magoffin 30–5–91–0; Robinson 30–11–72–3; Jordan 24–3–87–3; Liddle 24–0–119–2; Wells 23.3–4–77–0; Nash 5–0–28–0.

Sussex

*E. C. Joyce c Leaning b Rashid. 100	†B. C. Brown not out. 106
L. W. P. Wells b Rashid 43	C. J. Jordan not out 9
M. W. Machan c Leaning b Rashid. 0	B 12, l-b 10 22
C. D. Nash lbw b Plunkett. 18	
M. H. Yardy lbw b Sidebottom 124	1/110 (2) 2/110 (3) (7 wkts, 123 overs) 493
O. E. Robinson c Maxwell b Plunkett. 48	3/139 (4) 4/175 (1) 5/272 (6)
L. J. Wright b Patterson 23	6/326 (7) 7/461 (5)

S. J. Magoffin and C. J. Liddle did not bat.

Sidebottom 15–3–39–1; Bresnan 20–5–66–0; Patterson 19–6–63–1; Plunkett 24–4–90–2; Rashid 33–5–159–3; Maxwell 9–1–43–0; Leaning 3–1–11–0.

Umpires: N. L. Bainton and P. J. Hartley.

At Worcester, September 1–4. SUSSEX beat WORCESTERSHIRE by an innings and 63 runs.

SUSSEX v SOMERSET

At Hove, September 14–17. Drawn. Sussex 11pts, Somerset 13pts. Toss: Sussex.

On another flat pitch, Somerset did well to reduce Sussex to 171 for six, after the Overton twins became the second pair of brothers following Surrey's Currans in 2015 to share the new ball in a Championship match. But a stand of 137 between Yardy and Ashar Zaidi steered Sussex towards full batting points for the third successive game. Trescothick, who had just hit 153 against Hampshire, then cracked a sumptuous double-century – his sixth – though the loss of the third day to rain meant the game descended into a scramble for bonus points. A full-blooded hundred from Trego ensured Somerset also breezed past 400. A cheer went up from the home dressing-room after the close when news filtered through of Yorkshire's win at Southampton, meaning that Sussex were 16 points – and Somerset 18 – clear of Hampshire going into the final round. Back on the second day Yardy marked the last home match of a 17-season career with his 23rd first-class hundred. When he fell two deliveries later, the Somerset players shook his hand and, moments after they had taken to their feet to mark his century, the crowd gave Yardy a second and final standing ovation. It later emerged that Craig Overton had been overheard on the first day by both Yardy and umpire Alex Wharf muttering "Go back to your own fucking country", a comment thought to have been aimed at the Pakistan-born – but British-qualified – Zaidi. Overton was subsequently withdrawn from the game, with Somerset citing a hand injury, and found guilty of a level one offence. Previous misdemeanours meant he would serve a two-match ban, extending into 2016.

Close of play: first day, Sussex 303-6 (Yardy 60, Ashar Zaidi 90); second day, Somerset 114-2 (Trescothick 53, Hildreth 16); third day, no play.

Sussex

*E. C. Joyce c Ronchi b J. Overton 83	S. J. Magoffin c Cooper b Trego 13
L. W. P. Wells c Trescothick b Groenewald 13	L. J. Hatchett not out. 2
M. W. Machan c C. Overton b J. Overton . 21	
C. D. Nash c Trescothick b Trego 11	B 5, l-b 1, w 1, n-b 2 9
L. J. Wright c Trescothick b Allenby 20	
M. H. Yardy c Hildreth b Trego 104	1/24 (2) 2/67 (3) (104.1 overs) 409
†B. C. Brown c C. Overton b Leach 0	3/88 (4) 4/136 (5)
Ashar Zaidi lbw b J. Overton 91	5/162 (1) 6/171 (7) 7/308 (8)
C. J. Jordan c Ronchi b Groenewald 42	8/359 (6) 9/391 (10) 10/409 (9)

C. Overton 14–2–40–0; J. Overton 25–5–122–3; Groenewald 22.1–0–97–2; Trego 21–4–72–3; Allenby 17–4–55–1; Leach 5–1–17–1.

Somerset

*M. E. Trescothick not out	210	P. D. Trego not out	100
T. B. Abell b Jordan	13	L-b 10, n-b 6	16
T. L. W. Cooper c Brown b Magoffin	31		
J. C. Hildreth c Brown b Jordan	68	1/26 (2) 2/82 (3) (4 wkts dec, 100 overs)	438
J. Allenby c Nash b Jordan	0	3/256 (4) 4/262 (5)	

†L. Ronchi, C. Overton, T. D. Groenewald, J. Overton and M. J. Leach did not bat.

Magoffin 23–3–86–1; Jordan 24–2–110–3; Hatchett 17–0–93–0; Ashar Zaidi 25–0–82–0; Wells 8–0–46–0; Nash 3–0–11–0.

Umpires: I. J. Gould and A. G. Wharf.

At Leeds, September 22–25. SUSSEX lost to YORKSHIRE by 100 runs. *Sussex are relegated.*

WARWICKSHIRE

Muddling along in the Midlands

PAUL BOLTON

A season that promised so much fizzled out after Warwickshire failed to meet the high standards they had set for themselves in 2014, when they challenged for silverware in all three competitions. They effectively conceded the Championship to Yorkshire as early as the first week of July, after they were shot out by the title holders for 69, their lowest total since 1986 and the worst of the season anywhere in the country (apart from Australia's 60 all out in the Fourth Test at Trent Bridge). Although they bounced back to beat Durham and Somerset in their next two matches, their form remained erratic. They finished fifth.

Warwickshire's white-ball cricket was equally underwhelming and, while they reached finals day at Edgbaston for a second successive season, they meekly surrendered their title after Northamptonshire reduced them to 14 for four in the semi. The form of New Zealand captain Brendon McCullum, who had signed to great fanfare in the summer, was their Twenty20 campaign in microcosm: he plundered a competition-record 158 not out from 64 balls against Derbyshire, but failed to reach 50 again and, despite stating he would try to find time in his schedule, was unavailable for finals day.

They were mediocre in the Royal London One-Day Cup, losing heavily to Nottinghamshire and Essex, and finishing in the bottom half of their group. Dougie Brown, the director of cricket, claimed that poor scheduling had denied them the chance to prepare for the 50-over competition, yet they might still have reached the knockout stages had their final match against Kent not been washed out.

He might equally have blamed his top order: frequent collective failures meant that the rest were regularly left to dig Warwickshire out of trouble. "The disappointment is that we didn't quite manage to win the key moments in games in the second half of the season," said Brown. "And we didn't quite deliver the type of cricket that we had in 2014."

In the Championship, Warwickshire's runs tended to come from their less heralded batsmen. Ian Westwood was the only player to top 850 in first-class cricket, despite the distraction of a benefit season and missing two matches with a broken thumb. Laurie Evans recaptured his form of 2013, and made a maiden double-century in the turgid home draw with Sussex.

But the bigger names were disappointing. Jonathan Trott's retirement from international cricket did little to improve his form: he was unable to impose himself on county attacks as he once had, and his season dribbled away in a series of skittish cameos. Ireland captain William Porterfield made a one-day century against Sussex, but failed to make a Championship hundred for the fourth time in five seasons since joining Warwickshire. Varun Chopra began

Jeetan Patel

with centuries in the first two home matches, then passed 50 only twice in 19 innings; his captaincy also became more conservative as he battled for runs. In January, he was replaced by Ian Bell, who nevertheless insisted his England career was not over.

The younger contingent faced similar difficulties: Ateeq Javid, Jonathon Webb and Freddie Coleman struggled to make the transition from the Second XI. Tom Lewis and Pete McKay were released, as was Tom Milnes, who was signed by Derbyshire after a loan spell with them.

Sam Hain, who turned 20 in July, did show glimpses of quality, despite having his season disrupted by a shoulder injury. He scored a composed second-innings century in the defeat by Yorkshire, when others lacked his application against penetrative bowling.

The seam attack was frequently depleted by injuries: Chris Woakes, Boyd Rankin, Chris Wright and Keith Barker all missed chunks of the season. Woakes managed just three Championship appearances because of a knee injury or selection for England's one-day side. Rikki Clarke took up some of the slack with another solid all-round season.

Jeetan Patel, the former New Zealand off-spinner, proved a model overseas pro once more, taking over 50 first-class wickets for the fourth successive season, and often contributed valuable lower-order runs. He also sparked a debate, after the draw with Middlesex at Edgbaston in September, he said English spinners need to "practise a lot more".

The return of Test cricket to Edgbaston, after two season's absence, improved Warwickshire's financial situation after several eye-watering losses under Colin Povey, who stepped down as chief executive in December 2015 at the end of his tenth season in charge. A month later, the club announced a record operating profit of £2.26m. Povey deserves credit for driving through the pavilion development which replaced the decaying Victorian structure. His critics, of whom there were plenty, might argue that Warwickshire became less of a cricket club and more Edgbaston.com, during a period in which loyal members felt disconnected and undervalued.

Neil Snowball, who was head of sport operations at the 2012 London Olympics and chief operating officer of the organising committee for the 2015 Rugby World Cup, has the difficult tasks of rebuilding those relationships. But supporters will forgive much if the team starts winning trophies again.

The new year began with the shocking news that Tom Allin, a seamer who had played twice for the club, most recently in 2013, had been found dead beneath the Torridge Bridge, near Bideford, in north Devon. He was 28.

Championship attendance: 22,132.

WARWICKSHIRE RESULTS

All first-class matches – Played 16: Won 5, Lost 5, Drawn 6.
County Championship matches – Played 16: Won 5, Lost 5, Drawn 6.

LV= County Championship, 5th in Division 1;
NatWest T20 Blast, semi-finalists; Royal London One-Day Cup, 6th in Group B.

COUNTY CHAMPIONSHIP AVERAGES, BATTING AND FIELDING

Cap		Birthplace	M	I	NO	R	HS	100	Avge	Ct/St
	S. R. Hain	*Hong Kong*	10	17	2	547	106	2	36.46	8
2008	I. J. Westwood	*Birmingham†*	14	25	1	856	196	1	35.66	6
	L. J. Evans	*Lambeth*	15	27	3	826	213*	1	34.41	16
2013	K. H. D. Barker	*Manchester*	13	20	3	516	102*	1	30.35	2
2013	C. J. C. Wright	*Chipping Norton*	11	16	6	300	65	0	30.00	2
2007	T. R. Ambrose	*Newcastle, Australia*	14	22	0	651	153	2	29.59	34/5
2012	V. Chopra	*Barking*	15	25	1	658	119*	2	27.41	20
2012	J. S. Patel§	*Wellington, NZ*	16	23	2	543	98	0	25.85	10
2005	I. J. L. Trott	*Cape Town, SA*	11	18	0	451	87	0	25.05	6
2011	R. Clarke	*Orsett*	16	26	3	535	67	0	23.26	22
2014	W. T. S. Porterfield	*Londonderry, N. Ire*	6	11	0	196	61	0	17.81	7
2009	C. R. Woakes‡	*Birmingham†*	3	5	0	83	42	0	16.60	1
2013	W. B. Rankin	*Londonderry, N. Ire*	13	18	8	155	56*	0	15.50	4
	A. Javid	*Birmingham†*	4	6	0	64	27	0	10.66	4
	P. J. McKay	*Burton-upon-Trent*	2	4	0	24	17	0	6.00	6/1
	O. J. Hannon-Dalby	*Halifax*	4	6	1	24	8	0	4.80	0
	J. P. Webb	*Solihull†*	2	4	0	18	14	0	4.50	1

Also batted: M. R. Adair (*Belfast*) (1 match) 24*, 10*; I. R. Bell‡ (*Walsgrave†*) (cap 2001) (2 matches) 111, 12, 55 (4 ct); F. R. J. Coleman (*Edinburgh*) (1 match) 0, 0 (2 ct); R. A. Jones (*Stourbridge*) (1 match) 3; T. P. Milnes (*Stourbridge*) (1 match) 12*, 14*. J. E. Poysden (*Shoreham-by-Sea*) (1 match) did not bat.

† *Born in Warwickshire.* ‡ *ECB contract.* § *Official overseas player.*
¶ *Other non-England-qualified player.*

BOWLING

	Style	O	M	R	W	BB	5I	Avge
C. R. Woakes	RFM	74	20	217	11	3-48	0	19.72
J. S. Patel	OB	497.5	113	1,466	58	7-38	3	25.27
R. Clarke	RFM	387.3	83	1,206	47	5-62	1	25.65
W. B. Rankin	RFM	272.3	28	1,127	43	6-55	2	26.20
K. H. D. Barker	LFM	424.4	91	1,275	46	5-68	2	27.69
C. J. C. Wright	RFM	274.2	36	1,033	31	5-40	1	33.32

Also bowled: M. R. Adair (RFM) 15–3–61–1; L. J. Evans (RFM) 5–0–31–1; O. J. Hannon-Dalby (RFM) 116–23–406–8; A. Javid (RM/OB) 21–2–74–0; R. A. Jones (RFM) 17–1–68–4; T. P. Milnes (RFM) 30–3–120–4; J. E. Poysden (LBG) 40.4–4–165–1; I. J. L. Trott (RM) 34–6–108–1; I. J. Westwood (OB) 4–0–18–0.

LEADING ROYAL LONDON CUP AVERAGES (100 runs/4 wickets)

Batting	Runs	HS	Avge	SR	Ct/St
V. Chopra	217	88	54.25	71.14	3
A. Javid	143	42*	47.66	88.27	1
W. T. S. Porterfield	170	100	34.00	80.95	4
I. J. L. Trott	128	73*	32.00	64.97	0
T. R. Ambrose	155	59	31.00	75.60	12/1

Bowling	W	BB	Avge	ER
O. J. Hannon-Dalby	15	5-27	17.06	5.50
W. B. Rankin	4	3-33	24.75	4.95
K. H. D. Barker	4	2-51	35.50	5.46
J. E. Poysden	4	3-41	36.35	6.30
J. S. Patel	6	3-42	41.00	4.55

LEADING NATWEST T20 BLAST AVERAGES (120 runs/18 overs)

Batting	Runs	HS	Avge	SR	Ct/St
B. B. McCullum	270	158*	45.00	191.48	2
I. R. Bell	163	90	27.16	132.52	2
A. Javid	187	51*	37.40	124.66	1
L. J. Evans	312	50	20.80	119.54	11
W. T. S. Porterfield	313	55*	44.71	118.56	6
T. R. Ambrose	202	66*	28.85	118.12	9/3
R. Clarke	263	52*	23.90	118.18	12
V. Chopra	328	80	21.86	106.49	2

Bowling	W	BB	Avge	ER
R. Clarke	12	3-26	21.66	5.41
J. S. Patel	16	2-14	25.93	6.74
J. E. Poysden	8	4-51	28.37	7.09
A. Javid	6	2-29	36.33	7.78
W. B. Rankin	5	2-20	35.00	7.95
R. O. Gordon	21	4-20	19.85	8.34
O. J. Hannon-Dalby	20	4-29	24.65	9.10

FIRST-CLASS COUNTY RECORDS

Highest score for	501*	B. C. Lara v Durham at Birmingham	1994
Highest score against	322	I. V. A. Richards (Somerset) at Taunton	1985
Leading run-scorer	35,146	D. L. Amiss (avge 41.64)	1960–87
Best bowling for	10-41	J. D. Bannister v Comb. Services at Birmingham	1959
Best bowling against	10-36	H. Verity (Yorkshire) at Leeds	1931
Leading wicket-taker	2,201	W. E. Hollies (avge 20.45)	1932–57
Highest total for	810-4 dec	v Durham at Birmingham	1994
Highest total against	887	by Yorkshire at Birmingham	1896
Lowest total for	16	v Kent at Tonbridge	1913
Lowest total against	15	by Hampshire at Birmingham	1922

LIST A COUNTY RECORDS

Highest score for	206	A. I. Kallicharran v Oxfordshire at Birmingham	1984
Highest score against	172*	W. Larkins (Northamptonshire) at Luton	1983
Leading run-scorer	11,254	D. L. Amiss (avge 33.79)	1963–87
Best bowling for	7-32	R. G. D. Willis v Yorkshire at Birmingham	1981
Best bowling against	6-27	M. H. Yardy (Sussex) at Birmingham	2005
Leading wicket-taker	396	G. C. Small (avge 25.48)	1980–99
Highest total for	392-5	v Oxfordshire at Birmingham	1984
Highest total against	341-6	by Hampshire at Birmingham	2010
Lowest total for	59	v Yorkshire at Leeds	2001
Lowest total against	56	by Yorkshire at Birmingham	1995

TWENTY20 COUNTY RECORDS

Highest score for	158*	B. B. McCullum v Derbyshire at Birmingham	2015
Highest score against	100*	I. J. Harvey (Gloucestershire) at Birmingham	2003
Leading run-scorer	1,911	I. J. L. Trott (avge 39.81)	2003–14
Best bowling for	5-19	N. M. Carter v Worcestershire at Birmingham	2005
Best bowling against	5-25	D. J. Pattinson (Nottinghamshire) at Birmingham	2011
Leading wicket-taker	82	J. S. Patel (avge 20.93)	2009–15
Highest total for	242-2	v Derbyshire at Birmingham	2015
Highest total against	215-6	by Durham at Birmingham	2010
Lowest total for	73	v Somerset at Taunton	2013
Lowest total against	96	by Northamptonshire at Northampton	2011
	96	by Gloucestershire at Cheltenham	2013

ADDRESS

County Ground, Edgbaston, Birmingham B5 7QU; 0844 635 1902; info@edgbaston.com; www.edgbaston.com.

OFFICIALS

Captain 2015 V. Chopra
2016 I. R. Bell
Director of cricket D. R. Brown
Elite development manager P. Greetham
President Earl of Aylesford
Chairman N. Gascoigne

Chief executive 2015 C. Povey
2016 N. Snowball
Chairman, cricket committee J. H. Dodge
Head groundsman G. Barwell
Scorer M. D. Smith

At Birmingham, April 12–14 (not first-class). **Drawn.** ‡**Warwickshire 553** (124.2 overs) (I. J. Westwood 155, W. T. S. Porterfield 59, L. J. Evans 52, S. R. Hain 85, T. R. Ambrose 64; C. Bishnoi 4-105) **and 414-5 dec** (56 overs) (T. R. Ambrose 81, R. Clarke 102, W. T. S. Porterfield 93, S. R. Hain 96*); **Durham MCCU 220** (82.2 overs) (C. M. MacDonell 136; J. E. Poysden 3-41). *County debut: Sukhjit Singh. Of the three centuries in a run-saturated contest, the toughest was made by opener Charlie MacDonell, a psychology fresher, who achieved Durham MCCU's first against county opposition for two years, and was last man out, to the second new ball. Slow left-arm Sukhjit Singh came into the Warwickshire side on the final day as a replacement for Chris Wright, who was attending a funeral. A shuffled batting line-up sprinted along at more than seven an over in the second innings, with Clarke slamming seven sixes and Hain six.*

WARWICKSHIRE v HAMPSHIRE

At Birmingham, April 19–22. Drawn. Warwickshire 10pts, Hampshire 11pts. Toss: Warwickshire. County debut: A. R. Adams.

A match which promised an intriguing conclusion petered out on an increasingly docile pitch. Hampshire gave a debut to 39-year-old New Zealander Andre Adams, beginning a short spell with them before taking up a coaching job with Auckland. But Hampshire lacked the firepower to dislodge Chopra, who batted throughout the last day, when Ambrose kept him company for two hours. Warwickshire had wasted the new ball on the first morning, and allowed Wheater to strike a brisk 74, but the hostile Rankin fought back with a career-best six for 75. Warwickshire's batting faltered too, until Ambrose cut and pulled his way to a belligerent century. Although Jimmy Adams nicked the first ball of Hampshire's second innings, Carberry's 81, and a powerful hundred from Ervine, allowed them to set 379 in 107 overs. Hampshire's tight bowling ensured there was little chance of Warwickshire chasing down what would have been the highest total of the match.

Close of play: first day, Warwickshire 14-0 (Chopra 10, Westwood 4); second day, Hampshire 38-1 (Dawson 22, Carberry 14); third day, Warwickshire 47-0 (Chopra 10, Westwood 37).

Hampshire

*J. H. K. Adams c Clarke b Rankin	53	– c Ambrose b Barker	0
L. A. Dawson lbw b Wright	38	– c Hain b Clarke	27
M. A. Carberry b Wright	42	– b Clarke	81
J. M. Vince lbw b Rankin	8	– lbw b Clarke	0
W. R. Smith b Rankin	12	– st Ambrose b Patel	8
†A. J. A. Wheater c Chopra b Barker	74	– c Clarke b Patel	11
S. M. Ervine c Clarke b Rankin	0	– c Ambrose b Wright	102
G. K. Berg c Clarke b Rankin	8	– c Porterfield b Barker	36
D. R. Briggs lbw b Rankin	48	– c Patel b Wright	33
A. R. Adams c Chopra b Wright	6	– not out	13
J. A. Tomlinson not out	2	– c Patel b Rankin	11
B 9, l-b 11, w 2, n-b 6	28	B 8, l-b 3, n-b 6	17

1/94 (2) 2/121 (1) 3/137 (4)   (89.3 overs)   319   1/0 (1) 2/58 (2)   (94.2 overs)   339
4/169 (3) 5/178 (5) 6/194 (7)   3/58 (4) 4/86 (5)
7/206 (8) 8/309 (6) 9/317 (10) 10/319 (9)   5/108 (6) 6/194 (3) 7/254 (8)
                                                8/315 (9) 9/315 (7) 10/339 (11)

Barker 22–5–51–1; Wright 19–3–75–3; Clarke 18–3–59–0; Patel 14–2–39–0; Rankin 16.3–1–75–6. *Second innings*—Barker 23–4–68–2; Wright 14–2–59–2; Clarke 16–0–63–3; Rankin 12.2–1–40–1; Patel 28–5–96–2; Evans 1–0–2–0.

Warwickshire

*V. Chopra c Wheater b Berg	24	– not out		119
I. J. Westwood c Vince b Tomlinson	11	– lbw b A. R. Adams		40
W. T. S. Porterfield c Smith b Tomlinson	3	– c Wheater b Tomlinson		29
L. J. Evans lbw b Ervine	16	– c A. R. Adams b Tomlinson		9
S. R. Hain c Smith b A. R. Adams	25	– c Smith b Dawson		6
†T. R. Ambrose c J. H. K. Adams b Tomlinson	113	– c Berg b Smith		29
R. Clarke lbw b A. R. Adams	7	– not out		4
K. H. D. Barker c A. R. Adams b Ervine	31			
J. S. Patel b Briggs	30			
C. J. C. Wright not out	5			
W. B. Rankin c Vince b Berg	4			
B 4, l-b 5, n-b 2	11	B 1, w 5, n-b 2		8

1/39 (1) 2/39 (2) 3/42 (3)   (85.3 overs) 280
4/72 (4) 5/92 (5) 6/120 (7)
7/185 (8) 8/250 (9) 9/271 (6) 10/280 (11)

1/52 (2)   (5 wkts, 105.4 overs) 244
2/120 (3) 3/134 (4)
4/145 (5) 5/227 (6)

Tomlinson 17–3–53–3; Briggs 18–4–57–1; Berg 19.3–3–58–2; Ervine 13–3–43–2; A. R. Adams 16–4–54–2; Dawson 2–1–6–0. *Second innings*—Tomlinson 21–5–56–2; Berg 11–1–30–0; A. R. Adams 21–5–59–1; Briggs 15–3–33–0; Ervine 4–0–9–0; Smith 14–8–16–1; Dawson 17–9–28–1; Carberry 2.4–2–12–0.

Umpires: G. D. Lloyd and R. T. Robinson.

At Leeds, April 26–29. WARWICKSHIRE drew with YORKSHIRE.

WARWICKSHIRE v WORCESTERSHIRE

At Birmingham, May 9–12. Warwickshire won by 181 runs. Warwickshire 21pts, Worcestershire 3pts. Toss: Worcestershire.

Warwickshire's decision to leave on more grass than usual was rewarded with another comfortable victory over their local rivals, who had not won at Edgbaston since 1993. Batting proved tricky for all-comers, but Chopra's diligent 107 from 229 balls, his third hundred in successive Championship matches on this ground, put the game beyond Worcestershire. They were further frustrated by a ninth-wicket partnership of 114 between Wright and Rankin, who each moved up the order after Hain suffered a shoulder injury in the field. Rankin achieved two landmarks cherished by tailenders: his maiden first-class fifty, and his first six, off Ali, followed by two more, also against off-spinners and all down the ground. Ali had been freed to play by the ECB following a mixed Test series in the West Indies, but a five-man attack featuring him and another off-spinner, Senanayake, left Worcestershire unbalanced in conditions suited to swing and seam. Career-best figures for Leach's medium-pace in Warwickshire's first innings – and three acrobatic catches by Cox standing back – proved the point, but Evans and Hain nursed them to a reasonable position. After Mitchell was run out at the non-striker's end via Wright's fingertips, Worcestershire caved in to persistent bowling, and did so again in the second innings, when Gidman became Patel's 500th first-class wicket.

Close of play: first day, Warwickshire 258-8 (Barker 21, Wright 10); second day, Warwickshire 105-2 (Chopra 72, Evans 15); third day, Worcestershire 88-2 (Mitchell 16, Morris 0).

Warwickshire

*V. Chopra c Mitchell b Leach	3	– c Cox b Ali	107
I. J. Westwood lbw b Leach	8	– c Cox b Shantry	12
W. T. S. Porterfield c Cox b Shantry	29	– c Fell b Senanayake	4
L. J. Evans c Shantry b Leach	50	– c Mitchell b Leach	16
S. R. Hain lbw b Leach	82		
†T. R. Ambrose b Leach	1	– (5) c Shantry b Leach	6
R. Clarke c Ali b Morris	37	– (6) c and b Morris	1
K. H. D. Barker c Cox b Morris	21	– (7) lbw b Ali	43
J. S. Patel c Cox b Morris	9	– st Cox b Senanayake	8
C. J. C. Wright c Cox b Leach	16	– (8) not out	61
W. B. Rankin not out	0	– (10) not out	56
B 1, l-b 5, n-b 2	8	L-b 7	7

1/9 (1) 2/20 (2) 3/53 (3)   (101.3 overs) 264   1/30 (2)   (8 wkts dec, 109 overs) 321
4/140 (4) 5/142 (6) 6/215 (5)   2/60 (3) 3/106 (4)
7/215 (7) 8/231 (9) 9/258 (8) 10/264 (10)   4/124 (5) 5/125 (6)
                                                 6/191 (7) 7/196 (1) 8/207 (9)

Morris 27–5–79–3; Leach 26.3–6–73–6; Shantry 26–9–46–1; Senanayake 14–2–39–0; Ali 8–1–21–0. *Second innings*—Morris 27.8–8–73–1; Leach 24–4–61–2; Shantry 13–2–31–1; Senanayake 21–3–63–2; Ali 21–1–66–2; Mitchell 2–0–8–0; Kervezee 1–0–12–0.

Worcestershire

*D. K. H. Mitchell run out	1	– c Clarke b Rankin	38
R. K. Oliver c Westwood b Wright	13	– c Evans b Patel	33
M. M. Ali lbw b Wright	1	– c Ambrose b Barker	33
T. C. Fell c Clarke b Wright	36	– (5) lbw b Patel	33
A. P. R. Gidman b Barker	0	– (6) lbw b Patel	12
A. N. Kervezee c Porterfield b Barker	9	– (7) c Evans b Clarke	3
†O. B. Cox lbw b Clarke	45	– (8) c Ambrose b Patel	44
J. Leach c sub (T. P. Lewis) b Barker	18	– (9) not out	29
J. D. Shantry c Ambrose b Clarke	2	– (10) c Ambrose b Rankin	0
S. M. S. M. Senanayake c Chopra b Rankin	15	– (11) c Chopra b Barker	6
C. A. J. Morris not out	0	– (4) c Clarke b Barker	2
L-b 1, n-b 8	9	L-b 6, n-b 16	22

1/2 (1) 2/15 (3) 3/24 (2)   (42.5 overs) 149   1/52 (2) 2/88 (3)   (83 overs) 255
4/27 (5) 5/49 (6) 6/93 (4)   3/100 (4) 4/147 (1)
7/132 (8) 8/132 (7) 9/137 (9) 10/149 (10)   5/147 (5) 6/160 (6) 7/188 (7)
                                                 8/216 (8) 9/223 (10) 10/255 (11)

Barker 15–1–43–3; Wright 13–3–60–3; Clarke 9–2–15–2; Rankin 5.5–1–30–1. *Second innings*—Barker 19–5–42–3; Wright 12–2–38–0; Patel 22–7–69–4; Clarke 13–5–38–1; Rankin 17–2–62–2.

Umpires: D. J. Millns and M. J. Saggers.

WARWICKSHIRE v DURHAM

At Birmingham, May 17–20. Warwickshire won by eight wickets. Warwickshire 24pts, Durham 3pts. Toss: Warwickshire.

A bravura all-round performance from Barker tormented Durham, as he followed a hard-hit century from No. 8 with a match haul of nine for 157, taking his tally against them to 49 wickets in nine Championship games. Dropped off successive balls from Hastings on 16 and 20, Barker launched a brutal assault alongside Patel on the first evening, in a session which yielded 199 runs in 32 overs, undoing some impressive early work by Onions. His five-for had included Trott, who played positively in his first innings since announcing his international retirement – although there was little of the short stuff that hastened his demise in the Caribbean. Collingwood apart, Durham's batsmen were tentative, and they were made to follow on after folding against Barker and the aggressive Richard Jones, who had Stoneman caught on the hook with his second delivery of the

Championship season. A foot injury restricted Jones's workload in the second innings, but Durham could not escape Barker, despite a solid century from Stoneman. Trott was run out by a deflection at the bowler's end before Warwickshire knocked off their modest target.

Close of play: first day, Warwickshire 417-7 (Barker 86, Patel 50); second day, Durham 50-3 (Richardson 18, MacLeod 3); third day, Durham 189-4 (Stoneman 83, Collingwood 16).

Warwickshire

*V. Chopra c Mustard b Onions	13				
I. J. Westwood b Onions	88	– not out			32
W. T. S. Porterfield lbw b Rushworth	1	– (1) c sub (G. T. Main) b Rushworth			2
I. J. L. Trott lbw b Onions	42	– (3) run out			6
L. J. Evans c Mustard b Onions	45	– (4) not out			13
†T. R. Ambrose c Mustard b Hastings	13				
R. Clarke lbw b Rushworth	36				
K. H. D. Barker not out	102				
J. S. Patel run out	58				
R. A. Jones c Jennings b Onions	3				
W. B. Rankin c Borthwick b Hastings	6				
B 5, l-b 11, w 5, n-b 22	43	L-b 2, n-b 8			10

1/17 (1) 2/18 (3) 3/102 (4)   (107.4 overs) 450   1/2 (1)   (2 wkts, 17.4 overs) 63
4/208 (5) 5/209 (2) 6/227 (6)   2/12 (3)
7/330 (7) 8/427 (9) 9/435 (10) 10/450 (11)

Rushworth 27–5–84–2; Onions 29–4–85–5; Hastings 21.4–1–118–2; Coughlin 17–1–80–0; Collingwood 10–2–38–0; Borthwick 2–0–24–0; MacLeod 1–0–5–0. *Second innings*—Rushworth 7–1–16–1; Hastings 7–1–17–0; Borthwick 2–0–17–0; Coughlin 1.4–0–11–0.

Durham

M. D. Stoneman c Rankin b Jones	3	– run out			111
K. K. Jennings c Chopra b Barker	4	– c Clarke b Barker			3
S. G. Borthwick c Westwood b Jones	19	– lbw b Barker			14
M. J. Richardson c Porterfield b Barker	33	– c Chopra b Barker			47
C. S. MacLeod c Jones	3	– c Clarke b Rankin			16
*P. D. Collingwood b Rankin	68	– lbw b Clarke			19
†P. Mustard lbw b Barker	0	– c Porterfield b Barker			8
P. Coughlin b Barker	5	– c Porterfield b Clarke			49
J. W. Hastings lbw b Clarke	14	– c Trott b Clarke			23
C. Rushworth b Jones	15	– c Clarke b Barker			19
G. Onions not out	0	– not out			4
B 9, l-b 3, n-b 4, p 5	21	B 2, l-b 10, n-b 2			14

1/5 (1) 2/10 (2) 3/32 (3)   (40.5 overs) 185   1/5 (2) 2/29 (3)   (92.2 overs) 327
4/51 (5) 5/85 (4) 6/85 (7)   3/101 (4) 4/165 (5)
7/91 (8) 8/125 (9) 9/183 (10) 10/185 (6)   5/202 (6) 6/219 (7) 7/252 (1)
                                                 8/304 (8) 9/309 (9) 10/327 (10)

Barker 16–1–54–4; Jones 12–1–48–4; Clarke 6–1–24–1; Rankin 5.5–0–37–1; Patel 1–0–5–0. *Second innings*—Barker 27.2–2–103–5; Jones 5–0–20–0; Patel 25–10–57–0; Clarke 17–5–61–3; Trott 3–1–12–0; Rankin 15–0–62–1.

Umpires: N. G. C. Cowley and J. H. Evans.

At Hove, May 24–26. WARWICKSHIRE lost to SUSSEX by one wicket.

At Lord's, May 31–June 3. WARWICKSHIRE drew with MIDDLESEX.

At Worcester, June 14–15. WARWICKSHIRE beat WORCESTERSHIRE by an innings and 17 runs.

WARWICKSHIRE v SUSSEX

At Birmingham, June 28–July 1. Drawn. Warwickshire 9pts, Sussex 9pts. Toss: Sussex. County debut: P. I. Burgoyne. Championship debut: J. E. Poysden.

Warwickshire's decision to revisit a pitch already used for two Twenty20 games – in the belief that it would assist the spinners – backfired. The surface lacked pace and bounce, producing a torpid draw of statistical interest only. After just three wickets fell on the last two days, Mark Robinson, Sussex's coach, described the match as "atrocious"; his opposite number Dougie Brown admitted Warwickshire should have chosen a fresher strip offered by groundsman Gary Barwell. Against an attack featuring Sussex-born leg-spinner Josh Poysden, the visitors doubled their century tally for the season: it was the third time four of their batsmen had made a century in the same innings, after Northampton in 1938 and Horsham against Derbyshire in 2010. Ashar Zaidi relished the Pakistan-like conditions for his maiden Championship hundred. For the first time at Edgbaston, both sides topped 600. Warwickshire's total was their highest against Sussex at home, and included a county sixth-wicket record partnership of 327 from Evans and Ambrose, against some increasingly funky field-settings. Evans completed a maiden double-century and batted for almost eight hours, although by the end all 11 Sussex players, including wicketkeeper Brown, had turned their arm over.

Close of play: first day, Sussex 280-3 (Nash 112, Wright 43); second day, Warwickshire 62-3 (Trott 15, Wright 5); third day, Warwickshire 367-5 (Evans 103, Ambrose 65).

Sussex

*E. C. Joyce c Evans b Rankin	30		O. E. Robinson not out	19	
L. W. P. Wells c Clarke b Wright	68		B 1, w 1, n-b 4	6	
M. W. Machan c Wright b Poysden	22				
C. D. Nash st Ambrose b Patel	121		1/46 (1)	(6 wkts dec, 163.4 overs)	601
L. J. Wright b Patel	110		2/97 (3) 3/163 (2)		
†B. C. Brown not out	119		4/329 (4) 5/380 (5)		
Ashar Zaidi st Ambrose b Evans	106		6/571 (7)	110 overs: 348-4	

P. I. Burgoyne, S. J. Magoffin and M. E. Hobden did not bat.

Wright 18–1–73–1; Clarke 12–1–49–0; Patel 47–14–106–2; Rankin 15–1–79–1; Poysden 40.4–4–165–1; Javid 21–2–74–0; Trott 6–0–25–0; Evans 4–0–29–1.

Warwickshire

*V. Chopra c Brown b Magoffin	6		R. Clarke not out	41	
I. J. Westwood lbw b Wells	20				
A. Javid c Wright b Magoffin	0		B 23, l-b 11, n-b 12	46	
I. J. L. Trott b Hobden	68				
C. J. C. Wright c and b Ashar Zaidi	65		1/14 (1)	(6 wkts dec, 192 overs)	612
L. J. Evans not out	213		2/14 (3) 3/56 (2) 4/170 (4)		
†T. R. Ambrose c Robinson b Burgoyne	153		5/207 (5) 6/534 (7)	110 overs: 332-5	

J. S. Patel, J. E. Poysden and W. B. Rankin did not bat.

Magoffin 22–5–65–2; Robinson 17–4–62–0; Hobden 26–3–63–1; Burgoyne 37–5–113–1; Wells 26–1–85–1; Ashar Zaidi 31–10–62–1; Nash 14–2–59–0; Machan 6–0–28–0; Brown 8–0–31–0; Wright 1–0–2–0; Joyce 4–0–8–0.

Umpires: R. J. Bailey and D. J. Millns.

WARWICKSHIRE v YORKSHIRE

At Birmingham, July 5–8. Yorkshire won by 174 runs. Yorkshire 20pts, Warwickshire 3pts. Toss: Yorkshire.

Dougie Brown conceded the title was Yorkshire's to lose after the champions routed his side for the fourth time in three seasons. Yorkshire were spurred on by Bairstow's coruscating century and outstanding swing bowling from Sidebottom, whose match figures of 11 for 76 were the second-best of his long career. Bairstow made light of difficult early conditions by launching a counter-attack, though he had one let-off, on 37, when McKay – in the side for Tim Ambrose, who had a stomach bug – spilled a difficult leg-side chance as he hit the ground. Either side of a tropical thunderstorm

Bairstow raced on to his fourth century of the season, as Yorkshire finished on 213. Sidebottom then captured the first six wickets, before Brooks broke his monopoly, as Warwickshire were reduced to an eye-watering 37 for nine, with the follow-on still conceivable; they lost five of those wickets in 30 balls with the score on 35. Even though Clarke clumped 28 alongside former Yorkshire player Hannon-Dalby, Warwickshire were eventually dismissed for 69, their lowest score since 1986. Despite his illness, Ambrose alternated with Andy Umeed as a substitute wicketkeeper for part of Yorkshire's second innings after McKay hurt a finger. Yorkshire's sturdy approach, with Finch making a positive unbeaten 73, set up a declaration on the third evening, and only showers and a stylish century from Hain delayed the inevitable.

Close of play: first day, Warwickshire 11-2 (Westwood 8, Trott 2); second day, Yorkshire 125-1 (Rhodes 53, Leaning 28); third day, Warwickshire 43-1 (Westwood 17, Trott 25).

Yorkshire

A. Z. Lees st McKay b Patel	18	– c Chopra b Clarke		28
W. M. H. Rhodes b Wright	10	– c sub (T. R. Ambrose)		79
		b Hannon-Dalby		
J. A. Leaning c Patel b Wright	4	– c sub (T. R. Ambrose) b Rankin		46
*A. W. Gale c Chopra b Hannon-Dalby	1	– (5) b Patel		1
†J. M. Bairstow b Wright	108	– (6) c Westwood b Hannon-Dalby		23
A. J. Finch lbw b Clarke	28	– (4) not out		73
T. T. Bresnan c McKay b Clarke	10	– run out		1
J. D. Middlebrook c Clarke b Hannon-Dalby	5	– c Hain b Hannon-Dalby		2
S. A. Patterson c McKay b Wright	11	– not out		10
J. A. Brooks b Wright	8			
R. J. Sidebottom not out	2			
B 1, l-b 4, w 1, n-b 2	8	B 16, l-b 9, w 1		26

1/17 (2) 2/21 (3) 3/26 (4) (66.2 overs) 213   1/58 (1) (7 wkts dec, 80 overs) 289
4/55 (1) 5/129 (6) 6/153 (7)   2/152 (3) 3/219 (2)
7/170 (8) 8/195 (9) 9/208 (5) 10/213 (10)   4/222 (5) 5/259 (6) 6/263 (7) 7/267 (8)

Wright 16.2–4–40–5; Hannon-Dalby 22–4–60–2; Clarke 13–1–49–2; Rankin 11–3–50–0; Patel 4–0–9–1. *Second innings*—Wright 15–1–46–0; Hannon-Dalby 21–4–80–3; Patel 18–3–53–1; Clarke 10–3–18–1; Rankin 11–0–54–1; Trott 5–0–13–0.

Warwickshire

*V. Chopra b Sidebottom	0	– lbw b Sidebottom		0
I. J. Westwood b Sidebottom	14	– lbw b Sidebottom		40
C. J. C. Wright lbw b Sidebottom	0	– (9) b Brooks		6
I. J. L. Trott c Leaning b Brooks	18	– (3) b Sidebottom		29
L. J. Evans b Sidebottom	2	– (4) lbw b Sidebottom		0
S. R. Hain c Leaning b Sidebottom	0	– (5) lbw b Bresnan		106
†P. J. McKay lbw b Sidebottom	0	– (6) c Finch b Patterson		2
R. Clarke b Patterson	28	– (7) c Leaning b Middlebrook		18
J. S. Patel c Bairstow b Brooks	0	– (8) c Rhodes b Brooks		13
W. B. Rankin c Lees b Brooks	0	– (11) not out		9
O. J. Hannon-Dalby not out	5	– (10) b Sidebottom		5
L-b 2	2	B 16, l-b 10, n-b 2		28

1/0 (1) 2/0 (3) 3/29 (2) (28.1 overs) 69   1/0 (1) 2/58 (3) (85.5 overs) 259
4/35 (5) 5/35 (6) 6/35 (7)   3/58 (4) 4/109 (2)
7/35 (4) 8/35 (9) 9/37 (10) 10/69 (8)   5/123 (6) 6/170 (7) 7/189 (8)
                                               8/203 (9) 9/219 (10) 10/259 (5)

Sidebottom 12–6–34–6; Brooks 11–4–14–3; Bresnan 3–0–13–0; Patterson 2.1–0–6–1. *Second innings*—Sidebottom 19–6–42–5; Brooks 20–4–72–2; Patterson 12–4–30–1; Bresnan 14.5–3–43–1; Middlebrook 15–4–34–1; Rhodes 3–0–11–0; Finch 2–1–1–0.

Umpires: M. Burns and A. G. Wharf.

At Chester-le-Street, July 12–15. WARWICKSHIRE beat DURHAM by two wickets.

WARWICKSHIRE v SOMERSET

At Birmingham, July 18–21. **Warwickshire won by seven wickets.** Warwickshire 22pts, Somerset 4pts. Toss: Somerset.

Somerset were let down by their senior batsmen, and never recovered from an opening-day collapse on a pitch given a trim after being used for a Twenty20 match the previous evening. Patel teased out gentle turn to claim his first five-wicket haul of the summer, including Trescothick, who had appeared in no trouble until he carved to deep point. Even with resistance from the bottom four, Somerset's total felt 100 light, and Warwickshire's sensible application ensured the advantage was not wasted. The foundations were laid by Westwood and Trott, returning from paternity leave to make his highest first-class score since he quit international cricket in May, before Hain maintained the impressive start to his first-class career with his sixth century in 18 matches. Craig Overton persevered to pick up career-best figures, and Abell carried his bat for the second time in the season, but otherwise Somerset lacked composure against Patel's guile and Clarke's pace. Drizzle and bad light prevented Warwickshire from completing a win inside three days, but the formalities were over before lunch on the fourth.

Close of play: first day, Warwickshire 22-0 (Chopra 12, Westwood 8); second day, Warwickshire 319-8 (Hain 78, Patel 20); third day, Warwickshire 6-0 (Chopra 4, Westwood 2).

Somerset

*M. E. Trescothick c Evans b Patel	48	– lbw b Patel	15
T. B. Abell c Clarke b Patel	8	– not out	88
†M. D. Bates c Chopra b Patel	16	– lbw b Clarke	0
J. C. Hildreth c Chopra b Woakes	11	– b Clarke	0
T. L. W. Cooper c Clarke b Woakes	0	– lbw b Hannon-Dalby	17
J. Allenby c Patel b Clarke	37	– c Clarke b Woakes	11
P. D. Trego c Evans b Woakes	2	– lbw b Clarke	21
C. Overton c Hain b Patel	51	– c Trott b Clarke	9
Abdur Rehman c Westwood b Patel	13	– c Woakes b Patel	0
A. C. Thomas not out	32	– c Ambrose b Patel	1
T. D. Groenewald c Hain b Clarke	34	– c Ambrose b Patel	0
B 2, l-b 5, n-b 6	13	B 1, l-b 4, w 1, n-b 2	8

1/29 (2) 2/75 (3) 3/88 (1) (83.1 overs) 265
4/88 (5) 5/111 (4) 6/127 (7)
7/152 (6) 8/186 (9) 9/201 (8) 10/265 (11)

1/32 (1) 2/32 (3) (51.4 overs) 170
3/42 (4) 4/74 (5)
5/114 (6) 6/155 (7) 7/167 (8)
8/168 (9) 9/170 (10) 10/170 (11)

Barker 13–3–31–0; Woakes 15–1–48–3; Patel 24–3–89–5; Clarke 12.1–3–31–2; Hannon-Dalby 18–5–57–0; Trott 1–0–2–0. *Second innings*—Barker 10–3–34–0; Woakes 10–5–18–1; Clarke 12–2–43–4; Patel 14.4–2–47–4; Trott 1–1–0–0; Hannon-Dalby 4–1–23–1.

Warwickshire

*V. Chopra c Trego b Overton	33	– c Allenby b Thomas	4
I. J. Westwood b Thomas	66	– c Trescothick b Allenby	16
L. J. Evans lbw b Allenby	7	– not out	36
I. J. L. Trott c Bates b Overton	87	– c Groenewald b Overton	0
S. R. Hain not out	103	– not out	10
†T. R. Ambrose c Overton b Thomas	0		
R. Clarke c Cooper b Overton	1		
C. R. Woakes c Cooper b Overton	8		
K. H. D. Barker c Overton b Thomas	5		
J. S. Patel b Overton	41		
O. J. Hannon-Dalby c Thomas b Overton	0		
B 7, l-b 3, n-b 4	14	L-b 4, n-b 4	8

1/66 (1) 2/84 (3) 3/161 (2) (115.5 overs) 365
4/243 (4) 5/246 (6) 6/265 (7)
7/275 (8) 8/282 (9) 9/365 (10)
10/365 (11)   110 overs: 336-8

1/8 (1) (3 wkts, 28.3 overs) 74
2/35 (2) 3/36 (4)

Thomas 27–4–106–3; Groenewald 22–4–82–0; Abdur Rehman 28–10–58–0; Overton 23.5–2–74–6; Allenby 7–0–16–1; Trego 8–0–19–0. *Second innings*—Thomas 8–2–19–1; Groenewald 9–3–11–0; Allenby 6.3–1–28–1; Overton 5–1–12–1.

Umpires: P. K. Baldwin and B. J. Debenham.

At Southampton, August 7–10. WARWICKSHIRE lost to HAMPSHIRE by 216 runs.

At Nottingham, August 21–24. WARWICKSHIRE lost to NOTTINGHAMSHIRE by an innings and 123 runs.

WARWICKSHIRE v MIDDLESEX

At Birmingham, September 1–4. Drawn. Warwickshire 10pts, Middlesex 9pts. Toss: Middlesex.
  Jeetan Patel enjoyed his return to Edgbaston after two fruitless away matches, but the loss of the first day to rain, and further interruptions on the third, reduced the scope for a positive result. He had taken two for 339 in Warwickshire's defeats at Southampton and Nottingham, but exploited a pitch used on Twenty20 finals day to reel Middlesex in after a wayward start from the seamers, removing Compton lbw with his second ball, which looked leg-sideish. However, Dexter and Rayner shored up the innings, and Warwickshire found batting no easier until the busy Ambrose received support from the lower order. Patel briefly threatened to set up an unexpected win when he claimed three wickets on the final day, but Dexter's second disciplined innings of the match steered Middlesex to safety. Patel had some harsh words to say about English spinners, including Rayner, accusing them of not practising hard enough between matches.
  Close of play: first day, no play; second day, Warwickshire 21-1 (Chopra 10, Porterfield 1); third day, Warwickshire 224-8 (Ambrose 84, Wright 16).

Middlesex

P. R. Stirling c Clarke b Barker	41	– (2) lbw b Barker 4
S. D. Robson lbw b Clarke....................	14	– (1) b Barker 21
N. R. D. Compton lbw b Patel....................	18	– c sub (L. J. Evans) b Patel 28
D. J. Malan c Ambrose b Rankin	7	– lbw b Patel 10
*J. E. C. Franklin b Patel	8	– lbw b Patel 16
N. J. Dexter c Chopra b Patel....................	53	– c Clarke b Rankin 43
†J. A. Simpson lbw b Barker	1	– not out 14
O. P. Rayner c Chopra b Wright	24	– not out 21
J. A. R. Harris c Hain b Patel	7	
T. S. Roland-Jones not out	17	
T. J. Murtagh c Barker b Patel	12	
B 4, l-b 1	5	B 8, l-b 6, n-b 2 16

1/52 (2) 2/60 (1) 3/80 (4)   (79.1 overs) 207   1/17 (2)   (6 wkts, 62 overs) 173
4/80 (3) 5/107 (5) 6/114 (7)   2/40 (1) 3/63 (4)
7/165 (8) 8/174 (6) 9/185 (9) 10/207 (11)   4/72 (5) 5/105 (5) 6/149 (6)

Barker 16–5–23–2; Wright 10–1–52–1; Clarke 14–3–38–1; Rankin 14–5–30–1; Patel 25.1–7–59–5. *Second innings*—Barker 14–5–37–2; Wright 7–0–23–0; Patel 25–9–65–3; Clarke 5–2–3–0; Rankin 8–2–22–1; Westwood 3–0–9–0.

Warwickshire

*V. Chopra c Robson b Murtagh	44	J. S. Patel c Rayner b Murtagh	0
I. J. Westwood c Simpson b Rayner	7	C. J. C. Wright not out	32
W. T. S. Porterfield c Simpson b Rayner	1	W. B. Rankin lbw b Rayner	4
I. J. L. Trott c Simpson b Roland-Jones	10	L-b 12, n-b 4	16
S. R. Hain c Franklin b Murtagh	21		
†T. R. Ambrose c Rayner b Roland-Jones	89	1/9 (2) 2/21 (3) 3/52 (4) (96.3 overs)	254
R. Clarke c Rayner b Murtagh	0	4/85 (1) 5/86 (5) 6/86 (7)	
K. H. D. Barker c Rayner b Stirling	30	7/173 (8) 8/174 (9) 9/242 (6) 10/254 (11)	

Murtagh 25–6–55–4; Roland-Jones 25–4–59–2; Rayner 30.3–8–75–3; Harris 9–2–34–0; Stirling 7–1–19–1.

Umpires: P. K. Baldwin and A. G. Wharf.

WARWICKSHIRE v NOTTINGHAMSHIRE

At Birmingham, September 14–17. Drawn. Warwickshire 8pts, Nottinghamshire 12pts. Toss: Warwickshire.

Nottinghamshire assured themselves of a top-three finish by dominating their rivals for prize money in the scant play possible between the showers. Only four overs were bowled on the first two days, but the forecast rain did not arrive on the third, when James Taylor celebrated his inclusion in England's Test squad against Pakistan with a bustling 164. He was dropped four times, but his positive approach sparked a counter-attack after Barker had swung the ball extravagantly under cloud cover. Taylor passed 1,000 runs for the season, but there was little applause for his century from the Warwickshire players, who were convinced they had him caught behind on 99 off Trott. Jeetan Patel claimed his 50th wicket of the season when he ended Nottinghamshire's innings. Warwickshire then lost out in the race for bonus points by batting with little spirit against a young seam attack; Wood, Hutton and Ball notched up 100 wickets for the season between them.

Close of play: first day, no play; second day, Nottinghamshire 16-0 (B. R. M. Taylor 8, Hales 6); third day, Nottinghamshire 254-5 (J. W. A. Taylor 138, Read 50).

Nottinghamshire

B. R. M. Taylor lbw b Barker	24	L. J. Fletcher not out	24
A. D. Hales c Clarke b Barker	6	J. T. Ball lbw b Patel	0
S. J. Mullaney c Evans b Barker	0		
J. W. A. Taylor lbw b Barker	164	B 12, l-b 6, n-b 12	30
M. H. Wessels c Ambrose b Trott	9		
S. R. Patel b Barker	9	1/23 (2) 2/25 (3) (107.3 overs)	365
*†C. M. W. Read c Ambrose b Wright	63	3/46 (1) 4/105 (5)	
B. A. Hutton c Ambrose b Wright	0	5/130 (6) 6/285 (7) 7/285 (8)	
L. Wood b Patel	36	8/307 (4) 9/365 (9) 10/365 (11)	

Barker 30–8–68–5; Wright 21–2–83–2; Clarke 20–5–60–0; Rankin 16–1–90–0; Trott 12–3–24–1; Patel 8.3–3–22–2.

Warwickshire

*V. Chopra lbw b Hutton	25	J. S. Patel c Hales b Hutton	14
I. J. Westwood c Read b Wood	16	C. J. C. Wright c Read b Fletcher	14
L. J. Evans c Mullaney b Fletcher	34	W. B. Rankin not out	4
I. J. L. Trott c Wessels b Ball	31	L-b 7, n-b 10	17
S. R. Hain c Wessels b Ball	2		
†T. R. Ambrose c Hutton b Ball	8	1/44 (1) 2/44 (2) 3/103 (3) (46.2 overs)	187
R. Clarke lbw b Wood	11	4/114 (5) 5/130 (6) 6/139 (4)	
K. H. D. Barker c J. W. A. Taylor b Ball	11	7/153 (8) 8/153 (7) 9/183 (10) 10/187 (9)	

Ball 12–1–48–4; Wood 14–2–45–2; Hutton 11.2–2–47–2; Fletcher 9–1–40–2.

Umpires: N. G. B. Cook and M. J. Saggers.

At Taunton, September 22–25. WARWICKSHIRE lost to SOMERSET by 17 runs.

WORCESTERSHIRE

When they were up they were down . . .

JOHN CURTIS

Once again, Worcestershire demonstrated why they are considered cricket's yo-yo county: finishing bottom of Division One meant that, in the last 13 seasons, they have been promoted five times and relegated five times. Only in 2011 did they manage to avoid going straight back down, a feat described by Steve Rhodes as the best of his long career, as player and coach. The evidence suggests Worcestershire are too weak for the first division – and too strong for the second.

Yet relegation, which marred the county's 150th anniversary celebrations, was perhaps misleading. Generally, Worcestershire were competitive in the Championship: they achieved a first-innings lead in eight of their first ten matches; defeated Somerset, Hampshire and runners-up Middlesex, all by an innings; and have now claimed full bowling points in 41 of their last 44 Championship games, stretching back to May 2013. But they failed to exploit positions of strength, as in the home defeat by Durham, who were floundering at 103 for nine in their first innings. It was this lack of ruthlessness that did for Worcestershire, who finished just 12 points behind Hampshire, in seventh. Below-par periods, even if for only an hour, are severely punished in Division One.

Rhodes's ability to get the best from young players, and put together a competitive side – despite one of the smaller budgets of the 18 counties – was given wider recognition when he was elevated to the England Lions coaching set-up for their winter programme. One of his successes has been the seam attack. Joe Leach, Jack Shantry and Charlie Morris took a combined 160 Championship wickets – 19 more than in 2014. But that betrayed an overreliance on the trio, who were showing understandable signs of tiredness towards the end of the summer. Worcestershire were not helped by the recurrence of all-rounder Gareth Andrew's chronic back injury after only two matches. In eight seasons at New Road, he claimed 195 first-class wickets and hit a useful 2,413 runs, but his lack of fitness meant he was released in August.

The main difference between the team promoted in 2014 and the one relegated a year later was the loss of a match-winning overseas bowler. True, Saeed Ajmal appeared in both sides, but his potency had vanished with his old – and illegal – action. In 2014, Ajmal had scythed through line-ups, collecting 63 wickets in nine games at under 17. Twelve months on, his haul dwindled to 16 in eight; an average above 55 told a painful story.

Before Ajmal arrived in June, Worcestershire had turned to the Sri Lankan, Sachithra Senanayake, another off-spinner forced to adapt his action. But he fared only fractionally better, taking nine at 42. In a change of tack, Shannon Gabriel, a speedy West Indian seamer, was drafted in for the last two Championship games; he brought victory against Middlesex, but by then the season was beyond rescue. In 2016, the New Zealander Matt Henry is due to start, before handing over to South Africa's Kyle Abbott. Another New Zealander, spin-bowling all-rounder Mitchell Santner, was signed for the T20 Blast. In the boardroom, David Leatherdale stepped down after 27 years as player, commercial director and chief executive in order to become CEO of the Professional Cricketers' Association. Tom Scott, a former detective, was appointed chief executive in the short term.

Gareth Copley, Getty Images

Tom Fell

With Moeen Ali now an England fixture, skipper Daryl Mitchell and new signing Alex Gidman were expected to score the bulk of the runs. Instead, the 21-year-old Tom Fell was the shining light in the top six, passing 1,000 first-class runs and scoring three hundreds: two against Middlesex, one against Yorkshire. He was well supported by wicketkeeper Ben Cox, who made 778 and had his best season with the gloves, and by 19-year-old Joe Clarke, likened to Joe Root by batting coach Kevin Sharp – and selected for the Lions. Ross Whiteley also received a Lions call-up after proving he could translate his white-ball prowess into four-day cricket.

In the past, relegation has been greeted by mass exodus; this time, the club aimed for greater continuity, and several younger players signed new contracts. One who declined was opener Richard Oliver. He failed to build on the promise of his first season, and rejected a one-year deal after Worcestershire asked him to stay at home during the winter and work on his technique, rather than play grade cricket in Australia.

In the T20 Blast, which suited a young energetic side, Worcestershire finished runners-up in the North Group. For the second season in a row, Mitchell was their leading scorer, though Whiteley grabbed the headlines with his explosive hitting, and his tally of 29 sixes was matched only by Chris Gayle and Luke Wright; against Yorkshire he produced an astonishing unbeaten 91 from 35 balls. Tom Köhler-Cadmore also batted with flair and freedom, while Ajmal's powers were less dimmed in this format, and he took 21 wickets.

But in New Road's first T20 quarter-final, the lack of floodlights meant play was halted when Chris Wood, fielding for Hampshire, sustained a broken nose: he lost sight of the ball as he went for a catch. The light never improved, and Hampshire progressed on the Duckworth/Lewis method. Worcestershire and Derbyshire are the only counties never to reach finals day. The Royal London One-Day Cup was probably a competition too far. Worcestershire managed only one victory, though there was encouragement in Clarke's batting, not least when he made an unbroken 131 against Gloucestershire.

Championship attendance: 30,196.

WORCESTERSHIRE RESULTS

All first-class matches – Played 17: Won 4, Lost 10, Drawn 3.
County Championship matches – Played 16: Won 3, Lost 10, Drawn 3.

LV= County Championship, 9th in Division 1;
NatWest T20 Blast, quarter-finalists; Royal London One-Day Cup, 8th in Group A.

COUNTY CHAMPIONSHIP AVERAGES, BATTING AND FIELDING

Colours		Birthplace		M	I	NO	R	HS	100	Avge	Ct/St
2014	T. Köhler-Cadmore	Chatham		5	8	1	294	130*	1	42.00	5
2013	T. C. Fell	Hillingdon		16	26	0	1,084	171	3	41.69	20
2008	G. M. Andrew	Yeovil		2	4	0	152	70	0	38.00	0
2009	O. B. Cox	Wordsley†		16	26	5	778	109	1	37.04	43/2
2013	R. A. Whiteley	Sheffield		8	13	1	436	101	1	36.33	6
2015	J. M. Clarke	Shrewsbury		11	16	1	530	104*	1	35.33	3
2005	D. K. H. Mitchell	Badsey†		15	25	3	768	206*	2	34.90	18
2007	M. M. Ali	Birmingham		4	8	1	227	62	0	32.42	1
2012	J. Leach	Stafford		14	19	2	498	95	0	29.29	4
2012	B. L. D'Oliveira	Worcester†		7	11	0	267	49	0	24.27	4
2015	A. P. R. Gidman	High Wycombe		12	19	2	397	78	0	23.35	11
2009	A. N. Kervezee	Walvis Bay, Nam.		4	7	0	162	93	0	23.14	0
2014	R. K. Oliver	Stoke-on-Trent		12	21	0	452	101	1	21.52	8
2011	Saeed Ajmal§	Faisalabad, Pak		8	12	2	162	37	0	16.20	5
2015	S. M. S. M. Senanayake§	Colombo, SL		5	9	0	120	32	0	13.33	3
2009	J. D. Shantry	Shrewsbury		16	22	4	221	41*	0	12.27	4
2015	E. G. Barnard	Shrewsbury		4	4	1	35	17	0	11.66	2
2014	C. A. J. Morris	Hereford		14	21	10	85	24	0	7.72	2

Also batted: C. Munro§ (*Durban, SA*) (colours 2015) (1 match) 34. S. T. Gabriel§ (*Trinidad*) (colours 2015) (2 matches) did not bat.

† *Born in Worcestershire.*   ‡ *ECB contract.*   § *Official overseas player.*

BOWLING

	Style	O	M	R	W	BB	5I	Avge
J. D. Shantry	LFM	515.2	130	1,430	57	5-48	3	25.08
E. G. Barnard	RFM	100.1	20	345	12	3-63	0	28.75
J. Leach	RFM	467	74	1,772	59	6-73	2	30.03
C. A. J. Morris	RFM	470	90	1,510	44	5-71	1	34.31
B. L. D'Oliveira	LBG	103.4	17	407	11	5-48	1	37.00
Saeed Ajmal	OB	272.3	42	890	16	5-28	1	55.62

Also bowled: M. M. Ali (OB) 85–6–272–3; G. M. Andrew (RFM) 50.1–5–220–8; T. C. Fell (OB) 1–0–7–0; S. T. Gabriel (RFM) 40–3–183–9; A. P. R. Gidman (RM) 3–1–11–1; A. N. Kervezee (OB) 23–1–86–3; D. K. H. Mitchell (RM) 7–0–24–0; C. Munro 8–2–29–1; S. M. S. M. Senanayake (OB) 137–18–381–9; R. A. Whiteley (LM) 42–1–234–1.

LEADING ROYAL LONDON CUP AVERAGES (100 runs/4 wickets)

Batting

	Runs	HS	Avge	SR	Ct/St
J. M. Clarke	242	131*	80.66	101.25	1
T. C. Fell	215	63	35.83	74.39	1
D. K. H. Mitchell	168	59	33.60	63.63	5
R. A. Whiteley	172	77	28.66	100.58	0
O. B. Cox	110	38	22.00	106.79	9/2
T. Köhler-Cadmore	141	37	20.14	64.67	4
E. G. Barnard	102	51	17.00	121.42	3

Bowling

	W	BB	Avge	ER
A. Hepburn	6	4-34	13.00	4.14
J. D. Shantry	6	4-29	26.83	5.55
E. G. Barnard	12	3-59	29.25	5.75
J. Leach	7	4-30	30.14	5.27
Saeed Ajmal	3	3-33	40.12	4.70
C. A. J. Morris	5	3-46	43.60	5.76

LEADING NATWEST T20 BLAST AVERAGES (100 runs/18 overs)

Batting	Runs	HS	Avge	SR	Ct/St
R. A. Whiteley	315	91*	39.37	177.96	11
M. M. Ali	248	90	35.42	172.22	4
T. Köhler-Cadmore	365	75	30.41	134.19	11
B. L. D'Oliveira	116	56*	16.57	131.81	2
C. Munro	182	33	16.54	126.38	2
O. B. Cox	130	30*	26.00	125.00	4/4
D. K. H. Mitchell	412	58	34.33	116.05	6
R. K. Oliver	193	70*	24.12	114.88	4

Bowling	W	BB	Avge	ER
B. L. D'Oliveira	9	3-29	24.55	6.50
D. K. H. Mitchell	6	2-23	31.83	6.82
Saeed Ajmal	21	3-13	16.57	7.25
M. M. Ali	5	3-28	36.40	7.58
J. D. Shantry	16	2-26	29.43	8.56
E. G. Barnard	6	2-18	51.50	8.58
J. Leach	17	3-27	23.11	8.83

FIRST-CLASS COUNTY RECORDS

Highest score for	405*	G. A. Hick v Somerset at Taunton	1988
Highest score against	331*	J. D. B. Robertson (Middlesex) at Worcester	1949
Leading run-scorer	34,490	D. Kenyon (avge 34.18)	1946–67
Best bowling for	9-23	C. F. Root v Lancashire at Worcester	1931
Best bowling against	10-51	J. Mercer (Glamorgan) at Worcester	1936
Leading wicket-taker	2,143	R. T. D. Perks (avge 23.73)	1930–55
Highest total for	701-6 dec	v Surrey at Worcester	2007
Highest total against	701-4 dec	by Leicestershire at Worcester	1906
Lowest total for	24	v Yorkshire at Huddersfield	1903
Lowest total against	30	by Hampshire at Worcester	1903

LIST A COUNTY RECORDS

Highest score for	180*	T. M. Moody v Surrey at The Oval	1994
Highest score against {	158	W. Larkins (Northamptonshire) at Luton	1982
	158	R. A. Smith (Hampshire) at Worcester	1996
Leading run-scorer	16,416	G. A. Hick (avge 44.60)	1985–2008
Best bowling for	7-19	N. V. Radford v Bedfordshire at Bedford	1991
Best bowling against	7-15	R. A. Hutton (Yorkshire) at Leeds	1969
Leading wicket-taker	370	S. R. Lampitt (avge 24.52)	1987–2002
Highest total for	404-3	v Devon at Worcester	1987
Highest total against	399-4	by Sussex at Horsham	2011
Lowest total for	58	v Ireland v Worcester	2009
Lowest total against	45	by Hampshire at Worcester	1988

TWENTY20 COUNTY RECORDS

Highest score for	116*	G. A. Hick v Northamptonshire at Luton	2004
Highest score against	141*	C. L. White (Somerset) at Worcester	2006
Leading run-scorer	1,841	M. M. Ali (avge 24.87)	2007–15
Best bowling for	5-28	D. K. H. Mitchell v Northants at Northampton	2014
Best bowling against	6-21	A. J. Hall (Northamptonshire) at Northampton	2008
Leading wicket-taker	86	J. D. Shantry (avge 24.79)	2010–15
Highest total for	227-6	v Northamptonshire at Kidderminster	2007
Highest total against	229-4	by Lancashire at Worcester	2014
Lowest total for	86	v Northamptonshire at Worcester	2006
Lowest total against	93	by Gloucestershire at Bristol	2008

ADDRESS

County Ground, New Road, Worcester WR2 4QQ; 01905 748474; info@wccc.co.uk; www.wccc.co.uk.

OFFICIALS

Captain D. K. H. Mitchell
Director of cricket S. J. Rhodes
Academy coach E. J. Wilson
President Lord King of Lothbury
Chairman S. Taylor

Chief executive 2015 D. A. Leatherdale
Interim chief executive 2016 T. Scott
Head groundsman T. R. Packwood
Scorer S. Drinkwater

At Oxford, April 2–4. WORCESTERSHIRE beat OXFORD MCCU by an innings and 120 runs.

WORCESTERSHIRE v YORKSHIRE

At Worcester, April 12–14. Yorkshire won by ten wickets. Yorkshire 22pts, Worcestershire 6pts. Toss: Worcestershire. County debuts: S. M. S. M. Senanayake; C. A. Pujara. Championship debut: W. M. H. Rhodes.

The county champions were missing six players on England Test duty, plus captain Andrew Gale – completing his suspension for his contretemps with Ashwell Prince at Old Trafford in 2014. Club president Dickie Bird was none too pleased that four of the Yorkshire contingent were carrying the drinks in the Caribbean. But, after two nip-and-tuck days, Brooks collected career-best match figures of nine for 84 to launch a winning start to their title defence, a gutsy effort after Sidebottom was unable to bowl in the second innings because of a torn calf. Ali, proving his fitness before flying out for the Second Test in Grenada, got off the mark with a nick past Hodd and finished with 62, but the honours on a breezy opening day went to Fell, who made a determined century, his first in Division One. Worcestershire looked set for a sizeable lead when Andrew, in his first Championship appearance for 11 months, helped reduce Yorkshire to 193 for seven, still 118 in arrears. But clean striking from Bresnan all but eliminated the deficit. On the third morning, Bresnan and Brooks produced new-ball bowling of "Test-match quality" – in the words of Worcestershire coach Steve Rhodes – and Patterson mopped up the lower order for career-best figures of five for 11. Lees, with his second half-century as stand-in captain, and Will Rhodes, batting in Adam Lyth's opening spot, hurried Yorkshire to their small target.

Close of play: first day, Worcestershire 264-8 (Andrew 42, Senanayake 0); second day, Yorkshire 298-9 (Bresnan 78, Sidebottom 10).

Worcestershire

*D. K. H. Mitchell c Leaning b Brooks	4	– c Lees b Brooks	8
R. K. Oliver c Hodd b Brooks	1	– lbw b Bresnan	1
M. M. Ali c Hodd b Bresnan	62	– c Leaning b Brooks	4
T. C. Fell c Hodd b Bresnan	114	– c Lees b Patterson	14
A. P. R. Gidman lbw b Bresnan	7	– c Hodd b Brooks	4
T. Köhler-Cadmore b Brooks	3	– c Patterson b Brooks	24
†O. B. Cox c Bresnan b Sidebottom	9	– lbw b Patterson	0
G. M. Andrew c Lees b Brooks	59	– c Brooks b Patterson	16
J. D. Shantry lbw b Patterson	15	– not out	15
S. M. S. M. Senanayake c Rhodes b Brooks	13	– c Rhodes b Patterson	9
C. A. J. Morris not out	8	– lbw b Patterson	0
B 4, l-b 11, n-b 2	17	B 1, n-b 4	5

1/2 (2) 2/11 (1) 3/129 (3)   (93.3 overs) 311   1/3 (2) 2/10 (3)   (35.3 overs) 100
4/159 (5) 5/171 (6) 6/195 (7)   3/15 (1) 4/21 (5)
7/216 (4) 8/255 (9) 9/298 (8) 10/311 (10)   5/48 (4) 6/48 (7) 7/65 (6)
                                                                8/90 (8) 9/100 (10) 10/100 (11)

Sidebottom 22–6–77–1; Brooks 21.3–7–56–5; Bresnan 16–2–48–3; Patterson 19–7–40–1; Pyrah 3–2–14–0; Carver 6–0–36–0; Rhodes 5–1–19–0; Leaning 1–0–6–0. *Second innings*—Bresnan 13–4–44–1; Brooks 10–3–28–4; Patterson 7.3–3–11–5; Rhodes 5–1–16–0.

Yorkshire

*A. Z. Lees lbw b Andrew	87	– not out	52
W. M. H. Rhodes c Mitchell b Morris	0	– not out	45
C. A. Pujara c Fell b Andrew	0		
R. M. Pyrah c Mitchell b Shantry	43		
J. A. Leaning lbw b Shantry	10		
†A. J. Hodd c Mitchell b Andrew	30		
T. T. Bresnan c Fell b Andrew	83		
S. A. Patterson b Shantry	0		
R. J. Sidebottom not out	14		
J. A. Brooks c Cox b Andrew	26		
K. Carver c Oliver b Shantry	5		
B 1, l-b 6, n-b 2	9	B 8	8

1/2 (2) 2/3 (3) 3/111 (4)   (85.1 overs) 307   (no wkt, 17 overs) 105
4/127 (5) 5/172 (1) 6/186 (6)
7/193 (8) 8/274 (10) 9/293 (11) 10/307 (7)

In the first innings Sidebottom, when 10, retired hurt at 217-7 and resumed at 293-9.

Andrew 21.1–4–85–5; Morris 14–3–70–1; Shantry 23–5–65–4; Senanayake 18–2–47–0; Ali 9–0–33–0. *Second innings*—Andrew 4–0–25–0; Morris 4–1–14–0; Shantry 3–0–19–0; Senanayake 4–0–24–0; Ali 2–0–15–0.

Umpires: J. H. Evans and J. W. Lloyds.

At Hove, April 19–22. WORCESTERSHIRE lost to SUSSEX by 61 runs.

WORCESTERSHIRE v SOMERSET

At Worcester, May 3–5. Worcestershire won by an innings and 62 runs. Worcestershire 23pts, Somerset 5pts. Toss: Worcestershire.

Morris, who attended King's College, Taunton, and came through the Somerset age-groups, produced potent opening spells of 11–2–34–4 and 11–3–26–4 to decide the game inside three days, and give Worcestershire a confidence boost in their expected battle against the drop. He finished with career-best match figures of nine for 109, thanks to a relentless off-stump line, earning comparisons with his former team-mate Alan Richardson. "We've got a bit of soul-searching to do," said Trescothick. Worcestershire were still 51 behind in the first innings when Gidman was sixth out for a composed 78, his first half-century since joining from Gloucestershire. But Leach, who offered good support to Morris on his return to the side in plsace of the injured Gareth Andrew, made another telling contribution as he and Cox, with a career-best 109, plundered the second new ball during a seventh-wicket partnership of 168. Somerset appeared to have little stomach for the fight when they batted again, 152 behind. Trescothick had his off stump knocked back by Morris with the second ball of the third day, and there was no way back from 19 for five. Shantry's burst of four in 17 deliveries ended the game just after lunch.

Close of play: first day, Worcestershire 35-2 (Mitchell 20, Gidman 7); second day, Worcestershire 402.

Somerset

*M. E. Trescothick c Cox b Morris	10	– b Morris	0
J. G. Myburgh c Cox b Morris	11	– c Cox b Morris	6
T. L. W. Cooper c Cox b Morris	30	– b Morris	7
J. C. Hildreth c Cox b Leach	41	– lbw b Shantry	35
J. Allenby c Mitchell b Morris	7	– b Leach	1
†A. W. R. Barrow c Mitchell b Senanayake	26	– c Gidman b Leach	0
P. D. Trego c Mitchell b Leach	14	– c Senanayake b Morris	14
L. Gregory c Senanayake b Leach	30	– c Cox b Shantry	14
C. Overton c Cox b Morris	41	– lbw b Shantry	10
Abdur Rehman c Fell b Shantry	13	– not out	2
A. C. Thomas not out	12	– c Leach b Shantry	0
B 7, l-b 1, n-b 7	15	L-b 1	1

1/11 (1) 2/50 (2) 3/59 (3)　　　　　(75.1 overs) 250
4/71 (5) 5/142 (6) 6/134 (4)
7/169 (7) 8/221 (8) 9/227 (9) 10/250 (10)

1/0 (1) 2/13 (2)　　　　　(32 overs) 90
3/16 (3) 4/17 (5) 5/19 (6) 6/36 (7)
7/74 (8) 8/87 (4) 9/90 (9) 10/90 (11)

Shantry 15.1–8–43–1; Morris 24–5–71–5; Leach 22–4–76–3; Whiteley 3–0–13–0; Senanayake 10–0–38–1; Kervezee 1–0–1–0. *Second innings*—Morris 13–3–38–4; Leach 9–3–26–2; Shantry 8–2–15–4; Whiteley 2–0–10–0.

Worcestershire

*D. K. H. Mitchell lbw b Thomas	27	S. M. S. M. Senanayake c Trescothick	
R. K. Oliver c and b Gregory	3	b Trego	10
T. C. Fell c Trego b Thomas	1	C. A. J. Morris not out	3
A. P. R. Gidman c Myburgh b Overton	78	B 4, l-b 21, w 1, n-b 6	32
A. N. Kervezee b Trego	29		
R. A. Whiteley c Trescothick b Trego	11	1/14 (2) 2/19 (3) 3/44 (1)　(111.5 overs) 402	
†D. B. Cox c and b Gregory	109	4/103 (5) 5/135 (6) 6/199 (4)	
J. Leach c Trescothick b Thomas	95	7/367 (7) 8/379 (9) 9/392 (8)	
J. D. Shantry c Gregory b Thomas	4	10/402 (10)　　　　　110 overs: 398-9	

Thomas 23–5–81–4; Gregory 22–2–96–2; Trego 25.5–5–78–3; Overton 16–1–64–1; Allenby 15–5–28–0; Abdur Rehman 10–1–30–0.

Umpires: R. J. Evans and M. A. Gough.

At Birmingham, May 9–12. WORCESTERSHIRE lost to WARWICKSHIRE by 181 runs.

At Worcester, May 14–17. WORCESTERSHIRE lost to NEW ZEALANDERS by 15 runs (see New Zealand tour section).

WORCESTERSHIRE v DURHAM

At Worcester, May 24–27. Durham won by six wickets. Durham 19pts, Worcestershire 6pts. Toss: Durham.

Collingwood admitted his side had been outplayed for three-quarters of this game. But, having looked certain to follow on, Durham went top of the Championship with an emphatic win 45 minutes into the final day; Worcestershire were left to reflect on another one that got away. They had worked hard for a strong first-innings platform: Fell made a steady 78, and the last five wickets more than doubled the score. Durham were still 220 adrift when they lost their ninth wicket after lunch on the second day, under cloud cover and on a pitch showing some variable bounce. But Borthwick and Onions changed the momentum in a last-wicket stand of 95 and, although Worcestershire still claimed a lead of 125, the game ebbed away from them. Not for the first time, they collapsed in the second innings: Rushworth nipped out two with the new ball, and Hastings captured a career-best seven for 60. Despite Leach's brazen 76 from 53 balls, a target of 318 in more than five sessions left the door ajar for Durham to complete their recovery. The sun came out as they began their run-chase, and the pitch eased. Collingwood, watched by his parents on his 39th birthday, made his biggest Championship hundred since 2005, and ensured comfortable passage for Durham in century stands with Jennings and Richardson, who had taken the gloves from the out-of-form Phil Mustard. Senanayake, who went wicketless, was dropped for the next Championship match.

Close of play: first day, Durham 14-0 (Stoneman 4, Jennings 9); second day, Worcestershire 65-6 (Cox 0, Leach 0); third day, Durham 270-3 (Collingwood 111, Richardson 41).

Worcestershire

*D. K. H. Mitchell b Rushworth	0	– c Richardson b Hastings	24
R. K. Oliver b Onions	36	– lbw b Rushworth	11
T. C. Fell c Borthwick b Rushworth	78	– c Collingwood b Rushworth	10
A. P. R. Gidman lbw b Rushworth	12	– lbw b Hastings	6
A. N. Kervezee c Richardson b Coughlin	21	– c Collingwood b Hastings	0
R. A. Whiteley lbw b Coughlin	15	– c Richardson b Coughlin	0
†O. B. Cox c Richardson b Coughlin	67	– c Richardson b Hastings	32
J. Leach c MacLeod b Onions	24	– b Hastings	76
S. M. S. M. Senanayake c Richardson b Collingwood	16	– c Stoneman b Hastings	18
J. D. Shantry c Hastings b Coughlin	23	– c Richardson b Hastings	0
C. A. J. Morris not out	1	– not out	1
B 7, l-b 8, w 1, n-b 14	30	B 4, l-b 10	14

1/0 (1) 2/64 (2) 3/88 (4) (81.3 overs) 323
4/160 (5) 5/160 (3) 6/185 (6)
7/224 (8) 8/274 (9) 9/319 (10) 10/323 (7)

1/29 (2) 2/55 (3) (42.3 overs) 192
3/60 (1) 4/60 (5)
5/61 (6) 6/65 (4) 7/140 (7)
8/160 (9) 9/167 (10) 10/192 (8)

Rushworth 18–1–69–3; Onions 17–3–71–2; Hastings 18–5–72–0; Coughlin 16.3–4–70–4; Collingwood 12–5–26–1. *Second innings*—Rushworth 13–4–46–2; Onions 12–0–58–0; Coughlin 4–1–7–1; Hastings 12.3–2–60–7; Borthwick 1–0–7–0.

Durham

M. D. Stoneman b Leach	14	– c Cox b Leach	37
K. K. Jennings c Mitchell b Leach	12	– c Cox b Morris	61
S. G. Borthwick lbw b Shantry	103	– lbw b Shantry	4
*P. D. Collingwood lbw b Leach	3	– c Cox b Morris	127
†M. J. Richardson c Cox b Morris	5	– not out	66
G. J. Muchall lbw b Shantry	1	– not out	5
C. S. MacLeod c Oliver b Morris	3		
P. Coughlin c Fell b Shantry	6		
J. W. Hastings c Oliver b Shantry	0		
C. Rushworth c Gidman b Leach	8		
G. Onions not out	36		
L-b 4, w 1, n-b 2	7	B 8, l-b 10	18

1/24 (2) 2/37 (1) 3/47 (4) (72.3 overs) 198
4/59 (5) 5/68 (6) 6/73 (7)
7/86 (8) 8/94 (9) 9/103 (10) 10/198 (3)

1/53 (1) (4 wkts, 82 overs) 318
2/66 (3) 3/174 (2)
4/286 (4)

Morris 21–3–48–2; Leach 22–2–77–4; Senanayake 6–1–15–0; Shantry 21.3–8–39–4; Whiteley 2–0–15–0. *Second innings*—Morris 24–3–99–2; Leach 18–3–71–1; Shantry 23–3–78–1; Senanayake 12–1–26–0; Whiteley 2–0–17–0; Kervezee 1–0–1–0; Mitchell 2–0–8–0.

Umpires: G. D. Lloyd and M. J. Saggers.

At Southampton, May 31–June 3. WORCESTERSHIRE drew with HAMPSHIRE.

WORCESTERSHIRE v WARWICKSHIRE

At Worcester, June 14–15. Warwickshire won by an innings and 17 runs. Warwickshire 22pts, Worcestershire 4pts. Toss: Worcestershire.

Warwickshire chalked up their eighth successive Championship victory over their local rivals, after routing them for 80 in two and a half hours on the second day. That was Worcestershire's lowest total since 2012 – when Warwickshire sealed the title on this ground – and a procession of batsmen surrendered tamely to a well-honed attack. Worcestershire were competing strongly when Ambrose fell in the first over of the second morning, still 137 runs from parity. But Bell, despite a lean time at Test level, remained a cut above most county players, and made his 50th first-class hundred, adding 135 with Rikki Clarke. That was followed by brutal late hitting by Barker, much of it at the expense of Saeed Ajmal – who looked robbed of his old variations as he bowled with the red ball for the first time since remodelling his action – and Warwickshire built a lead of 97, despite more fine seam bowling from Leach and Shantry. Ali had been left out of England's one-day series against New Zealand in order to rediscover his bowling form, but he delivered just six overs to Ajmal's 17, to vocal displeasure in the crowd. Wright immediately sent Worcestershire on a downward spiral by removing the openers in his second over, and they were bundled out inside 33, amid a flurry of haywire shots. The match coincided with the 800th anniversary of the sealing of the Magna Carta between King John, who is buried in Worcester Cathedral, and a group of rebel barons. It was marked by four hours of bell-ringing from noon on the first day, during which 19-year-old Joe Clarke scored a maiden Championship fifty in just his second game.

Close of play: first day, Warwickshire 101-4 (Bell 46, Ambrose 31).

Worcestershire

*D. K. H. Mitchell c Javid b Wright	36	– c Bell b Wright	0
R. K. Oliver c Ambrose b Wright	27	– c Evans b Wright	2
M. M. Ali c Javid b Barker	45	– b Barker	7
T. C. Fell b Barker	4	– b Rankin	23
A. P. R. Gidman c Ambrose b Wright	4	– b Rankin	8
J. M. Clarke c Trott b Rankin	50	– c Bell b Barker	13
J. Leach c and b Rankin	22	– (8) b Patel	2
†O. B. Cox lbw b Patel	3	– (7) lbw b Rankin	14
J. D. Shantry lbw b Barker	17	– c Wright b Barker	0
Saeed Ajmal c Ambrose b Barker	10	– not out	3
C. A. J. Morris not out	5	– c Barker b Patel	1
B 10, l-b 2, n-b 8	20	W 1, n-b 6	7

1/38 (2) 2/104 (1) 3/119 (4)   (65.2 overs) 243   1/3 (1) 2/4 (2)   (32.5 overs) 80
4/124 (5) 5/126 (3) 6/179 (7)   3/24 (3) 4/35 (4)
7/197 (8) 8/225 (6) 9/238 (10) 10/243 (9)   5/50 (5) 6/61 (6) 7/66 (8)
                                               8/71 (9) 9/77 (7) 10/80 (11)

Barker 16.2–5–65–4; Wright 15–3–63–3; Clarke 9–4–29–0; Rankin 13–1–47–2; Patel 12–2–27–1. *Second innings*—Wright 7–3–14–2; Barker 10–2–26–3; Rankin 6–0–23–3; Clarke 4–0–11–0; Patel 5.5–3–6–2.

Warwickshire

*V. Chopra lbw b Leach	9	J. S. Patel c Saeed Ajmal b Shantry	17
A. Javid lbw b Leach	9	C. J. C. Wright lbw b Morris	16
I. R. Bell lbw b Shantry	111	W. B. Rankin lbw b Leach	13
I. J. L. Trott c Gidman b Shantry	0	B 8, l-b 8	16
L. J. Evans c Oliver b Leach	1		
†T. R. Ambrose c Cox b Shantry	31	1/20 (2) 2/31 (1) 3/34 (4) (91.5 overs) 340
R. Clarke lbw b Shantry	67	4/35 (5) 5/106 (6) 6/241 (3)
K. H. D. Barker not out	50	7/246 (7) 8/296 (9) 9/321 (10) 10/340 (11)

Morris 14–0–52–1; Leach 27.5–5–80–4; Shantry 27–1–92–5; Saeed Ajmal 17–1–82–0; Ali 6–0–18–0.

Umpires: B. J. Debenham and N. A. Mallender.

At Uxbridge, June 21–24. WORCESTERSHIRE drew with MIDDLESEX.

At Nottingham, June 29–July 2. WORCESTERSHIRE lost to NOTTINGHAMSHIRE by 113 runs.

WORCESTERSHIRE v HAMPSHIRE

At Worcester, July 6–9. Worcestershire won by an innings and 33 runs. Worcestershire 23pts, Hampshire 2pts. Toss: Worcestershire.

In this meeting of the bottom two, Worcestershire completed a thumping victory 25 minutes before lunch on the final day. Mitchell again showed his liking for the Hampshire attack, lasting more than nine hours to carry his bat for his second double-century, and enabling his side to recover from the loss of three early wickets in 12 balls from Bird. In the last four games between the counties, Mitchell had now scored 532 runs for once out. He shared century stands with Clarke, showing more signs of his huge potential, and Leach, before Saeed Ajmal enjoyed his most successful spell – five for 28 from 17 overs – with his new action, forcing Hampshire to follow on 295 behind. Shantry, astutely held back for the second innings after one short spell, then claimed his 50th first-class wicket of the season on his way to a five-for, just reward for his perseverance in relatively benign conditions. This was Hampshire's third consecutive defeat, and a weary Adams passed captaincy duties to Vince ahead of the next Championship game.

Close of play: first day, Worcestershire 228-5 (Mitchell 105, Cox 6); second day, Hampshire 86-3 (Vince 29, Smith 1); third day, Hampshire 164-6 (Gatting 28, Berg 12).

Worcestershire

*D. K. H. Mitchell not out	206	Saeed Ajmal st Wheater b Briggs	16
R. K. Oliver lbw b Bird	3	C. A. J. Morris c Wheater b Bird	9
T. C. Fell c Wheater b Bird	0		
T. Köhler-Cadmore b Bird	1	B 1, l-b 15, w 19, n-b 16	51
J. M. Clarke c Terry b Briggs	70		
B. L. D'Oliveira c Vince b Wheal	19	1/17 (2) 2/21 (3) 3/25 (4) (141 overs) 478	
†O. B. Cox b Wheal	23	4/167 (5) 5/216 (6) 6/259 (7)	
J. Leach c Berg b Briggs	59	7/382 (8) 8/423 (9) 9/461 (10)	
J. D. Shantry st Wheater b Smith	21	10/478 (11) 110 overs: 358-6	

Bird 35-2-146-4; Berg 24-5-58-0; Vince 4-0-15-0; Wheal 28-3-99-2; Briggs 41-10-123-3; Gatting 3-1-7-0; Smith 6-1-14-1.

Hampshire

*J. H. K. Adams lbw b Leach	20	– lbw b Shantry	6
S. P. Terry c Köhler-Cadmore b Morris	0	– c Cox b Shantry	37
M. A. Carberry lbw b Saeed Ajmal	36	– b Shantry	32
J. M. Vince b Leach	56	– b Saeed Ajmal	0
W. R. Smith not out	51	– c and b D'Oliveira	29
†A. J. A. Wheater c and b Saeed Ajmal	1	– c Cox b Morris	14
J. S. Gatting c Leach b Saeed Ajmal	4	– lbw b Saeed Ajmal	59
G. K. Berg b Leach	0	– b Saeed Ajmal	12
D. R. Briggs c Cox b Saeed Ajmal	7	– not out	42
B. Wheal c and b Saeed Ajmal	0	– b Shantry	10
J. M. Bird lbw b Leach	0	– c Cox b Shantry	10
B 6, l-b 2	8	B 8, l-b 3	11

1/1 (2) 2/44 (1) 3/75 (3)   (67 overs) 183   1/9 (1) 2/74 (2)   (88.3 overs) 262
4/118 (4) 5/119 (6) 6/131 (7)   3/77 (4) 4/77 (3)
7/131 (8) 8/148 (9) 9/152 (10) 10/183 (11)   5/97 (6) 6/138 (5) 7/164 (8)
                                        8/217 (7) 9/246 (10) 10/262 (11)

Morris 14–4–44–1; Leach 24–8–75–4; Shantry 5–1–14–0; D'Oliveira 7–3–14–0; Saeed Ajmal 17–9–28–5. *Second innings*—Morris 15–2–59–1; Shantry 20.3–5–51–5; Leach 13–1–47–0; Saeed Ajmal 29–5–72–3; D'Oliveira 11–2–22–1.

Umpires: N. L. Bainton and G. D. Lloyd.

At Scarborough, July 19–22. WORCESTERSHIRE lost to YORKSHIRE by seven wickets.

WORCESTERSHIRE v NOTTINGHAMSHIRE

At Worcester, August 7–10. Nottinghamshire won by five wickets. Nottinghamshire 22pts, Worcestershire 5pts. Toss: Worcestershire.

Nottinghamshire's upturn continued as they secured a tenth successive win in completed games across all formats, and a third in four Championship matches, having been bottom of the table in late June. A hamstring injury meant Daryl Mitchell ended a run of 68 consecutive Championship appearances. D'Oliveira stood in as opener, and Gidman as captain, top-scoring with 71 in his first Championship innings since suffering concussion when hit by a Ben Hilfenhaus bouncer at Trent Bridge six weeks earlier. Gidman eventually became Imran Tahir's first Championship wicket for his fifth county (and 23rd first-class team), in his only game in the competition before flying back to South Africa. Once again Nottinghamshire were indebted to Read after being five down for 128, despite Hales's first half-century in first-class cricket since April. Worcestershire lost three wickets wiping out the deficit, but the game took another twist as Whiteley made a responsible 78, adding 68 with Clarke and 73 with Cox. A target of 232 looked tricky when Nottinghamshire slumped to 37 for three, with Leach claiming his 50th wicket of the season. But James Taylor and Wessels put on 157, and the main threat to Nottinghamshire on the final day was the weather. Following a 75-minute delay, victory was secured after lunch.

Close of play: first day, Nottinghamshire 71-0 (B. R. M. Taylor 29, Hales 38); second day, Worcestershire 115-4 (Clarke 43, Whiteley 22); third day, Nottinghamshire 157-3 (J. W. A. Taylor 49, Wessels 70).

Worcestershire

R. K. Oliver c Read b Hutton	4	– c Read b Ball	4
B. L. D'Oliveira lbw b Gurney	18	– lbw b Hutton	19
T. C. Fell c Read b Ball	44	– b Hutton	4
J. M. Clarke lbw b Hutton	0	– b Ball	61
*A. P. R. Gidman c Read b Imran Tahir	71	– b Mullaney	21
R. A. Whiteley c Hutton b Ball	34	– b Patel	78
†O. B. Cox c Mullaney b Gurney	56	– c Mullaney b Imran Tahir	34
J. Leach c B. R. M. Taylor b Hutton	13	– c Read b Ball	40
J. D. Shantry lbw b Imran Tahir	4	– c B. R. M. Taylor b Imran Tahir	6
Saeed Ajmal b Gurney	7	– lbw b Ball	19
C. A. J. Morris not out	0	– not out	0
L-b 10, n-b 8	18	L-b 6	6

1/11 (1) 2/59 (2) 3/60 (4)   (68.1 overs) 269   1/4 (1) 2/9 (3)   (82.3 overs) 292
4/75 (3) 5/160 (6) 6/206 (5)   3/44 (2) 4/78 (5)
7/241 (8) 8/250 (9) 9/268 (7) 10/269 (10)   5/146 (4) 6/219 (7) 7/223 (6)
                                                      8/238 (9) 9/273 (10) 10/292 (8)

Ball 15–1–64–2; Hutton 18–3–58–3; Gurney 15.1–2–47–3; Imran Tahir 18–2–80–2; Mullaney 2–0–10–0. *Second innings*—Ball 15.3–0–67–4; Hutton 11–2–39–2; Gurney 15–1–46–0; Mullaney 6–2–18–1; Imran Tahir 18–3–65–2; Patel 17–2–51–1.

Nottinghamshire

B. R. M. Taylor lbw b Leach	31	– lbw b Morris	4
A. D. Hales b Shantry	85	– c Whiteley b Morris	9
S. J. Mullaney c Fell b Morris	21	– c D'Oliveira b Leach	24
J. W. A. Taylor b Morris	5	– c Gidman b Saeed Ajmal	66
M. H. Wessels lbw b Morris	0	– c Shantry b Saeed Ajmal	88
S. R. Patel run out	0	– not out	17
*†C. M. W. Read lbw b Shantry	90	– not out	19
B. A. Hutton c Cox b Whiteley	40		
J. T. Ball lbw b Saeed Ajmal	38		
Imran Tahir b D'Oliveira	2		
H. F. Gurney not out	2		
B 8, l-b 3, w 3, n-b 2	16	B 4, l-b 3	7

1/75 (1) 2/120 (3) 3/126 (4)   (81.3 overs) 330
4/126 (5) 5/128 (6) 6/175 (2)
7/258 (8) 8/318 (9) 9/321 (10) 10/330 (7)

1/4 (1)   (5 wkts, 71.4 overs) 234
2/33 (2) 3/37 (3)
4/194 (4) 5/200 (5)

Morris 16–6–48–3; Leach 18–2–78–1; Shantry 19.3–5–54–2; Saeed Ajmal 14–0–71–1; Whiteley 10–0–51–1; D'Oliveira 4–0–17–1. *Second innings*—Morris 15–2–45–2; Leach 10–0–61–1; Saeed Ajmal 17.4–3–61–2; Shantry 19–13–23–0; Whiteley 3–0–10–0; D'Oliveira 7–0–27–0.

Umpires: R. J. Bailey and S. A. Garratt.

At Taunton, August 21–24. WORCESTERSHIRE drew with SOMERSET.

WORCESTERSHIRE v SUSSEX

At Worcester, September 1–4. Sussex won by an innings and 63 runs. Sussex 24pts, Worcestershire 2pts. Toss: Worcestershire.

Sussex's crushing victory – their first since May – gave them some breathing space at the bottom, and all but ended Worcestershire's hopes of survival. When Worcestershire reached 93 for two, after choosing to bat on a mosaic-like pitch used twice for limited-overs games, they seemed to have battled their way through testing conditions. But they had no answer to the sustained hostility of Jordan, who captured his first five-wicket haul for a year and a half, in his second Championship match since returning from two months out with a side strain. Nash – standing in as captain for Joyce, who had a sore neck – retired hurt on the second afternoon as a precaution after top-edging Morris on to his helmet, but resumed after Wright and Brown had added 282 in 63 overs, the highest partnership in this fixture. Wright finished unbeaten on an explosive 226 from 274 balls, his first double-century, with seven sixes, though he was dropped three times. Worcestershire spilled half a dozen chances in all, with Saeed Ajmal going wicketless in his last match before leaving to undertake the Hajj. Sussex allowed Mitchell to open the batting after he returned from attending the birth of his daughter, but Worcestershire fared little better second time round, aside from the consolation of Clarke's maiden first-class hundred.

Close of play: first day, Worcestershire 185-9 (Gidman 37, Morris 1); second day, Sussex 251-3 (Wright 98, Brown 45); third day, Worcestershire 59-3 (Morris 4, Clarke 11).

Worcestershire

*D. K. H. Mitchell c Nash b Jordan	5	– c Jordan b Wells	10
B. L. D'Oliveira c Brown b Magoffin	38	– lbw b Magoffin	0
T. C. Fell b Jordan	6	– c Jordan b Ashar Zaidi	26
J. M. Clarke b Jordan	40	– (5) not out	104
A. P. R. Gidman not out	60	– (6) lbw b Ashar Zaidi	6
R. A. Whiteley c Yardy b Jordan	4	– (7) lbw b Jordan	2
†O. B. Cox b Jordan	4	– (8) b Robinson	31
J. Leach c Brown b Liddle	7	– (9) lbw b Ashar Zaidi	7
J. D. Shantry c Jordan b Robinson	15	– (10) lbw b Wells	13
Saeed Ajmal b Ashar Zaidi	22	– (11) b Magoffin	9
C. A. J. Morris b Wells	3	– (4) b Jordan	12
L-b 6	6	B 14, l-b 1, n-b 2	17

1/5 (1) 2/13 (3) 3/93 (4) (80 overs) 210
4/97 (2) 5/102 (6) 6/110 (7)
7/117 (8) 8/142 (9) 9/179 (10) 10/210 (11)

1/1 (2) 2/40 (1) (83.2 overs) 237
3/44 (3) 4/70 (4)
5/83 (6) 6/96 (7) 7/175 (8)
8/192 (9) 9/221 (10) 10/237 (11)

Magoffin 21–7–45–1; Jordan 22–4–68–5; Robinson 10–2–26–1; Liddle 11–1–31–1; Ashar Zaidi 12–4–17–1; Wells 4–0–17–1. *Second innings*—Magoffin 14.2–2–39–2; Jordan 21–4–59–2; Ashar Zaidi 22–6–55–3; Wells 13–5–21–2; Liddle 4–0–24–0; Robinson 9–1–24–1.

Sussex

M. H. Yardy c Fell b Shantry	13	Ashar Zaidi not out	15
L. W. P. Wells c Cox b Leach	10	B 6, l-b 15	21
M. W. Machan c Fell b Morris	32		
*C. D. Nash lbw b Leach	90	1/21 (1) (5 wkts dec, 116.4 overs) 510	
L. J. Wright not out	226	2/35 (2) 3/81 (3)	
†B. C. Brown c Saeed Ajmal b Morris	103	4/376 (6) 5/480 (4) 110 overs: 463-4	

C. J. Jordan, O. E. Robinson, S. J. Magoffin and C. J. Liddle did not bat.

Nash, when 38, retired hurt at 94-3 and resumed at 376-4.

Leach 25.4–5–113–2; Shantry 27–1–126–1; Saeed Ajmal 32–4–114–0; Morris 21–5–75–2; D'Oliveira 7–1–36–0; Whiteley 4–0–25–0.

Umpires: S. C. Gale and N. A. Mallender.

At Chester-le-Street, September 14–17. WORCESTERSHIRE lost to DURHAM by three wickets. *Worcestershire are relegated for the fourth time in nine seasons.*

WORCESTERSHIRE v MIDDLESEX

At Worcester, September 22–24. Worcestershire won by an innings and 128 runs. Worcestershire 24pts, Middlesex 1pt. Toss: Worcestershire.

Nottinghamshire's defeat by Hampshire meant Middlesex hung on to claim runners-up spot – worth an extra £81,000 – despite being bundled out twice inside 80 overs by relegated Worcestershire. The Trinidadian Shannon Gabriel marked his first and only home appearance with some hostile bowling which brought him five for 31, as Middlesex – put in on a helpful pitch – were routed for 98 after the first session was lost to rain. Middlesex's bowlers failed to make similar progress, and flatmates Fell and Köhler-Cadmore brought up personal milestones during a stand of 229. Fell completed 1,000 runs in a season for the first time during his career-best 171, while Köhler-Cadmore – the 2014 Wisden Schools Cricketer of the Year – showed no sign of nerves after resuming on the third morning on 97, completing his maiden hundred with his 12th four. Middlesex capitulated abjectly once more, losing all ten wickets between lunch and tea, with Dexter flashing to slip on 24 in his last innings before going to Leicestershire, and Simpson again left unbeaten.

Close of play: first day, Worcestershire 79-1 (D'Oliveira 38, Fell 37); second day, Worcestershire 329-3 (Fell 167, Köhler-Cadmore 97).

Middlesex

S. D. Robson c Fell b Gabriel	17	– (2) lbw b Barnard	16
P. R. Stirling c D'Oliveira b Leach	4	– (1) c Whiteley b Shantry	22
N. R. D. Compton c Cox b Leach	19	– c Cox b Barnard	4
D. J. Malan b Gabriel	0	– b Gabriel	25
N. J. Dexter c Mitchell b Shantry	0	– c Köhler-Cadmore b Shantry	24
*J. E. C. Franklin c Cox b Shantry	0	– b Gabriel	4
†J. A. Simpson not out	27	– not out	50
O. P. Rayner lbw b Gabriel	11	– b Shantry	0
J. A. R. Harris c Cox b Gabriel	0	– c Cox b Leach	7
T. S. Roland-Jones c Leach b Gabriel	0	– run out	2
T. J. Murtagh c Cox b Barnard	0	– run out	24
B 5, l-b 1, n-b 14	20	B 4, l-b 7, n-b 16	27

1/11 (2) 2/31 (1) 3/31 (4) (34.1 overs) 98
4/41 (5) 5/45 (6) 6/51 (3)
7/64 (8) 8/78 (9) 9/88 (10) 10/98 (11)

1/44 (2) 2/48 (3) (45 overs) 205
3/52 (1) 4/100 (5)
5/106 (4) 6/115 (6) 7/120 (8)
8/131 (9) 9/133 (10) 10/205 (11)

Leach 9–0–35–2; Gabriel 9–3–31–5; Barnard 8.1–2–21–1; Shantry 8–5–5–2. *Second innings—* Leach 8–0–34–1; Gabriel 9–0–40–2; Shantry 16–2–51–3; Barnard 9–2–39–2; D'Oliveira 3–0–30–0.

Worcestershire

*D. K. H. Mitchell c Rayner b Roland-Jones	0	†O. B. Cox not out	53
B. L. D'Oliveira c Franklin b Dexter	38	B 1, l-b 5, w 2, n-b 10	18
T. C. Fell c Harris b Dexter	171		
J. M. Clarke c Rayner b Murtagh	12	1/13 (1) (5 wkts dec, 114 overs) 431
T. Köhler-Cadmore not out	130	2/81 (2) 3/110 (4)
R. A. Whiteley c Murtagh b Dexter	9	4/339 (3) 5/353 (6) 110 overs: 409-5

J. Leach, E. G. Barnard, J. D. Shantry and S. T. Gabriel did not bat.

Murtagh 27–3–123–1; Roland-Jones 24–4–78–1; Dexter 23–8–51–3; Harris 15–0–82–0; Rayner 18–1–68–0; Franklin 6–1–19–0; Malan 1–0–4–0.

Umpires: I. J. Gould and R. T. Robinson.

YORKSHIRE

Second helping

DAVID WARNER

Not until they had won the battle to keep hold of their Championship crown did Yorkshire's swords sleep in their hands – and then only briefly. A triple-wicket maiden from Ryan Sidebottom to start the Middlesex game at Lord's, allied to events elsewhere, meant that by mid-afternoon on September 9 the title was secure, with 11 full playing days remaining. Perhaps the adrenalin which had surged all season temporarily abated: Middlesex achieved one of the Championship's great comebacks to inflict Yorkshire's only defeat of the summer, just as they had in 2014.

But this solitary setback concluded in a dream come true for captain Andrew Gale. He was able to hold the trophy aloft at the home of cricket – a short step from the ECB office which had decreed that he could not collect the spoils the previous year as he served a ban for his Roses spat with Ashwell Prince. For him it really was "My Sweet Lord's"; it would have been sweeter still had he not fallen for 98. It was the first time since the 1960s that Yorkshire had retained the Championship. For Brian Close, who led them to a hat-trick of titles from 1966, the news offered some comfort in the few days before his death.

Opposing captains conceded Yorkshire were the best team, and the statistics agreed: their 11 victories were a record for any county since the introduction of two divisions in 2000, as were their total of 286 points and winning margin of 68; there were only 67 between runners-up Middlesex and last-placed Worcestershire.

The recipe for Yorkshire's dominance came from a mix of good basic ingredients, rather than a complex variety of flavours. They had five top fast bowlers to choose from, while Jonny Bairstow was dazzling with the bat. He was well backed up in the first half of the season by the fast-emerging Jack Leaning, and later by Gale. When Gary Ballance was discarded by England, he also played some important innings, though Adam Lyth never really found his touch after his Ashes struggles; the ever-present Alex Lees averaged a respectable 33, though that was 11 down on 2014.

All this was overseen by Yorkshire's Australian coach, Jason Gillespie, and home-grown director of cricket, Martyn Moxon (there was an almost audible sigh of relief in May when England rejected Gillespie as their head coach in favour of another Australian, Trevor Bayliss). The pair complemented each other perfectly: Gillespie was mustard-keen and competitive, but not tied to the county's traditions; Moxon understood that the more Yorkshire-born players who made the grade, the more comfortable the fans would feel.

Of the battery of fast bowlers, Jack Brooks was again the leading wicket-taker, with 65 in the Championship. Tim Bresnan and the reliable Steven

Patterson each claimed 45, and the ageless Sidebottom had 41 from far fewer overs. He strained a calf muscle in the opening match at Worcester and missed the next five, but this helped preserve his strength. Sidebottom flattened Warwickshire at Edgbaston with 11 for 76, and was unplayable in the first innings at Lord's. Liam Plunkett, when not injured or wanted by England, was a handful; the spell which shattered Durham at Scarborough was among the fastest of the season.

Richard Sellers, Getty Images

Jonny Bairstow

Three Championship matches had been played by the time Bairstow was available – he was one of four Yorkshire players kicking their heels on England's Caribbean tour – and he swiftly embarked on a run of form that made it impossible for the selectors to continue ignoring him in the dozen. In his first dozen Championship innings, he hit 980 runs at 108, and he finished with 1,108 at 92, including a double-century, four other hundreds and five fifties from nine matches. It was batting of the highest order: his sequence of scores was up there with anything Geoffrey Boycott or Darren Lehmann could have produced in their prime.

Gillespie acknowledged that one of Yorkshire's soft spots was the top five's inability to score together consistently, but Bresnan was on hand to spark a revival when required, never more so than at Chester-le-Street in late June. He and Bairstow joined forces at 191 for six and added 366, a seventh-wicket record in England. Yorkshire went on to win by an innings and 47, gained top spot for the first time in 2015, and never looked back. Bresnan – who, like Lees, played in all 16 Championship matches – enjoyed his finest season with the bat, and would have averaged 50 had he managed one more run.

Mighty in the Championship, Yorkshire lagged in limited-overs cricket – winning only five of their 14 Twenty20 matches – and promised to identify and resolve the problems. They began before the season was out, when Lees replaced Gale as white-ball captain, to become Yorkshire's youngest leader since Lord Hawke. The Australian duo of Glenn Maxwell and, especially, Aaron Finch were disappointing, though 17-year-old quick bowler Matthew Fisher was superb. Maxwell – and Yorkshire – did better in the qualifying stages of the Royal London One-Day Cup, but without him they were trounced by Gloucestershire in the semi-final, despite a rousing start from Lyth. In August, it was announced that David Willey was to join on a three-year contract from Northamptonshire. And in the new year, Kane Williamson was signed for six weeks in midsummer after two previous successful stints at Headingley. Yorkshire were raising their sights, aiming not only to emulate Close's side with a third successive Championship, but to make history by pairing it with a one-day trophy.

Championship attendance: 59,109.

YORKSHIRE RESULTS

All first-class matches – Played 18: Won 12, Lost 1, Drawn 5.
County Championship matches – Played 16: Won 11, Lost 1, Drawn 4.

LV= County Championship, winners of Division 1;
NatWest T20 Blast, 8th in North Group; Royal London One-Day Cup, semi-finalists.

COUNTY CHAMPIONSHIP AVERAGES, BATTING AND FIELDING

Cap		Birthplace	M	I	NO	R	HS	100	Avge	Ct/St
2011	J. M. Bairstow.....	Bradford†	9	15	3	1,108	219*	5	92.33	29
	C. A. Pujara§.....	Rajkot, India	4	6	1	264	133*	1	52.80	2
2006	T. T. Bresnan.....	Pontefract†.....	16	22	5	849	169*	2	49.94	13
2000	R. J. Sidebottom....	Huddersfield†....	10	12	10	95	28	0	47.50	3
	A. J. Finch§......	Colac, Australia ..	3	4	1	124	73*	0	41.33	3
	G. J. Maxwell§....	Kew, Australia ...	4	7	1	244	140	1	40.66	3
2008	A. W. Gale.......	Dewsbury†.......	15	25	0	1,006	164	3	40.24	4
	J. A. Leaning.....	Bristol	15	25	2	922	123	3	40.08	19
2012	G. S. Ballance‡....	Harare, Zimbabwe.	8	13	0	458	165	1	35.23	7
2008	A. U. Rashid.....	Bradford†.......	7	10	0	347	127	1	34.70	3
2014	A. Z. Lees.......	Halifax†........	16	27	3	795	100	1	33.12	20
	W. M. H. Rhodes ...	Nottingham	9	15	2	388	79	0	29.84	3
2010	A. Lyth	Whitby†........	7	12	0	315	67	0	26.25	10
	A. J. Hodd.......	Chichester	8	10	2	180	54*	0	22.50	21/3
2012	S. A. Patterson ...	Beverley†.......	15	17	4	272	44*	0	20.92	3
2013	A. J. Brooks	Oxford	14	15	1	185	50*	0	13.21	4
2013	L. E. Plunkett‡....	Middlesbrough† .	5	8	0	96	28	0	12.00	4
	J. D. Middlebrook ...	Leeds†.........	6	7	0	49	23	0	7.00	1

Also batted: K. Carver (*Northallerton*†) (1 match) 5; M. D. Fisher (*York*†) (3 matches) 0, 0* (1 ct);
R. M. Pyrah (*Dewsbury*†) (cap 2010) (2 matches) 43, 37.

† *Born in Yorkshire.*			‡ *ECB contract.*			§ *Official overseas player.*

BOWLING

	Style	O	M	R	W	BB	5I	Avge
R. J. Sidebottom...................	LFM	248	65	734	41	6-34	3	17.90
J. A. Brooks	RFM	420.5	83	1,480	65	5-35	3	22.76
S. A. Patterson	RFM	431.1	142	1,128	45	5-11	2	25.06
J. D. Middlebrook	OB	126.3	22	441	17	5-82	1	25.94
A. U. Rashid.....................	LBG	222.1	31	813	29	4-48	0	28.03
T. T. Bresnan	RFM	422.5	112	1,390	45	5-85	0	30.88
L. E. Plunkett	RFM	115.1	17	459	14	4-61	0	32.78

Also bowled: K. Carver (SLA) 6–0–36–0; A. J. Finch (SLA) 2–1–1–0; M. D. Fisher (RFM)
73.5–18–243–5; J. A. Leaning (RFM) 23–3–141–1; A. Z. Lees (LBG) 4–0–12–0; A. Lyth (RM)
27.5–3–76–4; G. J. Maxwell (OB) 29–2–144–4; C. A. Pujara (LBG) 1–0–5–0; R. M. Pyrah (RM)
10–2–40–0; W. M. H. Rhodes (RFM) 80.5–17–271–8.

LEADING ROYAL LONDON CUP AVERAGES (100 runs/4 wickets)

Batting	Runs	HS	Avge	SR	Ct/St	Bowling	W	BB	Avge	ER
A. Lyth........	132	96	66.00	103.12	0	S. A. Patterson ...	13	5-24	19.84	4.42
G. J. Maxwell....	312	111	52.00	117.73	4	L. E. Plunkett ...	9	3-40	23.88	5.00
G. S. Ballance ..	296	77	42.28	74.37	3	W. M. H. Rhodes .	6	2-22	25.83	4.67
J. A. Leaning ...	249	72	35.57	78.05	4	M. D. Fisher	8	3-32	30.62	5.85
A. Z. Lees	247	75	27.44	64.65	3	T. T. Bresnan ...	8	2-41	33.12	5.21
W. M. H. Rhodes ...	132	46	22.00	70.21	2	A. U. Rashid ...	4	1-38	48.00	5.64
T. T. Bresnan ...	132	43	18.85	94.28	2					
A. J. Hodd	106	36	17.66	63.47	10/1					

LEADING NATWEST T20 BLAST AVERAGES (100 runs/18 overs)

Batting	Runs	HS	Avge	SR	Ct/St		Bowling		W	BB	Avge	ER
T. T. Bresnan ..	155	51	31.00	**158.16**	5		A. U. Rashid ..		6	2-26	29.00	**6.69**
G. J. Maxwell ..	229	92*	20.81	**155.78**	6		R. M. Pyrah ...		7	2-13	32.71	**7.38**
J. M. Bairstow ..	320	92	32.00	**134.45**	9/1		G. J. Maxwell ..		12	3-15	22.00	**7.76**
J. A. Leaning ...	338	60*	26.00	**134.12**	6		L. E. Plunkett..		11	3-49	22.00	**8.06**
A. J. Hodd	113	70	16.14	**117.70**	4		M. D. Fisher ...		16	5-22	22.62	**8.86**
A. Z. Lees	175	63	19.44	**115.13**	4		T. T. Bresnan ..		5	1-5	52.60	**10.11**
A. W. Gale	288	68*	26.18	**109.50**	2							

FIRST-CLASS COUNTY RECORDS

Highest score for	341	G. H. Hirst v Leicestershire at Leicester	1905
Highest score against	318*	W. G. Grace (Gloucestershire) at Cheltenham .	1876
Leading run-scorer	38,558	H. Sutcliffe (avge 50.20)	1919–45
Best bowling for	10-10	H. Verity v Nottinghamshire at Leeds	1932
Best bowling against	10-37	C. V. Grimmett (Australians) at Sheffield	1930
Leading wicket-taker	3,597	W. Rhodes (avge 16.02)	1898–1930
Highest total for	887	v Warwickshire at Birmingham.	1896
Highest total against	681-7 dec	by Leicestershire at Bradford	1996
Lowest total for	23	v Hampshire at Middlesbrough	1965
Lowest total against	13	by Nottinghamshire at Nottingham	1901

LIST A COUNTY RECORDS

Highest score for	191	D. S. Lehmann v Nottinghamshire at Scarborough	2001
Highest score against	177	S. A. Newman (Surrey) at The Oval	2009
Leading run-scorer	8,699	G. Boycott (avge 40.08).	1963–86
Best bowling for	7-15	R. A. Hutton v Worcestershire at Leeds.	1969
Best bowling against	7-32	R. G. D. Willis (Warwickshire) at Birmingham .	1981
Leading wicket-taker	308	C. M. Old (avge 18.96)	1967–82
Highest total for	411-6	v Devon at Exmouth.	2004
Highest total against	375-4	by Surrey at Scarborough.	1994
Lowest total for	54	v Essex at Leeds	2003
Lowest total against	23	by Middlesex at Leeds	1974

TWENTY20 COUNTY RECORDS

Highest score for	109	I. J. Harvey v Derbyshire at Leeds	2005
Highest score against	111	D. L. Maddy (Leicestershire) at Leeds	2004
Leading run-scorer	**2,260**	**A. W. Gale** (avge 25.39).	**2004–15**
Best bowling for	5-16	R. M. Pyrah v Durham at Scarborough	2011
Best bowling against	4-9	C. K. Langeveldt (Derbyshire) at Leeds	2008
Leading wicket-taker	**108**	**R. M. Pyrah** (avge 21.43).	**2005–15**
Highest total for	213-7	v Worcestershire at Leeds	2010
Highest total against	**231-4**	**by Lancashire at Manchester**	**2015**
Lowest total for	90-9	v Durham at Chester-le-Street	2009
Lowest total against	98	by Durham at Chester-le-Street	2006

ADDRESS

Headingley Cricket Ground, Leeds LS6 3BU; 0843 504 3099; cricket@yorkshireccc.com; www.yorkshireccc.com.

OFFICIALS

Captain A. W. Gale
    2016 (limited-overs) A. Z. Lees
Director of cricket M. D. Moxon
First-team coach J. N. Gillespie
Director of cricket development I. M. Dews

President H. D. Bird
Chairman S. J. Denison
Chief executive M. A. Arthur
Head groundsman A. Fogarty
Scorer J. T. Potter

At Abu Dhabi, March 22–24. YORKSHIRE beat MCC by nine wickets (see MCC section).

YORKSHIRE v LEEDS/BRADFORD MCCU

At Leeds, April 7–9. Drawn. Toss: Leeds/Bradford MCCU. First-class debut: S. F. G. Bullen.
Yorkshire were keen to run the rule over Championship contenders, given that six players were
with England in the Caribbean, and Gale was due to serve the last match of his ECB ban at Worcester.
Of the understudies, Pyrah and Hodd rescued their side from an uncomfortable 148 for five, after
Lees's solid half-century. But both were trapped by former Yorkshire colt Alex Lilley, who captured
four in all. The most memorable performance came from Joe Ellis-Grewal, who revived the students'
first innings with an energetic 42 from No. 10, before he too collected four wickets, unsettling
Yorkshire in a 33-over spell of left-arm spin broken by the close and lunch. Brooks had bowled
with control, and the county would probably have had time to win had they declared on the last day,
but Leeds/Bradford could feel satisfied with what they took from the game. Bresnan's first wicket
was his 400th in first-class cricket.

Close of play: first day, Leeds/Bradford MCCU 46-0 (Bullen 21, Thompson 21); second day,
Yorkshire 126-6 (Pyrah 1, Bresnan 6).

Yorkshire

A. Z. Lees c Wakefield b Pratt	63	– lbw b Lilley	8
W. M. H. Rhodes c Wakefield b Watkinson	1	– b Ellis-Grewal	19
D. M. Hodgson b Rouse	35	– lbw b Ellis-Grewal	19
*A. W. Gale lbw b Pratt	7	– c Weston b Rouse	32
J. A. Leaning b Lilley	8	– c Scott b Rouse	31
R. M. Pyrah lbw b Lilley	84	– c Weston b Ellis-Grewal	40
†A. J. Hodd lbw b Lilley	54	– lbw b Ellis-Grewal	5
T. T. Bresnan c Weston b Ellis-Grewal	8	– c Thompson b Watkinson	38
S. A. Patterson b Lilley	41	– c Weston b Pratt	30
K. Carver not out	7	– c Wakefield b Rouse	16
J. A. Brooks not out	0	– not out	38
L-b 5, w 3, n-b 13	21	B 11, l-b 5, w 1	17

1/4 (2) 2/76 (3)   (9 wkts dec, 82 overs) 329   1/8 (1) 2/47 (2)   (87.2 overs) 293
3/87 (4) 4/121 (5) 5/148 (1)   3/48 (3) 4/102 (4)
6/264 (7) 7/275 (6) 8/297 (8) 9/326 (9)   5/115 (5) 6/120 (7) 7/197 (6)
                                                           8/199 (8) 9/243 (10) 10/293 (9)

Lilley 20–4–65–4; Watkinson 14–2–52–1; Pratt 15–1–51–2; Rouse 14–2–60–1; Scott 7–1–54–0;
Ellis-Grewal 12–2–42–1. *Second innings*—Lilley 13–2–42–1; Watkinson 10–2–32–1; Rouse
13–1–45–3; Pratt 18.2–6–40–1; Ellis-Grewal 33–2–118–4.

Leeds/Bradford MCCU

S. F. G. Bullen b Brooks	36	– lbw b Carver	25
H. L. Thompson lbw b Bresnan	21	– c Leaning b Bresnan	3
W. T. Root b Patterson	18	– b Brooks	6
L. P. Weston c Hodd b Brooks	1	– c Hodgson b Carver	7
G. F. B. Scott c Hodd b Carver	11	– not out	1
H. P. Rouse c Hodd b Rhodes	23	– not out	5
†C. F. Wakefield lbw b Brooks	7		
L. Watkinson lbw b Patterson	20		
*A. E. Lilley run out	6		
J. S. E. Ellis-Grewal c Bresnan b Carver	42		
D. T. P. Pratt not out	2		
B 7, l-b 4, n-b 4	15	L-b 1	1

1/62 (2) 2/64 (1) 3/66 (4)   (74 overs) 202   1/3 (2) 2/10 (3)   (4 wkts, 33 overs) 48
4/89 (3) 5/115 (5) 6/123 (6)   3/33 (4) 4/42 (1)
7/130 (7) 8/141 (9) 9/172 (8) 10/202 (10)

Bresnan 15–5–35–1; Brooks 14–5–41–3; Patterson 15–6–38–2; Pyrah 8–0–27–0; Carver 15–8–33–2; Rhodes 4–2–6–1; Leaning 3–1–11–0. *Second innings*—Bresnan 6–3–3–1; Brooks 6–1–14–1; Carver 10–8–6–2; Rhodes 2–1–12–0; Patterson 5–2–6–0; Pyrah 3–1–6–0; Lees 1–1–0–0.

Umpires: P. J. Hartley and T. Lungley.

At Worcester, April 12–14. YORKSHIRE beat WORCESTERSHIRE by ten wickets.

At Nottingham, April 19–22. YORKSHIRE drew with NOTTINGHAMSHIRE.

YORKSHIRE v WARWICKSHIRE

At Leeds, April 26–29. Drawn. Yorkshire 9pts, Warwickshire 11pts. Toss: Warwickshire.
The champions and runners-up were both below strength, due to England calls and injuries. Warwickshire held the upper hand on a slow pitch, but lacked the conviction to send Yorkshire on a longer run-chase. When hail forced an early lunch, the target would have been 303 off 76 overs; they finally opted for 352 off 68. Yorkshire shut up shop on losing Pujara and Gale soon after tea. Westwood might have made history on the final morning, when he followed a serene, career-best 196 with 84. In sight of becoming the first man to score twin hundreds at Headingley, he was lbw for the second time to Middlebrook, who picked up eight in all on his return to his native county after 14 years, as a stand-in for Rashid (still twiddling his thumbs with England, but not his spinning fingers). Bresnan's five for 85 was his best return for three years, but controversy continued to plague Gale: trying to complete his century, he was caught off a waist-high full toss, whose legitimacy he queried. The decision stood, giving Rankin six in an innings in successive matches. Headingley's rose-shaped floodlights made their debut on the third evening.
Close of play: first day, Warwickshire 270-4 (Westwood 151, McKay 17); second day, Yorkshire 128-3 (Gale 17, Leaning 17); third day, Warwickshire 108-2 (Westwood 48, Evans 15).

Warwickshire

*V. Chopra c Hodd b Bresnan	0	– lbw b Bresnan	10
I. J. Westwood lbw b Middlebrook	196	– lbw b Middlebrook	84
W. T. S. Porterfield c Hodd b Bresnan	35	– c Pujara b Middlebrook	30
L. J. Evans lbw b Patterson	14	– lbw b Bresnan	15
S. R. Hain lbw b Bresnan	50	– b Middlebrook	24
†P. J. McKay b Bresnan	17	– st Hodd b Middlebrook	5
R. Clarke lbw b Fisher	39	– c Fisher b Middlebrook	36
K. H. D. Barker b Middlebrook	27	– not out	1
J. S. Patel c Patterson b Bresnan	31		
C. J. C. Wright not out	10		
W. B. Rankin lbw b Middlebrook	3		
L-b 13	13	B 1, l-b 5, n-b 8	14

1/0 (1) 2/95 (3) 3/136 (4) (143.3 overs) 435
4/228 (5) 5/278 (6) 6/360 (2)
7/380 (7) 8/404 (8) 9/426 (9)
10/435 (11)
110 overs: 309-5

1/12 (1) (7 wkts dec, 54.3 overs) 219
2/64 (3) 3/114 (4)
4/157 (2) 5/167 (6) 6/202 (5) 7/219 (7)

Bresnan 30–10–85–5; Brooks 25–7–66–0; Patterson 29–11–64–1; Fisher 17–2–70–1; Middlebrook 31.3–6–96–3; Rhodes 10–2–36–0; Pujara 1–0–5–0. *Second innings*—Bresnan 13–2–39–2; Brooks 9–2–35–0; Patterson 14–1–47–0; Fisher 2–0–10–0; Middlebrook 16.3–1–82–5.

Yorkshire

A. Z. Lees lbw b Patel	19	– c McKay b Clarke	21
W. M. H. Rhodes c Rankin b Patel	46	– lbw b Patel	29
C. A. Pujara c McKay b Rankin	23	– lbw b Patel	33
*A. W. Gale c Hain b Rankin	96	– c McKay b Patel	28
J. A. Leaning c Hain b Rankin	41	– not out	35
†A. J. Hodd b Porterfield b Rankin	12	– not out	54
T. T. Bresnan b Patel	2		
J. D. Middlebrook run out	2		
S. A. Patterson c McKay b Rankin	11		
J. A. Brooks c Evans b Rankin	21		
M. D. Fisher not out	0		
B 8, l-b 7, w 2, n-b 13	30	B 4, l-b 9, n-b 8	21

1/41 (1) 2/88 (2) 3/88 (3)   (98.3 overs) 303   1/48 (1)   (4 wkts, 64 overs) 221
4/185 (5) 5/207 (6) 6/222 (7)   2/82 (2) 3/129 (3)
7/224 (8) 8/249 (9) 9/303 (10) 10/303 (4)   4/136 (4)

Barker 22–4–74–0; Wright 18–1–63–0; Clarke 12–4–19–0; Patel 31–9–77–3; Rankin 15.3–0–55–6. *Second innings*—Barker 9–4–25–0; Wright 7–0–30–0; Patel 28–8–70–3; Clarke 11–0–48–1; Rankin 8–0–26–0; Westwood 1–0–9–0.

Umpires: S. A. Garratt and J. W. Lloyds.

YORKSHIRE v HAMPSHIRE

At Leeds, May 10–13. Yorkshire won by 305 runs. Yorkshire 23pts, Hampshire 4pts. Toss: Yorkshire. First-class debut: L. D. McManus. County debut: F. H. Edwards.

With their England tourists finally home, Yorkshire overwhelmed Hampshire with their ninth-biggest win by runs. They omitted Plunkett after he failed to attend a photocall and practice session, but three others who had been in the Caribbean played key roles: despite having no time to acclimatise, Bairstow compiled a fluent century, Lyth grafted sensibly towards a Test debut, and Rashid claimed four in each innings. Bairstow added 155 for the fifth wicket with Leaning, guaranteeing a useful total on a pitch offering bowlers some help, but Hampshire clung doggedly to their coat-tails until three careless moments shook them off. Carberry, trying to sweep his way to 100, found Pujara at deep midwicket; Ervine, who had partnered him in a reviving stand of 86, pulled straight to fine leg; and, in the last over of the second day, Adams perished slogging at Rashid. Having started his four-match Yorkshire career with a duck, Pujara ended it with a quality 133 to hasten the declaration, 448 ahead, with 21 overs plus a day to go. Brooks blasted three out in his first three overs, and only Will Smith and debutant keeper Lewis McManus – playing instead of the injured Adam Wheater – showed any resolve as Rashid mopped up again.

Close of play: first day, Yorkshire 333-7 (Leaning 77, Bresnan 23); second day, Hampshire 223-8 (McManus 10); third day, Hampshire 37-4 (Smith 18, Tomlinson 0).

Yorkshire

A. Lyth c McManus b Adams	53	– c McManus b Edwards	23
A. Z. Lees lbw b Tomlinson	1	– b Berg	16
C. A. Pujara c Ervine b Tomlinson	18	– not out	133
*A. W. Gale c Carberry b Adams	30	– c Tomlinson b Edwards	12
†J. M. Bairstow c McManus b Adams	102	– c Ervine b Dawson	59
J. A. Leaning lbw b Tomlinson	82	– not out	43
A. U. Rashid c Edwards b Berg	0		
W. M. H. Rhodes c Ervine b Berg	4		
T. T. Bresnan c Smith b Tomlinson	28		
S. A. Patterson not out	17		
J. A. Brooks c McManus b Edwards	9	B 4, l-b 2, w 1, n-b 12	19
B 1, l-b 17, n-b 8	26		

1/9 (2) 2/57 (3) 3/109 (1)   (112.3 overs) 370   1/35 (1)   (4 wkts dec, 69 overs) 305
4/114 (4) 5/269 (5) 6/274 (7)   2/57 (2) 3/80 (4)
7/279 (8) 8/343 (9) 9/354 (6)   4/210 (5)
10/370 (11)   110 overs: 359-9

Tomlinson 34–10–86–4; Edwards 15.3–3–77–1; Adams 30–9–68–3; Berg 19–4–49–2; Dawson 5–0–30–0; Ervine 9–1–42–0. *Second innings*—Tomlinson 9–2–33–0; Edwards 17–4–96–2; Berg 12–2–42–1; Adams 12–1–34–0; Dawson 12–0–63–1; Smith 7–0–31–0.

Hampshire

S. P. Terry lbw b Bresnan	0	– c Bresnan b Brooks	1
L. A. Dawson c Leaning b Rhodes	40	– lbw b Rashid	16
M. A. Carberry c Pujara b Rashid	97	– c Bairstow b Brooks	0
*J. M. Vince lbw b Brooks	6	– c Lyth b Brooks	2
W. R. Smith c Lyth b Brooks	0	– not out	64
S. M. Ervine c Patterson b Brooks	48	– (7) c Bairstow b Bresnan	5
†L. D. McManus lbw b Brooks	10	– (8) c Bairstow b Rhodes	28
G. K. Berg c Lyth b Rashid	10	– (9) c Brooks b Rashid	12
A. R. Adams c Gale b Rashid	0	– (10) c Bresnan b Rashid	0
J. A. Tomlinson lbw b Rashid	2	– (6) b Rashid	3
F. H. Edwards not out	2	– c Lees b Patterson	1
L-b 2, n-b 2	4	B 5, l-b 4, n-b 2	11

1/8 (1) 2/83 (2) 3/109 (4)   (80 overs) 227   1/1 (1) 2/1 (3)   (74.3 overs) 143
4/109 (5) 5/195 (3) 6/199 (6)   3/11 (4) 4/36 (2)
7/215 (8) 8/223 (9) 9/223 (7) 10/227 (10)   5/54 (6) 6/67 (7) 7/123 (8)
                                    8/138 (9) 9/138 (10) 10/143 (11)

Bresnan 17–7–33–1; Brooks 18–5–57–4; Patterson 17–9–35–0; Rhodes 8–2–29–1; Rashid 18–0–70–4; Lyth 2–1–1–0. *Second innings*—Bresnan 12–3–25–1; Brooks 17–7–31–3; Patterson 10.3–4–16–1; Rashid 26–9–48–4; Lyth 2–0–8–0; Rhodes 7–5–6–1.

Umpires: M. J. D. Bodenham and R. A. Kettleborough.

At Taunton, May 24–27. YORKHIRE drew with SOMERSET.

YORKSHIRE v MIDDLESEX

At Leeds, June 7–9. Yorkshire won by four wickets. Yorkshire 20pts, Middlesex 4pts. Toss: Middlesex.

This was a superb contest between the division's last unbeaten teams. It ebbed and flowed on a dry pitch, and was in doubt until the third evening, when Maxwell struck a straight six to win, ten balls into the extra half-hour. On the opening day, Compton had shored up Middlesex with three and a half hours' watchfulness until he became one of Brooks's five victims. At 142 for eight, Yorkshire looked second-best, but Patterson and Brooks hung around while Bairstow assumed total command with glorious batting that lifted his Championship aggregate to 402 in five innings and earned a lead of 17. "We're quite fortunate to have Jonny in this game," said coach Gillespie. "He should be with England." On 56 when Patterson arrived, Bairstow hit four sixes – all in a last-wicket stand of 59 with Brooks – to finish on 125, his tenth century for Yorkshire, one more than his late father David. The home bowlers gave little away – Patterson's 42 overs cost only 75 – but the Middlesex attack never gave an inch, either. Yorkshire could not relax until the ball found the middle of Maxwell's bat, after two runs in his previous three first-class innings.

Close of play: first day, Yorkshire 96-4 (Bairstow 25, Leaning 20); second day, Middlesex 127-4 (Malan 33, Franklin 26).

Middlesex

S. D. Robson b Brooks	41	– (2) lbw b Patterson		34
J. A. Burns lbw b Brooks	4	– (1) c Lyth b Brooks		20
N. R. D. Compton c Leaning b Brooks	70	– lbw b Brooks		0
D. J. Malan c Bairstow b Patterson	9	– c Bresnan b Lyth		35
N. J. Dexter c Bairstow b Brooks	0	– lbw b Bresnan		2
*J. E. C. Franklin c Leaning b Maxwell	3	– not out		55
†J. A. Simpson lbw b Maxwell	0	– b Bresnan		15
O. P. Rayner b Maxwell	20	– c Ballance b Patterson		28
J. A. R. Harris c Ballance b Brooks	22	– lbw b Rhodes		5
T. S. Roland-Jones lbw b Patterson	11	– c Ballance b Rhodes		4
T. J. Murtagh not out	17	– b Rhodes		13
B 12, l-b 3	15	B 8, l-b 4, n-b 6		18

1/6 (2) 2/68 (1) 3/83 (4) (68.5 overs) 212   1/51 (1) 2/51 (3)   (79.5 overs) 229
4/92 (5) 5/119 (6) 6/119 (7)   3/65 (2) 4/72 (5)
7/147 (8) 8/171 (3) 9/188 (10) 10/212 (9)   5/130 (4) 6/159 (7) 7/206 (8)
                                                 8/211 (9) 9/215 (10) 10/229 (11)

Bresnan 15–6–36–0; Brooks 18.5–4–44–5; Patterson 19–7–42–2; Rhodes 5–1–20–0; Maxwell 11–1–55–3. *Second innings*—Bresnan 17–5–51–2; Brooks 16–2–51–2; Patterson 23–12–33–2; Rhodes 9.5–0–42–3; Maxwell 4–0–19–0; Lyth 10–1–21–1.

Yorkshire

A. Lyth c Rayner b Roland-Jones	17	– c Simpson b Rayner		67
A. Z. Lees c Rayner b Murtagh	11	– lbw b Franklin		10
G. S. Ballance lbw b Murtagh	1	– st Simpson b Rayner		29
*A. W. Gale lbw b Harris	18	– b Murtagh		37
†J. M. Bairstow not out	125	– c Rayner b Roland-Jones		0
J. A. Leaning lbw b Roland-Jones	20	– c Rayner b Harris		25
G. J. Maxwell c Simpson b Roland-Jones	0	– not out		23
W. M. H. Rhodes c Simpson b Murtagh	11	– not out		10
T. T. Bresnan c Rayner b Harris	4			
S. A. Patterson b Roland-Jones	12			
J. A. Brooks c Simpson b Rayner	6			
B 1, l-b 3	4	B 4, l-b 8, n-b 2		14

1/29 (1) 2/29 (2) 3/36 (3)   (72.5 overs) 229   1/27 (2)   (6 wkts, 65.4 overs) 215
4/52 (5) 5/96 (6) 6/96 (7)   2/98 (3) 3/129 (1)
7/131 (8) 8/142 (9) 9/170 (10) 10/229 (11)   4/132 (5) 5/169 (6) 6/189 (4)

Murtagh 21–4–62–3; Roland-Jones 23–5–78–4; Harris 15–0–47–2; Dexter 11–2–19–0; Rayner 2.5–0–19–1. *Second innings*—Murtagh 13–3–36–1; Roland-Jones 16–5–32–1; Harris 12.4–2–56–1; Franklin 4–1–19–1; Rayner 17–6–52–2; Dexter 3–0–8–0.

Umpires: J. H. Evans and M. J. Saggers.

YORKSHIRE v NOTTINGHAMSHIRE

At Leeds, June 22–24. Yorkshire won by an innings and eight runs. Yorkshire 24pts, Nottinghamshire 3pts. Toss: Yorkshire.

Broad warmed up for the Ashes with five wickets and a robust fifty on the third and final day, his 29th birthday, but it was Yorkshire who celebrated: an emphatic victory pushed them into second spot, while Nottinghamshire propped up the table. Gillespie omitted both his fellow Australians – Glenn Maxwell rested and Aaron Finch sought form in the second team. After Yorkshire had won a good toss, Nottinghamshire struggled against a sharp attack, particularly on a damp and abbreviated first day; it took the tail to edge them past 200. Yorkshire also looked shaky when Broad dismissed their openers cheaply, but they were rescued by a rousing 255-run partnership between Gale and Leaning, a fourth-wicket record between these sides, beating 210 by Yorkshire's Ted Lester and Willie Watson at Trent Bridge in 1952. Broad removed both men early on the third morning, on his way to seven for 84, then the fourth-best figures of his career. But only his birthday bash saved his team-mates from greater humiliation as Sidebottom claimed four in the second innings. Acting-captain James Taylor was penalised for dissent when out for a duck on the first day: he had angrily waved his bat, then thumped an advertising hoarding.

Close of play: first day, Nottinghamshire 169-8 (Wood 19, Hilfenhaus 1); second day, Yorkshire 302-3 (Gale 144, Leaning 107).

Nottinghamshire

S. J. Mullaney c Hodd b Sidebottom	28	– c Bairstow b Sidebottom	9
B. R. M. Taylor c Lees b Patterson	29	– c Middlebrook b Sidebottom	0
M. J. Lumb lbw b Bresnan	7	– lbw b Bresnan	47
*J. W. A. Taylor c Hodd b Patterson	0	– lbw b Patterson	6
†M. H. Wessels lbw b Sidebottom	33	– c Bairstow b Bresnan	16
S. R. Patel lbw b Brooks	4	– c Lees b Sidebottom	4
W. R. S. Gidman lbw b Brooks	4	– c Ballance b Brooks	0
S. C. J. Broad c Leaning b Bresnan	34	– c Gale b Middlebrook	50
L. Wood b Brooks	38	– b Sidebottom	12
B. W. Hilfenhaus not out	28	– not out	17
J. T. Ball b Brooks	0	– c Sidebottom b Middlebrook	6
B 8, l-b 5, n-b 6	19	B 8, l-b 16, w 1, n-b 6	31

1/43 (2) 2/52 (3) 3/53 (4)   (59.5 overs) 224   1/1 (2) 2/20 (1)   (42.3 overs) 198
4/80 (1) 5/87 (6) 6/109 (7)   3/40 (4) 4/79 (5)
7/133 (5) 8/159 (8) 9/224 (9) 10/224 (11)   5/84 (3) 6/88 (7) 7/108 (6)
     8/126 (9) 9/186 (8) 10/198 (11)

Sidebottom 13–4–41–2; Brooks 14.5–2–56–4; Patterson 14–2–59–2; Bresnan 15–6–49–2; Middlebrook 3–1–6–0. *Second innings*—Sidebottom 11–3–39–4; Brooks 11–2–49–1; Bresnan 10–3–40–2; Patterson 7–0–34–1; Middlebrook 3.3–2–12–2.

Yorkshire

A. Lyth lbw b Broad	0	J. A. Brooks c B. R. M. Taylor b Broad	8
A. Z. Lees b Broad	15	R. J. Sidebottom lbw b Broad	0
G. S. Ballance c Patel b Hilfenhaus	14		
*A. W. Gale lbw b Broad	148	B 10, l-b 10, n-b 12	32
J. A. Leaning b Broad	110		
†J. M. Bairstow b Wood	15		430
T. T. Bresnan not out	52		
J. D. Middlebrook c Mullaney b Hilfenhaus	13		
S. A. Patterson c Wessels b Broad	23		

1/0 (1) 2/28 (3)   (114.4 overs) 430
3/51 (2) 4/306 (4) 5/325 (5)
6/325 (6) 7/368 (8) 8/418 (9)
9/430 (10) 10/430 (11)   110 overs: 418-7

Bairstow replaced †A. J. Hodd after returning from England's Twenty20 international.

Broad 26.4–5–84–7; Wood 18–3–73–1; Hilfenhaus 23–5–75–2; Ball 19–2–77–0; Gidman 7–1–28–0; Patel 18–2–60–0; Mullaney 3–0–13–0.

Umpires: G. D. Lloyd and D. J. Millns.

At Chester-le-Street, June 28–July 1. YORKSHIRE beat DURHAM by an innings and 47 runs.

At Birmingham, July 5–8. YORKSHIRE beat WARWICKSHIRE by 174 runs.

YORKSHIRE v WORCESTERSHIRE

At Scarborough, July 19–22. Yorkshire won by seven wickets. Yorkshire 24pts, Worcestershire 5pts. Toss: Yorkshire.

Victory extended Yorkshire's lead to 34 points with a game in hand, but it was only while Bairstow was in that they had complete mastery over a brave Worcestershire. His magnificent 139 made a Test recall inevitable – it was announced on the third day – and he followed it with a stunning unbeaten 51-ball 74, finishing as the first division's leading scorer with 980 at 108 from a dozen innings. Worcestershire had little luck, losing the toss and falling one short of avoiding the follow-on against the competition's strongest pace attack. Clarke, aged 19, showed wonderful promise in an unflustered career-best 88, and Whiteley completed a second-innings century, a week after thrashing 91 not out in 35 balls in a Twenty20 game at Leeds. Still, Bairstow's brilliance overshadowed everything, even Gale's faultless 164. Together they had added 254, overtaking not only Yorkshire's fourth-wicket best against these opponents – an unbroken 210 by Arthur Mitchell and Maurice Leyland at Worcester in 1933 – but the equivalent Worcestershire record, 243 by Maurice Nichol and Sidney Martin in the same match. Set 157 with showers threatening, Yorkshire stumbled to 44 for three before Lees and Bairstow, who smashed three sixes, raced home in a stand of 113.

Close of play: first day, Yorkshire 357-5 (Gale 127, Bresnan 17); second day, Worcestershire 195-6 (Clarke 76, Leach 13); third day, Worcestershire 221-6 (Whiteley 65, Leach 14).

Yorkshire

A. Z. Lees c Whiteley b Leach	12	– not out	58
W. M. H. Rhodes c Whiteley b Leach	9	– c Shantry b Saeed Ajmal	12
J. A. Leaning lbw b Leach	17	– lbw b Morris	4
*A. W. Gale c Mitchell b Shantry	164	– run out	4
†J. M. Bairstow c Fell b D'Oliveira	139	– not out	74
A. U. Rashid c Mitchell b Saeed Ajmal	6		
T. T. Bresnan c Whiteley b Leach	28		
L. E. Plunkett c Cox b Morris	10		
S. A. Patterson b Morris	1		
J. A. Brooks c Whiteley b Morris	0		
R. J. Sidebottom not out	8		
B 4, l-b 10, n-b 22	36	L-b 1, n-b 4	5

1/18 (2)　2/33 (1)　3/57 (3)　　　　　(108.2 overs) 430　　1/34 (2)　　　(3 wkts, 27.2 overs) 157
4/311 (5)　5/322 (6)　6/368 (7)　　　　　　　　　　　　2/40 (3)　3/44 (4)
7/385 (8)　8/387 (9)　9/391 (10)　10/430 (4)

Morris 30–4–90–3; Leach 27–3–139–4; Shantry 19.2–2–84–1; D'Oliveira 8–2–28–1; Saeed Ajmal 21–3–61–1; Whiteley 3–0–14–0. *Second innings*—Morris 9–1–49–1; Leach 3–0–24–0; Saeed Ajmal 11.2–3–50–1; Shantry 2–0–14–0; D'Oliveira 2–0–19–0.

Worcestershire

*D. K. H. Mitchell lbw b Patterson	14	– c Lees b Brooks	25
R. K. Oliver c Plunkett b Brooks	18	– lbw b Bresnan	14
T. C. Fell c Leaning b Plunkett	30	– c Bairstow b Brooks	23
J. M. Clarke c Lees b Sidebottom	88	– b Rashid	21
B. L. D'Oliveira c Bairstow b Patterson	13	– c Brooks b Plunkett	37
R. A. Whiteley c Leaning b Patterson	6	– lbw b Sidebottom	101
†O. B. Cox c Rashid b Brooks	15	– c Leaning b Plunkett	4
J. Leach lbw b Rashid	27	– c Plunkett b Patterson	27
J. D. Shantry c Lees b Rashid	17	– b Bresnan	8
Saeed Ajmal b Bresnan	37	– not out	12
C. A. J. Morris not out	3	– b Sidebottom	11
B 1, l-b 5, n-b 6	12	B 1, l-b 10, w 2, n-b 10	23

1/32 (2) 2/53 (1) 3/86 (3)   (75.3 overs) 280   1/18 (2) 2/65 (3)   (90.4 overs) 306
4/109 (5) 5/119 (6) 6/175 (7)   3/93 (1) 4/95 (4)
7/221 (4) 8/225 (8) 9/242 (9) 10/280 (10)   5/195 (6) 6/201 (7) 7/252 (8)
    8/280 (9) 9/280 (6) 10/306 (11)

Sidebottom 16–5–41–1; Brooks 15–2–65–2; Bresnan 10.3–4–34–1; Patterson 13–2–34–3; Plunkett 11–0–61–1; Rashid 10–1–39–2. *Second innings*—Sidebottom 12.4–2–37–2; Bresnan 14–2–48–1; Patterson 17–4–55–1; Plunkett 11–0–26–2; Brooks 15–0–41–3; Rashid 21–3–88–1.

Umpires: R. J. Evans and D. J. Millns.

YORKSHIRE v DURHAM

At Scarborough, August 7–9. Yorkshire won by 183 runs. Yorkshire 19pts, Durham 3pts. Toss: Yorkshire. First-class debut: J. T. A. Burnham.

On a green-tinged pitch with good carry for hungry bowlers, 25 wickets had toppled by lunch on the second day. When Gale provided Onions's 500th first-class victim with Yorkshire only 85 ahead, it looked as if the Scarborough festival would lose its last two days. But the next session brought 211 runs as Maxwell and Rashid shared a ground record sixth-wicket partnership; after tea, they extended it to 248, overhauling 201 by Phil Mead and George Thompson for Players v Gentlemen in 1911. Maxwell went on the rampage in a run-a-ball century, his first for Yorkshire, and Rashid kept pace in his first hundred of the summer. Set 447, Durham began well, as Borthwick completed 1,000 first-class runs for the season. But a dynamic spell from Plunkett ensured a fourth day was not needed. Newcomer Jack Burnham, aged 18, made up for a fourth-ball duck with a neat 50, Durham's only half-century of the game, before he was last out. The match was watched by 13,700 spectators, most of whom rejoiced in Yorkshire's sixth successive win – and their first double over Durham.

Close of play: first day, Yorkshire 10-0 (Hodd 2, Lees 6); second day, Yorkshire 420-9 (Patterson 18, Sidebottom 1).

Yorkshire

†A. J. Hodd lbw b Harrison	9	– c Richardson b Onions	21
A. Z. Lees b Rushworth	2	– c Richardson b Rushworth	19
J. A. Leaning c Muchall b Hastings	16	– c Stoneman b Harrison	13
*A. W. Gale c Borthwick b Rushworth	12	– c Richardson b Onions	1
G. S. Ballance c Muchall b Onions	6	– b Harrison	5
G. J. Maxwell c Richardson b Onions	36	– c Clark b Pringle	140
A. U. Rashid c Burnham b Onions	4	– c Clark b Rushworth	127
T. T. Bresnan b Harrison	47	– c Borthwick b Rushworth	28
L. E. Plunkett c Muchall b Rushworth	1	– lbw b Pringle	27
S. A. Patterson c Pringle b Rushworth	0	– b Onions	36
R. J. Sidebottom not out	17	– not out	1
L-b 4, n-b 8	12	L-b 15, w 1, n-b 6	22

1/13 (1) 2/15 (2) 3/27 (4)   (43 overs) 162   1/35 (2) 2/62 (3)   (103.2 overs) 440
4/46 (3) 5/54 (5) 6/91 (6)   3/66 (1) 4/73 (5)
7/94 (7) 8/95 (9) 9/95 (10) 10/162 (8)   5/79 (4) 6/327 (6) 7/369 (7)
    8/377 (8) 9/416 (9) 10/440 (10)

Rushworth 13–4–37–4; Harrison 9–0–42–2; Onions 11–0–41–3; Hastings 10–2–38–1. *Second innings*—Rushworth 23–8–53–3; Harrison 24–3–103–2; Onions 23.2–3–95–3; Hastings 9–2–47–0; Pringle 10–2–46–2; Borthwick 12–0–74–0; Muchall 2–0–7–0.

Durham

*M. D. Stoneman c Bresnan b Patterson	17	– c and b Bresnan	37
G. Clark c Ballance b Bresnan	6	– lbw b Plunkett	36
S. G. Borthwick lbw b Sidebottom	19	– c Maxwell b Plunkett	31
G. J. Muchall lbw b Patterson	0	– c Hodd b Plunkett	15
†M. J. Richardson c Hodd b Patterson	24	– lbw b Bresnan	48
J. T. A. Burnham b Plunkett	0	– c Gale b Plunkett	50
R. D. Pringle c Rashid b Sidebottom	40	– c Ballance b Rashid	4
J. W. Hastings c Lees b Sidebottom	13	– (9) lbw b Rashid	16
J. Harrison lbw b Rashid	0	– (8) run out	0
C. Rushworth c Maxwell b Sidebottom	6	– c Plunkett b Rashid	0
G. Onions not out	8	– not out	18
B 4, l-b 10, w 1, n-b 8	23	B 1, l-b 3, n-b 4	8

1/29 (2) 2/29 (1) 3/29 (4)   (43.2 overs) 156
4/65 (5) 5/66 (6) 6/91 (3)
7/131 (8) 8/132 (9) 9/148 (7) 10/156 (10)

1/54 (1) 2/107 (2)   (68.1 overs) 263
3/108 (3) 4/143 (4)
5/196 (5) 6/209 (7) 7/209 (8)
8/235 (6) 9/235 (10) 10/263 (6)

Sidebottom 13.2–3–44–4; Bresnan 10–1–50–1; Patterson 11–5–16–3; Plunkett 6–4–8–1; Rashid 3–0–24–1. *Second innings*—Sidebottom 11–1–54–0; Bresnan 11–1–35–2; Patterson 14–6–35–0; Plunkett 16.1–4–61–4; Rashid 14–2–66–3; Maxwell 2–0–8–0.

Umpires: N. G. B. Cook and J. W. Lloyds.

At Hove, August 21–24. YORKSHIRE drew with SUSSEX.

YORKSHIRE v SOMERSET

At Leeds, September 1–3. Yorkshire won by an innings and 126 runs. Yorkshire 22pts, Somerset 2pts. Toss: Yorkshire. Championship debut: L. Ronchi.

Yorkshire deserved this dominant win, and their only good fortune was to win the toss on a helpful, but far from spiteful, pitch. Somerset were eight down by lunch on the first day, and beaten by lunch on the third: it took the four home seamers only 82 overs to bowl them out twice. Brooks, unfit for the Durham game and left out at Hove, returned with five for 35, his best figures for Yorkshire, including his 50th Championship victim of the season; in between taking wickets, Patterson was also on song as nightwatchman, batting throughout the second morning and helping take the shine off the second new ball. Lyth and Ballance, both sent back to the drawing board after disappointing performances in the Ashes, had played comfortably to steer Yorkshire into the lead on the first evening. And Bairstow, also home after England duty, resumed his formidable Championship season, completing 1,000 runs in only 13 innings, fewer than anyone else in 2015. Yorkshire's ninth victory meant they needed only five points from three matches to retain their title.

Close of play: first day, Yorkshire 138-3 (Ballance 49, Patterson 2); second day, Somerset 44-2 (Cooper 12, Hildreth 18).

Somerset

*M. E. Trescothick b Sidebottom	5	– lbw b Sidebottom	5
T. B. Abell c Lees b Brooks	2	– c Finch b Brooks	4
T. L. W. Cooper c Lyth b Brooks	5	– c Bairstow b Patterson	28
J. C. Hildreth c Lyth b Sidebottom	3	– c Lyth b Brooks	57
J. Allenby b Brooks	0	– c Finch b Patterson	12
P. D. Trego c Bairstow b Bresnan	19	– c Bairstow b Patterson	13
†L. Ronchi c Bresnan b Brooks	25	– c Bairstow b Sidebottom	22
L. Gregory lbw b Brooks	24	– c Lyth b Bresnan	2
C. Overton c Bresnan b Patterson	10	– b Sidebottom	4
T. D. Groenewald not out	15	– c Ballance b Bresnan	1
M. J. Leach c Lyth b Patterson	2	– not out	0
		L-b 3, n-b 4	7

1/6 (2) 2/8 (1) 3/14 (3) (35 overs) 110   1/6 (2) 2/10 (1) (47.1 overs) 155
4/14 (5) 5/20 (4) 6/36 (6)   3/87 (3) 4/105 (5)
7/74 (8) 8/85 (9) 9/101 (7) 10/110 (11)   5/111 (4) 6/137 (6) 7/148 (7)
8/152 (9) 9/154 (8) 10/155 (10)

Sidebottom 8–3–17–2; Brooks 12–1–35–5; Bresnan 5–1–16–1; Patterson 10–1–42–2. *Second innings*—Sidebottom 11–2–32–3; Brooks 13–4–49–2; Bresnan 12.1–5–28–2; Patterson 11–3–43–3.

Yorkshire

A. Lyth c Gregory b Allenby	62	J. A. Brooks b Gregory	11
A. Z. Lees lbw b Overton	10	R. J. Sidebottom not out	0
G. S. Ballance c Trescothick b Overton	91		
*A. W. Gale b Leach	5	B 4, l-b 19	23
S. A. Patterson c Ronchi b Overton	44		
†J. M. Bairstow b Gregory	91	1/46 (2) 2/111 (1) (128.2 overs) 391
A. J. Finch lbw b Overton	13	3/133 (4) 4/223 (3) 5/236 (5)
T. T. Bresnan b Groenewald	18	6/279 (7) 7/304 (8) 8/364 (9)
J. D. Middlebrook c Trego b Gregory	23	9/390 (10) 10/391 (6) 110 overs: 305-7

Gregory 30.2–7–75–3; Groenewald 26–1–74–1; Overton 28–10–64–4; Trego 8–1–42–0; Allenby 22–8–46–1; Leach 14–2–67–1.

Umpires: S. A. Garratt and I. J. Gould.

At Lord's, September 9–12. YORKSHIRE lost to MIDDLESEX by 246 runs. *Yorkshire retain their Championship title on the opening day, suffer their only defeat of the season.*

At Southampton, September 14–17. YORKSHIRE beat HAMPSHIRE by five wickets.

YORKSHIRE v SUSSEX

At Leeds, September 22–25. Yorkshire won by 100 runs. Yorkshire 21pts, Sussex 4pts. Toss: Sussex. Yorkshire were already champions, but there were high stakes for Sussex, who needed a draw to preserve their first division status. Yorkshire, meanwhile, were hunting an 11th win (no county had beaten ten since the introduction of two divisions in 2000) and a record points haul (Somerset had amassed 266 in the second division in 2007). By 3.10 on the fourth day, Sussex were down – and the champions triumphant, having finished on 286 points. Their pace attack had blown apart the top half of the visitors' batting twice, though Yardy, in his last match before retirement, fought hard to keep them afloat. His gutsy and uncompromising 81-ball 70 brought near-parity in the first innings, and took his career aggregate against Yorkshire past 1,000 runs at 48. Under similar pressure on the final day, he was still able to shore things up, until a mis-hook at Bresnan made defeat inevitable. Yorkshire had also struggled against full-length bowling, particularly from Magoffin, but Gale's late burst of form enabled him to pass 1,000 for the season in his final innings. Six wickets for Brooks took him to 65 in 14 Championship games.

Close of play: first day, Yorkshire 241-7 (Bresnan 13, Plunkett 2); second day, Yorkshire 55-1 (Lyth 16, Ballance 39); third day, Yorkshire 298-9 (Bresnan 50).

Yorkshire

A. Lyth lbw b Jordan	3	– b Hatchett	39
A. Z. Lees lbw b Hatchett	29	– c and b Jordan	0
G. S. Ballance c Joyce b Liddle	55	– b Magoffin	45
*A. W. Gale b Magoffin	31	– c Jordan b Liddle	67
†J. M. Bairstow c Brown b Magoffin	1	– lbw b Jordan	36
J. A. Leaning c Jordan b Hatchett	36	– c Jordan b Liddle	9
A. U. Rashid c Brown b Liddle	53	– lbw b Magoffin	21
T. T. Bresnan c Jordan b Magoffin	16	– c Hatchett b Magoffin	55
L. E. Plunkett c Joyce b Magoffin	5	– c Machan b Jordan	4
J. A. Brooks c Yardy b Jordan	1	– c Brown b Hatchett	14
R. J. Sidebottom not out	0	– not out	2
B 4, l-b 7, n-b 10	21	L-b 9, n-b 4	13

1/3 (1) 2/55 (2) 3/106 (4) (83.2 overs) 251
4/108 (5) 5/140 (3) 6/212 (6)
7/238 (7) 8/250 (8) 9/251 (10) 10/251 (9)

1/0 (2) 2/65 (3) (104.3 overs) 305
3/123 (1) 4/190 (5)
5/202 (6) 6/217 (4) 7/238 (7)
8/255 (9) 9/298 (10) 10/305 (8)

Magoffin 24.2–6–57–4; Jordan 20–3–85–2; Hatchett 20–5–47–2; Liddle 15.4–4–44–2; Ashar Zaidi 4–1–7–0. *Second innings*—Magoffin 22.3–7–57–3; Jordan 24–3–73–3; Hatchett 21–4–66–2; Liddle 18–1–62–2; Ashar Zaidi 19–6–38–0.

Sussex

*E. C. Joyce c Bairstow b Brooks	2	– b Brooks	1
C. J. Jordan c and b Sidebottom	1	– lbw b Brooks	20
M. W. Machan c Bairstow b Brooks	26	– c Bairstow b Brooks	16
C. D. Nash c Bairstow b Bresnan	16	– b Bresnan	17
L. J. Wright c Lees b Plunkett	21	– c Bairstow b Bresnan	2
M. H. Yardy b Brooks	70	– c Lees b Bresnan	41
†B. C. Brown c Sidebottom b Bresnan	39	– c Leaning b Rashid	42
Ashar Zaidi lbw b Rashid	26	– lbw b Lyth	47
S. J. Magoffin c Bairstow b Plunkett	0	– lbw b Rashid	3
L. J. Hatchett c Bresnan b Lyth	25	– not out	8
C. J. Liddle not out	10	– lbw b Rashid	0
B 5, l-b 4, w 1, n-b 2	12	B 7, l-b 4	11

1/3 (1) 2/3 (2) 3/35 (3) (55.5 overs) 248
4/68 (4) 5/70 (5) 6/134 (7)
7/187 (8) 8/188 (9) 9/211 (6) 10/248 (10)

1/3 (1) 2/36 (2) (57.3 overs) 208
3/39 (3) 4/56 (4)
5/61 (5) 6/142 (6) 7/148 (7)
8/154 (9) 9/199 (8) 10/208 (11)

Sidebottom 11–3–32–1; Brooks 12–2–55–3; Bresnan 9–2–55–2; Plunkett 10–0–59–2; Rashid 12–4–34–1; Lyth 1.5–0–4–1. *Second innings*—Sidebottom 6–2–19–0; Brooks 11–1–39–3; Plunkett 14–1–53–0; Bresnan 12–5–30–3; Rashid 11.3–2–44–3; Lyth 3–1–12–1.

Umpires: M. A. Gough and D. J. Millns.

NATWEST T20 BLAST IN 2015

Review by Neville Scott

1 Lancashire   2 Northamptonshire   3= Hampshire, Warwickshire

In a tournament breathlessly marketed as a showcase for the global stars in Twenty20's expanding firmament, 133 scheduled matches came down to a final six balls bowled by a 21-year-old Merseyside seamer unknown to almost all of Edgbaston's merry throng. Indeed, Gavin Griffiths's opening over in the semi-final just hours earlier – a maiden, no less, to James Vince, whose 710 runs made him the competition's highest scorer in any summer – was the first of his Twenty20 career. Hampshire had lost that match limply, and Northamptonshire now failed to hit the 21 runs needed as Lancashire claimed a first knockout title for 16 years.

Twenty20 has been an integral part of youth and Second XI cricket for a whole generation; Griffiths was one of many to take the stage with remarkable ease. And his anonymity was apt: for all the hype about highly paid imports, it was arguably Kent, with a single player raised overseas (the Australian-born stalwart Mitch Claydon), who proved the side of the year. No team fielded more foreign-nurtured cricketers than Middlesex and Somerset, yet they were the first two knocked out in the South Group. The first three to reach the quarter-finals (Kent, Warwickshire and Worcestershire) had fewer men who learned the game outside the UK than 13 other counties.

There is a sports psychology dissertation to be written here. Twenty20 was briefly a slash-and-burn sideshow regarded seriously by few teams, but a new level of rigour, commitment and thought has allowed certain settled sides to triumph over opponents apparently better endowed with talent. And teams who do not subconsciously leave responsibility to affluent signings (or even resent their status) perhaps find the cohesion to succeed. Kent's domination of their group stage was stunning: it was as if the Folkestone film club had made movie shorts that outshone Hollywood blockbusters.

They fell in the quarter-finals, however, beaten by a Lancashire side who – after qualifying only on net run-rate – won at Canterbury by virtue of losing fewer wickets in a tied match, a cruel finish for Kent. Warwickshire overpowered Essex but then, plummeting to 14 for four, effectively lost to Northamptonshire in the first 20 legitimate balls (three of them successes for David Willey) of an uninspiring finals day. Worcestershire, the other prime performers in the group stage, shot themselves in the foot in the quarters: they failed to agree with the ECB about who should hire floodlights for a game that started at 5.30 – and ended in unlit farce, with defeat by Hampshire under Duckworth/Lewis.

It is not mean-spirited to Lancashire (their coach, Ashley Giles, conceded they were not the best Twenty20 side) to suggest there is something inherently wrong with a tournament that timetables 126 fixtures merely to reduce 18 teams to eight, half of whom then disappear in 150 minutes of a single match.

Midland express: Northamptonshire's David Willey rockets towards a 40-ball hundred in the quarter-final against Sussex at Hove.

Mike Hewitt, Getty Images

Not that the competition's integrity especially worries the ECB. With their hierarchy long drawn from retail and marketing, stacking shelves high with any product that sells remains the abiding concern. It would be quite possible to present two formats: an authentic league, comprising three groups of six, played home and away with promotion and relegation, and then a separate knockout cup. One of many tenable variants, this would entail only a 20% reduction in matches – but too much for the ECB to countenance, even as they talk of overcrowded summers.

Foreign Twenty20 stars – or, more accurately, big-name batsmen – undoubtedly increased crowds, though it is notable how few helped sides reach the last eight. The only two instances of genuinely match-winning batting in the seven knockout contests came, in fact, from Willey and Vince, who in the quarters hit the last two of the summer's 13 centuries. Willey's, from 40 balls, was the fastest by an Englishman in the competition's history. His second fifty needed only 13 deliveries, and one over from Michael Yardy was savaged for 34 runs in the Hove massacre. Vince, too, hit his maiden Twenty20 hundred, having finished unbeaten on 99 in mid-June when he struck the penultimate ball for four to win a group game against Kent. His undefeated 107 had probably done for Worcestershire, an hour before the embarrassment of the August gloom at New Road.

The club had earlier courted censure at Northampton, where wicketkeeper Ben Cox discarded his gloves and retreated to the fielding circle, becoming a cross between long stop and fly slip. This breached no law, but the umpires deliberated at length before ruling that it didn't flout the spirit of the game. Less trivial episodes led to an abandonment at Arundel, where Moises Henriques, Surrey's Australian all-rounder, suffered concussion and a broken jaw in a fielding collision with Rory Burns; and followed Lancashire's victory in the quarters, when a "bar brawl" (in the words of crime reporters) at Ashford left batsman Liam Livingstone, an innocent victim, needing around 20 stitches to his face.

It is often said that Twenty20 matches pivot on single, inspired innings. If sometimes true, this is no longer the norm. Almost unnoticed, bowlers (once mere fodder) are determining games, certainly in English conditions, acting as a unit to implement careful plans. And it has long been the case that batting partnerships, with support for key hitters right through the order, are at least as telling as high, individual scores.

Outstanding overseas batsmen did not generally confer success last year. Brendon McCullum's remarkable undefeated 158 from 64 balls – domestic Twenty20's highest tally – helped Warwickshire beat Derbyshire. Surprisingly, it was his county's first individual score above 90 (itself made only a month earlier, by Ian Bell against Durham) since the competition began in 2003. But McCullum's 112 runs from six other games were no more than marginal in four further wins. And, unforgettable as Chris Gayle's unbeaten 151 from 62 balls was, it did not lead to a Somerset victory over Kent at Taunton: Gayle, batting at the death, proved less significant than Sam Northeast, whose earlier 114 had been well supported by the top order; Claydon's unsung two for 23 proved more potent still. For Michael Klinger, Gloucestershire's Australian captain, fruitless runs might reasonably have led to despair. If not quite with the flamboyance of his television namesake, the cross-dressing orderly from *M*A*S*H*, Klinger became the first to hit three Twenty20 hundreds in a single English season – but only one took his county to victory. Two innings of 104 not out came on successive days, and he also hit 44, 61 and 75 – all in vain. Happily, his runs did help Gloucestershire triumph in the Royal London One-Day Cup, despite a duck in the final.

In a 14-match group stage (an inequitable format for leagues of nine, since some face the best only once), bowlers have a maximum aggregate of 56 overs. Of regulars completing at least half that number, ten sustained an economy-rate below seven per over. Four of these were stifling spinners, another four were medium-pacers. By taking pace off the ball, they proved difficult to smite. It is not a method likely to succeed in Tests but, against power hitting, decisive variations of speed almost defines good Twenty20 bowling.

The other two were Rikki Clarke, superb once more in allowing only 5.19 per over, and the left-arm James Faulkner, a man in the top four for both economy and strike-rate. He was probably the tournament's key foreign signing. And, after suspension by Australia for drink-driving, he remained available for Lancashire on finals day, bowling the penultimate over of the final, despite having earlier left the field with a dislocated finger. It seems no accident that eight of these ten played for sides who reached the quarters; they were arguably more significant, overall, than the sluggers who draw the crowds.

After a lopsided league phase – spread over 71 days – that often left unclear which games really mattered, the final round proved a washout; in vital contests, rain denied three teams their chance of progressing. As in previous seasons, only about a third of the group matches produced first-innings scores that are most likely to lead to tight finishes (somewhere between 150 and 180). Twenty20 retains popularity, especially in the South-East, albeit as a one-off, night-out spectacle for about half the crowd. But the big problem remains predictability: the outcome can too often be guessed too soon. The ECB have not yet found a way to guarantee sixes, nor neuter clever bowlers. Give them time. The day of universal, artificial pitches will surely arrive.

Prize money

£256,060 for winners: LANCASHIRE.
£123,934 for runners-up: NORTHAMPTONSHIRE.
£30,212 for losing semi-finalists: HAMPSHIRE, WARWICKSHIRE.
£4,500 for losing quarter-finalists: ESSEX, KENT, SUSSEX, WORCESTERSHIRE.
Match-award winners received £2,500 in the final, £1,000 in the semi-finals, £500 in the quarter-finals and £225 in the group games.

FINAL GROUP TABLES

	North Group	Played	Won	Lost	Tied	No result	Points	NRR
1	WARWICKSHIRE	14	10	4	0	0	20	0.20
2	WORCESTERSHIRE ...	14	9	4	0	1	19	0.68
3	NORTHAMPTONSHIRE	14	7	5	0	2	16	0.11
4	LANCASHIRE	14	7	6	0	1	15	0.46
5	Nottinghamshire.	14	7	6	0	1	15	0.01
6	Durham	14	5	8	0	1	11	−0.14
7	Leicestershire	14	4	7	1	2	11	−0.30
8	Yorkshire	14	5	8	1	0	11	−0.32
9	Derbyshire	14	4	10	0	0	8	−0.66

	South Group	Played	Won	Lost	Tied	No result	Points	NRR
1	KENT	14	9	4	0	1	19	0.16
2	SUSSEX	14	7	5	0	2	16	0.20
3	HAMPSHIRE	14	8	6	0	0	16	−0.12
4	ESSEX	14	7	6	0	1	15	0.20
5	Gloucestershire.	14	7	7	0	0	14	0.35
6	Glamorgan	14	7	7	0	0	14	−0.52
7	Surrey	14	5	6	0	3	13	−0.14
8	Somerset.	14	4	8	0	2	10	−0.18
9	Middlesex	14	4	9	0	1	9	0.03

Where counties finished equal on points, positions were decided by (a) net run-rate (runs scored per over minus runs conceded per over), (b) most points in head-to-head matches, and (c) drawing lots.

NATWEST T20 BLAST AVERAGES

BATTING (300 runs at 32.00)

		M	I	NO	R	HS	100	50	Avge	SR	4	6
1	†C. H. Gayle (*Somerset*)	3	3	2	328	151*	1	2	328.00	192.94	22	29
2	M. Klinger (*Glos*)	12	12	4	654	126*	3	4	81.75	142.17	54	21
3	J. M. Vince (*Hants*)	16	16	4	710	107*	1	5	59.16	134.46	87	14
4	L. J. Wright (*Sussex*)	14	14	3	564	111*	1	3	51.27	171.95	51	29
5	S. A. Northeast (*Kent*)	14	14	1	641	114	1	4	49.30	152.98	68	16
6	H. J. H. Marshall (*Glos*)	8	8	1	322	93	0	2	46.00	160.19	40	8
7	†J. A. Simpson (*Middx*)	13	11	3	367	84*	0	3	45.87	141.69	27	12
8	†W. T. S. Porterfield (*Warks*)	11	11	4	313	55*	0	1	44.71	118.56	29	9
9	S. J. Croft (*Lancs*)	16	16	5	478	94*	0	5	43.45	127.80	35	12
10	P. R. Stirling (*Middx*)	8	8	0	343	90	0	3	42.87	175.00	38	17
11	J. A. Leaning (*Yorks*)	14	14	6	338	60*	0	1	42.25	134.12	20	14
12	†J. A. Rudolph (*Glam*)	14	13	2	461	101*	1	3	41.90	127.34	61	4
13	†K. C. Sangakkara (*Surrey*)	9	9	1	332	58	0	1	41.50	149.54	33	11
14	†R. A. Whiteley (*Worcs*)	14	13	5	315	91*	0	1	39.37	177.96	11	29
15	I. A. Cockbain (*Glos*)	13	13	3	392	91*	0	2	39.20	149.61	35	17
16	S. R. Patel (*Notts*)	13	13	3	386	90*	0	1	38.60	129.53	25	13
17	T. Westley (*Essex*)	11	11	1	384	68	0	3	38.40	123.87	47	4
18	†A. J. Blake (*Kent*)	14	14	6	304	71*	0	3	38.00	167.03	28	14
19	J. P. Faulkner (*Lancs*)	13	13	5	302	73	0	1	37.75	141.12	9	15
20	C. D. Nash (*Sussex*)	13	13	1	444	88	0	5	37.00	133.33	56	8
21	R. E. Levi (*Northants*)	16	16	2	485	67*	0	3	34.64	143.49	61	15
22	D. K. H. Mitchell (*Worcs*)	14	14	2	412	58	0	3	34.33	116.05	44	0
23	M. H. Wessels (*Notts*)	13	13	0	439	97	0	3	33.76	150.34	43	21
24	W. J. Durston (*Derbys*)	14	14	1	431	88	0	3	33.15	138.14	49	12
25	J. M. Bairstow (*Yorks*)	11	11	1	320	92	0	1	32.00	134.45	23	15

BOWLING (12 wickets at 24.00)

		Style	O	M	R	W	BB	4I	Avge	SR	ER
1	S. T. Finn (*Middx*)	RFM	23	0	142	12	4-28	1	11.83	11.50	6.17
2	J. P. Faulkner (*Lancs*)	LFM	50.3	1	316	25	3-19	1	12.64	12.12	6.25
3	T. M. J. Smith (*Glos*)	SLA	43	1	302	23	5-39	1	13.13	11.21	7.02
4	U. Arshad (*Durham*)	RFM	37	0	292	22	3-18	0	13.27	10.09	7.89
5	S. D. Parry (*Lancs*)	SLA	57	0	392	25	4-16	1	15.68	13.68	6.87
6	R. S. Bopara (*Essex*)	RM	46.1	0	306	19	3-12	0	16.10	14.57	6.62
7	Saeed Ajmal (*Worcs*)	OB	48	1	348	21	3-13	0	16.57	13.71	7.25
8	D. J. Willey (*Northants*)	LFM	36	1	255	15	3-27	0	17.00	14.40	7.08
9	T. S. Mills (*Sussex*)	LF	45	1	358	19	4-22	1	18.84	14.21	7.95
10	J. E. C. Franklin (*Middx*)	LFM	26	0	232	12	5-21	1	19.33	13.00	8.92
11	S. W. Tait (*Essex*)	RF	53	0	445	23	3-28	0	19.34	13.82	8.39
12	A. M. Lilley (*Lancs*)	OB	49	0	317	16	3-31	0	19.81	18.37	6.46
13	R. O. Gordon (*Warwicks*)	RFM	50	0	417	21	4-20	1	19.85	14.28	8.34
14	M. E. Claydon (*Kent*)	RFM	53.1	0	406	20	3-16	0	20.30	15.95	7.63
15	J. Clark (*Lancs*)	RM	26.5	0	249	12	3-41	0	20.75	13.41	9.27
16	R. Clarke (*Warwicks*)	RFM	48	0	260	12	3-26	0	21.66	24.00	5.41
17	D. A. Cosker (*Glam*)	SLA	46.5	0	374	17	4-25	2	22.00	16.52	7.98
18	G. J. Maxwell (*Yorks*)	OB	34	0	264	12	3-15	0	22.00	17.00	7.76
19	D. A. Payne (*Glos*)	LFM	30.1	0	288	13	5-24	1	22.15	13.92	9.54
20	B. A. C. Howell (*Glos*)	RFM	52	1	377	17	3-18	0	22.17	18.35	7.25
21	M. D. Fisher (*Yorks*)	RFM	40.5	0	362	16	5-22	1	22.62	15.31	8.86
22	R. J. W. Topley (*Essex*)	LFM	40.4	0	367	16	3-25	0	22.93	15.25	9.02
23	D. R. Briggs (*Hants*)	SLA	59	0	414	18	3-21	0	23.00	19.66	7.01
24	J. Leach (*Worcs*)	RFM	44.3	0	393	17	3-27	0	23.11	15.70	8.83
25	S. J. Mullaney (*Notts*)	RFM	41	0	284	12	2-27	0	23.66	20.50	6.92
26	C. J. McKay (*Leics*)	RFM	45.3	0	332	14	4-24	1	23.71	19.50	7.29

LEADING WICKETKEEPERS

Dismissals	M		Dismissals	M	
16 (11 ct, 5 st)	16	A. J. A. Wheater (*Hants*)	10 (8 ct, 2 st)	9	N. J. O'Brien (*Leics*)
14 (11 ct, 3 st)	16	A. L. Davies (*Leics*)	10 (9 ct, 1 st)	11	J. M. Bairstow (*Yorks*)
12 (9 ct, 3 st)	16	T. R. Ambrose (*Warwicks*)	10 (7 ct, 3 st)	11	S. W. Billings (*Kent*)
11 (5 ct, 6 st)	14	G. O. Jones (*Glos*)	8 (4 ct, 4 st)	14	O. B. Cox (*Worcs*)

LEADING FIELDERS

Ct	M		Ct	M	
14	16	S. J. Croft (*Lancs*)	12	16	A. G. Prince (*Lancs*)
13	13	T. J. Wells (*Leics*)	11	14	T. Köhler-Cadmore (*Worcs*)
13	16	A. M. Lilley (*Lancs*)	11	14	R. A. Whiteley (*Worcs*)
12	14	R. N. ten Doeschate (*Essex*)	11	16	L. J. Evans (*Warwicks*)
12	16	R. Clarke (*Warwicks*)	10	14	B. A. C. Howell (*Glos*)

NORTH GROUP

DERBYSHIRE

At Derby, May 29 (floodlit). **Derbyshire won by five wickets.** Lancashire 127-9 (20 overs) (A. L. Davies 41; W. A. White 3-21); ‡Derbyshire 128-5 (17.4 overs) (H. M. Amla 51, T. M. Dilshan 38). *MoM: W. A. White. Attendance: 3,284. County debuts: T. M. Dilshan; J. P. Faulkner (Lancashire). The opening pair of Hashim Amla (the South African in his last game for Derbyshire) and Tillekeratne Dilshan (the Sri Lankan in his first) picked apart an inadequate Lancashire total with a partnership of 93 in 10.3 overs to set up their first win of the competition, following two away defeats.*

At Derby, June 5 (floodlit). **Durham won by five runs.** Durham 147-7 (20 overs) (P. D. Collingwood 41); ‡Derbyshire 142-9 (20 overs) (T. M. Dilshan 54; J. W. Hastings 3-29). *MoM: P. D. Collingwood. Attendance: 2,408. County debuts: N. J. Rimmington (Derbyshire); G. Clark (Durham). Dilshan's steady half-century took Derbyshire within sight of victory, but four late wickets for four runs betrayed an attack of the jitters. With only 14 to protect in the final two overs, John Hastings and Usman Arshad held their nerve.*

At Derby, June 18 (floodlit). **Derbyshire won by 17 runs.** Derbyshire 189-7 (20 overs) (W. J. Durston 88); ‡Leicestershire 172-7 (20 overs) (M. J. Cosgrove 44, T. J. Wells 64*). *MoM: W. J. Durston. Attendance: 2,139. Before this game four of Derbyshire's ten highest Twenty20 scores had been made by Wes Durston – appointed captain in this format at the start of the season – and he added a fifth with a forceful 88. It was a standard Leicestershire could not match, despite a late assault from Tom Wells, whose 64* came off 28 balls.*

At Derby, June 26 (floodlit). **Derbyshire won by 34 runs.** ‡Derbyshire 201-7 (20 overs) (H. D. Rutherford 37, C. F. Hughes 52; B. W. Hilfenhaus 3-29); Nottinghamshire 167 (19.1 overs) (M. H. Wessels 66, J. W. A. Taylor 33; N. J. Rimmington 3-24). *MoM: C. F. Hughes. Attendance: 4,268. Derbyshire ended a wait of ten years for a home win over their neighbours after Chesney Hughes pushed them towards a total of over 200 for only the second time. Riki Wessels countered powerfully, but Nottinghamshire lost momentum after he fell.*

At Chesterfield, July 5. **Northamptonshire won by three runs** (D/L). Northamptonshire 155-6 (20 overs) (R. E. Levi 42, J. J. Cobb 48); ‡Derbyshire 140-5 (18 overs) (W. J. Durston 60). *MoM: W. J. Durston. Attendance: 2,088. Derbyshire's target was revised to 144 in 18 overs, which they had reduced to 41 off 30 balls by the time Durston was out for 60. But the fifth-wicket pair of Scott Elstone and Tom Poynton were stifled, and could take only five from the final over when nine were needed. The Northamptonshire innings included a double-wicket maiden by Wayne White.*

At Chesterfield, July 12. **Derbyshire won by four wickets.** Yorkshire 146-9 (20 overs) (G. J. Maxwell 45, J. A. Leaning 37; W. J. Durston 3-14, S. J. Thakor 3-34); ‡Derbyshire 150-6 (18.5 overs) (H. D. Rutherford 40, W. L. Madsen 41). *MoM: W. J. Durston. Attendance: 4,454. In front of a bumper crowd, Derbyshire chased down a modest target to beat Yorkshire in a home*

Twenty20 fixture for the first time – something for their supporters to savour given their disastrous away campaign, in which they lost all seven games. Yorkshire were playing catch-up from 16-3 in the fifth over, after they looked to plunder Durston's off-spin, and came off second-best.

At Derby, July 17 (floodlit). **Worcestershire won by four wickets.** ‡Derbyshire 149-8 (20 overs) (W. J. Durston 32, B. A. Godleman 33); **Worcestershire 150-6** (19.3 overs) (R. K. Oliver 45, C. Munro 30). *MoM:* J. Leach. *Attendance:* 2,074. *Seamer Joe Leach gave Worcestershire the start they wanted by taking the first two Derbyshire wickets, and later provided the finish they needed with a calm 18 off 12 balls. That clinched victory with three balls to spare – and a place for Worcestershire in the quarter-finals.*

Derbyshire away matches

May 15: lost to Yorkshire by seven wickets.
May 22: lost to Leicestershire by seven wickets.
June 11: lost to Northamptonshire by six wickets.
June 12: lost to Lancashire by 67 runs.
June 19: lost to Worcestershire by eight wickets.
July 3: lost to Warwickshire by 60 runs.
July 10: lost to Nottinghamshire by two runs.

DURHAM

At Chester-le-Street, May 15. **Durham won by 41 runs** (D/L). **Durham 174-8** (20 overs) (P. Mustard 51, C. S. MacLeod 60); ‡Northamptonshire 47-5 (8 overs). *MoM:* C. S. MacLeod. *Attendance:* 2,940. *County debut:* Shahid Afridi (Northamptonshire). *Scotland international Calum MacLeod hit 11 fours in a 23-ball half-century. The light was already fading as Durham added only 28 in the last five overs, and deteriorated further as Northamptonshire stumbled before rain arrived.*

At Chester-le-Street, May 29 (floodlit). **Durham won by six runs. Durham 182-4** (20 overs) (P. Mustard 39, P. D. Collingwood 31, G. J. Muchall 34*, J. W. Hastings 37*); ‡Yorkshire 176-8 (20 overs) (A. W. Gale 41, T. T. Bresnan 30*; K. K. Jennings 4-37). *MoM:* J. W. Hastings. *Attendance:* 5,593. *In the first game under Durham's new floodlights, Keaton Jennings's rarely used medium-pace turned the match when the dangerous pair of Jonny Bairstow and Glenn Maxwell hit across straight balls. But the difference lay in the last over of each innings, with John Hastings involved in both. He hit Tim Bresnan's last four balls for three fours and a six, as 21 came off the final over – the same number Yorkshire required when Hastings came on to bowl the last six balls of the match. Bresnan had a chance of revenge but, with 12 needed off two, he missed the first.*

At Chester-le-Street, June 6. **Warwickshire won by seven wickets. Durham 163-7** (20 overs) (C. S. MacLeod 41, B. A. Stokes 40, G. J. Muchall 30*); ‡Warwickshire 164-3 (19.1 overs) (I. R. Bell 90, W. T. S. Porterfield 41*). *MoM:* I. R. Bell. *Attendance:* 3,854. *In a windswept contest, the holders were indebted to a masterclass from Ian Bell, whose 90 off 65 balls was briefly Warwickshire's highest Twenty20 score. It included two sixes – one driven, the other pulled – off the first two balls from Ben Stokes, who went for 44 in three overs.*

At Chester-le-Street, June 12 (floodlit). **Worcestershire won by five wickets.** ‡Worcestershire 159-5 (20 overs) (D. K. H. Mitchell 56, T. Köhler-Cadmore 53*); **Durham 156-7** (20 overs) (M. D. Stoneman 35, P. Mustard 43, G. J. Muchall 41*; Saeed Ajmal 3-16). *MoM:* D. K. H. Mitchell. *Attendance:* 3,728. *Chasing 160, Durham reached 40-0 in three overs, and were coasting at 79-1, only to lose momentum after Daryl Mitchell took two wickets in two balls. Mitchell had earlier enjoyed a stand of 76 with Tom Köhler-Cadmore, whose 53* was tarnished when he dropped his bat mid-pitch and team-mate Colin Munro tripped over it – and was run out.*

At Chester-le-Street, June 25 (floodlit). **Lancashire won by six wickets.** ‡Durham 141 (19.5 overs) (M. D. Stoneman 51; K. M. Jarvis 3-24; J. P. Faulkner 3-27); **Lancashire 143-4** (18.1 overs) (A. G. Prince 63*). *MoM:* A. G. Prince. *Attendance:* 3,335. *After they raced to 92-3 in ten overs, Durham were throttled by Lancashire's trio of spinners and added just 49. Ashwell Prince paced the reply in relative comfort, and only 12 were needed when James Faulkner was sensationally caught on the midwicket boundary, Ryan Pringle diving to hold the ball, then flipping it up as he slid towards the rope for Scott Borthwick to juggle a catch.*

At Chester-le-Street, July 3. **Durham won by 38 runs. Durham 163-5** (20 overs) (M. D. Stoneman 89*); ‡Leicestershire 125 (19.5 overs) (J. W. Hastings 3-10, U. Arshad 3-18). *MoM:* M. D. Stoneman. *Attendance:* 3,474. *Mark Stoneman's 89* was two short of Durham's record in this format. He and Mustard had 45 on the board after four overs, but 20-year-old off-spinner Rob Sayer* *stifled the innings with 4–0–16–2 on his Twenty20 debut. Usman Arshad helped a revival with a stand of 65* with Stoneman, then took two in two in the third over of the reply. Sunderland-born Ben Raine's 0-56 was the second-most-expensive return by a Leicestershire bowler.*

At Chester-le-Street, July 17 (floodlit). **Nottinghamshire won by 42 runs. Nottinghamshire 198-5** (20 overs) (M. J. Lumb 31, M. H. Wessels 97, J. W. A. Taylor 37); ‡**Durham 156-6** (20 overs) (G. J. Muchall 30*, J. W. Hastings 42). *MoM:* M. H. Wessels. *Attendance:* 4,574. *An innings of 97 off 51 balls by Riki Wessels, with five driven leg-side sixes, ended Durham's hopes of progress. With eight balls in which to become the second man to score a Twenty20 century at Riverside, he top-edged a sweep to the wicketkeeper.*

Durham away matches

May 22: beat Lancashire by 16 runs.
May 28: lost to Leicestershire by eight wickets.
May 31: lost to Nottinghamshire by 15 runs.
June 5: beat Derbyshire by five runs.

July 5: lost to Worcestershire by five wickets.
July 10: lost to Yorkshire by five wickets.
July 24: no result v Northamptonshire.

LANCASHIRE

At Manchester, May 15 (floodlit). **Lancashire won by five wickets** (D/L). ‡**Leicestershire 131-7** (15 overs) (K. J. O'Brien 47; G. A. Edwards 4-20); **Lancashire 142-5** (15 overs) (S. J. Croft 70*). *MoM:* S. J. Croft. *Attendance:* 5,196. *County debuts:* G. A. Edwards; G. D. Elliott, K. J. O'Brien (Leicestershire). *Lancashire's target was reduced to 140 in 15 overs, which they reached off the last ball as Steven Croft (70* from 39) cut Ben Raine to the boundary. Leicestershire were 105-2 after 11.2 overs when play was halted for 80 minutes. George Edwards, a 22-year-old fast bowler formerly with Surrey, took four wickets in 12 balls on debut.*

At Manchester, May 22 (floodlit). **Durham won by 16 runs.** ‡**Durham 155** (19.4 overs) (M. D. Stoneman 57, P. D. Collingwood 30); **Lancashire 139-9** (20 overs) (A. G. Prince 78). *MoM:* A. G. Prince. *Attendance:* 3,656. *Mark Stoneman made only his second Twenty20 half-century, though Durham lost their last eight for 50 in 8.2 overs. However, a hard-working performance in the field ensured their total was sufficient on an evening when Ashwell Prince shouldered the burden of Lancashire's reply. His wicket was one of four that fell in six balls.*

At Manchester, June 12 (floodlit). **Lancashire won by 67 runs. Lancashire 201-3** (20 overs) (S. J. Croft 94*, J. P. Faulkner 47*); ‡**Derbyshire 134** (18.2 overs) (C. F. Hughes 39; S. D. Parry 4-16). *MoM:* S. J. Croft. *Attendance:* 5,471. *County debut:* S. Mahmood (Lancashire). *Croft and James Faulkner put on 151* to set a Lancashire Twenty20 record for any wicket, 49 coming off the final two overs. Lancashire's three spinners shared six wickets, to leave Derbyshire with one win in six.*

At Manchester, June 18 (floodlit). **Worcestershire won by two wickets.** ‡**Lancashire 163-5** (20 overs) (A. G. Prince 33, K. R. Brown 42, S. J. Croft 31); **Worcestershire 164-8** (19.5 overs) (D. K. H. Mitchell 53). *MoM:* D. K. H. Mitchell. *Attendance:* 3,842. *Ben Cox's six over wide long-off Faulkner decided a fine match. Daryl Mitchell's 53 gave Worcestershire's pursuit of 164 a good start, backed up by a crucial stand of 37 in 20 balls between Cox and Brett D'Oliveira.*

At Manchester, June 26 (floodlit). **Warwickshire won by one run.** ‡**Warwickshire 137-8** (20 overs) (V. Chopra 40, W. T. S. Porterfield 35); **Lancashire 136-8** (20 overs) (J. P. Faulkner 34; R. O. Gordon 4-20). *MoM:* R. O. Gordon. *Attendance:* 7,227. *County debut:* B. B. McCullum (Warwickshire). *Recordo Gordon's mixture of cutters and slower-ball bouncers ultimately helped Warwickshire prevail on a slow surface. Lancashire needed 17 off the last over, and 21-year-old Liam Livingstone hit a four and a six before being run out off the final ball one short of a tie. Brendon McCullum's county debut was ended on 18 by a brilliant running catch from Croft.*

At Manchester, July 3 (floodlit). **Lancashire won by 29 runs. Lancashire 231-4** (20 overs) (A. G. Prince 59, K. R. Brown 69); ‡**Yorkshire 202-8** (20 overs) (A. W. Gale 35, A. J. Finch 33, T. T. Bresnan 51; S. D. Parry 3-29, A. M. Lilley 3-31). *MoM:* S. D. Parry. *Attendance:* 17,021. *In front of a full house, Lancashire completed a double over Yorkshire thanks to their highest Twenty20 total. Prince and Karl Brown pulverised a wayward attack, although 17-year-old seamer Matthew Fisher was an exception. In Yorkshire's reply, spinners Parry and Arron Lilley bowled astutely yet again, and Tim Bresnan's half-century gave the scorecard a patina of respectability which fooled nobody. Lancashire omitted Faulkner following his arrest for drink-driving the previous evening.*

At Manchester, July 15 (floodlit). **Nottinghamshire won by three wickets.** ‡**Lancashire 137-4** (20 overs) (K. R. Brown 51, S. J. Croft 51*, J. P. Faulkner 32*); **Nottinghamshire 140-7** (20 overs) (A. D. Hales 30, J. W. A. Taylor 33*). *MoM:* J. W. A. Taylor. *Attendance:* 8,564. *Victory would almost have guaranteed a quarter-final place, but Lancashire lost three wickets in the first 15 balls, and narrowly failed to defend a modest total. Nottinghamshire's own chances of progressing were revived by the coolest of innings from James Taylor, who hit the last two balls of the match for four.*

Lancashire away matches

May 29: lost to Derbyshire by five wickets.
June 5: beat Yorkshire by four wickets.
June 19: lost to Northamptonshire by four runs.
June 25: beat Durham by six wickets.

July 10: beat Leicestershire by 40 runs.
July 17: beat Warwickshire by eight runs.
July 24: no result v Worcestershire.

LEICESTERSHIRE

At Leicester, May 22. **Leicestershire won by seven wickets.** Derbyshire 163-6 (20 overs) (C. F. Hughes 59, B. A. Godleman 38*; J. K. H. Naik 3-23); ‡**Leicestershire 164-3** (19 overs) (E. J. H. Eckersley 39, K. J. O'Brien 31, N. J. O'Brien 47*). *MoM:* N. J. O'Brien. *Attendance:* 3,463. *A fourth-wicket stand of 69* between Grant Elliott and Niall O'Brien saw Leicestershire to a comfortable win. Off-spinner Jigar Naik had grabbed three wickets in six balls to rip out Derbyshire's middle order, before Chesney Hughes, with three sixes, lifted his side to a respectable total.*

At Leicester, May 28. **Leicestershire won by eight wickets.** ‡**Durham 123-5** (20 overs) (P. Mustard 45, G. J. Muchall 31*); **Leicestershire 124-2** (15.3 overs) (K. J. O'Brien 48*, G. D. Elliott 34*). *MoM:* K. J. O'Brien. *Attendance:* 1,542. *Kevin O'Brien's 48* from 34 balls took Leicestershire to an emphatic victory. O'Brien had also taken two wickets during a disciplined team bowling display: Durham managed no sixes.*

At Leicester, June 12. **No result** (D/L). **Northamptonshire 98-3** (11 overs) (B. M. Duckett 39*); ‡**Leicestershire 25-2** (3.1 overs). *Attendance:* 3,082. *Rain intervened after only seven balls, reducing the match to 11 overs a side. Leicestershire's target was revised to 101, but bad light descended.*

At Leicester, June 26. **Tied. Leicestershire 142-7** (20 overs) (A. P. Agathangelou 40); ‡**Yorkshire 142-8** (20 overs) (J. M. Bairstow 37, J. A. Leaning 48*; B. A. Raine 3-23). *MoM:* J. A. Leaning. *Attendance:* 3,520. *Yorkshire seemed on course for victory with Jack Leaning in full flow, and were strong favourites when they needed five runs from six balls. But Ben Raine produced an accurate last over and, with Leaning at the non-striker's end, trapped Adil Rashid lbw with the final ball to produce a tie. Andrea Agathangelou was the only Leicestershire batsman to find any fluency as an impressive Yorkshire attack shared the wickets.*

At Leicester, July 4. **Warwickshire won by eight runs.** ‡**Warwickshire 160-8** (20 overs) (T. R. Ambrose 34, R. Clarke 46; B. A. Raine 3-24); **Leicestershire 152-4** (20 overs) (M. J. Cosgrove 74). *MoM:* R. Clarke. *Attendance:* 4,248. *Leicestershire looked good for a win when Mark Cosgrove and Elliott took charge of the chase with a stand of 65 in 44 balls. But they lost impetus after Elliott was caught for 23, then Cosgrove was run out with five balls left and 17 required. Rikki Clarke, with 46 and 4–0–10–1, fully deserved the match award.*

At Leicester, July 10. **Lancashire won by 40 runs. Lancashire 191-5** (20 overs) (P. J. Horton 63, K. R. Brown 52, S. J. Croft 50); ‡**Leicestershire 151-8** (20 overs) (J. Clark 3-41). *MoM:* S. J. Croft. *Attendance:* 2,666. *Three individual fifties set Leicestershire an imposing target they came nowhere near challenging. Steven Croft, whose half-century took only 25 balls, conceded just 17 runs in four overs of off-spin.*

At Leicester, July 24. **Leicestershire v Nottinghamshire. Abandoned.**

Leicestershire away matches

May 15: lost to Lancashire by five wickets (D/L).
May 29: lost to Worcestershire by six wickets.
June 5: beat Nottinghamshire by six wickets.
June 18: lost to Derbyshire by 17 runs.

June 19: beat Warwickshire by seven wickets.
July 3: lost to Durham by 38 runs.
July 12: lost to Northamptonshire by nine wickets.

NORTHAMPTONSHIRE

At Northampton, May 29 (floodlit). **Warwickshire won by five wickets. ‡Northamptonshire 146-7** (20 overs) (R. E. Levi 58); **Warwickshire 150-5** (20 overs) (W. T. S. Porterfield 55*; Azharullah 3-30). *MoM:* W. T. S. Porterfield. *Attendance:* 3,460. *Needing nine from the final over, Warwickshire tied the scores with one ball remaining. Azharullah's final delivery beat both William Porterfield – who anchored his side's chase, much as Richard Levi had the Northamptonshire innings – and the wicketkeeper, Adam Rossington, who was standing up.*

At Northampton, June 5 (floodlit). **Worcestershire won by 14 runs. ‡Worcestershire 211-3** (20 overs) (M. M. Ali 90, D. K. H. Mitchell 43, T. Köhler-Cadmore 30*); **Northamptonshire 197-7** (20 overs) (R. E. Levi 42, J. J. Cobb 80; Saeed Ajmal 3-53). *MoM:* M. M. Ali. *Attendance:* 2,449. *Moeen Ali – dropped on nought – hit fives sixes and 11 fours in his 50-ball innings, while Josh Cobb cleared the boundary six times in 44 deliveries. But the main talking point was Worcestershire's decision to dispense with their wicketkeeper at the start of the 16th over of the Northamptonshire innings, bowled by Moeen Ali. Ben Cox shed his gloves and pads to become an extra fielder, and the umpires, after a lengthy consultation, allowed play to continue.*

At Northampton, June 11 (floodlit). **Northamptonshire won by six wickets. ‡Derbyshire 166-7** (20 overs) (W. J. Durston 77*, S. L. Elstone 37); **Northamptonshire 167-4** (17.5 overs) (D. J. Willey 60, A. G. Wakely 31*, Shahid Afridi 34). *MoM:* D. J. Willey. *Attendance:* 3,406. *Northamptonshire secured their first win thanks largely to David Willey, who had been released from the England ODI squad. Opening the innings, Willey hit 60 from 27 balls, including 24 off an over from Tillekeratne Dilshan. Wes Durston's 63-ball 77 was sedate by comparison.*

At Northampton, June 19 (floodlit). **Northamptonshire won by four runs. Northamptonshire 169-5** (20 overs) (J. J. Cobb 47, A. G. Wakely 36*); **‡Lancashire 165-8** (20 overs) (J. P. Faulkner 73, A. L. Davies 34; Azharullah 3-28). *MoM:* J. P. Faulkner. *Attendance:* 4,110. *James Faulkner (45 balls, four sixes) and Alex Davies added 91 runs off 52 deliveries, and looked like carrying Lancashire to their target. But Davies fell with 24 needed, and Faulkner could not manage 14 off the final over from Azharullah, top-edging the last ball back to the bowler to leave them just short.*

At Northampton, July 12. **Northamptonshire won by nine wickets.** Reduced to ten overs a side. **Leicestershire 111-4** (10 overs) (G. D. Elliott 56, B. A. Raine 32*); **‡Northamptonshire 115-1** (8.3 overs) (R. E. Levi 67*). *MoM:* R. E. Levi. *Attendance:* 3,719. *County debut:* Z. J. Chappell (Leicestershire). *A rollicking stand worth 65* off 30 balls between Levi and Ben Duckett earned Northamptonshire a comfortable victory in a rain-shortened match. Levi's 67* from 28 balls eclipsed Grant Elliott's 56 off 29.*

At Northampton, July 17 (floodlit). **Northamptonshire won by six wickets. Yorkshire 153-7** (20 overs) (A. Z. Lees 46); **‡Northamptonshire 156-4** (19 overs) (R. E. Levi 30, D. J. Willey 34, A. G. Wakely 46, B. M. Duckett 40*). *MoM:* D. J. Willey. *Attendance:* 6,253. *A relatively inexperienced Yorkshire side gave themselves a chance by plundering 27 off the last two overs against an otherwise tidy Northampton attack. But Duckett was outstanding, sharing a decisive partnership with the more circumspect Alex Wakely.*

At Northampton, July 24 (floodlit). **Northamptonshire v Durham. Abandoned.** *This washout, along with another at Leicester, took Northamptonshire into the quarter-finals.*

Northamptonshire away matches

May 15: lost to Durham by 41 runs (D/L).
June 12: no result v Leicestershire.
June 14: beat Yorkshire by eight wickets (D/L).
June 26: beat Worcestershire by two runs.

June 27: lost to Nottinghamshire by seven wickets.
July 5: beat Derbyshire by three runs (D/L).
July 22: lost to Warwickshire by one run.

NOTTINGHAMSHIRE

At Nottingham, May 15 (floodlit). **Nottinghamshire won by eight wickets. Nottinghamshire 141-7** (20 overs) (V. Chopra 80, L. J. Evans 35; L. J. Fletcher 3-24); **‡Nottinghamshire 142-2** (14.3 overs) (M. H. Wessels 30, A. D. Hales 86*). *MoM:* A. D. Hales. *Attendance:* 10,118. *County debuts:* G. P.

Smith (Nottinghamshire); T. P. Lewis (Warwickshire). *Luke Fletcher, Nottinghamshire's death-bowling specialist, produced yorkers at will to restrict Warwickshire. Alex Hales then hit eight sixes, six from consecutive balls, spread across two overs from Boyd Rankin and Ateeq Javid.*

At Nottingham, May 22 (floodlit). **Yorkshire won by six wickets. Nottinghamshire 143-7** (20 overs) (S. R. Patel 41, S. J. Mullaney 38); ‡**Yorkshire 146-4** (18.5 overs) (A. W. Gale 68*). *MoM:* A. W. Gale. *Attendance:* 9,375. *County debut:* G. J. Maxwell (Yorkshire). *Liam Plunkett's two wickets and 13 dot balls exemplified Yorkshire's discipline, as Nottinghamshire – with Hales now at the IPL – made a shallow total. It was comfortably overhauled thanks to Andrew Gale's easy-paced 68* and some meaty blows from Glenn Maxwell on Yorkshire debut.*

At Nottingham, May 31. **Nottinghamshire won by 15 runs. Nottinghamshire 175-7** (20 overs) (M. H. Wessels 67, S. R. Patel 46); ‡**Durham 160-6** (20 overs) (C. S. MacLeod 32, P. D. Collingwood 30, G. J. Muchall 42*). *MoM:* M. H. Wessels. *Attendance:* 6,802. *County debut:* D. J. G. Sammy (Nottinghamshire). *Riki Wessels mixed improvisation and power as he and Samit Patel gave substance to Nottinghamshire's innings with a stand of 100 in 11.3 overs. Durham's reply foundered after Darren Sammy, in his first match for the county, dismissed Calum MacLeod and Paul Collingwood with consecutive balls when both looked well set.*

At Nottingham, June 5 (floodlit). **Leicestershire won by six wickets. Nottinghamshire 148-7** (20 overs) (A. D. Hales 54, B. R. M. Taylor 47; C. J. McKay 4-24); ‡**Leicestershire 152-4** (18.5 overs) (Umar Akmal 76*; J. T. Ball 3-42). *MoM:* Umar Akmal. *Attendance:* 11,057. *County debut:* Umar Akmal. *Umar Akmal's 49-ball 76* crescendoed with three sixes in five deliveries from Fletcher, leaving Leicestershire needing three from seven. But the match ended without another ball bowled: the umpires realised Nottinghamshire would be unable to begin the last over at the required time, and awarded six penalty runs, taking Leicestershire past their target.*

At Nottingham, June 27. **Nottinghamshire won by seven wickets. ‡Northamptonshire 173-5** (20 overs) (J. J. Cobb 84, B. M. Duckett 30); **Nottinghamshire 175-3** (18.3 overs) (M. J. Lumb 45, S. R. Patel 58*, J. W. A. Taylor 38*). *MoM:* S. R. Patel. *Attendance:* 10,146. *Josh Cobb's Twenty20-best 84 helped Northamptonshire to a competitive total. But, from 80-3 in the tenth over, Patel and James Taylor fashioned a comfortable win by adding 95* to end Nottinghamshire's run of three defeats.*

At Nottingham, July 3 (floodlit). **Worcestershire won by 20 runs. ‡Worcestershire 173** (19.3 overs) (R. K. Oliver 31, T. Köhler-Cadmore 75; H. F. Gurney 3-25); **Nottinghamshire 153-9** (20 overs) (A. D. Hales 47; J. Leach 3-27). *MoM:* T. Köhler-Cadmore. *Attendance:* 10,123. *Tom Köhler-Cadmore punished shoddy Nottinghamshire bowling by hitting five sixes as he raced to 75 off 39 balls, his highest score in the format. It proved a platform for a Worcestershire win, despite losing their last five wickets for ten in 11 balls. Once Hales had gone, the Worcestershire bowlers offered few easy runs. Peter Moores, sacked as England coach in May, was denied a winning start after joining the Trent Bridge staff in a consultancy role.*

At Nottingham, July 10 (floodlit). **Nottinghamshire won by two runs. ‡Nottinghamshire 172-6** (20 overs) (A. D. Hales 54, S. R. Patel 52; S. J. Thakor 3-25); **Derbyshire 170-4** (20 overs) (H. D. Rutherford 62, W. L. Madsen 51*; J. T. Ball 3-36). *MoM:* J. T. Ball. *Attendance:* 13,582. *The local derby attracted a record Twenty20 crowd for Trent Bridge. A finely balanced match went to the last ball, when Harry Gurney, the left-arm seamer, won a battle of nerve against Derbyshire captain Wayne Madsen.*

Nottinghamshire away matches

June 7: beat Worcestershire by 11 runs.
June 12: lost to Warwickshire by seven wickets (D/L).
June 19: lost to Yorkshire by 40 runs.
June 26: lost to Derbyshire by 34 runs.

July 15: beat Lancashire by three wickets.
July 17: beat Durham by 42 runs.
July 24: no result v Leicestershire.

WARWICKSHIRE

At Birmingham, May 22 (floodlit). **Warwickshire won by 18 runs. Warwickshire 144-5** (20 overs); ‡**Worcestershire 126** (19.3 overs) (D. K. H. Mitchell 34, R. A. Whiteley 33; R. Clarke 3-26, R. O. Gordon 3-18). *MoM:* A. Javid. *Attendance:* 10,706. *County debut:* E. G. Barnard (Worcestershire). *Warwickshire maintained their home dominance of Worcestershire with a sixth win in seven matches* *at Edgbaston. Aggressive cameos from William Porterfield and Ateeq Javid topped and tailed their innings, and Recordo Gordon undermined Worcestershire's reply with two wickets in his first over.*

At Birmingham, June 12 (floodlit). **Warwickshire won by seven wickets** (D/L). **Nottinghamshire 149-9** (20 overs) (M. H. Wessels 39; O. J. Hannon-Dalby 4-29); ‡**Warwickshire 101-3** (10.2 overs) (I. R. Bell 38, W. T. S. Porterfield 37*). MoM: W. T. S. Porterfield. *Attendance: 5,572. Porterfield and Ian Bell eased Warwickshire to a revised target of 98 in 11 overs after Oliver Hannon-Dalby had throttled the visitors with his best Twenty20 figures. Darren Sammy's farewell innings for Nottinghamshire included a six off leg-spinner Josh Poysden that smashed a window in the third tier of the pavilion. James Taylor, released from England's ODI squad, captained Nottinghamshire after a three-and-a-half-hour drive from The Oval.*

At Birmingham, June 19 (floodlit). **Leicestershire won by seven wickets.** ‡**Warwickshire 160-5** (20 overs) (W. T. S. Porterfield 40, T. R. Ambrose 66*); **Leicestershire 164-3** (18.3 overs) (M. J. Cosgrove 44, N. J. O'Brien 40*, Umar Akmal 52*). MoM: B. A. Raine. *Attendance: 6,918. Umar Akmal finished his stint as Leicestershire's overseas locum by clobbering 52 from 38 balls and sharing a fourth-wicket stand of 93* in 70 with Niall O'Brien. Warwickshire's run of four wins ended.*

At Birmingham, June 21. **Warwickshire won by six wickets.** ‡**Yorkshire 132-7** (20 overs) (A. J. Finch 30, J. A. Leaning 45; R. O. Gordon 3-30); **Warwickshire 136-4** (18.4 overs) (W. T. S. Porterfield 42, T. R. Ambrose 46, L. J. Evans 32*). MoM: R. O. Gordon. *Attendance: 8,313. Yorkshire struggled to assess the pace of the pitch and were pinned down, first by Gordon and then Poysden, who ended Aaron Finch's scratchy innings. Porterfield and Tim Ambrose batted with greater fluency, and their third-wicket partnership of 66 doubled Warwickshire's total.*

At Birmingham, July 3 (floodlit). **Warwickshire won by 60 runs. Warwickshire 242-2** (20 overs) (V. Chopra 51, B. B. McCullum 158*); ‡**Derbyshire 182** (19.4 overs) (H. D. Rutherford 39, W. J. Durston 43; J. E. Poysden 4-51). MoM: B. B. McCullum. *Attendance: 8,393. On his home debut for Warwickshire, Brendon McCullum plundered the highest score in English Twenty20, and equalled the second-highest worldwide – his own 158* on the opening night of the first IPL, in 2008. He raced from 50 to 100 in 19 balls, and needed only 18 more to reach 150. His 64-ball innings contained 11 sixes, and his century – Warwickshire's first in Twenty20, but McCullum's seventh – dominated an opening partnership of 160 in 79 balls with Varun Chopra. The total of 242 was the best of the tournament, and Warwickshire's highest. Poysden profited from Derbyshire's brave attempt to chase a mammoth total to claim Twenty20-best figures.*

At Birmingham, July 17 (floodlit). **Lancashire won by eight runs. Lancashire 145-6** (20 overs) (S. J. Croft 64*); ‡**Warwickshire 137** (19.5 overs) (B. B. McCullum 41; J. P. Faulkner 3-19). MoM: S. J. Croft. *Attendance: 11,291. Ashley Giles, Lancashire's director of cricket, enjoyed victory on his return to Edgbaston thanks to a brilliant all-round contribution from Steven Croft. The Lancashire captain mastered a slow pitch with a well-paced innings, took the wickets of Tom Lewis and McCullum in successive balls, and held a stunning catch at backward point to dismiss Laurie Evans.*

At Birmingham, July 22 (floodlit). **Warwickshire won by one run. Warwickshire 154-5** (20 overs) (V. Chopra 52; S. P. Crook 3-30); ‡**Northamptonshire 153-6** (20 overs) (A. G. Wakely 51*; O. J. Hannon-Dalby 3-36). MoM: V. Chopra. *Attendance: 7,207. Warwickshire secured a home quarter-final by keeping their cool after Rory Kleinveldt struck sixes from the first two balls of Gordon's final over, from which Northamptonshire needed 23. Alex Wakely hit the last ball for two, when a boundary was required.*

Warwickshire away matches

May 15: lost to Nottinghamshire by eight wickets.
May 29: beat Northamptonshire by five wickets.
June 6: beat Durham by seven wickets.
June 26: beat Lancashire by one run.

July 4: beat Leicestershire by eight runs.
July 10: beat Worcestershire by five wickets.
July 24: lost to Yorkshire by eight wickets.

WORCESTERSHIRE

At Worcester, May 29. **Worcestershire won by six wickets. Leicestershire 147-6** (20 overs) (G. D. Elliott 33); ‡**Worcestershire 149-4** (17.4 overs) (D. K. H. Mitchell 58, O. B. Cox 30*). MoM: D. K. H. Mitchell. *Attendance: 2,113. Ross Whiteley's 26* off 11 balls powered Worcestershire to* *their first win, after skipper Daryl Mitchell had hit a 47-ball 58. On a sluggish pitch, Mitchell had also troubled the Leicestershire batsmen with his nagging medium-pace, conceding 13 in four overs; only 26 late-order runs from Tom Wells gave Leicestershire something to defend.*

At Worcester, June 7. **Nottinghamshire won by 11 runs. Nottinghamshire 169-5** (20 overs) (S. R. Patel 30, J. W. A. Taylor 35*, D. J. G. Sammy 39*); ‡**Worcestershire 158** (19.2 overs) (M. M. Ali 36, R. A. Whiteley 36; L. J. Fletcher 3-35, S. R. Patel 3-17). *MoM:* S. R. Patel. *Attendance:* 3,483. *County debut:* B. W. Hilfenhaus (Nottinghamshire). *Darren Sammy's clean, straight hitting brought 24 – including three sixes – from the final over of the Nottinghamshire innings. Samit Patel and Steven Mullaney tied Worcestershire down, and Whiteley's 36 off 18 balls was not enough.*

At Worcester, June 19. **Worcestershire won by eight wickets.** ‡**Derbyshire 136-7** (20 overs) (M. M. Ali 3-28); **Worcestershire 139-2** (12.5 overs) (M. M. Ali 65, D. K. H. Mitchell 33*). *MoM:* M. M. Ali. *Attendance:* 3,634. *County debut:* H. D. Rutherford (Derbyshire). *Derbyshire never recovered from losing a wicket in each of the first four overs. Moeen Ali then produced a display of brutal hitting (65 off 28 balls) to follow an effective spell of spin bowling as Worcestershire triumphed with 43 deliveries to spare.*

At Worcester, June 26. **Northamptonshire won by two runs. Northamptonshire 193-8** (20 overs) (D. J. Willey 31, S. P. Crook 56*, R. K. Kleinveldt 42); ‡**Worcestershire 191-6** (20 overs) (D. K. H. Mitchell 34, T. Köhler-Cadmore 36, C. Munro 33, R. A. Whiteley 41*). *MoM:* R. K. Kleinveldt. *Attendance:* 3,014. *In a high-scoring thriller, the task of making 14 from the final over was too much even for big-hitting left-hander Whiteley, as Azharullah bowled six precise yorkers to deny Worcestershire. At 133-7 in the 18th, Northamptonshire had been tottering, but the next 14 deliveries yielded 60 runs from the bats of Rory Kleinveldt and Steven Crook, including eight sixes.*

At Worcester, July 5. **Worcestershire won by five wickets. Durham 127-9** (20 overs) (P. Mustard 35; Saeed Ajmal 3-13); ‡**Worcestershire 128-5** (19 overs) (R. K. Oliver 70*). *MoM:* Saeed Ajmal. *Attendance:* 3,548. *The spin of Saeed Ajmal and Brett D'Oliveira kept a squeeze on a Durham innings hampered by three run-outs. When Worcestershire went out to bat, the biggest threat was the lightning that illuminated the sky over the cathedral, but the downpour never arrived. Richard Oliver's return to form ensured a win, though scoring was never easy on a slow pitch.*

At Worcester, July 10. **Warwickshire won by five wickets. Worcestershire 160-5** (20 overs) (T. Köhler-Cadmore 66, B. L. D'Oliveira 56*); ‡**Warwickshire 161-5** (19.3 overs) (R. Clarke 52*, L. J. Evans 35). *MoM:* R. Clarke. *Attendance:* 4,828. *Holders Warwickshire made sure of a quarter-final spot when Rikki Clarke (52 from 43 balls) led a recovery from 48-4. They had also found it difficult to score against Ajmal and D'Oliveira, but Clarke steadied the ship before steaming ahead. In the Worcestershire innings, only Academy products Köhler-Cadmore (61 from 51) and D'Oliveira (with his first fifty in any format) broke the spinners' stranglehold.*

At Worcester, July 24. **Worcestershire v Lancashire. Abandoned.** *A point gave Lancashire a place in the quarter-finals; Worcestershire were already sure of progressing.*

Worcestershire away matches

May 22: lost to Warwickshire by 18 runs.
June 5: beat Northamptonshire by 14 runs.
June 12: beat Durham by three runs.
June 18: beat Lancashire by two wickets.

July 3: beat Nottinghamshire by 20 runs.
July 14: beat Yorkshire by 74 runs.
July 17: beat Derbyshire by four wickets.

YORKSHIRE

At Leeds, May 15 (floodlit). **Yorkshire won by seven wickets. Derbyshire 128** (18.2 overs) (M. D. Fisher 5-22); ‡**Yorkshire 131-3** (16.4 overs) (A. W. Gale 41, J. M. Bairstow 40*). *MoM:* M. D. Fisher. *Attendance:* 5,381. *Seventeen-year-old fast bowler Matthew Fisher marked his first Twenty20 appearance with a display that showed why coaches raved about him. His 5-22 was Yorkshire's third-best analysis in the competition. A bright start hurried Derbyshire to 66-1 in the ninth over, before Fisher struck with his second ball – and from that point they were never in the game.*

At Leeds, June 5 (floodlit). **Lancashire won by four wickets. Yorkshire 185-8** (20 overs) (J. E. Root 55, G. S. Ballance 31; J. P. Faulkner 3-27); ‡**Lancashire 186-6** (20 overs) (A. G. Prince 32, J. C. Buttler 71*; G. J. Maxwell 3-15). *MoM:* J. C. Buttler. *Attendance:* 16,174. *Glenn Maxwell* *began this Roses thriller, played in front of a capacity crowd, by reverse-sweeping the first ball for six – and ended it missing a run-out from close range that would have tied the game. Lancashire's victory was brought about by the stupendous hitting of Jos Buttler, whose 71* came from 35 balls.*

At Leeds, June 14. **Northamptonshire won by eight wickets** (D/L). Reduced to 14 overs a side. **Yorkshire 82-7** (12 overs) (Shahid Afridi 3-15); **‡Northamptonshire 85-2** (7.4 overs) (R. E. Levi 35, B. M. Duckett 31*). *MoM:* Shahid Afridi. *Attendance:* 5,519. *Yorkshire had their two Australian big guns opening together for the first time, but Aaron Finch and Maxwell made only seven between them, and the other batsmen fared little better either side of a rain interruption. In a match already reduced to 14 overs a side, two more were lost at the end of the Yorkshire innings, and Northamptonshire's target was revised to 83 in 14. Richard Levi and Ben Duckett smacked 50 in four to inflict a third consecutive defeat on their opponents.*

At Leeds, June 19 (floodlit). **Yorkshire won by 40 runs. Yorkshire 209-4** (20 overs) (A. J. Hodd 70, G. J. Maxwell 92*); **‡Nottinghamshire 169-6** (20 overs) (S. R. Patel 90*, J. W. A. Taylor 32). *MoM:* G. J. Maxwell. *Attendance:* 8,359. *County debut:* D. T. Christian (Nottinghamshire). *After totalling 73 runs in eight innings in all competitions since joining Yorkshire, Maxwell burst into life by blasting a 48-ball 92*, then taking two wickets and two catches. Andy Hodd, who was plastering a wall at home when he received a late call-up to replace England-bound Jonny Bairstow, timed the ball perfectly as Maxwell's accomplice. Samit Patel struck a career-best 90, but was fighting a losing cause after Nottinghamshire slumped to 10-3.*

At Leeds, July 10 (floodlit). **Yorkshire won by five wickets. ‡Durham 191-6** (20 overs) (G. Clark 91*, J. W. Hastings 43*); **Yorkshire 194-5** (18.5 overs) (J. M. Bairstow 92, J. A. Leaning 39*). *MoM:* J. M. Bairstow. *Attendance:* 9,321. *County debut:* J. Shaw (Yorkshire). *While older brother Jordan was taking wickets for Lancashire, 22-year-old Graham Clark was making a name for himself with 91* from 57 balls in his third senior appearance for Durham. But he was pipped to the match award by the insatiable Bairstow (92 off 42). Both had explosive partners in the closing overs: John Hastings thrashed 43* from 12 balls, and Tim Bresnan 24* from eight.*

At Leeds, July 14 (floodlit). **Worcestershire won by 74 runs. ‡Worcestershire 191-6** (20 overs) (D. K. H. Mitchell 49, R. A. Whiteley 91*; L. E. Plunkett 3-49); **Yorkshire 117** (17 overs) (B. L. D'Oliveira 3-29). *MoM:* R. A. Whiteley. *Attendance:* 7,254. *Sheffield-born Ross Whiteley tore into his native county with some of the cleanest hitting seen at Headingley for years. Worcestershire were a shaky 63-4 until he took charge with a 35-ball aerial spectacular, which contained 11 sixes (and only two fours). Yorkshire's feeble reply ended their ambitions of qualifying, while their opponents breezed into the last eight.*

At Leeds, July 24 (floodlit). **Yorkshire won by eight wickets. ‡Warwickshire 145** (18.4 overs) (W. M. H. Rhodes 3-27); **Yorkshire 148-2** (19.3 overs) (A. Z. Lees 63, J. A. Leaning 60*). *MoM:* J. A. Leaning. *Attendance:* 6,908. *With Warwickshire topping the North Group, and Yorkshire doomed, this was a dead match. But Yorkshire turned the table on its head with an easy win, despite leaving out Maxwell "for unprofessional behaviour" after he turned up late for a Second XI match.*

Yorkshire away matches

May 22: beat Nottinghamshire by six wickets.
May 29: lost to Durham by six wickets.
June 21: lost to Warwickshire by six wickets.
June 26: tied with Leicestershire.

July 3: lost to Lancashire by 29 runs.
July 12: lost to Derbyshire by four wickets.
July 17: lost to Northamptonshire by six wickets.

SOUTH GROUP

ESSEX

At Chelmsford, May 16. **Surrey won by 44 runs. Surrey 205-5** (20 overs) (S. M. Davies 53, K. C. Sangakkara 58, G. C. Wilson 41, Z. S. Ansari 31*); **‡Essex 161** (20 overs) (G. M. Smith 44, R. N. ten Doeschate 40; T. K. Curran 4-35, J. E. Burke 3-23). *MoM:* T. K. Curran. *Attendance:* 3,896. *County debut:* J. E. Burke. *Surrey dominated a below-par Essex in all disciplines. Tom Curran broke a promising third-wicket stand of 71 between Greg Smith and Kishen Velani, and returned to polish off the innings as the final four wickets fell for 11 runs.*

At Chelmsford, May 29 (floodlit). **Somerset won by three wickets. Essex 176** (20 overs) (J. D. Ryder 54, T. Westley 68; A. C. Thomas 4-37, J. Allenby 3-10); ‡**Somerset 177-7** (20 overs) (C. H. Gayle 92). *MoM:* C. H. Gayle. *Attendance:* 4,996. *County debut:* C. H. Gayle. *Chris Gayle warmed the crowd on a bitterly cold night with a 59-ball 92 on his Somerset debut, three years after cancelling an agreement to play for them in this competition. Essex stuck to their task, but Lewis Gregory scrambled the winning run from the final ball. Jesse Ryder and Tom Westley had shared an opening stand of 90 in 48 deliveries for the hosts before wickets tumbled.*

At Chelmsford, June 11 (floodlit). **Essex won by 18 runs. Essex 181** (20 overs) (M. L. Pettini 68; T. M. J. Smith 3-26); ‡**Gloucestershire 163-7** (20 overs) (M. Klinger 104*; G. R. Napier 3-30). *MoM:* M. Klinger. *Attendance:* 3,988. *Michael Klinger struck an unbeaten Twenty20 century for the second time in a month against Essex, but on this occasion he lacked support: Gloucestershire stumbled to 92-7 in the 13th over. Klinger and James Fuller took 71 off the last 45 balls, but the surge came too late. Essex had relied on Mark Pettini (68 off 44) and some middle-order belligerence.*

At Chelmsford, June 19 (floodlit). **Essex won by 16 runs. Essex 187-7** (20 overs) (R. S. Bopara 52, N. L. J. Browne 38; M. G. Hogan 3-33); ‡**Glamorgan 171** (19.4 overs) (C. A. Ingram 70, G. G. Wagg 41; S. W. Tait 3-33, R. S. Bopara 3-25). *MoM:* R. S. Bopara. *Attendance:* 4,889. *Graham Napier's four sixes off Graham Wagg in the 19th over gave Essex much-needed impetus and ultimately proved the difference between the teams. Ravi Bopara followed up a well-constructed half-century with key wickets, and Glamorgan's hopes evaporated when Colin Ingram (70 from 46 balls) was dismissed by Napier with 30 required from ten.*

At Chelmsford, June 26 (floodlit). **Essex won by 78 runs. Essex 212-5** (20 overs) (M. L. Pettini 74, J. D. Ryder 107*); ‡**Hampshire 134** (18.3 overs) (R. J. W. Topley 3-25, R. S. Bopara 3-23). *MoM:* J. D. Ryder. *Attendance:* 5,048. *Jesse Ryder's first Twenty20 century propelled Essex to their third-highest total in the competition. Ryder, who hit eight sixes in his 55-ball 107, shared an opening stand of 126 with Pettini to take the game away from Hampshire, who lost a wicket in each of their first three overs. Bopara, playing his 100th Twenty20 match for Essex, and Reece Topley shared six wickets.*

At Chelmsford, July 17 (floodlit). **Essex won by four wickets.** ‡**Middlesex 150-5** (20 overs) (N. R. T. Gubbins 46); **Essex 151-6** (18.4 overs) (J. D. Ryder 59, T. Westley 45). *MoM:* J. D. Ryder. *Attendance:* 4,972. *Ryder's 21-ball half-century underpinned the Essex chase after Middlesex were restricted to a vulnerable total by a disciplined bowling performance. Shaun Tait took 2-19 from his four overs, including the wicket of Eoin Morgan, just as England's limited-overs captain was warming up.*

At Chelmsford, July 24 (floodlit). **Essex v Kent. Abandoned.** *One point took Essex to the knockout stages after Glamorgan's defeat by Gloucestershire on the same day. Kent finished top.*

Essex away matches

May 15: lost to Hampshire by 17 runs.
May 22: beat Glamorgan by five wickets.
May 24: lost to Gloucestershire by 34 runs.
June 5: beat Surrey by six wickets.

June 12: beat Sussex by seven wickets.
June 18: lost to Kent by six wickets.
July 10: lost to Middlesex by six wickets.

GLAMORGAN

At Cardiff, May 22 (floodlit). **Essex won by five wickets. Glamorgan 144-8** (20 overs) (J. A. Rudolph 30, C. B. Cooke 31; S. W. Tait 3-28); ‡**Essex 145-5** (17.4 overs) (R. S. Bopara 81*). *MoM:* R. S. Bopara. *Attendance:* 3,182. *Ravi Bopara's outstanding all-round performance (81* off 53 balls and 2–25) enabled Essex to cruise home on a quick pitch that suited their five-man pace attack. Glamorgan never recovered from a mid-innings collapse of five for 19.*

At Cardiff, May 29 (floodlit). **Hampshire won by 21 runs. Hampshire 148-8** (20 overs) (S. M. Ervine 49, W. R. Smith 30; G. G. Wagg 4-27); ‡**Glamorgan 127-8** (20 overs) (J. A. Rudolph 38, M. A. Wallace 37; C. P. Wood 4-16). *MoM:* G. G. Wagg. *Attendance:* 4,131. *County debut:* W. D. Parnell (Glamorgan). *Hampshire stumbled to 20-3 in the fifth over, but Sean Ervine and Will Smith built a useful total on a slow pitch. Glamorgan struggled to attack any of the Hampshire bowlers, Chris Wood starring with an outstanding 4–0–16–4.*

At Cardiff, June 5 (floodlit). **Glamorgan won by four runs. ‡Glamorgan 169-5** (20 overs) (J. A. Rudolph 60, C. A. J. Meschede 33, C. B. Cooke 39*); **Middlesex 165-5** (20 overs) (D. J. Malan 70, J. A. Simpson 31*). *MoM: C. A. J. Meschede. Attendance: 3,554. Middlesex were well placed at 74-1, but the tempo slackened after the dismissal of Dawid Malan, and they were unable to score 13 from the final over. Glamorgan were indebted to Craig Meschede, who shared a breezy 82-run opening stand with Jacques Rudolph and took two wickets with his medium-pace, including Malan.*

At Cardiff, June 13 (floodlit). **Glamorgan won by two runs** (D/L). **Somerset 159-5** (20 overs) (T. L. W. Cooper 84*); **‡Glamorgan 43-1** (6 overs). *MoM: T. L. W. Cooper. Attendance: 3,642. Glamorgan were narrowly ahead on D/L when the rain arrived after six overs. Tom Cooper, who hit six sixes in his 84*, had rescued Somerset after they slumped to 85-5 in the 16th over. In reply Meschede, on loan from Somerset, hit two sixes off Jim Allenby in the third over to put Glamorgan noses in front.*

At Cardiff, June 21. **Sussex won by ten wickets. Glamorgan 115-9** (20 overs) (C. B. Cooke 45, W. D. Parnell 32; O. E. Robinson 3-16); **‡Sussex 116-0** (12.2 overs) (C. D. Nash 53*, L. J. Wright 57*). *MoM: O. E. Robinson. Attendance: 3,284. County debut: G. J. Bailey (Sussex). Glamorgan coach Toby Radford described this ten-wicket trouncing by Sussex as their worst performance of the season. On a slow pitch, five of Glamorgan's top six made three runs between them – they were 23-5 in the seventh over – before Chris Cooke and Wayne Parnell averted a complete collapse. Chris Nash and Luke Wright sealed victory with 46 balls to spare.*

At Cardiff, June 26 (floodlit). **Surrey won by 19 runs. Surrey 146-8** (20 overs) (J. J. Roy 61; D. A. Cosker 4-25); **‡Glamorgan 127** (19.3 overs) (C. A. J. Meschede 31; Azhar Mahmood 3-14, S. M. Curran 3-17). *MoM: J. J. Roy. Attendance: 4,858. Outstanding performances from Jason Roy and Azhar Mahmood handed Glamorgan another home defeat. Roy, returning from England ODI duties, was the only player on either side to master another sluggish surface, while Azhar beat Meschede's bat six times in an over en route to figures of 4–1–14–3, as the Glamorgan top order flopped again.*

At Cardiff, July 24 (floodlit). **Gloucestershire won by eight wickets.** Reduced to five overs a side. **Glamorgan 45-1** (5 overs); **‡Gloucestershire 51-2** (3.5 overs). *MoM: C. D. J. Dent. Attendance: 3,276. Victory in this five-over shoot-out would have taken Glamorgan into the quarter-finals in place of Essex, whose fixture had been rained off. Colin Ingram hit 17 off the first over, but opening partner Graham Wagg failed to score from 12 of his 15 balls, two of which struck him on the helmet, the second forcing a retirement. Chris Dent's 28* eliminated Glamorgan.*

Glamorgan away matches

May 15: beat Surrey by 25 runs.
June 12: beat Gloucestershire by 19 runs.
June 19: lost to Essex by 16 runs.
June 28: beat Somerset by three runs.

July 3: beat Hampshire by 23 runs.
July 10: beat Sussex by eight wickets.
July 17: beat Kent by one run.

GLOUCESTERSHIRE

At Bristol, May 15. **Gloucestershire won by seven wickets. Middlesex 175-3** (20 overs) (N. R. D. Compton 78, P. R. Stirling 39, A. C. Voges 31*); **‡Gloucestershire 179-3** (19 overs) (H. J. H. Marshall 56, I. A. Cockbain 91*). *MoM: I. A. Cockbain. Attendance: 2,347. County debut: J. A. Burns (Middlesex). Captain in the absence of Michael Klinger, Ian Cockbain raised a whirlwind 91* to propel Gloucestershire to victory; he shared stands of 98 with Hamish Marshall and 61 with Geraint Jones. Nick Compton's 78 was his best in Twenty20 cricket.*

At Bristol, May 24. **Gloucestershire won by 34 runs. Gloucestershire 199-4** (20 overs) (M. Klinger 126*); **‡Essex 165** (18.4 overs) (T. Westley 67, R. N. ten Doeschate 54; D. A. Payne 3-24, T. M. J. Smith 5-39). *MoM: M. Klinger. Attendance: 2,087. Shrugging off the effects of jet lag, Klinger scored a brilliant 126* three days after arriving from Australia. His innings, the best for Gloucestershire, spanned 68 balls and included eight sixes, four of which came at Graham Napier's expense in the final over. Slipshod in the field, Essex were then undone by slow left-armer Tom Smith, whose five wickets included a hat-trick.*

At Bristol, June 12. **Glamorgan won by 19 runs. Glamorgan 191-3** (20 overs) (J. A. Rudolph 101*); **‡Gloucestershire 172-6** (20 overs) (M. Klinger 104*). *MoM: J. A. Rudolph. Attendance: 2,348. Glamorgan captain Jacques Rudolph produced a masterpiece of controlled aggression to* *register his first Twenty20 hundred, accruing 13 fours – but no sixes – in a superbly paced 71-ball innings. For the second day running, following Gloucestershire's trip to Chelmsford, Klinger hit 104* in defeat. It took his competition tally to 403 runs in four games without being dismissed. But he had scant support.*

At Bristol, June 19. **Somerset won by five wickets.** ‡Gloucestershire 165-8 (20 overs) (M. Klinger 44, I. A. Cockbain 34); **Somerset 166-5** (19.4 overs) (J. G. Myburgh 63). *MoM:* J. G. Myburgh. *Attendance:* 7,854. *Promoted to open in place of the omitted Marcus Trescothick, Johann Myburgh scored 63 from 50 deliveries as Somerset won with two balls to spare. Gloucestershire found the going tough in both powerplays: Somerset's seamers used clever variation, before Myburgh and Jim Allenby gave the reply early impetus.*

At Bristol, June 26. **Sussex won by three wickets.** ‡Gloucestershire 185-4 (20 overs) (H. J. H. Marshall 37, M. Klinger 61, I. A. Cockbain 30); **Sussex 188-7** (19.5 overs) (L. J. Wright 111*). *MoM:* L. J. Wright. *Attendance:* 3,029. *England cast-off Luke Wright smashed an astonishing 111* from 56 balls, and almost single-handedly guided Sussex to an unlikely victory. Defending 185, Gloucestershire appeared home and dry, until sloppy bowling leaked 77 in the last four overs. Fuller was the chief culprit: with 43 needed from 12 deliveries, he conceded 28 from five – and was then removed from the attack for two beamers.*

At Cheltenham, July 12. **Kent won by three wickets. Gloucestershire 166-7** (20 overs) (M. Klinger 75; M. E. Claydon 3-27); ‡Kent 170-7 (19.4 overs) (J. L. Denly 31, S. A. Northeast 49, A. J. Blake 59*; C. N. Miles 3-27). *MoM:* A. J. Blake. *Attendance:* 4,929. *Alex Blake bludgeoned a high-class 59* from 24 balls to take Kent into the knockout stages and all but end Gloucestershire's chances of qualifying. The in-form Klinger played beautifully for 75, but the innings fell away once he was out.*

At Cheltenham, July 14. **Gloucestershire won by five wickets. Hampshire 116** (20 overs) (J. M. Vince 32; C. N. Miles 3-25); ‡Gloucestershire 117-5 (18.4 overs) (B. A. C. Howell 31*, G. O. Jones 40). *MoM:* G. O. Jones. *Attendance:* 3,975. *A few days after announcing his impending retirement, Jones showed he still had much to offer with a match-winning 40 on his 39th birthday, rescuing Gloucestershire from 44-4.*

Gloucestershire away matches

May 17: lost to Sussex by six runs.
June 5: beat Kent by nine wickets.
June 11: lost to Essex by 18 runs.
June 14: beat Middlesex by 43 runs.

July 1: lost to Surrey by four wickets.
July 3: beat Somerset by eight wickets.
July 24: beat Glamorgan by eight wickets.

HAMPSHIRE

At Southampton, May 15 (floodlit). **Hampshire won by 17 runs.** ‡Hampshire 173-4 (20 overs) (M. A. Carberry 36, J. M. Vince 32, J. H. K. Adams 55*, O. A. Shah 32); **Essex 156** (19.3 overs) (G. M. Smith 30, R. N. ten Doeschate 68; Yasir Arafat 3-27). *MoM:* J. H. K. Adams. *Attendance:* 4,886. *County debuts: Yasir Arafat; C. J. Taylor (Essex). Jimmy Adams's 25-ball half-century was his fastest in Twenty20 cricket, in his 100th game. Ryan ten Doeschate hit 68 from 44, but fell in the last over, from which Essex had needed 24.*

At Southampton, May 22 (floodlit). **Kent won by five wickets.** ‡Hampshire 172-6 (20 overs) (J. M. Vince 66, A. J. A. Wheater 36); **Kent 178-5** (19.2 overs) (S. A. Northeast 60*, A. J. Blake 71*; W. R. Smith 3-24). *MoM:* A. J. Blake. *Attendance:* 4,347. *Kent were 70-5 after ten overs, before Sam Northeast and Alex Blake shared a match-winning stand of 108* in 56 balls. Blake's 71*, a career-best, came off 30 deliveries, included six sixes; and it eclipsed James Vince's slightly slower 66.*

At Southampton, June 4 (floodlit). **Hampshire won by 19 runs.** ‡Hampshire 172-3 (20 overs) (M. A. Carberry 57, O. A. Shah 58*, S. M. Ervine 42*); **Middlesex 153-6** (20 overs) (J. E. C. Franklin 31, J. A. Simpson 31). *MoM:* O. A. Shah. *Attendance:* 4,596. *County debut: J. M. Bird (Hampshire). Owais Shah and Sean Ervine put on 85* for Hampshire's fourth wicket, including 42 from the last two overs. Shah hit five sixes against his old county, for whom six batsmen made double figures, but none a telling contribution.*

At Southampton, June 19 (floodlit). **Sussex won by seven wickets. Hampshire 157-6** (20 overs) (J. M. Vince 41, O. A. Shah 36); ‡**Sussex 158-3** (18.4 overs) (C. Cachopa 89*, M. W. Machan 52*). *MoM:* C. Cachopa. *Attendance:* 7,891. *Sussex were 14-3 in the third over before Craig Cachopa, with a career-best 89*, put together a fourth-wicket stand of 144* in 95 balls with Matt Machan.*

At Southampton, July 3 (floodlit). **Glamorgan won by 23 runs.** ‡**Glamorgan 181-7** (20 overs) (J. A. Rudolph 77, C. A. J. Meschede 35*; G. K. Berg 3-34); **Hampshire 158-6** (20 overs) (M. A. Carberry 70). *MoM:* J. A. Rudolph. *Attendance:* 6,575. *Jacques Rudolph's 77, with 13 fours and no sixes, laid the platform before Craig Meschede's 35*, with no fours and four sixes, took the game away from Hampshire. Rudolph then claimed two wickets with his occasional leg-breaks as Glamorgan used 14 overs of spin; it was Hampshire's third successive defeat.*

At Southampton, July 10 (floodlit). **Hampshire won by 29 runs. Hampshire 186-5** (20 overs) (J. M. Vince 31, A. J. A. Wheater 78, O. A. Shah 37); ‡**Surrey 157-9** (20 overs) (V. S. Solanki 34, Azhar Mahmood 34; D. R. Briggs 3-21). *MoM:* A. J. A. Wheater. *Attendance:* 8,652. *County debut:* M. S. Crane (Hampshire). *Mason Crane, an 18-year-old leg-spinner from Shoreham, claimed Kumar Sangakkara as his first wicket on his senior debut. He was one of three slow bowlers who wreaked havoc on the Surrey batsmen after Adam Wheater's best Twenty20 score helped set a stiff target.*

At Southampton, July 23 (floodlit). **Hampshire won by six wickets.** ‡**Hampshire 143-7** (20 overs) (M. A. Carberry 57; M. T. C. Waller 3-17); **Somerset 137-8** (20 overs) (Yasir Arafat 4-37). *MoM:* Yasir Arafat. *Attendance:* 7,636. *County debut:* A. J. Hose (Somerset). *Hampshire reached the quarter-finals for the seventh successive season thanks to a fine performance from Yasir Arafat, supported by the spin of Danny Briggs and Will Smith. Michael Carberry was the only batsman to escape the twenties.*

Hampshire away matches

May 29: beat Glamorgan by 21 runs.
June 5: lost to Somerset by eight wickets.
June 12: beat Kent by six wickets.
June 18: beat Middlesex by 21 runs.

June 26: lost to Essex by 78 runs.
July 14: lost to Gloucestershire by five wickets.
July 17: beat Sussex by four runs.

KENT

At Canterbury, May 15 (floodlit). **Kent won by seven runs.** ‡**Kent 185-9** (20 overs) (J. L. Denly 37, S. A. Northeast 40, S. W. Billings 46; O. E. Robinson 3-35); **Sussex 178-6** (20 overs) (C. D. Nash 61, L. J. Wright 36, D. P. M. D. Jayawardene 39). *MoM:* O. E. Robinson. *Attendance:* 2,774. *County debut:* D. P. M. D. Jayawardene. *Seamers David Griffiths and Mitch Claydon held their nerve in a tense finish to secure Kent's first win of the season in any format. It looked uncertain as openers Luke Wright and Chris Nash put on 81, but Sussex lost their way once Mahela Jayawardene chipped to cow corner.*

At Beckenham, May 29. **Kent won by 23 runs.** ‡**Kent 193-8** (20 overs) (S. A. Northeast 96, F. K. Cowdrey 42; T. K. Curran 3-31); **Surrey 170-8** (20 overs) (K. C. Sangakkara 34, M. C. Henriques 63). *MoM:* S. A. Northeast. *Attendance:* 4,203. *County debut:* M. C. Henriques. *Sam Northeast hit 96 from 47 balls, adding 98 in 53 with Fabian Cowdrey, who then took 2-40 – and the catch that dismissed the dangerous Moises Henriques.*

At Beckenham, June 5 (floodlit). **Gloucestershire won by nine wickets.** ‡**Kent 156-6** (20 overs) (D. J. Bell-Drummond 31; B. A. C. Howell 3-18); **Gloucestershire 157-1** (17.2 overs) (M. Klinger 69*, I. A. Cockbain 54*). *MoM:* B. A. C. Howell. *Attendance:* 3,117. *The meeting between the two in-form teams in the South Group proved one-sided as Michael Klinger and Ian Cockbain shared 105* for the second wicket to see Gloucestershire home. Benny Howell took three wickets with his slingy seamers as the Kent innings fell away.*

At Canterbury, June 12 (floodlit). **Hampshire won by six wickets.** ‡**Kent 183-5** (18 overs) (S. A. Northeast 54, A. J. Blake 49*); **Hampshire 187-4** (17.5 overs) (J. M. Vince 99*, S. M. Ervine 37). *MoM:* J. M. Vince. *Attendance:* 3,180. *James Vince led from the front with a 57-ball 99* as Hampshire chased down Kent's 183-5 to win a thriller from the penultimate ball. After an hour's delay for rain made it an 18-over affair, Northeast hit his fourth fifty of the tournament, and Blake hammered 49 in Kent's decent total. Vince then slammed five sixes and eight fours, the last of which took Hampshire to victory, but left him stranded one short of a maiden century.*

At Canterbury, June 18 (floodlit). **Kent won by six wickets. Essex 173-6** (20 overs) (M. L. Pettini 56, R. S. Bopara 31); **‡Kent 174-4** (19.1 overs) (D. J. Bell-Drummond 61, S. A. Northeast 90). *MoM:* S. A. Northeast. *Attendance: 3,663. A second-wicket stand of 122 off 80 balls between Daniel Bell-Drummond and Northeast swept Kent to a comfortable win; Northeast now totalled 488 runs in eight innings. Matt Coles (2-28) and Twenty20 debutant Ivan Thomas (1-22) had bowled cleverly to limit Essex to a gettable total.*

At Canterbury, July 10 (floodlit). **Kent won by 22 runs. Kent 173-6** (20 overs) (D. J. Bell-Drummond 77, J. L. Denly 61; A. C. Thomas 3-28); **‡Somerset 151-9** (20 overs) (J. Overton 31, Abdur Rehman 30*). *MoM:* D. J. Bell-Drummond. *Attendance: 6,581. Kent went back to the top of the South Group with Bell-Drummond their eighth win in 11. On a sluggish pitch, Bell-Drummond made a competition-best 77 in an opening stand with Joe Denly worth 112, before Kent's innings tailed off. Somerset were crippled by regular wickets, though No. 10 Abdur Rehman helped wallop 34 off a nine-ball last over, from Coles.*

At Tunbridge Wells, July 17. **Glamorgan won by one run. ‡Glamorgan 179-7** (20 overs) (J. A. Rudolph 37, C. B. Cooke 36, G. G. Wagg 53*; M. D. Hunn 3-30); **Kent 178-8** (20 overs) (J. L. Denly 70, S. A. Northeast 38; M. G. Hogan 3-40). *MoM:* G. G. Wagg. *Attendance: 4,999. Glamorgan's fielders danced a jig of delight after a dramatic one-run win kept their hopes of qualification alive. Star performer was Australian seamer Michael Hogan, who took 2-1 in the 18th over, and defended 15 runs in the last. Denly aside, Kent's big hitters misfired. Glamorgan's innings had been given late heft by Graham Wagg's belligerent 53*.*

Kent away matches

May 22: beat Hampshire by five wickets.
May 28: lost to Middlesex by 115 runs.
May 31: beat Somerset by three runs.
June 19: beat Surrey by 54 runs.

July 3: beat Sussex by seven wickets.
July 12: beat Gloucestershire by three runs.
July 24: no result v Essex.

MIDDLESEX

At Lord's, May 28 (floodlit). **Middlesex won by 115 runs. ‡Middlesex 205-5** (20 overs) (P. R. Stirling 90, E. J. G. Morgan 54); **Kent 90** (14.4 overs) (J. E. C. Franklin 5-21). *MoM:* P. R. Stirling. *Attendance: 14,868. County debuts: K. J. Abbott, N. A. Sowter (Middlesex). After the destructive Paul Stirling had hit seven sixes in a 50-ball 90, James Franklin ripped through the Kent middle order to give Middlesex their largest Twenty20 victory by runs. It arrived when leg-spinner Nathan Sowter took two wickets from his first four balls in professional cricket.*

At Richmond, June 14. **Gloucestershire won by 43 runs. Gloucestershire 214-4** (20 overs) (I. A. Cockbain 75, B. A. C. Howell 57, G. O. Jones 34*); **‡Middlesex 171** (19.3 overs) (J. A. Simpson 74; D. A. Payne 5-24). *MoM:* I. A. Cockbain. *Attendance: 2,721. Middlesex's decision to bowl first on an unpredictable outground pitch backfired as Ian Cockbain struck 75 off 39 balls to take Gloucestershire past 200. For the hosts, John Simpson rewarded his elevation up the order with 74, and was the last to fall. Left-arm seamer David Payne produced Gloucestershire's best Twenty20 figures.*

At Lord's, June 18 (floodlit). **Hampshire won by 21 runs. ‡Hampshire 199-5** (20 overs) (M. A. Carberry 72*, O. A. Shah 64); **Middlesex 178-9** (20 overs) (P. R. Stirling 54, J. A. Simpson 35, J. E. C. Franklin 35). *MoM:* O. A. Shah. *Attendance: 17,746. Though starved of the strike, Michael Carberry led from the outset; Owais Shah hit a fifty at one of his former home grounds. Middlesex lacked explosion elsewhere – especially once Stirling departed for 54.*

At Uxbridge, June 26. **Somerset won by nine wickets. ‡Middlesex 171-7** (20 overs) (J. A. Simpson 84*; T. D. Groenewald 3-27); **Somerset 177-1** (18 overs) (J. G. Myburgh 53, J. Allenby 89*). *MoM:* J. Allenby. *Attendance: 2,651. County debut: L. Ronchi (Somerset). Somerset's opening stand of 118 helped make short work of a Middlesex total again indebted to Simpson. Jim Allenby, thriving in his new role at the top of the order, paced his innings comfortably.*

At Lord's, July 2 (floodlit). **Sussex won by seven wickets. Middlesex 133-8** (20 overs) (T. S. Mills 4-22); **‡Sussex 134-3** (15.2 overs) (L. J. Wright 47, M. W. Machan 30; M. J. McClenaghan 3-24). *MoM:* T. S. Mills. *Attendance: 19,721. County debut: M. J. McClenaghan. Tymal Mills's hostile* *bowling tormented Middlesex and left Sussex with a modest chase. The pitch, already used twice in the tournament, made timing difficult – and judging Mills's pace even more so. Fellow left-armer Mitchell McClenaghan, of New Zealand, prospered on his Middlesex debut.*

At Richmond, July 10. **Middlesex won by six wickets.** ‡**Essex 109** (18 overs) (J. S. Foster 33; S. T. Finn 4-28, J. E. C. Franklin 3-12); **Middlesex 110-4** (17 overs) (R. S. Bopara 3-12). *MoM:* S. T. Finn. *Attendance:* 2,941. *County debut:* G. F. B. Scott (Middlesex). *Essex struggled to read Richmond's slow pitch, allowing Middlesex to end a seven-match losing streak. Steven Finn took 4-28 on his first outing since an ECB-imposed break after the Twenty20 international against New Zealand on June 23.*

At Lord's, July 23 (floodlit). **Middlesex won by 43 runs.** ‡**Middlesex 185-5** (20 overs) (J. A. Simpson 53, E. J. G. Morgan 48, J. E. C. Franklin 41); **Surrey 142-9** (20 overs) (K. C. Sangakkara 32; S. T. Finn 3-17, N. J. Dexter 3-12). *MoM:* J. A. Simpson. *Attendance:* 26,533. *A huge crowd turned up for the London derby, but they had to make do with a lopsided contest as Surrey's batting wilted. After Finn and McClenaghan made early inroads, Surrey lost all hope when Kumar Sangakkara was caught at long-on in the 11th over. Simpson capped a fine Twenty20 season – 367 runs from 11 innings – with his third fifty.*

Middlesex away matches

May 15: lost to Gloucestershire by seven wickets.
May 29: beat Sussex by 42 runs.
June 4: lost to Hampshire by 19 runs.
June 5: lost to Glamorgan by four runs.

July 3: lost to Surrey by eight wickets.
July 17: lost to Essex by four wickets.
July 24: no result v Somerset.

SOMERSET

At Taunton, May 22. **Sussex won by five runs.** ‡**Sussex 175-6** (20 overs) (L. J. Wright 49, D. P. M. D. Jayawardene 36, C. J. Jordan 37); **Somerset 170-8** (20 overs) (J. Allenby 79; W. A. T. Beer 3-23). *MoM:* W. A. T. Beer. *Attendance:* 5,204. *County debut:* Sohail Tanvir (Somerset). *Chris Gayle's prolonged involvement in the IPL left Somerset's batting light, and they fell just short of a reachable target, despite a fine 79 by Jim Allenby in his first Twenty20 match for them. Tight mid-innings spells of spin from Will Beer and Michael Yardy were key.*

At Taunton, May 31. **Kent won by three runs.** ‡**Kent 227-7** (20 overs) (D. J. Bell-Drummond 51, S. A. Northeast 114; A. C. Thomas 3-46); **Somerset 224-7** (20 overs) (C. H. Gayle 151*). *MoM:* C. H. Gayle. *Attendance:* 6,288. *Gayle's sensational home debut featured 15 sixes – one short of Graham Napier's competition record and two shy of his own world record – yet it was not enough.*

TWO HUNDREDS IN A TWENTY20 MATCH

Worcs 227-6 (G. A. Hick 110) v Northants 222-3 (L. Klusener 111*) at Kidderminster . .	2007
Glos† 254-3 (K. J. O'Brien 119, H. J. H. Marshall 102) v Middlesex (149-8) at Uxbridge	2011
Kenya 194-2 (C. O. Obuya 100*) v Namibia 198-4 (C. G. Williams 125) at Windhoek. . .	2011-12
Auckland 202-4 (Azhar Mahmood 100*) v Canterbury 205-3 (R. J. Nicol 101*) at Auckland	2011-12
Lahore 224-2 (Imran Farhat 112*) v Hyderabad 166-5 (Sharjeel Khan 101*) at Lahore . .	2012-13
Essex 225-3 (T. Westley 109*) v Sussex 226-3 (L. J. Wright 153*) at Chelmsford	2014
Kent 227-7 (S. A. Northeast 114) v Somerset 224-7 (C. H. Gayle 151*) at Taunton. .	**2015**
Glam 191-3 (J. A. Rudolph 101*) v Glos 172-6 (M. Klinger 104*) at Bristol	**2015**
Knights 167-4 (T. B. de Bruyn 100) v Dolphins 170-1 (K. P. Pietersen 100*) at Kimberley	**2015-16**

† *The only instance of two hundreds in an innings.*

Fresh from his 92 at Chelmsford two days earlier, he regularly hit the ball out of the ground on his way to a 62-ball 151, of which 130 came in boundaries. His last 103 cascaded from 34 deliveries. But Somerset, attempting a record domestic chase of 228, needed 17 from the final six. With Gayle facing only four of them, it proved too many (he did strike the last ball into the River Tone, prompting* *a spectator to strip off and retrieve it; Gayle obligingly signed it for the new owner). Almost forgotten was a brilliant, match-winning hundred by Kent captain Sam Northeast – his first in Twenty20 cricket. He hit 16 fours and two sixes in a 58-ball 114. The other Kent hero was the wily Mitch Claydon, who bowled the final over and finished with 4–0–23–2 – extraordinary in the context.*

At Taunton, June 5. **Somerset won by eight wickets.** ‡**Hampshire 167-3** (20 overs) (J. M. Vince 64*, S. M. Ervine 30*); **Somerset 173-2** (18.3 overs) (C. H. Gayle 85*, P. D. Trego 51). *MoM:* C. H. Gayle. *Attendance:* 6,575. *Another Gayle masterclass ended with the packed crowd baying for him to clinch victory with a six. He obliged, with his eighth of the day, taking his tally to 29 sixes and 328 runs in three innings, two of them not out. The Hampshire batsmen had struggled for fluency, despite keeping wickets in hand.*

At Taunton, June 12. **Somerset v Surrey. Abandoned.**

At Taunton, June 28. **Glamorgan won by three runs. Glamorgan 170-4** (20 overs) (C. A. Ingram 96, G. G. Wagg 33*); ‡**Somerset 167-8** (20 overs) (P. D. Trego 39). *MoM:* C. A. Ingram. *Attendance:* 6,690. *Two marginal no-ball decisions for full tosses over waist height went Glamorgan's way in a tight contest – one resulting in Peter Trego's dismissal, the other denying Somerset a free hit at a crucial stage. Colin Ingram had smashed 96 on his return to Taunton after a brief stint there in 2014.*

At Taunton, July 3. **Gloucestershire won by eight wickets.** ‡**Somerset 174-6** (20 overs) (J. G. Myburgh 38, T. L. W. Cooper 38, L. Ronchi 49); **Gloucestershire 178-2** (19.2 overs) (M. Klinger 58, H. J. H. Marshall 93). *MoM:* H. J. H. Marshall. *Attendance:* 6,155. *An opening stand of 156 between Hamish Marshall and Michael Klinger helped Gloucestershire end a run of five Twenty20 defeats by their arch-rivals. Luke Ronchi had marked his home debut for Somerset with five sixes.*

At Taunton, July 24. **Somerset v Middlesex. Abandoned.**

Somerset away matches

May 29: beat Essex by three wickets.
June 13: lost to Glamorgan by two runs (D/L).
June 19: beat Gloucestershire by five wickets.
June 26: beat Middlesex by nine wickets.

July 10: lost to Kent by 22 runs.
July 17: lost to Surrey by 38 runs.
July 23: lost to Hampshire by six runs.

SURREY

At The Oval, May 15 (floodlit). **Glamorgan won by 25 runs. Glamorgan 240-3** (20 overs) (J. A. Rudolph 62, C. A. Ingram 91, C. B. Cooke 46*); ‡**Surrey 215** (19.3 overs) (S. M. Davies 58, K. C. Sangakkara 37, Z. S. Ansari 67*; D. A. Cosker 4-30). *MoM:* C. A. Ingram. *Attendance:* 18,194. *County debut:* Wahab Riaz (Surrey). *The tournament began in spectacular style with 455 runs: the highest aggregate for a domestic Twenty20 match in England. Surrey regretted giving Colin Ingram a life – they caught him off a no-ball when he had nine – as he and fellow South African left-hander Jacques Rudolph went on to hammer 141 off 72 deliveries. On his county debut, Wahab Riaz conceded 29 from the 19th over, which included three sixes by an inspired Chris Cooke (also born in South Africa). Surrey's batsmen made a spirited attempt, with Steven Davies and Zafar Ansari scoring at a brutal rate.*

HIGHEST MATCH AGGREGATES IN TWENTY20 CRICKET

469	Chennai Super Kings (246-5) v Rajasthan Royals (223-5) at Chennai	2009-10
467	South Africa (231-7) v West Indies (236-6) at Johannesburg	2014-15
457	Australia (248-6) v England (209-6) at Southampton	2013
455	**Glamorgan (240-3) v Surrey (215) at The Oval**	**2015**
451	Karachi Dolphins (243-2) v Lahore Eagles (208-8) at Lahore	2010-11
451	Essex (225-3) v Sussex (226-3) at Chelmsford	2014
451	**Kent (227-7) v Somerset (224-7) at Taunton**	**2015**
449	Worcestershire (227-6) v Northamptonshire (222-3) at Kidderminster	2007
449	**Colts CC (226-5) v Colombo CC (223-6) at Colombo (NCC)**	**2015-16**
447	Chennai Super Kings (240-5) v Kings XI (207-4) at Mohali	2007-08

At The Oval, June 5 (floodlit). **Essex won by six wickets.** ‡**Surrey 169-8** (20 overs) (K. C. Sangakkara 58, Z. S. Ansari 39*; R. S. Bopara 3-18); **Essex 170-4** (19.2 overs) (T. Westley 55, R. S. Bopara 57; M. P. Dunn 3-34). *MoM: R. S. Bopara. Attendance:* 20,004. *A third-wicket stand of 115 in 14 overs by Ravi Bopara and Tom Westley eased Essex towards a target that was no more than adequate. Bopara's cutters had frustrated Surrey, with Kumar Sangakkara and Ansari the only batsmen to find any freedom. Ansari's 16-ball blaze included four sixes.*

At The Oval, June 19 (floodlit). **Kent won by 54 runs.** ‡**Kent 231-7** (20 overs) (D. J. Bell-Drummond 38, S. A. Northeast 32, D. I. Stevens 90; T. E. Linley 4-45); **Surrey 177** (20 overs) (T. K. Curran 41, G. C. Wilson 55, Z. S. Ansari 33; D. I. Stevens 4-39, M. E. Claydon 3-16). *MoM: D. I. Stevens. Attendance:* 21,717. *County debut: S. M. Curran (Surrey). Darren Stevens added to his reputation as Surrey's bête noire, savaging 56 from his last 16 balls as Kent made their highest Twenty20 score. A makeshift attack – including the Curran brothers together for the first time – wilted under the assault, before Stevens returned to plough through Surrey's top order.*

At The Oval, July 1 (floodlit). **Surrey won by four wickets.** ‡**Gloucestershire 154-5** (20 overs) (H. J. H. Marshall 32, I. A. Cockbain 31, P. S. P. Handscomb 39, G. O. Jones 37*); **Surrey 155-6** (20 overs) (J. J. Roy 33, K. C. Sangakkara 34). *MoM: Azhar Mahmood. Attendance:* 15,511. *Azhar Mahmood brought the crowd to boiling point on the hottest July day on record by pulling the final ball of the match, from Craig Miles, for six over square leg to end a run of three home defeats. On a slow pitch, Surrey sweated over their chase, and left themselves 45 from the last five overs. They were let off the hook by a fusillade of extras in the final stages, and by Azhar's hitting.*

At The Oval, July 3 (floodlit). **Surrey won by eight wickets.** ‡**Middlesex 105-9** (20 overs) (D. J. Malan 40; Z. S. Ansari 3-17); **Surrey 106-2** (14.4 overs) (K. C. Sangakkara 40*). *MoM: Z. S. Ansari. Attendance:* 21,592. *A woeful Middlesex's seventh successive defeat was inflicted in clinical style in front of a large crowd – who seemed to take most pleasure from the London mascot derby, or from being chased round the outfield by stewards. Middlesex collapsed once Dawid Malan became the first of Ansari's three victims. Surrey, who were superb in the field, cruised to victory.*

At The Oval, July 17 (floodlit). **Surrey won by 38 runs.** ‡**Surrey 208-1** (20 overs) (J. J. Roy 122*, K. C. Sangakkara 31, R. J. Burns 46*); **Somerset 170-7** (20 overs) (J. C. Hildreth 51). *MoM: J. J. Roy. Attendance:* 20,585. *Jason Roy made Somerset pay for dropping him on 18 with a ferocious 122* from 65 balls – his second Twenty20 century, and the fourth-highest score by an Englishman. James Hildreth responded fluently, but the highlight was the dismissal of Tom Cooper, astonishingly caught one-handed by Ansari after he had sprinted 40 yards from deep midwicket.*

At The Oval, July 24 (floodlit). **Surrey v Sussex. Abandoned.** *Heavy rain wrecked Surrey's last chance of qualification, and assured Sussex of a home quarter-final.*

Surrey away matches

May 16: beat Essex by 44 runs.
May 29: lost to Kent by 23 runs.
June 12: no result v Somerset.
June 14: no result v Sussex.

June 26: beat Glamorgan by 19 runs.
July 10: lost to Hampshire by 29 runs.
July 23: lost to Middlesex by 43 runs.

SUSSEX

At Hove, May 17. **Sussex won by six runs. Sussex 167-5** (20 overs) (C. D. Nash 43, D. P. M. D. Jayawardene 43; T. M. J. Smith 3-23); ‡**Gloucestershire 161-9** (20 overs) (H. J. H. Marshall 45, J. M. R. Taylor 36; T. S. Mills 3-30). *MoM: W. A. T. Beer. Attendance:* 5,205. *Jack Taylor and Tom Smith had taken 32 off the 17th and 18th overs to give Gloucestershire a sniff, but Tymal Mills effectively ended their hopes when he yorked Taylor with the first ball of the final over. Will Beer won the match award for a lightning 22* and figures of 2-26.*

At Hove, May 29 (floodlit). **Middlesex won by 42 runs.** ‡**Middlesex 221-2** (20 overs) (D. J. Malan 115*, P. R. Stirling 88); **Sussex 179-9** (20 overs) (L. J. Wright 91, C. J. Jordan 35; K. J. Abbott 5-14, J. A. R. Harris 3-39). *MoM: D. J. Malan. Attendance:* 5,014. *Sussex had no answer to an opening partnership of 187 between Dawid Malan and Paul Stirling, the second-highest for any wicket in this competition. It took Middlesex to their biggest Twenty20 total. Stirling was explosive*

HIGHEST TWENTY20 PARTNERSHIPS IN THE UK

	Wkt			
192	1st	K. J. O'Brien and H. J. H. Marshall	Glos v Middx at Uxbridge............	2011
187	**1st**	**D. J. Malan and P. R. Stirling**	**Middx v Sussex at Hove**	**2015**
186	2nd	J. L. Langer and C. L. White	Somerset v Glos at Taunton	2006
175	1st	V. S. Solanki and G. A. Hick	Worcs v Northants at Kidderminster...	2007
170	2nd	M. J. Lumb and M. A. Carberry	Hants v Essex at Southampton	2009
169	1st	M. L. Pettini and A. N. Cook	Essex v Surrey at The Oval	2009
167	1st	B. J. Hodge and D. L. Maddy	Leics v Yorks at Leeds	2004
162*	2nd	V. V. S. Laxman and S. J. Croft	Lancs v Notts at Nottingham........	2009
160	2nd	M. B. Loye and B. J. Hodge	Lancs v Durham at Manchester......	2005
160	**1st**	**V. Chopra and B. B. McCullum**	**Warwicks v Derbys at Birmingham**	**2015**

during his 47-ball 88, while Malan went on to his second Twenty20 hundred, seven years after his first. South African fast bowler Kyle Abbott took four wickets in eight balls to end the contest, including Luke Wright for a pugnacious 91.

At Hove, June 12 (floodlit). **Essex won by seven wickets.** Sussex 140-9 (20 overs) (D. P. M. D. Jayawardene 53; S. W. Tait 3-29); ‡**Essex 144-3** (16.4 overs) (M. L. Pettini 48, T. Westley 47). *MoM:* T. Westley. *Attendance:* 5,035. *Mahela Jayawardene, who fell to the last ball, played a lone hand for Sussex, whose total on a slow pitch felt 30–40 short. Fourteen bowling changes kept Sussex guessing, and the canny Ravi Bopara didn't concede a boundary in four overs. Essex went to their third successive win with time to spare.*

At Arundel, June 14. **No result.** ‡Sussex 141-7 (18.4 overs) (C. D. Nash 41, D. P. M. D. Jayawardene 43; T. K. Curran 3-27, M. C. Henriques 3-23) v Surrey. *Attendance:* 7,103. *Play was abandoned after a horrific collision sent Surrey's Rory Burns and Moises Henriques to hospital. Burns suffered lacerations to his face and head, while Henriques needed extensive dental treatment after breaking his jaw when they ran into each other going for a catch. A stunned Arundel crowd watched as the players were treated on the outfield for 45 minutes, before being driven away in an ambulance. Neither team was in the mood to carry on, and the crowd applauded when the decision not to restart the match was announced.*

At Hove, July 3 (floodlit). **Kent won by seven wickets.** Sussex 136-8 (20 overs) (M. W. Machan 39, H. Z. Finch 35*; M. E. Claydon 3-40); ‡**Kent 137-3** (14.2 overs) (S. W. Billings 39*, A. J. Blake 52*). *MoM:* A. J. Blake. *Attendance:* 5,687. *After four successive away wins, Sussex again found life tough at home. Alex Blake and Sam Billings added 91 to make light work of a small target after James Tredwell and Darren Stevens had kept the lid on Sussex.*

At Hove, July 10 (floodlit). **Sussex won by eight wickets.** ‡Glamorgan 164-7 (20 overs) (B. J. Wright 63*; T. S. Mills 3-34); **Sussex 165-2** (14.5 overs) (C. D. Nash 50, L. J. Wright 92*). *MoM:* L. J. Wright. *Attendance:* 5,643. *For the third game in a row at Hove, the side batting second won. It was a canter for Sussex: after Mills had unsettled Glamorgan with his searing pace down the slope, Wright passed 500 Twenty20 runs for the season.*

At Hove, July 17 (floodlit). **Hampshire won by four runs. Hampshire 204-3** (20 overs) (J. M. Vince 90*, A. J. A. Wheater 51, O. A. Shah 40); ‡**Sussex 200-6** (20 overs) (C. D. Nash 88, L. J. Wright 42, G. J. Bailey 33; C. P. Wood 3-40). *MoM:* J. M. Vince. *Attendance:* 5,896. *On a flat pitch, Sussex were denied by their former colleague Yasir Arafat, who conceded five runs in the final over when ten were needed. The dismissal of Wright after a first-wicket stand of 98 was crucial, as was that of opening partner Chris Nash, for a career-best 88. Earlier, James Vince and Adam Wheater had pushed Hampshire past 200, setting up a win that kept their interest in the competition alive.*

Sussex away matches

May 16: lost to Kent by seven runs.
May 22: beat Somerset by five runs.
June 19: beat Hampshire by seven wickets.
June 21: beat Glamorgan by ten wickets.

June 26: beat Gloucestershire by three wickets.
July 2: beat Middlesex by seven wickets.
July 24: no result v Surrey.

QUARTER-FINALS

At Hove, August 12 (floodlit). **Northamptonshire won by seven wickets.** Sussex 165-7 (20 overs) (C. D. Nash 53, D. P. M. D. Jayawardene 50; D. J. Willey 3-27); ‡**Northamptonshire 166-3** (16 overs) (D. J. Willey 100). *MoM:* D. J. Willey. *Attendance:* 5,528. *David Willey's sensational 40-ball hundred included 34 off an over from Mike Yardy as Northamptonshire won with four overs to spare. Sussex were 92-1 in the tenth over, but struggled after Josh Cobb's startling one-handed catch at long leg removed Mahela Jayawardene. They bowled poorly at Willey, though a full house could only admire his power and placement as he cleared his front leg and lined up the midwicket boundary time and time again. Having put on 74 for the first wicket with Richard Levi inside eight overs, and 63 for the second with Cobb inside four, he finished with ten sixes and seven fours from 41 balls. "It was like watching Gayle," said Sussex captain Luke Wright.*

FASTEST TWENTY20 HUNDREDS IN THE UK

Balls

34	A. Symonds	Kent v Middlesex at Maidstone	2004
37	S. B. Styris	Sussex v Gloucestershire at Hove	2012
40	**D. J. Willey**	**Northamptonshire v Sussex at Hove**	**2015**
42	B. F. Smith	Worcestershire v Glamorgan at Worcester.	2005
42	**B. B. McCullum**	**Warwickshire v Derbyshire at Birmingham**	**2015**
44	G. A. Hick	Worcestershire v Northamptonshire at Kidderminster	2007
44	L. J. Wright	Sussex v Kent at Canterbury	2007
44	G. R. Napier	Essex v Sussex at Chelmsford	2008
44	K. J. O'Brien	Gloucestershire v Middlesex at Uxbridge	2011

At Birmingham, August 13 (floodlit). **Warwickshire won by 24 runs.** Warwickshire 189-5 (20 overs) (L. J. Evans 50, C. R. Woakes 48*); ‡Essex 165-6 (20 overs) (T. Westley 33, R. S. Bopara 32). *MoM:* C. R. Woakes. *Attendance:* 7,392. *Essex opted not to select Alastair Cook, who had been made available by the ECB, though he might not have made much difference. Essex were sloppy in the field: James Foster dropped two catches, including Laurie Evans before he had scored. Evans was then caught off a Shaun Tait no-ball (and off the subsequent free hit). He reached his fifty from 30 balls. Chris Woakes struck 48 from 23 before he helped stifle Essex's reply.*

At Worcester, August 14. **Hampshire won by 17 runs** (D/L). Hampshire 196-4 (20 overs) (M. A. Carberry 42, J. M. Vince 107*, A. J. A. Wheater 32); ‡Worcestershire 58-2 (8.1 overs). *MoM:* J. M. Vince. *Attendance:* 4,986. *Hampshire were on course for victory when bad light ended Worcestershire's reply after Chris Wood lost sight of the ball on the leg-side boundary and suffered a broken nose. Umpires Rob Bailey and Tim Robinson said conditions were dangerous, and took the players off. A disappointed home crowd wondered why the match had started at 5.30 on a ground without floodlights. In truth, James Vince had taken the game away from Worcestershire with a brilliant maiden Twenty20 century from 60 balls after Hampshire had been put in under threatening skies. It meant a fifth quarter-final defeat for Worcestershire, who were still to reach finals day.*

At Canterbury, August 15. **Lancashire won by virtue of losing fewer wickets.** Kent 142 (20 overs) (J. C. Tredwell 31*; S. D. Parry 3-31); ‡Lancashire 142-6 (20 overs) (A. G. Prince 62, J. C. Buttler 53; M. T. Coles 3-22). *MoM:* J. C. Buttler. *Attendance:* 6,460. *Without a super over to decide the outcome – the tie-breaker was having lost fewer wickets – Kent's supporters went home dissatisfied as Lancashire scraped through in a dramatic finish. Just six were needed from the final over, but Matt Coles struck twice in two balls – including the rampaging Jos Buttler. That left Lancashire needing five from two for outright victory; James Faulkner scrambled a brace of twos, which he knew was enough. On a slow, flat surface Kent limped into three figures, losing five for 33 in mid-innings to the spin of Stephen Parry and Arron Lilley. Ashwell Prince anchored the reply with 62, leaving Buttler to boost the rate with a muscular 53 from 37 balls. Lancashire's post-match celebrations were marred when Liam Livingstone suffered facial injuries during a bar brawl in Ashford.*

FINALS DAY REPORTS BY GEORGE DOBELL

SEMI-FINALS

WARWICKSHIRE v NORTHAMPTONSHIRE

At Birmingham, August 29. Northamptonshire won by five wickets. Toss: Northamptonshire.

In what was his last day's cricket for Northamptonshire before joining Yorkshire, David Willey effectively settled the match with his first eight deliveries. His second, full and swinging, trapped Chopra, Warwickshire's top-scorer in the competition, before Porterfield was bowled next ball; then, in his second over, Willey angled one across Bell to induce an edge. With Ambrose providing a return catch to Kleinveldt in between, the defending champions were 14 for four before they knew it. Clarke and Javid rebuilt in a fifth-wicket stand of 93, but tight bowling and a sluggish surface meant they did so sedately, eating up 15 overs. Even late impetus from Evans gave them little chance. Willey was well supported by the impressively sharp Stone, a 21-year-old who touched 90mph, while Kleinveldt and Shahid Afridi, who had been able to fly back to England thanks to the benevolence of a local sponsor, were both economical. Levi produced the measured innings required to keep Northamptonshire, the 2013 winners, on track. Despite a mid-innings stutter against Patel and Rankin, the experience of Afridi ensured there would be no mistake.

Man of the Match: R. E. Levi.

Attendance (for all three matches on finals day): 24,357.

Warwickshire

		B	4/6
1 *V. Chopra *lbw b 2*	2	5	0
2 I. R. Bell *c 4 b 2*	4	7	0
3 W. T. S. Porterfield *b 2*	0	1	0
4 †T. R. Ambrose *c and b 8*	5	5	1
5 R. Clarke *b 8*	41	44	2
6 A. Javid *not out*	51	50	3/1
7 L. J. Evans *run out*	18	8	1/2
B 4, l-b 3, w 3	10		

6 overs: 26-4   (20 overs) 131-6

1/5 2/6 3/12 4/14 5/107 6/131

8 C. R. Woakes, 9 J. S. Patel, 10 W. B. Rankin and 11 O. J. Hannon-Dalby did not bat.

Kleinveldt 4–0–16–2 (12); Willey 4–0–30–3 (13); Stone 4–0–26–0 (6); Shahid Afridi 4–0–21–0 (11); Azharullah 2–0–19–0 (3); White 2–0–12–0 (2).

Northamptonshire

		B	4/6
1 R. E. Levi *not out*	63	46	8/1
2 D. J. Willey *c 2 b 11*	12	12	1
3 J. J. Cobb *b 9*	15	17	1
4 †B. M. Duckett *c 4 b 10*	6	6	0
5 *A. G. Wakely *c 4 b 9*	0	1	0
6 S. P. Crook *c 2 b 10*	11	10	1
7 Shahid Afridi *not out*	19	16	1
L-b 5, w 4	9		

6 overs: 46-1   (18 overs) 135-5

1/27 2/67 3/74 4/80 5/95

8 R. K. Kleinveldt, 9 G. G. White, 10 O. P. Stone and 11 Azharullah did not bat.

Clarke 2–0–13–0 (6); Woakes 3–0–25–0 (7); Hannon-Dalby 3–0–30–1 (4); Patel 4–0–31–2 (7); Rankin 4–0–20–2 (10); Javid 2–0–11–0 (4).

Umpires: R. K. Illingworth and R. T. Robinson. Third umpire: R. J. Bailey.

HAMPSHIRE v LANCASHIRE

At Birmingham, August 29. Lancashire won by six wickets. Toss: Hampshire.

Hampshire's sixth successive finals day produced their fourth semi-final defeat in Birmingham, to go with tournament victories at Southampton in 2010 and Cardiff in 2012. This time, they failed to adapt to a slow pitch. Only Vince, with 69 of their 115 runs and nine of their 13 fours, achieved any fluency; and, with only two of his team-mates passing five, Hampshire were bowled out with a ball to go. It was a fine effort from an inexperienced Lancashire attack missing Kyle Jarvis with a broken hand, sustained in training the previous day. Gavin Griffiths, on Twenty20 debut, started with a maiden to Vince in the powerplay, while George Edwards accounted for Carberry and Wheater with successive deliveries. Parry and Lilley, Lancashire's two main spinners, then suffocated the innings, claiming combined figures of five for 32 in eight overs; Parry, in particular, found sharp turn, and beat Shah on the outside edge, before defeating Ervine and Dawson as they attempted to sweep. Faulkner – available because of his suspension by Australia following a drink-driving conviction – then showed his class in the final overs. In reply, Lancashire were 47 for one by the end of the powerplay, and the introduction of Hampshire's spinners came too late. Brown, with an unbeaten 45, calmly marshalled the chase to see Lancashire into the final for the second year in a row.

Man of the Match: S. D. Parry.

Hampshire

		B	4/6
1 M. A. Carberry *c 1 b 11*	13	11	2
2 *J. M. Vince *c 5 b 6*	69	60	9
3 †A. J. A. Wheater *c 5 b 11*	0	1	0
4 O. A. Shah *b 9*	12	10	2
5 S. M. Ervine *lbw b 9*	4	5	0
6 L. A. Dawson *lbw b 9*	3	7	0
7 W. R. Smith *b 6*	2	11	0
8 C. P. Wood *b 8*	2	5	0
9 Yasir Arafat *b 8*	0	1	0
10 D. R. Briggs *not out*	5	7	0
11 F. H. Edwards *c and b 6*	0	1	0
L-b 1, w 4	5		

6 overs: 37-2   (19.5 overs) 115

1/33 2/33 3/63 4/71 5/77 6/88 7/93 8/93 9/114

Croft 2–0–16–0 (4); Griffiths 3–1–21–0 (7); Edwards 3–0–16–2 (11); Faulkner 3.5–0–29–3 (8); Parry 4–0–21–3 (9); Lilley 4–0–11–2 (13).

Lancashire

		B	4/6
1 A. G. Prince *b 11*	14	10	2
2 A. L. Davies *lbw b 10*	18	17	1
3 K. R. Brown *not out*	45	43	4
4 *S. J. Croft *c 6 b 7*	9	20	0
5 †J. C. Buttler *c 5 b 10*	10	10	1
6 J. P. Faulkner *not out*	20	14	0/2
W 1, n-b 2	3		

6 overs: 47-1   (18.5 overs) 119-4

1/15 2/52 3/76 4/91

7 L. S. Livingstone, 8 A. M. Lilley, 9 S. D. Parry, 10 G. T. Griffiths and 11 G. A. Edwards did not bat.

Wood 2.5–0–27–0 (8); Edwards 3–0–24–1 (5); Yasir Arafat 2–0–15–0 (1); Dawson 4–1–19–0 (13); Briggs 4–0–19–2 (8); Smith 3–0–15–1 (7).

Umpires: R. J. Bailey and M. A. Gough.   Third umpire: R. K. Illingworth.

FINAL

LANCASHIRE v NORTHAMPTONSHIRE

At Birmingham, August 29 (floodlit). Lancashire won by 13 runs. Toss: Northamptonshire.

Lancashire had always denied their reputation as county cricket's answer to South Africa, but their chokers' tag had begun to fit all too neatly. Since 1999, and their last one-day silverware (the National League), they had been defeated 18 times in the latter stages – quarter-finals onwards – of limited-overs competitions. Five of those had come on Twenty20 finals days, when they had previously lost three semis and twice finished as runners-up.

Had Prince been caught before Lancashire had scored, they might have come second once more. But White was unable to get a hand on a tough chance at point, and the openers put on 77 in nine overs. Davies, standing outside his crease, produced the most fluent batting of the day, and never let the bowlers settle. He skipped down to the seam of Azharullah and the spin of White – driven for four and six in a first over that cost 15 – and, by the time he was out, Lancashire had the platform for a match-winning score. The nous of Shahid Afridi and skill of Willey dragged Northamptonshire back into the match as four wickets fell in eight balls. But Lilley helped plunder 24 from the final two overs, taking Lancashire to a total that – compared with the semi-finals' first-innings scores of 131 and 115 – looked imposing.

If Northamptonshire, plagued by financial trouble (and the only non-Test county at finals day), were to challenge it, they probably needed one of their openers to make a hefty contribution. But Faulkner plucked out Levi and Willey in his first two overs and, while Cobb kept hopes alive, Northamptonshire were never able to break free against an excellent spin attack. When Afridi slogged a slower ball from the admirably calm Griffiths to deep cover, the result was inevitable.

Pleasingly for Lancashire, their success came courtesy of locally developed youngsters: seven of their team could be described as home-grown. Victory also felt like vindication for their director of

Beginning of the end: Alex Davies gives Lancashire a strong start.

cricket, Ashley Giles. Jettisoned as England's limited-overs coach after they lost to the Netherlands 18 months earlier, he had been told not to bother applying when the head coach role became available in May. His return to Edgbaston – where he had led Warwickshire to the County Championship in 2012 – provided an eloquent reminder of his credentials.

Man of the Match: A. L. Davies.

Lancashire

		B	4/6
1 A. G. Prince *c 1 b 2*	43	45	4
2 A. L. Davies *b 3*	47	26	6/1
3 K. R. Brown *c 4 b 6*	0	3	0
4 †J. C. Buttler *c 3 b 2*	27	15	1/2
5 *S. J. Croft *run out*	9	10	0
6 J. P. Faulkner *c 1 b 6*	5	3	1
7 L. S. Livingstone *b 6*	0	1	0
8 A. M. Lilley *not out*	22	17	1/1
9 S. D. Parry *not out*	1	1	0
L-b 8, w 2, n-b 2	12		

6 overs: 52-0　　　(20 overs) 166-7

1/77 2/78 3/123 4/125 5/130 6/130 7/156

10 G. T. Griffiths and 11 G. A. Edwards did not bat.

Kleinveldt 3–0–29–0 (6); Willey 4–0–21–2 (10); Stone 2–0–20–0 (3); Azharullah 3–0–27–0 (4); White 2–0–31–0 (1); Shahid Afridi 4–0–14–3 (11); Cobb 2–0–16–1 (2).

Northamptonshire

		B	4/6
1 R. E. Levi *c 2 b 6*	16	12	3
2 D. J. Willey *c 8 b 6*	24	21	3/1
3 J. J. Cobb *not out*	44	37	2/1
4 †B. M. Duckett *lbw b 9*	20	16	3
5 S. P. Crook *c 8 b 5*	2	6	0
6 Shahid Afridi *c 7 b 10*	26	18	2/1
7 R. K. Kleinveldt *c 5 b 10*	11	8	2
8 *A. G. Wakely *not out*	4	2	1
L-b 4, w 2	6		

6 overs: 48-2　　　(20 overs) 153-6

1/32 2/45 3/74 4/81 5/133 6/148

9 G. G. White, 10 O. P. Stone and 11 Azharullah did not bat.

Croft 3–0–24–1 (4); Griffiths 3–0–23–2 (7); Edwards 3–0–34–0 (4); Faulkner 4–0–25–2 (11); Parry 4–0–23–1 (7); Lilley 3–0–20–0 (7).

Umpires: M. A. Gough and R. K. Illingworth.　　Third umpire: R. T. Robinson.

ROYAL LONDON ONE-DAY CUP IN 2015

REVIEW BY VITHUSHAN EHANTHARAJAH

1 Gloucestershire   2 Surrey   3= Nottinghamshire, Yorkshire

Every level of the game has a whiff of revolution these days, but prestige can get caught in the crossfire. The one-day competition was once domestic cricket's marquee event, with the Lord's curtain-closer offering a glimpse of two of the season's best teams. It was on terrestrial television as well, giving observers a chance to spy fresh talent, and bandwagons a chance to roll; one or two players might even book a winter touring spot.

At least Gloucestershire's triumph in September allowed cynics to remember fondly an era that is recent, yet almost feels bygone. The turn of the millennium belonged to the West, when an efficient one-day machine led by Mark Alleyne on the field and John Bracewell from the balcony won six trophies in six years.

By the time Gloucestershire began their dominance, in 1999, English attitudes to one-day cricket had already soured, with the national side's early departure from their own World Cup that summer confirming a fraught relationship. The flip-flopping between the length of domestic one-day matches hasn't helped, nor has the shoehorning of the competition into the summer-holiday portion of the season. That it occupies prime real estate in the schedule irks some, not least because it has meant stretching the more lucrative Twenty20 competition across four months.

Come the last week of July, with the players in various states of exhaustion, the second edition of the Royal London One-Day Cup sneaked up on everyone. Even the competition's Twitter team seemed to be reading off a limited script – gif after gif of some combination of "six" or "four" or "wicket", and Royal London's trademark pelican dressed as a country-club attendant.

Some teams were anxious to better their positions in the Championship, while others worried about the NatWest T20 Blast quarter-finals. The upshot was that some rested key players were rested for the 50-over competition. The commutes alone would take their toll. It was a competition few seemed to care about, cluttering an already crowded schedule, played by teams whose main aim, perhaps, was to emerge unscathed.

An alternative view came from the ECB's new director of cricket, Andrew Strauss: the tournament was, he said, a great opportunity for players to push for an England place. His comments were motivated by a desire to draw a line under the national team's perceived indifference to white-ball cricket. The run-soaked series against New Zealand in June had suggested English batsmen were not, in fact, totally out of tune with the rest of the world. But change had to come from the bottom up. Lo and behold, it did.

Despite the odd tired surface, a by-product of groundsmen having to spin too many plates, there was an emphasis on attacking cricket. Fourteen counties scored 300 or more in an innings at least once, while three chased down such targets – most notably when Kent overhauled 335 at Trent Bridge.

Stu Forster; Getty Images

Break in play: Jimmy Adams's helmet falls apart during the Glamorgan v Hampshire match at Cardiff. Moments later, the umpires decide the pitch is too dangerous for the game to continue.

Nottinghamshire had reduced them to 207 for five after 36 overs, whereupon Sam Billings powered his way to 118 from 89 balls. It was the only blemish on a Nottinghamshire campaign in which they won five of their six non-rain-affected Group B games. Kent's victory allowed them to sneak into the quarter-finals on net run-rate, after the last round of matches was washed out.

Essex, led by the home-grown talents of Tom Westley and Reece Topley, the competition's leading wicket-taker with 20, finished second in Group B, with Hampshire (who snapped up Topley for 2016) third. The highest total of the season came in the same group, as Middlesex racked up a club-record 367 for six against Sussex at Hove, with Dawid Malan and Nick Gubbins putting on 268.

There was controversy, too, as the game between Glamorgan and Hampshire at Sophia Gardens was abandoned because of a dangerous pitch after a good-length delivery from Michael Hogan clattered Jimmy Adams on the helmet. Hampshire were awarded the match, and Glamorgan deducted two points. The ECB later defied precedent and deemed the game would not count towards official List A statistics.

Group A provided the two finalists. It took just three rounds for the top four to assemble, and Surrey stood out. For so long their potential seemed to have been held back by off-field matters, but now something clicked. They quickly established a bat-first tactic, and dovetailed a mouth-watering top three of Steven Davies, Jason Roy and Kumar Sangakkara – who each made two hundreds – with an impressive seam attack. Jade Dernbach battled injury but still managed to play a key role, both up front and at the death, and he was aided by Tom Curran, given the responsibility to close out matches. Then there was Curran's younger brother Sam, a devilish left-arm-seaming all-rounder contained within the body of an extra from *The Inbetweeners*.

But while Surrey were earning the publicity, Gloucestershire were quietly going about their business. Led by Michael Klinger, who would finish as the competition's top run-scorer with 531 (only Glamorgan's Colin Ingram matched his three centuries), they turned themselves into a sum-of-their-parts juggernaut. Klinger was helped by three trusty seamers – David Payne, James Fuller and Benny Howell – who took 47 wickets between them. It was not particularly sexy, but when Gloucestershire needed someone to pull something out of the bag, they generally did. Take the quarter-final against Hampshire, where they required 51 from the last five overs: up stepped the former England wicketkeeper Geraint Jones, who matched his age with an undefeated 39, before all-rounder Jack Taylor looted 34 from 17 balls to complete the smash and grab. Then, in the semi-final against Yorkshire, Klinger's third ton made light work of a target of 264.

Meanwhile, Surrey had beaten Kent in the last eight, despite a late scare from Matt Coles who, after taking three wickets, bludgeoned nine sixes in a 71-ball hundred from No. 9; Kent still finished 18 short. It was back to The Oval for the semi, as Surrey and Nottinghamshire faced off in a match many felt would determine the champions. Sangakkara's masterful 166 trumped Greg Smith's 124, before Tom Curran's impressive last over sealed Surrey's four-run triumph.

The Lord's final was a modern classic, a match that played on every emotion. Dernbach snuffed out Klinger for a three-ball duck, and wickets continued to fall, before Jones – in his final game before retirement – scrapped to 50 to drag Gloucestershire to 220. Dernbach blew away the tail, becoming only the third bowler to take a hat-trick in a Lord's final. At 143 for two, Surrey were cruising. But Sangakkara fell to a full toss from Taylor, who also snared Burns and Tom Curran, before slow left-armer Tom Smith collected two more wickets. Sam Curran fought bravely, but – with seven needed off the final over – both he and skipper Gareth Batty provided catches, to send the Gloucestershire supporters delirious. It was their team's first limited-overs trophy since 2004. The players went to celebrate with them, before Jones was carried off the field. A competition that had started as an afterthought finished with one of the highlights of the season.

Prize money

£154,000 for winners: GLOUCESTERSHIRE.
£72,000 for runners-up: SURREY.
£23,150 for losing semi-finalists: NOTTINGHAMSHIRE, YORKSHIRE.
There was no financial reward for reaching the quarter-finals or winning group matches.

> **"** Needing to score at more than eight an over to scale the Himalayas, New Zealand never reached base camp."
> England v New Zealand in 2015, First One-Day International, page 319

FINAL GROUP TABLES

Group A	Played	Won	Lost	No result	Points	NRR
1 SURREY....................	8	6	1	1	13	1.07
2 GLOUCESTERSHIRE...........	8	5	2	1	11	0.06
3 YORKSHIRE.................	8	4	2	2	10	0.53
4 DURHAM...................	8	4	3	1	9	0.40
5 Northamptonshire...........	8	4	3	1	9	−0.45
6 Somerset..................	8	4	4	0	8	0.81
7 Derbyshire.................	8	4	4	0	8	0.15
8 Worcestershire.............	8	1	6	1	3	−0.62
9 Leicestershire..............	8	0	7	1	1	−1.91

Group B	Played	Won	Lost	No result	Points	NRR
1 NOTTINGHAMSHIRE...........	8	5	1	2	12	0.75
2 ESSEX....................	8	4	2	2	10	0.48
3 HAMPSHIRE................	8	4	3	1	9	0.55
4 KENT....................	8	3	3	2	8	0.03
5 Lancashire................	8	3	3	2	8	−0.03
6 Warwickshire..............	8	3	3	2	8	−0.76
7 Middlesex.................	8	3	4	1	7	−0.22
8 Glamorgan	8	2	3	3	3*	0.16
9 Sussex...................	8	0	5	3	3	−1.06

* *Glamorgan were deducted 4pts for preparing two poor pitches, one in the 2014 competition, and a second in August 2015.*

Where two or more counties finished with an equal number of points, the positions were decided by (a) most wins (b) net run-rate.

ROYAL LONDON ONE-DAY CUP AVERAGES

BATTING (250 runs at 45.00)

		M	I	NO	R	HS	100	50	Avge	SR	4	6
1	M. Klinger (*Glos*).........	8	8	3	531	137*	3	2	106.20	92.02	43	16
2	†C. A. Ingram (*Glam*)......	7	4	0	354	130	3	0	88.50	96.72	30	7
3	R. S. Bopara (*Essex*)......	8	7	3	301	101*	1	1	75.25	89.58	27	6
4	†D. J. Malan (*Middx*)......	7	7	1	406	156*	2	0	67.66	102.01	49	7
5	J. W. A. Taylor (*Notts*).....	9	9	3	401	109	1	3	66.83	91.76	31	11
6	L. A. Dawson (*Hants*)	8	6	1	324	85	0	4	64.80	86.40	20	5
7	D. T. Christian (*Notts*).....	7	5	1	251	72	0	3	62.75	135.67	18	11
8	†K. C. Sangakkara (*Surrey*)..	8	8	0	489	166	2	2	61.12	94.03	37	6
9	T. L. W. Cooper (*Somerset*)	8	8	2	359	104	1	1	59.83	100.56	40	6
10	†J. H. K. Adams (*Hants*)....	8	7	1	348	97	0	3	58.00	84.87	34	3
11	†S. M. Davies (*Surrey*)	9	9	0	509	115	2	2	56.55	93.05	46	4
12	†N. R. T. Gubbins (*Middx*) ..	6	6	0	339	141	1	2	56.50	104.30	26	13
13	D. J. Bell-Drummond (*Kent*)	8	7	2	272	80*	0	3	54.40	72.72	30	1
14	S. W. Billings (*Kent*)......	8	7	2	271	118*	1	2	54.20	103.04	31	3
15	G. J. Bailey (*Sussex*)	7	6	1	264	112	1	1	52.80	96.00	18	5
16	†R. J. Burns (*Surrey*)......	7	7	0	364	95	0	4	52.00	91.91	31	2
17	G. J. Maxwell (*Yorks*)	8	7	1	312	111	1	2	52.00	117.73	23	10
18	W. J. Durston (*Derbys*)	8	8	0	380	129	1	1	47.50	103.54	42	8
19	S. R. Patel (*Notts*)	10	8	2	284	124*	1	1	47.33	81.60	26	3
20	J. J. Roy (*Surrey*).........	9	9	0	411	112	2	1	45.66	102.75	53	2
21	J. J. Cobb (*Northants*)	8	7	0	318	104	1	2	45.42	70.35	33	4
22	T. Westley (*Essex*)	8	7	0	315	108	1	3	45.00	86.30	36	4
23	W. L. Madsen (*Derbys*)	8	8	1	315	106*	1	2	45.00	89.74	34	2

BOWLING (10 wickets at 30.00)

		Style	O	M	R	W	BB	4I	Avge	SR	ER
1	J. W. Hastings (*Durham*)	RFM	63.5	1	278	18	5-41	3	15.44	21.27	4.35
2	O. J. Hannon-Dalby (*Warwicks*)	RFM	46.3	0	256	15	5-27	1	17.06	18.60	5.50
3	R. J. W. Topley (*Essex*)	LFM	74.1	2	359	20	4-26	3	17.95	22.25	4.84
4	M. T. Coles (*Kent*)	RFM	60.5	5	304	16	4-34	1	19.00	22.81	4.99
5	S. A. Patterson (*Yorks*)	RFM	58.2	3	258	13	5-24	1	19.84	26.92	4.42
6	J. E. Burke (*Surrey*)	RFM	53.3	1	321	16	5-28	1	20.06	20.06	6.00
7	C. Overton (*Somerset*)	RFM	50.3	3	250	12	3-37	0	20.83	25.25	4.95
8	S. D. Parry (*Lancs*)	SLA	49.5	1	216	10	3-60	0	21.60	29.90	4.33
9	S. R. Patel (*Notts*)	SLA	55	1	287	13	4-11	1	22.07	25.38	5.21
10	J. W. Dernbach (*Surrey*)	RFM	82.5	3	423	19	6-35	1	22.26	26.15	5.10
11	S. G. Borthwick (*Durham*)	LBG	45.2	0	290	13	5-38	1	22.30	20.92	6.39
12	P. D. Trego (*Somerset*)	RFM	42.1	3	236	10	4-29	1	23.60	25.30	5.59
13	S. J. Thakor (*Derbys*)	RM	63	1	264	11	3-37	0	24.00	34.36	4.19
14	M. E. Claydon (*Kent*)	RFM	58.2	3	364	15	4-66	1	24.26	23.33	6.24
15	J. T. Ball (*Notts*)	RFM	67.3	2	327	13	4-47	1	25.15	31.15	4.84
16	O. P. Rayner (*Middx*)	OB	56	2	278	11	4-35	2	25.27	30.54	4.96
17	Z. S. Ansari (*Surrey*)	SLA	41	0	253	10	3-58	0	25.30	24.60	6.17
18	B. D. Cotton (*Derby*)	RFM	59	5	286	11	3-11	0	26.00	32.18	4.84
19	L. A. Dawson (*Hants*)	SLA	63	0	316	12	6-47	1	26.33	31.50	5.01
20	D. I. Stevens (*Kent*)	RM	66	3	305	11	4-29	1	27.72	36.00	4.62
21	B. A. C. Howell (*Glos*)	RM	85	2	420	15	3-37	0	28.00	34.00	4.94
22	C. N. Miles (*Glos*)	RFM	58.1	3	341	12	4-29	1	28.41	29.08	5.86
23	A. L. Hughes (*Derbys*)	RM	62	2	292	10	3-31	0	29.20	37.20	4.70
24	E. G. Barnard (*Worcs*)	RFM	61	3	351	12	3-59	0	29.25	30.50	5.75
25	J. K. Fuller (*Glos*)	RFM	87.2	4	448	15	3-26	0	29.86	34.93	5.12

GROUP A

DERBYSHIRE

At Derby, July 27, 2015 (day/night). **Yorkshire won by seven runs** (D/L). Reduced to 42 overs a side. **Yorkshire 239-6** (42 overs) (G. S. Ballance 69); ‡**Derbyshire 189-9** (29 overs) (H. D. Rutherford 56). *Attendance: 998. Derbyshire's target was revised to 197 in 29 overs. A fourth-wicket stand of 83 from 83 balls between Gary Ballance and Jack Leaning left Yorkshire well set in wet conditions, before a rain-delay recalculation and tight late bowling made a tricky chase for Derbyshire a little too tricky.*

At Derby, July 31, 2015 (day/night). **Derbyshire won by seven wickets. Northamptonshire 231** (50 overs) (J. J. Cobb 104; M. J. J. Critchley 4-48); ‡**Derbyshire 232-3** (48.2 overs) (B. A. Godleman 109*, W. L. Madsen 52). *Attendance: 791. Josh Cobb completed his first List A century since joining Northamptonshire, but they fell short in the second half of their innings, leg-spinner Matt Critchley taking 4-48. Billy Godleman's 109* – his first List A hundred – made them pay.*

At Derby, August 4, 2015 (day/night). **Derbyshire won by six wickets. Leicestershire 156** (41 overs); ‡**Derbyshire 159-4** (30.5 overs) (W. J. Durston 80). *Attendance: 732. After scoring a century in defeat two days earlier, Wes Durston's 80 sealed a Derbyshire victory with nearly 20 overs to spare. Alex Hughes's 3-31, a one-day best, left Leicestershire unable to defend a poor total.*

At Derby, August 18, 2015. **Derbyshire won by 49 runs** (D/L). ‡**Derbyshire 234-8** (50 overs) (S. J. Thakor 68, S. L. Elstone 52); **Worcestershire 181** (44 overs). *Attendance: 1,131. Worcestershire's target was revised to 231 in 48 overs. Progress was beyond both counties, but Derbyshire had the consolation of a closing victory. Half-centuries from Shiv Thakor and Scott Elstone set them on their way, while Charlie Morris took a one-day best 3-46 for Worcestershire.*

Derbyshire away matches

July 26: beat Somerset by 29 runs (D/L).

July 29: lost to Gloucestershire by six wickets (D/L).

Aug 2: lost to Surrey by 77 runs.

Aug 17: lost to Durham by 55 runs.

DURHAM

At Chester-le-Street, July 27, 2015. **Durham v Worcestershire. Abandoned.**

At Chester-le-Street, July 31, 2015. **Surrey won by 49 runs. Surrey 271-7** (50 overs) (S. M. Davies 98); ‡**Durham 222** (46.3 overs). *Attendance: 1,989. The teams went into the match as joint-leaders of Group A but, having fought back in the field after Surrey's flying start, Durham slipped to 222 all out. Surrey openers Steven Davies and Jason Roy had put on 78 inside 12 overs before Davies throttled back, holding the innings together with a responsible 98.*

At Chester-le-Street, August 2, 2015. **Yorkshire won by 32 runs** (D/L). Reduced to 43 overs a side. **Durham 224-7** (43 overs); ‡**Yorkshire 130-2** (24.3 overs) (G. J. Maxwell 65*). *Attendance: 3,240. A match already reduced to 43 overs a side was ended by more rain with Yorkshire well ahead on D/L. Liam Plunkett returned to haunt Durham, removing three of the top four. Glenn Maxwell made 65*, including most of the 36 runs conceded in three overs by Scott Borthwick.*

At Chester-le-Street, August 17, 2015. **Durham won by 55 runs. Durham 247-8** (50 overs) (M. J. Richardson 56); ‡**Derbyshire 192** (46.5 overs) (W. L. Madsen 77; J. W. Hastings 4-24). *Attendance: 2,024. Durham suffered three run-outs as they stumbled to 182-8. But Chris Rushworth – dropped on nine, 27 and 30 – made a one-day best 38* off 32 balls. His stand of 65* with Gordon Muchall proved decisive on a slow pitch: Michael Richardson reached 50 without hitting a boundary. Wayne Madsen made 77 for Derbyshire, but lacked support.*

Durham away matches

July 25: beat Northamptonshire by 54 runs.
July 29: beat Somerset by seven wickets.

August 4: lost to Gloucestershire by 71 runs (D/L).
August 6: beat Leicestershire by 146 runs.

GLOUCESTERSHIRE

At Bristol, July 29, 2015. **Gloucestershire won by six wickets** (D/L). **Derbyshire 274-5** (48 overs) (H. D. Rutherford 110, W. L. Madsen 106*); ‡**Gloucestershire 205-4** (35 overs) (G. H. Roderick 54). *Attendance: 957. Required to score an improbable 68 from 24 balls to reach a revised target of 204 in 35 overs, Gloucestershire achieved an astonishing victory thanks to a fifth-wicket stand of 53* between Jack Taylor and Benny Howell that spanned just 18 legitimate deliveries. With six wanted from the last, Taylor was caught at midwicket, only for umpire Alex Wharf to spot that Derbyshire had infringed the fielding regulations, which stipulated a maximum five fielders on the leg side, and Derbyshire had six. The single the batsmen completed, plus two for the no-ball, left Gloucestershire needing three off the free hit. Howell drove a four – to eclipse fine hundreds from Derbyshire's Hamish Rutherford and Wayne Madsen.*

At Bristol, August 2, 2015. **Gloucestershire won by three wickets.** ‡**Somerset 244-7** (50 overs) (J. C. Hildreth 85*, L. Gregory 62); **Gloucestershire 247-7** (49.4 overs) (M. Klinger 107). *Attendance: 2,973. Michael Klinger's 133-ball innings propelled Gloucestershire to their first List A victory over Somerset since 2008, as they chased down 245 with two balls to spare in a tense derby. James Hildreth had made 85* to rescue Somerset from the wreckage of 88-6, only to be upstaged by Klinger's superbly paced century.*

At Bristol, August 4, 2015. **Gloucestershire won by 71 runs** (D/L). ‡**Gloucestershire 289-7** (41 overs) (M. Klinger 135*, G. O. Jones 54); **Durham 214** (40.1 overs) (D. A. Payne 5-40). *Attendance: 1,219. Durham's target was revised to 286 in 41 overs. Klinger's seventh century of the season in all cricket came despite injury, and helped Gloucestershire register a fourth consecutive victory in the competition. Klinger – batting with a runner after damaging a hamstring on 92 – dominated stands of 132 with Geraint Jones and 68 with Benny Howell. David Payne claimed 5-40 as Durham steadily lost wickets.*

At Bristol, August 18, 2015. **Surrey won by 12 runs. Surrey 291-8** (50 overs) (R. J. Burns 95); ‡**Gloucestershire 279** (49.4 overs) (B. A. C. Howell 60; T. K. Curran 4-65). *Attendance: 1,882. Viewed mainly as a four-day cricketer, Rory Burns made a well-constructed 95 at almost a run a ball to help cement Surrey's position at the top of Group A and consign Gloucestershire to the* *runners-up spot in what proved to be a dress rehearsal for the final. Sam Curran and Gary Wilson weighed in with quick runs in a high-scoring contest, while Gloucestershire's James Fuller did his utmost to redress the balance, claiming 3-26 and hitting 45.*

Gloucestershire away matches

July 26: no result v Yorkshire.
July 31: beat Leicestershire by one run.

August 5: beat Worcestershire by four wickets (D/L).
August 18: lost to Northamptonshire by 146 runs.

LEICESTERSHIRE

At Leicester, July 26, 2015. **Leicestershire v Surrey. Abandoned.**

At Leicester, July 31, 2015. **Gloucestershire won by one run. Gloucestershire 315-6** (50 overs) (M. Klinger 50, G. H. Roderick 104, G. O. Jones 87); ‡**Leicestershire 314** (50 overs) (A. M. Ali 84). *Attendance: 702. Leicestershire took the game to the final ball thanks to a one-day best 84 from Aadil Ali and a hard-hit 42* from Rob Taylor. However, Gloucestershire clung on for a victory set up by Gareth Roderick's 104, his first century in one-day cricket.*

At Leicester, August 6, 2015. **Durham won by 146 runs. Durham 349-7** (50 overs) (M. D. Stoneman 98, S. G. Borthwick 87); ‡**Leicestershire 203** (37.3 overs) (L. J. Hill 86, N. J. O'Brien 50; S. G. Borthwick 5-38). *Attendance: 588. County debut: L. J. Hurt (Leicestershire) Scott Borthwick's all-round contribution helped Durham to an easy win. After Mark Stoneman hit 98, Borthwick belted 87 before grabbing 5-38 with his leg-spin as Leicestershire failed to challenge Durham's monumental 349-7.*

At Leicester, August 18, 2015. **Somerset won by nine wickets. Leicestershire 120** (39.4 overs); ‡**Somerset 122-1** (14.5 overs) (P. D. Trego 71*). *Attendance: 408. Somerset had victory in sight once they reduced Leicestershire to 6-3; they eventually dismantled them for a paltry 120. Peter Trego smote 71 from 31 balls as Somerset won inside 15 overs.*

Leicestershire away matches

July 29: lost to Northamptonshire by 55 runs.
August 3: lost to Yorkshire by 31 runs.

August 4: lost to Derbyshire by six wickets.
August 17: lost to Worcestershire by eight wickets.

NORTHAMPTONSHIRE

At Northampton, July 25, 2015. **Durham won by 54 runs. Durham 313-8** (50 overs) (P. Mustard 65, P. D. Collingwood 132); ‡**Northamptonshire 259** (46.2 overs) (R. E. Levi 87, B. M. Duckett 69; C. Rushworth 4-41, J. W. Hastings 4-35). *Attendance: 2,016. Durham opened the trophy defence of the trophy in convincing style, boosted by the highest List A score of Paul Collingwood's 21-season career, from just 97 balls. Chris Rushworth then rocked Northamptonshire's top order with three wickets in seven deliveries. Despite a face-saving 125-run stand between Richard Levi and Ben Duckett, they never came close.*

At Northampton, July 29, 2015 (day/night). **Northamptonshire won by 55 runs. ‡Northamptonshire 244-9** (50 overs) (J. J. Cobb 86, R. I. Keogh 50); **Leicestershire 189** (44.3 overs) (E. J. H. Eckersley 71). *Attendance: 927. County debut: M. G. K. Burgess (Leicestershire). Josh Cobb's 86 from 110 balls against his former county gave Northamptonshire a useful total, boosted by a late flourish – he not out from 13 deliveries – from Olly Stone, who then reduced Leicestershire to 7-3. Once Ned Eckersley's resistance was ended, the hosts won easily.*

At Northampton, August 3, 2015 (day/night). **Northamptonshire won by four wickets. ‡Somerset 247-8** (50 overs) (J. C. Hildreth 55; G. G. White 4-37); **Northamptonshire 249-6** (49 overs) (D. J. Willey 91, B. M. Duckett 61). *Attendance: 952. David Willey's run-a-ball 91 – he added 95 in 16 overs with Duckett – set Northamptonshire on course for victory, eventually achieved after a late wobble with an over to spare. Left-arm spinner Graeme White had found some turn, and Somerset were unable to cut loose, despite purposeful batting from James Hildreth and Tom Cooper.*

At Northampton, August 17, 2015. **Northamptonshire won by four wickets. ‡Gloucestershire 215** (49 overs) (G. H. Roderick 57, B. A. C. Howell 80; S. P. Crook 4-37); **Northamptonshire 217-6**

(41 overs) (J. J. Cobb 58). *Attendance: 729. Northamptonshire's comfortable win kept alive their quarter-final hopes. Benny Howell's careful innings – and an aggressive 31 from James Fuller down the order – ensured a respectable total for Gloucestershire. Northamptonshire then slumped from 111-1 to 170-6, but Alex Wakely and Kyle Coetzer completed the job.*

Northamptonshire away matches

July 27: lost to Surrey by 220 runs.

July 31: lost to Derbyshire by seven wickets.

August 2: beat Worcestershire by 21 runs.

August 18: no result v Yorkshire.

SOMERSET

At Taunton, July 26, 2015. **Derbyshire won by 29 runs** (D/L). Reduced to 14 overs a side. **Derbyshire 134-7** (14 overs); ‡**Somerset 74** (10 overs). *Attendance: 1,863. Rain interrupted a game already reduced to 14 overs a side, giving Somerset a revised target of 104 in ten. They had opted for a younger side after a dismal T20 campaign, but their white-ball woes continued when they were bowled out 30 short. Derbyshire deserved their win: Wayne Madsen's 45 off 27 balls helped them set a competitive total, and Ben Cotton took 3-11 as Somerset fell apart.*

At Taunton, July 29, 2015. **Durham won by seven wickets.** ‡**Somerset 327-8** (50 overs) (T. L. W. Cooper 104, P. D. Trego 53; J. W. Hastings 5-41); **Durham 331-3** (46.3 overs) (M. D. Stoneman 112, P. Mustard 98, S. G. Borthwick 66*). *Attendance: 3,643. Tom Cooper's maiden century for Somerset was eclipsed by a dynamic Durham run-chase: Mark Stoneman and Phil Mustard's 211-run opening stand was a county List A record for any wicket against first-class opposition. Scott Borthwick's 47-ball 66 ensured Durham's momentum was maintained and, in a batsman's match, confirmed the value of Hastings's five wickets.*

At Taunton, July 31, 2015. **Somerset won by 56 runs.** ‡**Somerset 305-7** (50 overs) (T. L. W. Cooper 93*); **Worcestershire 249** (45.2 overs) (E. G. Barnard 51). *Attendance: 4,309. Somerset's first win in any competition since June 27 was achieved thanks largely to a well-paced innings from Cooper, and three wickets each for Craig Overton and Jack Leach.*

At Taunton, August 17, 2015. **Somerset won by three wickets. Surrey 267** (49.5 overs) (S. M. Davies 111, R. J. Burns 76, G. C. Wilson 59); ‡**Somerset 273-7** (46.4 overs) (J. Allenby 53*). *Attendance: 6,004. A fine match offered more evidence of the exuberance of Somerset's young players. The Overton twins, Craig and Jamie, shared six wickets to restrict Surrey after a high-quality hundred from Steve Davies, and fifties from Rory Burns and Gary Wilson. Craig Overton then won the game with a six to reach 40 off 22 balls, but Allenby's 72-ball innings was as significant.*

Somerset away matches

August 2: lost to Gloucestershire by three wickets.

August 3: lost to Northamptonshire by four wickets.

August 5: beat Yorkshire by six wickets.

August 18: beat Leicestershire by nine wickets.

SURREY

At The Oval, July 27, 2015 (day/night). **Surrey won by 220 runs.** ‡**Surrey 343-5** (50 overs) (J. J. Roy 108, S. M. Davies 99); **Northamptonshire 123** (24 overs) (B. M. Duckett 56; S. M. Curran 4-32). *Attendance: 2,844. Surrey's opening stand of 195 by Jason Roy and Steve Davies was a record for any wicket in this fixture, and set up a massacre; Roy hit 15 fours and one six in 79 balls. In reply, Northamptonshire were in desperate straits at 45-6 against Sam Curran, and only Ben Duckett's late assault offered any consolation.*

At The Oval, July 29, 2015. **Surrey won by six runs.** ‡**Surrey 265-8** (50 overs) (Z. S. Ansari 66*); **Yorkshire 259-7** (50 overs) (G. J. Maxwell 55, G. S. Ballance 77). *Attendance: 4,907. Gary Ballance's 77 from 97 balls almost wrenched victory from Surrey's grasp but, when he fell, the task of scoring 22 from 16 proved too much. An eighth-wicket alliance worth 66 in seven overs between Zafar Ansari and Tom Curran, whose 44 came from 25 balls, had reinvigorated Surrey.*

At Guildford, August 2, 2015. **Surrey won by 77 runs. Surrey 326-6** (50 overs) (S. M. Davies 115, K. C. Sangakkara 109); ‡**Derbyshire 249** (41.5 overs) (W. J. Durston 129; J. E. Burke 5-28).

Attendance: 3,750. Wes Durston's spectacular 129 from 98 balls could not trump the efforts of Davies and Kumar Sangakkara, who had added 204 in 31 overs, a Surrey record against Derbyshire. Durston lacked support, and fell to a superb running catch at midwicket by Sam Curran off brother Tom's bowling; James Burke cleaned up.

At The Oval, August 4, 2015 (day/night). **Surrey won by 36 runs.** ‡**Surrey 328-7** (50 overs) (J. J. Roy 99, K. C. Sangakkara 76, R. J. Burns 61); **Worcestershire 292** (46.4 overs) (D. K. H. Mitchell 59, T. C. Fell 63, J. M. Clarke 54). *Attendance: 7,747. Surrey were given a scare before booking their quarter-final place. Roy's 95-ball 99 was backed up by Sangakkara and Rory Burns. But, when Tom Fell and Joe Clarke added 98 in 17 overs for Worcestershire's third wicket, the match was wide open. Burke and Sam Curran then caused a slide in which the last five fell for 34.*

Surrey away matches

July 26: no result v Leicestershire.
July 31: beat Durham by 49 runs.

August 17: lost to Somerset by three wickets.
August 18: beat Gloucestershire by 12 runs.

WORCESTERSHIRE

At Worcester, July 30, 2015. **Yorkshire won by 133 runs.** ‡**Yorkshire 345-6** (50 overs) (A. Z. Lees 67, G. J. Maxwell 111, J. A. Leaning 58*); **Worcestershire 212** (41.3 overs) (R. A. Whiteley 57; S. A. Patterson 5-24). *Attendance: 2,809. Glenn Maxwell's 76-ball assault set up Yorkshire's comfortable win. He made his second fifty off 25 deliveries, and gave Jack Leaning and Adil Rashid the ideal platform from which to add 102 for the sixth wicket in 11 overs. Despite Ross Whiteley's third half-century in a fortnight against Yorkshire, Worcestershire never came close. Steve Patterson's four wickets in 15 balls brought matters to a swift conclusion.*

At Worcester, August 2, 2015. **Northamptonshire won by 21 runs.** ‡**Northamptonshire 126** (35.1 overs) (J. Leach 4-30, J. D. Shantry 4-29); **Worcestershire 105** (31 overs) (Azharullah 4-22). *Attendance: 2,041. Joe Leach became the first player to take a hat-trick from the first three balls of a List A match in the UK – yet finished on the losing side. He dismissed Richard Levi, Rob Keogh and Ben Duckett on an unpredictable pitch and, after Jack Shantry also claimed three, Northamptonshire were 19-6. But thirties from Josh Cobb and Rory Kleinveldt gave them some hope, before Azharullah ripped through Worcestershire's top order. They were bowled out in 31 overs. Play was held up when a low-flying swan circled the square six times.*

At Worcester, August 5, 2015. **Gloucestershire won by four wickets (D/L). Worcestershire 264-8** (46 overs) (J. M. Clarke 131*); ‡**Gloucestershire 265-6** (44.5 overs) (W. A. Tavaré 61, G. H. Roderick 56, G. O. Jones 58). *Attendance: 1,945. Despite the absence of injured skipper Michael Klinger – and a brilliant hundred for Worcestershire by 19-year-old Joe Clarke – Gloucestershire's fifth straight win secured them a quarter-final place. By contrast, Worcestershire, who had returned from The Oval at 2am, had yet to win; Clarke, with 131* from 109 balls, was blameless. Openers Will Tavaré and Chris Dent put Gloucestershire on track with a stand of 106. Their target was subject to D/L, but the calculations left it unchanged at 265 from 46 overs.*

At Worcester, August 17, 2015. **Worcestershire won by eight wickets.** ‡**Leicestershire 172** (44.5 overs) (A. Hepburn 4-34); **Worcestershire 176-2** (32 overs) (T. C. Fell 60*, J. M. Clarke 51*). *Attendance: 1,681. Worcestershire ensured it was their opponents who took the wooden spoon in Group A. Leicestershire had relied on a ninth-wicket stand of 74 between Clint McKay, who made 42*, and Zak Chappell, who hit 31 in his first senior innings, to inch them towards a recovery after poor shot selection had let them down. Alex Hepburn, a 19-year-old Australian-born all-rounder, was the main beneficiary, taking 4-34 on List A debut. Saeed Ajmal's 3-33 was his best return since remodelling his action. Worcestershire cruised home.*

Worcestershire away matches

July 27: no result v Durham.
July 31: lost to Somerset by 56 runs.

August 4: lost to Surrey by 36 runs.
August 18: lost to Derbyshire by 49 runs (D/L).

YORKSHIRE

At Scarborough, July 26, 2015. **No result. ‡Yorkshire 227** (50 overs) (C. N. Miles 4-29); **Gloucestershire 5-0** (2 overs). *Attendance: 2,500. Five of Yorkshire's top six got starts – only to get themselves out. A ninth-wicket stand of 57 between Tim Bresnan and Steve Patterson took the total closer to respectability, but rain set in.*

At Leeds, August 3, 2015. **Yorkshire won by 31 runs. Yorkshire 277-9** (50 overs) (A. Z. Lees 75); **‡Leicestershire 246** (49.5 overs) (A. J. Robson 90). *Attendance: 3,970. A polished innings from acting-captain Alex Lees brought his highest score in any form of cricket since April. Angus Robson was as convincing for Leicestershire in reaching 90, a one-day best. But, once he was out, Yorkshire's bowlers were never under much pressure.*

At Scarborough, August 5, 2015. **Somerset won by six wickets. ‡Yorkshire 175** (49.5 overs) (P. D. Trego 4-29); **Somerset 178-4** (38.1 overs) (T. B. Abell 80). *Attendance: 4,967. Yorkshire fans expected a seaside cruise into the quarter-finals, but perhaps their team were unsettled by the injured Andrew Gale announcing before play that he was stepping down as one-day captain, in favour of Lees. Somerset, despite one win in five matches, bossed the game from start to finish. Jack Leaning and Will Rhodes staged a partial recovery from 22-4, but another collapse left Yorkshire 108-9, and it needed a last-wicket stand of 67 from youngsters Karl Carver and Matthew Fisher to preserve some dignity. Tom Abell stroked a career-best 80 in his fifth match.*

At Leeds, August 18, 2015. **‡Yorkshire v Northamptonshire. Abandoned.**

Yorkshire away matches

July 27: beat Derbyshire by seven runs (D/L).
July 29: lost to Surrey by six runs.
July 30: beat Worcestershire by 133 runs.
August 2: beat Durham by 32 runs (D/L).

GROUP B

ESSEX

At Chelmsford, July 27, 2015 (day/night). **Essex won by seven wickets. Lancashire 161-9** (50 overs) (R. S. Bopara 4-31); **‡Essex 163-3** (33 overs) (R. S. Bopara 101*). *Attendance: 2,092. The loss of Ashwell Prince to the third ball of the match, and a sedate approach by the other Lancashire batsmen, left Essex a straightforward task. Ravi Bopara's unbeaten century completed a fine all-round game, and weakened the argument that a poor pitch had caused Lancashire's modest total.*

At Chelmsford, July 29, 2015 (day/night). **Essex won by 152 runs. Essex 320-5** (50 overs) (M. L. Pettini 126, T. Westley 108); **‡Warwickshire 168** (40.2 overs) (I. J. L. Trott 51; R. J. W. Topley 4-29). *Attendance: 1,774. Eliminated from both cup competitions at the quarter-final stage by Warwickshire in 2014, Essex exacted some revenge. Openers Mark Pettini and Tom Westley provided a foundation for a substantial total with a stand of 191 in 34 overs. Faced with a daunting target, Warwickshire never recovered from the first-ball loss of Varun Chopra. Reece Topley claimed four wickets, while Kishen Velani equalled Essex's List A record of four outfield catches.*

At Chelmsford, August 2, 2015. **Nottinghamshire won by seven wickets. Essex 268-8** (50 overs) (M. L. Pettini 61, J. D. Ryder 81*); **‡Nottinghamshire 271-3** (48.4 overs) (J. W. A. Taylor 94*, S. R. Patel 124*). *Attendance: 3,983. County debut: Imran Tahir (Nottinghamshire). A Nottinghamshire record fourth-wicket stand of 215* – brought up in 35 overs by James Taylor and Samit Patel – made light of their chase. Essex had relied on the experienced pair of Pettini and Jesse Ryder.*

At Colchester, August 5, 2015. **Essex won by six wickets. Middlesex 296-5** (50 overs) (N. R. T. Gubbins 96, J. E. C. Franklin 63); **‡Essex 297-4** (47.1 overs) (T. Westley 56, R. S. Bopara 82*). *Attendance: 2,503. A fine one-day match was well supported by Colchester's cricket-lovers. Batsmen dominated: Nick Gubbins fell just short of three figures, then saw his efforts prove fruitless as Bopara guided Essex to victory.*

Essex away matches

July 26: no result v Kent.   August 4: beat Hampshire by six wickets.
July 31: lost to Glamorgan by 146 runs.   August 19: no result v Sussex.

GLAMORGAN

At Cardiff, July 28, 2015. **Glamorgan won by three wickets. Kent 317-7** (50 overs) (S. A. Northeast 74, S. W. Billings 56, D. I. Stevens 110); ‡**Glamorgan 321-7** (49.4 overs) (W. D. Bragg 59, C. A. Ingram 109, C. B. Cooke 94*). *Attendance:* 785. *Glamorgan achieved their highest run-chase at Sophia Gardens with two balls to spare. However, when rain had stopped play, with 112 needed from ten overs, they were 31 behind the D/L par. On the resumption, Chris Cooke launched a furious assault: his 94* came from only 54 balls, and built on good work from Colin Ingram and Will Bragg. In Kent's innings, Mark Wallace completed 1,000 dismissals for Glamorgan, and Darren Stevens struck a rapid century.*

At Cardiff, July 31, 2015. **Glamorgan won by 146 runs. Glamorgan 288-6** (50 overs) (C. A. Ingram 130, G. G. Wagg 62*); ‡**Essex 142** (37.1 overs). *Attendance:* 1,346. *Glamorgan easily defeated a team who had recently beaten them twice in the T20 Blast and once in the Championship. Ingram scored his second century in four days, and Graham Wagg struck 62 from 46 balls as Glamorgan made a competitive total. Essex never recovered from 16-3.*

At Cardiff, August 2, 2015. **No result.** ‡**Glamorgan 182-9** (50 overs) (C. A. Ingram 51); **Hampshire 26-0** (6.4 overs). *Attendance:* 1,494. *On what Glamorgan chief executive Hugh Morris described as "a dark day for the club", the match was called off 40 balls into Hampshire's reply because of a dangerous pitch. Jimmy Adams was struck on the helmet playing forward to Michael Hogan, while another rising ball smacked his partner, Michael Carberry, on the head. The match was awarded to Hampshire, and Glamorgan were fined £9,000, of which £5,000 was suspended. They were also docked two points, with a further two-point penalty to take effect if a pitch is rated unfit in 2016; it would also trigger the remainder of the fine. Glamorgan had already started the competition on minus two points after a similar transgression – involving the same strip – in 2014. They had, however, scored 288 runs on the very same pitch two days earlier. Following an internal investigation, the Cardiff groundsman, Keith Exton, left the club at the end of the month. In December, the ECB decreed that the game should not be considered an official List A match.*

At Swansea, August 5, 2015. **No result. Glamorgan 9-0** (6 overs) v ‡**Sussex.** *Attendance:* 405. *Only six overs were possible on the first day of the Swansea Festival.*

Glamorgan away matches

July 26: no result v Nottinghamshire.   August 17: lost to Middlesex by eight wickets.
August 3: lost to Warwickshire by nine wickets. August 19: no result v Lancashire.

HAMPSHIRE

At Southampton, July 27, 2015 (day/night). **Hampshire won by 87 runs.** ‡**Hampshire 343-6** (50 overs) (J. M. Vince 103, L. A. Dawson 73*); **Sussex 256** (41 overs) (L. J. Wright 58, M. W. Machan 93; L. A. Dawson 6-47). *Attendance:* 1,795. *County debut:* A. C. Thomas (Sussex). *James Vince's 103 was his first competitive century of the season, while Liam Dawson's bowling figures – his best in limited-overs cricket – completed a fine all-round performance after a brisk 73*. Hampshire's total, their best in List A matches at the Rose Bowl, proved too stiff for Sussex, despite Matt Machan's resistance. Well placed on 170-2, they lost seven for 54 in eight overs.*

At Southampton, August 1, 2015. **Hampshire won by ten wickets.** ‡**Middlesex 117** (32.4 overs) (M. S. Crane 4-30); **Hampshire 121-0** (22.5 overs) (M. A. Carberry 66*, J. H. K. Adams 53*). *Attendance:* 4,463. *Middlesex won the toss, but collapsed to 45-7 before James Harris and Ollie Rayner put on 55. Leg-spinner Mason Crane took the last four wickets. Hampshire needed only 84 minutes to wrap up a crushing victory.*

At Southampton, August 4, 2015 (day/night). **Essex won by six wickets.** ‡**Hampshire 209** (45.5 overs) (L. A. Dawson 85, W. R. Smith 63; R. J. W. Topley 4-26); **Essex 210-4** (42 overs) (M. L. Pettini 57, N. L. J. Browne 69, T. Westley 53). *Attendance:* 2,934. *Mark Pettini and Nick*

Browne put on 122 in 23 overs for the first wicket as Essex won with eight overs to spare. Hampshire had plummeted to 68-5 before Dawson and Will Smith added 124.

At Southampton, August 17, 2015 (day/night). **Lancashire won by 29 runs. ‡Lancashire 301-4** (50 overs) (A. G. Prince 102, A. N. Petersen 82); **Hampshire 272** (49.1 overs) (J. H. K. Adams 53, A. J. A. Wheater 111, L. A. Dawson 52). *Attendance:* 3,651. *Ashwell Prince and Alviro Petersen put on 147 for the second wicket as Lancashire reached a formidable 301, which proved enough to maintain their hopes of a place in the knockouts. Adam Wheater's second List A century was in vain.*

Hampshire away matches

July 30: lost to Kent by five wickets.
August 2: no result v Glamorgan.

August 5: beat Warwickshire by 23 runs (D/L).
August 19: no result v Nottinghamshire

KENT

At Tunbridge Wells, July 26, 2015. **Kent v Essex. Abandoned.**

At Canterbury, July 30, 2015 (day/night). **Kent won by five wickets. Hampshire 233** (47.5 overs) (M. A. Carberry 61); **‡Kent 236-5** (43 overs) (D. J. Bell-Drummond 80*, J. L. Denly 78). *Attendance:* 2,399. *Kent enjoyed a comfortable five-wicket win. After a flying start from the openers, Hampshire lost their way against spinners James Tredwell and Fabian Cowdrey, who picked up a one-day-best 3-32. Daniel Bell-Drummond anchored the pursuit with a steady 80*. He and Joe Denly put on 131 for the first wicket before Alex Blake polished things off with 34* from 24 balls.*

At Canterbury, August 2, 2015. **Kent won by eight wickets. Sussex 154** (44.3 overs) (D. I. Stevens 4-29); **‡Kent 155-2** (30.5 overs) (D. J. Bell-Drummond 55*). *Attendance:* 2,425. *Kent's niggardly seamers, especially Darren Stevens, proved too much for Sussex, for whom only two batsmen escaped the teens. Bell-Drummond ensured a toothless Sussex were crushed.*

At Canterbury, August 8, 2015. **Lancashire won by 51 runs. Lancashire 258-9** (50 overs) (S. J. Croft 55, L. S. Livingstone 91, A. L. Davies 57; M. T. Coles 4-34); **‡Kent 207** (37.4 overs) (A. J. Blake 89). *Attendance:* 2,308. *Liam Livingstone's hard-hit yet impudent 91 on List A debut steered Lancashire towards a comfortable win. He helped rescue them from 26-3, but fell to an ill-judged Dilscoop nine short of a hundred. The sprightly Alex Davies and watchful Steven Croft contributed contrasting fifties. Kent slid from 59-1 to 87-5, and Blake's one-day-best 89 was too late.*

Kent away matches

July 28: lost to Glamorgan by three wickets.
July 31: lost to Middlesex by 87 runs.

August 17: beat Nottinghamshire by five wickets.
August 19: no result v Warwickshire.

LANCASHIRE

At Blackpool, July 29, 2015. **Lancashire won by two wickets. Middlesex 161** (46.5 overs); **‡Lancashire 162-8** (48 overs). *Attendance:* 4,089. *County debut:* Junaid Khan (Middlesex). *Lancashire's first visit to Stanley Park since 2011 saw them prevail on a pitch requiring considerable skill – and a dose of fortune. Twelve batsmen reached double figures but no one made more than Karl Brown's fluent 36, which launched Lancashire's pursuit of 162. Junaid Khan, once of Lancashire, removed both openers, but Jordan Clark's skilful 29 set up the win. Middlesex had lurched to 111-8, before James Harris and Toby Roland-Jones shared the game's only fifty stand.*

At Manchester, August 2, 2015. **Warwickshire won by three wickets. Lancashire 265-7** (50 overs) (A. G. Prince 82, A. L. Davies 73*); **‡Warwickshire 268-7** (49.5 overs) (V. Chopra 88, T. R. Ambrose 59). *Attendance:* 3,081. *Warwickshire's victory – after two defeats and a washout – was the culmination of a thrilling chase, begun by Varun Chopra, maintained by Tim Ambrose and completed by Ateeq Javid, who cracked 32* from 21 balls. Lancashire had enjoyed another fine effort from Ashwell Prince, and a resourceful 63-ball 73* by Alex Davies that included a one-handed, backhand smash to the boundary. Boyd Rankin took three wickets in 12 balls to derail Lancashire.*

At Liverpool, August 4, 2015. **Nottinghamshire won by four wickets. Lancashire 216-8** (50 overs) (K. R. Brown 77); ‡**Nottinghamshire 217-6** (46.4 overs) (J. W. A. Taylor 56). *Attendance:* 3,089. *Brown's 77 guided Lancashire to 162-3 in the 42nd over, before Samit Patel took three quick wickets to rein them in. James Taylor's third fifty in a row sped Nottinghamshire towards their target, though the vital stand was the run-a-ball 71* added by Chris Read and Brett Hutton.*

At Manchester, August 19, 2015 (day/night). **No result. Lancashire 68-0** (8.4 overs) v ‡**Glamorgan.** *Attendance:* 1,448. *Four days after defeating Kent in the T20 Blast quarter-final, Lancashire hoped to deny them a place in the knockout stage of the Royal London Cup. But rain had the last word, and Kent, whose match at Edgbaston was also washed away, progressed at Lancashire's expense with a fractionally better net run-rate.*

Lancashire away matches

July 26: no result v Sussex.
July 27: lost to Essex by seven wickets.

August 8: beat Kent by 51 runs.
August 17: beat Hampshire by 29 runs.

MIDDLESEX

At Lord's, July 26, 2015. **Middlesex v Warwickshire. Abandoned.**

At Radlett, July 31, 2015. **Middlesex won by 87 runs.** ‡**Middlesex 260-9** (50 overs) (J. E. C. Franklin 50, N. R. T. Gubbins 56); **Kent 173** (41.2 overs) (S. W. Billings 68; O. P. Rayner 4-45). *Attendance:* 1,592. *Kent lost their last six for 18 as their composure deserted them on a slow track: off-spinner Ollie Rayner was destroyer-in-chief. Sam Billings, the mainstay of the Kent innings, had skyed a reverse sweep, triggering the collapse.*

At Lord's, August 6, 2015. **Nottinghamshire won by 49 runs. Nottinghamshire 295-9** (50 overs) (M. H. Wessels 132, S. J. Mullaney 51; O. P. Rayner 4-35); ‡**Middlesex 246** (48 overs) (S. D. Robson 88). *Attendance:* 3,071. *A switch-hit six brought up Riki Wessels's second List A century, his first since 2008, and ushered Nottinghamshire towards the knockouts. For the second time in a week, Rayner improved his best List A figures. From 152-1 in the 29th over, Middlesex came unstuck against the spin of Samit Patel and Imran Tahir.*

At Lord's, August 17, 2015. **Middlesex won by eight wickets.** ‡**Glamorgan 251-9** (50 overs) (J. A. Rudolph 58, C. A. Ingram 102; J. A. R. Harris 4-38); **Middlesex 255-2** (39.4 overs) (P. R. Stirling 58, D. J. Malan 156*). *Attendance:* 2,662. *Dawid Malan's highest limited-overs score (and his second century in four List A innings) eased Middlesex to victory after Colin Ingram's century had held Glamorgan together. Swansea-born James Harris chose not to celebrate his wickets; 4-38 was his best return in List A cricket.*

Middlesex away matches

July 29: lost to Lancashire by two wickets.
August 1: lost to Hampshire by ten wickets.

August 3: beat Sussex by three runs (D/L).
August 5: lost to Essex by six wickets.

NOTTINGHAMSHIRE

At Sookholme, July 25, 2015. **Nottinghamshire won by nine wickets. Warwickshire 220** (49.1 overs) (I. R. Bell 52; D. T. Christian 5-40); ‡**Nottinghamshire 221-1** (28.1 overs) (M. H. Wessels 85*, A. D. Hales 103). *Attendance:* 2,228. *Excellent swing bowling from Australian all-rounder Dan Christian, who finished with 5-40, and a 61-ball 103 from Alex Hales that included nine sixes hastened Nottinghamshire to a commanding victory. For the first time since 2004, when they played at Cleethorpes, they left Trent Bridge for a home fixture. The John Fretwell Sporting Complex, four miles north of Mansfield, was opened in 2008, and hosts Welbeck Colliery CC.*

At Sookholme, July 26, 2015. **No result. Nottinghamshire 83-3** (23 overs) v ‡**Glamorgan.** *Glamorgan's new-ball bowlers had Nottinghamshire in trouble before rain ended play.*

At Nottingham, August 17, 2015 (day/night). **Kent won by five wickets. Nottinghamshire 335** (49.2 overs) (A. D. Hales 81, J. W. A. Taylor 109, D. T. Christian 59; M. E. Claydon 4-66); ‡**Kent 340-5** (48.4 overs) (D. J. Bell-Drummond 73, F. K. Cowdrey 51, S. W. Billings 118*, A. J. Blake

50*). *Attendance: 4,341. Nottinghamshire failed to bat out their allocation, losing their last six wickets for four runs in ten balls as Coles took a hat-trick. Even so, a total of 335 – built around James Taylor's energetic 109 – looked daunting. Kent, however, overhauled it with eight balls to spare, thanks to a mature, measured 118* from Sam Billings.*

At Nottingham, August 19, 2015 (day/night). **No result. Nottinghamshire 256-3** (39 overs) (M. H. Wessels 81, A. D. Hales 58, D. T. Christian 72) v ‡Hampshire. *Attendance: 3,301. Already assured of a home quarter-final, Nottinghamshire were well placed when rain prevented them from setting what looked like being a commanding target. Christian hit five sixes in a 48-ball 72.*

Nottinghamshire away matches

July 30: beat Sussex by four wickets.
August 2: beat Essex by seven wickets.

August 4: beat Lancashire by four wickets.
August 6: beat Middlesex by 49 runs.

SUSSEX

At Horsham, July 26, 2015. **Sussex v Lancashire. Abandoned.** *Play was called off at 1pm. Organisers were expecting a crowd of 5,000, and the ladies' tea tent still managed to take £350.*

At Hove, July 30, 2015 (day/night). **Nottinghamshire won by four wickets.** ‡Sussex 282-9 (50 overs) (J. T. Ball 4-47); **Nottinghamshire 285-6** (46.2 overs) (J. W. A. Taylor 51, B. R. M. Taylor 62). *Attendance: 2,915. Chris Read became the first Nottinghamshire wicketkeeper to take six catches in a List A game, then calmed his team's nerves in a seventh-wicket stand of 56*. After their openers had walloped 96 in 12 overs, Sussex fell 20–30 short of par on a flat pitch.*

At Hove, August 3, 2015 (day/night). **Middlesex won by three runs (D/L). Middlesex 367-6** (50 overs) (D. J. Malan 131, N. R. T. Gubbins 141, J. A. Simpson 50); ‡Sussex 305-9 (40 overs) (L. J. Wright 72, G. J. Bailey 112). *Attendance: 3,064. Middlesex's biggest List A score was built around hundreds from Nick Gubbins and Dawid Malan, who put on 268, their county's second-best one-day partnership. Rain revised Sussex's target to 308 from 40 overs and, thanks to George Bailey's century, they came agonisingly close. He took eight from the first three balls of the last over, but was run out with eight more needed.*

At Hove, August 19, 2015 (day/night). **No result. Sussex 154-3** (32.3 overs) v ‡Essex. *Attendance: 2,816. County debut: P. D. Salt. Philip Salt, who opened the innings, became the 28th cricketer used by Sussex in 2015; he made his debut in a side containing no capped players. A point was enough to secure a home quarter-final for Essex; Sussex had long since given up any hope of progressing.*

Sussex away matches

July 27: lost to Hampshire by 87 runs.
August 2: lost to Kent by eight wickets.

August 5: no result v Glamorgan.
August 17: lost to Warwickshire by four wickets.

WARWICKSHIRE

At Birmingham, August 3, 2015 (day/night). **Warwickshire won by nine wickets.** ‡Glamorgan 179 (48.4 overs) (O. J. Hannon-Dalby 5-27); **Warwickshire 183-1** (38.1 overs) (V. Chopra 80*, I. J. L. Trott 73*). *Attendance: 2,349. Oliver Hannon-Dalby's figures, the best for Warwickshire in List A cricket since 2004, throttled Glamorgan, who struggled on the pitch used for the Third Ashes Test. A second-wicket stand of 157* between Varun Chopra and Jonathan Trott completed a thrashing.*

At Birmingham, August 5, 2015 (day/night). **Hampshire won by 23 runs (D/L). Hampshire 280-7** (50 overs) (L. A. Dawson 67, W. R. Smith 65); ‡Warwickshire 184-9 (31 overs). *Attendance: 2,865. Warwickshire's target, adjusted three times because of rain, was finally fixed at 208 in 31 overs, but they never came close. Liam Dawson, who had shared a fifth-wicket stand of 123 in 22 with Jimmy Adams, pinned Warwickshire's batsmen down with accurate left-arm spin and claimed three victims.*

At Rugby, August 17, 2015. **Warwickshire won by four wickets. Sussex 217** (46.5 overs) (G. J. Bailey 59); ‡**Warwickshire 218-6** (46.4 overs) (W. T. S. Porterfield 100). *Attendance: 1,914. After a washout here in 2014, the sun shone at this pleasant outground. Warwickshire remained in contention for a quarter-final thanks to William Porterfield's second List A century for them.*

At Birmingham, August 19, 2015 (day/night). **Warwickshire v ‡Kent. Abandoned.** *Attendance:* 1,903. *County debut: S. R. Dickson (Kent). A washout, after two abortive attempts to start, ended Warwickshire's quarter-final hopes.*

Warwickshire away matches

July 25: lost to Nottinghamshire by nine wickets.
July 26: no result v Middlesex.

July 29: lost to Essex by 152 runs.
August 2: beat Lancashire by three wickets.

QUARTER-FINALS

At Nottingham, August 25, 2015. **Nottinghamshire won by 49 runs (D/L). Nottinghamshire 170-4** (24 overs) (A. D. Hales 62); ‡**Durham 144** (21.2 overs) (S. R. Patel 4-11). *Attendance: 2,323. A five-hour rain delay left Durham chasing 194 in 24 overs after Nottinghamshire plundered 76 from the last 40 balls of their two-part innings. At 125-3 in the 16th, Durham were on course, but their last seven fell in 35 balls, Samit Patel accounting for four in 14 with his disciplined left-arm spin. Alex Hales had hit 62 from 54 for Nottinghamshire, and Dan Christian 48 from 35, while James Taylor's 29 included three consecutive sixes off Scott Borthwick's leg-spin.*

At Bristol, August 26, 2015. **Gloucestershire won by four wickets. Hampshire 217-7** (34 overs) (J. H. K. Adams 97, W. R. Smith 50); ‡**Gloucestershire 218-6** (33 overs) (M. Klinger 87). *Attendance: 1,235. In a game reduced to 34 overs a side, Klinger top-scored with 87 to take Gloucestershire to their first semi-final since 2009. He received support from Geraint Jones and Jack Taylor, whose explosive 34 off 17 balls secured a tense victory. Defeat was hard on Hampshire skipper Jimmy Adams, who contributed an intelligently paced 97; but he dropped Klinger at cover before he had scored.*

At The Oval, August 27, 2015. **Surrey won by 17 runs (D/L). ‡Surrey 273** (49.5 overs) (J. J. Roy 112); **Kent 233** (37.4 overs) (M. T. Coles 100). *Attendance: 5,263. Kent's target was revised to a demanding 251 in 40 overs, yet they almost snatched victory after all seemed lost. Entering at 101-7, Matt Coles bludgeoned a 73-ball century – his first in List A – with nine sixes and seven fours. Surrey looked incapable of containing Coles, who manipulated the strike superbly: in a tenth-wicket stand of 64, Matt Hunn made a single. Before an 80-minute rainbreak, Jason Roy's 116-ball innings had set Surrey on the way to a formidable total, though James Tredwell and Coles slowed their scoring.*

At Chelmsford, August 27, 2015. **Yorkshire won by 20 runs. Yorkshire 252-9** (50 overs) (J. A. Leaning 72; R. J. W. Topley 4-56); ‡**Essex 232** (47.5 overs) (T. Westley 54, R. N. ten Doeschate 52). *Attendance: 2,160. Liam Plunkett's fine all-round performance sent Yorkshire into the semis. They had plummeted from 163-3 to 195-7, before his 32-ball 49* sped them past 250. Plunkett then took the key Essex wickets of Tom Westley, Ravi Bopara and Jesse Ryder, as Yorkshire seized an initiative they never surrendered.*

SEMI-FINALS

YORKSHIRE v GLOUCESTERSHIRE

At Leeds, September 6, 2015. Gloucestershire won by eight wickets. Toss: Gloucestershire.

Whatever Klinger cost Gloucestershire in airfares was a sound investment. Their one-day captain had flown back to Australia after the quarter-final, but was persuaded to return for the semi and, as it turned out, the final. He hit a magnificent unbeaten 137, and shared an unbroken stand of 177 with Marshall – a one-day best for any Gloucestershire wicket against Yorkshire – to secure an unexpectedly easy victory. Yorkshire had seemed on course to improve a poor record of six wins from 21 cup semi-finals while Lyth was dominating a 103-run opening stand with Lees. But, when he top-edged a hook off Fuller and was caught at long leg for 96, from 88 balls, the bowlers tightened up. After surviving a first-ball lbw shout, Klinger never looked back, and Gloucestershire were already 90 for two when he was joined by Marshall. The pair skilfully pushed the ball around and punished anything loose.

Man of the Match: M. Klinger.   *Attendance:* 7,649.

Yorkshire

A. Lyth c Payne b Fuller	96		S. A. Patterson run out		9
*A. Z. Lees c and b Howell	21		M. D. Fisher not out		9
J. A. Leaning lbw b Howell	8		B 8, l-b 12, w 7		27
†J. M. Bairstow lbw b Norwell	34				
G. S. Ballance c and b Howell	27		1/103 (2) 2/127 (3)	(9 wkts, 50 overs)	263
W. M. H. Rhodes c Fuller b Taylor	4		3/159 (1) 4/198 (4)		
T. T. Bresnan c Klinger b Payne	27		5/208 (6) 6/226 (5)		
R. M. Pyrah c Klinger b Smith	1		7/245 (7) 8/249 (8) 9/263 (9)	10 overs: 60-0	

K. Carver did not bat.

Fuller 7–0–52–1; Payne 9–0–32–1; Norwell 9–0–46–1; Taylor 10–0–46–1; Howell 10–0–37–3; Smith 5–0–30–1.

Gloucestershire

C. D. J. Dent b Fisher		28
*M. Klinger not out		137
†G. H. Roderick c Leaning b Rhodes		18
H. J. H. Marshall not out		78
L-b 2, w 4		6
1/56 (1) 2/90 (3)	(2 wkts, 46.5 overs)	267
	10 overs: 56-1	

B. A. C. Howell, G. O. Jones, J. M. R. Taylor, J. K. Fuller, T. M. J. Smith, D. A. Payne and L. C. Norwell did not bat.

Patterson 8–0–52–0; Bresnan 7–0–40–0; Fisher 9.5–0–50–1; Rhodes 8–0–29–1; Carver 6–0–50–0; Pyrah 5–0–28–0; Lyth 3–0–16–0.

Umpires: J. W. Lloyds and N. A. Mallender.   Third umpire: D. J. Millns.

SURREY v NOTTINGHAMSHIRE

At The Oval, September 7, 2015. Surrey won by four runs. Toss: Surrey.

Kumar Sangakkara produced the highest score of the tournament, his innings a model of acceleration as he shot from 100 to 150 in 29 balls. He mixed drives and ramps in a command performance that lasted 138 deliveries, and came close to exhaustion because a huge boundary towards the gasometers, plus a slow pitch, limited him to 13 fours and a six. Foakes gave diligent assistance in a second-wicket partnership of 87, and Wilson helped Sangakkara up the pace in a stand of 149 for the fourth; Broad went wicketless in a rare county appearance. Nottinghamshire were quickly in trouble: Sam Curran struck twice in the second over, but Greg Smith – in his first List A game for them – steadily rebuilt the innings, first with Patel, then with the more muscular Christian. When Smith was run out, backing up too far at the non-striker's end, 27 were needed from 17 balls. Mullaney had been scoring freely but, with 19 required from two overs, Dernbach conceded five, as well as despatching Read with a superb slower ball. That left Nottinghamshire with too much to do.

Man of the Match: K. C. Sangakkara.   *Attendance:* 4,294.

Surrey

S. M. Davies c Wessels b Gurney	4
B. T. Foakes lbw b Mullaney	42
K. C. Sangakkara c Broad b Ball	166
R. J. Burns c Smith b Mullaney	23
†G. C. Wilson c Wessels b Ball	48
T. K. Curran not out	1
B 1, l-b 7, w 6, n-b 2	16

1/6 (1) 2/93 (2) (5 wkts, 50 overs) 300
3/145 (4) 4/294 (3)
5/300 (5) 10 overs: 37-1

A. Kapil, Z. S. Ansari, S. M. Curran, *G. J. Batty and J. W. Dernbach did not bat.

Gurney 8–1–58–1; Broad 8–1–40–0; Patel 10–0–62–0; Ball 9–0–52–2; Mullaney 10–0–49–2; Christian 5–0–31–0.

Nottinghamshire

M. J. Lumb c Davies b Dernbach	8	*†C. M. W. Read b Dernbach	3
M. H. Wessels b S. M. Curran	0	S. C. J. Broad not out	0
B. R. M. Taylor lbw b S. M. Curran	0	B 1, l-b 4, w 6	11
G. P. Smith run out	124		
S. R. Patel c Davies b Ansari	51	1/1 (2) 2/1 (3) (7 wkts, 50 overs) 296	
D. T. Christian c Ansari b Kapil	54	3/16 (1) 4/107 (5)	
S. J. Mullaney not out	42	5/219 (6) 6/274 (4) 7/284 (8) 10 overs: 36-3	

J. T. Ball and H. F. Gurney did not bat.

Dernbach 10–0–60–2; S. M. Curran 10–0–54–2; T. K. Curran 10–0–60–0; Ansari 9–0–42–1; Batty 7–0–44–0; Kapil 4–0–31–1.

Umpires: I. J. Gould and R. K. Illingworth.   Third umpire: N. G. B. Cook.

FINAL

GLOUCESTERSHIRE v SURREY

Hugh Chevallier

At Lord's, September 19. Gloucestershire won by six runs. Toss: Surrey.

It seemed churlish to grumble. At the stateliest of grounds and illuminated by glorious September sun, one of the masters of the modern game was showing off his skills. With Surrey chasing a meagre 221, Sangakkara saw no need for haste, so he deflected and dabbed, nudged and nurdled, as if his aim was to thread them to glory with minimal effort. He and the solid Burns had just celebrated a century partnership. At 143 for two, they needed another 78 – with more than 15 overs in which to finish their afternoon stroll.

There was no edge, no urgency, no contest: a showpiece final had become an exhibition match. The pitch wore a weary, autumnal complexion, and more than a handful of spectators had nodded off. The Gloucestershire attack, too, were losing their early vitality, after Roy – beaten more often than a wilful Victorian schoolboy – had mistimed to cover, and a hesitant Davies played on, both falling to the speedy Fuller. But then came 22 overs of risk-free batting, and the pall of predictability.

Out of nowhere, Sangakkara flumped a harmless full toss to midwicket off Taylor, who next over foxed Burns with the flight and turn of a proper off-break. No one was dozing now. Klinger, the Gloucestershire captain, had been geeing his side up all the while, but

Tom Shaw, Getty Images

Roaring back: Gloucestershire's Jack Taylor jumps for joy at the downfall of Tom Curran.

they had needed Sangakkara's error to worm their way back in. Wilson came and went, leaving the 17-year-old Sam Curran to keep Surrey going. Five wickets, 30 runs, 33 balls – nothing a cool head couldn't achieve. The 40-year-old Azhar Mahmood should have been just that but, like Burns, he shimmied down the wicket and was stumped, this time off Tom Smith's understated left-arm spin.

If the departures of Azhar, then Tom Curran shifted the momentum west, then it was swinging east again by the start of the 49th over: seven down, Surrey were 11 from victory – probably ten since the tie-breaker was wickets lost, and Gloucestershire had been all out. A tight line from Howell held Surrey to four from the first five balls, before Curran – eager to keep the strike – called his partner for a single. Burke hared for the other end, only for Dent's murderous throw from midwicket to polish him off. At least Curran would be facing.

Payne's first was on a tempting length, and rapid; it hurried Curran, who aimed for the Edrich Stand – and found long-on. Lord's, half empty, was at full volume. Five deliveries left. Batty kept out the next, then swished a shortish ball to midwicket, where Taylor cued West Country delirium by clinging on. Surrey's collapse was complete, which was hard on their No. 11.

The morning star had been Dernbach, bowling with more control than ever he found in an England shirt. Indeed, after Surrey chose to field, many thought he had wrapped up the business of the day with the third-ball dismissal of Klinger, who had averaged 132 in the tournament, but now wafted to Wilson. The batsmen went into their shell, partly because Dernbach and Azhar gave nothing away, partly because wickets were tumbling. At 108 for five in the 25th, Gloucestershire were sinking. Alas, Smith and Jones struggled for fluency, though they just about kept the innings afloat, scoring at three and a half an over in a stand 52.

Jones, in his last game before retirement, picked up speed with Taylor, the only player to use the meat of his bat; until he was athletically caught by Sam Curran at backward point, 250 seemed feasible. As Dernbach began the 48th over, Gloucestershire were 216 for seven. Jones cracked the first delivery for four to reach a crucial fifty, then fell to a

BEST FIGURES IN A LORD'S COUNTY FINAL

6-18	G. Chapple	Lancashire v Essex	1996
6-29	J. Garner	Somerset v Northamptonshire	1979
6-35	**J. W. Dernbach**	**Surrey v Gloucestershire**	**2015**
5-13	S. T. Jefferies	Hampshire v Derbyshire	1988
5-14	J. Garner	Somerset v Surrey	1981
5-26	P. A. J. DeFreitas	Lancashire v Northamptonshire	1990
5-27	R. J. Kirtley	Sussex v Lancashire	2006
5-29	G. R. Dilley	Worcestershire v Middlesex	1988
5-29	R. Illingworth	Yorkshire v Surrey	1965
5-34	I. J. Harvey	Gloucestershire v Glamorgan	2000
5-41	Imran Tahir	Warwickshire v Somerset	2010
5-55	P. W. Jarvis	Somerset v Gloucestershire	1999
5-65	M. J. Hoggard	Yorkshire v Somerset	2002
5-66	N. M. Carter	Warwickshire v Hampshire	2005

HAT-TRICKS IN A LORD'S COUNTY FINAL

K. Higgs	Leicestershire v Surrey	1974
J. M. M. Averis	Gloucestershire v Worcestershire	2004
J. W. Dernbach	**Surrey v Gloucestershire**	**2015**

brisk yorker; Miles edged an inswinger, and Payne failed to pick a slower ball to give Dernbach only the third hat-trick – and the third-best figures – in any Lord's final. Well though he bowled, he did not deserve the last wicket, a full toss missing leg by an embarrassing margin. It seemed the defining moment of drama – until Surrey's implosion.

Man of the Match: J. M. R. Taylor. *Attendance:* 16,578.

Gloucestershire

*M. Klinger c Wilson b Dernbach	0	
C. D. J. Dent c Azhar Mahmood b Dernbach	22	
†G. H. Roderick b Azhar Mahmood	39	
H. J. H. Marshall st Wilson b Batty	18	
B. A. C. Howell b Azhar Mahmood	9	
G. O. Jones b Dernbach	50	
T. M. J. Smith run out	20	
J. M. R. Taylor c S. M. Curran b Dernbach	35	
J. K. Fuller not out	3	

C. N. Miles c Wilson b Dernbach	0
D. A. Payne lbw b Dernbach	0
B 2, l-b 9, w 11, n-b 2	24

1/0 (1) 2/40 (2) 3/79 (4) (47.4 overs) 220
4/100 (5) 5/108 (3) 6/160 (7)
7/209 (8) 8/220 (6) 9/220 (10)
10/220 (11) 10 overs: 44-2

Dernbach 8.4–0–35–6; S. M. Curran 6–0–32–0; T. K. Curran 9–1–51–0; Batty 10–0–43–1; Azhar Mahmood 10–0–28–2; Burke 4–0–20–0.

Surrey

J. J. Roy c Smith b Fuller	11	
S. M. Davies b Fuller	13	
K. C. Sangakkara c sub (W. A. Tavaré) b Taylor	60	
R. J. Burns st Roderick b Taylor	56	
†G. C. Wilson c Klinger b Smith	8	
S. M. Curran c Howell b Payne	37	
Azhar Mahmood st Roderick b Smith	5	
T. K. Curran lbw b Payne	0	

J. E. Burke run out	11
*G. J. Batty c Taylor b Payne	0
J. W. Dernbach not out	0
B 2, l-b 4, w 5, n-b 2	13

1/13 (1) 2/42 (2) 3/143 (3) (49.3 overs) 214
4/148 (4) 5/165 (5) 6/191 (7)
7/192 (8) 8/214 (9) 9/214 (6)
10/214 (10) 10 overs: 28-1

Payne 8.3–0–36–2; Fuller 10–2–34–2; Miles 3–0–24–0; Taylor 10–0–43–3; Howell 8–0–29–0; Smith 10–0–42–2.

Umpires: R. J. Bailey and N. G. B. Cook. Third umpire: P. J. Hartley.

THE UNIVERSITIES IN 2015

RALPH DELLOR AND STEPHEN LAMB

CAMBRIDGE MCCU v NORTHAMPTONSHIRE

At Cambridge, April 2–4. Drawn. Toss: Cambridge MCCU. First-class debuts: J. B. T. Arksey, A. D. Blofield, R. J. Crichard, J. W. Tetley, A. R. Wright. County debut: J. J. Cobb.

Northamptonshire were reduced to 71 for four on the first morning, but a sixth-wicket partnership of 124 between Newton and Duckett steered them from danger. Both scored at a fair rate, sharing 30 boundaries. Northamptonshire declared after Duckett completed a 94-ball hundred, and still had 19 overs at Cambridge before the day was out. They reached 56 for one by the close, but only 35 balls were possible on the second day – enough for Philip Hughes to reach his first fifty against county opposition – and none at all on the third.

Close of play: first day, Cambridge MCCU 56-1 (Hughes 35); second day, Cambridge MCCU 82-3 (Hughes 55, Blofield 1).

Northamptonshire

S. D. Peters lbw b Crichard	24		D. J. Willey st Tetley b Wylie	31
J. J. Cobb b Pollock	10		S. P. Crook not out	10
*A. G. Wakely c Arksey b Arif	23		L-b 6, w 3, n-b 8	17
R. I. Keogh b Arif	9			
R. I. Newton c Hughes b Arksey	94		1/18 (2) (7 wkts dec, 72.5 overs)	357
†A. M. Rossington c Abbott b Shahzad	38		2/45 (1) 3/68 (4)	
B. M. Duckett not out	101		4/71 (3) 5/144 (6) 6/268 (5) 7/326 (8)	

O. P. Stone and Azharullah did not bat.

Shahzad 19–1–103–1; Pollock 17–5–46–1; Crichard 12–1–52–1; Arif 11–2–55–2; Blofield 6–0–48–0; Arksey 3.5–0–32–1; Wylie 4–0–15–1.

Cambridge MCCU

J. B. Abbott lbw b Crook	18	
P. H. Hughes not out	55	
A. R. Wright lbw b Azharullah	0	
†J. W. Tetley c Rossington b Willey	3	
A. D. Blofield not out	1	
B 1, l-b 4	5	

1/56 (1) 2/57 (3)   (3 wkts, 24.5 overs) 82
3/62 (4)

B. A. Wylie, Z. Shahzad, *A. W. Pollock, A. T. Arif, R. J. Crichard and J. B. T. Arksey did not bat.

Willey 6.5–1–36–1; Stone 6–2–18–0; Crook 6–1–10–1; Azharullah 6–2–13–1.

Umpires: M. Burns and N. A. Mallender.

At Cardiff, April 2–4. CARDIFF MCCU drew with GLAMORGAN.

At Southampton, April 2–4. LOUGHBOROUGH MCCU drew with HAMPSHIRE.

OXFORD MCCU v WORCESTERSHIRE

At Oxford, April 2–4. Worcestershire won by an innings and 120 runs. Toss: Worcestershire. First-class debuts: E. J. Ellis, J. O. Grundy, H. C. D. Hughes, M. B. Lake, J. N. McIver, L. A. Webb. County debut: A. P. R. Gidman.

Worcestershire's decision to flout tradition and field first was rewarded when they dismissed the students for 124, left-arm seamer Shantry thriving in helpful conditions. Six of the Oxford side were making their first-class debuts, but it was one of their more experienced members who took them past three figures: Lloyd Paternott made a patient 40 before he was stumped by Cox, standing up to Shantry. Worcestershire already had a small lead by stumps, and even the loss of the second day to rain could not save the students. The county side declared at 339 for six on the third afternoon, then took nine for 51 after tea to seal victory. Shantry returned remarkable match figures of 31.3–19–26–10, his best in first-class cricket, while former Oxford seamer Morris chipped in with six for 39.

Close of play: first day, Worcestershire 155-2 (Mitchell 51, Gidman 4); second day, no play.

Oxford MCCU

S. G. Leach b Andrew	22	– c Cox b Shantry	18
H. C. D. Hughes c Cox b Morris	2	– c Fell b Morris	1
L. M. Sabin b Morris	0	– c Mitchell b Shantry	26
L. C. Paternott st Cox b Shantry	40	– b Shantry	11
L. A. Webb c Gidman b Shantry	23	– c Köhler-Cadmore b Andrew	0
M. B. Lake b D'Oliveira	0	– lbw b Shantry	4
†E. J. Ellis c Köhler-Cadmore b Shantry	8	– c Gidman b Morris	8
*S. D. Weller c Fell b Shantry	7	– not out	6
J. N. McIver c Köhler-Cadmore b Shantry	0	– c Cox b Morris	4
J. O. Grundy c Mitchell b D'Oliveira	0	– c Cox b Morris	4
M. J. L. Kidd not out	4	– c Cox b Shantry	1
B 8, l-b 3, w 5, n-b 2	18	B 2, l-b 6, n-b 4	12

1/26 (2) 2/26 (3) 3/41 (1) (64.1 overs) 124
4/100 (5) 5/103 (4) 6/103 (6)
7/115 (7) 8/115 (9) 9/120 (8) 10/124 (10)

1/8 (2) 2/44 (3) (37.3 overs) 95
3/49 (1) 4/52 (5)
5/59 (6) 6/66 (4) 7/74 (7)
8/78 (9) 9/86 (10) 10/95 (11)

Andrew 17–5–44–1; Morris 15–8–22–2; Shantry 18–10–18–5; Gidman 3–1–6–0; D'Oliveira 11.1–3–23–2. *Second innings*—Andrew 11–2–47–1; Morris 9–1–17–4; D'Oliveira 4–2–15–0; Shantry 13.3–9–8–5.

Worcestershire

*D. K. H. Mitchell c Hughes b McIver	64	B. L. D'Oliveira not out	30
R. K. Oliver b Weller	42		
T. C. Fell st Ellis b McIver	43	B 9, l-b 3, n-b 20	32
A. P. R. Gidman b Lake	43		
A. N. Kervezee c Ellis b McIver	7		
T. Köhler-Cadmore not out	63		(6 wkts dec, 79 overs) 339
†O. B. Cox lbw b Lake	15		

G. M. Andrew, J. D. Shantry and C. A. J. Morris did not bat.

1/65 (2)   2/151 (3)   3/191 (1)
4/199 (5)   5/245 (4)   6/263 (7)

Weller 16–4–64–1; Grundy 18–3–79–0; Kidd 16–0–77–0; Lake 10–1–43–2; McIver 19–0–64–3.

Umpires: N. G. B. Cook and T. Lungley.

At Taunton, April 2–4. DURHAM MCCU drew with SOMERSET.

At Hove, April 2–4. LEEDS/BRADFORD MCCU drew with SUSSEX.

CAMBRIDGE MCCU v LEICESTERSHIRE

At Cambridge, April 7–9. Leicestershire won by 344 runs. Toss: Cambridge MCCU. County debuts: M. J. Cosgrove, N. D. Pinner.

Cambridge reduced Leicestershire to 161 for seven on the first day after Mark Cosgrove, making his debut for his new county as captain, was dismissed for a typically belligerent 92. It required 73 from Naik at No. 9 to sneak them past 300. Cambridge faltered badly against the seamers, with Freckingham taking five quick wickets to reduce them to 89 for nine, before a last-wicket stand of 51. Leicestershire pounded home their advantage in the second innings, Robson falling two short of a hundred, and Neil Pinner beginning a one-year contract in spectacular style with an unbeaten 165 from 203 balls. Cambridge then folded a second time.

Close of play: first day, Cambridge MCCU 64-4 (Ellison 22, Blofield 1); second day, Leicestershire 339-4 (Pinner 165, Wells 30).

Leicestershire

D. J. Redfern c Wylie b Shahzad	0	– c Tetley b Shahzad 3
A. J. Robson b Pollock	14	– c Abbott b Wylie 98
E. J. H. Eckersley b Pollock	1	– c Tetley b Pollock 15
*M. J. Cosgrove b Shahzad	92	
N. D. Pinner lbw b Crichard	32	– (4) not out 165
†N. J. O'Brien c Tetley b Arif	7	– (5) c Wright b Shahzad 18
T. J. Wells b Shahzad	1	– (6) not out 30
B. A. Raine c and b Wylie	44	
J. K. H. Naik c Crichard b Blofield	73	
O. H. Freckingham c Pollock b Blofield	15	
A. Sheikh not out	4	
B 6, l-b 7, w 1, n-b 6	20	L-b 2, n-b 8 10

1/0 (1) 2/15 (3) 3/22 (2) (74.2 overs) 303
4/100 (5) 5/127 (6) 6/129 (7)
7/161 (4) 8/249 (8) 9/298 (10) 10/303 (9)

1/14 (1) (4 wkts dec, 85 overs) 339
2/39 (3) 3/180 (2)
4/235 (5)

Shahzad 17–4–49–3; Pollock 19–5–75–2; Arif 6–0–36–1; Crichard 13–3–61–1; Blofield 10.2–0–33–2; Wylie 9–2–36–1. *Second innings*—Shahzad 17–4–40–2; Pollock 10–2–38–1; Arif 11–1–60–0; Blofield 19–1–100–0; Wylie 27–3–96–1; Crichard 1–0–3–0.

Cambridge MCCU

J. B. Abbott c O'Brien b Sheikh	2	– c Cosgrove b Sheikh 2
P. H. Hughes c Pinner b Raine	8	– lbw b Wells 19
†A. R. Wright lbw b Raine	0	– c Robson b Freckingham 8
J. W. Tetley lbw b Wells	21	– lbw b Naik 16
H. R. C. Ellison c O'Brien b Freckingham	24	– c Pinner b Freckingham 2
A. D. Blofield c Robson b Freckingham	2	– (7) not out 30
B. A. Wylie c Pinner b Freckingham	8	– (8) c O'Brien b Sheikh 4
Z. Shahzad c Cosgrove b Freckingham	0	– (9) lbw b Sheikh 0
*A. W. Pollock c Redfern b Freckingham	15	– (10) c Robson b Naik 15
A. T. Arif c Raine b Sheikh	39	– (6) lbw b Redfern 17
R. J. Crichard not out	11	– run out 0
B 8, l-b 7, w 1, n-b 12	28	B 10, l-b 20, n-b 15 45

1/2 (1) 2/5 (3) 3/16 (2) (38.5 overs) 140
4/45 (4) 5/68 (5) 6/70 (7)
7/74 (8) 8/78 (9) 9/89 (6) 10/140 (10)

1/16 (1) 2/63 (2) (38.5 overs) 158
3/63 (3) 4/73 (5)
5/97 (4) 6/101 (6) 7/121 (8)
8/121 (9) 9/146 (10) 10/158 (11)

Sheikh 10.5–1–48–2; Raine 10–4–17–2; Freckingham 11–2–39–5; Wells 7–3–21–1. *Second innings*—Sheikh 9–2–42–3; Raine 6–2–8–0; Wells 6–2–22–1; Freckingham 7–2–23–2; Naik 9.5–0–29–2; Redfern 1–0–4–1.

Umpires: N. G. C. Cowley and B. J. Debenham.

At Chester-le-Street, April 7–9. DURHAM MCCU lost to DURHAM by 379 runs.

At Bristol, April 7–9. CARDIFF MCCU lost to GLOUCESTERSHIRE by 217 runs.

At Nottingham, April 7–9. LOUGHBOROUGH MCCU drew with NOTTINGHAMSHIRE.

OXFORD MCCU v MIDDLESEX

At Oxford, April 7–9. Middlesex won by seven wickets. Toss: Oxford MCCU.

Oxford's brave decision to bat first backfired against a Middlesex attack including Finn, Murtagh and Harris, who shared eight wickets to dismiss the students for 124. Only Zimbabwean all-rounder Malcolm Lake offered any resistance, scoring more than half the runs with a counter-attacking 66. He then took two wickets with his medium-pace and, with seamers Abidine Sakande and Sam Weller each picking up three, a strong Middlesex line-up collapsed to 123 for nine, before Tom Helm and Finn put on 70. Oxford relied on their own last-wicket pairing to reach 218 in their second innings, but Middlesex, guided by a sensible unbeaten 60 from Malan, knocked off their target of 150 with ease.

Close of play: first day, Middlesex 98-6 (Simpson 2, Harris 1); second day, Oxford MCCU 168-8 (McIver 13, Sakande 5).

Oxford MCCU

S. G. Leach c Malan b Finn	7	– b Harris	41
H. C. D. Hughes c Malan b Murtagh	0	– lbw b Murtagh	4
L. M. Sabin lbw b Murtagh	6	– c and b Stirling	25
L. C. Paternott c Robson b Finn	2	– c Gubbins b Helm	3
L. A. Webb c Robson b Harris	13	– lbw b Stirling	32
M. B. Lake c Balbirnie b Murtagh	66	– c Simpson b Harris	12
†E. J. Ellis c Simpson b Finn	8	– c Simpson b Murtagh	2
*S. D. Weller c Simpson b Harris	1	– c Stirling b Murtagh	0
J. N. McIver b Stirling	4	– c Simpson b Helm	41
A. Sakande b Harris	0	– lbw b Finn	6
J. O. Grundy not out	11	– not out	21
B 4, n-b 2	6	B 12, l-b 14, w 1, n-b 4	31

1/1 (2) 2/13 (1) 3/15 (4)   (46.1 overs) 124
4/15 (3) 5/66 (5) 6/101 (7)
7/107 (6) 8/107 (6) 9/108 (10) 10/124 (9)

1/29 (2) 2/88 (3)   (77.2 overs) 218
3/99 (1) 4/101 (4)
5/121 (6) 6/134 (7) 7/138 (8)
8/156 (5) 9/169 (10) 10/218 (9)

Murtagh 13–3–26–3; Finn 10–2–25–3; Harris 13–4–35–2; Helm 9–3–34–1; Stirling 1.1–1–0–1.
Second innings—Murtagh 15–3–41–3; Finn 13–5–24–1; Harris 16–5–43–2; Helm 17.2–5–42–2; Stirling 31–8–31–2; Malan 3–0–11–0.

Middlesex

N. R. T. Gubbins c Ellis b Weller	32	– (2) c Ellis b Sakande	17
S. D. Robson lbw b Lake	24	– (1) b Weller	2
*N. R. D. Compton c Ellis b Sakande	9	– c Lake b Grundy	39
D. J. Malan lbw b Grundy	1	– not out	60
P. R. Stirling c McIver b Weller	11	– not out	19
†J. A. Simpson c Paternott b Lake	9		
A. Balbirnie b Sakande	5		
J. A. R. Harris c Paternott b Sakande	5		
T. J. Murtagh c Ellis b Weller	5		
T. G. Helm c Weller b Grundy	27		
S. T. Finn not out	41		
B 9, l-b 4, w 3, n-b 8	24	B 4, l-b 3, w 6	13

1/54 (2) 2/73 (1) 3/74 (4)   (73 overs) 193
4/85 (3) 5/85 (5) 6/91 (7)
7/107 (8) 8/112 (9) 9/123 (6) 10/193 (10)

1/11 (1)   (3 wkts, 38.4 overs) 150
2/31 (2) 3/94 (3)

Sakande 17–3–38–3; Weller 22–10–26–3; Grundy 13–1–41–2; Lake 15–3–41–2; McIver 6–1–34–0. *Second innings*—Sakande 12–0–44–1; Weller 8–1–31–1; Lake 6–1–30–0; Grundy 7–1–16–1; McIver 5–0–20–0; Leach 0.4–0–2–0.

Umpires: I. D. Blackwell and S. J. O'Shaughnessy.

At Leeds, April 7–9. LEEDS/BRADFORD MCCU drew with YORKSHIRE.

At Cambridge, April 12–13 (not first-class). **Derbyshire won by an innings and 264 runs.**
Derbyshire 535-6 dec (84 overs) (B. A. Godleman 60, M. J. Guptill 161, W. L. Madsen 133, S. J.
Thakor 60*; A. P. Hunt 3-112); ‡**Cambridge MCCU 95** (27 overs) (M. H. A. Footitt 4-35) **and 176**
(59.2 overs) (C. T. Lowen 53; W. J. Durston 3-27; S. J. Thakor 4-24). *County debut:* S. J. Thakor.
*The match was scheduled for three days but Cambridge did not last two. Put in, Derbyshire raced to
535-6 at more than six an over. New Zealander Martin Guptill smashed 161 from 108 balls; Wayne
Madsen's 155-ball 133 was sedate by comparison. Cambridge's first innings came and went in 27
overs. They made a slightly better fist of it after following on, opener Charles Lowen scoring 53, but
still fell to a huge defeat.*

At Chelmsford, April 12–14. CARDIFF MCCU drew with ESSEX.

At Canterbury, April 12–14. LOUGHBOROUGH MCCU drew with KENT.

At Manchester, April 12–14. LEEDS/BRADFORD MCCU drew with LANCASHIRE.

At Oxford, April 12–14 (not first-class). **Drawn.** ‡**Surrey 420-7 dec** (75 overs) (K. P. Pietersen 170,
G. C. Wilson 119*; S. D. Weller 3-81) **and 335-7 dec** (75 overs) (Z. S. Ansari 53, S. M. Davies 53,
J. J. Roy 85, G. J. Batty 68*; J. O. Grundy 4-78); **Oxford MCCU 224** (66.5 overs) (J. N. McIver
83; C. T. Tremlett 5-30) **and 212-2** (50 overs) (S. G. Leach 110*). *All the attention, including a
phalanx of cameras, was focused on Kevin Pietersen, who was playing red-ball cricket for the first
time since the 2013-14 Ashes, in a bid to regain his Test place. He did not disappoint, rescuing
Surrey from 113-5 with a dismissive 170 from 149 balls, and sharing a stand of 303 with Gary
Wilson. Chris Tremlett then ran through the Oxford top order, although Surrey were held up by
No. 9 Jack McIver before speeding to another declaration; Pietersen, his work done, looked on from
the pavilion. Oxford batted through 50 overs to save the match, with opener Steve Leach making
an unbeaten century.*

At Birmingham, April 12–14. DURHAM MCCU drew with WARWICKSHIRE.

THE UNIVERSITY MATCHES IN 2015

At Cambridge, June 12. **Cambridge University won by four wickets.** ‡**Oxford University 140**
(20 overs) (M. J. Winter 45; B. A. Wylie 3-20); **Cambridge University 141-6** (19 overs) (A. D.
Blofield 38, B. A. Wylie 37). *After washouts in 2013 and 2014, the Varsity Twenty20 match steered
clear of bad weather as Cambridge, inspired by slow-left-arm all-rounder Ben Wylie, completed a
comfortable win. Earlier, they had lost the women's match by 129 runs after Oxford wicketkeeper
Sian Kelly struck 127* off 72 balls during an unbroken opening partnership of 217 with Sarah
Attrill (57*).*

At Lord's, June 27. **Oxford University won by 43 runs.** ‡**Oxford University 202-8** (50 overs)
(S. A. Westaway 53; A. R. Patel 3-22); **Cambridge University 159** (34.2 overs) (O. J. Jones 4-27).
*Sam Westaway's half-century helped Oxford recover from 117-6 to reach 202-8, before medium-
pacer Owain Jones took 4-27 as Cambridge were bowled out in under 35 overs. Westaway claimed
seven victims behind the stumps to complete a fine all-round display, and clinch the 50-over game.*

CAMBRIDGE UNIVERSITY v OXFORD UNIVERSITY

At Cambridge, June 30–July 2. Cambridge University won by five wickets. Toss: Oxford University.
First-class debuts: D. Chohan, A. P. Hunt, A. R. Patel, P. J. A. Tice; T. H. Claughton, J. S. D.
Gnodde, M. S. T. Hughes.
 Cambridge's first victory in the four-day fixture since 2011 was achieved late on the third afternoon
when Alex Blofield cruised to an unbeaten 73 to cap an outstanding performance in which he made
his maiden first-class hundred, held four catches and took an important wicket. The foundations for

victory were laid on a sunny first day when seamers Alasdair Pollock and Ruari Crichard shared nine wickets as Oxford collapsed from 71 without loss to 156 all out. Blofield ensured Cambridge had a big lead, but their rivals were harder to budge in their second innings, as Matt Hughes added 112 with Matt Winter on his way to a debut first-class hundred. Blofield removed Winter in the second over of a much cooler third day, and the spin duo of Ben Wylie and Avish Patel worked their way through the rest. Cambridge lost three quick wickets to the impressive Owain Jones, but Blofield saw them home.

Close of play: first day, Cambridge University 99-3 (Hearne 43, Blofield 11); second day, Oxford University 160-1 (Hughes 77, Winter 56).

Oxford University

M. S. T. Hughes c Blofield b Hunt	41	– c Abbott b Patel	116
T. H. Claughton b Pollock	29	– lbw b Hunt	19
*M. J. Winter c Blofield b Pollock	0	– lbw b Blofield	56
O. J. Jones c Hunt b Crichard	32	– c Blofield b Patel	24
J. S. D. Gnodde b Pollock	3	– lbw b Patel	3
R. J. O'Grady c and b Crichard	15	– st Tice b Patel	11
†S. A. Westaway c Wylie b Crichard	14	– b Wylie	33
S. J. Cato not out	12	– c Abbott b Wylie	2
A. Sakande c Blofield b Crichard	0	– lbw b Wylie	33
J. Marsden lbw b Crichard	4	– not out	9
S. V. S. Mylavarapu b Pollock	4	– c Abbott b Patel	0
L-b 1, w 1	2	B 11, l-b 6, w 2	19

1/71 (2) 2/71 (3) 3/71 (1)   (45.5 overs) 156
4/78 (5) 5/117 (6) 6/122 (4)
7/143 (7) 8/143 (9) 9/149 (10) 10/156 (11)

1/48 (2) 2/160 (3)   (101.4 overs) 325
3/205 (4) 4/213 (5)
5/244 (1) 6/245 (6) 7/248 (8)
8/311 (9) 9/322 (7) 10/325 (11)

Pollock 18.5–7–43–4; Crichard 15–1–62–5; Hunt 7–1–38–1; Wylie 5–1–12–0. *Second innings—* Pollock 19–5–52–0; Crichard 12–0–65–0; Hunt 11–1–35–1; Wylie 14–8–14–3; Patel 29.4–2–88–5; Blofield 16–1–54–1.

Cambridge University

J. B. Abbott c Sakande b Jones	14	– lbw b Jones	19
P. H. Hughes lbw b Marsden	16	– c Mylavarapu b Jones	6
D. Chohan c Westaway b Cato	6	– lbw b Jones	0
A. G. Hearne c Westaway b Marsden	43	– b Hughes b Sakande	29
A. D. Blofield c Marsden b Sakande	105	– not out	73
*A. W. Pollock c Sakande b Jones	2	– c Winter b Cato	4
B. A. Wylie c Jones b Cato	26	– not out	1
A. R. Patel c Westaway b Marsden	61		
†P. J. A. Tice c Sakande b Jones	7		
R. J. Crichard c Hughes b Mylavarapu	21		
A. P. Hunt not out	19		
B 5, l-b 12, w 1, n-b 8	26	L-b 3, w 2, n-b 2	7

1/19 (1) 2/35 (2) 3/74 (3)   (107 overs) 346
4/107 (4) 5/109 (6) 6/162 (7)
7/293 (5) 8/301 (8) 9/308 (9) 10/346 (10)

1/12 (2)   (5 wkts, 37.2 overs) 139
2/13 (3) 3/27 (1)
4/106 (4) 5/130 (6)

Sakande 21–7–52–1; Jones 26–12–70–4; Marsden 21–4–72–2; Mylavarapu 25–5–71–1; Cato 12–2–43–2; Gnodde 2–0–21–0. *Second innings—* Jones 10–4–21–3; Mylavarapu 9–1–28–0; Cato 7–1–27–1; Marsden 6–1–27–0; Sakande 5.2–0–33–1.

Umpires: P. R. Pollard and R. J. Warren.

This was the 170th University Match, a first-class fixture dating back to 1827. Cambridge have won 59 and Oxford 55, with 56 drawn. It was played at Lord's until 2000.

MCC UNIVERSITIES CHAMPIONSHIP

		Played	Won	Lost	1st-inns wins	1st-inns losses	Drawn	Bonus Points	Points
1	Cardiff (3).............	5	1	0	2	0	2	43	90
2	Leeds/Bradford (2).....	5	0	0	4	0	1	39	84
3	Loughborough (1)	5	1	0	2	2	0	49	83*
4	Oxford (5).............	5	0	0	1	3	1	38	53
5	Cambridge (4)	5	0	2	2	1	0	30	50
6	Durham (6)...........	5	0	0	0	5	0	31	31

* *Loughborough were docked 3pts for a slow over-rate.*

*Outright win = 17pts; 1st-innings win in a drawn match = 10pts; no result on 1st innings = 5pts;
abandoned = 5pts.*

WINNERS

2001	Loughborough	2006	Oxford	2011	Cardiff
2002	Loughborough	2007	Cardiff/Glamorgan	2012	Cambridge
2003	Loughborough	2008	Loughborough	2013	Leeds/Bradford
2004	Oxford	2009	Leeds/Bradford	2014	Loughborough
2005	Loughborough	2010	Durham	2015	Cardiff

MCC UNIVERSITIES CHALLENGE FINAL

At Lord's, June 23. **Leeds/Bradford MCCU won by 117 runs. Leeds/Bradford MCCU 366-4**
(50 overs) (S. F. G. Bullen 86, W. T. Root 135, L. P. Weston 67*); ‡**Cardiff MCCU 249** (40.4 overs)
(H. P. Rouse 3-36). *Billy Root, Joe's left-handed younger brother, struck nine sixes in his 69-ball
135 against a Cardiff attack which included Kamau Leverock, the nephew of former Bermuda
spinner Dwayne. Leeds/Bradford's mammoth total was never under threat. Harry Rouse's three
wickets included that of younger sibling Tim; they embraced before Tim left the field.*

MCC IN 2015

S T E V E N   L Y N C H

The long-running argument over the redevelopment of Lord's continued to keep the lights burning late in the MCC committee room. Towards the end of the year, discussions centred on what action to take over a new £100m offer to build luxury flats on the land above the disused railway tunnels at the Nursery end of the ground.

Back in 1999, Railtrack decided to auction the leasehold of the land, which was acquired by a local developer, who offered more than MCC were prepared to pay. Ironically, Gerald Corbett, then Railtrack's chief executive, is now MCC's chairman, and playing a lead role in the negotiations, along with Roger Knight, the former MCC secretary who is the president for 2016.

MCC still have ambitious redevelopment plans, using their own money, although much depends on whether the next staging agreement for international cricket in England continues to allocate two Tests to Lord's each summer after 2019. With that uncertainty in mind it was decided to delay the rebuilding of the Tavern and Allen Stands, but work did start on the new Warner Stand, which was demolished over the winter. However, the unexpected discovery of asbestos deep in the foundations delayed construction of the replacement, and the new stand was not due to be ready for the first Test of the 2016 season.

MCC's world cricket committee, currently chaired by Mike Brearley, continued to act as an influential think tank for the global game. In 2015, they called for cricket to explore the possibility of becoming an Olympic sport, and also asked ICC to reconsider the decision to reduce the 2019 World Cup to ten teams. The committee's long-term advocacy of the pink ball for floodlit Test cricket was realised in November in Adelaide, where the first day/night Test was a success, particularly with the local public. New Zealand's captain in that game, Brendon McCullum – who will be playing Twenty20 cricket for Middlesex in 2016 – agreed to deliver the Cowdrey Spirit of Cricket Lecture during the summer, and was due to join the committee in October.

Two distinguished former MCC presidents died during the year: Tom Graveney, the first ex-professional cricketer to hold the post (in 2005), and Lord Griffiths (1990), who also chaired the working party that set up the ECB. Early in 2016 came more sad news, with the death of Tony Fleming, a popular administrator who was the first manager of the indoor school in 1977.

MCC's out-match list grew once again. In 2015, a total of 473 fixtures were arranged for men's teams, of which 225 were won, 117 lost, 73 drawn and two tied; 56 were abandoned or cancelled. MCC women's teams had 32 fixtures, of which 12 were won, six lost, two drawn, and 12 abandoned or cancelled.

New ground was broken during an MCC tour of Suriname and Panama, while other teams visited Denmark, Menorca, Nepal and – at the end of the year, to coincide with the senior England tour – South Africa.

MCC v YORKSHIRE

Ali Martin

At Abu Dhabi, March 22–24, 2015 (day/night). Yorkshire won by nine wickets. Toss: MCC. First-class debut: W. M. H. Rhodes.

In its sixth year in Abu Dhabi, played under floodlights and with a pink Kookaburra ball, the season-opening Champion County fixture saw Yorkshire efficiently despatch a strong MCC side inside three days. They also denied Cook time in the middle ahead of the Test series in the Caribbean. In an MCC team led by his former Test opening partner Compton – who nicked the first ball of the season – Cook was making his first appearance since the selectors dropped him from the one-day team shortly before the World Cup. To judge by his pre-match interview, in which he claimed "hindsight has probably proved them wrong", it was a decision that still rankled. On the field, he faced just six deliveries in the first innings, falling lbw when Sidebottom followed three outswingers with a straight one, and 30 in the second, when he duffed a pull off Brooks to midwicket. Instead, the bulk of Cook's match was spent watching from slip as Lyth hit his 15th first-class century, and an unbeaten 46 in a small fourth-innings chase, to make an early case for a Test debut; but, like Rashid – whose leg-spinning variations claimed six for 123 in the match – his role in the Caribbean would be limited to carrying drinks. For MCC, Hildreth and Mitchell produced compact half-centuries in the first innings, and Compton a characteristically watchful 74 in the second, but their attack was undermined by an early groin injury to Onions. Yorkshire's machine was better-oiled: Will Rhodes's first-class debut reaped three cheap wickets and a patient 61, and Lees – deputising while Andrew Gale served the rest of his suspension for the previous season's Ashwell Prince fracas – claimed his first victory as captain.

Close of play: first day, Yorkshire 82-2 (Lyth 53, Patterson 2); second day, MCC 13-0 (Compton 7, Cook 2).

MCC

*N. R. D. Compton c Bairstow b Sidebottom	0	– c Bairstow b Rhodes	74
A. N. Cook lbw b Sidebottom	3	– c Rashid b Brooks	5
M. A. Carberry c Lyth b Patterson	36	– c Bresnan b Lyth	23
J. C. Hildreth lbw b Bresnan	89	– lbw b Rashid	49
D. K. H. Mitchell lbw b Rhodes	54	– lbw b Rashid	9
Z. S. Ansari not out	24	– b Brooks	15
†S. W. Billings b Brooks	0	– c Bairstow b Brooks	26
C. Rushworth c Bairstow b Brooks	0	– lbw b Patterson	6
G. Onions lbw b Rhodes	1	– (11) c Rhodes b Rashid	0
A. E. N. Riley lbw b Rashid	3	– (9) not out	5
M. P. Dunn c Lyth b Rashid	1	– (10) c Rhodes b Rashid	0
B 6, n-b 4	10	B 2, l-b 6	8

1/0 (1) 2/7 (2) 3/81 (3)   (67.5 overs) 221   1/30 (2) 2/80 (3)   (76.5 overs) 220
4/160 (4) 5/185 (5) 6/186 (7)   3/125 (1) 4/140 (5)
7/186 (8) 8/196 (9) 9/215 (10) 10/221 (11)   5/176 (6) 6/193 (4) 7/210 (8)
                                                      8/213 (7) 9/220 (10) 10/220 (11)

Sidebottom 12–5–27–2; Brooks 12–2–57–2; Bresnan 10–2–33–1; Patterson 12–4–31–1; Rashid 14.5–1–51–2; Lyth 1–0–6–0; Rhodes 6–3–10–2. *Second innings*—Sidebottom 8–1–17–0; Brooks 13–6–22–3; Patterson 13–6–39–1; Bresnan 4–1–21–0; Rashid 22.5–3–72–4; Lyth 10–2–29–1; Rhodes 6–0–12–1.

" A few even cheered, which some thought rather poor form, until it was pointed out that the opposition were Australia, and the usual conventions did not apply."
Drink up! Drink up! And Miss the Game, page 27

Yorkshire

A. Lyth lbw b Riley	113	– not out	46
*A. Z. Lees c Billings b Dunn	11	– c Billings b Riley	8
J. A. Leaning c Mitchell b Ansari	14	– not out	13
S. A. Patterson b Riley	36		
†J. M. Bairstow lbw b Rushworth	0		
W. M. H. Rhodes c Cook b Rushworth	61		
A. J. Hodd c Billings b Dunn	57		
A. U. Rashid lbw b Carberry	42		
T. T. Bresnan c Cook b Riley	12		
R. J. Sidebottom not out	3		
J. A. Brooks c Hildreth b Ansari	2		
B 5, l-b 14, n-b 2	21	L-b 6	6

1/39 (2) 2/79 (3) 3/170 (4)   (114.1 overs) 372   1/42 (2)   (1 wkt, 20 overs) 73
4/173 (5) 5/195 (1) 6/299 (7)
7/319 (6) 8/348 (9) 9/369 (8) 10/372 (11)

Onions 3.5–0–8–0; Rushworth 22–7–69–2; Dunn 19.1–0–89–2; Riley 31–4–90–3; Ansari 28.1–4–74–2; Mitchell 8–1–23–0; Carberry 2–2–0–1. *Second innings*—Rushworth 6–2–12–0; Dunn 6–2–13–0; Carberry 3–1–6–0; Riley 4–0–28–1; Ansari 1–0–8–0.

Umpires: M. J. D. Bodenham and P. J. Hartley.

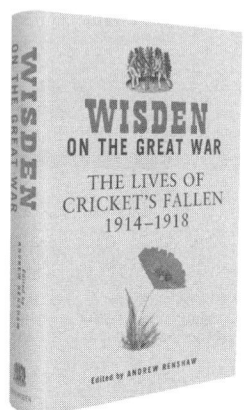

THE MINOR COUNTIES IN 2015

Philip August

Unlike the first-class game, Minor County cricket is awash with slow bowlers: the ten leading wicket-takers in the 2015 Championship comprised an off-spinner and, remarkably, nine slow left-armers. It all felt more like Bangladesh than Banbury. Since many pitches are batsman-friendly – Buckinghamshire pulled off chases of 490 for four and 352 for two – it would suggest the spinners possess some quality. Indeed, their success proves English cricket need not always be dominated by seamers and greentops.

Last summer the Minor Counties flirted with a Twenty20 tournament. Cheshire became the first winners and – after it was confirmed there would be no repeat in 2016 – the last, for now. Perhaps the fact that the clothes were white and the ball red symbolised the lack of commitment to the shortest format.

Cumberland headed the Eastern Division before defeating Oxfordshire in the Championship final to become Minor County champions for the third time. They won five games in the division, all by comfortable margins. In their first match, when they beat Northumberland by 131 runs, seamer Richard Gleeson and Toby Bulcock – a member of the slow-left army – shared 17 wickets; against Bedfordshire, Bulcock returned figures of 9.4–8–3–5. After crushing Cambridgeshire by an innings and 59 in their final division match, Cumberland headed the table by 31 points. Captain Gary Pratt became their leading century-maker, when he hit his 11th overall, against Lincolnshire.

In second place, having won their first three games, were **Buckinghamshire**. Their opening match was extraordinary. In answer to Hertfordshire's 487 for two declared, they were dismissed for 290. Hertfordshire chose to bat again, and set Buckinghamshire a monumental 490. Thanks to an unbeaten 244 from Tom Smith, they got there for the loss of four wickets. All told, 1,559 runs flowed in three days. Buckinghamshire then hunted down 352 to beat Bedfordshire by eight wickets, but lost heavily to Northumberland and Staffordshire.

Staffordshire played positive cricket under new captain Kadeer Ali, and Paul Byrne's slow left-arm was instrumental in their two biggest wins, taking six for 35 against Suffolk and seven for 82 against Buckinghamshire. In the Suffolk game, wicketkeeper Alex Mellor scored 208 not out and held 11 catches; Warwickshire gave him a contract for 2016.

Lincolnshire's fourth place should perhaps have been better after beginning with three wins in four games. Having come bottom in the previous two seasons, **Northumberland**, who won three and lost three, finished mid-table – an achievement that justified their strong partnership with Durham, and their commitment to fielding younger players. Captain Jacques du Toit scored heavily, while 18-year-old slow left-armer Ollie McGee took 34 wickets in five games.

The **Hertfordshire** all-rounder Tanveer Sikandar had an outstanding season, winning the Wilfred Rhodes Trophy for a batting average of 82. He made an unbeaten 209, and Eddie Ballard an undefeated 248, in the first innings of that match against Buckinghamshire; they put on 431 for the third wicket – the highest partnership since Minor County cricket began in 1895.

Bedfordshire recorded their first Championship win since 2010 when they beat Suffolk by five wickets in a nervy pursuit of 185. George Thurstance and Luke Thomas led the way, both scoring over 700 runs.

It was a discouraging summer for **Cambridgeshire**, who had been in the top three for the previous four years. They lost four games, but had the compensation of overcoming East Anglian rivals Norfolk and Suffolk. Captain Paul McMahon took 46 wickets at 14 to win the Frank Edwards Trophy. **Norfolk** were disappointed to come ninth, though Chris Brown took his 400th wicket, and the ever-reliable James Spelman passed 4,000 runs.

Suffolk had not finished in the bottom half of the table since 2001, so the wooden spoon was quite a comedown. The usually reliable Tom Huggins hit 168 and 132 against Bedfordshire, yet managed only 157 in his other ten innings as they suffered five defeats.

In the Western Division, **Oxfordshire** enjoyed success on all fronts. They lost their opening match, to Berkshire, before convincingly winning their next five. Aged just 15, Harrison Ward, making his debut against Herefordshire, became the youngest person ever to hit a century in the Minor County Championship, while off-spinner Harvey Eltham, aged 17, had the best average (13) by anyone claiming more than ten wickets.

Bottom and winless in 2014, unbeaten **Berkshire** were runners-up. Chris Peploe, yet another left-arm spinner, was alone in taking 50 wickets. There was an encouraging start for **Shropshire**, who brushed Cheshire aside in a two-day victory; Tom Weston, aged 20, and Ross Aucott, 19, put on a county-record 177 for the eighth wicket, but they had to wait until the last match for their next success, by ten wickets against Devon.

Cornwall had a solid summer, the highlight their triumph in the 50-over Trophy. In the Championship, they relied on new signing Brad Wadlan, from Herefordshire: he took 46 wickets with – inevitably – left-arm spin, and scored 560 runs. **Herefordshire** themselves had a mixed season, but drew motivation from comfortable victories over Devon and Cheshire, the bottom two teams.

For **Wales**, who climbed two places to sixth, the main achievement came at Usk, where they made 404 to beat Cornwall by five wickets, with Sean Griffiths hitting 133 not out. Their wins against Dorset and Herefordshire aside, **Wiltshire** secured only one batting point in four games. Although the bowlers prospered – Joe King, Tahir Afridi and Ed Young shared 74 wickets – they could not make up for their batsmen's failings.

Tom Hicks, the former **Dorset** captain, retired at the end of the season after amassing 2,245 runs and 256 wickets in 83 Championship games. They managed just one win, as did **Cheshire** who suffered from a lack of runs. A total of six batting points was the lowest in either division. Cheshire's use of 25 players in the Championship prevented a cohesive team spirit.

Winless **Devon** hit rock bottom; not since three-day fixtures were introduced in 2001 had they finished last in their division.

MINOR COUNTIES CHAMPIONSHIP, 2015

	Eastern Division	P	W	L	D	Bonus points Batting	Bonus points Bowling	Total points
1	CUMBERLAND (2)	6	5	0	1	17	24	125
2	Buckinghamshire (6)	6	4	2	0	12	18	94
3	Staffordshire (1)	6	3	2	1	18	20	90
4	Lincolnshire (4)	6	3	1	2	10	21	87
5	Northumberland (10)	6	3	3	0	14	24	86
6	Hertfordshire (8)	6	2	3	1	18	20	72*
7	Bedfordshire (9)	6	1	3	2	19	21	64
8	Cambridgeshire (3)	6	2	4	0	10	23	63*
9	Norfolk (7)	6	1	2	3	12	23	63
10	Suffolk (5)	6	1	5	0	16	22	54

	Western Division	P	W	L	D	Bonus points Batting	Bonus points Bowling	Total points
1	OXFORDSHIRE (7)	6	5	1	0	18	24	122
2	Berkshire (10)	6	4	0	2	13	24	109
3	Shropshire (6)	6	2	1	3	22	24	90
4	Cornwall (9)	6	3	2	1	15	22	89
5	Herefordshire (2)	6	2	3	1	17	22	75
6	Wales (8)	6	2	2	2	13	21	74
7	Wiltshire (1)	6	2	2	2	9	24	73
8	Dorset (5)	6	1	3	2	8	19	53*†
9	Cheshire (4)	6	1	4	1	6	20	50†
10	Devon (3)	6	0	4	2	16	24	48

Win = 16pts; draw = 4pts.

*   *2pt penalty for slow over-rate.*

†   *8pts awarded for a drawn game in which the first innings was not completed.*

Cambridgeshire finished above Norfolk by dint of having more wins.

LEADING AVERAGES, 2015

BATTING (300 runs in 6 completed innings, average 45.00)

		M	I	NO	R	HS	100	50	Avge	Ct/St
1	Tanveer Sikandar (*Hertfordshire*)	4	8	1	575	209*	1	5	82.14	1
2	G. R. Thurstance (*Bedfordshire*)	6	12	2	730	171	2	5	73.00	6
3	S. G. Leach (*Shropshire*)	6	11	1	702	170	1	4	70.20	4
4	L. W. Thomas (*Bedfordshire*)	6	12	1	763	171	4	0	69.36	6
5	J. du Toit (*Northumberland*)	6	12	0	770	144	3	5	64.16	7
6	G. J. Pratt (*Cumberland*)	7	10	3	435	156*	1	2	62.14	3
7	S. S. Arthurton (*Norfolk*)	6	10	0	612	172	2	4	61.20	8
8	S. W. Griffiths (*Wales*)	4	8	1	412	133*	1	3	58.85	1
9	C. M. MacDonell (*Buckinghamshire*)	5	10	1	510	99	0	6	56.66	8
10	W. D. C. Hale (*Cumberland*)	6	10	2	443	125	1	2	55.37	4
11	Asim Munir (*Cambridgeshire*)	6	12	1	585	123	2	3	53.18	13
12	E. G. C. Young (*Wiltshire*)	5	10	1	454	144	2	1	50.44	4
13	R. I. Kaufman (*Oxfordshire*)	6	11	3	400	103*	1	3	50.00	10
14	L. Gwynne (*Herefordshire*)	4	8	0	387	87	0	5	48.37	5
15	J. W. R. Miles (*Cumberland*)	6	9	1	386	106	1	3	48.25	3
16	N. V. Jeyaratnam (*Hertfordshire*)	5	8	1	335	98	0	3	47.85	6
17	J. A. J. Rishton (*Berkshire*)	4	8	1	334	127	1	2	47.71	7
18	B. L. Wadlan (*Cornwall*)	6	12	0	560	108	1	4	46.66	8
19	J. M. Spelman (*Norfolk*)	6	10	0	456	121	1	3	45.60	0

BOWLING (20 wickets at 25.00)

		Style	O	M	R	W	BB	5I	Avge
1	H. E. Eltham (*Oxfordshire*)	OB	85	21	276	21	5-31	1	13.14
2	P. J. McMahon (*Cambridgeshire*)	OB	280.4	86	657	46	8-96	6	14.28
3	L. C. Ryan (*Oxfordshire*)	SLA	186.5	43	512	35	5-37	1	14.62
4	T. Bulcock (*Cumberland*)	SLA	292.5	94	728	49	7-57	4	14.85
5	C. T. Peploe (*Berkshire*)	SLA	284.5	82	804	50	8-61	6	16.08
6	C. B. Keegan (*Oxfordshire*)	RFM	166.1	40	509	28	5-35	1	18.17
7	D. A. Woods (*Cheshire*)	SLA	191	40	602	32	6-55	3	18.81
8	E. G. C. Young (*Wiltshire*)	SLA	144.1	53	410	21	6-87	1	19.52
9	G. S. Randhawa (*Shropshire*)	SLA	260.5	60	688	35	7-119	2	19.65
10	O. F. McGee (*Northumberland*)	SLA	201.2	28	681	34	7-53	2	20.02
11	P. A. Byrne (*Staffordshire*)	SLA	236.2	70	603	30	7-82	2	20.10
12	B. L. Wadlan (*Cornwall*)	SLA	325.2	87	948	46	6-54	5	20.60
13	R. J. Gleeson (*Cumberland*)	RM	170.3	45	483	23	4-59	0	21.00
14	T. B. Huggins (*Suffolk*)	OB	195.5	44	596	28	7-38	2	21.28
15	T. M. Nugent (*Berkshire*)	RFM	194.2	39	636	28	5-51	2	22.71
16	D. O. Conway (*Herefordshire*)	RM	157.2	50	465	20	5-44	1	23.25
17	J. M. King (*Wiltshire*)	OB	216.4	48	687	29	5-79	1	23.68
18	B. J. France (*Norfolk*)	RM	176.1	46	514	21	5-95	1	24.47

S. A. Kazmi (Hertfordshire, SLA) took 34 wickets at 30.14.

CHAMPIONSHIP FINAL

At Carlisle, September 6–7. **Cumberland won by ten wickets.** Oxfordshire 85 (40.4 overs) (R. J. Gleeson 3-14, N. J. Longhurst 3-32, T. Bulcock 4-18) **and 89** (42 overs) (T. Bulcock 3-27, R. J. Gleeson 3-14); ‡Cumberland 170 (58.2 overs) (W. A. T. Beer 3-48, L. C. Ryan 5-37) **and 5-0** (0.2 overs). *A match scheduled for four days lasted barely four sessions. After heavy delay before the start, the ball swung, seamed and spun under cloudless skies. Asked to bat, Oxfordshire were bundled out for 85 in 40 overs by seamers Neil Longhurst and Richard Gleeson, and the prolific left-arm spin of Toby Bulcock. Richard Kaufman top-scored with 17 as his team-mates fell playing expansive drives. Cumberland showed more resolve – Will Hale and Josh Tolley put on 50 for the first wicket – and at 146-5 they were heading for a sizeable lead, until Luke Ryan, the captain and another slow left-armer, ran through the lower order. The 17-year-old Harvey Eltham was then promoted to open with Harrison Ward, aged just 15. Both knuckled down, Ward facing 53 balls for his two runs, though neither made double figures in the match. At 52-8, Oxfordshire faced an innings defeat. A slogged 29 from 16 deliveries by Chad Keegan averted that, but Cumberland needed two balls for victory.*

TROPHY FINAL

At Wormsley, August 26. **Cornwall won by seven wickets.** Northumberland 199-9 (42 overs) (G. R. Breese 50, C. T. Youldon 38*; A. D. Angove 3-30); ‡Cornwall 203-3 (29.4 overs) (M. L. Robins 42, A. D. Angove 43, T. G. Sharp 41*, B. L. Wadlan 36*). *Rain delayed the start until 3pm, and reduced the game to a 42-over contest. Northumberland lurched to 59-5, before a watchful 50 from Gareth Breese and a run-a-ball 38* from wicketkeeper Christopher Youldon steered them towards a respectable total. On a beautiful late-summer afternoon, Cornwall batted so positively that 12 overs went unbowled; Brad Wadlan hit three sixes in a stand of 71* with Tom Sharp.*

TWENTY20 FINAL

At Banbury, July 12. **Cheshire won by 119 runs.** ‡Cheshire 240-0 (20 overs) (W. M. Goodwin 132*, O. J. Law 101*); Oxfordshire 121 (16.1 overs) (R. Dixon 4-19, J. J. Williams 4-17). *Three counties qualified automatically for finals day by heading their groups. The fourth was determined by a play-off: Bedfordshire, winners of Group 5, overcame Cambridgeshire, who had topped Group 4. Cheshire edged Devon aside in the first semi, and Oxfordshire strolled home, despite the intervention of rain, in the second. The final was even more one-sided: Warren Goodwin (61 balls) and Ollie Law (59) batted throughout the Cheshire innings, which included 162 in boundaries. Oxfordshire, who promoted Chad Keegan, reached 44-0 in four overs, but from there it was downhill.*

SECOND ELEVEN CHAMPIONSHIP IN 2015

North Division	P	W	L	D	A	Bonus points Bat	Bowl	Pen	Total points
1 Nottinghamshire (2)......	9	4	0	5	0	19	34	0	142
2 Durham (8)	9	4	1	4	0	29	28	0	141
3 Lancashire (3)	9	3	1	5	0	25	30	0	128
4 Leicestershire (1)........	9	3	2	4	0	20	34	0	122
5 Warwickshire (6)........	9	3	1	3	1	14	24	−2	112*
6 Derbyshire (5)...........	9	2	2	5	0	19	23	0	99
7 Yorkshire (4)..........	9	2	4	3	0	10	29	0	86
8 Worcestershire (10)......	9	1	4	4	0	20	27	−0.5	82.5
9 MCC Universities	9	0	2	6	1	22	20	0	77
10 Northamptonshire	9	1	6	2	0	14	32	−1.5	70.5

South Division	P	W	L	D	A	Bonus points Bat	Bowl	Pen	Total points
1 Middlesex (3)...........	9	6	2	1	0	22	32	−1.5	153.5
2 Somerset (2)............	9	4	3	2	0	25	32	−1.5	129.5
3 Kent (6)	9	3	2	4	0	24	35	0	127
4 Surrey (4).............	9	4	4	1	0	26	29	0	124
5 Gloucestershire (7)......	9	4	4	1	0	25	26	0	120
6 Hampshire (9)	9	3	2	3	1	24	27	−0.5	118.5
7 Sussex (5)	9	3	3	3	0	26	29	0	118
8 Essex (1)	9	2	3	3	1	27	26	0	105
9 Glamorgan.............	9	2	4	3	0	16	21	0	84
10 MCC Young Cricketers...	9	0	5	4	0	25	24	0	74

In 2014, MCC Universities and Northamptonshire played in the South Division, when they finished tenth and eighth respectively; Glamorgan and MCC Young Cricketers played in the North Division, when they finished ninth and seventh.

Win = 16pts; draw/abandoned = 5pts.

* *Warwickshire gained an extra 3pts for batting when a match finished with the scores level. All penalties were for slow over-rates.*

LEADING AVERAGES, 2015

BATTING (480 runs)

	M	I	NO	R	HS	100	Avge	Ct/St
1 P. R. Stirling (*Middlesex*)	4	6	2	640	254	2	160.00	1
2 W. R. S. Gidman (*Nottinghamshire*)	8	10	4	561	94*	0	93.50	8
3 T. N. Cullen (*Leics, MCCU*)	6	9	3	511	135*	1	85.16	9/1
4 T. P. Alsop (*Hampshire*)	6	9	1	559	195	1	69.87	10/1
5 D. W. Lawrence (*Essex*).............	4	8	0	498	185	1	62.25	5
6 S. R. Dickson (*Kent*)...............	8	16	3	797	177	3	61.30	7
7 J. D. Libby (*Nottinghamshire*)	5	9	1	489	152*	3	61.12	0
8 J. T. A. Burnham (*Durham*)	7	11	2	538	116	1	59.77	4
9 S. Hicks (*MCCYC*)	9	15	4	620	177*	3	56.36	8
10 W. T. Root (*Nottinghamshire*)	8	14	4	562	166*	1	56.20	2
11 V. S. Solanki (*Surrey*).............	8	13	2	601	191	1	54.63	9
12 H. Hameed (*Lancashire*).............	6	10	0	532	104	1	53.20	1
13 C. J. Green (*Surrey*)	8	11	1	511	105	1	51.10	5
14 A. N. Kervezee (*Worcestershire*)	8	13	0	625	127	1	48.07	4
15 J. J. Weatherley (*Hampshire*)	8	11	0	502	150	2	45.63	2
16 S. S. Eskinazi (*Middlesex*)	10	17	1	687	126	1	42.93	29/1
17 L. S. Livingstone (*Lancashire*)........	8	14	1	538	118	1	41.38	7

		M	I	NO	R	HS	100	Avge	Ct/St
18	D. Murphy (*Northamptonshire*)	8	15	0	581	147	2	38.73	11
19	A. Kapil (*Surrey*)	9	13	0	481	105	2	37.00	2
20	C. F. Jackson (*Sussex*)	9	17	2	540	151*	1	36.00	29/4
21	H. Z. Finch (*Sussex*)	9	17	1	538	148*	2	33.62	15

BOWLING (18 wickets)

		Style	O	M	R	W	BB	5I	Avge
1	R. N. Gamble (*Somerset*)	RFM	170.1	54	486	28	5-54	1	17.35
2	H. W. Podmore (*Middlesex*)	RM	242	56	766	42	6-52	3	18.23
3	T. J. Lester (*Lancashire*)	LFM	125	18	438	24	6-35	2	18.25
4	G. S. Randhawa (*Durham*)	SLA	139	37	370	19	3-10	0	19.47
5	J. E. Poysden (*Warwickshire*)	LBG	117	23	429	22	4-16	1	19.50
6	B. A. Hutton (*Nottinghamshire*)	RM	118.5	21	438	22	5-52	1	19.90
7	N. A. Sowter (*Middlesex*)	LBG	100.4	12	420	21	6-70	1	20.00
8	P. I. Burgoyne (*Sussex*)	OB	224.3	34	764	38	7-171	2	20.10
9	T. P. Milnes (*Derbys, Warks*)	RFM	218.3	46	710	34	6-25	1	20.88
10	F. O. E. van den Bergh (*Surrey*) ...	SLA	236.1	48	776	36	5-31	4	21.55
11	G. S. Sandhu (*Middlesex*)	LFM	153	27	507	23	7-31	1	22.04
12	W. R. S. Gidman (*Nottinghamshire*) ..	RFM	168.3	45	485	22	3-38	0	22.04
13	K. A. Bull (*Glamorgan*)	OB	137.5	25	422	19	5-100	1	22.21
14	A. Hepburn (*Worcestershire*)	RM	137.4	37	421	18	5-66	1	23.38
15	Imran Qayyum (*Kent*)	SLA	187.3	19	697	29	5-18	1	24.03
16	J. R. Winslade (*Essex, MCCYC*)	RFM	158.1	38	515	20	6-43	1	25.75
17	T. R. G. Hampton (*Gloucestershire*) .	RFM	136	27	466	18	5-43	1	25.88
18	J. O. Grundy (*MCCU*)	LFM	131.4	27	552	21	3-56	0	26.28
19	M. A. Chambers (*Northamptonshire*)...	RFM	197	48	540	19	4-43	0	28.42
20	M. E. Milnes (*Durham, MCCU*)	RM	166	26	697	22	5-42	1	31.68
21	B. J. McCarthy (*Durham*)	RFM	167.4	31	660	20	5-34	1	33.00
22	Zain Shahzad (*Essex, MCCYC*)	RFM	214.2	35	933	18	3-65	0	51.83

SECOND ELEVEN CHAMPIONSHIP FINAL IN 2015

At Radlett, September 7–10. **Nottinghamshire won by four wickets. Middlesex 254** (76.5 overs) (S. S. Eskinazi 126, R. F. Higgins 34; L. J. Fletcher 3-35) **and 264** (70.1 overs) (M. K. Andersson 39, R. F. Higgins 63, N. A. Sowter 49, Extras 32; A. Carter 3-29, B. M. Kitt 3-77); ‡**Nottinghamshire 331** (100.4 overs) (A. Dal 31, W. R. S. Gidman 60, T. J. Moores 107; H. W. Podmore 6-90) **and 188-6** (51 overs) (S. K. W. Wood 33, W. R. S. Gidman 94*; R. H. Patel 3-58).

SECOND ELEVEN TROPHY FINAL IN 2015

At Chester-le-Street, August 27. **Derbyshire won by ten runs.** ‡**Derbyshire 247** (50 overs) (W. J. Durston 41, B. T. Slater 45, C. F. Hughes 69, T. C. Knight 32); **Durham 237** (50 overs) (P. Mustard 31, C. S. MacLeod 41, S. W. Poynter 35, W. J. Weighell 37; T. P. Milnes 3-43).

SECOND ELEVEN TWENTY20 FINAL IN 2015

At Arundel, July 16. **Middlesex won by four wickets.** ‡**Kent 115** (17.4 overs) (S. R. Dickson 40; H. W. Podmore 3-18, N. A. Sowter 3-33); **Middlesex 118-6** (17.1 overs) (R. F. Higgins 33*).

LEAGUE CRICKET IN 2015

Another Yorkshire success story

Geoffrey Dean

In the year Yorkshire retained the County Championship, the continued renaissance of club cricket in the county led to the sanctioning of an extra premier league. The current Yorkshire League will be split into two in 2016. The north division will contain six existing Yorkshire League clubs, as well as the top six from the York & District Senior League. The other group will be made up of the seven remaining Premier League teams, as well as the top four from the South Yorkshire Senior League and one from the Central Yorkshire League. Two will be relegated each year, and replaced by promoted clubs from feeder leagues. Meanwhile, the North Yorkshire & South Durham League will continue as part of the premier family, while the Bradford and Central Yorkshire leagues, which are amalgamating this year, hope to become the county's fourth premier league in 2017.

The oldest league in the world, the Birmingham & District, witnessed the highest score in its 127-year history – 246 by the Australian Alex Keath for Knowle & Dorridge against Berkswell. He amassed more than 1,000 runs, as did Kadeer Ali of West Bromwich Dartmouth. No one had managed the feat in the league since Andy Flower in 1996 (also for Dartmouth). For the third time in six years, the title went to Shrewsbury, who also won the 40-over knockout competition for the sixth successive summer.

One of the most dramatic final days of the season came in the East Anglian Premier League. The title awaited Swardeston if they overcame Copdock, but they fell well short of a target of 237, which meant second-placed Vauxhall Mallards would become champions if they won at Frinton. But Mallards' total of 153 was overhauled: they finished fourth, and Swardeston were able to celebrate a fourth successive championship. At the bottom, Woolpit staged a great escape to avoid the drop after two results went their way. First, they had to win, which they did, thanks to Michael Rippon's seven for 26 as Norwich collapsed for 65. Then Horsford had to beat Saffron Walden, and send them down instead. When Saffron Walden were shot out for 69, this looked a formality – but Horsford hit trouble too, before sneaking home with two wickets to spare.

In Wales, Ashley Wood took 56 wickets at 8.89 to spearhead Menai Bridge's successful retention of their North Wales League title. David Fox of Connah's Quay finished one short of 1,000, averaging 58 with three centuries. The highest innings of the season, 202 not out by the South African left-hander Francois Mostert, saved Bangor from relegation. They needed to win their final match, at Mochdre, to stay up, and victory was all but assured after Mostert and Andy Savage plundered 328 for the second wicket.

Roffey, who joined the Sussex League as recently as 2011, secured their second successive title. After 11 victories in 2014, they totted up 15 this time.

They still needed to win their final game to pip East Grinstead, and did so thanks to the 19-year-old Australian off-spinner Ben Manenti's five for 31 as Middleton were dismissed for 125. Wicketkeeper/batsman Matt Davies commuted each weekend from Spain to play.

Hampstead rounded off their 150th anniversary year by winning the Middlesex League, to the delight of their chairman Jim Carter, better known as Carson, the *Downton Abbey* butler. They clinched the title with a week to spare, which was just as well: they were skittled for 92 in their last match by Richmond, who drew level on points – but Hampstead had won more matches overall. Finchley were relegated for the first time.

Chris Aspin writes: England seamer Kate Cross became the first woman to play at senior level in the Central Lancashire League when she turned out for Heywood on the opening day of the season, and took three for 19 in seven overs against Clifton; she would have had a fourth had her brother Bobby not dropped a dolly. He made amends by hitting 75, and the match was won. A fortnight later, on May 10, Kate took eight for 47 in a six-wicket win over Unsworth, receiving a bigger collection than Bobby, who made 63. Exactly 35 years earlier, their father David helped West Ham beat Arsenal in the FA Cup final.

This was the CLL's final season, after 123 years, following a merger with the Saddleworth League. It will be called the Pennine League, though Heywood, Clifton and Unsworth have become founder members of the Greater Manchester League and will compete in their premiership division; Radcliffe and Elton will be in division one. The new league will have three divisions, each with 12 clubs.

Norden topped the Premiership, finishing nine points clear of Walsden and Monton & Weaste, and also took the Lees Wood Cup for the second year running, beating Royton in the final by six wickets. Their Australian professional Daniel Salpietro scored 1,060 runs at 70; he hit four centuries, including an unbeaten 166 against Royton.

Crompton, who gained promotion from the Championship along with Middleton, enjoyed their first major success since 1954, thanks largely to 68-year-old slow left-armer Mel Whittle, who started playing in the league before his colleagues were born. Mel announced his retirement in 2010 after taking 100 wickets for Oldham (see *Wisden 2011*, page 705), but returned in 2015 to the club where he first made his name. His 392.1 overs, by far the most in either division, brought him the most wickets – 81 at 12 each – and included eight for 32 against Oldham, the season's best return.

Records tumbled as Milnrow hammered 454 for four off 50 overs against Oldham. South African professional James Price, who faced 117 balls, hit 233, including 22 fours and nine sixes, and put on 323 for the first wicket with Lee Crabtree. Milnrow won by 223 runs. Price, who also made 208 as his side reached 331 for six against Elton, finished the season with 1,116 runs at 69. Another South African, slow left-armer Ernest Kemm of Middleton, topped the Championship bowling averages with 71 wickets at ten.

In the Lancashire League, Burnley became the first club to win the Worsley Cup three years running, beating Nelson in the final, and also carried off the championship, finishing 39 points clear of Enfield. In the cup quarter-final against Ramsbottom, Jonathan Clare crashed 199 off 104 deliveries as Burnley piled up 371 for seven. Clare, who had joined Derbyshire from Burnley in 2007, returned home to hit 14 sixes, losing several balls. In the final, Burnley made 206 before skittling Nelson for 88, with their professional – the local-born left-arm spinner Chris Holt – taking five for seven in six overs. Burnley's opening batsman Vishal Tripathi broke the club's amateur record with 1,138 runs at 47, and was only the 12th amateur to reach four figures since the league was formed in 1892. He was followed by his team-mate David Brown, formerly of Glamorgan and Gloucestershire, who made exactly 1,000 at 55. Holt, with 82 wickets at 11, was the league's leading bowler. All-conquering Burnley also won the Twenty20 competition and the Junior League.

The Pakistan international Bilawal Bhatti made an explosive debut for Todmorden, hitting 188 against Enfield off 115 balls, with a dozen sixes, then taking four for 45. Todmorden's 320 for five, which was enough for a 97-run victory, was their biggest home total. Alviro Petersen hammered 187 as Enfield's stand-in pro at Haslingden, to help his side to 324 for six. Haslingden chased hard, and were only 11 short when the overs ran out.

Despite missing the last four matches, Ramsbottom's Daryn Smit, one of the league's ten South African professionals, amassed 1,248 runs at 113 to set a new club record. He also picked up 74 wickets with his leg-breaks, at just eight apiece. Ockert Erasmus of Accrington scored 1,058 runs at 62, and claimed 70 wickets at 15. Against Rawtenstall, he took five for four after making an unbeaten 100.

Graeme Sneddon (Accrington) took the Rishton bowling for 152, and his team-mate Jake Clarke had the best amateur return – eight for 35 against Todmorden. Bacup's pro, Haseeb Azam, took eight for 26 at Nelson. Keith Roscoe, the league's oldest player at 53, harvested another 67 wickets for Rawtenstall at 12, taking his career total to 1,685. Kelly Smuts (160 not out) and Bradley Boddie shared an unbroken second-wicket stand of 220 in Rishton's home game against Bacup; left-hander Smuts ended the summer with 955 runs at 68.

The Lancashire League will continue for at least one more season in its current form, but there was talk of possible expansion to two divisions in 2017. This would affect several clubs in the Northern and Ribblesdale leagues. There were also concerns about increased travel.

Ramsbottom's Acre Bottom ground was flooded during the bad weather that hit the north late in 2015; the club launched an appeal to help pay for the restoration work required, which initial estimates put at £70,000.

" In his commentating days, his facility was not so much with words as with the way he never wasted them."
Richie Benaud 1930–2015, page 50

ECB PREMIER LEAGUE TABLES IN 2015

Birmingham & District League

		P	W	L	Pts
1	Shrewsbury	22	15	5	349
2	Berkswell	22	14	7	333
3	Knowle & Dorridge	22	13	6	327
4	Kidderminster Victoria	22	12	7	297
5	West Bromwich Dartmouth	22	12	7	289
6	Ombersley	22	12	8	288
7	Walmley	22	8	11	248
8	Barnt Green	22	9	11	236
9	Kenilworth Wardens	22	8	11	220
10	Wolverhampton	22	5	15	174
11	Brockhampton	22	4	16	169
12	Dorridge	22	5	16	168

Cheshire County League Premier Division

		P	W	L	Pts
1	**Hyde**	**22**	**15**	**5**	**413**
2	Nantwich	22	13	6	389
3	Toft	22	12	5	378
4	Alderley Edge	22	10	5	352
5	Chester Boughton Hall	22	9	5	349
6	Bowdon	22	8	8	276
7	Macclesfield	22	6	8	272
8	Cheadle	22	7	11	256
9	Bramhall	22	6	12	256
10	Neston	22	7	11	253
11	Marple	22	5	11	231
12	Grappenhall	22	2	13	174

Cornwall Premier Division

		P	W	L	Pts
1	**Werrington**	**18**	**12**	**4**	**278**
2	Truro	18	12	3	275
3	St Just	18	9	6	247
4	St Austell	18	7	5	235
5	Redruth	18	9	5	234
6	Grampound Road	18	9	6	232
7	Falmouth	18	6	9	192
8	Newquay	18	4	10	148
9	Penzance	18	2	13	144
10	Camborne	18	2	11	141

Derbyshire Premier League

		P	W	L	Pts
1	**Sandiacre Town**	**22**	**14**	**4**	**426**
2	Swarkestone	22	10	7	346
3	Chesterfield	22	7	4	339
4	Spondon	22	7	8	337
5	Ticknall	22	7	6	331
6	Ockbrook & Borrowash	22	9	5	330
7	Denby	22	7	6	321
8	Lullington Park	22	8	10	280
9	Eckington	22	6	9	276
10	Quarndon	22	8	11	258
11	Alvaston & Boulton	22	7	8	255
12	Dunstall	22	2	14	159

Devon League Premier Division

		P	W	L	Pts
1	**Torquay**	**18**	**15**	**2**	**318**
2	Sidmouth	18	13	4	270
3	North Devon	18	11	7	243
4	Exmouth	18	10	7	227
5	Bovey Tracey	18	8	8	222
6	Exeter	18	9	8	213
7	Plymouth	18	8	9	212
8	Heathcoat	18	7	11	197
9	Paignton	18	4	12	167
10	Plympton	18	0	15	95

East Anglian Premier League

		P	W	L	Pts
1	**Swardeston**	**22**	**12**	**7**	**384**
2	Frinton-on-Sea	22	10	5	376
3	Cambridge Granta	22	10	6	366
4	Vauxhall Mallards	22	10	7	364
5	Copdock & Old Ipswichian	22	9	6	356
6	Great Witchingham	22	9	7	331
7	Horsford	22	8	8	301
8	Burwell	22	7	13	296
9	Bury St Edmunds	22	6	9	282
10	Norwich	22	6	11	280
11	Woolpit	22	6	10	251
12	Saffron Walden	22	5	9	249

Essex League Premier Division

		P	W	L	Pts
1	**Chelmsford**	**18**	**14**	**3**	**310**
2	Brentwood	18	14	4	305
3	Wanstead & Snaresbrook	18	13	4	305
4	Colchester & East Essex	18	10	6	257
5	Chingford	18	9	9	226
6	South Woodford	18	5	11	172
7	Buckhurst Hill	18	6	8	166
8	Ilford	18	5	10	165
9	Loughton	18	4	13	153
10	Harold Wood	18	2	13	133

Home Counties Premier League Division One

		P	W	L	Pts
1	**High Wycombe**	**18**	**13**	**1**	**335**
2	Banbury	18	12	4	310
3	Henley	18	12	4	309
4	Reading	18	8	7	229
5	Slough	18	7	7	229
6	Burnham	18	6	8	216
7	Harefield	18	5	9	192
8	Tring Park	18	5	10	192
9	Horspath	18	5	9	191
10	Oxford	18	0	14	102

Kent League Premier Division

		P	W	L	Pts
1	**Hartley Country Club** ..	18	13	2	272
2	Sevenoaks Vine	18	12	3	252
3	Beckenham	18	8	5	228
4	Blackheath	18	8	5	212
5	Bexley	18	8	8	201
6	Lordswood	18	7	8	200
7	Tunbridge Wells	18	7	9	178
8	Bromley	18	4	11	152
9	Sandwich Town	18	4	9	141
10	Folkestone	18	2	12	103

Leics and Rutland League Premier Division

		P	W	L	Pts
1	**Kibworth**	22	17	2	486
2	Lutterworth	22	12	3	461
3	Sileby Town	22	9	6	415
4	Barrow Town	22	11	6	387
5	Loughborough Town	22	8*	8	353
6	Hinckley Town	22	8*	9	335
7	Syston Town	22	8	9	325
8	Market Harborough	22	8	8	316
9	Rothley Park	22	7	10	305
10	Leicester Ivanhoe	22	7	7	304
11	Kegworth Town	22	2	13	193
12	Thorpe Arnold	22	1	17	114

* *Plus one tie.*

Lincolnshire Cricket Board Premier League

		P	W	L	Pts
1	**Bracebridge Heath** ...	22	15	4	331
2	Sleaford	22	14	5	322
3	Woodhall Spa	22	10	4	308
4	Bourne	22	11	7	289
5	Louth	22	9	8	270
6	Market Deeping	22	10	7	260
7	Lindum	22	9	9	248
8	Skegness	22	7	11	222
9	Grantham	22	6	10	221
10	Grimsby Town	22	5	11	195
11	Market Rasen	22	5	12	182
12	Spalding	22	2	15	133

Liverpool & District Competition

		P	W	L	Pts
1	**New Brighton**	22	16	3	404
2	Ormskirk	22	13	7	346
3	Northern	22	10	5	313
4	Bootle	22	10	8	291
5	Formby	22	9	9	289
6	Birkenhead Park	22	9	9	278
7	Rainhill	22	8	11	270
8	Lytham	22	7	10	246
9	Leigh	22	7	8	236
10	Wallasey	22	6	10	221
11	Southport & Birkdale....	22	6	12	209
12	Highfield	22	5	14	183

Middlesex County League Division One

		P	W	L	Pts
1	**Hampstead**	18	11	5	119
2	Richmond	18	10	7	119
3	Stanmore	18	10	6	111
4	Ealing	18	10	5	106
5	North Middlesex	18	8	7	100
6	Twickenham	18	9	8	98
7	Southgate	18	8	8	97
8	Teddington	18	8	8	90
9	Finchley	18	5	13	64
10	Indian Gymkhana	18	3	15	32

Hampstead placed first by virtue of more wins.

Northamptonshire League Premier Division

		P	W	L	Pts
1	**Rushden Town**	22	17	2	507
2	Peterborough Town	22	15	5	472
3	Northampton Saints ...	22	15	6	439
4	Finedon Dolben	22	12	5	438
5	Old Northamptonians ..	22	10	7	372
6	Rushton	22	8	8	344
7	Oundle Town	22	7	8	315
8	Brixworth	22	4	12	266
9	Stony Stratford	22	6	13	245
10	Wollaston	22	4	13	239
11	Horton House	22	6	13	236
12	Geddington	22	2	14	196

North East Premier Division

		P	W	L	Pts
1	**South Northumberland** .	22	14	0	440
2	Chester-le-Street	22	8	3	382
3	Newcastle	22	11	4	365
4	Durham Academy	22	7	3	359
5	Benwell Hill	22	7	8	273
6	Hetton Lyons	22	5	9	271
7	Tynemouth	22	6	9	270
8	Whitburn	22	6	9	257
9	South Shields	22	5	9	237
10	Stockton	22	3	7	233
11	Gateshead Fell	22	6	10	232
12	Blaydon	22	3	10	209

Northern Premier League

		P	W	L	Pts
1	**Morecambe**	24	16	3	260
2	Fleetwood	24	15	6	239
3	Darwen	24	13	6	234
4	Blackpool	24	11	5	221
5	Leyland	24	11	5	212
6	Penrith	24	13	7	205
7	Barrow	24	9	9	178
8	Netherfield	24	8	12	178
9	Lancaster	24	8	11	172
10	Chorley	24	9*	11	169
11	St Annes	24	4	12	124
12	Kendal	24	5*	13	113
13	Preston	24	0	16	24

* *Plus one tie.*

North Staffs and South Cheshire League Premier Division

		P	W	L	Pts
1	**Stone**	**22**	**11**	**4**	**329**
2	Checkley	22	11	4	302
3	Whitmore	22	9	7	291
4	Knypersley	22	9	6	287
5	Leek	22	8*	8	278
6	J & G Meakin	22	6	8	267
7	Moddershall	22	7	5	263
8	Longton	22	6*	6	240
9	Porthill Park	22	5	9	237
10	Hem Heath	22	4	8	222
11	Little Stoke	22	4	9	212
12	Newcastle & Hartshill	22	4	10	202

* *Plus one tie.*

North Wales League Premier Division

		P	W	L	Pts
1	**Menai Bridge**	**22**	**16**	**3**	**260**
2	Connah's Quay	22	14	7	220
3	Brymbo	22	13	6	216
4	Mochdre	22	12	9	200
5	Hawarden Park	22	9	10	169
6	Denbigh	22	10	10	157
7	Pwllheli	22	8	12	153
8	Llandudno	22	9	11	151
9	Bangor	22	8	12	141
10	Pontblyddyn	22	7	13	133
11	St Asaph	22	6	14	132
12	Northop	22	7	13	127

North Yorkshire and South Durham League Premier Division

		P	W	L	Pts
1	**Richmondshire**	**26**	**14**	**4**	**413**
2	Great Ayton	26	11	6	380
3	Stokesley	26	12	4	373
4	Barnard Castle	26	11	7	371
5	Marske	26	12	6	366
6	Hartlepool	26	9	6	360
7	Middlesbrough	26	8	4	352
8	Darlington	26	9	7	329
9	Guisborough	26	8	11	266
10	Normandy Hall	26	5	11	257
11	Norton	26	4	11	233
12	Seaton Carew	26	5	12	232
13	Marton	26	4	13	217
14	Redcar	26	3	13	204

Nottinghamshire Cricket Board Premier League

		P	W	L	Pts
1	**Kimberley Institute**	**22**	**13**	**5**	**327**
2	Plumtree	22	10	4	305
3	Cuckney	22	8	5	300
4	Caythorpe	22	7	6	275
5	West Indian Cavaliers	22	10	6	274
6	Notts CCC Academy	22	8	7	269
7	Welbeck	22	9	6	264
8	Clifton Village	22	9	9	229
9	Radcliffe-on-Trent	22	7	10	210
10	Ordsall Bridon	22	5	10	204
11	Farnsfield	22	5	10	183
12	Attenborough	22	3	13	151

Southern Premier League

		P	W	L	Pts
1	**South Wilts**	**17**	**15**	**1**	**337**
2	Havant	17	11	5	291
3	Bashley (Rydal)	17	11	6	279
4	Hampshire Academy	17	8	8	245
5	Lymington	17	8	8	231
6	St Cross Symondians	17	7	9	210
7	Ventnor	17	7	9	203
8	Alton	17	5*	10	182
9	Burridge	17	4	12	161
10	Sarisbury Athletic	17	3*	11	159

* *Plus one tie.*

Surrey Championship Premier Division

		P	W	L	Pts
1	**Sunbury**	**18**	**13**	**4**	**303**
2	Normandy	18	12	4	282
3	Weybridge	18	11	6	274
4	Reigate Priory	18	11	3	273
5	Sutton	18	8	8	199
6	Wimbledon	18	8	8	194
7	Guildford	18	7	8	187
8	Beddington	18	5	10	148
9	Valley End	18	4	13	139
10	Leatherhead	18	1	15	86

Sussex League Premier Division

		P	W	L	Pts
1	**Roffey**	**19**	**15**	**3**	**471**
2	East Grinstead	19	14	3	467
3	Preston Nomads	19	11	3	423
4	Bexhill	19	10*	8	370
5	Horsham	19	8	8	331
6	Billingshurst	19	7	10	297
7	Brighton & Hove	19	6*	11	272
8	Cuckfield	19	5	9	265
9	Eastbourne	19	5	12	265
10	Middleton	19	5	12	259
11	Sussex Development XI	10	0	7	143†

* *Plus one tie.*

† *Played only ten games; their points were obtained by multiplying by 1.9.*

Swalec Premier League Division One

		P	W	L	Pts
1	**Bridgend Town**	**18**	**13**	**0**	**302**
2	Cardiff.	18	7	5	240
3	Port Talbot Town	18	8	4	227
4	Newport.	18	6	5	227
5	Ynysygerwn.	18	4	8	192
6	Pontarddulais	18	6	9	185
7	Neath.	18	5	3	182
8	Ammanford	18	4	8	175
9	Mumbles	18	2	7	166
10	St Fagans	18	3	9	156

West of England Premier League

		P	W	L	Pts
1	**Frocester**.	**18**	**14**	**4**	**301**
2	Clevedon	18	11	6	260
3	Bath	18	10	7	257
4	Corsham	18	9	7	242
5	Taunton St Andrews	18	9	9	231
6	Downend	18	8	10	219
7	Bridgwater	18	8	9	218
8	Bristol	18	7	9	216
9	Taunton Deane	18	6	11	185
10	Ilminster	18	3	13	139

Yorkshire Premier League

		P	W	L	Pts
1	**York**.	**24**	**18**	**4**	**144**
2	Barnsley	24	14	5	123
3	Yorkshire Academy.	24	13	7	114
4	Harrogate	24	12	7	111
5	Rotherham Town	24	13	7	110
6	Cleethorpes	24	9	11	85
7	Driffield Town	24	9	10	83
8	Appleby Frodingham. . . .	24	8	11	79
9	Doncaster Town	24	9	12	75
10	Castleford	24	8	11	75
11	Sheffield Collegiate	24	7	12	69
12	Sheffield United	24	4	15	48
13	Hull.	24	4	16	42

The following leagues do not have ECB Premier League status:

LANCASHIRE LEAGUE TABLES IN 2015

Lancashire League

		P	W	L	Pts
1	**Burnley**.	**26**	**21**	**3**	**257**
2	Enfield.	26	18	6	218
3	Ramsbottom.	26	16	8	211
4	Lowerhouse	26	16*	6	208
5	Church.	26	14*	9	185
6	Accrington.	26	14	10	179
7	Rawtenstall	26	12	12	161
8	Todmorden.	26	11	12	149
9	Haslingden.	26	8	14	138
10	Nelson.	26	8*	15	134
11	East Lancashire.	26	7*	15	114
12	Colne.	26	6	18	93
13	Rishton	26	6	16	92
14	Bacup	26	5	18	83

* *Plus one tie.*

Central Lancashire League – Premier Division

		P	W	L	Pts
1	**Norden**	**24**	**16**	**5**	**83**
2	Walsden.	24	14	5	74
3	Monton & Weaste	24	13	8	74
4	Littleborough	24	11	10	61
5	Heywood	24	9	11	53
6	Rochdale	24	8	11	53
7	Unsworth	24	7	12	48
8	Clifton	24	7	13	47
9	Royton.	24	5	14	37

Central Lancashire League – Championship Division

		P	W	L	Pts
1	**Crompton**	**24**	**17**	**3**	**92**
2	Middleton	24	12	8	71
3	Milnrow.	24	12	9	69
4	Radcliffe	24	12	8	69
5	Heyside	24	11	9	65
6	Elton	24	10	10	62
7	Ashton-under-Lyne	24	9	10	52
8	Werneth.	24	4	16	35
9	Oldham	24	3	17	25

OTHER LEAGUE WINNERS IN 2015

Airedale & Wharfedale	Otley	**Pembrokeshire**	Haverfordwest
Bolton Association	Edgworth	**Quaid-e-Azam**	Keighley RZM
Bolton League	Egerton	**Ribblesdale**	Clitheroe
Bradford	Pudsey St Lawrence	**Saddleworth**	Saddleworth
Cambs & Hunts	Godmanchester T	**Shropshire**	Newport
Central Yorkshire	Methley	**South Wales Association**	Llanelli
Hertfordshire	Radlett	**South Yorkshire**	Aston Hall
Huddersfield	Scholes	**Thames Valley**	Cookham Dean
Lancashire County	Prestwich	**Two Counties**	Sudbury
Norfolk Alliance	Fakenham	**Warwickshire**	Handsworth
North Essex	Mistley	**Worcestershire**	Pershore
North Lancs & Cumbria	Furness	**York Senior**	Sheriff Hutton
Northumberland &	Shotley Bridge		Bridge
Tyneside Senior			

LORD'S TAVERNERS CITY CUP IN 2015

James McCall

The City Cup was established because its organiser, *Wisden* editor Scyld Berry, believed that the towns of England and Wales were full of gifted young cricketers (many from South Asian backgrounds) who lacked only the opportunity to showcase their talent. If evidence was required, the founders could point to Luton's Monty Panesar.

Players of his ability do not evolve in isolation, and it always seemed likely Luton was harbouring other skilful players. This year, those suspicions were confirmed when they became City Cup champions after a six-run victory against Manchester at Grace Road. "Monty knew we were playing in the final, and he'll be made up that we won," said captain and wicketkeeper Suleiman Mohammed, a former team-mate of Panesar at Luton Indians.

Luton could thank their bowlers for taking them to the final. They defeated debutants Cardiff by six wickets in the first knockout match after restricting them to 116. The regional final against North London at Dunstable was less straightforward: in the last over, Luton – who had made 164 for six – needed seamer Essa Mohammed to hold his nerve and concede fewer than 12. He did – and they snatched a three-run victory.

Following the final, 24 players participated in an exhibition match in front of David Graveney, the national performance manager of the ECB Emerging Talent Programme. Five were selected to take part in further trials for the MCC Young Cricketers, including Bristol's Omar Randhawa, who led the competition's run-charts with 224 at a strike-rate of 138. North London's left-arm spinner Harindu Gunasekara also impressed with his control, despite possessing an unorthodox action that sees him release the ball on one leg while his body points toward silly mid-on.

Though it is an honour to represent MCC YC, selection is not a passport to the first-class game: only one in three go on to sign a county contract, and the 2015 team, which contained former City Cup players Janak Valand and Palash Joshi, finished the season winless and bottom of the South Division in the Second XI Championship. Financial constraints mean the tournament is unlikely to expand beyond 12 cities in the near future. The ECB need to invest more in the inner cities if they want to help develop the next Panesar; expanding the tournament to 16 towns, the objective when they took over its administration in 2013, would be a start.

NATIONAL KNOCKOUT FINAL

At Leicester, September 20. **Luton won by six runs.** ‡**Luton 166-7** (20 overs) (Suleiman Mohammed 54; A. Masood 3-29); **Manchester 160-7** (M. Bhada 81) (20 overs) (Suleiman Mohammed 54; A. Masood 3-29). *Luton opted to bat on a dry autumn afternoon. Captain Suleiman Mohammed led by example with a half-century, before No. 8 Mohammed Ismail struck a rapid 19. They were helped by the profligacy of Manchester's bowlers, who conceded 32 extras, including 20 in wides. In response, opener Mohammed Bhada, a veteran of last year's competition, hit 81, the second-highest score of the tournament. But the next best was 20 and, when wicketkeeper Ejaz Din was run out by Junaid Ashiq, Manchester's hopes of retaining their crown had gone.*

ROYAL LONDON CLUB CHAMPIONSHIP AND NATWEST CLUB T20 IN 2015

Paul Edwards

An encouraging feature of the national club knockouts in 2015 was the appearance of new teams in the latter stages of each competition. Exmouth and Pudsey Congs both made their debuts at Twenty20 finals day, while Northern became the first Liverpool Competition team to reach the final of the 45-over tournament. Playing on Sunday requires considerable commitment, particularly from those with families. Some teams, even the most successful in their leagues, baulk at playing two games every weekend deep into the summer. So knockout cricket often needs to be carefully embedded in a club's culture – which is clearly the case at Blackheath and Ealing, respective winners of the 45-over and Twenty20 knockouts in 2015.

The weather helped the smooth running of both. There were fewer concessions and rearranged matches than in previous years. The only disappointment was that Sky again chose to broadcast a one-hour highlights package of the Club T20 finals day, rather than the live coverage that gives players their moment in the limelight. Ealing's cricketers would have been especially sorry not to have seen the full battery of cameras at Cardiff: they dominated both their matches to win the competition for the second time in five years.

On the other hand, Caldy were doubtless relieved there was no broadcast of their 45-over game against Nantwich at Whitehouse Lane in April, when Lancashire's Liam Livingstone thrashed 350 from 138 balls in his side's 579 for seven. Livingstone hit 34 fours and 27 sixes, but was dismissed seven overs before the end of the Nantwich innings by 17-year-old Harry Daniel-Jones. "The ball was moving about a bit early on, and the third ball I faced nipped back through the gate and just missed the off stump," said Livingstone. "After that, I thought I'd try whacking a few." Caldy were dismissed for 79, thus losing by 500 runs.

ROYAL LONDON CLUB CHAMPIONSHIP FINAL

BLACKHEATH v NORTHERN

At Beckenham, September 20. Blackheath won by nine wickets. Toss: Northern.

Blackheath, the Kent Premier League club who had won this competition in 1971, enjoyed an emphatic triumph after Northern, their Merseyside opponents, chose to bat on a pitch retaining morning moisture. Blackheath made early inroads when experienced seamer Warren Lee took three wickets in his first six overs as Northern slipped to 42 for four. Ryan Maddock and Jack Boardman revived the innings with a fifth-wicket stand of 73 in 19 overs, but Northern's hopes of making a defendable total on a drying pitch were suffocated by James Hands, who had Boardman stumped on his way to figures of two for 13 from nine overs of skilful left-arm spin. Maddock was dismissed in the final over of the innings for a defiant 58. Helped by a Northern attack who showed little of the discipline that had got them this far, Blackheath's chase was a gentle stroll. Skipper Chris Willetts provided the bedrock with a composed half-century, while Tanveer Sikandar added 52 off 48 balls to take Blackheath home with more than 15 overs left.

Man of the match: W. W. Lee.

Northern

S. W. Lucas c Dipayan Paul b Lee	0	B. J. Sloan c Thornely b Tanveer Sikandar	4
D. J. Smith lbw b Ahmed	13	P. M. Park not out	16
L. B. Grey c Dipayan Paul b Lee	15	T. M. Sephton not out	0
*†J. Cole c Kerridge b Lee	7	B 2, l-b 5, w 7, n-b 2	16
R. Maddock c Lee b Dipayan Paul	58		
J. Boardman st Kerridge b Hands	28	1/0 (1) 2/20 (3) (9 wkts, 45 overs) 161
I. Carroll c Thornely b Hands	2	3/35 (4) 4/42 (2)
S. Cole c C. J. Willetts b Dipayan Paul	2	5/115 (6) 6/119 (7) 7/131 (8) 8/137 (9)
		9/158 (5)

Lee 7–1–25–3; Tanveer Sikandar 9–1–29–1; Ahmed 5–1–18–1; Mees 7–0–35–0; Hands 9–1–13–2; Dipayan Paul 8–1–34–2.

Blackheath

*C. J. Willetts not out	58
J. S. Ahmed c Boardman b Sephton	32
Tanveer Sikandar not out	52
L-b 8, w 12	20

1/67 (2)   (1 wkt, 29.4 overs) 162

M. A. Thornely, Dipayan Paul, D. Willetts, W. W. Lee, M. Mahfuzul, †J. Kerridge, J. M. Hands and T. Mees did not bat.

Maddock 7–1–24–0; S. Cole 3–0–22–0; Sephton 7–1–45–1; Grey 8.4–0–42–0; Park 4–0–21–0.

WINNERS 2005–2015

2005	Horsham	2011	Ealing
2006	South Northumberland	2012	York
2007	Bromley	2013	West Indian Cavaliers
2008	Kibworth	2014	Sandiacre Town
2009	Chester-le-Street	2015	Blackheath
2010	South Northumberland		

A full list of winners from 1969 to 2004 appears in Wisden 2005, *page 941.*

NATWEST CLUB T20

First semi-final   At Cardiff, September 1. **Exmouth won by five wickets. ‡Pudsey Congs 152-7** (20 overs) (A. Patel 44, A. D. Bairstow 44*; G. R. Chappell 4-24); **Exmouth 154-5** (19.5 overs) (D. F. Lye 65).

Second semi-final   At Cardiff, September 1. **Ealing won by ten wickets. Chester Boughton Hall 82** (18 overs) (C. H. Glasper 3-12, D. M. Lane 3-24); ‡**Ealing 82-0** (12 overs) (C. T. Peploe 40*).

Final   At Cardiff, September 1. **Ealing won by eight wickets. ‡Exmouth 174-7** (20 overs) (D. F. Lye 48, D. Pyle 41); **Ealing 177-2** (17.1 overs) (C. T. Peploe 70*, O. Wilkin 44, R. White 41*).

WINNERS 2008–2015

2008	South Northumberland	2012	Wimbledon
2009	Chester-le-Street	2013	Wimbledon
2010	Swardeston	2014	Chester Boughton Hall
2011	Ealing	2015	Ealing

DAVIDSTOW VILLAGE CUP IN 2015

BENJ MOOREHEAD

Within five days in September, Yorkshiremen twice stormed the Grace Gates and vanquished the southerners. First Yorkshire sealed the County Championship when they dismissed Middlesex for 106 in their first innings. Then Woodhouse Grange, the East Riding club, won the National Village Cup for a record fourth time, beating Foxton, of Cambridgeshire. Both county and club were repeating the success of the previous year. But, while another Yorkshire era may be dawning, Woodhouse Grange's stranglehold on the village game is at an end. In 2016 they will play in the new Yorkshire League North – an ECB Premier League – meaning they cannot compete in the Village Cup.

Dominance by a single team may not sit easily with a competition designed with the underdog at heart, but even romantics must recognise Grange's achievement in making seven village finals since 1995 – and five of the last nine. Nick Hadfield, the captain whose runs and wickets were again decisive, and Steve Burdett, who played with a damaged knee to make a crucial 58 in the semi, were both in their sixth final. Above all, it has been a triumph of unyielding focus, of keeping the same set of players committed to the outmoded notion of Sunday cricket, year after year.

A fourth title put Woodhouse Grange one ahead of St Fagans, from Cardiff, and Troon, who in 2015 were unable to raise a side for their regional game against Boconnoc. It was the third match Troon had forfeited in a week, and followed the club's decision to quit their Cornish league due to "player transfers, long-term injuries, and unavailability caused by family work and commitments".

Foxton were gallant losers, scoring the most runs by a team batting second in a Village final. Cei Sanderson, an opening batsman from Cheshire, made three successive hundreds before his 74 in the final, and 536 runs in all. Wickets were shared, led by the powerful figure of Jeffrey Douglas, a charismatic Jamaican-born cricketer whose all-round tenacity is in the mould of Ben Stokes. Douglas held his nerve in the last over of the helter-skelter semi-final against two-time winners Goatacre, when Ed Wilkins's counter-attacking 115 came within a whisker of taking his Wiltshire side to Lord's for the first time since 1990. Wilkins's godfather, Kevin Iles, played in that final and, at the age of 53, was an ever-present in 2015. Even Iles could not recall a comeback like the quarter-final win against Roche, from Cornwall, when Goatacre's No. 11 Matthew House, a naturalised seamer from New South Wales, smashed 66 from 23 balls during an unbroken last-wicket stand of 101 in seven overs. Goatacre finished on 231 for nine, and won by 98 runs.

Thirty years since the Fifers of Freuchie brought Scotland its one Village Cup, local rivals Falkland reached the last 16 with a stunning one-run victory against Ouseburn in Harrogate, a match of 613 runs. Welsh hopes evaporated after Bronwydd, of Camarthenshire, were beaten in an unsavoury quarter-final against Pelsall in Walsall. Supporters from a nearby football game burned a hole in the visitors' Welsh flag, and the Bronwydd chairman was headbutted.

It soured a fine run by Pelsall, whose home defeat by Woodhouse Grange in the semi-finals was watched by police.

There was no such cup run for Avoncroft, dismissed for 23 at Astwood Bank in the Worcestershire section in May. After their bowlers had been taken for 357 in 40 overs, with opener Sam Thomas making an unbeaten 205, Avoncroft's openers held tight for nearly seven overs – before they lost all ten for 11 runs in the next seven. The margin of 334 runs was the eighth-biggest in 44 years of the competition.

FINAL

FOXTON v WOODHOUSE GRANGE

At Lord's, September 13. Woodhouse Grange won by 19 runs. Toss: Woodhouse Grange.

A week after Shane Watson had driven Moeen Ali into the top tier of the Pavilion during the sell-out one-day international, Jeffrey Douglas almost emulated the feat in front of a cluster of spectators. The six, which hit the wall above the away dressing-room balcony on the lower tier, capped a barnstorming six overs in which Foxton's fourth-wicket pair of Douglas and Cei Sanderson took the score from 70 to 129 to give the underdogs a chance of overhauling Woodhouse Grange's 256. But Douglas skyed his next ball to midwicket, and Sanderson, who had stroked the first delivery of the innings through cover, was debilitated by a groin strain, eventually going for a classy 74. There were cameos down the order, but Foxton fell behind against accurate bowling. Batting first in overcast conditions, Grange openers Andrew Bilton and Nick Hadfield had seen off the new ball to put on 120. Tight spells of off-spin from David Fagan and Gareth Roots briefly stemmed the flow, and the irrepressible Douglas took an inspired diving catch to dismiss Hadfield, but otherwise Foxton's bowling and fielding lacked the efficiency Grange would show. Chris Bilton and Tom Young belted 69 chanceless runs from the last five overs to catapult Grange to the second-highest total in a Village final.

Man of the Match: C. R. Bilton.

Woodhouse Grange

A. J. Bilton c Douglas b Fagan	60	
*N. G. Hadfield c Douglas b Roots	64	
†C. R. Bilton not out	65	
T. S. Young not out	40	
L-b 6, w 21	27	

1/120 (1) 2/168 (2)   (2 wkts, 40 overs) 256

M. D. Hattee, S. D. Burdett, C. J. Suddaby, D. A. Suddaby, J. L. Jackson, A. Horner and T. S. Quinn did not bat.

Deas 5–0–27–0; Douglas 9–0–48–0; Fagan 9–1–39–1; Cambridge 2–0–22–0; Sanderson 5–0–29–0; Roots 7–0–59–1; Dean 3–0–26–0.

Foxton

C. B. Sanderson c Young b C. J. Suddaby	74	†J. Coe c Horner b C. J. Suddaby	18
*A. Webster lbw b Quinn	2	P. Dean not out	8
H. Hunter c Hattee b Hadfield	18	B 3, l-b 5, w 8, n-b 2	18
D. Fagan c C. R. Bilton b Jackson	1		
J. Douglas c Hattee b Jackson	47	1/27 (2) 2/48 (3) (8 wkts, 40 overs) 237	
D. G. Roots c C. R. Bilton b Burdett	22	3/53 (4) 4/130 (5)	
A. Akhter c Burdett b C. J. Suddaby	29	5/177 (1) 6/180 (6) 7/209 (8) 8/237 (7)	

A. Cambridge and T. S. Deas did not bat.

Horner 3–0–18–0; Quinn 9–0–26–1; Hadfield 6–1–40–1; Jackson 9–2–44–2; D. A. Suddaby 2–0–18–0; Burdett 6–0–43–1; C. J. Suddaby 5–0–40–3.

Umpires: D. Bull and C. Dunn.

DISABILITY CRICKET IN 2015

PAUL EDWARDS

"None of us have really understood what has happened over the course of the last fortnight. We've gone from setting off on tour with only our friends and family interested in what we were doing… to a point where the men's ODI team – and even David Cameron – were tweeting about us." This was the reaction of Iain Nairn, captain of England's Physical Disability team, on Sky TV after his side had won the five-nation tournament organised by the International Committee of the Red Cross. In fact, the significance of the victory carried far beyond Downing Street: it extended to all cricket-mad disabled children in the land, and offered reassurance that the game could include them too.

The Twenty20 tournament, held in Bangladesh in September, was the first multinational event between physically disabled teams. Suddenly, Sky were taking an interest, and the players were being lauded across the country. Ian Salisbury, the former England leg-spinner who was appointed coach in the summer, paid heart-warming tribute to the side at the end-of-season Cricket Writers' Club lunch.

Almost no one had foreseen England's breakthrough. Nairn's team lost their first game against the hosts, and needed to win the rest of their matches to secure the trophy. They accomplished this with relatively little fuss, winning their remaining three group games, before beating Pakistan by 19 runs in the final at Dhaka. Twenty-year-old Callum Flynn, who had hoped to play age-group cricket for Lancashire before bone cancer led to a knee replacement when he was 14, was named both Batsman and Player of the Series.

England's triumph reinforced the belief that disabled cricket has made more progress recently than even its most optimistic supporter could have predicted. The work of Sport England and the county boards is making the game available to more people, who are seizing their opportunities. "Physical disability cricket has moved further in the last 12 months than in the previous 15–20 years," said Ian Martin, the ECB's head of disability cricket. "The next goal is a world disability tournament running in the same season and at the same venue as an ICC tournament. I think we may do it in 2019.

"But I also want us to have a game which people can enjoy without necessarily being very good at it. And I don't think we're very far away from realising that goal. It's a Paralympic year in 2016, and we always have a challenge at such times, because the public's perception of disability sport is driven by the images they take from the podiums. But there is a great deal going on that is not in the Paralympics."

And a lot has been happening in elite disabled cricket. England's Visually Impaired team lost all five matches when India, the world champions, toured in May, but could take pride in improved performances since the previous winter's World Cup in South Africa. Luke Sugg, who scored four centuries in that tournament, was named disabled Player of the Year, and went on to make

Firoz Ahmed, ICRC

Proper recognition: England's Physical Disability team celebrate their triumph in Bangladesh.

a century and two fifties as the team regained the Ashes with a 4–1 victory in Australia in January 2016. Matthew Dean, the captain, made 96 not out, 116, 101 and 52 not out, while Ed Hossell's figures of five for 35 in the final 40-over match were the best by an England player. The Twenty20 series was drawn 1–1.

In March 2015 the Learning Disability team had also won in Australia. Chris Edwards led his side to a 5–1 victory, scoring his first international century in the sixth match, and averaging 97. International deaf cricket is going through a lull, though England compete in a four-team tournament in Dubai in the spring of 2016.

ENGLAND UNDER-19 v AUSTRALIA UNDER-19 IN 2015

BENJ MOOREHEAD

Under-19 Test (1): England 0, Australia 0
Under-19 one-day internationals (5): England 2, Australia 2

Four months on from their skirmishes in Perth, the return bout in England produced a similar tale, with Australia ahead on points, if not results. They had the better of the drawn Test at Chester-le-Street, where England were grateful for a sixth-wicket stand of 144 between Aaron Thomason and Ryan Davies, and – as at the WACA in April – second-innings resistance from Haseeb Hameed. This time Australia had to settle for parity over five one-day matches, one of which was abandoned. But their two victories were emphatic, and they were denied only by England's stunning chase of 295 in the final game, at Worcester, two days after the hosts had been rolled for 99.

An echo of the earlier series was the form of Australia's captain, Jake Doran. A compact, busy left-hander who also keeps wicket, he took his total to 773 runs in 12 innings across all matches on both tours. His timing was excellent: his second-innings 76 in Durham (after103 in the first) came the day after the senior Test side had been dismissed for 60 at Trent Bridge, leading former leg-spinner Stuart MacGill to demand his selection for the Fifth Test at The Oval. Graeme Hick, Australia's Under-19 coach, was more measured: "He's a lot more relaxed early in his innings, and he's playing shots he wouldn't have done a year ago. That's just a maturity and a confidence thing. Whether it's this year or next year, I'm sure we will hear a lot more from him."

Doran wasn't even Australia's top-scorer in England – Caleb Jewell, a tidy Tasmanian opener, made 401 runs overall, including two centuries; his only failure came at Leicester, where he was run out without facing. He was one of seven Australians called up, the selectors wanting players young enough for the 2015-16 Under-19 World Cup in Bangladesh – only for Cricket Australia to pull out on security grounds. England were unable to call on many first-choice players: Sam Curran (Surrey) and Saif Zaib (Northamptonshire) were on county duty, while the availability of Mason Crane (Hampshire) and Hameed (Lancashire) was limited. Other county first-teamers, such as 17-year-old Matthew Fisher at Yorkshire, were left out altogether. Eight members of the squad made their Championship debuts in 2015.

That was the good news. The seam attack was weaker for the absence of Saqib Mahmood, who strained a calf in the Test and then lost a fingernail on his return, at Derby. The one-day batting was again flaky: the imposing Essex opener Dan Lawrence made a pair of audacious hundreds, but of the rest only Jack Burnham passed 50. Less expected was the success of Staffordshire's Matt Parkinson, whose nine wickets in the four-day match – coupled with Crane's form at Hampshire – encouraged the thought that an English leg-spinner may yet hit the big time.

SQUADS

England *H. Hameed (Lancashire), A. H. T. Donald (Glamorgan), T. P. Alsop (Hampshire), H. R. Bernard (Kent), J. T. A. Burnham (Durham), M. S. Crane (Hampshire), S. M. Curran (Surrey), R. C. Davies (Kent), G. H. S. Garton (Sussex), B. G. F. Green (Somerset), A. J. Hickey (Durham), M. D. E. Holden (Middlesex), D. W. Lawrence (Essex), S. Mahmood (Lancashire), M. W. Parkinson (Staffordshire), B. J. Taylor (Hampshire), C. J. Taylor (Essex), A. D. Thomason (Warwickshire), J. D. Warner (Yorkshire), S. A. Zaib (Northamptonshire). *Coach:* A. Hurry.

Donald captained in the one-dayers. Alsop, Garton, Holden and Parkinson were selected for the Test match only; Bernard, Burnham, Donald and Hickey for the one-day series only.

Australia *J. R. Doran, J. A. S. Gauci, D. M. K. Grant, S. E. J. Grimwade, L. C. Hatcher, T. A. Healy, C. P. Jewell, A. Nair, J. R. Pattison, W. J. Pucovski, M. T. Renshaw, J. A. Richardson, F. A. Seymour, B. J. Taylor, H. T. R. Y. Thornton. *Coach:* G. A. Hick.

S. B Harper and P. C. Page were injured, and replaced by Renshaw and Seymour.

ENGLAND v AUSTRALIA

Under-19 Test Match

At Durham, August 4–7. Drawn. Toss: Australia Under-19.

Four gruelling days ended fairly in a draw, but the tourists always had their noses in front after England's wayward start in the field. Jake Doran, dropped on nought, then dismissed off a no-ball in the next over, shared stands of 77 with Jordan Gauci – who made a chanceless hundred – and, after a mini-collapse of three for six, 152 with Jhye Richardson. England's batsmen responded with gumption – both in the first innings against a fiery Richardson, and in the second, when a target of 308 in 47 overs was purely notional. In between, Caleb Jewell made a well-judged century, and Doran crafted 76 to ensure the match award. However, the game will also be remembered for a marathon effort from debutant leg-spinner Matthew Parkinson, a late replacement for the injured Brad Taylor. Parkinson's first-day workload amounted to 30.3 overs into a strong wind on an unresponsive pitch – yet he still managed five for 85, and finished with match figures of 71–16–222–9.

Close of play: first day, Australia Under-19 373-8 (Grant 10); second day, England Under-19 242-5 (Thomason 31, Davies 42); third day, Australia Under-19 91-3 (Jewell 38).

Australia Under-19

C. P. Jewell c Hameed b Parkinson	37	– (2) not out	109
J. R. Pattison c Davies b Mahmood	1	– (1) c Lawrence b Green	28
J. A. S. Gauci c Alsop b Green	111	– lbw b Parkinson	14
*J. R. Doran lbw b Parkinson	103	– (5) c Parkinson b Green	76
W. J. Pucovski c Davies b Parkinson	0	– (4) lbw b Parkinson	3
†T. A. Healy lbw b Green	1	– lbw b Green	6
J. A. Richardson c Warner b Parkinson	87	– st Davies b Parkinson	1
F. A. Seymour b Parkinson	1	– not out	2
D. M. K. Grant not out	46		
L. C. Hatcher b Parkinson	36		
S. E. J. Grimwade b Green	0		
B 5, l-b 3, w 9, n-b 6	23	B 3, l-b 2, w 3, n-b 6	14

1/2 (2) 2/108 (1) 3/185 (3) (110.5 overs) 446   1/56 (1) (6 wkts dec, 86 overs) 253
4/186 (5) 5/191 (6) 6/343 (4)   2/86 (3) 3/91 (4)
7/348 (8) 8/373 (7) 9/445 (10) 10/446 (11)   4/223 (5) 5/244 (6) 6/247 (7)

Mahmood 16–4–53–1; Warner 20–2–82–0; Green 15.5–1–72–3; Thomason 8–0–36–0; Taylor 3–0–25–0; Parkinson 38–10–130–6; Holden 10–1–40–0. *Second innings*—Thomason 10–2–24–0; Warner 12–3–30–0; Parkinson 33–6–92–3; Green 20–0–65–3; Taylor 2–0–7–0; Holden 6–1–21–0; Hameed 3–0–9–0.

England Under-19

T. P. Alsop lbw b Seymour	66	– c sub (M. T. Renshaw) b Grimwade .	39
M. D. E. Holden c Healy b Richardson	55	– c Doran b Grant	2
*H. Hameed lbw b Hatcher	21	– not out	72
D. W. Lawrence c Doran b Richardson	0	– c Healy b Seymour	27
C. J. Taylor b Richardson.	0	– not out	34
A. D. Thomason lbw b Seymour	67		
†R. C. Davies c Pucovski b Grant	73		
B. G. F. Green b Richardson	6		
J. D. Warner c Healy b Richardson	11		
M. W. Parkinson not out	32		
S. Mahmood b Grant	8		
B 22, l-b 20, w 5, n-b 6	53	B 5, w 6, n-b 1	12

1/95 (1) 2/143 (2) 3/143 (4)   (137.5 overs) 392   1/10 (2)   (3 wkts, 35 overs) 186
4/143 (5) 5/161 (3) 6/305 (7)   2/73 (1) 3/117 (4)
7/320 (6) 8/329 (8) 9/365 (9) 10/392 (11)

Richardson 26–9–75–5; Grant 25.5–10–62–2; Grimwade 38–12–86–0; Hatcher 16–6–40–1; Pattison 17–2–45–0; Seymour 14–8–41–2; Doran 1–0–1–0. *Second innings*—Richardson 7–2–32–0; Grant 6–1–19–1; Hatcher 7–1–48–0; Seymour 5–1–18–1; Grimwade 8–0–46–1; Doran 2–0–18–0.

Umpires: M. A. Gough and A. G. Wharf.

First Under-19 one-day international   At Gosforth, August 11. **Australia won by eight wickets.** ‡England 206 (45.1 overs) (C. J. Taylor 35, B. J. Taylor 33*; F. A. Seymour 4-56, A. J. Nair 4-33); Australia 207-2 (40.2 overs) (M. T. Renshaw 69*, C. P. Jewell 69, J. R. Doran 56*). *On a benign pitch England's batsmen got themselves in and out – four of the top six fell in the twenties – and it took a 36-ball innings from No. 9 Brad Taylor to raise 200. Tom Healy made two sharp stumpings: one standing up to Fletcher Seymour's medium-pace, the other to give a fourth wicket to Arjun Nair, a doosra-bowling off-spinner born to Indian parents but raised in Adelaide. Australia ticked off the runs at leisure, despite two wickets for Brad Taylor.*

Second Under-19 one-day international   At Chesterfield, August 14. **Abandoned.**

Third Under-19 one-day international   At Derby, August 17. **England won by three wickets.** ‡Australia 226-7 (50 overs) (C. P. Jewell 80, J. R. Doran 69, J. A. Richardson 30; H. R. Bernard 3-47, B. J. Taylor 3-50); England 229-7 (48.1 overs) (D. W. Lawrence 119, J. T. A. Burnham 33; D. M. K. Grant 3-46, J. R. Pattison 3-37). *Under lights and in front of the cameras, Dan Lawrence belted the highest Under-19 one-day score for England against Australia – beating Kevin Sharp's 107 at Arundel in 1977. Dropped on 27, he peppered the boundaries on both sides, hitting 18 fours and a six from 103 balls, before becoming the first of four wickets to fall for 12 runs as England staggered to their target. Earlier their bowlers had kept a lid on Australia's scoring-rate, crucially breaking a third-wicket stand of 137 between Jewell and Doran in the 40th over.*

Fourth Under-19 one-day international   At Leicester, August 20. ‡**Australia won by seven wickets.** England 99 (29.2 overs) (J. A. Richardson 3-33, L. C. Hatcher 6-27); ‡Australia 101-3 (20.2 overs) (M. T. Renshaw 39*). *England were rolled over by Liam Hatcher, who produced the best figures by an Australian at this level after England were inserted on a seaming pitch under heavy cloud. Richardson dismissed both openers before Hatcher engineered a collapse of 7-39. A last-wicket stand of 23 was the highest of the innings. Jewell was run out from the first ball of the reply, but opener Matthew Renshaw ensured Australia would take a 2–1 lead to New Road.*

Fifth Under-19 one-day international   At Worcester, August 22. **England won by four wickets.** Australia 294-6 (50 overs) (C. P. Jewell 106, J. A. S. Gauci 93; H. R. Bernard 3-52); ‡England 297-6 (49.4 overs) (D. W. Lawrence 106, A. J. Hickey 43, J. T. A. Burnham 53, A. H. T. Donald 38). *Another bold century from Lawrence inspired England towards their highest successful Under-19 run-chase – surpassing a pair of 272s, against India and New Zealand, both at Townsville in April 2012 – to square the series. Jewell and Jordan Gauci had begun with a stand of 196 for Australia on a good pitch. Lawrence led the reply, putting on 104 for the first wicket with Adam Hickey, and 101 for the second with Jack Burnham. But Lawrence was dismissed with 60 needed, and the chase went to the final over when Brad Taylor, whose ten overs had earlier gone for just 27, hit the winning boundary with two balls to spare to tarnish the homecoming of Australia's coach Graeme Hick.*

YOUTH CRICKET IN 2015

JAMES MCCALL

The ECB announced that the Kwik Cricket programme, designed to introduce the sport to Under-11s, was being reviewed "to ensure it is fit for purpose and achieving the outcome of getting more children playing more frequently in teams". The annual competition has been without a sponsor since January 2014 and, while the number of schools participating has risen since 2013, the number of children has declined.

There was better news from Chance to Shine, the charity that promotes cricket in state schools. They marked their tenth anniversary by announcing their aim of bringing the sport to another million children by 2020; the ECB estimate that the organisation have already introduced cricket to 2.5m children and 11,000 schools in England and Wales since 2005. In September's Chance to Shine Schools Cup national finals in Birmingham, 16 sides competed for honours at Under-15 and Under-13 level. Altrincham Grammar School for Boys claimed the Under-15 mixed competition after they won a dramatic bowlout against Haygrove School. South Dartmoor Community College were crowned girls Under-15 champions after they defeated South Hunsley, watched by England stars – and Chance to Shine ambassadors – Charlotte Edwards and Lydia Greenway.

The annual Bunbury Festival was hosted by Malvern College in Worcestershire, and was won by the South West. Lancashire's George Lavelle, who was selected for the North, stood out and claimed prizes – presented by Mike Gatting and England assistant coach Paul Farbrace – for best wicketkeeper, best all-rounder, most runs and most valuable player. Bunbury's ability to discover future international players remains second to none: 11 of the 13-man squad selected against Australia at Edgbaston in July had once taken part in the festival.

The third edition of the Super 4s tournament at Loughborough was won by the Midlands, who beat the North by 62 runs in the final. Nottinghamshire wicketkeeper Tom Keast was Player of the Tournament, making four stumpings against the South West and holding five catches against the North. In the third-place play-off, London & East chased down South West's 297 for seven to steal a two-wicket victory with three balls to spare.

In February, England Under-17 visited the UAE to take on Pakistan. They lost the one-day internationals 2–1, despite some promising all-round displays from captain Max Holden, and drew the three-day match.

Winners of age-group competitions – Under-17 County Championship Hampshire. **Under-17 County Cup** Surrey. **Under-17 B County Cup** Buckinghamshire. **Under-17 Girls County Championship** Lancashire. **Under-15 County Cup** Lancashire. **Under-15 Bunbury Festival** South West. **Under-15 B County Cup** Staffordshire and Middlesex. **Under-15 Girls County Championship** Yorkshire. **Under-15 Club Championship** Himley. **Under-13 Girls Chance to Shine Schools Cup** Urmston Grammar School. **Under-13 Mixed Chance to Shine Schools Cup** Hutton Grammar School. **Under-13 Club Championship** Guildford. **Under-13 Girls Championship** Yorkshire.

SCHOOLS CRICKET IN 2015

REVIEW BY DOUGLAS HENDERSON

Many people, especially of a certain age, struggle to watch schools cricket because of the on-field nonsense that now accompanies it: incessant noise, inane shouting, wides applauded with cries of "well bowled", and catches greeted as though they had just secured the World Cup… It's cheating, of course, the aim not to encourage team-mates but to intimidate the batsmen. In one match, the umpires instructed the fielding captain that the game would be conducted in complete silence, which it was.

The Spirit of Cricket is a preamble to the Laws rather than an integral part, though it does carry some weight, since Law 42 states that the "responsibility lies with the captains for ensuring that play is conducted within the spirit and traditions of the game, as described in The Preamble – The Spirit of Cricket, as well as within the Laws". That preamble is unambiguous, describing it as "against the Spirit of the Game… to indulge in cheating or any sharp practice, for instance… to seek to distract an opponent either verbally or by harassment with persistent clapping or unnecessary noise under the guise of enthusiasm and motivation of one's own side".

Even on finals day of the National Schools T20, the experienced umpires had to intervene several times, telling the captain to quieten things down. One of those umpires was Mark Williams, the new MCC Laws of Cricket Advisor, who is responsible for drafting the new code, due in 2017. One proposal is that elements of The Spirit of Cricket should be built into Law 42, and that umpires should have sanctions against misconduct. (Currently, cricket is the only major team sport in which the on-field officials are powerless to act against a persistent offender.)

Change may be afoot. "It is clear that players' behaviour has been deteriorating worldwide in amateur and junior cricket over the last few years," says Williams. "MCC are concerned about this and are seriously considering giving the umpires on-field sanctions to deal with misconduct. MCC are particularly concerned that young players should learn to play the game in an appropriate environment, where the expected standards of behaviour are high. Schoolmasters and coaches have a major responsibility to ensure this happens."

Since their trade does not translate neatly into numbers, wicketkeepers can get a raw deal. But if someone has many more stumpings than catches, it's a statistic that can't be ignored. After three seasons in the first team at Merchant Taylors', Crosby, 15-year-old George Lavelle had 40 stumpings and 32 catches. He captained Lancashire to the Under-15s championship and won several awards at the 2015 Bunbury Festival. He would probably have scored 1,000 runs for his school had he not missed several Saturday games playing for his club. As it was, he made 778 – and is a name to watch.

The most startling individual performance came at Under-14 level, when Robert Bassin of Bedford Modern took all ten wickets for nine runs in the

Jamie Pluck, courtesy of the *Saffron Walden Reporter*

Felsted's Ben Waring: the ninth Wisden Schools Cricketer of the Year.

Bedfordshire County Cup. Almost as striking was Lee Tyrrell, whose brisk inswingers claimed nine for three for Aldenham's senior team. Not since 2009 had anyone taken 50 wickets in a season, such are the restrictions on bowlers, either because of the prevalence of limited-overs games or because the ECB put a limit on spells for seamers. However, Felsted's slow left-armer Ben Waring ended with an astonishing 68 in normal games – at an average of 9.30. He has another year at school. The last player to reach 60 was Daniel Pheloung, another Felstedian, in 2005. Four others got to 40: Robert Bentley of Hampton, Tyler Meyer of Whitgift, Oundle's Benedict Graves and Aldenham's Tyrrell.

The season started with a bang: three double-centuries in the first three weeks. Brentwood's Rishi Patel hit 200 from 138 deliveries – including 31 fours and six sixes – and put on 320 with Harry Levy; next came Felsted's

Reece Hussain, nephew of Nasser, who made an unbeaten 200 en route to a Bradmanesque average of 95, boosted by seven not-outs; and Henry Gater of Taunton scored 206 in 44 overs, including nine sixes and 22 fours.

Four batsmen averaged over 100 (though no one did so from five or more completed innings): Martin Andersson of Reading Blue Coat School, James O'Neill from Birkenhead, Milan Mniszko of The Leys, and Bedford's Charlie Clarke. None of these totalled 500 for the season. O'Neill made an unbeaten 210, and Oundle's Tristan Tusa an undefeated 203, including a century in sixes. He shared a stand of 311 with opening partner Simon Fernandes, but his other 13 innings produced a total of just 144. Ten batsmen reached 1,000 for the summer — an indication that for most schools the weather wasn't too bad. Oliver Westbury of Shrewsbury struck six centuries, followed by Anshuman Rath of Harrow, who made five. Oundle's Graves hit four and a 99 not out.

It's trickier to rank all-rounders, but the best included Rath (1,075 runs and 37 wickets), Graves (894 and 40) and Tyrrell (708 and 40), as well as Whitgift's Ryan Patel (1,043 and 35).

For the second year running, Churcher's College in Petersfield boasted a 100% record — it's a shame they don't play more matches. Sir Thomas Rich's, a state grammar in Gloucester, enjoyed a 90% win-rate, including a defeat of the formidable RGS Worcester.

Records stretching across the entire sector are almost impossible to establish, though it seems likely that Caterham's 427 for five against Christ's Hospital was the highest score in a limited-overs match (beating the 425 made by Tiffin in 2004), since such games were few and far between in the last century. Led by captain Ross Powell, who made 158, Caterham scored at an electrifying rate in the 20 overs after lunch. Tiffin were themselves on the receiving end of an extraordinary score. Against decent bowling, Reed's amassed 375 for one in just 35 overs, with all three batsmen making hundreds: Sonny Cott, the captain, hit 139 in 85 balls; his opening partner Nathan Tilley, an Under-15, made 100 not out in 91; and Daniel Douthwaite, in an extraordinary innings containing only one dot ball, spanked an undefeated 125 from 35. He reached his hundred from his 31st delivery and clattered 34 from the last over, ending with 12 sixes and ten fours.

The National Schools T20 competition produced a sensational result in a regional final, when a north Bristol sixth-form college comfortably defeated Millfield. South Gloucestershire and Stroud College, based in Filton, have no home ground, though in former Gloucestershire opener Tim Hancock they have an experienced coach. Chasing a formidable 180, SGS were led to a famous victory by a 62-ball 107 from James Bracey. However, they stumbled against a strong Wellington College side, who progressed to finals day at Arundel.

Up against a Hurstpierpoint team boasting five Sussex Academy players, Wellington seemed likely to make a huge score so long as Sam Curran — with another year at school, yet about to become a Surrey regular — was flaying the ball to all corners. But he fell to a rash shot for 43, and Wellington set a target of 167 — demanding rather than daunting. George Garton struck the ball as cleanly as anyone and, after some nervous moments, Hurstpierpoint got home.

In the final, Malvern – who had overcome Sedbergh with ease – couldn't match the firepower of Hurstpierpoint, who deservedly won the trophy.

The choice of the 2015 Schools Cricketers of the Year was especially hard. Of at least three strong contenders, two – Hussain and Waring – both came from Felsted. Hussain scored 1,147 runs in 19 innings, while Winchester's Daniel Escott was only 51 behind from three fewer innings. In five years in the first XI, Escott did not miss a single game – a feat unmatched even by that illustrious Wykehamist, the Nawab of Pataudi. However, the Wisden Schools Cricketer of the Year is, for the first time, a bowler.

According to the former England Test batsman Jason Gallian, his coach at Felsted, Ben Waring is a slow left-armer who gives the ball good flight at a varied pace, and gets decent turn. He is also blessed with three of the most important qualities a spinner can possess: control, patience and an appetite for hard work. The winner of one of three cricket scholarships, Ben arrived at Felsted from Birchwood High School in Bishop's Stortford, having made his Hertfordshire debut at the age of 15. Bowling is unquestionably Ben's main suit, but he is athletic enough to field at backward point. His record confirms he has thrived on the extra opportunities, and there may soon be more: Essex have invited him to join their Academy.

WISDEN SCHOOLS CRICKETERS OF THE YEAR

2007	Jonathan Bairstow	St Peter's School, York
2008	James Taylor	Shrewsbury School
2009	Jos Buttler	King's College, Taunton
2010	Will Vanderspar	Eton College
2011	Daniel Bell-Drummond	Millfield School
2012	Thomas Abell	Taunton School
2013	Tom Köhler-Cadmore	Malvern College
2014	Dylan Budge	Woodhouse Grove
2015	**Ben Waring**	**Felsted School**

MCC Schools v ESCA

At Lord's, September 8. **MCC Schools won by two wickets. ESCA** 219-7 (50 overs) (H. C. Brook 34, T. J. Haines 63, J. L. N. Garrett 44, T. Banton 43); ‡**MCC Schools** 222-8 (49.5 overs) (B. Lynch 68, J. B. R. Keeping 34; R. R. Jafri 3-43).

ESCA *T. J. Haines (*Hurstpierpoint College*), L. Banks (*Newcastle Community HS*), T. Banton (*Bromsgrove School*), A. P. Beard (*Great Baddow HS, Chelmsford*), H. C. Brook (*Sedbergh School*), B. Claydon (*Bottisham Village College*), A. E. C. Dahl (*Cranleigh School*), J. L. N. Garrett (*Henry Box School*), R. R. Jafri (*Southborough HS*), F. S. Organ (*Canford School*), A. M. Thomas (*Merchant Taylors', Northwood*).

MCC *O. J. D. Pope (*Cranleigh School*), E. R. Bamber (*Mill Hill School*), Z. Crawley (*Tonbridge School*), D. A. Douthwaite (*Reed's School*), J. B. R. Keeping (*Stowe School*), B. Lynch (*King's College, Taunton*), J. I. McCoy (*Millfield School*), T. Z. Meyer (*Whitgift School*), S. D. Rimmer (*The King's School, Chester*), J. E. Smith (*Eastbourne College*), O. E. Westbury (*Shrewsbury School*).

Full coverage of the 2015 Eton v Harrow match can be found at wisden.com.

Schools who wish to be considered for inclusion should email *Wisden* at almanack@wisden.com. State schools and girls' schools are especially welcome.

Note: The following tables cover only those schools listed in the Schools A–Z section.

SCHOOLS AVERAGES

BEST BATTING AVERAGES (5 completed innings)

		I	NO	Runs	HS	100	Avge
1	R. Hussain (*Felsted School*)	19	7	1,147	200*	3	95.58
2	C. W. Holt (*Culford School*)	10	5	470	88*	0	94.00
3	R. J. Povey (*Rugby School*)	16	5	1,027	150	3	93.36
4	Z. Malik (*Malvern College*)	10	3	622	114*	3	88.85
5	J. A. Norman (*Monmouth School*)	11	1	847	184	4	84.70
6	Z. Crawley (*Tonbridge School*)	16	3	1,069	127*	4	82.23
7	O. M. D. Kolk (*Reed's School*)	15	6	740	181*	1	82.22
8	M. C. Erasmus (*Forest School*)	14	4	802	157*	4	80.20
9	T. R. A. Scriven (*Magdalen College School*)	16	6	799	132*	1	79.90
10	J. Tyrer (*Sir Thomas Rich's School*)	7	2	394	97*	0	78.80
11	D. A. Escott (*Winchester College*)	16	2	1,096	179	4	78.28
12	R. A. Udwadia (*Manchester GS*)	12	7	386	62*	0	77.20
13	B. J. Graff (*Westminster School*)	13	3	771	103*	2	77.10
14	C. O. Brain (*Kingswood School, Bath*)	14	3	843	160	1	76.63
15	R. R. Powell (*Caterham School*)	9	1	613	158	3	76.62
16	A. M. Andrady (*King's School, Chester*)	8	2	456	131*	1	76.00
17	O. J. D. Pope (*Cranleigh School*)	12	3	646	102	1	71.77
18	G. T. Hankins (*Millfield School*)	18	4	1,000	140	4	71.42
19	D. T. Lewis (*Clifton College*)	15	9	427	71*	0	71.16
20	L. Bedford (*Cranleigh School*)	16	5	780	107*	1	70.90
21	H. A. E. Hanford (*Caterham School*)	10	3	492	101*	1	70.28
22	B. W. M. Graves (*Oundle School*)	16	3	894	148	4	68.76
23	L. R. Henderson (*Durham School*)	19	8	750	113	1	68.18
24	E. I. Samuel (*Marlborough College*)	11	2	612	134	2	68.00
25	T. J. E. Weeks (*Bishop's Stortford College*)	10	3	472	103	1	67.42
26	A. A. Edekar (*St Edward's School, Oxford*)	13	5	536	126	1	67.00
27	C. R. Rule (*Ipswich School*)	12	0	786	154	4	65.50
28	T. R. Williamson (*Lancaster RGS*)	15	4	718	129	3	65.27

Four batsmen averaged over 100, but from fewer than five completed innings: M. K. Andersson (*Reading Blue Coat School*) 224.50; J. O'Neill (*Birkenhead School*) 203.50; M. A. Mniszko (*The Leys School*) 127.33; *and* C. R. Clarke (*Bedford School*) 103.00.

MOST RUNS

		I	NO	Runs	HS	100	Avge
1	R. Hussain (*Felsted School*)	19	7	1,147	200*	3	95.58
2	D. A. Escott (*Winchester College*)	16	2	1,096	179	4	78.28
3	A. Rath (*Harrow School*)	19	2	1,075	137*	5	63.23
4	Z. Crawley (*Tonbridge School*)	16	3	1,069	127*	4	82.23
5	O. E. Westbury (*Shrewsbury School*)	21	2	1,048	112	6	55.15
6	R. P. Patel (*Whitgift School*)	21	3	1,043	121	2	57.94
7	A. D. L. Russell (*Eton College*)	21	3	1,033	101*	1	57.38
8	R. J. Povey (*Rugby School*)	16	5	1,027	150	3	93.36
9	H. R. C. Came (*Bradfield College*)	20	4	1,003	139	3	62.68
10	G. T. Hankins (*Millfield School*)	18	4	1,000	140	4	71.42
11	C. M. Dickinson (*St Edward's School, Oxford*)	20	0	986	181	3	49.30
12	B. W. M. Graves (*Oundle School*)	16	3	894	148	4	68.76
13	A. D. Greenidge (*Dulwich College*)	18	1	889	186	4	52.29
14	J. E. Smith (*Eastbourne College*)	21	2	863	144	3	45.42
15	O. J. Grayson (*Felsted School*)	22	7	857	115*	2	57.13
16	J. A. Norman (*Monmouth School*)	11	1	847	184	4	84.70
17	C. O. Brain (*Kingswood School, Bath*)	14	3	843	160	1	76.63
18	F. R. Trenouth (*Clifton College*)	18	2	842	104*	2	52.62

		I	NO	Runs	HS	100	Avge
19	N. Welch (*Whitgift School*)	19	4	820	119	4	54.66
20	M. C. Erasmus (*Forest School*)	14	4	802	157*	4	80.20
21	T. R. A. Scriven (*Magdalen College School*)	16	6	799	132*	1	79.90
22	C. R. Rule (*Ipswich School*)	12	0	786	154	4	65.50
23	L. Bedford (*Cranleigh School*)	16	5	780	107*	1	70.90
24	G. I. D. Lavelle (*Merchant Taylors', Crosby*)	15	2	778	130*	1	59.84
25	B. J. Graff (*Westminster School*)	13	3	771	103*	2	77.10
26	J. H. Ludlow (*Hurstpierpoint College*)	14	1	760	176*	2	58.46
27	L. R. Henderson (*Durham School*)	19	8	750	113	1	68.18

BEST BOWLING AVERAGE (10 wickets)

		O	M	Runs	W	BB	Avge
1	F. H. Ambrose (*Canford School*)	54	9	167	26	5-17	6.42
2	C. J. Bridge (*Leeds Grammar School*)	60	16	135	19	3-20	7.10
3	J. Godfrey (*Woodhouse Grove School*)	23.2	3	82	11	5-16	7.45
4	A. W. G. Anderson (*George Heriot's School*)	19	4	78	10	3-8	7.80
5	L. H. I. Tyrrell (*Aldenham School*)	93.5	22	321	40	9-3	8.02
6	H. Aravinthan (*John Fisher School*)	49	5	145	18	6-12	8.05
7	J. D. Buckeridge (*Portsmouth Grammar School*)	68	12	191	23	5-52	8.30
8	D. Y. Pennington (*Wrekin College*)	48	11	143	17	7-28	8.41
9	V. Sharma (*The Grammar School at Leeds*)	32	8	95	11	3-5	8.63
10	O. D. Clarke (*Stowe School*)	28.2	0	130	15	4-24	8.66
11	P. Griffiths (*Wolverhampton Grammar School*)	46	3	218	25	3-12	8.72
12	B. R. A. Moulton (*St Lawrence College*)	33	3	114	13	5-35	8.76
13	R. R. Powell (*Caterham School*)	52	13	185	21	5-6	8.80
14	A. U. Rehman (*Dr Challoner's GS*)	42.3	6	161	18	5-19	8.94
15	W. K. Doerr (*Ellesmere College*)	55	10	179	20	5-16	8.95
16	S. P. Patel (*Bedford School*)	63.1	17	146	16	4-12	9.12
17	B. A. Waring (*Felsted School*)	170.5	50	628	68	6-81	9.23
18	R. W. P. Leader (*Glenalmond College*)	36	6	140	15	4-19	9.33
19	T. A. Dunn (*The Leys School*)	36	4	94	10	4-17	9.40
20	C. H. G. Baynes-Holden (*Denstone College*)	47	7	164	17	5-17	9.64
21	W. G. Kilbourn (*Mill Hill School*)	31	7	98	10	4-16	9.80
22	H. F. Dixon (*The Grammar School at Leeds*)	68	10	220	22	3-8	10.00

MOST WICKETS

		O	M	Runs	W	BB	Avge
1	B. A. Waring (*Felsted School*)	170.5	50	628	68	6-81	9.23
2	R. J. Bentley (*Hampton School*)	130	28	483	46	6-54	10.50
3	T. Meyer (*Whitgift School*)	155.5	32	475	45	7-24	10.55
4	L. H. I. Tyrrell (*Aldenham School*)	93.5	22	321	40	9-3	8.02
	B. W. M. Graves (*Oundle School*)	221.3	42	612	40	5-36	15.30
6	O. Birts (*Bradfield College*)	205	38	733	39	5-66	18.79
7	B. N. Evans (*Eastbourne College*)	131.3	27	495	38	6-24	13.02
8	A. Rath (*Harrow School*)	135.4	18	435	37	4-35	11.75
	R. A. Lock (*Whitgift School*)	168.4	26	587	37	4-13	15.86
	S. Shah (*Royal Grammar School, Worcester*)	165.2	17	626	37	4-25	16.91
11	L. J. Chapman (*Felsted School*)	167.4	35	577	36	4-10	16.02
12	C. G. Harrison (*King's College, Taunton*)	124	11	394	35	6-72	11.25
	R. P. Patel (*Whitgift School*)	136.4	16	453	35	4-31	12.94
	A. A. Cox (*Felsted School*)	147.4	35	498	35	4-19	14.22
	W. Jacks (*St George's College, Weybridge*)	145	20	575	35	5-11	16.42
16	J. M. P. Takavarasha (*Eton College*)	162	19	723	34	4-29	21.26
17	H. A. E. B. Portman (*Winchester College*)	141.0	23	394	33	5-22	11.93
	O. J. Brown (*George Watson's College*)	106	10	491	33	6-36	14.87
19	D. J. Clutterbuck (*Millfield School*)	155.4	20	475	32	5-26	14.84
	A. E. C. Dahl (*Cranleigh School*)	153.4	16	621	32	6-37	19.40

	O	M	Runs	W	BB	Avge
T. W. Loten (*Pocklington School*)	133	24	453	31	4-20	14.61
J. E. Smith (*Eastbourne College*)	147	16	549	31	6-34	17.70
J. P. Fischer (*Oundle School*)	183	30	638	31	6-76	20.58
D. J. Lloyd (*Shrewsbury School*)	199	28	663	31	4-42	21.38
B. A. Bhatti (*Tiffin School*)	14.5	23	663	31	7-33	21.38
S. A. Lakhani (*Haberdashers' Aske's BS*)	204.1	42	825	31	6-91	26.61

(row group label: 21)

OUTSTANDING SEASONS (minimum 7 matches)

	P	W	L	T	D	A	%W
Churcher's College	8	8	0	0	0	3	100.00
Bedford School	10	9	1	0	0	1	90.00
Sir Thomas Rich's School	10	9	1	0	0	3	90.00
Harrow School	19	17	2	0	0	0	89.47
Hurstpierpoint College	15	13	2	0	0	0	86.67
St Lawrence College	7	6	1	0	0	0	85.71
The Leys School	12	10	1	0	1	0	83.33
Whitgift School	21	17	2	0	2	0	80.95
Emanuel School	15	12	3	0	0	1	80.00
New Hall School	15	12	3	0	0	2	80.00
Millfield School	19	15	3	0	1	1	78.95
Ellesmere College	14	11	1	0	2	0	78.57
Felsted School	23	18	4	0	1	0	78.26
Birkenhead School	9	7	1	1	0	2	77.78
King's College, Taunton	18	14	3	0	1	1	77.78
St John's School, Leatherhead	13	10	3	0	0	0	76.92
Merchiston Castle School	13	10	3	0	0	0	76.92
St George's College, Weybridge	17	13	3	0	1	1	76.47
King's School, Worcester	17	13	3	0	1	2	76.47
Eastbourne College	21	16	4	0	1	1	76.19
Canford School	12	9	3	0	0	0	75.00
Silcoates School	12	9	3	0	0	2	75.00

The Grammar School at Leeds went unbeaten through the season, winning nine and drawing four of their 13 matches, giving a win-rate of 69.23%.

SCHOOLS A–Z

Counties have been included for all schools. Since cricket does not follow the current complex system of administrative division, *Wisden* has followed the county boundaries in existence before the dissolution of Middlesex in 1965. Those schools affected by the boundary changes of the last 50 years – such as Sedbergh, which was removed from Yorkshire and handed to Cumbria – are listed under their former county.

In the results line, A = abandoned without a ball bowled. An asterisk indicates captain. The qualification for the averages (which exclude Twenty20 and overseas tour games) is 150 runs or ten wickets.

Aldenham School *Hertfordshire*   P20 W11 L8 D1
Masters i/c C. S. Irish and M. I. Yeabsley   **Coach** D. G. Goodchild

From their 20 fixtures, Aldenham won 11 matches, including victories over Haileybury, Watford Grammar School and John Lyon. After five years in the first team, Lee Tyrrell passed 2,000 runs and reached 70 wickets – he took nine for three against Liverpool College. Daniel Murphy and the captain, Jonny Bryer, also did well. The school retained the Read Trophy and, for the first time, beat a John Dewes Invitational XI.

Batting L. H. I. Tyrrell 708 at 54.46; S. Woolley 151 at 50.33; D. S. G. Murphy 586 at 36.62; L. J. Prideaux 436 at 24.22; R. A. Kraushar 245 at 18.84; G. T. Ellingham 163 at 14.81; L. G. Hollett 231 at 13.58; *J. R. F. Bryer 164 at 10.93.

Bowling L. H. I. Tyrrell 40 at 8.02; U. Zeeshan-Lohya 10 at 12.00; S. Iqbal 17 at 23.29; S. Woolley 10 at 25.70; L. G. Hollett 14 at 33.71; J. R. F. Bryer 11 at 42.00.

Alleyn's School *Surrey*   P9 W6 L3

Master i/c R. N. Ody   **Coach** P. E. Edwards

Alleyn's enjoyed a good season, winning six of their nine games and finishing as runners-up in the London Cup. They were well led by Fergus Neve, who topped both averages.

Batting *F. S. Neve 347 at 38.55; J. J. Keeling 180 at 30.00; J. C. West 217 at 27.12.

Bowling F. S. Neve 11 at 15.00.

Bancroft's School *Essex*   P13 W6 L5 D2

Master i/c C. G. Greenidge

Some senior players believed it impossible to combine first-team cricket and exam success, and so the team was a young one. Samraj Sadra proved an able captain, and he enjoyed support from all-rounder Felix Edwards and colts Alex Agedah and Rishi Roy-Mukherjee. Results were auspicious.

Batting R. Roy-Mukherjee 170 at 42.50; F. Edwards 180 at 36.00; A. S. Nijjar 252 at 36.00; A. Agedah 270 at 30.00; V. Handa 269 at 26.90; *S. S. Sadra 238 at 26.44.

Bowling F. Edwards 22 at 14.45; V. Handa 13 at 15.07; R. Roy-Mukherjee 13 at 17.92; S. S. Sadra 13 at 18.76; H. Sohoye 13 at 20.84.

Barnard Castle School *Co. Durham*   P13 W3 L8 D2

Master i/c M. T. Pepper   **Coach** J. W. Lister

Although eight defeats suggest a disappointing season, many games were close, and – considering the age of the team – performances were most encouraging. Alex and Charlie Pearson, Toby Lush and Matthew Price are all good prospects.

Batting K. J. Atkinson 150 at 37.50; *T. F. Sowerby 300 at 33.33; T. J. Adamson 310 at 31.00.

Bowling C. L. Pearson 10 at 11.60; T. W. R. Lush 15 at 18.40; T. E. Stirke 10 at 23.10.

Bede's School *Sussex*   P17 W11 L6 A1

Master i/c A. P. Wells   **Coach** D. C. Gorringe

Despite some good individual performances the team did not play the consistent cricket of previous seasons. There were some outstanding victories, but overall it was a frustrating season from which lessons will be learned.

Batting J. Phelps 347 at 43.37; D. M. W. Rawlins 157 at 31.40; J. Billings 246 at 24.60; *C. Hodgson 195 at 24.37; D. Wilson 231 at 21.00.

Bowling D. M. W. Rawlins 14 at 10.92; J. Allen 15 at 17.13; J. Phelps 11 at 17.63; T. Gordon 12 at 22.08; T. Ogden 10 at 22.10; D. Wilson 13 at 22.61.

Bedford Modern School *Bedfordshire*   P13 W7 L6 A1

Master i/c P. J. Woodroffe

In an enjoyable summer with a winning record, Todd Pitkin was the leading batsman, while Ben Rodgers proved a talented all-rounder. Special mention goes to young wicketkeeper Matt Taylor, who held 16 catches and made five stumpings.

Batting A. Ali 155 at 38.75; T. B. Pitkin 376 at 34.18; B. R. Rodgers 238 at 26.44; R. J. Baxter 271 at 24.63; *T. H. J. Burman 164 at 20.50.

Bowling B. R. Rodgers 21 at 18.19; A. Ali 18 at 20.33; M. S. Rodgers 17 at 22.58; B. W. Jiggins 11 at 27.27.

Bedford School *Bedfordshire*   P10 W9 L1 A1

Master i/c I. G. S. Steer   **Coach** W. Montgomery

Quarter-final defeat in the National T20 Cup and a loss to Harrow were the only blemishes on another outstanding season. Openers Paddy McDuell and Jake Duxbury hit most runs, while the attack deserved great credit: Josh Selvey took six for 62 in their final game.

Batting C. R. Clarke 206 at 103.00; J. A. Duxbury 460 at 57.50; A. S. Momi 274 at 39.14; *P. R. J. McDuell 319 at 35.44; T. D. Bradbeer 156 at 26.00.

Bowling S. P. Patel 16 at 9.12; J. T. Selvey 19 at 17.31; P. R. J. McDuell 17 at 21.82; C. R. Clarke 12 at 23.16; B. Slawinski 16 at 27.00.

Berkhamsted School *Hertfordshire*   P17 W9 L6 D2

Master i/c G. R. A. Campbell

With nine wins and two draws from 17 matches, Berkhamsted enjoyed a solid season. Performances of note included a maiden hundred by 15-year-old Charlie Nicholls against Merchant Taylors', Matthew Pugh totalling 671 runs and Xavier Owen collecting 30 wickets.

Batting M. G. Pugh 671 at 39.47; C. A. Nicholls 509 at 33.93; J. D. Fosberry 231 at 25.66; A. Walters 176 at 25.14; X. G. Owen 310 at 20.66; W. Hughes 222 at 15.85; H. J. Robertson 158 at 14.36.

Bowling X. G. Owen 30 at 14.86; F. Thompson 11 at 15.00; H. Ormerod 17 at 19.58; O. Holdroyd 13 at 21.61; A. Walters 20 at 21.70; A. L. Nicholls 10 at 22.60; W. Hughes 11 at 24.81.

Birkenhead School *Cheshire*
Master i/c R. E. L. Lytollis   Coach G. J. Rickman

P9 W7 L1 T1 A2

The school produced several strong performances, including a tie against Manchester Grammar. James O'Neill was the leading batsman: his 210* against George Watson's broke the school record, and ensured a remarkable average. Ashley Watkins was the pick of the bowlers.

Batting J. O'Neill 407 at 203.50; *D. I. Smith 165 at 55.00; L. Filer 318 at 45.42; A. J. N. Rabot 253 at 42.16; W. Brewster 183 at 30.50.

Bowling T. Corran 10 at 13.80; A. Watkins 16 at 14.62.

Bishop's Stortford College *Hertfordshire*
Master i/c M. Drury   Coach N. D. Hughes

P12 W8 L4

The XI were well led by leading run-scorer Taylor Weeks, and a heartening season contained notable victories against the Perse and Colchester RGS. The highlight was a six-wicket win against MCC, aided by an undefeated century from Harry Bailey.

Batting *T. J. E. Weeks 472 at 67.42; H. M. Bailey 308 at 51.33; T. W. B. Langley-Jones 154 at 25.66; K. A. D. Henchie 214 at 17.83.

Bowling H. M. Bailey 10 at 13.60; S. R. Black 14 at 22.64; A. M. Sewell 11 at 23.63.

Bloxham School *Oxfordshire*
Master i/c B. Richmond   Coaches D. D. Finch and P. D. Atkins

P14 W4 L10 A2

A difficult season did at least allow the school to develop players for the future – and there was the achievement of reaching the second round of the National T20 Cup.

Batting *W. Gurney 276 at 25.09; J. Beever 245 at 17.50.

Bowling S. Manning 20 at 16.55; L. Webber 10 at 19.90.

Blundell's School *Devon*
Master i/c C. L. L. Gabbitass   Coach B. Barnes

P12 W7 L5 A2

The first team, captained by Dominic Bess (who joined the Somerset Academy), produced solid performances. Joel Harden was the leading run-scorer, while Dan Pyle emerged as an exciting, hard-hitting batsman.

Batting J. A. L. Maunder 288 at 41.14; D. R. Pyle 389 at 38.90; J. E. J. Harden 431 at 35.91; *D. M. Bess 220 at 27.50.

Bowling J. E. J. Harden 10 at 16.80; D. M. Bess 17 at 19.47; K. S. H. W. Watson 10 at 19.70; C. J. Fitzroy 12 at 32.25.

Bradfield College *Berkshire*
Master i/c M. S. Hill   Coach J. R. Wood

P21 W10 L7 D4

Harry Came broke the school batting record set in 1962 by Michael Mence (see *Wisden 2015*, page 203), becoming the first to reach 1,000 runs in a season. Sharp fielding suggested a good team spirit, and credit should be given to Oliver Birts, who captained a young side with intelligence and maturity.

Batting H. R. C. Came 1,003 at 62.68; A. A. P. Atkinson 512 at 28.44; J. R. Thompson 410 at 24.11; C. O. Gwynn 409 at 20.45; O. W. Baker 308 at 18.11; A. W. M. Higginson 306 at 18.00; S. T. Lines 161 at 13.41; *O. Birts 164 at 11.71.

Bowling A. A. P. Atkinson 17 at 12.76; O. Birts 39 at 18.79; S. T. Lines 14 at 22.64; C. O. Gwynne 20 at 26.70; H. R. C. Came 15 at 28.06; S. D. Waddington 11 at 37.36.

Bradford Grammar School *Yorkshire*
Master i/c A. G. Smith   Coach S. A. Kellett

P12 W3 L7 D2 A1

This was a testing season for a very young team. Kyme Tahirkheli dominated with bat and ball, but Milan Patel, Haroon Mahmood and Matt Handy all made significant improvement, while Under-15 batsman Robbie Williams showed great promise.

Batting K. K. Tahirkheli 381 at 31.75; *J. M. Celaire 185 at 16.81; M. D. Handy 180 at 16.36; H. A. Mahmood 164 at 13.66.

Bowling K. K. Tahirkheli 24 at 21.25; M. Patel 11 at 25.63; H. A. Mahmood 13 at 25.92.

Harry Came passed 1,000 runs for Bradfield; Fin Trenouth averaged over 50 for Clifton College.

Brentwood School *Essex*

P17 W11 L4 D2 A1

Master i/c B. R. Hardie   **Coach** S. Salisbury

A productive season saw batting records fall: Harry Levy and Rishi Patel shared a stand of 320, with Patel going on to 200. A well-balanced side comprised senior and younger players. Steve Hayward and Charlie Nowlan, who impressed many with their pace, return for 2016.

Batting H. Levy 532 at 59.11; R. K. Patel 687 at 53.00; K. Ali 429 at 48.00; R. Horswill 330 at 47.00; M. S. Bell 286 at 32.00.

Bowling C. J. A. Nowlan 15 at 11.60; K. Ali 14 at 18.21; R. K. Patel 15 at 20.80; M. S. Bell 13 at 26.00.

Brighton College *Sussex*

P14 W4 L10 A1

Master i/c M. P. Smethurst   **Coach** C. A. Esson

Four wins – one more than in 2014 – confirmed progress and spelt hope for the future. In his first full season as an off-spinner, Will Longley took 19 wickets, while Tom Anson led the seamers with 17. Captain Will Wright hit three half-centuries.

Batting *W. R. Wright 423 at 35.25; D. J. Sear 317 at 24.38; A. J. Bone 263 at 23.90.

Bowling T. M. Anson 17 at 21.70; T. A. Walker 10 at 28.50; W. S. Longley 19 at 29.73; J. Z. Montfort-Bebb 10 at 33.60.

Bristol Grammar School *Gloucestershire*

P16 W2 L13 D1 A1

Master i/c K. R. Blackburn

Winning only two games and losing 13 were proof of a poor season. Cam Scott and Harry Thompson leave after four years in the first team; for much of that time they have been mainstays. There are some good youngsters on the horizon.

Batting H. M. Thompson 313 at 34.77; T. J. Rowland 297 at 29.70; *C. J. Y. Scott 304 at 25.33; R. N. Panchal 257 at 21.41; M. J. M. Brewer 188 at 17.09; S. Canagarajah 175 at 13.46.

Bowling R. N. Panchal 16 at 26.93; C. J. Y. Scott 13 at 30.76; S. Gandhi 11 at 33.09; H. R. Patel 10 at 34.60.

Bromsgrove School *Worcestershire*   P10 W4 L5 D1 A1
Master i/c D. J. Fallows

Despite a much-improved fixture list, this was a frustrating season. Winning the Chesterton Cup at New Road was the main achievement.
Batting T. Banton 227 at 56.75; A. R. Wilkinson 151 at 50.33; J. Bewick 249 at 31.12; *H. F. Moberley 310 at 31.00; J. P. Kinder 199 at 19.90; B. E. I. Morgan 168 at 18.66.
Bowling B. E. I. Morgan 17 at 15.29; A. R. Wilkinson 14 at 29.85; J. P. Kinder 12 at 30.33.

Bryanston School *Dorset*   P12 W6 L6 A1
Master i/c S. J. Turrill   **Coach** P. J. Norton

Paddy Oakshott's youthful side gained invaluable experience from taking several games to a thrilling finish. He was well supported by Year 11s Owen Morris and Frank Turrill.
Batting *P. C. Oakshott 169 at 24.14; O. M. Thomas 187 at 23.37.
Bowling F. J. Turrill 20 at 14.05.

Canford School *Dorset*   P12 W9 L3
Master i/c S. L. C. Ives   **Coach** M. Keech

Victory in five of our seven games against other schools was just reward for a youthful side. Felix Ambrose again led from the front with bat and ball, and he left having made the honours board nine times.
Batting *F. H. Ambrose 263 at 87.66; F. S. Organ 198 at 49.50.
Bowling F. H. Ambrose 26 at 6.42.

Caterham School *Surrey*   P10 W5 L5 A1
Master i/c R. Smith   **Coach** C. A. Moore

Highlights of a magnificent season included a 50-over total of 427-5 against Christ's Hospital, and dismissing Reigate Grammar School for 57. Ross Powell hit 613 runs, with three centuries and a 98, and also had figures of five for five. Harry Hanford weighed in with 492 – and an unbeaten hundred.
Batting *R. R. Powell 613 at 76.62; H. A. E. Hanford 492 at 70.28; C. O. Nelson 230 at 57.50; W. Ireland 156 at 26.00; J. A. Foggin 186 at 20.66.
Bowling R. R. Powell 21 at 8.80; S. D. J. Thorpe 18 at 17.66; E. A. Chatfield 14 at 19.28; C. O. Nelson 10 at 27.00; J. S. Foggin 12 at 28.33.

Charterhouse *Surrey*   P19 W5 L12 D2 A1
Master i/c M. P. Bicknell

Once again Charterhouse suffered from a lack of runs. Only three players totalled 150, though Robbie Hughes hit two superb hundreds. However, the bowling was excellent: Tom Hurley was the pick, with 27 wickets, and 15-year-old George Barlow is a player to watch.
Batting *R. L. Hughes 439 at 43.90; T. E. W. Hurley 250 at 20.83; J. G. Hunter-Lees 240 at 17.14.
Bowling T. G. A. M. Brown 12 at 16.33; H. J. R. Browne 17 at 21.00; G. C. H. Barlow 15 at 21.20; T. E. W. Hurley 27 at 25.11; J. S. Charles 14 at 31.07.

Cheadle Hulme School *Cheshire*   P15 W5 L7 D3
Master i/c S. Burnage   **Coach** G. J. Clinton

Several new players, from Years 8 to 12, broke into the first team. Play often continued in the cold and the rain, and the team showed resilience when things were tough. A few close matches went to the opposition, and we look forward to improving that in 2016.
Batting B. Fluck 400 at 57.14; *B. D. Mesrie 231 at 38.50; W. M. F. Beckley 157 at 31.40.
Bowling D. W. Ray 10 at 12.10; W. M. F. Beckley 17 at 18.94; H. J. Firmston 13 at 21.53; B. D. Mesrie 11 at 24.36.

Chislehurst & Sidcup Grammar School *Kent*   P4 W2 L2 A4
Master i/c R. A. Wallbridge   **Coach** D. L. Pask

With exam pressure reducing availability, the school decided to organise a two-week end-of-term festival containing games against local schools and clubs, as well as a district side and the annual MCC match. It was largely a successful venture, and there are plans to improve it for 2016.
Batting The leading batsman was *T. W. Patrinos, who hit 102 runs at 34.00.
Bowling The leading bowler was B. E. Cartwright, who claimed nine wickets at 7.55.

Christ College, Brecon *Breconshire*
P14 W7 L7
Master i/c T. J. Trumper
Coach R. F. Evans

A century against the Old Boys from captain Iain Mitchell rounded off a fine season. Above average in all departments, the side gelled well, and their encouraging results included victories over King's Gloucester and – by nine wickets – Llandovery College.

Batting *I. H. Mitchell 448 at 40.72; W. J. C. Trumper 325 at 25.00; E. M. Barnett-Smith 198 at 15.23.

Bowling J. Newey 19 at 13.36; W. J. C. Trumper 13 at 15.15; I. H. Mitchell 21 at 16.61; C. W. Brayshaw 13 at 22.23; T. F. Clifford 10 at 28.20.

Christ's Hospital *Sussex*
P14 W3 L11 A2
Master i/c H. P. Holdsworth
Coach T. E. Jesty

An inexperienced side endured a difficult season, though they developed more confidence towards the end of term, when some promising colts stepped up. The batting should be less brittle in 2016, and the bowling more incisive.

Batting A. Walker 314 at 24.15; F. Burgess 270 at 22.50; W. E. Freeman 174 at 14.50.

Bowling J. J. Taylor-Edwards 10 at 20.80; A. Walker 14 at 22.50; A. P. Burgess 22 at 26.77; *F. Burgess 10 at 47.00.

Churcher's College *Hampshire*
P8 W8 A3
Master i/c R. Maier

This was another outstanding summer for a team whose unbeaten record spans two seasons. Since the core of the 2014 side returned, it was likely Churcher's would continue to have a strong outfit.

Batting *S. D. A. Head 154 at 25.66; F. J. M. McMillan 150 at 21.42.

Bowling B. D. Kelson 10 at 10.80; J. O. I. Campbell 10 at 11.10.

City of London Freemen's School *Surrey*
P16 W9 L7
Master i/c A. E. Buhagiar
Coach N. M. Stewart

A pre-season tour to South Africa helped the first team achieve a productive summer, with senior players instrumental in notable victories against MCC, Caterham and King's Bruton. Satbir Mann hit 101 against Tiffin, while the prolific Ben Sidwell took 29 wickets.

Batting S. Mann 408 at 34.00; B. D. Sidwell 240 at 20.00; T. A. I. Abraham 233 at 19.41; J. Symonds 259 at 18.50; *B. Lumsden 160 at 17.77; T. Newhouse 246 at 16.40; N. Hewitt 152 at 15.20.

Bowling B. D. Sidwell 29 at 10.17; S. Mann 17 at 15.23; T. Newhouse 10 at 18.50; J. Symonds 12 at 19.58; O. J. R. Williams 12 at 19.91; B. Lumsden 14 at 20.71; O. Graham 13 at 26.23.

Clayesmore School *Dorset*
P14 W7 L7 A1
Master i/c R. S. Miller
Coach D. O. Conway

The 2015 season was respectable in terms of results – and outstanding in the development of teamwork and camaraderie. Determined captaincy from Charlie Martin, plus support from a small senior group, enabled talent to flourish. Oliver Perrin led the way with bat and ball.

Batting O. W. C. R. Perrin 218 at 43.60; W. A. Hendy 277 at 27.70; O. G. Morgan 220 at 22.00; J. J. York 197 at 17.90; *C. M. Martin 178 at 17.80.

Bowling O. W. C. R. Perrin 12 at 14.08; J. E. Richardson 12 at 25.83; B. J. Thompson 16 at 29.68.

Clifton College *Gloucestershire*
P17 W12 L3 D2 A2
Master i/c J. C. Bobby
Coach P. W. Romaines

This was a hugely enjoyable and successful season for the Clifton XI. Fin Trenouth, who scored 842 runs, blazed a trail, while the most memorable performance was the seven-wicket win over Sherborne, the 150th anniversary of the fixture.

Batting D. T. Lewis 427 at 71.16; F. R. Trenouth 842 at 52.62; L. J. P. Shaw 446 at 29.73; T. M. Probert 327 at 29.72; A. D. Binnington Savage 315 at 28.63; *T. S. Costley 415 at 27.66; J. R. Barber 292 at 20.85; C. A. J. Spink 198 at 16.50.

Bowling L. J. P. Shaw 15 at 20.86; T. S. Costley 25 at 21.56; G. E. Jones 10 at 24.60; M. D. Hackett 11 at 26.45; T. M. Probert 18 at 28.05; V. Lakhani 22 at 28.54; T. C. C. Griffith 12 at 39.50.

Cranleigh School *Surrey*
P17 W12 L4 D1

Master i/c A. P. Forsdike　　　　　　　　　　**Coach** S. D. Welch

A young and talented team contained several who had won the Lord's Taverners Under-15 championship in 2014 – and many are available in 2016, too. Oliver Pope, a Year 12, guided his side to victories over Wellington College, Charterhouse and Tonbridge, among others.

Batting *O. J. D. Pope 646 at 71.77; L. Bedford 780 at 70.90; F. D. C. Austin 353 at 39.22; A. E. C. Dahl 256 at 25.60; J. A. Harris 240 at 20.00; M. P. Subba Row 254 at 19.53; O. W. Trower 212 at 19.27; R. J. D. Kennedy 157 at 15.70.

Bowling A. E. C. Dahl 32 at 19.40; J. Turner 14 at 20.71; E. J. Tristem 17 at 23.52; O. W. Trower 11 at 26.00; S. J. A. Dickson 14 at 29.78; M. P. Subba Row 11 at 40.27.

Culford School *Suffolk*
P11 W8 L2 D1

Master i/c A. H. Marsh

Culford enjoyed a successful season. Runs came quickly, and the bowling and fielding improved during the summer. The highlight was the win against MCC, courtesy of a sporting declaration after some poor weather.

Batting C. W. Holt 470 at 94.00; *K. D. Pask 515 at 64.37; M. J. Mitcham 313 at 34.77; A. D. Devoy 161 at 26.83.

Bowling C. W. Holt 15 at 11.00; K. D. Pask 18 at 11.27; D. T. Corbett 13 at 12.84; B. T. C. Milner 13 at 13.69; F. N. Statham 13 at 16.69.

Dame Allan's School *Northumberland*
P5 W3 L2 A2

Master i/c J. A. Benn

This was not the easiest of summers, with availability and fixtures causing an issue or two. Chris Smith led the batting and Chris Todd the bowling. Jack Hearn, the captain, deserved better than to finish his school career struggling with injury.

Batting C. J. Smith 157 at 52.33.

Bowling The leading bowler was C. J. Todd, who claimed eight wickets at 9.00.

Dauntsey's School *Wiltshire*
P20 W10 L8 D2

Master i/c A. J. Palmer　　　　　　　　　　**Coach** J. R. Ayling

With a team largely comprising confident Year 13 players, hopes were high. Performances, however, were sometimes disappointing, though there were gratifying wins against MCC and Repton. Rahul Patel, a Year 10, scored over 500 runs, while seamer Charlie Dale showed great control.

Batting R. N. Patel 526 at 37.57; M. H. Romer-Lee 394 at 32.83; A. S. Duckworth 494 at 29.05; O. D. Jackson 263 at 26.30; G. H. Rawson-Smith 217 at 21.70; C. H. Dale 209 at 19.00; W. J. Thomas 176 at 16.00.

Bowling *R. Duckworth 29 at 15.89; C. H. Dale 27 at 16.25; G. H. Rawson-Smith 18 at 16.27; A. S. Duckworth 25 at 20.04; M. H. Romer-Lee 20 at 25.85; H. J. W. Mangham 14 at 34.85.

Dean Close School *Gloucestershire*
P11 L9 D2

Master i/c A. G. A. Milne　　　　　　　　　　**Coach** R. J. Cunliffe

Results show this was not a vintage season for the Dean Close XI, captained by Gregor Lovatt. Several younger players gained valuable experience, and the Under-14 age group showed distinct promise. The cricket week in June, including a two-day match, was a success.

Batting O. S. Cahill 314 at 31.40; J. H. Richards 274 at 24.90; S. J. Wheatley 202 at 16.83; M. S. Court 163 at 16.30; S. W. P. Norwood 189 at 15.75.

Bowling S. J. Wheatley 18 at 21.38; O. S. Cahill 10 at 28.80.

Denstone College *Staffordshire*
P12 W8 L4 A2

Master i/c P. D. Brice　　　　　　　　　　**Coach** I. S. Trott

There were several defeats in a difficult start to the summer, but excellent bowling from Connor Baynes-Holden, Adam Pursell and Ben Motley, supported by powerful batting from Motley and Ben Burrows, ensured a rousing finale.

Batting B. A. Motley 314 at 34.88; *B. J. Burrows 319 at 31.90; E. M. R. Barlow 171 at 17.10.

Bowling C. H. G. Baynes-Holden 17 at 9.64; B. A. Motley 16 at 11.62; A. D. Pursell 24 at 12.70; J. M. R. Roche 16 at 20.75.

Dr Challoner's Grammar School *Buckinghamshire*
P11 W6 L3 D2 A2

Master i/c N. J. S. Buchanan

Dr Challoner's, led ably by captain and wicketkeeper Oliver Penton, fared well. The only defeats came when regulars were absent for exams, and there were fine wins over several local rivals. A young side should prosper in 2016.

Batting N. M. Aslam 191 at 38.20; D. J. Ogden 255 at 31.87.

Bowling A. U. Rehman 18 at 8.94; J. L. Anderson 10 at 12.80.

Dollar Academy *Clackmannanshire*
P12 W3 L8 D1 A1

Master i/c J. G. A. Frost

Dollar fought a number of tight games, with the highlights being victories over Stewart's Melville and Fettes, and a draw with MCC.

Batting C. P. Weir 367 at 40.77; K. Hinkson 300 at 37.50; B. Pearson 254 at 36.28.

Bowling H. Warr 11 at 17.36; E. Dawtrey 11 at 24.54.

Dover College *Kent*
P7 W1 L6 A3

Master i/c G. R. Hill

A young team, well led by Samraat Rai, developed considerably. Six of the team have another three seasons in the XI, and prospects are good.

Batting G. P. A. A. Cloake 263 at 52.60; *S. Rai 169 at 28.16.

Bowling G. P. A. A. Cloake 14 at 16.21.

Downside School *Somerset*
P10 W4 L5 D1

Master i/c H. P. A. Pike   **Coach** R. J. H. Lett

Downside School had a mixed season, though there were fine wins against Monkton Combe and Millfield's 2nd XI. Lawrie Graham scored heavily, Harry Ross spun his way to nearly 30 wickets, while the excellent wicketkeeper Patrick Hyams captained the side most capably.

Batting L. P. H. Graham 310 at 44.28; *P. J. H. Hyams 173 at 24.71.

Bowling H. J. Ross 18 at 11.88; J. McKechnie 10 at 12.20.

Dulwich College *Surrey*
P18 W6 L11 D1

Master i/c D. C. Shirazi   **Coach** C. W. J. Athey

A talented yet inconsistent team endured some frustration. Akil Greenidge was superb throughout, amassing 889 runs, while the spin of captain William Anthony and Janaom Rao proved effective.

Batting A. D. Greenidge 889 at 52.29; A. J. W. Rackow 547 at 32.17; J. P. Waugh 220 at 31.42; *W. Anthony 446 at 26.23; R. G. Marchant 238 at 15.86.

Bowling W. Anthony 21 at 14.80; J. K. Rao 23 at 18.95; F. G. Allocca 13 at 30.38; A. D. Purwar 19 at 30.73; T. H. Thornton 15 at 34.40.

Durham School *Co. Durham*
P21 W10 L10 D1

Master i/c M. B. Fishwick

A young squad won their first seven matches, but just three in the second half of the season, against Ampleforth, Sedbergh and Bromsgrove. Luke Henderson won the batting award, Piers Davison the bowling and Josh O'Brien the fielding. Davison was the most improved player, while Sam Taylor-Gell was named the best cricketer.

Batting L. R. Henderson 750 at 68.18; *S. Taylor-Gell 395 at 23.23; J. W. Kirkbride 183 at 18.30; J. O'Brien 221 at 17.00.

Bowling D. T. Scott 22 at 14.95; P. A. Davison 26 at 16.96; S. Taylor-Gell 26 at 17.65; M. Davison 11 at 35.18.

Eastbourne College *Sussex*
P21 W16 L4 D1 A1

Master i/c M. J. Banes   **Coach** R. S. Ferley

A total of 16 wins made this one of the best seasons in the college's history. Jacob Smith captained for a second year, leading the way with 863 runs and 31 wickets; Brad Evans offered invaluable all-round support.

Batting *J. E. Smith 863 at 45.42; B. N. Evans 701 at 35.05; G. S. Robinson 581 at 32.27; B. S. Twine 474 at 29.62; H. Lloyd 587 at 29.35; W. J. Corfield 244 at 22.18; R. Packham 174 at 19.33; J. W. Mackwood 219 at 16.84.

Bowling R. Packham 26 at 12.96; B. N. Evans 38 at 13.02; R. W. Sulke 24 at 14.91; J. E. Smith 31 at 17.70; B. S. Twine 26 at 22.88.

Dulwich College's Akil Greenidge – son of West Indies Test batsman Alvin – hit 889 runs, while Vansh Bajaj of Ellesmere College averaged 63 with the bat and 12 with the ball.

The Edinburgh Academy *Midlothian*   P12 W5 L6 D1
Master i/c R. W. Sales
A very young first team had an up-and-down summer. They developed well during the short season, and will benefit from more fixtures in 2016. Term ended on a high, with victories over Barnard Castle and Rossall, both strong schools.
Batting C. Chen 252 at 31.50; *R. Lopes 278 at 23.16; H. A. H. W. Simpson 209 at 19.00; S. O. Melvin-Farr 153 at 15.30; R. M. Milne 166 at 13.83.
Bowling C. D. Woodward 13 at 20.23; C. R. Clarkson 12 at 23.58; S. O. Melvin-Farr 12 at 24.16.

Elizabeth College, Guernsey *Channel Islands*   P6 W2 L4 A3
Master i/c T. Eisenhuth
Defeating Victoria College in Jersey was the highlight of the season. With captain Alex Bushell and three other senior players – Ryan Harris, Arun White and Jack Ingrouille – moving on, 2016 will be challenging.
Batting N. Guilbert 168 at 24.00.
Bowling N. Guilbert 11 at 23.36.

Ellesmere College *Shropshire*   P14 W11 L1 D2
Master i/c G. Owen   **Coach** R. Jones
In an excellent season, the school – calling on a large squad of talented players from Year 9 upwards – remained unbeaten in the longer format until the final week. The small number of senior cricketers provided exemplary support and leadership for the younger players.
Batting V. Bajaj 507 at 63.37; *W. K. Doerr 192 at 38.40; G. W. Newton 246 at 35.14; S. J. C. Ellis 166 at 27.66.
Bowling W. K. Doerr 20 at 8.95; J. Furnival 19 at 10.73; V. Bajaj 20 at 12.00; B. J. Gibbon 12 at 12.41; G. W. Newton 13 at 12.84.

Eltham College *Kent*
P10 W5 L3 D2 A3

Master i/c J. N. Batty

Results were mixed but, given the youth of the side, there is optimism for the future. There were good victories against Sevenoaks, Trinity, The Judd, Crawford College and Brighton Grammar. Hard-fought draws were achieved against Reed's and Ardingly.

Batting J. O. M. Williams 203 at 29.00; S. Smith 208 at 23.11; *A. J. S. Tawana 179 at 22.37.

Bowling A. Patel 15 at 16.53; D. J. Lester 12 at 16.91; I. Turner 11 at 21.72; S. R. Baker 11 at 26.54.

Emanuel School *Surrey*
P15 W12 L3 A1

Master i/c P. A. King   **Coach** M. J. Roberts

The first team went unbeaten against our usual school opposition, and the only defeats came against a strong MCC side and in a T20 festival. Captain Archie MacPherson led the way, scoring a hundred and seven half-centuries.

Batting *A. C. MacPherson 660 at 47.14; S. J. T. Eastaugh 389 at 29.92; J. L. Kremer 191 at 23.87; B. T. Casling 264 at 18.85; J. Hawley 234 at 16.71.

Bowling B. T. Casling 28 at 11.78; S. J. T. Eastaugh 24 at 14.91; W. P. R. Davis 10 at 29.50.

Epsom College *Surrey*
P17 W10 L7

Master i/c N. R. Taylor

A young team enjoyed a successful season. The leading lights were Liam Head with the ball and Ed Hughes with the bat – both Year 10s.

Batting E. D. Hughes 339 at 37.66; I. Z. B. Braithwaite 353 at 29.41; H. D. Williams 299 at 27.18; B. E. Holder 186 at 18.60; L. A. Head 153 at 17.00; M. A. Holder 200 at 14.28.

Bowling L. A. Head 27 at 12.59; H. D. Williams 18 at 16.44; B. E. Holder 21 at 16.90; *W. B. C. Joyce 15 at 19.66; P. B. O'Brien 18 at 20.44.

Eton College *Buckinghamshire*
P22 W16 L5 D1

Masters i/c R. R. Montgomerie/J. A. G. Fulton   **Coach** T. W. Roberts

A total of 16 wins – Eton's best in recent memory – was reward for adventurous, positive cricket. Led from the front by William Gordon Lennox, the team showed belief and commitment, and realised their potential. Alistair Russell in his third (and penultimate) year as wicketkeeper, was the second Etonian to score 1,000 runs in a season, after Will Vanderspar. Leading wicket-taker Jason Takavarasha and all-rounder Hector Hardman should also return for 2016.

Batting A. D. L. Russell 1,033 at 57.38; *W. R. C. Gordon Lennox 590 at 39.33; A. R. Treon 562 at 33.05; J. H. R. I. Hardman 490 at 28.82; N. C. Macdonagh 366 at 28.15; N. R. J. Harrington 336 at 24.00; E. J. Collins 419 at 22.05.

Bowling J. M. P. Takavarasha 34 at 21.26; O. J. W. Rogers 20 at 22.20; J. H. R. I. Hardman 30 at 22.60; W. J. E. Whipple 22 at 30.31; E. W. F. Fenwick 25 at 30.68; T. C. E. Wilkinson 22 at 31.36.

Exeter School *Devon*
P12 W8 L3 D1

Master i/c J. W. Fawkes

The school enjoyed a fine summer, winning two-thirds of their matches, thanks to an all-round squad effort. Batsmen George Hoult and Marcus Hoddinott fared well, while Ben Green – a role model for all pupils, including young leading wicket-taker Ben Hayes – played for England Under-19 against Australia.

Batting G. W. Hoult 332 at 55.33; *M. J. Hoddinott 417 at 52.12; T. A. Lammonby 207 at 41.40.

Bowling B. A. J. Hayes 12 at 15.41.

Felsted School *Essex*
P23 W18 L4 D1

Master i/c J. E. R. Gallian   **Coaches** C. S. Knightley/N. J. Lockhart

In an outstanding campaign, Felsted won 18 games. Under the leadership of Oliver Grayson, the first team showed great maturity and worked well together in the field. There were excellent performances from Reece Hussain, with over 1,100 runs, and Ben Waring, who took a school-record 68 wickets.

Batting R. Hussain 1,147 at 95.58; *O. J. Grayson 857 at 57.13; W. E. L. Buttleman 430 at 33.07; Y. A. Grant 425 at 30.35; A. Reardon 152 at 21.71; A. A. Cox 206 at 14.71.

Bowling B. A. Waring 68 at 9.23; A. A. Cox 35 at 14.22; E. H. J. Potter 15 at 15.60; L. J. Chapman 36 at 16.02; J. O. King 14 at 16.07; A. K. Minocha 17 at 18.05; J. A. Wisbey 10 at 25.20.

Reece Hussain, the leading scorer in schools cricket in 2015, hits out for Felsted.

Fettes College *Midlothian*   P14 W6 L5 D3
Master i/c A. B. Russell
An inexperienced team sometimes failed to convert starts into big scores, yet played good cricket. A varied and talented attack, well led by Harry West, gave hope for the future, while 15-year-old George Conner looked a batsman of promise.
Batting R. G. Darling 234 at 39.00; *R. C. Mather 241 at 26.77; G. G. Conner 313 at 22.35; R. T. Mather 229 at 19.08; M. D. Spencer 175 at 12.50.
Bowling H. G. E. West 16 at 20.12; B. M. Macleod 10 at 23.90; G. G. Conner 11 at 29.00; M. D. Spencer 13 at 32.61.

Forest School *Essex*   P16 W6 L6 D4 A1
Master i/c S. J. Foulds   **Coach** J. J. Kay
An indifferent summer came alive in the final fortnight with five wins in six games, including a thrilling last-ball victory against Brentwood School. The batting relied heavily on the excellent Matthew Erasmus; the bowling remained steady rather than threatening.
Batting M. C. Erasmus 802 at 80.20; A. C. Nicholls 407 at 33.91; W. R. Moss 163 at 27.16; A. Nair 190 at 27.14; M. C. Lavery 294 at 22.61; C. A. Hall 203 at 22.55; M. Batt 189 at 17.18.
Bowling U. Ashraf 23 at 21.73; C. A. Hall 21 at 23.04; A. C. Nicholls 14 at 37.35.

Framlingham College *Suffolk*   P11 W1 L7 D3
Master i/c B. J. France   **Coach** S. D. Greenall
Even allowing for the fact that all the team, bar Rob Goldsmith, should return for 2016, it was a tough season. A lack of runs meant the good work of the bowlers was often wasted. George Heldreich's eight wickets against the Gentlemen of Essex was the highlight.
Batting The leading batsman was J. S. P. Hulley, who hit 139 runs at 27.80.
Bowling J. S. P. Hulley 10 at 19.50; G. W. Heldreich 11 at 20.54; C. R. Greenhall 11 at 23.63.

George Heriot's School *Midlothian*   P7 W3 L4 A1
Master i/c E. L. Harrison
This was a mixed season, illuminated by an excellent win over Glasgow Academy. Alex Anderson, the captain, averaged 53 with the bat and less than eight with the ball.
Batting *A. W. G. Anderson 212 at 53.00.
Bowling A. W. G. Anderson 10 at 7.80.

George Watson's College *Midlothian* P15 W10 L3 T1 D1 A2
Master i/c M. J. Leonard **Coach** A. D. W. Patterson
After a successful Easter tour to Barbados, the first team enjoyed a strong season, winning the Scottish Cup for the first time. They batted aggressively, and were intelligently captained by Rory Evans. Oliver Brown bowled with accuracy to claim 33 wickets.
Batting A. M. Cockburn 545 at 45.41; C. J. Martin 297 at 29.70; M. Whitaker 183 at 22.87; J. M. W. Mullins 354 at 20.82; K. D. Arvind 212 at 19.27.
Bowling K. Bryce 12 at 14.75; O. J. Brown 33 at 14.87; T. D. Counsell 12 at 20.91; K. D. Arvind 17 at 21.47; A. M. Cockburn 13 at 22.92.

The Glasgow Academy *Lanarkshire* P8 W4 L2 D2 A2
Master i/c P. J. W. Smith **Coach** V. Hariharan
The development of younger players – and victory in the Glasgow Academy sixes tournament – were the major achievements of a good season. Cameron Russell proved a capable captain.
Batting J. L. Oliver 191 at 38.20; A. Khan 157 at 31.40.
Bowling F. M. Irfan 11 at 12.72.

The High School of Glasgow *Lanarkshire* P9 W1 L6 D2 A3
Master i/c D. N. Barrett **Coaches** N. R. Clarke/K. J. A. Robertson
The school negotiated a difficult summer with a competitive spirit. Perhaps the best cricket came on the end-of-season tour to Strathallan, Gordonstoun and Glenalmond, and there were also encouraging signs in the performances of Year 10 pupils Callum Coats and Murray Godsman.
Batting C. J. Coats 234 at 29.25; J. A. Stark 174 at 24.85.
Bowling The leading bowler was D. L. McKeating, who claimed seven wickets at 22.00.

Glenalmond College *Perthshire* P9 W5 L4 A2
Master i/c M. J. Davies
After a stuttering start, the XI hit their stride in the final six weeks of the season, and won their last four games. Blair Goodfellow and Thomas Stodart were the most prolific batsmen, Ruaraidh Leader the most incisive bowler.
Batting T. H. K. Stodart 302 at 37.75; *B. S. Goodfellow 249 at 31.12.
Bowling R. W. P. Leader 15 at 9.33.

Gordonstoun School *Morayshire* P9 W5 L1 D3 A3
Master i/c C. J. Barton **Coach** R. Denyer
A youthful XI completed a successful season and, with only one student leaving, 2016 looks encouraging. Special mention should go to Jack Harrison – 101* in his last game for the school – and Archie Houldsworth, who appears in these pages for the fourth year running.
Batting *A. J. Houldsworth 306 at 38.25; J. W. Harrison 177 at 35.40; T. J. Walton 205 at 29.28.
Bowling T. J. Walton 11 at 20.09; M. B. B. Rind 13 at 21.30.

Gresham's School *Norfolk* P14 W9 L4 D1 A2
Master i/c A. Horsley **Coach** M. J. Sorell
Jack Park led the team during a summer of achievement. Tatenda Chiradza hit most runs and took joint most wickets, while off-spinner Kieran Peters (Year 10) also had 17 victims; both were playing their first full season.
Batting A. Taylor 300 at 42.85; T. T. Chiradza 416 at 37.81; W. W. Wright 206 at 34.33; T. E. Sheridan 294 at 24.50; E. C. Parker 336 at 24.00.
Bowling K. T. Peters 17 at 19.06; T. T. Chiradza 17 at 21.58; W. W. Wright 13 at 22.38; *J. F. Park 11 at 25.18.

Haberdashers' Aske's Boys' School *Hertfordshire* P20 W10 L6 T1 D3 A1
Master i/c S. D. Charlwood **Coaches** D. H. Kerry/J. P. Hewitt
Jay Purohit skippered intelligently and – with support from wicketkeeper-batsman Alex Willis, opening batsman Ian Harris, and left-arm spinner Shaniel Lakhani – his young side fared better than expected, enjoying notable wins against Berkhamsted, MCC, St Albans and Exeter. The highlight was the T20 game on the Lord's Nursery Ground. Although Merchant Taylors' won easily, we had the better of the drawn two-day game against the same opposition.
Batting I. M. Harris 676 at 42.25; A. R. C. Willis 695 at 36.57; C. W. T. Mack 538 at 29.88; J. H. Urban 387 at 25.80; N. S. Amin 471 at 24.78; P. D. Sidwell 249 at 20.75; F. J. Wright 164 at 20.50.

Bowling A. Chatterjee 13 at 10.23; G. N. Lawrence 24 at 23.04; N. Rasakulasuriar 18 at 23.94; S. A. Lakhani 31 at 26.61; *J. Purohit 21 at 28.57; J. A. Navarajasegaran 10 at 31.20.

Haileybury *Hertfordshire*   P12 W2 L9 D1 A2
Master i/c Mrs E. L. Millo   **Coach** D. L. S. van Bunge
Despite appearances, the 2015 season was a success: there was leadership, application, teamwork and happiness in abundance. Every player remained available throughout – and long after – their exams, which is testament to a fresh and welcome cultural shift.
Batting *J. A. Brooking 405 at 25.31; G. M. McConachie 421 at 24.76; I. G. M. Dawes 297 at 16.50; F. J. R. Walker 188 at 15.66; B. G. A. Christensen 257 at 14.27.
Bowling I. G. M. Dawes 17 at 33.88; W. D. Vooght 12 at 37.08.

Hampton School *Middlesex*   P20 W10 L9 D1
Master i/c A. M. Banerjee   **Coach** C. P. Harrison
Life was never going to be easy for Robert Bentley's unseasoned batting line-up, but his players worked hard and will become a better side. Bentley was outstanding as batsman and bowler.
Batting *R. J. Bentley 487 at 25.63; T. E. G. Godfray 395 at 20.78; H. B. Mayes 346 at 19.22; T. M. Ryan 300 at 18.75; M. H. Starling 244 at 15.25; J. A. B. Williams 174 at 14.50; A. J. Lee 252 at 13.26.
Bowling R. J. Bentley 46 at 10.50; E. M. Ijaz 21 at 12.38; H. B. Mayes 21 at 16.52.

Harrow School *Middlesex*   P19 W17 L2
Master i/c R. S. C. Martin-Jenkins   **Coach** S. A. Jones
Anshy Rath was the player of the season, scoring five hundreds and claiming 37 wickets with his canny left-arm spin. Three others also scored centuries, including two from Year 11 Rahul Wijeratne. Three times the team passed 300. Abdullah Nazir, 15 years old, is one of the brightest young left-arm spinners in the country.
Batting A. Rath 1,075 at 63.23; *D. Steward 433 at 43.30; J. J. Cleverly 257 at 36.71; S. J. S. Assani 209 at 34.83; Rahul S. Wijeratne 537 at 31.58; F. W. A. Ruffell 426 at 26.62; A. A. Copestick 360 at 24.00; R. Sachin Wijeratne 249 at 22.63.
Bowling A. Rath 37 at 11.75; A. Nazir 27 at 14.77; M. G. Kellock 23 at 19.78; S. J. S. Assani 22 at 20.50; F. W. A. Ruffell 16 at 21.31; A. A. Copestick 13 at 25.84; T. M. Nevile 11 at 27.90.

The Harvey Grammar School *Kent*   P8 W4 L2 D2 A4
Master i/c S. Rowe   **Coach** P. M. Castle
Poor early-season weather curtailed the programme, but there were several cameo performances, including from Year 11 pupil Oliver Rhys-Jones.
Batting A. Leaver 156 at 39.00.
Bowling The leading bowler was D. J. Marsh, who claimed six wickets at 8.83.

Highgate School *Middlesex*   P11 W7 L4
Master i/c A. G. Tapp   **Coach** S. Patel
Middlesex cricketers Tom Waine and Jack Bruce featured strongly, with bat and ball. The young XI reached the final of the Middlesex Under-19 Cup.
Batting J. M. Bruce 367 at 45.87; T. F. Waine 240 at 26.66.
Bowling T. F. Waine 18 at 13.55; J. M. Bruce 14 at 14.14.

Hurstpierpoint College *Sussex*   P15 W13 L2
Master i/c N. J. K. Creed   **Coaches** J. Lewis/P. G. Hudson
A strong XI won the National Schools T20, the Langdale Trophy, the Woodard Festival and 13 of their 15 regular fixtures. Joseph Ludlow, the T20 captain, scored 1,267 runs in all forms of the game, while Dominic Keats took 34 wickets. George Garton, who captained in the longer formats, Thomas Haines, Jonty Jenner and Daniel Doram all played for Sussex Seconds.
Batting *J. H. Ludlow 760 at 58.46; J. J. Jenner 404 at 57.71; *G. H. S. Garton 431 at 53.87; T. J. Haines 325 at 27.08; B. M. Candfield 210 at 26.25; D. C. Keats 282 at 23.50; R. J. M. Whyte 167 at 15.18; J. M. Troak 172 at 13.23.
Bowling J. M. Troak 19 at 11.68; D. C. Keats 20 at 12.25; T. J. Haines 10 at 17.20; D. T. Doram 19 at 19.36; J. P. H. White 13 at 19.69; B. M. Candfield 16 at 26.87.

Leg-spinner Mason Crane, from Lancing, took a five-for in the Championship for Hampshire; Harrow's Anshuman Rath had a spectacular all-round season, with 1,075 runs and 37 wickets.

Hymers College *Yorkshire*
Master i/c G. Tipping

P12 W6 L5 D1 A3

Summer 2015 was a good one at Hymers College, with some outstanding batting from captain Tom Norman, Tom Jones and Lyndon Warkup.

Batting *T. H. R. Norman 494 at 61.75; L. J. Warkup 435 at 43.50; T. B. Jones 362 at 36.20; M. J. Caplin 156 at 15.60; T. G. Elstone 156 at 14.18.

Bowling I. Mohammed 10 at 16.80; T. H. R. Norman 18 at 20.94; M. C. Faulkner 12 at 24.50; J. A. Nettleton 14 at 28.35.

Ipswich School *Suffolk*
Master i/c A. K. Golding

P12 W5 L4 D3 A1

Coach R. E. East

Cameron Rule was the outstanding batsman, making four attacking centuries, while Ben Parker hit two. Year 9 Joshua Rymell also fared well. Sam Pace led the attack, and enjoyed useful support.

Batting *C. R. Rule 786 at 65.50; B. J. Parker 326 at 54.33; J. S. Rymell 287 at 23.91; S. G. Renshaw 211 at 21.10; J. A. C. Knight 166 at 18.44.

Bowling J. G. Stewart 10 at 15.10; S. D. Pace 14 at 23.14; C. T. Head 10 at 28.90; C. R. Rule 15 at 31.73.

The John Fisher School *Surrey*
Master i/c T. L. Vandoros

P11 W5 L6 A2

A young and vibrant team, thoughtfully captained by leading batsman Alex Dombrandt, had an exciting season. Harry Aravinthan offered excellent support with bat and ball. Every game contained the possibility of a win, and many kept spectators on the edge of their seats until the end.

Batting *A. J. Dombrandt 442 at 63.14; H. Aravinthan 300 at 33.33; C. Edgar 161 at 20.12.

Bowling H. Aravinthan 18 at 8.05.

The John Lyon School *Middlesex*
Master i/c A. S. Ling

P18 W10 L8

Coach C. T. Peploe

This represented a marked improvement from 2014. Seerone Kandasamy proved excellent with the bat, twice making it into the nineties. Thomas Marshall, the captain, and his younger brother Owen shared 45 wickets, while Kellan Ghelani collected 20.

Batting D. J. Maru 159 at 79.50; S. Kandasamy 384 at 38.40; D. M. Peerez 157 at 31.40; *T. B. W. Marshall 281 at 23.41; J. V. Gandhi 154 at 14.00.

Bowling T. B. W. Marshall 23 at 11.60; O. J. Marshall 22 at 16.31; K. D. Ghelani 20 at 19.00; J. C. R. Francis 12 at 26.83.

The Judd School *Kent*   P6 W1 L5 A1
Master i/c D. W. Joseph

Angus Willis, the team's outstanding batsman, skippered well in a disjointed season. The Tucker brothers, Owen and Matt, opened the bowling; Alex Jessop was the leading wicket-taker.

Batting The leading batsman was A. J. R. Willis, who hit 97 runs at 24.25.

Bowling The leading bowler was A. J. Jessop, who claimed eight wickets at 8.62.

Kimbolton School *Huntingdonshire*   P16 W5 L8 D3
Master i/c M. S. Gilbert   **Coach** W. Kerr-Dineen

There were plenty of runs, but with wickets harder to come by it was not an easy summer. The last-ball victory against MCC was memorable. Marcus Watkinson, Josh Smith and Jake Baynes stood out.

Batting *M. J. Watkinson 536 at 48.72; H. W. Peak 339 at 30.81; J. J. Smith 315 at 28.63; J. T. Baynes 385 at 25.66; J. Wright 224 at 16.00.

Bowling G. Napier 21 at 13.71; J. T. Baynes 14 at 17.42; D. Parekh-Hill 14 at 18.07; J. J. Smith 18 at 23.00; G. Wilkinson 10 at 37.30.

King Edward VI School, Southampton *Hampshire*   P10 W5 L4 D1
Master i/c D. Kent

After some good early victories, the failure to score consistently resulted in defeats later in the term. A hard-earned draw against the MCC was a high point. The leading bowler was Alec Damley-Jones, an Under-16; with only two players leaving before 2016.

Batting T. J. Smart 150 at 50.00; D. R. M. Damley-Jones 326 at 32.60; P. R. Holly 159 at 26.50; T. A. Fay 235 at 23.50.

Bowling O. T. Birnie 11 at 13.18; A. S. M. Damley-Jones 18 at 13.77; *E. F. I. Wright 14 at 22.71.

King Edward's School Birmingham *Warwickshire*   P17 W8 L7 D2 A1
Master i/c L. M. Roll   **Coach** D. Collins

A hard-working team made the most of their abilities to win more games than they lost.

Batting H. J. P. Lilburn 551 at 39.35; *S. J. Mubarik 525 at 35.00; T. Gupta 253 at 31.62; A. M. Georgevic 321 at 22.92; A. Hussain 205 at 22.77; H. Ajaib 189 at 21.00; J. Reddy 172 at 15.63.

Bowling H. Ajaib 21 at 16.19; S. Sawlani 15 at 18.80; R. R. Gandhewar 14 at 33.50; S. J. Mubarik 12 at 35.83; K. S. Gangurde 12 at 40.58.

King's College, Taunton *Somerset*   P18 W14 L3 D1 A1
Master i/c P. D. Lewis   **Coach** R. J. Woodman

In another busy and enjoyable summer, a strong team were well tested by the likes of Millfield, Exeter University and Cardiff MCCU. The runs were shared around, while Calvin Harrison led the bowlers. James Turpin was player of the season.

Batting *S. J. D. Underdown 327 at 54.50; B. Lynch 458 at 45.80; E. J. Byrom 447 at 44.70; J. R. Turpin 376 at 41.77; H. S. Thomas 342 at 38.00; C. J. Ayers 276 at 27.60.

Bowling C. G. Harrison 35 at 11.25; L. T. Redrup 18 at 14.22; J. R. Turpin 17 at 18.88.

King's College School, Wimbledon *Surrey*   P13 W5 L8 A3
Master i/c J. S. Gibson   **Coach** M. A. Stephenson

The highlight of the summer was captain George Thomas's century against Reigate. Led by Thomas and senior players Ed Blundell, Tom Weston and Bertie Lloyd, the team showed spirit, and learned much during a challenging season.

Batting E. J. Hawkins-Hooker 238 at 23.80; *G. M. Thomas 229 at 22.90; F. A. H. Freeman 271 at 22.58; E. R. Blundell 171 at 19.00; J. J. S. Hennessey 167 at 15.18; B. H. Lloyd 160 at 14.54.

Bowling T. A. R. Weston 13 at 22.76; K. M. Crichard 11 at 27.00; C. Reynolds 11 at 29.27; G. M. Thomas 12 at 34.16.

The King's School, Canterbury *Kent*   P18 W12 L3 D3 A1
Master i/c R. A. L. Singfield   **Coach** M. A. Ealham

The team played consistent, intelligent cricket, winning 12 of their 18 matches. Piers Richardson led the side superbly and young players developed well: Oliver Tikare, Will Heywood and Matthew Barker all scored accomplished centuries. Oliver Mann was the pick of the seam attack.

Batting O. B. S. Tikare 609 at 50.75; *P. B. Richardson 459 at 45.90; M. D. Barker 509 at 42.41;
W. J. Heywood 398 at 33.16; J. N. Leggett 323 at 32.30; E. C. S. Solly 194 at 19.40.

Bowling W. J. Heywood 11 at 11.45; P. B. Richardson 19 at 12.94; O. O. C. M. Kolade 13 at 14.00;
G. W. R. Meddings 10 at 14.00; O. J. D. Mann 23 at 15.60; J. J. Todd 22 at 17.63; W. J. Parker 10
at 19.10.

The King's School, Chester *Cheshire*   P11 W6 L2 D3 A4
Master i/c S. Neal   **Coach** N. R. Walker

A productive season was built on heavy scoring from Alastair Andrady and Stephen Rimmer at the
top of the order, skilful slow left-arm spin from Hansaj Singh, and Alec Davies's motivational
captaincy.

Batting A. M. Andrady 456 at 76.00; S. D. Rimmer 480 at 53.33; M. J. Thompson 183 at 18.30.

Bowling H. Singh 25 at 10.40.

The King's School in Macclesfield *Cheshire*   P14 W3 L9 D2 A3
Master i/c S. Moores   **Coach** A. Kennedy

Finlay McCance captained the team well in trying circumstances: poor weather, exams and injury all
added to the frustrations. There were some promising performances, with several Year 9 and 10 boys
representing the school.

Batting W. J. Hodgson 167 at 41.75; *F. J. McCance 327 at 29.72; O. R. Jones 171 at 28.50; T. A.
Key 231 at 25.66; C. McIlveen 191 at 15.91.

Bowling H. Elms 12 at 18.41; Z. W. H. Howdle 15 at 18.86; T. A. Key 18 at 22.38; C. McIlveen 12
at 24.58; A. F. L. Thorneycroft 13 at 25.38.

King's School, Rochester *Kent*   P9 W2 L6 D1 A3
Master i/c W. E. Smith   **Coach** C. H. Page

The team found it difficult to set competitive totals or chase a target, and paid the penalty. Fintan
Baker-Howard leaves after four years of service, including two as captain.

Batting T. J. O'Shea 174 at 21.75; J. W. Carslaw 155 at 19.37.

Bowling *F. E. Baker-Howard 15 at 12.60; C. A. Bentley 13 at 19.61.

The King's School, Worcester *Worcestershire*   P17 W13 L3 D1 A2
Master i/c D. P. Iddon   **Coach** A. A. D. Gillgrass

Opening batsmen Nick Hammond and Will Dovey again scored heavily in another successful season.
The bowling was varied: Cameron Stanley-Blakey and Will Burgoyne both performed
well in their first year in the XI.

Batting *N. A. Hammond 653 at 59.36; W. O. Dovey 550 at 50.00; W. T. Davies 203 at 29.00;
B. R. Sears 247 at 24.70; C. M. Norton 193 at 24.12; G. C. Howarth 206 at 22.88.

Bowling W. O. Dovey 10 at 19.30; W. Burgoyne 19 at 21.57; H. C. Wilde 24 at 22.37; J. Ham 15 at
24.00; C. Stanley-Blakey 22 at 25.77; G. C. Howarth 13 at 29.38.

Kingswood School, Bath *Somerset*   P15 W10 L3 D2 A1
Master i/c J. O. Brown

Kingswood enjoyed another strong season, claiming the Peak Sports League title with a 100%
record. Charlie Brain batted superbly, scoring 843 runs at 76, while George Postlethwaite, Osh
Devlin-Cook and Cameron Walker were at the heart of a strong bowling attack.

Batting C. O. Brain 843 at 76.63; *F. P. Barnard-Weston 370 at 41.11; O. W. Waters 465 at 38.75;
L. C. R. Reeman 285 at 20.35.

Bowling G. T. Postlethwaite 23 at 14.86; O. C. Devlin-Cook 20 at 17.45; C. G. Walker 19 at 17.94;
D. G. J. Mackenzie 13 at 26.15.

Kirkham Grammar School *Lancashire*   P12 W5 L5 D2 A5
Master i/c M. A. Whalley

The summer got off to a slow start, but an inexperienced team performed increasingly well. If the
team continue to develop, there will be much to look forward to.

Batting K. A. Wilkinson 253 at 25.30; *A. P. Whalley 174 at 24.85.

Bowling B. Anderson 11 at 13.00; N. Roux 10 at 13.10; A. A. Chiekrie 10 at 15.90; E. J. Bailey 13
at 21.76.

Lancaster Royal Grammar School *Lancashire*
P16 W4 L9 D3 A1

Master i/c I. W. Ledward   **Coach** I. Perryman

Too many games were lost by small margins, making it a disappointing season. On the plus side, there were strong victories over King's Macclesfield and RGS High Wycombe. Tom Williamson dominated the batting, while Will Fraser-Gray is developing as a pace bowler and explosive batsman.

Batting *T. R. Williamson 718 at 65.27; W. C. Fraser-Gray 316 at 35.11; A. W. H. Grunshaw 270 at 24.54; A. W. Derham 162 at 23.14; M. H. Bevan 161 at 23.00.

Bowling A. W. Derham 14 at 13.14; T. R. Williamson 23 at 15.39; W. C. Fraser-Gray 14 at 19.50; A. K. Nakhuda 11 at 22.36; M. H. Bevan 11 at 33.81; C. A. East 10 at 38.20.

Lancing College *Sussex*
P14 W8 L4 D2

Master i/c R. J. Maru

Lancing College endured a difficult start, losing four of their first five matches. But results improved, and in the end it became a good season. Leg-spinner Mason Crane was an astute captain, and he took ten Championship wickets in three outings for Hampshire.

Batting *M. S. Crane 310 at 38.75; M. C. Clarke 407 at 33.91; W. N. Fazakerley 292 at 32.44; R. T. Maskell 286 at 31.77; T. W. Nightingale 194 at 19.40.

Bowling M. S. Crane 23 at 11.21; O. J. John 19 at 15.78; W. N. Fazakerley 26 at 15.80; H. W. Smethurst 10 at 27.70; T. W. Nightingale 12 at 34.25.

The Grammar School at Leeds *Yorkshire*
P13 W9 D4 A4

Master i/c S. H. Dunn

Despite interruptions for weather and exams, the school went through the summer undefeated, thanks to the skilful captaincy of Jonny Haslem, and a solid all-round bowling attack led by Harry Dixon and well supported by Chris Bridge, Vikram Sharma and Tom Burton.

Batting *J. E. Haslem 321 at 32.10; E. B. Litvin 272 at 27.20; H. F. Dixon 171 at 24.42; O. F. J. Robinson 214 at 23.77

Bowling C. J. Bridge 19 at 7.10; V. Sharma 11 at 8.63; H. F. Dixon 22 at 10.00; T. B. J. Burton 15 at 14.73.

Leicester Grammar School *Leicestershire*
P8 W4 L3 T1 A2

Master i/c L. Potter

Performances were better than results suggested. Patrick Sadd has real potential as a left-arm fast bowler, while captain Jack O'Callaghan is a fine all-round cricketer.

Batting A. M. Tutt 201 at 28.71; M. Mulji 191 at 27.28; P. Sadd 168 at 24.00; *J. O. O'Callaghan 156 at 22.28; T. E. Rashid 151 at 21.57.

Bowling P. Sadd 11 at 16.18; J. O. O'Callaghan 10 at 20.10.

The Leys School *Cambridgeshire*
P12 W10 L1 D1

Master i/c R. I. Kaufman   **Coach** W. J. Earl

It was an outstanding summer for The Leys, who won ten of the 11 completed matches, and reached the last 16 of the National Schools T20 competition. Since the majority of the squad were Year 12 or below, the future is encouraging. Milan Mniszko was the star, scoring 602 runs and taking 31 wickets across all fixtures.

Batting M. A. Mniszko 382 at 127.33; A. S. B. Bramley 393 at 56.14; T. P. Cox 317 at 45.28; C. E. Hoole 307 at 30.70.

Bowling A. Dunn 10 at 9.40; J. A. Gunn Roberts 20 at 10.35; M. A. Mniszko 20 at 12.70; E. C. P. Fairey 14 at 18.21; S. J. Lawson 11 at 21.72.

Lord Wandsworth College *Hampshire*
P10 W3 L6 D1 A1

Master i/c D. M. Beven

The college recorded excellent wins against Oratory, Kingston Grammar and City of London Freemen's. The most notable performance came against MCC, when Hugo Hammond, a current England Disability international, hit 102 from 77 balls.

Batting H. D. Hammond 349 at 38.77; C. J. Young 317 at 28.81; S. H. R. Culmer 235 at 26.11; B. M. Wetherell 164 at 18.22.

Bowling R. Sriharan 13 at 20.76.

Loughborough Grammar School Leicestershire　　P14 W6 L6 T1 D1
Master i/c M. I. Gidley
Player availability was again hampered by exams, making an inconsistent season. Ben Mike batted well, and Ashish Trusz showed his all-round talent. The tie with the Old Boys proved a fitting finale.
Batting B. W. M. Mike 460 at 41.81; A. N. M. Trusz 323 at 40.37; *R. Chopra 331 at 36.77; R. J. Holland 224 at 24.88.
Bowling C. A. Royle 15 at 16.40; R. Chopra 18 at 20.05; A. N. M. Trusz 12 at 25.41.

Magdalen College School Oxfordshire　　P19 W6 L10 D3 A1
Master i/c D. Bebbington　　　　**Coach** A. J. Scriven
A young XI, captained by Hamish Currie (the team's only Year 13), learned to play as a unit. The vice-captain and Year 11, Tom Scriven, hit 799 runs, including 132 not out against MCC; he also claimed 13 wickets and 11 catches. He enjoyed good support from the entire batting line-up.
Batting T. R. A. Scriven 799 at 79.90; T. J. Price 228 at 45.60; A. Mayho 422 at 28.13; E. J. O. Smith 422 at 26.37; N. Devaney-Dykes 282 at 21.69; *H. F. W. Currie 189 at 21.00; F. M. K. Burton 188 at 12.53.
Bowling G. T. Westwood 10 at 14.40; T. R. A. Scriven 13 at 19.23; H. F. W. Currie 23 at 21.91; J. A. Beale 11 at 30.18; E. J. O. Smith 13 at 31.00; O. M. Mase 12 at 32.66; L. E. C. Richards 11 at 33.45.

Malvern College Worcestershire　　P14 W8 L3 D3
Master i/c M. A. Hardinges　　　　**Coach** N. A. Brett
Malvern had another good season, and reached the final of the National Schools T20 tournament for the first time. Ben Tegg and Zen Malik were the pick of the batsmen, scoring five hundreds between them and winning Malvern many games across all formats.
Batting Z. Malik 622 at 88.85; B. E. Tegg 628 at 62.80; J. A. Haynes 150 at 50.00; B. J. Twohig 210 at 42.00; J. L. Haynes 334 at 37.11; *F. G. F. Wynn 327 at 32.70.
Bowling J. L. Haynes 28 at 16.39; L. J. Smith 21 at 17.33; F. G. F. Wynn 11 at 20.54; G. R. M. Amphlett 11 at 21.00; B. J. Twohig 14 at 36.57.

The Manchester Grammar School Lancashire　　P14 W8 L2 T1 D3 A1
Master i/c M. Watkinson
Following a six-match tour to Sri Lanka, MGS enjoyed a successful season under the captaincy of Josh Dooler. Significant contributions by players of all ages augur well.
Batting R. A. Udwadia 386 at 77.20; *J. Dooler 471 at 47.10; S. J. Perry 446 at 40.54; J. A. Smith-Butler 401 at 40.10; O. G. F. Pooler 201 at 22.33; S. D. Povey 157 at 19.62.
Bowling A. J. P. Hamilton 16 at 20.31; R. A. Udwadia 12 at 23.66; J. A. Smith-Butler 12 at 23.75.

Marlborough College Wiltshire　　P12 W6 L5 D1 A1
Master i/c N. E. Briers
There were impressive wins against Radley, Sherborne, Canford and Magdalen College School, but the outstanding performance was the innings victory over Rugby in the two-day colours match, when 16-year-old Hampshire Academy player Elijah Samuel scored 134. It was the first decisive result at Marlborough since 1979, when Rugby prevailed, and at all since 2002, when Marlborough last won.
Batting E. I. Samuel 612 at 68.00; M. P. K. Read 235 at 33.57; S. W. Mead 327 at 29.72; B. C. Wilson 259 at 28.77; *A. J. Combe 231 at 21.00.
Bowling F. E. L. Campbell 27 at 16.92; S. W. Mead 15 at 19.66; F. J. Gordon 19 at 25.15; B. C. Wilson 12 at 29.91; J. N. A. Bunn 11 at 30.18.

Merchant Taylors' School, Crosby Lancashire　　P17 W10 L6 D1 A3
Master i/c S. P. Sutcliffe　　　　**Coach** J. Bell
The school had a successful season, and finished with three fine wins in their festival. George Lavelle was the pick of the batsmen, and also made more than 30 dismissals as wicketkeeper. He was well supported by captain Nick Knight. Of the bowlers, left-arm spinner Tom Hartley and the opening pair, Michael Sutcliffe and Josh Thompson, were the most consistent.
Batting G. I. D. Lavelle 778 at 59.84; *N. A. Knight 494 at 35.28; L. F. McLachlan 179 at 22.37.
Bowling A. D. J. Rankin 15 at 11.73; T. W. Hartley 28 at 12.28; J. J. Thompson 25 at 18.52; M. J. Sutcliffe 23 at 21.39.

Cyrus White came within a boundary of three hundreds for Sevenoaks School; Tom Scriven hit 799 at 79 (and took 13 wickets), and has two years left at Magdalen College School.

Merchant Taylors' School, Northwood *Hertfordshire* P18 W13 L4 D1 A2
Master i/c T. Webley
Some outstanding individual performances ensured an excellent summer. Highlights included Andrew Thomas's superb 115 not out to beat a strong Reed's XI, and Dylan Amin's impressive 77 to hasten victory against Haberdashers' Aske's on the Lord's Nursery Ground.
Batting A. M. Thomas 564 at 56.40; D. O'Sullivan 438 at 39.81; B. Close 173 at 28.83; D. Amin 321 at 22.92; N. S. Rawal 313 at 19.56; *S. R. B. Gates 175 at 17.50.
Bowling D. O'Sullivan 23 at 14.47; K. S. Singh 22 at 16.27; D. Patel 21 at 17.19; U. A. Khan 21 at 17.76; A. R. Amin 21 at 18.61.

Merchiston Castle School *Midlothian* P13 W10 L3
Master i/c R. D. McCann   **Coach** S. J. Horrocks
The first team, well captained by leading scorer Daniel Nutton, had a fine campaign, winning ten of their 13 matches.
Batting A. M. M. Hinton 182 at 60.66; *D. J. Nutton 415 at 51.87; A. B. White 181 at 20.11.
Bowling C. J. Fry 14 at 10.14; A. J. Chandrachud 14 at 12.00; A. W. J. Middleton 15 at 12.06.

Mill Hill School *Middlesex* P9 W5 L3 D1
Master i/c I. J. F. Hutchinson   **Coach** N. R. Hodgson
Capably led by Douglas McDougall, Mill Hill completed five wins, often against strong opposition. Top run-scorer and wicket-taker Ethan Bamber played for Middlesex Seconds. Sophia Dunkley and India Whitty also played for the school.
Batting E. R. Bamber 258 at 43.00; L. Vanhaesebroeck 156 at 26.00.
Bowling W. G. Kilbourn 10 at 9.80; E. R. Bamber 13 at 16.53.

Millfield School *Somerset* P19 W15 L3 D1 A1
Master i/c R. M. Ellison   **Coach** C. D. Gange
The first team had a dominant season, ending with 15 victories from a challenging fixture list. George Hankins scored exactly 1,000 runs, the first to reach the landmark in 25 years, and Dominic Clutterbuck took 32 wickets. Hankins and Tom Lace both hit four hundreds, and Josh McCoy one.

Batting *G. T. Hankins 1,000 at 71.42; T. C. Lace 681 at 45.40; G. A. Bartlett 328 at 36.44; T. J. Moores 400 at 36.36; K. O. Hopper 361 at 36.10; D. N. S. Scott 151 at 30.20; J. I. McCoy 213 at 26.62; J. Seward 194 at 24.25; J. O. Symes 151 at 16.77.
Bowling D. J. Clutterbuck 32 at 14.84; C. D. G. Carmichael 11 at 17.09; G. A. Bartlett 12 at 23.00; J. I. McCoy 16 at 26.87; M. J. Moroney 11 at 27.90; G. T. Hankins 21 at 29.33.

Monkton Combe School *Somerset*
P15 W5 L9 D1

Master i/c S. P. J. Palmer **Coach** B. Potter

A positive and enthusiastic side performed well sporadically. In the Peak Sports League, where the team finished third of seven, and George Leakey was the highest wicket-taker, results were excellent. Only two of those listed below are leavers, which encourages optimism for 2016.
Batting B. J. J. Wells 329 at 27.41; T. M. B. Salmon 322 at 23.00; E. J. Halse 222 at 20.18; C. L. Rose 219 at 18.25; W. F. A. Bishop 237 at 18.23; *G. A. Leakey 195 at 17.72.
Bowling G. A. Leakey 28 at 16.75; C. L. Rose 16 at 21.37; E. J. Halse 10 at 28.90; T. G. M. Wortelhock 13 at 34.00.

Monmouth School *Monmouthshire*
P14 W5 L7 D2 A1

Master i/c A. J. Jones **Coach** G. I. Burgess

Gabriel Warwick won the Rob Hastings Trew memorial cup as the Man of the Match against the Old Boys. Jamie Norman had a productive time, and hit more than 1,000 runs in all first-team cricket. Gareth Ansell missed many games because of his Glamorgan commitments.
Batting J. A. Norman 847 at 84.70; *G. Ansell 166 at 33.20; B. T. Wellington 327 at 27.25; H. M. Rose 300 at 21.42; O. D. Vickers 237 at 18.23; M. R. Kefalas 223 at 17.15.
Bowling A. G. Hamilton 11 at 15.18; D. M. Sharp 14 at 20.28; B. T. Wellington 15 at 27.66; H. M. Rose 14 at 29.14.

Mount Kelly College *Devon*
P8 W1 L6 D1

Master i/c B. W. Edge **Coach** R. A. F. Bache

It was a difficult, transitional year, but Harry Williams and Ben Grove showed real promise with bat and ball, and should return in 2016.
Batting The leading batsman was *H. S. Williams, who hit 148 runs at 21.14.
Bowling B. G. Grove 10 at 18.30.

New Hall School *Essex*
P15 W12 L3 A2

Master i/c G. D. James

The school had another fantastic year, which saw the emergence of some quality young players. The biggest achievements were the first victory over MCC, and sharing the Castle Festival.
Batting B. Allison 205 at 34.16; S. Sullivan 252 at 31.50; L. Pickering 356 at 29.66; J. Whetstone 237 at 26.33; C. Whetstone 256 at 25.60; *M. Jahanfar 208 at 16.00.
Bowling G. Spires 15 at 12.80; C. Whetstone 25 at 17.60; A. Gandhi 21 at 20.04; L. Pickering 13 at 25.53.

Newcastle-under-Lyme School *Staffordshire*
P14 W8 L5 D1 A3

Master i/c G. M. Breen **Coach** K. J. Barnett

The school won a record eight matches – and seven in a row between June 10 and 25. James Pokora, who represented Staffordshire Under-17s, scored 103 not out against Old Newcastilians and 119 against Wilmslow. William Clarke, a Year 9, took seven for 36 against Old Newcastilians.
Batting J. M. Pokora 277 at 92.33; *T. Y. Vickers 308 at 34.22; P. J. Vickers 246 at 22.36.
Bowling T. R. Cowling 21 at 15.04; T. Y. Vickers 12 at 17.66; P. J. Vickers 15 at 21.40; O. J. Tinsley 10 at 27.50.

Norwich School *Norfolk*
P9 W2 L5 T1 D1 A1

Master i/c R. W. Sims

With the first team containing six Year 11s, it was no surprise that 2015 was a summer of rebuilding. Sam Hunt was comfortably the most prolific batsman – and a joy to watch. Alfie Woodrow, consistent and gutsy, was the pick of the bowlers.
Batting S. S. E. T. Hunt 313 at 44.71; S. Gopaul 161 at 20.12.
Bowling A. B. Woodrow 15 at 16.53.

Nottingham High School *Nottinghamshire*   P11 W4 L6 D1 A1
Master i/c M. Baker
The team performed better in the shorter form of the game, where they limited opponents' totals with efficient bowling and fielding. And, despite some success in the 50-over format, they found it tricky to take early wickets or build an innings.
Batting S. Kulkarni 408 at 37.09; H. D. C. Llewelyn 256 at 32.00.
Bowling *C. L. Hurrell 10 at 16.10; L. J. Dickinson 12 at 25.58.

Oakham School *Rutland*   P17 W4 L7 D6
Master i/c J. P. Crawley   Coach F. C. Hayes
The early loss of captain and leading batsman Joseph Kendall to injury was a major blow to a young side that had to cope without an experienced run-scorer. It did not help that the attack was not especially penetrative; the upshot was just two school victories, over Stamford and Sedbergh.
Batting *J. S. Kendall 193 at 38.60; S. J. Wolstenholme 524 at 37.42; L. W. James 390 at 27.85; H. Merriman 315 at 26.25; W. J. Horrell 320 at 24.61; E. M. F. Tattersall 157 at 19.62.
Bowling E. M. F. Tattersall 28 at 15.53; J. Ilott 23 at 18.65; A. J. Radford 16 at 20.00; L. W. James 14 at 24.14; S. J. Wolstenholme 10 at 26.80.

The Oratory School *Oxfordshire*   P17 W8 L9
Master i/c S. C. B. Tomlinson   Coach C. B. Keegan
After a successful winter trip to Barbados, a young XI – ably led by Alfie Clifton – produced some pleasing performances. With nine of the 11 returning, there are high hopes for 2016.
Batting W. Legg 694 at 46.26; O. H. Tong-Jones 483 at 26.83; M. C. Baker-Smith 246 at 18.92; M. Price 266 at 15.64; *A. J. Clifton 210 at 15.00.
Bowling W. Legg 14 at 12.14; D. J. Williams 26 at 12.30; A. J. Clifton 22 at 12.45; C. L. Humphreys 17 at 16.35.

Oundle School *Northamptonshire*   P15 W6 L6 D3 A1
Master i/c J. R. Wake   Coach van der Merwe Genis
Benedict Graves was the outstanding all-rounder, topping both averages and hitting four centuries. One of the best all-rounders the school has produced, he led from the front, on and off the field. A highlight was the opening stand of 311 – struck against Loughborough Grammar School in just 28 overs – between Tristan Tusa (203 not out) and Simon Fernandes (102). Tusa's double, including a century in sixes, was only the fourth for Oundle since records began in 1876.
Batting *B. W. M. Graves 894 at 68.76; C. L. Fernandes 154 at 30.80; T. E. P. Tusa 347 at 28.91; J. P. Fischer 256 at 23.27; S. M. L. Fernandes 348 at 23.20; C. W. L. Fletcher 194 at 21.55; H. J. C. Lawes 203 at 20.30; B. A. Curry 177 at 14.75.
Bowling B. W. M. Graves 40 at 15.30; J. P. Fischer 31 at 20.58; J. Bourn 10 at 21.80; T. Lambton 14 at 23.35; F. D. Johnsrud 17 at 27.17.

The Perse School *Cambridgeshire*   P15 W4 L9 D2 A1
Master i/c S. Park   Coach J. C. Read
Term started badly when captain-elect Chris Pepper was sidelined with a knee injury. Akbar Akhter took charge of a young squad, but several close games went our opponents' way. Hosting a festival also involving Merchant Taylors' Crosby, Durham School and Bromsgrove School was the undoubted highlight.
Batting S. J. Abbasi 409 at 40.90; M. K. S. Pepper 364 at 33.09; *A. Akhter 375 at 26.78; A. W. C. Lockie 173 at 21.62; A. P. M. Mitchell 166 at 16.60; M. Chandraker 145 at 12.08.
Bowling M. K. S. Pepper 16 at 16.37; M. Chandraker 17 at 18.41; A. Akhter 14 at 22.57; D. C. C. Goyal 12 at 23.66.

Pocklington School *Yorkshire*   P18 W7 L3 D8
Master i/c D. Byas
An excellent season was marred only by losing to the Grammar School at Leeds, St Peter's and Birkenhead. The team were again well led by James Hanley.
Batting T. W. Loten 597 at 39.80; *J. R. Hanley 508 at 39.07; J. J. Atkinson 432 at 30.85; T. G. Foster 359 at 25.64.
Bowling T. W. Loten 31 at 14.61; J. R. Hanley 15 at 24.80; J. J. Atkinson 15 at 25.66; L. J. Medley 16 at 31.31.

Portsmouth Grammar School *Hampshire*
P14 W8 L6 A1
Master i/c S. J. Curwood   **Coach** S. D. Lavery

Centuries from Andy Gorvin, Jadon Buckeridge and Rory Prentice heralded victories over MCC, Brighton and King Edward VI School, Southampton. Ben Caldera scored back-to-back centuries in the pre-season Twenty20 competition.

Batting A. D. Gorvin 151 at 50.33; B. Caldera 244 at 40.66; J. D. Buckeridge 276 at 34.50; R. E. Prentice 185 at 26.42; S. Caldera 166 at 23.71.

Bowling J. D. Buckeridge 23 at 8.30; R. E. Prentice 15 at 12.00; D. S. Mugford 10 at 14.90; B. Caldera 10 at 17.70.

Prior Park College *Somerset*
P13 W7 L6 A1
Master i/c M. D. Bond   **Coach** M. E. Knights

With more ups than downs, 2015 was a fantastic season. Nick Lees and Fergus Nutt broke records when they shared a second-wicket stand worth 250. And in cricket week the school played their first two-day game – edging a thrilling match against Colston's in the penultimate over.

Batting F. R. Nutt 455 at 45.50; N. G. R. Lees 249 at 41.50; K. M. Kelly 275 at 25.00; A. T. Carruthers 258 at 23.45; *S. E. Jones 152 at 16.88.

Bowling A. J. Lord 17 at 12.64; M. A. Tonks 13 at 19.15; N. G. R. Lees 10 at 19.50; O. J. Williamson 12 at 21.83.

Queen Elizabeth Grammar School, Wakefield *Yorkshire*
P12 W5 L6 D1 A2
Master i/c I. A. Wolfenden   **Coach** C. Lawson

A youthful side admirably captained by Jacob Heseltine learned from a number of challenging experiences in a transitional season. Notable gains were made, and foundations for 2016 established.

Batting G. A. Thompson 240 at 34.28; H. J. Graham 266 at 24.18; *G. D. Heseltine 166 at 18.44.

Bowling M. J. Flathers 12 at 14.50; H. M. Longhurst 10 at 26.60.

Queen Elizabeth's Hospital *Gloucestershire*
P8 W1 L6 D1 A2
Master i/c P. E. Joslin   **Coach** D. Forder

It was an enjoyable season despite the results. The captain, Andy Barnsley, received support from fellow leavers Guy Sackett and Alex Agar. Edgar Thornton claimed most wickets, while youngsters Ed Wilson (who took a hat-trick) and Daaryoush Ahmed made excellent progress.

Batting G. M. J. Sackett 181 at 25.85.

Bowling E. J. D. Thornton 11 at 15.81.

Queen Mary's Grammar School, Walsall *Staffordshire*
P7 W2 L5
Master i/c B. T. Gibbons

After a couple of years in the wilderness, the team rose to the challenge of competing against established school sides in various tournaments. Despite a modest return by way of results, there was a renewed enthusiasm at senior level.

Batting A. P. Patel 160 at 26.66.

Bowling N. B. Patel 10 at 13.50.

Queen's College, Taunton *Somerset*
P16 W7 L8 D1 A2
Master i/c A. V. Suppiah   **Coach** A. G. Hamilton

The first team made totals of 200 or more on eight occasions, including a remarkable 321. Will MacDonagh and Stephen Doheny struck centuries, while Frank Spurway claimed 23 wickets. The squad looks most promising.

Batting S. T. P. Doheny 405 at 57.85; K. B. Joseph 339 at 26.07; *G. Shepherd 323 at 24.84; F. W. G. Spurway 336 at 22.40; W. P. MacDonagh 261 at 21.75; E. P. Trotman 152 at 19.00; S. B. Baxter 214 at 16.46.

Bowling S. T. P. Doheny 14 at 16.64; F. W. G. Spurway 23 at 28.13; O. R. Barrett 10 at 30.70; K. B. Joseph 13 at 33.46.

Radley College *Oxfordshire*
P13 W1 L11 D1
Master i/c S. H. Dalrymple   **Coach** A. R. Wagner

James Todd captained a young side in a tough campaign. Mungo Fawcett scored most runs and Charlie Purton took most wickets, while several younger players gained first-team experience that should prove hugely beneficial over the coming years.

Batting *J. M. I. Todd 245 at 22.27; M. L. P. Fawcett 281 at 21.61; R. W. M. Hanna 167 at 20.87; O. F. R. Martyn-Hemphill 158 at 17.55; R. A. Betley 188 at 17.09; J. B. J. Cunningham 159 at 14.45.
Bowling C. T. Purton 28 at 16.32; J. M. I. Todd 15 at 26.13; M. L. P. Fawcett 14 at 31.78.

Ratcliffe College *Leicestershire*
Master i/c E. O. Woodcock

P11 W5 L4 T1 D1 A4

The 2015 season produced more wins and more defeats than in many previous years, since the team played an attacking style of cricket that made draws a rarity. Sam and Jack Nightingale excelled in both batting and bowling, while James Lockton's left-arm spin again deceived many batsmen.
Batting *S. C. Nightingale 289 at 57.80; J. E. Nightingale 271 at 45.16; R. J. Thorne 162 at 23.14.
Bowling J. E. Nightingale 23 at 12.39; J. P. Lockton 23 at 13.65; S. C. Nightingale 13 at 19.30.

Reading Blue Coat School *Berkshire*
Master i/c G. C. Turner   Coach P. D. Wise

P14 W9 L5

A stronger fixture list provided a rewarding balance of success and challenge. In addition to his fine batting, Martin Andersson captained with maturity. Hamish Scott was the pick of the bowlers.
Batting *M. K. Andersson 449 at 224.50; M. T. Smart 217 at 31.00; T. A. Halson 277 at 30.77; S. J. Gemmill 273 at 33.33; N. E. Shaw 207 at 29.57; J. T. Kirkwood 244 at 22.18.
Bowling H. R. Scott 17 at 23.00; T. H. Stevenson 13 at 29.92; S. J. Gemmill 11 at 33.18.

Reed's School *Surrey*
Master i/c M. R. Dunn   Coach K. T. Medlycott

P18 W12 L3 D3

A record-breaking season reached its zenith against Tiffin: three batsmen – Sonny Cott, Nathan Tilley and Daniel Douthwaite – made centuries as Reed's closed on 375 for one. Douthwaite (whose bowling also comes at a serious pace) crashed 12 sixes and ten fours to make his hundred from 31 balls. In another match, Oskar Kolk hit 181, the school's highest score. It was no surprise that the team retained the South London 50/40 league title.
Batting O. M. D. Kolk 740 at 82.22; D. A. Douthwaite 483 at 60.37; H. G. D. Alderson 212 at 53.00; G. R. J. Mawhood 301 at 43.00; N. J. Tilley 429 at 42.90; *S. Cott 595 at 42.50; L. H. Bowerman 150 at 30.00; N. H. Spreeth 249 at 19.15.
Bowling B. T. Medlycott 13 at 21.30; O. M. D. Kolk 19 at 21.89; N. H. Spreeth 20 at 22.95; D. A. Douthwaite 23 at 23.21; W. G. Dawson 13 at 27.53; R. M. D. Strang 13 at 28.76; M. A. B. Mahne 11 at 29.72.

Reigate Grammar School *Surrey*
Master i/c P. W. Harrison   Coach J. E. Benjamin

P9 W2 L7

A new group of players negotiated a steep learning curve. Despite inexperience, David Gent led superbly. The team should develop well over the coming two years.
Batting *D. J. Gent 349 at 49.85; R. A. Haughton 244 at 34.85.
Bowling O. A. Simms 10 at 22.00.

Repton School *Derbyshire*
Master i/c I. M. Pollock   Coaches H. B. Dytham/J. A. Afford

P16 W8 L6 D2 A2

Although results were mixed, standards – on a tough fixture list – were high. The outstanding individual achievement came from Joss Morgan, who hit 97 not out and 110 in the same game. The 2016 season promises much, with just three of the first-choice XI leaving.
Batting S. O. Trotman 281 at 46.83; J. L. Morgan 530 at 40.76; E. J. Lawley 460 at 30.66; R. P. Brown 390 at 27.85; *J. P. Nijjar 302 at 25.16; E. J. Hibell 182 at 22.75.
Bowling S. O. Trotman 25 at 17.20; J. A. Wilkins 18 at 19.72; B. J. Mann 20 at 25.25; J. W. Bull 15 at 25.73; J. A. Bywater 18 at 26.16.

Royal Grammar School, Guildford *Surrey*
Master i/c C. J. L. Sandbach

P19 W10 L9

Winning the end-of-term RGS Cricket Festival was the pinnacle of the summer. Alex Sweet's performances with bat and ball were extremely pleasing, and it was sad to see the Year 13 boys leave, including captain Jonathan French and senior bowler Sam Jelley.
Batting M. H. James 240 at 40.00; A. R. I. Sweet 674 at 37.44; B. E. Thomas 298 at 33.11; *J. R. G. French 583 at 32.38; G. T. T. Mackenzie 352 at 23.46; H. L. Jones 197 at 21.88; R. G. Browning 191 at 19.10; L. R. Jones 224 at 18.66.

Alex Sweet combined 674 runs and 21 wickets for RGS Guildford.

Bowling A. R. I. Sweet 21 at 21.76; S. J. Jelley 26 at 23.46; B. M. Shaw 20 at 25.75; G. T. T. Mackenzie 21 at 26.28; D. J. R. Ashworth 17 at 26.70; J. R. G. French 14 at 30.92; J. C. Elder 13 at 31.07.

The Royal Grammar School, Worcester *Worcestershire* P20 W13 L6 D1 A1
Master i/c M. D. Wilkinson **Coach** P. J. Newport

Mark Jones led a successful team enthusiastically. With three centuries, Elliott Bartlett was the mainstay of an otherwise fragile batting side, but a decent seam attack – as well as three off-spinners – usually applied pressure. An exciting RGS Festival was the year's highlight.
Batting E. A. Bartlett 723 at 42.52; J. D. G. Taylor 691 at 34.55; K. D. Smith 309 at 30.90; J. M. Ridge 247 at 24.70; *M. D. Jones 393 at 23.11; S. Shah 367 at 21.58; G. S. Cook 198 at 19.80; J. J. Allen 202 at 18.36.
Bowling S. Shah 37 at 16.91; O. J. Saunders 14 at 18.78; M. D. Jones 17 at 24.29; A. S. Jawanda 25 at 24.92; J. D. G. Taylor 19 at 24.94; R. F. Watts 13 at 32.07.

Royal Hospital School *Suffolk* P13 W4 L5 D4
Master i/c T. D. Topley **Coach** D. W. Hawkley

Fine wins over Framlingham, Colchester RGS, Woodbridge and Norwich – as well as narrow defeats by MCC, XL Club and Gresham's – made for a challenging and satisfying season. The presence of two leg-spinning all-rounders proved fruitful, especially with captain Drew Felstead excelling behind the stumps. This was the 37th and final year of Don Hawkley's association with RHS cricket.
Batting M. W. Cowdrey 338 at 33.80; J. E. Allday 362 at 32.90; T. M. Allday 260 at 28.88; *D. W. Felstead 209 at 23.22.
Bowling M. W. Cowdrey 16 at 18.50; T. M. Allday 19 at 22.36; B. H. Tait 10 at 22.40; C. D. Gibson 14 at 25.57.

Rugby School *Warwickshire* P15 W9 L3 D3 A1
Master i/c P. J. Rosser **Coach** M. J. Powell

Rugby enjoyed a rewarding 2015, including an excellent win over Malvern and a hard-fought draw in the two-day fixture against Clifton College. Opening bat Robbie Povey became only the fifth Rugbeian to hit 1,000 runs in a summer.
Batting R. J. Povey 1,027 at 93.36; M. J. G. Taylor 519 at 37.07; L. A. Musiani Perez 459 at 30.60; E. W. Beard 375 at 25.00; J. D. Cutter 166 at 18.44; J. P. Rosser 212 at 15.14.
Bowling B. M. Hatton 13 at 23.23; E. W. Beard 13 at 24.46; M. J. G. Taylor 22 at 27.77; J. H. Woodhead 11 at 44.90.

Rydal Penrhos *Denbighshire*   P7 W3 L4 A3
Master i/c M. T. Leach
This was a satisfying season both in terms of results and exposing younger players to senior cricket.
Matthew Thomas led well and received good support, especially from William Sissons, who at 14
shows excellent potential.
Batting W. B. S. Sissons 224 at 56.00.
Bowling The leading bowler was W. B. S. Sissons, who claimed eight wickets at 14.12.

St Albans School *Hertfordshire*   P10 W4 L5 D1 A1
Master i/c M. C. Ilott
Alexander Cook, a talented batsman, bowler and fielder, enjoyed a fine summer. Across all formats,
the school played a total of 20 matches.
Batting A. S. Cook 244 at 48.80; C. F. Scott 244 at 30.50; *P. E. B. Scott 176 at 29.33; N. Lipschitz
180 at 22.50.
Bowling The leading bowler was P. E. B. Scott, who claimed nine wickets at 26.00.

St Benedict's School, Ealing *Middlesex*   P19 W8 L10 D1
Master i/c J. P. Thisanayagam
A young and dynamic side won their first Middlesex Cup. Exciting batsman Sam Allen and leading
wicket-takers Stefan Tsang and Theo Morris have two more seasons, so the future looks encouraging.
Batting S. J. L. Allen 395 at 39.50; J. J. Spanswick 394 at 32.83; B. D. P. Chippendale 337 at 25.92;
*L. J. Millman 297 at 22.84; T. A. Madden 203 at 13.53.
Bowling S. J. F. Tsang 25 at 16.80; T. O. A. Morris 19 at 24.57; B. D. P. Chippendale 10 at 26.10;
G. D. Yates 12 at 26.83.

St Edmund's School, Canterbury *Kent*   P9 W4 L5
Master i/c A. R. Jones   Coach C. Penn
Overall, it was a heartening season. A young side were strong in batting, thanks in part to stalwart
captain Thomas Phillis, and they were always competitive. However, a lack of real threat from the
bowlers limited their achievements.
Batting *T. J. W. Phillis 370 at 61.66; H. C. Rutherford-Roberts 279 at 34.87; U. Angdembe 151 at
18.87.
Bowling R. F. St John-Stevens 10 at 11.50; T. J. W. Phillis 11 at 15.00; A. Shipton 13 at 17.69;
U. Angdembe 11 at 22.81.

St Edward's School, Oxford *Oxfordshire*   P22 W14 L5 D3
Master i/c S. J. O. Roche   Coaches R. W. J. Howitt/R. C. Hooton
St Edward's run of form continued through a precocious season from a young side with only three
leavers. Calvin Dickinson and William Bull shared the captaincy with distinction. Outstanding
moments included Dickinson's 181 at Oratory, a partnership of 276 between Dickinson and
Alexander Woodland, and winning the John Harvey Cup for the third year in succession.
Batting A. A. Edekar 536 at 67.00; *C. M. Dickinson 986 at 49.30; A. J. Woodland 617 at 41.13;
*W. H. Bull 473 at 39.41; H. D. Ward 424 at 21.20; A. M. P. Wyles 174 at 19.33; W. N. Deasy 172
at 13.23.
Bowling A. C. P. Knott 13 at 14.00; R. H. M. Hipwell 20 at 16.90; S. P. Kennedy 19 at 19.84; A. A.
Edekar 14 at 20.14; A. J. Woodland 27 at 21.11; J. A. Curtis 21 at 22.09; A. M. P. Wyles 12 at
25.41; W. N. Deasy 10 at 26.40; W. H. Bull 15 at 27.20; H. D. Ward 14 at 35.85.

St George's College, Weybridge *Surrey*   P17 W13 L3 D1 A1
Master i/c O. J. Clayson   Coach R. Hall
This was a tremendous season for an experienced side who knew their roles. If no one stood head
and shoulders above their colleagues, everyone made a contribution.
Batting A. C. Firth 300 at 42.85; N. J. Christie 516 at 39.69; M. Garvey-Windrich 443 at 36.91;
W. Jacks 443 at 31.64; W. Arkell 345 at 28.75; J. Smith 276 at 23.00.
Bowling W. Jacks 35 at 16.42; A. Jackson 27 at 17.51; W. Arkell 23 at 18.00; A. R. Bartlett 20 at
20.45; J. Smith 26 at 21.38.

St John's School, Leatherhead *Surrey*
P13 W10 L3

Master i/c D. J. Hammond

Winning ten of 13 matches was proof of a highly talented outfit. Dimil Patel captained magnificently, leading the team to victory in the annual festival.

Batting H. D. Storey 532 at 40.92; *D. Patel 423 at 38.45; M. P. Denley 379 at 29.15; S. Budinger 369 at 28.38; M. A. R. James 216 at 21.60; A. J. Breakspear 189 at 14.53.

Bowling S. Budinger 22 at 23.63; M. A. R. James 21 at 25.00; D. Patel 21 at 25.23; R. A. MacFarlane 13 at 41.15; K. J. Klintworth 13 at 53.84.

St Lawrence College *Kent*
P7 W6 L1

Master i/c T. Moulton   **Coach** R. G. Coughtrie

Last summer turned out to be a good one for a young side, all of whom return in 2016. Ben Moulton's consistent batting, plus significant scores from B-J. Smith and Jake Smith – who led the side well – helped us win five games when chasing. These three were also the most potent bowlers.

Batting B. R. A. Moulton 225 at 45.00; B-J. Smith 151 at 25.16.

Bowling B. R. A. Moulton 13 at 8.76; B-J. Smith 11 at 10.09.

St Paul's School *Surrey*
P16 W10 L5 D1

Master i/c A. G. J. Fraser

The school's most rewarding victories came against RGS Guildford, KCS Wimbledon, Hampton and Epsom. All-rounders Niall Solomon and Thomas Powe enjoyed excellent seasons.

Batting T. B. Powe 556 at 50.54; *A. C. Dewhurst 437 at 43.70; N. G. Solomon 550 at 39.28.

Bowling A. M. C. Russell 28 at 11.85; N. G. Solomon 21 at 14.33; T. B. Powe 18 at 15.83.

St Peter's School, York *Yorkshire*
P19 W14 L4 D1 A1

Master i/c G. J. Sharp

Led brilliantly by Harry Stothard, St Peter's had an excellent summer. However, several valued senior players have departed, and Tom Spearman will lead a young, exciting side in 2016.

Batting W. M. S. Huffer 451 at 34.69; T. W. T. Latham 364 at 33.09; *H. A. Stothard 395 at 26.33; H. G. Adams 328 at 25.23; H. R. Contreras 342 at 24.42; W. L. A. Shaw 173 at 19.22; O. J. Leedham 205 at 18.63.

Bowling W. M. S. Huffer 14 at 10.85; C. J. Burdass 10 at 11.60; T. J. Patmore 26 at 14.46; T. R. Spearman 21 at 16.76; O. J. Leedham 20 at 18.35; S. C. Lodge 11 at 20.00; H. A. Stothard 17 at 20.70.

Sedbergh School *Yorkshire*
P14 W4 L10 A3

Master i/c C. P. Mahon   **Coach** M. P. Speight

A lop-sided campaign saw a young side struggle to finish off close games early in the term, before a marked improvement brought better results. They showed their real potential in cup competitions, reaching National Schools T20 finals day and the final of the National Under-17 Cup.

Batting H. C. Brook 661 at 50.84; G. R. Cameron 295 at 26.81; A. C. Simpson 309 at 23.76; *S. R. Croft 255 at 23.18; J. C. H. Park-Johnson 306 at 21.85; M. B. Silvester 190 at 17.27.

Bowling S. R. Croft 21 at 21.33; P. M. R. Phillips 12 at 22.66; J. C. H. Park-Johnson 10 at 27.25; W. J. Topham 10 at 35.50.

Sevenoaks School *Kent*
P12 W5 L6 D1

Master i/c C. J. Tavaré   **Coach** P. J. Hulston

After a slow start, a youthful first team finished strongly, winning four of their last five matches, including a four-wicket victory against MCC. The outstanding players were opening batsman Cyrus White, who hit two centuries and a 97, and left-arm swing bowler Tristan Flint, with 22 wickets.

Batting N. M. Bett 377 at 62.83; C. J. White 543 at 60.33; H. M. Gillis 162 at 20.25.

Bowling T. J. W. Flint 22 at 14.45; K. L. Joseph 11 at 27.81.

Sherborne School *Dorset*
P13 W7 L5 D1 A1

Master i/c T. O. Flowers   **Coach** A. Willows

Sherborne fared reasonably well in 2015, with wins over Canford, Blundell's and Taunton School. A narrow loss to Millfield, and heavier defeats by Cheltenham and Marlborough were disappointing. William Caldwell prospered in his debut season.

Batting W. R. H. Caldwell 696 at 63.27; G. J. R. Pope 356 at 27.38; *W. F. Cochrane-Dyet 313 at 24.07.

Bowling B. Weatherhead 16 at 18.18; J. M. T. Caldwell 15 at 23.86; W. R. H. Caldwell 14 at 24.28; D. F. P. Bell 10 at 25.40.

Shiplake College *Oxfordshire*   P15 W4 L11
Master i/c D. R. Miller   **Coaches** J. H. Howorth/C. Ellison
A young team managed four hard-fought wins, playing good cricket along the way, but a lack of runs undid them on several occasions. The first team return in 2016 with a season's experience. Joe Tucker, aged 15, hit 192 runs and took nine wickets.
Batting H. A. S. Ibbitson 196 at 21.77; J. W. Tucker 192 at 14.76; M. Tidswell 163 at 13.58.
Bowling T. McCooke 12 at 14.83.

Shrewsbury School *Shropshire*   P22 W16 L4 D2 A1
Master i/c A. S. Barnard   **Coach** A. P. Pridgeon
After a successful tour of South Africa and the UAE, Shrewsbury won the majority of their matches and retained the Silk Trophy for an unprecedented third year, overcoming Eton in their best performance of the summer.
Batting O. E. Westbury 1,048 at 55.15; G. P. Hargrave 742 at 49.46; *G. P. G. Lewis 606 at 35.64; H. R. D. Adair 646 at 34.00; G. D. Panayi 347 at 26.69; C. E. Home 238 at 26.44.
Bowling C. E. Home 28 at 14.75; G. D. Panayi 29 at 19.10; O. E. Westbury 28 at 20.32; D. J. Lloyd 31 at 21.38; P. J. Jacob 12 at 25.91; D. L. Durman 10 at 28.20; C. E. Cooke 12 at 42.66.

Silcoates School *Yorkshire*   P12 W9 L3 A2
Master i/c G. M. Roberts
Joe Seddon captained an experienced team to nine victories. Highlights included reaching the North East semi-final of the National Schools T20 and winning the end-of-season festival. Opening bowler Jonathan Donnelly was selected for Yorkshire Under-19s.
Batting J. M. Donnelly 421 at 52.62; C. Wallis 257 at 36.71; J. W. H. Seddon 394 at 32.83.
Bowling J. M. Donnelly 15 at 10.26; R. J. Lacey 14 at 13.92; J. W. H. Seddon 12 at 22.08.

Simon Langton Grammar School *Kent*   P5 W2 L2 D1 A3
Master i/c R. H. Green
A young side gained valuable experience at senior level, despite only five matches being played.
Batting The leading batsman was J. W. N. Gray, who hit 138 runs at 46.00.
Bowling The leading bowler was W. A. Hadler, who took eight wickets at 11.00.

Sir Thomas Rich's School *Gloucestershire*   P10 W9 L1 A3
Master i/c R. G. Williams   **Coach** N. D. O'Neil
This was a magnificent year for cricket at Sir Thomas Rich's. The school beat Dean Close by ten wickets in a two-day game, RGS Worcester by four, and Gloucestershire Gipsies by five. The outstanding player was Jack Tyrer.
Batting J. Tyrer 394 at 78.80; *H. A. Day 171 at 57.00; S. M. Rideout 191 at 47.75; J. A. Price 165 at 41.25.
Bowling H. Shahzad 13 at 12.15; S. M. Rideout 19 at 14.78; P. J. G. Carter 15 at 16.93.

Solihull School *Warwickshire*   P14 W6 L6 T1 D1 A5
Master i/c D. L. Maddy   **Coach** D. W. Smith
A young side took significant strides during the term, and there were several fine performances, including a two-day victory over Monmouth School, and maiden senior centuries from Fahd Janjua and William Rigg.
Batting F. K. Janjua 450 at 56.25; W. E. Rigg 433 at 39.36; J. G. Lankester 210 at 35.00; *W. G. Talbot-Davies 417 at 34.75; A. N. Szarmach 233 at 29.12; J. P. Hart 263 at 21.91.
Bowling R. M. Bradley 17 at 21.23; F. K. Janjua 12 at 31.66; W. G. Talbot-Davies 13 at 38.00.

Stamford School *Lincolnshire*   P10 W3 L6 D1 A1
Master i/c D. N. Jackson   **Coach** D. W. Headley
With each game, Sam Evison improved with bat, ball and in the art of captaincy. All-rounders Mohammed Danyaal and Harry Clarke, also Year 12s, and opener Jules Brahmachari should continue to develop. Year 8 opening batsmen Joey Evison and Year 10 opening bowler Nick Green seem likely to have long careers in the team.
Batting *S. H. G. Evison 364 at 52.00; J. A. Brahmachari 393 at 39.30; M. Danyaal 250 at 35.71.
Bowling S. H. G. Evison 10 at 37.90.

Oliver Westbury had a superb all-round reason for Shrewsbury School; Henry Gater scored a double-century for Taunton School against neighbours Queen's College.

Stewart's Melville College *Midlothian*   P15 W4 L7 D4 A4
Master i/c A. Ranson

A young team exceeded all expectations.

Batting S. O. Blain 428 at 42.80; J. M. Savage 151 at 25.16; M. A. G. Hancock 209 at 23.22; C. J. Miller 221 at 18.41; *J. P. B. Pennell 184 at 18.40.

Bowling F. M. Bell 13 at 10.53; A. L. Appleton 17 at 21.88; J. W. Stuart 15 at 23.33; J. P. B. Pennell 13 at 29.07.

Stonyhurst College *Lancashire*   P5 L5 A2
Master i/c G. Thomas   **Coach** J. J. Pienaar

The first three games were close – including defeats by one run and one wicket – but an inability to score runs, excepting Year 12 all-rounders Rhys Morgan and Michael Diamond, was the major weakness. Captain Will Metcalf made a strong contribution with the ball and in the field.

Batting The leading batsman was R. W. C. Morgan, who hit 142 runs at 28.40.

Bowling The leading bowler was J. N. Chitnis, who claimed six wickets at 18.50.

Stowe School *Buckinghamshire*   P20 W13 L1 D6 A2
Master i/c J. A. Knott   **Coach** P. R. Arnold

Everyone played their part in a highly rewarding and enjoyable season containing just one defeat. Eight of the 12-man squad return, giving cause for optimism for 2016. The team were strong in shorter formats, and the highlight was beating Menlo Park (national T20 champions in South Africa) in the final of our own T20 festival. Year 10 wicketkeeper-batsmen Adam King made his debut for Northamptonshire Seconds in the summer holidays and has joined their Academy.

Batting M. W. Hulbert 644 at 42.93; H. J. Hoare 515 at 34.33; J. B. R. Keeping 517 at 28.72; B. J. Lee 432 at 27.00; *T. E. Young 255 at 25.50; O. D. Clarke 153 at 21.85; A. E. King 188 at 20.88.

Bowling O. D. Clarke 15 at 8.66; G. A. Markham 24 at 12.66; H. J. Hoare 29 at 13.93; J. B. R. Keeping 28 at 20.46; S. Patel 18 at 22.77; T. E. Young 19 at 22.78; O. G. H. Woodward 13 at 27.69; S. R. J. Riley 13 at 31.61.

Sutton Valence School *Kent*   P14 W5 L3 D6
Master i/c V. J. Wells

An inexperienced first team, including only three Year 13s, performed well. Stuart Boltman and Ryan Jones were the top run-scorers, and the three spinners – Ollie Ridge, Alex Woodford and Year 11 Will Edwards – also shone.

Batting S. A. E. Boltman 333 at 37.00; R. L. N. Jones 438 at 33.69; S. F. Noss 167 at 27.83; J. R. Bevan-Thomas 234 at 19.50; T. H. Lennard 219 at 18.25; *A. Adil 211 at 17.58.

Bowling O. J. Ridge 11 at 24.54; W. M. Edwards 11 at 25.63; A. Adil 16 at 27.81; A. T. Woodford 13 at 31.76.

Taunton School *Somerset*
P17 W10 L7

Master i/c D. A. Jessep

On the back of a good winter tour to the UAE and Qatar, the first team produced some excellent cricket to win ten games. There were four centuries, including a magnificent 206 from the captain, Henry Gater, against Queen's Taunton. The wickets were shared, with leg-spinner Seb Horler claiming 21.

Batting *H. J. Gater 686 at 42.87; S. P. Whitefield 489 at 34.92; J. Harnett 267 at 33.37; S. W. Rixon 305 at 30.50; C. A. Smith 301 at 20.06; J. A. Spackman 256 at 17.06; D. J. Trapnell 192 at 14.76; E. Eminson 159 at 13.77.

Bowling C. A. Smith 16 at 21.00; S. P. Whitefield 18 at 22.33; S. M. Horler 21 at 24.47; D. H. Drew 13 at 26.69; J. A. Spackman 10 at 27.00.

Tiffin School *Surrey*
P19 W6 L11 D2 A2

Master i/c M. J. Williams

This was a difficult yet enjoyable season. All the side bar one returns in 2016. Vinay Samtani and Conor Fulton batted beautifully on occasion, but runs and wickets were hard to come by.

Batting V. K. Samtani 523 at 32.68; M. J. Talman 195 at 27.85; C. J. J. Fulton 461 at 27.11; *A. K. Rana 373 at 23.31; K. K. Sachdeva 326 at 20.37; B. A. Bhatti 172 at 14.33.

Bowling B. A. Bhatti 31 at 21.38; I. J. S. Shokar 22 at 25.63; T. J. Morse 12 at 25.91; D. L. S. Jones 14 at 26.21; K. K. Sachdeva 12 at 28.50; Y. I. M. Jackson 10 at 35.30.

Tonbridge School *Kent*
P16 W10 L5 D1

Master i/c A. R. Whittall   **Coach** I. Baldock

Tonbridge, captained again by Nick Winder, had an impressive season despite a relatively green side. Zak Crawley passed 1,000 runs, and Marcus O'Riordan took most wickets. Both are cricketers for the future, and have one more year at Tonbridge. Having won all but one match in the competition, Tonbridge narrowly missed taking the Cowdrey Cup.

Batting Z. Crawley 1,069 at 82.23; M. O'Riordan 461 at 32.92; H. A. Langham 367 at 30.58; C. McGregor 469 at 29.31; A. J. Bissett 263 at 29.22; E. R. B. Hyde 386 at 25.73; M. C. de Kock 234 at 21.27.

Bowling *N. J. Winder 27 at 23.74; A. J. Bissett 10 at 25.10; J. O. A. Prideaux 12 at 27.00; M. O'Riordan 30 at 29.43; Z. Crawley 13 at 35.15.

Trent College *Derbyshire*
P11 W4 L7 A1

Master i/c S. A. J. Boswell   **Coach** D. Hartley

A young XI had a challenging season in which the highlight was a strong team performance against Oakham School. Thomas Hill was the leading batsman, and Tim Wyatt – a lively opening bowler – caused problems with his pace.

Batting T. J. Hill 365 at 36.50; T. Wyatt 267 at 29.66; M. Young 198 at 18.00; D. Andrew 156 at 17.33.

Bowling J. E. Naylor 16 at 19.06; T. Wyatt 10 at 19.80; M. Davies 17 at 21.00; T. L. Naylor 11 at 25.09.

Trinity School *Surrey*
P16 W8 L8 A1

Master i/c R. J. Risebro   **Coach** I. D. K. Salisbury

George Jackson led the batting and bowling, while several younger players showed glimpses of what's to come in 2016.

Batting G. L. Jackson 332 at 36.88; D. J. Johnsen 254 at 28.22; J. M. Logan 337 at 25.92; J. T. W. Allen 301 at 23.15; J. W. Blake 261 at 20.07; M. T. Kelly 209 at 14.92; *J. B. Abrahams 233 at 14.56.

Bowling G. L. Jackson 19 at 15.78; H. S. Neale-Smith 21 at 17.23; A. H. Raza 16 at 19.37; M. T. Kelly 16 at 20.43; H. T. E. Fisher 12 at 24.25.

University College School *Middlesex*
P15 W3 L11 D1

Master i/c L. J. Greany   **Coach** A. R. Wilkes

Results were unkind, with several games narrowly lost, but there were some exceptional individual performances, especially from the four regular Year 10 players. Julius Raschke is a talent to watch, and a century from Michael Ettlinger ended the season on a high.

Batting J. F. Raschke 397 at 36.09; M. R. Ettlinger 275 at 34.37; A. S. Hamilton 163 at 16.30; D. A. S. Grabinar 192 at 16.00; A. W. Beckham 155 at 14.09.

Bowling A. S. Hamilton 17 at 16.70; R. Prabhakar 12 at 21.00; J. L. Driver 12 at 29.58; D. A. S. Grabinar 12 at 45.66.

Uppingham School *Rutland*   P14 W6 L2 T1 D5 A1
Master i/c T. Makhzangi   **Coaches** T. R. Ward/J. C. J. Sharrock
With six of the regular XI drawn from Year 11, a young team did well to win six games – it might have been more after they came close in a number of draws. The season also contained the 150th anniversary match against Repton, who ran out winners.
Batting W. Rogers 534 at 38.14; F. Tucker 394 at 32.83; G. Frankel 314 at 28.54; *L. S. W. Blakey 398 at 28.42; J. Maxwell 175 at 21.87; G. Loyd 268 at 20.61.
Bowling S. Chadge 13 at 22.00; G. Loyd 16 at 24.00; W. Rogers 24 at 30.75; S. Charlton 15 at 34.00.

Victoria College, Jersey *Channel Islands*   P12 W4 L7 D1 A1
Master i/c M. D. Smith   **Coach** C. E. Minty
William Harris and Solomon Warner, who threatened big scores on a number of occasions, shared a hundred stand to set up a good win over Elizabeth College. James Duckett was again the top wicket-taker, despite missing the start of the season with injury.
Batting S. O. T. Warner 287 at 26.09; D. D. De Klerk 188 at 23.50; E. B. Miles 230 at 23.00; W. P. Harris 240 at 20.00; R. W. Duckett 240 at 20.00.
Bowling J. N. Duckett 19 at 15.78; E. B. Miles 18 at 16.66; G. G. Donaldson 12 at 16.75; R. W. Duckett 11 at 23.63; D. Bourne 10 at 24.40.

Warwick School *Warwickshire*   P21 W13 L6 D2 A3
Master i/c S. R. G. Francis
This was an outstanding summer for a team who on paper had seemed slightly weaker. But they worked hard, and went undefeated in the longer format until their penultimate game. Charlie Blake and Rob Yates hit centuries, while Reuben Arnold and Charlie Pigott were the leading wicket-takers.
Batting R. M. Yates 540 at 45.00; *C. D. Blake 618 at 34.33; R. S. K. Arnold 543 at 31.94; D. Lynch 280 at 31.11; S. J. P. Forster 329 at 25.30.
Bowling R. S. K. Arnold 30 at 16.00; C. A. Pigott 22 at 20.54; R. M. Yates 13 at 24.07; J. G. Lynch 16 at 26.56; O. H. Richardson 15 at 35.86.

Wellingborough School *Northamptonshire*   P14 W8 L3 D3 A1
Master i/c G. E. Houghton   **Coach** D. J. Sales
Now under the guidance of ex-Northamptonshire batsman David Sales, the XI enjoyed another successful season, including fine wins against Oundle, Bloxham, Bedford Modern and the XL Club. With only two leavers, the side looks well placed for 2016.
Batting G. Groenland 480 at 53.33; B. T. Wall 426 at 42.60; L. J. Draper 250 at 41.66; *D. D. W. Brierley 370 at 37.00; S. J. Mulvey 228 at 25.33.
Bowling T. T. Mitchell 20 at 10.90; B. T. Wall 15 at 15.53; G. Groenland 15 at 21.73; M. R. Chalcraft 16 at 22.75.

Wellington College *Berkshire*   P18 W12 L3 T1 D2
Master i/c D. M. Pratt   **Coach** G. D. Franklin
There were victories in the Cowdrey Cup against Harrow, Radley and Charterhouse, while Wellington triumphed at the BOWS Festival, winning all three games. They also reached the semi-finals of the National Schools T20 competition.
Batting S. M. Curran 568 at 56.80; B. J. Curran 440 at 48.88; J. L. B. Davies 214 at 35.66; A. H. J. Dewes 439 at 33.76; P. G. N. Spriggs 269 at 33.62; A. W. Shoff 426 at 28.40; S. Kanwar 191 at 27.28; *C. P. A. Green 242 at 22.00; E. C. George 191 at 21.22; E. J. T. Bowcock 355 at 19.72; S. J. Sweetland 173 at 17.30.
Bowling L. J. M. Methley 30 at 17.43; S. M. Curran 22 at 18.31; G. C. Newson 13 at 19.15; C. P. A. Green 12 at 20.08; A. H. J. Dewes 23 at 21.17; P. G. N. Spriggs 13 at 26.23; B. J. Curran 13 at 27.92.

Wells Cathedral School *Somerset*   P13 W2 L8 D3
Master i/c J. A. Boot   **Coach** C. Keast
Some strong opponents included St Kentigern's College, New Zealand. The best performances were a nine-wicket win against Millfield Thirds and a narrow victory over Downside.
Batting R. E. Moss 241 at 30.12; *S. P. Betley 252 at 19.38; C. H. C. Gray 212 at 19.27; L. W. Boot 226 at 18.83; H. O. S. Connock 153 at 15.30.
Bowling H. J. Bench 10 at 16.80; M. A. Strachan-Stevens 15 at 22.20; L. W. Boot 10 at 34.40.

Barnaby Graff topped both sets of averages for Westminster School; Daniel Escott beat the Winchester College batting record, set by the Nawab of Pataudi in 1959, by scoring 1,096 runs.

Westminster School *Middlesex*   P13 W7 L4 D2
Master i/c J. D. Kershen   **Coach** S. K. Ranasinghe
Victory over Charterhouse was the most memorable achievement of a pleasing season in which a talented side could perhaps have won every game. Barnaby Graff, the star performer, hit 771 runs – beaten only once in the school's history – and topped the bowling too.
Batting B. J. Graff 771 at 77.10; I. A. Salim 255 at 23.18; S. R. Amin 228 at 19.00.
Bowling B. J. Graff 20 at 17.55; O. R. Lloyd Williams 12 at 22.16; *K. D. Amin 15 at 25.73; E. E. Daley 11 at 31.09.

Whitgift School *Surrey*   P21 W17 L2 D2
Master i/c D. M. Ward   **Coach** S. J. Woodward
Results reveal an excellent season in which all players made key contributions. Ryan Patel and Tyler Meyer were the outstanding contributors in all forms, with wickets and runs.
Batting R. P. Patel 1,043 at 57.94; N. Welch 820 at 54.66; *R. A. Lock 595 at 35.00; J. L. Smith 397 at 26.46; K. N. Beri 367 at 24.46; F. N. McManus 269 at 15.82.
Bowling T. Z. Meyer 45 at 10.55; R. P. Patel 35 at 12.94; R. A. Lock 37 at 15.86; J. E. Culff 25 at 23.52.

Winchester College *Hampshire*   P18 W8 L8 T1 D1 A1
Master i/c G. J. Watson   **Coach** P. N. Gover
It was a season of two halves: excellent before half-term, not so wonderful afterwards. Splendid early performances against Bradfield and Charterhouse were highlights; Daniel Escott excelled for a fourth year, and Henry Portman gave strong support with the ball.
Batting *D. A. Escott 1,096 at 78.28; S. M. Hussain 342 at 24.42; H. A. E. B. Portman 244 at 17.42; S. G. Byers 227 at 16.21; J. W. Mehrtens 182 at 14.00; R. M. C. Quinault 157 at 8.72.
Bowling H. A. E. B. Portman 33 at 11.93; A. A. Woodman 19 at 15.52; J. W. Mehrtens 14 at 22.42; A. H. J. Dodd 18 at 23.16; D. A. Escott 20 at 23.80; B. M. H. McCleery 16 at 35.68.

Wolverhampton Grammar School *Staffordshire*   P13 W9 L2 T1 D1
Master i/c T. King   **Coach** N. H. Crust
This was the best season for some years, thanks to a number of strong all-round team performances. Most squad members played a key role in at least one of the nine victories.
Batting A. O'Hara 250 at 83.33; C. Singh 382 at 38.20.

Bowling P. Griffiths 25 at 8.72; C. Singh 24 at 12.41; A. R. Carey 17 at 15.58; S. J. Timmins 14 at 20.50; K. Patel 10 at 25.10.

Woodbridge School *Suffolk* P7 W3 L4 A2
Master i/c D. A. Brous

A young team began with two wins, including a famous victory against MCC, thanks in part to a superb 95* from Ben Morgan. When half the regulars were absent because of exam pressure, victories dried up, but a promising team returned to winning ways once they were back to full strength.

Batting *B. M. J. Morgan 165 at 55.00; C. R. Askins 154 at 25.66.
Bowling C. R. Askins 10 at 21.30.

Woodhouse Grove School *Yorkshire* P12 W6 L2 D4 A4
Master i/c R. I. Frost   **Coach** A. Sidebottom

A good summer saw Woodhouse Grove go undefeated until the final week, and they narrowly missed out on a second successive appearance at the National Schools T20 finals day. Patrick Dixon, Bailey Worcester, Jibrael Malik and Nicky Bulcock all played for Yorkshire Under-19.

Batting J. Malik 476 at 47.60; *P. R. Dixon 517 at 47.00; G. S. A. Styles 221 at 36.83; B. J. Worcester 325 at 36.11; G. T. Newark 167 at 33.40.
Bowling J. Godfrey 11 at 7.45; A. H. Ahmed 16 at 13.68; J. Bulcock 16 at 16.68.

Worksop College *Nottinghamshire* P21 W14 L6 D1
Master i/c I. C. Parkin   **Coaches** A. Kettleborough/A. Parkin-Coates

Worksop enjoyed an excellent campaign. Major achievements included defeats of Repton, Trent, Nottinghamshire Under-17 and Leicestershire Under-17. Joseph Hayes and Tim Smith had good years with bat in hand, and Tom Keast represented Nottinghamshire Seconds, signing a development contract. Riecko Parker-Cole is one to watch.

Batting T. J. A. Smith 508 at 50.80; J. Hayes 524 at 43.66; R. M. Evans 267 at 26.70; L. A. Patterson-White 256 at 25.60; B. G. Holmes 327 at 25.15; T. G. Keast 270 at 24.54; D. L. McLean 158 at 17.55.
Bowling R. M. Evans 23 at 11.08; R. A. Parker-Cole 24 at 12.45; L. A. Patterson-White 24 at 12.62; S. G. Routledge 20 at 17.55; D. L. McLean 16 at 22.62.

Worth School *Sussex* P15 W9 L4 D2
Master i/c R. Chaudhuri

The captain, Toby Pullan, shone with the bat, and Harnoop Kalsi with the ball, making it a productive summer. The pre-season Dubai tour helped bring the team together.

Batting *T. M. C. Pullan 666 at 47.57; M. J. Rivers 568 at 43.69; L. R. Cummins 223 at 37.16; N. K. Amin 317 at 22.64.
Bowling H. S. Kalsi 21 at 20.95; L. R. Cummins 16 at 27.50; A. M. Ramani 11 at 40.00.

Wrekin College *Shropshire* P10 W6 L4 A2
Master i/c M. M. Winzor   **Coach** G. Davies

The first team did well in terms of results and player development; reaching the last 16 in the National Schools T20 was a first for the school. Dillon Pennington, the leading wicket-taker, made his debut for the Worcestershire Academy, aged 16.

Batting C. Dudley 476 at 52.88; R. T. J. Thomas 195 at 27.85; H. W. Chandler 214 at 26.75; T. O. Mackriel 164 at 23.42.
Bowling D. Y. Pennington 17 at 8.41.

Wycliffe College *Gloucestershire* P14 W3 L11 A2
Master i/c M. J. Kimber

A young squad struggled for consistency, but should have gained valuable experience. Highlights were 98 from captain Noah Cooper Llanes against MCC, and a first-team debut for Year 7 pupil Will Naish, the day after his 12th birthday.

Batting *N. S. Cooper Llanes 423 at 32.53; O. F. Carey 218 at 19.81; C. N. Trainor 250 at 19.23.
Bowling C. N. Trainor 13 at 24.15.

CRICKET IN IRELAND IN 2015

Life after Simmons

IAN CALLENDER

A planned year of consolidation proved to be one of change for Ireland, with a new coach at the helm, and a returning hero to ease the pain of Trent Johnston's retirement at the end of 2013. Johnston's absence was still being felt in 2015, when results fluctuated as much as off-field events. In February, Ireland chased down 305 to beat West Indies in the World Cup; five months later they suffered home Twenty20 defeats by Papua New Guinea and Hong Kong. Following their final World Cup match in March it was announced that Phil Simmons, Ireland's inspiration for eight years, would become head coach of his native West Indies. The team had flourished under his watch, qualifying for every major ICC tournament, and beating Test nations along the way. It was some act to follow for John Bracewell, the former New Zealand off-spinner, who in April was named as Ireland's fifth professional coach since 1995, with the stated goal of achieving Test status.

Bracewell had to contend with the retirements of the long-serving Alex Cusack and John Mooney. But better news arrived just before Christmas, when Boyd Rankin announced he had given up hope of playing for England again and was returning to lead the bowling attack. Ireland's prospects at the 2016 World Twenty20 were given a further boost when Tim Murtagh, the Middlesex seamer, reversed his decision to retire from the format.

The qualifying tournament, which Ireland co-hosted with Scotland in July, was the low point of 2015. Prior to the competition, Scotland won two Twenty20 games by six wickets, both at the new international venue of Bready in Northern Ireland. The defeats by Papua New Guinea and Hong Kong were Ireland's first against either nation in a competitive match and, though they managed to top their group and qualify for the World Twenty20, a semi-final loss to the Netherlands condemned them to third place, their lowest in an Associate tournament since 2010. It underlined how far Ireland had fallen in Twenty20 cricket. The batsmen, most of whom were returning from county duty, failed to adapt to their own, slow wickets; only captain William Porterfield and Paul Stirling scored fifties. To emphasise what Ireland will be missing, Mooney was the tournament's joint-leading wicket-taker with 14, and Cusack took ten.

The year had begun with victory in an ODI tri-series against Afghanistan and Scotland in the UAE. A month later, Ireland's victory over West Indies at Nelson meant they became the only team in the competition's history to chase down 300 or more on three occasions. But they were nearly beaten by the UAE in their next match, No. 10 George Dockrell hitting the winning runs with four balls to spare. The World Cup encapsulated Ireland's yo-yo year. Against South Africa they conceded more runs than ever before in a one-day international (411 for four), before making their highest ODI total (331 for eight), against Zimbabwe, who came within six runs of snatching victory.

India had it all their own way at Hamilton, and Ireland had to win their final group game at Adelaide to reach the quarter-finals. Despite a century from Porterfield, Pakistan coasted home. Nevertheless, two wins against Test opposition left a favourable impression. Ireland had an impact off the field as well, with senior players publicly criticising the ICC's decision to reduce the 2019 World Cup from 14 teams to ten.

Ireland did not escape the rain in 2015 – even a game at Dubai was washed out. Back home, a crowd in excess of 8,000 braved miserable weather for the biennial one-day international against England at Malahide, Porterfield's 200th match for his country overall. Only 18 overs were possible, and there was more rain in Belfast in August for the third visit in five years by Australia. Ed Joyce and Niall O'Brien had Ireland on target, but Glenn Maxwell removed both in successive overs as the world champions won by 23 runs.

In October, Ireland lost an ODI series in Zimbabwe 2–1, but the priority of the African trip was the subsequent Intercontinental Cup game against Namibia. The two-year competition offers a direct route to the top for Associate nations: in 2018 the winner will play a four-match series against the bottom-ranked Test side to determine whether they acquire Test status. Ireland thumped Namibia, having also beaten the UAE by an innings at Malahide in June to get Bracewell's reign off to a winning start. Joyce made double-hundreds in both matches, following up his 231 in Dublin – the highest by an Ireland player – with 205 at Windhoek, where Porterfield also made a career-best 186. Their stand of 326 was the country's second-highest for any wicket.

Ireland lost half their 24 completed matches across all three formats in 2015, and the fixture list is getting harder – as befits a team now officially recognised in the ODI rankings. In 2016 there will be a pair of two-match one-day series against Pakistan and Sri Lanka at Malahide, as well as ODIs against South Africa and Australia at Benoni in September.

Ireland Women enjoyed a successful year, despite three Twenty20 home defeats by Australia. In December, Isobel Joyce's side secured their place at the 2016 World Twenty20 after winning the qualifying event in Thailand, where they beat Bangladesh in the final.

The Under-19s made it through to their 50-over World Cup in Bangladesh – but only after they were invited to replace Australia, who withdrew on safety grounds. Ireland had initially missed out after losing to Nepal in the final of the qualifying event. They also finished runners-up in the European Under-19 Championship, won by Scotland.

At interprovincial level, the strong Leinster Lightning squad, captained for the last time by Mooney, finally completed a clean sweep of all three formats.

Winners of Irish Leagues and Cups
Irish Senior Cup Waringstown. **Leinster League and Senior Cup** Clontarf. **Munster League and Senior Cup** Cork County. **Northern League** Waringstown. **Northern Challenge Cup** CIYMS. **North West League** Coleraine. **North West Senior Cup** Donemana.

Ireland v Scotland

At Bready, June 18, 2015. **Scotland won by six wickets. ‡Ireland 146-5** (20 overs) (D. A. Rankin 34, K. J. O'Brien 30); **Scotland 150-4** (16.1 overs) (M. H. Cross 60; T. E. Kane 3-27). *T20I debuts: J. Anderson, T. E. Kane, G. J. McCarter, S. W. Poynter, D. A. Rankin, C. A. Young (Ireland); A. C. Evans, H. G. Munsey, M. R. J. Watt (Scotland). This series was designed to help the two host nations warm up for the Twenty20 Qualifier, although there was so much rain that warmth was a notable absentee. Boyd Rankin's brother David, one of five Ireland debutants in the absence of their England-based players, held the early batting together, and stand-in captain Kevin O'Brien offered some late welly. But Matthew Cross got Scotland going with 60 from 34 deliveries, and they won with 23 balls remaining.*

At Bready, June 19, 2015. **Ireland v ‡Scotland. Abandoned.** *T20I debuts: A. Balbirnie (Ireland); C. D. de Lange, G. T. Main (Scotland). Persistent rain eventually forced an abandonment; an additional match was arranged for the following day.*

At Bready, June 20, 2015. **Scotland won by six wickets. Ireland 166-6** (20 overs) (A. Balbirnie 31, A. D. Poynter 36, K. J. O'Brien 36); **‡Scotland 167-4** (18.1 overs) (K. J. Coetzer 34, M. H. Cross 48, P. L. Mommsen 47*; G. H. Dockrell 3-21). *Scotland clinched the series, overhauling another modest total with something to spare. After Harry Munsey was out in the first over of the chase, Kyle Coetzer put on 73 with Cross in 7.4 overs; Preston Mommsen finished things off with 47* from 29 balls.*

At Bready, June 21, 2015. **Scotland v ‡Ireland. Abandoned.** *MoS: M. H. Cross. Yet more rain thwarted attempts to start a five-over thrash at 5pm.*

IRELAND v AUSTRALIA

One-Day International

Ian Callender

At Belfast, August 27, 2015. Australia won by 23 runs (D/L). Toss: Australia. One-day international debut: J. A. Burns.

The class of Starc and the pace of Cummins proved the difference as Australia, playing their first one-day international since winning the World Cup five months earlier, beat Ireland in another rain-affected encounter. On their previous visit to Belfast, in June 2012, less than 11 overs had been possible; now, 64 were bowled between the showers. Even so, Ireland were on course for their adjusted target of 181 in 24 overs, and a first win over Australia, while Joyce and Niall O'Brien – whose injured brother Kevin was missing his first ODI for seven years – were putting on 86 for the third wicket at better than a run a ball. They departed in successive overs to Maxwell, but Ireland stayed in touch, and needed 46 from five overs with five wickets left. However, Wilson and Mooney – run out in a mix-up with Thompson – fell in the same Cummins over, and Starc soon ended Thompson's 16-ball cameo; Coulter-Nile mopped up. Smith, now full-time one-day captain, had surprisingly chosen to bat after the start was delayed to 12.30. But Burns, in his first ODI, and Warner justified his decision: they put on 139 inside 22 overs – Australia's highest partnership for any wicket against Ireland – before Young broke through, four overs after he had Burns caught behind on 61 off a no-ball. Murtagh then removed Warner for 84, and the middle order fell away before rain ended the innings.

Man of the Match: D. A. Warner.

Australia

J. A. Burns c O'Brien b Young	69	†M. S. Wade not out		2
D. A. Warner c Joyce b Murtagh	84			
*S. P. D. Smith c O'Brien b Thompson	21	B 1, l-b 3, w 1, n-b 1		6
G. J. Bailey b Murtagh	1			
G. J. Maxwell c O'Brien b McBrine	2	1/139 (1) 2/165 (2) (6 wkts, 40.2 overs)		222
S. R. Watson not out	26	3/167 (4) 4/170 (5)		
M. R. Marsh c Murtagh b Mooney	11	5/190 (3) 6/214 (7)	9 overs: 70-0	

N. M. Coulter-Nile, M. A. Starc and P. J. Cummins did not bat.

Young 6–0–49–1; Murtagh 10–1–45–2; Mooney 6–0–33–1; Thompson 6–1–37–1; McBrine 9–0–40–1; Stirling 3.2–0–14–0.

Ireland

*W. T. S. Porterfield b Starc	4	T. J. Murtagh not out		2
P. R. Stirling c Wade b Coulter-Nile	0	C. A. Young b Coulter-Nile		0
E. C. Joyce b Maxwell	44			
†N. J. O'Brien c Burns b Maxwell	45	B 6, l-b 1, w 5, n-b 1, p 5		18
A. Balbirnie c Coulter-Nile b Cummins	12			
G. C. Wilson c Wade b Cummins	1	1/5 (1) 2/7 (2) 3/93 (3) (23.4 overs)		157
S. R. Thompson c Wade b Starc	24	4/106 (4) 5/115 (5) 6/137 (6)		
J. F. Mooney run out	0	7/137 (8) 8/155 (7) 9/157 (9)		
A. R. McBrine c Cummins b Coulter-Nile	7	10/157 (11)	5 overs: 24-2	

Starc 5–0–34–2; Coulter-Nile 4.4–0–13–3; Cummins 5–0–19–2; Marsh 3–0–26–0; Maxwell 4–0–41–2; Watson 2–0–12–0.

Umpires: M. Hawthorne and J. S. Wilson.   Third umpire: S. Ravi.
Referee: J. J. Crowe.

CRICKET IN SCOTLAND IN 2015

Twitter storms and squally weather

WILLIAM DICK

If 2015 will be remembered for Scotland's latest failure to record a maiden World Cup victory, it was still a period of measured progress for the national side. That tiresome Caledonian talent for heroic sporting failure reared its head when Preston Mommsen's side appeared to be closing in on what would have been Scotland's greatest success on the global stage. The Scots, having scored 210, had Afghanistan on a plate in Dunedin at 97 for seven, only for Samiullah Shenwari to play the innings of his life and clinch an improbable one-wicket win.

Overall, Scotland performed with some distinction at the World Cup, displaying the attacking brand of cricket which is becoming their trademark under head coach Grant Bradburn, the former New Zealand international. Notable performances included Kyle Coetzer's 156 against Bangladesh, the highest score by an Associate batsman at any World Cup. Seamer Josh Davey was among the leading wicket-takers in the group stage, while Matthew Cross was one of the tournament's stand-out keepers.

The low point came off the field, when off-spinner Majid Haq responded to his omission from the penultimate fixture, against Sri Lanka in Hobart, by tweeting: "Always tougher when your [sic] in the minority!! #colour #race". He was immediately ordered home and suspended, but was later reinstated without explanation by Cricket Scotland, whose handling of the episode was questionable. Despite the reprieve, Haq's distinguished international career looked in jeopardy. His subtly flighted off-breaks have earned him 258 wickets in 210 games – both Scottish records – and he has occupied all 11 positions in the batting line-up, once scoring a first-class hundred against the Netherlands.

Equally in doubt was whether Scotland would play in another 50-over World Cup, given the reduction in the number of participating nations in 2019. Nevertheless, the door has not been completely shut, and the Scots made a reasonable start to the World Cricket League Championship, the first stage in a potentially circuitous route to the slimmed-down event. Two victories over Nepal in Ayr in July, together with a pair of washouts in Amstelveen, meant that, by the end of 2015, Scotland were level on points at the top of the table with Hong Kong, Kenya and the Netherlands.

It was not the first example of going Dutch last summer: Scotland and the Netherlands clinched their place at the 2016 ICC World Twenty20 as joint-winners of the Qualifier, when more inclement weather – this time at Malahide, near Dublin – saw the final abandoned without a ball bowled. Scotland had qualified the hard way, recovering from early defeats by the Netherlands and Afghanistan to win their group on net run-rate.

The opening fixture of a new Intercontinental Cup campaign was also weather-affected, with no play possible on the first day of their match against Afghanistan. Indeed, only 134 overs were bowled over the scheduled four days in Stirling, still enough for Scotland to claim a first-innings lead and 13 points in drawn game. However, this was followed by a first Intercontinental Cup defeat by the Dutch and, after the first two rounds, the Scots found themselves trailing leaders Ireland by 27 points. It was a disappointing end to another season in which the lack of regular high-profile fixtures on British soil was keenly felt. Media coverage, certainly in the written press, was as sparse as it has been for a quarter of a century.

Following the resignation of Roddy Smith and the interim leadership of Willie Donald, a new chief executive, Malcolm Cannon, took office. He should make it a priority to open negotiations with his ECB counterparts, with a view to restoring Scotland to one of the limited-overs county competitions. Cannon and a burgeoning administrative and coaching staff continue to be based in Edinburgh, following the scrapping of plans to build new headquarters in Stirling for financial reasons.

The North Sea Pro Series, with which Scottish and Dutch officials attempt to fill the county void, continued to be a damp squib. It was poorly promoted, and featured four teams who appear to lack any meaningful identity, even if they occasionally played some inspired white-ball cricket. The Highlanders – who, the uninitiated may be surprised to learn, feature players based in Edinburgh and the east – prevailed against their Scottish rivals, the Reivers, whose name offers little clue to the fact that Glasgow and the west provide the bulk of their squad. Sterner opposition came from the South Holland Seafarers, who finished second in the Pro50 tournament. In the T20 competition, the Highlanders also finished as champions.

The country's Under-19s won a thrilling last-day decider against Ireland in Jersey to clinch their place at this year's World Cup. Continuing improvement in the women's game was reflected in a semi-final place at the ICC Women's World Twenty20 Qualifier in Thailand, but defeat by Ireland means they didn't make it to the main event in India.

Domestically, Eastern Premier champions Grange maintained the east's dominance of the National Grand Final by beating Western Premier champions Clydesdale. Arbroath lifted the Scottish Cup for the first time, and there were also new winners of the Murgitroyd Twenty20 Cup in Forfarshire.

Winners of Scottish Leagues and Cups
Eastern Premier Division Grange. **Western Premier Division** Clydesdale. **National Champions** Grange. **Scottish Cup** Arbroath. **Murgitroyd Twenty20 Cup** Forfarshire. **Women's National League** Stirling County. **Women's Scottish Cup** George Watson's College.

CRICKET IN THE NETHERLANDS IN 2015

Roll on, Roelof

David Hardy

After the disappointment of losing one-day international status in 2014, the Netherlands began to put things right. Their first opportunity came in January, at the 50-over World Cricket League Division Two. The prize for the top two teams was promotion to the upper tiers of four-day and 50-over Associate cricket: the Intercontinental Cup and the WCL Championship. Despite losing two of their first three matches – including a 188-run defeat by hosts Namibia – big wins against Kenya and Uganda squeezed the Netherlands into second place. In the final, an eight-wicket win over Namibia was sweet revenge.

The Netherlands were back among the Associate elite, although results in the two premier competitions were mixed. Papua New Guinea visited in June, and were beaten comfortably in two 50-over matches, only to produce a shock victory in the four-day game. Dutch pride was restored three months later at The Hague, where the Netherlands beat Scotland – their first four-day win for seven years – but both 50-over games were rained off.

The weather had already prevented the Netherlands and Scotland from contesting the final of the World Twenty20 Qualifier, hosted by Ireland and Scotland in July. Four wins out of six group matches, and a tense victory in the play-off against Namibia, sealed qualification for India in 2016. Ireland were then beaten in the semi-final, before the washout at Malahide.

For much of the tournament the Netherlands had to do without Ahsan Malik Jamil, their leading seamer, who had been reported for a suspect action after the group-stage win over Scotland. He was cleared to return to international cricket at the start of 2016, after remedial work. His loss made the addition of South African international Roelof van der Merwe, whose Dutch ancestry allowed him to switch allegiances just in time for the World Twenty20 Qualifier, all the more welcome. He later played a crucial all-round role during the four-day defeat of Scotland, and helped ACC win the Twenty20 Cup, the Amstelveen club's first major trophy since 1954.

Elsewhere, young Dutch-born seamers Paul van Meekeren and Vivian Kingma made good progress, but there was no sign of a return for all-rounder Tim Gruijters, who had fallen out with the board after they replaced him with Tom Cooper for the 2014 World Twenty20, saying he was injured (Gruijters claimed he was fit). Cooper, busy with Somerset in 2015, was also missing.

Dosti United of Amsterdam won their first *Topklasse* (50-over) title with the help of South Africans Colin Ackermann, the captain, and Dwaine Pretorius, who hit ten sixes in an unbeaten 94 and took eight wickets in the two final play-off victories against Quick of The Hague. Quick's Wesley Barresi became the first batsman since 1996 to score 1,000 runs. The Netherlands women lost all five matches at the World Twenty20 Qualifiers in December.

The Netherlands v Nepal

At Amstelveen, June 30, 2015. **Netherlands won by 18 runs.** ‡**Netherlands 134-5** (20 overs) (S. J. Myburgh 67*); **Nepal 116-7** (20 overs) (P. Khadka 45*; M. A. A. Jamil 3-23). *T20I debuts*: P. S. Airee, K. C. Karan, A. Karn (Nepal). *This series formed part of the teams' preparations for the World Twenty20 Qualifier in Ireland and Scotland. The Netherlands were 32-3 after four overs, but Stephan Myburgh batted through the innings, scoring exactly half the runs and facing exactly half the balls. The target was too steep for Nepal, despite Paras Khadka's 45* from 42.*

At Amstelveen, July 1, 2015. **Netherlands won by 103 runs. Netherlands 172-4** (20 overs) (M. R. Swart 76*, B. N. Cooper 66); ‡**Nepal 69** (17.4 overs) (M. J. G. Rippon 3-11). *T20I debuts*: M. P. O'Dowd, M. B. van Schelven, T. P. Visée (Netherlands). *A second-wicket stand of 131 in 14 overs between Michael Swart and Ben Cooper set up another big chase – and Nepal fell way short.*

At Rotterdam, July 2, 2015. **Netherlands won by 18 runs.** ‡**Netherlands 149-6** (20 overs) (S. J. Myburgh 71*); **Nepal 131-9** (20 overs) (P. Khadka 36; M. A. A. Jamil 4-21). *T20I debut*: R. I. Ahmed (Netherlands). *Myburgh again batted through, for 71* from 56 balls, but no one else reached 20. Nepal built solidly, but the loss of Khadka – run out for 36 in the 19th over – spelt the end of their hopes. Three more wickets went down in the final over.*

At Rotterdam, July 3, 2015. **Nepal won by three wickets.** ‡**Netherlands 139-7** (20 overs) (R. E. van der Merwe 40*; S. Pun 3-26); **Nepal 141-7** (19.4 overs) (P. Khadka 54; M. A. A. Jamil 3-25). *T20I debut*: A. K. Mandal (Nepal). *MoS*: M. A. A. Jamil and P. Khadka. *Nepal pulled off a consolation victory in the last match, Khadka again the hero with 54 from 41 balls; this time, his dismissal in the 19th over was not fatal. The Netherlands won the series 3–1, with seamer Ahsan Malik Jamil taking 11-77 in the four matches.*

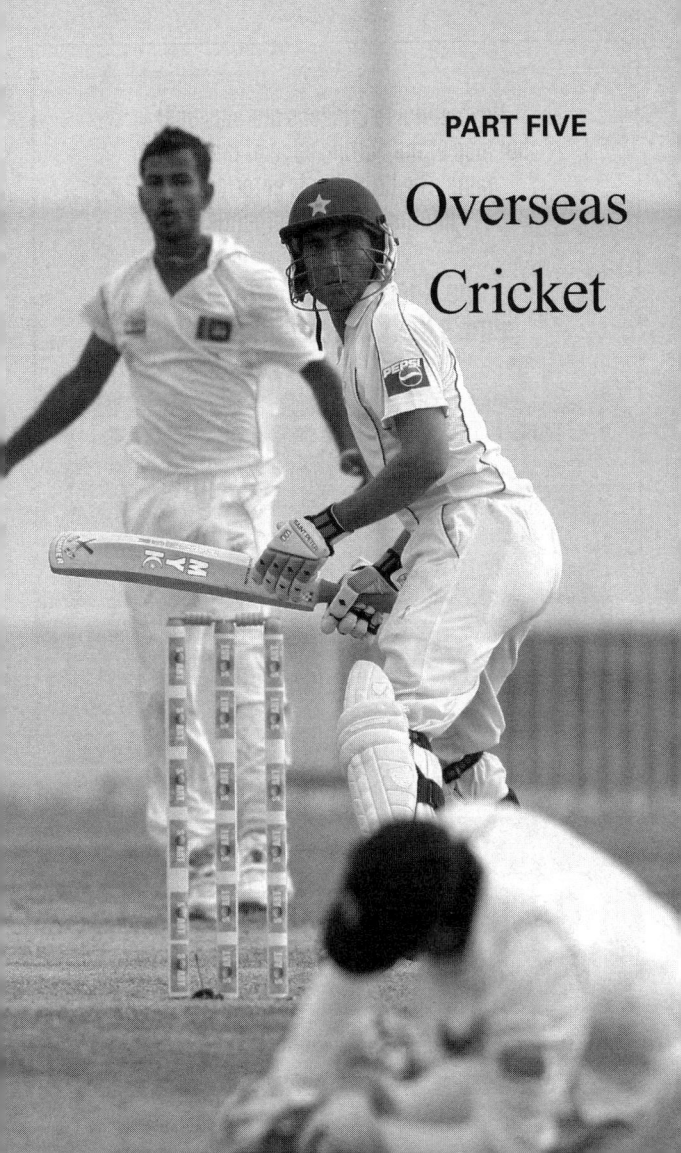

WORLD CRICKET IN 2015

Pretty in pink

SIMON WILDE

The first day/night Test, between Australia and New Zealand at Adelaide in November, was a significant success. Played on a grassy pitch designed to minimise abrasion on the pink ball, it lasted only three days, but resulted in a vibrant contest attended by 123,000 and generated record Australian TV viewing figures. It did what was hoped – putting bums on seats and engaging with a modern audience – and Cricket Australia expressed a desire to make it an annual occasion, including during the 2017-18 Ashes.

The idea of four-day Tests was also informally revisited as another means of halting the format's supposedly terminal decline in the face of Twenty20. Whether it was in as much trouble as some feared was debatable: 43 Tests were staged in 2015, more than in either of the previous two World Cup years of 2011 (39 Tests) and 2007 (31). England did their bit by playing 14, plus three more in South Africa in January 2016. An attendance of 50,000 on Boxing Day in Melbourne to watch a feeble West Indies side was cited as evidence of public disenchantment, but in the previous six years the MCG had witnessed the highest single-day Test attendances for the visits of England, India, Sri Lanka and Pakistan. Admittedly, without a healthy turnout from travelling England supporters, a grey Boxing Day in Durban would have been sparsely attended, and spectator numbers elsewhere were patchy.

World Cup years usually see brisk turnovers in captains and coaches, but 2015 was particularly busy. Michael Clarke, who stood down from one-day internationals after leading Australia to the trophy at Melbourne in March, retired from Tests after surrendering the Ashes in England five months later. New Zealand's Brendon McCullum announced his intention to go early in 2016, by which time Hashim Amla had resigned as South Africa's captain, in the middle of the Test series against England (and having just scored 201). Sri Lanka stalwart Kumar Sangakkara finally called it a day, as did Australia's 2013-14 Ashes hero Mitchell Johnson. Virender Sehwag quit the international game too, though he hadn't played for India since March 2013. Duncan Fletcher left after four years as India's head coach.

Against the odds, Alastair Cook, jettisoned from England's 50-over team late in 2014, not only survived as Test captain, but scored 1,364 runs and, in Abu Dhabi, played his country's longest-ever innings. But Peter Moores was sacked after only a year of his second term as head coach; his departure presaged a change in England's approach after another craven performance at the World Cup. With Andrew Strauss appointed director of cricket – and with Paul Farbrace as interim coach before the full-time appointment of the Australian Trevor Bayliss – they threw off the shackles in the short formats under Eoin Morgan, and also played more enterprising Test cricket, though of

Lakruwan Wanniarachchi, AFP/Getty Images

Old stagers: Younis Khan and Misbah-ul-Haq after guiding Pakistan to victory at Pallekele.

wildly fluctuating quality. **England** subsequently won six bilateral series across all formats, losing only the one-day games at home to Australia and the Tests in the United Arab Emirates to Pakistan, neither disgracefully. They ended 2015 with seven straight wins, including the Durban Test, and – for sheer entertainment (the World Cup excluded) – might even have pipped New Zealand as the team of the year.

By contrast, **West Indies** were mainly woeful, setting 21 defeats against only eight victories (including one against the UAE, and none in Tests), and failed to qualify for the 2017 Champions Trophy. Dwayne Bravo and Kieron Pollard were seen only in Twenty20s, in which West Indies topped the rankings in early 2016, and Chris Gayle disappeared after the World Cup, during which Jason Holder's dignified leadership made his replacement of Denesh Ramdin as Test captain inevitable. Shivnarine Chanderpaul, their most-capped Test player, was sidelined without ceremony. Ottis Gibson left as coach, only for his replacement, Phil Simmons, to be briefly suspended after criticising the continued absence of Bravo and Pollard. A Caricom report recommended that the West Indies board dissolve themselves, but they declined.

Home advantage was a frequent topic. **Australia** won the World Cup on their own soil, England's bowlers exploited classic seam-and-swing-friendly conditions to regain the Ashes, and India's Test spinners made fools of South Africa. New Zealand had a 19–3 record in all home internationals, and Pakistan, India, South Africa and Zimbabwe were all humbled in one-day series in **Bangladesh**, who looked a team on the up. Some Australians supported the idea of awarding the toss to the visiting side. No wonder: they lost seven out of 15 away (including six defeats in England), but went unbeaten in 17 completed home internationals. India made an unexpectedly strong defence of their World Cup title, at least until they met Australia in the Sydney semi. And Pakistan, still unable to play regularly at home, won five and lost one of eight Tests, their highlight a chase of 377 to beat Sri Lanka at Pallekele. Overall, away teams notched 12 Test wins and 20 defeats. Before they crashed spectacularly in India, South Africa had been unbeaten in 15 Test series on the road since 2006.

Nor were **South Africa** far from winning the World Cup. Weather hurt their chances in the narrow semi-final defeat by New Zealand, as did the decision – in accordance with Cricket South Africa guidelines – to play (the non-white) Vernon Philander ahead of (the white) Kyle Abbott. An aggressive transformation drive followed, despite disquiet in the dressing-room, which was blamed by some for South Africa not winning any of their subsequent Tests. But it did not prevent them securing a first one-day series win in India, and the policy received an overdue fillip in January 2016, when Temba Bavuma became his country's first black African to score a Test hundred, against England at Cape Town.

New Zealand, buoyed by a magical run to the World Cup final, were – like England – rarely dull. Across all formats, they won most games (27) and possessed the most complete batsman in Kane Williamson, who scored most runs (2,692, with eight hundreds); Ross Taylor made the highest Test score of the year (290 at Perth), and Martin Guptill the highest in ODIs (237 not out in the World Cup quarter-final against West Indies). They drew neutral support, as did **Pakistan**, who – until Mohammad Amir's imminent return from a five-year ban split the camp – played with unity and verve, though their one-day results were erratic. Leg-spinner Yasir Shah, before his three-month suspension for a failed drugs test, contributed at least seven wickets to each of Pakistan's five Test victories.

India managed a first Test series success under Virat Kohli's captaincy, coming from behind to win 2–1 in Sri Lanka, and owed most to Ravichandran Ashwin, the Player of the Series both there and at home to South Africa. Ashwin finished the year as the leading Test wicket-taker with 62, and was only one behind Australian left-arm seamer Mitchell Starc (88) in all internationals.

> **"**They disintegrated as if in homage to their previous tour of the UAE, in 2011-12, when their batsmen could scarcely leave their hotel rooms without wondering whether the corridors would take spin."
> Pakistan v England in 2015-16, Third Test, page 391

TEST MATCHES IN 2015

	Tests	Won	Lost	Drawn	% won	% lost	% drawn
Pakistan	8	5	1	2	**62.50**	12.50	25.00
Australia	13	8	3	2	**61.53**	23.07	15.38
India	9	5	1	3	**55.55**	11.11	33.33
New Zealand	8	4	3	1	**50.00**	37.50	12.50
England	14	6	6	2	**42.85**	42.85	14.28
Sri Lanka	11	4	7	0	**36.36**	63.63	00.00
South Africa	8	1	4	3	**12.50**	50.00	37.50
West Indies	10	1	8	1	**10.00**	80.00	10.00
Bangladesh	5	0	1	4	**0.00**	20.00	80.00
Totals	43	34	34	9	**79.06**	79.06	20.93

Zimbabwe played no Tests in 2015.

ONE-DAY INTERNATIONALS IN 2015

(Full Member matches only)

	ODIs	Won	Lost	NR	% won	% lost
Australia	16	12	3	1	**80.00**	20.00
Bangladesh	16	11	5	0	**68.75**	31.25
New Zealand	30	19	10	1	**65.51**	34.48
South Africa	22	13	9	0	**59.09**	40.90
India	21	11	9	1	**55.00**	45.00
Sri Lanka	23	10	12	1	**45.45**	54.54
England	23	10	13	0	**43.47**	56.52
Pakistan	25	10	14	1	**41.66**	58.33
West Indies	13	3	10	0	**23.07**	76.92
Zimbabwe	19	2	16	1	**11.11**	88.88
Totals	104	101	101	3		

The following teams also played official one-day internationals in 2015, some against Full Members (not included in the table above): Hong Kong (P2 W2); Afghanistan (P17 W8 L9); Ireland (P15 W6 L7 NR2); Scotland (P10 W1 L8 NR 1); United Arab Emirates (P8 L8). The % won and lost excludes no-results.

TWENTY20 INTERNATIONALS IN 2015

(Full Member matches only)

	T20Is	Won	Lost	% won	% lost
England	5	5	0	**100.00**	0.00
South Africa	9	6	3	**66.66**	33.33
Pakistan	10	6	4	**60.00**	40.00
West Indies	5	3	2	**60.00**	40.00
New Zealand	4	2	2	**50.00**	50.00
Bangladesh	5	2	3	**40.00**	60.00
India	4	1	3	**25.00**	75.00
Sri Lanka	4	1	3	**25.00**	75.00
Zimbabwe	9	2	7	**22.22**	77.77
Australia	1	0	1	**0.00**	100.00
Totals	28	28	28		

The following teams also played official Twenty20 internationals in 2015, some against Full Members (not included in the table above): Afghanistan (P11 W9 L2); Netherlands (P8 W6 L2); Scotland (P8 W4 L2 NR2); Papua New Guinea (P3 W2 L1); Hong Kong (P8 W5 L3); Oman (P7 W2 L5); United Arab Emirates (P4 W1 L3); Ireland (P8 W1 L5 NR2); Nepal (P7 W1 L6).

MRF TYRES ICC TEAM RANKINGS

TEST CHAMPIONSHIP (As at January 26, 2016)

		Matches	Points	Rating
1	India	32	3,535	110
2	Australia	40	4,376	109
3	South Africa	34	3,703	109
4	Pakistan	28	2,977	106
5	England	45	4,610	102
6	New Zealand	36	3,578	99
7	Sri Lanka	35	3,123	89
8	West Indies	33	2,504	76
9	Bangladesh	22	1,026	47
10	Zimbabwe	10	53	5

ONE-DAY CHAMPIONSHIP (As at January 6, 2016)

		Matches	Points	Rating
1	Australia	44	5,569	127
2	India	56	6,380	114
3	South Africa	57	6,362	112
4	New Zealand	52	5,767	111
5	Sri Lanka	67	6,956	104
6	England	56	5,639	101
7	Bangladesh	37	3,571	97
8	Pakistan	57	4,983	87
9	West Indies	38	3,256	86
10	Afghanistan	25	1,185	47
11	Ireland	15	683	46
12	Zimbabwe	55	2,466	45

TWENTY20 CHAMPIONSHIP (As at January 10, 2016)

		Matches	Points	Rating
1	West Indies	19	2,249	118
2	Australia	17	2,006	118
2	Sri Lanka	19	2,242	118
4	England	20	2,330	117
5	South Africa	25	2,879	115
6	Pakistan	27	3,085	114
7	New Zealand	21	2,393	114
8	India	14	1,537	110
9	Afghanistan	19	1,513	80
10	Bangladesh	12	831	69
11	Scotland	10	661	66
12	Hong Kong	11	675	61
13	Netherlands	14	859	61
14	Zimbabwe	18	907	50
15	Ireland	10	422	42

The following teams have ratings but have not yet played sufficient matches to achieve a ranking.

	Matches	Points	Rating
Papua New Guinea	3	210	70
Oman	7	190	27
United Arab Emirates	6	90	15

The ratings are based on all Test series, and one-day and Twenty20 internationals completed since August 1, 2012.

MRF TYRES ICC PLAYER RANKINGS

Introduced in 1987, the rankings have been backed by various sponsors, but were taken over by the International Cricket Council in January 2005. They rank cricketers on a scale up to 1,000 on their performances in Tests. The rankings take into account playing conditions, the quality of the opposition and the result of the matches. In August 1998, a similar set of rankings for one-day internationals was launched, and Twenty20 rankings were added in October 2011.

The leading players in the Test rankings on January 26, 2016, were:

Rank	Batsmen	Points	Rank	Bowlers	Points
1	S. P. D. Smith (*Australia*)	899	1	S. C. J. Broad (*England*)	872
2	J. E. Root (*England*)	889	2	R. Ashwin (*India*)	871
	K. S. Williamson (*New Zealand*)	889	3	Yasir Shah (*Pakistan*)	846
4	H. M. Amla (*South Africa*)	860	4	D. W. Steyn (*South Africa*)	841
5	D. A. Warner (*Australia*)	854	5	J. M. Anderson (*England*)	805
6	Younis Khan (*Pakistan*).	826	6	R. A. Jadeja (*India*)	789
7	A. B. de Villiers (*South Africa*) .	818	7	T. A. Boult (*New Zealand*)	787
8	A. D. Mathews (*Sri Lanka*)	808	8	J. R. Hazlewood (*Australia*) . . .	741
9	Misbah-ul-Haq (*Pakistan*)	764	9	T. G. Southee (*New Zealand*) . .	731
10	A. C. Voges (*Australia*)	753	10	M. Morkel (*South Africa*)	724
	A. M. Rahane (*India*).	753			

The leading players in the one-day international rankings on January 6, 2016, were:

Rank	Batsmen	Points	Rank	Bowlers	Points
1	A. B. de Villiers (*South Africa*) .	900	1	M. A. Starc (*Australia*)	713
2	V. Kohli (*India*)	804	2	T. A. Boult (*New Zealand*)	706
3	H. M. Amla (*South Africa*)	776	3	Shakib Al Hasan (*Bangladesh*) .	699
4	K. S. Williamson (*New Zealand*)	770	4	Imran Tahir (*South Africa*)	688
5	T. M. Dilshan (*Sri Lanka*)	760	5	D. W. Steyn (*South Africa*)	682
6	M. S. Dhoni (*India*)	741	6	M. G. Johnson (*Australia*)	672
7	S. Dhawan (*India*)	730	7	M. Morkel (*South Africa*)	666
8	M. J. Guptill (*New Zealand*) . . .	722	8	M. J. Henry (*New Zealand*)	650
9	L. R. P. L. Taylor (*New Zealand*)	720	9	Saeed Ajmal (*Pakistan*).	642
10	G. J. Maxwell (*Australia*)	717	10	R. Ashwin (*India*)	640

The leading players in the Twenty20 international rankings on January 10, 2016, were:

Rank	Batsmen	Points	Rank	Bowlers	Points
1	A. J. Finch (*Australia*)	854	1	S. Badree (*West Indies*)	751
2	V. Kohli (*India*)	845	2	R. Ashwin (*India*)	681
3	A. D. Hales (*England*)	795	3	S. M. S. M. Senanayake (*SL*). . .	671
4	F. du Plessis (*South Africa*)	758	4	Shahid Afridi (*Pakistan*)	670
5	C. H. Gayle (*West Indies*)	703	5	M. A. Starc (*Australia*)	659
	M. J. Guptill (*New Zealand*) . . .	703	6	S. L. Malinga (*Sri Lanka*)	657
7	B. B. McCullum (*New Zealand*)	684	7	Imran Tahir (*South Africa*)	641
8	Mohammad Shahzad (*Afghan*). .	681	8	Dawlat Zadran (*Afghanistan*) . .	636
9	M. D. K. J. Perera (*Sri Lanka*). .	678	9	K. M. D. N. Kulasekara (*SL*) . . .	628
10	E. J. G. Morgan (*England*).	665	10	Shakib Al Hasan (*Bangladesh*) .	626

TEST AVERAGES IN CALENDAR YEAR 2015

BATTING (400 runs)

	T	I	NO	R	HS	100	50	Avge	SR	Ct/St
†U. T. Khawaja (A)	3	5	1	504	174	3	1	126.00	69.61	0
K. S. Williamson (NZ)	8	16	3	1,172	242*	5	4	90.15	59.94	7
A. C. Voges (A)	12	18	6	1,028	269*	4	3	85.66	59.01	9
S. P. D. Smith (A)	13	24	4	1,474	215	6	5	73.70	62.08	15
†C. J. L. Rogers (A)	6	11	1	631	173	1	3	63.10	59.36	2
Younis Khan (P)	8	14	1	789	171*	3	1	60.69	56.72	12
J. E. Root (E)	14	26	3	1,385	182*	3	10	60.21	63.70	24
Mohammad Hafeez (P)	7	13	1	710	224	2	2	59.16	61.79	9
Azhar Ali (P)	6	10	0	576	226	2	2	57.60	46.19	13
†D. A. Warner (A)	13	24	0	1,317	253	4	5	54.87	81.85	11
†A. N. Cook (E)	14	26	1	1,364	263	3	8	54.56	43.67	16
Asad Shafiq (P)	8	13	0	706	131	3	3	54.30	51.83	6
†S. Dhawan (I)	6	10	1	485	173	2	0	53.88	54.18	2
Sarfraz Ahmed (P)	8	13	4	464	96	0	3	51.55	80.83	23/10
J. A. Burns (A)	6	11	0	555	129	2	3	50.45	68.26	6
A. B. de Villiers (SA)	6	10	0	492	148	1	2	49.20	50.87	12/2
B-J. Watling (NZ)	8	14	3	536	142*	2	2	48.72	48.33	32/3
M. Vijay (I)	7	12	1	522	150	1	3	47.45	49.06	6
L. D. Chandimal (SL)	11	20	1	901	162*	2	5	47.42	55.82	24/4
Misbah-ul-Haq (P)	8	14	1	616	102	1	6	47.38	52.07	5
A. M. Rahane (I)	9	15	2	593	127	3	1	45.61	53.76	20
†D. Elgar (SA)	8	13	3	438	118*	1	1	43.80	42.60	13
V. Kohli (I)	9	15	0	640	147	2	2	42.66	54.05	6
L. R. P. L. Taylor (NZ)	8	16	1	636	290	1	1	42.40	72.43	9
A. D. Mathews (SL)	11	21	1	845	122	3	4	42.25	53.17	14
†S. E. Marsh (A)	6	11	1	421	182	1	2	42.10	55.90	4
†K. C. Sangakkara (SL)	5	10	0	405	203	1	1	40.50	56.64	5
†F. D. M. Karunaratne (SL)	11	21	0	769	186	2	3	36.61	47.94	8
†T. W. M. Latham (NZ)	8	16	1	537	109*	1	3	35.80	47.14	12
†D. M. Bravo (WI)	9	18	0	644	108	1	5	35.77	45.00	10
†G. S. Ballance (E)	7	14	1	465	122	1	3	35.76	43.66	7
J. Blackwood (WI)	10	20	2	616	112*	1	4	34.22	54.60	14
M. J. Guptill (NZ)	7	14	0	475	156	1	3	33.92	53.19	6
B. B. McCullum (NZ)	8	15	1	425	80	0	3	30.35	79.88	5
†B. A. Stokes (E)	14	25	0	719	101	1	5	28.76	67.76	11
J. O. Holder (WI)	10	19	3	454	103*	1	2	28.37	66.27	8
M. N. Samuels (WI)	9	18	0	484	103	1	2	26.88	43.06	3
I. R. Bell (E)	13	24	2	571	143	1	4	25.95	43.85	12
J. K. Silva (SL)	9	16	0	413	125	1	3	25.81	37.57	5
†M. M. Ali (E)	13	23	0	563	77	0	4	24.47	54.13	8
K. C. Brathwaite (WI)	10	20	0	485	116	1	1	24.25	47.83	3
J. C. Buttler (E)	12	21	3	430	73	0	3	23.88	53.28	38

BOWLING (10 wickets)

	Style	O	M	R	W	BB	5I	Avge	SR
R. A. Jadeja (I)	SLA	140.5	56	249	23	5-21	2	10.82	36.73
A. Mishra (I)	LBG	122	16	346	22	4-43	0	15.72	33.27
R. Ashwin (I)	OB	376.4	94	1,067	62	7-66	7	17.20	36.45
J. L. Pattinson (A)	RFM	62.3	7	216	11	5-27	1	19.63	34.09
S. T. Finn (E)	RFM	108.5	22	361	18	6-79	1	20.05	36.27
Shoaib Malik (P)	OB	77.5	14	228	11	4-33	0	20.72	42.45
Imran Tahir (SA)	LBG	95	13	299	14	5-38	1	21.35	40.71

	Style	O	M	R	W	BB	5I	Avge	SR
D. W. Steyn (SA)	RF	127.1	26	371	17	4-70	0	21.82	44.88
J. M. Anderson (E)	RFM	393.3	114	1,042	46	6-42	2	22.65	51.32
Yasir Shah (P)	LBG	395	65	1,127	49	7-76	3	23.00	48.36
P. M. Siddle (A)	RFM	117.4	39	301	13	4-35	0	23.15	54.30
J. R. Hazlewood (A)	RFM	403.3	100	1,191	51	6-70	2	23.35	47.47
S. C. J. Broad (E)	RFM	450.3	111	1,334	56	8-15	2	23.82	48.26
M. R. Marsh (A)	RFM	130.4	27	485	20	4-61	0	24.25	39.20
K. T. G. D. Prasad (SL)	RFM	303.1	49	1,023	41	4-34	0	24.95	44.36
M. A. Starc (A)	LF	343.1	76	1,153	46	6-111	2	25.06	44.76
M. Morkel (SA)	RFM	191.3	46	498	19	4-76	0	26.21	60.47
Imran Khan, sen. (P)	RFM	109	22	344	13	5-58	1	26.46	50.30
P. V. D. Chameera (SL)	RF	126.5	9	509	18	5-47	1	28.27	42.27
N. M. Lyon (A)	OB	447.5	91	1,379	48	4-66	0	28.72	55.97
S. R. Harmer (SA)	OB	191.2	34	588	20	4-61	0	29.40	57.40
J. E. Taylor (WI)	RFM	233.4	46	837	28	6-47	1	29.89	50.07
T. A. Boult (NZ)	LFM	340	57	1,133	36	5-60	2	31.47	56.66
I. Sharma (I)	RFM	159	42	441	14	5-54	1	31.50	68.14
A. N. P. R. Fernando (SL)	RFM	285.5	42	934	28	4-62	0	33.35	61.25
M. G. Johnson (A)	LF	265	50	1,013	30	3-21	0	33.76	53.00
D. Bishoo (WI)	LBG	160.3	25	511	15	6-80	1	34.06	64.20
M. A. Wood (E)	RFM	254.3	59	860	25	3-39	0	34.40	61.08
H. M. R. K. B. Herath (SL)	SLA	442	64	1,317	37	7-48	2	35.59	71.67
Wahab Riaz (P)	LF	231	39	725	20	4-66	0	36.25	69.30
T. G. Southee (NZ)	RFM	342.1	63	1,095	29	4-26	0	37.75	70.79
D. L. Piedt (SA)	OB	108	13	386	10	5-153	1	38.60	64.80
P. H. T. Kaushal (SL)	OB	241.2	22	898	23	5-42	2	39.04	62.95
J. O. Holder (WI)	RFM	258.5	58	711	18	3-15	0	39.50	86.27
M. M. Ali (E)	OB	403.2	57	1,558	39	4-69	0	39.94	62.05
D. A. J. Bracewell (NZ)	RFM	213.4	36	686	17	3-18	0	40.35	75.41
S. T. Gabriel (WI)	RFM	120	22	439	10	2-47	0	43.90	72.00
M. D. Craig (NZ)	OB	241	45	915	20	4-53	0	45.75	72.30
U. T. Yadav (I)	RF	135	37	505	11	3-9	0	45.90	73.63
Zulfiqar Babar (P)	SLA	334	77	852	18	3-53	0	47.33	111.33
B. A. Stokes (E)	RFM	315.1	65	1,147	24	6-36	1	47.79	78.79
Taijul Islam (B)	SLA	147.4	10	544	11	6-163	1	49.45	80.54
M. J. Henry (NZ)	RFM	128.1	21	498	10	4-93	0	49.80	76.90

MOST DISMISSALS BY A WICKETKEEPER

Dis		T			Dis		T		
38	(38ct)	12	J. C. Buttler (E)		28	(22ct, 6st)	10	D. Ramdin (WI)	
36	(35ct, 1st)	9	P. M. Nevill (A)		25	(21ct, 4st)	7	L. D. Chandimal (SL)	
35	(32ct, 3st)	7	B-J. Watling (NZ)		17	(16ct, 1st)	4	B. J. Haddin (A)	
33	(23ct, 10st)	8	Sarfraz Ahmed (P)		15	(10ct, 5st)	8	W. P. Saha (I)	

Chandimal made three further catches in four Tests when not keeping wicket, and Watling none in one Test.

MOST CATCHES IN THE FIELD

Ct	T			Ct	T		
24	14	J. E. Root (E)		14	10	J. Blackwood (WI)	
20	9	A. M. Rahane (I)		14	11	J. M. Anderson (E)	
16	14	A. N. Cook (E)		14	11	A. D. Mathews (SL)	
15	13	S. P. D. Smith (A)					

ONE-DAY INTERNATIONAL AVERAGES IN CALENDAR YEAR 2015

BATTING (600 runs, average 35.00)

	M	I	NO	R	HS	100	50	Avge	SR	4	6
†K. C. Sangakkara (SL)	14	13	3	862	124	5	2	86.20	102.86	88	13
A. B. de Villiers (SA)	20	18	3	1,193	162*	5	5	79.53	137.91	91	58
Shoaib Malik (P)	15	15	6	607	112	1	4	67.44	108.39	49	17
F. du Plessis (SA)	20	19	4	884	133*	2	8	58.93	82.92	73	11
L. R. P. L. Taylor (NZ)	27	25	7	1,046	119*	4	4	58.11	81.65	85	12
K. S. Williamson (NZ)	27	26	2	1,376	118	3	9	57.33	89.87	149	12
M. J. Guptill (NZ)	32	32	5	1,489	237*	4	8	55.14	96.56	162	42
†D. A. Warner (A)	15	14	2	652	178	2	2	54.33	110.50	74	12
S. P. D. Smith (A)	19	17	2	805	105	2	5	53.66	86.09	71	7
T. M. Dilshan (SL)	25	24	1	1,207	161*	4	6	52.47	90.75	134	8
†Soumya Sarkar (B)	15	15	2	672	127*	1	4	51.69	102.28	88	15
Mushfiqur Rahim (B)	18	16	1	767	107	2	4	51.13	101.58	73	11
R. G. Sharma (I)	17	17	1	815	150	3	3	50.93	95.43	75	23
H. M. Amla (SA)	23	23	2	1,062	159	4	3	50.57	94.90	119	14
†R. R. Rossouw (SA)	17	16	2	681	132	2	3	48.64	98.55	63	19
†Tamim Iqbal (B)	18	18	2	742	132	2	5	46.37	81.62	89	10
M. N. Samuels (WI)	15	15	2	601	133*	2	3	46.23	84.76	52	16
J. W. A. Taylor (E)	21	20	5	691	101	1	4	46.06	82.06	54	9
G. J. Maxwell (A)	19	15	1	644	102	1	4	46.00	135.86	73	20
M. S. Dhoni (I)	20	17	3	640	92*	0	4	45.71	86.83	50	11
Azhar Ali (P)	17	17	0	775	102	2	5	45.58	84.23	77	6
†D. A. Miller (SA)	24	21	5	729	138*	2	1	45.56	109.45	58	21
G. D. Elliott (NZ)	27	24	5	850	104*	1	4	44.73	103.40	72	19
†E. J. G. Morgan (E)	25	23	1	967	121	2	7	43.95	93.79	82	30
†H. D. R. L. Thirimanne (SL)	25	24	4	861	139*	1	6	43.05	76.80	69	7
J. C. Buttler (E)	21	18	2	642	129	2	2	42.80	118.88	61	17
J. E. Root (E)	20	18	1	723	121	3	4	42.52	91.98	68	6
Mohammad Hafeez (P)	20	20	1	782	103	2	5	41.15	84.17	77	19
A. M. Rahane (I)	21	20	2	722	87	0	6	40.11	79.60	67	8
†S. C. Williams (Z)	26	25	2	893	102	1	7	38.82	87.63	70	13
†C. R. Ervine (Z)	22	21	3	698	130*	2	3	38.77	79.86	64	14
†S. Dhawan (I)	20	20	0	745	137	2	4	37.25	85.43	91	9
V. Kohli (I)	20	20	3	623	138	2	1	36.64	80.59	44	8
E. Chigumbura (Z)	27	26	4	772	117	2	1	35.09	81.69	54	15

BOWLING (20 wickets)

	Style	O	M	R	W	BB	4I	Avge	SR	ER
Mustafizur Rahman (B)	LFM	75.2	4	321	26	6-43	5	12.34	17.38	4.26
M. A. Starc (A)	LF	144.4	6	667	41	6-28	4	16.26	21.17	4.61
J. H. Davey (Scot)	RM	65.3	5	385	21	6-28	2	18.33	18.71	5.87
T. A. Boult (NZ)	LFM	160.1	19	712	36	5-27	4	19.77	26.69	4.44
K. Rabada (SA)	RF	87.1	5	425	21	6-16	2	20.23	24.90	4.87
C. J. Anderson (NZ)	LFM	83.1	1	533	25	4-52	1	21.32	19.96	6.40
M. Morkel (SA)	RF	134.1	6	630	28	4-39	1	22.50	28.75	4.69
P. J. Cummins (A)	RF	91.1	4	503	21	4-49	2	23.95	26.04	5.51
R. Ashwin (I)	OB	120.4	9	516	21	4-25	1	24.57	34.47	4.27
Imran Tahir (SA)	LBG	198.5	11	932	37	5-45	3	25.18	32.24	4.68
U. T. Yadav (I)	RF	110.2	6	632	25	4-31	2	25.28	26.48	5.72
Dawlat Zadran (Afg)	RFM	110.4	7	565	21	4-22	1	26.90	31.61	5.10
D. W. Steyn (SA)	RF	164.1	10	819	30	3-27	0	27.30	32.83	4.98
Wahab Riaz (P)	LF	166.5	6	878	32	4-45	3	27.43	31.28	5.26
J. E. Taylor (WI)	RFM	91.5	2	580	21	3-15	0	27.61	26.23	6.31

	Style	O	M	R	W	BB	4I	Avge	SR	ER
Shakib Al Hasan (B)	SLA	144	3	664	24	5-47	2	27.66	36.00	4.61
S. T. Finn (E)	RFM	149	10	858	31	5-33	3	27.67	28.83	5.75
M. Sharma (I)	RFM	115.4	5	651	23	3-48	0	28.30	30.17	5.62
Mashrafe bin Mortaza (B)	RFM	132	3	692	21	3-20	0	32.95	37.71	5.24
T. G. Southee (NZ)	RFM	154	9	929	28	7-33	1	33.17	33.00	6.03
M. M. Ali (E)	OB	162.4	2	768	23	3-32	0	33.39	42.43	4.72
Mohammad Irfan (P)	LFM	167	12	826	24	4-30	1	34.41	41.75	4.94
M. J. McClenaghan (NZ)	LFM	148.4	6	900	26	4-36	1	34.61	34.30	6.05
S. L. Malinga (SL)	RF	121.2	4	706	20	3-35	0	35.30	36.40	5.81
C. R. Woakes (E)	RFM	137.1	5	778	21	4-33	3	37.04	39.19	5.67
T. Panyangara (Z)	RFM	224.2	14	1,237	23	3-41	0	53.78	58.52	5.51

MOST DISMISSALS BY A WICKETKEEPER

Dis		M		Dis		M	
42	(38ct, 4st)	32	L. Ronchi (NZ)	24	(22ct, 2st)	16	Mushfiqur Rahim (B)
31	(29ct, 2st)	21	J. C. Buttler (E)	22	(22ct)	14	D. Ramdin (WI)
30	(27ct, 3st)	20	M. S. Dhoni (I)	21	(20ct, 1st)	17	Q. de Kock (SA)
27	(21ct, 6st)	22	Sarfraz Ahmed (P)				

Mushfiqur Rahim made no catches in two one-day internationals when not keeping wicket.

MOST CATCHES IN THE FIELD

Ct	M			Ct	M		
21	32	M. J. Guptill (NZ)		14	19	G. J. Maxwell (A)	
20	22	C. R. Ervine (Z)		14	23	H. M. Amla (SA)	
15	20	J. E. Root (E)		14	24	D. A. Miller (SA)	
14	15	Nasir Hossain (B)		14	27	L. R. P. L. Taylor (NZ)	

TWENTY20 INTERNATIONAL AVERAGES
IN CALENDAR YEAR 2015

BATTING (150 runs, strike-rate 110.00)

	M	I	NO	R	HS	100	50	Avge	SR	4	6
†C. H. Gayle (WI)	2	2	0	167	90	0	2	83.50	**231.94**	14	15
M. H. Cross (Scot)	8	5	0	206	60	0	1	41.20	**177.58**	28	7
P. L. Mommsen (Scot)	8	4	2	169	68*	0	1	84.50	**167.32**	13	9
†Najibullah Zadran (Afg)	8	7	2	172	44	0	0	34.40	**160.74**	7	13
F. du Plessis (SA)	6	6	1	272	119	1	1	54.40	**157.22**	27	8
Mohammad Shahzad (Afg) . .	11	11	0	297	75	0	3	27.00	**156.31**	31	15
†R. R. Rossouw (SA)	7	7	3	180	51*	0	1	45.00	**150.00**	16	8
P. W. Borren (Neth)	8	7	2	187	57	0	1	37.40	**146.09**	17	5
Mukhtar Ahmed (P)	6	6	0	192	83	0	2	32.00	**143.28**	23	5
W. Barresi (Neth)	8	8	0	158	75	0	1	19.75	**138.59**	17	7
M. N. van Wyk (SA)	5	5	1	157	114*	1	0	39.25	**137.71**	14	9
E. Chigumbura (Z)	10	10	0	171	54	0	1	17.10	**136.80**	13	8
Mohammad Nabi (Afg)	8	7	2	165	33*	0	0	33.00	**135.24**	8	8
A. B. de Villiers (SA)	6	6	0	160	51	0	1	26.66	**130.08**	22	5
Umar Akmal (P)	9	9	1	162	46	0	0	20.25	**129.60**	9	7
†S. C. Williams (Z)	10	10	2	246	58*	0	2	30.75	**127.46**	26	3
†B. N. Cooper (Neth)	8	8	1	223	66	0	2	31.85	**127.42**	16	11
Shoaib Malik (P)	8	8	1	219	75	0	1	31.28	**124.43**	18	4
†M. S. Chapman (HK)	8	8	1	226	63*	0	1	32.28	**122.82**	22	5
Babar Hayat (HK)	8	8	3	195	65*	0	1	39.00	**120.37**	12	8
Nawroz Mangal (Afg)	6	6	1	166	65*	0	2	33.20	**120.28**	12	7

	M	I	NO	R	HS	100	50	Avge	SR	4	6
Usman Ghani (Afg)	5	5	0	162	69	0	2	32.40	**119.11**	20	4
Sikandar Raza (Z).	11	10	0	181	59	0	1	18.10	**114.55**	17	3
†S. J. Myburgh (Neth)	6	6	2	168	71*	0	2	42.00	**113.51**	13	4
H. Masakadza (Z)	7	7	0	169	43	0	0	24.14	**113.42**	16	6
Samiullah Shenwari (Afg)	9	8	2	211	44	0	0	35.16	**112.83**	17	6

BOWLING (7 wickets, 20 overs)

	Style	O	M	R	W	BB	4I	Avge	SR	ER
Aizaz Khan (HK)	RFM	28.3	1	176	11	3-22	0	16.00	15.54	**6.17**
B. Regmi (Nepal)	SLA	24.1	0	155	10	4-16	1	15.50	14.50	**6.41**
Bilal Khan (Oman)	LFM	22.1	0	144	10	4-20	1	14.40	13.30	**6.49**
Mudassar Bukhari (Neth)	RFM	23.5	0	155	11	4-28	1	14.09	13.00	**6.50**
R. E. van der Merwe (Neth) . .	SLA	20	0	130	9	2-10	0	14.44	13.33	**6.50**
A. G. Cremer (Z)	LBG	33	1	217	14	3-18	0	15.50	14.14	**6.57**
A. C. Evans (Scot)	RFM	20	1	134	9	5-24	1	14.88	13.33	**6.70**
Mirwais Ashraf (Afg)	RFM	28	0	193	8	2-21	0	24.12	21.00	**6.89**
M. A. A. Jamil (Neth)	RFM	24.4	1	171	16	4-21	1	10.68	9.25	**6.93**
D. Wiese (SA)	RFM	23.2	0	165	14	5-23	1	11.78	10.00	**7.07**
Shahid Afridi (P)	LBG	37	0	266	7	3-15	0	38.00	31.71	**7.18**
Mohammad Nabi (Afg)	OB	32	0	231	8	3-25	0	28.87	24.00	**7.21**
Haseeb Amjad (HK)	RFM	29.2	2	213	14	4-16	1	15.21	12.57	**7.26**
Dawlat Zadran (Afg)	RFM	31	2	226	13	3-17	0	17.38	14.30	**7.29**
S. Kami (Nepal)	RM	25	0	185	7	2-24	0	26.42	21.42	**7.40**
S. C. Williams (Z)	SLA	36	0	272	9	3-28	0	30.22	24.00	**7.55**
Anwar Ali (P).	RFM	26	0	197	7	2-27	0	28.14	22.28	**7.57**
K. Rabada (SA)	RF	23	0	175	8	3-30	0	21.87	17.25	**7.60**
A. M. Phangiso (SA)	SLA	23	0	176	9	3-30	0	19.55	15.33	**7.65**
Sohail Tanvir (P)	LFM	31	1	241	11	3-29	0	21.90	16.90	**7.77**
S. M. Sharif (Scot)	RFM	23.1	0	191	8	3-29	0	23.87	17.37	**8.24**
K. J. Abbott (SA)	RFM	31.2	0	263	7	3-20	0	37.57	26.85	**8.39**

MOST DISMISSALS BY A WICKETKEEPER

Dis		M		Dis		M	
12	(7ct, 5st)	11	Mohammad Shahzad (Afg)	6	(6ct)	4	L. Ronchi (NZ)
8	(8ct)	7	Sultan Ahmed (Oman)	6	(5ct, 1st)	5	Mushfiqur Rahim (B)
7	(7ct)	4	J. J. Atkinson (HK)	6	(6ct)	8	M. H. Cross (Scot)

MOST CATCHES IN THE FIELD

Ct	M		Ct	M	
9	8	P. W. Borren (Neth)	6	7	R. R. Rossouw (SA)
8	11	Shafiqullah Shinwari (Afg)	6	10	S. C. Williams (Z)
7	11	Asghar Stanikzai (Afg)	6	11	Sikandar Raza (Z)
6	7	M. A. A. Jamil (Neth)			

S. W. Billings (E) and A. B. de Villiers (SA) both made six dismissals in all, some in the field and some as wicketkeeper.

INDEX OF TEST MATCHES

Nine earlier 2014-15 Test series – Zimbabwe v South Africa, West Indies v Bangladesh, Pakistan v Australia, Bangladesh v Zimbabwe, India v West Indies, Pakistan v New Zealand, Australia v India, South Africa v West Indies, New Zealand v Sri Lanka – appeared in *Wisden 2015*.

THE WORLD CUP IN 2014-15

Review by Gideon Haigh

1 Australia   2 New Zealand   3= India and South Africa

"Greatness is contagious" was the punchy, if regrettable, slogan for this World Cup – regrettable, because its launch in November 2014 coincided with the Ebola epidemic in West Africa. But one of the promotional images was at least uncannily prescient, showing the back of Michael Clarke as he walked into an MCG flooded with artificial light. For, shortly after 7.30pm on March 29, Australia's captain did exactly that, with his team 63 for two chasing 184 to beat New Zealand. By the time he returned 84 minutes later, having played his 223rd and last one-day international innings, his sparkling 74 had ensured he would bid the format farewell by lifting the trophy.

Clarke's well-led, well-drilled and well-chosen team were deserving victors, featuring Man of the Tournament Mitchell Starc, who swung the white ball at high pace throughout, and – in the final – Man of the Match James Faulkner, who baffled batsmen with a range of speeds and lengths. With Mitchell Johnson they formed a three-pronged left-arm pace attack of the highest quality, together taking 47 wickets at under 16 and an economy-rate of under 4.5; at times, the left-arm angle seemed the only countermeasure to otherwise overwhelming batting.

A month earlier at Eden Park, Brendon McCullum's **New Zealand** had beaten the Australians by one wicket in the tournament's outstanding match. But, if anything, that result spurred **Australia** to greater heights. Although it was their first defeat in any format since November, Clarke called it the "kick up the backside" they needed. The impression during the final was of a team reaching their best, against a team whose best had already been seen. Of the $US10.23m prize pool, the Australians shared $3.98m, the New Zealanders $1.75m.

Cricket's 11th World Cup was three times as long as the first, 40 years earlier. It contained nearly twice as many teams, and was watched in the flesh by more than six times as many spectators, the final setting an official record for a day's cricket, of 93,013. Television audiences were claimed to be the largest in history, helped by the presence in the last eight of four teams from South Asia, the sport's most populous market.

These included **Bangladesh**, the ICC's most recent Full Member, and a first-time quarter-finalist. They excluded England, one of the ICC's founder nations, despite the ECB having gone through the rigmarole of separating Ashes and World Cup cycles in order to enhance performances at each. It led instead to the worst of both worlds, but – the 5–0 whitewash of 2013-14 fresh in the memory – spread across two southern summers rather than just one. The losing semi-finalists were India, unbeaten until then and nourishing fantasies of back-to-back titles, and South Africa, who at last won a World Cup knockout game, only for rain to interrupt their late batting surge against New Zealand.

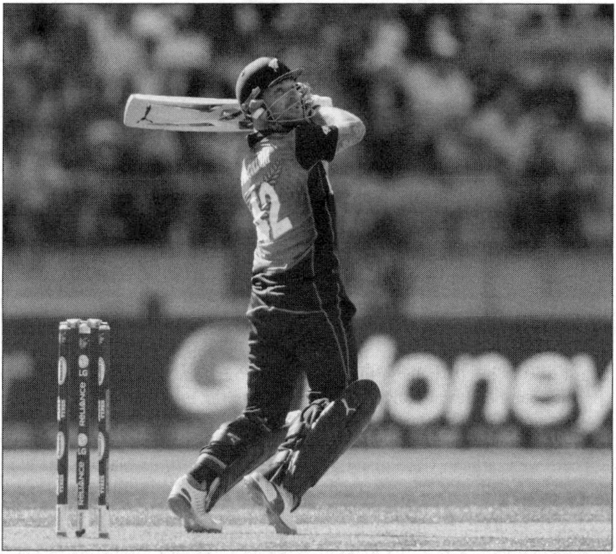

Shaun Botterill, Getty Images

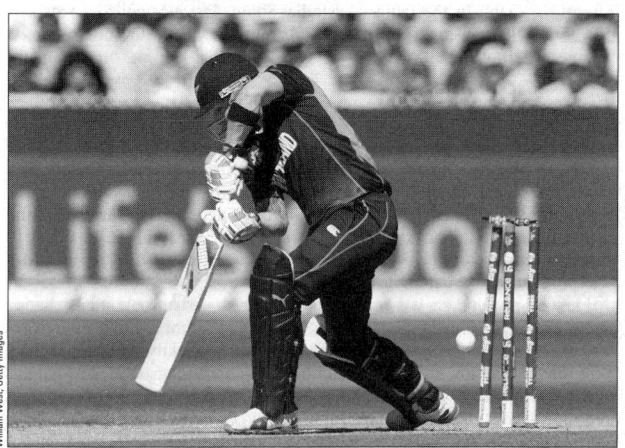

The hitter hit: Brendon McCullum had New Zealanders in raptures with his approach to the opening overs… until he ran into Mitchell Starc at Melbourne.

William West, Getty Images

These surges – South Africa had regularly scored at 12 an over for the last 15 – were the tournament's most noteworthy phenomenon. This was the second World Cup since the emergence of franchise Twenty20 – and specifically the IPL – as the game's fastest growing format, and its influence was obvious. So was the influence of the fielding restrictions applied in October 2012 to thin out boundary fielders, rendering them as ineffectual as widely spaced traffic cones; and of the modern bat, in its current stage of accelerated morphology.

There were 38 hundreds, nearly one every game, and 463 sixes, one every nine overs. In the fastest one-day international double-hundred, at Canberra's Manuka Oval, Chris Gayle struck 16 of them for West Indies against Zimbabwe. In making 237 *against* West Indies at Wellington's Westpac Stadium, Martin Guptill of New Zealand struck 11 – including the longest, measured at 110 metres. In the same match, Gayle hit eight sixes in a score of 61. West Indies were also on the receiving end when South Africa's captain A. B. de Villiers entered during the 30th over at the SCG, and raced to the fastest 150 – by 19 balls – finishing with 162 from 66. His West Indian opposite number Jason Holder was left nursing the most expensive ten-over analysis in World Cup history: one for 104. This time Gayle perished in the second over, whereupon the crowd began to disperse.

There were arguably too many games of this type. In 23 matches the side batting first compiled 300 or more; on 20 occasions it sufficed to secure victory, usually by a comfortable margin. The close result, traditionally the *sine qua non* of limited-overs cricket, towards which everything was contrived, became a rarity. In fact, the batting of World Cups past was made to seem archaic. In the 1987 final, Mike Gatting was pilloried for attempting a reverse sweep at a left-arm spinner; now Glenn Maxwell was even reverse-lapping left-arm seamers. In the fabled Australia–South Africa Super Six match of 1999, Steve Waugh slog-swept one, reverberating, six; now de Villiers seemed capable of doing it every other ball, over deep fine leg, and from a metre outside off stump.

To restrain the Twenty20-charged strokeplay by taking wickets, the best captains turned to Test-intensity bowling and field-settings. Angles mattered, and five of the 12 top wicket-takers came from the left: Starc and Johnson, plus New Zealand's Trent Boult and Daniel Vettori (the lone spinner), and Pakistan's Wahab Riaz. Wahab was responsible for the competition's most memorable spell, which would have removed a flinching Shane Watson in the quarter-final had Rahat Ali accepted a straightforward chance at fine leg. **Pakistan** had been the only team to defend fewer than 267, which they did twice, but lacked the batting to hurt the stronger teams.

Bouncers and yorkers were seen to advantage, not least from India's Umesh Yadav and Mohammed Shami, South Africa's Morne Morkel and New Zealand's Tim Southee. But miss your length even slightly and the penalties were mandatory: low full tosses, and bouncers achieving only chest height, vanished into the crowd. Nor was there much scope for spin, other than Vettori's native cunning, Imran Tahir's busy variations and Ravichandran Ashwin's beguiling loop. Slow-bowling ranks had been culled before the competition by the ICC's campaign against outré actions, which precluded the presence of Saeed Ajmal, Sunil Narine and Sohag Gazi, and restricted Sachithra Senanayake to a single, muted, appearance; Prosper Utseya had repackaged himself as a medium-paced cutter, but was not trusted with a game. Australia proved spin was a bonus rather than a necessity: they fielded the specialist slow left-armer Xavier Doherty only once, and otherwise subsisted on 45 overs from part-timers Maxwell, Clarke and Steven Smith.

MOST WICKETS FOR LEFT-ARM SEAMERS IN AN ODI

12	**New Zealand v Australia at Auckland**	**2014-15**
	T. A. Boult (5-27), C. J. Anderson (1-6); M. A. Starc (6-28)	
9	Australia v Sri Lanka at Sydney	2005-06
	N. W. Bracken (4-30); W. P. U. J. C. Vaas (4-56), P. D. R. L. Perera (1-72)	
9	India v Australia at Mumbai (Wankhede Stadium)	2007-08
	Zaheer Khan (1-22), R. P. Singh (2-59), I. K. Pathan (1-23); M. G. Johnson (3-46), N. W. Bracken (2-30)	
9	Australia v India at Adelaide	2007-08
	N. W. Bracken (2-21), M. G. Johnson (3-42); I. K. Pathan (4-41)	
9	India v Pakistan at Mohali	2010-11
	Zaheer Khan (2-58), A. Nehra (2-33); Wahab Riaz (5-46)	
9	**Pakistan v Zimbabwe at Brisbane**	**2014-15**
	Mohammad Irfan (4-30), Rahat Ali (1-37), Wahab Riaz (4-45)	
9	**Pakistan v South Africa at Auckland**	**2014-15**
	Mohammad Irfan (3-52), Rahat Ali (3-40), Wahab Riaz (3-45)	
9	**Australia v New Zealand at Melbourne**	**2014-15**
	M. A. Starc (2-20), M. G. Johnson (3-30), J. P. Faulkner (3-36); T. A. Boult (1-40)	

The cricket was not always of this character. There was batting along more orthodox lines from Sri Lanka's Kumar Sangakkara, who compiled an unprecedented four consecutive centuries with characteristic ease and grace; Bangladesh's Mahmudullah and Pakistan's Misbah-ul-Haq acted as stabilising cores to brittle teams. A glimpse of former ways could also be seen in the methods of the four Associate nations – Afghanistan, Ireland, Scotland and the UAE – who lacked the power for glory, and preferred more traditional virtues, even if they also inflicted some blows to remember. Afghanistan's Nawroz Mangal hit consecutive sixes – as high as they were long – off Mitchell Marsh at Perth; UAE tailender Mohammad Naveed fulfilled an ambition by lofting Dale Steyn deep into the Wellington terraces.

It was a satisfying World Cup in that the best four teams filled the last four places. Australia proved so strong they could leave Watson, their most experienced one-day all-rounder, out of one game, and barely use Marsh and George Bailey at all, despite important contributions to their opening victory, against England. Promoted to No. 3, Smith bounced back from a slow start; Maxwell, deployed when innings best suited him, was consistently destructive. Yet the outstanding contributor was indisputably Starc, who in December had struggled as a Test match change-bowler; he ended the tournament as the world's highest-ranked one-day bowler. Twelve of his 22 wickets at ten apiece were bowled, the last being the most important: McCullum, yorked third ball in the final.

To that point, McCullum had been devastating: from the mandatory powerplays he had looted 308 from 150 deliveries, with 42 fours and 17 sixes. His 77 from 25 balls against England, who had already been laid low by Southee's seven for 33, broke his own record for the fastest World Cup fifty. He carved a path for batting comrades Guptill, Kane Williamson, Ross Taylor, Grant Elliott and Corey Anderson; he set the tone, in the field with bold calls and elastic saves, and off the field with decorum and humility. Save perhaps for Allan Border in 1987, no World Cup captain can have been so popular. A photograph of the conclusion of the semi-final at Eden Park, where Elliott – having belted Steyn for six to win the game – is offering his prone opponent a consoling hand-up, was a fair representation of New Zealand's approach.

In need of a pick-me-up: New Zealand's Grant Elliott consoles South Africa's Dale Steyn after the Auckland semi-final.

The expressions of the vanquished, as it dawned on **South Africa** that the World Cup had again exceeded their grasp, were haunting, complete with tears of grief and thousand-yard stares. But, even after hammering **Sri Lanka** in the quarter-finals, they were never quite settled in their line-up, following the last-minute omission of all-rounder Ryan McLaren and the failure of left-arm seamer Wayne Parnell; Steyn and Hashim Amla contributed spasmodically, and opener Quinton de Kock barely at all, leaving too much to de Villiers. A team launched on a tide of national goodwill returned home to a further confrontation with their board over racial quotas in domestic cricket, and reports that officials had insisted on the inclusion of (non-white) Vernon Philander in the semi-final ahead of (white) Kyle Abbott.

India aroused false hope by beating Pakistan and South Africa, batting and bowling purposefully, fielding with exuberance and vitality, and attracting staggering proportions of live support – the crowds for their first two games raised the roofs of Adelaide Oval and the MCG. Seemingly somnolent through the Border–Gavaskar Trophy and the one-day tri-series with Australia and England, M. S. Dhoni suddenly looked engaged, animated and intuitive. Yet victories against the UAE, West Indies, Ireland, Zimbabwe and Bangladesh hardly tested them. Faced again with an Australian team who had repeatedly had the better of them over the summer, they squandered the advantages of a slow, turning pitch and another boisterously patriotic audience in Sydney.

It marked the end of Duncan Fletcher's tenure as head coach, after four mixed years.

The structure of twin pools and a quarter-final stage ensured it was a World Cup of two moods: 42 games to eliminate six of the 14 teams, and seven to reduce the remaining eight to one. "You'd have to have an absolute stinker not to make the quarter-finals," observed Stuart Broad in advance; **England** duly undershot even low expectations. Their campaign began as it would continue, with a feeble error: square leg Chris Woakes dropped the scoreless Aaron Finch, who went on to a power-packed hundred. Their bowling was largely impotent, their batting puny, their leadership moribund: a cipher with the bat, Eoin Morgan exercised negligible on-field authority following his late ascent to the captaincy at the expense of the sacked Alastair Cook; a grim, beleaguered coach, Peter Moores seemed unable to relieve the off-field atmosphere of staleness and rigidity, even fear. Two and a half years earlier, England had been ranked one-day cricket's No. 1 team; now they left the stage to the sound of their own feet. The only English player around for the concluding fortnight was Kevin Pietersen, basking in reflected inglory, as a commentator.

Shapoor Zadran approached the realms of folk hero

By contrast, the Associates won many friends, of whom 21,000 signed a petition protesting against the ICC's decision to downsize the 2019 World Cup to ten teams. It was **Ireland** who sprang the first surprise of sorts, comfortably defeating a lackadaisical **West Indies**, whose players seemed more concerned with the IPL auction, which took place on the same day. The omission of the experienced all-rounders Dwayne Bravo and Kieron Pollard, ostensibly because they were associated with previous failures – though both had played central roles in the players' strike in India a few months earlier – added to the sense of self-destruction. Gayle called it "victimisation" and "ridiculous selection".

Coached by West Indian Phil Simmons, the Irish beat three of their first four opponents, including Zimbabwe, another Full Member. But when their net run-rate was whipsawed by a heavy loss to South Africa, they failed to advance beyond the group stages. West Indies added insult to injury by recruiting Simmons as coach.

The Associates might have done still better. The **UAE** had Zimbabwe 167 for five, including Brendan Taylor, chasing 286 at Nelson; **Afghanistan** had Sri Lanka 51 for four, including Sangakkara, chasing 233 at Dunedin. In six innings each, the UAE's Shaiman Anwar made 311 runs – a record for an Associate batsman – Ireland's captain William Porterfield 275, and Afghanistan's Samiullah Shenwari 254; **Scotland's** medium-pacer Josh Davey took 15 wickets at 20. Shenwari and Davey were on opposite sides when their countries went to the last over and the last wicket in mutual pursuit of a maiden World Cup victory: the improbable pairing of Hamid Hassan and Shapoor Zadran added the decisive 19 runs from 16 balls before characteristically unrestrained celebrations. Shapoor approached the realms of folk hero.

The Cup's four juniors showed sufficient potential to justify their presence, and to impress the likes of Sachin Tendulkar and Rahul Dravid – significant,

It gives me great pleasure… ICC chairman N. Srinivasan elbowed aside president Mustafa Kamal to present the World Cup to Michael Clarke.

perhaps, given that the tournament's scale is the prerogative of India, the greatest contributor to, and beneficiary of, the global exchequer. Tendulkar himself suggested expanding future events to as many as 25 teams.

Otherwise, the ICC could claim to have had a satisfactory and trouble-free tournament. Player behaviour, after a preliminary warning, was good, New Zealand setting their high standard, and even Australia generally remaining within acceptable bounds, at least until the final, where Brad Haddin's send-offs left an acrid taste. If anything, match referees could have been a bit more liberal – the fines dished out to Watson and Wahab after the quarter-final seemed oversensitive. The umpiring was mainly adequate, the occasional howler apart. Although neither affected a match's outcome, Aleem Dar hashed two decisions at the MCG, depriving England's James Taylor of a hundred by being unaware that a ball is dead once a decision is reviewed, and gifting one to India's Rohit Sharma by deeming a waist-high full toss by Bangladesh's Rubel Hossain to have been a no-ball.

The Sharma decision had unintended consequences, for it provoked voluble protests from ICC president Mustafa Kamal of Bangladesh, who alleged a conspiracy to bring about a "pre-decided" win by the "Indian Cricket Council", and demanded an investigation to "inquire the issue to see if there's anything to it". This placed him on a collision course with his own chairman, India's Narayanaswami Srinivasan, who reacted by presenting the trophy to Clarke himself, and was booed by the Melbourne crowd. Further enraged, Kamal threatened to tell all: "My rights were dishonoured. After I go back home, I will let the whole world know what's happening in ICC. I will let the whole world know about those guys who are doing these mischievous things." Not long after, he resigned, now insisting he had no complaints against anyone, and unconvincingly playing the statesman: "Let the game of cricket under the leadership of ICC touch the hearts and minds of every cricket lover."

Apart from Clarke and Sangakkara signing off from one-day cricket, fans saw the last in the format of Vettori, Misbah, Mahela Jayawardene, Shahid Afridi and probably Brendan Taylor. The 29-year-old Taylor, named as twelfth man in the official ICC World Cup XI after a haul of 433 runs, left cricket in **Zimbabwe** holed beneath the waterline by signing a three-year Kolpak contract with Nottinghamshire. Needs must, of course. But it was a reminder that, while greatness may or may not be contagious, wealth assuredly isn't. The rich got richer at the 2015 World Cup; the rest were left to hope for higher-quality crumbs.

2014-15 WORLD CUP STATISTICS

Leading run-scorers

	M	I	NO	R	HS	100	Avge	SR	4	6
M. J. Guptill (NZ)	9	9	1	547	237*	2	68.37	104.58	59	16
†K. C. Sangakkara (SL)	7	7	2	541	124	4	108.20	105.87	57	7
A. B. de Villiers (SA)	8	7	2	482	162*	1	96.40	144.31	43	21
B. R. M. Taylor (Z)	6	6	0	433	138	2	72.16	106.91	43	12
†S. Dhawan (I)	8	8	0	412	137	2	51.50	91.75	48	9
S. P. D. Smith (A)	8	7	1	402	105	1	67.00	91.57	37	4
T. M. Dilshan (SL)	7	7	1	395	161*	2	65.83	96.57	46	3
F. du Plessis (SA)	7	7	1	380	109	1	63.33	84.63	28	4
Mahmudullah (B)	6	6	1	365	128*	2	73.00	81.83	30	6
Misbah-ul-Haq (P)	7	7	0	350	76	0	50.00	75.10	25	7
†D. A. Warner (A)	8	8	1	345	178	1	49.28	120.20	38	9
†C. H. Gayle (WI)	6	6	0	340	215	1	56.66	117.24	17	26
†S. C. Williams (Z)	6	6	1	339	96	0	67.80	109.00	29	6
H. M. Amla (SA)	8	8	0	333	159	1	41.62	95.14	35	5
R. G. Sharma (I)	8	8	1	330	137	1	47.14	91.66	33	9
B. B. McCullum (NZ)	9	9	0	328	77	0	36.44	188.50	44	17
G. J. Maxwell (A)	8	6	1	324	102	1	64.80	182.02	35	14
†D. A. Miller (SA)	8	7	2	324	138*	0	64.80	139.05	21	14
Shaiman Anwar (UAE)	6	6	0	311	106	1	51.83	91.47	34	4
G. D. Elliott (NZ)	9	8	1	310	84*	0	44.28	105.44	29	7
V. Kohli (I)	8	8	2	305	107	1	50.83	81.55	29	1
†H. D. R. L. Thirimanne (SL)	7	7	1	302	139*	1	50.33	84.83	29	2

Highest individual scores

Runs	Balls	4	6		
237*	163	24	11	M. J. Guptill	New Zealand v West Indies at Wellington
215	147	10	16	C. H. Gayle	West Indies v Zimbabwe at Canberra
178	133	19	5	D. A. Warner	Australia v Afghanistan at Perth
162*	66	17	8	A. B. de Villiers	South Africa v West Indies at Sydney
161*	146	22	0	T. M. Dilshan	Sri Lanka v Bangladesh at Melbourne
159	128	16	4	H. M. Amla	South Africa v Ireland at Canberra
156	134	17	4	K. J. Coetzer	Scotland v Bangladesh at Nelson
139*	143	13	2	H. D. R. L. Thirimanne	Sri Lanka v England at Wellington
138*	92	7	9	D. A. Miller	South Africa v Zimbabwe at Hamilton
138	110	15	5	B. R. M. Taylor	Zimbabwe v India at Auckland
137	146	16	2	S. Dhawan	India v South Africa at Melbourne
137	126	14	3	R. G. Sharma	India v Bangladesh at Melbourne

Runs	Balls	4	6			
135	128	12	3	A. J. Finch	Australia v England at Melbourne
133*	156	11	3	M. N. Samuels	West Indies v Zimbabwe at Canberra
128*	123	12	3	Mahmudullah	Bangladesh v New Zealand at Hamilton
128	107	12	5	M. M. Ali	England v Scotland at Christchurch
124	95	13	4	K. C. Sangakkara	Sri Lanka v Scotland at Hobart
121	108	14	2	J. E. Root	England v Sri Lanka at Wellington
121	91	11	4	B. R. M. Taylor	Zimbabwe v Ireland at Hobart

There were 19 other hundreds. The 38 centuries scored were a record for one World Cup, beating 24 in 2010-11.

Best strike-rates

	SR	Runs		SR	Runs
B. B. McCullum (NZ)	188.50	328	C. J. Anderson (NZ)	108.45	231
G. J. Maxwell (A)	182.02	324	B. R. M. Taylor (Z)	106.91	433
A. B. de Villiers (SA)	144.31	482	S. R. Watson (A)	106.12	208
D. A. Miller (SA)	139.05	324	K. C. Sangakkara (SL)	105.87	541
D. A. Warner (A)	120.20	345	Mushfiqur Rahim (B)	105.67	298
C. H. Gayle (WI)	117.24	340	M. M. Ali (E)	105.49	192
R. R. Rossouw (SA)	116.66	210	G. D. Elliott (NZ)	105.44	310
J. O. Holder (WI)	112.31	155	M. J. Guptill (NZ)	104.58	547
S. K. Raina (I)	110.07	284	J-P. Duminy (SA)	102.50	164
N. J. O'Brien (Ire)	109.34	199	M. S. Dhoni (I)	102.15	237
S. C. Williams (Z)	109.00	339	L. M. P. Simmons (WI)	101.16	173

Minimum 150 runs.

Leading wicket-takers

	Style	O	M	R	W	BB	4I	Avge	SR	ER
M. A. Starc (A)	LF	63.5	3	224	22	6-28	2	10.18	17.40	3.50
T. A. Boult (NZ)	LFM	85	14	371	22	5-27	2	16.86	23.18	4.36
U. T. Yadav (I)	RF	64.2	5	321	18	4-31	2	17.83	21.44	4.98
Mohammed Shami (I)	RFM	61	7	294	17	4-35	1	17.29	21.52	4.81
M. Morkel (SA)	RF	68.1	2	299	17	3-34	0	17.58	24.05	4.38
J. E. Taylor (WI)	RFM	57.3	2	328	17	3-15	0	19.29	20.29	5.70
Wahab Riaz (P)	LF	66.1	4	368	16	4-45	1	23.00	24.81	5.56
D. L. Vettori (NZ)	SLA	75.5	5	307	15	4-18	1	20.46	30.33	4.04
J. H. Davey (Sco)	RM	50	2	311	15	4-68	1	20.73	20.00	6.22
Imran Tahir (SA)	LBG	76.2	5	323	15	5-45	2	21.53	30.53	4.23
M. G. Johnson (A)	LF	63.3	2	326	15	4-22	1	21.73	25.40	5.13
T. G. Southee (NZ)	RFM	81	7	472	15	7-33	1	31.46	32.40	5.82
C. J. Anderson (NZ)	LFM	36.1	1	234	14	3-18	0	16.71	15.50	6.47
M. Sharma (I)	RFM	63	4	314	13	3-48	0	24.15	29.07	4.98
R. Ashwin (I)	OB	77	6	330	13	4-25	1	25.38	35.53	4.28
S. L. Malinga (SL)	RFM	63.4	1	354	12	3-35	0	29.50	31.83	5.56
Sohail Khan (P)	RFM	61.5	3	364	12	5-55	1	30.33	30.91	5.88

Best bowling analyses

7-33	T. G. Southee	New Zealand v England at Wellington
6-28	M. A. Starc	Australia v New Zealand at Auckland
5-27	T. A. Boult	New Zealand v Australia at Auckland
5-33	M. R. Marsh	Australia v England at Melbourne
5-45	Imran Tahir	South Africa v West Indies at Sydney
5-55	Sohail Khan	Pakistan v India at Adelaide
5-71	S. T. Finn	England v Australia at Melbourne
4-14	M. A. Starc	Australia v Scotland at Hobart

4-18	D. L. Vettori........	New Zealand v Afghanistan at Napier
4-21	K. J. Abbott	South Africa v Ireland at Canberra
4-22	M. G. Johnson	Australia v Afghanistan at Perth
4-25	R. Ashwin	India v UAE at Perth
4-26	Imran Tahir	South Africa v Sri Lanka at Sydney
4-27	J. O. Holder	West Indies v UAE at Napier
4-30	Mohammad Irfan	Pakistan v Zimbabwe at Brisbane

There were 13 other instances of a bowler taking four wickets in an innings.

Most economical bowlers

	ER	Overs		ER	Overs
M. A. Starc (A)	3.50	63.5	T. A. Boult (NZ)	4.36	85
D. L. Vettori (NZ)	4.04	75.5	M. Morkel (SA)..........	4.38	68.1
J. R. Hazlewood (A)........	4.10	42.5	H. M. R. K. B. Herath (SL) .	4.47	34.5
K. J. Abbott (SA)	4.19	31	Mohammad Irfan (P)	4.53	41
Imran Tahir (SA)	4.23	76.2	A. R. Cusack (Ire)	4.58	37.3
R. Ashwin (I)	4.28	77	J. P. Faulkner (A)........	4.70	41.5
Rahat Ali (P)	4.36	44	V. D. Philander (SA)	4.73	28.3

Minimum 20 overs.

Leading wicketkeepers

	Dis	M		Dis	M
B. J. Haddin (A)........	16 (16 ct)	8	Q. de Kock (SA)	10 (9 ct, 1 st)	8
M. S. Dhoni (I)	15 (15 ct)	8	Umar Akmal (P)	8 (8 ct)	4
D. Ramdin (WI).......	13 (13 ct)	7	J. C. Buttler (E)	8 (8 ct)	6
L. Ronchi (NZ)	13 (12 ct, 1 st)	9	Mushfiqur Rahim (B)...	8 (7 ct, 1 st)	6
M. H. Cross (Sco)	10 (9 ct, 1 st)	6	K. C. Sangakkara (SL)...	8 (5 ct, 3 st)	7

Umar Akmal made four further catches in three matches when not keeping wicket.

Most dismissals in a match

Sarfraz Ahmed	6 (6 ct)	Pakistan v South Africa at Auckland
Umar Akmal.............	5 (5 ct)	Pakistan v Zimbabwe at Brisbane
M. H. Cross	4 (4 ct)	Scotland v New Zealand at Dunedin
J. C. Buttler	4 (4 ct)	England v Scotland at Christchurch
Mushfiqur Rahim	4 (4 ct)	Bangladesh v England at Adelaide
M. S. Dhoni	4 (4 ct)	India v Bangladesh at Melbourne

Leading fielders

	Ct	M		Ct	M
R. R. Rossouw (SA)	9	6	H. M. Amla (SA)	6	8
U. T. Yadav (I)	8	8	A. B. de Villiers (SA)	6	8
J. E. Root (E).	7	6	A. J. Finch (A)	6	8
S. Dhawan (I)	7	8	S. K. Raina (I)	6	8
Soumya Sarkar (B)	6	6	D. L. Vettori (NZ)...............	6	9
F. du Plessis (SA)	6	7			

Highest totals

417-6	Australia v Afghanistan at Perth	341-6	South Africa v UAE at Wellington
411-4	South Africa v Ireland at Canberra	339-4	South Africa v Zimbabwe at Hamilton
408-5	South Africa v West Indies at Sydney	339-6	Pakistan v UAE at Napier
393-6	New Zealand v West Indies at Wellington	332-1	Sri Lanka v Bangladesh at Melbourne
376-9	Australia v Sri Lanka at Sydney	331-6	N Zealand v Sri Lanka at Christchurch
372-2	West Indies v Zimbabwe at Canberra	331-8	Ireland v Zimbabwe at Hobart
363-9	Sri Lanka v Scotland at Hobart	328-7	Australia v India at Sydney
342-9	Australia v England at Melbourne	326	Zimbabwe v Ireland at Hobart

There were 12 further totals of 300 or more.

Lowest completed totals

102	UAE v India at Perth	142	Afghanistan v Australia at Perth
123	England v New Zealand at Wellington	151	West Indies v South Africa at Sydney
130	Scotland v Australia at Hobart	151	Australia v New Zealand at Auckland
133	Sri Lanka v South Africa at Sydney	160	Pakistan v West Indies at Christchurch
142	Scotland v New Zealand at Dunedin	162	Afghanistan v Bangladesh at Canberra

A list of all-time World Cup records can be found on page 1370.

NATIONAL SQUADS

* Captain.   ‡ Did not play in World Cup.

Afghanistan *Mohammad Nabi, Afsar Zazai, Aftab Alam, Asghar Stanikzai, Dawlat Zadran, Gulbadeen Naib, Hamid Hassan, Javed Ahmadi, Mirwais Ashraf, Najibullah Zadran, Nasir Ahmadzai, Nawroz Mangal, Samiullah Shenwari, Shafiqullah, Shapoor Zadran, Usman Ghani. *Coach:* A. J. Moles.
    Mirwais Ashraf suffered a side strain, and was replaced in the squad by Shafiqullah.

Australia *M. J. Clarke, G. J. Bailey, P. J. Cummins, X. J. Doherty, J. P. Faulkner, A. J. Finch, B. J. Haddin, J. R. Hazlewood, M. G. Johnson, M. R. Marsh, G. J. Maxwell, S. P. D. Smith, M. A. Starc, D. A. Warner, S. R. Watson. *Coach:* D. S. Lehmann.

Bangladesh *Mashrafe bin Mortaza, ‡Al-Amin Hossain, Anamul Haque, Arafat Sunny, Imrul Kayes, Mahmudullah, Mominul Haque, Mushfiqur Rahim, Nasir Hossain, Rubel Hossain, Sabbir Rahman, ‡Shafiul Islam, Shakib Al Hasan, Soumya Sarkar, Taijul Islam, Tamim Iqbal, Taskin Ahmed. *Coach:* U. C. Hathurusinghe.
    Al-Amin Hossain was sent home for breaking a team curfew, and replaced by Shafiul Islam. Anamul Haque hurt his shoulder, and was replaced by Imrul Kayes.

England *E. J. G. Morgan, M. M. Ali, J. M. Anderson, G. S. Ballance, I. R. Bell, R. S. Bopara, S. C. J. Broad, J. C. Buttler, S. T. Finn, A. D. Hales, C. J. Jordan, J. E. Root, J. W. A. Taylor, J. C. Tredwell, C. R. Woakes. *Coach:* P. Moores.

India *M. S. Dhoni, R. Ashwin, Bhuvneshwar Kumar, ‡S. T. R. Binny, S. Dhawan, R. A. Jadeja, V. Kohli, Mohammed Shami, ‡A. R. Patel, A. M. Rahane, S. K. Raina, ‡A. T. Rayudu, M. Sharma, R. G. Sharma, U. T. Yadav. *Coach:* D. A. G. Fletcher.
    I. Sharma was originally selected in the 15-man squad, but did not recover from a knee injury and was replaced by M. Sharma.

Ireland *W. T. S. Porterfield, A. Balbirnie, ‡P. K. D. Chase, A. R. Cusack, G. H. Dockrell, E. C. Joyce, A. R. McBrine, J. F. Mooney, K. J. O'Brien, N. J. O'Brien, M. C. Sorensen, P. R. Stirling, S. R. Thompson, G. C. Wilson, ‡C. A. Young. *Coach:* P. V. Simmons.
    T. J. Murtagh was originally selected, but suffered a foot injury, and was replaced by Sorensen.

New Zealand *B. B. McCullum, C. J. Anderson, T. A. Boult, G. D. Elliott, M. J. Guptill, M. J. Henry, ‡T. W. M. Latham, M. J. McClenaghan, ‡N. L. McCullum, A. F. Milne, ‡K. D. Mills, L. Ronchi, T. G. Southee, L. R. P. L. Taylor, D. L. Vettori, K. S. Williamson. *Coach:* M. J. Hesson.
    Milne suffered a heel injury in the quarter-final against West Indies, and was replaced by Henry.

Pakistan *Misbah-ul-Haq, Ahmed Shehzad, Ehsan Adil, Haris Sohail, Mohammad Irfan, Nasir Jamshed, Rahat Ali, Sarfraz Ahmed, Shahid Afridi, Sohaib Maqsood, Sohail Khan, Umar Akmal, Wahab Riaz, Yasir Shah, Younis Khan. *Coach:* Waqar Younis.

Junaid Khan and Mohammad Hafeez were originally selected. Junaid suffered a thigh injury in New Zealand in February, and was replaced by Rahat Ali. Hafeez reported a calf injury on the same tour, and was replaced by Nasir Jamshed.

Scotland *P. L. Mommsen, R. D. Berrington, K. J. Coetzer, F. R. J. Coleman, M. H. Cross, J. H. Davey, A. C. Evans, H. J. W. Gardiner, R. M. Haq, M. A. Leask, M. W. Machan, C. S. MacLeod, ‡S. M. Sharif, R. M. L. Taylor, I. Wardlaw. *Coach:* G. E. Bradburn.

Haq was sent home for breaking the team's code of conduct on social media before the game against Sri Lanka.

South Africa *A. B. de Villiers, K. J. Abbott, H. M. Amla, F. Behardien, Q. de Kock, J-P. Duminy, F. du Plessis, Imran Tahir, D. A. Miller, M. Morkel, W. D. Parnell, ‡A. M. Phangiso, V. D. Philander, R. R. Rossouw, D. W. Steyn. *Coach:* R. C. Domingo.

Sri Lanka *A. D. Mathews, P. V. D. Chameera, L. D. Chandimal, T. M. Dilshan, H. M. R. K. B. Herath, D. P. M. D. Jayawardene, F. D. M. Karunaratne, P. H. T. Kaushal, K. M. D. N. Kulasekara, R. A. S. Lakmal, S. L. Malinga, B. M. A. J. Mendis, M. D. K. J. Perera, N. L. T. C. Perera, ‡K. T. G. D. Prasad, S. Prasanna, K. C. Sangakkara, S. M. S. M. Senanayake, W. U. Tharanga, H. D. R. L. Thirimanne. *Coach:* M. S. Atapattu.

Prasad fractured his hand, Mendis and Chandimal damaged their hamstrings, and Karunaratne and Herath sustained finger injuries. They were replaced by Chameera, Tharanga, M. D. K. J. Perera, Prasanna and Kaushal.

United Arab Emirates *Mohammad Tauqir, Amjad Ali, Amjad Javed, A. R. Berenger, Fahad Alhashmi, A. M. Guruge, Kamran Shazad, Khurram Khan, K. Krishnachandran, Mohammad Naveed, R. Mustafa, Nasir Aziz, S. P. Patil, Saqlain Haider, Shaiman Anwar. *Coach:* Aqib Javed.

West Indies *J. O. Holder, S. J. Benn, D. M. Bravo, J. L. Carter, J. Charles, ‡S. S. Cottrell, C. H. Gayle, N. O. Miller, D. Ramdin, K. A. J. Roach, A. D. Russell, D. J. G. Sammy, M. N. Samuels, L. M. P. Simmons, D. R. Smith, J. E. Taylor. *Coach:* S. C. Williams.

S. P. Narine was originally selected, but withdrew before departure, citing confidence issues with his remodelled bowling action; he was replaced by Miller. Bravo tore his left hamstring while batting against Pakistan, and was replaced by Charles.

Zimbabwe *E. Chigumbura, R. W. Chakabva, T. L. Chatara, C. J. Chibhabha, C. R. Ervine, T. Kamungozi, H. Masakadza, S. Matsikenyeri, S. F. Mire, T. Mupariwa, T. Panyangara, Sikandar Raza, B. R. M. Taylor, ‡P. Utseya, S. C. Williams. *Coach:* D. F. Whatmore.

POOL A

NEW ZEALAND v SRI LANKA

At Christchurch (Hagley Oval), February 14, 2015. New Zealand won by 98 runs. Toss: Sri Lanka.

As in 1992, New Zealand opened their home World Cup with victory. Back then they had stunned Australia, but this time the result came as no surprise: a display of efficiency and verve ensured they continued their recent dominance over Sri Lanka. After the New Zealanders had been put in on a drizzly, overcast morning, McCullum drove his first delivery through the covers en route to a 35-ball half-century; he and Guptill shared an opening stand of 111 in 16 overs that settled any nerves. Sri Lanka's pace bowling was initially poor, with Malinga – in his first competitive match since September – leaking 42 from four overs. Williamson, who was given a life first ball when Sangakkara failed to hold a tough chance, made 57; and, although Herath and Lakmal helped slow New Zealand's progress, the foundations had been laid. Anderson, dropped on 43 by Mendis, struck a forceful 75 off 46 balls as he and Ronchi closed the innings with 73 in six overs. The start of the chase suggested a close contest as Thirimanne hit a 45-ball fifty, but

Vettori bowled delightfully to remove Dilshan – after an opening stand of 67 – and Jayawardene when Sangakkara, after easing along at a run a ball, fell lbw to Boult, Sri Lanka had lost three for five in 12 balls. No one offered Mathews the support he needed to keep the game alive.   ANDREW McGLASHAN

Man of the Match: C. J. Anderson.   *Attendance:* 17,228.

New Zealand

M. J. Guptill c Sangakkara b Lakmal	49	†L. Ronchi not out	29	
*B. B. McCullum c Mendis b Herath	65	L-b 2, w 8, n-b 3	13	
K. S. Williamson c Karunaratne b Mendis	57			
L. R. P. L. Taylor st Sangakkara b Mendis	14	1/111 (2) 2/136 (1)	(6 wkts, 50 overs)	331
G. D. Elliott c Thirimanne b Lakmal	29	3/193 (3) 4/193 (4)		
C. J. Anderson c Lakmal b Kulasekara	75	5/258 (5) 6/331 (6)	10 overs: 77-0	

D. L. Vettori, A. F. Milne, T. G. Southee and T. A. Boult did not bat.

Kulasekara 8–0–78–1; Malinga 10–0–84–0; Mathews 6–0–28–0; Herath 9–0–37–1; Dilshan 5–0–35–0; Lakmal 10–0–62–2; Mendis 2–0–5–2.

Sri Lanka

H. D. R. L. Thirimanne b Boult	65	S. L. Malinga c Ronchi b Southee	0	
T. M. Dilshan c and b Vettori	24	R. A. S. Lakmal not out	7	
†K. C. Sangakkara lbw b Boult	39			
D. P. M. D. Jayawardene c Ronchi b Vettori	0	W 10, n-b 1	11	
F. D. M. Karunaratne b Milne	14			
*A. D. Mathews c Vettori b Southee	46	1/67 (2) 2/124 (1)	(46.1 overs)	233
B. M. A. J. Mendis c Ronchi b Milne	4	3/125 (4) 4/129 (3) 5/163 (5)		
K. M. D. N. Kulasekara c Elliott b Anderson	10	6/168 (7) 7/196 (8) 8/216 (6)		
H. M. R. K. B. Herath c Milne b Anderson	13	9/217 (10) 10/233 (9)	10 overs: 46-0	

Southee 10–1–43–2; Boult 10–0–64–2; Milne 10–0–56–2; Vettori 10–0–34–2; Elliott 2–0–11–0; Williamson 1–0–7–0; Anderson 3.1–0–18–2.

Umpires: M. Erasmus and N. J. Llong.   Third umpire: S. Ravi.
Referee: D. C. Boon.

AUSTRALIA v ENGLAND

At Melbourne, February 14, 2015 (day/night). Australia won by 111 runs. Toss: England.

Hours after a one-sided game had finished in controversy, the ICC confirmed that the officials had wrongly adjudged Anderson run out after Taylor, on 98, successfully reviewed his own dismissal for leg-before to Hazlewood. The ball should have been declared dead the moment Aleem Dar gave Taylor out, rendering Anderson's dash for a leg-bye irrelevant. But the game's most pertinent mistake was indisputably England's: from the fifth delivery, Finch flicked Anderson to square leg, where Woakes dropped a straightforward chance. Broad removed Warner and Watson with successive balls in the eighth over, and Woakes partially atoned by bowling Smith with an inswinger for five. But Finch went on to spank 135 from 128 deliveries – the first World Cup century for Australia against England, in their seventh meeting – and added 146 with Bailey, captain in place of the injured Michael Clarke. With Maxwell to the fore, Australia struck 76 from the last six overs to reach their highest total against England. Finn's last-gasp hat-trick hardly merited celebration: Haddin, Maxwell and Johnson were all caught on the slog to give him the second most expensive five-for in one-day internationals, after Scotland seamer Gordon Goudie's five for 73, also against Australia, at Edinburgh in 2009. England had abruptly changed their plans: the recalled Ballance had batted just once since

September, Taylor was shunted down three places to No. 6, and Woakes deprived of the new ball. Wickets soon tumbled, including Bell and Root in consecutive deliveries from Mitchell Marsh, who had taken only six wickets in 14 previous one-day internationals but now claimed five for 33. Morgan's poor run continued when he gloved Marsh down the leg side to be spectacularly held by Haddin, and Buttler fell to a brilliant catch by Smith, backpedalling from cover, to leave England facing annihilation at 92 for six. Taylor and Woakes doubled the score as Australia's intensity dropped, and Taylor was two short of a maiden international hundred when the umpires got it wrong.   RICHARD HOBSON

Man of the Match: A. J. Finch.   Attendance: 84,336.

Australia

D. A. Warner b Broad	22	M. G. Johnson c Anderson b Finn		0
A. J. Finch run out	135	M. A. Starc not out		0
S. R. Watson c Buttler b Broad	0	L-b 2, w 3		5
S. P. D. Smith b Woakes	5			
*G. J. Bailey b Finn	55	1/57 (1) 2/57 (3)	(9 wkts, 50 overs)	342
G. J. Maxwell c Root b Finn	66	3/70 (4) 4/216 (2)		
M. R. Marsh c Root b Finn	23	5/228 (5) 6/281 (7) 7/342 (8)		
†B. J. Haddin c Broad b Finn	31	8/342 (6) 9/342 (9)	10 overs: 66-2	

J. R. Hazlewood did not bat.

Anderson 10–0–67–0; Broad 10–0–66–2; Woakes 10–0–65–1; Finn 10–0–71–5; Ali 9–0–60–0; Root 1–0–11–0.

England

M. M. Ali c Bailey b Starc	10	S. T. Finn c b Johnson		1
I. R. Bell b Starc b Marsh	36	J. M. Anderson run out		8
G. S. Ballance c Finch b Marsh	10			
J. E. Root c Haddin b Marsh	5	L-b 5, w 11		16
*E. J. G. Morgan c Haddin b Marsh	0			
J. W. A. Taylor not out	98	1/25 (1) 2/49 (3) 3/66 (2)	(41.5 overs)	231
†J. C. Buttler c Smith b Marsh	10	4/66 (4) 5/73 (5) 6/92 (7)		
C. R. Woakes c Smith b Johnson	37	7/184 (8) 8/194 (9) 9/195 (10)		
S. C. J. Broad b Starc	0	10/231 (11)	10 overs: 50-2	

Starc 9–1–47–2; Hazlewood 6.5–0–45–0; Johnson 8–0–36–2; Marsh 9–0–33–5; Watson 3–0–13–0; Maxwell 4–0–33–0; Smith 2–0–19–0.

Umpires: Aleem Dar and H. D. P. K. Dharmasena.   Third umpire: B. F. Bowden.
Referee: J. J. Crowe.

NEW ZEALAND v SCOTLAND

At Dunedin, February 17, 2015. New Zealand won by three wickets. Toss: New Zealand.
Eight years after their last World Cup match, Scotland made a gruesome start. Dunedin, the Edinburgh of the South, should have felt like a home from home, but on a murky morning New Zealand's opening bowlers were inhospitable: Boult and Southee swung the ball prodigiously at high speed, and Scotland were soon 12 for four. To reach 142 was a gutsy effort. Machan, arriving at one for two, showed poise amid the chaos, counterpunching judiciously. He found an ally in Berrington, whose initial restraint gave way to a straight six off Vettori. They added 97 before Machan was caught trying to heave Anderson to midwicket, a shot that felt about ten overs premature. Scotland's second collapse – their last six fell for 33 – was even more dispiriting than the first, as it came under sunny skies, although Vettori bowled with guile. They equalled the World Cup record of five ducks in an innings; uniquely, four were first-ballers. New Zealand approached the chase brimming with intent. Scotland could have wilted, but Wardlaw and Davey found a threatening length outside off stump, and claimed three victims apiece. Even so, a three-wicket victory

hardly reflected New Zealand's dominance: they won with half their overs left. Yet, had Wardlaw caught Anderson at fine leg, they would have been 119 for six, and Scotland might have been dreaming of an extraordinary maiden World Cup win.   TIM WIGMORE

Man of the Match: T. A. Boult.   *Attendance:* 4,684.

Scotland

K. J. Coetzer c Elliott b Southee	1	R. M. Haq c Taylor b Vettori	0		
C. S. MacLeod lbw b Boult	0	I. Wardlaw lbw b Vettori	0		
H. J. W. Gardiner b Boult	0				
M. W. Machan c McCullum b Anderson	56	B 1, w 5	6		
*P. L. Mommsen lbw b Southee	0				
R. D. Berrington c Milne b Anderson	50	1/1 (2) 2/1 (3) 3/12 (1) (36.2 overs) 142			
†M. H. Cross c Ronchi b Anderson	14	4/12 (5) 5/109 (4) 6/117 (6)			
J. H. Davey not out	11	7/129 (7) 8/136 (9) 9/142 (10)			
R. M. L. Taylor st Ronchi b Vettori	4	10/142 (11) 10 overs: 22-4			

Southee 8–3–35–2; Boult 6–1–21–2; Milne 7–0–32–0; Vettori 8.2–1–24–3; Elliott 2–0–11–0; Anderson 5–1–18–3.

New Zealand

M. J. Guptill c Cross b Wardlaw	17	D. L. Vettori not out	8		
*B. B. McCullum c Cross b Wardlaw	15	A. F. Milne not out	1		
K. S. Williamson c Cross b Davey	38	L-b 1, w 5	6		
L. R. P. L. Taylor c Taylor b Haq	9				
G. D. Elliott c Cross b Wardlaw	29	1/18 (1) 2/48 (2) (7 wkts, 24.5 overs) 146			
C. J. Anderson c Wardlaw b Davey	11	3/66 (4) 4/106 (3)			
†L. Ronchi c Gardiner b Davey	12	5/117 (5) 6/133 (6) 7/137 (7) 10 overs: 66-2			

T. G. Southee and T. A. Boult did not bat.

Wardlaw 9.5–0–57–3; Taylor 4–0–27–0; Davey 7–0–40–3; Haq 4–0–21–1.

Umpires: S. D. Fry and N. J. Llong.   Third umpire: M. Erasmus.
Referee: D. C. Boon.

AFGHANISTAN v BANGLADESH

At Canberra, February 18, 2015 (day/night). Bangladesh won by 105 runs. Toss: Bangladesh.

Bangladeshi fans and their tiger mascots comfortably outnumbered supporters of Afghanistan, on their World Cup debut. And, proudly though the Afghan drums beat, they could not inspire an upset: Bangladesh, who had lost this fixture in the Asia Cup a year earlier, drew on their greater experience to ease to a routine win. Despite Soumya Sarkar's brisk cameo, Shapoor Zadran (a left-arm Shoaib Akhtar wannabe) and the miserly Mirwais Ashraf had Bangladesh treading water at 119 for four in the 30th over. Then two former captains wrested back the initiative: Shakib Al Hasan and Mushfiqur Rahim added 114 in 15.3 – Bangladesh's first century stand in a World Cup – including 48 from the batting powerplay. Afghanistan lost their way, and faced a much stiffer target than had seemed likely. When the canny Mashrafe bin Mortaza helped reduce them to three for three, the game was up. Afghanistan did manage two fifty partnerships but, of the established batsmen, only Mohammad Nabi, the captain, scored at anything like the required rate. Mortaza's figures of three for 20 reflected the assurance with which Bangladesh went about their task. The banana skin had been picked up and neatly placed in the bin.   DILEEP PREMACHANDRAN

Man of the Match: Mushfiqur Rahim.   *Attendance:* 10,972.

Bangladesh

Anamul Haque lbw b Mirwais Ashraf	29	Mominul Haque run out	3
Tamim Iqbal c Afsar Zazai b Mirwais Ashraf	19	Rubel Hossain not out	0
Soumya Sarkar lbw b Shapoor Zadran	28	Taskin Ahmed b Aftab Alam	1
Mahmudullah c Afsar Zazai			
b Shapoor Zadran	23	B 3, l-b 4, w 6	13
Shakib Al Hasan b Hamid Hassan	63		
†Mushfiqur Rahim c Samiullah Shenwari		1/47 (2) 2/52 (1) 3/102 (3) (50 overs) 267	
b Mohammad Nabi	71	4/119 (4) 5/233 (5) 6/241 (7)	
Sabbir Rahman b Hamid Hassan	3	7/247 (6) 8/263 (9) 9/263 (8)	
*Mashrafe bin Mortaza b Aftab Alam	14	10/267 (11) 10 overs: 38-0	

Hamid Hassan 10–0–61–2; Shapoor Zadran 7–1–20–2; Aftab Alam 9–0–55–2; Mirwais Ashraf 9–3–32–2; Mohammad Nabi 9–0–58–1; Javed Ahmadi 4.5–0–32–0; Samiullah Shenwari 1.1–0–2–0.

Afghanistan

Javed Ahmadi c and b Mashrafe bin Mortaza	1	Aftab Alam run out	14
†Afsar Zazai lbw b Rubel Hossain	1	Hamid Hassan c Anamul Haque	
Nawroz Mangal c Rubel Hossain		b Taskin Ahmed	0
b Mahmudullah	27	Shapoor Zadran not out	2
Asghar Stanikzai c Mahmudullah			
b Mashrafe bin Mortaza	1		
Samiullah Shenwari run out	42	L-b 1, w 2	3
*Mohammad Nabi c Soumya Sarkar			
b Mashrafe bin Mortaza	44	1/2 (1) 2/2 (2) 3/3 (4) (42.5 overs) 162	
Najibullah Zadran lbw b Shakib Al Hasan	17	4/65 (3) 5/78 (5) 6/136 (7)	
Mirwais Ashraf c Sabbir Rahman		7/136 (6) 8/154 (8) 9/154 (10)	
b Shakib Al Hasan	10	10/162 (11) 10 overs: 24-3	

Mashrafe bin Mortaza 9–2–20–3; Rubel Hossain 6–0–27–1; Taskin Ahmed 7–0–23–1; Shakib Al Hasan 8.5–0–43–2; Mahmudullah 8–1–31–1; Soumya Sarkar 3–0–13–0; Sabbir Rahman 1–0–4–0.

Umpires: S. J. Davis and J. S. Wilson.   Third umpire: Aleem Dar.
Referee: J. J. Crowe.

NEW ZEALAND v ENGLAND

At Wellington (Westpac Stadium), February 20, 2015 (day/night). New Zealand won by eight wickets. Toss: England.

England crashed to one of the worst defeats in World Cup history. Sent packing by Southee, they were then mauled by McCullum, who obliterated a target of 124 in 12.2 overs. "The ball swung late and they exposed us," said Morgan – none more so than Southee, who skilfully exploited the conditions after England had chosen to bat. Maintaining a full length, and with an occasional bouncer, he took seven for 33, the third-best figures in World Cups, and New Zealand's best in one-day internationals; England's last seven fell for 19 in 45 balls. Having already bowled Bell and set up Ali with a bouncer-yorker combination, Southee needed only two balls to breach Taylor's defence. Buttler and Woakes followed in his next over to deliveries moving away. As Root watched the destruction unfold, no dismissal was uglier than Broad's, backing away as he tried to hit over cover. McCullum then tore into England's bowlers, reaching the fastest World Cup fifty, from 18 balls, with the first of four successive sixes off Finn. After six overs the total was an extraordinary 96 and, when McCullum bottom-edged a Woakes full toss on to his stumps in the eighth over, he had made 77 from 25 balls, including seven sixes. New Zealand needed only 12 more runs come the mandatory meal break. England, having subsided to their joint-worst one-day loss in terms of balls remaining, resembled the last stragglers of Stalingrad, and sloped off to boos. RICHARD HOBSON

Man of the Match: T. G. Southee.   *Attendance*: 30,148.

England

I. R. Bell b Southee		8
M. M. Ali b Southee		20
G. S. Ballance c Williamson b Boult		10
J. E. Root c Vettori b Milne		46
*E. J. G. Morgan c Milne b Vettori		17
J. W. A. Taylor b Southee		0
†J. C. Buttler c Ronchi b Southee		3
C. R. Woakes b Southee		1
S. C. J. Broad c Vettori b Southee		4

S. T. Finn c Taylor b Southee		0
J. M. Anderson not out		1
L-b 6, w 7		13

1/18 (1) 2/36 (2)   (33.2 overs) 123
3/57 (3) 4/104 (5) 5/104 (6)
6/108 (7) 7/110 (8) 8/116 (9)
9/117 (10) 10/123 (4)   10 overs: 43-2

Southee 9–0–33–7; Boult 10–2–32–1; Milne 5.2–1–25–1; Vettori 7–0–19–1; Anderson 2–0–8–0.

New Zealand

M. J. Guptill b Woakes		22
*B. B. McCullum b Woakes		77
K. S. Williamson not out		9
L. R. P. L. Taylor not out		5
L-b 4, w 8		12

1/105 (2)   (2 wkts, 12.2 overs) 125
2/112 (1)   10 overs: 116-2

G. D. Elliott, C. J. Anderson, †L. Ronchi, D. L. Vettori, A. F. Milne, T. G. Southee and T. A. Boult did not bat.

Anderson 5–0–37–0; Broad 2.2–0–27–0; Finn 2–0–49–0; Woakes 3–1–8–2.

Umpires: P. R. Reiffel and R. J. Tucker.   Third umpire: B. N. J. Oxenford.
Referee: R. S. Mahanama.

AUSTRALIA v BANGLADESH

At Brisbane, February 21, 2015 (day/night). Abandoned.
    The tail end of Cyclone Marcia forced the abandonment of Australia's only game at the Gabba, and handed Bangladesh a crucial point. It also prevented Michael Clarke from making his competitive return after breaking down in the Adelaide Test in December.

AFGHANISTAN v SRI LANKA

At Dunedin, February 22, 2015. Sri Lanka won by four wickets. Toss: Sri Lanka.
    Dunedin is said to have only five Afghan families, but the locals adopted the underdogs, flourishing Afghan flags and imploring them to overcome Sri Lanka. They might have managed it but for Jayawardene's magisterial century – his 19th in one-day internationals and, it turned out, his last. Even having his bat snapped in two by a delivery from Shapoor Zadran did not perturb an innings full of magnificent drives and nonchalant flicks. Yet, when Jayawardene steered Hamid Hassan into the hands of third man, Sri Lanka still needed 55 from 52 balls, with only four wickets in hand. Afghanistan scented a famous win, but that was reckoning without Tissara Perera, who scythed his first ball through backward point and finished with a brutal unbeaten 47 off 26. Afghanistan's bowlers had created early mayhem: with Sri Lanka chasing a modest 233, Thirimanne was lbw to the first delivery of the reply, from Dawlat Zadran, and only an inaccurate throw saved Sangakkara from a run-out in the same over. A lifter from Shapoor then accounted for Dilshan – both openers gone first ball, for only the second time in one-day internationals, after Zimbabwe against West Indies in Georgetown in May 2006. Hassan became the third Afghan to strike in his opening over, castling Sangakkara with a lavish inswinger and celebrating with a cartwheel. Eighteen for three became 51 for four when Karunaratne nicked Hassan to slip, and Sri Lanka needed something special. (Soon afterwards, Hassan

pulled up with discomfort in his left boot, and swapped it with Shapoor's.) Jayawardene, adding 126 with the circumspect Mathews – who survived another run-out chance before facing a ball – provided it. After a run-a-ball fifty from Asghar Stanikzai, Afghanistan had frittered away a position of 157 for three in the 33rd over. Nabi's heave off Malinga launched a lamentable batting powerplay, which brought only ten runs.   TIM WIGMORE

Man of the Match: D. P. M. D. Jayawardene.   *Attendance:* 2,711.

Afghanistan

Javed Ahmadi c Herath b Lakmal	24	Hamid Hassan c Mendis b Mathews	0
Nawroz Mangal c Thirimanne b Mathews	10	Shapoor Zadran not out	1
Asghar Stanikzai c Mendis b Herath	54		
Samiullah Shenwari c Mathews b Perera	38	L-b 6, w 16, n-b 1	23
*Mohammad Nabi b Malinga	21		
Najibullah Zadran c Perera b Lakmal	10	1/34 (2) 2/40 (1) (49.4 overs)	232
†Afsar Zazai c Herath b Malinga	19	3/128 (3) 4/157 (4) 5/169 (5)	
Mirwais Ashraf c Lakmal b Malinga	28	6/175 (6) 7/221 (8) 8/227 (9)	
Dawlat Zadran b Mathews	4	9/227 (10) 10/232 (7) 10 overs: 40-2	

Malinga 9.4–1–41–3; Lakmal 10–1–36–2; Mathews 7–0–41–3; Perera 10–0–54–1; Herath 10–0–41–1; Mendis 3–0–13–0.

Sri Lanka

H. D. R. L. Thirimanne lbw b Dawlat Zadran	0	*A. D. Mathews run out	44
T. M. Dilshan c Afsar Zazai		B. M. A. J. Mendis not out	9
b Shapoor Zadran	0	N. L. T. C. Perera not out	47
†K. C. Sangakkara b Hamid Hassan	7	L-b 2, w 3, n-b 1	6
F. D. M. Karunaratne c Nawroz Mangal			
b Hamid Hassan	23	1/0 (1) 2/2 (2) (6 wkts, 48.2 overs)	236
D. P. M. D. Jayawardene		3/33 (3) 4/51 (4)	
c Nawroz Mangal b Hamid Hassan	100	5/177 (6) 6/178 (5) 10 overs: 35-3	

H. M. R. K. B. Herath, S. L. Malinga and R. A. S. Lakmal did not bat.

Dawlat Zadran 9–0–44–1; Shapoor Zadran 10–1–48–1; Hamid Hassan 9–0–45–3; Mirwais Ashraf 8.1–0–31–0; Mohammad Nabi 5.2–0–28–0; Asghar Stanikzai 0.5–0–6–0; Samiullah Shenwari 6–0–32–0.

Umpires: C. B. Gaffaney and R. K. Illingworth.   Third umpire: J. D. Cloete.
Referee: B. C. Broad.

ENGLAND v SCOTLAND

At Christchurch (Hagley Oval), February 23, 2015. England won by 119 runs. Toss: Scotland.

England played well enough for long enough to secure their first points of the tournament – but they were far from convincing. Success stemmed from a stand of 172 in 30 overs between Ali and Bell, England's best for the first wicket in World Cups. But there was a pronounced contrast: the fluent Ali hit five sixes in 107 deliveries and became the second England batsman to score a one-day international hundred in New Zealand after Chris Broad in 1987-88, while the laborious Bell managed only two fours in 85 balls. Scotland had shown early signs of nerves – Davey's first over included four wides – but England then lost Ali, the out-of-touch Ballance and Root in 11 deliveries. That flurry of wickets, coupled with a reluctance to promote Buttler, cost them the chance of accelerating towards 350; Haq's super-slow off-breaks were treated with excessive respect, and Davey recovered to claim four wickets. Even so, Scotland – whose assistant coach was the former England one-day captain Paul Collingwood – never threatened to make 304, and only Coetzer, with 71 from 84 balls, made any headway. Finn gradually built speed and rhythm, having removed Machan with his fourth ball, and conceded only 14 in his first eight overs. Some forlorn late hitting by Haq couldn't mask the fact that the cricket had been less competitive than the banter among spectators, in the first game between the sides since Scotland's independence referendum the previous September; Scottish taunts of "Your captain's Irish" were irrefutable.   RICHARD HOBSON

Man of the Match: M. M. Ali.   *Attendance:* 12,388.

England

M. M. Ali c Coleman b Haq	128	S. C. J. Broad not out 0
I. R. Bell c Coetzer b Berrington	54	S. T. Finn not out 1
G. S. Ballance b Evans	10	B 1, l-b 4, w 15, n-b 1 21
J. E. Root c Cross b Davey	1	
*E. J. G. Morgan c Mommsen b Davey	46	1/172 (2) 2/201 (1) (8 wkts, 50 overs) 303
J. W. A. Taylor st Cross b Davey	17	3/203 (3) 4/203 (4)
†J. C. Buttler c Davey b Wardlaw	24	5/252 (6) 6/297 (7)
C. R. Woakes c Mommsen b Davey	1	7/300 (5) 8/300 (8) 10 overs: 58-0

J. M. Anderson did not bat.

Wardlaw 10–1–60–1; Davey 10–0–68–4; Evans 10–1–46–1; Haq 10–0–51–1; Berrington 5–0–43–1; Machan 2–0–11–0; Coetzer 3–0–19–0.

Scotland

K. J. Coetzer c Woakes b Ali	71	A. C. Evans c Buttler b Anderson	9
C. S. MacLeod c Buttler b Anderson	4	I. Wardlaw not out 0
F. R. J. Coleman c Morgan b Woakes	7	
M. W. Machan c Buttler b Finn	5	L-b 5, w 2 7
*P. L. Mommsen c Broad b Root	26	
R. D. Berrington c Morgan b Ali	8	1/17 (2) 2/47 (3) 3/54 (4) (42.2 overs) 184
†M. H. Cross c Root b Finn	23	4/114 (5) 5/122 (1) 6/128 (6)
J. H. Davey c Buttler b Finn	9	7/150 (8) 8/160 (7) 9/184 (10)
R. M. Haq c Ballance b Woakes	15	10/184 (9) 10 overs: 47-1

Anderson 6–0–30–2; Broad 7–0–24–0; Woakes 5.2–0–25–2; Finn 9–3–26–3; Ali 10–0–47–2; Root 5–0–27–1.

Umpires: S. Ravi and R. J. Tucker.   Third umpire: M. Erasmus.
Referee: D. C. Boon.

AFGHANISTAN v SCOTLAND

At Dunedin, February 26, 2015. Afghanistan won by one wicket. Toss: Afghanistan.

In the final over of a pulsating match, and with Afghanistan needing four to win, last man Shapoor Zadran set off for an optimistic single. Scotland's first World Cup victory – in 11 attempts spanning nearly 16 years – was within their grasp: Machan had the stumps in his sights but, with Shapoor scrambling to regain his ground, missed with an underarm throw from a couple of yards. Shapoor flicked the next ball past short fine leg for four, dropped his bat and helmet, and ran 30 yards before slumping to his knees in joy: it had taken Afghanistan only three games to clinch a maiden win. Two sides who risked being culled if the World Cup were reduced to ten teams had produced a frenetic, harum-scarum encounter, the match of the tournament to date. When Berrington and Davey induced a collapse of five for 12, Afghanistan were reeling on 97 for seven. But Samiullah Shenwari, their most technically correct batsman, found allies down the order, adding 35 with Dawlat Zadran and 60 with Hamid Hassan. With 38 required from four overs, Shenwari heaved three sixes over midwicket off Haq, which would have cleared bigger grounds than the University Oval. But, four short of Afghanistan's first World Cup hundred, he perished attempting a fourth. The last pair, Shapoor and Hassan, needed 19 from 19 balls, and for the most part approached their task calmly. They had already worked hard for the win: with fellow pace bowler Dawlat they had collected eight for 99 in 30 overs. Six

Rob Jefferies, Getty Images

Winning run: Shapoor Zadran brings joy to Afghanistan.

Scotland batsmen fell between 23 and 31, but a careful ninth-wicket stand of 62 between Haq and Evans ensured a total to test Afghanistan. For so long, it seemed likely to beat them.   TIM WIGMORE

Man of the Match: Samiullah Shenwari.   *Attendance:* 3,229.

Scotland

K. J. Coetzer b Dawlat Zadran 25	R. M. Haq c Gulbadeen Naib
C. S. MacLeod c Najibullah Zadran	b Shapoor Zadran . 31
b Dawlat Zadran . 0	A. C. Evans c Mohammad Nabi
H. J. W. Gardiner lbw b Hamid Hassan . . . 5	b Shapoor Zadran . 28
M. W. Machan b Mohammad Nabi 31	I. Wardlaw not out 1
*P. L. Mommsen c Afsar Zazai	
b Gulbadeen Naib . 23	L-b 12, w 12, n-b 1 25
R. D. Berrington c Afsar Zazai	
b Dawlat Zadran . 25	1/7 (2) 2/38 (3) 3/40 (1) (50 overs) 210
†M. H. Cross c Afsar Zazai b Shapoor Zadran 15	4/93 (4) 5/95 (5) 6/132 (7)
J. H. Davey c Hamid Hassan	7/134 (8) 8/144 (6) 9/206 (9)
b Shapoor Zadran . 1	10/210 (10) 10 overs: 38-1

Shapoor Zadran 10–1–38–4; Dawlat Zadran 10–1–29–3; Hamid Hassan 10–1–32–1; Gulbadeen Naib 9–0–53–1; Mohammad Nabi 10–0–38–1; Javed Ahmadi 1–0–8–0.

Afghanistan

Javed Ahmadi c Machan b Berrington 51	Hamid Hassan not out 15
Nawroz Mangal b Evans 7	Shapoor Zadran not out 12
Asghar Stanikzai c Cross b Evans 4	
Samiullah Shenwari c Davey b Haq 96	L-b 1, w 10, n-b 1 12
*Mohammad Nabi lbw b Davey 1	
†Afsar Zazai lbw b Berrington 0	1/42 (2) 2/46 (3) (9 wkts, 49.3 overs) 211
Najibullah Zadran c Haq b Berrington 4	3/85 (1) 4/88 (5)
Gulbadeen Naib c Haq b Davey 0	5/89 (6) 6/96 (7) 7/97 (8)
Dawlat Zadran c Mommsen b Berrington . . 9	8/132 (9) 9/192 (4) 10 overs: 48-2

Wardlaw 9.3–0–61–0; Davey 10–1–34–2; Evans 10–1–30–2; Haq 10–0–45–1; Berrington 10–0–40–4.

Umpires: S. D. Fry and R. S. A. Palliyaguruge.   Third umpire: R. J. Tucker.
Referee: D. C. Boon.

BANGLADESH v SRI LANKA

At Melbourne, February 26, 2015 (day/night). Sri Lanka won by 92 runs. Toss: Sri Lanka.
Anamul Haque made three grabs at an edge from Thirimanne at first slip off the fourth
ball of the day, but couldn't hold on – and Bangladesh were batted out of their first
appearance at the MCG. Thirimanne profited from further good fortune as he nicked
between keeper and a wide slip on 22; after he was finally held at third man, with the total
on 122, Sri Lanka's advance was barely impeded. Dilshan had already begun to unfurl his
shots on a friendly surface; Sangakkara was fluent from the outset in his 400th one-day
international, ramping his first four over the slips, and soon outstripped his partner's
scoring-rate. They added 210, both stroking unbeaten hundreds. Dilshan reached his 21st
in one-day internationals off 115 balls, then, despite cramp, raised the tempo, striking four
fours off Taskin Ahmed in the 45th over, and finishing with Sri Lanka's highest World
Cup score. Sangakkara, who was dropped on 23 and 60, completed his 22nd in the final
over, off 73 balls, which made it his fastest – until three days later. Bangladesh needed
333, but Tamim Iqbal was bowled by Malinga's second delivery; though Soumya Sarkar
provided some early impetus, they were soon 100 for five. Senior batsmen down the order
played surer hands, but Sabbir Rahman alone passed 50, before Malinga returned to
dismiss him and last man Taskin with successive balls.   ANDREW FERNANDO
Man of the Match: T. M. Dilshan.   *Attendance:* 30,012.

Sri Lanka

H. D. R. L. Thirimanne c Taskin Ahmed	
b Rubel Hossain .	52
T. M. Dilshan not out	161
†K. C. Sangakkara not out	105
B 3, l-b 2, w 9	14

1/122 (1)   (1 wkt, 50 overs) 332
                           10 overs: 51-0

F. D. M. Karunaratne, D. P. M. D. Jayawardene, *A. D. Mathews, L. D. Chandimal, N. L. T. C. Perera, H. M. R. K. B. Herath, S. L. Malinga and R. A. S. Lakmal did not bat.

Mashrafe bin Mortaza 10–0–53–0; Rubel Hossain 9–0–62–1; Taskin Ahmed 10–1–82–0; Shakib Al Hasan 10–0–55–0; Mahmudullah 7–0–49–0; Sabbir Rahman 4–0–26–0.

Bangladesh

Tamim Iqbal b Malinga	0	Rubel Hossain not out	0
Anamul Haque run out	29	Taskin Ahmed lbw b Malinga	0
Soumya Sarkar c Sangakkara b Mathews . .	25		
Mominul Haque c Jayawardene b Lakmal .	1		
Mahmudullah c Herath b Perera	28	L-b 9, w 6	15
Shakib Al Hasan c Malinga b Dilshan . . .	46		
†Mushfiqur Rahim b Lakmal.	36	1/0 (1) 2/40 (3) 3/41 (4) (47 overs)	240
Sabbir Rahman c Sangakkara b Malinga. . .	53	4/84 (2) 5/100 (5) 6/164 (6)	
*Mashrafe bin Mortaza st Sangakkara		7/208 (7) 8/228 (9) 9/240 (8)	
b Dilshan .	7	10/240 (11) 10 overs: 60-3	

Malinga 9–0–35–3; Lakmal 8–0–49–2; Mathews 5.4–0–36–1; Herath 10–0–43–0; Perera 6.2–0–33–1; Dilshan 8–0–35–2.

Umpires: Aleem Dar and P. R. Reiffel.   Third umpire: R. A. Kettleborough.
Referee: J. J. Crowe.

WORLD CUP NOTES AND QUOTES

Moin Khan, Pakistan's chief selector, was ordered home by his board after being photographed visiting a casino in Christchurch four days after the defeat by India; the matter reached the upper house of parliament. Moin maintained he was there for dinner with his wife and friends – an explanation accepted by Pakistan Cricket Board chairman Shaharyar Khan.

Bangladesh seamer Al-Amin Hossain was also sent home, for breaking a 10pm team curfew in Brisbane. The Bangladesh management had been tipped off by the ICC's Anti-Corruption and Security Unit about his leaving the team hotel, although there was no suggestion of wrongdoing. "We don't even know where he went," said Nazmul Hassan, the Bangladesh Cricket Board president. "He is telling us different versions."

Shortly after Chris Gayle was out for four against Pakistan, a disgruntled West Indies fan tweeted: "Gayle goes... Can't buy a run. Let's give him a retirement package... Can't fail repeatedly and still front up based on reputation". That was retweeted by West Indies Cricket Board president Dave Cameron. The West Indies Players' Association said they were "extremely disturbed" by the retweet. Cameron later deleted it: "No offense intended. Full apologies extended. Rally round the West Indies." In his next innings, Gayle made 215 against Zimbabwe.

"I thought 275 was chaseable... we'll have to analyse the game data later," said England coach Peter Moores to Sky Sports' Nasser Hussain after they crashed out against Bangladesh. His comments were seized upon as evidence of England's preoccupation with statistics over intuition. But that was challenged by Mike Atherton in *The Times*, who had spoken to team analyst Nathan "Numbers" Leamon. "In this tournament, England have actually scaled right back their use of data-driven analysis," wrote Atherton. "The management, at the insistence of [Eoin] Morgan... felt that a younger, less experienced group of players would benefit from keeping things simple and reducing the clutter and information. So although every player is given an iPad with statistics and videos of opposition players, it is left entirely to them as to how much they access this information, if at all."

England's exit was ridiculed far and wide, even from below the World Cricket League. "Dear @ECB_cricket," tweeted the Japan Cricket Association, "this might not be a great time, but as there's room in your schedule, fancy a game in Japan on the way home? #challenge". Similar challenges from Malaysia and Singapore (ranked 23rd and 24th) were perhaps not so far-fetched: given a more expansionist ICC, they might have played England at the World Cup.

When Scotland's Majid Haq, whose loopy off-breaks were clocked at 41mph and inspired the online hashtag #things2dobetweenmajidreleasingballanditreachingbatsman, was left out of Scotland's penultimate game, against Sri Lanka, he tweeted: "Always tougher when your [sic] in the minority!! #colour #race". Haq was promptly sent home. He was already facing a three-game domestic ban at the start of the 2015 season for bashing his bat on the ground and using abusive language after being given lbw playing for Clydesdale in the 2014 Scottish Cup final, and subsequent comments he made on social media.

"Michael, you've had tremendous sex... success... as Australian captain," blurted the tongue-tied Stephan Shemilt, a BBC Sport website journalist, after Australia's semi-final victory over India. "Interesting," responded Clarke, as the press room descended into guffaws. "How well do you know me? That's a question for my wife."

Triple M radio caught up with a few of the celebrating Australian players in the early hours after their World Cup final win. Brad Haddin was introduced by Steven Smith as "the drunkest man in the team", and asked if his voice was so hoarse because of all the send-offs to New Zealand's batsmen. "You know what? They deserved it," he said. "They were that nice to us in New Zealand and we were that uncomfortable. In the team meeting, I said: 'I can't stand for this any more, we're going at them as hard as we can. I'm not playing cricket like this. If we get another crack at these guys in the final I'm letting everything [out]'. I'm not gonna play another one-dayer, so they can ban me for as long as they like." Haddin confirmed his retirement from ODIs in May.

Compiled by James Coyne

NEW ZEALAND v AUSTRALIA

At Auckland, February 28, 2015 (day/night). New Zealand won by one wicket. Toss: Australia.

Finally, two Test nations provided a contest worthy of the name. With New Zealand 146 for nine, chasing 152, at the start of the 24th over, Williamson calmly etched himself into folklore with six over long-on off Cummins. The resulting bedlam would normally have led to a noise-control call-out in this suburb of Mount Eden, but no New Zealander begrudged the decibel levels. Richard Hadlee handed McCullum the Chappell–Hadlee Trophy, which was at stake in this match. The theatre throughout reached Broadway standards, as 19 wickets fell in just 55.3 overs, 12 of them to left-arm seamers – comfortably a one-day international record. New Zealand were spearheaded by Boult, who claimed five in 17 legal balls without conceding a run off the bat. Australia had reached 80 for one in the 13th over, before Watson and Warner fell in successive deliveries to Vettori and Southee. Vettori had Smith caught behind to make it 95 for four. Then Boult took over. His first five, wicketless, overs had cost 24, but now he swung his way through a stunned Australian middle order, including Clarke, finally returning from back and hamstring problems. Eight fell for 26, and Haddin alone held up the one-way traffic, coaxing 45 out of the last wicket with Cummins. But, when New Zealand raced to 78 in the eighth over for the loss of Guptill, with McCullum charging at Starc and Johnson in a merciless 21-ball half-century, the Auckland crowd were taunting the Australians with chants of "You're worse than England." They sang too soon. Cummins removed McCullum, and Starc bowled Taylor and Elliott in consecutive balls. From 79 for four, Williamson and Anderson moved to 131. But Starc produced prodigious inswing on his way to six for 28 – like Boult, a career-best. Five wickets tumbled for 15 in three overs, leaving New Zealand still needing six. Williamson remained composed – and Eden Park went wild. ANDREW ALDERSON

Man of the Match: T. A. Boult.　　*Attendance:* 40,053.

Australia

A. J. Finch b Southee	14	M. G. Johnson c Williamson b Boult	1
D. A. Warner lbw b Southee	34	M. A. Starc b Boult	0
S. R. Watson c Southee b Vettori	23	P. J. Cummins not out	7
*M. J. Clarke c Williamson b Boult	12	B 4, l-b 2, w 6	12
S. P. D. Smith c Ronchi b Vettori	4		
G. J. Maxwell b Boult	1	1/30 (1) 2/80 (3) 3/80 (2) (32.2 overs)	151
M. R. Marsh b Boult	0	4/95 (5) 5/96 (6) 6/97 (7)	
†B. J. Haddin c sub (T. W. M. Latham)		7/104 (4) 8/106 (9) 9/106 (10)	
b Anderson	43	10/151 (8) 10 overs: 68-1	

Southee 9–0–65–2; Boult 10–3–27–5; Vettori 10–0–41–2; Milne 3–0–6–0; Anderson 0.2–0–6–1.

New Zealand

M. J. Guptill c Cummins b Starc	11	T. G. Southee b Starc	0
*B. B. McCullum c Starc b Cummins	50	T. A. Boult not out	0
K. S. Williamson not out	45		
L. R. P. L. Taylor b Starc	1	W 10, n-b 1	11
G. D. Elliott b Starc	0		
C. J. Anderson c Cummins b Maxwell	26	1/40 (1) 2/78 (2) (9 wkts, 23.1 overs)	152
†L. Ronchi c Haddin b Starc	6	3/79 (4) 4/79 (5)	
D. L. Vettori c Warner b Cummins	2	5/131 (6) 6/139 (7) 7/145 (8)	
A. F. Milne b Starc	0	8/146 (9) 9/146 (10) 10 overs: 81-4	

Johnson 6–1–68–0; Starc 9–0–28–6; Cummins 6.1–0–38–2; Marsh 1–0–11–0; Maxwell 1–0–7–1.

Umpires: M. Erasmus and R. K. Illingworth.　Third umpire: S. Ravi.
Referee: B. C. Broad.

ENGLAND v SRI LANKA

At Wellington (Westpac Stadium), March 1, 2015. Sri Lanka won by nine wickets. Toss:
England.

Sangakkara and Thirimanne – a constant thorn and a less familiar one – flayed England's
worst bowling of the tournament. Morgan later drew criticism for suggesting "275 to 280"
was par for the venue, especially since one-day cricket had moved on quickly in recent
months. Their total of 309 for six did seem competitive, but Sri Lanka enjoyed the easiest
of rides as they overtook it with 16 balls to spare, for the loss of only Dilshan. As against
Australia, England rued an early miss: the left-handed Thirimanne, on three, edged Broad
to first slip, where Root moved late, expecting wicketkeeper Buttler to claim the catch
instead. Thirimanne went on to a career-best unbeaten 139. The imperious Sangakkara,
who had scored 454 runs in seven one-day games at home against England before
Christmas, struck a second hundred in four days; from 70 balls, it was the fastest of his

---

NINE-WICKET WONDERS

Highest successful run-chases for the loss of one wicket in a one-day international:

362-1 (43.3 overs)	India v Australia at Jaipur	2013-14
312-1 (47.2)	**Sri Lanka v England at Wellington**	**2014-15**
267-1 (45.3)	Australia v Sri Lanka at Brisbane	2005-06
258-1 (41.5)	Australia v England at Centurion	2009-10
252-1 (42.5)	Sri Lanka v Bangladesh at Mirpur	2009-10
251-1 (39)	Pakistan v Australia at Rawalpindi	1994-95
249-1 (43.3)	West Indies v Australia at St George's, Grenada	2002-03
242-1 (47.3)	Pakistan v New Zealand at Manchester.	1999
241-1 (42.5)	West Indies v India at Trivandrum	1987-88

*The highest successful run-chase without losing a wicket is Sri Lanka's 231-0 (chasing 230) v
England in the 2010-11 World Cup quarter-final at R. Premadasa Stadium, Colombo.*

---

career. By the time Ali gave Thirimanne another life, on 98, England had lost any
semblance of control. Their own innings had been rescued by a mature performance from
Root, who capitalised on a reprieve from Jayawardene on two to succeed David Gower –
and mirror Thirimanne – as his country's youngest World Cup centurion. Frustration at
Morgan's dismissal approaching the powerplay was assuaged as Taylor gave Root
enterprising support in a fifth-wicket stand of 98 in 11 overs. An unbeaten 39 from 19
balls by Buttler embellished the total: he so unsettled Lakmal that the bowler was forced
off after a second beamer, leaving Dilshan to send down the final two balls of the innings.
The last two overs were thus delivered by four different bowlers: Perera had completed
the 49th, after Herath's left index finger was split by Buttler's rasping drive. But nothing
could stop Sri Lanka's top order. RICHARD HOBSON

Man of the Match: K. C. Sangakkara.   *Attendance:* 18,503.

England

M. M. Ali c Lakmal b Mathews	15	C. R. Woakes not out	9
I. R. Bell b Lakmal	49		
G. S. Ballance c and b Dilshan	6	B 4, l-b 3, w 9, n-b 2	18
J. E. Root lbw b Herath	121		
*E. J. G. Morgan c Dilshan b Perera	27	1/62 (1) 2/71 (3) (6 wkts, 50 overs) 309
J. W. A. Taylor c Dilshan b Malinga.	25	3/101 (2) 4/161 (5)
†J. C. Buttler not out	39	5/259 (6) 6/265 (4)
		10 overs: 62-1	

S. C. J. Broad, S. T. Finn and J. M. Anderson did not bat.

Malinga 10–0–63–1; Lakmal 7.4–0–71–1; Mathews 10–1–43–1; Dilshan 8.2–0–35–1; Herath 5.5–0–35–1; Perera 8.1–0–55–1.

Sri Lanka

H. D. R. L. Thirimanne not out	139
T. M. Dilshan c Morgan b Ali	44
†K. C. Sangakkara not out	117
B 8, l-b 1, w 3	12

1/100 (2)	(1 wkt, 47.2 overs)	312
	10 overs: 55-0	

D. P. M. D. Jayawardene, F. D. M. Karunaratne, *A. D. Mathews, L. D. Chandimal, N. L. T. C. Perera, H. M. R. K. B. Herath, S. L. Malinga and R. A. S. Lakmal did not bat.

Anderson 8–0–48–0; Broad 10–1–67–0; Woakes 9.2–0–72–0; Finn 8–0–54–0; Ali 10–0–50–1; Root 2–0–12–0.

Umpires: B. N. J. Oxenford and R. J. Tucker.   Third umpire: C. B. Gaffaney.
Referee: D. C. Boon.

AUSTRALIA v AFGHANISTAN

At Perth, March 4, 2015 (day/night). Australia won by 275 runs. Toss: Afghanistan.

The Afghan fast bowlers were drooling when they pitched up at Perth (the only thing that irked Shapoor Zadran was the run-up area in the nets, which wasn't long enough for him). These children of the refugee camps understood what the WACA meant to quick bowlers and, for six overs, they used the surface well. Finch couldn't handle them, and edged to slip. But Warner – who by his own admission had no idea who these bowlers were or how to pronounce their names – started punishing anything short. One shot struck a boy in the crowd; Warner sought him out later, apologised, and handed over a pair of batting gloves. He reached 150 by the 33rd over, and put on 260 with Smith, Australia's highest partnership for the second wicket in one-day internationals; Warner would finish with 178 off 133 balls. Shane Watson had been left out, but Maxwell had the freedom to reverse-lap, hook, pull and sweep 85mph seamers without fear; his 39-ball 88 included seven sixes. Clarke resisted the temptation for batting practice and promoted the bigger hitters instead; he was rewarded with the highest total at any World Cup, and the seventh-highest in the format. Dawlat Zadran, after an early wicket-maiden, finished as the seventh bowler to concede 100 or more in one-day internationals. The Afghan batsmen were unusually subdued, and slumped to the biggest defeat by runs at any World Cup as Johnson helped himself to four wickets. They had arrived knowing about the WACA's reputation; now they knew the reality too.   JARROD KIMBER

Man of the Match: D. A. Warner.   *Attendance:* 12,710.

Australia

D. A. Warner c Mohammad Nabi b Shapoor Zadran	178	
A. J. Finch c Nawroz Mangal b Dawlat Zadran	4	
S. P. D. Smith c Najibullah Zadran b Shapoor Zadran	95	
G. J. Maxwell c Mohammad Nabi b Dawlat Zadran	88	
J. P. Faulkner b Hamid Hassan	7	
M. R. Marsh c Najibullah Zadran b Nawroz Mangal	8	
†B. J. Haddin not out	20	
B 2, l-b 5, w 7, n-b 3	17	

1/14 (2) 2/274 (1)	(6 wkts, 50 overs)	417
3/339 (3) 4/382 (5)		
5/390 (4) 6/417 (6)	10 overs: 68-1	

*M. J. Clarke, M. G. Johnson, M. A. Starc and J. R. Hazlewood did not bat.

Dawlat Zadran 10–1–101–2; Shapoor Zadran 10–0–89–2; Hamid Hassan 10–0–70–1; Mohammad Nabi 10–0–84–0; Samiullah Shenwari 5–0–34–0; Javed Ahmadi 4–0–18–0; Nawroz Mangal 1–0–14–1.

Afghanistan

Javed Ahmadi c Clarke b Hazlewood	13	Hamid Hassan c Warner b Johnson	7
Usman Ghani c Faulkner b Johnson	12	Shapoor Zadran not out	0
Nawroz Mangal c Finch b Johnson	33		
Asghar Stanikzai c Smith b Johnson	4	B 4, l-b 5, w 10, n-b 1	20
Samiullah Shenwari c Johnson b Clarke	17		
*Mohammad Nabi c Clarke b Maxwell	2	1/30 (2) 2/32 (1) 3/46 (4) (37.3 overs)	142
Najibullah Zadran b Starc	24	4/94 (5) 5/94 (3) 6/103 (6)	
†Afsar Zazai c Haddin b Hazlewood	10	7/131 (7) 8/131 (9) 9/140 (8)	
Dawlat Zadran b Starc	0	10/142 (10) 10 overs: 44-2	

Starc 6–0–18–2; Hazlewood 8–1–25–2; Johnson 7.3–0–22–4; Clarke 5–0–14–1; Marsh 3–0–25–0; Faulkner 4–0–8–0; Maxwell 4–1–21–1.

Umpires: H. D. P. K. Dharmasena and M. A. Gough. Third umpire: B. F. Bowden.
Referee: R. S. Madugalle.

BANGLADESH v SCOTLAND

At Nelson, March 5, 2015. Bangladesh won by six wickets. Toss: Bangladesh.

Both sides passed 300 for the first time in a World Cup, but Bangladesh's hopes of a quarter-final rose after their self-assured batting saw them home with their highest second-innings total. In former days they might have panicked after Soumya Sarkar was caught down the leg side in the second over – which effectively made it five for two, as the regular

HIGHEST SUCCESSFUL WORLD CUP RUN-CHASES

329-7 (49.1 overs)	Ireland v England at Bangalore	2010-11
322-4 (48.1)	**Bangladesh v Scotland at Nelson**	**2014-15**
313-7 (49.2)	Sri Lanka v Zimbabwe at New Plymouth	1991-92
312-1 (47.2)	**Sri Lanka v England at Wellington (Westpac Stadium)**	**2014-15**
307-6 (45.5)	**Ireland v West Indies at Nelson**	**2014-15**
307-4 (47.4)	Ireland v Netherlands at Kolkata	2010-11
301-9 (49.5)	England v West Indies at Bridgetown	2006-07
300-7 (49.4)	South Africa v India at Nagpur	2010-11

Three other teams have made scores of 300-plus in the second innings of a World Cup match:

338-8 (50)	England tied with India at Bangalore	2010-11
326 (49.3)	**Zimbabwe lost to Ireland by five runs at Hobart**	**2014-15**
312 (46.2)	**Sri Lanka lost to Australia by 64 runs at Sydney**	**2014-15**

opener Anamul Haque had badly injured his shoulder while fielding, and didn't play again in the tournament. But Tamim Iqbal drove resplendently, falling five short of Bangladesh's first World Cup century, while the middle order took advantage of a flat pitch, short boundaries and some ragtag bowling. "The coach said we should bat like we're batting first," said Tamim, "not to think about the total." Coetzer's magnificent 156 in 134 balls, the highest World Cup score by an Associate player – beating Dave Houghton's 142 for Zimbabwe against New Zealand at Hyderabad in 1987 – deserved better. After an austere start as Scotland stuttered through soft dismissals for MacLeod and Gardiner, Coetzer showed that classical orthodoxy is no impediment to fast scoring. His straight-drives, often lofted, were struck with supreme timing and power: when he heaved Rubel Hossain over long-on for six, he brought up Scotland's maiden World Cup hundred, to trigger a spectacular assault on Bangladesh's seamers. Berrington and Cross then hit out in the death overs. Though 318 was over 100 clear of Scotland's highest total against a Full Member – among the Associates only Ireland had scored more in a World Cup game – another 20 runs might have brought that long-awaited victory. TIM WIGMORE

Man of the Match: K. J. Coetzer. *Attendance:* 3,491.

Scotland

K. J. Coetzer c Soumya Sarkar			
b Nasir Hossain .	156	†M. H. Cross c Sabbir Rahman	
C. S. MacLeod c Mahmudullah		b Taskin Ahmed .	20
b Mashrafe bin Mortaza .	11	J. H. Davey not out	4
H. J. W. Gardiner c Soumya Sarkar		R. M. Haq c Soumya Sarkar	
b Taskin Ahmed .	19	b Shakib Al Hasan .	1
M. W. Machan c and b Sabbir Rahman. . . .	35	A. C. Evans not out	0
*P. L. Mommsen c Soumya Sarkar		L-b 1, w 5, n-b 1	7
b Nasir Hossain .	39		
R. D. Berrington c Mushfiqur Rahim		1/13 (2) 2/38 (3) (8 wkts, 50 overs)	318
b Taskin Ahmed .	26	3/116 (4) 4/257 (5) 5/269 (1)	
		6/308 (6) 7/312 (7) 8/315 (9) 10 overs: 39-2	

I. Wardlaw did not bat.

Mashrafe bin Mortaza 8–0–60–1; Shakib Al Hasan 10–0–46–1; Taskin Ahmed 7–0–43–3; Rubel Hossain 8–0–60–0; Mahmudullah 5–0–29–0; Sabbir Rahman 7–0–47–1; Nasir Hossain 5–0–32–2.

Bangladesh

Tamim Iqbal lbw b Davey.	95	Sabbir Rahman not out	42
Soumya Sarkar c Cross b Davey	2	W 8, n-b 1	9
Mahmudullah b Wardlaw	62		
†Mushfiqur Rahim c MacLeod b Evans . .	60	1/5 (2) 2/144 (3) (4 wkts, 48.1 overs)	322
Shakib Al Hasan not out	52	3/201 (1) 4/247 (4) 10 overs: 62-1	

Anamul Haque, Nasir Hossain, *Mashrafe bin Mortaza, Rubel Hossain and Taskin Ahmed did not bat.

Wardlaw 9.1–0–75–1; Davey 10–0–68–2; Evans 10–1–67–1; Machan 7–0–45–0; Haq 10–0–49–0; Berrington 2–0–18–0.

Umpires: S. D. Fry and B. N. J. Oxenford.   Third umpire: R. J. Tucker.

Referee: D. C. Boon.

NEW ZEALAND v AFGHANISTAN

At Napier, March 8, 2015. New Zealand won by six wickets. Toss: Afghanistan.

Mohammad Nabi's decision to bat was greeted by audible sighs from the crowd. This was Napier's big day, and many feared that the combination of New Zealand's bowling and Afghanistan's batting would make it a short one. Prospects looked ominous when Boult snared Javed Ahmadi with the game's ninth ball, and Vettori – brought on for the third over to allow Boult and Southee to switch ends – bowled Usman Ghani with his first delivery. Skilfully varying his pace and flight, Vettori went on to claim four for 18, as his next three victims – including his 300th in one-day internationals – injudiciously tried to force off the back foot. His figures were the most economical ten-over spell in the tournament. At 59 for six, Afghanistan were flirting with ignominy. But the adhesive Samiullah Shenwari and belligerent left-hander Najibullah Zadran, who hit two huge sixes off Southee, added 86, and their contrasting fifties helped the total to 186, more than Australia or England had mustered against the same opposition. Afghanistan's pace attack operated with characteristic zest, but it was never likely to prevail against New Zealand's powerful line-up on a glorious day. McCullum began in his usual bristling fashion and, though there were fewer pyrotechnics after he edged a pull off Nabi on to his stumps, Guptill and Williamson batted serenely. A straightforward six-wicket win arrived with nearly 14 overs in hand, and the crowd happy that the match had at least extended past six o'clock.   TIM WIGMORE

Man of the Match: D. L. Vettori.   *Attendance:* 10,022.

Afghanistan

Javed Ahmadi lbw b Boult	1	Hamid Hassan c Milne b Anderson		16
Usman Ghani b Vettori	0	Shapoor Zadran not out		2
Nawroz Mangal b Vettori	27			
Asghar Stanikzai c Guptill b Boult	9	L-b 5, w 9		14
Samiullah Shenwari c Taylor b Anderson	54			
*Mohammad Nabi c Taylor b Vettori	6	1/5 (1) 2/6 (2) 3/24 (4)	(47.4 overs)	186
†Afsar Zazai lbw b Vettori	0	4/49 (3) 5/59 (6) 6/59 (7)		
Najibullah Zadran c Vettori b Milne	56	7/145 (8) 8/151 (9) 9/166 (5)		
Dawlat Zadran c Ronchi b Boult	1	10/186 (10)	10 overs: 33-3	

Southee 10–0–43–0; Boult 10.2–2–34–3; Vettori 10.4–4–18–4; Milne 10–0–38–1; Anderson 6.4–0–38–2; Elliott 1–0–10–0.

New Zealand

M. J. Guptill run out	57	C. J. Anderson not out		7
*B. B. McCullum b Mohammad Nabi	42			
K. S. Williamson c Samiullah Shenwari		L-b 2, w 4		6
b Shapoor Zadran	33			
L. R. P. L. Taylor not out	24	1/53 (2) 2/111 (3)	(4 wkts, 36.1 overs)	188
G. D. Elliott run out	19	3/143 (1) 4/175 (5)	10 overs: 68-1	

†L. Ronchi, D. L. Vettori, A. F. Milne, T. G. Southee and T. A. Boult did not bat.

Dawlat Zadran 9–0–51–0; Shapoor Zadran 10.2–0–45–1; Hamid Hassan 7–1–36–0; Mohammad Nabi 7.1–0–39–1; Samiullah Shenwari 3–0–15–0.

Umpires: J. D. Cloete and M. Erasmus.   Third umpire: S. J. Davis.
Referee: D. C. Boon.

AUSTRALIA v SRI LANKA

At Sydney, March 8, 2015 (day/night). Australia won by 64 runs. Toss: Australia.

Both teams beefed up their spin department, and three slow bowlers – Doherty, Senanayake and Prasanna – made World Cup debuts. But the turn never materialised, and it was batsmen who made merry, with Maxwell blasting a maiden international hundred in 51 balls to propel Australia to 376 for nine. Sri Lanka's only specialist quick, Malinga, had shared the new ball with the off-breaks of Senanayake: Australia were 41 for two in the ninth over, but Smith and Clarke quickly began to manoeuvre the spinners. They made smooth half-centuries, swelling their stand to 134 before yielding the stage to the middle-order hitters. Maxwell plundered runs all round the ground, treating spin and pace with equal brutality. He sped to 50 off 26 deliveries and was on track to become the fastest World Cup centurion; he seemed to have equalled Kevin O'Brien's record, for Ireland against England four years earlier, when he ran a single off his 50th ball, only to tell umpire Ian Gould it was a leg-bye. He reached three figures off 51 instead, a one-day record for Australia, while Watson battered 67 off 41 on his return to the side as they added a rampaging 160 for the fifth wicket in 82 deliveries. In Sri Lanka's reply, Sangakkara became the first batsman to hit three World Cup hundreds on the trot, while Dilshan struck six fours in an over against Johnson. The required rate was in sight for much of the innings, and a Sri Lankan win still appeared possible with Chandimal at the crease. But he strained his hamstring just before completing a 22-ball fifty, and had to retire in the next over. Sri Lanka's hopes departed with him.   ANDREW FERNANDO

Man of the Match: G. J. Maxwell.   *Attendance:* 39,951.

Australia

A. J. Finch st Sangakkara b Prasanna	24	M. A. Starc run out	0
D. A. Warner c Prasanna b Malinga	9	X. J. Doherty not out	0
S. P. D. Smith c Perera b Dilshan	72		
*M. J. Clarke b Malinga	68	B 1, l-b 1, w 4	6
G. J. Maxwell c Malinga b Perera	102		
S. R. Watson c Chandimal b Perera	67	1/19 (2) 2/41 (1) (9 wkts, 50 overs) 376	
J. P. Faulkner run out	0	3/175 (4) 4/177 (3)	
†B. J. Haddin c Perera b Mathews	25	5/337 (5) 6/338 (7) 7/368 (6)	
M. G. Johnson not out	3	8/373 (8) 9/374 (10) 10 overs: 49-2	

Malinga 10–0–59–2; Senanayake 9–0–59–0; Mathews 7–0–59–1; Prasanna 10–0–77–1; Perera 9–0–87–2; Dilshan 5–0–33–1.

Sri Lanka

H. D. R. L. Thirimanne c Haddin b Johnson	1	S. Prasanna b Starc	9
T. M. Dilshan lbw b Faulkner	62	S. M. S. M. Senanayake c Doherty b Starc	7
†K. C. Sangakkara c Finch b Faulkner	104	S. L. Malinga not out	0
D. P. M. D. Jayawardene run out	19	B 2, l-b 5, w 4	11
*A. D. Mathews c Haddin b Watson	35		
L. D. Chandimal retired hurt	52	1/5 (1) 2/135 (2) 3/188 (4) (46.2 overs) 312	
N. L. T. C. Perera c Doherty b Johnson	8	4/201 (3) 5/283 (5) 6/293 (7)	
W. U. Tharanga c Warner b Faulkner	4	7/305 (9) 8/307 (8) 9/312 (10) 10 overs: 69-1	

Chandimal retired hurt at 281-4.

Starc 8.2–0–29–2; Johnson 9–0–62–2; Watson 7–0–71–1; Doherty 7–0–60–0; Maxwell 6–0–35–0; Faulkner 9–0–48–3.

Umpires: Aleem Dar and I. J. Gould.   Third umpire: R. K. Illingworth.
Referee: J. J. Crowe.

BANGLADESH v ENGLAND

At Adelaide, March 9, 2015 (day/night). Bangladesh won by 15 runs. Toss: England.

England were eliminated after another anxious performance left coach Peter Moores conceding they had "let people down". But it was a memorable night for the jubilant Bangladeshis, who repeated their win over England at the 2011 World Cup in Chittagong to reach the quarter-finals for the first time. While Mahmudullah and Mushfiqur Rahim rescued Bangladesh from 99 for four with a stand of 141 (a national record for any wicket

A new low: Rubel Hossain castles James Anderson, knocking England out of the World Cup.

in the World Cup), England buckled. Bell grew inhibited after the needless run-out of Ali: in the same Rubel Hossain over, he nibbled behind, and Morgan pulled to long leg for his fifth duck in 11 one-day international innings. From 163 for six Buttler and Woakes put on 75 in ten overs – only for Buttler to undo the good work with a tentative waft. Next ball, with 38 needed from 25, Jordan fell to the tightest of calls: having thought better of a non-existent single, he dived back into his ground, but third umpire Simon Fry somehow ruled that the shoulder of his bat had bounced up as Shakib Al Hasan hit the stumps. There was still time for Tamim Iqbal to drop a sitter off Woakes at long-on, before Rubel – the quickest seamer on show – completed the job by bowling Broad and Anderson. It had all started brightly for England, as Anderson struck in each of his first two overs. But Mahmudullah chose the right balls to attack on his way to Bangladesh's first World Cup century, and the nuggety Mushfiqur chipped in, helping his side to their highest one-day total against England. As Bangladesh prepared for a quarter-final against India, England – with only a meaningless match against Afghanistan to come – steeled themselves for the post-mortem.   RICHARD HOBSON

Man of the Match: Mahmudullah.   *Attendance:* 11,963.

Bangladesh

Tamim Iqbal c Root b Anderson	2
Imrul Kayes c Jordan b Anderson	2
Soumya Sarkar c Buttler b Jordan	40
Mahmudullah run out	103
Shakib Al Hasan c Root b Ali	2
†Mushfiqur Rahim c Jordan b Broad	89
Sabbir Rahman c Morgan b Jordan	14

*Mashrafe bin Mortaza not out	6
Arafat Sunny not out	3
B 1, l-b 4, w 8, n-b 1	14

Rubel Hossain and Taskin Ahmed did not bat.

1/3 (2) 2/8 (1) (7 wkts, 50 overs) 275
3/94 (3) 4/99 (5) 5/240 (4)
6/261 (6) 7/265 (7) 10 overs: 32-2

Anderson 10–1–45–2; Broad 10–0–52–1; Jordan 10–0–59–2; Woakes 10–0–64–0; Ali 9–0–44–1; Root 1–0–6–0.

England

M. M. Ali run out	19	C. R. Woakes not out	42
I. R. Bell c Mushfiqur Rahim		C. J. Jordan run out	0
b Rubel Hossain .	63	S. C. J. Broad b Rubel Hossain	9
A. D. Hales c Mushfiqur Rahim		J. M. Anderson b Rubel Hossain	0
b Mashrafe bin Mortaza .	27		
J. E. Root c Mushfiqur Rahim			
b Mashrafe bin Mortaza .	29	L-b 4, n-b 1	5
*E. J. G. Morgan c Shakib Al Hasan			
b Rubel Hossain .	0	1/43 (1) 2/97 (3) (48.3 overs) 260
J. W. A. Taylor c Imrul Kayes		3/121 (2) 4/121 (5)	
b Taskin Ahmed .	1	5/132 (6) 6/163 (4)	
†J. C. Buttler c Mushfiqur Rahim		7/238 (7) 8/238 (9)	
b Taskin Ahmed .	65	9/260 (10) 10/260 (11) 10 overs: 50-1	

Mashrafe bin Mortaza 10–0–48–2; Rubel Hossain 9.3–0–53–4; Arafat Sunny 8–0–42–0; Shakib Al Hasan 10–0–41–0; Taskin Ahmed 9–0–59–2; Sabbir Rahman 2–0–13–0.

Umpires: B. F. Bowden and P. R. Reiffel.   Third umpire: S. D. Fry.
Referee: R. S. Madugalle.

SCOTLAND v SRI LANKA

At Hobart, March 11, 2015 (day/night). Sri Lanka won by 148 runs. Toss: Sri Lanka.

Sangakkara made history with his fourth one-day international hundred in a row; he was also the first to score four centuries in a single World Cup, and make 1,000 runs in all internationals in 2015. Sri Lanka exceeded 300 for the fourth match running, boosted by Sangakkara's third century partnership with Dilshan in that time, and their 20th in all one-day internationals; only Sachin Tendulkar and Sourav Ganguly had shared more (26). Joining forces in the sixth over, they were measured early on, as Scotland's seamers gleaned movement off the surface. But, once the threat eased, they began to crack boundaries, adding a brisk 195 in 29 overs, and completing their centuries off successive balls (Dilshan took 97, Sangakkara 86). Dilshan fell a few minutes later, whereupon Sangakkara became even more frenzied, hitting 23 off an over from Evans, before Davey dismissed Jayawardene and him in two deliveries; Sangakkara's final score was 124 off 95 balls, his highest in World Cups. Mathews reached 50 in 20, with his fourth consecutive leg-side six off Machan, but was dismissed next ball, attempting a fifth. Mommsen and Coleman struck bright half-centuries in Scotland's reply, but the required rate rose steeply, and their last six wickets fell for 26, five of them to Kulasekara and Chameera. ANDREW FERNANDO

Man of the Match: K. C. Sangakkara.   *Attendance:* 3,466.

Sri Lanka

H. D. R. L. Thirimanne c Mommsen b Evans	4	K. M. D. N. Kulasekara not out.	18
T. M. Dilshan c MacLeod b Davey	104	S. L. Malinga c Leask b Berrington	1
†K. C. Sangakkara c Cross b Davey	124	P. V. D. Chameera not out.	12
D. P. M. D. Jayawardene c MacLeod		L-b 3, w 10	13
b Davey .	2		
*A. D. Mathews c Coleman b Machan	51	1/21 (1) 2/216 (2) (9 wkts, 50 overs) 363
M. D. K. J. Perera c MacLeod b Taylor . .	24	3/244 (4) 4/244 (3)	
N. L. T. C. Perera c Coleman b Berrington .	7	5/289 (6) 6/326 (5) 7/328 (7)	
S. Prasanna c Coleman b Evans	3	8/331 (8) 9/336 (10) 10 overs: 46-1	

Taylor 10–0–46–1; Evans 10–0–72–2; Davey 8–0–63–3; Berrington 6.1–0–31–2; Leask 7–0–63–0; Coetzer 4.5–0–39–0; Machan 4–0–46–1.

Scotland

K. J. Coetzer c and b Malinga	0	R. M. L. Taylor c N. L. T. C. Perera	
C. S. MacLeod b Kulasekara	11	b Malinga	3
M. W. Machan lbw b Dilshan	19	J. H. Davey c Thirimanne b Chameera	4
*P. L. Mommsen c Thirimanne		A. C. Evans not out	1
b N. L. T. C. Perera	60	L-b 2, w 6, n-b 1	9
F. R. J. Coleman c N. L. T. C. Perera			
b Kulasekara	70	1/0 (1) 2/26 (2) 3/44 (3) (43.1 overs)	215
R. D. Berrington c Kulasekara b Chameera	29	4/162 (4) 5/189 (5) 6/192 (7)	
M. A. Leask c Sangakkara b Kulasekara	2	7/200 (8) 8/209 (9) 9/210 (6)	
†Mr.U. H. Cross c Sangakkara b Chameera	7	10/215 (10) 10 overs: 35-2	

Malinga 9–0–29–2; Kulasekara 7–0–20–3; N. L. T. C. Perera 7–0–41–1; Dilshan 5–0–15–1; Prasanna 8–0–57–0; Chameera 7.1–0–51–3.

Umpires: R. K. Illingworth and J. S. Wilson.   Third umpire: M. A. Gough.

Referee: J. J. Crowe.

NEW ZEALAND v BANGLADESH

At Hamilton, March 13, 2015 (day/night). New Zealand won by three wickets. Toss: New Zealand.

New Zealand pulled off their highest World Cup run-chase to end a sequence of seven one-day defeats by Bangladesh, six of them in Mirpur. Set 289, they quickly lost McCullum and Williamson, for his first single-figure dismissal in 24 one-day international innings. Both fell to Shakib Al Hasan, opening the bowling with his left-arm spin and captain in place of Mashrafe bin Mortaza, who had a sore throat and a calf injury (and was also in danger of an over-rate suspension). But Guptill, who finished with 105 from 100 balls, and the circumspect Taylor, whose 56 consumed 97, put on a steadying 131; Taylor passed 5,000 one-day international runs in his 144th innings, a record for New Zealand. Then Elliott and Anderson contributed 39 apiece to help ease them to their sixth win out of six, with three wickets and seven balls to spare. Bangladesh had lurched to 27 for two against Boult, before Mahmudullah – dropped third ball at second slip by Anderson off Southee – engineered a recovery with the help of Soumya Sarkar. The New Zealanders called for repellent after a swarm of insects invaded the pitch, amid reports that the bugs had caused local pharmacies to run out of spray. But Mahmudullah's concentration remained unbroken as he became only the second Bangladeshi, after Shahriar Nafees against Zimbabwe in 2006, to score successive ODI hundreds. ANDREW ALDERSON

Man of the Match: M. J. Guptill.   Attendance: 10,347.

Bangladesh

Tamim Iqbal c Anderson b Boult	13	Nasir Hossain c Taylor b Elliott	11
Imrul Kayes b Boult	2	Rubel Hossain not out	0
Soumya Sarkar c Anderson b Vettori	51	L-b 1, w 4	5
Mahmudullah not out	128		
*Shakib Al Hasan c Ronchi b Anderson	23	1/4 (2) 2/27 (1) (7 wkts, 50 overs)	288
†Mushfiqur Rahim c Ronchi b Anderson	15	3/117 (3) 4/151 (5)	
Sabbir Rahman c McCullum b Elliott	40	5/182 (6) 6/260 (7) 7/287 (8) 10 overs: 29-2	

Taijul Islam and Taskin Ahmed did not bat.

Southee 10–1–51–0; Boult 10–3–56–2; McClenaghan 8–0–68–0; Vettori 10–0–42–1; Anderson 10–0–43–2; Elliott 2–0–27–2.

New Zealand

M. J. Guptill c Rubel Hossain b Shakib Al Hasan .	105
*B. B. McCullum c Soumya Sarkar b Shakib Al Hasan .	8
K. S. Williamson c Tamim Iqbal b Shakib Al Hasan .	1
L. R. P. L. Taylor lbw b Nasir Hossain	56
G. D. Elliott c Taskin Ahmed b Rubel Hossain .	39
C. J. Anderson b Nasir Hossain	39

†L. Ronchi c Nasir Hossain b Shakib Al Hasan .	9
D. L. Vettori not out	16
T. G. Southee not out	12
L-b 1, w 4	5
1/27 (2) 2/33 (3) (7 wkts, 48.5 overs) 290	
3/164 (1) 4/210 (5)	
5/219 (4) 6/247 (7) 7/269 (6) 10 overs: 57-2	

T. A. Boult and M. J. McClenaghan did not bat.

Shakib Al Hasan 8.5–1–55–4; Taijul Islam 10–0–58–0; Rubel Hossain 8–1–40–1; Taskin Ahmed 8–0–49–0; Soumya Sarkar 4–0–19–0; Sabbir Rahman 2–0–14–0; Mahmudullah 3–0–22–0; Nasir Hossain 5–0–32–2.

Umpires: H. D. P. K. Dharmasena and R. A. Kettleborough.   Third umpire: N. J. Llong.
Referee: B. C. Broad.

AFGHANISTAN v ENGLAND

At Sydney, March 13, 2015 (day/night). England won by nine wickets (D/L). Toss: England.

Sporadic rain could not prevent England from finishing their doomed campaign with a hollow win. A desperately tepid occasion entered the realm of the bizarre when Morgan insisted he had "no regrets" about his side's performances throughout the tournament. Conditions closer to Keighley than Kabul had exposed the Afghans' techniques again, but did not douse the passion of a strong expat element in the crowd. Balls jagged and swung, and twice rain forced Afghanistan to restart their innings; then the longest of the showers ended it at 111 for seven in the 37th over. Edges were held efficiently, with Jordan and the recalled Bopara – Chris Woakes and Moeen Ali were injured – backing up the new-ball attack. Mohammad Nabi injected some urgency with a six over extra cover off Tredwell, making his first appearance in the tournament, and Shafiqullah played nicely before mistiming a sweep. Duckworth/Lewis set England 101 from 25 overs, which was never going to push them. Hales was dropped on nought and 12 by Najibullah Zadran at point off Shapoor Zadran, but Bell relished the low-pressure situation, and Taylor batted with the care of a man determined to be there at the end.   RICHARD HOBSON

Man of the Match: C. J. Jordan. *Attendance:* 9,203.

Afghanistan

Javed Ahmadi c Root b Broad	7
Nawroz Mangal c Root b Anderson	4
†Afsar Zazai c Buttler b Jordan	6
Nasir Ahmadzai c Buttler b Bopara	17
Samiullah Shenwari c Morgan b Jordan . . .	7
Shafiqullah c Bopara b Tredwell	30
*Mohammad Nabi c Tredwell b Bopara	16

Najibullah Zadran not out	12
Hamid Hassan not out	0
L-b 6, w 6	12
1/17 (2) 2/20 (1) (7 wkts, 36.2 overs) 111	
3/25 (3) 4/34 (5)	
5/65 (4) 6/93 (7) 7/101 (6) 10 overs: 24-2	

Dawlat Zadran and Shapoor Zadran did not bat.

Anderson 7–0–18–1; Broad 8–1–18–1; Jordan 6.2–2–13–2; Bopara 8–1–31–2; Tredwell 7–0–25–1.

England

A. D. Hales c Afsar Zazai b Hamid Hassan	37
I. R. Bell not out	52
J. W. A. Taylor not out	8
L-b 3, w 1	4

1/83 (1)   (1 wkt, 18.1 overs) 101
                                5 overs: 32-0

J. E. Root, *E. J. G. Morgan, †J. C. Buttler, R. S. Bopara, C. J. Jordan, J. C. Tredwell, S. C. J. Broad and J. M. Anderson did not bat.

Shapoor Zadran 4–0–25–0; Dawlat Zadran 3–0–23–0; Hamid Hassan 5–0–17–1; Mohammad Nabi 4.1–0–14–0; Samiullah Shenwari 2–0–19–0.

Umpires: B. F. Bowden and S. Ravi.   Third umpire: M. Erasmus.
Referee: D. C. Boon.

AUSTRALIA v SCOTLAND

At Hobart, March 14, 2015 (day/night). Australia won by seven wickets. Toss: Australia.
    Rain posed the main threat to Australia, who rushed to the win that would rule out a quarter-final with South Africa and a possible semi away to New Zealand. To the crowd's chagrin, Clarke chose to bowl under angry skies. Starc was glorious, chopping through the top and tail as Scotland, dazed by his accuracy and pace, equalled the World Cup record of five ducks for the second time in this tournament. MacLeod raced to a 19-ball 22 before cutting to point, but only Machan showed nous. Davey and Leask hit out lustily before light rain forced them off for half an hour, and on their return Starc wrapped things up in four deliveries. Clarke, seeking time in the middle, promoted himself to open: his 47 was fluent, but not quite quick enough to beat the rain. It arrived, heavily, as he holed out with Australia 39 runs short and 40 balls shy of the required 20 overs. Davey had become the highest Associate wicket-taker in a single World Cup when he had Watson caught behind, beating Eddo Brandes's 14 for Zimbabwe in 1992, just before they won Test status. Resuming after 95 minutes, Warner hit the first ball back for six. He and Faulkner – who sealed the win with another six – took two overs to finish the job and secure Australia's safe passage. The entire match lasted 41 overs, with none lost, despite the rain.   WILL MACPHERSON
    Man of the Match: M. A. Starc.   *Attendance:* 12,044.

Scotland

K. J. Coetzer c Smith b Starc	0	M. A. Leask not out		23
C. S. MacLeod c Warner b Starc	22	I. Wardlaw b Starc		0
M. W. Machan c Faulkner b Cummins	40			
*P. L. Mommsen c Starc b Watson	0	L-b 1, w 8		9
F. R. J. Coleman c Clarke b Johnson	0			
R. D. Berrington c Warner b Maxwell	1	1/8 (1) 2/36 (2) 3/37 (4)	(25.4 overs)	130
†M. H. Cross c Haddin b Cummins	9	4/50 (5) 5/51 (6) 6/78 (3)		
J. H. Davey b Starc	26	7/79 (7) 8/95 (9) 9/130 (8)		
R. M. L. Taylor c Haddin b Cummins	0	10/130 (11)	10 overs: 49-3	

Starc 4.4–1–14–4; Cummins 7–1–42–3; Watson 3–0–18–1; Johnson 4–1–16–1; Maxwell 4–0–24–1; Faulkner 3–0–15–0.

Australia

*M. J. Clarke c Leask b Wardlaw	47
A. J. Finch c Coleman b Taylor	20
S. R. Watson c Cross b Davey	24
J. P. Faulkner not out	16
D. A. Warner not out	21
L-b 2, w 3	5

1/30 (2) 2/88 (3)   (3 wkts, 15.2 overs) 133
3/92 (1)   10 overs: 63-1

S. P. D. Smith, G. J. Maxwell, †B. J. Haddin, M. G. Johnson, M. A. Starc and P. J. Cummins did not bat.

Wardlaw 5–0–57–1; Taylor 5–0–29–1; Davey 5–1–38–1; Leask 0.2–0–7–0.

Umpires: I. J. Gould and R. K. Illingworth.   Third umpire: J. S. Wilson.
Referee: J. J. Crowe.

POOL B

SOUTH AFRICA v ZIMBABWE

At Hamilton, February 15, 2015 (day/night). South Africa won by 62 runs. Toss: Zimbabwe.

The result might suggest a straightforward victory, but Zimbabwe were in contention for much of the match. When de Villiers departed to an acrobatic left-handed catch at long-off – Ervine clasped the ball, tossed it up while he stepped over the rope, and caught it again once safely back – South Africa were wobbling at 83 for four. But Miller and Duminy piled up a world-record fifth-wicket stand of 256, beating the 226 of Eoin Morgan and Ravi Bopara for England against Ireland at Malahide in 2013. Their attitude was confident, their running precise, their hitting clinical. But the bowling lacked thought: Zimbabwe's Plan A – a good length outside off stump – became as much of a liability in the closing overs as it had been an asset early on. Panyangara (6–2–17–1) and Chatara (5–1–13–1) had produced tight opening spells, but they were hammered at the death – though not quite as badly as Mire, whose final over cost 30 (644646), all to Miller, who ended up with nine sixes from 92 balls and a second one-day international century two matches after his first. Duminy reached his fourth hundred with a cheeky paddle-flick from the first ball of the last over, bowled by Panyangara; he rounded off the fun with a six and a four. After 28 runs off the opening powerplay, South Africa had thundered 146 off the last ten overs. Despite all this, Zimbabwe were on course at 191 for two, with their best batsmen in control. But Imran Tahir found Masakadza's leading edge in the 33rd over, Taylor slapped Morkel's slower ball to midwicket – and the initiative lurched back South Africa's way. Mire defiantly smashed Steyn and Morkel for six, but there was too much to do. NEIL MANTHORP

Man of the Match: D. A. Miller.   Attendance: 8,332.

South Africa

†Q. de Kock c Ervine b Chatara	7	J-P. Duminy not out	115
H. M. Amla b Panyangara	11	L-b 1, w 16, n-b 2	19
F. du Plessis c Taylor b Chigumbura	24		
*A. B. de Villiers c Ervine b Kamungozi	25	1/10 (1) 2/21 (2) (4 wkts, 50 overs) 339
D. A. Miller not out	138	3/67 (3) 4/83 (4) 10 overs: 28-2

F. Behardien, V. D. Philander, D. W. Steyn, M. Morkel and Imran Tahir did not bat.

Panyangara 10–2–73–1; Chatara 10–1–71–1; Mire 6–0–61–0; Chigumbura 4–0–30–1; Williams 8–0–44–0; Kamungozi 8–0–34–1; Sikandar Raza 3–0–19–0; Masakadza 1–0–6–0.

Zimbabwe

C. J. Chibhabha c Duminy b Imran Tahir . .	64	T. L. Chatara c and b Morkel	6
Sikandar Raza b Philander	5	T. Kamungozi not out	0
H. Masakadza c Amla b Imran Tahir	80		
†B. R. M. Taylor c Philander b Morkel.	40	L-b 13, w 9	22
S. C. Williams c de Kock b Duminy	8		
C. R. Ervine c de Villiers b Steyn	13	1/32 (2) 2/137 (1) (48.2 overs)	277
*E. Chigumbura run out	8	3/191 (3) 4/214 (4) 5/218 (5)	
S. F. Mire c de Villiers b Philander.	27	6/236 (7) 7/240 (6) 8/245 (9)	
T. Panyangara c de Villiers b Imran Tahir .	4	9/272 (8) 10/277 (10) 10 overs: 56-1	

Philander 8–0–30–2; Morkel 8.2–1–49–2; Steyn 9–0–64–1; Behardien 5–0–40–0; Duminy 8–0–45–1; Imran Tahir 10–0–36–3.

Umpires: R. E. J. Martinesz and R. J. Tucker. Third umpire: P. R. Reiffel.
Referee: R. S. Mahanama.

INDIA v PAKISTAN

At Adelaide, February 15, 2015 (day/night). India won by 76 runs. Toss: India.

Scarcely a hotel room was unoccupied as hordes of Indian supporters and a smaller – but equally vocal – Pakistani contingent descended on Adelaide. They would witness a game that ran to script: for the sixth time out of six since the sides first met in the World Cup, at Sydney in 1992, India won. Dhoni had chosen to bat on a pitch that was blameless at first but likely to slow up later, and India absorbed exacting early spells from Mohammad Irfan and Sohail Khan for the loss of only Rohit Sharma. Dhawan added 129 for the second wicket with Kohli, who found his range after failing to reach double figures in the tri-series with Australia and England. Kohli then put on 110 with Raina for the third, completing his 22nd one-day international century – and the first by an Indian against Pakistan in the World Cup. Sohail finished with five wickets as India were limited to an even 300, but the leg-breaks of Yasir Shah were treated contemptuously; he would not play again in the tournament. Pakistan's batting line-up felt the sum of spare parts, the result of trying to field five bowlers: Younis Khan made a rare appearance as an opener, and Umar Akmal kept wicket. A platform of 102 for two in the 24th over was serviceable, but three fell for one run, leaving Misbah-ul-Haq – not for the first time – to shoulder the burden. Unfairly, he took much of the blame on social media for Pakistan's latest World Cup misadventure against their most heated rivals. DANIEL BRETTIG

Man of the Match: V. Kohli. *Attendance:* 41,587.

India

R. G. Sharma c Misbah-ul-Haq b Sohail Khan .	15	A. M. Rahane b Sohail Khan.	0
S. Dhawan run out.	73	R. Ashwin not out	1
V. Kohli c Umar Akmal b Sohail Khan . . .	107	Mohammed Shami not out	3
S. K. Raina b Haris Sohail b Sohail Khan . .	74	L-b 2, w 3, n-b 1	6
*†M. S. Dhoni c Misbah-ul-Haq b Sohail Khan .	18	1/34 (1) 2/163 (2) (7 wkts, 50 overs)	300
R. A. Jadeja b Wahab Riaz	3	3/273 (3) 4/284 (4)	
		5/296 (6) 6/296 (5) 7/296 (7) 10 overs: 42-1	

M. Sharma and U. T. Yadav did not bat.

Mohammad Irfan 10–0–58–0; Sohail Khan 10–0–55–5; Shahid Afridi 8–0–50–0; Wahab Riaz 10–0–49–1; Yasir Shah 8–0–60–0; Haris Sohail 4–0–26–0.

Pakistan

Ahmed Shehzad c Jadeja b Yadav	47	Yasir Shah c Yadav b M. Sharma	13
Younis Khan c Dhoni b Mohammed Shami	6	Sohail Khan c Yadav b M. Sharma	7
Haris Sohail c Raina b Ashwin	36	Mohammad Irfan not out	1
*Misbah-ul-Haq c Rahane b Mohammed Shami	76	L-b 1, w 10, n-b 1	12
Sohaib Maqsood c Raina b Yadav	0		
†Umar Akmal c Dhoni b Jadeja	0		
Shahid Afridi c Kohli b Mohammed Shami	22		
Wahab Riaz c Dhoni b Mohammed Shami	4		

1/11 (2) 2/79 (3) 3/102 (1)   (47 overs) 224
4/102 (5) 5/103 (6) 6/149 (7)
7/154 (8) 8/203 (9) 9/220 (4)
10/224 (10)   10 overs: 46-1

Yadav 10–0–50–2; Mohammed Shami 9–1–35–4; M. Sharma 9–0–35–2; Raina 1–0–6–0; Ashwin 8–3–41–1; Jadeja 10–0–56–1.

Umpires: I. J. Gould and R. A. Kettleborough.   Third umpire: S. J. Davis.
Referee: R. S. Madugalle.

IRELAND v WEST INDIES

At Nelson, February 16, 2015. Ireland won by four wickets. Toss: Ireland.

Ireland's strong showing at previous World Cups meant that the scalp of another Full Member – their fourth, after Pakistan and Bangladesh in 2007, and England in 2011 – was

no great surprise. (They also became the first side in the tournament's history to chase down 300 or more on three occasions.) West Indies did not ooze invincibility: without the well-travelled Trinidadian all-rounders Dwayne Bravo and Kieron Pollard, who were omitted in the aftermath of the aborted tour of India, they were captained by the inexperienced Holder. Put in, they made 304, though on a small ground that left the door ajar. Joyce hit a classy 84 from 67 balls, sharing stands of 106 with Stirling – Man of the Match for his hard-hit 92 – and 96 with Niall O'Brien, who became the first Ireland batsman to score 500 World Cup runs. O'Brien steered them to a convincing victory, despite a wobble that, with 32 needed, saw four wickets tumble for 18 in five overs. There was no panic, however, and Mooney – as he had against England in 2011 – hit the winning four. Sammy, like Mooney fined for audible obscenities, had been instrumental in West Indies' recovery from 87 for five. He and Lendl Simmons added 154 as the innings picked up pace: Russell smashed 27 from 13 balls as the last ten overs yielded 124. Ireland's performance, described by Phil

Emerald smile: John Mooney and Niall O'Brien land another blow for Ireland.

Hagen Hopkins, Getty Images

Simmons (Lendl's uncle) as probably the best he had seen during his time with them, strengthened his hand as West Indies searched for a new coach; they appointed him a month later. IAN CALLENDER

Man of the Match: P. R. Stirling.   *Attendance:* 4,143.

THE CONTRACTION OF THE WORLD CUP

Ireland take on the old order

Tim Wigmore

"Best team in Europe" trumpeted a banner during Ireland's game against India at Hamilton. The previous night, Bangladesh's win over England had left Ireland as Europe's only hope of a quarter-finalist. They failed – but it couldn't detract from the mark they made.

When captain William Porterfield thumped Kemar Roach over square leg for six in the second over of Ireland's opening game, it set a template – a mix of controlled aggression, palpable self-belief and skill that brought them victories over West Indies, the UAE and Zimbabwe. In the last three World Cups, Ireland have beaten more Test teams (five) than England.

The Irish weren't afraid to take a chance. Against West Indies, they chose off-spinner Andy McBrine – who a year earlier had been belted for 25 in an over by the Netherlands at the World Twenty20 – to bowl to Chris Gayle in the powerplay. McBrine began with a maiden, and his meticulous line yielded just 26 runs from ten overs. Against Zimbabwe, Andy Balbirnie, who had just hit his first one-day international half-century, was promoted to No. 4 to avoid exposing two left-handers to off-spin. Emboldened, he swept and reverse-swept with panache in a magnificent 79-ball 97. England displayed no such flexibility: even when their openers put on 172 in 30 overs against Scotland, they persisted with Gary Ballance at No. 3; he slowed down the innings with an 18-ball ten.

The narrative of Irish flair and craic besting English rigidity became irresistible, but it was a little too cute. For all the references to data by coach Peter Moores and captain Eoin Morgan, England actually made less use of statistics than in previous years. Nor did they have a monopoly on conservatism. There was an obvious drawback in playing a battery of medium-pacers, yet Ireland chose not to pick the speedy Craig Young, despite his 16 ODI wickets at 14 apiece, or Peter Chase, whose extra bounce had attracted attention at Durham in 2014.

Still, while England – none more so than their Irish captain – seemed overwhelmed, Ireland embodied a quaint ideal: cricketers playing above themselves in their national colours. Although the schedule denied them fixtures in Sydney or Melbourne, the host cities with the biggest Irish-origin communities, crowds across Australasia embraced the men in green and their cheerleader Adrian Raftery, better known as Larry the Leprechaun.

But beneath the joy was a simmering anger. Ireland had played just nine ODIs against Full Member teams in the previous four years, and received an eighth of the ICC funding enjoyed by Zimbabwe. England not only poached their best players – Morgan and Boyd Rankin, who preferred an England Lions tour to a World Cup – but seemed determined to keep Ireland down. The ECB and their chairman Giles Clarke were privately leading the charge for the 2019 World Cup to be reduced to ten teams; they had already led the restructuring of the ICC, which was due to more than halve the proportion of revenue awarded to the 95 Associates and Affiliates; and they had not supported Cricket Ireland's bids for Full Membership.

Before the World Cup, Ireland's players resolved to draw attention to such inequity, painfully aware that – with the tournament contracting and the next two qualifying tournaments to be held in Bangladesh and Zimbabwe – this could well be their last. Porterfield queried why ICC membership had to be tiered into Full, Associate and Affiliate categories. And, after the ICC tweeted that Ireland's campaign was "memorable and inspiring", Porterfield replied: "So memorable and inspiring that you have decided to cut the next WC to 10 teams. What is your vision for the game of cricket?" Over 2,000 retweets suggested plenty agreed.

West Indies

D. R. Smith c Mooney b K. J. O'Brien	18	A. D. Russell not out	27
C. H. Gayle c K. J. O'Brien b Dockrell	36	*J. O. Holder not out	0
D. M. Bravo run out	0	L-b 1, w 9	10
M. N. Samuels lbw b Dockrell	21		
†D. Ramdin lbw b Dockrell	1	1/30 (1) 2/31 (3) (7 wkts, 50 overs)	304
L. M. P. Simmons c Dockrell b Sorensen	102	3/78 (2) 4/78 (4)	
D. J. G. Sammy c Dockrell b Mooney	89	5/87 (5) 6/241 (7) 7/302 (6) 10 overs: 40-2	

J. E. Taylor and K. A. J. Roach did not bat.

Mooney 7–1–59–1; Sorensen 8–0–64–1; McBrine 10–1–26–0; K. J. O'Brien 9–0–71–1; Dockrell 10–0–50–3; Stirling 6–0–33–0.

Ireland

*W. T. S. Porterfield c Ramdin b Gayle	23	J. F. Mooney not out	6
P. R. Stirling c Ramdin b Samuels	92		
E. C. Joyce c Bravo b Taylor	84	B 4, w 9	13
N. J. O'Brien not out	79		
A. Balbirnie c Bravo b Taylor	9	1/71 (1) 2/177 (2) (6 wkts, 45.5 overs)	307
†G. C. Wilson c Gayle b Taylor	1	3/273 (3) 4/285 (5)	
K. J. O'Brien run out	0	5/290 (6) 6/291 (7) 10 overs: 61-0	

G. H. Dockrell, M. C. Sorensen and A. R. McBrine did not bat.

Holder 9–1–44–0; Roach 6–0–52–0; Taylor 8.5–0–71–3; Russell 6–0–33–0; Gayle 8–0–41–1; Sammy 3–0–25–0; Samuels 4–0–25–1; Simmons 1–0–12–0.

Umpires: R. K. Illingworth and B. N. J. Oxenford.   Third umpire: C. B. Gaffaney.
Referee: B. C. Broad.

UNITED ARAB EMIRATES v ZIMBABWE

At Nelson, February 19, 2015. Zimbabwe won by four wickets. Toss: Zimbabwe.

Three days after Ireland's victory over West Indies, the UAE threatened to topple a Test nation for the first time. When Mire edged Mohammad Naveed behind, Zimbabwe were 167 for five, needing another 119 at nearly seven an over. But Williams and Ervine approached the equation with calmness and skill, and the batting powerplay yielded a risk-free 45. Even when Ervine fell, popping up a return catch to Krishnachandran, Williams's resolve remained unbroken. Shrewd placement and assiduous running defined his innings, though he sealed the win with a flourish: three consecutive fours off Naveed, who had bowled with bite on one of the tournament's most batsman-friendly grounds. Even in defeat, the UAE had proved a point. They were unrecognisable from the motley bunch who appeared in the 1996 World Cup, when Sultan Zarawani faced Allan Donald in a sunhat, and was hit on the head first ball. Their captain this time, Mohammad Tauqir – at 43 the oldest to lead a side at the World Cup – removed both openers, including Chakabva, whose back foot slipped on to the stumps as he worked him to leg. Chatara bowled with vim for Zimbabwe, but seven UAE players passed 20, aided by shoddy fielding; and though they repeatedly got out when set, 285 was their best ODI total. Batting too low at No. 6, Shaiman Anwar played with panache for 67, raising a 37-ball fifty with an emphatic straight six off Panyangara.   TIM WIGMORE

Man of the Match: S. C. Williams.   *Attendance:* 2,643.

United Arab Emirates

Amjad Ali c Ervine b Chatara	7	Amjad Javed not out	25
A. R. Berenger c Taylor b Mire	22	Mohammad Naveed not out	23
K. Krishnachandran c Chigumbura b Mire	34	B 4, l-b 6, w 15, n-b 1	26
Khurram Khan c Williams b Chatara	45		
†S. P. Patil c Chakabva b Williams	32	1/26 (1) 2/40 (2) (7 wkts, 50 overs) 285	
Shaiman Anwar c Ervine b Williams	67	3/122 (3) 4/134 (4)	
R. Mustafa c Taylor b Chatara	4	5/216 (5) 6/230 (7) 7/232 (6) 10 overs: 34-1	

Nasir Aziz and *Mohammad Tauqir did not bat.

Panyangara 9–0–66–0; Chatara 10–1–42–3; Mire 8–0–39–2; Kamungozi 10–0–53–0; Chigumbura 1–0–12–0; Williams 8–0–43–2; Sikandar Raza 3–0–11–0; Masakadza 1–0–9–0.

Zimbabwe

Sikandar Raza c Krishnachandran b Mohammad Tauqir	46	C. R. Ervine c and b Krishnachandran	42
R. W. Chakabva hit wkt b Mohammad Tauqir	35	*E. Chigumbura not out	14
H. Masakadza lbw b Amjad Javed	1	L-b 6, w 10	16
†B. R. M. Taylor lbw b Nasir Aziz	47	1/64 (1) 2/72 (3) (6 wkts, 48 overs) 286	
S. C. Williams not out	76	3/112 (2) 4/144 (4)	
S. F. Mire c Patil b Mohammad Naveed	9	5/167 (6) 6/250 (7) 10 overs: 55-0	

T. Panyangara, T. L. Chatara and T. Kamungozi did not bat.

Mohammad Naveed 10–1–60–1; Amjad Javed 9–0–49–1; Nasir Aziz 10–0–53–1; Mohammad Tauqir 9–0–51–2; Krishnachandran 9–0–59–1; Mustafa 1–0–8–0.

Umpires: J. D. Cloete and C. B. Gaffaney.   Third umpire: R. K. Illingworth.
Referee: B. C. Broad.

PAKISTAN v WEST INDIES

At Christchurch (Hagley Oval), February 21, 2015. West Indies won by 150 runs. Toss: Pakistan.

Nineteen balls was all it took for West Indies to dismantle Pakistan's top order. They soon condemned them to their second heavy defeat of the tournament, and boosted their own chances of a quarter-final place following their humbling loss to Ireland five days earlier. Set 311, Pakistan should have been in with a shout: the pitch was true, the square boundaries short, and the outfield fast. But they imploded horribly. Taylor made short work of the out-of-form Nasir Jamshed, inducing a miscued pull with a quick bouncer outside off from the second ball. Younis Khan was caught behind off the final delivery of the over, and Taylor scalped a third duck when Haris Sohail cut a short one not wide enough for the stroke and was caught at backward point. When Ahmed Shehzad sliced Holder to gully, Pakistan were one for four after 3.1 overs. No side had lost their first four wickets in a one-day international so cheaply (the previous worst was four, by Canada against Zimbabwe at Port-of-Spain in 2006). Misbah-ul-Haq fell to Russell to make it 25 for five, and half-centuries from Sohaib Maqsood and Umar Akmal merely limited the damage, as they went down to their heaviest defeat by West Indies. Earlier, most of the West Indian batsmen had made a start, thanks in part to some dismal fielding from Pakistan, who dropped four chances. Darren Bravo would not play again in the tournament after pulling a hamstring on 49 and departing the scene on a golf buggy, but Russell's 13-ball unbeaten 42 helped plunder 89 off the last six overs.   ANAND VASU

Man of the Match: A. D. Russell.   *Attendance:* 14,641.

West Indies

D. R. Smith c Harris Sohail b Sohail Khan	23	D. J. G. Sammy c Shahid Afridi	
C. H. Gayle c Wahab Riaz		b Wahab Riaz	30
b Mohammad Irfan	4	A. D. Russell not out	42
D. M. Bravo retired hurt	49	B 2, l-b 6, w 14, n-b 1	23
M. N. Samuels c sub (Yasir Shah)			
b Haris Sohail	38	1/17 (2) 2/28 (1) (6 wkts, 50 overs)	310
†D. Ramdin c sub (Yasir Shah) b Haris Sohail	51	3/103 (4) 4/194 (5)	
L. M. P. Simmons run out	50	5/259 (7) 6/310 (6) 10 overs: 46-2	

*J. O. Holder, J. E. Taylor and S. J. Benn did not bat.

Bravo retired hurt at 152-3.

Mohammad Irfan 10–0–44–1; Sohail Khan 10–1–73–1; Shahid Afridi 10–0–48–0; Haris Sohail 9–0–62–2; Wahab Riaz 10–0–67–1; Sohaib Maqsood 1–0–8–0.

Pakistan

Nasir Jamshed c Russell b Taylor	0	Sohail Khan c Ramdin b Benn	1
Ahmed Shehzad c Simmons b Holder	1	Mohammad Irfan not out	2
Younis Khan c Ramdin b Taylor	0		
Haris Sohail c sub (J. L. Carter) b Taylor	0	L-b 3, w 5, n-b 1	9
*Misbah-ul-Haq c Gayle b Russell	7		
Sohaib Maqsood c Benn b Sammy	50	1/0 (1) 2/1 (3) 3/1 (4) (39 overs)	160
†Umar Akmal c Smith b Russell	59	4/1 (2) 5/25 (5) 6/105 (6)	
Shahid Afridi c Holder b Benn	28	7/139 (7) 8/155 (9) 9/157 (8)	
Wahab Riaz c Ramdin b Russell	3	10/160 (10) 10 overs: 25-4	

Taylor 7–1–15–3; Holder 7–2–23–1; Russell 8–2–33–3; Sammy 8–0–47–1; Benn 9–0–39–2.

Umpires: M. Erasmus and N. J. Llong.   Third umpire: S. Ravi.
Referee: D. C. Boon.

INDIA v SOUTH AFRICA

At Melbourne, February 22, 2015 (day/night). India won by 130 runs. Toss: India.

A vast crowd, overwhelmingly backing India, and second in size in this tournament only to the final – enjoyed themselves as Dhawan compiled a slick, stylish century in his wife's home city. It was his seventh and highest one-day international century, with the pick of his 18 boundaries an audacious ramp off Parnell, followed next ball by a flourishing straight-drive. Dropped by Amla off Parnell at backward point on 53, Dhawan added 127 with Kohli, who looked in ominous form until smashing an Imran Tahir long-hop to midwicket. It had been exactly the sort of acceleration required after a cautious approach had brought India just 37 in the first 11 overs. Rahane's 79 from 60 balls was achieved in classic fashion, without a hint of improvisation, against an attack that lost Philander to a hamstring problem after he had bowled four overs. When South Africa batted, Mohammed Shami and Mohit Sharma followed predetermined plans for each batsman with precision, while a short back-stop for du Plessis, almost behind the keeper, cut off his signature lapsweep. There were two run-outs, and the last eight wickets tumbled for 69. India's victory was well prepared and ruthlessly executed. "I just want to feel sad in my room for a while," said de Villiers.   NEIL MANTHORP

Man of the Match: S. Dhawan.   *Attendance:* 86,876.

India

R. G. Sharma run out	0	R. Ashwin not out	5
S. Dhawan c Amla b Parnell	137	Mohammed Shami not out	4
V. Kohli c du Plessis b Imran Tahir	46	L-b 2, w 6, n-b 2	10
A. M. Rahane lbw b Steyn	79		
S. K. Raina c sub (R. R. Rossouw) b Morkel	6	1/9 (1) 2/136 (3) (7 wkts, 50 overs) 307
*†M. S. Dhoni c de Kock b Morkel	18	3/261 (2) 4/269 (5)
R. A. Jadeja run out	2	5/278 (4) 6/284 (7) 7/302 (6) 10 overs: 36-1

M. Sharma and U. T. Yadav did not bat.

Steyn 10–1–55–1; Philander 4–1–19–0; Duminy 7–0–39–0; Morkel 10–0–59–2; Imran Tahir 10–0–48–1; Parnell 9–0–85–1.

South Africa

H. M. Amla c Mohammed Shami		D. W. Steyn c Dhawan b Mohammed Shami	1
b M. Sharma .	22	M. Morkel b Ashwin	2
†Q. de Kock c Kohli b Mohammed Shami . .	7	Imran Tahir lbw b Jadeja	8
F. du Plessis c Dhawan b M. Sharma	55	L-b 1, w 6	7
*A. B. de Villiers run out	30		
D. A. Miller run out	22	1/12 (2) 2/40 (1) 3/108 (4) (40.2 overs) 177
J-P. Duminy c Raina b Ashwin	6	4/133 (3) 5/147 (6) 6/153 (5)
W. D. Parnell not out	17	7/153 (8) 8/158 (9) 9/161 (10)
V. D. Philander lbw b Ashwin.	0	10/177 (11) 10 overs: 38-1

Yadav 6–0–34–0; Mohammed Shami 8–1–30–2; M. Sharma 7–0–31–2; Jadeja 8.2–0–37–1; Ashwin 10–0–41–3; Raina 1–0–3–0.

Umpires: Aleem Dar and R. A. Kettleborough.   Third umpire: S. J. Davis.
Referee: J. J. Crowe.

WEST INDIES v ZIMBABWE

At Canberra, February 24, 2015 (day/night). West Indies won by 73 runs (D/L). Toss: West Indies.

With records tumbling like ninepins, it was easy to forget how close Gayle had come to another one-day failure. Zimbabwe were convinced he was lbw first ball, and the review foundered solely on the rock that is umpire's call. Had the decision fallen their way, Panyangara would have reduced West Indies to one for two in four balls. Instead Gayle, who had made one fifty in his 19 previous one-day internationals, accumulated steadily before peppering the stands with some characteristically monstrous hitting. His 215 – then the highest World Cup score, beating Gary Kirsten's 188 for South Africa against the UAE in 1996 – featured 16 sixes, equalling the ODI record; he and Samuels, relatively sedate in making 133 from 156 balls, put on all of West Indies' 372 runs, their highest

MOST SIXES IN A ONE-DAY INTERNATIONAL INNINGS

16	R. G. Sharma (209 from 158 balls)	India v Australia at Bangalore	2013-14
16	A. B. de Villiers (149 from 44)	South Africa v West Indies at Johannesburg. . .	2014-15
16	**C. H. Gayle (215 from 147)**	**West Indies v Zimbabwe at Canberra**	**2014-15**
15	S. R. Watson (185* from 96)	Australia v Bangladesh at Mirpur	2010-11
14	C. J. Anderson (131* from 47)	New Zealand v West Indies at Queenstown . . .	2013-14
12	X. M. Marshall (157* from 118)	West Indies v Canada at King City	2008
11	S. T. Jayasuriya (134 from 65)	Sri Lanka v Pakistan at Singapore. . .	1995-96
11	Shahid Afridi (102 from 40)	Pakistan v Sri Lanka at Nairobi.	1996-97
11	D. Ramdin (169 from 121)	West Indies v Bangladesh at Basseterre . . .	2014-15
11	**M. J. Guptill (237* from 163)**	**New Zealand v West Indies at Wellington . .**	**2014-15**
11	**A. B. de Villiers (119 from 61)**	**South Africa v India at Mumbai**	**2015-16**

one-day international total, and the highest partnership in List A cricket. In the 36th over, and with the score 166 for one, Gayle reached his 22nd one-day international hundred; it was the cue for such rapid acceleration that the opposition and the fans were left gobsmacked. He moved from 100 to 150 in 21 balls, then shot to 200 – the first non-Indian to reach the mark in ODIs, following Sachin Tendulkar, Virender Sehwag and Rohit Sharma (twice) – from a dozen more. West Indies cracked 152 in the last ten overs, before Gayle sliced the final delivery to deep point. Williams and Ervine hit classy half-centuries in a spirited Zimbabwe chase, interrupted briefly by rain that revised their target to 363 in 48 overs. But, with Gayle taking two wickets and a catch, the headlines were always going to be about one man. "This innings will ignite a lot of my passion," he promised. "It's a new beginning." DILEEP PREMACHANDRAN

Man of the Match: C. H. Gayle. *Attendance:* 5,544.

West Indies

D. R. Smith b Panyangara	0
C. H. Gayle c Chigumbura b Masakadza	215
M. N. Samuels not out	133
B 1, l-b 2, w 16, n-b 5	24

1/0 (1)	(2 wkts, 50 overs)	372
2/372 (2)	10 overs: 43-1	

J. L. Carter, †D. Ramdin, L. M. P. Simmons, D. J. G. Sammy, A. D. Russell, *J. O. Holder, J. E. Taylor and N. O. Miller did not bat.

Panyangara 9–0–82–1; Chatara 9.4–0–74–0; Williams 5–0–48–0; Chigumbura 7–0–44–0; Sikandar Raza 10–1–45–0; Kamungozi 3–0–37–0; Masakadza 6.2–0–39–1.

Zimbabwe

Sikandar Raza c Simmons b Holder	26	T. L. Chatara b Miller		16
R. W. Chakabva lbw b Holder	2	T. Kamungozi not out		6
H. Masakadza lbw b Taylor	5			
†B. R. M. Taylor c Ramdin b Samuels	37	L-b 9, w 14, n-b 2		25
S. C. Williams c Smith b Holder	76			
C. R. Ervine b Gayle	52	1/11 (2) 2/26 (3) 3/46 (1)	(44.3 overs)	289
S. Matsikenyeri lbw b Gayle	19	4/126 (4) 5/177 (5) 6/226 (6)		
*E. Chigumbura c Gayle b Taylor	21	7/239 (7) 8/254 (9) 9/266 (8)		
T. Panyangara c Ramdin b Taylor	4	10/289 (10)	9 overs: 50-3	

Taylor 10–0–38–3; Holder 7–0–48–3; Miller 6.3–0–48–1; Samuels 9–0–59–1; Russell 5–0–44–0; Sammy 1–0–8–0; Gayle 6–0–35–2.

Umpires: S. J. Davis and I. J. Gould. Third umpire: R. E. J. Martinesz.

Referee: R. S. Mahanama.

IRELAND v UNITED ARAB EMIRATES

At Brisbane, February 25, 2015 (day/night). Ireland won by two wickets. Toss: Ireland.

Ireland made it two out of two at the World Cup – and 11 in a row against the UAE in limited-overs cricket – though victory was not straightforward. Even Dockrell's winning hit, with four balls remaining, only narrowly eluded a fielder, summing up a run-chase full of thrills and near misses. Opening bowlers Mohammad Naveed and Guruge had found movement under the lights to limit Ireland to 50 for one in 14 overs; Amjad Javed clipped Joyce's off stump, only for the bail to wobble and settle back in the groove. Just after halfway, Ireland were an iffy 97 for four. Then Wilson, who had fallen in single figures in nine of his previous 14 one-day international innings, struck 80 from 69 balls. Even that was upstaged by Kevin O'Brien, who dominated their sixth-wicket stand of 72, smashing 50 from 25. His departure, aiming for a third six, threatened to cede the initiative, before

Dockrell settled matters. Earlier, the UAE recovered from 131 for six after 35 overs thanks largely to a maiden ODI hundred for 35-year-old Shaiman Anwar. The Irish bowlers lost their discipline in the batting powerplay, when the UAE added 47, and Shaiman reached three figures from 79 balls, sharing a World Cup record seventh-wicket stand of 107 with Javed in 12 overs. It was not quite enough.   IAN CALLENDER

Man of the Match: G. C. Wilson.   *Attendance:* 5,249.

United Arab Emirates

Amjad Ali c Sorensen b K. J. O'Brien	45	Mohammad Naveed c and b Cusack 13
A. R. Berenger c Porterfield b Stirling	13	*Mohammad Tauqir not out 2
K. Krishnachandran c K. J. O'Brien		A. M. Guruge not out 0
b Stirling .	0	B 1, l-b 4, w 11, n-b 1 17
Khurram Khan lbw b Dockrell	36	
†S. P. Patil c Stirling b K. J. O'Brien	2	1/49 (2) 2/53 (3) (9 wkts, 50 overs) 278
Shaiman Anwar c Wilson b Sorensen	106	3/73 (1) 4/78 (5)
R. Mustafa c Wilson b Cusack	2	5/125 (4) 6/131 (7) 7/238 (8)
Amjad Javed c Joyce b Sorensen........	42	8/269 (6) 9/276 (9) 10 overs: 44-0

Mooney 6–0–32–0; Sorensen 10–0–60–2; Cusack 10–0–54–2; Stirling 10–0–27–2; K. J. O'Brien 7–0–61–2; Dockrell 7–0–39–1.

Ireland

*W. T. S. Porterfield b Mohammad Tauqir..	37	J. F. Mooney c Amjad Ali b Amjad Javed .	2
P. R. Stirling c Patil b Guruge	3	A. R. Cusack not out 5
E. C. Joyce c Patil b Amjad Javed	37	G. H. Dockrell not out 7
N. J. O'Brien lbw b Mohammad Tauqir ...	17	
A. Balbirnie c sub (Saqlain Haider)		B 4, l-b 3, w 2, n-b 2 11
b Mohammad Naveed .	30	
†G. C. Wilson c Amjad Javed		1/4 (2) 2/72 (3) (8 wkts, 49.2 overs) 279
b Mohammad Naveed .	80	3/94 (1) 4/97 (4)
K. J. O'Brien c Mohammad Naveed		5/171 (5) 6/243 (7)
b Amjad Javed .	50	7/259 (8) 8/267 (6) 10 overs: 35-1

M. C. Sorensen did not bat.

Mohammad Naveed 9.2–1–65–2; Guruge 7–0–21–1; Amjad Javed 10–0–60–3; Mohammad Tauqir 9–0–38–2; Mustafa 9–0–45–0; Krishnachandran 5–0–43–0.

Umpires: M. A. Gough and N. J. Llong.   Third umpire: H. D. P. K. Dharmasena.
Referee: R. S. Madugalle.

SOUTH AFRICA v WEST INDIES

At Sydney, February 27, 2015 (day/night). South Africa won by 257 runs. Toss: South Africa.

South Africa were 146 for three when de Villiers entered in the 30th over, to face Gayle's off-spin with three men around the bat. Content to let Rossouw make the running, he eased to 36 from his first 26 deliveries, before belting 17 from the 40th. It was the cue for a carnival of savagery, as 150 spewed from the last ten overs. A fine golfer, de Villiers employed a classic drive to club four sixes over long-on, and added a couple of sweeps over fine leg from his opposite number, Holder; the 48th over cost 34, and the last 30. De Villiers needed 30 deliveries to reach 50, but his century came up in just 52, the second-quickest in World Cups. The 150, however, was without precedent in any one-day international, arriving from his 64th ball, and smashing the previous record – 83, by Shane Watson for Australia against Bangladesh at Mirpur in April 2011. It came only six weeks after de Villiers had plundered 149 from 44 balls against largely the same attack at Johannesburg. Now he finished with 162 from 66, with 17 fours and eight sixes. Holder's courage in bowling himself at the death brought up a century of his own: 104 from ten overs, the most expensive by a West Indian in ODIs, after starting with 5–2–9–1. The mayhem will not be readily forgotten, particularly a lap-swept six over fine leg off Russell from two feet outside off stump. Bewildered and broken, West Indies soon looked to be heading for more records. Gayle, fresh from the World Cup's first double-century, fell to his fourth ball, and they plummeted to 63 for seven in the face of some sublime leg-spin and googlies from Imran Tahir. Holder's defiant half-century could not avert his side's heaviest defeat, which also equalled the heaviest in World Cups – until Afghanistan outdid them against Australia a few days later. NEIL MANTHORP

Man of the Match: A. B. de Villiers. *Attendance:* 23,612.

South Africa

†Q. de Kock c Russell b Holder	12	F. Behardien not out		10
H. M. Amla lbw b Gayle	65	L-b 2, w 11, n-b 3		16
F. du Plessis c Ramdin b Gayle	62			
R. R. Rossouw c Ramdin b Russell	61	1/18 (1) 2/145 (3)	(5 wkts, 50 overs)	408
*A. B. de Villiers not out	162	3/146 (2) 4/280 (4)		
D. A. Miller c Taylor b Russell	20	5/328 (6)	10 overs: 30-1	

D. W. Steyn, K. J. Abbott, M. Morkel and Imran Tahir did not bat.

Taylor 8–1–64–0; Holder 10–2–104–1; Russell 9–0–74–2; Samuels 2–0–14–0; Benn 10–0–79–0; Sammy 7–0–50–0; Gayle 4–0–21–2.

West Indies

D. R. Smith c Miller b Imran Tahir	31	J. E. Taylor not out		15
C. H. Gayle b Abbott	3	S. J. Benn c Amla b Morkel		1
M. N. Samuels c de Kock b Abbott	0			
J. L. Carter c de Villiers b Morkel	10	L-b 5, w 3		8
†D. Ramdin b Imran Tahir	22			
L. M. P. Simmons lbw b Imran Tahir	0	1/12 (2) 2/16 (3) 3/52 (4)	(33.1 overs)	151
D. J. G. Sammy st de Kock b Imran Tahir	5	4/52 (1) 5/53 (6) 6/63 (7)		
A. D. Russell c Abbott b Imran Tahir	0	7/63 (8) 8/108 (5) 9/150 (9)		
*J. O. Holder c Amla b Steyn	56	10/151 (11)	10 overs: 47-2	

Steyn 7–0–24–1; Abbott 8–0–37–2; Morkel 5.1–0–23–2; Imran Tahir 10–2–45–5; du Plessis 3–0–17–0.

Umpires: S. J. Davis and I. J. Gould. Third umpire: R. E. J. Martinesz.
Referee: R. S. Mahanama.

INDIA v UNITED ARAB EMIRATES

At Perth, February 28, 2015 (day/night). India won by nine wickets. Toss: United Arab Emirates.

The UAE unravelled in haste, first against disciplined and energetic seam and swing, then against canny, skilful spin. Ashwin's off-breaks proved especially troublesome. Changing his pace and trajectory, but resorting to variations only sparingly, he winkled out the heart of the batting to finish with a career-best four for 25 – the best figures by a spinner in a one-day international at the WACA since 1991-92, when Ravi Shastri, now the Indian team director, took five for 15 against Australia. Krishnachandran popped a catch to leg slip to depart for a laboured four from 27 balls, Swapnil Patil edged an arm-ball, and Khurram Khan chose the wrong delivery to sweep, gloving to slip. A sprightly 35 from Shaiman Anwar, who put on 31 for the last wicket with Guruge – comfortably the highest stand of the innings – just about pushed the UAE into three figures, but not to a total that was going to trouble India. Dhawan fell early, before Rohit Sharma helped himself to an unbeaten 57; India got over the line with 187 balls to spare. Dhoni said the Associate nations deserved more opportunities against Full Members, before adding: "Not against India." ANAND VASU

Man of the Match: R. Ashwin. *Attendance:* 8,718.

United Arab Emirates

Amjad Ali c Dhoni b Bhuvneshwar Kumar	4	*Mohammad Tauqir b Jadeja		1
A. R. Berenger c Dhoni b Yadav	4	A. M. Guruge not out		10
K. Krishnachandran c Raina b Ashwin	4			
Khurram Khan c Raina b Ashwin	14	L-b 4, w 9		13
†S. P. Patil c Dhawan b Ashwin	7			
Shaiman Anwar b Yadav	35	1/7 (2) 2/13 (1) 3/28 (3)	(31.3 overs)	102
R. Mustafa lbw b M. Sharma	2	4/41 (5) 5/44 (4) 6/52 (7)		
Amjad Javed c Raina b Jadeja	2	7/61 (8) 8/68 (9) 9/71 (10)		
Mohammad Naveed b Ashwin	6	10/102 (6)	10 overs: 28-2	

Bhuvneshwar Kumar 5–0–19–1; Yadav 6.3–2–15–2; Ashwin 10–1–25–4; M. Sharma 5–1–16–1; Jadeja 5–0–23–2.

India

R. G. Sharma not out	57
S. Dhawan c Mustafa b Mohammad Naveed	14
V. Kohli not out	33

1/29 (2)	(1 wkt, 18.5 overs)	104
	10 overs: 52-1	

A. M. Rahane, S. K. Raina, *†M. S. Dhoni, R. A. Jadeja, R. Ashwin, Bhuvneshwar Kumar, M. Sharma and U. T. Yadav did not bat.

Mohammad Naveed 5–0–35–1; Guruge 6–1–19–0; Amjad Javed 2–0–12–0; Krishnachandran 3–0–17–0; Mohammad Tauqir 2.5–0–21–0.

Umpires: B. F. Bowden and M. A. Gough.   Third umpire: N. J. Llong.
Referee: R. S. Madugalle.

PAKISTAN v ZIMBABWE

At Brisbane, March 1, 2015 (day/night). Pakistan won by 20 runs. Toss: Pakistan.

Pakistan were glimpsing the exit door after defeats by India and West Indies. But a virtuoso all-round display from Wahab Riaz, plus a magnificent new-ball spell from Mohammad Irfan, inspired victory. Yet Zimbabwe, without a World Cup win over a Full Member nation since 1999, should have prevailed. Having limited Pakistan to 235, they were in charge at 128 for three. Then Taylor tickled Wahab down the leg side to end a stand of 54 from 49 balls with Williams, who batted with fluency until he cut to backward point as the collapse kicked in: 150 for four became 168 for eight. Chigumbura, nursing a torn quadriceps which had forced him off the field, inched Zimbabwe close, but the runs came too slowly. Pakistan's innings had depended on a stolid 121-ball 73 from Misbah-ul-Haq, and late impetus provided by Wahab's 46-ball unbeaten 54. Only 14 had come from the first ten overs as Misbah and Haris Sohail rebuilt from four for two in painstaking fashion, before Umar Akmal injected momentum. But a Williams-induced wobble – Shahid Afridi, on his 35th birthday, made his 30th one-day international duck, second only to Sanath Jayasuriya – left Pakistan in more strife. Chatara bowled superbly to end with three for 35, despite Wahab swinging his bat as 43 came from the last five overs. On a Gabba surface encouraging the quicks, that proved decisive. DILEEP PREMACHANDRAN

Man of the Match: Wahab Riaz. *Attendance:* 9,847.

Pakistan

Nasir Jamshed c Sikandar Raza b Chatara .	1	Wahab Riaz not out	54
Ahmed Shehzad c Taylor b Chatara	0	Sohail Khan not out	6
Haris Sohail c Williams b Sikandar Raza . .	27	L-b 3, w 17	20
*Misbah-ul-Haq c Williams b Chatara	73		
†Umar Akmal b Williams	33	1/1 (1) 2/4 (2) (7 wkts, 50 overs) 235
Shahid Afridi b Williams.	0	3/58 (3) 4/127 (5) 5/127 (6)
Sohaib Maqsood c and b Mupariwa	21	6/155 (7) 7/202 (4) 10 overs: 14-2

Rahat Ali and Mohammad Irfan did not bat.

Panyangara 10–1–49–0; Chatara 10–2–35–3; Mupariwa 8–1–36–1; Williams 10–1–48–2; Masakadza 3–0–14–0; Chigumbura 1–0–7–0; Sikandar Raza 7–0–34–1; Mire 1–0–9–0.

Zimbabwe

C. J. Chibhabha c Haris Sohail		*E. Chigumbura c Umar Akmal	
b Mohammad Irfan .	9	b Wahab Riaz .	35
Sikandar Raza c Haris Sohail		T. Mupariwa c Umar Akmal b Wahab Riaz	0
b Mohammad Irfan .	8	T. Panyangara run out	10
H. Masakadza c Misbah-ul-Haq		T. L. Chatara not out	0
b Mohammad Irfan .	29		
†B. R. M. Taylor c Umar Akmal		B 3, l-b 2, w 13, n-b 1	19
b Wahab Riaz .	50		
S. C. Williams c Ahmed Shehzad		1/14 (1) 2/22 (2) 3/74 (3) (49.4 overs) 215
b Rahat Ali .	33	4/128 (4) 5/150 (5) 6/166 (7)
C. R. Ervine c Umar Akmal b Wahab Riaz	14	7/168 (6) 8/168 (9) 9/215 (10)
S. F. Mire c Umar Akmal		10/215 (8) 10 overs: 28-2
b Mohammad Irfan .	8		

Mohammad Irfan 10–2–30–4; Sohail Khan 10–0–45–0; Rahat Ali 10–0–37–1; Wahab Riaz 9.4–1–45–4; Shahid Afridi 10–1–53–0.

Umpires: R. A. Kettleborough and J. S. Wilson.   Third umpire: P. R. Reiffel.
Referee: J. J. Crowe.

IRELAND v SOUTH AFRICA

At Canberra, March 3, 2015 (day/night). South Africa won by 201 runs. Toss: South Africa.

A final dash that produced 230 runs in the last 20 overs propelled South Africa past 400 for the second match in a row, an unprecedented feat in one-day internationals. Amla was in his element on a flat pitch and fast outfield, but owed his career-best score to the life he was afforded on ten by Joyce, who spilled a powerfully struck but routine chance at midwicket, off Kevin O'Brien's first delivery. Du Plessis dutifully worked his way to a foundation-laying run-a-ball century during a second-wicket stand of 247, while Amla managed four sixes. At the end it was Miller and Rossouw who did most of the damage, after off-spinner McBrine nabbed Amla (Joyce clinging on at long-off) and de Villiers (top-edging a reverse sweep for 24 off nine) in three balls. When Ireland batted, Abbott and Steyn were too fast and furious for the top order: they slipped to 48 for five, before Balbirnie and Kevin O'Brien stopped the rot. For the second match running, though, South Africa won by more than 200 runs – causing irreparable damage to Ireland's net run-rate.   NEIL MANTHORP

Man of the Match: H. M. Amla.   *Attendance:* 8,831.

South Africa

H. M. Amla c Joyce b McBrine	159	R. R. Rossouw not out		61
†Q. de Kock c Wilson b Mooney	1	B 1, w 7, n-b 3		11
F. du Plessis b K. J. O'Brien	109			
*A. B. de Villiers c N. J. O'Brien b McBrine	24	1/12 (2) 2/259 (3)	(4 wkts, 50 overs)	411
D. A. Miller not out	46	3/299 (1) 4/301 (4)	10 overs: 57-1	

F. Behardien, D. W. Steyn, K. J. Abbott, M. Morkel and Imran Tahir did not bat.

Mooney 7–2–52–1; Sorensen 6–0–76–0; K. J. O'Brien 7–0–95–1; Dockrell 10–0–56–0; Stirling 10–0–68–0; McBrine 10–0–63–2.

Ireland

*W. T. S. Porterfield c du Plessis b Abbott	12	M. C. Sorensen c de Kock b Morkel		22
P. R. Stirling c de Kock b Steyn	9	A. R. McBrine not out		2
E. C. Joyce c Amla b Steyn	0			
N. J. O'Brien c Amla b Abbott	14	L-b 3, w 9		12
A. Balbirnie c Rossouw b Morkel	58			
†G. C. Wilson lbw b Abbott	0	1/17 (2) 2/21 (1) 3/21 (3)	(45 overs)	210
K. J. O'Brien c Rossouw b Abbott	48	4/42 (4) 5/48 (6) 6/129 (5)		
J. F. Mooney b de Villiers	8	7/150 (8) 8/167 (7) 9/200 (10)		
G. H. Dockrell b Morkel	25	10/210 (9)	10 overs: 47-4	

Steyn 8–0–39–2; Abbott 8–0–21–4; Morkel 9–0–34–3; Imran Tahir 10–1–50–0; Behardien 2–0–13–0; Rossouw 2–0–13–0; du Plessis 4–0–30–0; de Villiers 2–0–7–1.

Umpires: S. J. Davis and R. E. J. Martinesz.   Third umpire: I. J. Gould.
Referee: R. S. Mahanama.

PAKISTAN v UNITED ARAB EMIRATES

At Napier, March 4, 2015 (day/night). Pakistan won by 129 runs. Toss: United Arab Emirates.

Pakistan have often swayed between crushing disappointments and staggering highs, but this routine win over a dogged UAE was neither. Invited to bat, they followed a sensible script against some handy bowling – accumulating early, then accelerating, before exploding at the death. Set 340, the UAE aimed merely to bat for 50 overs, which they did. After Pakistan opener Nasir Jamshed had failed again, Ahmed Shehzad and Haris Sohail put on 160 before falling in swift succession. Sohaib Maqsood and Misbah-ul-Haq took the reins and quickened the scoring – Misbah's fifty came from 39 deliveries – before Shahid Afridi crashed 21 off seven. Wahab Riaz faced just one ball, and clubbed it over McLean Park's short midwicket boundary. When the UAE slipped to 25 for three in ten overs, the game looked set for a premature end, but the middle order proved harder to displace. Two of their Pakistan-born players, Khurram Khan and Shaiman Anwar, batted resourcefully to add 83 in 19 overs. Shaiman – nicknamed "Sir Viv" by his team-mates – found himself the tournament's leading scorer with 270, two ahead of Kumar Sangakkara. Patil abandoned attack, but Amjad Javed launched a late assault, including two fours and two sixes in five balls from Sohail Khan, before both fell in the final over.   WILL MACPHERSON

Man of the Match: Ahmed Shehzad.   *Attendance:* 2,850.

Pakistan

Nasir Jamshed c Khurram Khan b Guruge .	4	Shahid Afridi not out.	21
Ahmed Shehzad run out	93	Wahab Riaz not out	6
Haris Sohail c Shaiman Anwar		L-b 3, w 12, n-b 1	16
b Mohammad Naveed .	70		
Sohaib Maqsood c Mustafa b Guruge	45	1/10 (1) 2/170 (3) (6 wkts, 50 overs) 339
*Misbah-ul-Haq c Mustafa b Guruge	65	3/176 (2) 4/251 (4)
†Umar Akmal c Amjad Ali b Guruge	19	5/312 (6) 6/312 (5) 10 overs: 41-1

Sohail Khan, Rahat Ali and Mohammad Irfan did not bat.

Mohammad Naveed 10–0–50–1; Guruge 8–0–56–4; Amjad Javed 9–0–76–0; Mohammad Tauqir 10–0–52–0; Khurram Khan 3–0–21–0; Krishnachandran 8–0–58–0; Mustafa 2–0–23–0.

United Arab Emirates

Amjad Ali b Rahat Ali.	14	Amjad Javed c Sohail Khan b Wahab Riaz	40
A. R. Berenger c Umar Akmal b Sohail Khan	2	Mohammad Naveed not out	0
K. Krishnachandran c Umar Akmal		*Mohammad Tauqir not out	0
b Sohail Khan .	0		
Khurram Khan c Wahab Riaz			
b Sohaib Maqsood .	43		
Shaiman Anwar c Nasir Jamshed		L-b 1, w 12	13
b Shahid Afridi .	62		
†S. P. Patil b Wahab Riaz	36	1/19 (1) 2/19 (2) (8 wkts, 50 overs) 210
R. Mustafa c Ahmed Shehzad		3/25 (3) 4/108 (4) 5/140 (5)
b Shahid Afridi .	0	6/140 (7) 7/208 (8) 8/210 (6) 10 overs: 25-3

A. M. Guruge did not bat.

Mohammad Irfan 3–1–2–0; Sohail Khan 9–2–54–2; Rahat Ali 10–0–30–1; Wahab Riaz 10–1–54–2; Shahid Afridi 10–1–35–2; Sohaib Maqsood 5–0–16–1; Haris Sohail 3–0–18–0.

Umpires: J. D. Cloete and S. Ravi.   Third umpire: R. K. Illingworth.
Referee: B. C. Broad.

INDIA v WEST INDIES

At Perth, March 6, 2015 (day/night). India won by four wickets. Toss: West Indies.

For those infuriated by the bloated World Cup schedule, this was a match to avoid. The first meeting between these teams since West Indies aborted their tour of India in October over a pay dispute ought to have been a politically charged occasion. But had both sides taken valium, put on their comfiest trousers and listened to trip-hop, they couldn't have shown less intent, interest or energy; Dhoni moved the field with the panache of a man showing an insurance document to a Friday-afternoon seminar. Against Mohammed Shami in particular, the West Indies top order seemed confused by the wooden things they held in their hands; Gayle's reluctance to consider singles resulted in the predictable run-out of Samuels. By the 25th over, they were 85 for seven, and it took a mix of brazen hitting and sheer bloody-mindedness from Holder, one man for whom playing for West Indies clearly meant something, to drag them to 182. That was at least a basis for negotiation on a helpful wicket, as their gesticulating bowling coach Curtly Ambrose – who once enjoyed a Test spell of seven for one here – was keen to ram home. And, for a while, they put up a fight. Taylor was excellent with the new ball, and India were six down with 49 to make. But, with nine overs still available for the four frontline seamers, Holder unaccountably turned to Samuels's remodelled off-spin and Dwayne Smith's enticing slow-medium. The game finished with these two spoon-feeding Dhoni and Ashwin in a way that no cricket lover should have had to endure. JARROD KIMBER

Man of the Match: Mohammed Shami.   *Attendance:* 17,557.

West Indies

D. R. Smith c Dhoni b Mohammed Shami .	6	*J. O. Holder c Kohli b Jadeja	57
C. H. Gayle c M. Sharma		J. E. Taylor c and b Yadav	11
b Mohammed Shami .	21	K. A. J. Roach not out	0
M. N. Samuels run out	2		
J. L. Carter c Mohammed Shami b Ashwin	21	L-b 5, w 16	21
†D. Ramdin b Yadav	0		
L. M. P. Simmons c Yadav b M. Sharma . .	9	1/8 (1) 2/15 (3) 3/35 (2) (44.2 overs) 182		
D. J. G. Sammy c Dhoni		4/35 (5) 5/67 (6) 6/71 (4)		
b Mohammed Shami .	26	7/85 (8) 8/124 (7) 9/175 (10)		
A. D. Russell c Kohli b Jadeja	8	10/182 (9) 10 overs: 38-4		

Mohammed Shami 8–2–35–3; Yadav 10–1–42–2; Ashwin 9–0–38–1; M. Sharma 9–2–35–1; Jadeja 8.2–0–27–2.

India

R. G. Sharma c Ramdin b Taylor	7	R. Ashwin not out	16
S. Dhawan c Sammy b Taylor	9		
V. Kohli c Samuels b Russell	33	B 1, l-b 3, w 19, n-b 3	26
A. M. Rahane c Ramdin b Roach	14		
S. K. Raina c Ramdin b Smith	22	1/11 (2) 2/20 (1) (6 wkts, 39.1 overs) 185		
*†M. S. Dhoni not out	45	3/63 (3) 4/78 (4)		
R. A. Jadeja c Samuels b Russell	13	5/107 (5) 6/134 (7) 10 overs: 41-2		

Mohammed Shami, M. Sharma and U. T. Yadav did not bat.

Taylor 8–0–33–2; Holder 7–0–29–0; Roach 8–1–44–1; Russell 8–0–43–2; Smith 5–0–22–1; Samuels 3.1–0–10–0.

Umpires: H. D. P. K. Dharmasena and N. J. Llong. Third umpire: B. F. Bowden.
Referee: R. S. Madugalle.

PAKISTAN v SOUTH AFRICA

At Auckland, March 7, 2015 (day/night). Pakistan won by 29 runs (D/L). Toss: South Africa.

The weapon of choice at this World Cup was a quick left-armer – and Pakistan had three. That proved decisive as Mohammad Irfan, Rahat Ali and Wahab Riaz (the quickest and most aggressive) compensated for a poor batting display with three wickets apiece to win a game that should have been South Africa's. Earlier, the recalled Sarfraz Ahmed – who went on to equal Adam Gilchrist's World Cup record of six dismissals – hoisted Duminy for three midwicket sixes in the 16th over. But it was a rare bright spot in Pakistan's innings: Younis Khan contrived to lob the part-time slows of de Villiers to cover, leaving the onus on Misbah-ul-Haq. Rain intervened twice during the innings, reducing the match to 47 overs a side. There was no late revival as Pakistan crashed to 222 all out, but they were well served by a Duckworth/Lewis equation which added nine runs to the target. De Kock fell second ball, though Amla and du Plessis appeared to have weathered the early storm at 67 for one. But both were beaten for pace and caught behind in the space of five balls, Rossouw flapped a rapid bouncer off his eyebrows to long leg, and Miller was trapped in front. De Villiers fought a dashing, daring but lone battle in pursuit of a gloriously unlikely win, hitting five sixes from 58 balls, but Pakistan's compelling bowling performance merited victory – their first over South Africa at the World Cup in four attempts. NEIL MANTHORP

Man of the Match: Sarfraz Ahmed. *Attendance:* 22,713.

Pakistan

†Sarfraz Ahmed run out	49	Rahat Ali c Imran Tahir b Steyn	1
Ahmed Shehzad c Steyn b Abbott	18	Mohammad Irfan not out	1
Younus Khan c Rossouw b de Villiers	37		
*Misbah-ul-Haq c Morkel b Steyn	56	L-b 7, w 6, n-b 1	14
Sohaib Maqsood c Rossouw b Abbott	8		
Umar Akmal c de Villiers b Morkel	13	1/30 (2) 2/92 (1) 3/132 (3) (46.4 overs) 222	
Shahid Afridi c Duminy b Steyn	22	4/156 (5) 5/175 (6) 6/212 (7)	
Wahab Riaz lbw b Imran Tahir	0	7/212 (8) 8/218 (4) 9/221 (10)	
Sohail Khan c Duminy b Morkel	3	10/222 (9) 10 overs: 35-1	

Steyn 10–3–30–3; Abbott 9–0–45–2; Morkel 9.4–0–25–2; Imran Tahir 9–1–38–1; de Villiers 6–0–43–1; Duminy 3–0–34–0.

South Africa

†Q. de Kock c Sarfraz Ahmed b Mohammad Irfan	0	K. J. Abbott c Younus Khan b Rahat Ali	12
H. M. Amla c Sarfraz Ahmed b Wahab Riaz	38	M. Morkel not out	6
F. du Plessis c Sarfraz Ahmed b Rahat Ali	27	Imran Tahir c Sarfraz Ahmed b Wahab Riaz	0
R. R. Rossouw c Sohail Khan b Wahab Riaz	6		
*A. B. de Villiers c Sarfraz Ahmed b Sohail Khan	77	L-b 1, w 7	8
D. A. Miller lbw b Rahat Ali	0	1/0 (1) 2/67 (3) (33.3 overs) 202	
J-P. Duminy c Wahab Riaz b Mohammad Irfan	12	3/67 (2) 4/74 (4)	
		5/77 (6) 6/102 (7)	
D. W. Steyn c Sarfraz Ahmed b Mohammad Irfan	16	7/138 (8) 8/172 (9)	
		9/200 (5) 10/202 (11) 9 overs: 67-1	

Mohammad Irfan 8–0–52–3; Sohail Khan 5–0–36–1; Rahat Ali 8–1–40–3; Shahid Afridi 5–0–28–0; Wahab Riaz 7.3–2–45–3.

Umpires: R. A. Kettleborough and B. N. J. Oxenford.   Third umpire: C. B. Gaffaney.
Referee: B. C. Broad.

IRELAND v ZIMBABWE

At Hobart, March 7, 2015 (day/night). Ireland won by five runs. Toss: Zimbabwe.

A nailbiting conclusion went Ireland's way thanks in part to a controversial catch. With Zimbabwe needing 32 from 20 balls, Williams launched Kevin O'Brien to deep midwicket, where Mooney, leaping high, clung on. It was difficult to tell whether he had touched the boundary; after umpteen replays some claimed the triangular foam had moved a fraction, but by then Williams had accepted Mooney's word and left the field. Had the umpires awarded a six, Williams would have reached three figures, and Zimbabwe would have been in the box seat. All the same, it looked as if Mupariwa, who took 18 off the penultimate over, might yet steal the game: Zimbabwe required seven from the last with two wickets remaining. But Chakabva played on, and Mupariwa skied to long-on, where Porterfield dived forward to take the catch – sparking scenes of Irish relief as much as celebration. Balbirnie, who had run himself out on 97 trying to keep the strike in the last over, put on 138 with Joyce, winner of the match award for an innings of 112 from 103 balls. Cusack, perhaps, had a stronger claim, holding his nerve at the death to claim four for 32, a World Cup best for Ireland. That included Taylor who, after passing 5,000 one-day international runs, was undone when he lofted a superb slower ball to mid-on. Ireland, whose highest one-day international total proved just enough, retained hopes of a quarter-final place. IAN CALLENDER

Man of the Match: E. C. Joyce.   *Attendance:* 4,048.

OVERSTEPPING THE MARK

"Alcoholic dumps Zim out of WC" was the Zimbabwean *Herald's* interpretation of their five-run defeat by Ireland. Robson Sharuko's opening paragraph began: "A recovering alcoholic, who was so depressed last year he even contemplated killing himself, was the Irishman who sealed Zimbabwe's fate at this World Cup in Hobart on Saturday night with a shameless piece of fielding dishonesty that has soiled this global cricket showcase." Sharuko was referring to John Mooney, who held a crucial catch to dismiss Sean Williams at deep square leg, possibly touching the boundary cushion as he held on. "[The cameras] zoomed in, and I thought it was pretty clear," said Zimbabwe captain Brendan Taylor. "But you've got to take the fielder's word." Sharuko suggested Mooney's history of clinical depression made it "very unlikely that, in the defining moment of such a big game, he could be trusted to have the honesty, let alone the decency, to concede that his foot touched the boundary". An embarrassed Taylor apologised "for this unacceptable article". Cricket Ireland reported it to the ICC, and considered legal action.

Ireland

*W. T. S. Porterfield c Masakadza b Williams	29	G. H. Dockrell not out		5
P. R. Stirling c Williams b Panyangara	10	A. R. Cusack not out		2
E. C. Joyce c Ervine b Chatara	112	L-b 4, w 8, n-b 3		15
A. Balbirnie run out	97			
K. J. O'Brien c Chakabva b Chatara	24	1/16 (2) 2/79 (1)	(8 wkts, 50 overs)	331
†G. C. Wilson c Chakabva b Williams	25	3/217 (3) 4/276 (5)		
J. F. Mooney b Williams	10	5/308 (6) 6/319 (7)		
N. J. O'Brien c Panyangara b Chatara	2	7/322 (8) 8/326 (4)	10 overs: 41-1	

A. R. McBrine did not bat.

Panyangara 9–0–69–1; Chatara 10–0–61–3; Mupariwa 10–0–56–0; Sikandar Raza 9–0–51–0; Williams 9–0–72–3; Masakadza 3–0–18–0.

Zimbabwe

C. J. Chibhabha c Porterfield b Cusack	18	T. Mupariwa c Porterfield b Cusack		18
Sikandar Raza c Stirling b Mooney	12	T. L. Chatara not out		1
S. F. Mire c Cusack b Dockrell	11			
H. Masakadza c Wilson b K. J. O'Brien	5	L-b 8, w 2, n-b 1		11
*†B. R. M. Taylor c K. J. O'Brien b Cusack	121			
S. C. Williams c Mooney b K. J. O'Brien	96	1/32 (2) 2/32 (1) 3/41 (4)	(49.3 overs)	326
C. R. Ervine c N. J. O'Brien b McBrine	11	4/74 (3) 5/223 (5) 6/259 (7)		
R. W. Chakabva b Cusack	17	7/300 (6) 8/305 (9) 9/325 (8)		
T. Panyangara c Porterfield b Mooney	5	10/326 (10)	10 overs: 41-2	

Cusack 9.3–2–32–4; Mooney 10–0–58–2; K. J. O'Brien 10–0–90–2; Dockrell 10–0–56–1; McBrine 8–0–56–1; Stirling 2–0–26–0.

Umpires: R. S. A. Palliyaguruge and P. R. Reiffel.   Third umpire: J. S. Wilson.
Referee: R. S. Mahanama.

INDIA v IRELAND

At Hamilton, March 10, 2015 (day/night). India won by eight wickets. Toss: Ireland.

With their vocal supporters packing Seddon Park's stands and banks, India brushed Ireland aside with clever spin bowling and powerful batting. They racked up their ninth successive World Cup win, to confirm top spot in Pool B. Ireland batted well before throwing away a fine start: Porterfield and Stirling took 60 off the first ten overs, the most

India conceded in the opening powerplay throughout the tournament. But Dhoni had introduced spin in the tenth, and India's four slow bowlers whiled away 22 overs in just 62 minutes. The Irish stalled, managing only 87 for two in that period, then playing rash shots when the seamers returned: their last seven tumbled for 53. Niall O'Brien scored an impressive run-a-ball 75, but was as guilty as any when he softly chipped Mohammed Shami to backward square leg; Balbirnie and Wilson had fallen sweeping. Ireland desperately needed early wickets, but Dhawan was dropped twice off Mooney (a return catch on five, and by the diving Porterfield at backward point on ten) on his way to a superb 84-ball century. He and Rohit Sharma went on to raise 174, India's largest opening stand in World Cup cricket, before Thompson – in his first match of the tournament – removed both.   WILL MACPHERSON

Man of the Match: S. Dhawan.   *Attendance:* 10,192.

Ireland

*W. T. S. Porterfield c Yadav b M. Sharma	67	G. H. Dockrell c Dhoni b Yadav		6
P. R. Stirling c Rahane b Ashwin	42	A. R. Cusack c Yadav b Mohammed Shami		11
E. C. Joyce b Raina	2			
N. J. O'Brien c Yadav b Mohammed Shami	75	L-b 2, w 9		11
A. Balbirnie c Mohammed Shami b Ashwin	24			
K. J. O'Brien c Dhoni b Mohammed Shami	1	1/89 (2) 2/92 (3) 3/145 (1)	(49 overs)	259
†G. C. Wilson c Rahane b Jadeja	6	4/206 (5) 5/208 (6) 6/222 (7)		
S. R. Thompson run out	2	7/226 (4) 8/227 (8) 9/238 (9)		
J. F. Mooney not out	12	10/259 (11)	10 overs: 60-0	

Yadav 4–0–34–1; Mohammed Shami 9–0–41–3; M. Sharma 6–0–38–1; Jadeja 7–0–45–1; Ashwin 10–1–38–2; Raina 10–0–40–1; R. G. Sharma 3–0–21–0.

India

R. G. Sharma b Thompson	64		
S. Dhawan c Porterfield b Thompson	100		
V. Kohli not out	44		
A. M. Rahane not out	33		
B 4, l-b 2, w 13	19		
1/174 (1)	(2 wkts, 36.5 overs)	260	
2/190 (2)	10 overs: 73-0		

S. K. Raina, *†M. S. Dhoni, R. A. Jadeja, R. Ashwin, Mohammed Shami, M. Sharma and U. T. Yadav did not bat.

Mooney 6–0–44–0; Cusack 8–0–43–0; Thompson 6–0–45–2; Dockrell 5–0–44–0; Stirling 5–0–36–0; K. J. O'Brien 6.5–0–42–0.

Umpires: H. D. P. K. Dharmasena and R. A. Kettleborough.   Third umpire: J. D. Cloete.
Referee: B. C. Broad.

SOUTH AFRICA v UNITED ARAB EMIRATES

At Wellington (Westpac Stadium), March 12, 2015 (day/night). South Africa won by 146 runs. Toss: United Arab Emirates.

There was plenty to admire – but little by way of suspense. The UAE were organised, determined, and unsurprisingly outclassed. Mohammad Naveed and Kamran Shazad were tidy with the new balls, while Mohammad Tauqir's off-spin proved awkward to get away. That was as good as it got, though it was a credit to the UAE bowlers that de Villiers faced as many as 82 deliveries for his 99 – only the third such score in the World Cup, after Adam Gilchrist in 2003 and J-P. Duminy in 2011 – before slapping Shazad to backward point. Miller also struggled for rhythm, with 49 from 48. "I don't see them scoring 400 against us," Tauqir had said before the match, and he was right; still, 341 was always going to be too many. It was unfortunate for the UAE's amateur batsmen that Morkel chose this match to produce his fastest, meanest performance of the tournament. He posed a constant physical threat: Khurram Khan and Tauqir – both 43 years old – were struck, and there were several further body blows. Amid the artillery Swapnil Patel displayed quick feet and a faultless technique to remain unbeaten on 57, although it took him 100 balls. Shaiman Anwar's 39 lifted his tournament tally to 309, two more than the previous record by an Associate batsman in a World Cup, set by Ryan ten Doeschate of the Netherlands in 2011. NEIL MANTHORP

Man of the Match: A. B. de Villiers. *Attendance:* 4,901.

South Africa

H. M. Amla c Amjad Ali		F. Behardien not out	64
b Mohammad Naveed	12	V. D. Philander not out	10
†Q. de Kock c Saqlain Haider b Amjad Javed	26		
R. R. Rossouw c and b Mohammad Tauqir	43	B 4, l-b 1, w 5, n-b 5	15
*A. B. de Villiers c Amjad Javed			
b Kamran Shazad	99	1/17 (1) 2/85 (2) (6 wkts, 50 overs)	341
D. A. Miller b Mohammad Naveed	49	3/96 (3) 4/204 (5)	
J-P. Duminy lbw b Mohammad Naveed	23	5/257 (4) 6/292 (6) 10 overs: 61-1	

D. W. Steyn, M. Morkel and Imran Tahir did not bat.

Mohammad Naveed 10–0–63–3; Kamran Shazad 8–0–59–1; Amjad Javed 10–0–87–1; Mohammad Tauqir 10–0–47–1; Fahad Alhashmi 7.2–0–45–0; Khurram Khan 4–0–31–0; Shaiman Anwar 0.4–0–4–0.

United Arab Emirates

Amjad Ali c Behardien b Duminy	21	*Mohammad Tauqir b Steyn	3
A. R. Berenger c Rossouw b Morkel	5	Kamran Shazad c Steyn b Philander	0
Khurram Khan c de Kock b Morkel	12	Fahad Alhashmi absent hurt	
Shaiman Anwar c Rossouw b Imran Tahir	39		
S. P. Patil not out	57	B 4, l-b 16, w 6, n-b 3	29
†Saqlain Haider c Rossouw b de Villiers	7		
Amjad Javed c sub (W. D. Parnell)		1/29 (2) 2/45 (1) (47.3 overs)	195
b de Villiers	5	3/45 (3) 4/108 (4) 5/118 (6)	
Mohammad Naveed c de Villiers		6/125 (7) 7/163 (8) 8/189 (9)	
b Philander	17	9/195 (10) 10 overs: 42-1	

Steyn 9–1–40–1; Philander 8.3–1–34–2; Morkel 10–2–23–2; Duminy 3–1–12–1; Behardien 4–1–11–0; Imran Tahir 10–0–40–1; de Villiers 3–0–15–2.

Umpires: S. J. Davis and R. J. Tucker. Third umpire: B. N. J. Oxenford.
Referee: R. S. Mahanama.

INDIA v ZIMBABWE

At Auckland, March 14, 2015 (day/night). India won by six wickets. Toss: India.

Taylor played the best 50-over innings of his career in his last match for Zimbabwe before committing himself to Nottinghamshire – but it was not enough to prevent India from completing their sixth win out of six. Reduced to 33 for three after being put in, Zimbabwe understood the value of keeping wickets in hand, as Taylor and Williams rebuilt with care in a stand of 93. Taylor then added 109 with Ervine, and timed his acceleration perfectly. His first 50, full of impudent reverse sweeps, came off 64 balls, his second off 35; off his next ten he thumped 37, finishing with five sixes and 15 fours. His eighth one-day international hundred made him the first Zimbabwean to score two in a row at a World Cup. India's three seamers shared nine wickets, though Ashwin and Jadeja, their two spinners, managed only one for 146. And now their batsmen needed a tricky 288. That looked even trickier when Panyangara removed both openers with 21 on the board, which soon became 92 for four. But Zimbabwe brought their part-time spinners on at the wrong time, allowing Raina and Dhoni a measure of the conditions. Raina was dropped by Masakadza at short fine leg on 47, and went on to a 104-ball 110, adding an increasingly fluent unbroken 196 with his captain. Dhoni had been in control from the moment he arrived, and finished with 85 from 76 balls, extending India's World Cup winning streak to ten. ANAND VASU

Man of the Match: S. K. Raina.   *Attendance:* 30,076.

Zimbabwe

C. J. Chibhabha c Dhawan b Mohammed Shami .	7	T. Panyangara c Yadav b Mohammed Shami	6
H. Masakadza c Dhoni b Yadav	2	T. Mupariwa not out	1
S. F. Mire c Dhoni b M. Sharma	9	T. L. Chatara b Yadav	0
*†B. R. M. Taylor c Dhawan b M. Sharma . .	138	L-b 2, w 7	9
S. C. Williams c and b Ashwin	50		
C. R. Ervine c and b M. Sharma	27	1/11 (2) 2/13 (1) 3/33 (3) (48.5 overs) 287	
Sikandar Raza b Mohammed Shami	28	4/126 (5) 5/235 (4) 6/241 (6)	
R. W. Chakabva c R. G. Sharma b Yadav . .	10	7/276 (7) 8/285 (9) 9/286 (8)	
		10/287 (11) 10 overs: 27-2	

Mohammed Shami 9–2–48–3; Yadav 9.5–1–43–3; M. Sharma 10–1–48–3; Ashwin 10–0–75–1; Jadeja 10–0–71–0.

India

R. G. Sharma c Sikandar Raza b Panyangara	16	*†M. S. Dhoni not out	85
S. Dhawan b Panyangara	4	B 1, l-b 2, w 12, n-b 1	16
V. Kohli b Sikandar Raza	38		
A. M. Rahane run out	19	1/21 (1) 2/21 (2) (4 wkts, 48.4 overs) 288	
S. K. Raina not out 110		3/71 (4) 4/92 (3) 10 overs: 35-2	

R. A. Jadeja, R. Ashwin, Mohammed Shami, M. Sharma and U. T. Yadav did not bat.

Panyangara 8.4–1–53–2; Chatara 10–1–59–0; Mupariwa 10–0–61–0; Mire 5–0–29–0; Williams 5–0–31–0; Sikandar Raza 8–0–37–1; Masakadza 2–0–15–0.

Umpires: C. B. Gaffaney and B. N. J. Oxenford.   Third umpire: R. J. Tucker.
Referee: R. S. Mahanama.

UNITED ARAB EMIRATES v WEST INDIES

At Napier, March 15, 2015. West Indies won by six wickets. Toss: West Indies.

West Indies left it to their last group match to qualify for the knockouts – though they had to wait a few hours for Pakistan to beat Ireland in Adelaide before their progress was confirmed. To complicate matters, Cyclone Pam was approaching New Zealand's north-east coast, prompting UAE captain Mohammad Tauqir to joke that his team were more

OLDEST CAPTAINS IN ONE-DAY INTERNATIONALS

Years	Days			
44	361	N. Gifford	England v Pakistan at Sharjah	1984-85
43	308	R. Sharma	Hong Kong v Pakistan at Colombo (SSC)	2004
43	**164**	**Khurram Khan**	**UAE v Afghanistan at Dubai (ICC Academy)**	**2014-15**
43	**60**	**Mohammad Tauqir**	**UAE v West Indies at Napier**	**2014-15**
42	347	S. W. Lubbers	Netherlands v South Africa at Rawalpindi	1995-96
42	114	C. E. B. Rice	South Africa v India at New Delhi	1991-92
42	68	R. B. Simpson	Australia v West Indies at Castries, St Lucia.	1977-78
41	186	D. B. Close	England v Australia at Birmingham	1972
41	42	R. Illingworth	England v New Zealand at Manchester.	1973
40	**296**	**Misbah-ul-Haq**	**Pakistan v Australia at Adelaide**	**2014-15**

worried about getting home than about West Indies: "Our employers are waiting for us." In the event, the UAE were blown away long before Pam arrived. Some seething short balls from Holder, and Taylor's pace and aggression, reduced them to 46 for six, including Krishnachandran's third duck of the tournament. And it needed a stand of 107 between Amjad Javed and Nasir Aziz – equalling the World Cup record for the seventh wicket, set 18 days earlier in Brisbane by Javed and Shaiman Anwar against Ireland – to avert a rout. It was the UAE's first century partnership for any wicket against a Test-playing nation. But 175 was hopelessly inadequate. Chris Gayle was left out to rest his back, and West Indies lost Dwayne Smith and Samuels to lazy wafts, but Charles – in his first ODI for 14 months – reached 50 in 34 balls, and Carter steered them home with his maiden international half-century.   FIRDOSE MOONDA

Man of the Match: J. O. Holder.   *Attendance:* 1,221.

United Arab Emirates

Amjad Ali lbw b Holder	5		*Mohammad Tauqir b Taylor		2
A. R. Berenger c Ramdin b Holder	7		A. M. Guruge not out		4
K. Krishnachandran c Smith b Holder	0				
Khurram Khan b Taylor	5		L-b 4, w 10		14
Shaiman Anwar b Taylor	2				
†S. P. Patil b Holder	6		1/13 (2) 2/16 (3) 3/17 (1)	(47.4 overs)	175
Amjad Javed b Russell	56		4/21 (4) 5/26 (5) 6/46 (6)		
Nasir Aziz c Holder b Samuels	60		7/153 (7) 8/167 (9) 9/167 (8)		
Mohammad Naveed b Russell	14		10/175 (10)	10 overs: 31-5	

Taylor 8.4–0–36–3; Holder 10–1–27–4; Roach 8–0–54–0; Russell 8–3–20–2; Samuels 10–4–25–1; Sammy 1–0–4–0; Smith 2–0–5–0.

West Indies

D. R. Smith c Patil b Guruge	15		†D. Ramdin not out		33
J. Charles c Krishnachandran b Amjad Javed	55		L-b 4, w 3		7
M. N. Samuels c Berenger b Guruge	9				
J. L. Carter not out	50		1/33 (1) 2/53 (3)	(4 wkts, 30.3 overs)	176
A. D. Russell c and b Amjad Javed	7		3/109 (2) 4/118 (5)	10 overs: 69-2	

L. M. P. Simmons, D. J. G. Sammy, *J. O. Holder, J. E. Taylor and K. A. J. Roach did not bat.

Nasir Aziz 6–0–47–0; Mohammad Naveed 6–0–34–0; Guruge 7.3–1–40–2; Mohammad Tauqir 3–0–22–0; Amjad Javed 8–0–29–2.

Umpires: Aleem Dar and R. E. J. Martinesz.   Third umpire: R. A. Kettleborough.
Referee: B. C. Broad.

IRELAND v PAKISTAN

At Adelaide, March 15, 2015 (day/night). Pakistan won by seven wickets. Toss: Ireland.
Pakistan's straightforward victory ended Ireland's involvement, and underlined the differences between teams playing regular one-day internationals and those restricted to one global 50-over event every four years: between the 2011 and 2015 tournaments, Ireland played nine ODIs against Full Member opponents, to Pakistan's 81. The Irish pace attack comprised Cusack, Mooney and Thompson, who barely tipped 80mph, while Pakistan boasted Sohail Khan, Rahat Ali and Wahab Riaz, all producing reverse swing at nearer 90. The outcome was clear long before the end, delayed by Umar Akmal blocking five balls in a row to allow Sarfraz Ahmed a century, his first, and Pakistan's only one of this World Cup. Porterfield had hit Ireland's second, to build a platform for a late assault.

But, once he was fifth out in the 39th over, the Pakistan bowlers proved too good, and the last five wickets added just 55. Openers Ahmed Shehzad and Sarfraz all but settled the contest by putting on 120 in 23 overs.   IAN CALLENDER

Man of the Match: Sarfraz Ahmed.   *Attendance:* 9,891.

Ireland

*W. T. S. Porterfield c Shahid Afridi	J. F. Mooney c Umar Akmal b Wahab Riaz 13
b Sohail Khan . 107	G. H. Dockrell run out 11
P. R. Stirling lbw b Ehsan Adil 3	A. R. Cusack not out 1
E. C. Joyce c Umar Akmal b Wahab Riaz . 11	
N. J. O'Brien c Umar Akmal b Rahat Ali . 12	L-b 2, w 10 12
A. Balbirnie c Shahid Afridi b Haris Sohail 18	
†G. C. Wilson b Wahab Riaz b Sohail Khan 29	1/11 (2) 2/56 (3) 3/86 (4) (50 overs) 237
K. J. O'Brien c Sohaib Maqsood	4/134 (5) 5/182 (1) 6/189 (6)
b Wahab Riaz . 8	7/204 (8) 8/216 (7) 9/230 (9)
S. R. Thompson c Umar Akmal b Rahat Ali 12	10/237 (10) 10 overs: 47-1

Sohail Khan 10–0–44–2; Ehsan Adil 7–0–31–1; Rahat Ali 10–0–48–2; Wahab Riaz 10–0–54–3; Shahid Afridi 10–0–38–0; Haris Sohail 3–0–20–1.

Pakistan

Ahmed Shehzad c Joyce b Thompson 63	
†Sarfraz Ahmed not out 101	
Haris Sohail run out 3	
*Misbah-ul-Haq hit wkt b Cusack 39	
Umar Akmal not out 20	
B 1, l-b 1, w 13 15	

1/120 (1) 2/126 (3)   (3 wkts, 46.1 overs) 241
3/208 (4)   10 overs: 65-0

Sohaib Maqsood, Shahid Afridi, Wahab Riaz, Sohail Khan, Rahat Ali and Ehsan Adil did not bat.

Cusack 10–1–43–1; Mooney 9–1–40–0; Thompson 10–0–59–1; Dockrell 6–0–43–0; K. J. O'Brien 10–0–49–0; Stirling 1.1–0–5–0.

Umpires: M. Erasmus and R. S. A. Palliyaguruge.   Third umpire: S. D. Fry.
Referee: R. S. Madugalle.

FINAL POOL TABLES

Pool A	Played	Won	Lost	No result	Points	Net run-rate
NEW ZEALAND	6	6	0	0	12	2.56
AUSTRALIA	6	4	1	1	9	2.25
SRI LANKA	6	4	2	0	8	0.37
BANGLADESH	6	3	2	1	7	0.13
England	6	2	4	0	4	–0.75
Afghanistan	6	1	5	0	2	–1.85
Scotland	6	0	6	0	0	–2.21

Pool B	Played	Won	Lost	No result	Points	Net run-rate
INDIA	6	6	0	0	12	1.82
SOUTH AFRICA	6	4	2	0	8	1.70
PAKISTAN	6	4	2	0	8	–0.08
WEST INDIES	6	3	3	0	6	–0.05
Ireland	6	3	3	0	6	–0.93
Zimbabwe	6	1	5	0	2	–0.52
United Arab Emirates	6	0	6	0	0	–2.03

QUARTER-FINALS

SOUTH AFRICA v SRI LANKA

At Sydney, March 18, 2015 (day/night). South Africa won by nine wickets. Toss: Sri Lanka. One-day international debut: P. H. T. Kaushal.

This was expected to be the tightest of the quarter-finals – but it proved the opposite, after a powerful bowling and fielding performance gave South Africa their first win in a World Cup knockout match, at the sixth attempt. Spinners Duminy and Imran Tahir claimed seven wickets between them, but it was the pace, accuracy and hostility of the seamers which set the tone. They did not bowl a loose delivery and, on the back of a record-breaking four consecutive centuries, Sangakkara found himself with just six runs from his first 42 balls. Vast experience taught him patience, but the release in pressure

SHORT WORK OF IT

Heaviest defeats (by balls unused) for Full Members at World Cups:

228	Bangladesh (108) v South Africa (109-0) at Bloemfontein	2002-03
226	Bangladesh (58) v West Indies (59-1) at Mirpur	2010-11
226	**England (123) v New Zealand (125-2) at Wellington**.	**2014-15**
215†	Sri Lanka (136) v England (137-1) at Leeds	1983
192	**Sri Lanka (133) v South Africa (134-1) at Sydney (quarter-final)**	**2014-15**
188†	England (93) v Australia (94-6) at Leeds (semi-final)	1975
184	England (154) v South Africa (157-1) at Bridgetown	2006-07
179	Pakistan (132) v Australia (133-2) at Lord's (final)	1999
175	West Indies (112) v Pakistan (113-0) at Mirpur (quarter-final)	2010-11

† *60-over match.*

never arrived. Thirimanne was the only Sri Lankan to look remotely comfortable, until Tahir's flight produced a return catch. Jayawardene was soon undone by a rapid skidder and chipped to midwicket. At the end of the 33rd over, Mathews whipped Duminy straight to midwicket as well. Kulasekara edged the first ball of Duminy's next over, then Tharindu Kaushal played back and was plumb in front, to complete the ninth hat-trick in World Cup history (two of them by Malinga, who later took the only South African wicket to fall). Sangakkara's long vigil ended with a slash to wide third man, ninth out with 45 from 96 deliveries; there wasn't a soul in the ground who believed his team were not condemned with his departure. Under no pressure, de Kock played his only substantial innings of the tournament, full of delightful cuts and drives, to hasten Sri Lanka's demise. The spindly off-spinner Kaushal was the second to make his one-day international debut in a World Cup knockout match after England's Wayne Larkins in the 1979 semi-final against New Zealand, but he made little impression. It was a sad way for Jayawardene and Sangakkara to end their one-day careers.   NEIL MANTHORP

Man of the Match: Imran Tahir.   *Attendance:* 27,259.

Sri Lanka

M. D. K. J. Perera c de Kock b Abbott	3
T. M. Dilshan c du Plessis b Steyn	0
†K. C. Sangakkara c Miller b Morkel	45
H. D. R. L. Thirimanne c and b Imran Tahir	41
D. P. M. D. Jayawardene c du Plessis	
b Imran Tahir . .	4
*A. D. Mathews c du Plessis b Duminy	19
N. L. T. C. Perera c Rossouw b Imran Tahir	0
K. M. D. N. Kulasekara c de Kock b Duminy	1

P. H. T. Kaushal lbw b Duminy 0
P. V. D. Chameera not out. 2
S. L. Malinga c Miller b Imran Tahir 3
B 4, l-b 2, w 7, n-b 2 15

1/3 (1) 2/4 (2) 3/69 (4)   (37.2 overs) 133
4/81 (5) 5/114 (6) 6/115 (7)
7/116 (8) 8/116 (9) 9/127 (3)
10/133 (11)   10 overs: 35-2

Steyn 7–2–18–1; Abbott 6–1–27–1; Morkel 7–1–27–1; Duminy 9–1–29–3; Imran Tahir
8.2–0–26–4.

South Africa

H. M. Amla c Kulasekara b Malinga 16
†Q. de Kock not out 78
F. du Plessis not out 21
          L-b 4, w 12, n-b 3 19

1/40 (1)   (1 wkt, 18 overs) 134
                            10 overs: 61-1

R. R. Rossouw, *A. B. de Villiers, D. A. Miller, J-P. Duminy, D. W. Steyn, K. J. Abbott, M. Morkel
and Imran Tahir did not bat.

Malinga 6–0–43–1; Dilshan 2–0–10–0; Kulasekara 1–0–13–0; Kaushal 6–0–25–0; Chameera
2–0–29–0; N. L. T. C. Perera 1–0–10–0.

Umpires: N. J. Llong and R. J. Tucker.   Third umpire: R. A. Kettleborough.
Referee: D. C. Boon.

BANGLADESH v INDIA

At Melbourne, March 19, 2015 (day/night). India won by 109 runs. Toss: India.
    Bangladesh's big adventure came to a predictable end as India maintained their 100%
tournament record. The Bangla Army joked beforehand that their side had won both their
previous one-day internationals against India in the month of March – one at the 2007
World Cup – but the only time the hat-trick seemed possible was while India rebuilt after
losing both openers in quick succession. The slippery Rubel Hossain started with
6–0–14–1, Kohli edging an expansive drive; and when Rahane was out in the 28th over

MOST CONSECUTIVE WORLD CUP WINS

		First	Last
25	Australia	v Pakistan at Lord's (F), 1999	v New Zealand at Nagpur, 2010-11
11	**India . . . .**	**v West Indies at Chennai, 2010-11**	**v Bangladesh at Melbourne (QF), 2014-15**
9	West Indies . .	v Sri Lanka at Manchester, 1975	v England at Lord's (F), 1979
8	India	v Zimbabwe at Harare, 2002-03	v Kenya at Durban (SF), 2002-03
8	**New Zealand**	**v Sri Lanka at Christchurch, 2014-15**	**v South Africa at Auckland (SF), 2014-15**
7	New Zealand	v Australia at Auckland, 1991-92	v England at Wellington, 1991-92
7	Pakistan	v Australia at Perth, 1991-92	v Netherlands at Lahore, 1995-96

the rate was fractionally above four. But Raina muscled 65 from 57 balls, and Rohit
Sharma took advantage of a controversial let-off: when 90, he swung Rubel's high full
toss to Imrul Kayes at deep midwicket, but Aleem Dar deemed it an above-the-waist no-
ball. Dar's call was marginal, and Sharma advanced to 137, spoiling Rubel's figures with
a six and two luscious fours in his ninth over, before he played on to the persistent Taskin
Ahmed. India's eventual 302 always looked enough: Tamim Iqbal started brightly but, the
ball after he was well caught by Dhoni, diving low to his left, Kayes tried to pinch a single
from Jadeja's misfield and was run out. Mahmudullah, fresh from back-to-back centuries,

was well held by Dhawan, tap-dancing perilously close to the boundary (the third official upheld the catch, fuelling Bangladeshi conspiracy theories about the umpiring). India's spinners exerted even more of a stranglehold – Ashwin whirred through his ten overs for 30 – and the game was up when Shakib Al Hasan sliced tamely to short third man. The last four wickets tumbled in 13 balls, as India claimed all ten for the seventh match in a row to complete Dhoni's 100th victory as one-day captain; only Allan Border and Ricky Ponting had more. STEVEN LYNCH

Man of the Match: R. G. Sharma. *Attendance:* 51,552.

India

R. G. Sharma b Taskin Ahmed	137	*†M. S. Dhoni c Nasir Hossain	
S. Dhawan st Mushfiqur Rahim		b Taskin Ahmed	6
b Shakib Al Hasan	30	R. A. Jadeja not out	23
V. Kohli c Mushfiqur Rahim		R. Ashwin not out	3
b Rubel Hossain	3	B 4, l-b 7, w 3, n-b 2	16
A. M. Rahane c Shakib Al Hasan			
b Taskin Ahmed	19	1/75 (2) 2/79 (3) (6 wkts, 50 overs)	302
S. K. Raina c Mushfiqur Rahim		3/115 (4) 4/237 (5)	
b Mashrafe bin Mortaza	65	5/273 (1) 6/296 (6)	10 overs: 51-0

Mohammed Shami, M. Sharma and U. T. Yadav did not bat.

Mashrafe bin Mortaza 10-0-69-1; Taskin Ahmed 10-0-69-3; Nasir Hossain 9-0-35-0; Mahmudullah 1-0-4-0; Rubel Hossain 10-0-56-1; Shakib Al Hasan 10-0-58-1.

Bangladesh

Tamim Iqbal c Dhoni b Yadav	25	Nasir Hossain c Ashwin b Jadeja	35
Imrul Kayes run out	5	*Mashrafe bin Mortaza c Dhoni b M. Sharma	1
Soumya Sarkar c Dhoni		Rubel Hossain c Ashwin b Yadav	0
b Mohammed Shami	29	Taskin Ahmed not out	0
Mahmudullah c Dhawan			
b Mohammed Shami	21	B 1, l-b 1, w 8	10
Shakib Al Hasan c Mohammed Shami			
b Jadeja	10	1/33 (1) 2/33 (2) 3/73 (4) (45 overs)	193
†Mushfiqur Rahim c Dhoni b Yadav	27	4/90 (3) 5/104 (5) 6/139 (6)	
Sabbir Rahman c Mohammed Shami		7/189 (8) 8/192 (9) 9/193 (10)	
b Yadav	30	10/193 (7)	10 overs: 44-2

Yadav 9-1-31-4; Mohammed Shami 8-1-37-2; M. Sharma 7-0-36-1; Ashwin 10-1-30-0; Raina 3-1-15-0; Jadeja 8-0-42-2.

Umpires: Aleem Dar and I. J. Gould. Third umpire: S. J. Davis.
Referee: R. S. Mahanama.

AUSTRALIA v PAKISTAN

At Adelaide, March 20, 2015 (day/night). Australia won by six wickets. Toss: Pakistan.

Australia's eventual gallop into the semi-finals meant this was not quite the World Cup's most engrossing fixture – but the duel between Wahab Riaz and Watson was without doubt its most arresting passage of play. Leading Pakistan's defence of a meagre 213, and riled by words of advice from Watson and Starc when he had batted, Wahab bent his back and bared heart and soul in an effort to sweep the competition favourites aside.

Shot, Shane! Wahab Riaz taunts Watson during their match-defining duel.

Warner was caught at third man, and Clarke could only fend a bouncer to short leg, leaving Watson to face up to a spell in which Wahab regularly crested 93mph. He struggled to cope with some venomous bouncers, prompting sarcastic applause from the bowler and a series of exchanges that would cost Wahab 50% of his match fee and Watson 15%. The turning point came when Watson, on four, top-edged a hook, only for Rahat Ali to drop a simple catch at fine leg that would have left Australia 83 for four. It drew the wind from Wahab's sails – and Watson breathed again. At the other end, Smith had been playing with an almost other-worldly assurance in the face of Wahab's fire; without Watson, however, he might not have had the partners to carry it through. After they added 89, Maxwell provided the decisive flourish. On a pitch offering something for everyone, Hazlewood earned the match award for bowling of great accuracy and subtle movement. But the pivotal moment of the Pakistan innings had come when Misbah-ul-Haq wasted a start by slogging Maxwell's modest off-break to Finch, the first of three Pakistani batsmen caught at deep midwicket. Such profligacy was made to look especially maddening when Wahab steamed in – but Australia held firm.   DANIEL BRETTIG

Man of the Match: J. R. Hazlewood.   *Attendance:* 35,516.

Pakistan

Ahmed Shehzad c Clarke b Hazlewood	5	Sohail Khan c Haddin b Hazlewood	4	
†Sarfraz Ahmed c Watson b Starc	10	Rahat Ali not out	6	
Haris Sohail c Haddin b Johnson	41			
*Misbah-ul-Haq c Finch b Maxwell	34	L-b 5, w 5	10	
Umar Akmal c Finch b Maxwell	20			
Sohaib Maqsood c Johnson b Hazlewood	29	(49.5 overs)	213	
Shahid Afridi c Finch b Hazlewood	23			
Wahab Riaz c Haddin b Starc	16			
Ehsan Adil c Starc b Faulkner	15			

1/20 (2) 2/24 (1) 3/97 (4) 4/112 (3) 5/124 (5) 6/158 (7) 7/188 (6) 8/188 (8) 9/195 (10) 10/213 (9)

10 overs: 37-2

Starc 10–1–40–2; Hazlewood 10–1–35–4; Johnson 10–0–42–1; Maxwell 7–0–43–2; Watson 5–0–17–0; Faulkner 7.5–0–31–1.

Australia

D. A. Warner c Rahat Ali b Wahab Riaz	24	G. J. Maxwell not out	44
A. J. Finch lbw b Sohail Khan	2		
S. P. D. Smith lbw b Ehsan Adil	65	W 9	9
*M. J. Clarke c Sohaib Maqsood b Wahab Riaz	8	(4 wkts, 33.5 overs)	216
S. R. Watson not out	64		

1/15 (2) 2/49 (1) 3/59 (4) 4/148 (3)

10 overs: 56-2

J. P. Faulkner, †B. J. Haddin, M. G. Johnson, M. A. Starc and J. R. Hazlewood did not bat.

Sohail Khan 7.5–0–57–1; Ehsan Adil 5–0–31–1; Rahat Ali 6–0–37–0; Wahab Riaz 9–0–54–2; Shahid Afridi 4–0–30–0; Haris Sohail 2–0–7–0.

Umpires: H. D. P. K. Dharmasena and M. Erasmus.   Third umpire: R. K. Illingworth.
Referee: R. S. Madugalle.

NEW ZEALAND v WEST INDIES

At Wellington (Westpac Stadium), March 21, 2015 (day/night). New Zealand won by 143 runs. Toss: New Zealand.

Guptill tore the West Indies bowling apart with an unbeaten 237 that sped New Zealand to a seventh World Cup semi-final. He surpassed his own 189 not out as their highest one-day international score, as well as Gayle's tournament-record 215, set a month earlier. West Indies were left to rue dropping him on four in the opening over, when Samuels spilled a low catch at square leg. McCullum had perished early, but Guptill steadied any jitters, adding 62 with Williamson and 143 with Taylor, and dominating every moment of the innings. His seventh ODI hundred came from 111 deliveries; his double needed just another 41, as 137 runs gushed from his last 52 balls. The tenth of his 11 sixes landed on

MOST SIXES IN A ONE-DAY INTERNATIONAL

38	India (19) v Australia (19) at Bangalore..................................	2013-14
31	New Zealand (13) v India (18) at Christchurch..........................	2008-09
31	**New Zealand (15) v West Indies (16) at Wellington**	**2014-15**
27*	**England (14) v New Zealand (13) at The Oval.**	**2015**
26	South Africa (12) v Australia (14) at Johannesburg......................	2005-06
26	New Zealand (10) v Australia (16) at Hamilton..........................	2006-07
26†	New Zealand (22) v West Indies (4) at Queenstown......................	2013-14
26‡	South Africa (17) v West Indies (9) at Centurion........................	2014-15
25	**South Africa (20) v India (5) at Mumbai**	**2015-16**
24	India (12) v Sri Lanka (12) at Rajkot..................................	2009-10

*   *England innings reduced to 46 overs.*   † *Reduced to 21 overs a side.*
‡   *Reduced to 42 overs a side.*

the roof over deep midwicket, and measured 110 metres; the closing 15 overs brought 206 as West Indies lost all control. During the onslaught Gayle offered Guptill a handshake and a congratulatory "Welcome to the 200 club." West Indies' only hope was for Gayle to respond in kind. Though struggling for mobility because of a persistent back problem that had jeopardised his place, he clubbed eight sixes on his way to 61 off 33 balls, all but his first run accumulated to leg. But the rest of the top order were blown away by the sustained pace and swing of Boult, who bowled his overs off the reel. Samuels, his third victim, was athletically caught by Vettori, seemingly defying gravity to intercept an upper-cut at third man. The tempo of the match was summed up when Sammy lofted Boult's penultimate ball for six, then was sent to the canvas ducking the next; both men smiled at each other, and Sammy mimicked a throat-slitting gesture. ANDREW McGLASHAN

Man of the Match: M. J. Guptill.   *Attendance:* 30,268.

New Zealand

M. J. Guptill not out	237	D. L. Vettori not out	8
*B. B. McCullum c Holder b Taylor......	12		
K. S. Williamson c Gayle b Russell	33	L-b 2, w 7, n-b 1	10
L. R. P. L. Taylor run out	42		
C. J. Anderson c Gayle b Russell	15	1/27 (2) 2/89 (3) (6 wkts, 50 overs)	393
G. D. Elliott lbw b Taylor.............	27	3/232 (4) 4/278 (5)	
†L. Ronchi c Benn b Taylor	9	5/333 (6) 6/365 (7)	

A. F. Milne, T. G. Southee and T. A. Boult did not bat.

Taylor 7–0–71–3; Holder 8–0–76–0; Benn 10–1–66–0; Russell 10–0–96–2; Sammy 8–0–38–0; Samuels 7–0–44–0.

West Indies

C. H. Gayle b Milne	61	J. E. Taylor c Guptill b Southee	11
J. Charles b Boult	3	S. J. Benn not out	9
L. M. P. Simmons c Guptill b Boult	12		
M. N. Samuels c Vettori b Boult	27		
†D. Ramdin lbw b Boult	0	W 6	6
J. L. Carter b Vettori	32	1/4 (2) 2/27 (3) 3/80 (4) (30.3 overs) 250	
D. J. G. Sammy c Ronchi b Anderson	27	4/80 (5) 5/120 (1) 6/166 (7)	
A. D. Russell b Southee	20	7/173 (6) 8/201 (8) 9/221 (10)	
*J. O. Holder c Anderson b Vettori	42	10/250 (9) 10 overs: 80-4	

Southee 8–1–82–2; Boult 10–3–44–4; Vettori 6.3–0–58–2; Milne 4–0–42–1; Anderson 2–0–24–1.

Umpires: R. A. Kettleborough and B. N. J. Oxenford.   Third umpire: R. J. Tucker.
Referee: B. C. Broad.

SEMI-FINALS

NEW ZEALAND v SOUTH AFRICA

At Auckland, March 24, 2015 (day/night). New Zealand won by four wickets (D/L). Toss: South Africa.

In what was immediately proclaimed the greatest cricketing moment on New Zealand soil, Elliott drove the penultimate ball over long-on for six to take the Black Caps into their first World Cup final. Thus ended a gripping contest on the ground where the All Blacks had lifted rugby's Webb Ellis Cup in 2011. South Africa's own World Cup wait went on. Steyn, the bowler, was left prostrate on the pitch, and de Villiers, the beaten captain, struggled to articulate his disappointment. That Elliott, who finished 84 not out from 73 balls, was born in Johannesburg and once scored a double-hundred for South Africa Under-19 merely twisted the knife; he had the good grace to offer Steyn his condolences. Rain had fallen at an unfortunate time for South Africa during their own innings, just as de Villiers was beginning to impose himself. But they also missed two

Mob-handed: J-P. Duminy clatters into Farhaan Behardien to give Grant Elliott a vital reprieve.

clear opportunities in the field. New Zealand, chasing a revised target of 298 in 43 overs, were given another blistering start by McCullum, who hit Philander out of the attack after one over; two days later, Cricket South Africa had to deny accusations that his selection ahead of Kyle Abbott, the team's most economical bowler in the tournament, was part of their transformation agenda. With 94 needed from 70 balls, and Anderson and Elliott well set, de Villiers failed to hold a poor throw from Rossouw, squandering a run-out chance. Then, with 14 required from seven, substitute Farhaan Berhardien stood underneath a mishit by Elliott at deep square leg, only for Duminy to run into his line of vision and cause a near-collision. So New Zealand entered the final over 12 runs away: Steyn needed treatment for cramp after two balls, Vettori edged the next to the third-man ropes, and a scampered bye preceded the hit that sparked euphoria among a capacity crowd. Earlier, du Plessis and Rossouw repaired the damage inflicted by Boult, operating at times with four slips and a gully; Henry also bowled aggressively after being thrust in for his World Cup debut following Adam Milne's heel injury. The acceleration sparked by de Villiers brought 87 runs from eight overs, before a heavy shower arrived at 216 for three from 38. Miller struck 49 from 18 balls following the resumption – a cameo that appeared decisive until the thrilling climax.   RICHARD HOBSON

Man of the Match: G. D. Elliott.   *Attendance:* 41,279.

South Africa

H. M. Amla b Boult	10	J-P. Duminy not out		8
†Q. de Kock c Southee b Boult	14	B 1, w 13		14
F. du Plessis c Ronchi b Anderson	82			
R. R. Rossouw c Guptill b Anderson	39	1/21 (1) 2/31 (2)	(5 wkts, 43 overs)	281
*A. B. de Villiers not out	65	3/114 (4) 4/217 (3)		
D. A. Miller c Ronchi b Anderson	49	5/272 (6)	10 overs: 39-2	

V. D. Philander, D. W. Steyn, M. Morkel and Imran Tahir did not bat.

Southee 9–1–55–0; Boult 9–0–53–2; Henry 8–2–40–0; Vettori 9–0–46–0; Williamson 1–0–5–0; Elliott 1–0–9–0; Anderson 6–0–72–3.

New Zealand

M. J. Guptill run out	34	D. L. Vettori not out		7
*B. B. McCullum c Steyn b Morkel	59			
K. S. Williamson b Morkel	6	B 6, l-b 2, w 5		13
L. R. P. L. Taylor c de Kock b Duminy	30			
G. D. Elliott not out	84	1/71 (2) 2/81 (3)	(6 wkts, 42.5 overs)	299
C. J. Anderson c du Plessis b Morkel	58	3/128 (1) 4/149 (4)		
†L. Ronchi c Rossouw b Steyn	8	5/252 (6) 6/269 (7)	9 overs: 81-2	

T. G. Southee, M. J. Henry and T. A. Boult did not bat.

Steyn 8.5–0–76–1; Philander 8–0–52–0; Morkel 9–0–59–3; Imran Tahir 9–1–40–0; Duminy 5–0–43–1; de Villiers 3–0–21–0.

Umpires: I. J. Gould and R. J. Tucker.   Third umpire: N. J. Llong.
Referee: D. C. Boon.

AUSTRALIA v INDIA

At Sydney, March 26, 2015 (day/night). Australia won by 95 runs. Toss: Australia.

Steven Smith had taken four Test hundreds off India in the southern summer, but his first one-day century against them – a wonderfully paced 93-ball 105 – proved the deepest cut, wresting India's grip from the World Cup they had won in 2011. Australia's progress to the last four had been stuttering, while India had gained seven straight wins. But, in front of a crowd awash with Indian tricolours, Australia coasted home. Smith and Finch – whose attritional 81 was chalk to his partner's gourmet cheese – added 182 in 31 overs for the second wicket, before Johnson landed devastating blows with bat and ball. India had dismissed their opponents in all seven victories but, after snaring Warner with a short delivery, they overdid the ploy. Yadav took four wickets, but went at eight an over; Mohammed Shami and Mohit Sharma proved almost as profligate, lessening the value of ten tight overs from Ashwin. From a healthy 232 for two, Australia could afford a wobble – they lost three for 16 – before Johnson's blistering nine-ball 27 smashed them well past 300. With Dhawan in swashbuckling form, India were on course until he picked out deep extra cover. Australia went for the throat: Kohli miscued a short one from Johnson, while Rohit Sharma played on, and a 70-run partnership between Rahane and Dhoni offered little more than nuisance value. Starc, fast and miserly, and Faulkner ensured India were dismissed for the only time in the tournament – a limp end to an otherwise excellent campaign. Asked about surrendering the trophy, a downcast Dhoni said: "It is something that doesn't really belong to anyone. We definitely took it from someone, so somebody took it from us." In 2011, that someone had been Australia. Four years on, they returned the favour, emphatically.   DILEEP PREMACHANDRAN

Man of the Match: S. P. D. Smith.   *Attendance:* 42,330.

Australia

A. J. Finch c Dhawan b Yadav	81	†B. J. Haddin not out		7
D. A. Warner c Kohli b Yadav	12	M. G. Johnson not out		27
S. P. D. Smith c R. G. Sharma b Yadav	105	B 1, l-b 7, w 6		14
G. J. Maxwell c Rahane b Ashwin	23			
S. R. Watson c Rahane b M. Sharma	28	1/15 (2) 2/197 (3)	(7 wkts, 50 overs)	328
*M. J. Clarke c R. G. Sharma b M. Sharma	10	3/232 (4) 4/233 (1)		
J. P. Faulkner b Yadav	21	5/248 (6) 6/284 (7) 7/298 (5)	10 overs: 56-1	

M. A. Starc and J. R. Hazlewood did not bat.

Mohammed Shami 10–0–68–0; Yadav 9–0–72–4; M. Sharma 10–0–75–2; Kohli 1–0–7–0; Jadeja 10–0–56–0; Ashwin 10–0–42–1.

India

R. G. Sharma b Johnson	34	M. Sharma b Faulkner		0
S. Dhawan c Maxwell b Hazlewood	45	U. T. Yadav b Starc		0
V. Kohli c Haddin b Johnson	1			
A. M. Rahane c Haddin b Starc	44	L-b 8, w 5, n-b 2		15
S. K. Raina c Haddin b Faulkner	7			
*†M. S. Dhoni run out	65	1/76 (2) 2/78 (3) 3/91 (1)	(46.5 overs)	233
R. A. Jadeja run out	16	4/108 (5) 5/178 (4) 6/208 (7)		
R. Ashwin b Faulkner	5	7/231 (6) 8/232 (8) 9/232 (10)		
Mohammed Shami not out	1	10/233 (11)	10 overs: 55-0	

Starc 8.5–0–28–2; Hazlewood 10–1–41–1; Johnson 10–0–50–2; Faulkner 9–1–59–3; Maxwell 5–0–18–0; Watson 4–0–29–0.

Umpires: H. D. P. K. Dharmasena and R. A. Kettleborough.   Third umpire: M. Erasmus.
Referee: R. S. Madugalle.

FINAL

AUSTRALIA v NEW ZEALAND

STEVEN LYNCH

At Melbourne, March 29, 2015 (day/night). Australia won by seven wickets. Toss: New Zealand.

Australia collected the World Cup for the fifth time, joining their predecessors India as home winners. Fittingly, the best innings was played by their captain, Clarke, who had just announced this would be his last one-day international. After a high-intensity, high-volume few weeks, it was a strangely old-fashioned match, decided by the ball and played

Outshone: Corey Anderson disappears into the shadows after Man of the Match James Faulkner bowls him for a duck.

out in front of an unusually restrained crowd, which nonetheless numbered 93,013 – a record for a single day's cricket outside the unaudited Kolkata terraces. It took the total attendance for the tournament to over a million.

Clarke's may have been the decisive innings, but the decisive passage came in the first over. McCullum, fresh from winning the toss, swished at his first delivery from Starc, charged at (and missed) the second, and was yorked by the third; he would later admit to not watching the ball. In their previous matches in the tournament – all at home – New Zealand's openers had averaged 56 together, at nine an over. Now it was one for one. A nation was left wondering whether their talisman, in different conditions, might have curbed his aggression for an over or two.

Guptill, the competition's leading scorer, missed a straight one from Maxwell – earning a send-off from Haddin that cost the Australians a few more friends – and New Zealand had to rebuild from 39 for three after Williamson chipped a return catch to Johnson. Elliott, one of the Cup's surprise stars, regrouped in a stand of 111 with the subdued Taylor, and the innings seemed back on course, until Taylor fell to the first ball of the 36th over. Could New Zealand's big-hitting middle order run riot in the last 15? The answer soon came: Anderson was undone by his second ball, from the inventive Faulkner, and Ronchi lasted only four before flashing to slip in the next over, from Starc.

There was not much more: in all the last seven wickets crashed for 33 in ten overs, including Elliott for a fighting 83 from 82 balls; he departed to another ugly volley from Haddin, as well as Faulkner. Australia's left-arm quicks took eight for 86; their right-armoury managed one for 90.

Boult hurried Finch into a leading edge – his 22nd wicket of the tournament, putting him level with Starc – but New Zealand needed more early strikes if they were to emulate India's success in defending 183 at Lord's in 1983. Australia resolutely refused to play ball. Warner collected the first 28 runs off the bat, including three successive fours in Southee's third over (later, the off-colour Southee would concede four in a row to Clarke). Warner eventually hoisted Henry to deep square, which brought in Clarke, to avid applause. He started stiffly, his correct strokeplay seemingly an anachronism in these days of windmilling wonderbats – but soon realised this was the sort of game he was used to, more Test-match chase than one-day slogfest.

The introduction of Vettori, in his final international appearance, slowed things down, until Clarke launched him over long-off in the 25th over, a clean six born of inbuilt timing rather than gym-built muscle. By halfway Australia needed just 54. Clarke seemed set to take them home, but chopped Henry on with nine required, having made 74 from 72 balls. Meanwhile, Smith, his heir apparent, had carried quietly on to his fifth successive score above 50 since Vettori snared him for four in the pool game. New Zealand's breathless one-wicket victory then had sealed the match of the tournament; this one, sadly, followed several previous World Cup finals in failing to provide much excitement.

Australia's team and fans were not bothered by that, and the loudest roar of the night came when Smith pulled Henry for the winning boundary with 16.5 overs to spare. Now it was time for fireworks, glitter and a lap of honour in front of those who had stayed to the triumphant end of a long and emotional season for Australian cricket.

Man of the Match: J. P. Faulkner.   *Attendance:* 93,013.

Man of the Tournament: M. A. Starc.   *Tournament attendance:* 1,016,421.

New Zealand

M. J. Guptill b Maxwell	15	M. J. Henry c Starc b Johnson	0
*B. B. McCullum b Starc	0	T. A. Boult not out	0
K. S. Williamson c and b Johnson	12		
L. R. P. L. Taylor c Haddin b Faulkner	40	L-b 7, w 6	13
G. D. Elliott c Haddin b Faulkner	83		
C. J. Anderson b Faulkner	0	1/1 (2) 2/33 (1) 3/39 (3) (45 overs) 183	
†L. Ronchi c Clarke b Starc	0	4/150 (4) 5/150 (6) 6/151 (7)	
D. L. Vettori b Johnson	9	7/167 (8) 8/171 (5) 9/182 (10)	
T. G. Southee run out	11	10/183 (9) 10 overs: 31-1	

Starc 8–0–20–2; Hazlewood 8–2–30–0; Johnson 9–0–30–3; Maxwell 7–0–37–1; Faulkner 9–1–36–3; Watson 4–0–23–0.

Australia

D. A. Warner c Elliott b Henry	45
A. J. Finch c and b Boult	0
S. P. D. Smith not out	56
*M. J. Clarke b Henry	74
S. R. Watson not out	2
L-b 3, w 6	9

1/2 (2) 2/63 (1) (3 wkts, 33.1 overs) 186
3/175 (4) 10 overs: 56-1

G. J. Maxwell, J. P. Faulkner, †B. J. Haddin, M. G. Johnson, M. A. Starc and J. R. Hazlewood did not bat.

Southee 8–0–65–0; Boult 10–0–40–1; Vettori 5–0–25–0; Henry 9.1–0–46–2; Anderson 1–0–7–0.

Umpires: H. D. P. K. Dharmasena and R. A. Kettleborough.   Third umpire: M. Erasmus.
Referee: R. S. Madugalle.

AUSTRALIAN CRICKET IN 2015

One lousy session

Daniel Brettig

Eighteen overs and three balls – and 94 minutes. In that time, Australia's cricketers endured a debacle that was to overshadow much of the other 364 days, 22 hours and 26 minutes of 2015. It was a year in which they won a home World Cup, three Test series and two other one-day tournaments. It was also a year in which they bade farewell to Ryan Harris, Michael Clarke, Chris Rogers, Shane Watson, Brad Haddin and Mitchell Johnson from Test cricket. But all that had to compete in the memory with being skittled for 60 on the first morning at Trent Bridge to give up the Ashes – the nadir of a tour that had promised much, yet ultimately delivered more pain and missed opportunities than any Australian trip to England since 1981.

A more triumphant note had been struck at the World Cup in February and March, a tournament in which Clarke's team fulfilled expectations in almost

AUSTRALIA IN 2015

	Played	Won	Lost	Drawn/No result
Tests	13	8	3	2
One-day internationals	20	15	3	2
Twenty20 internationals	1	–	1	–

DECEMBER JANUARY	4 Tests (h) v India	(see *Wisden 2015*, page 840)
FEBRUARY	Triangular ODI tournament (h) v England and India	(page 273)
MARCH	ICC World Cup (in Australia and New Zealand)	(page 860)
APRIL		
MAY		
JUNE	2 Tests (a) v West Indies	(page 1149)
JULY AUGUST SEPTEMBER	5 Tests, 5 ODIs and 1 T20I (a) v England 1 ODI (a) v Ireland	(page 327) (page 840)
OCTOBER		
NOVEMBER	3 Tests (h) v New Zealand	(page 930)
DECEMBER JANUARY	3 Tests (h) v West Indies	(page 945)

For a review of Australian domestic cricket from the 2014-15 season, see page 960.

every respect. Their preparation had been affected by speculation over whether Clarke would be fit after hamstring surgery; obvious tension between the captain and the selectors had even compelled Cricket Australia chief executive James Sutherland to reassure Clarke of his commission.

A smooth return owed much to stand-in captain George Bailey after he led his men to a vast victory over England in the tournament opener, before uncomplainingly giving up his place in the side for the rest of the event. There was one hiccup, against New Zealand at Eden Park, but even then the power of Mitchell Starc's swinging yorkers was underlined when he turned a modest chase into a cliffhanger. When the two sides met in the final, it was defined as much by Starc's first-over rocket into Brendon McCullum's off stump as by some ungracious send-offs and celebrations from the Australians.

Two days after the World Cup, the selection chairman Rod Marsh announced the squad for the tours of the West Indies and England. In retrospect, it was the day many of the troubles subsequently seen during the Ashes had their genesis. The same 17 were chosen for widely contrasting conditions, meaning the likes of Haddin and Watson were guaranteed their spots, despite questionable form. It was also a squad chosen exclusively for the now; a judge as wise as Jason Gillespie soon called the 2015 Australians "Dad's Army".

Not that this had much impact in the Caribbean. On the contrary, the know-how of Adam Voges was vital in extricating the Australians from an awkward second day in Dominica; at 35, he became the oldest debut centurion in Tests. Against a West Indian side wrong-footed by the muddled exit of Shivnarine Chanderpaul, and distracted by the looming Caribbean Premier League, Voges's innings set up the series, before Steve Smith's fine 199 at Sabina Park ensured a comprehensive 2–0 margin.

Australia's early days in England coincided with a burst of sunny weather, and a pair of comfortable tour-match victories. But trouble soon arose in the shape of Harris's knee, which was so compromised in Canterbury that he suffered a leg fracture trying to bowl on it, and said an emotional goodbye to the game. Coach Darren Lehmann had not expected Harris to play every Test, but to lose him for all five was a blow; it was never quite shrugged off. He was badly missed in Cardiff, where a lack of precision contrasted with English plans for every visiting batsman, which brought victory in four days.

At Lord's, a flat pitch and Clarke's correct call at the toss set up an Australian triumph redolent of 2013-14, as Rogers and Smith made big runs before Johnson, Starc and Josh Hazlewood rumbled out heavy-legged Englishmen. At their London base in Kensington, Australia's players, staff and administrators celebrated the thumping 405-run victory like Ashes winners.

But as Marsh would ruefully note: "We were so wrong." Edgbaston brought a fresher surface and James Anderson's wobble ball, a slim first innings and a heavy defeat. By this point the Australians were no longer the happiest bunch, as private concerns about the treatment of Haddin – who had stood down for personal reasons at Lord's but was not reinstated – left players and selectors at odds. Clarke's batting, meanwhile, had deteriorated alarmingly, leading to ever more strident denials that he was thinking of retirement.

Bowling with altitude: Mitchell Starc in the World Cup final.

It all came crashing down on a slightly damp morning in Nottingham, as Stuart Broad hit exactly the right length to lure the Australians into repeated errors. The shortest opening innings in Test history was over before lunch on the first day, the series before lunch on the third. Five careers instantly lost their happy ending, and Clarke began the retirement procession within moments of the final wicket. As the old captain lay low in London, Smith was inked in as the new leader in the modest surrounds of Northampton, where belated, frank conversations took place. Equally belated was the inclusion of Peter Siddle, who would go on to add balance to the bowling attack in a victory at The Oval which was also the result of much-improved play by Smith and Voges against England's seamers. Too late.

Coming home to face New Zealand and West Indies, Smith and his remodelled team were able to accomplish a pair of series victories that underlined Australia's pre-eminence in their own backyard, even if the inaugural day/night Test – in more seam-friendly conditions at Adelaide – noticeably closed the gap with McCullum's side.

There was no such closeness against West Indies, who had to contend with the sight of many of their best players performing in the Big Bash. That competition enjoyed a breakthrough season, attracting enormous crowds and television ratings. Rested from BBL duty to protect a sore knee, Smith was left with one lesson at the forefront of his mind, taken primarily from Trent Bridge: to win abroad, the Australian way needed rethinking.

AUSTRALIA v NEW ZEALAND IN 2015-16

Geoff Lemon

Test matches (3): Australia 2, New Zealand 0

This series will be remembered as the birth of day/night Test cricket, so newly delivered as to feel slick with caul. Its infant health proved sufficiently robust to avoid abandonment on a hillside but, depending on your perspective, the weanling could grow up to be either cricket's saviour or the monster that devours it. Either scenario places a lot of responsibility on a newborn.

Destruction, at least, won't be attributable to the format's pink ball. The lurid Kookaburra with the pine-green stitching stood up staunchly to everything asked of it on its first Test outing, during the third match, at Adelaide. The grassy pitch designed to preserve the ball's condition also helped preserve the sanity of onlookers, providing a more balanced contest after the Perth Test was dominated by the bat. As for concerns about visibility, ask the fan who pulled off a spectacular catch from the first pink-ball six, at deep square leg, at dusk.

When this series had first been scheduled, New Zealand's Test side were so weak they were designated as the warm-up act for the touring clown show that is the modern West Indies. But Brendon McCullum had overseen New Zealand's resurgence. Australia had lost badly in the UAE and England over the previous 13 months, while the New Zealanders had fought creditably in both countries for 1–1 draws.

Yet, as it turned out, their new breed retained a mental block. They were talked up for their first Trans-Tasman win since the days of Richard Hadlee but, as in the 2015 World Cup, their arrival in Australia changed the story. They were barely present for the First Test, nor for the opening day of the Second, and with that the chance of a series win was gone. While they fought back in Perth to draw, and were denied a potentially match-winning lead in Adelaide by an error from third umpire Nigel Llong, it was the first time since their tour of England in 2013, eight series earlier, that New Zealand had tasted overall defeat.

Even so, there was plenty to cheer. As his Test average marched towards 50, Kane Williamson filled one of the few remaining holes in his résumé by taking a hundred – in fact two – off the Australians, to finish the series with 428 runs at 85. Appreciation for his class belatedly overcame the myopia of local fans and pundits. Ross Taylor's Perth 290, meanwhile, was the highest Test score by a visiting batsman in Australia. Doug Bracewell bowled impressive spells, and Trent Boult came close to winning the Third Test with five for 60. McCullum was admired, and his every dismissal – in what turned out to be his final overseas series – cheered with a tinge of relief.

For Australia the series was about renewal. A few months earlier, Ryan Harris had retired before a ball of the 2015 Ashes was bowled. Shane Watson and Brad Haddin had lasted one Test. Michael Clarke shouldn't have lasted five. Chris Rogers called time on himself. Back home, Mitchell Johnson realised he'd had enough.

Two seasons earlier, 11 Australians surged through the 2013-14 Ashes whitewash unchanged. Only three were ever-present then and now. Against England, Steve Smith, David Warner and Nathan Lyon had been junior parties. Now they were captain, vice-captain, and the "GOAT" – designated mirthfully

Threading it neatly: Ross Taylor at Perth.

Paul Kane, Getty Images

by team-mates as the Greatest Of All Time after becoming the nation's most prolific off-spinner. The nickname wasn't pure irony: he would soon become the first Australian offie to play 50 Tests and, in terms of spin wickets, trailed only the leg-break cartel of Shane Warne, Richie Benaud, Clarrie Grimmett and Stuart MacGill.

Warner embraced responsibility, making three consecutive centuries for the second time in his career, including his first double and his two longest innings. He finished with 592 runs; only Graham Gooch (752), Brian Lara (688) and Mohammad Yousuf (665) had compiled more in a series of three Tests. Usman Khawaja scored two tons on his return to the side before tweaking his hamstring, while newly anointed opener Joe Burns also hit a maiden hundred, in the First Test. Adam Voges proved his worth as a late-blooming selection with 285 runs at 71.

Johnson's abrupt retirement after Perth fundamentally changed the fast-bowling attack. Australia's coach Darren Lehmann saw no contradiction in coveting extreme pace – playing the erratic pair of Johnson and Mitchell Starc – while lamenting a lack of control. The sensible and economical choice of Peter Siddle had been forced on the selectors come Adelaide, where Starc's injured ankle allowed Josh Hazlewood a turn as attack leader.

Off the field, there was plenty of talk about "nice guys". New Zealand were built up as paragons of deference and decency, and Australians accused them of hamming it up. As a couple of bemused New Zealanders explained when the cameras were off, this was nothing to do with illustrating their opponents' faults: they were simply behaving the way they'd been taught. Taking into account the preceding weeks of the rugby World Cup, and the All Blacks' respect for even the most lowly opponent, that was hard to dispute.

If the Australians were shown up for a lack of class, it was their own behaviour that made them vulnerable. ABC commentator Dirk Nannes met hostility for saying that the team's historically poor reputation meant the current lot needed to try to change it. The response to his comments only proved his point. In the end the nice guys did finish last, leaving Australia hopeful that their own new era would work out. But New Zealand left with reputation intact, and renewed determination to boss the return series in February.

NEW ZEALAND TOURING PARTY

*B. B. McCullum, T. A. Boult, D. A. J. Bracewell, M. D. Craig, M. J. Guptill, M. J. Henry, T. W. M. Latham, M. J. McClenaghan, J. D. S. Neesham, L. Ronchi, H. D. Rutherford, M. J. Santner, T. G. Southee, L. R. P. L. Taylor, N. Wagner, B-J. Watling, K. S. Williamson. *Coach:* M. J. Hesson.

C. J. Anderson was replaced by Santner before the tour. Wagner and McClenaghan joined the squad after Southee and Neesham either developed or aggravated injuries in the First Test. All three suffered back problems.

TEST MATCH AVERAGES

AUSTRALIA – BATTING AND FIELDING

	T	I	NO	R	HS	100	50	Avge	Ct/St
†U. T. Khawaja	2	3	1	304	174	2	0	152.00	0
†D. A. Warner	3	6	0	592	253	3	0	98.66	2
A. C. Voges	3	6	2	285	119	1	1	71.25	1
†M. A. Starc	3	4	3	52	28*	0	0	52.00	1
S. P. D. Smith	3	6	0	281	138	1	1	46.83	7
J. A. Burns	3	6	0	265	129	1	1	44.16	3
P. M. Nevill	3	4	0	130	66	0	1	32.50	11/1
†J. R. Hazlewood	3	3	2	14	8*	0	0	14.00	1
M. R. Marsh	3	5	0	69	34	0	0	13.80	2

Played in three Tests: N. M. Lyon 4*, 34 (3 ct). Played in two Tests: †M. G. Johnson 2, 29 (2 ct). Played in one Test: †S. E. Marsh 2, 49; P. M. Siddle 0, 9*.

BOWLING

	Style	O	M	R	W	BB	5I	Avge
M. A. Starc	LF	89.5	20	302	13	4-57	0	23.23
M. R. Marsh	RFM	52	7	210	7	3-59	0	30.00
J. R. Hazlewood	RFM	119.1	20	411	13	6-70	1	31.61
N. M. Lyon	OB	107.5	14	329	10	3-63	0	32.90
M. G. Johnson	LF	74	13	340	7	3-105	0	48.57

Also bowled: P. M. Siddle (RFM) 31–11–89–2; S. P. D. Smith (LBG) 6–0–19–0; A. C. Voges (SLA) 1–0–3–0.

NEW ZEALAND – BATTING AND FIELDING

	T	I	NO	R	HS	100	50	Avge	Ct/St
K. S. Williamson	3	6	1	428	166	2	1	85.60	3
L. R. P. L. Taylor	3	6	1	405	290	1	0	81.00	4
†T. W. M. Latham	3	6	0	187	50	0	1	31.16	4
B. B. McCullum	3	5	0	137	80	0	1	27.40	1
†M. D. Craig	3	5	1	91	26*	0	0	22.75	1
T. A. Boult	3	5	3	45	23*	0	0	22.50	1
B-J. Watling	3	5	0	83	32	0	0	16.60	9/2
D. A. J. Bracewell	3	5	0	66	27*	0	0	16.50	1
T. G. Southee	3	5	0	69	21	0	0	13.80	3
M. J. Guptill	3	6	0	82	23	0	0	13.66	2

Played in one Test: M. J. Henry 6; †J. D. S. Neesham 3, 3; †M. J. Santner 31, 45 (1 ct).

BOWLING

	Style	O	M	R	W	BB	5I	Avge
T. A. Boult	LFM	115	15	489	13	5-60	1	37.61
D. A. J. Bracewell	RFM	106.1	15	368	7	3-18	0	52.57
T. G. Southee	RFM	111	20	363	6	4-97	0	60.50
M. D. Craig	OB	102	5	513	8	3-78	0	64.12

Also bowled: M. J. Guptill (OB) 3–0–7–0; M. J. Henry (RFM) 42–9–158–2; B. B. McCullum (RM) 2–0–16–0; J. D. S. Neesham (RFM) 20–1–111–1; M. J. Santner (SLA) 18–1–62–2; K. S. Williamson (OB) 12.2–0–58–1.

At Canberra, October 23, 2015 (day/night). **New Zealanders won by 102 runs. ‡New Zealanders 307-8** (50 overs) (M. J. Guptill 94, T. W. M. Latham 131; J. P. Behrendorff 3-56); **Prime Minister's XI 205** (45.2 overs) (A. C. Voges 55, R. G. L. Carters 74; T. A. Boult 3-27, J. D. S. Neesham 3-23). *Martin Guptill and Tom Latham opened with a stand of 196 in 33.5 overs and, although they then lost 3-3, the New Zealanders went on to pass 300. The PM's XI struggled to 13-3 against the pink ball and, after Jimmy Neesham removed the Hussey brothers – Mike (captain for the day) and David – it was left to Adam Voges and wicketkeeper Ryan Carters to save embarrassment. Voges added to criticism of the pink-ball experiment: "The one that got hit on to the roof [by Guptill] and didn't come back was 28 overs old and it looked like it was 68. To be honest, it didn't hold up very well at all tonight… There were bits of pink left, but it was more green than pink by the end."*

At Canberra, October 24–25, 2015. **Drawn. ‡Cricket Australia XI 325-4 dec** (90 overs) (J. A. Burns 102, U. T. Khawaja 111*); **New Zealanders 368-8** (82 overs) (K. S. Williamson 68, B. B. McCullum 58, M. D. Craig 60). *The CA XI chose from 12 players, the New Zealanders from 13. Joe Burns and Usman Khawaja pressed their cases for inclusion in the First Test by scoring centuries; Burns eventually retired, but Khawaja was still there at the close, after hitting 20 fours. The New Zealanders batted solidly the following day: Guptill made a duck, but everyone else reached double figures. Only one other batsman was actually dismissed – the other six all retired out. Ashton Agar's hopes of a Test recall were dented by figures of 22–1–111–0.*

At Sydney (Blacktown International Sportspark), October 29–30, 2015. **Drawn. ‡Cricket Australia XI 503-1 dec** (121.1 overs) (R. G. L. Carters 209, A. J. Finch 288*) **v New Zealanders.** *In one of first-class cricket's strangest games, the Cricket Australia XI openers, Ryan Carters and Aaron Finch (who hit 24 fours and seven sixes), shared a stand of 503 – the highest on Australian soil, beating 464* by the Waugh twins for New South Wales's fifth wicket against Western Australia at Perth in 1990-91. But when they were finally separated, shortly before lunch on the second of the scheduled three days, the match was abandoned as the pitch was breaking up and had become dangerous; Brendon McCullum did not use his faster bowlers on the second day. "I'd describe it as a jigsaw with half the pieces missing," observed New Zealand's coach Mike Hesson. "They're unable to grow any grass here at this time of year so it was basically like rolled mud with a little topping. As it dried, it baked and bits started falling out." A spokesman for CA said: "Preparation of the wicket was compromised by poor weather conditions in Sydney early this week."*

AUSTRALIA v NEW ZEALAND

First Test Match

At Brisbane, November 5–9, 2015. Australia won by 208 runs. Toss: Australia.

You could understand why people fancied New Zealand. Australia's new opener Burns had boshed a few one-day runs in the build-up. Steve Smith, their sole success at first drop since Ricky Ponting, was forced down to No. 4 by the return of Khawaja, a previous failure, which in turn placed extra pressure on Khawaja himself. Voges was lucky to have made it to seven Tests. And Mitchell Marsh had not proved himself more than a bowling slogger.

Arrayed against this disorder were Southee and Boult, both of whom had spent most of the World Cup hooping the white ball into the stumps of defenceless batsmen. A muggy tropical morning, you imagined, and they might cause havoc. That remained in the imagination. For the first 20 minutes Southee bent a few, including one just past Burns's off stump. But, once that brief shadow passed, the pattern of so many Gabba Tests was imposed once more, as Australia chugged relentlessly to 556 for four, and New Zealand delivered lengths that made scoring simple.

As a batsman, if not always in his personal interactions, Warner the batsman likes to get off on the right foot. For the third home season in a row, he struck a century in Australia's opening match. And, for the second season in a row, he did it in both innings, joining Ponting and Sunil Gavaskar as the only batsmen to make twin Test tons on three occasions. Until now, the longest innings of Warner's Test career had been 174 balls. Before the series, he had spoken about wanting to improve that. Here, he passed 200 balls for the first time.

Burns made a confident 71 before edging Southee and, with 161 on the board, Khawaja – in his first Test for more than two years – was granted easy passage. He lofted Craig's off-spin for two sixes from four balls, and had matched his previous Test best of 65 by the time Warner fell for 163. Khawaja's maiden century came to generous home-ground applause just before stumps, with Australia's 389 for two the biggest first-day score at the Gabba.

Smith was bowled by some good left-arm swing from Boult next morning but, with Southee sidelined early in the day by a back injury, Khawaja and Voges added 157. Khawaja felt emboldened enough to reverse-sweep Williamson, but only provided a catch to point, provoking Smith's declaration with Voges on 83.

From Williamson to Williamson it went, New Zealand's No. 3 providing the only resistance after the long drag in the field. His 140 out of 317 was a Test knock of the finest standard, especially when the three below him mustered nine runs between them; it made him the first to pass 2,000 international runs in 2015. Latham's 47 and some low-order stubbornness were Williamson's main support but, his strokeplay was on another plane. He started by flicking Hazlewood through midwicket and Lyon over it, before driving Johnson straight and pulling Marsh square. By stumps, he had 55.

It was his work through cover and point that thrilled the most, the immaculate timing of each cut, late cut and drive, the way the ball flew from his bat to the fence. Analysts recorded his percentage of controlled strokes at 92, but that felt insultingly low. He made nearly a century in boundaries alone, and was caught behind only when the need to shield No. 11 Boult from Starc disrupted his rhythm.

With a lead of 509 and liberty to swing, Burns and Warner became the first Australian openers to put on 100 in each innings of a Test. Warner had now been involved in four successive opening stands of 100-plus, following 113 at Trent Bridge and 110 at The Oval, both with Chris Rogers; no team had ever boasted four in a row. The only other instance of a pair sharing two stands of 150-plus in a Test was by Paul Gibb and Eddie Paynter, who put on 184 and 168 for England's second wicket at Johannesburg in 1938-39. Burns reached his first century in Tests with two sixes in three balls off Craig under stormy skies that brought a brief interruption; Warner followed in a blaze of shots. Four slogged wickets before play ended meant little for New Zealand, but summed up a Test in which runs came at 4.17 an over – a record in Australia, at least until the West Indians arrived.

Set 504 on the fourth morning, New Zealand could opt only for a go-slow. Rain and bad light limited the day to 53 overs, as Latham stonewalled for more than an hour and a half, and Guptill for more than three. But they were prised out and, while Williamson batted as fluidly as his first attempt, he was adjudged leg-before to a ball from Lyon that the review showed would have been lucky to kiss the bail. It was two overs before tea, after which play was abandoned.

McCullum entertained everyone next day with a run-a-ball 80, as did last man Boult with his crane-kick batting: a bowler-puzzling method of exposing his stumps before blocking the ball while balancing on one leg, with movement across the crease in either direction, and occasional whacks for four through the line. Vaudeville stuff, but you couldn't help feeling flat at a finale played out in front of a few hundred people on a Monday morning, and at the contest that never materialised.

Man of the Match: D. A. Warner.   *Attendance:* 53,572.

Close of play: first day, Australia 389-2 (Khawaja 102, Smith 41); second day, New Zealand 157-5 (Williamson 55, Watling 14); third day, Australia 264-4 (Khawaja 9, Voges 1); fourth day, New Zealand 142-3 (Taylor 20, McCullum 4).

Australia

J. A. Burns c Watling b Southee	71	– c Taylor b Craig 129
D. A. Warner c Taylor b Neesham	163	– c Boult b Craig 116
U. T. Khawaja c Guptill b Williamson	174	– not out 9
*S. P. D. Smith b Boult	48	– c Williamson b Boult 1
A. C. Voges not out	83	– (6) not out. 1
M. R. Marsh (did not bat)		– (5) c McCullum b Craig 2
L-b 7, w 4, n-b 6	17	L-b 1, w 1, n-b 4 6

1/161 (1) 2/311 (2)   (4 wkts dec, 130.2 overs) 556   1/237 (2)   (4 wkts dec, 42 overs) 264
3/399 (4) 4/556 (3)   2/254 (1) 3/258 (4)
4/263 (5)

†P. M. Nevill, M. G. Johnson, M. A. Starc, J. R. Hazlewood and N. M. Lyon did not bat.

Southee 24–8–70–1; Boult 29–3–127–1; Bracewell 27–3–107–0; Craig 31–3–156–0; Neesham 11–1–50–1; Williamson 8.2–0–39–1. *Second innings*—Boult 8–0–61–1; Bracewell 11–1–63–0; Neesham 9–0–61–0; Craig 14–0–78–3.

New Zealand

M. J. Guptill c Warner b Hazlewood	23	– (2) c Smith b Lyon 23
T. W. M. Latham c Lyon b Starc	47	– (1) lbw b Starc 29
K. S. Williamson c Nevill b Starc	140	– lbw b Lyon 59
L. R. P. L. Taylor c Smith b Johnson	0	– c Smith b Hazlewood 26
*B. B. McCullum c Voges b Johnson	6	– c Smith b Marsh 80
J. D. S. Neesham b Starc	3	– c Burns b Johnson 3
†B-J. Watling c Nevill b Johnson	32	– lbw b Lyon 14
M. D. Craig c Marsh b Lyon	24	– not out 26
D. A. J. Bracewell b Marsh	16	– lbw b Marsh 0
T. G. Southee b Starc	14	– c Nevill b Hazlewood 5
T. A. Boult not out	0	– c Nevill b Starc 15
L-b 4, w 1, n-b 7	12	B 7, l-b 5, w 2, n-b 1 15

1/56 (1) 2/102 (2) 3/105 (4)   (82.2 overs) 317   1/44 (1) 2/98 (2)   (88.3 overs) 295
4/114 (5) 5/118 (6) 6/185 (7)   3/136 (3) 4/165 (4)
7/231 (8) 8/273 (9) 9/310 (10) 10/317 (3)   5/205 (6) 6/242 (7) 7/243 (5)
8/243 (9) 9/249 (10) 10/295 (11)

Starc 17.2–4–57–4; Johnson 21–3–105–3; Hazlewood 21–5–70–1; Lyon 17–3–46–1; Marsh 5–0–32–1; Voges 1–0–3–0. *Second innings*—Starc 20.3–5–69–2; Johnson 19–6–58–1; Hazlewood 18–3–68–2; Marsh 10–3–25–2; Lyon 21–3–63–3.

Umpires: R. K. Illingworth and N. J. Llong.   Third umpire: S. Ravi.
Referee: R. S. Mahanama.

> ❝ Benaud's was the blue-chip stock in every portfolio, the household brand in every home.❞
> Richie Benaud 1930–2015, page 44

AUSTRALIA v NEW ZEALAND

Second Test Match

At Perth, November 13–17, 2015. Drawn. Toss: Australia.

It is Perthian pre-match tradition to talk things up. This, we are told every year, will be a return to the old WACA pitch: pace, carry, bounce, lightning, nostalgia. But, as so often, looking to the past leads to disappointment. The 2015 edition was more kitchen sponge than trampoline. Nicks, even in the opening overs, didn't carry. Runs were plonked at will. The bowlers couldn't work on swing because the ball kept going out of shape. "Things fall apart; the centre cannot hold," warned W. B. Yeats. And so the icons fell: the WACA dead, the Kookaburra plucked and, some time on the third day, Australia's fourth-highest wicket-taker looked around and asked "What's the point?"

Not since South Africa's visit in December 2005 had a Test here finished as a draw. The malaise was general. The groundsman skulked around with his tail between his legs. Ball-manufacturing reps held hushed conversations with journalists. The sightscreen broke down for 17 minutes, and administrators failed to see the humour in the ABC's light-hearted interview with Sunny Munn, its operator.

The same administrators had bragged about record crowds for a Brisbane match devoid of atmosphere and priced beyond reason and, while the WACA better suits lower numbers, it suffered the same fate. On that first day in Brisbane, Ryan Harris had a lap of honour around a ground barely a third full; on the fifth in Perth, Mitchell Johnson's Test career petered out in front of a few Tuesday spectators.

WHACKING IT AT THE WACA

The highest aggregates in Test matches at Perth:

Runs	Wkts		
1,672	**28**	**Aus (559-9 dec and 385-7 dec) drew with NZ (624 and 104-2)**	**2015-16**
1,522	35	NZ (534-9 dec and 256-9 dec) drew with Aus (351 and 381-7)	2001-02
1,468	37	India (402 and 330-9 dec) lost to Aus (394 and 342-8)	1977-78
1,427	36	WI (449 and 349-9 dec) beat Aus (395-8 dec and 234).	1988-89
1,389	30	Eng (592-8 dec and 199-8 dec) drew with Aus (401 and 197-4).	1986-87
1,389	34	Aus (375 and 319) lost to SA (281 and 414-4)	2008-09
1,369	33	Aus (258 and 528-8 dec) drew with SA (296 and 287-5)	2005-06
1,358	36	Aus (385 and 369-6 dec) beat Eng (251 and 353).	2013-14
1,336	35	Aus (244 and 527-5 dec) beat Eng (215 and 350)	2006-07
1,306	24	Aus (398 and 323-1 dec) drew with NZ (419-9 dec and 166-4)	1993-94

There have been three higher aggregates elsewhere in Australia, the highest 1,764 in the draw between West Indies (276 and 616) and Australia (533 and 339-9) at Adelaide in 1968-69.

But, for fans of batting, there were achievements on display beyond the merely substantial. Again, Smith won the toss; again, New Zealand bowled poorly. This time, Warner went even bigger, scoring more runs on the first day of a Test – 244 – than anyone bar Don Bradman, who made 309 at Leeds in 1930 (and 244 himself at The Oval in 1934). Having faced 200 balls for the first time at Brisbane, Warner followed up with a new personal-best, out early on the second morning from his 286th. Nor was his innings a whirlwind: it was measured and controlled, balancing risk against reward. Until Taylor trumped him, it was the WACA's second-highest Test score, after Matthew Hayden's then-world-record 380 against Zimbabwe in 2003-04. Khawaja added a century of his own on the first day in a partnership of 302, with the stumps score 416 for two; but he would injure a hamstring in the field the following day, and take no further part in the series.

MITCHELL JOHNSON RETIRES FROM INTERNATIONAL CRICKET

The boy with the curl

GREG BAUM

Mitchell Johnson's final Test, on a WACA pitch so lifeless the coroner ought to have been called, felt like a recapitulation of all his previous 72 matches. In the first innings, he took one for 157. Retirement had been exercising his mind for months, and that day it dawned on him that he no longer enjoyed the grind. In the second innings, with only formalities remaining and nothing weighing on him, he briefly tapped into a rich old vein, blasting out both Kiwi openers with short, fast balls, and finishing with two for 20. It meant that oh-so-recognisable face could depart with a smile.

Johnson's trademark effect was his pantomime villain's moustache, but he also had a figurative curl in the middle of his forehead. For most of his career, he was either very good indeed – or horrid. Only in his last year did he have the sort of games that are normal for other workaday trundlers, bowling respectably enough, but with scant reward. It was not for him.

His debut was the first after Glenn McGrath's retirement. And he was everything McGrath was not: quick, left-arm, fearsome to behold, obvious. He was, and remained, extraordinarily athletic, which was manifest in his batting and fielding. But bowling is more mechanical, and Johnson wrestled all his career with control of his slinging action.

When it held together, he terrified Test batsmen as no one has since the West Indians in their heyday, and no Australian since Jeff Thomson. Mike Hussey faced Johnson at peak pace in a Sheffield Shield match and said he saw his arm, but not the ball in flight. It just appeared at his end, like a firework; he could only hope he had the appropriate reflex.

But when Johnson's action came apart, he became a laughing stock, the Barmy Army's favourite target. It hurt him, and affected his bowling. Here was Johnson's essential contradiction: outwardly a bruiser, inwardly delicate. He was a private man in a more public and accountable role than any elected official. On his last day, he went with the least fuss posterity would permit.

After an injury-delayed start in Test cricket, Johnson seemed to be approaching his zenith against South Africa in 2008-09. After breaking his toe in 2011-12, he played only four Tests in the next two years, and seemed to be off the books. But he returned in 2013-14 with a rare vengeance, taking 59 wickets in eight Tests at 15 apiece. Even those figures do not begin to reflect the terror he struck among English and South African batsmen. On both sides of the fence, he set pulses racing as only a fast bowler can. Graeme Swann retired midway through the Ashes whitewash, and later said there had been nothing wrong until Johnson took off his blindfold.

He was more resilient than imagined: outside that two-year hiatus, he missed just two other Tests. But he regained his ballistic level only fleetingly – one morning at Edgbaston in 2015, an afternoon at the Gabba later that year. Instability in the Australian attack forced him too often into the stock role to which he was patently unsuited.

Another force was at work. At Adelaide in 2014-15, in the first Test after the death of Phillip Hughes, Johnson hit India's Virat Kohli, who had just come to the crease, on the helmet. Kohli was shaken, Johnson distraught. It was a harbinger: within a year, he had retired. He did so lying fourth on Australia's all-time list, with 313 wickets, behind Shane Warne, McGrath and Dennis Lillee. It is some company. At his best, Johnson was not out of place.

New Zealand fought back admirably on the second day, bowling tighter lines to a side looking to push on, and defying the conditions to take seven for 143. Henry had some success as the injured Jimmy Neesham's replacement, while Craig profited from Australia's slap-happy approach, but Smith's declaration denied them the satisfaction of bowling his side out.

Deep into the fifth session of the match, New Zealand's batsmen could easily have fallen over. Guptill went fifth ball, and Latham for 36, but this time Williamson found support in Taylor, who had looked so bad in Brisbane that his very career seemed in danger. But the treatment he had received between matches on a growth on his eye had an immediate effect. He relied on thumps through cover, and the pair settled in for a partnership that would reach 265 before Williamson miscued Hazlewood halfway through the third day.

Starc unleashed a terrifically fast new-ball spell, the speed gun alleging 160.4kph (99.66mph), but Taylor fought fire with fire, slashing six boundaries in Starc's six-over burst. With a series of partners in support, he passed Martin Crowe's 188 in 1985-86 to reach the highest New Zealand score against Australia, and started his third day of batting on 235. He finished with 290 – including 43 fours – the highest by an overseas batsman in Australia, passing Englishman Tip Foster's 287, set at Sydney on his debut way back in 1903-04.

With 624, New Zealand had a 65-run lead. It was during this batathon that Johnson found himself, ball in hand, wondering why he was still doing this. If ever a pitch was going to prompt an existential crisis, this was it. Only a mighty collapse would produce a result. Instead, Smith and Voges made centuries in a stand of 224, and Johnson announced his retirement on the final morning.

Australia batted until after lunch, before setting a nominal 321. For a champion player's farewell, such conservative captaincy was tone-deaf. The sparse crowd could only cheer Johnson's last few boundaries with the bat, and his final wickets as he removed New Zealand's openers with two farewell bouncers. But then it was back to Taylor and Williamson, condemning Johnson's last outing to a conclusion as flat as the pitch that hosted it.

Man of the Match: L. R. P. L. Taylor.   *Attendance:* 40,288.

Close of play: first day, Australia 416-2 (Warner 244, Smith 5); second day, New Zealand 140-2 (Williamson 70, Taylor 26); third day, New Zealand 510-6 (Taylor 235, Craig 7); fourth day, Australia 258-2 (Smith 131, Voges 101).

Australia

J. A. Burns b Henry	40	– c Taylor b Southee	0
D. A. Warner c Craig b Boult	253	– c Latham b Boult	24
U. T. Khawaja c Latham b Bracewell	121		
*S. P. D. Smith c Watling b Henry	27	– (3) c Watling b Boult	138
A. C. Voges c Watling b Boult	41	– (4) lbw b Southee	119
M. R. Marsh c and b Bracewell	34	– (5) lbw b Bracewell	1
†P. M. Nevill st Watling b Craig	19	– (6) c Watling b Southee	35
M. G. Johnson st Watling b Craig	2	– (7) c Watling b Southee	29
M. A. Starc c Latham b Craig	0	– (8) not out	28
J. R. Hazlewood not out	8	– (9) not out	2
N. M. Lyon not out	4		
B 4, l-b 1, w 1, n-b 4	10	B 4, l-b 3, w 1, n-b 1	9

1/101 (1) 2/403 (3)   (9 wkts dec, 133 overs) 559   1/8 (1)   (7 wkts dec, 103 overs) 385
3/427 (2) 4/462 (4) 5/512 (5)   2/46 (2) 3/270 (3)
6/539 (6) 7/547 (7) 8/547 (9) 9/547 (8)   4/277 (5) 5/294 (4) 6/355 (7) 7/366 (6)

Southee 29–6–88–0; Boult 26–2–123–2; Henry 22–2–105–2; Bracewell 25–1–81–2; Craig 23–0–123–3; Williamson 3–0–11–0; Guptill 3–0–7–0; McCullum 2–0–16–0. *Second innings*— Southee 25–4–97–4; Boult 19–2–77–2; Bracewell 20–5–62–1; Henry 20–7–53–0; Craig 18–1–81–0; Williamson 1–0–8–0.

New Zealand

M. J. Guptill lbw b Starc	1	– (2) c Burns b Johnson	17
T. W. M. Latham c Smith b Lyon	36	– (1) c Hazlewood b Johnson	15
K. S. Williamson c Johnson b Hazlewood	166	– not out	32
L. R. P. L. Taylor c sub (J. W. Wells) b Lyon	290	– not out	36
*B. B. McCullum b Marsh	27		
†B-J. Watling c Lyon b Starc	1		
D. A. J. Bracewell c Nevill b Johnson	12		
M. D. Craig c Johnson b Lyon	15		
M. J. Henry b Lyon	6		
T. G. Southee c and b Starc	21		
T. A. Boult not out	23		
B 7, l-b 11, w 5, n-b 3	26	B 4	4

1/6 (1) 2/87 (2) 3/352 (3)	(153.5 overs)	624	1/34 (1) (2 wkts, 28 overs) 104
4/432 (5) 5/447 (6) 6/485 (7)			2/44 (2)
7/525 (8) 8/554 (9) 9/587 (10) 10/624 (4)			

Starc 37–7–119–4; Hazlewood 32–2–134–1; Johnson 28–2–157–1; Lyon 37.5–6–107–3; Marsh 15–1–73–1; Smith 4–0–16–0. *Second innings*—Starc 6–1–33–0; Hazlewood 6–3–3–0; Johnson 6–2–20–2; Lyon 7–0–35–0; Marsh 3–0–9–0.

Umpires: N. J. Llong and S. Ravi. Third umpire: R. K. Illingworth.
Referee: R. S. Mahanama.

At Perth, November 21–22, 2015 (day/night). **Drawn.** ‡**Western Australia XI 345-13** (90 overs) (W. G. Bosisto 78, S. M. Whiteman 117; N. Wagner 5-62, M. J. Santner 4-62); **New Zealanders 426-11** (89.2 overs) (M. J. Guptill 103, B-J. Watling 81; J. S. Paris 3-31, A. J. Tye 4-40). *The New Zealanders chose from 15 players and the Western Australians 12. The tourists' final preparation for the day/night pink-ball Test went well. Mitchell Santner bowled himself into the side for Adelaide, working his way through a self-regenerating WA batting line-up – three went in again, which allowed Wagner to trap Jonathan Wells lbw twice. Yorkshire-born Sam Whiteman made 117 before falling late in the evening: "My previous best score against the pink ball was about ten," he said. "I think it's a little bit tougher under lights, but definitely bearable." On the second day the New Zealanders amassed 426, Guptill hitting four sixes in a 109-ball century. Latham and Watling batted twice, while WA wicketkeeper Josh Inglis claimed seven catches and a stumping.*

AUSTRALIA v NEW ZEALAND

Third Test Match

At Adelaide, November 27–29, 2015 (day/night). Australia won by three wickets. Toss: New Zealand. Test debut: M. J. Santner.

Pink ball, pink skies, pink champagne. It was the season of the "rosé ball", as commentary troupe White Line Wireless dubbed it, inferring that the new projectile was *the* choice for those summer sessions that linger between afternoon and dusk.

Adelaide and Lord's rank as cricket's greatest social grounds. A stroll through town hours before play revealed a buzz, pubs overflowing ahead of the 2.00 start. Of 47,441 attending the first day, perhaps a quarter were never in their seats. They were out the back, on the tennis courts and the lawns, in the pop-up carnival of vodka bars, sparkling-wine marquees, Pimm's pavilions and craft-beer tents that sprawled around the ground's flank. Strings of lights, strings of flags, strings of expletives when the day wore on and the drinks failed to wear off.

McCullum finally won a toss, and Starc prepared to send down Test cricket's first delivery with a pink ball. Its colour glowed in the afternoon sunlight, a fragment of a hazard warning or a rave party flickering at the grandstands. And Guptill became its first victim, leg-before to Hazlewood in the fourth over. Afternoon gave way to the crepuscular spectacular, sunset painting the sky, and so to darkness and its new tactical intrigue: rightly or not, no one wanted to bat under lights.

THE FIRST PINK-BALL TEST

All right on the day/night

Daniel Brettig

In January 1993, Adelaide Oval hosted a Test unrepresentative of its tradition – a low-scoring classic on a lively pitch, won by West Indies by what the local *Advertiser* called "one measly run". Nothing of its like was seen again until November 2015, when another finely balanced contest unfolded in South Australia's capital. The inaugural day/night Test featured a pink ball, a prime-time final session and mighty crowds, surpassing the expectations of administrators, enthusing spectators, and accepted by players in a spirit of experimentation, if not total approval.

Despite more than six years' testing, the ball had been a source of consternation, notably when torn to pieces by an abrasive Canberra pitch in New Zealand's fixture against the Prime Minister's XI. Adam Voges expressed his dissatisfaction that night, while Wally Edwards and David Peever – Cricket Australia's chairmen past and present – pored over the chewed-up projectiles as though they were the Dead Sea Scrolls.

Adelaide won hosting rights, largely because of a newly developed stadium and a modular playing surface. The curator, Damian Hough, had prepared a drop-in pitch for the previous month's day/night pink-ball Sheffield Shield match between South Australia and New South Wales that served as a dress rehearsal, and the ground had hosted the rock band AC/DC only a few days before the Test. Hough was encouraged by the board to leave plenty of grass on the pitch, and lushness in the square and outfield, the better to preserve the ball.

Questions about how the public would respond were answered swiftly. Ticket sales were comparable to an Ashes summer, and the three-day attendance of 123,736 was a record for any Adelaide Test not involving England. Most were entranced by the contest, which ebbed and flowed before climaxing in a tense but television-friendly Sunday-night conclusion. Viewing figures peaked at 3.19m, which made it one of the year's top five TV sporting events in Australia (the World Cup final had peaked at 4.21m).

It was undoubtedly compelling. The players loved the atmosphere, and appreciated the micromanagement to ensure the ball would last. But there were reservations, summed up by New Zealand captain Brendon McCullum: "Day/night Test cricket is meant to allow Test cricket to be played at night. It is not meant to change how Test cricket should play. I think there was a fraction too much grass."

In stating that the game "exceeded expectations on every front", CA's chief executive James Sutherland pointed to a wider benefit. While many home boards produce pitches favouring their team, here was an environment for the best game of cricket in the circumstances – even if it brought New Zealand's seam and swing attack into play.

"There's no reason why we can't prepare pitches that do provide that balance," he said. "At times there's an overemphasis on preparing a wicket to suit the home team rather than the audience. Those conditions probably suited the New Zealanders more than the Australians, but it was a captivating contest from ball one."

New Zealand were planning their own floodlit Test against Bangladesh in late 2016, and both South Africa and Pakistan may find themselves playing under lights in Australia next season, having also expressed interest in hosting one themselves. "With the raging success of this year we'd clearly be disappointed if we didn't get at least one Test match next year played as a day/night," he said. "And I don't see any reason why we won't be going down the path of pursuing it for an Ashes Test or two as well."

Morne de Klerk, Getty Images

The future's bright: cricket's new dawn under Adelaide's sunset.

What a contest and what a contrast: from duelling scores of 200 between batsmen in Perth, to 200 between *teams* in Adelaide. The grass on the pitch merely kept bowlers in the game: plenty of batsmen caused their own demise. Both sides were in it for the duration, and every player was in it when he had his chance.

New Zealand gave a debut to their spinning all-rounder Mitchell Santner. Australia replaced the injured Usman Khawaja with Shaun Marsh, ahead of candidates with greater claims, to renewed and strident public protest. Back came Siddle, who quickly showed his worth by drying up Williamson with some tight seam bowling, setting up his dismissal by Starc's yorker.

The tea break included a photo tribute at 4.08 to mark the anniversary of Phillip Hughes's death – 408 was his Test number – at his adopted home ground. In accordance with his family's wishes, the moment was understated, and the cricket pressed on. Latham notched a fine fifty, his first of the series, but Lyon made the breakthrough, as he so often does. Taylor edged Siddle, McCullum was done for pace by Starc, Nevill had three catches in 11 balls, and a steady 94 for two had become a shaky 98 for five.

Santner square-drove his first delivery for four, and his enterprising innings led a brief recovery with Watling, but all out for 202 soon after the 40-minute dinner break looked well short. On the flip side for Australia, Starc had left the field with an ankle problem. They lost Warner and Burns in the evening session, but it was the bright light of the second day that saw things unravel. Voges was done in by beautiful swing, Shaun Marsh by ugly running – McCullum brilliantly throwing down the stumps while prone, after a diving save at mid-off – and Mitchell Marsh to a plain prod. Australia were 80 for five – and New Zealand circling.

Smith had been in command, but aimed a strange slog at Craig, who then removed Siddle in the same over. Santner was appealing for his first Test wicket when he was informed that the supposed caught-behind had in fact brushed Hazlewood's stumps. And Australia should have been 118 for nine, with the hobbled Starc to come, when Lyon swept Santner. The ball clipped the back of his bat, and was caught by Williamson at second slip via Lyon's shoulder. Umpire Ravi said not out, but New Zealand immediately asked for a review. The deviation was clear, as was Hot Spot, but Lyon's forward lunge and body position obscured the stump mike and meant Snicko did not register a sound. Nor did it register when the ball struck his shoulder, nor did third umpire Nigel Llong register any of that information. Instead he crawled back and forth for five minutes, said the mark on Hot Spot "could have come from anywhere", watched an Eagle Eye prediction of the wrong delivery, and declared it not out. Lyon, standing by the boundary with pink cheeks and a pink mark on his bat, was more surprised than anyone.

The ICC later admitted Llong had got it wrong, but that was too late for a New Zealand side whose focus had been shaken. Lyon batted as if in the cricket version of *It's a Wonderful Life*, and Nevill went with him. The 74 they slogged would be the highest partnership of the match, and Starc rode that momentum to help add another 34. A potential 84-run deficit had become a 22-run lead. Just as importantly, minutes of relatively benign afternoon batting had been soaked up: New Zealand were very soon playing under lights.

They lost five for 116 that evening, before next day Santner helped drag the score past 200. Hazlewood relished his chance as attack leader, taking a Test-best six for 70, while Mitchell Marsh got Williamson and McCullum. A total of 208 was perhaps 60 short. Australia needed 187, with a session of daylight before a session at night.

Boult had struggled for rhythm and pace, but finally came to life. After a fast start, Australia crashed to 66 for three and, with the edgy Shaun Marsh under scrutiny, the collapse was on. This time, he refused to go. He did edge a few, but survived. The suffocating spells of Boult and Bracewell had to end, and McCullum could partner Southee only with Craig's unthreatening spin. Batting with state team-mate Voges, Marsh grew in stature.

They were 72 from winning when Voges edged Boult, and 26 short when Mitchell Marsh holed out. It looked done by then, but there was still time for Boult to get Shaun Marsh, then Nevill. With two required and the limping Starc inexplicably sent in, there were nervous moments for Siddle with seven slips yet no quick singles. Eventually he squeezed the runs, completing a 2–0 series victory. Far bigger was the win for Cricket Australia and their boss James Sutherland, whose years of advocacy of day/night Tests had finally borne fruit. It was no guarantee that the concept would always work, but compelling proof that it could. There would surely be no going back.

Man of the Match: J. R. Hazlewood.   *Attendance:* 123,736.

Man of the Series: D. A. Warner.

Close of play: first day, Australia 54-2 (Smith 24, Voges 9); second day, New Zealand 116-5 (Santner 13, Watling 7).

New Zealand

M. J. Guptill lbw b Hazlewood	1	– (2) c M. R. Marsh b Hazlewood	17
T. W. M. Latham c Nevill b Lyon	50	– (1) c Nevill b Hazlewood	10
K. S. Williamson lbw b Starc	22	– c Nevill b M. R. Marsh	9
L. R. P. L. Taylor c Nevill b Siddle	21	– lbw b Hazlewood	32
*B. B. McCullum c Nevill b Starc	4	– lbw b M. R. Marsh	20
M. J. Santner b Starc	31	– st Nevill b Lyon	45
†B-J. Watling c Smith b Hazlewood	29	– c Smith b Hazlewood	7
M. D. Craig b Lyon	11	– c Nevill b Hazlewood	15
D. A. J. Bracewell c Burns b Siddle	11	– not out	27
T. G. Southee c Warner b Hazlewood	16	– c Lyon b M. R. Marsh	13
T. A. Boult not out	2	– b Hazlewood	5
L-b 1, w 2, n-b 1	4	B 6, l-b 2	8

1/7 (1) 2/59 (3) 3/94 (2)   (65.2 overs) 202
4/98 (4) 5/98 (5) 6/142 (6)
7/164 (8) 8/184 (7) 9/194 (9) 10/202 (10)

1/29 (2) 2/32 (1)   (62.5 overs) 208
3/52 (3) 4/84 (5)
5/98 (4) 6/116 (7) 7/140 (8)
8/175 (6) 9/192 (10) 10/208 (11)

Starc 9–3–24–3; Hazlewood 17.2–2–66–3; Siddle 17–5–54–2; Lyon 15–1–42–2; M. R. Marsh 5–1–12–0; Smith 2–0–3–0. *Second innings*—Hazlewood 24.5–5–70–6; Siddle 14–6–35–0; M. R. Marsh 14–2–59–3; Lyon 10–1–36–1.

Australia

J. A. Burns b Bracewell	14	– (2) lbw b Boult	11
D. A. Warner c Southee b Boult	1	– (1) c Southee b Bracewell	35
*S. P. D. Smith c Watling b Craig	53	– lbw b Boult	14
A. C. Voges c Guptill b Southee	13	– c Southee b Boult	28
S. E. Marsh run out	2	– c Taylor b Boult	49
M. R. Marsh c Watling b Bracewell	4	– c Williamson b Santner	28
†P. M. Nevill c Santner b Bracewell	66	– c Watling b Boult	10
P. M. Siddle c Latham b Craig	0	– not out	9
J. R. Hazlewood b Santner	4		
N. M. Lyon c Williamson b Boult	34		
M. A. Starc not out	24	– (9) not out	0
B 5, l-b 3, w 1	9	L-b 2, w 1	3

1/6 (2) 2/34 (1) 3/63 (4)   (72.1 overs) 224
4/67 (5) 5/80 (6) 6/109 (3)
7/109 (8) 8/116 (9) 9/190 (10) 10/224 (7)

1/34 (2)   (7 wkts, 51 overs) 187
2/62 (1) 3/66 (3)
4/115 (4) 5/161 (6) 6/176 (5) 7/185 (7)

Southee 17–1–50–1; Boult 17–5–41–2; Bracewell 12.1–3–18–3; Santner 16–1–54–1; Craig 10–1–53–2. *Second innings*—Southee 16–1–58–0; Boult 16–3–60–5; Bracewell 11–2–37–1; Craig 6–0–22–0; Santner 2–0–8–1.

Umpires: R. K. Illingworth and S. Ravi. Third umpire: N. J. Llong.
Referee: R. S. Mahanama.

AUSTRALIA v WEST INDIES IN 2015-16

Adam Collins

Test matches (3): Australia 2, West Indies 0

It is said that to hang a lantern on your problems is to begin solving them. The solution may be distant, but West Indies cricket had the biggest, brightest floodlights trained on its troubles, as the team were annihilated in the premier time slot of the Australian summer. Across three Test matches the tourists served as glorified bowling machines – and their batting fared little better.

Questions abounded. Why were the prime matches allocated to West Indies, and not New Zealand, who had toured at the beginning of the season? And how could public interest be generated in a series against an opponent thrashed by a makeshift team of emerging players ahead of the First Test at Hobart? For Tasmanian administrators already on notice that they might lose their Test because of poor attendances, it was cause for real concern.

This series came 20 years after West Indies lost the No. 1 mantle to Australia, a stark reminder of their demise ever since. Off the field, some big names from the past were working hard: Richie Richardson was team manager, Curtly Ambrose bowling coach, and Clive Lloyd chairman of selectors. Phil Simmons, meanwhile, had been reinstated as head coach following his suspension for criticising selection policy a few weeks earlier. It mattered little. Before long, they bucked against the scrutiny, banning broadcaster Fazeer Mohammed from interviewing players because of perceived unfair reporting. Whatever the gripe, it was clumsy treatment of their sole travelling journalist.

As usual, West Indies were, for various reasons, missing some of their strongest players, not least the trio of Chris Gayle, Dwayne Bravo and Andre Russell, all enjoying themselves in Australia's Big Bash League while the Test team wilted. So lopsided was the series that entertainment had to be sought elsewhere. Australians were fascinated that the touring party contained two men named Brathwaite, so nearly shared with an iconic local pop star of yesteryear. In fact, Daryl Braithwaite was invited to sing at a Big Bash game the day before the Third Test, which seemed at odds with Cricket Australia's slogan for a cringeworthy campaign telling Test crowds "Don't be a Daryl" (their ad featured a man named Daryl who misses the cricket because he's out shopping for tiles).

The statistics were no less absurd. Adam Voges lifted his average against West Indies to 542 in five Tests (and his overall figure to 85). In a welcome counter-attack at Hobart, Kraigg Brathwaite briefly threatened Charles Bannerman's record for the highest proportion of runs in a completed innings (67.34%), dating back to the very first Test match, in 1877; he had to settle for fourth on the list, having made 94 out of West Indies' 148 all out – or 63.51%. At Melbourne, four Australians made centuries in an innings for the third time. And only a promotion up the order on the final day of the Third Test saved wicketkeeper Peter Nevill from registering a "did not bat" through an entire

HIGHEST TEST AVERAGE AGAINST ONE OPPONENT

		T	I	NO	Runs	HS	100	Avge
A. C. Voges (A).	**v WI (2015–2015-16)**	**5**	**4**	**3**	**542**	**269***	**3**	**542.00**
D. G. Bradman (A)	v SA (1931-32)	5	5	1	806	299*	4	201.50
D. G. Bradman (A)	v India (1947-48)	5	6	2	715	201	4	178.75
J. C. Adams (WI).	v India (1994-95)	3	6	3	520	174*	2	173.33
S. P. D. Smith (A).	**v WI (2015–2015-16)**	**5**	**7**	**4**	**497**	**199**	**2**	**165.66**
D. L. Houghton (Z)	v SL (1994-95)	3	3	0	466	266	2	155.33
C. A. Davis (WI)	v India (1970-71)	4	8	4	529	125*	2	132.25
Misbah-ul-Haq (P).	v India (2007-08)	3	6	2	464	161*	1	116.00
W. R. Hammond (E) . . .	v NZ (1931–1946-47)	9	11	2	1,015	336*	4	112.77
S. M. Nurse (WI).	v NZ (1968-69)	3	5	0	558	258	2	111.60

Minimum 400 runs, all opponents except *Bangladesh and Zimbabwe.*

series. In all, Australia scored 1,489 runs for the loss of 12 wickets, to West Indies' 1,254 for 48.

This isn't to say the series didn't matter to individuals. An understated story was the elevation of 31-year-old slow left-armer Stephen O'Keefe to the Australian team for the Third Test, in which he looked the part, and put himself in contention for the second spinner's role for the tour of Sri Lanka in 2016.

On the batting front, the Australian selectors made a tough – but justified – decision to drop Shaun Marsh after his 182 at Hobart. Instead, they kept faith with Usman Khawaja, returning from a hamstring injury, and Joe Burns, both of whom had been picked against New Zealand at the start of the summer; each made a century at Melbourne. Khawaja admitted thinking he would never play for Australia again after suffering a serious knee injury at the end of 2014. Now he was one of the most in-form players on the planet.

West Indies did, though, have one or two bright spots. Darren Bravo's refusal to accept the status quo at Melbourne, where he made a dogged 81, was as impressive as his classy century at Hobart. Kraigg Brathwaite looked up to the task of being a Test opener, while his unrelated namesake Carlos added much-needed spunk as a big-hitting all-rounder down the order. Jason Holder, the captain, showed himself to be a capable cricketer with visible determination, speaking with eloquence and purpose. He bowled better than his numbers suggested, and his batting may demand a promotion to bolster a fragile middle order in which Marlon Samuels registered 35 runs, and about as many hapless half-attempts in the field.

But we could laud green shoots for the rest of our lives. It's more serious than that now. A fight for the very survival of Test cricket in the Caribbean awaits. It's not going to be pretty.

WEST INDIES TOURING PARTY

*J. O. Holder, D. Bishoo, J. Blackwood, C. R. Brathwaite, K. C. Brathwaite, D. M. Bravo, R. Chandrika, S. O. Dowrich, S. T. Gabriel, S. D. Hope, D. Ramdin, K. A. J. Roach, M. N. Samuels, J. E. Taylor, J. A. Warrican. *Coach:* P. V. Simmons.

Gabriel sustained an ankle injury in the First Test and was replaced by M. L. Cummins.

TEST MATCH AVERAGES

AUSTRALIA – BATTING AND FIELDING

	T	I	NO	R	HS	100	50	Avge	Ct
S. P. D. Smith............	3	3	2	214	134*	1	1	214.00	6
†D. A. Warner	3	4	1	226	122*	1	1	75.33	3
J. A. Burns	3	4	0	192	128	1	0	48.00	5
M. R. Marsh..............	3	3	2	40	21	0	0	40.00	0

Played in three Tests: P. M. Nevill 7* (8 ct); A. C. Voges 269*, 106*; †J. R. Hazlewood (1 ct), N. M. Lyon (5 ct) and †J. L. Pattinson (2 ct) did not bat. Played in two Tests: †U. T. Khawaja 144, 56 (1 ct); P. M. Siddle did not bat. Played in one Test: †S. E. Marsh 182; S. N. J. O'Keefe did not bat.

BOWLING

	Style	O	M	R	W	BB	5I	Avge
S. N. J. O'Keefe	SLA	26.1	7	63	3	3-63	0	21.00
J. L. Pattinson	RFM	80.3	10	292	13	5-27	1	22.46
N. M. Lyon................	OB	121	33	331	13	4-66	0	25.46
J. R. Hazlewood	RFM	87.3	25	216	8	4-45	0	27.00
M. R. Marsh	RFM	38.3	8	141	5	4-61	0	28.20
P. M. Siddle	RFM	49	11	145	5	2-36	0	29.00

Also bowled: S. P. D. Smith (LBG) 5–1–26–0.

WEST INDIES – BATTING AND FIELDING

	T	I	NO	R	HS	100	50	Avge	Ct/St
†D. M. Bravo	3	5	0	247	108	1	1	49.40	1
K. C. Brathwaite	3	5	0	229	94	0	2	45.80	1
C. R. Brathwaite	2	3	0	130	69	0	2	43.33	0
D. Ramdin	3	5	0	133	62	0	2	26.60	3/1
R. Chandrika	2	4	0	87	37	0	0	21.75	0
J. O. Holder	3	5	0	101	68	0	1	20.20	1
K. A. J. Roach	3	5	0	82	31	0	0	16.40	1
J. Blackwood	3	5	0	58	28	0	0	11.60	2
J. E. Taylor...............	3	5	0	40	15	0	0	8.00	0
M. N. Samuels	3	5	0	35	19	0	0	7.00	1
J. A. Warrican	3	5	5	44	21*	0	0	–	0

Played in one Test: S. D. Hope 9; S. T. Gabriel did not bat.

BOWLING

	Style	O	M	R	W	BB	5I	Avge
J. A. Warrican	SLA	77	4	380	5	3-158	0	76.00

Also bowled: J. Blackwood (OB) 6–0–25–0; C. R. Brathwaite (RFM) 43–4–162–1; K. C. Brathwaite (OB) 35–1–150–1; S. T. Gabriel (RFM) 10–1–59–1; J. O. Holder (RFM) 61–12–186–2; K. A. J. Roach (RFM) 41–2–247–0; J. E. Taylor (RFM) 46–2–257–2.

At Brisbane (Allan Border Field), December 2–5, 2015. **Cricket Australia XI won by ten wickets.** ‡**West Indians 243** (90.5 overs) (D. M. Bravo 51; S. Milenko 5-76) **and 210** (58.2 overs) (J. O. Holder 65; R. A. Lees 3-68, C. J. Boyce 4-84); **Cricket Australia XI 444** (104.2 overs) (J. M. Carder 58, J. J. Peirson 64, M. W. Short 76, J. J. Bazley 50; J. O. Holder 4-76) **and 13-0** (2.5 overs). *The West Indians were routed by a hotchpotch team of six first-class debutants and nine players under 24 – and it would have been worse but for a wagging tail. They were 115-6 in their first innings and 97-7 in their second, and only some late-order runs averted an innings defeat. Queensland team-mates Simon Milenko (5-76 with his medium pace in the first innings) and leg-spinner Cameron Boyce (six in the match) were the chief destroyers. There was no respite for West Indies in the field: eight of the Cricket Australia XI reached 30 as they racked up 444.*

AUSTRALIA v WEST INDIES

First Test Match

At Hobart, December 10–12, 2015. Australia won by an innings and 212 runs. Toss: Australia.

Snow rested on top of Hobart's Mount Wellington on the third and final afternoon of the First Test. It felt appropriate, given the latest cold snap in Caribbean cricket's endless winter. Twelve West Indian wickets fell on the day to complete a hiding in half the allotted time. Every fear about the gulf between these teams had been realised.

Things began to unravel for the tourists from the moment the coin came down and Smith said: "We'll bat, mate." Holder admitted he would have bowled first on a pitch which was green on top but flat underneath. West Indies had talked up their fast bowlers, but both Taylor and Roach began with a no-ball, and Australia's openers rattled off 75 in 11 overs. There were 16 boundaries in the opening hour, and Warner raised his fifty from 40 deliveries.

But, to their credit, West Indies fought back to have Australia three down by lunch, with the key wickets of Warner and Smith falling to Jomel Warrican, a 23-year-old left-arm spinner playing only his second Test. This brought together Voges and Shaun Marsh. They had spent more than a decade at Western Australia longing to join forces at international level; now they made it count. Initially restrained, Voges broke free with four boundaries in an over from Warrican, using his feet to drive straight and his timing to flick to leg. Feasting on the wayward Taylor, he made his third Test century a formality. It came at a run a ball – Hobart's fastest Test hundred – and was his most fluent innings for Australia. But Voges wasn't done yet.

HIGHEST PROPORTION OF A COMPLETED TEST INNINGS

Runs	Total	%			
165*	245	67.34	C. Bannerman	Australia v England at Melbourne.......	1876-77
123	184	66.84	M. J. Slater	Australia v England at Sydney	1998-99
167	261	63.98	V. V. S. Laxman	India v Australia at Sydney	1999-2000
94	**148**	**63.51**	**K. C. Brathwaite**	**West Indies v Australia at Hobart**	**2015-16**
134	211	63.50	C. G. Greenidge	West Indies v England at Manchester ...	1976
52*	82	63.41	A. P. Gurusinha	Sri Lanka v India at Chandigarh	1990-91
100	159	62.89	J. R. Reid	New Zealand v England at Christchurch..	1962-63
258	417	61.87	S. M. Nurse	West Indies v New Zealand at Christchurch	1968-69
60	97	61.85	M. Amarnath	†India v West Indies at Kingston	1975-76
121	198	61.11	G. N. Yallop	Australia v England at Sydney	1978-79
154*	252	61.11	G. A. Gooch	England v West Indies at Leeds	1991

† *Five men absent.*

At the other end Marsh was content to watch and accumulate. Later, against the fast bowlers, he struck cover-drives so perfect you wondered why his talents had not reaped more. Marsh pulled Roach to the rope to raise his own third Test hundred, and his first at home. Voges' 150 came next, via a reverse sweep. By stumps Australia had amassed 438 for three, the most conceded in a day by West Indies.

Holder's problems had been compounded by an injury to Gabriel, who damaged his left ankle and arrived at the ground on crutches next morning. Voges flogged the rest of the attack, moving from his overnight 174 to an unbeaten 269 (a first-class best) by lunch, having faced 285 balls and hit 33 fours. By the time Marsh slog-swept Warrican to deep midwicket for 182 (also a first-class best), their alliance was worth 449 and

Coach's delight: Adam Voges plays in the V – and out of the manual.

had broken all sorts of records. It was the highest fourth-wicket stand in Tests (beating 437 between Mahela Jayawardene and Thilan Samaraweera for Sri Lanka against Pakistan at Karachi in 2008-09), the highest for any wicket in Australia (beating 405 between Sid Barnes and Don Bradman for the fifth, against England at Sydney in 1946-47), and the highest against West Indies (beating 411 between Peter May and Colin Cowdrey at Edgbaston in 1957). Only five other partnerships in Test history had yielded more. Over lunch, Voges – who had already surpassed Doug Walters's 242 at Sydney in 1968-69 as the highest score for Australia against West Indies – sportingly agreed to forego the chance of a triple-century, allowing Smith to declare and unleash his bowlers.

Hazlewood made the initial incision, but the wickets really started to tumble after Lyon came on. First he deceived Chandrika in the flight, then in a single over took a stunning return catch to dismiss Samuels, and had Blackwood snaffled at short leg for the first half of a pair. The collapse was in full swing when Siddle trapped Holder to make it 116 for six.

All the while Bravo was showing the responsibility and class missing from the rest of the top order. At last he found support in Roach, and the pair nursed their side to 207 for six by the close. But, with Gabriel absent injured, it took Australia just five overs to wrap up the innings on the third morning, with Hazlewood leading the way. It was time enough for Bravo, ninth out, to reach his seventh Test hundred, including 20 boundaries, many of which crashed into the cover fence.

Pattinson, returning to the Test team after 21 injury-blighted months, had been wicketless and expensive. But, the follow-on enforced, there was a second chance against a wounded opponent. He responded with a burst of four wickets in his first four overs to set off an even more spectacular collapse, and finished with his joint-best Test figures of five for 27. Kraigg Brathwaite hit out with enterprise, but the mismatch was over when his stumps were bent back by Hazlewood for 94 before tea on the third day, condemning West Indies to their heaviest defeat by Australia for almost 85 years.

Man of the Match: A. C. Voges. *Attendance:* 15,313.

Close of play: first day, Australia 438-3 (Voges 174, S. E. Marsh 139); second day, West Indies 207-6 (Bravo 94, Roach 31).

Australia

J. A. Burns b Gabriel	33		
D. A. Warner c Ramdin b Warrican	64		
*S. P. D. Smith c Blackwood b Warrican	10		
A. C. Voges not out	269		
S. E. Marsh c Bravo b Warrican	182		
M. R. Marsh not out	1		
B 4, l-b 3, w 3, n-b 14	24		

1/75 (1)   (4 wkts dec, 114 overs)   **583**
2/104 (3)   3/121 (2)
4/570 (5)

†P. M. Nevill, P. M. Siddle, J. L. Pattinson, J. R. Hazlewood and N. M. Lyon did not bat.

Taylor 17–0–108–0; Roach 16–1–99–0; Gabriel 10–1–59–1; Holder 24–3–75–0; Warrican 28–1–158–3; Brathwaite 13–0–52–0; Blackwood 6–0–25–0.

West Indies

K. C. Brathwaite lbw b Hazlewood	2	– b Hazlewood	94
R. Chandrika c Smith b Lyon	25	– c Smith b Pattinson	0
D. M. Bravo c Lyon b Siddle	108	– b Pattinson	4
M. N. Samuels c and b Lyon	9	– c Warner b Pattinson	4
J. Blackwood c Burns b Lyon	0	– b Pattinson	0
†D. Ramdin c Hazlewood	8	– c Warner b M. R. Marsh	4
*J. O. Holder lbw b Siddle	15	– c Nevill b Pattinson	17
K. A. J. Roach c Nevill b Hazlewood	31	– c Nevill b Hazlewood	3
J. E. Taylor b Hazlewood	0	– c Pattinson b Hazlewood	12
J. A. Warrican not out	2	– not out	6
S. T. Gabriel absent hurt		– absent hurt	
B 7, l-b 10, w 1, n-b 5	23	L-b 1, w 1, n-b 3	5

1/17 (1)   2/58 (2)   3/78 (4)   (70 overs)   223   1/2 (2)   2/20 (3)   (36.3 overs)   148
4/78 (5)   5/89 (6)   6/116 (7)   3/24 (4)   4/24 (5)   5/30 (6)
7/215 (8)   8/215 (9)   9/223 (3)   6/60 (7)   7/91 (8)   8/117 (9)   9/148 (1)

Hazlewood 18–5–45–4; Pattinson 15–0–68–0; Siddle 15–5–36–2; Lyon 19–6–43–3; M. R. Marsh 3–1–14–0. *Second innings*—Hazlewood 10.3–3–33–3; Pattinson 8–2–27–5; Siddle 7–1–34–0; M. R. Marsh 7–0–36–1; Lyon 4–0–17–0.

Umpires: M. Erasmus and I. J. Gould.   Third umpire: C. B. Gaffaney.
Referee: B. C. Broad.

At Geelong, December 19–20, 2015 (not first-class). **Drawn. West Indians 303-8 dec** (90 overs) (K. C. Brathwaite 78, J. Blackwood 69; J. W. Hart 4-93); **‡Victoria XI 169-3** (58 overs) (J. C. Hancock 80*). *Both sides chose from 12 players. In stifling heat, against a Victoria attack with no first-class experience, the West Indies top order fired for the first time on the tour. Kraigg Brathwaite retired to allow others some batting time, but his departure induced a slide of six for 43, with four wickets for leg-spinner Jeremy Hart. The tourists struggled to make inroads next day, not helped by Taylor, who had his back turned and was leaning on the fence beyond the fine-leg boundary when a mis-hook came his way. "It can't be a good look," said West Indies coach Phil Simmons. "It's a team trying to gain respect, so we have to make sure we cut out things like that." The beneficiary was opener Jake Hancock, on 22, who reached 80 before rain washed out the final session.*

AUSTRALIA v WEST INDIES

Second Test Match

At Melbourne, December 26–29, 2015. Australia won by 177 runs. Toss: West Indies. Test debut: C. R. Brathwaite.

All the talk on the eve of the Boxing Day Test was how long it would take Australia to go 2–0 up. Some even considered bringing forward their travel plans for the New Year celebrations. So when West Indies stretched the match deep into the fourth day, it felt as if they had exceeded expectations.

On a damp first morning, the covers had been peeled back to reveal a pitch green enough to persuade Holder to bowl – or perhaps he was shielding his fragile batsmen. In any case, it didn't take long for Australia to pick up the tune of the First Test, as Warner struck five of his first eight deliveries, from Roach and Taylor, for four: Merry Christmas! He holed out soon after, but the point had been made.

Khawaja, returning from a hamstring tear, and Burns, preferred to the unlucky Shaun Marsh, each had plenty to play for, and neither hurried. A rhythm more in keeping with Test cricket prevailed until lunch. In the afternoon, both batsmen shifted gears with limited risk, going toe to toe as they went to their fifties and beyond. A thrash past point brought Burns his second Test hundred. The first had come at Brisbane in November, when he had walked out to bat in the second innings with Australia miles in front. This was different: a quintessential day-one opener's hand, where you earn your keep.

Two balls later, Khawaja reached his third century in his last three Tests – and the 1,000th scored for Australia in all internationals (England were next, on 964, followed by India, on 688). If the two against New Zealand had been defined by how hard he hit the ball, this was the result of exploiting the MCG's vast expanses to scamper between the wickets, with no sign of the hamstring injury; just 30 of his 144 came in boundaries. Both men fell to tired shots after a long day of graft, but their stand of 258 left Australia impregnable at the close, which was taken at 345 for three.

Resuming on the second day, Smith was desperate to join in the run-fest after missing out at Hobart, while Voges was too savvy to pass up an opportunity against shrunken bowlers. Like Khawaja, Smith found the gaps and ran breathlessly; Voges cut and flicked any time the bowlers mislaid their length, passing 1,000 Test runs in just 18 innings; before him, only Australia's Mark Taylor (1,219 in 1989) and England's Alastair Cook (1,013 in 2006) had reached the mark in their first calendar year in Test cricket. Smith's sixth century in 2015, and his fifth in eight Tests as captain, meant he would finish the year with more runs (1,474) than anyone. Voges joined him on three figures – making it four hundreds from the top five for only the third time in a Test innings – with a trademark clip past mid-on, after which Australia declared at 551 for three. It took his average against West Indies to a ridiculous 542, the highest for any player against any team, beating South African Jacques Rudolph's 293 against Bangladesh.

It felt like Hobart all over again. As before, Lyon's early introduction was the catalyst for another batting debacle, after he had Kraigg Brathwaite caught at short leg. Pattinson's reverse swing was too much for Chandrika and Samuels, while the you-miss-I-hit approach of Siddle accounted for Holder first ball. At stumps, West Indies were 91 for six.

Once more Bravo was watching it all unfold from the other end. Finally, on the third day, he received help in the big, determined shape of Barbadian debutant Carlos Brathwaite. Twice Pattinson dismissed him with no-balls, but a half-century was appropriate recognition for his toil. Not for the first time, the West Indies tail fared better than the frontline batsmen, offering admirable support to Bravo, who was last to fall for 81, having faced 204 balls in a shade over six hours.

Khawaja and Smith enjoyed a game of target practice for a session before Australia declared for the third innings in succession, setting West Indies 460 to win or, more to the point, two days to survive. Chandrika embodied a more committed effort with an innings of two and three-quarter hours that could be his making. Every other specialist got a start but none progressed, as West Indies slipped to 150 for five. There followed a spirited stand of 100 between Holder and Ramdin, his predecessor as captain, and for a moment it seemed possible Australia would be deprived of their day off. It was not to be. Mitchell Marsh, who had barely featured in the series until now, bowled with genuine pace to dismiss both en route to a Test-best four for 61, as the tail fell in a flurry. For the 11th time in a row, the Frank Worrell Trophy was Australia's.

As for West Indies, Trinidadian commentator Fazeer Mohammed lamented that it might be their last appearance at the Boxing Day Test for a long time. Sadly, he was almost certainly correct.

Man of the Match: N. M. Lyon.   *Attendance:* 127,069.

Close of play: first day, Australia 345-3 (Smith 32, Voges 10); second day, West Indies 91-6 (Bravo 13, C. R. Brathwaite 3); third day, Australia 179-3 (Smith 70, Marsh 18).

Australia

J. A. Burns st Ramdin b K. C. Brathwaite	128	– c K. C. Brathwaite b Holder	5
D. A. Warner c Samuels b Taylor	23	– c Holder b C. R. Brathwaite	17
U. T. Khawaja c Ramdin b Taylor	144	– c Ramdin b Holder	56
*S. P. D. Smith not out	134	– not out	70
A. C. Voges not out	106		
M. R. Marsh (did not bat)		– (5) not out	18
L-b 10, w 4, n-b 2	16	L-b 6, w 2, n-b 5	13

1/29 (2) 2/287 (1)   (3 wkts dec, 135 overs) 551   1/7 (1)   (3 wkts dec, 32 overs) 179
3/328 (3)   2/46 (2) 3/123 (3)

†P. M. Nevill, P. M. Siddle, J. L. Pattinson, J. R. Hazlewood and N. M. Lyon did not bat.

Taylor 22–2–97–2; Roach 17–1–97–0; Holder 22–7–47–0; C. R. Brathwaite 30–3–109–0; Warrican 26–2–113–0; K. C. Brathwaite 18–1–78–1. *Second innings*—Taylor 3–0–25–0; Holder 11–1–49–2; C. R. Brathwaite 6–1–30–1; Roach 4–0–22–0; Warrican 8–0–47–0.

West Indies

K. C. Brathwaite c Burns b Lyon	17	– c Smith b Lyon	31
R. Chandrika lbw b Pattinson	25	– lbw b Pattinson	37
D. M. Bravo c Smith b Pattinson	81	– c Nevill b Siddle	21
M. N. Samuels lbw b Pattinson	0	– c Nevill b Marsh	19
J. Blackwood c and b Lyon	28	– lbw b Lyon	20
†D. Ramdin c Burns b Siddle	0	– c Nevill b Marsh	59
*J. O. Holder b Siddle	0	– c Hazlewood b Marsh	68
C. R. Brathwaite c and b Lyon	59	– b Lyon	2
K. A. J. Roach lbw b Pattinson	22	– c Warner b Pattinson	11
J. E. Taylor c Nevill b Lyon	15	– c Pattinson b Marsh	0
J. A. Warrican not out	11	– not out	4
B 5, l-b 5	13	L-b 7, w 1, n-b 2	10

1/35 (1) 2/50 (2) 3/50 (4)   (100.3 overs) 271   1/35 (1) 2/83 (3)   (88.3 overs) 282
4/82 (5) 5/83 (6) 6/83 (7)   3/91 (2) 4/118 (4)
7/173 (8) 8/215 (9) 9/239 (10) 10/271 (3)   5/150 (5) 6/250 (6) 7/253 (8)
                                                          8/274 (7) 9/278 (9) 10/282 (10)

Hazlewood 21–6–49–0; Pattinson 22.3–1–72–4; Lyon 29–8–66–4; Siddle 18–3–40–2; Marsh 7–4–15–0; Smith 3–0–21–0. *Second innings*—Hazlewood 20–6–40–0; Pattinson 17–4–49–2; Lyon 23–7–85–3; Siddle 9–2–35–1; Marsh 17.3–2–61–4; Smith 2–1–5–0.

Umpires: M. Erasmus and C. B. Gaffaney.   Third umpire: I. J. Gould.
Referee: B. C. Broad.

AUSTRALIA v WEST INDIES

Third Test Match

At Sydney, January 3–7, 2016. Drawn. Toss: West Indies.

Torrents of rain not seen at a Sydney Test for a quarter of a century denied Australia the chance of a 3–0 series victory. After events at the MCG, Holder simply had to bat when he won the toss. The previous Test had shown that the West Indian batsmen could compete in patches; now they had to do it from the start. Certainly there was improvement, but too often wickets were lost just as a partnership was blossoming. It was Kraigg Brathwaite's turn to be the trunk of the innings while the branches snapped off around him; Samuels's comical run-out, stranded after Brathwaite dropped his bat mid-pitch, then returned to safety, summed up his tour and the frustration for those around him.

This was a track suited to the twirlers from the first day. Lyon's hard-spun delivery to bowl Blackwood pitched so far outside off stump that the batsman offered no shot. The selectors had got it right in picking O'Keefe, the slow left-armer playing his second Test. He removed Holder, caught one-handed by Burns at short leg as West Indies finished the day on 207 for six.

Then came the rain. Only 11.2 overs were possible on the second day, though at least they were entertaining, Carlos Brathwaite twice smashing Pattinson over the fence, including an audacious slay over extra cover, on his way to 69 from 71 balls. After the third and fourth days were washed out, decisions had to be made. Smith suggested a mix of forfeited innings and declaration bowling, but Holder was keen for his side to pass 300 for the first time in the series. And so they did, guided by Ramdin's 62, an innings that spanned all five days. Three wickets apiece for Australia's spin twins was just reward. Warner had been the only member of Australia's top five yet to notch a century in the series, but he made amends with a hundred from 82 balls, the fastest in Tests at the SCG.

A damp, limp match to end the dampest, limpest series felt about right.

Man of the Match: D. A. Warner. *Attendance:* 62,555.

Man of the Series: A. C. Voges.

Close of play: first day, West Indies 207-6 (Ramdin 23, C. R. Brathwaite 35); second day, West Indies 248-7 (Ramdin 30, Roach 0); third day, no play; fourth day, no play.

West Indies

K. C. Brathwaite c Smith b Lyon	85	J. E. Taylor c Lyon b O'Keefe	13
S. D. Hope c Nevill b Hazlewood	9	J. A. Warrican not out	21
D. M. Bravo c Khawaja b Pattinson	33		
M. N. Samuels run out	4	B 5, l-b 2, n-b 1	8
J. Blackwood b Lyon	10		
†D. Ramdin c Smith b O'Keefe	62	1/13 (2) 2/104 (3) (112.1 overs)	330
*J. O. Holder c Burns b O'Keefe	1	3/115 (4) 4/131 (5)	
C. R. Brathwaite b Pattinson	69	5/158 (1) 6/159 (7) 7/246 (8)	
K. A. J. Roach c Burns b Lyon	15	8/296 (6) 9/300 (9) 10/330 (10)	

Hazlewood 18-5-49-1; Pattinson 18-3-76-2; Lyon 46-12-120-3; Marsh 4-1-15-0; O'Keefe 26.1-7-63-3.

Australia

D. A. Warner not out	122	
J. A. Burns c Roach b Warrican	26	
M. R. Marsh c Blackwood b Warrican	21	
†P. M. Nevill not out	7	
1/100 (2) (2 wkts dec, 38 overs)	176	
2/154 (3)		

U. T. Khawaja, *S. P. D. Smith, A. C. Voges, S. N. J. O'Keefe, J. L. Pattinson, J. R. Hazlewood and N. M. Lyon did not bat.

Taylor 4-0-27-0; Holder 4-1-15-0; Roach 4-0-29-0; Warrican 15-1-62-2; C. R. Brathwaite 7-0-23-0; K. C. Brathwaite 4-0-20-0.

Umpires: C. B. Gaffaney and I. J. Gould. Third umpire: M. Erasmus.
Referee: B. C. Broad.

AUSTRALIA UNDER-19 v ENGLAND UNDER-19 IN 2014-15

Benj Moorehead

Under-19 Test (1): Australia 0, England 0
Under-19 one-day internationals (5): Australia 3, England 2

Matches between the senior England and Australia teams come around thicker and faster, but this was the first Under-19 series between the two countries in 12 years. Played in Western Australia at the back end of the southern summer, the tour was a rough ride for England's teenagers. On true pitches often spiced with moisture, they were mostly outperformed by opponents who had the better of the drawn Test, and won the one-day series with a game to spare.

But results are not everything at this level – which is, after all, the point of Under-19 matches. "To play against an Australian side in conditions our guys are not used to was always going to be tough," said Andy Hurry, the England coach. "Their quality has stretched our players and presented real moments of pressure – and therefore learning opportunities."

Sometimes England responded well. At the WACA, scene of the Test match, they trailed by 283 on first innings after two torrid days with bat and ball. But Haseeb Hameed, a throwback to an age of dogged top-order batsmen, camped at one end through most of the next day, while his emboldened colleagues played freely around him. With England 59 ahead and five down going into the fourth, it was a pity rain prevented an acid test of their character.

There was more riding on the one-day internationals, given the World Cup that loomed in early 2016, though these were hardly conditions to prepare for a tournament in Bangladesh. Time and again the England batsmen were exposed by extra bounce off a full length: following their narrow victory in the first match, Nos 1–3 failed to score more than two in nine of their combined 12 innings, and they were dismissed twice for under 150. Only Aaron Thomason (with three fifties) and Callum Taylor (two) found any form. A seam-bowling all-rounder from Norfolk, Taylor also made a regal 72 in the Test, and took four wickets in the first 50-over game.

Australia's next generation, coached by Graeme Hick, appeared in good order. They had the player of the series in their captain, Jake Doran, who in January had become the youngest debutant in Australian domestic Twenty20 cricket. He followed 169 at the WACA with 248 runs in five one-day innings while being dismissed only three times. Yet arguably the greater damage was done by the new-ball pair of Henry Thornton and Jhye Richardson. They tormented England's frontline batsmen throughout, taking 13 wickets each.

There was a blast from the past when a wicketkeeper called Healy – Tom, son of Ian (and cousin of Alyssa, wicketkeeper for Australia's women) – made 66 and took six catches in the Test. Further down the ranks was another name to chill English souls: Austin Waugh, son of ice-man Steve, was selected for the Under-16 side.

ENGLAND UNDER-19 TOURING PARTY

England *J. J. Weatherley (Hampshire), H. R. Bernard (Kent), M. S. Crane (Hampshire), R. C. Davies (Kent), W. S. Davis (Derbyshire), A. H. T. Donald (Glamorgan), B. G. F. Green (Somerset), H. Hameed (Lancashire), M. D. E. Holden (Middlesex), M. Hussain (Yorkshire), S. Mahmood (Lancashire), M. W. Parkinson (Staffordshire), B. J. Taylor (Hampshire), C. J. Taylor (Essex), A. D. Thomason (Warwickshire), J. D. Warner (Yorkshire). *Coach:* A. Hurry.

AUSTRALIA v ENGLAND

Under-19 Test Match

At Perth, April 6–9, 2015. Drawn. Toss: England Under-19.

The young tourists were relishing the prospect of playing at the WACA, but it didn't take them long to find out why the senior team had won just once in 13 Tests there. They were 11 for four inside the first hour, then 32 for five, the batsmen falling victim to the infamous Perth bounce and the pace of Henry Thornton. Then, on day two, Sam Heazlett and Jake Doran bloodied the England attack with a fourth-wicket partnership of 218 in just over a session. After Heazlett went for 160, Doran added 138 in 24 overs with Tom Healy. At 133 for three in their second innings, England still trailed by 150 – but they were saved by an innings of Boltonian resolve from Haseeb Hameed, who blunted the Australians for five and a half hours. He found support in sparkling innings from Callum Taylor and Ryan Davies, whose counter-attacking 61 in the first innings had averted a capitulation. But, with England 59 ahead and only five wickets left, rain washed out the final day.

Close of play: first day, Australia Under-19 103-3 (Heazlett 68, Doran 4); second day, England Under-19 38-0 (Weatherley 14, Holden 19); third day, England Under-19 342-5 (Hameed 91, Thomason 12).

England Under-19

*J. J. Weatherley c Ayre b Thornton	3	– c Healy b Walker	68
M. D. E. Holden c Healy b Thornton	4	– c Healy b Grant	24
H. Hameed c Healy b Grant	0	– not out	91
M. Hussain c Heazlett b Thornton	0	– c Thornton b Grant	8
C. J. Taylor c Healy b Guthrie	9	– c Morgan b Thornton	72
†R. C. Davies c Short b Ayre	61	– c Short b Thornton	42
A. D. Thomason c and b Grant	40	– not out	12
B. G. F. Green not out	23		
B. J. Taylor lbw b Ayre	7		
J. D. Warner c Morgan b Short	1		
S. Mahmood c Healy b Thornton	10		
B 4, l-b 4, n-b 6	14	L-b 8, w 12, n-b 5	25

1/6 (1) 2/7 (2) 3/7 (3)   (62.1 overs) 172
4/11 (4) 5/32 (5) 6/116 (6)
7/122 (7) 8/141 (9) 9/143 (10) 10/172 (11)

1/47 (2)   (5 wkts, 113 overs) 342
2/122 (1) 3/133 (4)
4/253 (5) 5/321 (6)

Thornton 13.1–8–17–4; Grant 13–4–27–2; Walker 6–0–35–0; Guthrie 6–0–26–1; Short 12–4–33–1; Ayre 12–3–26–2. *Second innings*—Thornton 25–6–91–2; Grant 23–3–73–2; Guthrie 16–2–61–0; Short 10–3–21–0; Ayre 29–8–69–0; Walker 10–2–19–1.

Australia Under-19

J. M. Carder lbw b Mahmood	0	R. R. Ayre not out	1
S. D. Heazlett b B. J. Taylor	160		
*J. Morgan c Davies b Green	19	B 7, l-b 8, w 3, n-b 6	24
M. W. Short c Weatherley b C. J. Taylor	8		
J. R. Doran lbw b B. J. Taylor	169	1/0 (1) (7 wkts dec, 105.3 overs) 455
†T. A. Healy c Thomason b B. J. Taylor	66	2/44 (3) 3/85 (4)
G. L. Walker c C. J. Taylor b Mahmood	8	4/303 (2) 5/441 (5) 6/450 (6) 7/455 (7)

H. T. R. Y. Thornton, D. M. K. Grant and L. Guthrie did not bat.

Mahmood 21.3–0–69–2; Warner 16–1–82–0; Thomason 7–0–47–0; Green 18–2–84–1; C. J. Taylor 11–1–37–1; B. J. Taylor 22–4–78–3; Holden 10–1–43–0.

Umpires: S. A. J. Craig and S. A. Lightbody.
Referee: R. W. Stratford.

First Under-19 one-day international   At Bunbury, April 13, 2015. **England won by two wickets.** ‡**Australia 219** (48.4 overs) (J. R. Doran 82, P. C. Page 30; C. J. Taylor 4-49); **England 220-8** (49.3 overs) (A. H. T. Donald 32, M. Hussain 76). *The teams travelled just over 100 miles south for the first two one-day games. Somerset's Ben Green (20*) held his nerve in a tight finish after a collapse of 4-28 risked wasting a fine 76 from Mosun Hussain. Australia had been kept in check by a bowling attack which – 19 wides aside – offered control and incision. Jake Doran carried over his Test form, but only 17 runs were added in 43 deliveries after he was dismissed by Callum Taylor in the 42nd over.*

Second Under-19 one-day international   At Bunbury, April 15, 2015. **Australia won by eight wickets.** ‡**England 109** (45.2 overs) (C. J. Taylor 50; J. A. Richardson 3-37, H. T. R. Y. Thornton 3-9); **Australia 112-2** (25.3 overs) (J. Morgan 38). *England were blown away by an inspired opening spell from local boy Jhye Richardson, ably supported by new-ball partner Henry Thornton (7.2–4–9–3) and slow left-armer Riley Ayre (10–4–10–2). A battling fifty from the in-form Callum Taylor helped England draw out the innings, with 60 runs scraped together in 27 overs from the depths of 49-6. Australia skipped to their target with few alarms, although Matt Parkinson claimed both openers in a tidy spell of leg-spin.*

Third Under-19 one-day international   At Perth (Murdoch University), April 18, 2015. **Australia won by three wickets.** England 241-7 (50 overs) (J. J. Weatherley 47, A. H. T. Donald 48, C. J. Taylor 67, A. D. Thomason 66*; J. A. Richardson 3-56); ‡**Australia 242-7** (49.5 overs) (S. B. Harper 67, J. R. Doran 102; S. Mahmood 3-54). *A third-wicket stand of 150 between Sam Harper and Doran – whose century took his tour tally to 382 in four innings – was making light work of a challenging target, but Australia wobbled on the finishing line and a seesaw contest was settled only when Thornton took 12 runs off the first five balls of the last over, bowled by Jared Warner. England captain Joe Weatherly and Glamorgan's Aneurin Donald had overseen a recovery from 22-2, before fluent innings from Callum Taylor (61 in 67 balls) and Aaron Thomason (66* in 76) carried the tourists to a testing 241-7.*

Fourth Under-19 one-day international   At Perth (Murdoch University), April 21, 2015. **Australia won by seven wickets.** England 138 (49.5 overs) (A. D. Thomason 70; J. A. Richardson 4-33); ‡**Australia 139-3** (28 overs) (J. M. Carder 52*, S. D. Heazlett 47). *Australia took the series with another clinical spell of fast bowling from Richardson, on his home ground. He was on a hat-trick in the first over after removing Weatherley and Donald for ducks, and claimed two more as England's brittle batting order struggled on a juicy surface. Thomason saved some face with a resilient half-century, before Jake Carder marshalled Australia to victory with 22 overs to spare. Hampshire all-rounder Brad Taylor took two wickets with his off-breaks, to go with a stubborn 14 from 56 balls.*

Fifth Under-19 one-day international   At Perth (Murdoch University), April 23, 2015. **England won by 82 runs.** England 232-8 (50 overs) (R. C. Davies 81, A. H. T. Donald 38, A. D. Thomason 63, B. J. Taylor 34; H. T. R. Y. Thornton 4-46); ‡**Australia 150** (40.1 overs) (T. A. Healy 58*; H. R. Bernard 5-14). *In only his second appearance of the series, Hugh Bernard took three early wickets to set England on course for a consolation win. Doran (27) flickered briefly, and Tom Healy held out to the end, but Bernard – reaping the rewards of a good length – returned to claim the only five-wicket haul of the tour. England, on the brink of another embarrassment at 8-3, were rescued by 81 from Ryan Davies and a third consecutive half-century by Thomason.*

KFC T20 BIG BASH LEAGUE IN 2014-15

Jesse Hogan

Against the backdrop of a limited-overs arms race, in which totals spiral ever higher, it was refreshing to see **Perth Scorchers** retain their title thanks to disciplined bowling. The pace trio of Jason Behrendorff, Yasir Arafat and Andrew Tye finished in the tournament's top four wicket-takers. Yet, rather than blast teams out, the Scorchers – also including Brad Hogg, the impossibly evergreen left-arm wrist-spinner who turned 44 just after the final – preferred to strangle the run-rate, picking up wickets when batsmen took a risk too far.

Perth conceded 150 only three times in ten matches, and on four occasions won despite setting a target of 145 or under – most significantly against Melbourne Stars, whom they defeated in the semi-finals for the third time in four years. The Stars' recruitment of England outcast Kevin Pietersen helped ensure they were pre-tournament favourites, but they lost their first three matches – only to turn things round in style, winning their next five to make the knockout stage with ease.

Each of those three early defeats featured a notable individual contribution. In the season opener against Adelaide Strikers, Pietersen's dashing 66 – one of his three half-centuries in an impressive tournament – was eclipsed by Adelaide wicketkeeper Tim Ludeman's unbeaten 92 from 44 balls. In their next match, **Hobart Hurricanes'** West Indies all-rounder Darren Sammy blasted 38 not out from a mere 12. Then one of their own, Glenn Maxwell, provided the image of the tournament – for the wrong reasons. Struggling for form, he shouldered arms to his first ball, a full delivery from Brisbane's Ryan Duffield. It clattered into his stumps, leaving Maxwell a target of derision; to his credit, he adopted the photograph as his social-media profile image.

Sydney Thunder, the previous year's whipping boys, improved their credibility slightly, thanks to Jacques Kallis. He cracked 235 runs at a strike-rate of 136, chipped in with five wickets, and was named Player of the Tournament. Against **Brisbane Heat**, who replaced them at the bottom, he and fellow 39-year-old Mike Hussey enjoyed an opening stand of 160, comfortably the highest of the competition for any wicket.

The progress of **Sydney Sixers** and **Melbourne Stars**, the glamour teams of Australia's biggest cities, was helped by last-ball derby victories. And, when the teams met at the MCG, the Stars cut things fine again: James Faulkner enhanced his reputation as a nerveless finisher by hitting Brett Lee, in his farewell Big Bash, for two sixes in a super over.

Against Perth, meanwhile, Peter Handscomb walloped two last-over sixes to speed the Stars into the semis, and raise his hundred (the only other one in the tournament came from Perth's redoubtable Michael Klinger). Needing 66 from five overs, and with five wickets down, the Stars had seemed out of contention until Handscomb engineered a dramatic comeback – though perhaps not the most dramatic of the evening. A seagull strolling at deep midwicket had been struck by a powerful pull from Adam Voges, leaving the nearest fielder – the caring, if sombre, Rob Quiney – to pick up the motionless bird and gingerly place it beyond the boundary. A couple of minutes later, the seagull groggily stood up and, to a tumultuous reception, flew a short distance before resuming its post on the outfield.

The "spin to win" mantra long espoused by Adelaide coach Darren Berry was supported by the stats. Of those to send down 20 overs, the three stingiest were all slow bowlers: Hogg, Fawad Ahmed of **Melbourne Renegades** and the Stars' Michael Beer. And the old saw that Twenty20 would be no place for wrist-spinners was belied by the presence of three – Hogg, Fawad and Adelaide's Adam Zampa – among the meanest six.

The success of spin was perhaps Berry's sole cause for a smile. The **Adelaide Strikers** emulated the Stars in 2013-14, and the Renegades the year before, in finishing at least a game ahead at the top of the table, before capitulating in a home semi-final. Adelaide Oval had rivalled the much smaller WACA for the best atmosphere, and expectations were high among a whopping crowd of 52,633. But Adelaide crumbled, triggering the end of Berry's tenure.

It was known before the competition began that no team would enjoy home advantage in the final, since Cricket Australia had given the match to Canberra: the approaching World Cup meant many stadiums were unavailable, and a neutral venue was deemed the fairest policy. All the same, Perth were displeased with a choice of ground far closer to their opponents, Sydney Sixers, than to their own WACA – which in previous years would have been used because Perth finished the league phase in the higher place.

The near-capacity crowd of 11,741 at Manuka Oval were treated to yet another last-ball finish, the fifth of the season. Perth required eight at the start of the final over, and knocked off seven from the first three, before Lee came within a whisker of forcing an unlikely super over. He bowled Nathan Coulter-Nile and Sam Whiteman, but Arafat chanced a harum-scarum single that would have brought a run-out had Moises Henriques not fumbled the return. It denied Lee the perfect send-off, but was no more than Perth, who coped with pressure better than anyone, deserved.

KFC T20 BIG BASH LEAGUE, 2014-15

	Played	Won	Lost	No result	Points	Net run-rate
ADELAIDE STRIKERS	8	6	1	1	13	1.15
PERTH SCORCHERS	8	5	3	0	10	0.70
MELBOURNE STARS	8	5	3	0	10	0.33
SYDNEY SIXERS	8	5	3	0	10	0.00
Hobart Hurricanes	8	3	5	0	6	−0.28
Melbourne Renegades	8	3	5	0	6	−0.35
Sydney Thunder	8	2	5	1	5	−0.48
Brisbane Heat	8	2	6	0	4	−1.11

Teams tied on points were separated on net run-rate (calculated by subtracting runs conceded per over from runs scored per over).

First semi-final   At Adelaide, January 24, 2015. **Sydney Sixers won by 87 runs.** ‡Sydney Sixers **181-4** (20 overs) (M. J. Lumb 32, N. J. Maddinson 85); **Adelaide Strikers 94** (14.3 overs) (D. E. Bollinger 3-21). *MoM*: N. J. Maddinson. *Attendance*: 52,633. *Sydney's Nic Maddinson struck*

85 from 48 balls to help ensure that, for the third year in a row, the fourth-placed team beat the first. The attendance was the largest at Adelaide Oval and – at the time – for any match in the Big Bash.

Second semi-final   At Perth, January 25, 2015. **Perth Scorchers won by 18 runs.** ‡**Perth Scorchers 144-7** (20 overs) (S. E. Marsh 35, M. A. Carberry 50; J. W. Hastings 3-27); **Melbourne Stars 126** (19.5 overs) (L. J. Wright, 31, K. P. Pietersen 31; A. J. Tye 4-18). *MoM*: A. J. Tye. *Attendance: 19,289. The momentum seemed to have tipped towards the Stars after Clint McKay conceded no runs in the 20th over of the Perth innings. But Andrew Tye, who had been booed while swinging and missing, then strangled the Stars' response. Perth had now qualified for all four Big Bash finals; the Stars had been eliminated in four semis.*

FINAL

PERTH SCORCHERS v SYDNEY SIXERS

At Canberra, January 28, 2015. Perth Scorchers won by four wickets. Toss: Sydney Sixers.

The last over started with Perth needing eight to retain their Big Bash crown; after three balls, Michael Carberry had levelled the scores, but lost the strike. Brett Lee, now 38 and in the final over of his professional career, then seared in successive yorkers to find himself on a hat-trick. Another full delivery zeroed in on the stumps: Yasir Arafat managed to get some bat on it – and hared for the far end. There was never a run, but Moises Henriques failed to gather the ball cleanly, and broke the stumps with empty hands. Henriques had earlier dug the Sixers out of a hole, steering them from seven for two after three overs – and 49 for four in the tenth – to give them a chance.

Man of the Match: S. E. Marsh.   *Attendance:* 11,837.

Man of the Tournament: J. H. Kallis.

Sydney Sixers		*B*	*4/6*
1 M. J. Lumb *b* 6	3	8	0
2 M. H. Wessels *b* 10	2	4	0
3 N. J. Maddinson *b* 8	19	22	2
4 *M. C. Henriques *run out*	77	57	5/2
5 J. C. Silk *b* 11	3	4	0
6 †R. G. L. Carters *not out*	35	25	4
L-b 3, w 5	8		
6 overs: 29-2 (20 overs) 147-5			

1/5 2/7 3/44 4/49 5/147

7 S. A. Abbott, 8 S. N. J. O'Keefe, 9 N. M. Lyon, 10 B. Lee and 11 D. E. Bollinger did not bat.

Behrendorff 4–0–19–1 (11); Coulter-Nile 4–0–32–1 (9); Tye 4–0–31–0 (6); Yasir Arafat 4–0–37–1 (6); Hogg 4–0–25–1 (8).

Perth Scorchers		*B*	*4/6*
1 S. E. Marsh *c 7 b 9*	73	59	3/3
2 M. Klinger *c 7 b 10*	33	37	4
3 *A. C. Voges *c 6 b 11*	20	13	1
4 M. A. Carberry *not out*	9	7	1
5 A. J. Turner *c 7 b 9*	0	1	0
6 N. M. Coulter-Nile *b 10*	7	3	0/1
7 †S. M. Whiteman *b 10*	0	1	0
8 Yasir Arafat *not out*	1	1	0
L-b 2, w 1, n-b 2	5		
6 overs: 41-0 (20 overs) 148-6			

1/70 2/113 3/131 4/132 5/147 6/147

9 A. J. Tye, 10 J. P. Behrendorff and 11 G. B. Hogg did not bat.

Lee 4–0–25–3 (13); Abbott 3–0–26–0 (3); Lyon 4–0–34–2 (9); Bollinger 3–0–27–1 (4); O'Keefe 2–0–13–0 (4); Henriques 4–0–21–0 (9).

Umpires: M. D. Martell and P. Wilson.   Third umpire: S. J. Nogajski.

Referee: R. W. Stratford.

DOMESTIC CRICKET IN AUSTRALIA IN 2014-15

Peter English

The Sheffield Shield was overshadowed, for very different reasons, at both ends of the summer. In November, Phillip Hughes was fatally injured playing for South Australia against his old team, New South Wales, at Sydney; all games in progress were called off, and the tournament paused until after his funeral. In the closing stages, with the World Cup occupying the major grounds, the states headed inland to new venues at Wagga Wagga and Alice Springs, while the final, between Victoria and Western Australia, was held at Tasmania's Bellerive Oval. It was the choice of table-leaders Victoria, who needed only a draw to claim the Shield; Western Australia, fearing Hobart's reputation for wet weather, were furious, briefly threatening legal action. Colin Barnett, the state premier, described it as a "stupid, stupid decision".

Western Australia – now officially titled the "Alcohol. Think Again Western Warriors" – were fighting for an unprecedented clean sweep. In October, they had won the one-day cup, their first major trophy since 2003-04; in January, their sister team, the **Perth Scorchers**, retained the Twenty20 Big Bash title. All three finals were played away from home, but it was the flat, mostly lifeless pitch in Hobart that killed their hopes. They took first-innings lead and set a target of 334, but coach Justin Langer said he knew 20 wickets would be "almost impossible"; his men managed 14, with Victoria stubbornly blocking their way on the fifth afternoon. **Victoria** catapulted from last in the previous season to their 29th Shield. They headed the table with six wins, and also collected most batting and bowling points under a revised system: it offered bonus points in the opening 100 overs of each first innings, and one point for a draw, but no reward for first-innings lead.

Shortly before Victoria's triumph, it was announced that the final would be their last match under coach Greg Shipperd, whose contract was not renewed despite four Shield trophies in 11 years; he was replaced by David Saker, returning from his job as England bowling coach. Victoria's road to the final relied on 48 wickets from leg-spinner Fawad Ahmed – the most in the tournament – and prolific batting: seven men passed 500 runs, led by Marcus Stoinis, with 785.

Yet it was Western Australia's batsmen who filled the top three spots in the Shield run list. Adam Voges flooded 1,358 at 104, a state record, with six centuries, peaking with 249 against South Australia; Michael Klinger enjoyed his move from Adelaide to Perth, hitting four hundreds in an aggregate of 1,046, while Cameron Bancroft scored 896. Seamer Nathan Rimmington and slow left-armer Ashton Agar took 66 wickets between them.

There were no prizes left for the remaining states. **New South Wales** fell short in the one-day final for the second time running, and narrowly missed the Shield final. Their bowlers thrived – Steve O'Keefe, Doug Bollinger, Nathan Lyon and Sean Abbott earned more than 20 wickets apiece – but they found run-scoring more difficult: wicketkeeper Peter Nevill finished with 764, almost 300 more than his nearest team-mate.

Queensland underperformed, and sacked coach Stuart Law, a hero from his playing days, mid-season. All-rounder James Hopes, who stood out with 30 wickets and 356 runs, signalled another change when he stepped down as captain after five years. For **Tasmania**, the consistent opener Ed Cowan registered four centuries in his 815 runs, but returned to New South Wales for 2015-16. Andrew Fekete, an import from Victoria, swung his way to 37 wickets, second only to Fawad. Ben Dunk became the first batsman to score a double-hundred in the one-day tournament, with 229 against Queensland.

The campaign was a disaster for **South Australia**, last for the fifth time in six Shield seasons, and bottom of the one-day tournament. In their defence, priorities were altered following Hughes's death. In early February, Johan Botha resigned as captain and was replaced by 21-year-old Travis Head. Further upheaval occurred when the coach Darren Berry departed with a year left on his contract; former captain Jamie Siddons took over.

FIRST-CLASS AVERAGES, 2014-15

BATTING (450 runs, average 30.00)

	M	I	NO	R	HS	100	Avge	Ct/St
S. P. D. Smith (*Australia*)	4	8	2	769	192	4	128.16	6
A. C. Voges (*Western Australia*)	11	20	7	1,358	249	6	104.46	18
V. Kohli (*India*)	4	8	0	692	169	4	86.50	2
P. M. Nevill (*New South Wales*)	10	14	4	764	235*	2	76.40	29/5
D. J. Hussey (*Victoria*).	7	10	2	532	142	2	66.50	13
M. Vijay (*India*)	4	8	0	482	144	1	60.25	4
M. Klinger (*Western Australia*)	11	20	2	1,046	190	4	58.11	7
†M. S. Wade (*Victoria*)	9	11	1	572	152	2	57.20	34/2
*S. E. Marsh (*Western Aus/Australia*). . . .	14	22	5	960	164*	3	56.47	15
P. S. P. Handscomb (*Victoria*)	10	13	1	647	134	3	53.91	14
†N. J. Maddinson (*New South Wale*)	7	9	0	483	118	1	53.66	4
C. J. Ferguson (*South Australia*)	10	19	3	836	140	4	52.25	5
†C. J. L. Rogers (*Victoria/Australia*)	12	19	1	936	112	2	52.00	4
D. T. Christian (*Victoria*).	10	15	4	560	105*	2	50.90	11
J. A. Burns (*Queensland/Australia*)	12	21	2	939	183	2	49.42	8
M. P. Stoinis (*Victoria*)	10	17	1	785	99	0	49.06	0
†E. J. M. Cowan (*Tasmania*)	9	17	0	815	158	4	47.94	3
C. T. Bancroft (*Western Australia*)	11	19	0	896	211	3	47.15	14
†R. J. Quiney (*Victoria*).	11	17	1	687	125	2	42.93	9
†M. J. Cosgrove (*South Australia*).	9	17	0	686	103	1	40.35	3
†T. M. Head (*South Australia*).	10	17	0	641	85	0	37.70	3
†C. D. Hartley (*Queensland*)	10	16	2	522	142*	2	37.28	38/2
T. L. W. Cooper (*South Australia*)	10	19	2	626	121	2	36.82	10
†M. S. Harris (*Western Australia*)	10	17	2	548	158*	1	36.53	5
†S. O. Henry (*New South Wales*)	10	15	1	471	142	1	33.64	6
P. J. Forrest (*Queensland*)	10	16	1	457	93	0	30.46	20

BOWLING (15 wickets, average 50.00)

	Style	O	M	R	W	BB	5I	Avge
J. R. Hopes (*Queensland*)	RFM	302.4	101	658	30	5-60	1	21.93
P. M. Siddle (*Victoria/Australia*)	RFM	242.4	69	677	30	8-54	2	22.56
S. N. J. O'Keefe (*New South Wales*)	SLA	285.2	83	650	28	5-24	1	23.21
A. L. Fekete (*Tasmania*)	RFM	296.5	69	892	37	5-66	2	24.10
N. J. Rimmington (*Western Australia*) . . .	RFM	300.2	81	848	35	5-27	2	24.22
Fawad Ahmed (*Victoria*)	LBG	359	51	1,193	48	8-89	3	24.85
D. E. Bollinger (*New South Wales*)	LFM	215.5	50	603	24	5-56	1	25.12
M. A. Starc (*NSW/Australia*)	LF	152.3	34	466	18	4-64	0	25.88
S. A. Abbott (*New South Wales*)	RFM	196.5	46	626	23	6-14	1	27.21
R. J. Harris (*Queensland/Australia*)	RFM	171.5	43	503	17	4-59	0	29.58
N. M. Coulter-Nile (*Western Australia*) . . .	RFM	196.3	53	504	17	3-34	0	29.64
M. G. Hogan (*Western Australia*)	RFM	223.5	64	623	21	4-64	0	29.66
S. P. Mackin (*Western Australia*)	RFM	217.4	69	626	21	4-36	0	29.80
S. M. Boland (*Victoria*)	RFM	244.5	52	753	25	6-67	1	30.12
B. W. Hilfenhaus (*Tasmania*)	RFM	177.2	48	484	16	5-11	1	30.25
A. C. Agar (*Western Australia*)	SLA	318.1	77	945	31	5-81	2	30.48
S. L. Rainbird (*Tasmania*)	LFM	170.4	36	568	18	4-83	0	31.55
N. M. Lyon (*NSW/Australia*)	OB	501	93	1,468	46	7-152	2	31.91
J. R. Hazlewood (*NSW/Australia*)	RFM	162.2	37	491	15	5-68	1	32.73
J. M. Bird (*Tasmania*)	RFM	189.5	52	599	18	4-55	0	33.27
P. R. George (*Queensland*)	RFM	216.2	46	666	20	5-78	0	33.30
Mohammed Shami (*India*).	RFM	126.3	15	537	15	5-112	1	35.80
C. P. Tremain (*Victoria*).	RFM	209.5	43	677	16	3-31	0	42.31
G. S. Sandhu (*New South Wales*)	RFM	204.1	40	709	15	4-69	0	47.26

SHEFFIELD SHIELD, 2014-15

| | | | | *Bonus points* | | |
	Played	*Won*	*Lost*	*Drawn*	*Batting*	*Bowling*	*Points*
VICTORIA	10	6	3	1	9.43	11*	57.43
WESTERN AUSTRALIA	10	5	1	4	6.84*	9	49.84
New South Wales	10	5	3	2	6.76	8.5	47.26
Queensland	10	4	5	1	7.99	6.5*	38.99†
Tasmania.	10	2	6	2	4.11*	9.5	27.61
South Australia	10	2	6	2	7.91	3.5	24.91†

* *Four teams had their bonus points annulled in the matches called off after Phillip Hughes's
injury on November 25: Victoria lost 0.5, Western Australia 0.87, Queensland 1.5, Tasmania 0.17.
Neither New South Wales nor South Australia had received any points when the accident occurred.*

† *0.5 deducted for a slow over-rate.*

*Outright win = 6pts; draw = 1pt. Bonus points awarded for the first 100 overs of each team's first
innings: 0.01 batting points for every run over the first 200 runs; 0.5 bowling points for the fifth
wicket taken and for every subsequent two.*

At Adelaide, October 31–November 3, 2014. **South Australia won by eight wickets. ‡Queensland
443-8 dec** (N. G. Stevens 158, C. D. Hartley 147*) **and 152** (C. J. Sayers 6-34); **South Australia
368-4 dec** (C. J. Ferguson 100*) **and 228-2.** *South Australia 7.12pts, Queensland 1.24pts. Chadd
Sayers claimed a hat-trick in Queensland's first innings, before Nick Stevens, whose career record
was 27 in four innings, and Chris Hartley fought back with 256 for the fifth wicket. But, after Johan
Botha declared 75 behind, Sayers routed Queensland with a career-best 6-34 to set up South
Australia's first home victory since February 2013.*

At Melbourne, October 31–November 3, 2014. **Victoria won by nine wickets. New South Wales
366** (S. M. Boland 6-67) **and 271; ‡Victoria 507-5 dec** (D. J. Hussey 129, P. S. P. Handscomb
108*, D. T. Christian 105*) **and 131-1.** *Victoria 8.85pts, New South Wales 1.26pts. Scott Boland
took a career-best six on the opening day. Victoria then registered three centuries: Peter Handscomb
and Daniel Christian added 206* for the sixth wicket after David Hussey's 129. On the last day Ben
Rohrer of New South Wales was felled when a bouncer from Chris Tremain struck his right ear, and
driven off on a motorised stretcher. Severe concussion kept him out for several weeks.*

At Perth, October 31–November 3, 2014. **Western Australia won by seven wickets. ‡Tasmania
215** (N. J. Rimmington 5-38) **and 242** (E. J. M. Cowan 100); **Western Australia 353** (C. T. Bancroft
129; A. L. Fekete 5-80) **and 105-3.** *Western Australia 8.67pts, Tasmania 1.15pts. Nathan
Rimmington's career-best return and Cameron Bancroft's maiden hundred helped ensure that all
three games in the opening round were won by the home side.*

At Adelaide, November 8–11, 2014 (day/night). **New South Wales won by 168 runs. ‡New South
Wales 230** (J. Botha 6-34) **and 392-5 dec** (N. C. R. Larkin 130, S. O. Henry 142); **South Australia
293** (T. L. W. Cooper 121) **and 161** (S. N. J. O'Keefe 5-24). *New South Wales 7.77pts, South
Australia 2.43pts. Matches in this round used a pink ball, continuing trials for day/night Tests. Nick
Larkin, who had played for Ireland v Sri Lanka A in July, scored a century in his second first-class
game, and shared three-figure stands in both innings with Scott Henry. Left-arm spinner Steve
O'Keefe returned from his Test debut in the UAE to wrap up victory with 25–14–24–5.*

At Hobart, November 8–11, 2014 (day/night). **Tasmania won by eight wickets. ‡Victoria 279 and
173; Tasmania 253** (E. J. M. Cowan 105) **and 200-2.** *Tasmania 8.03pts, Victoria 2.29pts. Victoria's
Chris Rogers withdrew, citing fatigue after the Tests in the UAE, plus previous problems as a colour-
blind batsman against the pink ball. Ed Cowan scored a second successive hundred, and Jordan Silk
led Tasmania home early on the final morning with 97*.*

At Perth, November 8–10, 2014 (day/night). **Western Australia won by eight wickets. ‡Queensland
163** (N. J. Rimmington 5-27) **and 210** (J. P. Behrendorff 7-70); **Western Australia 357** (S. E. Marsh
111; J. R. Hopes 5-60) **and 18-2.** *Western Australia 8.12pts. Western Australia won again:
Rimmington improved his career-best, Bancroft fell one short of a second successive hundred, and
Jason Behrendorff's career-best 7-70 gave him 10-110, the tournament's best match return.*

At Brisbane, November 16–19, 2014. **Queensland won by 188 runs. ‡Queensland 472-9 dec** (J. A. Burns 183) **and 200-8 dec; New South Wales 302** (N. J. Maddinson 118; L. W. Feldman 5-83) **and 182.** *Queensland 8.86pts, New South Wales 1.02pts. Joe Burns, with a career-best, and Peter Forrest (93) added 254 for Queensland's third wicket. Team-mate Ryan Harris bowled 32.5 overs across two innings for seven wickets, in his first outing since knee surgery in March.*

At Adelaide, November 16–19, 2014. **Victoria won by an innings and 46 runs. ‡South Australia 431-8 dec** (C. J. Ferguson 140, T. P. Ludeman 106) **and 130** (P. M. Siddle 5-31); **Victoria 607-7 dec** (C. J. L. Rogers 107, P. S. P. Handscomb 134). *Victoria 7.24pts, South Australia 1.19pts. Callum Ferguson and Tim Ludeman added 208 for South Australia's fifth wicket. Handscomb and Christian (89) followed up Rogers's century with 179 for Victoria's sixth. Peter Siddle had a hand in South Australia's first six second-innings wickets, catching the one he didn't take himself.*

At Hobart, November 16–19, 2014. **Drawn. Western Australia 301** (M. Klinger 100) **and 270-6 dec** (A. C. Voges 109*); **‡Tasmania 247 and 215-8.** *Tasmania 1.47pts, Western Australia 2.85pts. Set 325 in 71 overs, Tasmania slumped to 190-8 in 56.1, but James Faulkner (63*) and Sam Rainbird (0* in 40 balls) survived an hour for the draw.*

At Sydney, November 25–28, 2014. **Drawn. ‡South Australia 136-2 v New South Wales.** *New South Wales 1pt, South Australia 1pt. The match ended on the first afternoon when Phillip Hughes, on 63*, was hit on the neck by a bouncer which burst an artery. He collapsed and was taken to hospital, but died two days later.*

At Brisbane (Allan Border Field), November 25–28, 2014. **Drawn. ‡Tasmania 217; Queensland 73-1.** *Queensland 1pt, Tasmania 1pt. This match and the one at Melbourne were called off after the first day because of Phillip Hughes's collapse at Sydney. All bonus points were cancelled.*

At Melbourne, November 25–28, 2014. **Drawn. ‡Western Australia 287-5** (C. T. Bancroft 132, S. E. Marsh 134*) **v Victoria.** *Victoria 1pt, Western Australia 1pt. Bancroft and Shaun Marsh added 244 for Western Australia's fourth wicket.*

At Sydney, December 9–12, 2014. **New South Wales won by an innings and 80 runs. ‡Queensland 268 and 99** (S. A. Abbott 6-14); **New South Wales 447** (R. G. L. Carters 198, K. R. Patterson 126). *New South Wales 8.07pts, Queensland 0.68pts. Shield cricket resumed, four days behind schedule, after Phillip Hughes's funeral. Abbott, who was applauded by the crowd, bowled a bouncer in his first over, and in the second innings collected a career-best 7–3–14–6 to ensure victory. In New South Wales's innings, Ryan Carters and Kurtis Patterson added 212 for the fourth wicket.*

At Hobart, December 9–12, 2014. **Tasmania won by 313 runs. ‡Tasmania 362** (E. J. M. Cowan 147; T. L. Lawford 5-82) **and 298-8 dec** (E. J. M. Cowan 158); **South Australia 302 and 45** (B. W. Hilfenhaus 5-11). *Tasmania 8.73pts, South Australia 2.02pts. Cowan hit a pair of centuries before South Australia succumbed for 45, the seventh-lowest Shield total, and the worst since their own 29 at Sydney ten years earlier. Ben Hilfenhaus's analysis was 14–11–11–5, Andrew Fekete's 11–6–9–3; Tasmania completed their third-biggest win by runs.*

At Perth, December 9–12, 2014. **Victoria won by 117 runs. Victoria 350 and 341-3 dec** (D. T. Christian 105*); **‡Western Australia 287** (A. C. Voges 101) **and 287** (A. C. Voges 139*). *Victoria 8.83pts, Western Australia 1.37pts. Adam Voges hit twin hundreds, but Victoria's win displaced Western Australia at the head of the Shield table. Christian's 99-ball 105* helped set a target of 405.*

At Brisbane, February 7–9, 2015. **Queensland won by an innings and 13 runs. ‡Victoria 260** (M. S. Wade 152; P. R. George 5-78) **and 239; Queensland 512** (C. A. Lynn 250, C. D. Hartley 123). *Queensland 9.56pts, Victoria 1.1pts. Matthew Wade scored two-thirds of Victoria's runs after coming in at 31-4. Queensland were then 33-4 before Chris Lynn and Chris Hartley added 273, a state fifth-wicket record. Lynn, in his first Shield game since March after shoulder surgery, closed the second day on 250*, his maiden double-hundred, including ten sixes and 21 fours in 329 balls and seven hours 40 minutes. Next morning, he set a world record for the highest overnight score ended without addition, beating Misbah-ul-Haq's 247 for Sui Northen Gas Pipelines v Sui Southern Gas Corporation at Sheikhupura, 2008-09.*

At Hobart, February 7–10, 2015. **New South Wales won by an innings and 91 runs. ‡Tasmania 272 and 213** (D. E. Bollinger 5-56); **New South Wales 576-9 dec** (P. M. Nevill 235*). *New South Wales 8.91pts, Tasmania 1.72pts. New South Wales went from 66-5 to 576-9, thanks to stands of 87, 82, 180, 50 and 111*, only the second known instance of a team adding at least 50 for each of their last five wickets, following Victoria (177-5 to 550) v Tasmania at Launceston in 1921-22. Peter*

Nevill featured in all five stands (one up on Bill Ponsford in the earlier match); he faced 379 balls in eight hours 56 minutes for 235*, his maiden double-hundred, and the second-highest Shield score by a keeper, after 321 by Billy Murdoch, also for New South Wales, v Victoria in 1881-82. O'Keefe, who helped add 180 for the eighth wicket, fell one short of a maiden century. Tasmania lost their last nine for 65 on the final day.

At Perth, February 7–10, 2015. **Western Australia won by eight wickets. ‡South Australia 328 and 260; Western Australia 467** (M. Klinger 190, A. C. Voges 101) **and 122-2.** *Western Australia 9.14pts, South Australia 1.28pts. Travis Head became South Australia's youngest captain at 21 years 40 days; in Shield cricket he was second only to Cameron White, who led Victoria aged 20. Michael Klinger, who hit five sixes, and Voges, with his third successive hundred, added 215 for Western Australia's third wicket, as they regained first place in the table.*

At Wagga Wagga, February 15–17, 2015. **New South Wales won by 156 runs. ‡New South Wales 206 and 233; Victoria 114 and 169.** *New South Wales 7.56pts, Victoria 1.5pts. This was the first Shield game in the country city of Wagga Wagga, staged at the Robertson Oval. Doug Bollinger of hosts New South Wales became the first man to take a second Shield hat-trick (his first was at Perth in 2007-08). Nathan Lyon and O'Keefe spun out Victoria to put NSW top.*

At Adelaide (Glenelg Oval), February 16–19, 2015. **Drawn. ‡South Australia 469** (A. C. Agar 5-133) **and 238** (A. C. Agar 5-81); **Western Australia 633** (M. Klinger 151, A. C. Voges 249) **and 72-4.** *South Australia 2.21pts, Western Australia 2.79pts. Western Australia's 633, the biggest total of the tournament, was their second-highest in all, after 654 v Victoria in 1986-87; Klinger and Voges, whose second, career-best double-hundred lasted seven hours 45 minutes and 366 balls, added 311 for the third wicket. It was Voges' fifth century in seven innings. Former Test spinner Ashton Agar (still only 21) followed 64 in 47 balls by claiming ten wickets for the first time, to set up a target of 75 in eight overs. Shaun Marsh needed four off the final ball but managed only a single.*

At Hobart, February 16–17, 2015. **Queensland won by an innings and 50 runs. Tasmania 149 and 121** (S. Milenko 5-15); **‡Queensland 320.** *Queensland 8.7pts, Tasmania 1.5pts. Queensland captain James Hopes took four wickets and hit 98 to put them on course for a two-day win, completed by Simon Milenko's 5-15 in his second first-class match.*

At Adelaide (Glenelg Oval), February 24–27, 2015. **South Australia won by five wickets. ‡Tasmania 364 and 219-5 dec; South Australia 295** (T. L. W. Cooper 104) **and 291-5** (C. J. Ferguson 117*). *South Australia 7.36pts, Tasmania 2.14pts. South Australia were 2-3 in the first innings after their top three fell for ducks, but completed their second victory of the season after Tasmania declared to set them 289.*

At Newcastle, February 25–28, 2015. **Western Australia won by seven wickets. ‡New South Wales 345** (P. M. Nevill 112) **and 97; Western Australia 300 and 143-3.** *Western Australia 7.27pts, New South Wales 1.42pts. Voges reached 1,000 first-class runs in the season in Western Australia's second innings, and completed 10,000 career runs just before their victory, which was all but certain once Agar (4-22) bowled out New South Wales for 97.*

At Alice Springs, February 25–27, 2015. **Victoria won by an innings and 14 runs. ‡Queensland 207** (Fawad Ahmed 5-50) **and 168; Victoria 389** (R. J. Quiney 111; M. A. Philipson 7-107). *Victoria 8.68pts, Queensland 0.57pts. This match, a home fixture for Victoria, was the first first-class game at Traeger Park, in Northern Territory's Alice Springs. Off-spinner Michael Philipson took 7-107 in his third first-class appearance, but finished on the wrong end of a three-day innings defeat.*

At Sydney (Bankstown Oval), March 5–8, 2015. **New South Wales won by ten wickets. ‡Tasmania 237 and 183; New South Wales 394 and 27-0.** *New South Wales 7.81pts, Tasmania 1.37pts. Tailenders Gurinder Sandhu (97*, including five sixes) and Lyon (42) both made career-bests as they added 100 for New South Wales's ninth wicket; Lyon also claimed three in each innings.*

At Brisbane (Allan Border Field), March 5–8, 2015. **Western Australia won by 95 runs. Western Australia 417-7 dec** (S. E. Marsh 164*, S. M. Whiteman 120) **and 173; ‡Queensland 279-7 dec and 216.** *Western Australia 7.27pts, Queensland 0.79pts. Marsh and Sam Whiteman added 255 for Western Australia's fifth wicket; in the second innings, Queensland wicketkeeper Hartley made five dismissals for the third time in the tournament, which gave him seven in the match. Queensland declared behind, attempting to force a win to stay in the race for the final, but in vain.*

At Adelaide (Glenelg Oval), March 5–8, 2015. **Victoria won by an innings and one run. ‡Victoria 534-6 dec** (R. J. Quiney 125, D. J. Hussey 142); **South Australia 175** (P. M. Siddle 8-54) **and 358.** *Victoria 9.05pts. Victoria completed their second innings victory over South Australia in* *the season – both at Adelaide grounds, because they had been displaced from Melbourne by the World Cup. Jake Lehmann, son of Australian national coach Darren and nephew of former England player Craig White, scored 54 on first-class debut as South Australia succumbed to Peter Siddle's career-best 8-54, which was also the best return of the tournament.*

At Brisbane, March 13–16, 2015. **Queensland won by five wickets. South Australia 230 and 458** (M. J. Cosgrove 103, C. J. Ferguson 107; B. C. J. Cutting 5-88); ‡**Queensland 390** (C. R. Hemphrey 118) **and 301-5** (J. A. Burns 135*). *Queensland 8.09pts, South Australia 0.8pts. Mark Cosgrove hit 103 in 97 balls. South Australian keeper Tim Ludeman made seven dismissals in the match, while Queensland fielder Peter Forrest held six catches – both for the second time in the season.*

At Alice Springs, March 13–15, 2015. **Victoria won by 400 runs.** ‡**Victoria 449** (P. S. P. Handscomb 104, M. S. Wade 101; A. L. Fekete 5-66) **and 230-2 dec; Tasmania 145** (J. M. Holland 6-41) **and 134** (Fawad Ahmed 5-35). *Victoria 8.89pts, Tasmania 0.5pts. The second match at Alice Springs produced Victoria's fourth-biggest win by runs, and their sixth of the season. Spinners Jon Holland and Fawad Ahmed rolled over Tasmania twice to secure first place in the table.*

At Perth, March 13–16, 2015. **Drawn.** ‡**New South Wales 407** (M. C. Henriques 145); **Western Australia 483-4 dec** (C. T. Bancroft 211, M. Klinger 161). *Western Australia 1.36pts, New South Wales 2.44pts. Bancroft, who batted 13 hours 17 minutes and faced 567 balls to convert his third century into a maiden double, added 324 with Klinger, a Western Australian second-wicket record. With New South Wales needing victory to reach the final, the draw saw Western Australia through.*

FINAL

VICTORIA v WESTERN AUSTRALIA

At Hobart, March 21–25, 2015. Drawn. Victoria won the Sheffield Shield by virtue of leading the qualifying table. Toss: Western Australia.

Second-placed Western Australia needed a significant total, and Voges marched purposefully to 107, his sixth century of the campaign. For once, Klinger failed, though he was the second, after Voges, to reach 1,000 first-class runs in the season. Western Australia were 372 for five on the second morning, but fell away as leg-spinner Fawad Ahmed returned eight for 89 from 40 overs – the best figures in a Shield final, or by a spinner in the competition for 22 years. Rogers signed off from Australian domestic cricket with 112, and bad light and rain helped stretch Victoria's first innings into the fourth day, when they were all out 40 behind. Harris scored a rapid, career-best 158 to set up a target of 334, but Victoria concentrated on the draw which would guarantee their title. Hussey, in his last match before retiring, and his captain Wade made sure with an unbroken stand of 35 in 30 overs, including a passage of 50 balls without a run. Afterwards, Wade unveiled a tattoo of Phillip Hughes on his right arm.

Man of the Match: M. S. Harris.

Close of play: first day, Western Australia 310-4 (Voges 100, Whiteman 37); second day, Victoria 135-0 (Quiney 48, Rogers 79); third day, Victoria 288-3 (Stoinis 43, Handscomb 16); fourth day, Western Australia 240-2 (Harris 129, Voges 15).

Western Australia

C. T. Bancroft c Wade b Siddle	55	– c Quiney b Siddle	38
M. S. Harris b Fawad Ahmed	81	– not out	158
M. Klinger c Wade b Fawad Ahmed	18	– c and b Boland	45
*A. C. Voges b Siddle	107	– not out	36
S. E. Marsh c Wade b Fawad Ahmed	6		
†S. M. Whiteman b Fawad Ahmed	72		
A. C. Agar not out	44		
N. M. Coulter-Nile c Handscomb b Fawad Ahmed	9		
N. J. Rimmington c Christian b Fawad Ahmed	3		
A. J. Tye c Hussey b Fawad Ahmed	5		
S. P. Mackin c Christian b Fawad Ahmed	0		
B 4, l-b 10, w 5, n-b 2	21	B 4, l-b 9, n-b 3	16

1/130 (1) 2/154 (2) 3/163 (3)   (134 overs) 421   1/123 (1)   (2 wkts dec, 55 overs) 293
4/205 (5) 5/328 (4) 6/372 (6)   2/212 (3)
7/394 (8) 8/411 (9) 9/421 (10) 10/421 (11)

Pattinson 26–3–101–0; Siddle 30–11–67–2; Boland 24–3–85–0; Stoinis 6–0–21–0; Fawad Ahmed 40–9–89–8; Christian 5–0–29–0; Hussey 3–0–15–0. *Second innings*—Siddle 16–3–67–1; Pattinson 5.5–0–30–0; Boland 10–0–59–1; Fawad Ahmed 10–0–51–0; Stoinis 3.1–0–14–0; Christian 8–0–50–0; Quiney 2–0–9–0.

Victoria

R. J. Quiney c Voges b Coulter-Nile	69	– (2) c Whiteman b Tye	53
C. J. L. Rogers lbw b Agar	112	– (1) b Coulter-Nile	17
M. P. Stoinis b Agar	47	– c and b Agar	8
D. J. Hussey lbw b Mackin	33	– not out	37
P. S. P. Handscomb c and b Rimmington	48	– b Coulter-Nile	13
*†M. S. Wade lbw b Agar	0	– not out	9
D. T. Christian b Tye	27		
J. L. Pattinson not out	13		
P. M. Siddle c Harris b Voges	3		
S. M. Boland lbw b Rimmington	7		
Fawad Ahmed b Rimmington	0		
B 6, l-b 11, w 1, n-b 4	22	B 17, l-b 2, n-b 2	21

1/185 (2) 2/197 (1) 3/259 (4)	(153.5 overs)	381	1/50 (1)	(4 wkts, 95 overs) 158
4/299 (3) 5/299 (6) 6/338 (5)			2/70 (3) 3/98 (2)	
7/352 (7) 8/359 (9) 9/377 (10) 10/381 (11)			4/123 (5)	

Coulter-Nile 28–6–82–1; Mackin 30–13–51–1; Tye 26–10–48–1; Agar 44–15–100–3; Rimmington 23.5–1–79–3; Voges 2–1–4–1. *Second innings*—Coulter-Nile 18.5–5–30–2; Mackin 15–9–20–0; Rimmington 18–9–23–0; Agar 23–11–29–1; Tye 16–7–37–1; Marsh 2–2–0–0; Voges 2–2–0–0; Harris 1–1–0–0.

Umpires: S. D. Fry and M. D. Martell.   Third umpire: J. D. Ward.
Referee: P. L. Marshall.

CHAMPIONS

Sheffield Shield					
1892-93	Victoria	1921-22	Victoria	1953-54	New South Wales
1893-94	South Australia	1922-23	New South Wales	1954-55	New South Wales
1894-95	Victoria	1923-24	Victoria	1955-56	New South Wales
1895-96	New South Wales	1924-25	Victoria	1956-57	New South Wales
1896-97	New South Wales	1925-26	New South Wales	1957-58	New South Wales
1897-98	Victoria	1926-27	South Australia	1958-59	New South Wales
1898-99	Victoria	1927-28	Victoria	1959-60	New South Wales
1899-1900	New South Wales	1928-29	New South Wales	1960-61	New South Wales
1900-01	Victoria	1929-30	Victoria	1961-62	New South Wales
1901-02	New South Wales	1930-31	Victoria	1962-63	Victoria
1902-03	New South Wales	1931-32	New South Wales	1963-64	South Australia
1903-04	New South Wales	1932-33	New South Wales	1964-65	New South Wales
1904-05	New South Wales	1933-34	Victoria	1965-66	New South Wales
1905-06	New South Wales	1934-35	Victoria	1966-67	Victoria
1906-07	New South Wales	1935-36	South Australia	1967-68	Western Australia
1907-08	Victoria	1936-37	Victoria	1968-69	South Australia
1908-09	New South Wales	1937-38	New South Wales	1969-70	Victoria
1909-10	South Australia	1938-39	South Australia	1970-71	South Australia
1910-11	New South Wales	1939-40	New South Wales	1971-72	Western Australia
1911-12	New South Wales	1940–46	*No competition*	1972-73	Western Australia
1912-13	South Australia	1946-47	Victoria	1973-74	Victoria
1913-14	New South Wales	1947-48	Western Australia	1974-75	Western Australia
1914-15	Victoria	1948-49	New South Wales	1975-76	South Australia
1915–19	*No competition*	1949-50	New South Wales	1976-77	Western Australia
1919-20	New South Wales	1950-51	Victoria	1977-78	Western Australia
1920-21	New South Wales	1951-52	New South Wales	1978-79	Victoria
		1952-53	South Australia	1979-80	Victoria

1980-81	Western Australia	1994-95	Queensland	2004-05	New South Wales*
1981-82	South Australia	1995-96	South Australia	2005-06	Queensland
1982-83	New South Wales*	1996-97	Queensland*	2006-07	Tasmania
1983-84	Western Australia	1997-98	Western Australia	2007-08	New South Wales
1984-85	New South Wales	1998-99	Western Australia*		
1985-86	New South Wales			*Sheffield Shield*	
1986-87	Western Australia	*Pura Milk Cup*		2008-09	Victoria
1987-88	Western Australia	1999-2000	Queensland	2009-10	Victoria
1988-89	Western Australia			2010-11	Tasmania
1989-90	New South Wales	*Pura Cup*		2011-12	Queensland
1990-91	Victoria	2000-01	Queensland	2012-13	Tasmania
1991-92	Western Australia	2001-02	Queensland	2013-14	New South Wales
1992-93	New South Wales	2002-03	New South Wales*	2014-15	Victoria
1993-94	New South Wales	2003-04	Victoria		

New South Wales have won the title 46 times, Victoria 29, Western Australia 15, South Australia 13, Queensland 7, Tasmania 3.

* *Second in table but won final. Finals were introduced in 1982-83.*

MATADOR BBQs ONE-DAY CUP, 2014-15

50-over league plus play-off and final

	Played	Won	Lost	No result	Bonus points	Points	Net run-rate
WESTERN AUSTRALIA	7	5	1	1	0	25	0.93
QUEENSLAND...............	7	5	2	0	4	24	1.10
NEW SOUTH WALES........	7	4	2	1	0	18	−0.22
Tasmania	7	2	4	1	2	12	−0.08
Victoria	7	2	5	0	0	7.5*	−1.20
South Australia	7	1	5	1	0	6	−0.57

* *0.5pt deducted for slow over-rate.*

Win = 4pts; no result/abandoned = 2pts; 1 bonus pt awarded for achieving victory with a run-rate 1.25 times that of the opposition.

Net run-rate was calculated by subtracting runs conceded per over from runs scored per over.

Play-off At Sydney (Olympic Park), October 24, 2014 (day/night). **New South Wales won by two wickets.** ‡**Queensland 225-8** (50 overs); **New South Wales 229-8** (49.4 overs). *MoM:* J. R. Hopes. *Queensland captain James Hopes (72) and Ben Cutting (52) added 112 to rescue them from 95-6, but it was not enough to stop New South Wales.*

Final At Sydney, October 26, 2014 (day/night). **Western Australia won by 64 runs.** ‡**Western Australia 255-6** (50 overs); **New South Wales 191** (44.1 overs) (J. P. Behrendorff 5-27). *MoM:* M. Klinger. *MoS:* C. L. White (Victoria). *Western Australia claimed the one-day title for the first time since 2003-04. Michael Klinger was out for 96 in the final over of their innings. Opening bowler Joel Paris broke down with a quad injury in the fourth over of New South Wales's reply; captain Adam Voges took over and immediately had Peter Nevill lbw. Shane Watson (83) and Kurtis Patterson (44) added 115 for New South Wales's third wicket, but left-armer Jason Behrendorff's career-best five wound up the innings early.*

The KFC T20 Big Bash League has its own section (page 957).

BANGLADESH CRICKET IN 2015

Tigers burning bright

UTPAL SHUVRO

It's not often Bangladesh fans can be called spoiled, but 2015 brought a glut of remarkable home performances as their side beat Pakistan, India and South Africa in one-day series for the first time. If getting the better of their two Asian rivals was gratifying, it was the turnaround against South Africa that really showed the Bangladeshis' quality. After losing both Twenty20s and the first one-day international, they fought back to win the next two matches convincingly, earning themselves a place in the 2017 Champions Trophy – the first time they had qualified since 2006. After dismissing their more illustrious opponents with aplomb, the one-day whitewash of Zimbabwe in November felt routine.

It was Bangladesh's performance in the World Cup that sowed the seeds of their incredible run. They thrived on lively, antipodean wickets, and dumped England out on their way to the knockout stages. Their own exit was controversial: in the quarter-final against India, Rohit Sharma was caught off a

BANGLADESH IN 2015

Tests	Played	Won	Lost	Drawn/No result
Tests	5	–	1	4
One-day internationals	19	13	5	1
Twenty20 internationals	5	2	3	–

JANUARY		
FEBRUARY	ICC World Cup (in Australia and New Zealand)	(page 860)
MARCH		
APRIL	2 Tests, 3 ODIs and 1 T20I (h) v Pakistan	(page 970)
MAY		
JUNE	1 Test and 3 ODIs (h) v India	(page 976)
JULY	2 Tests, 3 ODIs and 2 T20Is (h) v South Africa	(page 979)
AUGUST		
SEPTEMBER		
OCTOBER		
NOVEMBER	3 ODIs and 2 T20Is (h) v Zimbabwe	(page 984)
DECEMBER		

For a review of Bangladesh domestic cricket from the 2014-15 season, see page 986.

delivery that was no-balled for height in the 39th over. Replays suggested it would have reached the batsman below his waist, but on-field officials Ian Gould and Aleem Dar chose not to refer the decision to the third umpire. Sharma then helped India reach a target of 302, and Bangladesh's batsmen cracked under scoreboard pressure.

The decision caused outrage back home. Effigies of Gould and Dar were burned at Dhaka University, and Prime Minister Sheikh Hasina claimed her side had been "made to lose". Mustafa Kamal, the ICC president and a minister for planning in the Bangladesh government, announced that an investigation should be held to determine if the match officials had "an agenda". As a result of his outburst, he was deprived by ICC chairman N. Srinivasan of the honour of presenting the World Cup trophy to the eventual winners, Australia. A furious Kamal later resigned.

Back on the field, the experience of Shakib Al Hasan, Tamim Iqbal and Mushfiqur Rahim was key to Bangladesh's limited-overs success, while Mashrafe bin Mortaza captained with aggression and utilised his seam bowlers shrewdly. All-rounder Soumya Sarkar emerged as a carefree stroke-maker, while the 19-year-old left-arm seamer Mustafizur Rahman caused havoc with his cutters, becoming the first player to be named Man of the Match on both ODI and Test debut.

It was harder to judge Bangladesh's form in the red-ball game. They lost the Second Test against Pakistan by 328 runs at Mirpur, but drew their other four, the last three of which were severely affected by rain. Bangladesh had been forced to play matches in the monsoon months of June and July in order to accommodate the schedules of India and South Africa. But the weather had nothing to do with the draw at Khulna, where they pulled off the greatest escape in their history. Faced with a first-innings deficit of 296 against Pakistan, Tamim and Imrul Kayes put on 312, the largest opening partnership in any Test team's second innings, to help their side reach 555 for six. Tamim's 206 was Bangladesh's highest individual score.

Off-field events took some of the gloss off the year. Cricket Australia postponed the senior side's October tour, and announced that the Under-19 team would not participate in the 2016 World Cup in Bangladesh because of security concerns; the South African women's side also cancelled their visit in November, following an increase in Islamist violence. It was a cruel end to 2015, raising concerns that Bangladesh could struggle to host future internationals.

In September, seamer Shahadat Hossain was suspended by the Bangladesh Cricket Board after he was alleged to have tortured his 11-year-old live-in housemaid. Shahadat and his wife, also accused, went into hiding, but were arrested in early October. He was granted bail until March 31.

BANGLADESH v PAKISTAN IN 2014-15

MOHAMMAD ISAM

One-day internationals (3): Bangladesh 3, Pakistan 0
Twenty20 international (1): Bangladesh 1, Pakistan 0
Test matches (2): Bangladesh 0, Pakistan 1

Before this tour, Bangladesh had not beaten Pakistan since the 1999 World Cup, after which they had lost 40 games to them in all formats, including all eight Tests. So to sweep the limited-overs matches was a result to savour. Building on their quarter-final place at the World Cup, the Bangladeshis gained crucial points in their bid to break into the top eight of the ICC one-day international rankings – and qualify automatically for the 2017 Champions Trophy and the 2019 World Cup. Pakistan were in danger of missing out on the first of those.

They arrived with a new look: Misbah-ul-Haq and Shahid Afridi had now retired from the 50-over format, and Azhar Ali was the surprise choice as captain, having been out of the one-day set-up for more than two years. His form was good, but he was unable to lift a team in flux, which contained two off-spinners – Saeed Ajmal and Mohammad Hafeez – restored after doubts about their actions. Afridi returned for the Twenty20 game, but had little impact.

The highlights for Bangladesh were centuries in the first two one-day matches for Tamim Iqbal, and a maiden hundred in the third for Soumya Sarkar, a silky 22-year-old left-hander. Mushfiqur Rahim also batted well, while there was some assured captaincy from Mashrafe bin Mortaza.

It was a different story in the Tests, for which Pakistan were bolstered by the return of Misbah and Younis Khan. Bangladesh saved the First by batting through the last five sessions, mainly thanks to a monumental opening partnership between Tamim, who made a national-record 206, and Imrul Kayes. But Pakistan's left-arm seamers Wahab Riaz and Junaid Khan cashed in on a sportier pitch for the Second, at Mirpur. Bangladesh handicapped themselves by choosing only two regular seamers, and were left almost impotent when Shahadat Hossain limped off in the first over. Pakistan ran up another big total, featuring Younis's 29th Test hundred and Azhar's first double. Seven wickets for leg-spinner Yasir Shah – preferred to Ajmal, not the same bowler after remodelling his action – ensured Pakistan took the series.

The tour had been in doubt until a week before it started, as the two boards bickered about terms. The arguments had begun back in 2011, with a disagreement over nominations for the ICC presidency, and continued the following year when Bangladesh twice cancelled a trip to Pakistan. This visit went ahead after the BCB agreed to pay $US325,000 as compensation for those cancellations. It felt like a price worth paying.

PAKISTAN TOURING PARTY

Misbah-ul-Haq (T), Ahmed Shehzad (20), Asad Shafiq (T/50), Azhar Ali (T/50), Babar Azam (T), Bilawal Bhatti (T), Ehsan Adil (50), Fawad Alam (50), Haris Sohail (T/50/20), Imran Khan, sen. (T/20), Junaid Khan (T/50), Mohammad Hafeez (T/50/20), Mohammad Rizwan (50/20), Mukhtar Ahmed (20), Rahat Ali (50), Saad Nasim (50/20), Saeed Ajmal (T/50/20), Sami Aslam (T/50), Sarfraz Ahmed (T/50/20), Shahid Afridi (20), Sohail Tanvir (20), Umar Gul (50/20), Wahab Riaz (T/50/20), Yasir Shah (T), Younis Khan (T), Zulfiqar Babar (T/50). Coach: Waqar Younis.

Azhar Ali captained in the one-day internationals, and Shahid Afridi in the Twenty20 game. Sohail Khan missed the tour with a back injury, Sohaib Maqsood and Yasir Shah withdrew from the limited-overs matches with hand injuries (though Yasir was fit for the Tests), and Ehsan Adil and Rahat Ali tweaked hamstring injuries during the 50-over series. They were replaced by Junaid Khan (previously only in the Test squad), Saad Nasim (originally picked for the Twenty20 match), Zulfiqar Babar and Umar Gul.

At Fatullah, April 15, 2015. **Bangladesh Cricket Board XI won by one wicket.** ‡**Pakistanis 268-9** (50 overs) (Mohammad Hafeez 85, Fawad Alam 67*; Shuvagata Hom 3-39); **Bangladesh Cricket Board XI 270-9** (48.5 overs) (Sabbir Rahman 123; Junaid Khan 4-38). *Both sides chose from 13 players. Fawad Alam, with 67* from 58 balls, helped the Pakistanis to a reasonable total. The Board XI made a poor start, but Sabbir Rahman, who hit eight sixes and seven fours from 99 balls, got them back on course. Sohag Gazi (36 from 28) steered his side towards victory.*

First one-day international   At Mirpur, April 17, 2015 (day/night). **Bangladesh won by 79 runs.** ‡**Bangladesh 329-6** (50 overs) (Tamim Iqbal 132, Mushfiqur Rahim 106, Shakib Al Hasan 31; Wahab Riaz 4-59); **Pakistan 250** (45.2 overs) (Azhar Ali 72, Haris Sohail 51, Mohammad Rizwan 67; Taskin Ahmed 3-42, Arafat Sunny 3-47). *MoM:* Mushfiqur Rahim. *ODI debuts:* Mohammad Rizwan, Saad Nasim. *A third-wicket stand of 178 in 21.4 overs – a national all-wicket record in ODIs – propelled Bangladesh to their highest total, beating 326-3 against the same opposition at Mirpur in March 2014. Tamim Iqbal, driving fluently, made his fifth ODI century, and Mushfiqur Rahim his third, from just 69 balls. Pakistan were in touch for the first 30 overs – debutant Mohammad Rizwan opened his account with three successive fours – but lost their last six wickets for 33. This was Bangladesh's first victory over Pakistan since the 1999 World Cup, after which they had lost eight Tests, 25 ODIs and seven T20s.*

Second one-day international   At Mirpur, April 19, 2015 (day/night). **Bangladesh won by seven wickets.** ‡**Pakistan 239-6** (50 overs) (Azhar Ali 36, Haris Sohail 44, Saad Nasim 77*, Wahab Riaz 51*); **Bangladesh 240-3** (38.1 overs) (Tamim Iqbal 116*, Mushfiqur Rahim 65). *MoM:* Tamim Iqbal. *Bangladesh clinched the series with another convincing win. This one was set up by the bowlers – who reduced Pakistan to 77-5, before Saad Nasim and Wahab Riaz added 85* for the seventh wicket – and rubber-stamped by another fine partnership between Tamim and Mushfiqur. They added 118 in 22 overs, Tamim becoming the third Bangladeshi (after Shahriar Nafees in 2006-07 and Mahmudullah in the 2015 World Cup) to score successive ODI centuries.*

Third one-day international   At Mirpur, April 22, 2015 (day/night). **Bangladesh won by eight wickets.** ‡**Pakistan 250** (49 overs) (Azhar Ali 101, Sami Aslam 45, Haris Sohail 52); **Bangladesh 251-2** (39.3 overs) (Tamim Iqbal 64, Soumya Sarkar 127*, Mushfiqur Rahim 49*). *MoM:* Soumya Sarkar. *MoS:* Tamim Iqbal. *ODI debut:* Sami Aslam (Pakistan). *Azhar Ali continued his fine form since assuming the captaincy with his maiden ODI hundred. He put on 91 for the first wicket with debutant Sami Aslam, a 19-year-old left-hander, and 98 for the third with Haris Sohail – but the last seven wickets could scrape together only 47. Tamim was on song again, although he was outdone by Soumya Sarkar, another left-hander, whose 127* – also a maiden ODI hundred – included six sixes. They put on 145 for the first wicket in 25.3 overs to hasten the whitewash.*

Twenty20 international   At Mirpur, April 24, 2015 (floodlit). **Bangladesh won by seven wickets.** ‡**Pakistan 141-5** (20 overs) (Mukhtar Ahmed 37, Haris Sohail 30*); **Bangladesh 143-3** (16.2 overs) (Shakib Al Hasan 57*, Sabbir Rahman 51*). *MoM:* Sabbir Rahman. *T20I debuts:* Mustafizur Rahman, Soumya Sarkar (Bangladesh); Mohammad Rizwan, Mukhtar Ahmed (Pakistan). *The return of Shahid Afridi briefly threatened to derail Bangladesh, but two deliveries after blasting a six he was undone by Mustafizur Rahman, a 19-year-old debutant left-arm seamer. Afridi looked miffed at the caught-behind decision, even asking if DRS was available (it wasn't). Pakistan's eventual total looked light, and so it proved, although Bangladesh declined to 38-3 before Shakib Al Hasan and Sabbir Rahman wrapped things up with a stand of 105*.*

BANGLADESH v PAKISTAN

First Test Match

At Khulna, April 28–May 2, 2015. Drawn. Toss: Bangladesh. Test debuts: Mohammad Shahid, Soumya Sarkar; Sami Aslam.

This Test was played in the shadow of a devastating earthquake that badly affected Nepal. It struck three days before the game and killed over 9,000, including four in Bangladesh. While at practice the following day, the teams felt an aftershock, despite being more than 400 miles from the epicentre. It was a sobering reminder of cricket's place in the grand scheme.

At first it was business as usual: Pakistan restricted the home batsmen on a docile pitch and then ran up a big lead. Bangladesh appeared to be having trouble readjusting to five-day cricket after the limited-overs series: the top eight all got into double figures, but no one made a century. Mominul Haque, who had missed the shorter games, top-scored with 80, though he fell to the last ball of the first day, and next morning the innings crumbled from a promising position; in all, the last seven fell for 96. Wahab Riaz and leg-spinner Yasir Shah, who took three wickets apiece, were a constant threat.

Mohammad Hafeez, who had looked out of sorts in the one-day matches, returned to form with a bang, converting his eighth Test century into his first double, five months after 197 against New Zealand. Strong off the back foot, he put on 227 with Azhar Ali, who made 83, and there were also eighties for Asad Shafiq and Sarfraz Ahmed, who put on 126 for the sixth wicket.

The loss of the last five for 34 on the fourth morning kept the lead under 300 – just. Slow left-armer Taijul Islam finished with an expensive six-for, his last wicket a stumping

MOST RUNS BY OPENING BATSMEN IN A TEST

811	England (261) v South Africa (550) at Birmingham	2003
749	India (392) v South Africa (357) at Chennai	2007-08
706	West Indies (232) v Australia (474) at Bridgetown	1964-65
679	England (536) v India (143) at Lord's	1990
676	**Bangladesh (432) v Pakistan (244) at Khulna**	**2014-15**
662	West Indies (195) v England (467) at Kingston	1929-30
662	West Indies (197) v Pakistan (465) at Bridgetown	1957-58
634	South Africa (291) v England (343) at Johannesburg	2004-05
619	West Indies (317) v South Africa (302) at St John's	2004-05
612	India (380) v Sri Lanka (232) at Mumbai (Brabourne)	2009-10

by Mahmudullah, who was keeping wicket as Mushfiqur Rahim had injured his right ring finger, and Imrul Kayes, the original stand-in, needed a rest after 120 overs behind the stumps. Mahmudullah was only the second man to collect a stumping and a five-for in Tests (he took five for 51 with his off-breaks against West Indies in St Vincent in 2009), after New Zealand's John Reid.

Seasoned Bangladesh-watchers feared a collapse in the face of a deficit of 296 with five sessions to survive, but they could hardly have been more wrong. Tamim Iqbal and Imrul batted through the rest of the fourth day, scorching past their own national first-wicket record (224 against Zimbabwe at Chittagong in November 2014). Tamim purred to his half-century by reverse-sweeping Zulfiqar Babar for four, and celebrated by smashing the next ball over long-on for six; later he struck Yasir for successive sixes to the same area.

Imrul, meanwhile, zipped past 1,000 runs, in his 20th Test, with a six of his own off Yasir. The spinners extracted some turn, but the openers countered it well, and continued next morning to 312, a Bangladesh record for any wicket, beating 267 for the fifth by Mohammad Ashraful and Mushfiqur against Sri Lanka at Galle in 2012-13. It was the highest opening partnership in any Test team's second innings, surpassing 290 by Colin Cowdrey and Geoff Pullar against South Africa at The Oval in 1960. And it was the second-highest stand in Tests between two left-handers, after the 322 by Brian Lara and Jimmy Adams for West Indies' fifth wicket against Australia at Kingston in 1998-99.

Crucially, there was no major wobble after Zulfiqar removed Imrul for a career-best 150. Tamim sailed on to 206, batting nearly seven and a half hours in all. He struck seven sixes, as well as 17 fours, and eclipsed Mushfiqur's 200 in that Galle match as the highest Test score for Bangladesh; their eventual 555 for six was comfortably their best second-innings total, and they finished with more runs – 887 – than they had previously managed in a Test. Shakib Al Hasan ensured the draw with a patient unbeaten 76, finding time for a slanging match with Wahab for which both were fined. A delighted Mushfiqur hailed the result as "a very big turning point in Bangladesh cricket ... the last two days have proved that we are a very competitive side".

Man of the Match: Tamim Iqbal.

Close of play: first day, Bangladesh 236-4 (Shakib Al Hasan 19); second day, Pakistan 227-1 (Mohammad Hafeez 137, Azhar Ali 65); third day, Pakistan 537-5 (Asad Shafiq 51, Sarfraz Ahmed 51); fourth day, Bangladesh 273-0 (Tamim Iqbal 138, Imrul Kayes 132).

Bangladesh

Tamim Iqbal c Azhar Ali b Yasir Shah	25	– st Sarfraz Ahmed b Mohammad Hafeez	206
Imrul Kayes c and b Mohammad Hafeez	51	– c sub (Babar Azam) b Zulfiqar Babar	150
Mominul Haque lbw b Zulfiqar Babar	80	– b Junaid Khan	21
Mahmudullah c Sarfraz Ahmed b Wahab Riaz	49	– lbw b Junaid Khan	40
Shakib Al Hasan c Asad Shafiq b Zulfiqar Babar	25	– not out	76
*†Mushfiqur Rahim c Misbah-ul-Haq b Yasir Shah	32	– lbw b Mohammad Hafeez	0
Soumya Sarkar c Asad Shafiq b Mohammad Hafeez	33	– c Mohammad Hafeez b Asad Shafiq	33
Shuvagata Hom not out	12	– not out	20
Taijul Islam b Yasir Shah	1		
Mohammad Shahid c Misbah-ul-Haq b Wahab Riaz	10		
Rubel Hossain c Sarfraz Ahmed b Wahab Riaz	2		
L-b 5, n-b 7	12	L-b 4, w 2, n-b 3	9

1/52 (1)   2/92 (2)   3/187 (4)   (120 overs) 332   1/312 (2)   (6 wkts, 136 overs) 555
4/236 (3)   5/243 (5)   6/305 (7)   2/345 (3)   3/399 (1)
7/310 (6)   8/312 (9)   9/329 (10)   10/332 (11)   4/463 (4)   5/464 (6)   6/524 (7)

Junaid Khan 16–2–40–0; Wahab Riaz 26–7–55–3; Mohammad Hafeez 18–5–47–2; Zulfiqar Babar 32–3–99–2; Yasir Shah 28–4–86–3. *Second innings*—Junaid Khan 21–5–88–2; Zulfiqar Babar 32–1–125–1; Mohammad Hafeez 20–0–82–2; Wahab Riaz 20–3–75–0; Yasir Shah 30–2–123–0; Azhar Ali 6–1–26–0; Asad Shafiq 7–0–32–1.

Pakistan

Mohammad Hafeez c Mahmudullah b Shuvagata Hom . 224	Wahab Riaz b Taijul Islam 0
Sami Aslam c Mushfiqur Rahim b Taijul Islam . 20	Yasir Shah lbw b Taijul Islam 13
Azhar Ali b Shuvagata Hom 83	Zulfiqar Babar st Mahmudullah b Taijul Islam . 11
Younis Khan b Taijul Islam 33	Junaid Khan not out 0
*Misbah-ul-Haq c Rubel Hossain b Taijul Islam . 59	B 5, l-b 8, w 3, n-b 4 20
Asad Shafiq c and b Shakib Al Hasan 83	1/50 (2) 2/277 (3) (168.4 overs) 628
†Sarfraz Ahmed c sub (Liton Das) b Mohammad Shahid . 82	3/339 (4) 4/402 (1)
	5/468 (5) 6/594 (7) 7/595 (8)
	8/617 (6) 9/617 (9) 10/628 (10)

Rubel Hossain 22–3–82–0; Mohammad Shahid 19–4–59–1; Taijul Islam 46.4–4–163–6; Shuvagata Hom 34–1–120–2; Shakib Al Hasan 37–4–146–1; Mahmudullah 4–0–30–0; Soumya Sarkar 1–0–2–0; Mominul Haque 5–0–13–0.

Umpires: N. J. Llong and R. E. J. Martinesz.   Third umpire: P. R. Reiffel.
Referee: J. J. Crowe.

BANGLADESH v PAKISTAN

Second Test Match

At Mirpur, May 6–9, 2015. Pakistan won by 328 runs. Toss: Bangladesh.

Normal service was resumed after the defiance of Khulna, with Pakistan easing to their ninth victory in ten Tests against Bangladesh. Pakistan again ran up a big total – and this time, on a quicker pitch, the home batsmen could not dig in for the duration.

Bangladesh's decision to choose only two seamers looked suspect when Mushfiqur Rahim opted to bowl – and even more so when Shahadat Hossain limped off in the opening over after tripping while delivering the first ball. Though he returned briefly, he further damaged his knee ligaments while practising in the lunch interval, and faced a six-month lay-off. Azhar Ali made hay against a lop-sided attack, extending his eighth Test century to his first double. His 226 was the record score between these sides, sneaking past Mohammad Hafeez's 224 in the previous match.

Azhar shared a stand of 250 with Younis Khan, who equalled Don Bradman with his 29th Test century. Both survived being caught off what replays showed were no-balls. In all, Azhar – who also put on 207 with Asad Shafiq – batted for 562 minutes, faced 428 balls, and hit 20 fours and two sixes. The features of his diligent innings were front-foot drives and sweet timing, although he had a lucky escape on 157 – a score on which he had twice previously fallen in Tests – when he edged off-spinner Shuvagata Hom just past the wicketkeeper and through the vacant slip area.

The spinners could do little to stem the flow, and Misbah-ul-Haq eventually declared at tea on the second day. He then watched his own bowlers make the most of the pitch. Junaid Khan removed Tamim Iqbal with the fourth ball and, after Imrul Kayes stroked him for four boundaries in an over, had Mominul Haque caught behind. Yasir Shah's third delivery – a big leg-break – knocked back Imrul's leg stump, and two more wickets left Bangladesh floundering at 107 for five by the close.

With Wahab Riaz disconcerting the batsmen with his bounce, the innings lasted less than 20 overs next morning, and it was a surprise when Misbah decided to bat again, despite a lead of 354. Hafeez fell for a fourth-ball duck, but Misbah led the way himself with 82 from 72 deliveries, before calling a halt.

Bangladesh were left to score 550 in more than two days, but there was no repeat of the openers' Khulna heroics. Imrul again fell to Yasir, and Tamim – having become the second Bangladeshi, after Habibul Bashar, to pass 3,000 Test runs – departed quickly on the fourth morning, swishing at a wide one from Imran Khan. Earlier, Imran had become the first player not to face a ball in his first four Tests.

Mominul stood firm, reaching 50 for the 11th Test in a row (only A. B. de Villiers, with 12, had a longer sequence). But wickets fell regularly at the other end, and when Mominul finally drove low to cover it was 143 for seven, with Shahadat unable to bat. The impressive Yasir hastened the end with four more wickets. After a month in Bangladesh, Pakistan had finally won a game – and with it the Test series.

Man of the Match: Azhar Ali.   *Man of the Series:* Azhar Ali.
Close of play: first day, Pakistan 323-3 (Azhar Ali 127, Misbah-ul-Haq 9); second day, Bangladesh 107-5 (Shakib Al Hasan 14); third day, Bangladesh 63-1 (Tamim Iqbal 32, Mominul Haque 15).

Pakistan

Mohammad Hafeez c Mushfiqur Rahim b Mohammad Shahid .	8	– c Mushfiqur Rahim b Mohammad Shahid .	0
Sami Aslam c Shahadat Hossain b Taijul Islam ...	19	– c Mahmudullah b Mohammad Shahid	8
Azhar Ali c Mahmudullah b Shuvagata Hom	226	– c Shuvagata Hom b Soumya Sarkar .	25
Younus Khan c Shuvagata Hom b Mohammad Shahid .	148	– c and b Taijul Islam	39
*Misbah-ul-Haq b Shakib Al Hasan	9	– c sub (Abul Hasan) b Mahmudullah .	82
Asad Shafiq c Mahmudullah b Shuvagata Hom . . .	107	– b Shuvagata Hom	15
†Sarfraz Ahmed not out	21	– not out	18
Wahab Riaz c Imrul Kayes b Taijul Islam	4		
Yasir Shah lbw b Taijul Islam	0		
L-b 8, w 2, n-b 5	15	L-b 2, w 6	8

1/9 (1) 2/58 (2)   (8 wkts dec, 152 overs) 557   1/0 (1)   (6 wkts dec, 41.1 overs) 195
3/308 (4) 4/323 (5) 5/530 (3)   2/25 (2) 3/49 (3)
6/545 (6) 7/552 (8) 8/557 (9)   4/107 (4) 5/140 (6) 6/195 (5)

Junaid Khan and Imran Khan, sen. did not bat.

Shahadat Hossain 0.2–0–4–0; Soumya Sarkar 17.4–1–57–0; Mohammad Shahid 31–10–72–2; Taijul Islam 51–3–179–3; Shuvagata Hom 16–0–76–2; Shakib Al Hasan 30–3–136–1; Mominul Haque 3–0–12–0; Mahmudullah 2–0–12–0; Imrul Kayes 1–0–1–0. *Second innings*—Mohammad Shahid 10–4–23–2; Taijul Islam 10–0–56–1; Soumya Sarkar 9–0–45–1; Shakib Al Hasan 8–0–43–0; Shuvagata Hom 2–0–18–1; Mahmudullah 2.1–0–8–1.

Bangladesh

Tamim Iqbal lbw b Junaid Khan	4	– c Sarfraz Ahmed b Imran Khan	42
Imrul Kayes b Yasir Shah	32	– b Yasir Shah	16
Mominul Haque c Sarfraz Ahmed b Junaid Khan . .	13	– c Asad Shafiq b Yasir Shah	68
Mahmudullah c Azhar Ali b Wahab Riaz	28	– c Younus Khan b Imran Khan	2
Shakib Al Hasan not out	89	– c Wahab Riaz b Mohammad Hafeez .	13
*†Mushfiqur Rahim b Yasir Shah	12	– b Yasir Shah	0
Soumya Sarkar c Azhar Ali b Wahab Riaz	3	– c Sarfraz Ahmed b Wahab Riaz	1
Shuvagata Hom c Asad Shafiq b Wahab Riaz	0	– b Junaid Khan	39
Taijul Islam b Mohammad Hafeez	15	– c Sami Aslam b Yasir Shah	10
Mohammad Shahid c Azhar Ali b Yasir Shah	1	– not out	14
Shahadat Hossain absent hurt		– absent hurt	
L-b 2, w 2, n-b 2	6	B 4, l-b 4, n-b 8	16

1/4 (1) 2/38 (3) 3/69 (2)   (47.3 overs) 203   1/48 (2) 2/86 (1)   (56.5 overs) 221
4/85 (4) 5/107 (6) 6/113 (7)   3/95 (4) 4/121 (5)
7/119 (8) 8/140 (9) 9/203 (10)   5/126 (6) 6/139 (7)
                                                             7/143 (3) 8/177 (9) 9/221 (8)

Junaid Khan 6–2–26–2; Imran Khan 7–0–31–0; Wahab Riaz 15–2–73–3; Yasir Shah 15.3–4–58–3; Mohammad Hafeez 4–1–13–1. *Second innings*—Junaid Khan 10.5–1–45–1; Imran Khan 11–1–56–2; Yasir Shah 21–3–73–4; Wahab Riaz 11–1–36–1; Mohammad Hafeez 3–0–3–1.

Umpires: N. J. Llong and P. R. Reiffel.   Third umpire: R. E. J. Martinesz.
Referee: J. J. Crowe.

BANGLADESH v INDIA IN 2015

S A U R A B H S O M A N I

Test match (1): Bangladesh 0, India 0
One-day internationals (3): Bangladesh 2, India 1

Few gave Bangladesh much chance when India arrived for a flying visit, but they ended up taking the one-day series, their first bilateral victory over them in four attempts. This trip was firmed up only after Bangladesh voted in favour of the Indian-led reorganisation of the ICC in 2014. India's jam-packed schedule meant it had to take place in June, monsoon time in Bangladesh – and the weather ruined the one-off Test, the first between the sides for more than five years (though India still had not hosted Bangladesh).

But rain mostly stayed away during the 50-over games, in which Bangladesh outperformed a jaded Indian side. Abandoning their usual reliance on spin at home, they unleashed Rubel Hossain and Taskin Ahmed – two slippery bowlers who could hurry the batsmen – and introduced the feisty 19-year-old left-arm cutter Mustafizur Rahman. He started with two five-fors, and ended up with 13 wickets, a world record for a three-match one-day series. The batsmen also performed consistently, with relative newcomers Soumya Sarkar, Sabbir Rahman and Liton Das doing well.

Murali Vijay and Shikhar Dhawan shared a huge opening stand in the Test, but just about the only plus point for India in the one-dayers was M. S. Dhoni's decision to promote himself after the opening game to No. 4, where he made 47 and 69, taking his average in that position to 68. But Dhoni was involved in an ugly incident in the first match, when he shoulder-charged Mustafizur, who had got in his way as he tried a quick single. Both were fined.

INDIAN TOURING PARTY

*V. Kohli (T/50), V. R. Aaron (T), R. Ashwin (T/50), Bhuvneshwar Kumar (T/50), S. T. R. Binny (50), S. Dhawan (T/50), M. S. Dhoni (50), Harbhajan Singh (T), R. A. Jadeja (50), D. S. Kulkarni (50), A. R. Patel (50), C. A. Pujara (T), A. M. Rahane (T/50), S. K. Raina (50), A. T. Rayudu (50), W. P. Saha (T), I. Sharma (T), K. V. Sharma (T), M. Sharma (50), R. G. Sharma (T/50), M. Vijay (T), U. T. Yadav (T/50). *Coach:* R. J. Shastri.

Dhoni captained in the one-day games. K. L. Rahul withdrew from the Test squad with illness.

BANGLADESH v INDIA

Test Match

At Fatullah, June 10–14, 2015. Drawn. Toss: India. Test debut: Liton Das.

There had never previously been a Test match in Bangladesh in June, and it soon became apparent why: heavy rain was rarely far away, with at least one session washed out every day, and all three on the second. Only 184.2 overs were bowled, little more than the equivalent of two full days. A draw was inevitable – only the second time in eight meetings that Bangladesh had escaped defeat by India, following a similarly soggy encounter at Chittagong in May 2007.

What play there was possible showed the gulf between the sides at this level. Kohli, India's new Test captain, had promised attacking cricket. It was a call enjoyed by Vijay and Dhawan, who put on 283 – India's fourth-highest opening stand, and their best for any wicket against Bangladesh. They scored at more than four an over, against an unbalanced attack containing four frontline spinners but only one regular seamer. Dhawan, who might not have played had Lokesh Rahul been available, scorched to 150 on the truncated first day, and was first out, for 173, on the second. Vijay was more sedate, lasting 401 minutes for 150, his sixth Test century. After three wickets fell for 27, Rahane hit an attractive 98, before attempting a third successive four off Shakib Al Hasan, and gifting him his fourth wicket. After another downpour ended the third day, Kohli declared.

Only one session was possible on the fourth, when Tamim Iqbal overtook Habibul Bashar (3,026) as Bangladesh's leading Test scorer. Mominul Haque, though, could not extend his run of Tests with at least one fifty to a record-equalling 12. Liton Das – making his debut as wicketkeeper to reduce the load on Mushfiqur Rahim, as he recovered from an injured finger – cracked 44 from 45 balls, but fell just when it seemed the follow-on might be averted. With Ashwin teasing and looping to his best figures outside India, and Harbhajan Singh grabbing three wickets in his first Test for more than two years, Bangladesh did have to bat again. But, with time for only 15 more overs, there was no danger of defeat.

Man of the Match: S. Dhawan.

Close of play: first day, India 239-0 (Vijay 89, Dhawan 150); second day, no play; third day, India 462-6 (Ashwin 2, Harbhajan Singh 7); fourth day, Bangladesh 111-3 (Imrul Kayes 59, Shakib Al Hasan 0).

India

M. Vijay lbw b Shakib Al Hasan	150	Harbhajan Singh not out	7
S. Dhawan c and b Shakib Al Hasan	173		
R. G. Sharma b Shakib Al Hasan	6	B 4, l-b 1, n-b 1	6
*V. Kohli b Jubair Hossain	14		
A. M. Rahane b Shakib Al Hasan	98	1/283 (2) (6 wkts dec, 103.3 overs)	462
†W. P. Saha b Jubair Hossain	6	2/291 (3) 3/310 (4)	
R. Ashwin not out	2	4/424 (1) 5/445 (6) 6/453 (5)	

U. T. Yadav, V. R. Aaron and I. Sharma did not bat.

Mohammad Shahid 22–2–88–0; Soumya Sarkar 3–0–11–0; Shuvagata Hom 14–0–52–0; Shakib Al Hasan 24.3–1–105–4; Taijul Islam 20–0–85–0; Jubair Hossain 19–1–113–2; Imrul Kayes 1–0–3–0.

Bangladesh

Tamim Iqbal st Saha b Ashwin	19	– not out	16
Imrul Kayes st Saha b Harbhajan Singh	72	– not out	7
Mominul Haque c Yadav b Harbhajan Singh	30		
*Mushfiqur Rahim c R. G. Sharma b Ashwin	2		
Shakib Al Hasan c Saha b Ashwin	9		
Soumya Sarkar b Aaron	37		
†Liton Das c R. G. Sharma b Ashwin	44		
Shuvagata Hom c R. G. Sharma b Ashwin	9		
Taijul Islam not out	16		
Mohammad Shahid c Dhawan b Harbhajan Singh	6		
Jubair Hossain run out	0		
L-b 9, n-b 3	12		
1/27 (1) 2/108 (3) 3/110 (4) (65.5 overs)	256	(no wkt, 15 overs)	23
4/121 (5) 5/172 (6) 6/176 (6)			
7/219 (8) 8/232 (7) 9/246 (10) 10/256 (11)			

I. Sharma 7–0–24–0; Ashwin 25–6–87–5; Yadav 7–0–45–0; Aaron 9–0–27–1; Harbhajan Singh 17.5–2–64–3. *Second innings*—Yadav 2–1–4–0; Ashwin 6–2–8–0; Harbhajan Singh 5–2–11–0; Vijay 1–1–0–0; Dhawan 1–1–0–0.

Umpires: H. D. P. K. Dharmasena and N. J. Llong.   Third umpire: Sharfuddoula.

Referee: A. J. Pycroft.

First one-day international   At Mirpur, June 18, 2015 (day/night). **Bangladesh won by 79 runs.** ‡**Bangladesh 307** (49.4 overs) (Tamim Iqbal 60, Soumya Sarkar 54, Shakib Al Hasan 52, Sabbir Rahman 41, Nasir Hossain 34; R. Ashwin 3-51); **India 228** (46 overs) (R. G. Sharma 63, S. Dhawan 30, S. K. Raina 40, R. A. Jadeja 32; Mustafizur Rahman 5-50). *MoM:* Mustafizur Rahman. *ODI debuts:* Liton Das, Mustafizur Rahman (Bangladesh). *After an opening stand of 102 in 13.4 overs, Bangladesh survived a Ravichandran Ashwin-inspired wobble to pass 300 against India for the first time in a one-day international. India also made a good start, as Rohit Sharma added 95 with Shikhar Dhawan in 16 overs, but were derailed by Bangladesh's pacemen: Taskin Ahmed removed Dhawan and Virat Kohli in three balls; later Mustafizur Rahman, a 19-year-old left-armer from Satkhira, claimed three in five. Mustafizur's debut five-for – only the second for Bangladesh, after Taskin's 5-28 against India here in June 2014 – earned him the match award, although he did feature in an unsavoury clash with M. S. Dhoni, who shoulder-charged him out of the way while trying a quick single. After delivering the ball, Mustafizur had wandered across the pitch into the batsman's line, as he had done earlier to impede Sharma, and briefly left the field. Dhoni said it was accidental – "a typical kind of a street clash" – but referee Andy Pycroft disagreed, fining him 75% and Mustafizur 50% of their match fees.*

Second one-day international   At Mirpur, June 21, 2015 (day/night). **Bangladesh won by six wickets** (D/L). ‡**India 200** (45 overs) (S. Dhawan 53, M. S. Dhoni 47, S. K. Raina 34; Mustafizur Rahman 6-43); **Bangladesh 200-4** (38 overs) (Soumya Sarkar 34, Liton Das 36, Mushfiqur Rahim 31, Shakib Al Hasan 51*). *MoM:* Mustafizur Rahman. *Mustafizur followed his fine debut with an even more impressive performance, demolishing India for 200 with six wickets. Only Zimbabwe's Brian Vitori, against Bangladesh in August 2011, had previously taken five-fors in his first two ODIs. Two showers interrupted India's innings, reducing the match to 47 overs a side (Bangladesh's target was minimally adjusted to 200). Rohit Sharma fell to the second ball of the game – Mustafizur's first wicket – but Dhawan and Kohli (23) repaired the damage in a stand of 74. Later Nasir Hossain removed both; then, after Dhoni and Suresh Raina had lifted the score to 163-4, Mustafizur returned, to mop up with 5-10 from his last 28 balls. Ashwin again bowled well, but consistent batting ensured no slip-ups as Bangladesh clinched their first series victory over India. "This is one of the biggest achievements," said their captain, Mashrafe bin Mortaza. "I think the boys are playing fearless cricket. This is the significant change."*

Third one-day international   At Mirpur, June 24, 2015 (day/night). **India won by 77 runs. India 317-6** (50 overs) (S. Dhawan 75, M. S. Dhoni 69, A. T. Rayudu 44, S. K. Raina 38; Mashrafe bin Mortaza 3-76); ‡**Bangladesh 240** (47 overs) (Soumya Sarkar 40, Liton Das 34, Sabbir Rahman 43, Nasir Hossain 32; S. K. Raina 3-45). *MoM:* S. K. Raina. *MoS:* Mustafizur Rahman. *A fluent 73-ball 75 from Dhawan, a forthright innings from Dhoni, and a late flourish from Raina (38 from 21 balls) ensured India avoided an embarrassing whitewash. Bangladesh's new self-belief meant chasing down 318 wasn't out of the question, but the early loss of Tamim Iqbal set them back, before tight bowling from the spinners – Ashwin, Raina and Akshar Patel had combined figures of 27–2–124–6 – put India firmly in charge. Mustafizur Rahman (2-57) took his haul for the series to 13 wickets, a record for any three-match rubber (Ryan Harris picked up 13 in three for Australia against Pakistan in 2009-10, but missed two games of the five-match series).*

BANGLADESH v SOUTH AFRICA IN 2015

Neil Manthorp

Twenty20 internationals (2): Bangladesh 0, South Africa 2
One-day internationals (3): Bangladesh 2, South Africa 1
Test matches (2): Bangladesh 0, South Africa 0

It was a tour dominated by one question: were Bangladesh really as good as their run to a World Cup quarter-final, and subsequent one-day beatings of Pakistan and India, suggested? The answer was yes. This looked like the most talented crop of players in the country's 15 years as an ICC Full Member. Bangladesh also broke new ground during the one-day series: their victory in the second game confirmed their place in the 2017 Champions Trophy, now restricted to the eight top-ranked teams. And, while they remained better suited to the shorter formats, there seemed every reason to believe they would finally be able to compete at Test level.

A second question cropped up repeatedly too: why had cricket been scheduled in the middle of the Asian monsoon? Two of the three ODIs were affected by rain, though all produced easy wins for the team batting second after losing the toss on turning pitches. However, just four days' Test cricket went ahead out of a possible ten. The boards of both countries responded with a shrug, lamenting the lack of windows in the fixture list, especially for the smaller nations; locals also pointed out that the last two monsoon seasons had been unusually dry. The South Africans were left vexed when their lead at the top of the Test rankings was cut by five points, punishment for drawing against a lower-ranked team.

They had arrived seeking a new Test opener and a frontline spinner, as well as a one-day all-rounder to come in at No. 7. Ryan McLaren and Wayne Parnell were widely tipped to go head to head for that spot, but McLaren never played a match and both were dropped on their return home. Farhaan Behardien played instead in all three games. Stiaan van Zyl made a strong impression as Dean Elgar's new Test opening partner – his medium-pace was a bonus – and off-spinner Simon Harmer looked steady at the highest level, even if he reaffirmed the impression that he was unlikely to bowl many teams out.

The selectors were hoping that Quinton de Kock would return to form in all formats. They clearly had their doubts, though, and included Dane Vilas, another wicketkeeper-batsman, in the Test party. De Kock's batting was patchy against the white ball and, despite his glovework looking neater than ever in the First Test, he made a duck and had a physical set-to with Tamim Iqbal; it was no surprise when Vilas made his debut at Mirpur. A. B. de Villiers, meanwhile, had already returned home after the two Twenty20s, ending his run of 98 consecutive Tests – a record from debut, but some way short of Allan Border's all-time mark of 153.

De Kock was not the only one to lose his temper. Rilee Rossouw got involved in a shoulder-barging incident, again with Tamim, during the one-day series, and was swiftly punished. Sekandar Ali, a reporter for newspaper *Alokito Bangladesh*, was assaulted by security personnel for not having media accreditation during a Bangladesh training session, even though none had been issued. And, before the series had started, the Bangladesh Cricket Board asked Cricket South Africa to stop flying a camera drone which had been filming for their YouTube channel, because Bangladeshi law did not permit unmanned objects in its airspace.

SOUTH AFRICAN TOURING PARTY

*H. M. Amla (T/50), K. J. Abbott (50/20), T. Bavuma (T), F. Behardien (50), Q. de Kock (T/50/20), A.B de Villiers (20), J-P. Duminy (T/50/20), F. du Plessis (T/50/20), D. Elgar (T), S. R. Harmer (T), B. E. Hendricks (20), R. R. Hendricks (T), Imran Tahir (50), E. Leie (20), R. McLaren (50), D. A. Miller (50/20), M. Morkel (T/50), C. H. Morris (50/20), W. D. Parnell (50/20), A. M. Phangiso (T/50/20), V. D. Philander (T), K. Rabada (T/50/20), R. R. Rossouw (50/20), D. W. Steyn (T), S van Zyl (T), D. J. Vilas (T), D. Wiese (20). *Coach:* R. C. Domingo.

Du Plessis captained in the Twenty20s. De Villiers was originally selected, as captain, for the one-day series, but returned home ahead of paternity leave.

At Fatullah, July 3, 2015. **South Africans won by eight wickets. ‡Bangladesh Cricket Board XI 99** (18 overs) (D. Wiese 3-13); **South Africans 101-2** (12 overs) (Q. de Kock 35). *The BCB XI chose from 12 players and the South Africans 14 for this 20-over game. Free entry meant a packed stadium and, after the authorities closed the gates, three children were injured attempting to scale a wall. The South Africans gave nine players a bowl, and bundled the Bangladeshis out for 99. The home side picked up their only wickets when Quinton de Kock and A. B. de Villiers (25) retired out after hitting 64 in seven overs.*

First Twenty20 international   At Mirpur, July 5, 2015. **South Africa won by 52 runs. ‡South Africa 148-4** (20 overs) (F. du Plessis 79*, R. R. Rossouw 31*); **Bangladesh 96** (18.5 overs). *MoM:* F. du Plessis. *T20I debut:* Liton Das (Bangladesh). *Faf du Plessis read the conditions perfectly, pacing his own, and his team's, innings on a dry, slow pitch which cried out for graft. Rilee Rossouw muscled two fours and two sixes to boost the total, but the Bangladeshis, employing four slow bowlers – one of them, off-spinner Sohag Gazi, returning with a remodelled action – and just two seamers, might have believed that keeping the South Africans below 150 was a job well done. Kyle Abbott and Kagiso Rabada applied a short-pitched attack unusual for Twenty20s, but the spinners profited most as the surface deteriorated, with J-P. Duminy's 2-11 eye-catching in its control and deception. The match marked the introduction of new ICC international regulations: Mustafizur Rahman became the first bowler to have a no-ball for height penalised with a free hit, which Rossouw could only shovel for a single to midwicket.*

Second Twenty20 international   At Mirpur, July 7, 2015. **South Africa won by 31 runs. ‡South Africa 169-4** (20 overs) (Q. de Kock 44, A. B. de Villiers 40, D. A. Miller 30*); **Bangladesh 138** (19.2 overs) (Soumya Sarkar 37; K. J. Abbott 3-20, E. Leie 3-16, A. M. Phangiso 3-30). *MoM:* E. Leie. *MoS:* F. du Plessis (South Africa). *T20I debuts:* Rony Talukdar (Bangladesh); E. Leie. *A rollicking opening partnership of 95 in 10.3 overs between de Kock and de Villiers laid the foundation for a total well beyond Bangladesh's reach. The pitch offered generous, if slow, turn, as it had 48 hours earlier, but the pair made light work of the spinners, showing power and imagination with a series of well-placed late cuts and dabs. The Gauteng spin pair of Aaron Phangiso and Eddie Leie, bamboozling the batsmen with his leg-break variations, then swept up six for 46 between them.*

First one-day international   At Mirpur, July 10, 2015 (day/night). **South Africa won by eight wickets. ‡Bangladesh 160** (36.3 overs) (Shakib Al Hasan 48, Nasir Hossain 31; K. Rabada 6-16); **South Africa 164-2** (31.1 overs) (Q. de Kock 35, F. du Plessis 63*, R. R. Rossouw 45*). *MoM:* K. Rabada. *ODI debut:* K. Rabada. *Rabada, preferred to Morne Morkel and Wayne Parnell, made a sensational entrance into one-day internationals with a hat-trick in his second over: Tamim Iqbal was beaten for pace and bowled for a 13-ball duck, Liton Das flicked a leg-side delivery to short midwicket, and Mahmudullah was trapped by a length ball to fall lbw. "I went for the yorker and missed it by miles," said Rabada. "But I'll take it." He was the second bowler to claim a hat-trick on ODI debut, after Taijul Islam against Zimbabwe on this ground seven months earlier. Rabada's eventual return of 6-16 from eight overs in a match reduced to 40 a side – including a second spell* *of 3–2–2–2 – were the best figures for any debutant, surpassing West Indian Fidel Edwards's 6-22 at Harare in 2003-04. Du Plessis and Rossouw were clinical in the pressure-free environment of a small run-chase – a contrast to the apparent overconfidence that had brought down a Bangladesh line-up after wins over Pakistan and India.*

Second one-day international At Mirpur, July 12, 2015 (day/night). **Bangladesh won by seven wickets. ‡South Africa 162** (46 overs) (F. du Plessis 41, F. Behardien 36; Mustafizur Rahman 3-38, Nasir Hossain 3-26); **Bangladesh 167-3** (27.4 overs) (Soumya Sarkar 88*, Mahmudullah 50). *MoM:* Soumya Sarkar. *A return to traditional strengths on a dry pitch served Bangladesh well, as spinners Shakib Al Hasan and Nasir Hossain strangled the middle order with tight lines and clever field-placings. The experienced Shakib goaded the batsmen with tantalising flight while conceding only 30 in ten overs, and his frugality contributed to a career-best 3-26 for off-spinner Nasir. Rossouw and David Miller reflected the almost catatonic state of the South African batting, scratching their way to four and nine from 24 balls apiece. Mustafizur reprised some of the unusual skills which had brought him 13 wickets against India a month earlier, with his cutters and slower balls too wily for most. Rabada briefly gave South Africa hope with two quick wickets – Tamim donated the first with an unnecessary heave – but Soumya Sarkar's aerial counter-attack made sure of a win which sealed Bangladesh's place in the 2017 Champions Trophy. In a naive attempt to intimidate the home side, Rossouw led a physical and verbal assault at the beginning of the run-chase, brushing shoulders with Tamim after he was dismissed. Rossouw was fortunate it cost him only half his match fee.*

Third one-day international At Chittagong, July 15, 2015 (day/night). **Bangladesh won by nine wickets** (D/L). **‡South Africa 168-9** (40 overs) (D. A. Miller 44, J-P. Duminy 51; Shakib Al Hasan 3-33); **Bangladesh 170-1** (26.1 overs) (Tamim Iqbal 61*, Soumya Sarkar 90). *MoM:* Soumya Sarkar. *MoS:* Soumya Sarkar. *Local media had described Bangladesh's series-levelling victory three days earlier as a "once-in-a-generation result". But that was a closely fought contest compared to the decider, in which South Africa were humiliated. Hashim Amla had rarely struggled quite like this, labouring on a two-paced pitch against the excellent left-armers Mustafizur and Shakib (who reached 200 ODI wickets, as did captain Mashrafe bin Mortaza). At 50-4, South Africa's ambitions extended no further than respectability, but even that eluded them: Miller and Duminy proved too conscious of keeping wickets in hand once rain intervened at 78-4 after 23 overs. Bangladesh romped to their adjusted target of 170 from 40 overs without care or concern. Rabada and Morkel were caned, particularly by Soumya Sarkar, who gave an exhibition of how to play fast bowling. Tamim seemed intent on enjoying the South Africans' discomfort for as long as possible, even if it meant prolonging the run-chase.*

BANGLADESH v SOUTH AFRICA

First Test Match

At Chittagong, July 21–25, 2015. Drawn. Toss: South Africa. Test debut: Mustafizur Rahman.

South Africa's first Test for six months was intriguingly poised heading into the fourth day. The world's No. 1 team had started rustily, before fighting their way back to parity, only for the monsoon to wipe out the last two days. A draw at least allowed Bangladesh to end their 100% losing record against South Africa but, given their position in the match, they might have hoped for better.

Bangladesh's early approach with the ball had been optimistic and overly aggressive: with South Africa 104 for one at lunch, Amla's decision to bat looked a good one. However, Bangladesh changed tack and bowled dry. Mohammad Shahid sent down seven consecutive maidens, five of them in one spell, mostly at du Plessis, whose determination to absorb the pressure did not pay off with a big score. Bangladesh's new discovery Mustafizur Rahman, a 19-year-old left-arm swinger and cutter, then tore out the middle order with three wickets in four balls: Amla became his maiden Test wicket when he edged a drive, Duminy was plumb in front, and de Kock shakily survived the hat-trick delivery, before losing his off stump to a stunning awayswinger which kept a touch low. Mustafizur's four for 37 were the second-best by a Bangladeshi seamer on debut, after Manjural Islam's six for 81 at Bulawayo in 2000-01.

Fortunately for South Africa, Bavuma did far more than just hang around: he was bustling and proactive, showing a willingness to hit the ball rather than push it. He did everything possible in the team's interests, and perished that way, too, hitting out with only the last man for company.

Bangladesh went on to claim a lead of 78, their biggest in a Test in which they had batted second – but it could have been much more. Tamim Iqbal missed a full toss from Elgar's occasional left-arm spin on 57, and Shakib Al Hasan's slog off Harmer high to midwicket was grim. Tamim, who had brushed shoulders with Rilee Rossouw in the one-day series, became wrapped up in a similar altercation with de Kock who, after being restrained by his captain, was fined 75% of his match fee. In the stands, two young spectators were detained by security services for shouting racial obscenities at the South African players.

When Bangladesh reached 179 for four at the close of day two, South Africa were under real pressure, but Steyn finally discovered some rhythm next morning, and the last six fell for 131. Only 12 overs were possible after tea, during which South Africa's new opening pair of van Zyl and Elgar narrowed the deficit to 17 before the weather closed in.

Man of the Match: Mustafizur Rahman.

Close of play: first day, Bangladesh 7-0 (Tamim Iqbal 1, Imrul Kayes 5); second day, Bangladesh 179-4 (Mushfiqur Rahim 16, Shakib Al Hasan 1); third day, South Africa 61-0 (van Zyl 33, Elgar 28); fourth day, no play.

South Africa

D. Elgar c Liton Das b Taijul Islam	47	– (2) not out........... 28
S. van Zyl c Liton Das b Mahmudullah	34	– (1) not out........... 33
F. du Plessis lbw b Shakib Al Hasan	48	
*H. M. Amla c Liton Das b Mustafizur Rahman	13	
T. Bavuma c Jubair Hossain b Mustafizur Rahman	54	
J-P. Duminy lbw b Mustafizur Rahman	0	
†Q. de Kock b Mustafizur Rahman	0	
V. D. Philander c Shakib Al Hasan b Jubair Hossain	24	
S. R. Harmer c Mominul Haque b Jubair Hossain	9	
D. W. Steyn c Tamim Iqbal b Jubair Hossain	2	
M. Morkel not out	3	
B 8, l-b 5, n-b 1	14	

1/58 (2) 2/136 (1) 3/136 (3)　　　(83.4 overs) 248　　　(no wkt, 21.1 overs)　61
4/173 (4) 5/173 (6) 6/173 (7)
7/208 (8) 8/237 (9) 9/239 (10) 10/248 (5)

Mohammad Shahid 17–9–34–0; Mustafizur Rahman 17.4–6–37–4; Shakib Al Hasan 14–2–45–1; Mahmudullah 3–0–9–1; Taijul Islam 18–3–57–1; Jubair Hossain 14–1–53–3. *Second innings*— Mustafizur Rahman 5–0–21–0; Taijul Islam 2–0–4–0; Mahmudullah 1–1–0–0; Shakib Al Hasan 5–0–19–0; Mohammad Shahid 6–1–12–0; Jubair Hossain 2.1–1–5–0.

Bangladesh

Tamim Iqbal b Elgar	57	Mustafizur Rahman c Duminy b Steyn	3
Imrul Kayes st de Kock b van Zyl	26	Jubair Hossain not out	0
Mominul Haque b Harmer	6		
Mahmudullah lbw b Philander	67	L-b 7, n-b 1	8
*Mushfiqur Rahim lbw b Steyn	28		
Shakib Al Hasan c Duminy b Harmer	47	1/46 (2) 2/55 (3)　　(116.1 overs) 326	
†Liton Das c de Kock b Harmer	50	3/144 (1) 4/178 (4)	
Mohammad Shahid c van Zyl b Philander	25	5/195 (5) 6/277 (6) 7/311 (8)	
Taijul Islam c Elgar b Steyn	9	8/319 (7) 9/325 (9) 10/326 (10)	

Steyn 22.1–5–78–3; Philander 20–2–40–2; Morkel 19–2–52–0; Harmer 35–8–105–3; van Zyl 13–4–23–1; Elgar 3–0–6–1; Duminy 4–0–15–0.

Umpires: R. A. Kettleborough and J. S. Wilson.　　Third umpire: P. R. Reiffel.
Referee: B. C. Broad.

BANGLADESH v SOUTH AFRICA
Second Test Match

At Mirpur, July 30–August 3, 2015. Drawn. Toss: Bangladesh. Test debut: D. J. Vilas.

Steyn became the 13th bowler to take 400 Test wickets on the first – and only – day's play, as Bangladesh reached 246 for eight on a bone-dry surface. That was a better score than it looked but, once again, everyone was left frustrated by the weather. Tamim Iqbal was the man to oblige Steyn, flashing at a wide, cross-seam delivery to provide

FASTEST TO 400 TEST WICKETS

Balls		Tests	From	To
16,634	**D. W. Steyn (SA)**	**80**	**2004-05**	**2015**
20,453†	R. J. Hadlee (NZ)	80	1972-73	1989-90
20,526	G. D. McGrath (A)	87	1993-94	2002-03
21,200	Wasim Akram (P)	96	1984-85	2000
21,695	C. E. L. Ambrose (WI)	97	1987-88	2000
23,096	**J. M. Anderson (E)**	**104**	**2003**	**2015**
23,165†	C. A. Walsh (WI)	107	1984-85	1998-99
23,285	S. M. Pollock (SA)	103	1995-96	2006-07
24,061	M. Muralitharan (SL)	72	1992-93	2001-02
24,967†	Kapil Dev (I)	115	1978-79	1991-92
25,329	S. K. Warne (A)	92	1991-92	2001
26,776	A. Kumble (I)	85	1990	2004-05
26,961	Harbhajan Singh (I)	96	1997-98	2011

† *In the absence of detailed scoresheets for the Tests in which Hadlee, Walsh and Kapil Dev took their 400th wickets, the balls shown are those at the end of the innings.*

Amla with a regulation head-high catch at first slip. Steyn was sporting a white headband to keep his long locks in place, making him appear more like Björn Borg, until he whipped it off to oblige the photographers. Rain meant the pitch had been under covers 48 hours before the start, which was too late to water it or prepare it adequately. Bangladesh made a familiar glut of thirties and forties, though Mushfiqur Rahim was rewarded for his application and technique.

Man of the Match: Mushfiqur Rahim.   *Man of the Series:* D. W. Steyn.

Close of play: first day, Bangladesh 246-8 (Nasir Hossain 13); second day, no play; third day, no play; fourth day, no play.

Bangladesh

Tamim Iqbal c Amla b Steyn	6	Nasir Hossain not out		13
Imrul Kayes lbw b Duminy	30	Mohammad Shahid b Steyn		1
Mominul Haque c Vilas b Duminy	40	B 5, l-b 11, n-b 2		18
Mahmudullah c Bavuma b Steyn	35			
*Mushfiqur Rahim c Vilas b Elgar	65	1/12 (1) 2/81 (3) (8 wkts, 88.1 overs)		246
Shakib Al Hasan c Bavuma b Morkel	35	3/86 (2) 4/180 (4)		
†Liton Das c Elgar b Morkel	3	5/215 (5) 6/220 (7) 7/245 (6) 8/246 (9)		

Mustafizur Rahman and Jubair Hossain did not bat.

Steyn 16.1–4–30–3; Philander 11–2–25–0; Morkel 14–2–45–1; Harmer 23–3–76–0; van Zyl 2–1–5–0; Elgar 7–0–22–1; Duminy 15–4–27–3.

South Africa

D. Elgar, S. van Zyl, F. du Plessis, *H. M. Amla, T. Bavuma, J-P. Duminy, †D. J. Vilas, V. D. Philander, S. R. Harmer, D. W. Steyn, M. Morkel.

Umpires: R. A. Kettleborough and P. R. Reiffel.   Third umpire: J. S. Wilson.
Referee: B. C. Broad.

BANGLADESH v ZIMBABWE IN 2015-16

Neil Manthorp

One-day internationals (3): Bangladesh 3, Zimbabwe 0
Twenty20 internationals (2): Bangladesh 1, Zimbabwe 1

The cancellation by Australia of their two-Test series because of security fears had created a window in Bangladesh's calendar. It needed to be filled, for commercial as much as philanthropic reasons, in a nation whose passionate supporters had finally begun to see their team beating the world's top sides.

One-day victories over Pakistan, India and South Africa had led to a belief that, 15 years after Test admission, Bangladesh's cricketers were finally doing their country justice. The Australian tour was going to be a test of their worth. The disappointment was palpable when security reports suggested the visit would be unsafe, although just weeks later the Australian football team visited Dhaka for a World Cup qualifier. And confusion was followed by anger. The gap was filled by the ever-eager Zimbabweans, who had also been willing to tour Pakistan five months earlier, despite security advice to the contrary. Safety was just about the last concern for a team who had grown almost as familiar with Dhaka as they had with Harare or Bulawayo.

Bangladesh grabbed the opportunity to confirm they had moved on, and left the sides' recent rivalry behind. For their part, Zimbabwe had a chance to show that their busiest international home season had improved their game. They soon found the answer: as always, the Zimbabweans played fine shots, bowled good balls and held excellent catches. But they could also slog wildly, deliver a pie every over, and drop dollies. Most worrying was their naivety in match situations that most club teams would recognise and understand better. Thanks to Malcolm Waller, they did at least round off the tour with a win, which squared the Twenty20 series after a 50-over whitewash.

Bangladesh looked clinical and complete. The fact that their unprecedented run of five series wins were all at home was not their fault: rather it was an indictment of the embarrassment which passes for an international schedule. The major nations say Bangladesh tours lose money, so they don't invite them. That may have been the case in the past, but the current team, more than any other, deserve a chance to prove their worth overseas.

ZIMBABWE TOURING PARTY

*E. Chigumbura, R. W. Chakabva, C. J. Chibhabha, T. S. Chisoro, A. G. Cremer, C. R. Ervine, L. M. Jongwe, N. Madziva, W. P. Masakadza, C. T. Mutombodzi, R. Mutumbami, T. Muzarabani, J. C. Nyumbu, T. Panyangara, Sikandar Raza, M. N. Waller, S. C. Williams. *Coach:* D. F. Whatmore. Mutumbami injured his ankle during the first ODI, and was replaced by Mutombodzi.

At Fatullah, November 5, 2015. **Zimbabweans won by seven wickets. Bangladesh Cricket Board XI 277-8** (50 overs) (Imrul Kayes 56, Anamul Haque 52, Mushfiqur Rahim 81*; A. G. Cremer 3-21, L. M. Jongwe 3-20); ‡**Zimbabweans 281-3** (46.4 overs) (C. R. Ervine 95, S. C. Williams 54 ret hurt, E. Chigumbura 64*). *The Zimbabweans chose from 16 players, and the Board XI from 14. After an opening partnership of 105, Mushfiqur Rahim lifted the Board XI to 277, putting on 90 for the* *fifth wicket with Shahriar Nafees (38), back in the mix for national selection after topping the run-charts in the National Cricket League. The tourists reached their target with ease: Craig Ervine and Sean Williams added 125 for the third wicket, before Williams retired at a drinks break; Elton Chigumbura cracked 64* from 49 balls.*

First one-day international At Mirpur, November 7, 2015 (day/night). **Bangladesh won by 145 runs. Bangladesh 273-9** (50 overs) (Tamim Iqbal 40, Mushfiqur Rahim 107, Sabbir Rahman 57); ‡**Zimbabwe 128** (36.1 overs) (L. M. Jongwe 39, E. Chigumbura 41; Shakib Al Hasan 5-47). *MoM:* Mushfiqur Rahim. *Soft of hand and quick of foot, Mushfiqur Rahim set up Bangladesh's win with a calm hundred, his fourth in ODIs. Sabbir Rahman added a brisk half-century. Zimbabwe were never in touch. Luke Jongwe displayed flashes of talent after being promoted to open, then Chigumbura struck two defiant sixes – but Shakib Al Hasan tossed up some tempting offerings, and finished with career-best figures. Zimbabwe's wicketkeeper Richmond Mutumbami was hit on the ankle in the field, and unable to bat; he later returned home.*

Second one-day international At Mirpur, November 9, 2015 (day/night). **Bangladesh won by 58 runs. Bangladesh 241-9** (50 overs) (Imrul Kayes 76, Sabbir Rahman 33, Nasir Hossain 41; T. Panyangara 3-41); ‡**Zimbabwe 183** (43.2 overs) (E. Chigumbura 47, Sikandar Raza 33; Mustafizur Rahman 3-33). *MoM:* Imrul Kayes. *When Imrul Kayes's responsible innings ended with a catch to backward point, Bangladesh seemed vulnerable at 151-5 – but they were rescued by Sabbir and Nasir Hossain. Zimbabwe were also looking good at 151-4 in the 34th over, but Al-Amin Hossain removed Sikandar Raza and Chigumbura in quick succession after a stand of 73, and the tail once more failed to make much impression. The slippery left-armer Mustafizur Rahman again showed his class, with three wickets – and several nods of appreciation and shakes of the head from the batsmen who survived him.*

Third one-day international At Mirpur, November 11, 2015 (day/night). **Bangladesh won by 61 runs.** ‡**Bangladesh 276-9** (50 overs) (Tamim Iqbal 73, Imrul Kayes 73, Mahmudullah 52); **Zimbabwe 215** (43.3 overs) (S. C. Williams 64, E. Chigumbura 45, M. N. Waller 32; Mustafizur Rahman 5-34). *MoM:* Tamim Iqbal. *MoS:* Mushfiqur Rahim. *Bangladesh were well set for a 3–0 whitewash after an untroubled opening stand of 147 in 29.3 overs, but wobbled to 226-6 after 44; the first three wickets all fell to stumpings by Regis Chakabva, a first for ODIs. Then came an incident which left the tourists fuming: on 32, Mahmudullah seemed to be run out by yards by Sikandar Raza's direct hit. He kept going towards the pavilion, only to stop when the decision was referred to the third umpire, Enamul Haque. He spotted that Chakabva had knocked off a bail while preparing to gather the return, so pressed the "not out" button. However Chakabva, realising he might have broken the wicket, had also collected the ball and removed a stump – but the umpires ruled this had taken place after the decision was referred, and the ball was therefore dead. Play was held up for several minutes while the players debated the issue, and at one stage it seemed possible they would walk off. Mustafizur eventually rendered discussion academic with another eye-catching performance, returning to add three wickets after Zimbabwe had reached a competitive 186-4 in the 36th over.*

First Twenty20 international At Mirpur, November 13, 2015 (floodlit). **Bangladesh won by four wickets. Zimbabwe 131** (19.3 overs) (M. N. Waller 68); ‡**Bangladesh 136-6** (17.4 overs) (Tamim Iqbal 31; A. G. Cremer 3-29). *MoM:* M. N. Waller. *T20I debut:* Jubair Hossain (Bangladesh). *Zimbabwe were struggling at 38-4 in the ninth over, before Malcolm Waller blitzed 68 from 31 balls, with six sixes. He piled on 67 with Craig Ervine (20), but no one else passed 15. Bangladesh lost Anamul Haque in the first over, and later shrugged off the departures of Nasir and Tamim Iqbal in the 11th over to ease home with 14 balls to spare, despite spinners Graeme Cremer and Tendai Chisoro sharing five wickets.*

Second Twenty20 international At Mirpur, November 15, 2015 (floodlit). **Zimbabwe won by three wickets.** ‡**Bangladesh 135-9** (20 overs) (Anamul Haque 47; T. Panyangara 3-30); **Zimbabwe 136-7** (19.5 overs) (L. M. Jongwe 34, M. N. Waller 40; Al-Amin Hossain 3-20). *MoM:* N. Madziva. *MoS:* M. N. Waller. *Zimbabwe rounded off an otherwise dismal tour with a last-gasp victory to share the T20 series. Mashrafe bin Mortaza had used up his frontline bowlers, so off-spinner Nasir had to bowl the last, with 18 wanted. Waller was caught in the deep from the first delivery, but Neville Madziva (28*) sliced the next over extra cover for six; finally, with the target reduced to six from two, he smashed Nasir 20 yards over the straight boundary, and celebrated by flinging his bat away and jumping into the arms of his team-mates. Earlier, Anamul Haque had been unable to locate top gear: he entered in the fourth over and was run out in the last, finishing with 47 from 51 balls.*

DOMESTIC CRICKET IN BANGLADESH IN 2014-15

Utpal Shuvro

For most Test nations, the fact that the domestic tournaments ran with few hitches would not be worth mentioning. For Bangladesh, smooth scheduling and timely finishes were a welcome change, all the more remarkable in one of the most volatile years in the nation's history. A three-month transport blockade called by the opposition paralysed the economy, but domestic cricket marched on.

This did not mean it escaped controversy. At the climax of the first-class National Cricket League, Khulna accused Dhaka Metropolis of throwing their match against Rangpur, when a draw would have given Khulna the title. Entering the final round, Rangpur, Khulna and Dhaka Division were tied on 96 points: all three won, with the extra point for a first-innings lead, so the title was settled on bonus points. Rangpur had collected the maximum eight, Khulna seven, and Dhaka six. But **Rangpur's** victory, to earn their first title, came only after they claimed Dhaka Metropolis's last wicket with four minutes to spare. The BCB's Anti-Corruption Unit investigated Khulna's allegations, but announced in August that they could find no proof of wrongdoing. It was only Rangpur's fourth first-class season, after their regional division became independent of Rajshahi – who had won four successive titles up to 2011-12 but finished fifth this time, meaning they would be in the second tier when the tournament split in 2015-16.

Batsmen dominated the NCL, with 62 centuries and nine doubles in 28 matches (the previous records were 39 and three). Rangpur's Liton Das led the way with style and consistency: his 1,024 NCL runs were another record, surpassing Minhazul Abedin's 1,012 in 2001-02, and he became the first to score five centuries in one tournament; he made his debut for Bangladesh in June. Another international debutant was Rony Talukdar of Dhaka Division, who scored 777 NCL runs, including three consecutive centuries, though he did not establish himself in the Bangladesh side as strongly as Liton. He was the leading scorer in the one-day Dhaka Premier League, with 714 for Prime Doleshwar, just ahead of Liton's 686 for Abahani. Three other batsmen reached 1,000 in all first-class cricket. Alok Kapali headed the averages with 1,156 runs at 88, with double-hundreds for Sylhet and East Zone; to his dismay, chief selector Faruque Ahmed remarked that the 31-year-old Kapali wasn't even in their Plan B. Shahriar Nafees made 1,092 without winning a recall, and there was no senior call-up as yet for his Barisal team-mate, Mosaddek Hossain, aged 19. He scored 1,033 at 86, with four hundreds, including 250 and 282 in successive innings, and featured in a 423-run stand.

As usual, left-arm spinners dominated the bowling. Out-of-favour Elias Sunny was the highest wicket-taker in the NCL, with 42 for Dhaka Metropolis, and in the Dhaka Premier League, with 31 for Prime Doleshwar. Abdur Razzak, another discarded slow left-armer, took most wickets in all first-class cricket, with 41 for Khulna, plus 18 for South Zone in the four-day Bangladesh Cricket League.

He helped **South Zone** retain their title in the third BCL, contested by zonal franchises. A one-day competition for the same franchise teams was introduced to prepare the national players for Pakistan's visit, though it was uncertain whether it would be repeated; the winners were **East Zone**. There was no Twenty20 competition, though the BPL was to return in 2015-16.

The Dhaka Premier League, which had gained List A status the previous year, was decided on the last day, when **Prime Bank** claimed their first title. The League was marred by umpiring controversies, which were not unusual, except in their scale: three club officials from Legends of Rupganj were handed bans for alleging that BCB officials were involved in manipulating the umpires. Legends of Rupganj – who had won the previous competition as Gazi Tank Cricketers – caused a more welcome stir at the beginning of the season when they flew in Sachin Tendulkar to unveil the rebranded club's logo.

FIRST-CLASS AVERAGES, 2014-15

BATTING (550 runs)

	M	I	NO	R	HS	100	Avge	Ct/St
Alok Kapali (*Sylhet/East Zone*).	10	16	3	1,156	228	3	88.92	13
Mosaddek Hossain (*Barisal/South Zone*)	8	12	0	1,033	282	4	86.08	5
Tushar Imran (*Khulna/South Zone*).	9	13	3	836	203*	3	83.60	4
Liton Das (*Bangladesh A/Rangpur/E Zone*) . .	9	17	1	1,232	175	5	77.00	13
Tasamul Haque (*Chittagong/East Zone*).	7	13	4	640	131*	3	71.11	4
†Shahriar Nafees (*Bang A/Barisal/S Zone*) . . .	10	17	0	1,092	219	2	64.23	5
Ziaur Rahman (*Khulna/South Zone*).	9	13	2	687	164	3	62.45	3
Abdul Mazid (*Dhaka/Central Zone*)	9	15	1	840	253*	3	60.00	5
†Tamim Iqbal (*Bangladesh*)	5	10	0	585	206	3	58.50	1
Naeem Islam (*Bang A/Rangpur/N Zone*)	12	20	4	922	147	3	57.62	20
†Imrul Kayes (*Bangladesh/Khulna/S Zone*) . . .	11	19	1	983	166	4	54.61	16
†Shadman Islam (*Bang A/Dhaka Met/E Zone*) .	9	15	0	816	140	1	54.40	5
†Fazle Mahmud (*Barisal*)	7	12	1	593	100*	1	53.90	1
Rony Talukdar (*Dhaka/Central Zone*)	10	17	0	901	227	4	53.00	8
Rajin Saleh (*Sylhet/East Zone*)	10	16	2	730	201*	3	52.14	16
†Junaid Siddique (*Rajshahi/North Zone*)	10	18	1	780	193	3	45.88	9
†Mehrab Hossain (*Dhaka Metropolis/C Zone*) . .	10	18	1	776	108	2	45.64	6
Raqibul Hasan (*Bang A/Dhaka/C Zone*)	12	21	2	815	145	2	42.89	17
Shuvagata Hom (*Bangladesh/Dhaka/C Zone*) . .	12	24	1	697	135	3	41.00	15
Asif Ahmed (*Dhaka Metropolis/East Zone*) . . .	9	16	1	615	103	1	41.00	7/1
Farhad Hossain (*Bang A/Rajshahi/N Zone*) . . .	9	16	2	552	87	0	39.42	8
Marshall Ayub (*Bang A/Dhaka Met/C Zone*) .	12	22	0	692	113	1	31.45	15

BOWLING (20 wickets, average 35.00)

	Style	O	M	R	W	BB	5I	Avge
Mustafizur Rahman (*Khulna/S Zone*)	LFM	185.4	52	469	26	5-28	1	18.03
Shuvagata Hom (*Bang/Dhaka/C Zone*)	OB	244.3	41	874	37	6-22	3	23.62
Abdur Razzak (*Khulna/South Zone*)	SLA	588.4	162	1,523	59	8-100	5	25.81
Elias Sunny (*Dhaka Met/C Zone*)	SLA	422.5	105	1,355	51	7-73	5	26.56
Mosharraf Hossain (*Dhaka/C Zone*)	SLA	372.5	73	1,056	39	7-173	4	27.07
Rahatul Ferdous (*Sylhet*)	SLA	197.3	39	581	21	4-56	0	27.66
Saqlain Sajib (*Bang A/Rajshahi/N Z*)	SLA	500	94	1,520	52	9-82	5	29.23
Jubair Hossain (*Bang A/Bang/Dhaka*)	LBG	315.4	29	1,147	38	5-96	1	30.18
Taijul Islam (*Bang A/Dhaka/North Zone*)	SLA	346	45	1,161	37	8-39	3	31.37
Mahmudul Hasan (*Rangpur/N Zone*)	OB	322.4	73	973	31	5-76	2	31.38
Mukhtar Ali (*Rajshahi/North Zone*)	RFM	218.3	47	758	24	5-58	1	31.58
Sadiqur Rahman (*Sylhet/East Zone*)	OB	231.5	44	695	22	4-27	0	31.59
Shakib Al Hasan (*Bangladesh*)	SLA	204.5	36	654	20	6-59	3	32.70
Mohammad Shahid (*Bangladesh A/ Dhaka Met/Bangladesh/C Zone*).	RFM	275.5	55	904	27	4-100	0	33.48
Suhrawadi Shuvo (*Rangpur*)	SLA	236	54	690	20	5-88	1	34.50

WALTON NATIONAL CRICKET LEAGUE, 2014-15

	P	W	L	D	1st-inns points	Bonus points Batting	Bowling	Pts
Rangpur	7	4	0	3	5	24	19	121
Khulna	7	4	1	2	6	25	19	120
Dhaka.	7	4	0	3	5	24	17	119
Dhaka Metropolis	7	2	2	3	4	20	18	83
Rajshahi	7	2	4	1	3	16	17	71
Sylhet	7	1	2	4	3	14	17	62
Barisal.	7	0	4	3	2	15	13	39
Chittagong	7	0	4	3	0	8	14	31

Outright win = 16pts; draw = 3pts; first-innings lead = 1pt. First-innings bonus points were awarded as follows for the first 110 overs of each team's first innings: one batting point for the first 200 runs and then for 250, 300, 350 and 400; one bowling point for the third wicket taken and then for the sixth and ninth.

At Fatullah (KSOA), January 25–28, 2015. **Rangpur won by 225 runs. Rangpur 269** (Naeem Islam 107) **and 257-5 dec** (Liton Das 150); ‡**Chittagong 107 and 194.** *Rangpur 22pts, Chittagong 2pts. Chittagong wicketkeeper Irfan Sukkur held five catches in Rangpur's first innings and seven in the match. Liton Das hit 150 in 142 balls.*

At Mirpur, January 25–27, 2015. **Dhaka won by an innings and 413 runs. Barisal 139** (Mohammad Sharif 6-24) **and 99** (Shuvagata Hom 6-22); ‡**Dhaka 651-5 dec** (Rony Talukdar 227, Raqibul Hasan 145, Taibur Rahman 106*). *Dhaka 25pts, Barisal 1pt. Rony Talukdar scored his maiden double-hundred, putting on 197 for Dhaka's first wicket with Abdul Mazid (76) and 226 for the second with Raqibul Hasan, to build a 512-run lead. Career-best returns from Mohammad Sharif and Shuvagata Hom (9.4–3–22–6) ensured the biggest victory in Bangladeshi cricket.*

At Savar (BKSP No. 3), January 25–28, 2015. **Dhaka Metropolis won by 285 runs. ‡Dhaka Metropolis 302** (Mehdi Hasan 141) **and 375** (Mehrab Hossain 108; Saqlain Sajib 6-120); **Rajshahi 218 and 174** (Saikat Ali 5-45). *Dhaka Metropolis 23pts, Rajshahi 4pts.*

At Savar (BKSP No. 2), January 25–28, 2015. **Khulna won by an innings and 178 runs. Khulna 536-8 dec** (Tushar Imran 177*, Nurul Hasan 115); ‡**Sylhet 184 and 174** (Abdur Razzak 7-71). *Khulna 24pts, Sylhet 1pt. Tushar Imran and Nurul Hasan put on 238 for Khulna's fifth wicket.*

At Savar (BKSP No. 2), February 1–4, 2015. **Khulna won by six wickets. ‡Barisal 271** (Abdur Razzak 8-100) **and 402** (Shahriar Nafees 219); **Khulna 390** (Imrul Kayes 166; Sohag Gazi 5-94) **and 287-4** (Imrul Kayes 127*). *Khulna 24pts, Barisal 4pts. Abdur Razzak's 8-100 was the best return of this tournament; in all he took 11-254. Imrul Kayes scored a century in each innings; in the second, he put on 122* for the fifth wicket in 10.1 overs with Ziaur Rahman, whose 31-ball 65 included seven sixes, as they chased 284 against the clock. In between, Shahriar Nafees compiled a maiden double-century, adding 238 for Barisal's second wicket with Fazle Mahmud (74).*

At Fatullah (KSOA Outer), February 1–4, 2015. **Rajshahi won by nine wickets. ‡Chittagong 209** (Farhad Reza 5-45) **and 298** (Mukhtar Ali 5-58); **Rajshahi 411** (Junaid Siddique 113; Iftekhar Sajjad 8-112) **and 100-1.** *Rajshahi 25pts, Chittagong 4pts. Rajshahi were 231-7 in their first innings, before Mukhtar Ali (96) and Sanjamul Islam (88) added 166 for the eighth wicket – but Iftekhar Sajjad took 8-112 in his second match.*

At Fatullah (KSOA), February 1–4, 2015. **Dhaka won by an innings and 24 runs. Dhaka 525** (Abdul Mazid 253*, Rony Talukdar 163); ‡**Dhaka Metropolis 90** (Shuvagata Hom 5-17) **and 411.** *Dhaka 25pts, Dhaka Metropolis 1pt. Abdul Mazid batted nine hours 35 minutes for his maiden double-hundred – all but five balls of the innings, as he retired hurt at 525-8. He and Rony Talukdar had put on 314 for Dhaka's first wicket, a Bangladeshi domestic record. Shuvagata Hom (7.2–2–17–5) made Dhaka Metropolis follow on 435 behind, and even a ninth-wicket stand of 115 between Zabid Hossain (58*) and Abu Haider (68) could not avert an innings defeat.*

At Savar (BKSP No. 3), February 1–4, 2015. **Drawn. ‡Rangpur 367** (Enamul Haque 5-107) **and 301-8 dec** (Liton Das 116); **Sylhet 261 and 326-6.** *Rangpur 11pts, Sylhet 8pts. In Rangpur's second innings, No. 7 Ariful Haque hit 51* in 28 balls.*

At Savar (BKSP No. 3), February 8–11, 2015. **Dhaka won by an innings and 174 runs. ‡Chittagong 155** (Mosharraf Hossain 5-37) **and 287** (Tasamul Haque 114); **Dhaka 616-5 dec** (Abdul Mazid 113, Rony Talukdar 201, Shuvagata Hom 119). *Dhaka 25pts, Chittagong 1pt. Rony Talukdar hit seven sixes as he scored his third hundred in successive innings, two of them doubles; all three led to totals of 500-plus and innings victories for Dhaka. Rony and Abdul Mazid put on 304 for Dhaka's first wicket, taking their average opening stand in this season to 271.*

At Fatullah (KSOA), February 8–11, 2015. **Drawn. ‡Dhaka Metropolis 400** (Shadman Islam 140; Al-Amin 5-49) **and 247-8 dec; Barisal 261** (Elias Sunny 7-73) **and 267-2** (Fazle Mahmud 100*). *Dhaka Metropolis 10pts, Barisal 7pts.*

At Mirpur, February 8–11, 2015. **Rangpur won by 193 runs. Rangpur 310 and 259-8 dec; ‡Khulna 213** (Mahmudul Hasan 5-76) **and 163.** *Rangpur 23pts, Khulna 4pts. Rangpur moved above Khulna into second place with a victory which would prove decisive at the end of the campaign.*

At Savar (BKSP No. 2), February 8–11, 2015. **Drawn. ‡Rajshahi 482** (Maisuqur Rahman 158, Junaid Siddique 112); **Sylhet 324** (Sanjamul Islam 5-84) **and 335-3** (Rahatul Ferdous 106*). *Rajshahi 11pts, Sylhet 7pts. Sylhet's Enamul Haque became the first Bangladeshi to take 400 first-class wickets, in his 14th season.*

At Savar (BKSP No. 3), February 16–19, 2015. **Drawn. Rangpur 518-9 dec** (Liton Das 175, Naeem Islam 147) **and 65-0; ‡Barisal 668** (Mosaddek Hossain 250, Al-Amin 199). *Barisal 10pts, Rangpur 7pts. Mosaddek Hossain, whose previous first-class record was 34 runs from four matches, scored 250, and added 423 with Al-Amin, who also reached a maiden century in his fifth game – and fell one short of a double. It was the fifth-highest stand for the fifth wicket in all first-class cricket (though only the second-highest in Bangladeshi domestic cricket) and led to this tournament's biggest total.*

At Fatullah (KSOA), February 16–19, 2015. **Drawn. Sylhet 500** (Rajin Saleh 181, Alok Kapali 175; Mosharraf Hossain 5-109); **‡Dhaka 202 and 175-5.** *Dhaka 5pts, Sylhet 11pts. Rajin Saleh and Alok Kapali both reached career-bests and shared a stand of 348, a national fourth-wicket record.*

At Savar (BKSP No. 2), February 16–19, 2015. **Drawn. ‡Dhaka Metropolis 496** (Marshall Ayub 113, Mohammad Shahid 102; Noor Hossain 6-150); **Chittagong 274** (Tasamul Haque 131*; Elias Sunny 5-80) **and 376-6** (Nazimuddin 108*). *Dhaka Metropolis 11pts, Chittagong 7pts. Mohammad Shahid hit a maiden century, at No. 10, in 102 balls, including seven sixes, and put on 114 for Dhaka Metropolis's last wicket with Asif Hasan, who contributed 20*.*

At Mirpur, February 16–19, 2015. **Khulna won by an innings and 183 runs. Khulna 560-6 dec** (Tushar Imran 203*, Ziaur Rahman 164); **‡Rajshahi 225 and 152** (Abdur Razzak 5-52). *Khulna 23pts, Rajshahi 2pts. Tushar Imran reached a maiden double-century, adding 295, a national sixth-wicket record, with Ziaur Rahman, who hit seven sixes.*

At Savar (BKSP No. 2), February 23–26, 2015. **Drawn. ‡Barisal 597-9 dec** (Mosaddek Hossain 282); **Chittagong 339** (Nafees Iqbal 108; Sohag Gazi 5-133) **and 324-3** (Tasamul Haque 120*, Irfan Sukkur 104*). *Barisal 11pts, Chittagong 8pts. Mosaddek Hossain's second double-hundred in successive innings was the fourth-highest score on Bangladeshi soil, and the third-highest by a Bangladeshi. His 282 took only 309 balls; he added 138 for the sixth wicket with Sohag Gazi (94), 127 for the seventh with Salman Hossain (37) and 134 for the ninth with Kamrul Islam (23*).*

At Fatullah (KSOA), February 23–26, 2015. **Drawn. ‡Dhaka 366** (Shuvagata Hom 135) **and 216-2** (Abdul Mazid 104); **Khulna 600-9 dec** (Tushar Imran 158, Mithun Ali 126, Ziaur Rahman 110). *Dhaka 6pts, Khulna 11pts. Tushar Imran and Mithun Ali put on 222 for Khulna's fourth wicket.*

At Mirpur, February 23–26, 2015. **Dhaka Metropolis won by 135 runs. ‡Dhaka Metropolis 264 and 264-8 dec** (Shamsur Rahman 103; Nabil Samad 6-59); **Sylhet 171 and 222.** *Dhaka Metropolis 22pts, Sylhet 3pts.*

At Savar (BKSP No. 3), February 23–26, 2015. **Rangpur won by an innings and one run. ‡Rajshahi 263 and 263; Rangpur 527-6 dec** (Liton Das 173, Naeem Islam 138*). *Rangpur 24pts, Rajshahi 3pts. In Rajshahi's first innings, Mukhtar Ali (85) hit eight sixes, four of them off consecutive deliveries from Sanjit Saha. He added four more in a second-innings 70*.*

At Savar (BKSP No. 2), March 2–5, 2015. **Rajshahi won by four wickets. ‡Barisal 235** (Saqlain Sajib 5-81) **and 364** (Sanjamul Islam 5-126); **Rajshahi 247** (Sohag Gazi 5-106) **and 353-6.** *Rajshahi 21pts, Barisal 4pts. Rajshahi captain Farhad Reza took them within touching distance of their 353-run target by smashing 50 in 32 deliveries – they won with nine balls to spare.*

At Fatullah (KSOA), March 2–5, 2015. **Drawn. ‡Sylhet 507-8 dec** (Rajin Saleh 111, Alok Kapali 211*) **and 88-3; Chittagong 332** (Iftekhar Sajjad 126*). *Chittagong 6pts, Sylhet 9pts. Alok Kapali scored a maiden double-century, adding 191 for Sylhet's fourth wicket with Rajin Saleh.*

At Mirpur, March 2–5, 2015. **Drawn. Dhaka 335** (Raqibul Hasan 130) **and 259; ‡Rangpur 306 and 100-1.** *Dhaka 10pts, Rangpur 9pts. Rony Talukdar made a three-ball duck in Dhaka's first innings, but his younger brother Jony scored 90 on debut. Rangpur keeper Dhiman Ghosh held five catches in that innings, and seven in all. The teams finished level on 96 points, along with Khulna.*

At Savar (BKSP No. 3), March 2–5, 2015. **Drawn. ‡Khulna 416** (Mehedi Hasan 140) **and 331-8 dec** (Shamsur Rahman 5-69); **Dhaka Metropolis 341** (Abdur Razzak 5-135). *Dhaka Metropolis 8pts, Khulna 10pts. Dhaka Metropolis's Mohammad Shahid was banned from bowling in Khulna's first innings after running on the pitch.*

At Mirpur, March 9–12, 2015. **Sylhet won by ten wickets. Barisal 167 and 390; ‡Sylhet 486-9 dec** (Rajin Saleh 201*) **and 75-0.** *Sylhet 23pts, Barisal 2pts. Rajin Saleh reached a maiden double-hundred, and added 115 for Sylhet's ninth wicket with Enamul Haque (50).*

At Savar (BKSP No. 3), March 9–11, 2015. **Khulna won by an innings and 24 runs. ‡Chittagong 190 and 155** (Mustafizur Rahman 5-28); **Khulna 369** (Ziaur Rahman 122). *Khulna 24pts, Chittagong 3pts. Coming in at 72-5, Ziaur Rahman hit ten sixes in his 122. After winning in three days, Khulna had to wait for results elsewhere to find out whether they were champions.*

At Fatullah (KSOA), March 9–12, 2015. **Dhaka won by 134 runs. ‡Dhaka 318** (Shuvagata Hom 111) **and 332-9 dec** (Nadif Chowdhury 100*); **Rajshahi 291 and 225** (Mosharraf Hossain 5-84). *Dhaka 23pts, Rajshahi 5pts. Dhaka finished third after dropping two batting points, while defeat condemned Rajshahi to the second tier of the revamped 2015-16 tournament.*

At Savar (BKSP No. 2), March 9–12, 2015. **Rangpur won by 102 runs. ‡Rangpur 491** (Liton Das 107, Ariful Haque 112*; Elias Sunny 6-156) **and 306** (Elias Sunny 5-78); **Dhaka Metropolis 437** (Mehdi Hasan 138, Mehrab Hossain 103; Suhrawadi Shuvo 5-88) **and 258** (Mahmudul Hasan 5-89). *Rangpur 25pts, Dhaka Metropolis 8pts. Rangpur won the National Cricket League for the first time, by a single point, though runners-up Khulna accused Dhaka Metropolis of throwing the game after their last wicket fell within four minutes to go. On the opening day, Liton Das hit his fifth hundred of the tournament; in his second-innings 77, he became the second man to score 1,000 in an NCL season. Next morning, Ariful Haque reached his century in 54 balls; he hit 12 sixes from 56 balls in all. On the final day, he was banned from bowling in Dhaka Metropolis's second innings after running on the pitch. Slow left-armer Elias Sunny took 11-234.*

NATIONAL CRICKET LEAGUE WINNERS

†1999-2000	Chittagong	2004-05	Dhaka	2010-11	Rajshahi
2000-01	Biman Bangladesh	2005-06	Rajshahi	2011-12	Rajshahi
	Airlines	2006-07	Dhaka	2012-13	Khulna
2001-02	Dhaka	2007-08	Khulna	2013-14	Dhaka
2002-03	Khulna	2008-09	Rajshahi	2014-15	Rangpur
2003-04	Dhaka	2009-10	Rajshahi		

† The National Cricket League was not first-class in 1999-2000.

Dhaka and Rajshahi have won the title 5 times, Khulna 3 times, Biman Bangladesh Airlines, Chittagong and Rangpur 1.

BANGLADESH CRICKET LEAGUE, 2014-15

					1st-inns	Bonus points		
	P	W	L	D	points	Batting	Bowling	Pts
South Zone	3	1	0	2	3	13	8	46
East Zone	3	1	0	2	2	7	9	40
Central Zone	3	1	1	1	1	5	8	33
North Zone	3	0	2	1	0	7	7	17

Outright win = 16pts; draw = 3pts; first-innings lead = 1pt. First-innings bonus points were awarded as follows for the first 110 overs of each team's first innings: one batting point for the first 200 runs and then for 250, 300, 350 and 400; one bowling point for the third wicket taken and then for the sixth and ninth.

At Fatullah (KSOA), April 21–24, 2015. **South Zone won by 216 runs. ‡South Zone 352** (Sohag Gazi 108; Ariful Haque 6-75) **and 266-3 dec** (Anamul Haque 111); **North Zone 235 and 167** (Abdur Razzak 6-69). *South Zone 24pts, North Zone 4pts. Sohag Gazi came in at 213-6 on the first day and scored 108 out of 139 for the last two wickets. Abdur Razzak, who took 10-136 in all, and North Zone's Saqlain Sajib both claimed their 50th wicket of the season.*

At Chittagong (ZAC), April 30–May 3, 2015. **East Zone won by three wickets. Central Zone 179 and 348-9 dec; ‡East Zone 304** (Elias Sunny 7-124) **and 227-7.** *East Zone 23pts, Central Zone 3pts. Slow left-armer Elias Sunny's 7-124 took him past 50 wickets for the season. East Zone achieved a target of 224 in the 31st over, in fading light.*

At Fatullah (KSOA), May 7–10, 2015. **Drawn. ‡Central Zone 413** (Rony Talukdar 106) **and 69-4; South Zone 541** (Shahriar Nafees 161, Mosaddek Hossain 153, Sohag Gazi 106; Mosharraf Hossain 7-173). *Central Zone 8pts, South Zone 11pts. Rony Talukdar hit 102* before lunch on the first day; Mosharraf Hossain (89) and Elias Sunny (58*) added 137 for the ninth wicket. Mosharraf later took seven wickets with his left-arm spin, but South Zone pulled ahead during a 185-run seventh-wicket stand between Mosaddek Hossain, who hit seven sixes, and Sohag Gazi, who hit eight.*

At Chittagong (ZAC), May 7–10, 2015. **Drawn. East Zone 473** (Alok Kapali 228, Asif Ahmed 103) **and 106-4; ‡North Zone 384** (Junaid Siddique 193). *East Zone 10pts, North Zone 8pts. Alok Kapali reached his second double-century of the season, passing 1,000 runs. He hit seven sixes in eight hours 49 minutes, and added 191 for the fifth wicket with Asif Ahmed. Junaid Siddique was run out seven short of a maiden double.*

At Mirpur, May 24–27, 2015. **Central Zone won by 80 runs. ‡Central Zone 289** (Mahmudullah 113; Taijul Islam 5-113) **and 200; North Zone 287** (Shuvagata Hom 5-78) **and 122.** *Central Zone 22pts, North Zone 5pts. In a difficult match for the top order, the fourth wicket fell at 62, 61, 74 and 51 across the four innings.*

At Chittagong (ZAC), May 24–27, 2015. **Drawn. South Zone 385 and 452** (Soumya Sarkar 127, Mosaddek Hossain 119); **‡East Zone 247 and 166-3.** *East Zone 7pts, South Zone 11pts. The two leading teams in this competition fought it out in the last round, and a first-innings lead of 138 gave the title to South Zone. Shahriar Nafees and Mithun Ali narrowly missed centuries in that first innings, after putting on 174 for South's third wicket, though Shahriar passed 1,000 runs in the season; so did Mosaddek Hossain in their second innings, when he added 176 for the fifth with Soumya Sarkar, who reached a maiden century. In East Zone's second, Liton Das's 74 was his tenth score of 50-plus in the season, in his ninth game.*

DHAKA PREMIER DIVISION, 2014-15

50-over league plus super league and relegation league

Prelim League	P	W	L	Pts	Super League	P	W	L	Pts
ABAHANI	11	9	2	18	Prime Bank	16	13	3	26
PRIME BANK	11	9	2	18	Prime Doleshwar	16	12	4	24
KALA BAGAN	11	7	4	14	Kala Bagan	16	10	6	20
PRIME DOLESHWAR	11	7	4	14	Abahani	16	10	6	20
LEGENDS OF RUPGANJ	11	7	4	14	Legends of Rupganj	16	8	8	16
MOHAMMEDAN	11	7	4	14	Mohammedan	16	8	8	16
Victoria	11	7	4	14					
Brothers Union	11	5	6	10					
Shkh Jamal Dhanmondi	11	4	7	8	**Relegation**	P	W	L	Pts
Kala Bagan Krira Chak	11	2	9	4	Kala Bagan Krira Ch.	13	4	9	8
Partex	11	2	9	4	Partex	13	3	10	6
Old DOHS	11	0	11	0	Old DOHS	13	0	13	0

BANGLADESH ONE-DAY CRICKET LEAGUE, 2014-15

50-over league plus final

	Played	Won	Lost	No result	Points	Net run-rate
East Zone	3	2	0	1	5	2.06
North Zone	3	2	0	1	5	0.92
South Zone	3	1	2	0	2	–1.36
Central Zone	3	0	3	0	0	–0.75

Final At Mirpur, April 12 (day/night). **East Zone won by three wickets** (D/L). **North Zone 291-9** (50 overs) (Mahmudul Hasan 107); **‡East Zone 281-7** (45 overs). *MoM: Abul Hasan. Mahmudul Hasan and Nasir Hossain (96) added 140 for North Zone's fourth wicket. In reply, Liton Das (50) and Mominul Haque (78) shared a second-wicket stand of 102 in 13 overs and, after East Zone's run-chase was interrupted by rain and their target revised to 278 off 46, Nos 8 and 9 Abul Hasan and Arafat Sunny smashed 40 in 16 balls to see them home with an over in hand.*

INDIAN CRICKET IN 2015

A whiff of altruism

DILEEP PREMACHANDRAN

Twelve months on from a dismal 2014, Indian cricket found itself in a better place on the field. But the turmoil behind the scenes only intensified, with a former board president removed from his post at the ICC, his successor dying in office, and two IPL franchises – including the most popular – suspended for two years.

The new set-up of captain Virat Kohli and team director Ravi Shastri presided over five wins in the nine Tests India played, including series victories in Sri Lanka, for the first time since 1993-94, and at home to South Africa, who hadn't lost away in nine years. When South Africa then lost to England in early 2016, India found themselves back on top of the Test rankings for the first time since 2011. In the 50-over format, where M. S. Dhoni still held the reins, there was a sterling defence of the World Cup crown, with seven straight wins broken by Australia in the semi-final at Sydney.

INDIA IN 2015

	Played	Won	Lost	Drawn/No result
Tests	9	5	1	3
One-day internationals	23	13	9	1
Twenty20 internationals	5	1	3	1

DECEMBER / JANUARY	4 Tests (a) v Australia	(see *Wisden 2015* page 840)
FEBRUARY	Triangular ODI tournament (in Australia) v Australia and England	(page 273)
MARCH	ICC World Cup (in Australia and New Zealand)	(page 860)
APRIL		
MAY		
JUNE	1 Test and 3 ODIs (a) v Bangladesh	(page 976)
JULY	3 ODIs and 2 T20Is (a) v Zimbabwe	(page 1163)
AUGUST	3 Tests (a) v Sri Lanka	(page 1121)
SEPTEMBER		
OCTOBER / NOVEMBER / DECEMBER	4 Tests, 5 ODIs and 3 T20Is (h) v South Africa	(page 996)

For a review of Indian domestic cricket from the 2014-15 season, see page 1018.

With open arms: Virat Kohli embraces India's new spirit of adventure in Test cricket. South Africa's Hashim Amla is the batsman to fall, at Mohali.

But, in the larger scheme of things, any cricketing excellence was eclipsed by decisions taken by courts, judicial commissions and the board's own working committee. Narayanaswami Srinivasan, the most powerful man in the game for nearly half a decade, was the figure most buffeted by the winds of change. Having been asked to step aside as BCCI president while the courts investigated the spot-fixing scandal of 2013, he had found refuge as ICC chairman. But, in November 2015, after Shashank Manohar's return as BCCI president, and with Anurag Thakur making his presence felt following his election to secretary in March, the board relieved Srinivasan of his ICC role, too. Manohar, a peripheral figure since himself leaving the president's post in 2011, took his place.

That he did so was due to the death of Jagmohan Dalmiya in September. Lalit Modi and Srinivasan may have filled Indian cricket's vault with vast riches, but it had been Dalmiya who installed the safe and, initially, lined it with deposits. Having fallen foul of Sharad Pawar, Modi and cohorts in 2005, he had been on the fringes – until the board turned to him once they were in disarray. He took over as president in March, winning an election nearly a decade after he was shunted aside. Despite poor health and frequent memory lapses, he set about trying to change public perception of the BCCI. The media policy was brought into the 21st century, and officials and selectors abandoned the tradition of behaving like the old Soviet Politburo.

Manohar went even further, suggesting that the Big Three takeover of the ICC, which Srinivasan had masterminded with the help of England and

VIRENDER SEHWAG RETIRES

Test cricket's Robespierre

Tunku Varadarajan

It is no exaggeration to say that Virender Sehwag, of rugged farming stock, from a scruffy town near Delhi, was cricket's first true trendsetter of Indian origin since Ranjitsinhji, a Victorian royal from a scruffy principality in Gujarat.

Ranji, whose gift to cricket was the un-Christian stroke – which liberated batting from the tyranny of the "V" – played his first Test 105 years before "Viru". Sehwag, for his part, redefined opening batsmanship in Tests, turning the role from an engineer who oversees the foundation of a fortress, into a cavalryman who charges deep into enemy territory.

Unlike Ranji, Sehwag's role in history was not immediately apparent. He batted at No. 6 in his first Test, scoring – it's true – a ton against a handy South African attack. But it was not until his sixth match, at Lord's in 2002, that he opened India's batting in the longer game, scoring 84 off 96 balls in an early display of the fireworks that were to light up his 12-year career. When he announced his international retirement in October 2015, it was more than two years since he had played for his country. But he is not easily forgotten.

Sehwag's genius lay in his audacity to bat in Tests the way he batted in limited-overs cricket. When he scored 195 off 233 balls on Boxing Day at the MCG in 2003, he was Test cricket's Robespierre, a ruthless top-order revolutionary. Numbers, famously, tell only part of cricket's story; but, with Sehwag, they do so without narrative inflation. His scoring rate of 82 runs per 100 balls in 104 Tests is second only to the 86 in 27 of Shahid Afridi, who had late-order licence to run amok, and averaged 36 to Sehwag's 49. (By the end of 2015, New Zealand's Tim Southee could boast 86 too, but from down the order.)

Sehwag, remember, scorched his runs against the best fast bowlers, when the ball was new. His strike-rate is the highest for any opener in Tests. Gordon Greenidge, whom many recall as a marauder, managed only 49. Others were quicker than that, but still far slower than Sehwag: Sanath Jayasuriya's strike-rate was 65, Matthew Hayden's and Chris Gayle's 60. Even a middle-order giant such as Viv Richards fell short, with 69 (although he and Greenidge played a few innings where the balls faced are not known).

David Warner, whom Sehwag counselled during their time together at the IPL, is the opener who comes closest, with 76. But, while he draws gasps for his hitting, the boorish Warner has little of the public affection enjoyed by the genial Sehwag, who sledged only with his bat.

The numbers go on: the three highest scores by an Indian in Tests are Sehwag's, including the fastest triple-century in Test history, from 278 deliveries. Of the six fastest-known Test double-hundreds, three are Sehwag's; of the 11 fastest, five. He hit the most fours by a Test opener (1,163), yet he never played for the record books the way his idol Sachin Tendulkar is thought by some to have done.

On 295 at Multan in March 2004, and on the brink of becoming India's first triple-centurion, he clattered Saqlain Mushtaq for six. On 254 at Lahore in January 2006, his opening partnership with Rahul Dravid then worth 410 – three short of the all-time first-wicket record – he flashed and was caught behind. This compound of ruthlessness and insouciance was Sehwag's formula. He turned Test cricket inside out, driving bowlers to despair – yet never once looked at a scorecard with anything other than amusement.

Australia, hadn't been in the best interests of the game. In early 2016, he presided over an ICC meeting which concluded that everything the Big Three stood for needed to be reviewed. That followed the publication of the report on the IPL by a committee headed by R. M. Lodha, a former Chief Justice of India. It recommended sweeping changes to the structures of the Indian game, all aimed at greater transparency and accountability. Altruism was in the air.

One of Manohar's first acts as president had been to confirm the suspension of Chennai Super Kings and Rajasthan Royals from the IPL, based on an earlier suggestion of the Lodha committee. His view – that cricket had been brought into disrepute by individuals who were associated with the franchises and had been accused of corruption – left the BCCI with no room for manoeuvre.

Things weren't as bleak for the national team, who rode on the confidence gained by thumping Pakistan in the World Cup's opening game to reach the last four, bowling out every team they played on the way. In non-World Cup one-day internationals, India won six and lost eight, again showing their preference for the big stage.

In the longest format, the pugnacious attitude favoured by Kohli and Shastri, who had taken charge once Duncan Fletcher's contract wasn't renewed after the World Cup, was tested in Sri Lanka, where they lost at Galle, having dominated for three days. But they showed resolve to swamp their hosts in the next two Tests, the first of which ruined Kumar Sangakkara's farewell. Ravichandran Ashwin, who had worked hard on his consistency, was the star turn, and things were no different back home, where he took 31 wickets at 11 apiece to lead the 3–0 rout of South Africa. He finished 2015 as Test cricket's leading wicket-taker, with 62, including seven five-wicket hauls, four more than anyone else. Nine other Indian bowlers managed 89 between them, in the year left-arm seamer Zaheer Khan announced his retirement from the international game after 610 wickets in all formats.

South Africa had won the Twenty20s 2–0, and completed a 3–2 win in the 50-over games after piling up 438 in the decider in Mumbai. That placid surface, which provoked sarcastic comments from Shastri to the curator, enraged the Indians. It was an unusually dry pitch that greeted South Africa for the First Test in Mohali, where Ravindra Jadeja, back in the side after strong displays in domestic cricket, took five for 21 to set the tone for a series he would finish with 23 wickets at ten each. South Africa lost Dale Steyn to a groin injury in Mohali, and crossed 200 just once in seven innings. In Nagpur, on a pitch the ICC declared poor, they again lost in three days; in Delhi, the India spin tourniquet eventually had its way, after South Africa batted 143.1 overs for 143 in the second innings. The classy Ajinkya Rahane, who scored two hundreds, showed what was possible.

Next day, it was announced that Pune and Rajkot would replace Chennai and Rajasthan in the IPL. Pune picked Dhoni, in many ways the face of the league after playing 153 matches in Chennai's vivid yellow. Four days earlier, it had been announced that Chennai, home to Srinivasan, would not host a single men's game during the World Twenty20 in 2016. The big-ticket matches went to Nagpur (Manohar's fiefdom) and Dharmasala (Thakur's). It was a symbolic way to bookend the most tumultuous of years.

INDIA v SOUTH AFRICA IN 2015-16

REVIEW BY NEIL MANTHORP

Twenty20 internationals (3): India 0, South Africa 2
One-day internationals (5): India 2, South Africa 3
Test matches (4): India 3, South Africa 0

This tour hardly needed hype, but there were some pretty good ingredients nonetheless: revenge, status, and a proud unbeaten record. The former BCCI president Narayanaswami Srinivasan's unilateral decision to slash India's last visit to South Africa, in 2013-14, from a full tour to the bare bones of two Tests and three one-day internationals still left a bitter taste. India were fired up too. Virat Kohli's demonstrative love of Test cricket made a refreshing change from M. S. Dhoni's apparent indifference, and he spoke often in the lead-up about the importance of toppling the best team in the world, and ending South Africa's eight-year record of 15 consecutive unbeaten series away from home, stretching back to 2007 in Pakistan.

And when they did end it, with a victory in the Third Test at Nagpur as emphatic as in the First at Mohali, Kohli could not disguise his anger that so much attention was focused on the pitch, which offered spectacular turn for the spinners from about half an hour after the toss. His emotions understandably clouded his judgment, for the surface demanded scrutiny; that some of it was ill-informed, and based on even stronger emotions, was unfortunate. Kohli grew frustrated, and team director Ravi Shastri stroppy.

The majority of the media, including the Indian contingent, were critical of the ploy of preparing a dry and broken surface, but it was the flurry of social-media sarcasm from former players, notably Australians and Englishmen watching from afar, which set Shastri off. "To hell with five-day Tests," he ranted. The South Africans, meanwhile, stuck to their pre-tour pledge and didn't murmur a word of dissent, even through gritted teeth. But for four days of rain in Bangalore, they knew they could easily have been whitewashed.

India's victories in the First and Third Tests were both achieved inside three days, just like their previous three home Tests, way back in 2013 (two against West Indies, one against Australia). Since 1950, when all Tests have been scheduled for four or more days, no side had previously enjoyed more than three successive three-day home wins. It was no great surprise that India utilised home advantage – most countries do – but they did so to a rare extreme. They also batted, bowled and fielded better than South Africa, a simple fact easily forgotten amid the bluster.

But, rightly or wrongly, there was no semblance of the fair contest between bat and ball (which many irate South Africans and self-proclaimed Test purists seemed to think was enshrined in some constitution). After the Third Test, match referee Jeff Crowe reported the Nagpur pitch as poor, and the BCCI appealed against his verdict. Two weeks later that was rejected by the

Ajay Aggarwal, *Hindustan Times*/Getty Images

In the palm of his hand: Ravichandran Ashwin toyed with South Africa, taking 31 wickets at 11.

ICC, and both the board and the Vidarbha Cricket Association received an official warning.

It left some tricky questions. Do the BCCI have a responsibility to care about anything other than the result? Can India, who were helped considerably by winning all four tosses, win series abroad – particularly in England, Australia and South Africa – with such an approach on home soil? That said, in the final Test at Delhi they showed they could still prevail on more traditional pitches.

Emotional or not, Kohli was right to be frustrated, because there were some outstanding performances from his players. Conditions may have been helpful, but it would be harsh to place an asterisk next to the figures of off-spinner Ravichandran Ashwin (Man of the Series for his 31 wickets at 11) and slow left-armer Ravindra Jadeja (23 at ten). Even Amit Mishra's moderate leg-spin collected seven wickets at 17. The trio accounted for all but eight of the South African wickets claimed by Indian bowlers.

Only four half-centuries were scored in the first three Tests, two of them by A. B. de Villiers, a statistic bandied around by some of the South Africans as justification for their inadequacy. "It's not only us who have struggled," said the captain and coaches, missing the point that cricket isn't about scoring fifties or hundreds, but scoring more runs than your opponents. India tidied that one up anyway, when Ajinkya Rahane made a century in each innings at Delhi. Kohli added 88 in one of the most fluent innings of the series, and became the first captain to lift the new Freedom Trophy, dedicated to Mahatma Gandhi and Nelson Mandela.

It was all a far cry from the high-quality entertainment served up during the preceding limited-overs matches, in which – contrary to predictions – South Africa prevailed in both formats. The 50-over series went down to the last game in Mumbai, where three South Africans smashed centuries in a total of 438, to the undisguised fury of that man Shastri.

SOUTH AFRICAN TOURING PARTY

*H. M. Amla (T/50/20), K. J. Abbott (T/50/20), T. Bavuma (T), F. Behardien (50/20), Q. de Kock (50/20), M. de Lange (T/20), A. B. de Villiers (T/50/20), J-P. Duminy (T/50/20), F. du Plessis (T/50/20), D. Elgar (T/50), S. R. Harmer (T), Imran Tahir (T/50/20), E. Leie (20), D. A. Miller (50/20), J. A. Morkel (20), M. Morkel (T/50), C. H. Morris (50/20), A. M. Phangiso (50), V. D. Philander (T), D. L. Piedt (T), K. Rabada (T/50/20), D. W. Steyn (T/50), S. van Zyl (T), D. J. Vilas (T), K. Zondo (50/20). *Coach:* R. C. Domingo.

Du Plessis captained in the Twenty20 matches, and de Villiers in the one-day internationals. D. Wiese was originally named for the Twenty20s, but broke his hand and was replaced by J. A. Morkel. R. R. Rossouw was in the original squad for the 50-over matches but failed to recover from a foot injury and was replaced by Zondo, who had originally been chosen only for the Twenty20s. Elgar, due to arrive for the Tests, was summoned early after Duminy injured his hand in the third ODI. De Lange, who had been in the Twenty20 squad, was recalled after Steyn suffered a groin injury in the First Test. Philander injured his ankle playing football before the Second, and was replaced by Abbott.

TEST MATCH AVERAGES

INDIA – BATTING AND FIELDING

	T	I	NO	R	HS	100	50	Avge	Ct/St
A. M. Rahane	4	6	1	266	127	2	0	53.20	10
M. Vijay	4	7	1	210	75	0	1	35.00	1
C. A. Pujara	4	6	0	202	77	0	1	33.66	3
V. Kohli	4	6	0	200	88	0	1	33.33	3
R. Ashwin	4	5	1	101	56	0	1	25.25	1
†S. Dhawan	4	7	1	150	45*	0	0	25.00	
†R. A. Jadeja	4	5	0	109	38	0	0	21.80	5
W. P. Saha	4	6	1	83	32	0	0	16.60	5/2
U. T. Yadav	2	3	1	16	10*	0	0	8.00	
R. G. Sharma	2	4	0	26	23	0	0	6.50	1
A. Mishra	2	4	0	25	14	0	0	6.25	0
I. Sharma	3	3	2	1	1*	0	0	1.00	1

Played in two Tests: V. R. Aaron 0, 1*. Played in one Test: S. T. R. Binny did not bat (1 ct).

BOWLING

	Style	O	M	R	W	BB	5I	Avge
R. A. Jadeja	SLA	140.5	56	249	23	5-21	2	10.82
R. Ashwin	OB	164.4	56	345	31	7-66	4	11.12
U. T. Yadav	RF	42	20	60	5	3-9	0	12.00
A. Mishra	LBG	43	5	121	7	3-51	0	17.28

Also bowled: V. R. Aaron (RF) 20–1–72–2; S. T. R. Binny (RFM) 3–2–1–0; S. Dhawan (OB) 3–1–9–0; V. Kohli (RM) 1–1–0–0; C. A. Pujara (LBG) 1–0–2–0; I. Sharma (RFM) 62–27–115–1; M. Vijay (OB) 2–0–2–0.

SOUTH AFRICA – BATTING AND FIELDING

	T	I	NO	R	HS	100	50	Avge	Ct
A. B. de Villiers	4	7	0	258	85	0	2	36.85	4
†D. Elgar	4	7	0	137	38	0	0	19.57	4
H. M. Amla	4	7	0	118	43	0	0	16.85	8
†J-P. Duminy	3	5	0	70	35	0	0	14.00	2
S. R. Harmer	2	4	1	39	13	0	0	13.00	0
†S. van Zyl	3	5	0	56	36	0	0	11.20	0
†M. Morkel	3	5	1	38	22	0	0	9.50	0
F. du Plessis	4	7	0	60	39	0	0	8.57	2
D. J. Vilas	4	7	0	60	15	0	0	8.57	6
†K. Rabada	3	5	3	14	6*	0	0	7.00	0
K. J. Abbott	2	3	0	18	14	0	0	6.00	0
Imran Tahir	4	7	2	21	8	0	0	4.20	1

Played in one Test: T. Bavuma 22, 34; V. D. Philander 3, 1; D. L. Piedt 5, 1; D. W. Steyn 6, 2 (1 ct).

BOWLING

	Style	O	M	R	W	BB	5I	Avge
K. J. Abbott	RFM	52.5	17	105	6	5-40	1	17.50
V. D. Philander	RFM	27	8	61	3	2-38	0	20.33
M. Morkel	RF	78.1	24	186	9	3-19	0	20.66
Imran Tahir	LBG	95	13	299	14	5-38	1	21.35
S. R. Harmer	OB	83.2	11	254	10	4-61	0	25.40
D. Elgar	SLA	43	3	136	5	4-22	0	27.20
D. L. Piedt	OB	56	7	170	4	4-117	0	42.50

Also bowled: J-P. Duminy (OB) 9–0–51–1; K. Rabada (RF) 49–17–111–2; D. W. Steyn (RF) 11–3–30–0; S. van Zyl (RM) 4–1–5–1.

At Delhi (Palam), September 29, 2015 (floodlit). **India A won by eight wickets.** ‡**South Africans 189-3** (20 overs) (A. B. de Villiers 37, F. du Plessis 42 ret hurt, J-P. Duminy 68*); **India A 193-2** (19.4 overs) (M. Vohra 56, M. A. Agarwal 87, S. V. Samson 31*). *Both sides chose from 12 players. A whirlwind innings from J-P. Duminy, who hit six sixes from 32 balls, took the South Africans to a decent score – but an India A side containing only one international (Manish Pandey, who wasn't required to bat) chased well. Manan Vohra put on 119 for the first wicket with Mayank Agarwal, who hit 60 in boundaries from 49 balls, then 20-year-old Sanju Samson ensured the initiative was not surrendered.*

LIMITED-OVERS MATCH REPORTS BY DILEEP PREMACHANDRAN

INDIA v SOUTH AFRICA

First Twenty20 International

At Dharmasala, October 2, 2015 (floodlit). South Africa won by seven wickets. Toss: South Africa. Twenty20 international debut: S. Aravind.

Only five times in Twenty20 internationals had a team chased down 200 or more to win. Now, in the Himalayan foothills of Dharmasala, Duminy – helped by Behardien – did just that, in the process eclipsing Rohit Sharma's wonderful 66-ball 106. India once won the World Twenty20 when the unheralded Joginder Sharma bowled the final over, but there was no such reprise when Sreenath Aravind, a 31-year-old debutant slow left-armer from Bangalore, was given the responsibility to defend ten off the last. Duminy's third-ball six all but settled the issue. He had already grabbed back the initiative – after de Villiers and du Plessis fell in the space of five deliveries – with three sixes in a row in the 16th over, from Patel. It was the sort of late impetus India's innings had lacked, as a relatively modest 41 came from their final five overs. Rohit Sharma and Kohli, who became the quickest to 1,000 runs in the format (from 27 innings, five fewer than Kevin Pietersen and Alex Hales), had imperiously added 138 – an Indian all-wicket record – from 74 balls. But, after both departed in the same Abbott over, the charge never came. Duminy timed his perfectly, eventually hitting seven of the game's 20 sixes, a record for a Twenty20 international in India.

Man of the Match: J-P. Duminy.

India

		B	4/6
1 R. G. Sharma c 7 b 9	106	66	12/5
2 S. Dhawan run out	3	4	0
3 V. Kohli c 4 b 9	43	27	1/3
4 S. K. Raina lbw b 7	14	8	0/2
5 *†M. S. Dhoni not out	20	12	2/1
6 A. T. Rayudu run out	0	1	0
7 A R. Patel not out	2	3	0
L-b 2, w 8, n-b 1	11		

6 overs: 46-1   (20 overs) **199-5**

1/22 2/160 3/162 4/184 5/184

8 Bhuvneshwar Kumar, 9 R. Ashwin, 10 S. Aravind and 11 M. Sharma did not bat.

Abbott 4–0–29–2 (10); Rabada 4–0–32–0 (12); de Lange 4–0–47–0 (7); Morris 4–0–35–0 (4); Imran Tahir 3–0–35–0 (4); Duminy 1–0–8–0 (0).

South Africa

		B	4/6
1 H. M. Amla run out	36	24	5
2 †A. B. de Villiers b 9	51	32	7/1
3 *F. du Plessis b 10	4	5	0
4 J-P. Duminy not out	68	34	1/7
5 F. Behardien not out	32	23	4/1
L-b 5, w 4	9		

6 overs: 67-0   (19.4 overs) **200-3**

1/77 2/93 3/95

6 D. A. Miller, 7 C. H. Morris, 8 K. Rabada, 9 K. J. Abbott, 10 M. de Lange and 11 Imran Tahir did not bat.

Bhuvneshwar Kumar 4–0–40–0 (8); Aravind 3.4–0–44–1 (4); M. Sharma 4–0–40–0 (7); Patel 4–0–45–0 (8); Ashwin 4–0–26–1 (9).

Umpires: V. A. Kulkarni and C. Shamshuddin.   Third umpire: A. K. Chaudhary.
Referee: B. C. Broad.

INDIA v SOUTH AFRICA

Second Twenty20 International

At Cuttack, October 5, 2015 (floodlit). South Africa won by six wickets. Toss: South Africa.

If Dharmasala was disappointing for India, this defeat, which handed the series to South Africa, was abject. On a Cuttack pitch as full of cracks as a shattered mirror, Albie Morkel – with a career-best three for 12 in his 50th Twenty20 international – and Imran Tahir skittled India for 92. An irate crowd hurled plastic bottles on to the pitch, forcing two stoppages, before South Africa eased to victory with 17 balls in hand. Duminy, with an unconquered 30, was once again the calming influence, after Ashwin had dismissed the top three in a tidy spell to become India's leading Twenty20 wicket-taker, with 29. For India, both Kohli and Rohit Sharma were run out, and no one passed 22. In his first international appearance for 18 months, Morkel had Dhoni – formerly his Chennai Super Kings captain – edging behind and, once Tahir's googly did for Raina and Harbhajan Singh, India tumbled to their second-lowest Twenty20 total. The bottles, which far outnumbered India's runs, kept the players off for 51 minutes. But, after the upper stands were cleared, Duminy did the rest.

Man of the Match: J. A. Morkel.

India

	B	4/6
1 R. G. Sharma *run out*	22	24 2
2 S. Dhawan *lbw b 7*	11	12 2
3 V. Kohli *run out*	1	1 0
4 S. K. Raina *c 2 b 11*	22	24 3
5 A. T. Rayudu *b 8*	0	2 0
6 *†M. S. Dhoni *c 1 b 10*	5	8 0
7 A. R. Patel *c 3 b 10*	9	12 0
8 Harbhajan Singh *b 11*	0	1 0
9 R. Ashwin *b 7*	11	15 1
10 Bhuvneshwar Kumar *b 10*	0	2 0
11 M. Sharma *not out*	0	4 0
L-b 1, w 9, n-b 1	11	

6 overs: 35-2　　(17.2 overs)　92

1/28 2/30 3/43 4/45 5/67 6/69 7/69 8/85 9/85

Abbott 3–0–21–0 (11); Imran Tahir 4–0–24–2 (10); Rabada 4–0–18–1 (10); Morris 2.2–0–16–2 (6); Morkel 4–0–12–3 (13).

South Africa

	B	4/6
1 †A. B. de Villiers *b 9*	19	21 2
2 H. M. Amla *c 1 b 9*	2	3 0
3 *F. du Plessis *c 11 b 9*	16	14 2/1
4 J-P. Duminy *not out*	30	39 3
5 F. Behardien *lbw b 7*	11	18 0
6 D. A. Miller *not out*	10	8 0/1
L-b 3, w 5	8	

6 overs: 38-2　　(17.1 overs)　96-4

1/13 2/38 3/49 4/76

7 C. H. Morris, 8 K. Rabada, 9 K. J. Abbott, 10 J. A. Morkel and 11 Imran Tahir did not bat.

Bhuvneshwar Kumar 2–0–13–0 (7); Ashwin 4–0–24–3 (13); Harbhajan Singh 4–0–20–0 (12); M. Sharma 1–0–7–0 (2); Raina 3.1–0–12–0 (10); Patel 3–0–17–1 (6).

Umpires: C. K. Nandan and C. Shamshuddin.　　Third umpire: V. A. Kulkarni.
Referee: B. C. Broad.

INDIA v SOUTH AFRICA

Third Twenty20 International

At Kolkata, October 8, 2015 (floodlit). Abandoned.
Heavy rain the day before the match left the Eden Gardens outfield waterlogged. After three inspections, it was called off at 9.30.
Man of the Series: J-P. Duminy.

INDIA v SOUTH AFRICA

First One-Day International

At Kanpur, October 11, 2015. South Africa won by five runs. Toss: South Africa.
The change in format did not affect Rohit Sharma. Yet again he made a masterful century: 150 in 133 balls, with 13 fours and six sixes. But, yet again, India's lack of hitting depth was exposed as South Africa held on for a five-run win. India had needed 35 from four overs, with seven wickets in hand, when a tired Sharma was caught and bowled by Imran Tahir. Raina followed in the same over, and India were left wanting 11 off the last. Step forward the 20-year-old Kagiso Rabada. He had conceded nine in his previous over, but now induced miscues from Dhoni – unable to reprise his finishing heroics of yore – and Binny, and gave away only five. India, who had been 191 for one, were left to reflect on another botched chase, and a marvellous hundred from de Villiers that ensured the first 300-plus total at Green Park. Having taken a relatively sedate 54 balls over his half-century, de Villiers – who walked in to chants of "AB! AB!" – raced to three figures in a further 19 with his sixth six. India, who lost Ashwin to a side strain in his fifth over, conceded 53 in the last three. De Villiers's day was slightly tarnished when he was fined 40% of his match fee for South Africa's slow over-rate.
Man of the Match: A. B. de Villiers.

South Africa

†Q. de Kock c Raina b Ashwin	29	F. Behardien not out	35
H. M. Amla b Mishra	37	L-b 3, w 5	8
F. du Plessis lbw b Yadav	62		
*A. B. de Villiers not out	104	1/45 (1) 2/104 (2) (5 wkts, 50 overs)	303
D. A. Miller st Dhoni b Mishra	13	3/152 (3) 4/197 (5)	
J-P. Duminy c Dhoni b Yadav	15	5/238 (6) 10 overs: 48-1	

D. W. Steyn, K. Rabada, Imran Tahir and M. Morkel did not bat.

Bhuvneshwar Kumar 10–0–67–0; Yadav 10–0–71–2; Ashwin 4.4–0–14–1; Mishra 10–0–47–2; Binny 8–0–63–0; Raina 7–0–37–0; Kohli 0.2–0–1–0.

India

R. G. Sharma c and b Imran Tahir	150	Bhuvneshwar Kumar not out	1
S. Dhawan lbw b Morkel	23	A. Mishra not out	0
A. M. Rahane c Miller b Behardien	60	L-b 4, w 13	17
V. Kohli c Morkel b Steyn	11		
*†M. S. Dhoni c and b Rabada	31	1/42 (2) 2/191 (3) (7 wkts, 50 overs)	298
S. K. Raina c Duminy b Imran Tahir	3	3/214 (4) 4/269 (1)	
S. T. R. Binny c Amla b Rabada	2	5/273 (6) 6/297 (5) 7/297 (7) 10 overs: 59-1	

R. Ashwin and U. T. Yadav did not bat.

Steyn 10–0–54–1; Rabada 10–0–58–2; Behardien 6–0–38–1; Morkel 10–0–51–1; Duminy 4–0–36–0; Imran Tahir 10–0–57–2.

Umpires: Aleem Dar and V. A. Kulkarni.   Third umpire: C. Shamshuddin.
Referee: B. C. Broad.

INDIA v SOUTH AFRICA

Second One-Day International

At Indore, October 14, 2015 (day/night). India won by 22 runs. Toss: India.

Three days after copping vociferous criticism for his failure to close out the game in Kanpur, Dhoni was a man apart as India levelled the series with a comfortable victory in a low-scoring game. They had been 82 for three when he arrived and, despite Rahane's sprightly half-century, limped to 165 for seven in the 40th over. But Dhoni brought back memories of his halcyon years, finishing with an unbeaten 92 from 86 balls, including four sixes. South Africa were cruising as du Plessis and Duminy added 82 for the third wicket. Once Patel dismissed both in consecutive overs on his way to format-best figures of three for 39, however, the pressure was on de Villiers to take his side home. Instead, he flat-batted Mohit Sharma to short cover, where Kohli took an exceptional catch. As South Africa's slide continued, Behardien fell victim to a catch that never was, wrongly given out caught behind down the leg side off Harbhajan Singh; the umpire, Vineet Kulkarni, had been the subject of an Indian complaint after the previous game. Behind the stumps, the usually phlegmatic Dhoni was an animated as he had ever been. This was his 20th match award in one-day internationals (including one for an Asia XI), but his first since July 2013.

Man of the Match: M. S. Dhoni.

India

R. G. Sharma b Rabada	3	U. T. Yadav c de Kock b Steyn	4
S. Dhawan c Duminy b Morkel	23	M. Sharma not out	0
A. M. Rahane b Imran Tahir	51		
V. Kohli run out	12	L-b 2, w 10, n-b 1	13
*†M. S. Dhoni not out	92		
S. K. Raina c de Kock b Morkel	0	1/3 (1) 2/59 (2) (9 wkts, 50 overs)	247
A. R. Patel lbw b Steyn	13	3/82 (4) 4/102 (3)	
Bhuvneshwar Kumar b Imran Tahir	14	5/104 (6) 6/124 (7) 7/165 (8)	
Harbhajan Singh c de Kock b Steyn	22	8/221 (9) 9/225 (10) 10 overs: 44-1	

Steyn 10–0–49–3; Rabada 10–1–49–1; Morkel 10–0–42–2; Duminy 9–0–59–0; Imran Tahir 10–1–42–2; Behardien 1–0–4–0.

South Africa

H. M. Amla st Dhoni b Patel	17		Imran Tahir c Dhoni b Bhuvneshwar Kumar	9
†Q. de Kock c M. Sharma b Harbhajan Singh	34		M. Morkel c Raina b Bhuvneshwar Kumar	4
F. du Plessis c Kohli b Patel	51			
J-P. Duminy lbw b Patel	36		L-b 3, w 2	5
*A. B. de Villiers c Kohli b M. Sharma	19			
D. A. Miller c Dhoni b Bhuvneshwar Kumar	0		1/40 (1) 2/52 (2)	(43.4 overs) 225
F. Behardien b Dhoni b Harbhajan Singh	18		3/134 (4) 4/141 (3) 5/142 (6)	
D. W. Steyn c Kohli b Yadav	13		6/167 (5) 7/186 (8) 8/200 (7)	
K. Rabada not out	19		9/221 (10) 10/225 (11)	10 overs: 56-2

Bhuvneshwar Kumar 8.4–0–41–3; Yadav 8–0–52–1; Harbhajan Singh 10–0–51–2; Patel 10–0–39–3; M. Sharma 5–0–21–1; Raina 2–0–18–0.

Umpires: Aleem Dar and V. A. Kulkarni. Third umpire: C. K. Nandan.

Referee: B. C. Broad.

INDIA v SOUTH AFRICA

Third One-Day International

At Rajkot, October 18, 2015 (day/night). South Africa won by 18 runs. Toss: South Africa.

For the third game in succession, the chasing team got themselves into a good position, only for a middle-order fumble to hand victory to the opposition. De Kock's fourth one-day century against India, and his third-wicket partnership of 118 with du Plessis – caught off a Mohit Sharma no-ball on 16 en route to a fluent 60 off 63 balls – had given South Africa impetus, though India's spinners kept them to 270. Hostile and accurate short-pitched bowling from Morne Morkel once again exposed Indian vulnerabilities, draining the final overs of any real tension. Kohli, restored to No. 3, made 77, and Dhoni 47, but neither looked especially fluent, eating up 160 deliveries between them. South Africa's pace bowlers aimed back of a length to great effect, and the required rate ballooned. Rohit Sharma had made an assured 65 but, with Raina's wretched run continuing, there was no lower-order heft to get India across the line once Morkel – who finished with four for 39 – prised out Dhoni, Kohli and Rahane in his final spell. As at Indore, spectators created an impromptu light show, turning on the torches on their mobile phones during the eighth over of India's innings to create a scene that was more rock concert than run-chase.

Man of the Match: M. Morkel.

South Africa

†Q. de Kock run out	103		D. W. Steyn run out	12
D. A. Miller c Rahane b Harbhajan Singh	33		K. Rabada not out	0
H. M. Amla st Dhoni b Mishra	5			
F. du Plessis c Bhuvneshwar Kumar b M. Sharma	60		W 5, n-b 1	6
*A. B. de Villiers lbw b Patel	4		1/72 (2) 2/87 (3)	(7 wkts, 50 overs) 270
J-P. Duminy c Raina b M. Sharma	14		3/205 (4) 4/210 (1)	
F. Behardien not out	33		5/210 (5) 6/241 (6) 7/264 (8)	10 overs: 59-0

Imran Tahir and M. Morkel did not bat.

Bhuvneshwar Kumar 10–1–65–0; M. Sharma 9–0–62–2; Harbhajan Singh 10–0–41–1; Mishra 10–0–38–1; Patel 9–0–51–1; Raina 2–0–13–0.

India

R. G. Sharma c and b Duminy	65	Harbhajan Singh not out	20
S. Dhawan c de Villiers b Morkel	13		
V. Kohli c Miller b Morkel	77	B 2, l-b 1, w 8	11
*†M. S. Dhoni c Steyn b Morkel	47		
S. K. Raina c Miller b Imran Tahir	0	1/41 (2) 2/113 (1) (6 wkts, 50 overs)	252
A. M. Rahane c Miller b Morkel	4	3/193 (4) 4/206 (5)	
A. R. Patel not out	15	5/216 (3) 6/216 (6) 10 overs: 40-0	

Bhuvneshwar Kumar, A. Mishra and M. Sharma did not bat.

Steyn 10–0–65–0; Rabada 10–0–39–0; Morkel 10–1–39–4; Duminy 8–0–46–1; Imran Tahir 10–0–51–1; Behardien 2–0–9–0.

Umpires: Aleem Dar and C. Shamsuddin.   Third umpire: C. K. Nandan.
Referee: B. C. Broad.

INDIA v SOUTH AFRICA

Fourth One-Day international

At Chennai, October 22, 2015 (day/night). India won by 35 runs. Toss: India.
This was a tale of two centuries, as Kohli's 140-ball 138 outdid de Villiers's 107-ball 112. South Africa, who needed an even 300 to clinch the series with a game to go, couldn't manage a partnership more sizeable than 56. With India's three-pronged spin attack dictating terms, not even de Villiers could change their fate. Among his team-mates, only de Kock went past 22 and, with the asking-rate soaring, de Villiers finally edged a pull off Bhuvneshwar Kumar to Dhoni in the 45th over. His 22nd one-day international hundred was a South African record, surpassing Amla and Herschelle Gibbs; de Villiers also overtook Gibbs's tally of 8,094, leaving only Jacques Kallis (11,550) ahead. Kohli, whose century was his 23rd, had enjoyed the support that de Villiers lacked: Rahane helped him add 104 for the third wicket, and Raina – after three runs in three innings – made a 52-ball 53 in a partnership worth 127. Kohli struck five sixes, scampered between the wickets, and batted from the fifth over until the 49th, when he was claimed by a combination of cramp and Rabada. India managed just 29 for four in the last five overs but, once South Africa slid to 88 for four, even de Villiers's magic was inadequate.
Man of the Match: V. Kohli.

India

R. G. Sharma c du Plessis b Morris	21	Bhuvneshwar Kumar run out	0
S. Dhawan c de Kock b Rabada	7		
V. Kohli c de Kock b Rabada	138	L-b 3, w 12, n-b 1	16
A. M. Rahane c de Kock b Steyn	45		
S. K. Raina c de Villiers b Steyn	53	1/28 (1) 2/35 (2) (8 wkts, 50 overs)	299
*†M. S. Dhoni c de Villiers b Steyn	15	3/139 (4) 4/266 (5)	
Harbhajan Singh b Rabada	0	5/291 (3) 6/291 (7)	
A. R. Patel not out	4	7/299 (6) 8/299 (9) 10 overs: 43-2	

A. Mishra and M. Sharma did not bat.

Steyn 10–0–61–3; Rabada 10–0–54–3; Morris 9–0–55–1; Phangiso 9–0–51–0; Imran Tahir 9–0–58–0; Behardien 3–0–17–0.

South Africa

†Q. de Kock c Rahane b Harbhajan Singh ..	43
H. M. Amla c Dhawan b M. Sharma......	7
F. du Plessis c Dhoni b Patel...........	17
*A. B. de Villiers c Dhoni	
b Bhuvneshwar Kumar.	112
D. A. Miller lbw b Harbhajan Singh......	6
F. Behardien lbw b Mishra.............	22
C. H. Morris run out.................	9
A. M. Phangiso c Patel	
b Bhuvneshwar Kumar.	20

D. W. Steyn c Rahane	
b Bhuvneshwar Kumar.	6
K. Rabada not out....................	8
Imran Tahir not out..................	4
L-b 3, w 5, n-b 2	10

1/36 (2) 2/67 (1)   (9 wkts, 50 overs) 264
3/79 (3) 4/88 (5)
5/144 (6) 6/185 (7) 7/233 (4)
8/250 (8) 9/250 (9)   10 overs: 63-1

Bhuvneshwar Kumar 10–0–68–3; M. Sharma 10–0–48–1; Harbhajan Singh 10–0–50–2; Patel 10–0–40–1; Mishra 10–1–55–1.

Umpires: S. Ravi and C. Shamshuddin.   Third umpire: A. K. Chaudhary.
Referee: B. C. Broad.

INDIA v SOUTH AFRICA

Fifth One-Day International

At Mumbai (Wankhede), October 25, 2015 (day/night). South Africa won by 214 runs. Toss: South Africa.

By the time de Villiers had scored his third century of the series, from just 57 deliveries, it was as good as over. De Kock had already helped himself to a 78-ball hundred, his fifth against India in only nine innings, and du Plessis followed suit, smashing 133 from 115 before retiring with cramp. The de Villiers assault was the final indignity for an Indian attack on a placid Wankhede Stadium pitch; Bhuvneshwar Kumar leaked 106, second only to Australian Mick Lewis's 113, on the last occasion South Africa made 438, at Johannesburg in March 2006. This, then, became the joint-third-highest total in one-day internationals, and the most conceded by India. The tourists also equalled their own record, set nine months earlier against West Indies at Johannesburg, of three batsmen making centuries in the same innings (de Villiers had reached three figures that day too). In all, 169 runs came from the last 12 overs, as de Villiers finished with 11 sixes and South Africa with 20 (only New Zealand, with 22 against West Indies at Queenstown in 2013-14, had managed more in an ODI). For a while, as Dhawan stroked a run-a-ball 60, and Rahane Catherine-wheeled his way to 87 from 58, India threatened to make a match of it. But Rabada made key incisions, and Steyn saw off Rahane to seal South Africa's biggest win over India in terms of runs (previously 157 at Durban in 2006-07). India's support staff made up for the lack of fight by getting into a war of words with the curator, the former Test opener Sudhir Naik. The team's think tank had asked for a pitch that would take sharp turn but, once South Africa's batsmen had enjoyed their romp, team director Ravi Shastri was alleged to have said: "Well done, Sudhir, very good wicket." The sarcasm was unmistakable, though he insisted there had been no abuse. That was the lot of his poor bowlers, as South Africa claimed the series 3–2.

Man of the Match: Q. de Kock.   *Man of the Series:* A. B. de Villiers.

South Africa

†Q. de Kock c Kohli b Raina.............	109
H. M. Amla c Dhoni b M. Sharma	23
F. du Plessis retired hurt	133
*A. B. de Villiers c Dhoni	
b Bhuvneshwar Kumar.	119
D. A. Miller not out...................	22

F. Behardien c Raina b Harbhajan Singh ..	16
D. Elgar not out.....................	5
L-b 2, w 9	11

1/33 (2) 2/187 (1)   (4 wkts, 50 overs) 438
3/398 (4) 4/430 (6)   10 overs: 73-1

K. Rabada, D. W. Steyn, K. J. Abbott and Imran Tahir did not bat.

Du Plessis retired hurt at 351-2.

Bhuvneshwar Kumar 10–0–106–1; M. Sharma 7–0–84–1; Harbhajan Singh 10–0–70–1; Patel 8–0–65–0; Mishra 10–0–78–0; Raina 3–0–19–1; Kohli 2–0–14–0.

India

R. G. Sharma c Imran Tahir b Abbott	16	Bhuvneshwar Kumar c Miller b Imran Tahir	1
S. Dhawan c Amla b Rabada	60	A. Mishra lbw b Rabada	4
V. Kohli c de Kock b Rabada	7	M. Sharma not out	0
A. M. Rahane c Behardien b Steyn	87	L-b 1, w 4	5
S. K. Raina b Rabada	12		
*†M. S. Dhoni b Imran Tahir	27	1/22 (1) 2/44 (3) 3/156 (2) (36 overs)	224
A. R. Patel c Miller b Steyn	5	4/172 (5) 5/185 (4) 6/195 (7)	
Harbhajan Singh c sub (C. H. Morris)		7/201 (8) 8/210 (9) 9/219 (6)	
b Steyn	0	10/224 (10) 10 overs: 51-2	

Steyn 7–0–38–3; Rabada 7–0–41–4; Abbott 7–0–39–1; Behardien 8–0–55–0; Imran Tahir 7–1–50–2.

Umpires: A. K. Chaudhary and H. D. P. K. Dharmasena.   Third umpire: V. A. Kulkarni.
Referee: B. C. Broad.

At Mumbai (Brabourne), October 30–31, 2015. **Drawn. ‡Indian Board President's XI 296** (78.5 overs) (K. L. Rahul 72, N. V. Ojha 52; D. W. Steyn 43; S. R. Harmer 3-41) **and 92-0** (30 overs); **South Africans 302** (69.2 overs) (A. B. de Villiers 112, D. J. Vilas 54; S. N. Thakur 4-70). *The President's XI chose from 13 players, the South Africans from 14. Both sides recovered from poor starts: the President's XI were 27-3 before Lokesh Rahul, who hit 13 fours, added 105 with Karun Nair (44). In turn, the South Africans slipped to 57-5 before de Villiers made his third century in three innings, and his fourth of the tour. He put on 115 with Dane Vilas; later Dale Steyn slapped 37 from 28 balls to give his side a narrow lead.*

INDIA v SOUTH AFRICA

First Test Match

TELFORD VICE

At Mohali, November 5–7, 2015. India won by 108 runs. Toss: India. Test debut: K. Rabada.

India won through a masterful display of spin by Ashwin, who opened the bowling in both innings and returned match figures of nine for 90. It was also a confident start for Kohli, whose first home Test as India's captain began when he won the toss on his 27th birthday. Who needs Bollywood when cricket does the job?

South Africa had effectively lost four days before a ball was even bowled, when du Plessis admitted: "We are expecting the worst; we are expecting the ball to spin on day one." It did – and on days two and three as well. And that was that: game over, in less time than the South Africans (whose previous three-day defeat had come seven years earlier, at Kanpur) had fretted about being beaten. Du Plessis managed nought and one.

Kohli also got drawn into the pitch-bitching, but remained on the front foot. "Whenever we travel abroad there's never been any focus on the pitch," he said. "The focus has always been how we are going to struggle against their bowlers, or how our bowlers are going to be hit around the park. So I don't really care what's been said or written."

But the words of India's team director Ravi Shastri to the Mumbai groundsman, after South Africa had clinched the one-day series on a surface that was more Wanderers than Wankhede, were crucial. Though a complaint of verbal abuse was laid against him – and later withdrawn – the message had been delivered. Mohali was not a dangerous pitch, but it did take batting and seam bowling out of the equation to a degree that could be considered unfair. Batsmen became butterflies awaiting the piercing of the pin.

"There were quite a few dismissals from both teams because of a lack of turn rather than an excess," said Amla. "Sometimes those are the more difficult pitches to play on." He and du Plessis, South Africa's most careful batsmen, proved that point by offering no stroke at – and being bowled by – deliveries that did not venture far off the straight. It was clear from the early exchanges that the team whose batsmen were less timid and clumsy would hold the advantage. And that team was India.

Little was pretty about their first innings, and even less about Elgar's left-arm spin. After winning the toss, India were bowled out for 201 an hour after tea, with Elgar – who had taken only six wickets in his previous 17 Tests – picking up four for 22. In an innings that produced three ducks and a mere single for Kohli, who drove the debutant fast bowler Kagiso Rabada to cover, Vijay alone looked like he knew what he was doing, with a flinty, composed 75. Elgar didn't look like he knew what he was doing beyond going through the motions. But, given the pitch, that did not matter. He celebrated his successes with a downward glance.

By stumps, South Africa had slipped to 28 for two, and before tea next day they had been bowled out, 17 behind. That they managed to venture that close was because Elgar, Amla and de Villiers dug in for nearly seven hours between them. No one else made it into double figures, as the batsmen tried to shake off the shackles by playing strokes too big for the occasion. Predictably, they failed, allowing Ashwin to rip and roar his way to five for 51. Referring to his dismissal of Elgar, who ran out of grit and carved a carpenter's cut to backward point, Ashwin said: "I made a point of telling him it's not Johannesburg, unfortunately. I saw it coming, I knew he was going to play that shot."

Eighteen of the 22 wickets that had fallen by the close on the second day – with India, led by Pujara, 142 ahead – belonged to spinners, though Steyn had been ruled out of bowling in the second innings (and, it transpired, the rest of the series) because of a groin strain. Next day India lost their last eight for 39 inside 20 overs as leg-spinner Imran Tahir and off-spinner Harmer finished with four each, taking to 15 the number of wickets claimed by South Africa's slow bowlers – their most in a Test since 1952-53.

Even so, a target of 218 looked beyond them: among visiting sides only West Indies, at Delhi in 1987-88, had chased more to win a Test in India. Philander opened with Elgar, which was more of a surprise than a five-wicket haul for Jadeja's brisk left-arm spin, less flashy than Ashwin but more accurate. His match return of eight for 76 was a Test-best. South Africa's second defeat in 22 away Tests was confirmed an hour after tea, when Tahir was smacked flush on the boot in front of off stump by Jadeja. Like many of his team-mates throughout the game, he knew little about the delivery.

Man of the Match: R. A. Jadeja.

Close of play: first day, South Africa 28-2 (Elgar 13, Amla 9); second day, India 125-2 (Pujara 63, Kohli 11).

India

M. Vijay lbw b Harmer	75	– c sub (T. Bavuma) b Imran Tahir....	47
S. Dhawan c Amla b Philander	0	– c de Villiers b Philander.	0
C. A. Pujara lbw b Elgar	31	– c Amla b Imran Tahir.	77
*V. Kohli c Elgar b Rabada	1	– c Vilas b van Zyl	29
A. M. Rahane c Amla b Elgar	15	– c sub (T. Bavuma) b Harmer	2
†W. P. Saha c Amla b Elgar.	0	– c Vilas b Imran Tahir.	20
R. A. Jadeja lbw b Philander	38	– lbw b Harmer	8
A. Mishra c Steyn b Elgar	6	– c du Plessis b Harmer.	2
R. Ashwin not out	20	– c Amla b Imran Tahir.	3
U. T. Yadav b Imran Tahir.	5	– b Harmer	1
V. R. Aaron b Imran Tahir.	0	– not out	1
B 6, l-b 1, n-b 3	10	B 9, l-b 1	10

1/0 (2) 2/63 (3) 3/65 (4)　　　　(68 overs) 201　　1/9 (2) 2/95 (1)　　　　(75.3 overs) 200
4/102 (5) 5/102 (6) 6/140 (1)　　　　　　　　　　　3/161 (4) 4/164 (3)
7/154 (8) 8/196 (7) 9/201 (10) 10/201 (11)　　　5/164 (5) 6/178 (7) 7/182 (8)
　　　　　　　　　　　　　　　　　　　　　　　　　8/185 (9) 9/188 (10) 10/200 (6)

Steyn 11–3–30–0; Philander 15–5–38–2; Harmer 14–1–51–1; Rabada 10–0–30–1; Elgar 8–1–22–4; Imran Tahir 10–3–23–2. *Second innings*—Philander 12–3–23–1; Harmer 24–5–61–4; Elgar 7–1–34–0; Imran Tahir 16.3–1–48–4; Rabada 12–7–19–0; van Zyl 4–1–5–1.

South Africa

D. Elgar c Jadeja b Ashwin	37	– c Kohli b Aaron	16
S. van Zyl lbw b Ashwin	5	– (6) c Rahane b Ashwin	36
F. du Plessis b Jadeja	0	– c Rahane b Ashwin	1
*H. M. Amla st Saha b Ashwin	43	– b Jadeja	0
A. B. de Villiers b Mishra	63	– b Mishra	16
†D. J. Vilas c Jadeja b Ashwin	1	– (7) b Jadeja	7
V. D. Philander c Rahane b Jadeja	3	– (2) lbw b Jadeja	1
S. R. Harmer lbw b Mishra	7	– c Rahane b Jadeja	11
D. W. Steyn st Saha b Jadeja	6	– c Vijay b Ashwin	2
K. Rabada not out	1	– not out	1
Imran Tahir c Pujara b Ashwin	4	– lbw b Jadeja	4
B 6, l-b 7, n-b 1	14	B 8, l-b 5, w 1	14

1/9 (2) 2/9 (3) 3/85 (1)   (68 overs) 184   1/8 (2) 2/9 (3)   (39.5 overs) 109
4/105 (4) 5/107 (6) 6/136 (7)   3/10 (4) 4/32 (5)
7/170 (8) 8/179 (9) 9/179 (5) 10/184 (11)   5/45 (1) 6/60 (7) 7/102 (8)
                                             8/102 (6) 9/105 (9) 10/109 (11)

Ashwin 24–5–51–5; Yadav 6–1–12–0; Aaron 8–1–18–0; Jadeja 18–0–55–3; Mishra 12–3–35–2. *Second innings*—Ashwin 14–5–39–3; Jadeja 11.5–4–21–5; Mishra 8–0–26–1; Aaron 3–0–3–1; Yadav 3–0–7–0.

Umpires: H. D. P. K. Dharmasena and R. A. Kettleborough.   Third umpire: V. A. Kulkarni.
Referee: J. J. Crowe.

INDIA v SOUTH AFRICA

Second Test Match

Neil Manthorp

At Bangalore, November 14–18, 2015. Drawn. Toss: India.

Only a single day's play was possible before a depressing, grey drizzle descended – and refused to abate. The match therefore represented no more than a couple of pieces in the series jigsaw, but those inclined towards forensic investigation might conclude they were significant. Wet weather prevented the groundsman fulfilling his pre-match instructions, even though a marquee was erected over the square to keep it as dry as possible. Kohli had expected far more seam movement after choosing to bowl first, and South Africa found themselves on a trustworthy pitch not dissimilar, in terms of pace and bounce, to many of their own.

But, de Villiers apart, they made a mess of things. Then, for four days, the scoreboard stood unmoved as a reminder of their inadequacy. Ashwin and Jadeja dominated the batsmen, taking four wickets apiece. Van Zyl left a straight one, and du Plessis was smartly caught at short leg off an inside edge. Amla was cleaned up by a beauty from Aaron – a rare wicket for an Indian seamer – then Elgar was bowled trying an aggressive sweep in the first over after lunch, after battling through the morning session.

In a peculiar twist of logistical fate, de Villiers was playing his 100th Test in the city and stadium where his IPL exploits for the Royal Challengers have made him not just a household name, but as revered and cheered as any Indian. He was in glorious touch, too, and would surely have celebrated the occasion with a century had he received a semblance of meaningful support. Instead he was left with the tail, and finally fell for 85, via the faintest of touches off the glove, after a solo effort to rescue an embarrassing total. The ease with which Dhawan and Vijay cruised to 80 was equally embarrassing for South Africa – but happy confirmation for India that they were in control of the series.

Close of play: first day, India 80-0 (Vijay 28, Dhawan 45); second day, no play; third day, no play; fourth day, no play.

South Africa

S. van Zyl lbw b Ashwin	10		K. Rabada c Pujara b Jadeja		0
D. Elgar b Jadeja	38		M. Morkel c Binny b Ashwin		22
F. du Plessis c Pujara b Ashwin	0		Imran Tahir not out		0
*H. M. Amla b Aaron	7		L-b 2, n-b 6		8
A. B. de Villiers c Saha b Jadeja	85				
J-P. Duminy c Rahane b Ashwin	15		1/15 (1) 2/15 (3) 3/45 (4) (59 overs)		214
†D. J. Vilas c and b Jadeja	15		4/78 (2) 5/120 (6) 6/159 (7)		
K. J. Abbott run out	14		7/177 (5) 8/177 (9) 9/214 (10) 10/214 (8)		

Sharma 13–3–40–0; Binny 3–2–1–0; Ashwin 18–2–70–4; Aaron 9–0–51–1; Jadeja 16–2–50–4.

India

M. Vijay not out	28
S. Dhawan not out	45
B 4, n-b 3	7

(no wkt, 22 overs)   80

C. A. Pujara, *V. Kohli, A. M. Rahane, †W. P. Saha, R. A. Jadeja, S. T. R. Binny, R. Ashwin, V. R. Aaron and I. Sharma did not bat.

Morkel 7–1–23–0; Abbott 6–1–18–0; Rabada 5–1–17–0; Duminy 2–0–9–0; Imran Tahir 2–0–9–0.

Umpires: I. J. Gould and R. A. Kettleborough.   Third umpire: C. Shamshuddin.
Referee: J. J. Crowe.

INDIA v SOUTH AFRICA

Third Test Match

NEIL MANTHORP

At Nagpur, November 25–27, 2015. India won by 124 runs. Toss: India.

A pitch which looked and behaved as though it had already hosted a week's play was a spinners' jackpot. Scores of 20 or 30 seemed to be worth double, and it was India's batsmen who were able to produce most of those. South Africa, on the other hand, appeared clueless: when they cascaded to 12 for five early on the second day, the contest was virtually over. Duminy's 35 from 65 balls was one of his most skilled innings, but even that swelled the total only to 79 – South Africa's lowest since 1956-57, when they made 72 against England at both Johannesburg and Cape Town.

Vijay had made best use of the game's first hour, when South Africa used pace from both ends for the first 40 minutes before introducing Harmer's gentle off-spin. Vijay knew what was coming, and drove the seamers at every opportunity. Occasionally he was a little loose, but every run was precious. The openers put on 50 and, although India later slipped to 125 for six, Saha and Jadeja dug in.

Saha was the beggar, taking anything on offer, pickpocketing singles and fighting for survival for 145 minutes and 32 runs. Jadeja chanced his arm, and smacked six fours in his 73-minute 34. It was already apparent to the South Africans that they were in trouble; body language betrayed their concern.

Every scoring opportunity felt as if it could affect the outcome of the match, and the South African bowlers provided too many. By contrast, Ashwin and Jadeja were so accurate that batsmen were limited to two or three shots – but into areas where there was an abundance of fielders, especially in the second innings, during which South Africa mostly abandoned thoughts of run-scoring in favour of survival and pride-salvation.

India's lead of 136 had given them control, and useful contributions from Dhawan and Pujara took the game emphatically beyond South Africa's reach. Imran Tahir celebrated his second-innings five-for in typically ebullient style with a kiss of the pitch, but the reality was different: it was relatively meaningless, as the advantage had tiptoed past 300. It was 218 before Amla even brought Tahir on, and his wickets came from catches in the deep and a slashed long-hop to backward point, while the unfortunate Saha bottom-edged a cut which bounced to slip via the boot of wicketkeeper Vilas.

SLOW TORTURE

Most wickets in a Test by Indian spinners:

20	v England at Madras	1972-73		19	v Australia at Delhi	1969-70
20	v New Zealand at Auckland	1975-76		19	v England at Calcutta	1972-73
20	v Australia at Chennai	2012-13		19	v England at Bangalore	1976-77
20	**v South Africa at Nagpur**	**2015-16**		19	v West Indies at Madras	1987-88
19	v Australia at Kanpur	1959-60		**19**	**v South Africa at Mohali**	**2015-16**

South Africa's first innings had lasted only 33.1 overs, but they made a mess of the argument that the pitch was unplayable by surviving almost 90 in their second, though scoring at little more than two an over. Not even the intoxicated or insane – never mind the merely optimistic – pretended there was any chance of overhauling the target of 310, despite three days in which to do it.

Amla batted with a suitable grimness, as did du Plessis, but Amla's captaincy betrayed the pressure he was under. In both innings he sent the hapless Tahir out as nightwatchman in his stead, and both times had to come out and face the final few deliveries anyway, as Tahir was quickly tossed aside by the spinners.

Ashwin thrived on the extra workload which South Africa's second-innings application afforded him, enjoying the opportunity to set batsmen up with his enchanting carrom ball and top-spinner, instead of seeing them merely surrender to his off-breaks. He finished with a career-best seven for 66, the best by an Indian against South Africa. Also in their element were Jadeja and Mishra, whose leg-spin might have been third in the pecking order but would almost certainly have yielded equally impressive results had it been promoted.

Kohli's annoyance that a thumping victory and famous series win were put down to the pitch – which was later censured by the ICC – was understandable, but naive. Never mind the players: there were 40-year veterans of the Indian game who could not recall such a surface. But Kohli was right in one respect: he had been prepared to gamble, with the backing of his players, and achieved a resounding success. And the victory was down to the superior skills of his team, not the toss of a coin or the broken soil.

Man of the Match: R. Ashwin.

Close of play: first day, South Africa 11-2 (Elgar 7, Amla 0); second day, South Africa 32-2 (Elgar 10, Amla 3).

India

M. Vijay lbw b Morkel	40	– c Amla b Morkel	5
S. Dhawan c and b Elgar	12	– c Vilas b Imran Tahir	39
C. A. Pujara lbw b Harmer	21	– b Duminy	31
*V. Kohli c Vilas b Morkel	22	– c du Plessis b Imran Tahir	16
A. M. Rahane b Morkel	13	– c Duminy b Imran Tahir	9
R. G. Sharma c de Villiers b Harmer	2	– c Elgar b Morkel	23
†W. P. Saha c Duminy b Harmer	32	– c Amla b Imran Tahir	7
R. A. Jadeja b Rabada	34	– b Harmer	5
R. Ashwin b Imran Tahir	15	– lbw b Morkel	7
A. Mishra lbw b Harmer	3	– b Imran Tahir	14
I. Sharma not out	0	– not out	1
B 15, l-b 3, w 2, n-b 1	21	B 8, l-b 5, n-b 3	16

1/50 (2) 2/69 (1) 3/94 (3) (78.2 overs) 215
4/115 (5) 5/116 (4) 6/125 (6)
7/173 (8) 8/201 (7) 9/215 (9) 10/215 (10)

1/8 (1) 2/52 (3) (46.3 overs) 173
3/97 (2) 4/102 (4)
5/108 (5) 6/122 (7) 7/128 (8)
8/150 (9) 9/171 (6) 10/173 (10)

Morkel 16.1–7–35–3; Rabada 17–8–30–1; Harmer 27.2–2–78–4; Elgar 4–0–7–1; Imran Tahir 12.5–1–41–1; Duminy 1–0–6–0. *Second innings*—Morkel 10–5–19–3; Harmer 18–3–64–1; Rabada 5–1–15–0; Duminy 2–0–24–1; Imran Tahir 11.3–2–38–5.

South Africa

D. Elgar b Ashwin	7	– lbw b Ashwin	18
S. van Zyl c Rahane b Ashwin	0	– c R. G. Sharma b Ashwin	5
Imran Tahir b Jadeja	4	– lbw b Mishra	8
*H. M. Amla c Rahane b Ashwin	1	– c Kohli b Mishra	39
A. B. de Villiers c and b Jadeja	0	– lbw b Ashwin	9
F. du Plessis b Jadeja	10	– b Mishra	39
J-P. Duminy lbw b Mishra	35	– lbw b Mishra	19
†D. J. Vilas b Jadeja	13	– c Saha b Ashwin	12
S. R. Harmer b Ashwin	13	– not out	8
K. Rabada not out	6	– c Kohli b Ashwin	6
M. Morkel c and b Ashwin	1	– b Ashwin	4
L-b 1	1	B 9, l-b 5, n-b 4	18

1/4 (2) 2/9 (3) 3/11 (1) (33.1 overs) 79
4/12 (4) 5/12 (5) 6/35 (6)
7/47 (8) 8/66 (9) 9/76 (7) 10/79 (11)

1/17 (2) 2/29 (3) (89.5 overs) 185
3/40 (1) 4/58 (5)
5/130 (4) 6/135 (6) 7/164 (7)
8/167 (8) 9/177 (10) 10/185 (11)

I. Sharma 2–1–4–0; Ashwin 16.1–6–32–5; Jadeja 12–3–33–4; Mishra 3–0–9–1. *Second innings*—I. Sharma 15–6–20–0; Ashwin 29.5–7–66–7; Jadeja 25–12–34–0; Mishra 20–2–51–3.

Umpires: I. J. Gould and B. N. J. Oxenford. Third umpire: A. K. Chaudhary.
Referee: J. J. Crowe.

INDIA v SOUTH AFRICA

Fourth Test Match

NEIL MANTHORP

At Delhi, December 3–7, 2015. India won by 337 runs. Toss: India.

South Africa sensed a real chance of consolation, if not redemption, when the off-spinner Dane Piedt, in his first Test of the series, bowled with the precision and patience of India's slow men to claim four wickets before tea on the first day. By then – with Abbott, also restored to the side, helping out – India were 139 for six. But, without the injured Dale Steyn to attack the tail, India were slowly able to rebuild. Rahane received proactive support from Jadeja and Ashwin, who was dropped by Amla at slip on 14 en route to a half-century. Ashwin hung around while 136 were added, and India's eventual total looked about that many above par on a track which, while less spiteful than Mohali and Nagpur, also helped the spinners.

Rahane's delightful century – the first of the series – was memorable for his ability to deflate any pressure the South Africans were able to apply. His four sixes were not the result of bad deliveries, but a desire to assert his authority when necessary. Each time the momentum of the game tilted back towards India.

Jadeja's unrelenting accuracy and unreadable changes of pace then earned him five wickets, but Yadav and Ashwin might easily have collected more than two apiece on another day, such was South Africa's disarray. Kohli waived the follow-on, despite a lead

---

DOUBLING UP

Two centuries in a Test for India:

V. S. Hazare (116 and 145)	v Australia at Adelaide	1947-48
S. M. Gavaskar (124 and 220)	v West Indies at Port-of-Spain	1970-71
S. M. Gavaskar (111 and 137)	v Pakistan at Karachi.	1978-79
S. M. Gavaskar (107 and 182*)	v West Indies at Calcutta	1978-79
R. Dravid (190 and 103*)	v New Zealand at Hamilton	1999-99
R. Dravid (110 and 135)	v Pakistan at Kolkata	2004-05
V. Kohli (115 and 141)	v Australia at Adelaide	2014-15
A. M. Rahane (127 and 100*)	**v South Africa at Delhi**	**2015-16**

---

of 213, and when his side then slipped to 57 for four some local pessimists – and others of a delusional disposition – contemplated a twist. It could have been worse: two overs later Kohli was given out caught behind, but Imran Tahir had overstepped. Replays subsequently confirmed there was no contact between bat and ball, which may also explain why Kohli escaped sanction for an obvious display of dissent.

His subsequent path towards an apparently inevitable hundred was cut short at 88 by an Abbott inswinger, but Kohli allowed Rahane to complete a memorable Test with a second century before a declaration which represented the balance of the series: chasing 481 with around 160 overs left, South Africa had the option neither of victory nor a draw.

Still, they made an admirable effort to stave off defeat, taking bloody-mindedness to another level. Dull Test cricket in the 1950s and '60s was boring because it moved at a glacial pace when there was actually something to play for. This was entirely different, and became utterly absorbing in a macabre yet impressive way. On the fourth evening, with South Africa 72 for two after 72 overs, Yadav was almost at a loss for words: "Defending is one thing, but when they are blocking half-volleys and full tosses, that is something we have never seen before."

The innings contained the three slowest partnerships in Test history of over 200 balls. Bavuma, promoted to open in only his fifth Test, rattled along with 34 from 117 balls (he even hit a six). But his stand of 44 with Amla took 38 overs. Then Amla and de Villiers dropped a gear, adding 27 in 42, a staggering performance given their usual scoring-rates. Amla finally fell on the final morning, after making 25 from 244 balls in 289 minutes. But de Villiers stayed put, adding 35 at a run an over with du Plessis.

At tea on the final day, South Africa had inched to 136 for five from 138 overs, but Vilas fell to the fifth ball after the resumption, and two deliveries later Ashwin removed de Villiers, after 354 minutes of abstinence had produced 43 runs. He scored off only 21 of his 297 balls: it was the longest-known Test innings under 50. The end was not so easily delayed, as the last five wickets added only seven runs between them in 31 balls after tea.

The 143.1 overs South Africa faced was the most in a fourth innings by any team in Asia. But it wasn't quite enough, and India claimed the series 3–0.

Man of the Match: A. M. Rahane.   *Man of the Series:* R. Ashwin.

Close of play: first day, India 231-7 (Rahane 89, Ashwin 6); second day, South Africa 121; third day, India 190-4 (Kohli 83, Rahane 52); fourth day, South Africa 72-2 (Amla 23, de Villiers 11).

India

M. Vijay c Amla b Piedt	12	– c Vilas b Morkel	3
S. Dhawan lbw b Piedt	33	– b Morkel	21
C. A. Pujara b Abbott	14	– (4) b Imran Tahir	28
*V. Kohli c Vilas b Piedt	44	– (5) lbw b Abbott	88
A. M. Rahane c de Villiers b Imran Tahir	127	– (6) not out	100
R. G. Sharma c Imran Tahir b Piedt	1	– (3) b Morkel	0
†W. P. Saha b Abbott	1	– not out	23
R. A. Jadeja c Elgar b Abbott	24		
R. Ashwin c de Villiers b Abbott	56		
U. T. Yadav not out	10		
I. Sharma lbw b Abbott	0		
B 8, w 1, n-b 3	12	L-b 2, n-b 2	4

1/30 (1) 2/62 (2) 3/66 (3)   (117.5 overs) 334   1/4 (1)   (5 wkts dec, 100.1 overs) 267
4/136 (4) 5/138 (6) 6/139 (7)   2/8 (3) 3/53 (2)
7/198 (8) 8/296 (5) 9/334 (9) 10/334 (11)   4/57 (4) 5/211 (5)

Morkel 24–5–58–0; Abbott 24.5–7–40–5; Piedt 38–6–117–4; Imran Tahir 16–2–66–1; Elgar 11–0–33–0; Duminy 4–0–12–0. *Second innings*—Morkel 21–6–51–3; Abbott 22–9–47–1; Piedt 18–1–53–0; Imran Tahir 26.1–4–74–1; Elgar 13–1–40–0.

South Africa

D. Elgar c Saha b Yadav	17	– c Rahane b Ashwin	4
T. Bavuma b Jadeja	22	– b Ashwin	34
*H. M. Amla c Saha b Jadeja	3	– b Jadeja	25
A. B. de Villiers c I. Sharma b Jadeja	42	– c Jadeja b Ashwin	43
F. du Plessis c Rahane b Jadeja	0	– lbw b Jadeja	10
J-P. Duminy b Yadav	1	– lbw b Ashwin	0
†D. J. Vilas b I. Sharma	11	– b Yadav	13
K. J. Abbott lbw b Ashwin	4	– b Yadav	0
D. L. Piedt c Rahane b Jadeja	5	– c Saha b Yadav	1
M. Morkel not out	9	– b Ashwin	2
Imran Tahir c sub (K. L. Rahul) b Ashwin	1	– not out	0
B 5, n-b 1	6	B 8, l-b 3	11

1/36 (1) 2/40 (2) 3/56 (3)   (49.3 overs) 121   1/5 (1) 2/49 (2)   (143.1 overs) 143
4/62 (5) 5/65 (6) 6/79 (7)   3/76 (3) 4/111 (5)
7/84 (8) 8/103 (9) 9/118 (4) 10/121 (11)   5/112 (6) 6/136 (7) 7/136 (4)
                                            8/140 (8) 9/143 (9) 10/143 (10)

I. Sharma 12–5–28–1; Yadav 12–3–32–2; Ashwin 13.3–5–26–2; Jadeja 12–2–30–5. *Second innings*—I. Sharma 20–12–23–0; Ashwin 49.1–26–61–5; Jadeja 46–33–26–2; Yadav 21–16–9–3; Dhawan 3–1–9–0; Vijay 2–0–2–0; Kohli 1–1–0–0; Pujara 1–0–2–0.

Umpires: H. D. P. K. Dharmasena and B. N. J. Oxenford.   Third umpire: C. K. Nandan.
Referee: J. J. Crowe.

THE PEPSI INDIAN PREMIER LEAGUE IN 2014-15

Anand Vasu

Not for the first time, the IPL's cricket was overshadowed by its politics. On July 14, less than two months after Mumbai Indians had claimed their second title, Gurunath Meiyappan (the former team principal of Chennai Super Kings) and Raj Kundra (co-owner of Rajasthan Royals) were finally banned for life from the sport after a Supreme Court committee headed by the former Indian Chief Justice R. M. Lodha ruled that both were guilty of placing bets on the 2013 tournament.

The Chennai and Rajasthan franchises, who between them had won three of the IPL's first four editions, were both suspended for two years, while Meiyappan's father-in-law, Narayanaswami Srinivasan, was finally forced out of the position of power he had created for himself – not only in Indian cricket, where he had been president of the BCCI, but in the world game too, as he lost his post as chairman of the ICC. "Disrepute has been brought to cricket, the BCCI and the IPL to such an extent," said Lodha, "that doubts abound in the public consciousness about whether games are clean or not."

Pune and Rajkot were chosen to replace the banned teams, and – in December 2015 – the former Chennai and Rajasthan players were involved in a special draft auction. The ninth edition of the IPL will feature the unfamiliar sight of Chennai totem M. S. Dhoni turning out for Pune, who were picked up by the New Rising consortium, owned by prominent businessman Sanjiv Goenka. Rajkot, who were bought by Intex, a mobile phone company, snapped up local boy Ravindra Jadeja, as well as Suresh Raina, Dwayne Bravo and Brendon McCullum.

By contrast, IPL8 had been comfortably the most uneventful yet: it was actually about bat and ball. **Mumbai Indians** regained the title they had relinquished to Kolkata Knight Riders the previous year, beating off a strong Chennai in the final. But, for the first half of the competition, their timid approach ensured more was said about the support staff than the players. With Ricky Ponting, Jonty Rhodes, Robin Singh and Shane Bond in the coaching ranks, Mumbai certainly drew attention to themselves.

After losing their first four matches, and managing only one victory in six, Mumbai won seven of their last eight games to guarantee a play-off place. Ponting told them to treat each one like a final, which was easier said than done. Yet they came together when it mattered. Rohit Sharma repeatedly lifted the team, Lendl Simmons went from being occasionally savage to dependably resolute, Harbhajan Singh bowled with a skill that had apparently gone missing, and Kieron Pollard graduated from a primitive punisher of bad balls to a senior pro who controlled the tempo of the game. By the end of the tournament, they were well above the rest.

Delhi Daredevils won only five games, but were spared a third successive wooden spoon by the dismal efforts of **Kings XI Punjab**. They had lit up the previous tournament, but now struck a discordant note from the get-go, and lost 11 out of 14.

The 2015 IPL lacked a tangible feel-good story, which in the past had often been provided by **Rajasthan Royals**. They were early contenders for glory, with five consecutive wins, before a swift tapering-off was arrested only when Shane Watson's blistering 59-ball century against Kolkata. But one Watson does not an IPL make, and even the emergence of Karun Nair and Deepak Hooda as home-grown talents could not realise Rajasthan's dream.

Royal Challengers Bangalore discovered, once again, that Chris Gayle, A. B. de Villiers and Virat Kohli did not guarantee success. Gayle was so off-colour that he was dropped twice (both times against Chennai), and de Villiers showed his true self too infrequently. When he was good, though, he was irresistible – as in Mumbai where, after playing out five dot balls, he creamed 133 from the next 54. But, when a team depend so much on their top three, it becomes impossible to manufacture results when they fail, an inevitable occurrence in a competition lasting the best part of two months. **Sunrisers Hyderabad** had the tournament's leading scorer – David Warner, with 562 runs, including seven fifties from 14 innings – but were otherwise just off the pace, winning and losing seven.

Kolkata Knight Riders were keen, though rather too keen for their own good. Gautam Gambhir, surplus to requirements at national level, seemed driven to the point of obsession, and the joy of playing the game stayed in the dressing-room. At press conferences, Gambhir – once shy and charming – was only too ready to spar, even if no offence was intended. The one player who managed to stay in a happy bubble was Jamaican Andre Russell, pleased to be given the chance to show the world what he could do. With 326 runs from 11 innings, he did not make it into the top 20 run-getters' list, but his runs came at the ridiculous strike-rate of 192. No other batsman with more than four innings came close, and the fact that Russell managed to keep the bullet boundaries coming on a slow Eden Gardens surface was testament to his muscularity.

Chennai Super Kings had come close to mastering the Twenty20 template in previous IPL seasons and, for a while, were the smoothest-running machine once more. They had been nurtured superbly over the years, with a core group of high-quality players backing up Dhoni, their captain, who understood the dynamics of limited-overs cricket perhaps better than anyone in its history. Chennai headed the table, before a red-hot Mumbai enjoyed a better day, and walked away with the trophy. Following the Supreme Court's ruling, Chennai will not get another chance until 2018.

INDIAN PREMIER LEAGUE, 2014-15

	Played	Won	Lost	No result	Points	Net run-rate
CHENNAI SUPER KINGS	14	9	5	0	18	0.70
MUMBAI INDIANS	14	8	6	0	16	-0.04
ROYAL CHALLENGERS BANGALORE	14	7	5	2	16	1.03
RAJASTHAN ROYALS	14	7	5	2	16	0.06
Kolkata Knight Riders	14	7	6	1	15	0.25
Sunrisers Hyderabad	14	7	7	0	14	-0.23
Delhi Daredevils	14	5	8	1	11	-0.04
Kings XI Punjab	14	3	11	0	6	-1.43

First qualifying final   At Mumbai (Wankhede), May 19, 2015 (floodlit). **Mumbai Indians won by 25 runs. ‡Mumbai Indians 187-6** (20 overs) (L. M. P. Simmons 65, P. A. Patel 35, K. A. Pollard 41; D. J. Bravo 3-40); **Chennai Super Kings 162** (19 overs) (F. du Plessis 45; S. L. Malinga 3-23). *MoM:* K. A. Pollard. *Lendl Simmons, who hit five sixes, and Parthiv Patel kicked off Mumbai's innings with 90 in 10.4 overs, then Kieron Pollard also larruped five sixes, in a 17-ball 41. Chennai lost Dwayne Smith for a duck, to a leg-side lbw, but recovered to 86-2 in the 11th over, before Harbhajan Singh removed Suresh Raina and M. S. Dhoni with successive balls. Mumbai went on to their eighth win in nine games; Chennai lived to fight another day, in the second qualifying final against the winner of the next match.*

Elimination final   At Gahunje, May 20, 2015 (floodlit). **Royal Challengers Bangalore won by 71 runs. ‡Royal Challengers Bangalore 180-4** (20 overs) (A. B. de Villiers 66, Mandeep Singh 54*); **Rajasthan Royals 109** (19 overs) (A. M. Rahane 42). *MoM:* A. B. de Villiers. *De Villiers, whose 66 took only 38 balls, added 113 for the third wicket in 11 overs with Mandeep Singh (54* off 34) to propel Bangalore to an imposing total. Rajasthan needed 15 more than any side had chased to win an IPL game on this ground, and were never on terms: Ajinkya Rahane lasted 14 overs for 42, but no one else managed more than 12.*

Second qualifying final   At Ranchi, May 22, 2015 (floodlit). **Chennai Super Kings won by three wickets. Royal Challengers Bangalore 139-8** (20 overs) (C. H. Gayle 41, S. N. Khan 31; A. Nehra 3-28); **‡Chennai Super Kings 140-7** (19.5 overs) (M. E. K. Hussey 56). *MoM:* A. Nehra. *On a testing pitch in Dhoni's home town, Chris Gayle was forced to dig in after Bangalore dipped to 36-3; his 41 used up 43 balls. Dinesh Karthik (28) and 17-year-old Sarfaraz Khan (31 from 21) helped muscle the total to 139. Chennai were set back by the loss of Faf du Plessis and Raina in three balls in the tenth over, but Mike Hussey took them close with 56 from 46. At 135-4 in the 19th over it looked all over, but Pawan Negi and Dwayne Bravo fell to successive deliveries, leaving five needed from the 20th. Dhoni collected two twos off medium-pacer Harshal Patel, but was then caught behind – before Ravichandran Ashwin put Chennai into the final for the sixth time out of eight. He had earlier taken 1-13 in his four overs, and was the only regular bowler in IPL8 to concede less than a run a ball.*

FINAL

CHENNAI SUPER KINGS v MUMBAI INDIANS

At Kolkata, May 24, 2015 (floodlit). Mumbai Indians won by 41 runs. Toss: Chennai Super Kings.

Mumbai Indians surged to their second title in three years, shrugging off the first-over run-out of Patel to post a sizeable score after being sent in, a departure from Dhoni's usual Twenty20 tactics. Simmons rounded off a fine tournament with a robust 68; only David Warner, with 562 for Sunrisers Hyderabad, made more runs overall than his 540 (Ajinkya Rahane also made 540, for Rajasthan Royals). Simmons and Rohit Sharma, whose 50 occupied just 26 balls, piled on 119 in 11 overs. Pollard and Rayudu then smacked three sixes apiece to lift Mumbai past 200. Only Chennai, with 205 in 2011, had made a higher total in the IPL final – but they couldn't match that this time. Regular wickets meant they fell well short, despite a responsible 57 from Dwayne Smith. McClenaghan, the New Zealand left-arm paceman, snuffed out Hussey and Bravo, and later removed Ashwin to finish with the best figures of the day. "We always had the talent," he said. "It was just ensuring the guys believed in each other, and realised they were playing for the mate next to them and not just themselves."

Man of the Match: R. G. Sharma. *Man of the Tournament:* A. D. Russell (Kolkata Knight Riders).

Mumbai Indians

		B	4/6
1 L. M. P. Simmons *b 1*	68	45	8/3
2 †P. A. Patel *run out*	0	3	0
3 *R. G. Sharma *c 8 b 5*	50	26	6/2
4 K. A. Pollard *c 3 b 10*	36	18	2/3
5 A. T. Rayudu *not out*	36	24	0/3
6 H. H. Pandya *c 3 b 5*	0	2	0
7 Harbhajan Singh *not out*	6	3	0/1
B 1, l-b 4, n-b 1	6		

6 overs: 61-1   (20 overs) 202-5

1/1 2/120 3/120 4/191 5/191

8 J. Suchith, 9 R. Vinay Kumar, 10 M. J. McClenaghan and 11 S. L. Malinga did not bat.

Nehra 4–0–41–0 (10); Sharma 4–0–38–1 (9); Ashwin 2–0–21–0 (6); Jadeja 2–0–26–0 (3); Negi 2–0–18–0 (2); Bravo 4–0–36–2 (8); Smith 2–0–17–1 (4).

Chennai Super Kings

		B	4/6
1 D. R. Smith *lbw b 7*	57	48	9/1
2 M. E. K. Hussey *c 8 b 10*	4	9	1
3 S. K. Raina *st 2 b 7*	28	19	3/1
4 *†M. S. Dhoni *b 11*	18	13	1/1
5 D. J. Bravo *c 1 b 10*	9	6	0/1
6 P. Negi *c 6 b 11*	3	5	0
7 F. du Plessis *c 3 b 9*	1	3	0
8 R. A. Jadeja *not out*	11	8	1
9 R. Ashwin *c 8 b 10*	2	4	0
10 M. Sharma *not out*	21	7	1/2
L-b 2, w 3, n-b 2	7		

6 overs: 31-1   (20 overs) 161-8

1/22 2/88 3/99 4/108 5/124 6/125 7/134 8/137

11 A. Nehra did not bat.

Malinga 4–0–25–2 (11); McClenaghan 4–0–25–3 (15); Vinay Kumar 4–0–39–1 (10); Pandya 4–0–36–0 (9); Harbhajan Singh 4–0–34–2 (7).

Umpires: H. D. P. K. Dharmasena and R. K. Illingworth.   Third umpire: V. A. Kulkarni.
Referee: R. S. Madugalle.

IPL FINALS

2007-08	RAJASTHAN ROYALS beat Chennai Super Kings by three wickets at Mumbai.
2008-09	DECCAN CHARGERS beat Royal Challengers Bangalore by six runs at Johannesburg.
2009-10	CHENNAI SUPER KINGS beat Mumbai Indians by 22 runs at Mumbai.
2010-11	CHENNAI SUPER KINGS beat Royal Challengers Bangalore by 58 runs at Chennai.
2011-12	KOLKATA KNIGHT RIDERS beat Chennai Super Kings by five wickets at Chennai.
2012-13	MUMBAI INDIANS beat Chennai Super Kings by 23 runs at Kolkata.
2013-14	KOLKATA KNIGHT RIDERS beat Kings XI Punjab by three wickets at Bangalore.
2014-15	MUMBAI INDIANS beat Chennai Super Kings by 41 runs at Kolkata.

DOMESTIC CRICKET IN INDIA IN 2014-15

R. Mohan

Karnataka won an unprecedented second successive treble, sweeping the Ranji Trophy, the Irani Cup and the Vijay Hazare 50-over tournament for the second year running. The cricketers from Bangalore, the world's IT back-office, are a tenacious lot – in a city where traffic jams can mean it takes three hours to cover ten kilometres, they probably have to be. But a fine temperament for the game could also be considered a legacy of the days of stylish batsman Gundappa Viswanath and off-spinner Erapalli Prasanna, who helped Karnataka win their first Ranji titles in the 1970s. Vinay Kumar's treble-winning side sported the same qualities of confidence and motivation.

They prided themselves on blending secure stalwarts and hungry youngsters, with the seniors Robin Uthappa, the tournament's top scorer with 912 runs, and Vinay Kumar himself, joint-leading wicket-taker with 48, showing the way. The presence of four proficient seamers was the key to sustained success; domestic cricket in India has witnessed a significant shift towards pace as spin bowling has declined.

The prolific 22-year-old Lokesh Rahul scored 838 Ranji runs at 93, despite playing only five games because he was called up for India's tour of Australia – but, with 336 at 112 in the Duleep Trophy, he passed 1,000 first-class runs for the second successive season. Only Himachal Pradesh's Paras Dogra averaged more. Rahul became the first to score a triple-hundred for Karnataka, though he was followed a few weeks later by 23-year-old Karun Nair in the final. In thrashing **Tamil Nadu**, another southern side, Karnataka pulled ahead of Delhi's seven Ranji titles to place themselves second only to runaway leaders Mumbai, who have triumphed 40 times in the tournament's 81 seasons.

For **Mumbai**, it was a tough season. Their Ranji campaign began with a shock defeat by Jammu & Kashmir, traditionally one of the weakest teams, who had the additional handicap of being forced to play all their games away from home because of devastating floods. Mumbai also suffered an innings loss at the hands of Tamil Nadu, their first by any Ranji side since 1950-51. They still scraped into the knockout, thanks to Shardul Thakur, who was to tie with Vinay Kumar on 48 wickets, but were bowled out for 44 by Karnataka in the semi-final.

Karnataka's tenacity was tested in the Irani Cup match between the Ranji champions and the Rest of India: they fell 20 behind on first innings, but got their batting together second time round, thanks to a composed unbeaten 123 by Manish Pandey. A young Rest XI needed 403 to win, but Abhimanyu Mithun reduced them to eight for three in an impressive new-ball spell.

Karnataka had won their first trophy back in November. Because of the World Cup, the interstate Vijay Hazare tournament had been brought forward, and they beat Punjab by 156 runs in the final. They had faced a stiffer test in the semi against Bengal, who needed 13 off 14 balls with five wickets in hand; but Mithun made the breakthrough, and Karnataka ended up bowling Bengal out in the final over. Punjab lost another limited-overs final in April, when **Gujarat** beat them by two wickets in a tense chase in the Twenty20 Syed Mushtaq Ali Trophy.

In the Duleep Trophy in October, Rahul had presented his credentials for a national call-up with a century in each innings in the final. Despite his efforts, **South Zone** went down by nine runs in a sensational finish, with **Central Zone** winning the closest final in the competition's history. At the start of the last day, South were cruising at 203 for one in pursuit of 301. Then seam bowler Pankaj Singh struck twice in five balls, and the spinners ran through the rest to fashion Central's first Duleep title for ten years. The competition, whose importance as a Test trial has faded, was suspended for the following season, though it was expected to return in 2016-17.

In the 50-over zonal tournament, **East Zone** ended **West's** run of three successive titles, with 16-year-old Virat Singh scoring a fifty in the final.

FIRST-CLASS AVERAGES, 2014-15

BATTING (650 runs)

	M	I	NO	R	HS	100	Avge	Ct/St
P. Dogra (*Himachal Pradesh/Rest of India*)	8	10	2	839	230*	4	104.87	7
K. L. Rahul (*South Zone/Karnataka*)	7	12	0	1,174	337	4	97.83	5
G. H. Vihari (*South Zone/Hyderabad*) . .	9	13	2	856	263	3	77.81	6/1
I. R. Jaggi (*Jharkhand*)	8	12	3	670	201*	2	74.44	1
S. P. Jackson (*Saurashtra*)	8	14	2	819	181*	3	68.25	0
N. V. Ojha (*C Zone/Madhya Pradesh/Rest*)	9	15	1	879	217	3	62.78	29/6
Gurkeerat Singh (*Punjab*)	8	14	2	677	101*	1	56.41	3
†Yuvraj Singh (*North Zone/Punjab*).	8	13	0	718	182	3	55.23	6
G. Satish (*Vidarbha*)	9	17	4	707	167	2	54.38	9
K. Srikar Bharat (*Andhra*)	9	15	1	758	308	2	54.14	45/1
C. G. Khurana (*Maharashtra*)	10	15	2	698	130*	2	53.69	4
†G. Gambhir (*Delhi*)	10	15	1	736	167	2	52.57	2
R. Samarth (*Karnataka*)	8	14	0	726	180	2	51.85	6
S. S. Iyer (*Mumbai*)	10	17	1	809	153	2	50.56	6
R. V. Uthappa (*South Zone/Karnataka*) . . .	14	24	1	1,158	156	3	50.34	22/1
K. K. Nair (*South Zone/Karnataka*) . .	12	19	1	880	328	1	48.88	4
†S. S. Tiwary (*East Zone/Jharkhand*)	10	17	2	721	162	4	48.06	11
K. D. Karthik (*South Zone/Tamil Nadu*). .	13	22	3	893	129	4	47.00	17/5
A. R. Bawne (*West Zone/Maharashtra*) . .	11	18	3	705	124	4	47.00	8
R. Shreyas Gopal (*Karnataka*).	13	19	4	693	145	2	46.20	6
J. S. Saxena (*Central Zone/Madhya Pradesh*).	10	17	0	768	144	2	45.17	3
†A. Mukund (*Tamil Nadu*)	11	20	1	858	140	2	45.15	9
R. N. B. Indrajith (*Tamil Nadu*)	11	17	1	713	101	1	44.56	13/1
R. D. Bist (*Central Zone/Rajasthan*). . . .	10	19	4	652	124*	2	43.46	3
†S. D. Chatterjee (*East Zone/Bengal*)	10	17	0	736	192	1	43.29	3
S. A. Yadav (*West Zone/Mumbai*)	11	20	2	738	135	2	41.00	23
M. K. Pandey (*South Zone/Karnataka*) . . .	13	20	2	722	193	2	40.11	21

BOWLING (30 wickets)

	Style	O	M	R	W	BB	5I	Avge
D. Sivakumar (*Andhra*)	RFM	277.1	106	627	44	7-30	4	14.25
B. C. Mohanty (*East Zone/Odisha*)	RFM	308.4	89	755	44	6-42	2	17.15
R. B. Kalaria (*Gujarat*).	LFM	241.1	80	567	33	6-45	3	17.18
S. P. Purkayastha (*Assam*)	OB	249.2	67	631	36	8-29	5	17.52
S. Aravind (*Karnataka*)	LM	336.4	100	797	44	4-9	0	18.11
J. Yadav (*Haryana/Rest of India*)	OB	186.1	28	613	33	7-64	3	18.57
D. R. Behera (*Odisha*)	RM	261.1	79	625	33	4-22	0	18.93
A. A. Sanklecha (*Maharashtra*)	RFM	234	43	651	32	5-93	1	20.34
R. Vinay Kumar (*South Zone/Karnataka*) . .	RFM	415.4	110	1,160	55	6-20	3	21.09
V. C. Stephen (*Andhra*)	LFM	266.5	67	806	37	6-32	1	21.78
P. M. Datey (*Madhya Pradesh*)	RM	230.2	59	677	31	5-86	2	21.83
Pankaj Singh (*Central Zone/Rajasthan*)	RFM	316.3	72	948	43	5-109	1	22.04
S. B. Wagh (*Vidarbha*)	LM	283.5	82	743	33	5-43	1	22.51
S. M. Fallah (*Maharashtra*)	LM	390	103	882	39	5-36	2	22.61
S. N. Thakur (*West Zone/Mumbai/Rest*) . . .	RFM	427	107	1,292	57	6-53	6	22.66
K. Anureet Singh (*Railways*)	RFM	288.4	86	735	32	5-43	2	22.96
A. Mithun (*South Zone/Karnataka*)	RFM	392.3	108	1,173	47	5-31	1	24.95
R. Dhawan (*N Zone/Himachal Pr/Rest*) . . .	RM	454.4	109	1,290	47	7-93	4	27.44
R. Shreyas Gopal (*S Zone/Karnataka*). . . .	LBG	302	47	1,120	40	4-39	0	28.00
M. Rangarajan (*Tamil Nadu*)	OB	347	74	1,035	36	7-135	2	28.75
A. B. Dinda (*East Zone/Bengal*)	RFM	314	70	995	32	7-87	1	31.09
S. S. Mundhe (*West Zone/Maharashtra*)	RM	363.3	67	1,082	30	6-38	1	36.06

DULEEP TROPHY, 2014-15

Quarter-final At Rohtak, October 15–18, 2014. **East Zone won by 102 runs. East Zone 278** (M. K. Tiwary 100*) **and 281-7 dec** (S. S. Tiwary 109); ‡**West Zone 322** (A. R. Bawne 105; R. K. Datta 5-60) **and 135.** *Despite slipping to 47-4 on a seaming pitch, West Zone took a first-innings lead of 44. But there was no recovery in the second innings after Manoj Tiwary set a target of 238.*

Semi-final At Rohtak, October 22–24, 2014. **South Zone won by an innings and 118 runs. South Zone 264** (R. V. Uthappa 120); ‡**East Zone 84 and 62.** *East Zone could not reach three figures in either innings on another green pitch, and lost with nearly two days to spare.*

Semi-final At Mohali, October 22–25, 2014. **Drawn.** Central Zone qualified for the final by virtue of their first-innings lead. ‡**Central Zone 538** (J. S. Saxena 110, N. V. Ojha 217) **and 312** (M. Rawat 116); **North Zone 457** (G. Gambhir 167) **and 24-1.** *Naman Ojha's 217, his fourth double-hundred, was his fourth century in four innings, following three for India A in Australia.*

Final At Delhi (Feroz Shah Kotla), October 29–November 2, 2014. **Central Zone won by nine runs.** ‡**Central Zone 276 and 403** (R. D. Bist 112*); **South Zone 379** (K. L. Rahul 185) **and 291** (K. L. Rahul 130). *Lokesh Rahul scored twin centuries, including a career-best 185, but finished on the losing side. He and Baba Apparajith (56) had steered South Zone to 203-1, chasing 301, but the last nine fell for 88. It was the closest victory in any Duleep final.*

RANJI TROPHY, 2014-15

Group A	Played	Won	Lost	Drawn	1st-inns points	Bonus points	Points	Quotient
KARNATAKA	8	4	0	4	8	1	33	1.633
TAMIL NADU	8	4	1	3	3	2	29	1.244
MUMBAI	8	2	2	4	8	0	20	0.937
Madhya Pradesh	8	1	1	6	12	1	19	1.143
Baroda	8	1	2	5	11	1	18	1.078
Railways	8	0	2	6	16	0	16	0.922
Uttar Pradesh	8	2	3	3	3	0	15	0.760
Bengal	8	0	1	7	13	0	13	0.820
Jammu & Kashmir	8	1	3	4	6	0	12	0.601

Group B	Played	Won	Lost	Drawn	1st-inns points	Bonus points	Points	Quotient
DELHI	8	5	1	2	4	3	37	1.471
MAHARASHTRA	8	3	2	3	7	1	26	1.290
VIDARBHA	8	2	1	5	11	1	24	1.468
Gujarat	8	2	2	4	12	0	24	0.965
Odisha	8	3	3	2	2	0	20	0.790
Punjab	8	2	3	3	7	0	19	0.947
Rajasthan	8	2	3	3	5	1	18	0.821
Haryana	8	2	4	2	4	1	17	0.875
Saurashtra	8	1	3	4	4	0	10	0.668

Group C	Played	Won	Lost	Drawn	1st-inns points	Bonus points	Points	Quotient
ASSAM	8	5	1	2	4	4	38	1.325
ANDHRA	8	4	1	3	3	2	29	1.454
Himachal Pradesh	8	2	0	6	14	2	28	1.677
Jharkhand	8	2	1	5	9	0	21	1.171
Hyderabad	8	1	1	6	14	0	20	1.123
Kerala	8	1	1	6	14	0	20	0.908
Tripura	8	0	3	5	9	0	9	0.635
Services	8	0	4	4	8	0	8	0.773
Goa	8	0	3	5	5	0	5	0.575

Outright win = 6pts; lead on first innings in a drawn match = 3pts; deficit on first innings in a drawn match = 1pt; no decision on first innings = 1pt. Teams tied on points were ranked on most wins, and then on quotient (runs scored per wicket divided by runs conceded per wicket).

The top three teams from Groups A and B and the top two from Group C advanced to the quarter-finals. The bottom teams from Groups A and B transferred to C for 2015-16, and were replaced by the Group C qualifiers.

Group A

At Vadodara (Reliance), December 7–10, 2014. **Drawn. ‡Bengal 455** (S. D. Chatterjee 192; Swapnil Singh 5-99) **and 246-9 dec** (L. R. Shukla 105*); **Baroda 354** (D. Hooda 114). *Baroda 1pt, Bengal 3pts. Baroda wicketkeeper Pinal Shah made six dismissals in Bengal's first innings (5ct, 1st), before 19-year-old Deepak Hooda scored 114 on first-class debut.*

At Bangalore (Chinnaswamy), December 7–10, 2014. **Karnataka won by 285 runs. Karnataka 290 and 351-5 dec; ‡Tamil Nadu 274 and 82.** *Karnataka 6pts. Left-armer Sreenath Aravind took a hat-trick in Tamil Nadu's second-innings collapse.*

At Mumbai (Wankhede), December 7–10, 2014. **Jammu & Kashmir won by four wickets. ‡Mumbai 236 and 254** (S. A. Yadav 115; R. Punia 5-76); **Jammu & Kashmir 254** (S. Khajuria 107) **and 237-6.** *Jammu & Kashmir 6pts. In one of the great Ranji upsets, Jammu & Kashmir won the first match they had ever played against 40-times champions Mumbai. It was only their 21st victory in 56 years as a first-class team – and it was to be their sole win in this tournament.*

At Delhi (Karnail Singh), December 7–10, 2014. **Drawn. Madhya Pradesh 181** (K. Anureet Singh 5-43) **and 310; ‡Railways 280** (A. N. Ghosh 120; P. M. Datey 5-86) **and 43-3.** *Railways 3pts, Madhya Pradesh 1pt. Railways wicketkeeper Mahesh Rawat made nine dismissals in all (8ct, 1st).*

At Kolkata (Eden Gardens), December 14–17, 2014. **Karnataka won by nine wickets. Karnataka 408** (R. Shreyas Gopal 145; A. B. Dinda 7-87) **and 71-1; ‡Bengal 251 and 227** (R. Vinay Kumar 6-34). *Karnataka 6pts. Shreyas Gopal and Aravind (29*) put on 148 for Karnataka's tenth wicket.*

At Indore (Holkar), December 14–17, 2014. **Uttar Pradesh won by four wickets. Madhya Pradesh 296 and 63** (A. Mishra 6-26); **‡Uttar Pradesh 180 and 183-6.** *Uttar Pradesh 6pts. Madhya Pradesh equalled their third-lowest total as they collapsed against Amit Mishra (not the Test player) and Praveen Kumar (3-16). Harpreet Singh scored a two-hour 37, but no one else passed seven.*

At Delhi (Karnail Singh), December 14–17, 2014. **Drawn. Railways 242** (S. N. Thakur 6-59) **and 136-4; ‡Mumbai 101.** *Railways 3pts, Mumbai 1pt.*

At Natham, December 14–16, 2014. **Tamil Nadu won by 277 runs. ‡Tamil Nadu 254** (Waseem Raza 5-68) **and 286-5 dec** (A. Mukund 137); **Jammu & Kashmir 132 and 131** (R. Aushik Srinivas 5-12). *Tamil Nadu 6pts. The first first-class match at NPR College of Engineering and Technology.*

At Vadodara (Reliance), December 21–24, 2014. **Drawn. Jammu & Kashmir 497** (Parvez Rasool 136; R. Punia 124*; Swapnil Singh 6-152) **and 147-9** (S. S. Mangalorkar 6-46); **‡Baroda 426** (S. P. Wakaskar 172). *Baroda 1pt, Jammu & Kashmir 3pts. Baroda's Yusuf Pathan slapped a spectator for "indecent comments" directed at him and team-mates.*

At Delhi (Karnail Singh), December 21–24, 2014. **Karnataka won by 136 runs. ‡Karnataka 247** (K. R. Upadhyay 7-98) **and 174-5 dec; Railways 171 and 114** (A. Mithun 5-31). *Karnataka 6pts.*

At Chennai (Chidambaram), December 21–24, 2014. **Drawn. ‡Madhya Pradesh 437** (J. S. Saxena 144, D. Bundela 104; M. Rangarajan 7-135) **and 112-4; Tamil Nadu 248** (A. N. Sharma 5-103) **and 369** (K. D. Karthik 129; S. S. Jain 5-50). *Tamil Nadu 1pt, Madhya Pradesh 3pts. Dinesh Karthik hit 129 in 115 balls.*

At Kanpur (Modi), December 21–24, 2014. **Mumbai won by eight wickets. Uttar Pradesh 206** (S. N. Thakur 6-53) **and 161; ‡Mumbai 270 and 98-2.** *Mumbai 6pts.*

At Kolkata (Eden Gardens), December 28–31, 2014. **Drawn. Mumbai 414** (S. S. Iyer 153); **‡Bengal 210** (S. N. Thakur 5-59) **and 129-0.** *Bengal 1pt, Mumbai 3pts.*

At Gwalior, December 28–31, 2014. **Drawn. Baroda 358** (P. M. Datey 5-101); **‡Madhya Pradesh 178** (Gagandeep Singh 5-41) **and 119-6.** *Madhya Pradesh 1pt, Baroda 3pts.*

At Chennai (Chidambaram), December 28–31, 2014. **Drawn. ‡Tamil Nadu 213** (A. K. Yadav 6-68) **and 133-3 dec; Railways 236.** *Tamil Nadu 1pt, Railways 3pts. Railways' Rohan Bhosale was hit on the neck at short leg and carried off, but came in at 212-9 to help them take first-innings points.*

At Kanpur (Modi), December 28–31, 2014. **Drawn. ‡Uttar Pradesh 299-5 dec; Jammu & Kashmir 199-8** (I. Dev Singh 103*). *Uttar Pradesh 1pt, Jammu & Kashmir 1pt.*

At Kolkata (Eden Gardens), January 5–8, 2015. **Drawn. Tamil Nadu 246 and 327-5** (K. D. Karthik 103*); **‡Bengal 454-9 dec** (A. R. Easwaran 150*). *Bengal 3pts, Tamil Nadu 1pt.*

At Hubli, January 5–7, 2015. **Karnataka won by an innings and 30 runs. Jammu & Kashmir 160 and 233; ‡Karnataka 423-9 dec** (R. V. Uthappa 156). *Karnataka 7pts. Karnataka had now won all their four matches of the season, to make it 12 victories in 13 first-class games since November 2013.*

At Mumbai (Wankhede), January 5–8, 2015. **Drawn. Mumbai 404** (S. A. Yadav 135; Y. B. Rawat 5-74) **and 311-4** (S. S. Iyer 142*); **‡Madhya Pradesh 538-7 dec** (N. V. Ojha 155, D. Bundela 115). *Mumbai 1pt, Madhya Pradesh 3pts. Naman Ojha and Devendra Bundela added 258 for Madhya Pradesh's fourth wicket.*

At Lucknow, January 5–8, 2015. **Baroda won by ten wickets. ‡Baroda 498** (K. H. Devdhar 146) **and 33-0; Uttar Pradesh 223** (T. M. Srivastava 112; Y. K. Pathan 6-67) **and 307** (Swapnil Singh 6-91). *Baroda 7pts.*

At Kolkata (Eden Gardens), January 13–16, 2015. **Drawn. ‡Bengal 387** (W. P. Saha 166) **and 264-5 dec; Jammu & Kashmir 315 and 219-2** (Imran Haroon 102*). *Bengal 3pts, Jammu & Kashmir 1pt. Imran Haroon scored 102* on first-class debut.*

At Indore (Holkar), January 13–16, 2015. **Drawn. ‡Madhya Pradesh 303 and 277-3** (A. R. Shrivastava 108*, N. V. Ojha 115); **Karnataka 522** (M. K. Pandey 193, R. Shreyas Gopal 124). *Madhya Pradesh 1pt, Karnataka 3pts. Aditya Shrivastava scored 91 and 108* on first-class debut, while Ojha hit nine sixes in his 81-ball 115.*

At Delhi (Karnail Singh), January 13–16, 2015. **Drawn. ‡Baroda 298 and 240-5; Railways 263.** *Railways 1pt, Baroda 3pts.*

At Chennai (Chidambaram), January 13–15, 2015. **Tamil Nadu won by an innings and 49 runs. ‡Uttar Pradesh 182** (R. S. Shah 5-63) **and 169** (M. Rangarajan 5-42); **Tamil Nadu 400** (A. Mukund 140). *Tamil Nadu 7pts.*

At Mysore (Srikantadatta Narasimha Raja Wadeyar), January 21–24, 2015. **Drawn. ‡Baroda 335** (D. Hooda 142) **and 254; Karnataka 302 and 153-7.** *Karnataka 1pt, Baroda 3pts. Mysore's fifth first-class ground. Karnataka remained unbeaten despite being 50-6 on the final day.*

At Delhi (Karnail Singh), January 21–24, 2015. **Drawn. Railways 234-5 dec and 18-0; ‡Jammu & Kashmir 114** (K. Anureet Singh 5-48). *Railways 3pts, Jammu & Kashmir 1pt.*

At Chennai (Chidambaram), January 21–23, 2015. **Tamil Nadu won by an innings and 44 runs. ‡Mumbai 141** (R. S. Shah 7-34) **and 232; Tamil Nadu 417** (R. N. B. Indrajith 101). *Tamil Nadu 7pts. This was Mumbai's first innings defeat since losing to the Rest of India in 1977-78, and their first in the Ranji Trophy since Gujarat beat them in 1950-51.*

At Mohan Nagar, January 21–24, 2015. **Drawn. Bengal 141-4 v ‡Uttar Pradesh.** *Uttar Pradesh 1pt, Bengal 1pt.*

At Vadodara (Moti Bagh), January 29–February 1, 2015. **Mumbai won by 169 runs. ‡Mumbai 287** (A. P. Tare 127*) **and 304-9 dec** (Y. K. Pathan 5-80); **Baroda 184 and 238** (S. N. Thakur 5-39). *Mumbai 6pts. Baroda's Kedar Devdhar was hit on the helmet at short leg and did not return until the final day; he scored 58* as Baroda succumbed to Thakur's fourth five-wicket haul of the season.*

At Kolkata (Eden Gardens), January 29–February 1, 2015. **Drawn. ‡Bengal 268 and 298-8 dec; Railways 302** (S. S. Lahiri 5-99) **and 198-8.** *Bengal 1pt, Railways 3pts.*

At Bangalore (Chinnaswamy), January 29–February 1, 2015. **Drawn. Karnataka 719-9 dec** (K. L. Rahul 337, A. A. Kazi 117*; P. Kumar 5-88) **and 215; ‡Uttar Pradesh 220 and 42-2.** *Karnataka 3pts, Uttar Pradesh 1pt. Lokesh Rahul scored Karnataka's first triple-hundred. He batted for 448 balls and 11 hours 11 minutes, striking 212 runs in boundaries (47 fours and four sixes), and added 225 for the seventh wicket with Abrar Kazi, who had never reached 50 before. Karnataka led by 499 but did not enforce the follow-on; they were already sure of heading the group.*

At Indore (Holkar), January 29–31, 2015. **Madhya Pradesh won by an innings and 97 runs.** ‡**Madhya Pradesh 371** (R. Punia 5-65); **Jammu & Kashmir 177 and 97** (A. N. Sharma 5-35, J. S. Saxena 5-35). *Madhya Pradesh 7pts. A crushing defeat relegated Jammu & Kashmir.*

At Vadodara (Moti Bagh), February 6–9, 2015. **Tamil Nadu won by seven wickets. Baroda 149 and 245;** ‡**Tamil Nadu 188** (S. S. Mangalorkar 7-49) **and 207-3** (M. Vijay 104*). *Tamil Nadu 6pts. Tamil Nadu ensured their place in the quarter-finals.*

At Indore (Holkar), February 6–9, 2015. **Drawn. Madhya Pradesh 514-6 dec** (A. R. Shrivastava 151, J. S. Saxena 109); ‡**Bengal 219** (Y. B. Rawat 5-65) **and 303-8.** *Madhya Pradesh 3pts, Bengal 1pt. Shrivastava and Jalaj Saxena put on 222 for Madhya Pradesh's first wicket. Bengal ended the tournament with their seventh draw; they never won, but avoided relegation by a single point.*

At Mumbai (Wankhede), February 6–9, 2015. **Drawn.** ‡**Mumbai 436** (S. D. Lad 106, N. A. Patil 106) **and 223-8 dec; Karnataka 415** (R. Samarth 180; H. S. Baddhan 6-139) **and 110-1.** *Mumbai 3pts, Karnataka 1pt. Mumbai scraped into the quarter-finals thanks to first-innings points after Karnataka lost their last six wickets for 78, though they remained unbeaten since November 2012.*

At Delhi (Karnail Singh), February 6–9, 2015. **Uttar Pradesh won by seven wickets.** ‡**Railways 345** (M. Rawat 146; P. Kumar 6-74) **and 189** (P. P. Chawla 5-67); **Uttar Pradesh 292** (R. L. Mali 5-66) **and 246-3** (E. R. Dwivedi 102*). *Uttar Pradesh 6pts. Eklavya Dwivedi hit 102* in 73 balls.*

Group B

At Delhi (Roshanara), December 7–10, 2014. **Delhi won by nine wickets. Delhi 442** (G. Gambhir 147) **and 19-1;** ‡**Saurashtra 217 and 240.** *Delhi 7pts.*

At Gahunje, December 7–10, 2014. **Drawn.** ‡**Odisha 311** (B. B. Samantray 106) **and 178-5; Maharashtra 371.** *Maharashtra 3pts, Odisha 1pt.*

At Patiala (Dhruve Pandove), December 7–10, 2014. **Punjab won by 120 runs.** ‡**Punjab 273** (J. Yadav 6-85) **and 330-6 dec** (Yuvraj Singh 130); **Haryana 283 and 200.** *Punjab 6pts. This was the first first-class match at the Dhruve Pandove Stadium for 17 years.*

At Jaipur (Sawai Mansingh), December 7–10, 2014. **Drawn. Gujarat 340 and 266-7 dec** (P. K. Panchal 110); ‡**Rajasthan 195 and 271-8** (R. D. Bist 124*). *Rajasthan 1pt, Gujarat 3pts.*

At Rohtak, December 14–17, 2014. **Haryana won by 53 runs. Haryana 136** (S. M. Fallah 5-36) **and 176;** ‡**Maharashtra 105** (A. Hooda 5-27) **and 154** (M. Sharma 5-45). *Haryana 6pts.*

At Cuttack (Dhaneswar Rath), December 14–17, 2014. **Gujarat won by eight wickets. Odisha 225** (R. B. Kalaria 6-59) **and 248** (A. R. Mallick 126; R. B. Kalaria 6-45); ‡**Gujarat 372** (B. H. Merai 134) **and 105-2.** *Gujarat 6pts. Rush Kalaria improved his career-best figures twice in his 12-104.*

At Jaipur (Sawai Mansingh), December 14–17, 2014. **Drawn. Rajasthan 437-5 dec** (V. A. Saxena 118, A. L. Menaria 100*); ‡**Saurashtra 269 and 117-3.** *Rajasthan 3pts, Saurashtra 1pt.*

At Nagpur (VCA Stadium), December 14–17, 2014. **Drawn. Punjab 195 and 255** (G. Khera 100); ‡**Vidarbha 158** (S. Sharma 5-51, S. Kaul 5-49) **and 143-3.** *Vidarbha 1pt, Punjab 3pts.*

At Delhi (Feroz Shah Kotla), December 21–24, 2014. **Delhi won by an innings and seven runs.** ‡**Rajasthan 141 and 232; Delhi 380-6 dec** (U. Chand 146). *Delhi 7pts.*

At Rohtak, December 21–24, 2014. **Drawn. Vidarbha 154** (J. Sharma 5-46) **and 23-2;** ‡**Haryana 156.** *Haryana 3pts, Vidarbha 1pt.*

At Gahunje, December 21–24, 2014. **Punjab won by three wickets. Maharashtra 210 and 384** (K. M. Jadhav 109, R. A. Tripathi 103); ‡**Punjab 391** (Yuvraj Singh 136) **and 205-7** (S. M. Fallah 5-60). *Punjab 6pts. Punjab wicketkeeper Gitansh Khera held nine catches in the match. Samad Fallah was fined 10% of his fee for excessive appealing and dissent at their rejection.*

At Rajkot (Khandheri), December 21–24, 2014. **Drawn.** ‡**Saurashtra 207 and 364-5 dec** (S. P. Jackson 156); **Gujarat 248** (S. K. Patel 105; D. A. Jadeja 5-74) **and 130-2.** *Saurashtra 1pt, Gujarat 3pts. Aarpit Vasavada (88) and Sheldon Jackson added 212 for Saurashtra's third wicket.*

At Delhi (Feroz Shah Kotla), December 28–31, 2014. **Delhi won by an innings and 109 runs.** ‡**Delhi 425-6 dec** (U. Chand 105, V. Sehwag 105); **Gujarat 150 and 166** (V. Sood 6-43). *Delhi 7pts. Delhi's third win put them on top of the group with a game in hand.*

At Rohtak, December 28–31, 2014. **Odisha won by seven wickets. Haryana 127 and 143; ‡Odisha 232-9 dec** (J. Yadav 6-91) **and 41-3.** *Odisha 6pts.*

At Jaipur (Sawai Mansingh), December 28–31, 2014. **Drawn. Vidarbha 296** (S. U. Shrivastava 130; Pankaj Singh 5-109) **and 296-4 dec** (S. Badrinath 152*); **‡Rajasthan 188** (R. D. Thakur 5-50) **and 236-7.** *Rajasthan 1pt, Vidarbha 3pts.*

At Rajkot (Khandheri), December 28–31, 2014. **Drawn. ‡Punjab 659-7 dec** (Mandeep Singh 235, Yuvraj Singh 182, Gurkeerat Singh 101*) **and 15-0; Saurashtra 559** (S. D. Jogiyani 145, S. P. Jackson 181*). *Saurashtra 1pt, Punjab 3pts. Mandeep Singh hit his second double-hundred and added 379 for the fourth wicket with Yuvraj Singh, helping Punjab to reach their third-highest total.*

At Rohtak, January 5–8, 2015. **Drawn. Delhi 278** (V. Sehwag 147) **and 134-5; ‡Haryana 188.** *Haryana 1pt, Delhi 3pts. Mohit Sharma ended Delhi's first innings with a hat-trick in the first over of the second morning. Delhi might have made it four wins in four but for losing a day to fog.*

At Sambalpur, January 5–8, 2015. **Drawn. Vidarbha 240 and 165-2 dec; ‡Odisha 137-9 dec and 117-6.** *Odisha 1pt, Vidarbha 3pts.*

At Jaipur (Sawai Mansingh), January 5–8, 2015. **Rajasthan won by nine wickets. Rajasthan 433** (P. I. Sharma 140) **and 93-1; ‡Punjab 274 and 247.** *Rajasthan 6pts. This was Rajasthan's first victory over Punjab; they had met seven times, all since 1998-99.*

At Rajkot (Khandheri), January 5–8, 2015. **Maharashtra won by an innings and 48 runs. ‡Maharashtra 519** (A. R. Bawne 124; K. R. Makwana 5-120); **Saurashtra 273** (S. P. Jackson 102; C. G. Khurana 5-70) **and 198** (A. A. Darekar 7-72). *Maharashtra 7pts. Jackson scored his third century in three innings.*

At Delhi (Feroz Shah Kotla), January 13–15, 2015. **Delhi won by an innings and 150 runs. ‡Delhi 353** (U. Chand 117; B. C. Mohanty 5-76); **Odisha 118 and 85** (M. Sharma 6-24). *Delhi 7pts. Delhi's fourth win in five games was their third by an innings.*

At Ahmedabad (Motera), January 13–16, 2015. **Drawn. ‡Gujarat 513-8 dec** (R. H. Bhatt 150); **Punjab 362** (R. H. Bhatt 5-44) **and 120-1.** *Gujarat 3pts, Punjab 1pt. Off-spinning all-rounder Rujul Bhatt combined a 150 with 5-44.*

At Gahunje, January 13–15, 2015. **Maharashtra won by nine wickets. Rajasthan 270** (P. R. Yadav 127) **and 106** (S. S. Mundhe 6-38); **‡Maharashtra 274 and 105-1.** *Maharashtra 6pts.*

At Nagpur (VCA Stadium), January 13–16, 2015. **Drawn. ‡Vidarbha 583-9 dec** (F. Y. Fazal 107, G. Satish 167) **and 116-2; Saurashtra 309** (C. A. Pujara 114; A. A. Wakhare 5-89). *Vidarbha 3pts, Saurashtra 1pt. Faiz Fazal and Ganesh Satish added 217 for Vidarbha's second wicket.*

At Surat, January 21–24, 2015. **Vidarbha won by 120 runs. ‡Vidarbha 236** (R. R. Powar 5-87) **and 307-8 dec** (S. U. Shrivastava 101; R. R. Powar 5-99); **Gujarat 248** (A. A. Wakhare 6-92) **and 175** (A. A. Wakhare 7-70). *Vidarbha 6pts. Off-spinner Akshay Wakhare claimed 13-162.*

At Gahunje, January 21–24, 2015. **Drawn. Maharashtra 330** (S. M. Gugale 174) **and 366** (S. S. Mundhe 104); **‡Delhi 307 and 78-3.** *Maharashtra 3pts, Delhi 1pt.*

At Balangir, January 21–23, 2015. **Rajasthan won by ten wickets. Rajasthan 305** (V. A. Saxena 106) **and 42-0; ‡Odisha 144 and 199.** *Rajasthan 7pts. This was the first first-class match in Balangir, at the Gandhi Stadium.*

At Rajkot (Khandheri), January 21–23, 2015. **Saurashtra won by 62 runs. ‡Saurashtra 238** (J. Yadav 7-64) **and 213** (J. Yadav 6-90); **Haryana 226** (K. R. Makwana 6-87) **and 163** (D. A. Jadeja 6-63). *Saurashtra 6pts. Jayant Yadav was one of three off-spinners to take 13 wickets in a match in this tournament; he was also the game's top scorer, with 97 in Haryana's first innings, but still lost as Dharmendrasinh Jadeja and Kamlesh Makwana claimed 19 wickets between them.*

At Valsad, January 29–February 1, 2015. **Drawn. ‡Gujarat 429** (Y. Venugopal Rao 104, R. B. Kalaria 106; A. A. Sanklecha 5-93); **Maharashtra 262 and 429-3 dec** (C. G. Khurana 130*, A. R. Bawne 100*). *Gujarat 3pts, Maharashtra 1pt. Kalaria and Mehul Patel (62) added 172 for Gujarat's eighth wicket.*

At Rohtak, January 29–31, 2015. **Haryana won by an innings and 119 runs. Haryana 373** (H. Rana 149, N. Saini 100; A. V. Choudhary 5-83); **‡Rajasthan 180** (H. V. Patel 6-69) **and 74** (J. Sharma 5-27, H. V. Patel 5-43). *Haryana 7pts. Himanshu Rana, a 16-year-old in his third match,* *scored a maiden hundred; he and Nitin Saini rescued Haryana from 66-4 with a stand of 205. Rajasthan shed 15 wickets on the second day and lost early on the third.*

At Mohali, January 29–31, 2015. **Odisha won by six wickets. Punjab 167 and 141** (B. C. Mohanty 6-42); ‡**Odisha 183** (S. Kaul 5-34) **and 127-4.** *Odisha 6pts.*

At Nagpur (VCA Stadium), January 29–31, 2015. **Vidarbha won by an innings and 93 runs.** ‡**Vidarbha 370** (G. Satish 163; S. Sharma 5-67); **Delhi 154** (S. B. Wagh 5-46) **and 123.** *Vidarbha 7pts. Despite Delhi's only group defeat, they were now sure of their place in the quarter-finals.*

At Ahmedabad (Sardar Vallabhbhai Patel), February 6–7, 2015. **Gujarat won by nine wickets.** ‡**Haryana 129** (R. R. Powar 5-40) **and 110** (R. B. Kalaria 5-26); **Gujarat 125** (A. Mishra 5-37) **and 115-1.** *Gujarat 6pts. Gujarat won in two days, after 26 wickets fell on the first. But it was the loss of one wicket in their second innings that cost them a place in the knockout; the bonus point for a ten-wicket win would have seen them through ahead of Vidarbha.*

At Gahunje, February 6–9, 2015. **Maharashtra won by six wickets. Maharashtra 342** (A. R. Bawne 100*) **and 168-4;** ‡**Vidarbha 114** (D. J. Muthuswami 5-19) **and 391.** *Maharashtra 6pts. Maharashtra wicketkeeper Rohit Motwani held nine catches in the match. Both teams qualified for the quarter-finals, Vidarbha on quotient after finishing level with Gujarat.*

At Cuttack (Barabati), February 6–9, 2015. **Odisha won by two wickets. Saurashtra 218 and 152;** ‡**Odisha 88** (S. Tyagi 5-24) **and 283-8.** *Odisha 6pts. Saurashtra took a 130-run first-innings lead in this relegation battle, but Odisha fought back to send them down.*

At Patiala (Dhruve Pandove), February 6–8, 2015. **Delhi won by 90 runs.** ‡**Delhi 249 and 192; Punjab 263 and 88** (M. Sharma 5-31). *Delhi 6pts. Delhi's fifth win in eight.*

Group C

At Visakhapatnam (Rajasekhara Reddy), December 7–10, 2014. **Drawn. Hyderabad 522;** ‡**Andhra 369** (D. B. Prasanth Kumar 124) **and 215-2** (K. Srikar Bharat 130*). *Andhra 1pt, Hyderabad 3pts. Ashish Reddy (95) and Chama Milind (97*, after six runs in two previous first-class matches) added 162 for Hyderabad's ninth wicket.*

At Wayanad, December 7–10, 2014. **Drawn. Goa 367 and 179-1** (S. K. Kamat 103*); ‡**Kerala 393** (A. A. Verma 129, N. Surendran 123). *Kerala 3pts, Goa 1pt. The first first-class game staged in Wayanad, at the Krishnagiri Stadium.*

At Delhi (Palam), December 7–10, 2014. **Himachal Pradesh won by an innings and 29 runs. Services 226 and 224;** ‡**Himachal Pradesh 479.** *Himachal Pradesh 7pts.*

At Guwahati (Nehru), December 7–9, 2014. **Assam won by ten wickets. Tripura 135 and 155** (K. S. Das 7-50); ‡**Assam 275** (M. B. Murasingh 5-70) **and 18-0.** *Assam 7pts.*

At Vizianagram (Dr P. V. G. Raju), December 14–17, 2014. **Andhra won by seven wickets. Kerala 229 and 129** (P. D. Vijaykumar 5-33); ‡**Andhra 141 and 221-3.** *Andhra 6pts.*

At Guwahati (Nehru), December 14–17, 2014. **Drawn. Assam 191 and 235-9 dec;** ‡**Jharkhand 217 and 78-4.** *Assam 1pt, Jharkhand 3pts. Debutant wicketkeeper-batsman Ishan Kishan, aged 16, scored 60 opening in Jharkhand's first innings.*

At Hyderabad (Uppal), December 14–17, 2014. **Drawn. Hyderabad 568-7 dec** (T. D. Agarwal 135, G. H. Vihari 179, S. A. Quadri 115*); ‡**Goa 269 and 181-2** (A. S. Desai 100*). *Hyderabad 3pts, Goa 1pt. Tanmay Agarwal, a 19-year-old left-hander, scored 135 on first-class debut, and shared a second-wicket stand of 304 with Hanuma Vihari.*

At Delhi (Palam), December 14–17, 2014. **Drawn. Tripura 430;** ‡**Services 368-2** (R. Paliwal 139*, Yashpal Singh 101*). *Services 1pt, Tripura 1pt.*

At Porvorim, December 21–24, 2014. **Drawn.** ‡**Goa 357 and 184; Himachal Pradesh 381** (A. Kalsi 115). *Goa 1pt, Himachal Pradesh 3pts. Batting at No. 9 in Goa's first innings, Robin D'Souza hit seven sixes in a 73-ball 67.*

At Dhanbad (Jawaharlal Nehru), December 21–24, 2014. **Drawn.** ‡**Jharkhand 142** (R. K. Datta 5-64) **and 409-8 dec** (I. R. Jaggi 201*); **Tripura 362 and 12-0.** *Jharkhand 1pt, Tripura 3pts. The first first-class game at the Jawaharlal Nehru Stadium. Jharkhand were 18-4 in their first innings, and 41-4 in their second, before Ishank Jaggi scored the second double-hundred of his career.*

At Wayanad, December 21–24, 2014. **Drawn. Hyderabad 270** (P. U. Anthaf 5-61) **and 249-1** (T. D. Agarwal 110, P. Akshath Reddy 104*); ‡**Kerala 447-7 dec** (S. Baby 200*). *Kerala 3pts, Hyderabad 1pt. Kerala's captain, Sachin Baby, converted a maiden century into a double. Agarwal, with another hundred, and Akshath Reddy ensured the draw with an opening stand of 235.*

At Delhi (Palam), December 21–24, 2014. **Drawn. Andhra 234 and 19-1;** ‡**Services 286.** *Services 3pts, Andhra 1pt.*

At Guwahati (Barsapara), December 28–31, 2014. **Himachal Pradesh won by an innings and 133 runs.** ‡**Himachal Pradesh 549-4 dec** (A. Bains 156, P. Dogra 230*); **Assam 218 and 198** (R. Dhawan 5-53). *Himachal Pradesh 7pts. Paras Dogra scored his fourth double-hundred.*

At Hyderabad (Uppal), December 28–31, 2014. **Drawn.** ‡**Services 306 and 285** (A. A. Bhandari 5-109); **Hyderabad 338** (G. H. Vihari 119) **and 52-1.** *Hyderabad 3pts, Services 1pt.*

At Dhanbad (Jawaharlal Nehru), December 28–31, 2014. **Drawn.** ‡**Jharkhand 337** (Virat Singh 100) **and 337-5** (S. S. Tiwary 125*); **Kerala 383.** *Jharkhand 1pt, Kerala 3pts. Virat Singh, three weeks past his 17th birthday, scored 100 in his second first-class match.*

At Agartala, December 28–31, 2014. **Drawn. Goa 251** (R. K. Datta 6-64) **and 238-9 dec;** ‡**Tripura 265 and 113-1.** *Tripura 3pts, Goa 1pt.*

At Vizianagram (Dr P. V. G. Raju), January 5–8, 2015. **Andhra won by nine wickets. Jharkhand 246 and 104** (V. C. Stephen 6-32); ‡**Andhra 304 and 47-1.** *Andhra 6pts.*

At Guwahati (Barsapara), January 5–7, 2015. **Assam won by five wickets.** ‡**Services 113** (A. K. Das 5-40) **and 170** (S. P. Purkayastha 5-29); **Assam 257 and 27-5.** *Assam 6pts.*

At Dharmasala, January 5–8, 2015. **Drawn. Kerala 196** (R. Dhawan 5-57) **and 252-8** (P. Rohan Prem 101*); ‡**Himachal Pradesh 517** (P. Dogra 166, B. Sharma 118). *Himachal Pradesh 3pts, Kerala 1pt.*

At Agartala, January 5–8, 2015. **Hyderabad won by nine wickets. Tripura 184** (Anwar Ahmed 5-53) **and 351;** ‡**Hyderabad 491-9 dec** (P. Akshath Reddy 174, D. B. Ravi Teja 100*) **and 48-1.** *Hyderabad 6pts.*

At Ongole (C. S. R. Sarma), January 13–15, 2015. **Andhra won by an innings and eight runs. Tripura 151** (D. Sivakumar 7-30) **and 151;** ‡**Andhra 310** (M. Kaif 109; M. B. Murasingh 5-70). *Andhra 7pts.*

At Dharmasala, January 13–16, 2015. **Drawn. Himachal Pradesh 304** (A. Bains 129) **and 91-6;** ‡**Jharkhand 232** (R. Dhawan 5-90). *Himachal Pradesh 3pts, Jharkhand 1pt. Ankush Bains and Ankit Kalsi (80) added 203 for Himachal Pradesh's second wicket.*

At Hyderabad (Uppal), January 13–16, 2015. **Assam won by an innings and 56 runs.** ‡**Assam 393; Hyderabad 215** (S. P. Purkayastha 5-59) **and 122** (S. P. Purkayastha 8-29). *Assam 7pts. Off-spinner Sarupam Purkayastha routed Hyderabad with a career-best 29–16–29–8, and 13-88 in the match – both the best returns of this tournament.*

At Delhi (Palam), January 13–16, 2015. **Drawn. Goa 304 and 26-0;** ‡**Services 381** (A. H. Gupta 125, H. R. Sethi 132*; M. G. Gawas 5-111). *Services 3pts, Goa 1pt. Hardik Sethi scored 132* on first-class debut.*

At Porvorim, January 21–24, 2015. **Assam won by ten wickets. Goa 175** (S. P. Purkayastha 5-69) **and 268** (S. P. Purkayastha 6-76); ‡**Assam 435-8 dec** (Tarjinder Singh 119*) **and 12-0.** *Assam 7pts. Purkayastha's 11-145 gave him 29 wickets in his last five innings. His team-mate Tarjinder Singh held five catches in the field in Goa's first innings.*

At Dharmasala, January 21–24, 2015. **Drawn. Andhra 336-8 dec** (M. U. B. Sriram 105); ‡**Himachal Pradesh 186-7.** *Himachal Pradesh 1pt, Andhra 1pt.*

At Ranchi (Jharkhand SCA Oval), January 21–24, 2015. **Drawn.** ‡**Jharkhand 556-9 dec** (S. S. Tiwary 100, I. R. Jaggi 201*) **and 189-4 dec; Hyderabad 455** (P. Akshath Reddy 133, A. Ashish Reddy 104; V. R. Aaron 5-131) **and 7-0.** *Jharkhand 3pts, Hyderabad 1pt. The first first-class match at the Jharkhand State CA Oval. Jaggi scored a third double-hundred, his second in a month.*

At Agartala, January 21–24, 2015. **Drawn. Tripura 179 and 295-9** (A. A. Verma 5-61); ‡**Kerala 301-9 dec.** *Tripura 1pt, Kerala 3pts.*

At Guwahati (Barsapara), January 29–February 1, 2015. **Assam won by ten wickets. Andhra 137 and 198** (J. Syed Mohammad 5-27); ‡**Assam 312** (S. P. Purkayastha 108*) **and 25-0**. *Assam 7pts. This was Assam's third ten-wicket victory of the season – they also won one by an innings – and it saw them into the quarter-finals with a round to go. Purkayastha scored a maiden hundred, at No. 8.*

At Porvorim, January 29–February 1, 2015. **Jharkhand won by eight wickets.** ‡**Jharkhand 385** (S. S. Tiwary 162) **and 55-2; Goa 215 and 223** (S. S. Quadri 5-82). *Jharkhand 6pts.*

At Thalassery, January 29–February 1, 2015. **Kerala won by nine wickets. Kerala 483** (S. V. Samson 207; S. Yadav 5-94) **and 10-1;** ‡**Services 318** (R. Paliwal 157; A. A. Verma 5-92) **and 174** (A. R. Chandran 6-39). *Kerala 6pts. Sanju Samson hit his second double-hundred.*

At Agartala, January 29–February 1, 2015. **Drawn. Himachal Pradesh 535-5 dec** (P. Dogra 204*, B. Sharma 119*); ‡**Tripura 346** (B. B. Ghosh 100; R. Dhawan 7-93) **and 239**. *Tripura 1pt, Himachal Pradesh 3pts. Dogra scored his fifth double-century and second of the season, adding 218* for Himachal Pradesh's sixth wicket with Bipul Sharma.*

At Ongole (C. S. R. Sarma), February 6–8, 2015. **Andhra won by an innings and 136 runs. Andhra 548-5 dec** (K. Srikar Bharat 308, M. U. B. Sriram 144); ‡**Goa 198 and 214** (D. Sivakumar 5-38). *Andhra 7pts. Srikar Bharat converted his maiden double-century into 308 from 311 balls, with six sixes; it was Andhra's first triple-hundred. He put on 333 with Muramalla Sriram for the second wicket and later held four catches in each innings behind the stumps. A comprehensive victory turned out to be enough to take Andhra into the quarter-finals.*

At Hyderabad (Uppal), February 6–9, 2015. **Drawn. Himachal Pradesh 511** (P. Dogra 137, B. Sharma 176); ‡**Hyderabad 524-5** (T. D. Agarwal 105, G. H. Vihari 263). *Hyderabad 3pts, Himachal Pradesh 1pt. On the first day, Test slow left-armer Pragyan Ojha, who had been suspended since December while the BCCI investigated his action, marked his comeback with three wickets in an over. Himachal Pradesh passed 500 for the fourth time in this tournament, and Hyderabad for the third. Dogra – with his fourth century in six innings – and Bipul Sharma added 249 for Himachal's sixth wicket, while Agarwal and Vihari put on 224 for Hyderabad's second. Agarwal ended his first season as he began it, with a century, before Vihari batted ten hours and one minute for his second double-hundred. By taking first-innings points, Hyderabad kept Himachal out of the quarter-finals.*

At Jamshedpur, February 6–8, 2015. **Jharkhand won by nine wickets. Services 230 and 235** (S. S. Quadri 6-102); ‡**Jharkhand 387** (S. P. Gautam 150) **and 84-1**. *Jharkhand 6pts.*

At Thalassery, February 6–9, 2015. **Drawn.** ‡**Assam 344 and 188-6; Kerala 266** (A. A. Verma 142). *Kerala 1pt, Assam 3pts.*

Knockouts

Quarter-final At Rohtak, February 16–18, 2015. **Maharashtra won by 75 runs.** ‡**Maharashtra 91** (D. Sivakumar 6-41) **and 223** (D. Sivakumar 6-79); **Andhra 138 and 101.** *Maharashtra were bowled out in double figures on the opening day, with Duwarapu Sivakumar on his way to 12-120, but went on to win with two days to spare.*

Quarter-final At Indore (Holkar), February 16–20, 2015. **Drawn.** Karnataka qualified for the semi-finals by virtue of their first-innings lead. **Karnataka 452** (R. V. Uthappa 153) **and 415-5 dec** (R. Samarth 178); ‡**Assam 185 and 338-4** (G. K. Sharma 127*). *Rahul (91 and 73) shared two century opening partnerships, 194 with Robin Uthappa in Karnataka's first innings, and 124 with Ravikumar Samarth in their second, when Uthappa, batting at No. 4 after taking over the injured keeper's gloves, passed 1,000 first-class runs in the season. Gokul Sharma and Arun Karthik (94) added 203 for Assam's fourth wicket in the final innings, but a target of 683 was impossible.*

Quarter-final At Cuttack (Dhaneswar Rath), February 16–20, 2015. **Mumbai won by 204 runs. Mumbai 156 and 450** (A. A. Herwadkar 161); ‡**Delhi 166** (S. N. Thakur 5-54) **and 236**. *Delhi seamer Rajat Bhatia had first-innings figures of 12–9–3–1, while his team-mate, wicketkeeper Rahul Yadav, held nine catches in the match. But Shardul Thakur's fifth five-wicket haul of the season pinned Delhi back, and 20-year-old Akhil Herwadkar's maiden century helped Mumbai to set 441.*

Quarter-final At Jaipur (Sawai Mansingh), February 16–20, 2015. **Drawn.** Tamil Nadu qualified for the semi-finals by virtue of their first-innings lead. **Tamil Nadu 403** (V. Shankar 111) **and 266;** ‡**Vidarbha 259 and 142-8**. *Vijay Shankar, backed up by Murali Vijay (96) and Baba Indrajith (97), ensured a substantial first-innings lead to see Tamil Nadu through.*

Semi-final   At Bangalore (Chinnaswamy), February 25–28, 2015. **Karnataka won by 112 runs.** ‡**Karnataka 202 and 286; Mumbai 44** (R. Vinay Kumar 6-20) **and 332.** *The opening day produced 21 wickets as Mumbai crashed for 44 (with Abhishek Nayar absent after suffering concussion in the field). It was the second-lowest total in their history, after 42 against Gujarat in 1977-78. Vinay Kumar bowled unchanged for 8–1–20–6. Next day, Thakur took his 50th wicket of the season, but Karnataka left a target of 445 and won with more than five sessions to spare.*

Semi-final   At Kolkata (Eden Gardens), February 25–March 1, 2015. **Drawn.** Tamil Nadu qualified for the final by virtue of their first-innings lead. ‡**Tamil Nadu 549** (K. D. Karthik 151) **and 119-0 dec; Maharashtra 454** (S. M. Gugale 154, C. G. Khurana 125). *For Tamil Nadu, Nos 4 to 8 all passed 65; for Maharashtra, although Swapnil Gugale and Chirag Khurana added 270 for the second wicket, the last five fell for 43, conceding the decisive first-innings lead. Maharashtra No. 11 Fallah collected his third successive duck, and sixth of the season; he had also made 0* three times. Tamil Nadu wicketkeeper Karthik was fined 40% of his match fee for excessive appealing.*

Final   At Mumbai (Wankhede), March 8–12, 2015. **Karnataka won by an innings and 217 runs. Tamil Nadu 134** (R. Vinay Kumar 5-34) **and 411** (V. Shankar 103, K. D. Karthik 120); ‡**Karnataka 762** (K. L. Rahul 188, K. K. Nair 328, R. Vinay Kumar 105*). *Karnataka retained their title. Early on the second day they were 84-5, but they added 678 for their last five wickets, a world record, beating 652 (260-5 to 912-6) by Tamil Nadu v Goa in 1988-89. Opener Rahul, who had retired hurt after pulling a hamstring in the field, resumed – hobbling – to pass 1,000 first-class runs for the season and add 386 for the sixth wicket with Karun Nair, who batted 14 hours 32 minutes and 560 balls for 328, the highest score in a Ranji final; Nair later put on 142 for the eighth wicket with captain Vinay Kumar. Only Rahul had scored more for Karnataka, with his 337 a few weeks earlier; this was also Karnataka's second-highest total, after 791-6 against Bengal in 1990-91. Tamil Nadu needed 628 to make them bat again and, despite brave efforts, could not get near. On the opening day Vinay Kumar took his 50th first-class wicket of the season.*

RANJI TROPHY WINNERS

1934-35	Bombay	1961-62	Bombay	1988-89	Delhi
1935-36	Bombay	1962-63	Bombay	1989-90	Bengal
1936-37	Nawanagar	1963-64	Bombay	1990-91	Haryana
1937-38	Hyderabad	1964-65	Bombay	1991-92	Delhi
1938-39	Bengal	1965-66	Bombay	1992-93	Punjab
1939-40	Maharashtra	1966-67	Bombay	1993-94	Bombay
1940-41	Maharashtra	1967-68	Bombay	1994-95	Bombay
1941-42	Bombay	1968-69	Bombay	1995-96	Karnataka
1942-43	Baroda	1969-70	Bombay	1996-97	Mumbai
1943-44	Western India	1970-71	Bombay	1997-98	Karnataka
1944-45	Bombay	1971-72	Bombay	1998-99	Karnataka
1945-46	Holkar	1972-73	Bombay	1999-2000	Mumbai
1946-47	Baroda	1973-74	Karnataka	2000-01	Baroda
1947-48	Holkar	1974-75	Bombay	2001-02	Railways
1948-49	Bombay	1975-76	Bombay	2002-03	Mumbai
1949-50	Baroda	1976-77	Bombay	2003-04	Mumbai
1950-51	Holkar	1977-78	Karnataka	2004-05	Railways
1951-52	Bombay	1978-79	Delhi	2005-06	Uttar Pradesh
1952-53	Holkar	1979-80	Delhi	2006-07	Mumbai
1953-54	Bombay	1980-81	Bombay	2007-08	Delhi
1954-55	Madras	1981-82	Delhi	2008-09	Mumbai
1955-56	Bombay	1982-83	Karnataka	2009-10	Mumbai
1956-57	Bombay	1983-84	Bombay	2010-11	Rajasthan
1957-58	Baroda	1984-85	Bombay	2011-12	Rajasthan
1958-59	Bombay	1985-86	Delhi	2012-13	Mumbai
1959-60	Bombay	1986-87	Hyderabad	2013-14	Karnataka
1960-61	Bombay	1987-88	Tamil Nadu	2014-15	Karnataka

Bombay/Mumbai have won the Ranji Trophy 40 times, Karnataka 8, Delhi 7, Baroda 5, Holkar 4, Bengal, Hyderabad, Madras/Tamil Nadu, Maharashtra, Railways and Rajasthan 2, Haryana, Nawanagar, Punjab, Uttar Pradesh and Western India 1.

IRANI CUP, 2014-15

Ranji Trophy Champions (Karnataka) v Rest of India

At Bangalore (Chinnaswamy), March 17–20, 2015. **Karnataka won by 246 runs. Karnataka 244** (V. R. Aaron 6-63) **and 422** (M. K. Pandey 123*; S. N. Thakur 5-86); ‡**Rest of India 264 and 156.** *Wicketkeeper Naman Ojha held six catches in Karnataka's first innings and eight in the match. Shardul Thakur took five for the sixth time in the season. Despite Karnataka trailing by 20, Karun Nair (80) and Manish Pandey helped set up a huge target, then Abhimanyu Mithun reduced the Rest to 8-3. Karnataka collected a third trophy, for the second successive season.*

VIJAY HAZARE TROPHY, 2014-15

Five 50-over zonal leagues plus knockout

Semi-final At Ahmedabad (Motera C), November 23, 2014. **Karnataka won by six runs. Karnataka 268-9** (50 overs); ‡**Bengal 262** (49.5 overs). *Vinay Kumar and Abhimanyu Mithun played crucial roles at the end of both innings. First, they shared a last-wicket stand of 46; then they claimed four of the five wickets which fell for six runs in 13 balls as Bengal finished just short.*

Semi-final At Ahmedabad (Motera B), November 23, 2014. **Punjab won by seven wickets. Odisha 238-7** (50 overs); ‡**Punjab 244-3** (48.3 overs). *Amitoze Singh (91) and Mandeep Singh (81) added 167 for Punjab's second wicket; Yuvraj Singh and Taruwar Kohli completed the job.*

Final At Ahmedabad (Motera), November 25, 2014 (day/night). **Karnataka won by 156 runs. Karnataka 359-7** (50 overs) (M. A. Agarwal 125); ‡**Punjab 203** (38.2 overs). *Karnataka retained their title; Mayank Agarwal hit 125 in 100 balls, sharing stands of 162 with Robin Uthappa (87) and 85 with Karun Nair for the first two wickets. Punjab declined swiftly from 91-1 in the 15th over.*

DEODHAR TROPHY, 2014-15

50-over knockout

Quarter-final At Mumbai (Wankhede), November 29, 2014. **South Zone won by 116 runs. South Zone 296-9** (50 overs) (R. N. B. Apparajith 113; Pankaj Singh 5-45); ‡**Central Zone 180** (36.3 overs). *Baba Apparajith hit 113 in 105 balls and added 124 for South's fourth wicket with Karun Nair (74); Pankaj Singh struck three times in their final over, before Central's batsmen folded.*

Semi-final At Mumbai (Wankhede), November 30, 2014. **East Zone won by 52 runs. East Zone 273-8** (50 overs) (M. K. Tiwary 151); ‡**North Zone 221** (47.1 overs). *Manoj Tiwary hit a one-day-best 151 in 121 balls, and North Zone struggled to recover from 29-3.*

Semi-final At Mumbai (Wankhede), December 1, 2014. **West Zone won by two wickets. South Zone 314-7** (50 overs); ‡**West Zone 319-8** (47.1 overs). *Mayank Agarwal (86) steered South Zone to a solid 180-1 before being stumped off a wide. Akshar Patel (64* in 38 balls) rallied West Zone from 174-6, adding 70 in six overs with Suryakumar Yadav (80) and 50 in six with Shardul Thakur (31*), to secure their seventh successive final.*

Final At Mumbai (Wankhede), December 3, 2014 (day/night). **East Zone won by 24 runs.** ‡**East Zone 269-8** (50 overs); **West Zone 245** (47.2 overs). *West Zone hoped for a fourth successive title, but 16-year-old Virat Singh (54) and Tiwary (75) put on 135 for East's third wicket, then Ashok Dinda reduced West to 37-3. Though Kedar Jadhav hit a 91-ball 97, their last six fell for 50.*

SYED MUSHTAQ ALI TROPHY, 2014-15

Five 20-over zonal leagues, two super leagues plus final

Final At Bhubaneswar, April 7, 2015. **Gujarat won by two wickets. Punjab 117-9** (20 overs); ‡**Gujarat 123-8** (19.5 overs). *Rohit Dahiya pinned back Punjab with 4-15. In reply Gujarat were a shaky 60-5 in the 12th over, but opener Smit Patel reached 50* to complete a tight victory with a ball to spare – their second Syed Mushtaq Ali Trophy in three seasons.*

NEW ZEALAND CRICKET IN 2015

The year of the Kiwi

ANDREW ALDERSON

Brendon McCullum spoke of his team enjoying "the time of our lives" during a World Cup in which they reached the final for the first time in 11 attempts. And, for Kiwi fans, his statement echoed across most of 2015.

The New Zealand team earned respect which transcended mere nationalism. At home, a rugby-obsessed public embraced the cricketers' camaraderie. Overseas, their sportsmanship turned friendly competitiveness from oxymoron to *raison d'être*. They marched on a diet of diligence, talent and humility, and the absorption of pressure produced self-belief. "The brand of cricket has captivated New Zealand," said McCullum, "and is starting to make people around the world sit up and take notice."

NEW ZEALAND IN 2015

	Played	Won	Lost	Drawn/No result
Tests	8	4	3	1
One-day internationals	32	21	10	1
Twenty20 internationals	4	2	2	–

DECEMBER JANUARY	2 Tests and 7 ODIs (h) v Sri Lanka 2 ODIs (h) v Pakistan	(see *Wisden 2015* page 970) (page 1033)
FEBRUARY MARCH	ICC World Cup (in Australia and New Zealand)	(page 860)
APRIL		
MAY JUNE	2 Tests, 5 ODIs and 1 T20I (a) v England	(page 300)
JULY		
AUGUST	3 ODIs and 1 T20I (a) v Zimbabwe 3 ODIs and 2 T20Is (a) v South Africa	(page 1166) (page 1080)
SEPTEMBER		
OCTOBER		
NOVEMBER	3 Tests (a) v Australia	(page 931)
DECEMBER JANUARY	2 Tests, 5 ODIs and 2 T20Is (h) v Sri Lanka	(page 1036)

For a review of New Zealand domestic cricket from the 2014-15 season, see page 1048.

Taste of success: Ross Taylor celebrates a double-century against Australia at the WACA.

In Tests, New Zealand equalled their 1987–91 record of 13 undefeated matches at home. An engrossing 1–1 draw in England – including their first Test victory there since 1999 – maintained a record run of seven series without defeat. And, although that came to an end in Australia in November, the year started and finished with 2–0 defeats of Sri Lanka. Kane Williamson was at times ranked as the No. 1 batsman in the world, and Trent Boult reached No. 2 in the bowling charts. On the down side, New Zealand didn't win either of their Test series away from home, and lost the one-dayers in England 3–2, even though they scored more overall, and more quickly, in a run-soaked series.

The high point of the year came in the World Cup, with Grant Elliott's six to win the semi-final off the penultimate ball against South Africa at Eden Park. Elliott walloped Dale Steyn over long-on to trigger local euphoria – but had the good grace to extend a hand to the prone Steyn in the moment of victory. Sadly for New Zealand, they were overwhelmed by Australia in the final at Melbourne, perhaps not coincidentally their first match away from the comforts of home.

There were other highlights for the co-hosts. Williamson's nerveless six clinched a high-octane pool match against Australia by one wicket, after Boult had taken five for 27. Tim Southee demolished England with seven for 33, New Zealand's best one-day figures, and Martin Guptill spanked 237 not out – a World Cup record – in the quarter-final against West Indies. McCullum himself hurtled along at a phenomenal strike-rate of 188. Last but not least, Daniel Vettori rolled back the years with an acrobatic catch at third man to send back Marlon Samuels in the quarter-final. Vettori bowed out after the final, his 437th international match for New Zealand, in which he scored 6,929 runs and took 696 wickets.

Dame Therese Walsh, in charge of the New Zealand leg of the Cup, also earned plaudits. She had given the sport oxygen for the next generation by negotiating to host 23 of the 49 matches. All 23 were sold out, and the boost to the economy was estimated at $NZ110m. New Zealand Cricket reported a surplus of $23.7m for the 2014-15 financial year, allied to an increase in attendances, viewership and participation. Public expectations of success and failure changed: New Zealand were expected to win.

In one respect, their limited-overs prowess harmed the side. Nine players were signed up by IPL teams, which restricted their preparation for the England tour that started in May. A total of 523 at Lord's initially looked like a triumph, but it became the highest opening innings from which a Test had been lost in 131 matches there. They rebounded to win the Second Test, with B-J. Watling scoring New Zealand's first Headingley hundred.

A lack of preparation time also hampered things in Australia in November. Aside from Williamson's 140, New Zealand looked short of match practice in losing the Brisbane Test. Ross Taylor's 290 at Perth ensured the Second Test was drawn, but New Zealand went down 2–0 after the inaugural day/night Test at Adelaide. A collective losing purse of $A400,000 anaesthetised most of the quibbles about the pink ball and the transition to dusk.

Williamson was the team benchmark, his batting perfection speaking where an acute modesty wouldn't. He scored the most Test runs (1,172 in 16 innings at 90) and centuries (five) in a calendar year by any New Zealander, while his 2,692 runs in all international formats had been bettered in a year only by Kumar Sangakkara (2,868 in 2014) and Ricky Ponting (2,833 in 2005). He became the first Kiwi to be anointed *Wisden's* Leading Cricketer in the World.

Elsewhere, Chris Cairns's perjury trial threatened to overshadow the on-field and administrative advances. He always maintained the match-fixing allegations against him were "despicable lies", and was eventually found not guilty at Southwark Crown Court. Several of New Zealand's finest from the previous generation – and McCullum from the current one – underwent a judicial laparoscopy as witnesses. Lou Vincent, who also testified, remains the only New Zealand player to admit to cheating, but the underlying theme was that Kiwis are as vulnerable as anyone to the practice.

McCullum sprung a surprise by announcing he would retire after the home series against Australia in February, which included his own 100th Test – and Test cricket's fastest century, off 54 balls, in Christchurch. Only 34, he will be next to impossible to replace. He hit his 100th Test six during 2015, equalling Adam Gilchrist's mark, and quipped it was his only record that Williamson wouldn't eventually break; in early 2016, he hit his 200th in ODIs too. Nathan McCullum, his brother, also announced his retirement after almost 150 limited-overs internationals, while the long-serving seamer Kyle Mills joined Vettori in stepping down after the World Cup.

Coach Mike Hesson thus had a lot to consider at the end of a momentous year, as it fell to a new generation to continue the impetus and inspiration which McCullum had provided since taking over as captain in 2012.

NEW ZEALAND v PAKISTAN IN 2014-15

Andrew Alderson

One-day internationals (2): New Zealand 2, Pakistan 0

This two-match series was arranged to tune up both teams for the World Cup. New Zealand's victory was their fourth in five one-day series, while Pakistan lost their fourth in a row since reaching the final of the Asia Cup in March 2014; they were even beaten in two practice games.

The tour had an unusual start when a feverish Haris Sohail was unnerved by what he said was a supernatural presence shaking his bed at a Christchurch hotel. During the first one-day international, at Wellington, the ground announcer teased him by blasting the *Ghostbusters* theme from the speakers on his entry and dismissal.

New Zealand had to dispel demons of their own. At 7ft 1in, Mohammad Irfan revelled in the extra bounce he could generate outside the United Arab Emirates, while Shahid Afridi created the odd unplayable delivery. Even so, the series ended with at least one half-century for all of New Zealand's top five except captain Brendon McCullum, and wickets for all their bowlers. In contrast, Pakistan's middle order failed and, Irfan aside, their pace bowling looked more buffet than à la carte.

PAKISTAN TOURING PARTY

*Misbah-ul-Haq, Ahmed Shehzad, Bilawal Bhatti, Ehsan Adil, Haris Sohail, Mohammad Hafeez, Mohammad Irfan, Sarfraz Ahmed, Shahid Afridi, Sohaib Maqsood, Sohail Khan, Umar Akmal, Wahab Riaz, Yasir Shah, Younis Khan. *Coach:* Waqar Younis.

Junaid Khan was originally selected, but withdrew with a thigh injury and was replaced by Bilawal Bhatti.

At Lincoln (Bert Sutcliffe Oval), January 25, 2015. **New Zealand Cricket President's XI won by six wickets.** ‡Pakistanis 313 (49.3 overs) (Misbah-ul-Haq 107, Umar Akmal 68); **New Zealand Cricket President's XI 317-4** (49.2 overs) (H. M. Nicholls 104, T. L. Seifert 115*). *The NZC President's XI chose from 12 players. Misbah-ul-Haq and Umar Akmal added 105 for the Pakistanis' fifth wicket, before Wahab Riaz and Ehsan Adil clattered 36 in two overs for the ninth to lift them past 300. But the locals were not daunted. Henry Nicholls put on 93 with opening partner Michael Pollard (35), and 85 with Tim Seifert, who hit 115* in 89 balls, including a six and a four to clinch victory in the final over.*

At Lincoln (Bert Sutcliffe Oval), January 27, 2015. **New Zealand Cricket President's XI won by one wicket.** ‡Pakistanis 267-7 (50 overs) (Umar Akmal 77, Misbah-ul-Haq 88*); **New Zealand Cricket XI 269-9** (49.5 overs) (M. A. Pollard 153). *The NZC President's XI chose from 13 players – including the tourists' Ehsan Adil, who went on to bowl Umar Akmal. The Pakistanis were 79-5 before another century stand between Umar and Misbah, this time 116. But Pollard swung the match with 153 in 132 balls; none of his team-mates reached 30, though the tail finished the job after he was seventh out with 24 required from 22 deliveries.*

❝ Scottish taunts of 'Your captain's Irish' were irrefutable.❞
England v Scotland, World Cup, page 878

NEW ZEALAND v PAKISTAN

First One-Day International

At Wellington (Westpac Stadium), January 31, 2015 (day/night). New Zealand won by seven wickets. Toss: New Zealand.

New Zealand maintained control throughout, but for the blip of a Shahid Afridi cameo. They passed a target of 211 with more than ten overs in hand, thanks to an unbeaten 112 for the fourth wicket between Taylor, who anchored the innings, and Elliott, whose international redemption continued. The pair quelled the bounce generated by Mohammad Irfan's height, which Elliott described as "like batting on a trampoline", and used their feet deftly to Afridi's spin. Earlier, Afridi had entered with Pakistan 127 for six, but refused to surrender, lashing 67 off 29 balls. In a stand of 71 with Misbah-ul-Haq, he scored 62, Misbah six and Extras three. The Pakistanis' baseball-style pinstripes seemed appropriate as three Afridi strikes cleared the rope, and nine more were spanked for four. His dynamism distracted from respectable bowling which kept Pakistan 40 or 50 short of par, according to their batting coach, Grant Flower. Returning after a groin injury, Mills claimed two for 29 in ten overs – though he was finished by the 22nd over, and able to achieve rhythm in an Afridi-free zone.

Man of the Match: G. D. Elliott.

Pakistan

Mohammad Hafeez b Mills	0	Ehsan Adil c B. B. McCullum b Elliott	6
Ahmed Shehzad c Ronchi b Boult	15	Mohammad Irfan not out	1
Younis Khan lbw b Mills	9	L-b 3, w 9, n-b 1	13
*Misbah-ul-Haq c Latham b Elliott	58		
Haris Sohail c Guptill b Anderson	23	1/0 (1) 2/29 (2) 3/32 (3) (45.3 overs) 210
Umar Akmal b Elliott	13	4/81 (5) 5/113 (6) 6/127 (7)
†Sarfraz Ahmed c Latham b Anderson	5	7/198 (4) 8/203 (9) 9/203 (8)
Shahid Afridi c Guptill b Milne	67	10/210 (10) 10 overs: 30-2
Bilawal Bhatti c Guptill b Boult	0	

Mills 10–2–29–2; Boult 9–0–25–2; Milne 10–0–43–1; N. L. McCullum 6–0–37–0; Anderson 6–0–47–2; Elliott 4.3–0–26–3.

New Zealand

M. J. Guptill c Bilawal Bhatti b Mohammad Irfan	39	L. R. P. L. Taylor not out	59
		G. D. Elliott not out	64
*B. B. McCullum c Ahmed Shehzad b Bilawal Bhatti	17	L-b 3, w 8	11
T. W. M. Latham c Sarfraz Ahmed b Shahid Afridi	23	1/31 (2) 2/75 (3) (3 wkts, 39.3 overs) 213
		3/101 (1) 10 overs: 61-1

C. J. Anderson, †L. Ronchi, N. L. McCullum, K. D. Mills, A. F. Milne and T. A. Boult did not bat.

Mohammad Irfan 10–2–60–1; Bilawal Bhatti 8–0–51–1; Ehsan Adil 7.3–0–44–0; Shahid Afridi 10–0–39–1; Haris Sohail 4–0–16–0.

Umpires: C. B. Gaffaney and M. A. Gough.   Third umpire: R. J. Tucker.
Referee: J. Srinath.

NEW ZEALAND v PAKISTAN

Second One-Day International

At Napier, February 3, 2015 (day/night). New Zealand won by 119 runs. Toss: New Zealand.

Williamson was the architect of New Zealand's 369 for five, with 112 off 88 balls, while Taylor's unbeaten 102 from 70 provided the landscaping. Taylor completed his century with a four off the innings' last delivery; it came in his 150th one-day international and was New Zealand's 100th hundred in the format. Guptill had ended a tepid run with 76, a riposte to Pearl Jam's "Can't find a better man" blaring from the loudspeakers as he strode out. Pakistan's bowlers were punished through the short square boundaries: only Mohammad Irfan and Shahid Afridi conceded less than a run a ball. But Sarfraz Ahmed missed two stumpings off Afridi, one when Taylor had 25. New Zealand's total was the second-highest in one-day internationals at McLean Park, and Pakistan struggled with the rising run-rate. Openers Ahmed Shehzad and Mohammad Hafeez did accelerate, but New Zealand patience triumphed. The slide began at 111, and the result was a fait accompli by the time the most economical bowler, Vettori, had delivered 31 dot balls.

Man of the Match: K. S. Williamson.

New Zealand

M. J. Guptill c Bilawal Bhatti b Ahmed Shehzad .	76	N. L. McCullum not out		9
*B. B. McCullum b Shahid Afridi.	31			
K. S. Williamson c Haris Sohail b Mohammad Irfan .	112	L-b 6, w 5		11
L. R. P. L. Taylor not out	102			
G. D. Elliott c Haris Sohail b Ehsan Adil . .	28	1/43 (2) 2/171 (1) (5 wkts, 50 overs)		369
†L. Ronchi c Sarfraz Ahmed b Mohammad Irfan .	0	3/250 (3) 4/322 (5)		
		5/340 (6) 10 overs: 48-1		

D. L. Vettori, T. G. Southee, A. F. Milne and T. A. Boult did not bat.

Mohammad Irfan 10–0–52–2; Bilawal Bhatti 10–0–93–0; Shahid Afridi 10–0–57–1; Ehsan Adil 8–0–68–1; Haris Sohail 6–0–47–0; Younis Khan 2–0–17–0; Ahmed Shehzad 4–0–29–1.

Pakistan

Mohammad Hafeez c Milne b Elliott	86	Ehsan Adil c Ronchi b Boult.		1
Ahmed Shehzad c Milne b N. L. McCullum	55	Mohammad Irfan not out.		0
Younis Khan c Southee b N. L. McCullum	11			
*Misbah-ul-Haq c Taylor b Southee	45	L-b 2, w 6, n-b 1		9
Shahid Afridi c Elliott b Vettori	11			
Umar Akmal b Milne	4	1/111 (2) 2/130 (3) (43.1 overs)		250
Haris Sohail c B. B. McCullum b Milne . . .	6	3/173 (1) 4/187 (5) 5/194 (6)		
†Sarfraz Ahmed c B. B. McCullum b Elliott	13	6/206 (7) 7/227 (8) 8/248 (9)		
Bilawal Bhatti c Guptill b Southee	9	9/250 (4) 10/250 (10) 10 overs: 50-0		

Southee 8–0–52–2; Boult 8.1–0–35–1; Vettori 10–0–41–1; Milne 8–0–52–2; N. L. McCullum 5–0–33–2; Elliott 4–0–35–2.

Umpires: R. J. Tucker and D. J. Walker.   Third umpire: M. A. Gough.
Referee: J. Srinath.

NEW ZEALAND v SRI LANKA IN 2015-16

Mark Geenty

Test matches (2): New Zealand 2, Sri Lanka 0
One-day internationals (5): New Zealand 3, Sri Lanka 1
Twenty20 internationals (2): New Zealand 2, Sri Lanka 0

By the time Sri Lanka's weary, wounded cricketers departed in mid-January, they had spent more than 100 days in New Zealand over the previous 13 months, across two tours and a World Cup. This was no ticket to success: in fact, familiarity very nearly bred contempt. A solitary victory from nine internationals was the tourists' lot on their latest visit, and by the final Twenty20 game in Auckland there was minimal resistance from a team who looked as if they couldn't wait for the plane home. Even without some key players, it was a highly disappointing tour.

It always looked a tough task against a New Zealand side which had not lost a home Test since March 2012, and had just been steeled by a tough series in Australia. The itinerary did Sri Lanka few favours either, after the initial oasis of a three-day warm-up in Queenstown. They moved to the antarctic climes of Dunedin in December for the First Test, and the players struggled to regain warmth in their hands for the rest of the trip.

The portents weren't good even before a ball was bowled in Dunedin. Wicketkeeper-batsman Kusal Perera was sent home after he tested positive for an unspecified banned substance, while seamer Dammika Prasad suffered a back injury in the warm-up and was ruled out of the tour. Cruelly, the Sri Lankans watched on television as their two best batsmen of recent years – Kumar Sangakkara and Mahela Jayawardene – strutted their stuff in Twenty20 franchise cricket.

How they could have done with them here. None of the visiting batsmen managed a century: their captain Angelo Mathews's 95 in the final one-day international was the highest individual innings. Many a promising fightback was undone by a flurry of loose shots. Mathews, Dimuth Karunaratne and Dinesh Chandimal (given the gloves in Perera's absence) all showed resistance at times, but not for long enough.

The one shining light was the wiry fast bowler Dushmantha Chameera who, but for a horror second-innings batting collapse, might have bowled Sri Lanka to a Test victory at Hamilton, where he took nine wickets. Chameera was fast, hostile and durable, but the others found success hard to come by.

New Zealand's opener Martin Guptill was the standout figure, reaching 50 seven times in 11 innings, and averaging 63 in the Tests and 82 in the one-dayers. Then he blasted 121 off 59 deliveries in two Twenty20 innings, including a national-record 19-ball half-century at Auckland. That stood for barely 20 minutes before Colin Munro bettered it – or battered it – by five. Kane Williamson wasn't far behind. Following his match-winning century at Hamilton, he ate his Christmas dinner as the world's top-ranked Test batsman.

Post haste: Colin Munro sprints towards New Zealand's fastest international fifty, at Auckland.

Life after Brendon McCullum also loomed into view. He led them to victory in both Tests, then confirmed he would be retiring after the home series against Australia in February. Shortly after that, he aggravated his old back injury, hurling himself across the rope and slamming into an advertising board at Hagley Oval. McCullum missed the last three ODIs and the Twenty20s, but New Zealand had plenty of firepower without him.

SRI LANKAN TOURING PARTY

*A. D. Mathews (T/50/20), P. V. D. Chameera (T/50/20), L. D. Chandimal (T/50/20), T. M. Dilshan (50/20), A. N. P. R. Fernando (T/50), M. V. T. Fernando (T), M. D. Gunathilleke (50/20), H. M. R. K. B. Herath (T), M. D. U. S. Jayasundera (T), D. S. N. F. G. Jayasuriya (20), C. K. Kapugedera (50/20), F. D. M. Karunaratne (T), K. M. D. N. Kulasekara (50/20), R. A. S. Lakmal (T/50/20), S. L. Malinga (50), B. A. W. Mendis (50), B. K. G. Mendis (T), M. D. K. Perera (T), M. D. K. J. Perera (T), N. L. T. C. Perera (50/20), K. T. G. D. Prasad (T), S. M. S. M. Senanayake (50/20), J. K. Silva (T), T. A. M. Siriwardene (T/50/20), H. D. R. L. Thirimanne (50), I. Udana (20), J. D. F. Vandersay (T/50/20), K. D. K. Vithanage (T/50/20). *Coach:* J. L. Jayaratne.

M. D. K. J. Perera left before the First Test after failing a drugs test; he was replaced by Silva for the Tests, and Vithanage for the 50-over matches. When Prasad injured his back, M. V. T. Fernando was called up for the Tests, and Kulasekara for the 50-over matches. S. L. Malinga was selected for both limited-overs squads, but failed to recover from a knee injury; he was replaced by N. L. T. C. Perera (and Chandimal as Twenty20 captain). Gunathilleke and Lakmal, not originally in the Twenty20 squad, were kept on.

At Queenstown, December 3–5 (not first-class). **Drawn. Sri Lankans 193** (72.5 overs) (F. D. M. Karunaratne 93; N. Wagner 3-31, T. G. Johnston 4-43) **and 226-6** (71 overs) (M. D. U. S. Jayasundera 63, K. D. K. Vithanage 61, A. D. Mathews 54*); ‡**New Zealand Cricket President's XI 399-8 dec** (84.3 overs) (B. Popli 79, B. S. Smith 81, S. Hicks 79*, T. G. Johnston 62; P. V. D. Chameera 4-57). *The President's XI chose from 13 players, and the Sri Lankans from 15. The tourists received an early indication of tough times ahead, struggling against a side containing only one Test player (seamer Neil Wagner). Dimuth Karunaratne batted for almost five hours in the first innings, when* *the next-best was Rangana Herath's 34 from No. 9. The President's XI openers, Delhi-born Bharat Popli and Ben Smith, put on 179, and the lead was swelled by 20-year-old Shawn Hicks and Tim Johnston. Dammika Prasad bowled only four overs before limping out of the tour with a back injury. The Sri Lankans batted better in their second innings, and avoided defeat.*

NEW ZEALAND v SRI LANKA

First Test Match

At Dunedin (University Oval), December 10–14, 2015. New Zealand won by 122 runs. Toss: Sri Lanka. Test debut: M. D. U. S. Jayasundera.

It's a long way from Colombo to Dunedin, geographically and climatically. And, as Sri Lanka assembled for the opening Test, it must have felt like a circumnavigation of the globe for their youngsters. It was 18 years since their previous Test in the world's southernmost venue, across town at Carisbrook: back in March 1997, the New Zealand opener Bryan Young had hit 267 not out, and Sri Lanka crashed to a heavy defeat. This time, woollen hats, jackets and several sweaters were mandatory as the University Oval welcomed them with a polar blast. From there the match went largely to the same script.

Mathews smiled when he called correctly, but such delight was rare over the next five days. New Zealand's batsmen seized control, then their attack toiled hard on an unresponsive surface, before clinching victory on the final afternoon.

As Mathews found out, a thick covering of grass didn't automatically mean a seamer's haven. The Dunedin wicket has always been slow and lifeless, needing grass cover to add some zing, but it remained sluggish, with worryingly variable bounce. Guptill's second-innings dismissal to Herath – bowled by one that shot along the ground – was a concern for a venue whose Test credentials were under scrutiny.

New Zealand were in control from the first morning, once Guptill stood tall and starting driving some overpitched offerings. Little went right for the bowlers, who were short of a gallop; Nuwan Pradeep Fernando snared four wickets, but went for almost five an over. Mathews turned down the chance to review an lbw appeal when Chameera pinned Guptill on 78; replays showed he would have been out. Guptill ploughed on, making the most of his first Test appearance on home soil since March 2012. He reached his third Test century – the first for 41 innings – during a stand of 173 with Williamson, then watched McCullum conduct a typical late-afternoon assault of 75 from 57 balls. After just over six hours Guptill finally wafted Mathews to Chandimal, who was keeping wicket because Kusal Perera had been sent home. By the close New Zealand already had 409 on the board, their third-highest total on the first day of a Test.

They had chosen four pacemen, with Wagner recalled for his first Test in almost a year, alongside the inexperienced spinner Santner. And all of them had to put in the hard yards in the victory push, as Sri Lanka survived 212 overs in total. Opener Karunaratne, who had done well in New Zealand a year earlier, dug in for more than four hours, while Chandimal settled in for nearly five – but they overdid the caution, perhaps unsurprisingly as they lacked support. The first innings ended after lunch on the third day with Sri Lanka 137 behind, even though they had batted for 21 overs longer than New Zealand.

Watling, the reliable wicketkeeper, was the central figure in the hosts' slow march towards all 20 wickets. He would eventually catch nine of them, to equal the national record for dismissals already shared by him and McCullum, and become only the third keeper to take nine catches in a Test twice, after Mark Boucher and Brad Haddin.

Before that, Latham extended the lead, with his third Test century, batting throughout the five-hour innings before the declaration left a target of 405 in around 140 overs. McCullum's brief innings occupied only six balls, but included two sixes – the second of which was his 100th in Tests, to equal Adam Gilchrist's record. "It's the only record of mine Kane Williamson won't break," he joked.

The weather was a more likely winner than Sri Lanka, especially when hailstones cascaded on to the outfield on the final day and threatened to whisk the covers away to the nearby athletics track. But, either side of that, the seamers worked their way through the batting, helped by an important strike from Santner, who removed top scorer Chandimal for 58. Southee bowled full and induced early edges, then Wagner charged in and tried the short-pitched approach. His lively old-ball spell ruffled the batsmen, notably Mathews, whose odd dismissal was the beginning of the end. Casually pushing the pad forward to let a full delivery pass down the leg side, Mathews was mortified to see it cannon into his stumps.

Chandimal fell at the same score and, although Vithanage and Siriwardene put on 48 in eight overs, it was all done and dusted midway through the second session.

Man of the Match: M. J. Guptill.

Close of play: first day, New Zealand 409-8 (Bracewell 32, Wagner 0); second day, Sri Lanka 197-4 (Chandimal 83, Vithanage 10); third day, New Zealand 171-1 (Latham 72, Williamson 48); fourth day, Sri Lanka 109-3 (Chandimal 31).

New Zealand

M. J. Guptill	c Chandimal b Mathews	156	– (2) b Herath		46
T. W. M. Latham	c and b Lakmal	22	– (1) not out		109
K. S. Williamson	c Karunaratne b Fernando	88	– b Chameera		71
L. R. P. L. Taylor	lbw b Fernando	8	– b Herath		15
*B. B. McCullum	c Vithanage b Siriwardene	75	– not out		17
M. J. Santner	c Chandimal b Chameera	12			
†B-J. Watling	c Vithanage b Chameera	5			
D. A. J. Bracewell	lbw b Fernando	47			
T. G. Southee	c Siriwardene b Lakmal	2			
N. Wagner	c Jayasundera b Fernando	7			
T. A. Boult	not out	0			
	B 4, l-b 3, w 1, n-b 1	9	B 4, n-b 5		9

1/56 (2) 2/229 (3) 3/245 (4) (96.1 overs) 431 | 1/79 (2) (3 wkts dec, 65.4 overs) 267
4/334 (5) 5/359 (6) 6/365 (7) | 2/220 (3) 3/247 (4)
7/394 (1) 8/399 (9) 9/426 (10) 10/431 (8)

Lakmal 16–1–69–2; Fernando 23.1–2–112–4; Mathews 9–2–28–1; Chameera 20–2–112–2; Herath 19–1–46–0; Jayasundera 5–0–33–0; Siriwardene 4–0–24–1. *Second innings*—Lakmal 13–0–40–0; Mathews 4–1–4–0; Chameera 14–0–61–1; Fernando 13–1–52–0; Herath 11.4–1–62–2; Siriwardene 8–0–32–0; Jayasundera 2–0–12–0.

Sri Lanka

F. D. M. Karunaratne	c Watling b Santner	84	– c Watling b Southee		29
B. K. G. Mendis	c Watling b Boult	8	– c Watling b Southee		46
M. D. U. S. Jayasundera	c Watling b Wagner	1	– c Watling b Wagner		3
†L. D. Chandimal	c Guptill b Southee	83	– lbw b Santner		58
*A. D. Mathews	c Watling b Southee	2	– b Wagner		25
K. D. K. Vithanage	c Watling b Southee	22	– lbw b Southee		38
T. A. M. Siriwardene	c Taylor b Wagner	35	– c McCullum b Boult		29
H. M. R. K. B. Herath	c Boult b Wagner	15	– c Guptill b Boult		6
P. V. D. Chameera	c Taylor b Boult	14	– b Santner		14
R. A. S. Lakmal	not out	18	– c and b Bracewell		23
A. N. P. R. Fernando	c Watling b Santner	3	– not out		4
	B 1, l-b 4, n-b 4	9	B 2, l-b 4, w 1		7

1/19 (2) 2/29 (3) 3/151 (1) (117.1 overs) 294 | 1/54 (1) 2/64 (3) (95.2 overs) 282
4/156 (5) 5/198 (4) 6/209 (6) | 3/109 (2) 4/165 (5)
7/252 (7) 8/273 (8) 9/287 (9) 10/294 (11) | 5/165 (4) 6/213 (6) 7/236 (8)
8/249 (7) 9/268 (9) 10/282 (10)

Boult 22–7–52–2; Southee 27–4–71–3; Bracewell 21–6–42–0; Wagner 25–5–87–3; Santner 21.1–8–37–2; Williamson 1–1–0–0. *Second innings*—Boult 15–2–58–2; Southee 21–6–52–3; Bracewell 19.2–5–46–1; Santner 22–6–53–2; Wagner 17–5–56–2; Williamson 1–0–11–0.

Umpires: R. A. Kettleborough and N. J. Llong.   Third umpire: P. R. Reiffel.
Referee: D. C. Boon.

NEW ZEALAND v SRI LANKA

Second Test Match

At Hamilton, December 18–21, 2015. New Zealand won by five wickets. Toss: New Zealand.

Two years previously, New Zealand had been alarmed to find the Seddon Park pitch dry, and providing help to West Indies' spinners. There was no such problem this time: coach Mike Hesson's pre-series call for green surfaces had been heard loud and clear. Not since India's tour of 2002-03, when the third day featured parts of all four innings, had the Hamilton pitch looked quite so similar to the outfield. As often happens in New Zealand, though, it didn't offer as much seam movement as the verdancy suggested, but the new track – relaid the previous year – still ensured a spicy time for batsmen. Steep bounce was their greatest enemy, prompting spectacular collapses and sore fingers on both sides. But Williamson's class told, coolly guiding New Zealand home, despite a fine display from the speedy Chameera.

Their bowlers had tried too hard after being given first use of the inviting green carpet – the 16th Test in a row in New Zealand in which the captain winning the toss had bowled first – and Sri Lanka's total of 292 looked competitive. Kusal Mendis, in only his third Test, had an exciting time: dropped second ball by Taylor at slip, he had advanced to 20 when Bracewell hit the off stump hard (replays showed it moving) but the bail refused to drop. Mendis made it to 31 before edging Southee again, and Watling caught it. Chandimal scored a breezy 47, but Mathews and Siriwardene tucked in as Wagner overdid the short stuff. Both collected three sixes, and cracked 138 in 30 overs before Boult claimed two in an over. Running out of partners, Mathews poked to third slip, and the innings soon closed, just short of 300 rather than well past it, as had seemed likely at one stage.

Guptill and Latham put on 81, helped by Mathews's mysterious reluctance to try Chameera, his fastest bowler. He eventually came on as third change, immediately after lunch, and had Latham caught at leg gully in his second over. Williamson followed in his next, skying a pull, and Taylor edged a fizzer in the one after that. With Herath removing Guptill in between, New Zealand had lost four for eight.

In his 99th Test – all consecutive from debut, breaking A. B. de Villiers's record – McCullum buckled down, surviving 80 minutes for 18; the promising Santner followed suit, making 38 in two and a half hours. Bracewell hung around too, but Chameera finished with five for 47 as Sri Lanka took a lead of 55, and sniffed a chance of squaring the series.

Chameera's success, however, had shown New Zealand what to do, and the Sri Lankans were subjected to a short-pitched barrage on the springy surface. Karunaratne and Mendis started brightly with a stand of 71, but after that the bounce began to play on the batsmen's minds, and all ten wickets tumbled for 62 in 14 overs. Southee claimed seven wickets in the match, and 13 in the series. A fascinating Test had been turned on its head, as New Zealand eyed a target of 189 to maintain their unbeaten home Test record since losing to South Africa in March 2012 – here at Hamilton.

Chameera was given the new ball this time, and by the end of his third over had removed both openers. It was game on. Williamson, though, was equal to the task: he had learned from his brief first innings, and now shelved the pull or hook when Chameera dropped short. In tricky conditions, with the match on the line, it was another batting masterclass – driving, cutting, deflecting.

He added 67 with Taylor, and 52 with McCullum – both falling to Chameera, who ended with nine in the match. But he could not confound Williamson a second time, and his 13th Test century ensured New Zealand's 2–0 series triumph. This innings briefly took him to the top of the ICC rankings for Test batsmen, having scored 1,172 Test runs, eight more than McCullum's previous national record from the year before. New Zealand had now gone 13 home Tests without defeat, equalling their longest such run, between 1986-87 and 1990-91. This was their fourth win in a row at home, all against Sri Lanka.

Man of the Match: K. S. Williamson.

Close of play: first day, Sri Lanka 264-7 (Mathews 63, Chameera 0); second day, New Zealand 232-9 (Bracewell 30); third day, New Zealand 142-5 (Williamson 78, Watling 0).

Sri Lanka

F. D. M. Karunaratne c Watling b Southee	12	– c Southee b Bracewell	27
B. K. G. Mendis c Watling b Southee	31	– c Santner b Southee	46
M. D. U. S. Jayasundera run out	26	– c Watling b Bracewell	0
†L. D. Chandimal c Watling b Bracewell	47	– c Guptill b Wagner	4
*A. D. Mathews c Latham b Southee	77	– c Watling b Southee	2
T. A. M. Siriwardene c Taylor b Boult	62	– c Boult b Wagner	26
K. D. K. Vithanage c McCullum b Boult	0	– c Bracewell b Wagner	9
H. M. R. K. B. Herath run out	4	– b Southee	0
P. V. D. Chameera c McCullum b Bracewell	4	– run out	2
R. A. S. Lakmal c Williamson b Wagner	4	– not out	1
A. N. P. R. Fernando not out	2	– c Watling b Southee	0
L-b 11, w 12	23	B 4, l-b 2, w 7, n-b 3	16

1/39 (1) 2/44 (2) 3/115 (3)   (80.1 overs) 292
4/121 (4) 5/259 (6) 6/259 (7)
7/264 (8) 8/284 (5) 9/288 (10) 10/292 (9)

1/71 (1) 2/71 (3)   (36.3 overs) 133
3/77 (4) 4/87 (2)
5/110 (5) 6/123 (6) 7/123 (8)
8/131 (7) 9/133 (9) 10/133 (11)

Boult 20–2–51–2; Southee 21–5–63–3; Bracewell 22.1–4–81–2; Wagner 9–1–51–1; Santner 7–0–34–0; Williamson 1–0–1–0. *Second innings*—Boult 7–1–30–0; Southee 12.3–2–26–4; Bracewell 8–1–31–2; Wagner 9–2–40–3.

New Zealand

M. J. Guptill c Mathews b Herath	50	– (2) c Karunaratne b Chameera	1
T. W. M. Latham c Karunaratne b Chameera	28	– (1) c Fernando b Chameera	4
K. S. Williamson c Lakmal b Chameera	1	– not out	108
L. R. P. L. Taylor c Chandimal b Chameera	0	– c sub (J. D. F. Vandersay) b Chameera	35
*B. B. McCullum c Mendis b Herath	18	– c Mathews b Chameera	18
M. J. Santner c Chandimal b Fernando	38	– c Chandimal b Lakmal	4
†B-J. Watling c Vithanage b Lakmal	28	– not out	13
D. A. J. Bracewell not out	35		
T. G. Southee c Jayasundera b Chameera	4		
N. Wagner c Vithanage b Chameera	17		
T. A. Boult c Herath b Fernando	0		
L-b 3, w 8, n-b 7	18	L-b 1, n-b 5	6

1/81 (2) 2/83 (3) 3/86 (1)   (79.4 overs) 237
4/89 (4) 5/128 (5) 6/168 (6)
7/196 (7) 8/201 (9) 9/232 (10) 10/237 (11)

1/4 (1)   (5 wkts, 54.3 overs) 189
2/11 (2) 3/78 (4)
4/130 (5) 5/142 (6)

Lakmal 16–4–48–1; Mathews 11–7–25–0; Fernando 17.4–4–39–2; Herath 22–1–75–2; Chameera 13–3–47–5. *Second innings*—Chameera 17–1–68–4; Lakmal 12–4–20–1; Herath 11–0–48–0; Fernando 12–1–43–0; Mathews 1–0–4–0; Siriwardene 1.3–0–5–0.

Umpires: N. J. Llong and P. R. Reiffel.   Third umpire: R. A. Kettleborough.
Referee: D. C. Boon.

NEW ZEALAND v SRI LANKA

First One-Day International

At Christchurch (Hagley Oval), December 26, 2015. New Zealand won by seven wickets. Toss: Sri Lanka. One-day international debut: H. M. Nicholls.

Ten months on from the World Cup opener, the two combatants from that chilly, giddy afternoon reconvened at the same venue. New Zealand won again, but even more emphatically, roaring into top gear as Sri Lanka stalled. A festive crowd of 8,200 basked on the hill, and saw the contest effectively decided inside ten overs. With Trent Boult and Tim Southee both rested, Mathews opted to bat first – but the young tearaways did the damage. Bowling full and shaping the ball away, Henry – whose opening spell on his home ground was 7–1–26–4 – and Milne reduced Sri Lanka to 27 for five. There was no way back, although Siriwardene and Kulasekara put on 98 to lift the total near to 200. New Zealand sensed an early finish, and 108 came from the first ten overs. Guptill hit four sixes in his 79 from 56 balls, while McCullum slammed a trademark 55 off 25, with 50 in boundaries. It was left to Henry Nicholls, the local left-hander on international debut, to finish things off with successive fours off Ajantha Mendis, and 29 overs to spare.

Man of the Match: M. J. Henry.

Sri Lanka

M. D. Gunathilleke c Ronchi b Milne	8		B. A. W. Mendis c Ronchi b McClenaghan	4
T. M. Dilshan c Nicholls b Henry	9		P. V. D. Chameera not out	13
H. D. R. L. Thirimanne lbw b Henry	1		R. A. S. Lakmal c Latham b Bracewell	8
†L. D. Chandimal c Taylor b Henry	5			
*A. D. Mathews c Latham b Henry	0		W 8	8
T. A. M. Siriwardene c McCullum				
b Bracewell	66		1/13 (1) 2/20 (2) 3/23 (3) (47 overs)	188
C. K. Kapugedera c Santner b Bracewell	8		4/23 (5) 5/27 (4) 6/65 (7)	
K. M. D. N. Kulasekara c Ronchi			7/163 (6) 8/164 (8) 9/167 (9)	
b McClenaghan	58		10/188 (11) 10 overs: 29-5	

Milne 10–0–30–1; Henry 10–1–49–4; McClenaghan 10–2–40–2; Bracewell 9–1–37–3; Santner 8–0–32–0.

New Zealand

M. J. Guptill c Kulasekara b Siriwardene	79
*B. B. McCullum c Lakmal b Siriwardene	55
T. W. M. Latham b Dilshan	18
L. R. P. L. Taylor not out	5
H. M. Nicholls not out	23
L-b 1, w 10	11

1/108 (2) 2/162 (3)   (3 wkts, 21 overs) 191
3/164 (1)

10 overs: 108-0

M. J. Santner, †L. Ronchi, D. A. J. Bracewell, A. F. Milne, M. J. Henry and M. J. McClenaghan did not bat.

Kulasekara 3–0–27–0; Lakmal 3–0–24–0; Mathews 1–0–17–0; Mendis 5–0–49–0; Siriwardene 5–0–45–2; Chameera 2–0–18–0; Dilshan 2–0–10–1.

Umpires: M. A. Gough and P. D. Jones.   Third umpire: R. K. Illingworth.
Referee: A. J. Pycroft.

> **"** Rogers provided a sturdy counterpoint to the swash in Smith's buckle."
> Five Cricketers of the Year, page 102

NEW ZEALAND v SRI LANKA

Second One-Day International

At Christchurch (Hagley Oval), December 28, 2015. New Zealand won by ten wickets. Toss: Sri Lanka. One-day international debut: J. D. F. Vandersay.

If Boxing Day had been a stroll in the park for New Zealand, this was almost a sleepwalk. Henry again haunted the top order, before Guptill monstered the bowling. Sri Lanka folded once more after choosing to bat, as Henry collected another four-for, and McClenaghan took three. This time there was no partial recovery: Sri Lanka's top score was 19, by Kulasekara from No. 8. And the match was over even more quickly: Guptill scorched to his half-century in 17 balls, one short of the world record, clouting eight sixes – and nine fours – in his unbeaten 93 from 30; his strike-rate of 310 had been bettered only by A. B. de Villiers (338, in his 149 from 44 against West Indies at Johannesburg in 2014-15) in an innings of 25 balls or more. Jeffrey Vandersay, Sri Lanka's debutant leg-spinner, had a cruel introduction, conceding 34 from his two overs as New Zealand careered to victory in 40 minutes to complete what Sri Lanka's coach Jerome Jayaratne called "a really humiliating day". The caterers were left to rustle up an early lunch, as the entire match – New Zealand's 12th successive win at home – lasted only 36 overs.

Man of the Match: M. J. Guptill.

Sri Lanka

M. D. Gunathilleke c Santner b Henry	17	S. M. S. M. Senanayake b Henry	0
T. M. Dilshan c Taylor b Henry	7	P. V. D. Chameera c Ronchi b Sodhi	9
H. D. R. L. Thirimanne c Henry		J. D. F. Vandersay not out	7
b McClenaghan	1		
†L. D. Chandimal lbw b Bracewell	9	L-b 4, w 2, n-b 1	7
*A. D. Mathews c Ronchi b McClenaghan	17		
T. A. M. Siriwardene c Nicholls		1/20 (2) 2/29 (3) 3/31 (1) (27.4 overs) 117	
b McClenaghan	12	4/54 (4) 5/56 (5) 6/81 (6)	
C. K. Kapugedera run out	12	7/81 (7) 8/81 (9) 9/94 (10)	
K. M. D. N. Kulasekara c Latham b Henry	19	10/117 (8) 10 overs: 40-3	

Bracewell 6–2–31–1; Henry 9.4–2–33–4; McClenaghan 8–0–32–3; Santner 1–0–5–0; Sodhi 3–0–12–1.

New Zealand

M. J. Guptill not out	93
T. W. M. Latham not out	17
L-b 2, w 6	8

(no wkt, 8.2 overs) 118

*B. B. McCullum, L. R. P. L. Taylor, H. M. Nicholls, M. J. Santner, †L. Ronchi, D. A. J. Bracewell, M. J. Henry, I. S. Sodhi and M. J. McClenaghan did not bat.

Chameera 2–0–41–0; Kulasekara 2–0–19–0; Senanayake 2.2–0–22–0; Vandersay 2–0–34–0.

Umpires: R. K. Illingworth and D. J. Walker.   Third umpire: M. A. Gough.
Referee: A. J. Pycroft.

NEW ZEALAND v SRI LANKA

Third One-Day International

At Nelson, December 31, 2015. Sri Lanka won by eight wickets. Toss: New Zealand.

Sri Lanka finally found some semblance of form, and rescued the tour from disaster with a fine batting display. Williamson returned for New Zealand after missing the previous two matches with a knee niggle, and took over as captain from McCullum, who had aggravated a back injury trying to prevent a boundary in the previous game. He top-scored with 59, but Saxton Oval had been a batsman's paradise during the World Cup, and New Zealand's total – with Chameera outstanding and Vandersay applying the brakes after his nightmare debut – looked underwhelming. Still, the verve with which Sri Lanka took on the challenge was refreshing after their recent collapses. Gunathilleke started with four sixes in his 65 from 45 balls, putting on 98 with Dilshan, who kept the rate under control with a run-a-ball 91. He added 111 with Thirimanne, who calmly collected the rest with Chandimal. New Zealand missed Henry, strangely sent back to domestic cricket.

Man of the Match: M. D. Gunathilleke.

New Zealand

M. J. Guptill c Dilshan b Chameera	30	A. F. Milne not out		17
T. W. M. Latham c Fernando b Vandersay	42	T. G. Southee not out		18
*K. S. Williamson c Chameera b Siriwardene	59			
L. R. P. L. Taylor c Mathews b Vandersay	0	L-b 4, w 10, n-b 1		15
H. M. Nicholls b Chameera	20			
M. J. Santner run out	38	1/42 (1) 2/102 (2)	(8 wkts, 50 overs)	276
†L. Ronchi c Kapugedera b Fernando	7	3/102 (4) 4/143 (5)		
D. A. J. Bracewell c sub		5/163 (3) 6/191 (7)		
(S. M. S. M. Senanayake) b Fernando	30	7/215 (6) 8/257 (8)	10 overs: 47-1	

M. J. McClenaghan did not bat.

Fernando 10–0–55–2; Chameera 10–0–38–2; Dilshan 8–1–43–0; Kulasekara 5–0–31–0; Mathews 2–0–17–0; Vandersay 10–1–55–2; Siriwardene 5–0–33–1.

Sri Lanka

M. D. Gunathilleke c Taylor b McClenaghan	65
T. M. Dilshan run out	91
H. D. R. L. Thirimanne not out	87
†L. D. Chandimal not out	27
W 6, n-b 1	7
1/98 (1) 2/209 (2) (2 wkts, 46.2 overs)	277
10 overs: 83-0	

*A. D. Mathews, T. A. M. Siriwardene, C. K. Kapugedera, K. M. D. N. Kulasekara, P. V. D. Chameera, A. N. P. R. Fernando and J. D. F. Vandersay did not bat.

Southee 6–0–44–0; Milne 6–0–50–0; Bracewell 6.2–0–45–0; McClenaghan 9–0–39–1; Santner 10–0–59–0; Williamson 8–0–38–0; Guptill 1–0–2–0.

Umpires: B. F. Bowden and M. A. Gough. Third umpire: R. K. Illingworth.
Referee: A. J. Pycroft.

NEW ZEALAND v SRI LANKA

Fourth One-Day International

At Nelson, January 2, 2016. No result. Toss: Sri Lanka.

Nelson boasts some of the highest sunshine hours in New Zealand, but couldn't rustle up two bright days for its New Year double-header. Early rain had already shortened this one to a 24-over match, which was interestingly poised when another downpour forced the players off for good. There was time for Guptill to wallop three sixes off Chameera in an over costing 26.

New Zealand

M. J. Guptill lbw b Kulasekara	....	27
T. W. M. Latham c Chandimal b Perera	..	9
*K. S. Williamson c and b Chameera	......	12
L. R. P. L. Taylor not out	....	20
H. M. Nicholls not out	....	4
W 2, n-b 1	....	3

1/37 (2) 2/45 (1)   (3 wkts, 9 overs)   75
3/53 (3)   5 overs: 46-2

M. J. Santner, †L. Ronchi, A. F. Milne, M. J. Henry, I. S. Sodhi and M. J. McClenaghan did not bat.

Chameera 3–0–32–1; Perera 2–0–13–1; Kulasekara 1–0–4–1; Siriwardene 2–0–11–0; Vandersay 1–0–15–0.

Sri Lanka

M. D. Gunathilleke, T. M. Dilshan, H. D. R. L. Thirimanne, †L. D. Chandimal, *A. D. Mathews, N. L. T. C. Perera, T. A. M. Siriwardene, C. K. Kapugedera, K. M. D. N. Kulasekara, P. V. D. Chameera and J. D. F. Vandersay.

Umpires: B. F. Bowden and R. K. Illingworth.   Third umpire: M. A. Gough.
Referee: A. J. Pycroft.

NEW ZEALAND v SRI LANKA

Fifth One-Day International

At Mount Maunganui, January 5, 2016. New Zealand won by 36 runs. Toss: Sri Lanka.
     Sri Lanka still had a chance to level the series, but were thwarted again by Henry. Restored after missing the first Nelson match, he sliced through the order to finish with five for 40, and 13 wickets in the series at nine apiece. After Dilshan sent a trademark scoop straight to the keeper, Henry got going with the scalps of Thirimanne and Gunathilleke. A stand of 93 between Chandimal and Mathews was broken by the rusty Boult, back after a break, then Henry returned at the death to claim three more wickets, the key one being Mathews, who hooked to deep square, where Nicholls took a good high catch which would have carried for six. Mathews's 95 was Sri Lanka's highest individual score of the tour. Earlier, after Latham fell in the first over, Guptill's tenth one-day international century was the backbone of New Zealand's substantial innings, helped by 61s from Williamson and Taylor. Guptill finished the series with 331 runs, a strike-rate of 139, and 19 sixes.
     Man of the Match: M. J. Henry.

New Zealand

M. J. Guptill c Perera b Kulasekara	....	102
T. W. M. Latham c Chandimal b Fernando		0
*K. S. Williamson c Chandimal b Dilshan	..	61
L. R. P. L. Taylor c Siriwardene		
b Kulasekara	.	61
H. M. Nicholls c Dilshan b Kulasekara	....	2
†L. Ronchi not out	....	37

M. J. Santner not out	....	21
L-b 5, w 5	....	10

1/3 (2) 2/125 (3)   (5 wkts, 50 overs)   294
3/206 (1) 4/215 (5)
5/262 (4)   10 overs: 55-1

A. F. Milne, M. J. Henry, I. S. Sodhi and T. A. Boult did not bat.

Fernando 10–1–69–1; Chameera 9–0–41–0; Perera 6–0–45–0; Kulasekara 10–0–53–3; Dilshan 10–0–49–1; Siriwardene 5–0–32–0.

Sri Lanka

M. D. Gunathilleke c Sodhi b Henry	15
T. M. Dilshan c Ronchi b Boult	5
H. D. R. L. Thirimanne b Henry	2
†L. D. Chandimal c Williamson b Boult	50
*A. D. Mathews c Nicholls b Henry	95
N. L. T. C. Perera c Taylor b Milne	15
T. A. M. Siriwardene c Nicholls b Santner .	39
C. K. Kapugedera c Milne b Henry	10
K. M. D. N. Kulasekara c Santner b Boult . .	15

P. V. D. Chameera b Henry	0
A. N. P. R. Fernando not out	0
L-b 1, w 11	12
1/12 (2) 2/15 (3) 3/33 (1) (47.1 overs) 258	
4/126 (4) 5/161 (6) 6/223 (7)	
7/237 (8) 8/252 (5) 9/253 (10)	
10/258 (9) 10 overs: 33-3	

Boult 8.1–0–43–3; Henry 10·1–1–40–5; Milne 9–0–54–1; Santner 9–1–54–1; Sodhi 9–0–55–0; Williamson 2–0–11–0.

Umpires: B. F. Bowden and M. A. Gough.   Third umpire: R. K. Illingworth.
Referee: A. J. Pycroft.

NEW ZEALAND v SRI LANKA

First Twenty20 International

At Mount Maunganui, January 7, 2016. New Zealand won by three runs. Toss: Sri Lanka. Twenty20 international debut: M. D. Gunathilleke.

With nearly 8,000 crammed in, the gates were closed at the Bay Oval. New Zealand – ranked a lowly eighth in the format, while Sri Lanka were first – reached 182, mainly thanks to an opening stand of 101 between Guptill and Williamson, although the later batsmen failed to capitalise. Henry and Boult took two early wickets apiece, reducing Sri Lanka to 42 for four after five overs, but Gunathilleke and Siriwardene kept blazing away. It boiled down to 13 off the last over, which was entrusted to Elliott, making an international comeback after breaking his arm in the nets in November. But Kulasekara slogged the third ball to deep midwicket, Kapugedera was run out, and New Zealand hung on.

Man of the Match: T. A. Boult.

New Zealand

		B	4/6
1 M. J. Guptill run out	58	34	4/4
2 *K. S. Williamson c 11 b 9 . . .	53	42	5/1
3 C. Munro c and b 9	36	26	2/2
4 C. J. Anderson c 6 b 10	2	3	0
5 L. R. P. L. Taylor not out	22	9	3/1
6 G. D. Elliott not out	10	6	1
W 1	1		

6 overs: 62-0   (20 overs)   182-4

1/101   2/131   3/135   4/163

7 †L. Ronchi, 8 M. J. Henry, 9 M. J. McClenaghan, 10 I. S. Sodhi and 11 T. A. Boult did not bat.

Lakmal 3–0–39–0 (4); Perera 3–0–39–0 (4); Kulasekara 4–0–26–2 (8); Jayasuriya 4–0–28–0 (8); Vandersay 4–0–30–1 (6); Dilshan 2–0–20–0 (0).

Sri Lanka

		B	4/6
1 M. D. Gunathilleke c 5 b 10 . . .	46	29	3/2
2 T. M. Dilshan c 7 b 11	0	1	0
3 *†L. D. Chandimal c 10 b 8 . . .	7	7	1
4 D. S. N. F. G. Jayasuriya c 7 b 11	4	3	0
5 A. D. Mathews c 6 b 8	4	5	1
6 T. A. M. Siriwardene c 9 b 11 . .	42	31	2/2
7 N. L. T. C. Perera c 1 b 8	28	19	3/1
8 C. K. Kapugedera run out	17	15	2
9 K. M. D. N. Kulasekara c 11 b 6	14	10	0/1
10 J. D. F. Vandersay not out	4	1	1
11 R. A. S. Lakmal not out	1	1	0
L-b 6, w 4, n-b 2	12		

6 overs: 56-4   (20 overs)   179-9

1/10   2/27   3/33   4/42   5/84   6/133   7/153   8/173
9/174

Henry 4–0–44–3 (10); Boult 4–0–21–3 (10); McClenaghan 4–0–40–0 (6); Elliott 2–0–18–1 (3); Sodhi 4–0–33–1 (5); Munro 2–0–17–0 (3).

Umpires: P. D. Jones and D. J. Walker.   Third umpire: B. F. Bowden.
Referee: A. J. Pycroft.

NEW ZEALAND v SRI LANKA

Second Twenty20 International

At Auckland, January 10, 2016. New Zealand won by nine wickets. Toss: New Zealand.

Sri Lanka's dispiriting tour ended with another shellacking from New Zealand's batsmen, to the delight of a crowd of 17,000. Mathews, with 81 not out from 49 balls, was the lone star of Sri Lanka's innings, but then had to watch helplessly as Guptill zoomed to his half-century in 19 balls,

ANYTHING YOU CAN DO...

The fastest half-centuries in Twenty20 internationals:

Balls

12	Yuvraj Singh (58)	India v England at Durban.	2007-08
14	**C. Munro (50*)**	**New Zealand v Sri Lanka at Auckland**	**2015-16**
17	P. R. Stirling (79)	Ireland v Afghanistan at Dubai	2011-12
17	S. J. Myburgh (63)	Netherlands v Ireland at Sylhet	2013-14
17	**C. H. Gayle (77)**	**West Indies v South Africa at Cape Town**	**2014-15**
18	D. A. Warner (67)	Australia v West Indies at Sydney.	2009-10
18	G. J. Maxwell (74)	Australia v Pakistan at Mirpur.	2013-14
19	†D. A. Warner (89)	Australia v South Africa at Melbourne	2008-09
19	G. Gambhir (55)	India v Sri Lanka at Nagpur.	2009-10
19	**M. J. Guptill (63)**	**New Zealand v Sri Lanka at Auckland**	**2015-16**

† *On debut.*

breaking by four the national record he already shared with Aaron Redmond. But Guptill owned the record for about 20 minutes, as Munro slammed a fifty from just 14 deliveries, winning the match with his seventh six, from the last ball of the tenth over. "I'm not sure what these two had for breakfast," said Williamson. "But it was unbelievable to watch."

Man of the Match: C. Munro.

Sri Lanka

		B	*4/6*
1 M. D. Gunathilleke *b 9*	8	6	1
2 T. M. Dilshan *c 10 b 6*	28	26	4
3 D. S. N. F. G. Jayasuriya *c 2 b 9*	3	10	0
4 *†L. D. Chandimal *c 5 b 8*	2	4	0
5 A. D. Mathews *not out*	81	49	7/4
6 T. A. M. Siriwardene *c 11 b 8* . .	0	1	0
7 K. D. K. Vithanage *c 9 b 6*	1	4	0
8 N. L. T. C. Perera *c 1 b 6*	6	10	0
9 I. Udana *c 2 b 6*	0	2	0
10 J. D. F. Vandersay *not out*	8	8	1
L-b 2, w 3	5		

6 overs: 37-2   (20 overs) 142-8

1/11 2/33 3/39 4/63 5/66 6/70 7/98 8/103

11 P. V. D. Chameera did not bat.

Boult 4–0–36–0 (8); Milne 4–0–36–2 (8); McClenaghan 4–0–22–0 (11); Santner 4–0–24–2 (13); Elliott 4–0–22–4 (8).

New Zealand

		B	*4/6*
1 M. J. Guptill *c 4 b 8*	63	25	6/5
2 *K. S. Williamson *not out*	32	21	3
3 C. Munro *not out*	50	14	1/7
W 2	2		

6 overs: 82-0   (10 overs) 147-1

1/89

4 C. J. Anderson, 5 L. R. P. L. Taylor, 6 G. D. Elliott, 7 †L. Ronchi, 8 M. J. Santner, 9 A. F. Milne, 10 M. J. McClenaghan and 11 T. A. Boult did not bat.

Udana 3–0–34–0 (4); Chameera 3–0–46–0 (2); Vandersay 2–0–41–0 (2); Perera 2–0–26–1 (5).

Umpires: B. F. Bowden and P. D. Jones.   Third umpire: D. J. Walker.
Referee: A. J. Pycroft.

DOMESTIC CRICKET IN NEW ZEALAND IN 2014-15

Mark Geenty

With only six teams chasing the spoils, securing back-to-back first-class titles might appear relatively straightforward. But **Canterbury's** successful defence of the Plunket Shield in 2014-15 was the first instance since Auckland managed it in 2002-03. In between, every team except Otago has hoisted the trophy. This even spread is helped by New Zealand Cricket's contracting model: each major association rank 14 players, and those unhappy with their rating can look elsewhere.

Canterbury's third Shield in five years was a testament to a solid core of experienced former internationals, led by opener Peter Fulton, and some rising talent from the Christchurch production line under coach Gary Stead. They sealed their latest title in the final round, with their sixth win: 21-year-old left-armer Ed Nuttall set up victory over Northern Districts with six for 35, before Fulton added the polish with 91 not out off 53 balls. Fulton, Andrew Ellis and Neil Broom each topped 800 runs, while Ellis also snared 29 wickets. Leg-spinner Todd Astle, still waiting to add to his one Test cap, was second on the wicket-taking charts, with 44 – one behind 20-year-old Otago seamer Jacob Duffy. Earlier in the season, some supporters were dismayed when the team, rebranded Canterbury Kings, played the Twenty20 competition in a purple and gold strip rather than their traditional red and black.

Auckland were runners-up in all three formats, losing both limited-overs finals, but winning their last Plunket Shield game to clinch second place. Colin Munro hit a world-record 23 sixes, seven clear of the previous mark, in his 281 off 167 balls against Central in Napier. But Auckland coach Matt Horne was asked to reapply for his job after the season ended; he declined, and Mark O'Donnell, who had held the post for seven seasons up to 2008-09, was reinstated.

In the Georgie Pie Super Smash Twenty20 competition, **Wellington** won their second final in eight months, after breaking a decade-long title drought with the 50-over trophy in April 2014. Victory over Auckland qualified them for a lucrative first Champions League appearance – until the news that it was being scrapped. All-rounder Grant Elliott was dominant with bat and ball, his rejuvenated form spurring him into the World Cup squad. Wellington had less success in the longer formats, but Stephen Murdoch broke the province's first-class record when he topped the run list with 998. At the season's end they lost captain and coach: James Franklin signed with Middlesex as a non-overseas player via his Irish ancestry, meaning he could return to Wellington only as an import, while Jamie Siddons went back to South Australia after four years; Michael Papps and Bruce Edgar succeeded them.

Central Districts won the 50-over Ford Trophy; they headed the league, lost the first preliminary final to Auckland, beat Otago in the third, then took revenge on Auckland in the deciding final. That victory marked the end of former Test opener Jamie How's career, dismissed first ball in his last innings. George Worker was the tournament's leading run-scorer, with 538, including three centuries. His 194 against Canterbury in Timaru was the second-highest one-day innings in New Zealand until Martin Guptill's World Cup double-hundred against West Indies overtook How's 222 from two years earlier. But Central failed in the Plunket Shield and the T20.

Northern Districts headed the Twenty20 league but bowed out in the play-offs. They were fourth in the Plunket Shield, where Dean Brownlie, who had moved from Canterbury to warmer climes in Tauranga, set a Northern record with 334 against Central at New Plymouth's idyllic amphitheatre, Pukekura Park – the fifth-highest first-class score by a New Zealander.

Former England all-rounder Dimitri Mascarenhas had a tough first season coaching **Otago**, third in the first-class competition and last in the T20; he left to become New Zealand bowling coach, while his assistant Nathan King replaced him.

FIRST-CLASS AVERAGES, 2014-15

BATTING (500 runs)

	M	I	NO	R	HS	100	Avge	Ct/St
B. Cachopa (*Auckland*)	10	16	5	783	135*	3	71.18	39
D. G. Brownlie (*Northern Districts*)	6	11	0	691	334	2	62.81	7
T. C. Bruce (*Central Districts*)	7	12	1	632	112*	1	57.45	10
†C. Munro (*Auckland*)	9	16	0	899	281	3	56.18	7
P. G. Fulton (*Canterbury*)	10	19	3	879	209*	3	54.93	20
W. A. Young (*Central Districts*)	10	17	0	909	132	1	53.47	0
A. M. Ellis (*Canterbury*)	10	18	2	853	171	2	53.31	3
S. J. Murdoch (*Wellington*)	10	20	1	998	155*	3	52.52	10
D. C. de Boorder (*Otago*)	10	17	5	604	146	1	50.33	36/1
†A. P. Devcich (*Northern Districts*)	8	15	0	744	132	2	49.60	7
†J. A. Raval (*Auckland*)	10	19	1	876	148	2	48.66	18
†J. E. C. Franklin (*Wellington*)	7	14	2	561	139	1	46.75	11
N. T. Broom (*Canterbury*)	10	19	1	820	123	2	45.55	11
†H. M. Nicholls (*Canterbury*)	10	18	0	778	119	2	43.22	8
†M. G. Bracewell (*Otago*)	10	17	0	726	147	1	42.70	5
B. S. Wilson (*Northern Districts*)	6	12	0	511	165	1	42.58	7
C. F. K. van Wyk (*Central Districts*)	9	16	4	510	74*	0	42.50	39/1
B-J. Watling (*N Districts/New Zealand*) . .	10	18	2	639	142*	1	39.93	35/1
G. R. Hay (*Central Districts*)	10	18	1	632	157	1	37.17	5
M. H. W. Papps (*Wellington*)	10	20	0	738	171	2	36.90	17
†H. D. Rutherford (*Otago/New Zealand*) . .	9	17	0	599	87	0	35.23	11
†M. J. Santner (*Northern Districts*)	10	19	2	545	101	1	32.05	12
M. A. Pollard (*Wellington*)	10	20	1	503	82	0	26.47	11
†R. M. Hira (*Canterbury*)	10	20	0	501	100	1	25.05	6

BOWLING (15 wickets, average 40.00)

	Style	O	M	R	W	BB	5I	Avge
T. A. Boult (*N Districts/New Zealand*)	LFM	116.4	24	305	18	5-37	1	16.94
H. K. Bennett (*Canterbury*)	RFM	114.5	18	381	19	4-43	0	20.05
T. G. Southee (*N Districts/N Zealand*)	RFM	114.4	26	310	15	4-18	0	20.66
M. R. Quinn (*Auckland*)	RFM	184	39	628	29	4-41	0	21.65
J. D. Baker (*Northern Districts*)	RFM	275.2	73	736	33	6-75	2	22.30
E. J. Nuttall (*Canterbury*)	LFM	145.1	31	471	21	6-35	1	22.42
L. H. Ferguson (*Auckland*)	RFM	144.2	27	491	21	5-58	1	23.38
T. D. Astle (*Canterbury*)	LBG	327.2	51	1,042	44	5-46	1	23.68
J. A. Duffy (*Otago*)	RFM	373.4	104	1,083	45	6-83	3	24.06
B. J. Arnel (*Wellington*)	RFM	367	99	1,017	39	6-52	3	26.07
G. W. Aldridge (*Northern Districts*)	RFM	306.1	68	1,025	39	5-52	2	26.28
D. A. J. Bracewell (*C Dists/N Zealand*) . . .	RFM	319.1	61	1,055	38	6-41	2	27.76
M. B. McEwan (*Wellington*)	RFM	273.4	67	874	31	5-87	1	28.19
M. J. Henry (*Canterbury*)	RFM	189.3	44	571	20	4-29	0	28.55
M. D. Bates (*Auckland*)	LFM	328.2	77	1,035	36	4-47	0	28.75
B. M. Wheeler (*Central Districts*)	LFM	288.1	72	806	27	3-34	0	29.85
D. J. Bartlett (*Auckland*)	RFM	155.4	26	540	18	4-39	0	30.00
A. J. McKay (*Wellington*)	LFM	196.1	43	697	22	4-91	0	31.68
T. S. Nethula (*Auckland*)	LBG	314	38	1,042	32	4-24	0	32.56
A. M. Ellis (*Canterbury*)	RFM	314	70	955	29	4-75	0	32.93
N. Wagner (*Otago/New Zealand*)	LFM	408.2	94	1,306	39	5-73	0	33.48
D. J. Grobbelaar (*Auckland*)	LM	204.4	36	654	18	3-33	0	36.33
S. C. Kuggeleijn (*Northern Districts*)	RFM	283.1	60	988	27	4-104	0	36.59
C. M. Smith (*Otago*)	LM	203	53	632	17	3-30	0	37.17

PLUNKET SHIELD, 2014-15

	Played	Won	Lost	Drawn	Bonus points Batting	Bonus points Bowling	Points	Net avge runs/wkt
Canterbury	10	6	4	0	14	36	122	5.64
Auckland	10	5	4	1	16	39	115	5.42
Otago	10	4	4	2	17	34	99	–3.06
Northern Districts......	10	4	4	2	16	34	98	–1.61
Wellington	10	4	4	2	8	37	93	–3.32
Central Districts	10	2	5	3	13	32	69	–3.80

Outright win = 12pts. Bonus points were awarded as follows for the first 110 overs of each team's first innings: one batting point for the first 250 runs, and then for 300, 350 and 400; one bowling point for the third wicket taken, and then for the fifth, seventh and ninth. Net average runs per wicket is calculated by subtracting average runs conceded per wicket from average runs scored per wicket.

At Whangarei (Cobham Oval), October 23–26, 2014. **Auckland won by five wickets. ‡Northern Districts 253 and 241; Auckland 284** (G. W. Aldridge 5-52) **and 211-5.** *Auckland 17pts, Northern Districts 5pts.*

At Christchurch (Hagley Oval), October 25–28, 2014. **Wellington won by four wickets. Canterbury 242 and 407-7 dec** (H. M. Nicholls 119); **‡Wellington 343 and 308-6** (S. J. Murdoch 155*). *Wellington 18pts, Canterbury 4pts. Stephen Murdoch steered Wellington to victory with a career-best 155* in 164 balls.*

At Napier (Nelson Park), October 26–29, 2014. **Central Districts won by an innings and 94 runs. ‡Otago 207 and 134** (D. A. J. Bracewell 5-57); **Central Districts 435-6 dec** (B. S. Smith 112). *Central Districts 18pts, Otago 1pt. Central Districts wicketkeeper Kruger van Wyk held ten catches in the match, six in Otago's second-innings collapse.*

At Christchurch (Hagley Oval), December 11–14, 2014. **Canterbury won by 102 runs. Canterbury 269** (D. A. J. Bracewell 6-41) **and 412-7 dec** (P. G. Fulton 209*); **‡Central Districts 305 and 274.** *Canterbury 17pts, Central Districts 6pts. Peter Fulton hit his third double-hundred to set a target of 377.*

At Dunedin (University Oval), December 11–14, 2014. **Northern Districts won by 27 runs. Northern Districts 380 and 310-4 dec** (J. F. Carter 125); **‡Otago 189** (I. S. Sodhi 5-27) **and 474** (M. G. Bracewell 147, M. D. Craig 104). *Northern Districts 19pts, Otago 4pts. Set 502, Otago were 372-9 before last pair Mark Craig and Jacob Duffy (27*) added 102; with 28 needed from 7.3 overs, Craig is bowled, having scored a maiden century. Even so, 474 was the third-highest fourth-innings total in New Zealand.*

At Wellington (Basin Reserve), December 11–14, 2014. **Auckland won by six wickets. Wellington 199 and 133; ‡Auckland 205-8 dec and 128-4.** *Auckland 16pts, Wellington 3pts. In Wellington's first innings, nine batsmen were caught by the Cachopa brothers: five by wicketkeeper Brad (who added a sixth in the second innings), three by Craig and one by Carl (who also took five wickets in the match with his medium-pace).*

Wellington

B. J. Barnett lbw b Quinn	6
*M. H. W. Papps c Craig Cachopa b Bates..	5
S. J. Murdoch c B. Cachopa b Quinn	29
M. A. Pollard c B. Cachopa b Bartlett.....	10
†T. A. Blundell c B. Cachopa b Quinn	18
H. A. Walsh c Craig Cachopa b Bates	17
L. J. Woodcock c B. Cachopa b Carl Cachopa .	49
M. B. McEwan c Carl Cachopa b Bartlett .	11

M. R. Gillespie c Craig Cachopa b Quinn .	16
M. J. Tugaga c B. Cachopa b Carl Cachopa	8
B. J. Arnel not out	6
B 16, l-b 7, n-b 1	24

1/7 (2)   2/25 (1)   3/39 (4)   (60 overs)   199
4/64 (3)   5/82 (5)   6/101 (6)
7/142 (8)   8/171 (9)   9/190 (7)   10/199 (10)

M. D. Bates 13–4–38–2; M. R. Quinn 18–8–41–4; D. J. Grobbelaar 14–4–42–0; D. J. Bartlett 10–2–34–2; T. S. Nethula 2–0–16–0; Carl Cachopa 3–1–5–2.

At Auckland (Eden Park Outer Oval), December 18–21, 2014. **Central Districts won by 245 runs. Central Districts 159 and 333;** ‡**Auckland 117 and 130.** *Central Districts 16pts, Auckland 4pts.*

At Rangiora, December 18–21, 2014. **Otago won by 82 runs. Otago 369 and 139;** ‡**Canterbury 210** (R. M. Hira 100; N. Wagner 5-76) **and 216.** *Otago 19pts, Canterbury 4pts.*

At Hamilton, December 18–20, 2014. **Northern Districts won by 395 runs. Northern Districts 223 and 347-6 dec** (D. R. Flynn 112); ‡**Wellington 117** (T. A. Boult 5-37) **and 58.** *Northern Districts 16pts, Wellington 4pts. Northern Districts completed easily their biggest win by runs after Wellington crumbled for 58, their lowest Plunket Shield total since 1957-58, sliding from 24-1 to 24-6 in 19 balls against Tim Southee (4-18) and Trent Boult (2-13).*

At Auckland (Colin Maiden Park), February 6–9, 2015. **Drawn. Auckland 356** (B. Cachopa 104; J. D. Baker 6-75) **and 209-8 dec;** ‡**Northern Districts 212 and 316-9.** *Auckland 6pts, Northern Districts 3pts. Jimmy Baker took 10-128 in the match, then helped to save it, coming in at No. 11 with nine balls to go.*

At Queenstown, February 6–9, 2015. **Drawn. Central Districts 289** (D. A. J. Bracewell 105; N. Wagner 5-92); ‡**Otago 13-0.** *Otago 4pts, Central Districts 1pt. Only 78.3 overs survived the rain, most of them on the third day when Doug Bracewell reached a maiden Plunket century in 93 balls.*

At Wellington (Basin Reserve), February 6–9, 2015. **Canterbury won by nine wickets. Wellington 263** (T. D. Astle 5-46) **and 264;** ‡**Canterbury 356** (A. M. Ellis 171; B. J. Arnel 5-95) **and 172-1.** *Canterbury 19pts, Wellington 5pts. Andrew Ellis and Fred Anderson (54) added 178 for Canterbury's seventh wicket to give them a decisive lead.*

At New Plymouth, February 15–18, 2015. **Drawn. Northern Districts 556-9 dec** (D. G. Brownlie 334, M. J. Santner 101); ‡**Central Districts 401** (G. R. Hay 157) **and 268-5.** *Northern Districts 3pts, Northern Districts 6pts. Dean Brownlie almost doubled his career-best, 171, after completing*

TRIPLE-HUNDREDS BY NEW ZEALANDERS

385	B. Sutcliffe	Otago v Canterbury at Christchurch	1952-53
355	B. Sutcliffe	Otago v Auckland at Dunedin	1949-50
341	C. M. Spearman	Gloucestershire v Middlesex at Gloucester	2004
338*	R. C. Blunt	Otago v Canterbury at Christchurch	1931-32
334	**D. G. Brownlie**	**N. Districts v C. Districts at New Plymouth**	**2014-15**
317	K. R. Rutherford	New Zealanders v D. B. Close's XI at Scarborough	1986
311*	G. M. Turner	Worcestershire v Warwickshire at Worcester	1982
306	M. H. Richardson	New Zealanders v Zimbabwe A at Kwekwe	2000-01
302	B. B. McCullum	New Zealand v India at Wellington	2013-14
301*	P. G. Fulton	Canterbury v Auckland at Christchurch	2002-03

Northern Districts' first triple-hundred. He reached 222* on the first day, and in all batted nine hours 12 minutes and hit 40 fours and eight sixes in 398 balls, adding 217 for the sixth wicket with Mitchell Santner. It was Northern Districts' fifth total of 550-plus, all in the last six seasons.

At Rangiora, February 16–19, 2015. **Auckland won by ten wickets. Canterbury 268 and 266;** ‡**Auckland 491** (J. A. Raval 126) **and 44-0.** *Auckland 18pts, Canterbury 3pts.*

At Wellington (Karori Park), February 16–19, 2015. **Otago won by six wickets. Wellington 272 and 318** (J. E. C. Franklin 139); ‡**Otago 377** (J. D. Ryder 108, D. C. de Boorder 146) **and 214-4.** *Otago 19pts, Wellington 5pts. This match started a day late, because of a wet patch on the pitch and a sandy patch on the bowler's run-up; this meant new umpires on the final day, when the original pair were unavailable. A further game scheduled for Karori Park on March 8–11 was transferred from Wellington to New Plymouth.*

At Whangarei (New Cobham Oval), February 27–March 2, 2015. **Northern Districts won by 43 runs.** ‡**Northern Districts 374 and 273-8 dec; Central Districts 300-6 dec** (W. A. Young 132) and 304. *Northern Districts 17pts, Central Districts 6pts. Northern Districts set a total of 348 in 110 overs, and bowled Central Districts out with 3.5 to spare.*

At Queenstown, February 28–March 3, 2015. **Drawn. Wellington 297** (S. J. Murdoch 121; N. Wagner 5-73) **and 255-5** (M. H. W. Papps 110); ‡**Otago 251-8 dec.** *Otago 5pts, Wellington 4pts. Ten Otago players, though not the keeper, bowled in Wellington's second innings.*

At Auckland (Colin Maiden Park), March 1–4, 2015. **Canterbury won by four wickets.** ‡**Auckland 294** (B. Cachopa 131*) **and 407-6 dec** (C. Munro 137); **Canterbury 340** (H. M. Nicholls 102) **and 362-6** (P. G. Fulton 101). *Canterbury 18pts, Auckland 5pts. In Auckland's second innings Colin Munro completed his century in 98 balls, and hit seven sixes in all, but Fulton helped Canterbury home with eight deliveries to spare.*

At New Plymouth, March 8–11, 2015. **Wellington won by three wickets.** ‡**Central Districts 229** (M. B. McEwan 5-87) **and 252** (B. J. Arnel 6-52); **Wellington 242 and 240-7.** *Wellington 16pts, Central Districts 4pts.*

At Christchurch (Hagley Oval), March 9–12, 2015. **Canterbury won by 301 runs. Canterbury 381** (J. D. Baker 5-90) **and 338-6 dec** (P. G. Fulton 123*); ‡**Northern Districts 234 and 184.** *Canterbury 19pts, Northern Districts 4pts.*

At Dunedin (University Oval), March 9–12, 2015. **Otago won by four wickets. Auckland 335 and 280** (J. A. Duffy 5-57); ‡**Otago 360-8 dec** (M. G. Bracewell 126) **and 258-6.** *Otago 19pts, Auckland 4pts. Otago knocked off a target of 256 in 38.3 overs, a rate of 6.7 an over.*

At Auckland (Colin Maiden Park), March 17–20, 2015. **Wellington won by 213 runs. Wellington 344 and 387-5 dec** (M. H. W. Papps 171); ‡**Auckland 350-7 dec** (J. A. Raval 148, C. Munro 108) **and 168.** *Wellington 17pts, Auckland 7pts. Wellington were helped to their first-innings 344 by a 110-run eighth-wicket stand between Brady Barnett (65) and Matt McEwan (52) – both maiden fifties. But Jeet Raval and Munro fought back with 201 for Auckland's third wicket, giving them a narrow lead before a last-day collapse.*

At Nelson (Saxton Oval), March 17–20, 2015. **Canterbury won by 183 runs. Canterbury 463-9 dec** (A. M. Ellis 112) **and 305-5 dec** (N. T. Broom 123); ‡**Central Districts 350-9 dec** (T. C. Bruce 112*) **and 235.** *Canterbury 20pts, Central Districts 7pts.*

At Hamilton, March 18–21, 2015. **Northern Districts won by 49 runs.** ‡**Northern Districts 464-8 dec** (D. G. Brownlie 128, B. S. Wilson 165) **and 254** (A. P. Devcich 123; J. A. Duffy 6-83); **Otago 363 and 306** (G. W. Aldridge 5-57). *Northern Districts 20pts, Otago 4pts. Brownlie and Brad Wilson opened with 214 for Northern Districts. On the last day, Jesse Ryder took umbrage when umpire Gary Baxter gave him out for 25 in Otago's second innings. He did not dispute a charge of serious dissent, including offensive language, and was suspended from the final round in April.*

At Napier (Nelson Park), March 24–27, 2015. **Auckland won by an innings and 64 runs. Auckland 668-7 dec** (C. Munro 281, B. Cachopa 135*); ‡**Central Districts 233 and 371** (L. H. Ferguson 5-58). *Auckland 20pts, Central Districts 2pts. Munro hit a world-record 23 sixes (plus 17 fours) in his 281 from 167 balls, which took less than four hours. The previous record was 16 sixes, shared by Andrew Symonds, Graham Napier, Jesse Ryder and Mukhtar Ali; Symonds's record of 20 sixes in a match was also broken. He reached 50 in 30 balls, 100 in 68, and 200 in 133; it was his second double-century, and only nine short of the Auckland record. Munro added 214 for the fourth wicket in 26 overs with Robert O'Donnell (42). Auckland's total of 668-7 was their second-highest, and the fourth-highest in Plunket Shield cricket.*

At Dunedin (University Oval), March 25–28, 2015. **Otago won by four wickets. Canterbury 247** (N. T. Broom 117) **and 144** (J. A. Duffy 5-58); ‡**Otago 250-8 dec and 142-6.** *Otago 17pts, Canterbury 3pts. Canterbury were looking to seal the title with a fourth consecutive win, but Otago's victory left them only ten points clear of the field.*

At Wellington (Basin Reserve), March 25–27, 2015. **Wellington won by six wickets. Northern Districts 240** (A. P. Devcich 132; B. J. Arnel 6-62) **and 214;** ‡**Wellington 287** (D. Joon 113) **and 169-4.** *Wellington 17pts, Northern Districts 4pts.*

At Auckland (Colin Maiden Park), April 1–4, 2015. **Auckland won by six wickets. Otago 387 and 143;** ‡**Auckland 344 and 187-4.** *Auckland 18pts, Otago 7pts. Auckland keeper Brad Cachopa held five catches in an innings again, in Otago's second, and eight in the match, though this time his brothers missed out. Although Auckland completed their fifth win, they finished in second place, seven points behind Canterbury.*

At Napier (McLean Park), April 1–4, 2015. **Drawn. Wellington 227 and 439-7 dec** (S. J. Murdoch 112); ‡**Central Districts 355 and 86-1.** *Central Districts 6pts, Wellington 4pts. Murdoch's second-innings century ended when he was only two runs short of 1,000 for the season, but he broke Luke Woodcock's Wellington record of 988 in 2009-10.*

At Mount Maunganui, April 1–3, 2015. **Canterbury won by nine wickets. Northern Districts 256-8 dec and 101** (E. J. Nuttall 6-35); ‡**Canterbury 213-8 dec and 150-1.** *Canterbury 15pts, Northern Districts 4pts. The first first-class match played at the Bay Oval confirmed Canterbury's title, with their sixth win. On the third day, which turned out to be the last, left-armer Ed Nuttall collected a career-best 6-35, the best return of this tournament, and Fulton raced to victory with 91* in 53 balls, including seven sixes.*

CHAMPIONS

	Plunket Shield	1957-58	Otago	1988-89	Auckland
1921-22	Auckland	1958-59	Auckland	1989-90	Wellington
1922-23	Canterbury	1959-60	Canterbury	1990-91	Auckland
1923-24	Wellington	1960-61	Wellington	1991-92	Central Districts Northern Districts
1924-25	Otago	1961-62	Wellington		
1925-26	Wellington	1962-63	Northern Districts	1992-93	Northern Districts
1926-27	Auckland	1963-64	Auckland	1993-94	Canterbury
1927-28	Wellington	1964-65	Canterbury	1994-95	Auckland
1928-29	Auckland	1965-66	Wellington	1995-96	Auckland
1929-30	Wellington	1966-67	Central Districts	1996-97	Canterbury
1930-31	Canterbury	1967-68	Central Districts	1997-98	Canterbury
1931-32	Wellington	1968-69	Auckland	1998-99	Central Districts
1932-33	Otago	1969-70	Otago	1999-2000	Northern Districts
1933-34	Auckland	1970-71	Central Districts	2000-01	Wellington
1934-35	Canterbury	1971-72	Otago		
1935-36	Wellington	1972-73	Wellington		*State Championship*
1936-37	Auckland	1973-74	Wellington	2001-02	Auckland
1937-38	Auckland	1974-75	Otago	2002-03	Auckland
1938-39	Auckland			2003-04	Wellington
1939-40	Auckland		*Shell Trophy*	2004-05	Auckland
1940-45	*No competition*	1975-76	Canterbury	2005-06	Central Districts
1945-46	Canterbury	1976-77	Otago	2006-07	Northern Districts
1946-47	Auckland	1977-78	Auckland	2007-08	Canterbury
1947-48	Otago	1978-79	Otago	2008-09	Auckland
1948-49	Canterbury	1979-80	Northern Districts		
1949-50	Wellington	1980-81	Auckland		*Plunket Shield*
1950-51	Otago	1981-82	Wellington	2009-10	Northern Districts
1951-52	Canterbury	1982-83	Wellington	2010-11	Canterbury
1952-53	Otago	1983-84	Canterbury	2011-12	Northern Districts
1953-54	Central Districts	1984-85	Wellington	2012-13	Central Districts
1954-55	Wellington	1985-86	Otago	2013-14	Canterbury
1955-56	Canterbury	1986-87	Central Districts	2014-15	Canterbury
1956-57	Wellington	1987-88	Otago		

Auckland have won the title outright 22 times, Wellington 20, Canterbury 18, Otago 13, Central Districts 8, Northern Districts 7. Central Districts and Northern Districts also shared the title once.

THE FORD TROPHY, 2014-15

50-over league plus knockout

	Played	Won	Lost	No result	Bonus points	Points	Net run-rate
CENTRAL DISTRICTS	8	6	2	0	2	26	1.16
AUCKLAND	8	5	3	0	4	24	0.84
OTAGO	8	3	3	2	1	17	0.25
NORTHERN DISTRICTS ...	8	4	4	0	0	16	−0.75
Canterbury	8	2	4	2	1	13	−0.86
Wellington	8	2	6	0	1	9	−0.83

Preliminary finals 1st v 2nd: Auckland beat Central Districts by 45 runs. **3rd v 4th:** Otago beat Northern Districts by three wickets. **Final play-off:** Central Districts beat Otago by 49 runs.

Final   At Auckland (Colin Maiden Park), February 1, 2015. Central Districts won by 78 runs. ‡**Central Districts 271-7** (50 overs); **Auckland 193** (38.2 overs). *In his final match before retirement, Jamie How was out first ball, but his Central Districts team-mates built a solid total; of the seven batsmen dismissed, six were caught or run out by the Cachopa brothers, Brad, Craig and Carl. But Bevan Small then removed all three Cachopas before Andrew Mathieson (4-22) worked through Auckland's middle order; the highest stand of the innings was 81 for the ninth wicket by Donovan Grobbelaar and Michael Bates.*

STATE OF ORIGIN MATCH

At Hamilton, October 31, 2014 (floodlit). South Island won by 15 runs. South Island 139-8 (20 overs); ‡**North Island 124-8** (20 overs). *This match was a curtain-raiser for the domestic Twenty20 competition. Neil Broom and Michael Papps opened with 41 for South Island, the highest stand of the match, whereas the North openers fell in the first nine balls of their reply; their colleagues never quite caught up.*

GEORGIE PIE SUPER SMASH, 2014-15

20-over league plus knockout

	Played	Won	Lost	NR/A	Points	Net run-rate
NORTHERN DISTRICTS	10	7	2	1	30	0.43
WELLINGTON	10	5	3	2	24	0.23
AUCKLAND	10	5	4	1	22	0.43
Canterbury	10	5	5	0	20	0.53
Central Districts	10	3	6	1	14	−0.51
Otago	10	2	7	1	10	−1.12

Preliminary finals   1st v 2nd: Wellington beat Northern Districts by eight wickets. **Loser of 1st play-off v 3rd:** Auckland beat Northern Districts by six wickets.

Final   At Hamilton, December 7, 2014. Wellington won by six runs. Wellington 186-6 (20 overs); ‡**Auckland 180-9** (20 overs). *In a high-scoring final, Wellington opener Michael Pollard hit 76 in 56 balls, with six sixes, before Grant Elliott smashed 40 in 17; he shared a seventh-wicket stand of 39* in 2.1 overs with Luke Woodcock, whose share was four. Auckland made a storming start, but lacked an anchor and slipped from 125-3 to 126-6 in four deliveries. Their last pair could not manage 14 off the final over.*

PAKISTAN CRICKET IN 2015

The road home

OSMAN SAMIUDDIN

It hardly mattered that the first ball of international cricket bowled on Pakistani soil for 2,272 days was less eventful than the previous one. On March 2, 2009, at Lahore's Gaddafi Stadium, some swift work from Mahela Jayawardene had run out Salman Butt. The umpires called time, but terror struck the next morning with the attack on the Sri Lankan team bus.

The drought was broken on May 22, 2015, by a leg-side half-volley from Anwar Ali to Zimbabwe's Hamilton Masakadza, and the delivery should consider itself fortunate not to have been hit for four. It hardly befitted the occasion, but who cared? A packed Gaddafi Stadium, an ecstatic Lahore and a rapt Pakistan were too busy acknowledging the immensity of the moment. It was hugely emotional: the first tiny steps on the long road back to Pakistan hosting international cricket.

How fraught that journey would be was evident a week later, when a blast on the outer reaches of the heavy security perimeter around the stadium –

PAKISTAN IN 2015

	Played	Won	Lost	Drawn/No result
Tests	8	5	1	2
One-day internationals	27	12	14	1
Twenty20 internationals	10	6	4	–

JANUARY — FEBRUARY	2 ODIs (a) v New Zealand	(page 1033)
FEBRUARY — MARCH	ICC World Cup (in Australia and New Zealand)	(page 860)
APRIL — MAY	2 Tests, 3 ODIs and 1 T20I (a) v Bangladesh 3 ODIs and 2 T20Is (h) v Zimbabwe	(page 970) (page 1058)
JUNE — JULY — AUGUST	3 Tests, 5 ODIs and 2 T20Is (a) v Sri Lanka	(page 1105)
SEPTEMBER — OCTOBER — NOVEMBER	3 ODIs and 2 T20Is (a) v Zimbabwe 3 Tests, 4 ODIs and 3 T20Is (h) v England (in UAE)	(page 1168) (page 375)
DECEMBER		

For a review of Pakistan domestic cricket from the 2014-15 season, see page 1064.

Service with a smile: Captain Misbah-ul-Haq oversees success against England.

nearly 800 metres from the ground – killed two people. At first, security officials claimed it was a malfunctioning electricity transformer. Next day, the federal information minister revealed it was a suicide attack, foiled by a police official. Zimbabwe stayed on for the remaining fixture, but it would have done nothing to ease the trepidation they had felt before they arrived. The Pakistan Cricket Board, it emerged, had to pay each touring player a hardship fee of $US12,500 before they agreed to come.

That series, however, nestled into the tapestry of a reassuring and redemptive year. As it closed, the long-gestating Pakistan Super League was finally on the brink of delivery. The PCB had been cultivating plans for their own franchise-based Twenty20 league since 2007; two earlier attempts to launch it had failed. But in December they sold five franchises (representing Karachi, Lahore, Islamabad, Peshawar and Quetta) and held a players' draft that attracted some of the game's biggest names – Chris Gayle, Kevin Pietersen and Shane Watson among them. The first few tournaments were likely to be played in the UAE. If all went to plan, PCB officials hoped for profits of $US50,000-60,000 over ten years.

That would represent a significant new revenue stream, one to offset the absence of India from their international schedule. The Indians were supposed to resume bilateral ties in December 2015, with Pakistan hosting a full series in the UAE. It would have been their first Test encounter for eight years. Yet the BCCI prevaricated, partly hindered by their own administrative troubles. The two boards held hastily scheduled meetings, and meetings about meetings;

as time ran out, they chopped down the itinerary, and – without ever explaining their reasons – the BCCI demanded another neutral venue, such as Sri Lanka. Around the same time, the Indian and Pakistani governments were agreeing to peace talks, but even that could not conjure a series.

If the hankering for matches with India sometimes seemed unbecoming, it was justified. This was a series signed, sealed and waiting to be delivered, following the horse-trading that accompanied the Big Three takeover at the ICC, but all Pakistan ended up with was the higher moral ground.

Redemption was a theme of the year, not least in the return of Mohammad Amir. In January 2015, after persistent PCB lobbying, the ICC had decided to allow Amir, now 23, to return to domestic cricket, seven months before the official end of his five-year ban for spot-fixing on Pakistan's tour of England in 2010. As he made a gradual return to competitive cricket, it seemed he had lost none of his teenage vim. Less than a year after the ban was lifted, he was good enough to be back in the Pakistan squad, on a trip to New Zealand in January 2016.

Not everyone was happy about it. Azhar Ali, the one-day captain, and Mohammad Hafeez, both part of that 2010 tour, felt strongly enough to boycott a training camp which he attended. Azhar offered his resignation (which was refused), and Hafeez said Amir had "hurt my country's integrity". They sorted out their differences, reportedly after Amir apologised to them.

All of which left the actual cricket. Pakistan won each of their three Test series, including their first victory in Sri Lanka for nine years. That was clinched in Pallekele in memorable style, with Younis Khan's 171 steering them past a target of 377 to Pakistan's highest fourth innings, and the sixth-highest ever to win. A 2–0 victory against England, with Misbah-ul-Haq to the fore, maintained their dominance in the UAE, where they have not lost a Test series since it became their second home in 2010. The result saw them rise – briefly but giddily – to second in the Test rankings. In all, seven of their batsmen averaged 47 or more.

Pakistan were awful in green: dumped out of the World Cup quarter-finals, whitewashed in Bangladesh and thrashed by England. They missed the continuity of selection of the Test side, burning through new players and never settling on an XI. They were so bad they almost missed the cut for the Champions Trophy, squeezing in behind Bangladesh.

It wasn't enough to dampen a generally bright year. This being Pakistan, however, there had to be a sting: it came with a failed dope test for leg-spinner Yasir Shah, who was later banned for three months. Despite playing only seven Tests, Yasir was the fourth-highest Test wicket-taker in 2015, his 49 victims crucial to their successes. Here was the necessary reminder that, if things are going too well for Pakistan, they never go too well for too long.

PAKISTAN v ZIMBABWE IN 2015

Shahid Hashmi

Twenty20 internationals (2): Pakistan 2, Zimbabwe 0
One-day internationals (3): Pakistan 2, Zimbabwe 0

The Pakistan Cricket Board's promotional hook for the country's first full international series in more than six years spoke for itself: "Igniting a passion that brings together a nation #cricketcomeshome". On May 22, at Lahore's Gaddafi Stadium – where play had been suspended on March 3, 2009 following the terrorist attack on buses carrying the Sri Lankan team and match officials – the wheel came full circle.

The response of the Pakistani cricketing public went beyond all expectations. The stands were packed at the 27,000-capacity stadium for all five games, even against Zimbabwe. Spectators lined up five or six hours before the start of the first Twenty20 – a routine maintained until the last one-day international, despite multiple security checks and temperatures hovering around 42°C. Inside the ground, the sights and sounds were exhilarating. Fans chanted "Pakistan is safe for cricket" and "We want more cricket". Pakistan's famous supporter Abdul Jalil – better known as "Chacha Cricket" – described the occasion as his "rebirth".

The Zimbabweans were accorded a heroes' welcome for showing the courage to come to a country which had been a no-go destination for so long. Alistair Campbell, the managing director of Zimbabwe Cricket, declared his board's solidarity with Pakistan. "It was," he said, "one of the rare occasions in the subcontinent when the opposition were also embraced."

Zimbabwe certainly had every opportunity to walk away. A week before they arrived, a sectarian massacre on a bus in Karachi killed more than 40, prompting ZC to briefly announce the tour had been suspended. Both the Zimbabwean government and the Federation of International Cricketers' Associations, the world players' union, advised them to cancel it altogether. To add to the sense of isolation, the ICC confirmed they would not be sending any of their umpires; the Zimbabwean Russell Tiffin stood alongside Pakistani colleagues.

The tour proceeded peacefully until the second one-day international, when an explosion 800 metres from the stadium killed two people and injured several others. To avoid panic, the police initially claimed the blast was an accident with an electricity transformer, but it soon emerged that a suicide bomber had detonated a gas cylinder on an autorickshaw. The Zimbabweans chose to honour the schedule, a move criticised by Tony Irish, FICA's executive chairman. "This was a tragic loss of life over cricket, and demonstrates that the security situation remains unmanageable and the risks of touring Pakistan are unacceptable," he said. "I am very surprised Zimbabwe are staying on to play the third ODI."

There was undoubtedly an element of expediency behind Zimbabwe's decision. They were desperate for more top-level cricket, having played substantially fewer internationals than any other Full Member between the last two World Cups. Reports suggested that each Zimbabwe player was paid $US12,500 by the PCB – roughly two months' salary on a ZC national contract – at a time when many were still waiting for their World Cup dues. In all, Pakistan's board topped up Zimbabwe's empty coffers by $500,000.

As for the security, nothing was left to chance. The Pakistanis provided the touring players and delegation – headed by Ozias Bvute, the controversial former ZC managing director – with measures normally reserved for heads of state. There were 4,000 police guarding the stadium and the surrounding sports complex – more were added after the explosion – and the teams' journeys to and from the ground had air surveillance.

Lessons will be learned, though: if and when the next tour takes place, the security may be less asphyxiating. Perceptions about Pakistan will change, slowly – provided there is no major terrorism. But, for the time being, fans were simply grateful to watch some international cricket.

Pakistan's one-day form had dipped so alarmingly that they risked failing to qualify for the 2017 Champions Trophy. Following their 3–0 whitewash in Bangladesh, they could not afford the slightest slip-up against a team ranked below them, and their top-order batsmen – led by captain Azhar Ali, with 227 runs – fired in all three matches. Most encouraging of all, the assured performances of 22-year-old Mukhtar Ahmed in the Twenty20 matches, and 20-year-old Babar Azam in the last ODI, demonstrated that Pakistan were still producing exciting young cricketers. For Zimbabwe, Elton Chigumbura's century in the first ODI typified an opposition stronger than some expected.

ZIMBABWEAN TOURING PARTY

*E. Chigumbura, C. J. Chibhabha, C. K. Coventry, A. G. Cremer, C. R. Ervine, R. Kaia, H. Masakadza, C. B. Mpofu, T. Mupariwa, R. Mutumbami, T. Panyangara, V. Sibanda, Sikandar Raza, P. Utseya, B. V. Vitori, S. C. Williams. *Coach:* D. F. Whatmore.

First Twenty20 international   At Lahore, May 22, 2015 (floodlit). **Pakistan won by five wickets. ‡Zimbabwe 172-6** (20 overs) (H. Masakadza 43, E. Chigumbura 54; Mohammad Sami 3-36); **Pakistan 173-5** (19.3 overs) (Mukhtar Ahmed 83, Ahmed Shehzad 55). *MoM:* Mukhtar Ahmed. *T20I debut:* R. Mutumbami (Zimbabwe). *A full house at the Gaddafi Stadium included the country's president, Mamnoon Hussain, and witnessed the return of international cricket to Pakistan after 2,271 days. It was a poignant occasion for one of the Pakistani umpires, Ahsan Raza, who had sustained serious injuries in the March 2009 attack. Five Pakistanis – Ahmed Shehzad, Anwar Ali, Bilawal Bhatti, Mukhtar Ahmed and, after 186 appearances elsewhere, Umar Akmal – were playing an international match on home soil for the first time. Anwar bowled the first delivery, which rapped harmlessly into Hamilton Masakadza's pads – and raised the roof. Masakadza and Vusi Sibanda opened with 58 inside seven overs, before Mohammad Sami, in his first international for three years, removed both with successive balls. Elton Chigumbura steered Zimbabwe to their highest Twenty20 total against Pakistan with a 35-ball 54. But Pakistan were lifted by an opening partnership between Mukhtar and Shehzad of 142 – equalling their first-wicket record – and the match went down to the last over, with six needed. Shahid Afridi thumped his first ball, a full toss from Tinashe Panyangara, for the winning boundary, sending the crowd into raptures.*

Second Twenty20 international   At Lahore, May 24, 2015 (floodlit). **Pakistan won by two wickets.** ‡**Zimbabwe 175-3** (20 overs) (V. Sibanda 49, H. Masakadza 39, S. C. Williams 58*); **Pakistan 176-8** (19.4 overs) (Mukhtar Ahmed 62, Umar Akmal 30). *MoM*: Mukhtar Ahmed. *MoS*: Mukhtar Ahmed. *T20I debuts*: Imad Wasim, Nauman Anwar (Pakistan). *Imran Khan, the former Pakistan captain and now leader of the opposition Tehreek-e-Insaf party, was in attendance as another tight finish enthralled a packed house. Pakistan gave a debut to Imad Wasim, a spin-bowling all-rounder born in Swansea. Zimbabwe, spared facing Wahab Riaz – who had hurt his hand dropping a return chance in the first match – began with 68 in 8.3 overs between Masakadza and Sibanda, before Sean Williams's career-best 58*, from 32 balls. Three sixes from Chigumbura in the 18th over, bowled by Mohammad Sami, helped send Zimbabwe past their total two days earlier. Mukhtar Ahmed launched the reply with a 40-ball 62 – meaning he had top-scored in his first three Twenty20 internationals – but then Pakistan slumped, losing five for 44 in five overs. They looked down and out, until No. 10 Bilawal Bhatti smashed six, two and four off the final over, bowled by Brian Vitori.*

First one-day international   At Lahore, May 26, 2015 (day/night). **Pakistan won by 41 runs.** ‡**Pakistan 375-3** (50 overs) (Mohammad Hafeez 86, Azhar Ali 79, Shoaib Malik 112, Haris Sohail 89*); **Zimbabwe 334-5** (50 overs) (Sikandar Raza 36, H. Masakadza 73, E. Chigumbura 117, S. C. Williams 36; Wahab Riaz 3-47). *MoM*: Shoaib Malik. *Shoaib Malik put his derailed international career back on track with his first century for six years. He lifted Pakistan to a crucial victory on their return to one-day cricket following the shock 3–0 defeat in Bangladesh. Azhar Ali, continuing his sumptuous form since taking on the captaincy, made a slick start in an opening stand of 170 in 26 overs with Mohammad Hafeez. Malik and Haris Sohail built on that with 201 in the last 23, guiding Pakistan to their second-highest ODI total, and highest at home. It was the first time four batsmen had all made 70 or more in an ODI innings. Zimbabwe stayed in touch until their captain Chigumbura, who profited from two drops to make his first century in his 174th ODI, was yorked by Wahab Riaz, bowling with venom at the death. Only three men had played more ODIs before scoring their first hundred: Shaun Pollock (285th), Mark Boucher (220th), and Steve Waugh (187th). In conditions where the other pace bowlers were travelling at seven an over, Wahab finished with 3-47. To make things worse for Zimbabwe, Chigumbura was suspended for the next two games for a slow over-rate.*

Second one-day international   At Lahore, May 29, 2015 (day/night). **Pakistan won by six wickets.** **Zimbabwe 268-7** (50 overs) (C. J. Chibhabha 99, Sikandar Raza 100*); ‡**Pakistan 269-4** (47.2 overs) (Azhar Ali 102, Asad Shafiq 39, Haris Sohail 52*, Shoaib Malik 36*). *MoM*: Azhar Ali. *Azhar Ali led Pakistan to their first bilateral one-day series win in six attempts. They needed a solid innings to overhaul 268, and Azhar stood up with the second century of his tenure – and the first by a Pakistan captain in a successful run-chase – while Haris Sohail and Shoaib Malik ensured they did not let up. Umpire Shozab Raza had been involved in two contentious decisions, giving out Zimbabwe's stand-in captain Masakadza and Chamu Chibhabha – one short of a maiden hundred – to close catches while sweeping; replays suggested bat was not involved in either case. Late impetus was provided by the Sialkot-born Sikandar Raza, who took the attack to the Pakistan bowlers in an 84-ball century. An explosion on an autorickshaw just outside the first entry checkpoint into the sports complex caused some unease in the stands, but Pakistan's chase continued uninterrupted. The bomber and a police sub-inspector were killed, and several others injured.*

Third one-day international   At Lahore, May 31, 2015 (day/night). **No result.** ‡**Pakistan 296-9** (50 overs) (Mohammad Hafeez 80, Azhar Ali 46, Babar Azam 54, Anwar Ali 38*; Sikandar Raza 3-59); **Zimbabwe 68-0** (9 overs) (C. J. Chibhabha 39*). *MoS*: Azhar Ali. *ODI debuts*: Babar Azam (Pakistan); R. Kaia (Zimbabwe). *Rain wiped out Pakistan's hopes of a first one-day series whitewash for more than three years – though defeat would have left them further adrift of eighth place in the race for the last spot at the Champions Trophy. They were well served again by Azhar Ali and Mohammad Hafeez, who put on 115 in the first 20 overs, but Sikandar Raza's part-time off-spin unsettled the middle order, and three run-outs did not help. It took a mature fifty from debutant Babar Azam and two sixes from Anwar Ali to lift Pakistan towards 300. Sibanda and Chibhabha then raced to 62 in eight overs, suggesting another close finish. But floodlight failure and a dust storm forced the players off, and just one more over was possible before drizzle ended play for good. Soon afterwards, the Zimbabweans were boarding their bus for the airport.*

PAKISTAN A v ENGLAND LIONS IN THE UAE IN 2015-16

A-team Twenty20 internationals (5): Pakistan A 2, England Lions 3
A-team one-day internationals (5): Pakistan A 3, England Lions 2

In a tour of two halves – the Twenty20 internationals were played before Christmas, and the one-dayers afterwards – the teams proved well matched. The deciding T20 game ended in a tie: England Lions edged it in a super over. The 50-over rubber also went down to the wire, with Pakistan A coming back from 2–0 down to win 3–2.

The Lions' star performer was Middlesex's 28-year-old left-hander Dawid Malan, who had not appeared at this level before. He made 253 runs in the Twenty20 matches, and 211 in the 50-over games, one of which he missed through illness. "He's a beautiful timer of the ball," said Andy Flower, England's technical director of elite coaching, who oversaw the tour. "He's been really consistent, but he's also been explosive at times."

Sam Billings scored well too, collecting 391 runs all told, while captain James Vince atoned for a miserable first half – just 26 runs in the five T20s – by topping the run-charts with 236 in the longer format after Christmas. Both made the cut for the World Twenty20 in India early in 2016, though Malan missed out.

The final place in that squad went to Liam Dawson, the Hampshire slow left-armer, who took 12 wickets in the international games, going for little more than six an over in the Twenty20s. He also scored useful runs, which helped edge him ahead of Stephen Parry in the pecking order.

The trip was preceded by a 12-day batting and spin camp in November in Dubai – part of the England Performance Programme – attended by several of the tourists (a similar exercise for the fast bowlers took place in South Africa at the same time). The Lions visit also gave Steven Finn a chance to regain fitness after suffering a stress fracture of the foot during England's senior tour of the region. After spending most of the previous month sporting a moon boot, Finn tucked some overs under his belt and was able to return to Test duty in South Africa.

Pakistan A, usually led by Junaid Khan, did well to recover to win the one-day series, although their side had more international experience than their opponents. Apart from Junaid and his deputy Fawad Alam, a pair with 25 Test and 90 senior one-day caps between them, the Pakistanis also included Khurram Manzoor, who had scored a Test century against South Africa in 2013-14. But there was no sign of the rehabilitated Mohammad Amir, even though the national coach Waqar Younis had been keen to include him. During the Twenty20 leg, he was allowed to play for Chittagong Vikings in the Bangladesh Premier League instead. By the time the 50-over matches started in January, he was touring New Zealand with the senior team.

ENGLAND LIONS TOURING PARTY

*J. M. Vince (Hampshire; 50/20), J. T. Ball (Nottinghamshire (50/20), D. J. Bell-Drummond (Kent; 50/20), S. W. Billings (Kent; 50/20), D. R. Briggs (Hampshire; 20), J. M. Clarke (Worcestershire; 50/20), T. K. Curran (Surrey; 50/20), L. A. Dawson (Hampshire; 50/20), S. T. Finn (Middlesex; 20), B. T. Foakes (Surrey; 50/20), D. J. Malan (Middlesex; 50/20), T. S. Mills (Sussex; 20), C. Overton (Somerset; 50), J. Overton (Somerset; 50/20), S. D. Parry (Lancashire; 50/20), L. E. Plunkett (Yorkshire; 50), T. S. Roland-Jones (Middlesex; 50), R. J. W. Topley (Hampshire; 20), T. Westley (Hampshire; 50/20), R. A. Whiteley (Worcestershire; 50/20).

Head coach: A. Flower (50/20). *Assistant coach:* S. J. Rhodes (50/20). *Manager:* G. A. M. Jackson (20), D. Feist (50). *Observer selectors:* M. Newell (20), A. R. C. Fraser (50). *Batting coach:* G. P. Thorpe (20). *Fast-bowling coach:* R. L. Johnson (20), G. Welch (50). *Spin-bowling coach:* P. M. Such (20). *Fielding coach:* C. G. Taylor (50). *Consultant coaches:* D. L. Vettori (20), G. Kirsten (50). *Physiotherapist:* B. T. Langley (50/20). *Strength and conditioning coach:* P. T. Atkinson (50/20). *Analyst:* K. Stuart (50/20). *Security manager:* L. F. Attrill (20), C. Timmerman (50). *Media relations manager:* A. J. Wilson (50/20).

From the originally selected team, Z. S. Ansari (Surrey) and L. Gregory (Somerset) withdrew injured, D. J. Willey (Yorkshire) was allowed to play in the T20 Big Bash in Australia instead, and C. J. Jordan (Sussex) was called up to the senior squad in the UAE after Finn suffered a stress fracture in his left foot; Finn was added to the Lions party to aid his recuperation. Briggs, Curran, Mills and J. Overton were named as replacements.

At Dubai (ICC Academy), December 4, 2015. **England Lions won by two wickets. ‡United Arab Emirates 132-6** (20 overs) (Ghulam Shabber 56); **England Lions 136-8** (20 overs) (B. T. Foakes 49; Farhan Ahmed 3-20). *The Lions made a meal of their first warm-up, against a team containing eight Twenty20 debutants. After recovering from 39-4, the Lions wobbled again at the end, losing two wickets – including top-scorer Ben Foakes – to leave the ninth-wicket pair needing three from the final three balls. They got there when Jake Ball hit the last, from Waheed Ahmed, to the boundary.*

First A-Team Twenty20 international At Dubai (ICC Academy), December 7, 2015. **Pakistan A won by seven wickets. ‡England Lions 145-6** (20 overs) (D. J. Malan 51, S. W. Billings 31); **Pakistan A 149-3** (19 overs) (Iftikhar Ahmed 66*, Babar Azam 53*). *MoM:* Iftikhar Ahmed. *Dawid Malan hit 51 from 44 balls to shepherd the Lions towards a handy total, which looked better still when Pakistan A slipped to 25-3 in the fifth over. But Iftikhar Ahmed and Babar Azam combined in a stand of 124* which brought their side victory with an over to spare.*

Second A-Team Twenty20 international At Dubai (ICC Academy), December 10, 2015 (day/night). **England Lions won by 41 runs. England Lions 164-5** (20 overs) (D. J. Malan 80); **‡Pakistan A 123** (19.3 overs) (Sohaib Maqsood 40, Babar Azam 35; J. Overton 3-26). *MoM:* D. J. Malan. *Malan, who faced only 56 balls, again led the way with the bat for the Lions – and this time Pakistan A could not bounce back from 27-3. The new-ball pair of Reece Topley and Jamie Overton finished with combined figures of 4-45 from eight overs.*

Third A-Team Twenty20 international At Dubai (ICC Academy), December 11, 2015 (day/night). **Pakistan A won by four wickets. ‡England Lions 142-6** (20 overs) (D. J. Malan 35, L. A. Dawson 45*); **Pakistan A 146-6** (19.4 overs) (Sharjeel Khan 70, Saad Nasim 33; S. T. Finn 3-22). *MoM:* Sharjeel Khan. *Steven Finn took two wickets in two balls to set back Pakistan A's chase, but Sharjeel Khan made 70 from 50, before he was out in the 17th over. By then the target was down to 20 from 19, and Pakistan A took it easy.*

Fourth A-Team Twenty20 international At Dubai (ICC Academy), December 13, 2015 (day/night). **England Lions won by five wickets. Pakistan A 116-9** (20 overs) (Sohaib Maqsood 38); **‡England Lions 119-5** (18.1 overs) (S. W. Billings 61*, L. A. Dawson 37; Junaid Khan 3-9). *MoM:* S. W. Billings. *The Lions squared the series thanks to Sam Billings, who took charge after his side dipped to 9-3 in the fourth over. He hit 61* from 48 balls, and put on 94 with Liam Dawson. Earlier, tight seam bowling from Topley (2-21) and Tom Curran (2-15 on his representative debut), plus two wickets for Malan's leg-breaks, restricted Pakistan A to a below-par 116.*

Fifth A-Team Twenty20 international At Dubai (ICC Academy), December 16, 2015. **England Lions won after an eliminator over, following a tie. Pakistan A 165-3** (20 overs) (Sohaib Maqsood 40); **‡England Lions 165-4** (20 overs) (D. J. Malan 81, S. W. Billings 50). *MoM:* D. J. Malan. *A solid all-round batting performance lifted Pakistan A to the highest score of the series, but the in-form Malan made 81 from 55 balls, adding 93 for the third wicket with Billings to take his side* *close. Malan was run out from the last delivery, going for the winning run – but stayed in the middle for the super over, in which consecutive fours off Junaid Khan took the score to 12-0. Pakistan A could manage only 8-1, so the Lions pinched the 20-over series 3–2.*

At Dubai (ICC Academy), January 14, 2016. **England Lions won by five wickets. United Arab Emirates XI 210-9** (50 overs) (Mohammad Shehzad 46); ‡**England Lions 211-5** (42 overs) (J. M. Vince 88, T. Westley 57*). *Both sides chose from 15 players. James Vince and Tom Westley – neither of whom had enjoyed much luck in the pre-Christmas portion of the tour – combined to take the Lions close to victory in the first warm-up match for the 50-over series.*

At Dubai (ICC Academy), January 16, 2016. **United Arab Emirates XI won by two wickets. ‡England Lions 222-9** (50 overs) (J. M. Vince 58, J. Overton 57*; Amjad Javed 3-55, Mohammad Shehzad 3-49); **United Arab Emirates XI 223-8** (49.4 overs) (S. P. Patil 50; L. E. Plunkett 3-29). *Both sides chose from 15 players. The Lions slumped to 141-8, despite Vince's equable 58, and were indebted to No. 10 Jamie Overton's 57* from 35 balls for a competitive total; he hit 22 (444442) off the last over, from Mohammad Shehzad. Although Swapnil Patil made 50, three wickets for Liam Plunkett helped reduce the UAE to 185-8 in the 44th over – but the ninth-wicket pair, Rohan Mustafa and Ahmed Raza, added 38* to seal a notable victory.*

First A-Team one-day international At Dubai (ICC Academy), January 20, 2016. **England Lions won by five wickets. Pakistan A 192** (47 overs) (Fawad Alam 51; T. K. Curran 3-29); ‡**England Lions 194-5** (41.1 overs) (J. M. Vince 70, D. J. Malan 41, S. W. Billings 35*). *Pakistan A found scoring difficult: none of the visiting bowlers conceded more than 4.33 per over. Vince and Malan ignited the chase with 103 in 20.2 overs, after which the Lions could shrug off the first-ball loss of Westley and saunter to victory.*

Second A-Team one-day international At Dubai (ICC Academy), January 22, 2016. **England Lions won by 69 runs. England Lions 314-5** (50 overs) (D. J. Malan 114, S. W. Billings 31, L. A. Dawson 33, R. A. Whiteley 50*; Mohammad Nawaz 3-57); ‡**Pakistan A 245** (44.1 overs) (Fakhar Zaman 61, Fawad Alam 31, Mohammad Nawaz 51; T. S. Roland-Jones 3-48, L. A. Dawson 3-36). *MoM:* D. J. Malan. *Malan continued his superb run, gliding to 114 from 109 balls. When he departed, Ross Whiteley hit 50* from 30, and Joe Clarke clobbered three sixes in 25* to whizz the Lions past 300; the last five overs brought 66. Pakistan A reached 100-2 in the 18th, but lost wickets regularly.*

Third A-Team one-day international At Dubai (ICC Academy), January 25, 2016. **Pakistan A won by 17 runs. Pakistan A 288-5** (50 overs) (Khurram Manzoor 113, Fakhar Zaman 51, Fawad Alam 40*); ‡**England Lions 271** (48.5 overs) (J. M. Vince 102, T. Westley 34. S. W. Billings 51, L. A. Dawson 41; Mohammad Nawaz 3-57). *MoM:* Khurram Manzoor. *Led by Khurram Manzoor, who had a Test century to his name, Pakistan A kept the series alive. Khurram put on 100 with Fakhar Zaman, then captain Fawad Alam took the total close to 300. Even without the unwell Malan, the Lions looked on course at 223-3 after 41 overs, but Vince was out after completing a fine century. Although Dawson made a run-a-ball 41, he received little support.*

Fourth A-Team one-day international At Dubai (ICC Academy), January 28, 2016. **Pakistan A won by six wickets. England Lions 181** (44.3 overs) (J. M. Vince 32, D. J. Malan 56); ‡**Pakistan A 182-4** (46.3 overs) (Asif Zakir 68*, Zohaib Khan 42*). *MoM:* Asif Zakir. *Vince and the fit-again Malan put on 60 for the first wicket in 9.3 overs, before Vince was run out by a direct hit from Mohammad Abbas for the second match in a row. But it was a struggle after that, and no one else passed 20. Pakistan A also found scoring difficult and, when Fawad Alam was bowled by Westley, they were 66-4 in the 24th over. But Asif Zakir bedded down, adding 116* with Zohaib Khan to square the series.*

Fifth A-Team one-day international At Dubai (ICC Academy), January 30, 2016. **Pakistan A won by three wickets. ‡England Lions 216** (49.1 overs) (S. W. Billings 89, L. A. Dawson 48; Fakhar Zaman 5-27); **Pakistan A 217-7** (47.5 overs) (Khurram Manzoor 39, Fakhar Zaman 62). *MoM:* Fakhar Zaman. *Pakistan A completed a come-from-behind 3–2 win. The Lions had recovered from 52-4 thanks to a fifth-wicket stand of 106 between Billings, who reined himself in to make 89 from 101 balls, and Dawson. But, with slow left-armer Fakhar Zaman taking five wickets, the tail could not wag. Zaman then cracked 62 from 65 deliveries to set his side on the way; despite a late wobble, when Tom Curran took two wickets with successive balls to reduce them to 187-7, Pakistan A completed victory with 13 deliveries to spare.*

DOMESTIC CRICKET IN PAKISTAN IN 2014-15

Abid Ali Kazi

For a sixth season Pakistan had to play most of their international cricket abroad, but there were small advances: visits from Afghanistan and Kenya, building up to a one-day series with Zimbabwe. The first-class programme, however, remained entirely domestic.

Its structure underwent yet another reshuffle (only once this century have the first-class competitions retained the same format and number of teams from one year to the next). After two seasons in which the regional sides contested the Quaid-e-Azam Trophy, and the departmental sides the President's Trophy, they were once again lumped into a single Quaid-e-Azam tournament, with two leagues.

The Gold League featured 12 teams, six each from the previous Quaid-e-Azam and President's competitions. The second tier, the Silver League, had 14 (the remainder, plus one) in two groups, each with four regional and three departmental sides. All the regional teams played first-class cricket under the animal names already used in limited-overs competitions (Karachi Dolphins, Lahore Lions, etc). But, by 2015-16, they had reverted to their traditional names, and the number of first-class sides in the Quaid-e-Azam – still mingling departmental and regional – had been cut from 26 to 16.

As usual the departmental teams, which pay better, finished on top. In the Gold League, there was a three-way battle to qualify for the final, with Port Qasim Authority squeezed out in the last group round. **Sui Northern Gas Pipelines** won the final by claiming a first-innings lead of 303, thanks to a 251-run stand between Mohammad Rizwan and Khurram Shehzad. **National Bank** fought back in the second innings, when three individual hundreds helped them past 500, to deny Sui Northern an outright win, but it was too late to shake their grip on the trophy.

The Silver League final had a similar plot, with **Habib Bank** securing first-innings lead, before State Bank amassed 527 second time round, with Babar Azam extending a maiden century to 266. But State Bank came closer to turning the match on its head. They set a target of 334, with more than a day to take ten wickets for an outright victory, but managed only seven. Pakistan International Airlines had cruised through the Silver League, winning seven out of seven until State Bank knocked them out in the semi-final.

The board applied the same principles in revamping the one-day tournaments, with a dozen teams from the 2013-14 regional and departmental competitions taking part in the President's Gold Cup, and the rest in the Silver Cup. Coincidentally, the two losing first-class finalists reached the Gold Cup final: **State Bank** beat National Bank with a ball to spare. **WAPDA** had a much more decisive win in the Silver Cup final, passing Hyderabad Hawks' 117 in the 28th over.

There was a third List A competition, the Pentangular One-Day Cup, for four provincial sides and a federal team: **Khyber Pakhtunkhwa Fighters** headed the table on net run-rate and beat Baluchistan Warriors in the final.

The four provincial sides had started a Twenty20 tournament in August 2014, which was cancelled halfway through because of security concerns. It was followed in September by a Twenty20 cup for 18 regional teams (with the previous season's entrants joined by Azad Jammu & Kashmir Jaguars, from the Pakistani territory adjoining the Indian state of Jammu & Kashmir). **Peshawar Panthers** were champions; the top eight went on to a further Twenty20 tournament in May, won by **Sialkot Stallions**.

Naeemuddin, of Quaid-e-Azam champions Sui Northern Gas, was the only player who reached 1,000 first-class runs, with 1,045 at 55; Usman Salahuddin of State Bank headed the averages, with 649 at 72. Six bowlers claimed 50 wickets, led by Sohail Khan of Port Qasim Authority, with 64 at 22; the averages were topped by Ali Imran of PIA, who took 38 at just 14.

FIRST-CLASS AVERAGES, 2014-15

BATTING (600 runs, average 35.00)

	M	I	NO	R	HS	100	Avge	Ct/St
Usman Salahuddin (*State Bank*)	9	14	5	649	154*	2	72.11	7
†Fawad Alam (*National Bank*)	8	11	1	719	201	2	71.90	9
Mohammad Rizwan (*Sui Northern Gas*). .	9	12	1	659	224	2	59.90	22/1
†Ali Asad (*United Bank*).	11	17	1	902	150*	3	56.37	8
Faisal Khan (*Sialkot Stallions*)	6	12	1	612	149*	2	55.63	5
†Naeemuddin (*Sui Northern Gas*)	12	23	4	1,045	211*	5	55.00	6
Mohammad Waqas (*Karachi Dolphins*) . . .	9	15	1	762	205*	3	54.42	4
Kamran Akmal (*National Bank*)	12	17	0	900	275	3	52.94	40/2
†Imad Wasim (*Islamabad Leopards*)	9	14	2	601	207	1	50.08	3
Iftikhar Ahmed (*WAPDA*)	10	17	1	789	150*	3	49.31	5
†Umar Siddiq (*Lahore Lions*)	11	20	2	862	166	3	47.88	10
Khurram Shehzad (*Sui Northern Gas*)	11	18	3	680	120	3	45.33	11
Aamer Sajjad (*WAPDA*)	10	16	2	611	121	2	43.64	22
†Saad Ali (*Karachi Dolphins*)	9	16	2	608	105	2	43.42	11
Shahid Yousuf (*ZTBL*)	11	20	2	770	121*	2	42.77	11
Fazal Subhan (*Karachi Dolphins*)	9	17	1	674	207	1	42.12	5
†Ali Waqas (*Sui Northern Gas*)	12	21	5	660	104*	1	41.25	11
†Sarmad Bhatti (*Islamabad Leopards*)	11	19	3	651	86	0	40.68	13
†Mohammad Nawaz (*National Bank*)	10	17	2	610	102	1	40.66	5
†Umar Amin (*Port Qasim Authority*)	10	18	2	642	103	1	40.12	6
Akbar Badshah (*Peshawar Panthers*)	11	18	2	634	117	1	39.62	4
†Adnan Raees (*WAPDA*)	11	19	2	669	141*	2	39.35	7
†Ali Sarfraz (*Islamabad Leopards*)	11	20	2	697	112*	1	38.72	10
†Ayaz Tasawwar (*WAPDA*)	11	18	2	616	95	0	38.50	6
Zahid Mansoor (*Rawalpindi Rams*)	10	19	2	647	165*	1	38.05	22
Khalid Latif (*Port Qasim Authority*)	11	19	1	680	123*	1	37.77	16

BOWLING (35 wickets, average 24.00)

	Style	O	M	R	W	BB	5I	Avge
Ali Imran (*PIA*)	RFM	187	39	561	38	6-45	2	14.76
Najaf Shah (*PIA*)	LFM	246.1	68	638	42	6-21	2	15.19
Hammad Azam (*National Bank*)	RM	225.2	72	552	35	8-26	2	15.77
Shahzaib Ahmed (*Karachi Dolphins*)	LBG	223.4	35	681	43	8-122	4	15.83
Mansoor Ahmed (*Karachi Zebras*)	LBG	250.2	64	656	38	7-16	4	17.26
Abdul Rauf (*Port Qasim Authority*)	RFM	292.5	70	831	48	7-69	6	17.31
Mohammad Ali (*WAPDA*)	RFM	285.4	64	800	46	7-43	3	17.39
Mir Hamza (*Karachi Dolphins*)	LFM	349.2	87	1,011	58	7-73	6	17.43
Rumman Raees (*United Bank*)	LFM	260	73	633	36	6-70	1	17.58
Sadaf Hussain (*KRL*)	LFM	255.2	77	644	36	5-31	2	17.88
Hamza Nadeem (*Islamabad Leopards*). . . .	RFM	323.1	83	860	48	5-35	2	17.91
Imran Khalid (*Sui Northern Gas*)	SLA	255	68	692	38	6-146	2	18.21
Waqas Maqsood (*WAPDA*)	LFM	311.1	73	939	50	5-37	3	18.78
Tabish Khan (*Sui Southern Gas*)	RFM	294.3	79	828	42	7-39	4	19.71
Mohammad Irfan (*Sui Southern Gas*)	SLA	228.2	50	714	35	5-47	3	20.40
Majid Ali (*Multan Tigers*)	LFM	285.2	33	1,046	51	6-92	3	20.50
Kashif Bhatti (*State Bank*)	SLA	353.2	88	849	41	7-85	3	20.70
Mohammad Abbas (*Pakistan TV*)	RFM	279	80	829	38	7-57	3	21.81
Sohail Khan (*Port Qasim Authority*)	RFM	381.4	61	1,414	64	8-91	6	22.09
Taj Wali (*Peshawar Panthers*)	LFM	321	75	951	43	7-63	4	22.11
Azizullah (*Peshawar Panthers*)	RFM	305.1	66	921	41	7-52	3	22.46
Rizwan Akbar (*Rawalpindi Rams*)	RFM	382	102	1,152	51	6-60	3	22.58
Zohaib Ahmed (*Islamabad Leopards*)	RFM	233.4	52	843	37	6-80	2	22.78
Shehzad Azam (*Islamabad Leopards*)	RFM	316.1	48	1,198	52	7-80	4	23.03

QUAID-E-AZAM TROPHY GOLD LEAGUE, 2014-15

	Played	Won	Lost	Drawn	1st-inns points	Points	Net run-rate
SUI NORTHERN GAS	11	8	1	2	24	72	0.21
NATIONAL BANK	11	6†	1	4	27	65	0.68
Port Qasim Authority	11	6*	1	4‡	21	59	−0.14
WAPDA	11	5†	2	4‡	12	45	0.02
United Bank	11	4†	3	4	18	44	−0.11
Karachi Dolphins	11	4*	4	3‡	18	44	0.12
Islamabad Leopards	11	4	2	5	18	42	0.10
Rawalpindi Rams	11	4	4	3	12	36	0.11
Peshawar Panthers	11	2*	7	2	12	25	0.19
Lahore Lions	11	2	8	1	9	21	−0.75
ZTBL	11	2*	5	4	6	19	0.16
Multan Tigers	11	0	9	2	3	3	−0.82

WAPDA = Water and Power Development Authority;
ZTBL = Zarai Taraqiati Bank Limited (formerly ADBP).

*   One innings win.   † Two innings win.   ‡ One draw after following on.

Outright win = 6pts; win by an innings = 1pt extra; lead on first innings in a won or drawn game = 3pts; draw after following on = 1pt. Teams tied on points were ranked on most wins, then fewest losses, then on net run-rate (runs conceded per over from runs scored per over).

At Islamabad (Diamond), October 12–15, 2014. **Drawn.** ZTBL 193 (Shehzad Azam 7-80) **and 12-0;** ‡Islamabad Leopards 209 (Usman Shinwari 6-66). *Islamabad Leopards 3pts.*

At Karachi (National), October 12–15, 2014. **Port Qasim Authority won by 153 runs. Port Qasim Authority 220 and 321-7 dec;** ‡Karachi Dolphins 222 (Mohammad Sami 5-47) **and** 166 (Abdur Rauf 5-39). *Port Qasim Authority 6pts.*

At Lahore (Gaddafi), October 12–15, 2014. **WAPDA won by an innings and 98 runs. WAPDA 542-6 dec** (Mohammad Saad 157, Aamer Sajjad 121); **‡Lahore Lions 288** (Mohammad Ali 5-37) **and 156.** *WAPDA 10pts.*

At Multan (Cricket), October 12–15, 2014. **Sui Northern Gas won by seven wickets. Multan Tigers 219** (Abdul Rehman Muzammil 124*) **and** 155 (Yasir Shah 5-47); ‡Sui Northern Gas 157 (Majid Ali 5-69) **and 218-3.** *Sui Northern Gas 6pts.*

At Peshawar (Arbab Niaz), October 12–15, 2014. **Drawn.** ‡National Bank 170 (Afaq Ahmed 5-52); **Peshawar Panthers 228-6.** *Peshawar Panthers 3pts.*

At Rawalpindi (Cricket), October 12–15, 2014. **United Bank won by an innings and 62 runs. Rawalpindi Rams 130 and 60;** ‡United Bank 252-3 dec (Ali Asad 101). *United Bank 10pts. Rawalpindi collapsed for 60 on the final day of a rain-affected game; only opener Shoaib Nasir and Extras reached double figures. United Bank wicketkeeper Bismillah Khan held six catches, giving him nine in the match.*

At Islamabad (Diamond), October 18–20, 2014. **Islamabad Leopards won by one wicket. United Bank 95** (Mudassar Ali 5-24) **and 228** (Hamza Nadeem 5-35); ‡Islamabad Leopards 151 and 173-9 (Junaid Ilyas 5-56). *Islamabad Leopards 9pts. Three bowlers took maiden five-fors. Islamabad captain Imad Wasim steered his side to a one-wicket, three-day win with 75*.*

At Lahore (Gaddafi), October 18–20, 2014. **ZTBL won by an innings and 25 runs.** Lahore Lions 226 (Sohail Tanvir 5-42) **and** 180; ‡ZTBL 431 (Sohail Tanvir 163). *ZTBL 10pts. Sohail Tanvir followed up 5-42 with a career-best 163 in 161 balls, with seven sixes, from No. 7.*

At Multan (Cricket), October 18–21, 2014. **Port Qasim Authority won by 179 runs.** ‡Port Qasim Authority 324 (Umar Amin 103) **and** 253 (Mohammad Rameez 5-102); **Multan Tigers 255 and** 143 (Sohail Khan 6-81). *Port Qasim Authority 9pts.*

At Peshawar (Arbab Niaz), October 18–20, 2014. **WAPDA won by an innings and 99 runs. Peshawar Panthers 109 and 70;** ‡WAPDA 278 (Iftikhar Ahmed 107; Azizullah 5-74). *WAPDA 10pts.*

At Rawalpindi (Cricket), October 18–21, 2014. **National Bank won by nine wickets. Rawalpindi Rams 282 and 201; ‡National Bank 444** (Fawad Alam 201) **and 40-1.** *National Bank 9pts. Fawad Alam was last out in National Bank's first innings – a sixth catch for Rawalpindi wicketkeeper Talha Qureshi – for 201 in 227 balls, his second double-hundred.*

At Karachi (National), October 19–22, 2014. **Karachi Dolphins won by 234 runs. ‡Karachi Dolphins 205** (Saad Ali 105) **and 402-7 dec** (Imran Khalid 6-146); **Sui Northern Gas 203** (Shahzaib Ahmed 6-67) **and 170.** *Karachi Dolphins 9pts. This was Sui Northern Gas's only defeat of the tournament – chasing 405, they fell well short.*

At Islamabad (Diamond), October 24–27, 2014. **Drawn. National Bank 167 and 128** (Shehzad Azam 5-62); **‡Islamabad Leopards 148** (Hammad Azam 8-26) **and 122-6.** *National Bank 3pts. Hammad Azam achieved career-best figures, while Islamabad wicketkeeper Naeem Anjum held ten catches in the match.*

At Karachi (National), October 24–27, 2014. **Drawn. Karachi Dolphins 222** (Shoaib Malik 5-70) **and 458-8 dec** (Fazal Subhan 207); **‡ZTBL 118** (Adeel Malik 5-27) **and 337-6** (Yasir Hameed 114). *Karachi Dolphins 3pts. Fazal Subhan scored a maiden double-hundred.*

At Lahore (Gaddafi), October 24–27, 2014. **Sui Northern Gas won by five wickets. Lahore Lions 232 and 241** (Umar Siddiq 131*); **‡Sui Northern Gas 370** (Imran Butt 189*; Mohammad Bilawal 6-86) **and 109-5.** *Sui Northern Gas 9pts. Imran Butt carried his bat through Sui Northern's first innings for a career-best 189*.*

At Multan (Cricket), October 24–27, 2014. **WAPDA won by 159 runs. WAPDA 185 and 354-6 dec** (Iftikhar Ahmed 132, Adnan Raees 122); **‡Multan Tigers 291** (Waqas Maqsood 5-86) **and 89** (Mohammad Ali 7-43). *WAPDA 6pts.*

At Peshawar (Arbab Niaz), October 24–27, 2014. **United Bank won by ten wickets. Peshawar Panthers 98 and 251** (Jamaluddin 116); **‡United Bank 340** (Hamza Paracha 111; Afaq Ahmed 6-66) **and 10-0.** *United Bank 9pts. Hamza Pancha and Ali Asad (94) added 202 for United Bank's second wicket.*

At Rawalpindi (Cricket), October 24–27, 2014. **Drawn. Port Qasim Authority 240-9 dec** (Asim Kamal 101*; Rizwan Akbar 5-87) **and 299-4** (Khalid Latif 123*); **‡Rawalpindi Rams 308.** *Rawalpindi Rams 3pts.*

At Islamabad (Diamond), October 30–November 2, 2014. **Sui Northern Gas won by 112 runs. ‡Sui Northern Gas 262** (Shehzad Azam 7-82) **and 315-6 dec** (Naeemuddin 126); **Islamabad Leopards 236 and 229.** *Sui Northern Gas 9pts.*

At Karachi (National), October 30–November 2, 2014. **WAPDA won by three wickets. Karachi Dolphins 80** (Mohammad Ali 5-42, Waqas Maqsood 5-37) **and 311** (Babar Hussain 120); **‡WAPDA 303** (Adnan Raees 141*) **and 89-7** (Mir Hamza 5-33). *WAPDA 9pts. WAPDA completed their fourth straight win, despite losing seven wickets achieving an apparently simple target of 89.*

At Lahore (Gaddafi), October 30–November 2, 2014. **United Bank won by an innings and 54 runs. Lahore Lions 216 and 201** (Ali Zahid 5-27); **‡United Bank 471-9 dec** (Saeed Bin Nasir 120, Wajihuddin 164). *United Bank 10pts. Saeed Bin Nasir and Wajihuddin added 234 for United Bank's fifth wicket.*

At Multan (Cricket), October 30–November 1, 2014. **National Bank won by an innings and 42 runs. Multan Tigers 68 and 280; ‡National Bank 390** (Kamran Akmal 126, Akbar-ur-Rehman 113*). *National Bank 10pts.*

At Peshawar (Arbab Niaz), October 30–November 1, 2014. **Port Qasim Authority won by 196 runs. Port Qasim Authority 166** (Azizullah 5-50) **and 376-9 dec**; **‡Peshawar Panthers 126** (Mohammad Sami 7-35) **and 220** (Abdur Rauf 7-69). *Port Qasim Authority 9pts. Mohammad Sami followed up his 7-35 with a 62-ball 65, including five sixes.*

At Rawalpindi (Cricket), October 30–November 2, 2014. **Rawalpindi Rams won by three wickets. ZTBL 205 and 243** (Shahid Yousuf 121*); **‡Rawalpindi Rams 205** (Kashif Daud 5-65) **and 244-7.** *Rawalpindi Rams 6pts.*

At Islamabad (Diamond), November 6–9, 2014. **Drawn. Islamabad Leopards 229 and 219; ‡WAPDA 196 and 101-3.** *Islamabad Leopards 3pts.*

At Karachi (National), November 6–9, 2014. **National Bank won by six wickets. Karachi Dolphins 207** (Mohammad Waqas 105; Ataullah 6-45) **and 197; ‡National Bank 271** (Mir Hamza 7-73) **and**

134-4. *National Bank 9pts. Mohammad Waqas, with a maiden century, and Yasir Mushtaq (58) contributed 152 for Dolphins' fifth wicket, out of 207; only one other man reached double figures.*

At Lahore (Gaddafi), November 6–9, 2014. **Drawn. Lahore Lions 457-7 dec** (Umar Siddiq 166); ‡**Port Qasim Authority 155 and 195-2** (Shahzaib Hasan 107). *Lahore Lions 3pts, Port Qasim Authority 1pt.*

At Multan (Cricket), November 6–9, 2014. **Drawn.** ‡**Multan Tigers 403** (Abdul Rehman Muzammil 111, Mohammad Ali 104; Adil Raza 5-103) **and 145-4; United Bank 567-4 dec** (Ahsan Ali 224, Ammar Hasan 107*). *United Bank 3pts. Ahsan Ali and Ammar Hasan, who put on 226 for United's second wicket, scored maiden hundreds, and Ahsan converted his into a double.*

At Peshawar (Arbab Niaz), November 6–9, 2014. **ZTBL won by four wickets. Peshawar Panthers 160 and 445** (Musadiq Ahmed 170; Zohaib Khan 5-104); ‡**ZTBL 467** (Rameez Alam 148) **and 141-6.** *ZTBL 9pts.*

At Rawalpindi (Cricket), November 6–9, 2014. **Sui Northern Gas won by nine wickets. Rawalpindi Rams 158 and 97** (Asad Ali 6-39); ‡**Sui Northern Gas 189** (Rizwan Akbar 6-60) **and 69-1.** *Sui Northern Gas 9pts.*

At Islamabad (Diamond), November 12–15, 2014. **Port Qasim Authority won by 45 runs.** ‡**Port Qasim Authority 170** (Shehzad Azam 5-86) **and 312; Islamabad Leopards 158** (Sohail Khan 8-91) **and 279** (Abdur Rauf 5-71). *Port Qasim Authority 9pts.*

At Karachi (National), November 12–15, 2014. **Drawn. Karachi Dolphins 411** (Adil Raza 5-87) **and 376-3** (Yasir Mushtaq 151*, Saad Ali 104*); ‡**United Bank 291** (Mir Hamza 5-74). *Karachi Dolphins 3pts. Yasir Mushtaq, who scored a maiden century, and Saad Ali added 205* for Karachi's fourth wicket in their second innings.*

At Lahore (Gaddafi), November 12–14, 2014. **National Bank won by an innings and 157 runs. National Bank 542-9 dec** (Kamran Akmal 275); ‡**Lahore Lions 159** (Hammad Azam 6-39) **and 226** (Ahmed Jamal 6-82). *National Bank 10pts. Kamran Akmal hit nine sixes in a career-best 275, his second double-hundred.*

At Multan (Cricket), November 12–15, 2014. **Drawn. ZTBL 244 and 315-9 dec;** ‡**Multan Tigers 282** (Ahmed Rasheed 120; Mohammad Khalil 6-85) **and 175-5.** *Multan Tigers 3pts.*

At Peshawar (Arbab Niaz), November 12–15, 2014. **Sui Northern Gas won by four wickets. Peshawar Panthers 120** (Samiullah Khan 6-31) **and 237;** ‡**Sui Northern Gas 135** (Taj Wali 6-42) **and 225-6** (Naeemuddin 113*). *Sui Northern Gas 9pts. Left-arm seamer Samiullah Khan wrapped up Peshawar's first innings with a hat-trick; their last five wickets all fell on 120.*

At Rawalpindi (Cricket), November 12–15, 2014. **Rawalpindi Rams won by three wickets. WAPDA 316** (Atlas Khan 5-114) **and 162;** ‡**Rawalpindi Rams 270 and 209-7.** *Rawalpindi Rams 6pts.*

At Islamabad (Diamond), November 18–21, 2014. **Drawn. Rawalpindi Rams 351 and 261-8 dec;** ‡**Islamabad Leopards 253** (Haseeb Azam 5-74) **and 152-4.** *Rawalpindi Rams 3pts.*

At Lahore (Gaddafi), November 18–20, 2014. **Peshawar Panthers won by nine wickets. Lahore Lions 221** (Taj Wali 7-63) **and 166** (Taj Wali 5-58); ‡**Peshawar Panthers 345** (Jamaluddin 116, Akbar Badshah 117) **and 45-1.** *Peshawar Panthers 9pts. Left-arm seamer Taj Wali took 12-121 in the match, ending Lahore's first innings with a hat-trick which gave him a career-best 7-63; he had been the second victim in Samiullah's hat-trick a week earlier.*

At Multan (Cricket), November 18–20, 2014. **Karachi Dolphins won by an innings and 182 runs. Multan Tigers 46** (Mir Hamza 6-16) **and 222** (Shahzaib Ahmed 5-53); ‡**Karachi Dolphins 450.** *Karachi Dolphins 10pts. On the opening morning Multan collapsed for 46, the season's lowest total, including six ducks. Five men were bowled and four lbw as Adeel Malik (4-21) and Mir Hamza bowled unchanged through 13.5 overs.*

At Rawalpindi (Cricket), November 18–21, 2014. **Drawn. National Bank 399** (Sami Aslam 162); ‡**WAPDA 231** (Zia-ul-Haq 5-55) **and 311-8** (Iftikhar Ahmed 150*). *National Bank 3pts, WAPDA 1pt.*

At Islamabad (National), November 18–21, 2014. **Port Qasim Authority won by an innings and 17 runs. Port Qasim Authority 508** (Khurram Manzoor 139); ‡**ZTBL 218** (Sohail Khan 5-55) **and 273** (Abdur Rauf 6-108). *Port Qasim Authority 10pts.*

At Islamabad (Marghzar), November 18–21, 2014. **Sui Northern Gas won by 169 runs.** ‡**Sui Northern Gas 289** (Prince Abbas 5-81) **and 268-8 dec** (Naeemuddin 101; Ali Zahid 5-72); **United Bank 266 and 122.** *Sui Northern Gas 9pts. United Bank wicketkeeper Bismillah Khan held seven catches in Sui Northern Gas's first innings. This was Sui Northern's fifth consecutive win, and their sixth in all.*

At Lahore (LCCA), November 24–25, 2014. **Lahore Lions won by nine wickets. Karachi Dolphins 132** (Mohammad Saeed 5-47) **and 135;** ‡**Lahore Lions 236** (Adeel Malik 5-83) **and 32-1.** *Lahore Lions 9pts.*

At Islamabad (Diamond), November 24–27, 2014. **Drawn. National Bank 451-9 dec** (Umar Waheed 120) **and 168-4 dec;** ‡**United Bank 310** (Ali Asad 129) **and 201-4.** *National Bank 3pts.*

At Peshawar (Arbab Niaz), November 24–27, 2014. **Islamabad Leopards won by nine wickets. Islamabad Leopards 402** (Faizan Riaz 114) **and 53-1;** ‡**Peshawar Panthers 251 and 201** (Imad Wasim 6-47). *Islamabad Leopards 9pts.*

At Lahore (Gaddafi), November 24–27, 2014. **Drawn.** ‡**Port Qasim Authority 379** (Daniyal Ahsan 122*) **and 303; WAPDA 278** (Aamer Sajjad 103; Abdur Rauf 6-52). *Port Qasim Authority 3pts.*

At Rawalpindi (Cricket), November 24–26, 2014. **Rawalpindi Rams won by 72 runs. Rawalpindi Rams 137** (Majid Ali 5-46) **and 197;** ‡**Multan Tigers 70 and 192** (Rashid Latif 5-67). *Rawalpindi Rams 9pts. Multan were bowled out in double figures for the second game in a row and the fourth time in the season.*

At Islamabad (Marghzar), November 24–27, 2014. **Drawn.** ‡**Sui Northern Gas 306** (Khurram Shehzad 109) **and 254-4 dec; ZTBL 138 and 296-6.** *Sui Northern Gas 3pts.*

At Islamabad (Diamond), November 30–December 3, 2014. **Drawn. Islamabad Leopards 384** (Mohammad Irfan 131; Mir Hamza 5-91); ‡**Karachi Dolphins 185 and 383** (Mohammad Waqas 205*; Hamza Nadeem 5-48). *Islamabad Leopards 3pts, Karachi Dolphins 1pt. Mohammad Waqas followed a first-ball duck by batting eight hours 52 minutes in the follow-on for his maiden double-hundred. Islamabad's Shehzad Azam claimed his 50th first-class wicket of the season.*

At Lahore (LCCA), November 30–December 2, 2014. **Lahore Lions won by nine wickets. Multan Tigers 162** (Mohammad Bilawal 5-58) **and 181** (Mustafa Iqbal 6-22); ‡**Lahore Lions 300** (Sadaf Mehdi 5-104) **and 44-1.** *Lahore Lions 9pts.*

At Faisalabad (Iqbal), November 30–December 3, 2014. **Sui Northern Gas won by nine wickets.** ‡**Sui Northern Gas 506-7 dec** (Naeemuddin 156, Khurram Shehzad 107) **and 29-1; National Bank 191 and 340.** *Sui Northern Gas 9pts.*

At Lahore (Gaddafi), November 30–December 2, 2014. **Port Qasim Authority won by eight wickets. United Bank 84** (Sohail Khan 6-26) **and 254** (Naved Sarwar 127; Abdur Rauf 5-71, Sohail Khan 5-111); ‡**Port Qasim Authority 276** (Prince Abbas 5-90) **and 63-2.** *Port Qasim Authority 9pts. Sohail Khan's 11-137 was his third match return of ten or more in the season, and included his 50th wicket.*

At Rawalpindi (Cricket), November 30–December 3, 2014. **Drawn.** ‡**Rawalpindi Rams 340** (Zahid Mansoor 165*, Yasim Murtaza 120) **and 302-8; Peshawar Panthers 350** (Ashfaq Ahmed 146; Rizwan Akbar 5-81). *Peshawar Panthers 3pts. In Rawalpindi's first innings, Zahid Mansoor and Yasim Murtaza added 236 for the seventh wicket; no one else passed 12 and there were five ducks.*

At Multan (Multan CC), November 30–December 3, 2014. **WAPDA won by 168 runs. WAPDA 193** (Mohammad Khalil 5-51) **and 291** (Sajjad Hussain 6-61); ‡**ZTBL 185** (Waqas Maqsood 5-68) **and 131.** *WAPDA 9pts. This was the first first-class match at the old Multan Cricket Club ground for 18 years, as it had been largely superseded by the new Multan Cricket Stadium. Waqas Maqsood reached 50 first-class wickets in the season.*

At Hyderabad (Niaz), December 6–8, 2014. **Rawalpindi Rams won by seven wickets. Lahore Lions 129** (Abid Hussain 6-47) **and 219** (Haseeb Azam 5-70); ‡**Rawalpindi Rams 222** (Aftab Azwar 5-79) **and 127-3.** *Rawalpindi Rams 9pts.*

At Multan (Multan CC), December 6–8, 2014. **Islamabad Leopards won by 303 runs. Islamabad Leopards 54** (Mohammad Asif 8-19) **and 575** (Faizan Riaz 158, Imad Wasim 207; Sadaf Mehdi 5-158); ‡**Multan Tigers 121 and 205** (Zohaib Ahmed 6-80). *Islamabad Leopards 6pts. Islamabad pulled off an astonishing victory. Put in, they were bowled out for 54, with only No. 9 Naeem Anjum and Extras reaching double figures as off-spinner Mohammad Asif (not the Test seamer) claimed*

LARGEST DIFFERENCE BETWEEN ONE TEAM'S TOTALS

551	Barbados (175 and 726-7 dec) v Trinidad at Bridgetown (won)	1926-27
551	Pakistan (106 and 657-8 dec) v West Indies at Bridgetown (drawn)	1957-58
551	Middlesex (83 and 634-7 dec) v Essex at Chelmsford (drawn)	1983
543	Somerset (87 and 630) v Yorkshire at Leeds (won)	1901
540	Northamptonshire (172 and 712) v Glamorgan at Northampton (drawn)	1998
540	KwaZulu-Natal (214 and 754) v Northerns at Durban (drawn)	2001-02
531	Free Foresters (65 and 596-8 dec) v Cambridge University at Cambridge (drawn) .	1919
528	Somerset (126 and 654-6 dec) v Hampshire at Taunton (drawn)	2008
526	New South Wales (235 and 761-8 dec) v Queensland at Sydney (won)	1929-30
524	Cambridge University (179 and 703-9 dec) v Sussex at Hove (drawn)	1890
521	Punjab (580 and 59) v Mumbai at Mumbai (Wankhede) (drawn)	2012-13
521	**Islamabad Leopards (54 and 575) v Multan Tigers at Multan CC (won)**	**2014-15**

7.1–2–19–8. But, by the close of the first day, when 22 wickets fell, they were 26 ahead. Their second innings stretched to 575 – the highest total of the season – thanks in part to Imad Wasim, who hit a maiden double-hundred and added 323 for Islamabad's sixth wicket with Faizan Riaz. Asif finished with 12-170, but Zohaib Ahmed (10-131) wrapped up a massive 303-run win on the fourth morning.

At Karachi (NBP), December 6–9, 2014. **National Bank won by nine wickets. ZTBL 323** (Shahid Yousuf 115; Mohammad Asghar 5-89) **and 162; ‡National Bank 416-9 dec** (Mohammad Nawaz 102, Fawad Alam 164) **and 70-1.** *National Bank 9pts. ZTBL keeper Zulqarnain Haider held seven catches in National Bank's first innings. Zohaib Khan carried his bat for 64* in ZTBL's second.*

At Karachi (National), December 6–9, 2014. **Drawn. Sui Northern Gas 278** (Mohammad Rizwan 105; Sohail Khan 5-124) **and 539-3** (Naeemuddin 211*, Azhar Ali 154, Ali Waqas 104*); **‡Port Qasim Authority 307.** *Port Qasim Authority 3pts. Naeemuddin batted eight minutes short of ten hours for his second double-hundred – and fifth century of the season – adding 277 for Sui Northern's second wicket with Azhar Ali. Though Sui Northern failed to take first-innings points, they were now assured of a place in the final.*

At Karachi (UBL), December 6–9, 2014. **Drawn. ‡United Bank 277** (Mohammad Irfan 6-60) **and 284-9 dec** (Ali Asad 150*; Azhar Attari 5-52); **WAPDA 212** (Rumman Raees 6-70) **and 175-3.** *United Bank 3pts.*

At Karachi (Arabian Sea), December 7–9, 2014. **Karachi Dolphins won by ten wickets. ‡Peshawar Panthers 86** (Shahzaib Ahmed 6-24) **and 307** (Shahzaib Ahmed 8-122); **Karachi Dolphins 340 and 57-0.** *Karachi Dolphins 9pts. This was the first first-class match at the Arabian Sea Country Club. Leg-spinner Shahzaib Ahmed improved best bowling figures twice on his way to 14-146, the best match analysis of the season.*

At Hyderabad (Niaz), December 12–15, 2014. **Karachi Dolphins won by 120 runs. Karachi Dolphins 325** (Mohammad Waqas 128) **and 165** (Haseeb Azam 6-52); **‡Rawalpindi Rams 253** (Babar Rehman 5-67) **and 117** (Mir Hamza 6-41). *Karachi Dolphins 9pts. Karachi wicketkeeper Mohammad Hasan held nine catches in the match. Mir Hamza and Rawalpindi's Rizwan Akbar both reached 50 wickets for the season.*

At Karachi (National), December 13–16, 2014. **Islamabad Leopards won by five wickets. Lahore Lions 149** (Zohaib Ahmed 5-66) **and 325** (Umar Siddiq 113); **‡Islamabad Leopards 204** (Mohammad Saeed 6-66) **and 271-5** (Ali Sarfraz 112*). *Islamabad Leopards 9pts.*

At Multan (Multan CC), December 13–16, 2014. **Peshawar Panthers won by an innings and 75 runs. Peshawar Panthers 403** (Aimal Khan 113*; Majid Ali 6-92); **‡Multan Tigers 113** (Azizullah 7-52) **and 215** (Taj Wali 5-78). *Peshawar Panthers 10pts. Majid Ali passed 50 first-class wickets in the season during his career-best 6-92.*

At Karachi (NBP), December 13–16, 2014. **National Bank won by 135 runs. ‡National Bank 249** (Tabish Nawab 5-65) **and 279** (Qaiser Abbas 111; Tabish Nawab 5-156); **Port Qasim Authority 91** (Mohammad Nawaz 7-31) **and 302** (Daniyal Ahsan 102). *National Bank 9pts. This was a straight fight to join Sui Northern in the final; thanks to Mohammad Nawaz's 11-93, National Bank overtook Port Qasim Authority to claim second place in the table. Sohail Khan's four wickets for Port Qasim Authority took him to 64 in the season.*

At Karachi (Arabian Sea), December 13–14, 2014. **Sui Northern Gas won by eight wickets.** ‡**WAPDA 90** (Manzoor Khan 5-22) **and 108** (Imran Khalid 5-43); **Sui Northern Gas 133** (Khalid Usman 6-42) **and 66-2.** *Sui Northern Gas 9pts. Sui Northern's Naeemuddin passed 1,000 first-class runs for the season during a two-day win, their eighth in all, which ensured they headed the table.*

At Karachi (UBL), December 13–16, 2014. **United Bank won by 72 runs.** ‡**United Bank 254** (Kashif Daud 7-30) **and 214;** ZTBL **185 and 211** (Ali Zahid 5-61). *United Bank 9pts.*

Final At Karachi (National), December 22–26, 2014. **Drawn.** Sui Northern Gas won the Quaid-e-Azam Trophy by virtue of their first-innings lead. **National Bank 242** (Manzoor Khan 5-43) **and 508** (Sami Aslam 122, Kamran Akmal 137, Raza Hasan 123; Imran Ali 5-85); ‡**Sui Northern Gas 543** (Mohammad Rizwan 224, Khurram Shehzad 120) **and 28-0.** *Mohammad Rizwan effectively made sure of the Quaid-e-Azam Trophy when he batted eight hours 38 minutes for his maiden double-hundred, putting on 251 for Sui Northern's fifth wicket with Khurram Shehzad. National Bank had been bowled out on the first day but, at their second attempt, also passed 500, with Sami Aslam and Kamran Akmal adding 220 for the fourth wicket, and Raza Hasan scoring a maiden century from No. 9. It was too late: Sui Northern's 301-run first-innings lead secured the title.*

QUAID-E-AZAM TROPHY WINNERS

1953-54	Bahawalpur	1977-78	Habib Bank	1996-97	Lahore City
1954-55	Karachi	1978-79	National Bank	1997-98	Karachi Blues
1956-57	Punjab	1979-80	PIA	1998-99	Peshawar
1957-58	Bahawalpur	1980-81	United Bank	1999-2000	PIA
1958-59	Karachi	1981-82	National Bank	2000-01	Lahore City Blues
1959-60	Karachi	1982-83	United Bank	2001-02	Karachi Whites
1961-62	Karachi Blues	1983-84	National Bank	2002-03	PIA
1962-63	Karachi A	1984-85	United Bank	2003-04	Faisalabad
1963-64	Karachi Blues	1985-86	Karachi	2004-05	Peshawar
1964-65	Karachi Blues	1986-87	National Bank	2005-06	Sialkot
1966-67	Karachi	1987-88	PIA	2006-07	Karachi Urban
1968-69	Lahore	1988-89	ADBP	2007-08	Sui Northern Gas
1969-70	PIA	1989-90	PIA	2008-09	Sialkot
1970-71	Karachi Blues	1990-91	Karachi Whites	2009-10	Karachi Blues
1972-73	Railways	1991-92	Karachi Whites	2010-11	Habib Bank
1973-74	Railways	1992-93	Karachi Whites	2011-12	PIA
1974-75	Punjab A	1993-94	Lahore City	2012-13	Karachi Blues
1975-76	National Bank	1994-95	Karachi Blues	2013-14	Rawalpindi
1976-77	United Bank	1995-96	Karachi Blues	2014-15	Sui Northern Gas

The competition has been contested sometimes by regional teams, sometimes by departments, and sometimes by a mixture of the two. Karachi teams have won the Quaid-e-Azam Trophy 20 times, PIA 7, National Bank 5, Lahore teams and United Bank 4, Bahawalpur, Habib Bank, Peshawar, Punjab, Railways, Sialkot and Sui Northern Gas 2, ADBP, Faisalabad and Rawalpindi 1.

QUAID-E-AZAM TROPHY SILVER LEAGUE, 2014-15

Group One	P	W	L	D	Pts
PIA	6	6*	0	0	52
KRL	6	4*	1	1	34
PAKISTAN TV	6	3*	2	1	28
HYDERABAD HAWKS	6	2	3	1	18
Karachi Zebras	6	2	3	1	15
Lahore Eagles	6	0	4	2	6
Quetta Bears	6	0	4	2	3

Group Two	P	W	L	D	Pts
HABIB BANK	6	4‡	1	1	42
SUI SOUTHERN GAS	6	3*	1	2	34
STATE BANK	6	2*	1	3	28
BAHAWALPUR STAGS	6	1	1	4‡	16
Sialkot Stallions	6	1	2	3	6
Faisalabad Wolves	6	1	3	2	6
Abbottabad Falcons	6	0	3	3	3

PIA = Pakistan International Airlines; KRL = Khan Research Laboratories.

* *One innings win.* † *Three innings wins.* ‡ *One draw after following on.*

Outright win = 6pts; win by an innings = 1pt extra; lead on first innings in a won or drawn game = 3pts; draw after following on = 1pt. Teams tied on points were ranked on most wins, then fewest losses, then on net run-rate (runs conceded per over from runs scored per over).

Group One

At Hyderabad (Niaz), October 12–15, 2014. **Hyderabad Hawks won by 40 runs. Hyderabad Hawks** 248 (Lal Kumar 103*) **and 357-6 dec** (Shoaib Laghari 106*); ‡**Pakistan Television 126** (Babar Khan 5-48) **and 439** (Rehan Afridi 157*). *Hyderabad Hawks 9pts. Set 480 to win in a day and a half, Pakistan Television recovered from 23-3 to score 439 (then a national record for the fourth innings), thanks to a career-best 157* from Rehan Afridi.*

At Karachi (NBP), October 12–15, 2014. **PIA won by 100 runs. PIA 224** (Zohaib Shera 5-36) **and 249-4 dec** (Faisal Iqbal 106*); ‡**Karachi Zebras 79** (Aizaz Cheema 6-26) **and 294.** *PIA 9pts. Fahad Iqbal (89) and Faisal Iqbal added 204 for PIA's fourth wicket.*

At Lahore (LCCA), October 12–15, 2014. **KRL won by five wickets. Lahore Eagles 252 and 154** (Fahad-ul-Haq 108; Sadaf Hussain 5-31); ‡**KRL 172** (Asif Raza 5-54) **and 235-5.** *KRL 6pts.*

At Hyderabad (Niaz), October 18–20, 2014. **PIA won by ten wickets. Hyderabad Hawks 173 and 242** (Hazrat Shah 5-68); ‡**PIA 415-8 dec** (Shehzar Mohammad 107) **and 4-0.** *PIA 9pts.*

At Karachi (NBP), October 18–20, 2014. **Pakistan Television won by six wickets. ‡Karachi Zebras 261 and 139** (Mohammad Abbas 7-57); **Pakistan Television 191** (Mansoor Ahmed 5-45) **and 211-4.** *Pakistan Television 6pts.*

At Rawalpindi (KRL), October 18–20, 2014. **KRL won by ten wickets. Quetta Bears 168 and 91** (Yasir Ali 5-22); ‡**KRL 220 and 42-0.** *KRL 9pts.*

At Karachi (UBL), October 24–27, 2014. **KRL won by seven wickets. Karachi Zebras 83 and 324** (Zeeshan Jamil 112); ‡**KRL 268** (Basit Ali 5-49, Mansoor Ahmed 5-104) **and 140-3.** *KRL 9pts. Zeeshan Jamil and Jahid Ali (78) added 206 for Karachi's fourth wicket, but could not make up for their collapse to 17-5 on the opening morning.*

At Lahore (LCCA), October 24–27, 2014. **PIA won by five wickets. Lahore Eagles 206 and 166** (Tahir Khan 6-40); ‡**PIA 264 and 110-5.** *PIA 9pts.*

At Islamabad (National), October 24–26, 2014. **Pakistan Television won by an innings and 62 runs. ‡Quetta Bears 194 and 51** (Waqar Ahmed 6-38); **Pakistan Television 307.** *Pakistan Television 10pts. After a first-day washout, Quetta effectively lost inside two days; they collapsed for 51 as Waqar Ahmed and Mohammad Abbas (4-13) bowled unchanged through 16.5 overs.*

At Hyderabad (Niaz), October 30–November 2, 2014. **KRL won by an innings and 51 runs. Hyderabad Hawks 213 and 232;** ‡**KRL 496** (Saeed Anwar 113, Luqman Butt 111). *KRL 10pts.*

At Lahore (LCCA), October 30–November 2, 2014. **Pakistan Television won by 226 runs. Pakistan Television 294** (Bilawal Iqbal 5-60) **and 292-6 dec** (Hasan Raza 109); ‡**Lahore Eagles 213** (Mohammad Abbas 5-66) **and 147** (Mohammad Abbas 5-46). *Pakistan Television 9pts. Nineteen-year-old Hasan Raza scored 109 on first-class debut.*

At Islamabad (National), October 30–November 1, 2014. **PIA won by 102 runs. PIA 179 and 222;** ‡**Quetta Bears 186** (Hazrat Shah 5-61) **and 113** (Najaf Shah 6-21). *PIA 6pts.*

At Karachi (UBL), November 6–8, 2014. **Karachi Zebras won by six wickets. Hyderabad Hawks 260 and 93** (Mansoor Ahmed 7-16); ‡**Karachi Zebras 176** (Babar Khan 5-41) **and 178-4.** *Karachi Zebras 6pts.*

At Rawalpindi (KRL), November 6–9, 2014. **Drawn. Pakistan Television 260 and 206** (Sadaf Hussain 5-62); ‡**KRL 253** (Usman Arshad 101*) **and 141-6.** *Pakistan Television 3pts.*

At Lahore (LCCA), November 6–9, 2014. **Drawn. ‡Lahore Eagles 229 and 222-2 dec** (Fahad-ul-Haq 100*); **Quetta Bears 142** (Shahid Nawaz 5-30) **and 90-3.** *Lahore Eagles 3pts.*

At Hyderabad (Niaz), November 12–15, 2014. **Hyderabad Hawks won by 21 runs. Hyderabad Hawks 196 and 160** (Nazar Hussain 9-60); ‡**Quetta Bears 180 and 155** (Aslam Sattar 6-44). *Hyderabad Hawks 9pts. Left-arm seamer Nazar Hussain's 9-60 was the best return of the season, but it was leg-spinner Aslam Sattar's career-best 6-44 that won the day.*

At Rawalpindi (KRL), November 12–15, 2014. **PIA won by four wickets. KRL 107** (Ali Imran 6-45) **and 337;** ‡**PIA 241** (Nauman Ali 5-74) **and 204-6.** *PIA 9pts.*

At Lahore (LCCA), November 12–14, 2014. **Karachi Zebras won by seven runs. Karachi Zebras 257** (Shahid Nawaz 5-45) **and 105;** ‡**Lahore Eagles 198** (Ahmed Iqbal 5-15) **and 157** (Basit Ali

5-44). *Karachi Zebras 9pts. Shahid Nawaz took a hat-trick as Karachi's last four wickets fell at 257 in the first innings. Chasing 165, Lahore were 152-7 but lost their last three for five.*

At Karachi (NBP), November 18–21, 2014. **Drawn. ‡Karachi Zebras 187** (Gohar Faiz 5-56) **and 342-8 dec** (Arsalan Bashir 114, Owais Rehmani 114); **Quetta Bears 268** (Mansoor Ahmed 7-80) **and 142-8.** *Quetta Bears 3pts. Arsalan Bashir scored 114 on first-class debut, and added 223 with captain Owais Rehmani, who also scored 114, after making five dismissals in Quetta's first innings.*

At Lahore (LCCA), November 18–21, 2014. **Drawn. Lahore Eagles 334** (Fahad-ul-Haq 138; Babar Khan 5-114) **and 290-6 dec** (Mohammad Waheed 110); **‡Hyderabad Hawks 238 and 213-8.** *Lahore Eagles 3pts.*

At Sialkot (Jinnah), November 18–20, 2014. **PIA won by an innings and 18 runs. Pakistan Television 133** (Najaf Shah 6-31) **and 317** (Raheel Majeed 174); **‡PIA 468-6 dec** (Sheharyar Ghani 152*, Shoaib Khan 114*). *PIA 10pts. PIA finished top of their group with six wins out of six, after Sheharyar Ghani and Shoaib Khan added 244* for their seventh wicket.*

Group Two

At Bahawalpur, October 12–15, 2014. **Drawn. ‡Sui Southern Gas 519** (Usman Tariq 111, Awais Zia 164) **and 24-2 dec; Bahawalpur Stags 199** (Mohammad Irfan 5-47) **and 186-4.** *Sui Southern Gas 3pts. Sui Southern Gas returned to first-class status after four seasons in second-class tournaments.*

At Faisalabad (Iqbal), October 12–15, 2014. **Drawn. ‡State Bank 305** (Faisal Yasin 5-86) **and 122-5; Faisalabad Wolves 222.** *State Bank 3pts.*

At Sialkot (Jinnah), October 12–15, 2014. **Drawn. Sialkot Stallions 351** (Atiq-ur-Rehman 103; Umar Gul 5-90) **and 146-8; ‡Habib Bank 430.** *Habib Bank 3pts.*

At Abbottabad, October 18–20, 2014. **Habib Bank won by an innings and 14 runs. Abbottabad Falcons 185** (Umar Gul 5-41) **and 117; ‡Habib Bank 316** (Imran Farhat 113; Shakeel Ahmed 5-42). *Habib Bank 10pts.*

At Bahawalpur, October 18–21, 2014. **Drawn. ‡State Bank 525-6 dec** (Mukhtar Ahmed 144, Naved Yasin 173); **Bahawalpur Stags 274** (Kashif Bhatti 7-85) **and 262-8** (Faisal Mubashir 104*). *Bahawalpur Stags 1pt, State Bank 3pts. After adding 176 with Mukhtar Ahmed for State Bank's second wicket – both achieved career-bests – Naved Yasin held five catches in the field in Bahawalpur's first innings and eight in the match.*

At Faisalabad (Iqbal), October 18–20, 2014. **Sui Southern Gas won by an innings and 243 runs. Faisalabad Wolves 118 and 100; ‡Sui Southern Gas 461-9 dec** (Tariq Haroon 137). *Sui Southern Gas 10pts. Nos 8 and 9 Tariq Haroon and Tabish Khan (67) added 182 for Sui Southern's eighth wicket to set up the biggest victory of the season.*

At Abbottabad, October 24–27, 2014. **State Bank won by eight wickets. Abbottabad Falcons 219** (Saad Altaf 5-64) **and 250; ‡State Bank 284 and 186-2** (Mukhtar Ahmed 101*). *State Bank 9pts.*

At Faisalabad (Iqbal), October 24–26, 2014. **Habib Bank won by an innings and 70 runs. Habib Bank 332; ‡Faisalabad Wolves 166 and 96** (Abdur Rehman 5-53). *Habib Bank 10pts.*

At Sialkot (Jinnah), October 24–27, 2014. **Sui Southern Gas won by 175 runs. Sui Southern Gas 210** (Hasan Ali 5-97) **and 413-8 dec** (Haris Ali 121, Awais Zia 108); **‡Sialkot Stallions 81** (Tabish Khan 6-33) **and 367** (Faisal Khan 149*; Mohammad Irfan 5-66). *Sui Southern Gas 9pts. In Sialkot's first innings, only Atiq-ur-Rehman (41) reached double figures. In Sui Southern's second, 20-year-old Haris Ali scored 121 on first-class debut.*

At Abbottabad, October 30–November 2, 2014. **Drawn. Abbottabad Falcons 223** (Tabish Khan 5-43) **and 359** (Waqar Orakzai 138*); **‡Sui Southern Gas 297** (Saifullah Bangash 148*) **and 141-7.** *Sui Southern Gas 3pts.*

At Bahawalpur, October 30–November 2, 2014. **Habib Bank won by nine wickets. Bahawalpur Stags 221 and 309** (Rehan Rafiq 102; Abdur Rehman 6-98); **‡Habib Bank 442** (B. M. Shafayat 145) **and 91-1.** *Habib Bank 9pts.*

At Sialkot (Jinnah), October 30–November 2, 2014. **Drawn. Sialkot Stallions 342** (Bilal Asif 111, Faisal Khan 121) **and 378-6** (Ahmed Butt 106*); **‡State Bank 343** (Kashif Bhatti 158; Hasan Ali

8-107). *State Bank 3pts. Sialkot wicketkeeper Ahmed Butt followed five catches in State Bank's innings with a maiden century – the third of the match, after Bilal Asif and Kashif Bhatti. Bilal and Faisal Khan had added 215 for Sialkot's fourth wicket; Kashif and Mohtashim Ali (82) put on 193 for State Bank's seventh.*

At Abbottabad, November 6–9, 2014. **Drawn. Faisalabad Wolves 232** (Fahim Ashraf 105) **and 278-5 dec; ‡Abbottabad Falcons 353 and 9-0.** *Abbottabad Falcons 3pts. Faisalabad were 84-8 on the first day before Fahim Ashraf and Sadaqat Ali (62) added 131 for the ninth wicket.*

At Islamabad (Marghzar), November 6–8, 2014. **Habib Bank won by an innings and 40 runs. ‡State Bank 120 and 138; Habib Bank 298** (Aamer Yamin 5-92). *Habib Bank 10pts.*

At Sialkot (Jinnah), November 6–9, 2014. **Drawn. Sialkot Stallions 185** (Imranullah Aslam 5-37) **and 268; ‡Bahawalpur Stags 293** (Bilal Asif 5-60) **and 114-6.** *Bahawalpur Stags 3pts.*

At Bahawalpur, November 12–15, 2014. **Drawn. ‡Abbottabad Falcons 383** (Waqar Orakzai 110; Ahmed Raza 7-92) **and 238-8** (Imranullah Aslam 5-81); **Bahawalpur Stags 529** (Imranullah Aslam 127, Faisal Mubashir 127, Bilal Khilji 114; Inam Khan 5-149). *Bahawalpur Stags 3pts. Imranullah Aslam and Adeel Basit (81) opened for Bahawalpur with 216, before Faisal Mubashir and Bilal Khilji added 226 for the third wicket. Imranullah followed his 127 by taking 5-81 with his leg-spin.*

At Islamabad (Marghzar), November 12–15, 2014. **Sui Southern Gas won by 26 runs. Sui Southern Gas 152 and 288** (Mohammad Waqas 140); **‡Habib Bank 112** (Tabish Khan 7-39) **and 302.** *Sui Southern Gas 9pts.*

At Sialkot (Jinnah), November 12–15, 2014. **Faisalabad Wolves won by five wickets. Sialkot Stallions 210 and 384** (Bilal Hussain 157; Naseer Akram 5-102); **‡Faisalabad Wolves 154 and 444-5** (Imran Ali 182*). *Faisalabad Wolves 6pts. Faisalabad overhauled a target of 441 – a national fourth-innings record, beating Pakistan Television's 439 (to lose) a month earlier.*

At Abbottabad, November 18–20, 2014. **Sialkot Stallions won by six wickets. Abbottabad Falcons 229 and 91** (Waqas Ahmed 7-37); **‡Sialkot Stallions 208 and 114-4.** *Sialkot Stallions 6pts.*

At Faisalabad (Iqbal), November 18–20, 2014. **Bahawalpur Stags won by six wickets. ‡Faisalabad Wolves 76** (Zahir Siddiqi 6-36) **and 154; Bahawalpur Stags 198** (Sadaqat Ali 7-78) **and 35-4.** *Bahawalpur Stags 9pts.*

At Sargodha, November 18–21, 2014. **State Bank won by an innings and 21 runs. Sui Southern Gas 312** (Zafar Gohar 5-80) **and 155** (Kashif Bhatti 5-43, Zafar Gohar 5-60); **‡State Bank 488** (Usman Salahuddin 129*, Rizwan Haider 107; Mohammad Irfan 5-144). *State Bank 10pts.*

Knockouts

Quarter-final At Mirpur, November 23–26, 2014. **Habib Bank won by 18 runs. Habib Bank 128** (Mir Ali 5-39) **and 423-5 dec** (B. M. Shafayat 201*); **‡Hyderabad Hawks 266 and 267** (Azeem Ghumman 121). *Bilal Shafayat, the former Nottinghamshire batsman, came in at 5-2 in Habib Bank's second innings, still 133 behind, to turn the match with a maiden double-hundred.*

Quarter-final At Faisalabad (Iqbal), November 23–25, 2014. **State Bank won by an innings and 47 runs. KRL 176 and 171; ‡State Bank 394** (Usman Salahuddin 154*).

Quarter-final At Sialkot (Jinnah), November 23–25, 2014. **PIA won by six wickets. Bahawalpur Stags 137 and 96; ‡PIA 104 and 132-4.** *PIA's seventh successive win in this tournament was their eighth in all, going back to January 2014.*

Quarter-final At Islamabad (National), November 23–26, 2014. **Sui Southern Gas won by 235 runs. ‡Sui Southern Gas 266** (Waqar Ahmed 5-53) **and 373; Pakistan Television 222** (Atif Maqbool 6-82) **and 182** (Tabish Khan 5-55).

Semi-final At Mirpur, November 28–December 1, 2014. **Drawn.** Habib Bank qualified for the final by virtue of their first-innings lead. **Habib Bank 417** (Rameez Aziz 169) **and 201-4; ‡Sui Southern Gas 415** (Asif Zakir 204*). *Asif Zakir batted nine hours 16 minutes for his second double-hundred, but ran out of partners with Sui Southern three short of the first-innings lead which would determine the finalists in this drawn match.*

Semi-final At Sialkot (Jinnah), November 28–December 1, 2014. **State Bank won by three wickets. PIA** 120 (Rizwan Haider 6-57) **and** 279 (Rizwan Haider 5-101); ‡**State Bank 172 and 229-7** (Ali Imran 6-47). *State Bank ended PIA's winning run to reach the final.*

Final At Faisalabad (Iqbal), December 3–7, 2014. **Drawn.** Habib Bank won the Silver League by virtue of their first-innings lead. ‡**State Bank 162 and 527-8 dec** (Babar Azam 266); **Habib Bank 356** (Kashif Bhatti 5-113) **and 211-7.** *After State Bank's inadequate first innings, Babar Azam converted his maiden hundred into 266, batting 12 minutes short of ten hours, to help set Habib Bank a target of 334. They were seven down with 11 overs to go, but batted out time to claim the title on first-innings lead.*

COOL AND COOL PRESENTS HAIER PENTANGULAR ONE-DAY CUP, 2014-15

50-over league plus final

	Played	Won	Lost	Points	Net run-rate
KHYBER PAKHTUNKHWA FIGHTERS	4	3	1	6	0.76
BALUCHISTAN WARRIORS	4	3	1	6	0.06
Punjab Badshahs	4	3	1	6	0.03
Federal United	4	1	3	2	−0.53
Sind Knights	4	0	4	0	−0.33

Final At Karachi (National), January 11, 2015 (day/night). **Khyber Pakhtunkhwa Fighters won by six wickets. Baluchistan Warriors 238** (47 overs) (Sami Aslam 119; Junaid Khan 5-45); ‡**Khyber Pakhtunkhwa Fighters 242-4** (47 overs) (Mohammad Rizwan 103*). *MoM: Junaid Khan. Junaid Khan worked through Baluchistan's batting for a one-day best, and Mohammad Rizwan completed victory with 103* in 87 balls.*

HAIER PRESIDENT'S ONE-DAY GOLD CUP, 2014-15

Two 50-over leagues plus knockout

Semi-final At Karachi (National), January 29, 2015. **State Bank won by nine wickets. Karachi Dolphins 214** (43.2 overs); ‡**State Bank 215-1** (36.3 overs) (Babar Azam 142*). *Babar Azam's one-day-best 142* in 120 balls swept State Bank into their second final of the season with more than 13 overs to spare.*

Semi-final At Karachi (National), January 30, 2015. **National Bank won by 48 runs. National Bank 340-5** (50 overs); ‡**KRL 292** (49.2 overs). *Kamran Akmal dominated National Bank's innings with 90 in 75 balls.*

Final At Karachi (National), February 1, 2015. **State Bank won by two wickets. National Bank 279-6** (50 overs); ‡**State Bank 283-8** (49.5 overs). *Mohammad Nawaz struck 93 in 67 balls, adding 139 for National Bank's sixth wicket with Qaiser Abbas (46*). But a fourth-wicket century stand between Mukhtar Ahmed and Naved Yasin put State Bank on course for victory, though No. 9 Kashif Bhatti had to hit two fours in the final over to complete it.*

HAIER PRESIDENT'S ONE-DAY SILVER CUP, 2014-15

Three 50-over leagues plus triangular super league and final

Final At Lahore (Gaddafi), February 8, 2015. **WAPDA won by eight wickets. Hyderabad Hawks 117** (43.5 overs); ‡**WAPDA 121-2** (27.3 overs). *Mohammad Irfan, a 19-year-old seamer in his first one-day match, reduced Hyderabad to 31-5 and finished with 4-12. Ayaz Tasawwar and Aamer Sajjad then added 98* for WAPDA's third wicket to secure the cup with 22.3 overs to go.*

TAQREEBAT-E-AZADI T20 TOURNAMENT, 2014-15

20-over league

	Played	Won	Lost	Cancelled	Points	Net run-rate
Baluchistan.	3	1	0	2	4	5.35
Punjab	3	1	0	2	4	0.48
Khyber Pakhtunkhwa.	3	1	1	1	3	–0.10
Sind	3	0	2	1	1	–2.81

This tournament was called off after six matches for security reasons.

BANK ALBARAKA PRESENTS HAIER T20 CUP, 2014-15

Four 20-over leagues plus knockout

Semi-final　At Karachi (National), September 27, 2014. **Peshawar Panthers won by six runs. Peshawar Panthers 156-7** (20 overs); ‡**Sialkot Stallions 150-7** (20 overs). *Peshawar captain Zohaib Khan scored 30 in 19 balls, then dismissed Sialkot's two leading scorers.*

Semi-final　At Karachi (National), September 27, 2014 (floodlit). **Lahore Lions won by nine runs.** ‡**Lahore Lions 179-7** (20 overs); **Multan Tigers 170** (20 overs). *Kamran Akmal opened for Lahore with 77 in 43 balls, adding 114 with Imam-ul-Haq (50) for the second wicket; Mohammad Aftab followed up with four top-order Multan wickets.*

Final　At Karachi (National), September 28, 2014 (floodlit). **Peshawar Panthers won by seven wickets.** ‡**Lahore Lions 133-9** (20 overs); **Peshawar Panthers 134-3** (19.2 overs). *Taj Wali (3-30) removed both Lahore openers, including Kamran for four, and Iftikhar Ahmed guided Peshawar home with 50*.*

COOL AND COOL PRESENTS HAIER SUPER EIGHT T20, 2014-15

Two 20-over leagues plus knockout

Semi-final　At Faisalabad (Iqbal), May 17, 2015 (floodlit). **Sialkot Stallions won by 65 runs. Sialkot Stallions 167** (19.4 overs); ‡**Karachi Dolphins 102** (17 overs). *Sialkot opener Nauman Anwar scored 80 in 43 balls in a game where no one else reached 30. Sialkot lost their last six for 17, and Karachi for 16.*

Semi-final　At Faisalabad (Iqbal), May 17, 2015 (floodlit). **Lahore Lions won by four wickets.** ‡**Rawalpindi Rams 100-8** (20 overs); **Lahore Lions 105-6** (19.1 overs). *Ahmed Shehzad batted throughout Lahore's innings for 58*, more than double the next-best score on either side.*

Final　At Faisalabad (Iqbal), May 18, 2015 (floodlit). **Sialkot Stallions won by 74 runs.** ‡**Sialkot Stallions 197-9** (20 overs); **Lahore Lions 123-8** (20 overs). *Nauman Anwar improved his best Twenty20 score for the second time in two days with 97 in 54 balls, including six sixes, and added 111 for Sialkot's fourth wicket with Haris Sohail (47).*

SOUTH AFRICAN CRICKET IN 2015

Falling from grace

Colin Bryden

After losing four Tests and winning only one in 2015 – against a weak West Indies at the start of the year – South Africa finally gave up top spot in the rankings when England triumphed at Johannesburg early in 2016. Alarm bells should perhaps have sounded in July, when South Africa were bowled out for 248 at Chittagong, and conceded a first-innings lead to Bangladesh. But the tour was scheduled at the end of the monsoon season, and six of the remaining seven days of the Tests were rained off.

By the end of the year, though, that total against Bangladesh remained South Africa's highest in ten completed innings after the West Indies series; there were only two more above 200, and Temba Bavuma's 54 at Chittagong was

SOUTH AFRICA IN 2015

	Played	Won	Lost	Drawn/No result
Tests	8	1	4	3
One-day internationals	24	15	9	–
Twenty20 internationals	10	6	3	1

DECEMBER – JANUARY	3 Tests, 5 ODIs and 3 T20Is (h) v West Indies	(see *Wisden 2015*, page 1047)
FEBRUARY – MARCH	ICC World Cup (in Australia and New Zealand)	(page 860)
APRIL		
MAY		
JUNE		
JULY	2 Tests, 3 ODIs and 2 T20Is (a) v Bangladesh	(page 979)
AUGUST	3 ODIs and 2 T20Is (h) v New Zealand	(page 1080)
SEPTEMBER		
OCTOBER – NOVEMBER – DECEMBER	4 Tests, 5 ODIs and 2 T20Is (a) v India	(page 996)
JANUARY – FEBRUARY	4 Tests, 5 ODIs and 2 T20Is (h) v England	(page 403)

For a review of South African domestic cricket from the 2014-15 season, see page 1090.

one of just four half-centuries, of which only one – Dean Elgar's bat-carrying 118 in the Boxing Day Test against England – was converted into three figures. The mood did not improve when, in January 2016, Gulam Bodi – who played three limited-overs internationals in 2007 – was banned for 20 years for trying to fix matches in the Ram Slam T20 tournament.

Four Tests in India had proved an exercise in humiliation against spin. The surface for the Third Test at Nagpur – where South Africa were skittled for 79 in their first innings – was condemned as poor by the ICC. But, even when tracks were reasonable, as at Bangalore and Delhi, batsmen struggled. South Africa's 3–0 defeat was their first away from home since 2006 in Sri Lanka.

The calendar-year averages told a distressing tale. A. B. de Villiers averaged 49 and Elgar 43, but the next-best was Hashim Amla, with 22. Faf du Plessis and J-P. Duminy averaged 16 and 14 respectively. After 11 Test innings without a half-century, Amla collected 201 against England at Cape Town in January 2016 – and promptly resigned the captaincy, which passed to de Villiers, who had just relinquished the gloves after only one Test back behind the stumps. One weakness was the lack of a specialist opener to partner Elgar, a malaise summed up by Stiaan van Zyl's travails against England.

The bowlers enjoyed reasonable success, although injuries took their toll. Dale Steyn, for so long the leader of the attack, suffered a groin problem in the First Test in India, then strained his shoulder in his comeback match against England. In between, he took his 400th Test wicket while dodging the downpours in Bangladesh. Vernon Philander hurt an ankle playing football ahead of the Second Test in India, and did not play again for the rest of the year. Still, the attack was rarely mastered. Steyn took 17 wickets at 21, and Morne Morkel 19 at 26, although off-spinner Simon Harmer was the leading wicket-taker, with 20. When his bowling looked anodyne in India, Harmer was replaced by Dane Piedt, another off-spinner. Leg-spinner Imran Tahir took 14 wickets in India but, at 36, might have come to the end of his long-delayed Test career.

If the batting struggled in Tests, it was often scintillating in one-day internationals. De Villiers, captain in the format, was phenomenal, hitting 1,193 runs at an average of 79 and a strike-rate of 137. He made five centuries, all at better than a run a ball. That included the fastest ODI hundred, from just 31 deliveries, against West Indies at Johannesburg. He repeated the dose against them in the World Cup, reaching three figures from 52, and spanked another, from 57, against India in Mumbai. Amla also reached 1,000 runs.

South Africa went past 400 on four occasions, which helped them win 15 of their 50-over matches, against nine defeats. The most traumatic loss, as so often, came in the World Cup. It was controversial, too. After Sri Lanka were convincingly beaten in the quarter-final, the team and management wanted the same XI to play in the semi, against New Zealand at Auckland. But politics intervened. The target for South African teams in international matches is a minimum of four non-white players, and there had been only three against Sri Lanka. With Philander recovered from injury after missing that game, the management were pressured into picking him for the semi ahead of Kyle Abbott, one of the successes of the tournament. Cricket South Africa, while not confirming any direct interference, acknowledged that Haroon Lorgat, their

Julian Finney, Getty Images

Lost in thought: Hashim Amla's batting suffered during his time as captain

chief executive, had impressed upon the convener of selectors and the coach "the need to properly consider the best XI bearing in mind the transformation guidelines". Philander took none for 52, and New Zealand won when Grant Elliott smashed the penultimate ball, from Steyn, over long-on for six.

Whether such issues had any bearing on the decline of the Test team was difficult to assess, especially as the one-day side went on to enjoy success after the World Cup, beating New Zealand at home and India away. But there was a lack of international experience in the coaching staff, while the only Test player among the selectors was Ashwell Prince, a newcomer to the panel.

Apparently unabashed by the World Cup controversy, CSA almost immediately announced an even more aggressive transformation policy for domestic cricket, with franchise teams compelled to include six non-white players, three of whom had to be black Africans. This led to some unbalanced teams at the start of the season, with high-profile players having to sit out.

Perhaps the most encouraging harbingers of an uncertain future were the emergence of fast bowler Kagiso Rabada, followed by Bavuma's century against England at Cape Town in January. Two months after his 20th birthday, Rabada took a hat-trick in the second over of his debut, in a one-dayer against Bangladesh at Mirpur in July, and finished with six for 16. He soon graduated to Test cricket, and claimed 13 wickets in South Africa's consolation win over England at Centurion. The son of middle-class parents and the product of an exclusive school, he cannot really be claimed as a product of CSA's development programme – but he is black, and genuinely talented.

SOUTH AFRICA v NEW ZEALAND IN 2015-16

Neil Manthorp

Twenty20 internationals (2): South Africa 1, New Zealand 1
One-day internationals (3): South Africa 2, New Zealand 1

In those areas of South Africa where rain falls largely in the summer months, cricket at junior and club level is not unusual during the winter. But series of two Twenty20 and three one-day internationals that coincided with the start of rugby's Currie Cup had fans scratching their heads. What was the point?

Money.

Since the takeover of the game's finances by the Big Three, Cricket South Africa have felt obliged to generate whatever revenue they can, whenever they can. Yet, beyond making some cash, this short tour – which had begun in Zimbabwe – was bereft of meaning.

Not even the marketeers' old favourite of "revenge" – these teams had fought an epic semi-final in the World Cup back in March – would wash, since New Zealand, victors that night in Auckland, were a substantially different team in South Africa. They were without the captain, Brendon McCullum, who was rested, along with Tim Southee. Also missing were Ross Taylor (after sustaining a groin injury in Zimbabwe), Trent Boult and Corey Anderson (both recovering from stress-related back problems), and Daniel Vettori (retired). The South Africans, too, were suffering some high-profile absentees. Faf du Plessis was nursing a damaged knee, while J-P. Duminy and Morne Morkel – after playing the first Twenty20 international – were with their pregnant wives.

In the event – and with some irony, given the main goal of the series – CSA failed to sell coverage to Sky NZ, who claimed the price was too high; CSA said all they had wanted was a "market-related rights fee", which was not forthcoming. Neutral observers might have pointed out that there was no market precedent for a series at this time of year. Supporters in New Zealand were eventually offered a free internet link to live streaming of the games. Both series were close: the Twenty20 games were shared, and South Africa took the decisive third one-dayer.

NEW ZEALAND TOURING PARTY

*K. S. Williamson, D. A. J. Bracewell, G. D. Elliott, M. J. Guptill, M. J. Henry, T. W. M. Latham, M. J. McClenaghan, N. L. McCullum, A. F. Milne, C. Munro, J. D. S. Neesham, L. Ronchi, I. S. Sodhi, B. M. Wheeler, G. H. Worker. *Coach:* M. J. Hesson.

Before the tour, which began in Zimbabwe, M. J. Santner withdrew with a broken thumb, and was replaced by Worker. L. R. P. L. Taylor injured his groin in Zimbabwe, and returned home; he was not replaced.

> **"** I only ever had one pair of pads. That did me, my whole career."
> Last Men In, page 68

SOUTH AFRICA v NEW ZEALAND

First Twenty20 International

At Durban, August 14, 2015. South Africa won by six wickets. Toss: South Africa.

At 68 without loss in the eighth over – and at 100 for one after 12 – New Zealand seemed destined for a substantial total. But some intelligent left-arm spin from Phangiso and a moment of sloppiness from Guptill shifted the game South Africa's way. Phangiso ripped one past a charging Williamson to give a straightforward stumping to van Wyk, whose eagle eyes later spotted Guptill coasting for what should have been a straightforward single and, embarrassingly, failing to run his bat in. When Phangiso trapped the left-handed Worker with a curving arm-ball, New Zealand had subsided to 125 for five, having lost four wickets in 19 deliveries. They never regained momentum. The game was there for South Africa's taking and, thanks to the meticulous Amla and the more ruthless de Villiers and Rossouw, they got home easily.

Man of the Match: A. M. Phangiso.

New Zealand		B	4/6
1 M. J. Guptill *run out*	42	37	5
2 *K. S. Williamson *st 1 b 8*.....	42	21	8
3 G. H. Worker *lbw b 8*.........	28	26	3/1
4 C. Munro *c 3 b 7*	0	1	0
5 G. D. Elliott *c 4 b 7*	5	4	1
6 †L. Ronchi *run out*...........	5	9	0
7 T. W. M. Latham *c 11 b 9*	12	10	1
8 N. L. McCullum *c 3 b 9*......	2	8	0
9 D. A. J. Bracewell *not out*	7	2	0/1
10 A. F. Milne *not out*..........	2	2	0
B 3, l-b 2, w 1	6		

6 overs: 56-0   (20 overs)   151-8

1/68 2/102 3/102 4/118 5/125 6/138 7/142 8/142

11 M. J. McClenaghan did not bat.

Abbott 4–0–27–0 (11); Rabada 4–0–29–2 (11); Morkel 4–0–37–0 (7); Wiese 4–0–24–2 (9); Phangiso 4–0–29–2 (9).

South Africa		B	4/6
1 †M. N. van Wyk *c 3 b 9*	19	21	2/1
2 H. M. Amla *c 7 b 10*	48	41	4/1
3 *A. B. de Villiers *c 8 b 3*.....	33	21	5
4 R. R. Rossouw *c 6 b 11*.......	38	20	4/2
5 D. A. Miller *not out*..........	2	3	0
6 F. Behardien *not out*	4	2	1
L-b 5, w 2, n-b 1	8		

6 overs: 40-1   (17.5 overs)   152-4

1/35 2/85 3/144 4/147

7 D. Wiese, 8 A. M. Phangiso, 9 K. Rabada, 10 K. J. Abbott and 11 M. Morkel did not bat.

Bracewell 3–0–17–1 (10); Milne 3.5–0–23–1 (12); McClenaghan 3–0–33–1 (6); Worker 2–0–19–1 (4); McCullum 4–0–34–0 (4); Elliott 1–0–12–0 (1); Williamson 1–0–9–0 (0).

Umpires: J. D. Cloete and S. George.   Third umpire: A. T. Holdstock.
Referee: R. S. Mahanama.

SOUTH AFRICA v NEW ZEALAND

Second Twenty20 International

At Centurion, August 16, 2015. New Zealand won by 32 runs. Toss: New Zealand.

New Zealand openers Guptill and Williamson again reached 50 at almost ten an over. This time, though, their companions used the foundation to build a match-winning score against bowlers unable to repeat the spirited comeback of two days earlier. Guptill cover-drove the first ball for four and twice lobbed Leie's leg-breaks back over the bowler's head for six; another disappeared over long-on off Abbott. Neesham struck the ball cleanly at the end, though not as explosively as Munro, who hit three fours and a six before falling to his seventh fifty-six. Chasing 178, South Africa never quite settled and, though they had 75 after ten overs, the top four were gone. Off-spinner McCullum and the rapid Milne had given little away with the new ball; left-armer McClenaghan and leg-spinner Sodhi even less in the middle overs.

Man of the Match: M. J. Guptill.   *Man of the Series: M. J. Guptill.*

New Zealand

		B	4/6
1 M. J. Guptill c 6 b 5	60	35	6/3
2 *K. S. Williamson c 10 b 9 . .	25	17	4/1
3 T. W. M. Latham c 1 b 11	3	8	0
4 G. D. Elliott lbw b 8	20	17	2
5 J. D. S. Neesham b 9	28	19	3/1
6 †L. Ronchi c 6 b 7	6	8	0
7 C. Munro c 3 b 9	18	7	3/1
8 N. L. McCullum *not out*.	1	2	0
9 A. F. Milne *not out*.	10	7	1
L-b 1, w 5	6		

6 overs: 53-1   (20 overs) 177-7

1/52 2/70 3/104 4/113 5/146 6/166 7/166

10 M. J. McClenaghan and 11 I. S. Sodhi did not bat.

Phangiso 4–0–40–1 (6); Abbott 4–0–44–0 (11); Rabada 4–0–30–3 (12); Wiese 4–0–26–1 (9); Leie 3–0–32–1 (4); Behardien 1–0–4–1 (2).

South Africa

		B	4/6
1 H. M. Amla c 7 b 9	14	13	2
2 †M. N. van Wyk c 6 b 10	3	5	0
3 *A. B. de Villiers c 5 b 8	15	9	2/1
4 R. R. Rossouw c 2 b 11	26	23	4
5 F. Behardien c 1 b 8	36	27	3/1
6 D. A. Miller c 7 b 10	29	20	2/1
7 D. Wiese c 8 b 11	2	4	0
8 A. M. Phangiso c 2 b 5	2	5	0
9 K. Rabada *not out*	5	6	0
10 K. J. Abbott *not out*	9	8	1
W 4	4		

6 overs: 40-2   (20 overs) 145-8

1/15 2/19 3/47 4/75 5/112 6/115 7/123 8/131

11 E. Leie did not bat.

McCullum 4–0–31–2 (6); Milne 4–0–27–1 (12); McClenaghan 4–0–28–2 (12); Neesham 3–0–22–1 (6); Sodhi 4–0–27–2 (7); Elliott 1–0–10–0 (0).

Umpires: J. D. Cloete and S. George.   Third umpire: A. T. Holdstock.
Referee: R. S. Mahanama.

SOUTH AFRICA v NEW ZEALAND

First One-Day International

At Centurion, August 19, 2015. South Africa won by 20 runs. Toss: New Zealand. One-day international debut: D. Wiese.

In just his 116th innings, Amla hit his 21st one-day international hundred, equalling the South African record set by Herschelle Gibbs (from 236). A second-wicket stand of 185 with Rossouw was more effective than attractive, with Amla's customary style neutered by a slow, awkward pitch on which Rossouw failed to score from 63 of his 112 balls. The total might have been higher had Milne not dismissed de Villiers and Amla in the 45th over – one caught at midwicket and the other yorked, but both undone by rare speed. Steyn, apparently unfazed by the South African bowling plans being pushed under the wrong hotel door by the team analyst – they were later published on Facebook – had chances dropped off the first and fourth deliveries of the innings, before Ronchi was caught at slip off the sixth. Latham made a careful 60 after his first-ball reprieve, but no one else hung around for long, and the game looked up when he departed at 158 for five. Neesham and Munro swung selectively in a stand of 71, and the tailenders kept going, but wickets fell too regularly.

Man of the Match: H. M. Amla.

South Africa

†M. N. van Wyk c McCullum b McClenaghan .	16
H. M. Amla b Milne	124
R. R. Rossouw b McClenaghan.	89
*A. B. de Villiers c Latham b Milne	9
D. A. Miller c Milne b Neesham.	14
F. Behardien run out	15
D. Wiese run out	14
V. D. Philander *not out*	0
B 4, l-b 4, w 15	23

1/46 (1) 2/231 (3)   (7 wkts, 50 overs) 304
3/252 (4) 4/258 (2)
5/286 (5) 6/304 (6) 7/304 (7)   10 overs: 47-1

K. Rabada, D. W. Steyn and Imran Tahir did not bat.

McCullum 5–0–29–0; Milne 10–0–51–2; McClenaghan 10–1–72–2; Neesham 7–0–47–1; Sodhi 10–1–55–0; Elliott 4–0–23–0; Munro 4–0–19–0.

New Zealand

T. W. M. Latham lbw b Philander	60	A. F. Milne not out	15

T. W. M. Latham lbw b Philander 60
†L. Ronchi c Amla b Steyn 1
*K. S. Williamson c sub (D. Elgar) 47
    b Imran Tahir
M. J. Guptill c Miller b Wiese 25
G. D. Elliott c Miller b Philander 4
J. D. S. Neesham c van Wyk b Wiese 41
C. Munro lbw b Imran Tahir 33
N. L. McCullum c Behardien b Rabada . . . 10

A. F. Milne not out 15
M. J. McClenaghan b Steyn 16
I. S. Sodhi run out 0
    B 5, l-b 15, w 10, n-b 2 32

1/3 (2) 2/107 (3)   (48.1 overs) 284
3/148 (4) 4/156 (5) 5/158 (1)
6/229 (6) 7/243 (7) 8/251 (8)
9/283 (10) 10/284 (11)   10 overs: 33-1

Steyn 9–0–50–2; Philander 10–1–51–2; Rabada 9.1–0–49–1; Imran Tahir 10–0–40–2; Wiese 7–0–63–2; Behardien 3–0–11–0.

Umpires: J. D. Cloete and I. J. Gould.   Third umpire: A. T. Holdstock.
Referee: R. S. Mahanama.

SOUTH AFRICA v NEW ZEALAND

Second One-Day International

At Potchefstroom, August 23, 2015. New Zealand won by eight wickets. Toss: South Africa. One-day international debut: G. H. Worker.

Starved of international cricket, the people of Potchefstroom turned up in droves – unlike their team, who didn't turn up at all. The New Zealanders were outstanding, the South Africans insipid and indecisive. The pitch, so slow that batsmen facing anything except a half-volley or full toss were spoilt for choice, wasn't great either. In the closing overs Guptill received some help from the debutant, George Worker, to ensure he reached a deserved century. He and Latham had put on 126, a New Zealand record for the first wicket against South Africa (surpassing 114 at the 1992 World Cup between Latham's father, Rod, and Mark Greatbatch). But, for all the runs from the top of the order, the win – as Guptill admitted – had been engineered by the bowlers. Milne was fast and accurate once again, and Bracewell swung the ball with skill and precision. However, it was the mixed-up, gentle medium-pace of Elliott that did most to stifle the home batting.

Man of the Match: M. J. Guptill.

South Africa

H. M. Amla c Elliott b Milne 8
†M. N. van Wyk b Milne 2
R. R. Rossouw c Williamson b Bracewell . 39
*A. B. de Villiers c Guptill b Elliott 31
D. A. Miller c Munro b Bracewell 5
F. Behardien c Williamson b Bracewell . . 70
D. Wiese lbw b Sodhi 8
V. D. Philander not out 30
A. M. Phangiso run out 1

D. W. Steyn run out. 2
Imran Tahir run out 4

    L-b 3, w 1 4

1/9 (1) 2/20 (2)   (49.3 overs) 204
3/68 (3) 4/76 (5) 5/107 (4)
6/134 (7) 7/188 (6) 8/192 (9)
9/195 (10) 10/204 (11)   10 overs: 48-2

Wheeler 9.3–1–39–0; Milne 10–0–39–2; Bracewell 10–0–31–3; Sodhi 10–0–59–1; Elliott 7–0–25–1; Worker 1–0–5–0; Munro 2–0–3–0.

New Zealand

M. J. Guptill not out 103
T. W. M. Latham c Rossouw b Imran Tahir 64
*K. S. Williamson b Phangiso 7
G. H. Worker not out 20
    L-b 3, w 10 13

1/126 (2) 2/140 (3) (2 wkts, 44.3 overs) 207
                      10 overs: 56-0

G. D. Elliott, C. Munro, †L. Ronchi, D. A. J. Bracewell, A. F. Milne, B. M. Wheeler and I. S. Sodhi did not bat.

Philander 6–0–21–0; Phangiso 10–1–37–1; Steyn 8–1–38–0; Wiese 4–0–23–0; Imran Tahir 10–1–42–1; Behardien 2–0–18–0; Rossouw 2.3–0–14–0; de Villiers 2–0–11–0.

Umpires: S. George and I. J. Gould. Third umpire: J. D. Cloete.
Referee: R. S. Mahanama.

SOUTH AFRICA v NEW ZEALAND

Third One-Day International

At Durban, August 26, 2015. South Africa won by 62 runs. Toss: South Africa.

South Africa based their decision to bat on local knowledge, since van Wyk was captain of Dolphins, the Durban franchise. He knew the well-grassed pitch would become more difficult under lights – and so it did. Van Wyk was less fluent in his innings of 58 from 100 balls than he would have wished, but an opening partnership of 89 set the stage for de Villiers, who unfurled a typical array of classic and unusual shots, one of which sped him to 8,000 one-day international runs in his 182nd innings, 18 fewer than India's Sourav Ganguly, the previous fastest. Miller, another Durban lad, ran hard to atone for his lack of timing, while Behardien finished an encouraging series at No. 6 with 40 from 28 balls. After Guptill's early departure, Latham and Williamson established a solid platform for New Zealand. But the balance shifted in the 24th over, when Imran Tahir sneaked a googly past Williamson, and again in the 28th, when Latham was unseated by an underarm throw from Miller, running in from deep square leg. Wiese collected three wickets with his seamers, but it was the miserliness of Tahir and the speedy Rabada which caused the run-chase to fail.

Man of the Match: A. B. de Villiers. *Man of the Series:* H. M. Amla.

South Africa

†M. N. van Wyk c Latham b Elliott	58		K. J. Abbott not out		3
H. M. Amla c and b Elliott	44				
R. R. Rossouw c Latham b Wheeler	6		B 4, l-b 3, w 13		20
*A. B. de Villiers b Bracewell	64				
D. A. Miller c Ronchi b Milne	36		1/89 (2) 2/96 (3)	(7 wkts, 50 overs)	283
F. Behardien c Williamson b Wheeler	40		3/134 (1) 4/220 (4)		
D. Wiese c Sodhi b Wheeler	12		5/232 (5) 6/258 (7) 7/283 (6)	10 overs: 49–0	

K. Rabada, D. W. Steyn and Imran Tahir did not bat.

Wheeler 10–0–71–3; Milne 10–1–44–1; Bracewell 10–1–54–1; Sodhi 8–0–55–0; Elliott 10–0–41–2; Munro 2–0–11–0.

New Zealand

M. J. Guptill c van Wyk b Steyn	10		B. M. Wheeler not out		13
T. W. M. Latham run out	54		I. S. Sodhi c Rossouw b Abbott		5
*K. S. Williamson b Imran Tahir	39				
G. H. Worker b Wiese	21		L-b 1, w 5		6
G. D. Elliott c Rabada b Wiese	20				
C. Munro b Wiese	35		1/18 (1) 2/102 (3)	(49.2 overs)	221
†L. Ronchi c Amla b Rabada	1		3/114 (2) 4/141 (4) 5/152 (5)		
D. A. J. Bracewell c Amla b Imran Tahir	13		6/156 (7) 7/187 (8) 8/201 (9)		
A. F. Milne c Miller b Rabada	0		9/201 (6) 10/221 (11)	10 overs: 40–1	

Steyn 10–0–41–1; Rabada 10–1–33–2; Wiese 9–0–58–3; Abbott 9.2–0–43–1; Imran Tahir 10–0–36–2; Behardien 1–0–9–0.

Umpires: J. D. Cloete and I. J. Gould. Third umpire: S. George.
Referee: R. S. Mahanama.

ENGLAND LIONS IN SOUTH AFRICA IN 2014-15

A-team Test matches (2): South Africa A 0, England Lions 0
A-team one-day internationals (5): South Africa A 1, England Lions 3

This tour played out simultaneously with England's World Cup preparations in Australia, and the senior side did not compare favourably. As the England batsmen were being carpeted in a one-day tri-series by Mitchell Starc and Mitchell Johnson – admittedly a tougher proposition, in much bigger stadiums – the young Lions were tearing into highly regarded South African seamers. Even before the World Cup campaign descended into debacle, critics were rounding on the selectors for their lack of faith in the kind of six-hitters needed to prosper under the current one-day regulations at the time. As if to ram home the point, A. B. de Villiers slammed 16 of them in 44 balls against West Indies at the Wanderers while the Lions were in the country.

With a sense of abandon that continued to elude England's elders, Jason Roy and James Vince helped clatter South Africa A for 376 in the second one-day match, at Kimberley. Lions head coach Mark Robinson said Roy's 141 from 110 balls "couldn't be matched", only for Ben Stokes to trump it with 151 not out from 86 balls two games later. Stokes conceded that a couple of his 15 sixes might have been caught on a bigger ground, but there was no stopping the bandwagon set in motion by his omission from the World Cup squad. "The thing that frustrates me is that England were batting him at No. 8," said Paul Collingwood, his captain at Durham. "What England did is like telling Cristiano Ronaldo to play at right-back."

For good measure, Stokes captured eight wickets at 14 in the one-day series – which the Lions won 3–1 – against a powerful line-up headed by Reeza Hendricks and Dean Elgar. Harry Gurney, briefly considered by England as a successor to Ryan Sidebottom, took six in three games, having already missed the cut for a World Cup in which left-arm quicks would thrive. Mark Wood, whose previous Lions tour, in Sri Lanka, had been curtailed by a side strain after one match, confirmed his hostility in the two four-day games, both of which were drawn.

The most intriguing selection was Jonathan Trott, cleared by ECB medical staff to take part in his first representative series since leaving the 2013-14 Ashes tour with a stress-related condition. The oldest player in the squad by three years, he captained the Lions in the red-ball matches, before departing for a family holiday in Florida. Trott's presence was interpreted as a three-way shoot-out between him, Adam Lyth and Sam Robson, the two openers here, for the chance to partner Alastair Cook in the Test series in the Caribbean in April. Trott seemed back to his vintage best when – despite a spell of short stuff – he settled in for close to 11 hours on the flattest of pitches at Paarl. The South Africans took note, and he succumbed to a trap set at leg slip in the next match at Bloemfontein.

Otherwise, the tour reflected Yorkshire's pre-eminence in the English game. Seven of the 21 players were drawn from the reigning county champions, not to mention four Yorkshiremen among the backroom staff. During the tour, Colin Graves announced his intention to stand as ECB chairman, and Geoffrey Boycott invited Lyth and Jonny Bairstow round for dinner at his house near Paarl. Boycott's oft-stated belief that Yorkshire could beat the current England crop came a step closer to reality when a Yorkshire VII triumphed over The Rest in a training-ground game of touch rugby; Castleford Tigers devotee Tim Bresnan scored the winning try.

Rather than the cosseted experience of most modern international tours, this trip provided an insight into southern Africa. No sooner had the Lions arrived for their first training session than a thunderstorm had them scurrying into the Wanderers indoor school. Paarl was uncomfortably hot; in the games played inland at altitude, the ball flew off the bat. Two of the fixtures were at township grounds in Soweto and Mamelodi, and the players used their downtime to visit wildlife sanctuaries and donate kit to young cricketers.

ENGLAND LIONS TOURING PARTY

*I. J. L. Trott (Warwickshire, FC), J. M. Bairstow (Yorkshire, FC/50), S. W. Billings (Kent, FC/50), T. T. Bresnan (Yorkshire, 50), J. A. Brooks (Yorkshire, FC/50), M. P. Dunn (Surrey, FC), H. F. Gurney (Nottinghamshire, 50), A. Z. Lees (Yorkshire, FC/50), A. Lyth (Yorkshire, FC/50), C. Overton (Somerset, FC), S. D. Parry (Lancashire, 50), S. R. Patel (Nottinghamshire, 50), L. E. Plunkett (Yorkshire, FC/50), W. B. Rankin (Warwickshire, FC/50), A. U. Rashid (Yorkshire, FC/50), A. E. N. Riley (Kent, FC), S. D. Robson (Middlesex, FC), J. J. Roy (Surrey, 50), B. A. Stokes (Durham, 50), J. M. Vince (Hampshire, FC/50), M. A. Wood (Durham, FC/50).

Vince captained in the one-day series. G. S. Ballance (Yorkshire) was originally selected, but then chosen for England's World Cup squad. Dunn flew home after the first four-day game with a groin strain. Wood was added to the one-day squad after Overton returned home for ankle surgery after the first-class games. Bresnan joined the squad for the third one-day match onwards.

Coach: M. A. Robinson. *Manager:* G. A. M. Jackson. *Batting coach:* G. P. Thorpe. *Fast bowling coaches:* C. E. W. Silverwood/O. D. Gibson. *Technical director of elite coaching:* A. Flower. *Physiotherapist:* B. T. Langley. *Strength and conditioning coach:* P. Atkinson. *Team doctor:* Harjinder Singh. *Analyst:* G. T. Lindsay. *Security manager:* T. Minish. *Media relations manager:* A. J. Wilson.

At Soweto (University of Johannesburg), January 5–7, 2015 (not first-class). **Drawn. England Lions 443** (112.3 overs) (A. Lyth 106, S. D. Robson 109, A. Z. Lees 85, J. M. Bairstow 62; Z. Pongolo 3-70) **and 176-5 dec** (44 overs) (I. J. L. Trott 79*, S. W. Billings 53); ‡**Gauteng Invitation XI 179** (49.3 overs) (M. A. Wood 4-29) **and 120-8** (42 overs). *Each team chose from 15 players. An England side returned to Soweto for the first time since the ground-breaking 1995-96 tour – when Nelson Mandela met the team – but this game took place in the slightly less evocative surroundings of the university campus ground. Adam Lyth and Sam Robson each retired out with hundreds, exploiting some conservative field settings as the day dragged on. Mark Wood's pace unsettled a young Gauteng Invitation side, ripping out the last three wickets in nine balls. The tourists' lead was topped up by a reassuring 79* from Jonathan Trott, and a first Lions fifty for Sam Billings. They were two wickets from victory, with half an hour remaining, when the match was abandoned because of an approaching electrical storm.*

SOUTH AFRICA A v ENGLAND LIONS

First A-Team Test

At Paarl, January 11–14, 2015. Drawn. Toss: South Africa A.

The Boland Park curator left some grass on top of a notorious featherbed in an attempt to conjure some kind of a contest, but it made no difference. The Lions ran headlong into a well-drilled set of batsmen midway through their domestic season: Gihahn Cloete and Stiaan van Zyl opened with 122, surviving a threatening spell from Wood, before Theunis de Bruyn cashed in with an unflustered maiden double-century. The Lions dipped to 67 for three on the second afternoon, but Trott clipped his first ball, from old friend and opposing captain Rory Kleinveldt, through his favoured midwicket, and knuckled down to organise a recovery, in conditions he knew well from his childhood in the Western Cape. He survived a drop on seven by wicketkeeper Rudi Second off Ryan McLaren, and a short barrage from Kleinveldt with a man set back on the hook, to bat for ten hours 47 minutes, sharing in four consecutive century partnerships. Brooks's joy at swishing a career-best unbeaten 53 was short-lived: he resorted to bowling off-cutters until, in unrelenting heat, the teams shook hands with a session remaining.

Close of play: first day, South Africa A 379-4 (de Bruyn 126, Second 25); second day, England Lions 169-3 (Trott 57, Vince 43); third day, England Lions 507-6 (Trott 176, Plunkett 31).

South Africa A

G. L. Cloete c Robson b Rankin	123	– lbw b Rankin	29
S. van Zyl c Lees b Plunkett	65	– c Bairstow b Rashid	39
A. G. Puttick c Lees b Plunkett	0	– not out	9
T. B. de Bruyn not out	202	– not out	6
K. Zondo st Bairstow b Lyth	21		
†R. S. Second lbw b Wood	27		
R. McLaren b Plunkett	36		
C. H. Morris b Plunkett	2		
*R. K. Kleinveldt b Wood	5		
D. L. Piedt not out	0		
B 4, l-b 2, w 5, n-b 12	23	W 7, n-b 2	9

1/122 (2) 2/132 (3) 　　(8 wkts dec, 130 overs) 504　　1/64 (1)　　(2 wkts, 32 overs) 92
3/282 (1) 4/318 (5) 5/382 (6)　　　　　　　　　　　2/77 (2)
6/472 (7) 7/480 (8) 8/499 (9)

B. E. Hendricks did not bat.

Brooks 23–1–94–0; Wood 30–3–99–2; Plunkett 26–4–91–4; Rankin 24–4–67–1; Rashid 19–0–109–0; Vince 4–1–11–0; Lyth 4–0–27–1. *Second innings*—Wood 7–1–22–0; Plunkett 9–0–35–0; Brooks 6–0–17–0; Rankin 5–2–7–1; Rashid 5–1–11–1.

England Lions

A. Lyth lbw b Morris	7	J. A. Brooks not out	53
S. D. Robson b Kleinveldt	41		
A. Z. Lees b Kleinveldt	9	B 4, l-b 3, w 2, n-b 15	24
*I. J. L. Trott not out	211		
J. M. Vince c Puttick b Kleinveldt	78	1/13 (1)　　(8 wkts dec, 160 overs) 624
†J. M. Bairstow b Kleinveldt	63	2/52 (3) 3/67 (2)
A. U. Rashid b McLaren	78	4/232 (5) 5/335 (6)
L. E. Plunkett c Cloete b Morris	55	6/446 (7) 7/552 (8)
M. A. Wood b Piedt	5	8/561 (9)

W. B. Rankin did not bat.

Hendricks 29–4–110–0; Morris 27–4–98–2; Kleinveldt 30–4–127–4; McLaren 19.5–6–60–1; Piedt 46–1–187–1; van Zyl 8–0–35–0; Zondo 0.1–0–0–0.

Umpires: B. P. Jele and B. M. White.　　Referee: S. B. Lambson.

SOUTH AFRICA A v ENGLAND LIONS

Second A-Team Test

At Bloemfontein, January 18–21, 2015. Drawn. Toss: England Lions.

The Lions clung on for a draw, thanks in part to two bad misses by the South Africans on the third day. The tourists were yet to erase a first-innings deficit of 161 when Vince was dropped behind on four by Second; then van Zyl made a hash of an easy chance squirted to gully by Trott off a Kleinveldt slower ball. Not long after, a spectacular thunderstorm rolled in, forcing the players off for two hours. Just one more wicket fell by the close, and Wood mucked in on the last day alongside Vince, who extended his first Lions century past 150 before play was ended around tea. South Africa A had made all the early running: Trott flicked his fourth delivery, an inducker from Chris Morris, off his pads into the hands of leg slip, and it took gritty innings from four Yorkshiremen to scrape the Lions to 260. Cloete was bowled shouldering arms to Wood first ball next morning, and the South Africans were themselves 29 for three. But de Bruyn – dropped on 31 by Trott at slip from off-spinner Riley – put on 210 with the 5ft 3in Temba Bavuma, who said he was unable to see the ball when Rankin's hand strayed above the sightscreen. Rankin became the first bowler to dismiss de Bruyn in the series, but not until he had faced 470 balls, or gone past 1,000 career first-class runs in just his 20th innings.

Close of play: first day, South Africa A 29-1 (Hendricks 20, Cloete 6); second day, South Africa A 389-7 (Second 21, Kleinveldt 1); third day, England Lions 212-4 (Vince 61, Bairstow 2).

England Lions

A. Lyth c Second b van Zyl	65	– c Hendricks b Rabada	37
S. D. Robson c Second b Kleinveldt	5	– b Kleinveldt	0
A. Z. Lees c Ontong b Kleinveldt	5	– b Rabada	39
*I. J. L. Trott c Hendricks b Morris	0	– lbw b Piedt	53
J. M. Vince c Ontong b Piedt	31	– not out	152
†J. M. Bairstow b Kleinveldt	47	– c Second b Kleinveldt	7
A. U. Rashid c Second b Morris	68	– c Hendricks b Rabada	32
L. E. Plunkett lbw b Piedt	24	– b Morris	13
M. A. Wood c Hendricks b Rabada	5	– not out	44
A. E. N. Riley c and b Piedt	0		
W. B. Rankin not out	0		
B 3, l-b 5, w 1, n-b 1	10	B 13, l-b 2, w 2, n-b 8	25

1/7 (2) 2/15 (3) 3/16 (4) (76.5 overs) 260
4/82 (5) 5/160 (1) 6/164 (6)
7/211 (8) 8/223 (9) 9/226 (10) 10/260 (7)

1/1 (2) (7 wkts dec, 116 overs) 402
2/78 (1) 3/81 (3)
4/196 (4) 5/227 (6) 6/308 (7) 7/330 (8)

Kleinveldt 14–2–53–3; Morris 15.5–3–51–2; Rabada 17–6–36–1; Piedt 25–4–100–3; van Zyl 5–2–12–1. *Second innings*—Kleinveldt 28–6–82–2; Morris 23–5–73–1; Piedt 29–3–97–1; Rabada 25–5–94–3; van Zyl 8–1–28–0; Ontong 2–0–8–0; Bavuma 1–0–5–0.

South Africa A

R. R. Hendricks c Lyth b Rankin	20	K. Rabada c Bairstow b Plunkett	5
S. van Zyl b Wood	1	D. L. Piedt b Plunkett	0
G. L. Cloete b Wood	6		
T. B. de Bruyn c Bairstow b Rankin	161	B 4, l-b 4, w 2, n-b 6	16
T. Bavuma c Rashid b Vince	102		
*J. L. Ontong c Lees b Plunkett	54	1/1 (2) 2/29 (3) (110 overs) 421
†R. S. Second not out	27	3/29 (1) 4/239 (5)
C. H. Morris c Bairstow b Rankin	7	5/338 (4) 6/371 (6) 7/381 (8)
R. K. Kleinveldt c Bairstow b Rankin	22	8/410 (9) 9/421 (10) 10/421 (11)

Wood 27–7–92–2; Plunkett 22–4–75–3; Riley 13–1–80–0; Rankin 27–10–78–4; Vince 9–1–38–1; Rashid 7–0–40–0; Trott 5–2–10–0.

Umpires: A. Paleker and B. M. White. Referee: S. B. Lambson.

First A-team one-day international   At Bloemfontein, January 25, 2015. **England Lions won by four wickets. South Africa A** 172 (39.3 overs) (B. A. Stokes 4-22); ‡**England Lions 173-6** (34.3 overs). *England Lions warmed up for the one-day series with a trip to the Bagamoya Wildlife Estate, where some of the players dared to enter an enclosure of (real) lions. Their five-man seam attack then dismantled South Africa A on a helpful pitch. It was a good day for two bowlers culled from the World Cup reckoning: Harry Gurney (3-26) and Ben Stokes each struck in their first over and shared seven wickets. The Lions slipped to 134-6 in the 29th over, but Samit Patel (17*) and Liam Plunkett (22*) steered them to a modest target.*

Second A-team one-day international   At Kimberley, January 28, 2015 (day/night). **England Lions won by 70 runs. England Lions 376-6** (50 overs) (J. J. Roy 141, J. M. Vince 99; K. Rabada 4-67); ‡**South Africa A 306** (44.1 overs) (R. R. Hendricks 141, D. Elgar 66). *Jason Roy took full toll of a pristine pitch with 141 from 110 deliveries. James Vince, another strokemaker yet to be tried in one-day internationals, put on 198 with him for the second wicket before falling lbw for 99. The South Africans picked up eight wickets in the last 10.4 overs, and carried the momentum into their innings, with Reeza Hendricks and Dean Elgar crashing 142 in the opening 18, as the dew under lights helped the ball come on more quickly. Hendricks matched Roy's score, from four fewer balls. But Stephen Parry (2-44), fresh from the Big Bash, slowed the chase with the wickets of Elgar and Dane Vilas.*

Third A-team one-day international   At Potchefstroom, January 31, 2015. **No result. South Africa A 1-0** (1.2 overs) v ‡**England Lions.** *Tim Bresnan's return to England colours for the first time since the 2014 World Twenty20 lasted just eight balls before rain swept in. In an attempt to keep the series alive, the home side had drafted in Quinton de Kock, Wayne Parnell and Aaron Phangiso from South Africa's series victory over West Indies.*

Fourth A-Team one-day international   At Pretoria (Mamelodi Oval), February 2, 2015. **England Lions won by 89 runs. England Lions 378-6** (50 overs) (J. J. Roy 67, B. A. Stokes 151*, S. W. Billings 56); ‡**South Africa A 289** (42.5 overs) (D. Elgar 79, C. H. Morris 58*). *The Lions team bus snaked through the Mamelodi township to this small ground, where locals danced and sang, even as the tourists piled on the runs. After Roy's third helpful score of the series, Stokes put on a phenomenal display with 151 from 86 balls, thumping nine sixes off the last 14 legitimate deliveries he faced. He struck 15 in all, several of which sailed into the township; one had to be fished out of the stream behind the ground. Stokes and Sam Billings put on 132 in just 64 deliveries. The series was as good as sewn up, though Chris Morris exacted a little revenge with 58* from 33.*

MOST SIXES IN A LIST A INNINGS

17	G. Snyman (196)	Namibia v UAE at Windhoek	2007-08
16	R. G. Sharma (209)	India v Australia at Bangalore	2013-14
16	**A. B. de Villiers (149)**	**South Africa v West Indies at Johannesburg**	**2014-15**
16	**C. H. Gayle (215)**	**West Indies v Zimbabwe at Canberra**	**2014-15**
15	S. R. Watson (185*)	Australia v Bangladesh at Mirpur	2010-11
15	R. N. ten Doeschate (180)	Essex v Scotland at Chelmsford	2013
15	**B. A. Stokes (151*)**	**England Lions v South Africa A at Pretoria**	**2014-15**
14	C. J. Anderson (131*)	New Zealand v West Indies at Queenstown	2013-14
14	**J. M. How (177)**	**Central Districts v Canterbury at New Plymouth**. . . .	**2014-15**

Fifth A-Team one-day international   At Benoni, February 5, 2015 (day/night). **South Africa A won by 78 runs. South Africa A 287-6** (50 overs) (R. R. Hendricks 107, D. Elgar 66); ‡**England Lions 209** (42.4 overs) (J. M. Bairstow 64, S. R. Patel 55; K. Rabada 4-51). *The Lions surrendered their unbeaten tour record, following another big opening stand between Hendricks and Elgar, who put on 149 in 28.2 overs. Jack Brooks (3-55) stemmed the flow with three quick wickets; Stokes was not used. Initially, the Willowmoore Park floodlights, among the oldest in world cricket, were not bright enough for the Lions to begin their reply, and play was held up for 35 minutes while an electrician got two of them up to full power. Openers Billings and Roy fell in the first four overs, and the Lions never quite recovered. Kagiso Rabada, 19, took his second four-wicket haul of the series.*

DOMESTIC CRICKET IN SOUTH AFRICA IN 2014-15

Colin Bryden

The **Highveld Lions** climbed from last in all competitions the previous season to claim their first four-day title since the franchise teams were introduced in 2004. With virtually the same playing staff who had won only four matches out of 34 across all formats (including the Champions League in India) in 2013-14, they won seven of their ten Sunfoil Series fixtures and finished almost 40 points ahead of the field.

Of all the franchises, the Lions had least trouble meeting Cricket South Africa's requirement that all teams should include at least three black Africans in 2015-16. Batsman Temba Bavuma, pace bowler Kagiso Rabada, leg-spinner Eddie Leie and wicketkeeper Thami Tsolekile were regulars in the first-class side, while left-armer Lonwabo Tsotsobe was a key figure in limited-overs games.

The 19-year-old Rabada, a star when South Africa won the Under-19 World Cup in 2014, generated surprising pace from a lissom, seemingly effortless action, and produced the bowling performance of the season: nine for 33 against the Dolphins in Johannesburg, to complete a match haul of 14 for 105, a record for the franchise era. A seam attack of Rabada and the bustling Hardus Viljoen, plus Chris Morris and Dwaine Pretorius, took 130 wickets, all averaging under 22, while Leie made useful contributions when spin was needed. Stephen Cook showed flair as a captain, always aiming for outright wins, and led the tournament's run-scorers with 889 at 63, converting five of his six fifties into centuries. Neil McKenzie, aged 39, made 690 runs at 69 in his final first-class season, signing off with an unbeaten 203 against the Warriors. Bavuma also averaged 69, and earned a Test debut against West Indies.

The **Cape Cobras** put up a poor defence of the first-class title they had won in four of the previous five seasons; only a decisive victory on the final day hauled them as high as fourth. National calls were a factor, while injuries disrupted the bowling. Even so, they had the competition's leading wicket-taker, fast bowler Dane Paterson, who collected 42 at 22. The Cobras did top both limited-overs tables for the second year running, winning eight matches in the Ram Slam T20 Challenge league, before beating the **Knights** in the final. West Indian imports played crucial roles for both finalists: Kieron Pollard dominated the tournament with his big hitting, canny medium-pace and excellent fielding for the Cobras, while Andre Russell was almost as effective for the Knights, who had a disappointing season in the longer formats.

The Cobras also looked well placed to win the final of the Momentum One-Day Cup when Richard Levi and Andrew Puttick put on 180 for the first wicket, though they failed to build on that platform and finished on 285 for eight. By contrast, the **Titans** recovered from a poor start – losing their first four for 60 – as Albie Morkel and Dean Elgar hit centuries to ensure the title. The Titans were runners-up in the Sunfoil Series, but bottom of the Twenty20 league, with just two wins.

The **Dolphins**, who were T20 champions in 2013-14, failed to reach the knockout, but did better in the one-day competition, where captain Morné van Wyk and Cameron Delport pummelled the Knights for an unbeaten 367 at Bloemfontein – a world-record opening partnership in one-day cricket. They finished second, but were well beaten by the Titans in the play-off. The Dolphins were third in the four-day competition, where van Wyk topped the batting averages with 714 at 79, and young fast bowlers Matt Pillans and Daryn Dupavillon made significant progress, taking 55 wickets between them.

The **Warriors** struggled in all competitions, despite some excellent batting by Colin Ingram, their captain; they finished bottom of the four-day tournament and failed to reach the knockout in either limited-overs format.

Gauteng and **Northerns** shared the three-day title for the provincial teams; Gauteng also won the Twenty20 league, and **Border** the 50-over trophy.

FIRST-CLASS AVERAGES, 2014-15

BATTING (650 runs)

	M	I	NO	R	HS	100	Avge	Ct/St
G. L. van Buuren (*Northerns/Titans*) .	9	13	4	780	235	3	86.66	3
M. N. van Wyk (*Dolphins*).	8	13	4	714	122	2	79.33	29/1
N. D. McKenzie (*Lions*).	8	11	1	690	203*	3	69.00	17
S. C. Cook (*Lions/Gauteng*).	11	19	3	1,072	156	6	67.00	5
†M. N. Erlank (*Free State/Knights*) . . .	11	14	3	732	163*	2	66.54	10
H. Klaasen (*Northerns*).	11	14	2	783	201	1	65.25	31/1
†D. Elgar (*Titans/South Africa*)	9	15	3	775	208*	3	64.58	5
T. Bavuma (*Lions/South Africa/SA A*)	10	14	3	682	153	3	62.00	5
N. J. van den Bergh (*North West*)	10	17	6	661	141*	2	60.09	25/1
T. B. de Bruyn (*Titans/S Africa A*). . . .	11	19	2	984	202*	2	57.88	6
A. R. Swanepoel (*Griqualand West*) . . .	9	17	3	795	124	2	56.78	6
†S. van Zyl (*WP/SA/SA A/C Cobras*). .	11	16	2	775	107	3	55.35	5
†P. Botha (*Free State/Knights*)	11	15	2	719	103	2	55.30	11
R. E. van der Merwe (*Titans*)	10	16	2	774	205*	3	55.28	9
†C. A. Ingram (*Warriors*)	10	19	3	852	131*	3	53.25	14
B. J. Pelser (*Lions/North West*)	11	20	3	897	176	1	52.76	11
P. J. van Biljon (*Knights/Free State*) . .	10	18	2	787	175	3	49.18	10
†O. A. Ramela (*Cape Cobras*)	10	16	1	724	202*	2	48.26	8
†M. C. Kleinveldt (*W Prov/C Cobras*) . .	11	17	1	766	101	1	47.87	9
C. N. Ackermann (*Warriors/E Prov*). .	9	18	2	731	107*	1	45.68	7
P. J. Malan (*W Province/Cape Cobras*)	11	18	1	746	182	2	43.88	12
†D. A. Hendricks (*Lions/Gauteng*)	15	24	3	900	105	1	42.85	11
†D. P. Conway (*Lions/Gauteng*)	13	21	2	763	102	2	40.15	16
A. J. N. Price (*Eastern Province*)	10	18	1	664	167	3	39.05	12
R. S. Second (*Knights/South Africa A*)	11	19	1	694	113	1	38.55	29/2
†I. Khan (*KZN Inland/Dolphins*)	16	30	1	1,026	127	3	35.37	6
†D. J. van Wyk (*KZN/Dolphins*)	18	31	0	1,081	171	2	34.87	16
†G. L. Cloete (*Knights/Griq W/SA A*). .	16	29	0	905	135	2	31.20	19/1

BOWLING (35 wickets)

	Style	O	M	R	W	BB	5I	Avge
Z. Pongolo (*Gauteng*)	RM	227.1	55	701	43	5-50	2	16.30
G. C. Viljoen (*Lions*).	RF	239.3	55	797	39	7-32	2	20.43
G. R. Rabie (*South Western Districts*)	RFM	315	103	853	41	5-41	1	20.80
D. Paterson (*W Province/Cape Cobras*) . .	RFM	317.1	73	971	45	5-60	2	21.57
K. Rabada (*Lions/South Africa A*).	RF	318	77	954	43	9-33	2	22.18
D. R. Deeb (*Gauteng/Lions*)	SLA	416.1	88	1,096	48	6-57	1	22.83
T. Muller (*W Province/Cape Cobras*). . . .	RFM	264	65	821	35	5-44	1	23.45
S. H. Jamison (*Gauteng/Lions*)	RFM	297.5	75	945	40	4-44	0	23.62
C. H. Morris (*Lions/South Africa A*)	RFM	278.5	71	877	37	4-35	0	23.70
R. R. Richards (*Titans/Northerns*)	LFM	346.5	73	1,102	46	5-31	2	23.95
D. Klein (*North West*)	LFM	247	32	985	41	8-72	1	24.02
D. Olivier (*Free State/Knights*).	RF	320.5	88	898	37	5-61	2	24.27
M. W. Pillans (*KZN Inland/Dolphins*) . . .	RF	401.5	70	1,289	53	6-67	1	24.32
D. M. Dupavillon (*KZN/Dolphins*)	RF	357.2	65	1,205	49	6-62	2	24.59
A. C. R. Birch (*Warriors*)	RFM	316	87	914	37	5-43	1	24.70
T. Bokako (*Eastern Province*).	RF	241	47	903	36	5-14	2	25.08
K. A. Maharaj (*KwaZulu-Natal/Dolphins*)	SLA	384.4	75	1,152	44	6-58	2	26.18
C. A. Dry (*Knights/Free State*)	RFM	322.4	82	941	35	5-44	1	26.88
G. F. Linde (*W Province/Cape Cobras*) . . .	SLC	373.3	78	1,213	37	6-81	3	32.78
S. von Berg (*Titans/Northerns*).	LBG	380.5	62	1,274	38	6-117	2	33.52
S. R. Harmer (*Warriors/South Africa*) . . .	OB	414.2	82	1,282	35	4-82	0	36.62

Averages include CSA Provincial Three-Day Challenge matches played in Namibia.

SUNFOIL SERIES, 2014-15

					Bonus points		
	Played	Won	Lost	Drawn	Batting	Bowling	Points
Lions	10	7	1	2	44.64	37	151.64
Titans	10	4	4	2	40.76	31	111.76
Dolphins	10	4	4	2	37.76	30	107.76
Cape Cobras	10	2	4	4	39.88	29	87.88†
Knights	10	3	4	3	28.80	27	85.80
Warriors	10	2	5	3	23.48	28	71.48

†   *1pt deducted for slow over-rate.*

Outright win = 10pts. Bonus points awarded for the first 100 overs of each team's first innings. One batting point was awarded for the first 150 runs and 0.02 of a point for every subsequent run. One bowling point was awarded for the third wicket taken and for every subsequent two.

At Bloemfontein, September 25–27, 2014. **Knights won by 128 runs.** ‡**Knights 140 and 327** (R. S. Second 113); **Warriors 137** (C. A. Dry 5-44) **and 202.** *Knights 14pts, Warriors 4pts. Knights crashed to 32-8 in the first innings before Nos 9 and 10 Corné Dry and Quinton Friend scored 51 apiece; they went on to take a first-innings lead early on the second day. No team had won a first-class match in South Africa after losing their first eight wickets so cheaply.*

At Johannesburg, September 25–28, 2014. **Lions won by 190 runs.** ‡**Lions 401 and 155-5 dec; Titans 197 and 169** (G. C. Viljoen 7-32). *Lions 18.18pts, Titans 3.94pts. Hardus Viljoen bowled Lions to their first victory with 7-32, including all six wickets to fall on the final day.*

At Potchefstroom, October 2–5, 2014. **Knights won by 143 runs. Knights 267 and 381** (G. L. Cloete 135; G. C. Viljoen 5-77); ‡**Lions 368** (T. L. Tsolekile 113; D. du Preez 5-54) **and 137.** *Knights 16.34pts, Lions 7.98pts. Knights inflicted Lions' only first-class defeat of the season, despite trailing by 101 on first innings.*

At Benoni, October 2–5, 2014. **Titans won by 170 runs.** ‡**Titans 539-6 dec** (R. E. van der Merwe 205*) **and 165-5 dec; Warriors 291** (C. A. Ingram 111) **and 243** (R. R. Richards 5-31). *Titans 18.76pts, Warriors 5.82pts. In his ninth season, Roelof van der Merwe converted a maiden hundred to 205*, setting up a win completed by a hat-trick from left-arm seamer Rowan Richards.*

At Cape Town, December 18–21, 2014. **Lions won by 213 runs.** ‡**Lions 413** (N. D. McKenzie 125) **and 223-9 dec** (G. F. Linde 5-84); **Cape Cobras 306 and 117.** *Lions 18.3pts, Cape Cobras 6.12pts. Dominic Hendricks (99) and Neil McKenzie added 210 for Lions' third wicket.*

At Pietermaritzburg, December 18–21, 2014. **Drawn.** ‡**Warriors 353** (M. L. Price 113) **and 277-9 dec; Dolphins 370** (R. McLaren 121*) **and 145-5.** *Dolphins 7.4pts, Warriors 7.92pts. Leg-spinner Imran Tahir was officially suspended for Warriors' next game, on January 8–11, after confronting the umpires, who had removed him from the attack for running on the pitch. The suspension did not apply to international cricket, however, and he played two Twenty20s for South Africa v West Indies during that match.*

At Bloemfontein, December 18–21, 2014. **Titans won by 152 runs. Titans 366** (H. G. Kuhn 132) **and 367-7 dec** (R. E. van der Merwe 121); ‡**Knights 185** (R. R. Richards 5-38) **and 396** (P. J. van Biljon 113; M. de Lange 6-108). *Titans 19.32pts, Knights 5.7pts.*

At Paarl, December 27–30, 2014. **Drawn.** ‡**Knights 570-5 dec** (R. R. Hendricks 157, P. J. van Biljon 175, A. J. Pienaar 136*); **Cape Cobras 514** (M. Y. Vallie 117). *Cape Cobras 4.54pts, Knights 6.48pts. Pite van Biljon and Obus Pienaar added 240 for Knights' fifth wicket.*

At Durban, December 27–30, 2014. **Dolphins won by an innings and 54 runs. Dolphins 508-8 dec** (R. McLaren 126*); ‡**Titans 208 and 246** (K. J. Abbott 5-49). *Dolphins 19.68pts, Titans 4.16pts.*

At Potchefstroom, January 8–11, 2015. **Lions won by an innings and 35 runs. Cape Cobras 300 and 140;** ‡**Lions 475** (S. C. Cook 147*). *Lions 17.94pts, Cape Cobras 5pts. Stephen Cook retired not out on the third morning, after the birth of his daughter, and a full substitute replaced him.*

At East London, January 8–11, 2015. **Warriors won by 109 runs. Warriors 458-6 dec** (C. A. Ingram 131*) **and 167-2 dec;** ‡**Dolphins 200 and 316** (I. Khan 103). *Warriors 18.18pts, Dolphins 4pts.*

At Kimberley, January 15–18, 2015. **Dolphins won by 242 runs. ‡Dolphins 452** (I. Khan 127, C. Chetty 101*; P. Botha 7-89) **and 171-3 dec; Knights 255 and 126** (D. M. Dupavillon 5-38). *Dolphins 17.06pts, Knights 4.1pts.*

At Benoni, January 15–18, 2015. **Drawn. ‡Lions 485-7 dec** (S. C. Cook 122); **Titans 550-5 dec** (H. G. Kuhn 244*, M. Q. Adams 101). *Titans 6.82pts, Lions 6.44pts. Heino Kuhn's third and biggest double-hundred was the highest score of the season; he batted 11 hours and 53 minutes.*

At Port Elizabeth, January 15–18, 2015. **Warriors won by 16 runs. Warriors 203 and 317; ‡Cape Cobras 199 and 305.** *Warriors 16.06pts, Cape Cobras 5.98pts.*

At Kimberley, February 19–22, 2015. **Drawn. ‡Cape Cobras 294** (A. G. Puttick 100) **and 299-7 dec** (A. G. Puttick 101*); **Knights 304 and 263-9** (T. Muller 5-44). *Knights 8.08pts, Cape Cobras 7.42pts.*

At Johannesburg, February 19–22, 2015. **Lions won by ten wickets. ‡Dolphins 302** (C. Chetty 106; K. Rabada 5-72) **and 134** (K. Rabada 9-33); **Lions 421** (S. C. Cook 122) **and 19-0.** *Lions 20.28pts, Dolphins 6.96pts. Aged only 19, Kagiso Rabada improved his career-best figures twice: his 9-33 was the best innings return of the season, and 14-105 the best match figures in the franchise system's 11 years. In between, Cook scored his third century in successive innings.*

At Port Elizabeth, February 19–21, 2015. **Titans won by ten wickets. ‡Titans 448** (R. E. van der Merwe 100) **and 4-0; Warriors 148** (N. E. Mbhalati 6-38) **and 300** (C. A. Ingram 115*). *Titans 19.06pts, Warriors 2pts. Ethy Mbhalati's career-best 6-38 forced Warriors to follow on 300 behind; they slumped once more, to 84-6, but Colin Ingram and Basheer Walters (55) added 102 for the last wicket and just managed to make Titans bat again. Titans wicketkeeper Mangaliso Mosehle took nine catches in the match.*

At Paarl, February 26–March 1, 2015. **Cape Cobras won by 170 runs. ‡Cape Cobras 308 and 341-7 dec** (D. J. Vilas 100*); **Titans 175** (M. Shezi 6-51) **and 304** (D. Paterson 5-63). *Cape Cobras 18.16pts, Titans 5.5pts.*

At Durban, February 26–March 1, 2015. **Drawn. ‡Dolphins 455-5 dec** (D. J. van Wyk 171, M. N. van Wyk 103*); **Knights 237** (M. W. Pillans 6-67) **and 234-9.** *Dolphins 7.04pts, Knights 3.74pts. Divan and Morné van Wyk provided the second instance of brothers scoring centuries in the same first-class innings in South Africa, after Gary and Peter Kirsten for Western Province v Eastern Province in the Currie Cup final at Port Elizabeth in 1989-90.*

At East London, February 26–March 1, 2015. **Drawn. Warriors 287 and 272** (G. C. Viljoen 5-70); **‡Lions 462-8 dec** (S. C. Cook 152, T. Bavuma 109*) **and 81-4.** *Warriors 4.74pts, Lions 7.66pts. Cook scored his fourth hundred in five innings, and put on 192 for Lions' first wicket with Rassie van der Dussen (74). Chasing 98, his team needed 17 off 14 overs when bad light ended the match.*

At Cape Town, March 5–7, 2015. **Dolphins won by eight wickets. ‡Cape Cobras 156** (K. A. Maharaj 6-58) **and 253** (S. van Zyl 107); **Dolphins 270** (D. Paterson 5-60) **and 142-2.** *Dolphins 17.4pts, Cape Cobras 5.12pts.*

At Cape Town, March 12–15, 2015. **Drawn. ‡Warriors 288 and 256-3; Cape Cobras 545** (O. A. Ramela 129). *Cape Cobras 9pts, Warriors 4.76pts. Darryl Brown (63) and Simon Harmer (94) rescued Warriors from 111-6 on the first day by adding 161 for the seventh wicket.*

At Bloemfontein, March 12–15, 2015. **Lions won by ten wickets. ‡Knights 248 and 289; Lions 441** (N. D. McKenzie 108; W. L. Coetsee 5-78) **and 99-0.** *Lions 18.16pts, Knights 3.96pts. Lions' second ten-wicket win in a month left them 16 points clear with two rounds to go.*

At Centurion, March 12–15, 2015. **Dolphins won by three wickets. ‡Titans 267 and 261** (D. Elgar 122); **Dolphins 352 and 178-7.** *Dolphins 18.72pts, Titans 7.34pts. Dolphins' Divan van Wyk passed 1,000 first-class runs in the season in a first-innings 87, his tenth score of 50-plus.*

At Durban, March 19–22, 2015. **Lions won by 178 runs. Lions 395** (T. Bavuma 153) **and 355-6 dec** (S. C. Cook 143); **‡Dolphins 280** (D. Pretorius 5-64) **and 292.** *Lions 18.48pts, Dolphins 5.6pts. Lions' sixth win secured the title. Cook scored his fifth century of the tournament and passed 1,000 first-class runs for the season. Earlier, Dolphins' Imraan Khan had also reached 1,000, and his team-mate, pace bowler Mathew Pillans, taken his 50th first-class wicket of the summer.*

At Benoni, March 19–22, 2015. **Drawn. Cape Cobras 484** (O. A. Ramela 202*; R. R. Richards 5-114); **‡Titans 421-3** (D. Elgar 208*). *Titans 6.8pts, Cape Cobras 5.92pts. Four of the five double-centuries in this tournament were scored at Willowmore Park: this rain-shortened match produced* *a maiden double for Omphile Ramela, who batted for ten hours three minutes, while Dean Elgar completed his third before retiring hurt on the final day. Titans keeper Mosehle made five catches in an innings for the third time in this tournament; he had also caught four and stumped one in an innings playing for Easterns in November.*

At East London, March 19–22, 2015. **Knights won by 93 runs.** ‡**Knights 223 and 253-7 dec** (P. J. van Biljon 102*; A. C. R. Birch 5-43); **Warriors 145 and 238.** *Knights 16.46pts, Warriors 4pts. Dillon du Preez had figures of 16.3–11–13–3 in Warriors' first innings.*

At Pietermaritzburg, March 26–29, 2015. **Cape Cobras won by an innings and 117 runs. Cape Cobras 597** (J. L. Ontong 166, J. M. Kemp 143; D. Smit 5-75); ‡**Dolphins 245** (K. Zondo 120) **and 235** (M. N. van Wyk 122). *Cape Cobras 21.62pts, Dolphins 3.9pts. Cobras jumped from bottom to fourth. They passed 500 for the third time since December, advancing to the highest total of this tournament and a record for their franchise. In reply, Dolphins collapsed to 40-4, then 8-4 when they followed on, with left-armer Mpilo Njoloza completing a hat-trick that straddled both innings.*

At Johannesburg, March 26–29, 2015. **Lions won by an innings and 51 runs. Warriors 200 and 213** (G. C. Viljoen 5-59); ‡**Lions 464-9 dec** (N. D. McKenzie 203*). *Lions 18.22pts, Warriors 4pts. Lions completed their seventh win, and third in succession. Neil McKenzie announced his retirement from first-class cricket after scoring the third double-hundred of his career, which was also his 53rd century. He was the tenth man to reach 200 in his final first-class innings; the only other South African was Jack Siedle, for Natal against Western Province in 1936-37.*

At Centurion, March 26–29, 2015. **Titans won by eight wickets.** ‡**Titans 452-9 dec** (H. Davids 122, D. Wiese 107) **and 24-2; Knights 297** (D. Wiese 6-58) **and 178.** *Titans 20.06pts, Knights 6.94pts. David Wiese's century and eight wickets helped Titans to their fourth win; they leapfrogged Dolphins to finish as runners-up.*

CHAMPIONS

Currie Cup		
1889-90	Transvaal
1890-91	Kimberley
1892-93	Western Province
1893-94	Western Province
1894-95	Transvaal
1896-97	Western Province
1897-98	Western Province
1902-03	Transvaal
1903-04	Transvaal
1904-05	Transvaal
1906-07	Transvaal
1908-09	Western Province
1910-11	Natal
1912-13	Natal
1920-21	Western Province
1921-22	{ Transvaal / Natal / Western Province
1923-24	Transvaal
1925-26	Transvaal
1926-27	Transvaal
1929-30	Transvaal
1931-32	Western Province
1933-34	Natal
1934-35	Transvaal
1936-37	Natal
1937-38	{ Natal / Transvaal
1946-47	Natal
1947-48	Natal
1950-51	Transvaal
1951-52	Natal

1952-53	Western Province
1954-55	Natal
1955-56	Western Province
1958-59	Transvaal
1959-60	Natal
1960-61	Natal
1962-63	Natal
1963-64	Natal
1965-66	{ Natal / Transvaal
1966-67	Natal
1967-68	Natal
1968-69	Transvaal
1969-70	{ Transvaal / Western Province
1970-71	Transvaal
1971-72	Transvaal
1972-73	Transvaal
1973-74	Natal
1974-75	Western Province
1975-76	Natal
1976-77	Natal
1977-78	Western Province
1978-79	Transvaal
1979-80	Transvaal
1980-81	Natal
1981-82	Western Province
1982-83	Transvaal
1983-84	Transvaal
1984-85	Transvaal
1985-86	Western Province
1986-87	Transvaal
1987-88	Transvaal

1988-89	Eastern Province	2001-02	KwaZulu-Natal
1989-90 {	Eastern Province	2002-03	Easterns
	Western Province	2003-04	Western Province
		2004-05 {	Dolphins
Castle Cup			Eagles
1990-91	Western Province	2005-06 {	Dolphins
1991-92	Eastern Province		Titans
1992-93	Orange Free State	2006-07	Titans
1993-94	Orange Free State	2007-08	Eagles
1994-95	Natal	2008-09	Titans
1995-96	Western Province	2009-10	Cape Cobras
		2010-11	Cape Cobras
SuperSport Series		2011-12	Titans
1996-97	Natal		
1997-98	Free State	*Sunfoil Series*	
1998-99	Western Province	2012-13	Cape Cobras
1999-2000	Gauteng	2013-14	Cape Cobras
2000-01	Western Province	2014-15	Lions

Transvaal/Gauteng have won the title outright 25 times, Natal/KwaZulu-Natal 21, Western Province 18, Cape Cobras 4, Orange Free State/Free State and Titans 3, Eastern Province 2, Eagles, Easterns, Kimberley and Lions 1. The title has been shared seven times as follows: Transvaal 4, Natal and Western Province 3, Dolphins 2, Eagles, Eastern Province and Titans 1.

From 1971-72 to 1990-91, the non-white South African Cricket Board of Control (later the South African Cricket Board) organised their own three-day tournaments. These are now recognised as first-class (see *Wisden 2006*, pages 79–80). A list of winners appears in *Wisden 2007*, page 1346.

SUNFOIL THREE-DAY CHALLENGE, 2014-15

Pool A	P	W	L	D	Pts		Pool B	P	W	L	D	Pts
NORTHERNS	10	6	2	2	131.48		GAUTENG	10	5	1	4	124.78
North West......	10	4	0	6	120.34		Free State.......	10	3	1	6	111.06
Western Province .	10	3	2	5	104.56		KZN Inland	10	4	2	4	103.34
SW Districts......	10	3	2	5	94.18		Eastern Province .	10	3	2	5	94.22
Griqualand West ..	10	2	5	3	83.22‡		Easterns........	10	3	4	3	90.38
Border	10	2	4	4	81.16		Boland	10	1	6	3	62.82†
KwaZulu-Natal ...	10	1	3	6	69.28‡		Namibia	10	0	6	4	48.30

† *1pt deducted for slow over-rate.*   ‡ *2pts deducted for slow over-rate.*

Outright win = 10pts. Bonus points awarded for the first 100 overs of each team's first innings. One batting point was awarded for the first 150 runs and 0.02 of a point for every subsequent run. One bowling point was awarded for the third wicket taken and for every subsequent one.

The teams were divided into two pools of seven. Each played the other six in their pool, plus four teams from the other pool; all these results counted towards the final table. The two pool leaders met in a final.

Pool A

At Durban, October 2–4, 2014. **Drawn. KwaZulu-Natal 128 and 208-2** (M. R. Ramsaroop 100*); ‡**Western Province 230-7 dec.** *KwaZulu-Natal 3pts, Western Province 6.6pts.*

At Oudtshoorn, October 9–11, 2014. **Northerns won by two wickets. South Western Districts 214 and 211;** ‡**Northerns 164** (G. R. Rabie 5-41) **and 262-8.** *Northerns 15.28pts, South Western Districts 6.28pts.*

At East London, October 16–18, 2014. **Drawn. South Western Districts 258; ‡Border 56-2.** *Border 4pts, South Western Districts 3.16pts.*

At Centurion, October 16–18, 2014. **KwaZulu-Natal won by seven wickets. Northerns 191 and 261** (K. A. Maharaj 5-70); **‡KwaZulu-Natal 366** (S. Muthusamy 104*; S. von Berg 6-117) **and 90-3.** *KwaZulu-Natal 17.48pts, Northerns 4.82pts.*

At Oudtshoorn, October 23–25, 2014. **Drawn. Western Province 295-4 dec** (P. J. Malan 120*) **and 221-3 dec; ‡South Western Districts 364-9 dec** (L. L. Mnyanda 109). *South Western Districts 6.28pts, Western Province 7.9pts.*

At East London, October 30–November 1, 2014. **Drawn. North West 187 and 68-3; ‡Border 197.** *Border 5.94pts, North West 5.74pts.*

At East London, November 13–15, 2014. **Border won by nine wickets. Griqualand West 258 and 224; ‡Border 421-9 dec** (M. D. Walters 161, M. J. Nqolo 137) **and 66-1.** *Border 19.1pts, Griqualand West 4.16pts. Martin Walters and Jerry Nqolo added 294 for Border's fourth wicket.*

At Pretoria, November 13–14, 2014. **Northerns won by eight wickets. Western Province 90** (S. F. Mofokeng 5-33) **and 139; ‡Northerns 201 and 29-2.** *Northerns 16.02pts, Western Province 4pts.*

At Potchefstroom, November 20–22, 2014. **Drawn. North West 335** (N. Bredenkamp 134*) **and 200-6 dec; ‡KwaZulu-Natal 262 and 163-7.** *North West 8.7pts, KwaZulu-Natal 7.24pts.*

At Potchefstroom, December 18–20, 2014. **Drawn. North West 243 and 375-6 dec** (N. J. van den Bergh 100*); **‡Northerns 250** (D. Klein 8-72) **and 241-5.** *North West 6.86pts, Northerns 7pts. Dieter Klein's 8-72 was the best innings return of this tournament.*

At Kimberley, January 8–10, 2015. **North West won by 163 runs. North West 351** (B. J. Pelser 176) **and 248** (R. C. Williams 5-42); **‡Griqualand West 247 and 189** (B. C. Fortuin 5-33). *North West 19.02pts, Griqualand West 6.94pts.*

At Centurion, January 15–17, 2015. **Northerns won by an innings and nine runs. Griqualand West 193 and 258; ‡Northerns 460-6 dec** (G. L. van Buuren 150*). *Northerns 20.96pts, Griqualand West 3.86pts.*

At Cape Town, January 15–17, 2015. **North West won by seven wickets. Western Province 260 and 108; ‡North West 224** (S. Khan 6-56) **and 148-3.** *North West 16.48pts, Western Province 7.2pts.*

At Durban, January 22–24, 2015. **Drawn. KwaZulu-Natal 154 and 306; ‡Border 226 and 114-4.** *KwaZulu-Natal 5.08pts, Border 6.52pts.*

At Potchefstroom, January 22–24, 2015. **Drawn. South Western Districts 177** (D. Klein 6-81) **and 478-6 dec** (R. D. McMillan 204); **‡North West 326** (N. J. van den Bergh 141*) **and 231-6.** *North West 8.52pts, South Western Districts 5.54pts. Ross McMillan reached a maiden double-hundred.*

At Cape Town, January 22–24, 2015. **Drawn. ‡Griqualand West 258 and 274-6** (A. R. Swanepoel 114*); **Western Province 403-8 dec** (G. F. Linde 103*). *Western Province 8.08pts, Griqualand West 6.16pts.*

At East London, January 29–31, 2015. **Northerns won by ten wickets. Border 158 and 182; ‡Northerns 187** (P. Fojela 5-33) **and 154-0.** *Northerns 15.74pts, Border 5.16pts.*

At Durban, January 29–31, 2015. **Drawn. KwaZulu-Natal 406-8 dec** (D. J. van Wyk 117); **‡Griqualand West 252 and 192-3.** *KwaZulu-Natal 9.32pts, Griqualand West 6.04pts.*

At Oudtshoorn, February 12–13, 2015. **Griqualand West won by an innings and 77 runs. South Western Districts 88** (J. N. Frylinck 7-32) **and 101; ‡Griqualand West 266.** *Griqualand West 17.32pts, South Western Districts 4pts.*

At Rondebosch, February 12–14, 2015. **Drawn. Border 262** (S. Seyibokwe 101) **and 312-7** (M. Marais 104*); **‡Western Province 374.** *Western Province 9.3pts, Border 6.24pts.*

At Oudtshoorn, February 19–21, 2015. **Drawn. KwaZulu-Natal 279 and 264-6** (R. Minnie 107*); **‡South Western Districts 286.** *South Western Districts 7.72pts, KwaZulu-Natal 7.58pts.*

Pool B

At Johannesburg (Bottom Oval), October 2–4, 2014. **Drawn. Eastern Province 273** (L. R. Walters 115) **and 212** (A. J. N. Price 108); ‡**Gauteng 323-7 dec and 60-2.** *Gauteng 8.46pts, Eastern Province 6.46pts.*

At Benoni, October 9–11, 2014. **Gauteng won by five wickets. Easterns 224 and 230;** ‡**Gauteng 284 and 174-5.** *Gauteng 17.68pts, Easterns 6.48pts.*

At Windhoek, October 16–18, 2014. **Eastern Province won by nine wickets.** ‡**Eastern Province 400-9 dec** (K. R. Smuts 148) **and 71-1; Namibia 125 and 343.** *Eastern Province 20pts, Namibia 4pts.*

At Benoni, October 23–25, 2014. **Drawn. Boland 156** (T. Shamsi 6-24) **and 297-8;** ‡**Easterns 343-7 dec** (G. M. Thomson 144). *Easterns 8.72pts, Boland 4.12pts.*

At Pietermaritzburg, October 23–25, 2014. **Drawn. Free State 406-6 dec;** ‡**KwaZulu-Natal Inland 67 and 280-5** (A. L. Ndlovu 126*). *KwaZulu-Natal Inland 2pts, Free State 8.08pts. KwaZulu-Natal Inland followed on 339 behind, but batted out the last day to draw.*

At Port Elizabeth (Union), November 6–8, 2014. **Drawn. Eastern Province 231 and 260-4** (C. N. Ackermann 107*); ‡**Easterns 304** (P. Yiba 6-61). *Eastern Province 6.62pts, Easterns 7.54pts.*

At Port Elizabeth (Union), November 20–22, 2014. **Eastern Province won by four wickets. Boland 248 and 91** (S. Gidana 5-25, T. Bokako 5-14); ‡**Eastern Province 246 and 94-6** (J. G. Dill 6-34). *Eastern Province 16.92pts, Boland 6.96pts.*

At Bloemfontein, November 20–22, 2014. **Drawn.** ‡**Gauteng 190** (G. A. Vries 5-22) **and 187-3; Free State 385-9 dec** (C. A. Dry 142). *Free State 9.2pts, Gauteng 4.8pts. Corné van Dry, who reached a maiden century, and Michael Erlank (78) added 192 for Free State's seventh wicket.*

At Paarl, November 27–29, 2014. **Drawn. Free State 347-6 dec and 25-1 dec;** ‡**Boland 157.** *Boland 3.14pts, Free State 8.4pts.*

At Windhoek, December 4–6, 2014. **Drawn. KwaZulu-Natal Inland 303-9 dec and 194-2 dec** (I. Khan 108); ‡**Namibia 132 and 224-4.** *Namibia 4pts, KwaZulu-Natal Inland 8.06pts.*

At Bloemfontein, December 11–13, 2014. **Free State won by an innings and 47 runs.** ‡**Namibia 174 and 190; Free State 411-8 dec** (M. N. Erlank 163*). *Free State 20.1pts, Namibia 4.48pts.*

At Johannesburg, December 18–20, 2014. **Gauteng won by 99 runs. Gauteng 224 and 150;** ‡**KwaZulu-Natal Inland 184 and 91.** *Gauteng 16.48pts, KwaZulu-Natal Inland 5.68pts.*

At Port Elizabeth (Union), January 8–10, 2015. **KwaZulu-Natal Inland won by 95 runs.** ‡**KwaZulu-Natal Inland 305** (S. Gidana 5-52) **and 213-9 dec; Eastern Province 171 and 252** (K. R. Smuts 122; A. H. Razak 5-47). *KwaZulu-Natal Inland 18.1pts, Eastern Province 5.42pts.*

At Pietermaritzburg, January 15–17, 2015. **Drawn.** ‡**Easterns 307 and 249-6 dec** (W. B. Marshall 103); **KwaZulu-Natal Inland 336-9 dec** (N. Hendrie 104; G. M. Thomson 5-71) **and 128-4.** *KwaZulu-Natal Inland 8.72pts, Easterns 8.14pts.*

At Paarl, January 22–23, 2015. **Gauteng won by nine wickets. Boland 135 and 173;** ‡**Gauteng 295** (D. P. Conway 100) **and 15-1.** *Gauteng 17.9pts, Boland 4pts. Boland wicketkeeper Soyisile Pono made six catches in Gauteng's first innings.*

At Benoni, January 22–24, 2015. **Easterns won by five wickets. Free State 173** (G. M. Thomson 5-51) **and 217;** ‡**Easterns 267** (E. H. Kemm 133*) **and 125-5.** *Easterns 16.64pts, Free State 4.46pts. Ernest Kemm carried his bat, adding 149 for Easterns' ninth wicket with Clayton August (63).*

At Bloemfontein (OFS University), January 29–31, 2015. **Drawn.** ‡**Eastern Province 372** (A. J. N. Price 144; T. Ntuli 5-96) **and 184-6 dec; Free State 255** (P. Botha 103) **and 143-4.** *Free State 7.1pts, Eastern Province 9.44pts.*

At Johannesburg (Top Oval), January 29–31, 2015. **Drawn. Namibia 235** (Z. Pongolo 5-50) **and 73-2;** ‡**Gauteng 379.** *Gauteng 9.58pts, Namibia 6.7pts.*

At Windhoek, February 5–6, 2015. **Easterns won by an innings and 19 runs. Namibia 128 and 135;** ‡**Easterns 282.** *Easterns 17.26pts, Namibia 3pts.*

At Pietermaritzburg, February 12–14, 2015. **KwaZulu-Natal Inland won by six runs. KwaZulu-Natal Inland 213 and 220;** ‡**Boland 187 and 240.** *KwaZulu-Natal Inland 16.26pts, Boland 5.74pts.*

At Paarl, February 19–21, 2015. **Drawn. Namibia 212 and 263;** ‡**Boland 287** (B. M. Scholtz 8-116) **and 153-9** (B. M. Scholtz 5-66). *Boland 7.54pts, Namibia 6.24pts. Slow left-armer Bernard Scholtz took 13-182, the best match figures of the tournament, and the best ever for Namibia. His 8-116 was Namibia's second-best innings return, after Ian van Zyl's 8-34 v Ireland at Dublin in 2006.*

Cross Pool

At Kimberley, October 2–4, 2014. **KwaZulu-Natal Inland won by 47 runs. KwaZulu-Natal Inland 257 and 250;** ‡**Griqualand West 305** (A. R. Swanepoel 124; K. Nipper 5-58) **and 155.** *KwaZulu-Natal Inland 17.14pts, Griqualand West 8.1pts.*

At Port Elizabeth (Union), October 9–11, 2014. **Eastern Province won by 56 runs.** ‡**Eastern Province 153** (D. L. Brown 5-14) **and 280** (A. J. N. Price 167); **Border 280** (K. R. Smuts 5-66) **and 97** (T. Bokako 5-24). *Eastern Province 15.06pts, Border 7.6pts.*

At Windhoek, October 9–11, 2014. **Drawn.** ‡**Western Province 484-5 dec** (M. C. Kleinveldt 101, M. Z. Hamza 202*); **Namibia 275** (G. F. Linde 5-94) **and 227-9** (R. van Schoor 103*; G. F. Linde 6-81). *Namibia 4.5pts, Western Province 9.16pts. Zubayr Hamza advanced from a maiden hundred to a double, after adding 184 for Western Province's fourth wicket with Matthew Kleinveldt.*

At Kimberley, October 16–18, 2014. **Drawn.** ‡**Griqualand West 316** (D. Olivier 5-67) **and 111-2; Free State 346-9 dec** (V. L. Orros 109). *Griqualand West 8.32pts, Free State 8.92pts.*

At Potchefstroom, October 16–18, 2014. **Drawn. North West 368;** ‡**Gauteng 516-7** (D. A. Hendricks 105, D. P. Conway 102, D. R. Deeb 112). *North West 6.38pts, Gauteng 7.68pts. Dominic Hendricks and Devon Conway put on 202 for Gauteng's second wicket.*

At Windhoek, October 23–25, 2014. **North West won by seven wickets.** ‡**Namibia 269** (N. R. P. Scholtz 116) **and 247; North West 373-9 dec** (A. J. Malan 166*) **and 144-3.** *North West 19.46pts, Namibia 7.38pts.*

At Paarl, October 30–November 1, 2014. **Western Province won by seven wickets. Boland 159 and 341** (E. C. Kriek 133*; B. J. Young 5-68); ‡**Western Province 384 and 118-3.** *Western Province 18.14pts, Boland 4.18pts.*

At Bloemfontein, October 30–November 1, 2014. **Drawn. Northerns 247** (D. Olivier 5-61) **and 4-0;** ‡**Free State 324-9 dec** (M. N. Erlank 118; E. L. Hawken 5-36). *Free State 8.26pts, Northerns 5.94pts.*

At Chatsworth, October 30–November 1, 2014. **Drawn.** ‡**KwaZulu-Natal 308-6 dec** (S. Muthusamy 135*); **Eastern Province 100 and 82-3.** *KwaZulu-Natal 8.16pts, Eastern Province 2pts. Senuran Muthusamy added 206 for KwaZulu-Natal's sixth wicket with Chad Bowes (91).*

At Oudtshoorn, October 30–November 1, 2014. **South Western Districts won by an innings and 18 runs. Namibia 130 and 94;** ‡**South Western Districts 242.** *South Western Districts 16.84pts, Namibia 4pts.*

At Johannesburg, November 6–8, 2014. **Gauteng won by ten wickets.** ‡**KwaZulu-Natal 159 and 118; Gauteng 258** (D. M. Dupavillon 6-62) **and 23-0.** *Gauteng 17.16pts, KwaZulu-Natal 5.18pts.*

At Pietermaritzburg, November 13–15, 2014. **Drawn.** ‡**South Western Districts 172 and 242-7 dec; KwaZulu-Natal Inland 162 and 124-6.** *KwaZulu-Natal Inland 5.24pts, South Western Districts 5.44pts. SWD wicketkeeper Brendon Louw made six catches in KwaZulu-Natal's first innings.*

At Potchefstroom, November 13–15, 2014. **North West won by seven wickets. Boland 156 and 297** (K. D. Petersen 142; V. C. M. Mazibuko 5-57); ‡**North West 322 and 133-3.** *North West 18.44pts, Boland 5.12pts.*

At Benoni, November 27–29, 2014. **South Western Districts won by 228 runs. South Western Districts 264 and 289-2 dec** (W. Lategan 138*); ‡**Easterns 163 and 162.** *South Western Districts 17.28pts, Easterns 5.26pts.*

At Johannesburg, November 27–29, 2014. **Gauteng won by seven wickets. Gauteng 359-8 dec** (S. C. Cook 156) **and 152-3;** ‡**Border 193 and 314** (G. V. J. Koopman 108; Z. Pongolo 5-67). *Gauteng 19.18pts, Border 4.86pts.*

At Pietermaritzburg, November 27–29, 2014. **KwaZulu-Natal Inland won by 100 runs. ‡KwaZulu-Natal Inland 197 and 167; KwaZulu-Natal 123 and 141** (G. I. Hume 5-18). *KwaZulu-Natal Inland 15.94pts, KwaZulu-Natal 4pts.*

At Cape Town, December 4–6, 2014. **Western Province won by eight wickets. ‡Western Province 419-5 dec** (P. J. Malan 182) **and 234-2** (S. van Zyl 104*); **Easterns 252 and 399-4 dec** (J. Snyman 150). *Western Province 17.2pts, Easterns 3.04pts. Stiaan van Zyl hit 104* in 87 balls as Western Province rushed to victory on the final evening.*

At Paarl, December 11–13, 2014. **South Western Districts won by an innings and 23 runs. ‡Boland 103 and 356; South Western Districts 482-7 dec** (C. Jonker 201*). *South Western Districts 21.64pts, Boland 3pts. Christiaan Jonker reached his maiden double-hundred in 182 balls, hitting 12 fours and 12 sixes.*

At East London, December 11–13, 2014. **Border won by seven wickets. Easterns 114** (A. Gqamane 6-30) **and 257; ‡Border 287** (G. M. Thomson 6-46) **and 85-3.** *Border 17.74pts, Easterns 4pts. Ayabulela Gqamane's full first-innings figures were 8.2–2–30–6.*

At Kimberley, December 11–13, 2014. **Griqualand West won by 11 runs. Griqualand West 270** (D. R. Deeb 6-57) **and 172; ‡Gauteng 193-8 dec and 238** (D. de Koker 5-54). *Griqualand West 16.4pts, Gauteng 5.86pts. Chasing 250, Gauteng were 217-3, but collapsed as Desmond de Koker took five wickets in 18 deliveries.*

At Kimberley, December 18–20, 2014. **Boland won by seven wickets. ‡Griqualand West 296** (D. S. Rosier 137) **and 219; Boland 401 and 115-3.** *Boland 20.02pts, Griqualand West 7.92pts.*

At Benoni, January 8–10, 2015. **Easterns won by 67 runs. Easterns 303** (W. Coulentianos 116*) **and 27-1 dec; ‡Northerns first inns forfeited and 263.** *Easterns 13.3pts, Northerns 3pts.*

At Chatsworth, January 15–17, 2015. **Free State won by 154 runs. ‡Free State 375-9 dec** (J. L. du Plooy 107*) **and 116-5 dec; KwaZulu-Natal 162** (S. M. Khomari 5-34) **and 175.** *Free State 18.72pts, KwaZulu-Natal 4.24pts. Four days after his 20th birthday, and batting at No. 8, Leus du Plooy scored a century on first-class debut. Shadley van Schalkwyk claimed a hat-trick in KwaZulu-Natal's second innings to help Free State to victory.*

At Port Elizabeth, February 12–14, 2015. **Drawn. North West 437-9 dec** (R. H. Frenz 157, N. J. van den Bergh 111); **‡Eastern Province 295-9.** *Eastern Province 7.9pts, North West 10.74pts. Nicky van den Bergh hit 111 in 99 balls.*

At Pretoria, February 12–13, 2015. **Northerns won by an innings and 229 runs. Northerns 492** (G. L. van Buuren 130, H. Klaasen 201); **‡Namibia 119** (S. von Berg 5-33) **and 144** (S. A. Mothoa 6-29). *Northerns 21.84pts, Namibia 4pts. Heinrich Klassen, who scored 201, his first double-century, in 143 balls with 15 fours and 13 sixes, joined forces with Graeme van Buuren at 124-5 to put on 237 for Northerns' sixth wicket.*

At Bloemfontein, February 19–20, 2015. **Free State won by an innings and 56 runs. Border 99 and 136; ‡Free State 291** (P. Botha 102; Y. Pangabantu 5-69). *Free State 17.82pts, Border 4pts.*

At Centurion, February 19–21, 2015. **Northerns won by an innings and 123 runs. ‡Eastern Province 220 and 230** (L. R. Walters 101); **Northerns 573-8 dec** (G. L. van Buuren 235). *Northerns 20.94pts, Eastern Province 4.4pts. Van Buuren scored his third century in successive innings, and advanced to a maiden double. He also took six wickets in the match, helping Northerns to their third innings win in four games (they won the other by ten wickets).*

At Rondebosch, February 19–21, 2015. **Western Province won by seven wickets. ‡KwaZulu-Natal Inland 210 and 163** (M. B. Njoloza 5-42); **Western Province 249** (M. Z. Hamza 128*) **and 125-3.** *Western Province 16.98pts, KwaZulu-Natal Inland 6.2pts.*

Final At Centurion, February 27–March 1, 2015. **Drawn. Gauteng 292 and 225-4 dec; ‡Northerns 269 and 42-3.** *Gauteng and Northerns shared the title.*

MOMENTUM ONE-DAY CUP, 2014-15

50-over league plus knockout

	Played	Won	Lost	NR/A	Bonus points	Points	Net run-rate
CAPE COBRAS	10	6	3	1	3	29	0.39
DOLPHINS	10	5	2	3	0	26	0.15
TITANS	10	5	4	1	1	21	0.17
Warriors	10	5	5	0	1	21	−0.04
Lions	10	3	6	1	1	15	−0.25
Knights	10	2	6	2	1	15	−0.41

The match between Titans and Knights was called off after 19 overs because of a dangerous pitch; though it was a no result, Knights were awarded 4pts and Titans 0pts, rather than 2pts each.

Titans and Warriors tied on head-to-head points; Titans qualified for the play-off on net run-rate.

Play-off   At Durban, February 10, 2015 (day/night). **Titans won by 58 runs.** ‡Titans 267-6 (50 overs) (D. Elgar 100); **Dolphins** 209 (44.3 overs). *MoM:* D. Elgar. *Dean Elgar added 92 for Titans' sixth wicket with David Wiese, who hit 71* in 33 balls with five sixes.*

Final   At Cape Town, February 13, 2015 (day/night). **Titans won by five wickets.** ‡Cape Cobras 285-8 (50 overs) (R. E. Levi 104); **Titans 288-5** (47.1 overs) (D. Elgar 100, J. A. Morkel 134*). *MoM:* J. A. Morkel. *Richard Levi and Andrew Puttick opened for Cobras with 180 in 31 overs. Titans slumped to 60-4 in reply, but Elgar, with his second successive hundred, and Albie Morkel, who hit 134* – his maiden one-day century, in 103 balls with seven sixes – added 195 in 31 overs to take them within sight of victory.*

RAM SLAM T20 CHALLENGE, 2014-15

	Played	Won	Lost	Tied	NR/A	Bonus points	Points	Net run-rate
CAPE COBRAS	10	8	1	0	1	3	37	1.14
LIONS	10	6	3	0	1	2	28	0.01
KNIGHTS	10	4	3	0	3	2	24	1.20
Dolphins	10	3	6	0	1	2	16	0.05
Warriors	10	3	6	1	0	0	15	−1.34
Titans	10	2	7	1	0	0	11	−0.70

Play-off   At Johannesburg, December 7, 2014. **Knights won by eight wickets.** ‡Lions 148-5 (20 overs); **Knights 150-2** (17.5 overs). *MoM:* R. R. Hendricks and M. P. Siboto (both Knights). *Reeza Hendricks and Rilee Rossouw added 115 in 13 overs for Knights' second wicket.*

Final   At Cape Town, December 12, 2014 (day/night). **Cape Cobras won by 33 runs.** ‡Cape Cobras 158-4 (20 overs); **Knights** 125-9 (20 overs). *MoM:* D. Paterson and O. A. Ramela (both Cobras). *Dane Paterson took 4-33 in Knights' run-chase.*

CSA PROVINCIAL ONE-DAY CHALLENGE, 2014-15

50-over league

Pool A	P	W	L	NR	Pts	Pool B	P	W	L	NR	Pts
BORDER	6	4	2	0	17	FREE STATE	6	3	0	3	20
Northerns	6	3	2	1	17	KwaZulu-Natal Inland	6	4	2	0	18
KwaZulu-Natal	6	3	2	1	16	Boland	6	3	2	1	14
North West	6	3	3	0	13	Eastern Province	6	2	2	2	13
Griqualand West	6	2	3	1	11	Gauteng	6	2	3	1	11
Western Province	6	2	3	1	10	Namibia	6	2	4	0	9
South Western Districts	6	2	4	0	9	Easterns	6	1	4	1	7

Border qualified for the final because they had more wins than Northerns.

Final   At Bloemfontein, March 7, 2015. **Border won by five wickets.** Reduced to 47 overs a side. Free State 110 (32.3 overs); ‡Border 111-5 (34.2 overs). *In a low-scoring match, Free State were 47-6 after 13 overs; Border seamers Phaphama Fojela and Lundi Mbane finished with four apiece.*

CSA PROVINCIAL T20, 2014-15

20-over league plus final

	Played	Won	Lost	NR/A	Bonus points	Points	Net run-rate
Gauteng	4	4	0	0	1	17	1.22
Northerns	4	3	1	0	1	13	0.62
Namibia	4	3	1	0	0	12	0.53
Griqualand West	4	3	1	0	0	12	0.16
KwaZulu-Natal	4	2	1	1	2	12	1.30
Western Province	4	2	2	0	1	9	0.43
Border	4	2	2	0	1	9	0.11
South Western Districts	4	2	2	0	0	8	−0.07
North West	4	1	2	1	1	7	1.10
KwaZulu-Natal Inland	4	1	2	1	0	6	−0.77
Eastern Province	4	1	2	1	0	6	−0.82
Easterns	4	1	3	0	0	4	−0.96
Boland	4	1	3	0	0	4	−1.85
Free State	4	0	4	0	0	0	−0.83

Namibia and Griqualand West finished ahead of KwaZulu-Natal by dint of more wins; all other tied teams were separated on net-run-rate.

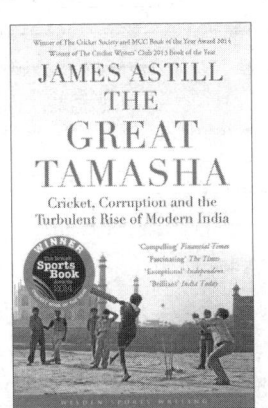

SRI LANKA CRICKET IN 2015

In the footsteps of giants

SA'ADI THAWFEEQ

A year of transition was dominated by the departure of Kumar Sangakkara, who bade goodbye to a glorious career during August's home Tests against India. It was a more sombre farewell than Sri Lanka wanted: India won his last Test by 278 runs, and his final contributions were 32 and 18. That left him with an aggregate of 12,400 Test runs, fifth on the all-time list; only Don Bradman has scored more than his 11 double-centuries.

Sangakkara's limited-overs career had a more fitting conclusion, when he scored four consecutive hundreds, a one-day international record, at the World Cup earlier in the year. He finished as the leading wicketkeeper in that format, with 482 dismissals, including a record 98 stumpings. Mahela Jayawardene, who played his last international game during the World Cup, had bowed out of Test cricket the previous year, and Tillekeratne Dilshan, though still

SRI LANKA IN 2015

	Played	Won	Lost	Drawn/ No result
Tests	11	4	7	–
One-day internationals	25	12	12	1
Twenty20 internationals	4	1	3	–

DECEMBER — JANUARY	2 Tests and 7 ODIs (a) v New Zealand	(see *Wisden 2015*, page 970)
FEBRUARY — MARCH	ICC World Cup (in Australia and New Zealand)	(page 860)
APRIL		
MAY		
JUNE — JULY	3 Tests, 5 ODIs and 2 T20Is (h) v Pakistan	(page 1105)
AUGUST	3 Tests (h) v India	(page 1121)
SEPTEMBER		
OCTOBER — NOVEMBER	2 Tests, 3 ODIs and 2 T20Is (h) v West Indies	(page 1130)
DECEMBER — JANUARY	2 Tests, 5 ODIs and 2 T20Is (a) v New Zealand	(page 1036)

For a review of Sri Lankan domestic cricket from the 2014-15 season, see page 1138.

available for limited-overs, had given up Tests in 2013. The loss of those three icons created a big hole in Sri Lanka's batting, which they struggled to fill.

The heirs apparent, Lahiru Thirimanne and Dinesh Chandimal, found it difficult to live up to expectations. Thirimanne managed just 310 runs at 23 in eight Tests, though he did better in ODIs, with 861 at 43. By contrast Chandimal, down the order because of wicketkeeping duties, had a fairly good run in Tests, with 901 at 47, but managed only 325 one-day runs at 36. Captain Angelo Mathews suffered slightly from having to shoulder extra batting responsibilities, but still totalled 845 in his 11 Tests, with three centuries. Among the younger brigade, opener Dimuth Karunaratne scored a promising 769 Test runs. Dilshan's one-day tally of 1,207 was his highest yet in a calendar year.

On the bowling front, the most impressive development came from seamer Dammika Prasad. By the end of 2014, he had taken 34 wickets from 16 Tests over an injury-hit six years. But he worked assiduously on his fitness, and became the spearhead of the Test attack, collecting 41 wickets at 24 from nine games before a back strain ended his tour of New Zealand. Prasad's form compensated for the loss of fellow pace bowler Shaminda Eranga, who suffered a series of recurring injuries – back, groin and hamstring – and did not play a Test in 2015.

Left-arm spinner Rangana Herath, who had borne the brunt of the bowling since Muttiah Muralitharan retired in 2010, managed 37 wickets in ten Tests, but was left out of the final Test against Pakistan, whose batsmen had worked out how to counter him after years of torment. Young off-spinner Tharindu Kaushal was touted as Herath's successor after taking 22 wickets in his first six Tests of the year, but in September his doosra was deemed illegal. He played one more Test, against West Indies, before being dropped.

Kusal Perera looked as if he could become Sri Lanka's most thrilling batsman since Sanath Jayasuriya, until a positive result in a dope test taken during the West Indies series resulted in an abrupt recall from New Zealand, and left him fighting to save his career. The emergence of all-rounder Milinda Siriwardene and fiery fast bowler Dushmantha Chameera gave Sri Lanka some hope. A late developer, Siriwardene made his international debut in all three formats at the age of 29, and displayed his talent with free-flowing hits and useful left-arm spin. Chameera was an exciting find, consistently topping 87mph, and unsettling batsmen with his pace and bounce.

But results were disappointing. Sri Lanka lost Test series in New Zealand at either end of 2015, and at home to Pakistan and India in between; their only series win came against West Indies, and they slipped to seventh in the ICC rankings. Despite Sangakkara's batting, they were knocked out of the World Cup in the quarter-final. At the start of 2016, two defeats by New Zealand cost them top spot in the Twenty20 rankings.

On the administrative front, Sri Lanka Cricket failed to hold board elections by the legal deadline of the end of March, blaming the World Cup. Sports minister Navin Dissanayake replaced Jayantha Dharmadasa's regime with a nine-member interim committee, headed by former Test cricketer Sidath Wettimuny, with a brief to get rid of "system corruption" at SLC. The

Rob Jefferies, Getty Images

Into the fray: Dushmantha Chameera lets rip against New Zealand in Dunedin.

committee cut down severely on unnecessary expenditure, diverting it towards the development of the game's infrastructure. The ICC were unhappy, however, pointing out that their articles of association empowered them to suspend members whose government interfered in cricket administration. They delayed the payment owing from the World Cup, and insisted elections be held as soon as possible.

With a new sports minister, Dayasiri Jayasekera, in office after August's change of government, the SLC election was held on January 3, 2016, and was free and fair, allowing all candidates to contest the posts without political interference. An alliance between Thilanga Sumathipala (now deputy speaker of parliament) and his former rival Dharmadasa won the day; both were determined to defeat the former secretary Nishantha Ranatunga, who had been involved in a running battle with Dharmadasa while he was president. Sumathipala beat Ranatunga 88–56 to become president for the fourth time, while Dharmadasa and Kangadaran Mathivanan were elected vice-presidents, keeping out Nishantha's brother Arjuna, the former World Cup-winning captain who was now minister for ports and shipping.

Jayananda Warnaweera, the former Test spinner and long-serving curator at Galle, had survived from Dharmadasa's administration to serve on the interim committee, but stepped down in October. The following month, SLC suspended him from all cricket activity for two years, after he failed to attend two interviews during the ICC's Anti-Corruption Unit's investigations into alleged match-fixing; in January 2016, the ICC imposed a three-year ban (to run concurrently with SLC's) for his refusal to co-operate.

SRI LANKA v PAKISTAN IN 2015

Andrew Fernando

Test matches (3): Sri Lanka 1, Pakistan 2
One-day internationals (5): Sri Lanka 2, Pakistan 3
Twenty20 internationals (2); Sri Lanka 0, Pakistan 2

As the teams convened for their seventh Test series in little more than six years, Pakistan considered how to handle a familiar problem: Sri Lanka's spinners, especially their slow left-armer Rangana Herath, who had taken 88 wickets against them in 17 matches. On the eve of the First Test, Misbah-ul-Haq's assertion that his side had worked out "an answer for Herath" was greeted with mild scepticism: for years, visiting captains had claimed to have watched enough footage, pored over enough stats, or hired enough witch doctors, to neutralise him. And, for years, Herath would finish the series picking his teeth with the bones of his opponents, legs crossed, in a hammock.

But, as the series opener at Galle wound into its later stages, Pakistan's batsmen were slinking down the track to drive, or hanging back in the crease to sweep. Herath, who had long delayed surgery on both knees, seemed to be pivoting more gingerly than usual in his delivery stride, and extracted less bite out of a pitch that had historically been kind to him. It was here, and in the second innings in Colombo, where Pakistan laid the foundations for their record-breaking victory at Pallekele that gave them the series 2–1. Herath took just one wicket in each of the first two Tests, and was left out of the Third. Angelo Mathews discovered that, even if he could do without Kumar Sangakkara (who missed the decider as part of his retirement plan) and Mahela Jayawardene, he would struggle to live without Herath.

In the event, Pakistan's own slow men outshone Sri Lanka's, particularly Yasir Shah, the leg-spinner with the melted-velvet action and seemingly laser-guided control. He appeared to know when a batsman would venture down the track, and pulled his length back or slipped in a quicker one. Yasir provoked three stumpings in the third innings in Galle; and, on the first day at Pallekele, two men perished trying to lift him over mid-off or mid-on.

So complete was his hold that, even when the tracks offered meagre turn, the batsmen committed to more wrong lines than a karaoke drunk. He took 24 wickets in the three Tests, behind only Shane Warne's 26 in 2003-04 among visiting bowlers in Sri Lanka. The hosts didn't prosper until Yasir tired on the third day at Pallekele – and that might not have happened had he not already sent down almost 150 overs in the series, thanks in part to Wahab Riaz's hand injury on the first day of the Second Test. Sri Lanka's top wicket-taker, unusually, was a seamer – Dammika Prasad, with 14. Both top orders proved fragile, one reason why all three Tests ended in positive results.

The groundsmen also deserved praise. Even Galle humoured the seamers early on, before descending into its usual cantankerous spinning mood. The P. Sara Oval did not discriminate, providing bounce and movement for all; and

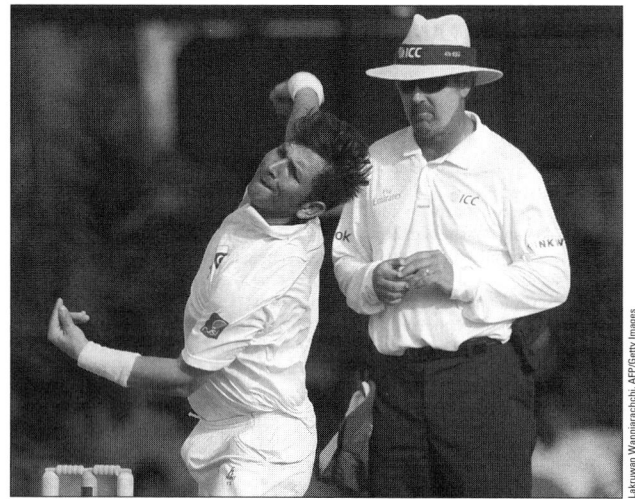

Lakruwan Wanniarachchi, AFP/Getty Images

Sleight of hand: Yasir Shah, watched by umpire Richard Illingworth, bamboozles the Sri Lankans.

both teams strapped three seamers to the plough for the Pallekele decider. Mathews felt the surface had flattened a bit by the time Shan Masood and Younis Khan mastered his attack, but the pitch took seam and spin throughout.

Pakistan completed a rare clean sweep by winning the one-day and Twenty20 series. Their batting gave them the upper hand in the 50-over games, the top order dominating an attack led by the fading Lasith Malinga. Sri Lanka's two victories were built on Kusal Perera's aggression. The T20s were almost a foregone conclusion, as Sri Lanka tried out several youngsters in the hope of uncovering some rough diamonds for the World Twenty20 in 2016.

All the matches – particularly the Tests – were played in good spirit, and many will remember Younis Khan's sublime 171 to complete Pakistan's monumental run-chase at Pallekele. Not long after he took off his pads, he was sitting in the dug-out with Kaushal Silva, Sri Lanka's opener, who was lapping up wisdom at the feet of the old man. But the tour was defined by the contributions of a spinner. And it was Yasir Shah who was left picking his teeth with the bones of his opponents, legs crossed, in a hammock.

PAKISTAN TOURING PARTY

*Misbah-ul-Haq (T), Ahmed Shehzad (T/50/20), Anwar Ali (50/20), Asad Shafiq (T/50), Azhar Ali (T/50), Babar Azam (T/50), Bilal Asif (50), Ehsan Adil (T/50), Haris Sohail (T), Imad Wasim (50/20), Imran Khan, sen. (T), Junaid Khan (T), Mohammad Hafeez (T/50/20), Mohammad Irfan (50/20), Mohammad Rizwan (50/20), Mukhtar Ahmed (50/20), Nauman Anwar (20), Rahat Ali (T/50), Sarfraz Ahmed (T/50/20), Shahid Afridi (20), Shan Masood (T), Shoaib Malik (50/20),

Sohail Tanvir (20), Umar Akmal (20), Wahab Riaz (T), Yasir Shah (T/50/20), Younis Khan (T), Zia-ul-Haq (20), Zulfiqar Babar (T). *Coach:* Waqar Younis.

Haris Sohail (knee) and Wahab Riaz (broken hand) were replaced during the Test series by Babar Azam and Rahat Ali. Wahab was expected to return for the Twenty20 matches, but was not fully fit; Zia-ul-Haq replaced him. Azhar Ali captained in the 50-over matches, and Shahid Afridi in the Twenty20s.

TEST MATCH AVERAGES

SRI LANKA – BATTING AND FIELDING

	T	I	NO	R	HS	100	50	Avge	Ct/St
A. D. Mathews............	3	6	1	269	122	1	1	53.80	1
†F. D. M. Karunaratne.........	3	6	0	318	130	1	2	53.00	2
J. K. Silva...............	3	5	0	222	125	1	1	44.40	0
L. D. Chandimal............	3	5	0	153	67	0	1	30.60	11/3
†K. C. Sangakkara..........	2	4	0	102	50	0	1	25.50	4
†H. M. R. K. B. Herath	2	3	2	25	18*	0	0	25.00	0
†H. D. R. L. Thirimanne	3	6	1	90	44	0	0	18.00	0
P. H. T. Kaushal...........	2	3	0	44	18	0	0	14.66	0
†K. D. K. Vithanage..........	2	4	0	56	34	0	0	14.00	1
K. T. G. D. Prasad..........	3	5	0	37	35	0	0	7.40	0
A. N. P. R. Fernando........	2	4	2	8	4*	0	0	4.00	0

Played in one Test: P. V. D. Chameera 2; R. A. S. Lakmal 6*, 0; †J. Mubarak 25, 35; M. D. K. Perera 15, 0; †W. U. Tharanga 46, 48.

BOWLING

	Style	O	M	R	W	BB	5I	Avge
P. V. D. Chameera	RF	28.5	1	86	4	3-53	0	21.50
K. T. G. D. Prasad	RFM	107.3	13	379	14	4-92	0	27.07
A. N. P. R. Fernando	RFM	53	9	169	5	3-29	0	33.80
P. H. T. Kaushal..............	OB	80.5	5	308	9	5-42	1	34.22
M. D. K. Perera	OB	34.1	3	153	4	4-122	0	38.25

Also bowled: H. M. R. K. B. Herath (SLA) 68.2–11–218–2; R. A. S. Lakmal (RFM) 33–6–112–1; A. D. Mathews (RFM) 43–13–80–2; J. Mubarak (OB) 3.1–0–16–0; K. D. K. Vithanage (LBG) 3–0–21–0.

PAKISTAN – BATTING AND FIELDING

	T	I	NO	R	HS	100	50	Avge	Ct/St
Sarfraz Ahmed	3	4	1	204	96	0	2	68.00	9/5
Younis Khan	3	5	1	267	171*	1	0	66.75	4
Asad Shafiq	3	4	0	175	131	1	0	43.75	1
Azhar Ali	3	5	0	208	117	1	1	41.60	7
Zulfiqar Babar	2	3	1	68	56	0	1	34.00	2
Mohammad Hafeez	2	4	1	98	46*	0	0	32.66	3
Ahmed Shehzad	3	6	1	143	69	0	1	28.60	0
Misbah-ul-Haq	3	5	1	114	59*	0	1	28.50	2
Yasir Shah	3	4	0	56	23	0	0	14.00	2
Junaid Khan	2	3	2	11	6*	0	0	11.00	0
Wahab Riaz	2	3	0	24	14	0	0	8.00	0

Played in one Test: Ehsan Adil 0; Imran Khan, sen. 0; Rahat Ali 2; †Shan Masood 13, 125.

BOWLING

	Style	O	M	R	W	BB	5I	Avge
Yasir Shah	LBG	176.3	28	464	24	7-76	3	19.33
Imran Khan, sen.	RFM	36.4	6	109	5	5-58	1	21.80
Wahab Riaz	LF	51	9	139	5	3-74	0	27.80
Rahat Ali	LFM	42	7	156	5	3-74	0	31.20
Mohammad Hafeez	OB	34	5	103	3	2-40	0	34.33
Zulfiqar Babar	SLA	81	20	219	6	3-64	0	36.50

Also bowled: Azhar Ali (LBG) 12–1–49–2; Ehsan Adil (RFM) 31–7–103–1; Junaid Khan (LFM) 56–11–180–1.

At Colombo (Colts), June 11–13, 2015. **Drawn.** ‡**Pakistanis 247** (73.3 overs) (Ahmed Shehzad 82, Younis Khan 64; J. D. F. Vandersay 5-73) **and 257-7 dec** (69.4 overs) (Shan Masood 69; J. D. F. Vandersay 3-94); **Sri Lanka Board President's XI 241** (89.1 overs) (J. K. Silva 101; Zulfiqar Babar 6-31) **and 129-3** (27 overs) (W. U. Tharanga 50, F. D. M. Karunaratne 54). *The Pakistanis chose from 15 players, and the President's XI 14. Pakistan's batsmen gave little sign of the mastery they would eventually attain over Sri Lanka's spinners, struggling on the first day against the leg-breaks of Jeffrey Vandersay. Kaushal Silva warmed up for the Tests with a diligent century, although his opening partner Dimuth Karunaratne was out second ball. Vandersay added three more wickets in the second innings, while leaking five an over. The President's XI were set 264, but there was time for only 27 overs.*

SRI LANKA v PAKISTAN

First Test Match

At Galle, June 17–21, 2015. Pakistan won by ten wickets. Toss: Pakistan.

With Pakistan trussed up at 96 for five in response to a serviceable 300, Sri Lanka's worst-case scenario appeared to be a draw, especially as the first day had been lost to rain. But the lower-middle order cut loose and tore the home bowlers to pieces. On a ground that had once been a fortress, Sri Lanka eventually slid to a big defeat, their first at home by Pakistan in nine Tests since April 2006.

Yasir Shah and Asad Shafiq played substantial roles in the heist, but it was Sarfraz Ahmed's combative 96 from 86 balls that really picked the match from Sri Lanka's pockets, quelling Pakistan's crisis with fast hands and even quicker feet. Sarfraz whipped his third ball to the square-leg boundary, and gaps in the field seemed to open up. He was slapping balls through the covers, slashing them behind point, and fiercely sweeping the spinners – all the while flitting around the crease to manipulate the bowlers' lines and lengths. Prasad and Herath, the leaders of this Sri Lankan attack, were handled with particular severity.

After reaching 1,000 Test runs in his 28th innings, a record for a Pakistan wicketkeeper, Sarfraz was bowled by Prasad on the sweep, but he had helped bend Sri Lanka out of shape. Pakistan were still 65 adrift when he was out, but the game's course had been changed.

If Sarfraz had been rapacious, Shafiq was restrained, working carefully to consolidate his team's rapid gains, with more help from the tail. He held firm through Herath's long, probing spells, pushed the seamers into spaces when they erred, and left the ambitious shots to his team-mates. His most memorable moment was a lofted drive down the ground to reach his seventh Test hundred, but that was one of only five boundaries in his eventual 131, compiled in six and a quarter hours. Pakistan took the lead while Shafiq had Yasir for company, but it was his ninth-wicket stand of 101 with Zulfiqar Babar that swelled the advantage into three figures. Zulfiqar, who had managed only 50 runs in eight previous Tests, reached a maiden half-century with his second six.

Earlier, once play had finally got under way, Silva struck a patient second Test hundred. Dropped by Yasir at backward point off Wahab Riaz on nine, he batted for almost seven and a half hours, but his 125 was by a distance Sri Lanka's most substantial innings of the match; and his stand of 112 with Sangakkara, who made a subdued 50, was their only century partnership.

Sri Lanka's second innings began on the fourth evening. But, as so often at Galle, a spinner sent the match hurtling to a conclusion. Yasir was not just aggressive – giving the ball plenty of air, and achieving dramatic, fast turn – but, for a wrist-spinner, uncommonly accurate. The batsmen attempted to block him at first, perhaps reasoning they no longer stood a chance of winning. But, after he began his charge, they tried to subdue him with some big strokes. Neither plan worked.

On the final day, once Wahab had broken through with the wicket of Thirimanne, Yasir was irresistible. He had removed Sangakkara the previous night, and now hemmed in an inexperienced middle order, teasing out some rash strokes. Three batsmen were stumped – the most in a Sri Lankan Test innings – and two more slogged to leg. Mathews might have been unfortunate to be given out caught at short leg: replays were inconclusive, so Richard Illingworth's original decision stood. Yasir's seven for 76 were the best figures for a visiting bowler in Sri Lanka, beating Shane Warne's seven for 94 for Australia against Pakistan at the P. Sara Oval in 2002-03.

After bundling Sri Lanka out for 206, Pakistan had a session to score 90, which the openers knocked off in 11.2 overs. Mohammad Hafeez was there at the end, although his delight was soon clouded when his bowling action was reported once again.

Man of the Match: Sarfraz Ahmed.

Close of play: first day, no play; second day, Sri Lanka 178-3 (Silva 80, Mathews 10); third day, Pakistan 118-5 (Asad Shafiq 14, Sarfraz Ahmed 15); fourth day, Sri Lanka 63-2 (Karunaratne 36, Perera 0).

Sri Lanka

F. D. M. Karunaratne c Sarfraz Ahmed b Wahab Riaz .	21	– (2) st Sarfraz Ahmed b Yasir Shah . . .	79
J. K. Silva c Sarfraz Ahmed b Zulfiqar Babar	125	– (1) c Azhar Ali b Wahab Riaz	5
K. C. Sangakkara c Younis Khan b Wahab Riaz	50	– c Azhar Ali b Yasir Shah	18
H. D. R. L. Thirimanne c Zulfiqar Babar b Mohammad Hafeez .	8	– (5) c Younis Khan b Wahab Riaz	44
*A. D. Mathews b Wahab Riaz	19	– (6) c Azhar Ali b Yasir Shah	5
†L. D. Chandimal b Zulfiqar Babar	23	– (7) st Sarfraz Ahmed b Yasir Shah . .	38
K. D. K. Vithanage c and b Mohammad Hafeez . . .	18	– (8) c Zulfiqar Babar b Yasir Shah . . .	1
M. D. K. Perera c Sarfraz Ahmed b Yasir Shah	15	– (4) b Yasir Shah	0
K. T. G. D. Prasad lbw b Zulfiqar Babar	0	– st Sarfraz Ahmed b Zulfiqar Babar . .	2
H. M. R. K. B. Herath not out	6	– c Mohammad Hafeez b Yasir Shah . .	1
A. N. P. R. Fernando c and b Yasir Shah	4	– not out	0
L-b 5, w 2, n-b 4	11	B 5, l-b 1, w 6, n-b 1	13

1/30 (1) 2/142 (3) 3/154 (4)   (109.3 overs) 300
4/189 (5) 5/226 (6) 6/261 (7)
7/277 (8) 8/288 (9) 9/291 (2) 10/300 (11)

1/18 (1) 2/63 (3)   (77.1 overs) 206
3/63 (4) 4/132 (5)
5/144 (6) 6/167 (2) 7/175 (8)
8/200 (9) 9/203 (10) 10/206 (7)

Junaid Khan 16–5–38–0; Wahab Riaz 26–3–74–3; Zulfiqar Babar 27–8–64–3; Yasir Shah 30.3–6–79–2; Mohammad Hafeez 10–0–40–2. *Second innings*—Wahab Riaz 16–4–46–2; Junaid Khan 7–1–23–0; Yasir Shah 30.1–6–76–7; Mohammad Hafeez 10–3–24–0; Zulfiqar Babar 14–4–31–1.

Pakistan

Mohammad Hafeez c Karunaratne b Prasad	2	– not out	46
Ahmed Shehzad lbw b Prasad	9	– not out	43
Azhar Ali lbw b Herath	8		
Younis Khan b Perera	47		
*Misbah-ul-Haq c Sangakkara b Fernando	20		
Asad Shafiq st Chandimal b Perera	131		
†Sarfraz Ahmed b Prasad	96		
Wahab Riaz b Perera	14		
Yasir Shah c Chandimal b Fernando	23		
Zulfiqar Babar c Vithanage b Perera	56		
Junaid Khan not out	6		
L-b 1, w 1, n-b 3	5	B 3	3

1/2 (1) 2/11 (2) 3/35 (3)   (113.1 overs) 417   (no wkt, 11.2 overs) 92
4/86 (4) 5/96 (5) 6/235 (7)
7/273 (8) 8/302 (9) 9/403 (10) 10/417 (6)

Prasad 24–4–91–3; Fernando 19–1–71–2; Herath 30–4–99–1; Perera 31.1–3–122–4; Mathews 6–1–12–0; Vithanage 3–0–21–0. *Second innings*—Herath 4.2–0–30–0; Prasad 2–1–10–0; Fernando 2–0–18–0; Perera 3–0–31–0.

Umpires: R. K. Illingworth and P. R. Reiffel.   Third umpire: C. B. Gaffaney.
Referee: B. C. Broad.

SRI LANKA v PAKISTAN

Second Test Match

At Colombo (PSO), June 25–29, 2015. Sri Lanka won by seven wickets. Toss: Pakistan. Test debut: P. V. D. Chameera.

Sri Lanka shook up their side after the setback at Galle, and two vibrant young bowlers set them on course for a series-squaring win. In the first innings, 22-year-old off-spinner Tharindu Kaushal gutted the lower order, claiming a maiden five-for. In the second, 23-year-old debutant Dushmantha Chameera rattled the Pakistanis with his pace.

In only his second Test, Kaushal gleaned considerable turn from the first-day pitch, and Pakistan's batsmen struggled to counter him. Mohammad Hafeez was Exhibit A: he prodded at Kaushal, offering a genial handshake, but the ball was leaning in for the kiss on both cheeks. It turned far more than he expected, and clipped the inner half of the bat before wriggling on to leg stump. Asad Shafiq had his inside edge beaten completely and was out leg-before. Sarfraz Ahmed did manage to get bat on the ball that dismissed him, only for the deflection to fly off his pads to first slip. Kaushal finished with five for 42 and, with Prasad having claimed three top-order wickets, Pakistan were skittled for 138.

Sri Lanka's response was slow but steady. Silva's 80 took almost five and a half hours, though he was lucky to escape a reviewed decision for a catch off Zulfiqar Babar at slip when 13: replays indicated no contact, but Paul Reiffel, the third umpire, omitted to check for lbw, and it was later shown that the ball was hitting the stumps. So Silva survived – and no one else was in any great rush either. Mathews made the only other half-century of the innings, using up 153 deliveries over his 77, as Sri Lanka amassed a lead of 177. Yasir Shah took another six wickets, but had to toil through more than 40 overs, with Wahab Riaz able to bowl only nine because his hand had been broken by Chameera when he batted.

Azhar Ali then outdid even Silva for patience, surviving eight and a half hours for 117 as he led a much stronger Pakistan response. He put on 120 for the second wicket with Ahmed Shehzad, and 73 for the third with Younis Khan, who was winning his 100th cap. But, after Younis departed for 40, Azhar had to watch wickets tumble at the other end.

Misbah-ul-Haq was the first victim of Prasad's canny use of the second new ball, shortly before lunch on the fourth day, trapped by one that seamed in. Prasad later had Sarfraz Ahmed caught behind, then yorked Yasir. The remainder of the lower order surrendered to Chameera, who nudged 150kph during the afternoon. Finally, running out of partners, Azhar was stumped after reaching his fifth Test century against Sri Lanka, and ninth in all. Pakistan's last six fell for 55, with Prasad adding four for 92 to his three first-innings scalps. Chandimal made six dismissals in the innings, equalling Amal Silva's national record, set against India at the SSC in 1985-86.

Sri Lanka needed only 153 for their 50th Test win on home soil, but could not start until the fifth morning because of rain. And, with more bad weather forecast for the afternoon, they looked to collect the runs quickly against an attack lacking Wahab. Vithanage, sent in to open, whipped his first delivery over midwicket, and hit three more fours, plus successive sixes off Zulfiqar Babar, in his 23-ball 34. Karunaratne stroked a smooth fifty and, though Sangakkara was out for a golden duck in his final innings against long-suffering Pakistan – he finished with 2,911 runs against them in 23 Tests at an average of 74 – Mathews and Thirimanne settled matters before the weather could make a difference.

Man of the Match: K. T. G. D. Prasad.

Close of play: first day, Sri Lanka 70-1 (Silva 21, Sangakkara 18); second day, Sri Lanka 304-9 (Herath 10, Chameera 0); third day, Pakistan 171-2 (Azhar Ali 64, Younis Khan 23); fourth day, Pakistan 329.

Pakistan

Mohammad Hafeez b Kaushal	42	– c Sangakkara b Mathews	8
Ahmed Shehzad c Sangakkara b Prasad	1	– c Chandimal b Prasad	69
Azhar Ali c Chandimal b Prasad	26	– st Chandimal b Herath	117
Younis Khan c Chandimal b Prasad	6	– c Chandimal b Mathews	40
*Misbah-ul-Haq run out	7	– lbw b Prasad	22
Asad Shafiq lbw b Kaushal	2	– c Chandimal b Chameera	27
†Sarfraz Ahmed c Mathews b Kaushal	14	– c Chandimal b Prasad	16
Wahab Riaz lbw b Kaushal	6	– (11) lbw b Chameera	6
Yasir Shah c Sangakkara b Kaushal	15	– (8) b Prasad	0
Zulfiqar Babar b Chameera	5	– (9) not out	7
Junaid Khan not out	2	– (10) c Chandimal b Chameera	3
L-b 4, w 3, n-b 7	14	B 2, l-b 2, w 5, n-b 5	14

1/5 (2) 2/51 (3) 3/74 (4) (42.5 overs) 138   1/9 (1) 2/129 (2) (118.2 overs) 329
4/89 (1) 5/95 (6) 6/96 (5)   3/202 (4) 4/234 (5)
7/113 (7) 8/117 (8) 9/124 (10) 10/138 (9)   5/274 (6) 6/301 (7) 7/303 (8)
  8/313 (3) 9/323 (10) 10/329 (11)

Prasad 13–2–43–3; Mathews 9–4–16–0; Chameera 10–0–33–1; Kaushal 10.5–0–42–5. *Second innings*—Prasad 29.3–3–92–4; Mathews 11–5–15–2; Herath 34–7–89–1; Chameera 18.5–1–53–3; Kaushal 25–3–76–0.

Sri Lanka

F. D. M. Karunaratne c Sarfraz Ahmed		– lbw b Yasir Shah	50
b Junaid Khan	28		
J. K. Silva run out	80		
K. C. Sangakkara c Asad Shafiq b Zulfiqar Babar	34	– c Azhar Ali b Yasir Shah	0
H. D. R. L. Thirimanne c Azhar Ali b Yasir Shah	7	– (5) not out	20
*A. D. Mathews lbw b Yasir Shah	77	– (4) not out	43
†L. D. Chandimal b Yasir Shah	1		
K. D. K. Vithanage b Yasir Shah	3	– (2) c Mohammad Hafeez	
		b Zulfiqar Babar	34
K. T. G. D. Prasad lbw b Mohammad Hafeez	35		
H. M. R. K. B. Herath not out	18		
P. H. T. Kaushal c Misbah-ul-Haq b Yasir Shah	18		
P. V. D. Chameera c Younis Khan b Yasir Shah	2		
B 6, l-b 4, w 1, n-b 1	12	L-b 6	6

1/47 (1) 2/98 (3) 3/119 (4)   (121.3 overs) 315   1/49 (2)   (3 wkts, 26.3 overs) 153
4/191 (2) 5/194 (6) 6/202 (7)   2/49 (3) 3/121 (1)
7/275 (8) 8/275 (5) 9/303 (10) 10/315 (11)

Wahab Riaz 9–2–19–0; Junaid Khan 29–5–89–1; Zulfiqar Babar 32–8–82–1; Yasir Shah
41.3–5–96–6; Mohammad Hafeez 10–2–19–1. *Second innings*—Junaid Khan 4–0–30–0;
Mohammad Hafeez 4–0–20–0; Zulfiqar Babar 8–0–42–1; Yasir Shah 10.3–0–55–2.

Umpires: R. K. Illingworth and S. Ravi. Third umpire: P. R. Reiffel.
Referee: B. C. Broad.

SRI LANKA v PAKISTAN

Third Test Match

At Pallekele, July 3–7, 2015. Pakistan won by seven wickets. Toss: Pakistan.

The odds were resolutely against Pakistan when they started their chase of 377 to snatch the series. They had never made so many to win a Test – only five higher targets had ever been reached – and were soon 13 for two. But, with Younis Khan buckling down for a superb unbeaten 171, they skated home, losing only one more wicket.

The ease of Pakistan's eventual victory belied the manner in which batsmen had struggled on a demanding deck. Seeing live grass on the first day, both sides included three seamers, with Sri Lanka contentiously dropping Rangana Herath, the cornerstone of their attack since the retirement of Muttiah Muralitharan in 2010. Dushmantha Chameera was also missing, after picking up a side strain during his impressive debut in Colombo.

Misbah-ul-Haq opted to bowl first, and was rewarded with the wicket of the in-form Silva. But Pakistan were held up by Karunaratne, who left judiciously and put away the bad ball. He added 91 for the second wicket with Tharanga – given the unenviable task of replacing Kumar Sangakkara at No. 3 – but it turned out to be the most substantial partnership of the innings.

Once again, Yasir Shah was the destroyer: after removing Tharanga, he dismissed Thirimanne and Mathews (both driving uppishly to the substitute, Babar Azam) as Sri Lanka declined to 137 for four. Karunaratne held firm for his second Test century, but the rest made only minor contributions, none more than 25 from Mubarak, recalled for his 11th Test at 34, after seven years out of the side.

Pakistan were batting early on the second morning, but they were also undone by swing and seam under still-heavy skies, and were soon 45 for three. Pradeep Fernando contributed several probing spells, finishing with three for 29, but Sarfraz Ahmed made a forthright unbeaten 78. He and Azhar Ali were the only batsmen to survive for more than an hour, and a total of 215 looked insufficient. Wahab Riaz's replacement, Imran Khan – on strike for the first time, in his fifth Test – made an eight-ball duck.

Sri Lanka led by 63, but again started poorly, slipping to 80 for four before being rescued by Mathews' fifth Test century. He added 81 with Mubarak, then 117 with the lively Chandimal, apparently putting his side firmly in charge. At last, Sri Lanka seemed to have worked out how to counter Yasir, who would claim only two wickets.

Last out, Mathews batted for 397 minutes, and reined himself in to hit only 12 fours and a six. It didn't seem to matter that the last five wickets tumbled for 35, all of them to Imran, who hustled to his maiden five-for in 33 balls. As Mathews admitted: "I thought we were sitting pretty with a lead of 376."

By the middle of the fourth day, with Ahmed Shehzad out for a duck and Azhar Ali for five, Sri Lanka were sitting even prettier. But now Younis joined Shan Masood, and booked in for the rest of the match. They saw off the new ball, then attacked the off-breaks of young Kaushal, Sri Lanka's only spinner. He proved easily rattled: as the batsmen came down the track, he served up too many full tosses, then over-compensated with long-hops. Masood and Younis were happy to take advantage. As the pitch lost its venom, both reached three figures not long before the fourth-day close. Masood, playing only because Mohammad Hafeez had flown to India to undergo tests on his bowling action, made his maiden century in his fifth Test, while Younis purred to his 30th, passing Don Bradman.

And, although Masood finally fell in the 11th over of the fifth day, dancing down to Kaushal once too often after a stand of 242, Younis found an equally determined partner in Misbah. It was remarkably smooth sailing: they continued to attack Kaushal and milk the seamers, and whisked Pakistan home without further loss, surpassing the 315 for nine they had made to beat Australia at Karachi in October 1994. Sri Lanka looked bedraggled, and Mathews clearly missed Herath's control.

Younis batted for more than seven hours and, though he was clearly tired towards the end, his sweeping remained sublime. This was the highest of his five fourth-innings Test hundreds – a world record – and the best by a Pakistani, beating 155 by Salim Malik in Colombo in 1996-97. Misbah adopted his more aggressive avatar towards the end, striking successive fours off Kaushal, then launching the first ball of the next over, from Mubarak, over long-on for six to complete a stunning series victory. "The key factor was to keep calm," he said. "We have lost a couple of Tests in Sri Lanka when we panicked." Pakistan's reward was third place in the ICC Test rankings, while Sri Lanka remained seventh.

Man of the Match: Younis Khan. *Man of the Series:* Yasir Shah.

Close of play: first day, Sri Lanka 272-8 (Kaushal 17, Lakmal 1); second day, Pakistan 209-9 (Sarfraz Ahmed 72, Imran Khan 0); third day, Sri Lanka 228-5 (Mathews 77, Chandimal 39); fourth day, Pakistan 230-2 (Shan Masood 114, Younis Khan 101).

Sri Lanka

F. D. M. Karunaratne st Sarfraz Ahmed b Azhar Ali	130	– b Rahat Ali 10
J. K. Silva c Sarfraz Ahmed b Rahat Ali	9	– c Misbah-ul-Haq b Ehsan Adil...... 3
W. U. Tharanga c Younis Khan b Yasir Shah	46	– c Azhar Ali b Yasir Shah 48
H. D. R. L. Thirimanne c sub (Babar Azam) b Yasir Shah.	11	– b Rahat Ali..................... 0
*A. D. Mathews c sub (Babar Azam) b Yasir Shah..	3	– c Sarfraz Ahmed b Imran Khan ..122
J. Mubarak st Sarfraz Ahmed b Yasir Shah	25	– c Azhar Ali b Yasir Shah 35
†L. D. Chandimal lbw b Rahat Ali...............	24	– lbw b Imran Khan 67
K. T. G. D. Prasad c Yasir Shah b Azhar Ali......	0	– c Sarfraz Ahmed b Imran Khan 0
P. H. T. Kaushal lbw b Rahat Ali...............	18	– c Sarfraz Ahmed b Imran Khan 8
R. A. S. Lakmal not out	6	– c Sarfraz Ahmed b Imran Khan 0
A. N. P. R. Fernando lbw b Yasir Shah	0	– not out 4
L-b 3, w 3	6	B 4, l-b 9, w 3.............. 16

1/15 (2) 2/106 (3) 3/133 (4)   (89.5 overs) 278
4/137 (5) 5/204 (6) 6/248 (1)
7/248 (8) 8/264 (7) 9/277 (9) 10/278 (11)

1/12 (1) 2/22 (2)   (95.4 overs) 313
3/35 (4) 4/80 (3)
5/161 (6) 6/278 (7) 7/278 (8)
8/290 (9) 9/306 (10) 10/313 (5)

Rahat Ali 21–4–74–3; Ehsan Adil 14–3–37–0; Imran Khan 16–3–51–0; Yasir Shah 31.5–4–78–5; Azhar Ali 7–0–35–2. *Second innings*—Rahat Ali 21–3–82–2; Ehsan Adil 17–4–66–1; Imran Khan 20.4–3–58–5; Yasir Shah 32–7–80–2; Azhar Ali 5–1–14–0.

Pakistan

Shan Masood lbw b Prasad	13	– st Chandimal b Kaushal	125
Ahmed Shehzad c Chandimal b Fernando	21	– b Lakmal	0
Azhar Ali c Karunaratne b Fernando	52	– c Chandimal b Prasad	5
Younis Khan run out	3	– not out	171
Asad Shafiq lbw b Prasad	15		
†Sarfraz Ahmed not out	78		
*Misbah-ul-Haq lbw b Fernando	6	– (5) not out	59
Ehsan Adil lbw b Kaushal	0		
Yasir Shah c Chandimal b Prasad	18		
Rahat Ali lbw b Kaushal	2		
Imran Khan, sen. b Kaushal	0		
L-b 4, w 1, n-b 2	7	B 5, l-b 10, w 2, n-b 5	22

1/32 (1) 2/40 (2) 3/45 (4)   (66 overs) 215   1/0 (2)   (3 wkts, 103.1 overs) 382
4/91 (5) 5/135 (3) 6/151 (7)   2/13 (3) 3/255 (1)
7/152 (8) 8/197 (9) 9/202 (10) 10/215 (11)

Prasad 19–1–78–3; Lakmal 14–1–64–0; Fernando 15–5–29–3; Mathews 4–1–3–0; Kaushal 14–1–37–3. *Second innings*—Prasad 20–2–65–1; Lakmal 19–5–48–1; Fernando 17–3–51–0; Mathews 13–2–34–0; Kaushal 31–1–153–1; Mubarak 3.1–0–16–0.

Umpires: I. J. Gould and P. R. Reiffel.   Third umpire: S. Ravi.
Referee: B. C. Broad.

SRI LANKA v PAKISTAN

First One-Day International

At Dambulla, July 11, 2015. Pakistan won by six wickets. Toss: Pakistan. One-day international debut: T. A. M. Siriwardene.

Mohammad Hafeez had just returned from the third test on his bowling action inside a year, but provided an immediate reminder of his worth as a batsman, setting Pakistan on track for a six-wicket win with his tenth century in one-day internationals. Earlier, as he awaited news from Chennai on the legality of his off-breaks, he had taken a career-best four wickets as Sri Lanka were restricted to 255. Dilshan was caught off what turned out to be a no-ball from Mohammad Irfan in the third over, then spooned the free hit to mid-on. He survived to make 38, but was one of several batsmen to waste a decent start: each of the top six reached 20, but only Chandimal passed 50. The debutant Milinda Siriwardene contributed a brisk 22 at the death. Pakistan's openers began rapidly before both fell in quick succession, then Hafeez took control. He had cracked Mathews through cover point to get under way, and maintained an even pace, tonking Prasanna's leg-spin for successive sixes in the 29th over. He put on 58 with Babar Azam, then 75 with Shoaib Malik (the only other man to score a hundred and take four wickets in the same ODI for Pakistan), before chipping a return catch. But Malik kicked off what would prove a fine series with an unbeaten half-century, completing the chase with a six.

Man of the Match: Mohammad Hafeez.

Sri Lanka

M. D. K. J. Perera c Mohammad Rizwan b Mohammad Hafeez.	26
T. M. Dilshan b Mohammad Hafeez	38
H. D. R. L. Thirimanne c Sarfraz Ahmed b Anwar Ali.	23
W. U. Tharanga st Sarfraz Ahmed b Mohammad Hafeez.	20
*A. D. Mathews c Babar Azam b Yasir Shah	38
†L. D. Chandimal not out	65
N. L. T. C. Perera c Mohammad Rizwan b Mohammad Hafeez.	1
T. A. M. Siriwardene c Mohammad Rizwan b Rahat Ali.	22
S. Prasanna c Mohammad Hafeez b Rahat Ali.	0
S. L. Malinga not out.	4
B 4, l-b 7, w 6, n-b 1	18

(8 wkts, 50 overs) 255

1/44 (1) 2/82 (3) 3/111 (4) 4/118 (2) 5/200 (5) 6/204 (7) 7/244 (8) 8/245 (9)

10 overs: 48-1

R. A. S. Lakmal did not bat.

Mohammad Irfan 10–0–41–0; Rahat Ali 8–0–44–2; Anwar Ali 7–0–38–1; Mohammad Hafeez 10–1–41–4; Yasir Shah 10–0–46–1; Shoaib Malik 5–0–34–0.

Pakistan

*Azhar Ali c Chandimal b Mathews	21
Ahmed Shehzad c Chandimal b Lakmal	29
Mohammad Hafeez c and b N. L. T. C. Perera.	103
Babar Azam lbw b Dilshan	25
Shoaib Malik not out.	55
Mohammad Rizwan not out	20
L-b 1, w 5	6

(4 wkts, 45.2 overs) 259

1/47 (1) 2/65 (2) 3/123 (4) 4/198 (3)

10 overs: 51-1

†Sarfraz Ahmed, Yasir Shah, Rahat Ali, Anwar Ali and Mohammad Irfan did not bat.

Malinga 8–0–56–0; Lakmal 5–1–21–1; N. L. T. C. Perera 8–0–32–1; Mathews 5–0–22–1; Prasanna 9–0–72–0; Dilshan 8.2–0–45–1; Siriwardene 2–0–10–0.

Umpires: I. J. Gould and R. E. J. Martinesz. Third umpire: R. J. Tucker.
Referee: J. Srinath.

SRI LANKA v PAKISTAN

Second One-Day International

At Pallekele, July 15, 2015 (day/night). Sri Lanka won by two wickets. Toss: Pakistan. One-day international debut: S. S. Pathirana.

Kusal Perera's manic 68 from 25 balls gave his side the impetus needed to attack a big target: only one higher total had been successfully chased in Sri Lanka, when Pakistan's 288 was overhauled at Dambulla in August 2009. Perera has often been compared to Sanath Jayasuriya, and his assault here matched Jayasuriya's national record for the fastest fifty, which he reached in just 17 deliveries. He edged his second ball over the slips for four, then in the second over walloped three fours and a six off Rahat Ali, before cracking Mohammad Irfan for three fours in successive legal deliveries. Azhar Ali turned to spin, but Perera was severe on Mohammad Hafeez as well, collecting consecutive fours to hurtle past 50. When he finally holed out in the ninth over, having clobbered 13 fours and two sixes, Sri Lanka already had 92 on the board. Rahat slowed things down with three wickets, but Chandimal took control of the final push. He put on 52 with Sachith Pathirana – another debutant, who had earlier taken two expensive wickets – but the late loss of Tissara Perera made for a tense finish. Azhar Ali had underpinned Pakistan's total, which was swelled by Mohammad Rizwan's 52 from 38 balls.

Man of the Match: M. D. K. J. Perera.

Pakistan

*Azhar Ali c Siriwardene b Dilshan	79	Yasir Shah c Siriwardene b Malinga	1	
Ahmed Shehzad b Pathirana	30	Rahat Ali not out	0	
Mohammad Hafeez c Mathews b Pathirana	9	B 4, l-b 3, w 9, n-b 1	17	
Babar Azam b Siriwardene	12			
Shoaib Malik b Mathews	51	1/59 (2) 2/75 (3)	(8 wkts, 50 overs)	287
Mohammad Rizwan lbw b Fernando	52	3/96 (4) 4/179 (5)		
†Sarfraz Ahmed lbw b Malinga	7	5/197 (1) 6/217 (7)		
Anwar Ali not out	29	7/273 (6) 8/278 (9)	10 overs: 44-0	

Mohammad Irfan did not bat.

Mathews 10–2–36–1; Fernando 8–1–42–1; N. L. T. C. Perera 2–0–15–0; Malinga 10–0–64–2;
Pathirana 9–0–70–2; Siriwardene 5–0–22–1; Dilshan 6–0–31–1.

Sri Lanka

M. D. K. J. Perera c Yasir Shah b Mohammad Irfan	68	S. S. Pathirana st Sarfraz Ahmed b Mohammad Hafeez	33	
T. M. Dilshan b Rahat Ali	47	N. L. T. C. Perera c Shoaib Malik b Anwar Ali	15	
W. U. Tharanga b Rahat Ali	28	S. L. Malinga not out	2	
*A. D. Mathews run out	8	L-b 2, w 7	9	
H. D. R. L. Thirimanne c Anwar Ali b Rahat Ali	4			
†L. D. Chandimal not out	48	1/92 (1) 2/140 (3)	(8 wkts, 48.1 overs)	288
T. A. M. Siriwardene lbw b Mohammad Hafeez	26	3/155 (2) 4/157 (4) 5/159 (5)		
		6/196 (7) 7/248 (8) 8/285 (9)	10 overs: 98-1	

A. N. P. R. Fernando did not bat.

Mohammad Irfan 10–0–61–1; Rahat Ali 9.1–0–73–3; Mohammad Hafeez 10–0–61–2; Anwar Ali
7–0–33–1; Yasir Shah 10–0–51–0; Shoaib Malik 2–0–7–0.

Umpires: R. E. J. Martinesz and R. J. Tucker.   Third umpire: I. J. Gould.
Referee: J. Srinath.

SRI LANKA v PAKISTAN

Third One-Day International

At Colombo (RPS), July 19, 2015 (day/night). Pakistan won by 135 runs. Toss: Pakistan. One-day
international debut: Imad Wasim.

It was not a proud evening for Sri Lanka. Pummelled by Pakistan, they also had to endure an
outbreak of violence among the crowd, which forced a half-hour delay. Rocks were thrown inside
the south-eastern stand and, when some of the offenders – thought to be Sri Lankan Muslims cheering
for Pakistan – were ejected from the ground, more projectiles came in from outside the stadium,
through the back of the same open stand. One big stone reached the field, and play was suspended
until the situation was brought under control. Pakistan's victory was set up by a commanding batting
performance, featuring a lively opening stand, brisk fifties from Mohammad Hafeez and Sarfraz
Ahmed, and a late sprint that lifted them well past 300. Sarfraz pilfered singles and rarely allowed a
poor ball to go unpunished, ending with 77 from 74 deliveries, before he was run out in a mix-up
with Shoaib Malik, who then piled on 59 with Mohammad Rizwan in less than six overs. Sri Lanka
were never on terms after losing Dilshan and Kusal Perera in successive overs from Anwar Ali, and
subsided for 181. Yasir Shah, their nemesis in the Tests, claimed a one-day best of four for 29.

Man of the Match: Sarfraz Ahmed.

Pakistan

Ahmed Shehzad c Pathirana b Malinga. . . .	44	Mohammad Rizwan not out	35
*Azhar Ali run out.	49		
Mohammad Hafeez c M. D. K. J. Perera		B 4, l-b 1, w 8, n-b 2	15
b Pathirana .	54		
†Sarfraz Ahmed run out	77	1/93 (1) 2/124 (2) (4 wkts, 50 overs)	316
Shoaib Malik not out.	42	3/196 (3) 4/257 (4) 10 overs: 55-0	

Imad Wasim, Anwar Ali, Yasir Shah, Rahat Ali and Mohammad Irfan did not bat.

Mathews 8–0–52–0; Fernando 9–0–47–0; Malinga 10–0–80–1; Pathirana 10–0–49–1; N. L. T. C. Perera 10–0–63–0; Dilshan 3–0–20–0.

Sri Lanka

M. D. K. J. Perera c Sarfraz Ahmed		T. A. M. Siriwardene run out	2
b Anwar Ali .	20	S. S. Pathirana c Anwar Ali b Yasir Shah . .	19
T. M. Dilshan c Azhar Ali b Anwar Ali . . .	14	S. L. Malinga b Imad Wasim.	6
H. D. R. L. Thirimanne c Sarfraz Ahmed		A. N. P. R. Fernando not out	3
b Rahat Ali .	56	B 4, l-b 1, w 5, n-b 1	11
W. U. Tharanga st Sarfraz Ahmed			
b Yasir Shah	16	1/33 (2) 2/42 (1) (41.1 overs)	181
*A. D. Mathews c Shoaib Malik b Yasir Shah	4	3/82 (4) 4/93 (5) 5/130 (6)	
†L. D. Chandimal b Imad Wasim	18	6/142 (3) 7/144 (8) 8/170 (7)	
N. L. T. C. Perera c Anwar Ali b Yasir Shah	12	9/172 (9) 10/181 (10) 10 overs: 52-2	

Mohammad Irfan 7–1–32–0; Anwar Ali 5–0–24–2; Rahat Ali 7–0–35–1; Shoaib Malik 5–0–28–0; Yasir Shah 10–1–29–4; Imad Wasim 7.1–0–28–2.

Umpires: I. J. Gould and R. R. Wimalasiri.   Third umpire: R. J. Tucker.
Referee: J. Srinath.

SRI LANKA v PAKISTAN

Fourth One-Day International

At Colombo (RPS), July 22, 2015 (day/night). Pakistan won by seven wickets. Toss: Sri Lanka.

Pakistan clinched the series, their batsmen encountering few obstacles as they hustled to victory with more than nine overs to spare. Their bowlers had started well, too: Mohammad Irfan dismissed the dangerous Kusal Perera for a duck, although that was followed by a stand of 109 between Dilshan and Thirimanne. But wickets went down regularly after that, as six successive batsmen made between 12 and 20. Pakistan never looked back after a rapid opening stand of 75; Malinga's first three overs cost 20, and slow left-armer Pathirana went for 24 in his first two. Ahmed Shehzad motored to 95 from 90 balls, and put on 115 with Mohammad Hafeez – banned two days before the third ODI from bowling for a year after ICC experts deemed his action illegal.

Man of the Match: Ahmed Shehzad.

Sri Lanka

M. D. K. J. Perera c Imad Wasim		S. S. Pathirana run out.	14
b Mohammad Irfan .	0	S. L. Malinga c Mohammad Rizwan	
T. M. Dilshan b Imad Wasim	50	b Mohammad Irfan .	17
H. D. R. L. Thirimanne c Ahmed Shehzad		R. A. S. Lakmal not out.	1
b Yasir Shah .	90	A. N. P. R. Fernando not out	0
*A. D. Mathews c Yasir Shah b Rahat Ali . .	12		
†L. D. Chandimal c Yasir Shah		B 4, l-b 1, w 8, n-b 2	15
b Mohammad Irfan .	20	1/0 (1) 2/109 (2) (9 wkts, 50 overs)	256
S. M. A. Priyanjan c Mohammad Hafeez		3/143 (4) 4/170 (5)	
b Anwar Ali .	18	5/186 (3) 6/215 (7) 7/228 (6)	
T. A. M. Siriwardene		8/243 (8) 9/252 (9)	
c Mohammad Rizwan b Anwar Ali .	19	10 overs: 48-1	

Mohammad Irfan 10–0–50–3; Anwar Ali 7–0–41–2; Rahat Ali 7–0–39–1; Yasir Shah 10–0–50–1; Azhar Ali 2–0–13–0; Imad Wasim 10–0–43–1; Shoaib Malik 4–0–15–0.

Pakistan

*Azhar Ali c sub (S. M. S. M. Senanayake)		Shoaib Malik not out	29
b Malinga .	33	B 4, w 9	13
Ahmed Shehzad c Perera b Lakmal	95		
Mohammad Hafeez c Chandimal		1/75 (1) 2/190 (2) (3 wkts, 40.5 overs) 257	
b Siriwardene .	70	3/213 (3)	
†Sarfraz Ahmed not out	17	10 overs: 69-0	

Mohammad Rizwan, Imad Wasim, Anwar Ali, Yasir Shah, Rahat Ali and Mohammad Irfan did not bat.

Malinga 9–2–46–1; Lakmal 8–0–50–1; Pathirana 10–0–81–0; Fernando 2.2–0–9–0; Mathews 2.4–0–9–0; Siriwardene 5.5–0–28–1; Dilshan 3–0–30–0.

Umpires: R. J. Tucker and R. R. Wimalasiri.   Third umpire: I. J. Gould.
Referee: J. Srinath.

SRI LANKA v PAKISTAN

Fifth One-Day International

At Hambantota, July 26, 2015 (day/night). Sri Lanka won by 165 runs. Toss: Sri Lanka.

Kusal Perera hammered 116, his second one-day international century, at better than a run a ball to set up a score that even Pakistan's in-form batsmen couldn't threaten, despite a placid pitch. Perera put on 164 with Dilshan, who – aged 38 and in his 319th one-day international – became the 11th to score 10,000 runs. He was the fourth from Sri Lanka, after Kumar Sangakkara (14,234), Sanath Jayasuriya (13,430) and Mahela Jayawardene (12,650). Mathews and Siriwardene weighed in at the end, clouting five sixes between them as they added 114 in the last nine overs. Sri Lanka's 368 was their second-highest at home, behind 398 for five against Kenya in the 1996 World Cup; they had only once made more against a Test-playing nation anywhere (411 for eight against India at Rajkot in 2009-10, when they still lost). Mohammad Hafeez was the most fluent of Pakistan's batsmen, easing boundaries square of the wicket, and stepping out to send Senanayake over long-off. But it wasn't enough; the run-rate only briefly touched six, and was regularly set back by wickets, three of them to Senanayake, in his first match of the series.

Man of the Match: M. D. K. J. Perera. Man of the Series: Mohammad Hafeez.

Sri Lanka

M. D. K. J. Perera run out	116	*A. D. Mathews not out	70
T. M. Dilshan run out	62	T. A. M. Siriwardene not out	52
H. D. R. L. Thirimanne		L-b 6, w 3	9
c Mohammad Rizwan b Rahat Ali .	30		
†L. D. Chandimal c Sarfraz Ahmed		1/164 (2) 2/212 (1) (4 wkts, 50 overs) 368	
b Rahat Ali .	29	3/219 (3) 4/254 (4) 10 overs: 64-0	

S. M. A. Priyanjan, N. L. T. C. Perera, S. M. S. M. Senanayake, R. A. S. Lakmal and P. L. S. Gamage did not bat.

Mohammad Irfan 10–1–73–0; Anwar Ali 9–0–71–0; Rahat Ali 10–0–74–2; Imad Wasim 3–0–27–0; Shoaib Malik 10–0–44–0; Yasir Shah 8–0–73–0.

Pakistan

*Azhar Ali run out		35
Ahmed Shehzad st Chandimal		
b Senanayake		18
Mohammad Hafeez lbw b Mathews		37
†Sarfraz Ahmed run out		27
Shoaib Malik c Thirimanne		
b N. L. T. C. Perera		11
Mohammad Rizwan c Chandimal		
b N. L. T. C. Perera		29
Imad Wasim c and b Senanayake		15

Anwar Ali c N. L. T. C. Perera b Gamage		11
Yasir Shah c N. L. T. C. Perera b Senanayake		9
Rahat Ali c Senanayake b Siriwardene		0
Mohammad Irfan not out		4
L-b 1, w 2, n-b 4		7

1/51 (2) 2/71 (1)   (37.2 overs) 203
3/116 (3) 4/121 (4) 5/140 (5)
6/170 (7) 7/178 (6) 8/197 (9)
9/197 (8) 10/203 (10)   10 overs: 52-1

Gamage 10–0–62–1; Lakmal 6–0–35–0; Senanayake 8–1–39–3; N. L. T. C. Perera 8–0–38–2; Mathews 3–0–9–1; Siriwardene 2.2–0–19–1.

Umpires: I. J. Gould and R. E. J. Martinesz. Third umpire: R. J. Tucker.
Referee: J. Srinath.

SRI LANKA v PAKISTAN

First Twenty20 International

At Colombo (RPS), July 30, 2015 (floodlit). Pakistan won by 29 runs. Toss: Pakistan. Twenty20 international debuts: D. M. de Silva, B. Fernando, T. A. M. Siriwardene, J. D. F. Vandersay.

Ahmed Shehzad set the platform before his ramp flew straight to fine leg, then Shoaib Malik and Umar Akmal blasted 81 from 45 balls, taking Malinga for 37 from three overs. These three, who all scored 46, lifted Pakistan to a total which the inexperienced Sri Lankan line-up never looked like reaching. They slipped to 19 for three in the fourth over, and could not recover, despite sprightly knocks from Siriwardene, who made a promising 35 from 18 deliveries, and Kapugedera. Sohail Tanvir was the prime destroyer with the new ball, finishing with three for 29. One of Sri Lanka's four debutants, leg-spinner Jeffrey Vandersay, went for just 25 from his four overs.

Man of the Match: Sohail Tanvir.

Pakistan

		B	4/6
1 Mukhtar Ahmed c 10 b 5		2	8 0
2 Ahmed Shehzad c 11 b 8		46	38 4
3 Mohammad Hafeez c 4 b 8		17	14 2
4 Shoaib Malik not out		46	31 4
5 Umar Akmal lbw b 11		46	24 3/3
6 *Shahid Afridi b 9		8	4 0/1
7 Anwar Ali not out		0	1 0
L-b 3, w 7		10	

6 overs: 42-1   (20 overs) 175-5

1/10 2/52 3/83 4/164 5/175

8 †Mohammad Rizwan, 9 Imad Wasim, 10 Sohail Tanvir and 11 Mohammad Irfan did not bat.

Fernando 4–0–38–1 (9); Mathews 4–0–33–1 (8); Malinga 4–0–46–1 (7); Vandersay 4–0–25–0 (4); N. L. T. C. Perera 4–0–30–2 (7).

Sri Lanka

		B	4/6
1 †M. D. K. J. Perera c 6 b 7		4	3 0
2 T. M. Dilshan c 8 b 10		6	5 1
3 D. M. de Silva c 2 b 4		31	32 1
4 K. D. K. Vithanage b 10		1	4 0
5 A. D. Mathews b 9		23	26 1
6 T. A. M. Siriwardene c 7 b 10		35	18 3/2
7 C. K. Kapugedera not out		31	16 1/3
8 N. L. T. C. Perera c 8 b 7		2	4 0
9 B. Fernando not out		8	12 1
B 1, l-b 3, w 1		5	

6 overs: 35-3   (20 overs) 146-7

1/4 2/13 3/19 4/55 5/92 6/116 7/121

10 J. D. F. Vandersay and 11 *S. L. Malinga did not bat.

Anwar Ali 4–0–27–2 (10); Sohail Tanvir 4–0–29–3 (9); Mohammad Irfan 4–0–25–0 (12); Shahid Afridi 4–0–31–0 (4); Imad Wasim 3–0–21–1 (7); Shoaib Malik 1–0–9–1 (3).

Umpires: R. E. J. Martinesz and R. S. A. Palliyaguruge. Third umpire: R. R. Wimalasiri.
Referee: J. Srinath.

SRI LANKA v PAKISTAN

Second Twenty20 International

At Colombo (RPS), August 1, 2015 (floodlit). Pakistan won by one wicket. Toss: Sri Lanka. Twenty20 international debuts: D. S. N. F. G. Jayasuriya, M. D. Shanaka.

Sri Lanka looked set to square the series when Pakistan dipped to 107 for seven in the 15th over – itself something of a recovery from 40 for five, as Shahid Afridi belted four sixes in his 45. But the inexperience of a home side with six men playing their first or second 20-over international proved crucial: Anwar Ali, down at No. 9, brought the chase to life with two sixes and a four from the debutant off-spinner Shehan Jayasuriya in the 17th over, before treating Tissara Perera and Malinga with similar disdain to take Pakistan to within eight of victory. Malinga did then dismiss Anwar, for 46 from 17 balls, but Imad Wasim had enough in the tank to get them over the line. His six off Binura Fernando sealed only the third one-wicket win in T20 internationals, after England's over Australia at Adelaide in 2010-11, and the Netherlands against Bangladesh in The Hague in 2012. The victory triggered great delight among the tourists, who had now won all three series. Earlier, Kapugedera had also walloped four sixes to propel Sri Lanka to an imposing total.

Man of the Match: Anwar Ali. Man of the Series: Shoaib Malik.

Sri Lanka

		B	4/6
1 †M. D. K. J. Perera *b 4*	. . . . . .	19	14 3
2 T. M. Dilshan *c 3 b 9*	. . . .	10	8 2
3 D. S. N. F. G. Jayasuriya *c 8 b 10*	40	32 3/2
4 D. M. de Silva *b 7*	. . . .	14	15 1
5 N. L. T. C. Perera *st 6 b 4*	. . . . .	1	3 0
6 T. A. M. Siriwardene *c 1 b 11*	. .	23	19 1/1
7 C. K. Kapugedera *not out*	. . . . .	48	25 2/4
8 M. D. Shanaka *run out*	. . . .	7	4 1
L-b 3, w 7		10	

6 overs: 48-2   (20 overs) 172-7

1/24 2/32 3/61 4/64 5/90 6/145 7/172

9 B. Fernando, 10 J. D. F. Vandersay and 11 *S. L. Malinga did not bat.

Anwar Ali 4–0–40–1 (7); Sohail Tanvir 4–0–44–1 (8); Shoaib Malik 3–0–16–2 (10); Mohammad Irfan 4–0–31–1 (8); Shahid Afridi 4–0–30–1 (9); Imad Wasim 1–0–8–0 (3).

Pakistan

		B	4/6
1 Mukhtar Ahmed *c 7 b 9*	. . . . . .	4	7 0
2 Ahmed Shehzad *b 9*	. . . .	7	8 1
3 Mohammad Hafeez *run out*	. . . .	11	12 1
4 Shoaib Malik *st 1 b 6*	. . . .	8	12 0
5 Umar Akmal *run out*	. . . .	4	4 0
6 †Mohammad Rizwan *b 5*	. . . . . .	17	18 1
7 *Shahid Afridi *b 3*	. . . .	45	22 1/4
8 Imad Wasim *not out*	. . . .	24	14 2/1
9 Anwar Ali *c 1 b 11*	. . . .	46	17 3/4
10 Sohail Tanvir *run out*	. . . .	1	1 0
11 Mohammad Irfan *not out*	. . . .	1	1 0
L-b 1, w 5		6	

6 overs: 34-3   (19.2 overs) 174-9

1/11 2/16 3/33 4/40 5/40 6/101 7/107 8/165 9/167

Fernando 3.2–0–33–2 (6); Jayasuriya 4–0–37–1 (7); N. L. T. C. Perera 4–0–27–1 (12); Siriwardene 2–0–17–1 (3); Vandersay 2–0–19–0 (3); Malinga 4–0–40–1 (4).

Umpires: R. S. A. Palliyaguruge and R. R. Wimalasiri.   Third umpire: R. E. J. Martinesz.
Referee: J. Srinath.

SRI LANKA v INDIA IN 2015-16

R. KAUSHIK

Test matches (3): Sri Lanka 1, India 2

The first Test series between these teams for five years – either side of 24 one-day internationals – found both in a state of renewal. Virat Kohli could finally get his teeth into a full assignment as Test captain, having previously led India on one-off occasions at Adelaide, Sydney and Fatullah. And the future under Kohli looked compelling: after being tripped up in an epic opening match at Galle, India pulled off a pair of wins in Colombo to claim their first Test series victory in Sri Lanka since 1993-94, and their first overseas since 2011, in the West Indies. They also became the first Indian side to win an away series having fallen 1–0 behind.

Sri Lanka, meanwhile, had to go through the process of bidding farewell to the most successful batsman in their history, when Kumar Sangakkara retired from international cricket after the Second Test. He went into the series with a phenomenal home record, and motivated by the possibility of equalling Don Bradman's 12 Test double-centuries. But Sangakkara was flummoxed by Ravichandran Ashwin, unsure whether to come forward or go back to his stock off-break, and was dismissed by him in all four innings for a total of 95. As part of the deal struck with Sri Lanka Cricket, he missed the last match in order to help Surrey for the rest of the English season, and finished a Test series without a half-century for only the third time in almost a decade.

Politically, the series was something of a sop from the BCCI to old boardroom allies. The previous October, an internal pay dispute had prompted West Indies to abandon their tour of India, with a one-day international, a Twenty20 and three Tests left to play; Sri Lanka swiftly stepped in, sending their players over for five fill-in ODIs. In return, the BCCI agreed to switch the venue for these three Tests from India to Sri Lanka, ensuring SLC some much-needed revenue.

However, the matches attracted less than expected. Where series involving India had previously earned nearly $2m a Test, Sony now bought the rights for all three matches for just $3.25m, after a bid of $1.4m from Ten Sports, SLC's long-standing broadcast partners, was turned down. The First Test was brought forward to avoid a clash with the country's general elections, and the Third moved to Colombo from Pallekele, which was deemed vulnerable to August rain.

The cricket itself wasn't always of the highest order, but there was no disputing the stronger side. India were beset by injuries – Shikhar Dhawan, Murali Vijay and Wriddhaman Saha all returned home – yet overcame the odds under Kohli, for whom aggression is the default state. India rejigged their top order throughout, picking a different opening combination in each Test, yet five batsmen struck a century.

Kohli's declared faith in a five-man attack also paid off with the full 60 wickets. Ashwin led the way with 21 at 18, complemented by 15 at 15 from leg-spinner Amit Mishra on his return to Test cricket after four years. Ishant Sharma took eight on a helpful surface in the decisive match at the Sinhalese Sports Club.

Sri Lanka were badly let down by their batting. Too often Angelo Mathews waged a solitary battle, making both his hundreds in losing causes. All but 67 of Dinesh Chandimal's tally of 288 came at Galle, where his magical unbeaten 162 in the second innings helped Sri Lanka turn a 192-run deficit into a 63-run victory. Dammika Prasad bowled tirelessly and ferociously, but India worked out a way to keep Rangana Herath at bay – at least after the First Test, when he took a phenomenal seven for 48 to crush their hopes of chasing 176.

India–Sri Lanka encounters had often been characterised by bonhomie, but there was little love lost this time. Sharma, eager to have a word with batsmen he had just dismissed, was slapped with a one-Test ban for three breaches of the ICC Code of Conduct; Chandimal was suspended for a one-day international after making physical contact with him in the Third Test; and several others were fined. The absence of the DRS played its part in tempers fraying, and the unrelenting schedule cannot have helped.

INDIAN TOURING PARTY

*V. Kohli, V. R. Aaron, R. Ashwin, Bhuvneshwar Kumar, S. T. R. Binny, S. Dhawan, Harbhajan Singh, A. Mishra, K. K. Nair, N. V. Ojha, C. A. Pujara, A. M. Rahane, K. L. Rahul, W. P. Saha, I. Sharma, R. G. Sharma, M. Vijay, U. T. Yadav. *Coach:* R. J. Shastri.

Dhawan fractured his right hand during the First Test, and flew home. Binny was brought into the squad for the last two Tests. Vijay and Saha were ruled out of the Third with hamstring injuries, and replaced by Nair and Ojha.

TEST MATCH AVERAGES

SRI LANKA – BATTING AND FIELDING

	T	I	NO	R	HS	100	50	Avge	Ct/St
L. D. Chandimal	3	6	1	288	162*	1	1	57.60	5/1
A. D. Mathews	3	6	0	339	110	2	1	56.50	3
†K. C. Sangakkara	2	4	0	95	40	0	0	23.75	0
†H. D. R. L. Thirimanne	3	6	0	142	62	0	1	23.66	1
†H. M. R. K. B. Herath	3	6	1	89	49	0	0	17.80	1
†J. Mubarak	2	4	0	71	49	0	0	17.75	2
J. K. Silva	3	6	0	87	51	0	1	14.50	3
†F. D. M. Karunaratne	3	6	0	67	46	0	0	11.16	3
P. H. T. Kaushal	3	6	1	35	16	0	0	7.00	1
K. T. G. D. Prasad	3	6	0	41	27	0	0	6.83	1
A. N. P. R. Fernando	2	4	2	5	3	0	0	2.50	1

Played in one Test: P. V. D. Chameera 0*, 4 (1 ct); †M. D. K. J. Perera 55, 70 (3 ct, 1 st); †W. U. Tharanga 4, 0 (4 ct).

BOWLING

	Style	O	M	R	W	BB	5I	Avge
A. D. Mathews	RFM	41	18	75	4	2-24	0	18.75
K. T. G. D. Prasad	RFM	110	20	354	15	4-43	0	23.60
A. N. P. R. Fernando	RFM	71	13	220	8	4-62	0	27.50
H. M. R. K. B. Herath	SLA	157.1	20	465	15	7-48	1	31.00
P. H. T. Kaushal	OB	135.3	10	496	13	5-134	1	38.15

Also bowled: P. V. D. Chameera (RFM) 34–2–135–2.

INDIA – BATTING AND FIELDING

	T	I	NO	R	HS	100	50	Avge	Ct/St
W. P. Saha	2	4	1	131	60	0	2	43.66	2/1
V. Kohli	3	6	0	233	103	1	1	38.83	3
R. G. Sharma	3	6	0	202	79	0	2	33.66	3
A. M. Rahane	3	6	0	178	126	1	0	29.66	10
A. Mishra	3	6	0	157	59	0	1	26.16	1
K. L. Rahul	3	6	0	126	108	1	0	21.00	9
S. T. R. Binny	2	4	0	76	49	0	0	19.00	2
R. Ashwin	3	6	0	94	58	0	1	15.66	1
I. Sharma	3	5	2	23	10	0	0	7.66	0
U. T. Yadav	2	4	2	14	4*	0	0	7.00	0

Played in one Test: V. R. Aaron 4, 1*; †S. Dhawan 134, 28 (1 ct); Harbhajan Singh 14, 1; N. V. Ojha 21, 35 (4 ct, 1 st); C. A. Pujara 145*, 0 (1 ct); M. Vijay 0, 82 (2 ct).

BOWLING

	Style	O	M	R	W	BB	5I	Avge
A. Mishra	LBG	79	11	225	15	4-43	0	15.00
R. Ashwin	OB	115	20	380	21	6-46	2	18.09
I. Sharma	RFM	90	15	302	13	5-54	1	23.23
S. T. R. Binny	RFM	40	10	117	3	2-24	0	39.00
U. T. Yadav	RF	54	11	214	5	2-65	0	42.80

Also bowled: V. R. Aaron (RF) 18–0–107–2; Harbhajan Singh (OB) 25–1–90–1.

At Colombo (RPS), August 6–8, 2015 (not first-class). **Drawn. Indians 351** (88.1 overs) (S. Dhawan 62, A. M. Rahane 109; C. A. K. Rajitha 5-68) **and 180** (58.4 overs); ‡**Sri Lanka Board President's XI 121** (31 overs) (I. Sharma 5-23) **and 200-6** (54 overs) (J. K. Silva 83*, W. U. Tharanga 52; R. Ashwin 3-38). *Each side chose from 15 players. Against a young attack, Lokesh Rahul (43) and Shikhar Dhawan began with a century stand, before Ajinkya Rahane strengthened India's position with 109 from 127 balls. An experienced home batting unit staggered to 10-5 against Ishant Sharma, swinging the Kookaburra prodigiously. The Indians were far enough ahead after two days for Cheteshwar Pujara (31) and Rahul (47) to retire out overnight; the President's XI were set 411, and Test opener Kaushal Silva negotiated Ravichandran Ashwin until stumps.*

SRI LANKA v INDIA

First Test Match

At Galle, August 12–15, 2015. Sri Lanka won by 63 runs. Toss: Sri Lanka.

Years from now, when Virat Kohli finally puts his feet up, he will wonder how this one got away. The numbers spoke of Indian dominance. They bowled Sri Lanka out on the first day for 183, and boasted two of the game's three centuries, a bowler with match figures of ten for 160 and a fielder who broke the record for most catches in a Test. And yet they were soundly beaten with nearly a day and a half to spare. There could be no better advert for the capriciousness of Test cricket. Even accounting for Chandimal's wondrous 162, this will go down as a match that India lost, rather than Sri Lanka won.

The Indians had ticked all the boxes over the first two days, despite Mathews winning what seemed an important toss. With Ashwin at the top of his game, making the most of unexpectedly inconsistent bounce, Sri Lanka were sent into a tailspin, stemmed only by a sparkling partnership of 79 for the sixth wicket between Mathews and Chandimal. They were bundled out inside 50 overs, with Ashwin fetching six for 46, ably supported by Mishra in his first Test since The Oval in 2011.

Sri Lanka's spinners couldn't find the same purchase. India were missing their regular opener Murali Vijay, laid low with a hamstring injury, and lost Rahul and Rohit Sharma cheaply. But Dhawan and Kohli first defied the bowling, then dictated terms in a third-wicket stand of 227. Kohli was imposing as he made his fourth hundred in four Tests as

ABOUT-TURN

Biggest first-innings deficit before going on to win:

291	Australia (256) beat Sri Lanka (547-8 dec) by 16 runs at Colombo (SSC)	1992-93
274	India (171) beat Australia (445) by 171 runs at Kolkata	2000-01
261	England (325) beat Australia (586) by ten runs at Sydney	1894-95
236	Australia (75) beat South Africa (311) by five wickets at Durban	1949-50
227	England (174) beat Australia (401-9 dec) by 18 runs at Leeds	1981
206	Australia (127) beat Pakistan (333) by 36 runs at Sydney	2009-10
192	**Sri Lanka (183) beat India (375) by 63 runs at Galle**	**2015-16**

At Centurion in 1999-2000, England declared their first innings on 0-0 and South Africa (248-8 dec) forfeited their second to set up a run-chase. At The Oval in 2006, England trailed Pakistan by 331 runs on first innings; they were awarded victory after Pakistan refused to take the field.

captain, while Dhawan put mind over matter, battling through an injury to his right hand sustained when dropping Silva. An X-ray later revealed two hairline cracks, forcing him out of the series. Saha, who had earlier fluffed the simplest of catches off Chandimal, made amends with his maiden Test fifty as India opened a lead of 192; off-spinner Tharindu Kaushal's five wickets were no more than a footnote, and he served up a surfeit of full tosses.

When Ashwin and Mishra removed Sri Lanka's openers for ducks in the four overs before stumps, a three-day finish loomed. That feeling was reinforced next morning, when they lurched to 95 for five, with Sangakkara flashing a drive to slip. Then Thirimanne joined Chandimal, and the game turned on its head. Both batsmen benefited early in their innings from umpiring errors on close catches, and made them count. Chandimal effortlessly transferred the pressure back to the Indians, who did not react quickly enough to strokeplay that was incandescent and innovative, yet devoid of desperation. Orthodox drives dovetailed with cheeky sweeps as he helped erase the deficit in a stand of 125 with Thirimanne, then put on 82 with Mubarak, before India regrouped to winkle out the tail. Rahane was a key accomplice throughout both innings, holding eight catches – six at slip off the spinners, and two at gully off the quicks – to break a record shared by five others.

India were left to make 176 in more than two days, on a track which had slowed up considerably. Only once, at Bridgetown in 1996-97, had they lost when chasing under 200. But, by going into their shells, they played into Herath's hands. After a quiet first innings, he drew blood early in the second – and was all over the Indians. He devastated them with a relentless wicket-to-wicket line, finishing with seven for 48, the second-best figures at Galle, after seven for 46 by Muttiah Muralitharan against England in 2003-04. Sri Lanka's near-certain defeat had been transformed into a memorable victory.

Man of the Match: L. D. Chandimal.

Close of play: first day, India 128-2 (Dhawan 53, Kohli 45); second day, Sri Lanka 5-2 (Prasad 3, Sangakkara 1); third day, India 23-1 (Dhawan 13, I. Sharma 5).

Sri Lanka

F. D. M. Karunaratne c Rahane b I. Sharma	9	– b Ashwin	0
J. K. Silva c Dhawan b Aaron	5	– b Mishra	0
H. D. R. L. Thirimanne c Rahane b Ashwin	13	– (7) c Rahane b Ashwin	44
K. C. Sangakkara c Rahul b Ashwin	5	– c Rahane b Ashwin	40
*A. D. Mathews c R. G. Sharma b Ashwin	64	– c Rahul b Mishra	39
J. Mubarak c Rahul b Ashwin	0	– (8) c Rahane b Harbhajan Singh	49
†L. D. Chandimal c Rahane b Mishra	59	– (6) not out	162
K. T. G. D. Prasad lbw b Ashwin	0	– (3) c Rahane b Aaron	3
H. M. R. K. B. Herath b Ashwin	23	– c Rahane b Mishra	1
P. H. T. Kaushal c R. G. Sharma b Mishra	0	– c Saha b I. Sharma	7
A. N. P. R. Fernando not out	0	– b Ashwin	3
B 1, l-b 1, n-b 3	5	B 3, w 8, n-b 8	19

1/15 (1) 2/15 (2) 3/27 (4)	(49.4 overs) 183	1/0 (1) 2/1 (2)	(82.2 overs) 367
4/54 (3) 5/60 (6) 6/139 (5)		3/5 (3) 4/92 (4)
7/155 (8) 8/179 (7) 9/179 (10) 10/183 (9)		5/95 (5) 6/220 (7) 7/302 (8)
		8/319 (9) 9/360 (10) 10/367 (11)

I. Sharma 11–3–30–1; Aaron 11–0–68–1; Ashwin 13.4–2–46–6; Mishra 6–1–20–2; Harbhajan Singh 8–1–17–0. *Second innings*—Ashwin 28.2–6–114–4; Mishra 17–2–61–3; Harbhajan Singh 17–0–73–1; Aaron 7–0–39–1; I. Sharma 13–0–77–1.

India

K. L. Rahul lbw b Prasad	7	– lbw b Herath	5
S. Dhawan b Fernando	134	– c and b Kaushal	28
R. G. Sharma lbw b Mathews	9	– (4) b Herath	4
*V. Kohli lbw b Kaushal	103	– (5) c Silva b Kaushal	3
A. M. Rahane lbw b Kaushal	0	– (6) c Mathews b Herath	36
†W. P. Saha c Chandimal b Fernando	60	– (7) st Chandimal b Herath	2
R. Ashwin b Fernando	7	– (9) c Prasad b Herath	3
Harbhajan Singh b Kaushal	14	– c Silva b Herath	1
A. Mishra b Kaushal	10	– (10) c Karunaratne b Kaushal	15
I. Sharma not out	3	– (3) lbw b Herath	10
V. R. Aaron c Mathews b Kaushal	4	– not out	1
L-b 10, w 3, n-b 11	24	L-b 2, w 1, n-b 1	4

1/14 (1) 2/28 (3) 3/255 (4)	(117.4 overs) 375	1/12 (1) 2/30 (3)	(49.5 overs) 112
4/257 (5) 5/294 (2) 6/302 (7)		3/34 (4) 4/45 (5)
7/330 (8) 8/344 (9) 9/366 (6) 10/375 (11)		5/60 (2) 6/65 (7) 7/67 (8)
		8/81 (9) 9/102 (6) 10/112 (10)

Prasad 22–4–54–1; Fernando 26–2–98–3; Mathews 4–1–12–1; Kaushal 32.4–2–134–5; Herath 33–4–67–0. *Second innings*—Prasad 4–2–4–0; Herath 21–6–48–7; Kaushal 17.5–1–47–3; Fernando 3–8–0–0; Mathews 1–0–3–0.

Umpires: N. J. Llong and B. N. J. Oxenford.   Third umpire: R. E. J. Martinesz.
Referee: A. J. Pycroft.

SRI LANKA v INDIA

Second Test Match

At Colombo (PSO), August 20–24, 2015. India won by 278 runs. Toss: India.

Kumar Sangakkara's final international appearance confirmed the suspicion that sport and fairytale finishes rarely coincide. His 134th Test delivered neither personal glory nor collective success as India came roaring back to square the series. At Galle, he had struggled to come to terms with Ashwin, who now accounted for him in both innings with turning, bouncing deliveries which he could only prod to slip. India celebrated Kohli's first win as Test captain, and their first in ten Tests since shocking England at Lord's more than a year earlier.

After Kohli had won the toss, Vijay's comeback innings lasted just four deliveries before he was trapped by Prasad, who quickly accounted for Rahane, pushed up to No. 3. But, from 12 for two, Kohli joined Rahul in a stand of 164 that tipped the balance India's way. Rahul made the most of being dropped on 11 by Mubarak at gully, reaching his second century in his fourth Test, while Kohli and Rohit Sharma, happier in the middle order, both hit seventies, and Saha another fifty.

Despite losing Karunaratne early again, Sri Lanka held firm, countering Ashwin's threat with greater confidence on a surface providing little assistance to the spinners. Silva contributed a gritty half-century, but the real thrust came from a wonderful hundred by Mathews, who added 127 for the fourth wicket with Thirimanne. Mathews eventually became a prize maiden Test wicket for Binny, who had toiled without reward for three matches in England in 2014, but was now preferred to Harbhajan Singh. Thirimanne's dismissal for 62, adjudged caught behind off Ishant Sharma, gave India an opening, before Ashwin and Mishra swept through the lower order as Sri Lanka lost their last seven for just 65. Sharma's send-offs to Thirimanne and Chandimal earned the disapproval of match referee Andy Pycroft, who docked him 65% of his fee; Thirimanne lost 30% of his for showing surprise at Bruce Oxenford's decision.

India built on their lead of 87 thanks to Rahane's polished 126 and his alliance of 140 for the second wicket with Vijay. But the innings had its distractions: Saha retired hurt with a painful hamstring (meaning Rahul stood in as wicketkeeper in the second innings, and Naman Ojha was called up for the last Test); and, on the fourth day, reserve umpire Ranmore Martinesz asked a traditional *papare* band in the stands to stop playing during overs, so his on-field colleagues could stand a better chance of judging bat–pad decisions.

By the time Kohli declared, 412 ahead, Sri Lanka needed to score more than they ever had in the fourth innings to win. Their recent batting travails suggested it would be beyond them, and they were rolled over for 134. Ashwin did the early damage on his way to a third five-for in three Tests, and Mishra's googly bamboozled the tail. The P. Sara Oval, the venue of both Sri Lanka's inaugural Test and their first win, was swamped by a sea of well-wishers, among them the president and prime minister, eager to say goodbye to an emotional Sangakkara. It was a bittersweet farewell.

Man of the Match: K. L. Rahul.

Close of play: first day, India 319-6 (Saha 19); second day, Sri Lanka 140-3 (Thirimanne 28, Mathews 19); third day, India 70-1 (Vijay 39, Rahane 28); fourth day, Sri Lanka 72-2 (Karunaratne 25, Mathews 23).

India

M. Vijay lbw b Prasad	0	– lbw b Kaushal	82
K. L. Rahul c Chandimal b Chameera	108	– b Prasad	2
A. M. Rahane c Karunaratne b Prasad	4	– c Chandimal b Kaushal	126
*V. Kohli c Mathews b Herath	78	– lbw b Kaushal	10
R. G. Sharma lbw b Mathews	79	– c Mubarak b Kaushal	34
S. T. R. Binny c Chameera b Herath	10	– c Thirimanne b Prasad	17
†W. P. Saha lbw b Herath	56	– not out	13
R. Ashwin c Silva b Mathews	2	– c Chandimal b Prasad	19
A. Mishra c Chandimal b Chameera	24	– c Mubarak b Prasad	10
I. Sharma lbw b Herath	2		
U. T. Yadav not out	2	– (10) not out	4
B 8, l-b 13, w 4, n-b 3	28	L-b 4, w 3, n-b 1	8

1/4 (1) 2/12 (3) 3/176 (4)   (114 overs) **393**   1/3 (2)   (8 wkts dec, 91 overs) **325**
4/231 (2) 5/267 (6) 6/319 (5)   2/143 (1) 3/171 (4)
7/321 (8) 8/367 (9) 9/386 (7) 10/393 (10)   4/256 (5) 5/262 (3)
                                           6/283 (6) 7/311 (8) 8/318 (9)

In the second innings Saha, when 5, retired hurt at 267-5 and resumed at 311-7.

Prasad 24–7–84–2; Mathews 15–7–24–2; Chameera 20–2–72–2; Herath 25–3–81–4; Kaushal 30–2–111–0. *Second innings*—Prasad 15–0–43–4; Herath 29–4–96–0; Chameera 14–0–63–0; Mathews 2–1–1–0; Kaushal 31–1–118–4.

Sri Lanka

F. D. M. Karunaratne lbw b Yadav	1	– (2) b Ashwin 46
J. K. Silva c Ashwin b Mishra	51	– (1) c Binny b Ashwin 1
K. C. Sangakkara c Rahane b Ashwin	32	– c Vijay b Ashwin 18
H. D. R. L. Thirimanne c Saha b I. Sharma	62	– (6) c sub (C. A. Pujara) b Ashwin .. 11
*A. D. Mathews c Vijay b Binny	102	– (4) c Rahul b Yadav 23
†L. D. Chandimal c Rahul b I. Sharma	11	– (5) b Mishra 15
J. Mubarak b Mishra	22	– c Kohli b I. Sharma 0
K. T. G. D. Prasad c Rahane b Mishra	5	– c Mishra b Ashwin 0
H. M. R. K. B. Herath lbw b Mishra	1	– not out 4
P. H. T. Kaushal st Saha b Mishra	6	– lbw b Mishra 5
P. V. D. Chameera not out	0	– lbw b Mishra 4
B 2, l-b 6, n-b 5	13	L-b 4, w 1, n-b 2 7

1/1 (1) 2/75 (3) 3/114 (2) (108 overs) 306 1/8 (1) 2/33 (3) (43.4 overs) 134
4/241 (4) 5/259 (6) 6/284 (5) 3/72 (4) 4/91 (5)
7/289 (8) 8/300 (7) 9/306 (9) 10/306 (10) 5/106 (6) 6/111 (7) 7/114 (8)
8/123 (2) 9/128 (10) 10/134 (11)

I. Sharma 21–3–68–2; Yadav 19–5–67–1; Binny 18–4–44–1; Ashwin 29–3–76–2; Mishra 21–3–43–4. *Second innings*—Ashwin 16–6–42–5; Yadav 7–1–18–1; I. Sharma 11–2–41–1; Mishra 9.4–3–29–3.

Umpires: B. N. J. Oxenford and R. J. Tucker.   Third umpire: R. S. A. Palliyaguruge.
Referee: A. J. Pycroft.

SRI LANKA v INDIA

Third Test Match

At Colombo (SSC), August 28–September 1, 2015. India won by 117 runs. Toss: Sri Lanka. Test debuts: M. D. K. J. Perera; N. V. Ojha.

One of the golden rules in the subcontinent, no matter how tempting the alternative, is to bat first. But, carried away by a generous and rare covering of grass on a relaid pitch, at a ground notorious for high-scoring draws, Mathews gambled and threw India in. While his decision wasn't decisive, it did play some part in the result, which secured India's first overseas series in more than four years, and their first in Sri Lanka in five attempts since 1993-94. It was also Sri Lanka's first defeat at the Sinhalese Sports Club for 15 Tests.

They were exposed to the harsh reality of life without Kumar Sangakkara. Only Mathews, with a battling hundred in a forlorn cause, and Kusal Perera, who became the third wicketkeeper to make twin half-centuries on Test debut – after Chandimal at Durban in 2011-12, and India's Dilawar Hussain against England at Calcutta in 1933-34 – offered any resistance. Otherwise, the Sri Lankans were blown away by the pace of Ishant Sharma, also the central figure in a series of ugly spats which earned him a one-Test ban.

Those incidents, involving Sharma, Prasad and Chandimal, did nothing for cricket's image. Near the end of India's second innings, Sharma reacted to several bouncers from

Prasad, Sri Lanka's most threatening bowler, by running down the pitch tapping his helmet. Chandimal walked over from slip and brushed shoulders with Sharma, incurring a one-match suspension, to apply in a one-day international. And, when Ashwin was out to end the innings, Prasad ran after Sharma at full pelt towards the dressing-rooms to continue the argument. A fired-up Sharma then gave send-offs to Tharanga – picked to replace Sangakkara – and Chandimal, having already been fined for the same offence in the Second Test.

While there were many heroes in India's victory, Pujara stood head and shoulders above them all. His reputation for durability had taken a serious knock in England in 2014. But injuries to Shikhar Dhawan and Murali Vijay earned him a recall in the role of opener, where he had averaged more than 100 in four previous innings. Still, liberal seam movement, coupled with thick cloud cover, made this a tough challenge.

After rain limited the first day to 15 overs, Prasad made light of a sore neck to harry the Indian batsmen. But Pujara handled him with class on his way to an unbeaten 145, becoming only the fourth Indian to carry his bat. He put on 104 for the eighth wicket with Mishra, resilient and forceful, to steer India to 312, an extremely good total in the conditions. It was boosted by five penalty runs when Perera, diving to his left, dropped a nick off Kohli, and the ball trickled on to the helmet behind him.

India's bowlers were stunning, none more than Sharma, but they were helped by a series of ill-judged strokes. Shortly after lunch on the third day, Sri Lanka were reeling at 47 for six, then Prasad was temporarily forced to retire from a blow on the hand from Sharma. Perera rallied them with a combative fifty, having been reprieved on nine by Rahul at slip, but India gained a lead of 111. They slipped to seven for three in the second innings, but much of the juice had drained from the surface, and the lower order were able to steer them to an adequate 274, setting Sri Lanka a stiff target of 386. Kaushal had his action reported, and was later banned from bowling his doosra.

After Sharma and Yadav fired out the top order, Mathews and Perera had dug deep to add 135. But it always felt as if one wicket would bring a few and, once Perera reverse-swept Ashwin to point, the end arrived swiftly. Sri Lanka lost their last five for 26, Sharma trappings the admirable Mathews lbw with the second new ball to end their slim hopes.

Man of the Match: C. A. Pujara.   *Man of the Series:* R. Ashwin.

Close of play: first day, India 50-2 (Pujara 19, Kohli 14); second day, India 292-8 (Pujara 135, I. Sharma 2); third day, India 21-3 (Kohli 1, R. G. Sharma 14); fourth day, Sri Lanka 67-3 (Silva 24, Mathews 22).

India

K. L. Rahul b Prasad	2	– (2) b Fernando	2
C. A. Pujara not out	145	– (1) b Prasad	0
A. M. Rahane lbw b Fernando	8	– lbw b Fernando	4
*V. Kohli c Perera b Mathews	18	– c Tharanga b Fernando	21
R. G. Sharma c Tharanga b Prasad	26	– c Tharanga b Prasad	50
S. T. R. Binny lbw b Prasad	0	– c Tharanga b Prasad	49
†N. V. Ojha c Tharanga b Kaushal	21	– c Karunaratne b Herath	35
R. Ashwin c Perera b Prasad	5	– (9) c Perera b Prasad	58
A. Mishra st Perera b Herath	59	– (8) run out	39
I. Sharma b Herath	6	– (11) not out	2
U. T. Yadav b Herath	4	– (10) c Herath b Fernando	4
L-b 2, w 4, n-b 7, p 5	18	B 1, l-b 1, w 3, n-b 5	10

1/2 (1) 2/14 (3) 3/64 (4)   (100.1 overs) 312   1/0 (1) 2/2 (2)   (76 overs) 274
4/119 (5) 5/119 (6) 6/173 (7)   3/7 (3) 4/64 (4)
7/180 (8) 8/284 (9) 9/298 (10) 10/312 (11)   5/118 (5) 6/160 (6) 7/179 (7)
                                                       8/234 (8) 9/269 (10) 10/274 (9)

Prasad 26–4–100–4; Fernando 22–6–52–1; Mathews 13–6–24–1; Herath 27.1–3–84–3; Kaushal 12–2–45–1. *Second innings*—Prasad 19–3–69–4; Fernando 17–2–62–4; Herath 22–0–89–1; Mathews 6–3–11–0; Kaushal 12–2–41–0.

Sri Lanka

W. U. Tharanga c Rahul b I. Sharma	4	– c Ojha b I. Sharma	0
J. K. Silva b Yadav	3	– c Pujara b Yadav	27
F. D. M. Karunaratne c Rahul b Binny	11	– c Ojha b Yadav	0
L. D. Chandimal lbw b Binny	23	– c Kohli b I. Sharma	18
*A. D. Mathews c Ojha b I. Sharma	1	– lbw b I. Sharma	110
H. D. R. L. Thirimanne c Rahul b I. Sharma	0	– c Rahul b Ashwin	12
†M. D. K. J. Perera c Kohli b I. Sharma	55	– c R. G. Sharma b Ashwin	70
K. T. G. D. Prasad st Ojha b Mishra	27	– (10) c Binny b Ashwin	6
H. M. R. K. B. Herath c Ojha b I. Sharma	49	– (8) lbw b Ashwin	11
P. H. T. Kaushal lbw b Mishra	16	– (9) not out	1
A. N. P. R. Fernando not out	2	– lbw b Mishra	0
L-b 1, w 2, n-b 7	10	B 4, l-b 2, n-b 7	13

1/11 (1) 2/11 (2) 3/40 (4)   (52.2 overs) 201
4/45 (5) 5/47 (3) 6/47 (6)
7/127 (7) 8/156 (10) 9/183 (9) 10/201 (8)

1/1 (1) 2/2 (3)   (85 overs) 268
3/21 (4) 4/74 (2)
5/107 (6) 6/242 (7) 7/249 (5)
8/257 (8) 9/263 (10) 10/268 (11)

In the first innings Prasad, when 1, retired hurt at 48-6 and resumed at 156-8.

I. Sharma 15-2-54-5; Yadav 13-2-64-1; Binny 9-3-24-2; Ashwin 8-1-33-0; Mishra 7.2-1-25-2. *Second innings*—I. Sharma 19-5-32-3; Yadav 15-3-65-2; Binny 13-3-49-0; Mishra 18-1-47-1; Ashwin 20-2-69-4.

Umpires: N. J. Llong and R. J. Tucker.   Third umpire: R. R. Wimalasiri.
Referee: A. J. Pycroft.

SRI LANKA v WEST INDIES IN 2015-16

Sa'adi Thawfeeq

Test matches (2): Sri Lanka 2, West Indies 0
One-day internationals (3): Sri Lanka 3, West Indies 0
Twenty20 internationals (2): Sri Lanka 1, West Indies 1

After successive home defeats by Pakistan and India, the Sri Lankans kicked off a new era – their first series without both Mahela Jayawardene and Kumar Sangakkara – by winning their two Tests against West Indies. They swept the one-day internationals, too, before West Indies salvaged something from a miserable tour with victory in the second Twenty20 game.

It was a tough assignment for 23-year-old Jason Holder, who had replaced Denesh Ramdin as the Test captain after some impressive one-day showings. As ever, West Indies were in a state of flux: this was their first tour for years without the steadying influence of Shivnarine Chanderpaul, while Chris Gayle was not sighted at all after undergoing surgery on his troublesome back in August. Dwayne Bravo and Kieron Pollard were selected only for the Twenty20 leg, angering the new coach Phil Simmons, who had wanted them for the 50-over games as well. He blamed their absence on "too much interference from outside in the selection", comments which meant he was suspended by the West Indian board; Eldine Baptiste took temporary charge.

Sri Lanka were also under new command, following Marvan Atapattu's surprise resignation early in September after the India series: Jerome Jayaratne, who had a modest first-class career as an all-rounder in the 1990s, took over as interim coach, and presided over such a happy atmosphere in the dressing-room that the players asked the board to keep him on.

As so often in Sri Lanka, spin was the visitors' undoing. Rangana Herath claimed ten wickets in the innings victory at Galle, and five more in the Second Test, to take him close to 300 overall. He had promising support from Milinda Siriwardene, another slow left-armer and, at 29, a latecomer to Test cricket. But there was a setback for off-spinner Tharindu Kaushal, a prolific domestic wicket-taker, who managed only one expensive scalp at Galle. He had been reported for a suspect action after the series against India, which seemed to affect his confidence.

The West Indian batsmen struggled in both Tests – their highest total in four attempts was 251 – and managed only three half-centuries, two of them by Darren Bravo. The bowling was equally uninspiring, though a remarkable burst by part-time off-spinner Kraigg Brathwaite set up an outside chance of victory in the Second Test. Brathwaite had claimed only three previous first-class victims – and just one in Tests – but now took six for 29. West Indies were left needing 244 to square the series, but subsided to 171.

Sri Lanka's 2–0 victory made them the first holders of a new trophy between the sides, named after Garry Sobers and Michael Tissera, a Sri Lankan captain from pre-Test days. Sobers flew in for the Second Test, and gave a tearful speech: "My whole obligation was to West Indies cricket. I never made a run for me. I always played for the West Indies teams. Records meant nothing. I don't think we have that kind of person today."

WEST INDIES TOURING PARTY

*J. O. Holder (T/50/20), D. Bishoo (T/50/20), J. Blackwood (T/50), C. R. Brathwaite (T/50/20), K. C. Brathwaite (T), D. J. Bravo (20), D. M. Bravo (T/50/20), J. L. Carter (50/20), R. Chandrika (T), J. Charles (50/20), S. O. Dowrich (T), A. D. S. Fletcher (50/20), S. T. Gabriel (T), S. D. Hope (T), J. N. Mohammed (50), S. P. Narine (50/20), K. A. Pollard (20), D. Ramdin (T/50/20), R. Rampaul (50/20), K. A. J. Roach (T), A. D. Russell (T/50/20), D. J. G. Sammy (20), M. N. Samuels (T/50/20), J. E. Taylor (T/50/20), J. A. Warrican (T). *Interim coach:* E. A. E. Baptiste.

Sammy captained in the Twenty20 matches. S. Badree was originally selected for the Twenty20 squad, but withdrew suffering from dengue fever, and was replaced by Bishoo.

At Colombo (SSC), October 9–11, 2015. **Drawn.** ‡**West Indians 209** (65.3 overs) (C. R. Brathwaite 54; S. Randiv 5-73); **Sri Lanka Board President's XI 455-7** (107 overs) (M. D. U. S. Jayasundera 142, M. B. Ranasinghe 101, T. A. M. Siriwardene 105*). *Both sides chose from 15 players. The West Indians made hard work of their only warm-up game, in which all three days were affected by the weather. First they slipped to 136-8, before No. 10 Carlos Brathwaite smacked four sixes in his 54; then, after Kemar Roach took wickets with the first two balls of the reply, three of the President's XI batsmen made centuries. Test prospect Udara Jayasundera put on 214 with 20-year-old Minod Bhanuka Ranasinghe, a left-hander with only two first-class matches under his belt, then Milinda Siriwardene made a successful Test case of his own, scoring 105*.*

SRI LANKA v WEST INDIES

First Test Match

At Galle, October 14–17, 2015. Sri Lanka won by an innings and six runs. Toss: Sri Lanka. Test debut: T. A. M. Siriwardene.

Sri Lanka were easy winners in the end, running up a huge total, then letting their spinners loose on the ever-helpful Galle pitch. But it might have been different had West Indies not dropped five catches – two of them off Chandimal, who went on to make 151.

The hosts had started carefully on a sluggish surface, and reached 100 in the 41st over, when Thirimanne became the first of leg-spinner Bishoo's four expensive victims. But Karunaratne, the cautious left-hander, and the more adventurous Chandimal batted through the rest of a hot and humid first day, and opened out next morning to complete the first 200 partnership by either side in this fixture. Karunaratne, who reached three figures with a six off Bishoo, was eventually out for a chanceless career-best 186, compiled in 482 minutes. Chandimal put on 86 with Mathews in 20 overs, before the last seven wickets tumbled for 59, Bishoo taking three in 12 balls.

It wasn't long before Sri Lanka's spinners got stuck in. Herath came on for the sixth over, and Brathwaite was given out lbw to his third ball; a review saved him but, when he was trapped in front again next over, he didn't bother going upstairs. Hope and Samuels soon followed, but Bravo – who had scored 58 on Test debut at Galle five years previously – made another studied half-century, before falling to a superb catch by Chandimal, diving goalkeeper-style at short midwicket. No one else could make much headway, although Ramdin survived for 99 minutes and Roach for 108. Herath finished with six for 68, his eighth five-for at Galle, and ended the game with 78 wickets here in 14 Tests.

West Indies had prolonged their first innings past tea on the third day, but Mathews still enforced the follow-on. This time it was the other slow left-armer, the debutant Milinda Siriwardene, who made the breakthrough, as Hope dragged on an attempted leg-side force. Samuels failed again – a miserable match got worse when his bowling action was reported for the third time in his career – and, when Bravo wafted a catch behind, West Indies were sinking fast at 88 for five. Blackwood counter-attacked, hitting three sixes on his way to 92, but only delayed the inevitable. He was last out, midway through the fourth day, as Sri Lanka completed the ninth win in their last 14 Tests at Galle, dating back to July 2009.

The pitch was the first for 18 years not prepared by Jayananda Warnaweera, the Test-bowler-turned-Galle-groundsman, who was about to be suspended for two years by Sri Lanka Cricket after failing to appear before an ICC Anti Corruption Unit probe. The ICC later imposed their own three-year ban, stating: "Warnaweera failed, on two separate occasions, to attend a scheduled interview with the ACU in relation to an ongoing investigation, and failed to provide documents required from him. He also failed to respond in any manner to the charge and he is consequently deemed to have accepted that he committed the offence charged."

Man of the Match: H. M. R. K. B. Herath.

Close of play: first day, Sri Lanka 250-2 (Karunaratne 135, Chandimal 72); second day, West Indies 66-2 (Bravo 15, Samuels 7); third day, West Indies 67-2 (Bravo 20, Bishoo 6).

Sri Lanka

F. D. M. Karunaratne c and b Samuels	186	H. M. R. K. B. Herath lbw b Bishoo	0
J. K. Silva c Ramdin b Roach	17	P. H. T. Kaushal not out	9
H. D. R. L. Thirimanne		A. N. P. R. Fernando c Gabriel b Bishoo	0
c sub (R. Chandrika) b Bishoo	16	B 4, l-b 5, w 5, n-b 6	20
L. D. Chandimal c Blackwood b Taylor	151		
*A. D. Mathews c and b Holder	48	1/56 (2) 2/101 (3) (152.3 overs) 484	
T. A. M. Siriwardene c Ramdin b Taylor	1	3/339 (1) 4/425 (4)	
†M. D. K. J. Perera b Gabriel	23	5/427 (6) 6/448 (5) 7/467 (8)	
K. T. G. D. Prasad c Holder b Bishoo	13	8/467 (9) 9/475 (7) 10/484 (11)	

Taylor 20–4–65–2; Roach 19–3–57–1; Holder 21–4–36–1; Gabriel 20–2–76–1; Samuels 27–4–84–1; Bishoo 40.3–2–143–4; Brathwaite 5–0–14–0.

West Indies

K. C. Brathwaite lbw b Herath	19	– lbw b Herath	34
S. D. Hope b Herath	23	– b Siriwardene	6
D. M. Bravo c Chandimal b Herath	50	– c Perera b Fernando	31
M. N. Samuels b Herath	11	– (5) lbw b Herath	0
J. Blackwood c Siriwardene b Prasad	11	– (6) c Silva b Prasad	92
†D. Ramdin c Perera b Fernando	23	– (7) c Silva b Siriwardene	11
*J. O. Holder c Perera b Prasad	19	– (8) run out	18
K. A. J. Roach st Perera b Herath	22	– (9) st Perera b Herath	5
J. E. Taylor c Mathews b Kaushal	31	– (10) lbw b Prasad	5
D. Bishoo not out	23	– c Mathews b Herath	10
S. T. Gabriel b Herath	0	– not out	7
B 5, l-b 6, w 1, n-b 7	19	L-b 3, w 2, n-b 3	8

1/33 (1) 2/49 (2) 3/70 (4)   (82 overs) 251   1/18 (2) 2/60 (1)   (68.3 overs) 227
4/111 (5) 5/132 (3) 6/165 (7)   3/74 (4) 4/74 (5)
7/171 (6) 8/217 (9) 9/251 (8) 10/251 (11)   5/88 (3) 6/136 (7) 7/172 (8)
                                                 8/178 (9) 9/189 (10) 10/227 (6)

Prasad 15–6–38–2; Fernando 15–4–56–1; Herath 33–9–68–6; Kaushal 14–4–65–1; Siriwardene 5–2–13–0. *Second innings*—Prasad 9.3–3–28–2; Herath 22–5–79–4; Fernando 14–1–28–1; Siriwardene 12–1–60–2; Kaushal 11–3–29–0.

Umpires: M. Erasmus and R. K. Illingworth.   Third umpire: S. D. Fry.
Referee: D. C. Boon.

SRI LANKA v WEST INDIES

Second Test Match

At Colombo (PSO), October 22–26, 2015. Sri Lanka won by 72 runs. Toss: Sri Lanka. Test debuts: B. K. G. Mendis; J. A. Warrican.

In front of Sir Garfield Sobers, and hordes of schoolchildren admitted free, West Indies twice threatened to square the series, only for their batsmen to fall short again. They owed the chance of their first Test win in 11 attempts in Sri Lanka to two unheralded bowlers: Jomel Warrican, a slow left-armer from Barbados making his debut, took four wickets on the opening day as Sri Lanka were bowled out for 200, then Kraigg Brathwaite, whose rarely seen off-breaks had claimed a solitary wicket in 23 previous Tests, polished off the second innings with a five-for.

However, West Indies' batting would have made Sobers wince: all out for 163 in the first innings to concede a lead of 37, then – needing a modest 244 for victory on a track that was turning, but not prodigiously – all out for 171. It was a team effort by Sri Lanka's bowlers: slow left-armers Herath and Siriwardene, and paceman Prasad, took five wickets apiece, while off-spinner Dilruwan Perera claimed four.

Siriwardene also starred with the bat, his 68 on the first afternoon – a maiden Test half-century – proving to be the highest score of the match after Sri Lanka had slipped to 90 for five. West Indies vastly improved their fielding from the First Test, the highlight being Brathwaite's low catch at second slip to account for Mathews. Warrican, who had received his cap from Sobers before play, started with a long-hop, settled down with an unbroken 14-over spell, and took four of the last five wickets.

Prasad set West Indies back with three quick strikes and, although Brathwaite lasted 163 minutes for 47, no one else exceeded Holder's 21. Sri Lanka tried to build on their slender lead, but were pegged back: Taylor struck with the first ball of the innings, then the accurate Warrican flummoxed Mendis and Silva (the first of a Test-record-equalling five outfield catches in an innings for Blackwood) when they looked set. However, a decisive advantage still seemed likely when Mathews and Siriwardene took Sri Lanka 188 in front – only for the unsung Brathwaite to up-end the innings with six cheap wickets for his rusty off-breaks as Sri Lanka collapsed in a heap. Brathwaite had to badger Holder for a chance: "Jason knows I like to bowl," he said. "I was always in his ear telling him I could get the breakthrough. It came to a point where he said he'd give me a try."

West Indies needed 244, but Brathwaite's big day ended in disappointment when he fell to the final delivery. Rain wiped out the fourth, but Hope and Bravo took the total to 80 when play resumed on the fifth morning. Then the wheels fell off: Siriwardene had Hope stumped for a doughty 35, before Samuels and Blackwood departed for single figures. Herath had been having a quiet match, with just one wicket in 32 overs, but virtually decided the issue in his 33rd, when Ramdin and Bravo (after battling 155 minutes for 61) both edged to Mathews at slip. Three more wickets tumbled – five went down in 46 balls in all – and, although Roach and Warrican closed the gap a little, Herath finally sealed a 2–0 series win. It was the 11th successive positive result in a Test at the P. Sara Oval, though only Sri Lanka's second victory in the last six.

Man of the Match: T. A. M. Siriwardene.   *Man of the Series:* H. M. R. K. B. Herath.
Close of play: first day, West Indies 17-1 (Brathwaite 4, Bishoo 5); second day, Sri Lanka 76-2 (Silva 31, Chandimal 5); third day, West Indies 20-1 (Hope 17); fourth day, no play.

Sri Lanka

F. D. M. Karunaratne lbw b Holder	13	– c Bishoo b Taylor	0
J. K. Silva c Ramdin b Taylor	0	– c Blackwood b Warrican	32
B. K. G. Mendis c Ramdin b Roach	13	– c Ramdin b Warrican	39
L. D. Chandimal b Taylor	25	– c Ramdin b Taylor	12
*A. D. Mathews c Brathwaite b Holder	14	– c Blackwood b Brathwaite	46
T. A. M. Siriwardene c Taylor b Warrican	68	– c Blackwood b Brathwaite	42
†M. D. K. J. Perera c and b Warrican	16	– c Ramdin b Brathwaite	5
M. D. K. Perera st Ramdin b Bishoo	5	– (9) c Roach b Brathwaite	7
H. M. R. K. B. Herath not out	26	– (8) c Blackwood b Brathwaite	18
K. T. G. D. Prasad c Ramdin b Warrican	7	– not out	1
A. N. P. R. Fernando lbw b Warrican	0	– c Blackwood b Brathwaite	0
B 10, l-b 3	13	B 2, l-b 2	4

1/1 (2) 2/34 (1) 3/34 (3)   (66 overs) 200   1/0 (1) 2/55 (3)   (75.3 overs) 206
4/59 (5) 5/90 (4) 6/127 (7)   3/84 (2) 4/84 (4)
7/149 (8) 8/173 (6) 9/200 (10) 10/200 (11)   5/151 (6) 6/165 (7) 7/195 (8)
                                                        8/203 (9) 9/206 (5) 10/206 (11)

Taylor 15–2–50–2; Roach 12–4–30–1; Holder 11–1–22–2; Warrican 20–2–67–4; Bishoo 8–0–18–1. *Second innings*—Taylor 8–3–26–2; Roach 6–1–15–0; Holder 5–1–9–0; Warrican 25–2–62–2; Bishoo 20–3–61–0; Brathwaite 11.3–4–29–6.

West Indies

K. C. Brathwaite c M. D. K. J. Perera b Siriwardene	47	– lbw b Prasad	3
S. D. Hope lbw b Prasad	4	– st M. D. K. J. Perera b Siriwardene	35
D. Bishoo c M. D. K. J. Perera b Prasad	13	– (10) run out	0
D. M. Bravo b Prasad	2	– (3) c Mathews b Herath	61
M. N. Samuels c Mathews b Siriwardene	13	– (4) c Mathews b M. D. K. Perera	6
J. Blackwood c M. D. K. J. Perera b Prasad	16	– (5) lbw b Siriwardene	4
†D. Ramdin b Herath	14	– (6) c Mathews b Herath	10
*J. O. Holder c Mathews b M. D. K. Perera	21	– (7) lbw b Siriwardene	7
K. A. J. Roach not out	17	– (8) lbw b Herath	13
J. E. Taylor lbw b M. D. K. Perera	1	– (9) c Siriwardene b Herath	1
J. A. Warrican c and b M. D. K. Perera	1	– not out	20
B 9, l-b 3, w 1, n-b 1	14	B 3, l-b 1, w 1, n-b 6	11

1/7 (2) 2/33 (3) 3/37 (4)   (64.2 overs) 163   1/20 (1) 2/80 (2)   (65.5 overs) 171
4/76 (5) 5/89 (1) 6/105 (6)   3/97 (4) 4/102 (5)
7/137 (7) 8/149 (8) 9/151 (10) 10/163 (11)   5/124 (6) 6/125 (3) 7/133 (7)
                                                         8/136 (9) 9/138 (10) 10/171 (8)

Prasad 12–3–34–4; Fernando 11–3–24–0; Herath 20–5–39–1; M. D. K. Perera 11.2–3–28–3; Siriwardene 10–2–26–2. *Second innings*—Prasad 12–2–38–1; Fernando 3–0–11–0; Herath 19.5–5–56–4; M. D. K. Perera 20–4–31–1; Siriwardene 13–1–25–3.

Umpires: S. D. Fry and R. J. Tucker.   Third umpire: M. Erasmus.
Referee: D. C. Boon.

At Colombo (Colts), October 29, 2015. **West Indians won by 43 runs** (D/L). **West Indians 318** (48.4 overs) (A. D. Russell 89, C. R. Brathwaite 113; B. Fernando 3–71); ‡**Sri Lanka Board President's XI 103-3** (21 overs). *The West Indian top order failed again, crashing to 109-7 after 30 overs, before an astonishing eighth-wicket stand of 193 in 16.3 overs saved the day. Andre Russell hit six sixes and six fours, but was outdone by Carlos Brathwaite, who reached 100 in just 50 balls, slamming seven sixes and ten fours in all. The President's XI reply was cut short by rain after 21 overs, at which point their D/L target was 147.*

First one-day international   At Colombo (RPS), November 1, 2015 (day/night). **Sri Lanka won by one wicket** (D/L). **West Indies 159-8** (26 overs) (D. M. Bravo 38, A. D. Russell 41, J. O. Holder 36; R. A. S. Lakmal 3-15); ‡**Sri Lanka 164-9** (24.5 overs) (T. M. Dilshan 59; S. P. Narine 3-21). *MoM:* T. M. Dilshan. ODI debuts: M. D. Gunathilleke, D. S. N. F. G. Jayasuriya (Sri Lanka).

Sri Lanka's last pair pinched a close game, after coming together with 11 needed from 14 balls to overhaul a revised target of 163 in 26 overs. A leg injury to Andre Russell meant West Indies were a bowler short. Perhaps encouraged by Kraigg Brathwaite's unexpected success in the Second Test, Jason Holder entrusted the penultimate over to the medium-pace of Johnson Charles, who had never bowled in 32 previous one-day appearances. After conceding three from his first four balls, Charles overstepped – and Ajantha Mendis then smashed the free hit over the long-on boundary to win the match. It was tough on Sunil Narine, who took 3-21 in his first international for more than a year. Earlier, West Indies had been floundering at 42-4, before Russell clouted 41 from 24 balls, and Holder 36 from 13; both hit three sixes. Tillekeratne Dilshan gave the chase an explosive start with 59 from 32. Holder was suspended from the next match for a slow over-rate.

Second one-day international   At Colombo (RPS), November 4, 2015 (day/night). **Sri Lanka won by eight wickets** (D/L). ‡**West Indies 214** (37.4 overs) (J. Charles 83, M. N. Samuels 63); **Sri Lanka 225-2** (36.3 overs) (M. D. K. J. Perera 99, H. D. R. L Thirimanne 81*). MoM: M. D. K. J. Perera. *ODI debut: J. Blackwood (West Indies). Charles did his best to atone for his first-match bowling by spanking 83 from 70 balls, but a rainbreak in the 27th over, which lopped 12 off each innings, was untimely for West Indies, who then lost six for 65 in 11 – four of them to silly run-outs. After a worrying time with injuries, Lasith Malinga looked back to full fitness: he had Andre Fletcher caught behind with his second ball, dismissed Jason Mohammed as well, and hit the stumps for two of the run-outs. Stand-in captain Marlon Samuels made 63, but could do little in the field as Kusal Perera and Lahiru Thirimanne piled on 156 for the second wicket, taking Sri Lanka close to their revised target of 225 in 38 overs. Samuels should not have been permitted to bowl, as the 14-day grace period since his action was reported had run out. But West Indies had chosen their team after being incorrectly advised by the ICC that Samuels could bowl.*

Third one-day international   At Pallekele, November 7, 2015 (day/night). **Sri Lanka won by 19 runs** (D/L). **West Indies 206-9** (36 overs) (M. N. Samuels 110*); ‡**Sri Lanka 180-5** (32.3 overs) (M. D. K. J. Perera 50). MoM: M. N. Samuels. MoS: M. D. K. J. Perera. *Rain again played spoilsport, interrupting West Indies' innings twice, then making a final appearance late on with Sri Lanka ahead of the par score of 161. It meant they swept the one-day series 3–0. West Indies had nosedived to 18-4 in the sixth over, and were indebted to Samuels's ninth century in one-day internationals. Returning to form in style after a miserable run, he finished with 110* from 95 balls. But his team-mates mustered only 74 between them. With Perera scurrying to 50 from 47, Sri Lanka stayed in front, reaching 100 in the 18th over, and the rain finally ended proceedings in the 33rd. There was more bad news for West Indies after the match: Narine's action was reported again, and he was banned from bowling in international cricket three weeks later.*

First Twenty20 international   At Pallekele, November 9, 2015 (floodlit). **Sri Lanka won by 30 runs. Sri Lanka 215-3** (20 overs) (M. D. K. J. Perera 40, T. M. Dilshan 56, D. S. N. F. G. Jayasuriya 36, L. D. Chandimal 40*, A. D. Mathews 37*); ‡**West Indies 185** (19.5 overs) (A. D. S. Fletcher 57; S. M. S. M. Senanayake 4-46). MoM: S. M. S. M. Senanayake. *T20I debut: P. V. D. Chameera. Sri Lanka shot along at more than ten an over, and passed 200 for the first time in a home Twenty20 international. Perera and Dilshan put on 91 in 9.4, Shehan Jayasuriya chipped in, and Dinesh Chandimal and Angelo Mathews kept swinging. In all, 84 came from the last five. West Indies lost Charles to Malinga's second delivery, but Fletcher clobbered six sixes to keep his side in the hunt. Russell faced only eight balls but muscled two of them over the boundary, and West Indies sniffed a chance when Dwayne Bravo and Kieron Pollard – restored to the side for the shortest format – put on 51. But both fell in the space of four balls, before the dangerous pair of Darren Sammy and Holder succumbed to successive deliveries from Sachithra Senanayake.*

Second Twenty20 international   At Colombo (RPS), November 11, 2015 (floodlit). **West Indies won by 23 runs.** ‡**West Indies 162-6** (20 overs) (J. Charles 34, D. J. Bravo 31, D. Ramdin 34*); **Sri Lanka 139** (20 overs) (T. M. Dilshan 52, D. S. N. F. G. Jayasuriya 30; R. Rampaul 3-20, D. J. Bravo 4-28). MoM: D. J. Bravo. MoS: T. M. Dilshan. *West Indies broke their international duck for the tour at the last gasp, squaring the Twenty20 series mainly thanks to Dwayne Bravo, who followed a run-a-ball 31 with four wickets as Sri Lanka – at one stage 93-1 – lost their last nine for 46. Fletcher and Charles had started the match with 62 in 6.2 overs, then the unsung Ramdin's brisk unbeaten 34 pushed his side well past 150. Dilshan began in typically belligerent fashion, and put on 70 with Jayasuriya, but after that only Milinda Siriwardene could manage double figures. West Indies' fielding finally hit the heights: Russell sprinted to his left from long-on to cling on superbly to Jayasuriya's lofted drive. "It always makes your job easier when you have Russell, Sammy, Pollard – some of the best fielders in the world – in one team," said Bravo.*

SRI LANKA UNDER-19 TRI-SERIES IN 2015-16

BENJ MOOREHEAD

1 India   2 Sri Lanka   3 England

Four matches on typical subcontinental pitches before Christmas did not bode well for England's chances at the Under-19 World Cup in Bangladesh which followed a month later. Three ended in defeat, while rain in the fourth, against hosts Sri Lanka, ended their slim hopes of making the final.

Runs were hard to come by on slow surfaces at Colombo's R. Premadasa Stadium. Newcomer George Bartlett made 70 during a creditable chase against India in England's third game, but – as they had been against Australia in the summer – they were too reliant on Essex's Dan Lawrence, who made a pair of 55s at the top of the order.

The bowlers fared better. Captain Brad Taylor and part-timer Lawrence gave little away with their off-spin, while Mason Crane claimed seven victims with his leg-breaks. Of the seamers, Somerset's Ben Green varied his pace effectively, and Sam Curran of Surrey took six wickets in his first two appearances for the Under-19s.

India, coached by Rahul Dravid, were streets ahead of both opponents, winning all five of their matches and appearing strong in all disciplines. Washington Sundar, a 16-year-old left-handed opener from Chennai, topped the charts with 208 runs in four innings, including three half-centuries. Whatever his future, his name will be hard to forget.

ENGLAND UNDER-19 TOURING PARTY

*B. J. Taylor (Hampshire), G. A. Bartlett (Somerset), H. R. Bernard (Kent), J. T. A. Burnham (Durham), M. S. Crane (Hampshire), S. M. Curran (Surrey), R. C. Davies (Somerset), B. G. F. Green (Somerset), H. Hameed (Lancashire), A. J. Hickey (Durham), M. D. E. Holden (Middlesex), D. W. Lawrence (Essex), S. Mahmood (Lancashire), T. J. Moores (Nottinghamshire), C. J. Taylor (Essex), J. D. Warner (Yorkshire). *Coach:* A. Hurry.

G. H. S. Garton (Sussex) was later added as cover.

At Colombo (RPS), December 11, 2015. **India won by 86 runs** (D/L). Reduced to 34 overs a side. **India 254-7** (34 overs) (Anmolpreet Singh 56, S. N. Khan 84; B. F. Green 3-28); ‡**England 159-9** (29 overs) (D. W. Lawrence 55; M. K. Lomror 4-10). *England's target was revised to 246 in 29 overs. Needing almost 8.5 an over, they had progressed to 95-2 in the 16th, but two wickets in three deliveries – including Dan Lawrence for a 46-ball 55 – exposed the rest to 16-year-old slow left-armer Mahipal Lomror. Sarfaraz Khan's 66-ball 84, including six sixes, had helped India to a formidable total.*

At Colombo (RPS), December 12, 2015. **India won by four runs** (D/L). ‡**India 284-7** (50 overs) (M. S. Washington Sundar 77, I. P. Kishan 33, A. N. Khare 102, Virat Singh 30; A. M. Fernando 3-54); **Sri Lanka 250-5** (47 overs) (W. I. A. Fernando 75, K. I. C. Asalanka 74). *Sri Lanka's target was revised to 255 in 47 overs. Amandeep Khare's century had pushed India to 266-2 in the 47th over, but Sri Lanka took 5-18 from the last 19 balls, then came within a whisker of victory after seventies from Avishka Fernando and Charith Asalanka. They needed seven off the last three balls, but Kanishk Seth removed Wanidu Hasaranga de Silva, and the final two deliveries yielded only two.*

At Colombo (RPS), December 14, 2015. **Sri Lanka won by 52 runs.** ‡**Sri Lanka 191** (49.1 overs) (K. I. C. Asalanka 48, S. Ashan 38; B. J. Taylor 4-34); **England 139** (38.3 overs) (J. T. A. Burnham

32). *At 64-1 in the 12th over, England were well placed to chase a small total, but an assortment of spinners helped reduce them to 94-7, and two run-outs summed up the panic. The dismal batting undid England's fine performance in the field, led by their captain Brad Taylor, who took four of the first six wickets to fall as Sri Lanka subsided from 110-2.*

At Colombo (RPS), December 15, 2015. **India won by 20 runs.** ‡**India 261** (50 overs) (H. J. Rana 50, R. R. Pant 71, R. K. Bhui 42, Virat Singh 38; M. S. Crane 3-51); **England 241** (49.3 overs) (D. W. Lawrence 55, G. A. Bartlett 70, M. D. E. Holden 45; M. Dagar 3-27, R. R. Batham 3-24). *England fell to their third successive defeat but, chasing again, were much improved. Another express start from Lawrence was backed up by George Bartlett's 70, but pressure told on the tail. The bowlers, of whom eight were used, had done well to restrict India from 201-2 in the 39th over.*

At Colombo (RPS), December 17, 2015. **India won by four wickets. Sri Lanka 221-9** (50 overs) (W. M. K. Bandara 74, P. H. K. D. Mendis 65; K. K. Ahmed 4-55); ‡**India 223-6** (47.5 overs) (M. S. Washington Sundar 61, Virat Singh 60*, M. K. Lomror 32). *India were rocking at 119-5 before Virat Singh and Lomror nudged and nurdled them towards a fourth win in four matches. Sri Lanka's innings had been underpinned by a patient fourth-wicket stand of 91 between Kaveen Bandara and Kamindu Mendis, but left-arm seamer Khaleel Ahmed removed both to avert a late onslaught.*

At Colombo (RPS), December 18, 2015. **No result.** Reduced to 45 overs a side. ‡**Sri Lanka 227** (45 overs) (W. M. K. Bandara 36, P. H. K. D. Mendis 52, P. V. R. de Silva 34; S. M. Curran 4-52); **England 41-2** (10 overs). *England needed an unlikely 228 in 28 overs to reach the final on net run-rate, but the weather denied them the chance. Sri Lanka's total had been restricted by the spin of Brad Taylor and Lawrence, who together conceded only 59 runs in 18 overs, and Sam Curran's fine spell of reverse swing at the death.*

India 8pts, Sri Lanka 3pts, England 1pt.

Final At Colombo (RPS), December 21, 2015. **India won by five wickets.** ‡**Sri Lanka 158** (47.2 overs) (P. V. R. de Silva 58; K. K. Ahmed 3-29); **India 159-5** (33.5 overs) (M. S. Washington Sundar 56, R. R. Pant 35; B. A. D. N. Silva 3-18). *India dominated the final, as they had the tournament. Batting first, Sri Lanka were sliced open by the new-ball pair of Aavesh Khan and Khaleel, losing 4-4 from 19-0, before a relative recovery led by wicketkeeper Vishad Randika (58 from 75 balls). India's openers Washington Sundar and Rishabh Pant began with a brisk 89, and victory came with more than 16 overs remaining.*

DOMESTIC CRICKET IN SRI LANKA IN 2014-15

Sa'adi Thawfeeq

Ports Authority sprang a major surprise when they overcame several of the better-fancied clubs to bag the plum trophy, the Premier League, though defending champions Nondescripts took them to the wire. Formerly known as Seeduwa Raddoluwa, the club were taken over in 2011 by the Sri Lankan Ports Authority, whose chairman, Priyath Bandu Wickrama Munige, became their president and had played two first-class matches for them with the aim of qualifying to compete for office at Sri Lanka Cricket. He could have captured a wicket with his first delivery, on debut against Colombo in 2012-13, aged 39, but dropped a return catch offered by Nimesh Perera.

Including their time as Seeduwa Raddoluwa, this was Ports Authority's seventh season in the Premier League. It was the second year running they had qualified for the Super Eight, though in 2013-14 they went on to finish bottom. This time they comfortably headed Group B, but started the Super Eight more than ten points behind Group A leaders **Nondescripts**, who had a better record against fellow qualifiers: Nondescripts faltered in the later stages, however, whereas Ports Authority won their last three games. The two met in the final round, with Nondescripts still a few points ahead; Ports Authority overtook them with a thumping 193-run victory. In all, they had won seven of their ten games, and lost only one.

Their top batsmen, both passing 750 runs, were their only current internationals, Ashan Priyanjan and Dhananjaya de Silva, who made his Sri Lanka debut in a Twenty20 game against Pakistan a few months later. Left-arm spinner Malinda Pushpakumara, who joined from Moors, took 70 wickets at 16, more than anyone in the tournament. As in 2013-14, he finished second in the overall first-class list, behind Nondescripts off-spinner Tharindu Kaushal, who had 75, including 15 in three innings against West Indies A.

Kaushal had made his Test debut in Christchurch a few weeks before the Premier League began, and played in the World Cup quarter-final (though his doosra was later found to be illegal); his Nondescripts team-mate Jehan Mubarak earned a Test recall against Pakistan in July, after nearly eight years' absence. Left-hander Mubarak passed 1,000 first-class runs for the second successive season, just behind Badureliya captain Milinda Siriwardene, who headed the averages with 1,144 at 67.

Tamil Union's Kithuruwan Vithanage scored 351 in one innings, a record in Sri Lankan domestic cricket, against Air Force – who failed to win a single first-class match, and were later relegated from the Premier League after an extraordinary play-off against **Galle**, the winners of the non-first-class Emerging Trophy. Galle were bowled out for 31 on the opening day, and conceded a first-innings lead of 184, but fought back so strongly that they beat Air Force by four runs. **Ragama** won the Plate League, for the six teams not qualifying for the Super Eight.

Colombo Colts beat Sinhalese in the final of the Premier Limited-Overs Tournament, which was badly affected by the December weather: nine games were abandoned or no-results. Sinhalese also found themselves on the losing end in the SLC Twenty20 final, when **Badureliya** beat them by ten runs. Badureliya had already got the better of Sinhalese in a group match, after Amal Athulathmudali hit ten sixes in his 94, and were involved in a rare tie, against Ragama.

The ECB arranged for several players from the England Performance Programme to appear for Sri Lankan clubs during the season; following Moeen Ali's success with Moors three years earlier, it was hoped they would benefit from exposure to Asian conditions. The most successful was Scott Borthwick, who scored a hundred for Chilaw Marians against Moors. Ben Foakes, Will Tavaré, Tom Westley, Greg Smith and Michael Richardson also took part in the Premier League or Limited-Overs Tournament. West Indian Kieran Powell played four matches for Tamil Union.

FIRST-CLASS AVERAGES, 2014-15

BATTING (550 runs)

	M	I	NO	R	HS	100	Avge	Ct/St
†T. A. M. Siriwardene (*Badureliya*)........	10	19	2	1,144	185*	3	67.29	9
†M. D. U. S. Jayasundera (*Ragama*)	9	15	2	842	205*	4	64.76	7
D. A. S. Gunaratne (*Army*)	8	15	1	850	136	4	60.71	5
†J. Mubarak (*Sri Lanka A/Nondescripts*).....	12	22	3	1,112	161	3	58.52	10
†R. J. M. G. M. Rupasinghe (*Badureliya*)	8	14	3	598	105	1	54.36	3
†M. L. R. Buddika (*Tamil Union*)	10	18	3	800	154	3	53.33	7
P. K. J. R. N. Nonis (*Ragama*)	8	13	1	622	101	1	51.83	5
†K. D. K. Vithanage (*SL A/Tamil Union*)	10	18	1	881	351	5	51.82	12
S. M. A. Priyanjan (*SL A/Ports Authority*). .	12	20	3	850	150*	2	50.00	11
K. P. S. P. Karunanayake (*Army*)	10	20	3	815	150*	2	47.94	8
†N. T. Paranavitana (*Sinhalese*)	9	14	1	604	124	1	46.46	8
D. M. de Silva (*Ports Authority*)..........	10	18	1	772	156	4	45.41	7
S. C. Serasinghe (*Ports Authority*)	10	16	2	603	103	1	43.07	9
L. P. C. Silva (*Colombo*)	10	19	1	763	128	2	42.38	13
†D. S. N. F. G. Jayasuriya (*Colts*)	9	16	2	575	92	0	41.07	5
T. M. U. S. Karunaratne (*Saracens*)	9	17	1	643	106	1	40.18	15
†W. U. Tharanga (*Sri Lanka A/Nondescripts*).	9	16	1	598	135	1	39.86	10
†K. P. A. Perera (*Bloomfield*)	10	19	2	677	166	1	39.82	3
B. O. P. Fernando (*Moors*)	10	18	2	611	119	1	38.18	6
M. S. Warnapura (*Sri Lanka A/Bloomfield*). .	11	20	3	625	131	2	36.76	5
H. G. Kumara (*Saracens*)	9	17	1	581	200*	1	36.31	6
H. Dumindu (*Colombo*)	10	19	1	645	150*	1	35.83	6
D. M. Sarathchandra (*Tamil Union*)	10	19	1	632	133	1	35.11	28/9
L. Abeyratne (*Colombo*).	10	19	3	561	126	2	35.06	24/10
D. P. W. Diminguwa (*Tamil Union*)	10	19	1	624	164	2	34.66	9
A. K. Perera (*Nondescripts*)	10	18	0	573	92	0	31.83	7
R. J. I. Udayanga (*Badureliya*)	10	19	0	571	60	0	30.05	12
†D. P. D. N. Dickwella (*SL A/Nondescripts*). .	13	23	0	691	209	2	30.04	33/15

BOWLING (25 wickets, average 25.00)

	Style	O	M	R	W	BB	5I	Avge
P. M. Pushpakumara (*Ports Authority*).....	SLA	363.2	67	1,171	70	8-97	4	16.72
P. L. S. Gamage (*SL A/Chilaw Marians*)....	RFM	298	44	963	57	7-58	5	16.89
B. Fernando (*Sinhalese*)	LFM	134	17	482	28	9-70	2	17.21
J. G. A. Janoda (*Colombo*)	RFM	184.5	35	472	27	6-47	2	17.48
J. U. Chaturanga (*Moors*)	SLA	138.5	28	443	25	8-76	3	17.72
P. H. T. Kaushal (*SL A/Nondescripts*)......	OB	369.4	42	1,343	75	8-131	10	17.90
A. N. P. R. Fernando (*SL A/Bloomfield*)	RFM	226.5	46	757	40	5-63	2	18.92
M. D. K. Perera (*Colts*)	OB	283.1	56	778	40	7-101	3	19.45
H. I. A. Jayaratne (*Colts*)	RFM	143.2	20	497	25	4-52	0	19.88
W. R. Palleguruge (*Army*)	SLA	190.4	29	583	28	6-63	2	20.82
M. A. Aponso (*Ragama*)	SLA	197.2	28	648	31	5-44	2	20.90
H. M. C. M. Bandara (*Badureliya*)	LBG	144.1	25	553	26	6-70	2	21.26
M. V. T. Fernando (*SL A/Bloomfield*)	LFM	253.5	48	937	44	5-71	2	21.29
G. S. M. Ekanayake (*Ports Authority*)	RFM	177.4	42	547	25	5-39	1	21.88
C. W. Vidanapathirana (*Nondescripts*)	RFM	212	43	713	32	5-36	2	22.28
L. H. D. Dilhara (*Moors*)	RFM	238.4	45	726	32	5-44	1	22.68
T. M. U. S. Karunaratne (*Saracens*)	OB	259.1	38	806	35	6-50	4	23.02
J. D. F. Vandersay (*Sinhalese*)	LBG	185	25	654	28	6-69	2	23.35
M. N. M. Dilshad (*Badureliya*)	LFM	198.4	23	794	34	7-54	1	23.35
D. K. R. C. Jayatissa (*Army*).	OB	154.2	17	592	25	6-54	2	23.68
E. M. C. D. Edirisinghe (*Tamil Union*)	SLA	277.2	42	905	38	8-108	3	23.81
P. A. D. L. R. Sandakan (*Colombo*)	SLC	269	22	1,093	45	5-58	3	24.28
S. Prasanna (*Sri Lanka A/Army*)	LBG	274.3	45	840	34	7-38	1	24.70

PREMIER LEAGUE, 2014-15

Group A	P	W	L	D	Pts
NONDESCRIPTS CC	6	4	0	2	92.475
TAMIL UNION	6	3	1	2	62.475
BADURELIYA SC	6	0	2	4	54.420
BLOOMFIELD	6	2	1	3	54.155
Ragama CC	6	1	0	5	50.615
Colts CC	6	1	3	2	44.575
Air Force SC	6	0	4	2	19.275

Group B	P	W	L	D	Pts
PORTS AUTHORITY	6	4	0	2	88.905
MOORS SC	6	1	0	5	67.980
COLOMBO CC	6	3	1	2	66.345
ARMY SC	6	2	1	3	46.675
Sinhalese SC	6	1	1	4	42.705
Saracens SC	6	0	3	3	30.110
Chilaw Marians CC	6	0	5	1	29.570

Super Eight	P	W	L	D	Pts
Ports Authority	7	4	1	2	92.350
Nondescripts CC	7	4	2	1	85.970
Moors SC	7	3	0	4	83.615
Bloomfield	7	2	2	3	65.270
Colombo CC	7	3	2	2	63.605
Army SC	7	1	2	4	56.560
Tamil Union	7	1	4	2	39.915
Badureliya SC	7	0	5	2	33.415

Plate	P	W	L	D	Pts
Ragama CC	5	2	0	3	57.840
Colts CC	5	2	0	3	49.960
Saracens SC	5	0	0	5	43.000
Sinhalese SC	5	2	0	3	41.015
Chilaw Marians CC	5	1	3	1	36.940
Air Force SC	5	0	4	1	16.200

The top four teams from each group advanced to the Super Eight, carrying forward their results against fellow qualifiers, then played the other four qualifiers. The bottom three from each group entered the Plate competition, run on the same principles. The bottom-placed Plate team faced a relegation play-off against the Emerging Trophy winners.

Outright win = 12pts; win by an innings = 2pts extra; lead on first innings in a drawn game = 8pts. Bonus points were awarded as follows: 0.1pt for each wicket taken and 0.005pt for each run scored, up to 400 runs per innings.

Group A

At Katunayake (Air Force), January 16–18, 2015. **Colts won by nine wickets. Air Force 190 and 266; ‡Colts 365 and 92-1.** *Colts 16.285pts, Air Force 3.38pts.*

At Colombo (Bloomfield), January 16–18, 2015. **Drawn. ‡Bloomfield 293 and 200-5; Ragama 463-6 dec** (M. D. U. S. Jayasundera 171). *Bloomfield 3.065pts, Ragama 11.5pts.*

At Colombo (NCC), January 16–18, 2015. **Nondescripts won by an innings and 114 runs. Badureliya 179** (P. H. T. Kaushal 5-66) **and 337** (A. D. Solomons 104; P. H. T. Kaushal 5-106); **‡Nondescripts 630-6 dec** (D. P. D. N. Dickwella 209, W. U. Tharanga 135, J. Mubarak 124). *Nondescripts 18pts, Badureliya 3.18pts. Niroshan Dickwella, who reached a maiden double-century in 181 balls, and Pawan Wickramasinghe (70) shared an opening stand of 253 for Nondescripts; Upul Tharanga and Jehan Mubarak followed up with 215 for the third wicket. Andy Solomons hit 104 in 80 balls, with seven sixes, before becoming one of Tharindu Kaushal's ten victims.*

At Colombo (Bloomfield), January 23–25, 2015. **Drawn. Bloomfield 156 and 340-4** (K. P. A. Perera 166, M. S. Warnapura 100*); **‡Badureliya 471-8 dec** (T. A. M. Siriwardene 145, R. J. M. G. M. Rupasinghe 105). *Bloomfield 3.28pts, Badureliya 11.4pts. Milinda Siriwardene, who hit nine sixes in his 145, added 208 for Badureliya's second wicket with Imesh Udayanga (59). In reply, Primosh Perera and Madawa Warnapura put on 210 for Bloomfield's second.*

At Colombo (Colts), January 23–25, 2015. **Tamil Union won by 182 runs. Tamil Union 207 and 400-8 dec** (D. P. W. Diminguwa 164, K. D. K. Vithanage 103); **‡Colts 296** (E. M. C. D. Edirisinghe 5-74) **and 129.** *Tamil Union 17.035pts, Colts 3.925pts. Kithuruwan Vithanage hit 103 in 79 balls.*

At Colombo (NCC), January 23–25, 2015. **Drawn. Nondescripts 404** (M. A. Aponso 5-100) **and 299-4** (J. Mubarak 106*); **‡Ragama 311** (R. S. S. S. de Zoysa 125*; P. H. T. Kaushal 7-95). *Nondescripts 12.495pts, Ragama 2.955pts.*

At Katunayake (Air Force), January 30–February 1, 2015. **Bloomfield won by nine wickets. Air Force 144** (S. Randiv 5-30) **and 267; ‡Bloomfield 305 and 107-1.** *Bloomfield 16.06pts, Air Force 3.155pts.*

At Maggona, January 30–February 1, 2015. **Drawn. Badureliya 304** (T. A. M. Siriwardene 180*) **and 171; ‡Colts 247 and 194-7.** *Badureliya 12.075pts, Colts 4.205pts.*

At Colombo (PSO), January 30–February 1, 2015. **Nondescripts won by six wickets. Tamil Union 252 and 167; ‡Nondescripts 344** (D. P. D. N. Dickwella 108, P. D. Wickramasinghe 103; E. M. C. D. Edirisinghe 8-108) **and 76-4.** *Nondescripts 16.1pts, Tamil Union 3.495pts.*

At Colombo (PSO), February 5–7, 2015. **Drawn. Tamil Union 290 and 281** (D. M. Sarathchandra 133; H. M. C. M. Bandara 6-70); **‡Ragama 381** (B. K. E. L. Milantha 110) **and 17-0.** *Tamil Union 3.855pts, Ragama 11.99pts.*

At Maggona, February 6–8, 2015. **Drawn. Badureliya 305 and 229-9 dec** (K. L. Rukmal 5-53); **‡Air Force 188 and 218-9** (R. M. G. K. Sirisoma 7-46). *Badureliya 12.57pts, Air Force 3.93pts.*

At Colombo (NCC), February 6–8, 2015. **Nondescripts won by 49 runs. ‡Nondescripts 309** (A. N. P. R. Fernando 5-103) **and 174; Bloomfield 209** (P. H. T. Kaushal 5-78) **and 225.** *Nondescripts 16.415pts, Bloomfield 4.17pts.*

At Katunayake (Air Force), February 13–15, 2015. **Tamil Union won by an innings and 287 runs. ‡Tamil Union 650-8 dec** (K. D. K. Vithanage 351, M. L. R. Buddika 105); **Air Force 167 and 196** (D. M. Wickramanayaka 5-37). *Tamil Union 18pts, Air Force 2.615pts. Vithanage converted a maiden double-hundred into 351, hitting 37 fours and 14 sixes in 283 balls. It was a Sri Lankan domestic record, though Mahela Jayawardene made 374 in a Test against South Africa in 2006. Vithanage added 329 for Tamil Union's fourth wicket with Rumesh Buddika, plus century stands for the fifth and sixth, helping his side to this tournament's highest total and biggest victory.*

At Colombo (Bloomfield), February 13–15, 2015. **Drawn. Ragama 191 and 301-6 dec** (M. D. U. S. Jayasundera 122); **‡Badureliya 208 and 182-6.** *Badureliya 11.55pts, Ragama 4.06pts.*

At Colombo (Colts), February 13–15, 2015. **Nondescripts won by 70 runs. Nondescripts 338** (D. S. Weerakkody 108) **and 177; ‡Colts 245 and 200.** *Nondescripts 16.575pts, Colts 4.225pts.*

At Colombo (Bloomfield), February 20–22, 2015. **Bloomfield won by three wickets. ‡Colts 220** (A. N. P. R. Fernando 5-63) **and 138** (M. V. T. Fernando 5-71); **Bloomfield 119** (M. D. K. Perera 5-26) **and 242-7.** *Bloomfield 15.805pts, Colts 3.49pts.*

At Colombo (Moors), February 20–22, 2015. **Ragama won by 171 runs. Ragama 288** (C. G. Wijesinghe 141) **and 232-6 dec** (P. K. J. R. N. Nonis 101); **‡Air Force 159** (M. A. Aponso 5-44) **and 190** (H. M. C. M. Bandara 5-102). *Ragama 16.6pts, Air Force 3.345pts.*

At Colombo (PSO), February 20–22, 2015. **Tamil Union won by 149 runs. Tamil Union 189** (M. N. M. Dilshad 7-54) **and 309-9 dec; ‡Badureliya 205 and 144.** *Tamil Union 16.49pts, Badureliya 3.645pts.*

At Colombo (Colts), February 27–March 1, 2015. **Drawn. ‡Colts 485-6 dec** (A. J. A. D. D. L. A. Jayasinghe 100*, S. S. Pathirana 113*) **and 209-1 dec** (M. D. K. J. Perera 108*); **Ragama 342** (B. K. E. L. Milantha 116; M. D. K. Perera 7-101) **and 220-4.** *Colts 12.445pts, Ragama 3.51pts. Sachith Pathirana hit 106* on the second morning, finishing with 113* from 87 balls, including eight sixes; he added 186* for the seventh wicket with Angelo Jayasinghe. In Colts' second innings, Kusal Perera hit 108* in 69 balls, with seven sixes.*

At Colombo (NCC), February 27–March 1, 2015. **Drawn. ‡Nondescripts 378** (L. U. Igalagamage 119; W. S. C. Wanigasekera 5-57) **and 428-9 dec** (M. W. L. S. Lakmal 5-84); **Air Force 190.** *Nondescripts 12.89pts, Air Force 2.85pts. Lahiru Udara Igalagamage and Tharindu Kaushal (80) added 196 for Nondescripts' seventh wicket; both scored career-bests, and Kaushal later took his 50th wicket of the season, in his eighth match.*

At Colombo (PSO), February 27–March 1, 2015. **Drawn. Bloomfield 216 and 319** (E. M. C. D. Edirisinghe 5-65); **‡Tamil Union 179 and 141-1.** *Tamil Union 3.6pts, Bloomfield 11.775pts.*

Group B

At Katunayake (FTZ), January 16–18, 2015. **Drawn. ‡Army 299 and 227-7; Sinhalese 477-9 dec** (N. T. Paranavitana 124, S. H. T. Kandamby 124; S. Prasanna 5-140). *Army 3.53pts, Sinhalese 11.7pts. Tharanga Paranavitana and Thilina Kandamby added 222 for Sinhalese's fourth wicket. In the Army's second innings, Seekkuge Prasanna hit a 19-ball fifty.*

At Colombo (CCC), January 16–17, 2015. **Ports Authority won by an innings and three runs. ‡Colombo 103** (P. M. Pushpakumara 5-37) **and 116** (G. S. M. Ekanayake 5-39); **Ports Authority 222** (P. A. D. L. R. Sandakan 5-80). *Ports Authority 17.11pts, Colombo 2.095pts.*

At Katunayake (FTZ), January 16–18, 2015. **Drawn. ‡Saracens 243** (L. H. D. Dilhara 5-44) **and 304; Moors 289** (K. P. Gajasinghe 105*) **and 5-0.** *Moors 11.47pts, Saracens 3.735pts.*

At Colombo (CCC), January 23–25, 2015. **Colombo won by five wickets. Chilaw Marians 71** (J. G. A. Janoda 5-13) **and 244; ‡Colombo 181** (P. L. S. Gamage 5-63) **and 135-5.** *Colombo 15.58pts, Chilaw Marians 3.075pts. Durham's Scott Borthwick scored seven on debut for Chilaw Marians in their first-innings collapse, when Arosh Janoda had figures of 11–5–13–5.*

At Colombo (Moors), January 23–25, 2015. **Drawn. Moors 365 and 206-6 dec** (W. R. Palleguruge 6-63); **‡Army 281 and 121-4.** *Moors 12.255pts, Army 3.61pts. In Moors' first innings, debutant Shanuka Dulaj Withanawasam and Ranil Dhammika scored 54 each, adding 113 for the last wicket.*

At Katunayake (FTZ), January 23–25, 2015. **Drawn. ‡Saracens 272** (T. M. U. S. Karunaratne 106; J. D. F. Vandersay 6-69) **and 291** (M. D. Gunathilleke 6-70); **Sinhalese 198** (T. M. U. S. Karunaratne 6-66) **and 221-6** (N. T. Paranavitana 104*). *Saracens 12.415pts, Sinhalese 4.095pts. Umesh Karunaratne followed up his century with 6-66 from his off-spin.*

At Colombo (RPS), January 30–February 1, 2015. **Moors won by 22 runs. Moors 355** (D. D. M. Rajakaruna 143) **and 208-8 dec; ‡Chilaw Marians 260** (J. U. Chaturanga 8-76) **and 281** (S. G. Borthwick 115). *Moors 16.815pts, Chilaw Marians 4.505pts. Chasing 304, Chilaw Marians reached 258-4 thanks to Borthwick, who scored 115 in 107 balls, but lost their last six for 23.*

At Colombo (CCC), January 30–February 1, 2015. **Colombo won by 96 runs. Colombo 181 and 330-6 dec** (L. Abeyratne 101*); **‡Saracens 192 and 223** (M. A. Liyanapathiranage 6-44). *Colombo 16.555pts, Saracens 3.675pts.*

At Colombo (NCC), January 30–February 1, 2015. **Ports Authority won by four wickets. Sinhalese 185 and 256; ‡Ports Authority 286 and 159-6.** *Ports Authority 16.225pts, Sinhalese 3.805pts.*

At Colombo (RPS), February 6–8, 2015. **Army won by 68 runs. Army 136 and 253** (P. L. S. Gamage 7-63); **‡Chilaw Marians 122 and 199.** *Army 15.945pts, Chilaw Marians 3.605pts.*

At Colombo (CCC), February 6–8, 2015. **Ports Authority won by ten wickets. ‡Saracens 210** (P. M. Pushpakumara 5-57) **and 140; Ports Authority 329-9 dec** (D. M. de Silva 109) **and 25-0.** *Ports Authority 15.77pts, Saracens 2.65pts.*

At Colombo (SSC), February 6–8, 2015. **Drawn. Sinhalese 224 and 329-7; ‡Moors 328** (L. H. D. Dilhara 113). *Sinhalese 3.765pts, Moors 11.34pts. Kosala Kulasekara (28) and Dilhara Lokuhettige added 135 for Moors' eighth wicket.*

At Panagoda, February 13–15, 2015. **Army won by two wickets. Saracens 187** (B. A. W. Mendis 5-37) **and 202** (A. J. C. Silva 5-52); **‡Army 226** (T. M. U. S. Karunaratne 6-50) **and 168-8.** *Army 15.97pts, Saracens 3.745pts. In the Army's run-chase, Seekkuge Prasanna hit a 25-ball fifty.*

At Colombo (RPS), February 13–15, 2015. **Ports Authority won by 215 runs. ‡Ports Authority 356** (D. M. de Silva 156; P. L. S. Gamage 6-97) **and 250-3 dec** (S. M. A. Priyanjan 150*); **Chilaw Marians 226** (P. M. Pushpakumara 6-69) **and 165.** *Ports Authority 17.03pts, Chilaw Marians 3.255pts.*

At Colombo (Moors), February 13–15, 2015. **Drawn. ‡Moors 275 and 260** (D. Hettiarachchi 6-84); **Colombo 133** (J. U. Chaturanga 5-30) **and 267-9** (J. U. Chaturanga 5-86). *Moors 12.575pts, Colombo 4pts.*

At Colombo (CCC), February 20–22, 2015. **Drawn. Army 324 and 234-5** (K. P. S. P. Karunanayake 150*); **‡Ports Authority 521-9 dec** (D. M. de Silva 116, S. C. Serasinghe 103). *Army 3.69pts, Ports Authority 11.5pts. Shalika Karunanayake hit 150* in 104 balls, with ten fours and 14 sixes.*

At Katunayake (FTZ), February 20–22, 2015. **Drawn. Chilaw Marians 314** (T. R. Priyan 5-94) **and 211-9 dec** (T. M. U. S. Karunaratne 6-75); **‡Saracens 221 and 177-4.** *Chilaw Marians 12.025pts, Saracens 3.89pts.*

At Colombo (SSC), February 20–22, 2015. **Drawn. Sinhalese 179 and 267-5; ‡Colombo 406** (L. P. C. Silva 120, K. H. R. K. Fernando 106; B. Fernando 5-84). *Sinhalese 3.23pts, Colombo 11.5pts.*

At Panagoda, February 27–March 1, 2015. **Colombo won by 137 runs. Colombo 324 and 199** (W. R. Palleguruge 5-70); **‡Army 220 and 166** (M. A. Liyanapathiranage 6-68). *Colombo 16.615pts, Army 3.93pts.*

At Colombo (RPS), February 27–March 1, 2015. **Sinhalese won by ten wickets. Chilaw Marians 269** (J. D. F. Vandersay 5-47) **and 152; ‡Sinhalese 278 and 144-0.** *Sinhalese 16.11pts, Chilaw Marians 3.105pts.*

At Colombo (Moors), February 27–March 1, 2015. **Drawn. Moors 180 and 305-9 dec; ‡Ports Authority 229** (L. J. P. Gunaratne 6-79) **and 45-1.** *Moors 3.525pts, Ports Authority 11.27pts.*

Super Eight

At Hambantota, March 5–8, 2015. **Moors won by an innings and 156 runs. Moors 574** (I. S. S. Samarasooriya 147, K. P. Gajasinghe 150); **‡Badureliya 221 and 197.** *Moors 18pts, Badureliya 3.09pts. In Badureliya's second innings, Moors wicketkeeper Denuwan Rajakaruna held five catches for the third time in the tournament.*

At Pallekele, March 5–8, 2015. **Bloomfield won by ten wickets. Ports Authority 223 and 257; ‡Bloomfield 426** (W. A. A. M. Silva 113, B. K. G. Mendis 108) **and 56-0.** *Bloomfield 16.28pts, Ports Authority 3.4pts. Ports Authority's only defeat in this tournament.*

At Colombo (RPS), March 5–8, 2015. **Colombo won by six wickets. Tamil Union 377** (K. D. K. Vithanage 102, M. L. R. Buddika 154; J. G. A. Janoda 6-47) **and 221; ‡Colombo 259 and 341-4** (H. Dumindu 150*). *Colombo 17pts, Tamil Union 4.39pts.*

At Galle, March 5–8, 2015. **Nondescripts won by three wickets. ‡Army 293** (D. A. S. Gunaratne 134; C. W. Vidanapathirana 5-36) **and 171** (P. H. T. Kaushal 5-60); **Nondescripts 227** (D. K. R. C. Jayatissa 6-108) **and 238-7.** *Nondescripts 16.325pts, Army 4.02pts.*

At Colombo (NCC), March 12–15, 2015. **Drawn. Army 334** (K. P. S. P. Karunanayake 146) **and 265-7 dec** (D. A. S. Gunaratne 100); **‡Tamil Union 207** (D. K. R. C. Jayatissa 6-54) **and 151-4.** *Army 12.395pts, Tamil Union 3.49pts. Asela Gunaratne (97) and Karunanayake came together at 25-3 in the Army's first innings and added 240 for the fourth wicket. Gunaratne reached 100 second time round.*

At Colombo (Bloomfield), March 12–15, 2015. **Ports Authority won by eight wickets. ‡Ports Authority 367** (R. M. G. K. Sirisoma 7-113) **and 52-2; Badureliya 211 and 207.** *Ports Authority 16.095pts, Badureliya 3.29pts. Shanuka Dissanayake (94) and Malinda Pushpakumara (74) added 128 for Ports Authority's eighth wicket. Later, Pushpakumara took his 50th wicket of the season, in his eighth match, with his left-arm spin.*

At Colombo (Colts), March 12–15, 2015. **Drawn. ‡Moors 362** (M. V. T. Fernando 5-94) **and 80-1; Bloomfield 390** (W. A. A. M. Silva 118, M. S. Warnapura 131). *Bloomfield 11.05pts, Moors 3.21pts. Ashen Silva and Warnapura added 230 for Bloomfield's second wicket.*

At Panagoda, March 12–15, 2015. **Drawn. ‡Colombo 304** (L. P. C. Silva 128; S. C. D. Boralessa 5-111) **and 218-6; Nondescripts 463** (J. Mubarak 161). *Colombo 3.61pts, Nondescripts 11.6pts. Jehan Mubarak passed 1,000 first-class runs for the season in his 161.*

At Colombo (NCC), March 19–22, 2015. **Drawn. ‡Army 415** (D. A. S. Gunaratne 122) **and 277-7 dec; Badureliya 239** (N. K. Liyanapathirana 5-94) **and 394-5** (T. A. M. Siriwardene 185*). *Badureliya 4.865pts, Army 12.885pts. Milinda Siriwardene passed 1,000 first-class runs for the season in his career-best 185*.*

At Colombo (PSO), March 19–21, 2015. **Bloomfield won by eight wickets. Colombo 235 and 85; ‡Bloomfield 238** (B. M. D. K. Mendis 5-73, P. A. D. L. R. Sandakan 5-75) **and 83-2.** *Bloomfield 15.605pts, Colombo 2.8pts.*

At Colombo (RPS), March 19–22, 2015. **Moors won by 221 runs. Moors 296** (P. C. de Silva 107; C. W. Vidanapathirana 5-65) **and 340-8 dec** (B. O. P. Fernando 119); **‡Nondescripts 195 and 220.** *Moors 17.18pts, Nondescripts 3.875pts.*

At Colombo (Colts), March 19–21, 2015. **Ports Authority won by six wickets. ‡Tamil Union 198 and 268** (P. M. Pushpakumara 8-97); **Ports Authority 370** (S. M. A. Priyanjan 122) **and 101-4.** *Ports Authority 16.355pts, Tamil Union 3.73pts.*

1144 Overseas Cricket – Sri Lanka

At Colombo (RPS), March 26–29, 2015. **Colombo won by 282 runs. Colombo 297 and 414-8 dec** (L. Abeyratne 126); ‡**Badureliya 194** (P. A. D. L. R. Sandakan 5-58) **and 235.** *Colombo 17.485pts, Badureliya 3.945pts. Badureliya's Siriwardene finished the season with 84 and 58 – giving him 12 scores of 50 or more in this tournament.*

At Colombo (Moors), March 26–28, 2015. **Army won by nine wickets.** ‡**Bloomfield 189 and 213** (S. Prasanna 7-38); **Army 335** (D. A. S. Gunaratne 136; S. K. C. Randunu 5-108) **and 71-1.** *Army 16.03pts, Bloomfield 3.11pts. Gunaratne's 136 was his seventh successive score of 50 or more, and his fourth century in successive matches.*

At Colombo (CCC), March 26–29, 2015. **Moors won by 30 runs.** ‡**Moors 315** (R. L. B. Rambukwella 5-41) **and 259; Tamil Union 348** (D. P. W. Diminguwa 111, M. L. R. Buddika 106) **and 196.** *Moors 16.87pts, Tamil Union 4.72pts. Pabasara Waduge Diminguwa and Buddika added 206 for Tamil Union's second wicket.*

At Colombo (PSO), March 26–29, 2015. **Ports Authority won by 193 runs. Ports Authority 243** (P. H. T. Kaushal 5-51) **and 281** (D. M. de Silva 127; P. H. T. Kaushal 8-131); ‡**Nondescripts 214 and 117.** *Ports Authority 16.62pts, Nondescripts 3.655pts. Defending champions Nondescripts headed the Super Eight table at the start of the final round, but Ports Authority swept away their advantage to take the title with their third successive win, despite Kaushal's 13-182. It was the best match return of the season, giving him 60 in eight games in this tournament.*

CHAMPIONS

Lakspray Trophy	1995-96	Colombo CC	2005-06 Sinhalese SC
1988-89 { Nondescripts CC / Sinhalese SC	1996-97	Bloomfield C&AC	2006-07 Colombo CC
	1997-98	Sinhalese SC	2007-08 Sinhalese SC
1989-90 Sinhalese SC			2008-09 Colts CC
	Premier League		2009-10 Chilaw Marians
P. Saravanamuttu Trophy	1998-99	Bloomfield C&AC	2010-11 Bloomfield C & AC
1990-91 Sinhalese SC	1999-2000	Colts CC	2011-12 Colts CC
1991-92 Colts CC	2000-01	Nondescripts CC	2012-13 Sinhalese SC
1992-93 Sinhalese SC	2001-02	Colts CC	2013-14 Nondescripts CC
1993-94 Nondescripts CC	2002-03	Moors SC	2014-15 Ports Authority CC
1994-95 { Bloomfield C&AC / Sinhalese SC	2003-04	Bloomfield C&AC	
	2004-05	Colts CC	

Sinhalese have won the title outright 7 times, Colts 6, Bloomfield 4, Nondescripts 3, Colombo 2, Chilaw Marians, Moors and Ports Authority 1. Sinhalese have shared it twice, Bloomfield and Nondescripts once.

Plate

At Colombo (Colts), March 6–7, 2015. **Ragama won by six wickets.** ‡**Chilaw Marians 127** (S. Weerakoon 5-50) **and 132; Ragama 176 and 85-4.** *Ragama 15.305pts, Chilaw Marians 2.695pts.*

At Colombo (Bloomfield), March 6–8, 2015. **Drawn.** ‡**Saracens 232 and 310-9 dec** (M. N. M. Aslam 104*); **Colts 214 and 177-5.** *Colts 3.855pts, Saracens 12.21pts.*

At Colombo (Moors), March 6–8, 2015. **Sinhalese won by six wickets.** ‡**Air Force 185** (B. Fernando 9-70) **and 255; Sinhalese 374** (M. D. Shanaka 125) **and 68-4.** *Sinhalese 16.21pts, Air Force 3.6pts. Binura Fernando's 9-70 was the season's best return. Dasun Shanaka, with a maiden century, and Kasun Madushanka (33) added 106 for Sinhalese's ninth wicket.*

At Katunayake (FTZ), March 13–15, 2015. **Chilaw Marians won by six wickets. Air Force 112** (P. L. S. Gamage 5-25) **and 119;** ‡**Chilaw Marians 149** (D. H. A. Isanka 5-23) **and 85-4.** *Chilaw Marians 15.17pts, Air Force 2.555pts.*

At Dambulla, March 13–15, 2015. **Drawn.** ‡**Sinhalese 320** (M. D. Shanaka 127; M. D. K. Perera 5-65) **v Colts.** *Colts 1pt, Sinhalese 1.6pts.*

At Colombo (CCC), March 13–15, 2015. **Drawn. Ragama 401-4 dec** (M. D. U. S. Jayasundera 205*) **and 85-3;** ‡**Saracens 215** (S. Nanayakkare 5-73). *Ragama 11.425pts, Saracens 1.775pts. Udara Jayasundera hit his second double-century and put on 220 for Ragama's first wicket with Nilushan Nonis (94).*

At Colombo (Moors), March 20–22, 2015. **Colts won by 86 runs.** ‡**Colts 301** (P. L. S. Gamage 7-58) **and 174; Chilaw Marians 160** (D. S. N. F. G. Jayasuriya 5-42) **and 229.** *Colts 16.375pts, Chilaw Marians 3.945pts. Lahiru Gamage's career-best 7-58 included his 50th wicket of the season.*

At Colombo (Bloomfield), March 20–22, 2015. **Drawn.** ‡**Ragama 487** (M. D. U. S. Jayasundera 127); **Sinhalese 403** (M. B. Ranasinghe 128, J. K. Silva 104). *Ragama 11pts, Sinhalese 3pts. Minod Bhanuka Ranasinghe and Kaushal Silva opened with 226 for Sinhalese – in reply to 195 from Ragama openers Jayasundera and Nonis (76). First-innings points secured the Plate for Ragama.*

At Katunayake (FTZ), March 20–22, 2015. **Drawn.** ‡**Saracens 353 and 389-9** (H. G. Kumara 200*); **Air Force 284** (T. M. U. S. Karunaratne 5-116). *Saracens 12.71pts, Air Force 3.32pts. Geeth Kumara scored a maiden century in 55 balls, and went on to 200* in 170, with 15 sixes.*

Relegation Play-off

At Panagoda, April 10–12, 2015. **Galle won by four runs. Galle 31** (D. M. A. D. Karunaratne 5-21) **and 295** (K. I. C. Asalanka 114); ‡**Air Force 215 and 107** (K. M. M. de Silva 6-46). *There was confusion about whether this match had first-class status. If it did, Galle's 31 was the lowest total by a winning team in a first-class match since 1924 (the lowest ever was 15 by Hampshire against Warwickshire in 1922). Second time round, Charith Asalanka's century helped to set Air Force a target of 112, and slow left-armer Malith de Silva bowled them out just short. Both were (probably) making their first-class debuts.*

PREMIER LIMITED-OVERS TOURNAMENT, 2014-15

Two 50-over leagues plus knockout

Semi-final   At Colombo (RPS), December 18, 2014. **Colts won by 65 runs** (D/L). **Ragama 189-9** (50 overs); ‡**Colts 126-2** (21.1 overs). *Rain ended play with Colts 65 ahead of the par score of 61; Kusal Perera (62*) and Bhanuka Rajapaksa (43*) had added 91 in 16 overs.*

Semi-final   At Colombo (RPS), December 19, 2014. **Sinhalese won by five runs** (D/L). **Moors 230-8** (50 overs); ‡**Sinhalese 161-5** (37 overs). *Janaka Gunaratne (64*) had rallied Moors from 143-7, but Thilina Kandamby's 47* kept Sinhalese ahead when rain ended play.*

Final   At Colombo (RPS), December 21, 2014. **Colts won by 56 runs. Colts 251-9** (50 overs) (N. L. T. C. Perera 5-34); ‡**Sinhalese 195** (41.3 overs). *Perera (55) and Rajapaksa (80) dominated Colts' innings again, despite Tissara Perera's five middle-order victims, before Nuwan Kulasekara and off-spinner Shehan Jayasuriya claimed four Sinhalese wickets each.*

SRI LANKA CRICKET TWENTY20 TOURNAMENT, 2014-15

20-over league plus semi-final and final

Semi-final   At Colombo (SSC), April 9, 2015. **Badureliya won by five wickets. Nondescripts 135-9** (20 overs); ‡**Badureliya 139-5** (19.2 overs). *Mohomed Dilshad and Andy Solomons reduced Nondescripts to 40-4, and Milinda Siriwardene (31*) ensured Badureliya's place in the final.*

Semi-final   At Colombo (SSC), April 9, 2015. **Sinhalese won by eight wickets. Colts 118** (19.1 overs); ‡**Sinhalese 119-2** (13.3 overs). *Binura Fernando (4-26) had Colts reeling on 9-4. Minod Bhanuka Ranasinghe steered Sinhalese home with 70 in 48 balls, and 39 balls to spare.*

Final   At Colombo (SSC), April 10, 2015. **Badureliya won by ten runs. Badureliya 176-4** (20 overs); ‡**Sinhalese 166-9** (20 overs). *Gihan Rupasinghe (74*) and Siriwardene (66 in 37 balls) added 122 for Badureliya's fourth wicket, before Kasun Rajitha and Solomons each dismissed four Sinhalese batsmen to ensure the title.*

WEST INDIES CRICKET IN 2015

Better together?

Tony Cozier

Hardly a month has passed in the 21st century without West Indian cricket, once the epitome of sporting excellence and the pride of its people, suffering vicious infighting at board level and ignominy on the pitch. The latest decline was even more pronounced than usual, with the abject performance of the players intrinsically linked to troubles off the field.

The selectors' decision not to take the 41-year-old Shivnarine Chanderpaul on the December tour of Australia drew widespread fury, not least from his native Guyana, whose cricket board called it "ridiculous" and "unfathomable". Chanderpaul announced his retirement from international cricket in January, ending a career that had lasted 21 years and 164 Tests.

Head coach Phil Simmons's claim that "interference from outside" had caused Dwayne Bravo and Kieron Pollard to be excluded from the

WEST INDIES IN 2015

	Played	Won	Lost	Drawn/No result
Tests	10	1	8	3
One-day internationals	15	4	11	–
Twenty20 internationals	5	3	2	–

DECEMBER — JANUARY	3 Tests, 5 ODIs and 3 T20Is (a) v South Africa	(see *Wisden 2015*, page 1047)
FEBRUARY — MARCH	ICC World Cup (in Australia and New Zealand)	(page 860)
APRIL — MAY	3 Tests (h) v England	(page 283)
JUNE	2 Tests (h) v Australia	(page 1149)
JULY		
AUGUST		
SEPTEMBER		
OCTOBER — NOVEMBER	2 Tests, 3 ODIs and 2 T20Is (a) v Sri Lanka	(page 1130)
DECEMBER — JANUARY	3 Tests (a) v Australia	(page 945)

For a review of West Indian domestic cricket from the 2014-15 season, see page 1155.

Uneasy lies the head: Jason Holder had a tough start as West Indies' second-youngest Test captain.

one-day squad for the tour of Sri Lanka had already led to his being suspended by the board, in late September. The ban came just six months after Simmons had been appointed head coach following eight successful years in charge of Ireland.

The controversy did nothing for West Indies' form. Under the temporary control of Eldine Baptiste, they lost both Tests and all three one-day internationals, though the T20 series was shared. Simmons's reinstatement in November was no panacea: West Indies suffered a humiliating ten-wicket loss to a fledgling Cricket Australia XI at Brisbane, before being soundly beaten in two of the three Tests.

Further distractions included the contentious re-election of Jamaican financier Dave Cameron for a second term as West Indies Cricket Board president; the lingering uncertainty over the $US42m compensation claim by the Indian board following the abandonment of West Indies' tour there in late 2013; and the suspension from international cricket of Sunil Narine, their leading limited-overs spinner, because of an illegal action.

The change in the Test captaincy in September, from Denesh Ramdin to Jason Holder, a 23-year-old all-rounder appointed one-day leader in December 2014, added to the sense of flux. Predictably, Holder endured a difficult initiation; he wasn't helped by the declining contributions of senior batsman Marlon Samuels, and fast bowlers Jerome Taylor and Kemar Roach.

Against such a backdrop, the West Indies were beaten in eight of their ten Tests in 2015, and won only once – a hopeful, but fleeting, triumph to level the series against England in Barbados. Their record in 15 one-day internationals – four victories, 11 defeats – was little better, and in September their failure to qualify for the 2017 Champions Trophy was confirmed after they dropped out of the top eight of the 50-over rankings. Even if their jump to the top of the Twenty20 rankings in early 2016 was caused by the demotion of Sri Lanka – who suffered 2–0 defeats against Pakistan and New Zealand – it was a morale boost all the same. Significantly, the T20 team included several global franchise players no longer available for West Indies in other formats, including Bravo and Darren Sammy.

The Caribbean Community's sub-committee on cricket arranged a meeting with the WICB in April, during which a team of eminent West Indians agreed to review the structure of the board. The findings of a wide-ranging report were fiercely critical of the WICB, and the recommendation – that "the board should be immediately dissolved and all current members resign" – was unequivocal. An interim board would then be appointed in order to "install a new governance framework".

The proposals were predictably rejected, just like two previous studies, published in 2007 and 2012. Cameron was adamant that the organisation needed to be "free of interference from governments". His comments triggered a heated exchange with Keith Mitchell, prime minister of Grenada and chairman of the Caricom cricket group. There seemed little prospect of a speedy resolution.

It is hard to guess at the future of West Indies cricket, except that all the signs are negative. Indeed, there were doubts that the team would survive, as it has done for over 100 years, as the only entity unifying the English-speaking Caribbean – or split into its scattered, minuscule components, as was the case with the brief political union, the West Indies Federation, in 1962.

Baldath Mahabir, who became the first and only director to resign from the "unprofessional" WICB in November, was worried that the younger generation would turn from a West Indies team "that has taken a battering for the last two decades" to support their own territorial sides.

Cameron's return as president in March provided an example of the insularity that could lead to such a split. After the Jamaica Cricket Association directors backed his rival, Barbados CA president Joel Garner, the membership overturned the choice, and Cameron gained the votes needed.

Meanwhile, the West Indies women continued to hold their own. After defeating Pakistan in all three T20s at home in October and November, they stayed fifth in the ICC rankings. Six victories in eight one-day internationals meant they finished the year second in the Women's Championship. By the end of 2015, captain Stafanie Taylor was fourth in the one-day batting rankings, with off-spinner Anisa Mohammed third among the bowlers in both the 50- and 20-over formats. By contrast, the highest-ranked male West Indian batsman in Tests – once Chanderpaul had quit – was Darren Bravo, at No. 25; Roach was the leading male bowler, at No. 21.

At the moment, women's cricket doesn't rate highly with the Caribbean public. It may do if such discrepancies with the ailing men's game persist.

WEST INDIES v AUSTRALIA IN 2015

Daniel Brettig

Test matches (2): West Indies 0, Australia 2

Twenty years after Mark Taylor's team wrested the Frank Worrell Trophy – and Test cricket supremacy – from Richie Richardson's West Indians, the same contest was more footnote than final frontier. Australia were on their way to the Ashes, and the West Indians a matter of days away from the third edition of the Caribbean Premier League.

There was an optimism about West Indies cricket thanks to a Test series shared 1–1 with England, the emergence of Jason Holder as an exciting all-rounder and one-day captain, and the appointment of the respected Phil Simmons as coach. But much of this good feeling evaporated with the decision to drop the venerable and venerated Shivnarine Chanderpaul after a pair of lean series against South Africa and England, apparently ending a 21-year Test career. Stories revealing the exchanges between Chanderpaul and the selectors did not help, and a team that had been buzzing after the win over England at Barbados were now beset by questions about their middle-order rock. Whatever Chanderpaul's recent failings, some felt he deserved to depart at a time of his own choosing. Subsequent events showed that the quality of the youth beneath him was modest, at best.

Australia, lacking only Ryan Harris, at home for the birth of his first child and to rest his troublesome knee, outpointed West Indies in all departments, from Michael Clarke's agile captaincy to razor-sharp fielding. Josh Hazlewood and Mitchell Starc showed that Australian pace bowling would be in good hands even after Harris and Mitchell Johnson, now 35 and 33, exit the stage.

Meanwhile, an outstanding century from debutant Adam Voges, also 35, was a strong endorsement of his know-how; he had waited nearly a decade since being twelfth man for the 2006-07 Perth Ashes Test, and had been told a year before the 2015 World Cup that he would play no part in it. Steve Smith was promoted to No. 3, and soared to an innings of 199 at Sabina Park that lost little by comparison with anyone who had batted there for Australia. He also soared to the top of the Test batting rankings.

Simmons wanted to repair relationships with the region's IPL players, and after these two Tests it looked a wise decision. Save for some sparkling displays by Holder, Devendra Bishoo and Jerome Taylor, and a sure-footed debut by Shane Dowrich, the West Indian performance was lamentable. Ramdin looked a leaden captain, Kraigg Brathwaite an opener out of his depth against high pace, and Kemar Roach a sadly diminished figure after his own pace had marked the corresponding series in 2012.

The Australians knew any resistance would be momentary, and swarmed over their opponents at the slightest sign of weakness. Perhaps most troubling was the thought that, if a series could be so one-sided in the Caribbean, what chance of a contest in Australia in 2015-16?

AUSTRALIAN TOURING PARTY

*M. J. Clarke, Fawad Ahmed, B. J. Haddin, J. R. Hazlewood, M. G. Johnson, N. M. Lyon, M. R. Marsh, S. E. Marsh, P. M. Nevill, C. J. L. Rogers, P. M. Siddle, S. P. D. Smith, M. A. Starc, A. C. Voges, D. A. Warner, S. R. Watson. *Coach:* D. S. Lehmann.

At North Sound, Antigua, May 27–29, 2015. **Drawn.** ‡**West Indies Cricket Board President's XI 382** (114 overs) (R. Chandrika 74, S. O. Dowrich 78, R. L. Chase 76, J. N. Mohammed 55, C. R. Brathwaite 50*) **and 161-4** (48 overs) (S. O. Dowrich 53*, R. L. Chase 55*; J. R. Hazlewood 3-4); **Australians 250** (104 overs) (S. E. Marsh 118, A. C. Voges 52; C. R. Brathwaite 3-39, J. Warrican 3-93). *The Australians left out Test regulars David Warner, Steve Smith, Mitchell Johnson and Mitchell Starc, who instead practised against each other in the nets. Josh Hazlewood took two wickets in his opening spell, and Fawad Ahmed one in his first over, but after that the Australians were made to toil in humid conditions. Fifties for Rajendra Chandrika and Shane Dowrich put them in the Test frame. After Shaun Marsh and Adam Voges had added 116 for the third wicket, the Australians plunged to 217-8 against the Barbadian pair of Carlos Brathwaite and Jomel Warrican, and only just went past the follow-on target. Hazlewood then struck in each of his first three overs, before the slow bowlers were brought on to see out time.*

WEST INDIES v AUSTRALIA

First Test Match

At Roseau, Dominica, June 3–5, 2015. Australia won by nine wickets. Toss: West Indies. Test debuts: S. O. Dowrich; A. C. Voges.

For a time on the second day it appeared as though West Indies would, at the very least, make it difficult for Australia to win, and perhaps even emerge as winners themselves. The sharp spin extracted by Bishoo had confounded most of the batsmen: Smith was stumped, and a statuesque Haddin bowled by a ball that pitched outside leg before screwing back to strike the top of off. However, the long-awaited debutant, Western Australia and Middlesex captain Adam Voges, produced an innings of rare quality, and found willing allies down the order. An unbeaten 130 made him the oldest debut centurion in Test history.

The more travelled members of Australia's side were grateful, for until that point they had looked decidedly rusty. They had been unbalanced by the decision to rule out Chris Rogers because of concussion suffered at the hands of a local net bowler, Anderson Burton, and there was a patchiness about the Australian bowling on the first day that a better side might have exploited.

It was largely a combination of sharp fielding and poor batting that rounded up West Indies for 148 in the first two sessions: it was difficult to fathom that no one had passed 36 in the best batting conditions of the match. The absence of Shivnarine Chanderpaul was

OLDEST TO HIT A CENTURY ON TEST DEBUT

Years	Days			
35	**243**	**A. C. Voges (130*)**	**Australia v West Indies at Roseau**............	**2015**
35	118	D. L. Houghton (121)	Zimbabwe v India at Harare.................	1992-93
33	240	S. C. Griffith (140)	England v West Indies at Port-of-Spain........	1947-48
32	334	H. L. Collins (104)	Australia v England at Sydney.............	1920-21
32	283	Aminul Islam (145)	Bangladesh v India at Dhaka.............	2000-01
32	50	W. G. Grace (152)	England v Australia at The Oval.............	1880
30	119	C. A. Milton (104*)	England v New Zealand at Leeds.............	1958

A SELECT BAND

Best Test innings figures by West Indies leg-spinners:

33–10–80–6	**D. Bishoo**	**v Australia at Roseau**	**2015**
34.2–4–92–6	W. Ferguson	v England at Port-of-Spain.	1947-48
8.1–1–23–5	D. A. J. Holford	v India at Bridgetown.	1975-76
13.4–2–34–5	†B. F. Butcher	v England at Port-of-Spain.	1967-68
31.5–10–78–5	D. Ramnarine	v South Africa at Bridgetown.	2000-01
25–6–90–5	D. Bishoo	v Bangladesh at Mirpur	2011-12
40–6–116–5	W. Ferguson	v England at Georgetown.	1947-48

† *His only wickets in 44 Tests.*

noticeable, with neither Samuels nor Bravo able to step up in the way Ramdin or the selectors had hoped. The muddle was symbolised by the stumps, which still carried the promotional stickers from West Indies' previous Test series, with "England" crossed out in blue marker pen.

Australia lost Warner in the third over to a Taylor delivery that leapt at his gloves and slipped to 126 for six before Voges intervened, with help from the tail. Because of the 12-hour time difference between Perth and Roseau, Voges' family had been informed of his selection before he was, so they could be filmed offering a message of support. Suitably fortified, he played with commendable patience to get used to a slow, turning pitch and testing bowling, before accelerating with some panache as he neared his hundred. He was on 77, and the total just 221, when joined by last man Hazlewood, who stuck around stubbornly to help put on a further 97. Bishoo, on his way to capturing the best Test figures for a West Indian leg-spinner, was unable to maintain his initial threat; a bruised and bloodied spinning finger meant he would miss the Second Test.

Voges' performance had an impact on the scoreboard, and also on West Indian morale. Faced with an unexpected deficit of 170, they were quickly in trouble at 37 for three. A determined stand of 144 between Samuels and the game's other debutant, Shane Dowrich of Barbados, raised hope of a meaningful fourth-innings target, but their dismissals signalled the start of a familiar batting slide; in all, six were out in single figures. The chief architects were Starc, near unplayable when he was able to swing the ball, and Hazlewood. The Australians were able to dash off their target of 47 before the light worsened, and had retained the Frank Worrell Trophy inside three days.

Comprehensive: Denesh Ramdin is castled by Mitchell Johnson as West Indies are bundled out before tea on the first day.

Clarke was under no illusions that the decisiveness of the margin obscured numerous kinks – namely, the consistency of the bowlers and the application of the batsmen. Ramdin was pointedly critical of Samuels for getting "sucked in": for all his resistance on day three, he had contrived to get out hooking in each innings.

Man of the Match: A. C. Voges.

Close of play: first day, Australia 85-3 (Smith 17, Voges 20); second day, West Indies 25-2 (Bravo 3, Dowrich 1).

West Indies

K. C. Brathwaite c Haddin b Hazlewood	10	– b Starc	15
S. D. Hope c Marsh b Johnson	36	– c Clarke b Johnson	2
D. M. Bravo c Clarke b Lyon	19	– c Warner b Hazlewood	5
S. O. Dowrich b Hazlewood	15	– c Watson b Hazlewood	70
M. N. Samuels c Hazlewood b Starc	7	– c Starc b Johnson	74
J. Blackwood c Haddin b Hazlewood	2	– st Haddin b Lyon	12
*†D. Ramdin b Johnson	19	– b Lyon	3
J. O. Holder c Marsh b Starc	21	– not out	12
J. E. Taylor c Voges b Smith	6	– lbw b Starc	0
D. Bishoo not out	9	– b Starc	1
S. T. Gabriel c Clarke b Johnson	2	– b Starc	0
W 1, n-b 1	2	B 11, l-b 10, w 1	22

1/23 (1) 2/63 (3) 3/75 (2) (53.5 overs) 148   1/21 (2) 2/21 (1) (86 overs) 216
4/85 (4) 5/87 (6) 6/91 (5)   3/37 (3) 4/181 (4)
7/121 (7) 8/133 (8) 9/144 (9) 10/148 (11)   5/198 (6) 6/198 (5) 7/206 (7)
    8/206 (9) 9/216 (10) 10/216 (11)

Johnson 13.5–2–34–3; Hazlewood 15–7–33–3; Starc 15–5–48–2; Lyon 6–1–20–1; Watson 3–1–11–0; Smith 1–0–2–1. *Second innings*—Johnson 15–3–38–2; Starc 18–7–28–4; Hazlewood 16–7–17–2; Lyon 24–7–67–2; Smith 2–0–16–0; Watson 7–3–6–0; Voges 2–0–15–0; Clarke 2–0–8–0.

Australia

D. A. Warner c Blackwood b Taylor	8	– (2) c Bravo b Taylor	28
S. E. Marsh c Bravo b Holder	19	– (1) not out	13
S. P. D. Smith st Ramdin b Bishoo	25	– not out	5
*M. J. Clarke c Ramdin b Bishoo	18		
A. C. Voges not out	130		
S. R. Watson c Holder b Bishoo	11		
†B. J. Haddin b Bishoo	8		
M. G. Johnson c Samuels b Bishoo	20		
M. A. Starc b Bishoo	0		
N. M. Lyon lbw b Gabriel	22		
J. R. Hazlewood b Samuels	39		
B 9, l-b 3, w 1, n-b 5	18	N-b 1	1

1/13 (1) 2/38 (2) 3/61 (4) (107 overs) 318   1/42 (2) (1 wkt, 5 overs) 47
4/97 (3) 5/112 (6) 6/126 (7)
7/178 (8) 8/178 (9) 9/221 (10) 10/318 (11)

Taylor 20–0–72–1; Gabriel 15–3–38–1; Holder 14–3–30–1; Bishoo 33–10–80–6; Samuels 22–2–71–1; Blackwood 3–0–15–0. *Second innings*—Taylor 3–0–22–1; Gabriel 2–0–25–0.

Umpires: Aleem Dar and R. A. Kettleborough. Third umpire: I. J. Gould.
Referee: R. S. Mahanama.

WEST INDIES v AUSTRALIA

Second Test Match

At Kingston, Jamaica, June 11–14, 2015. Australia won by 277 runs. Toss: West Indies. Test debut: R. Chandrika.

    Not much could be expected of a West Indies side that had to rule out Devendra Bishoo (bruised finger) and Marlon Samuels and Shannon Gabriel (illness) only a few hours before play, and it was no surprise when they delivered little. Taylor and Holder provided brief glimmers, but the class of Smith and the incisive work of Hazlewood and Starc overwhelmed them.

The Australians played a sturdier brand of cricket than in Dominica, and toasted Smith's fifth hundred in six Tests, and his first at No. 3. He was needed in the first over of the match, after Warner was again surprised by a short ball from Taylor, the owner of an enviable record at Sabina Park. The pitch had more pace and bounce than Dominica, and Taylor's opening spell of 5–5–0–2 took full advantage, also accounting for Shaun Marsh, still in the team while Chris Rogers convalesced. But, curiously, Ramdin did not call on Taylor again until the penultimate over of the session, another maiden; in between, Smith and Clarke established a bridgehead.

Clarke's innings was sketchy – Roach held a return catch when he had just three, only to be no-balled – but his calculated risks moved the scoreboard along. Smith's steady acceleration was accompanied by deep concentration and just the right amount of respect for an attack that could not maintain Taylor's early excellence. No one else reached 50, but useful stands down the order allowed Australia to near 400, when Taylor forced a yorker through Smith's defences to trip him up one short of a maiden Test double-century; for the second time in four Tests, he was out in the 190s. Taylor posed for photographs with three metal plates from the scoreboard – 6, 4 and 7 – to mark career-best figures.

The worrying state of Caribbean batsmanship was underlined when Guyana's Rajendra Chandrika, possessing a first-class average of 25 and no hundred, walked out to face Starc – and walked back inside three overs. Lyon quickly removed Brathwaite to surpass Hugh Trumble's tally of 141 Test wickets and become Australia's most prolific off-spinner, and Hazlewood was incisive in claiming his second Test five-for.

Holder's bold show on the third morning, driving and cutting with skill, served to avoid a follow-on mark the Australians would have been unlikely to enforce anyway. And, after a cautious third-innings accumulation that allowed Smith to rack up another half-century, Clarke gave West Indies more than two days to chase 392.

They did not get even a third of the way there, melting away in a manner that was disheartening even when allowances were made for Australia's excellence. Before the end of the day, both West Indies openers had bagged ducks in the same innings for the first time in 32 years. Chandrika's pair was the first for a West Indian debutant since Alf Valentine at Old Trafford in 1950, and only the fourth for any opener in his maiden Test – after New Zealand's Ken Rutherford, Saeed Anwar of Pakistan and Zimbabwe's Dirk Viljoen.

Hazlewood deservedly took the series award, having moved the ball both ways, in the air and off the seam. For Australia, this felt like an Ashes warm-up match; for West Indies, perhaps just an old-world distraction ahead of the glitz of the Caribbean Premier League.

Man of the Match: S. P. D. Smith. *Man of the Series:* J. R. Hazlewood.

Close of play: first day, Australia 258-4 (Smith 135, Watson 20); second day, West Indies 143-8 (Holder 13); third day, West Indies 16-2 (Bravo 8, Dowrich 1).

Australia

D. A. Warner c Hope b Taylor	0	– (2) c Ramdin b Roach	62
S. E. Marsh lbw b Taylor	11	– (1) c Holder b Permaul	69
S. P. D. Smith lbw b Taylor	199	– not out	54
*M. J. Clarke c Ramdin b Holder	47	– not out	14
A. C. Voges c Ramdin b Taylor	37		
S. R. Watson b Taylor	25		
†B. J. Haddin b Taylor	22		
M. G. Johnson c Bravo b Roach	5		
M. A. Starc b Holder	6		
J. R. Hazlewood c Blackwood b Permaul	24		
N. M. Lyon not out	5		
B 5, l-b 7, n-b 6	18	B 9, l-b 4	13

1/0 (1) 2/16 (2) 3/134 (4)   (126.5 overs) 399   1/117 (2)   (2 wkts dec, 65 overs) 212
4/210 (5) 5/264 (6) 6/296 (7)   2/163 (1)
7/306 (8) 8/330 (9) 9/393 (3) 10/399 (10)

Taylor 25–10–47–6; Roach 25–2–113–1; Holder 22–3–64–2; Permaul 34.5–7–124–1; Brathwaite 19–2–39–0; Blackwood 1–1–0–0. *Second innings*—Taylor 10–2–24–0; Roach 9–2–26–1; Permaul 21–3–83–1; Holder 10–2–24–0; Brathwaite 11–3–23–0; Blackwood 4–1–19–0.

West Indies

K. C. Brathwaite b Lyon	4	– b Starc	0
R. Chandrika c Haddin b Starc	0	– c Marsh b Starc	0
D. M. Bravo lbw b Lyon	14	– c Marsh b Hazlewood	11
S. O. Dowrich c Haddin b Hazlewood	13	– b Starc	4
S. D. Hope c Haddin b Lyon	26	– b Johnson	16
J. Blackwood c Warner b Hazlewood	51	– b Hazlewood	0
*†D. Ramdin lbw b Hazlewood	8	– c Clarke b Johnson	29
J. O. Holder not out	82	– c Starc b Watson	1
V. Permaul c Haddin b Johnson	0	– not out	23
K. A. J. Roach c Haddin b Hazlewood	7	– c Smith b Lyon	3
J. E. Taylor lbw b Hazlewood	0	– b Lyon	0
B 6, l-b 2, w 1, n-b 1, p 5	15	B 13, l-b 11, w 2, n-b 1	27

1/1 (2) 2/9 (1) 3/25 (3)   (59.5 overs) 220   1/0 (1) 2/1 (2)   (42 overs) 114
4/44 (4) 5/77 (5) 6/119 (7)   3/20 (4) 4/27 (3)
7/142 (6) 8/143 (9) 9/220 (10) 10/220 (11)   5/33 (6) 6/55 (5) 7/62 (8)
                                            8/111 (7) 9/114 (10) 10/114 (11)

Starc 14–2–50–1; Hazlewood 15.5–8–38–5; Lyon 14–4–55–3; Johnson 14–2–54–1; Watson 2–0–10–0. *Second innings*—Starc 13–5–34–3; Hazlewood 10–5–18–2; Lyon 7–3–12–2; Johnson 8–1–23–2; Watson 4–2–3–1.

Umpires: I. J. Gould and R. A. Kettleborough.   Third umpire: Aleem Dar.
Referee: R. S. Mahanama.

DOMESTIC CRICKET IN THE WEST INDIES IN 2014-15

Haydn Gill

Another attempt by West Indian authorities to lift the standard of Caribbean cricket produced only marginal improvement. The regional first-class tournament was rebranded as the Professional Cricket League, to be contested by the six traditional territories under a franchise system, while Combined Campuses & Colleges, who had taken part over the previous seven seasons, appeared only in the 50-over competition. The West Indian Cricket Board created a pool of 90 players (excluding contracted internationals) who were guaranteed a basic income of $US15,600–36,000, plus up to $18,000 from match fees and prize money – making the first-class game fully professional.

Franchises were to choose ten players from their own territory and five from a cross-territorial pool, to spread talent. In fact, only two teams hired a foreigner. Trinidad & Tobago signed the Guyanese ex-Test player Ramnaresh Sarwan, who then withdrew, citing personal reasons, while Guyana picked Barbados all-rounder Raymon Reifer. The competition was expanded to include home and away rounds (last tried in 2004-05 and 2008-09), played between November and March, with a break in January for the 50-over tournament. There was no knockout stage.

WICB president Dave Cameron called it "a revolutionary introduction" but, despite the development of a handful of young players, the quality of the cricket still looked amateurish. Of the 30 matches, 25 produced outright results, and nine ended inside three days. The number of centuries rose from 21 the previous season to 26 (matching the increase in fixtures); there were six totals of 400-plus, up from four, and 35 totals under 200, up by three.

The season was a triumph for **Guyana**, who won the league with a round to spare: it was their first first-class trophy since a shared title in 1997-98, and their first outright since 1992-93. A year earlier, they could not win one of their six games; this time, they won eight out of ten. The title was effectively decided in an enthralling seventh-round game with defending champions **Barbados**, who led by 91 on their first innings. Guyana chased down 333 with time running out, thanks largely to a 144-run stand between their most experienced batsmen, Shivnarine Chanderpaul and Narsingh Deonarine.

Guyana's batting was usually solid – except for an astonishing collapse as they pursued 69 in their earlier match with Barbados – but their trump cards were slow left-armer Veerasammy Permaul and leg-spinner Devendra Bishoo. In another season dominated by slow bowlers (seven of the top ten wicket-takers were spinners), Permaul and Bishoo headed the list, with 128 at 15 between them. Both earned a recall to the Test team.

The Barbados selectors emphasised younger players, including a few who won international call-ups. Captain Kraigg Brathwaite, aged 22, had another outstanding season, passing 600 runs, as did team-mates Shai Hope (21) and Shane Dowrich (23). The only batsmen with more runs were the experienced Devon Smith, with 822, and his fellow Windwards opener, Tyrone Theophile, with 689. **Windward Islands** finished in the top three for the third year running, and might have challenged for their first title had they been more consistent (they won five and lost four).

Jamaica, champions for five successive years from 2007-08 to 2011-12, were a disappointing fourth. Test batsman Marlon Samuels was left out of the squad for breaching selection rules: his association said he had failed to play in 80% of domestic fixtures as required when not on international duty.

Trinidad & Tobago, who won the 50-over tournament in January and the third Caribbean Premier League in July, slipped down the four-day table after finishing a close second the previous year. As well as Sarwan pulling out, five others – including Dwayne Bravo and Sunil Narine – withdrew from the first-class squad, to concentrate on limited-overs cricket or recover from injuries. **Leeward Islands** finished bottom for the third time in four seasons, losing eight matches on the trot before two consolation wins.

FIRST-CLASS AVERAGES, 2014-15

BATTING (300 runs, average 20.00)

	M	I	NO	R	HS	100	Avge	Ct/St
J. E. Root (*England*)	3	5	1	358	182*	1	89.50	4
†G. S. Ballance (*England*)	3	6	1	331	122	1	66.20	2
S. O. Dowrich (*Barbados*)	10	15	3	615	131*	2	51.25	15/5
K. C. Brathwaite (*Barbados/West Indies*)	11	19	2	846	182	4	49.76	7
†D. S. Smith (*Windward Islands/West Indies*)	11	20	1	915	151	2	48.15	19
J. Charles (*Windward Islands*)	5	8	1	333	151	1	47.57	11
R. L. Chase (*Barbados*)	8	13	1	534	120*	1	44.50	6
T. Theophile (*Windward Islands*)	10	17	1	689	136	2	43.06	8
†N. Deonarine (*Guyana*)	9	14	2	514	139	2	42.83	2
A. D. S. Fletcher (*Windward Islands*)	6	9	1	326	120	1	40.75	12/1
S. D. Hope (*Barbados/West Indies*)	10	17	1	642	211	2	40.12	11
†V. A. Singh (*Guyana*)	8	14	2	479	141	1	39.91	6
J. Blackwood (*Jamaica/West Indies*)	11	20	2	716	112*	1	39.77	5
C. D. Barnwell (*Guyana*)	10	15	3	471	148	1	39.25	6
†Y. Cariah (*Trinidad & Tobago*)	8	14	2	431	71	0	35.91	2
†S. Chanderpaul (*Guyana/West Indies*)	11	19	1	631	119	1	35.05	6
R. Chandrika (*Guyana*)	9	15	0	525	83	0	35.00	6
J. N. Mohammed (*Trinidad & Tobago*)	10	20	3	587	143*	2	34.52	3
†L. R. Johnson (*Guyana*)	8	14	0	465	78	0	33.21	15
†K. Y. Ottley (*Trinidad & Tobago*)	5	10	0	312	99	0	31.20	3
R. R. S. Cornwall (*Leeward Islands*)	7	14	1	357	101*	1	27.46	7
†J. D. Campbell (*Jamaica*)	9	16	0	423	83	0	26.43	10
D. C. Thomas (*Leeward Islands*)	10	20	1	473	99*	0	24.89	14
T. L. Lambert (*Jamaica*)	10	18	1	404	87	0	23.76	4
K. Y. G. Ottley (*Trinidad & Tobago*)	9	17	1	351	82	0	21.93	7

BOWLING (15 wickets)

	Style	O	M	R	W	BB	5I	Avge
N. O. Miller (*Jamaica*)	SLA	128	40	239	17	7-63	1	14.05
K. K. Peters (*Windward Islands*)	LM	217.4	62	524	37	6-24	4	14.16
J. A. Warrican (*Barbados*)	SLA	298.4	87	734	49	8-72	5	14.97
V. Permaul (*Guyana/West Indies*)	SLA	492.5	171	1,072	71	8-26	4	15.09
M. Matthew (*Windward Islands*)	RFM	218.5	57	512	31	5-19	2	16.51
J. M. Anderson (*England*)	RFM	119.2	38	306	17	6-42	1	18.00
C. R. Brathwaite (*Barbados*)	RFM	132.2	35	357	19	4-18	0	18.78
D. K. Jacobs (*Jamaica*)	LBG	320.3	68	855	48	7-54	4	17.81
D. Bishoo (*Guyana/West Indies*)	LBG	441.1	92	1,250	65	6-74	4	19.23
G. C. Tonge (*Leeward Islands*)	RFM	198.2	58	602	30	5-57	1	20.06
A. B. W. Bobb (*Windward Islands*)	SLA	285.3	55	666	31	6-45	3	21.48
I. Khan (*Trinidad & Tobago*)	SLA	392	67	1,226	56	6-13	4	21.89
J. O. Dawes (*Jamaica*)	RF	154.3	48	426	18	4-57	0	23.66
M. J. Mindley (*Jamaica*)	RFM	186.1	51	477	19	5-35	1	25.10
M. L. Cummins (*Barbados*)	RF	143.2	23	468	18	5-63	1	26.00
S. Shillingford (*Windward Islands*)	OB	348	69	945	36	6-31	3	26.25
M. K. A. Richards (*Trinidad & Tobago*)	RFM	232.5	59	720	27	4-42	0	26.66
R. R. S. Cornwall (*Leeward Islands*)	OB	250.1	57	781	29	7-96	1	26.93
D. E. Bernard (*Jamaica*)	RFM	164.5	28	509	18	5-57	1	28.27
R. R. Beaton (*Guyana*)	RFM	179	43	541	19	4-40	0	28.47
A. R. Nurse (*Barbados*)	OB	247.1	37	729	25	4-56	0	29.16
L. A. S. Sebastien (*Windward Islands*)	OB	200.4	44	524	17	5-39	2	30.82
D. E. Johnson (*Windward Islands*)	LF	136	19	494	15	3-48	0	32.93
S. T. Gabriel (*Trinidad & Tobago/WI*)	RFM	194	45	644	19	3-40	0	33.89
O. V. Brown (*Jamaica*)	LBG	166.3	24	516	15	3-37	0	34.40

Averages include England's tour in April–May but not Australia's in May–June.

WICB PROFESSIONAL CRICKET LEAGUE, 2014-15

				Bonus points		
	Played	Won	Lost	Drawn	Batting	Bowling	Points
Guyana Jaguars	10	8	1	1	21	28	148
Barbados Pride	10	5	1	4	18	27	117
Windward Islands Volcanoes	10	5	4	1	23	23	109
Jamaica Scorpion	10	3	5	2	6	27	75
Trinidad & Tobago Red Force	10	2	6	2	10	25	65
Leeward Islands Hurricanes .	10	2	8	0	6	24	54

Win = 12pts; draw = 3pts. Bonus points were awarded as follows for the first 110 overs of each team's first innings: one batting point for the first 200 runs and then for 250, 300, 350 and 400; one bowling point for the third wicket taken and then for the sixth and ninth.

At Providence, Guyana, November 14–16, 2014. **Guyana won by an innings and ten runs. ‡Guyana 343** (N. Deonarine 110*); **Leeward Islands 94 and 239.** *Guyana 17pts, Leeward Islands 2pts. Guyana's three-day win might have been even more one-sided but for Jahmar Hamilton (74) and Gavin Tonge (49): with Leewards 118-6 in the follow-on, still 131 behind, they added 102.*

At Kingston, Jamaica, November 14–16, 2014. **Jamaica won by 13 runs. ‡Jamaica 208** (A. B. W. Bobb 6-45) **and 162** (A. B. W. Bobb 5-48); **Windward Islands 110** (M. J. Mindley 5-35) **and 247** (D. K. Jacobs 7-72). *Jamaica 16pts, Windward Islands 3pts. Seamer Marquino Mindley, only 20, took 5-35 on first-class debut.*

At Port-of-Spain, Trinidad, November 14–17, 2014. **Drawn. Barbados 360** (K. C. Brathwaite 182); **‡Trinidad & Tobago 96 and 213-5.** *Trinidad & Tobago 5pts, Barbados 8pts.*

At Bridgetown (Kensington Oval), Barbados, November 21–24, 2014. **Drawn. Jamaica 111-4 dec; ‡Barbados 6-2 dec.** *Barbados 4pts, Jamaica 3pts. Rain prevented any play before the final day.*

At Providence, Guyana, November 21–24, 2014. **Guyana won by 92 runs. ‡Guyana 291** (N. Deonarine 139; K. K. Peters 5-36) **and 175-6 dec; Windward Islands 184** (N. Deonarine 5-24) **and 190** (V. Permaul 8-36). *Guyana 17pts, Windward Islands 1pt. Narsingh Deonarine scored his second hundred in two games, then ensured first-innings lead with five wickets; slow left-armer Veerasammy Permaul completed victory with a career-best 31.2–20–36–8.*

At Basseterre, St Kitts, November 21–24, 2014. **Trinidad & Tobago won by six wickets. Leeward Islands 202 and 130** (I. Khan 6-13); **‡Trinidad & Tobago 130 and 203-4.** *Trinidad & Tobago 15pts, Leeward Islands 4pts.*

At Providence, Guyana, November 28–December 1, 2014. **Barbados won by two runs. Guyana 261 and 66** (D. R. Smith 5-17); **‡Barbados 101** (V. Permaul 8-26) **and 228.** *Barbados 15pts, Guyana 5pts. Guyana collapsed in astonishing fashion on the last day, falling just short of a target of 69 thanks to Dwayne Smith's career-best 5-17. Their 66 was this tournament's lowest total. Guyana's only defeat of the season was tough on Permaul, who had forced Barbados to follow on by improving his career-best for the second time in two matches: his 15.2–5–26–8, the season's best return, included the last four in seven balls. He then added four more to finish with 12-101, and 28 in the first three games. Barbados became the first team to win after following on in the West Indies since the start of the first-class competition in 1965-66. There were two earlier instances, also involving Barbados, who lost to R. S. Lucas's XI in 1894-95 and to Jamaica in 1958.*

At Port-of-Spain, Trinidad, November 28–December 1, 2014. **Jamaica won by 37 runs. ‡Jamaica 173** (I. Khan 6-52) **and 196; Trinidad & Tobago 131** (S. S. Cottrell 5-42) **and 201** (N. O. Miller 7-63). *Jamaica 15pts, Trinidad & Tobago 3pts. In their first innings, 145 of their runs came in a fifth-wicket stand between Tamar Lambert (87) and David Bernard (65); no one else passed six.*

At St George's (Queen's Park New), Grenada, November 28–December 1, 2014. **Windward Islands won by nine wickets. ‡Leeward Islands 109** (L. A. S. Sebastien 5-39) **and 334** (O. Peters 104; L. A. S. Sebastien 5-50); **Windward Islands 308-5 dec** (D. S. Smith 145) **and 138-1.** *Windward Islands 18pts, Leeward Islands 1pt. Devon Smith's century led to victory and earned him a call-up to South Africa to replace the injured Chris Gayle.*

At Kingston, Jamaica, December 5–8, 2014. **Jamaica won by four wickets. Leeward Islands 103** (D. K. Jacobs 5-27) **and 313; ‡Jamaica 222** (G. C. Tonge 5-57) **and 195-6.** *Jamaica 16pts, Leeward*

Islands 3pts. Jamaica were 87-7 on the opening day, when 17 wickets fell, but Nikita Miller (62) and Damion Jacobs (41) added 100 for the eighth to help them to a crucial lead. In Leewards' second innings, Rahkeem Cornwall scored 95 on first-class debut.

At Port-of-Spain, Trinidad, December 5–8, 2014. **Guyana won by an innings and 60 runs. ‡Trinidad & Tobago 198 and 234; Guyana 492-8 dec** (V. A. Singh 141). *Guyana 18pts, Trinidad & Tobago 1pt. Guyana's Anthony Bramble caught three and stumped two in Trinidad & Tobago's first innings. Chris Barnwell (65*) and Permaul (50*) added 112* for Guyana's ninth wicket, taking them to the tournament's highest total. Guyana led the table by seven points at the break.*

At Arnos Vale, St Vincent, December 5–8, 2014. **Barbados won by 11 runs. ‡Barbados 352** (R. L. Chase 120*) **and 128** (S. Shillingford 5-46); **Windward Islands 274** (J.A. Charles 151; J. A. Warrican 5-75) **and 195.** *Barbados 17pts, Windward Islands 4pts. Barbados batsman Omar Phillips was hit on the head at the non-striker's end, failing to evade a drive from Shai Hope, and was knocked unconscious. His helmet prevented serious damage, but he was out of action until March. On the third day, an invasion by a large swarm of bees forced players and umpires to duck for cover.*

At Bridgetown (Kensington Oval), Barbados, February 6–8, 2015. **Barbados won by an innings and 190 runs. Barbados 406-6 dec** (S. O. Dowrich 131*); **‡Leeward Islands 136 and 80.** *Barbados 16pts, Leeward Islands 1pt. In the most crushing result of the season, Leewards lost their top five batsmen for 50 in the first innings and 27 in the second.*

At Kingston, Jamaica, February 6–9, 2015. **Guyana won by 105 runs. Guyana 314 and 202; ‡Jamaica 177 and 234.** *Guyana 18pts, Jamaica 3pts. Permaul hit a career-best 86 in 107 balls in Guyana's first innings. Jamaican keeper Carlton Baugh caught the top five in their second.*

At Gros Islet, St Lucia, February 6–9, 2015. **Windward Islands won by an innings and 148 runs. ‡Windward Islands 400-8 dec** (T. Theophile 136); **Trinidad & Tobago 177** (K. K. Peters 5-21) **and 75.** *Windward Islands 20pts, Trinidad & Tobago 2pts. In all, Devon Smith held seven catches in the field for Windwards.*

At Bridgetown (Kensington Oval), Barbados, February 13–16, 2015. **Barbados won by 222 runs. Barbados 275 and 278-5 dec** (S. D. Hope 111*); **‡Trinidad & Tobago 218 and 113.** *Barbados 17pts, Trinidad & Tobago 4pts. Barbados' fourth consecutive win – featuring Hope's maiden hundred – was Trinidad & Tobago's fourth consecutive defeat.*

At North Sound, Antigua, February 13–15, 2015. **Guyana won by eight wickets. Leeward Islands 139 and 200** (D. Bishoo 6-82); **‡Guyana 267** (R. R. S. Cornwall 7-96) **and 73-2.** *Guyana 17pts, Leeward Islands 3pts. Cornwall's off-spin claimed 7-96 in his third first-class match.*

At Arnos Vale, St Vincent, February 13–15, 2015. **Windward Islands won by an innings and 22 runs. ‡Jamaica 204** (A. B. W. Bobb 5-38) **and 102** (S. Shillingford 6-31); **Windward Islands 328** (A. D. S. Fletcher 120; D. E. Bernard 5-57). *Windward Islands 18pts, Jamaica 4pts.*

At Bridgetown (Kensington Oval), Barbados, February 20–23, 2015. **Guyana won by four wickets. Barbados 312** (K. C. Brathwaite 102; D. Bishoo 6-94) **and 241-6 dec** (K. C. Brathwaite 112); **‡Guyana 221** (M. L. Cummins 5-63) **and 335-6.** *Guyana 15pts, Barbados 5pts. Kraigg Brathwaite scored a century in each innings, but Barbados suffered their only defeat of the season, despite a first-innings lead of 91; Deonarine (90) and Shivnarine Chanderpaul (64) added 144 for Guyana's fourth wicket, before Raymon Reifer (41*) saw them past a target of 333.*

At Kingston, Jamaica, February 20–22, 2015. **Trinidad & Tobago won by 179 runs. Trinidad & Tobago 277 and 246; ‡Jamaica 167 and 177** (I. Khan 6-24). *Trinidad & Tobago 17pts, Jamaica 3pts. In the fourth innings, Jamaica were 177-5 before slow left-armer Imran Khan took four wickets in an over; Akeal Hosein added the last, still at the same score.*

At Gros Islet, St Lucia, February 20–22, 2015. **Windward Islands won by nine wickets. Leeward Islands 161** (K. K. Peters 6-24) **and 170** (M. Matthew 5-32); **‡Windward Islands 249 and 84-1.** *Windward Islands 16pts, Leeward Islands 3pts.*

At Providence, Guyana, March 6–8, 2015. **Guyana won by five wickets. ‡Jamaica 258** (V. Permaul 5-77) **and 138** (V. Permaul 5-33); **Guyana 236** (D. K. Jacobs 5-67) **and 163-5.** *Guyana 16pts, Jamaica 5pts. Permaul collected ten or more in a match for the third time in this tournament – including his 50th of the season – while Bramble made four dismissals in each innings (5ct, 3st).*

At Basseterre, St Kitts, March 6–8, 2015. **Barbados won by nine wickets. ‡Leeward Islands 215** (J. A. Warrican 8-88) **and 150** (J. A. Warrican 5-50); **Barbados 353** (S. O. Dowrich 106) **and 13-1.**

Barbados 18pts, Leewards Islands 3pts. Slow left-armer Jomel Warrican converted his career-best 8-88 into 13-138, the best match return of the season. It was Leewards' eighth consecutive defeat.

At Couva, Trinidad, March 6–9, 2015. **Windward Islands won by 175 runs. ‡Windward Islands 350** (I. Khan 6-127) **and 249** (K. A. Pollard 5-36); **Trinidad & Tobago 299** (J. N. Mohammed 100; K. K. Peters 6-59) **and 125** (M. Matthew 5-19). *Windward Islands 18pts, Trinidad & Tobago 4pts.*

At Bridgetown (Kensington Oval), Barbados, March 13–16, 2015. **Drawn. ‡Barbados 480** (S. D. Hope 211, S. S. J. Brooks 124) **and 167-5 dec; Windward Islands 416** (D. Smith 151, T. Theophile 125) **and 101-6** (J. A. Warrican 5-29). *Barbados 8pts, Windward Islands 8pts. Hope batted nine and a half hours for a maiden double-hundred, the only one in this tournament. Barbados had been 2-2 after winning the toss, before he and Sharmarh Brooks, with a maiden century, added 237. Smith and Tyrone Theophile responded with an opening stand of 269. Barbados set Windwards 232, and Warrican reduced them to 85-6, but the hosts could not finish the job.*

At Providence, Guyana, March 13–16, 2015. **Drawn. ‡Guyana 291 and 266-5 dec; Trinidad & Tobago 340** (D. Bishoo 6-79) **and 99-3.** *Guyana 7pts, Trinidad & Tobago 9pts. Guyana sealed the title despite the draw; their 22pt lead was unassailable with one round to go. Bishoo's 6-79 took him to 50 wickets in the season; T&T's Imran Khan also reached the mark.*

At Basseterre, St Kitts, March 13–16, 2015. **Leeward Islands won by four wickets. ‡Jamaica 175 and 274** (A. Martin 5-76); **Leeward Islands 285** (S. P. Peters 136; D. K. Jacobs 7-54) **and 168-6.** *Leeward Islands 17pts, Jamaica 3pts. Leewards finally ended their losing streak, while Jamaica's extended to five, despite leg-spinner Damion Jacobs's 10-110.*

At Kingston, Jamaica, March 20–23, 2015. **Drawn. ‡Barbados 310** (S. S. J. Brooks 100) **and 303-9; Jamaica 228** (J. A. Warrican 8-72). *Jamaica 7pts, Barbados 9pts. Warrican improved his career-best again, taking his tally in March to 26 wickets in five innings.*

At Couva, Trinidad, March 20–23, 2015. **Leeward Islands won by five wickets. ‡Trinidad & Tobago 291** (J. N. Mohammed 143*) **and 226; Leeward Islands 277 and 245-5** (R. R. S. Cornwall 101*). *Leeward Islands 17pts, Trinidad & Tobago 5pts. Cornwall combined a maiden century with six wickets in the match to help Leewards win again.*

At Roseau, Dominica, March 20–23, 2015. **Guyana won by an innings and ten runs. Windward Islands 283** (D. Bishoo 6-74) **and 134; ‡Guyana 427** (S. Chanderpaul 119, C. D. Barnwell 148; S. Shillingford 5-118). *Guyana 18pts, Windward Islands 3pts. Chanderpaul, with his 71st century, and Barnwell, with his first, added 251 for Guyana's sixth wicket. Their team-mate Bramble finished with 41 dismissals (33ct, 8st), more than twice as many as the next-best keeper in the tournament.*

REGIONAL CHAMPIONS

Shell Shield		1985-86	Barbados	2001-02	Jamaica
1965-66	Barbados	1986-87	Guyana		
1966-67	Barbados			*Carib Beer Cup*	
1967-68	No competition	*Red Stripe Cup*		2002-03	Barbados
1968-69	Jamaica	1987-88	Jamaica	2003-04	Barbados
1969-70	Trinidad	1988-89	Jamaica	2004-05	Jamaica
1970-71	Trinidad	1989-90	Leeward Islands	2005-06	Trinidad & Tobago
1971-72	Barbados	1990-91	Barbados	2006-07	Barbados
1972-73	Guyana	1991-92	Jamaica	2007-08	Jamaica
1973-74	Barbados	1992-93	Guyana		
1974-75	Guyana	1993-94	Leeward Islands	*Headley–Weekes Trophy*	
1975-76 {	Trinidad	1994-95	Barbados	2008-09	Jamaica
	Barbados	1995-96	Leeward Islands	2009-10	Jamaica
1976-77	Barbados	1996-97	Barbados	2010-11	Jamaica
1977-78	Barbados			2011-12	Jamaica
1978-79	Barbados	*President's Cup*		2012-13	Barbados
1979-80	Barbados	1997-98 {	Leeward Islands		
1980-81	Combined Islands		Guyana	*President's Trophy*	
1981-82	Barbados			2013-14	Barbados
1982-83	Guyana	*Busta Cup*			
1983-84	Barbados	1998-99	Barbados	*WICB Professional Cricket*	
1984-85	Trinidad & Tobago	1999-2000	Jamaica	*League*	
		2000-01	Barbados	2014-15	Guyana

Barbados have won the title outright 21 times, Jamaica 12, Guyana 6, Trinidad/Trinidad & Tobago 4, Leeward Islands 3, Combined Islands 1. Barbados, Guyana, Leeward Islands and Trinidad have also shared the title.

NAGICO REGIONAL SUPER50, 2014-15

50-over league plus knockout

Zone A	P	W	L	NR	Pts		Zone B	P	W	L	NR	Pts
GUYANA	3	2	1	0	9		TRINIDAD & TOBAGO	3	3	0	0	14
CAMPUS/COLLEGES . .	3	1	0	2	8		JAMAICA	3	2	1	0	10
Windward Islands	3	1	1	1	6		Leeward Islands	3	1	2	0	5
Barbados	3	0	2	1	2		West Indies Under-19 . . .	3	0	3	0	0

Semi-final At Port-of-Spain, Trinidad, January 22, 2015 (day/night). **Guyana won by six wickets. Jamaica 188-9** (50 overs); ‡**Guyana 189-4** (48.1 overs). MoM: S. Chanderpaul (Guyana). *Shivnarine Chanderpaul batted throughout Guyana's innings for 98*, adding 99* with Royston Crandon (45*).*

Semi-final At Port-of-Spain, Trinidad, January 23, 2015 (day/night). **Trinidad & Tobago won by 41 runs** (D/L). **Trinidad & Tobago 159** (31.3 overs) (C. M. Powell 5-22); ‡**Combined Campuses & Colleges 114** (30.4 overs). MoM: R. Rampaul (T&T). *Rain reduced the match to 32 overs a side; Campuses & Colleges' D/L target was 156, but they crumbled against Ravi Rampaul (3-17) and Dwayne Bravo (3-22). Christopher Powell took five wickets in his second senior match.*

Final At Port-of-Spain, Trinidad, January 25, 2015 (day/night). **Trinidad & Tobago won by 135 runs. Trinidad & Tobago 200-8** (50 overs) (J. N. Mohammed 117*) ‡**Guyana 65** (23.5 overs) (S. P. Narine 6-9). MoM: J. N. Mohammed and S. P. Narine. *Jason Mohammed, whose maiden one-day hundred included six sixes, single-handedly outscored Guyana, who collapsed in less than half the allotted overs as Sunil Narine's off-spin claimed career-best figures of 8–3–9–6. Only opener Trevon Griffith (first out, for 31 out of 36) passed seven.*

CARIBBEAN PREMIER LEAGUE, 2015

20-over league plus knockout

	Played	Won	Lost	NR/A	Points	NRR
BARBADOS TRIDENTS	10	6	4	0	12	0.18
GUYANA AMAZON WARRIORS	10	5	4	1	11	0.58
TRINIDAD & TOBAGO RED STEEL.	10	5	4	1	11	−0.07
JAMAICA TALLAWAHS	10	4	5	1	9	−0.42
ST LUCIA ZOUKS	10	4	5	1	9	−0.67
ST KITTS AND NEVIS PATRIOTS . . .	10	4	6	0	8	0.22

Play-off At Port-of-Spain, Trinidad, July 23, 2015 (floodlit). **Trinidad & Tobago Red Steel won by 27 runs.** ‡**Trinidad & Tobago Red Steel 152-6** (20 overs); **Jamaica Tallawahs 125** (19.3 overs) (D. J. Bravo 5-23). MoM: D. M. Bravo (T&T). *Darren Bravo hit six sixes in his 63-ball 86*, before his brother Dwayne grabbed five wickets in 17 deliveries – both career-bests in the format.*

Semi-final At Port-of-Spain, Trinidad, July 25, 2015 (floodlit). **Trinidad & Tobago Red Steel won by six wickets.** ‡**Guyana Amazon Warriors 108-9** (20 overs); **Trinidad & Tobago Red Steel 109-4** (18.3 overs). MoM: Kamran Akmal (T&T). *Lendl Simmons (64) batted for all but five balls of Guyana's innings, but Kamran Akmal's 49 steered Trinidad & Tobago towards a final against the defending champions. His brother Umar made a duck for Guyana.*

Final At Port-of-Spain, Trinidad, July 26, 2015 (floodlit). **Trinidad & Tobago Red Steel won by 20 runs. Trinidad & Tobago Red Steel 178-5** (20 overs); **Barbados Tridents 158-4** (20 overs). MoM: Kamran Akmal (T&T). MoS: D. J. Bravo (T&T). *Cameron Delport (50 in 38 balls) and Kamran Akmal (60 in 46) set up victory by adding 102 for Trinidad & Tobago's second wicket.*

ZIMBABWE CRICKET IN 2015

Quantity, not quality

MEHLULI SIBANDA

Zimbabwe played 42 international matches in 2015, their second-most in any calendar year – but the figure was misleading, because it did not include a single Test. A decade earlier, they had voluntarily withdrawn from Tests after a dispute with players left them so weak that the ICC agreed they should focus on one-day cricket – a temporary measure which dragged on for six years. This time, they simply could not persuade any other Full Member to find space for more than a handful of limited-overs games. Even Bangladesh, who originally scheduled three Tests for Zimbabwe's visit in 2015-16, first cut them back to two, then postponed them altogether, substituting four extra T20 internationals as preparation for the World Twenty20.

The year began with a poor display at the World Cup. Zimbabwe finished sixth out of seven in their pool, their only victory coming against the UAE.

ZIMBABWE IN 2015

	Played	Won	Lost	Drawn/No result
Tests	–	–	–	–
One-day internationals	31	7	23	1
Twenty20 internationals	11	2	9	–

JANUARY		
FEBRUARY	ICC World Cup (in Australia and New Zealand)	(page 860)
MARCH		
APRIL		
MAY	3 ODIs and 2 T20Is (a) v Pakistan	(page 1058)
JUNE		
JULY	3 ODIs and 2 T20Is (h) v India	(page 1163)
AUGUST	3 ODIs and 1 T20I (h) v New Zealand	(page 1166)
SEPTEMBER	3 ODIs and 2 T20Is (h) v Pakistan	(page 1168)
	3 ODIs (h) v Ireland	(page 1170)
OCTOBER	5 ODIs and 2 T20Is (h) v Afghanistan	(page 1172)
NOVEMBER	3 ODIs and 2 T20Is (a) v Bangladesh	(page 984)
DECEMBER	5 ODIs and 2 T20Is (a) v Afghanistan (in the UAE)	(page 1194)
JANUARY		

For a review of Zimbabwean domestic cricket from the 2014-15 season, see page 1175.

Afterwards, coach Dav Whatmore signed a new four-year contract, but former captain Brendan Taylor walked away, joining Nottinghamshire on a three-year Kolpak contract. He had scored 433 runs at the World Cup – a Zimbabwean record – including centuries against Ireland and India, which took him to another national record, of eight ODI hundreds, passing Alistair Campbell.

Zimbabwe's highest-profile games of the year came in May, when they became the first Full Member to tour Pakistan since the Sri Lankan team bus was attacked by terrorists in 2009. They played two Twenty20 matches and three one-day internationals at Lahore's Gaddafi Stadium, completing the tour despite an explosion outside the ground during the penultimate game: two people died, one of them apparently a suicide bomber. Pakistan won four matches before the last was ended by rain.

Although the Pakistan Cricket Board paid the permanently cash-strapped Zimbabwe Cricket $US500,000, the trip was highly controversial. The players' union had advised that the risks of touring Pakistan were still unmanageable, and Zimbabwe's Sports & Recreation Commission had refused to give it the green light. In November, the commission barred Wilson Manase, the ZC chairman at the time of the tour, from holding office in any national sports association for four years, ruling that he had unilaterally approved it after they had denied authorisation. Angrily insisting that the decision had been made by the entire ZC board, and the delegation led by ZC's one-time managing director Ozias Bvute, he contested the ban in court.

Manase had already lost his role as chairman, which he had taken on an interim basis in July 2014 when the long-serving Peter Chingoka resigned. He expected to be confirmed in the board elections of August 2015, but was voted out and replaced by former vice-chairman Tavengwa Mukuhlani.

Campbell had been appointed managing director of cricket under Manase, but his powers were reduced after the change. He resigned in October, a few months after Zimbabwe's off-spinner and ex-captain Prosper Utseya had accused him of "racism and victimisation", and of keeping him out of the World Cup. There was further fallout when Mark Vermeulen, a white batsman with a history of mental health issues, attacked Utseya's move in an online rant that referred to black people as "apes". He deleted it and claimed Utseya had accepted an apology, but Vermeulen was banned from all cricket by ZC. A Cornish club which hired him as their professional for 2016 faced protests.

On the field, Zimbabwe hosted India, New Zealand and Pakistan, all for a brief programme of one-day and Twenty20 internationals; they won a single match against each of them. They did manage a 2–1 victory in a one-day series against Ireland in October, but later that month made history as the first Full Member to lose a series to an Associate. In five 50-over games, Afghanistan defeated them 3–2, and they followed up by winning the Twenty20 internationals 2–0. (This was the first international cricket in Zimbabwe's second-largest city, Bulawayo, for more than a year.) In case this appeared a fluke, Afghanistan achieved identical series results when Zimbabwe played them again in Sharjah at the turn of the year. In between, the Zimbabweans visited Bangladesh for the Test-less series, and were again put to the sword: their only victory came with a ball to spare in the final Twenty20 game.

ZIMBABWE v INDIA IN 2015

Tristan Holme

One-day internationals (3): Zimbabwe 0, India 3
Twenty20 internationals (2): Zimbabwe 1, India 1

Zimbabwe had grown accustomed to receiving watered-down Indian teams. So there was no great surprise when India rested six senior players, left two others at home for an A-team series against Australia, and allowed team director Ravi Shastri to take an Ashes punditry job with Sky Sports. Zimbabwe were simply relieved that the tour went ahead at all: the BCCI's concern over player burnout, and distaste for the series broadcaster, Ten Sports – whose parent company, the Essel Group, had been in talks about a rebel Twenty20 league – had delayed its confirmation until the eleventh hour.

So low-key was the contest that the African satellite channel SuperSport, which for years had screened all Zimbabwe's home matches, showed the World Twenty20 qualifying tournament, featuring Kenya and Namibia, instead. This at least meant live cricket returned to Zimbabwean free-to-air television for the first time in more than a decade, on the state-owned Zimbabwe Broadcasting Corporation – although the excitement was tempered by the C-rate production and regular musical interludes.

Still, viewers of the first one-day international received good value when Elton Chigumbura's hundred ensured a thrilling finish. Thereafter the tour reverted largely to type, as India comfortably swept the ODI series and won the first Twenty20. It required a chivvying display in the field from Sikandar Raza – standing in as captain for the injured Chigumbura – to rouse Zimbabwe to a series-levelling win in the second.

The ODIs saw the introduction of the ICC's latest playing conditions, which attempted to make life a fraction easier for the bowlers by relaxing the fielding restrictions. But the more interesting development was an experiment with Dukes balls for the first time in Zimbabwean cricket. Whereas the white Kookaburra had usually given the side bowling first a huge advantage in games starting at 9am, the Dukes was liable to swing even in the afternoon, lessening Chigumbura's success at the toss in all three matches.

With Ravi Jadeja dropped altogether, Ambati Rayudu, Kedar Jadhav, Stuart Binny and Manish Pandey all made a case for inclusion in India squads, while Ajinkya Rahane, deputising as captain for M. S. Dhoni, led astutely despite the tour being overshadowed by events back home. During the third ODI the verdict of the Justice Lodha Committee, assigned to investigate corruption in the IPL, filtered through, leaving five of the squad, including Rahane, to worry about their futures with Rajasthan Royals and Chennai Super Kings, the two suspended franchises.

There were off-field distractions for Zimbabwe, too: a letter sent by Prosper Utseya to the board, in which he alleged racism by their managing director, Alistair Campbell was leaked. It had been written before the tour of Pakistan in May, so it was not news to everyone; in any case, locals were used to such political controversies. Utseya played the day after the letter was made public – and Zimbabwe recorded a notable victory, briefly reviving memories of their late-1990s heyday.

INDIAN TOURING PARTY

*A. M. Rahane, Bhuvneshwar Kumar, S. T. R. Binny, Harbhajan Singh, K. M. Jadhav, D. S. Kulkarni, M. K. Pandey, A. R. Patel, A. T. Rayudu, S. V. Samson, M. Sharma, S. Sharma, M. K. Tiwary, R. V. Uthappa, M. Vijay. *Coaches:* B. Arun, S. B. Bangar, R. Sridhar.

    K. V. Sharma was originally selected, but fractured a finger before departure. Rayudu suffered a thigh injury during the second ODI, and was replaced by Samson.

First one-day international   At Harare, July 10, 2015. **India won by four runs. India 255-6** (50 overs) (A. M. Rahane 34, A. T. Rayudu 124*, S. T. R. Binny 77); ‡**Zimbabwe 251-7** (50 overs) (H. Masakadza 34, E. Chigumbura 104*, Sikandar Raza 37). *MoM:* A. T. Rayudu. *A seesaw game ended with Elton Chigumbura requiring six from the final three balls, off Bhuvneshwar Kumar. He turned down two singles, but failed to hit the last delivery for six. Thanks to Bhuvneshwar's excellent death bowling, India had escaped with a narrow victory. They recovered from 87-5 through a 160-run stand between Ambati Rayudu and Stuart Binny – an India record for the sixth wicket – as the pair absorbed what little pressure the hosts were able to apply, before 90 came from the final ten overs. India were also left wondering how they had allowed Chigumbura to drag his side back into the match. Zimbabwe had looked dead and buried at 160-6 in the 38th over, but No. 8 Graeme Cremer (27) managed to keep his captain company for the next 11, in which they chipped off 86. Chigumbura hammered a second consecutive ODI century but, as with his maiden hundred, in his 174th match, in Pakistan in May, he was unable to carry his team over the line, and a previously buoyant crowd quickly dispersed.*

Second one-day international   At Harare, July 12, 2015. **India won by 62 runs. India 271-8** (50 overs) (A. M. Rahane 63, M. Vijay 72, A. T. Rayudu 41; N. Madziva 4-49); ‡**Zimbabwe 209** (49 overs) (C. J. Chibhabha 72, R. Mutumbami 32; Bhuvneshwar Kumar 4-33). *MoM:* M. Vijay. *After their top-order collapse in the first game, India adopted a more circumspect approach on a slow surface. Openers Ajinkya Rahane and Murali Vijay managed just 70 in the first 19 overs, but extended that to 112 in the next seven. Vijay struck his maiden ODI fifty, while Rayudu, who later injured his thigh, had lucky escapes on 16, when an lbw shout from Chamu Chibhahha was turned down (there was no DRS), and 26, when Brian Vitori dropped him at long-on, and also suffered a thigh injury. The only time India didn't have it all their own way was in their last ten overs, when Neville Madziva showed skill with the reversing ball to record career-best figures. Bhuvneshwar's double strike in a superb opening spell reduced Zimbabwe to 43-3, and they never recovered, with Sean Williams having to bat through tendonitis of the knee. Chibhabha stroked a pleasing 72 but, when he was smartly run out by Rahane, Zimbabwe's meagre hopes left with him.*

Third one-day international   At Harare, July 14, 2015. **India won by 83 runs. India 276-5** (50 overs) (R. V. Uthappa 31, M. K. Pandey 71, K. M. Jadhav 105*); ‡**Zimbabwe 193** (42.4 overs) (C. J. Chibhabha 82; S. T. R. Binny 3-55). *MoM:* K. M. Jadhav. *MoS:* A. T. Rayudu (India). *ODI debut:* M. K. Pandey. *Timid captaincy and a woeful dropped catch by Chigumbura let India off the hook. With the tourists 82-4 in the 22nd over, Chigumbura allowed medium-pacers Hamilton Masakadza and Prosper Utseya (no longer bowling off-breaks after his action was ruled illegal) to complete their ten-over allocations, giving Manish Pandey and Kedar Jadhav time to settle. When leg-spinner Cremer was eventually introduced, Chigumbura put down Jadhav at backward point; he added 63 from his last 30 balls, finishing with a maiden century in his fourth ODI. Their assault left Zimbabwe shellshocked: Chibhabha made another fifty but, with the required rate climbing and his team-mates abandoning him, he was caught in the deep with more than 100 still needed. "Please bear with us," pleaded Dav Whatmore, after his tenth defeat in 11 completed ODIs since taking over as Zimbabwe's coach before the World Cup.*

First Twenty20 international   At Harare, July 17, 2015. **India won by 54 runs.** ‡**India 178-5** (20 overs) (A. M. Rahane 33, M. Vijay 34, R. V. Uthappa 39*; C. B. Mpofu 3-33); **Zimbabwe 124-7** (20 overs) (A. R. Patel 3-17). *MoM:* A. R. Patel. *T20I debuts:* N. Madziva, T. Muzarabani (Zimbabwe); S. T. R. Binny, K. M. Jadhav, M. K. Pandey, A. R. Patel, S. Sharma (India). *India* *fielded five Twenty20 international debutants, but it did not mean a lack of experience. Their IPL know-how was evident as Vijay and Rahane set the tone with 64 in seven overs, and Robin Uthappa steered the rest of the innings. Only Chris Mpofu's accurate burst kept India in check late on. Masakadza and Chibhabha made a steady start against the seamers, but were quickly undone by the spin of Akshar Patel and Harbhajan Singh (2-29). They took care of the top five as Zimbabwe sank from 55-0 to 90-6, before limping through the last few overs with no purpose beyond survival.*

Second Twenty20 international   At Harare, July 19, 2015. **Zimbabwe won by ten runs.** ‡**Zimbabwe 145-7** (20 overs) (C. J. Chibhabha 67); **India 135-9** (20 overs) (R. V. Uthappa 42; A. G. Cremer 3-18). *MoM:* C. J. Chibhabha. *MoS:* C. J. Chibhabha. *T20I debut:* S. V. Samson (India). *Sikandar Raza was handed the captaincy at short notice after an injury to Chigumbura, and injected some much-needed energy into Zimbabwe's cricket, leading them to their first Twenty20 international win in Harare. It was also their first over India in any format since twice humbling them in a home tri-series in 2010. Helped by the absence of Harbhajan Singh, who made way for the debutant Sanju Samson, Chibhabha hit a career-best 67 from 51 balls in an underwhelming total, and Cremer's excellent first spell of 3–0–14–2 suffocated India's middle order. But there was no doubting their inspiration: Sikandar geed up his team and convinced them they could defend a small total. A string of sublime catches and unlikely run-outs followed, Zimbabwe's enthusiasm building with each one. India wilted, tumbling from 57-1 to 69-5 in the space of three overs. Sikandar took no credit, and made no claim on the captaincy, but the identity of Zimbabwe's best leader was now clear.*

ZIMBABWE v NEW ZEALAND IN 2015-16

Austin Karonga

One-day internationals (3): Zimbabwe 1, New Zealand 2
Twenty international (1): Zimbabwe 0, New Zealand 1

After warming up with some strong displays against India – including a share of the Twenty20 games – Zimbabwe harboured hopes of a first one-day series victory over a Test-playing nation other than Bangladesh for more than 14 years.

New Zealand were lacking Brendon McCullum, who was given the tour off, as well as their usual new-ball pair of Trent Boult (back trouble) and Tim Southee (rested); they also lost Ross Taylor to a groin injury after the second one-dayer. And the alarm bells were ringing when Zimbabwe chased down 304 to win the first 50-over game, thanks to a superb maiden one-day century from Craig Ervine.

After that, though, Zimbabwe's old frailties resurfaced. Although Hamilton Masakadza and Chamu Chibhabha formed a useful opening partnership, the middle order was less cohesive, the bowling unpenetrative, and the fielding fallible. In the second ODI, Zimbabwe were 146 for eight before a determined century from Sikandar Raza dragged them to a reasonable total – but New Zealand's openers knocked off their target as Martin Guptill and Tom Latham both scored unbeaten hundreds. Then, after another bright start to their chase in the decider, Zimbabwe fell away – a disappointment after a better display of out-cricket had restricted New Zealand to 273. The solitary Twenty20 game was one-sided.

Kane Williamson cut an impressive figure standing in as New Zealand's captain, making 97 and 90 in his two one-day innings.

NEW ZEALAND TOURING PARTY

*K. S. Williamson, D. A. J. Bracewell, G. D. Elliott, M. J. Guptill, M. J. Henry, T. W. M. Latham, M. J. McClenaghan, N. L. McCullum, A. F. Milne, C. Munro, J. D. S. Neesham, L. Ronchi, I. S. Sodhi, L. R. P. L. Taylor, B. M. Wheeler, G. H. Worker. *Coach:* M. J. Hesson.

   M. J. Santner was originally selected, but broke his thumb and was replaced by Worker.

The tour started with two warm-up games in Pretoria. Then, after playing in Zimbabwe, the New Zealanders retuned to South Africa for more limited-overs matches. For details of those games, see page 1080.

First one-day international   At Harare, August 2, 2015. **Zimbabwe won by seven wickets. New Zealand 303-4** (50 overs) (K. S. Williamson 97, L. R. P. L. Taylor 112*, G. D. Elliott 43); ‡**Zimbabwe 304-3** (49 overs) (H. Masakadza 84, C. J. Chibhabha 42, C. R. Ervine 130*; N. L. McCullum 3-62). *MoM:* C. R. Ervine. *ODI debut:* I. S. Sodhi (New Zealand). *New Zealand, playing in shirts emblazoned with "Aoteaora" (the country's Maori name) to celebrate Maori Language Week at home, looked secure after Kane Williamson and Ross Taylor, who hit his 15th century in one-day internationals, propelled them towards 303. Zimbabwe had only once scored more to win an ODI (329-9 against New Zealand at Bulawayo in October 2011, after Williamson and Taylor both made hundreds). But Chamu Chibhabha started with a sprightly 42, Hamilton Masakadza and Craig Ervine took the score to 194 in the 35th over, and there were no late wobbles. Ervine glided* *to his maiden ODI hundred in 99 balls, and finished with 11 fours and five sixes from 108. He brought the scores level with four and six from the last two balls of the 49th over, from Jimmy Neesham, and the match was won when the first delivery of the final over, from Nathan McCullum, was a wide. "They outplayed us in all areas," admitted Williamson.*

Second one-day international   At Harare, August 4, 2015. **New Zealand won by ten wickets. ‡Zimbabwe 235-9** (50 overs) (C. J. Chibhabha 42, Sikandar Raza 100*, T. Panyangara 33; I. S. Sodhi 3-38); **New Zealand 236-0** (42.2 overs) (M. J. Guptill 116*, T. W. M. Latham 100*). *MoM:* M. J. Guptill and T. W. M. Latham. *New Zealand levelled the series with an emphatic victory, their seventh by ten wickets in ODIs. Martin Guptill and Tom Latham shared their second-highest opening partnership, after the 274 of James Marshall and Brendon McCullum against Ireland at Aberdeen in 2008; it was also the second-highest against Zimbabwe, behind 282 by Upul Tharanga and Tillekeratne Dilshan for Sri Lanka at Pallekele in 2010-11. Latham's century was his first in ODIs, in his 28th match, while Guptill passed 4,000 runs in the course of his eighth. For the second game in a row, the winning run was a wide (this time from Sean Williams). Earlier, Zimbabwe had slumped to 146-8 before Sikandar Raza, whose third ODI hundred included four sixes (two off successive balls from Williamson), and Tinashe Panyangara put on 89 for the ninth wicket, beating one of Zimbabwe's oldest records – the 55 added by Kevin Curran and Peter Rawson against West Indies in only their sixth official international, during the 1983 World Cup at Edgbaston.*

Third one-day international   At Harare, August 7, 2015. **New Zealand won by 38 runs. New Zealand 273-6** (50 overs) (M. J. Guptill 42, K. S. Williamson 90, G. D. Elliott 36, J. D. S. Neesham 37*; A. G. Cremer 3-44); **‡Zimbabwe 235** (47.4 overs) (H. Masakadza 57, C. J. Chibhabha 32, C. R. Ervine 32, S. C. Williams 63; M. J. McClenaghan 3-36). *MoM:* K. S. Williamson. *MoS:* K. S. Williamson. *A rare series victory for Zimbabwe looked a possibility after a fine display in the field limited New Zealand to 273; Graeme Cremer took three wickets with his leg-breaks, and off-spinner John Nyumbu two. Williamson reached 50 for the sixth successive innings in ODIs, but was out in the nineties for the fifth time in 2015 (only Sachin Tendulkar, with six in 2007, had more in a calendar year), after an athletic juggling act by Ervine on the long-on boundary. Masakadza and Chibhabha took advantage of some nervy bowling to give Zimbabwe another good start, but both fell in the space of 11 balls, and after that only Williams could make much progress. From 159-3 the last seven wickets went down for 76, and New Zealand filched the series 2–1.*

Twenty20 international   At Harare, August 9, 2015. **New Zealand won by 80 runs. New Zealand 198-5** (20 overs) (M. J. Guptill 33, G. H. Worker 62; S. C. Williams 3-28); **‡Zimbabwe 118-8** (20 overs) (C. R. Ervine 42). *MoM:* G. H. Worker. *T20I debut:* G. H. Worker. *A muscular 62 from 38 deliveries by the 25-year-old debutant George Worker set New Zealand on the way to a target that proved far too much. The only serious resistance came from Ervine, dropped first ball by wicketkeeper Luke Ronchi off the pacy Adam Milne (4–0–10–2), who later smacked Ervine on the helmet. After taking eight deliveries to get off the mark, Worker clouted four sixes; Zimbabwe managed only one, from Chris Mpofu, off the last ball of the match.*

ZIMBABWE v PAKISTAN IN 2015-16

Neil Manthorp

Twenty20 internationals (2): Zimbabwe 0, Pakistan 2
One-day internationals (3): Zimbabwe 1, Pakistan 2

Cynicism and under-the-table deals in scheduling are nothing new in cricket, but this tour hit a laughable new low. Pakistan's board were committed to repaying Zimbabwe for becoming, earlier in 2015, the first Test-playing nation to venture into their country for six years. Despite that, they postponed the return trip for a fortnight, in order to ensure their participation in the Champions Trophy in England in 2017. The top eight nations in the ICC's one-day table at the cut-off date of September 30 were due to qualify. But that deadline coincided with the original dates for this trip, and Pakistan – placed eighth, behind Bangladesh and only one point ahead of West Indies – would have missed out if they had lost the one-day series to Zimbabwe. So they simply turned up later. It meant five matches were rattled off in nine days, allowing Pakistan to get to the UAE in time for England's visit.

Zimbabwe ordered dry, lifeless pitches for the first three games, presumably to nullify Pakistan's fast bowlers and encourage their own spinners. But the cricket was appallingly dull, and Pakistan's slow men were too potent anyway. One of them, 30-year-old Bilal Asif from Sialkot, had an interesting time. Drafted in because Mohammad Hafeez had been banned from bowling, Bilal made his debut as an off-spinning opening batsman, and claimed five for 25 in his second match – only for his action to be reported too. He was sent off for tests, and was eventually cleared.

Pakistan won both Twenty20 games, which followed almost identical patterns, and might have swept the 50-over series but for the decision to halt the second match, with just two overs left, because of bad light. Pakistan were behind on Duckworth/Lewis, but needed 21 more, with Shoaib Malik and Yasir Shah well set. Zimbabwe's fortuitous victory did at least keep the series alive until the final match, when they collapsed again.

After a decade in which their side had been selected along predictable lines, Zimbabwe began looking to the future. Vusi Sibanda did not appear at all, and the remodelled Prosper Utseya only in the Twenty20s, while Hamilton Masakadza was jettisoned for the final one-dayer. Opener Brian Chari and seamer Luke Jongwe, meanwhile, made promising starts.

PAKISTAN TOURING PARTY

*Azhar Ali (50), Aamer Yamin (50/20), Ahmed Shehzad (50/20), Asad Shafiq (50), Babar Azam (50), Bilal Asif (50/20), Imad Wasim (50/20), Imran Khan, jun. (20), Mohammad Hafeez (50/20), Mohammad Irfan (50/20), Mohammad Rizwan (50/20), Mukhtar Ahmed (20), Rahat Ali (50), Sarfraz Ahmed (50), Shahid Afridi (20), Shoaib Malik (50/20), Sohaib Maqsood (50/20), Sohail Tanvir (20), Umar Akmal (20), Wahab Riaz (50/20), Yasir Shah (50). *Coach:* Waqar Younis.

Shahid Afridi captained in the Twenty20 games. Anwar Ali was originally named in the one-day squad, but withdrew with a groin strain and was replaced by Aamer Yamin. Bilal Asif, initially chosen only for the T20s, was added to the one-day squad.

First Twenty20 international At Harare, September 27, 2015. **Pakistan won by 13 runs. ‡Pakistan 136-8** (20 overs) (Shoaib Malik 35, Mohammad Rizwan 33*; C. J. Chibhabha 3-18); **Zimbabwe 123-9** (20 overs) (E. Chigumbura 31; Imad Wasim 4-11). *MoM:* Imad Wasim. *T20I debuts:* L. M. Jongwe (Zimbabwe); Imran Khan, jun. (Pakistan). *On a dreadfully slow pitch, Shoaib Malik provided the only batting flair, and even he managed only two fours and a heaved six from 24 balls. Mohammad Rizwan struggled, but his runs proved important. Elton Chigumbura's bowling changes were peculiar: his seamers claimed 5-35 in seven overs, the spinners 2-67 in nine. Zimbabwe dipped to 90-8 in the 16th, although Chigumbura gave them hope before he was run out in the final over. Slow left-armer Imad Wasim opened the bowling and returned 4–0–11–4, then added two run-outs.*

Second Twenty20 international At Harare, September 29, 2015. **Pakistan won by 15 runs. ‡Pakistan 136-6** (20 overs) (Umar Akmal 38*); **Zimbabwe 121-7** (20 overs) (S. C. Williams 40*, Sikandar Raza 36). *MoM:* Umar Akmal. *MoS:* Imad Wasim. *Rarely can successive games have followed such similar patterns. Pakistan matched their total from two days earlier, this time indebted to Umar Akmal's 28-ball 38*. Zimbabwe's bowlers again looked disciplined, but their batsmen floundered against an attack who must have felt at home: on a dry, slow pitch, the chase never really started in earnest. From 24-4 in the seventh over, Sean Williams mistimed his way to 40*, while Sikandar Raza largely mis-slogged 36 – but seamers Sohail Tanvir and Mohammad Irfan were too cunning, and Imad (4–0–14–1) almost impossible to get away.*

First one-day international At Harare, October 1, 2015. **Pakistan won by 131 runs. Pakistan 259-6** (50 overs) (Sarfraz Ahmed 44, Shoaib Malik 31, Mohammad Rizwan 75*, Imad Wasim 61); **‡Zimbabwe 128** (37 overs) (Yasir Shah 6-26). *MoM:* Yasir Shah. *ODI debuts:* B. B. Chari (Zimbabwe); Aamer Yamin (Pakistan). *Watching paint dry would have been more entertaining than this contest, which never threatened to come to life on another atrociously slow pitch. Sarfraz Ahmed worked hard to repair some early damage but, when he lost patience and carted leg-spinner Graeme Cremer to deep midwicket, Pakistan were 128-5. Rizwan and Imad both made their highest scores, although neither timed anything terribly well, apart from their running between the wickets. Only in the final moments of their 128-run sixth-wicket stand did batting look less difficult than hitting a rock with a hockey stick. When Pakistan's spinners came on, it was men against boys. They claimed all ten Zimbabwean wickets, with Yasir Shah producing a fine exhibition of variation and control for a career-best 6-26.*

Second one-day international At Harare, October 3, 2015. **Zimbabwe won by five runs** (D/L). **Zimbabwe 276-6** (50 overs) (C. J. Chibhabha 90, B. B. Chari 39, E. Chigumbura 67, Sikandar Raza 32; Wahab Riaz 4-63); **‡Pakistan 256-8** (48 overs) (Shoaib Malik 96*, Aamer Yamin 62, Yasir Shah 32*). *MoM:* E. Chigumbura. *ODI debut:* Bilal Asif (Pakistan). *A different pitch – one with some grass on it – produced a compelling spectacle. Zimbabwe ran up an excellent total, then reduced Pakistan to 76-6 – but they fought back superbly, and were 21 short of victory when the sun literally set on their chances. The umpires took the players off, with Shoaib Malik in sight of a century, and Pakistan marginally adrift on Duckworth/Lewis. Earlier, Chamu Chibhabha anchored Zimbabwe's innings, which was transformed by an extraordinary incident in the 43rd over: Wahab Riaz's last-ball bouncer hit Chigumbura so flush on the forehead that the ball was caught at midwicket. Far from being incapacitated, Zimbabwe's captain was galvanised: he raced from 35 to 67 in his next 17 deliveries, lashing out with bruised fury. When Pakistan batted, Tinashe Panyangara and Luke Jongwe bowled with control, but horrible shots accounted for four of the first six wickets, and there was a silly run-out. Shoaib Malik was serenely indifferent to the chaos, and turned from defence to attack once he realised Aamer Yamin was intent on hitting out. A seventh-wicket stand of 111 was followed by 63* for the ninth in six overs with the cool Yasir – but neither he nor Shoaib could control the falling sun, or Zimbabwe's slow over-rate.*

Third one-day international At Harare, October 5, 2015. **Pakistan won by seven wickets. Zimbabwe 161** (38.5 overs) (C. J. Chibhabha 48, R. Mutumbami 67; Imad Wasim 3-36, Bilal Asif 5-25); **‡Pakistan 162-3** (34 overs) (Ahmed Shehzad 32, Bilal Asif 38, Asad Shafiq 38*, Shoaib Malik 34*). *MoM:* Bilal Asif. *MoS:* Shoaib Malik. *As so often with Zimbabwe, a step forward was followed by two steps back: from 89-0 in the 21st over, they lost all ten for 72, with only No. 9 Jongwe (16*) reaching double figures after the openers. Off-spinner Bilal Asif was the architect of the destruction, with five wickets in his second ODI, but his bowling action was reported after the match. Bilal then showed he could bat too, making a breezy 38 as Pakistan claimed the series.*

ZIMBABWE v IRELAND IN 2015-16

Ian Callender

One-day internationals (3): Zimbabwe 2, Ireland 1

This was Ireland's first three-match one-day series against a Test-playing nation for five years – and all the games were close, proving there was little between the teams. Zimbabwe's victory meant they swapped places with Ireland in the ICC's one-day rankings, moving back up to tenth, but the tourists' success in the final ensured the result was the same as on their previous visit, in September 2010.

Zimbabwe were fresh from a series against Pakistan, as well as recent flying visits from India and New Zealand, while Ireland had played just two one-day internationals (one of them rain-ruined) since the World Cup in March. And being match-fit certainly helped: Craig Ervine, who had made his maiden century against New Zealand in August, scored another – the only hundred in the three games – while Sikandar Raza was named Player of the Series, after marrying 143 runs to three wickets the only time he bowled.

The team winning the toss won all three matches after choosing to bowl. Ireland were too reliant on Gary Wilson and Paul Stirling for their runs, and hamstrung when their spinners proved ineffective on slow, dry pitches. They had turned down the chance of a tri-series, also involving Afghanistan, preferring to prepare for their Intercontinental Cup match in Namibia. With that in mind they stayed in Harare for a four-day game against Zimbabwe A, in which Stuart Poynter – kept on only after an injury to Max Sorensen – scored his maiden first-class century.

IRELAND TOURING PARTY

W. T. S. Porterfield, A. Balbirnie, G. H. Dockrell, E. C. Joyce, A. R. McBrine, J. F. Mooney, T. J. Murtagh, K. J. O'Brien, N. J. O'Brien, S. W. Poynter, M. C. Sorensen, P. R. Stirling, S. R. Thompson, G. C. Wilson, C. A. Young. Coach: J. G. Bracewell.

Sorensen injured his back during the tour and returned home; Poynter, who had been due to leave after the one-day internationals, remained with the team.

First one-day international   At Harare, October 9, 2015. **Zimbabwe won by two wickets. Ireland 219-8** (50 overs) (E. C. Joyce 53, G. C. Wilson 70*); ‡**Zimbabwe 222-8** (49 overs) (C. R. Ervine 60, Sikandar Raza 60*). *MoM:* Sikandar Raza. *ODI debut:* W. P. Masakadza (Zimbabwe). *Zimbabwe gained revenge for their World Cup defeat at Hobart in March, although they scraped home with little to spare. When they declined to 171-7 in the 40th over, Ireland were slight favourites, but Sikandar Raza stayed cool. Like Craig Ervine, he enjoyed the Irish seamers, who went for 100 in a combined 19 overs on a slow pitch. Earlier, Ed Joyce and Gary Wilson had rebuilt diligently from 54-3 but, when Joyce's 88-ball innings ended in the 36th over, the total was only 137; some late hitting from Andy McBrine lifted it past 200. Slow left-armer Wellington Masakadza joined his brothers Hamilton and Shingirai (neither of whom played here) as an international cricketer.*

Second one-day international   At Harare, October 11, 2015. **Zimbabwe won by five wickets. Ireland 268-7** (50 overs) (P. R. Stirling 72, N. J. O'Brien 50, G. C. Wilson 65; Sikandar Raza 3-49); ‡**Zimbabwe 270-5** (48.3 overs) (C. J. Chibhabha 30, C. R. Ervine 101*, S. C. Williams 43, Sikandar Raza 33). *MoM:* C. R. Ervine. *Ervine's unbeaten century ensured Zimbabwe won the series, and moved above Ireland to tenth in the ICC rankings. He batted for more than 40 overs in stifling heat* *before finishing the match with a four off John Mooney – but he had been dropped on 64 by Niall O'Brien, standing up to Mooney. Both teams had 202-4 after 40 overs, but Ireland's innings seized up after that. Paul Stirling, Wilson and O'Brien all gave their wickets away after passing 50.*

Third one-day international At Harare, October 13, 2015. **Ireland won by two wickets. Zimbabwe 187** (49.2 overs) (S. C. Williams 51, E. Chigumbura 34, Sikandar Raza 50; T. J. Murtagh 4-32); ‡**Ireland 189-8** (46.5 overs) (P. R. Stirling 50). *MoM:* T. J. Murtagh. *MoS:* Sikandar Raza. *ODI debut:* T. Muzarabani (Zimbabwe). Ireland gained a consolation victory, though it looked unlikely when they dipped to 160-8 in the 43rd over, chasing a modest target after Zimbabwe's last six wickets had tumbled for 28. But Tim Murtagh, who had restricted Zimbabwe with his first ODI four-for, kept his head, adding 29* for the ninth wicket with McBrine, whose thick-edged four off the debutant seamer Taurai Muzarabani clinched the match. Earlier, William Porterfield had begun the chase with three fours in Muzarabani's first over, which cost 18 in all.*

At Harare, October 17–20, 2015. **Drawn.** ‡**Zimbabwe A 392** (P. J. Moor 52, R. W. Chakabva 104, M. N. Waller 138; C. A. Young 4-107, J. F. Mooney 4-74) **and 346-6 dec** (R. W. Chakabva 101, M. N. Waller 118); **Ireland 353** (S. W. Poynter 125; T. N. Garwe 4-61) **and 271-5** (K. J. O'Brien 56*, J. F. Mooney 65*). *Ireland warmed up for their Intercontinental Cup match in Namibia with a high-scoring four-day game. Zimbabwe A were rescued twice by the Test pair of Regis Chakabva and Malcolm Waller, who added 198 for the fifth wicket in the first innings, and 199 for the fourth in*

DOUBLING UP

Two batsmen from the same side scoring twin centuries in a first-class match:

W. L. Foster (140, 172*)/R. E. Foster (134, 101*)	Worcs v Hants at Worcester	1939
C. C. Dacre (119, 125*)/W. R. Hammond (122, 111*)	Glos v Worcs at Worcester	1933
C. L. Badcock (120, 102)/R. A. Hamence (130, 103*)	S. Aust v Vic. at Melbourne	1940-41
U. M. Merchant (143, 156)/D. G. Phadkar (131, 160)	Bombay v M'rashtra at Poona . .	1948-49
I. M. Chappell (145, 121)/G. S. Chappell (247*, 133)	Aust v NZ at Wellington.	1973-74
Azhar Ali (109, 100*)/Misbah-ul-Haq (101, 101*)	Pak v Aust at Abu Dhabi	2014-15
R. W. Chakabva (104, 101)/M. N. Waller (138, 118)	**Zim A v Ireland at Harare. . . .**	**2015-16**

the second. They became only the seventh pair of batsmen to score twin hundreds for the same side in a first-class match, and the first outside a Test since 1948-49. Stuart Poynter replied with a maiden century. Ireland never threatened a lofty target of 386, but were rescued from 141-5 by a responsible stand of 130* in 36 overs between Kevin O'Brien, who lasted 138 balls, and John Mooney, who hit 11 fours from 106.

For Ireland's match against Namibia (October 25–27) see Intercontinental Cup section (page 1187).

see Intercontinental Cup section (page 1187)

ZIMBABWE v AFGHANISTAN IN 2015-16

Liam Brickhill

One-day internationals (5): Zimbabwe 2, Afghanistan 3
Twenty20 internationals (2): Zimbabwe 0, Afghanistan 2

Zimbabwe's busy season concluded with a tour by Afghanistan, the fifth visitors since July. On slow, low pitches which were more Middle East than Matabeleland, the Afghans outdid Zimbabwe with their stroke-playing top order, nagging spinners and reverse-savvy seamers, and secured a historic victory in the 50-over matches – the first time an Associate side had beaten a Full Member in a bilateral series. For good measure, Afghanistan then won both Twenty20 games.

Their top three led the way, with Mohammad Nabi enjoying a move up to No. 3, despite a golden duck at No. 5 in the first match. In his first outing up the order he contributed a maiden century, and in all made 233 runs, winning the Man of the Series award. Backing him up was a steady bowling attack, particularly Dawlat Zadran, who filled the role of senior man with aplomb, providing control with the new ball and reverse swing at good pace with the old. Afghanistan also unearthed a 17-year-old leg-spinner of great promise in Rashid Khan. The icing on the cake came when Inzamam-ul-Haq, their distinguished new coach, agreed a two-year contract.

For Zimbabwe, just about the only players to enjoy the conditions were their own spinners: the two slow left-armers, Tendai Chisoro and Wellington Masakadza, collected 19 wickets in the 50-over matches at less than 20 apiece. It was a particularly fine start for Chisoro, who until recently had been a quick bowler. The batting, though, struggled for fluency after the first game, which Zimbabwe won easily.

As so often, they were unsettled by off-field wrangling. Rumours about the former captain Alistair Campbell's frustration at his diminishing role as managing director for cricket were borne out when he resigned after the tour, while Andy Waller was sacked as batting coach.

AFGHANISTAN TOURING PARTY

*Asghar Stanikzai (50/20), Aftab Alam (50/20), Dawlat Zadran (50), Fareed Ahmad (50/20), Gulbadeen Naib (20), Hamza Hotak (50/20), Hashmatullah Shahidi (50), Karim Sadiq (20), Mirwais Ashraf (50/20), Mohammad Nabi (50/20), Mohammad Shahzad (50/20), Najibullah Zadran (50), Nawroz Mangal (50/20), Noor Ali Zadran (50), Rashid Khan (50/20), Samiullah Shenwari (50/20), Shafiqullah Shinwari (50/20), Shapoor Zadran (50/20), Usman Ghani (20). *Coach:* Inzamam-ul-Haq.

At Bulawayo, October 8, 2015. **Afghanistan XI won by 70 runs.** ‡**Afghanistan XI 356-5** (50 overs) (Noor Ali Zadran 98, Nawroz Mangal 62, Mohammad Shahzad 78, Mohammad Nabi 45*; T. S. Chisoro 3-48); **Zimbabwe Chairman's XI 286** (48.1 overs) (K. T. Kasuza 80, R. W. Chakabva 42, P. J. Moor 43, K. L. Sauramba 42). *Both sides chose from 15 players. Noor Ali Zadran and Nawroz Mangal put on 134 for the first wicket in 25.5 overs, then Mohammad Nabi propelled the Afghans to a big total, adding 61* in the last 20 balls with Najibullah Zadran, who made 33* off eight. The Chairman's XI fell away after reaching 168-1.*

At Bulawayo, October 10, 2015. **Afghanistan XI won by 22 runs.** ‡**Afghanistan XI 226** (49 overs) (Mohammad Shahzad 72; T. Mufudza 3-57); **Zimbabwe Chairman's XI 204** (44.1 overs) (T. S. Chisoro 63, D. T. Tiripano 44*). *Both sides chose from 15 players. The Chairman's XI seemed to be sliding to defeat at 95-9, but Tendai Chisoro and Donald Tiripano took them close with a last-ditch stand of 109. Nabi eventually ended the fun, becoming the fifth Afghan bowler to take two wickets in the innings.*

At Bulawayo, October 12, 2015. **Zimbabwe Chairman's XI won by 34 runs. Zimbabwe Chairman's XI 215** (49 overs) (R. W. Chakabva 92; Fareed Ahmad 3-27); ‡**Afghanistan XI 181** (45.3 overs) (Samiullah Shenwari 57; D. T. Tiripano 3-15, T. S. Chisoro 3-43). *Both sides chose from 15 players. After their batting heroics in the previous match, Tiripano and Chisoro now joined forces with the ball to make sure Afghanistan did not win all three warm-ups.*

First one-day international At Bulawayo, October 16, 2015. **Zimbabwe won by eight wickets.** ‡**Afghanistan 122** (34.1 overs) (L. M. Jongwe 3-16, W. P. Masakadza 4-21, T. S. Chisoro 3-16); **Zimbabwe 126-2** (23.2 overs) (R. Mutumbami 30, C. J. Chibhabha 58). *MoM:* W. P. Masakadza. *ODI debut:* T. S. Chisoro (Zimbabwe). *Afghanistan hit early trouble when seamer Luke Jongwe nipped out both openers in his third over, and the slips were given plenty of work; Craig Ervine finished with four catches. Mohammad Shahzad's brief rally was ended when he swung across a straight one from Wellington Masakadza, whose fellow slow left-armer Chisoro collected three wickets on debut on a helpful surface. Dawlat Zadran's hitting helped lift the total, but Richmond Mutumbami set the chase on course with an enterprising knock.*

Second one-day international At Bulawayo, October 18, 2015. **Afghanistan won by 58 runs.** ‡**Afghanistan 271-6** (50 overs) (Noor Ali Zadran 60, Mohammad Nabi 116, Asghar Stanikzai 39); **Zimbabwe 213** (46.4 overs) (R. Mutumbami 35, C. R. Ervine 43, L. M. Jongwe 46). *MoM:* Mohammad Nabi. *ODI debut:* Rashid Khan (Afghanistan). *Promoted to No. 3, Nabi hit his maiden ODI century in his 53rd match to set up a hefty total. He and Noor Ali added 133 for the second wicket in 28 overs; Nabi hit only three fours, but ended up with six sixes, one of which cleared the three-storey building at the City End. Slog-sweeping to good effect, Mutumbami hit three sixes of his own in reply, but Zimbabwe's middle order stumbled to 143-6 against the slow men, including the 17-year-old leg-spinning debutant Rashid Khan. Jongwe's fleet-footed 46 from 33 balls briefly threatened a fightback but, after his stumps were rattled by Dawlat, Afghanistan soon squared the series.*

Third one-day international At Bulawayo, October 20, 2015. **Zimbabwe won by six wickets.** ‡**Afghanistan 223-8** (50 overs) (Noor Ali Zadran 56, Mohammad Shahzad 30, Shafiqullah Shenwari 35); **Zimbabwe 229-4** (49.4 overs) (R. Mutumbami 74, S. C. Williams 39, E. Chigumbura 49*; Hamza Hotak 3-47). *MoM:* R. Mutumbami. *Batting first again, Afghanistan sailed to 124-1 in the 31st over before losing three wickets in six balls without addition. Nabi, trying a single after a misfield, was run out soon afterwards, before Shafiqullah Shenwari organised a recovery to 223. But it wasn't enough on another surface which encouraged the spinners. Left-arm spinner Hamza Hotak opened the attack for Afghanistan, and took the only three wickets that fell to bowlers. The one that didn't was an oddity: Chamu Chibhabha inside-edged towards his stumps, but swatted the ball away with his glove, and was given out handled the ball. He was the third player to suffer the fate in one-day internationals, after India's Mohinder Amarnath at Melbourne in 1985-86, and South Africa's Daryll Cullinan against West Indies at Durban in 1998-99. Mutumbami anchored the first half of the chase with a career-best 74, before Elton Chigumbura and Sikandar Raza (29*) finished the job in the final over.*

Fourth one-day international At Bulawayo, October 22, 2015. **Afghanistan won by three wickets.** ‡**Zimbabwe 184-8** (50 overs) (Sikandar Raza 86; Dawlat Zadran 3-37); **Afghanistan 185-7** (46.4 overs) (Mohammad Shahzad 80, Asghar Stanikzai 32; T. S. Chisoro 3-38). *MoM:* Mohammad Shahzad. *Two quick wickets from Dawlat set Zimbabwe back, then the spinners tightened the noose: in all they took 4-120 in 34 overs. Sikandar overcame uncomfortable stiffness in his right knee and a withering blow to the groin during his battling 86; no one else made more than 26. After a cautious start to the chase, Shahzad opened up, clattering three sixes on his way to 80, before he sliced Chisoro into the covers. That made it 119-3, but skipper Asghar Stanikzai hung on grimly for 60 deliveries and, although he was out in the 45th over, making it a nervous 178-7, Rashid's straight six off Sean Williams soon levelled the series at 2–2.*

Fifth one-day international At Bulawayo, October 24, 2015. **Afghanistan won by 73 runs. Afghanistan 245-9** (50 overs) (Noor Ali Zadran 54, Mohammad Nabi 53, Asghar Stanikzai 38; W. P. Masakadza 3-31, Sikandar Raza 3-40); ‡**Zimbabwe 172** (44.1 overs) (S. C. Williams 102;

Dawlat Zadran 4-22, Hamza Hotak 3-41). *MoM:* S. C. Williams and Dawlat Zadran. *MoS:* Mohammad Nabi. *A big crowd turned out for the final match, with vuvuzelas and flags lending it a charged atmosphere. Afghanistan appeared the more inspired, calmly defending 245 to secure their historic win, the first by an Associate team in a bilateral series against a Test-playing nation. Noor Ali's third fifty of the series was the adhesive for Afghanistan's top order; he added 97 for the second wicket with Nabi, and two huge sixes from Mirwais Ashraf helped boost the total from 202-7. Dawlat again made two early incisions, and Zimbabwe were soon 51-5; Williams was left to play a lone hand, sweeping, dabbing and swiping to a maiden century in his 95th ODI. But the next-highest was Jongwe's 16 and, when Williams was finally stumped off Rashid, Afghanistan's players celebrated their triumph in style.*

First Twenty20 international At Bulawayo, October 26, 2015. **Afghanistan won by six wickets.** ‡**Zimbabwe 153-5** (20 overs) (Sikandar Raza 59, C. J. Chibhabha 54; Dawlat Zadran 3-29); **Afghanistan 154-4** (19.1 overs) (Mohammad Shahzad 34, Mohammad Nabi 33*, Najibullah Zadran 37*). *MoM:* Dawlat Zadran. *T20I debuts:* T. S. Chisoro, W. P. Masakadza (Zimbabwe); Rashid Khan, Usman Ghani (Afghanistan). *Zimbabwe looked set for a formidable total when Sikandar and Chibhabha raced to 100 in the 13th over, but Dawlat's superb control over the old ball scuppered the charge. In the first over of his second spell he removed Chibhabha, then dismissed Williams and Ervine with successive deliveries in his next. Shahzad, with 34 from 21 balls, ensured Afghanistan kept up with the required rate and, after a wobble to 85-4 after 11 overs, Nabi and Najibullah coolly added 69*.*

Second Twenty20 international At Bulawayo, October 28, 2015. **Afghanistan won by five wickets.** ‡**Zimbabwe 190-7** (20 overs) (S. C. Williams 54, R. Mutumbami 43, E. Chigumbura 33); **Afghanistan 191-5** (19.5 overs) (Usman Ghani 65, Gulbadeen Naib 56*). *MoM:* Gulbadeen Naib. *A confident Afghanistan won the 20-over series too, knocking off a big total with a ball to spare. Chibhabha had fallen to the second delivery of the day, but Williams spanked a 21-ball fifty. Zimbabwe's pacemen then tried a short-pitched assault, only for the 18-year-old opener Usman Ghani took them on; he slapped three sixes in his 45-ball 65, although a couple of mis-hooks only just evaded the wicketkeeper. Gulbadeen Naib's inventive strokeplay brought him a maiden T20I fifty as well, and his ability to find unlikely gaps behind the wicket carried Afghanistan to victory.*

DOMESTIC CRICKET IN ZIMBABWE IN 2014-15

John Ward

The 2014-15 domestic season was more peaceful than some of its predecessors. The opening round of the Logan Cup did start a day late, due to another players' strike, but this one was quickly resolved, and no further problems between cricketers and administrators intruded on the field of play.

Only four franchises took part. Southern Rocks, from the small city of Masvingo, had been disbanded, a blow to the growing number of cricket-lovers there, though Zimbabwe Cricket's reasons – serious financial constraints and a shrinking pool of genuine first-class talent – could hardly be rebutted. Officially, they merged with Mountaineers; in practice, all this seemed to mean was that Mountaineers signed several of their leading players.

It was unfortunate that the Logan Cup matches clashed with Zimbabwe's overseas tours, ruling out the regular international players – which reduced standards, as well as depriving them of time in the middle. This resulted in a close competition, however, as form fluctuated and every team were capable of beating any other. The bowling was usually much stronger than the batting: each side had at least two good seamers, and spinners often reaped harvests on pitches that turned from the start or crumbled later. Batsmen rarely managed to build an innings; when they did, it tended to win the match.

The Logan Cup champions were **Matabeleland Tuskers**, for the fourth time in five seasons. In an unusual hat-trick, the last three of these titles were secured in the penultimate match before an anticlimactic defeat. They suffered less than other franchises from national call-ups, and were given a fine start by Sean Williams, controversially omitted from the tour of Bangladesh and determined to make somebody pay. When he went to the World Cup, his team seemed temporarily to lose confidence, suffering two defeats before recovering to take the trophy. They had rebuilt their traditionally strong pace attack, with Tawanda Mupariwa in superb form, collecting 15 wickets at 14 before the World Cup. He was backed by Steve Chimhamhiwa, the promising all-rounder Luke Jongwe (formerly with Southern Rocks) and Brian Vitori, who found his best form late on, after recovering from a car accident. Keith Dabengwa, now 34, had one of his best seasons with the bat.

Runners-up **Mid West Rhinos** were a surprise package. On paper they seemed to have less depth than their rivals, but they benefited greatly when Vusi Sibanda and Malcolm Waller were left out of the World Cup squad. Welsh professional Brad Wadlan had a valuable all-round season, and was the leading wicket-taker with 39; Carl Mumba, a 19-year-old pace bowler, took 25 at 14 each, and looked a good prospect.

Mashonaland Eagles were captained by Greg Lamb, returning after a season away from first-class cricket. They produced occasional strong individual performances amid mediocrity. Tino Mutombodzi struck a monumental 230 in Mutare, while Joylord Gumbie kept wicket capably and finished with an impressive century in Bulawayo. Trevor Garwe, like Mike Chinouya of Mid West Rhinos, often bowled without the rewards he deserved. The team did win the Pro50 Championship, beating Matabeleland Tuskers, who had easily dominated the group stage, in the final. For the second year running, there was no domestic Twenty20 tournament – this time, apparently, because of the lack of a sponsor.

Mountaineers, the previous season's double champions, plunged to the bottom of the Logan Cup table, despite two futile victories. They suffered from international calls, but had picked up some good players, mainly from Southern Rocks. Several of those who remained, however – notably Tino Mawoyo, Shingi Masakadza and Donald Tiripano (who had a niggling injury) – were below par.

The strange career of Mark Vermeulen finally seemed to have ended. After some strong batting against Afghanistan, he returned to Test cricket after a ten-year gap, playing South Africa in August 2014 – but, after a disappointing tour of Bangladesh with Zimbabwe A, abruptly announced his retirement and moved to South Africa. He had played franchise cricket for five seasons, each for a different team.

FIRST-CLASS AVERAGES, 2014-15

BATTING (300 runs, average 25.00)

	M	I	NO	R	HS	100	Avge	Ct/St
V. Sibanda (*Mid West Rhinos*)	6	10	1	610	173	2	67.77	11
M. L. Pettini (*Mashonaland Eagles*)	4	6	0	302	142	1	50.33	4
†K. M. Dabengwa (*Matabeleland Tuskers*)	8	14	1	619	141	2	47.61	10
G. A. Lamb (*Mashonaland Eagles*)	7	12	3	358	86	0	39.77	5
C. T. Mutombodzi (*Mashonaland Eagles*) . . .	9	17	1	630	230	1	39.37	18
F. Mutizwa (*Mountaineers*)	9	16	3	508	127*	1	39.07	22/4
R. Mutumbami (*Matabeleland Tuskers*)	6	12	1	391	86	0	35.54	15
M. N. Waller (*Mid West Rhinos*)	7	11	0	376	141	1	34.18	2
†P. S. Masvaure (*Mid West Rhinos*)	8	15	1	472	77	0	33.71	3
†R. P. Burl (*Mashonaland Eagles*)	8	14	1	433	92	0	33.30	7
J. Gumbie (*Mashonaland Eagles*)	9	16	4	392	168*	1	32.66	20
†B. L. Wadlan (*Mid West Rhinos*)	9	17	1	509	77	0	31.81	9
L. M. Jongwe (*Matabeleland Tuskers*)	9	14	2	379	118	1	31.58	7
G. A. T. Mamhiyo (*Matabeleland Tuskers*)	9	15	2	400	82	0	30.76	4
S. P. Gupo (*Mashonaland Eagles*)	7	13	1	366	89	0	30.50	0
B. T. Mujuru (*Matabeleland Tuskers*)	8	14	0	420	96	0	30.00	5
K. T. Kasuza (*Mountaineers*)	9	17	0	469	80	0	27.58	5
C. Kunje (*Mountaineers*)	6	12	0	327	115	1	27.25	5
†N. Mpofu (*Matabeleland Tuskers*)	9	16	0	428	71	0	26.75	7
†B. M. Chapungu (*Mid West Rhinos*)	7	13	0	332	78	0	25.53	2

BOWLING (15 wickets)

	Style	O	M	R	W	BB	5I	Avge
T. Mupariwa (*Matabeleland Tuskers*)	RFM	100	35	212	15	3-32	0	14.13
C. T. Mumba (*Mid West Rhinos*)	RFM	157.1	39	366	25	5-27	2	14.64
L. M. Jongwe (*Matabeleland Tuskers*)	RM	227.3	59	615	34	5-32	2	18.08
W. P. Masakadza (*Mashonaland Eagles*)	SLA	178.2	46	473	25	5-47	2	18.92
B. L. Wadlan (*Mid West Rhinos*)	SLA	254	50	751	39	7-39	1	19.25
T. Muzarawetu (*Mashonaland Eagles*)	RM	162.5	39	556	26	5-75	1	21.38
T. Mufudza (*Mountaineers*)	OB	140.3	29	431	19	7-31	1	22.68
N. Madziva (*Mid West Rhinos*)	RM	154.3	41	369	15	3-21	0	24.60
S. D. Chimhamhiwa (*Matabeleland Tuskers*) . .	RFM	184.5	46	568	23	4-66	0	24.69
N. M'shangwe (*Mountaineers*)	LBG	191.4	30	648	25	5-50	1	25.92
T. N. Garwe (*Mashonaland Eagles*)	RFM	205.5	44	551	21	4-24	0	26.23
J. C. Nyumbu (*Matabeleland Tuskers*)	OB	211.5	35	649	24	6-96	1	27.04
G. A. Lamb (*Mashonaland Eagles*)	OB	146	25	426	15	4-42	0	28.40
B. V. Vitori (*Matabeleland Tuskers*)	LFM	196	41	661	23	4-30	0	28.73
S. W. Masakadza (*Mountaineers*)	RFM	181	41	594	19	5-74	1	31.26
T. S. Chisoro (*Mid West Rhinos*)	LFM	176.2	33	514	16	3-38	0	32.12
T. I. Mupunga (*Mountaineers*)	RM	241	50	790	24	4-87	0	32.91

LOGAN CUP, 2014-15

	Played	Won	Lost	Drawn	1st-inns points	Points
Matabeleland Tuskers	9	5	3	1	6	38
Mid West Rhinos	9	5	4	0	5	35
Mashonaland Eagles	9	4	4	1	4	30
Mountaineers	9	2	5	2	2	18

Win = 6pts; draw = 2pts; lead on first innings = 1pt.

At Harare (Old Hararians), November 12–14, 2014. **Mid West Rhinos won by 17 runs. ‡Mid West Rhinos 228 and 213; Mashonaland Eagles 309 and 115** (B. L. Wadlan 7-39). *Mid West Rhinos 6pts, Mashonaland Eagles 1pt. Mashonaland Eagles led by 81 on first innings but, chasing 133, collapsed against the left-arm spin of Brad Wadlan, who took 10-88 in the match, and also scored 55 as opener in Mid West Rhinos' second innings.*

At Bulawayo (Queens), November 12–15, 2014. **Drawn. ‡Mountaineers 158 and 348-9** (C. Kunje 115); **Matabeleland Tuskers 351-9 dec** (K. M. Dabengwa 102, S. C. Williams 101). *Matabeleland Tuskers 3pts, Mountaineers 2pts. Both matches in this round started a day later than scheduled because of a players' strike.*

At Kwekwe, November 24–27, 2014. **Matabeleland Tuskers won by an innings and 95 runs. ‡Mid West Rhinos 255 and 111; Matabeleland Tuskers 461-9 dec.** *Matabeleland Tuskers 7pts. Matabeleland Tuskers' innings was the ninth in all first-class cricket to include three batsmen dismissed in the nineties: Bornaparte Mujuru (96), Sean Williams (96) and Brian Chari (99).*

At Mutare, November 24–27, 2014. **Mashonaland Eagles won by 336 runs. ‡Mashonaland Eagles 401 and 311-8 dec; Mountaineers 261 and 115.** *Mashonaland Eagles 7pts. Eagles' Cephas Zhuwao hit 12 sixes in the match – five in a 35-ball 45, followed by seven in his career-best 75 from 50.*

At Bulawayo (Queens), December 9–12, 2014. **Matabeleland Tuskers won by 230 runs. Matabeleland Tuskers 405-9 dec** (W. P. Masakadza 5-109) **and 94-4 dec; ‡Mashonaland Eagles 112 and 157.** *Matabeleland Tuskers 7pts. Keith Dabengwa's left-arm spin brought him second-innings figures of 14–6–15–3 for Tuskers.*

At Kwekwe, December 9–12, 2014. **Mountaineers won by nine wickets. Mid West Rhinos 193 and 169** (T. Mufudza 7-31); **‡Mountaineers 317** (K. D. Bhasikoro 5-37) **and 46-1.** *Mountaineers 7pts. Mid West Rhinos were 105-9 on the first day, before Mike Chinouya (who had reached double figures only three times in 74 innings, for a career average of 4.48) and Kudakwashe Bhasikoro put on 88, Chinouya hit 40*. But Natsai M'shangwe saw Mountaineers past 300, hitting six sixes in his 61, before off-spinner Tapiwa Mufudza, whose career-best 7-31 was the best return of the season, set up a straightforward win.*

At Harare (Sports Club), January 27–30, 2015. **Mountaineers won by 76 runs. ‡Mountaineers 193 and 319-8 dec** (I. Kaia 106); **Mashonaland Eagles 191 and 245.** *Mountaineers 7pts. Mountaineers captain and keeper Forster Mutizwa made eight dismissals (7ct, 1st) in the match.*

At Bulawayo (Queens), January 27–30, 2015. **Mid West Rhinos won by six wickets. Mid West Rhinos 415** (V. Sibanda 115, M. N. Waller 141; L. M. Jongwe 5-71) **and 154-4; ‡Matabeleland Tuskers 219 and 346** (L. M. Jongwe 118). *Mid West Rhinos 7pts. Vusi Sibanda and Malcolm Waller added 225 for Mid West Rhinos' fourth wicket; both fell to 19-year-old Luke Jongwe, who followed a career-best 5-71 with his second century.*

At Harare (Sports Club), February 8–11, 2015. **Mashonaland Eagles won by nine wickets. Matabeleland Tuskers 307** (K. M. Dabengwa 141; T. Muzarabani 5-63) **and 127; ‡Mashonaland Eagles 382 and 54-1.** *Mashonaland Eagles 7pts. Mashonaland Eagles' Taurai Muzarabani claimed career-bests with ball and bat. He took a hat-trick in Matabeleland Tuskers' first innings, then turned the match around with 70* from No. 11, adding 140 with Brighton Mugochi – the game's only century stand.*

At Mutare, February 8–11, 2015. **Mid West Rhinos won by nine wickets. Mid West Rhinos 419 and 102-1; ‡Mountaineers 206 and 310** (F. Mutizwa 127*). *Mid West Rhinos 7pts.*

At Kwekwe, February 15–18, 2015. **Mashonaland Eagles won by five wickets. ‡Mid West Rhinos 351** (T. Muzarawetu 5-75) **and 128; Mashonaland Eagles 297 and 185-5.** *Mashonaland Eagles 6pts, Mid West Rhinos 1pt.*

At Mutare, February 15–18, 2015. **Matabeleland Tuskers won by 94 runs. ‡Matabeleland Tuskers 194 and 267; Mountaineers 171 and 196.** *Matabeleland Tuskers 7pts.*

At Kwekwe, February 22–25, 2015. **Matabeleland Tuskers won by 141 runs. Matabeleland Tuskers 367 and 211-7 dec; ‡Mid West Rhinos 249 and 188.** *Matabeleland Tuskers 7pts. In Matabeleland Tuskers' second innings, No. 9 Brian Vitori hit 33* off 16 balls, with five sixes.*

At Mutare, February 22–25, 2015. **Drawn. ‡Mashonaland Eagles 478-7 dec** (M. L. Pettini 142, C. T. Mutombodzi 230); **Mountaineers 391-8.** *Mountaineers 2pts, Mashonaland Eagles 2pts. Mark Pettini of Essex and Tino Mutombodzi, whose maiden double-hundred was the only one of the* *season, added 352 for Mashonaland Eagles' third wicket. It was a Zimbabwean domestic all-wicket record, beating 342 for the second by Paul Horton (of Lancashire) and Gavin Ewing for Matabeleland Tuskers against Southern Rocks in 2010-11.*

At Harare (Old Hararians), March 3–5, 2015. **Mid West Rhinos won by an innings and 26 runs. Mashonaland Eagles 133** (C. T. Mumba 5-27) **and 233;** ‡**Mid West Rhinos 392** (V. Sibanda 173). *Mid West Rhinos 7pts. Sibanda and Tendai Chisoro added 165 for Mid West's seventh wicket.*

At Bulawayo (Queens), March 3–6, 2015. **Matabeleland Tuskers won by six wickets. Mountaineers 150** (L. M. Jongwe 5-32) **and 275** (J. C. Nyumbu 6-96); ‡**Matabeleland Tuskers 289** (S. W. Masakadza 5-74) **and 140-4.** *Matabeleland Tuskers 7pts. Matabeleland Tuskers secured the title with their fifth win, as Jongwe improved on his career-best bowling again, and off-spinner John Nyumbu claimed six in the second innings.*

At Bulawayo (Queens), March 12–15, 2015. **Mashonaland Eagles won by six wickets.** ‡**Matabeleland Tuskers 252** (W. P. Masakadza 5-47) **and 174; Mashonaland Eagles 356** (J. Gumbie 168*) **and 75-4.** *Mashonaland Eagles 7pts. Joylord Gumbie batted seven and a half hours for a maiden century, helping Mashonaland Eagles defeat the champions. Wellington Masakadza's left-arm spin claimed 9-90 in the match.*

At Kwekwe, March 12–14, 2015. **Mid West Rhinos won by 181 runs.** ‡**Mid West Rhinos 314 and 196-9 dec** (N. M'shangwe 5-50); **Mountaineers 165 and 164** (C. T. Mumba 5-44). *Mid West Rhinos 7pts. Mid West Rhinos made sure of second place with their fifth win.*

LOGAN CUP WINNERS

1993-94	Mashonaland U24	2001-02	Mashonaland	2009-10	Mashonaland Eagles
1994-95	Mashonaland	2002-03	Mashonaland	2010-11	Matabeleland Tuskers
1995-96	Matabeleland	2003-04	Mashonaland	2011-12	Matabeleland Tuskers
1996-97	Mashonaland	2004-05	Mashonaland	2012-13	Matabeleland Tuskers
1997-98	Mashonaland	2005-06	*No competition*	2013-14	Mountaineers
1998-99	Matabeleland	2006-07	Easterns	2014-15	Matabeleland Tuskers
1999-2000	Mashonaland	2007-08	Northerns		
2000-01	Mashonaland	2008-09	Easterns		

Mashonaland/Northerns/Mashonaland Eagles have won the title 11 times, Matabeleland/Matabeleland Tuskers 6, Easterns/Mountaineers 3, Mashonaland Under-24 1.

PRO50 CHAMPIONSHIP, 2014-15

50-over league plus final

	Played	Won	Lost	Bonus points	Points	Net run-rate
Matabeleland Tuskers	9	7	2	3	31	0.41
Mashonaland Eagles	9	5	4	1	21	-0.10
Mountaineers	9	4	5	3	19	0.27
Mid West Rhinos	9	2	7	1	9	-0.58

Final At Bulawayo (Queens), March 21, 2015. **Mashonaland Eagles won by four wickets.** ‡**Matabeleland Tuskers 266-7** (50 overs); **Mashonaland Eagles 268-6** (49.3 overs). MoM: C. T. Mutombodzi. *Mashonaland captain Tino Mutombodzi hit a one-day-best 79 in 76 deliveries to see his side most of the way to victory, which was completed by Wellington Masakadza's 14-ball 24*.*

OTHER FIRST-CLASS TOURS

PAKISTAN A IN SRI LANKA IN 2014-15

Pakistan A, captained by Fawad Alam, toured Sri Lanka in April and May 2015, playing six representative matches. Sri Lanka A won the one-day series 2–1, while all three four-day games were drawn. Sri Lanka's wicketkeeper-batsman Kusal Perera made two centuries and an 87 in the one-day matches, then added hundreds in the first and third unofficial Tests.

At Matara, April 26, 2015. **Sri Lanka A won by eight wickets. ‡Pakistan A 203** (48.1 overs) (Fawad Alam 58); **Sri Lanka A 204-2** (32.2 overs) (M. D. K. J. Perera 114*, S. M. A. Priyanjan 57*).

At Hambantota, April 29, 2015. **Sri Lanka A won by seven runs** (D/L). **Sri Lanka A 265-9** (50 overs) (M. D. K. J. Perera 110); **‡Pakistan A 213-7** (40 overs) (Khurram Manzoor 69, Fawad Alam 65). *Pakistan A's target was revised to 221 in 40 overs.*

At Colombo (RPS), May 2, 2015. **Pakistan A won by six wickets. Sri Lanka A 277** (47.2 overs) (M. D. K. J. Perera 87, D. S. N. F. G. Jayasuriya 67; Imad Wasim 4-29); **‡Pakistan A 281-4** (48.1 overs) (Mukhtar Ahmed 96, Fawad Alam 76*).

At Colombo (RPS), May 6–9, 2015. **Drawn. Pakistan A 401** (Khurram Manzoor 82, Umar Amin 99, Fawad Alam 72; P. H. T. Kaushal 6-117); **‡Sri Lanka A 313-5** (M. D. K. J. Perera 119*, D. A. S. Gunaratne 64*; Mir Hamza 3-58).

At Pallekele, May 13–16, 2015. **Drawn. Sri Lanka A 327** (D. M. de Silva 96, K. D. K. Vithanage 96; Imad Wasim 4-44) **and 206-3** (M. D. U. S. Jayasundera 92, M. S. Warnapura 80); **‡Pakistan A 333** (Usman Salahuddin 86, Fawad Alam 64; P. L. S. Gamage 3-71, P. H. T. Kaushal 3-88).

At Dambulla, May 20–23, 2015. **Drawn. Sri Lanka A 273** (M. D. K. J. Perera 90, N. T. Gamage 76; Shehzad Azam 3-54, Fawad Alam 4-40) **and 411-5** (M. D. U. S. Jayasundera 56, K. D. K. Vithanage 136, S. M. A. Priyanjan 54, M. D. K. J. Perera 102*); **‡Pakistan A 580-8 dec** (Shan Masood 182, Umar Amin 127, Ali Asad 89, Adnan Akmal 54*; P. L. S. Gamage 4-112).

AUSTRALIA A AND SOUTH AFRICA A IN INDIA IN 2015

Australia A, captained by Usman Khawaja, and South Africa A, led by Dane Vilas, toured India in July and August 2015. Both sides played two unofficial Tests, in addition to a triangular one-day series, which was won by India A. Left-arm spinner Steve O'Keefe took 14 wickets in the two four-day games, helping Australia A win 1–0. India A fared better against South Africa, bowling them out for 76 to win the second unofficial Test, with slow left-armer Axar Patel returning figures of 6–6–0–4. Mayank Agarwal's 409 runs in the one-day series included 176 and 130 against South Africa, while Ashton Agar, another left-arm spinner, took 12 wickets for Australia A at 12 apiece.

At Chennai, July 22–25, 2015. **Drawn. ‡India A 301** (K. L. Rahul 96, C. A. Pujara 55, V. Shankar 51*; S. N. J. O'Keefe 6-82) **and 206-8 dec; Australia A 268** (P. S. P. Handscomb 91, M. P. Stoinis 77; P. P. Ojha 5-85, A. Mishra 3-55) **and 161-4** (C. T. Bancroft 51, T. M. Head 50).

At Chennai, July 29–August 1, 2015. **Australia A won by ten wickets. ‡India A 135** (K. K. Nair 50; G. S. Sandhu 3-25) **and 274** (A. Mukund 59; G. S. Sandhu 4-76, S. N. J. O'Keefe 4-88); **Australia A 349** (C. T. Bancroft 150, C. J. Ferguson 54; P. P. Ojha 4-107, R. N. B. Apparajith 5-86) **and 62-0.**

At Chennai, August 5, 2015. **Australia A won by nine wickets. ‡South Africa A 171** (48.4 overs); **Australia A 175-1** (31 overs) (U. T. Khawaja 73, J. A. Burns 63*). *MoM:* U. T. Khawaja.

At Chennai, August 7, 2015. **Australia A won by 119 runs. ‡Australia A 334-4** (50 overs) (U. T. Khawaja 100, J. A. Burns 154); **India A 215** (42.3 overs) (U. Chand 52, K. M. Jadhav 50; G. S. Sandhu 4-28, A. Zampa 4-49). *MoM:* J. A. Burns.

At Chennai, August 9, 2015. **India A won by eight wickets. ‡South Africa A 244** (50 overs) (Q. de Kock 108, D. J. Vilas 50; R. Dhawan 4-49); **India A 247-2** (37.4 overs) (M. A. Agarwal 130, U. Chand 90). *MoM:* M. A. Agarwal.

At Chennai, August 10, 2015. **Australia A won by three wickets. ‡India A 258-9** (50 overs) (M. A. Agarwal 61, M. K. Pandey 50; A. C. Agar 5-39); **Australia A 262-7** (48.3 overs) (C. A. Lynn 63, A. Zampa 54). *MoM:* A. C. Agar.

At Chennai, August 12, 2015. **Australia A won by 108 runs. ‡Australia A 272** (47.2 overs) (M. S. Wade 130, P. S. P. Handscomb 52); **South Africa A 164** (37.1 overs) (D. Elgar 64). *MoM:* M. S. Wade.

At Chennai, August 13, 2015. **India A won by 34 runs. India A 371-3** (50 overs) (M. A. Agarwal 176, U. Chand 64, M. K. Pandey 108*); **‡South Africa A 337-6** (50 overs) (Q. de Kock 113, R. R. Hendricks 76, K. Zondo 86). *MoM:* M. A. Agarwal.

Final At Chennai, August 14, 2015. **India A won by four wickets. ‡Australia A 226-9** (50 overs) (U. T. Khawaja 76); **India A 229-6** (43.3 overs) (Gurkeerat Singh 87*). *MoM:* Gurkeerat Singh.

At Wayanad, August 18–21, 2015. **Drawn. ‡South Africa A 542** (R. R. Hendricks 50, O. A. Ramela 112, T. Bavuma 66, Q. de Kock 113, D. J. Vilas 75; A. R. Patel 4-115) **and 105-1 dec** (R. R. Hendricks 61); **India A 204** (D. L. Piedt 5-85) **and 309-4** (A. Mukund 65, K. K. Nair 114*, V. Shankar 74*).

At Wayanad, August 25–28, 2015. **India A won by an innings and 81 runs. ‡South Africa A 260** (S. van Zyl 96; A. R. Patel 5-92, J. Yadav 3-53) **and 76** (A. R. Patel 4-0); **India A 417-8 dec** (Jiwanjot Singh 52, A. Mukund 72, A. T. Rayudu 71, A. R. Patel 69*; D. L. Piedt 5-191).

BANGLADESH A IN INDIA IN 2015-16

Bangladesh A, captained by Mominul Haque, made a short tour of southern India in September 2015, playing three one-day matches – which India A won 2–1 – and two first-class games. India A won the only unofficial Test by an innings, with Shikhar Dhawan making 150. Nasir Hossain was the leading run-scorer (176) and wicket-taker (eight) in the one-day series; he hit a century and took five wickets in the match Bangladesh A won.

At Bangalore, September 16, 2015. **India A won by 96 runs. India A 322-7** (50 overs) (M. A. Agarwal 56, S. V. Samson 73, Gurkeerat Singh 65, R. Dhawan 56*); **‡Bangladesh A 226** (42.3 overs) (Liton Das 75, Nasir Hossain 52; Gurkeerat Singh 5-29).

At Bangalore, September 18, 2015. **Bangladesh A won by 65 runs. Bangladesh A 252-8** (50 overs) (Nasir Hossain 102*); **‡India A 187** (42.2 overs) (U. Chand 56; Rubel Hossain 4-33, Nasir Hossain 5-36).

At Bangalore, September 20, 2015. **India A won by 75 runs** (D/L method). **‡India A 297-6** (50 overs) (S. V. Samson 90, S. K. Raina 104); **Bangladesh A 141-6** (32 overs). *Bangladesh A's target was revised to 217 in 32 overs.*

At Mysore, September 22–24, 2015. **Karnataka won by four wickets. ‡Bangladesh A 158** (Liton Das 50, Shuvagata Hom 55; P. M. Krishna 5-49) **and 309** (Anamul Haque 89, Shuvagata Hom 50*; J. Suchith 6-60); **Karnataka 287** (S. A. Bhavane 88; Saqlain Sajib 4-85, Shuvagata Hom 4-45) **and 185-6**.

At Bangalore, September 27–29, 2015. **India A won by an innings and 32 runs. Bangladesh A 228** (Sabbir Rahman 122*, Shuvagata Hom 62; V. R. Aaron 4-45, J. Yadav 4-28) **and 151** (Mominul Haque 54; I. C. Pandey 3-28, J. Yadav 3-48); **‡India A 411-5 dec** (S. Dhawan 150, K. K. Nair 71, V. Shankar 86).

SRI LANKA A IN NEW ZEALAND IN 2015-16

Sri Lanka A, captained by Ashan Priyanjan, toured New Zealand in October 2015, little more than a month before the senior side went there. New Zealand A won all four one-day games, and one of the two unofficial Tests. Kithuruwan Vithanage made the only century of the one-day series, and was added to the team for the full tour. Henry Nicholls, a left-hander from Canterbury, scored hundreds in each of the unofficial Tests – in which leg-spinners Todd Astle and Jeffrey Vandersay both took 12 wickets.

At Christchurch (Hagley Oval), October 5, 2015. **New Zealand A won by eight wickets. Sri Lanka A 214** (45.3 overs) (M. D. Gunathilleke 57, K. D. K. Vithanage 58; M. J. Santner 4-38); ‡**New Zealand A 216-2** (39.3 overs) (M. A. Pollard 59, G. H. Worker 83*).

At Christchurch (Hagley Oval), October 7, 2015. **New Zealand A won by 15 runs. New Zealand A 305-4** (50 overs) (M. A. Pollard 54, M. G. Bracewell 83, H. M. Nicholls 79*); ‡**Sri Lanka A 290** (48.3 overs) (M. D. Gunathilleke 65, K. D. K. Vithanage 120).

At Lincoln, October 10, 2015. **New Zealand A won by 117 runs. New Zealand A 302-9** (50 overs) (W. A. Young 85); ‡**Sri Lanka A 185** (40.5 overs) (D. P. D. N. Dickwella 50).

At Lincoln, October 13, 2015. **New Zealand A won by 172 runs.** Reduced to 45 overs a side. ‡**New Zealand A 299-5** (45 overs) (M. G. Bracewell 53, M. J. Santner 70*); **Sri Lanka A 127** (25.4 overs).

At Christchurch (Hagley Oval), October 17–20, 2015. **Drawn. New Zealand A 470** (J. A. Raval 152, D. G. Brownlie 68, H. M. Nicholls 144*; J. D. F. Vandersay 5-107) **and 229-6 dec** (H. M. Nicholls 88, D. C. de Boorder 86*; M. V. T. Fernando 3-72); ‡**Sri Lanka A 358** (M. D. U. S. Jayasundera 99, D. P. D. N. Dickwella 128; A. F. Milne 3-52, C. Munro 3-37) **and 274-6** (K. D. K. Vithanage 88, A. R. S. Silva 120*; N. Wagner 4-79).

At Lincoln, October 24–26, 2015. **New Zealand A won by nine wickets. Sri Lanka A 303** (M. D. U. S. Jayasundera 52, K. D. K. Vithanage 62, D. A. S. Gunaratne 79; T. D. Astle 4-55) **and 234** (M. B. Ranasinghe 69, K. D. K. Vithanage 84; T. D. Astle 7-78); ‡**New Zealand A 519** (J. A. Raval 65, D. G. Brownlie 113, H. M. Nicholls 137, W. A. Young 66, D. C. de Boorder 58*; M. A. Aponso 3-133, J. D. F. Vandersay 5-128) **and 20-1**.

BANGLADESH A IN ZIMBABWE IN 2015-16

Bangladesh A, captained by Shuvagata Hom, toured South Africa and Zimbabwe in November 2015. After four warm-up games in Pretoria, they travelled to Harare, where they came out on top in all three one-day games against Zimbabwe A; they also won one of the unofficial Tests, with the other drawn. Mithun Ali amassed 226 runs in the one-dayers, while Zimbabwe A's Peter Moor scored centuries in both unofficial Tests; he shared a second-wicket stand of 229 with Brian Chari in the second of them.

At Harare, November 2, 2015. **Bangladesh A won by 138 runs. Bangladesh A 252-9** (50 overs) (Shadman Islam 58, Mithun Ali 100); ‡**Zimbabwe A 114** (37 overs) (Mahmudul Hasan 4-30).

At Harare, November 4, 2015. **Bangladesh A won by 36 runs. Bangladesh A 282-6** (50 overs) (Mithun Ali 66, Mosaddek Hossain 50*); ‡**Zimbabwe A 246-9** (50 overs) (B. B. Chari 69, C. T. Mutombodzi 57).

At Harare, November 6, 2015. **Bangladesh A won by 122 runs. Bangladesh A 286-8** (50 overs) (Rony Talukdar 77, Mithun Ali 60); ‡**Zimbabwe A 164** (41.3 overs).

At Harare, November 9–12, 2015. **Bangladesh A won by 14 runs.** ‡**Bangladesh A 268** (Mosaddek Hossain 66; V. Sibanda 3-32) **and 211** (Nurul Hasan 79*; T. N. Garwe 5-41); **Zimbabwe A 336** (H. Masakadza 64, P. J. Moor 104, R. P. Burl 78; Mohammad Shahid 3-56, Taijul Islam 4-80, Abu Jayed 3-75) **and 129** (Mohammad Shahid 5-45, Saqlain Sajib 3-30).

At Harare, November 15–18, 2015. **Drawn.** ‡**Zimbabwe A 303** (H. Masakadza 50, P. J. Moor 62, J. Gumbie 70) **and 376-5 dec** (B. B. Chari 128, P. J. Moor 103, R. P. Burl 51*, G. A. T. Mamhiyo 50); **Bangladesh A 402** (Tasamul Haque 102, Shuvagata Hom 92, Mosaddek Hossain 85, Nurul Hasan 52; D. T. Tiripano 3-89, N. M'shangwe 3-70) **and 88-4** (V. M. Nyauchi 3-23).

For the England Lions tour of South Africa in 2014-15, see page 1085; for their matches against Pakistan in the UAE in 2015-16, see page 1061.

ICC WORLD TWENTY20 QUALIFIER IN 2015

Tim Brooks

1= Netherlands, Scotland   3 Ireland   4 Hong Kong   5 Afghanistan   6 Oman

The surge in interest, profile and global coverage of the World Twenty20 Qualifier in Ireland and Scotland in July 2015 showed that fans were increasingly engaging with international cricket below the highest level. Fourteen teams – whittled down from an entry list of more than 60 Associates and Affiliates – fought for the right to party in the preliminary round of the World Twenty20 itself, in India in March 2016.

Shortly before the tournament started, the ICC confirmed their depressingly short-termist decision to restrict the 50-over World Cup to ten teams from 2019. With the World Twenty20 now set to take place every four years (rather than biennially, as before), this meant most of the Associates would now have only one realistic crack (rather than three) at playing in a global tournament every four years. And, with qualifying teams earning $US250,000 from the ICC, failure to progress was simply unthinkable. It ensured some nail-biting cricket.

Previous tournaments had been too predictable but, from the first round of games, it was clear the established order was changing. Many assumed Ireland and Afghanistan would benefit from an ever-growing gap in funding, and remain unchallenged. But the Afghans surprisingly lost to Oman, then had two matches washed out, while Ireland were rebuilding after the Twenty20 retirements of Trent Johnston and Ed Joyce. Both sides had come to see the lower-ranked Test nations as their natural opposition: it was as if they hadn't bargained for the chasing pack. Both qualified in the end, but neither made the final, which was washed out by a Dublin downpour, denying Scotland and the Netherlands a tilt at the trophy.

Frequent rain made amateur mathematicians out of twitchy fans: nerves jangle when a single boundary or wicket can be the difference between a bright future or four years of oblivion, and the twittersphere was transfixed. At the climax of a compelling group stage Kenya fell agonisingly short: had they won their last game against the Netherlands, they would have qualified directly; instead they missed out altogether.

Apart from the finalists, Hong Kong, Ireland, Afghanistan and Oman all booked their passage to India. Oman had been pre-tournament outsiders, but in the course of three weeks they went from obscurity to near-celebrity, earning official Twenty20 international status – and the funding boost. The former England all-rounder Derek Pringle, Oman's technical advisor, wore a broad smile.

Jersey also emerged with enormous credit. A stunning win over Hong Kong, and the scintillating form of 17-year-old Jonty Jenner – who hit an unbeaten 90 from 52 balls against Namibia – showed that a small Associate team could still prosper. Despite that loss, Hong Kong also made it through, thanks in part to the performances against Namibia of brothers Irfan (who scored 98) and

Nadeem Ahmed (who took five for 12). The USA were spirited and competitive, rising above the farcical governance of their domestic game, which was about to lead to the suspension of their national body by the ICC. But there was heartbreak for Nepal, who proved listless and lost their coveted Twenty20 International status.

Namibia's all-rounder Bernard Scholtz was named Player of the Tournament, while team-mate Stephan Baard topped the run-charts with 309. However, Namibia lost the vital play-off for a World T20 place to Oman. Alasdair Evans of Scotland and Ireland's John Mooney joined Scholtz with 14 wickets apiece.

To the ICC's credit, some 20 games were broadcast, while their excellent app helped generate unprecedented interest on social media. They championed the tournament as a showcase for their commitment to a "bigger, better global game", even if that sits uncomfortably with a ten-team World Cup. Several captains used post-match interviews to vent their frustration at the lack of opportunities, while Ireland's John Mooney wore a black armband to symbolise the death of cricket's global development. But, the politics and rhetoric aside, this was an absorbing competition, which showed there is plenty to admire below Test level.

FINAL GROUP TABLES

Group A	Played	Won	Lost	No result	Points	Net run-rate
IRELAND	6	4	2	0	8	1.35
HONG KONG	6	3	2	1	7	0.61
NAMIBIA	6	3	2	1	7	0.31
PAPUA NEW GUINEA	6	3	2	1	7	0.11
United States of America	6	3	3	0	6	−0.32
Jersey	6	2	4	0	4	−0.52
Nepal	6	1	4	1	3	−1.49

Group B	Played	Won	Lost	No result	Points	Net run-rate
SCOTLAND	6	4	2	0	8	1.20
NETHERLANDS	6	4	2	0	8	1.15
AFGHANISTAN	6	3	1	2	8	0.69
OMAN	6	3	2	1	7	0.37
Kenya	6	3	2	1	7	−0.64
United Arab Emirates	6	1	4	1	3	−1.68
Canada	6	0	5	1	1	−1.29

Win = 2pts. No result = 1pt.

The two group winners progressed to the semi-finals, and qualified directly for the World Twenty20 in India early in 2016. The second- and third-placed teams engaged in play-offs, the winners of which also progressed to the World T20. The fourth-placed teams played the losers of the play-offs, with the winners taking the final two places in the main event.

Group matches

Of the 42 group games, only those between the sides with official Twenty20 international status before the tournament (Afghanistan, Hong Kong, Ireland, Nepal, the Netherlands, Papua New Guinea, Scotland and the United Arab Emirates) are shown below. After the qualification process, Nepal lost this status, and Oman gained it. Full scores from the other matches can be found at cricketarchive.com.

Group A

At Bready, July 13, 2015. **Hong Kong v Papua New Guinea. Abandoned.**

At Belfast, July 13, 2015. **Ireland won by eight wickets. Nepal 53** (14.3 overs) (S. R. Thompson 3-10, K. J. O'Brien 3-8); ‡**Ireland 54-2** (8 overs). *MoM:* K. J. O'Brien. *Nepal crashed to the second-lowest total in T20 internationals, after the Netherlands' 39 against Sri Lanka at Chittagong in March 2014. On an overcast day with rain in the Stormont air, Ireland's seamers did the damage: Alex Cusack's first over was a wicket maiden, and Stuart Thompson and Kevin O'Brien had combined figures of 7.3–0–18–3. Gyanendra Malla, one of Nepal's better players of spin, was dropped to No. 5 in the order to give him more chance of facing the slow men – but in the event the seamers did all the bowling.*

At Belfast, July 13, 2015. **Papua New Guinea won by two wickets.** ‡**Ireland 123-9** (20 overs) (W. T. S. Porterfield 57; W. T. Gavera 3-17); **Papua New Guinea 124-8** (18.5 overs) (A. Vala 32; T. E. Kane 3-19). *MoM:* N. Vanua. *T20I debuts:* C. J. A. Amini, M. D. Dai, W. T. Gavera, L. Nou, K. Pala, J. B. Reva, L. Siaka, T. P. Ura, A. Vala, N. Vanua, J. N. T. Vare (PNG). *In their first official Twenty20 international, PNG made a winning start, upsetting the tournament favourites. Apart from William Porterfield, only Gary Wilson (10) and last man Cusack (13*) made it into double figures in Ireland's underwhelming total. PNG were wobbling at 93-8 – six men were out in single figures, three of them to seamer Tyrone Kane – but Norman Vanua (28*) muscled four sixes from ten balls to drag his side over the line. "I was in shock," said Vanua. "It's the best feeling ever."*

At Belfast, July 15, 2015. **Hong Kong won by five wickets. Nepal 109** (20 overs) (Haseeb Amjad 4-16); ‡**Hong Kong 110-5** (19.1 overs) (B. Regmi 4-16). *MoM:* Haseeb Amjad. *T20I debut:* Anshuman Rath (Hong Kong). *Nepal recovered from 31-5 to reach 109, which never looked enough, despite four wickets for slow left-armer Basant Regmi. Earlier, Hong Kong seamer Aizaz Khan had figures of 4–0–7–1.*

At Malahide, July 17, 2015. **Papua New Guinea won by eight wickets. Nepal 93** (19.4 overs); ‡**Papua New Guinea 99-2** (14.1 overs) (T. P. Ura 32, A. Vala 34*). *MoM:* A. Vala. *Nepal's batsmen underperformed again, losing their last six wickets for 19, before PNG cruised home.*

At Malahide, July 17, 2015. **Hong Kong won by five runs. Hong Kong 129-8** (20 overs) (M. S. Chapman 30; K. J. O'Brien 3-32); ‡**Ireland 124-8** (20 overs) (P. R. Stirling 34; Irfan Ahmed 3-11). *MoM:* Irfan Ahmed. *Hong Kong, who had lost their first match to Jersey, gave themselves a chance of reaching the later stages by handing another defeat to Ireland, leaving them the task of beating Jersey themselves to qualify (they did). Hong Kong's attack had stymied Ireland's chase: Tanvir Afzal bowled his four overs off the reel, conceding only nine, before fellow seamer Irfan Ahmed chipped in with 3-11. Ireland struggled to 105-4 in the 18th over, then lost Porterfield and Thompson to successive balls; Stuart Poynter and George Dockrell fell in the 19th, from Irfan, and 23 off the last proved beyond John Mooney.*

Group B

At Edinburgh, July 9, 2015. **Scotland won by nine wickets. United Arab Emirates 109** (18.1 overs) (M. R. J. Watt 3-28, M. A. Leask 3-20); ‡**Scotland 110-1** (10 overs) (H. G. Munsey 62*, K. J. Coetzer 39). *MoM:* H. G. Munsey. *T20I debuts:* Abdul Shakoor, Mohammad Naveed, Mohammad Shehzad, Mohammad Tauqir, Umair Ali (UAE). *Scotland's spinners – Michael Leask and Mark Watt – strangled the UAE's innings, in which No. 10 Mohammad Naveed top-scored with 19. George Munsey, who hit 11 fours and a six from 36 balls, and Kyle Coetzer (nine fours from 16 deliveries) kick-started the chase with 96 in eight overs. At 43 years 176 days, Mohammad Tauqir became the oldest man, debutant and captain to appear in Twenty20 internationals.*

At Edinburgh, July 9, 2015. **Afghanistan won by 32 runs. Afghanistan 162-7** (20 overs) (Samiullah Shenwari 44, Mohammad Nabi 33, Najibullah Zadran 33; M. A. A. Jamil 3-36); ‡**Netherlands 130** (19.4 overs) (B. N. Cooper 36; Dawlat Zadran 3-17, Sharafuddin Ashraf 3-27). *MoM:* Sharafuddin Ashraf. *T20I debut:* Sharafuddin Ashraf. *Four sixes from Najibullah Zadran, who faced only 11 balls for his 33*, propelled Afghanistan to a handy total, although the Netherlands looked well set at 66-1 in the ninth over. But three wickets for the 20-year-old debutant slow left-armer Sharafuddin Ashraf, starting with top-scorer Ben Cooper from his second delivery, proved decisive.*

At Edinburgh, July 10, 2015. **Afghanistan won by eight wickets.** ‡**United Arab Emirates 164-6** (20 overs) (Mohammad Shehzad 43, Shaiman Anwar 35); **Afghanistan 168-2** (17.2 overs) (Mohammad Shehzad 74, Asghar Stanikzai 44*, Samiullah Shenwari 30*). *MoM:* Mohammad Shahzad (Afghanistan). *The UAE's total of 164, which included eight sixes, looked competitive – until Mohammad Shahzad got going for Afghanistan, slamming 74 from 37 balls, with seven fours and five sixes of his own.*

At Edinburgh, July 11, 2015. **Netherlands won by 32 runs.** ‡**Netherlands 191-6** (20 overs) (W. Barresi 75, P. W. Borren 47; A. C. Evans 5-24); **Scotland 159** (19.5 overs) (P. L. Mommsen 68*; Mudassar Bukhari 3-22). *MoM:* A. C. Evans. *Wesley Barresi slammed 75 from 40 balls, with seven fours and five sixes, to raise a total proved decisive, despite the efforts of Carlton seamer Alasdair Evans, born in Kent to Scottish parents, who took Scotland's first five-for in Twenty20 internationals. Scotland lost Munsey for a duck in the first over, and slipped to 79-7 in the 12th before skipper Preston Mommsen made 68* from 44 balls.*

At Edinburgh, July 12, 2015. **Netherlands won by seven wickets. United Arab Emirates 119-7** (20 overs) (S. P. Patil 34); ‡**Netherlands 125-3** (17.1 overs) (B. N. Cooper 50*). *MoM:* R. E. van der Merwe (Netherlands). *T20I debuts:* Fayyaz Ahmed, Nasir Aziz (UAE). *The former South African international Roelof van der Merwe took 2-10 in his four overs, and Ahsan Jamil Malik 2-17, as the UAE were kept in check. Cooper supervised the chase with 50* from 38 balls.*

At Edinburgh, July 12, 2015. **Afghanistan won by 37 runs.** ‡**Afghanistan 210-5** (20 overs) (Mohammad Shahzad 75, Asghar Stanikzai 34, Najibullah Zadran 37, Mohammad Nabi 33*); **Scotland 173** (19.2 overs) (M. H. Cross 37, P. L. Mommsen 44; Hamid Hasan 3-29). *MoM:* Mohammad Shahzad. *Afghanistan's third straight win gave them every chance of progressing, although they suffered a surprise defeat to Oman and two washouts in their remaining group games. Mohammad Shahzad was again the star, biffing seven sixes in his 36-ball 75. Scotland were in with a shout at 162-5 in the 17th over, but lost their last five wickets for 11.*

Qualifying play-offs

At Malahide, July 21, 2015. **Hong Kong won by five wickets.** ‡**Afghanistan 161-7** (20 overs) (Nawroz Mangal 53; Haseeb Amjad 3-28); **Hong Kong 162-5** (20 overs) (J. J. Atkinson 47, M. S. Chapman 40). *MoM:* Nawroz Mangal. *Hong Kong ensured their place at the World Twenty20 with a surprise victory that meant Afghanistan had to win a play-off to qualify too. It boiled down to the last over, from Mohammad Nabi, from which Hong Kong needed 16. Mark Chapman (40 from 25 balls) was caught at midwicket from the first delivery, but Babar Hayat smacked a six and a four, then a three. Tanvir Afzal was run out off the fifth ball, but Hayat faced the last, with two wanted – and drove it past cover for the required runs. The ICC's Anti-Corruption Unit investigated the match after reports of irregular betting patterns, but found nothing untoward.*

At Malahide, July 21, 2015. **Netherlands won by four wickets.** ‡**Namibia 135-6** (20 overs) (C. G. Williams 43, N. R. P. Scholtz 37); **Netherlands 137-6** (19.2 overs) (S. J. Myburgh 31; B. M. Scholtz 3-15). *MoM:* B. M. Scholtz. *The Netherlands booked a spot in the World Twenty20, taking control from the first over – in which the potentially explosive Gerrie Snyman was run out without facing – although a tight spell from slow left-armer Bernard Scholtz induced a few butterflies during the chase, which had started badly when Barresi was out first ball. Namibia's paceman Jason Davidson was later banned from bowling when his action was deemed illegal.*

At Malahide, July 23, 2015. **Afghanistan won by six wickets.** ‡**Papua New Guinea 127-6** (20 overs) (C. J. A. Amini 37*); **Afghanistan 128-4** (18.2 overs) (Nawroz Mangal 65*). *MoM:* Nawroz Mangal. *T20I debuts:* V. V. Morea, C. A. Soper (PNG). *Afghanistan finally made sure they would be playing in the World Twenty20. PNG dipped to 55-5, but Chris Amini dragged them to 127. Mohammad Shahzad fell to the first ball of the chase, but Nawroz Mangal stood firm, and was still there when Najibullah Zadran clinched the match with a six.*

At Malahide, July 23, 2015. **Oman won by five wickets. Namibia 148-9** (20 overs) (S. J. Baard 62, R. van Schoor 34; M. Ansari 3-23); ‡**Oman 150-5** (19 overs) (Jatinder Singh 33, Zeeshan Siddiqui 51*). *MoM:* Zeeshan Siddiqui. *The final qualifying spot went to Oman, who had started the competition as rank outsiders. Namibia looked in charge at 126-3, only to lose six for 22, and again when Oman lost two wickets in four balls to be 130-5 in the 16th over, needing 19 more off 15* *deliveries. But Zeeshan Siddiqui kept his cool, finishing the match with a four that brought up his own half-century from 32 balls. "Oman have made history," said Pankaj Khimji of the Oman Cricket Association. "To make it to fifth or sixth position is inexplicable."*

First semi-final At Malahide, July 25, 2015. **Scotland won by five wickets. Hong Kong 116** (19.4 overs) (Aizaz Khan 31; A. C. Evans 3-17, S. M. Sharif 3-29, R. M. L. Taylor 3-17); ‡**Scotland 117-5** (12.2 overs) (K. J. Coetzer 33, M. H. Cross 39). *MoM:* R. M. L. Taylor (Scotland). *Some fine seam bowling – Alasdair Evans, Safyaan Sharif and Rob Taylor had combined figures of 12–1–63–9 – sank Hong Kong. Kyle Coetzer took 16 off the first over of the reply, and the Scots sailed into the final.*

Fifth place play-off At Clontarf, July 25, 2015. **Afghanistan won by five wickets. Oman 127-9** (20 overs); ‡**Afghanistan 130-5** (18.5 overs) (Samiullah Shenwari 40*, Najibullah Zadran 44). *MoM:* Najibullah Zadran. *T20I debuts:* Aamer Ali, Aamer Kaleem, M. S. Ansari, Jatinder Singh, Khawar Ali, Mehran Khan, Mohammad Nadeem, R. J. Ranpura, Sultan Ahmed, Zeeshan Maqsood, Zeeshan Siddiqui (Oman). *In their first official T20 international, Oman sniffed another upset after reducing Afghanistan to 7-3 in the fourth over of their chase – but experience won out, with Samiullah Shenwari anchoring the innings.*

Second semi-final At Malahide, July 25, 2015. **Netherlands won by five wickets. Ireland 128** (19.5 overs) (A. Balbirnie 31, K. J. O'Brien 33; Mudassar Bukhari 4-28); ‡**Netherlands 129-5** (18.1 overs) (B. N. Cooper 43, P. W. Borren 36*; K. J. O'Brien 3-26). *MoM:* Mudassar Bukhari. *Ireland made a decent start, reaching 70-2 in the 12th over – but 112-4 became 128 all out, which looked insufficient. So it proved: the Netherlands overcame a rocky start (16-2 after three overs) and had something in hand at the end, despite O'Brien's three wickets.*

Third place play-off At Malahide, July 26, 2015. **Ireland v Hong Kong. Abandoned.** *No play was possible. Ireland were ranked third because of their superior record in the group stage.*

Final At Malahide, July 26, 2015. **Netherlands v Scotland. Abandoned.** *Rain, which had not cost a single over in any of the earlier matches in Ireland, hung around throughout the last day of the tournament. The third-place play-off was abandoned at 12.45pm, and another downpour meant the final was called off at 2.55. The teams shared the trophy.*

ICC INTERCONTINENTAL CUP, 2015–17

The ICC's first-class competition for the leading Associate teams resumed in 2015, with a tangible prize at the end of the three-year tournament: the winners will contest a four-match play-off in 2018 against the bottom-ranked Full Member nation, with the promise of Test cricket – starting with one against England at Lord's – should they prevail. Ireland, who had won four of the six previous tournaments – including the most recent, which finished in 2013 – were the early favourites for the plum play-off spot. The 37-year-old Ed Joyce reacted well to the idea of a belated Test debut: he scored 231 in his first match, against the UAE, and 205 in the second, in Namibia. Ireland won both by an innings to take an early lead in the table.

INTERCONTINENTAL CUP TABLE

	Played	Won	Lost	Drawn	First-innings lead	Points
Ireland	2	2	0	0	2	40
Netherlands	2	1	1	0	2	26
Afghanistan	2	1	0	1	0	21
Hong Kong	2	1	1	0	1	20
Papua New Guinea	2	1	1	0	1	20
Namibia	2	1	1	0	1	20
Scotland	2	0	1	1	1	13
United Arab Emirates	2	0	2	0	0	0

As at December 31, 2015.
Win = 14pts. Tie = 7pts. Draw with more than ten hours lost to weather = 7pts. Draw with less than ten hours lost = 3pts. First-innings lead = 6pts. Tie on first innings = 3pts. Abandoned = 10pts.

At Windhoek (Wanderers), May 10–13, 2015. **Namibia won by 114 runs.** ‡Namibia 272 (R. van Schoor 52, S. F. Burger 52, N. R. P. Scholtz 85*; Tanvir Afzal 3-60, Haseeb Amjad 5-49) **and 232-5 dec** (R. A. H. Pitchers 105*; Hong Kong 203 (Nizakat Khan 58, Tanvir Afzal 52; S. F. Burger 3-28, J. J. Smit 4-57) **and 187** (B. M. Scholtz 3-53). *Namibia 20pts. MoM: R. A. H. Pitchers. First-class debuts: Babar Hayat, Ehsan Nawaz, Haseeb Amjad, J. P. R. Lamsam, Nizakat Khan, Skhawat Ali, Tanvir Afzal, Waqas Barkat (Hong Kong). This was Hong Kong's first first-class match since the second Intercontinental Cup, in 2005, but Namibia made home advantage count. Their 21-year-old opener Xander Pitchers scored his third first-class hundred, while captain Nicolaas Scholtz ended the match by taking wickets with his only two deliveries in the second innings.*

At Malahide, June 2–5, 2015. **Ireland won by an innings and 26 runs.** Ireland 492 (P. R. Stirling 146, E. C. Joyce 231; Amjad Javed 4-117); ‡United Arab Emirates 213 (Shaiman Anwar 57; C. A. Young 4-51, J. F. Mooney 3-36, G. H. Dockrell 3-48) **and 253** (Saqib Ali 51, S. P. Patil 63; C. A. Young 3-59, G. H. Dockrell 4-93). *Ireland 20pts. MoM: E. C. Joyce. Ireland took control on the first day – which they finished at 420-3 – through a second-wicket partnership of 231 in 47 overs between Paul Stirling and Ed Joyce, who continued to his third double-century, and highest score. The bowlers then worked their way through the UAE batting: slow left-armer George Dockrell, who failed to take a wicket in the County Championship in 2015, managed seven.*

At Stirling, June 2–5, 2015. **Drawn. Scotland 233** (P. L. Mommsen 77; Rahmat Shah 3-30, Samiullah Shenwari 3-23); ‡Afghanistan 135 (Samiullah Shenwari 51*; C. D. de Lange 3-21). *Scotland 13pts, Afghanistan 7pts. MoM: Samiullah Shenwari. First-class debut: A. R. I. Umeed (Scotland). Rain, which washed out the first day and truncated the others, ensured a draw. Both sides received four extra points as more than ten hours' play was lost.*

At Amstelveen, June 16–18, 2015. **Papua New Guinea won by five wickets. Netherlands 209** (L. Nou 5-49) **and 223** (T. van der Gugten 57; W. T. Gavera 3-52, J. B. Reva 4-42); ‡Papua New Guinea 128 (T. van der Gugten 6-29) **and 305-5** (A. Vala 124*, M. D. Dai 91; P. A. van Meekeren 3-44). *Papua New Guinea 14pts, Netherlands 6pts. MoM: A. Vala. First-class debuts: M. P. O'Dowd*

(Netherlands); C. J. A. Amini, M. D. Dai, W. T. Gavera, V. V. Morea, L. Nou, J. B. Reva, L. Siaka, T. P. Ura, A. Vala, N. Vanua, J. N. T. Vare (PNG). *Papua New Guinea came from behind – a first-innings deficit of 81 after Timm van der Gugten's 17–10–29–6 – to win their maiden first-class match. Set 305, they were 82-4 before Mahuru Dai, who had top-scored in a disappointing first innings with 26, joined No. 3 Asad Vala. They put on 200, with Vala reaching PNG's first century; Dai just missed his, but shortly after he was lbw for 91 the islanders were celebrating victory: their captain, Jack Vare, hit the winning boundary.*

At Voorburg, September 8–11, 2015. **Netherlands won by 44 runs. Netherlands 210** (R. E. van der Merwe 73; J. H. Davey 3-36) **and 123** (J. H. Davey 3-43); ‡**Scotland 133** (V. J. Kingma 4-36) **and 156** (R. D. Berrington 59, R. M. L. Taylor 52; R. E. van der Merwe 3-52, P. W. Borren 4-1). *Netherlands 20pts. First-class debuts:* R. I. Ahmed, B. N. Cooper (Netherlands). *Chasing 201, Scotland recovered from 52-5 through a partnership of 93 between Richie Berrington and Rob Taylor. But the end came quickly once Michael Rippon broke through: medium-pacer Peter Borren, the Dutch captain, had his first bowl of the match, and claimed 3.2–2–1–4.*

At Windhoek (Wanderers), October 24–27, 2015. **Ireland won by an innings and 107 runs.** ‡**Namibia 251** (J-P. Kotze 78) **and 212** (T. J. Murtagh 4-18, G. H. Dockrell 3-55); **Ireland 570-6 dec** (W. T. S. Porterfield 186, E. C. Joyce 205, J. F. Mooney 53*). *Ireland 20pts. MoM:* E. C. Joyce. *Ireland's second thumping victory was set up by another double-century from Joyce – who hit 26 fours and six sixes – and his second-wicket stand of 326 with William Porterfield. John Mooney, in his last match for Ireland, hit a quick fifty and took two wickets.*

At Dubai (ICC Academy), November 11–14, 2015. **Hong Kong won by 276 runs.** ‡**Hong Kong 378** (K. D. Shah 62, Babar Hayat 113, Tanvir Afzal 104; Asif Iqbal 3-38) **and 184** (Babar Hayat 73; Nasir Aziz 4-90, Ahmed Raza 5-61); **United Arab Emirates 181** (S. P. Patil 75; A. Rath 4-34) **and 105** (L. Sreekumar 61; Nadeem Ahmed 4-40, Haseeb Amjad 4-10). *Hong Kong 20pts. MoM:* Babar Hayat. *First-class debuts:* Aizaz Khan, Anshuman Rath, C. Carter, K. D. Shah (Hong Kong); Y. Punja, Qais Farooq, Raja Adeel, L. Sreekumar (UAE). *Maiden centuries for the Pakistan-born pair of Babar Hayat and Tanvir Afzal, the captain, propelled Hong Kong to a substantial total and set up a maiden first-class victory. The UAE needed 382, but that was academic once they had plunged to 6-5. Laxman Sreekumar averted humiliation, clouting ten fours in 61, but Qais Farooq (26) was the only other batsman to reach double figures.*

At Sharjah, November 21–24, 2015. **Afghanistan won by 201 runs.** ‡**Afghanistan 144** (N. Vanua 4-36) **and 540** (Mohammad Shahzad 116, Hashmatullah Shahidi 112, Asghar Stanikzai 127, Gulbadeen Naib 75, Mirwais Ashraf 54); **Papua New Guinea 295** (A. Vala 62, M. D. Dai 129; Yamin Ahmadzai 3-64, Zahir Khan 3-44) **and 188** (A. Vala 81; Yamin Ahmadzai 4-41, Zahir Khan 4-25). *Afghanistan 14pts, Papua New Guinea 6pts. MoM:* Asghar Stanikzai. *First-class debuts:* Zahir Khan (Afghanistan); S. Bau, C. A. Soper (PNG). *An upset seemed possible when a century from Dai – who hit five sixes – took PNG to a lead of 151 after Afghanistan's first-day collapse. But the Afghans regrouped well: Hashmatullah Shahidi put on 150 with Mohammad Shahzad, then 178 with captain Asghar Stanikzai, whose 127 included six sixes. The lower order pushed the lead to 389, and PNG never recovered from 54-4, despite another useful innings from Vala.*

ICC WORLD CRICKET LEAGUE CHAMPIONSHIP, 2015–17

The first division of the ICC's World Cricket League was reconfigured for 2015. The top teams will qualify for the World Cup Qualifier in 2018, where they will join Afghanistan and Ireland, who have pre-qualified by virtue of previous results; they were not included in this edition of the WCL. The remaining four with official one-day international status – Hong Kong, Papua New Guinea, Scotland and the United Arab Emirates – were joined in Division One by the top four from WCL's Division Two, which was held in January 2015. Hosts Namibia, Kenya, Nepal and the Netherlands all made it through. Hong Kong and Kenya, with three wins out of four, were the early leaders, although Scotland and the Netherlands joined them on six points after both their matches in June were washed out. Hong Kong's Mark Chapman became the first player from an Associate nation to score a century on ODI debut, with an unbeaten 124 against the UAE in Dubai.

WORLD CRICKET LEAGUE CHAMPIONSHIP TABLE

	Played	Won	Lost	Tied	No Result	Points	Net run-rate
Hong Kong	4	3	1	0	0	6	1.45
Kenya	4	3	1	0	0	6	0.66
Netherlands	4	2	0	0	2	6	1.66
Scotland	4	2	0	0	2	6	1.06
Papua New Guinea	4	2	2	0	0	4	−0.63
Namibia	4	1	3	0	0	2	−0.81
United Arab Emirates	4	1	3	0	0	2	−1.28
Nepal	4	0	4	0	0	0	−0.36

As at December 31, 2015.

Win = 2pts. Tie/no result = 1pt. Where teams were level on points, standings are decided by (a) most wins, (b) net run-rate. Only the matches between Hong Kong and the United Arab Emirates in 2015 were official one-day internationals.

At Windhoek (Wanderers), May 15, 2015. **Namibia won by one wicket. Hong Kong 194-9** (50 overs) (Irfan Ahmed 40; N. R. P. Scholtz 4-42); ‡**Namibia 195-9** (49.2 overs) (R. van Schoor 31, S. F. Burger 52, N. R. P. Scholtz 40, J-P. Kotze 31*; Nadeem Ahmed 4-27). *MoM:* N. R. P. Scholtz. *Namibia slumped to 13-4 in the sixth over, and even after Sarel Burger organised a revival they were 153-8. But wicketkeeper Jean-Pierre Kotze got them home in the last over, after Bernard Scholtz was run out from the previous ball.*

At Windhoek (Wanderers), May 17, 2015. **Hong Kong won by eight wickets.** ‡**Namibia 109** (36.1 overs) (R. van Schoor 36*; Tanvir Afzal 5-17); **Hong Kong 113-2** (36.2 overs) (Irfan Ahmed 36, J. P. R. Lamsam 41*). *MoM:* Tanvir Afzal. *In another shocking collapse, Namibia nosedived to 15-7 in the 12th over as Tanvir Afzal ran riot; it was soon 30-8. Raymond van Schoor dragged them to three figures, but it was never enough.*

At Rotterdam, June 22, 2015. **Netherlands won by five wickets** (D/L method). **Papua New Guinea 122-9** (24 overs) (M. A. A. Jamil 4-37); ‡**Netherlands 125-5** (18.1 overs) (M. R. Swart 38, B. N. Cooper 37*; C. J. A. Amini 3-26). *Rain delayed the start, reducing this to a 30-overs match, then a shower in PNG's innings lopped a further six off each side's allocation. The PNG batsmen struggled in the conditions, and the Netherlands' target was only minimally revised, to 124 in 24 overs; three late wickets made the result look closer than it was.*

At Amstelveen, June 24, 2015. **Netherlands won by 85 runs. Netherlands 297-6** (50 overs) (S. J. Myburgh 34, P. W. Borren 105*, Mudassar Bukhari 51*); ‡**Papua New Guinea 212** (40.3 overs) (S. Bau 41, K. Pala 56). *The Dutch completed a double, with their captain Peter Borren's maiden List A century setting up a tall target. PNG tried gamely – Kila Pala hit 56 from 42 balls, with 42 in boundaries – but fell short.*

At Southampton (Nursery), June 25, 2015. **United Arab Emirates won by five wickets. Kenya 171** (40.5 overs) (C. O. Obuya 36, N. N. Odhiambo 62; Mohammad Naveed 4-36, A. M. Guruge 3-29); ‡**United Arab Emirates 173-5** (41.4 overs) (Amjad Ali 49, S. P. Patil 38). *This match, and the next, was played in the unlikely surroundings of the Rose Bowl, as both teams were preparing for the World Twenty20 Qualifier, in Ireland and Scotland in July. Nehemiah Odhiambo's 62 from No. 7 seemed to have given Kenya a chance, especially when the UAE dipped to 119-5, but Mohammad Shahzad and Amjad Javed put on 54* to claim the points.*

At Southampton (Nursery), June 27, 2015. **Kenya won by 65 runs. Kenya 270-6** (50 overs) (N. K. Patel 32, I. A. Karim 67, R. R. Patel 59*, S. O. Ngoche 56*); ‡**United Arab Emirates 205** (44.3 overs) (Shaiman Anwar 43, Mohammad Tauqir 54; J. O. Ngoche 5-26). *Kenya laboured to 149-6 in the 39th over, but were boosted by a stand of 121* in 11.1 between skipper Rakep Patel and Shem Ngoche, who belted four fours and four sixes from 36 balls.*

At Ayr, July 29, 2015. **Scotland won by three runs.** Reduced to 36 overs a side. **Scotland 235-7** (K. J. Coetzer 41, P. L. Mommsen 78, C. D. de Lange 55*); ‡**Nepal 232-5** (A. K. Mandal 100,

P. Khadka 70). *Scotland were given an almighty scare by Anil Mandal, who hit a maiden century, and shared a third-wicket stand of 139 with Paras Khadka. Nepal needed 17 from the last over of a match shortened to 36 by rain, but Mandal fell to the first ball and, although Sompal Kami lofted Alasdair Evans for six and four, the Scots just held on. They had earlier been labouring at 101-5, before Preston Mommsen and Con de Lange put on 113 in 13 overs.*

At Ayr, July 31–August 1, 2015. **Scotland won by nine wickets** (D/L method). **Nepal 167** (49.1 overs) (S. Vesawkar 30; A. C. Evans 3-18); ‡**Scotland 111-1** (13.5 overs) (H. G. Munsey 40*, M. H. Cross 51*). *Nepal's batsmen struggled to pierce the field on an overcast day. Rain delayed Scotland's reply, their target being reduced to 110 in 22 overs – but after the restart only ten balls were possible before rain drove the players off again. They returned on the reserve day, when George Munsey (40*) and Matthew Cross hurried home with a stand of 91*.*

At Amstelveen, September 14–15, 2015. **No result. Netherlands 161-6** (43 overs) (R. E. van der Merwe 62*, P. M. Seelaar 68; J. H. Davey 3-22) **v ‡Scotland.** *Scotland continued to be dogged by rain: only 23.3 overs were possible on the first day, and 19.3 on the reserve. Netherlands were 35-5 before Roelof van der Merwe and Pieter Seelaar put on 126.*

At Amstelveen, September 16–17, 2015. **Netherlands v Scotland. Abandoned.** *More rain forced an abandonment at noon on the reserve day.*

At Windhoek (Wanderers), October 30, 2015. **Kenya won by 11 runs.** ‡**Kenya 287-7** (50 overs) (A. A. Obanda 52, C. O. Obuya 32, R. R. Patel 80, S. O. Ngoche 35*); **Namibia 276** (49 overs) (S. J. Baard 132, J-P. Kotze 33; S. O. Ngoche 3-53). *Another solid batting performance from Kenya, in which Patel smote 80 from 58 balls, proved too much for Namibia, even though captain and opener Stephan Baard cracked 132 from 106.*

At Windhoek (Wanderers), November 1–2, 2015. **Kenya won by 92 runs.** ‡**Kenya 215** (50 overs) (N. M. Odhiambo 46, Gurdeep Singh 39, L. N. Oluoch 33); **Namibia 123** (38.3 overs) (J. J. Smit 31*). *Kenya recovered from 68-5, but their eventual total hardly looked imposing – until Namibia crashed to 67-9. The last pair, J. J. Smit and Chris Coombe (28), almost doubled the score, but it was nowhere near enough.*

At Abu Dhabi, November 16, 2015. **Papua New Guinea won by two wickets.** ‡**Nepal 232-8** (50 overs) (S. P. Khakurel 63, S. Vesawkar 78; A. Vala 3-32); **Papua New Guinea 235-8** (49.3 overs) (T. P. Ura 30, A. Vala 87, C. J. A. Amini 35). *MoM: A. Vala. It was a busy time in the Gulf: England were in the middle of their one-day series against Pakistan, while down the road in Dubai the UAE were taking on Hong Kong. Nepal lost Mandal to the first ball of the match, but recovered to 223 thanks to fellow opener Subash Khakurel, who batted to the 35th over, and late impetus from Sharad Vesawkar. PNG looked up against it at 138-6 in the 30th, but Asad Vala took them close with 87, and John Reva clinched victory by hitting the first three balls of the last over for two, two and four.*

At Dubai (ICC Academy), November 16, 2015. **Hong Kong won by 89 runs.** ‡**Hong Kong 298-4** (50 overs) (A. Rath 36, K. D. Shah 34*, Babar Hayat 45, M. S. Chapman 124*); **United Arab Emirates 209** (42.3 overs) (Shaiman Anwar 76; Haseeb Amjad 3-49, A. Rath 3-22). *MoM:* M. S. Chapman. *ODI debuts:* C. Carter, M. S. Chapman (Hong Kong); Abdul Shakoor, Asif Iqbal, Y. Punja, L. Sreekumar, Umair Ali, Zaheer Maqsood (UAE). *The 21-year-old left-hander Mark Chapman became the first player from an Associate nation to score a century on ODI debut (Eoin Morgan hit 99 in his first match, for Ireland in 2006). Hong Kong's total proved too steep, despite Shaiman Anwar's 64-ball 76.*

At Abu Dhabi, November 18, 2015. **Papua New Guinea won by three wickets.** ‡**Nepal 224-8** (50 overs) (S. Pun 47, G. Malla 36, P. Khadka 58, S. Vesawkar 42; N. Vanua 3-49, A. Vala 3-36); **Papua New Guinea 225-7** (49.4 overs) (S. Bau 36, J. N. T. Vare 76*, J. B. Reva 31*; S. Kami 3-51). *MoM:* J. N. T. Vare. *Nepal lost both openers in the first over for ducks, but Khadka organised a recovery to 224. PNG's opener Lega Siaka also failed to score, and things looked bad at 141-7. But skipper Vare and Reva (31* from 45) added 84* to pull off another last-over victory.*

At, Dubai (ICC Academy), November 18, 2015. **Hong Kong won by 136 runs.** ‡**Hong Kong 282-8** (50 overs) (A. Rath 53, Tanvir Afzal 73, Aizaz Khan 37*); **United Arab Emirates 146** (40.1 overs) (Shaiman Anwar 71; Tanvir Afzal 3-31, Nadeem Ahmed 3-32). *MoM:* Tanvir Afzal. *ODI debuts:* Waqas Khan (Hong Kong); Qadeer Ahmed, Usman Mushtaq (UAE). *Tanvir Afzal and Aizaz Khan (37*) continued the tournament trend for lower-order comebacks, their eighth-wicket stand of 101 dragging Hong Kong to 282. Only Shaiman Anwar scored more than 20 as the UAE subsided to their third defeat out of four.*

OTHER INTERNATIONAL MATCHES IN 2015

Associates Tri-Series in the United Arab Emirates

This 50-over series formed part of the warm-up for the World Cup for Afghanistan, Scotland and Ireland, who emerged victorious. Javed Ahmadi of Afghanistan led the run-scorers with 189, while his team-mate Najibullah Zadran made 129, including 94 in boundaries.

At Dubai (ICC Academy), January 8, 2015. **Afghanistan won by eight wickets.** Reduced to 45 overs a side. **Scotland 237-8** (45 overs) (H. J. W. Gardiner 96; Dawlat Zadran 3-41); ‡**Afghanistan 240-2** (38 overs) (Javed Ahmadi 74, Usman Ghani 48, Afsar Zazai 48*, Nasir Ahmadzai 52*). MoM: Javed Ahmadi. *Hamish Gardiner, who had scored 89 in his most recent ODI, in September 2014, underpinned Scotland's innings. But Afghanistan's openers shot out of the blocks, Javed Ahmadi and Usman Ghani putting on 121 in 17.3 overs, and the target was reached with few alarms.*

At Dubai (International), January 10, 2015 (day/night). **Ireland won by three wickets. Afghanistan 180** (44.2 overs) (Javed Ahmadi 81, Najibullah Zadran 45; G. H. Dockrell 4-35); ‡**Ireland 181-7** (43.2 overs) (E. C. Joyce 51, K. J. O'Brien 30, A. Balbirnie 31*; Javed Ahmadi 4-37). MoM: Javed Ahmadi. *The only one of the top six to make it into double figures, Ahmadi fought a lone hand, at least until No. 7 Najibullah Zadran supplied some late aggression. Ireland slipped to 29-3, before recovering to claim victory with more than six overs to spare, despite four wickets for Ahmadi, and a second successive match award.*

At Dubai (International), January 12, 2015 (day/night). **Ireland won by three wickets. Scotland 216-9** (50 overs) (M. W. Machan 86, Extras 30; C. A. Young 3-27); ‡**Ireland 220-7** (46.3 overs) (N. J. O'Brien 80*, J. F. Mooney 36; I. Wardlaw 3-49). MoM: N. J. O'Brien. *The early batsmen struggled again: Scotland were 45-4, Ireland 7-2. Matt Machan guided the Scots past 200, but Niall O'Brien paced the chase well. He collected only five boundaries (two of them sixes) from 106 balls, and put on 61 for the seventh wicket with John Mooney.*

At Abu Dhabi, January 14, 2015 (day/night). **Scotland won by 150 runs. ‡Scotland 213-7** (50 overs) (P. L. Mommsen 31, R. D. Berrington 62, J. H. Davey 53*; Aftab Alam 3-48); **Afghanistan 63** (18.3 overs) (I. Wardlaw 4-22, J. H. Davey 6-28). MoM: J. H. Davey. *Scotland recovered from 108-6 thanks to Richie Berrington and Josh Davey, who put on 99. Davey and Iain Wardlaw then both returned career-bests as Afghanistan collapsed from 38-0 to 63 all out, their lowest in ODIs at the time (previously 88 against Kenya in 2010-11; they would be bowled out for 58 by Zimbabwe in January 2016).*

At Dubai (International), January 17, 2015. **Afghanistan won by 71 runs. Afghanistan 246-8** (50 overs) (Asghar Stanikzai 44, Samiullah Shenwari 50, Najibullah Zadran 83; C. A. Young 3-45, K. J. O'Brien 3-49); ‡**Ireland 175** (43.3 overs) (P. R. Stirling 36, N. J. O'Brien 33; Hamid Hassan 3-24). MoM: Najibullah Zadran. *Afghanistan rebounded well from the batting horrors of the previous match. Najibullah again provided late thrust with 83 from 50 balls, including six sixes. Ireland never quite got going in reply: six batsmen reached double figures, but Paul Stirling's 36 was the highest.*

At Dubai (ICC Academy), January 19, 2015. **Scotland v ‡Ireland. Abandoned.** *ODI debut: P. K. D. Chase (Ireland). The match was all set for a delayed start when the rain returned. It meant a frustrating international baptism for fast bowler Peter Chase, who had played for Durham in 2014.*

Ireland 5pts, Afghanistan 4pts, Scotland 3pts.

Associates Twenty20 internationals in the United Arab Emirates

Three of the Associate teams who had qualified for the World Twenty20 in India early in 2016 contested a series of matches in November that also included the hosts, the UAE. Oman surprised Hong Kong, winning two of their three games, but went down to the UAE and a weakened Afghanistan side – who lost their match against Hong Kong. Bilal Khan, Oman's Pakistan-born left-arm seamer, took ten for 144 in six games.

At Abu Dhabi, November 21, 2015. **Oman won by six wickets. Hong Kong 106-9** (20 overs) (Bilal Khan 3-29); ‡**Oman 107-4** (18.3 overs) (Zeeshan Siddiqui 33*, Sultan Ahmed 37*). *T20I debuts: C. Carter (Hong Kong); Aaqib Sulehri, Adnan Ilyas, Bilal Khan, A. V. Lalcheta (Oman). Oman tasted victory in only their second official Twenty20 international (they had lost the first, to*

Afghanistan in Dublin in July), after Hong Kong's batsmen struggled: no one reached 20. Oman were rocking at 43-4, before Zeeshan Siddiqui and skipper Sultan Ahmed put on 64*.

At Abu Dhabi, November 22, 2015. **United Arab Emirates won by seven wickets. Oman 133-8** (20 overs) (Zeeshan Maqsood 44; R. Mustafa 3-9); ‡**United Arab Emirates 134-3** (18.2 overs) (R. Mustafa 41, Shaiman Anwar 54). *T20I debuts: Amjad Gul, Qadeer Ahmed, Zaheer Maqsood (UAE). Shaiman Anwar, the UAE's leading batsman in the World Cup, anchored his side to victory in this one-off international with 54 from 43 balls. Off-spinner Rohan Mustafa had figures of 4–2–9–3, then went in and made 41.*

At Abu Dhabi, November 25, 2015. **Oman won by four runs. Oman 131-6** (20 overs) (Adnan Ilyas 37, Aamer Kaleem 42*; Aizaz Khan 3-22); ‡**Hong Kong 127** (19.5 overs) (Bilal Khan 4-20, Zeeshan Maqsood 3-22). *Oman clinched their three-match series against Hong Kong with another close-run win. Bilal Khan, who had removed both openers, started the last over with six needed – but took two more wickets and conceded only a single.*

At Abu Dhabi, November 26, 2015. **Hong Kong won by eight wickets. Oman 149-4** (20 overs) (Adnan Ilyas 49, Aamer Kaleem 46*); ‡**Hong Kong 155-2** (18.3 overs) (Babar Hayat 65*, M. S. Chapman 63*). *T20I debut: Sufyan Mehmood (Oman). Hong Kong's batsmen finally hit their stride, Babar Hayat and Mark Chapman putting on 127* in 14 overs. Earlier, Khawar Ali's 18 for Oman had included four successive fours off Tanvir Afzal; Aaqib Sulehri retired hurt after being hit on the leg first ball. From 48-3, Adnan Ilyas and Aamir Kaleem added 101 in 12 overs.*

At Abu Dhabi, November 28, 2015. **Hong Kong won by four wickets.** ‡**Afghanistan 162-6** (20 overs) (Asghar Stanikzai 51, Samiullah Shenwari 34, Shafiqullah Shinwari 30); **Hong Kong 166-6** (19.4 overs) (Babar Hayat 35, Tanvir Afzal 42). *T20I debuts: M. Nasim Baras, Rokhan Barakzai (Afghanistan). Hong Kong surprised below-strength Afghanistan in this one-off game, despite captain Asghar Stanikzai's 51 from 37 balls. Hayat responded with 35 from 18; both he and Tanvir clouted three sixes.*

At Abu Dhabi, November 29, 2015. **Afghanistan won by 27 runs. Afghanistan 159-8** (20 overs) (Usman Ghani 69; Mehran Khan 3-30); ‡**Oman 132** (18.1 overs) (Adnan Ilyas 34; Sayed Shirzad 3-16). *T20I debuts: Sayed Shirzad, Yamin Ahmadzai (Afghanistan). With 33 needed from three overs, Oman sniffed an upset, but the debutant left-arm seamer Sayed Shirzad struck twice in three balls, and the last wicket fell in the next over. Afghanistan's wicketkeeper Mohammad Shahzad, who was out second ball for four, made five dismissals (three catches and two stumpings), a record for a Twenty20 international innings.*

At Abu Dhabi, November 30, 2015. **Afghanistan won by 12 runs. Afghanistan 160-4** (20 overs) (Mohammad Shahzad 60, Shafiqullah Shinwari 32*); ‡**Oman 148-8** (20 overs) (Khawar Ali 38; Yamin Ahmadzai 3-34). *Shahzad's 60 from 46 balls ensured a tall target, and Oman were never really on terms. Afghanistan won the series 2–0.*

CRICKET IN AFGHANISTAN IN 2015

Bedding in with the big boys

SHAHID HASHMI

Afghanistan's rise continued apace. In February, they won their first match at a World Cup, beating Scotland by one wicket amid euphoric scenes in Dunedin. Yet this was trumped by one-day and Twenty20 series victories against Zimbabwe, home and away, towards the end of the year – the first time an Associate team had won a series against a Test nation in either format.

As a result, Afghanistan moved into tenth place in the one-day rankings – their highest position – while batsman Mohammad Shahzad and fast bowler Dawlat Zadran broke into the top ten of the Twenty20 rankings. Shahzad, left out of the World Cup squad for being overweight, celebrated his return with the highest ODI score by an Afghan player (131 not out), and what was at the time the fourth-highest in all Twenty20 internationals (118 not out) – both against Zimbabwe at Sharjah. No wonder Nasimullah Danish described his first year as chairman of the Afghanistan Cricket Board as "one of the best" in the country's brief history.

There were significant developments off the field. The team attracted a main sponsor for the first time in two years, and in December the ACB announced that their cricketers would be moving their base from Sharjah to a newly completed stadium close to Delhi. The Greater Noida ground had yet to be granted international status, but was cleared to host games between Associate nations; the players will benefit from superior facilities, as well as exposure to leading Indian coaches and former players.

The Under-19 side marked the new era with a series against Zimbabwe at their new home just days after the announcement. "India's support is massive because they are the superpowers of the game," said Danish. Ties between the countries were strengthened when ex-Indian seamer Manoj Prabhakar was appointed bowling coach a week before Christmas.

Prabhakar will work alongside Inzamam-ul-Haq, the former Test batsman who became Afghanistan's third Pakistani coach on the eve of the Zimbabwe tour, following the ACB's decision not to renew the one-year contract of Andy Moles. Inzamam was an instant success. In October, Afghanistan came from behind to win the ODI series at Bulawayo 3–2 – a scoreline they repeated in the return bout at Sharjah two months later. Chasing 249 in the deciding match there, Afghanistan collapsed to 146 for six, before Gulbadeen Naib (82 not out off 68 balls) saw them home with two balls to spare. Afghanistan swept to victory in all four Twenty20 matches. "The only thing I have done is to channel their passion and aggression in the right direction," said Inzamam. "They are still a work in progress."

There had been more change when Mohammad Nabi ended his two-year reign as captain after the World Cup, and was succeeded by Asghar Stanikzai.

Back in the rank and file, Nabi thrived, scoring his maiden one-day international century at Bulawayo in October.

Afghanistan's performance at the World Twenty20 Qualifier in June was one of the few disappointments. Although they booked their place for India in 2016, defeats by Oman and Hong Kong meant a fifth-place finish. Their first appearance at a World Cup was also a sobering experience, despite the win against Scotland. Sri Lanka were pushed hard at Dunedin, but there were heavy defeats against the four other Test nations in their group, including a 275-run thumping by Australia – the largest loss by runs in a World Cup match.

The ultimate goal remains Test cricket, and there now exists a tangible path to the top, with the winners of the first-class Intercontinental Cup due to take on the lowest-ranked Test side in 2018. Rain had the last word in Afghanistan's first fixture of the two-year competition, away to Scotland in June. Less than six months later, they overturned a first-innings deficit of 151 to beat Papua New Guinea at Sharjah.

The deal with India has not diverted the ACB from their ambition to play their matches in Afghanistan, with Danish claiming the country now has "seven proper cricket grounds to host an international team". Three more – in Kandahar, Laghman and Zabul – are under construction.

Kabul hosted every match of the domestic Shpageeza Twenty20 tournament, which again drew large crowds. Speenghar took the T20 title, while Mis Ainak retained the four-day crown.

AFGHANISTAN v ZIMBABWE IN THE UAE IN 2015-16

Paul Radley

One-day internationals (5): Afghanistan 3, Zimbabwe 2
Twenty20 internationals (2): Afghanistan 2, Zimbabwe 0

Two months after Afghanistan travelled to Zimbabwe and became the first Associate side to beat a Test nation in a bilateral one-day series, they showed it was no fluke by replicating the results on what passes for home soil in Sharjah. Afghanistan took a 2–0 lead in the one-dayers before Zimbabwe hit back. The decider went down to the wire, but Afghanistan won with two balls and two wickets to spare. "It's a historic day," said their captain Asghar Stanikzai. The win moved them up to tenth in the ICC rankings, ahead of Ireland and Zimbabwe. For good measure, they then won both Twenty20 games too, as they had at Bulawayo in October.

The decisive 50-over match was a triumph for Gulbadeen Naib, in his first game of the series. He had not passed 31 in 15 previous ODIs, but now – coming in at No. 7 – zoomed to 82 not out, with six sixes, the last of which sealed victory. Gulbadeen thought he had won the match from the previous delivery, and embarked on a lap of honour before the umpires brought him down to earth. He quickly recovered his composure, and flicked the next ball over the ropes at deep square.

Afghanistan's other hero was their hard-hitting opener Mohammad Shahzad, who collected 388 runs in the seven matches, including a hundred in each format. Back in favour after missing the 2015 World Cup on fitness grounds, he paid tribute to the influence of the coach, former Pakistan captain Inzamam-ul-Haq, built along similarly comfortable lines.

Another sobering defeat for Zimbabwe was leavened by the return to form of Hamilton Masakadza: restored to the side for the last four 50-over games, he made 266 runs, and was unfortunate that his run-a-ball 110 in the final match did not lead to victory.

The series started on Christmas Day, which is not widely observed in the Islamic emirate of Sharjah. But the matches did have a festive feel at times, particularly when Afghanistan had the upper hand, giving their passionate supporters reason to celebrate. They regularly performed the *attan*, a traditional folk dance, while Afghan flags were flourished proudly. The revelry was at its most fevered when Shahzad pummelled Afghanistan's first Twenty20 international century in the final game.

ZIMBABWE TOURING PARTY

*E. Chigumbura (50/20), C. J. Chibhabha (50/20), T. S. Chisoro (50/20), A. G. Cremer (50/20), C. R. Ervine (50/20), L. M. Jongwe (50/20), N. Madziva (50/20), H. Masakadza (50/20), W. P. Masakadza (50/20), P. J. Moor (50/20), R. Mutumbami (50/20), T. Muzarabani (50/20), T. Panyangara (50), Sikandar Raza (50/20), D. T. Tiripano (20), M. N. Waller (50/20). *Coach:* D. F. Whatmore.

S. C. Williams was originally selected, but withdrew with a groin injury. He was replaced by Chisoro in the 50-over squad, and W. P. Masakadza for the Twenty20 series. Panyangara failed to shake off a leg injury, and was replaced by Tiripano for the Twenty20s.

First one-day international At Sharjah, December 25, 2015 (day/night). **Afghanistan won by 49 runs.** ‡**Afghanistan 131** (38.5 overs) (Noor Ali Zadran 63; A. G. Cremer 5-20); **Zimbabwe 82** (30.5 overs) (Hamza Hotak 4-17, Mohammad Nabi 3-15). *MoM:* Hamza Hotak. *ODI debut:* Yamin Ahmadzai (Afghanistan). *Zimbabwe seemed to have sewn up some Christmas Day cheer when they bowled Afghanistan out for 131 on a turning track, only to collapse themselves, eight men scoring 18 runs between them (including four ducks). Noor Ali Zadran was the only batsman on either side to exceed Zimbabwe captain Elton Chigumbura's 28. Slow left-armer Hamza Hotak took the new ball and claimed his best one-day figures.*

Second one-day international At Sharjah, December 29, 2015 (day/night). **Afghanistan won by four wickets.** ‡**Zimbabwe 253-7** (50 overs) (P. J. Moor 50, H. Masakadza 47, C. R. Ervine 73; Dawlat Zadran 3-57); **Afghanistan 254-6** (47.4 overs) (Noor Ali Zadran 31, Mohammad Shahzad 131*, Mohammad Nabi 33; E. Chigumbura 3-32). *MoM:* Mohammad Shahzad. *ODI debut:* Rokhan Barakzai (Afghanistan). *Mohammad Shahzad clouted eight sixes (and seven fours) in Afghanistan's highest ODI score, beating Nawroz Mangal's 129 against the UAE in Dubai in 2014-15. His stands of 82 for the first wicket with Noor Ali, and 87 for the second with Mohammad Nabi, enabled Afghanistan to reach the highest total of the series.*

Third one-day international At Sharjah, January 2, 2016 (day/night). **Zimbabwe won by 117 runs.** ‡**Zimbabwe 175** (48.3 overs) (H. Masakadza 83, A. G. Cremer 58; Mirwais Ashraf 3-20); **Afghanistan 58** (16.1 overs) (Mohammad Shahzad 31; N. Madziva 3-27, L. M. Jongwe 5-6). *MoM:* H. Masakadza. *Zimbabwe lost both openers for ducks, and were 49-7 before a decisive partnership of 104 between Hamilton Masakadza, who faced 138 balls, and Graeme Cremer, who hit a maiden international half-century in his 75th innings. Afghanistan were also 0-2, but there was no recovery as they slipped to their lowest ODI total, undercutting 63 against Scotland at Abu Dhabi in 2014-15. Only Shahzad, who biffed 31 in 22 balls, reached double figures. Once he was out, making it 39-4, just 19 more were added, with medium-pacer Luke Jongwe collecting 5.1–1–6–5.*

Fourth one-day international At Sharjah, January 4, 2016 (day/night). **Zimbabwe won by 65 runs.** ‡**Zimbabwe 226** (49.1 overs) (P. J. Moor 52, C. J. Chibhabha 53; Dawlat Zadran 3-54, Rashid Khan 3-43); **Afghanistan 161** (45 overs) (Mohammad Shahzad 45, Hashmatullah Shahidi 31; C. J.

Chibhabha 4-25). *MoM: C. J. Chibhabha. The outfield was slowed by a rare tropical downpour the day before the match, so Zimbabwe's total was better than it looked. Openers Peter Moor and Chamu Chibhabha – both out for ducks in the previous game – made half-centuries this time, and added 92. Chibhabha later dismissed Shahzad to set Afghanistan back, and added three more wickets with his gentle seamers for career-best figures as the series was squared.*

Fifth one-day international At Sharjah, January 6, 2016 (day/night). **Afghanistan won by two wickets.** ‡**Zimbabwe 248** (49.5 overs) (P. J. Moor 42, H. Masakadza 110, R. Mutumbami 40; Hamza Hotak 3-41); **Afghanistan 254-8** (49.4 overs) (Noor Ali Zadran 30, Hashmatullah Shahidi 32, Gulbadeen Naib 82*, Rashid Khan 31; L. M. Jongwe 3-50). *MoM: Gulbadeen Naib. MoS: Mohammad Shahzad. Masakadza's fourth ODI century – but his first for more than six years – lifted Zimbabwe to a handy total, helped by some erratic fielding; Afghanistan's coach Inzamam-ul-Haq was visibly annoyed. He was even more worried later when they dipped to 146-6, but the recalled Gulbadeen Naib saved the day, putting on 85 with Rashid Khan then – with ten needed from the last over – hit Neville Madziva for two twos and a four to level the scores (there was also a wide). Gulbadeen ran off in celebration, before realising one more was needed; he deposited his next ball over square leg for his sixth six. Afghanistan won the Alokozay Cup 3–2.*

First Twenty20 international At Sharjah, January 8, 2016 (floodlit). **Afghanistan won by five runs.** ‡**Afghanistan 187-7** (20 overs) (Mohammad Shahzad 33, Usman Ghani 42, Gulbadeen Naib 37; A. G. Cremer 3-17); **Zimbabwe 182-7** (20 overs) (H. Masakadza 33, M. N. Waller 49*; Dawlat Zadran 3-32). *MoM: Gulbadeen Naib. T20I debuts: P. J. Moor, D. T. Tiripano (Zimbabwe). Gulbadeen reprised his heroics of the previous match with 37 from 20 balls to propel Afghanistan to a total that proved just beyond Zimbabwe. They started the final over needing 21, but Dawlat Zadran sent down a wide and two high no-balls, then Luke Jongwe slammed a four and a six. However, needing another six off the final delivery, he sliced a catch to Gulbadeen at deep cover. Earlier, Shahzad had smashed 33 from 17, losing two balls out of the ground, before Cremer's leg-breaks slowed things down. Masakadza objected to the send-off he received from wicketkeeper Shahzad when he was bowled in the 12th over, and had to be guided away from the celebratory Afghan huddle by the umpire.*

Second Twenty20 international At Sharjah, January 10, 2016 (floodlit). **Afghanistan won by 81 runs.** **Afghanistan 215-6** (20 overs) (Mohammad Shahzad 118*); ‡**Zimbabwe 134** (18.1 overs) (H. Masakadza 63, P. J. Moor 35). *MoM: Mohammad Shahzad. MoS: Mohammad Shahzad. Shahzad hit 88 in boundaries – ten fours and eight sixes – on the way to 118* from 67 balls, Afghanistan's first century in Twenty20 internationals. Zimbabwe were soon 34-5 and, although Masakadza launched five sixes, putting on 77 with Moor, no one else managed more than ten. Afghanistan took the T20 series 2–0.*

CRICKET IN HONG KONG IN 2015

Keeping up appearances

Alvin Sallay

A year after being awarded one-day international status, Hong Kong's cricketers made sure standards didn't slip. The highlight was qualification for the 2016 World Twenty20 in India, following victories over Nepal, Ireland and Afghanistan in July. Hong Kong lost to Scotland in the semi-finals, while the Irish weather prevented them from playing off for third place against the hosts. But qualification meant a second successive World Twenty20 appearance, after they stunned Bangladesh at Chittagong in 2014. Haseeb Amjad finished the tournament with ten wickets – second only to Ireland's Kevin O'Brien – at 9.90 apiece, with fellow seamer Irfan Ahmed claiming eight at 12.

The good work continued in November, when – after eight 50-over defeats out of eight in official one-day internationals stretching back to July 2004 – Hong Kong brushed aside the United Arab Emirates twice in the space of three days in Dubai. In the first of those games, the talented left-hander Mark Chapman made a superb unbeaten 124 from 116 balls, becoming the tenth player to score a century on one-day international debut – a list that includes Desmond Haynes, Andy Flower and Phillip Hughes – but the first from an Associate nation. The 21-year-old Chapman, whose father is from New Zealand and mother from China, had missed the early stages of the UAE tour to sit his engineering finals at Auckland University. But the Hong Kong Cricket Association hope he will continue to play for the country of his birth – and become the face of the sport in the region.

The second match against the UAE was dominated by Tanvir Afzal, who followed a hard-hit 73 from 33 balls, including seven sixes, with three for 31. Tanvir had assumed the captaincy in May, after Jamie Atkinson stepped down to concentrate on his own game. Atkinson, a cool-headed wicketkeeper-batsman, had played a leading role in Hong Kong's development, presiding over their qualification for the 2014 World Twenty20 and their ascent to ODI status.

Under Tanvir, Hong Kong achieved their first win in the Intercontinental Cup, thrashing the UAE in Dubai in November to put behind them a disappointing defeat by Namibia at Windhoek in May. The Pakistan-born Babar Hayat made 113 and 73 from No. 3, while Tanvir contributed a first-innings 104 to set up a crushing 276-run victory.

That game followed a 50-over defeat by an England XI in Abu Dhabi, in which Hayat managed 78. Later that month, Hong Kong were also beaten by a Pakistan XI, but not before Chapman had contributed a 39-ball 50. In between, the team lost focus, going down 2–1 in a Twenty20 series against Oman, and dropping a place to 11th in the ICC rankings – though they remained above Zimbabwe, and recovered well to beat Afghanistan.

In early 2016, Hong Kong finally hosted a home international after a ten-year hiatus caused by the ICC's ruling that established venues such as Hong Kong Cricket Club and the Kowloon Cricket Club were too small. With land at a premium, and following lengthy discussions, the governing body approved the use of the Mission Road ground in Mong Kok, situated next to the Hong Kong Softball Association. After their four-day game against Scotland was abandoned due to rain, the hosts thrashed the Scots by 109 runs in a one-day international, part of the ICC's World Cricket League Championship.

For Hong Kong's matches in the ICC World Twenty20 Qualifier, see page 1182; for the Intercontinental Cup, see page 1187; for the World Cricket League Championship, see page 1202; and for their T20 series against Oman in the UAE, see page 1191.

CRICKET IN PAPUA NEW GUINEA IN 2015

Mind games

Tim Wigmore

Papua New Guinea's players suppressed tears as they walked off the pitch at Malahide on July 23. They had been defeated by Afghanistan in a play-off to reach the World Twenty20, and did not need reminding of the consequences: no access to the $250,000 available for the six qualifiers, and no chance of facing a Test nation for the first time. Their last realistic hope of making an ICC global event this decade had gone.

They had squandered a prime opportunity. After winning three of their first four matches (the other, against Hong Kong, was abandoned), PNG needed just one more victory to secure a spot in India in March 2016. First they were thrashed by Namibia, then – most gallingly – they lost to the United States. Against Afghanistan, PNG's total of 127 for six provided a reminder of the limitations of their batting, before some rudimentary fielding errors – crucial dropped catches, and conceding a no-ball because three fielders were behind square on the leg side – spoke of nerves and naivety. Greg Campbell, the former Australian Test bowler now acting as Cricket PNG's general manager, admitted his side lacked "composure when under pressure in those crucial moments".

This was not the first time that the Barramundis, as they are known, had made an electric start to a qualification tournament, then collapsed with their prize in sight. In the months after their latest disappointment, the players worked with a sports psychologist, and were scheduled to do so more extensively in 2016.

Yet the year still contained several landmark moments, and they marked their debut first-class match by chasing 305 against the Netherlands in the Intercontinental Cup at Amstelveen in June. Asad Vala, their best batsman in 2015, scored an unbeaten 124, having put on 200 for the fifth wicket with Mahuru Dai, who hit 91.

It also fell to PNG to end Ireland's long winning run in World Twenty20 Qualifiers. Their game at Belfast distilled the best of Papuan cricket. Tigerish fielding and unrelentingly accurate medium-pace combined to restrict Ireland to 123 for nine. Then, as PNG faltered in reply, burly No. 9 Norman Vanua harrumphed four sixes in six balls. It showed what the side, who remain among the youngest in Associate cricket, could achieve. That PNG were yet to play a one-day international against a Test nation two years on from gaining ODI status was a source of frustration.

But there is no obscuring the strides made by a team who, as recently as 2011, were in World Cricket League Division Three. It is hoped that Kenya's visit for the 50-over World Cricket League Championship fixtures in May will be the first official international staged in the country. Amini Park, in Port Moresby, could then host ODIs in 2017, when Scotland tour.

Meanwhile, Australia continued to provide support. The Barrumundis played in the South Australian Premier League for the third year running, and hope to compete against state Second XIs in 2016-17, while there are plans to increase the flow of young Papuan players to Australian clubs. There are welcome signs, too, that the women's team are progressing. In December they came fifth in the World Twenty20 Qualifier, and captain Norma Ovasuru received a rookie contract in Australia's inaugural Women's Big Bash League.

CRICKET IN THE UNITED ARAB EMIRATES IN 2015

The last part-timers

PAUL RADLEY

At the start of the year, the UAE were preparing to travel to the World Cup. After the World Twenty20 in 2014, it was their second global event in quick succession. But the results – six matches, six defeats – suggested they were glorified tourists in Australia and New Zealand. And, by the end of the year, the antiquated system that had spawned their side was being torn down.

It was a bleak time for Emirates cricket. The great progress of the previous two years was checked. And, once the old guard who had been propping up the national team started to move on, the nation's cricket was shown up as being out of date. The nadir came when a young Hong Kong side whitewashed the UAE across all formats in Dubai in November. "We have been lucky to have had some really talented individuals, but the opposition is moving far ahead of us and we are playing catch-up," said David East, the former Essex wicketkeeper who is now the chief executive of the Emirates Cricket Board. "We have to adapt and channel our energies into supporting full-time cricketers."

Chief among the changes is the implementation of central contracts, so the UAE will have its first batch of professional cricketers, accountable to the board. The selectors will also be paid, a national academy is due to be inaugurated, and there is a plan to overhaul the domestic game. But there is likely to be pain at national level for some time yet.

"We are the only part-timers," said Aqib Javed, the UAE's coach. "All other teams are full-time. In the past two and a half years, those teams have improved a lot. If somebody wants to compete with a professional, you have to act like one."

The most notable figure to take his leave in 2015 was Khurram Khan, the former captain and a mainstay of the side for a dozen years. He retired, aged 43, after finally making it to a World Cup at the fifth attempt. The end was a little unsavoury: Khurram, a Pakistani expat, was relieved of the captaincy on the eve of the tournament, and replaced by Mohammad Tauqir, an Emirati only seven months his junior. Typically, Khurram made little fuss, and went to the World Cup, though he lacked his usual brio with the bat, and hardly bowled at all.

But he earned an unexpected reward in retirement, when he was bought for $US22,000 at the Masters Champions League auction in December – a more-than-decent payout for someone whose day job is as part of the Emirates airline cabin crew.

For the UAE's matches in the World Cup, see page 860; for the ICC World Twenty20 Qualifier, see page 1182; for the Intercontinental Cup, see page 1187; and for the World Cricket League Championship, see page 1202.

CRICKET IN NEPAL IN 2015

The earthquake's shadow

UJJWAL ACHARYA

The 7.8-magnitude earthquake on April 25 that killed over 8,000 people also badly damaged Nepal's cricket infrastructure, including the international grounds at Mulpani and Tribhuvan University. The disaster occurred just two weeks after Nepal had hosted a 63-over memorial game in honour of the Australian batsman Phillip Hughes; tremors from the earthquake triggered an avalanche at Everest Base Camp that scuppered an attempt by Chhurim Sherpa to carry some of Hughes's kit to the summit. In order to raise money for the relief effort, the Cricket Association of Nepal launched "Bat for Nepal", with the national side due to play eight charity games against international opponents over a two-year period.

A month earlier, they had produced a sequence of torpid displays at the World Twenty20 Qualifier in Scotland and Ireland. After an opening victory against the USA, Nepal lost four of their next five, and finished bottom of Group A, which cost them their Twenty20 international status, awarded only the previous year. Their pre-tournament tour of Europe in June had been equally disappointing. They lost to Gloucestershire's Second XI at Bath, then went down 3–1 in a T20 series to the Netherlands. A change in format did not help, and Nepal were beaten twice in the one-day ICC World Cricket League by both Scotland and Papua New Guinea.

It wasn't only the players who underperformed. The board have experienced infighting ever since their former president Tanka Angbuhang and 18 other members of the organisation were accused of embezzling Rs14.31m (£90,000) in June 2014. Though all 19 were found not guilty in December, the decision could not prevent the board from splitting into pro- and anti-Angbuhang factions during the end-of-year AGM. In October, popular head coach Pubudu Dassanayake had left the national set-up for "personal reasons", following months of uncertainty about his contract.

The Under-19 side restored some pride at their World Cup qualifying tournament in Malaysia, which had been due to take place in Nepal before the earthquake. They were crowned champions after left-arm spinner Lalit Rajbanshi's figures of 10–1–36–4 helped them overcome Ireland in the final.

CRICKET IN OMAN IN 2015

No mirage

PAUL BIRD

After Oman had slipped from the ICC World Cricket League Division Two in 2007 to Division Five at the start of the 2016 season, no one expected them to qualify for this year's World Twenty20. Even after they had won the Asian Cricket Council Twenty20 Cup in January 2015 – earning themselves a place at the World Twenty20 qualification event – they were still one of the least fancied sides in Scotland and Ireland. In a land where the majority are more interested in football and cars, few Omanis were aware that their team were involved in a major tournament.

But Oman's success in a damp northern European summer was nothing short of miraculous. They demolished Canada, the Netherlands and Afghanistan in the league stages, before grabbing the last qualification place with a win against Namibia; Zeeshan Siddiqui was the hero, guiding his team home with an unbeaten 51 from 32 balls, but there were headlines too for former England all-rounder Derek Pringle, hired as a technical adviser.

At home, the country's cricket board began the process of expanding the Amerat National Cricket Centre, the site of one of the finest cricket pitches in the Middle East. A second grass pitch is due to be installed by September, and a new pavilion and indoor training centre should open by the end of the year. With floodlights and TV cables in place, the governing body want to see international matches played beneath the Amerat basin's impressive mountains before 2020.

Yet Oman's most successful international sport is still seen by many locals as a minority activity played by a migrant South Asian workforce. Persuading talented Omanis to carry on past Under-19 level remains a challenge. Limited progress is being made: over 300 Omanis had registered to play league cricket in 2016, while the 2015-16 edition of the Omani Premier League included one team made up entirely of locals. But if officials continue to beg the ICC to shorten qualification periods for overseas players, and OPL teams sign the likes of ex-Pakistan wicketkeeper Zulqarnain Haider, it seems unlikely that cricket can truly be brought into the mainstream.

CRICKET ROUND THE WORLD IN 2015

COMPILED BY JAMES COYNE AND TIMOTHY ABRAHAM

ICC WORLD CRICKET LEAGUE

Both the year's World Cricket League tournaments were beset by accusations of player ineligibility and doubts over the structure. The cost of staging these events, believed to be around $US18,000 in Europe, was unpopular with administrators from the Big Three, who had led the financial overhaul of the ICC in January 2014. By the end of 2015, the WCL – which once spanned eight divisions – had been cut back to five.

Plenty was at stake in Division Two in January 2015: a top-two finish would be rewarded with inclusion in the next Intercontinental Cup and WCL Championship, plus a High Performance grant of up to $450,000. Four teams still had a chance heading into the last round of group games, but things went against Nepal and Canada, who were each put in, then watched Kenya and hosts Namibia chase down middling totals. Nepal finished third, and dragged themselves off the field in tears, under the impression they had missed out – only for the ICC Board to spring a surprise a few days later. Their decision to elevate Afghanistan and Ireland, the two highest-ranking Associates, to the 2019 World Cup qualification standings meant that Nepal and Kenya (who had finished fourth) were added to the WCL Championship. The Division Two title went to the Netherlands, who had squeezed into the final with three wins from five, and went on to beat Namibia, despite missing several of their bigger-name imports because of eligibility rules.

Confusion surrounded two Uganda players, Mpho Selowa and Lepono Ndlovu – both 28-year-old wicketkeepers born in Pretoria, who had sometimes played under different names. The Uganda Cricket Association insisted the pair held dual Ugandan and South African citizenship. Ndlovu turned up a month later opening the batting – as a homegrown player – for KwaZulu-Natal Inland in South African first-class cricket. Their selection made little difference to Uganda's fortunes: they were relegated to Division Three, alongside Canada.

There was further intrigue in Division Six, hosted by Essex in September. Saudi Arabia's failure to secure UK visas handed Vanuatu an easy passage to the semi-finals, where they unexpectedly lost to Suriname. It was a hugely significant result: soon after the tournament it was confirmed that, because of the cutbacks, a top-two finish would be needed to stay in the WCL.

But, even before Suriname had landed in England, there were rumblings that the make-up of their squad featured several with Guyanese roots. A dossier, submitted to ICC head of legal Iain Higgins after the tournament, cast doubt on the eligibility of at least six influential players, among them Gavin Singh, whose 189 runs and 13 wickets had landed him the Man of the Tournament award, and Muneshwar Patandin, who took five for 18 in the pivotal semi-final. Vanuatu put the matter to the ICC, and investigations were ongoing in early 2016.   JAMES COYNE

ALBANIA

C. B. Fry would surely have bestowed a cricketing heritage on Albania had he accepted the country's throne. Instead, Sir Norman Wisdom has provided late inspiration. Wisdom, who died in 2010, remains a revered figure in Albania, as his were the only western films allowed during the communist dictatorship of Enver Hoxha. And, among the celebrations last year for the centenary of Wisdom's birth, was a cricket match, believed to be the first formal game in Albania since the country won independence in 1912. The Albanian Eagles and the International Lions met for the Sir Norman Wisdom Trophy in May, on a synthetic pitch provided by third division football team Internacional Tirana. "It was certainly one of the more unusual requests," said Wisdom's son Nicholas, who played two first-class games for Sussex in 1974, when contacted for permission to use the family name. "My father was an occasional cricket watcher and turned out once in a while in celebrity matches. I'm sure he'd have been delighted to play a part in Albania's cricket history." The plan was executed by two Englishmen, David Smith and Phil Griffiths, who were in Tirana advising the Albanians on the modernisation of their customs and tax administrations. Griffiths had also coached the Albanian national rugby team in his spare time, and persuaded several of the squad to pick up a bat, ensuring that – unusually for European cricket – the majority of the players were natives. The Lions scored 79 from their 20 overs and, after a tea of *bukë gruri* (corn bread) and *qofte të fërguara* (meatballs), the Eagles knocked off the target, nine wickets down, in a tense finish.

Fry once quipped that cricket might have prevented Mussolini's invasion of Albania in April 1939. "It would have been ideal at the end of March for English cricket teams to come out in a favourable climate and get some practice in the sun before the county season," he wrote. "And damn it, nobody would have dared invade Albania with county cricket going on. The British Navy would have been absolutely obliged to step in and prevent it." Fry's opportunity to become Charles III of Albania apparently came about in 1924, when his England and Sussex team-mate Ranjitsinhji, one of India's three representatives at the League of Nations, took him along to Geneva as a speechwriter. But the Anglo-French poet Hilaire Belloc, a contemporary of Fry at Oxford, warned him against it. "Do not accept the crown of Albania," he said. "Be content with a cellar of wine and the society of those who love you." In any case, the job spec included an annual unearned income of £10,000, which Fry did not have. Four years later, Zog I proclaimed himself Albania's king, a position he retained until fleeing the Italian occupiers.

This made Prince Leka II – Zog's grandson – an appropriate choice to bowl the ceremonial first ball 76 years later. Educated in South Africa and at Sandhurst, the man who would be king should the Republic of Albania decide to restore the monarchy is a cricket enthusiast. "A great honour," said Leka. "There might not be a league or national team in Albania for years to come, but cricket has to start somewhere." The opening ball was faced by writer, comedian and captain of the Lions XI, Tony Hawks, who had a top 20 single in the country in 2002 with "Big in Albania", co-written with Wisdom and Sir Tim Rice after a bet. More fixtures are planned in Tirana this summer, including a game against the Old Albanians, featuring Rice and some former class-mates from St Albans School. Timothy Abraham

BELGIUM

A match played under 1815 Laws, complete with period dress and equipment, and no boundaries, was among the highlights of four days of cricket to mark the bicentenary of the Battle of Waterloo. The Guards CC – a team of Foot Guards in the Queen's Household Division – mastered the underarm, four-ball-over format, triumphing over Royal Brussels CC at their ground in Ohain. Cricket had provided a footnote in the lead-up to Waterloo. In his seminal book *The Cricket-Field*, James Pycroft noted that, six days before the battle, the Duke of Wellington had escorted Lady Jane Lennox, the 16-year-old daughter of the Duke of Richmond – himself a renowned first-class batsman, who provided the finance for Thomas Lord's grounds in Marylebone – to Enghien to watch cricket between officers in The Guards. The match was reportedly halted by the arrival of the Prince of Orange. On June 18, 2015, the exact anniversary of the battle, a Royal Brussels Chairman's XI met The Guards in a day-long declaration game. This time the home side prevailed, spurred on by a fiery opening spell and an explosive 62 from the former Zimbabwe Test bowler Brighton Watambwa, now resident in Belgium and captain of the national side. A triangular Twenty20 series, also involving MCC, was played over the next two days. Teams and guests then made the short walk to the battlefield to watch a poignant re-enactment. Charles Fellows-Smith

BERMUDA

Bermudian cricket is in disarray. An undisciplined squad, lacking rudimentary skills, are overseen by a Bermuda Cricket Board riven with infighting and self-interest, and seemingly without a realistic plan for the future. During last season's Champion of Champions final, a scrap broke out between Jason Anderson, the Cleveland County wicketkeeper, and George O'Brien, batting for Willow Cuts, prompting an invasion of supporters, officials and security staff which held up play for 15 minutes until the police arrived. The incident was filmed on camera, and quickly went viral, attracting the attention of even *The Washington Post*. Anderson was banned for life for instigating the fight; O'Brien for the better part of the 2016 season for swinging at him with his bat. The incident was the nadir of a domestic season littered with bad behaviour and a decline in standards, which the BCB did little to combat until it was too late.

Cricket's infrastructure is falling apart: the square at the National Sports Centre, which once had one-day international status, has been termed unfit for purpose by the ICC, to the extent that domestic finals can no longer be played there; neither the BCB nor the government have the funds to resolve the problem. While the future of Bermuda's national teams, junior and senior, is bleak, players continue to make some impact overseas: Kamau Leverock (Glamorgan), Delray Rawlins (Sussex) and Jordan Smith (Warwickshire) were all part of county set-ups at various levels in 2015. LeiLanni Nesbeth, meanwhile, was included in the Sussex women's Under-15 squad after the BCB helped her get a scholarship to Bede's School. No Bermudian players were deemed good enough to make the ICC Americas Combine squad for the West Indies 50-over competition beginning in January 2016, a decision that did not bode well ahead of WCL Division Four. Nine years and millions of wasted dollars since Bermuda's participation in the 2007 World Cup, there is no telling how far they have left to fall.   JOSH BALL

CANADA

Through a witch's brew of ignorance, negligence, incompetence, unaccountability and even spite, Canada's administrators have run the game into the frozen ground. An incendiary outburst from national captain Rizwan Cheema provided the year's only heat. The list of grievances was long – from team-mates who allegedly faked injuries, to others who hid them so they could be selected for tours, to board officials who didn't step down when they failed to deliver on their commitments. Airing Canada's dirty linen in public could hasten the end of Cheema's international career, which would probably hurt more if the team had any fixtures scheduled. This was the year Canada slipped to Division Three of the World Cricket League, surrendering any pretence to remain as a top-flight Associate. They travelled to Division Two at least hoping to retain their position, but lost a crucial match to Nepal, and went on to finish last. Gallingly, the Nepalese were coached by Pubudu Dassanayake, whose four years with Canada between 2007 and 2011 now looks like a golden age. They went winless in the World Twenty20 Qualifier too – a flameout of such proportions that Cheema felt he had no option but to let rip. Canada had begun 2015 with four 50-over matches in Harare against Zimbabwe A, losing 3–1. That Cricket Canada's Twitter feed persisted in referring to these as "ODIs" (they had lost one-day international status a year earlier in any case) was careless at best. Canada at least won ICC Americas Twenty20 Division One in May, although the only semblance of competition came from fellow ne'er-do-wells USA and Bermuda.   FARAZ SARWAT

COOK ISLANDS

The legacy of the whalers and missionaries who brought cricket to the Cook Islands in the 19th century lives on. The internationally recognised version of cricket is now played on 12 of the 15 islands, while the 500 or so inhabitants of Pukapuka – said to descend from the survivors of a cyclone which struck around 1700 – also play their own local variant, *pole wale*, loosely related to Samoan *kilikiti*. There is no limit on the number of players, and bowling can be done from both ends, depending on the end to which the fielder returns the ball. Batsmen stand still after their shots, and have runners who use long *kikau* branches to get from crease to crease more quickly. The Cook Islands Cricket mission statement is: "More Kids, More Cricket, Better Performance". All senior cricket is Twenty20, which has helped integrate youngsters who have come up through school Sixes and holiday coaching programmes. On the main island of Rarotonga, where a cricket association has existed since 1910, seven women's sides have sprung up over the last five years; Muri Girls went through the last season unbeaten. In the inter-island domestic tournament, women play alongside men and bat first. The playing base is encouragingly local, with only 3% expats, rising to 10% on Rarotonga. Dodging wild chickens, or picking their remains off the field, is part of the game. Fielding on Aitutaki inevitably involves retrieving the ball from a lagoon which forms the boundary on one side. Religious observance means no play on a Sunday (and, on Aitutaki, on Saturday as well). Delayed starts, usually blamed on "island time", are now subject to docked overs. The deterrent has worked a treat. CHRIS DRURY

THE GAMBIA

The 130 or so members of Sussex Seniors have been supporting cricket in Africa's smallest mainland country since 2007. We have toured twice, staging coaching sessions, and shipped out more than £50,000 of equipment. This has helped the Gambia Cricket Association, led by their president Jonny Gomez, to give hundreds of boys and girls the opportunity to play the game. A few of them clearly have ability, but their opportunities are limited to the occasional African regional tournament. With this in mind, Mbye Dumbuya and Ismalia Tamba, Gambia's captain and vice-captain, were invited to play league and friendly cricket with Sussex clubs Heathfield Park and Fletching last summer. Their trip was to be fully sponsored, with accommodation and all expenses paid. All the requested documentation, plus £85 per player for a six-month sports visa, was forwarded to the relevant government departments. But their applications were refused. On appeal, we were advised to approach players from the European Union, as they could be in the country tomorrow. Advised to reapply, we attached another £85 per player, but were again refused by James Brokenshire, the immigration minister. He did not believe the pair's intention in the UK was to play cricket; nor that they would be accommodated and financed; nor that they would return to The Gambia when their visas expired. All subsequent letters to Brokenshire, home secretary Theresa May and prime minister David Cameron have gone unanswered, and the Home Office does not comment on individual cases. This has left hundreds of Sussex cricketers frustrated. ANDREW SHANKS

Andrew Shanks plays for Sussex Over-70s.

GERMANY

The Deutscher Cricket Bund are hoping that men such as Arif Jamal can be the role model for integrating recent South Asian migrants into German society. Jamal arrived from Afghanistan aged 15 with his brother, and ended up in a children's home in Essen, in the industrial north-west. He entered Germany's Under-19 set-up, grafted for his coaching badges, and now works part-time as a youth officer for the DCB, coaching the next generation of teenage arrivals in Essen. Even before the migrant influx of 2015, Germany was one of world cricket's growth areas: participation had doubled over the previous four years to 3,000 registered players – more than anywhere on the continent except the Netherlands – with the majority of women and youths drawn from German families not historically connected to the game. And, of the projected million-plus migrants arriving last year alone, it is estimated that a fifth might be from Afghanistan, Pakistan and

Bangladesh. "Most are males between 14 to 40, and every second one seems to be a cricketer," says Brian Mantle, the DCB managing director. At the height of the influx in September and October, the DCB were receiving around 25 messages a day from new arrivals or local authorities, mainly requesting equipment or guidance on where to play. "We've been dealing with this on a smaller scale for years, but now it's overwhelming," says Mantle. "We're helping as much as we can, getting boxes of kit out to people. And we've been helped by our generous neighbours and sponsors. But because of our limited funds and personnel we're not able to even scratch the surface."

The changes brought about after the Big Three takeover means that Associates such as Germany no longer have ICC regional support funding – a situation exacerbated in May when artificial pitches in Bonn and Cologne, each worth €12,000, were set alight by vandals. League matches continued, but then someone carved holes in the wicket at Bonn. It was initially feared that the perpetrator was from the far right, and hostile to a sport played by Asian immigrants. "The fact that it was cut on a length suggests it was done by someone who knows their cricket," says Mantle. "But we can't prove anything." The 16 teams in the Rhineland responded with defiance, coming together to set down two replacement pitches. JAMES COYNE

Donations of equipment can be made by emailing Brian Mantle at manager@cricket.de.

INDONESIA

Cricket in the world's fourth-most populous country has been transformed from a mainly expat pastime to a slicker operation giving unprecedented opportunities to some of society's poorest. Tribute should be paid to a group of Indonesian coaches – all ICC Level One-qualified – who have nurtured young players in four provinces over 15 years. All this is overseen by a national committee with strong political support. The government's recognition of cricket as a national sport has had far-reaching consequences: the formation of provincial bodies; more funding; higher numbers of Indonesian nationals playing the game; the development of provincial, local and school leagues; the increased participation of women; involvement of national teams in ICC East Asia–Pacific tournaments; and the marrying of expat competitions and leagues into the national calendar. The Bali International Sixes, an annual favourite and a starting point for many Indonesian players, reaches its 20th anniversary in 2016, and ten of the country's 37 provinces are expected to be entering teams. One sad story has been the scrapping of the Bajo 20s, which took place near the National Komodo Park in Flores until 2009. After disputes between the cricketers and footballers, the concrete wicket was smashed up with pickaxes. But there has been one positive outcome: Fernandes Nato, a former star of Bajo 20s, has gone on to represent Indonesia, and now runs a cricket centre in Jakarta. ALAN WILSON

MEXICO

For Cancún's cricketers, a classical loft through the off side is met with complaints and catcalls from team-mates rather than applause. To retrieve the ball from beyond the shortest boundary at the ground, located at the Instituto Americano Leonardo Da Vinci, on the outskirts of this popular tropical holiday resort, is to risk all manner of hazards. "It is pure jungle in there," explains Phillip Barkhuizen, captain, groundsman and indispensable organiser-in-chief of cricket in Cancún. "There are snakes of all different colours, panthers, pumas… You may even get the odd crocodile straying from the lagoon." The Mayan name for Cancún translates as "nest of snakes", and new arrivals are made aware of the club's four-step rule: if you cannot see the ball within four paces of the boundary, it is given up for lost. Cricket spread to Cancún in 2008, when a game was staged to coincide with the visit at the nearby El Rey polo club of the UK ambassador to Mexico, Giles Paxman, younger brother of BBC presenter Jeremy. The facilities were top-notch, but the playing surface was littered with horse manure. Cancún White Tigers CC were quickly formed

WOMEN'S CRICKET IN EUROPE

Sister act

ROD LYALL

The complexities of assembling the best female players from Europe's smaller cricketing countries have not deterred Patrick Demaerschalk from building a platform for their talent. Although emerging women's national teams have started meeting up in recent years, there is currently no ICC Europe-administered tournament beneath the annual round robin between Ireland, Scotland and the Netherlands. But in June, with ICC Europe's blessing, a Continental Women's XI put together by Demaerschalk, a Belgian cricket coach, played against a Netherlands Invitation XI in Utrecht. Demaerschalk's contention, one shared by the players themselves, was that they seldom had the chance to pit themselves against challenging opposition of their own sex, as most play in men's leagues back home. "I would like to see a pool of, say, 25 players who could be invited to take part," he said. "A bit like the Barbarians in rugby." The team were captained by Claudia Balogh of Hungary – who trained with England Women at Edgbaston in 2014 – and featured Andrea-Mae Zepeda (Austria), Shweta Sinha (Belgium), Anne Lund Østergård, Camilla Østergård and Line Østergård (Denmark), Rebecca Blake and Emma Chancé (France), and Agatha Acris and Christine McNally (Gibraltar). Players from Italy and Germany were unable to take part because of prior commitments. After a spectacular storm disrupted the first day, the schedule was tweaked to a Twenty20 followed by a two-innings match (limited to 15 overs each). The tourists lost the T20 by 93 runs, but claimed a first-innings lead in the second game, before losing by 16 runs. Ultimately, the international experience of Dutch teenagers Sterre Kalis – with 118 runs across both matches without being dismissed – and Lisa Klokgieters, who took three wickets in the second game, saw the Netherlands XI home.

and, after briefly sharing facilities with the city's baseball team, Tigres de Quintana Roo, they moved to their present home. The playing standard is good, but numbers fluctuate depending on those working in the tourist industry; the current state of the club nets – overgrown with jungle – hints at a recent decline. The only possible cut or pull shot would be with a machete. TIMOTHY ABRAHAM

SERBIA

The migrant crisis prompted several EU countries to put up the shutters, but Serbia's cricketers view the influx differently. Over the last few years, coaches from the Serbian Cricket Federation have been heading into a detention centre near Belgrade to stage tapeball competitions with Pakistani and Afghan asylum seekers. Serbian cricket has grown up a great deal since the first hit-ups took place on a footpath beneath Belgrade's Kalemegdan fortress in 2007. Their big breakthrough came when the SCF began leasing a field from the Aeronautical Union of Serbia at Lisičji Jarak aerodrome (loosely translated as "Fox Ditch"), just north of Belgrade. Recreational gliders and parachutists land over midwicket's shoulder, while umpires are advised not to wear traditional long white coats on account of possible confusion with staff and inmates at the psychiatric hospital and low-security prison just down the road. Now the Belgrade pioneers are being challenged by Bački Monoštor, a small village in the ethnic melting-pot of Vojvodina, yards from where the Danube divides Serbia and Croatia. A few years back, Miloš Zikić, a local

Triumphant lionesses: Sierra Leone celebrate their victory in the North-West Africa Women's Twenty20 tournament.

cheesemaker, succeeded in getting cricket on the bill at the Bodrog Fest – an annual celebration of the medieval town of Bodrog, on which the present-day village is built. There it caught the eye of the Beashi community, native Romanian speakers who trace their lineage to Roma slaves taken by Vlad II Dracul, the father of Vlad the Impaler, in the 15th century. After honing their techniques at the village recreation ground, Bodrog Deers entered the national 40-over and Twenty20 leagues in 2013. Sebastijan Balog, one of five cricket-playing brothers and cousins from the village, is one of the best wicketkeepers in Serbia. The villagers of Bački Monoštor could scarcely have guessed how profound their impact could be. Last June, the ICC approved Serbia's application for Affiliate Membership, making them the first admission since the Big Three realignment. The new ground and players provided by Bački Monoštor were thought to be pivotal in meeting the ICC's tightened development criteria. JAMES COYNE

SIERRA LEONE

Sierra Leone were emphatic winners of the first North-West Africa Women's Twenty20 tournament, less than three months after their government lifted the Ebola-related public ban on sporting events. They won all their six matches in The Gambia, helped by a £20,000 donation of equipment from cricketers in Lancashire. In 2007, ICC Africa made it mandatory for all members to initiate a women's development programme. But it proved difficult for the North-West Africa Cricket Conference to get an international tournament off the ground, largely due to lack of funds. Sierra Leone and Nigeria were invited to the 2011 ICC Africa Women's Twenty20 in Uganda, but couldn't compete with the East African nations. Since then, the NWACC have focused on developing the skills and fitness of their female cricketers. Eventually it was agreed that The Gambia would host an international round robin, with teams from Ghana, Mali and Sierra Leone. Getting them all there was fraught with complications: Sierra Leone had to travel more than 700 miles by road, passing through Guinea, because of a lack of direct flights from Freetown to Banjul as a result of Ebola restrictions. Mali drove through Senegal, while Ghana took an indirect flight via Lagos, but faced delays and turned up late in dribs and drabs. Although the July 22 Square ground in Banjul played well enough, the Medical Research Council Oval at Bakau was in poor shape, and the thick grass made it difficult to score more than a single. Sierra Leone's attack was well led by Ann-Marie and Aminata Kamara, while Linda Bull took 15 economical wickets. The Gambia lost to Sierra Leone by nine and ten wickets, but won their other four games, twice reaching 100 in the first innings, and produced the Player of the Tournament, Aminata Mendi. Ghana twice proved too strong for Mali, and have asked to host the second edition in 2016, but the organisers need substantial sponsorship in order for it to become an annual event.   FRANCIS SAMURA

THAILAND

Suleeporn Laomi's beaming face embodied Thailand's reputation as the "Land of Smiles" after she secured the chance of a lifetime at the ICC Women's World Twenty20 Qualifier in Bangkok. It was announced after the Qualifier that a promising young player from each of the eight competing nations would spend two weeks with a franchise in the Women's Big Bash League rookie programme in Australia. Laomi, a 17-year-old leg-spinner, impressed the selection panel with her control and composure, taking five wickets in five games at her team's best economy-rate. She has made steady progress since playing in the Asian Cricket Council Under-19 Championships aged just 12, and making her senior debut at 16. The Cricket Association of Thailand also demonstrated they could host an official ICC tournament, even if the on-field performance of the young home side was a slight letdown after their breakthrough showing at the 2013 Qualifier in Ireland. The semi-finals decided the last two positions in the 2016 tournament proper, and the final between Ireland and Bangladesh was the first official Twenty20 international in Thailand. CAT provided the scorers, Duckworth/Lewis managers and scoreboard operators; a team of 14 were involved at the two grounds, and were soon on the field themselves, playing for Thailand Flash in a local T20 competition. Laomi attended CPP School in Doi Saket, near Chiang Mai, which operates as a centre of excellence for young Thai cricketers, many from hill-tribe backgrounds, and also enjoyed access to regular tournament experience provided by CAT and the ACC. It is essential for the future of Thai cricket that these openings do not wither away. The ICC's winding-down of the ACC for cost reasons has meant opportunities have dried up for regional members such as Thailand. The senior men have not been involved in any competition since 2012, and the Under-19s since 2013. CAT have tried to fill the void with women's tournaments in Chiang Mai, and the annual National Youth Championships across the provinces. And touring sides continue to come from all over the world to play in the popular Sixes competitions, which give further opportunities for young Thais to hone their skills, and raise money for coaching programmes.   RICHARD LOCKWOOD

USA

After several years of ever more egregious governance violations, a third ICC suspension since 2005 for the USA Cricket Association seemed to be a matter of when, not if. Sure enough, the penalty was imposed at June's ICC Annual Conference in Barbados. The previous January, ICC chairman N. Srinivasan had outlined a range of issues deemed worthy of suspension, including repeatedly delayed elections in violation of USACA's own constitution; a membership base which no longer made up the majority of cricket stakeholders in the country (predominantly because of the presence of a rival body, the American Cricket Federation); deterioration in performance of the men's national team (relegated to Division Four of the World Cricket League in October 2014); and a failure to hire a chief executive following Darren Beazley's resignation in March 2014. The subsequent case presented in Barbados accused USACA of being "unprofessional" and "not trustworthy", and contained further allegations of 11 ghost leagues and a failure to open their financial accounts for review. However, many of these were subjective measures, and hard to prove.

HAWAII

The Three Ws of the Pacific

Ravi Chaturvedi

The iconic Diamond Head volcano and the date palms and banyan trees flanking the Pacific Ocean, provide a stunning backdrop for the Honolulu Cricket Club at Kapiolani Park. The Three Ws here are winds, waves and wings – specifically the nene goose, Hawaii's national bird. The luminescent lights of the seafront even allow for the novelty of night matches in summertime, when the weather is usually warm enough for umpires to stand in traditional Hawaiian shirts. Cricket has been played in Hawaii since British missionaries and sugar cultivators pitched up in the 1840s, more than 100 years before the islands were absorbed into the United States. Back then, J. C. Penny was a ferocious fast bowler, taking seven wickets in a local competition and once sending the bails flying 32 yards. Honolulu CC and Maui CC are the traditional rivals, competing for the Hawaiian Friendship Cup – or, its full title, the Alexander Liholiho Ipu Pilialoha O Hawaii Cup – in honour of King Kamehameha IV, an Anglophile who patronised the early game, and played cricket in his palace grounds before dying of chronic asthma aged 29. More recently, the Hawaiian T20 Premier League was launched in 2008, and the current holders are Sunset Slashers, who beat Hawaiian Super Kings by one run in a sensational final. Honolulu CC are trying to persuade Hawaii's governor and the city mayor to have a second matting wicket installed at Kapiolani Park, in anticipation of increased international competition. Irked by what they consider stepmotherly treatment from USACA towards cricket in the 50th state of the Union, Honolulu CC have asked the ICC – so far without success – to allow Hawaii to compete separately in East Asia–Pacific regional tournaments against the likes of Papua New Guinea and Samoa. They have also invited them to Honolulu for a pan-Polynesian tournament.

In the end, the smoking gun came in the form of the ICC's $200,000 loan to USACA in June 2013, ostensibly to fund national-team activities, but which administrators in Dubai suspected was used to pay off mounting debts racked up from fighting multiple lawsuits. USACA had not paid back the loan, nor had they provided sufficient receipts or bank statements to prove where the money went.

Though their officials were suspended, the USA national team were not prevented from competing. Even so, their training camps before the World Twenty20 Qualifier were cancelled, and the ICC had to buy the tickets to fly them to Ireland, where the USA came within one win of making the knockouts – without their best player, wicketkeeper-batsman Steven Taylor, who withdrew at the eleventh hour to join Caribbean Premier League team Barbados Tridents. Taylor became the second American-born player, after Sri Lanka's Jehan Mubarak, to earn a full contract with a major Twenty20 franchise league.

In September, the first ICC Americas Combine was held at the new cricket facility at World Sports Park in Indianapolis, and was widely praised by those involved. Of several hundred applications, 103 players were invited and 88 attended the evaluation process for a 15-man combined squad to compete in the West Indies' 2016 domestic 50-over competition. Fast bowler Ali Khan, who had never been picked by USACA selectors, made the cut. He was one of nine USA and six Canada players deemed good enough by a panel including former Test bowlers Courtney Walsh and Venkatapathy Raju.

Shane Warne's and Sachin Tendulkar's Cricket All-Stars venture brought the year to a noisy conclusion. Top-drawer batsmen still in their thirties, such as Kumar Sangakkara,

Mahela Jayawardene and Virender Sehwag, toyed with former cannon-armed quicks from the 1990s, such as Allan Donald and Curtly Ambrose, who were now little more than cannon fodder. The quality of cricket was panned by most media outlets. Warne declared the event a rousing success, and claimed more than 100,000 people cheered the players on at New York's Citi Field, Houston's Minute Maid Park, and the Dodger Stadium in Los Angeles, all ballparks using drop-in pitches. In fact, the combined turnstile attendance was 65,116 – a figure severely impacted by the price of tickets, which began at $50 and went up to $325 in LA. Fewer than half the seats were filled across the three venues. Still, Cricket Australia announced their interest in staging international cricket in the USA, eager to capitalise on the expat fan base.

The All-Stars tour was littered with problems behind the scenes. Eyebrows were raised five days before the opening match, when promoters Leverage Agency issued a joint press release with USACA – by now suspended – titled "Cricket All-Stars team up with USACA to promote cricket development". According to sources close to the event, the process of distributing complimentary tickets to local leagues and youth clinics in New York and Houston went haywire with USACA's involvement. Their links with the All-Stars were curbed in time for the final game in Los Angeles, one of several cities visited by ICC officials in November for town-hall meetings aimed at charting a path forward for cricket in the country. The ICC laid out 39 terms and conditions for USACA to satisfy in order to be reinstated as their member board. It was clear they were still a long way off. PETER DELLA PENNA

VANUATU

Mark Stafford, the president of Vanuatu Cricket, was preparing for the official opening of the association's new nets when Cyclone Pam arrived. The category-five storm ripped through the South Pacific archipelago in March 2015, killing 16 people, leaving thousands homeless and destroying vital infrastructure. "It certainly set us back a bit," says Stafford, an Australian who has lived in Vanuatu for 30 years. UNESCO estimated in May that $US268m will be needed to repair the damage. The ICC, Cricket Australia and New Zealand Cricket contributed $200,000 from 2015 World Cup proceeds to the relief effort, and Cricket Papua New Guinea pledged $7,500 to help Vanuatu's first-team players, at least half of whom are unemployed or have part-time jobs. The International Olympic Committee also pitched in to help rebuild facilities. "We have recovered and managed to stage a full programme through the second half of 2015," says Stafford. In a symbolic moment, the new training facility in Port Vila eventually opened in September, when the national team returned from World Cricket League Division Six in England, having just missed out on promotion (see page 1202). In July, Vanuatu's men took home the gold medal from the Pacific Games Twenty20 tournament, twice beating an experimental PNG side. The women just missed out on a medal. JAMIE SMYTH

VATICAN CITY

St Peter's CC, the team of priests and seminarians studying in the Vatican, broke more new ground with a match against an all-Muslim team. Mount CC, from Batley in West Yorkshire, travelled to Rome in October, motivated by a desire to improve interfaith relations, and provide St Peter's CC with a second ecclesiastic challenge, following the historic Anglican v Catholic fixture at the St Lawrence Ground in Canterbury in September 2014. The Mount touring party of 33, mainly British Pakistanis, also visited the Vatican Museums and St Peter's Basilica, and attended Sunday mass led by Pope Francis. St Peter's CC won the inaugural Sir John Major Friendship Cup tie by four runs at the Capannelle hippodrome. Later that month, St Peter's claimed the Augustine Cup from the Archbishop of Canterbury's XI by winning their second encounter by 42 runs at Capannelle – a game coinciding with the conclusion of the Catholic Church's Synod on the Family. Unfortunately, the scheduled trip by Caacupe de la Villa, a young team from impoverished backgrounds in Buenos Aires, had to be postponed because of funding problems, although there was hope their visit would go ahead in 2016. Jorge Maria Bergoglio served as archbishop of Buenos Aires from 1998 until his election at the 2013 papal conclave. "They remember seeing their archbishop walking around the streets," said Father Eamonn O'Higgins, St Peter's team manager and spiritual director. "And he blessed their cricket ground." JOHN McCARTHY

ICC GLOBAL TOURNAMENTS IN 2015

WORLD CRICKET LEAGUE

Competition	Date	Winner	Runner-up	Others (in finishing order)
WCL Div Two	Jan	Netherlands	Namibia	Kenya, Nepal, Uganda, Canada
WCL Div Six†	Sept	Suriname	Guernsey	Vanuatu, Norway, Fiji, Botswana, Cayman Islands

† *Saudi Arabia did not participate after failing to meet visa requirements.*

REGIONAL TWENTY20 TOURNAMENTS

Competition	Date	Winner	Runner-up	Others (in finishing order)
Africa Div One	Mar/Apr	Namibia	Kenya	Uganda, Ghana, Botswana, Tanzania
Americas Div One	May	Canada	USA	Bermuda, Suriname
ACC Twenty20 Cup	Jan	Oman	Kuwait	Saudi Arabia, Singapore, Malaysia, Maldives
European Div One	May	Jersey	Denmark	Italy, Guernsey, Norway, France
Pacific Games	July	Vanuatu	PNG	Tonga, New Caledonia

WOMEN'S TOURNAMENTS

Competition	Date	Winner	Runner-up	Others (in finishing order)
World Twenty20 Qualifier	Nov/Dec	Ireland	Bangladesh	Zimbabwe, Scotland, PNG, China, Thailand, Netherlands
Pacific Games	July	Samoa	PNG	Fiji, Vanuatu, Cook Islands, New Caledonia

Women's Cricket

WOMEN'S INTERNATIONAL CRICKET IN 2015

MELINDA FARRELL

Never has a rebel Twenty20 league been so warmly welcomed by cricket administrators. The very words are usually enough to make them shudder, so it was ironic that a sporting goods franchise called "rebel" won the naming rights to the inaugural Women's Big Bash League in Australia. Its launch in December 2015 capped a groundbreaking year for women's cricket. A Test – England v Australia – was televised for the first time in history; the Ashes attracted unprecedented crowds; and the ECB announced plans for their own revamped Twenty20 competition in 2016, the Women's Super League.

The biggest successes resulted from a long-term view and sound investment. Cricket Australia were believed to have offset the cost of broadcasting eight WBBL games on free-to-air television to the tune of around $A500,000. That paid immediate dividends: the first match to be broadcast drew a TV audience of 250,000. Similar ratings for the next game inspired the Ten Network to experiment with upgrading some matches from their secondary digital channel to the premier station – where the Melbourne derby pulled a peak audience of 439,000 – and then to show two more fixtures. Cricketers from England, New Zealand, South Africa and the West Indies secured contracts ranging from $3,000 to $10,000. Though modest compared with the men's game, they were a significant step in the women's march towards professionalism.

But increased viewing numbers bring higher scrutiny. The pressure on female players to deliver an entertaining match had already become clear in the Ashes Test at Canterbury in August, when the very existence of women's Test cricket was questioned. The batting, apart from a fine 99 from Australia's Jess Jonassen, was uninspiring, and the bowling often pedestrian. It did little to advance the women's case for more long-form cricket.

In fairness, the pitch gave them little to work with. If good surfaces are important to the men's game, they are especially so for women who, equipped with less raw power, fare better on pitches offering pace which both bowlers and batsmen can exploit. Three months later, conditions were engineered in Adelaide to give the first day/night men's Test the best chance of success; the same effort should have been made for the first televised women's Test.

No matter the conditions, there was no disguising the fact England were falling behind Australia. Losing the Ashes precipitated a change of coach – Mark Robinson succeeding Paul Shaw – but England's problems might not be so easily fixed. In 2014, the ECB had followed Cricket Australia by awarding central contracts to their leading players. The Australians, however, also invested money in state contracts, so that decent state players can now be semi-professional, too, whereas many county players even pay for net sessions.

The most common path for players to reach the England side is via the Academy. As a result, there appears to be a relatively small pool of players competing for an England shirt. There is undoubtedly talent outside the high-performance model, but how does it rise to the top? Australia's strong domestic structure ensures late bloomers can push for selection. It's hard to imagine England calling up a 30-year-old for the Ashes on the strength of her domestic performances, as Australia did with leg-spinner Kristen Beams.

The ECB are attempting to address their weaker domestic base by consolidating county cricket and introducing their 20-over Women's Super League, with 50-over matches to be added in 2017. And the problem is by no means theirs alone. There is a danger that Australia's superior long-term investment in female cricketers could see them open a gap that all other nations find difficult to close – as their easy dominance in the first year and a half of the ICC Women's Championship suggested.

Yet some of the best performances in the WBBL came from international signings. Stafanie Taylor of West Indies, Marizanne Kapp from South Africa, and England's Sarah Taylor and Charlotte Edwards all showed there is talent to match the best Australians, given the right environment. The Indians were notable absentees. Though the BCCI have sought to protect the IPL by preventing contracted players joining other Twenty20 leagues, they have no equivalent female competition to provide an excuse for keeping Jhulan Goswami and Mithali Raj away from the WBBL.

But, if two of the Big Three are investing in T20 leagues, what could a women's IPL, featuring the world's best players, do for the profile of the game worldwide? The outstanding ratings for the WBBL, which so impressed the Ten Network, prove that if you invest in a prominent shop window more people are likely to buy. Then, it's up to the players to deliver.

ICC WOMEN'S CHAMPIONSHIP, 2014–2016

In 2014, the ICC introduced a Women's Championship as a qualifying tournament for the next World Cup. It was also intended to create a more meaningful international programme for the leading teams. Each of the eight sides who had contested the 2012-13 World Cup were to play each other in three one-day internationals over two and a half years. The top four at the conclusion of the Championship in November 2016 will qualify directly for the 2017 World Cup in England; the bottom four will join six regional qualifiers in a further competition to settle the final four places. Teams were free to arrange extra bilateral fixtures within the same series, and could choose which three one-day internationals counted towards the Championship. Australia led the way by the end of 2015, their only defeat coming in England, who lay fifth, after 2–1 losses to New Zealand and Australia.

ICC WOMEN'S CHAMPIONSHIP

	Played	Won	Lost	No result	Points	Net run-rate
Australia	12	10	2	0	20	0.86
West Indies	12	8	4	0	16	0.55
New Zealand	12	7	5	0	14	0.35
South Africa	12	6	5	1	13	−0.01
England	12	6	5	1	13	−0.02
Pakistan	12	4	8	0	8	−0.38
India	12	3	8	1	7	−0.41
Sri Lanka	12	2	9	1	5	−1.03

As at February 14, 2016. Win = 2pts; no result = 1pt. Where teams are tied on points, their position is determined on net run-rate.

THE LEADING WOMAN CRICKETER IN THE WORLD, 2015

Suzie Bates

Raf Nicholson

Back in 2011, Suzie Bates faced a crossroads. Cricket or basketball? White Ferns or Tall Ferns? She had played both from a young age, and represented New Zealand at basketball at the 2008 Beijing Olympics. For a time, she balanced the two. But, in July 2011, the White Ferns offered her the captaincy – a full-time commitment. "I took a while to decide," she recalls.

We should all be glad she chose cricket. Bates has been making waves ever since her international debut in March 2006 – not least with a glorious 168 off 105 balls against Pakistan in the 2009 World Cup semi-final – and one of the marks of her captaincy has been the continued flow of runs.

She was Player of the Tournament at the 2013 World Cup, and was later named the ICC's one-day Player of the Year. Her unbeaten 94 off 61 balls against Pakistan during the 2014 World Twenty20 was the highest score by a New Zealand woman in the format; and she finished 2015 fourth on the all-time list of run-scorers in Twenty20 internationals. She is also a useful medium-pace death bowler, and back in 2014 was selected to captain the Rest of the World against MCC Women at Lord's, which she considers the highlight of her career. It's little wonder she was one of the top overseas picks for the inaugural Women's Big Bash League in Australia in 2015-16.

At 5ft 8in, with an athletic body honed on the basketball court, Bates spent 2015 consolidating her status as one of the power hitters of the women's game, finishing the year just behind her opening partner Rachel Priest on the 50-over runs list, with 585 at 48. She made 258 while being dismissed only twice during the 5–0 one-day whitewash of Sri Lanka in November, and 69 off 58 balls in the second of the three Twenty20 games against them. Thirteen cheap one-day wickets underlined her importance. Her favourite moment, though, came when New Zealand won two of their three ICC Women's Championship matches against England in February; in the first of them, she hit her sixth ODI century. "It was a good few days," she grins.

Born in 1987 in Dunedin, Bates learned the game in the backyard with her two older brothers. Much of her early club cricket was spent alongside boys, though she was talent-spotted during a national competition for the Otago Girls' High School. By the time she was 15, she was representing Otago Sparks in the national women's league.

While Bates now considers herself a full-time cricketer – in April 2013 she was among the first New Zealand women to earn a professional contract – she also works as an ambassador for the New Zealand Olympic Committee, visiting schools to talk about her sporting experiences. "I love basketball and I do miss it," she says. "But, with the Big Bash and English Super League and a full international schedule, I want to make the most of my career as a cricketer. With where the women's game is heading, it's really exciting to be part of it."

MRF TYRES ICC WOMEN'S RANKINGS

TEAM RANKINGS (as at December 31, 2015)

		Matches	Points	Rating
1	Australia	41	5,490	134
2	England	39	4,851	124
3	New Zealand	45	5,023	112
4	India	29	3,034	105
5	West Indies	48	4,885	102
6	South Africa	40	3,668	92
7	Pakistan	47	3,767	80
8	Sri Lanka	45	3,218	72
9	Bangladesh	18	845	47
10	Ireland	16	493	31

The ratings are based on all women's Tests, one-day and Twenty20 internationals played since October 1, 2012.

PLAYER RANKINGS

In October 2008, the ICC launched a set of rankings for women cricketers, on the same principles as those for men, based on one-day international performances. Twenty20 rankings were added in September 2012. There are no Test rankings.

The leading players in the women's one-day international rankings on December 31, 2015, were:

Rank	Batsmen	Points	Rank	Bowlers	Points
1	M. M. Lanning (*Australia*)	796	1	J. Goswami (*India*)	765
2	S. W. Bates (*New Zealand*)	717	2	K. H. Brunt (*England*)	656
2	S. J. Taylor (*England*)	717	2	A. Mohammed (*West Indies*)	656
4	S. R. Taylor (*West Indies*)	702	4	S. R. Taylor (*West Indies*)	647
5	C. M. Edwards (*England*)	695	5	E. A. Perry (*Australia*)	608
6	M. Raj (*India*)	679	6	S. Ismail (*South Africa*)	583
7	H. Kaur (*India*)	643	7	J. L. Gunn (*England*)	582
8	E. A. Perry (*Australia*)	640	8	D. van Niekerk (*South Africa*)	579
9	R. H. Priest (*New Zealand*)	589	9	E. A. Osborne (*Australia*)	552
10	A. J. Blackwell (*Australia*)	570	10	Sana Mir (*Pakistan*)	550

The leading players in the women's Twenty20 international rankings on December 31, 2015, were:

Rank	Batsmen	Points	Rank	Bowlers	Points
1	M. M. Lanning (*Australia*)	687	1	A. Shrubsole (*England*)	678
2	C. M. Edwards (*England*)	655	2	D. Hazell (*England*)	646
3	S. J. Taylor (*England*)	636	3	A. Mohammed (*West Indies*)	616
4	S. W. Bates (*New Zealand*)	627	4	M. J. G. Nielsen (*New Zealand*)	603
5	M. Raj (*India*)	623	5	Salma Khatun (*Bangladesh*)	601
6	S. R. Taylor (*West Indies*)	616	6	E. A. Perry (*Australia*)	580
7	D. J. S. Dottin (*West Indies*)	600	7	S. Ismail (*South Africa*)	578
8	Bismah Maroof (*Pakistan*)	577	8	J. L. Jonassen (*Australia*)	573
9	E. J. Villani (*Australia*)	555	9	S. J. Coyte (*Australia*)	559
10	S. F. M. Devine (*New Zealand*)	553	10	K. D. U. Prabodhani (*Sri Lanka*)	557

WOMEN'S ONE-DAY INTERNATIONAL AVERAGES IN CALENDAR YEAR 2015

BATTING (150 runs)

	M	I	NO	R	HS	100	50	Avge	SR	Ct/St
S. R. Taylor (WI)	8	8	3	399	98*	0	3	79.80	72.02	4
M. M. Lanning (A.)	3	3	0	195	104	1	1	65.00	95.12	1
E. A. Perry (A.)	3	3	0	193	78	0	2	64.33	85.77	0
R. H. Priest (NZ)	15	13	2	592	157	2	4	53.81	80.87	13/2
†M. D. Thirush Kamini (I)	4	4	1	158	62*	0	1	52.66	66.66	0
S. W. Bates (NZ)	15	14	2	585	106	1	4	48.75	81.47	16
Javeria Khan (P)	12	12	2	467	133*	1	2	46.70	61.36	6
S. J. Taylor (E.)	8	8	1	319	93	0	2	45.57	86.44	2/3
C. M. Edwards (E.)	8	8	1	288	65	0	3	41.14	68.24	2
M. R. Aguilleira (WI)	8	8	2	232	68	0	2	38.66	62.87	2/2
D. J. S. Dottin (WI)	8	8	2	228	84*	0	2	38.00	75.00	1
Sana Mir (P)	12	12	5	257	52	0	2	36.71	51.50	6
†Bismah Maroof (P)	11	11	1	365	99	0	2	36.50	55.89	4
†A. E. Satterthwaite (NZ)	15	13	3	352	76*	0	1	35.20	65.91	5
†A. C. Jayangani (SL)	10	10	0	341	99	0	3	34.10	67.92	1
S. F. M. Devine (NZ)	15	12	0	363	89	0	2	30.25	69.80	4
K. T. Perkins (NZ)	15	12	5	209	70*	0	1	29.85	72.56	9
N. R. Sciver (E)	8	7	1	169	66	0	2	28.16	78.60	7
†L. S. Greenway (E.)	7	6	0	168	53	0	1	28.00	63.39	2
Asmavia Iqbal (P)	12	9	3	157	44*	0	0	26.16	72.68	5
H. C. Knight (E.)	8	8	0	188	79	0	1	23.50	59.87	2
Marina Iqbal (P)	10	10	0	213	69	0	1	21.30	52.72	5
Nain Abidi (P)	12	12	0	243	48	0	0	20.25	52.37	5
H. A. S. D. Siriwardene (SL)	10	10	2	161	42*	0	0	20.12	50.78	3
†W. P. M. Weerakkody (SL)	10	10	0	199	42	0	0	19.90	49.13	8/4
M. A. D. D. Surangika (SL)	11	11	0	170	43	0	0	15.45	52.63	0

BOWLING (7 wickets)

	Style	O	M	R	W	BB	4I	Avge	SR	ER
S. Luus (SA)	LBG	24.4	1	74	10	5-20	2	7.40	14.80	3.00
Anam Amin (P)	SLA	87	20	222	25	4-7	3	8.88	20.88	2.55
A. M. Peterson (NZ)	RM	43.4	8	140	10	4-25	1	14.00	26.20	3.20
H. K. Matthews (WI)	OB	59	4	196	13	3-7	0	15.07	27.23	3.32
R. S. Gayakwad (I)	SLA	45.2	8	125	8	3-25	0	15.62	34.00	2.75
E. M. Bermingham (NZ)	LBG	75.4	6	268	17	4-16	1	15.76	26.70	3.54
L. M. Kasperek (NZ)	OB	65.2	16	187	11	4-27	1	17.00	35.63	2.86
A. Mohammed (WI)	OB	71.2	8	202	11	2-15	0	18.36	38.90	2.83
K. L. Cross (E.)	RFM	36	3	149	8	5-24	1	18.62	27.00	4.13
Bismah Maroof (P)	LBG	49	2	176	9	3-14	0	19.55	32.66	3.59
S. W. Bates (NZ)	RM	72.5	4	273	13	3-21	0	21.00	33.61	3.74
I. Ranaweera (SL)	SLA	83.5	13	347	14	4-53	1	24.78	35.92	4.13
M. J. G. Nielsen (E.)	LM	101	10	355	14	5-21	1	25.35	43.28	3.51
S. F. M. Devine (NZ)	RM	103.3	17	392	15	3-40	0	26.13	41.40	3.78
B. M. S. M. Kumari (SL)	SLA	52.3	2	196	7	3-24	0	28.00	45.00	3.73
R. L. Grundy (E)	SLA	60	3	236	8	3-36	0	29.50	45.00	3.93
Asmavia Iqbal (P)	RFM	72.2	6	327	11	3-28	0	29.72	39.45	4.52
H. C. Knight (E.)	OB	67	3	303	10	4-47	1	30.30	40.20	4.52
H. A. S. D. Siriwardene (SL)	RFM	78.4	2	341	11	4-30	1	30.90	42.90	4.32
Sana Mir (P)	OB	108.5	14	375	11	2-22	0	34.09	59.36	3.44
A. Shrubsole (E)	RFM	55	5	239	7	4-36	1	34.14	47.14	4.34
L. M. Tahuhu (NZ)	RFM	100.2	8	381	11	3-25	0	34.63	54.72	3.79
H. A. M. Samuddika (SL)	RM	71	7	270	7	2-16	0	38.57	60.85	3.80

WOMEN'S INTERNATIONAL SERIES IN 2015

PAKISTAN v SRI LANKA IN THE UAE IN 2014-15

One-day internationals (3): Pakistan 3, Sri Lanka 0
Twenty20 internationals (3): Pakistan 1, Sri Lanka 2

After losing all eight games on a recent tour of Australia, Pakistan were on more comfortable ground when they hosted Sri Lanka in the United Arab Emirates, and their whitewash of the one-day internationals briefly lifted them to fourth place in the ICC Women's Championship. Javeria Khan hit an unbeaten 133, their highest one-day score, in the final game. But Sri Lanka fought back to win the Twenty20 series, despite lurching from their highest 20-over score to their lowest on successive days. Their captain, Chamari Atapattu Jayangani, scored 239 runs at 39 across the six matches, to Javeria's 230 at 46; Pakistan captain Sana Mir collected 11 wickets in all, including a Twenty20 hat-trick.

First one-day international   At Sharjah, January 9, 2015. **Pakistan won by five wickets.** ‡**Sri Lanka 178-8** (50 overs) (A. C. Jayangani 49, M. A. D. D. Surangika 43); **Pakistan 180-5** (48.4 overs) (Marina Iqbal 69, Javeria Khan 30, Nida Dar 37*; I. Ranaweera 3-28). *PoM:* Marina Iqbal. *Pakistan opener Marina Iqbal batted into the 45th over for a maiden fifty, which took her side within 30 runs of their first victory in the Women's Championship; Nida Dar's run-a-ball 37* finished the job.*

Second one-day international   At Sharjah, January 11, 2015. **Pakistan won by 12 runs.** ‡**Pakistan 138-9** (50 overs) (Sana Mir 34; B. M. S. M. Kumari 3-24); **Sri Lanka 126** (45.1 overs) (M. A. D. D. Surangika 38; Sadia Yousuf 3-28, Bismah Maroof 3-14). *PoM:* Sana Mir. *ODI debut:* B. M. S. M. Kumari (Sri Lanka). *In a match dominated by the spinners, debutant slow left-armer Sugandika Kumari helped restrict Pakistan to 138 – then, coming in at 108-9, batted nearly eight overs with Inoka Ranaweera, before she was caught behind, with Sri Lanka still 13 short.*

Third one-day international   At Sharjah, January 13, 2015. **Pakistan won by seven wickets.** ‡**Sri Lanka 242-5** (50 overs) (A. C. Jayangani 99, W. P. M. Weerakkody 32, H. A. S. D. Siriwardene 39*); **Pakistan 245-3** (47.2 overs) (Javeria Khan 133*, Sana Mir 51*). *PoM:* Javeria Khan. *Chamari Atapattu Jayangani scored 99 in 109 balls, and Shashikala Siriwardene followed up with 39* in 28, to set Pakistan 243, more than they had ever managed batting second. But Javeria Khan compiled a maiden international hundred – and a Pakistan record – batting 141 balls in all and adding 127 in 21 overs with Sana Mir; she completed their 3–0 victory with her 12th four.*

Women's Championship: Pakistan 6pts, Sri Lanka 0pts.

First Twenty20 international   At Sharjah, January 15, 2015. **Sri Lanka won by eight runs.** ‡**Sri Lanka 151-5** (20 overs) (A. C. Jayangani 31, M. A. D. D. Surangika 50*); **Pakistan 143-8** (20 overs) (Javeria Khan 40, Bismah Maroof 50*). *PoM:* M. A. D. D. Surangika. *T20I debuts:* M. G. M. C. P. Gunawardene, B. M. S. M. Kumari (Sri Lanka). *Dilani Manodara Surangika reached her maiden international half-century off her 40th ball, the last of Sri Lanka's innings, as they passed 150 for the first time in this format, helped by a five-run penalty when a ball hit a parked helmet in the third over. Pakistan fell away from 87-2, and suffered four run-outs, though there was time for Bismah Maroof to reach her own 50 from 45 deliveries.*

Second Twenty20 international   At Sharjah, January 16, 2015. **Pakistan won by 55 runs.** ‡**Pakistan 124-6** (20 overs) (Sana Mir 48*; H. A. M. Samuddika 3-25); **Sri Lanka 69** (15.3 overs) (Sana Mir 4-14). *PoM:* Sana Mir. *T20I debut:* Naila Nazir (Pakistan). *Pakistan captain Sana Mir levelled the series with a career-best 48*, followed by a hat-trick as Sri Lanka collapsed for their lowest Twenty20 total, the day after their highest.*

Third Twenty20 international   At Sharjah, January 17, 2015. **Sri Lanka won by five wickets.** ‡**Pakistan 110-9** (20 overs) (Bismah Maroof 46); **Sri Lanka 112-5** (17.5 overs) (A. C. Jayangani 44). *PoM:* A. C. Jayangani. *Sri Lanka took the series 2–1 after Jayangani steered them to within 18 runs of victory with a run-a-ball 44; her team-mates had plenty of time to complete the win. Earlier, two wickets and a run-out from Udeshika Prabodhani had reduced Pakistan to 11-3 in the third over; Bismah Maroof supervised the addition of 76 for the next two wickets, but a target of 111 posed no problems.*

NEW ZEALAND v ENGLAND IN 2014-15

Martin Davies

One-day internationals (5): New Zealand 2, England 3
Twenty20 internationals (3): New Zealand 1, England 2

England's trip to New Zealand looked like a success on paper, though some of the gloss was taken off by the hosts' winning two of the first three 50-over games – which counted towards the ICC Championship – and emerging with four points to England's two.

After those three matches the teams switched to Twenty20 mode. England won 2–1, and kept the momentum going when the one-dayers resumed, snatching the last two. It was their third successive 50-over bilateral series win in New Zealand.

The final two games produced batting masterclasses from England's No. 3 Sarah Taylor, who hit 89 not out and 93 to finish with 245 runs at 61 and the Player of the Series award. She made 30 more than the next-best, Charlotte Edwards, who still averaged 53 and – in the deciding Twenty20 game, at Lincoln – notched up her 200th game as England captain. It was a milestone that seemed to create more media interest than any other aspect of the tour. Typically self-effacing, Edwards was more interested in winning the match (which her team did) than any celebrations.

New Zealand's stars were openers Rachel Priest and Suzie Bates, the captain, who began the one-day series with a stand of 157 at Mount Maunganui. After England's bowlers had helped square the series two days later, Priest ensured New Zealand would claim the lion's share of the Women's Championship points, thanks to an unbroken second-wicket stand of 153 with Amy Satterthwaite.

ENGLAND TOURING PARTY

*C. M. Edwards (Kent), K. H. Brunt (Yorkshire), K. L. Cross (Lancashire), L. S. Greenway (Kent), R. L. Grundy (Warwickshire), J. L. Gunn (Nottinghamshire), D. Hazell (Yorkshire), A. E. Jones (Warwickshire), H. C. Knight (Berkshire), L. A. Marsh (Sussex), N. R. Sciver (Surrey), A. Shrubsole (Somerset), S. J. Taylor (Sussex), L. Winfield (Yorkshire), D. N. Wyatt (Nottinghamshire). *Coach:* P. F. Shaw.

First one-day international At Mount Maunganui, February 11, 2015. **New Zealand won by 67 runs. New Zealand 240-8** (50 overs) (S. W. Bates 106, R. H. Priest 52; H. C. Knight 4-47); ‡**England 173** (45.2 overs). *PoM:* S. W. Bates. *ODI debut:* R. L. Grundy (England). *Charlotte Edwards chose to bowl on a green pitch, but openers Suzie Bates and Rachel Priest (in her 50th one-day international) put on 157 in 31 overs. Bates had reached her sixth ODI hundred when she became the third to fall, sparking a collapse of 4-4 as off-spinner Heather Knight collected career-best figures. But Katie Perkins guided the lower order through the last ten overs, before the run-outs of openers Knight and Edwards set England back. Only some late hitting by Anya Shrubsole, who top-scored with 29, took them beyond 150. It was New Zealand's first 50-over victory against England in seven games, stretching back to July 2010 at Lord's.*

Second one-day international At Mount Maunganui, February 13, 2015. **England won by 90 runs.** ‡**England 194** (49.2 overs) (C. M. Edwards 65, S. J. Taylor 45; A. M. Peterson 4-25); **New Zealand 104** (36.1 overs) (A. Shrubsole 4-36). *PoM:* C. M. Edwards. *England's bowlers levelled the series, despite another indifferent performance from their batsmen on a good pitch. Edwards and Sarah Taylor contributed 110, but the other nine managed only 69; medium-pacer Anna Peterson was the main beneficiary, with 4-25, including the key wicket of Taylor. New Zealand started brightly, with Priest crashing three boundaries in Shrubsole's first over, but Edwards's run-out of Bates soon pegged them back. Tight bowling made it 47-3 in the 16th over, and Shrubsole removed Kate Broadmore and Sara McGlashan in the 22nd; she finished with 4-36 as New Zealand slipped to a heavy defeat.*

Third one-day international At Mount Maunganui, February 15, 2015. **New Zealand won by nine wickets.** ‡**England 217-9** (50 overs) (C. M. Edwards 40, H. C. Knight 79; E. M. Bermingham

3-35, A. E. Satterthwaite 3-37); **New Zealand 219-1** (48.4 overs) (S. W. Bates 39, R. H. Priest 96*, A. E. Satterthwaite 76*). PoM: R. H. Priest. *England subsided badly from 133-1 in the 33rd over, with Nos 4, 5 and 6 managing only six between them. Knight made a well-crafted 79 but, without Katherine Brunt's 26 off 24 balls, they would not have reached 200. Bates and Priest began at a lick, taking 28 off Brunt's first three overs, and were comfortably placed at 51-0 after ten. Bates then clipped Shrubsole to midwicket, but Priest and Amy Satterthwaite took their time in a stand of 153*.*

Women's Championship: New Zealand 4pts, England 2pts.

First Twenty20 international   At Whangarei, February 19, 2015. **England won by eight wickets.** ‡**New Zealand 60** (19.4 overs) (H. C. Knight 3-10, A. Shrubsole 3-6); **England Women 61-2** (11.4 overs) (C. M. Edwards 32*). PoM: H. C. Knight. *New Zealand got themselves into a mess trying to attack Knight, who opened the bowling with her off-breaks. After Brunt removed Bates in the second over, Knight picked up 3-2, including a magnificent one-handed boundary catch by Lydia Greenway to get rid of Sophie Devine. When Danielle Hazell struck twice to reduce New Zealand to 18-6, they were threatening the lowest total in women's T20Is (Sri Lanka's 57 against Bangladesh at Guangzhou in China in 2012-13). But Erin Bermingham's dogged 20 helped avoid that ignominy – just. England lost Lauren Winfield early, but breezed home in the 12th over.*

Second Twenty20 international   At Whangarei, February 20, 2015. **New Zealand won by six wickets.** ‡**England 122-5** (20 overs) (L. Winfield 48, H. C. Knight 30); **New Zealand 124-4** (19.2 overs) (R. H. Priest 41). PoM: R. H. Priest. *England's innings never quite got going after Edwards fell for an eight-ball duck. Winfield went in the 17th over, for 48 from 59 balls, though Knight's brutal 30 off 15 – including 19 off the last over, from Devine – dragged them to a competitive total. Bates and Priest set another good platform for New Zealand with 64 inside ten overs and, though McGlashan and Satterthwaite went cheaply, Devine hit 29 off 20 balls to square the series.*

Third Twenty20 international   At Lincoln, February 24, 2015. **England won by five wickets.** **New Zealand 97-9** (20 overs) (S. F. M. Devine 37); ‡**England 102-5** (18.4 overs) (L-M. M. Tahuhu 3-28). PoM: H. C. Knight. PoS: H. C. Knight. T20I debut: A. M. Peterson (New Zealand). *This was Edwards's 200th game in charge of England. Once again, New Zealand's batsmen found ways to get out – eight of the nine wickets fell to catches – and England took the series 2–1 without needing to locate top gear. Only Devine, with 37 off 31 balls, showed much fluency as New Zealand laboured to 97-9. Hazell passed Holly Colvin's England record of 63 T20I wickets, as she and fellow off-spinners Knight and Laura Marsh each struck twice. Lea Tahuhu's career-best 3-28 left England 55-3 in the tenth over, but Greenway and Natalie Sciver put on 38, and Brunt sealed victory with a six.*

Fourth one-day international   At Lincoln, February 26, 2015. **England won by nine wickets.** **New Zealand 168** (50 overs) (K. L. Cross 5-24, R. L. Grundy 3-36); ‡**England 169-1** (32.1 overs) (C. M. Edwards 64*, S. J. Taylor 89*). PoM: K. L. Cross. ODI debut: H. M. Rowe (New Zealand). *The one-day games resumed with the series (but no Women's Championship points) up for grabs. A career-best five-for for Kate Cross, and four catches for Jenny Gunn, set up a simple England run-chase, after New Zealand staggered to 168 on a benign pitch. But for the last two wickets adding 69, they would barely have reached three figures. Knight fell in the third over, but Edwards and the increasingly fluent Taylor, who passed 3,000 ODI runs, batted with ease in a stand of 158* to set up the tour's second decider.*

Fifth one-day international   At Lincoln, February 28, 2015. **England won by five wickets. New Zealand 230-8** (50 overs) (S. F. M. Devine 58, K. T. Perkins 70*, R. L. Grundy 3-36); ‡**England 232-5** (45 overs) (S. J. Taylor 93, N. R. Sciver 65*). PoM: S. J. Taylor. PoS: S. J. Taylor. *England rounded off their trip with another comprehensive win to edge the ODI series 3–2. New Zealand's batsmen again lost patience after being sent in but, from 101-5, Devine rebuilt the innings with Katie Perkins, who hit a career-best 70* from 88 and helped take 46 from the last five overs. Knight departed to the fifth ball of the reply, then Edwards and Danni Wyatt fell in quick succession. Stability came from Taylor, with 93 from 99 balls, and Sciver, who hit a career-best 65* from 63. Taylor took 15 off the 33rd over, but was eventually run out by Satterthwaite from the deep. Five down, England still needed 64, but Brunt helped Sciver knock off the runs with five overs to spare.*

PAKISTAN v SOUTH AFRICA IN THE UAE IN 2014-15

One-day internationals (3): Pakistan 1, South Africa 2
Twenty20 internationals (3): Pakistan 2, South Africa 1

Ten wickets for leg-spinner Suné Luus helped South Africa claim the one-day series, before Pakistan reversed the score in the Twenty20s. Asmavia Iqbal shone with both bat and ball.

First one-day international   At Sharjah, March 13, 2015. **Pakistan won by 57 runs. ‡Pakistan 216-6** (50 overs) (Javeria Khan 49, Bismah Maroof 99, Asmavia Iqbal 35*; S. Luus 4-38); **South Africa 159-9** (50 overs) (T. Chetty 32; Anam Amin 3-24). PoM: Bismah Maroof. *A career-best 99 from Bismah Maroof inspired Pakistan to only their third win in 13 completed one-day internationals against South Africa. They overcame a mid-innings wobble against leg-spinner Suné Luus, then – led by Anam Amin's left-arm spin – kept the reply in check.*

Second one-day international   At Sharjah, March 15, 2015. **South Africa won by three wickets. ‡Pakistan 133** (48.4 overs) (Javeria Khan 34, Sana Mir 35*; S. Ismail 3-15, S. Luus 5-20); **South Africa 134-7** (48.4 overs) (T. Chetty 33, D. van Niekerk 34*; Anam Amin 4-9). PoM: S. Luus. *South Africa squared the series after Luus improved her career-best figures for the second time in three days. She received good support from opening bowler Shabnim Ismail (9–4–15–3) as Pakistan lost their last eight for 61. Amin proved unhittable once more, taking 4-9 in ten overs, but Dane van Niekerk dragged South Africa over the line with eight balls to spare.*

Third one-day international   At Sharjah, March 17, 2015. **South Africa won by five wickets. ‡Pakistan 153-9** (50 overs) (Sana Mir 52); **South Africa 156-5** (46.4 overs) (M. du Preez 43, L. Lee 54). PoM: L. Lee. PoS: S. Luus. *A fourth-wicket stand of 79 between Mignon du Preez and Lizelle Lee broke the back of South Africa's pursuit of a modest 154 and clinched their side the series. Only Sana Mir had shown much resistance for Pakistan.*

Women's Championship: South Africa 4pts, Pakistan 2pts.

First Twenty20 international   At Sharjah, March 19, 2015. **Pakistan won by five wickets. South Africa 101-7** (20 overs) (M. du Preez 41; Asmavia Iqbal 3-23); **‡Pakistan 103-5** (18.3 overs) (Marina Iqbal 42; S. Luus 3-14). PoM: Asmavia Iqbal. *An all-round display from Asmavia Iqbal earned Pakistan victory with nine balls to go. She followed 3-23 with 23* off 18 balls, after opener Marina Iqbal had given the chase impetus with 42.*

Second Twenty20 international   At Sharjah, March 20, 2015. **Pakistan won by six wickets. ‡South Africa 83-6** (20 overs); **Pakistan 84-4** (17.5 overs) (Bismah Maroof 30*). PoM: Asmavia Iqbal. *Asmavia was again to the fore as Pakistan claimed the series. Her figures of 4–0–12–2 helped limit South Africa to 83-6, before she hit a 14-ball 21.*

Third Twenty20 international   At Sharjah, March 22, 2015. **South Africa won by seven wickets. Pakistan 106-7** (20 overs) (Bismah Maroof 34, Asmavia Iqbal 31; D. van Niekerk 3-12); **‡South Africa 107-3** (19.5 overs) (D. van Niekerk 67). PoM: D. van Niekerk. PoS: Asmavia Iqbal. *South Africa finished the tour with a consolation win inspired by van Niekerk. First she took 3-12 with her leg-breaks to keep Pakistan's innings within chaseable proportions, then made 67 as the South Africans won with a ball to spare.*

SRI LANKA v WEST INDIES IN 2014-15

One-day internationals (4): Sri Lanka 1, West Indies 3
Twenty20 internationals (3): Sri Lanka 1, West Indies 2

West Indies, led for the last time by Merissa Aguilleira, toured Sri Lanka, the lowest-ranked side in the table, and emerged with victories in both the one-day and Twenty20 series. The last three 50-over matches counted towards the ICC Women's Championship. Stafanie Taylor, who took over as captain later in the year, spearheaded the batting, along with the hard-hitting Deandra Dottin.

First one-day international   At Colombo (RPS), May 13, 2015. **West Indies won by five wickets.**
‡**Sri Lanka 149** (49.5 overs) (W. P. M. Weerakkody 42; H. K. Matthews 3-19); **West Indies 153-5**
(40.1 overs) (D. J. S. Dottin 84*, M. R. Aguilleira 30). *PoM:* D. J. S. Dottin. *ODI debut:*
M. G. M. C. P. Gunawardene (Sri Lanka). *Prasadini Weerakkody and Lasanthi Madushani (23)
started with a stand of 79, but both fell in the space of three balls, and the remaining batsmen could
manage only a further 70; there were four run-outs. Eshani Kaushalya, captaining in place of the
injured Chamari Atapattu Jayangani, grabbed two quick wickets as West Indies slipped to 41-4 –
but, oddly, did not bowl again, finishing with 3–1–4–2. Deandra Dottin stopped the rot, putting on
70 with Merissa Aguilleira.*

Second one-day international   At Colombo (RPS), May 15, 2015. **Sri Lanka won by six wickets.**
‡**West Indies 124** (42.3 overs) (S. R. Taylor 43; H. A. S. D. Siriwardene 4-30); **Sri Lanka 127-4**
(39.2 overs) (H. A. S. D. Siriwardene 42*). *PoM:* H. A. S. D. Siriwardene. *Now it was West Indies'
turn to collapse, as they reached 95-2 in the 31st over, only to lose eight for 29. Off-spinner
Shashikala Siriwardene took four wickets, then ensured victory with 42* from 72 balls.*

Third one-day international   At Colombo (RPS), May 18, 2015. **West Indies won by 18 runs.**
(D/L). ‡**West Indies 215-3** (50 overs) (K. A. Knight 34, S. R. Taylor 86*, D. J. S. Dottin 69*;
B. M. S. M. Kumari 3-48); **Sri Lanka 170-8** (40.2 overs) (M. D. N. Hansika 50*). *PoM:* S. R.
Taylor. *A fourth-wicket stand of 151* in 28 overs between Stafanie Taylor and Dottin lifted West
Indies to a handy score. A shower in the 25th over of the reply meant Sri Lanka's target was revised
to 209 in 46, but another downpour ended play with them adrift of the D/L par score of 188, despite
Nipuni Hansika's maiden international half-century.*

Fourth one-day international   At Colombo (RPS), May 20, 2015. **West Indies won by 31 runs.**
‡**West Indies 156** (47.3 overs) (B. Cooper 46; S. S. Weerakkody 3-37, I. Ranaweera 3-17); **Sri
Lanka 125** (45.2 overs) (L. E. Kaushalya 30; H. K. Matthews 3-7). *PoM:* B. Cooper. *Only Britney
Cooper, with a career-best 46, made much headway as West Indies creaked to 156; slow left-armer
Inoka Ranaweera had figures of 10–4–17–3. But Sri Lanka struggled too, and were polished off by
17-year-old Hayley Matthews (who had earlier made 24 as opener). She took the last three wickets
in 14 balls with her off-breaks as West Indies clinched the series.*

Women's Championship: West Indies 4pts, Sri Lanka 2pts.

First Twenty20 international   At Colombo (RPS), May 23, 2015. **Sri Lanka won by five runs**
(D/L). **West Indies 109-6** (20 overs) (S. R. Taylor 40); ‡**Sri Lanka 88-6** (15.2 overs). *PoM:* S. S.
Weerakkody. *Sripali Weerakkody struck twice in the opening over – the first four balls went 4W4W
– before Taylor and Aguilleira (28*) doubled the score from 45-4. Dilani Manodara Surangika got
Sri Lanka moving with 28 from 21 deliveries and, although four wickets tumbled in 12, they were
just ahead on D/L when the weather closed in.*

Second Twenty20 international   At Colombo (RPS), May 25, 2015. **West Indies won by eight
wickets.** ‡**Sri Lanka 124-5** (20 overs) (M. A. D. D. Surangika 30); **West Indies 125-2** (18.5 overs)
(S. R. Taylor 59*, D. J. S. Dottin 51). *PoM:* S. R. Taylor. *West Indies squared the series, chiefly
through a second-wicket partnership of 101 in 14.4 overs between Taylor and Dottin.*

Third Twenty20 international   At Colombo (RPS), May 26, 2015. **West Indies won by nine
wickets. Sri Lanka 74-9** (20 overs) (A. C. Jayangani 43; H. K. Matthews 4-10); ‡**West Indies 75-1**
(11.2 overs) (H. K. Matthews 32*, S. R. Taylor 40). *PoM:* H. K. Matthews. *Sri Lanka struggled
against the off-spin of Anisa Mohammed (4–2–7–2) and Matthews (4–0–10–4); Jayangani hit six
fours from 48 balls, but of the others only Chathurani Gunawardene (10) reached double figures or
found the boundary. Aguilleira pulled off three stumpings. Openers Matthews and Taylor galloped
to 74 in the 12th over, although Taylor was out with West Indies one short of clinching the series.*

INDIA v NEW ZEALAND IN 2015

*One-day internationals (5): India 3, New Zealand 2
Twenty20 internationals (3): India 1, New Zealand 2*

India took the 50-over series, but New Zealand gained more Women's Championship
points after winning two of the first three matches – and claimed the Twenty20 series too.

First one-day international   At Bangalore, June 28, 2015. **India won by 17 runs.** ‡**India 142**
(44.3 overs) (J. N. Goswami 57; L-M. M. Tahuhu 3-25, M. J. G. Nielsen 3-24, L. M. Kasperek

3-39); **New Zealand 125** (45.3 overs) (S. Rana 3-26). *ODI debuts:* R. V. Kalpana (India); L. M. Kasperek (New Zealand). *Jhulan Goswami's maiden one-day international fifty, in her 139th game, helped India recover from 87-8. Their eventual 142 proved beyond the tourists, for whom captain Suzie Bates top-scored with just 28. Earlier, Edinburgh-born off-spinner Leigh Kasperek took three wickets on her New Zealand debut; she had previously played for Scotland, but qualified after spending three seasons in New Zealand domestic cricket.*

Second one-day international   At Bangalore, July 1, 2015. **New Zealand won by three wickets.** ‡**India 163** (49.3 overs) (M. D. Thirush Kamini 61, H. Kaur 31; S. W. Bates 3-21); **New Zealand 164-7** (44.2 overs) (S. F. M. Devine 33, K. T. Perkins 30). *New Zealand squared the series, despite faltering in pursuit of 164. At 132-7, the game could have gone either way, but Anna Peterson took charge with two fours and a six in an over from Sneh Rana. India's total was built around 61 from opener Thirush Kamini.*

Third one-day international   At Bangalore, July 3, 2015. **New Zealand won by six wickets.** ‡**India 182-9** (50 overs) (M. D. Raj 30, V. Krishnamurthy 63; S. F. M. Devine 3-40); **New Zealand 186-4** (45.4 overs) (S. W. Bates 59, R. H. Priest 64). *New Zealand sealed crucial Championship points after an opening stand of 125 between Bates – caught at slip on one from a Goswami no-ball – and Rachel Priest took the edge off their pursuit of 183. For India, only Veda Krishnamurthy passed 30.*

Women's Championship: New Zealand 4pts, India 2pts.

Fourth one-day international   At Bangalore, July 6, 2015. **India won by eight wickets.** ‡**New Zealand 220** (49.5 overs) (A. E. Satterthwaite 43, S. F. M. Devine 89; N. Niranjana 3-35, R. S. Gayakwad 3-25); **India 221-2** (44.2 overs) (M. D. Thirush Kamini 31, S. S. Mandhana 66, M. D. Raj 81*, H. Kaur 32*). *India captain Mithali Raj inspired her side to their second-highest successful chase, behind 230-5 against England at Lord's in 2012. She added 124 for the second wicket with Smriti Mandhana, and finished with 81* off 88 balls, her 37th half-century in the format. New Zealand had collapsed from 135-3, despite Sophie Devine's 89, which included three sixes. The result left the series all-square at 2–2.*

Fifth one-day international   At Bangalore, July 8, 2015. **India won by nine wickets.** ‡**New Zealand 118** (41 overs) (S. W. Bates 42); **India 121-1** (27.2 overs) (M. D. Thirush Kamini 62*, D. B. Sharma 44*). *India's bowlers set up a series-clinching win as New Zealand lost eight for 57. Kamini and Deepti Sharma sealed victory with 103* for the second wicket.*

First Twenty20 international   At Bangalore, July 11, 2015. **New Zealand won by eight wickets.** **India 125** (19.5 overs) (M. D. Raj 35; M. J. G. Nielsen 3-30, K. E. Broadmore 3-16); ‡**New Zealand 126-2** (12.3 overs) (A. E. Satterthwaite 39*, S. F. M. Devine 70). *T20I debuts:* N. C. Dodd, L. M. Kasperek (New Zealand). *Devine cracked 70* off only 22 balls, including the fastest half-century in the format, from 18. Her eight sixes included four in an over from Rana that cost 32, while her third-wicket stand of 89* in less than five overs with Amy Satterthwaite took New Zealand home with 45 balls to spare. India's total of 125 would have been more anaemic but for Raj's 23-ball 35 at the top of the order.*

Second Twenty20 international   At Bangalore, July 13, 2015. **New Zealand won by six wickets.** **India 136-6** (20 overs) (V. R. Vanitha 41, H. Kaur 30); ‡**New Zealand 139-4** (17.5 overs) (R. H. Priest 60). *T20I debut:* H. M. Rowe (New Zealand). *New Zealand claimed the series thanks to Priest's domineering 60 from 34 balls, with 52 runs coming in boundaries; it was her first fifty in Twenty20 internationals.*

Third Twenty20 international   At Bangalore, July 15, 2015. **India won by three wickets. New Zealand 126-8** (20 overs) (S. W. Bates 34; R. S. Gayakwad 3-17); ‡**India 128-7** (19 overs) (V. Krishnamurthy 34). *India avoided a clean sweep after their spinners slowed New Zealand down from 59-1 in the sixth over. Sushma Verma made four stumpings, equalling the record for a Twenty20 international innings. The home batsmen then inched across the line.*

THE WOMEN'S ASHES IN 2015

Raf Nicholson

One-day internationals (3): England 1, Australia 2
Test match (1): England 0, Australia 1
Twenty20 internationals (3): England 2, Australia 1
Overall Ashes points: England 6, Australia 10

This was the most hotly anticipated women's bilateral series ever, with history made before a ball had even been bowled. For the first time, all the matches were held at first-class grounds, and every ball was broadcast live on Sky; never before had a women's Test been televised in full. A change in the scoring system, with two fewer points for the Test win than had been the case in 2013-14, appeared to favour Australia, world champions in both one-day and Twenty20 cricket. In the event, the tweak made little difference. Australia followed victory in the 50-over matches – which also formed part of the Women's International Championship – with a comprehensive win in the lone Test, at Canterbury. That meant England needed to win all three Twenty20 games to retain the Ashes. They won the first, but lost the second, leaving Charlotte Edwards's side trailing 10–4, and posing serious questions about the state of the women's game in the UK. Victory in the dead rubber at Cardiff was no consolation.

The truth, despite the hype, was that the series was not a classic. In particular, there were calls for the abolition of all women's Tests after England played out 34 maidens and 436 dot balls on the second day. While it was fair that both teams, now fully professional, should expect increased scrutiny, the indictment of an 81-year-old format on the basis of one game seemed short-sighted; some felt Canterbury was the least uncompetitive Ashes Test, played by either gender, of the summer. Clare Connor, the ECB's head of women's cricket, was unequivocal in her continued support for the format: "I would never want to be part of an administration that strikes a line through Test cricket."

The series, though, revealed some glaring issues with England's batting, both technical and psychological, arguably the result of a dearth of quality at domestic level. They suffered bad collapses in the second and third one-dayers, were rolled over on the last afternoon of the Test for 101, and relinquished the Ashes in similarly sad fashion during the second T20 at Hove, where they would have kept their hopes alive had they surpassed Australia's 107 for seven, but were skittled for 87. Natalie Sciver's 66 in the first match, at Taunton, was England's highest score in the seven games; the failure to shine of Sarah Taylor, who made a pair in the Tests, was a serious blow. There was also a feeling that the refreshing and innovative approach to captaincy shown by 23-year-old Meg Lanning outshone Edwards, more than 12 years her senior. Stephen Brenkley in *The Independent* even called for Edwards's resignation the day after the final Twenty20 game.

Suggestions by television pundits that the Australians looked more athletic in the field were less justified. While errors were made by England – including missed chances to dismiss Lanning early during the Bristol and Worcester ODIs – they often appeared fitter than before, particularly during the T20 series, when they limited Australia to 25 boundaries across the three games. Australia's top order also underperformed, a testament to the effectiveness of England's strike bowlers, Katherine Brunt and Anya Shrubsole. Brunt's 75mph four-over spell on day three at Canterbury, in which she conceded just nine runs and removed Elyse Villani and Lanning for ducks, was the best of the series. Australia once again relied heavily on Ellyse Perry with both bat and ball: she finished as the leading run-scorer and wicket-taker on either side.

While the cricket may not be remembered in years to come, the series as a whole will go down as a watershed moment for the women's game. Certainly the record crowds – 22,000 attended the matches – suggested it was now a valued product in its own right.

AUSTRALIAN TOURING PARTY

*M. M. Lanning, K. M. Beams, A. J. Blackwell, N. E. Bolton, J. E. Cameron, S. J. Coyte, R. M. Farrell, H. L. Ferling, G. M. Harris, A. J. Healy, J. L. Jonassen, B. L. Mooney, E. A. Osborne, E. A. Perry, M. L. Schutt, E. J. Villani. *Coach:* M. P. Mott.

D. M. Kimmince was originally scheduled to replace Bolton for the Twenty20 internationals, but suffered a back injury and was herself replaced by Harris. Mooney also joined the squad as cover.

First one-day international   At Taunton, July 21, 2015. **England won by four wickets. ‡Australia 238-9** (50 overs) (E. A. Perry 78, A. J. Blackwell 58; K. H. Brunt 3-48); **England 240-6** (45.4 overs) (S. J. Taylor 30, L. S. Greenway 53, N. R. Sciver 66; E. A. Osborne 3-39). *England 2pts. PoM:* N. R. Sciver. *England shook things up by bringing in wicketkeeper-batsman Amy Jones and all-rounder Georgia Elwiss (for her first ODI since February 2013). Australia, meanwhile, were forced to open with Jess Jonassen, after Nicole Bolton suffered concussion in the nets the day before the game. A jet-lagged Australia were quickly in trouble after a ferocious spell from Katherine Brunt left them 25-2 in the ninth over. A fourth-wicket partnership of 121 between Ellyse Perry, who passed 1,000 ODI runs, and Alex Blackwell helped rescue them, but England closed out the game with a superb performance in the field that produced four run-outs. A total of 238 was below-par on a good batting pitch, and a strong performance from England's middle order, including 66 from Natalie Sciver (her highest ODI score), saw them home with 26 balls to spare.*

Second one-day international   At Bristol, July 23, 2015. **Australia won by 63 runs. Australia 259-6** (50 overs) (E. J. Villani 35, N. E. Bolton 37, M. M. Lanning 104, E. A. Perry 48); **‡England 196** (43 overs) (C. M. Edwards 58, H. C. Knight 38, S. J. Taylor 43; M. L. Schutt 4-47). *Australia 2pts. PoM:* M. M. Lanning. *Embarrassingly, the powerplay circle had to be adjusted two overs in, as it had been set at 30 yards (the distance for a men's international) instead of 25. With Bolton back in the side, Australia started with an opening stand of 65. The stage was set for Meg Lanning's sixth ODI century, which came off 98 balls and left England – who had never knocked off more than 242 – chasing a formidable 260. They began well, with openers Charlotte Edwards and Heather Knight putting on 92 in 20 overs, until Knight was superbly run out by a direct hit from a kneeling Lanning at short midwicket. Lanning's quiet word to her bowlers during the drinks break, in which she instructed them to aim full and straight, paid dividends: England collapsed from 122-1 to 196 all out inside 18 overs, the last nine all falling either bowled or lbw, as the accuracy of Megan Schutt helped wrap up the tail.*

Third one-day international   At Worcester, July 26–27, 2015. **Australia won by 89 runs. Australia 241-7** (50 overs) (N. E. Bolton 40, M. M. Lanning 85, E. A. Perry 67); **‡England 152** (43.1 overs) (H. C. Knight 38, L. S. Greenway 45, K. H. Brunt 31; K. M. Beams 3-13). *Australia 2pts. PoM:* E. A. Perry. *PoS:* E. A. Perry. *The third ODI took place on the reserve day after rain prevented play on the Sunday. England tried to shore up their batting, reinstating all-rounder Jenny Gunn alongside Lauren Winfield, who was averaging 205 in county cricket before the series started. But it was Australia's batsmen who shone once more. Despite the slowest of outfields, Lanning and Perry helped take their side to 241. England responded poorly, with Edwards – caught behind in Perry's first over – setting the tone for another collapse. Only Knight, Lydia Greenway, Brunt – who hit the first six of the series – and Extras reached double figures, as leg-spinner Kristen Beams, billed as Australia's secret weapon, finally got into her stride.*

Women's Championship: Australia 4pts, England 2pts.

ENGLAND v AUSTRALIA

Test Match

At Canterbury, August 11–14, 2015. Australia won by 161 runs. Australia 4pts. Toss: Australia. Test debuts: G. A. Elwiss; K. M. Beams, N. E. Bolton, J. L. Jonassen.

Lanning chose to bat, but Edwards's assertion that she would have bowled anyway was vindicated when Australia found themselves 99 for five just after lunch. Spells either side of the break from Shrubsole did the damage, her inswingers removing the top four for nine runs in 27 balls. However, a ninth-wicket partnership of 68 between two Test debutants, Jonassen and Beams, took Australia to 274 – a position of strength they never relinquished.

Jonassen's dismissal after a delayed start next morning, trapped in front by Brunt, prompted the declaration. She was only the third to fall for 99 in a women's Test, following **England's stasis was summed up by Shrubsole's 68-minute duck** England's Betty Snowball (against Australia at The Oval in 1937) and Jill Kennare of Australia (against India in Bombay in 1983-84). Perry then took two wickets in two balls after lunch and, though Edwards avoided the hat-trick – eventually passing the England record for most Test runs against Australia, held by her first international opening partner Jan Brittin (1,024) – her side got stuck in a rut. They didn't pass the follow-on target of 125 until an hour after tea, and lost wickets steadily along the way. Brunt top-scored from No. 9 with an enterprising 39, but England's stasis was summed up by Shrubsole's 68-minute duck. With Perry and Schutt sharing seven wickets, they were all out for 168, a deficit of 106.

A pumped-up Brunt quickly reduced Australia to two for two on the third morning, including the prize wicket of Lanning, for a second failure. Rain wiped out almost two sessions but, after play finally resumed at 3.45, the tourists slipped further to 51 for four – only for Blackwell and Jonassen to resurrect the innings. The final session saw the use of technology for the first time in a women's Test, as the umpires reviewed Knight's low catch at slip when Blackwell had nine – and concluded it had not been taken cleanly. On the fourth day, England needed early wickets, but the overnight pair extended their stand to 92, and Australia declared on 156 for six, setting England 263 in 89 overs. That was quickly exposed as a fantasy, as Perry and Schutt combined in devastating fashion to leave them 29 for five, including the disappointing Taylor for a five-ball pair.

Greenway and Elwiss put on 51 in 32 overs as England tried to dig in for the draw but, when Greenway was bowled by Perry (whose six for 32 gave her match figures of nine for 70), their hopes disappeared. Seven overs later, they were all out for 101 – and Australia were celebrating a mammoth 161-run victory. Their 8–2 lead meant England needed to win all three Twenty20 matches to come off the ledger and retain the Ashes.

Player of the Match: J. L. Jonassen.

Close of play: first day, Australia 268-8 (Jonassen 95, Beams 24); second day, England 168; third day, Australia 90-4 (Blackwell 15, Jonassen 29).

Australia

E. J. Villani c Knight b Shrubsole	33	– b Brunt	0
N. E. Bolton b Shrubsole	36	– c Brunt b Cross	25
*M. M. Lanning c Knight b Shrubsole	3	– lbw b Brunt	0
E. A. Perry c Taylor b Shrubsole	5	– c Taylor b Shrubsole	13
A. J. Blackwell lbw b Brunt	7	– not out	47
J. L. Jonassen lbw b Brunt	99	– c Greenway b Marsh	54
†A. J. Healy lbw b Marsh	39	– b Knight	9
S. J. Coyte c Taylor b Cross	3		
M. L. Schutt lbw b Marsh	11		
K. M. Beams not out	26		
H. L. Ferling not out	0		
B 5, l-b 1, w 6	12	B 4, l-b 4	8

1/66 (1) 2/70 (3)   (9 wkts dec, 101 overs) 274   1/0 (1)   (6 wkts dec, 55.5 overs) 156
3/84 (2) 4/87 (4) 5/99 (5)   2/2 (3) 3/19 (4)
6/176 (7) 7/187 (8) 8/206 (9) 9/274 (6)   4/51 (2) 5/143 (6) 6/156 (7)

Brunt 24–10–60–2; Shrubsole 25–4–63–4; Cross 16–2–59–1; Elwiss 3–0–11–0; Marsh 21–8–42–2; Knight 11–2–23–0; Sciver 1–0–10–0. *Second innings*—Brunt 14–2–41–2; Shrubsole 18–9–28–1; Cross 6–2–9–1; Marsh 14–1–53–1; Knight 3.5–0–17–1.

England

H. C. Knight c Lanning b Coyte	14	– lbw b Coyte	5
L. Winfield c Healy b Perry	1	– lbw b Schutt	12
†S. J. Taylor lbw b Perry	0	– b Perry	0
*C. M. Edwards b Schutt	30	– c Healy b Perry	1
L. S. Greenway lbw b Perry	22	– b Perry	16
N. R. Sciver lbw b Schutt	35	– c Healy b Schutt	2
G. A. Elwiss b Jonassen	17	– c Schutt b Perry	46
L. A. Marsh c Healy b Schutt	0	– b Perry	0
K. H. Brunt b Coyte	39	– c Healy b Perry	6
A. Shrubsole lbw b Schutt	0	– lbw b Coyte	1
K. L. Cross not out	2	– not out	4
L-b 3, n-b 5	8	B 1, l-b 5, n-b 2	8

1/7 (2) 2/7 (3) 3/34 (1)   (84.4 overs) 168
4/61 (4) 5/93 (5) 6/125 (6)
7/125 (7) 8/129 (8) 9/166 (9) 10/168 (10)

1/11 (1) 2/12 (3)   (59.1 overs) 101
3/16 (4) 4/27 (2)
5/29 (6) 6/80 (5) 7/80 (8)
8/92 (9) 9/97 (7) 10/101 (10)

Perry 17–5–38–3; Schutt 18.4–11–26–4; Coyte 18–8–30–2; Ferling 14–3–33–0; Jonassen 16–7–36–1; Lanning 1–0–2–0. *Second innings*—Perry 13–5–32–6; Schutt 7–1–15–2; Coyte 12.1–5–15–2; Jonassen 8–4–15–0; Beams 11–3–12–0; Ferling 4–2–5–0; Lanning 4–3–1–0.

Umpires: N. A. Mallender and A. G. Wharf.   Third umpire: M. J. Saggers.
Referee: D. T. Jukes.

First Twenty20 international   At Chelmsford, August 26, 2015 (floodlit). **England won by seven wickets.** Australia 122-8 (20 overs) (E. A. Perry 30); ‡**England 125-3** (17.3 overs) (C. M. Edwards 39, S. J. Taylor 50). *England 2pts. PoM: S. J. Taylor. England's last-ditch bid to hang on to the Ashes began at Chelmsford, where they had never lost. They recalled Danielle Hazell and Danni Wyatt, and a tight performance in the field kept the pressure on Australia, as both Lanning and Perry struggled to get the ball off the square. The innings included three late run-outs. Sarah Taylor responded to her Test failures with a fluent 43-ball 50, having added 77 with Edwards, as England romped to victory with 15 deliveries to spare.*

Second Twenty20 international   At Hove, August 28, 2015 (floodlit). **Australia won by 20 runs.** Australia 107-7 (20 overs); ‡**England 87** (19.1 overs) (R. M. Farrell 3-17). *Australia 2pts. PoM: R. M. Farrell. Needing only 108 to take things to the wire in Cardiff, England surrendered the Ashes after collapsing to 28-5 in six overs of gruesome shot selection. Greenway did her best, but ran out of partners and time, and England subsided to their lowest total in 90 T20Is. Australia's batsmen had struggled too, with Shrubsole and Becky Grundy reducing them to 77-5 in the 16th over. But a 17-ball 21* by Jess Cameron spirited them past 100 – and her runs would prove crucial.*

Third Twenty20 international   At Cardiff, August 31, 2015. **England won by five wickets.** Australia 111 (20 overs) (A. Shrubsole 4-11, N. R. Sciver 4-15); ‡**England 114-5** (18.1 overs) (N. R. Sciver 47). *England 2pts. PoM: N. R. Sciver. PoS: E. A. Perry and A. Shrubsole. The final game of the series, part of a double-header with the men, earned England a consolation victory as Australia's batting failed to fire. They were bowled out for the first time in any format on the tour, and required the hitting of Grace Harris, who launched three sixes in successive overs, to get them to a semi-respectable total. Rene Farrell reduced England to 22-3, but Sciver – who had earlier taken four wickets – added 55 with Brunt, and Greenway applied the finishing touches to complete a bittersweet victory.*

IRELAND v AUSTRALIA IN 2015

Twenty20 internationals (3): Ireland 0, Australia 3

After winning the one-off Test against England at Canterbury, the Australians made a quick trip to Ireland, where they played three Twenty20 internationals as a warm-up for the climax of the women's Ashes. Meg Lanning's side predictably proved too strong for the locals, winning the matches by increasingly comfortable margins. Grace Harris, a

21-year-old all-rounder from Queensland, made a confident start in international cricket, and collected the Player of the Series award.

First Twenty20 international   At Dublin (YMCA), August 19, 2015. **Australia won by 25 runs. Australia 140-5** (20 overs) (E. J. Villani 32, M. M. Lanning 43); ‡**Ireland 115-8** (20 overs). *T20I debut: G. M. Harris (Australia). Jess Jonassen, who had hit 99 and 54 in the Ashes Test victory, was out early this time – but Meg Lanning made 43 from 38 balls to ensure a serviceable total. Australia's bowlers then kept things quiet, and Ireland never recovered from losing three wickets on 51.*

Second Twenty20 international   At Dublin (YMCA), August 21, 2015. **Australia won by 55 runs.** ‡**Australia 131-6** (20 overs) (E. A. Perry 39; K. J. Garth 3-17); **Ireland 76-7** (20 overs). *Entering after Lanning fell to make it 38-4 in the seventh over, Ellyse Perry cracked 39 from 32 balls – and Grace Harris 19* from seven – as Australia again posted a total that proved well beyond Ireland. Their captain Isobel Joyce top-scored with 24, before being run out by Jonassen, who took 4–0–8–2 with her left-arm spin.*

Third Twenty20 international   At Dublin (YMCA), August 22, 2015. **Australia won by 99 runs.** ‡**Australia 186-1** (20 overs) (E. J. Villani 80, E. A. Perry 55*, G. M. Harris 39*); **Ireland 87-7** (20 overs) (K. J. Garth 30*). *PoS: G. M. Harris. Australia swept the series after another one-sided game. Elyse Villani hit 80 from 53 balls and put on 121 with Perry in 14 overs. Ireland lost both openers for ducks in the first over, and were never on terms with an asking-rate of more than nine an over. Jonassen again proved impossible to get away, finishing with 4–2–7–2 (and 12–1–37–5 in the series).*

PAKISTAN v BANGLADESH IN 2015-16

Twenty20 internationals (2): Pakistan 2, Bangladesh 0
One-day internationals (2): Pakistan 2, Bangladesh 0

Women's cricket returned to Pakistan for the first time since January 2006, four months after Zimbabwe's men visited in May. Only Sana Mir, Pakistan's captain, and Asmavia Iqbal had previously played an international on home soil, and the series received plenty of media attention. Pakistan won all four matches comfortably as their opponents struggled to score at the required rate. Bangladesh's team manager Shafiqul Haq caused controversy after he reprimanded all-rounder Salma Khatun for using Urdu in a press conference: the BCB later confirmed that the Bangladeshi government had asked their players to use only Bengali and English when speaking to journalists.

First Twenty20 international   At Karachi (Southend), September 30, 2015. **Pakistan won by 29 runs.** ‡**Pakistan 124-5** (20 overs) (Javeria Khan 44, Bismah Maroof 65); **Bangladesh 95-7** (20 overs). *PoM: Bismah Maroof. T20I debuts: Nahida Akter, Nigar Sultana (Bangladesh). A second-wicket stand of 87 between Javeria Khan and Bismah Maroof was enough to put Pakistan in control, despite the best efforts of Bangladesh's wicketkeeper Nigar Sultana, who produced a run-out, two stumpings and a catch. Bangladesh were reasonably placed at 49-1 from ten overs, but were unable to up the rate as wickets fell regularly.*

Second Twenty20 international   At Karachi (Southend), October 1, 2015. **Pakistan won by 34 runs.** ‡**Pakistan 114-6** (20 overs) (Marina Iqbal 33, Bismah Maroof 44); **Bangladesh 80-7** (20 overs). *PoM: Bismah Maroof. PoS: Bismah Maroof. For the second match running, Bangladesh failed to reach 100, despite finishing with wickets in hand. Marina Iqbal and Maroof got Pakistan off to a steady start, before Aliya Riaz struck a lively 20 off 15 deliveries. Bangladesh were never in contention, crashing to 28-4 in the tenth over, and lacking the power to put Pakistan under pressure.*

First one-day international   At Karachi (Southend), October 4, 2015. **Pakistan won by 20 runs.** ‡**Pakistan 214** (49.5 overs) (Bismah Maroof 92; Salma Khatun 3-31); **Bangladesh 194-9** (50 overs) (Rumana Ahmed 70; Anam Amin 3-25). *PoM: Bismah Maroof. ODI debuts: Diana Baig (Pakistan), Nahida Akter (Bangladesh). After electing to bat, Pakistan were struggling at 38-2 in the 13th over, but were rescued by Maroof's 128-ball 92. Salma Khatun's off-spin brought her three economical wickets. The Bangladeshi chase limped to 60-3 in the 18th, before Fargana Hoque and Rumana Ahmed put on 44. Rumana, who finished with 70, added another 44, this time for the eighth wicket with Jahanara Alam, before both fell to the spinners with overs running out.*

Second one-day international   At Karachi (Southend), October 6, 2015. **Pakistan won by six wickets.** ‡Bangladesh 123-9 (50 overs) (Ayasha Rahman 39, Nigar Sultana 30*; Asmavia Iqbal 3-28, Anam Amin 4-7); **Pakistan 124-4** (38.3 overs) (Marina Iqbal 31, Bismah Maroof 41). *PoM:* Anam Amin. *PoS:* Bismah Maroof. *ODI debut:* Nigar Sultana (Bangladesh). *Pakistan's bowlers dominated Bangladesh. Asmavia Iqbal reduced the visitors to 24-3, before left-arm spinner Anam Amin produced remarkable figures of 10–5–7–4. Only Sultana and Ritu Moni, who added 47 for the eighth wicket, batted with any application. Maroof again top-scored, with 41, as Pakistan cruised to a six-wicket win in the 39th over.*

WEST INDIES v PAKISTAN IN 2015-16

One-day internationals (4): West Indies 3, Pakistan 1
Twenty20 internationals (3): West Indies 3, Pakistan 0

Stafanie Taylor was appointed West Indies captain, succeeding Merissa Aguilleira, who had done the job for six years. Taylor scored 321 runs at 80 across their seven matches with Pakistan, leading her side to victory in all but one, though the final Twenty20 game was not settled until the sixth delivery of an eliminator over. It was agreed that the last three of the four one-day internationals should count towards the Women's Championship – which worked out well for West Indies, as their only defeat had come in the first. Pakistan later travelled to Fort Lauderdale, where they outclassed the USA in two Twenty20 matches, winning by 184 runs and ten wickets.

First one-day international   At Gros Islet, St Lucia, October 16, 2015 (day/night). **Pakistan won by six wickets.** West Indies 222-9 (50 overs) (M. R. Aguilleira 67*, B. Cooper 37); ‡Pakistan 225-4 (48.1 overs) (Javeria Khan 90, Nain Abidi 31). *PoM:* Javeria Khan. *Merissa Aguilleira steered West Indies from 96-5 to a respectable total, but Javeria Khan and Nain Abidi, who added 79 in 13 overs for the third wicket, put Pakistan on course for what was to be their only win in the Caribbean.*

Second one-day international   At Gros Islet, St Lucia, October 18, 2015 (day/night). **West Indies won by three wickets.** Pakistan 149 (46.1 overs) (Nain Abidi 48); ‡West Indies 150-7 (46.5 overs) (S. R. Taylor 49; Anam Amin 4-27). *PoM:* A. Mohammed (West Indies). *Pakistan collapsed from 127-3, but left-arm spinner Anam Amin reduced West Indies to 106-7 in the 34th over, before Kyshona Knight and Anisa Mohammed added the 44 needed to win.*

Third one-day international   At Gros Islet, St Lucia, October 21, 2015 (day/night). **West Indies won by 109 runs.** West Indies 281-5 (50 overs) (H. K. Matthews 35, S. R. Taylor 98*, M. R. Aguilleira 68, Kyshona A. Knight 45); ‡Pakistan 172-9 (50 overs) (Javeria Khan 73*; S. R. Taylor 3-26). *PoM:* S. R. Taylor. *In another uncertain start, West Indies were 57-3 before Stafanie Taylor and Aguilleira, her predecessor as captain, put on 130. Taylor then deployed her off-breaks to good effect: she left Pakistan on 125-6, needing more than 12 an over.*

Fourth one-day international   At Gros Islet, St Lucia, October 24, 2015 (day/night). **West Indies won by six wickets.** Pakistan 182-5 (50 overs) (Bismah Maroof 41, Asmavia Iqbal 44*; S. S. Connell 3-32); ‡West Indies 183-4 (42.2 overs) (S. R. Taylor 87*, M. R. Aguilleira 37). *PoM:* S. R. Taylor. *PoS:* S. R. Taylor. *ODI debut:* Ayesha Zafar (Pakistan). *Asmavia Iqbal's 43-ball 44* lifted Pakistan after Shamilia Connell had them in trouble on 107-5. Taylor and Aguilleira combined again to add 94 for West Indies' fourth wicket, taking them within three runs of victory. West Indies won the series 3–1, but took all six Championship points, rising from third place to second – tied on 16pts with Australia, who had played three fewer games.*

Women's Championship: West Indies 6pts, Pakistan 0pts.

First Twenty20 international   At St George's (Queen's Park), Grenada, October 29, 2015. **West Indies won by eight wickets.** Pakistan 74-9 (20 overs); ‡West Indies 78-2 (16.2 overs) (D. J. S. Dottin 38*). *PoM:* D. J. S. Dottin. *T20I debut:* Ayesha Zafar (Pakistan). *Tremayne Smartt helped reduce Pakistan to 24-5; though they recovered slightly to set a target of 75, Deandra Dottin hit a run-a-ball 38* to take West Indies home with 22 deliveries in hand.*

Second Twenty20 international   At St George's (Queen's Park), Grenada, October 31, 2015. **West Indies won by 11 runs** (D/L method). Pakistan 95-7 (20 overs) (Nain Abidi 35; D. J. S. Dottin 3-20); ‡West Indies 91-3 (17.4 overs) (S. R. Taylor 48*). *PoM:* S. R. Taylor. *Dottin contributed* *three wickets and a run-out as Pakistan failed to reach three figures again. When rain ended play in West Indies' 18th over, Taylor's 48* in 43 balls had ensured they were ahead of par.*

Third Twenty20 international   At St George's (Queen's Park), Grenada, November 1, 2015. **West Indies won after an eliminator over, following a tie** (D/L). **West Indies 88** (19.5 overs) (Kycia A. Knight 49; Sana Mir 4-14); ‡**Pakistan 77** (17 overs) (Bismah Maroof 30). *PoM:* Sana Mir. *PoS:* D. J. S. Dottin. *T20I debut:* Diana Baig (Pakistan). *It was West Indies' turn to be put in, and they were bowled out cheaply, only Kycia Knight passing eight as Pakistan captain Sana Mir's off-spin claimed 4-14. She then helped Bismah Maroof add 39 for the fourth wicket as they chased a revised target of 78 in 17 overs. They needed two from their last three balls, only to lose three wickets (two to run-outs) while scrambling a single to tie. Pakistan managed 3-2 from their eliminator over; Kyshona Knight hit West Indies' final delivery for four, to complete a 3–0 series victory.*

NEW ZEALAND v SRI LANKA IN 2015-16

One-day internationals (5): New Zealand 5, Sri Lanka 0
Twenty20 internationals (3): New Zealand 3, Sri Lanka 0

In their first bilateral series in New Zealand, Sri Lanka's women lost all their matches – and their captain, Shashikala Siriwardene, who fractured her thumb and had to hand the job back to Chamari Atapattu Jayangani. Meanwhile, New Zealand captain Suzie Bates and her opening partner Rachel Priest went on a batting rampage. Bates scored 363 runs at 90 across the eight international games, and Priest 404 at 101, even though both sat out a couple of innings to give their team-mates a chance. In the three one-day matches where New Zealand chased a target, they won with more than 30 overs to spare. For Sri Lanka, only Jayangani showed much consistency: she scored 250 runs in nine games (including a warm-up, which was also lost), nearly twice as many as any of her colleagues.

First one-day international   At Lincoln, November 3, 2015. **New Zealand won by 96 runs. New Zealand 283-9** (50 overs) (S. W. Bates 38, R. H. Priest 108, A. E. Satterthwaite 69; I. Ranaweera 4-53); ‡**Sri Lanka 187-9** (50 overs) (A. C. Jayangani 75; L. M. Kasperek 4-27). *PoM:* R. H. Priest. *ODI debut:* N. N. D. Silva (Sri Lanka). *Rachel Priest hit 108 in 116 balls, her maiden century for New Zealand, adding 131 for the second wicket with Amy Satterthwaite. Slow left-armer Inoka Ranaweera claimed a hat-trick with the last three deliveries of the innings, before Chamara Atapattu Jayangani set Sri Lanka on course for what would remain their highest total of the series. It was well short.*

Second one-day international   At Lincoln, November 5, 2015. **New Zealand won by ten wickets. Sri Lanka 126** (46.5 overs) (M. A. D. D. Surangika 31, P. R. C. S. Kumarihami 35; S. W. Bates 3-27); ‡**New Zealand 130-0** (14.3 overs) (S. W. Bates 70*, R. H. Priest 51*). *PoM:* S. W. Bates. *Sri Lanka lost their first four wickets for 26, and their last four for 22, Suzie Bates picking up three, before smashing 70* from 44 balls. She and Priest romped home with more than 35 overs in hand.*

Third one-day international   At Lincoln, November 7, 2015. **New Zealand won by 188 runs.** ‡**New Zealand 326-5** (50 overs) (S. W. Bates 80, R. H. Priest 157, S. J. McGlashan 39); **Sri Lanka 138** (41.5 overs) (E. M. Bermingham 3-26). *PoM:* R. H. Priest. *Priest plundered 157 from 146 balls, her second century in five days, as she and Bates amassed 196 by the 32nd over, a record opening stand for New Zealand in ODIs, beating the 180 of Barb Bevege and Lesley Murdoch against an International XI in Auckland in 1981-82. Leg-spinner Erin Bermingham wound up Sri Lanka's reply, in which captain Shashikala Siriwardene's right thumb was fractured, ending her tour. New Zealand moved third in the Women's Championship.*

Women's Championship: New Zealand 6pts, Sri Lanka 0pts.

Fourth one-day international   At Lincoln, November 10, 2015. **New Zealand won by ten wickets.** ‡**Sri Lanka 126** (46.2 overs) (A. C. Jayangani 56, K. A. D. A. Kanchana 31; M. J. G. Nielsen 5-21); **New Zealand 127-0** (18.3 overs) (S. W. Bates 70*, A. E. Satterthwaite 49*). *PoM:* M. J. G. Nielsen. *ODI debut:* W. G. A. K. K. Kulasuriya (Sri Lanka). *Bates had a new opening partner in Satterthwaite, but it made little difference; she hit 70* in 51 balls and shared New Zealand's third successive century stand for the first wicket. Earlier, left-arm seamer Morna Nielsen had run through Sri Lanka with a career-best 5-21.*

Fifth one-day international At Christchurch (Hagley Oval), November 13, 2015. **New Zealand won by eight wickets.** ‡**Sri Lanka 99** (47.5 overs) (E. M. Bermingham 4-16); **New Zealand 102-2** (17.3 overs) (S. J. McGlashan 39). *PoM:* E. M. Bermingham. *Bermingham improved her best international figures by collecting the last four wickets of Sri Lanka's innings and, though New Zealand shuffled their order, they completed a 5–0 whitewash with more than 32 overs to spare.*

First Twenty20 international At Christchurch (Hagley Oval), November 15, 2015. **New Zealand won by 102 runs.** ‡**New Zealand 188-3** (20 overs) (S. W. Bates 36, R. H. Priest 49, S. F. M. Devine 54); **Sri Lanka 86-6** (20 overs) (O. U. Ranasinghe 34*). *PoM:* S. F. M. Devine. *T20I debut:* T. M. M. Newton (New Zealand). *Bates and Priest resumed their partnership to run up 82 in the first eight overs, but for once they were outscored: Sophie Devine struck four sixes in a 35-ball 54. Sri Lanka were 29-4 by the ninth over, though only two more fell as Oshadi Ranasinghe batted out the next 11.*

Second Twenty20 international At Nelson, November 20, 2015. **New Zealand won by 11 runs.** ‡**New Zealand 114-7** (20 overs) (S. W. Bates 69; K. A. D. A. Kanchana 3-22); **Sri Lanka 103-8** (20 overs) (A. C. Jayangani 47; L. M. Kasperek 3-7, S. W. Bates 3-23). *PoM:* S. W. Bates. *In the closest match of the tour, Ama Kanchana helped restrict New Zealand to 114, before Jayangani and Prasadini Weerakkody opened with 64, Sri Lanka's biggest stand in either series. They started the final over on 103-5, needing 12, but off-spinner Leigh Kasperek produced a triple-wicket maiden.*

Third Twenty20 international At Nelson, November 22, 2015. **New Zealand won by nine wickets. Sri Lanka 86-9** (20 overs) (T. M. M. Newton 3-9); ‡**New Zealand 90-1** (9.2 overs) (A. E. Satterthwaite 33, R. H. Priest 37*). *PoM:* T. M. M. Newton. *PoS:* S. W. Bates. *T20I debut:* W. G. A. K. K. Kulasuriya (Sri Lanka). *After two early run-outs, 20-year-old Thamsyn Newton reduced Sri Lanka to 70-7. Priest rounded off the series with 37* in 23 balls as New Zealand needed less than half their allocation of overs to canter to a 3–0 win.*

ICC WORLD TWENTY20 QUALIFIER IN 2015-16

1. Ireland   2. Bangladesh   3. Zimbabwe   4. Scotland

Eight teams converged on Bangkok late in 2015, to compete for the two available places at the Women's World Twenty20 in India early the following year. The favourites eased through: Bangladesh and Ireland both won all three of their group games, and contested a hard-fought final, which Ireland's Lucy O'Reilly, just 16, clinched with a single off the last ball.

Zimbabwe beat Scotland to take third place, but there was a surprise lower down the pecking order. China, whose team contained only home-grown players, beat the Netherlands, then overcame hosts Thailand to reach the date final, where they lost to Papua New Guinea. Thailand overcame a poor start – they were demolished for 32 by Bangladesh in the opening game – to take seventh place by beating the Dutch by nine wickets.

China's captain Huang Zhuo made 122 runs overall; only Cecelia Joyce, Ireland's skipper, made more (152). Rumana Ahmed, the Bangladesh leg-spinner, took 14 wickets at the remarkable average of 3.64.

Final At Bangkok, December 5, 2015. **Ireland won by two wickets.** ‡**Bangladesh 105-3** (20 overs) (Nigar Sultana 41, Rumana Ahmed 38*; C. J. Metcalfe 3-14); **Ireland 106-8** (20 overs) (C. N. I. M. Joyce 32). *PoM:* Rumana Ahmed. *PoS:* Rumana Ahmed. *T20I debuts:* C. C. Dalton, R. A. Lewis (Ireland). *Both teams had already qualified for the World Twenty20, so only honour was at stake in the first official international match at the Terdthai ground in Bangkok. Bangladesh reached three figures mainly thanks to a third-wicket stand of 74 between Nigar Sultana and Rumana Ahmed, the Player of the Tournament after taking 14-51 overall. Ireland reached the last delivery needing one to win, whereupon non-striker Laura Delany (26*) survived an attempt to run her out while backing up, after a lengthy discussion between the umpires. When Salma Khatun finally sent down the last ball, 16-year-old Lucy O'Reilly hit it for the winning single.*

ENGLISH DOMESTIC CRICKET IN 2015

Four days after Yorkshire's men secured the County Championship, their women's team made it a double. Yorkshire dominated the women's Championship in the 1990s, but had not claimed the title since 2002. This time, however, they ended the 12-year duopoly of Sussex and Kent by winning the tournament (now the Royal London Women's One-Day Cup) on the final day.

Defending champions Kent started the round ahead, but had already completed their fixtures. Yorkshire needed 17 points to overtake them, and Sussex the maximum 18 to draw level. As it was, Sussex lost to Berkshire, while Yorkshire – reinforced by Lauren Winfield and Katherine Brunt after the Ashes – trounced Lancashire, their sixth victory. Kent, who had five, would have triumphed again had the ECB upheld their protest against their match with Sussex in May being declared a tie (they argued the ball was dead before Sussex ran the crucial single).

Yorkshire captain Winfield missed half the campaign, but scored 270 for once out in her four innings, and Katie Levick collected 20 wickets at nine apiece. Only her fellow leg-spinner Sarah Clarke had more, with 23 for Surrey, where she was one of the first women to be formally capped by the club, along with England all-rounder Natalie Sciver, Katherine Robson and Cecily Scutt.

Lancashire, who lost every game, dropped straight back to Division Two. But with two-up/two-down promotion and relegation now automatic, Somerset – the only unbeaten team in the top three tiers – returned to Division One, after being thwarted twice in the play-offs. They were powered by 323 runs from Sophie Luff; and Staffordshire, also promoted, by 331 from Evelyn Jones.

Sussex won the NatWest Women's Twenty20 Cup, which replaced 2014's complicated structure with straightforward round robins in all but the fourth division. They tied on points with Yorkshire and Kent, and each had won one of their head-to-head matches, so Sussex took the title on net run-rate. Yorkshire retained the Under-15 and Under-13 County Cups, and Lancashire won the Under-17 Cup.

Southern League champions Bath Wanderers won the national final of the Regional Leagues competition, with Luff and Izzy Westbury overwhelming a young J&G Meakin side from the Midlands. Bath had beaten Northern champions and perennial semi-finalists New Farnley the previous day, while J&G Meakin had defeated Newport, from the South West League.

The season's biggest news was the announcement of a 20-over Women's Cricket Super League, to begin in 2016 (alongside the county competitions), with a 50-over tournament to be added in 2017. Though it was not on the scale of the inaugural Australian WBBL in 2015-16, in which several England players appeared, the ECB were investing £3m over four years, including the first prize money for an English women's domestic competition. There would be six teams, with two overseas players each, and in January their hosts were named as Hampshire Cricket, Lancashire County Cricket Board, Loughborough University, South West (Somerset, Gloucestershire and Exeter University), Surrey and Yorkshire; the first tournament was to run in August. If the League takes off, the days of the County Championship could be numbered.

ROYAL LONDON WOMEN'S ONE-DAY CUP IN 2015

50-over league

Division One

	Played	Won	Lost	NR	A	Batting	Bowling	Points	Avge pts
Yorkshire	8	6	1	0	1	25	22	107	15.28
Kent	8	5*	1	0	1	24	26	105	15.00
Sussex	8	4*	2	0	1	25	24	94	13.42
Berkshire	8	4	2	0	2	21	19	80	13.33
Middlesex	8	3	4	0	1	22	22	74	10.57
Surrey	8	3	5	0	0	25	28	83	10.37
Warwickshire	8	3	4	0	1	19	22	71	10.14
Nottinghamshire	8	3	4	0	1	16	22	68	9.71
Lancashire	8	0	8	0	0	17	6	23	2.87

Division Two

	Played	Won	Lost	NR	A	Batting	Bowling	Points	Avge pts
SOMERSET	8	6	0	0	2	21	24	105	17.50
STAFFORDSHIRE	8	5	1	0	2	22	21	93	15.50
Worcestershire	8	4	3	0	1	24	21	85	12.14
Ireland	8	3	3	1	1	13	21	64	10.66
Essex	8	3	4	0	1	15	24	69	9.85
Wales	8	2	4	1	1	19	18	57	9.50
Devon	8	3	5	0	0	24	21	75	9.37
Durham	8	3	5	0	0	16	22	68	8.50
Scotland	8	1	5	0	2	13	20	43	7.16

Division Three

	Played	Won	Lost	NR	A	Batting	Bowling	Points	Avge pts
HAMPSHIRE	8	6	1	0	1	23	26	109	15.57
LEICESTERSHIRE	8	5	3	0	0	26	25	101	12.62
Derbyshire	8	4	3	0	1	21	20	81	11.57
Oxfordshire	8	3*	2	1	1	16	18	69	11.50
Cheshire	8	3	3	1	1	17	18	65	10.83
Netherlands	8	3	3	1	1	18	17	65	10.83
Northamptonshire	8	3	4	0	1	10	17	57	8.14
Hertfordshire	8	2	4	1	1	15	9	44	7.33
Suffolk	8	0*	6	0	1	16	17	38	5.42

* Plus one tie.

Division Four

North and East: NORFOLK avge pts 17.00, Cumbria 13.75, Cambs & Hunts 8.00, Northumberland 7.75. Lincolnshire 7.25.

South and West: GLOUCESTERSHIRE avge pts 17.75, Shropshire 14.50, Cornwall 13.00, Wiltshire 7.33, Dorset 7.00, Buckinghamshire 4.50.

Win = 10pts; tie = 5pts. Up to four batting and four bowling points are available to each team in each match. Final points are divided by the number of matches played (excluding no-results and abandoned games) to calculate the average number of points.

The top two teams in Divisions Two to Three plus the two group winners in Division Four were promoted; the bottom two in Divisions One to Three were relegated. Ireland withdrew in 2016.

DIVISION ONE AVERAGES

BATTING (200 runs)

	M	I	NO	R	HS	100	50	Avge	Ct/St
L. Winfield (*Yorks*)	4	4	3	270	99*	0	3	270.00	6/1
H. C. Knight (*Berkshire*)	5	5	1	305	162*	1	1	76.25	2
F. C. Wilson (*Middx*)	6	6	1	301	110	1	1	60.20	2
C. M. Edwards (*Kent*)	5	5	1	220	88*	0	2	55.00	5
G. M. Hennessy (*Warwicks*)	6	6	2	200	70*	0	2	50.00	2
S. J. Taylor (*Sussex*)	5	5	0	216	77	0	2	43.20	5/1
B. L. Morgan (*Middx*)	7	6	0	243	77	0	3	40.50	4
A. J. Macleod (*Berkshire*)	5	5	0	202	107	1	1	40.40	2
T. T. Beaumont (*Kent*)	6	6	0	203	67	0	1	33.83	7/1

BOWLING (10 wickets)

	Style	O	M	R	W	BB	4I	Avge	SR	ER
K. A. Levick (*Yorks*)	LBG	62.5	8	193	20	6-25	2	9.65	18.85	3.07
H. L. Colvin (*Sussex*)	SLA	66	12	180	18	5-33	2	10.00	22.00	2.72
S. L. Clarke (*Surrey*)	LBG	74.4	6	235	23	4-11	2	10.21	19.47	3.14
R. H. Candy (*Surrey*)	RM	44.3	7	125	10	4-21	1	12.50	26.70	2.80
J. L. Gunn (*Notts*)	RFM	51	8	147	11	3-26	0	13.36	27.81	2.88
D. L. Warren (*Middx*)	RS	63.3	7	213	15	5-34	2	14.20	25.40	3.35
R. L. Grundy (*Warwicks*)	SLA	44.1	4	156	10	4-28	1	15.60	26.50	3.53
I. M. G. Westbury (*Middx*)	OB	60.3	3	223	14	3-15	0	15.92	25.92	3.68
E. L. Burt (*Sussex*)	RM	52	9	180	11	3-41	0	16.36	28.36	3.46
R. J. Widdowson (*Notts*)	RM	51.2	6	165	10	3-24	0	16.50	30.80	3.21
M. S. Belt (*Kent*)	OB	62.3	5	217	13	4-24	2	16.69	28.84	3.47

NATWEST WOMEN'S TWENTY20 CUP IN 2015

Final placings

Division One: SUSSEX 24pts, Yorkshire 24, Kent 24, Middlesex 20, Ireland 13, Nottinghamshire 12, Berkshire 12, Somerset 9, Surrey 2.
Division Two: LANCASHIRE 32pts, WARWICKSHIRE 24, Essex 20, Netherlands 16, Staffordshire 16, Wales 12, Durham 9, Cheshire 8, Derbyshire 5.
Division Three: WORCESTERSHIRE 32pts, HAMPSHIRE 28, Devon 24, Scotland 20, Northamptonshire 12, Cornwall 12, Oxfordshire 8, Gloucestershire 8, Buckinghamshire 0.
Division Four: *Group A:* Leicestershire 16pts, Suffolk 12, Norfolk 4, Cambridgeshire 0; *Group B:* Hertfordshire 24, Dorset 8, Wiltshire 4; *Group C:* Shropshire 15, Cumbria 11, Lincolnshire 7, Northumberland 3. The three group winners advanced to a mini-league.
Division Four Finals Day: HERTFORDSHIRE 8, SHROPSHIRE 4, Leicestershire 0.

The top two teams in Divisions Two to Four were promoted; the bottom two in Divisions One to Three were relegated. Ireland and the Netherlands withdrew in 2016.

NATIONAL KNOCKOUT CUP REGIONAL LEAGUE FINAL

At Kibworth, September 20. **Bath Wanderers won by 235 runs. ‡Bath Wanderers 307-4** (50 overs) (I. M. Imlach 34, S. N. Luff 152*, A. Shrubsole 46*, Extras 37); **J&G Meakin 72** (33.4 overs) (E. Jones 30; I. M. G. Westbury 6-7). *Bath stormed to victory with more than 16 overs to spare. Sophie Luff plundered 152* in 132 balls, though team-mate Anya Shrubsole had to visit hospital after being hit on the elbow by a fielder's throw. Izzy Westbury had gone for a duck, but made up for it by wrecking J&G Meakin's batting with figures of 6.4-3-7-6.*

PART SEVEN

Records
and
Registers

FEATURES OF 2015

This section covers the calendar year. Some of the features listed occurred in matches reported in *Wisden 2015* and some will be reported in *Wisden 2017*; these items are indicated by [W15] or [W17].

A dagger (†) indicates a national record.

Double-Hundreds (96)

	Mins	Balls	4	6		
355*	450	396	36	15	K. P. Pietersen	Surrey v Leicestershire at The Oval.
351		283	37	14	K. D. K. Vithanage . .	Tamil Union v Air Force at Katunayake.
337	671	448	47	4	K. L. Rahul	Karnataka v Uttar Pradesh at Bangalore.
334	552	398	40	8	D. G. Brownlie	N Districts v C Districts at New Plymouth.
328	872	560	46	1	K. K. Nair	Karnataka v Tamil Nadu at Mumbai.
308	504	311	38	6	K. Srikar Bharat	Andhra v Goa at Ongole.
291	501	385	39	2	J. W. A. Taylor	Nottinghamshire v Sussex at Horsham.
290	567	374	43	0	L. R. P. L. Taylor . . .	New Zealand v Australia (2nd Test) at Perth.
288*	458	363	24	7	A. J. Finch	Cricket Australia XI v NZ at Sydney. [W17]
286	494	376	35	2	A. N. Petersen	Lancashire v Glamorgan at Colwyn Bay.
282	433	309	37	5	‡Mosaddek Hossain .	Barisal v Chittagong at Savar.
281	236	167	17	23	C. Munro	Auckland v Central Districts at Napier.
269*	410	285	33	0	‡A. C. Voges	Australia v West Indies (1st Test) at Hobart.
268	490	347	34	2	C. D. J. Dent	Gloucestershire v Glamorgan at Bristol.
263	601	419	31	2	‡G. H. Vihari	Hyderabad v Himachal Prad. at Hyderabad.
263	836	528	18	0	A. N. Cook	England v Pakistan (1st Test) at Abu Dhabi.
261	358	258	35	7	‡A. G. Prince	Lancashire v Glamorgan at Colwyn Bay.
255*	686	453	19	4	N. B. Behera	Orissa v Haryana at Rohtak. [W17]
253*	575	383	26	2	Abdul Mazid	Dhaka v Dhaka Metropolis at Fatullah.
253	409	286	24	2	D. A. Warner	Australia v New Zealand (2nd Test) at Perth.
250	460	329	21	10	C. A. Lynn	Queensland v Victoria at Brisbane.
250	519	448	21	5	‡Mosaddek Hossain .	Barisal v Rangpur at Savar.
249	465	366	31	0	‡A. C. Voges	Western Australia v S Australia at Adelaide.
247	519	335	36	0	Taufeeq Umar	Sui N Gas v Lahore Blues at Karachi. [W17]
245	639	420	24	4	Shoaib Malik	Pakistan v England (1st Test) at Abu Dhabi.
244*	713	515	20	1	H. G. Kuhn	Titans v Lions at Benoni.
244	518	368	29	1	B. S. Smith	Central Districts v Otago at Napier. [W17]
242*	623	438	18	0	K. S. Williamson	N Zealand v SL (2nd Test) at Wellington. [W15]
239	451	322	37	0	Mominul Haque	Chittagong v Barisal at Bogra. [W17]
236	366	282	38	1	A. D. Hales	Nottinghamshire v Yorkshire at Nottingham.
235*	536	379	25	1	P. M. Nevill	New South Wales v Tasmania at Hobart.
235	350	250	30	4	G. L. van Buuren . . .	Northerns v Eastern Province at Centurion.
232	518	360	28	3	S. A. Asnodkar	Goa v Jammu & Kashmir at Jammu. [W17]
231		232	29	3	‡E. C. Joyce	Ireland v United Arab Emirates at Dublin.
230	384	277	28	2	C. T. Mutombodzi . . .	Mash. Eagles v Mountaineers at Mutare.
230	460	349	28	2	‡A. G. Prince	Lancashire v Derbyshire at Southport.
228	529	382	17	7	‡Alok Kapali	East Zone v North Zone at Chittagong.
227	351	266	26	3	‡Rony Talukdar	Dhaka v Barisal at Mirpur.
227	266	176	29	11	M. J. Guptill	Derbyshire v Gloucestershire at Bristol.
227*	437	280	18	8	‡P. Dogra	Himachal Prad. v Services at Dharmasala. [W17]
226*	370	274	28	7	L. J. Wright	Sussex v Worcestershire at Worcester.
226	562	428	20	2	Azhar Ali	Pakistan v Bangladesh (2nd Test) at Mirpur.
224*	422	289	32	0	Fawad Alam	Nat. Bank v Karachi Whites at Karachi. [W17]
224	464	332	23	3	Mohammad Hafeez .	Pakistan v Bangladesh (1st Test) at Khulna.
221	594	435	24	0	Sami Aslam	Lahore Whites v FATA at Lahore. [W17]
220*	405	304	29	1	J. C. Hildreth	Somerset v Worcestershire at Worcester.
220*	483	343	23	1	R. D. Bist	Himachal P v Hyderabad at Dharmasala. [W17]
219*	358	268	31	1	J. M. Bairstow	Yorkshire v Durham at Chester-le-Street.
219	346	307	32	0	Shahriar Nafees	Barisal v Khulna at Savar.
219	555	447	22	2	‡G. H. Vihari	Hyderabad v Tripura at Hyderabad. [W17]

	Mins	Balls	4	6			
217	318	225	30	5	T. G. Mokoena	. . . . .	Easterns v Eastern Province at Benoni. [W17]
215	503	346	25	1	S. P. D. Smith	. . . . . .	Australia v England (2nd Test) at Lord's.
215	606	423	20	1	U. A. Sharma	. . . .	Uttar Pradesh v Baroda at Greater Noida. [W17]
213*	478	396	24	0	L. J. Evans	. . . . .	Warwickshire v Sussex at Birmingham.
213		295	33	0	C. J. Ferguson	. . . . . .	South Australia v Tasmania at Hobart. [W17]
211*	450	346	18	3	‡Alok Kapali	. . . . . .	Sylhet v Chittagong at Fatullah.
211*	647	403	17	0	I. J. L. Trott	. . . . .	England Lions v South Africa A at Paarl.
211	797	567	22	1	C. T. Bancroft	. . . . .	Western Australia v NSW at Perth.
211	570	452	15	1	S. D. Hope	. . . . .	Barbados v Windward Islands at Bridgetown.
210*	389	272	26	1	M. E. Trescothick	. . . .	Somerset v Sussex at Hove.
210	341	270	26	6	G. H. Worker	. . . . .	Central Districts v Wellington at Nelson. [W17]
209*	324	242	23	6	‡P. Dogra	. . . . . .	Himachal Prad. v Tripura at Dharmasala. [W17]
209*	392	283	27	4	S. S. Tiwary	. . . . .	Jharkhand v Hyderabad at Hyderabad. [W17]
209		193	20	5	D. P. D. N. Dickwella	. . .	Nondescripts v Badureliya at Colombo.
209	458	364	18	0	R. G. L. Carters	. . . . .	Cricket Australia XI v NZ at Sydney. [W17]
208*	445	277	26	2	D. Elgar	. . . .	Titans v Cape Cobras at Benoni.
208	592	452	19	3	P. Rohan Prem	. . . .	Kerala v Hyderabad at Hyderabad. [W17]
207	404	264	27	4	S. V. Samson	. . . .	Kerala v Services at Thalassery.
206*	542	413	25	0	D. K. H. Mitchell	. . .	Worcestershire v Hampshire at Worcester.
206	448	278	17	7	Tamim Iqbal	. . . . .	Bangladesh v Pakistan (1st Test) at Khulna.
205*		286	18	6	M. D. U. S. Jayasundera	. .	Ragama v Saracens at Colombo.
205	314	218	30	1	Fakhar Zaman	. . . .	Habib Bank v FATA at Sialkot. [W17]
205	259	201	26	6	‡E. C. Joyce	. . . .	Ireland v Namibia at Windhoek. [W17]
205		242	31	0	J. S. Lehmann	. . . .	South Australia v Tasmania at Hobart. [W17]
204*	430	282	19	4	‡P. Dogra	. . . . . .	Himachal Pradesh v Tripura at Agartala.
204	390	304	24	1	R. D. McMillan	. . . .	SW Districts v North West at Potchefstroom.
203*	523	394	24	2	N. D. McKenzie	. . . .	Lions v Warriors at Johannesburg.
203*	461	372	23	0	Tushar Imran	. . . .	Khulna v Rajshahi at Mirpur.
203	412	306	18	3	K. C. Sangakkara	. .	Sri Lanka v NZ (2nd Test) at Wellington. [W15]
203	497	382	18	1	C. R. Ervine	. . . .	Mat. Tuskers v Mountaineers at Bulawayo. [W17]
203	437	321	20	7	N. Gangta	. . . .	Himachal Pradesh v J&K at Dharmasala. [W17]
203	404	266	26	3	R. Paliwal	. . . . . .	Services v Tripura at Agartala. [W17]
202*	404	275	30	0	T. B. de Bruyn	. . . .	South Africa A v England Lions at Paarl.
202*	603	403	27	2	O. A. Ramela	. . . .	Cape Cobras v Titans at Benoni.
202*		401	24	1	M. Klinger	. . . . . .	Western Australia v Tasmania at Hobart. [W17]
202	381	256	28	1	Akbar-ur-Rehman	. . .	Nat. Bank v Sui Southern Gas at Karachi. [W17]
201*	514	342	21	4	I. R. Jaggi	. . . .	Jharkhand v Hyderabad at Ranchi.
201*	446	331	20	3	Rajin Saleh	. . . . .	Sylhet v Barisal at Mirpur.
201*	268	207	25	5	Gurkeerat Singh	. . . .	Punjab v Railways at Mohali. [W17]
201	200	143	15	13	H. Klaasen	. . . . .	Northerns v Namibia at Pretoria.
201	347	240	22	7	‡Rony Talukdar	. . . .	Dhaka v Chittagong at Savar.
200*		171	11	15	H. G. Kumara	. . .	Saracens v Air Force at Katunayake.
200*	383	290	23	0	S. M. Davies	. . . .	Surrey v Glamorgan at Cardiff.
200*		245	15	7	‡Mosaddek Hossain	. .	Barisal v Sylhet at Khulna. [W17]
200	253	216	21	11	G. G. Wagg	. . . .	Glamorgan v Surrey at Guildford.
200	292	176	25	5	S. S. Iyer	. . . . .	Mumbai v Punjab at Mumbai. [W17]

‡ *Dogra and Mosaddek Hossain scored three double-hundreds, while Alok Kapali, Joyce, Prince,*
Rony Talukdar, Vihari and Voges each scored two.

Hundred on First-Class Debut

128		Almas Saukat	. . . . . .	Uttar Pradesh v Madhya Pradesh at Moradabad. [W17]
114		K. I. C. Asalanka	. . .	Galle v Air Force at Panagoda.
154* and 109*		T. J. Dean	. . . .	Victoria v Queensland at Melbourne. [W17]
107*		J. L. du Plooy	. . . . .	Free State v KwaZulu-Natal at Chatsworth.
129		S. D. Heazlett	. . . .	Queensland v Tasmania at Hobart. [W17]
116		M. S. T. Hughes	. . . .	Oxford University v Cambridge University at Cambridge.
102*		Imran Haroon	. . . . . .	Jammu & Kashmir v Bengal at Kolkata.
101		R. M. Patidar	. . . .	Madhya Pradesh v Baroda at Vadodara. [W17]

110	O. E. Robinson	Sussex v Durham at Chester-le-Street.
132*	H. R. Sethi	Services v Goa at Delhi.
119	A. D. Shanware	Vidarbha v Orissa at Nagpur. [W17]
108*	A. R. Shrivastava . . .	Madhya Pradesh v Karnataka at Indore.
124*	A. Vala	Papua New Guinea v Netherlands at Amstelveen.

Three Hundreds in Successive Innings

| D. A. Warner (Australia) . . . . | 163 and 116 | v New Zealand (1st Test) at Brisbane. |
| | 253 | v New Zealand (2nd Test) at Perth. |

Hundred in Each Innings of a Match

K. C. Brathwaite	102	112	Barbados v Guyana at Bridgetown.
R. W. Chakabva	104	101	Zimbabwe A v Ireland at Harare. [W17]
T. J. Dean	154*	109*	Victoria v Queensland at Melbourne. [W17]
B. A. Godleman	108	105*	Derbyshire v Kent at Derby.
A. Harinath	120	104	Surrey v Glamorgan at Guildford.
Imrul Kayes	166	127*	Khulna v Barisal at Savar.
Marshall Ayub	107	115*	Dhaka Metropolis v Khulna at Mirpur. [W17]
R. Paliwal	121	103	Services v Saurashtra at Delhi. [W17]
A. G. Puttick	100	101*	Cape Cobras v Knights at Kimberley.
A. M. Rahane	127	100*	India v South Africa (4th Test) at Delhi.
Shahriar Nafees	168	174*	Barisal v Chittagong at Bogra. [W17]
Umar Siddiq	113	174	United Bank v Port Qasim Authority at Islamabad. [W17]
M. N. Waller	138	118	Zimbabwe A v Ireland at Harare. [W17]
D. A. Warner	163	116	Australia v New Zealand (1st Test) at Brisbane.

Carrying Bat through Completed Innings

T. B. Abell	76*	Somerset (200) v Nottinghamshire at Taunton.
T. B. Abell	88*	Somerset (170) v Warwickshire at Birmingham.
S. C. Cook	53*	South Africa A (136) v England XI at Pietermaritzburg. [W17]
D. Elgar	118*	South Africa (214) v England (1st Test) at Durban.
D. A. Hendricks	142*	Gauteng (313) v North West at Johannesburg. [W17]
E. H. Kemm	133*	Easterns (267) v Free State at Benoni.
I. Khan	146*	KwaZulu-Natal Inland (271) v E Province at Pietermaritzburg. [W17]
D. K. H. Mitchell	206*	Worcestershire (478) v Hampshire at Worcester.
C. A. Pujara	145*	India (312) v Sri Lanka (3rd Test) at Colombo.
V. A. Saxena	66*	Rajasthan (198) v Bengal at Kolkata. [W17]

Hundred before Lunch

Ariful Haque	112*	Rangpur v Dhaka Metropolis at Savar.
S. S. Pathirana	7* to 113*	Colts v Ragama at Colombo.
Rony Talukdar	102*	Central Zone v South Zone at Fatullah.
J. J. Roy	21* to 132*	Surrey v Lancashire at The Oval.

Most Sixes in an Innings

23‡	C. Munro (281)	Auckland v Central Districts at Napier.
15†	H. G. Kumara (200*)	Saracens v Air Force at Katunayake.
15	K. P. Pietersen (355*)	Surrey v Leicestershire at The Oval.
14	K. P. S. P. Karunanayake (150*)	Army v Ports Authority at Colombo.
14	K. D. K. Vithanage (351)	Tamil Union v Air Force at Katunayake.
13	H. Klaasen (201)	Northerns v Namibia at Pretoria.
12	Ariful Haque (112*)	Rangpur v Dhaka Metropolis at Savar.

11	M. J. Guptill (227)	Derbyshire v Gloucestershire at Bristol.
11	G. G. Wagg (200)	Glamorgan v Surrey at Guildford.
10	C. A. Lynn (250)	Queensland v Victoria at Brisbane.
10	Ziaur Rahman (122)	Khulna v Chittagong at Savar.

‡ *World record.*

Most Runs in Boundaries

	4	6		
234	36	15	K. P. Pietersen (355*)	Surrey v Leicestershire at The Oval.
232	37	14	K. D. K. Vithanage (351)	Tamil Union v Air Force at Katunayake.
212	47	4	K. L. Rahul (337)	Karnataka v Uttar Pradesh at Bangalore.
208	40	8	D. G. Brownlie (334)	Northern Districts v C Districts at New Plymouth.
206	17	23	C. Munro (281)	Auckland v Central Districts at Napier.

Longest Innings

Mins

872	K. K. Nair (328)	Karnataka v Tamil Nadu at Mumbai.
836†	A. N. Cook (263)	England v Pakistan (1st Test) at Abu Dhabi.
797†	C. T. Bancroft (211)	Western Australia v New South Wales at Perth.
713	H. G. Kuhn (244*)	Titans v Lions at Benoni.
686	N. B. Behera (255*)	Orissa v Haryana at Rohtak. W17
671	K. L. Rahul (337)	Karnataka v Uttar Pradesh at Bangalore.
647	I. J. L. Trott (211*)	England Lions v South Africa A at Paarl.
639	Shoaib Malik (245)	Pakistan v England (1st Test) at Abu Dhabi.

Unusual Dismissals

Handled the Ball
I. Khan (29) . . . . Dolphins v Lions at Johannesburg.

Obstructing the Field
W. E. Bell (44). . . . . Northern Cape v Border at Kimberley. W17

First-Wicket Partnership of 100 in Each Innings

194	124	R. V. Uthappa (1st inns)/R. Samarth (2nd)/K. L. Rahul, Karnataka v Assam at Indore.
130	123	C. T. Bancroft/M. S. Harris, Western Australia v Victoria at Hobart.
144	193	Nazmul Hossain/Junaid Siddique, Rajshahi v Chittagong at Rajshahi. W17
161	237	J. A. Burns/D. A. Warner, Australia v New Zealand (1st Test) at Brisbane.

Highest Wicket Partnerships

First Wicket

503†	R. G. L. Carters/A. J. Finch, Cricket Australia XI v New Zealanders at Sydney. W17
314	Abdul Mazid/Rony Talukdar, Dhaka v Dhaka Metropolis at Fatullah.
312	Tamim Iqbal/Imrul Kayes, Bangladesh v Pakistan (1st Test) at Khulna.
304	Abdul Mazid/Rony Talukdar, Dhaka v Chittagong at Savar.
291	Imran Butt/Naeemuddin, Sui Northern Gas v Peshawar at Peshawar. W17
283	M. Vijay/S. Dhawan, India v Bangladesh (Only Test) at Fatullah.

Second Wicket

333	K. Srikar Bharat/M. U. B. Sriram, Andhra v Goa at Ongole.
326†	W. T. S. Porterfield/E. C. Joyce, Ireland v Namibia at Windhoek. W17
324	C. T. Bancroft/M. Klinger, Western Australia v New South Wales at Perth.
302	D. A. Warner/U. T. Khawaja, Australia v New Zealand (2nd Test) at Perth.
284	C. J. L. Rogers/S. P. D. Smith, Australia v England (2nd Test) at Lord's.
283	Shahriar Nafees/Fazle Mahmud, Barisal v Chittagong at Bogra. W17
282	N. B. Behera/Ranjit Singh, Orissa v Haryana at Rohtak. W17

Third Wicket

501	A. N. Petersen/A. G. Prince, Lancashire v Glamorgan at Colwyn Bay.
352†	M. L. Pettini/C. T. Mutombodzi, Mashonaland Eagles v Mountaineers at Mutare.
311	M. Klinger/A. C. Voges, Western Australia v South Australia at Adelaide.
290	M. W. Machan/C. D. Nash, Sussex v Somerset at Taunton.

Fourth Wicket

449	A. C. Voges/S. E. Marsh, Australia v West Indies (1st Test) at Hobart.
378	C. J. Ferguson/J. S. Lehmann, South Australia v Tasmania at Hobart. W17
348†	Rajin Saleh/Alok Kapali, Sylhet v Dhaka at Fatullah.
304	Jahid Ali/Faisal Iqbal, Karachi Whites v United Bank at Karachi. W17
294	K. C. Sangakkara/S. M. Davies, Surrey v Glamorgan at Cardiff.
287	Mohammad Saif/S. N. Khan, Uttar Pradesh v Madhya Pradesh at Moradabad. W17
282‡	L. J. Wright/B. C. Brown, Sussex v Worcestershire at Worcester.

‡ *295 runs were added for Sussex's fourth wicket v Worcestershire, C. D. Nash retiring hurt after 13 had been added.*

Fifth Wicket

423	Mosaddek Hossain/Al-Amin, Barisal v Rangpur at Savar.
273	C. A. Lynn/C. D. Hartley, Queensland v Victoria at Brisbane.
255	S. E. Marsh/S. M. Whiteman, Western Australia v Queensland at Brisbane.

Sixth Wicket

386	K. K. Nair/K. L. Rahul, Karnataka v Tamil Nadu at Mumbai.
365*	K. S. Williamson/B-J. Watling, New Zealand v Sri Lanka (2nd Test) at Wellington. W15
365	J. W. A. Taylor/C. M. W. Read, Nottinghamshire v Sussex at Horsham.
327	L. J. Evans/T. R. Ambrose, Warwickshire v Sussex at Birmingham.
306*	Gurkeerat Singh/G. Khera, Punjab v Railways at Mohali. W17
295†	Tushar Imran/Ziaur Rahman, Khulna v Rajshahi at Mirpur.

Seventh Wicket

366*†	J. M. Bairstow/T. T. Bresnan, Yorkshire v Durham at Chester-le-Street.
225	K. L. Rahul/A. A. Kazi, Karnataka v Uttar Pradesh at Bangalore.
214	M. Klinger/A. C. Agar, Western Australia v Tasmania at Hobart. W17
212	R. L. Jangid/A. A. Sarwate, Vidarbha v Haryana at Nagpur. W17

Eighth Wicket

180	P. M. Nevill/S. N. J. O'Keefe, New South Wales v Tasmania at Hobart.
175	D. J. Malan/J. A. R. Harris, Middlesex v Nottinghamshire at Nottingham.
172	R. B. Kalaria/M. B. Patel, Gujarat v Maharashtra at Valsad.

Ninth Wicket

154	Khalid Latif/Zohaib Shera, Port Qasim Authority v United Bank at Islamabad. W17

Tenth Wicket

164	O. E. Robinson/M. E. Hobden, Sussex v Durham at Chester-le-Street.
140	B. Mugochi/T. Muzarabani, Mashonaland Eagles v Matabeleland Tuskers at Harare.
139	K. P. Pietersen/M. P. Dunn, Surrey v Leicestershire at The Oval.
134	G. H. Worker/A. W. Mathieson, Central Districts v Wellington at Nelson. W17
119	J. D. Unadkat/D. A. Jadeja, Saurashtra v Jammu & Kashmir at Jammu. W17
114	Mohammad Shahid/Asif Hasan, Dhaka Metropolis v Chittagong at Savar.
113	S. D. Withanawasam/D. G. R. Dhammika, Moors v Army at Colombo.
111*	P. M. Nevill/D. E. Bollinger, New South Wales v Tasmania at Hobart.
105	G. G. Wagg/M. G. Hogan, Glamorgan v Surrey at Guildford.
104	L. V. van Beek/W. S. A. Williams, Canterbury v Otago at Christchurch. W17
102	C. A. Ingram/B. D. Walters, Warriors v Titans at Port Elizabeth.
100	A. L. Davies/K. M. Jarvis, Lancashire v Derbyshire at Derby.

Most Wickets in an Innings

9-33	K. Rabada	Lions v Dolphins at Johannesburg.
9-34	J. A. R. Harris	Middlesex v Durham at Lord's.
9-70	B. Fernando.	Sinhalese v Air Force at Colombo.
8-15	S. C. J. Broad	England v Australia (4th Test) at Nottingham.
8-29	S. P. Purkayastha	Assam v Hyderabad at Hyderabad.
8-42	Imran Tahir	Dolphins v Knights at Kimberley. [W17]
8-54	P. M. Siddle	Victoria v South Australia at Adelaide.
8-58	J. S. Saxena.	Madhya Pradesh v Railways at Gwalior. [W17]
8-72	J. A. Warrican	Barbados v Jamaica at Kingston.
8-76	J. U. Chaturanga	Moors v Chilaw Marians at Colombo.
8-88	J. A. Warrican	Barbados v Leeward Islands at Basseterre.
8-89	Fawad Ahmed.	Victoria v Western Australia at Hobart.
8-96	J. S. Saxena.	Madhya Pradesh v Railways at Gwalior. [W17]
8-97	P. M. Pushpakumara . . .	Ports Authority v Tamil Union at Colombo.
8-97	V. Khanna	Punjab v Railways at Mohali. [W17]
8-100	Abdur Razzak	Khulna v Barisal at Savar.
8-106	Sanjamul Islam	Rajshahi v Chittagong at Chittagong. [W17]
8-108	E. M. C. D. Edirisinghe	Tamil Union v Nondescripts at Colombo.
8-111	S. Randiv	Galle v Army at Galle. [W17]
8-112	Iftekhar Sajjad.	Chittagong v Rajshahi at Fatullah.
8-116	B. M. Scholtz	Namibia v Boland at Paarl.
8-131	P. H. T. Kaushal	Nondescripts v Ports Authority at Colombo.
8-151	R. H. Bhatt	Gujarat v Punjab at Mohali. [W17]
8-179	J. K. H. Naik	Leicestershire v Lancashire at Manchester.

Most Wickets in a Match

16-154	J. S. Saxena.	Madhya Pradesh v Railways at Gwalior. [W17]
14-105	K. Rabada	Lions v Dolphins at Johannesburg.
13-83	D. Pathania	Services v Jharkhand at Delhi. [W17]
13-88	S. P. Purkayastha	Assam v Hyderabad at Hyderabad.
13-103	J. A. R. Harris	Middlesex v Durham at Lord's.
13-108	A. N. Sharma	Madhya Pradesh v Andhra at Indore. [W17]
13-126	R. A. Jadeja.	Saurashtra v Jharkhand at Rajkot. [W17]
13-135	R. A. Jadeja.	Saurashtra v Hyderabad at Rajkot. [W17]
13-138	J. A. Warrican	Barbados v Leeward Islands at Basseterre.
13-154	J. Yadav	Haryana v Saurashtra at Rajkot.
13-162	A. A. Wakhare	Vidarbha v Gujarat at Surat.
13-182	P. H. T. Kaushal	Nondescripts v Ports Authority at Colombo.
13-182	B. M. Scholtz	Namibia v Boland at Paarl.
12-85	T. Shamsi	Titans v Cape Cobras at Benoni. [W17]
12-98	R. Ashwin	India v South Africa (3rd Test) at Nagpur.
12-120	D. Sivakumar	Andhra v Maharashtra at Rohtak.
12-133	Imran Tahir.	Dolphins v Knights at Kimberley. [W17]
12-159	S. J. Magoffin	Sussex v Nottinghamshire at Nottingham.
12-175	V. V. Dabholkar	Mumbai v Tamil Nadu at Mumbai. [W17]

Outstanding Innings Analyses

2–2–0–4	K. S. Monish.	Kerala v Himachal Pradesh at Perintalmanna. [W17]
6–6–0–4	A. R. Patel.	India A v South Africa A at Wayanad.

Four Wickets in Four Balls

Taj Wali		Peshawar v Port Qasim Authority at Peshawar. [W17]

Hat-Tricks (14)

Azizullah	Sui Northern Gas v WAPDA at Karachi. [W17]
G. J. Batty	Surrey v Derbyshire at The Oval.
D. E. Bollinger	New South Wales v Victoria at Wagga Wagga.
J. P. Faulkner	Lancashire v Leicestershire at Manchester.
B. C. Mohanty	Orissa v Delhi at Bhubaneswar.
T. Muzarabani	Mashonaland Eagles v Matabeleland Tuskers at Harare.
M. B. Njoloza.	Cape Cobras v Dolphins at Pietermaritzburg.
S. Prasanna	Army v Sinhalese at Colombo. [W17]
C. Rushworth	Durham v Hampshire at Southampton.
H. S. Sharath	Karnataka v Haryana at Mysore. [W17]
M. Sharma	Haryana v Delhi at Rohtak.
Taj Wali	Peshawar v Port Qasim Authority at Peshawar. [W17]
S. C. van Schalkwyk	Free State v KwaZulu-Natal at Chatsworth.
U. T. Yadav	Vidarbha v Rajasthan at Nagpur. [W17]

Four Wickets in Five Balls

C. Rushworth	Durham v Hampshire at Southampton.

Wicket with First Ball in First-Class Career

P. M. Krishna	Karnataka v Bangladesh A at Bangalore. [W17]
Ibraheem Gul	FATA v WAPDA at Sialkot. [W17]

Match Double (100 runs and 10 wickets)

R. L. Jangid	110; 4-44, 7-59	Vidarbha v Haryana at Nagpur. [W17]
J. Yadav	97, 35; 7-64, 6-90	Haryana v Saurashtra at Rajkot.

Most Wicketkeeping Dismissals in an Innings

7 (7ct)	Bismillah Khan	WAPDA v Karachi Whites at Karachi. [W17]
7 (7ct)	L. Ronchi.	Somerset v Hampshire at Taunton.
7 (6ct, 1st)	A. V. Ubarhande	Vidarbha v Bengal at Kolkata. [W17]
6 (6ct)	S. W. Billings	Kent v Lancashire at Manchester.
6 (5ct, 1st)	L. D. Chandimal	Sri Lanka v Pakistan (2nd Test) at Colombo.
6 (6ct)	T. Chieckley	Western Province v Boland at Cape Town. [W17]
6 (6ct)	S. D. Jogiyani	Saurashtra v Jammu & Kashmir at Jammu. [W17]
6 (5ct, 1st)	Kamran Akmal	National Bank v United Bank at Karachi. [W17]
6 (4ct, 2st)	G. Khera	Punjab v Mumbai at Mumbai. [W17]
6 (6ct)	B. I. Louw	SW Districts v Free State at Oudtshoorn. [W17]
6 (6ct)	R. H. Motwani.	Maharashtra v Vidarbha at Gahunje.
6 (3ct, 3st)	W. A. S. Niroshan	Badureliya v Air Force at Maggona.
6 (6ct)	N. V. Ojha	Rest of India v Karnataka at Bangalore.
6 (6ct)	S. Pono	Boland v Gauteng at Paarl.
6 (6ct)	G. H. Roderick.	Gloucestershire v Northamptonshire at Northampton.
6 (5ct, 1st)	P. R. Shah	Baroda v Karnataka at Mysore.
6 (6ct)	D. Smit.	Dolphins v Lions at Johannesburg. [W17]
6 (5ct, 1st)	K. Srikar Bharat.	Andhra v Madhya Pradesh at Indore. [W17]
6 (6ct)	B-J. Watling.	New Zealand v Sri Lanka (1st Test) at Dunedin.
6 (6ct)	R. M. Yadav	Delhi v Mumbai at Cuttack.

Most Wicketkeeping Dismissals in a Match

10 (10ct)	C. D. Hartley	Queensland v South Australia at Brisbane. W17
10 (8ct, 2st)	P. R. Shah	Baroda v Karnataka at Mysore.
10 (10ct)	D. Smit	Dolphins v Lions at Johannesburg. W17
9 (9ct)	T. Chieckty	Western Province v Boland at Cape Town. W17
9 (8ct, 1st)	J. Gumbie	Zimbabwe A v Bangladesh A at Harare. W17
9 (7ct, 2st)	Kamran Akmal	National Bank v United Bank at Karachi. W17
9 (9ct)	M. Mosehle	Titans v Warriors at Port Elizabeth.
9 (9ct)	R. H. Motwani	Maharashtra v Vidarbha at Gahunje.
9 (9ct)	N. J. O'Brien	Leicestershire v Glamorgan at Leicester.
9 (7ct, 2st)	A. V. Ubarhande	Vidarbha v Bengal at Kolkata. W17
9 (9ct)	B-J. Watling	New Zealand v Sri Lanka (1st Test) at Dunedin.
9 (9ct)	R. M. Yadav	Delhi v Mumbai at Cuttack.

Most Catches in an Innings in the Field

5	J. Blackwood	West Indies v Sri Lanka (2nd Test) at Colombo.
5	P. J. Forrest	Queensland v South Australia at Brisbane.
5	A. M. Rahane	India v Sri Lanka (1st Test) at Galle.
5	Tarjinder Singh	Assam v Goa at Porvorim.
5	K. D. V. Wimalasekara	Badureliya v Bloomfield at Colombo.

Most Catches in a Match in the Field

8	A. M. Rahane	India v Sri Lanka (1st Test) at Galle.
7	D. S. Smith	Windward Islands v Trinidad & Tobago at Gros Islet.
6	C. J. Anderson	Northern Districts v Auckland at Auckland. W17
6	S. D. Atitkar	Maharashtra v Saurashtra at Rajkot.
6	P. J. Forrest	Queensland v Victoria at Brisbane.
6	P. J. Forrest	Queensland v South Australia at Brisbane.
6	K. Kantasingh	Trinidad & Tobago v Leeward Islands at Basseterre. W17
6	S. E. Marsh	Western Australia v South Australia at Perth.
6	C. H. Morris	Lions v Dolphins at Durban.
6	A. R. Nurse	Barbados v Leeward Islands at Basseterre.
6	C. A. Pujara	Saurashtra v Haryana at Rajkot.
6	Shuvagata Hom	Dhaka v Chittagong at Savar.
6	M. H. Yardy	Sussex v Middlesex at Hove.

No Byes Conceded in Total of 500 or More

S. W. Billings	Kent v Australians (507-8 dec) at Canterbury.
E. R. Dwivedi	Uttar Pradesh v Mumbai (610-9 dec) at Mumbai. W17
Farhan Khan	Lahore Blues v Sui Northern Gas (512) at Karachi. W17
J. S. Foster	Essex v Kent (633-8 dec) at Tunbridge Wells.
G. Khera	Punjab v Mumbai (569-8 dec) at Mumbai. W17
T. P. Ludeman	South Australia v Victoria (534-6 dec) at Adelaide.
Mushfiqur Rahim	Bangladesh v Pakistan (557-8 dec) (2nd Test) at Mirpur.
N. V. Ojha	Madhya Pradesh v Tamil Nadu (596-9 dec) at Indore. W17
D. Ramdin	West Indies v Australia (551-3 dec) (2nd Test) at Melbourne.
W. P. Saha	India v Australia (572-7 dec) (4th Test) at Sydney. W15
W. P. Saha	Bengal v Karnataka (537-9 dec) at Bangalore. W17
N. Saini	Haryana v Vidarbha (504-7 dec) at Nagpur. W17
Sarfraz Ahmed	Pakistan v Bangladesh (555-6) (1st Test) at Khulna.
C. F. K. van Wyk	Central Districts v Northern Districts (556-9 dec) at New Plymouth.
K. A. Vaz	Goa v Andhra (548-5 dec) at Ongole.
B-J. Watling	New Zealand v Australia (556-4 dec) (1st Test) at Brisbane.
Zabid Hossain	Dhaka Metropolis v Dhaka (525) at Fatullah.
Zeeshan Gul	Hyderabad v Sui Southern Gas (529) at Hyderabad. W17

Highest Innings Totals

762	Karnataka v Tamil Nadu at Mumbai.
719-9 dec	Karnataka v Uttar Pradesh at Bangalore.
707-8 dec	Himachal Pradesh v Hyderabad at Dharmasala. [W17]
698-5 dec	Lancashire v Glamorgan at Colwyn Bay.
686-7 dec	Uttar Pradesh v Madhya Pradesh at Moradabad. [W17]
668-7 dec	Auckland v Central Districts at Napier.
668	Barisal v Rangpur at Savar.
651-5 dec	Dhaka v Barisal at Mirpur.
650-8 dec	Tamil Union v Air Force at Katunayake.
650-8 dec	Central Districts v Otago at Napier. [W17]
633-8 dec	Kent v Essex at Tunbridge Wells.
633	Western Australia v South Australia at Adelaide.
630-6 dec	Nondescripts v Badureliya at Colombo.
630-9 dec	Somerset v Hampshire at Taunton.
628	Pakistan v Bangladesh (1st Test) at Khulna.
624-8 dec	England Lions v South Africa A at Paarl.
624	New Zealand v Australia (2nd Test) at Perth.

Lowest Innings Totals

31	Galle v Air Force at Panagoda.
37	Orissa v Bengal at Kalyani. [W17]
44‡	Mumbai v Karnataka at Bangalore.
45	Jharkhand v Services at Delhi. [W17]
47	Eastern Province v KwaZulu-Natal Inland at Pietermaritzburg. [W17]
51	Rajasthan v Orissa at Jaipur. [W17]
56	Andhra v Madhya Pradesh at Indore. [W17]
58	Uttar Pradesh v Railways at Ghaziabad. [W17]
58	Free State v Northern Cape at Bloemfontein. [W17]
58	Lahore Whites v Karachi Whites at Lahore. [W17]
60	Australia v England (4th Test) at Nottingham.
61	Tripura v Goa at Porvorim. [W17]
68	Tamil Nadu v Punjab at Natham. [W17]
68	Namibia v Border at East London. [W17]
69	Warwickshire v Yorkshire at Birmingham.
69	Saurashtra v Kerala at Perintalmanna. [W17]
69	Port Qasim Authority v Sui Northern Gas at Faisalabad. [W17]
69	Tamil Nadu v Punjab at Natham. [W17]
70	Hyderabad v Sui Southern Gas at Hyderabad. [W17]

‡   *One batsman absent hurt.*

Highest Fourth-Innings Totals

405-5	Middlesex v Somerset at Taunton (set 402).
402-8	Somerset v Nottinghamshire at Taunton (set 401).

Match Aggregate of 1,500 Runs

1,672 for 28	Australia (559-9 dec and 385-7 dec) v NZ (624 and 104-2) (2nd Test) at Perth.
1,610 for 40	England (389 and 478) v New Zealand (523 and 220) (1st Test) at Lord's.
1,550 for 30	Australia (572-7 dec and 251-6 dec) v India (475 and 252-7) (4th Test) at Sydney. [W15]
1,547 for 33	Leicestershire (292 and 480) v Surrey (557 and 218-3) at The Oval.
1,515 for 26	Bangladesh (332 and 555-6) v Pakistan (628) (1st Test) at Khulna.

Matches Dominated by Batting (1,200 runs at 80 runs per wicket)

1,213-12 (101.08) Sussex (601-6 dec) v Warwickshire (612-6 dec) at Birmingham.
1,214-14 (86.71) Uttar Pradesh (686-7 dec) v Madhya Pradesh (528-7) at Moradabad. [W17]

Four Individual Hundreds in an Innings

Sussex (601-6 dec) v Warwickshire at Birmingham.
Punjab (604-5 dec) v Railways at Mohali. [W17]
Australia (551-3 dec) v West Indies (2nd Test) at Melbourne.

Six Individual Fifties in an Innings

Australia (572-7 dec) v India (4th Test) at Sydney. [W15]
England Lions (624-8 dec) v South Africa A at Paarl.
Nondescripts (404) v Ragama at Colombo.
Dhaka Metropolis (411) v Dhaka at Fatullah.
Essex (610-8 dec) v Surrey at The Oval.
Kent (633-8 dec) v Essex at Tunbridge Wells.
Gujarat (505) v Baroda at Valsad.
Mumbai (610-9 dec) v Uttar Pradesh at Mumbai. [W17]
Bengal (528-8 dec) v Maharashtra at Gahunje. [W17]
Knights (491-9 dec) v Cape Cobras at Cape Town. [W17]

Large Margin of Victory

Dhaka (651-5 dec) beat Barisal (139 and 99) at Mirpur by an innings and 413 runs.†
Australia (566-8 dec and 254-2 dec) beat England (312 and 103) (2nd Test) at Lord's by 405 runs.
Victoria (449 and 230-2 dec) beat Tasmania (145 and 134) at Alice Springs by 400 runs.

Eleven Bowlers in an Innings

Sussex v Warwickshire (612-6 dec) at Birmingham.
Rangpur v Dhaka Metropolis (352-7 dec) at Khulna. [W17]

Most Extras in an Innings

	b	l-b	w	n-b	
67	26	34	6	1	New Zealand (523) v England (First Test) at Lord's.
62	9	22	1	30	Middlesex (269) v Sussex at Hove.
61	11	5	1	44	Glamorgan (513-9 dec) v Leicestershire at Leicester.
61	12	20	3	26	Surrey (315) v Derbyshire at Derby.
57	26	18	7	6	Cape Cobras (597) v Dolphins at Pietermaritzburg.
57	21	24	0	12	Lancashire (368) v Leicestershire at Leicester.
56	13	8	1	34	Gloucestershire (411) v Derbyshire at Bristol.

Career Aggregate Milestones

25,000 runs	S. Chanderpaul.
15,000 runs	Misbah-ul-Haq, C. M. W. Read, I. J. L. Trott, Younis Khan.
10,000 runs	N. R. D. Compton, M. J. Cosgrove, H. A. P. W. Jayawardene, M. Klinger, J. Mubarak, J. L. Ontong, M. H. W. Papps, Saeed Bin Nasir, J. K. Silva, Taufeeq Umar, A. C. Voges, M. A. Wallace.
500 wickets	S. C. J. Broad, S. J. Magoffin, G. Onions, J. S. Patel, C. E. Shreck.
1,000 dismissals	C. M. W. Read.
500 dismissals	T. R. Ambrose, C. D. Hartley.

RECORDS

COMPILED BY PHILIP BAILEY

This section covers
- first-class records to December 31, 2015 (page 1255).
- List A one-day records to December 31, 2015 (page 1283).
- List A Twenty20 records to December 31, 2015 (page 1286).
- Test records to January 26, 2016, the end of the South Africa v England series (page 1288).
- Test records series by series (page 1321).
- one-day international records to January 6, 2016 (page 1361).
- World Cup records (page 1370).
- Twenty20 international records to January 10, 2016 (page 1376).
- miscellaneous other records to January 5, 2016 (page 1381).
- women's Test records, one-day international and Twenty20 international records to December 31, 2015 (page 1385).

The sequence
- Test series records begin with those involving England, arranged in the order their opponents entered Test cricket (Australia, South Africa, West Indies, New Zealand, India, Pakistan, Sri Lanka, Zimbabwe, Bangladesh). Next come all remaining series involving Australia, then South Africa – and so on until Zimbabwe v Bangladesh records appear on page 1358.

Notes
- Unless otherwise stated, all records apply only to first-class cricket. This is considered to have started in 1815, after the Napoleonic War.
- mid-year seasons taking place outside England are given simply as 2014, 2015, etc.
- (E), (A), (SA), (WI), (NZ), (I), (P), (SL), (Z) or (B) indicates the nationality of a player or the country in which a record was made.
- in career records, dates in italic indicate seasons embracing two different years (i.e. non-English seasons). In these cases, only the first year is given, e.g. *2014* for 2014-15.

See also
- up-to-date records on www.wisdenrecords.com.
- Features of 2015 (page 1238).

CONTENTS

FIRST-CLASS RECORDS

BATTING RECORDS

LIST A ONE-DAY RECORDS

LIST A TWENTY20 RECORDS

TEST RECORDS

BATTING RECORDS

BOWLING RECORDS

ALL-ROUND RECORDS

WICKETKEEPING RECORDS

FIELDING RECORDS

TEAM RECORDS

PLAYERS

UMPIRES

TEST SERIES

ONE-DAY INTERNATIONAL RECORDS

TWENTY20 INTERNATIONAL RECORDS

MISCELLANEOUS RECORDS

WOMEN'S TEST AND OTHER INTERNATIONAL RECORDS

NOTES ON RECORDS

Assaults on the summit

Rob Smyth

The volume of Test cricket is such that cumulative records are under constant attack. In 2015, Alastair Cook and James Anderson became England's leading run-scorer and wicket-taker respectively, while Younis Khan and Tamim Iqbal broke the records for most Test runs for Pakistan and Bangladesh. Dale Steyn became only the second South African to take 400 Test wickets, and needs 16 to overtake Shaun Pollock. Cook requires 36 runs, and Younis 884, to reach 10,000.

Other records revealed the game's contemporary brand. In February 2016, New Zealand captain Brendon McCullum made the fastest Test century of all time, from 54 balls, against Australia in his farewell match; the previous month Ben Stokes had smashed the second-fastest double, off 163, against South Africa, while adding 399 with Jonny Bairstow, which raised the sixth-wicket Test record for the third time since February 2014. There was a new fourth-wicket record, with Adam Voges and Shaun Marsh putting on 449 against West Indies – Australia's second-highest partnership for any wicket, two short of Bill Ponsford and Don Bradman at The Oval in 1934. By the end of Australia's tour of New Zealand in February, Voges was averaging 95.50, from 21 Test innings, second only to Bradman.

Chris Gayle and Marlon Samuels added 372 for West Indies against Zimbabwe at the World Cup, an all-wicket record in one-day internationals; Gayle's 215 was the highest World Cup score for 25 days, until Martin Guptill struck 237 not out in New Zealand's quarter-final against West Indies.

Other achievements included India's Ajinkya Rahane taking eight catches against Sri Lanka, a Test record for an outfielder, and Colin Munro obliterating the record for most sixes in a first-class innings – and, indeed, match – hammering 23 for Auckland against Central Districts.

The most eye-widening achievement of all came in January 2016, when Pranav Dhanawade, a 15-year-old from a suburb of Mumbai, scored 1,009 in one innings (see page 119), beating 628 not out by 13-year-old A. E. J. Collins in 1899 as the highest recorded score in any cricket match. Few records are safe these days, but it should be a while before Dhanawade's is broken.

ROLL OF DISHONOUR

The following players have either been banned after being found guilty of some form of corruption, or have admitted to some form of on-field corruption:

Amit Singh (I), Ata-ur-Rehman (P), M. Azharuddin (I), A. Bali (I), G. H. Bodi (SA), A. A. Chavan (I), P. Cleary (A), W. J. Cronje (SA), Danish Kaneria (P), H. H. Gibbs (SA), A. Jadeja (I), K. S. Lokuarachchi (SL), M. D. Mishra (I), Mohammad Amir (P), Mohammad Ashraful (B), Mohammad Asif (P), Naved Arif (P), M. O. Odumbe (K), M. Prabhakar (I), Salim Malik (P), Salman Butt (P), M. N. Samuels (WI), H. N. Shah (I), Shariful Haque (B), Ajay Sharma (I), S. Sreesanth (I), S. J. Srivastava (I), T. P. Sudhindra (I), S. K. Trivedi (I), L. Vincent (NZ), M. S. Westfield (E), H. S. Williams (SA), A. R. Yadav (I).

FIRST-CLASS RECORDS

This section covers first-class cricket to December 31, 2015. Bold type denotes performances in the calendar year 2015 or, in career figures, players who appeared in first-class cricket in that year.

BATTING RECORDS

HIGHEST INDIVIDUAL INNINGS

In all first-class cricket, there have been **203** individual scores of 300 or more. The highest are:

501*	B. C. Lara	Warwickshire v Durham at Birmingham	1994
499	Hanif Mohammad	Karachi v Bahawalpur at Karachi	1958-59
452*	D. G. Bradman	NSW v Queensland at Sydney	1929-30
443*	B. B. Nimbalkar	Maharashtra v Kathiawar at Poona	1948-49
437	W. H. Ponsford	Victoria v Queensland at Melbourne	1927-28
429	W. H. Ponsford	Victoria v Tasmania at Melbourne	1922-23
428	Aftab Baloch	Sind v Baluchistan at Karachi	1973-74
424	A. C. MacLaren	Lancashire v Somerset at Taunton	1895
405*	G. A. Hick	Worcestershire v Somerset at Taunton	1988
400*	B. C. Lara	West Indies v England at St John's	2003-04
394	Naved Latif	Sargodha v Gujranwala at Gujranwala	2000-01
390	S. C. Cook	Lions v Warriors at East London	2009-10
385	B. Sutcliffe	Otago v Canterbury at Christchurch	1952-53
383	C. W. Gregory	NSW v Queensland at Brisbane	1906-07
380	M. L. Hayden	Australia v Zimbabwe at Perth	2003-04
377	S. V. Manjrekar	Bombay v Hyderabad at Bombay	1990-91
375	B. C. Lara	West Indies v England at St John's	1993-94
374	D. P. M. D. Jayawardene	Sri Lanka v South Africa at Colombo	2006
369	D. G. Bradman	South Australia v Tasmania at Adelaide	1935-36
366	N. H. Fairbrother	Lancashire v Surrey at The Oval	1990
366	M. V. Sridhar	Hyderabad v Andhra at Secunderabad	1993-94
365*	C. Hill	South Australia v NSW at Adelaide	1900-01
365*	G. S. Sobers	West Indies v Pakistan at Kingston	1957-58
364	L. Hutton	England v Australia at The Oval	1938
359*	V. M. Merchant	Bombay v Maharashtra at Bombay	1943-44
359	R. B. Simpson	NSW v Queensland at Brisbane	1963-64
357*	R. Abel	Surrey v Somerset at The Oval.	1899
357	D. G. Bradman	South Australia v Victoria at Melbourne	1935-36
356	B. A. Richards	South Australia v Western Australia at Perth	1970-71
355*	G. R. Marsh	Western Australia v South Australia at Perth	1989-90
355	**K. P. Pietersen**	**Surrey v Leicestershire at The Oval**	**2015**
355	B. Sutcliffe	Otago v Auckland at Dunedin	1949-50
353	V. V. S. Laxman	Hyderabad v Karnataka at Bangalore.	1999-2000
352	W. H. Ponsford	Victoria v NSW at Melbourne	1926-27
352	C. A. Pujara	Saurashtra v Karnataka at Rajkot	2012-13
351	**K. D. K. Vithanage**	**Tamil Union v Air Force at Katunayake**	**2014-15**
350	Rashid Israr	Habib Bank v National Bank at Lahore	1976-77

A fuller list can be found in Wisdens up to 2011.

DOUBLE-HUNDRED ON DEBUT

227	T. Marsden	Sheffield & Leicester v Nottingham at Sheffield. . . .	1826
207	N. F. Callaway†	New South Wales v Queensland at Sydney	1914-15
240	W. F. E. Marx	Transvaal v Griqualand West at Johannesburg	1920-21
200*	A. Maynard	Trinidad v MCC at Port-of-Spain	1934-35
232*	S. J. E. Loxton	Victoria v Queensland at Melbourne.	1946-47
215*	G. H. G. Doggart	Cambridge University v Lancashire at Cambridge . . .	1948

202	J. Hallebone	Victoria v Tasmania at Melbourne	1951-52
230	G. R. Viswanath	Mysore v Andhra at Vijayawada.	1967-68
260	A. A. Muzumdar	Bombay v Haryana at Faridabad	1993-94
209*	A. Pandey	Madhya Pradesh v Uttar Pradesh at Bhilai	1995-96
210*	D. J. Sales	Northamptonshire v Worcestershire at Kidderminster	1996
200*	M. J. Powell	Glamorgan v Oxford University at Oxford	1997
201*	M. C. Juneja	Gujarat v Tamil Nadu at Ahmedabad	2011-12
213	Jiwanjot Singh	Punjab v Hyderabad at Mohali	2012-13

†   *In his only first-class innings. He was killed in action in France in 1917.*

TWO SEPARATE HUNDREDS ON DEBUT

148	and 111	A. R. Morris	New South Wales v Queensland at Sydney	1940-41
152	and 102*	N. J. Contractor	Gujarat v Baroda at Baroda	1952-53
132*	and 110	Aamer Malik	Lahore A v Railways at Lahore	1979-80
130	and 100*	Noor Ali	Afghanistan v Zimbabwe XI at Mutare	2009
158	and 103*	K. H. T. Indika	Police v Seeduwa Raddoluwa at Colombo	2010-11
126	and 112	V. S. Awate	Maharashtra v Vidarbha at Nagpur	2012-13
154*	**and 109***	**T. J. Dean**	**Victoria v Queensland at Melbourne**	**2015-16**

TWO DOUBLE-HUNDREDS IN A MATCH

| A. E. Fagg . . . . | 244 | 202* | Kent v Essex at Colchester . . . . | 1938 |

TRIPLE-HUNDRED AND HUNDRED IN A MATCH

| G. A. Gooch. . . . . | 333 | 123 | England v India at Lord's. . . . . | 1990 |
| K. C. Sangakkara. . . . . | 319 | 105 | Sri Lanka v Bangladesh at Chittagong. . . . . . | 2013-14 |

DOUBLE-HUNDRED AND HUNDRED IN A MATCH

In addition to Fagg, Gooch and Sangakkara, there have been **60** further instances of a batsman scoring a double-hundred and a hundred in the same first-class match. The most recent are:

Younis Khan	106	202*	Yorkshire v Hampshire at Southampton	2007
M. W. Goodwin	119	205*	Sussex v Surrey at Hove	2007
V. Sibanda.	209	116*	Zimbabwe XI v Kenya at Kwekwe.	2009-10
Y. K. Pathan	108	210*	West Zone v South Zone at Hyderabad.	2009-10
S. M. Ervine	208	160	Southern Rocks v MW Rhinos at Masvingo . .	2009-10
C. J. L. Rogers.	200	140*	Derbyshire v Surrey at The Oval.	2010
M. R. Ramprakash	223	103*	Surrey v Middlesex at The Oval	2010
N. V. Ojha	219*	101*	India A v Australia A at Brisbane	2014

Zaheer Abbas achieved the feat four times, for Gloucestershire between 1976 and 1981, and was not out in all eight innings. M. R. Hallam did it twice for Leicestershire, in 1959 and 1961; N. R. Taylor twice for Kent, in 1990 and 1991; G. A. Gooch for England in 1990 (see above) and Essex in 1994; M. W. Goodwin twice for Sussex, in 2001 and 2007; and C. J. L. Rogers for Northamptonshire in 2006 and for Derbyshire in 2010.

TWO SEPARATE HUNDREDS IN A MATCH MOST TIMES

R. T. Ponting	8	J. B. Hobbs.	6	M. L. Hayden	5
Zaheer Abbas	8	G. M. Turner	6	G. A. Hick	5
W. R. Hammond	7	C. B. Fry	5		
M. R. Ramprakash	7	G. A. Gooch	5		

W. Lambert scored 107 and 157 for Sussex v Epsom at Lord's in 1817, and it was not until W. G. Grace made 130 and 102 for South of the Thames v North of the Thames at Canterbury in 1868 that the feat was repeated.*

FIVE HUNDREDS OR MORE IN SUCCESSION

D. G. Bradman (1938-39)	6	B. C. Lara (1993-94/1994)	5
C. B. Fry (1901)	6	P. A. Patel (2007/2007-08)	5
M. J. Procter (1970-71)	6	E. D. Weekes (1955-56)	5
M. E. K. Hussey (2003)	5		

Bradman also scored four hundreds in succession twice, in 1931-32 and 1948/1948-49; W. R. Hammond did it in 1936-37 and 1945/1946, and H. Sutcliffe in 1931 and 1939.

T. W. Hayward (Surrey v Nottinghamshire and Leicestershire), D. W. Hookes (South Australia v Queensland and New South Wales) and V. Sibanda (Zimbabwe XI v Kenya and Mid West v Southern Rocks) are the only players to score two hundreds in each of two successive matches. Hayward scored his in six days, June 4-9, 1906.

The most fifties in consecutive innings is ten – by E. Tyldesley in 1926, by D. G. Bradman in the 1947-48 and 1948 seasons and by R. S. Kaluwitharana in 1994-95.

MOST HUNDREDS IN A SEASON

D. C. S. Compton (1947)	18	T. W. Hayward (1906)	13
J. B. Hobbs (1925)	16	E. H. Hendren (1923)	13
W. R. Hammond (1938)	15	E. H. Hendren (1927)	13
H. Sutcliffe (1932)	14	E. H. Hendren (1928)	13
G. Boycott (1971)	13	C. P. Mead (1928)	13
D. G. Bradman (1938)	13	H. Sutcliffe (1928)	13
C. B. Fry (1901)	13	H. Sutcliffe (1931)	13
W. R. Hammond (1933)	13		
W. R. Hammond (1937)	13		

Since 1969 (excluding G. Boycott – above)

G. A. Gooch (1990)	12	M. R. Ramprakash (1995)	10
S. J. Cook (1991)	11	M. R. Ramprakash (2007)	10
Zaheer Abbas (1976)	11	G. M. Turner (1970)	10
G. A. Hick (1988)	10	Zaheer Abbas (1981)	10
H. Morris (1990)	10		

The most outside England is nine by V. Sibanda in Zimbabwe (2009-10), followed by eight by D. G. Bradman in Australia (1947-48), D. C. S. Compton (1948-49), R. N. Harvey and A. R. Morris (both 1949-50) all three in South Africa, M. D. Crowe in New Zealand (1986-87), Asif Mujtaba in Pakistan (1995-96), V. V. S. Laxman in India (1999-2000) and M. G. Bevan in Australia (2004-05).

The most double-hundreds in a season is six by D. G. Bradman (1930), five by K. S. Ranjitsinhji (1900) and E. D. Weekes (1950), and four by Arun Lal (1986-87), C. B. Fry (1901), W. R. Hammond (1933 and 1934), E. H. Hendren (1929-30), V. M. Merchant (1944-45), C. A. Pujara (2012-13) and G. M. Turner (1971-72).

MOST DOUBLE-HUNDREDS IN A CAREER

D. G. Bradman	37	W. H. Ponsford	13	G. Boycott	10
W. R. Hammond	36	J. T. Tyldesley	13	R. Dravid	10
E. H. Hendren	22	P. Holmes	12	M. W. Gatting	10
M. R. Ramprakash	17	Javed Miandad	12	S. M. Gavaskar	10
H. Sutcliffe	17	J. L. Langer	12	J. Hardstaff, jun	10
C. B. Fry	16	**K. C. Sangakkara**	**12**	V. S. Hazare	10
G. A. Hick	16	R. B. Simpson	12	B. J. Hodge	10
J. B. Hobbs	16	J. W. Hearne	11	D. P. M. D. Jayawardene	10
C. G. Greenidge	14	L. Hutton	11	I. V. A. Richards	10
K. S. Ranjitsinhji	14	D. S. Lehmann	11	A. Shrewsbury	10
G. A. Gooch	13	V. M. Merchant	11	R. T. Simpson	10
W. G. Grace	13	**C. J. L. Rogers**	**11**	G. M. Turner	10
B. C. Lara	13	A. Sandham	11	Zaheer Abbas	10
C. P. Mead	13	**Younis Khan**	**11**		

MOST HUNDREDS IN A CAREER

(100 or more)

		Total	Total Inns	100th 100 Season	Inns	400+	300+	200+
1	J. B. Hobbs	197	1,315	1923	821	0	1	16
2	E. H. Hendren	170	1,300	1928-29	740	0	1	22
3	W. R. Hammond	167	1,005	1935	680	0	4	36
4	C. P. Mead	153	1,340	1927	892	0	0	13
5	G. Boycott	151	1,014	1977	645	0	0	10
6	H. Sutcliffe	149	1,088	1932	700	0	1	17
7	F. E. Woolley	145	1,532	1929	1,031	0	1	9
8	G. A. Hick	136	871	1998	574	1	3	16
9	L. Hutton	129	814	1951	619	0	1	11
10	G. A. Gooch	128	990	1992-93	820	0	1	13
11	W. G. Grace	126	1,493	1895	1,113	0	3	13
12	D. C. S. Compton	123	839	1952	552	0	1	9
13	T. W. Graveney	122	1,223	1964	940	0	0	7
14	D. G. Bradman	117	338	1947-48	295	1	6	37
15 {	I. V. A. Richards	114	796	1988-89	658	0	1	10
	M. R. Ramprakash	114	764	2008	676	0	1	17
17	Zaheer Abbas	108	768	1982-83	658	0	0	10
18 {	A. Sandham	107	1,000	1935	871	0	1	11
	M. C. Cowdrey	107	1,130	1973	1,035	0	1	3
20	T. W. Hayward	104	1,138	1913	1,076	0	1	8
21 {	G. M. Turner	103	792	1982	779	0	1	10
	J. H. Edrich	103	979	1977	945	0	1	4
23 {	L. E. G. Ames	102	951	1950	916	0	0	9
	E. Tyldesley	102	961	1934	919	0	0	7
	D. L. Amiss	102	1,139	1986	1,081	0	0	3

In the above table, 200+, 300+ and 400+ include all scores above those figures.

    G. A. Gooch's record includes his century in South Africa in 1981-82, which is no longer accepted by the ICC. Zaheer Abbas and G. Boycott scored their 100th hundreds in Test matches.

Current Players

The following who played in 2015 have scored 40 or more hundreds.

C. J. L. Rogers	73	A. N. Cook	51	A. G. Prince	45
S. Chanderpaul	71	Wasim Jaffer	51	H. M. Amla	44
M. E. Trescothick	58	I. R. Bell	50	E. C. Joyce	42
K. C. Sangakkara	55	K. P. Pietersen	50	Misbah-ul-Haq	42
R. W. T. Key	54	J. A. Rudolph	49	V. Sehwag	42
N. D. McKenzie	53	M. J. Clarke	45		
Younis Khan	52	D. J. Hussey	45		

MOST RUNS IN A SEASON

	Season	I	NO	R	HS	100	Avge
D. C. S. Compton	1947	50	8	3,816	246	18	90.85
W. J. Edrich	1947	52	8	3,539	267*	12	80.43
T. W. Hayward	1906	61	8	3,518	219	13	66.37
L. Hutton	1949	56	6	3,429	269*	12	68.58
F. E. Woolley	1928	59	4	3,352	198	12	60.94

	Season	I	NO	R	HS	100	Avge
H. Sutcliffe.............	1932	52	7	3,336	313	14	74.13
W. R. Hammond	1933	54	5	3,323	264	13	67.81
E. H. Hendren........	1928	54	7	3,311	209*	13	70.44
R. Abel................	1901	68	8	3,309	247	7	55.15

3,000 in a season has been surpassed on 19 other occasions (a full list can be found in Wisden 1999 and earlier editions). W. R. Hammond, E. H. Hendren and H. Sutcliffe are the only players to achieve the feat three times. K. S. Ranjitsinhji was the first batsman to reach 3,000 in a season, with 3,159 in 1899. M. J. K. Smith (3,245 in 1959) and W. E. Alley (3,019 in 1961) are the only players except those listed above to have reached 3,000 since World War II.

W. G. Grace scored 2,739 runs in 1871 – the first batsman to reach 2,000 in a season. He made ten hundreds including two double-hundreds, with an average of 78.25 in all first-class matches.

The highest aggregate in a season since the reduction of County Championship matches in 1969 is 2,755 by S. J. Cook (42 innings) in 1991, and the last batsman to achieve 2,000 was M. R. Ramprakash (2,026 in 2007).

2,000 RUNS IN A SEASON MOST TIMES

J. B. Hobbs.............	17	F. E. Woolley..........	13	C. P. Mead..........	11
E. H. Hendren.........	15	W. R. Hammond	12	T. W. Hayward........	10
H. Sutcliffe............	15	J. G. Langridge........	11		

Since the reduction of County Championship matches in 1969, G. A. Gooch is the only batsman to have reached 2,000 runs in a season five times.

1,000 RUNS IN A SEASON MOST TIMES

Includes overseas tours and seasons.

W. G. Grace..........	28	A. Jones..............	23	G. Gunn..............	20
F. E. Woolley	28	T. W. Graveney	22	T. W. Hayward	20
M. C. Cowdrey.......	27	W. R. Hammond	22	G. A. Hick...........	20
C. P. Mead..........	27	D. Denton	21	James Langridge.....	20
G. Boycott...........	26	J. H. Edrich	21	J. M. Parks..........	20
J. B. Hobbs..........	26	G. A. Gooch	21	M. R. Ramprakash....	20
E. H. Hendren.......	25	W. Rhodes	21	A. Sandham.........	20
D. L. Amiss..........	24	D. B. Close	20	M. J. K. Smith	20
W. G. Quaife.........	24	K. W. R. Fletcher	20	C. Washbrook........	20
H. Sutcliffe	24	M. W. Gatting	20		

F. E. Woolley reached 1,000 runs in 28 consecutive seasons (1907–1938), C. P. Mead in 27 (1906–1936).

Outside England, 1,000 runs in a season has been reached most times by D. G. Bradman (in 12 seasons in Australia).

Three batsmen have scored 1,000 runs in a season in each of four different countries: G. S. Sobers in West Indies, England, India and Australia; M. C. Cowdrey and G. Boycott in England, South Africa, West Indies and Australia.

HIGHEST AGGREGATES OUTSIDE ENGLAND

	Season	I	NO	R	HS	100	Avge
In Australia							
D. G. Bradman...........	1928-29	24	6	1,690	340*	7	93.88
In South Africa							
J. R. Reid...............	1961-62	30	2	1,915	203	7	68.39
In West Indies							
E. H. Hendren	1929-30	18	5	1,765	254*	6	135.76
In New Zealand							
M. D. Crowe	1986-87	21	3	1,676	175*	8	93.11

	Season	I	NO	R	HS	100	Avge
In India							
C. G. Borde	1964-65	28	3	1,604	168	6	64.16
In Pakistan							
Saadat Ali	1983-84	27	1	1,649	208	4	63.42
In Sri Lanka							
R. P. Arnold	1995-96	24	3	1,475	217*	5	70.23
In Zimbabwe							
V. Sibanda	2009-10	26	4	1,612	215	9	73.27
In Bangladesh							
Liton Das	**2014-15**	**17**	**1**	**1,232**	**175**	**5**	**77.00**

In more than one country, the following aggregates of over 2,000 runs have been recorded:

M. Amarnath (P/I/WI)	1982-83	34	6	2,234	207	9	79.78
J. R. Reid (SA/A/NZ)	1961-62	40	2	2,188	203	7	57.57
S. M. Gavaskar (I/P)	1978-79	30	6	2,121	205	10	88.37
R. B. Simpson (I/P/A/WI) . . .	1964-65	34	4	2,063	201	8	68.76
M. H. Richardson (Z/SA/NZ) .	2000-01	34	3	2,030	306	4	65.48

LEADING BATSMEN IN AN ENGLISH SEASON

(Qualification: 8 completed innings)

Season	Leading scorer	Runs	Avge	Top of averages	Runs	Avge
1946	D. C. S. Compton	2,403	61.61	W. R. Hammond	1,783	84.90
1947	D. C. S. Compton	3,816	90.85	D. C. S. Compton	3,816	90.85
1948	L. Hutton	2,654	64.73	D. G. Bradman	2,428	89.92
1949	L. Hutton	3,429	68.58	J. Hardstaff	2,251	72.61
1950	R. T. Simpson	2,576	62.82	E. D. Weekes	2,310	79.65
1951	J. D. Robertson	2,917	56.09	P. B. H. May	2,339	68.79
1952	L. Hutton	2,567	61.11	D. S. Sheppard	2,262	64.62
1953	W. J. Edrich	2,557	47.35	R. N. Harvey	2,040	65.80
1954	D. Kenyon	2,636	51.68	D. C. S. Compton	1,524	58.61
1955	D. J. Insole	2,427	42.57	D. J. McGlew	1,871	58.46
1956	T. W. Graveney	2,397	49.93	K. Mackay	1,103	52.52
1957	T. W. Graveney	2,361	49.18	P. B. H. May	2,347	61.76
1958	P. B. H. May	2,231	63.74	P. B. H. May	2,231	63.74
1959	M. J. K. Smith	3,245	57.94	V. L. Manjrekar	755	68.63
1960	M. J. K. Smith	2,551	45.55	R. Subba Row	1,503	55.66
1961	W. E. Alley	3,019	56.96	W. M. Lawry	2,019	61.18
1962	J. H. Edrich	2,482	51.70	R. T. Simpson	867	54.18
1963	J. B. Bolus	2,190	41.32	G. S. Sobers	1,333	47.60
1964	T. W. Graveney	2,385	54.20	K. F. Barrington	1,872	62.40
1965	J. H. Edrich	2,319	62.67	M. C. Cowdrey	2,093	63.42
1966	A. R. Lewis	2,198	41.47	G. S. Sobers	1,349	61.31
1967	C. A. Milton	2,089	46.42	K. F. Barrington	2,059	68.63
1968	B. A. Richards	2,395	47.90	G. Boycott	1,487	64.65
1969	J. H. Edrich	2,238	69.93	J. H. Edrich	2,238	69.93
1970	G. M. Turner	2,379	61.00	G. S. Sobers	1,742	75.73
1971	G. Boycott	2,503	100.12	G. Boycott	2,503	100.12
1972	Majid Khan	2,074	61.00	G. Boycott	1,230	72.35
1973	G. M. Turner	2,416	67.11	G. M. Turner	2,416	67.11
1974	R. T. Virgin	1,936	56.94	C. H. Lloyd	1,458	63.39
1975	G. Boycott	1,915	73.65	R. B. Kanhai	1,073	82.53
1976	Zaheer Abbas	2,554	75.11	Zaheer Abbas	2,554	75.11
1977	I. V. A. Richards	2,161	65.48	G. Boycott	1,701	68.04

Season	Leading scorer	Runs	Avge	Top of averages	Runs	Avge
1978	D. L. Amiss...........	2,030	53.42	C. E. B. Rice...........	1,871	66.82
1979	K. C. Wessels.......	1,800	52.94	G. Boycott...........	1,538	102.53
1980	P. N. Kirsten.......	1,895	63.16	A. J. Lamb...........	1,797	66.55
1981	Zaheer Abbas.......	2,306	88.69	Zaheer Abbas.......	2,306	88.69
1982	A. I. Kallicharran	2,120	66.25	G. M. Turner........	1,171	90.07
1983	K. S. McEwan.......	2,176	64.00	I. V. A. Richards.....	1,204	75.25
1984	G. A. Gooch.......	2,559	67.34	C. G. Greenidge	1,069	82.23
1985	G. A. Gooch.......	2,208	71.22	I. V. A. Richards.....	1,836	76.50
1986	C. G. Greenidge	2,035	67.83	C. G. Greenidge	2,035	67.83
1987	G. A. Hick........	1,879	52.19	M. D. Crowe........	1,627	67.79
1988	G. A. Hick........	2,713	77.51	R. A. Harper........	622	77.75
1989	S. J. Cook........	2,241	60.56	D. M. Jones........	1,510	88.82
1990	G. A. Gooch.......	2,746	101.70	G. A. Gooch.......	2,746	101.70
1991	S. J. Cook........	2,755	81.02	C. L. Hooper........	1,501	93.81
1992	{ P. D. Bowler........	2,044	65.93	Salim Malik........	1,184	78.93
	{ M. A. Roseberry	2,044	56.77			
1993	G. A. Gooch.......	2,023	63.21	D. C. Boon........	1,437	75.63
1994	B. C. Lara........	2,066	89.82	J. D. Carr........	1,543	90.76
1995	M. R. Ramprakash ...	2,258	77.86	M. R. Ramprakash ...	2,258	77.86
1996	G. A. Gooch.......	1,944	67.03	S. C. Ganguly	762	95.25
1997	S. P. James........	1,775	68.26	G. A. Hick........	1,524	69.27
1998	J. P. Crawley.......	1,851	74.04	J. P. Crawley.......	1,851	74.04
1999	S. G. Law........	1,833	73.32	S. G. Law........	1,833	73.32
2000	D. S. Lehmann	1,477	67.13	M. G. Bevan........	1,124	74.93
2001	M. E. K. Hussey	2,055	79.03	D. R. Martyn........	942	104.66
2002	I. J. Ward...........	1,759	62.82	R. Dravid........	773	96.62
2003	S. G. Law........	1,820	91.00	S. G. Law........	1,820	91.00
2004	R. W. T. Key.......	1,896	79.00	R. W. T. Key.......	1,896	79.00
2005	O. A. Shah........	1,728	66.46	M. E. K. Hussey	1,074	76.71
2006	M. R. Ramprakash ...	2,278	103.54	M. R. Ramprakash	2,278	103.54
2007	M. R. Ramprakash ...	2,026	101.30	M. R. Ramprakash	2,026	101.30
2008	S. C. Moore........	1,451	55.80	T. Frost........	1,003	83.58
2009	M. E. Trescothick ...	1,817	75.70	M. R. Ramprakash ...	1,350	90.00
2010	M. R. Ramprakash ...	1,595	61.34	J. C. Hildreth	1,440	65.45
2011	M. E. Trescothick ...	1,673	79.66	I. R. Bell........	1,091	90.91
2012	N. R. D. Compton ...	1,494	99.60	N. R. D. Compton	1,494	99.60
2013	C. J. L. Rogers	1,536	51.20	S. M. Katich........	1,097	73.13
2014	A. Lyth........	1,619	70.39	J. E. Root........	1,052	75.14
2015	**J. C. Hildreth........**	**1,758**	**56.70**	**J. M. Bairstow........**	**1,226**	**72.11**

The highest average recorded in an English season was 115.66 (2,429 runs, 26 innings) by D. G. Bradman in 1938.

In 1953, W. A. Johnston averaged 102.00 from 17 innings, 16 not out.

MOST RUNS

Dates in italics denote the first half of an overseas season; i.e. *1945* denotes the 1945-46 season.

		Career	R	I	NO	HS	100	Avge
1	J. B. Hobbs.........	1905–1934	61,237	1,315	106	316*	197	50.65
2	F. E. Woolley.......	1906–1938	58,959	1,532	85	305*	145	40.75
3	E. H. Hendren.......	1907–1938	57,611	1,300	166	301*	170	50.80
4	C. P. Mead	1905–1936	55,061	1,340	185	280*	153	47.67
5	W. G. Grace	1865–1908	54,896	1,493	105	344	126	39.55
6	W. R. Hammond	1920–1951	50,551	1,005	104	336*	167	56.10
7	H. Sutcliffe........	1919–1945	50,138	1,088	123	313	149	51.95
8	G. Boycott........	1962–1986	48,426	1,014	162	261*	151	56.83
9	T. W. Graveney	1948–*1971*	47,793	1,223	159	258	122	44.91
10	G. A. Gooch........	1973–2000	44,846	990	75	333	128	49.01
11	T. W. Hayward......	1893–1914	43,551	1,138	96	315*	104	41.79

		Career	R	I	NO	HS	100	Avge
12	D. L. Amiss	1960–1987	43,423	1,139	126	262*	102	42.86
13	M. C. Cowdrey	1950–1976	42,719	1,130	134	307	107	42.89
14	A. Sandham	1911–1937	41,284	1,000	79	325	107	44.82
15	G. A. Hick	1983–2008	41,112	871	84	405*	136	52.23
16	L. Hutton	1934–1960	40,140	814	91	364	129	55.51
17	M. J. K. Smith	1951–1975	39,832	1,091	139	204	69	41.84
18	W. Rhodes	1898–1930	39,802	1,528	237	267*	58	30.83
19	J. H. Edrich	1956–1978	39,790	979	104	310*	103	45.47
20	R. E. S. Wyatt	1923–1957	39,405	1,141	157	232	85	40.04
21	D. C. S. Compton	1936–1964	38,942	839	88	300	123	51.85
22	E. Tyldesley	1909–1936	38,874	961	106	256*	102	45.46
23	J. T. Tyldesley	1895–1923	37,897	994	62	295*	86	40.66
24	K. W. R. Fletcher	1962–1988	37,665	1,167	170	228*	63	37.77
25	C. G. Greenidge	1970–1992	37,354	889	75	273*	92	45.88
26	J. W. Hearne	1909–1936	37,252	1,025	116	285*	96	40.98
27	L. E. G. Ames	1926–1951	37,248	951	95	295	102	43.51
28	D. Kenyon	1946–1967	37,002	1,159	59	259	74	33.63
29	W. J. Edrich	1934–1958	36,965	964	92	267*	86	42.39
30	J. M. Parks	1949–1976	36,673	1,227	172	205*	51	34.76
31	M. W. Gatting	1975–1998	36,549	861	123	258	94	49.52
32	D. Denton	1894–1920	36,479	1,163	70	221	69	33.37
33	G. H. Hirst	1891–1929	36,323	1,215	151	341	60	34.13
34	I. V. A. Richards	1971–1993	36,212	796	63	322	114	49.40
35	A. Jones	1957–1983	36,049	1,168	72	204*	56	32.89
36	W. G. Quaife	1894–1928	36,012	1,203	185	255*	72	35.37
37	R. E. Marshall	1945–1972	35,725	1,053	59	228*	68	35.94
38	M. R. Ramprakash . . .	1987–2012	35,659	764	93	301*	114	53.14
39	G. Gunn	1902–1932	35,208	1,061	82	220	62	35.96

Some works of reference provide career figures which differ from those in this list, owing to the exclusion or inclusion of matches recognised or not recognised as first-class by Wisden. *A fuller list can be found in* Wisdens *up to 2011.*

Current Players with 20,000 Runs

	Career	R	I	NO	HS	100	Avge
S. Chanderpaul	1991–2015	25,399	570	103	303*	71	54.38
C. J. L. Rogers	1998–2015	24,460	529	38	319	73	49.81
M. E. Trescothick	1993–2015	23,531	591	31	284	58	42.01

HIGHEST CAREER AVERAGE

(Qualification: 10,000 runs)

Avge		Career	I	NO	R	HS	100
95.14	D. G. Bradman	1927–1948	338	43	28,067	452*	117
71.22	V. M. Merchant	1929–1951	229	43	13,248	359*	44
67.46	Ajay Sharma	1984–2000	166	16	10,120	259*	38
65.18	W. H. Ponsford	1920–1934	235	23	13,819	437	47
64.99	W. M. Woodfull	1921–1934	245	39	13,388	284	49
58.24	A. L. Hassett	1932–1953	322	32	16,890	232	59
58.19	V. S. Hazare	1934–1966	365	45	18,621	316*	60
57.84	S. R. Tendulkar	1988–2013	490	51	25,396	248*	81
57.83	D. S. Lehmann	1987–2007	479	33	25,795	339	82
57.32	M. G. Bevan	1989–2006	400	66	19,147	216	68
57.22	A. F. Kippax	1918–1935	256	33	12,762	315*	43
56.83	G. Boycott	1962–1986	1,014	162	48,426	261*	151
56.55	C. L. Walcott	1941–1963	238	29	11,820	314*	40
56.37	K. S. Ranjitsinhji	1893–1920	500	62	24,692	285*	72
56.22	R. B. Simpson	1952–1977	436	62	21,029	359	60

Avge		Career	I	NO	R	HS	100
56.10	W. R. Hammond	1920–1951	1,005	104	50,551	336*	167
56.02	M. D. Crowe	1979–1995	412	62	19,608	299	71
55.90	R. T. Ponting	1992–2013	494	62	24,150	257	82
55.51	L. Hutton	1934–1960	814	91	40,140	364	129
55.34	E. D. Weekes	1944–1964	241	24	12,010	304*	36
55.33	R. Dravid	1990–2011	497	67	23,794	270	68
55.11	S. V. Manjrekar	1984–1997	217	31	10,252	377	31

G. A. Headley scored 9,921 runs, average 69.86, between 1927-28 and 1954.

FASTEST FIFTIES

Minutes
11	C. I. J. Smith (66)	Middlesex v Gloucestershire at Bristol	1938
13	Khalid Mahmood (56)	Gujranwala v Sargodha at Gujranwala	2000-01
14	S. J. Pegler (50)	South Africans v Tasmania at Launceston	1910-11
14	F. T. Mann (53)	Middlesex v Nottinghamshire at Lord's	1921
14	H. B. Cameron (56)	Transvaal v Orange Free State at Johannesburg	1934-35
14	C. I. J. Smith (52)	Middlesex v Kent at Maidstone	1935

The number of balls taken to achieve fifties was rarely recorded until recently. C. I. J. Smith's two fifties (above) may have taken only 12 balls each. Khalid Mahmood reached his fifty in 15 balls.

Fifties scored in contrived circumstances and with the bowlers' compliance are excluded from the above list, including the fastest of them all, in 8 minutes (13 balls) by C. C. Inman, Leicestershire v Nottinghamshire at Nottingham, 1965, and 10 minutes by G. Chapple, Lancashire v Glamorgan at Manchester, 1993.

FASTEST HUNDREDS

Minutes
35	P. G. H. Fender (113*)	Surrey v Northamptonshire at Northampton	1920
40	G. L. Jessop (101)	Gloucestershire v Yorkshire at Harrogate	1897
40	Ahsan-ul-Haq (100*)	Muslims v Sikhs at Lahore	1923-24
42	G. L. Jessop (191)	Gentlemen of South v Players of South at Hastings	1907
43	A. H. Hornby (106)	Lancashire v Somerset at Manchester	1905
43	D. W. Hookes (107)	South Australia v Victoria at Adelaide	1982-83
44	R. N. S. Hobbs (100)	Essex v Australians at Chelmsford	1975

The fastest recorded authentic hundred in terms of balls received was scored off 34 balls by D. W. Hookes (above). Research of the scorebook has shown that P. G. H. Fender scored his hundred from between 40 and 46 balls. He contributed 113 to an unfinished sixth-wicket partnership of 171 in 42 minutes with H. A. Peach.

E. B. Alletson (Nottinghamshire) scored 189 out of 227 runs in 90 minutes against Sussex at Hove in 1911. It has been estimated that his last 139 runs took 37 minutes.

Hundreds scored in contrived circumstances and with the bowlers' compliance are excluded, including the fastest of them all, in 21 minutes (27 balls) by G. Chapple, Lancashire v Glamorgan at Manchester, 1993, 24 minutes (27 balls) by M. L. Pettini, Essex v Leicestershire at Leicester, 2006, and 26 minutes (36 balls) by T. M. Moody, Warwickshire v Glamorgan at Swansea, 1990.

FASTEST DOUBLE-HUNDREDS

Minutes
113	R. J. Shastri (200*)	Bombay v Baroda at Bombay	1984-85
120	G. L. Jessop (286)	Gloucestershire v Sussex at Hove	1903
120	C. H. Lloyd (201*)	West Indians v Glamorgan at Swansea	1976
130	G. L. Jessop (234)	Gloucestershire v Somerset at Bristol	1905
131	V. T. Trumper (293)	Australians v Canterbury at Christchurch	1913-14

FASTEST TRIPLE-HUNDREDS

Minutes

181	D. C. S. Compton (300)	MCC v North Eastern Transvaal at Benoni	1948-49
205	F. E. Woolley (305*)	MCC v Tasmania at Hobart	1911-12
205	C. G. Macartney (345)	Australians v Nottinghamshire at Nottingham	1921
213	D. G. Bradman (369)	South Australia v Tasmania at Adelaide	1935-36

MOST RUNS IN A DAY BY ONE BATSMAN

390*	B. C. Lara	Warwickshire v Durham at Birmingham	1994
345	C. G. Macartney	Australians v Nottinghamshire at Nottingham	1921
334	W. H. Ponsford	Victoria v New South Wales at Melbourne	1926-27
333	K. S. Duleepsinhji	Sussex v Northamptonshire at Hove	1930
331*	J. D. Robertson	Middlesex v Worcestershire at Worcester	1949
325*	B. A. Richards	South Australia v Western Australia at Perth	1970-71

These scores do not necessarily represent the complete innings. See pages 1255.

*There have been another **14** instances of a batsman scoring 300 in a day, most recently 319 by R. R. Rossouw, Eagles v Titans at Centurion in 2009-10 (see Wisden 2003, page 278, for full list).*

LONGEST INNINGS

Hrs Mins

16	55	R. Nayyar (271)	H. Pradesh v Jammu & Kashmir at Chamba . . .	1999-2000
16	10	Hanif Mohammad (337)	Pakistan v West Indies at Bridgetown	1957-58
		Hanif believes he batted 16 hours 39 minutes.		
15	7	V. A. Saxena (257)	Rajasthan v Tamil Nadu at Chennai	2011-12
14	38	G. Kirsten (275)	South Africa v England at Durban	1999-2000
14	**32**	**K. K. Nair (328)**	**Karnataka v Tamil Nadu at Mumbai**	**2014-15**
13	56	S. C. Cook (390)	Lions v Warriors at East London	2009-10
13	**56**	**A. N. Cook (263)**	**England v Pakistan at Abu Dhabi**	**2015-16**
13	43	T. Kohli (300*)	Punjab v Jharkhand at Jamshedpur	2012-13
13	41	S. S. Shukla (178*)	Uttar Pradesh v Tamil Nadu at Nagpur	2008-09
13	32	A. Chopra (301*)	Rajasthan v Maharashtra at Nasik	2010-11

1,000 RUNS IN MAY

	Runs	*Avge*
W. G. Grace, May 9 to May 30, 1895 (22 days)	1,016	112.88
Grace was 46 years old.		
W. R. Hammond, May 7 to May 31, 1927 (25 days)	1,042	74.42
Hammond scored his 1,000th run on May 28, thus equalling		
Grace's record of 22 days.		
C. Hallows, May 5 to May 31, 1928 (27 days)	1,000	125.00

1,000 RUNS IN APRIL AND MAY

	Runs	*Avge*
T. W. Hayward, April 16 to May 31, 1900	1,074	97.63
D. G. Bradman, April 30 to May 31, 1930	1,001	143.00
On April 30 Bradman was 75 not out.		
D. G. Bradman, April 30 to May 31, 1938	1,056	150.85
Bradman scored 258 on April 30, and his 1,000th run on May 27.		
W. J. Edrich, April 30 to May 31, 1938	1,010	84.16
Edrich was 21 not out on April 30. All his runs were scored at Lord's.		
G. M. Turner, April 24 to May 31, 1973	1,018	78.30
G. A. Hick, April 17 to May 29, 1988	1,019	101.90
Hick scored a record 410 runs in April, and his 1,000th run on May 28.		

MOST RUNS SCORED OFF AN OVER

(All instances refer to six-ball overs)

36	G. S. Sobers	off M. A. Nash, Nottinghamshire v Glamorgan at Swansea (six sixes).	1968
36	R. J. Shastri	off Tilak Raj, Bombay v Baroda at Bombay (six sixes).	1984-85
34	E. B. Alletson	off E. H. Killick, Nottinghamshire v Sussex at Hove (46604446; including two no-balls).	1911
34	F. C. Hayes	off M. A. Nash, Lancashire v Glamorgan at Swansea (646666)	1977
34†	A. Flintoff	off A. J. Tudor, Lancashire v Surrey at Manchester (64444660; including two no-balls).	1998
34	C. M. Spearman	off S. J. P. Moreton, Gloucestershire v Oxford UCCE at Oxford (666646) *Moreton's first over in first-class cricket.* .	2005
32	I. T. Botham	off I. R. Snook, England XI v Central Districts at Palmerston North (466466).	1983-84
32	P. W. G. Parker	off A. I. Kallicharran, Sussex v Warwickshire at Birmingham (466664).	1982
32	I. R. Redpath	off N. Rosendorff, Australians v Orange Free State at Bloemfontein (666644).	1969-70
32	C. C. Smart	off G. Hill, Glamorgan v Hampshire at Cardiff (664664).	1935
32	Khalid Mahmood	off Naved Latif, Gujranwala v Sargodha at Gujranwala (666662).	2000-01

† *Altogether 38 runs were scored off this over, the two no-balls counting for two extra runs each under ECB regulations.*

The following instances have been excluded because of the bowlers' compliance: 34 – M. P. Maynard off S. A. Marsh, Glamorgan v Kent at Swansea, 1992; 34 – G. Chapple off P. A. Cottey, Lancashire v Glamorgan at Manchester, 1993; 34 – F. B. Touzel off F. J. J. Viljoen, Western Province B v Griqualand West at Kimberley, 1993-94. Chapple scored a further 32 off Cottey's next over.

There were 35 runs off an over received by A. T. Reinholds off H. T. Davis, Auckland v Wellington at Auckland 1995-96, but this included 16 extras and only 19 off the bat.

In a match against KwaZulu-Natal at Stellenbosch in 2006-07, W. E. September (Boland) conceded 34 in an over: 27 to M. Bekker, six to K. Smit, plus one no-ball.

In a match against Canterbury at Christchurch in 1989-90, R. H. Vance (Wellington) deliberately conceded 77 runs in an over of full tosses which contained 17 no-balls and, owing to the umpire's understandable miscalculation, only five legitimate deliveries.

The greatest number of runs scored off an eight-ball over is 34 (40446664) by R. M. Edwards off M. C. Carew, Governor-General's XI v West Indians at Auckland, 1968-69.

MOST SIXES IN AN INNINGS

23	**C. Munro (281)**	**Auckland v Central Districts at Napier**.	**2014-15**
16	A. Symonds (254*)	Gloucestershire v Glamorgan at Abergavenny.	1995
16	G. R. Napier (196)	Essex v Surrey at Croydon	2011
16	J. D. Ryder (175)	New Zealanders v Australia A at Brisbane.	2011-12
16	Mukhtar Ali (168)	Rajshahi v Chittagong at Savar.	2013-14
15	J. R. Reid (296)	Wellington v Northern Districts at Wellington.	1962-63
15	Ziaur Rahman (152*)	South Zone v Central Zone at Mirpur.	2012-13
15	**H. G. Kumara (200*)**	**Saracens v Air Force at Katunayake**.	**2014-15**
15	**K. P. Pietersen (355*)**	**Surrey v Leicestershire at The Oval**	**2015**

*There have been **15** further instances of 13 or more sixes in an innings, including 13 by F. B. Touzel (128*) for Western Province B v Griqualand West in contrived circumstances at Kimberley in 1993-94.*

MOST SIXES IN A MATCH

23	C. Munro (281)	Auckland v Central Districts at Napier	2014-15
20	A. Symonds (254*, 76)	Gloucestershire v Glam at Abergavenny	1995
17	W. J. Stewart (155, 125)	Warwickshire v Lancashire at Blackpool	1959
17	K. P. S. P. Karunanayake (52, 150*)	Army v Ports Authority at Colombo	2014-15

MOST SIXES IN A SEASON

80	I. T. Botham	1985	49	I. V. A. Richards	1985
66	A. W. Wellard	1935	48	A. W. Carr	1925
57	A. W. Wellard	1936	48	J. H. Edrich	1965
57	A. W. Wellard	1938	48	A. Symonds	1995
51	A. W. Wellard	1933			

MOST BOUNDARIES IN AN INNINGS

	4s/6s			
72	62/10	B. C. Lara (501*)	Warwickshire v Durham at Birmingham	1994
68	68/–	P. A. Perrin (343*)	Essex v Derbyshire at Chesterfield	1904
65	64/1	A. C. MacLaren (424)	Lancashire v Somerset at Taunton	1895
64	64/–	Hanif Mohammad (499)	Karachi v Bahawalpur at Karachi	1958-59
57	52/5	J. H. Edrich (310*)	England v New Zealand at Leeds	1965
57	52/5	Naved Latif (394)	Sargodha v Gujranwala at Gujranwala	2000-01
56	54/2	K. M. Jadhav (327)	Maharashtra v U. Pradesh at Gahunje	2012-13
55	55/–	C. W. Gregory (383)	NSW v Queensland at Brisbane	1906-07
55	53/2	G. R. Marsh (355*)	W. Australia v S. Australia at Perth	1989-90
55	51/3†	S. V. Manjrekar (377)	Bombay v Hyderabad at Bombay	1990-91
55	52/3	D. S. Lehmann (339)	Yorkshire v Durham at Leeds	2006
55	54/1	D. K. H. Mitchell (298)	Worcestershire v Somerset at Taunton	2009
55	54/1	S. C. Cook (390)	Lions v Warriors at East London	2009-10
55	47/8	R. R. Rossouw (319)	Eagles v Titans at Centurion	2009-10

† *Plus one five.*   ‡ *Plus three fives.*

PARTNERSHIPS OVER 500

624	for 3rd	K. C. Sangakkara (287)/D. P. M. D. Jayawardene (374), Sri Lanka v South Africa at Colombo	2006
580	for 2nd	Rafatullah Mohmand (302*)/Aamer Sajjad (289), WAPDA v Sui Southern Gas at Sheikhupura	2009-10
577	for 4th	V. S. Hazare (288)/Gul Mahomed (319), Baroda v Holkar at Baroda	1946-47
576	for 2nd	S. T. Jayasuriya (340)/R. S. Mahanama (225), Sri Lanka v India at Colombo	1997-98
574*	for 4th	F. M. M. Worrell (255*)/C. L. Walcott (314*), Barbados v Trinidad at Port-of-Spain	1945-46
561	for 1st	Waheed Mirza (324)/Mansoor Akhtar (224*), Karachi Whites v Quetta at Karachi	1976-77
555	for 1st	P. Holmes (224*)/H. Sutcliffe (313), Yorkshire v Essex at Leyton	1932
554	for 1st	J. T. Brown (300)/J. Tunnicliffe (243), Yorks v Derbys at Chesterfield	1898
539	for 3rd	S. D. Jogiyani (282)/R. A. Jadeja (303*), Saurashtra v Gujarat at Surat	2012-13
523	for 3rd	M. A. Carberry (300*)/N. D. McKenzie (237), Hants v Yorks at Southampton	2011
520*	for 5th	C. A. Pujara (302*)/R. A. Jadeja (232*), Saurashtra v Orissa at Rajkot	2008-09
503	for 1st	R. G. L. Carters (209)/A. J. Finch (288*), Cricket Australia XI v New Zealanders at Sydney	2015-16
502*	for 4th	F. M. M. Worrell (308*)/J. D. C. Goddard (218*), Barbados v Trinidad at Bridgetown	1943-44
501	for 3rd	A. N. Petersen (286)/A. G. Prince (261), Lancs v Glam at Colwyn Bay	2015

HIGHEST PARTNERSHIPS FOR EACH WICKET

First Wicket

561	Waheed Mirza/Mansoor Akhtar, Karachi Whites v Quetta at Karachi.	1976-77
555	P. Holmes/H. Sutcliffe, Yorkshire v Essex at Leyton.	1932
554	J. T. Brown/J. Tunnicliffe, Yorkshire v Derbyshire at Chesterfield	1898
503	**R. G. L. Carters/A. J. Finch, Cricket Aust. XI v New Zealanders at Sydney**	**2015-16**
490	E. H. Bowley/J. G. Langridge, Sussex v Middlesex at Hove	1933

Second Wicket

580	Rafatullah Mohmand/Aamer Sajjad, WAPDA v Sui S. Gas at Sheikhupura	2009-10
576	S. T. Jayasuriya/R. S. Mahanama, Sri Lanka v India at Colombo	1997-98
480	D. Elgar/R. R. Rossouw, Eagles v Titans at Centurion.	2009-10
475	Zahir Alam/L. S. Rajput, Assam v Tripura at Gauhati	1991-92
465*	J. A. Jameson/R. B. Kanhai, Warwicks v Gloucestershire at Birmingham.	1974

Third Wicket

624	K. C. Sangakkara/D. P. M. D. Jayawardene, Sri Lanka v SA at Colombo.	2006
539	S. D. Jogiyani/R. A. Jadeja, Saurashtra v Gujarat at Surat	2012-13
523	M. A. Carberry/N. D. McKenzie, Hampshire v Yorks at Southampton	2011
501	**A. N. Petersen/A. G. Prince, Lancashire v Glamorgan at Colwyn Bay**	**2015**
467	A. H. Jones/M. D. Crowe, New Zealand v Sri Lanka at Wellington	1990-91

Fourth Wicket

577	V. S. Hazare/Gul Mahomed, Baroda v Holkar at Baroda.	1946-47
574*	C. L. Walcott/F. M. M. Worrell, Barbados v Trinidad at Port-of-Spain.	1945-46
502*	F. M. M. Worrell/J. D. C. Goddard, Barbados v Trinidad at Bridgetown	1943-44
470	A. I. Kallicharran/G. W. Humpage, Warwicks v Lancs at Southport	1982
462*	D. W. Hookes/W. B. Phillips, South Australia v Tasmania at Adelaide	1986-87

Fifth Wicket

520*	C. A. Pujara/R. A. Jadeja, Saurashtra v Orissa at Rajkot	2008-09
494	Marshall Ayub/Mehrab Hossain, Central Zone v East Zone at Bogra	2012-13
479	Misbah-ul-Haq/Usman Arshad, Sui N. Gas v Lahore Shalimar at Lahore	2009-10
464*	M. E. Waugh/S. R. Waugh, New South Wales v Western Australia at Perth. . . .	1990-91
423	**Mosaddek Hossain/Al-Amin, Barisal v Rangpur at Savar**	**2014-15**

Sixth Wicket

487*	G. A. Headley/C. C. Passailaigue, Jamaica v Lord Tennyson's XI at Kingston. .	1931-32
428	W. W. Armstrong/M. A. Noble, Australians v Sussex at Hove	1902
417	W. P. Saha/L. R. Shukla, Bengal v Assam at Kolkata	2010-11
411	R. M. Poore/E. G. Wynyard, Hampshire v Somerset at Taunton	1899
386	**K. K. Nair/K. L. Rahul, Karnataka v Tamil Nadu at Mumbai**	**2014-15**

Seventh Wicket

460	Bhupinder Singh, jun./P. Dharmani, Punjab v Delhi at Delhi	1994-95
371	M. R. Marsh/S. M. Whiteman, Australia A v India A at Brisbane	2014
366*	**J. M. Bairstow/T. T. Bresnan, Yorkshire v Durham at Chester-le-Street** . . .	**2015**
347	D. St E. Atkinson/C. C. Depeiza, West Indies v Australia at Bridgetown	1954-55
347	Farhad Reza/Sanjamul Islam, Rajshahi v Chittagong at Savar.	2013-14

Eighth Wicket

433	A. Sims and V. T. Trumper, A. Sims' Aust. XI v Canterbury at Christchurch...	1913-14
392	A. Mishra/J. Yadav, Haryana v Karnataka at Hubli	2012-13
332	I. J. L. Trott/S. C. J. Broad, England v Pakistan at Lord's	2010
313	Wasim Akram/Saqlain Mushtaq, Pakistan v Zimbabwe at Sheikhupura	1996-97
292	R. Peel/Lord Hawke, Yorkshire v Warwickshire at Birmingham.	1896

Ninth Wicket

283	A. Warren/J. Chapman, Derbyshire v Warwickshire at Blackwell............	1910
268	J. B. Commins/N. Boje, South Africa A v Mashonaland at Harare	1994-95
261	W. L. Madsen/T. Poynton, Derbyshire v Northants at Northampton	2012
251	J. W. H. T. Douglas/S. N. Hare, Essex v Derbyshire at Leyton	1921
249*†	A. S. Srivastava/K. Seth, Madhya Pradesh v Vidarbha at Indore	2000-01

† *276 unbeaten runs were scored for this wicket in two separate partnerships; after Srivastava retired hurt, Seth and N. D. Hirwani added 27.*

Tenth Wicket

307	A. F. Kippax/J. E. H. Hooker, New South Wales v Victoria at Melbourne	1928-29
249	C. T. Sarwate/S. N. Banerjee, Indians v Surrey at The Oval	1946
239	Aqeel Arshad/Ali Raza, Lahore Whites v Hyderabad at Lahore	2004-05
235	F. E. Woolley/A. Fielder, Kent v Worcestershire at Stourbridge	1909
233	Ajay Sharma/Maninder Singh, Delhi v Bombay at Bombay	1991-92

There have been only 13 last-wicket stands of 200 or more.

UNUSUAL DISMISSALS

Handled the Ball

There have been **60** instances in first-class cricket. The most recent are:

D. J. Watson	Dolphins v Eagles at Bloemfontein	2004-05
M. Zondeki	Cape Cobras v Eagles at Bloemfontein	2006-07
L. N. Mosena	Free State v Limpopo at Bloemfontein	2006-07
W. S. A. Williams	Canterbury v Otago at Dunedin	2012-13
E. Lewis	Trinidad & Tobago v Leeward Islands at Port-of-Spain ...	2013-14
C. A. Pujara	Derbyshire v Leicestershire at Derby	2014
I. Khan	**Dolphins v Lions at Johannesburg**	**2014-15**

Obstructing the Field

There have been **25** instances in first-class cricket. T. Straw of Worcestershire was given out for obstruction v Warwickshire in both 1899 and 1901. The most recent are:

K. N. S. Fernando	Lankan v Army at Welisara	2006-07
H. R. Jadhav	Baroda v Uttar Pradesh at Baroda	2006-07
Riaz Kail	Abbottabad v Quetta at Abbottabad	2009-10
M. R. Ramprakash	Surrey v Gloucestershire at Cheltenham	2011
Z. E. Surkari	Canada v Afghanistan at King City	2011
Nasir Ahmadzai	Afghanistan v Zimbabwe A at Harare	2014
W. E. Bell	**Northern Cape v Border at Kimberley.**	**2015-16**

Hit the Ball Twice

There have been **21** instances in first-class cricket. The last occurrence in England involved J. H. King of Leicestershire v Surrey at The Oval in 1906. The most recent are:

Aziz Malik	Lahore Division v Faisalabad at Sialkot.	1984-85
Javed Mohammad	Multan v Karachi Whites at Sahiwal	1986-87
Shahid Pervez	Jammu & Kashmir v Punjab at Srinagar	1986-87
Ali Naqvi	PNSC v National Bank at Faisalabad	1998-99
A. George	Tamil Nadu v Maharashtra at Pune	1998-99
Maqsood Raza	Lahore Division v PNSC at Sheikhupura.	1999-2000
D. Mahajan	Jammu & Kashmir v Bihar at Jammu	2005-06

Timed Out

There have been **five** instances in first-class cricket:

A. Jordaan	Eastern Province v Transvaal at Port Elizabeth (SACB match).	1987-88
H. Yadav	Tripura v Orissa at Cuttack.	1997-98
V. C. Drakes	Border v Free State at East London	2002-03
A. J. Harris	Nottinghamshire v Durham UCCE at Nottingham.	2003
R. A. Austin	Combined Campuses & Colleges v Windward Is at Arnos Vale	2013-14

BOWLING RECORDS

TEN WICKETS IN AN INNINGS

In the history of first-class cricket, there have been **80** instances of a bowler taking all ten wickets in an innings, plus a further three instances of ten wickets in 12-a-side matches. Occurrences since the Second World War:

	O	M	R		
*W. E. Hollies (Warwickshire).	20.4	4	49	v Notts at Birmingham	1946
J. M. Sims (East).	18.4	2	90	v West at Kingston	1948
T. E. Bailey (Essex).	39.4	9	90	v Lancashire at Clacton.	1949
J. K. Graveney (Glos.)	18.4	2	66	v Derbyshire at Chesterfield	1949
R. Berry (Lancashire)	36.2	9	102	v Worcestershire at Blackpool	1953
S. P. Gupte (President's XI)	24.2	7	78	v Combined XI at Bombay	1954-55
J. C. Laker (Surrey).	46	18	88	v Australians at The Oval	1956
J. C. Laker (England)	51.2	23	53	v Australia at Manchester	1956
G. A. R. Lock (Surrey)	29.1	18	54	v Kent at Blackheath.	1956
K. Smales (Nottinghamshire)	41.3	20	66	v Gloucestershire at Stroud.	1956
P. M. Chatterjee (Bengal).	19	11	20	v Assam at Jorhat	1956-57
J. D. Bannister (Warwickshire).	23.3	11	41	v Comb. Services at Birmingham†	1959
A. J. G. Pearson (Cambridge U.)	30.3	8	78	v Leics at Loughborough	1961
N. I. Thomson (Sussex).	34.2	19	49	v Warwickshire at Worthing.	1964
P. J. Allan (Queensland)	15.6	3	61	v Victoria at Melbourne	1965-66
I. J. Brayshaw (W. Australia)	17.6	4	44	v Victoria at Perth	1967-68
Shahid Mahmood (Karachi Whites)	25	5	58	v Khairpur at Karachi	1969-70
E. E. Hemmings (International XI)	49.3	14	175	v West Indies XI at Kingston	1982-83
P. Sunderam (Rajasthan).	22	5	78	v Vidarbha at Jodhpur.	1985-86
S. T. Jefferies (W. Province).	22.5	7	59	v Orange Free State at Cape Town	1987-88
Imran Adil (Bahawalpur)	22.5	3	92	v Faisalabad at Faisalabad	1989-90
G. P. Wickremasinghe (Sinhalese)	19.2	5	41	v Kalutara at Colombo	1991-92
R. L. Johnson (Middlesex)	18.5	6	45	v Derbyshire at Derby.	1994
Naeem Akhtar (Rawalpindi B)	21.3	10	28	v Peshawar at Peshawar	1995-96
A. Kumble (India).	26.3	9	74	v Pakistan at Delhi	1998-99

	O	M	R		
D. S. Mohanty (East Zone)	19	5	46	v South Zone at Agartala	2000-01
O. D. Gibson (Durham)	17.3	1	47	v Hampshire at Chester-le-Street	2007
M. W. Olivier (Warriors)	26.3	4	65	v Eagles at Bloemfontein	2007-08
Zulfiqar Babar (Multan)	39.4	3	143	v Islamabad at Multan	2009-10

*   *W. E. Hollies bowled seven and had three lbw. The only other instance of a bowler achieving the feat without the direct assistance of a fielder came in 1850 when J. Wisden bowled all ten, for North v South at Lord's.*

†   *Mitchells & Butlers Ground.*

OUTSTANDING BOWLING ANALYSES

	O	M	R	W		
H. Verity (Yorkshire)	19.4	16	10	10	v Nottinghamshire at Leeds	1932
G. Elliott (Victoria)	19	17	2	9	v Tasmania at Launceston	1857-58
Ahad Khan (Railways)	6.3	4	7	9	v Dera Ismail Khan at Lahore	1964-65
J. C. Laker (England)	14	12	2	8	v The Rest at Bradford	1950
D. Shackleton (Hampshire)	11.1	7	4	8	v Somerset at Weston-s-Mare	1955
E. Peate (Yorkshire)	16	11	5	8	v Surrey at Holbeck	1883
K. M. Dabengwa (Westerns)	4.4	3	1	7	v Northerns at Harare	2006-07
F. R. Spofforth (Australians)	8.3	6	3	7	v England XI at Birmingham	1884
W. A. Henderson (NE Transvaal)	9.3	7	4	7	v OFS at Bloemfontein	1937-38
Rajinder Goel (Haryana)	7	4	4	7	v Jammu & Kashmir at Chandigarh	1977-78
N. W. Bracken (NSW)	7	5	4	7	v South Australia at Sydney	2004-05
V. I. Smith (South Africans)	4.5	3	1	6	v Derbyshire at Derby	1947
S. Cosstick (Victoria)	21.1	20	1	6	v Tasmania at Melbourne	1868-69
Israr Ali (Bahawalpur)	11	10	1	6	v Dacca U. at Bahawalpur	1957-58
A. D. Pougher (MCC)	3	3	0	5	v Australians at Lord's	1896
G. R. Cox (Sussex)	6	6	0	5	v Somerset at Weston-s-Mare	1921
R. K. Tyldesley (Lancashire)	5	5	0	5	v Leicestershire at Manchester	1924
P. T. Mills (Gloucestershire)	6.4	6	0	5	v Somerset at Bristol	1928

MOST WICKETS IN A MATCH

19-90	J. C. Laker	England v Australia at Manchester	1956
17-48†	C. Blythe	Kent v Northamptonshire at Northampton	1907
17-50	C. T. B. Turner	Australians v England XI at Hastings	1888
17-54	W. P. Howell	Australians v Western Province at Cape Town	1902-03
17-56	C. W. L. Parker	Gloucestershire v Essex at Gloucester	1925
17-67	A. P. Freeman	Kent v Sussex at Hove	1922
17-89	W. G. Grace	Gloucestershire v Nottinghamshire at Cheltenham	1877
17-89	F. C. L. Matthews	Nottinghamshire v Northants at Nottingham	1923
17-91	H. Dean	Lancashire v Yorkshire at Liverpool	1913
17-91†	H. Verity	Yorkshire v Essex at Leyton	1933
17-92	A. P. Freeman	Kent v Warwickshire at Folkestone	1932
17-103	W. Mycroft	Derbyshire v Hampshire at Southampton	1876
17-106	G. R. Cox	Sussex v Warwickshire at Horsham	1926
17-106†	T. W. J. Goddard	Gloucestershire v Kent at Bristol	1939
17-119	W. Mead	Essex v Hampshire at Southampton	1895
17-137	W. Brearley	Lancashire v Somerset at Manchester	1905
17-137	J. M. Davison	Canada v USA at Fort Lauderdale	2004
17-159	S. F. Barnes	England v South Africa at Johannesburg	1913-14
17-201	G. Giffen	South Australia v Victoria at Adelaide	1885-86
17-212	J. C. Clay	Glamorgan v Worcestershire at Swansea	1937

†   *Achieved in a single day.*

H. Arkwright took 18-96 for MCC v Gentlemen of Kent in a 12-a-side match at Canterbury in 1861.
   *There have been **58** instances of a bowler taking 16 wickets in an 11-a-side match, the most recent being 16-100 by J. U. Chaturanga for Singha v Antonians at Gampaha, 2010-11.*

FOUR WICKETS WITH CONSECUTIVE BALLS

There have been **42** instances in first-class cricket. R. J. Crisp achieved the feat twice, for Western Province in 1931-32 and 1933-34. A. E. Trott took four in four balls and another hat-trick in the same innings for Middlesex v Somerset in 1907, his benefit match. Occurrences since 2005:

C. M. Willoughby	Cape Cobras v Dolphins at Durban	2005-06
Tabish Khan	Karachi Whites v ZTBL at Karachi	2009-10
Kamran Hussain	Habib Bank v Lahore Shalimar at Lahore	2009-10
N. Wagner	Otago v Wellington at Queenstown	2010-11
Khalid Usman	Abbottabad v Karachi Blues at Karachi	2011-12
Mahmudullah	Central Zone v North Zone at Savar	2013-14
A. C. Thomas	Somerset v Sussex at Taunton	2014
Taj Wali	**Peshawar v Port Qasim Authority at Peshawar**	**2015-16**

In their match with England at The Oval in 1863, Surrey lost four wickets in the course of a four-ball over from G. Bennett.

Sussex lost five wickets in the course of the final (six-ball) over of their match with Surrey at Eastbourne in 1972. P. I. Pocock, who had taken three wickets in his previous over, captured four more, taking in all seven wickets with 11 balls, a feat unique in first-class matches. (The eighth wicket fell to a run-out.)

In 1996, K. D. James took four in four balls for Hampshire against Indians at Southampton and then scored a century, a feat later emulated by Mahmudullah.

HAT-TRICKS

Double Hat-Trick

Besides Trott's performance, which is mentioned in the preceding section, the following instances are recorded of players having performed the hat-trick twice in the same match, Rao doing so in the same innings.

A. Shaw	Nottinghamshire v Gloucestershire at Nottingham	1884
T. J. Matthews	Australia v South Africa at Manchester	1912
C. W. L. Parker	Gloucestershire v Middlesex at Bristol	1924
R. O. Jenkins	Worcestershire v Surrey at Worcester	1949
J. S. Rao	Services v Northern Punjab at Amritsar	1963-64
Amin Lakhani	Combined XI v Indians at Multan	1978-79

Five Wickets in Six Balls

W. H. Copson	Derbyshire v Warwickshire at Derby	1937
W. A. Henderson	N.E. Transvaal v Orange Free State at Bloemfontein	1937-38
P. I. Pocock	Surrey v Sussex at Eastbourne	1972
Yasir Arafat	Rawalpindi v Faisalabad at Rawalpindi	2004-05
N. Wagner	Otago v Wellington at Queenstown	2010-11

Yasir Arafat's five wickets were spread across two innings and interrupted only by a no-ball. Wagner was the first to take five wickets in a single over.

Most Hat-Tricks

D. V. P. Wright	7	R. G. Barlow	4	T. G. Matthews	4
T. W. J. Goddard	6	Fazl-e-Akbar	4	M. J. Procter	4
C. W. L. Parker	6	A. P. Freeman	4	T. Richardson	4
S. Haigh	5	J. T. Hearne	4	F. R. Spofforth	4
V. W. C. Jupp	5	J. C. Laker	4	F. S. Trueman	4
A. E. G. Rhodes	5	G. A. R. Lock	4		
F. A. Tarrant	5	G. G. Macaulay	4		

Hat-Trick on Debut

There have been **18** instances in first-class cricket. Occurrences since 2000:

S. M. Harwood	Victoria v Tasmania at Melbourne	2002-03
P. Connell	Ireland v Netherlands at Rotterdam	2008
A. Mithun	Karnataka v Uttar Pradesh at Meerut	2009-10
Zohaib Shera	Karachi Whites v National Bank at Karachi	2009-10

R. R. Phillips (Border) took a hat-trick in his first over in first-class cricket (v Eastern Province at Port Elizabeth, 1939-40) having previously played in four matches without bowling.

250 WICKETS IN A SEASON

	Season	O	M	R	W	Avge
A. P. Freeman	1928	1,976.1	423	5,489	304	18.05
A. P. Freeman	1933	2,039	651	4,549	298	15.26
T. Richardson	1895‡	1,690.1	463	4,170	290	14.37
C. T. B. Turner	1888†	2,427.2	1,127	3,307	283	11.68
A. P. Freeman	1931	1,618	360	4,307	276	15.60
A. P. Freeman	1930	1,914.3	472	4,632	275	16.84
T. Richardson	1897‡	1,603.4	495	3,945	273	14.45
A. P. Freeman	1929	1,670.5	381	4,879	267	18.27
W. Rhodes	1900	1,553	455	3,606	261	13.81
J. T. Hearne	1896‡	2,003.1	818	3,670	257	14.28
A. P. Freeman	1932	1,565.5	404	4,149	253	16.39
W. Rhodes	1901	1,565	505	3,797	251	15.12

†   *Indicates 4-ball overs.*   ‡   *5-ball overs.*

In four consecutive seasons (1928–1931), A. P. Freeman took 1,122 wickets, and in eight consecutive seasons (1928–1935), 2,090 wickets. In each of these eight seasons he took over 200 wickets.

   T. Richardson took 1,005 wickets in four consecutive seasons (1894–1897).

   The earliest date by which any bowler has taken 100 wickets in an English season is June 12, achieved by J. T. Hearne in 1896 and C. W. L. Parker in 1931, when A. P. Freeman did it on June 13.

100 WICKETS IN A SEASON MOST TIMES

(Includes overseas tours and seasons)

W. Rhodes 23	C. W. L. Parker 16	G. H. Hirst 15
D. Shackleton 20	R. T. D. Perks 16	A. S. Kennedy 15
A. P. Freeman 17	F. J. Titmus 16	
T. W. J. Goddard 16	J. T. Hearne 15	

D. Shackleton reached 100 wickets in 20 successive seasons – 1949–1968.

   Since the reduction of County Championship matches in 1969, D. L. Underwood (five times) and J. K. Lever (four times) are the only bowlers to have reached 100 wickets in a season more than twice. The highest aggregate in a season since 1969 is 134 by M. D. Marshall in 1982.

   The most instances of 200 wickets in a season is eight by A. P. Freeman, who did it in eight successive seasons – 1928 to 1935 – including 304 in 1928. C. W. L. Parker did it five times, T. W. J. Goddard four times, and J. T. Hearne, G. A. Lohmann, W. Rhodes, T. Richardson, M. W. Tate and H. Verity three times each.

   The last bowler to reach 200 wickets in a season was G. A. R. Lock (212 in 1957).

An expanded and regularly updated online version of the Records can be found at www.wisdenrecords.com

100 WICKETS IN A SEASON OUTSIDE ENGLAND

W		Season	Country	R	Avge
116	M. W. Tate	1926-27	India/Ceylon	1,599	13.78
113	Kabir Khan	1998-99	Pakistan	1,706	15.09
107	Ijaz Faqih	1985-86	Pakistan	1,719	16.06
106	C. T. B. Turner	1887-88	Australia	1,441	13.59
106	R. Benaud	1957-58	South Africa	2,056	19.39
105	Murtaza Hussain	1995-96	Pakistan	1,882	17.92
104	S. F. Barnes	1913-14	South Africa	1,117	10.74
104	Sajjad Akbar	1989-90	Pakistan	2,328	22.38
103	Abdul Qadir	1982-83	Pakistan	2,367	22.98

LEADING BOWLERS IN AN ENGLISH SEASON

(Qualification: 10 wickets in 10 innings)

Season	Leading wicket-taker	Wkts	Avge	Top of averages	Wkts	Avge
1946	W. E. Hollies	184	15.60	A. Booth.	111	11.61
1947	T. W. J. Goddard	238	17.30	J. C. Clay	65	16.44
1948	J. E. Walsh	174	19.56	J. C. Clay	41	14.17
1949	R. O. Jenkins	183	21.19	T. W. J. Goddard	160	19.18
1950	R. Tattersall	193	13.59	R. Tattersall	193	13.59
1951	R. Appleyard	200	14.14	R. Appleyard	200	14.14
1952	J. H. Wardle	177	19.54	F. S. Trueman.	61	13.78
1953	B. Dooland	172	16.58	C. J. Knott	38	13.71
1954	B. Dooland	196	15.48	J. B. Statham	92	14.13
1955	G. A. R. Lock	216	14.49	R. Appleyard	85	13.01
1956	D. J. Shepherd	177	15.36	G. A. R. Lock	155	12.46
1957	G. A. R. Lock	212	12.02	G. A. R. Lock	212	12.02
1958	G. A. R. Lock	170	12.08	H. L. Jackson	143	10.99
1959	D. Shackleton.	148	21.55	J. B. Statham	139	15.01
1960	F. S. Trueman	175	13.98	J. B. Statham	135	12.31
1961	J. A. Flavell	171	17.79	J. A. Flavell	171	17.79
1962	D. Shackleton.	172	20.15	C. Cook	58	17.13
1963	D. Shackleton.	146	16.75	C. C. Griffith	119	12.83
1964	D. Shackleton.	142	20.40	J. A. Standen	64	13.00
1965	D. Shackleton.	144	16.08	H. J. Rhodes.	119	11.04
1966	D. L. Underwood	157	13.80	D. L. Underwood	157	13.80
1967	T. W. Cartwright	147	15.52	D. L. Underwood	136	12.39
1968	R. Illingworth.	131	14.36	O. S. Wheatley.	82	12.95
1969	R. M. H. Cottam.	109	21.04	A. Ward	69	14.82
1970	D. J. Shepherd	106	19.16	Majid Khan	11	18.81
1971	L. R. Gibbs.	131	18.89	G. G. Arnold	83	17.12
1972	T. W. Cartwright	98	18.64	I. M. Chappell	10	10.60
	B. Stead	98	20.38			
1973	B. S. Bedi.	105	17.94	T. W. Cartwright	89	15.84
1974	A. M. E. Roberts	119	13.62	A. M. E. Roberts	119	13.62
1975	P. G. Lee	112	18.45	A. M. E. Roberts	57	15.80
1976	G. A. Cope	93	24.13	M. A. Holding	55	14.38
1977	M. J. Procter.	109	18.04	R. A. Woolmer.	19	15.21
1978	D. L. Underwood	110	14.49	D. L. Underwood	110	14.49
1979	D. L. Underwood	106	14.85	J. Garner.	55	13.83
	J. K. Lever	106	17.30			
1980	R. D. Jackman	121	15.40	J. Garner.	49	13.93
1981	R. J. Hadlee	105	14.89	R. J. Hadlee	105	14.89
1982	M. D. Marshall.	134	15.73	R. J. Hadlee	61	14.57
1983	J. K. Lever	106	16.28	Imran Khan	12	7.16
	D. L. Underwood	106	19.28			
1984	R. J. Hadlee	117	14.05	R. J. Hadlee	117	14.05

Season	Leading wicket-taker	Wkts	Avge	Top of averages	Wkts	Avge
1985	N. V. Radford	101	24.68	R. M. Ellison	65	17.20
1986	C. A. Walsh	118	18.17	M. D. Marshall	100	15.08
1987	N. V. Radford	109	20.81	R. J. Hadlee	97	12.64
1988	F. D. Stephenson	125	18.31	M. D. Marshall	42	13.16
1989	D. R. Pringle	94	18.64	T. M. Alderman	70	15.64
1989	S. L. Watkin	94	25.09			
1990	N. A. Foster	94	26.61	I. R. Bishop	59	19.05
1991	Waqar Younis	113	14.65	Waqar Younis	113	14.65
1992	C. A. Walsh	92	15.96	C. A. Walsh	92	15.96
1993	S. L. Watkin	92	22.80	Wasim Akram	59	19.27
1994	M. M. Patel	90	22.86	C. E. L. Ambrose	77	14.45
1995	A. Kumble	105	20.40	A. A. Donald	89	16.07
1996	C. A. Walsh	85	16.84	C. E. L. Ambrose	43	16.67
1997	A. M. Smith	83	17.63	A. A. Donald	60	15.63
1998	C. A. Walsh	106	17.31	V. J. Wells	36	14.27
1999	A. Sheriyar	92	24.70	Saqlain Mushtaq	58	11.37
2000	G. D. McGrath	80	13.21	C. A. Walsh	40	11.42
2001	R. J. Kirtley	75	23.32	G. D. McGrath	40	15.60
2002	M. J. Saggers	83	21.51	C. P. Schofield	18	18.38
2002	K. J. Dean	83	23.50			
2003	Mushtaq Ahmed	103	24.65	Shoaib Akhtar	34	17.05
2004	Mushtaq Ahmed	84	27.59	D. S. Lehmann	15	17.40
2005	S. K. Warne	87	22.50	M. Muralitharan	36	15.00
2006	Mushtaq Ahmed	102	19.91	Naved-ul-Hasan	35	16.71
2007	Mushtaq Ahmed	90	25.66	Harbhajan Singh	37	18.54
2008	J. A. Tomlinson	67	24.76	M. Davies	41	14.63
2009	Danish Kaneria	75	23.69	G. Onions	69	19.95
2010	A. R. Adams	68	22.17	J. K. H. Naik	35	17.68
2011	D. D. Masters	93	18.13	T. T. Bresnan	29	17.68
2012	G. Onions	72	14.73	G. Onions	72	14.73
2013	G. Onions	73	18.92	T. A. Copeland	45	18.26
2014	M. H. A. Foottit	84	19.19	G. R. Napier	52	15.63
2015	**C. Rushworth**	**90**	**20.54**	**R. J. Sidebottom**	**43**	**18.09**

MOST WICKETS

Dates in italics denote the first half of an overseas season; i.e. *1970* denotes the 1970-71 season.

		Career	W	R	Avge
1	W. Rhodes	1898–1930	4,187	69,993	16.71
2	A. P. Freeman	1914–1936	3,776	69,577	18.42
3	C. W. L. Parker	1903–1935	3,278	63,817	19.46
4	J. T. Hearne	1888–1923	3,061	54,352	17.75
5	T. W. J. Goddard	1922–1952	2,979	59,116	19.84
6	W. G. Grace	1865–1908	2,876	51,545	17.92
7	A. S. Kennedy	1907–1936	2,874	61,034	21.23
8	D. Shackleton	1948–1969	2,857	53,303	18.65
9	G. A. R. Lock	1946–*1970*	2,844	54,709	19.23
10	F. J. Titmus	1949–1982	2,830	63,313	22.37
11	M. W. Tate	1912–1937	2,784	50,571	18.16
12	G. H. Hirst	1891–1929	2,739	51,282	18.72
13	C. Blythe	1899–1914	2,506	42,136	16.81

Some works of reference provide career figures which differ from those in this list, owing to the exclusion or inclusion of matches recognised or not recognised as first-class by Wisden. A fuller list can be found in Wisdens up to 2011.

Current Players with 750 Wickets

	Career	W	R	Avge
G. Chapple	1992–2015	985	26,314	26.71
H. M. R. K. B. Herath	1996–2015	921	23,368	25.37
D. Hettiarachchi	1994–2015	856	19,478	22.75
Yasir Arafat	1997–2015	787	18,851	23.95
Harbhajan Singh	1997–2015	776	22,400	28.86
S. Weerakoon	1995–2014	775	16,478	21.26

ALL-ROUND RECORDS

REMARKABLE ALL-ROUND MATCHES

V. E. Walker	20*	108	10-74	4-17	England v Surrey at The Oval	1859
W. G. Grace	104		2-60	10-49	MCC v Oxford University at Oxford .	1886
G. Giffen	271		9-96	7-70	South Australia v Victoria at Adelaide	1891-92
B. J. T. Bosanquet	103	100*	3-75	8-53	Middlesex v Sussex at Lord's	1905
G. H. Hirst	111	117*	6-70	5-45	Yorkshire v Somerset at Bath	1906
F. D. Stephenson	111	117	4-105	7-117	Notts v Yorkshire at Nottingham.	1988

E. M. Grace, for MCC v Gentlemen of Kent in a 12-a-side match at Canterbury in 1862, scored 192* and took 5-77 and 10-69.

HUNDRED AND HAT-TRICK

G. Giffen, Australians v Lancashire at Manchester	1884
*W. E. Roller, Surrey v Sussex at The Oval	1885
W. B. Burns, Worcestershire v Gloucestershire at Worcester	1913
V. W. C. Jupp, Sussex v Essex at Colchester	1921
R. E. S. Wyatt, MCC v Ceylonese at Colombo	1926-27
L. N. Constantine, West Indians v Northamptonshire at Northampton	1928
D. E. Davies, Glamorgan v Leicestershire at Leicester	1937
V. M. Merchant, Dr C. R. Pereira's XI v Sir Homi Mehta's XI at Bombay	1946-47
M. J. Procter, Gloucestershire v Essex at Westcliff-on-Sea.	1972
M. J. Procter, Gloucestershire v Leicestershire at Bristol	1979
†K. D. James, Hampshire v Indians at Southampton.	1996
J. E. C. Franklin, Gloucestershire v Derbyshire at Cheltenham.	2009
Sohag Gazi, Barisal v Khulna at Khulna	2012-13
Sohag Gazi, Bangladesh v New Zealand at Chittagong	2013-14
†Mahmudullah, Central Zone v North Zone at Savar	2013-14

* *W. E. Roller is the only player to combine 200 with a hat-trick.*

† *K. D. James and Mahmudullah both combined 100 with four wickets in four balls (Mahmudullah's split between two innings).*

THE DOUBLE

The double was traditionally regarded as 1,000 runs and 100 wickets in an English season. The feat became exceptionally rare after the reduction of County Championship matches in 1969.

Remarkable Seasons

	Season	R	W		Season	R	W
G. H. Hirst	1906	2,385	208	J. H. Parks	1937	3,003	101

1,000 Runs and 100 Wickets

W. Rhodes	16	W. G. Grace	8	F. J. Titmus	8
G. H. Hirst	14	M. S. Nichols	8	F. E. Woolley	7
V. W. C. Jupp	10	A. E. Relf	8	G. E. Tribe	7
W. E. Astill	9	F. A. Tarrant	8		
T. E. Bailey	8	M. W. Tate	8†		

† *M. W. Tate also scored 1,193 runs and took 116 wickets on the 1926-27 MCC tour of India and Ceylon.*

R. J. Hadlee (1984) and F. D. Stephenson (1988) are the only players to perform the feat since the reduction of County Championship matches in 1969. A complete list of those performing the feat before then may be found on page 202 of the 1982 Wisden. T. E. Bailey (1959) was the last player to achieve 2,000 runs and 100 wickets in a season; M. W. Tate (1925) the last to reach 1,000 runs and 200 wickets. Full lists may be found in Wisdens up to 2003.

Wicketkeeper's Double

The only wicketkeepers to achieve 1,000 runs and 100 dismissals in a season were L. E. G. Ames (1928, 1929 and 1932, when he scored 2,482 runs) and J. T. Murray (1957).

WICKETKEEPING RECORDS

MOST DISMISSALS IN AN INNINGS

9 (8ct, 1st)	Tahir Rashid	Habib Bank v PACO at Gujranwala	1992-93
9 (7ct, 2st)	W. R. James*	Matabeleland v Mashonaland CD at Bulawayo	1995-96
8 (all ct)	A. T. W. Grout	Queensland v Western Australia at Brisbane	1959-60
8 (all ct)†	D. E. East	Essex v Somerset at Taunton	1985
8 (all ct)	S. A. Marsh‡	Kent v Middlesex at Lord's	1991
8 (6ct, 2st)	T. J. Zoehrer	Australians v Surrey at The Oval	1993
8 (7ct, 1st)	D. S. Berry	Victoria v South Australia at Melbourne	1996-97
8 (7ct, 1st)	Y. S. S. Mendis	Bloomfield v Kurunegala Youth at Colombo	2000-01
8 (7ct, 1st)	S. Nath§	Assam v Tripura at Guwahati	2001-02
8 (all ct)	J. N. Batty¶	Surrey v Kent at The Oval	2004
8 (all ct)	Golam Mabud	Sylhet v Dhaka at Dhaka	2005-06
8 (all ct)	A. Z. M. Dyili	Eastern Province v Free State at Port Elizabeth	2009-10
8 (all ct)	D. C. de Boorder	Otago v Wellington at Wellington	2009-10
8 (all ct)	R. S. Second	Free State v North West at Bloemfontein	2011-12
8 (all ct)	T. L. Tsolekile	South Africa A v Sri Lanka A at Durban	2012

*There have been **101** further instances of seven dismissals in an innings. R. W. Taylor achieved the feat three times, and G. J. Hopkins, Kamran Akmal, I. Khaleel, S. A. Marsh, K. J. Piper, Shahin Hossain, T. L. Tsolekile and Wasim Bari twice. Khaleel did it twice in the same match. Marsh's and Tsolekile's two instances both included one of eight dismissals – see above. H. Yarnold made six stumpings and one catch in an innings for Worcestershire v Scotland at Dundee in 1951. A fuller list can be found in Wisdens before 2004.*

*	*W. R. James also scored 99 and 99 not out.*	†	*The first eight wickets to fall.*
‡	*S. A. Marsh also scored 108 not out.*	§	*On his only first-class appearance.*
¶	*J. N. Batty also scored 129.*		

WICKETKEEPERS' HAT-TRICKS

W. H. Brain, Gloucestershire v Somerset at Cheltenham, 1893 – three stumpings off successive balls from C. L. Townsend.

G. O. Dawkes, Derbyshire v Worcestershire at Kidderminster, 1958 – three catches off successive balls from H. L. Jackson.

R. C. Russell, Gloucestershire v Surrey at The Oval, 1986 – three catches off successive balls from C. A. Walsh and D. V. Lawrence (2).

MOST DISMISSALS IN A MATCH

14 (11ct, 3st)	I. Khaleel	Hyderabad v Assam at Guwahati	2011-12
13 (11ct, 2st)	W. R. James*	Matabeleland v Mashonaland CD at Bulawayo	1995-96
12 (8ct, 4st)	E. Pooley	Surrey v Sussex at The Oval	1868
12 (9ct, 3st)	D. Tallon	Queensland v New South Wales at Sydney	1938-39
12 (9ct, 3st)	H. B. Taber	New South Wales v South Australia at Adelaide	1968-69
12 (all ct)	P. D. McGlashan	Northern Districts v Central Districts at Whangarei	2009-10
12 (11ct, 1st)	T. L. Tsolekile	Lions v Dolphins at Johannesburg	2010-11
12 (all ct)	Kashif Mahmood	Lahore Shalimar v Abbottabad at Abbottabad	2010-11
12 (all ct)	R. S. Second	Free State v North West at Bloemfontein	2011-12

* *W. R. James also scored 99 and 99 not out.*

100 DISMISSALS IN A SEASON

128 (79ct, 49st)	L. E. G. Ames	1929	104 (82ct, 22st)	J. T. Murray	1957
122 (70ct, 52st)	L. E. G. Ames	1928	102 (69ct, 33st)	F. H. Huish	1913
110 (63ct, 47st)	H. Yarnold	1949	102 (95ct, 7st)	J. T. Murray	1960
107 (77ct, 30st)	G. Duckworth	1928	101 (62ct, 39st)	F. H. Huish	1911
107 (96ct, 11st)	J. G. Binks	1960	101 (85ct, 16st)	R. Booth	1960
104 (40ct, 64st)	L. E. G. Ames	1932	100 (91ct, 9st)	R. Booth	1964

L. E. G. Ames achieved the two highest stumping totals in a season: 64 in 1932, and 52 in 1928.

MOST DISMISSALS

Dates in italics denote the first half of an overseas season; i.e. *1914* denotes the 1914-15 season.

			Career	M	Ct	St
1	R. W. Taylor	1,649	1960–1988	639	1,473	176
2	J. T. Murray	1,527	1952–1975	635	1,270	257
3	H. Strudwick	1,497	1902–1927	675	1,242	255
4	A. P. E. Knott	1,344	1964–1985	511	1,211	133
5	R. C. Russell	1,320	1981–2004	465	1,192	128
6	F. H. Huish	1,310	1895–1914	497	933	377
7	B. Taylor	1,294	1949–1973	572	1,083	211
8	S. J. Rhodes	1,263	1981–2004	440	1,139	124
9	D. Hunter	1,253	1888–1909	548	906	347
10	H. R. Butt	1,231	1890–1912	550	954	277

Current Players with 500 Dismissals

		Career	M	Ct	St
1,007	C. M. W. Read	1997–2015	321	957	50
804	Kamran Akmal	1997–2015	210	742	62
785	J. S. Foster	2000–2015	257	727	58
709	M. A. Wallace	1999–2015	249	654	55
669	H. A. P. W. Jayawardene	*1997–2014*	249	550	119
648	B. J. Haddin	*1999–2015*	184	608	40
644	P. Mustard	2002–2015	188	625	19
635	G. O. Jones	2001–2015	203	599	36
553	Zulfiqar Jan	*1999–2015*	152	525	28
535	T. L. Tsolekile	*1999–2014*	160	499	36
531	T. R. Ambrose	2001–2015	195	498	33
522	C. D. Hartley	*2003–2015*	118	506	16

Some of these figures include catches taken in the field.

FIELDING RECORDS

excluding wicketkeepers

MOST CATCHES IN AN INNINGS

7	M. J. Stewart	Surrey v Northamptonshire at Northampton	1957
7	A. S. Brown	Gloucestershire v Nottinghamshire at Nottingham	1966
7	R. Clarke	Warwickshire v Lancashire at Liverpool.	2011

MOST CATCHES IN A MATCH

10	W. R. Hammond†	Gloucestershire v Surrey at Cheltenham	1928
9	R. Clarke	Warwickshire v Lancashire at Liverpool.	2011
8	W. B. Burns	Worcestershire v Yorkshire at Bradford	1907
8	F. G. Travers	Europeans v Parsees at Bombay	1923-24
8	A. H. Bakewell	Northamptonshire v Essex at Leyton	1928
8	W. R. Hammond	Gloucestershire v Worcestershire at Cheltenham	1932
8	K. J. Grieves	Lancashire v Sussex at Manchester	1951
8	C. A. Milton	Gloucestershire v Sussex at Hove	1952
8	G. A. R. Lock	Surrey v Warwickshire at The Oval	1957
8	J. M. Prodger	Kent v Gloucestershire at Cheltenham	1961
8	P. M. Walker	Glamorgan v Derbyshire at Swansea.	1970
8	Masood Anwar	Rawalpindi v Lahore Division at Rawalpindi	1983-84
8	M. C. J. Ball	Gloucestershire v Yorkshire at Cheltenham	1994
8	J. D. Carr	Middlesex v Warwickshire at Birmingham.	1995
8	G. A. Hick	Worcestershire v Essex at Chelmsford	2005
8	Naved Yasin	State Bank v Bahawalpur Stags at Bahawalpur.	2014-15
8	**A. M. Rahane**	**India v Sri Lanka at Galle. . . . .**	**2015-16**

† *Hammond also scored a hundred in each innings.*

MOST CATCHES IN A SEASON

78	W. R. Hammond.	1928		71	P. J. Sharpe	1962
77	M. J. Stewart	1957		70	J. Tunnicliffe.	1901
73	P. M. Walker.	1961				

The most catches by a fielder since the reduction of County Championship matches in 1969 is 59 by
G. R. J. Roope in 1971.

MOST CATCHES

Dates in italics denote the first half of an overseas season; i.e. *1970* denotes the 1970-71 season.

		Career	M			Career	M
1,018	F. E. Woolley	1906–1938	979	784	J. G. Langridge. . .	1928–1955	574
887	W. G. Grace	1865–1908	879	764	W. Rhodes	1898–1930	1,107
830	G. A. R. Lock. . . .	1946–*1970*	654	758	C. A. Milton	1948–1974	620
819	W. R. Hammond .	1920–1951	634	754	E. H. Hendren. . . .	1907–1938	833
813	D. B. Close.	1949–1986	786				

*The most catches by a current player is **479** by **M. E. Trescothick** between 1993 and 2015.*

TEAM RECORDS

HIGHEST INNINGS TOTALS

1,107	Victoria v New South Wales at Melbourne	1926-27
1,059	Victoria v Tasmania at Melbourne	1922-23
952-6 dec	Sri Lanka v India at Colombo.	1997-98
951-7 dec	Sind v Baluchistan at Karachi.	1973-74
944-6 dec	Hyderabad v Andhra at Secunderabad	1993-94
918	New South Wales v South Australia at Sydney	1900-01
912-8 dec	Holkar v Mysore at Indore	1945-46
912-6 dec†	Tamil Nadu v Goa at Panjim	1988-89
910-6 dec	Railways v Dera Ismail Khan at Lahore	1964-65
903-7 dec	England v Australia at The Oval	1938
900-6 dec	Queensland v Victoria at Brisbane	2005-06

† *Tamil Nadu's total of 912-6 dec included 52 penalty runs from their opponents' failure to meet the required bowling rate.*

The highest total in a team's second innings is 770 by New South Wales v South Australia at Adelaide in 1920-21.

HIGHEST FOURTH-INNINGS TOTALS

654-5	England v South Africa at Durban	1938-39
	After being set 696 to win. The match was left drawn on the tenth day.	
604	Maharashtra (*set 959 to win*) v Bombay at Poona.	1948-49
576-8	Trinidad (*set 672 to win*) v Barbados at Port-of-Spain	1945-46
572	New South Wales (*set 593 to win*) v South Australia at Sydney.	1907-08
541-7	West Zone (*won*) v South Zone at Hyderabad	2009-10
529-9	Combined XI (*set 579 to win*) v South Africans at Perth	1963-64
518	Victoria (*set 753 to win*) v Queensland at Brisbane	1926-27
513-9	Central Province (*won*) v Southern Province at Kandy.	2003-04
507-7	Cambridge University (*won*) v MCC and Ground at Lord's	1896
506-6	South Australia (*won*) v Queensland at Adelaide	1991-92
503-4	South Zone (*won*) v England A at Gurgaon	2003-04
502-6	Middlesex (*won*) v Nottinghamshire at Nottingham	1925
502-8	Players (*won*) v Gentlemen at Lord's	1900
500-7	South African Universities (*won*) v Western Province at Stellenbosch	1978-79

MOST RUNS IN A DAY (ONE SIDE)

721	Australians (721) v Essex at Southend (1st day).	1948
651	West Indians (651-2) v Leicestershire at Leicester (1st day)	1950
649	New South Wales (649-7) v Otago at Dunedin (2nd day)	1923-24
645	Surrey (645-4) v Hampshire at The Oval (1st day)	1909
644	Oxford U. (644-8) v H. D. G. Leveson Gower's XI at Eastbourne (1st day) . . .	1921
640	Lancashire (640-8) v Sussex at Hove (1st day).	1937
636	Free Foresters (636-7) v Cambridge U. at Cambridge (1st day).	1938
625	Gloucestershire (625-6) v Worcestershire at Dudley (2nd day)	1934

MOST RUNS IN A DAY (BOTH SIDES)

(excluding the above)

685	North (169-8 and 255-7), South (261-8 dec) at Blackpool (2nd day)	1961
666	Surrey (607-4), Northamptonshire (59-2) at Northampton (2nd day).	1920
665	Rest of South Africa (339), Transvaal (326) at Johannesburg (1st day)	1911-12
663	Middlesex (503-4), Leicestershire (160-2) at Leicester (2nd day)	1947
661	Border (201), Griqualand West (460) at Kimberley (1st day).	1920-21
649	Hampshire (570-8), Somerset (79-3) at Taunton (2nd day)	1901

HIGHEST AGGREGATES IN A MATCH

Runs	Wkts		
2,376	37	Maharashtra v Bombay at Poona	1948-49
2,078	40	Bombay v Holkar at Bombay	1944-45
1,981	35	South Africa v England at Durban	1938-39
1,945	18	Canterbury v Wellington at Christchurch	1994-95
1,929	39	New South Wales v South Australia at Sydney	1925-26
1,911	34	New South Wales v Victoria at Sydney	1908-09
1,905	40	Otago v Wellington at Dunedin	1923-24

In Britain

Runs	Wkts		
1,815	28	Somerset v Surrey at Taunton	2002
1,808	20	Sussex v Essex at Hove	1993
1,795	34	Somerset v Northamptonshire at Taunton	2001
1,723	31	England v Australia at Leeds	1948
1,706	23	Hampshire v Warwickshire at Southampton	1997

LOWEST INNINGS TOTALS

12†	Oxford University v MCC and Ground at Oxford	1877
12	Northamptonshire v Gloucestershire at Gloucester	1907
13	Auckland v Canterbury at Auckland	1877-78
13	Nottinghamshire v Yorkshire at Nottingham	1901
14	Surrey v Essex at Chelmsford	1983
15	MCC v Surrey at Lord's	1839
15†	Victoria v MCC at Melbourne	1903-04
15†	Northamptonshire v Yorkshire at Northampton	1908
15	Hampshire v Warwickshire at Birmingham	1922
	Following on, Hampshire scored 521 and won by 155 runs.	
16	MCC and Ground v Surrey at Lord's	1872
16	Derbyshire v Nottinghamshire at Nottingham	1879
16	Surrey v Nottinghamshire at The Oval	1880
16	Warwickshire v Kent at Tonbridge	1913
16	Trinidad v Barbados at Bridgetown	1942-43
16	Border v Natal at East London (first innings)	1959-60
17	Gentlemen of Kent v Gentlemen of England at Lord's	1850
17	Gloucestershire v Australians at Cheltenham	1896
18	The Bs v England at Lord's	1831
18†	Kent v Sussex at Gravesend	1867
18	Tasmania v Victoria at Melbourne	1868-69
18†	Australians v MCC and Ground at Lord's	1896
18	Border v Natal at East London (second innings)	1959-60
18†	Durham MCCU v Durham at Chester-le-Street	2012

† *One man absent.*

At Lord's in 1810, The Bs, with one man absent, were dismissed by England for 6.

LOWEST TOTALS IN A MATCH

34	(16 and 18) Border v Natal at East London	1959-60
42	(27† and 15†) Northamptonshire v Yorkshire at Northampton	1908

† *Northamptonshire batted one man short in each innings.*

LOWEST AGGREGATE IN A COMPLETED MATCH

Runs	Wkts		
85	11†	Quetta v Rawalpindi at Islamabad............................	2008-09
105	31	MCC v Australians at Lord's................................	1878

† *Both teams forfeited their first innings.*

The lowest aggregate in a match in which the losing team was bowled out twice since 1900 is 157 for 22 wickets, Surrey v Worcestershire at The Oval, 1954.

LARGEST VICTORIES

Largest Innings Victories

Inns and 851 runs	Railways (910-6 dec) v Dera Ismail Khan at Lahore............	1964-65
Inns and 666 runs	Victoria (1,059) v Tasmania at Melbourne.....................	1922-23
Inns and 656 runs	Victoria (1,107) v New South Wales at Melbourne..............	1926-27
Inns and 605 runs	New South Wales (918) v South Australia at Sydney............	1900-01
Inns and 579 runs	England (903-7 dec) v Australia at The Oval..................	1938
Inns and 575 runs	Sind (951-7 dec) v Baluchistan at Karachi....................	1973-74
Inns and 527 runs	New South Wales (713) v South Australia at Adelaide..........	1908-09
Inns and 517 runs	Australians (675) v Nottinghamshire at Nottingham............	1921

Largest Victories by Runs Margin

685 runs	New South Wales (235 and 761-8 dec) v Queensland at Sydney ..	1929-30
675 runs	England (521 and 342-8 dec) v Australia at Brisbane...........	1928-29
638 runs	New South Wales (304 and 770) v South Australia at Adelaide ...	1920-21
609 runs	Muslim Comm. Bank (575 and 282-0 dec) v WAPDA at Lahore ..	1977-78

Victory Without Losing a Wicket

Lancashire (166-0 dec and 66-0) beat Leicestershire by ten wickets at Manchester......	1956
Karachi A (277-0 dec) beat Sind A by an innings and 77 runs at Karachi	1957-58
Railways (236-0 dec and 16-0) beat Jammu & Kashmir by ten wickets at Srinagar......	1960-61
Karnataka (451-0 dec) beat Kerala by an innings and 186 runs at Chikmagalur........	1977-78

*There have been **30** wins by an innings and 400 runs or more, the most recent being **an innings and 413 runs by Dhaka v Barisal at Mirpur in 2014-15**.*

*There have been **21** wins by 500 runs or more, the most recent being 541 runs by Nottinghamshire v Durham MCCU at Durham in 2013.*

*There have been **32** wins by a team losing only one wicket, the most recent being by Rawalpindi v Quetta at Islamabad in 2008-09.*

TIED MATCHES

Since 1948, a tie has been recognised only when the scores are level with all the wickets down in the fourth innings. There have been **34** instances since then, including two Tests (see Test record section). Sussex have featured in five of those, Essex and Kent in four each.

The most recent instances are:

Somerset v West Indies A at Taunton	†2002
Warwickshire v Essex at Birmingham..	2003
Worcestershire v Zimbabweans at Worcester	2003
Habib Bank v WAPDA at Lahore	2011-12
Border v Boland at East London	2012-13

† *Somerset (453) made the highest total to tie a first-class match.*

MATCHES COMPLETED ON FIRST DAY

(Since 1946)

Derbyshire v Somerset at Chesterfield, June 11.	1947
Lancashire v Sussex at Manchester, July 12	1950
Surrey v Warwickshire at The Oval, May 16	1953
Somerset v Lancashire at Bath, June 6 (H. F. T. Buse's benefit).	1953
Kent v Worcestershire at Tunbridge Wells, June 15	1960
Griqualand West v Easterns at Kimberley, March 10	2010-11

SHORTEST COMPLETED MATCHES

Balls

121	Quetta (forfeit and 41) v Rawalpindi (forfeit and 44-1) at Islamabad	2008-09
350	Somerset (35 and 44) v Middlesex (86) at Lord's	1899
352	Victoria (82 and 57) v Tasmania (104 and 37-7) at Launceston	1850-51
372	Victoria (80 and 50) v Tasmania (97 and 35-2) at Launceston	1853-54

An expanded and regularly updated online version of the Records can be found at www.wisdenrecords.com

LIST A ONE-DAY RECORDS

List A is a concept intended to provide an approximate equivalent in one-day cricket of first-class status. It was introduced by the Association of Cricket Statisticians and Historians and is now recognised by the ICC, with a separate category for Twenty20 cricket. Further details are available at stats.acscricket.how/ListA/Description.html. List A games comprise:

(a) One-day internationals.
(b) Other international matches (e.g. A-team internationals).
(c) Premier domestic one-day tournaments in Test-playing countries.
(d) Official tourist matches against the main first-class teams (e.g. counties, states, provinces and national Board XIs).

The following matches are excluded:

(a) Matches originally scheduled as less than 40 overs per side (e.g. Twenty20 games).
(b) World Cup warm-up games.
(c) Tourist matches against teams outside the major domestic competitions (e.g. universities).
(d) Festival games and pre-season friendlies.

This section covers one-day cricket to December 31, 2015. Bold type denotes performances in the calendar year 2015 or, in career figures, players who appeared in List A cricket in that year.

BATTING RECORDS

HIGHEST INDIVIDUAL INNINGS

268	A. D. Brown	Surrey v Glamorgan at The Oval	2002
264	R. G. Sharma	India v Sri Lanka at Kolkata	2014-15
248	S. Dhawan	India A v South Africa A at Pretoria	2013
237*	**M. J. Guptill**	**New Zealand v West Indies at Wellington**	**2014-15**
229*	B. R. Dunk	Tasmania v Queensland at Sydney.	2014-15
222*	R. G. Pollock	Eastern Province v Border at East London	1974-75
222	J. M. How	Central Districts v Northern Districts at Hamilton	2012-13
219	V. Sehwag	India v West Indies at Indore	2011-12
215	**C. H. Gayle**	**West Indies v Zimbabwe at Canberra**	**2014-15**
209	R. G. Sharma	India v Australia at Bangalore	2013-14
207	Mohammad Ali	Pakistan Customs v DHA at Sialkot	2004-05
206	A. I. Kallicharran	Warwickshire v Oxfordshire at Birmingham	1984
204*	Khalid Latif	Karachi Dolphins v Quetta Bears at Karachi	2008-09
203	A. D. Brown	Surrey v Hampshire at Guildford.	1997
202*	A. Barrow	Natal v SA African XI at Durban.	1975-76
202*	P. J. Hughes	Australia A v South Africa A at Darwin	2014
202	**T. M. Head**	**South Australia v Western Australia at Sydney**	**2015-16**
201*	R. S. Bopara	Essex v Leicestershire at Leicester.	2008
201	V. J. Wells	Leicestershire v Berkshire at Leicester	1996
200*	S. R. Tendulkar	India v South Africa at Gwalior.	2009-10

MOST RUNS

	Career	M	I	NO	R	HS	100	Avge
G. A. Gooch.	1973–1997	614	601	48	22,211	198*	44	40.16
G. A. Hick	1983–2008	651	630	96	22,059	172*	40	41.30
S. R. Tendulkar	1989–2011	551	538	55	21,999	200*	60	45.54
K. C. Sangakkara	**1997–2015**	**512**	**484**	**51**	**18,630**	**169**	**36**	**43.02**
I. V. A. Richards	1973–1993	500	466	61	16,995	189*	26	41.96
R. T. Ponting	1992–2013	456	445	53	16,363	164	34	41.74
C. G. Greenidge.	1970–1992	440	436	33	16,349	186*	33	40.56
S. T. Jayasuriya	1989–2011	557	542	25	16,128	189	31	31.19
A. J. Lamb.	1972–1995	484	463	63	15,658	132*	19	39.14
D. L. Haynes	1976–1996	419	416	44	15,651	152*	28	42.07
S. C. Ganguly	1989–2011	437	421	43	15,622	183	31	41.32

	Career	M	I	NO	R	HS	100	Avge
K. J. Barnett	1979–2005	527	500	54	15,564	136	17	34.89
R. Dravid	1992–2011	449	416	55	15,271	153	21	42.30
D. P. M. D. Jayawardene	**1995–2014**	**541**	**504**	**50**	**15,124**	**163***	**20**	**33.31**
M. G. Bevan	1989–2006	427	385	124	15,103	157*	13	57.86

HIGHEST PARTNERSHIP FOR EACH WICKET

367*	for 1st	M. N. van Wyk and C. S. Delport, Dolphins v Knights at Bloemfontein .	2014-15
372	**for 2nd**	**C. H. Gayle and M. N. Samuels, West Indies v Zimbabwe at Canberra**	**2014-15**
309*	for 3rd	T. S. Curtis and T. M. Moody, Worcestershire v Surrey at The Oval. . .	1994
276	for 4th	Mominul Haque and A. R. S. Silva, Prime Dol. v Abahani at Bogra	2013-14
267*	for 5th	Minhazul Abedin and Khaled Mahmud, Bangladeshis v Bahawalpur at Karachi	1997-98
267*	**for 6th**	**G. D. Elliott and L. Ronchi, New Zealand v Sri Lanka at Dunedin .**	**2014-15**
203*	for 7th	S. H. T. Kandamby and H. M. R. K. B. Herath, Sri Lanka A v South Africa A at Benoni	2008-09
203	for 8th	Shahid Iqbal and Haaris Ayaz, Karachi Whites v Hyderabad at Karachi . .	1998-99
155	for 9th	C. M. W. Read and A. J. Harris, Notts v Durham at Nottingham	2006
128	for 10th	A. Ashish Reddy and M. Ravi Kiran, Hyderabad v Kerala at Secunderabad	2014-15

BOWLING RECORDS

BEST BOWLING ANALYSES

8-15	R. L. Sanghvi	Delhi v Himachal Pradesh at Una	1997-98
8-19	W. P. U. J. C. Vaas	Sri Lanka v Zimbabwe at Colombo	2001-02
8-20*	D. T. Kottehewa	Nondescripts v Ragama at Colombo	2007-08
8-21	M. A. Holding	Derbyshire v Sussex at Hove	1988
8-26	K. D. Boyce	Essex v Lancashire at Manchester	1971
8-30	G. D. R. Eranga	Burgher v Army at Colombo	2007-08
8-31	D. L. Underwood	Kent v Scotland at Edinburgh	1987
8-43	S. W. Tait	South Australia v Tasmania at Adelaide	2003-04
8-52	K. A. Stoute	West Indies A v Lancashire at Manchester	2010
8-66	S. R. G. Francis	Somerset v Derbyshire at Derby	2004

* *Including two hat-tricks.*

MOST WICKETS

	Career	M	B	R	W	BB	4I	Avge
Wasim Akram.	1984–2003	594	29,719	19,303	881	5-10	46	21.91
A. A. Donald.	1985–2003	458	22,856	14,942	684	6-15	38	21.84
M. Muralitharan	1991–2010	453	23,734	15,270	682	7-30	29	22.39
Waqar Younis.	1988–2003	412	19,841	15,098	675	7-36	44	22.36
J. K. Lever	1968–1990	481	23,208	13,278	674	5-8	34	19.70
J. E. Emburey	1975–2000	536	26,399	16,811	647	5-23	26	25.98
I. T. Botham	1973–1993	470	22,899	15,264	612	5-27	18	24.94

WICKETKEEPING AND FIELDING RECORDS

MOST DISMISSALS IN AN INNINGS

8	(all ct)	D. J. S. Taylor	Somerset v Combined Universities at Taunton . . .	1982
8	(5ct, 3st)	S. J. Palframan	Boland v Easterns at Paarl	1997-98
8	(all ct)	D. J. Pipe	Worcestershire v Hertfordshire at Hertford	2001
7	(6ct, 1st)	R. W. Taylor	Derbyshire v Lancashire at Manchester	1975
7	(4ct, 3st)	Rizwan Umar	Sargodha v Bahawalpur at Sargodha	1991-92

7	(all ct)	A. J. Stewart	Surrey v Glamorgan at Swansea	1994
7	(all ct)	I. Mitchell	Border v Western Province at East London	1998-99
7	(6ct, 1st)	M. K. P. B. Kularatne	Galle v Colts at Colombo	2001-02
7	(5ct, 2st)	T. R. Ambrose	Warwickshire v Middlesex at Birmingham	2009
7	(3ct, 4st)	W. A. S. Niroshan	Chilaw Marians v Saracens at Katunayake	2009-10
7	(all ct)	M. Rawat	Railways v Madhya Pradesh at Nagpur	2011-12
7	(all ct)	H. C. Madushan	Badureliya v Colombo at Colombo	2013-14
7	(6ct, 1st)	P. A. Patel	West Zone v Central Zone at Visakhapatnam	2013-14
7	(all ct)	D. J. Vilas	Cape Cobras v Knights at Kimberley	2014-15

MOST CATCHES IN AN INNINGS IN THE FIELD

5	V. J. Marks	Combined Universities v Kent at Oxford	1976
5	J. M. Rice	Hampshire v Warwickshire at Southampton	1978
5	A. J. Kourie	Transvaal v Western Province at Johannesburg	1979-80
5	J. N. Rhodes	South Africa v West Indies at Bombay	1993-94
5	J. W. Wilson	Otago v Auckland at Dunedin	1993-94
5	K. C. Jackson	Boland v Natal at Durban	1995-96
5	Mohammad Ramzan	PNSC v PIA at Karachi	1998-99
5	Amit Sharma	Punjab v Jammu & Kashmir at Ludhiana	1999-2000
5	B. E. Young	South Australia v Tasmania at Launceston	2001-02
5	Hasnain Raza	Bahawalpur v Pakistan Customs at Karachi	2002-03
5	D. J. Sales	Northamptonshire v Essex at Northampton	2007
5	L. N. Mosena	Free State v North West at Bloemfontein	2007-08
5	A. R. McBrine	Ireland v Sri Lanka A at Belfast	2014

TEAM RECORDS

HIGHEST INNINGS TOTALS

496-4	(50 overs)	Surrey v Gloucestershire at The Oval	2007
443-9	(50 overs)	Sri Lanka v Netherlands at Amstelveen	2006
439-2	**(50 overs)**	**South Africa v West Indies at Johannesburg**	**2014-15**
438-4	**(50 overs)**	**South Africa v India at Mumbai**	**2014-15**
438-5	(50 overs)	Surrey v Glamorgan at The Oval	2002
438-9	(49.5 overs)	South Africa v Australia at Johannesburg	2005-06
434-4	(50 overs)	Australia v South Africa at Johannesburg	2005-06
433-3	(50 overs)	India A v South Africa A at Pretoria	2013
429	(49.5 overs)	Glamorgan v Surrey at The Oval	2002
424-5	(50 overs)	Buckinghamshire v Suffolk at Dinton	2002
424-7	(50 overs)	New Zealand A v Northamptonshire at Northampton	2014

LOWEST INNINGS TOTALS

18	(14.3 overs)	West Indies Under-19 v Barbados at Blairmont	2007-08
19	(10.5 overs)	Saracens v Colts at Colombo	2012-13
23	(19.4 overs)	Middlesex v Yorkshire at Leeds	1974
30	(20.4 overs)	Chittagong v Sylhet at Dhaka	2002-03
31	(13.5 overs)	Border v South Western Districts at East London	2007-08
34	(21.1 overs)	Saurashtra v Mumbai at Mumbai	1999-2000
35	(18 overs)	Zimbabwe v Sri Lanka at Harare	2003-04
35	(20.2 overs)	Cricket Coaching School v Abahani at Fatullah	2013-14
35	(15.3 overs)	Rajasthan v Railways at Nagpur	2014-15
36	(25.4 overs)	Leicestershire v Sussex at Leicester	1973
36	(18.4 overs)	Canada v Sri Lanka at Paarl	2002-03
38	(15.4 overs)	Zimbabwe v Sri Lanka at Colombo	2001-02
39	(26.4 overs)	Ireland v Sussex at Hove	1985
39	(15.2 overs)	Cape Cobras v Eagles at Paarl *(one man absent)*	2008-09
39	(24.4 overs)	Namibia v United Arab Emirates at Sharjah	2013-14

LIST A TWENTY20 RECORDS

This section covers Twenty20 cricket to December 31, 2015. Bold type denotes performances in the calendar year 2015 or, in career figures, players who appeared in Twenty20 cricket in that year.

BATTING RECORDS

HIGHEST INDIVIDUAL INNINGS

175*	C. H. Gayle	RC Bangalore v Pune Warriors at Bangalore	2012-13
158*	B. B. McCullum	Kolkata Knight Riders v RC Bangalore at Bangalore . .	2007-08
158*	**B. B. McCullum**	**Warwickshire v Derbyshire at Birmingham**	**2015**
156	A. J. Finch	Australia v England at Southampton	2013
153*	L. J. Wright	Sussex v Essex at Chelmsford	2014
152*	G. R. Napier	Essex v Sussex at Chelmsford	2008
151*	**C. H. Gayle**	**Somerset v Kent at Taunton**	**2015**
145	L. P. van der Westhuizen	Namibia v Kenya at Windhoek	2011-12
141*	C. L. White	Somerset v Worcestershire at Worcester	2006
140*	P. J. Malan	Western Province v Easterns at Cape Town	2014-15
130	Tamim Iqbal	UCB BCB XI v Mohammedan at Mirpur	2013-14

MOST RUNS

	Career	M	I	NO	R	HS	100	Avge
C. H. Gayle	*2005–2015*	229	225	33	8,473	175*	16	44.13
B. J. Hodge	*2003–2015*	247	233	50	6,781	106	2	37.05
B. B. McCullum	*2004–2015*	219	216	22	6,311	158*	7	32.53
K. A. Pollard	*2006–2015*	299	267	80	5,887	89*	0	31.48
D. J. Hussey	*2004–2015*	251	239	47	5,871	100*	1	30.57
D. A. Warner	*2006–2015*	195	194	19	5,835	135*	5	33.34
S. K. Raina	*2006–2015*	205	195	32	5,549	109*	3	34.04
Shoaib Malik	*2004–2015*	213	201	56	5,548	95*	0	38.26
O. A. Shah	*2003–2015*	230	217	49	5,509	84	0	32.79
D. R. Smith	*2005–2015*	239	232	20	5,489	110*	3	25.89
R. N. ten Doeschate	*2003–2015*	266	235	52	5,356	121*	2	29.26
L. J. Wright	*2004–2015*	231	212	21	5,327	153*	5	27.89
R. G. Sharma	*2006–2015*	204	193	35	5,223	109*	3	33.05

HIGHEST PARTNERSHIP FOR EACH WICKET

201	for 1st	P. J. Ingram and J. M. How, C. Dist. v Wellington at New Plymouth.	2011-12
215*	**for 2nd**	**V. Kohli and A. B. de Villiers, RC Bangalore v Mumbai Indians at Mumbai**.	**2014-15**
162	for 3rd	Abdul Razzaq and Nasir Jamshed, Lahore Lions v Quetta Bears at Lahore . .	2009
202*	for 4th	M. C. Juneja and A. Malik, Gujarat v Kerala at Indore	2012-13
149	for 5th	Y. V. Takawale and S. V. Bahutule, Maharashtra v Gujarat at Mumbai. . . .	2006-07
126*	for 6th	C. S. MacLeod and J. W. Hastings, Durham v Nhants at Chester-le-St	2014
100	**for 7th**	**J. Suchith and Harbhajan Singh, Mumbai Indians v KXI Punjab at Mumbai**.	**2014-15**
120	for 8th	Azhar Mahmood and I. Udana, Wayamba v Uva at Colombo	2012
64	for 9th	K. Magage and H. S. M. Zoysa, Burgher v Panadura at Colombo	2011-12
59	for 10th	H. H. Streak and J. E. Anyon, Warwickshire v Worcs at Birmingham	2005

BOWLING RECORDS

BEST BOWLING ANALYSES

6-5	A. V. Suppiah	Somerset v Glamorgan at Cardiff....................	2011
6-6	Shakib Al Hasan	Barbados v Trinidad & Tobago at Bridgetown	2013
6-7	S. L. Malinga	Melbourne Stars v Perth Scorchers at Perth	2012-13
6-8	B. A. W. Mendis	Sri Lanka v Zimbabwe at Hambantota.................	2012-13
6-9	P. Fojela	Border v Easterns at East London.	2014-15
6-14	Sohail Tanvir	Rajasthan Royals v Chennai Superstars at Jaipur........	2007-08
6-14	**D. Punia**	**Services v Haryana at Delhi.................**	**2014-15**
6-15	S. R. Abeywardene	Panadura v Air Force at Colombo	2005-06

MOST WICKETS

	Career	M	B	R	W	BB	4I	Avge
S. L. Malinga	*2004–2015*	220	4,811	5,367	295	6-7	11	18.19
D. J. Bravo	*2005–2015*	272	4,992	6,654	280	4-23	7	23.76
Yasir Arafat	*2005–2015*	217	4,499	5,983	277	4-5	10	21.59
A. C. Thomas	*2003–2015*	225	4,558	5,739	263	5-24	5	21.82
D. P. Nannes	*2007–2014*	215	4,624	5,719	257	5-31	9	22.25
Azhar Mahmood ..	*2003–2015*	223	4,689	5,947	250	5-24	3	23.78
Saeed Ajmal	*2004–2015*	168	3,772	4,041	234	4-14	7	17.26
J. A. Morkel	*2003–2015*	285	4,667	5,933	228	4-25	3	26.02
S. P. Narine......	*2010–2015*	168	3,856	3,552	216	5-19	11	16.44

WICKETKEEPING AND FIELDING RECORDS

MOST DISMISSALS IN AN INNINGS

7 (all ct)	E. F. M. U. Fernando Lankan v Moors at Colombo	2005-06

MOST CATCHES IN AN INNINGS IN THE FIELD

5	Manzoor Ilahi	Jammu & Kashmir v Delhi at Delhi	2010-11
5	J. M. Vince	Hampshire v Leeward Islands at North Sound	2010-11
5	J. L. Ontong	Cape Cobras v Knights at Cape Town	2014-15
5	**A. K. V. Adikari**	**Chilaw Marians v Bloomfield at Colombo**	**2014-15**
5	**P. G. Fulton**	**Canterbury v Northern Districts at Hamilton**	**2015-16**

TEAM RECORDS

HIGHEST INNINGS TOTALS

263-5	(20 overs)	RC Bangalore v Pune Warriors at Bangalore	2012-13
260-6	(20 overs)	Sri Lanka v Kenya at Johannesburg.	2007-08
254-3	(20 overs)	Gloucestershire v Middlesex at Uxbridge	2011
250-3	(20 overs)	Somerset v Gloucestershire at Taunton	2006

LOWEST INNINGS TOTALS

30	(11.1 overs)	Tripura v Jharkhand at Dhanbad	2009-10
39	(10.3 overs)	Netherlands v Sri Lanka at Chittagong.	2013-14
44	(12.5 overs)	Leeward Islands v Trinidad & Tobago at North Sound	2011-12
44	(14.4 overs)	Boland v North West at Potchefstroom	2014-15
45	(8.4 overs)	Mohammedan v Prime Bank at Sylhet..................	2013-14

TEST RECORDS

This section covers all Tests up to January 26, 2016. Bold type denotes performances since January 1, 2015, or, in career figures, players who have appeared in Test cricket since that date.

BATTING RECORDS

HIGHEST INDIVIDUAL INNINGS

400*	B. C. Lara	West Indies v England at St John's	2003-04
380	M. L. Hayden	Australia v Zimbabwe at Perth	2003-04
375	B. C. Lara	West Indies v England at St John's	1993-94
374	D. P. M. D. Jayawardene	Sri Lanka v South Africa at Colombo (SSC)	2006
365*	G. S. Sobers	West Indies v Pakistan at Kingston	1957-58
364	L. Hutton	England v Australia at The Oval	1938
340	S. T. Jayasuriya	Sri Lanka v India at Colombo (RPS)	1997-98
337	Hanif Mohammad	Pakistan v West Indies at Bridgetown	1957-58
336*	W. R. Hammond	England v New Zealand at Auckland	1932-33
334*	M. A. Taylor	Australia v Pakistan at Peshawar	1998-99
334	D. G. Bradman	Australia v England at Leeds	1930
333	G. A. Gooch	England v India at Lord's	1990
333	C. H. Gayle	West Indies v Sri Lanka at Galle	2010-11
329*	M. J. Clarke	Australia v India at Sydney	2011-12
329	Inzamam-ul-Haq	Pakistan v New Zealand at Lahore	2002
325	A. Sandham	England v West Indies at Kingston	1929-30
319	V. Sehwag	India v South Africa at Chennai	2007-08
319	K. C. Sangakkara	Sri Lanka v Bangladesh at Chittagong	2013-14
317	C. H. Gayle	West Indies v South Africa at St John's	2004-05
313	Younis Khan	Pakistan v Sri Lanka at Karachi	2008-09
311*	H. M. Amla	South Africa v England at The Oval	2012
311	R. B. Simpson	Australia v England at Manchester	1964
310*	J. H. Edrich	England v New Zealand at Leeds	1965
309	V. Sehwag	India v Pakistan at Multan	2003-04
307	R. M. Cowper	Australia v England at Melbourne	1965-66
304	D. G. Bradman	Australia v England at Leeds	1934
302	L. G. Rowe	West Indies v England at Bridgetown	1973-74
302	B. B. McCullum	New Zealand v India at Wellington	2013-14

There have been 62 further instances of 250 or more runs in a Test innings.

The highest innings for the countries not mentioned above are:

266	D. L. Houghton	Zimbabwe v Sri Lanka at Bulawayo	1994-95
206	**Tamim Iqbal**	**Bangladesh v Pakistan at Khulna**	**2014-15**

HUNDRED ON TEST DEBUT

C. Bannerman (165*)	Australia v England at Melbourne	1876-77
W. G. Grace (152)	England v Australia at The Oval	1880
H. Graham (107)	Australia v England at Lord's	1893
†K. S. Ranjitsinhji (154*)	England v Australia at Manchester	1896
†P. F. Warner (132*)	England v South Africa at Johannesburg	1898-99
†R. A. Duff (104)	Australia v England at Melbourne	1901-02
§R. E. Foster (287)	England v Australia at Sydney	1903-04
G. Gunn (119)	England v Australia at Sydney	1907-08
†R. J. Hartigan (116)	Australia v England at Adelaide	1907-08
†H. L. Collins (104)	Australia v England at Sydney	1920-21
W. H. Ponsford (110)	Australia v England at Sydney	1924-25
A. A. Jackson (164)	Australia v England at Adelaide	1928-29
†G. A. Headley (176)	West Indies v England at Bridgetown	1929-30

J. E. Mills (117)	New Zealand v England at Wellington	1929-30
Nawab of Pataudi sen. (102)	England v Australia at Sydney	1932-33
B. H. Valentine (136)	England v India at Bombay	1933-34
†L. Amarnath (118)	India v England at Bombay	1933-34
†P. A. Gibb (106)	England v South Africa at Johannesburg	1938-39
S. C. Griffith (140)	England v West Indies at Port-of-Spain	1947-48
A. G. Ganteaume (112)	West Indies v England at Port-of-Spain	1947-48
†J. W. Burke (101*)	Australia v England at Adelaide	1950-51
P. B. H. May (138)	England v South Africa at Leeds	1951
R. H. Shodhan (110)	India v Pakistan at Calcutta	1952-53
B. H. Pairaudeau (115)	West Indies v India at Port-of-Spain	1952-53
†O. G. Smith (104)	West Indies v Australia at Kingston	1954-55
A. G. Kripal Singh (100*)	India v New Zealand at Hyderabad	1955-56
C. C. Hunte (142)	West Indies v Pakistan at Bridgetown	1957-58
C. A. Milton (104*)	England v New Zealand at Leeds	1958
†A. A. Baig (112)	India v England at Manchester	1959
Hanumant Singh (105)	India v England at Delhi	1963-64
Khalid Ibadulla (166)	Pakistan v Australia at Karachi	1964-65
B. R. Taylor (105)	New Zealand v India at Calcutta	1964-65
K. D. Walters (155)	Australia v England at Brisbane	1965-66
J. H. Hampshire (107)	England v West Indies at Lord's	1969
†G. R. Viswanath (137)	India v Australia at Kanpur	1969-70
G. S. Chappell (108)	Australia v England at Perth	1970-71
‡§L. G. Rowe (214, 100*)	West Indies v New Zealand at Kingston	1971-72
A. I. Kallicharran (100*)	West Indies v New Zealand at Georgetown	1971-72
R. E. Redmond (107)	New Zealand v Pakistan at Auckland	1972-73
†F. C. Hayes (106*)	England v West Indies at The Oval	1973
†C. G. Greenidge (107)	West Indies v India at Bangalore	1974-75
†L. Baichan (105*)	West Indies v Pakistan at Lahore	1974-75
G. J. Cosier (109)	Australia v West Indies at Melbourne	1975-76
S. Amarnath (124)	India v New Zealand at Auckland	1975-76
Javed Miandad (163)	Pakistan v New Zealand at Lahore	1976-77
†A. B. Williams (100)	West Indies v Australia at Georgetown	1977-78
†D. M. Wellham (103)	Australia v England at The Oval	1981
†Salim Malik (100*)	Pakistan v Sri Lanka at Karachi	1981-82
K. C. Wessels (162)	Australia v England at Brisbane	1982-83
W. B. Phillips (159)	Australia v Pakistan at Perth	1983-84
¶M. Azharuddin (110)	India v England at Calcutta	1984-85
D. S. B. P. Kuruppu (201*)	Sri Lanka v New Zealand at Colombo (CCC)	1986-87
†M. J. Greatbatch (107*)	New Zealand v England at Auckland	1987-88
M. E. Waugh (138)	Australia v England at Adelaide	1990-91
A. C. Hudson (163)	South Africa v West Indies at Bridgetown	1991-92
R. S. Kaluwitharana (132*)	Sri Lanka v Australia at Colombo (SSC)	1992-93
D. L. Houghton (121)	Zimbabwe v India at Harare	1992-93
P. K. Amre (103)	India v South Africa at Durban	1992-93
†G. P. Thorpe (114*)	England v Australia at Nottingham	1993
G. S. Blewett (102*)	Australia v England at Adelaide	1994-95
S. C. Ganguly (131)	India v England at Lord's	1996
†Mohammad Wasim (109*)	Pakistan v New Zealand at Lahore	1996-97
Ali Naqvi (115)	Pakistan v South Africa at Rawalpindi	1997-98
Azhar Mahmood (128*)	Pakistan v South Africa at Rawalpindi	1997-98
M. S. Sinclair (214)	New Zealand v West Indies at Wellington	1999-2000
†Younis Khan (107)	Pakistan v Sri Lanka at Rawalpindi	1999-2000
Aminul Islam (145)	Bangladesh v India at Dhaka	2000-01
†H. Masakadza (119)	Zimbabwe v West Indies at Harare	2001
T. T. Samaraweera (103*)	Sri Lanka v India at Colombo (SSC)	2001
Taufeeq Umar (104)	Pakistan v Bangladesh at Multan	2001-02
†Mohammad Ashraful (114)	Bangladesh v Sri Lanka at Colombo (SSC)	2001-02
V. Sehwag (105)	India v South Africa at Bloemfontein	2001-02
L. Vincent (104)	New Zealand v Australia at Perth	2001-02
S. B. Styris (107)	New Zealand v West Indies at St George's	2002

J. A. Rudolph (222*)	South Africa v Bangladesh at Chittagong	2003
‡Yasir Hameed (170, 105).	Pakistan v Bangladesh at Karachi	2003
†D. R. Smith (105*).	West Indies v South Africa at Cape Town	2003-04
A. J. Strauss (112)	England v New Zealand at Lord's	2004
M. J. Clarke (151)	Australia v India at Bangalore	2004-05
†A. N. Cook (104*)	England v India at Nagpur	2005-06
M. J. Prior (126*).	England v West Indies at Lord's	2007
M. J. North (117).	Australia v South Africa at Johannesburg	2008-09
†Fawad Alam (168).	Pakistan v Sri Lanka at Colombo (PSS).	2009
†I. J. L. Trott (119)	England v Australia at The Oval	2009
Umar Akmal (129).	Pakistan v New Zealand at Dunedin	2009-10
†A. B. Barath (104)	West Indies v Australia at Brisbane	2009-10
A. N. Petersen (100)	South Africa v India at Kolkata	2009-10
S. K. Raina (120).	India v Sri Lanka at Colombo (SSC)	2010
K. S. Williamson (131)	New Zealand v India at Ahmedabad	2010-11
†K. A. Edwards (110)	West Indies v India at Roseau	2011
S. E. Marsh (141).	Australia v Sri Lanka at Pallekele	2011-12
Abul Hasan (113).	Bangladesh v West Indies at Khulna	2012-13
†F. du Plessis (110*)	South Africa v Australia at Adelaide	2012-13
H. D. Rutherford (171)	New Zealand v England at Dunedin.	2012-13
S. Dhawan (187)	India v Australia at Mohali.	2012-13
R. G. Sharma (177)	India v West Indies at Kolkata	2013-14
†J. D. S. Neesham (137*)	New Zealand v India at Wellington	2013-14
S. van Zyl (101*).	South Africa v West Indies at Centurion	2014-15
A. C. Voges (130*)	**Australia v West Indies at Roseau**	**2015**
S. C. Cook (115)	**South Africa v England at Centurion**	**2015-16**

†   *In his second innings of the match.*
‡   *L. G. Rowe and Yasir Hameed are the only batsmen to score a hundred in each innings on debut.*
§   *R. E. Foster (287, 19) and L. G. Rowe (214, 100*) are the only batsmen to score 300 on debut.*
¶   *M. Azharuddin is the only batsman to score hundreds in each of his first three Tests.*

  L. Amarnath and S. Amarnath were father and son.
  Ali Naqvi and Azhar Mahmood achieved the feat in the same innings.
  Only Bannerman, Houghton and Aminul Islam scored hundreds in their country's first Test.

TWO SEPARATE HUNDREDS IN A TEST

Triple-Hundred and Hundred in a Test

| G. A. Gooch (England) . . . . | 333 and 123 v India at Lord's . . . . | 1990 |
| K. C. Sangakkara (Sri Lanka) . . . . . | 319 and 105 v Bangladesh at Chittagong . . . . | 2013-14 |

The only instances in first-class cricket. M. A. Taylor (Australia) scored 334* and 92 v Pakistan at Peshawar in 1998-99.

Double-Hundred and Hundred in a Test

K. D. Walters (Australia).	242 and 103 v West Indies at Sydney	1968-69
S. M. Gavaskar (India).	124 and 220 v West Indies at Port-of-Spain	1970-71
†L. G. Rowe (West Indies)	214 and 100* v New Zealand at Kingston	1971-72
G. S. Chappell (Australia)	247* and 133 v New Zealand at Wellington	1973-74
B. C. Lara (West Indies)	221 and 130 v Sri Lanka at Colombo (SSC)	2001-02

†   *On Test debut.*

Two Hundreds in a Test

There have been **81** instances of a batsman scoring two separate hundreds in a Test, including the seven listed above. The most recent was by **A. M. Rahane for India v South Africa at Delhi in 2015-16.**
  S. M. Gavaskar (India), R. T. Ponting (Australia) and **D. A. Warner** (Australia) all achieved the feat three times. C. L. Walcott scored twin hundreds twice in one series, for West Indies v Australia in 1954-55. L. G. Rowe and Yasir Hameed both did it on Test debut.

MOST DOUBLE-HUNDREDS

D. G. Bradman (A) 12	M. S. Atapattu (SL) 6	R. Dravid (I) 5
K. C. Sangakkara (SL) . . **11**	Javed Miandad (P) 6	G. C. Smith (SA) 5
B. C. Lara (WI) 9	R. T. Ponting (A) 6	**Younis Khan (P)** **5**
W. R. Hammond (E) 7	V. Sehwag (I) 6	
D. P. M. D. Jayawardene (SL) 7	S. R. Tendulkar (I) 6	

M. J. Clarke (Australia) scored four double-hundreds in the calendar year 2012.

MOST HUNDREDS

S. R. Tendulkar (I). . . 51	**A. N. Cook (E)** **28**	**I. R. Bell (E)** **22**
J. H. Kallis (SA) 45	A. R. Border (A) 27	G. Boycott (E). 22
R. T. Ponting (A). 41	G. C. Smith (SA) 27	M. C. Cowdrey (E) 22
K. C. Sangakkara (SL) . **38**	G. S. Sobers (WI) 26	W. R. Hammond (E) 22
R. Dravid (I) 36	**H. M. Amla (SA)** **25**	D. C. Boon (A) 21
S. M. Gavaskar (I) 34	Inzamam-ul-Haq (P) 25	**A. B. de Villiers (SA)** . . **21**
D. P. M. D. Jayawardene (SL) 34	G. S. Chappell (A) 24	R. N. Harvey (A) 21
B. C. Lara (WI) 34	Mohammad Yousuf (P). . . 24	G. Kirsten (SA) 21
S. R. Waugh (A) 32	I. V. A. Richards (WI) . . . 24	A. J. Strauss (E) 21
Younis Khan (P) **31**	Javed Miandad (P). 23	K. F. Barrington (E) 20
S. Chanderpaul (WI). . . **30**	J. L. Langer (A) 23	P. A. de Silva (SL). 20
M. L. Hayden (A) 30	K. P. Pietersen (E) 23	G. A. Gooch (E) 20
D. G. Bradman (A) 29	V. Sehwag (I) 23	M. E. Waugh (A). 20
M. J. Clarke (A). **28**	M. Azharuddin (I) 22	

*The most hundreds for New Zealand is 17 by M. D. Crowe, the most for Zimbabwe is 12 by A. Flower, and the most for Bangladesh is 7 by **Tamim Iqbal.***

MOST HUNDREDS AGAINST ONE TEAM

D. G. Bradman. . . 19	Australia v England	**K. C. Sangakkara 10**	**Sri Lanka v Pakistan**
S. M. Gavaskar . . 13	India v West Indies	G. S. Sobers. 10	West Indies v England
J. B. Hobbs 12	England v Australia	S. R. Waugh. 10	Australia v England
S. R. Tendulkar . . 11	India v Australia		

MOST DUCKS

	0s	Inns		0s	Inns
C. A. Walsh (WI)	43	185	**I. Sharma (I)**	**22**	**100**
C. S. Martin (NZ)	36	104	M. S. Atapattu (SL)	22	156
G. D. McGrath (A)	35	138	S. R. Waugh (A)	22	260
S. K. Warne (A)	34	199	S. J. Harmison (E).	21	86
M. Muralitharan (SL)	33	164	M. Ntini (SA)	21	116
Zaheer Khan (I)	29	127	Waqar Younis (P)	21	120
M. Dillon (WI)	26	68	M. S. Panesar (E)	20	68
C. E. L. Ambrose (WI).	26	145	B. S. Bedi (I)	20	101
Danish Kaneria (P)	25	84	D. L. Vettori (NZ/World) . . .	20	174
D. K. Morrison (NZ).	24	71	M. A. Atherton (E)	20	212
B. S. Chandrasekhar (I)	23	80			

CARRYING BAT THROUGH TEST INNINGS

(Figures in brackets show team's total)

A. B. Tancred	26*	(47)	South Africa v England at Cape Town.	1888-89
J. E. Barrett	67*	(176)†	Australia v England at Lord's.	1890
R. Abel	132*	(307)	England v Australia at Sydney	1891-92
P. F. Warner	132*	(237)†	England v South Africa at Johannesburg	1898-99
W. W. Armstrong	159*	(309)	Australia v South Africa at Johannesburg . . .	1902-03

J. W. Zulch	43*	(103)	South Africa v England at Cape Town	1909-10
W. Bardsley	193*	(383)	Australia v England at Lord's	1926
W. M. Woodfull	30*	(66)§	Australia v England at Brisbane	1928-29
W. M. Woodfull	73*	(193)‡	Australia v England at Adelaide	1932-33
W. A. Brown	206*	(422)	Australia v England at Lord's	1938
L. Hutton	202*	(344)	England v West Indies at The Oval	1950
L. Hutton	156*	(272)	England v West Indies at Adelaide	1950-51
Nazar Mohammad¶	124*	(331)	Pakistan v India at Lucknow	1952-53
F. M. M. Worrell¶	191*	(372)	West Indies v England at Nottingham	1957
T. L. Goddard	56*	(99)	South Africa v Australia at Cape Town	1957-58
D. J. McGlew	127*	(292)	South Africa v New Zealand at Durban	1961-62
C. C. Hunte	60*	(131)	West Indies v Australia at Port-of-Spain	1964-65
G. M. Turner	43*	(131)	New Zealand v England at Lord's	1969
W. M. Lawry	49*	(107)	Australia v India at Delhi	1969-70
W. M. Lawry	60*	(116)‡	Australia v England at Sydney	1970-71
G. M. Turner	223*	(386)	New Zealand v West Indies at Kingston	1971-72
I. R. Redpath	159*	(346)	Australia v New Zealand at Auckland	1973-74
G. Boycott	99*	(215)	England v Australia at Perth	1979-80
S. M. Gavaskar	127*	(286)	India v Pakistan at Faisalabad	1982-83
Mudassar Nazar¶	152*	(323)	Pakistan v India at Lahore	1982-83
S. Wettimuny	63*	(144)	Sri Lanka v New Zealand at Christchurch	1982-83
D. C. Boon	58*	(103)	Australia v New Zealand at Auckland	1985-86
D. L. Haynes	88*	(211)	West Indies v Pakistan at Karachi	1986-87
G. A. Gooch	154*	(252)	England v West Indies at Leeds	1991
D. L. Haynes	75*	(176)	West Indies v England at The Oval	1991
A. J. Stewart	69*	(175)	England v Pakistan at Lord's	1992
D. L. Haynes	143*	(382)	West Indies v Pakistan at Port-of-Spain	1992-93
M. H. Dekker	68*	(187)	Zimbabwe v Pakistan at Rawalpindi	1993-94
M. A. Atherton	94*	(228)	England v New Zealand at Christchurch	1996-97
G. Kirsten	100*	(239)	South Africa v Pakistan at Faisalabad	1997-98
M. A. Taylor	169*	(350)	Australia v South Africa at Adelaide	1997-98
G. W. Flower	156*	(321)	Zimbabwe v Pakistan at Bulawayo	1997-98
Saeed Anwar	188*	(316)	Pakistan v India at Calcutta	1998-99
M. S. Atapattu	216*	(428)	Sri Lanka v Zimbabwe at Bulawayo	1999-2000
R. P. Arnold	104*	(231)	Sri Lanka v Zimbabwe at Harare	1999-2000
Javed Omar	85*	(168)†‡	Bangladesh v Zimbabwe at Bulawayo	2000-01
V. Sehwag	201*	(329)	India v Sri Lanka at Galle	2008
S. M. Katich	131*	(268)	Australia v New Zealand at Brisbane	2008-09
C. H. Gayle	165*	(317)	West Indies v Australia at Adelaide	2009-10
Imran Farhat	117*	(223)	Pakistan v New Zealand at Napier	2009-10
R. Dravid	146*	(300)	India v England at The Oval	2011
T. M. K. Mawoyo	163*	(412)	Zimbabwe v Pakistan at Bulawayo	2011-12
D. A. Warner	123*	(233)	Australia v New Zealand at Hobart	2011-12
C. A. Pujara	**145***	**(312)**	**India v Sri Lanka at Colombo (SSC)**	**2015-16**
D. Elgar	**118***	**(214)**	**South Africa v England at Durban**	**2015-16**

† *On debut.*   ‡ *One man absent.*   § *Two men absent.*   ¶ *Father and son.*

G. M. Turner (223) holds the record for the highest score by a player carrying his bat through a Test innings. He was also the youngest at 22 years 63 days old when he first did it in 1969.*

D. L. Haynes, who is alone in achieving this feat on three occasions, also opened the batting and was last man out in each innings for West Indies v New Zealand at Dunedin, 1979-80.

MOST RUNS IN A SERIES

	T	I	NO	R	HS	100	Avge		
D. G. Bradman	5	7	0	974	334	4	139.14	A v E	1930
W. R. Hammond	5	9	1	905	251	4	113.12	E v A	1928-29
M. A. Taylor	6	11	1	839	219	2	83.90	A v E	1989
R. N. Harvey	5	9	0	834	205	4	92.66	A v SA	1952-53

	T	I	NO	R	HS	100	Avge		
I. V. A. Richards...	4	7	0	829	291	3	118.42	WI v E	1976
C. L. Walcott	5	10	0	827	155	5	82.70	WI v A	1954-55
G. S. Sobers	5	8	2	824	365*	3	137.33	WI v P	1957-58
D. G. Bradman	5	9	0	810	270	3	90.00	A v E	1936-37
D. G. Bradman	5	5	1	806	299*	4	201.50	A v SA	1931-32

MOST RUNS IN A CALENDAR YEAR

	T	I	NO	R	HS	100	Avge	Year
Mohammad Yousuf (P)......	11	19	4	1,788	202	9	99.33	2006
I. V. A. Richards (WI).......	11	19	0	1,710	291	7	90.00	1976
G. C. Smith (SA)..........	15	25	2	1,656	232	6	72.00	2008
M. J. Clarke (A)...........	11	18	3	1,595	329*	5	106.33	2012
S. R. Tendulkar (I).........	14	23	3	1,562	214	7	78.10	2010
S. M. Gavaskar (I).........	18	27	1	1,555	221	5	59.80	1979
R. T. Ponting (A)..........	15	28	5	1,544	207	6	67.13	2005
R. T. Ponting (A)..........	11	18	3	1,503	257	6	100.20	2003

M. Amarnath reached 1,000 runs in 1983 on May 3, in his ninth Test of the year.
   The only case of 1,000 in a year before World War II was C. Hill of Australia: 1,060 in 1902.
   M. L. Hayden (Australia) scored 1,000 runs in each year from 2001 to 2005.

MOST RUNS

		T	I	NO	R	HS	100	Avge
1	S. R. Tendulkar (India)	200	329	33	15,921	248*	51	53.78
2	R. T. Ponting (Australia)	168	287	29	13,378	257	41	51.85
3	J. H. Kallis (South Africa/World)	166	280	40	13,289	224	45	55.37
4	R. Dravid (India/World)	164	286	32	13,288	270	36	52.31
5	**K. C. Sangakkara (Sri Lanka) ..**	**134**	**233**	**17**	**12,400**	**319**	**38**	**57.40**
6	B. C. Lara (West Indies/World) ..	131	232	6	11,953	400*	34	52.88
7	**S. Chanderpaul (West Indies) ..**	**164**	**280**	**49**	**11,867**	**203***	**30**	**51.37**
8	D. P. M. D. Jayawardene (SL) ..	149	252	15	11,814	374	34	49.84
9	A. R. Border (Australia)	156	265	44	11,174	205	27	50.56
10	S. R. Waugh (Australia)	168	260	46	10,927	200	32	51.06
11	S. M. Gavaskar (India)	125	214	16	10,122	236*	34	51.12
12	**A. N. Cook (England)**	**126**	**226**	**12**	**9,964**	**294**	**28**	**46.56**
13	G. C. Smith (South Africa/Wld) .	117	205	13	9,265	277	27	48.25
14	**Younis Khan (Pakistan)**	**104**	**186**	**17**	**9,116**	**313**	**31**	**53.94**
15	G. A. Gooch (England)	118	215	6	8,900	333	20	42.58
16	Javed Miandad (Pakistan)	124	189	21	8,832	280*	23	52.57
17	Inzamam-ul-Haq (Pakistan/World)	120	200	22	8,830	329	25	49.60
18	V. V. S. Laxman (India)	134	225	34	8,781	281	17	45.97
19	**M. J. Clarke (Australia)**	**115**	**198**	**22**	**8,643**	**329***	**28**	**49.10**
20	M. L. Hayden (Australia)	103	184	14	8,625	380	30	50.73
21	V. Sehwag (India/World)	104	180	6	8,586	319	23	49.34
22	I. V. A. Richards (West Indies)...	121	182	12	8,540	291	24	50.23
23	A. J. Stewart (England)........	133	235	21	8,463	190	15	39.54
24	D. I. Gower (England).........	117	204	18	8,231	215	18	44.25
25	K. P. Pietersen (England)	104	181	8	8,181	227	23	47.28
26	G. Boycott (England)	108	193	23	8,114	246*	22	47.72
27	**A. B. de Villiers (South Africa)** .	**106**	**176**	**16**	**8,074**	**278***	**21**	**50.46**
28	G. S. Sobers (West Indies)	93	160	21	8,032	365*	26	57.78
29	M. E. Waugh (Australia)........	128	209	17	8,029	153*	20	41.81
30	M. A. Atherton (England)	115	212	7	7,728	185*	16	37.69
31	**I. R. Bell (England)**	**118**	**205**	**24**	**7,727**	**235**	**22**	**42.69**
32	J. L. Langer (Australia)	105	182	12	7,696	250	23	45.27
33	M. C. Cowdrey (England)	114	188	15	7,624	182	22	44.06
34	C. G. Greenidge (West Indies) ...	108	185	16	7,558	226	19	44.72

		T	I	NO	R	HS	100	Avge
35	Mohammad Yousuf (Pakistan) . . .	90	156	12	7,530	223	24	52.29
36	M. A. Taylor (Australia)	104	186	13	7,525	334*	19	43.49
37	C. H. Lloyd (West Indies)	110	175	14	7,515	242*	19	46.67
38	D. L. Haynes (West Indies)	116	202	25	7,487	184	18	42.29
39	D. C. Boon (Australia)	107	190	20	7,422	200	21	43.65
40	**H. M. Amla (South Africa)**	**92**	**156**	**13**	**7,358**	**311***	**25**	**51.45**
41	G. Kirsten (South Africa)	101	176	15	7,289	275	21	45.27
42	W. R. Hammond (England).	85	140	16	7,249	336*	22	58.45
43	C. H. Gayle (West Indies)	103	182	11	7,214	333	15	42.18
44	S. C. Ganguly (India)	113	188	17	7,212	239	16	42.17
45	S. P. Fleming (New Zealand)	111	189	10	7,172	274*	9	40.06
46	G. S. Chappell (Australia)	87	151	19	7,110	247*	24	53.86
47	A. J. Strauss (England)	100	178	6	7,037	177	21	40.91
48	D. G. Bradman (Australia)	52	80	10	6,996	334	29	99.94
49	S. T. Jayasuriya (Sri Lanka)	110	188	14	6,973	340	14	40.07
50	L. Hutton (England)	79	138	15	6,971	364	19	56.67

MOST RUNS FOR EACH COUNTRY

ENGLAND

A. N. Cook	**9,964**	A. J. Stewart	8,463	K. P. Pietersen	8,181
G. A. Gooch	8,900	D. I. Gower	8,231	G. Boycott	8,114

AUSTRALIA

R. T. Ponting	13,378	S. R. Waugh	10,927	M. L. Hayden	8,625
A. R. Border	11,174	**M. J. Clarke**	**8,643**	M. E. Waugh	8,029

SOUTH AFRICA

J. H. Kallis†	13,206	**A. B. de Villiers**	**8,074**	G. Kirsten	7,289
G. C. Smith†	9,253	**H. M. Amla**	**7,358**	H. H. Gibbs	6,167

† J. H. Kallis also scored 44 and 39 and G. C. Smith 12 and 0 for the World XI v Australia (2005-06 Super Series Test).*

WEST INDIES

B. C. Lara†	11,912	I. V. A. Richards	8,540	C. G. Greenidge	7,558
S. Chanderpaul	**11,867**	G. S. Sobers	8,032	C. H. Lloyd	7,515

† B. C. Lara also scored 5 and 36 for the World XI v Australia (2005-06 Super Series Test).

NEW ZEALAND

S. P. Fleming	7,172	M. D. Crowe	5,444	**L. R. P. L. Taylor** . . .	**5,232**
B. B. McCullum	**6,273**	J. G. Wright	5,334	N. J. Astle	4,702

INDIA

S. R. Tendulkar	15,921	S. M. Gavaskar	10,122	V. Sehwag†	8,503
R. Dravid†	13,265	V. V. S. Laxman	8,781	S. C. Ganguly	7,212

† R. Dravid also scored 0 and 23 and V. Sehwag 76 and 7 for the World XI v Australia (2005-06 Super Series Test).

PAKISTAN

Younis Khan **9,116**	Inzamam-ul-Haq† 8,829	Salim Malik 5,768
Javed Miandad 8,832	Mohammad Yousuf . . 7,530	Zaheer Abbas 5,062

† *Inzamam-ul-Haq also scored 1 and 0 for the World XI v Australia (2005-06 Super Series Test).*

SRI LANKA

K. C. Sangakkara . . .**12,400**	S. T. Jayasuriya. 6,973	M. S. Atapattu. 5,502
D. P. M. D. Jayawardene 11,814	P. A. de Silva 6,361	**T. M. Dilshan**. **5,492**

ZIMBABWE

A. Flower 4,794	A. D. R. Campbell . . . 2,858	H. H. Streak 1,990
G. W. Flower 3,457	G. J. Whittall. 2,207	H. Masakadza. 1,712

BANGLADESH

Tamim Iqbal **3,118**	**Shakib Al Hasan** **2,823**	**Mushfiqur Rahim** . . . **2,650**
Habibul Bashar. 3,026	Mohammad Ashraful 2,737	Javed Omar. 1,720

HIGHEST CAREER AVERAGE

(Qualification: 20 innings)

Avge		T	I	NO	R	HS	100
99.94	D. G. Bradman (A)	52	80	10	6,996	334	29
60.97	R. G. Pollock (SA)	23	41	4	2,256	274*	7
60.83	G. A. Headley (WI)	22	40	4	2,190	270*	10
60.73	H. Sutcliffe (E)	54	84	9	4,555	194	16
59.23	E. Paynter (E)	20	31	5	1,540	243	4
58.67	K. F. Barrington (E)	82	131	15	6,806	256	20
58.61	E. D. Weekes (WI)	48	81	5	4,455	207	15
58.45	W. R. Hammond (E).	85	140	16	7,249	336*	22
57.90	**S. P. D. Smith (A)**	**39**	**72**	**10**	**3,590**	**215**	**13**
57.78	G. S. Sobers (WI)	93	160	21	8,032	365*	26
57.40	**K. C. Sangakkara (SL)**	**134**	**233**	**17**	**12,400**	**319**	**38**
56.94	J. B. Hobbs (E)	61	102	7	5,410	211	15
56.68	C. L. Walcott (WI)	44	74	7	3,798	220	15
56.67	L. Hutton (E)	79	138	15	6,971	364	19
56.00	**Mominul Haque (B)**	**17**	**30**	**4**	**1,456**	**181**	**4**
55.37	J. H. Kallis (SA/World)	166	280	40	13,289	224	45
55.00	E. Tyldesley (E)	14	20	2	990	122	3

S. G. Barnes (A) scored 1,072 runs at 63.05 from 19 innings.

BEST CAREER STRIKE-RATES

(Runs per 100 balls. Qualification: 1,000 runs)

SR		T	I	NO	R	100	Avge
86.97	Shahid Afridi (P)	27	48	1	1,716	5	36.51
86.78	**T. G. Southee (NZ)**.	**46**	**74**	**6**	**1,156**	**0**	**17.00**
82.22	V. Sehwag (I).	104	180	6	8,586	23	49.34
81.98	A. C. Gilchrist (A).	96	137	20	5,570	17	47.60
77.07	**D. A. Warner (A)**	**49**	**91**	**4**	**4,467**	**16**	**51.34**
76.49	G. P. Swann (E).	60	76	14	1,370	0	22.09

SR		T	I	NO	R	100	Avge
74.56	**Sarfraz Ahmed (P)**..............	21	37	9	1,296	3	46.28
70.74	**B. A. Stokes (E)**	23	41	0	1,383	3	33.73
70.28	M. Muralitharan (SL)	133	164	56	1,261	0	11.67
67.88	D. J. G. Sammy (WI).........	38	63	2	1,323	1	21.68
66.60	**S. C. J. Broad (E)**............	91	130	18	2,565	1	22.90
65.98	Umar Akmal (P)	16	30	2	1,003	1	35.82
65.54	T. M. Dilshan (SL)	87	145	11	5,492	16	40.98
65.13*	S. T. Jayasuriya (SL)..........	110	188	14	6,973	14	40.07

* *The above figures are complete except for Jayasuriya, who played one innings for which the balls faced are not recorded. Comprehensive data on balls faced has been available only in recent decades, and its introduction varied from country to country. Among earlier players for whom partial data is available, Kapil Dev (India) had a strike-rate of 80.91 and I. V. A. Richards (West Indies) 70.19 in those innings which were fully recorded.*

HIGHEST PERCENTAGE OF TEAM'S RUNS OVER TEST CAREER

(Qualification: 20 Tests)

	Tests	Runs	Team Runs	% of Team Runs
D. G. Bradman (Australia)........	52	6,996	28,810	24.28
G. A. Headley (West Indies)....	22	2,190	10,239	21.38
B. C. Lara (West Indies).	131	11,953	63,328	18.87
L. Hutton (England)	79	6,971	38,440	18.13
J. B. Hobbs (England)	61	5,410	30,211	17.90
A. D. Nourse (South Africa)	34	2,960	16,659	17.76
E. D. Weekes (West Indies)......	48	4,455	25,667	17.35
B. Mitchell (South Africa).......	42	3,471	20,175	17.20
H. Sutcliffe (England)	54	4,555	26,604	17.12
K. C. Sangakkara (Sri Lanka) ...	134	**12,400**	72,779	17.03
B. Sutcliffe (New Zealand)	42	2,727	16,158	16.87

The percentage shows the proportion of a team's runs scored by that player in all Tests in which he played, including team runs in innings in which he did not bat.

FASTEST FIFTIES

Minutes

24	Misbah-ul-Haq	Pakistan v Australia at Abu Dhabi	2014-15
27	Mohammad Ashraful	Bangladesh v India at Mirpur	2007
28	J. T. Brown	England v Australia at Melbourne	1894-95
29	S. A. Durani	India v England at Kanpur	1963-64
30	E. A. V. Williams	West Indies v England at Bridgetown.......	1947-48
30	B. R. Taylor	New Zealand v West Indies at Auckland	1968-69

The fastest fifties in terms of balls received (where recorded) are:

Balls

21	Misbah-ul-Haq	Pakistan v Australia at Abu Dhabi	2014-15
24	J. H. Kallis	South Africa v Zimbabwe at Cape Town	2004-05
25	S. Shillingford...............	West Indies v New Zealand at Kingston.....	2014
26	Shahid Afridi.................	Pakistan v India at Bangalore	2004-05
26	Mohammad Ashraful	Bangladesh v India at Mirpur	2007
26	D. W. Steyn................	South Africa v West Indies at Port Elizabeth .	2014-15

An expanded and regularly updated online version of the Records can be found at
www.wisdenrecords.com

FASTEST HUNDREDS

Minutes

70	J. M. Gregory	Australia v South Africa at Johannesburg....	1921-22
74	Misbah-ul-Haq	Pakistan v Australia at Abu Dhabi	2014-15
75	G. L. Jessop	England v Australia at The Oval	1902
78	R. Benaud	Australia v West Indies at Kingston	1954-55
80	J. H. Sinclair	South Africa v Australia at Cape Town	1902-03
81	I. V. A. Richards	West Indies v England at St John's	1985-86
86	B. R. Taylor	New Zealand v West Indies at Auckland	1968-69

The fastest hundreds in terms of balls received (where recorded) are:

Balls

56	I. V. A. Richards	West Indies v England at St John's	1985-86
56	Misbah-ul-Haq	Pakistan v Australia at Abu Dhabi	2014-15
57	A. C. Gilchrist	Australia v England at Perth	2006-07
67	J. M. Gregory	Australia v South Africa at Johannesburg....	1921-22
69	S. Chanderpaul	West Indies v Australia at Georgetown	2002-03
69	D. A. Warner	Australia v India at Perth	2011-12
70	C. H. Gayle	West Indies v Australia at Perth	2009-10

In February 2016, after the deadline for this section, B. B. McCullum reached 100 in 54 balls for New Zealand v Australia at Christchurch, in his final Test.

FASTEST DOUBLE-HUNDREDS

Minutes

214	D. G. Bradman	Australia v England at Leeds	1930
217	N. J. Astle	New Zealand v England at Christchurch.....	2001-02
223	S. J. McCabe	Australia v England at Nottingham	1938
226	V. T. Trumper	Australia v South Africa at Adelaide	1910-11
234	D. G. Bradman	Australia v England at Lord's	1930
240	W. R. Hammond	England v New Zealand at Auckland	1932-33

The fastest double-hundreds in terms of balls received (where recorded) are:

Balls

153	N. J. Astle	New Zealand v England at Christchurch.....	2001-02
163	**B. A. Stokes**	**England v South Africa at Cape Town**	**2015-16**
168	V. Sehwag	India v Sri Lanka at Mumbai (BS)	2009-10
182	V. Sehwag	India v Pakistan at Lahore	2005-06
186	B. B. McCullum	New Zealand v Pakistan at Sharjah	2014-15
194	V. Sehwag	India v South Africa at Chennai	2007-08

FASTEST TRIPLE-HUNDREDS

Minutes

288	W. R. Hammond	England v New Zealand at Auckland	1932-33
336	D. G. Bradman	Australia v England at Leeds	1930

The fastest triple-hundred in terms of balls received (where recorded) is:

Balls

278	V. Sehwag	India v South Africa at Chennai	2007-08

MOST RUNS SCORED OFF AN OVER

28	B. C. Lara (466444)	off R. J. Peterson	WI v SA at Johannesburg ..	2003-04
28	G. J. Bailey (462466)	off J. M. Anderson	A v E at Perth	2013-14
27	Shahid Afridi (666621)	off Harbhajan Singh	P v I at Lahore	2005-06
26	C. D. McMillan (444464)	off Younis Khan	NZ v P at Hamilton	2000-01
26	B. C. Lara (406664)	off Danish Kaneria	WI v P at Multan	2006-07
26	M. G. Johnson (446066)	off P. L. Harris	A v SA at Johannesburg	2009-10
26	B. B. McCullum (466046)	off R. A. S. Lakmal	NZ v SL at Christchurch ...	2014-15

MOST RUNS IN A DAY

309	D. G. Bradman	Australia v England at Leeds	1930
295	W. R. Hammond	England v New Zealand at Auckland	1932-33
284	V. Sehwag	India v Sri Lanka at Mumbai	2009-10
273	D. C. S. Compton	England v Pakistan at Nottingham	1954
271	D. G. Bradman	Australia v England at Leeds	1934

MOST SIXES IN A CAREER

A. C. Gilchrist (A)	100		I. V. A. Richards (WI)	84
B. B. McCullum (NZ)	**100**		A. Flintoff (E/World)	82
C. H. Gayle (WI)	98		M. L. Hayden (A)	82
J. H. Kallis (SA/World)	97		K. P. Pietersen (E)	81
V. Sehwag (I/World)	91		M. S. Dhoni (I)	78
B. C. Lara (WI)	88		R. T. Ponting (A)	73
C. L. Cairns (NZ)	87		C. H. Lloyd (WI)	70

SLOWEST INDIVIDUAL BATTING

0	in 101 minutes	G. I. Allott, New Zealand v South Africa at Auckland	1998-99
4*	in 110 minutes	Abdul Razzaq, Pakistan v Australia at Melbourne	2004-05
6	in 137 minutes	S. C. J. Broad, England v New Zealand at Auckland	2012-13
9*	in 184 minutes	Arshad Khan, Pakistan v Sri Lanka at Colombo (SSC)	2000
18	in 194 minutes	W. R. Playle, New Zealand v England at Leeds	1958
19*	in 217 minutes	M. D. Crowe, New Zealand v Sri Lanka at Colombo (SSC)	1983-84
25	**in 289 minutes**	**H. M. Amla, South Africa v India at Delhi**	**2015-16**
35	in 332 minutes	C. J. Tavaré, England v India at Madras	1981-82
43	**in 354 minutes**	**A. B. de Villiers, South Africa v India at Delhi**	**2015-16**
60	in 390 minutes	D. N. Sardesai, India v West Indies at Bridgetown	1961-62
62	in 408 minutes	Ramiz Raja, Pakistan v West Indies at Karachi	1986-87
68	in 458 minutes	T. E. Bailey, England v Australia at Brisbane	1958-59
86	in 474 minutes	Shoaib Mohammad, Pakistan v West Indies at Karachi	1990-91
99	in 505 minutes	M. L. Jaisimha, India v Pakistan at Kanpur	1960-61
104	in 529 minutes	S. V. Manjrekar, India v Zimbabwe at Harare	1992-93
105	in 575 minutes	D. J. McGlew, South Africa v Australia at Durban	1957-58
114	in 591 minutes	Mudassar Nazar, Pakistan v England at Lahore	1977-78
120*	in 609 minutes	J. J. Crowe, New Zealand v Sri Lanka at Colombo (CCC)	1986-87
136*	in 675 minutes	S. Chanderpaul, West Indies v India at St John's	2001-02
163	in 720 minutes	Shoaib Mohammad, Pakistan v New Zealand at Wellington	1988-89
201*	in 777 minutes	D. S. B. P. Kuruppu, Sri Lanka v NZ at Colombo (CCC)	1986-87
275	in 878 minutes	G. Kirsten, South Africa v England at Durban	1999-2000
337	in 970 minutes	Hanif Mohammad, Pakistan v West Indies at Bridgetown	1957-58

SLOWEST HUNDREDS

557 minutes	Mudassar Nazar, Pakistan v England at Lahore	1977-78
545 minutes	D. J. McGlew, South Africa v Australia at Durban	1957-58
535 minutes	A. P. Gurusinha, Sri Lanka v Zimbabwe at Harare	1994-95
516 minutes	J. J. Crowe, New Zealand v Sri Lanka at Colombo (CCC)	1986-87
500 minutes	S. V. Manjrekar, India v Zimbabwe at Harare	1992-93
488 minutes	P. E. Richardson, England v South Africa at Johannesburg	1956-57

The slowest hundred for any Test in England is 458 minutes (329 balls) by K. W. R. Fletcher, England v Pakistan, The Oval, 1974.

The slowest double-hundred in a Test was scored in 777 minutes (548 balls) by D. S. B. P. Kuruppu for Sri Lanka v New Zealand at Colombo (CCC), 1986-87, on his debut.

PARTNERSHIPS OVER 400

624	for 3rd	K. C. Sangakkara (287)/D. P. M. D. Jayawardene (374)	SL v SA	Colombo (SSC)	2006
576	for 2nd	S. T. Jayasuriya (340)/R. S. Mahanama (225)	SL v I	Colombo (RPS)	1997-98
467	for 3rd	A. H. Jones (186)/M. D. Crowe (299)	NZ v SL	Wellington	1990-91
451	for 2nd	W. H. Ponsford (266)/D. G. Bradman (244)	A v E	The Oval	1934
451	for 3rd	Mudassar Nazar (231)/Javed Miandad (280*)	P v I	Hyderabad	1982-83
449	**for 4th**	**A. C. Voges (269*)/S. E. Marsh (182)**	**A v WI**	**Hobart**	**2015-16**
446	for 2nd	C. C. Hunte (260)/G. S. Sobers (365*)	WI v P	Kingston	1957-58
438	for 2nd	M. S. Atapattu (249)/K. C. Sangakkara (270)	SL v Z	Bulawayo	2003-04
437	for 4th	D. P. M. D. Jayawardene (240)/T. T. Samaraweera (231)	SL v P	Karachi	2008-09
429*	for 3rd	J. A. Rudolph (222*)/H. H. Dippenaar (177*)	SA v B	Chittagong	2003
415	for 1st	N. D. McKenzie (226)/G. C. Smith (232)	SA v B	Chittagong	2007-08
413	for 1st	V. Mankad (231)/Pankaj Roy (173)	I v NZ	Madras	1955-56
411	for 4th	P. B. H. May (285*)/M. C. Cowdrey (154)	E v WI	Birmingham	1957
410	for 1st	V. Sehwag (254)/R. Dravid (128*)	I v P	Lahore	2005-06
405	for 5th	S. G. Barnes (234)/D. G. Bradman (234)	A v E	Sydney	1946-47

415 runs were added for the third wicket for India v England at Madras in 1981-82 by D. B. Vengsarkar (retired hurt), G. R. Viswanath and Yashpal Sharma. 408 runs were added for the first wicket for India v Bangladesh at Mirpur in 2007 by K. D. Karthik (retired hurt), Wasim Jaffer (retired hurt), R. Dravid and S. R. Tendulkar.

HIGHEST PARTNERSHIPS FOR EACH WICKET

First Wicket

415	N. D. McKenzie (226)/G. C. Smith (232)	SA v B	Chittagong	2007-08
413	V. Mankad (231)/Pankaj Roy (173)	I v NZ	Madras	1955-56
410	V. Sehwag (254)/R. Dravid (128*)	I v P	Lahore	2005-06
387	G. M. Turner (259)/T. W. Jarvis (182)	NZ v WI	Georgetown	1971-72
382	W. M. Lawry (210)/R. B. Simpson (201)	A v WI	Bridgetown	1964-65

Second Wicket

576	S. T. Jayasuriya (340)/R. S. Mahanama (225)	SL v I	Colombo (RPS)	1997-98
451	W. H. Ponsford (266)/D. G. Bradman (244)	A v E	The Oval	1934
446	C. C. Hunte (260)/G. S. Sobers (365*)	WI v P	Kingston	1957-58
438	M. S. Atapattu (249)/K. C. Sangakkara (270)	SL v Z	Bulawayo	2003-04
382	L. Hutton (364)/M. Leyland (187)	E v A	The Oval	1938

Third Wicket

624	K. C. Sangakkara (287)/D. P. M. D. Jayawardene (374)	SL v SA	Colombo (SSC)	2006
467	A. H. Jones (186)/M. D. Crowe (299)	NZ v SL	Wellington	1990-91
451	Mudassar Nazar (231)/Javed Miandad (280*)	P v I	Hyderabad	1982-83
429*	J. A. Rudolph (222*)/H. H. Dippenaar (177*)	SA v B	Chittagong	2003
397	Qasim Omar (206)/Javed Miandad (203*)	P v SL	Faisalabad	1985-86

Fourth Wicket

449	**A. C. Voges (269*)/S. E. Marsh (182)**	**A v WI**	**Hobart**	**2015-16**
437	D. P. M. D. Jayawardene (240)/T. T. Samaraweera (231)	SL v P	Karachi	2008-09
411	P. B. H. May (285*)/M. C. Cowdrey (154)	E v WI	Birmingham	1957
399	G. S. Sobers (226)/F. M. M. Worrell (197*)	WI v E	Bridgetown	1959-60
388	W. H. Ponsford (181)/D. G. Bradman (304)	A v E	Leeds	1934

Fifth Wicket

405	S. G. Barnes (234)/D. G. Bradman (234)	A v E	Sydney	1946-47
385	S. R. Waugh (160)/G. S. Blewett (214)	A v SA	Johannesburg	1996-97
376	V. V. S. Laxman (281)/R. Dravid (180)	I v A	Kolkata	2000-01
338	G. C. Smith (234)/A. B. de Villiers (164)	SA v P	Dubai	2013-14
334*	M. J. Clarke (329*)/M. E. K. Hussey (150*)	A v I	Sydney	2011-12

Sixth Wicket

399	**B. A. Stokes (258)/J. M. Bairstow (150*)**	**E v SA**	**Cape Town**	**2015-16**
365*	**K. S. Williamson (242*)/B-J. Watling (142*)**	**NZ v SL**	**Wellington**	**2014-15**
352	B. B. McCullum (302)/B-J. Watling (124)	NZ v I	Wellington	2013-14
351	D. P. M. D. Jayawardene (275)/			
	H. A. P. W. Jayawardene (154*).	SL v I	Ahmedabad	2009-10
346	J. H. Fingleton (136)/D. G. Bradman (270)	A v E	Melbourne	1936-37

Seventh Wicket

347	D. St E. Atkinson (219)/C. C. Depeiza (122)	WI v A	Bridgetown	1954-55
308	Waqar Hassan (189)/Imtiaz Ahmed (209)	P v NZ	Lahore	1955-56
280	R. G. Sharma (177)/R. Ashwin (124)	I v WI	Kolkata	2013-14
259*	V. V. S. Laxman (143*)/M. S. Dhoni (132*)	I v SA	Kolkata	2009-10
248	Yousuf Youhana (203)/Saqlain Mushtaq (101*) . . .	P v NZ	Christchurch	2000-01

Eighth Wicket

332	I. J. L. Trott (184)/S. C. J. Broad (169).	E v P	Lord's	2010
313	Wasim Akram (257*)/Saqlain Mushtaq (79)	P v Z	Sheikhupura	1996-97
256	S. P. Fleming (262)/J. E. C. Franklin (122*)	NZ v SA	Cape Town	2005-06
253	N. J. Astle (156*)/A. C. Parore (110)	NZ v A	Perth	2001-02
246	L. E. G. Ames (137)/G. O. B. Allen (122)	E v NZ	Lord's	1931

Ninth Wicket

195	M. V. Boucher (78)/P. L. Symcox (108).	SA v P	Johannesburg	1997-98
190	Asif Iqbal (146)/Intikhab Alam (51).	P v E	The Oval	1967
184	Mahmudullah (76)/Abul Hasan (113).	B v WI	Khulna	2012-13
180	J-P. Duminy (166)/D. W. Steyn (76)	SA v A	Melbourne	2008-09
163*	M. C. Cowdrey (128*)/A. C. Smith (69*)	E v NZ	Wellington	1962-63

Tenth Wicket

198	J. E. Root (154*)/J. M. Anderson (81)	E v I	Nottingham	2014
163	P. J. Hughes (81*)/A. C. Agar (98).	A v E	Nottingham	2013
151	B. F. Hastings (110)/R. O. Collinge (68*)	NZ v P	Auckland	1972-73
151	Azhar Mahmood (128*)/Mushtaq Ahmed (59)	P v SA	Rawalpindi	1997-98
143	D. Ramdin (107*)/T. L. Best (95).	WI v E	Birmingham	2012

HIGHEST PARTNERSHIPS FOR EACH COUNTRY

ENGLAND

359	for 1st	L. Hutton (158)/C. Washbrook (195)	v SA	Johannesburg	1948-49
382	for 2nd	L. Hutton (364)/M. Leyland (187)	v A	The Oval	1938
370	for 3rd	W. J. Edrich (189)/D. C. S. Compton (208)	v SA	Lord's	1947
411	for 4th	P. B. H. May (285*)/M. C. Cowdrey (154)	v WI	Birmingham	1957
254	for 5th	K. W. R. Fletcher (113)/A. W. Greig (148)	v I	Bombay	1972-73
399	**for 6th**	**B. A. Stokes (258)/J. M. Bairstow (150*)**	**v SA**	**Cape Town**	**2015-16**
197	for 7th	M. J. K. Smith (96)/J. M. Parks (101*)	v WI	Port-of-Spain	1959-60
332	for 8th	I. J. L. Trott (184)/S. C. J. Broad (169)	v P	Lord's	2010
163*	for 9th	M. C. Cowdrey (128*)/A. C. Smith (69*)	v NZ	Wellington	1962-63
198	for 10th	J. E. Root (154*)/J. M. Anderson (81)	v I	Nottingham	2014

AUSTRALIA

382	for 1st	W. M. Lawry (210)/R. B. Simpson (201)	v WI	Bridgetown	1964-65
451	for 2nd	W. H. Ponsford (266)/D. G. Bradman (244)	v E	The Oval	1934
315	for 3rd	R. T. Ponting (206)/D. S. Lehmann (160)	v WI	Port-of-Spain	2002-03
449	**for 4th**	**A. C. Voges (269*)/S. E. Marsh (182)**	**v WI**	**Hobart**	**2015-16**
405	for 5th	S. G. Barnes (234)/D. G. Bradman (234)	v E	Sydney	1946-47
346	for 6th	J. H. Fingleton (136)/D. G. Bradman (270)	v E	Melbourne	1936-37
217	for 7th	K. D. Walters (250)/G. J. Gilmour (101)	v NZ	Christchurch	1976-77
243	for 8th	R. J. Hartigan (116)/C. Hill (160)	v E	Adelaide	1907-08
154	for 9th	S. E. Gregory (201)/J. McC. Blackham (74)	v E	Sydney	1894-95
163	for 10th	P. J. Hughes (81*)/A. C. Agar (98)	v E	Nottingham	2013

SOUTH AFRICA

415	for 1st	N. D. McKenzie (226)/G. C. Smith (232)	v B	Chittagong	2007-08
315*	for 2nd	H. H. Gibbs (211*)/J. H. Kallis (148*)	v NZ	Christchurch	1998-99
429*	for 3rd	J. A. Rudolph (222*)/H. H. Dippenaar (177*)	v B	Chittagong	2003
308	for 4th	H. M. Amla (208)/A. B. de Villiers (152)	v WI	Centurion	2014-15
338	for 5th	G. C. Smith (234)/A. B. de Villiers (164)	v P	Dubai	2013-14
271	for 6th	A. G. Prince (162*)/M. V. Boucher (117)	v B	Centurion	2008-09
246	for 7th	D. J. McGlew (255*)/A. R. A. Murray (109)	v NZ	Wellington	1952-53
150	for 8th {	N. D. McKenzie (103)/S. M. Pollock (111)	v SL	Centurion	2000-01
		G. Kirsten (130)/M. Zondeki (59)	v E	Leeds	2003
195	for 9th	M. V. Boucher (78)/P. L. Symcox (108)	v P	Johannesburg	1997-98
107*	for 10th	A. B. de Villiers (278*)/M. Morkel (35*)	v P	Abu Dhabi	2010-11

WEST INDIES

298	for 1st	C. G. Greenidge (149)/D. L. Haynes (167)	v E	St John's	1989-90
446	for 2nd	C. C. Hunte (260)/G. S. Sobers (365*)	v P	Kingston	1957-58
338	for 3rd	E. D. Weekes (206)/F. M. M. Worrell (167)	v E	Port-of-Spain	1953-54
399	for 4th	G. S. Sobers (226)/F. M. M. Worrell (197*)	v E	Bridgetown	1959-60
322	for 5th†	B. C. Lara (213)/J. C. Adams (94)	v A	Kingston	1998-99
282*	for 6th	B. C. Lara (400*)/R. D. Jacobs (107*)	v E	St John's	2003-04
347	for 7th	D. St E. Atkinson (219)/C. C. Depeiza (122)	v A	Bridgetown	1954-55
148	for 8th	J. C. Adams (101*)/F. A. Rose (69)	v Z	Kingston	1999-2000
161	for 9th	C. H. Lloyd (161*)/A. M. E. Roberts (68)	v I	Calcutta	1983-84
143	for 10th	D. Ramdin (107*)/T. L. Best (95)	v E	Birmingham	2012

† 344 runs were added between the fall of the 4th and 5th wickets: P. T. Collins retired hurt when he and Lara had added 22 runs.

NEW ZEALAND

387	for 1st	G. M. Turner (259)/T. W. Jarvis (182)	v WI	Georgetown	1971-72
297	for 2nd	B. B. McCullum (202)/K. S. Williamson (192)	v P	Sharjah	2014-15
467	for 3rd	A. H. Jones (186)/M. D. Crowe (299)	v SL	Wellington	1990-91
271	for 4th	L. R. P. L. Taylor (151)/J. D. Ryder (201) . . .	v I	Napier	2008-09
222	for 5th	N. J. Astle (141)/C. D. McMillan (142)	v Z	Wellington	2000-01
365*	**for 6th**	**K. S. Williamson (242*)/B.-J. Watling (142*)**	**v SL**	**Wellington**	**2014-15**
225	for 7th	C. L. Cairns (158)/J. D. P. Oram (90).	v SA	Auckland	2003-04
256	for 8th	S. P. Fleming (262)/J. E. C. Franklin (122*) . .	v SA	Cape Town	2005-06
136	for 9th	I. D. S. Smith (173)/M. C. Snedden (22)	v I	Auckland	1989-90
151	for 10th	B. F. Hastings (110)/R. O. Collinge (68*)	v P	Auckland	1972-73

INDIA

413	for 1st	V. Mankad (231)/Pankaj Roy (173)	v NZ	Madras	1955-56
370	for 2nd	M. Vijay (167)/C. A. Pujara (204).	v A	Hyderabad	2012-13
336	for 3rd†	V. Sehwag (309)/S. R. Tendulkar (194*).	v P	Multan	2003-04
353	for 4th	S. R. Tendulkar (241*)/V. V. S. Laxman (178) .	v A	Sydney	2003-04
376	for 5th	V. V. S. Laxman (281)/R. Dravid (180)	v A	Kolkata	2000-01
298*	for 6th	D. B. Vengsarkar (164*)/R. J. Shastri (121*). .	v A	Bombay	1986-87
280	for 7th	R. G. Sharma (177)/R. Ashwin (124)	v WI	Kolkata	2013-14
161	for 8th	A. Kumble (88)/M. Azharuddin (109)	v SA	Calcutta	1996-97
149	for 9th	P. G. Joshi (52*)/R. B. Desai (85)	v P	Bombay	1960-61
133	for 10th	S. R. Tendulkar (248*)/Zaheer Khan (75) . . .	v B	Dhaka	2004-05

† *415 runs were scored for India's 3rd wicket v England at Madras in 1981-82, in two partnerships: D. B. Vengsarkar and G. R. Viswanath put on 99 before Vengsarkar retired hurt, then Viswanath and Yashpal Sharma added a further 316.*

PAKISTAN

298	for 1st	Aamir Sohail (160)/Ijaz Ahmed, sen. (151) . . .	v WI	Karachi	1997-98
291	for 2nd	Zaheer Abbas (274)/Mushtaq Mohammad (100)	v E	Birmingham	1971
451	for 3rd	Mudassar Nazar (231)/Javed Miandad (280*) .	v I	Hyderabad	1982-83
350	for 4th	Mushtaq Mohammad (201)/Asif Iqbal (175) . .	v NZ	Dunedin	1972-73
281	for 5th	Javed Miandad (163)/Asif Iqbal (166)	v NZ	Lahore	1976-77
269	for 6th	Mohammad Yousuf (223)/Kamran Akmal (154)	v E	Lahore	2005-06
308	for 7th	Waqar Hassan (189)/Imtiaz Ahmed (209)	v NZ	Lahore	1955-56
313	for 8th	Wasim Akram (257*)/Saqlain Mushtaq (79) . .	v Z	Sheikhupura	1996-97
190	for 9th	Asif Iqbal (146)/Intikhab Alam (51).	v E	The Oval	1967
151	for 10th	Azhar Mahmood (128*)/Mushtaq Ahmed (59)	v SA	Rawalpindi	1997-98

SRI LANKA

335	for 1st	M. S. Atapattu (207*)/S. T. Jayasuriya (188). .	v P	Kandy	2000
576	for 2nd	S. T. Jayasuriya (340)/R. S. Mahanama (225) .	v I	Colombo (RPS)	1997-98
624	for 3rd	K. C. Sangakkara (287)/ D. P. M. D. Jayawardene (374).	v SA	Colombo (SSC)	2006
437	for 4th	D. P. M. D. Jayawardene (240)/ T. T. Samaraweera (231)	v P	Karachi	2008-09
280	for 5th	T. T. Samaraweera (138)/T. M. Dilshan (168) .	v B	Colombo (PSS)	2005-06
351	for 6th	D. P. M. D. Jayawardene (275)/ H. A. P. W. Jayawardene (154*)	v I	Ahmedabad	2009-10
223*	for 7th	H. A. P. W. Jayawardene (120*)/ W. P. U. J. C. Vaas (100*)	v B	Colombo (SSC)	2007
170	for 8th	D. P. M. D. Jayawardene (237)/ W. P. U. J. C. Vaas (69)	v SA	Galle	2004
118	for 9th	T. T. Samaraweera (83)/B. A. W. Mendis (78) .	v I	Colombo (PSS)	2010
79	for 10th	W. P. U. J. C. Vaas (68*)/M. Muralitharan (43)	v A	Kandy	2003-04

ZIMBABWE

164	for 1st	D. D. Ebrahim (71)/A. D. R. Campbell (103) .	v WI	Bulawayo	2001
160	for 2nd	Sikandar Raza (82)/H. Masakadza (81)	v B	Chittagong	2014-15
194	for 3rd	A. D. R. Campbell (99)/D. L. Houghton (142).	v SL	Harare	1994-95
269	for 4th	G. W. Flower (201*)/A. Flower (156)	v P	Harare	1994-95
277*	for 5th	M. W. Goodwin (166*)/A. Flower (100*)	v P	Bulawayo	1997-98
165	for 6th	D. L. Houghton (121)/A. Flower (59).	v I	Harare	1992-93
154	for 7th	H. H. Streak (83*)/A. M. Blignaut (92)	v WI	Harare	2001
168	for 8th	H. H. Streak (127*)/A. M. Blignaut (91)	v WI	Harare	2003-04
87	for 9th	P. A. Strang (106*)/B. C. Strang (42)	v P	Sheikhupura	1996-97
97*	for 10th	A. Flower (183*)/H. K. Olonga (11*)	v I	Delhi	2000-01

BANGLADESH

312	**for 1st**	**Tamim Iqbal (206)/Imrul Kayes (150)**	**v P**	**Khulna**	**2014-15**
232	for 2nd	Shamsur Rahman (106)/Imrul Kayes (115) . . .	v SL	Chittagong	2013-14
157	for 3rd	Tamim Iqbal (70)/Mominul Haque (126*) . . .	v NZ	Chittagong	2013-14
167	for 4th	Naeem Islam (108)/Shakib Al Hasan (89) . . .	v WI	Mirpur	2012-13
267	for 5th	Mohammad Ashraful (190)/Mushfiqur Rahim (200).	v SL	Galle	2012-13
191	for 6th	Mohammad Ashraful (129*)/Mushfiqur Rahim (80).	v SL	Colombo (PSS)	2007
145	for 7th	Shakib Al Hasan (87)/Mahmudullah (115) . . .	v NZ	Hamilton	2009-10
113	for 8th	Mushfiqur Rahim (79)/Naeem Islam (38). . . .	v E	Chittagong	2009-10
184	for 9th	Mahmudullah (76)/Abul Hasan (113)	v WI	Khulna	2012-13
69	for 10th	Mohammad Rafique (65)/Shahadat Hossain (3*)	v A	Chittagong	2005-06

UNUSUAL DISMISSALS

Handled the Ball

W. R. Endean	South Africa v England at Cape Town	1956-57
A. M. J. Hilditch	Australia v Pakistan at Perth.	1978-79
Mohsin Khan	Pakistan v Australia at Karachi.	1982-83
D. L. Haynes	West Indies v India at Bombay.	1983-84
G. A. Gooch	England v Australia at Manchester	1993
S. R. Waugh	Australia v India at Chennai.	2000-01
M. P. Vaughan	England v India at Bangalore	2001-02

Obstructing the Field

| L. Hutton | England v South Africa at The Oval . . . . | 1951 |

There have been no cases of Hit the Ball Twice or Timed Out in Test cricket.

BOWLING RECORDS

MOST WICKETS IN AN INNINGS

10-53	J. C. Laker	England v Australia at Manchester	1956
10-74	A. Kumble	India v Pakistan at Delhi.	1998-99
9-28	G. A. Lohmann	England v South Africa at Johannesburg	1895-96
9-37	J. C. Laker	England v Australia at Manchester	1956
9-51	M. Muralitharan.	Sri Lanka v Zimbabwe at Kandy	2001-02
9-52	R. J. Hadlee	New Zealand v Australia at Brisbane	1985-86
9-56	Abdul Qadir	Pakistan v England at Lahore	1987-88
9-57	D. E. Malcolm.	England v South Africa at The Oval.	1994
9-65	M. Muralitharan.	Sri Lanka v England at The Oval	1998

9-69	J. M. Patel	India v Australia at Kanpur	1959-60
9-83	Kapil Dev	India v West Indies at Ahmedabad	1983-84
9-86	Sarfraz Nawaz	Pakistan v Australia at Melbourne	1978-79
9-95	J. M. Noreiga	West Indies v India at Port-of-Spain	1970-71
9-102	S. P. Gupte	India v West Indies at Kanpur	1958-59
9-103	S. F. Barnes	England v South Africa at Johannesburg	1913-14
9-113	H. J. Tayfield	South Africa v England at Johannesburg	1956-57
9-121	A. A. Mailey	Australia v England at Melbourne	1920-21
9-127	H. M. R. K. B. Herath . . .	Sri Lanka v Pakistan at Colombo (SSC)	2014

There have been 73 instances of eight wickets in a Test innings.

The best bowling figures for the countries not mentioned above are:

| 8-39 | Taijul Islam . . . . | Bangladesh v Zimbabwe at Mirpur . . . . | 2014-15 |
| 8-109 | P. A. Strang . . . . | Zimbabwe v New Zealand at Bulawayo . . . . | 2000-01 |

OUTSTANDING BOWLING ANALYSES

	O	M	R	W		
J. C. Laker (E)	51.2	23	53	10	v Australia at Manchester	1956
A. Kumble (I)	26.3	9	74	10	v Pakistan at Delhi	1998-99
G. A. Lohmann (E)	14.2	6	28	9	v South Africa at Johannesburg	1895-96
J. C. Laker (E)	16.4	4	37	9	v Australia at Manchester	1956
G. A. Lohmann (E)	9.4	5	7	8	v South Africa at Port Elizabeth . . .	1895-96
J. Briggs (E)	14.2	5	11	8	v South Africa at Cape Town	1888-89
S. C. J. Broad (E)	**9.3**	**5**	**15**	**8**	**v Australia at Nottingham**	**2015**
S. J. Harmison (E)	12.3	8	12	7	v West Indies at Kingston	2003-04
J. Briggs (E)	19.1	11	17	7	v South Africa at Cape Town	1888-89
M. A. Noble (A)	7.4	2	17	7	v England at Melbourne	1901-02
W. Rhodes (E)	11	3	17	7	v Australia at Birmingham	1902

WICKET WITH FIRST BALL IN TEST CRICKET

Batsman dismissed

T. P. Horan	W. W. Read	A v E	Sydney	1882-83
A. Coningham	A. C. MacLaren	A v E	Melbourne	1894-95
W. M. Bradley	F. Laver	E v A	Manchester	1899
E. G. Arnold	V. T. Trumper	E v A	Sydney	1903-04
A. E. E. Vogler	E. G. Hayes	SA v E	Johannesburg	1905-06
J. N. Crawford	A. E. E. Vogler	E v SA	Johannesburg	1905-06
G. G. Macaulay	G. A. L. Hearne	E v SA	Cape Town	1922-23
M. W. Tate	M. J. Susskind	E v SA	Birmingham	1924
M. Henderson	E. W. Dawson	NZ v E	Christchurch	1929-30
H. D. Smith	E. Paynter	NZ v E	Christchurch	1932-33
T. F. Johnson	W. W. Keeton	WI v E	The Oval	1939
R. Howorth	D. V. Dyer	E v SA	The Oval	1947
Intikhab Alam	C. C. McDonald	P v A	Karachi	1959-60
R. K. Illingworth	P. V. Simmons	E v WI	Nottingham	1991
N. M. Kulkarni	M. S. Atapattu	I v SL	Colombo (RPS)	1997-98
M. K. G. C. P. Lakshitha	Mohammad Ashraful	SL v B	Colombo (SSC)	2002
N. M. Lyon	K. C. Sangakkara	A v SL	Galle	2011-12
R. M. S. Eranga	S. R. Watson	SL v A	Colombo (SSC)	2011-12
D. L. Piedt	M. A. Vermeulen	SA v Z	Harare	2014-15
G. C. Viljoen	**A. N. Cook**	**SA v E**	**Johannesburg**	**2015-16**

HAT-TRICKS

Most Hat-Tricks

S. C. J. Broad	**2**	H. Trumble............	2
T. J. Matthews†	2	Wasim Akram‡	2

† *T. J. Matthews did the hat-trick in each innings of the same match.*
‡ *Wasim Akram did the hat-trick in successive matches.*

Hat-Tricks

There have been **41** hat-tricks in Tests, including the above. Occurrences since 2007:

R. J. Sidebottom	England v New Zealand at Hamilton...................	2007-08
P. M. Siddle............	Australia v England at Brisbane	2010-11
S. C. J. Broad...........	England v India at Nottingham	2011
Sohag Gazi†	Bangladesh v New Zealand at Chittagong................	2013-14
S. C. J. Broad...........	England v Sri Lanka at Leeds	2014

† *Sohag Gazi also scored 101 not out.*

M. J. C. Allom, P. J. Petherick and D. W. Fleming did the hat-trick on Test debut. D. N. T. Zoysa took one in the second over of a Test (his first three balls); I. K. Pathan in the first over of a Test.

FOUR WICKETS IN FIVE BALLS

M. J. C. Allom.......	England v New Zealand at Christchurch...................	1929-30
	On debut, in his eighth over: W-WWW	
C. M. Old...........	England v Pakistan at Birmingham	1978
	Sequence interrupted by a no-ball: WW-WW	
Wasim Akram.......	Pakistan v West Indies at Lahore (*WW-WW*)	1990-91

MOST WICKETS IN A TEST

19-90	J. C. Laker	England v Australia at Manchester............	1956
17-159	S. F. Barnes	England v South Africa at Johannesburg	1913-14
16-136†	N. D. Hirwani..........	India v West Indies at Madras.............	1987-88
16-137†	R. A. L. Massie	Australia v England at Lord's...............	1972
16-220	M. Muralitharan	Sri Lanka v England at The Oval	1998

† *On Test debut.*

There have been 18 further instances of 14 or more wickets in a Test match.

The best bowling figures for the countries not mentioned above are:

15-123	R. J. Hadlee	New Zealand v Australia at Brisbane	1985-86
14-116	Imran Khan	Pakistan v Sri Lanka at Lahore	1981-82
14-149	M. A. Holding	West Indies v England at The Oval	1976
13-132	M. Ntini	South Africa v West Indies at Port-of-Spain.....	2004-05
12-200	Enamul Haque, jun......	Bangladesh v Zimbabwe at Dhaka	2004-05
11-255	A. G. Huckle	Zimbabwe v New Zealand at Bulawayo........	1997-98

MOST BALLS BOWLED IN A TEST

S. Ramadhin (West Indies) sent down 774 balls in 129 overs against England at Birmingham, 1957, the most delivered by any bowler in a Test, beating H. Verity's 766 for England against South Africa at Durban, 1938-39. In this match Ramadhin also bowled the most balls (588) in any first-class innings, since equalled by Arshad Ayub, Hyderabad v Madhya Pradesh at Secunderabad, 1991-92.

MOST WICKETS IN A SERIES

	T	R	W	Avge		
S. F. Barnes	4	536	49	10.93	England v South Africa	1913-14
J. C. Laker	5	442	46	9.60	England v Australia	1956
C. V. Grimmett	5	642	44	14.59	Australia v South Africa . . .	1935-36
T. M. Alderman	6	893	42	21.26	Australia v England	1981
R. M. Hogg	6	527	41	12.85	Australia v England	1978-79
T. M. Alderman	6	712	41	17.36	Australia v England	1989
Imran Khan	6	558	40	13.95	Pakistan v India	1982-83
S. K. Warne	5	797	40	19.92	Australia v England	2005

The most for South Africa is 37 by H. J. Tayfield against England in 1956-57, for West Indies 35 by M. D. Marshall against England in 1988, for India 35 by B. S. Chandrasekhar against England in 1972-73 (all in five Tests), for New Zealand 33 by R. J. Hadlee against Australia in 1985-86, for Sri Lanka 30 by M. Muralitharan against Zimbabwe in 2001-02, for Zimbabwe 22 by H. H. Streak against Pakistan in 1994-95 (all in three Tests), and for Bangladesh 18 by Enamul Haque, jun. against Zimbabwe in 2004-05 (two Tests) and 18 by Shakib Al Hasan against Zimbabwe in 2014-15 (three Tests).

MOST WICKETS IN A CALENDAR YEAR

	T	R	W	Avge	5I	10M	Year
S. K. Warne (Australia)	15	2,114	96	22.02	6	2	2005
M. Muralitharan (Sri Lanka)	11	1,521	90	16.89	9	5	2006
D. K. Lillee (Australia).	13	1,781	85	20.95	5	2	1981
A. A. Donald (South Africa)	14	1,571	80	19.63	7	–	1998
M. Muralitharan (Sri Lanka)	12	1,699	80	21.23	7	4	2001
J. Garner (West Indies).	15	1,604	77	20.83	4	–	1984
Kapil Dev (India)	18	1,739	75	23.18	5	1	1983
M. Muralitharan (Sri Lanka)	10	1,463	75	19.50	7	3	2000

MOST WICKETS

		T	Balls	R	W	Avge	5I	10M	SR
1	M. Muralitharan (SL/World).	133	44,039	18,180	800	22.72	67	22	55.04
2	S. K. Warne (Australia).	145	40,704	17,995	708	25.41	37	10	57.49
3	A. Kumble (India).	132	40,850	18,355	619	29.65	35	8	65.99
4	G. D. McGrath (Australia) . .	124	29,248	12,186	563	21.64	29	3	51.95
5	C. A. Walsh (West Indies) . .	132	30,019	12,688	519	24.44	22	3	57.84
6	Kapil Dev (India)	131	27,740	12,867	434	29.64	23	2	63.91
7	**J. M. Anderson (England)** .	**113**	**25,185**	**12,638**	**433**	**29.18**	**18**	**2**	**58.16**
8	R. J. Hadlee (New Zealand) .	86	21,918	9,611	431	22.29	36	9	50.85
9	S. M. Pollock (South Africa)	108	24,353	9,733	421	23.11	16	1	57.84
10	**Harbhajan Singh (India)** .	**103**	**28,580**	**13,537**	**417**	**32.46**	**25**	**5**	**68.53**
11	Wasim Akram (Pakistan) . .	104	22,627	9,779	414	23.62	25	5	54.65
12	**D. W. Steyn (South Africa)** .	**82**	**16,956**	**9,150**	**406**	**22.53**	**25**	**5**	**41.76**
13	C. E. L. Ambrose (WI)	98	22,103	8,501	405	20.99	22	3	54.57
14	M. Ntini (South Africa). . . .	101	20,834	11,242	390	28.82	18	4	53.42
15	I. T. Botham (England)	102	21,815	10,878	383	28.40	27	4	56.95
16	M. D. Marshall (West Indies)	81	17,584	7,876	376	20.94	22	4	46.76
17	Waqar Younis (Pakistan) . . .	87	16,224	8,788	373	23.56	22	5	43.49
18	Imran Khan (Pakistan)	88	19,458	8,258	362	22.81	23	6	53.75
18	D. L. Vettori (NZ/World) . .	113	28,814	12,441	362	34.36	20	3	79.59
20	D. K. Lillee (Australia)	70	18,467	8,493	355	23.92	23	7	52.01
20	W. P. U. J. C. Vaas (SL) . . .	111	23,438	10,501	355	29.58	12	2	66.02
22	**S. C. J. Broad (England)** . . .	**91**	**18,885**	**9,545**	**333**	**28.66**	**15**	**2**	**56.71**
23	A. A. Donald (South Africa).	72	15,519	7,344	330	22.25	20	3	47.02
24	R. G. D. Willis (England) . . .	90	17,357	8,190	325	25.20	16	–	53.40

		T	Balls	R	W	Avge	5I	10M	SR
25	**M. G. Johnson** (Australia) .	73	**16,001**	**8,891**	313	**28.40**	12	3	**51.12**
26	Zaheer Khan (India)	92	18,785	10,247	311	32.94	11	1	60.40
27	B. Lee (Australia)	76	16,531	9,554	310	30.81	10	–	53.32
28	L. R. Gibbs (West Indies) . . .	79	27,115	8,989	309	29.09	18	2	87.75
29	F. S. Trueman (England). . . .	67	15,178	6,625	307	21.57	17	3	49.43

MOST WICKETS FOR EACH COUNTRY

ENGLAND

J. M. Anderson **433**	**S. C. J. Broad** **333**	F. S. Trueman 307
I. T. Botham 383	R. G. D. Willis 325	D. L. Underwood 297

AUSTRALIA

S. K. Warne 708	D. K. Lillee 355	B. Lee 310
G. D. McGrath 563	**M. G. Johnson** **313**	C. J. McDermott 291

SOUTH AFRICA

S. M. Pollock 421	M. Ntini 390	J. H. Kallis† 291
D. W. Steyn **406**	A. A. Donald 330	**M. Morkel** **242**

† *J. H. Kallis also took 0-35 and 1-3 for the World XI v Australia (2005-06 Super Series Test).*

WEST INDIES

C. A. Walsh 519	M. D. Marshall 376	J. Garner 259
C. E. L. Ambrose 405	L. R. Gibbs 309	M. A. Holding 249

NEW ZEALAND

R. J. Hadlee 431	C. S. Martin 233	**T. G. Southee** **163**
D. L. Vettori† 361	C. L. Cairns 218	D. K. Morrison 160

† *D. L. Vettori also took 1-73 and 0-38 for the World XI v Australia (2005-06 Super Series Test).*

INDIA

A. Kumble 619	**Harbhajan Singh** **417**	B. S. Bedi 266
Kapil Dev 434	Zaheer Khan 311	B. S. Chandrasekhar 242

PAKISTAN

Wasim Akram 414	Imran Khan 362	Abdul Qadir 236
Waqar Younis 373	Danish Kaneria 261	Saqlain Mushtaq 208

SRI LANKA

M. Muralitharan† 795	**H. M. R. K. B. Herath** . .**297**	C. R. D. Fernando 100
W. P. U. J. C. Vaas 355	S. L. Malinga 101	S. T. Jayasuriya 98

† *M. Muralitharan also took 2-102 and 3-55 for the World XI v Australia (2005-06 Super Series Test).*

ZIMBABWE

H. H. Streak 216	P. A. Strang 70	B. C. Strang 56
R. W. Price. 80	H. K. Olonga 68	A. M. Blignaut 53

BANGLADESH

Shakib Al Hasan. 147	Mashrafe bin Mortaza . . . 78	Enamul Haque, jun. 44
Mohammad Rafique. 100	**Shahadat Hossain. 72**	Sohag Gazi 38

BEST CAREER AVERAGES

(Qualification: 75 wickets)

Avge		T	W	Avge		T	W
10.75	G. A. Lohmann (E)	18	112	18.63	C. Blythe (E)	19	100
16.43	S. F. Barnes (E)	27	189	20.39	J. H. Wardle (E)	28	102
16.53	C. T. B. Turner (A)	17	101	20.53	A. K. Davidson (A)	44	186
16.98	R. Peel (E)	20	101	20.94	M. D. Marshall (WI)	81	376
17.75	J. Briggs (E)	33	118	20.97	J. Garner (WI)	58	259
18.41	F. R. Spofforth (A)	18	94	20.99	C. E. L. Ambrose (WI)	98	405
18.56	F. H. Tyson (E)	17	76				

BEST CAREER STRIKE-RATES

(Balls per wicket. Qualification: 75 wickets)

SR		T	W	SR		T	W
34.19	G. A. Lohmann (E)	18	112	45.74	Shoaib Akhtar (P)	46	178
38.75	S. E. Bond (NZ)	18	87	46.76	M. D. Marshall (WI)	81	376
41.65	S. F. Barnes (E)	27	189	47.02	A. A. Donald (SA)	72	330
41.76	**D. W. Steyn (SA)**	**82**	**406**	**47.44**	**S. T. Finn (E)**	**29**	**113**
43.49	Waqar Younis (P)	87	373	**48.13**	**V. D. Philander (SA)**	**32**	**126**
44.52	F. R. Spofforth (A)	18	94	**48.44**	**Yasir Shah (P)**	**12**	**76**
45.12	J. V. Saunders (A)	14	79	48.78	Mohammad Asif (P)	23	106
45.18	J. Briggs (E)	33	118	49.32	C. E. H. Croft (WI)	27	125
45.42	F. H. Tyson (E)	17	76	49.43	F. S. Trueman (E)	67	307
45.46	C. Blythe (E)	19	100				

BEST CAREER ECONOMY-RATES

(Runs per six balls. Qualification: 75 wickets)

ER		T	W	ER		T	W
1.64	T. L. Goddard (SA)	41	123	1.94	W. J. O'Reilly (A)	27	144
1.67	R. G. Nadkarni (I)	41	88	1.94	H. J. Tayfield (SA)	37	170
1.88	H. Verity (E)	40	144	1.95	A. L. Valentine (WI)	36	139
1.88	G. A. Lohmann (E)	18	112	1.95	F. J. Titmus (E)	53	153
1.89	J. H. Wardle (E)	28	102	1.97	S. Ramadhin (WI)	43	158
1.91	R. Illingworth (E)	61	122	1.97	R. Peel (E)	20	101
1.93	C. T. B. Turner (A)	17	101	1.97	A. K. Davidson (A)	44	186
1.94	M. W. Tate (E)	39	155	1.98	L. R. Gibbs (WI)	79	309

HIGHEST PERCENTAGE OF TEAM'S WICKETS OVER TEST CAREER

(Qualification: 20 Tests)

	Tests	Wkts	Team Wkts	% of Team Wkts
M. Muralitharan (Sri Lanka/World).	133	800	2,070	38.64
S. F. Barnes (England).	27	189	494	38.25
R. J. Hadlee (New Zealand).	86	431	1,255	34.34
C. V. Grimmett (Australia)	37	216	636	33.96
Fazal Mahmood (Pakistan)	34	139	410	33.90
R. Ashwin (India).	**32**	**176**	**536**	**32.83**
W. J. O'Reilly (Australia)	27	144	446	32.28
S. P. Gupte (India)	36	149	470	31.70
Saeed Ajmal (Pakistan)	35	178	575	30.95
Mohammad Rafique (Bangladesh).	33	100	328	30.48
A. V. Bedser (England)	51	236	777	30.37

Excluding the Super Series Test, Muralitharan took 795 out of 2,050 wickets in his 132 Tests for Sri Lanka, a percentage of 38.78.

The percentage shows the proportion of a team's wickets taken by that player in all Tests in which he played, including team wickets in innings in which he did not bowl.

ALL-ROUND RECORDS

HUNDRED AND FIVE WICKETS IN AN INNINGS

England

A. W. Greig	148	6-164	v West Indies	Bridgetown	1973-74
I. T. Botham	103	5-73	v New Zealand	Christchurch	1977-78
I. T. Botham	108	8-34	v Pakistan	Lord's	1978
I. T. Botham	114	6-58, 7-48	v India	Bombay.	1979-80
I. T. Botham	149*	6-95	v Australia	Leeds.	1981
I. T. Botham	138	5-59	v New Zealand	Wellington	1983-84

Australia

C. Kelleway	114	5-33	v South Africa	Manchester	1912
J. M. Gregory	100	7-69	v England.	Melbourne.	1920-21
K. R. Miller	109	6-107	v West Indies	Kingston	1954-55
R. Benaud	100	5-84	v South Africa	Johannesburg	1957-58

South Africa

J. H. Sinclair	106	6-26	v England.	Cape Town	1898-99
G. A. Faulkner	123	5-120	v England.	Johannesburg . . .	1909-10
J. H. Kallis	110	5-90	v West Indies	Cape Town	1998-99
J. H. Kallis	139*	5-21	v Bangladesh	Potchefstroom. . .	2002-03

West Indies

D. St E. Atkinson	219	5-56	v Australia	Bridgetown	1954-55
O. G. Smith	100	5-90	v India	Delhi	1958-59
G. S. Sobers	104	5-63	v India	Kingston	1961-62
G. S. Sobers	174	5-41	v England	Leeds.	1966

New Zealand

B. R. Taylor†	105	5-86	v India	Calcutta.	1964-65

India

V. Mankad	184	5-196	v England	Lord's	1952
P. R. Umrigar	172*	5-107	v West Indies	Port-of-Spain	1961-62
R. Ashwin	103	5-156	v West Indies	Mumbai	2011-12

Pakistan

Mushtaq Mohammad	201	5-49	v New Zealand	Dunedin	1972-73
Mushtaq Mohammad	121	5-28	v West Indies	Port-of-Spain	1976-77
Imran Khan	117	6-98, 5-82	v India	Faisalabad	1982-83
Wasim Akram	123	5-100	v Australia	Adelaide	1989-90

Zimbabwe

| P. A. Strang | 106* | 5-212 | v Pakistan | Sheikhupura | 1996-97 |

Bangladesh

Shakib Al Hasan	144	6-82	v Pakistan	Mirpur	2011-12
Sohag Gazi	101*	6-77‡	v New Zealand	Chittagong	2013-14
Shakib Al Hasan	137	5-80, 5-44	v Zimbabwe	Khulna	2014-15

†   *On debut.*   ‡   *Including a hat-trick; Sohag Gazi is the only player to score a hundred and take a hat-trick in the same Test.*

HUNDRED AND FIVE DISMISSALS IN AN INNINGS

D. T. Lindsay	182	6ct	SA v A	Johannesburg	1966-67
I. D. S. Smith	113*	4ct, 1st	NZ v E	Auckland	1983-84
S. A. R. Silva	111	5ct	SL v I	Colombo (PSS)	1985-86
A. C. Gilchrist	133	4ct, 1st	A v E	Sydney	2002-03
M. J. Prior	118	5ct	E v A	Sydney	2010-11
A. B. de Villiers	103*	6ct and 5ct	SA v P	Johannesburg	2012-13
M. J. Prior	110*	5ct	E v NZ	Auckland	2012-13
B-J. Watling	124	5ct	NZ v I	Wellington	2013-14
B-J. Watling	**142***	**4ct, 1st**	**NZ v SL**	**Wellington**	**2014-15**

100 RUNS AND TEN WICKETS IN A TEST

A. K. Davidson	44	5-135	} A v WI	Brisbane	1960-61
	80	6-87			
I. T. Botham	114	6-58	} E v I	Bombay	1979-80
		7-48			
Imran Khan	117	6-98	} P v I	Faisalabad	1982-83
		5-82			
Shakib Al Hasan	137	5-80	} B v Z	Khulna	2014-15
	6	5-44			

Wicketkeeper A. B. de Villiers scored 103 and held 11 catches for South Africa against Pakistan at Johannesburg in 2012-13.*

2,000 RUNS AND 200 WICKETS

	Tests	Runs	Wkts	Tests for 1,000/100 Double
R. Benaud (Australia)	63	2,201	248	32
†I. T. Botham (England)	102	5,200	383	21
S. C. J. Broad (England)	**91**	**2,565**	**333**	**35**
C. L. Cairns (New Zealand)	62	3,320	218	33

	Tests	Runs	Wkts	Tests for 1,000/100 Double
A. Flintoff (England/World)	79	3,845	226	43
R. J. Hadlee (New Zealand).	86	3,124	431	28
Harbhajan Singh (India)	**103**	**2,224**	**417**	**62**
Imran Khan (Pakistan).	88	3,807	362	30
M. J. Johnson (Australia)	**73**	**2,065**	**313**	**37**
†J. H. Kallis (South Africa/World)	166	13,289	292	53
Kapil Dev (India).	131	5,248	434	25
A. Kumble (India)	132	2,506	619	56
S. M. Pollock (South Africa)	108	3,781	421	26
†G. S. Sobers (West Indies)	93	8,032	235	48
W. P. U. J. C. Vaas (Sri Lanka)	111	3,089	355	47
D. L. Vettori (New Zealand/World).	113	4,531	362	47
†S. K. Warne (Australia)	145	3,154	708	58
Wasim Akram (Pakistan).	104	2,898	414	45

H. H. Streak scored 1,990 runs and took 216 wickets in 65 Tests for Zimbabwe.

†   *J. H. Kallis also took 200 catches, S. K. Warne 125, I. T. Botham 120 and G. S. Sobers 109. These four and C. L. Hooper (5,762 runs, 114 wickets and 115 catches for West Indies) are the only players to have achieved the treble of 1,000 runs, 100 wickets and 100 catches in Test cricket.*

WICKETKEEPING RECORDS

MOST DISMISSALS IN AN INNINGS

7 (all ct)	Wasim Bari.	Pakistan v New Zealand at Auckland	1978-79
7 (all ct)	R. W. Taylor.	England v India at Bombay.	1979-80
7 (all ct)	I. D. S. Smith	New Zealand v Sri Lanka at Hamilton	1990-91
7 (all ct)	R. D. Jacobs	West Indies v Australia at Melbourne	2000-01

The first instance of seven wicketkeeping dismissals in a Test innings was a joint effort for Pakistan v West Indies at Kingston in 1976-77. Majid Khan made four catches, deputising for the injured wicketkeeper Wasim Bari, who made three more catches on his return.

*There have been **29** instances of players making six dismissals in a Test innings, the most recent being **J. M. Bairstow (all ct)** for **England v South Africa at Johannesburg in 2015-16**.*

MOST STUMPINGS IN AN INNINGS

5	K. S. More	India v West Indies at Madras	1987-88

MOST DISMISSALS IN A TEST

11 (all ct)	R. C. Russell.	England v South Africa at Johannesburg . . .	1995-96
11 (all ct)	A. B. de Villiers	South Africa v Pakistan at Johannesburg . . .	2012-13
10 (all ct)	R. W. Taylor.	England v India at Bombay.	1979-80
10 (all ct)	A. C. Gilchrist	Australia v New Zealand at Hamilton	1999-2000

*There have been 25 instances of players making nine dismissals in a Test, the most recent being **J. M. Bairstow (all ct)** for **England v South Africa at Johannesburg in 2015-16**. S. A. R. Silva made 18 in two successive Tests for Sri Lanka against India in 1985-86.*

The most stumpings in a match is 6 by K. S. More for India v West Indies at Madras in 1987-88.

J. J. Kelly (8ct) for Australia v England in 1901-02 and L. E. G. Ames (6ct, 2st) for England v West Indies in 1933 were the only keepers to make eight dismissals in a Test before World War II.

MOST DISMISSALS IN A SERIES

(Played in 5 Tests unless otherwise stated)

29 (all ct)	B. J. Haddin	Australia v England	2013
28 (all ct)	R. W. Marsh	Australia v England	1982-83
27 (25ct, 2st)	R. C. Russell	England v South Africa	1995-96
27 (25ct, 2st)	I. A. Healy	Australia v England (6 Tests)	1997

S. A. R. Silva made 22 dismissals (21ct, 1st) in three Tests for Sri Lanka v India in 1985-86.
*　H. Strudwick, with 21 (15ct, 6st) for England v South Africa in 1913-14, was the only wicketkeeper to make as many as 20 dismissals in a series before World War II.*

MOST DISMISSALS

			T	Ct	St
1	M. V. Boucher (South Africa/World)	555	147	532	23
2	A. C. Gilchrist (Australia)	416	96	379	37
3	I. A. Healy (Australia)	395	119	366	29
4	R. W. Marsh (Australia)	355	96	343	12
5	M. S. Dhoni (India)	294	90	256	38
6	**B. J. Haddin (Australia)**	**270**	**66**	**262**	**8**
	P. J. L. Dujon (West Indies)	270	79	265	5
8	A. P. E. Knott (England)	269	95	250	19
9	M. J. Prior (England)	256	79	243	13
10	A. J. Stewart (England)	241	82	227	14
11	Wasim Bari (Pakistan)	228	81	201	27
12	R. D. Jacobs (West Indies)	219	65	207	12
	T. G. Evans (England)	219	91	173	46
14	**D. Ramdin (West Indies)**	**217**	**74**	**205**	**12**
15	Kamran Akmal (Pakistan)	206	53	184	22
16	A. C. Parore (New Zealand)	201	67	194	7

The record for P. J. L. Dujon excludes two catches taken in two Tests when not keeping wicket; A. J. Stewart's record likewise excludes 36 catches taken in 51 Tests and A. C. Parore's three in 11 Tests.
*　Excluding the Super Series Test, M. V. Boucher made 553 dismissals (530ct, 23st in 146 Tests) for South Africa, a national record.*
*　W. A. Oldfield made 52 stumpings, a Test record, in 54 Tests for Australia; he also took 78 catches.*

The most dismissals by a wicketkeeper playing for the countries not mentioned above are:

		T	Ct	St
K. C. Sangakkara (Sri Lanka)	151	48	131	20
A. Flower (Zimbabwe)	151	55	142	9
Khaled Mashud (Bangladesh)	87	44	78	9

K. C. Sangakkara's record excludes 51 catches taken in 86 matches when not keeping wicket but includes two catches taken as wicketkeeper in a match where he took over when the designated keeper was injured; A. Flower's record excludes nine catches in eight Tests when not keeping wicket.

FIELDING RECORDS

(Excluding wicketkeepers)

MOST CATCHES IN AN INNINGS

5	V. Y. Richardson	Australia v South Africa at Durban	1935-36
5	Yajurvindra Singh	India v England at Bangalore	1976-77
5	M. Azharuddin	India v Pakistan at Karachi	1989-90
5	K. Srikkanth	India v Australia at Perth	1991-92
5	S. P. Fleming	New Zealand v Zimbabwe at Harare	1997-98
5	G. C. Smith	South Africa v Australia at Perth	2012-13
5	D. J. G. Sammy	West Indies v India at Mumbai	2013-14

5	D. M. Bravo	West Indies v Bangladesh at Arnos Vale	2014-15
5	**A. M. Rahane**	**India v Sri Lanka at Galle**	**2015-16**
5	**J. Blackwood**	**West Indies v Sri Lanka at Colombo (PSO)**	**2015-16**

MOST CATCHES IN A TEST

8	**A. M. Rahane**	**India v Sri Lanka at Galle**	**2015-16**
7	G. S. Chappell	Australia v England at Perth	1974-75
7	Yajurvindra Singh	India v England at Bangalore	1976-77
7	H. P. Tillekeratne	Sri Lanka v New Zealand at Colombo (SSC)	1992-93
7	S. P. Fleming	New Zealand v Zimbabwe at Harare	1997-98
7	M. L. Hayden	Australia v Sri Lanka at Galle	2003-04

*There have been **28** instances of players taking six catches in a Test, the most recent being D. M. Bravo for West Indies v Bangladesh at Arnos Vale, 2014-15.*

MOST CATCHES IN A SERIES

(Played in 5 Tests unless otherwise stated)

15	J. M. Gregory	Australia v England	1920-21
14	G. S. Chappell	Australia v England (6 Tests)	1974-75
13	R. B. Simpson	Australia v South Africa	1957-58
13	R. B. Simpson	Australia v West Indies	1960-61
13	B. C. Lara	West Indies v England (6 Tests)	1997-98
13	R. Dravid	India v Australia (4 Tests)	2004-05
13	B. C. Lara	West Indies v India (4 Tests)	2005-06

MOST CATCHES

Ct	T		Ct	T	
210	164†	R. Dravid (India/World)	157	104	M. A. Taylor (Australia)
205	149	D. P. M. D. Jayawardene (SL)	156	156	A. R. Border (Australia)
200	166†	J. H. Kallis (SA/World)	135	134	V. V. S. Laxman (India)
196	168	R. T. Ponting (Australia)	**134**	**115**	**M. J. Clarke (Australia)**
181	128	M. E. Waugh (Australia)	128	103	M. L. Hayden (Australia)
171	111	S. P. Fleming (New Zealand)	**125**	**126**	**A. N. Cook (England)**
169	117†	G. C. Smith (SA/World)	125	145	S. K. Warne (Australia)
164	131†	B. C. Lara (West Indies/World)			

† *Excluding the Super Series Test, Dravid made 209 catches in 163 Tests for India, Kallis 196 in 165 Tests for South Africa, and Lara 164 in 130 Tests for West Indies, all national records. G. C. Smith made 166 catches in 116 Tests for South Africa.*

*The most catches in the field for other countries are: Pakistan 117 in 104 Tests (**Younis Khan**); Zimbabwe 60 in 60 Tests (A. D. R. Campbell); Bangladesh **28** in 27 Tests (**Mahmudullah**).*

TEAM RECORDS

HIGHEST INNINGS TOTALS

952-6 dec	Sri Lanka v India at Colombo (RPS)	1997-98
903-7 dec	England v Australia at The Oval	1938
849	England v West Indies at Kingston	1929-30
790-3 dec	West Indies v Pakistan at Kingston	1957-58
765-6 dec	Pakistan v Sri Lanka at Karachi	2008-09
760-7 dec	Sri Lanka v India at Ahmedabad	2009-10
758-8 dec	Australia v West Indies at Kingston	1954-55
756-5 dec	Sri Lanka v South Africa at Colombo (SSC)	2006
751-5 dec	West Indies v England at St John's	2003-04

The highest innings totals for the countries not mentioned above are:

726 dec	India v Sri Lanka at Mumbai (BS)	2009-10
690	New Zealand v Pakistan at Sharjah	2014-15
682-6 dec	South Africa v England at Lord's	2003
638	Bangladesh v Sri Lanka at Galle	2012-13
563-9 dec	Zimbabwe v West Indies at Harare	2001

HIGHEST FOURTH-INNINGS TOTALS

To win

418-7	West Indies (needing 418) v Australia at St John's	2002-03
414-4	South Africa (needing 414) v Australia at Perth	2008-09
406-4	India (needing 403) v West Indies at Port-of-Spain	1975-76
404-3	Australia (needing 404) v England at Leeds	1948

To tie

347	India v Australia at Madras	1986-87

To draw

654-5	England (needing 696 to win) v South Africa at Durban	1938-39
450-7	South Africa (needing 458 to win) v India at Johannesburg	2013-14
429-8	India (needing 438 to win) v England at The Oval	1979
423-7	South Africa (needing 451 to win) v England at The Oval	1947

To lose

451	New Zealand (lost by 98 runs) v England at Christchurch	2001-02
445	India (lost by 47 runs) v Australia at Adelaide	1977-78
440	New Zealand (lost by 38 runs) v England at Nottingham	1973
431	New Zealand (lost by 121 runs) v England at Napier	2007-08

MOST RUNS IN A DAY (BOTH SIDES)

588	England (398-6), India (190-0) at Manchester (2nd day)	1936
522	England (503-2), South Africa (19-0) at Lord's (2nd day)	1924
509	Sri Lanka (509-9) v Bangladesh at Colombo (PSS) (2nd day)	2002
508	England (221-2), South Africa (287-6) at The Oval (3rd day)	1935

MOST RUNS IN A DAY (ONE SIDE)

509	Sri Lanka (509-9) v Bangladesh at Colombo (PSS) (2nd day)	2002
503	England (503-2) v South Africa at Lord's (2nd day)	1924
494	Australia (494-6) v South Africa at Sydney (1st day)	1910-11
482	Australia (482-5) v South Africa at Adelaide (1st day)	2012-13
475	Australia (475-2) v England at The Oval (1st day)	1934

MOST WICKETS IN A DAY

27	England (18-3 to 53 all out and 62) v Australia (60) at Lord's (2nd day)	1888
25	Australia (112 and 48-5) v England (61) at Melbourne (1st day)	1901-02

HIGHEST AGGREGATES IN A TEST

Runs	Wkts			Days played
1,981	35	South Africa v England at Durban	1938-39	10†
1,815	34	West Indies v England at Kingston	1929-30	9‡
1,764	39	Australia v West Indies at Adelaide	1968-69	5
1,753	40	Australia v England at Adelaide	1920-21	6
1,747	25	Australia v India at Sydney	2003-04	5
1,723	31	England v Australia at Leeds	1948	5
1,702	28	Pakistan v India at Faisalabad	2005-06	5

† *No play on one day.* ‡ *No play on two days.*

LOWEST INNINGS TOTALS

26	New Zealand v England at Auckland	1954-55
30	South Africa v England at Port Elizabeth	1895-96
30	South Africa v England at Birmingham	1924
35	South Africa v England at Cape Town	1898-99
36	Australia v England at Birmingham	1902
36	South Africa v Australia at Melbourne	1931-32
42	Australia v England at Sydney	1887-88
42	New Zealand v Australia at Wellington	1945-46
42†	India v England at Lord's	1974
43	South Africa v England at Cape Town	1888-89
44	Australia v England at The Oval	1896
45	England v Australia at Sydney	1886-87
45	South Africa v Australia at Melbourne	1931-32
45	New Zealand v South Africa at Cape Town	2012-13

The lowest innings totals for the countries not mentioned above are:

47	West Indies v England at Kingston	2003-04
49	Pakistan v South Africa at Johannesburg	2012-13
51	Zimbabwe v New Zealand at Napier	2011-12
62	Bangladesh v Sri Lanka at Colombo (PSS)	2007
71	Sri Lanka v Pakistan at Kandy	1994-95

FEWEST RUNS IN A FULL DAY'S PLAY

95	Australia (80), Pakistan (15-2) at Karachi (1st day, 5½ hrs)	1956-57
104	Pakistan (0-0 to 104-5) v Australia at Karachi (4th day, 5½ hrs)	1959-60
106	England (92-2 to 198) v Australia at Brisbane (4th day, 5 hrs)	1958-59
	England were dismissed five minutes before the close of play, leaving no	
	time for Australia to start their second innings.	
111	S. Africa (48-2 to 130-6 dec), India (29-1) at Cape Town (5th day, 5½ hrs) . . .	1992-93
112	Australia (138-6 to 187), Pakistan (63-1) at Karachi (4th day, 5½ hrs)	1956-57
115	Australia (116-7 to 165 and 66-5 after following on) v Pakistan at Karachi (4th	
	day, 5½ hrs)	1988-89
117	India (117-5) v Australia at Madras (1st day, 5½ hrs)	1956-57
117	New Zealand (6-0 to 123-4) v Sri Lanka at Colombo (SSC) (5th day, 5¾ hrs) .	1983-84

In England

151	England (175-2 to 289), New Zealand (37-7) at Lord's (3rd day, 6 hrs)	1978
158	England (211-2 to 369-9) v South Africa at Manchester (5th day, 6 hrs)	1998
159	Pakistan (208-4 to 350), England (17-1) at Leeds (3rd day, 6 hrs)	1971

LOWEST AGGREGATES IN A COMPLETED TEST

Runs	Wkts			Days played
234	29	Australia v South Africa at Melbourne	1931-32	3†
291	40	England v Australia at Lord's	1888	2
295	28	New Zealand v Australia at Wellington	1945-46	2
309	29	West Indies v England at Bridgetown	1934-35	3
323	30	England v Australia at Manchester	1888	2

† *No play on one day.*

LARGEST VICTORIES

Largest Innings Victories

Inns & 579 runs	England (903-7 dec) v Australia (201 & 123†) at The Oval	1938
Inns & 360 runs	Australia (652-7 dec) v South Africa (159 & 133) at Johannesburg . .	2001-02
Inns & 336 runs	West Indies (614-5 dec) v India (124 & 154) at Calcutta	1958-59
Inns & 332 runs	Australia (645) v England (141 & 172) at Brisbane	1946-47
Inns & 324 runs	Pakistan (643) v New Zealand (73 & 246) at Lahore	2002
Inns & 322 runs	West Indies (660-5 dec) v New Zealand (216 & 122) at Wellington . .	1994-95
Inns & 310 runs	West Indies (536) v Bangladesh (139 & 87) at Dhaka	2002-03
Inns & 301 runs	New Zealand (495-7 dec) v Zimbabwe (51 & 143) at Napier	2011-12

† *Two men absent in both Australian innings.*

Largest Victories by Runs Margin

675 runs	England (521 & 342-8 dec) v Australia (122 & 66†) at Brisbane	1928-29
562 runs	Australia (701 & 327) v England (321 & 145‡) at The Oval	1934
530 runs	Australia (328 & 578) v South Africa (205 & 171§) at Melbourne	1910-11
491 runs	Australia (381 & 361-5 dec) v Pakistan (179 & 72) at Perth	2004-05
465 runs	Sri Lanka (384 and 447-6 dec) v Bangladesh (208 and 158) at Chittagong . . .	2008-09
425 runs	West Indies (211 & 411-5 dec) v England (71 & 126) at Manchester	1976
409 runs	Australia (350 & 460-7 dec) v England (215 & 186) at Lord's	1948
408 runs	West Indies (328 & 448) v Australia (203 & 165) at Adelaide	1979-80
405 runs	**Australia (566-8 dec & 254-2 dec) v England (312 & 103) at Lord's**	**2015**

† *One man absent in Australia's first innings; two men absent in their second.*
‡ *Two men absent in England's first innings; one man absent in their second.*
§ *One man absent in South Africa's second innings.*

TIED TESTS

West Indies (453 & 284) v Australia (505 & 232) at Brisbane	1960-61
Australia (574-7 dec & 170-5 dec) v India (397 & 347) at Madras	1986-87

MOST CONSECUTIVE TEST VICTORIES

16	Australia	1999-2000–2000-01	9	South Africa	2001-02–2003
16	Australia	2005-06–2007-08	8	Australia	1920-21–1921
11	West Indies	1983-84–1984-85	8	England	2004–2004-05
9	Sri Lanka	2001–2001-02			

MOST CONSECUTIVE TESTS WITHOUT VICTORY

44	New Zealand	1929-30–1955-56	23	New Zealand	1962-63–1967-68
34	Bangladesh	2000-01–2004-05	22	Pakistan	1958-59–1964-65
31	India	1981-82–1984-85	21	Sri Lanka	1985-86–1992-93
28	South Africa	1935–1949-50	20	West Indies	1968-69–1972-73
24	India	1932–1951-52	20	West Indies	2004-05–2007
24	Bangladesh	2004-05–2008-09			

WHITEWASHES

Teams winning every game in a series of four Tests or more:

Five-Test Series

Australia beat England 1920-21	West Indies beat England 1985-86
Australia beat South Africa. 1931-32	South Africa beat West Indies 1998-99
England beat India 1959	Australia beat West Indies 2000-01
West Indies beat India. 1961-62	Australia beat England 2006-07
West Indies beat England 1984	Australia beat England 2013-14

Four-Test Series

Australia beat India. 1967-68	England beat India 2011
South Africa beat Australia. 1969-70	Australia beat India. 2011-12
England beat West Indies 2004	India beat Australia. 2012-13

The winning team in each instance was at home, except for West Indies in England, 1984.

PLAYERS

YOUNGEST TEST PLAYERS

Years	Days			
15	124	Mushtaq Mohammad	Pakistan v West Indies at Lahore	1958-59
16	189	Aqib Javed	Pakistan v New Zealand at Wellington.	1988-89
16	205	S. R. Tendulkar	India v Pakistan at Karachi	1989-90

The above table should be treated with caution. All birthdates for Bangladesh and Pakistan (after Partition) must be regarded as questionable because of deficiencies in record-keeping. Hasan Raza was claimed to be 14 years 227 days old when he played for Pakistan against Zimbabwe at Faisalabad in 1996-97; this age was rejected by the Pakistan Cricket Board, although no alternative has been offered. Suggestions that Enamul Haque jun. was 16 years 230 days old when he played for Bangladesh against England in Dhaka in 2003-04 have been discounted by well-informed local observers, who believe he was 18.

The youngest Test players for countries not mentioned above are:

Years	Days			
17	122	J. E. D. Sealy.	West Indies v England at Bridgetown	1929-30
17	128	Mohammad Sharif	Bangladesh v Zimbabwe at Bulawayo	2000-01
17	189	C. D. U. S. Weerasinghe .	Sri Lanka v India at Colombo (PSS).	1985-86
17	239	I. D. Craig.	Australia v South Africa at Melbourne.	1952-53
17	352	H. Masakadza	Zimbabwe v West Indies at Harare.	2001
18	10	D. L. Vettori	New Zealand v England at Wellington.	1996-97
18	149	D. B. Close	England v New Zealand at Manchester	1949
18	340	P. R. Adams	South Africa v England at Port Elizabeth . . .	1995-96

OLDEST PLAYERS ON TEST DEBUT

Years	Days			
49	119	J. Southerton.	England v Australia at Melbourne	1876-77
47	284	Miran Bux.	Pakistan v India at Lahore	1954-55
46	253	D. D. Blackie	Australia v England at Sydney	1928-29
46	237	H. Ironmonger.	Australia v England at Brisbane	1928-29
42	242	N. Betancourt	West Indies v England at Port-of-Spain	1929-30
41	337	E. R. Wilson	England v Australia at Sydney	1920-21
41	27	R. J. D. Jamshedji	India v England at Bombay	1933-34
40	345	C. A. Wiles	West Indies v England at Manchester.	1933
40	295	O. Henry	South Africa v India at Durban.	1992-93

Years	Days			
40	216	S. P. Kinneir	England v Australia at Sydney	1911-12
40	110	H. W. Lee	England v South Africa at Johannesburg	1930-31
40	56	G. W. A. Chubb	South Africa v England at Nottingham	1951
40	37	C. Ramaswami	India v England at Manchester	1936

The oldest Test player on debut for New Zealand was H. M. McGirr, 38 years 101 days, v England at Auckland, 1929-30; for Sri Lanka, D. S. de Silva, 39 years 251 days, v England at Colombo (PSS), 1981-82; for Zimbabwe, A. C. Waller, 37 years 84 days, v England at Bulawayo, 1996-97; for Bangladesh, Enamul Haque, sen. 35 years 58 days, v Zimbabwe at Harare, 2000-01. A. J. Traicos was 45 years 154 days old when he made his debut for Zimbabwe (v India at Harare, 1992-93) having played three Tests for South Africa in 1969-70.

OLDEST TEST PLAYERS

(Age on final day of their last Test match)

Years	Days			
52	165	W. Rhodes	England v West Indies at Kingston	1929-30
50	327	H. Ironmonger	Australia v England at Sydney	1932-33
50	320	W. G. Grace	England v Australia at Nottingham	1899
50	303	G. Gunn	England v West Indies at Kingston	1929-30
49	139	J. Southerton	England v Australia at Melbourne	1876-77
47	302	Miran Bux	Pakistan v India at Peshawar	1954-55
47	249	J. B. Hobbs	England v Australia at The Oval	1930
47	87	F. E. Woolley	England v Australia at The Oval	1934
46	309	D. D. Blackie	Australia v England at Adelaide	1928-29
46	206	A. W. Nourse	South Africa v England at The Oval	1924
46	202	H. Strudwick	England v Australia at The Oval	1926
46	41	E. H. Hendren	England v West Indies at Kingston	1934-35
45	304	A. J. Traicos	Zimbabwe v India at Delhi	1992-93
45	245	G. O. B. Allen	England v West Indies at Kingston	1947-48
45	215	P. Holmes	England v India at Lord's	1932
45	140	D. B. Close	England v West Indies at Manchester	1976

MOST TEST APPEARANCES

200	S. R. Tendulkar (India)		133	A. J. Stewart (England)
168	R. T. Ponting (Australia)		132	A. Kumble (India)
168	S. R. Waugh (Australia)		132	C. A. Walsh (West Indies)
166	J. H. Kallis (South Africa/World)		131	Kapil Dev (India)
164	**S. Chanderpaul (West Indies)**		131	B. C. Lara (West Indies/World)
164	R. Dravid (India/World)		128	M. E. Waugh (Australia)
156	A. R. Border (Australia)		**126**	**A. N. Cook (England)**
149	D. P. M. D. Jayawardene (Sri Lanka)		125	S. M. Gavaskar (India)
147	M. V. Boucher (South Africa/World)		124	Javed Miandad (Pakistan)
145	S. K. Warne (Australia)		124	G. D. McGrath (Australia)
134	V. V. S. Laxman (India)		121	I. V. A. Richards (West Indies)
134	**K. C. Sangakkara (Sri Lanka)**		120	Inzamam-ul-Haq (Pakistan/World)
133	M. Muralitharan (Sri Lanka/World)			

Excluding the Super Series Test, J. H. Kallis has made 165 appearances for South Africa, a national record. The most appearances for New Zealand is 112 by D. L. Vettori; for Zimbabwe, 67 by G. W. Flower; and for Bangladesh 61 by Mohammad Ashraful.

MOST CONSECUTIVE TEST APPEARANCES FOR A COUNTRY

153	A. R. Border (Australia)		March 1979 to March 1994
124	**A. N. Cook (England)**		**May 2006 to January 2016**
107	M. E. Waugh (Australia)		June 1993 to October 2002
106	S. M. Gavaskar (India)		January 1975 to February 1987
99†	**B. B. McCullum (New Zealand)**		**March 2004 to December 2015**

98	A. B. de Villiers (South Africa)................	December 2004 to January 2015
96†	A. C. Gilchrist (Australia).....................	November 1999 to January 2008
93	R. Dravid (India)............................	June 1996 to December 2005
93	D. P. M. D. Jayawardene (Sri Lanka)...........	November 2002 to January 2013

The most consecutive Test appearances for the countries not mentioned above are:

85	G. S. Sobers (West Indies)...................	April 1955 to April 1972
56	A. D. R. Campbell (Zimbabwe)................	October 1992 to September 2001
53	Javed Miandad (Pakistan)....................	December 1977 to January 1984
46	**Mushfiqur Rahim (Bangladesh)**.............	**July 2007 to August 2015**

†   *Complete Test career.*

Bold type denotes sequence which was still in progress after January 1, 2016.

MOST TESTS AS CAPTAIN

	P	W	L	D		P	W	L	D
G. C. Smith (SA/World)	109	53	29*	27	A. Ranatunga (SL)	56	12	19	25
A. R. Border (A)	93	32	22	38†	M. A. Atherton (E)	54	13	21	20
S. P. Fleming (NZ)	80	28	27	25	W. J. Cronje (SA)	53	27	11	15
R. T. Ponting (A)	77	48	16	13	M. P. Vaughan (E)	51	26	11	14
C. H. Lloyd (WI)	74	36	12	26	I. V. A. Richards (WI)	50	27	8	15
M. S. Dhoni (I)	60	27	18	15	M. A. Taylor (A)	50	26	13	11
S. R. Waugh (A)	57	41	9	7	A. J. Strauss (E)	50	24	11	15

*   *Includes defeat as World XI captain in Super Series Test against Australia.*   †   *One tie.*

Most Tests as captain of other countries:

	P	W	L	D
Imran Khan (P)	48	14	8	26
A. D. R. Campbell (Z)	21	2	12	7
Mushfiqur Rahim (B)	**24**	**4**	**11**	**9**

A. R. Border captained Australia in 93 consecutive Tests.

    W. W. Armstrong (Australia) captained his country in the most Tests without being defeated: ten matches with eight wins and two draws.

    Mohammad Ashraful (Bangladesh) captained his country in the most Tests without ever winning: 12 defeats and one draw.

UMPIRES

MOST TESTS

		First Test	Last Test
128	S. A. Bucknor (West Indies)	1988-89	2008-09
108	R. E. Koertzen (South Africa)	1992-93	2010
101	**Aleem Dar (Pakistan)**	**2003-04**	**2015-16**
95	D. J. Harper (Australia)	1998-99	2011
92	D. R. Shepherd (England)	1985	2004-05
84	**B. F. Bowden (New Zealand)**	**1999-2000**	**2014-15**
78	D. B. Hair (Australia)	1991-92	2008
74	S. J. A. Taufel (Australia)	2000-01	2012
73	S. Venkataraghavan (India)	1992-93	2003-04
66	H. D. Bird (England)	1973	1996
57	**S. J. Davis (Australia)**	**1997-98**	**2014-15**

SUMMARY OF TESTS

To January 26, 2016

	Opponents	Tests					Won by							Tied	Drawn
			E	A	SA	WI	NZ	I	P	SL	Z	B	Wld		
England	Australia	**341**	108	140	–	–	–	–	–	–	–	–	–	–	93
	South Africa	**145**	58	–	32	–	–	–	–	–	–	–	–	–	55
	West Indies	**151**	46	–	–	54	–	–	–	–	–	–	–	–	51
	New Zealand	**101**	48	–	–	–	9	–	–	–	–	–	–	–	44
	India	**112**	43	–	–	–	–	21	–	–	–	–	–	–	48
	Pakistan	**77**	22	–	–	–	–	–	18	–	–	–	–	–	37
	Sri Lanka	**28**	10	–	–	–	–	–	–	8	–	–	–	–	10
	Zimbabwe	**6**	3	–	–	–	–	–	–	–	–	–	–	–	3
	Bangladesh	**8**	8	–	–	–	–	–	–	–	–	0	–	–	0
Australia	South Africa	**91**	–	50	21	–	–	–	–	–	–	–	–	–	20
	West Indies	**116**	–	58	–	32	–	–	–	–	–	–	–	1	25
	New Zealand	**55**	–	29	–	–	8	–	–	–	–	–	–	–	18
	India	**90**	–	40	–	–	–	24	–	–	–	–	–	1	25
	Pakistan	**59**	–	28	–	–	–	–	14	–	–	–	–	–	17
	Sri Lanka	**26**	–	17	–	–	–	–	–	1	–	–	–	–	8
	Zimbabwe	**3**	–	3	–	–	–	–	–	–	0	–	–	–	0
	Bangladesh	**4**	–	4	–	–	–	–	–	–	–	0	–	–	0
	ICC World XI	**1**	–	1	–	–	–	–	–	–	–	–	0	–	0
South Africa	West Indies	**28**	–	–	18	3	–	–	–	–	–	–	–	–	7
	New Zealand	**40**	–	–	23	–	4	–	–	–	–	–	–	–	13
	India	**33**	–	–	13	–	–	10	–	–	–	–	–	–	10
	Pakistan	**23**	–	–	12	–	–	–	4	–	–	–	–	–	7
	Sri Lanka	**22**	–	–	11	–	–	–	–	5	–	–	–	–	6
	Zimbabwe	**8**	–	–	7	–	–	–	–	–	0	–	–	–	1
	Bangladesh	**10**	–	–	8	–	–	–	–	–	–	0	–	–	2
West Indies	New Zealand	**45**	–	–	–	13	13	–	–	–	–	–	–	–	19
	India	**90**	–	–	–	30	–	16	–	–	–	–	–	–	44
	Pakistan	**46**	–	–	–	15	–	–	16	–	–	–	–	–	15
	Sri Lanka	**17**	–	–	–	3	–	–	–	8	–	–	–	–	6
	Zimbabwe	**8**	–	–	–	6	–	–	–	–	0	–	–	–	2
	Bangladesh	**12**	–	–	–	8	–	–	–	–	–	2	–	–	2
New Zealand	India	**54**	–	–	–	–	10	18	–	–	–	–	–	–	26
	Pakistan	**53**	–	–	–	–	8	–	24	–	–	–	–	–	21
	Sri Lanka	**32**	–	–	–	–	14	–	–	8	–	–	–	–	10
	Zimbabwe	**15**	–	–	–	–	9	–	–	–	0	–	–	–	6
	Bangladesh	**11**	–	–	–	–	8	–	–	–	–	0	–	–	3
India	Pakistan	**59**	–	–	–	–	–	9	12	–	–	–	–	–	38
	Sri Lanka	**38**	–	–	–	–	–	16	–	7	–	–	–	–	15
	Zimbabwe	**11**	–	–	–	–	–	7	–	–	2	–	–	–	2
	Bangladesh	**8**	–	–	–	–	–	6	–	–	–	0	–	–	2
Pakistan	Sri Lanka	**51**	–	–	–	–	–	–	19	14	–	–	–	–	18
	Zimbabwe	**17**	–	–	–	–	–	–	10	–	3	–	–	–	4
	Bangladesh	**10**	–	–	–	–	–	–	9	–	–	0	–	–	1
Sri Lanka	Zimbabwe	**15**	–	–	–	–	–	–	–	10	0	–	–	–	5
	Bangladesh	**16**	–	–	–	–	–	–	–	14	–	0	–	–	2
Zimbabwe	Bangladesh	**14**	–	–	–	–	–	–	–	–	6	5	–	–	3
		2,200	346	370	145	164	83	127	126	75	11	7	0	2	744

	Tests	Won	Lost	Drawn	Tied	% Won	Toss Won
England	969	346	282	341	–	35.70	466
Australia	786†	370†	208	206	2	47.07	398
South Africa	400	145	134	121	–	36.25	192
West Indies	513	164	177	171	1	31.96	264
New Zealand	406	83	163	160	–	20.44	204
India	495	127	157	210	1	25.65	250
Pakistan	395	126	111	158	–	31.89	188
Sri Lanka	245	75	90	80	–	30.61	134
Zimbabwe	97	11	60	26	–	11.34	56
Bangladesh	93	7	71	15	–	7.52	48
ICC World XI	1	0	1	0	–	0.00	0

† *Includes Super Series Test between Australia and ICC World XI.*

ENGLAND v AUSTRALIA

	Captains					
Season	*England*	*Australia*	*T*	*E*	*A*	*D*
1876-77	James Lillywhite	D. W. Gregory	2	1	1	0
1878-79	Lord Harris	D. W. Gregory	1	0	1	0
1880	Lord Harris	W. L. Murdoch	1	1	0	0
1881-82	A. Shaw	W. L. Murdoch	4	0	2	2
1882	A. N. Hornby	W. L. Murdoch	1	0	1	0

THE ASHES

	Captains						
Season	*England*	*Australia*	*T*	*E*	*A*	*D*	*Held by*
1882-83	Hon. Ivo Bligh	W. L. Murdoch	4*	2	2	0	E
1884	Lord Harris[1]	W. L. Murdoch	3	1	0	2	E
1884-85	A. Shrewsbury	T. P. Horan[2]	5	3	2	0	E
1886	A. G. Steel	H. J. H. Scott	3	3	0	0	E
1886-87	A. Shrewsbury	P. S. McDonnell	2	2	0	0	E
1887-88	W. W. Read	P. S. McDonnell	1	1	0	0	E
1888	W. G. Grace[3]	P. S. McDonnell	3	2	1	0	E
1890†	W. G. Grace	W. L. Murdoch	2	2	0	0	E
1891-92	W. G. Grace	J. McC. Blackham	3	1	2	0	A
1893	W. G. Grace[4]	J. McC. Blackham	3	1	0	2	E
1894-95	A. E. Stoddart	G. Giffen[5]	5	3	2	0	E
1896	W. G. Grace	G. H. S. Trott	3	2	1	0	E
1897-98	A. E. Stoddart[6]	G. H. S. Trott	5	1	4	0	A
1899	A. C. MacLaren[7]	J. Darling	5	0	1	4	A
1901-02	A. C. MacLaren	J. Darling[8]	5	1	4	0	A
1902	A. C. MacLaren	J. Darling	5	1	2	2	A
1903-04	P. F. Warner	M. A. Noble	5	3	2	0	E
1905	Hon. F. S. Jackson	J. Darling	5	2	0	3	E
1907-08	A. O. Jones[9]	M. A. Noble	5	1	4	0	A
1909	A. C. MacLaren	M. A. Noble	5	1	2	2	A
1911-12	J. W. H. T. Douglas	C. Hill	5	4	1	0	E
1912	C. B. Fry	S. E. Gregory	3	1	0	2	E
1920-21	J. W. H. T. Douglas	W. W. Armstrong	5	0	5	0	A
1921	Hon. L. H. Tennyson[10]	W. W. Armstrong	5	0	3	2	A
1924-25	A. E. R. Gilligan	H. L. Collins	5	1	4	0	A
1926	A. W. Carr[11]	H. L. Collins[12]	5	1	0	4	E
1928-29	A. P. F. Chapman[13]	J. Ryder	5	4	1	0	E
1930	A. P. F. Chapman[14]	W. M. Woodfull	5	1	2	2	A
1932-33	D. R. Jardine	W. M. Woodfull	5	4	1	0	E
1934	R. E. S. Wyatt[15]	W. M. Woodfull	5	1	2	2	A
1936-37	G. O. B. Allen	D. G. Bradman	5	2	3	0	A
1938†	W. R. Hammond	D. G. Bradman	4	1	1	2	A
1946-47	W. R. Hammond[16]	D. G. Bradman	5	0	3	2	A
1948	N. W. D. Yardley	D. G. Bradman	5	0	4	1	A
1950-51	F. R. Brown	A. L. Hassett	5	1	4	0	A
1953	L. Hutton	A. L. Hassett	5	1	0	4	E
1954-55	L. Hutton	I. W. Johnson[17]	5	3	1	1	E
1956	P. B. H. May	I. W. Johnson	5	2	1	2	E
1958-59	P. B. H. May	R. Benaud	5	0	4	1	A
1961	P. B. H. May[18]	R. Benaud[19]	5	1	2	2	A
1962-63	E. R. Dexter	R. Benaud	5	1	1	3	A
1964	E. R. Dexter	R. B. Simpson	5	0	1	4	A
1965-66	M. J. K. Smith	R. B. Simpson[20]	5	1	1	3	A
1968	M. C. Cowdrey[21]	W. M. Lawry[22]	5	1	1	3	A
1970-71†	R. Illingworth	W. M. Lawry[23]	6	2	0	4	E
1972	R. Illingworth	I. M. Chappell	5	2	2	1	E

Captains

Season	England	Australia	T	E	A	D	Held by
1974-75	M. H. Denness[24]	I. M. Chappell	6	1	4	1	A
1975	A. W. Greig[25]	I. M. Chappell	4	0	1	3	A
1976-77‡	A. W. Greig	G. S. Chappell	1	0	1	0	—
1977	J. M. Brearley	G. S. Chappell	5	3	0	2	E
1978-79	J. M. Brearley	G. N. Yallop	6	5	1	0	E
1979-80‡	J. M. Brearley	G. S. Chappell	3	0	3	0	—
1980‡	I. T. Botham	G. S. Chappell	1	0	0	1	—
1981	J. M. Brearley[26]	K. J. Hughes	6	3	1	2	E
1982-83	R. G. D. Willis	G. S. Chappell	5	1	2	2	A
1985	D. I. Gower	A. R. Border	6	3	1	2	E
1986-87	M. W. Gatting	A. R. Border	5	2	1	2	E
1987-88‡	M. W. Gatting	A. R. Border	1	0	0	1	—
1989	D. I. Gower	A. R. Border	6	0	4	2	A
1990-91	G. A. Gooch[27]	A. R. Border	5	0	3	2	A
1993	G. A. Gooch[28]	A. R. Border	6	1	4	1	A
1994-95	M. A. Atherton	M. A. Taylor	5	1	3	1	A
1997	M. A. Atherton	M. A. Taylor	6	2	3	1	A
1998-99	A. J. Stewart	M. A. Taylor	5	1	3	1	A
2001	N. Hussain[29]	S. R. Waugh[30]	5	1	4	0	A
2002-03	N. Hussain	S. R. Waugh	5	1	4	0	A
2005	M. P. Vaughan	R. T. Ponting	5	2	1	2	E
2006-07	A. Flintoff	R. T. Ponting	5	0	5	0	A
2009	A. J. Strauss	R. T. Ponting	5	2	1	2	E
2010-11	A. J. Strauss	R. T. Ponting[31]	5	3	1	1	E
2013	A. N. Cook	M. J. Clarke	5	3	0	2	E
2013-14	A. N. Cook	M. J. Clarke	5	0	5	0	A
2015	**A. N. Cook**	**M. J. Clarke**	**5**	**3**	**2**	**0**	**E**

	T	E	A	D
In Australia	175	57	91	27
In England	**166**	**51**	**49**	**66**
Totals	**341**	**108**	**140**	**93**

* *The Ashes were awarded in 1882-83 after a series of three matches which England won 2–1. A fourth match was played and this was won by Australia.*
† *The matches at Manchester in 1890 and 1938 and at Melbourne (Third Test) in 1970-71 were abandoned without a ball being bowled and are excluded.*
‡ *The Ashes were not at stake in these series.*

The following deputised for the official touring captain or were appointed by the home authority for only a minor proportion of the series:
[1]A. N. Hornby (First). [2]W. L. Murdoch (First), H. H. Massie (Third), J. McC. Blackham (Fourth). [3]A. G. Steel (First). [4]A. E. Stoddart (First). [5]J. McC. Blackham (First). [6]A. C. MacLaren (First, Second and Fifth). [7]W. G. Grace (First). [8]H. Trumble (Fourth and Fifth). [9]F. L. Fane (First, Second and Third). [10]J. W. H. T. Douglas (First and Second). [11]A. P. F. Chapman (Fifth). [12]W. Bardsley (Third and Fourth). [13]J. C. White (Fifth). [14]R. E. S. Wyatt (Fifth). [15]C. F. Walters (First). [16]N. W. D. Yardley (Fifth). [17]A. R. Morris (Second). [18]M. C. Cowdrey (First and Second). [19]R. N. Harvey (Second). [20]B. C. Booth (First and Third). [21]T. W. Graveney (Fourth). [22]B. N. Jarman (Fourth) [23]I. M. Chappell (Seventh). [24]J. H. Edrich (Fourth). [25]M. H. Denness (First). [26]I. T. Botham (First and Second). [27]A. J. Lamb (First). [28]M. A. Atherton (Fifth and Sixth). [29]M. A. Atherton (Second and Third). [30]A. C. Gilchrist (Fourth). [31]M. J. Clarke (Fifth).

HIGHEST INNINGS TOTALS

For England in England: 903-7 dec at The Oval	....	1938
in Australia: 644 at Sydney	....	2010-11
For Australia in England: 729-6 dec at Lord's.	....	1930
in Australia: 659-8 dec at Sydney	....	1946-47

LOWEST INNINGS TOTALS

For England in England: 52 at The Oval 1948
 in Australia: 45 at Sydney 1886-87

For Australia in England: 36 at Birmingham 1902
 in Australia: 42 at Sydney 1887-88

DOUBLE-HUNDREDS

For England (13)

364	L. Hutton at The Oval	1938	227	K. P. Pietersen at Adelaide	2010-11
287	R. E. Foster at Sydney	1903-04	216*	E. Paynter at Nottingham	1938
256	K. F. Barrington at Manchester . .	1964	215	D. I. Gower at Birmingham . . .	1985
251	W. R. Hammond at Sydney	1928-29	207	N. Hussain at Birmingham	1997
240	W. R. Hammond at Lord's	1938	206	P. D. Collingwood at Adelaide . .	2006-07
235*	A. N. Cook at Brisbane	2010-11	200	W. R. Hammond at Melbourne .	1928-29
231*	W. R. Hammond at Sydney	1936-37			

For Australia (24)

334	D. G. Bradman at Leeds	1930	232	S. J. McCabe at Nottingham	1938
311	R. B. Simpson at Manchester . . .	1964	225	R. B. Simpson at Adelaide	1965-66
307	R. M. Cowper at Melbourne	1965-66	219	M. A. Taylor at Nottingham	1989
304	D. G. Bradman at Leeds	1934	**215**	**S. P. D. Smith at Lord's . . . . . .**	**2015**
270	D. G. Bradman at Melbourne . . .	1936-37	212	D. G. Bradman at Adelaide	1936-37
266	W. H. Ponsford at The Oval	1934	211	W. L. Murdoch at The Oval	1884
254	D. G. Bradman at Lord's	1930	207	K. R. Stackpole at Brisbane	1970-71
250	J. L. Langer at Melbourne.	2002-03	206*	W. A. Brown at Lord's	1938
244	D. G. Bradman at The Oval	1934	206	A. R. Morris at Adelaide.	1950-51
234	S. G. Barnes at Sydney	1946-47	201*	J. Ryder at Adelaide	1924-25
234	D. G. Bradman at Sydney	1946-47	201	S. E. Gregory at Sydney	1894-95
232	D. G. Bradman at The Oval	1930	200*	A. R. Border at Leeds	1993

INDIVIDUAL HUNDREDS

In total, England have scored **239** hundreds against Australia, and Australia have scored **304** against England. The players with at least five hundreds are as follows:

For England

12: J. B. Hobbs.
9: D. I. Gower, W. R. Hammond.
8: H. Sutcliffe.
7: G. Boycott, J. H. Edrich, M. Leyland.
5: K. F. Barrington, D. C. S. Compton, M. C. Cowdrey, L. Hutton, F. S. Jackson, A. C. MacLaren.

For Australia

19: D. G. Bradman.
10: S. R. Waugh.
9: G. S. Chappell.
8: A. R. Border, A. R. Morris, R. T. Ponting.
7: D. C. Boon, **M. J. Clarke**, W. M. Lawry, M. J. Slater.
6: R. N. Harvey, M. A. Taylor, V. T. Trumper, M. E. Waugh, W. M. Woodfull.
5: M. L. Hayden, J. L. Langer, C. G. Macartney, W. H. Ponsford, **S. P. D. Smith**.

RECORD PARTNERSHIPS FOR EACH WICKET

For England

323 for 1st	J. B. Hobbs and W. Rhodes at Melbourne.........................	1911-12
382 for 2nd†	L. Hutton and M. Leyland at The Oval	1938
262 for 3rd	W. R. Hammond and D. R. Jardine at Adelaide	1928-29
310 for 4th	P. D. Collingwood and K. P. Pietersen at Adelaide..............	2006-07
206 for 5th	E. Paynter and D. C. S. Compton at Nottingham	1938
215 for 6th	{ L. Hutton and J. Hardstaff jun. at The Oval	1938
	{ G. Boycott and A. P. E. Knott at Nottingham	1977
143 for 7th	F. E. Woolley and J. Vine at Sydney	1911-12
124 for 8th	E. H. Hendren and H. Larwood at Brisbane	1928-29
151 for 9th	W. H. Scotton and W. W. Read at The Oval.....................	1884
130 for 10th	R. E. Foster and W. Rhodes at Sydney	1903-04

For Australia

329 for 1st	G. R. Marsh and M. A. Taylor at Nottingham....................	1989
451 for 2nd†	W. H. Ponsford and D. G. Bradman at The Oval	1934
276 for 3rd	D. G. Bradman and A. L. Hassett at Brisbane....................	1946-47
388 for 4th	W. H. Ponsford and D. G. Bradman at Leeds	1934
405 for 5th‡	S. G. Barnes and D. G. Bradman at Sydney	1946-47
346 for 6th†	J. H. Fingleton and D. G. Bradman at Melbourne................	1936-37
165 for 7th	C. Hill and H. Trumble at Melbourne	1897-98
243 for 8th†	R. J. Hartigan and C. Hill at Adelaide	1907-08
154 for 9th†	S. E. Gregory and J. McC. Blackham at Sydney	1894-95
163 for 10th†	P. J. Hughes and A. C. Agar at Nottingham	2013

†   *Record partnership against all countries.*   ‡   *World record.*

MOST RUNS IN A SERIES

England in England	............732 (average 81.33)	D. I. Gower	1985
England in Australia	............905 (average 113.12)	W. R. Hammond	1928-29
Australia in England	............974 (average 139.14)	D. G. Bradman	1930
Australia in Australia	............810 (average 90.00)	D. G. Bradman	1936-37

MOST WICKETS IN A MATCH

In total, England bowlers have taken ten or more wickets in a match **40** times against Australia, and Australian bowlers have done it **43** times against England. The players with at least 12 in a match are as follows:

For England

19-90 (9-37, 10-53)	J. C. Laker at Manchester	1956
15-104 (7-61, 8-43)	H. Verity at Lord's...	1934
15-124 (7-56, 8-68)	W. Rhodes at Melbourne......................................	1903-04
14-99 (7-55, 7-44)	A. V. Bedser at Nottingham	1953
14-102 (7-28, 7-74)	W. Bates at Melbourne	1882-83
13-163 (6-42, 7-121)	S. F. Barnes at Melbourne	1901-02
13-244 (7-168, 6-76)	T. Richardson at Manchester	1896
13-256 (5-130, 8-126)	J. C. White at Adelaide	1928-29
12-102 (6-50, 6-52)†	F. Martin at The Oval	1890
12-104 (7-36, 5-68)	G. A. Lohmann at The Oval	1886
12-136 (6-49, 6-87)	J. Briggs at Adelaide	1891-92

There are a further 12 instances of 11 wickets in a match, and 17 instances of ten.

For Australia

16-137 (8-84, 8-53)†	R. A. L. Massie at Lord's	1972
14-90 (7-46, 7-44)	F. R. Spofforth at The Oval	1882
13-77 (7-17, 6-60)	M. A. Noble at Melbourne	1901-02
13-110 (6-48, 7-62)	F. R. Spofforth at Melbourne	1878-79
13-148 (6-97, 7-51)	B. A. Reid at Melbourne	1990-91
13-236 (4-115, 9-121)	A. A. Mailey at Melbourne	1920-21
12-87 (5-44, 7-43)	C. T. B. Turner at Sydney	1887-88
12-89 (6-59, 6-30)	H. Trumble at The Oval	1896
12-107 (5-57, 7-50)	S. C. G. MacGill at Sydney	1998-99
12-173 (8-65, 4-108)	H. Trumble at The Oval	1902
12-175 (5-85, 7-90)†	H. V. Hordern at Sydney	1911-12
12-246 (6-122, 6-124)	S. K. Warne at The Oval	2005

There are a further 13 instances of 11 wickets in a match, and 18 instances of ten.

† *On first appearance in England–Australia Tests.*

A. V. Bedser, J. Briggs, J. C. Laker, T. Richardson, R. M. Hogg, A. A. Mailey, H. Trumble and C. T. B. Turner took ten wickets or more in successive Tests.

MOST WICKETS IN A SERIES

England in England	46 (average 9.60)	J. C. Laker	1956
England in Australia	38 (average 23.18)	M. W. Tate	1924-25
Australia in England	42 (average 21.26)	T. M. Alderman (6 Tests)	1981
Australia in Australia	41 (average 12.85)	R. M. Hogg (6 Tests)	1978-79

WICKETKEEPING – MOST DISMISSALS

	M	Ct	St	Total
†R. W. Marsh (Australia)	42	141	7	148
I. A. Healy (Australia)	33	123	12	135
A. P. E. Knott (England)	34	97	8	105
A. C. Gilchrist (Australia)	20	89	7	96
†W. A. Oldfield (Australia)	38	59	31	90
A. A. Lilley (England)	32	65	19	84
B. J. Haddin (Australia)	**20**	**79**	**1**	**80**
A. J. Stewart (England)	26	76	2	78
A. T. W. Grout (Australia)	22	69	7	76
T. G. Evans (England)	31	64	12	76

† *The number of catches by R. W. Marsh (141) and stumpings by W. A. Oldfield (31) are respective records in England–Australia Tests.*

Stewart held a further six catches in seven matches when not keeping wicket.

SCORERS OF OVER 2,500 RUNS

	T	I	NO	R	HS	100	Avge
D. G. Bradman (Australia)	37	63	7	5,028	334	19	89.78
J. B. Hobbs (England)	41	71	4	3,636	187	12	54.26
A. R. Border (Australia)	47	82	19	3,548	200*	8	56.31
D. I. Gower (England)	42	77	4	3,269	215	9	44.78
S. R. Waugh (Australia)	46	73	18	3,200	177*	10	58.18
G. Boycott (England)	38	71	9	2,945	191	7	47.50
W. R. Hammond (England)	33	58	3	2,852	251	9	51.85
H. Sutcliffe (England)	27	46	5	2,741	194	8	66.85
C. Hill (Australia)	41	76	1	2,660	188	4	35.46
J. H. Edrich (England)	32	57	3	2,644	175	7	48.96
G. A. Gooch (England)	42	79	0	2,632	196	4	33.31
G. S. Chappell (Australia)	35	65	8	2,619	144	9	45.94

BOWLERS WITH 100 WICKETS

	T	Balls	R	W	5I	10M	Avge
S. K. Warne (Australia)	36	10,757	4,535	195	11	4	23.25
D. K. Lillee (Australia).	29	8,516	3,507	167	11	4	21.00
G. D. McGrath (Australia)	30	7,280	3,286	157	10	0	20.92
I. T. Botham (England)	36	8,479	4,093	148	9	2	27.65
H. Trumble (Australia)	31	7,895	2,945	141	9	3	20.88
R. G. D. Willis (England).	35	7,294	3,346	128	7	0	26.14
M. A. Noble (Australia)	39	6,895	2,860	115	9	2	24.86
R. R. Lindwall (Australia).	29	6,728	2,559	114	6	0	22.44
W. Rhodes (England).	41	5,790	2,616	109	6	1	24.00
S. F. Barnes (England)	20	5,749	2,288	106	12	1	21.58
C. V. Grimmett (Australia).	22	9,224	3,439	106	11	2	32.44
D. L. Underwood (England). . . .	29	8,000	2,770	105	4	2	26.38
A. V. Bedser (England)	21	7,065	2,859	104	7	2	27.49
G. Giffen (Australia)	31	6,391	2,791	103	7	1	27.09
W. J. O'Reilly (Australia)	19	7,864	2,587	102	8	3	25.36
C. T. B. Turner (Australia)	17	5,179	1,670	101	11	2	16.53
R. Peel (England)	20	5,216	1,715	101	5	1	16.98
T. M. Alderman (Australia)	17	4,717	2,117	100	11	1	21.17
J. R. Thomson (Australia)	21	4,951	2,418	100	5	0	24.18

RESULTS ON EACH GROUND

In England

	Matches	England wins	Australia wins	Drawn
The Oval.	37	16	7	14
Manchester.	29	7	7	15†
Lord's.	36	7	15	14
Nottingham	22	6	7	9
Leeds	24	7	9	8
Birmingham	14	6	3	5
Sheffield	1	0	1	0
Cardiff	2	1	0	1
Chester-le-Street.	1	1	0	0

† *Excludes two matches abandoned without a ball bowled.*

In Australia

	Matches	England wins	Australia wins	Drawn
Melbourne	55	20	28	7†
Sydney	55	22	26	7
Adelaide.	31	9	17	5
Brisbane				
Exhibition Ground	1	1	0	0
Woolloongabba	20	4	11	5
Perth.	13	1	9	3

† *Excludes one match abandoned without a ball bowled.*

ENGLAND v SOUTH AFRICA

	Captains					
Season	England	South Africa	T	E	SA	D
1888-89	C. A. Smith[1]	O. R. Dunell[2]	2	2	0	0
1891-92	W. W. Read	W. H. Milton	1	1	0	0
1895-96	Lord Hawke[3]	E. A. Halliwell[4]	3	3	0	0

Captains

Season	England	South Africa	T	E	SA	D
1898-99	Lord Hawke	M. Bisset	2	2	0	0
1905-06	P. F. Warner	P. W. Sherwell	5	1	4	0
1907	R. E. Foster	P. W. Sherwell	3	1	0	2
1909-10	H. D. G. Leveson Gower[5]	S. J. Snooke	5	2	3	0
1912	C. B. Fry	F. Mitchell[6]	3	3	0	0
1913-14	J. W. H. T. Douglas	H. W. Taylor	5	4	0	1
1922-23	F. T. Mann	H. W. Taylor	5	2	1	2
1924	A. E. R. Gilligan[7]	H. W. Taylor	5	3	0	2
1927-28	R. T. Stanyforth[8]	H. G. Deane	5	2	2	1
1929	J. C. White[9]	H. G. Deane	5	2	0	3
1930-31	A. P. F. Chapman	H. G. Deane[10]	5	0	1	4
1935	R. E. S. Wyatt	H. F. Wade	5	0	1	4
1938-39	W. R. Hammond	A. Melville	5	1	0	4
1947	N. W. D. Yardley	A. Melville	5	3	0	2
1948-49	F. G. Mann	A. D. Nourse	5	2	0	3
1951	F. R. Brown	A. D. Nourse	5	3	1	1
1955	P. B. H. May	J. E. Cheetham[11]	5	3	2	0
1956-57	P. B. H. May	C. B. van Ryneveld[12]	5	2	2	1
1960	M. C. Cowdrey	D. J. McGlew	5	3	0	2
1964-65	M. J. K. Smith	T. L. Goddard	5	1	0	4
1965	M. J. K. Smith	P. L. van der Merwe	3	0	1	2
1994	M. A. Atherton	K. C. Wessels	3	1	1	1
1995-96	M. A. Atherton	W. J. Cronje	5	0	1	4
1998	A. J. Stewart	W. J. Cronje	5	2	1	2
1999-2000	N. Hussain	W. J. Cronje	5	1	2	2
2003	M. P. Vaughan[13]	G. C. Smith	5	2	2	1

THE BASIL D'OLIVEIRA TROPHY

Captains

Season	England	South Africa	T	E	SA	D	Held by
2004-05	M. P. Vaughan	G. C. Smith	5	2	1	2	E
2008	M. P. Vaughan[14]	G. C. Smith	4	1	2	1	SA
2009-10	A. J. Strauss	G. C. Smith	4	1	1	2	SA
2012	A. J. Strauss	G. C. Smith	3	0	2	1	SA
2015-16	**A. N. Cook**	**H. M. Amla[15]**	**4**	**2**	**1**	**1**	**E**

In South Africa			81	31	19	31
In England			64	27	13	24
Totals			**145**	**58**	**32**	**55**

The following deputised for the official touring captain or were appointed by the home authority for only a minor proportion of the series:

[1]M. P. Bowden (Second). [2]W. H. Milton (Second). [3]Sir T. C. O'Brien (First). [4]A. R. Richards (Third). [5]F. L. Fane (Fourth and Fifth). [6]L. J. Tancred (Second and Third). [7]J. W. H. T. Douglas (Fourth). [8]G. T. S. Stevens (Fifth). [9]A. W. Carr (Fourth and Fifth). [10]E. P. Nupen (First), H. B. Cameron (Fourth and Fifth). [11]D. J. McGlew (Third and Fourth). [12]D. J. McGlew (Second). [13]N. Hussain (First). [14]K. P. Pietersen (Fourth). [15]A. B. de Villiers (Third and Fourth).

SERIES RECORDS

Highest score	E	**258**	B. A. Stokes at Cape Town	2015-16
	SA	311*	H. M. Amla at The Oval	2012
Best bowling	E	9-28	G. A. Lohmann at Johannesburg	1895-96
	SA	9-113	H. J. Tayfield at Johannesburg	1956-57
Highest total	E	654-5	at Durban	1938-39
	SA	682-6 dec	at Lord's	2003
Lowest total	E	76	at Leeds	1907
	SA {	30	at Port Elizabeth	1895-96
		30	at Birmingham	1924

ENGLAND v WEST INDIES

Captains

Season	England	West Indies	T	E	WI	D
1928	A. P. F. Chapman	R. K. Nunes	3	3	0	0
1929-30	Hon. F. S. G. Calthorpe	E. L. G. Hoad[1]	4	1	1	2
1933	D. R. Jardine[2]	G. C. Grant	3	2	0	1
1934-35	R. E. S. Wyatt	G. C. Grant	4	1	2	1
1939	W. R. Hammond	R. S. Grant	3	1	0	2
1947-48	G. O. B. Allen[3]	J. D. C. Goddard[4]	4	0	2	2
1950	N. W. D. Yardley[5]	J. D. C. Goddard	4	1	3	0
1953-54	L. Hutton	J. B. Stollmeyer	5	2	2	1
1957	P. B. H. May	J. D. C. Goddard	5	3	0	2
1959-60	P. B. H. May[6]	F. C. M. Alexander	5	1	0	4

THE WISDEN TROPHY

Captains

Season	England	West Indies	T	E	WI	D	Held by
1963	E. R. Dexter	F. M. M. Worrell	5	1	3	1	WI
1966	M. C. Cowdrey[7]	G. S. Sobers	5	1	3	1	WI
1967-68	M. C. Cowdrey	G. S. Sobers	5	1	0	4	E
1969	R. Illingworth	G. S. Sobers	3	2	0	1	E
1973	R. Illingworth	R. B. Kanhai	3	0	2	1	WI
1973-74	M. H. Denness	R. B. Kanhai	5	1	1	3	WI
1976	A. W. Greig	C. H. Lloyd	5	0	3	2	WI
1980	I. T. Botham	C. H. Lloyd[8]	5	0	1	4	WI
1980-81†	I. T. Botham	C. H. Lloyd	4	0	2	2	WI
1984	D. I. Gower	C. H. Lloyd	5	0	5	0	WI
1985-86	D. I. Gower	I. V. A. Richards	5	0	5	0	WI
1988	J. E. Emburey[9]	I. V. A. Richards	5	0	4	1	WI
1989-90‡	G. A. Gooch[10]	I. V. A. Richards[11]	4	1	2	1	WI
1991	G. A. Gooch	I. V. A. Richards	5	2	2	1	WI
1993-94	M. A. Atherton	R. B. Richardson[12]	5	1	3	1	WI
1995	M. A. Atherton	R. B. Richardson	6	2	2	2	WI
1997-98§	M. A. Atherton	B. C. Lara	6	1	3	2	WI
2000	N. Hussain[13]	J. C. Adams	5	3	1	1	E
2003-04	M. P. Vaughan	B. C. Lara	4	3	0	1	E
2004	M. P. Vaughan	B. C. Lara	4	4	0	0	E
2007	M. P. Vaughan[14]	R. R. Sarwan[15]	4	3	0	1	E
2008-09§	A. J. Strauss	C. H. Gayle	5	0	1	4	WI
2009	A. J. Strauss	C. H. Gayle	2	2	0	0	E
2012	A. J. Strauss	D. J. G. Sammy	3	2	0	1	E
2014-15	**A. N. Cook**	**D. Ramdin**	**3**	**1**	**1**	**1**	**E**
	In England..........................		83	32	29	22	
	In West Indies		**68**	**14**	**25**	**29**	
	Totals		151	46	54	51	

†   *The Second Test, at Georgetown, was cancelled owing to political pressure and is excluded.*
‡   *The Second Test, at Georgetown, was abandoned without a ball being bowled and is excluded.*
§   *The First Test at Kingston in 1997-98 and the Second Test at North Sound in 2008-09 were called off on their opening days because of unfit pitches and are shown as draws.*

The following deputised for the official touring captain or were appointed by the home authority for only a minor proportion of the series:
[1]N. Betancourt (Second), M. P. Fernandes (Third), R. K. Nunes (Fourth). [2]R. E. S. Wyatt (Third). [3]K. Cranston (First). [4]G. A. Headley (First), G. E. Gomez (Second). [5]F. R. Brown (Fourth). [6]M. C. Cowdrey (Fourth and Fifth). [7]M. J. K. Smith (First), D. B. Close (Fifth). [8]I. V. A. Richards (Fifth). [9]M. W. Gatting (First), C. S. Cowdrey (Fourth), G. A. Gooch (Fifth). [10]A. J. Lamb (Fourth and Fifth). [11]D. L. Haynes (Third). [12]C. A. Walsh (Fifth). [13]A. J. Stewart (Second). [14]A. J. Strauss (First). [15]S. Ganga (Third and Fourth).

SERIES RECORDS

Highest score	E	325	A. Sandham at Kingston	1929-30
	WI	400*	B. C. Lara at St John's.....................	2003-04
Best bowling	E	8-53	A. R. C. Fraser at Port-of-Spain	1997-98
	WI	8-45	C. E. L. Ambrose at Bridgetown	1989-90
Highest total	E	849	at Kingston	1929-30
	WI	751-5 dec	at St John's	2003-04
Lowest total	E	46	at Port-of-Spain	1993-94
	WI	47	at Kingston	2003-04

ENGLAND v NEW ZEALAND

	Captains					
Season	*England*	*New Zealand*	*T*	*E*	*NZ*	*D*
1929-30	A. H. H. Gilligan	T. C. Lowry	4	1	0	3
1931	D. R. Jardine	T. C. Lowry	3	1	0	2
1932-33	D. R. Jardine[1]	M. L. Page	2	0	0	2
1937	R. W. V. Robins	M. L. Page	3	1	0	2
1946-47	W. R. Hammond	W. A. Hadlee	1	0	0	1
1949	F. G. Mann[2]	W. A. Hadlee	4	0	0	4
1950-51	F. R. Brown	W. A. Hadlee	2	1	0	1
1954-55	L. Hutton	G. O. Rabone	2	2	0	0
1958	P. B. H. May	J. R. Reid	5	4	0	1
1958-59	P. B. H. May	J. R. Reid	2	1	0	1
1962-63	E. R. Dexter	J. R. Reid	3	3	0	0
1965	M. J. K. Smith	J. R. Reid	3	3	0	0
1965-66	M. J. K. Smith	B. W. Sinclair[3]	3	0	0	3
1969	R. Illingworth	G. T. Dowling	3	2	0	1
1970-71	R. Illingworth	G. T. Dowling	2	1	0	1
1973	R. Illingworth	B. E. Congdon	3	2	0	1
1974-75	M. H. Denness	B. E. Congdon	2	1	0	1
1977-78	G. Boycott	M. G. Burgess	3	1	1	1
1978	J. M. Brearley	M. G. Burgess	3	3	0	0
1983	R. G. D. Willis	G. P. Howarth	4	3	1	0
1983-84	R. G. D. Willis	G. P. Howarth	3	0	1	2
1986	M. W. Gatting	J. V. Coney	3	0	1	2
1987-88	M. W. Gatting	J. J. Crowe[4]	3	0	0	3
1990	G. A. Gooch	J. G. Wright	3	1	0	2
1991-92	G. A. Gooch	M. D. Crowe	3	2	0	1
1994	M. A. Atherton	K. R. Rutherford	3	1	0	2
1996-97	M. A. Atherton	L. K. Germon[5]	3	2	0	1
1999	N. Hussain[6]	S. P. Fleming	4	1	2	1
2001-02	N. Hussain	S. P. Fleming	3	1	1	1
2004	M. P. Vaughan[7]	S. P. Fleming	3	3	0	0
2007-08	M. P. Vaughan	D. L. Vettori	3	2	1	0
2008	M. P. Vaughan	D. L. Vettori	3	2	0	1
2012-13	A. N. Cook	B. B. McCullum	3	0	0	3
2013	A. N. Cook	B. B. McCullum	2	2	0	0
2015	**A. N. Cook**	**B. B. McCullum**	**2**	**1**	**1**	**0**
	In New Zealand		47	18	4	25
	In England		**54**	**30**	**5**	**19**
	Totals		**101**	**48**	**9**	**44**

The following deputised for the official touring captain or were appointed by the home authority for only a minor proportion of the series:

[1]R. E. S. Wyatt (Second). [2]F. R. Brown (Third and Fourth). [3]M. E. Chapple (First). [4]J. G. Wright (Third). [5]S. P. Fleming (Third). [6]M. A. Butcher (Third). [7]M. E. Trescothick (First).

SERIES RECORDS

Highest score	E	336*	W. R. Hammond at Auckland.............		1932-33
	NZ	222	N. J. Astle at Christchurch		2001-02
Best bowling	E	7-32	D. L. Underwood at Lord's.............		1969
	NZ	7-74	B. L. Cairns at Leeds.................		1983
Highest total	E	593-6 dec	at Auckland.........................		1974-75
	NZ	551-9 dec	at Lord's		1973
Lowest total	E	64	at Wellington.......................		1977-78
	NZ	26	at Auckland		1954-55

ENGLAND v INDIA

		Captains					
Season	*England*		*India*	*T*	*E*	*I*	*D*
1932	D. R. Jardine		C. K. Nayudu	1	1	0	0
1933-34	D. R. Jardine		C. K. Nayudu	3	2	0	1
1936	G. O. B. Allen		Maharaj of Vizianagram	3	2	0	1
1946	W. R. Hammond		Nawab of Pataudi sen.	3	1	0	2
1951-52	N. D. Howard[1]		V. S. Hazare	5	1	1	3
1952	L. Hutton		V. S. Hazare	4	3	0	1
1959	P. B. H. May[2]		D. K. Gaekwad[3]	5	5	0	0
1961-62	E. R. Dexter		N. J. Contractor	5	0	2	3
1963-64	M. J. K. Smith		Nawab of Pataudi jun.	5	0	0	5
1967	D. B. Close		Nawab of Pataudi jun.	3	3	0	0
1971	R. Illingworth		A. L. Wadekar	3	0	1	2
1972-73	A. R. Lewis		A. L. Wadekar	5	1	2	2
1974	M. H. Denness		A. L. Wadekar	3	3	0	0
1976-77	A. W. Greig		B. S. Bedi	5	3	1	1
1979	J. M. Brearley		S. Venkataraghavan	4	1	0	3
1979-80	J. M. Brearley		G. R. Viswanath	1	1	0	0
1981-82	K. W. R. Fletcher		S. M. Gavaskar	6	0	1	5
1982	R. G. D. Willis		S. M. Gavaskar	3	1	0	2
1984-85	D. I. Gower		S. M. Gavaskar	5	2	1	2
1986	M. W. Gatting[4]		Kapil Dev	3	0	2	1
1990	G. A. Gooch		M. Azharuddin	3	1	0	2
1992-93	G. A. Gooch[5]		M. Azharuddin	3	0	3	0
1996	M. A. Atherton		M. Azharuddin	3	1	0	2
2001-02	N. Hussain		S. C. Ganguly	3	0	1	2
2002	N. Hussain		S. C. Ganguly	4	1	1	2
2005-06	A. Flintoff		R. Dravid	3	1	1	1
2007	M. P. Vaughan		R. Dravid	3	0	1	2
2008-09	K. P. Pietersen		M. S. Dhoni	2	0	2	1
2011	A. J. Strauss		M. S. Dhoni	4	4	0	0
2012-13	A. N. Cook		M. S. Dhoni	4	2	1	1
2014	A. N. Cook		M. S. Dhoni	5	3	1	1
	In England			57	30	6	21
	In India			55	13	15	27
	Totals			112	43	21	48

* *Since 1951-52, series in India have been for the De Mello Trophy. Since 2007, series in England have been for the Pataudi Trophy.*

The following deputised for the official touring captain or were appointed by the home authority for only a minor proportion of the series:
[1]D. B. Carr (Fifth). [2]M. C. Cowdrey (Fourth and Fifth). [3]Pankaj Roy (Second). [4]D. I. Gower (First). [5]A. J. Stewart (Second).

The 1932 Indian touring team was captained by the Maharaj of Porbandar but he did not play in the Test match.

SERIES RECORDS

Highest score	E	333	G. A. Gooch at Lord's....................		1990
	I	224	V. G. Kambli at Bombay..................		1992-93
Best bowling	E	8-31	F. S. Trueman at Manchester..............		1952
	I	8-55	V. Mankad at Madras....................		1951-52
Highest total	E	710-7 dec	at Birmingham.........................		2011
	I	664	at The Oval		2007
Lowest total	E	101	at The Oval		1971
	I	42	at Lord's.............................		1974

ENGLAND v PAKISTAN

		Captains				
Season	*England*	*Pakistan*	*T*	*E*	*P*	*D*
1954	L. Hutton[1]	A. H. Kardar	4	1	1	2
1961-62	E. R. Dexter	Imtiaz Ahmed	3	1	0	2
1962	E. R. Dexter[2]	Javed Burki	5	4	0	1
1967	D. B. Close	Hanif Mohammad	3	2	0	1
1968-69	M. C. Cowdrey	Saeed Ahmed	3	0	0	3
1971	R. Illingworth	Intikhab Alam	3	1	0	2
1972-73	A. R. Lewis	Majid Khan	3	0	0	3
1974	M. H. Denness	Intikhab Alam	3	0	0	3
1977-78	J. M. Brearley[3]	Wasim Bari	3	0	0	3
1978	J. M. Brearley	Wasim Bari	3	2	0	1
1982	R. G. D. Willis[4]	Imran Khan	3	2	1	0
1983-84	R. G. D. Willis[5]	Zaheer Abbas	3	0	1	2
1987	M. W. Gatting	Imran Khan	5	0	1	4
1987-88	M. W. Gatting	Javed Miandad	3	0	1	2
1992	G. A. Gooch	Javed Miandad	5	1	2	2
1996	M. A. Atherton	Wasim Akram	3	0	2	1
2000-01	N. Hussain	Moin Khan	3	1	0	2
2001	N. Hussain[6]	Waqar Younis	2	1	1	0
2005-06	M. P. Vaughan[7]	Inzamam-ul-Haq	3	0	2	1
2006†	A. J. Strauss	Inzamam-ul-Haq	4	3	0	1
2010	A. J. Strauss	Salman Butt	4	3	1	0
2011-12U	A. J. Strauss	Misbah-ul-Haq	3	0	3	0
2015-16U	**A. N. Cook**	**Misbah-ul-Haq**	**3**	**0**	**2**	**1**
	In England		47	20	9	18
	In Pakistan		24	2	4	18
	In United Arab Emirates..........		**6**	**0**	**5**	**1**
	Totals.........................		**77**	**22**	**18**	**37**

† *In 2008, the ICC changed the result of the forfeited Oval Test of 2006 from an England win to a draw, in contravention of the Laws of Cricket, only to rescind their decision in January 2009.*
U Played in United Arab Emirates.

The following deputised for the official touring captain or were appointed by the home authority for only a minor proportion of the series:
[1]D. S. Sheppard (Second and Third). [2]M. C. Cowdrey (Third). [3]G. Boycott (Third). [4]D. I. Gower (Second). [5]D. I. Gower (Second and Third). [6]A. J. Stewart (Second). [7]M. E. Trescothick (First).

SERIES RECORDS

Highest score	E	278	D. C. S. Compton at Nottingham		1954
	P	274	Zaheer Abbas at Birmingham		1971
Best bowling	E	8-34	I. T. Botham at Lord's....................		1978
	P	9-56	Abdul Qadir at Lahore....................		1987-88
Highest total	E	598-9 dec	**at Abu Dhabi**		**2015-16**
	P	708	at The Oval		1987
Lowest total	E	72	at Abu Dhabi		2011-12
	P	72	at Birmingham.........................		2010

ENGLAND v SRI LANKA

				Captains				
Season	*England*			*Sri Lanka*	*T*	*E*	*SL*	*D*
1981-82	K. W. R. Fletcher			B. Warnapura	1	1	0	0
1984	D. I. Gower			L. R. D. Mendis	1	0	0	1
1988	G. A. Gooch			R. S. Madugalle	1	1	0	0
1991	G. A. Gooch			P. A. de Silva	1	1	0	0
1992-93	A. J. Stewart			A. Ranatunga	1	0	1	0
1998	A. J. Stewart			A. Ranatunga	1	0	1	0
2000-01	N. Hussain			S. T. Jayasuriya	3	2	1	0
2002	N. Hussain			S. T. Jayasuriya	3	2	0	1
2003-04	M. P. Vaughan			H. P. Tillekeratne	3	0	1	2
2006	A. Flintoff			D. P. M. D. Jayawardene	3	1	1	1
2007-08	M. P. Vaughan			D. P. M. D. Jayawardene	3	0	1	2
2011	A. J. Strauss			T. M. Dilshan[1]	3	1	0	2
2011-12	A. J. Strauss			D. P. M. D. Jayawardene	2	1	1	0
2014	A. N. Cook			A. D. Mathews	2	0	1	1
	In England				15	6	3	6
	In Sri Lanka				13	4	5	4
	Totals				28	10	8	10

The following deputised for the official touring captain for only a minor proportion of the series:
[1]K. C. Sangakkara (Third).

SERIES RECORDS

Highest score	E	203	I. J. L. Trott at Cardiff	2011
	SL	213*	D. P. M. D. Jayawardene at Galle	2007-08
Best bowling	E	7-70	P. A. J. DeFreitas at Lord's	1991
	SL	9-65	M. Muralitharan at The Oval	1998
Highest total	E	575-9 dec	at Lord's.	2014
	SL	628-8 dec	at Colombo (SSC)	2003-04
Lowest total	E	81	at Galle.	2007-08
	SL	81	at Colombo (SSC)	2000-01

ENGLAND v ZIMBABWE

			Captains				
Season	*England*		*Zimbabwe*	*T*	*E*	*Z*	*D*
1996-97	M. A. Atherton		A. D. R. Campbell	2	0	0	2
2000	N. Hussain		A. Flower	2	1	0	1
2003	N. Hussain		H. H. Streak	2	2	0	0
	In England			4	3	0	1
	In Zimbabwe			2	0	0	2
	Totals			6	3	0	3

SERIES RECORDS

Highest score	E	137	M. A. Butcher at Lord's	2003
	Z	148*	M. W. Goodwin at Nottingham.	2000
Best bowling	E	6-33	R. L. Johnson at Chester-le-Street.	2003
	Z	6-87	H. H. Streak at Lord's	2000
Highest total	E	472	at Lord's	2003
	Z	376	at Bulawayo.	1996-97
Lowest total	E	147	at Nottingham	2000
	Z	83	at Lord's	2000

ENGLAND v BANGLADESH

			Captains				
Season	*England*		*Bangladesh*	*T*	*E*	*B*	*D*
2003-04	M. P. Vaughan		Khaled Mahmud	2	2	0	0
2005	M. P. Vaughan		Habibul Bashar	2	2	0	0
2009-10	A. N. Cook		Shakib Al Hasan	2	2	0	0
2010	A. J. Strauss		Shakib Al Hasan	2	2	0	0
	In England			4	4	0	0
	In Bangladesh.			4	4	0	0
	Totals			8	8	0	0

SERIES RECORDS

Highest score	E	226	I. J. L. Trott at Lord's	2010
	B	108	Tamim Iqbal at Manchester.	2010
Best bowling	E	5-35	S. J. Harmison at Dhaka	2003-04
	B	5-98	Shahadat Hossain at Lord's	2010
Highest total	E	599-6 dec	at Chittagong	2009-10
	B	419	at Mirpur	2009-10
Lowest total	E	295	at Dhaka.	2003-04
	B	104	at Chester-le-Street	2005

AUSTRALIA v SOUTH AFRICA

		Captains				
Season	*Australia*	*South Africa*	*T*	*A*	*SA*	*D*
1902-03S	J. Darling	H. M. Taberer[1]	3	2	0	1
1910-11A	C. Hill	P. W. Sherwell	5	4	1	0
1912E	S. E. Gregory	F. Mitchell[2]	3	2	0	1
1921-22S	H. L. Collins	H. W. Taylor	3	1	0	2
1931-32A	W. M. Woodfull	H. B. Cameron	5	5	0	0
1935-36S	V. Y. Richardson	H. F. Wade	5	4	0	1
1949-50S	A. L. Hassett	A. D. Nourse	5	4	0	1
1952-53A	A. L. Hassett	J. E. Cheetham	5	2	2	1
1957-58S	I. D. Craig	C. B. van Ryneveld[3]	5	3	0	2
1963-64A	R. B. Simpson[4]	T. L. Goddard	5	1	1	3
1966-67S	R. B. Simpson	P. L. van der Merwe	5	1	3	1
1969-70S	W. M. Lawry	A. Bacher	4	0	4	0
1993-94A	A. R. Border	K. C. Wessels[5]	3	1	1	1
1993-94S	A. R. Border	K. C. Wessels	3	1	1	1
1996-97S	M. A. Taylor	W. J. Cronje	3	2	1	0
1997-98A	M. A. Taylor	W. J. Cronje	3	1	0	2
2001-02A	S. R. Waugh	S. M. Pollock	3	3	0	0
2001-02S	S. R. Waugh	M. V. Boucher	3	2	1	0
2005-06A	R. T. Ponting	G. C. Smith	3	2	0	1
2005-06S	R. T. Ponting	G. C. Smith[6]	3	3	0	0
2008-09A	R. T. Ponting	G. C. Smith	3	1	2	0
2008-09S	R. T. Ponting	G. C. Smith[7]	3	2	1	0
2011-12S	M. J. Clarke	G. C. Smith	2	1	1	0
2012-13A	M. J. Clarke	G. C. Smith	3	0	1	2
2013-14S	M. J. Clarke	G. C. Smith	3	2	1	0
	In South Africa.		50	28	13	9
	In Australia.		38	20	8	10
	In England		3	2	0	1
	Totals		91	50	21	20

S Played in South Africa.   A Played in Australia.   E Played in England.

The following deputised for the official touring captain or were appointed by the home authority for only a minor proportion of the series:
[1]J. H. Anderson (Second), E. A. Halliwell (Third). [2]L. J. Tancred (Third). [3]D. J. McGlew (First). [4]R. Benaud (First). [5]W. J. Cronje (Third). [6]J. H. Kallis (Third). [7]J. H. Kallis (Third).

SERIES RECORDS

Highest score	A	299*	D. G. Bradman at Adelaide	1931-32
	SA	274	R. G. Pollock at Durban.	1969-70
Best bowling	A	8-61	M. G. Johnson at Perth	2008-09
	SA	7-23	H. J. Tayfield at Durban.	1949-50
Highest total	A	652-7 dec	at Johannesburg	2001-02
	SA	651	at Cape Town.	2008-09
Lowest total	A	47	at Cape Town.	2011-12
	SA	36	at Melbourne	1931-32

AUSTRALIA v WEST INDIES

		Captains					
Season	*Australia*	*West Indies*	*T*	*A*	*WI*	*T*	*D*
1930-31A	W. M. Woodfull	G. C. Grant	5	4	1	0	0
1951-52A	A. L. Hassett[1]	J. D. C. Goddard[2]	5	4	1	0	0
1954-55W	I. W. Johnson	D. St E. Atkinson[3]	5	3	0	0	2

THE FRANK WORRELL TROPHY

		Captains						
Season	*Australia*	*West Indies*	*T*	*A*	*WI*	*T*	*D*	*Held by*
1960-61A	R. Benaud	F. M. M. Worrell	5	2	1	1	1	A
1964-65W	R. B. Simpson	G. S. Sobers	5	1	2	0	2	WI
1968-69A	W. M. Lawry	G. S. Sobers	5	3	1	0	1	A
1972-73W	I. M. Chappell	R. B. Kanhai	5	2	0	0	3	A
1975-76A	G. S. Chappell	C. H. Lloyd	6	5	1	0	0	A
1977-78W	R. B. Simpson	A. I. Kallicharran[4]	5	1	3	0	1	WI
1979-80A	G. S. Chappell	C. H. Lloyd[5]	3	0	2	0	1	WI
1981-82A	G. S. Chappell	C. H. Lloyd	3	1	1	0	1	WI
1983-84W	K. J. Hughes	C. H. Lloyd[6]	5	0	3	0	2	WI
1984-85A	A. R. Border[7]	C. H. Lloyd	5	1	3	0	1	WI
1988-89A	A. R. Border	I. V. A. Richards	5	1	3	0	1	WI
1990-91W	A. R. Border	I. V. A. Richards	5	1	2	0	2	WI
1992-93A	A. R. Border	R. B. Richardson	5	1	2	0	2	WI
1994-95W	M. A. Taylor	R. B. Richardson	4	2	1	0	1	A
1996-97A	M. A. Taylor	C. A. Walsh	5	3	2	0	0	A
1998-99W	S. R. Waugh	B. C. Lara	4	2	2	0	0	A
2000-01A	S. R. Waugh[8]	J. C. Adams	5	5	0	0	0	A
2002-03W	S. R. Waugh	B. C. Lara	4	3	1	0	0	A
2005-06A	R. T. Ponting	S. Chanderpaul	3	3	0	0	0	A
2007-08W	R. T. Ponting	R. R. Sarwan[9]	3	2	0	0	1	A
2009-10A	R. T. Ponting	C. H. Gayle	3	2	0	0	1	A
2011-12W	M. J. Clarke	D. J. G. Sammy	3	2	0	0	1	A
2015W	**M. J. Clarke**	**D. Ramdin**	**2**	**2**	**0**	**0**	**0**	**A**
2015-16A	**S. P. D. Smith**	**J. O. Holder**	**3**	**2**	**0**	**0**	**1**	**A**
	In Australia		66	37	18	1	10	
	In West Indies		50	21	14	0	15	
	Totals		116	58	32	1	25	

A   Played in Australia.   W   Played in West Indies.

The following deputised for the official touring captain or were appointed by the home authority for only a minor proportion of the series:

[1]A. R. Morris (Third). [2]J. B. Stollmeyer (Fifth). [3]J. B. Stollmeyer (Second and Third). [4]C. H. Lloyd (First and Second). [5]D. L. Murray (First). [6]I. V. A. Richards (Second). [7]K. J. Hughes (First and Second). [8]A. C. Gilchrist (Third). [9]C. H. Gayle (Third).

SERIES RECORDS

Highest score	A	**269***	**A. C. Voges** at Hobart	**2015-16**
	WI	277	B. C. Lara at Sydney	1992-93
Best bowling	A	8-71	G. D. McKenzie at Melbourne	1968-69
	WI	7-25	C. E. L. Ambrose at Perth	1992-93
Highest total	A	758-8 dec	at Kingston	1954-55
	WI	616	at Adelaide	1968-69
Lowest total	A	76	at Perth	1984-85
	WI	51	at Port-of-Spain	1998-99

AUSTRALIA v NEW ZEALAND

		Captains					
Season	Australia		New Zealand	T	A	NZ	D
1945-46N	W. A. Brown		W. A. Hadlee	1	1	0	0
1973-74A	I. M. Chappell		B. E. Congdon	3	2	0	1
1973-74N	I. M. Chappell		B. E. Congdon	3	1	1	1
1976-77N	G. S. Chappell		G. M. Turner	2	1	0	1
1980-81A	G. S. Chappell		G. P. Howarth[1]	3	2	0	1
1981-82N	G. S. Chappell		G. P. Howarth	3	1	1	1

TRANS-TASMAN TROPHY

		Captains						
Season	Australia		New Zealand	T	A	NZ	D	Held by
1985-86A	A. R. Border		J. V. Coney	3	1	2	0	NZ
1985-86N	A. R. Border		J. V. Coney	3	0	1	2	NZ
1987-88A	A. R. Border		J. J. Crowe	3	1	0	2	A
1989-90A	A. R. Border		J. G. Wright	1	0	0	1	A
1989-90N	A. R. Border		J. G. Wright	1	0	1	0	NZ
1992-93N	A. R. Border		M. D. Crowe	3	1	1	1	NZ
1993-94A	A. R. Border		M. D. Crowe[2]	3	2	0	1	A
1997-98A	M. A. Taylor		S. P. Fleming	3	2	0	1	A
1999-2000N	S. R. Waugh		S. P. Fleming	3	3	0	0	A
2001-02A	S. R. Waugh		S. P. Fleming	3	0	0	3	A
2004-05A	R. T. Ponting		S. P. Fleming	2	2	0	0	A
2004-05N	R. T. Ponting		S. P. Fleming	3	2	0	1	A
2008-09A	R. T. Ponting		D. L. Vettori	2	2	0	0	A
2009-10N	R. T. Ponting		D. L. Vettori	2	2	0	0	A
2011-12A	M. J. Clarke		L. R. P. L. Taylor	2	1	1	0	A
2015-16A	**S. P. D. Smith**		**B. B. McCullum**	**3**	**2**	**0**	**1**	**A**
	In Australia			31	17	3	11	
	In New Zealand			24	12	5	7	
	Totals			**55**	**29**	**8**	**18**	

A Played in Australia.   N Played in New Zealand.

The following deputised for the official touring captain: [1]M. G. Burgess (Second). [2]K. R. Rutherford (Second and Third).

SERIES RECORDS

Highest score	A	**253**	**D. A. Warner at Perth**	**2015-16**
	NZ	**290**	**L. R. P. L. Taylor at Perth**	**2015-16**
Best bowling	A	6-31	S. K. Warne at Hobart	1993-94
	NZ	9-52	R. J. Hadlee at Brisbane	1985-86
Highest total	A	607-6 dec	at Brisbane	1993-94
	NZ	**624**	**at Perth**	**2015-16**
Lowest total	A	103	at Auckland	1985-86
	NZ	42	at Wellington	1945-46

AUSTRALIA v INDIA

		Captains					
Season	*Australia*		*India*	*T*	*A*	*I*	*T*	*D*
1947-48*A*	D. G. Bradman		L. Amarnath	5	4	0	0	1
1956-57*I*	I. W. Johnson[1]		P. R. Umrigar	3	2	0	0	1
1959-60*I*	R. Benaud		G. S. Ramchand	5	2	1	0	2
1964-65*I*	R. B. Simpson		Nawab of Pataudi jun.	3	1	1	0	1
1967-68*A*	R. B. Simpson[2]		Nawab of Pataudi jun.[3]	4	4	0	0	0
1969-70*I*	W. M. Lawry		Nawab of Pataudi jun.	5	3	1	0	1
1977-78*A*	R. B. Simpson		B. S. Bedi	5	3	2	0	0
1979-80*I*	K. J. Hughes		S. M. Gavaskar	6	0	2	0	4
1980-81*A*	G. S. Chappell		S. M. Gavaskar	3	1	1	0	1
1985-86*A*	A. R. Border		Kapil Dev	3	0	0	0	3
1986-87*I*	A. R. Border		Kapil Dev	3	0	0	1	2
1991-92*A*	A. R. Border		M. Azharuddin	5	4	0	0	1

THE BORDER–GAVASKAR TROPHY

		Captains						
Season	*Australia*		*India*	*T*	*A*	*I*	*T*	*D*	*Held by*
1996-97*I*	M. A. Taylor		S. R. Tendulkar	1	0	1	0	0	I
1997-98*I*	M. A. Taylor		M. Azharuddin	3	1	2	0	0	I
1999-2000*A*	S. R. Waugh		S. R. Tendulkar	3	3	0	0	0	A
2000-01*I*	S. R. Waugh		S. C. Ganguly	3	1	2	0	0	I
2003-04*A*	S. R. Waugh		S. C. Ganguly	4	1	1	0	2	I
2004-05*I*	R. T. Ponting[4]		S. C. Ganguly[5]	4	2	1	0	1	A
2007-08*A*	R. T. Ponting		A. Kumble	4	2	1	0	1	A
2008-09*I*	R. T. Ponting		A. Kumble[6]	4	0	2	0	2	I
2010-11*I*	R. T. Ponting		M. S. Dhoni	2	0	2	0	0	I
2011-12*A*	M. J. Clarke		M. S. Dhoni[7]	4	4	0	0	0	A
2012-13*I*	M. J. Clarke[8]		M. S. Dhoni	4	0	4	0	0	I
2014-15*A*	**M. J. Clarke[9]**		**M. S. Dhoni[10]**	**4**	**2**	**0**	**0**	**2**	**A**
	In Australia			44	28	5	0	11	
	In India			46	12	19	1	14	
	Totals			**90**	**40**	**24**	**1**	**25**	

A Played in Australia.   *I Played in India.*

The following deputised for the official touring captain or were appointed by the home authority for only a minor proportion of the series:
[1]R. R. Lindwall (Second). [2]W. M. Lawry (Third and Fourth). [3]C. G. Borde (First). [4]A. C. Gilchrist (First, Second and Third). [5]R. Dravid (Third and Fourth). [6]M. S. Dhoni (Second and Fourth). [7]V. Sehwag (Fourth). [8]S. R. Watson (Fourth). [9]S. P. D. Smith (Second, Third and Fourth). [10]V. Kohli (First and Fourth).

SERIES RECORDS

Highest score	A	329*	M. J. Clarke at Sydney....................	2011-12
	I	281	V. V. S. Laxman at Kolkata...............	2000-01
Best bowling	A	8-215	J. J. Krejza at Nagpur...................	2008-09
	I	9-69	J. M. Patel at Kanpur...................	1959-60
Highest total	A	674	at Adelaide...........................	1947-48
	I	705-7 dec	at Sydney............................	2003-04
Lowest total	A	83	at Melbourne.........................	1980-81
	I	58	at Brisbane..........................	1947-48

AUSTRALIA v PAKISTAN

<table>
<tr><td colspan="2"></td><td align="center">Captains</td><td></td><td></td><td></td><td></td></tr>
<tr><td>Season</td><td>Australia</td><td>Pakistan</td><td>T</td><td>A</td><td>P</td><td>D</td></tr>
<tr><td>1956-57P</td><td>I. W. Johnson</td><td>A. H. Kardar</td><td>1</td><td>0</td><td>1</td><td>0</td></tr>
<tr><td>1959-60P</td><td>R. Benaud</td><td>Fazal Mahmood[1]</td><td>3</td><td>2</td><td>0</td><td>1</td></tr>
<tr><td>1964-65P</td><td>R. B. Simpson</td><td>Hanif Mohammad</td><td>1</td><td>0</td><td>0</td><td>1</td></tr>
<tr><td>1964-65A</td><td>R. B. Simpson</td><td>Hanif Mohammad</td><td>1</td><td>0</td><td>0</td><td>1</td></tr>
<tr><td>1972-73A</td><td>I. M. Chappell</td><td>Intikhab Alam</td><td>3</td><td>3</td><td>0</td><td>0</td></tr>
<tr><td>1976-77A</td><td>G. S. Chappell</td><td>Mushtaq Mohammad</td><td>3</td><td>1</td><td>1</td><td>1</td></tr>
<tr><td>1978-79A</td><td>G. N. Yallop[2]</td><td>Mushtaq Mohammad</td><td>2</td><td>1</td><td>1</td><td>0</td></tr>
<tr><td>1979-80P</td><td>G. S. Chappell</td><td>Javed Miandad</td><td>3</td><td>0</td><td>1</td><td>2</td></tr>
<tr><td>1981-82A</td><td>G. S. Chappell</td><td>Javed Miandad</td><td>3</td><td>2</td><td>1</td><td>0</td></tr>
<tr><td>1982-83P</td><td>K. J. Hughes</td><td>Imran Khan</td><td>3</td><td>0</td><td>3</td><td>0</td></tr>
<tr><td>1983-84A</td><td>K. J. Hughes</td><td>Imran Khan[3]</td><td>5</td><td>2</td><td>0</td><td>3</td></tr>
<tr><td>1988-89P</td><td>A. R. Border</td><td>Javed Miandad</td><td>3</td><td>0</td><td>1</td><td>2</td></tr>
<tr><td>1989-90A</td><td>A. R. Border</td><td>Imran Khan</td><td>3</td><td>1</td><td>0</td><td>2</td></tr>
<tr><td>1994-95P</td><td>M. A. Taylor</td><td>Salim Malik</td><td>3</td><td>0</td><td>1</td><td>2</td></tr>
<tr><td>1995-96A</td><td>M. A. Taylor</td><td>Wasim Akram</td><td>3</td><td>2</td><td>1</td><td>0</td></tr>
<tr><td>1998-99P</td><td>M. A. Taylor</td><td>Aamir Sohail</td><td>3</td><td>1</td><td>0</td><td>2</td></tr>
<tr><td>1999-2000A</td><td>S. R. Waugh</td><td>Wasim Akram</td><td>3</td><td>3</td><td>0</td><td>0</td></tr>
<tr><td>2002-03S/U</td><td>S. R. Waugh</td><td>Waqar Younis</td><td>3</td><td>3</td><td>0</td><td>0</td></tr>
<tr><td>2004-05A</td><td>R. T. Ponting</td><td>Inzamam-ul-Haq[4]</td><td>3</td><td>3</td><td>0</td><td>0</td></tr>
<tr><td>2009-10A</td><td>R. T. Ponting</td><td>Mohammad Yousuf</td><td>3</td><td>3</td><td>0</td><td>0</td></tr>
<tr><td>2010E</td><td>R. T. Ponting</td><td>Shahid Afridi[5]</td><td>2</td><td>1</td><td>1</td><td>0</td></tr>
<tr><td>2014-15U</td><td>M. J. Clarke</td><td>Misbah-ul-Haq</td><td>2</td><td>0</td><td>2</td><td>0</td></tr>
<tr><td></td><td colspan="2">In Pakistan ....</td><td>20</td><td>3</td><td>7</td><td>10</td></tr>
<tr><td></td><td colspan="2">In Australia........................</td><td>32</td><td>21</td><td>4</td><td>7</td></tr>
<tr><td></td><td colspan="2">In Sri Lanka ....</td><td>1</td><td>1</td><td>0</td><td>0</td></tr>
<tr><td></td><td colspan="2">In United Arab Emirates ....</td><td>4</td><td>2</td><td>2</td><td>0</td></tr>
<tr><td></td><td colspan="2">In England ....</td><td>2</td><td>1</td><td>1</td><td>0</td></tr>
<tr><td></td><td colspan="2">Totals ....</td><td>59</td><td>28</td><td>14</td><td>17</td></tr>
</table>

P Played in Pakistan.   A Played in Australia.
S/U First Test played in Sri Lanka, Second and Third Tests in United Arab Emirates.
E Played in England.

The following deputised for the official touring captain or were appointed by the home authority for only a minor proportion of the series:

[1]Imtiaz Ahmed (Second). [2]K. J. Hughes (Second). [3]Zaheer Abbas (First, Second and Third). [4]Yousuf Youhana *later known as Mohammad Yousuf* (Second and Third). [5]Salman Butt (Second).

An expanded and regularly updated online version of the Records can be found at
www.wisdenrecords.com

SERIES RECORDS

Highest score	A	334*	M. A. Taylor at Peshawar	1998-99
	P	237	Salim Malik at Rawalpindi	1994-95
Best bowling	A	8-24	G. D. McGrath at Perth	2004-05
	P	9-86	Sarfraz Nawaz at Melbourne	1978-79
Highest total	A	617	at Faisalabad	1979-80
	P	624	at Adelaide	1983-84
Lowest total	A	80	at Karachi	1956-57
	P	53	at Sharjah	2002-03

AUSTRALIA v SRI LANKA

		Captains				
Season	*Australia*		*Sri Lanka*	*T*	*A*	*SL*	*D*
1982-83*S*	G. S. Chappell		L. R. D. Mendis	1	1	0	0
1987-88*A*	A. R. Border		R. S. Madugalle	1	1	0	0
1989-90*A*	A. R. Border		A. Ranatunga	2	1	0	1
1992-93*S*	A. R. Border		A. Ranatunga	3	1	0	2
1995-96*A*	M. A. Taylor		A. Ranatunga[1]	3	3	0	0
1999-2000*S*	S. R. Waugh		S. T. Jayasuriya	3	0	1	2
2003-04*S*	R. T. Ponting		H. P. Tillekeratne	3	3	0	0
2004*A*	R. T. Ponting[2]		M. S. Atapattu	2	1	0	1

THE WARNE–MURALITHARAN TROPHY

		Captains					
Season	*Australia*		*Sri Lanka*	*T*	*A*	*SL*	*D*	*Held by*
2007-08*A*	R. T. Ponting		D. P. M. D. Jayawardene	2	2	0	0	A
2011-12*S*	M. J. Clarke		T. M. Dilshan	3	1	0	2	A
2012-13*A*	M. J. Clarke		D. P. M. D. Jayawardene	3	3	0	0	A
	In Australia			13	11	0	2	
	In Sri Lanka			13	6	1	6	
	Totals			26	17	1	8	

A   Played in Australia.   S   Played in Sri Lanka.

The following deputised for the official touring captain or was appointed by the home authority for only a minor proportion of the series:
[1]P. A. de Silva (Third). [2]A. C. Gilchrist (First).

SERIES RECORDS

Highest score	A	219	M. J. Slater at Perth	1995-96
	SL	192	K. C. Sangakkara at Hobart	2007-08
Best bowling	A	7-39	M. S. Kasprowicz at Darwin	2004
	SL	7-157	H. M. R. K. B. Herath at Colombo (SSC)	2011-12
Highest total	A	617-5 dec	at Perth	1995-96
	SL	547-8 dec	at Colombo (SSC)	1992-93
Lowest total	A	120	at Kandy	2003-04
	SL	97	at Darwin	2004

AUSTRALIA v ZIMBABWE

		Captains				
Season	*Australia*	*Zimbabwe*	T	A	Z	D
1999-2000Z	S. R. Waugh	A. D. R. Campbell	1	1	0	0
2003-04A	S. R. Waugh	H. H. Streak	2	2	0	0
	In Australia....................		2	2	0	0
	In Zimbabwe		1	1	0	0
	Totals		3	3	0	0

A   Played in Australia.   Z   Played in Zimbabwe.

SERIES RECORDS

Highest score	A	380	M. L. Hayden at Perth....................	2003-04
	Z	118	S. V. Carlisle at Sydney.................	2003-04
Best bowling	A	6-65	S. M. Katich at Sydney	2003-04
	Z	6-121	R. W. Price at Sydney	2003-04
Highest total	A	735-6 dec	at Perth...........................	2003-04
	Z	321	at Perth...........................	2003-04
Lowest total	A	403	at Sydney	2003-04
	Z	194	at Harare	1999-2000

AUSTRALIA v BANGLADESH

		Captains				
Season	*Australia*	*Bangladesh*	T	A	B	D
2003A	S. R. Waugh	Khaled Mahmud	2	2	0	0
2005-06B	R. T. Ponting	Habibul Bashar	2	2	0	0
	In Australia....................		2	2	0	0
	In Bangladesh..................		2	2	0	0
	Totals		4	4	0	0

A   Played in Australia.   B   Played in Bangladesh.

SERIES RECORDS

Highest score	A	201*	J. N. Gillespie at Chittagong	2005-06
	B	138	Shahriar Nafees at Fatullah	2005-06
Best bowling	A	8-108	S. C. G. MacGill at Fatullah	2005-06
	B	5-62	Mohammad Rafique at Fatullah.............	2005-06
Highest total	A	581-4 dec	at Chittagong	2005-06
	B	427	at Fatullah	2005-06
Lowest total	A	269	at Fatullah	2005-06
	B	97	at Darwin	2003

AUSTRALIA v ICC WORLD XI

Season	*Australia*	*ICC World XI*	T	A	ICC	D
2005-06A	R. T. Ponting	G. C. Smith	1	1	0	0

A   Played in Australia.

SERIES RECORDS

Highest score	A	111	M. L. Hayden at Sydney	2005-06
	Wld	76	V. Sehwag at Sydney	2005-06
Best bowling	A	5-43	S. C. G. MacGill at Sydney	2005-06
	Wld	4-59	A. Flintoff at Sydney	2005-06
Highest total	A	345	at Sydney	2005-06
	Wld	190	at Sydney	2005-06
Lowest total	A	199	at Sydney	2005-06
	Wld	144	at Sydney	2005-06

SOUTH AFRICA v WEST INDIES

Season	South Africa	Captains West Indies	T	SA	WI	D	
1991-92W	K. C. Wessels	R. B. Richardson	1	0	1	0	
1998-99S	W. J. Cronje	B. C. Lara	5	5	0	0	

SIR VIVIAN RICHARDS TROPHY

Season	South Africa	Captains West Indies	T	SA	WI	D	Held by
2000-01W	S. M. Pollock	C. L. Hooper	5	2	1	2	SA
2003-04S	G. C. Smith	B. C. Lara	4	3	0	1	SA
2004-05W	G. C. Smith	S. Chanderpaul	4	2	0	2	SA
2007-08 S	G. C. Smith	C. H. Gayle[1]	3	2	1	0	SA
2010W	G. C. Smith	C. H. Gayle	3	2	0	1	SA
2014-15S	**H. M. Amla**	**D. Ramdin**	**3**	**2**	**0**	**1**	**SA**
	In South Africa		**15**	**12**	**1**	**2**	
	In West Indies		13	6	2	5	
	Totals		**28**	**18**	**3**	**7**	

S   Played in South Africa.   W   Played in West Indies.

The following deputised for the official touring captain:
  [1]D. J. Bravo (Third).

SERIES RECORDS

Highest score	SA	**208**	**H. M. Amla at Centurion**	**2014-15**
	WI	317	C. H. Gayle at St John's	2004-05
Best bowling	SA	7-37	M. Ntini at Port-of-Spain	2004-05
	WI	7-84	F. A. Rose at Durban	1998-99
Highest total	SA	658-9 dec	at Durban	2003-04
	WI	747	at St John's	2004-05
Lowest total	SA	141	at Kingston	2000-01
	WI	102	at Port-of-Spain	2010

SOUTH AFRICA v NEW ZEALAND

Season	South Africa	Captains New Zealand	T	SA	NZ	D
1931-32N	H. B. Cameron	M. L. Page	2	2	0	0
1952-53N	J. E. Cheetham	W. M. Wallace	2	1	0	1
1953-54S	J. E. Cheetham	G. O. Rabone[1]	5	4	0	1
1961-62S	D. J. McGlew	J. R. Reid	5	2	2	1
1963-64N	T. L. Goddard	J. R. Reid	3	0	0	3
1994-95S	W. J. Cronje	K. R. Rutherford	3	2	1	0
1994-95N	W. J. Cronje	K. R. Rutherford	1	1	0	0

Season	South Africa	Captains New Zealand	T	SA	NZ	D
1998-99*N*	W. J. Cronje	D. J. Nash	3	1	0	2
2000-01*S*	S. M. Pollock	S. P. Fleming	3	2	0	1
2003-04*N*	G. C. Smith	S. P. Fleming	3	1	1	1
2005-06*S*	G. C. Smith	S. P. Fleming	3	2	0	1
2007-08*S*	G. C. Smith	D. L. Vettori	2	2	0	0
2011-12*N*	G. C. Smith	L. R. P. L. Taylor	3	1	0	2
2012-13*S*	G. C. Smith	B. B. McCullum	2	2	0	0
	In New Zealand		17	7	1	9
	In South Africa		23	16	3	4
	Totals		40	23	4	13

N Played in New Zealand.   S Played in South Africa.

The following deputised for the official touring captain:
[1]B. Sutcliffe (Fourth and Fifth).

SERIES RECORDS

Highest score	SA	275*	D. J. Cullinan at Auckland	1998-99
	NZ	262	S. P. Fleming at Cape Town	2005-06
Best bowling	SA	8-53	G. B. Lawrence at Johannesburg..........	1961-62
	NZ	6-60	J. R. Reid at Dunedin	1963-64
Highest total	SA	621-5 dec	at Auckland	1998-99
	NZ	595	at Auckland	2003-04
Lowest total	SA	148	at Johannesburg.........................	1953-54
	NZ	45	at Cape Town	2012-13

SOUTH AFRICA v INDIA

Season	South Africa	Captains India	T	SA	I	D
1992-93*S*	K. C. Wessels	M. Azharuddin	4	1	0	3
1996-97*I*	W. J. Cronje	S. R. Tendulkar	3	1	2	0
1996-97*S*	W. J. Cronje	S. R. Tendulkar	3	2	0	1
1999-2000*I*	W. J. Cronje	S. R. Tendulkar	2	2	0	0
2001-02*S*†	S. M. Pollock	S. C. Ganguly	2	1	0	1
2004-05*I*	G. C. Smith	S. C. Ganguly	2	0	1	1
2006-07*S*	G. C. Smith	R. Dravid	3	2	1	0
2007-08*I*	G. C. Smith	A. Kumble[1]	3	1	1	1
2009-10*I*	G. C. Smith	M. S. Dhoni	2	1	1	0
2010-11*S*	G. C. Smith	M. S. Dhoni	3	1	1	1
2013-14*S*	G. C. Smith	M. S. Dhoni	2	1	0	1

THE FREEDOM TROPHY

Season	South Africa	Captains India	T	SA	I	D	Held by
2015-16*I*	H. M. Amla	**V. Kohli**	4	0	3	1	I
	In South Africa		17	8	2	7	
	In India		16	5	8	3	
	Totals		33	13	10	10	

S Played in South Africa.   I Played in India.

† *The Third Test at Centurion was stripped of its official status by the ICC after a disciplinary dispute and is excluded.*

The following was appointed by the home authority for only a minor proportion of the series:
[1]M. S. Dhoni (Third).

SERIES RECORDS

Highest score	SA	253*	H. M. Amla at Nagpur...............	2009-10
	I	319	V. Sehwag at Chennai...............	2007-08
Best bowling	SA	8-64	L. Klusener at Calcutta.............	1996-97
	I	**7-66**	**R. Ashwin at Nagpur**.............	**2015-16**
Highest total	SA	620-4 dec	at Centurion......................	2010-11
	I	643-6 dec	at Kolkata........................	2009-10
Lowest total	SA	**79**	**at Nagpur**......................	**2015-16**
	I	66	at Durban.........................	1996-97

SOUTH AFRICA v PAKISTAN

		Captains					
Season	*South Africa*	*Pakistan*	*T*	*SA*	*P*	*D*
1994-95S	W. J. Cronje	Salim Malik	1	1	0	0
1997-98P	W. J. Cronje	Saeed Anwar	3	1	0	2
1997-98S	W. J. Cronje[1]	Rashid Latif[2]	3	1	1	1
2002-03S	S. M. Pollock	Waqar Younis	2	2	0	0
2003-04P	G. C. Smith	Inzamam-ul-Haq[3]	2	0	1	1
2006-07S	G. C. Smith	Inzamam-ul-Haq	3	2	1	0
2007-08P	G. C. Smith	Shoaib Malik	2	1	0	1
2010-11U	G. C. Smith	Misbah-ul-Haq	2	0	0	2
2012-13S	G. C. Smith	Misbah-ul-Haq	3	3	0	0
2013-14U	G. C. Smith	Misbah-ul-Haq	2	1	1	0
	In South Africa..................		12	9	2	1
	In Pakistan		7	2	1	4
	In United Arab Emirates		4	1	1	2
	Totals..........................		23	12	4	7

S Played in South Africa. P Played in Pakistan. U Played in United Arab Emirates.

The following deputised for the official touring captain or were appointed by the home authority for only a minor proportion of the series:
[1]G. Kirsten (First). [2]Aamir Sohail (First and Second). [3]Yousuf Youhana *later known as Mohammad Yousuf* (First).

SERIES RECORDS

Highest score	SA	278*	A. B. de Villiers at Abu Dhabi..............	2010-11
	P	146	Khurram Manzoor at Abu Dhabi.............	2013-14
Best bowling	SA	7-29	K. J. Abbott at Centurion.................	2012-13
	P	6-78	Mushtaq Ahmed at Durban.................	1997-98
		6-78	Waqar Younis at Port Elizabeth............	1997-98
Highest total	SA	620-7 dec	at Cape Town......................	2002-03
	P	456	at Rawalpindi	1997-98
Lowest total	SA	124	at Port Elizabeth	2006-07
	P	49	at Johannesburg....................	2012-13

SOUTH AFRICA v SRI LANKA

		Captains					
Season	*South Africa*	*Sri Lanka*	*T*	*SA*	*SL*	*D*
1993-94SL	K. C. Wessels	A. Ranatunga	3	1	0	2
1997-98SA	W. J. Cronje	A. Ranatunga	2	2	0	0
2000SL	S. M. Pollock	S. T. Jayasuriya	3	1	1	1
2000-01SA	S. M. Pollock	S. T. Jayasuriya	3	2	0	1
2002-03SA	S. M. Pollock	S. T. Jayasuriya[1]	2	2	0	0

		Captains				
Season	*South Africa*	*Sri Lanka*	*T*	*SA*	*SL*	*D*
2004*SL*	G. C. Smith	M. S. Atapattu	2	0	1	1
2006*SL*	A. G. Prince	D. P. M. D. Jayawardene	2	0	2	0
2011-12*SA*	G. C. Smith	T. M. Dilshan	3	2	1	0
2014*SL*	H. M. Amla	A. D. Mathews	2	1	0	1
	In South Africa..........................		10	8	1	1
	In Sri Lanka.............................		12	3	4	5
	Totals.............................		22	11	5	6

SA   Played in South Africa.   SL   Played in Sri Lanka.

The following deputised for the official captain:
  [1]M. S. Atapattu (Second).

SERIES RECORDS

Highest score	SA	224	J. H. Kallis at Cape Town..................	2011-12
	SL	374	D. P. M. D. Jayawardene at Colombo (SSC)...	2006
Best bowling	SA	7-81	M. de Lange at Durban...................	2011-12
	SL	7-84	M. Muralitharan at Galle.................	2000
Highest total	SA	580-4 dec	at Cape Town......................	2011-12
	SL	756-5 dec	at Colombo (SSC).....................	2006
Lowest total	SA	168	at Durban........................	2011-12
	SL	95	at Cape Town......................	2000-01

SOUTH AFRICA v ZIMBABWE

		Captains				
Season	*South Africa*	*Zimbabwe*	*T*	*SA*	*Z*	*D*
1995-96*Z*	W. J. Cronje	A. Flower	1	1	0	0
1999-2000*S*	W. J. Cronje	A. D. R. Campbell	1	1	0	0
1999-2000*Z*	W. J. Cronje	A. Flower	1	1	0	0
2001-02*Z*	S. M. Pollock	H. H. Streak	2	1	0	1
2004-05*S*	G. C. Smith	T. Taibu	2	2	0	0
2014-15*Z*	H. M. Amla	B. R. M. Taylor	1	1	0	0
	In Zimbabwe......................		5	4	0	1
	In South Africa...................		3	3	0	0
	Totals.........................		8	7	0	1

S   Played in South Africa.   Z   Played in Zimbabwe.

SERIES RECORDS

Highest score	SA	220	G. Kirsten at Harare......................	2001-02
	Z	199*	A. Flower at Harare......................	2001-02
Best bowling	SA	8-71	A. A. Donald at Harare...................	1995-96
	Z	5-101	B. C. Strang at Harare...................	1995-96
Highest total	SA	600-3 dec	at Harare........................	2001-02
	Z	419-9 dec	at Bulawayo......................	2001-02
Lowest total	SA	346	at Harare........................	1995-96
	Z	54	at Cape Town.....................	2004-05

SOUTH AFRICA v BANGLADESH

Season	South Africa	Captains Bangladesh	T	SA	B	D
2002-03S	S. M. Pollock[1]	Khaled Mashud	2	2	0	0
2003B	G. C. Smith	Khaled Mahmud	2	2	0	0
2007-08B	G. C. Smith	Mohammad Ashraful	2	2	0	0
2008-09S	G. C. Smith	Mohammad Ashraful	2	2	0	0
2015B	**H. M. Amla**	**Mushfiqur Rahim**	**2**	**0**	**0**	**2**
	In South Africa....................		4	4	0	0
	In Bangladesh....................		**6**	**4**	**0**	**2**
	Totals.........................		**10**	**8**	**0**	**2**

S   Played in South Africa.   B   Played in Bangladesh.

The following deputised for the official captain:
[1]M. V. Boucher (First).

SERIES RECORDS

Highest score	SA	232	G. C. Smith at Chittagong	2007-08
	B	75	Habibul Bashar at Chittagong	2003
Best bowling	SA	5-19	M. Ntini at East London	2002-03
	B	6-27	Shahadat Hossain at Mirpur...............	2007-08
Highest total	SA	583-7 dec	at Chittagong	2007-08
	B	**326**	**at Chittagong**	**2015**
Lowest total	SA	170	at Mirpur	2007-08
	B	102	at Dhaka................................	2003

WEST INDIES v NEW ZEALAND

Season	West Indies	Captains New Zealand	T	WI	NZ	D
1951-52N	J. D. C. Goddard	B. Sutcliffe	2	1	0	1
1955-56N	D. St E. Atkinson	J. R. Reid[1]	4	3	1	0
1968-69N	G. S. Sobers	G. T. Dowling	3	1	1	1
1971-72W	G. S. Sobers	G. T. Dowling[2]	5	0	0	5
1979-80N	C. H. Lloyd	G. P. Howarth	3	0	1	2
1984-85W	I. V. A. Richards	G. P. Howarth	4	2	0	2
1986-87N	I. V. A. Richards	J. V. Coney	3	1	1	1
1994-95W	C. A. Walsh	K. R. Rutherford	2	1	0	1
1995-96W	C. A. Walsh	L. K. Germon	2	1	0	1
1999-2000N	B. C. Lara	S. P. Fleming	2	0	2	0
2002W	C. L. Hooper	S. P. Fleming	2	0	1	1
2005-06N	S. Chanderpaul	S. P. Fleming	3	0	2	1
2008-09N	C. H. Gayle	D. L. Vettori	2	0	0	2
2012W	D. J. G. Sammy	L. R. P. L. Taylor	2	2	0	0
2013-14N	D. J. G. Sammy	B. B. McCullum	3	0	2	1
2014W	D. Ramdin	B. B. McCullum	3	1	2	0
	In New Zealand..................		27	7	10	10
	In West Indies..................		18	6	3	9
	Totals		45	13	13	19

N   Played in New Zealand.   W   Played in West Indies.

The following deputised for the official touring captain or were appointed by the home authority for only a minor proportion of the series:
[1]H. B. Cave (First). [2]B. E. Congdon (Third, Fourth and Fifth).

SERIES RECORDS

Highest score	WI	258	S. M. Nurse at Christchurch	1968-69
	NZ	259	G. M. Turner at Georgetown	1971-72
Best bowling	WI	7-37	C. A. Walsh at Wellington	1994-95
	NZ	7-27	C. L. Cairns at Hamilton	1999-2000
Highest total	WI	660-5 dec	at Wellington	1994-95
	NZ	609-9 dec	at Dunedin (University)	2013-14
Lowest total	WI	77	at Auckland	1955-56
	NZ	74	at Dunedin	1955-56

WEST INDIES v INDIA

	Captains					
Season	*West Indies*	*India*	T	WI	I	D
1948-49*I*	J. D. C. Goddard	L. Amarnath	5	1	0	4
1952-53*W*	J. B. Stollmeyer	V. S. Hazare	5	1	0	4
1958-59*I*	F. C. M. Alexander	Ghulam Ahmed[1]	5	3	0	2
1961-62*W*	F. M. M. Worrell	N. J. Contractor[2]	5	5	0	0
1966-67*I*	G. S. Sobers	Nawab of Pataudi jun.	3	2	0	1
1970-71*W*	G. S. Sobers	A. L. Wadekar	5	0	1	4
1974-75*I*	C. H. Lloyd	Nawab of Pataudi jun.[3]	5	3	2	0
1975-76*W*	C. H. Lloyd	B. S. Bedi	4	2	1	1
1978-79*I*	A. I. Kallicharran	S. M. Gavaskar	6	0	1	5
1982-83*W*	C. H. Lloyd	Kapil Dev	5	2	0	3
1983-84*I*	C. H. Lloyd	Kapil Dev	6	3	0	3
1987-88*I*	I. V. A. Richards	D. B. Vengsarkar[4]	4	1	1	2
1988-89*W*	I. V. A. Richards	D. B. Vengsarkar	4	3	0	1
1994-95*I*	C. A. Walsh	M. Azharuddin	3	1	1	1
1996-97*W*	C. A. Walsh[5]	S. R. Tendulkar	5	1	0	4
2001-02*W*	C. L. Hooper	S. C. Ganguly	5	2	1	2
2002-03*I*	C. L. Hooper	S. C. Ganguly	3	0	2	1
2005-06*W*	B. C. Lara	R. Dravid	4	0	1	3
2011*W*	D. J. G. Sammy	M. S. Dhoni	3	0	1	2
2011-12*I*	D. J. G. Sammy	M. S. Dhoni	3	0	2	1
2013-14*I*	D. J. G. Sammy	M. S. Dhoni	2	0	2	0
	In India		45	14	11	20
	In West Indies		45	16	5	24
	Totals		90	30	16	44

I Played in India.   *W Played in West Indies.*

The following deputised for the official touring captain or were appointed by the home authority for only a minor proportion of the series:
[1]P. R. Umrigar (First), V. Mankad (Fourth), H. R. Adhikari (Fifth). [2]Nawab of Pataudi jun. (Third, Fourth and Fifth). [3]S. Venkataraghavan (Second). [4]R. J. Shastri (Fourth). [5]B. C. Lara (Third).

SERIES RECORDS

Highest score	WI	256	R. B. Kanhai at Calcutta	1958-59
	I	236*	S. M. Gavaskar at Madras	1983-84
Best bowling	WI	9-95	J. M. Noreiga at Port-of-Spain	1970-71
	I	9-83	Kapil Dev at Ahmedabad	1983-84
Highest total	WI	644-8 dec	at Delhi	1958-59
	I	644-7 dec	at Kanpur	1978-79
Lowest total	WI	103	at Kingston	2005-06
	I	75	at Delhi	1987-88

WEST INDIES v PAKISTAN

Captains

Season	West Indies	Pakistan	T	WI	P	D
1957-58*W*	F. C. M. Alexander	A. H. Kardar	5	3	1	1
1958-59*P*	F. C. M. Alexander	Fazal Mahmood	3	1	2	0
1974-75*P*	C. H. Lloyd	Intikhab Alam	2	0	0	2
1976-77*W*	C. H. Lloyd	Mushtaq Mohammad	5	2	1	2
1980-81*P*	C. H. Lloyd	Javed Miandad	4	1	0	3
1986-87*P*	I. V. A. Richards	Imran Khan	3	1	1	1
1987-88*W*	I. V. A. Richards[1]	Imran Khan	3	1	1	1
1990-91*P*	D. L. Haynes	Imran Khan	3	1	1	1
1992-93*W*	R. B. Richardson	Wasim Akram	3	2	0	1
1997-98*P*	C. A. Walsh	Wasim Akram	3	0	3	0
1999-2000*W*	J. C. Adams	Moin Khan	3	1	0	2
2001-02*U*	C. L. Hooper	Waqar Younis	2	0	2	0
2004-05*W*	S. Chanderpaul	Inzamam-ul-Haq[2]	2	1	1	0
2006-07*P*	B. C. Lara	Inzamam-ul-Haq	3	0	2	1
2010-11*W*	D. J. G. Sammy	Misbah-ul-Haq	2	1	1	0
	In West Indies		23	11	5	7
	In Pakistan		21	4	9	8
	In United Arab Emirates		2	0	2	0
	Totals		46	15	16	15

P   Played in Pakistan.   W   Played in West Indies.   U   Played in United Arab Emirates.

The following were appointed by the home authority or deputised for the official touring captain for a minor proportion of the series:
[1]C. G. Greenidge (First). [2]Younis Khan (First).

SERIES RECORDS

Highest score	WI	365*	G. S. Sobers at Kingston	1957-58
	P	337	Hanif Mohammad at Bridgetown	1957-58
Best bowling	WI	8-29	C. E. H. Croft at Port-of-Spain	1976-77
	P	7-80	Imran Khan at Georgetown	1987-88
Highest total	WI	790-3 dec	at Kingston	1957-58
	P	657-8 dec	at Bridgetown	1957-58
Lowest total	WI	53	at Faisalabad	1986-87
	P	77	at Lahore	1986-87

WEST INDIES v SRI LANKA

Captains

Season	West Indies	Sri Lanka	T	WI	SL	D
1993-94*S*	R. B. Richardson	A. Ranatunga	1	0	0	1
1996-97*W*	C. A. Walsh	A. Ranatunga	2	1	0	1
2001-02*S*	C. L. Hooper	S. T. Jayasuriya	3	0	3	0
2003*W*	B. C. Lara	H. P. Tillekeratne	2	1	0	1
2005*S*	S. Chanderpaul	M. S. Atapattu	2	0	2	0
2007-08*W*	C. H. Gayle	D. P. M. D. Jayawardene	2	1	1	0
2010-11*S*	D. J. G. Sammy	K. C. Sangakkara	3	0	0	3

THE SOBERS–TISSERA TROPHY

		Captains						
Season	*West Indies*	*Sri Lanka*	*T*	*WI*	*SL*	*D*		*Held by*
2015-16S	J. O. Holder	A. D. Mathews	2	0	2	0		**SL**
	In West Indies		6	3	1	2		
	In Sri Lanka		**11**	**0**	**7**	**4**		
	Totals..........................		17	3	8	6		

W Played in West Indies.   SL Played in Sri Lanka.

SERIES RECORDS

Highest score	WI	333	C. H. Gayle at Galle	2010-11
	SL	204*	H. P. Tillekeratne at Colombo (SSC)	2001-02
Best bowling	WI	7-57	C. D. Collymore at Kingston..............	2003
	SL	8-46	M. Muralitharan at Kandy................	2005
Highest total	WI	580-9 dec	at Galle	2010-11
	SL	627-9 dec	at Colombo (SSC).....................	2001-02
Lowest total	WI	113	at Colombo (SSC).....................	2005
	SL	150	at Kandy	2005

WEST INDIES v ZIMBABWE

		Captains				
Season	*West Indies*	*Zimbabwe*	*T*	*WI*	*Z*	*D*
1999-2000W	J. C. Adams	A. Flower	2	2	0	0

THE CLIVE LLOYD TROPHY

		Captains						
Season	*West Indies*	*Zimbabwe*	*T*	*WI*	*Z*	*D*		*Held by*
2001Z	C. L. Hooper	H. H. Streak	2	1	0	1		WI
2003-04Z	B. C. Lara	H. H. Streak	2	1	0	1		WI
2012-13W	D. J. G. Sammy	B. R. M. Taylor	2	2	0	0		WI
	In West Indies		4	4	0	0		
	In Zimbabwe		4	2	0	2		
	Totals		8	6	0	2		

W Played in West Indies.   Z Played in Zimbabwe.

SERIES RECORDS

Highest score	WI	191	B. C. Lara at Bulawayo	2003-04
	Z	127*	H. H. Streak at Harare	2003-04
Best bowling	WI	6-49	S. Shillingford at Bridgetown	2012-13
	Z	6-73	R. W. Price at Harare..................	2003-04
Highest total	WI	559-6 dec	at Bulawayo........................	2001
	Z	563-9 dec	at Harare	2001
Lowest total	WI	128	at Bulawayo........................	2003-04
	Z	63	at Port-of-Spain	1999-2000

WEST INDIES v BANGLADESH

		Captains				
Season	*West Indies*	*Bangladesh*	*T*	*WI*	*B*	*D*
2002-03*B*	R. D. Jacobs	Khaled Mashud	2	2	0	0
2003-04*W*	B. C. Lara	Habibul Bashar	2	1	0	1
2009*W*	F. L. Reifer	Mashrafe bin Mortaza[1]	2	0	2	0
2011-12*B*	D. J. G. Sammy	Mushfiqur Rahim	2	1	0	1
2012-13*B*	D. J. G. Sammy	Mushfiqur Rahim	2	2	0	0
2014-15*W*	D. Ramdin	Mushfiqur Rahim	2	2	0	0
	In West Indies		6	3	2	1
	In Bangladesh.....................		6	5	0	1
	Totals		12	8	2	2

B   Played in Bangladesh.   W   Played in West Indies.

The following deputised for the official touring captain for a minor proportion of the series:
[1]Shakib Al Hasan (Second).

SERIES RECORDS

Highest score	*WI*	261*	R. R. Sarwan at Kingston	2003-04
	B	128	Tamim Iqbal at St Vincent................	2009
Best bowling	*WI*	6-3	J. J. C. Lawson at Dhaka...................	2002-03
	B	6-74	Sohag Gazi at Mirpur	2012-13
Highest total	*WI*	648-9 dec	at Khulna	2012-13
	B	556	at Mirpur	2012-13
Lowest total	*WI*	181	at St Vincent	2009
	B	87	at Dhaka.................................	2002-03

NEW ZEALAND v INDIA

		Captains				
Season	*New Zealand*	*India*	*T*	*NZ*	*I*	*D*
1955-56*I*	H. B. Cave	P. R. Umrigar[1]	5	0	2	3
1964-65*I*	J. R. Reid	Nawab of Pataudi jun.	4	0	1	3
1967-68*N*	G. T. Dowling[2]	Nawab of Pataudi jun.	4	1	3	0
1969-70*I*	G. T. Dowling	Nawab of Pataudi jun.	3	1	1	1
1975-76*N*	G. M. Turner	B. S. Bedi[3]	3	1	1	1
1976-77*I*	G. M. Turner	B. S. Bedi	3	0	2	1
1980-81*N*	G. P. Howarth	S. M. Gavaskar	3	1	0	2
1988-89*I*	J. G. Wright	D. B. Vengsarkar	3	1	2	0
1989-90*N*	J. G. Wright	M. Azharuddin	3	1	0	2
1993-94*N*	K. R. Rutherford	M. Azharuddin	1	0	0	1
1995-96*I*	L. K. Germon	M. Azharuddin	3	0	1	2
1998-99*N*†	S. P. Fleming	M. Azharuddin	2	1	0	1
1999-2000*I*	S. P. Fleming	S. R. Tendulkar	3	0	1	2
2002-03*N*	S. P. Fleming	S. C. Ganguly	2	2	0	0
2003-04*I*	S. P. Fleming	S. C. Ganguly[4]	2	0	0	2
2008-09*N*	D. L. Vettori	M. S. Dhoni[5]	3	0	1	2
2010-11*I*	D. L. Vettori	M. S. Dhoni	3	0	1	2
2012-13*I*	L. R. P. L. Taylor	M. S. Dhoni	2	0	2	0

	Captains					
Season	*New Zealand*	*India*	*T*	*NZ*	*I*	*D*
2013-14*N*	B. B. McCullum	M. S. Dhoni	2	1	0	1
	In India............................		31	2	13	16
	In New Zealand		23	8	5	10
	Totals............................		54	10	18	26

I Played in India.   *N* Played in New Zealand.

† *The First Test at Dunedin was abandoned without a ball being bowled and is excluded.*

The following deputised for the official touring captain or were appointed by the home authority for a minor proportion of the series:

¹Ghulam Ahmed (First). ²B. W. Sinclair (First). ³S. M. Gavaskar (First). ⁴R. Dravid (Second). ⁵V. Sehwag (Second).

SERIES RECORDS

Highest score	NZ	302	B. B. McCullum at Wellington............	2013-14
	I	231	V. Mankad at Madras	1955-56
Best bowling	NZ	7-23	R. J. Hadlee at Wellington	1975-76
	I	8-72	S. Venkataraghavan at Delhi............	1964-65
Highest total	NZ	680-8 dec	at Wellington.........................	2013-14
	I	583-7 dec	at Ahmedabad	1999-2000
Lowest total	NZ	94	at Hamilton	2002-03
	I	81	at Wellington.........................	1975-76

NEW ZEALAND v PAKISTAN

	Captains					
Season	*New Zealand*	*Pakistan*	*T*	*NZ*	*P*	*D*
1955-56*P*	H. B. Cave	A. H. Kardar	3	0	2	1
1964-65*P*	J. R. Reid	Hanif Mohammad	3	0	0	3
1964-65*P*	J. R. Reid	Hanif Mohammad	3	0	2	1
1969-70*P*	G. T. Dowling	Intikhab Alam	3	1	0	2
1972-73*N*	B. E. Congdon	Intikhab Alam	3	0	1	2
1976-77*P*	G. M. Turner¹	Mushtaq Mohammad	3	0	2	1
1978-79*N*	M. G. Burgess	Mushtaq Mohammad	3	0	1	2
1984-85*P*	J. V. Coney	Zaheer Abbas	3	0	2	1
1984-85*N*	G. P. Howarth	Javed Miandad	3	2	0	1
1988-89*N*†	J. G. Wright	Imran Khan	2	0	0	2
1990-91*P*	M. D. Crowe	Javed Miandad	3	0	3	0
1992-93*N*	K. R. Rutherford	Javed Miandad	1	0	1	0
1993-94*N*	K. R. Rutherford	Salim Malik	3	1	2	0
1995-96*N*	L. K. Germon	Wasim Akram	1	0	1	0
1996-97*P*	L. K. Germon	Saeed Anwar	2	1	1	0
2000-01*N*	S. P. Fleming	Moin Khan²	3	1	1	1
2002*P*‡	S. P. Fleming	Waqar Younis	1	0	1	0
2003-04*N*	S. P. Fleming	Inzamam-ul-Haq	2	0	1	1
2009-10*N*	D. L. Vettori	Mohammad Yousuf	3	1	1	1

Season	New Zealand	Captains	Pakistan	T	NZ	P	D
2010-11N	D. L. Vettori		Misbah-ul-Haq	2	0	1	1
2014-15U	B. B. McCullum		Misbah-ul-Haq	3	1	1	1
	In Pakistan			21	2	13	6
	In New Zealand			29	5	10	14
	In United Arab Emirates			3	1	1	1
	Totals			53	8	24	21

N   Played in New Zealand.   P   Played in Pakistan.   U   Played in United Arab Emirates.

†   *The First Test at Dunedin was abandoned without a ball being bowled and is excluded.*
‡   *The Second Test at Karachi was cancelled owing to civil disturbances.*

The following were appointed by the home authority for only a minor proportion of the series or deputised for the official touring captain:
¹J. M. Parker (Third). ²Inzamam-ul-Haq (Third).

SERIES RECORDS

Highest score	NZ	204*	M. S. Sinclair at Christchurch................	2000-01
	P	329	Inzamam-ul-Haq at Lahore...................	2002
Best bowling	NZ	7-52	C. Pringle at Faisalabad	1990-91
	P	7-52	Intikhab Alam at Dunedin...................	1972-73
Highest total	NZ	690	at Sharjah	2014-15
	P	643	at Lahore.................................	2002
Lowest total	NZ	70	at Dacca.................................	1955-56
	P	102	at Faisalabad	1990-91

NEW ZEALAND v SRI LANKA

Season	New Zealand	Captains	Sri Lanka	T	NZ	SL	D
1982-83N	G. P. Howarth		D. S. de Silva	2	2	0	0
1983-84S	G. P. Howarth		L. R. D. Mendis	3	2	0	1
1986-87S†	J. J. Crowe		L. R. D. Mendis	1	0	0	1
1990-91N	M. D. Crowe¹		A. Ranatunga	3	0	0	3
1992-93S	M. D. Crowe		A. Ranatunga	2	0	1	1
1994-95N	K. R. Rutherford		A. Ranatunga	2	0	1	1
1996-97N	S. P. Fleming		A. Ranatunga	2	2	0	0
1997-98S	S. P. Fleming		A. Ranatunga	3	1	2	0
2003S	S. P. Fleming		H. P. Tillekeratne	2	0	0	2
2004-05N	S. P. Fleming		M. S. Atapattu	2	1	0	1
2006-07N	S. P. Fleming		D. P. M. D. Jayawardene	2	1	1	0
2009S	D. L. Vettori		K. C. Sangakkara	2	0	2	0
2012-13S	L. R. P. L. Taylor		D. P. M. D. Jayawardene	2	1	1	0
2014-15N	**B. B. McCullum**		**A. D. Mathews**	**2**	**2**	**0**	**0**
2015-16N	**B. B. McCullum**		**A. D. Mathews**	**2**	**2**	**0**	**0**
	In New Zealand			17	10	2	5
	In Sri Lanka			15	4	6	5
	Totals...........................			32	14	8	10

N   Played in New Zealand.   S   Played in Sri Lanka.

†   *The Second and Third Tests were cancelled owing to civil disturbances.*

The following was appointed by the home authority for only a minor proportion of the series:
¹I. D. S. Smith (Third).

Test Records – New Zealand v Sri Lanka 1351

SERIES RECORDS

Highest score	NZ	299	M. D. Crowe at Wellington	1990-91
	SL	267	P. A. de Silva at Wellington	1990-91
Best bowling	NZ	7-130	D. L. Vettori at Wellington	2006-07
	SL	6-43	H. M. R. K. B. Herath at Galle	2012-13
Highest total	NZ	671-4	at Wellington	1990-91
	SL	498	at Napier	2004-05
Lowest total	NZ	102	at Colombo (SSC)	1992-93
	SL	93	at Wellington	1982-83

NEW ZEALAND v ZIMBABWE

	Captains					
Season	*New Zealand*	*Zimbabwe*	*T*	*NZ*	*Z*	*D*
1992-93Z	M. D. Crowe	D. L. Houghton	2	1	0	1
1995-96N	L. K. Germon	A. Flower	2	0	0	2
1997-98Z	S. P. Fleming	A. D. R. Campbell	2	0	0	2
1997-98N	S. P. Fleming	A. D. R. Campbell	2	2	0	0
2000-01Z	S. P. Fleming	H. H. Streak	2	2	0	0
2000-01N	S. P. Fleming	H. H. Streak	1	0	0	1
2005-06Z	S. P. Fleming	T. Taibu	2	2	0	0
2011-12Z	L. R. P. L. Taylor	B. R. M. Taylor	1	1	0	0
2011-12N	L. R. P. L. Taylor	B. R. M. Taylor	1	1	0	0
	In New Zealand		6	3	0	3
	In Zimbabwe		9	6	0	3
	Totals		15	9	0	6

N Played in New Zealand.   Z Played in Zimbabwe.

SERIES RECORDS

Highest score	NZ	157	M. J. Horne at Auckland	1997-98
	Z	203*	G. J. Whittall at Bulawayo	1997-98
Best bowling	NZ	6-26	C. S. Martin at Napier	2011-12
	Z	8-109	P. A. Strang at Bulawayo	2000-01
Highest total	NZ	495-7 dec	at Napier	2011-12
	Z	461	at Bulawayo.	1997-98
Lowest total	NZ	207	at Harare	1997-98
	Z	51	at Napier	2011-12

NEW ZEALAND v BANGLADESH

	Captains					
Season	*New Zealand*	*Bangladesh*	*T*	*NZ*	*B*	*D*
2001-02N	S. P. Fleming	Khaled Mashud	2	2	0	0
2004-05N	S. P. Fleming	Khaled Mashud	2	2	0	0
2007-08N	D. L. Vettori	Mohammad Ashraful	2	2	0	0
2008-09B	D. L. Vettori	Mohammad Ashraful	2	1	0	1
2009-10N	D. L. Vettori	Shakib Al Hasan	1	1	0	0
2013-14B	B. B. McCullum	Mushfiqur Rahim	2	0	0	2
	In New Zealand		5	5	0	0
	In Bangladesh.		6	3	0	3
	Totals		11	8	0	3

B Played in Bangladesh.   N Played in New Zealand.

SERIES RECORDS

Highest score	NZ	202	S. P. Fleming at Chittagong	2004-05
	B	181	Mominul Haque at Chittagong	2013-14
Best bowling	NZ	7-53	C. L. Cairns at Hamilton	2001-02
	B	7-36	Shakib Al Hasan at Chittagong	2008-09
Highest total	NZ	553-7 dec	at Hamilton	2009-10
	B	501	at Chittagong	2013-14
Lowest total	NZ	171	at Chittagong	2008-09
	B	108	at Hamilton	2001-02

INDIA v PAKISTAN

		Captains					
Season	*India*	*Pakistan*	*T*	*I*	*P*	*D*
1952-53*I*	L. Amarnath	A. H. Kardar	5	2	1	2
1954-55*P*	V. Mankad	A. H. Kardar	5	0	0	5
1960-61*I*	N. J. Contractor	Fazal Mahmood	5	0	0	5
1978-79*P*	B. S. Bedi	Mushtaq Mohammad	3	0	2	1
1979-80*I*	S. M. Gavaskar[1]	Asif Iqbal	6	2	0	4
1982-83*P*	S. M. Gavaskar	Imran Khan	6	0	3	3
1983-84*I*	Kapil Dev	Zaheer Abbas	3	0	0	3
1984-85*P*	S. M. Gavaskar	Zaheer Abbas	2	0	0	2
1986-87*I*	Kapil Dev	Imran Khan	5	0	1	4
1989-90*P*	K. Srikkanth	Imran Khan	4	0	0	4
1998-99*I*	M. Azharuddin	Wasim Akram	2	1	1	0
1998-99*I*†	M. Azharuddin	Wasim Akram	1	0	1	0
2003-04*P*	S. C. Ganguly[2]	Inzamam-ul-Haq	3	2	1	0
2004-05*I*	S. C. Ganguly	Inzamam-ul-Haq	3	1	1	1
2005-06*P*	R. Dravid	Inzamam-ul-Haq[3]	3	0	1	2
2007-08*I*	A. Kumble	Shoaib Malik[4]	3	1	0	2
	In India		33	7	5	21
	In Pakistan		26	2	7	17
	Totals		59	9	12	38

I Played in India.   P Played in Pakistan.

† *This Test was part of the Asian Test Championship and was not counted as part of the preceding bilateral series.*

The following were appointed by the home authority for only a minor proportion of the series or deputised for the official touring captain:
[1]G. R. Viswanath (Sixth). [2]R. Dravid (First and Second). [3]Younis Khan (Third). [4]Younis Khan (Second and Third).

SERIES RECORDS

Highest score	I	309	V. Sehwag at Multan	2003-04
	P	280*	Javed Miandad at Hyderabad	1982-83
Best bowling	I	10-74	A. Kumble at Delhi	1998-99
	P	8-60	Imran Khan at Karachi	1982-83
Highest total	I	675-5 dec	at Multan	2003-04
	P	699-5	at Lahore	1989-90
Lowest total	I	106	at Lucknow	1952-53
	P	116	at Bangalore	1986-87

INDIA v SRI LANKA

Captains

Season	India	Sri Lanka	T	I	SL	D
1982-83*I*	S. M. Gavaskar	B. Warnapura	1	0	0	1
1985-86*S*	Kapil Dev	L. R. D. Mendis	3	0	1	2
1986-87*I*	Kapil Dev	L. R. D. Mendis	3	2	0	1
1990-91*I*	M. Azharuddin	A. Ranatunga	1	1	0	0
1993-94*S*	M. Azharuddin	A. Ranatunga	3	1	0	2
1993-94*I*	M. Azharuddin	A. Ranatunga	3	3	0	0
1997-98*S*	S. R. Tendulkar	A. Ranatunga	2	0	0	2
1997-98*I*	S. R. Tendulkar	A. Ranatunga	3	0	0	3
1998-99*S*†	M. Azharuddin	A. Ranatunga	1	0	0	1
2001*S*	S. C. Ganguly	S. T. Jayasuriya	3	1	2	0
2005-06*I*	R. Dravid[1]	M. S. Atapattu	3	2	0	1
2008*S*	A. Kumble	D. P. M. D. Jayawardene	3	1	2	0
2009-10*I*	M. S. Dhoni	K. C. Sangakkara	3	2	0	1
2010*S*	M. S. Dhoni	K. C. Sangakkara	3	1	1	1
2015-16*S*	**V. Kohli**	**A. D. Mathews**	**3**	**2**	**1**	**0**
	In India		17	10	0	7
	In Sri Lanka		**21**	**6**	**7**	**8**
	Totals		**38**	**16**	**7**	**15**

I   Played in India.   S   Played in Sri Lanka.

†   *This Test was part of the Asian Test Championship.*

The following was appointed by the home authority for only a minor proportion of the series:
[1]V. Sehwag (Third).

SERIES RECORDS

Highest score	*I*	293	V. Sehwag at Mumbai (BS)	2009-10
	SL	340	S. T. Jayasuriya at Colombo (RPS)	1997-98
Best bowling	*I*	7-51	Maninder Singh at Nagpur	1986-87
	SL	8-87	M. Muralitharan at Colombo (SSC)	2001
Highest total	*I*	726-9 dec	at Mumbai (BS)	2009-10
	SL	952-6 dec	at Colombo (RPS)	1997-98
Lowest total	*I*	**112**	**at Galle**	**2015-16**
	SL	82	at Chandigarh	1990-91

INDIA v ZIMBABWE

Captains

Season	India	Zimbabwe	T	I	Z	D
1992-93*Z*	M. Azharuddin	D. L. Houghton	1	0	0	1
1992-93*I*	M. Azharuddin	D. L. Houghton	1	1	0	0
1998-99*Z*	M. Azharuddin	A. D. R. Campbell	1	0	1	0
2000-01*I*	S. C. Ganguly	H. H. Streak	2	1	0	1
2001*Z*	S. C. Ganguly	H. H. Streak	2	1	1	0
2001-02*I*	S. C. Ganguly	S. V. Carlisle	2	2	0	0
2005-06*Z*	S. C. Ganguly	T. Taibu	2	2	0	0
	In India		5	4	0	1
	In Zimbabwe		6	3	2	1
	Totals		11	7	2	2

I   Played in India.   Z   Played in Zimbabwe.

SERIES RECORDS

Highest score	I	227	V. G. Kambli at Delhi	1992-93
	Z	232*	A. Flower at Nagpur	2000-01
Best bowling	I	7-59	I. K. Pathan at Harare.	2005-06
	Z	6-73	H. H. Streak at Harare	2005-06
Highest total	I	609-6 dec	at Nagpur	2000-01
	Z	503-6	at Nagpur	2000-01
Lowest total	I	173	at Harare.	1998-99
	Z	146	at Delhi.	2001-02

INDIA v BANGLADESH

		Captains				
Season	*India*	*Bangladesh*	*T*	*I*	*B*	*D*
2000-01*B*	S. C. Ganguly	Naimur Rahman	1	1	0	0
2004-05*B*	S. C. Ganguly	Habibul Bashar	2	2	0	0
2007*B*	R. Dravid	Habibul Bashar	2	1	0	1
2009-10*B*	M. S. Dhoni[1]	Shakib Al Hasan	2	2	0	0
2015*B*	**V. Kohli**	**Mushfiqur Rahim**	**1**	**0**	**0**	**1**
	In Bangladesh		**8**	**6**	**0**	**2**

B   Played in Bangladesh.

The following deputised for the official touring captain for a minor proportion of the series:
  [1]V. Sehwag (First).

SERIES RECORDS

Highest score	I	248*	S. R. Tendulkar at Dhaka	2004-05
	B	158*	Mohammad Ashraful at Chittagong	2004-05
Best bowling	I	7-87	Zaheer Khan at Mirpur	2009-10
	B	6-132	Naimur Rahman at Dhaka	2000-01
Highest total	I	610-3 dec	at Mirpur	2007
	B	400	at Dhaka.	2000-01
Lowest total	I	243	at Chittagong	2009-10
	B	91	at Dhaka.	2000-01

PAKISTAN v SRI LANKA

		Captains				
Season	*Pakistan*	*Sri Lanka*	*T*	*P*	*SL*	*D*
1981-82*P*	Javed Miandad	B. Warnapura[1]	3	2	0	1
1985-86*P*	Javed Miandad	L. R. D. Mendis	3	2	0	1
1985-86*S*	Imran Khan	L. R. D. Mendis	3	1	1	1
1991-92*P*	Imran Khan	P. A. de Silva	3	1	0	2
1994-95*S*†	Salim Malik	A. Ranatunga	2	2	0	0
1995-96*P*	Ramiz Raja	A. Ranatunga	3	1	2	0
1996-97*S*	Ramiz Raja	A. Ranatunga	2	0	0	2
1998-99*P*‡	Wasim Akram	H. P. Tillekeratne	1	0	0	1
1998-99*B*‡	Wasim Akram	P. A. de Silva	1	1	0	0
1999-2000*P*	Saeed Anwar[2]	S. T. Jayasuriya	3	1	2	0
2000*S*	Moin Khan	S. T. Jayasuriya	3	2	0	1
2001-02*P*‡	Waqar Younis	S. T. Jayasuriya	1	0	1	0
2004-05*P*	Inzamam-ul-Haq	M. S. Atapattu	2	1	1	0
2005-06*S*	Inzamam-ul-Haq	D. P. M. D. Jayawardene	2	1	0	1
2008-09*P*§	Younis Khan	D. P. M. D. Jayawardene	2	0	0	2
2009*S*	Younis Khan	K. C. Sangakkara	3	0	2	1
2011-12*U*	Misbah-ul-Haq	T. M. Dilshan	3	1	0	2

		Captains				
Season	*Pakistan*	*Sri Lanka*	*T*	*P*	*SL*	*D*
2012S	Misbah-ul-Haq[3]	D. P. M. D. Jayawardene	3	0	1	2
2013-14U	Misbah-ul-Haq	A. D. Mathews	3	1	1	1
2014S	Misbah-ul-Haq	A. D. Mathews	2	0	2	0
2015S	**Misbah-ul-Haq**	**A. D. Mathews**	**3**	**2**	**1**	**0**
	In Pakistan		21	8	6	7
	In Sri Lanka		**23**	**8**	**7**	**8**
	In Bangladesh.		1	1	0	0
	In United Arab Emirates		6	2	1	3
	Totals.		**51**	**19**	**14**	**18**

P   Played in Pakistan.   S   Played in Sri Lanka.   B   Played in Bangladesh.
U   Played in United Arab Emirates.

† *One Test was cancelled owing to the threat of civil disturbances following a general election.*
‡ *These Tests were part of the Asian Test Championship.*
§ *The Second Test ended after a terrorist attack on the Sri Lankan team bus on the third day.*

The following deputised for the official touring captain or were appointed by the home authority for only a minor proportion of the series:
[1]L. R. D. Mendis (Second). [2]Moin Khan (Third). [3]Mohammad Hafeez (First).

SERIES RECORDS

Highest score	P	313	Younis Khan at Karachi	2008-09
	SL	253	S. T. Jayasuriya at Faisalabad	2004-05
Best bowling	P	8-58	Imran Khan at Lahore	1981-82
	SL	9-127	H. M. R. K. B. Herath at Colombo (SSC)	2014
Highest total	P	765-6 dec	at Karachi.	2008-09
	SL	644-7 dec	at Karachi.	2008-09
Lowest total	P	90	at Colombo (PSS)	2009
	SL	71	at Kandy.	1994-95

PAKISTAN v ZIMBABWE

		Captains				
Season	*Pakistan*	*Zimbabwe*	*T*	*P*	*Z*	*D*
1993-94P	Wasim Akram[1]	A. Flower	3	2	0	1
1994-95Z	Salim Malik	A. Flower	3	2	1	0
1996-97P	Wasim Akram	A. D. R. Campbell	2	1	0	1
1997-98Z	Rashid Latif	A. D. R. Campbell	2	1	0	1
1998-99P†	Aamir Sohail[2]	A. D. R. Campbell	2	0	1	1
2002-03Z	Waqar Younis	A. D. R. Campbell	2	2	0	0
2011-12Z	Misbah-ul-Haq	B. R. M. Taylor	1	1	0	0
2013-14Z	Misbah-ul-Haq	B. R. M. Taylor[3]	2	1	1	0
	In Pakistan		7	3	1	3
	In Zimbabwe		10	7	2	1
	Totals		17	10	3	4

P   Played in Pakistan.   Z   Played in Zimbabwe.

† *The Third Test at Faisalabad was abandoned without a ball being bowled and is excluded.*

The following were appointed by the home authority for only a minor proportion of the series:
[1]Waqar Younis (First). [2]Moin Khan (Second). [3]H. Masakadza (First).

SERIES RECORDS

Highest score	P	257*	Wasim Akram at Sheikhupura	1996-97
	Z	201*	G. W. Flower at Harare	1994-95
Best bowling	P	7-66	Saqlain Mushtaq at Bulawayo	2002-03
	Z	6-90	H. H. Streak at Harare	1994-95
Highest total	P	553	at Sheikhupura	1996-97
	Z	544-4 dec	at Harare	1994-95
Lowest total	P	103	at Peshawar	1998-99
	Z	120	at Harare	2013-14

PAKISTAN v BANGLADESH

	Captains					
Season	*Pakistan*	*Bangladesh*	*T*	*P*	*B*	*D*
2001-02*P*†	Waqar Younis	Naimur Rahman	1	1	0	0
2001-02*B*	Waqar Younis	Khaled Mashud	2	2	0	0
2003-04*P*	Rashid Latif	Khaled Mahmud	3	3	0	0
2011-12*B*	Misbah-ul-Haq	Mushfiqur Rahim	2	2	0	0
2014-15*B*	**Misbah-ul-Haq**	**Mushfiqur Rahim**	**2**	**1**	**0**	**1**
	In Pakistan		4	4	0	0
	In Bangladesh		**6**	**5**	**0**	**1**
	Totals		**10**	**9**	**0**	**1**

P Played in Pakistan.   B   Played in Bangladesh.

† *This Test was part of the Asian Test Championship.*

SERIES RECORDS

Highest score	P	**226**	**Azhar Ali at Mirpur**	**2014-15**
	B	**206**	**Tamim Iqbal at Khulna**	**2014-15**
Best bowling	P	7-77	Danish Kaneria at Dhaka	2001-02
	B	6-82	Shakib Al Hasan at Mirpur	2011-12
Highest total	P	**628**	**at Khulna**	**2014-15**
	B	**555-6**	**at Khulna**	**2014-15**
Lowest total	P	175	at Multan	2003-04
	B	96	at Peshawar	2003-04

SRI LANKA v ZIMBABWE

	Captains					
Season	*Sri Lanka*	*Zimbabwe*	*T*	*SL*	*Z*	*D*
1994-95*Z*	A. Ranatunga	A. Flower	3	0	0	3
1996-97*S*	A. Ranatunga	A. D. R. Campbell	2	2	0	0
1997-98*S*	A. Ranatunga	A. D. R. Campbell	2	2	0	0
1999-2000*Z*	S. T. Jayasuriya	A. Flower	3	1	0	2
2001-02*S*	S. T. Jayasuriya	S. V. Carlisle	3	3	0	0
2003-04*Z*	M. S. Atapattu	T. Taibu	2	2	0	0
	In Sri Lanka		7	7	0	0
	In Zimbabwe		8	3	0	5
	Totals		15	10	0	5

S Played in Sri Lanka.   Z Played in Zimbabwe.

SERIES RECORDS

Highest score	SL	270	K. C. Sangakkara at Bulawayo	2003-04
	Z	266	D. L. Houghton at Bulawayo..............	1994-95
Best bowling	SL	9-51	M. Muralitharan at Kandy	2001-02
	Z	5-106	P. A. Strang at Colombo (RPS)...........	1996-97
Highest total	SL	713-3 dec	at Bulawayo.........................	2003-04
	Z	462-9 dec	at Bulawayo.........................	1994-95
Lowest total	SL	218	at Bulawayo.........................	1994-95
	Z	79	at Galle............................	2001-02

SRI LANKA v BANGLADESH

		Captains					
Season	*Sri Lanka*		*Bangladesh*	*T*	*SL*	*B*	*D*
2001-02S†	S. T. Jayasuriya		Naimur Rahman	1	1	0	0
2002S	S. T. Jayasuriya		Khaled Mashud	2	2	0	0
2005-06S	M. S. Atapattu		Habibul Bashar	2	2	0	0
2005-06B	D. P. M. D. Jayawardene		Habibul Bashar	2	2	0	0
2007S	D. P. M. D. Jayawardene		Mohammad Ashraful	3	3	0	0
2008-09B	D. P. M. D. Jayawardene		Mohammad Ashraful	2	2	0	0
2012-13S	A. D. Mathews		Mushfiqur Rahim	2	1	0	1
2013-14B	A. D. Mathews		Mushfiqur Rahim	2	1	0	1
	In Sri Lanka........................			10	9	0	1
	In Bangladesh			6	5	0	1
	Totals................................			16	14	0	2

S   Played in Sri Lanka.   B   Played in Bangladesh.

†   *This Test was part of the Asian Test Championship.*

SERIES RECORDS

Highest score	SL	319	K. C. Sangakkara at Chittagong.............	2013-14
	B	200	Mushfiqur Rahim at Galle	2012-13
Best bowling	SL	7-89	H. M. R. K. B. Herath at Colombo (RPS)	2012-13
	B	5-70	Shakib Al Hasan at Mirpur	2008-09
Highest total	SL	730-6 dec	at Mirpur	2013-14
	B	638	at Galle.............................	2012-13
Lowest total	SL	293	at Mirpur	2008-09
	B	62	at Colombo (PSS)	2007

An expanded and regularly updated online version of the Records can be found at
www.wisdenrecords.com

ZIMBABWE v BANGLADESH

		Captains				
Season	*Zimbabwe*	*Bangladesh*	*T*	*Z*	*B*	*D*
2000-01Z	H. H. Streak	Naimur Rahman	2	2	0	0
2001-02B	B. A. Murphy[1]	Naimur Rahman	2	1	0	1
2003-04Z	H. H. Streak	Habibul Bashar	2	1	0	1
2004-05B	T. Taibu	Habibul Bashar	2	0	1	1
2011-12Z	B. R. M. Taylor	Shakib Al Hasan	1	1	0	0
2012-13Z	B. R. M. Taylor	Mushfiqur Rahim	2	1	1	0
2014-15B	B. R. M Taylor	Mushfiqur Rahim	3	0	3	0

	T	*Z*	*B*	*D*
In Zimbabwe	7	5	1	1
In Bangladesh.	7	1	4	2
Totals	14	6	5	3

Z   Played in Zimbabwe.   B   Played in Bangladesh.

The following deputised for the official touring captain:

[1]S. V. Carlisle (Second).

SERIES RECORDS

Highest score	Z	171	B. R. M. Taylor at Harare	2012-13
	B	137	Shakib Al Hasan at Khulna	2014-15
Best bowling	Z	6-59	D. T. Hondo at Dhaka	2004-05
	B	8-39	Taijul Islam at Mirpur	2014-15
Highest total	Z	542-7 dec	at Chittagong	2001-02
	B	503	at Chittagong	2014-15
Lowest total	Z	114	at Mirpur	2014-15
	B	107	at Dhaka.	2001-02

TEST GROUNDS

in chronological order

	City and Ground	*First Test Match*		*Tests*
1	**Melbourne, Melbourne Cricket Ground**	**March 15, 1877**	A v E	108
2	**London, Kennington Oval**	**September 6, 1880**	E v A	98
3	**Sydney, Sydney Cricket Ground (No. 1)**	**February 17, 1882**	A v E	104
4	Manchester, Old Trafford	July 11, 1884	E v A	76
5	**London, Lord's**	**July 21, 1884**	E v A	131
6	**Adelaide, Adelaide Oval**	**December 12, 1884**	A v E	74
7	Port Elizabeth, St George's Park	March 12, 1889	SA v E	26
8	**Cape Town, Newlands**	**March 25, 1889**	SA v E	53
9	Johannesburg, Old Wanderers	March 2, 1896	SA v E	22
	Now the site of Johannesburg Railway Station.			
10	**Nottingham, Trent Bridge**	**June 1, 1899**	E v A	61
11	**Leeds, Headingley**	**June 29, 1899**	E v A	74
12	**Birmingham, Edgbaston**	**May 29, 1902**	E v A	48
13	Sheffield, Bramall Lane	July 3, 1902	E v A	1
	Sheffield United Football Club have built a stand over the cricket pitch.			
14	Durban, Lord's	January 21, 1910	SA v E	4
	Ground destroyed and built on.			
15	**Durban, Kingsmead**	**January 18, 1923**	SA v E	41
16	Brisbane, Exhibition Ground	November 30, 1928	A v E	2
	No longer used for cricket.			
17	Christchurch, Lancaster Park	January 10, 1930	NZ v E	40
	Also known under sponsors' names.			

	City and Ground	*First Test Match*		*Tests*
18	**Bridgetown, Kensington Oval**	**January 11, 1930**	**WI v E**	**51**
19	**Wellington, Basin Reserve**	**January 24, 1930**	**NZ v E**	**57**
20	Port-of-Spain, Queen's Park Oval	February 1, 1930	WI v E	59
21	Auckland, Eden Park	February 14, 1930	NZ v E	49
22	Georgetown, Bourda	February 21, 1930	WI v E	30
23	**Kingston, Sabina Park**	**April 3, 1930**	**WI v E**	**48**
24	**Brisbane, Woolloongabba**	**November 27, 1931**	**A v SA**	**58**
25	Bombay, Gymkhana Ground	December 15, 1933	I v E	1
	No ground used for first-class cricket.			
26	Calcutta (*now Kolkata*), Eden Gardens	January 5, 1934	I v E	39
27	Madras (*now Chennai*), Chepauk (Chidambaram Stadium)	February 10, 1934	I v E	31
28	**Delhi, Feroz Shah Kotla**	**November 10, 1948**	**I v WI**	**33**
29	Bombay (*now Mumbai*), Brabourne Stadium	December 9, 1948	I v WI	18
	Rarely used for first-class cricket.			
30	Johannesburg, Ellis Park	December 27, 1948	SA v E	6
	Mainly a football and rugby stadium, no longer used for cricket.			
31	Kanpur, Green Park (Modi Stadium)	January 12, 1952	I v E	21
32	Lucknow, University Ground	October 25, 1952	I v P	1
	Ground destroyed, now partly under a river bed.			
33	Dacca (*now Dhaka*), Dacca (*now Bangabandhu*) Stadium	January 1, 1955	P v I	17
	Originally in East Pakistan, now Bangladesh, no longer used for cricket.			
34	Bahawalpur, Dring (*now Bahawal*) Stadium	January 15, 1955	P v I	1
	Still used for first-class cricket.			
35	Lahore, Lawrence Gardens (Bagh-e-Jinnah)	January 29, 1955	P v I	3
	Still used for club and occasional first-class matches.			
36	Peshawar, Services Ground	February 13, 1955	P v I	1
	Superseded by new stadium.			
37	Karachi, National Stadium	February 26, 1955	P v I	41
38	Dunedin, Carisbrook	March 11, 1955	NZ v E	10
39	Hyderabad, Fateh Maidan (Lal Bahadur Stadium)	November 19, 1955	I v NZ	3
40	Madras, Corporation Stadium	January 6, 1956	I v NZ	9
	Superseded by rebuilt Chepauk Stadium.			
41	**Johannesburg, Wanderers**	**December 24, 1956**	**SA v E**	**36**
42	Lahore, Gaddafi Stadium	November 21, 1959	P v A	40
43	Rawalpindi, Pindi Club Ground	March 27, 1965	P v NZ	1
	Superseded by new stadium.			
44	Nagpur, Vidarbha C.A. Ground	October 3, 1969	I v NZ	9
	Superseded by new stadium.			
45	**Perth, Western Australian C.A. Ground**	**December 11, 1970**	**A v E**	**42**
46	Hyderabad, Niaz Stadium	March 16, 1973	P v E	5
47	**Bangalore, Karnataka State C.A. Ground (Chinnaswamy Stadium)**	**November 22, 1974**	**I v WI**	**21**
48	Bombay (*now Mumbai*), Wankhede Stadium	January 23, 1975	I v WI	24
49	Faisalabad, Iqbal Stadium	October 16, 1978	P v I	24
50	Napier, McLean Park	February 16, 1979	NZ v P	10
51	Multan, Ibn-e-Qasim Bagh Stadium	December 30, 1980	P v WI	1
	Superseded by new stadium.			
52	St John's (Antigua), Recreation Ground	March 27, 1981	WI v E	22
53	**Colombo, P. Saravanamuttu Stadium/ P. Sara Oval**	**February 17, 1982**	**SL v E**	**20**
54	Kandy, Asgiriya Stadium	April 22, 1983	SL v A	21
55	Jullundur, Burlton Park	September 24, 1983	I v P	1
56	Ahmedabad, Sardar Patel (Gujarat) Stadium	November 12, 1983	I v WI	12
57	**Colombo, Sinhalese Sports Club Ground**	**March 16, 1984**	**SL v NZ**	**39**
58	Colombo, Colombo Cricket Club Ground	March 24, 1984	SL v NZ	3
59	Sialkot, Jinnah Stadium	October 27, 1985	P v SL	4
60	Cuttack, Barabati Stadium	January 4, 1987	I v SL	2
61	Jaipur, Sawai Mansingh Stadium	February 21, 1987	I v P	1
62	**Hobart, Bellerive Oval**	**December 16, 1989**	**A v SL**	**12**

	City and Ground	First Test Match		Tests
63	Chandigarh, Sector 16 Stadium	November 23, 1990	I v SL	1
	Superseded by Mohali ground.			
64	**Hamilton, Seddon Park**	**February 22, 1991**	**NZ v SL**	**21**
	Also known under various sponsors' names.			
65	Gujranwala, Municipal Stadium	December 20, 1991	P v SL	1
66	Colombo, R. Premadasa (Khettarama) Stadium	August 28, 1992	SL v A	8
67	Moratuwa, Tyronne Fernando Stadium	September 8, 1992	SL v A	4
68	Harare, Harare Sports Club	October 18, 1992	Z v I	32
69	Bulawayo, Bulawayo Athletic Club	November 1, 1992	Z v NZ	1
	Superseded by Queens Sports Club ground.			
70	Karachi, Defence Stadium	December 1, 1993	P v Z	1
71	Rawalpindi, Rawalpindi Cricket Stadium	December 9, 1993	P v Z	8
72	Lucknow, K. D. "Babu" Singh Stadium	January 18, 1994	I v SL	1
73	Bulawayo, Queens Sports Club	October 20, 1994	Z v SL	19
74	**Mohali, Punjab Cricket Association Stadium**	**December 10, 1994**	**I v WI**	**12**
75	Peshawar, Arbab Niaz Stadium	September 8, 1995	P v SL	6
76	**Centurion (*ex Verwoerdburg*), Centurion Park**	**November 16, 1995**	**SA v E**	**21**
77	Sheikhupura, Municipal Stadium	October 17, 1996	P v Z	2
78	St Vincent, Arnos Vale	June 20, 1997	WI v SL	3
79	**Galle, International Stadium**	**June 3, 1998**	**SL v NZ**	**27**
80	Bloemfontein, Springbok Park	October 29, 1999	SA v Z	4
	Also known under various sponsors' names.			
81	Multan, Multan Cricket Stadium	August 29, 2001	P v B	5
82	Chittagong, Chittagong Stadium	November 15, 2001	B v Z	8
	Also known as M. A. Aziz Stadium.			
83	**Sharjah, Sharjah Cricket Association Stadium**	**January 31, 2002**	**P v WI**	**8**
84	**St George's, Grenada, Queen's Park New Stadium**	**June 28, 2002**	**WI v NZ**	**3**
85	East London, Buffalo Park	October 18, 2002	SA v B	1
86	Potchefstroom, North West Cricket Stadium	October 25, 2002	SA v B	1
	Now known under sponsor's name.			
87	Chester-le-Street, Riverside Ground	June 5, 2003	E v Z	5
	Also known under sponsor's name.			
88	Gros Islet, St Lucia, Beausejour Stadium	June 20, 2003	WI v SL	4
89	Darwin, Marrara Cricket Ground	July 18, 2003	A v B	2
90	Cairns, Cazaly's Football Park	July 25, 2003	A v B	2
	Also known under sponsor's name.			
91	**Chittagong, Chittagong Divisional Stadium**	**February 28, 2006**	**B v SL**	**14**
	Also known as Bir Shrestha Shahid Ruhul Amin Stadium / Zohur Ahmed Chowdhury Stadium.			
92	Bogra, Shaheed Chandu Stadium	March 8, 2006	B v SL	1
93	**Fatullah, Narayanganj Osmani Stadium**	**April 9, 2006**	**B v A**	**2**
94	Basseterre, St Kitts, Warner Park	June 22, 2006	WI v I	3
95	**Mirpur (Dhaka), Shere Bangla Nat'l Stadium**	**May 25, 2007**	**B v I**	**14**
96	Dunedin, University Oval	January 4, 2008	NZ v B	7
97	Providence Stadium, Guyana	March 22, 2008	WI v SL	2
98	**North Sound, Antigua, Sir Vivian Richards Stadium**	**May 30, 2008**	**WI v A**	**4**
99	**Nagpur, Vidarbha C. A. Stadium, Jamtha**	**November 6, 2008**	**I v A**	**5**
100	**Cardiff, Sophia Gardens**	**July 8, 2009**	**E v A**	**3**
	Now known under sponsor's name.			
101	Hyderabad, Rajiv Gandhi Int'l Stadium	November 12, 2010	I v NZ	3
102	**Dubai, Dubai Sports City Stadium**	**November 12, 2010**	**P v SA**	**9**
103	**Abu Dhabi, Sheikh Zayed Stadium**	**November 20, 2010**	**P v SA**	**8**
104	**Pallekele, Muttiah Muralitharan Stadium**	**December 1, 2010**	**SL v WI**	**4**
105	Southampton, Rose Bowl	June 16, 2011	E v SL	2
106	**Roseau, Dominica, Windsor Park**	**July 6, 2011**	**WI v I**	**4**
107	**Khulna, Khulna Division Stadium**	**November 21, 2012**	**B v WI**	**2**
	Also known as Bir Shrestha Shahid Flight Lt Motiur Rahman / Shaikh Abu Naser Stadium.			
108	Christchurch, Hagley Oval	December 26, 2014	NZ v SL	1

Bold type denotes grounds used for Test cricket since January 1, 2015.

ONE-DAY INTERNATIONAL RECORDS

Matches in this section do not have first-class status.

This section covers one-day international cricket to January 6, 2016. Bold type denotes performances since January 1, 2015, or, in career figures, players who have appeared in one-day internationals since that date.

SUMMARY OF ONE-DAY INTERNATIONALS

1970-71 to January 6, 2016

	Opponents	Matches	Won by														Tied	NR
			E	A	SA	WI	NZ	I	P	SL	Z	B	Ass	Asia	Wld	Afr		
England	Australia	136	51	80	–	–	–	–	–	–	–	–	–	–	–	–	2	3
	South Africa	51	22	–	25	–	–	–	–	–	–	–	–	–	–	–	1	3
	West Indies	88	42	–	–	42	–	–	–	–	–	–	–	–	–	–	–	4
	New Zealand	83	36	–	–	–	41	–	–	–	–	–	–	–	–	–	2	4
	India	93	38	–	–	–	–	50	–	–	–	–	–	–	–	–	2	3
	Pakistan	76	45	–	–	–	–	–	29	–	–	–	–	–	–	–	–	2
	Sri Lanka	64	30	–	–	–	–	–	–	34	–	–	–	–	–	–	–	–
	Zimbabwe	30	21	–	–	–	–	–	–	–	8	–	–	–	–	–	–	1
	Bangladesh	16	13	–	–	–	–	–	–	–	–	3	–	–	–	–	–	–
	Associates	22	19	–	–	–	–	–	–	–	–	–	1	–	–	–	–	2
Australia	South Africa	88	–	46	39	–	–	–	–	–	–	–	–	–	–	–	3	–
	West Indies	135	–	70	–	59	–	–	–	–	–	–	–	–	–	–	3	3
	New Zealand	127	–	86	–	–	35	–	–	–	–	–	–	–	–	–	–	6
	India	118	–	68	–	–	–	40	–	–	–	–	–	–	–	–	–	10
	Pakistan	93	–	58	–	–	–	–	31	–	–	–	–	–	–	–	1	3
	Sri Lanka	91	–	56	–	–	–	–	–	31	–	–	–	–	–	–	–	4
	Zimbabwe	30	–	27	–	–	–	–	–	–	2	–	–	–	–	–	–	1
	Bangladesh	19	–	18	–	–	–	–	–	–	–	1	–	–	–	–	–	–
	Associates	22	–	21	–	–	–	–	–	–	–	–	0	–	–	–	–	1
	ICC World XI	3	–	3	–	–	–	–	–	–	–	–	–	–	0	–	–	–
South Africa	West Indies	58	–	–	43	13	–	–	–	–	–	–	–	–	–	–	1	1
	New Zealand	65	–	–	38	–	22	–	–	–	–	–	–	–	–	–	–	5
	India	76	–	–	45	–	–	28	–	–	–	–	–	–	–	–	–	3
	Pakistan	72	–	–	47	–	–	–	24	–	–	–	–	–	–	–	–	1
	Sri Lanka	60	–	–	29	–	–	–	–	29	–	–	–	–	–	–	1	1
	Zimbabwe	38	–	–	35	–	–	–	–	–	2	–	–	–	–	–	–	1
	Bangladesh	17	–	–	14	–	–	–	–	–	–	3	–	–	–	–	–	–
	Associates	22	–	–	22	–	–	–	–	–	–	–	0	–	–	–	–	–
West Indies	New Zealand	61	–	–	–	30	24	–	–	–	–	–	–	–	–	–	–	7
	India	116	–	–	–	60	–	53	–	–	–	–	–	–	–	–	1	2
	Pakistan	127	–	–	–	69	–	–	55	–	–	–	–	–	–	–	3	–
	Sri Lanka	54	–	–	–	27	–	–	–	24	–	–	–	–	–	–	–	3
	Zimbabwe	45	–	–	–	35	–	–	–	–	9	–	–	–	–	–	–	1
	Bangladesh	28	–	–	–	19	–	–	–	–	–	7	–	–	–	–	–	2
	Associates	22	–	–	–	19	–	–	–	–	–	–	2	–	–	–	–	1
New Zealand	India	93	–	–	–	–	41	46	–	–	–	–	–	–	–	–	1	5
	Pakistan	96	–	–	–	–	40	–	53	–	–	–	–	–	–	–	1	2
	Sri Lanka	95	–	–	–	–	45	–	–	41	–	–	–	–	–	–	1	8
	Zimbabwe	38	–	–	–	–	27	–	–	–	9	–	–	–	–	–	1	1
	Bangladesh	25	–	–	–	–	17	–	–	–	–	8	–	–	–	–	–	–
	Associates	15	–	–	–	–	15	–	–	–	–	–	0	–	–	–	–	–
India	Pakistan	127	–	–	–	–	–	51	72	–	–	–	–	–	–	–	–	4
	Sri Lanka	149	–	–	–	–	–	83	–	54	–	–	–	–	–	–	1	11
	Zimbabwe	60	–	–	–	–	–	48	–	–	10	–	–	–	–	–	2	–
	Bangladesh	32	–	–	–	–	–	26	–	–	–	5	–	–	–	–	–	1
	Associates	27	–	–	–	–	–	25	–	–	–	–	2	–	–	–	–	–
Pakistan	Sri Lanka	147	–	–	–	–	–	–	84	58	–	–	–	–	–	–	1	4
	Zimbabwe	54	–	–	–	–	–	–	47	–	4	–	–	–	–	–	1	2
	Bangladesh	35	–	–	–	–	–	–	31	–	–	4	–	–	–	–	–	–
	Associates	28	–	–	–	–	–	–	26	–	–	–	1	–	–	–	1	–
Sri Lanka	Zimbabwe	47	–	–	–	–	–	–	–	39	7	–	–	–	–	–	–	1
	Bangladesh	38	–	–	–	–	–	–	–	33	–	4	–	–	–	–	–	1
	Associates	20	–	–	–	–	–	–	–	19	–	–	1	–	–	–	–	–

	Opponents	Matches	E	A	SA	WI	NZ	I	P	SL	Z	B	Ass	Asia	Wld	Afr	Tied	NR
			Won by															
Zimbabwe	Bangladesh	67	–	–	–	–	–	–	–	–	28	39	–	–	–	–	–	–
	Associates	62	–	–	–	–	–	–	–	43	–	–	16	–	–	–	1	2
Bangladesh	Associates	35	–	–	–	–	–	–	–	–	–	24	11	–	–	–	–	–
Associates	Associates	179	–	–	–	–	–	–	–	–	–	–	171	–	–	–	1	7
Asian CC XI	ICC World XI	1	–	–	–	–	–	–	–	–	–	–	–	0	1	–	–	–
	African XI	6	–	–	–	–	–	–	–	–	–	–	–	4	–	1	–	1
		3,772	317	533	337	373	307	450	452	362	122	98	205	4	1	1	32	128

Associate and Affiliate Members of ICC who have played one-day internationals are Afghanistan, Bermuda, Canada, East Africa, Hong Kong, Ireland, Kenya, Namibia, Netherlands, Papua New Guinea, Scotland, United Arab Emirates and USA. Sri Lanka, Zimbabwe and Bangladesh played one-day internationals before gaining Test status; these are not counted as Associate results.

RESULTS SUMMARY OF ONE-DAY INTERNATIONALS

1970-71 to January 6, 2016 (3,722 matches)

	Matches	Won	Lost	Tied	No Result	% Won (excl. NR)
Australia	862	533	289	9	31	64.68
South Africa	547	337	189	6	15	63.90
Pakistan	855	452	377	8	18	54.48
India	891	450	395	7	39	53.22
West Indies	734	373	329	8	24	53.09
England	659	317	313	7	22	50.31
Sri Lanka	765	362	366	4	33	49.72
New Zealand	698	307	347	6	38	46.96
Bangladesh	312	98	210	–	4	31.81
Zimbabwe	471	122	334	5	10	27.00
Papua New Guinea	2	2	–	–	–	100.00
Asian Cricket Council XI	7	4	2	–	1	66.66
Afghanistan	61	31	30	–	–	50.81
Ireland	101	45	47	3	6	48.94
Netherlands	76	28	44	1	3	39.04
Scotland	80	26	50	–	4	34.21
Kenya	154	42	107	–	5	28.18
ICC World XI	4	1	3	–	–	25.00
Canada	77	17	58	–	2	22.66
Bermuda	35	7	28	–	–	20.00
Hong Kong	10	2	8	–	–	20.00
African XI	6	1	4	–	1	20.00
United Arab Emirates	26	5	21	–	–	19.23
USA	2	–	2	–	–	0.00
East Africa	3	–	3	–	–	0.00
Namibia	6	–	6	–	–	0.00

Matches abandoned without a ball bowled are not included except (from 2004) where the toss took place, in accordance with an ICC ruling. Such matches, like those called off after play began, are now counted as official internationals in their own right, even when replayed on another day. In the percentages of matches won, ties are counted as half a win.

BATTING RECORDS

HIGHEST INDIVIDUAL INNINGS

264	R. G. Sharma	India v Sri Lanka at Kolkata	2014-15
237*	**M. J. Guptill**	**New Zealand v West Indies at Wellington**	**2014-15**
219	V. Sehwag	India v West Indies at Indore	2011-12
215	**C. H. Gayle**	**West Indies v Zimbabwe at Canberra**	**2014-15**

209	R. G. Sharma	India v Australia at Bangalore	2013-14
200*	S. R. Tendulkar	India v South Africa at Gwalior	2009-10
194*	C. K. Coventry	Zimbabwe v Bangladesh at Bulawayo	2009
194	Saeed Anwar	Pakistan v India at Chennai	1997-98
189*	I. V. A. Richards	West Indies v England at Manchester	1984
189*	M. J. Guptill	New Zealand v England at Southampton	2013
189	S. T. Jayasuriya	Sri Lanka v India at Sharjah	2000-01
188*	G. Kirsten	South Africa v UAE at Rawalpindi	1995-96
186*	S. R. Tendulkar	India v New Zealand at Hyderabad	1999-2000
185*	S. R. Watson	Australia v Bangladesh at Mirpur	2010-11
183*	M. S. Dhoni	India v Sri Lanka at Jaipur	2005-06
183	S. C. Ganguly	India v Sri Lanka at Taunton	1999
183	V. Kohli	India v Pakistan at Mirpur	2011-12
181*	M. L. Hayden	Australia v New Zealand at Hamilton	2006-07
181	I. V. A. Richards	West Indies v Sri Lanka at Karachi	1987-88
178*	H. Masakadza	Zimbabwe v Kenya at Harare	2009-10
178	**D. A. Warner**	**Australia v Afghanistan at Perth.**	**2014-15**
177	P. R. Stirling	Ireland v Canada at Toronto	2010
175*	Kapil Dev	India v Zimbabwe at Tunbridge Wells	1983
175	H. H. Gibbs	South Africa v Australia at Johannesburg	2005-06
175	S. R. Tendulkar	India v Australia at Hyderabad	2009-10
175	V. Sehwag	India v Bangladesh at Mirpur	2010-11
175	C. S. MacLeod	Scotland v Canada at Christchurch	2013-14

The highest individual scores for other Test countries are:

| 167* | R. A. Smith | England v Australia at Birmingham . . . . | 1993 |
| 154 | Tamim Iqbal | Bangladesh v Zimbabwe at Bulawayo . . . . | 2009 |

MOST HUNDREDS

S. R. Tendulkar (I) 49	H. H. Gibbs (SA) 21	Mohammad Yousuf (P/As) . 15
R. T. Ponting (A/World) . . 30	Saeed Anwar (P) 20	V. Sehwag (I/Wld/Asia) . . 15
S. T. Jayasuriya (SL/Asia) . 28	**D. P. M. D. Jayawardene 19**	**L. R. P. L. Taylor (NZ) . . 15**
K. C. Sangakkara (SL) . 25	**(SL/Asia)**	
V. Kohli (I) 23	B. C. Lara (WI/World) . . . 19	*Most hundreds for other*
A. B. de Villiers (SA) . . . 23	M. E. Waugh (A) 18	*Test countries:*
T. M. Dilshan (SL) 22	D. L. Haynes (WI) 17	M. E. Trescothick (E) . . . 12
S. C. Ganguly (I/Asia) . . . 22	J. H. Kallis (SA/Wld/Af) . . 17	**B. R. M. Taylor (Z) 8**
C. H. Gayle (WI/World) 22	N. J. Astle (NZ) 16	**Shakib Al Hasan (B) . . . 6**
H. M. Amla (SA) 21	A. C. Gilchrist (A/World) . . 16	**Tamim Iqbal (B) 6**

Ponting's total includes one for the World XI, the only hundred for a combined team.

MOST RUNS

		M	I	NO	R	HS	100	Avge
1	S. R. Tendulkar (India)	463	452	41	18,426	200*	49	44.83
2	**K. C. Sangakkara (SL/Asia/World) . . . .**	**404**	**380**	**41**	**14,234**	**169**	**25**	**41.98**
3	R. T. Ponting (Australia/World)	375	365	39	13,704	164	30	42.03
4	S. T. Jayasuriya (Sri Lanka/Asia)	445	433	18	13,430	189	28	32.36
5	**D. P. M. D. Jayawardene (SL/Asia) . . . .**	**448**	**418**	**39**	**12,650**	**144**	**19**	**33.37**
6	Inzamam-ul-Haq (Pakistan/Asia)	378	350	53	11,739	137*	10	39.52
7	J. H. Kallis (S. Africa/World/Africa)	328	314	53	11,579	139	17	44.36
8	S. C. Ganguly (India/Asia)	311	300	23	11,363	183	22	41.02
9	R. Dravid (India/World/Asia)	344	318	40	10,889	153	12	39.16
10	B. C. Lara (West Indies/World)	299	289	32	10,405	169	19	40.48
11	**T. M. Dilshan (Sri Lanka)**	**327**	**300**	**41**	**10,216**	**161***	**22**	**39.44**

The leading aggregates for players who have appeared for other Test countries are:

	M	I	NO	R	HS	100	Avge
S. P. Fleming (New Zealand/World)	280	269	21	8,037	134*	8	32.40
A. Flower (Zimbabwe).	213	208	16	6,786	145	4	35.34
I. R. Bell (England).	161	157	14	5,416	141	4	37.87
Tamim Iqbal (Bangladesh)	153	152	3	4,713	154	6	31.63

*Excluding runs for combined teams, the record aggregate for Sri Lanka is **13,975** in 397 matches by* **K. C. Sangakkara**; *for Australia, 13,589 in 374 matches by R. T. Ponting; for Pakistan, 11,701 in 375 matches by Inzamam-ul-Haq; for South Africa, 11,550 in 323 matches by J. H. Kallis; for West Indies, 10,348 in 295 matches by B. C. Lara; and for New Zealand, 8,007 in 279 matches by S. P. Fleming.*

BEST CAREER STRIKE-RATES BY BATSMEN

(Runs per 100 balls. Qualification: 1,000 runs)

SR		Position	M	I	R	Avge
126.44	G. J. Maxwell (A)	5/6	55	50	1,535	34.88
120.75	L. Ronchi (A/NZ).	7	65	49	1,094	26.68
117.26	J. C. Buttler (E).	6/7	65	56	1,644	34.97
117.00	Shahid Afridi (P/World/Asia) . . .	2/7	398	369	8,064	23.57
108.77	N. L. T. C. Perera (SL)	7/8	110	81	1,178	17.32
104.33	V. Sehwag (I/World/Asia)	1/2	251	245	8,273	35.05
100.28	A. B. de Villiers (SA).	4/5	195	187	8,403	54.21
100.05	D. J. G. Sammy (WI).	7/8	126	105	1,871	24.94
100.00	D. A. Miller (SA).	5/6	82	73	1,819	34.98

Position means a batsman's most usual position(s) in the batting order.

FASTEST ONE-DAY INTERNATIONAL FIFTIES

Balls			
16	A. B. de Villiers	**South Africa v West Indies at Johannesburg**.	**2014-15**
17	S. T. Jayasuriya	Sri Lanka v Pakistan at Singapore	1995-96
17	M. D. K. J. Perera	**Sri Lanka v Pakistan at Pallekele**	**2015**
17	M. J. Guptill.	**New Zealand v Sri Lanka at Christchurch**	**2015-16**
18	S. P. O'Donnell	Australia v Sri Lanka at Sharjah	1989-90
18	Shahid Afridi	Pakistan v Sri Lanka at Nairobi	1996-97
18	Shahid Afridi	Pakistan v Netherlands at Colombo (SSC)	2002
18	G. J. Maxwell	Australia v India at Bangalore	2013-14
18	Shahid Afridi	Pakistan v Bangladesh at Mirpur	2013-14
18	B. B. McCullum.	**New Zealand v England at Wellington**	**2014-15**

FASTEST ONE-DAY INTERNATIONAL HUNDREDS

Balls			
31	A. B. de Villiers	South Africa v West Indies at Johannesburg.	2014-15
36	C. J. Anderson.	New Zealand v West Indies at Queenstown.	2013-14
37	Shahid Afridi	Pakistan v Sri Lanka at Nairobi	1996-97
44	M. V. Boucher.	South Africa v Zimbabwe at Potchefstroom	2006-07
45	B. C. Lara	West Indies v Bangladesh at Dhaka	1999-2000
45	Shahid Afridi	Pakistan v India at Kanpur	2004-05
46	J. D. Ryder	New Zealand v West Indies at Queenstown.	2013-14
46	J. C. Buttler	**England v Pakistan at Dubai**.	**2015-16**
48	S. T. Jayasuriya	Sri Lanka v Pakistan at Singapore	1995-96

HIGHEST PARTNERSHIP FOR EACH WICKET

286	for 1st	W. U. Tharanga and S. T. Jayasuriya	SL v E	Leeds	2006
372	**for 2nd**	**C. H. Gayle and M. N. Samuels**	**WI v Z**	**Canberra**	**2014-15**
258	for 3rd	D. M. Bravo and D. Ramdin	WI v B	Basseterre.	2014-15
275*	for 4th	M. Azharuddin and A. Jadeja	I v Z	Cuttack.	1997-98
256*	**for 5th**	**D. A. Miller and J-P. Duminy**	**SA v Z**	**Hamilton**	**2014-15**
267*	**for 6th**	**G. D. Elliott and L. Ronchi**	**NZ v SL**	**Dunedin**	**2014-15**
177	**for 7th**	**J. C. Buttler and A. U. Rashid**	**E v NZ**	**Birmingham**	**2015**
138*	for 8th	J. M. Kemp and A. J. Hall	SA v I	Cape Town.	2006-07
132	for 9th	A. D. Mathews and S. L. Malinga	SL v A	Melbourne	2010-11
106*	for 10th	I. V. A. Richards and M. A. Holding	WI v E	Manchester.	1984

BOWLING RECORDS

BEST BOWLING ANALYSES

8-19	W. P. U. J. C. Vaas	Sri Lanka v Zimbabwe at Colombo (SSC)	2001-02
7-12	Shahid Afridi	Pakistan v West Indies at Providence	2013
7-15	G. D. McGrath	Australia v Namibia at Potchefstroom	2002-03
7-20	A. J. Bichel	Australia v England at Port Elizabeth	2002-03
7-30	M. Muralitharan	Sri Lanka v India at Sharjah	2000-01
7-33	**T. G. Southee**	**New Zealand v England at Wellington**	**2014-15**
7-36	Waqar Younis	Pakistan v England at Leeds	2001
7-37	Aqib Javed	Pakistan v India at Sharjah	1991-92
7-51	W. W. Davis	West Indies v Australia at Leeds	1983

The best analyses for other Test countries are:

6-4	S. T. R. Binny	India v Bangladesh at Mirpur	2014
6-16	**K. Rabada**	**South Africa v Bangladesh at Mirpur**	**2015**
6-19	H. K. Olonga	Zimbabwe v England at Cape Town	1999-2000
6-26	Mashrafe bin Mortaza	Bangladesh v Kenya at Nairobi	2006
6-26	Rubel Hossain	Bangladesh v New Zealand at Mirpur	2013-14
6-31	P. D. Collingwood	England v Bangladesh at Nottingham	2005

HAT-TRICKS

Four Wickets in Four Balls

S. L. Malinga	Sri Lanka v South Africa at Providence.	2006-07

Four Wickets in Five Balls

Saqlain Mushtaq	Pakistan v Zimbabwe at Peshawar.	1996-97

Most Hat-Tricks

S. L. Malinga	3		W. P. U. J. C. Vaas†	2
Saqlain Mushtaq	2		Wasim Akram	2

† *W. P. U. J. C. Vaas took the second of his two hat-tricks, for Sri Lanka v Bangladesh at Pietermaritzburg in 2002-03, with the first three balls of the match.*

Hat-Tricks

There have been **39** hat-tricks in one-day internationals, including the above. Those since 2013-14:

Rubel Hossain	Bangladesh v New Zealand at Mirpur	2013-14
P. Utseya	Zimbabwe v South Africa at Harare.	2014-15
Taijul Islam†	Bangladesh v Zimbabwe at Mirpur	2014-15

J-P. Duminy	**South Africa v Sri Lanka at Sydney**	2014-15
S. T. Finn	**England v Australia at Melbourne**	2014-15
K. Rabada	**South Africa v Bangladesh at Mirpur**	2015

† *On one-day international debut – a unique feat.*

MOST WICKETS

		M	*Balls*	*R*	*W*	*BB*	*4I*	*Avge*
1	M. Muralitharan (SL/World/Asia)	350	18,811	12,326	534	7-30	25	23.08
2	Wasim Akram (Pakistan).	356	18,186	11,812	502	5-15	23	23.52
3	Waqar Younis (Pakistan).	262	12,698	9,919	416	7-36	27	23.84
4	W. P. U. J. C. Vaas (SL/Asia)	322	15,775	11,014	400	8-19	13	27.53
5	**Shahid Afridi (Pakistan/World/Asia)** .	**398**	**17,670**	**13,635**	**395**	**7-12**	**13**	**34.51**
6	S. M. Pollock (SA/World/Africa)	303	15,712	9,631	393	6-35	17	24.50
7	G. D. McGrath (Australia/World)	250	12,970	8,391	381	7-15	16	22.02
8	B. Lee (Australia)	221	11,185	8,877	380	5-22	23	23.36
9	A. Kumble (India/Asia).	271	14,496	10,412	337	6-12	10	30.89
10	S. T. Jayasuriya (Sri Lanka/Asia)	445	14,874	11,871	323	6-29	12	36.75
11	J. Srinath (India)	229	11,935	8,847	315	5-23	10	28.08
12	**D. L. Vettori (New Zealand/World)**. . .	**295**	**14,060**	**9,674**	**305**	**5-7**	**10**	**31.71**
13	S. K. Warne (Australia/World)	194	10,642	7,541	293	5-33	13	25.73
14	**S. L. Malinga (Sri Lanka)**	**191**	**9,207**	**8,082**	**291**	**6-38**	**16**	**27.77**
15 {	Saqlain Mushtaq (Pakistan).	169	8,770	6,275	288	5-20	17	21.78
	A. B. Agarkar (India).	191	9,484	8,021	288	6-42	12	27.85
17	Zaheer Khan (India/Asia)	200	10,097	8,301	282	5-42	8	29.43
18	J. H. Kallis (S. Africa/World/Africa). . . .	328	10,750	8,680	273	5-30	4	31.79
19	A. A. Donald (South Africa)	164	8,561	5,926	272	6-23	13	21.78
20 {	**J. M. Anderson (England)**	**194**	**9,584**	**7,861**	**269**	**5-23**	**13**	**29.22**
	Abdul Razzaq (Pakistan/Asia).	265	10,941	8,564	269	6-35	11	31.83
	Harbhajan Singh (India/Asia)	**236**	**12,479**	**8,973**	**269**	**5-31**	**5**	**33.35**
23	M. Ntini (South Africa/World)	173	8,687	6,559	266	6-22	12	24.65
24	Kapil Dev (India).	225	11,202	6,945	253	5-43	4	27.45

The leading aggregates for players who have appeared for other Test countries are:

H. H. Streak (Zimbabwe)	189	9,468	7,129	239	5-32	8	29.82
C. A. Walsh (West Indies)	205	10,882	6,918	227	5-1	7	30.47
Abdur Razzak (Bangladesh)	153	7,965	6,065	207	5-29	9	29.29

Excluding wickets taken for combined teams, the record for Sri Lanka is 523 in 343 matches by M. Muralitharan; for South Africa, 387 in 294 matches by S. M. Pollock; for Australia, 380 in 249 matches by G. D. McGrath; for India, 334 in 269 matches by A. Kumble; for New Zealand, 297 in 291 matches by **D. L. Vettori**; *and for Zimbabwe, 237 in 187 matches by H. H. Streak.*

BEST CAREER STRIKE-RATES BY BOWLERS

(Balls per wicket. Qualification: 1,500 balls)

SR		*M*	*W*
24.28	**M. A. Starc (A)**	**46**	**90**
26.95	Mohammed Shami (I).	47	87
27.22	S. W. Tait (A).	35	62
27.32	**B. A. W. Mendis (SL)**	**87**	**152**
28.48	M. J. McClenaghan (NZ)	47	82
28.72	R. N. ten Doeschate (Netherlands)	33	55
29.21	S. E. Bond (NZ)	82	147
29.34	**M. Morkel (SA/Africa)**	**103**	**176**
29.38	G. I. Allott (NZ)	31	52
29.43	B. Lee (A).	221	380
29.58	L. S. Pascoe (A)	29	53

BEST CAREER ECONOMY-RATES

(Runs conceded per six balls. Qualification: 50 wickets)

ER		M	W
3.09	J. Garner (WI)	98	146
3.28	R. G. D. Willis (E)	64	80
3.30	R. J. Hadlee (NZ)	115	158
3.32	M. A. Holding (WI)	102	142
3.40	A. M. E. Roberts (WI)	56	87
3.48	C. E. L. Ambrose (WI)	176	225

WICKETKEEPING AND FIELDING RECORDS

MOST DISMISSALS IN AN INNINGS

6 (all ct)	A. C. Gilchrist	Australia v South Africa at Cape Town	1999-2000
6 (all ct)	A. J. Stewart	England v Zimbabwe at Manchester	2000
6 (5ct, 1st)	R. D. Jacobs	West Indies v Sri Lanka at Colombo (RPS)	2001-02
6 (5ct, 1st)	A. C. Gilchrist	Australia v England at Sydney	2002-03
6 (all ct)	A. C. Gilchrist	Australia v Namibia at Potchefstroom	2002-03
6 (all ct)	A. C. Gilchrist	Australia v Sri Lanka at Colombo (RPS)	2003-04
6 (all ct)	M. V. Boucher	South Africa v Pakistan at Cape Town	2006-07
6 (5ct, 1st)	M. S. Dhoni	India v England at Leeds	2007
6 (5ct, 1st)	A. C. Gilchrist	Australia v India at Vadodara	2007-08
6 (all ct)	M. J. Prior	England v South Africa at Nottingham	2008
6 (all ct)	J. C. Buttler	England v South Africa at The Oval	2013
6 (all ct)	M. H. Cross	Scotland v Canada at Christchurch	2013-14
6 (5ct, 1st)	Q. de Kock	S. Africa v New Zealand at Mount Maunganui	2014-15
6 (all ct)	**Sarfraz Ahmed**	**Pakistan v South Africa at Auckland**	**2014-15**

MOST DISMISSALS

			M	Ct	St
1	482	K. C. Sangakkara (Sri Lanka/World/Asia)	360	384	98
2	472	A. C. Gilchrist (Australia/World)	282	417	55
3	424	M. V. Boucher (South Africa/Africa)	294	402	22
4	342	M. S. Dhoni (India/Asia)	270	254	88
5	287	Moin Khan (Pakistan)	219	214	73
6	242	B. B. McCullum (New Zealand)	185	227	15
7	234	I. A. Healy (Australia)	168	195	39
8	220	Rashid Latif (Pakistan)	166	182	38
9	206	R. S. Kaluwitharana (Sri Lanka)	186	131	75
10	204	P. J. L. Dujon (West Indies)	169	183	21

The leading aggregates for players who have appeared for other Test countries are:

	165	A. Flower (Zimbabwe)	186	133	32
	163	A. J. Stewart (England)	138	148	15
	162	**Mushfiqur Rahim (Bangladesh)**	**147**	**124**	**38**

*Excluding dismissals for combined teams, the most for Sri Lanka is **473** (378ct, 95st) in 353 matches by **K. C. Sangakkara**; for Australia, 470 (416ct, 54st) in 281 matches by A. C. Gilchrist; for South Africa, 415 (394ct, 21st) in 289 matches by M. V. Boucher; and for India, **336** (251ct, 85st) in 267 matches by **M. S. Dhoni**.*

K. C. Sangakkara's list excludes 19 catches taken in 44 one-day internationals when not keeping wicket; M. V. Boucher's record excludes 1 in 2; B. B. McCullum's excludes 32 in 71; R. S. Kaluwitharana's 1 in 3; A. Flower's 8 in 27; A. J. Stewart's 11 in 32; Mushfiqur Rahim's 2 in 11. A. C. Gilchrist played five one-day internationals without keeping wicket, but made no catches in those games. R. Dravid (India) made 210 dismissals (196ct, 14st) in 344 one-day internationals but only 86 (72ct, 14st) in 74 as wicketkeeper (including one where he took over during the match).

MOST CATCHES IN AN INNINGS IN THE FIELD

5   J. N. Rhodes . . . .   South Africa v West Indies at Bombay   1993-94

There have been 33 instances of four catches in an innings.

MOST CATCHES

Ct	M		Ct	M	
218	**448**	**D. P. M. D. Jayawardene (SL/Asia)**	127	273	A. R. Border (Australia)
160	375	R. T. Ponting (Australia/World)	**127**	**398**	**Shahid Afridi (Pak/World/Asia)**
156	334	M. Azharuddin (India)			
140	463	S. R. Tendulkar (India)			*Most catches for other Test countries:*
133	280	S. P. Fleming (New Zealand/World)	120	227	C. L. Hooper (West Indies)
131	328	J. H. Kallis (SA/World/Africa)	108	197	P. D. Collingwood (England)
130	**262**	**Younis Khan (Pakistan)**	86	221	G. W. Flower (Zimbabwe)
130	350	M. Muralitharan (SL/World/Asia)	**50**	**160**	**Mashrafe bin Mortaza (Ban/As)**

Excluding catches taken for combined teams, the record aggregate for Sri Lanka is 213 in 442 matches by D. P. M. D. Jayawardene; for Australia, 158 in 374 by R. T. Ponting; for New Zealand, 132 in 279 by S. P. Fleming; for South Africa, 131 in 323 by J. H. Kallis; and for Bangladesh, 49 in 158 by Mashrafe bin Mortaza.

Younis Khan's record excludes five catches made in three one-day internationals as wicketkeeper.

TEAM RECORDS

HIGHEST INNINGS TOTALS

443-9	(50 overs)	Sri Lanka v Netherlands at Amstelveen	2006
439-2	**(50 overs)**	**South Africa v West Indies at Johannesburg**	**2014-15**
438-4	**(50 overs)**	**South Africa v India at Mumbai**	**2015-16**
438-9	(49.5 overs)	South Africa v Australia at Johannesburg	2005-06
434-4	(50 overs)	Australia v South Africa at Johannesburg	2005-06
418-5	(50 overs)	South Africa v Zimbabwe at Potchefstroom	2006-07
418-5	(50 overs)	India v West Indies at Indore	2011-12
417-6	**(50 overs)**	**Australia v Afghanistan at Perth**	**2014-15**
414-7	(50 overs)	India v Sri Lanka at Rajkot	2009-10
413-5	(50 overs)	India v Bermuda at Port-of-Spain	2006-07
411-4	**(50 overs)**	**South Africa v Ireland at Canberra**	**2014-15**
411-8	(50 overs)	Sri Lanka v India at Rajkot	2009-10
408-5	**(50 overs)**	**South Africa v West Indies at Sydney**	**2014-15**
408-9	**(50 overs)**	**England v New Zealand at Birmingham**	**2015**
405-5	(50 overs)	India v Sri Lanka at Kolkata	2014-15
402-2	(50 overs)	New Zealand v Ireland at Aberdeen	2008
401-3	(50 overs)	India v South Africa at Gwalior	2009-10

The highest totals by other Test countries are:

385-7	(50 overs)	Pakistan v Bangladesh at Dambulla	2010
372-2	**(50 overs)**	**West Indies v Zimbabwe at Canberra**	**2014-15**
351-7	(50 overs)	Zimbabwe v Kenya at Mombasa	2008-09
329-6	**(50 overs)**	**Bangladesh v Pakistan at Mirpur**	**2014-15**

HIGHEST TOTALS BATTING SECOND

438-9	(49.5 overs)	South Africa v Australia at Johannesburg (*Won by 1 wicket*) . .	2005-06
411-8	(50 overs)	Sri Lanka v India at Rajkot (*Lost by 3 runs*)	2009-10
365-9	**(45 overs)**	**England v New Zealand at The Oval** (*Lost by 13 runs D/L*) .	**2015**
362-1	(43.3 overs)	India v Australia at Jaipur (*Won by 9 wickets*)	2013-14
351-4	(49.3 overs)	India v Australia at Nagpur (*Won by 6 wickets*)	2013-14
350-3	**(44 overs)**	**England v New Zealand at Nottingham** (*Won by 7 wickets*) .	**2015**
350-9	(49.3 overs)	New Zealand v Australia at Hamilton (*Won by 1 wicket*)	2006-07

HIGHEST MATCH AGGREGATES

872-13	(99.5 overs)	South Africa v Australia at Johannesburg	2005-06
825-15	(100 overs)	India v Sri Lanka at Rajkot	2009-10
763-14	**(96 overs)**	**England v New Zealand at The Oval**	**2015**
730-9	**(100 overs)**	**South Africa v West Indies at Johannesburg**	**2014-15**
726-14	(95.1 overs)	New Zealand v India at Christchurch	2008-09
721-6	(93.3 overs)	India v Australia at Jaipur	2013-14
709-16	(95.1 overs)	India v Australia at Bangalore	2013-14
709-8	**(100 overs)**	**Pakistan v Zimbabwe at Lahore**	**2015**
701-10	(99.3 overs)	India v Australia at Nagpur	2013-14

LOWEST INNINGS TOTALS

35	(18 overs)	Zimbabwe v Sri Lanka at Harare	2003-04
36	(18.4 overs)	Canada v Sri Lanka at Paarl	2002-03
38	(15.4 overs)	Zimbabwe v Sri Lanka at Colombo (SSC)	2001-02
43	(19.5 overs)	Pakistan v West Indies at Cape Town	1992-93
43	(20.1 overs)	Sri Lanka v South Africa at Paarl	2011-12
44	(24.5 overs)	Zimbabwe v Bangladesh at Chittagong	2009-10
45	(40.3 overs)	Canada v England at Manchester	1979
45	(14 overs)	Namibia v Australia at Potchefstroom	2002-03

The lowest totals by other Test countries are:

54	(26.3 overs)	India v Sri Lanka at Sharjah	2000-01
54	(23.2 overs)	West Indies v South Africa at Cape Town	2003-04
58	(18.5 overs)	Bangladesh v West Indies at Mirpur	2010-11
58	(17.4 overs)	Bangladesh v India at Mirpur	2014
64	(35.5 overs)	New Zealand v Pakistan at Sharjah	1985-86
69	(28 overs)	South Africa v Australia at Sydney	1993-94
70	(25.2 overs)	Australia v England at Birmingham	1977
70	(26.3 overs)	Australia v New Zealand at Adelaide	1985-86
86	(32.4 overs)	England v Australia at Manchester	2001

LARGEST VICTORIES

290 runs	New Zealand (402-2 in 50 overs) v Ireland (112 in 28.4 ov) at Aberdeen	2008
275 runs	**Australia (417-6 in 50 overs) v Afghanistan (142 in 37.3 overs) at Perth**	**2014-15**
272 runs	South Africa (399-6 in 50 overs) v Zimbabwe (127 in 29 overs) at Benoni	2010-11
258 runs	South Africa (301-8 in 50 overs) v Sri Lanka (43 in 20.1 overs) at Paarl	2011-12
257 runs	India (413-5 in 50 overs) v Bermuda (156 in 43.1 overs) at Port-of-Spain	2006-07
257 runs	**South Africa (408-5 in 50 overs) v West Indies (151 in 33.1 overs) at Sydney**	**2014-15**
256 runs	Australia (301-6 in 50 overs) v Namibia (45 in 14 overs) at Potchefstroom	2002-03
256 runs	India (374-4 in 50 overs) v Hong Kong (118 in 36.5 overs) at Karachi	2008

*There have been **48** instances of victory by ten wickets.*

TIED MATCHES

There have been **32** tied one-day internationals. Australia have tied nine matches; Bangladesh are the only Test country never to have tied. The most recent ties are:

India (338 in 49.5 overs) v England (338-8 in 50 overs) at Bangalore	2010-11
India (280-5 in 50 overs) v England (270-8 in 48.5 overs) at Lord's (D/L)	2011
Australia (220 in 49.5 overs) v West Indies (220 in 49.4 overs) at St Vincent	2011-12
Sri Lanka (236-9 in 50 overs) v India (236-9 in 50 overs) at Adelaide	2011-12
South Africa (230-6 in 31 overs) v West Indies (190-6 in 26.1 overs) at Cardiff (D/L)	2013
Ireland (268-5 in 50 overs) v Netherlands (268-9 in 50 overs) at Amstelveen	2013
Pakistan (229-6 in 50 overs) v West Indies (229-9 in 50 overs) at Gros Islet	2013
Pakistan (266-5 in 47 overs) v Ireland (275-5 in 47 overs) at Dublin (D/L)	2013
New Zealand (314 in 50 overs) v India (314-9 in 50 overs) at Auckland	2013-14

OTHER RECORDS

MOST APPEARANCES

463 S. R. Tendulkar (I)	334 M. Azharuddin (I)
448 D. P. M. D. Jayawardene (SL/Asia)	328 J. H. Kallis (SA/World/Africa)
445 S. T. Jayasuriya (SL/Asia)	**327 T. M. Dilshan (SL)**
404 K. C. Sangakkara (SL/World/Asia)	325 S. R. Waugh (A)
398 Shahid Afridi (P/World/Asia)	322 W. P. U. J. C. Vaas (SL/Asia)
378 Inzamam-ul-Haq (P/Asia)	311 S. C. Ganguly (I/Asia)
375 R. T. Ponting (A/World)	308 P. A. de Silva (SL)
356 Wasim Akram (P)	303 S. M. Pollock (SA/World/Africa)
350 M. Muralitharan (SL/World/Asia)	300 T. M. Dilshan (SL)
344 R. Dravid (I/World/Asia)	

*Excluding appearances for combined teams, the record for Sri Lanka is 441 by S. T. Jayasuriya; for Pakistan, **393** by **Shahid Afridi**; for Australia, 374 by R. T. Ponting; for South Africa, 323 by J. H. Kallis; for West Indies, 295 by B. C. Lara; for New Zealand, **291** by **D. L. Vettori**; for Zimbabwe, 221 by G. W. Flower; for England, 197 by P. D. Collingwood; and for Bangladesh, 177 by Mohammad Ashraful.*

MOST MATCHES AS CAPTAIN

	P	W	L	T	NR		P	W	L	T	NR
R. T. Ponting (A/World)	230	165	51	2	12	S. C. Ganguly (I/Asia)	147	76	66	0	5
S. P. Fleming (NZ)	218	98	106	1	13	Imran Khan (P)	139	75	59	1	4
A. Ranatunga (SL)	193	89	95	1	8	W. J. Cronje (SA)	138	99	35	1	3
M. S. Dhoni (I)	**181**	**101**	**65**	**4**	**11**	D. P. M. D. Jayawardene (SL/Asia)	138	99	35	1	3
A. R. Border (A)	178	107	67	1	3		129	71	49	1	8
M. Azharuddin (I)	174	90	76	2	6	B. C. Lara (WI)	125	59	59	1	7
G. C. Smith (SA/Af)	150	92	51	1	6						

WORLD CUP RECORDS

Throughout this section, bold type denotes performances in the 2014-15 World Cup or, in career figures, players who appeared in that tournament.

WORLD CUP FINALS

1975	WEST INDIES (291-8) beat Australia (274) by 17 runs	Lord's
1979	WEST INDIES (286-9) beat England (194) by 92 runs	Lord's
1983	INDIA (183) beat West Indies (140) by 43 runs	Lord's
1987	AUSTRALIA (253-5) beat England (246-8) by seven runs	Calcutta
1992	PAKISTAN (249-6) beat England (227) by 22 runs	Melbourne
1996	SRI LANKA (245-3) beat Australia (241-7) by seven wickets	Lahore
1999	AUSTRALIA (133-2) beat Pakistan (132) by eight wickets	Lord's
2003	AUSTRALIA (359-2) beat India (234) by 125 runs	Johannesburg
2007	AUSTRALIA (281-4) beat Sri Lanka (215-8) by 53 runs (D/L method)	Bridgetown
2011	INDIA (277-4) beat Sri Lanka (274-6) by six wickets	Mumbai
2015	**AUSTRALIA (186-3) beat New Zealand (183) by seven wickets**	**Melbourne**

TEAM RESULTS

	Rounds reached				Matches			
	W	F	SF	P	W	L	T	NR
Australia (11)	5	7	7	84	62	20	1	1
New Zealand (11)	–	1	7	79	48	30	–	1
India (11)	2	3	6	75	46	27	1	1
England (11)	–	3	5	72	41	29	1	1
West Indies (11)	2	3	4	71	41	29	–	1
Pakistan (11)	1	2	6	71	40	29	–	2
South Africa (7)	–	–	4	55	35	18	2	–
Sri Lanka (11)	1	3	4	73	35	35	1	2
Bangladesh (5)	–	–	–	32	11	20	–	1
Zimbabwe (9)	–	–	–	57	11	42	1	3
Ireland (3)	–	–	–	21	7	13	1	–
Kenya (5)	–	–	1	29	6	22	–	1
Canada (4)	–	–	–	18	2	16	–	–
Netherlands (4)	–	–	–	20	2	18	–	–
Afghanistan (1)	–	–	–	6	1	5	–	–
United Arab Emirates (2)	–	–	–	11	1	10	–	–
Bermuda (1)	–	–	–	3	–	3	–	–
East Africa (1)	–	–	–	3	–	3	–	–
Namibia (1)	–	–	–	6	–	6	–	–
Scotland (3)	–	–	–	14	–	14	–	–

The number of tournaments each team has played in is shown in brackets. Matches abandoned or cancelled without a ball bowled are not included.

BATTING RECORDS

Highest Scores

237*	**M. J. Guptill**	**New Zealand v West Indies at Wellington**	**2014-15**
215	**C. H. Gayle**	**West Indies v Zimbabwe at Canberra**	**2014-15**
188*	G. Kirsten	South Africa v United Arab Emirates at Rawalpindi . . .	1995-96
183	S. C. Ganguly	India v Sri Lanka at Taunton	1999
181	I. V. A. Richards	West Indies v Sri Lanka at Karachi	1987-88
178	**D. A. Warner**	**Australia v Afghanistan at Perth**	**2014-15**
175*	Kapil Dev	India v Zimbabwe at Tunbridge Wells	1983
175	V. Sehwag	India v Bangladesh at Mirpur	2010-11
172*	C. B. Wishart	Zimbabwe v Namibia at Harare	2002-03
171*	G. M. Turner†	New Zealand v East Africa at Birmingham	1975
162*	**A. B. de Villiers**	**South Africa v West Indies at Sydney**	**2014-15**
161*	**T. M. Dilshan**	**Sri Lanka v Bangladesh at Melbourne**	**2014-15**
161	A. C. Hudson	South Africa v Netherlands at Rawalpindi	1995-96
160	Imran Nazir	Pakistan v Zimbabwe at Kingston	2006-07

Highest scores for other Test-playing countries:

158	A. J. Strauss	England v India at Bangalore	2010-11
128*	**Mahmudullah**	**Bangladesh v New Zealand at Hamilton**	**2014-15**

† *Turner scored 171* on the opening day of the inaugural World Cup in 1975.*

Most Hundreds

6, S. R. Tendulkar (I); **5,** R. T. Ponting (A) and **K. C. Sangakkara (SL); 4, A. B. de Villiers (SA), T. M. Dilshan (SL),** S. C. Ganguly (I), **D. P. M. D. Jayawardene (SL)** and M. E. Waugh (A); 3, M. L. Hayden (A), S. T. Jayasuriya (SL), Ramiz Raja (P), I. V. A. Richards (WI) and Saeed Anwar (P).

Most Runs in a Tournament

673, S. R. Tendulkar (I) 2002-03; 659, M. L. Hayden (A) 2006-07; 548, D. P. M. D. Jayawardene (SL) 2006-07; **547, M. J. Guptill (NZ) 2014-15; 541, K. C. Sangakkara (SL) 2014-15**; 539, R. T. Ponting (A) 2006-07; 523, S. R. Tendulkar (I) 1995-96; 500, T. M. Dilshan (SL) 2010-11.

Most Runs

	M	I	NO	R	HS	100	Avge
S. R. Tendulkar (India).	45	44	4	2,278	152	6	56.95
R. T. Ponting (Australia)	46	42	4	1,743	140*	5	45.86
K. C. Sangakkara (Sri Lanka) .	**37**	**35**	**8**	**1,532**	**124**	**5**	**56.74**
B. C. Lara (West Indies)	34	33	4	1,225	116	2	42.24
A. B. de Villiers (South Africa) .	**23**	**22**	**3**	**1,207**	**162***	**4**	**63.52**
S. T. Jayasuriya (Sri Lanka).	38	37	3	1,165	120	3	34.26
J. H. Kallis (South Africa)	36	32	7	1,148	128*	1	45.92
T. M. Dilshan (Sri Lanka)	**27**	**25**	**4**	**1,112**	**161***	**4**	**52.95**
D. P. M. D. Jayawardene (SL) . .	**40**	**34**	**3**	**1,100**	**115***	**4**	**35.48**
A. C. Gilchrist (Australia)	31	31	1	1,085	149	1	36.16
Javed Miandad (Pakistan)	33	30	5	1,083	103*	1	43.32
S. P. Fleming (New Zealand).	33	33	3	1,075	134*	2	35.83
H. H. Gibbs (South Africa)	25	23	4	1,067	143	2	56.15
P. A. de Silva (Sri Lanka)	35	32	3	1,064	145	2	36.68
I. V. A. Richards (West Indies) . .	23	21	5	1,013	181	3	63.31
S. C. Ganguly (India).	21	21	3	1,006	183	4	55.88
M. E. Waugh (Australia)	22	22	3	1,004	130	4	52.84

Highest Partnership for Each Wicket

282	for 1st	W. U. Tharanga and T. M. Dilshan . . . . SL v Z	Pallekele	2010-11
372	**for 2nd**	**C. H. Gayle and M. N. Samuels.** . . . . . WI v Z	**Canberra**	**2014-15**
237*	for 3rd	R. Dravid and S. R. Tendulkar. . . . . . . I v K	Bristol	1999
204	for 4th	M. J. Clarke and B. J. Hodge . . . . A v Neth	Basseterre	2006-07
256*	**for 5th**	**D. A. Miller and J. P. Duminy** . . . . . . SA v Z	**Hamilton**	**2014-15**
162	for 6th	K. J. O'Brien and A. R. Cusack . . . . . . Ire v E	Bangalore	2010-11
107	**for 7th** {	**Shaiman Anwar and Amjad Javed** . . UAE v Ire	**Brisbane**	**2014-15**
		Amjad Javed and Nasir Aziz. . . . . . . UAE v WI	**Napier**	**2014-15**
117	for 8th	D. L. Houghton and I. P. Butchart . . . . Z v NZ	Hyderabad (India)	1987-88
126*	for 9th	Kapil Dev and S. M. H. Kirmani . . . . . . I v Z	Tunbridge Wells	1983
71	for 10th	A. M. E. Roberts and J. Garner . . . . WI v I	Manchester	1983

BOWLING RECORDS

Best Bowling

7-15	G. D. McGrath	Australia v Namibia at Potchefstroom	2002-03
7-20	A. J. Bichel	Australia v England at Port Elizabeth	2002-03
7-33	**T. G. Southee**	**New Zealand v England at Wellington**	**2014-15**
7-51	W. W. Davis	West Indies v Australia at Leeds	1983
6-14	G. J. Gilmour	Australia v England at Leeds	1975
6-23	A. Nehra	India v England at Durban	2002-03
6-23	S. E. Bond	New Zealand v Australia at Port Elizabeth	2002-03
6-25	W. P. U. J. C. Vaas	Sri Lanka v Bangladesh at Pietermaritzburg	2002-03
6-27	K. A. J. Roach	West Indies v Netherlands at Delhi	2010-11
6-28	**M. A. Starc**	**Australia v New Zealand at Auckland**	**2014-15**
6-38	S. L. Malinga	Sri Lanka v Kenya at Colombo (RPS)	2010-11
6-39	K. H. MacLeay	Australia v India at Nottingham	1983

Best analyses for other Test-playing countries:

5-16	Shahid Afridi	Pakistan v Kenya at Hambantota	2010-11
5-18	A. J. Hall	South Africa v England at Bridgetown	2006-07
5-21	P. A. Strang	Zimbabwe v Kenya at Patna.	1995-96
5-39	V. J. Marks	England v Sri Lanka at Taunton.	1983
4-21	Shafiul Islam	Bangladesh v Ireland at Mirpur	2010-11

Other Bowling Records

Hat-tricks: Chetan Sharma, India v New Zealand at Nagpur, 1987-88; Saqlain Mushtaq, Pakistan v Zimbabwe at The Oval, 1999; W. P. U. J. C. Vaas, Sri Lanka v Bangladesh at Pietermaritzburg, 2002-03 (the first three balls of the match); B. Lee, Australia v Kenya at Durban, 2002-03; S. L. Malinga, Sri Lanka v South Africa at Providence, 2006-07 (four wickets in four balls); K. A. J. Roach, West Indies v Netherlands at Delhi, 2010-11; S. L. Malinga, Sri Lanka v Kenya at Colombo (RPS), 2010-11; **S. T. Finn, England v Australia at Melbourne, 2014-15; J-P. Duminy, South Africa v Sri Lanka at Sydney, 2014-15**.

Most economical bowling (minimum 10 overs): 12–8–6–1, B. S. Bedi, India v East Africa at Leeds, 1975.

Most expensive bowling (minimum 10 overs): 12–1–105–2, M. C. Snedden, New Zealand v England at The Oval, 1983; **10–2–104–1, J. O. Holder, West Indies v South Africa at Sydney, 2014-15; 10–1–101–2, Dawlat Zadran, Afghanistan v Australia at Perth, 2014-15.**

Most Wickets in a Tournament

26, G. D. McGrath (A) 2006-07; 23, M. Muralitharan (SL) 2006-07, S. W. Tait (A) 2006-07 and W. P. U. J. C. Vaas (SL) 2002-03; **22, T. A. Boult (NZ) 2014-15,** B. Lee (A) 2002-03, **M. A. Starc (A) 2014-15;** 21, G. B. Hogg (A) 2006-07, G. D. McGrath (A) 2002-03, Shahid Afridi (P) 2010-11 and Zaheer Khan (I) 2010-11; 20, G. I. Allott (NZ) 1999 and S. K. Warne (A) 1999.

Most Wickets

	M	B	R	W	BB	4I	Avge
G. D. McGrath (Australia)	39	1,955	1,292	71	7-15	2	18.19
M. Muralitharan (Sri Lanka) . .	40	2,061	1,335	68	4-19	4	19.63
Wasim Akram (Pakistan)	38	1,947	1,311	55	5-28	3	23.83
W. P. U. J. C. Vaas (Sri Lanka)	31	1,570	1,040	49	6-25	2	21.22
Zaheer Khan (India)	23	1,193	890	44	4-42	1	20.22
J. Srinath (India)	34	1,700	1,224	44	4-30	2	27.81
S. L. Malinga (Sri Lanka) . . .	**22**	**1,024**	**908**	**43**	**6-38**	**2**	**21.11**
A. A. Donald (South Africa) . .	25	1,313	913	38	4-17	2	24.02
J. D. P. Oram (New Zealand) .	23	1,094	768	36	4-39	2	21.33
D. L. Vettori (New Zealand) .	**32**	**1,689**	**1,168**	**36**	**4-18**	**2**	**32.44**
B. Lee (Australia)	17	825	629	35	5-42	3	17.97
G. B. Hogg (Australia)	21	951	654	34	4-27	2	19.23
Imran Khan (Pakistan)	28	1,017	655	34	4-37	2	19.26
S. W. Tait (Australia)	18	819	731	34	4-39	1	21.50
T. G. Southee (New Zealand)	**17**	**920**	**784**	**33**	**7-33**	**1**	**23.75**
S. K. Warne (Australia)	28	1,166	624	32	4-29	4	19.50
C. Z. Harris (New Zealand) . . .	17	977	861	32	4-7	1	26.90

WICKETKEEPING RECORDS

Most Dismissals in an Innings

6 (6ct)	A. C. Gilchrist	Australia v Namibia at Potchefstroom	2002-03
6 (6ct)	**Sarfraz Ahmed . . . .**	**Pakistan v South Africa at Auckland . . . .**	**2014-15**
5 (5ct)	S. M. H. Kirmani	India v Zimbabwe at Leicester	1983
5 (4ct, 1st)	J. C. Adams	West Indies v Kenya at Pune	1995-96
5 (4ct, 1st)	Rashid Latif	Pakistan v New Zealand at Lahore	1995-96
5 (5ct)	R. D. Jacobs	West Indies v New Zealand at Southampton	1999
5 (4ct, 1st)	N. R. Mongia	India v Zimbabwe at Leicester	1999
5 (5ct)	**Umar Akmal . . . .**	**Pakistan v Zimbabwe at Brisbane . . . .**	**2014-15**

Most Dismissals in a Tournament

21, A. C. Gilchrist (A) 2002-03; 17, A. C. Gilchrist (A) 2006-07 and K. C. Sangakkara (SL) 2002-03; **16**, R. Dravid (I) 2002-03, P. J. L. Dujon (WI) 1983, **B. J. Haddin (A) 2014-15** and Moin Khan (P) 1999; **15, M. S. Dhoni (I) 2014-15**, D. J. Richardson (SA) 1991-92, K. C. Sangakkara (SL) 2006-07.

Most Dismissals

K. C. Sangakkara (SL)	**54 (41ct, 13st)**		**D. Ramdin (WI)**	**26 (all ct)**
A. C. Gilchrist (A)	52 (45ct, 7st)		A. J. Stewart (E)	23 (21ct, 2st)
M. S. Dhoni (I)	**32 (27ct, 5st)**		R. D. Jacobs (WI)	22 (21ct, 1st)
B. B. McCullum (NZ)	32 (30ct, 2st)		Wasim Bari (P)	22 (18ct, 4st)
M. V. Boucher (SA)	31 (all ct)		A. Bagai (Canada)	21 (19ct, 2st)
Moin Khan (P)	30 (23ct, 7st)		I. A. Healy (A)	21 (18ct, 3st)
B. J. Haddin (A)	**29 (all ct)**		P. J. L. Dujon (WI)	20 (19ct, 1st)

B. B. McCullum took a further two catches in nine matches when not keeping wicket.

FIELDING RECORDS

Most Catches

28, R. T. Ponting (A); 18, S. T. Jayasuriya (SL); **16**, C. L. Cairns (NZ), Inzamam-ul-Haq (P), **D. P. M. D. Jayawardene (SL)** and B. C. Lara (WI); 15, G. C. Smith (SA); **14**, P. A. de Silva (SL), A. Kumble (I), **W. T. S. Porterfield (Ire)** and S. R. Waugh (A).

MOST APPEARANCES

46, R. T. Ponting (A); 45, S. R. Tendulkar (I); **40, D. P. M. D. Jayawardene (SL)** and M. Muralitharan (SL); 39, G. D. McGrath (A); 38, S. T. Jayasuriya (SL) and Wasim Akram (P); **37, K. C. Sangakkara (SL)**; 36, J. H. Kallis (SA); 35, P. A. de Silva (SL) and Inzamam-ul-Haq (P); **34**, B. C. Lara (WI), **B. B. McCullum (NZ)** and J. Srinath (I); 33, S. P. Fleming (NZ), Javed Miandad (P) and S. R. Waugh (A); **32, D. L. Vettori (NZ)**.

TEAM RECORDS

Highest Totals

417-6	**(50 overs)**	**Australia v Afghanistan at Perth**	**2014-15**
413-5	(50 overs)	India v Bermuda at Port-of-Spain	2006-07
411-4	**(50 overs)**	**South Africa v Ireland at Canberra**	**2014-15**
408-5	**(50 overs)**	**South Africa v West Indies at Sydney**	**2014-15**
398-5	(50 overs)	Sri Lanka v Kenya at Kandy	1995-96
393-6	**(50 overs)**	**New Zealand v West Indies at Wellington**	**2014-15**
377-6	(50 overs)	Australia v South Africa at Basseterre	2006-07
376-9	**(50 overs)**	**Australia v Sri Lanka at Sydney**	**2014-15**
373-6	(50 overs)	India v Sri Lanka at Taunton	1999
372-2	**(50 overs)**	**West Indies v Zimbabwe at Canberra**	**2014-15**
370-4	(50 overs)	India v Bangladesh at Mirpur	2010-11

Highest totals for other Test-playing countries:

349	(49.5 overs)	Pakistan v Zimbabwe at Kingston	2006-07
340-2	(50 overs)	Zimbabwe v Namibia at Harare	2002-03
338-8	(50 overs)	England v India at Bangalore	2010-11
322-4	**(48.1 overs)**	**Bangladesh v Scotland at Nelson**	**2014-15**

Highest total batting second:

338-8	(50 overs)	England v India at Bangalore	2010-11

Lowest Totals

36	(18.4 overs)	Canada v Sri Lanka at Paarl	2002-03
45	(40.3 overs)	Canada v England at Manchester	1979
45	(14 overs)	Namibia v Australia at Potchefstroom.	2002-03
58	(18.5 overs)	Bangladesh v West Indies at Mirpur	2010-11
68	(31.3 overs)	Scotland v West Indies at Leicester.	1999
69	(23.5 overs)	Kenya v New Zealand at Chennai.	2010-11
74	(40.2 overs)	Pakistan v England at Adelaide.	1991-92
77	(27.4 overs)	Ireland v Sri Lanka at St George's	2006-07
78	(24.4 overs)	Bermuda v Sri Lanka at Port-of-Spain	2006-07
78	(28 overs)	Bangladesh v South Africa at Mirpur	2010-11

Highest Aggregate

688-18	**(96.2 overs)**	**Australia v Sri Lanka at Sydney**	**2014-15**

RESULTS

Largest Victories

10 wkts	India beat East Africa at Leeds	1975
10 wkts	West Indies beat Zimbabwe at Birmingham.	1983
10 wkts	West Indies beat Pakistan at Melbourne	1991-92
10 wkts	South Africa beat Kenya at Potchefstroom	2002-03
10 wkts	Sri Lanka beat Bangladesh at Pietermaritzburg	2002-03
10 wkts	South Africa beat Bangladesh at Bloemfontein	2002-03
10 wkts	Australia beat Bangladesh at North Sound	2006-07
10 wkts	New Zealand beat Kenya at Chennai	2010-11
10 wkts	New Zealand beat Zimbabwe at Ahmedabad	2010-11
10 wkts	Pakistan beat West Indies at Mirpur	2010-11
10 wkts	Sri Lanka beat England at Colombo (RPS).	2010-11
275 runs	**Australia beat Afghanistan at Perth**	**2014-15**
257 runs	India beat Bermuda at Port-of-Spain	2006-07
257 runs	**South Africa beat West Indies at Sydney**	**2014-15**
256 runs	Australia beat Namibia at Potchefstroom	2002-03

Narrowest Victories

1 wkt	West Indies beat Pakistan at Birmingham	1975
1 wkt	Pakistan beat West Indies at Lahore	1987-88
1 wkt	South Africa beat Sri Lanka at Providence.	2006-07
1 wkt	England beat West Indies at Bridgetown	2006-07
1 wkt	**Afghanistan beat Scotland at Dunedin**	**2014-15**
1 wkt	**New Zealand beat Australia at Auckland**	**2014-15**
1 run	Australia beat India at Madras	1987-88
1 run	Australia beat India at Brisbane	1991-92
2 runs	Sri Lanka beat England at North Sound	2006-07

Ties

Australia v South Africa at Birmingham	1999
South Africa v Sri Lanka (D/L) at Durban.	2002-03
Ireland v Zimbabwe at Kingston	2006-07
India v England at Bangalore.	2010-11

TWENTY20 INTERNATIONAL RECORDS

Matches in this section do not have first-class status.

This section covers Twenty20 international cricket to January 10, 2016. Bold type denotes performances since January 1, 2015, or, in career figures, players who have appeared in Twenty20 internationals since that date.

RESULTS SUMMARY OF TWENTY20 INTERNATIONALS

2004-05 to January 10, 2016 (477 matches)

	Matches	Won	Lost	No Result	% Won (excl. NR)
Sri Lanka	73	44*	28	1	61.11
South Africa	82	49	32	1	60.49
Pakistan	95	57*	38†	–	60.00
India	57	32*	24	1	57.14
England	79	39*	36	4	52.00
Australia	78	40	37†	1	51.94
West Indies	71	35†	34*	2	50.72
New Zealand	85	42†	41‡	2	50.60
Bangladesh	46	13	32	1	28.88
Zimbabwe	44	9*	35	–	20.45
Papua New Guinea	3	2	1	–	66.66
Afghanistan	38	23	15	–	60.52
Netherlands	37	21	15	1	58.33
Hong Kong	12	7	5	–	58.33
Ireland	45	21	19	5	52.50
Scotland	33	12	18	3	40.00
Kenya	29	10	19	–	34.48
Oman	7	2	5	–	28.57
Nepal	11	3	8	–	27.27
Canada	19	4	15*	–	21.05
United Arab Emirates	7	1	6	–	14.28
Bermuda	3	–	3	–	0.00

* *Includes one game settled by a tie-break.* † *Includes two settled by a tie-break.*
‡ *Includes three settled by a tie-break. Ties were decided by bowling contests or one-over eliminators.*

Matches abandoned without a ball bowled are not included except where the toss took place, when they are shown as no result.

BATTING RECORDS

HUNDREDS

156	A. J. Finch	Australia v England at Southampton	2013
123	B. B. McCullum	New Zealand v Bangladesh at Pallekele	2012-13
119	**F. du Plessis**	**South Africa v West Indies at Johannesburg**	**2014-15**
118*	**Mohammad Shahzad**	**Afghanistan v Zimbabwe at Sharjah**	**2015-16**
117*	R. E. Levi	South Africa v New Zealand at Hamilton	2011-12
117	C. H. Gayle	West Indies v South Africa at Johannesburg	2007-08
116*	B. B. McCullum	New Zealand v Australia at Christchurch	2009-10
116*	A. D. Hales	England v Sri Lanka at Chittagong	2013-14
114*	**M. N. van Wyk**	**South Africa v West Indies at Durban**	**2014-15**
111*	Ahmed Shehzad	Pakistan v Bangladesh at Mirpur	2013-14
106	**R. G. Sharma**	**India v South Africa at Dharmasala**	**2015-16**
104*	T. M. Dilshan	Sri Lanka v Australia at Pallekele	2011-12

101*	M. J. Guptill	New Zealand v South Africa at East London	2012-13
101	S. K. Raina	India v South Africa at Gros Islet, St Lucia	2010
100	D. P. M. D. Jayawardene	Sri Lanka v Zimbabwe at Providence	2010
100	R. D. Berrington	Scotland v Bangladesh at Voorburg	2012

MOST RUNS

		M	I	NO	R	HS	100	Avge
1	B. B. McCullum (New Zealand)	71	70	10	2,140	123	2	35.66
2	T. M. Dilshan (Sri Lanka)	68	67	10	1,618	104*	1	28.38
3	M. J. Guptill (New Zealand)	54	52	6	1,535	101*	1	33.36
4	J-P. Duminy (South Africa)	63	58	18	1,528	96*	0	38.20
5	D. P. M. D. Jayawardene (Sri Lanka)	55	55	8	1,493	100	1	31.76
6	D. A. Warner (Australia)	53	53	3	1,448	90*	0	28.96
7	Mohammad Hafeez (Pakistan)	68	66	3	1,432	86	0	22.73
8	Umar Akmal (Pakistan)	68	65	11	1,421	94	0	26.31
9	C. H. Gayle (West Indies)	45	43	3	1,406	117	1	35.15
10	K. C. Sangakkara (Sri Lanka)	56	53	9	1,382	78	0	31.40
11	E. J. G. Morgan (England)	54	52	10	1,285	85*	0	30.59
12	Shahid Afridi (Pakistan)	87	81	12	1,275	54*	0	18.47
13	Shoaib Malik (Pakistan)	67	63	14	1,178	75	0	24.04
14	K. P. Pietersen (England)	37	36	5	1,176	79	0	37.93
15	A. B. de Villiers (South Africa)	63	60	9	1,167	79*	0	22.88
16	S. R. Watson (Australia)	49	47	3	1,164	81	0	26.45
17	L. R. P. L. Taylor (New Zealand)	66	59	11	1,159	63	0	24.14
18	A. D. Hales (England)	37	37	5	1,111	116*	1	34.71
18	Mohammad Shahzad (Afghanistan)	38	38	2	1,111	118*	1	30.86
20	H. Masakadza (Zimbabwe)	40	40	1	1,098	79	0	28.15
21	V. Kohli (India)	30	28	5	1,016	78*	0	44.17

FASTEST TWENTY20 INTERNATIONAL FIFTIES

Balls

12	Yuvraj Singh	India v England at Durban	2007-08
14	**C. Munro**	**New Zealand v Sri Lanka at Auckland**	**2015-16**
17	P. R. Stirling	Ireland v Afghanistan at Dubai	2011-12
17	S. J. Myburgh	Netherlands v Ireland at Sylhet	2013-14
17	**C. H. Gayle**	**West Indies v South Africa at Cape Town**	**2014-15**
18	D. A. Warner	Australia v West Indies at Sydney	2009-10
18	G. J. Maxwell	Australia v Pakistan at Mirpur	2013-14

FASTEST TWENTY20 INTERNATIONAL HUNDREDS

Balls

45	R. E. Levi	South Africa v New Zealand at Hamilton	2011-12
46	**F. du Plessis**	**South Africa v West Indies at Johannesburg**	**2014-15**
47	A. J. Finch	Australia v England at Southampton	2013
50	C. H. Gayle	West Indies v South Africa at Johannesburg	2007-08
50	B. B. McCullum	New Zealand v Australia at Christchurch	2009-10

HIGHEST PARTNERSHIP FOR EACH WICKET

170	for 1st	G. C. Smith and L. L. Bosman	SA v E	Centurion	2009-10
166	for 2nd	D. P. M. D. Jayawardene and			
		K. C. Sangakkara	SL v WI	Bridgetown	2010
152	for 3rd	A. D. Hales and E. J. G. Morgan	E v SL	Chittagong	2013-14
112	for 4th	K. P. Pietersen and E. J. G. Morgan	E v P	Dubai	2009-10
119*	for 5th	Shoaib Malik and Misbah-ul-Haq	P v A	Johannesburg	2007-08
101*	for 6th	M. E. K. Hussey and C. L. White	A v SL	Bridgetown	2010
91	for 7th	P. D. Collingwood and M. H. Yardy	E v WI	The Oval	2007
80	**for 8th**	**P. L. Mommsen and S. M. Sharif**	**Scot v Neth**	**Edinburgh**	**2015**
63	for 9th	Sohail Tanvir and Saeed Ajmal	P v SL	Dubai	2013-14
31*	for 10th	Wahab Riaz and Shoaib Akhtar	P v NZ	Auckland	2010-11

BOWLING RECORDS

BEST BOWLING ANALYSES

6-8	B. A. W. Mendis	Sri Lanka v Zimbabwe at Hambantota	2012-13
6-16	B. A. W. Mendis	Sri Lanka v Australia at Pallekele.	2011-12
5-3	H. M. R. K. B. Herath	Sri Lanka v New Zealand at Chittagong	2013-14
5-6	Umar Gul	Pakistan v New Zealand at The Oval	2009
5-6	Umar Gul	Pakistan v South Africa at Centurion	2012-13
5-13	Elias Sunny	Bangladesh v Ireland at Belfast	2012
5-13	Samiullah Shenwari	Afghanistan v Nepal at Sharjah	2013-14
5-18	T. G. Southee	New Zealand v Pakistan at Auckland	2010-11
5-19	R. McLaren	South Africa v West Indies at North Sound	2010
5-19	M. A. A. Jamil	Netherlands v South Africa at Chittagong	2013-14
5-20	N. N. Odhiambo	Kenya v Scotland at Nairobi	2009-10
5-23	**D. Wiese**	**South Africa v West Indies at Durban**	**2014-15**
5-24	**A. C. Evans**	**Scotland v Netherlands at Edinburgh**	**2015**
5-26	D. J. G. Sammy	West Indies v Zimbabwe at Port-of-Spain	2009-10
5-31	S. L. Malinga	Sri Lanka v England at Pallekele	2012-13

HAT-TRICKS

B. Lee	Australia v Bangladesh at Cape Town	2007-08
J. D. P. Oram	New Zealand v Sri Lanka at Colombo	2009
T. G. Southee	New Zealand v Pakistan at Auckland	2010-11

MOST WICKETS

		M	B	R	W	BB	4I	Avge
1	Shahid Afridi (Pakistan)	87	1,904	2,084	88	4-11	3	23.68
2	Saeed Ajmal (Pakistan)	64	1,430	1,516	85	4-19	4	17.83
3	Umar Gul (Pakistan)	58	1,167	1,387	83	5-6	6	16.71
4	S. L. Malinga (Sri Lanka)	61	1,283	1,556	74	5-31	1	21.02
5	B. A. W. Mendis (Sri Lanka)	39	885	952	66	6-8	5	14.42
6	S. C. J. Broad (England).	56	1,173	1,491	65	4-24	1	22.93
7	D. W. Steyn (South Africa)	38	817	879	55	4-9	2	15.98
	N. L. McCullum (New Zealand)	61	1,093	1,257	55	4-16	2	22.85
9	G. P. Swann (England)	39	810	859	51	3-13	0	16.84
10	K. M. D. N. Kulasekara (Sri Lanka) . .	44	931	1,125	48	4-32	1	23.43
11	Sohail Tanvir (Pakistan)	50	1,053	1,268	47	3-12	0	26.97
12	Mohammad Hafeez (Pakistan)	68	1,004	1,120	46	4-10	1	24.34
	T. G. Southee (New Zealand).	38	822	1,182	46	5-18	1	25.69
14	Shakib Al Hasan (Bangladesh)	38	841	910	45	4-21	2	20.22
	M. Morkel (South Africa)	39	832	1,022	45	4-17	2	22.71

WICKETKEEPING AND FIELDING RECORDS

MOST DISMISSALS IN AN INNINGS

5 (3ct, 2st)	**Mohammad Shahzad**	Afghanistan v Oman at Abu Dhabi	**2015-16**
4 (all ct)	A. C. Gilchrist	Australia v Zimbabwe at Cape Town.	2007-08
4 (all ct)	M. J. Prior	England v South Africa at Cape Town.	2007-08
4 (all ct)	A. C. Gilchrist	Australia v New Zealand at Perth.	2007-08
4 (all st)	Kamran Akmal	Pakistan v Netherlands at Lord's	2009
4 (3ct, 1st)	N. J. O'Brien	Ireland v Sri Lanka at Lord's	2009
4 (2ct, 2st)	A. B. de Villiers	South Africa v West Indies at North Sound	2010
4 (all ct)	M. S. Dhoni	India v Afghanistan at Gros Islet	2010
4 (3ct, 1st)	G. C. Wilson	Ireland v Kenya at Dubai	2011-12
4 (all ct)	A. B. de Villiers	South Africa v Zimbabwe at Hambantota	2012-13
4 (all ct)	M. S. Dhoni	India v Pakistan at Colombo (RPS)	2012-13
4 (all ct)	W. Barresi	Netherlands v Kenya at Dubai	2013-14
4 (2ct, 2st)	Q. de Kock	South Africa v Pakistan at Dubai	2013-14
4 (all st)	D. Ramdin	West Indies v Pakistan at Mirpur	2013-14

MOST DISMISSALS

			M	*Ct*	*St*
1	60	Kamran Akmal (Pakistan)	53	28	32
2	**48**	**D. Ramdin (West Indies)**	**52**	**30**	**18**
3	45	K. C. Sangakkara (Sri Lanka).	56	25	20
4	**40**	**Mushfiqur Rahim (Bangladesh)**	**43**	**19**	**21**
5	**36**	**M. S. Dhoni (India)**	**52**	**25**	**11**
6	**33**	**Mohammad Shahzad (Afghanistan)**	**37**	**19**	**14**
7	32	B. B. McCullum (New Zealand).	42	24	8

B. B. McCullum's record excludes 11 catches taken in 28 matches when not keeping wicket. Kamran Akmal and Mohammad Shahzad both played one match in which they did not keep wicket and did not take a catch.

MOST CATCHES IN AN INNINGS IN THE FIELD

4	D. J. G. Sammy	West Indies v Ireland at Providence	2010

MOST CATCHES

Ct	M		Ct	M	
41	66	L. R. P. L. Taylor (New Zealand)	28	60	D. J. G. Sammy (West Indies)
37	39	A. B. de Villiers (South Africa)	28	63	J-P. Duminy (South Africa)
32	48	Umar Akmal (Pakistan)	27	67	Shoaib Malik (Pakistan)
30	55	D. J. Bravo (West Indies)	26	35	P. W. Borren (Netherlands)
29	53	D. A. Warner (Australia)	25	63	T. M. Dilshan (Sri Lanka)
28	54	M. J. Guptill (New Zealand)	25	87	Shahid Afridi (Pakistan)

A. B. de Villiers' record excludes 27 dismissals (21ct, 6st) in 24 matches when keeping wicket; Umar Akmal's excludes 13 (11ct, 2st) in 20 matches and Dilshan's 7 (5ct, 2st) in 5.

TEAM RECORDS

HIGHEST INNINGS TOTALS

260-6	(20 overs)	Sri Lanka v Kenya at Johannesburg	2007-08
248-6	(20 overs)	Australia v England at Southampton	2013
241-6	(20 overs)	South Africa v England at Centurion	2009-10
236-6	**(19.2 overs)**	**West Indies v South Africa at Johannesburg**	**2014-15**
231-7	**(20 overs)**	**South Africa v West Indies at Johannesburg**	**2014-15**
225-7	(20 overs)	Ireland v Afghanistan at Abu Dhabi	2013-14
221-5	(20 overs)	Australia v England at Sydney	2006-07

LOWEST INNINGS TOTALS

39	(10.3 overs)	Netherlands v Sri Lanka at Chittagong	2013-14
53	**(14.3 overs)**	**Nepal v Ireland at Belfast**	**2015**
56	(18.4 overs)	Kenya v Afghanistan at Sharjah	2013-14
60†	(15.3 overs)	New Zealand v Sri Lanka at Chittagong	2013-14
67	(17.2 overs)	Kenya v Ireland at Belfast	2008
68	(16.4 overs)	Ireland v West Indies at Providence	2010
69	(17 overs)	Hong Kong v Nepal at Chittagong	2013-14
69	**(17.4 overs)**	**Nepal v Netherlands at Amstelveen**	**2015**
70	(20 overs)	Bermuda v Canada at Belfast	2008

† *One man absent.*

OTHER RECORDS

MOST APPEARANCES

87	**Shahid Afridi (Pakistan)**		64	**Saeed Ajmal (Pakistan)**
71	**B. B. McCullum (New Zealand)**		63	**A. B. de Villiers (South Africa)**
68	**T. M. Dilshan (Sri Lanka)**		63	**J-P. Duminy (South Africa)**
68	**Mohammad Hafeez (Pakistan)**		61	**N. L. McCullum (New Zealand)**
68	**Umar Akmal (Pakistan)**		61	**S. L. Malinga (Sri Lanka)**
67	**Shoaib Malik (Pakistan)**		60	**D. J. G. Sammy (West Indies)**
66	**L. R. P. L. Taylor (New Zealand)**			

WORLD TWENTY20 FINALS

2007-08	INDIA (157-5) beat Pakistan (152) by five runs	Johannesburg
2009	PAKISTAN (139-2) beat Sri Lanka (138-6) by eight wickets	Lord's
2010	ENGLAND (148-3) beat Australia (147-6) by seven wickets	Bridgetown
2012-13	WEST INDIES (137-6) beat Sri Lanka (101) by 36 runs	Colombo (RPS)
2013-14	SRI LANKA (134-4) beat India (130-4) by six wickets	Mirpur

An expanded and regularly updated online version of the Records can be found at
www.wisdenrecords.com

MISCELLANEOUS RECORDS

LARGE ATTENDANCES

Test Series

943,000	Australia v England (5 Tests)	1936-37

In England

549,650	England v Australia (5 Tests)	1953

Test Matches

†‡465,000	India v Pakistan, Calcutta	1998-99
350,534	Australia v England, Melbourne (Third Test)	1936-37

Attendance at India v England at Calcutta in 1981-82 may have exceeded 350,000.

In England

158,000+	England v Australia, Leeds	1948
140,111	England v India, Lord's	2011
137,915	England v Australia, Lord's	1953

Test Match Day

‡100,000	India v Pakistan, Calcutta (first four days)	1998-99
91,112	Australia v England, Melbourne (Fourth Test, first day)	2013-14
90,800	Australia v West Indies, Melbourne (Fifth Test, second day)	1960-61
89,155	Australia v England, Melbourne (Fourth Test, first day)	2006-07

Other First-Class Matches in England

93,000	England v Australia, Lord's (Fourth Victory Match, 3 days)	1945
80,000+	Surrey v Yorkshire, The Oval (3 days)	1906
78,792	Yorkshire v Lancashire, Leeds (3 days)	1904
76,617	Lancashire v Yorkshire, Manchester (3 days)	1926

One-Day Internationals

‡100,000	India v South Africa, Calcutta	1993-94
‡100,000	India v West Indies, Calcutta	1993-94
‡100,000	India v West Indies, Calcutta	1994-95
‡100,000	India v Sri Lanka, Calcutta (World Cup semi-final)	1995-96
‡100,000	India v Australia, Kolkata	2003-04
93,013	**Australia v New Zealand, Melbourne (World Cup final)**	**2014-15**
‡90,000	India v Pakistan, Calcutta	1986-87
‡90,000	India v South Africa, Calcutta	1991-92
87,182	England v Pakistan, Melbourne (World Cup final)	1991-92
86,133	Australia v West Indies, Melbourne	1983-84

Twenty20 International

84,041	Australia v India, Melbourne	2007-08

† *Estimated.*
‡ *No official attendance figures were issued for these games, but capacity at Calcutta (now Kolkata) is believed to have reached 100,000 following rebuilding in 1993.*

LORD'S CRICKET GROUND

Lord's and the Marylebone Cricket Club were founded in London in 1787. The Club has enjoyed an uninterrupted career since that date, but there have been three grounds known as Lord's. The first (1787–1810) was situated where Dorset Square now is; the second (1809–13), at North Bank, had to be abandoned owing to the cutting of the Regent's Canal; and the third, opened in 1814, is the present one at St John's Wood. It was not until 1866 that the freehold of Lord's was secured by MCC. The present pavilion was erected in 1890 at a cost of £21,000.

MINOR CRICKET

HIGHEST INDIVIDUAL SCORES

1,009*	**P. P. Dhanawade, K. C. Gandhi English School v Arya Gurukul at Kalyan**	**2015-16**
	Dhanawade faced 327 balls in 6 hours 36 minutes and hit 129 fours and 59 sixes	
628*	A. E. J. Collins, Clark's House v North Town at Clifton College.	
	A junior house match. His innings of 6 hours 50 minutes was spread over four	
	afternoons	1899
566	C. J. Eady, Break-o'-Day v Wellington at Hobart	1901-02
546	P. P. Shaw, Rizvi Springfield School v St Francis D'Assisi School at Mumbai . . .	2013-14
515	D. R. Havewalla, B. B. and C. I. Railways v St Xavier's at Bombay	1933-34
506*	J. C. Sharp, Melbourne GS v Geelong College at Melbourne	1914-15
502*	Chaman Lal, Mohindra Coll., Patiala v Government Coll., Rupar at Patiala.	1956-57
498	Arman Jaffer, Rizvi Springfield School v IES Raja Shivaji School at Mumbai. . .	2010-11
486*	S. Sankruth Sriram, JSS Intl School U16 v Hebron School U16 at Ootacamund .	2014-15
485	A. E. Stoddart, Hampstead v Stoics at Hampstead.	1886
475*	Mohammad Iqbal, Muslim Model HS v Government HS, Sialkot at Gujranwala.	1958-59
473	Arman Jaffer, Rizvi Springfield School v IES VN Sule School at Mumbai.	2012-13
466*	G. T. S. Stevens, Beta v Lambda (University College School house match) at	
	Neasden. *Stevens scored his 466 and took 14 wickets on one day*	1919
461*	Ali Zorain Khan, Nagpur Cricket Academy v Reshimbagh Gymkhana at Nagpur	2010-11
459	J. A. Prout, Wesley College v Geelong College at Geelong	1908-09
451*	V. H. Mol, Maharashtra Under-19 v Assam Under-19 at Nasik	2011-12

The highest score in a Minor County match is 323 by F. E. Lacey for Hampshire v Norfolk at Southampton in 1887; the highest in the Minor Counties Championship is 282 by E. Garnett for Berkshire v Wiltshire at Reading in 1908.*

HIGHEST PARTNERSHIPS

721* for 1st	B. Manoj Kumar and M. S. Tumbi, St Peter's High School v St Philip's	
	High School at Secunderabad	2006-07
664* for 3rd	V. G. Kambli and S. R. Tendulkar, Sharadashram Vidyamandir School v	
	St Xavier's High School at Bombay	1987-88

Manoj Kumar and Tumbi reportedly scored 721 in 40 overs in an Under-13 inter-school match; they hit 103 fours between them, but no sixes. Their opponents were all out for 21 in seven overs.
Kambli was 16 years old, Tendulkar 14. Tendulkar made his Test debut 21 months later.

MOST WICKETS WITH CONSECUTIVE BALLS

There are **two** recorded instances of a bowler taking nine wickets with consecutive balls. Both came in school games: Paul Hugo, for Smithfield School v Aliwal North at Smithfield, South Africa, in 1930-31, and Stephen Fleming (not the future Test captain), for Marlborough College A v Bohally School at Blenheim, New Zealand, in 1967-68. There are five further verified instances of eight wickets in eight balls, the most recent by Mike Walters for the Royal Army Educational Corps v Joint Air Transport Establishment at Beaconsfield in 1979.

TEN WICKETS FOR NO RUNS

There are **24** recorded instances of a bowler taking all ten wickets in an innings for no runs, the most recent by David Morton, for Bayside Muddies v Ranatungas in Brisbane in 1998-99. The previous instance was also in Australia, by the schoolgirl Emma Liddell, for Metropolitan East v West at Penrith (Sydney) in 1995-96. When Jennings Tune did it, for the Yorkshire club Cliffe v Eastrington at Cliffe in 1923, all ten of his victims were bowled.

NOUGHT ALL OUT

In minor matches, this is more common than might be imagined. The historian Peter Wynne-Thomas says the first recorded example was in Norfolk, where an Eleven of Fakenham, Walsingham and Hempton were dismissed for nought by an Eleven of Licham, Dunham and Brisley in July 1815.

MOST DISMISSALS IN AN INNINGS

The only recorded instance of a wicketkeeper being involved in all ten dismissals in an innings was by Welihinda Badalge Bennett, for Mahinda College against Richmond College in Ceylon (now Sri Lanka) in 1952-53. His feat comprised six catches and four stumpings. There are three other known instances of nine dismissals in the same innings, one of which – by H. W. P. Middleton for Priory v Mitre in a Repton School house match in 1930 – included eight stumpings. Young Rangers' innings against Bohran Gymkhana in Karachi in 1969-70 included nine run-outs.

The widespread nature – and differing levels of supervision – of minor cricket matches mean that record claims have to be treated with caution. Additions and corrections to the above records for minor cricket will only be considered for inclusion in Wisden *if they are corroborated by independent evidence of the achievement.*

Research: Steven Lynch

RECORD HIT

The Rev. W. Fellows, while at practice on the Christ Church ground at Oxford in 1856, drove a ball bowled by Charles Rogers 175 yards from hit to pitch.

BIGGEST HIT AT LORD'S

The only known instance of a batsman hitting a ball over the present pavilion at Lord's occurred when A. E. Trott, appearing for MCC against Australians on July 31, August 1, 2, 1899, drove M. A. Noble so far and high that the ball struck a chimney pot and fell behind the building.

THROWING THE CRICKET BALL

140 yards 2 feet, Robert Percival, on the Durham Sands racecourse, Co. Durham.		c1882
140 yards 9 inches, Ross Mackenzie, at Toronto		1872
140 yards, "King Billy" the Aborigine, at Clermont, Queensland		1872

Extensive research by David Rayvern Allen has shown that these traditional records are probably authentic, if not necessarily wholly accurate. Modern competitions have failed to produce similar distances although Ian Pont, the Essex all-rounder who also played baseball, was reported to have thrown 138 yards in Cape Town in 1981. There have been speculative reports attributing throws of 150 yards or more to figures as diverse as the South African Test player Colin Bland, the Latvian javelin thrower Janis Lusis, who won a gold medal for the Soviet Union in the 1968 Olympics, and the British sprinter Charley Ransome. The definitive record is still awaited.

COUNTY CHAMPIONSHIP

MOST APPEARANCES

762	W. Rhodes	Yorkshire	1898–1930
707	F. E. Woolley	Kent	1906–1938
668	C. P. Mead	Hampshire	1906–1936
617	N. Gifford	Worcestershire (484), Warwickshire (133)	1960–1988
611	W. G. Quaife	Warwickshire	1895–1928
601	G. H. Hirst	Yorkshire	1891–1921

MOST CONSECUTIVE APPEARANCES

423	K. G. Suttle...	Sussex...	1954–1969
412	J. G. Binks...	Yorkshire...	1955–1969

J. Vine made 417 consecutive appearances for Sussex in all first-class matches (399 of them in the Championship) between July 1900 and September 1914.

J. G. Binks did not miss a Championship match for Yorkshire between making his debut in June 1955 and retiring at the end of the 1969 season.

UMPIRES

MOST COUNTY CHAMPIONSHIP APPEARANCES

570	T. W. Spencer...	1950–1980	517	H. G. Baldwin...	1932–1962
531	F. Chester...	1922–1955	511	A. G. T. Whitehead...	1970–2005
523	D. J. Constant...	1969–2006			

MOST SEASONS ON ENGLISH FIRST-CLASS LIST

38	D. J. Constant...	1969–2006	27	B. Dudleston...	1984–2010
36	A. G. T. Whitehead...	1970–2005	27	J. W. Holder...	1983–2009
31	K. E. Palmer...	1972–2002	27	J. Moss...	1899–1929
31	T. W. Spencer...	1950–1980	26	W. A. J. West...	1896–1925
30	R. Julian...	1972–2001	25	H. G. Baldwin...	1932–1962
30	P. B. Wight...	1966–1995	25	A. Jepson...	1960–1984
29	H. D. Bird...	1970–1998	25	J. G. Langridge...	1956–1980
28	F. Chester...	1922–1955	25	B. J. Meyer...	1973–1997
28	B. Leadbeater...	1981–2008	25	D. R. Shepherd...	1981–2005
28	R. Palmer...	1980–2007			

An expanded and regularly updated online version of the Records can be found at www.wisdenrecords.com

WOMEN'S TEST RECORDS

This section covers all women's Tests to December 31, 2015. Bold type denotes performances in the calendar year 2015 or, in career figures, players who appeared in women's Tests in that year.

BATTING RECORDS

HIGHEST INDIVIDUAL INNINGS

242	Kiran Baluch	Pakistan v West Indies at Karachi	2003-04
214	M. D. Raj	India v England at Taunton	2002
209*	K. L. Rolton	Australia v England at Leeds	2001
204	K. E. Flavell	New Zealand v England at Scarborough	1996
204	M. A. J. Goszko	Australia v England at Shenley	2001
200	J. Broadbent	Australia v England at Guildford	1998

1,000 RUNS IN A CAREER

R	T		R	T	
1,935	27	J. A. Brittin (England)	1,110	13	S. Agarwal (India)
1,676	**23**	**C. M. Edwards (England)**	1,078	12	E. Bakewell (England)
1,594	22	R. Heyhoe-Flint (England)	1,030	15	S. C. Taylor (England)
1,301	19	D. A. Hockley (New Zealand)	1,007	14	M. E. Maclagan (England)
1,164	18	C. A. Hodges (England)	1,002	14	K. L. Rolton (Australia)

BOWLING RECORDS

BEST BOWLING ANALYSES

8-53	N. David	India v England at Jamshedpur	1995-96
7-6	M. B. Duggan	England v Australia at Melbourne	1957-58
7-7	E. R. Wilson	Australia v England at Melbourne	1957-58
7-10	M. E. Maclagan	England v Australia at Brisbane	1934-35
7-18	A. Palmer	Australia v England at Brisbane	1934-35
7-24	L. Johnston	Australia v New Zealand at Melbourne	1971-72
7-34	G. E. McConway	England v India at Worcester	1986
7-41	J. A. Burley	New Zealand v England at The Oval	1966

MOST WICKETS IN A MATCH

13-226	Shaiza Khan	Pakistan v West Indies at Karachi	2003-04

50 WICKETS IN A CAREER

W	T		W	T	
77	17	M. B. Duggan (England)	60	19	S. Kulkarni (India)
68	11	E. R. Wilson (Australia)	57	16	R. H. Thompson (Australia)
63	20	D. F. Edulji (India)	55	15	J. Lord (New Zealand)
60	13	C. L. Fitzpatrick (Australia)	50	12	E. Bakewell (England)
60	14	M. E. Maclagan (England)			

WICKETKEEPING RECORDS

SIX DISMISSALS IN AN INNINGS

8 (6ct, 2st)	L. Nye	England v New Zealand at New Plymouth	1991-92
6 (2ct, 4st)	B. A. Brentnall	New Zealand v South Africa at Johannesburg	1971-72

25 DISMISSALS IN A CAREER

		T	Ct	St
58	C. Matthews (Australia)	20	46	12
43	J. Smit (England)	21	39	4
36	S. A. Hodges (England)	11	19	17
28	B. A. Brentnall (New Zealand)	10	16	12

TEAM RECORDS

HIGHEST INNINGS TOTALS

569-6 dec	Australia v England at Guildford	1998
525	Australia v India at Ahmedabad	1983-84
517-8	New Zealand v England at Scarborough	1996
503-5 dec	England v New Zealand at Christchurch	1934-35

LOWEST INNINGS TOTALS

35	England v Australia at Melbourne	1957-58
38	Australia v England at Melbourne	1957-58
44	New Zealand v England at Christchurch	1934-35
47	Australia v England at Brisbane	1934-35
50	Netherlands v South Africa at Rotterdam	2007

WOMEN'S ONE-DAY INTERNATIONAL RECORDS

This section covers women's one-day international cricket to December 31, 2015. Bold type denotes performances in the calendar year 2015 or, in career figures, players who appeared in women's one-day internationals in that year.

BATTING RECORDS

HIGHEST INDIVIDUAL INNINGS

229*	B. J. Clark	Australia v Denmark at Mumbai	1997-98
173*	C. M. Edwards	England v Ireland at Pune	1997-98
171	S. R. Taylor	West Indies v Sri Lanka at Mumbai	2012-13
168	S. W. Bates	New Zealand v Pakistan at Sydney	2008-09
157	**R. H. Priest**	**New Zealand v Sri Lanka at Lincoln**	**2015-16**
156*	L. M. Keightley	Australia v Pakistan at Melbourne	1996-97
156*	S. C. Taylor	England v India at Lord's	2006
154*	K. L. Rolton	Australia v Sri Lanka at Christchurch	2000-01
153*	J. Logtenberg	South Africa v Netherlands at Deventer	2007
151	K. L. Rolton	Australia v Ireland at Dublin	2005

MOST RUNS IN A CAREER

R	M		R	M	
5,885	**188**	**C. M. Edwards (England)**	4,814	141	K. L. Rolton (Australia)
5,029	**158**	**M. D. Raj (India)**	4,101	126	S. C. Taylor (England)
4,844	118	B. J. Clark (Australia)	4,064	118	D. A. Hockley (New Zealand)

BOWLING RECORDS

BEST BOWLING ANALYSES

7-4	Sajjida Shah............	Pakistan v Japan at Amsterdam.................	2003
7-8	J. M. Chamberlain.......	England v Denmark at Haarlem	1991
7-14	A. Mohammed...........	West Indies v Pakistan at Mirpur	2011-12
7-24	S. Nitschke...........	Australia v England at Kidderminster	2005
6-10	J. Lord	New Zealand v India at Auckland.............	1981-82
6-10	M. Maben	India v Sri Lanka at Kandy	2003-04
6-10	S. Ismail.............	South Africa v Netherlands at Savar	2011-12

MOST WICKETS IN A CAREER

W	M		W	M	
180	109	C. L. Fitzpatrick (Australia)	**108**	**88**	**S. R. Taylor (West Indies)**
173	**143**	**J. N. Goswami (India)**	103	90	H. A. S. D. Siriwardene
146	125	L. C. Sthalekar (Australia)			(Sri Lanka)
141	97	N. David (India)	102	105	C. E. Taylor (England)
126	**90**	**A. Mohammed (W. Indies)**	101	83	I. T. Guha (England)
117	**126**	**J. L. Gunn (England)**	100	78	N. Al Khader (India)

WICKETKEEPING RECORDS

MOST DISMISSALS IN AN INNINGS

6 (4ct, 2st)	S. L. Illingworth	New Zealand v Australia at Beckenham	1993
6 (1ct, 5st)	V. Kalpana..........	India v Denmark at Slough	1993
6 (2ct, 4st)	Batool Fatima	Pakistan v West Indies at Karachi.............	2003-04
6 (4ct, 2st)	Batool Fatima	Pakistan v Sri Lanka at Colombo	2010-11

MOST DISMISSALS IN A CAREER

		M	Ct	St
133	R. J. Rolls (New Zealand)	104	90	43
114	J. Smit (England)	109	69	45
113†	**S. J. Taylor (England)**	**98**	**73**	**40**
111†	**T. Chetty (South Africa)**	**70**	**79**	**32**
100†	J. C. Price (Australia).............	84	70	30

† *Taylor's total includes two catches in eight matches and Chetty's two in two matches while not keeping wicket, and Price's one taken in the field after giving up the gloves in mid-game.*

TEAM RECORDS

HIGHEST INNINGS TOTALS

455-5	New Zealand v Pakistan at Christchurch	1996-97
412-3	Australia v Denmark at Mumbai	1997-98
397-4	Australia v Pakistan at Melbourne	1996-97
376-2	England v Pakistan at Vijayawada	1997-98
375-5	Netherlands v Japan at Schiedam	2003
373-7	New Zealand v Pakistan at Sydney	2008-09
368-8	West Indies v Sri Lanka at Mumbai.......................	2012-13

LOWEST INNINGS TOTALS

22	Netherlands v West Indies at Deventer	2008
23	Pakistan v Australia at Melbourne	1996-97
24	Scotland v England at Reading	2001
26	India v New Zealand as St Saviour	2002
27	Pakistan v Australia at Hyderabad (India)........................	1997-98
28	Japan v Pakistan at Amsterdam	2003
29	Netherlands v Australia at Perth	1988-89

WOMEN'S WORLD CUP WINNERS

1973	England	1993	England	2008-09	England
1977-78	Australia	1997-98	Australia	2012-13	Australia
1981-82	Australia	2000-01	New Zealand		
1988-89	Australia	2004-05	Australia		

WOMEN'S TWENTY20 INTERNATIONAL RECORDS

This section covers women's Twenty20 international cricket to December 31, 2015. Bold type denotes performances in the calendar year 2015 or, in career figures, players who appeared in women's Twenty20 internationals in that year.

BATTING RECORDS

HIGHEST INDIVIDUAL INNINGS

126	M. M. Lanning......	Australia v Ireland at Sylhet	2013-14
116*	S. A. Fritz	South Africa v Netherlands at Potchefstroom	2010-11
112*	D. J. S. Dottin	West Indies v South Africa at Basseterre	2010
96*	K. L. Rolton	Australia v England at Taunton	2005
94*	S. W. Bates	New Zealand v Pakistan at Sylhet..................	2013-14
92*	C. M. Edwards.......	England v Australia at Hobart	2013-14

MOST RUNS IN A CAREER

R	M		R	M	
2,354	87	C. M. Edwards (England)	1,303	49	M. D. Raj (India)
1,874	65	S. R. Taylor (West Indies)	1,187	80	L. S. Greenway (England)
1,805	73	S. J. Taylor (England)	1,150	62	Bismah Maroof (Pakistan)
1,803	75	S. W. Bates (New Zealand)	1,113	79	A. J. Blackwell (Australia)
1,541	79	D. J. S. Dottin (West Indies)	1,033	53	S. F. M. Devine (New Zealand)
1,517	55	M. M. Lanning (Australia)	1,018	68	S. J. McGlashan (New Zealand)

BOWLING RECORDS

BEST BOWLING ANALYSES

6-17	A. E. Satterthwaite......	New Zealand v England at Taunton	2007
5-10	A. Mohammed..........	West Indies v South Africa at Cape Town	2009-10
5-11	J. N. Goswami..........	India v Australia at Visakhapatnam.............	2011-12
5-11	A. Shrubsole	England v New Zealand at Wellington...........	2011-12
5-12	A. Mohammed..........	West Indies v New Zealand at Bridgetown.......	2013-14
5-15	S. F. Daley.............	West Indies v Sri Lanka at Colombo (RPS)	2012-13

MOST WICKETS IN A CAREER

W	M		W	M	
92	**77**	**A. Mohammed (West Indies)**	56	39	A. Shrubsole (England)
72	68	S. F. Daley (West Indies)	56	58	L. A. Marsh (England)
67	63	D. Hazell (England)	56	63	Sana Mir (Pakistan)
67	69	E. A. Perry (Australia)	56	65	S. R. Taylor (West Indies)
63	50	H. L. Colvin (England)	56	84	J. L. Gunn (England)
60	54	L. C. Sthalekar (Australia)			

WICKETKEEPING RECORDS

MOST DISMISSALS IN AN INNINGS

5 (1ct, 4st)	Kycia A. Knight	West Indies v Sri Lanka at Colombo (RPS)		2012-13
5 (1ct, 4st)	Batool Fatima	Pakistan v Ireland at Dublin		2013
5 (1ct, 4st)	Batool Fatima	Pakistan v Ireland at Dublin (semi-final)		2013

MOST DISMISSALS IN A CAREER

		M	Ct	St
62	**S. J. Taylor (England)**	**73†**	**20**	**42**
54	**R. H. Priest (New Zealand)**	**56†**	**29**	**25**
51*	**J. L. Gunn (England)**	**84**	**51**	
50	Batool Fatima (Pakistan)	45	11	39
50*	**L. S. Greenway (England)**	**80**	**50**	

* *Catches made by non-wicketkeeper in the field.*

† *Taylor's total includes two matches and Priest's one in the field where they made no catches.*

TEAM RECORDS

HIGHEST INNINGS TOTALS

205-1	South Africa v Netherlands at Potchefstroom	2010-11
191-4	West Indies v Netherlands at Potchefstroom	2010-11
191-4	Australia v Ireland at Sylhet	2013-14
188-3	**New Zealand v Sri Lanka at Christchurch**	**2015-16**
186-1	**Australia v Ireland at Dublin**	**2015**
186-7	New Zealand v South Africa at Taunton	2007
185-2	Australia v Pakistan at Sylhet	2013-14
184-4	West Indies v Ireland at Dublin	2008
180-5	England v South Africa at Taunton	2007
180-5	New Zealand v West Indies at Gros Islet, St Lucia	2010

LOWEST INNINGS TOTALS

57	Sri Lanka v Bangladesh at Guanggong	2012-13
60	Pakistan v England at Taunton	2009
60	**New Zealand v England at Whangarei**	**2014-15**
62	India v Australia at Billericay	2011
62	Bangladesh v Sri Lanka at Guanggong	2012-13
63	Pakistan v India at Guanggong	2012-13

WOMEN'S WORLD TWENTY20 WINNERS

2009	England	2012-13	Australia
2010	Australia	2013-14	Australia

BIRTHS AND DEATHS

TEST CRICKETERS

Full list from 1876-77 to January 26, 2016

In the Test career column, dates in italics indicate seasons embracing two different years (i.e. non-English seasons). In these cases, only the first year is given, e.g. 1876 for 1876-77. Some non-English series taking place outside the host country's normal season are dated by a single year.

The Test career figures are complete up to January 26, 2016; the one-day international totals up to January 6, 2016, and the Twenty20 international totals up to January 10, 2016. Career figures are for one national team only; those players who have appeared for more than one Test team are listed on page 1473, and for more than one one-day international or Twenty20 international team on page 1475.

The forename by which a player is known is underlined if it is not his first name.

Family relationships are indicated by superscript numbers; where the relationship is not immediately apparent from a shared name, see the notes at the end of this section. (CY 1889) signifies that the player was a Wisden Cricketer of the Year in the 1889 Almanack. The 5/10 column indicates instances of a player taking five wickets in a Test innings and ten wickets in a match. O/T signifies number of one-day and Twenty20 internationals played.

1 Father and son(s). 2 Brothers. 3 Grandfather, father and son. 4 Grandfather and grandson. 5 Great-grandfather and great-grandson.

† Excludes matches for another Test team. ‡ Excludes matches for another ODI or T20I team.

ENGLAND (669 players)

	Born	Died	Tests	Test Career	Runs	HS	100s	Avge	Wkts	BB	5/10	Avge	Ct/St	O/T
Abel Robert (CY 1890)	30.11.1857	10.12.1936	13	1888–1902	744	132*	2	37.20	–	–	–/–	–	13	
Absolom Charles Alfred	7.6.1846	30.7.1889	1	1878	58	52	0	29.00	–	–	–/–	–	0	
Adams Christopher John (CY 2004)	6.5.1970		5	1999	104	31	0	13.00	1	1-42	0/0	59.00	6	5
Afzaal Usman	9.6.1977		3	2001	83	54	0	16.60	1	1-49	0/0	49.00	0	
Agnew Jonathan Philip (CY 1988)	4.4.1960		3	1984–1985	10	5	0	10.00	4	2-51	0/0	93.25	0	3
Ali Kabir	24.11.1980		1	2003	10	9	0	5.00	5	3-80	0/0	27.20	0	14
Ali Moeen Munir (CY 2015)	18.6.1987		23	2014–2015	949	108*	1	27.91	64	6-67	1/0	39.76	13	31/10
Allen David Arthur	29.10.1935	24.5.2014	39	1959–1966	918	88	1	25.50	122	5-30	4/0	30.97	10	
Allen Sir George Oswald Browning ('Gubby')	31.7.1902	29.11.1989	25	1930–1947	750	122	1	24.19	81	7-80	5/1	29.37	20	
Allom Maurice James Carrick	23.3.1906	8.4.1995	5	1929–1930	14	8*	0	14.00	14	5-38	1/0	18.92	0	
Allott Paul John Walter	14.9.1956		13	1981–1985	213	52*	0	14.20	26	6-61	1/0	41.69	4	13
Ambrose Timothy Raymond	1.12.1982		11	2007–2008	447	102	1	29.80	–	–	–/–	–	31	5/1
Ames Leslie Ethelbert George CBE (CY 1929)	3.12.1905	27.2.1990	47	1929–1938	2,434	149	8	40.56	–	–	–/–	–	74/23	

Name	Born	Died	Tests	Test Career	Runs	HS	100s	Avge	Wkts	BB	5/10	Avge	Ct/St	O/T
Amiss Denis Leslie MBE (CY 1975)	7.4.1943		50	1966–1977	3,612	262*	11	46.30	–	–	–/–	–	24	18
Anderson James Michael (CY 2009)	30.7.1982		113	2003–2015	1,032	81	0	10.32	433	7-43	18/2	29.18	73	194/19
Andrew Keith Vincent	15.12.1929	27.12.2010	2	1954–1963	29	15	0	9.66			–/–		8/1	
Appleyard Robert MBE (CY 1952)	27.6.1924	17.3.2015	9	1954–1956	51	19*	0	17.00	31	5-51	1/0	17.87	4	
Archer Alfred German	6.12.1871	15.7.1935	1	1898	31	24*	0	31.00			–/–		1	
Armitage Thomas	25.4.1848	21.9.1922	2	1876	33	21	0	16.50	0	0-15	0/0	–	1	
Arnold Edward George	7.11.1876	25.10.1942	10	1903–1907	160	40	0	13.33	31	5-37	1/0	25.41	8	
Arnold Geoffrey Graham (CY 1972)	3.9.1944		34	1967–1975	421	59	0	12.02	115	6-45	6/0	28.29	9	14
Arnold John	30.11.1907	4.4.1984	1	1931	34	34	0	17.00			–/–		0	
Astill William Ewart (CY 1933)	1.3.1888	10.2.1948	9	1927–1929	190	40	0	12.66	25	4-58	0/0	34.24	7	
Atherton Michael Andrew OBE (CY 1991)	23.3.1968		115	1989–2001	7,728	185*	16	37.69	2	1-20	0/0	151.00	83	54
Athey Charles William Jeffrey	27.9.1957		23	1980–1988	919	123	1	22.97			–/–		13	31
Attewell William (CY 1892)	12.6.1861	11.6.1927	10	1884–1891	150	43*	0	16.66	28	4-42	0/0	22.35	9	
Bailey Robert John	28.10.1963		4	1988–1989	119	43	0	14.87			–/–		4	4
Bailey Trevor Edward CBE (CY 1950)	3.12.1923	10.2.2011	61	1949–1958	2,290	134*	1	29.74	132	7-34	5/1	29.21	32	
Bairstow David Leslie	1.9.1951	5.1.1998	4	1979–1980	125	59	0	20.83			–/–		12/1	21
[1] **Bairstow Jonathan Marc** (CY 2016)	26.9.1989		24	2012–2015	1,204	150*	1	32.54			–/–		42/1	12/19
Bakewell Alfred Harry (CY 1934)	2.11.1908	23.1.1983	6	1931–1935	409	107	0	45.44			–/–		3	
Balderstone John Christopher	16.11.1940	6.3.2000	2	1976	39	35	0	9.75	1	1-80	0/0	80.00	1	
Ballance Gary Simon (CY 2015)	22.11.1989		15	2013–2015	1,194	156	4	47.76			–/–		14	16
Barber Robert William (1967)	26.9.1935		28	1960–1968	1,495	185	1	35.59	42	4-132	0/0	43.00	21	
Barber Wilfred	18.4.1901	10.9.1968	2	1935	83	44	0	20.75			–/–		1	
Barlow Graham Derek	26.3.1950		3	1976–1977	17	7*	0	4.25	1	1-0	0/0	0.00	1	6
Barlow Richard Gorton	28.5.1851	31.7.1919	17	1881–1886	591	62	0	22.73	34	7-40	3/0	22.55	14	
Barnes Sydney Francis (CY 1910)	19.4.1873	26.12.1967	27	1901–1914	242	38*	0	8.06	189	9-103	24/7	16.43	12	
Barnes William (CY 1890)	27.5.1852	24.3.1899	21	1880–1890	725	134	1	23.38	51	6-28	3/0	15.54	19	
Barnett Charles John (CY 1937)	3.7.1910	28.5.1993	20	1933–1948	1,098	129	2	35.41	0	0-1	0/0	–	14	
Barnett Kim John (CY 1989)	17.7.1960		4	1988–1989	207	80	0	29.57			–/–		2	1
Barratt Fred	12.4.1894	29.1.1947	5	1929–1930	28	17	0	9.33	5	1-8	0/0	47.00	1	
Barrington Kenneth Frank (CY 1960)	24.11.1930	14.3.1981	82	1955–1968	6,806	256	20	58.67	29	3-4	0/0	44.82	58	
Barton Victor Alexander	6.10.1867	23.3.1906	1	1891	23	23	0	23.00	0	0-32	0/0	–	1	
Bates Willie	19.11.1855	8.1.1900	15	1881–1886	656	64	0	27.33	50	7-28	4/1	16.42	9	
Batty Gareth Jon	13.10.1977		7	2003–2005	144	38	0	20.57	11	3-55	0/0	66.63	3	10/1
Bean George	7.3.1864	16.3.1923	3	1891	92	50	0	18.40			–/–		4	
Bedser Sir Alec Victor CBE (CY 1947)	4.7.1918	4.4.2010	51	1946–1955	714	79	0	12.75	236	7-44	15/5	24.89	26	
Bell Ian Ronald MBE (CY 2008)	11.4.1982		118	2004–2015	7,727	235	22	42.69	1	1-33	0/0	76.00	100	161/8

Name	Born	Died	Test Career	Tests	Runs	HS	100s	Avge	Wkts	BB	Avge	5/10	Ct/St	O/T
Benjamin Joseph Emmanuel	2.2.1961		1994	1	0	0	0	0.00	4	4-42	20.00	0/0	0	2
Benson Mark Richard	6.7.1958		1986	1	51	30	0	25.50	–	–	–	–/–	0	1
Berry Robert	29.1.1926	2.12.2006	1950	2	6	4*	0	3.00	9	5-63	25.33	1/0	2	
Bicknell Martin Paul *(CY 2001)*	14.1.1969		1993–2003	4	45	15	0	6.42	14	4-84	38.78	0/0	2	7
Binks James Graham *(CY 1969)*	5.10.1935		1963	2	91	55	0	22.75	–	–	–	–/–	8	
Bird Morice Carlos	25.3.1888	9.12.1933	1909–1913	10	280	61	0	18.66	8	3-11	15.00	0/0	5	
Birkenshaw Jack MBE	13.11.1940		1972–1973	5	148	64	0	21.14	13	5-57	36.07	1/0	3	
Blackwell Ian David	10.6.1978		2005	1	4	4	0	4.00	0	0-28	–	0/0	0	34
Blakey Richard John	15.1.1967		1992	2	7	6	0	1.75	–	–	–	–/–	2	3
Bligh *Hon.* Ivo Francis Walter	13.3.1859	10.4.1927	1882	4	62	19	0	10.33	–	–	–	–/–	7	
Blythe Colin *(CY 1904)*	30.5.1879	8.11.1917	1901–1909	19	183	27	0	9.63	100	8-59	18.63	9/4	6	
Board John Henry	23.2.1867	15.4.1924	1898–1905	6	108	29	0	10.80	–	–	–	–/–	8/3	
Bolus John Brian	31.1.1934		1963–1963	7	496	88	0	41.33	–	0-16	–	0/0	2	
Booth Major William *(CY 1914)*	10.12.1886	1.7.1916	1913	2	46	32	0	23.00	7	4-49	18.57	0/0	0	
Bopara Ravinder Singh	4.5.1985		2007–2012	13	575	143	3	31.94	1	1-39	290.00	0/0	6	120/38
Borthwick Scott George	19.4.1990		2013	1	5	4	0	2.50	4	3-33	20.50	0/0	2	2/1
Bosanquet Bernard James Tindal *(CY 1905)*	13.10.1877	12.10.1936	1903–1905	7	147	27	0	13.36	25	8-107	24.16	2/0	9	
Botham *Sir* Ian Terence OBE *(CY 1978)*	24.11.1955		1977–1992	102	5,200	208	14	33.54	383	8-34	28.40	27/4	120	116
Bowden Montague Parker	1.11.1865	19.2.1892	1888	2	25	25	0	12.50	–	–	–	–/–	1	
Bowes William Eric *(CY 1932)*	25.7.1908	4.9.1987	1932–1946	15	28	10*	0	4.66	68	6-33	22.33	6/0	2	
Bowley Edward Henry *(CY 1930)*	6.6.1890	9.7.1974	1929–1929	5	252	109	1	36.00	0	0-7	–	0/0	2	
Boycott Geoffrey OBE *(CY 1965)*	21.10.1940		1964–1981	108	8,114	246*	22	47.72	7	3-47	54.57	0/0	33	36
Bradley Walter Morris	2.1.1875	19.6.1944	1899	2	23	23*	0	23.00	6	5-67	38.83	1/0	0	
Braund Leonard Charles *(CY 1902)*	18.10.1875	23.12.1955	1901–1907	23	987	104	3	25.97	47	8-81	38.51	3/0	39	
Brearley John Michael OBE *(CY 1977)*	28.4.1942		1976–1981	39	1,442	91	0	22.88	–	–	–	–/–	52	25
Brearley Walter *(CY 1909)*	11.3.1876	30.1.1937	1905–1912	4	21	11*	0	7.00	17	5-110	21.11	1/0	0	
Brennan Donald Vincent	10.2.1920	9.1.1985	1951	2	16	16	0	8.00	–	–	–	–/–	0/1	
Bresnan Timothy Thomas *(CY 2012)*	28.2.1985		2009–2013	23	575	91	0	26.13	72	5-48	32.73	1/0	8	85/34
Briggs John *(CY 1889)*	3.10.1862	11.1.1902	1884–1899	33	815	121	0	18.11	118	8-11	17.75	9/4	12	
Broad Brian Christopher	29.9.1957		1984–1989	25	1,661	162	6	39.54	–	0-4	–	0/0	10	34
Broad Stuart Christopher John *(CY 2010)*	24.6.1986		2007–2015	91	2,565	169	1	22.90	333	8-15	28.66	15/2	26	119/56
Brockwell William *(CY 1895)*	21.11.1865	30.6.1935	1893–1899	7	202	49	0	16.83	5	3-33	61.80	0/0	6	
Bromley-Davenport Hugh Richard	18.8.1870	23.5.1954	1895–1898	4	128	84	0	21.33	4	2-46	24.50	0/0	1	
Brookes Dennis *(CY 1957)*	29.10.1915	9.3.2006	1947	1	17	10	0	8.50	–	–	–	–/–	0	
Brown Alan	17.10.1935		1961	2	3	3*	0	–	3	3-27	50.00	0/0	1	
Brown David John	30.1.1942		1965–1969	26	342	44*	0	11.79	79	5-42	28.31	2/0	7	

	Born	Died	Tests	Test Career	Runs	HS	100s	Avge	Wkts	BB	5/10	Avge	Ct/St	OIT
Brown Frederick Richard MBE (CY 1933)	16.12.1910	24.7.1991	22	1931-1953	734	79	0	25.31	45	5-49	1/0	31.06	22	
Brown George	6.10.1887	3.12.1964	7	1921-1922	299	84	0	29.90	0	–	–/–	–	9/3	
Brown John Thomas (CY 1895)	20.8.1869	4.11.1904	8	1894-1899	470	140	1	36.15	0	0-22	0/0	–	7	
Brown Simon John Emmerson	29.6.1969		1	1996	11	10*	0	11.00	2	1-60	0/0	69.00	1	
Buckenham Claude Percival	16.1.1876	23.2.1937	4	1909	43	17	0	6.14	21	5-115	1/0	28.23	2	
¹ Butcher Alan Raymond (CY 1991)	7.1.1954		1	1979	34	20	0	17.00	0	0-9	0/0	–	1	1
Butcher Mark Alan	23.8.1972		71	1997-2004	4,288	173*	8	34.58	15	4-42	0/0	36.06	61	
Butcher Roland Orlando	14.10.1953		3	1980	71	32	0	14.20		–	–/–	–	3	3
Butler Harold James	12.3.1913	17.7.1991	2	1947-1947	15	15*	0	15.00	12	4-34	0/0	17.91	1	
Butt Henry Rigden	27.12.1865	21.12.1928	3	1895	22	13	0	7.33		–	–/–	–	1/1	
Buttler Joseph Charles	8.9.1990		15	2014-2015	630	85	0	30.00		–	–/–	–	49	65/40
Caddick Andrew Richard (CY 2001)	21.11.1968		62	1993-2003	861	49*	0	10.37	234	7-46	13/1	29.91	21	54
Calthorpe *Hon.* Frederick Somerset Gough-	27.5.1892	19.11.1935	4	1929-1930	129	49	0	18.42	1	1-38	0/0	91.00	3	
Capel David John	6.2.1963		15	1987-1989	374	98	0	15.58	21	3-88	0/0	50.66	6	23
Carberry Michael Alexander	29.9.1980		6	2009-2013	345	60	0	28.75	0	–	–/–	–	7	6/1
Carr Arthur William (CY 1923)	21.5.1893	7.2.1963	11	1922-1929	237	63	0	19.75	0	–	–/–	–	3	
Carr Donald Bryce OBE (CY 1960)	28.12.1926		2	1951	135	76	0	33.75	2	2-84	0/0	70.00	0	
Carr Douglas Ward (CY 1910)	17.3.1872	23.3.1950	1	1909	0	0	0	0.00	7	5-146	1/0	40.28	0	
Cartwright Thomas William MBE	22.7.1935	30.4.2007	5	1964-1965	26	9	0	5.20	15	6-94	1/0	36.26	2	
Chapman Arthur Percy Frank (CY 1919)	3.9.1900	16.9.1961	26	1924-1930	925	121	1	28.90	1	0-10	0/0	10.00	32	
Charlwood Henry Rupert James	19.12.1846	6.6.1888	2	1876	63	36	0	15.75		–	–/–	–	1	
Chatterton William	27.12.1861	19.3.1913	1	1891	48	48	0	48.00	0	–	–/–	–	0	
Childs John Henry (CY 1987)	15.8.1951		2	1988	2	2*	0	–	3	1-13	0/0	61.00	0	
Christopherson Stanley	11.11.1861	6.4.1949	1	1884	17	17	0	17.00	1	1-52	0/0	69.00	0	
Clark Edward Winchester	9.8.1902	28.4.1982	8	1929-1934	36	10	0	9.00	32	5-98	1/0	28.09	1	20
Clarke Rikki	29.9.1981		2	2003	96	55	0	32.00	4	2-7	0/0	15.00	1	
Clay John Charles	18.3.1898	11.8.1973	1	1935	–	–	–	–	0	0-30	0/0	–	0	3
Close Dennis Brian CBE (CY 1964)	24.2.1931	14.9.2015	22	1949-1976	887	70	0	25.34	18	4-35	0/0	29.55	24	
Coldwell Leonard John	10.1.1933	6.8.1996	7	1962-1964	9	6*	0	4.50	22	6-85	1/0	27.72	1	
Collingwood Paul David MBE (CY 2007)	26.5.1976		68	2003-2010	4,259	206	10	40.56	17	3-23	0/0	59.88	96	197/35
⁴ Compton Denis Charles Scott CBE (CY 1939)	23.5.1918	23.4.1997	78	1937-1956	5,807	278	17	50.06	25	5-70	1/0	56.40	49	
⁴ Compton Nicholas Richard Denis (CY 2013)	26.6.1983		13	2012-2015	724	117	2	31.47	0	–	–/–	–	5	
Cook Alastair Nathan MBE (CY 2012)	25.12.1984		126	2005-2015	9,964	294	28	46.56	0	1-6	0/0	7.00	125	92/4
Cook Cecil ("Sam")	23.8.1921	5.9.1996	1	1947	4	4	0	2.00	0	0-40	0/0	–	0	6
Cook Geoffrey	9.10.1951		7	1981-1982	203	66	0	15.61	0	0-4	0/0	–	9	3
Cook Nicholas Grant Billson	17.6.1956		15	1983-1989	179	31	0	8.52	52	6-65	4/1	32.48	5	

	Born	Died	Tests	Test Career	Runs	HS	100s	Avge	Wkts	BB	5/10	Avge	Ct/St	O/T
Cope Geoffrey Alan	23.2.1947		3	1977	40	22	0	13.33	8	3-102	0/0	34.62	1	2
Copson William Henry (CY 1937)	27.4.1908	13.9.1971	3	1939–1947	6	6	0	6.00	15	5-85	1/0	19.80	1	
Cork Dominic Gerald (CY 1996)	7.8.1971		37	1995–2002	864	59	0	18.00	131	7-43	5/0	29.81	18	32
Cornford Walter Latter	25.12.1900	6.2.1964	4	1929	36	18	0	9.00			–/–		5/3	
Cottam Robert Michael Henry	16.10.1944		4	1968–1972	27	13	0	6.75	14	4-50	0/0	23.35	2	
Coventry *Hon.* Charles John	26.2.1867	2.6.1929	2	1888	13	12	0	13.00					2	
Cowans Norman George	17.4.1961		19	1982–1985	175	36	0	7.95	51	6-77	2/0	39.27	9	23
Cowdrey Christopher Stuart	20.10.1957		6	1984–1988	101	38	0	14.42	4	2-65	0/0	77.25	5	3
Cowdrey Lord [Michael Colin] CBE (CY 1956)	24.12.1932	4.12.2000	114	1954–1974	7,624	182	22	44.06	0	0-1	0/0		120	1
Coxon Alexander	18.1.1916	22.1.2006	1	1948	19	19	0	19.00	3	2-90	0/0	57.33	0	
Cranston James	9.1.1859	10.12.1904	1	1890	31	16	0	15.50					0	
Cranston Kenneth	20.10.1917	8.1.2007	8	1947–1948	209	45	0	14.92	18	4-12	0/0	25.61	1	
Crapp John Frederick	14.10.1912	13.2.1981	7	1948–1948	319	56	0	29.00			–/–		7	
Crawford John Neville (CY 1907)	1.12.1886	2.5.1963	12	1905–1907	469	74	0	22.33	39	5-48	3/0	29.48	13	13
Crawley John Paul	21.9.1971		37	1994–2002	1,800	156*	4	34.61			–/–		29	
Croft Robert Damien Bale MBE	25.5.1970		21	1996–2001	421	37*	0	16.19	49	5-95	1/0	37.24	10	50
Curtis Timothy Stephen	15.1.1960		5	1988–1989	140	41	0	15.55	0	0-7	0/0		3	
Cuttell Willis Robert (CY 1898)	13.9.1863	9.12.1929	2	1898	65	21	0	16.25	6	3-17	0/0	12.16	2	
Dawson Edward William	13.2.1904	4.6.1979	5	1927–1929	175	55	0	19.44					3	
Dawson Richard Kevin James	4.8.1980		7	2001–2002	114	19*	0	11.40	11	4-134	0/0	61.54	3	
Dean Harry	13.8.1884	12.3.1957	3	1912	10	8	0	5.00	11	4-19	0/0	13.90	2	
DeFreitas Phillip Anthony Jason (CY 1992)	18.2.1966		44	1986–1995	934	88	0	14.82	140	7-70	4/0	33.57	14	103
Denness Michael Henry OBE (CY 1975)	1.12.1940	19.4.2013	28	1969–1975	1,667	188	4	39.69			–/–		28	12
Denton David (CY 1906)	4.7.1874	16.2.1950	11	1905–1909	424	104	1	20.19					8	
Dewes John Gordon	11.10.1926	12.5.2015	5	1948–1950	121	67	0	12.10					0	
Dexter Edward Ralph CBE (CY 1961)	15.5.1935		62	1958–1968	4,502	205	9	47.89	66	4-10	0/0	34.93	29	36
Dilley Graham Roy	18.5.1959	5.10.2011	41	1979–1989	521	56	0	13.35	138	6-38	6/0	29.76	10	36
Dipper Alfred Ernest	9.11.1885	7.11.1945	1	1921	51	40	0	25.50					0	
Doggart George Hubert Graham OBE	18.7.1925		2	1950	76	29	0	19.00					3	
D'Oliveira Basil Lewis CBE (CY 1967)	4.10.1931	18.11.2011	44	1966–1972	2,484	158	5	40.06	47	3-46	0/0	39.55	29	4
Dollery Horace Edgar ("Tom") (CY 1952)	14.10.1914	20.1.1987	4	1947–1950	72	37	0	10.28					1	
Dolphin Arthur	24.12.1885	23.10.1942	1	1920	1	1	0	0.50					1	
Douglas John William Henry Tyler (CY 1915)	3.9.1882	19.12.1930	23	1911–1924	962	119	1	29.15	45	5-46	1/0	33.02	9	
Downton Paul Rupert	4.4.1957		30	1980–1988	785	74	0	19.62			–/–		70/5	28
Druce Norman Frank (CY 1898)	1.1.1875	27.10.1954	5	1897	252	64	0	28.00					5	
Ducat Andrew (CY 1920)	16.2.1886	23.7.1942	1	1921	5	3	0	2.50						

	Born	Died	Tests	Test Career	Runs	HS	100s	Avge	Wkts	BB	5/10	Avge	Ct/St	O/T
Duckworth George (CY 1929)	9.5.1901	5.11.1966	24	1924–1936	234	39*	0	14.62	–	–	–/–	–	45/15	
Duleepsinhji Kumar Shri (CY 1930)	13.6.1905	5.12.1959	12	1929–1931	995	173	3	58.52	0	–	0–7	–	10	
Durston Frederick John	11.7.1893	8.4.1965	1	1921	8	6*	0	8.00	5	4-102	0/0	27.20	0	
Ealham Mark Alan	27.8.1969		8	1996–1998	210	53*	0	21.00	17	4-21	0/0	28.70	4	64
Edmonds Philippe-Henri . . .	8.3.1951		51	1975–1987	875	64	0	17.50	125	7-66	2/0	34.18	42	29
Edrich John Hugh MBE (CY 1966) .	21.6.1937		77	1963–1976	5,138	310*	12	43.54	0	0-6	0/0	–	43	7
Edrich William John (CY 1940) . .	26.3.1916	24.4.1986	39	1938–1954	2,440	219	6	40.00	41	4-68	–/–	41.29	39	
Elliott John	2.11.1891	2.2.1976	4	1927–1933	61	37*	0	15.25	0	–	–/–	–	8/3	
Ellison Richard Mark (CY 1986) . .	21.9.1959		11	1984–1986	202	41	0	13.46	35	6-77	3/1	29.94	2	14
Emburey John Ernest (CY 1984) . .	20.8.1952		64	1978–1995	1,713	75	0	22.53	147	7-78	6/0	38.40	34	61
Emmett George Malcolm	2.12.1912	18.12.1976	1	1948	10	10	0	5.00	0	–	–/–	–	0	
Emmett Thomas	3.9.1841	29.6.1904	7	1876–1881	160	48	0	13.33	9	7-68	1/0	31.55	9	
Evans Alfred John	1.5.1889	18.9.1960	1	1921	18	14	0	9.00	0	–	–/–	–	0	
Evans Thomas Godfrey CBE (CY 1951)	18.8.1920	3.5.1999	91	1946–1959	2,439	104	2	20.49	0	–	–/–	–	173/46	
Fagg Arthur Edward	18.6.1915	13.9.1977	5	1936–1939	150	39	0	18.75	0	–	–/–	–	5	
Fairbrother Neil Harvey	9.9.1963		10	1987–1992	219	83	0	15.64	0	–	–/–	–	4	75
Fane Frederick Luther	27.4.1875	27.11.1960	14	1905–1909	682	143	1	26.23	0	0-9	–/–	–	6	
Farnes Kenneth (CY 1939)	8.7.1911	20.10.1941	15	1934–1938	58	20	0	4.83	60	6-96	3/1	28.65	1	
Farrimond William	23.5.1903	15.11.1979	4	1930–1935	116	35	0	16.57	0	–	–/–	–	5/2	
Fender Percy George Herbert (CY 1915)	22.8.1892	15.6.1985	13	1920–1929	380	60	0	19.00	29	5-90	2/0	40.86	14	
Ferris John James	21.5.1867	17.11.1900	1†	1891	16	16	0	16.00	13	7-37	2/1	7.00	4	
Fielder Arthur (CY 1907)	19.7.1877	30.8.1949	6	1903–1907	78	20	0	11.17	26	6-82	1/0	27.34	4	
Finn Steven Thomas	4.4.1989		29	2010–2015	190	56	0	11.75	113	6-79	5/0	28.34	6	65/21
Fishlock Laurence Barnard (CY 1947) .	2.1.1907	25.6.1986	4	1936–1946	47	19*	0	11.75	0	–	–/–	–	1	
Flavell John Alfred (CY 1965) . . .	15.5.1929	25.2.2004	4	1961–1964	31	14	0	7.75	7	2-65	0/0	52.42	0	
Fletcher Keith William Robert OBE (CY 1974)	20.5.1944		59	1968–1981	3,272	216	7	39.90	1	1-6	0/0	96.50	54	24
Flintoff Andrew MBE (CY 2004) . .	6.12.1977		79§	1998–2009	3,795	167	5	31.89	219	5-58	3/0	33.34	52	138‡/7
Flowers Wilfred	7.12.1856	1.11.1926	8	1884–1893	254	56	0	18.14	14	5-46	1/0	21.14	2	
Ford Francis Gilbertson Justice . .	14.12.1866	7.2.1940	5	1894	168	48	0	18.66	1	1-47	0/0	129.00	5	
Foster Frank Rowbotham (CY 1912) .	31.1.1889	3.5.1958	11	1911–1912	330	71	0	23.57	45	6-91	4/0	20.57	11	26
Foster James Savin	15.4.1980		7	2001–2002	226	48	0	25.11	0	–	–/–	–	17/1	11/5
Foster Neil Alan (CY 1988)	6.5.1962		29	1983–1993	446	39	0	11.73	88	8-107	5/1	32.85	7	48
Foster Reginald Erskine ("Tip") (CY 1900)	16.4.1878	13.5.1914	8	1903–1907	602	287	1	46.30	0	–	–/–	–	13	
Fothergill Arnold James	26.8.1854	1.8.1932	2	1888	33	32	0	16.50	8	4-19	0/0	11.25	1	
Fowler Graeme	20.4.1957		21	1982–1984	1,307	201	3	35.32	0	0-0	–/–	–	10	26

§ *Flintoff's figures exclude 50 runs and seven wickets for the ICC World XI v Australia in the Super Series Test in 2005-06.*

Name	Born	Died	Tests	Test Career	Runs	HS	100s	Avge	Wkts	BB	5/10	Avge	Ct/St	O/T
Fraser Angus Robert Charles MBE (CY 1996)	8.8.1965		46	1989–1998	388	32	0	7.46	177	8-53	13/2	27.32	9	42
Freeman Alfred Percy ("Tich") (CY 1923)	17.5.1888	28.1.1965	12	1924–1929	154	50*	0	14.00	66	7-71	5/3	25.86	4	
French Bruce Nicholas	13.8.1959		16	1986–1987	308	59	0	18.11		–	–/–	–	38/1	13
Fry Charles Burgess (CY 1895)	25.4.1872	7.9.1956	26	1895–1912	1,223	144	2	32.18	0	0-3	0/0	–	17	
Gallian Jason Edward Riche	25.6.1971		3	1995–1995	74	28	0	12.33	0	0-6	0/0	–	–	
Gatting Michael William OBE (CY 1984)	6.6.1957		79	1977–1994	4,409	207	10	35.55	4	1-14	0/0	79.25	59	92
Gay Leslie Hewitt	24.3.1871	1.11.1949	1	1894	37	–	0	18.50		–	–/–	–	3/1	
Geary George (CY 1927)	9.7.1893	6.3.1981	14	1924–1934	249	66	0	15.56	46	7-70	4/1	29.41	13	
Gibb Paul Antony	11.7.1913	7.12.1977	8	1938–1946	581	120	2	44.69		–	–/–	–	30/3	
Giddins Edward Simon Hunter	20.7.1971		4	1999–2000	10	7	0	2.50	12	5-15	1/0	20.00	0	
Gifford Norman MBE (CY 1975)	30.3.1940		15	1964–1973	179	25*	0	16.27	33	5-55	1/0	31.09	8	
Giles Ashley Fraser MBE (CY 2005)	19.3.1973		54	1998–2006	1,421	59	0	20.89	143	5-57	5/0	40.60	33	62
[2] Gilligan Alfred Herbert Harold	29.6.1896	5.5.1978	1	1929	71	32	0	17.75		–	–/–	–	–	
[2] Gilligan Arthur Edward Robert (CY 1924)	23.12.1894	5.9.1976	11	1922–1924	209	39*	0	16.07	36	6-7	2/1	29.05	3	
[2] Gimblett Harold (CY 1953)	19.10.1914	30.3.1978	3	1936–1939	129	67*	0	32.25		–	–/–	–	1	
Gladwin Clifford	3.4.1916	9.4.1988	8	1947–1949	170	51*	0	28.33	15	3-21	0/0	38.06	3	
Goddard Thomas William John (CY 1938)	1.10.1900	22.5.1966	8	1930–1939	13	8	0	6.50	22	6-29	1/0	26.72	2	
Gooch Graham Alan OBE (CY 1980)	23.7.1953		118	1975–1994	8,900	333	20	42.58	23	3-39	0/0	46.47	103	125
Gough Darren (CY 1999)	18.9.1970		58	1994–2003	855	65	0	12.57	229	6-42	9/0	28.39	13	158‡/2
Gover Alfred Richard MBE (CY 1937)	29.2.1908	7.10.2001	4	1936–1946	36	2*	0	–	8	3-85	0/0	44.87	–	
Gower David Ivon OBE (CY 1979)	1.4.1957		117	1978–1992	8,231	215	18	44.25	1	1-1	–/–	20.00	74	114
Grace Edward Mills	28.11.1841	20.5.1911	1	1880	36	36	0	18.00		–	–/–	–	1	
Grace George Frederick	13.12.1850	22.9.1880	1	1880	0	0	0	0.00		–	–/–	–	2	
[2] Grace William Gilbert (CY 1896)	18.7.1848	23.10.1915	22	1880–1899	1,098	170	2	32.29	9	2-12	0/0	26.22	39	
Graveney Thomas William OBE (CY 1953)	16.6.1927	3.11.2015	79	1951–1969	4,882	258	11	44.38	1	1-34	0/0	167.00	80	
Greenhough Thomas	9.11.1931	15.9.2009	4	1959–1960	4	4	0	1.33	16	5-35	1/0	22.31	1	
Greenwood Andrew	20.8.1847	12.2.1889	2	1876	77	49	0	19.25		–	–/–	–	2	
[2] Greig Anthony William (CY 1975)	6.10.1946	29.12.2012	58	1972–1977	3,599	148	8	40.43	141	8-86	6/2	32.20	87	22
[2] Greig Ian Alexander	8.12.1955		2	1982	26	14	0	6.50	4	4-53	0/0	28.50	0	2
Grieve Basil Arthur Firebrace	28.5.1864	19.11.1917	2	1888	40	14*	0	40.00		–	–/–	–	–	
Griffith Stewart Cathie CBE ("Billy")	16.6.1914	7.4.1993	3	1947–1948	157	140	0	31.40		–	–/–	–	5	
[2] Gunn George (CY 1914)	13.6.1879	29.6.1958	15	1907–1929	1,120	122*	2	40.00	0	0-8	0/0	–	15	
Gunn John Richmond (CY 1904)	19.7.1876	21.8.1963	6	1901–1905	85	24	0	10.62	18	5-76	1/0	21.50	3	
Gunn William (CY 1890)	4.12.1858	29.1.1921	11	1886–1899	392	102*	2	21.77		–	–/–	–	5	
Habib Aftab	7.2.1972		2	1999	26	19	0	8.66		–	–/–	–	6	
Haig Nigel Esmé	12.12.1887	27.10.1966	5	1921–1929	126	47	0	14.00	13	3-73	0/0	34.46	4	

	Born	Died	Tests	Test Career	Runs	HS	100s	Avge	Wkts	BB	Avge	5/10	Ct/St	O/T
Haigh Schofield (CY 1901)	19.3.1871	27.2.1921	11	1898–1912	113	25	0	7.53	24	6-11	25.91	1/0	8	24/37
Hales Alexander Daniel	3.1.1989		4	2015	136	60	0	17.00	–	–	–	–/–	1	–
Hallows Charles (CY 1928)	4.4.1895	10.11.1972	2	1921–1928	42	26	0	42.00	0	0-2	–	–/–	0	0‡
Hamilton Gavin Mark	16.9.1974		1	1999	0	0	0	0.00	0	0-63	–	–/–	0	–
Hammond Walter Reginald (CY 1928)	19.6.1903	1.7.1965	85	1927–1946	7,249	336*	22	58.45	83	5-36	37.80	2/0	110	3
Hampshire John Harry	10.2.1941		8	1969–1975	403	107	1	26.86	–	–	–	–/–	9	
Hardinge Harold Thomas William ("Wally") (CY 1915)	25.2.1886	8.5.1965	1	1921	30	25	0	15.00	–	–	–	–/–	0	
¹ Hardstaff Joseph, sen (CY 1938)	9.11.1882	2.4.1947	5	1907	311	72	0	31.10	–	–	–	–/–	1	
¹ Hardstaff Joseph, jun (CY 1938)	3.7.1911	1.11.1990	23	1935–1948	1,636	205*	4	46.74	–	–	–	–/–	9	
Harmison Stephen James MBE (CY 2005) §	23.10.1978		63§	2002–2009	742	49*	0	12.16	222	7-12	31.94	8/1	7	58/2
Harris Lord [George Robert Canning]	3.2.1851	24.3.1932	4	1878–1884	145	52	0	29.00	0	0-14	–	0/0	2	
Hartley John Cabourn	15.11.1874	8.3.1963	2	1905	15	9	0	3.75	1	1-62	115.00	0/0	2	
Hawke Lord [Martin Bladen] (CY 1909)	16.8.1860	10.10.1938	5	1895–1898	55	30	0	7.85	–	–	–	–/–	3	
Hayes Ernest George (CY 1907)	6.11.1876	2.12.1953	5	1905–1912	86	35	0	10.75	1	1-28	52.00	0/0	2	
Hayes Frank Charles	6.12.1946		9	1973–1976	244	106*	1	15.25	–	–	–	–/–	2	
Hayward Thomas Walter (CY 1895)	29.3.1871	19.7.1939	35	1899–1909	1,999	137	3	34.46	14	4-22	36.71	0/0	19	
² Headley Dean Warren	27.1.1970		15	1997–1999	186	31	0	8.45	60	6-60	27.85	1/0	7	13
² Hearne Alec (CY 1894)	22.7.1863	16.5.1952	1	1891	9	9	0	9.00	–	–	–	–/–	–	
¹,² Hearne Frank	23.11.1858	14.7.1949	2‡	1888	47	27	0	23.50	–	–	–	–/–	–	
² Hearne George Gibbons	7.7.1856	13.2.1932	1	1891	0	0	0	0.00	–	–	–	–/–	–	
Hearne John Thomas (CY 1892)	3.5.1867	17.4.1944	12	1891–1899	126	40	0	9.00	49	6-41	22.08	4/1	4	
Hearne John William (CY 1912)	11.2.1891	14.9.1965	24	1911–1926	806	114	1	26.00	30	5-49	48.73	1/0	13	
Hegg Warren Kevin	23.2.1968		2	1998	30	15	0	7.50	–	–	–	–/–	8	
Hemmings Edward Ernest	20.2.1949		16	1982–1990	383	95	0	22.52	43	6-58	42.44	1/0	5	33
Hendren Elias Henry ("Patsy") (CY 1920)	5.2.1889	4.10.1962	51	1920–1934	3,525	205*	7	47.63	1	1-27	31.00	0/0	33	
Hendrick Michael (CY 1978)	22.10.1948		30	1974–1981	128	15	0	6.40	87	4-28	25.83	0/0	25	22
Heseltine Christopher	26.11.1869	13.6.1944	2	1895	18	18	0	9.00	5	5-38	16.80	1/0	1	
Hick Graeme Ashley MBE (CY 1987)	23.5.1966		65	1991–2001	3,383	178	6	31.32	23	4-126	56.78	0/0	90	120
Higgs Kenneth (CY 1968)	14.1.1937		15	1965–1968	185	63	0	11.56	71	6-91	20.74	2/0	4	
Hill Allen	14.11.1843	28.8.1910	2	1876	101	49	0	50.50	7	4-27	18.57	0/0	1	
Hill Arthur James Ledger	26.7.1871	6.9.1950	3	1895	251	124	1	62.75	4	4-8	2.00	0/0	1	
Hilton Malcolm Jameson (CY 1957)	2.8.1928	8.7.1990	4	1950–1951	37	15	0	7.40	14	5-61	34.07	1/0	1	
Hirst George Herbert (CY 1901)	7.9.1871	10.5.1954	24	1897–1909	790	85	0	22.57	59	5-48	30.00	3/0	18	
Hitch John William (CY 1914)	7.5.1886	7.7.1965	7	1911–1921	103	51*	0	14.71	7	2-31	46.42	0/0	4	

§ Harmison's figures exclude one run and four wickets for the ICC World XI v Australia in the Super Series Test in 2005-06.

Records and Registers

Player	Born	Died	Test Career	Tests	Runs	HS	100s	Avge	Wkts	BB	5/10	Avge	Ct/St	OIT
Hobbs Sir John Berry (CY 1909)	16.12.1882	21.12.1963	1907–1930	61	5,410	211	15	56.94	1	1-19	0/0	165.00	17	
Hobbs Robin Nicholas Stuart	8.5.1942		1967–1971	7	34	15*	0	6.80	12	3-25	0/0	40.08	8	
Hoggard Matthew James MBE (CY 2006)	31.12.1976		2000–2007	67	473	38	0	7.27	248	7-61	7/1	30.50	24	26
Hollies William Eric (CY 1955)	5.6.1912	16.4.1981	1934–1950	13	37	18*	0	5.28	44	7-50	5/0	30.27	2	
[2]Holioake Adam John (CY 2003)	5.9.1971		1997–1998	2	65	45	0	10.83	2	2-31	0/0	33.50	4	35
Holioake Benjamin Caine	11.11.1977	23.3.2002	1997–1998	2	44	28	0	11.00	4	2-105	0/0	49.75	2	20
Holmes Errol Reginald Thorold (CY 1936)	21.8.1905	3.9.1971	1934–1935	5	114	85*	0	16.28	2	1-10	0/0	38.00	4	
Holmes Percy (CY 1920)	25.11.1886	3.9.1971	1921–1932	7	357	88	0	27.46	—	—	—/—	—	3	
Hone Leland	30.1.1853	31.12.1896	1878	1	13	7	0	6.50	—	—	—/—	—	0	
Hopwood John Leonard	30.10.1903	15.6.1985	1934	2	12	8	0	6.00	0	0-16	0/0	—	0	
Hornby Albert Neilson ("Monkey")	10.2.1847	17.12.1925	1878–1884	3	21	9	0	3.50	1	1-0	0/0	0.00	0	
Horton Martin John	21.4.1934	3.4.2011	1959	2	60	58	0	30.00	2	2-24	0/0	29.50	0	
Howard Nigel David	18.5.1925	31.5.1979	1951	4	86	23	0	17.20	—	—	—/—	—	0	
Howell Henry	29.11.1890	9.7.1932	1920–1924	5	15	5	0	7.50	7	4-115	0/0	79.85	4	
Howorth Richard	26.4.1909	2.4.1980	1947–1947	5	145	45*	0	18.12	19	6-124	1/0	33.42	2	
Humphries Joseph	19.5.1876	7.5.1946	1907	3	44	16	0	8.80	—	—	—/—	—	7	
Hunter Joseph	3.8.1855	4.1.1891	1884	5	93	39*	0	18.60	—	—	—/—	—	8/3	
Hussain Nasser OBE (CY 2003)	28.3.1968		1989–2004	96	5,764	207	14	37.18	0	0-15	0/0	—	67	88
Hutchings Kenneth Lotherington (CY 1907)	7.12.1882	9.1.1916	1907–1909	7	341	126	1	28.41	1	1-5	0/0	81.00	9	
[1]Hutton Sir Leonard (CY 1938)	23.6.1916	6.9.1990	1937–1954	79	6,971	364	19	56.67	3	1-2	0/0	77.33	57	
Hutton Richard Anthony	6.9.1942		1971	5	219	81	0	36.50	9	3-72	0/0	28.55	9	4
Iddon John	8.1.1902	17.4.1946	1934–1935	5	170	73	0	28.33	0	0-3	0/0	—		
Igglesden Alan Paul	8.10.1964		1989–1993	3	6	3*	0	3.00	6	2-91	0/0	54.83	1	
Ikin John Thomas	7.3.1918	15.9.1984	1946–1955	18	606	60	0	20.89	3	1-38	0/0	118.00	31	
Illingworth Raymond CBE (CY 1960)	8.6.1932		1958–1973	61	1,836	113	2	23.24	122	6-29	3/0	31.20	45	3
Illingworth Richard Keith	23.8.1963		1991–1995	9	128	28	0	18.28	19	4-96	0/0	32.36	5	25
Ilott Mark Christopher	27.8.1970		1993–1995	5	28	15	0	7.00	12	3-48	0/0	45.16	5	
Insole Douglas John CBE (CY 1956)	18.4.1926		1950–1957	9	408	110*	1	27.20	—	—	—/—	—	8	
Irani Ronald Charles	26.10.1971		1996–1999	3	86	41	0	17.20	3	1-22	0/0	37.33	2	31
Jackman Robin David (CY 1981)	13.8.1945		1980–1982	4	42	17	0	7.00	14	4-110	0/0	31.78	0	15
Jackson Sir Francis Stanley (CY 1894)	21.11.1870	9.3.1947	1893–1905	20	1,415	144*	5	48.79	24	5-52	1/0	33.29	10	
Jackson Herbert Leslie (CY 1959)	7.9.1921	25.4.2007	1949–1961	2	15	8	0	15.00	7	2-26	0/0	22.14	0	
James Stephen Peter	7.9.1967		1998	2	71	36	0	17.75	—	—	—/—	—		
Jameson John Alexander	30.6.1941		1971–1973	4	214	82	0	26.75	1	1-17	0/0	17.00	1	3
Jardine Douglas Robert (CY 1928)	23.10.1900	18.6.1958	1928–1933	22	1,296	127	1	48.00	0	0-10	0/0	—	26	
Jarvis Paul William	29.6.1965		1987–1992	9	132	29*	0	10.15	21	4-107	0/0	45.95	2	16

	Born	Died	Tests	Test Career	Runs	HS	100s	Avge	Wts	BB	5/10	Avge	Ct/St	O/T
Jenkins, Roland Oliver (CY 1950)	24.11.1918	22.7.1995	9	1948–1952	198	39	0	18.00	32	5-116	1/0	34.31	4	–
Jessop, Gilbert Laird (CY 1898)	19.5.1874	11.5.1955	18	1899–1912	569	104	1	21.88	10	4-68	0/0	35.40	11	–
Johnson, Richard Leonard	29.12.1974	–	3	2003–2003	59	26	0	14.75	16	6-33	2/0	17.18	0	10
Jones, Arthur Owen	16.8.1872	21.12.1914	12	1899–1909	291	34	0	13.85	3	3-73	0/0	44.33	15	–
Jones, Geraint Owen MBE	14.7.1976	–	34	2003–2006	1,172	100	1	23.91	–	–	–/–	–	128/5	49/2
Jones, Ivor Jeffrey	10.12.1941	–	15	1963–1967	38	16	0	4.75	44	6-118	1/0	40.20	4	–
Jones, Simon Philip MBE (CY 2006)	25.12.1978	–	18	2002–2005	205	44	0	15.76	59	6-53	3/0	28.23	4	8
Jordan, Christopher James	4.10.1988	–	8	2014–2014	180	35	0	18.00	21	4-18	0/0	35.80	14	24/9
Jupp, Henry	19.11.1841	8.4.1889	2	1876	68	63	0	17.00	0	–	–/–	–	2	–
Jupp, Vallance William Crisp (CY 1928)	27.3.1891	9.7.1960	8	1921–1928	208	38	0	17.33	28	4-37	0/0	22.00	5	–
Keeton, William Walter (CY 1940)	30.4.1905	10.10.1980	2	1934–1939	57	25	0	14.25	0	–	–/–	–	0	–
Kennedy, Alexander Stuart (CY 1933)	24.1.1891	15.11.1959	5	1922	93	41*	0	15.50	31	5-76	2/0	19.32	5	–
Kenyon, Donald	15.5.1924	12.11.1996	8	1951–1955	192	87	0	12.80	0	–	–/–	–	5	–
Kerrigan, Simon Christopher	10.5.1989	–	1	2013	1	1*	0	–	0	0-53	0/0	–	–	–
Key, Robert William Trevor (CY 2005)	12.5.1979	–	15	2002–2004	775	221	1	31.00	0	–	–/–	–	11	5/1
Khan, Amjad	14.10.1980	–	1	2008	–	–	–	–	1	1-111	0/0	122.00	2	–
Killick, *Rev.* Edgar Thomas	9.5.1907	18.5.1953	2	1929	81	31	0	20.25	0	–	–/–	–	2	–
Kilner, Roy (CY 1924)	17.10.1890	5.4.1928	9	1924–1926	233	74	0	33.28	24	4-51	0/0	30.58	6	–
King, John Herbert	16.4.1871	18.11.1946	1	1909	64	60	0	32.00	1	1-99	0/0	99.00	1	–
Kinneir, Septimus Paul (CY 1912)	13.5.1871	16.10.1928	1	1911	52	30	0	26.00	0	–	–/–	–	–	–
Kirtley, Robert James	10.1.1975	–	4	2003–2003	32	12	0	5.33	19	6-34	1/0	29.52	1	11/1
Knight, Albert Ernest (CY 1904)	8.10.1872	25.4.1946	3	1903	81	70*	0	16.20	0	–	–/–	–	3	–
Knight, Barry Rolfe	18.2.1938	–	29	1961–1969	812	127	2	26.19	70	4-38	0/0	31.75	14	–
Knight, Donald John (CY 1915)	12.5.1894	5.1.1960	2	1921	54	27	0	13.50	–	–	–/–	–	–	–
Knight, Nicholas Christopher	28.11.1969	–	17	1995–2001	719	113	3	23.96	0	–	–/–	–	26	100
Knott, Alan Philip Eric (CY 1970)	9.4.1946	–	95	1967–1981	4,389	135	5	32.75	–	–	–/–	–	250/19	20
Knox, Neville Alexander (CY 1907)	10.10.1884	3.3.1935	2	1907	24	8*	0	8.00	3	2-39	0/0	35.00	0	–
Laker, James Charles (CY 1952)	9.2.1922	23.4.1986	46	1947–1958	676	63	0	14.08	193	10-53	9/3	21.24	12	–
Lamb, Allan Joseph (CY 1981)	20.6.1954	–	79	1982–1992	4,656	142	14	36.09	1	1-6	0/0	23.00	75	122
Langridge, James (CY 1932)	10.7.1906	10.9.1966	8	1933–1946	242	70	0	26.88	19	7-56	0/0	21.73	6	–
Larkins, Wayne	22.11.1953	–	13	1979–1990	493	64	0	20.54	0	–	–/–	–	8	25
Larter, John David Frederick	24.4.1940	–	10	1962–1965	16	10	0	3.20	37	5-57	2/0	25.43	5	–
Larwood, Harold MBE (CY 1927)	14.11.1904	22.7.1995	21	1926–1932	485	98	0	19.40	78	6-32	4/1	28.35	15	–
Lathwell, Mark Nicholas	26.12.1971	–	2	1993	78	33	0	19.50	0	–	–/–	–	0	–
Lawrence, David Valentine ("Syd")	28.11.1964	17.4.2011	5	1988–1991	60	34	0	10.00	18	5-106	1/0	37.55	0	–
Leadbeater, Edric	15.8.1927	–	2	1951	40	38	0	20.00	2	1-38	0/0	109.00	3	1

Name	Born	Died	Tests	Test Career	Runs	HS	Avge	100s	Wkts	Avge	BB	5/10	Ct/St	O/T
Lee Henry William	26.11.1890	21.4.1981	1	1930	19	18	9.50	0				-/-	0	
Lees Walter Scott (CY 1906)	25.12.1875	10.9.1924	5	1905	66	25*	11.00	0	26	17.96	6-78	2/0	2	
Legge Geoffrey Bevington	26.1.1903	21.11.1940	5	1927–1929	299	196	49.83	1	0		0-34	0/0	1	
Leslie Charles Frederick Henry	8.12.1861	12.2.1921	4	1882	106	54	15.14	0	4		4-31	0/0		
Lever John Kenneth MBE (CY 1979)	24.2.1949		21	1976–1986	306	53	11.76	0	73	26.72	7-46	3/1	11	22
Lever Peter	17.9.1940		17	1970–1975	350	88*	21.87	0	41	36.80	6-38	2/0	11	10
Leveson Gower Sir Henry Dudley Gresham	8.5.1873	1.2.1954	3	1909	95	31	23.75	0				-/-	1	
Levett William Howard Vincent ("Hopper")	25.1.1908	1.12.1995	1	1933	7	5	7.00	0				-/-	3	
Lewis Anthony Robert CBE	6.7.1938		9	1972–1973	457	125	32.64	1				-/-	0	
Lewis Clairmonte Christopher	14.2.1968		32	1990–1996	1,105	117	23.02	1	93	37.52	6-111	3/0	25	53
Lewis Jonathan	26.8.1975		1	2006	27	20	13.50	0	3	40.66	3-68	0/0	0	13/2
Leyland Maurice (CY 1929)	20.7.1900	1.1.1967	41	1928–1938	2,764	187	46.06	9	6	97.50	3-91	0/0	13	
Lilley Arthur Frederick Augustus ("Dick") (CY 1897)	28.11.1866	17.11.1929	35	1896–1909	903	84	20.52	0	1	23.00	1-23	0/0	70/22	
Lillywhite James	23.2.1842	25.10.1929	2	1876	16	10	8.00	0	8	15.75	4-70	1/0	1	
Lloyd David	18.3.1947		9	1974–1974	552	214*	42.46	1	0		0-4	-/-	11	8
Lloyd Timothy Andrew	5.11.1956		1	1984	10	10*	–	0	0			-/-	0	3
Loader Peter James (CY 1958)	25.10.1929	15.3.2011	13	1954–1958	76	17	5.84	0	39	22.51	6-36	1/0	2	
Lock Graham Anthony Richard (CY 1954)	5.7.1929	30.3.1995	49	1952–1967	742	89	13.74	0	174	25.58	7-35	9/3	59	
Lockwood William Henry (CY 1899)	25.3.1868	26.4.1932	12	1893–1902	231	52*	17.76	0	43	20.53	7-71	5/1	4	
Lohmann George Alfred (CY 1889)	2.6.1865	1.12.1901	18	1886–1896	213	62*	8.87	0	112	10.75	9-28	9/5	28	
Lowson Frank Anderson	1.7.1925	8.9.1984	7	1951–1955	245	68	18.84	0				-/-	5	
Lucas Alfred Perry	20.2.1857	12.10.1923	5	1878–1884	157	55	19.62	0	0		0-23	0/0	11	
Luckhurst Brian William (CY 1971)	5.2.1939	1.3.2005	21	1970–1974	1,298	131	36.05	2	1	32.00	1-9	0/0	14	3
Lyth Adam (CY 2015)	25.9.1987		7	2015	265	107	20.38	1	0			-/-	8	
Lyttelton Hon. Alfred	7.2.1857	5.7.1913	4	1880–1884	94	31	15.66	0	4	4.75	4-19	0/0	2	
Macaulay George Gibson (CY 1924)	7.12.1897	13.12.1940	8	1922–1933	112	76	18.66	0	24	27.58	5-64	1/0	5	
MacBryan John Crawford William (CY 1925)	22.7.1892	14.7.1983	1	1924	–	–	–	0				-/-	0	
McCague Martin John	24.5.1969		3	1993–1994	21	11	4.20	0	6	65.00	4-121	0/0	5	
McConnon James Edward	21.6.1922	26.1.2003	2	1954	18	11	9.00	0	4	18.50	3-19	0/0	4	
McGahey Charles Percy (CY 1902)	12.2.1871	10.1.1935	2	1901	38	18	9.50	0				-/-	3	
McGrath Anthony	6.10.1975		4	2003	201	81	40.20	0	4	14.00	3-16	0/0	3	14
MacGregor Gregor (CY 1891)	31.8.1869	20.8.1919	8	1890–1893	96	31	12.00	0				-/-	14/3	
McIntyre Arthur John William (CY 1958)	14.5.1918	26.12.2009	3	1950–1955	19	7	3.16	0				-/-	8	
MacKinnon Francis Alexander	9.4.1848	27.2.1947	1	1878	5	5	2.50	0	0			-/-	0	
MacLaren Archibald Campbell (CY 1895)	1.12.1871	17.11.1944	35	1894–1909	1,931	140	33.87	5				-/-	29	

	Born	Died	Tests	Test Career	Runs	HS	100s	Avge	Wkts	BB	5/10	Avge	Ct/St	OT
McMaster Joseph Emile Patrick	16.3.1861	7.6.1929	1	1888	0	0	0	0.00					0	8/4
Maddy Darren Lee	23.5.1974		3	1999–1999	46	24	0	11.50	0	0-40	0/0	–	4	26/4
Mahmood Sajid Iqbal	21.12.1981		8	2006–2006	81	34	0	8.10	20	4-22	0/0	38.10	0	
Makepeace Joseph William Henry	22.8.1881	19.12.1952	4	1920	279	117	1	34.87			–/–		0	
Malcolm Devon Eugene (CY 1995)	22.2.1963		40	1989–1997	236	29	0	6.05	128	9-57	5/2	37.09	7	10
Mallender Neil Alan	13.8.1961		2	1992	8	4	0	2.66	10	5-50	1/0	21.50	0	
†Mann Francis George CBE	6.9.1917	8.8.2001	7	1948–1949	376	136*	1	37.60	–		–/–		3	
†Mann Francis Thomas	3.3.1888	6.10.1964	5	1922	281	84	0	35.12	–		–/–		4	
Marks Victor James	25.6.1955		6	1982–1983	249	83	0	27.66	11	3-78	0/0	44.00	1	34
Marriott Charles Stowell ("Father")	14.9.1895	13.10.1966	1	1933	0	0	0	0.00	11	6-59	2/1	8.72	2	
Martin Frederick (CY 1892)	12.10.1861	13.12.1921	2	1890–1891	14	13	0	7.00	14	6-50	2/1	10.07	2	
Martin John William	16.2.1917	4.1.1987	1	1947	26	26	0	13.00	10	1-111	0/0	129.00	0	
Martin Peter James	15.11.1968		8	1995–1997	115	29	0	8.84	17	4-60	0/0	34.11	6	20
Mason John Richard (CY 1898)	26.3.1874	15.10.1958	5	1897	129	32	0	12.90	2	1-8	0/0	74.50	5	
Matthews Austin David George	3.5.1904	29.7.1977	1	1937	2	2*	0	–	2	1-13	0/0	32.50	1	
May Peter Barker Howard CBE (CY 1952)	31.12.1929	27.12.1994	66	1951–1961	4,537	285*	13	46.77	–		–/–		42	
Maynard Matthew Peter (CY 1998)	21.3.1966		4	1988–1993	87	35	0	10.87	–		–/–		3	14
Mead Charles Philip (CY 1912)	9.3.1887	26.3.1958	17	1911–1928	1,185	182*	4	49.37	–		–/–		4	
Mead Walter (CY 1904)	1.4.1868	18.3.1954	1	1899	7	7	0	–	1	1-91	0/0	91.00	1	
Midwinter William Evans	19.6.1851	3.12.1890	4†	1881	95	36	0	13.57	10	4-81	0/0	27.20	5	
Milburn Colin ("Ollie") (CY 1967)	23.10.1941	28.2.1990	9	1966–1968	654	139	2	46.71	–		–/–		5	
Miller Audley Montague	19.10.1869	26.6.1959	1	1895	24	20*	0	–	–		–/–		0	
Miller Geoffrey OBE	8.9.1952		34	1976–1984	1,213	98*	0	25.80	60	5-44	1/0	30.98	17	25
Milligan Frank William	19.3.1870	31.3.1900	2	1898	58	38*	0	14.50	0	0-12	0/0	–	1	
Millman Geoffrey	2.10.1934	6.4.2005	6	1961–1962	60	32*	0	12.00	–		–/–		13/2	
Milton Clement Arthur (CY 1959)	10.3.1928	25.4.2007	6	1958–1959	204	104*	1	25.50	0	0-4	0/0	–	5	
Mitchell Arthur	13.9.1902	25.12.1976	6	1933–1936	298	72	0	29.80	0		–/–		9	
Mitchell Frank (CY 1902)	13.8.1872	11.10.1935	2‡	1898	88	41	0	22.00	–		–/–		2	
Mitchell Thomas Bignall	4.9.1902	27.1.1996	5	1932–1935	20	9	0	5.00	8	2-49	0/0	62.25	1	
Mitchell-Innes Norman Stewart ("Mandy")	7.9.1914	28.12.2006	1	1935	5	5	0	5.00	–		–/–		0	
Mold Arthur Webb (CY 1892)	27.5.1863	29.4.1921	3	1893	0	0*	0	0.00	7	3-44	0/0	33.42	1	
Moon Leonard James	9.2.1878	23.11.1916	4	1905	182	36	0	22.75	–		–/–		4	
Morgan Eoin Joseph Gerard (CY 2011)	10.9.1986		16	2010–2011	700	130	2	30.43	–		–/–		11	132‡/54
Morley Frederick	16.12.1850	28.9.1884	4	1880–1882	6	2*	0	1.50	16	5-56	1/0	18.50	4	
Morris Hugh	5.10.1963		3	1991	115	44	0	19.16	–		–/–		3	
Morris John Edward	1.4.1964		3	1990	71	32	0	23.66	–		–/–		3	8

	Born	Died	Tests	Test Career	Runs	HS	100s	Avge	Wkts	BB	5/10	Avge	Ct/St	O/T
Mortimore John Brian	14.5.1933	13.2.2014	9	1958–1964	243	73*	0	24.30	13	3-36	0/0	56.38	3	
Moss Alan Edward	14.11.1930		9	1953–1960	61	26	0	10.16	21	4-35	0/0	29.80	3	
Moxon Martyn Douglas (CY 1993)	4.5.1960		10	1986–1989	455	99	0	28.43	0	0-3	0/0	–	10	8
Mullally Alan David	12.7.1969		19	1996–2001	127	24	0	5.52	58	5-105	1/0	31.24	6	50
Munton Timothy Alan (CY 1995)	30.7.1965		2	1992	25	25*	0	25.00	4	2-22	0/0	50.00	0	
Murdoch William Lloyd	18.10.1854	18.2.1911	1†	1891	12	12	0	12.00	–	–	–/–	–	0/1	
Murray John Thomas MBE (CY 1967)	1.4.1935		21	1961–1967	506	112	1	22.00	–	–	–/–	–	52/3	
Newham William	12.12.1860	26.6.1944	1	1887	26	17	0	13.00	–	–	–/–	–	1	
Newport Philip John	11.10.1962		3	1988–1990	110	40*	0	27.50	10	4-87	0/0	41.70	2	
Nichols Morris Stanley (CY 1934)	6.10.1900	26.1.1961	14	1930–1939	355	78*	0	29.58	41	6-35	2/0	28.09	11	
Oakman Alan Stanley Myles	20.4.1930		2	1956	14	10	0	7.00	0	0-21	0/0	–	7	
O'Brien Sir Timothy Carew	5.11.1861	9.12.1948	5	1884–1895	59	20	0	7.37	–	–	–/–	–	4	
O'Connor Jack	6.11.1897	22.2.1977	4	1929–1930	153	51	0	21.85	1	1-31	0/0	72.00	2	
Old Christopher Middleton (CY 1979)	22.12.1948		46	1972–1981	845	65	0	14.82	143	7-50	4/0	28.11	22	32
Oldfield Norman	5.5.1911	19.4.1996	1	1939	99	80	0	49.50	–	–	–/–	–	0	
Onions Graham (CY 2010)	9.9.1982		9	2009–2012	30	17*	0	10.00	32	5-38	1/0	29.90	0	4
Ormond James	20.8.1977		2	2001	38	18	0	12.66	2	1-70	0/0	92.50	0	
Padgett Douglas Ernest Vernon	20.7.1934		2	1960	51	31	0	12.75	0	0-8	0/0	–	5	
Paine George Alfred Edward (CY 1935)	11.6.1908	30.3.1978	4	1934	97	49	0	16.16	17	5-168	1/0	27.47	2	
Palairet Lionel Charles Hamilton (CY 1893)	27.5.1870	27.3.1933	2	1902	49	20	0	12.25	–	–	–/–	–	0	
Palmer Charles Henry CBE	15.5.1919	31.3.2005	1	1953	22	22	0	11.00	0	0-15	0/0	–	0	
Palmer Kenneth Ernest MBE	22.4.1937		1	1964	10	10	0	10.00	1	1-113	0/0	189.00	4	
Panesar Mudhsuden Singh ("Monty") (CY 2007)	25.4.1982		50	2006–2013	220	26	0	4.88	167	6-37	12/2	34.71	10	26/1
Parfitt Peter Howard (CY 1963)	8.12.1936		37	1961–1972	1,882	131*	7	40.91	12	2-5	0/0	47.83	42	
Parker Charles Warrington Leonard (CY 1923)	14.10.1882	11.7.1959	1	1921	3	3*	0	–	2	2-32	0/0	16.00	5	
Parker Paul William Giles	15.1.1956		1	1981	13	13	0	6.50	–	–	–/–	–	0	
Parkhouse William Gilbert Anthony	12.10.1925	10.8.2000	7	1950–1959	373	78	0	28.69	–	–	–/–	–	3	
Parkin Cecil Harry (CY 1924)	18.2.1886	15.6.1943	10	1920–1924	160	36	0	12.30	32	5-38	2/0	35.25	3	
[1]Parks James Horace (CY 1938)	12.5.1903	21.11.1980	1	1937	29	22	0	14.50	3	2-26	0/0	12.00	3	
[1]Parks James Michael (CY 1968)	21.10.1931		46	1954–1967	1,962	108*	2	32.16	1	1-43	0/0	51.00	103/11	
[1]Pataudi Iftikhar Ali Khan, Nawab of (CY 1932)	16.3.1910	5.1.1952	3†	1932–1934	144	102	1	28.80	–	–	–/–	–	2	
Patel Minal Mahesh	7.7.1970		2	1996	45	27	0	22.50	2	1-101	0/0	180.00	0	
[1]Patel Samit Rohit	30.11.1984		6	2011–2015	151	42	0	16.77	7	2-27	0/0	60.14	3	36/18
[2]Pattinson Darren John	2.8.1979		1	2008	21	13	0	10.50	2	2-95	0/0	48.00	0	
Paynter Edward (CY 1938)	5.11.1901	5.2.1979	20	1931–1939	1,540	243	4	59.23	–	–	–/–	–	7	
Peate Edmund	2.3.1855	11.3.1900	9	1881–1886	70	13	0	11.66	31	6-85	2/0	22.03	2	

	Born	Died	Tests	Test Career	Runs	HS	100s	Avge	Wkts	BB	5/10	Avge	Ct/St	O/T
Peebles Ian Alexander Ross (CY 1931)	20.1.1908	27.2.1980	13	1927-1931	98	26	0	10.88	45	6-63	3/0	30.91	5	
Peel Robert (CY 1889)	12.2.1857	12.8.1941	20	1884-1896	427	83	0	14.72	101	7-31	5/1	16.98	17	
Penn Frank	7.3.1851	26.12.1916	1	1880	50	27*	0	50.00	0	0-2	0/0	–	–	
Perks Reginald Thomas David	4.10.1911	22.11.1977	2	1938-1939	3	2*	0	–	11	5-100	2/0	32.27	–	
Philipson Hylton	8.6.1866	4.12.1935	5	1891-1894	63	30	0	9.00	0	–	–/–	–	8/3	
Pietersen Kevin Peter MBE (CY 2006)	27.6.1980		104	2005-2013	8,181	227	23	47.28	10	3-52	0/0	88.60	62	134‡/37
Pigott Anthony Charles Shackleton	4.6.1958		2	1983	12	8*	0	12.00	2	2-75	0/0	37.50	0	–
Pilling Richard (CY 1891)	11.8.1855	28.3.1891	8	1881-1888	91	23	0	7.58	–	–	–/–	–	10/4	
Place Winston	7.12.1914	25.1.2002	3	1947	144	107	1	28.80	–	–	–/–	–	0	
Plunkett Liam Edward	6.4.1985		13	2005-2014	238	55*	0	15.86	41	5-64	1/0	37.46	3	34/3
Pocock Patrick Ian	24.9.1946		25	1967-1984	206	33	0	6.24	67	6-79	3/0	44.41	15	1
Pollard Richard	19.6.1912	16.12.1985	4	1946-1948	13	10*	0	13.00	15	5-24	1/0	25.20	3	
Poole Cyril John	13.3.1921	11.2.1996	3	1951	161	69*	0	40.25	0	0-9	0/0	–	1	
Pope George Henry	27.1.1911	29.10.1993	1	1947	8	8*	0	–	1	1-49	0/0	85.00	0	
Pougher Arthur Dick	19.4.1865	20.5.1926	1	1891	17	17	0	17.00	3	3-26	0/0	8.66	2	
Price John Sidney Ernest	22.7.1937		15	1963-1972	66	32	0	7.33	40	5-73	1/0	35.02	7	
Price Wilfred Frederick Frank	25.4.1902	13.1.1969	1	1938	6	6	0	3.00	0	0-0	0/0	–	2	
Prideaux Roger Malcolm	31.7.1939		3	1968-1968	102	64	0	20.40	0	0-0	0/0	–		
Pringle Derek Raymond	18.9.1958		30	1982-1992	695	63	0	15.10	70	5-95	3/0	35.97	10	44
Prior Matthew James (CY 2010)	26.2.1982		79	2007-2014	4,099	131*	7	40.18	–	–	–/–	–	243/13	68/10
Pullar Geoffrey (CY 1960)	1.8.1935	26.12.2014	28	1959-1962	1,974	175	4	43.86	1	1-1	0/0	37.00	2	
Quaife William George (CY 1902)	17.3.1872	13.10.1951	7	1899-1901	228	68	0	19.00	0	0-6	0/0	–	4	
Radford Neal Victor (CY 1986)	7.6.1957		3	1986-1987	21	12*	0	7.00	4	2-131	0/0	87.75	0	6
Radley Clive Thornton MBE (CY 1979)	13.5.1944		8	1977-1978	481	158	2	48.10	–	–	–/–	–	4	4
Ramprakash Mark Ravin MBE (CY 2007)	5.9.1969		52	1991-2001	2,350	154	2	27.32	4	1-2	0/0	119.25	39	18
Randall Derek William (CY 1980)	24.2.1951		47	1976-1984	2,470	174	7	33.37	0	0-1	0/0	–	31	49
Ranjitsinhji Kumar Shri (CY 1897)	10.9.1872	2.4.1933	15	1896-1902	989	175	2	44.95	1	1-23	0/0	39.00	13	
Rankin William Boyd	5.7.1984		1	2013	13	13	0	6.50	1	1-47	0/0	81.00	0	7/2‡
Rashid Adil Usman	17.2.1988		3	2015	103	61	0	20.60	8	5-64	1/0	69.50	0	20/10
Read Christopher Mark Wells (CY 2011)	10.8.1978		15	1999-2006	360	55	0	18.94	–	–	–/–	–	48/6	36/1
Read Holcombe Douglas ("Hopper")	28.1.1910	5.1.2000	1	1935				–	6	4-136	0/0	33.33	–	
Read John Maurice (CY 1890)	9.2.1859	17.2.1929	17	1882-1893	461	57	0	17.07	0	0-27	0/0	–	8	
Read Walter William (CY 1893)	23.11.1855	6.1.1907	18	1882-1893	720	117	1	27.69	0	1-4	0/0	–	16	
Reeve Dermot Alexander OBE (CY 1996)	2.4.1963		3	1991	124	59	0	24.80	2	1-4	0/0	30.00	1	29
Relf Albert Edward (CY 1914)	26.6.1874	26.3.1937	13	1903-1913	416	63	0	23.11	25	5-85	1/0	24.96	14	
Rhodes Harold James	22.7.1936		2	1959	0	0*	0	–	9	4-50	0/0	27.11	0	

Name	Born	Died	Tests	Test Career	Runs	HS	100s	Avge	Wkts	BB	5/10	Avge	Ct/St	O/T
Rhodes Steven John (CY 1995)	17.6.1964		11	1994–1994	294	65*	0	24.50			—/—		46/3	9
Rhodes Wilfred (CY 1899)	29.10.1877	8.7.1973	58	1899–1929	2,325	179	2	30.19	127	8-68	6/1	26.96	60	22
Richards Clifton James ("Jack")	10.8.1934		8	1986–1988	285	133	1	21.92			—/—		20/1	
[2]Richardson Derek Walter ("Dick")	3.11.1934		1	1957	33	33	0	33.00			—/—		1	
[2]Richardson Peter Edward (CY 1957)	4.7.1931		34	1956–1963	2,061	126	5	37.47	3	2-10	0/0	16.00	6	
[2]Richardson Thomas (CY 1897)	11.8.1870	2.7.1912	14	1893–1897	177	25*	0	11.06	88	8-94	11/4	25.22	5	
Richmond Thomas Leonard	23.6.1890	29.12.1957	1	1921	6	4	0	3.00	2	2-69	0/0	43.00	1	
Ridgway Frederick	10.8.1923	26.9.2015	5	1951	49	24	0	8.16	7	4-83	0/0	54.14	3	
Robertson John David Benbow (CY 1948)	22.2.1917	12.10.1996	11	1947–1951	881	133	2	46.36	2	2-17	0/0	29.00	6	
Robins Robert Walter Vivian (CY 1930)	3.6.1906	12.12.1968	19	1929–1937	612	108	1	26.60	64	6-32	1/0	27.46	12	26
Robinson Robert Timothy (CY 1986)	21.11.1958		29	1984–1989	1,601	175	4	36.38	0	0-0	0/0		8	
Robson Samuel David	1.7.1989		7	2014	336	127	0	30.54			—/—		5	
Roope Graham Richard James	12.7.1946	26.11.2006	21	1972–1978	860	77	0	30.71	0	0-2	0/0		35	8
Root Charles Frederick	16.4.1890	20.1.1954	3	1926			0		8	4-84	0/0	24.25	0	
Root Joseph Edward (CY 2014)	30.12.1990		39	2012–2015	3,406	200*	9	54.93	12	2-9	0/0	51.08	41	63/12
Rose Brian Charles (CY 1980)	4.6.1950		9	1977–1980	358	70	0	25.57			—/—		4	2
Royle Vernon Peter Fanshawe Archer	29.1.1854	21.5.1929	1	1878	21	18	0	10.50			—/—		2	
Rumsey Frederick Edward	4.12.1935		5	1964–1965	30	21*	0	15.00	17	4-25	0/0	27.11	0	
Russell Albert Charles ("Jack") (CY 1923)	7.10.1887	23.3.1961	10	1920–1922	910	140	5	56.87			—/—		8	
Russell Robert Charles ("Jack") (CY 1990)	15.8.1963		54	1988–1997	1,897	128*	2	27.10			—/—		153/12	40
Russell William Eric	3.7.1936		10	1961–1967	362	70	0	21.29	0	0-19	0/0		4	
Saggers Martin John	23.5.1972		3	2003–2004	1	1	0	0.33	7	2-29	0/0	35.28	0	
Salisbury Ian David Kenneth (CY 1993)	21.11.1970		15	1992–2000	368	50	0	16.72	20	4-163	0/0	76.95	5	4
Sandham Andrew (CY 1923)	6.7.1890	20.4.1982	14	1921–1929	879	325	2	38.21			—/—		4	
Schofield Christopher Paul	6.10.1978		2	2000	67	57	0	22.33	0	0-73	0/0		0	0/4
Schultz Sandford Spence	29.8.1857	18.12.1937	1	1878	20	20	0	20.00	1	1-16	0/0	26.00	0	
Scotton William Henry	15.1.1856	9.7.1893	15	1881–1886	510	90	1	22.17	0	0-20	0/0		2	
Selby John	1.7.1849	11.3.1894	6	1876–1881	256	70	0	23.27			—/—		1	
Selvey Michael Walter William	25.4.1948		3	1976–1976	15	5*	0	7.50	6	4-41	0/0	57.16	0	
Shackleton Derek (CY 1959)	12.8.1924	28.9.2007	7	1950–1963	113	42	0	18.83	18	4-72	0/0	42.66	1	
Shah Owais Alam	22.10.1978		6	2005–2008	269	88	0	26.90	0	0-12	0/0		2	71/17
Shahzad Ajmal	27.7.1985		1	2010	5	5	0	5.00	4	3-45	0/0	15.75	1	11/3
Sharp John	15.2.1878	28.1.1938	3	1909	188	105	1	47.00	3	3-67	0/0	37.00	2	
Sharpe John William (CY 1892)	9.12.1866	19.6.1936	3	1890–1891	44	26	0	22.00	11	6-84	1/0	27.72	2	
Sharpe Philip John (CY 1963)	27.12.1936	19.5.2014	12	1963–1969	786	111	1	46.23			—/—		17	
Shaw Alfred	29.8.1842	16.1.1907	7	1876–1881	111	40	0	10.09	12	5-38	1/0	23.75	4	

	Born	Died	Tests	Test Career	Runs	HS	100s	Avge	Wks	BB	Avge	5/10	Ct/St	OIT
Sheppard Rt Rev. Lord [David Stuart] (CY 1953)	6.3.1929	5.3.2005	22	1950–1962	1,172	119	3	37.80	–	–	–	–/–	12	–
Sherwin Mordecai (CY 1891)	26.2.1851	3.7.1910	3	1886–1888	30	21*	0	15.00	0	0-2	–	–/–	5/2	–
Shrewsbury Arthur (CY 1890)	11.4.1856	19.5.1903	23	1881–1893	1,277	164	3	35.47	0	–	–	0/0	29	–
Shuter John	9.2.1855	5.7.1920	1	1888	28	28	0	28.00	–	–	–	–/–	1	–
Shuttleworth Kenneth	13.11.1944		5	1970–1971	46	21	0	7.66	12	5-47	35.58	1/0	1	–
Sidebottom Arnold	1.4.1954		1	1985	2	2	0	2.00	1	1-65	65.00	0/0	–	–
[1] Sidebottom Ryan Jay (CY 2008)	15.1.1978		22	2001–2009	313	31	0	15.65	79	7-47	28.24	5/1	5	25/18
Silverwood Christopher Eric Wilfred	5.3.1975		6	1996–2002	29	10	0	7.25	11	5-91	40.36	1/0	2	7
Simpson Reginald Thomas (CY 1950)	27.2.1920	24.11.2013	27	1948–1954	1,401	156*	4	33.35	2	2-4	11.00	0/0	5	–
Simpson-Hayward George Hayward Thomas	7.6.1875	2.10.1936	5	1909	105	29*	0	15.00	23	6-43	18.26	2/0	1	–
Sims James Morton	13.5.1903	27.4.1973	4	1935–1936	16	12	0	4.00	11	5-73	43.63	1/0	6	–
Sinfield Reginald Albert	24.12.1900	17.3.1988	1	1938	6	6	0	6.00	2	1-51	61.50	0/0	1	–
Slack Wilfred Norris	12.12.1954	15.11.1989	3	1985–1986	81	52	0	13.50	0	–	–	–/–	3	2
Smailes Thomas Francis	27.3.1910	1.12.1970	1	1946	25	25	0	25.00	3	3-44	20.66	0/0	–	–
Small Gladstone Cleophas CBE.	18.10.1961		17	1986–1990	263	59	0	15.47	55	5-48	34.01	2/0	3	53
Smith Alan Christopher CBE.	25.10.1936		6	1962	118	69*	0	29.50	0	–	–	–/–	20	–
Smith Andrew Michael	1.10.1967		1	1997	4	4*	0	4.00	0	0-89	–	0/0	–	–
Smith Cedric Ivan James (CY 1935)	25.8.1906	8.2.1979	5	1934–1937	102	27	0	10.20	15	5-16	26.20	1/0	–	–
Smith Sir Charles Aubrey	21.7.1863	20.12.1948	1	1888	3	3	0	3.00	7	5-19	8.71	1/0	–	–
[2] Smith Christopher Lyall (CY 1984)	15.10.1958		8	1983–1986	392	91	0	30.15	3	2-31	13.00	0/0	4	4
Smith David Mark	9.1.1956		2	1985	80	47	0	20.00	–	–	–	–/–	1	2
Smith David Robert	5.10.1934	17.12.2003	5	1961	38	34	0	9.50	6	2-60	59.83	0/0	2	–
Smith Denis (CY 1935)	24.1.1907	12.9.1979	2	1935	128	57	0	32.00	1	1-12	97.00	0/0	1	–
Smith Donald Victor	14.6.1923		3	1957	25	16*	0	8.33	–	–	–	–/–	–	–
Smith Edward Thomas	19.7.1977		3	2003	87	64	0	17.40	–	–	–	–/–	5	–
Smith Ernest James ("Tiger")	6.2.1886	31.8.1979	11	1911–1913	113	22	0	8.69	–	–	–	–/–	17/3	–
Smith Harry	21.5.1891	12.11.1937	1	1928	7	7	0	7.00	–	–	–	–/–	1	–
[2] Smith Michael John Knight OBE (CY 1960)	30.6.1933		50	1958–1972	2,278	121	3	31.63	1	1-10	128.00	0/0	53	–
Smith Robin Arnold (CY 1990)	13.9.1963		62	1988–1995	4,236	175	9	43.67	0	0-6	–	0/0	39	71
Smith Thomas Peter Bromley (CY 1947)	30.10.1908	4.8.1967	4	1946–1946	33	24	0	6.60	3	2-172	106.33	0/0	0	–
Smithson Gerald Arthur	1.11.1926	6.9.1970	2	1947	70	35	0	23.33	–	–	–	–/–	–	–
Snow John Augustine (CY 1973)	13.10.1941		49	1965–1976	772	73	0	13.54	202	7-40	26.66	8/1	16	9
Southerton James	16.11.1827	16.6.1880	2	1876	7	6	0	3.50	7	4-46	15.28	0/0	2	–
Spooner Reginald Herbert (CY 1905)	21.10.1880	2.10.1961	10	1905–1912	481	119	1	32.06	0	–	–	–/–	4	–
Spooner Richard Thompson	30.12.1919	20.12.1997	7	1951–1955	354	92	0	27.23	–	–	–	–/–	10/2	–
Stanyforth Ronald Thomas	30.5.1892	20.2.1964	4	1927	13	6*	0	2.60	–	–	–	–/–	7/2	–

	Born	Died	Tests	Test Career	Runs	HS	100s	Avge	Wkts	BB	5/10	Avge	Ct/St	OIT
Staples Samuel James (CY 1929)	18.9.1892	4.6.1950	3	1927	65	39	0	13.00	15	3-50	0/0	29.00	0	
Statham John Brian CBE (CY 1955)	17.6.1930	10.6.2000	70	1950–1965	675	38	0	11.44	252	7-39	9/1	24.84	28	1
Steel Allan Gibson	24.9.1858	15.6.1914	13	1880–1888	600	148	2	35.29	29	3-27	0/0	20.86	5	
Steele David Stanley OBE (CY 1976)	29.9.1941		8	1975–1976	673	106	1	42.06	2	1-1	0/0	19.50	7	
Stephenson John Patrick	14.3.1965		1	1989	36	25	0	18.00	0	—	–/–	—	0	
Stevens Greville Thomas Scott (CY 1918)	7.1.1901	19.9.1970	10	1922–1929	263	69	0	15.47	20	5-90	2/1	32.40	9	
Stevenson Graham Barry	16.12.1955		2	1979–1980	28	27*	0	28.00	5	3-111	0/0	36.60	0	4
Stewart Alec James OBE (CY 1993)	8.4.1963		133	1989–2003	8,463	190	15	39.54	0	0-5	0/0	—	263/14	170
Stewart Michael James OBE (CY 1958)	16.9.1932		8	1962–1963	385	87	0	35.00	0	—	–/–	—	6	
Stoddart Andrew Ernest (CY 1893)	11.3.1863	3.4.1915	16	1887–1897	996	173	2	35.57	2	1-10	0/0	47.00	6	
Stokes Benjamin Andrew (CY 2016)	4.6.1991		23	2013–2015	1,383	258	3	33.73	57	6-36	2/0	38.07	15	34/9
Storer William (CY 1899)	25.11.1867	28.2.1912	6	1897–1899	215	51	0	19.54	2	1-24	0/0	54.00	11	
Strauss Andrew John OBE (CY 2005)	2.3.1977		100	2004–2012	7,037	177	21	40.91	0	—	–/–	—	121	127/4
Street George Benjamin	6.12.1889	24.4.1924	1	1922	11	7*	0	11.00	0	—	–/–	—	0/1	
Strudwick Herbert (CY 1912)	28.1.1880	14.2.1970	28	1909–1926	230	24	0	7.93	0	—	–/–	—	61/12	
Studd Charles Thomas	2.12.1860	16.7.1931	5	1882–1882	160	48	0	20.00	3	2-35	0/0	32.66	5	
Studd George Brown	20.10.1859	13.2.1945	4	1882	31	9*	0	4.42	0	—	–/–	—	8	
Subba Row Raman CBE (CY 1961)	29.1.1932		13	1958–1961	984	137	3	46.85	0	0-2	0/0	—	5	
Such Peter Mark	12.6.1964		11	1993–1999	67	14*	0	6.09	37	6-67	2/0	33.56	4	
Sugg Frank Howe (CY 1890)	11.1.1862	29.5.1933	2	1888	55	31	0	27.50	0	—	–/–	—	0	
Sutcliffe Herbert (CY 1920)	24.11.1894	22.1.1978	54	1924–1935	4,555	194	16	60.73	0	—	–/–	—	23	
Swann Graeme Peter (CY 2010)	24.3.1979		60	2008–2013	1,370	85	0	22.09	255	6-65	17/3	29.96	54	79/39
Swetman Roy	25.10.1933		11	1958–1959	254	65	0	16.93	0	—	–/–	—	24/2	
Tate Frederick William	24.7.1867	24.2.1943	1	1902	9	5*	0	9.00	2	2-7	0/0	25.50	2	
Tate Maurice William (CY 1924)	30.5.1895	18.5.1956	39	1924–1935	1,198	100*	1	25.48	155	6-42	7/1	26.16	11	
Tattersall Roy	17.8.1922	9.12.2011	16	1950–1954	50	10*	0	5.00	58	7-52	4/1	26.08	8	
Tavaré Christopher James	27.10.1954		31	1980–1989	1,755	149	2	32.50	0	0-0	0/0	—	20	
Taylor James William Arthur	6.1.1990		7	2012–2015	312	76	0	26.00	0	—	–/–	—	6	29
Taylor Jonathan Paul	8.8.1964		2	1992–1994	34	17*	0	17.00	3	1-18	0/0	52.00	0	27
Taylor Kenneth	21.8.1935		3	1959–1964	57	24	0	11.40	0	0-6	0/0	—	1	1
Taylor Leslie Brian	25.10.1953		2	1985		1*	0	—	4	2-34	0/0	44.50	0	
Taylor Robert William MBE (CY 1977)	17.7.1941		57	1970–1983	1,156	97	0	16.28	0	0-6	0/0	—	167/7	2
Tennyson *Lord* Lionel Hallam (CY 1914)	7.11.1889	6.6.1951	9	1913–1921	345	74*	0	31.36	0	0-1	0/0	—	6	27
Terry Vivian Paul	14.1.1959		2	1984	16	8	0	5.33	0	—	–/–	—	2	
Thomas John Gregory	12.8.1960		5	1985–1986	83	31*	0	13.83	10	4-70	0/0	50.40	5	
Thompson George Joseph (CY 1906)	27.10.1877	3.3.1943	6	1909–1909	273	63	0	30.33	23	4-50	0/0	27.73	5	3

	Born	Died	Tests	Test Career	Runs	HS	100s	Avge	Wts	BB	5/10	Avge	Ct/St	O/T
Thomson Norman Ian	23.1.1929		5	1964	69	39	0	23.00	9	2-55	0/0	63.11	3	
Thorpe Graham Paul MBE (CY 1998)	1.8.1969		100	1993–2005	6,744	200*	16	44.66	0	0-0	0/0		105	82
Titmus Frederick John MBE (CY 1963)	24.11.1932	23.3.2011	53	1955–1974	1,449	84*	0	22.29	153	7-79	7/0	32.22	35	2
Tolchard Roger William	15.6.1946		4	1976	129	67	0	25.80			–/–		5	1
[1]**Townsend** Charles Lucas (CY 1899)	7.11.1876	17.10.1958	2	1899	51	38	0	17.00	3	3-50	0/0	25.00	1	
[1]**Townsend** David Charles Humphery	20.4.1912	17.1.1997	3	1934	77	36	0	12.83	0	0-9	0/0		2	
[1]**Townsend** Leslie Fletcher (CY 1934)	8.6.1903	17.2.1993	4	1929–1933	97	40	0	16.16	6	2-22	0/0	34.16	2	
Tredwell James Cullum	27.2.1982		2	2009–2014	45	37	0	22.50	11	4-47	2/0	29.18	2	45/17
Tremlett Christopher Timothy	2.9.1981		12	2007–2013	113	25*	0	10.27	53	6-48	0/0	27.00	4	15/1
[4]**Tremlett** Maurice Fletcher	5.7.1923	30.7.1984	3	1947	20	18*	0	6.66	4	2-98	0/0	56.50	0	
Trescothick Marcus Edward MBE (CY 2005)	25.12.1975		76	2000–2006	5,825	219	14	43.79	1	1-34	0/0	155.00	95	123/3
[2]**Trott** Albert Edwin (CY 1899)	6.2.1873	30.7.1914	2‡	1898	23	16	0	5.75	17	5-49	1/0	11.64	4	
Trott Ian Jonathan Leonard (CY 2011)	22.4.1981		52	2009–2014	3,835	226	9	44.08	5	1-5	0/0	80.00	29	68/7
Trueman Frederick Sewards OBE (CY 1953)	6.2.1931	1.7.2006	67	1952–1965	981	39*	0	13.81	307	8-31	17/3	21.57	64	
Tudor Alex Jeremy	23.10.1977		10	1998–2002	229	99*	0	19.08	28	5-44	1/0	34.39	3	3
Tufnell Neville Charsley	13.6.1887	3.8.1951	1	1909	14	14	0	14.00			–/–		0/1	
Tufnell Philip Clive Roderick	29.4.1966		42	1990–2001	153	22*	0	5.10	121	7-47	5/2	37.68	12	20
Turnbull Maurice Joseph Lawson (CY 1931)	16.3.1906	5.8.1944	9	1929–1936	224	61	0	20.36			–/–		1	
[2]**Tyldesley** [George] Ernest (CY 1920)	5.2.1889	5.5.1962	14	1921–1928	990	122	3	55.00	0	0-2	0/0		2	
[2]**Tyldesley** John Thomas (CY 1902)	22.11.1873	27.11.1930	31	1898–1909	1,661	138	4	30.75	0		0/0		16	
[4]**Tyldesley** Richard Knowles (CY 1925)	11.3.1897	17.9.1943	7	1924–1930	47	29	0	7.83	19	3-50	0/0	32.57	1	
Tylecote Edward Ferdinando Sutton	23.6.1849	15.3.1938	6	1882–1886	152	66	0	19.00			–/–		5/5	
Tyler Edwin James	13.10.1864	25.1.1917	1	1895	0	0	0	0.00	4	3-49	0/0	16.25		
Tyson Frank Holmes (CY 1956)	6.6.1930	27.9.2015	17	1954–1958	230	37*	0	10.95	76	7-27	4/1	18.56	4	
Udal Shaun David	18.3.1969		4	2005	109	33*	0	18.16	8	4-14	1/0	43.00		11
Ulyett George	21.10.1851	18.6.1898	25	1876–1890	949	149	1	24.33	50	7-36	1/0	20.40	19	
Underwood Derek Leslie MBE (CY 1969)	8.6.1945		86	1966–1981	937	45*	0	11.56	297	8-51	17/6	25.83	44	26
Valentine Bryan Herbert	17.1.1908	2.2.1983	7	1933–1938	454	136	2	64.85			–/–		2	
Vaughan Michael Paul OBE (CY 2003)	29.10.1974		82	1999–2008	5,719	197	18	41.44	6	2-71	0/0	93.50	42	86/2
Verity Hedley (CY 1932)	18.5.1905	31.7.1943	40	1931–1939	669	66*	0	20.90	144	8-43	5/2	24.37	30	
Vernon George Frederick	20.6.1856	10.8.1902	1	1882	14	11*	0	14.00			–/–		0	
Vine Joseph (CY 1906)	15.5.1875	25.4.1946	2	1911	46	36	0	46.00	0		0/0		0	
Voce William (CY 1933)	8.8.1909	6.6.1984	27	1929–1946	308	66	0	13.39	98	7-70	3/2	27.88	15	
Waddington Abraham	4.2.1893	28.10.1959	2	1920	16	7	0	4.00	1	1-35	0/0	119.00	1	
Wainwright Edward (CY 1894)	8.4.1865	28.10.1919	5	1893–1897	132	49	0	14.66	0	0-11	0/0		2	
Walker Peter Michael	17.2.1936		3	1960	128	52	0	32.00	0	0-8	0/0		5	

	Born	Died	Tests	Test Career	Runs	HS	100s	Avge	Wkts	BB	5/10	Avge	Ct/St	OIT
Walters Cyril Frederick (CY 1934)	28.8.1905	23.12.1992	11	1933–1934	784	102	1	52.26	–	–	–/–	–	6	–
Ward Alan	10.8.1947		5	1969–1976	40	21	0	8.00	14	4-61	0/0	32.35	3	–
Ward Albert (CY 1890)	21.11.1865	6.1.1939	7	1893–1894	487	117	1	37.46	–	–	–/–	–	1	–
Ward Ian James	30.9.1972		5	2001	129	39	0	16.12	–	–	–/–	–	1	–
Wardle John Henry (CY 1954)	8.1.1923	23.7.1985	28	1947–1957	653	66	0	19.78	102	7-36	5/1	20.39	12	4
Warner Sir Pelham Francis (CY 1904).	2.10.1873	30.1.1963	15	1898–1912	622	132*	1	23.92	–	–	–/–	–	3	–
Warr John James	16.7.1927		2	1950	4	4	0	1.00	1	1-76	0/0	281.00	0	–
Warren Arnold.	2.4.1875	3.9.1951	1	1905	7	7	0	7.00	6	5-57	1/0	18.83	1	–
Washbrook Cyril CBE (CY 1947).	6.12.1914	27.4.1999	37	1937–1956	2,569	195	6	42.81	1	1-25	0/0	33.00	12	–
Watkin Steven Llewellyn (CY 1994).	15.9.1964		3	1991–1993	25	13	0	5.00	11	4-65	0/0	27.72	1	–
Watkins Albert John ("Allan").	21.4.1922	3.8.2011	15	1948–1952	810	137*	2	40.50	11	3-20	0/0	50.36	17	–
Watkinson Michael	1.8.1961		4	1995–1995	167	82*	0	33.40	10	3-64	0/0	34.80	1	–
Watson Willie (CY 1954).	7.3.1920	23.4.2004	23	1951–1958	879	116	2	25.85	–	–	–/–	–	8	–
Webbe Alexander Josiah.	16.11.1855	19.2.1941	1	1878	4	4	0	2.00	–	–	–/–	–	2	–
Wellard Arthur William (CY 1936).	8.4.1902	31.12.1980	2	1937–1938	47	38	0	11.75	7	4-81	0/0	33.85	2	–
Wells Alan Peter	2.10.1961		1	1995	3	3*	0	3.00	–	–	–/–	–	0	1
Wharton Alan	30.4.1923	26.8.1993	1	1949	20	13	0	10.00	–	–	–/–	–	0	–
Whitaker John James (CY 1987).	5.5.1962		1	1986	11	11	0	11.00	–	–	–/–	–	1	2
White Craig	16.12.1969		30	1994–2002	1,052	121	1	24.46	59	5-32	3/0	37.62	14	51
White David William ("Butch")	14.12.1935	1.8.2008	2	1961	0	0	0	0.00	4	3-65	0/0	29.75	0	–
White John Cornish (CY 1929).	19.2.1891	2.5.1961	15	1921–1930	239	29	0	18.38	49	8-126	3/1	32.26	6	–
Whysall William Wilfrid (CY 1925)	31.10.1887	11.11.1930	4	1924–1930	209	76	0	29.85	0	0-9	0/0	–	7	–
Wilkinson Leonard Litton	5.11.1916	3.9.2002	3	1938	3	2	0	3.00	7	2-12	0/0	38.71	0	–
Willey Peter	6.12.1949		26	1976–1986	1,184	102*	2	26.90	7	2-73	0/0	65.14	3	26
Williams Neil FitzGerald.	2.7.1962	27.3.2006	1	1990	38	38*	0	38.00	2	2-148	0/0	74.00	0	–
Williams Robert George Dylan MBE (CY 1978).	30.5.1949		90	1970–1984	840	28*	0	11.50	325	8-43	16/0	25.20	39	64
[2] Wilson Clement Eustace Macro.	15.5.1875	8.2.1944	2	1898	42	18	0	14.00	–	–	–/–	–	1	–
Wilson Donald	7.8.1937	21.7.2012	6	1963–1970	75	42	0	12.50	11	2-17	0/0	42.36	1	13
[2] Wilson Evelyn Rockley	25.3.1879	21.7.1957	1	1920	10	5	0	5.00	3	2-28	0/0	12.00	0	–
Woakes Christopher Roger.	2.3.1989		6	2013–2015	129	26*	0	21.50	8	3-30	0/0	63.75	3	7/1
Wood Arthur (CY 1939).	25.8.1898	1.4.1973	4	1938–1939	80	53	0	20.00	–	–	–/–	–	10/1	–
Wood Barry	26.12.1942		12	1972–1978	454	90	0	21.61	0	0-2	0/0	–	6	–
Wood George Edward Charles	22.8.1893	18.3.1971	3	1924	7	6	0	3.50	–	–	–/–	–	5/1	–
Wood Henry (CY 1891).	14.12.1853	30.4.1919	4	1888–1891	204	134*	0	68.00	–	–	–/–	–	2/1	–
Wood Mark Andrew	11.11.1990		8	2015–2015	185	32*	0	20.55	25	3-39	0/0	34.40	2	–
Wood Reginald	7.3.1860	6.1.1915	1	1886	6	6	0	3.00	–	–	–/–	–	0	–

Name	Born	Died	Tests	Test Career	Runs	HS	100s	Avge	Wkts	BB	5/10	Avge	Ct/St	O/T
Woods Samuel Moses James (CY 1889)	13.4.1867	30.4.1931	3†	1895	122	53	0	30.50	5	3-28	0/0	25.80	4	
Woolley Frank Edward (CY 1911)	27.5.1887	18.10.1978	64	1909–1934	3,283	154	5	36.07	83	7-76	4/1	33.91	64	6
Woolmer Robert Andrew (CY 1976)	14.5.1948	18.3.2007	19	1975–1981	1,059	149	3	33.09	4	1-8	0/0	74.75	10	
Worthington Thomas Stanley (CY 1937)	21.8.1905	31.8.1973	9	1929–1936	321	128	1	29.18	8	2-19	0/0	39.50	8	
Wright Charles William	27.5.1863	10.11.1936	3	1895	125	71	0	31.25	–	–	–/–	–	0	
Wright Douglas Vivian Parson (CY 1940)	21.8.1914	13.11.1998	34	1938–1950	289	45	0	11.11	108	7-105	6/1	39.11	10	
Wyatt Robert Elliott Storey (CY 1930)	2.5.1901	20.4.1995	40	1927–1936	1,839	149	2	31.70	18	3-4	0/0	35.66	16	
Wynyard Edward George	1.4.1861	30.10.1936	3	1896–1905	72	30	0	12.00	0	0-2	0/0	–	1	
Yardley Norman Walter Dransfield (CY 1948)	19.3.1915	3.10.1989	20	1938–1950	812	99	0	25.37	21	3-67	0/0	33.66	14	
Young Harding Isaac ("Sailor")	5.2.1876	12.12.1964	2	1899	43	43	0	21.50	12	4-30	0/0	21.83	1	
Young John Albert	14.10.1912	5.2.1993	8	1947–1949	28	10*	0	5.60	17	3-65	0/0	44.52	5	
Young Richard Alfred	16.9.1885	1.7.1968	2	1907	27	13	0	6.75	–	–	–/–	–	6	

AUSTRALIA (443 players)

Name	Born	Died	Tests	Test Career	Runs	HS	100s	Avge	Wkts	BB	5/10	Avge	Ct/St	O/T
a'Beckett Edward Lambert	11.8.1907	2.6.1989	4	1928–1931	143	41	0	20.42	3	1-41	0/0	105.66	4	
Agar Ashton Charles	14.10.1993		2	2013	130	98	0	32.50	2	2-82	0/0	124.00	0	2
Alderman Terence Michael (CY 1982)	12.6.1956		41	1981–1990	203	26*	0	6.54	170	6-47	14/1	27.15	27	65
Alexander George	22.4.1851	6.11.1930	2	1880–1884	52	33	0	13.00	2	2-69	0/0	46.50	2	
Alexander Harry Houston	9.6.1905	15.4.1993	1	1932	17	17*	0	17.00	1	1-129	0/0	154.00	0	
Allan Francis Erskine	2.12.1849	9.2.1917	1	1878	5	5	0	5.00	4	2-30	0/0	20.00	0	
Allen Peter John	31.12.1935		1	1965	–	–	–	–	2	2-58	0/0	41.50	0	
Allen Reginald Charles	2.7.1858	2.5.1952	1	1886	44	30	0	22.00	–	–	–/–	–	2	
Andrews Thomas James Edwin	26.8.1890	28.1.1970	16	1921–1926	592	94	0	26.90	1	1-23	0/0	116.00	12	
Angel Jo	22.4.1968		4	1992–1994	35	11	0	5.83	10	3-54	0/0	46.30	1	3
[2] **Archer** Kenneth Alan	17.1.1928		5	1950–1951	234	48	0	26.00	–	–	–/–	–	0	
[2] **Archer** Ronald Graham	25.10.1933	27.5.2007	19	1952–1956	713	128	1	24.58	48	5-53	1/0	27.45	20	3
Armstrong Warwick Windridge (CY 1903)	22.5.1879	13.7.1947	50	1901–1921	2,863	159*	6	38.68	87	6-35	3/0	33.59	44	
Badcock Clayvel Lindsay ("Jack")	10.4.1914	13.12.1982	7	1936–1938	160	118	1	14.54	–	–	–/–	–	3	
Bailey George John	7.9.1982		5	2013	183	53	0	26.14	–	–	–/–	–	10	63/28
[2] **Bannerman** Alexander Chalmers	21.3.1854	19.9.1924	28	1878–1893	1,108	94	0	23.08	4	3-111	0/0	40.75	21	
[2] **Bannerman** Charles	23.7.1851	20.8.1930	3	1876–1878	239	165*	1	59.75	–	–	–/–	–	0	
Bardsley Warren (CY 1910)	6.12.1882	20.1.1954	41	1909–1926	2,469	193*	6	40.47	–	–	–/–	–	12	

	Born	Died	Tests	Test Career	Runs	HS	100s	Avge	Wkts	BB	5/10	Avge	Ct/St	O/T
Barnes Sidney George.	5.6.1916	16.12.1973	13	1938–1948	1,072	234	3	63.05	4	2-25	–/–	54.50	14	
Barnet Benjamin Arthur.	23.3.1908		4	1938	195	57	0	27.85	–	–	–/–	–	3/2	
Barrett John Edward.	15.10.1866	6.2.1916	2	1890	80	67*	0	26.66	–	–	–/–	–	1	
Beard Graeme Robert	19.8.1950		3	1979	114	49	0	22.80	1	1-26	0/0	109.00	0	2
Beer Michael Anthony.	9.6.1984		2	2010–2011	6	2*	0	3.00	3	2-56	0/0	59.33	1	
Benaud John	11.5.1944		3	1972	223	142	1	44.60	0	2-12	0/0	6.00	0	
Benaud Richard OBE (CY 1962) . .	6.10.1930	10.4.2015	63	1952–1964	2,201	122	3	24.45	248	7-72	16/1	27.03	65	
Bennett Murray John.	6.10.1956		3	1984–1985	71	23	0	23.66	6	3-79	0/0	54.16	5	8
Bevan Michael Gwyl.	8.5.1970		18	1994–1997	785	91	0	29.07	29	6-82	1/1	24.24	8	232
Bichel Andrew John	27.8.1970		19	1996–2003	355	71	0	16.90	58	5-60	1/0	32.24	16	67
Bird Jackson Munro	11.12.1986		3	2012–2013	7	6*	0	7.00	13	4-41	1/0	23.30	0	
Blackham John McCarthy (CY 1891).	11.5.1854	28.12.1932	35	1876–1894	800	74	0	15.68	–	–	–/–	–	37/24	
Blackie Donald Dearness	5.4.1882	18.4.1955	3	1928	24	11*	0	8.00	14	6-94	1/0	31.71	2	
Blewett Gregory Scott.	28.10.1971		46	1994–1999	2,552	214	4	34.02	14	2-9	0/0	51.42	45	32
Bollinger Douglas Erwin	24.7.1981		12	2008–2010	54	21	0	7.71	50	5-28	2/0	25.92	2	39/9
Bonnor George John.	25.2.1855	27.6.1912	17	1880–1888	512	128	1	17.06	2	1-5	0/0	42.00	16	
Boon David Clarence MBE (CY 1994).	29.12.1960		107	1984–1995	7,422	200	21	43.65	0	0-0	0/0	–	99	181
Booth Brian Charles MBE	19.10.1933		29	1961–1965	1,773	169	5	42.21	3	2-33	0/0	48.66	17	
Border Allan Robert (CY 1982) . .	27.7.1955		156	1978–1993	11,174	205	27	50.56	39	7-46	2/1	39.10	156	273
Boyle Henry Frederick.	10.12.1847	21.11.1907	12	1878–1884	153	36*	0	12.75	32	6-42	1/0	20.03	10	
Bracken Nathan Wade.	12.9.1977		5	2003–2005	70	37	0	17.50	12	4-48	0/0	42.08	2	116/19
Bradman Sir Donald George AC (CY 1931).	27.8.1908	25.2.2001	52	1928–1948	6,996	334	29	99.94	2	1-8	0/0	36.00	32	
Bright Raymond James	13.7.1954		25	1977–1986	445	33	0	14.35	53	7-87	4/1	41.13	13	11
Bromley Ernest Harvey.	2.9.1912	1.2.1967	2	1932–1934	38	26	0	9.50	–	0-19	0/0	–	2	
Brown William Alfred (CY 1939). .	31.7.1912	16.3.2008	22	1934–1948	1,592	206*	4	46.82	–	–	–/–	–	14	
Bruce William	22.5.1864	3.8.1925	14	1884–1894	702	80	0	29.25	12	3-88	0/0	36.66	12	
Burge Peter John Parnell (CY 1965).	17.5.1932	5.10.2001	42	1954–1965	2,290	181	4	38.16	–	–	–/–	–	23	
Burke James Wallace (CY 1957). .	12.6.1930	2.2.1979	24	1950–1958	1,280	189	3	34.59	8	4-37	0/0	28.75	18	
Burn Edwin James Kenneth (K.E.). .	17.9.1862	20.7.1956	2	1890	41	19	0	10.25	–	–	–/–	–	0	
Burns Joseph Antony	6.9.1989		8	2014–2015	603	129	2	43.07	–	–	–/–	9	6	
Burton Frederick John.	2.11.1865	25.8.1929	2	1886–1887	4	2*	0	2.00	–	–	–/–	–	1/1	
Callaway Sydney Thomas	6.2.1868	25.11.1923	3	1891–1894	87	41	0	17.40	6	5-37	1/0	23.66	1	
Callen Ian Wayne	2.5.1955		1	1977	26	22*	0	–	6	3-83	0/0	31.83	1	5
Campbell Greg Dale.	10.3.1964		4	1989–1989	10	6*	0	2.50	13	3-79	0/0	38.69	1	12
Carkeek William ("Barlow"). . . .	17.10.1878	20.2.1937	6	1912	16	6*	0	5.33	–	–	–/–	–	6/2	
Carlson Phillip Henry	8.8.1951		2	1978	23	21	0	5.75	2	2-41	0/0	49.50	2	4

	Born	Died	Tests	Test Career	Runs	HS	100s	Avge	Wkts	BB	5/10	Avge	Ct/St	O/T
Carter Hanson	15.3.1878	8.6.1948	28	1907-1921	873	72	0	22.97					44/21	
Casson Beau	7.12.1982		1	2007	10	10	0	10.00	3	3-86	0/0	43.00	2	
[2,4] Chappell Gregory Stephen MBE (CY 1973)	7.8.1948		87	1970-1983	7,110	247*	24	53.86	47	5-61	1/0	40.70	122	74
[2,4] Chappell Ian Michael (CY 1976)	26.9.1943		75	1964-1979	5,345	196	14	42.42	20	2-21	0/0	65.80	105	16
[2,4] Chappell Trevor Martin	21.10.1952		3	1981	79	27	0	15.80					2	20
Charlton Percie Chater	9.4.1867	30.9.1954	2	1890	29	11	0	7.25	3	3-18	0/0	8.00	0	
Chipperfield Arthur Gordon	17.11.1905	29.7.1987	14	1934-1938	552	109	1	32.47	5	3-91	0/0	87.40	15	
Clark Stuart Rupert	28.9.1975		24	2005-2009	248	39	0	10.78	94	5-32	2/0	23.86	4	39/9
Clark Wayne Maxwell	19.9.1953		10	1977-1978	98	33	0	5.76	44	4-46	0/0	28.75	6	
Clarke Michael John (CY 2010)	2.4.1981		115§	2004-2015	8,643	329*	28	49.10	31	6-9	0/0	38.19	134	245/34
Colley David John	15.3.1947		3	1972	84	54	0	21.00	6	3-83	0/0	52.00	1	1
Collins Herbert Leslie	21.1.1888	28.5.1959	19	1920-1926	1,352	203	4	45.06	4	2-47	0/0	63.00	13	
Coningham Arthur	14.7.1863	13.6.1939	1	1894	13	10	0	6.50	2	2-17	0/0	38.00	0	
Connolly Alan Norman	29.6.1939		29	1963-1970	260	37	0	10.40	102	6-47	4/0	29.22	17	
Cook Simon Hewitt	29.1.1972		2	1997	18	15	0		7	5-39	1/0	25.11	0	
Cooper Bransby Beauchamp	15.3.1844	7.8.1914	1	1876	18	15	0	9.00					2	
[5] Cooper William Henry	11.9.1849	5.4.1939	2	1881-1884	13	7	0	6.50	9	6-120	1/0	37.83	1	
Copeland Trent Aaron	14.3.1986		3	2011	39	23*	0	13.00	6	2-24	0/0	28.50	2	
Corling Grahame Edward	13.7.1941		5	1964	5	3	0	1.66	12	4-60	0/0	37.25	14	
Cosier Gary John	25.4.1953		18	1975-1978	897	168	2	28.93	5	2-26	0/0	68.20	14	9
Cottam John Thomas	5.9.1867	30.1.1897	1	1886	4	3	0	2.00					0	
Cotter Albert ("Tibby")	3.12.1883	31.10.1917	21	1903-1911	457	45	0	13.05	89	7-148	7/0	28.64	8	
Coulthard George	1.8.1856	22.10.1883	1	1881	6	6*	0						0	
Cowan Edward James McKenzie	16.6.1982		18	2011-2013	1,001	136	1	31.28					24	
Cowper Robert Maskew	5.10.1940		27	1964-1968	2,061	307	5	46.84	36	4-48	0/0	31.63	21	
Craig Ian David	12.6.1935	16.11.2014	11	1952-1957	358	53	0	19.88					2	
Crawford William Patrick Anthony	3.8.1933	21.1.2009	4	1956-1957	53	34	0	17.66	7	3-28	0/0	15.28	2	
Cullen Daniel James	10.4.1984		1	2005	15	13*	0	15.00	1	1-25	0/0	54.00	0	5
Cummins Patrick James	8.5.1993		2	2011	6	6*	0	2.00	7	6-79	1/0	16.71	2	18/15
Dale Adam Craig	30.12.1968		2	1997-1998	5	5	0	2.50	6	3-71	0/0	31.16	1	30
Darling Joseph (CY 1900)	21.11.1870	2.1.1946	34	1894-1905	1,657	178	3	28.56					27	
Darling Leonard Stuart	14.8.1909	24.6.1992	12	1932-1936	474	85	0	27.88	0	0-3	0/0		8	
Darling Warwick Maxwell	1.5.1957		14	1977-1979	697	91	0	26.80					5	18
Davidson Alan Keith MBE (CY 1962)	14.6.1929		44	1953-1962	1,328	80	0	24.59	186	7-93	14/2	20.53	42	
Davis Ian Charles	25.6.1953		15	1973-1977	692	105	1	26.61					9	3

§ Clarke's figures include 44 runs and one catch for Australia v the ICC World XI in the Super Series Test in 2005-06.

Name	Born	Died	Tests	Test Career	Runs	HS	100s	Avge	Wkts	BB	5/10	Avge	Ct/St	O/T
Davis Simon Peter	8.11.1959	–	1	1985	0	0	0	0.00	–	–	–/–	–	0	39
De Courcy James Harry	18.4.1927	20.6.2000	3	1953	81	41	0	16.20	–	–	–/–	–	3	
Dell Anthony Ross	6.8.1947		2	1970–1973	6	3*	0		6	3-65	0/0	26.66	0	
Dodemaide Anthony Ian Christopher	5.10.1963		10	1987–1992	202	50	0	22.44	34	6-58	1/0	28.02	6	24
Doherty Xavier John	22.12.1982		4	2010–2012	51	18*	0	12.75	7	3-131	0/0	78.28	2	60/11
Donnan Henry	12.11.1864	13.8.1956	5	1891–1896	75	15	0	8.33	0	0-22	0/0		2	
Doolan Alexander James	29.11.1985		4	2013–2014	191	89	0	23.87	–	–	–/–	–	4	
Dooland Bruce (CY 1955)	1.11.1923	8.9.1980	3	1946–1947	76	29	0	19.00	9	4-69	0/0	46.55	3	
Duff Reginald Alexander	17.8.1878	13.12.1911	22	1901–1905	1,317	146	2	35.59	4	2-43	0/0	21.25	14	
Duncan John Ross Frederick	25.3.1944		1	1970	3	3	0	3.00	0	0-30	0/0		0	
Dyer Gregory Charles	16.3.1959		6	1986–1987	131	60	0	21.83	–	–	–/–	–	22/2	23
Dymock Geoffrey	21.7.1945		21	1973–1979	236	31*	0	9.44	78	7-67	5/1	27.12	10	15
Dyson John	11.6.1954		30	1977–1984	1,359	127*	2	26.64	–	–	–/–	–	10	29
Eady Charles John	29.10.1870	20.12.1945	2	1896–1901	20	10*	0	6.66	7	3-30	0/0	16.00	0	
Eastwood Kenneth Humphrey	23.11.1935		1	1970	5	5	0	2.50	1	1-21	0/0	21.00	0	
Ebeling Hans Irvine	1.1.1905	12.1.1980	1	1934	43	41	0	21.50	3	3-74	0/0	29.66	0	
Edwards John Dunlop	12.6.1860	31.7.1911	3	1888	48	26	0	9.60	–	–	–/–	–	1	
Edwards Ross	1.12.1942		20	1972–1975	1,171	170*	2	40.37	0	0-20	0/0		7	9
Edwards Walter John	23.12.1949		3	1974	68	30	0	11.33	–	–	–/–	–	14	
Elliott Matthew Thomas Gray (CY 1998)	28.9.1971		21	1996–2004	1,172	199	3	33.48	0	0-0	0/0		14	1
Emery Philip Allen	25.6.1964		1	1994	8	8*	0		–	–	–/–	–	5/1	1
Emery Sidney Hand	15.10.1885	7.1.1967	4	1912	6	5	0	3.00	5	2-46	0/0	49.80	2	1
Evans Edwin	26.3.1849	2.7.1921	6	1881–1886	82	33	0	10.25	7	3-64	0/0	47.42	5	
Fairfax Alan George	16.6.1906	17.5.1955	10	1928–1930	410	65	0	51.25	21	4-31	0/0	30.71	15	
Faulkner James Peter	29.4.1990		1	2013	45	23	0	22.50	6	4-51	0/0	16.33	0	44/11
Favell Leslie Ernest MBE	6.10.1929	14.6.1987	19	1954–1960	757	101	1	27.03	–	–	–/–	–	9	
Ferris John James (CY 1889)	21.5.1867	17.11.1900	8†	1886–1890	98	20*	0	8.16	48	5-26	4/0	14.25	4	
Fingleton John Henry Webb OBE	28.4.1908	22.11.1981	18	1931–1938	1,189	136	5	42.46	–	–	–/–	–	13	
Fleetwood-Smith Leslie O'Brien ("Chuck")	30.3.1908	16.3.1971	10	1935–1938	54	16*	0	9.00	42	6-110	2/1	37.38	0	
Fleming Damien William	24.4.1970		20	1994–2000	305	71*	0	19.06	75	5-30	3/0	25.89	9	88
Francis Bruce Colin	18.2.1948		3	1972	52	27	0	10.40	–	–	–/–	–	5	
Freeman Eric Walter	13.7.1944		11	1967–1969	345	76	0	19.16	34	4-52	0/0	33.17	5	
Freer Frederick Alfred William	4.12.1915	2.11.1998	1	1946	28	28*	0		3	2-49	0/0	24.66	0	
Gannon John Bryant ('Sam')	8.2.1947		3	1977	3	3*	0	3.00	11	4-77	0/0	32.81	0	
Garrett Thomas William	26.7.1858	6.8.1943	19	1876–1887	339	51*	0	12.55	36	6-78	2/0	26.94	3	
Gaunt Ronald Arthur	26.2.1934	30.3.2012	3	1957–1963	6	3	0	3.00	7	3-53	0/0	44.28	1	

	Born	Died	Tests	Test Career	Runs	HS	100s	Avge	Wkts	BB	5/10	Avge	Ct/St	O/T
Gehrs Donald Raeburn Algernon	29.11.1880	25.6.1953	6	1903–1910	221	67	0	20.09	–	–	–	–	6	
George Peter Robert	16.10.1986		1	2010	2	2	0	1.00	2	2-48	0/0	38.50		
[2] Giffen George (CY 1894)	27.3.1859	29.11.1927	31	1881–1896	1,238	161	1	23.55	103	7-117	7/1	27.09	24	
[2] Giffen Walter Frank	20.9.1861	28.6.1949	3	1886–1891	11	11	0	1.83	–	–	–	–	1	
Gilbert David Robert	29.12.1960		9	1985–1986	57	15	0	7.12	16	3-48	0/0	52.68	0	14
Gilchrist Adam Craig (CY 2002) §	14.11.1971		96	1999–2007	5,570	204*	17	47.60	–	–	–	–	379/37	287/13
Gillespie Jason Neil (CY 2002)	19.4.1975		71	1996–2005	1,218	201*	1	18.73	259	7-37	8/0	26.13	27	97/1
Gilmour Gary John	26.6.1951	10.6.2014	15	1973–1976	483	101	0	23.00	54	6-85	3/0	26.03	8	5
Gleeson John William	14.3.1938		29	1967–1972	395	45	0	10.39	93	5-61	3/0	36.20	17	
Graham Henry	22.11.1870	7.2.1911	6	1893–1896	301	107	2	30.10	–	–	–	–	3	
[2] Gregory David William	15.4.1845	4.8.1919	3	1876	60	43	0	20.00	0	0-9	0/0	–	0	
[1,2] Gregory Edward James	29.5.1839	22.4.1899	1	1876	11	11	0	5.50	–	–	–	–	0	
[1,2] Gregory Jack Morrison (CY 1922)	14.8.1895	7.8.1973	24	1920–1928	1,146	119	2	36.96	85	7-69	4/0	31.15	37	
Gregory Ross Gerald	28.2.1916	10.6.1942	2	1936	153	80	0	51.00	0	0-14	0/0	–	1	
[2] Gregory Sydney Edward (CY 1897)	14.4.1870	31.7.1929	58	1890–1912	2,282	201	4	24.53	0	0-4	0/0	–	25	
Grimmett Clarence Victor (CY 1931)	25.12.1891	2.5.1980	37	1924–1935	557	50	0	13.92	216	7-40	21/7	24.21	17	
Groube Thomas Underwood	2.9.1857	5.8.1927	1	1880	11	11	0	5.50	–	–	–	–	0	
Grout Arthur Theodore Wallace	30.3.1927	9.11.1968	51	1957–1965	890	74	0	15.08	–	–	–	–	163/24	
Guest Colin Ernest John	7.10.1937		1	1962	11	11	0	11.00	0	0-8	0/0	–	0	
Haddin Bradley James	23.10.1977		66	2007–2015	3,265	169	4	32.97	–	–	–	–	262/8	126/34
Hamence Ronald Arthur	25.11.1915	24.3.2010	3	1946–1947	81	30*	0	27.00	–	–	–	–	2	
Hammond Jeffrey Roy	19.4.1950		5	1972	28	19	0	9.33	15	4-38	0/0	32.53	2	
Harris Ryan James (CY 2014)	11.10.1979		27	2009–2014	603	74	0	21.53	113	7-117	5/0	23.52	13	21/3
Harry John	1.8.1857	27.10.1919	1	1894	8	6	0	4.00	–	–	–	–	1	
Hartigan Roger Joseph	12.12.1879	7.6.1958	2	1907	170	116	1	42.50	–	–	–	–	2	
Hartkopf Albert Ernst Victor	28.12.1889	20.5.1968	1	1924	80	80	0	40.00	1	1-120	0/0	134.00	0	
[2] Harvey Mervyn Roye	29.4.1918	18.3.1995	1	1946	43	31	0	21.50	–	–	–	–	0	
[2] Harvey Robert Neil MBE (CY 1954)	8.10.1928		79	1947–1962	6,149	205	21	48.41	3	1-8	0/0	40.00	64	
Hassett Arthur Lindsay MBE (CY 1949)	28.8.1913	16.6.1993	43	1938–1953	3,073	198*	10	46.56	0	0-1	0/0	–	30	
Hastings John Wayne	4.11.1985		1	2012	52	32	0	26.00	1	1-51	0/0	153.00		13/3
Hauritz Nathan Michael	18.10.1981		17	2004–2010	426	75	0	25.05	63	5-53	2/0	34.98	3	58/3
Hawke Neil James Napier	27.6.1939	25.12.2000	27	1962–1968	365	45*	0	16.59	91	7-105	6/1	29.41	9	
Hayden Matthew Lawrence (CY 2003) §	29.10.1971		103	1993–2008	8,625	380	30	50.73	0	0-7	0/0	–	128	161/9
Hazlewood Josh Reginald	8.1.1991		15	2014–2015	154	39	0	25.66	61	6-70	3/0	24.54	6	13/4

§ Gilchrist's figures include 95 runs, five catches and two stumpings, and Hayden's 188 runs and three catches, for Australia v the ICC World XI in the Super Series Test in 2005-06.

	Born	Died	Tests	Test Career	Runs	HS	100s	Avge	Wkts	BB	5/10	Avge	Ct/St	O/T
Hazlitt Gervys Rignold	4.9.1888	30.10.1915	9	1907–1912	89	34*	0	11.12	23	7-25	1/0	27.08	4	
Healy Ian Andrew (CY 1994)	30.4.1964		119	1988–1999	4,356	161*	4	27.39	–	–	–/–	–	366/29	168
Hendry Hunter Scott Thomas Laurie ("Stork")	24.5.1895	16.12.1988	11	1921–1928	335	112	1	20.93	16	3-36	0/0	40.00	10	
Henriques Moises Constantino	1.2.1987		3	2012	156	81*	0	31.20	2	1-48	0/0	77.50	1	6/4
Hibbert Paul Anthony	23.7.1952	27.11.2008	1	1977	15	13	0	7.50	–	–	–/–	–	–	
Higgs James Donald	11.7.1950		22	1977–1980	111	16	0	5.55	66	7-143	2/0	31.16	3	
Hilditch Andrew Mark Jefferson	20.5.1956		18	1978–1985	1,073	119	2	31.55	–	–	–/–	–	13	8
Hilfenhaus Benjamin William	15.3.1983		27	2008–2012	355	56*	0	13.65	99	5-75	2/0	28.50	7	25/7
Hill Clement (CY 1900)	18.3.1877	5.9.1945	49	1896–1911	3,412	191	7	39.21	–	–	–/–	–	33	
Hill John Charles	25.6.1923	11.8.1974	3	1953–1954	21	8*	0	7.00	8	3-35	0/0	34.12	2	
Hoare Desmond Edward	19.10.1934		1	1960	35	35	0	17.50	2	2-68	0/0	78.00	2	
Hodge Bradley John	29.12.1974		6	2005–2007	503	203*	1	55.88	0	0-8	0/0	–	9	25/15
Hodges John Robart	11.8.1855	d unknown	2	1876	10	8	0	3.33	6	2-7	0/0	14.00	0	
Hogan Tom George	23.9.1956		7	1982–1983	205	42*	0	18.63	15	5-66	1/0	47.06	2	16
Hogg George Bradley	6.2.1971		7	1996–2007	186	79	0	26.57	17	2-40	0/0	54.88	7	123/15
Hogg Rodney Malcolm	5.3.1951		38	1978–1984	439	52	0	9.75	123	6-74	6/2	28.47	7	71
Hohns Trevor Victor	23.1.1954		7	1988–1989	136	40	0	22.66	17	3-59	0/0	34.11	3	
Hole Graeme Blake	6.1.1931	14.2.1990	18	1950–1954	789	66	0	25.45	3	1-9	0/0	42.00	21	
Holland Robert George	19.10.1946		11	1984–1985	35	10	0	3.18	34	6-54	3/2	39.76	5	2
Hookes David William	3.5.1955	19.1.2004	23	1976–1985	1,306	143*	1	34.36	1	1-4	0/0	41.00	12	39
Hopkins Albert John Young	3.5.1874	25.4.1931	20	1901–1909	509	43	0	16.41	26	4-81	0/0	26.76	11	
Horan Thomas Patrick	8.3.1854	16.4.1916	15	1876–1884	471	124	1	18.84	11	6-40	1/0	13.00	6	
Hordern Herbert Vivian MBE	10.2.1883	17.6.1938	7	1910–1911	254	50	0	23.09	46	7-90	5/2	23.36	6	
Hornibrook Percival Mitchell	27.7.1899	25.8.1976	6	1928–1930	60	26	0	10.00	17	7-92	1/0	39.05	7	
Howell William Peter	29.12.1869	14.7.1940	18	1897–1903	158	35	0	7.52	49	5-81	1/0	28.71	12	
Hughes Kimberley John (CY 1981)	26.1.1954		70	1977–1984	4,415	213	9	37.41	0	0-0	0/0	–	50	97
Hughes Mervyn Gregory (CY 1994)	23.11.1961		53	1985–1993	1,032	72*	0	16.64	212	8-87	7/1	28.38	23	33
Hughes Phillip Joel	30.11.1988	27.11.2014	26	2008–2013	1,535	160	3	32.65	–	–	–/–	–	15	25/1
Hunt William Alfred	26.8.1908	30.12.1983	1	1931	0	0	0	0.00	0	0-14	0/0	–	0	
Hurst Alan George	15.7.1950		12	1973–1979	102	26	0	6.00	43	5-28	2/0	27.90	3	8
Hurwood Alexander	17.6.1902	26.9.1982	2	1930	5	5	0	2.50	11	4-22	0/0	15.45	2	
Hussey Michael Edward Killeen	27.5.1975		79	2005–2012	6,235	195	19	51.52	7	1-0	0/0	43.71	85	185/38
Inverarity Robert John	31.1.1944		6	1968–1972	174	56	0	17.40	4	3-26	0/0	23.25	4	
Iredale Francis Adams	19.6.1867	15.4.1926	14	1894–1899	807	140	2	36.68	0	0-3	0/0	–	16	
Ironmonger Herbert	7.4.1882	31.5.1971	14	1928–1932	42	12	0	2.62	74	7-23	4/2	17.97	3	
Iverson John Brian	27.7.1915	24.10.1973	5	1950	3	1*	0	0.75	21	6-27	1/0	15.23	2	

Name	Born	Died	Tests	Test Career	Runs	HS	100s	Avge	Wkts	BB	5/10	Avge	Ct/St	O/T
Jackson Archibald Alexander	5.9.1909	16.2.1933	8	1928-1930	474	164	1	47.40	–	–	–/–	–	7	
Jaques Philip Anthony	3.5.1979		11	2005-2007	902	150	3	47.47	–	–	–/–	–	7	6
Jarman Barrington Noel	17.2.1936		19	1959-1968	400	78	0	14.81	–	–	–/–	–	50/4	
Jarvis Arthur Harwood	19.10.1860	15.11.1933	11	1884-1894	303	82	0	16.83	–	–	–/–	–	9/9	
Jenner Terrence James	8.9.1944	24.5.2011	9	1970-1975	208	74	0	23.11	24	5-90	1/0	31.20	5	
Jennings Claude Burrows	5.6.1884	20.6.1950	6	1912	107	32	0	17.83	–	–	–/–	–	5	
Johnson Ian William Geddes CBE	8.12.1917	9.10.1998	45	1945-1956	1,000	77	0	18.51	109	7-44	3/0	29.19	30	
Johnson Leonard Joseph	18.3.1919	20.4.1977	1	1947	25	25*	0	–	6	3-8	0/0	12.33	0	
Johnson Mitchell Guy	2.11.1981		73	2007-2015	2,065	123*	1	22.20	313	8-61	12/3	28.40	27	153/30
Johnston William Arras (CY 1949)	26.2.1922	25.5.2007	40	1947-1954	273	29	0	11.37	160	6-44	7/0	23.91	16	
Jones Dean Mervyn (CY 1990)	24.3.1961		52	1983-1992	3,631	216	11	46.55	1	1-5	0/0	64.00	34	164
Jones Ernest	30.9.1869	23.11.1943	19	1894-1902	126	20	0	5.04	64	7-88	3/1	29.01	21	
Jones Samuel Percy	1.8.1861	14.7.1951	12	1881-1887	428	87	0	21.40	6	4-47	0/0	18.66	12	
Joslin Leslie Ronald	13.12.1947		1	1967	9	7	0	4.50	–	–	–/–	–	0	
Julian Brendon Paul	10.8.1970		7	1992-1995	128	56*	0	16.00	15	4-36	0/0	39.93	4	25
Kasprowicz Michael Scott	10.2.1972		38	1996-2005	445	25	0	10.59	113	7-36	4/0	32.88	16	43/2
Katich Simon Mathew	21.8.1975		56§	2001-2010	4,188	157	10	45.03	21	6-65	1/0	30.23	39	45/3
Kelleway Charles	25.4.1886	16.11.1944	26	1910-1928	1,422	147	3	37.42	52	5-33	1/0	32.36	24	
Kelly James Joseph (CY 1903)	10.5.1867	14.8.1938	36	1896-1905	664	46*	0	17.02	–	–	–/–	–	43/20	
Kelly Thomas Joseph Dart	3.5.1844	20.7.1893	2	1876-1878	64	35	0	21.33	–	–	–/–	–	2	
Kendall Thomas Kingston	24.8.1851	17.8.1924	2	1876	39	17*	0	13.00	14	7-55	1/0	15.35	2	
Kent Martin Francis	23.11.1953		3	1981	171	54	0	28.50	–	–	–/–	–	6	5
Kerr Robert Byers	16.6.1961		2	1985	31	17	0	7.75	–	–	–/–	–	1	4
Khawaja Usman Tariq	18.12.1986		13	2010-2015	881	174	2	46.36	–	–	–/–	–	6	3
Kippax Alan Falconer	25.5.1897	5.9.1972	22	1924-1934	1,192	146	2	36.12	0	0-2	0/0	–	13	
Kline Lindsay Francis	29.9.1934	2.10.2015	13	1957-1960	58	15*	0	8.28	34	7-75	1/1	22.82	9	
Krejza Jason John	14.11.1983		2	2008	71	32	0	23.66	13	8-215	1/1	43.23	4	
Laird Bruce Malcolm	21.11.1950		21	1979-1982	1,341	92	0	35.28	0	0-3	0/0	–	16	23
Langer Justin Lee (CY 2001)	21.11.1970		105§	1992-2006	7,696	250	23	45.27	0	0-3	0/0	–	73	8
Langley Gilbert Roche Andrews (CY 1957)	14.9.1919	14.5.2001	26	1951-1956	374	53	0	14.96	–	–	–/–	–	83/15	
Laughlin Trevor John	30.1.1951		3	1977-1978	87	35	0	17.40	6	5-101	1/0	43.66	6	6
Laver Frank Jonas	7.12.1869	24.9.1919	15	1899-1909	196	45	0	11.52	37	8-31	2/0	26.05	8	
Law Stuart Grant (CY 1998)	12.10.1968		1	1995	54	54*	0	–	0	0-40	0/0	–	1	54
Lawry William Morris (CY 1962)	11.2.1937		67	1961-1970	5,234	210	13	47.15	0	0-9	0/0	–	30	1
Lawson Geoffrey Francis	7.12.1957		46	1980-1989	894	74	0	15.96	180	8-112	11/2	30.56	10	79

§ Katich's figures include two runs and one catch, and Langer's 22 runs and one catch, for Australia v the ICC World XI in the Super Series Test in 2005-06.

	Born	Died	Tests	Test Career	Runs	HS	100s	Avge	Wkts	BB	5/10	Avge	Ct/St	O/T
Lee Brett (CY 2006)	8.11.1976		76	1999–2008	1,451	64	0	20.15	310	5-30	10/0	30.81	23	221/25
Lee Philip Keith	15.9.1904	9.8.1980	2	1931–1932	57	42	0	19.00	5	4-111	0/0	42.40	11	
Lehmann Darren Scott (CY 2001)	5.2.1970		27	1997–2004	1,798	177	5	44.95	15	3-42	0/0	27.46	11	117
Lillee Dennis Keith (CY 1973)	18.7.1949		70	1970–1983	905	73*	0	13.71	355	7-83	23/7	23.92	23	63
Lindwall Raymond Russell MBE (CY 1949)	3.10.1921	23.6.1996	61	1945–1959	1,502	118	2	21.15	228	7-38	12/0	23.03	26	
Love Hampden Stanley Bray	10.8.1895	22.7.1969	1	1932	8	5	0	4.00	–	–	–/–	–	3	
Love Martin Lloyd	30.3.1974		5	2002–2003	233	100*	1	46.60	–	–	–/–	–	7	
Loxton Samuel John Everett OBE	29.3.1921	3.12.2011	12	1947–1950	554	101	1	36.93	8	3-55	0/0	43.62	7	
Lyon Nathan Michael	20.11.1987		52	2011–2015	492	40*	0	15.37	185	7-94	7/1	33.42	27	8
Lyons John James	21.5.1863	21.7.1927	14	1886–1897	731	134	1	27.07	6	5-30	0/0	24.83	3	
McAlister Peter Alexander	11.7.1869	10.5.1938	8	1903–1909	252	41	0	16.80	–	–	–/–	–	10	
Macartney Charles George (CY 1922)	27.6.1886	9.9.1958	35	1907–1926	2,131	170	7	41.78	45	7-58	2/1	27.55	17	
McCabe Stanley Joseph (CY 1935)	16.7.1910	25.8.1968	39	1930–1938	2,748	232	6	48.21	36	4-13	0/0	42.86	41	
McCool Colin Leslie	9.12.1916	5.4.1986	14	1945–1949	459	104*	1	35.30	36	5-41	3/0	26.61	14	
McCormick Ernest Leslie	16.5.1906	28.6.1991	12	1935–1938	54	17*	0	6.00	36	4-101	0/0	29.97	8	
McCosker Richard Bede (CY 1976)	11.12.1946		25	1974–1979	1,622	127	4	39.56	–	–	–/–	–	21	14
McDermott Craig John (CY 1986)	14.4.1965		71	1984–1995	940	42*	0	12.20	291	8-97	14/2	28.63	19	138
McDonald Andrew Barry	15.6.1981		4	2008	107	68	0	21.40	9	3-25	0/0	33.33	2	
McDonald Colin Campbell	17.11.1928		47	1951–1961	3,107	170	5	39.32	0	0-3	0/0	–	14	
McDonald Edgar Arthur (CY 1922)	6.1.1891	22.7.1937	11	1920–1921	116	36	0	16.57	43	5-32	2/0	33.27	3	
McDonnell Percy Stanislaus	13.11.1858	24.9.1896	19	1880–1888	955	147	3	28.93	0	0-11	0/0	–	6	
McGain Bryce Edward	25.3.1972		1	2008	2	2	0	1.00	0	0-149	0/0	–	0	
MacGill Stuart Charles Glyndwr	25.2.1971		44§	1997–2007	349	43	0	9.69	208	8-108	12/2	29.02	16	3
McGrath Glenn Donald (CY 1998)	9.2.1970		124§	1993–2006	641	61	0	7.36	563	8-24	29/3	21.64	38	249½/2
McIlwraith John	7.9.1857	5.7.1938	1	1886	9	7	0	4.50	–	–	–/–	–	0	
McIntyre Peter Edward	27.4.1966		2	1994–1996	22	16	0	7.33	5	3-103	0/0	38.80	0	
McKay Clinton James	22.2.1983		1	2009	10	10	0	10.00	1	1-56	0/0	101.00	0	59/6
Mackay Kenneth Donald MBE	24.10.1925	13.6.1982	37	1956–1962	1,507	89	0	33.48	50	6-42	2/0	34.42	16	
McKenzie Graham Douglas (CY 1965)	24.6.1941		60	1961–1970	945	76	0	12.27	246	8-71	16/3	29.78	34	1
McKibbin Thomas Robert	10.12.1870	15.12.1939	5	1894–1897	88	28*	0	14.66	17	7-35	0/0	29.17	4	
McLaren John William	22.12.1886	17.11.1921	1	1911	0	0*	0	–	–	–	–/–	–	0	
Maclean John Alexander	27.4.1946		4	1978	79	33*	0	11.28	–	–	–/–	–	18	
McLeod Charles Edward	24.10.1869	26.11.1918	17	1894–1905	573	112	1	23.87	33	5-65	2/0	40.15	9	2
McLeod Robert William	19.1.1868	14.6.1907	6	1891–1893	146	31	0	13.27	12	5-53	1/0	31.83	3	

§ *Lee's figures include four runs, two wickets and one catch, MacGill's no runs and nine wickets and McGrath's two runs and three wickets, for Australia v the ICC World XI in the Super Series Test in 2005-06.*

	Born	Died	Tests	Test Career	Runs	HS	100s	Avge	Wkts	BB	5/10	Avge	Ct/St	O/T
McShane Patrick George..........	18.4.1858	11.12.1903	3	1884–1887	26	12*	0	5.20	1	1-39	0/0	48.00	2	–
Maddocks Leonard Victor.........	24.5.1926		7	1954–1956	177	69	0	17.70	–	–	–	–	19/1	23
Maguire John Norman............	15.9.1956		3	1983	28	15*	0	7.00	10	4-57	0/0	32.30	2	–
Mailey Arthur Alfred............	3.1.1886	31.12.1967	21	1920–1926	222	46*	0	11.10	99	9-121	6/2	33.91	14	–
Mallett Ashley Alexander.........	13.7.1945		38	1968–1980	430	43*	0	11.62	132	8-59	6/1	29.84	30	9
Malone Michael Francis..........	9.10.1950		1	1977	46	46	0	46.00	6	5-63	0/0	12.83	0	10
Mann Anthony Longford..........	8.11.1945		4	1977	189	105	1	23.62	4	3-12	0/0	79.00	2	–
Manou Graham Allan............	23.4.1979		1	2009	21	13*	0	21.00	–	–	–	–	3	4
Marr Alfred Percy..............	28.3.1862	15.3.1940	1	1884	5	5	0	2.50	0	0-3	0/0	–	2	–
[1]Marsh Geoffrey Robert.........	31.12.1958		50	1985–1991	2,854	138	6	33.18	–	–	–	–	38	117
[1,2]Marsh Mitchell Ross..........	20.10.1991		13	2014–2015	419	87	0	24.64	21	4-61	0/0	31.61	5	23/4
[1,2]Marsh Rodney William MBE (CY 1982)..	4.11.1947		96	1970–1983	3,633	132	3	26.51	0	0-3	0/0	–	343/12	92
[1,2]Marsh Shaun Edward..........	9.7.1983		17	2011–2015	1,094	182	3	37.72	–	–	–	–	12	46/13
Martin John Wesley.............	28.7.1931	16.7.1992	8	1960–1966	214	55	0	17.83	17	3-56	0/0	48.94	5	–
Martyn Damien Richard (CY 2002)...	21.10.1971		67	1992–2006	4,406	165	13	46.37	2	1-0	0/0	84.00	36	208/4
Massie Hugh Hamon.............	11.4.1854	12.10.1938	9	1881–1884	249	55	0	15.56	–	–	–	–	5	–
Massie Robert Arnold Lockyer (CY 1973).	14.4.1947		6	1972–1972	78	42	0	11.14	31	8-53	2/1	20.87	1	3
Matthews Christopher Darrell......	22.9.1962		3	1986–1988	54	32	0	10.80	6	3-95	0/0	52.16	1	–
Matthews Gregory Richard John....	15.12.1959		33	1983–1992	1,849	130	4	41.08	61	5-103	2/1	28.22	17	59
Matthews Thomas James..........	3.4.1884	14.10.1943	8	1911–1912	153	53	0	17.00	16	4-29	0/0	26.18	7	–
Maxwell Glenn James............	14.10.1988		3	2012–2014	80	37	0	13.33	7	4-127	0/0	38.71	2	55/25
May Timothy Brian Alexander......	26.1.1962		24	1987–1994	225	42*	0	14.06	75	5-9	3/0	34.74	6	47
Mayne Edgar Richard............	2.7.1882	26.10.1961	4	1912–1921	64	25*	0	21.33	0	0-1	0/0	–	2	–
Mayne Lawrence Charles..........	23.1.1942		6	1964–1969	76	13	0	9.50	19	4-43	0/0	33.05	3	–
Meckiff Ian...................	6.1.1935		18	1957–1963	154	45*	0	11.84	45	6-38	2/0	31.62	9	–
Meuleman Kenneth Douglas........	5.9.1923	10.9.2004	1	1945	0	0	0	0.00	–	–	–	–	–	–
Midwinter William Evans.........	19.6.1851	3.12.1890	8†	1876–1886	174	37	0	13.38	14	5-78	1/0	23.78	5	–
Miller Colin Reid..............	6.2.1964		18	1998–2000	174	43	0	8.28	69	5-32	3/1	26.15	6	–
Miller Keith Ross MBE (CY 1954)....	28.11.1919	11.10.2004	55	1945–1956	2,958	147	7	36.97	170	7-60	7/1	22.97	38	–
Minnett Roy Baldwin............	13.6.1888	21.10.1955	9	1911–1912	391	90	0	26.00	11	4-34	0/0	26.36	9	–
Misson Francis Michael..........	19.11.1938		5	1960–1961	38	25*	0	19.00	16	4-58	0/0	38.50	6	76
Moody Thomas Masson (CY 2000)....	2.10.1965		8	1989–1992	456	106	2	32.57	2	1-17	0/0	73.50	9	–
Moroney John.................	24.7.1917	1.7.1999	7	1949–1951	383	118	2	34.81	–	–	–	–	0	–
Morris Arthur Robert MBE (CY 1949)..	19.1.1922	22.8.2015	46	1946–1954	3,533	206	12	46.48	2	1-5	0/0	25.00	15	–
Morris Samuel................	22.6.1855	20.9.1931	1	1884	14	10*	0	14.00	2	2-73	0/0	36.50	0	–
Moses Henry.................	13.2.1858	7.12.1938	6	1886–1894	198	33	0	19.80	–	–	–	–	1	–

Name	Born	Died	Tests	Test Career	Runs	HS	100s	Avge	Wkts	BB	5/10	Avge	Ct/St	O/T
Moss Jeffrey Kenneth	29.6.1947		1	1978	60	38*	0	60.00	–	–	–/–	–	0	1
Moule William Henry	31.1.1858	24.8.1939	1	1880	40	34	0	20.00	3	3-23	0/0	7.66	1	–
Muller Scott Andrew	11.7.1971		2	1999	6	6*	0	–	7	3-68	0/0	36.85	2	–
Murdoch William Lloyd	18.10.1854	18.2.1911	18†	1876–1890	896	211	2	32.00	–	–	–/–	–	14	–
Musgrove Henry Alfred	27.11.1858	2.11.1931	1	1884	13	9	0	6.50	–	–	–/–	–	0	–
Nagel Lisle Ernest	6.3.1905	23.11.1971	1	1932	21	21*	0	21.00	2	2-110	0/0	55.00	0	–
Nash Laurence John	2.5.1910	24.7.1986	2	1931–1936	30	17	0	15.00	10	4-18	0/0	12.60	6	–
Nevill Peter Michael	13.10.1985		10	2015–2015	280	66	0	28.00	–	–	–/–	–	36/1	–
Nicholson Matthew James	2.10.1974		1	1998	14	9	0	7.00	4	3-56	0/0	28.75	0	–
Nitschke Homesdale Carl ("Jack")	14.4.1905	29.9.1982	2	1931	53	47	0	26.50	–	–	–/–	–	3	–
Noble Montague Alfred (CY 1900)	28.1.1873	22.6.1940	42	1897–1909	1,997	133	1	30.25	121	7-17	9/2	25.00	26	–
Noblet Geffery	14.9.1916	16.8.2006	3	1949–1952	22	13*	0	7.33	7	3-21	0/0	26.14	1	–
North Marcus James	28.7.1979		21	2008–2010	1,171	128	5	35.48	14	6-55	1/0	42.21	17	2/1
Nothling Otto Ernest	1.8.1900	26.9.1965	1	1928	52	44	0	26.00	0	0-12	0/0	–	0	–
O'Brien Leo Patrick Joseph	2.7.1907	13.3.1997	5	1932–1936	211	61	0	26.37	–	–	–/–	–	3	–
O'Connor John Denis Alphonsus	9.9.1875	23.8.1941	4	1907–1909	86	20	0	12.28	13	5-40	1/0	26.15	3	–
O'Donnell Simon Patrick	26.1.1963		6	1985–1985	206	48	0	29.42	6	3-37	0/0	84.00	4	87
Ogilvie Alan David	3.6.1951		5	1977	178	47	0	17.80	–	–	–/–	–	5	–
O'Keefe Stephen Norman John	9.12.1984		2	2014–2015	6	6	0	6.00	7	3-63	0/0	40.28	1	0/7
O'Keeffe Kerry James	25.11.1949		24	1970–1977	644	85	0	25.76	53	5-101	1/0	38.07	15	2
Oldfield William Albert Stanley MBE (CY 1927)	9.9.1894	10.8.1976	54	1920–1936	1,427	65*	0	22.65	–	–	–/–	–	78/52	–
²O'Neill Norman Clifford Louis (CY 1962)	19.2.1937	3.3.2008	42	1958–1964	2,779	181	6	45.55	17	4-41	0/0	39.23	21	–
O'Reilly William Joseph OBE (CY 1935)	20.12.1905	6.10.1992	27	1931–1945	410	56*	0	12.81	144	7-54	11/3	22.59	7	–
Oxenham Ronald Keven	28.7.1891	16.8.1939	7	1928–1931	151	48	0	15.10	14	4-39	0/0	37.28	4	–
Paine Timothy David	8.12.1984		4	2010–2010	287	92	0	35.87	–	–	–/–	–	16/1	26/5
Palmer George Eugene	22.2.1859	22.8.1910	17	1880–1886	296	48	0	14.09	78	7-65	6/2	21.51	13	–
Park Roy Lindsay	30.7.1892	23.1.1947	1	1920	0	0	0	0.00	1	0-9	0/0	–	0	–
Pascoe Leonard Stephen	13.2.1950		14	1977–1981	106	30*	0	10.60	64	5-59	1/0	26.06	2	29
Pattinson James Lee	3.5.1990		16	2011–2015	331	42	0	30.09	64	5-27	4/0	26.14	3	15/4
Pellew Clarence Everard ("Nip")	21.9.1893	9.5.1981	10	1920–1921	484	116	2	37.23	0	0-3	0/0	–	4	–
Phillips Wayne Bentley	1.3.1958		27	1983–1985	1,485	159	2	32.28	–	–	–/–	–	52	48
Phillips Wayne Norman	7.11.1962		1	1991	22	14	0	11.00	–	–	–/–	–	0	–
Philpott Peter Ian	21.11.1934		8	1964–1965	93	22	0	10.33	26	5-90	1/0	38.46	5	–
Ponsford William Harold MBE (CY 1935)	19.10.1900	6.4.1991	29	1924–1934	2,122	266	7	48.22	–	–	–/–	–	21	–
Ponting Ricky Thomas (CY 2006)	19.12.1974		168§	1995–2012	13,378	257	41	51.85	5	1-0	0/0	55.20	196	374‡/17

§ *Ponting's figures include 100 runs and one catch for Australia v the ICC World XI in the Super Series Test in 2005-06.*

	Born	Died	Tests	Test Career	Runs	HS	100s	Avge	Wkts	BB	5/10	Avge	Ct/St	O/T
Pope Roland James	18.2.1864	27.7.1952	1	1884	3	3	0	1.50	0	0-3	–/–	–	0	
Quiney Robert Gray	20.8.1982		2	2012	9	9	0	3.00	0	–	0/0	–	0	
Rackemann Carl Gray	3.6.1960		12	1982–1990	53	15*	0	5.30	39	6-86	3/1	29.15	2	52
Ransford Vernon Seymour (CY 1910)	20.3.1885	19.3.1958	20	1907–1911	1,211	143*	1	37.84	1	1-9	0/0	28.00	10	
Redpath Ian Ritchie MBE	11.5.1941		66	1963–1975	4,737	171	8	43.45	0	0-0	0/0	–	83	5
Reedman John Cole	9.10.1865	25.3.1924	1	1894	21	17	0	10.50	1	1-12	0/0	24.00	1	
Reid Bruce Anthony	14.3.1963		27	1985–1992	93	13	0	4.65	113	7-51	5/2	24.63	5	61
Reiffel Paul Ronald	19.4.1966		35	1991–1997	955	79*	0	26.52	104	6-71	5/0	26.96	15	92
Renneberg David Alexander	23.9.1942		8	1966–1967	22	9	0	3.66	23	5-39	2/0	36.08	2	
Richardson Arthur John	24.7.1888	23.12.1973	9	1924–1926	403	100	1	31.00	12	2-20	0/0	43.41	1	
Richardson Victor York OBE	7.9.1894	30.10.1969	19	1924–1935	706	138	1	23.53	–	–	–	–	24	
Rigg Keith Edward	21.5.1906	28.2.1995	8	1930–1936	401	127	1	33.41	–	–	–	–	5	
Ring Douglas Thomas	14.10.1918	23.6.2003	13	1947–1953	426	67	0	22.42	35	6-72	2/0	37.28	5	
Ritchie Gregory Michael	23.1.1960		30	1982–1986	1,690	146	3	35.20	0	0-10	0/0	–	14	44
Rixon Stephen John	25.2.1954		13	1977–1984	394	54	0	18.76	–	–	–/–	–	42/5	6
Robertson Gavin Ron	28.5.1966		4	1997–1998	140	57	0	20.00	13	4-72	0/0	39.61	1	13
Robertson William Roderick	6.10.1861	24.6.1938	1	1884	2	2	0	1.00	0	0-24	0/0	–	0	
Robinson Richard Daryl	8.6.1946		3	1977	100	34	0	16.66	–	–	–/–	–	4	2
Robinson Rayford Harold	26.3.1914	10.8.1965	1	1936	5	3	0	2.50	–	–	–	–	0	
Rogers Christopher John Llewellyn (CY 2014)	31.8.1977		25	2007–2015	2,015	173	5	42.87	–	–	–/–	–	15	
Rorke Gordon Frederick	27.6.1938		4	1958–1959	9	7	0	4.50	10	3-23	0/0	20.30	1	
Rutherford John Walter	25.9.1929		1	1956	30	30	0	30.00	1	1-11	0/0	15.00	0	
Ryder John	8.8.1889	3.4.1977	20	1920–1928	1,394	201*	3	51.62	17	2-20	0/0	43.70	17	
Saggers Ronald Arthur	15.5.1917	17.3.1987	6	1948–1949	30	14	0	10.00	–	–	–/–	–	16/8	
Saunders John Victor	21.3.1876	21.12.1927	14	1901–1907	39	11*	0	2.29	79	7-34	6/0	22.73	5	
Scott Henry James Herbert	26.12.1858	23.9.1910	8	1884–1886	359	102	1	27.61	0	0-9	0/0	–	8	
Sellers Reginald Hugh Durning	20.8.1940		1	1964	0	0	0	0.00	0	0-17	0/0	–	0	
Serjeant Craig Stanton	1.11.1951		12	1977–1978	522	124	1	23.72	–	–	–	–	13	3
Sheahan Andrew Paul	30.9.1946		31	1967–1973	1,594	127	2	33.91	–	–	–	–	17	3
Shepherd Barry Kenneth	23.4.1937	17.9.2001	9	1962–1964	502	96	0	41.83	0	0-3	0/0	–	2	
Siddle Peter Matthew	25.11.1984		60	2008–2015	983	51	0	14.04	205	6-54	8/0	29.99	16	17/2
Sievers Morris William	13.4.1912	10.5.1968	3	1936	67	25*	0	13.40	9	5-21	1/0	17.88	4	
Simpson Robert Baddeley (CY 1965)	3.2.1936		62	1957–1977	4,869	311	10	46.81	71	5-57	2/0	42.26	110	2
Sincock David Keith	1.2.1942		3	1964–1965	80	29	0	26.66	8	3-67	0/0	51.25	2	
Slater Keith Nichol	12.3.1936		1	1958	1	1*	0	–	2	2-40	0/0	50.50	0	
Slater Michael Jonathon	21.2.1970		74	1993–2001	5,312	219	14	42.83	1	1-4	0/0	10.00	33	42

Name	Born	Died	Tests	Test Career	Runs	HS	100s	Avge	Wkts	BB	5/10	Avge	Ct/St	O/T
Sleep Peter Raymond	4.5.1957		14	1978–1989	483	90	0	24.15	31	5-72	–/–	45.06	4	
Slight James	20.10.1855	9.12.1930	1	1880	11	11	0	5.50	–				0	
Smith David Bertram Miller	14.9.1884	29.7.1963	2	1912	30	24*	0	15.00	–				0	
Smith Steven Barry	18.10.1961		3	1983	41	12	0	8.20	–				–	28
Smith Steven Peter Devereux (CY 2016)	2.6.1989		39	2010–2015	3,590	215	13	57.90	16	3-18	0/0	52.31	38	64/22
Spofforth Frederick Robert	9.9.1853	4.6.1926	18	1876–1886	217	50	0	9.43	94	7-44	7/4	18.41	11	
Stackpole Keith Raymond MBE (CY 1973)	10.7.1940		43	1965–1973	2,807	207	7	37.42	15	2-33	0/0	66.73	47	6
Starc Mitchell Aaron	13.1.1990		25	2011–2015	700	99	0	26.92	91	6-111	4/0	30.58	13	46/20
Stevens Gavin Byron	29.2.1932		4	1959	112	28	0	16.00	–				2	
Symonds Andrew	9.6.1975		26	2003–2008	1,462	162*	2	40.61	24	3-50	0/0	37.33	22	198/14
Taber Hedley Brian	29.4.1940		16	1966–1969	353	48	0	16.04	–				56/4	
Tait Shaun William	22.2.1983		3	2005–2007	20	8	0	6.66	5	3-97	–/–	60.40	1	35/19
Tallon Donald (CY 1949)	17.2.1916	7.9.1984	21	1945–1953	394	92	0	17.13	–				50/8	
Taylor John Morris	10.10.1895	12.5.1971	20	1920–1926	997	108	1	35.60	1	1-25	0/0	45.00	11	
Taylor Mark Anthony (CY 1990)	27.10.1964		104	1988–1998	7,525	334*	19	43.49	1	1-11	0/0	26.00	157	113
Taylor Peter Laurence	22.8.1956		13	1986–1991	431	87	0	26.93	27	6-78	1/0	39.55	10	83
Thomas Grahame	21.3.1938		8	1964–1965	325	61	0	29.54	–				3	
Thomas George Ronald	22.3.1927	29.8.2003	1	1951	44	28	0	22.00	–				0	
Thomson Alan Lloyd ("Froggy")	2.12.1945		4	1970	22	12*	0	22.00	12	3-79	0/0	54.50	0	1
Thomson Jeffrey Robert	16.8.1950		51	1972–1985	679	49	0	12.81	200	6-46	8/0	28.00	20	50
Thomson Nathaniel Frampton Davis	29.5.1839	2.9.1896	2	1876	67	41	0	16.75	1	1-14	0/0	31.00	3	
Thurlow Hugh Motley ("Pud")	10.1.1903	3.12.1975	1	1931	0	0	0	0.00	–	0-33	0/0		0	
Toohey Peter Michael	20.4.1954		15	1977–1979	893	122	1	31.89	–	0-4	0/0		9	5
Toshack Ernest Raymond Herbert	8.12.1914	11.5.2003	12	1945–1948	73	20*	0	14.60	47	6-29	4/1	21.04	4	
Travers Joseph Patrick Francis	10.1.1871	15.9.1942	1	1901	10	9	0	5.00	1	1-14	0/0	14.00	0	
Tribe George Edward (CY 1955)	4.10.1920	5.4.2009	3	1946	35	25*	0	17.50	2	2-48	0/0	165.00	0	
2Trott Albert Edwin (CY 1899)	6.2.1873	30.7.1914	3†	1894	205	85*	0	102.50	9	8-43	1/0	21.33	4	
2Trott George Henry Stevens (CY 1894)	5.8.1866	10.11.1917	24	1888–1897	921	143	1	21.92	29	4-71	0/0	35.13	21	
2Trumble Hugh (CY 1897)	12.5.1867	14.8.1938	32	1890–1903	851	70	0	19.79	141	8-65	9/3	21.78	45	
2Trumble John William	16.9.1863	17.8.1944	7	1884–1886	243	59	0	20.25	10	3-29	0/0	22.20	3	
Trumper Victor Thomas (CY 1903)	2.11.1877	28.6.1915	48	1899–1911	3,163	214*	8	39.04	8	3-60	0/0	39.62	31	
Turner Alan	23.7.1950		14	1975–1976	768	136	1	29.53	–				15	6
Turner Charles Thomas Biass (CY 1889)	16.11.1862	1.1.1944	17	1886–1894	323	29	0	11.53	101	7-43	11/2	16.53	8	
Veivers Thomas Robert	6.4.1937		21	1963–1966	813	88	0	31.26	33	4-68	0/0	41.66	7	
Veletta Michael Robert John	30.10.1963		8	1987–1989	207	39	0	18.81	–				12	20
Voges Adam Charles	4.10.1979		13	2015–2015	1,028	269*	4	85.66	0	0-3	0/0		9	31/7

	Born	Died	Tests	Test Career	Runs	HS	100s	Avge	Wkts	BB	5/10	Avge	Ct/St	O/T
Wade Matthew Scott	26.12.1987		12	2011–2012	623	106	2	34.61	0	0-0	0/0	–	33/3	53/23
Waite Mervyn George	7.1.1911	16.12.1985	2	1938	11	8	–	3.66	1	1-150	0/0	190.00		
Walker Maxwell Henry Norman ("Tim")	12.9.1948		34	1972–1977	586	78*	–	19.53	138	8-143	6/0	27.47	12	17
Wall Thomas Welbourn ("Tim")	13.5.1904	26.3.1981	18	1928–1934	121	20	–	6.36	56	5-14	3/0	35.89	11	
Walters Francis Henry	9.2.1860	1.6.1922	1	1884	12	7	–	6.00	–	–	–/–	–	2	
Walters Kevin Douglas MBE.	21.12.1945		74	1965–1980	5357	250	15	48.26	49	5-66	1/0	29.08	43	28
Ward Francis Anthony	23.2.1906	25.3.1974	4	1936–1938	36	18	–	6.00	11	6-102	2/0	52.18		
Warne Shane Keith (CY 1994).	13.9.1969		145	1992–2007	3154	99	–	17.32	708	8-71	37/10	25.41	125	193‡
Warner David Andrew	27.10.1986		49	2011–2015	4467	253	16	51.34	4	2-45	0/0	63.50	37	65/53
Watkins John Russell	16.4.1943		1	1972	39	36	–	39.00	0	0-21	0/0	–		
Watson Graeme Donald	8.3.1945		5	1966–1972	97	50	–	10.77	6	2-67	0/0	42.33	4	2
Watson Shane Robert	17.6.1981		59	2005–2015	3731	176	4	35.19	75	6-33	3/0	33.68	45	190/49
Watson William James	31.1.1931		4	1954	106	30	–	17.66	0	0-5	0/0	–		
[2] Waugh Mark Edward (CY 1991).	2.6.1965		128	1990–2002	8029	153*	20	41.81	59	5-40	1/0	41.16	181	244
Waugh Stephen Rodger (CY 1989)	2.6.1965		168	1985–2003	10927	200	32	51.06	92	5-28	3/0	37.44	112	325
Wellham Dirk Macdonald	13.3.1959		6	1981–1986	257	103	1	23.36	0	–	–/–	–		17
Wessels Kepler Christoffel (CY 1995)	14.9.1957		24†	1982–1985	1761	179	4	42.95	0	0-2	0/0	–	18	54‡
Whatmore Davenell Frederick	16.3.1954		7	1978–1979	293	77	–	22.53	0	0-11	0/0	–	13	
White Cameron Leon	18.8.1983		4	2008	146	46	–	29.20	5	2-71	0/0	68.40		88/47
Whitney Michael Roy	24.2.1959		12	1981–1992	68	13	–	6.18	39	7-27	2/1	33.97	2	38
Whitty William James	15.8.1886	30.1.1974	14	1909–1912	161	39*	–	13.41	65	6-17	3/0	21.12	4	
Wiener Julien Mark	1.5.1955		6	1979	281	93	–	25.54	0	0-19	0/0	–	4	7
Williams Brad Andrew	20.11.1974		4	2003	23	10*	–	7.66	9	4-53	0/0	45.11		25
Wilson John William	20.8.1921	13.10.1985	1	1956	0	0*	–	–	1	1-25	0/0	64.00		
Wilson Paul	12.1.1972		1	1998	–	–	–	–	0	0-50	0/0	–		
Wood Graeme Malcolm	6.11.1956		59	1977–1988	3374	172	9	31.83	–	–	–/–	–	41	83
Woodcock Ashley James	27.2.1947		1	1973	27	27	–	27.00	–	–	–/–	–		
Woodfull William Maldon OBE (CY 1927).	22.8.1897	11.8.1965	35	1926–1934	2300	161	7	46.00	–	–	–/–	–	7	
Woods Samuel Moses James (CY 1889).	13.4.1867	30.4.1931	3†	1888	32	18	–	5.33	5	2-35	0/0	24.20	1	4
Woolley Roger Douglas	16.9.1954		2	1982–1983	21	13	–	10.50	–	–	–/–	–		
Worrall John	20.6.1860	17.11.1937	11	1884–1899	478	76	–	25.15	1	1-97	0/0	127.00	13	
Wright Kevin John	27.12.1953		10	1978–1979	219	55*	–	16.84	–	–	–/–	–	31/4	
Yallop Graham Neil	7.10.1952		39	1977–1984	2756	268	8	41.13	1	1-21	0/0	116.00	23	
Yardley Bruce	5.9.1947		33	1977–1982	978	74	–	19.56	126	7-98	6/1	31.63	31	
Young Shaun	13.6.1970		1	1997	4	4*	–	4.00	0	0-5	0/0	–		
Zoehrer Timothy Joseph	25.9.1961		10	1985–1986	246	52*	–	20.50	–	–	–/–	–	18/1	22

§ Warne's figures include 12 runs and six wickets, and Watson's 34 runs and no wicket, for Australia v the ICC World XI in the Super Series Test in 2005-06.

SOUTH AFRICA (326 players)

	Born	Died	Tests	Test Career	Runs	HS	100s	Avge	Wkts	BB	5/10	Avge	Ct/St	O/T
Abbott Kyle John	18.6.1987		7	2012–2015	59	16	0	6.55	21	7-29	2/0	25.57	3	20/14
Ackerman Hylton Deon	14.2.1973		4	1997	161	57	0	20.12				–	1	
Adams Paul Regan	20.1.1977		45	1995–2003	360	35	0	9.00	134	7-128	4/1	32.87	29	24
Adcock Neil Amwin Treharne (CY 1961) . .	8.3.1931	6.1.2013	26	1953–1961	146	24	0	5.40	104	6-43	5/0	21.10	4	
Amla Hashim Mahomed (CY 2013) . .	31.3.1983		92	2004–2015	7,358	311*	25	51.45	0	0-4		–	78	126/30
Anderson James Henry	26.4.1874	11.3.1926	1	1902	43	32	0	21.50				–	1	
Ashley William Hare	10.2.1862	14.7.1930	1	1888	1	1	0	0.50	7	7-95	1/0	13.57	0	
Bacher Adam Marc	29.10.1973		19	1996–1999	833	96	0	26.03				–	11	13
Bacher Aron ("Ali")	24.5.1942		12	1965–1969	679	73	0	32.33				–	10	
Balaskas Xenophon Constantine . .	15.10.1910	12.5.1994	9	1930–1938	174	122*	1	14.50	22	5-49	1/0	36.63	5	
Barlow Edgar John	12.8.1940	30.12.2005	30	1961–1969	2,516	201	6	45.74	40	5-85	1/0	34.05	35	
Baumgartner Harold Vane	17.11.1883	8.4.1938	1	1913	19	16	0	9.50	2	2-99		49.50	–	
Bavuma Temba	17.5.1990		9	2014–2015	383	102*	1	38.30				–	5	
Beaumont Rolland	4.2.1884	25.5.1958	5	1912–1913	70	31	0	7.77				–	2	
Begbie Denis Warburton	12.12.1914	10.3.2009	5	1948–1949	138	48	0	19.71	1	1-38	0/0	130.00	2	
Bell Alexander John	15.4.1906	1.8.1985	16	1929–1935	69	26*	0	6.27	48	6-99	4/0	32.64	6	
Bisset *Sir* Murray	14.4.1876	24.10.1931	3	1898–1909	103	35	0	25.75				–	2/1	
Bissett George Finlay	5.11.1905	14.11.1965	4	1927	38	23	0	19.00	25	7-29	2/0	18.76	1	
Blanckenberg James Manuel . . .	31.12.1892	d unknown	18	1913–1924	455	59	0	19.78	60	6-76	4/0	30.28	9	
Bland Kenneth Colin (CY 1966) . .	5.4.1938		21	1961–1966	1,669	144*	3	49.08	2	2-16	0/0	62.50	10	
Bock Ernest George	17.9.1908	5.9.1961	1	1935	11	9*	0	–	0	0-42	0/0	–	0	
Boje Nico	20.3.1973		43	1999–2006	1,312	85	0	25.23	100	5-62	3/0	42.65	18	113½/1
Bond Gerald Edward	5.4.1909	27.8.1965	1	1938	0	0	0	0.00	0	0-16	0/0	–	0	
Bosch Tertius	14.3.1966	14.2.2000	1	1991	5	5*	0	–	3	2-61	0/0	34.66	0	2
Botha Johan	2.5.1982		5	2005–2010	83	25	0	20.75	17	4-56	0/0	33.70	3	76½/40
Botten James Thomas ("Jackie") . .	21.6.1938	14.5.2006	3	1965	65	33	0	10.83	8	2-56	0/0	42.12	1	
Boucher Mark Verdon (CY 2009) . .	3.12.1976		146§	1997–2011	5,498	125	5	30.54	1	1-6	0/0	6.00	530/23	290½/25
Brann William Henry	4.4.1899	22.9.1953	3	1922	71	50	0	14.20				–	2	
Briscoe Arthur Wellesley ("Dooley") . .	6.2.1911	22.4.1941	2	1935–1938	33	16	0	11.00				–	–	
Bromfield Harry Dudley	26.6.1932		9	1961–1965	59	21	0	11.80	17	5-88	1/0	35.23	13	
Brown Lennox Sidney	24.11.1910	1.9.1983	2	1931	17	8	0	5.66	3	1-30	0/0	63.00	0	
Burger Christopher George de Villiers . .	12.7.1935	5.6.2014	2	1957	62	37*	0	20.66				–	1	

§ *Boucher's figures exclude 17 runs and two catches for the ICC World XI v Australia in the Super Series Test in 2005-06.*

	Born	Died	Tests	Test Career	Runs	HS	100s	Avge	Wkts	BB	5/10	Avge	Ct/St	O/T
Burke Sydney Frank	11.3.1934		2	1961–1964	42	20	0	14.00	11	6-128	2/1	23.36	0	
Buys Isaac Daniel	4.2.1895	d unknown	1	1922	4	4*	0	4.00	0	0-20	0/0	–	0	
Cameron Horace Brakenridge ("Jock") (CY 1936)	5.7.1905	2.11.1935	26	1927–1935	1,239	90	0	30.21	–	–	–/–	–	39/12	
Campbell Thomas	9.2.1882	5.10.1924	5	1909–1912	90	48	0	15.00	–	–	–/–	–	7/1	
Carlstein Peter Rudolph	28.10.1938		8	1957–1963	190	42	0	14.61	–	–	–/–	–	3	
Carter Claude Paglett	23.4.1881	8.11.1952	10	1912–1924	181	45	0	18.10	28	6-50	2/0	24.78	2	
Catterall Robert Hector (CY 1925)	10.7.1900	3.11.1961	24	1922–1930	1,555	120	3	37.92	7	3-15	0/0	23.14	12	
Chapman Horace William	30.6.1890	1.12.1941	1	1913–1921	39	17	0	13.00	1	1-51	0/0	104.00	0	
Cheetham John Erskine	26.5.1920	21.8.1980	24	1948–1955	883	89	1	23.86	0	0-2	0/0	–	13	
Chevalier Grahame Anton	9.3.1937		1	1969	0	0*	0	0.00	5	3-68	0/0	20.00	0	
Christy James Alexander Joseph	12.12.1904	1.2.1971	10	1929–1931	618	103	1	34.33	2	1-15	0/0	46.00	3	
Chubb Geoffrey Walter Ashton	12.4.1911	28.8.1982	5	1951	63	15*	0	10.50	21	6-51	2/0	27.47	1	
Cochran John Alexander Kennedy	15.7.1909	15.6.1987	1	1930	4	4	0	4.00	0	0-47	0/0	–	0	
Coen Stanley Keppel ("Shunter")	14.10.1902	29.1.1967	2	1927	101	41*	0	50.50	0	0-7	0/0	–	1	
Commaille John McIllwaine Moore ("Mick")	21.2.1883	28.7.1956	12	1909–1927	355	47	0	16.90	–	–	–/–	–	2	
Commins John Brian	19.2.1965		3	1994	125	45	0	25.00	–	–	–/–	–	1	4
Conyngham Dalton Parry	10.5.1897	7.7.1979	1	1922	6	6*	0	–	2	1-40	0/0	51.50	0	
Cook Frederick James	1870	30.11.1915	1	1895	7	7	0	3.50	–	–	–/–	–	2	
Cook Stephen Craig	29.11.1982		3	2015	140	115	1	70.00	–	–	–/–	–	2	
Cook Stephen James (CY 1990)	31.7.1953		3	1992–1993	107	43	0	17.83	–	–	–/–	–	1	
Cooper Alfred Henry Cecil	2.9.1893	18.7.1963	3	1913	6	6	0	3.00	4	2-74	0/0	61.25	1	
Cox Joseph Lovell	28.6.1886	4.7.1971	3	1913	17	12*	0	3.40	0	0-23	0/0	–	0	
Cripps Godfrey	19.10.1865	27.7.1943	1	1891	21	18	0	10.50	–	–	–/–	–	0	
Crisp Robert James	28.5.1911	2.3.1994	9	1935–1936	123	35	0	10.25	20	5-99	1/0	37.35	3	
Cronje Wessel Johannes ("Hansie")	25.9.1969	1.6.2002	68	1991–1999	3,714	135	6	36.41	43	3-14	0/0	29.95	33	188
Cullinan Daryll John	4.3.1967		70	1992–2000	4,554	275*	14	44.21	2	1-10	0/0	35.50	67	138
Curnow Sydney Harry	16.12.1907	28.7.1986	7	1930–1931	168	47	0	12.00	–	–	–/–	–	5	
Dalton Eric Londesbrough	2.12.1906	26.3.1981	15	1929–1938	698	117	2	31.72	12	4-59	0/0	40.83	5	
Davies Eric Quail	26.8.1909	11.11.1976	5	1935–1938	9	3	0	1.80	7	4-75	0/0	68.71	1	
Dawson Alan Charles	27.11.1969		2	2003	10	10	0	10.00	10	5-20	1/0	23.40	2	19
Dawson Oswald Charles	1.9.1919	22.12.2008	9	1947–1948	293	55	0	20.92	3	2-57	0/0	57.80	10	
Deane Hubert Gouvaine ("Nummy")	21.7.1895	21.10.1939	17	1924–1930	628	93	0	25.12	–	–	–/–	–	8	
de Bruyn Zander	5.7.1975		3	2004	155	83	0	38.75	3	2-32	0/0	30.66	1	
de Kock Quinton	17.12.1992		8	2013–2015	407	129*	1	45.22	–	–	–/–	–	31/2	52/22
de Lange Marchant	13.10.1990		2	2011	9	9	0	4.50	9	7-81	1/0	30.77	1	3/6

	Born	Died	Tests	Test Career	Runs	HS	100s	Avge	Wkts	BB	5/10	Avge	Ct/St	O/T
de Villiers Abraham Benjamin	17.2.1984		106	2004–2015	8,074	278*	21	50.46	2	2-49	0/0	52.00	197/5	190½/63
de Villiers Petrus Stephanus ("Fanie")	13.10.1964		18	1993–1997	359	67*	0	18.89	85	6-23	5/2	24.27	11	83
de Wet Friedel	26.6.1980		2	2009	20	20	0	10.00	6	4-55	0/0	31.00	1	101‡/1
Dippenaar Hendrik Human ("Boeta")	14.6.1977		38	1999–2006	1,718	177*	3	30.14	–	–	–/–	–	27	
Dixon Cecil Donovan	12.2.1891	9.9.1969	1	1913	0	0	0	0.00	3	2-62	0/0	39.33	1	
Donald Allan Anthony (CY 1992)	20.10.1966		72	1991–2001	652	37	0	10.68	330	8-71	20/3	22.25	18	164
Dower Robert Reid	4.6.1876	15.9.1964	1	1898	9	9	0	4.50	–	–	–/–	–	2	
Draper Ronald George	24.12.1926		2	1949	25	15	0	8.33	–	–	–/–	–	0	
Duckworth Christopher Anthony Russell	22.3.1933		2	1956	28	13	0	7.00	–	–	–/–	–	3	
Dumbrill Richard	19.11.1938		5	1965–1966	153	36	0	15.30	9	4-30	0/0	37.33	3	
Duminy Jacobus Petrus	16.12.1897	31.1.1980	3	1927–1929	30	12	0	5.00	1	1-17	0/0	39.00	2	
Duminy Jean-Paul	14.4.1984		34	2008–2015	1,423	166	4	32.34	37	4-73	0/0	37.29	26	146/63
Dunell Owen Robert	15.7.1856	21.10.1929	2	1888	42	26*	0	14.00	–	–	–/–	–	–	
du Plessis Francois	13.7.1984		29	2012–2015	1,682	137	4	41.02	0	0-1	0/0	–	15	82/26
du Preez John Harcourt	14.11.1942		2	1966	0	0	0	0.00	3	2-22	0/0	17.00	1	
du Toit Jacobus Francois	2.4.1869	10.7.1909	1	1891	2	2*	0	–	1	1-47	0/0	47.00	–	
Dyer Dennis Victor	2.5.1914	16.6.1990	3	1947	96	62	0	16.00	–	–	–/–	–	1	
Eksteen Clive Edward	2.12.1966		7	1993–1999	91	22	0	10.11	8	3-12	0/0	61.75	5	6
Elgar Dean	11.6.1987		25	2012–2015	1,249	121	4	36.73	13	4-22	0/0	40.76	27	6
Elgie Michael Kelsey ("Kim")	6.3.1933		3	1961	75	56	0	12.50	0	0-18	0/0	–	1	
Elworthy Steven	23.2.1965		2	1998–2002	72	48	0	18.00	13	4-66	0/0	34.15	0	39
Endean William Russell	31.5.1924	28.6.2003	28	1951–1957	1,630	162*	3	33.95	–	–	–/–	–	41	
Farrer William Stephen ("Buster")	8.12.1936		6	1961–1963	221	40	0	27.62	–	–	–/–	–	2	
Faulkner George Aubrey	17.12.1881	10.9.1930	25	1905–1924	1,754	204	4	40.79	82	7-84	4/0	26.58	20	
Fellows-Smith Jonathan Payn	3.2.1932		4	1960	166	35	0	27.66	0	0-13	0/0	–	2	
Fichardt Charles Gustav	20.3.1870	30.5.1923	2	1891–1895	15	10	0	3.75	–	–	–/–	–	2	
Finlason Charles Edward	19.2.1860	31.7.1917	1	1888	6	6	0	3.00	0	0-7	0/0	–	0	
Floquet Claude Eugene	3.11.1884	22.11.1963	1	1909	12	11*	0	12.00	0	0-24	0/0	–	0	
Francis Howard Henry	26.5.1868	7.1.1936	2	1898	39	29	0	9.75	–	–	–/–	–	0	
Francois Cyril Matthew	20.6.1897	26.5.1944	5	1922	252	72	0	31.50	6	3-23	0/0	37.50	5	
Frank Charles Newton	27.1.1891	25.12.1961	3	1921	236	152	1	39.33	–	–	–/–	–	0	
Frank William Hughes Bowker	23.11.1872	16.2.1945	2	1895	7	5	0	3.50	–	–	–/–	–	0	
Fuller Edward Russell Henry	2.8.1931	19.7.2008	7	1952–1957	64	17	0	8.00	22	5-66	1/0	30.36	3	
Fullerton George Murray	8.12.1922	19.11.2002	7	1947–1951	325	88	0	25.00	–	–	–/–	–	10/2	
Funston Kenneth James	3.12.1925	15.4.2005	18	1952–1957	824	92	0	25.75	–	–	–/–	–	7	
Gamsy Dennis	17.2.1940		2	1969	39	30*	0	19.50	–	–	–/–	–	5	

Name	Born	Died	Tests	Test Career	Runs	HS	100s	Avge	Wkts	BB	5/10	Avge	Ct/St	O/T
Gibbs Herschelle Herman	23.2.1974	–	90	1996–2007	6,167	228	14	41.95	–	0-4	–/–	–	94	248/23
Gleeson Robert Anthony	6.12.1873	27.9.1919	1	1895	4	3	0	4.00	1	1-28	0/0	28.00	2	–
Glover George Keyworth	13.5.1870	15.11.1938	1	1895	21	18*	0	21.00	–	–	0/0	–	0	–
Goddard Trevor Leslie	1.8.1931	–	41	1955–1969	2,516	112	1	34.46	123	6-53	5/0	26.22	48	–
Gordon Norman	6.8.1911	2.9.2014	5	1938	6	7*	0	1.50	20	5-103	2/0	40.35	–	–
Graham Robert	16.9.1877	21.4.1946	2	1898	6	4	0	–	3	2-22	0/0	42.33	–	–
Grieveson Ronald Eustace	24.8.1909	24.7.1998	2	1938	114	75	0	57.00	–	–	–	–	7/3	–
Griffin Geoffrey Merton	12.6.1939	16.11.2006	2	1960	25	14	0	6.25	8	4-87	0/0	24.00	0	–
Hall Alfred Ewart	23.1.1896	1.1.1964	7	1922–1930	11	5	0	1.83	40	7-63	3/1	22.15	4	–
Hall Andrew James	31.7.1975	–	21	2001–2006	760	163	1	26.20	45	3-1	0/0	35.93	16	88/2
Hall Glen Gordon	24.5.1938	26.6.1987	1	1964	0	0	0	0.00	1	1-94	0/0	94.00	–	–
Halliwell Ernest Austin (CY 1905)	7.9.1864	2.10.1919	8	1891–1902	188	57	0	12.53	–	–	–	–	10/2	–
Halse Clive Gray	28.2.1935	2.8.2002	3	1963	30	19*	0	–	6	3-50	0/0	43.33	1	3
[2] Hands Philip Albert Myburgh	18.3.1890	27.4.1951	5	1913–1924	300	83	0	25.00	–	0-1	–	–	3	–
[2] Hands Reginald Harry Myburgh	26.7.1888	–	1	1913	7	7	0	3.50	1	1-57	0/0	88.00	0	–
Hanley Martin Andrew	10.11.1918	2.6.2000	1	1948	0	0	0	0.00	–	–	–	–	–	–
Harmer Simon Ross	10.2.1989	–	5	2014–2015	58	13	0	11.60	20	4-61	0/0	29.40	1	3
Harris Paul Lee	2.11.1978	–	37	2006–2010	460	46	0	10.69	103	6-127	3/0	37.87	16	–
Harris Terence Anthony	27.8.1916	7.3.1993	3	1947–1948	100	60	0	25.00	–	–	–	–	1	–
Hartigan Gerald Patrick Desmond	30.12.1884	7.1.1955	5	1912–1913	114	51	0	11.40	1	1-72	0/0	141.00	0	–
Harvey Robert Lyon	14.9.1911	20.7.2000	2	1935	51	28	0	12.75	–	–	–	–	0	–
Hathorn Christopher Maitland Howard	7.4.1878	17.5.1920	12	1902–1910	325	102	1	17.10	–	–	–	–	5	–
Hayward Mornantau ("Nantie")	6.3.1977	–	16	1999–2004	66	14	0	7.33	54	5-56	1/0	29.79	4	21
Hearne Frank	23.11.1858	14.11.1949	4†	1891–1895	121	30	0	15.12	2	2-40	0/0	20.00	3	–
[1,2] Hearne George Alfred Lawrence	27.3.1888	–	3	1922–1924	59	28	0	–	–	–	–	–	8	–
Heine Peter Samuel	28.6.1928	4.2.2005	14	1955–1961	209	31	0	11.80	58	6-58	4/0	25.08	8	–
Henderson Claude William	14.6.1972	–	7	2001–2002	65	30	0	9.95	22	4-116	0/0	42.18	2	4
Henry Omar	23.11.1952	–	3	1992	53	34	0	9.28	3	2-56	0/0	63.00	0	3
Hime Charles Frederick William	24.10.1869	6.12.1940	1	1895	8	8	0	17.66	1	1-20	0/0	31.00	–	–
Hudson Andrew Charles	17.3.1965	–	35	1991–1997	2,007	163	4	33.45	–	–	–	–	36	89
Hutchinson Philip	25.1.1862	30.9.1925	2	1888	14	11	0	4.00	–	–	–	–	–	–
Imran Tahir	27.3.1979	–	20	2011–2015	130	29*	0	18.50	57	5-32	2/0	40.24	8	49/18
Ironside David Ernest James	2.5.1925	21.8.2005	3	1953	37	13	0	18.50	15	5-51	1/0	18.33	2	–
Irvine Brian Lee	9.3.1944	–	4	1969	353	102	1	50.42	–	–	–	–	1	–
Jack Steven Douglas	4.8.1970	–	2	1994	7	7	0	3.50	8	4-69	0/0	24.50	1	2
Johnson Clement Lecky	31.3.1871	31.5.1908	1	1895	10	7	0	5.00	0	0-57	0/0	–	1	–

Name	Born	Died	Tests	Test Career	Runs	HS	100s	Avge	Wkts	BB	5/10	Avge	Ct/St	O/T
Kallis Jacques Henry (CY 2013)	16.10.1975		165‡	1995–2013	13,206	224	45	55.25	291	6-54	5/0	32.63	196	323‡/25
Keith Headley James	25.10.1927	17.11.1997	8	1952–1956	318	73	0	21.20	0	0-19	0/0	–	9	
Kemp Justin Miles	2.10.1977			2000–2005	80	55	0	13.33	9	3-33	0/0	24.66	1	79‡/8
Kempis Gustav Adolph	4.8.1865	19.5.1890	1	1888	0	0*	0	0.00	4	3-53	0/0	19.00	1	
Khan Imran	27.4.1984		1	2008	20	20	0	20.00	2	1-0	0/0	71.00	0	
[2] Kirsten Gary (CY 2004)	23.11.1967		101	1993–2003	7,289	275	21	45.27	0	0-5	0/0	–	83	185
Kirsten Peter Noel	14.5.1955		12	1991–1994	626	104	1	31.30			–/–		8	40
Kleinveldt Rory Keith	15.3.1983		4	2012	27	17*	0	9.00	10	3-65	0/0	42.20	0	10/6
Klusener Lance (CY 2000)	4.9.1971		49	1996–2004	1,906	174	4	32.86	80	8-64	1/0	37.91	34	171
Kotze Johannes Jacobus ("Kodgee")	7.8.1879	7.7.1931	3	1902–1907	2	2	0	0.40	6	3-64	0/0	40.50	3	
Kuiper Adrian Paul	24.8.1959		1	1991	34	34	0	17.00	0	0-5	–/–	–	3	25
Kuys Frederick	21.3.1870	12.9.1953	1	1898	26	26	0	13.00	2	2-31	0/0	15.50	0	
Lance Herbert Roy ("Tiger")	6.6.1940	10.11.2010	13	1961–1969	591	70	0	28.14	12	3-30	0/0	39.91	7	
Langeveldt Charl Kenneth	17.12.1974		6	2004–2005	16	10	0	8.00	16	5-46	1/0	37.06	2	72/9
Langton Arthur Chudleigh Beaumont ("Chud")	2.3.1912	27.11.1942	15	1935–1938	298	73*	0	15.68	40	5-58	1/0	45.67	8	
Lawrence Godfrey Bernard	31.3.1932		5	1961	141	43	0	17.62	28	8-53	2/0	28.14	2	
le Roux Frederick Louis	5.2.1882	22.9.1963	1	1913	1	1	0	0.50	0	0-7	–/–	–	0	
Lewis Percy Tyson	2.10.1884	30.1.1976	1	1913	0	0	0	0.00	0	0-20	–/–	–	0	
Liebenberg Gerhardus Frederick Johannes	7.4.1972		5	1997–1998	104	45	0	13.00			–/–		7	4
[3] Lindsay Denis Thomson	4.9.1939	30.11.2005	19	1963–1969	1,130	182	3	37.66			–/–		57/2	
[4] Lindsay John Dixon	8.9.1908	31.8.1990	3	1947	21	21	0	7.00			–/–		4/1	
Lindsay Nevil Vernon	30.7.1886	2.2.1976	1	1921	35	29	0	17.50			–/–		1	
Ling William Victor Stone	3.10.1891	26.9.1960	6	1921–1922	168	38	0	16.80	0	0-1	–/–	–	1	
Llewellyn Charles Bennett (CY 1911)	26.9.1876	7.6.1964	15	1895–1912	544	90	0	20.14	48	6-92	4/1	29.60	7	
Lundie Eric Balfour	15.3.1888	12.9.1917	1	1913	1	1	0	1.00	4	4-101	0/0	26.75	0	
Macaulay Michael John	19.4.1939		1	1964	33	21	0	16.50	2	2-72	0/0	36.50	0	
McCarthy Cuan Neil	24.3.1929	14.8.2000	15	1948–1951	28	5	0	3.11	36	6-43	2/0	41.94	6	
McGlew Derrick John ("Jackie") (CY 1956)	11.3.1929	9.6.1998	34	1951–1961	2,440	255*	7	42.06	0	0-7	–/–	–	18	
McKenzie Neil Douglas (CY 2009)	24.11.1975		58	2000–2008	3,253	226	5	37.39	0	0-20	–/–	–	54	64/2
McKinnon Atholl Henry	20.8.1932	2.12.1983	8	1960–1966	107	27	0	17.83	26	4-128	0/0	35.57	0	
McLaren Ryan	9.2.1983		2	2009–2013	47	33*	0	23.50		2-72	0/0	54.00	0	54/12
McLean Roy Alastair (CY 1961)	9.7.1930	26.8.2007	40	1951–1964	2,120	142	5	30.28	0	0-1	–/–	–	23	
McMillan Brian Mervin	22.12.1963		38	1992–1998	1,968	113	3	39.36	75	4-65	0/0	33.82	49	78
McMillan Quintin	23.6.1904	3.7.1948	13	1929–1931	306	50*	0	18.00	36	5-66	2/0	34.52	8	
Mann Norman Bertram Fleetwood ("Tufty")	28.12.1920	31.7.1952	19	1947–1951	400	52	0	13.33	58	6-59	1/0	33.10	8	

§ Kallis's figures exclude 83 runs, one wicket and four catches for the ICC World XI v Australia in the Super Series Test in 2005-06.

	Born	Died	Tests	Test Career	Runs	HS	100s	Avge	Wkts	BB	5/10	Avge	Ct/St	O/T
Mansell Percy Neville Frank MBE	16.3.1920	9.5.1995	13	1951–1955	355	90	0	17.75	11	3-58	0/0	66.90	15	
Markham Lawrence Anderson	12.9.1924	5.8.2000	1	1948	20	20	0	20.00	1	1-34	0/0	72.00	0	
Marx Waldemar Frederick Eric	4.7.1895		3	1921	125	36	0	20.83	4	1-85	0/0	36.00	0	56
Matthews Craig Russell	15.2.1965		18	1992–1995	348	62*	0	18.31	52	5-42	2/0	28.88	4	
Meintjes Douglas James	9.6.1890	17.7.1979	2	1922	43	21	0	14.33	2	3-38	0/0	19.16	2	
Melle Michael George	3.6.1930	28.12.2003	7	1949–1952	68	17	0	8.50	26	6-71	2/0	32.73	4	
Melville Alan (CY 1948)	19.5.1910	18.4.1983	11	1938–1948	894	189	4	52.58			–/–		8	
Middleton James	30.9.1865	23.12.1913	6	1895–1902	52	22	0	7.42	24	5-51	2/0	18.41	1	
Mills Charles Henry	26.11.1867	26.7.1948	1	1891	25	21	0	12.50	2	2-83	0/0	41.50	1	
Milton Sir William Henry	3.12.1854	6.3.1930	3	1888–1891	68	21	0	11.33	2	1-5	0/0	24.00	2	
Mitchell Bruce (CY 1936)	8.1.1909	1.7.1995	42	1929–1948	3,471	189*	8	48.88	27	5-87	1/0	51.11	56	
Mitchell Frank (CY 1902)	13.8.1872	11.10.1935	3†	1912	28	12	0	4.66	–	–	–/–		8	
Morkel Denijs Paul Beck	25.11.1906	6.10.1980	16	1927–1931	663	88	0	24.55	18	4-93	0/0	45.61	13	56‡/50
²Morkel Johannes Albertus	10.6.1981		1	2008	58	58	0	58.00	1	1-44	0/0	132.00	1	100‡/53
²Morkel Morne	6.10.1984		71	2006–2015	775	40	0	11.56	242	6-23	6/0	29.33	19	8/4
Morris Christopher Henry	30.4.1987		2	2015	98	69	0	32.66	4	1-8	0/0	63.25	2	
Murray Anton Ronald Andrew	30.4.1922	17.4.1995	10	1952–1953	289	109	0	22.23	18	4-169	0/0	39.44	3	
Nel Andre	15.7.1977		36	2001–2008	337	34	0	9.91	123	6-32	3/1	31.86	16	79/2
Nel John Desmond	10.7.1928			1949–1957	150	38	0	13.63			–/–		3	
Newberry Claude	1889	1.8.1916	4	1913	62	16	0	7.75	11	4-72	0/0	24.36	3	
Newson Edward Serrurier OBE	2.12.1910	24.4.1988	3	1930–1938	30	16	0	7.50	4	2-58	0/0	66.25	3	
Ngam Mfuneko	29.1.1979		3	2000	0	0*	–		11	3-26	0/0	17.18	1	
Nicholson John Fairless William	19.7.1899	13.12.1935	3	1927	179	78	0	35.80	–	–	–/–		3	
Norton Norman Ogilvie	11.5.1881	27.6.1968	1	1909	9	7	0	4.50	4	4-47	0/0	11.75	0	
¹Nourse Arthur Dudley (CY 1948)	12.11.1910	14.8.1981	34	1935–1951	2,960	231	9	53.81			–/–		12	
¹Nourse Arthur William ("Dave")	25.1.1879	8.7.1948	45	1902–1924	2,234	111	1	29.78	41	4-25	0/0	37.87	43	
Ntini Makhaya	6.7.1977		101	1997–2009	699	32*	0	9.84	390	7-37	18/4	28.82	25	172‡/10
Nupen Eiulf Peter ("Buster")	1.1.1902	29.1.1977	17	1921–1935	348	69	0	14.50	50	6-46	5/1	35.76	9	
Ochse Arthur Edward	11.3.1870	11.4.1918	2	1888	16	8	0	4.00			–/–		0	
Ochse Arthur Lennox	11.10.1899	5.5.1949	3	1927–1929	11	4*	0	3.66	10	4-79	0/0	36.20	1	
O'Linn Sidney	5.5.1927		7	1960–1961	297	98	0	27.00	1	1-79	0/0	133.00	4	
Ontong Justin Lee	4.1.1980		2	2001–2004	57	32	0	19.00	–	–	–/–		1	27‡/14
Owen-Smith Harold Geoffrey ("Tuppy") (CY 1930)	18.2.1909	28.2.1990	5	1929	252	129	1	42.00	0	0-3	0/0	–	4	
Palm Archibald William	8.6.1901	17.8.1966	1	1927	15	13	0	7.50	–	–	–/–		1	

	Born	Died	Tests	Test Career	Runs	HS	100s	Avge	Wkts	BB	5/10	Avge	Ct/St	O/T
Parker George Macdonald	27.5.1899	1.5.1969	2	1924	3	2*	0	1.50	8	6-152	1/0	34.12	0	0
Parkin Durant Clifford	20.2.1873	20.3.1936	1	1891	6	6	0	3.00	3	3-82	0/0	27.33	1	
Parnell Wayne Dillon	30.7.1989		4	2009-2013	44	22	0	14.66	7	2-17	0/0	36.85	1	46/35
Partridge Joseph Titus	9.12.1932	6.6.1988	11	1963-1964	73	13*	0	10.42	44	7-91	3/0	31.20	6	
Pearse Charles Ormerod Cato	10.10.1884	7.5.1953	3	1910	55	31	0	9.16	3	3-56	0/0	35.33		
Pegler Sidney James	28.7.1888	10.9.1972	16	1909-1924	356	35*	0	15.47	47	7-65	2/0	33.44	5	
Petersen Alviro Nathan	25.11.1980		36	2009-2014	2,093	182	5	34.88	1	1-2	0/0	62.00	31	21/2
Peterson Robin John	4.8.1979		15	2003-2013	464	84	0	27.29	38	5-33	1/0	37.26	9	79/21
Philander Vernon Darryl	24.6.1985		32	2011-2015	725	74	0	25.00	126	6-44	9/2	22.08	8	30/7
Piedt Dane Lee-Roy	6.3.1990		5	2014-2015	39	19	0	6.50	22	5-153	1/0	35.31	4	
[2]Pithey Anthony John	17.7.1933	17.11.2006	17	1956-1964	819	154	1	31.50	0	0-5	0/0	–	3	
[2]Pithey David Bartlett	4.10.1936		8	1963-1966	138	55	0	12.54	12	6-58	1/0	48.08	6	
Plimsoll Jack Bruce	27.10.1917	11.11.1999	1	1947	16	8*	0	16.00	3	3-128	0/0	47.66	0	
[1,2]Pollock Peter Maclean (CY 1966)	30.6.1941		28	1961-1969	607	75*	0	21.67	116	6-38	9/1	24.18	9	
[2]Pollock Robert Graeme (CY 1966)	27.2.1944		23	1963-1969	2,256	274	7	60.97	4	2-50	0/0	51.00	17	
Pollock Shaun Maclean (CY 2003)	16.7.1973		108	1995-2007	3,781	111	2	32.31	421	7-87	16/1	23.11	72	294¾/12
Poore Robert Montagu (CY 1900)	20.3.1866	14.7.1938	3	1895	76	20	0	12.66	1	1-4	0/0	4.00	3	
Potbecary James Edward	6.12.1933		3	1960	26	12	0	6.50	9	4-58	0/0	39.33	2	
Powell Albert William	18.7.1873	11.9.1948	1	1898	16	11	0	8.00	1	1-10	0/0	10.00	2	
Pretorius Dewald	6.12.1977		4	2001-2003	22	9	0	7.33	6	4-115	0/0	71.66	0	
Prince Ashwell Gavin	28.5.1977		66	2001-2011	3,665	162*	11	41.64	1	1-2	0/0	47.00	47	49¾/1
Prince Charles Frederick Henry	11.9.1874	2.2.1949	1	1898	6	5	0	3.00	–	–	–/–	–	0	
Pringle Meyrick Wayne	22.6.1966		4	1991-1995	67	33	0	16.75	5	2-62	0/0	54.00	0	17
Procter Michael John (CY 1970)	15.9.1946		7	1966-1969	226	48	0	25.11	41	6-73	1/0	15.02	4	
Promnitz Henry Louis Ernest	23.2.1904	7.9.1983	2	1927	14	5	0	3.50	8	5-58	1/0	20.12	2	
Quinn Neville Anthony	21.2.1908	5.8.1934	12	1929-1931	90	28	0	6.00	35	6-92	3/1	32.71	2	
Rabada Kagiso	25.5.1995		6	2015	56	24	0	11.20	24	7-112	2/1	24.70	1	10/8
Reid Norman	26.12.1890	6.6.1947	1	1921	17	11	0	8.50	2	2-63	0/0	31.50	0	
Rhodes Jonathan Neil (CY 1999)	27.7.1969		52	1992-2000	2,532	117	3	35.66	0	0-0	–/–	–	34	245
[2]Richards Alfred Renfrew	14.12.1867	9.1.1904	1	1895	–	–	–	–	–	–	–/–	–	0	
Richards Barry Anderson (CY 1969)	21.7.1945		4	1969	508	140	2	72.57	1	1-12	0/0	26.00	3	
[2]Richards William Henry Matthews	26.3.1862	4.1.1903	1	1888	4	4	0	2.00	–	–	–/–	–	0	
Richardson David John	16.9.1959		42	1991-1997	1,359	109	0	24.26	–	–	–/–	–	150/2	122
Robertson John Benjamin	5.6.1906	5.7.1985	3	1935	51	17	0	10.20	6	3-143	0/0	53.50	2	
Rose-Innes Albert	16.2.1868	22.11.1946	2	1888	14	13	0	3.50	5	5-43	1/0	17.80	2	
Routledge Thomas William	18.4.1867	9.5.1927	4	1891-1895	72	24	0	9.00	–	–	–/–	–	2	

	Born	Died	Tests	Test Career	Runs	HS	100s	Avge	Wkts	BB	5/10	Avge	Ct/St	O/T
² Rowan Athol Matthew Burchell	7.2.1921	22.2.1998	15	1947–1951	290	41	0	17.05	54	5-68	4/0	38.59	7	–
² Rowan Eric Alfred Burchell (CY 1952)	20.7.1909	30.4.1993	26	1935–1951	1,965	236	3	43.66	0	0-0	0/0	–	14	–
Rowe George Alexander	15.6.1874	8.1.1950	5	1895–1902	26	13*	0	4.33	15	5-115	1/0	30.40	4	43‡/1
Rudolph Jacobus Andries	4.5.1981	–	48	2003–2012	2,622	222*	6	35.43	4	1-1	0/0	108.00	29	4
Rushmere Mark Weir	7.1.1965	–	1	1991	6	3	0	3.00	–	–	–/–	–	0	–
Samuelson Sivert Vause	21.11.1883	18.11.1958	1	1909	22	15	0	11.00	0	0-64	0/0	–	0	–
Schultz Brett Nolan	26.8.1970	–	9	1992–1997	9	6	0	1.50	37	5-48	2/0	20.24	2	–
Schwarz Reginald Oscar (CY 1908)	4.5.1875	18.11.1918	20	1905–1912	374	61	0	13.85	55	6-47	2/0	25.76	18	1
Seccull Arthur William	14.9.1868	20.7.1945	1	1895	23	17*	0	23.00	2	2-37	0/0	18.50	1	–
Seymour Michael Arthur ("Kelly")	5.6.1936	–	7	1963–1969	84	36	0	12.00	9	3-80	0/0	65.33	2	–
Shalders William Alfred	12.2.1880	18.3.1917	12	1898–1907	355	42	0	16.13	1	1-6	0/0	6.00	2	–
Shepstone George Harold	9.4.1876	3.7.1940	2	1895–1898	38	21	0	9.50	0	0-8	0/0	–	2	–
Sherwell Percy William	17.8.1880	17.4.1948	13	1905–1910	427	115	1	23.72	–	–	–/–	–	20/16	–
Siedle Ivan Julian ("Jack")	11.1.1903	24.8.1982	18	1927–1935	977	141	1	28.73	1	1-7	0/0	7.00	7	–
Sinclair James Hugh	16.10.1876	23.2.1913	25	1895–1911	1,069	106	3	23.23	63	6-26	1/0	31.68	9	–
Smith Charles James Edward	25.12.1872	27.3.1947	1	1902	106	45	0	21.20	–	–	–/–	–	2	–
Smith Frederick William	31.3.1861	17.4.1914	3	1888–1895	45	12	0	9.00	2	2-145	0/0	110.62	2	–
Smith Graeme Craig (CY 2004)	1.2.1981	–	116§	2001–2013	9,253	277	27	48.70	8	4-143	0/0	64.08	166	196‡/33
Smith Vivian Ian	22.9.1925	25.8.2015	9	1947–1957	39	11*	0	3.90	–	–	–/–	–	3	–
Snell Richard Peter	12.9.1968	–	26	1991–1994	95	48	0	13.57	19	4-74	0/0	28.31	24	42
² Snooke Sibley John ("Tip")	1.2.1881	14.8.1966	26	1905–1922	1,008	103	1	22.40	35	8-70	1/1	20.05	24	–
Snooke Stanley de la Courtte	11.11.1878	6.4.1959	1	1907	4	2	0	0.00	–	–	–/–	–	1	–
Solomon William Rodger Thomson	23.4.1872	13.7.1964	1	1898	2	2	0	2.00	–	–	–/–	–	0	–
Stewart Robert Burnard	3.9.1856	12.9.1913	1	1888	13	9	0	6.50	–	–	–/–	–	0	–
Steyn Dale Willem (CY 2013)	27.6.1983	–	82	2004–2015	1,143	76	1	14.11	406	7-51	25/5	22.53	22	110‡/38
Steyn Philippus Jeremia Rudolf	30.6.1967	–	3	1994	127	46	0	21.16	–	–	–/–	–	3	1
Stricker Louis Anthony	26.5.1884	5.2.1960	13	1909–1912	344	48	0	14.33	1	1-36	0/0	105.00	3	–
Strydom Pieter Coenraad	10.6.1969	–	2	1999	35	30	0	11.66	1	0-27	0/0	–	0	10
Susskind Manfred John	8.6.1891	9.7.1957	5	1924	268	65	0	33.50	–	–	–/–	–	5	–
Symcox Patrick Leonard	14.4.1960	–	20	1993–1998	741	108	1	28.50	37	4-69	0/0	43.32	5	80
Taberer Henry Melville	7.10.1870	5.6.1932	1	1902	2	2	0	2.00	–	–	–/–	–	0	–
² Tancred Augustus Bernard	20.8.1865	23.11.1911	2	1888	87	29	0	29.00	–	–	–/–	–	2	–
² Tancred Louis Joseph	7.10.1876	28.7.1934	14	1902–1913	530	97	0	21.20	1	1-25	0/0	48.00	3	–
² Tancred Vincent Maximilian	7.7.1875	3.6.1904	1	1898	25	4	0	12.50	–	–	–/–	–	0	–
² Tapscott George Lancelot ("Dusty")	7.11.1889	13.12.1940	1	1913	5	4	0	2.50	–	–	–/–	–	1	–

§ G. C. Smith's figures exclude 12 runs and three catches for the ICC World XI v Australia in the Super Series Test in 2005-06.

	Born	Died	Tests	Test Career	Runs	HS	100s	Avge	Wks	BB	Avge	5/10	Ct/St	O/T
[2]Tapscott Lionel Eric ("Doodles")	18.3.1894	7.7.1934	2	1922	58	50*	0	29.00	0	0-2	25.91	0/0	0	
Tayfield Hugh Joseph (CY 1956)	30.1.1929	24.2.1994	37	1949–1960	862	75	0	16.90	170	9-113	21.86	14/2	26	
Taylor Alistair Innes ("Scotch")	25.7.1925	7.2.2004	2	1956	18	12	0	–	–	–	–	–	0	
[2]Taylor Daniel	9.1.1887	24.1.1957	2	1913	85	36	0	21.25	–	–	–	–	0	
[2]Taylor Herbert Wilfred (CY 1925)	5.5.1889	8.2.1973	42	1912–1931	2,936	176	7	40.77	5	3-15	31.20	0/0	19	4
Terbrugge David John	31.1.1977		7	1998–2003	16	4*	0	5.33	20	5-46	25.85	1/0	4	
Theunissen Nicolaas Hendrik Christiaan de Jong	4.5.1867	9.11.1929	1	1888	2	2*	0	2.00	–	0-51	–	–	1	
Thornton George	24.12.1867	31.1.1939	1	1902	1	1*	0	–	1	1-20	20.00	0/0	1	
Tomlinson Denis Stanley	4.9.1910	11.7.1993	1	1935	9	9	0	9.00	–	0-38	–	0/0	0	
Traicos Athanasios John	17.5.1947		3‡	1969	8	5*	0	4.00	4	2-70	51.75	0/0	4	0‡
Trimborn Patrick Henry Joseph	18.5.1940		4	1966–1969	13	11*	0	6.50	11	3-12	23.36	0/0	7	
Tsolekile Thami Lungisa	9.10.1980		3	2004	47	22	0	9.40	–	–	–	–	6	
Tsotsobe Lonwabo Lennox	7.3.1984		5	2010–2010	19	8*	0	6.33	9	3-43	49.77	0/0	–	61/23
[1]Tuckett Lindsay Thomas Delville	6.2.1919		9	1947–1948	131	40*	0	11.90	19	5-68	51.57	1/0	11	
[1]Tuckett Lindsay Richard ("Len")	19.4.1885	8.4.1963	1	1913	0	0*	0	0.00	0	0-24	–	0/0	9	
Twentyman-Jones Percy Sydney	13.9.1876	8.3.1954	1	1902	0	0	0	0.00	–	–	–	–	2	
van der Bijl Pieter Gerhard Vincent	21.10.1907	16.2.1973	5	1938	460	125	1	51.11	–	–	–	–	5	
van der Merwe Edward Alexander	9.11.1903	26.2.1971	2	1929–1935	27	19	0	9.00	–	–	–	–	1	
van der Merwe Peter Laurence	14.3.1937		15	1963–1966	533	76	0	25.38	1	1-6	22.00	0/0	11	
van Jaarsveld Martin	18.6.1974		9	2002–2004	397	73	0	30.53	0	0-28	–	0/0	14	11
van Ryneveld Clive Berrange	19.3.1928		19	1951–1957	724	83	0	26.81	17	4-67	39.47	0/0	14	
van Zyl Stiaan	19.9.1987		11	2014–2015	355	101*	1	27.30	6	3-20	23.83	0/0	5	
Varnals George Derek	24.7.1935		3	1964	97	23	0	16.16	–	–	–	–	5	
Vilas Dane James	10.6.1985		5	2015–2015	94	26	0	10.44	–	–	–	–	13	0/1
Viljoen G. C. ("Hardus")	6.3.1989		1	2015	26	20*	0	26.00	1	1-79	94.00	0/0		
Viljoen Kenneth George	14.5.1910	21.1.1974	27	1930–1948	1,365	124	2	28.43	2	0-10	–	0/0	5	
Vincent Cyril Leverton	16.2.1902	24.8.1968	25	1927–1935	526	60	0	20.23	84	6-51	31.32	3/0	27	
Vincent Charles Henry	2.9.1866	28.9.1943	1	1888–1891	26	9	0	4.33	4	3-88	48.25	0/0	20	
Vogler Albert Edward Ernest (CY 1908)	28.11.1876	9.8.1946	15	1905–1910	340	65	0	17.00	64	7-94	22.73	5/1	20	
[2]Wade Herbert Frederick	14.9.1905	23.11.1980	10	1935–1935	327	40*	0	20.43	–	–	–	–	4	
[2]Wade Walter Wareham ("Billy")	18.6.1914	31.5.2003	11	1938–1949	511	125	1	28.38	–	–	–	–	15/2	
Waite John Henry Bickford	19.1.1930	22.6.2011	50	1951–1964	2,405	134	4	30.44	–	–	–	–	124/17	
Walter Kenneth Alexander	5.11.1939	13.9.2003	2	1961	11	10	0	3.66	6	4-63	32.83	0/0	3	
Ward Thomas Alfred	2.8.1887	16.2.1936	23	1912–1924	459	64	0	13.90	–	–	–	–	19/13	
Watkins John Cecil	10.4.1923		15	1949–1956	612	92	0	23.53	29	4-22	28.13	0/0	12	
Wesley Colin	5.9.1937		3	1960	49	35	0	9.80	–	–	–	–	1	

	Born	Died	Tests	Test Career	Runs	HS	100s	Avge	Wkts	BB	5/10	Avge	Ct/St	O/T
Wessels Kepler Christoffel (CY 1995)	14.9.1957		16†	1991–1994	1,027	118	2	38.03	—	—	-/-	—	12	55‡
Westcott Richard John	19.9.1927		5	1953–1957	166	62	0	18.44	0	0-22	0/0	—	10	
White Gordon Charles	5.2.1882	17.10.1918	17	1905–1912	872	147	2	30.06	9	4-47	0/0	33.44	10	
Willoughby Charl Myles	3.12.1974		2	2003	—	—	0	—	1	1-47	0/0	125.00	0	3
Willoughby Joseph Thomas	7.11.1874	11.3.1952	2	1895	8	5	0	2.00	2	2-37	0/0	26.50	0	
Wimble Clarence Skelton	22.4.1861	28.1.1930	2	1891	0	0	0	0.00	—	—	-/-	—	0	
Winslow Paul Lyndhurst	21.5.1929	24.5.2011	5	1949–1955	186	108	1	20.66	—	—	-/-	—	3	
Wynne Owen Edgar	1.6.1919	13.7.1975	6	1948–1949	219	50	0	18.25	—	—	-/-	—	1	
Zondeki Monde	25.7.1982		6	2003–2008	82	59	0	16.40	19	6-39	1/0	25.26	1	11/1
Zulch Johan Wilhelm	2.1.1886	19.5.1924	16	1909–1921	983	150	2	32.76	0	0-2	0/0	—	4	

WEST INDIES (306 players)

	Born	Died	Tests	Test Career	Runs	HS	100s	Avge	Wkts	BB	5/10	Avge	Ct/St	O/T
Achong Ellis Edgar	16.2.1904	30.8.1986	6	1929–1934	81	22	0	8.10	8	2-64	0/0	47.25	5	
Adams James Clive	9.1.1968		54	1991–2000	3,012	208*	6	41.26	27	5-17	1/0	49.48	48	127
Alexander Franz Copeland Murray ("Gerry")	2.11.1928	16.4.2011	25	1957–1960	961	108	1	30.03	—	—	-/-	—	85/5	
Ali Imtiaz	28.7.1954		1	1975	1	1*	0	—	2	2-37	0/0	44.50	0	
Ali Inshan	25.9.1949	24.6.1995	12	1970–1976	172	25	0	10.75	34	5-59	1/0	47.67	7	
Allan David Walter	5.11.1937		5	1961–1966	75	40*	0	12.50	—	—	-/-	—	15/3	
Allen Ian Basil Alston	6.10.1965		2	1991	5	4*	0	—	5	2-69	0/0	36.00	0	
Ambrose Sir Curtly Elconn Lynwall (CY 1992)	21.9.1963		98	1987–2000	1,439	53	0	12.40	405	8-45	22/3	20.99	18	176
Arthurton Keith Lloyd Thomas	21.2.1965		33	1988–1995	1,382	157*	2	30.71	1	1-17	0/0	183.00	22	105
Asgarali Nyron Sultan	28.12.1920	5.11.2006	2	1957	62	29	0	15.50	—	—	-/-	—	1	
Atkinson Denis St Eval	9.8.1926	9.11.2001	22	1948–1957	922	219	2	31.79	47	7-53	3/0	35.04	11	
Atkinson Eric St Eval	6.11.1927	29.5.1998	8	1957–1958	126	37	0	15.75	25	5-42	1/0	23.56	2	
Austin Richard Arkwright	5.9.1954	7.2.2015	2	1977	22	20	0	11.00	0	0-5	0/0	—	2	1
Austin Ryan Anthony	15.11.1981		2	2009	39	19	0	9.75	3	1-29	0/0	51.66	2	
Bacchus Sheik Faoud Ahamul Faisel	31.11.1954		19	1977–1981	782	250	1	26.06	0	0-3	0/0	—	17	29
Baichan Leonard	12.5.1946		3	1974–1975	184	105*	0	46.00	—	—	-/-	—	2	
Baker Lionel Sionne	6.9.1984		4	2008–2009	23	17	0	11.50	5	2-39	0/0	79.00	1	10/3
Banks Omari Ahmed Clemente	17.7.1982		10	2002–2005	318	50*	0	26.50	28	4-87	0/0	48.82	6	5
Baptiste Eldine Ashworth Elderfield	12.3.1960		10	1983–1989	233	87*	0	23.30	16	3-31	0/0	35.18	2	43
Barath Adrian Boris	14.4.1990		15	2009–2012	657	104	1	23.46	0	0-3	0/0	—	13	14/2
Barrett Arthur George	4.4.1944		6	1970–1974	40	19	0	6.66	13	3-43	0/0	46.38	0	

	Born	Died	Tests	Test Career	Runs	HS	100s	Avge	Wkts	BB	Avge	5/10	Avge	Ct/St	O/T
Barrow Ivanhoe Mordecai	16.1.1911	2.4.1979	11	1929-1939	276	105	1	16.23	–	–		–/–		17/5	
Bartlett Edward Lawson	10.3.1906	21.12.1976	5	1928-1930	131	84	0	18.71	–	–		–/–		2	
Baugh Carlton Seymour	23.6.1982		21	2002-2011	610	68	0	17.94	–	–		–/–		43/5	47/3
Benjamin Kenneth Charlie Griffith	8.4.1967		26	1991-1997	222	43*	0	7.92	92	6-66	30.27	4/1		12	26
Benjamin Winston Keithroy Matthew	31.12.1964		21	1987-1994	470	85	0	18.80	61	4-46	27.01	0/0		14	85
Benn Sulieman Jamaal	22.7.1981		26	2007-2014	486	42	0	14.29	87	6-81	39.10	6/0		0	34/18
Bernard David Eddison	19.7.1981		3	2002-2009	202		0	40.40	4	2-30		0/0		0	20/1
Bess Brandon Jeremy	13.12.1987			2010	11	11*	0	11.00	1	1-65	92.00	0/0			
Best Carlisle Alonza	14.5.1959		8	1985-1990	342	164	1	28.50	–	–		–/–		8	24
Best Tino la Bertram	26.8.1981		25	2002-2013	401	95	0	12.53	57	6-40	40.19	2/0		6	26/6
Betancourt Nelson	4.6.1887	12.10.1947	1	1929	52	39	0	26.00	–	–		–/–			
Binns Alfred Philip	24.7.1929		5	1952-1955	64	27	0	9.14	–	–		–/–		14/3	
Birkett Lionel Sydney	14.4.1905	16.1.1998	4	1930	136	64	0	17.00	1	1-16	71.00	0/0		4	
Bishoo Devendra	6.11.1985		15	2010-2015	244	30	0	15.25	55	6-80	38.05	2/0		9	13/5
Bishop Ian Raphael	24.10.1967		43	1988-1997	632	48	0	12.15	161	6-40	24.27	6/0		8	84
Black Marlon Ian	7.6.1975		6	2000-2001	21		0	2.62	12	4-83	49.75	0/0			5
Blackwood Jermaine	20.11.1991		15	2014-2015	800	112*	1	33.33	2	2-14	78.50	0/0		17	5
Boyce Keith David (CY 1974)	11.10.1943	11.10.1996	21	1970-1975	657	95*	0	24.33	60	6-77	30.01	2/1		5	8
Bradshaw Ian David Russell	9.7.1974		5	2005	96	33	0	13.71	9	3-73	60.00	0/0		0	62/1
Brathwaite Carlos Ricardo	18.7.1988		2	2015	130	69	0	43.33	1	1-30	162.00	0/0		3	7/2
Brathwaite Kraigg Clairmonte	1.12.1992		27	2010-2015	1,686	212	4	34.40	9	6-29	5.00	1/0		10	
[2]Bravo Dwayne John	7.10.1983		40	2004-2010	2,200	113	3	31.42	86	6-55	39.83	0/0		41	164/55
[2]Bravo Darren Michael	6.2.1989		42	2010-2015	2,988	218	7	41.50	0	0-2		–/–		41	84/12
Breese Gareth Rohan	9.1.1976		1	2002	5	5	0	2.50	2	2-108	67.50	0/0			
Browne Courtney Oswald	7.12.1970		20	1994-2004	387	68	0	16.12	–	–		–/–		79/2	46
Browne Cyril Rutherford	8.10.1890	12.1.1964	4	1928-1929	176	70*	0	25.14	6	2-72	39.50	0/0			
Butcher Basil Fitzherbert (CY 1970)	3.9.1933	1.9.2009	44	1958-1969	3,104	209*	7	43.11	5	5-34	18.00	0/0		15	
Butler Lennox Stephen	9.2.1929		1	1954	16	16	0	16.00	2	2-151	75.50	0/0		0	
Butts Clyde Godfrey	8.7.1957		7	1984-1987	108	38	0	15.42	10	4-73	59.50	1/0		2	
Bynoe Michael Robin	23.2.1941		4	1958-1966	111	48	0	18.50	0			0/0		4	
Camacho George Stephen	15.10.1945	2.10.2015	11	1967-1970	640	87	0	29.09	–	–		–/–		0	
Cameron Francis James	22.6.1923	10.6.1994	5	1948	151	75*	0	25.16	3	0-12	92.66	0/0		4	
[2]Cameron John Hemsley	8.4.1914	13.2.2000	2	1939	6	5	0	2.00	3	2-74	29.33	0/0		0	
Campbell Sherwin Legay	1.11.1970		52	1994-2001	2,882	208	4	32.38	0	3-66		0/0		47	90
Carew George McDonald	4.6.1910	9.12.1974	4	1934-1948	170	107	1	28.33	0	0-2		–/–			
[2]Carew Michael Conrad ("Joey")	15.9.1937	8.1.2011	19	1963-1971	1,127	109	1	34.15	8	1-11	54.62	0/0		13	

	Born	Died	Tests	Test Career	Runs	HS	100s	Avge	Wkts	BB	5/10	Avge	Ct/St	OIT
Challenor George	28.6.1888	30.7.1947	3	1928	101	46	0	16.83	–	–	–/–	–	0	–
Chanderpaul Shivnarine (CY 2008)	16.8.1974		164	1993–2014	11,867	203*	30	51.37	9	1-2	0/0	98.11	66	268/22
Chandrika Rajindra	8.8.1989		3	2015–2015	87	37	0	14.50	–	–	–/–	–	6	
Chang Herbert Samuel	2.7.1952		1	1978	8	8	0	4.00	–	–	–/–	–	0	
Chattergoon Sewnarine	3.4.1981		4	2007–2008	127	46	0	18.14	–	–	–/–	–	4	18
Christiani Cyril Marcel	28.10.1913	4.4.1938	4	1934	98	32*	0	19.60	–	–	–/–	–	6/1	
2 Christiani Robert Julian	19.7.1920	4.1.2005	22	1947–1953	896	107	1	26.35	3	3-52	0/0	36.00	19/2	
Clarke Carlos Bertram OBE	7.4.1918	14.10.1993	3	1939	3	2	0	1.00	6	3-59	0/0	43.50	0	10
Clarke Sylvester Theophilus	11.12.1954	4.12.1999	11	1977–1981	172	35*	0	15.63	42	5-126	1/0	27.85	2	30
2 Collins Pedro Tyrone	12.8.1976		32	1998–2005	235	24	0	5.87	106	6-53	3/0	34.63	7	30
Collymore Corey Delanelo	21.12.1977		30	1998–2007	197	16*	0	7.88	93	7-57	4/1	32.30	6	84
Constantine *Lord* [Learie Nicholas] MBE (CY 1940)	21.9.1901	1.7.1971	18	1928–1939	635	90	0	19.24	58	5-75	2/0	30.10	28	
Cottrell Sheldon Shane	19.8.1989		2	2013–2014	11	5	0	2.75	2	1-72	0/0	98.00	0	2/6
Croft Colin Everton Hunte	15.3.1953		27	1976–1981	158	33	0	10.53	125	8-29	3/0	23.30	8	19
Cuffy Cameron Eustace	8.2.1970		15	1994–2002	58	15	0	4.14	43	4-82	0/0	33.83	5	41
Cummins Anderson Cleophas	7.5.1966		5	1992–1994	98	50	0	19.60	48	4-54	0/0	42.75	1	63‡
Da Costa Oscar Constantine	11.9.1907	1.10.1936	5	1929–1934	153	39	0	19.12	3	1-14	0/0	58.33	5	
Daniel Wayne Wendell	16.1.1956		10	1975–1983	46	11	0	6.57	36	5-39	1/0	25.27	4	18
2 Davis Bryan Allan	2.5.1940		4	1964	245	68	0	30.62	–	–	–/–	–	1	
2 Davis Charles Allan	1.1.1944		15	1968–1972	1,301	183	4	54.20	2	1-27	0/0	165.00	4	
Davis Winston Walter	18.9.1958		15	1982–1987	202	77	0	13.46	45	4-19	0/0	32.71	10	35
De Caires Francis Ignatius	12.5.1909	2.2.1959	3	1929	232	80	0	38.66	0	0-9	0/0	–	1	
Deonarine Narsingh	16.8.1983		18	2004–2013	725	82	0	25.89	24	4-37	0/0	29.70	16	31/8
Depeiza Cyril Clairmonte	10.10.1928	10.11.1995	5	1954–1955	187	122	1	31.16	0	0-3	0/0	–	7/4	
Dewdney David Thomas	23.10.1933		9	1954–1957	17	5*	0	2.42	21	5-21	1/0	38.42	2	
Dhanraj Rajindra	6.2.1969		4	1994–1995	17	9	0	4.25	8	2-49	0/0	74.37	1	
Dillon Mervyn	5.6.1974		38	1996–2003	549	43	0	8.44	131	5-71	2/0	33.57	16	6
Dowe Uton George	29.3.1949		4	1970–1972	8	5*	0	8.00	12	4-69	0/0	44.50	3	108
Dowlin Travis Montague	24.2.1977		6	2009–2010	343	95	0	31.18	0	0-3	0/0	–	5	11/2
Dowrich Shane Omari	30.10.1991		2	2015	102	70	0	25.50	–	–	–/–	–	5	
Drakes Vasbert Conniel	5.8.1969		12	2002–2003	386	67	0	21.44	33	5-93	1/0	41.27	2	34
2 Dujon Peter Jeffrey Leroy (CY 1989)	28.5.1956		81	1981–1991	3,322	139	5	31.94	–	–	–/–	–	267/5	169
2 Edwards Fidel Henderson	6.2.1982		55	2003–2012	394	30	0	6.56	165	7-87	5/0	37.87	10	50/20
Edwards Kirk Anton	3.11.1984		17	2011–2014	986	121	2	31.80	2	0-19	0/0	–	15	16
Edwards Richard Martin	3.6.1940		5	1968	65	22	0	9.28	18	5-84	0/0	34.77	0	

	Born	Died	Tests	Test Career	Runs	HS	100s	Avge	Wkts	BB	5/10	Avge	Ct/St	O/T
Ferguson Wilfred	14.12.1917	23.2.1961	8	1947–1953	200	75	0	28.57	34	6-92	3/1	34.26	11	–
Fernandes Maurius Pacheco	12.8.1897	8.5.1981	2	1928–1929	49	22	0	12.25	–	–	–/–	–	0	–
Findlay Thaddeus Michael MBE	19.10.1943		10	1969–1972	212	44*	0	16.30	–	–	–/–	–	19/2	2
Foster Maurice Linton Churchill	9.5.1943		14	1969–1977	580	125	1	30.52	9	2-41	0/0	66.66	3	–
Francis George Nathaniel	11.12.1897	12.1.1942	10	1928–1933	81	19*	0	5.78	23	4-40	0/0	33.17	7	–
Frederick Michael Campbell	6.5.1927	18.6.2014	1	1953	30	30	0	15.00	–	–	–/–	–	0	–
Fredericks Roy Clifton (CY 1974)	11.11.1942	5.9.2000	59	1968–1976	4,334	169	8	42.49	7	1-12	0/0	78.28	62	12
Fudadin Assad Badyr	1.8.1985		3	2012	122	55	0	30.50	0	0-11	0/0	–	4	–
Fuller Richard Livingston	30.1.1913	3.5.1987	1	1934	1	1	0	1.00	0	0-2	0/0	–	0	–
Furlonge Hammond Allan	19.6.1934		3	1954–1955	99	64	0	19.80	–	–	–/–	–	0	–
Gabriel Shannon Terry	28.4.1988		16	2012–2015	53	20*	0	4.41	34	3-10	0/0	37.67	9	0/2
Ganga Daren	14.1.1979		48	1998–2007	2,160	135	3	25.71	1	1-20	0/0	106.00	30	35/1
Ganteaume Andrew Gordon	22.1.1921	17.2.2016	1	1947	112	112	1	112.00	–	–	–/–	–	2	–
Garner Joel MBE (CY 1980)	16.12.1952		58	1976–1986	672	60	0	12.44	259	6-56	7/0	20.97	42	98
Garrick Leon Vivian	11.11.1976		2	2000	27	27	0	13.50	–	–	–/–	–	1	3
Gaskin Berkeley Bertram McGarrell	21.3.1908	2.5.1979	2	1947	17	10	0	5.66	2	1-15	0/0	79.00	2	–
Gayle Christopher Henry	21.9.1979		103	1999–2014	7,214	333	15	42.18	73	5-34	2/0	42.73	96	266/45
Gibbs Glendon Lionel	27.12.1925	21.2.1979	1	1954	12	12	0	6.00	0	0-2	0/0	–	0	–
Gibbs Lancelot Richard (CY 1972)	29.9.1934		79	1957–1975	488	25	0	6.97	309	8-38	18/2	29.09	52	3
Gibson Ottis Delroy (CY 2008)	16.3.1969		2	1995–1998	93	37	0	23.25	3	2-81	0/0	91.66	0	15
Gilchrist Roy	28.6.1934	18.7.2001	13	1957–1958	60	12	0	5.45	57	6-55	1/0	26.68	4	–
Gladstone Morais George	14.1.1901	19.5.1978	1	1929	12	12*	0	–	1	1-139	0/0	189.00	0	–
Goddard John Douglas Claude OBE	21.4.1919	26.8.1987	27	1947–1957	859	83*	0	30.67	33	5-31	1/0	31.81	22	–
Gomes Hilary Angelo ("Larry") (CY 1985)	13.7.1953		60	1976–1986	3,171	143	9	39.63	15	2-20	0/0	62.00	18	83
Gomez Gerald Ethridge	10.10.1919	6.8.1996	29	1939–1953	1,243	101	1	30.31	58	7-55	1/1	27.41	18	–
² Grant George Copeland ("Jackie")	9.5.1907	26.10.1978	12	1930–1934	413	71*	0	25.81	0	0-1	0/0	–	10	–
² Grant Rolph Stewart	15.12.1909	18.10.1977	7	1934–1939	220	77	0	22.00	11	3-68	0/0	32.09	13	–
Gray Anthony Hollis	23.5.1963		5	1986	48	12*	0	8.00	22	4-39	0/0	17.13	6	25
Greenidge Alvin Ethelbert	20.8.1956		6	1977–1978	222	69	0	22.20	–	–	–/–	–	5	1
Greenidge Cuthbert Gordon MBE (CY 1977)	1.5.1951		108	1974–1990	7,558	226	19	44.72	0	0-4	0/0	–	96	128
Greenidge Geoffrey Alan	26.5.1948		5	1971–1972	209	50	0	29.85	0	0-2	0/0	–	3	–
Grell Mervyn George	18.12.1899	11.11.1976	1	1929	34	21	0	17.00	0	0-7	0/0	–	1	–
Griffith Adrian Frank Gordon	19.11.1971		14	1996–2000	638	114	1	24.53	–	–	–/–	–	13	–
Griffith Charles Christopher (CY 1964)	14.12.1938		28	1959–1968	530	54	0	16.56	94	6-36	5/0	28.54	16	9
Griffith Herman Clarence	1.12.1893	18.3.1980	13	1928–1933	91	18	0	5.05	44	6-103	2/0	28.25	4	–
Guillen Simpson Clairmonte ("Sammy")	24.9.1924	2.3.2013	5†	1951	104	54	0	26.00	–	–	–/–	–	9/2	–

Name	Born	Died	Tests	Test Career	Runs	HS	100s	Avge	Wkts	BB	5/10	Avge	Ct/St	O/T
Hall Sir Wesley Winfield	12.9.1937		48	1958–1968	818	50*	0	15.73	192	7-69	9/1	26.38	11	
Harper Roger Andrew	17.3.1963		25	1983–1993	535	74	0	18.44	46	6-57	1/0	28.06	36	105
Haynes Desmond Leo (CY 1991)	15.2.1956		116	1977–1993	7,487	184	18	42.29	1	1-2	0/0	8.00	65	238
[3]Headley George Alphonso MBE (CY 1934)	30.5.1909	30.11.1983	22	1929–1953	2,190	270*	10	60.83	0	0-0	-/-		14	1
[3]Headley Ronald George Alphonso	29.6.1939		2	1973	62	42	0	15.50					2	1
Hendriks John Leslie	21.12.1933		20	1961–1969	447	64	0	18.62					42/5	
Hinds Ryan O'Neal	17.2.1981		5	2001–2009	505	84	0	21.04	13	2-45	0/0	66.92	16	14
Hinds Wavell Wayne	7.9.1976		45	1999–2005	2,608	213	5	33.01	16	3-79	0/0	36.87	32	119/5
Hoad Edward Lisle Goldsworthy	29.1.1896	5.3.1986	4	1928–1933	98	36	0	12.25					10	
Holder Jason Omar	5.11.1991		13	2014–2015	546	103*	1	27.30	21	3-15	0/0	39.00	10	35/4
Holder Roland Irwin Christopher	22.12.1967		11	1997–1998	380	91	0	25.33					9	37
Holder Vanburn Alonzo	8.10.1945		40	1969–1978	682	42	0	14.20	109	6-28	3/0	33.27	22	12
Holding Michael Anthony (CY 1977)	16.2.1954		60	1975–1986	910	73	0	13.78	249	8-92	13/2	23.68	22	102
Holford David Anthony Jerome	16.4.1940		24	1966–1976	768	105*	1	22.58	51	5-23	1/0	39.39	18	
Holt John Kenneth Constantine	12.8.1923	3.6.1997	17	1953–1958	1,066	166	2	36.75	1	1-20	0/0	20.00	8	
Hooper Carl Llewellyn	15.12.1966		102	1987–2002	5,762	233	13	36.46	114	5-26	4/0	49.42	115	227
Hope Shai Diego	10.11.1993		6	2015	171	36	0	15.54					2	
Howard Anthony Bourne	27.8.1946		1	1971					2	2-140	0/0	70.00	0	
Hunte Sir Conrad Cleophas (CY 1964)	9.5.1932	3.12.1999	44	1957–1966	3,245	260	8	45.06	2	1-17	0/0	55.00	16	
Hunte Errol Ashton Clairmonte	3.10.1905	26.6.1967	3	1929	166	58	0	33.00						
Hylton Leslie George	29.3.1905	17.5.1955	6	1934–1939	70	19	0	11.66	16	4-27	0/0	26.12		
Jacobs Ridley Detamore	26.11.1967		65	1998–2004	2,577	118	3	28.31					207/12	147
Jaggernauth Amit Sheldon	16.11.1983		1	2007	0*	0*	0	0.00	1	1-74	0/0	96.00		
Johnson Hophnie Hobah Hines	13.7.1910	24.6.1987	3	1947–1950	38	22	0	9.50	13	5-41	2/1	18.30	1	
Johnson Leon Rayon	8.8.1987		4	2014	275	66	0	39.28					3	6
Johnson Tyrell Fabian	10.1.1917	5.4.1985	1	1939	9	9*	0		3	2-53	0/0	43.00		
Jones Charles Ernest Llewellyn	3.11.1902	10.12.1959	4	1929–1934	63	19*	0	9.00	0	0-2			1	
Jones Prior Erskine Waverley	6.6.1917	27.11.1991	9	1947–1951	47	10*	0	5.22	25	5-85	1/0	30.04	4	
Joseph David Rolston Emmanuel	15.11.1969		1	1998	141	50	0	20.14						
Joseph Sylvester Cleofoster	5.9.1978		5	2004–2007	147	45	0	14.70	0	0-8			3	13
Julien Bernard Denis	13.3.1950		24	1973–1976	866	121	2	30.92	50	5-57	1/0	37.36	14	12
Jumadeen Raphick Rasif	12.4.1948		12	1971–1978	84	56	0	21.00	29	4-72	0/0	39.34	4	
Kallicharran Alvin Isaac (CY 1983)	21.3.1949		66	1971–1980	4,399	187	12	44.43	4	2-16	0/0	39.50	51	31
Kanhai Rohan Bholalall (CY 1964)	26.12.1935		79	1957–1973	6,227	256	15	47.53	0	0-1			50	7
Kentish Esmond Seymour Maurice	21.11.1916	10.6.2011	2	1947–1953	1*	1*	0	1.00	8	5-49	1/0	22.25		
King Collis Llewellyn	11.6.1951		9	1976–1980	418	100*	1	32.15	5	1-30	0/0	94.00	5	18

Name	Born	Died	Tests	Test Career	Runs	HS	100s	Avge	Wkts	BB	5/10	Avge	Ct/St	O/T
King Frank McDonald	14.12.1926	23.12.1990	14	1952-1955	116	21	0	8.28	29	5-74	1/0	39.96	5	
King Lester Anthony	27.2.1939	9.7.1998	2	1961-1967	41	20	0	10.25	9	5-46	1/0	17.11	5	
King Reon Dane	6.10.1975		19	1998-2004	66	12*	0	3.47	53	5-51	1/0	32.69	2	50
Lambert Clayton Benjamin	10.2.1962		5	1991-1998	284	104	1	31.55	1	1-4	0/0	5.00	2	11‡
Lara Brian Charles (CY 1995)	2.5.1969		130§	1990-2006	11,912	400*	34	53.17	0	0-0	0/0	—	164	295‡
Lashley Patrick Douglas ("Peter")	11.2.1937		4	1960-1966	159	49	0	22.71	1	1-1	0/0	1.00	4	
Lawson Jermaine Jay Charles	13.1.1982		13	2002-2005	52	14	0	3.46	51	7-78	2/0	29.64	—	13
Legall Ralph Archibald	1.12.1925	2003	4	1952	50	23	0	10.00	—	—	—	—	8/1	
Lewis Desmond Michael	21.2.1946		3	1970	259	88	0	86.33	—	—	—	—	8	
Lewis Rawl Nicholas	5.9.1974		5	1997-2007	89	40	0	8.90	4	2-42	0/0	114.00	8	28/1
Lloyd Clive Hubert CBE (CY 1971)	31.8.1944		110	1966-1984	7,515	242*	19	46.67	10	2-13	0/0	62.20	90	87
Logie Augustine Lawrence	28.9.1960		52	1982-1991	2,470	130	2	35.79	0	0-0	0/0	—	57	158
McGarrell Neil Christopher	12.7.1972		4	2000-2001	61	33	0	15.25	17	4-23	0/0	26.64	—	17
McLean Nixon Alexei McNamara	20.7.1973		19	1997-2000	368	46	0	12.26	44	3-53	0/0	42.56	2	45
McMorris Easton Dudley Ashton St John	4.4.1935		13	1957-1966	564	125	2	26.85	—	—	—	—	5	
McWatt Clifford Aubrey	1.2.1922	20.7.1997	6	1953-1954	202	54	0	28.85	1	1-16	0/0	16.00	9/1	
Madray Ivan Samuel	2.7.1934	23.4.2009	2	1957	3	2	0	1.00	0	0-12	0/0	—	5	
Marshall Malcolm Denzil (CY 1983)	18.4.1958	4.11.1999	81	1978-1991	1,810	92	0	18.85	376	7-22	22/4	20.94	25	136
[2] Marshall Norman Edgar	27.2.1924	11.8.2007	1	1954	8	8	0	4.00	2	1-22	0/0	31.00	—	
[2] Marshall Roy Edwin (CY 1959)	25.4.1930	27.10.1992	4	1951	143	30	0	20.42	0	0-3	0/0	—	1	
Marshall Xavier Melbourne	27.3.1986		7	2005-2008	243	85	0	20.25	0	0-0	0/0	—	7	24/6
Martin Frank Reginald	12.10.1893	23.11.1967	9	1928-1930	486	123*	1	28.58	8	3-91	0/0	77.37	7	
Martindale Emmanuel Alfred	25.11.1909	17.3.1972	10	1933-1939	58	22	0	5.27	37	5-22	3/0	21.72	5	
Mattis Everton Hugh	11.4.1957		4	1980	145	71	0	29.00	0	0-4	0/0	—	—	
Mendonca Ivor Leon	13.7.1934	14.6.2014	2	1961	81	78	0	40.50	—	—	—	—	8/2	
Merry Cyril Arthur	20.1.1911	19.4.1964	2	1933	34	13	0	8.50	—	—	—	—	1	
Miller Nikita O'Neil	16.5.1982		1	2009	5	5	0	2.50	0	0-27	0/0	—	1	46/9
Miller Roy	24.12.1924		1	1952	23	23	0	23.00	0	0-28	0/0	—	0	
Mohammed Dave	8.10.1979		5	2003-2006	225	52	0	32.14	13	3-98	0/0	51.38	0	7
Moodie George Horatio	26.11.1915	8.6.2002	1	1934	5	5	0	5.00	3	2-23	0/0	13.33	—	
Morton Runako Shakur	22.7.1978	4.3.2012	15	2005-2007	573	70*	0	22.03	0	0-4	0/0	—	20	56/7
Moseley Ezra Alphonsa	5.1.1958		2	1989	35	26	0	8.75	6	2-70	0/0	43.50	—	9
Murray David Anthony	29.5.1950		19	1977-1981	601	84	0	21.46	—	—	—	—	57/5	10
Murray Deryck Lance	20.5.1943		62	1963-1980	1,993	91	0	22.90	—	—	—	—	181/8	26
Murray Junior Randalph	20.1.1968		33	1992-2001	918	101*	0	22.39	—	—	—	—	99/3	55

§ Lara's figures exclude 41 runs for the ICC World XI v Australia in the Super Series Test in 2005-06.

	Born	Died	Tests	Test Career	Runs	HS	100s	Avge	Wkts	BB	5/10	Avge	Ct/St	O/T
Nagamootoo Mahendra Veeren	9.10.1975		5	2000–2002	185	68	0	26.42	12	3-119	0/0	53.08	2	24
Nanan Rangy	29.5.1953		4	1980	16	8	0	8.00	4	2-37	0/0	22.75	2	
Narine Sunil Philip	26.5.1988		6	2012–2013	40	22*	0	8.00	21	6-91	2/0	40.52	2	55/34
Nash Brendan Paul	14.12.1977		21	2008–2011	1,103	114	2	33.42	2	1-21	0/0	123.50	6	9
Neblett James Montague	13.11.1901	28.3.1959	1	1934	16	11*	0	16.00	1	1-44	0/0	75.00	0	
Noreiga Jack Mollinson	15.4.1936	8.8.2003	4	1970	11	9	0	3.66	17	9-95	2/0	29.00	2	
Nunes Robert Karl	7.6.1894	23.7.1958	4	1928–1929	245	92	0	30.62			–/–		2	
Nurse Seymour MacDonald (CY 1967)	10.11.1933		29	1959–1968	2,523	258	6	47.60	0	0-0	0/0	–	21	
Padmore Albert Leroy	17.12.1946		2	1975–1976	8	8*	0	8.00	1	1-36	0/0	135.00	0	
Pagon Donovan Jomo	13.9.1982		2	2004	37	35	0	12.33			–/–		0	
Pairaudeau Bruce Hamilton	14.4.1931		13	1952–1957	454	115	1	21.61	0	0-3	0/0	–	6	
Parchment Brenton Anthony	24.6.1982		2	2007	55	20	0	13.75			–/–		–	7/1
Parry Derick Recaldo	22.12.1954		12	1977–1979	381	65	0	22.41	23	5-15	1/0	40.69	4	6
Pascal Nelon Troy	25.4.1987		1	2010–2010	12	10	0	6.00	0	0-27	0/0	–	–	1
Passailaigue Charles Clarence	4.8.1901	7.1.1972	1	1929	46	44	0	46.00	0	0-15	0/0	–	3	
Patterson Balfour Patrick	15.9.1961		28	1985–1992	145	21*	0	6.59	93	5-24	5/0	30.90	5	59
Payne Thelston Rodney O'Neale	13.2.1957		1	1985	5	5	0	5.00			–/–		5	7
Permaul Veerasammy	11.8.1989		6	2012–2015	98	23*	0	12.25	18	3-32	0/0	43.77	2	6
Perry Nehemiah Odolphus	16.6.1968		4	1998–1999	74	26	0	12.33	10	5-70	1/0	44.60	4	21
Peters Keon Kenroy	24.2.1982		1	2014	0	0	0	0.00	2	2-69	0/0	34.50	0	
Phillip Norbert	12.6.1948		9	1977–1978	297	47	0	29.70	28	4-48	0/0	37.17	5	
Phillips Omar Jamel	12.10.1986		2	2009	160	94	0	40.00			–/–		1	
Pierre Lancelot Richard	5.6.1921	14.4.1989	1	1947					0	0-9	0/0	–	0	
Powell Daren Brentlyle	15.4.1978		37	2002–2008	407	36*	0	7.82	85	5-25	1/0	47.85	8	55/5
Powell Kieran Omar Akeem	6.3.1990		21	2011–2014	1,072	134	3	27.48			–/–		19	28/1
Powell Ricardo Lloyd	16.12.1978		2	1999–2003	53	30	0	17.66	0	0-13	0/0	–	1	109
Rae Allan Fitzroy	30.9.1922	27.2.2005	15	1948–1952	1,016	109	4	46.18			–/–		10	
Ragoonath Suruj	22.3.1968		2	1998	13	9	0	4.33			–/–		1	
Ramadhin Sonny (CY 1951)	1.5.1929		43	1950–1960	361	44	0	8.20	158	7-49	10/1	28.98	9	1
Ramdass Ryan Rakesh	3.7.1983		1	2005	26	23	0	13.00			–/–		2	
Ramdin Denesh	13.3.1985		74	2005–2015	2,898	166	4	25.87			–/–		205/12	129/52
Rammarine Dinanath	4.6.1975		12	1997–2001	106	35*	0	6.23	45	5-78	1/0	30.73	3	4
Rampaul Ravindranath	15.10.1984		18	2009–2012	335	40*	0	14.56	49	4-48	0/0	34.79	6	92/23
Reifer Floyd Lamonte	23.7.1972		6	1996–2009	111	29	0	9.25			–/–		3	8/1
Richards Dale Maurice	16.7.1976		3	2009–2010	125	69	0	20.83			–/–		4	8/1
Richards Sir Isaac Vivian Alexander (CY 1977)	7.3.1952		121	1974–1991	8,540	291	24	50.23	32	2-17	0/0	61.37	122	187

Name	Born	Died	Tests	Test Career	Runs	HS	100s	Avge	Wkts	BB	5/10	Avge	Ct/St	O/T
Richardson *Sir* Richard Benjamin (CY 1992)	12.1.1962		86	1983–1995	5,949	194	16	44.39	0	0-0	-/-	-	90	224
Rickards Kenneth Roy	22.8.1923	21.8.1995	2	1947–1951	104	67	0	34.66					0	
Roach Clifford Archibald	13.3.1904	16.4.1988	16	1928–1934	952	209	2	30.70	2	1-18	0/0	51.50	5	
Roach Kemar Andre Jamal	30.6.1988		37	2009–2015	509	41	0	10.38	122	6-48	6/1	30.23	10	67/11
Roberts Alphonso Theodore	18.9.1937	24.7.1996	1	1955	28	28	0	14.00					0	
Roberts *Sir* Anderson Montgomery Everton *CBE* (CY 1975)	29.1.1951		47	1973–1983	762	68	0	14.94	202	7-54	11/2	25.61	9	56
Roberts Lincoln Abraham	4.9.1974		1	1998	0	0	0	0.00					0	
Rodriguez William Vicente	25.6.1934	d unknown	5	1961–1967	96	50	0	13.71	7	3-51	0/0	53.42	3	
Rose Franklyn Albert	1.2.1972		19	1996–2000	344	69	0	13.23	53	7-84	2/0	30.88	4	27
Rowe Lawrence George	8.1.1949		30	1971–1979	2,047	302	7	43.55	0	0-1	0/0	-	17	11
Russell Andre Dwayne	29.4.1988		1	2010	2	2	0	2.00	1	1-73	0/0	104.00	0	51/35
[2] St Hill Edwin Lloyd	9.3.1904	21.5.1957	2	1929	18	12	0	4.50	3	2-110	0/0	73.66	1	
[2] St Hill Wilton H	6.7.1893		3	1928–1929	117	38	0	19.50	0	0-9	0/0	-	0	
Sammy Darren Julius Garvey	20.12.1983		38	2007–2013	1,323	106	1	21.68	84	7-66	4/0	35.79	65	126/60
[2] Samuels Marlon Nathaniel (CY 2013)	5.1.1981		64	2000–2015	3,622	260	7	33.53	41	4-13	0/0	59.63	27	177/40
[2] Samuels Robert George	13.3.1971		6	1995–1996	372	125	1	37.20					8	8
Sanford Adam	12.7.1975		11	2001–2003	72	18*	0	4.80	30	4-132	0/0	43.86	4	
Sarwan Ramnaresh Ronnie	23.6.1980		87	1999–2011	5,842	291	15	40.01	23	4-37	0/0	50.56	53	181/18
Scarlett Reginald Osmond	15.8.1934		3	1959	54	29*	0	18.00	2	1-46	0/0	104.50	2	
[1] Scott Alfred Homer Patrick	29.7.1934	15.6.1961	1	1952	5	5	0	5.00	0	0-52	0/0	-	0	
[1] Scott Oscar Charles ("Tommy")	14.8.1892	12.9.1963	8	1928–1930	171	35	0	17.10	22	5-266	1/0	42.04	0	
Sealey Benjamin James	12.8.1899	3.11.1982	1	1933	41	29	0	20.50	1	1-10	0/0	10.00	0	
Sealy James Edward Derrick	11.9.1912		11	1929–1939	478	92	1	28.11					6/1	
Shepherd John Neil (CY 1979)	9.11.1943		5	1969–1970	77	32	0	9.62	19	5-104	1/0	31.33	2	2
Shillingford Grayson Cleophas	25.9.1944		4	1969–1971	57	25	0	8.14	15	3-63	0/0	25.21	2	
Shillingford Irvine Theodore	18.4.1944		4	1976–1977	218	120	1	31.14					9	
Shillingford Shane	22.2.1983		16	2010–2014	266	53*	0	13.30	70	6-49	6/2	34.55	6	
Shivnarine Sewdatt	13.5.1952	23.12.2009	8	1977–1978	379	63	0	29.15	1	1-13	0/0	167.00	5	
Simmons Lendl Mark Platter	25.1.1985		8	2008–2011	278	49	0	17.37	1	1-60	0/0	147.00	26	68/34
Simmons Philip Verant (CY 1997)	18.4.1963		26	1987–1997	1,002	110	1	22.26	4	2-34	0/0	64.25	26	143
Singh Charran Kamkaran	27.11.1935	19.11.2015	2	1959	11	11	0	3.66	5	2-28	0/0	33.20	3	
Small Joseph A.	3.11.1892	26.4.1958	3	1928–1929	79	52	0	13.16	3	2-67	0/0	61.33	3	
Small Milton Aster	12.2.1964		2	1983–1984	3	3*	0		4	3-40	0/0	38.25	0	2
Smith Cameron Wilberforce	29.7.1933		5	1960–1961	222	55	0	24.66					4/1	
Smith Devon Sheldon	21.10.1981		38	2002–2014	1,593	108	1	24.50	0	0-3	-/-	-	30	47/6

	Born	Died	Test Career	Tests	Runs	HS	100s	Avge	Wkts	BB	5/10	Avge	Ct/St	O/T
Smith Dwayne Romel	12.4.1983		2003–2005	10	320	105*	1	24.61	7	3-71	0/0	49.14	9	105/33
Smith O'Neil Gordon ("Collie") (CY 1958)	5.5.1933	9.9.1959	1954–1958	26	1,331	168	4	31.69	48	5-90	0/0	33.85	9	1
Sobers Sir Garfield St Aubrun (CY 1964)	28.7.1936		1953–1973	93	8,032	365*	26	57.78	235	6-73	6/0	34.03	109	
Solomon Joseph Stanislaus	26.8.1930		1958–1964	27	1,326	100*	1	34.00	4	1-20	0/0	67.00	13	
Stayers Sven Conrad ("Charlie")	9.6.1937	6.1.2005	1961	4	58	35*	0	19.33	9	3-65	0/0	40.44	0	
[2]**Stollmeyer Jeffrey Baxter**	11.3.1921	10.9.1989	1939–1954	32	2,159	160	4	42.33	13	3-32	0/0	39.00	20	
[2]**Stollmeyer Victor Humphrey**	24.1.1916	21.9.1999	1939	1	96	96	0	96.00					1	
Stuart Colin Ellsworth Laurie	28.9.1973		2000–2001	6	24	12*	0	3.42	20	3-33	0/0	31.40	2	5
Taylor Jaswick Ossie	3.1.1932	13.11.1999	1957–1958	3	4	4*	0	2.00	10	5-109	1/0	27.30	2	
Taylor Jerome Everton	22.6.1984		2003–2015	46	856	106	1	12.96	130	6-47	4/0	34.46	8	81/19
Thompson Patterson Ian Chesterfield	26.9.1971		1995–1996	2	17	10*	0	8.50	5	2-58	0/0	43.00	0	2
Tonge Gavin Courtney	13.2.1983		2009	2	25	23*	0	12.50	1	1-28	0/0	113.00	1	5/1
Trim John	25.1.1915	12.11.1960	1947–1951	4	21	12	0	5.25	18	5-34	1/0	16.16	2	
Valentine Alfred Louis (CY 1951)	28.4.1930	11.5.2004	1950–1961	36	141	14	0	4.70	139	8-104	8/2	30.32	13	
Valentine Vincent Adolphus	4.4.1908	6.7.1972	1933	2	35	19*	0	11.66	1	1-55	0/0	104.00	0	
Walcott Sir Clyde Leopold (CY 1958)	17.1.1926	26.8.2006	1947–1959	44	3,798	220	15	56.68	11	3-50	0/0	37.09	53/11	
Walcott Leslie Arthur	18.1.1894	27.2.1984	1929	1	40	24	0	40.00	1	1-17	0/0	32.00	0	
Wallace Philo Alphonso	2.8.1970		1997–1998	7	279	92	0	21.46					9	33
[1]**Walsh Courtney Andrew (CY 1987)**	30.10.1962		1984–2000	132	936	30*	0	7.54	519	7-37	22/3	24.44	29	205
Walton Chadwick Antonio Kirkpatrick	3.7.1985		2009	1	13	10	0	3.25					10	5/2
Warrican Jomel Andrel	20.5.1992		2015	4	65	21*	0	65.00	11	4-67	0/0	46.27	1	
Washington Dwight Marlon	5.3.1983		2004	1	7	7*	0	–	0	0-20	0/0	–	0	
Watson Chester Donald	1.7.1938		1959–1961	7	12	5	0	2.40	19	4-62	0/0	38.10	3	
[1]**Weekes Sir Everton de Courcy (CY 1951)**	26.2.1925		1947–1957	48	4,455	207	15	58.61	1	1-8	0/0	77.00	49	
White Kenneth Hunnell	24.1.1912	9.2.1998	1939	2	173	57*	0	57.66					1	
White Anthony Wilbur	20.11.1938		1964	2	71	65	0	23.66	3	2-34	0/0	50.66	1	
Wight Claude Vibart	28.7.1902	4.10.1969	1928–1929	2	67	23	0	22.33	0	0-6	0/0	–	0	
Wight George Leslie	28.5.1929	4.1.2004	1952	1	21	21	0	21.00					0	
Wiles Charles Archibald	11.8.1892	4.11.1957	1933	1	2	2	0	1.00					0	
Willett Elquemedo Tonito	1.5.1953		1972–1974	5	74	26	0	14.80	11	3-33	0/0	43.81	0	
Williams Alvadon Basil	21.11.1949	25.10.2015	1977–1978	7	469	111	2	39.08					1	
Williams David	4.11.1963		1991–1997	11	242	65	0	13.44					40/2	36
Williams Ernest Albert Vivian ("Foffie")	10.4.1914	13.4.1997	1939–1947	4	113	72	0	18.83	9	3-51	0/0	26.77	2	
Williams Stuart Clayton	12.8.1969		1993–2001	31	1,183	128	1	24.14	0	0-19	0/0	–	27	57
Wishart Kenneth Leslie	28.11.1908	18.10.1972	1934	1	52	26	0	26.00					0	
[1]**Worrell Sir Frank Mortimer Maglinne (CY 1951)**	1.8.1924	13.3.1967	1947–1963	51	3,860	261	9	49.48	69	7-70	2/0	38.72	43	

NEW ZEALAND (268 players)

Name	Born	Died	Tests	Test Career	Runs	HS	100s	Avge	Wkts	BB	5/10	Avge	Ct/St	O/T
Adams Andre Ryan	17.1.1975		1	2001	18	11	0	9.00	6	3-44	0/0	17.50	1	42/4
Alabaster John Chaloner	11.7.1930		21	1955–1971	272	34	0	9.71	49	4-46	0/0	38.02	7	
Allcott Cyril Francis Walter	7.10.1896	19.11.1973	6	1929–1931	113	33	0	22.60	6	2-102	0/0	90.16	3	
Allott Geoffrey Ian	24.12.1971		10	1995–1999	27	8*	0	3.37	19	4-74	0/0	58.47	2	31
Anderson Corey James	13.12.1990		13	2013–2015	533	116	1	31.35	13	3-47	0/0	38.46	5	35/17
Anderson Robert Wickham	2.10.1948		9	1976–1978	423	92	0	23.50	–	–	–/–	–	–	2
[1] **Anderson William McDougall**	8.10.1919	21.12.1979	1	1945	5	4	0	2.50	–	–	–/–	–	1	
Andrews Bryan	4.4.1945		2	1973	22	17	0	22.00	2	2-40	0/0	77.00	1	
Arnel Brent John	3.1.1979		6	2009–2011	45	8*	0	5.62	9	4-95	0/0	62.88	3	
Astle Nathan John	15.9.1971		81	1995–2006	4,702	222	11	37.02	51	3-27	0/0	42.01	70	223/4
Astle Todd Duncan	24.9.1986		1	2012	38	35	0	19.00	1	1-56	0/0	97.00	1	
Badcock Frederick Theodore ("Ted")	9.8.1897	19.9.1982	7	1929–1932	137	64	0	19.57	16	4-80	0/0	38.12	1	
Barber Richard Trevor	3.6.1925	7.8.2015	1	1955	17	12	0	8.50	–	–	–/–	–	–	
Bartlett Gary Alex	3.2.1941		10	1961–1967	263	40	0	15.47	24	6-38	1/0	33.00	8	
Barton Paul Thomas	9.10.1935		7	1961–1962	285	109	1	20.35	–	–	–/–	–	4	
Beard Donald Derek	14.1.1920	15.7.1982	4	1951–1955	101	31	0	20.20	9	3-22	0/0	33.55	2	
[1] **Beck John Edward Francis**	1.8.1934	23.4.2000	8	1953–1955	394	99	0	26.26	–	–	–/–	–	0	
Bell Matthew David	25.2.1977		18	1998–2007	729	107	2	24.30	–	–	–/–	–	19	
Bell William	5.9.1931	23.7.2002	2	1953	21	21*	0	–	2	1-54	0/0	117.50	1	
Bennett Hamish Kyle	22.2.1987		1	2010	4	4	0	4.00	0	0-47	0/0	–	–	14
Bilby Grahame Paul	7.5.1941		2	1965	55	28	0	13.75	–	–	–/–	–	3	
Blain Tony Elston	17.2.1962		11	1986–1993	456	78	0	26.82	–	–	–/–	–	19/2	38
Blair Robert William	23.6.1932	22.6.1966	19	1952–1963	189	64*	0	6.75	43	4-85	0/0	35.23	5	
Blunt Roger Charles (CY 1928)	3.11.1900		9	1929–1931	330	96	0	27.50	12	3-17	0/0	39.33	5	
Bolton Bruce Alfred	31.5.1935		2	1958	59	33	0	19.66	–	–	–/–	–	1	
Bond Shane Edward	7.6.1975		18	2001–2009	168	41*	0	12.92	87	6-51	5/1	22.09	8	82/20
Boock Stephen Lewis	20.9.1951		30	1977–1988	207	37	0	6.27	74	7-87	4/0	34.64	14	14
Boult Trent Alexander	22.7.1989		33	2011–2015	392	52*	0	15.68	142	6-40	5/1	28.28	15	28/9
Bracewell Brendon Paul	14.9.1959		6	1978–1984	24	8	0	2.40	14	3-110	0/0	41.78	1	1
[1,2] **Bracewell Douglas Alexander John**	28.9.1990		24	2011–2015	501	47	0	13.54	67	6-40	2/0	37.29	8	12/14
[2] **Bracewell John Garry**	15.4.1958		41	1980–1990	1,001	110	1	20.42	102	6-32	4/1	35.81	31	53
Bradburn Grant Eric	26.5.1966		7	1990–2000	105	30*	0	13.12	6	3-134	0/0	76.66	6	11
[1] **Bradburn Wynne Pennell**	24.11.1938	25.9.2008	2	1963	62	32	0	15.50	–	–	–/–	–	2	

	Born	Died	Tests	Test Career	Runs	HS	100s	Avge	Wkts	BB	5/10	Avge	Ct/St	O/T
Brown Vaughan Raymond	3.11.1959		2	1985	51	36*	0	25.50	1	1-17	0/0	176.00	3	3
Brownlie Dean Graham	30.7.1984		14	2011–2013	711	109	0	29.62	1	1-13	0/0	52.00	17	105
Burgess Mark Gordon	17.7.1944		50	1967–1980	2,684	119*	5	31.20	6	3-23	0/0	35.33	34	26
Burke Cecil	27.3.1914	4.8.1997	1	1945	4	3	0	2.00	–	–	–	–	2	
Burtt Thomas Browning	22.1.1915	24.5.1988	10	1946–1952	252	42	0	21.00	33	6-162	3/0	35.45	2	26/19
Butler Ian Gareth	24.11.1981		8	2001–2004	76	26	0	9.50	24	6-46	1/0	36.83	4	
Butterfield Leonard Arthur	29.8.1913	5.7.1999	1	1945	0	0	0	0.00	–	0-24	0/0	–	–	
1 **Cairns** Bernard Lance	10.10.1949		43	1973–1985	928	64	0	16.28	130	7-74	6/1	32.91	30	78
1 **Cairns** Christopher Lance (CY 2000)	13.6.1970		62	1989–2004	3,320	158	5	33.53	218	7-27	13/1	29.40	14	214/2
Cameron Francis James MBE	1.6.1932		19	1961–1965	116	27*	0	11.60	62	5-34	3/0	29.82	1	
Cave Henry Butler	10.10.1922	15.9.1989	19	1949–1958	229	22*	0	8.80	34	4-21	0/0	43.14	8	
Chapple Murray Ernest	25.7.1930	31.7.1985	14	1952–1965	497	76	0	19.11	–	1-24	0/0	84.00	10	
Chatfield Ewen John MBE	3.7.1950		43	1974–1988	180	21*	0	8.57	123	6-73	3/1	32.17	7	114
Cleverley Donald Charles	23.12.1909	16.2.2004	2	1931–1945	19	10*	0	19.00	–	0-51	0/0	–	0	
Collinge Richard Owen	2.4.1946		35	1964–1978	533	68*	0	14.40	116	6-63	3/0	29.25	10	15
Colquhoun Ian Alexander	8.6.1924	26.2.2005	2	1954	1	1*	0	0.50	–	–	–	–	4	
Coney Jeremy Vernon MBE (CY 1984)	21.6.1952		52	1973–1986	2,668	174*	3	37.57	27	3-28	0/0	35.77	64	88
Congdon Bevan Ernest OBE (CY 1974)	11.2.1938		61	1964–1978	3,448	176	7	32.22	59	5-65	1/0	36.50	44	11
Cowie John OBE	30.3.1912	3.6.1994	9	1937–1949	90	45	0	10.00	45	6-40	4/1	21.53	3	
Craig Mark Donald	23.3.1987		13	2014–2015	512	67	0	36.57	46	7-94	1/1	44.21	12	
Cresswell George Fenwick	22.3.1915	10.1.1966	3	1949–1950	14	12*	0	7.00	13	6-168	1/0	22.46	0	
Cromb Ian Burns	25.6.1905	6.3.1984	5	1931–1931	123	51*	0	20.50	8	3-113	0/0	55.25	1	
2 **Crowe** Jeffrey John	14.9.1958		39	1982–1989	1,601	128	3	26.24	–	0-0	0/0	–	41	75
2 **Crowe** Martin David OBE (CY 1985)	22.9.1962		77	1981–1995	5,444	299	17	45.36	14	2-25	0/0	48.28	71	143
Cumming Craig Derek	31.8.1975		11	2004–2007	441	74	0	25.94	–	–	–	–		13
Cunis Robert Smith	5.1.1941	9.8.2008	20	1963–1971	295	51	0	12.82	51	6-76	1/0	37.00	1	
D'Arcy John William	23.4.1936		5	1958	136	33	0	13.60	–	–	–	–	0	
Davis Heath Te-Ihi-O-Te-Rangi	30.11.1971		5	1994–1997	20	8*	0	6.66	17	5-63	1/0	29.35	4	11
de Groen Richard Paul	5.8.1962		5	1993–1994	45	26	0	7.50	11	3-40	0/0	45.90	0	12
Dempster Charles Stewart (CY 1932)	15.11.1903	14.2.1974	10	1929–1932	723	136	2	65.72	–	0-10	0/0	–	2	
Dempster Eric William MBE	25.1.1925	15.8.2011	5	1952–1953	106	47	0	17.66	2	1-24	0/0	109.50	1	
Dick Arthur Edward	10.10.1936		17	1961–1965	370	50*	0	14.23	–	–	–	–	47/4	
Dickinson George Ritchie	11.3.1903	17.3.1978	3	1929–1931	31	11	0	6.20	8	3-66	0/0	30.62	3	
Donnelly Martin Paterson (CY 1948)	17.10.1917	22.10.1999	7	1937–1949	582	206	1	52.90	–	0-20	0/0	–	7	
Doull Simon Blair	6.8.1969		32	1992–1999	570	46	0	14.61	98	7-65	6/0	29.30	16	42
Dowling Graham Thorne OBE	4.3.1937		39	1961–1971	2,306	239	3	31.16	1	1-19	0/0	19.00	23	

	Born	Died	Tests	Test Career	Runs	HS	Avge	100s	Wkts	BB	Avge	5/10	Ct/St	O/T
Drum Christopher James	10.7.1974		5	2000–2001	10	4	3.33	0	16	3-36	30.12	0/0	4	5
Dunning John Angus	6.2.1903	24.6.1971	4	1932–1937	38	19	7.60	0	5	2-35	98.60	0/0	2	–
Edgar Bruce Adrian	23.11.1956		39	1978–1986	1,958	161	30.59	3	0	0-3	–	0/0	14	64
Edwards Graham Neil ("Jock")	27.5.1955		8	1976–1980	377	55	25.13	0				–/–	7	6
Elliott Grant David	21.3.1979		5	2007–2009	86	25	10.75	0	4	2-8	35.00	0/0	2	78/8
Emery Raymond William George	28.3.1915	18.12.1982	2	1951	46	28	11.50	0	2	2-52	26.00	0/0	0	–
Fisher Frederick Eric	28.7.1924	19.6.1996	1	1952	23	14	11.50	0	1	1-78	78.00	0/0	0	–
Fleming Stephen Paul	1.4.1973		111	1993–2007	7,172	274*	40.06	9	0		–		171	279‡/5
Flynn Daniel Raymond	16.4.1985		24	2008–2012	1,038	95	25.95	0			–		10	20/5
Foley Henry	28.1.1906	16.10.1948	1	1929	4	2	2.00	0			–		0	–
Franklin James Edward Charles	7.11.1980		31	2000–2012	808	122*	20.71	1	82	6-119	33.97	3/0	12	110/38
Franklin Trevor John	15.3.1962		21	1983–1990	828	101	23.00	1			–		8	3
Freeman Douglas Linford	8.9.1914	31.5.1994	2	1932	2	1	1.00	0	1	1-91	169.00	0/0	–	–
Fulton Peter Gordon	1.2.1979		23	2005–2014	967	136	25.44	2	0		–		25	49/12
Gallichan Norman	3.6.1906	25.3.1969	1	1937	32	30	16.00	0	3	3-99	37.66	0/0	1	–
Gedye Sidney Graham	2.5.1929		4	1963–1964	193	55	24.12	0			–		2	–
Germon Lee Kenneth	4.11.1968		12	1995–1996	382	55	21.22	0			–		27/2	37
Gillespie Mark Raymond	17.10.1979		5	2007–2011	76	27	10.85	0	22	6-113	28.68	3/0	1	32/11
Gillespie Stuart Ross	2.3.1957		1	1985	28	28	28.00	0	1	1-79	79.00	0/0	0	19
Gray Evan John	18.11.1954		10	1983–1988	248	50	15.50	0	17	3-73	52.11	0/0	6	10
Greatbatch Mark John	11.12.1963		41	1987–1996	2,021	146*	30.62	3	0	0-0	–	0/0	27	84
Guillen Simpson Clairmonte ("Sammy")	24.9.1924	2.3.2013	3†	1955	98	41	16.33	0			–		4/1	–
Guptill Martin James	30.9.1986		38	2008–2015	2,193	189	30.45	3	5	3-37	53.00	0/0	39	124/54
Guy John William	29.8.1934		12	1955–1961	440	102	20.95	1			–		8	–
[1,2] **Hadlee** Dayle Robert	6.1.1948		26	1969–1977	530	56	14.32	0	71	4-30	33.64	0/0	8	11
[1,2] **Hadlee** Sir Richard John (CY 1982)	3.7.1951		86	1972–1990	3,124	151*	27.16	2	431	9-52	22.29	36/9	39	115
[1] **Hadlee** Walter Arnold CBE	4.6.1915	29.9.2006	11	1937–1950	543	116	30.16	1			–		6	–
Harford Noel Sherwin	30.8.1930	30.3.1981	8	1955–1958	229	93	15.26	0			–		6	–
Harford Roy Ivan	30.5.1936		3	1967	7	6	2.33	0			–		11	–
Harris Chris Zinzan	20.11.1969		23	1992–2002	777	71	20.44	0	16	2-16	73.12	0/0	14	250
[2] **Harris** Parke Gerald Zinzan	18.7.1927	1.12.1991	9	1955–1964	378	101	22.23	1	0	0-14	–	0/0	6	–
Harris Roger Meredith	27.7.1933		2	1958	31	13	10.33	0			–		0	–
Hart Matthew Norman	16.5.1972		14	1993–1995	353	45	17.65	0	29	5-77	49.58	1/0	9	13
[2] **Hart** Robert Garry	2.12.1974		11	2002–2003	260	57*	16.25	0			–		29/1	2
Hartland Blair Robert	22.10.1966		9	1991–1994	303	52	16.83	0			–		5	16
Haslam Mark James	26.9.1972		4	1992–1995	4	3	4.00	0	2	1-33	122.50	0/0	2	1

	Born	Died	Tests	Test Career	Runs	HS	100s	Avge	Wkts	BB	5/10	Avge	Ct/St	O/T
Hastings Brian Frederick	23.3.1940		31	1968–1976	1,510	117*	4	30.20		0-3	0/0		23	11
Hayes John Arthur	11.1.1927	25.12.2007	15	1950–1958	73	19*	0	4.86	30	4-36	0/0	40.56	3	
Henderson Matthew	2.8.1895	17.6.1970	1	1929	8	6	0	8.00	2	2-38	0/0	32.00		
Henry Matthew James	14.12.1991		3	2015–2015	65	27	0	21.66	10	4-93	0/0	49.80	1	20/4
Hopkins Gareth James	24.11.1976		1	2008–2010	71	15	0	11.83					9	25/10
2 Horne Matthew Jeffery	5.12.1970		35	1996–2003	1,788	157	4	28.38	0	0-4	0/0		17	50
2 Horne Philip Andrew	21.1.1960		4	1986–1990	71	27	0	10.14					3	
Hough Kenneth William	24.10.1928	20.9.2009	2	1958	62	31*	0	62.00	6	3-79	0/0	29.16		4
How Jamie Michael	19.5.1981		19	2005–2008	772	92	0	22.70	0	0-0	0/0		18	41/5
2 Howarth Geoffrey Philip OBE	29.3.1951		47	1974–1984	2,531	147	6	32.44	3	1-13	0/0	90.33	29	70
2 Howarth Hedley John	25.12.1943	7.11.2008	30	1969–1976	291	61	0	12.12	86	5-34	2/0	36.95	33	9
Ingram Peter John	25.10.1978		2	2009	61	42	0	15.25						8/3
James Kenneth Cecil	12.3.1904	21.8.1976	11	1929–1932	52	14	0	4.72					11/5	
Jarvis Terrence Wayne	29.7.1944		13	1964–1972	625	182	1	29.76	1	1-40	0/0	194.00	3	
Jones Andrew Howard	9.5.1959		39	1986–1994	2,922	186	7	44.27	1		0/0		25	87
Jones Richard Andrew	22.10.1973		1	2003	23	16	0	11.50					2	5
Kennedy Robert John	3.6.1972		4	1995	28	22	0	7.00	6	3-28	0/0	63.33		7
Kerr John Lambert	28.12.1910	27.5.2007	7	1931–1937	212	59	0	19.27					4	
Kuggeleijn Christopher Mary	10.5.1956		2	1988	7	7	0	1.75	1	1-50	0/0	67.00		16
Larsen Gavin Rolf	27.9.1962		8	1994–1995	127	26*	0	14.11	24	3-57	0/0	28.70	5	121
1 Latham Rodney Terry	12.6.1961		4	1991–1992	219	119	1	31.28	1	0-6	0/0		1	33
1 Latham Thomas William Maxwell MBE	2.4.1992		16	2013–2015	1,180	137	3	39.33		0-4	0/0		17	37/12
Lees Warren Kenneth MBE	19.3.1952		21	1976–1983	778	152	1	23.57		0-6	0/0		52/7	31
Legat Ian Bruce	7.6.1930	24.1.1973	1	1953	2	1*	0	1.00					2	
Legat John Gordon	27.5.1926	9.3.1973	9	1951–1955	351	61	0	21.93					1	
Lissette Allen Fisher	6.11.1919	24.1.1973	2	1955	4	4*	0	1.00	3	2-73	0/0	41.33	0	
Loveridge Greg Riaka	15.1.1975		1	1995	4	4*	0		0	0-0	0/0		1	
Lowry Thomas Coleman	17.2.1898	20.7.1976	7	1929–1931	223	80	0	27.87		1-1	0/0		8	
McCullum Brendon Barrie (CY 2016)	27.9.1981		99	2003–2015	6,273	302	11	38.48	1	1-1	0/0	85.00	194/11	256/71
McEwan Paul Ernest	19.12.1953		4	1979–1984	96	40*	0	16.00	1	1-6	0/0		5	17
MacGibbon Anthony Roy	28.8.1924	6.4.2010	26	1950–1958	814	66	0	19.85	70	5-64	1/0	30.85	13	
McGirr Herbert Mendelson	5.11.1891	14.4.1964	2	1929	51	51	0	51.00	1	1-65	0/0	115.00	0	
McGregor Spencer Noel	18.12.1931	21.11.2007	25	1954–1964	892	111	2	19.82					9	
McIntosh Timothy Gavin	4.12.1979		17	2008–2010	854	136	2	27.54					0	
McKay Andrew John	17.4.1980		1	2010	25	20*	0	25.00	1	1-120	0/0	120.00	0	
McLeod Edwin George	14.10.1900	14.9.1989	1	1929	18	16	0	18.00	0	0-5	0/0		0	19/2

	Born	Died	Tests	Test Career	Runs	HS	100s	Avge	Wkts	BB	5/10	Avge	Ct/St	O/T
McMahon Trevor George	8.11.1929		5	1955	7	4*	0	2.33	–	–	–/–	–	7/1	–
McMillan Craig Douglas	13.9.1976		55	1997–2004	3,116	142	6	38.46	28	3-48	0/0	44.89	22	197/8
McRae Donald Alexander Noel	25.12.1912	10.8.1986	1	1945	8	8	0	4.00	0	0-44	0/0	–	0	–
[2] Marshall Hamish John Hamilton	15.2.1979		13	2000–2005	652	160	1	38.35	0	0-4	0/0	–	1	66/3
[2] Marshall James Andrew Hamilton	15.2.1979		7	2004–2008	218	52	0	19.81	–	–	–/–	–	5	10/3
Martin Bruce Philip	25.4.1980		5	2012–2013	74	41	0	14.80	12	4-43	0/0	53.83	0	–
Martin Christopher Stewart	10.12.1974		71	2000–2012	123	12*	0	2.36	233	6-26	10/1	33.81	14	20/6
Mason Michael James	27.8.1974			2003	3	3	0	1.50	0	0-32	0/0	–	0	26/3
Matheson Alexander Malcolm	27.2.1906	31.12.1985	2	1929–1931	7	7	0	7.00	2	2-7	0/0	68.00	0	–
Meale Trevor	11.11.1928		2	1958	21	10	0	5.25	–	–	–/–	–	0	–
Merritt William Edward	18.8.1908	21.5.2010	6	1929–1931	73	19	0	10.42	12	4-104	0/0	51.41	2	–
Meuli Edgar Milton	20.2.1926	15.4.2007	1	1952	38	23	0	19.00	–	–	–/–	–	2	–
Milburn Barry Douglas	24.11.1943		3	1968	8	4*	0	8.00	–	–	–/–	–	6/2	–
Miller Lawrence Somerville Martin	31.3.1923	17.12.1996	13	1952–1958	346	47	0	13.84	0	0-1	0/0	–	1	–
Mills John Ernest	3.9.1905	11.12.1972	7	1929–1932	241	117	1	26.77	–	–	–/–	–	1	–
Mills Kyle David	15.3.1979		19	2004–2008	289	57	0	11.56	44	4-16	0/0	33.02	4	170/42
Moir Alexander McKenzie	17.7.1919	17.6.2000	17	1950–1958	327	41*	0	14.86	28	6-155	2/0	50.64	2	–
Mooney Denis Andrew Robert ("Sonny")	11.8.1910	15.7.1942	3	1937	156	64	0	26.00	0	0-9	0/0	–	3	–
Mooney Francis Leonard Hugh	26.5.1921	8.3.2004	14	1949–1953	343	46	0	17.15	–	–	–/–	–	22/8	–
Morgan Ross Winston	12.2.1941		20	1964–1971	734	97	0	22.24	5	1-16	0/0	121.80	12	–
Morrison Bruce Donald	17.12.1933		1	1962	10	10	0	5.00	2	2-129	0/0	64.50	1	–
Morrison Danny Kyle	3.2.1966		48	1987–1996	379	42	0	8.42	160	7-89	10/0	34.68	14	96
Morrison John Francis MacLean	27.8.1947		17	1973–1981	656	117	1	22.62	2	2-52	0/0	35.50	9	18
Motz Richard Charles (*CY 1966*)	12.1.1940	29.4.2007	32	1961–1969	612	60	0	11.54	100	6-63	5/0	31.48	9	–
Munro Colin	11.3.1987		1	2012	15	15	0	7.50	2	2-40	0/0	20.00	0	12/20
Murray Bruce Alexander Grenfell	18.9.1940		13	1967–1970	598	90	0	23.92	1	1-0	0/0	0.00	21	–
Murray Darrin James	4.9.1967		8	1994	303	52	0	20.20	–	–	–/–	–	0	1
Nash Dion Joseph	20.11.1971		32	1992–2001	729	89*	0	23.51	93	6-27	3/1	28.48	13	81
Neesham James Douglas Sheehan	17.9.1990		9	2013–2015	612	137*	2	38.25	12	3-42	0/0	39.33	7	19/13
Newman *Sir* Jack	3.7.1902	23.9.1996	3	1931–1932	33	19	0	8.25	2	2-76	0/0	127.00	0	–
Nicol Robert James	28.5.1983		2	2011	28	19	0	7.00	0	0-5	0/0	–	2	22/21
O'Brien Iain Edward	10.7.1976		22	2004–2009	219	31	0	7.55	73	6-75	1/0	33.27	7	10/4
O'Connor Shayne Barry	15.11.1973		19	1997–2001	103	20	0	5.72	53	5-51	1/0	32.52	6	38
Oram Jacob David Philip	28.7.1978		33	2002–2009	1,780	133	5	36.32	60	4-41	0/0	33.05	15	160/36
O'Sullivan David Robert	16.11.1944		11	1972–1976	158	23*	0	9.29	18	5-148	1/0	67.83	2	3
Overton Guy William Fitzroy	8.6.1919	7.9.1993	3	1953	8	3*	0	1.60	9	3-65	0/0	28.66	1	–

	Born	Died	Tests	Test Career	Runs	HS	100s	Avge	Wkts	BB	5/10	Avge	Ct/St	O/T
Owens Michael Barry	11.11.1969	–	8	1992–1994	16	8*	0	2.66	17	4-99	0/0	34.41	3	1
Page Milford Laurenson ("Curly")	8.5.1902	13.2.1987	14	1929–1937	492	104	1	24.60	5	2-21	0/0	46.20	6	–
Papps Michael Hugh William	2.7.1979	–	8	2003–2007	246	86	0	16.40	–	–	–/–	–	11	6
[2]**Parker John Morton**	21.2.1951	–	36	1972–1980	1,498	121	3	24.55	1	1-24	0/0	24.00	30	24
[2]**Parker Norman Murray**	28.8.1948	–	3	1976	89	40	0	14.83	–	–	–/–	–	2	–
Parore Adam Craig	23.1.1971	–	78	1990–2001	2,865	110	2	26.28	–	–	–/–	–	197/7	179
Patel Dipak Narshibhai	25.10.1958	–	37	1986–1996	1,200	99	0	20.68	75	6-50	3/0	42.05	15	75
Patel Jeetan Shashi (CY 2015).	7.5.1980	–	19	2005–2012	276	27*	0	12.00	52	5-110	1/0	48.46	12	39/11
Petherick Peter James	25.9.1942	7.6.2015	6	1976	34	13	0	4.85	16	3-90	0/0	42.81	4	–
Petrie Eric Charlton	22.5.1927	14.8.2004	14	1955–1965	258	55	0	12.90	–	–	–/–	–	25	–
Playle William Rodger	1.12.1938	–	8	1958–1962	151	65	0	10.06	–	–	–/–	–	4	–
Pocock Blair Andrew	18.6.1971	–	15	1993–1997	665	85	0	22.93	0	0-10	0/0	–	5	–
Pollard Victor	7.9.1945	–	32	1964–1973	1,266	116	2	24.34	40	3-3	0/0	46.32	19	3
Poore Matt Beresford	1.6.1930	–	14	1952–1955	355	45	0	15.43	9	2-28	0/0	40.77	1	–
Priest Mark Wellings	12.8.1961	–	3	1990–1997	56	26	0	14.00	3	2-42	0/0	52.66	0	18
Pringle Christopher	26.1.1968	–	14	1990–1994	175	30	0	10.29	30	7-52	1/1	46.30	3	64
Puna Narotam ("Tom").	28.10.1929	7.6.1996	3	1965	31	18*	0	15.50	4	2-40	0/0	60.00	1	–
Rabone Geoffrey Osborne	6.11.1921	19.1.2006	12	1949–1954	562	107	1	31.22	16	6-68	1/0	39.68	5	–
Redmond Aaron James	23.9.1979	–	8	2008–2013	325	83	0	21.66	3	2-47	0/0	26.66	5	6/7
Redmond Rodney Ernest	29.12.1944	–	1	1972	163	107	1	81.50	–	–	–/–	–	0	2
Reid John Fulton	3.3.1956	–	19	1978–1985	1,296	180	6	46.28	0	0-0	0/0	–	9	25
Reid John Richard OBE (CY 1959)	3.6.1928	–	58	1949–1965	3,428	142	6	33.28	85	6-60	1/0	33.35	43/1	–
Richardson Mark Hunter	11.6.1971	–	38	2000–2004	2,776	145	4	44.77	7	2-9	0/0	21.00	26	4
Roberts Albert William	20.8.1909	13.5.1978	5	1929–1937	248	66*	0	27.55	7	4-101	0/0	29.85	4	–
Roberts Andrew Duncan Glenn	6.5.1947	26.10.1989	7	1975–1976	254	84*	0	23.09	4	1-12	0/0	45.50	4	1
Robertson Gary Keith	15.7.1960	–	1	1985	12	12	0	12.00	1	1-91	0/0	91.00	4	10
Ronchi Luke	23.4.1981	–	4	2015	119	88	0	59.50	–	–	–/–	–	11	6½/18‡
Rowe Charles Gordon	30.6.1915	9.6.1995	1	1945	0	0	0	0.00	0	0-2	0/0	–	0	–
Rutherford Hamish Duncan	27.4.1989	–	16	2012–2014	755	171	1	26.96	–	–	–/–	–	11	4/7
Rutherford Kenneth Robert	26.10.1965	–	56	1984–1994	2,465	107*	3	27.08	1	1-38	0/0	161.00	32	121
Ryder Jesse Daniel	6.8.1984	–	18	2008–2011	1,269	201	3	40.93	5	2-7	0/0	31.00	12	48/22
Santner Mitchell Josef	5.2.1992	–	1	2015	130	45	0	26.00	1	1-74	0/0	74.00	0	10/2
Scott Roy Hamilton	6.3.1917	5.8.2005	1	1946	18	18	0	18.00	0	0-5	0/0	–	0	–
Scott Verdun John	31.7.1916	2.8.1980	10	1945–1951	458	84	0	28.62	–	–	–/–	–	7	–
Sewell David Graham	20.10.1977	–	1	1997	1	1*	0	–	0	0-9	0/0	–	0	–
Shrimpton Michael John Froud	23.6.1940	13.6.2015	10	1962–1973	265	46	0	13.94	5	3-35	0/0	31.60	2	–

Name	Born	Died	Tests	Test Career	Runs	HS	100s	Avge	Wkts	BB	5/10	Avge	Ct/St	O/T
Sinclair Barry Whitley	23.10.1936		21	1962–1967	1,148	138	3	29.43	2	2-32	0/0	16.00	8	–
Sinclair Ian McKay	1.6.1933		2	1955	25	18*	0	8.33	1	1-79	0/0	120.00	1	–
Sinclair Mathew Stuart	9.11.1975		33	1999–2009	1,635	214	3	32.05	0	0-1	0/0	–	31	54/2
Smith Frank Brunton	13.3.1922	6.7.1997	4	1946–1951	237	96	0	47.40	1	1-113	0/0	113.00	0	–
Smith Horace Dennis	8.1.1913	25.1.1986	1	1932	4	4	0	4.00	0	0-5	–/–	–	0	–
Smith Ian David Stockley MBE	28.2.1957		63	1980–1991	1,815	173	2	25.56	0	0-46	0/0	–	168/8	98
Snedden Colin Alexander	7.1.1918	23.4.2011	1	1946	–	–	–	–	0	–	–/–	–	1	–
Snedden Martin Colin	23.11.1958		25	1980–1990	327	33*	0	14.86	58	5-68	1/0	37.91	7	93
Sodhi Inderbir Singh ("Ish")	31.10.1992		11	2013–2014	337	63	0	25.92	27	4-96	0/0	52.81	7	9/5
Southee Timothy Grant	11.12.1988		46	2007–2015	1,156	77*	0	17.00	163	7-64	4/1	31.47	29	99/38
Sparling John Trevor	24.7.1938		11	1958–1963	229	50	0	12.72	5	1-9	0/0	65.40	4	–
Spearman Craig Murray	4.7.1972		19	1995–2000	922	112	1	26.34	–	–	–/–	–	21	51
Stead Gary Raymond	9.1.1972		5	1998–1999	278	78	0	34.75	0	0-1	0/0	–	–	–
Stirling Derek Alexander	5.10.1961		6	1984–1986	108	26	0	15.42	13	4-88	0/0	46.23	2	6
Styris Scott Bernard	10.7.1975		29	2002–2007	1,586	170	5	36.04	20	3-28	0/0	50.75	23	188/31
Su'a Murphy Logo	7.11.1966		13	1991–1994	165	44	0	12.69	36	5-73	2/0	38.25	8	12
Sutcliffe Bert MBE (CY 1950)	17.11.1923	20.4.2001	42	1946–1965	2,727	230*	5	40.10	4	2-38	0/0	86.00	40	–
Taylor Bruce Richard	12.7.1943		30	1964–1973	898	124	2	20.40	111	7-74	4/0	26.60	10	2
Taylor Donald Dougald	2.3.1923	5.12.1980	3	1946–1955	159	77	0	31.80	0	–	–/–	–	2	–
Taylor Luteru Ross Poutoa Lote	8.3.1984		69	2007–2015	5,232	290	13	45.49	2	2-4	0/0	24.00	112	171/66
Thomson Keith	26.2.1941		2	1967	94	69	0	31.33	2	1-9	0/0	9.00	7	–
Thomson Shane Alexander	27.1.1969		19	1989–1995	958	120*	1	30.90	19	3-63	0/0	50.15	7	56
Tindill Eric William Thomas	18.12.1910	1.8.2010	15	1937–1946	73	37*	0	9.12	–	–	–/–	–	6/1	–
Troup Gary Bertram	3.10.1952		15	1976–1985	55	13*	0	4.58	39	6-95	1/1	37.28	2	22
Truscott Peter Bennetts	14.8.1941		1	1964	29	26	0	14.50	–	–	–/–	–	–	–
Tuffey Daryl Raymond	11.6.1978		26	1999–2009	427	80*	0	16.42	77	6-54	2/0	31.75	15	94/3
Turner Glenn Maitland (CY 1971)	26.5.1947		41	1968–1982	2,991	259	7	44.64	0	0-5	0/0	–	42	41
Twose Roger Graham	17.4.1968		16	1995–1999	628	94	0	25.12	3	2-36	0/0	43.33	5	87
Vance Robert Howard	31.3.1955		4	1987–1989	207	68	0	29.57	–	–	–/–	–	4	8
Van Wyk Cornelius Francois Kruger	7.2.1980		9	2011–2012	341	71	0	21.31	–	–	–/–	–	23/1	–
Vaughan Justin Thomas Caldwell	30.8.1967		6	1992–1996	201	44	0	18.27	11	4-27	0/0	40.90	2	18
Vettori Daniel Luca	27.11.1978		112‡	1996–2014	4,523	140	6	30.15	361	7-87	20/3	34.15	58	291‡/34
Vincent Lou	11.11.1978		23	2001–2007	1,332	224	4	34.15	0	0-5	0/0	–	19	102/9
Vivian Graham Ellery	28.2.1946		5	1964–1971	110	43	0	18.33	1	1-14	0/0	107.00	3	–
Vivian Henry Gifford	4.11.1912	12.8.1983	7	1931–1937	421	100	0	42.10	17	4-58	0/0	37.23	1	–

§ Vettori's figures exclude eight runs and one wicket for the ICC World XI v Australia in the Super Series Test in 2005-06.

	Born	Died	Tests	Test Career	Runs	HS	100s	Avge	Wts	BB	5/10	Avge	Ct/St	O/T
Wadsworth Kenneth John	30.11.1946	19.8.1976	33	1969–1975	1,010	80	0	21.48	–	–	–/–	–	92/4	13
Wagner Neil	13.3.1986		18	2012–2015	224	37	0	11.78	67	5-64	1/0	33.34	4	
Walker Brooke Graeme Keith	25.3.1977		5	2000–2002	118	27*	0	19.66	5	2-92	0/0	79.80	0	11
Wallace Walter Mervyn	19.12.1916	21.3.2008	13	1937–1952	439	66	0	20.90	0	0-5	0/0	–	5	
Walmsley Kerry Peter	23.8.1973		3	1994–2000	13	5	0	2.60	9	3-70	0/0	43.44	0	2
Ward John Thomas	11.3.1937		8	1963–1967	75	35*	0	12.50	–	–	–/–	–	16/1	
Watling Bradley-John	9.7.1985		36	2009–2015	1,961	142*	5	37.71	–	–	0/0	–	119/5	22/5
Watson William	31.8.1965		15	1986–1993	60	11	0	5.00	40	6-78	1/0	34.67	4	61
Watt Leslie	17.9.1924	15.11.1996	1	1954	2	2	0	1.00	–	–	–/–	–	0	
Webb Murray George	22.6.1947		3	1970–1973	12	12	0	6.00	4	2-114	0/0	117.75	0	
Webb Peter Neil	14.7.1957		2	1979	11	5	0	3.66	0	0-1	0/0	–	2	5
Weir Gordon Lindsay	2.6.1908	31.10.2003	11	1929–1937	416	74*	0	29.71	7	3-38	0/0	29.85	3	
White David John	26.6.1961		2	1990	31	18	0	7.75	0	0-5	0/0	–	3	3
Whitelaw Paul Erskine	10.2.1910	28.8.1988	2	1932	64	30	0	32.00	–	–	–/–	–	1	
Williamson Kane Stuart (CY 2016)	8.8.1990		46	2010–2015	3,895	242*	13	49.93	28	4-44	0/0	38.39	39	88/27
Wiseman Paul John	4.5.1970		25	1997–2004	366	36	0	14.07	61	5-82	2/0	47.59	11	15
Wright John Geoffrey MBE	5.7.1954		82	1977–1992	5,334	185	12	37.82	0	0-1	0/0	–	38	149
Young Bryan Andrew	3.11.1964		35	1993–1998	2,034	267*	2	31.78	–	–	–/–	–	54	74
Young Reece Alan	15.9.1979		5	2010–2011	169	57	0	24.14	–	–	–/–	–	8	
Yuile Bryan William	29.10.1941		17	1962–1969	481	64	0	17.81	34	4-43	0/0	35.67	12	

INDIA (285 players)

	Born	Died	Tests	Test Career	Runs	HS	100s	Avge	Wts	BB	5/10	Avge	Ct/St	O/T
Aaron Varun Raymond	29.10.1989		9	2011–2015	35	9	0	3.88	18	3-97	0/0	52.61	1	9
Abid Ali Syed	9.9.1941		29	1967–1974	1,018	81	0	20.36	47	6-55	1/0	42.12	32	5
Adhikari Hemchandra Ramachandra	31.7.1919	25.10.2003	21	1947–1958	872	114*	1	31.14	3	3-68	0/0	27.33	8	
Agarkar Ajit Bhalchandra	4.12.1977		26	1998–2005	571	109*	1	16.79	58	6-41	1/0	47.32	6	191/4
[2] Amar Singh Ladha	4.12.1910	21.5.1940	7	1932–1936	292	51	0	22.46	28	7-86	2/0	30.64	3	
[1,2] Amarnath Mohinder (CY 1984)	24.9.1950		69	1969–1987	4,378	138	11	42.50	32	4-63	0/0	55.68	47	85
[1,2] Amarnath Nanik ("Lala")	11.9.1911	5.8.2000	24	1933–1952	878	118	1	24.38	45	5-96	2/0	32.91	13	
[1,2] Amarnath Surinder	30.12.1948		10	1975–1978	550	124	1	30.55	1	1-5	0/0	5.00	4	3
Amir Elahi	1.9.1908	28.12.1980	1†	1947	17	13	0	8.50	–	–	–/–	–	0	
Amre Pravin Kalyan	14.8.1968		11	1992–1993	425	103	1	42.50	–	–	–/–	–	9	37
Ankola Salil Ashok	1.3.1968		1	1989	6	6	0	6.00	2	1-35	0/0	64.00	0	20

Name	Born	Died	Tests	Test Career	Runs	HS	100s	Avge	Wkts	BB	5/10	Avge	Ct/St	O/T
² Apte Arvindrao Laxmanrao	24.10.1934	5.8.2014	1	1959	15	8	0	7.50	–	–	–/–	–	0	–
² Apte Madhavrao Laxmanrao	5.10.1932		7	1952	542	163*	1	49.27	0	0-3	–/–	–	2	–
Arshad Ayub	2.8.1958		13	1987–1989	257	57	0	17.13	41	5-50	3/0	35.07	2	32
Arun Bharathi	14.12.1962		1	1986	4	2*	0	4.00	4	3-76	0/0	29.00	2	4
Arun Lal	1.8.1955		16	1982–1988	729	93	0	26.03	0	0-0	0/0	–	13	13
Ashwin Ravichandran	17.9.1986		32	2011–2015	1,204	124	2	31.68	176	7-66	16/4	25.39	13	100/28
Azad Kirtivardhan	2.1.1959		7	1980–1983	135	24	0	11.25	3	2-84	0/0	124.33	3	25
Azharuddin Mohammad (CY 991)	8.2.1963		99	1984–1999	6,215	199	22	45.03	0	0-4	0/0	–	105	334
Badani Hemang Kamal	14.11.1976		4	2001	94	38	0	15.66	0	0-17	0/0	–	6	40
Badrinath Subramaniam	30.8.1980		2	2009	63	56	0	21.00	–	–	–/–	–	2	7/1
Bahutule Sairaj Vasant	6.1.1973		2	2000–2001	39	21*	0	13.00	3	1-32	0/0	67.66	1	8
Baig Abbas Ali	19.3.1939		10	1959–1966	428	112	1	23.77	0	0-2	0/0	–	6	–
Balaji Lakshmipathy	27.9.1981		8	2003–2004	51	31	0	5.66	27	5-76	1/0	37.18	0	30/5
Banerjee Sarobindu Nath ("Shute")	3.10.1911	14.10.1980	1	1948	13	8	0	6.50	5	4-54	0/0	25.40	0	–
Banerjee Subroto Tara	13.2.1969		1	1991	3	3	0	3.00	3	3-47	0/0	15.66	0	6
Banerjee Sudangsu Abinash	1.11.1917	14.9.1992	1	1948	0	0	0	0.00	5	4-120	0/0	36.20	3	–
Bangar Sanjay Bapusaheb	11.10.1972		12	2001–2002	470	100*	0	29.37	7	2-23	0/0	49.00	4	15
Baqa Jilani Mohammad	20.7.1911	2.7.1941	1	1936	16	12	0	16.00	0	0-55	0/0	–	0	–
Bedi Bishan Singh	25.9.1946		67	1966–1979	656	50*	0	8.98	266	7-98	14/1	28.71	26	10
Bhandari Prakash	27.11.1935		3	1954–1956	77	39	0	19.25	0	0-12	0/0	–	1	–
Bharadwaj Raghvendrarao Vijay	15.8.1975		3	1999	28	22	0	9.33	1	1-26	0/0	107.00	3	10
Bhat Adwai Raghuram	16.4.1958		2	1983	6	6	0	3.00	4	2-65	0/0	37.75	0	–
Bhuvneshwar Kumar	5.2.1990		12	2012–2014	393	63*	0	26.20	29	6-82	2/0	35.00	4	55/13
¹ Binny Roger Michael Humphrey	19.7.1955		27	1979–1986	830	83*	0	23.05	47	6-56	2/0	32.63	11	72
Binny Stuart Terence Roger	3.6.1984		6	2014–2015	194	78	0	21.55	3	2-24	0/0	86.00	4	14/2
Borde Chandrakant Gulabrao	21.7.1934		55	1958–1969	3,061	177*	5	35.59	52	5-88	1/0	46.48	37	–
Chandrasekhar Bhagwat Subramanya (CY 1972)	17.5.1945		58	1963–1979	167	22	0	4.07	242	8-79	16/2	29.74	25	1
Chauhan Chetandra Pratap Singh	21.7.1947		40	1969–1980	2,084	97	0	31.57	2	1-4	0/0	53.00	38	1
Chauhan Rajesh Kumar	19.12.1966		21	1992–1997	98	23	0	7.00	47	4-48	0/0	39.51	12	35
Chawla Piyush Pramod	24.12.1988		3	2005–2012	6	4	0	2.00	7	4-69	0/0	38.57	1	25/7
Chopra Aakash	19.9.1977		10	2003–2004	437	60	0	23.00	0	–	–/–	–	15	–
Chopra Nikhil	26.12.1973		1	1999	7	4	0	3.50	0	0-78	0/0	–	0	–
Chowdhury Nirode Ranjan	23.5.1923	14.12.1979	2	1948–1951	3	3*	0	3.00	1	1-130	0/0	205.00	0	–
Colah Sorabji Hormasji Munchersha	22.9.1902	11.9.1950	2	1932–1933	69	31	0	17.25	–	–	–/–	–	2	–
Contractor Nariman Jamshedji	7.3.1934		31	1955–1961	1,611	108	1	31.58	1	1-9	0/0	80.00	18	39

Name	Born	Died	Tests	Test Career	Runs	HS	100s	Avge	Wkts	BB	5/10	Avge	Ct/St	O/T
Dahiya Vijay	10.5.1973		2	2000-2001	2	2*	0	–					6	19
Dani Hemchandra Tukaram	24.5.1933	19.12.1999	1	1952	–	–	–	–	1	1-9	0/0	19.00		
Das Shiv Sunder	5.11.1977		23	2000-2002	1,326	110	2	34.89	0	0-7	0/0	–	34	4
Dasgupta Deep	7.6.1977		8	2001-2002	344	100	1	28.66					13	5
Desai Ramakant Bhikaji	20.6.1939	27.4.1998	28	1958-1967	418	85	0	13.48	74	6-56	2/0	37.31	9	
Dhawan Shikhar (CY 2014)	5.12.1985		19	2013-2015	1,308	187	4	40.87	0	0-0	0/0	–	15	69/8
Dhoni Mahendra Singh	7.7.1981		90	2005-2014	4,876	224	6	38.09	0	0-1	0/0	–	256/38	267‡/52
Dighe Sameer Sudhakar	8.10.1968		6	2000-2001	141	47	0	15.66					12/2	23
Dilawar Hussain	19.3.1907	26.8.1967	3	1933-1936	254	59	0	42.33					6/1	
Divecha Ramesh Vithaldas	18.10.1927	11.2.2003	5	1951-1952	60	26	0	12.00	11	3-102	0/0	28.09		
Doshi Dilip Rasiklal	22.12.1947		33	1979-1983	129	20	0	4.60	114	6-102	6/0	34.60	10	15
Dravid Rahul (CY 2000)	11.1.1973		164§	1996-2012	13,265	270	36	52.63	1	1-18	0/0	39.00	209	340/1
Durani Salim Aziz	11.12.1934		29	1960-1973	1,202	104	1	25.04	75	6-73	3/1	35.42	14	
Engineer Farokh Maneksha	25.2.1938		46	1961-1975	2,611	121	2	31.08					66/16	5
Gadkari Chandrasekhar Vaman	3.2.1928	11.1.1998	6	1952-1955	129	50*	0	21.50	0	0-8	0/0	–	6	
Gaekwad Anshuman Dattajirao	23.9.1952		40	1974-1985	1,985	201	2	30.07	2	1-4	0/0	93.50	15	15
[1] Gaekwad Dattajirao Krishnarao	27.10.1928		11	1952-1961	350	52	0	18.42	0	0-4	0/0	–	5	
[1] Gaekwad Hiralal Ghasulal	29.8.1923	2.1.2003	1	1952	22	14	0	11.00	0	0-47	0/0	–	0	
Gambhir Gautam	14.10.1981		56	2004-2014	4,046	206	9	42.58	0	0-4	0/0	–	38	147/37
Gandhi Devang Jayant	6.9.1971		4	1999-2000	204	88	0	34.00					0	
Gandotra Ashok	24.11.1948		2	1969-1970	54	18	0	13.50					0	
Ganesh Doddanarsiah	30.6.1973		4	1997	25	8	0	6.25	5	2-28	0/0	57.40	1	1
Ganguly Sourav Chandidas	8.7.1972		113	1996-2008	7,212	239	16	42.17	32	3-28	0/0	52.53	71	308‡
Gavaskar Sunil Manohar (CY 1980)	10.7.1949		125	1971-1987	10,122	236*	34	51.12	1	1-34	0/0	206.00	108	108
Ghavri Karsan Devjibhai	28.2.1951		39	1974-1981	913	86	0	21.23	109	5-33	4/0	33.54	16	19
Ghorpade Jayasinghrao Mansinghrao	2.10.1930	29.3.1978	8	1952-1959	229	41	0	15.26					4	
Ghulam Ahmed	4.7.1922	28.10.1998	22	1948-1959	192	50	0	8.72	68	7-49	4/1	30.17	3	
Gopalan Morappakam Joysam	6.6.1909	21.12.2003	1	1933-1934	18	11*	0	18.00	1	1-39	0/0	39.00	3	
Gopinath Coimbatarao Doraikannu	1.3.1930		8	1951-1960	242	50*	0	22.00	1	1-11	0/0	11.00	2	
Guard Ghulam Mustafa	12.12.1925	13.3.1978	2	1958-1961	11	7	0	5.50	3	2-69	0/0	60.66	2	
Guha Subrata	31.1.1946		4	1967-1970	17	6	0	3.40	3	2-55	0/0	103.66	2	
Gul Mahomed	15.10.1921	8.5.1992	8†	1946-1952	166	34	0	11.06	2	2-21	0/0	12.00	3	
[2] Gupte Balkrishna Pandharinath	30.8.1934	12.12.2005	3	1960-1964	28	17*	0	28.00	3	1-54	0/0	116.33	0	
[2] Gupte Subhashchandra Pandharinath ("Fergie")	11.12.1929	31.5.2002	36	1951-1961	183	21	0	6.31	149	9-102	12/1	29.55	14	
Gursharan Singh	8.3.1963		1	1990	18	18	0	18.00						

§ Dravid's figures exclude 23 runs and one catch for the ICC World XI v Australia in the Super Series Test in 2005-06.

Name	Born	Died	Tests	Test Career	Runs	HS	100s	Avge	Wkts	BB	5/10	Avge	Ct/St	O/T
Hafeez Abdul (see Kardar)														
Hanumant Singh	29.3.1939	29.11.2006	14	1963–1969	686	105	1	31.18	–	0-5	0/0	–	11	–
Harbhajan Singh	3.7.1980		103	1997–2015	2,224	115	2	18.22	417	8-84	25/5	32.46	42	234‡/27
Hardikar Manohar Shankar	8.2.1936	4.2.1995	2	1958	56	32*	0	18.66	1	1-9	0/0	55.00	3	–
Harvinder Singh	23.12.1977		3	1997–2001	6	6	0	2.00	4	2-62	0/0	46.25	1	16
Hazare Vijay Samuel	11.3.1915	18.12.2004	30	1946–1952	2,192	164*	7	47.65	20	4-29	0/0	61.00	11	–
Hindlekar Dattaram Dharmaji	1.1.1909	30.3.1949	4	1936–1946	71	26	0	14.20	–	–	–/–	–	3	–
Hirwani Narendra Deepchand	18.10.1968		17	1987–1996	54	17	0	5.40	66	8-61	4/1	30.10	5	18
Ibrahim Khanmohammad Cassumbhoy	26.1.1919	12.11.2007	4	1948	169	85	0	21.12	–	–	–/–	–	5	–
Indrajitsinhji Kumar Shri	15.6.1937	12.3.2011	4	1964–1969	51	23	0	8.50	–	–	–/–	–	6/3	–
Irani Jamshed Khudadad	8.8.1923	25.2.1982	2	1947	3	2*	0	3.00	–	–	–/–	–	2/1	–
Jadeja Ajaysinhji	1.2.1971		15	1992–1999	576	96	0	26.18	–	–	–/–	–	5	196
[3]Jadeja Ravindrasinh Anirudhsinh	6.12.1988		16	2012–2015	473	68	0	23.76	68	6-138	4/0	–	16	121/22
Jahangir Khan Mohammad	1.2.1910	23.7.1988	4	1932–1936	39	13	0	4.00	4	4-60	0/0	63.75	4	–
Jai Laxmidas Purshottamdas	1.4.1902	29.1.1968	1	1933	19	19	0	9.50	–	–	–/–	–	–	–
Jaisimha Motganhalli Laxmanarsu	3.3.1939	6.7.1999	39	1959–1970	2,056	129	3	30.68	9	2-54	0/0	92.11	17	–
Jamshedji Rustomji Jamshedji Dorabji	18.11.1892	5.4.1976	1	1933	5	4*	0	5.00	3	3-137	0/0	45.66	2	–
Jayantilal Kenia	13.1.1948		1	1970	5	5	0	5.00	–	–	–/–	–	2	–
Johnson David Jude	16.10.1971		2	1996	8	5	0	4.00	3	2-52	0/0	47.66	0	–
Joshi Padmanabh Govind	27.10.1926	8.1.1987	12	1951–1960	207	52*	0	10.89	–	–	–/–	–	18/9	–
Joshi Sunil Bandacharya	6.6.1969		15	1996–2000	352	92	0	20.70	41	5-142	2/0	35.85	8	69
Kaif Mohammad	1.12.1980		13	1999–2005	624	148*	1	32.84	–	–	–/–	–	14	125
Kambli Vinod Ganpat	18.1.1972		17	1992–1995	1,084	227	4	54.20	–	0-4	0/0	–	7	104
Kanitkar Hemant Shamsunder	8.12.1942	9.6.2015	2	1974	74	65	0	18.50	–	–	–/–	–	–	–
Kanitkar Hrishikesh Hemant	14.11.1974		2	1999–2000	111	45	0	27.75	–	0-2	0/0	–	1	34
Kapil Dev (CY 1983)	6.1.1959		131	1978–1993	5,248	163	8	31.05	434	9-83	23/2	29.64	64	225
Kapoor Aashish Rakesh	25.3.1971		4	1994–1996	97	42	0	19.40	6	2-19	0/0	42.50	2	17
Kardar Abdul Hafeez	17.1.1925	21.4.1996	3†	1946	80	43	0	16.00	–	–	–/–	–	–	–
Karim Syed Saba	14.11.1967		1	2000	15	15	0	15.00	–	–	–/–	–	3	34
Karthik Krishankumar Dinesh	1.6.1985		23	2004–2015	1,000	129	1	27.77	–	–	–/–	–	51/5	71/9
Kartik Murali	11.9.1976		8	1999–2004	88	43	0	9.77	24	4-44	0/0	34.16	2	37/1
Kenny Ramnath Baburao	29.9.1930	21.11.1985	5	1958–1959	245	62	0	27.22	1	1-9	0/0	13.00	1	–
Kirmani Syed Mujtaba Hussein	29.12.1949		88	1975–1985	2,759	102	2	27.04	–	–	–/–	–	160/38	49
Kishenchand Gogumal	14.4.1925	16.4.1997	5	1947–1952	89	44	0	8.90	–	–	–/–	–	4	–
Kohli Virat	5.11.1988		41	2011–2015	2,994	169	11	44.02	–	0-0	0/0	–	36	166/30
[4]Kripal Singh Amritsar Govindsingh	6.8.1933	22.7.1987	14	1955–1964	422	100*	1	28.13	10	3-43	0/0	58.40	4	–

	Born	Died	Tests	Test Career	Runs	HS	100s	Avge	Wkts	BB	5/10	Avge	Ct/St	O/T
Krishnamurthy Pochiah	12.7.1947	28.1.1999	5	1970	33	20	0	5.50	–	–	–/–	–	7/1	10
Kulkarni Nilesh Moreshwar	3.4.1973		3	1997–2000	5	4	0	5.00	2	1-70	0/0	166.00	1	10
Kulkarni Rajiv Ramesh	25.9.1962		3	1986	2	2	0	1.00	5	3-85	0/0	45.40	1	10
Kulkarni Umesh Narayan	7.3.1942		4	1967	13	7	0	4.33	5	2-37	0/0	47.60	0	
Kumar Praveen	2.10.1986		6	2011	149	40	0	14.90	27	5-106	1/0	25.81	2	68/10
Kumar Vaman Viswanath	22.6.1935		2	1960–1961	6	6	0	3.00	7	5-64	1/0	28.85	2	
Kumble Anil (CY 1996)	17.10.1970		132	1990–2008	2,506	110*	1	17.77	619	10-74	35/8	29.65	60	269*
Kunderan Budhisagar Krishnappa	2.10.1939	23.6.2006	18	1959–1967	981	192	2	32.70	0	0-13	0/0	–	23/7	
Kuruvilla Abey	8.8.1968		10	1996–1997	66	35*	0	6.60	25	5-68	1/0	35.68	0	25
Lall Singh	16.12.1909	19.11.1985	1	1932	44	29	0	22.00	–	–	–/–	–	1	
Lamba Raman	2.1.1960	22.2.1998	4	1986–1987	102	53	0	20.40	–	–	–/–	–	5	32
Laxman Vangipurappu Venkata Sai (CY 2002)	1.11.1974		134	1996–2011	8,781	281	17	45.97	2	1-2	0/0	63.00	135	86
Madan Lal	20.3.1951		39	1974–1986	1,042	74	0	22.65	71	5-23	4/0	40.08	15	67
Maka Ebrahim Suleman	5.3.1922	7.9.1994	2	1952	2	2*	0	–	–	–	–/–	–	2/1	
Malhotra Ashok Omprakash	26.1.1957		7	1981–1984	226	72*	0	25.11	0	0-0	0/0	–	9	20
Maninder Singh	13.6.1965		35	1982–1992	99	15	0	3.80	88	7-27	3/2	37.36	9	59
¹Manjrekar Sanjay Vijay	12.7.1965		37	1987–1996	2,043	218	4	37.14	0	0-4	0/0	–	25/1	74
¹Manjrekar Vijay Laxman	26.9.1931	18.10.1983	55	1951–1964	3,208	189*	7	39.12	1	1-16	0/0	44.00	19/2	
¹Mankad Ashok Vinoo	12.10.1946	1.8.2008	22	1969–1977	991	97	0	25.41	0	0-0	0/0	–	12	67
¹Mankad Mulvantrai Himmatlal ("Vinoo") (CY 1947)	12.4.1917	21.8.1978	44	1946–1958	2,109	231	5	31.47	162	8-52	8/2	32.32	33	
Mantri Madhav Krishnaji	1.9.1921	23.5.2014	4	1951–1954	67	39	0	9.57	–	–	–/–	–	8/1	
Meherhomji Khershedji Rustomji	9.8.1911	10.2.1982	1	1936	0	0*	0	–	–	–	–/–	–	1	
Mehra Vijay Laxman	12.3.1938	25.8.2006	8	1955–1963	329	62	0	25.30	0	0-1	0/0	–	1	
Merchant Vijay Madhavji (CY 1937)	12.10.1911	27.10.1987	10	1933–1951	859	154	3	47.72	0	0-17	0/0	–	7	
Mhambrey Paras Laxmikant	20.6.1972		2	1996	58	28	0	29.00	2	1-43	0/0	74.00	0	3
²Milkha Singh Amritsar Govindsingh	31.12.1941		4	1959–1961	92	35	0	15.33	0	0-2	0/0	–	2	
Mishra Amit	24.11.1982		18	2008–2015	574	84	0	21.25	65	5-71	1/0	33.96	7	31/7
Mithun Abhimanyu	25.10.1989		4	2010–2011	120	46	0	24.00	9	4-105	0/0	50.66	0	5
Modi Rustomji Sheriyar	11.11.1924	17.5.1996	10	1946–1952	736	112	1	46.00	0	0-14	0/0	–	3	
Mohammed Shami	3.9.1990		12	2013–2014	166	51*	0	12.76	47	5-47	2/0	36.14	4	47/4
Mohanty Debasis Sarbeswar	20.7.1976		2	1997	0	0*	0	–	4	4-78	0/0	59.75	0	45
Mongia Nayan Ramlal	19.12.1969		44	1993–2000	1,442	152	1	24.03	–	–	–/–	–	99/8	140
More Kiran Shankar	4.9.1962		49	1986–1993	1,285	73	0	25.70	0	0-12	0/0	–	110/20	94
Muddiah Venatappa Musandra	8.6.1929	1.10.2009	2	1959–1960	11	11	0	5.50	3	2-40	0/0	44.66	0	
Mukund Abhinav	6.1.1990		5	2011	211	62	0	21.10	–	–	–/–	–	5	

	Born	Died	Tests	Test Career	Runs	HS	100s	Avge	Wkts	BB	5/10	Avge	Ct/St	O/T
Mushtaq Ali Syed	17.12.1914	18.6.2005	11	1933–1951	612	112	2	32.21	3	1-45	0/0	67.33	7	
Nadkarni Rameshchandra Gangaram ("Bapu")	4.4.1933		41	1955–1967	1,414	122*	1	25.70	88	6-43	4/1	29.07	22	
Naik Sudhir Sakharam	21.2.1945		3	1974–1974	141	77	0	23.50	–	–	–/–	–	0	
Naoomal Jeoomal	17.4.1904	28.7.1980	3	1932–1933	108	43	0	27.00	2	1-4	0/0	34.00	0	2
Narasimha Rao Modireddy Venkateshwar	11.8.1954		4	1978–1979	46	20*	0	9.20	3	2-46	0/0	75.66	8	
Navle Janardan Gyanoba	7.12.1902	7.9.1979	2	1932–1933	42	13	0	10.50	–	–	–/–	–	1	
Nayak Surendra Vithal	20.10.1954		2	1982	19	11	0	9.50	1	1-16	0/0	132.00	1	
²Nayudu Cottari Kanakaiya (CY 1933)	31.10.1895	14.11.1967	7	1932–1936	350	81	0	25.00	9	3-40	0/0	42.88	4	4
²Nayudu Cottari Subbanna	18.4.1914	22.11.2002	11	1933–1951	147	36	0	9.18	2	1-19	0/0	179.50	3	
²Nazir Ali Syed	8.6.1906	18.2.1975	2	1932–1933	30	13	0	7.50	4	4-83	0/0	20.75	0	
Nehra Ashish	29.4.1979		17	1998–2003	77	19	0	5.50	44	4-72	0/0	42.40	5	117‡/8
Nissar Mohammad	1.8.1910	11.3.1963	6	1932–1936	55	14	0	6.87	25	5-90	3/0	28.28	2	
Nyalchand Sukhlal Shah	14.9.1915	3.1.1997	1	1952	7	6*	0	7.00	3	3-97	0/0	32.33	–	
Ojha Naman Vijaykumar	20.7.1983		1	2015	56	35	0	28.00	–	–	–/–	–	4/1	1/2
Ojha Pragyan Prayish	5.9.1986		24	2009–2013	89	18*	0	8.90	113	6-47	7/1	30.26	10	18/6
Pai Ajit Manohar	28.4.1945		1	1969	10	9	0	5.00	2	2-29	0/0	15.50	0	
Palia Phiroze Edulji	5.9.1910	9.9.1981	2	1932–1936	29	16	0	9.66	0	0-2	0/0	–	0	
Pandit Chandrakant Sitaram	30.9.1961		5	1986–1991	171	39	0	24.42	–	–	–/–	–	14/2	36
Pankaj Singh	6.5.1985		2	2014	10	9	0	3.33	2	2-113	0/0	146.00	2	
Parkar Ghulam Ahmed	25.10.1955		1	1982	7	6	0	3.50	–	–	–/–	–	2	10
Parkar Ramnath Dhondu	31.10.1946	11.8.1999	2	1972	80	35	0	20.00	–	–	–/–	–	1	
Parsana Dhiraj Devshibhai	2.12.1947		2	1978	1	1	0	0.50	1	1-32	0/0	50.00	0	
Patankar Chandrakant Trimbak	24.11.1930		1	1955	14	13	0	14.00	–	–	–/–	–	3/1	
¹Pataudi Iftikhar Ali Khan, Nawab of (CY 1932)	16.3.1910	5.1.1952	3†	1946	55	22	0	11.00	–	–	–/–	–	0	
¹Pataudi Mansur Ali Khan, Nawab of (CY 1968)	5.1.1941	22.9.2011	46	1961–1974	2,793	203*	6	34.91	1	1-10	0/0	88.00	27	120/24
Patel Brijesh Parsuram	24.11.1952		21	1974–1977	972	115*	1	29.45	–	–	–/–	–	17	
Patel Jasubhai Motibhai	26.11.1924	12.12.1992	7	1954–1959	25	12	0	2.77	29	9-69	2/1	21.96	2	10
Patel Munaf Musa	12.7.1983		13	2005–2011	60	15*	0	7.50	35	4-25	0/0	38.54	6	70/3
Patel Parthiv Ajay	9.3.1985		20	2002–2008	683	69	0	29.69	–	–	–/–	–	41/8	38/2
Patel Rashid	1.6.1964		1	1988	0	0	0	0.00	0	0-14	0/0	–	0	1
Pathan Irfan Khan	27.10.1984		29	2003–2007	1,105	102	1	31.57	100	7-59	7/2	32.26	8	120/24
Patiala Maharajah of (Yadavendra Singh)	17.1.1913	17.6.1974	1	1933	84	60	0	42.00	–	–	–/–	–	2	
Patil Sadashiv Raoji	10.10.1933		1	1955	14	14*	0	–	2	1-15	0/0	25.50	1	
Patil Sandeep Madhusudan	18.8.1956		29	1979–1984	1,588	174	4	36.93	9	2-28	0/0	26.66	12	45
Phadkar Dattatraya Gajanan	12.12.1925	17.3.1985	31	1947–1958	1,229	123	2	32.34	62	7-159	3/0	36.85	21	31
Powar Ramesh Rajaram	20.5.1978		2	2007	13	7	0	6.50	6	3-33	0/0	19.66	0	

	Born	Died	Tests	Test Career	Runs	HS	100s	Avge	Wkts	BB	5/10	Avge	Ct/St	O/T
Prabhakar Manoj	15.4.1963		39	1984–1995	1,600	120	1	32.65	96	6-132	3/0	37.30	20	130
Prasad Bapu Krishnarao Venkatesh	5.8.1969		33	1996–2001	203	30*	0	7.51	96	6-33	7/1	35.00	6	161
Prasad Mannava Sri Kanth	24.4.1975		6	1999	106	19	0	11.77			—/—	—	15	17
Prasanna Erapalli Anatharao Srinivas	22.5.1940		49	1961–1978	735	37	0	11.48	189	8-76	10/2	30.38	18	
Pujara Cheteshwar Arvind	25.1.1988		32	2010–2015	2,420	206*	6	47.45	0	0-2	0/0	—	24	5
Punjab Panamal Hotchand	20.9.1921	4.10.2011	5	1954	164	33	0	16.40			—/—	—	5	
Rahane Ajinkya Madhukar	6.6.1988		22	2012–2015	1,619	147	6	44.97	0	0-64	0/0	—	27	63/13
Rahul Kannur Lokesh	18.4.1992		5	2014–2015	256	110	2	25.60			—/—	—	10	
Rai Singh Kanwar	24.2.1922	12.11.1993	1	1947	26	24	0	13.00			—/—	—	0	
Raina Suresh Kumar	27.11.1986		18	2010–2014	768	120	1	26.48	13	2-1	0/0	46.38	23	223/46
Rajinder Pal	18.11.1937		1	1963	6	3*	0	6.00	1	0-3	0/0	—	0	
Rajindernath Vijay	7.1.1928	22.11.1989	1	1952	—	—	—	—			—/—	—	0/4	
Rajput Lalchand Sitaram	18.12.1961		2	1985	105	61	0	26.25			—/—	—	4	4
Raju Sagi Lakshmi Venkatapathy	9.7.1969		28	1989–2000	240	31	0	10.00	93	6-12	5/1	30.72	6	53
Raman Woorkeri Venkat	23.5.1965		11	1987–1996	448	96	0	24.88	2	1-7	0/0	64.50	6	27
Ramaswami Cotar	16.6.1896	1.1990	1	1936	170	60	0	56.66			—/—	—	0	
Ramchand Gulabrai Sipahimalani	26.7.1927	8.9.2003	33	1952–1959	1,180	109	1	24.58	41	6-49	1/0	46.31	20	
Ramesh Sadagoppan	16.10.1975		19	1998–2001	1,367	143	2	37.97	0	0-5	0/0	—	18	24
[2] Ranji Ladha	10.2.1900	20.12.1948	1	1933	1	1	0	0.50	0	0-64	0/0	—	1	
Rangachari Commandur Rajagopalachari	14.4.1916	9.10.1993	4	1947–1948	8	8*	0	2.66	9	5-107	1/0	54.77	1	
Rangnekar Khanderao Moreshwar	27.6.1917	11.10.1984	3	1947	33	18	0	5.50			—/—	—	1	
Ranjane Vasant Baburao	22.7.1937	22.12.2011	7	1958–1964	40	16	0	6.66	19	4-72	0/0	34.15	1	
Rathore Vikram	26.3.1969		6	1996–1996	131	44	0	13.10			—/—	—	12	7
Ratra Ajay	13.12.1981		6	2001–2002	163	115*	0	18.11	0	0-1	0/0	—	11/2	12
Razdan Vivek	25.8.1969		2	1989	6	6*	0	6.00	5	5-79	1/0	28.20	0	3
Reddy Bharath	12.11.1954		4	1979	38	21	0	9.50			—/—	—	9/2	3
Rege Madhusudan Ramachandra	18.3.1924	16.12.2013	1	1948	15	15	0	7.50			—/—	—	1	
Roy Ambar	5.6.1945	19.9.1997	4	1969	91	48	0	13.00			—/—	—	0	
[1] Roy Pankaj	31.5.1928	4.2.2001	43	1951–1960	2,442	173	5	32.56	1	1-6	0/0	66.00	16	
[1] Roy Pranab	10.2.1957		2	1981	71	60*	0	35.50			—/—	—	0	
Saha Wriddhaman Prasanta	24.10.1984		11	2009–2015	367	60	0	21.58			—/—	—	14/5	9
Sandhu Balwinder Singh	3.8.1956		8	1982–1983	214	71	0	30.57	10	3-87	0/0	55.70	1	22
Sanghvi Rahul Laxman	3.9.1974		1	2000–2001	2	2	0	1.00	2	2-67	0/0	39.00	0	10
Sarandeep Singh	21.10.1979		3	2000–2001	43	39*	0	43.00	10	4-136	0/0	43.00	1	16
Sardesai Dilip Narayan	8.8.1940	2.7.2007	30	1961–1972	2,001	212	5	39.23	0	0-3	0/0	—	4	
Sarwate Chandrasekhar Trimbak	22.7.1920	23.12.2003	9	1946–1951	208	37	0	13.00	3	1-16	0/0	124.66	0	

	Born	Died	Tests	Test Career	Runs	HS	100s	Avge	Wkts	BB	5/10	Avge	Ct/St	OIT
Saxena Ramesh Chandra	20.9.1944	16.8.2011	1	1967	25	16	0	12.50	–	0-11	0/0	–	–	–
Sehwag Virender	20.10.1978		104	2001–2012	8,503	319	23	49.43	40	5-104	1/0	47.35	90	241‡/19
Sekhar Thirumalai Ananthanpillai	28.3.1956		2	1982	0	0*	0	–	0	0-43	0/0	–	0	–
Sen Probir Kumar ("Khokhan")	31.5.1926	27.1.1970	14	1947–1952	165	25	0	11.78	–	–	–	–	20/11	–
Sen Gupta Apoorva Kumar	3.8.1939	14.9.2013	1	1958	9	8	0	4.50	–	–	–	–	0	–
Sharma Ajay Kumar	3.4.1964		1	1987	53	30	0	26.50	0	0-9	0/0	–	–	31
Sharma Chetan	3.1.1966		23	1984–1988	396	54	0	22.00	61	6-58	4/1	35.45	7	65
Sharma Gopal	3.8.1960		5	1984–1990	11	10*	0	3.66	10	4-88	0/0	41.80	7	11
Sharma Ishant	2.9.1988		68	2007–2015	550	31*	0	8.87	201	7-74	7/1	36.90	14	76/14
Sharma Karan Vinod	23.10.1987		1	2014	8	4*	0	8.00	2	2-95	0/0	59.50	0	2/1
Sharma Parthasarathy Harishchandra	5.1.1948	20.10.2010	5	1974–1976	187	54	0	18.70	0	0-2	0/0	–	0	2
Sharma Rohit Gurunath	30.4.1987		16	2013–2015	896	177	2	33.18	2	1-26	0/0	98.50	17	143/44
Sharma Sanjeev Kumar	25.8.1965		2	1988–1990	56	38	0	28.00	10	3-37	0/0	41.16	–	23
Shastri Ravishankar Jayadritha	27.5.1962		80	1980–1992	3,830	206	11	35.79	151	5-75	2/0	40.96	36	150
Shinde Sadashiv Ganpatrao	18.8.1923	22.6.1955	7	1946–1952	85	14	0	14.16	12	6-91	1/0	59.75	–	–
Shodhan Roshan Harshadlal ("Deepak")	18.10.1928		3	1952	181	110	1	60.33	0	0-1	0/0	–	0	–
Shukla Rakesh Chandra	4.2.1948		1	1982	29	24	0	29.00	2	2-82	0/0	76.00	0	–
Siddiqui Iqbal Rashid	26.12.1974		1	2001	–	–	–	–	1	1-32	0/0	48.00	0	–
Sidhu Navjot Singh	20.10.1963		51	1983–1998	3,202	201	9	42.13	–	0-9	0/0	–	9	136
Singh Rabindra Ramanarayan ("Robin")	14.9.1963		1	1998	27	15	0	13.50	–	0-16	0/0	–	5	136
Singh Robin	1.1.1970		1	1998	0	0	0	0.00	3	–	0/0	58.66	–	–
Singh Rudra Pratap	6.12.1985		14	2005–2011	116	30	0	7.25	40	5-59	1/0	42.05	6	58/10
Singh Vikram Rajvir	17.9.1984		5	2005–2007	47	29	0	11.75	8	3-48	0/0	53.37	1	2
Sivaramakrishnan Laxman	31.12.1965		9	1982–1985	130	25	0	16.25	26	6-64	3/1	44.03	9	16
Sohoni Sriranga Wasudev	5.3.1918	19.5.1993	4	1946–1951	83	29*	0	16.60	2	1-16	0/0	101.00	–	–
Solkar Eknath Dhondu	18.3.1948	26.6.2005	27	1969–1976	1,068	102	1	25.42	18	3-28	0/0	59.44	53	7
Sood Man Mohan	6.7.1939		1	1959	3	3	0	1.50	–	–	–	–	2	–
Sreesanth Shanthakumaran	6.2.1983		27	2005–2011	281	35	0	10.40	87	5-40	3/0	37.59	–	53/10
Srikkanth Krishnamachari	21.12.1959		43	1981–1991	2,062	123	2	29.88	0	0-1	0/0	–	40	146
Srinath Javagal	31.8.1969		67	1991–2002	1,009	76	0	14.21	236	8-86	10/1	30.49	22	229
Srinivasan Thirumalai Echambadi	26.10.1950	6.12.2010	1	1980	48	29	0	24.00	–	–	–	–	–	–
Subramanya Venkataraman	16.7.1936	20.6.2010	9	1964–1967	263	75	0	18.78	3	2-32	0/0	67.00	9	–
Sunderam Gundihal Rama	29.3.1930	5.5.2012	2	1955	4	3*	0	–	3	2-46	0/0	55.33	9	–
Surendranath	4.1.1937	13.1.2013	11	1958–1960	136	27	0	10.46	26	5-75	2/0	40.50	4	–
Surti Rusi Framroze	25.5.1936		26	1960–1969	1,263	99	0	28.70	42	5-74	1/0	46.71	26	–

§ Sehwag's figures exclude 83 runs and one catch for the ICC World XI v Australia in the Super Series Test in 2005-06.

	Born	Died	Tests	Test Career	Runs	HS	100s	Avge	Wts	BB	5/10	Avge	Ct/St	O/T
Swamy Venkatraman Narayan	23.5.1924	1.5.1983	1	1955	–	–	–	–	–	–	0/0	–	0	
Tamhane Narendra Shankar	4.8.1931	19.3.2002	21	1954–1960	225	54*	0	10.22	–	–	–/–	–	35/16	
Tarapore Keki Khurshedji	17.12.1910	15.6.1986	1	1948	2	2	0	2.00	0	0-72	0/0	–	0	
Tendulkar Sachin Ramesh (CY 1997)	24.4.1973		200	1989–2013	15,921	248*	51	53.78	46	3-10	0/0	54.17	115	463/1
Umrigar Pahlanji Ratanji ("Polly")	28.3.1926	7.11.2006	59	1948–1961	3,631	223	12	42.22	35	6-74	2/0	42.08	33	
Unadkat Jaydev Dipakbhai	18.10.1991		1	2010	2	1*	0	2.00	0	0-101	0/0	–	0	7
Vengsarkar Dilip Balwant (CY 1987)	6.4.1956		116	1975–1991	6,868	166	17	42.13	0	0-3	0/0	–	78	129
Venkataraghavan Srinivasaraghavan	21.4.1945		57	1964–1983	748	64	0	11.68	156	8-72	3/1	36.11	44	15
Venkataramana Margashayam	24.4.1966		1	1988	0	0*	0	–	1	1-10	0/0	58.00	1	1
Vijay Murali	1.4.1984		37	2008–2015	2,630	167	6	41.09	1	1-12	0/0	107.00	31	179
Vinay Kumar Ranganath	12.2.1984		1	2011	11	6	0	5.50	1	1-73	0/0	73.00	0	319
Viswanath Gundappa Rangnath	12.2.1949		91	1969–1982	6,080	222	14	41.93	1	1-11	0/0	46.00	63	25
Viswanath Sadanand	29.11.1962		3	1985	31	20	0	6.20			–/–		11	22
Vizianagram Maharajkumar of (Sir Vijaya Anand)	28.12.1905	2.12.1965	3	1936	33	19*	0	8.25	0	0-0	0/0	–	1	
Wadekar Ajit Laxman	1.4.1941		37	1966–1974	2,113	143	1	31.07	0	0-0	0/0	–	46	2
Wasim Jaffer	16.2.1978		31	1999–2007	1,944	212	5	34.10	2	2-18	0/0	9.00	27	2
Wassan Atul Satish	23.3.1968		4	1989–1990	94	53	0	23.50	10	4-108	0/0	50.40	1	9
1,2 Wazir Ali Syed	15.9.1903	17.6.1950	7	1932–1936	237	42	0	16.92	0	0-0	0/0	–	–	7
Yadav Nandlal Shivlal	26.1.1957		35	1979–1986	403	43	0	14.39	102	5-76	3/0	35.09	10	7
Yadav Umeshkumar Tilak	25.10.1987		17	2011–2015	109	30	0	7.78	53	5-93	1/0	36.05	4	52/1
Yadav Vijay	14.3.1967		1	1992	30	30	0	30.00	0		–/–	–	1/2	19
Yajurvindra Singh	1.8.1952		4	1976–1979	109	43*	0	18.16	0	0-2	0/0	–	11	
Yashpal Sharma	11.8.1954		37	1979–1983	1,606	140	2	33.45	1	1-6	0/0	17.00	16	42
Yograj Singh	25.3.1958		1	1980	10	6	0	5.00	1	1-63	0/0	63.00	0	6
1 Yohanan Tinu	18.2.1979		3	2001–2002	13	8*	0	–	5	2-56	0/0	51.20	1	3
Yuvraj Singh	12.12.1981		40	2003–2012	1,900	169	3	33.92	9	2-9	0/0	60.77	31	290/40
Zaheer Khan (CY 2008)	7.10.1978		92	2000–2013	1,231	75	0	11.95	311	7-87	11/1	32.94	19	194/17

PAKISTAN (221 players)

	Born	Died	Tests	Test Career	Runs	HS	100s	Avge	Wkts	BB	5/10	Avge	Ct/St	O/T
Aamer Malik	3.1.1963		14	1987–1994	565	117	2	35.31	1	1-0	0/0	89.00	15/1	24
Aamir Nazir	2.1.1971		6	1992–1995	31	11	0	6.20	20	5-46	1/0	29.85	1/0	9
Aamir Sohail	14.9.1966		47	1992–1999	2,823	205	5	35.28	25	4-54	0/0	41.96	36	156
Abdul Kadir	10.5.1944		4	1964	272	95	0	34.00	–	–	–/–	–	0/1	
Abdul Qadir	15.9.1955		67	1977–1990	1,029	61	0	15.59	236	9-56	15/5	32.80	15	104
Abdul Razzaq	2.12.1979		46	1999–2006	1,946	134	3	28.61	100	5-35	1/0	36.94	15	261½/32
Abdur Rauf	9.12.1978		3	2009–2009	52	31	0	8.66	6	2-59	0/0	46.33	0	4/1
Abdur Rehman	1.3.1980		22	2007–2014	395	60	0	14.10	99	6-25	2/0	29.39	8	31/8
²Adnan Akmal	13.3.1985		21	2010–2013	591	64	0	24.62	–	–	–/–	–	66/11	5
Afaq Hussain	31.12.1939	25.2.2002	2	1961–1964	66	35*	0	–	1	1-40	0/0	–	2	
Aftab Baloch	1.4.1953		2	1969–1974	97	60*	0	48.50	0	0-2	0/0	–	0	
Aftab Gul	31.3.1946		6	1968–1971	182	33	0	22.75	0	0-4	0/0	–	3	
Agha Saadat Ali	21.6.1929	25.10.1995	1	1955	8	8*	0	–	–	–	–/–	–	–	
Agha Zahid	7.1.1953		1	1974	15	14	0	7.50	–	–	–/–	–	0	
Ahmed Shehzad	23.11.1991		11	2013–2015	861	176	3	43.05	0	0-8	0/0	–	3	73/37
Aizaz Cheema	5.9.1979		7	2011–2012	1	1*	0	–	20	4-24	0/0	31.90	1	14/5
Akram Raza	22.11.1964		9	1989–1994	153	32	0	15.30	13	3-46	0/0	56.30	8	49
Ali Hussain Rizvi	6.1.1974		1	1997	–	–	–	–	2	2-72	0/0	36.00	0	
Ali Naqvi	19.3.1977		5	1997	242	115	1	30.25	0	0-11	0/0	–	1	
Alim-ud-Din	15.12.1930	12.7.2012	25	1954–1962	1,091	109	2	25.37	1	1-17	0/0	75.00	8	
Amir Elahi	1.9.1908	28.12.1980	5†	1952	65	47	0	10.83	7	4-134	0/0	35.42	0	
Anil Dalpat	20.9.1963		9	1983–1984	167	52	0	15.18	–	–	–/–	–	22/3	15
Anwar Hussain	16.7.1920	9.10.2002	4	1952	42	17	0	7.00	1	1-25	0/0	29.00	0	
Anwar Khan	24.12.1955		1	1978	15	12	0	15.00	0	0-12	0/0	–	0	
Aqib Javed	5.8.1972		22	1988–1998	101	28*	0	5.05	54	5-84	1/0	34.70	2	163
Arif Butt	17.5.1944	10.7.2007	3	1964	59	20	0	11.80	14	6-89	1/0	20.57	2	
Arshad Khan	22.3.1971		9	1997–2004	31	9*	0	5.16	32	5-38	1/0	30.00	0	58
Asad Shafiq	28.1.1986		41	2010–2015	2,597	137	8	43.28	1	1-32	0/0	51.00	36	58/10
Asif Ahmed	6.6.1973		1	1993	1	1*	0	1.00	2	2-31	0/0	26.50	0	3
Ashraf Ali	22.4.1958		8	1981–1987	229	65	0	45.80	–	–	–/–	–	17/5	16
Asif Iqbal (CY 1968)	6.6.1943		58	1964–1979	3,575	175	11	38.85	53	5-48	2/0	28.33	36	10
Asif Masood	23.11.1946		16	1968–1976	93	30*	0	10.33	38	5-111	0/0	41.26	5	7
Asif Mujtaba	4.11.1967		25	1986–1996	928	65*	0	24.42	4	1-0	0/0	75.75	19	66

Name	Born	Died	Tests	Test Career	Runs	HS	100s	Avge	Wkts	BB	5/10	Avge	Ct/St	O/T
Asim Kamal	31.5.1976		12	2003–2005	717	99	0	37.73	–	–	–/–	–	10	30
Ata-ur-Rehman	28.3.1975		13	1992–1996	76	19	0	8.44	31	4-50	0/0	34.54	2	30
Atif Rauf	3.3.1964		1	1993	25	16	0	12.50	–	–	–/–	–	–	3
Atiq-uz-Zaman	20.7.1975		1	1999	26	25	0	13.00	–	–	–/–	–	5	6
Azam Khan	1.3.1969		1	1996	14	14	0	14.00	–	–	–/–	–	–	15
Azeem Hafeez	29.7.1963		18	1983–1984	134	24	0	8.37	63	6-46	4/0	34.98	1	31
Azhar Ali	19.2.1985		45	2010–2015	3,427	226	11	43.37	4	2-35	0/0	53.50	48	109
Azhar Khan	7.9.1955		1	1979	14	14	0	14.00	1	1-1	0/0	2.00	–	2
Azhar Mahmood	28.2.1975		21	1997–2001	900	136	1	30.00	39	4-50	0/0	35.94	14	143
[2]Azmat Rana	3.11.1951	30.5.2015	1	1979	49	49	0	49.00	–	–	–/–	–	–	50
Basit Ali	13.12.1970		19	1992–1995	858	103	1	26.81	0	0-6	0/0	–	6	50
[3]Bazid Khan	25.3.1981		1	2005	32	23	0	16.00	–	–	–/–	–	–	5
Bilawal Bhatti	17.9.1991		2	2013	70	32	0	35.00	6	3-65	0/0	48.50	0	18
Danish Kaneria	16.12.1980		61	2000–2010	360	29	0	7.05	261	7-77	15/2	34.79	18	18
D'Souza Antao	17.11.1939		6	1958–1962	76	23*	0	38.00	17	5-112	1/0	43.82	0	6
Ehsan Adil	15.3.1993		3	2012–2015	21	12	0	5.25	5	2-54	0/0	52.60	0	6
Ehtesham-ud-Din	4.9.1950		5	1979–1982	2	2	0	1.00	16	5-47	1/0	23.43	2	18
Faisal Iqbal	30.12.1981		26	2000–2009	1,124	139	1	26.76	0	0-7	0/0	–	22	18
Farhan Adil	25.9.1977		1	2003	33	25	0	16.50	–	–	–/–	–	0	
Farooq Hamid	3.3.1945		1	1964	3	3	0	1.50	1	1-82	0/0	107.00	0	
Farrukh Zaman	2.4.1956		1	1976	–	–	–	–	0	0-7	0/0	–	3	
Fawad Alam	8.10.1985		3	2009	250	168	1	41.66	–	–	–/–	–	11	38/24
Fazal Mahmood (CY 1955)	18.2.1927	30.5.2005	34	1952–1962	620	60	0	14.09	139	7-42	13/4	24.70	11	
Fazl-e-Akbar	20.10.1980		5	1997–2003	52	25	0	13.00	11	3-85	0/0	46.45	–	2
Ghazali Mohammad Ebrahim Zainuddin	15.6.1924	26.4.2003	1	1954	32	18	0	8.00	–	–	–/–	–	0	
Ghulam Abbas	1.5.1947		1	1967	12	12	0	6.00	–	–	–/–	–	0	
Gul Mahomed	15.10.1921	8.5.1992	1†	1956	39	27*	0	39.00	0	0-18	0/0	–	0	
[1,2]Hanif Mohammad (CY 1968)	21.12.1934		55	1952–1969	3,915	337	12	43.98	1	1-1	0/0	95.00	40	12
Haroon Rashid	25.3.1953		23	1976–1982	1,217	153	3	34.77	0	0-3	0/0	–	16	16
Hasan Raza	11.3.1982		7	1996–2005	235	68	0	21.36	0	0-1	0/0	–	5	
Haseeb Ahsan	15.7.1939	8.3.2013	12	1957–1961	61	14	0	6.77	27	6-202	2/0	49.25	1	5
[2]Humayun Farhat	24.1.1981		1	2000	54	28	0	27.00	–	–	–/–	–	3	
Ibadulla Khalid ("Billy")	20.12.1935		4	1964–1967	253	166	1	31.62	1	1-42	0/0	99.00	3	
Iftikhar Anjum	1.12.1980		1	2005	9	9*	0	–	2	0-3	0/0	–	0	62/2
Ijaz Ahmed, sen.	20.9.1968		60	1986–2000	3,315	211	12	37.67	2	1-9	0/0	38.50	45	250
Ijaz Ahmed, jun.	2.2.1969		2	1995	29	16	0	9.66	0	0-1	0/0	–	3	2

	Born	Died	Tests	Test Career	Runs	HS	100s	Avge	Wkts	BB	5/10	Avge	Ct/St	O/T
Ijaz Butt	10.3.1938		8	1958–1962	279	58	0	19.92	4	1-38	0/0	74.75	5	27
Ijaz Faqih	24.3.1956		5	1980–1987	183	105	1	26.14	3	2-69	0/0	94.66	0	0
Imran Farhat	20.5.1982		40	2000–2012	2,400	128	3	32.00					40	58/7
Imran Khan (CY 1983)	25.11.1952		88	1971–1992	3,807	136	6	37.69	362	8-58	23/6	22.81	28	175
Mohammad Imran Khan	15.7.1987		7	2014–2015	0	0*	0	0.00	20	5-58	1/0	28.10	0	0
Imran Nazir	16.12.1981		8	1998–2002	427	131	2	32.84					2	79/25
Imtiaz Ahmed	5.1.1928		41	1952–1962	2,079	209	3	29.28	0	0-0	0/0		77/16	
Intikhab Alam	28.12.1941		47	1959–1976	1,493	138	1	22.28	125	7-52	5/2	35.95	20	4
§ Inzamam-ul-Haq	3.3.1970		119	1992–2007	8,829	329	25	50.16	0	0-8	0/0		81	375/1
Iqbal Qasim	6.8.1953		50	1976–1988	549	56	0	13.07	171	7-49	8/2	28.11	42	15
Irfan Fazil	2.11.1981		1	1999	4	3	0	4.00	2	1-30	0/0	32.50	2	1
Israr Ali	1.5.1927	1.2.2016	4	1952–1959	33	10	0	4.71	6	2-29	0/0	27.50	2	
Jalal-ud-Din	12.6.1959		6	1982–1985	3	2	0	3.00	11	3-77	0/0	48.81	0	8
Javed Akhtar	21.11.1940		1	1962	4	2*	0	4.00	0	0-52	0/0		0	
Javed Burki	8.5.1938		25	1960–1969	1,341	140	3	30.47	0	0-2	0/0		7	
Javed Miandad (CY 1982)	12.6.1957		124	1976–1993	8,832	280*	23	52.57	17	3-74	0/0	40.11	93/1	233
Junaid Khan	24.12.1989		22	2011–2015	122	17	0	7.17	71	5-38	5/0	31.73	4	52/9
Kabir Khan	12.4.1974		4	1994	24	10	0	8.00	9	3-26	0/0	41.11	4	10
[2] Kamran Akmal	13.1.1982		53	2002–2010	2,648	158*	6	30.79					184/22	154/54
[2] Kardar Abdul Hafeez	17.1.1925	21.4.1996	23†	1952–1957	847	93	0	24.91	21	3-35	0/0	45.42	15	
Khalid Hassan	14.7.1937	3.12.2013	1	1954	17	10	0	17.00	2	2-116	0/0	58.00	0	
Khalid Wazir	27.4.1936		2	1954	14	9*	0	7.00					0	
Khan Mohammad	1.1.1928	4.7.2009	13	1952–1957	100	26*	0	10.00	54	6-21	4/0	23.92	4	
Khurram Manzoor	10.6.1986		16	2008–2014	817	146	1	28.17					8	7
Liaqat Ali	21.5.1955		5	1974–1978	28	12	0	7.00	6	3-80	0/0	59.83	2	3
Mahmood Hussain	2.4.1932	25.12.1991	27	1952–1962	336	35	0	10.18	68	6-67	2/0	38.64	5	
[2] Majid Jahangir Khan (CY 1970)	28.9.1946		63	1964–1982	3,931	167	8	38.92	27	4-45	0/0	53.92	70	23
Mansoor Akhtar	25.12.1957		19	1980–1989	655	111	0	25.19					9	41
Manzoor Elahi	15.4.1963		6	1984–1994	123	52	0	15.37	7	2-38	0/0	27.71	7	54
Maqsood Ahmed	26.3.1925	4.1.1999	16	1952–1955	507	99	0	19.50	3	2-12	0/0	63.66	13	
Masood Anwar	12.12.1967		1	1990	39	37	0	19.50	3	2-59	0/0	34.00	0	
Mathias Wallis	4.2.1935	1.9.1994	21	1955–1962	783	77	0	23.72	0	0-20	0/0		22	
Miran Bux	20.4.1907	8.2.1991	2	1954	1	1*	0	1.00	2	2-82	0/0	57.50	0	
Misbah-ul-Haq	28.5.1974		61	2000–2015	4,352	161*	10	48.89					44	162/39
Mohammad Akram	10.9.1974		9	1995–2000	24	10*	0	2.66	17	5-138	1/0	50.52	4	23

§ Inzamam-ul-Haq's figures exclude one run for the ICC World XI v Australia in the Super Series Test in 2005-06.

	Born	Died	Tests	Test Career	Runs	HS	100s	Avge	Wkts	BB	5/10	Avge	Ct/St	O/T
Mohammad Amir (formerly Mohammad Aamer)	13.4.1992		14	2009–2010	278	30*	0	12.63	51	6-84	3/0	29.09	3	15/18
Mohammad Asif	20.12.1982		23	2004–2010	141	29	0	5.64	106	6-41	7/1	24.36	3	35/11
Mohammad Aslam Khokhar	5.1.1920	22.1.2011	1	1954	34	18	0	17.00			–/–		1	
Mohammad Ayub	13.9.1979		1	2012	47	25	0	23.50			–/–		0	
Mohammad Farooq	8.4.1938		7	1960–1964	85	47	0	17.00	21	4-70	0/0	32.47	1	
Mohammad Hafeez	17.10.1980		47	2003–2015	3,350	224	9	40.85	52	4-16	0/0	33.90	38	173/68
Mohammad Hussain	8.10.1976		2	1996–1998	18	17	0	6.00	3	2-66	0/0	29.00	1	14
Mohammad Ilyas	19.3.1946		10	1964–1968	441	126	1	23.21	0	0-1	0/0		6	
Mohammad Irfan	6.6.1982		4	2012–2013	28	14	0	5.60	10	3-44	0/0	38.90	0	57/13
Mohammad Khalil	11.11.1982		2	2004	9	5	0	3.00	3	0-38	0/0	31.00	0	3
Mohammad Munaf	2.11.1935		4	1959–1961	63	19	0	12.60	11	4-42	0/0	33.05	0	4
Mohammad Nazir	8.3.1946		14	1969–1983	144	29*	0	18.00	34	7-99	3/0	30.11	4	4
Mohammad Ramzan	25.12.1970		1	1997	36	29	0	18.00			–/–			
Mohammad Salman	7.8.1981		2	2010	25	13	0	6.25			–/–		2/1	7/1
Mohammad Sami	24.2.1981		36	2000–2012	487	49	0	11.59	85	5-36	2/0	52.74	7	87/7
Mohammad Talha	15.10.1988		4	2008–2014	34	19	0	8.50	9	3-65	0/0	56.00	0	3
Mohammad Wasim	8.8.1977		18	1996–2000	783	192	2	30.11			–/–		22	25
Mohammad Yousuf (CY 2007) (formerly Yousuf Youhana)	27.8.1974		90	1997–2010	7,530	223	24	52.29		0-3	0/0		65	281/3
Mohammad Zahid	2.8.1976		5	1996–2002	7	6*	0	1.40	15	7-66	1/1	33.46	0	11
Mohsin Kamal	16.6.1963		9	1983–1994	37	13*	0	9.25	24	4-116	0/0	34.25	4	19
Mohsin Khan	15.3.1955		48	1977–1986	2,709	200	7	37.10		0-0	0/0		34	75
[3]Moin Khan	23.9.1971		69	1990–2004	2,741	137	4	28.55			–/–		128/20	219
Mudassar Nazar	6.4.1956		76	1976–1988	4,114	231	10	38.09	66	6-32	1/0	38.36	48	122
Mufasir-ul-Haq	16.8.1944	27.7.1983	1	1964	8	8*	0		3	2-50	0/0	28.00	1	
Munir Malik	10.7.1934	30.11.2012	3	1959–1962	7	4	0	2.33	9	5-128	1/0	39.77	0	
Mushtaq Ahmed (CY 1997)	28.6.1970		52	1989–2003	656	59	0	11.71	185	7-56	10/3	32.97	23	144
[2]Mushtaq Mohammad (CY 1963)	22.11.1943		57	1958–1978	3,643	201	10	39.17	79	5-28	3/0	29.22	42	10
Nadeem Abbasi	15.4.1964		3	1989	46	36	0	23.00			–/–		6	
Nadeem Ghauri	12.10.1962		1	1989	0	0	0	0.00	0	0-20	0/0		0	6
[2]Nadeem Khan	10.12.1969		2	1992–1998	34	25	0	17.00	2	2-147	0/0	115.00	1	2
Nasim-ul-Ghani	14.5.1941		29	1957–1972	747	101	1	16.60	52	6-67	2/0	37.67	11	
Nasir Jamshed	6.12.1989		2	2012	51	46	0	12.75			–/–		0	48/18
Naushad Ali	1.10.1943		6	1964	156	39	0	14.18			–/–		9	
Naved Anjum	27.7.1963		2	1989–1990	44	22	0	14.66	4	2-57	0/0	40.50	0	13
Naved Ashraf	4.9.1974		2	1998–1999	64	32	0	21.33			–/–		0	

	Born	Died	Tests	Test Career	Runs	HS	100s	Avge	Wkts	BB	5/10	Avge	Ct/St	O/T
Naved Latif	21.2.1976		1	2001	20	20	0	10.00	0	–	–/–	–	0	11
Naved-ul-Hasan	28.2.1978		9	2004–2006	239	42*	0	19.91	18	3-30	0/0	58.00	3	74/4
¹ Nazar Mohammad	5.3.1921	12.7.1996	5	1952	277	124*	1	39.57	0	0-4	0/0	–	7	
Niaz Ahmed	11.11.1945		2	1967–1968	17	16*	0	–	3	2-72	0/0	–	1	
² Pervez Sajjad	30.8.1942	12.4.2000	19	1964–1972	123	24	0	13.66	59	7-74	3/0	23.89	9	
Qaiser Abbas	7.5.1982		1	2000	2	2	0	2.00	0	0-35	0/0	–	1	
Qasim Omar	9.2.1957		26	1983–1986	1,502	210	3	36.63	0	0-0	0/0	–	15	31
Rahat Ali	12.9.1988		14	2012–2015	98	35*	0	8.16	40	6-127	2/0	36.25	7	13
² Ramiz Raja	14.8.1962		57	1983–1996	2,833	122	2	31.83	0	–	–/–	–	34	198
Rashid Khan	15.12.1959		4	1981–1984	155	59	0	31.66	8	3-129	0/0	45.00	2	29
Rashid Latif	14.10.1968		37	1992–2003	1,381	150	0	28.77	1	0-10	0/0	–	119/11	166
Rehman Sheikh Fazalur	11.6.1935		1	1957	10	8	0	5.00	0	1-43	0/0	–	0	
Riaz Afridi	21.1.1985		1	2004	9	9	0	9.00	2	2-42	0/0	43.50	0	
Rizwan-uz-Zaman	4.9.1961		11	1981–1988	345	60	0	19.16	4	3-26	0/0	11.50	4	3
² Sadiq Mohammad	3.5.1945		41	1969–1980	2,579	166	5	35.81	0	0-0	0/0	–	28	19
Saeed Ahmed	1.10.1937		41	1957–1972	2,991	172	5	40.41	22	4-64	0/0	36.45	13	
Saeed Ajmal	14.10.1977		35	2009–2014	451	50	0	11.00	178	7-55	10/4	28.10	11	113/64
Saeed Anwar (CY 1997)	6.9.1968		55	1990–2001	4,052	188*	11	45.52	0	0-0	0/0	–	18	247
Salah-ud-Din	14.2.1947		5	1964–1969	117	34*	0	19.50	7	2-36	0/0	26.71	3	
Saleem Jaffer	19.11.1962		14	1986–1991	42	10*	0	5.25	36	5-40	1/0	31.63	3	39
Salim Altaf	19.4.1944		21	1967–1978	276	53*	0	14.52	46	4-11	0/0	37.17	5	6
² Salim Elahi	21.11.1976		13	1995–2002	436	72	0	18.95	0	–	–/–	–	10/1	48
Salim Malik (CY 1988)	16.4.1963		103	1981–1998	5,768	237	15	43.69	5	1-3	0/0	82.80	65	283
Salim Yousuf	7.12.1959		32	1981–1990	1,055	91*	0	27.05	–	–	–/–	–	91/13	86
Salman Butt	7.10.1984		33	2003–2010	1,889	122	3	30.46	1	1-36	0/0	106.00	12	78/24
Sami Aslam	12.12.1995		2	2014	47	35*	0	15.66	0	–	–/–	–	1	
Saqlain Mushtaq (CY 2000)	29.12.1976		49	1995–2003	927	101*	1	14.48	208	8-164	13/3	29.83	15	169
Sarfraz Ahmed	22.5.1987		21	2009–2015	1,296	112	3	46.28	0	–	–/–	–	46/17	56/10
Sarfraz Nawaz	1.12.1948		55	1968–1983	1,045	90	0	17.71	177	9-86	4/1	32.75	26	45
Shabbir Ahmed	21.4.1976		10	2003–2005	88	24*	0	8.80	51	5-48	2/0	23.03	3	32/1
Shadab Kabir	12.11.1977		5	1996–2001	148	55	0	21.14	0	0-9	0/0	–	11	3
Shafiq Ahmed	28.3.1949		6	1974–1980	99	27*	0	11.00	0	0-1	0/0	–	3	3
² Shafqat Rana	10.8.1943		5	1964–1969	221	95	0	31.57	0	1-2	0/0	9.00	5	
² Shahid Afridi	1.3.1980		27	1998–2010	1,716	156	5	36.51	48	5-52	1/0	35.60	10	393‡/87
Shahid Israr	1.3.1950	29.4.2013	1	1976	7	7*	0	–	–	–	–/–	–	2	
Shahid Mahboob	25.8.1962		1	1989	–	–	–	–	2	2-131	0/0	65.50	0	10

	Born	Died	Tests	Test Career	Runs	HS	100s	Avge	Wts	BB	5/10	Avge	Ct/St	O/T
Shahid Mahmood	17.3.1939		1	1962	25	16	-	12.50	0	0-23	0/0	-	5	
Shahid Nazir	4.12.1977		15	1996–2006	194	40	-	12.12	36	5-53	1/0	35.33	5	17
Shahid Saeed	6.1.1966		1	1989	12	12	-	12.00	0	0-7	0/0	-	0	10
Shakeel Ahmed, sen.	12.2.1966		1	1998	1	1	-	1.00	-	-	-/-	-	1	
Shakeel Ahmed, jun.	12.11.1971		3	1992–1994	74	33	-	14.80	4	4-91	0/0	34.75	-	2
Shan Masood	14.10.1989		7	2013–2015	361	125	-	25.78	-	-	-/-	-	6	
Sharpe Duncan Albert	3.8.1937		3	1959	134	56	-	22.33	-	-	-/-	-	2	
Shoaib Akhtar	13.8.1975		46	1997–2007	544	47	-	10.07	178	6-11	12/2	25.69	12	158‡/15
Shoaib Malik	1.2.1982		35	2001–2015	1,898	245	3	35.14	32	4-33	0/0	47.46	18	231/67
[1]Shoaib Mohammad	8.1.1961		45	1983–1995	2,705	203*	7	44.34	5	2-8	0/0	34.00	22	63
Shuja-ud-Din Butt	10.4.1930	7.2.2006	19	1954–1961	395	47	-	15.19	20	3-18	0/0	40.05	8	
Sikander Bakht	25.8.1957		26	1976–1982	146	22*	-	6.34	67	8-69	3/1	36.00	7	27
Sohail Khan	6.3.1984		2	2008–2011	11	11	-	11.00	1	1-62	0/0	245.00	0	12/3
Sohail Tanvir	12.12.1984		2	2007	17	13	-	5.66	5	3-83	0/0	63.20	3	62/50
Tahir Naqqash	6.6.1959		15	1981–1984	300	57	-	21.42	34	5-40	2/0	41.11	3	40
Talat Ali Malik	29.5.1950		10	1972–1978	370	61	-	23.12	0	0-1	0/0	-	4	
Tanvir Ahmed	20.12.1978		5	2010–2012	170	57	-	34.00	17	6-120	1/0	26.64	1	2/1
Taslim Arif	1.5.1954	13.3.2008	6	1979–1980	501	210*	1	62.62	1	1-28	0/0	28.00	6/3	2
Taufeeq Umar	20.6.1981		44	2001–2014	2,963	236	7	37.98	-	-	-/-	-	48	22
Tauseef Ahmed	10.5.1958		34	1979–1993	318	35*	-	17.66	93	6-45	3/0	31.72	9	70
Umar Akmal	26.5.1990		16	2009–2011	1,003	129	1	35.82	-	-	-/-	-	12	111/68
Umar Amin	16.10.1989		4	2010	99	33	-	12.37	3	1-7	0/0	21.00	1	15/10
Umar Gul	14.4.1984		47	2003–2012	577	65*	-	9.94	163	6-135	4/0	34.06	11	126/58
Wahab Riaz	28.6.1985		15	2010–2015	149	27	-	8.76	43	5-63	1/0	34.16	3	67/12
Wajahatullah Wasti	11.11.1974		6	1998–1999	329	133	1	36.55	0	0-0	0/0	-	7	15
[2]Waqar Hassan	12.9.1932		21	1952–1959	1,071	189	1	31.50	0	0-10	0/0	-	10	
Waqar Younis (CY 1992)	16.11.1971		87	1989–2002	1,010	45	-	10.20	373	7-76	22/5	23.56	18	262
Wasim Akram (CY 1993)	3.6.1966		104	1984–2001	2,898	257*	3	22.64	414	7-119	25/5	23.62	44	356
Wasim Bari	23.3.1948		81	1967–1983	1,366	85	-	15.88	0	0-2	0/0	-	201/27	51
Wasim Raja	3.7.1952	23.8.2006	57	1972–1984	2,821	125	4	36.16	51	4-50	0/0	35.80	20	54
[2]Wazir Mohammad	22.12.1929		20	1952–1959	801	189	2	27.62	0	0-2	0/0	-	5	
Yasir Ali	15.10.1985		1	2003	1	1*	-	-	2	1-12	0/0	27.50	0	
Yasir Arafat	12.3.1982		3	2007–2008	94	50*	-	47.00	9	5-161	1/0	48.66	0	11/13
Yasir Hameed	28.2.1978		25	2003–2010	1,491	170	2	32.41	0	0-0	0/0	-	20	56
Yasir Shah	2.5.1986		12	2014–2015	136	25	-	10.46	76	7-76	4/0	24.17	7	15/2
[2]Younis Ahmed	20.10.1947		4	1969–1986	177	62	-	29.50	0	0-6	0/0	-	0	2

	Born	Died	Tests	Test Career	Runs	HS	100s	Avge	Wkts	BB	5/10	Avge	Ct/St	O/T
Younis Khan	29.11.1977		104	1999–2015	9,116	313	31	53.94	9	2-23	0/0	54.55	117	265/25
Yousuf Yousuf (see Mohammad Yousuf)														
Zaheer Abbas (CY 1972)	24.7.1947		78	1969–1985	5,062	274	12	44.79	3	2-21	0/0	44.00	34	62
Zahid Fazal	10.11.1973		9	1990–1995	288	78	0	18.00	–	–	–/–	–	5	19
[2]Zahoor Elahi	1.3.1971		2	1996	30	22	0	10.00	–	–	–/–	–	1	14
[2]Zakir Khan	3.4.1963		2	1985–1989	9	9*	0	–	5	3-80	0/0	–	–	17
Zulfiqar Ahmed	22.11.1926	3.10.2008	9	1952–1956	200	63*	0	33.33	20	6-42	2/1	18.30	5	
Zulfiqar Babar	10.12.1978		13	2013–2015	128	56	0	16.00	51	5-74	2/0	38.82	3	16
Zulqarnain	25.5.1962		3	1985	24	13	0	6.00	–	–	–/–	–	8/2	5/7
Zulqarnain Haider	23.4.1986		1	2010	88	88	0	44.00	–	–	–/–	–	2	4/3

SRI LANKA (133 players)

	Born	Died	Tests	Test Career	Runs	HS	100s	Avge	Wkts	BB	5/10	Avge	Ct/St	O/T
Ahangama Franklyn Saliya	14.9.1959		3	1985	11	11	0	5.50	18	5-52	1/0	19.33	1	1
Amalean Kaushik Nuginda	7.4.1965		2	1985–1987	11	7*	0	9.00	7	4-97	0/0	22.28	1	8
Amerasinghe Amerasinghe Mudalige Jayantha Gamini	2.2.1954		2	1983	54	34	0	18.00	3	2-73	0/0	50.00	3	–
Amerasinghe Merenna Koralage Don Ishara	5.3.1978		1	2007	0	0*	0	–	1	1-62	0/0	105.00	0	8
Anurasiri Sangarange Don	5.3.1966		18	1985–1997	91	24	0	5.35	41	4-71	0/0	37.75	4	45
Arnold Russel Premakumaran	25.10.1973		44	1996–2004	1,821	123	3	28.01	11	3-76	0/0	54.36	51	180/1
Atapattu Marvan Samson	22.11.1970		90	1990–2007	5,502	249	16	39.02	1	1-9	0/0	24.00	58	268/2
Bandara Herath Mudiyanselage Charitha Malinga	31.12.1979		8	1997–2005	124	43	0	15.50	16	3-84	0/0	39.56	4	31/4
Bandaratilleke Mapa Rallage Chandima Niroshan	16.5.1975		7	1997–2001	93	25	0	11.62	23	5-36	1/0	30.34	0	3
Chameera Pathira Vasan Dushmantha	11.1.1992		4	2015–2015	40	14	0	6.66	18	5-47	1/0	28.27	7	9/3
Chandana Umagiliya Durage Upul	7.5.1972		16	1998–2004	616	92	0	26.78	37	6-179	3/1	41.48		147
Chandimal Lokuge Dinesh	18.11.1989		25	2011–2015	1,835	162*	5	45.87	–	–	–/–	–	46/8	107/31
Dassanayake Pubudu Buthiya	11.7.1970		11	1993–1994	196	36	0	13.06	–	–	–/–	–	19/5	16
de Alwis Ronald Guy	15.2.1959	12.1.2013	11	1982–1987	152	28	0	8.00	–	–	–/–	–	21/2	31
de Mel Ashantha Lakdasa Francis	9.5.1959		17	1981–1986	326	34	0	14.17	59	6-109	3/0	36.94	9	57
de Saram Samantha Indika	2.9.1973		4	1999	117	39	0	23.40	–	–	–/–	–	4/1	15/1
de Silva Ashley Matthew	3.12.1963		7	1992–1993	10	9	0	3.33	–	–	–/–	–		4
de Silva Dandeniyage Somachandra	11.6.1942		12	1981–1984	406	61	0	21.36	37	5-59	1/0	36.40	5	41

	Born	Died	Test Career	Tests	Runs	HS	100s	Avge	Wkts	BB	5/10	Avge	Ct/St	O/T
de Silva Ellawalakankanamge Asoka Ranjit	28.3.1956		1985–1990	10	185	50	0	15.41	8	2-67	0/0	129.00	4	28
de Silva Ginigalgodage Ramba Ajit	12.12.1952		1981–1982	4	41	14	0	8.20	7	2-38	0/0	55.00	0	6
de Silva Karunakalage Sajeewa Chanaka	11.1.1971		1996–1998	8	65	27	0	9.28	16	5-85	1/0	55.56	5	38
de Silva Pinnaduwage Aravinda (CY 1996)	17.10.1965		1984–2002	93	6,361	267	20	42.97	29	3-30	0/0	41.65	43	308
de Silva Sanjeewa Kumara Lanka	29.7.1975		1997	3	36	20*	0	18.00	–	–	–/–	–	1	11
de Silva Weddikkara Ruwan Sujeewa	7.10.1979		2002–2007	3	10	5*	0	10.00	11	4-35	0/0	19.00	1	–
Dharmasena Handunnettige Deepthi Priyantha Kumar	24.4.1971		1993–2003	31	868	62*	0	19.72	69	6-72	3/0	42.31	14	141
Dias Roy Luke	18.10.1952		1981–1986	20	1,285	109	3	36.71	0	0-17	0/0	–	6	58
Dickwella Dickwella Patabandige Dilantha Niroshan	23.6.1993		2014–2014	4	144	72	0	20.57	–	–	–/–	–	15/2	–
Dilshan Tillekeratne Mudiyanselage	14.10.1976		1999–2012	87	5,492	193	16	40.98	39	4-10	0/0	43.87	88	327/68
Dunusinghe Chamara Iroshan	19.10.1970		1994–1995	5	160	91	0	16.00	–	–	–/–	–	13/2	7
Eranga Ranaweera Mudiyanselage Shaminda	23.6.1986		2011–2014	16	186	45*	0	16.90	52	4-49	0/0	34.88	5	17/3
Fernando Aththachchi Nuwan Pradeep Roshan	19.10.1986		2011–2015	17	75	17*	0	3.94	42	4-62	0/0	46.50	3	–
Fernando Congenige Randhi Dilhara	19.7.1979		2000–2012	40	249	39*	0	8.30	100	5-42	3/0	37.84	10	146½/17
Fernando Ellekutige Rufus Nemesion Susil	19.12.1955		1982–1983	5	112	46	0	11.20	4	3-63	0/0	27.00	2	7
Fernando Kandage Hasantha Ruwan Kumara	14.10.1979		2002	2	38	24	0	9.50	1	1-29	0/0	107.00	0	7
Fernando Kandana Arachchige Dinusha Manoj	10.8.1979		2003	3	56	51*	0	28.00	18	4-27	0/0	44.00	4	17
Fernando Thudellage Charitha Buddhika	22.8.1980		2001–2002	9	132	45	0	26.40	0	0-24	0/0	–	4	3
Gallage Indika Sanjeewa	22.11.1975		1999	5	3	3	0	3.00	0	–	–/–	–	0	3
Goonatillake Hettiarachige Mahes	16.8.1952		1981–1982	5	177	56	0	22.12	0	–	–/–	–	10/3	6
Gunasekera Yohan	8.11.1957		1982	2	48	23	0	12.00	0	–	–/–	–	6	3
Gunawardene Dihan Avishka	26.5.1977		1998–2005	6	181	43	0	16.45	0	–	–/–	–	2	61
Gunaratne Roshan Punyajith Wijesinghe	16.1.1962	21.7.2005	1982	1	0	0*	0	–	0	0-84	0/0	34.05	0	–
Gurusinha Asanka Pradeep	16.9.1966		1985–1996	41	2,452	143	7	38.92	20	2-7	0/0	34.05	33	147
Hathurusinghe Upul Chandika	13.9.1968		1990–1998	26	1,274	83	0	29.62	17	4-66	0/0	46.41	7	35
Herath Herath Mudiyanselage Rangana	19.3.1978		1999–2015	67	1,049	80*	0	13.62	297	9-127	23/5	29.87	17	71/9
Hettiarachi Dinuka	15.7.1976		2000	1	0	0*	0	0.00	2	2-36	0/0	20.50	0	–
Jayasekera Rohan Stanley Amarasinhwardene	7.12.1957		1981	1	2	2	0	1.00	0	–	–/–	–	0	2
Jayasundera Madurawelage Don Udara Supeksha	3.1.1991		2015	2	30	26	0	7.50	0	0-12	0/0	–	2	–
Jayasuriya Sanath Teran (CY 1997)	30.6.1969		1990–2007	110	6,973	340	14	40.07	98	5-34	2/0	34.34	78	441½/31
Jayawardene Denagamage Proboth Mahela de Silva (CY 2007)	27.5.1977		1997–2014	149	11,814	374	34	49.84	6	2-32	0/0	51.66	205	443½/55

	Born	Died	Tests	Test Career	Runs	HS	100s	Avge	Wkts	BB	5/10	Avge	Ct/St	O/T
Jayawardene Hewasandatchige Asiri Prasanna														
Wishvanath.............	9.10.1979		58	2000–2014	2,124	154*	4	29.50	–	–	–/–	–	124/32	6
Jeganathan Sridharan........	11.7.1951		2	1982	19	8	0	4.75	–	–	0/0	–	0	5
John Vinothen Bede.........	27.5.1960		6	1982–1984	53	27*	0	10.60	28	5-60	2/0	21.92	2	45
Jurangpathy Baba Roshan.....	25.6.1967		2	1985–1986	1	1	0	0.25	1	1-69	0/0	93.00	2	
Kalaviitigoda Shantha........	23.12.1977		2	2004	8	7	0	4.00	–	–	–/–	–	2	
Kalpage Ruwan Senani.......	19.2.1970		11	1993–1998	294	63	0	18.37	12	2-27	0/0	64.50	10	86
² Kaluhalamulla H. K. S. R. (see Randiv, Suraj)														
² Kaluperuma Lalith Wasantha Silva	25.6.1949		2	1981	12	11*	0	4.00	0	0-24	0/0	–	2	4
² Kaluperuma Sanath Mohan Silva	22.10.1961		4	1983–1987	88	23	0	11.00	2	2-17	0/0	62.00	6	2
Kaluwitharana Romesh Shantha	24.11.1969		49	1992–2004	1,933	132*	3	26.12	–	–	–/–	–	93/26	189
Kapugedera Chamara Kantha..	24.4.1987		8	2006–2009	418	96	0	34.83	0	0-9	0/0	–	6	97/26
Karunaratne Frank Dimuth Madushanka	28.4.1988		25	2012–2015	1,622	186	3	35.26	0	0-5	0/0	–	19	17
Kaushal Paskuwal Handi Tharindu	5.3.1993		7	2014–2015	106	18	0	10.60	25	5-42	2/0	44.20	3	1
Kulasekara Chamith Kosala Bandara	15.7.1985		1	2011	22	15	0	11.00	1	1-65	0/0	80.00	0	4
Kulasekara Kulasekara Mudiyanselage Dinesh														
Nuwan.............	22.7.1982		21	2004–2014	391	64	0	14.48	48	4-21	0/0	37.37	8	173/44
Kuruppu Don Sardha Brendon Priyantha.	5.1.1962		4	1986–1991	320	201*	1	53.33	–	–	–/–	–	1	54
Kuruppuarachchi Ajith Kosala.	1.11.1964		2	1985–1986	0	0*	0	–	8	5-44	1/0	18.62	0	
Labrooy Graeme Fredrick.....	7.6.1964		9	1986–1990	158	70*	0	14.36	27	5-133	1/0	44.22	3	44
Lakmal Ranasinghe Arachchige Suranga.	10.3.1987		26	2010–2015	196	23	0	8.16	54	4-78	0/0	49.16	6	42/5
Lakshitha Materba Kanatha Gamage Chamila														
Premanath.............	4.1.1979		2	2002–2002	42	40	0	14.00	3	3-60	0/0	31.60	1	7
Liyanage Dulip Kapila.......	6.6.1972		9	1992–2001	69	23	0	7.66	17	4-56	0/0	39.17	4	16
Lokuarachchi Kaushal Samaraweera	20.5.1982		4	2003–2003	94	28*	0	23.50	5	2-47	0/0	59.00	1	2l/2
Madugalle Ranjan Senerath....	22.4.1959		21	1981–1988	1,029	103	1	29.40	0	0-0	0/0	–	9	63
Madurasinghe Madurasinghe Arachchige														
Wijayasiri Ranjith........	30.1.1961		3	1988–1992	24	11	0	4.80	3	3-60	0/0	57.33	0	12
Mahanama Roshan Siriwardene.	31.5.1966		52	1985–1997	2,576	225	4	29.27	0	0-3	0/0	–	56	213
Maharoof Mohamed Farveez...	7.9.1984		22	2003–2011	556	72	0	18.53	25	4-52	0/0	65.24	7	104/7
Malinga Separamadu Lasith...	28.8.1983		30	2004–2010	275	64	0	11.45	101	5-50	3/0	33.15	7	191/61
Mathews Angelo Davis (CY 2015)	2.6.1987		56	2009–2015	4,015	160	7	50.18	30	4-44	0/0	49.56	37	169/59
Mendis Balapuwaduge Ajantha Winslo	11.3.1985		19	2008–2014	213	78	0	16.38	70	6-99	4/1	34.77	2	87/39
Mendis Balapuwaduge Kusal Gimhan.	2.2.1995		3	2015	183	46	0	30.50	–	–	–/–	–	1	
Mendis Louis Rohan Duleep..	25.8.1952		24	1981–1988	1,329	124	4	31.64	–	–	–/–	–	9	79
Miranda Magina Thilan Thushara.	1.3.1981		10	2003–2010	94	15*	0	8.54	28	5-83	1/0	37.14	3	38/6
		14.5.1996												

Name	Born	Died	Test Career	Tests	Runs	HS	100s	Avge	Wkts	BB	5/10	Avge	Ct/St	O/T
Muharak Jehan	10.1.1981		2002–2015	13	385	49	0	17.50	0	0-1	0/0		15	40/16
Muralitharan Muttiah (CY 1999)	17.4.1972		1992–2010	132§	1,259	67	0	11.87	795	9-51	67/22	22.67	70	343‡/12
Nawaz Mohamed Naveed	20.9.1973		2002	1	99	78*	0	99.00						3
Nissanka Ratnayake Arachchige Prabath	25.10.1980		2003	4	18	12*	0	6.00	10	5-64	1/0	36.60	0	23
Paranavitana Nishad Tharanga	15.4.1982		2008–2012	32	1,792	111	2	32.58	1	1-26	0/0	86.00	27	
Perera Anhettige Suresh Asanka	16.2.1978		1998–2001	3	77	43*	0	25.66	1	1-104	0/0	180.00	6	20
Perera Mahawaduge Dilruwan Kamalaneth	22.7.1982		2013–2015	9	155	95	0	11.07	44	5-69	3/0	29.56	6	5/3
Perera Mathurage Don Kusal Janith	17.8.1990		2015	3	169	70	0	33.80			-/-		9/4	51/22
Perera Narangoda Liyanaarachchilage Tissara Chiranth	3.4.1989		2011–2012	6	203	75	0	20.30	11	4-63	0/0	59.36	1	110/42
Perera Panagodage Don Ruchira Laksiri	6.4.1977		1998–2002	8	33	11*	0	11.00	17	3-40	0/0	38.88	2	19/2
Prasad Kariyawasam Tirana Gamage Dammika	30.5.1983		2008–2015	25	476	47	0	12.86	75	5-50	1/0	35.97	6	24/1
Prasanna Seekkuge	27.6.1985		2011	1	5	5	0	5.00	0	0-80	0/0		0	25/3
Pushpakumara Karuppiahyage Ravindra	21.7.1975		1994–2001	23	166	44	0	8.73	58	7-116	4/0	38.65	10	31
Ramanayake Champaka Priyadarshana Hewage	8.1.1965		1987–1993	18	143	34*	0	9.53	44	5-82	1/0	42.72	6	62
Ramyakumara Wijekoon Mudiyanselage Gayan	21.12.1976		2005	2	38	14	0	12.66	2	2-49	0/0	33.00	0	0/3
Ranasinghe Anura Nandana	13.10.1956	9.11.1998	1981–1982	2	88	77	0	22.00	1	1-23	0/0	69.00	0	9
² Ranatunga Arjuna (CY 1999)	1.12.1963		1981–2000	93	5,105	135*	4	35.69	16	2-17	0/0	65.00	47	269
² Ranatunga Dammika	12.10.1962		1989	2	87	45	0	29.00			-/-		0	4
² Ranatunga Sanjeeva	25.4.1969		1994–1996	9	531	118	2	33.18			-/-		2	13
Randiv Suraj (Hewa Kaluhalamullage Suraj Randiv Kaluhalamulla; formerly M. M. M. Suraj)	30.1.1985		2010–2012	12	147	39	0	9.18	43	5-82	1/0	37.51	1	30/7
Ratnayake Rumesh Joseph	2.1.1964		1982–1991	23	433	56	0	14.43	73	6-66	5/0	35.10	9	70
Ratnayeke Joseph Ravindran	2.5.1960		1981–1989	22	807	93	0	25.21	56	8-83	4/0	35.21	11	78
Samarasekera Maitipage Athula Rohitha	5.8.1961		1988–1991	4	118	57	0	16.85	3	2-38	0/0	34.66	3	39
Samaraweera Dulip Prasanna	12.2.1972		1993–1994	7	211	42	0	15.07			-/-		5	5
² Samaraweera Thilan Thusara	22.9.1976		2001–2012	81	5,462	231	14	48.76	15	4-49	0/0	45.93	45	53
Sangakkara Kumar Chokshanada (CY 2012)	27.10.1977		2000–2015	134	12,400	319	38	57.40	0	0-4	0/0		182/20	397‡/56
Senanayake Charith Panduka	19.12.1962		1990	3	97	64	0	19.40			-/-		2	
Senanayake Senanayake Mudiyanselage Sachithra Madhushanka	9.2.1985		2013	1	5	5	0	5.00	0	0-30	0/0			49/19
Silva Kelaniyage Jayantha Kaushal	27.5.1986		2011–2015	24	1,404	139	2	31.90	0		-/-		25/1	
Silva Kelanyage Jayantha	2.6.1973		1995–1997		6	6*	0	2.00	20	4-16	0/0	32.35	1	1

§ *Muralitharan's figures exclude two runs, five wickets and two catches for the ICC World XI v Australia in the Super Series Test in 2005-06.*

	Born	Died	Tests	Test Career	Runs	HS	100s	Avge	Wks	BB	5/10	Avge	Ct/St	O/T
Silva Lindamullage Prageeth Chamara	14.12.1979		11	2006–2007	537	152*	1	33.56	1	1-57	0/0	65.00	7	75/16
Silva Sampathawaduge Amal Rohitha	12.12.1960		9	1982–1988	353	111	2	25.21		–	–/–	–	33/1	20
Siriwardene Tissa Appuhamilage Milinda	4.12.1985		4	2015	263	68	0	37.57		–	0/0	–	3	13/6
Tharanga Warushavithana Upul	2.2.1985		21	2005–2015	1,117	165	1	30.18	8	3-25	–/–	23.12	17	179±/10
Thirimanne Hettige Don Rumesh Lahiru	8.9.1989		23	2011–2015	969	155*	1	24.84	0	0-5	0/0	–	9	107/22
Tillekeratne Hashan Prasantha	14.7.1967		83	1989–2003	4,545	204*	11	42.87	0	0-0	0/0	–	122/2	200
Upashantha Kalutarage Eric Amila	10.6.1972		2	1998–2002	10	6	0	3.33	4	2-41	0/0	50.00	0	12
Vaas Warnakulasuriya Patabendige Ushantha Joseph Chaminda	27.1.1974		111	1994–2009	3,089	100*	1	24.32	355	7-71	12/2	29.58	31	321±/6
Vandort Michael Graydon	19.1.1980		20	2001–2008	1,144	140	4	36.90		–	–/–	–	6	1
Vithanage Kasun Disi Kithuruwan	26.2.1991		10	2012–2015	370	103*	1	26.42	1	1-73	0/0	133.00	10	6/3
Warnapura Bandula	1.3.1953		4	1981–1982	96	38	0	12.00	1	0-1	0/0	–	2	12
Warnapura Basnayake Shalith Malinda	26.5.1979		14	2007–2009	821	120	2	35.69	0	0-40	0/0	–	14	3
Warnaweera Kahakatchchi Patabandige Jayananda	23.11.1960		10	1985–1994	39	20	0	4.33	32	4-25	0/0	31.90	0	6
Weerasinghe Colombage Don Udesh Sanjeewa	1.3.1968		1	1985	3	3	0	3.00	0	0-8	0/0	–	0	
Welagedara Uda Walawwe Mahim Bandaralage Chanaka Asanka	20.3.1981		21	2007–2014	218	48	0	9.08	55	5-52	2/0	41.32	5	10/2
[2]Wettimuny Mithra de Silva	11.6.1951		2	1982	28	17	0	7.00		–	–/–	–	2	1
[2]Wettimuny Sidath (CY 1985)	12.8.1956		23	1981–1986	1,221	190	2	29.07	0	0-16	0/0	–	10	35
Wickremasinghe Anguppulige Gamini Dayananda	27.12.1965		3	1989–1992	17	13*	0	8.50	0		–/–	–	9/1	4
Wickremasinghe Gallage Pramodya	14.8.1971		40	1991–2000	555	51	0	9.40	85	6-60	3/0	41.87	18	134
Wijegunawardene Kapila Indaka Weerakkody	23.11.1964		2	1991–1991	14	6*	0	4.66	7	4-51	0/0	21.00	0	26
Wijesuriya Roger Gerard Christopher Ediriweera	18.2.1960		4	1981–1985	22	8	0	4.40	1	1-68	0/0	294.00	1	8
Wijetunge Piyal Kashyapa	6.8.1971		1	1993	10	10	0	5.00	2	1-58	0/0	59.00	0	
Zoysa Demuni Nuwan Tharanga	13.5.1978		30	1996–2004	288	28*	0	8.47	64	5-20	1/0	33.70	4	9

ZIMBABWE (95 players)

	Born	Died	Tests	Test Career	Runs	HS	100s	Avge	Wkts	BB	5/10	Avge	Ct/St	O/T
Arnott Kevin John	8.3.1961		4	1992	302	101*	1	43.14	–	–	–/–	–	4	13
Blignaut Arnoldus Mauritius ("Andy")	1.8.1978		19	2000–2005	886	92	0	26.84	53	5-73	3/0	37.05	13	54/1
Brain David Hayden	4.10.1964		9	1992–1994	115	28	0	10.45	30	5-42	1/0	30.50	1	23
Brandes Eddo André	5.3.1963		10	1992–1999	121	39	0	10.08	26	3-45	0/0	36.57	4	59
Brent Gary Bazil	13.2.1976		4	1999–2001	35	25	0	5.83	7	3-21	0/0	44.85	1	70/3
Briant Gavin Aubrey	11.4.1969		1	1992	17	16	0	8.50	–	–	–/–	–	0	5
Bruk-Jackson Glen Keith	25.4.1969		2	1993	39	31	0	9.75	–	–	–/–	–	0	
Burmester Mark Greville	24.1.1968		3	1993	54	30*	0	27.00	3	3-78	0/0	75.66	1	8
Butchart Iain Peter	9.5.1960		1	1994	23	15	0	11.50	0	0-11	0/0	–	1	20
Campbell Alistair Douglas Ross	23.9.1972		60	1992–2002	2,858	103	2	27.21	0	0-1	0/0	–	60	188
Carlisle Stuart Vance	10.5.1972		37	1994–2005	1,615	118	1	26.91	–	–	–/–	–	34	111
Chakabva Regis Wiriranai	20.9.1987		8	2011–2014	495	101	1	33.00	–	–	–/–	–	9	34/5
Chari Brian Bara	14.2.1992		2	2014	29	25	0	7.25	0	0-9	0/0	–	0	
Chatara Tendai Larry	28.2.1991		7	2012–2014	82	22	0	6.83	20	5-61	1/0	29.25	0	27/7
Chigumbura Elton	14.3.1986		14	2003–2014	569	88	0	21.07	21	5-54	1/0	46.00	6	196½/39
Coventry Charles Kevin	8.3.1983		2	2005	88	37	0	22.00	–	–	–/–	–	3	39/13
Cremer Alexander Graeme	19.9.1986		11	2004–2012	216	43	0	10.80	24	4-4	0/0	45.62	6	61/20
Crocker Gary John	16.5.1962		3	1992	69	33	0	23.00	5	2-65	0/0	72.33	6	6
Dabengwa Keith Mbusi	17.8.1980		3	2005	90	25	0	15.00	5	3-127	0/0	49.80	1	37/8
Dekker Mark Hamilton	5.12.1969		14	1993–1996	333	68*	0	15.85	0	0-5	0/0	–	12	23
Duffin Terrence	20.3.1982		2	2005	80	56	0	20.00	–	–	–/–	–	1	23
Ebrahim Dion Digby	7.8.1980		29	2000–2005	1,226	94	0	22.70	–	–	–/–	–	16	82
Ervine Craig Richard	19.8.1985		7	2011–2014	286	49	0	23.83	9	4-146	0/0	43.11	8	47/16
[2] Ervine Sean Michael	6.12.1982		5	2003–2003	261	86	0	32.62	0	0-8	0/0	–	7	53
Evans Craig Neil	29.11.1969		3	1996–2003	52	22	0	8.66	2	1-27	0/0	130.00	1	7
Ewing Gavin Mackie	21.11.1981		3	2003–2005	108	71	0	18.00	–	–	–/–	–	0	
Ferreira Neil Robert	3.6.1979		1	2005	21	16	0	10.50	–	–	–/–	–	0	
[2] Flower Andrew OBE (CY 2002)	28.4.1968		63	1992–2002	4,794	232*	12	51.54	0	0-0	0/0	–	151/9	213
[2] Flower Grant William	20.12.1970		67	1992–2003	3,457	201*	6	29.54	25	4-41	0/0	61.48	43	221
Friend Travis John	7.1.1981		13	2001–2003	447	81	0	29.80	25	5-31	1/0	43.60	2	51
Goodwin Murray William	11.12.1972		19	1997–2000	1,414	166*	3	42.84	0	0-3	0/0	–	10	71
Gripper Trevor Raymond	28.12.1975		20	1999–2003	809	112	1	21.86	6	2-91	0/0	84.83	14	8
Hondo Douglas Tafadzwa	7.7.1979		9	2001–2004	83	19	0	9.22	21	6-59	1/0	36.85	5	56

	Born	Died	Tests	Test Career	Runs	HS	100s	Avge	Wkts	BB	5/10	Avge	Ct/St	O/T
Houghton David Laud	23.6.1957		22	1992–1997	1,464	266	4	43.05	0	0-0	0/0	–	17	63
Huckle Adam George	21.9.1971		8	1997–1998	74	28*	0	6.72	25	6-109	2/1	34.88	3	19
James Wayne Robert	27.8.1965		4	1993–1994	61	33	0	15.25	–	–	–/–	–	16	11
Jarvis Kyle Malcolm	16.2.1989		8	2011–2012	58	25*	0	7.25	30	5-54	2/0	31.73	3	249
Jarvis Malcolm Peter	6.12.1955		5	1992–1994	4	2*	0	2.00	11	3-30	0/0	35.72	2	12
Johnson Neil Clarkson	24.1.1970		13	1998–2000	532	107	1	24.18	15	4-77	0/0	39.60	12	48
Kamungozi Tafadzwa Paul	8.6.1987		1	2014	5	5	0	2.50	1	1-51	0/0	58.00	0	14/1
Lamb Gregory Arthur	4.3.1980		1	2011	46	39	0	23.00	3	3-120	0/0	47.00	2	15/5
Lock Alan Charles Ingram	10.9.1962	11.6.2001	1	1995	8	8*	0	8.00	5	3-68	0/0	21.00	0	8
Madondo Trevor Nyasha	22.11.1976		3	1997–2000	90	74*	0	30.00	–	–	–/–	–	1	13
Mahwire Ngonidzashe Blessing	31.7.1982		10	2002–2005	147	50*	0	13.36	18	4-92	0/0	50.83	1	23
Maregwede Alester	4.8.1981		2	2003	74	28	0	18.50	–	–	–/–	–	3	11
Marillier Douglas Anthony	24.4.1978		5	2000–2001	185	73	0	30.83	11	4-57	0/0	29.27	2	48
Maruma Timycen	19.4.1988		1	2012	20	10	0	10.00	–	–	–/–	–	0	16/9
²Masakadza Hamilton	9.8.1983		29	2001–2014	1,712	158	4	30.57	13	3-24	0/0	27.69	18	165/40
²Masakadza Shingirai Winston	4.9.1986		5	2011–2014	88	24	0	11.00	16	4-32	0/0	32.18	2	167
Matambanadzo Everton Zvikomborero.	13.4.1976		3	1996–1999	17	7	0	4.25	4	2-62	0/0	62.50	0	7
Matsikenyeri Stuart	3.5.1983		8	2003–2004	351	57	0	23.40	2	1-58	0/0	172.50	7	113/10
Mawoyo Tinotenda Mbiri Kanayi	8.1.1986		8	2011–2013	454	163*	1	30.26	–	–	–/–	–	6	7
Mbangwa Mpumelelo ("Pommie")	26.6.1976		15	1996–2000	34	8	0	2.00	32	3-23	0/0	31.43	6	29
Meth Keegan Orry	8.2.1988		1	2012	72	31*	0	24.00	–	–	–/–	–	0	9
Mpofu Christopher Bobby	27.11.1985		9	2004–2011	27	8	0	2.45	20	4-92	0/0	44.45	2	68/20
Mupariwa Tawanda	16.4.1985		2	2003	15	14	0	15.00	4	2-41	0/0	24.50	0	39/4
Murphy Brian Andrew	1.12.1976		11	1999–2001	123	30	0	10.25	28	4-67	0/0	51.25	11	31
Mushangwe Natsai	9.2.1991		2	2014	8	8	0	2.00	–	–	–/–	–	0	6/5
Mutendera David Travolta	25.1.1979		1	2000	10	10	0	5.00	7	4-82	0/0	61.83	2	9
Mutizwa Forster	24.8.1985		1	2011	24	18	0	12.00	0	0-29	0/0	–	0	17/3
Mutumbami Richmond	11.6.1989		6	2012–2014	217	43	0	19.72	–	–	–/–	–	17/2	28/7
Mwayenga Waddington	20.6.1984		1	2005	15	14*	0	15.00	1	1-79	0/0	79.00	0	3
Ncube Njabulo	14.10.1989		1	2011	17	14	0	8.50	1	1-80	0/0	121.00	1	
Nkala Mluleki Luke	14.1.1981		10	2000–2004	187	47	0	14.38	11	3-82	0/0	66.09	4	50/1
Nyumbu John Curtis	1.3.1983		2	2014	30	24	0	7.50	8	5-157	1/0	50.00	1	19
Olonga Henry Khaaba	3.7.1976		30	1994–2002	184	40*	0	5.41	68	5-70	2/0	38.52	10	50
Panyangara Tinashe	21.10.1985		9	2003–2014	201	30	0	16.75	31	5-59	2/0	26.22	3	64/11
Peall Stephen Guy	2.9.1969		9	1993–1994	60	30	0	15.00	4	2-89	0/0	75.75	1	21
Price Raymond William	12.6.1976		22	1999–2012	261	36	0	8.70	80	6-73	5/1	36.06	4	102/16

	Born	Died	Tests	Test Career	Runs	HS	100s	Avge	Wkts	BB	5/10	Avge	Ct/St	O/T
Pycroft Andrew John	6.6.1956		3	1992	152	60	0	30.40		–	–/–		2	20
Ranchod Ujesh	17.5.1969		1	1992	8	7	0	4.00	1	1-45	0/0	45.00	0	3
² **Rennie** Gavin James	12.1.1976		23	1997–2001	1,023	93	0	22.73	1	1-40	0/0	84.00	13	40
² **Rennie** John Alexander	29.7.1970		4	1993–1997	62	22	0	12.40	3	2-22	0/0	97.66	1	44
Rogers Barney Guy	20.8.1982		4	2004	90	29	0	11.25	0	0-17	0/0		1	15
Shah Ali Hassimshah	7.8.1959		3	1992–1996	122	62	0	24.40	1	1-46	0/0	125.00	0	28
Sibanda Vusimuzi	10.10.1983		14	2003–2014	591	93	0	21.10		–	–/–		16	122‡/18
Sikandar Raza	24.4.1986		4	2013–2014	327	82	0	40.87	5	3-123	0/0	60.60	2	55/18
² **Strang** Bryan Colin	9.6.1972		26	1994–2001	465	53	0	12.91	56	5-101	1/0	39.33	11	49
² **Strang** Paul Andrew	28.7.1970		24	1994–2001	839	106*	1	27.06	70	8-109	4/1	36.02	15	95
Streak Heath Hilton	16.3.1974		65	1993–2005	1,990	127*	1	22.35	216	6-73	7/0	28.14	17	187‡
Taibu Tatenda	14.5.1983		28	2001–2011	1,546	153	1	30.31	1	1-27	0/0	27.00	57/5	149‡/17
Taylor Brendan Ross Murray	6.2.1986		23	2004–2014	1,493	171	4	34.72	0	0-6	0/0		23	167/10
Tiripano Donald Tatenda	17.3.1988		1	2014	20	15*	0	20.00	2	2-65	0/0	32.50	1	7/2
Traicos Athanasios John	17.5.1947		4†	1992	11	5	0	2.75	14	5-86	1/0	40.14	4	27
Utseya Prosper	26.3.1985		4	2003–2013	107	45	0	15.28	10	3-60	0/0	41.00	2	164/35
Vermeulen Mark Andrew	2.3.1979		9	2002–2014	449	118	1	24.94	0	0-5	0/0		6	43
Viljoen Dirk Peter	11.3.1977		2	1997–2000	57	38	0	14.25	1	1-14	0/0	65.00	1	53
Vitori Brian Vitalis	22.2.1990		12	2011–2013	52	19*	0	10.40	12	5-61	1/0	38.66	2	19/8
¹ **Waller** Andrew Christopher	25.9.1959		2	1996	69	50	0	23.00		–	–/–		2	39
¹ **Waller** Malcolm Noel	28.9.1984		9	2011–2014	396	72*	0	23.29	6	4-59	0/0	22.00	6	56/18
Watambwa Brighton Tonderai	9.6.1977		6	2000–2001	11	4*	0	3.66	14	4-64	0/0	35.00	0	63
Whittall Andrew Richard	28.3.1973		10	1996–1999	114	17	0	7.60	7	3-73	0/0	105.14	8	147
Whittall Guy James	5.9.1972		46	1993–2002	2,207	203*	4	29.42	51	4-18	0/0	40.94	19	147
Williams Sean Colin	26.9.1986		2	2012–2014	64	31	0	16.00	2	2-95	0/0	56.50	1	95/18
Wishart Craig Brian	9.1.1974		27	1995–2005	1,098	114	0	22.40		–	–/–		15	90

BANGLADESH (78 players)

	Born	Died	Tests	Test Career	Runs	HS	100s	Avge	Wks	BB	5/10	Avge	Ct/St	O/T
Abdur Razzak	15.6.1982		12	2005–2013	245	43	0	17.50	23	3-93	0/0	67.39	4	153/34
Abul Hasan	5.8.1992		3	2012	165	113	1	82.50	3	2-80	0/0	123.66	3	64
Aftab Ahmed	10.11.1985		16	2004–2009	582	82*	0	20.78	5	2-31	0/0	47.40	7	85/11
Akram Khan	1.11.1968		8	2000–2003	259	44	0	16.18		–	–/–		3	44
Al-Amin Hossain	1.1.1990		6	2013–2014	68	32*	0	22.66	6	3-80	0/0	76.66	0	14/11

	Born	Died	Tests	Test Career	Runs	HS	100s	Avge	Wkts	BB	5/10	Avge	Ct/St	O/T
Al Sahariar	23.4.1978		15	2000–2003	683	71	0	22.76	–	–	–/–	–	10	29
Alamgir Kabir	10.1.1981		3	2002–2003	8	4	0	2.00	6	0-39	0/0	–	0	0
Alok Kapali	1.1.1984		17	2002–2005	584	85	0	17.69	1	3-3	0/0	–	5	69/7
Aminul Islam	2.2.1968		13	2000–2002	530	145	1	21.20	1	1-66	0/0	–	5	39
Anamul Haque	16.12.1992		4	2012–2014	73	22	0	9.12	0	–	–/–	–	2	30/13
Anwar Hossain Monir	31.12.1981		3	2003–2005	22	13	0	7.33	0	0-95	0/0	–	0	1
Anwar Hossain Piju	10.12.1983		1	2002	14	12	0	7.00	–	–	–/–	–	0	–
Bikash Ranjan Das	14.7.1982		1	2000	2	2	0	1.00	1	1-64	0/0	72.00	0	1
Ehsanul Haque	1.12.1979		1	2002	7	5	0	3.50	0	0-18	0/0	–	1	–
Elias Sunny	2.8.1986		4	2011–2012	38	20*	0	7.60	12	6-94	1/0	43.16	1	6
Enamul Haque, sen.	27.2.1966		10	2000–2003	180	24*	0	12.00	18	4-136	0/0	57.05	1	4/7
Enamul Haque, jun.	5.12.1986		15	2003–2012	59	13	0	5.90	44	7-95	3/1	40.61	3	29
Fahim Muntasir	1.11.1980		7	2001–2002	52	33	0	8.66	5	3-131	0/0	68.40		10
Faisal Hossain	26.10.1978		1	2003	7	5	0	3.50	0	–	–/–	–	0	3
Habibul Bashar	17.8.1972		50	2000–2007	3,026	113	3	30.87	0	0-1	0/0	–	22	111
Hannan Sarkar	1.12.1982		17	2002–2004	662	76	0	20.06	0	–	–/–	–	7	20
Hasibul Hossain	3.6.1977		5	2000–2001	97	31	0	10.77	6	2-125	0/0	95.16	1	32
Imrul Kayes	2.2.1987		24	2008–2015	1,252	150	3	27.82	0	0-1	0/0	–	20	58/5
Jahurul Islam	12.12.1986		7	2009–2012	347	48	0	26.69	0	–	–/–	–	7	14/3
Javed Omar Belim	25.11.1976		40	2000–2007	1,720	119	1	22.05	0	–	–/–	–	10	59
Jubair Hossain	12.9.1995		6	2014–2015	13	7*	0	4.33	16	5-96	1/0	30.81	2	3/1
Junaid Siddique	30.10.1987		19	2007–2012	969	106	1	26.18	0	0-2	0/0	–	11	54/7
Khaled Mahmud	26.7.1971		12	2001–2003	266	45	0	12.09	13	4-37	0/0	64.00	7	77
Khaled Mashud	8.2.1976		44	2000–2007	1,409	103*	1	19.04	–	–	–/–	–	78/9	126
Liton Das	13.10.1994		3	2015	97	50	0	32.33	–	–	–/–	–	3	9/3
Mahbubul Alam	1.12.1983		4	2008	5	5	0	1.25	5	2-62	0/0	62.80	3	5
Mahmudullah	4.2.1986		27	2009–2015	1,506	115	1	31.37	37	5-51	1/0	45.40	28/1	125/37
Manjural Islam	7.11.1979	16.3.2007	17	2000–2003	81	21	0	3.68	28	6-81	1/0	57.32	4	34
Manjural Islam Rana	4.5.1984		6	2003–2004	257	69	0	25.70	5	3-84	0/0	80.20	3	25
Marshall Ayub	5.12.1988		5	2013	125	41	0	20.83	4	0-15	0/0	–	2	–
Mashrafe bin Mortaza	5.10.1983		36	2001–2009	797	79	0	12.85	78	4-60	0/0	41.52	9	158/33
Mehrab Hossain, sen.	22.9.1978		9	2000–2003	241	71	0	13.38	0	0-5	0/0	–	6	18
Mehrab Hossain, jun.	8.7.1987		9	2007–2008	243	83	0	20.25	2	2-29	0/0	70.25	9	18/2
Mohammad Ashraful	9.9.1984		61	2001–2012	2,737	190	6	24.00	21	2-42	0/0	60.52	25	175/23
Mohammad Rafique	5.9.1970		33	2000–2007	1,059	111	1	18.57	100	6-77	7/0	40.76	7	123/1
Mohammad Salim	15.10.1981		2	2003	49	26	0	16.33	–	–	–/–	–	3/1	1

	Born	Died	Test Career	Tests	Runs	HS	100s	Avge	Wkts	BB	5/10	Avge	Ct/St	O/T
Mohammad Shahid	1.11.1993		2014–2015	5	57	25	0	11.40	5	2-23	0/0	57.60	0	9
Mohammad Sharif	12.12.1983		2000–2007	10	122	24*	0	7.17	14	4-98	0/0	79.00	5	26/6
Mominul Haque	29.9.1991		2012–2015	17	1,456	181	4	56.00	–	–	–/–	–	13	158/43
Mushfiqur Rahim	1.9.1988		2005–2015	48	2,650	200	3	32.31	1	1-10	0/0	192.00	76/11	28
Mushfiqur Rahman	1.1.1980		2000–2004	10	232	46*	0	13.64	13	4-65	0/0	63.30	6	9/5
Mustafizur Rahman	6.9.1995		2015	2	3	3	0	3.00	4	4-37	0/0	14.50	0	–
Naeem Islam	31.12.1986		2008–2012	11	416	108	0	32.00	1	1-11	0/0	303.00	2	59/10
[2] Nafis Iqbal	31.1.1985		2004–2005	11	518	121	1	23.54	–	–	–/–	–	2	16
Naimur Rahman	19.9.1974		2000–2002	8	210	48	0	15.00	12	6-132	1/0	59.83	4	29
Nasir Hossain	30.11.1991		2011–2015	17	971	100	1	37.34	8	3-52	0/0	51.62	10	56/29
Nazimuddin	1.10.1985		2011–2012	3	125	78	0	20.83	–	–	–/–	–	0	11/7
Nazmul Hossain	5.10.1987		2004–2011	2	16	8*	0	8.00	5	2-61	0/0	38.80	0	38/4
Rafiqul Islam	7.11.1977		2002	1	7	8*	0	3.50	–	–	–/–	–	0	1
Rajin Saleh	20.11.1983		2003–2008	24	1,141	89	0	25.93	2	1-9	0/0	134.00	15	43
Raqibul Hasan	8.10.1987		2008–2011	9	336	65	0	19.76	1	1-0	0/0	17.00	5	55/5
Robiul Islam	20.10.1986		2010–2014	9	99	33	0	9.00	25	6-71	2/0	39.68	5	3/1
Rubel Hossain	1.1.1990		2009–2014	23	197	45*	0	8.95	32	5-166	1/0	75.90	11	67/11
Sajidul Islam	18.1.1988		2007–2012	3	18	6	0	3.00	5	2-71	0/0	77.33	0	0/1
Sanwar Hossain	5.8.1973		2001–2003	9	345	49	0	19.16	5	2-128	0/0	62.00	2	27
Shafiul Islam	6.10.1989		2009–2014	8	183	53	0	13.07	15	3-86	0/0	50.53	1	52/11
Shahadat Hossain	7.8.1986		2005–2014	38	521	40	0	10.01	72	6-27	4/0	51.81	2	51/6
Shahriar Hossain	1.6.1976		2000–2003	3	99	48	0	19.80	–	–	–/–	–	0/1	20
Shahriar Nafees	1.5.1985		2005–2012	24	1,267	138	1	26.39	–	–	–/–	–	19	75/1
Shakib Al Hasan	24.3.1987		2007–2015	42	2,823	144	3	39.76	147	7-36	14/1	33.31	19	157/38
Shamsur Rahman	5.6.1988		2013–2014	6	305	106	1	25.41	–	–	–/–	–	7	10/9
Shuvagata Hom	11.11.1986		2014–2015	7	213	50	0	21.30	8	2-66	0/0	59.12	5	4
Sohag Gazi	5.8.1991		2012–2015	10	325	101*	1	21.66	38	6-74	2/0	42.07	5	20/10
Soumya Sarkar	25.2.1993		2014–2015	3	107	37	0	21.40	4	1-45	0/0	115.00	0	16/3
Subrawadi Shuvo	21.11.1988		2011	1	15	15	0	7.50	4	3-73	0/0	36.50	0	17/1
Syed Rasel	3.7.1984		2005–2007	6	37	19	0	4.62	12	4-129	0/0	47.75	6	52/8
Taijul Islam	7.2.1992		2014–2015	9	137	32	0	11.41	36	8-39	3/0	33.94	1	–
Talha Jubair	10.12.1985		2002–2004	7	52	31	0	6.50	14	3-135	0/0	55.07	1	6
[2] Tamim Iqbal (CY 2011)	20.3.1989		2007–2015	42	3,118	206	7	39.46	1	0-1	0/0	–	11	153/41
Tapash Baisya	25.12.1982		2002–2005	21	384	66	0	11.29	36	4-72	0/0	59.36	6	56
Tareq Aziz	4.9.1983		2003–2004	3	22	10*	0	11.00	1	1-76	0/0	261.00	1	10
Tushar Imran	10.12.1983		2002–2007	5	89	28	0	8.90	0	0-48	0/0	–	1	41
Ziaur Rahman	2.12.1986		2012	1	14	14	0	7.00	4	4-63	0/0	17.75	0	13/14

Notes

*Family relationships in the above lists are indicated by superscript numbers; the following list
   contains only those players whose relationship is not apparent from a shared name.*

In one Test, A. and G. G. Hearne played for England; their brother, F. Hearne, for South Africa.
The Waughs and New Zealand's Marshalls are the only instance of Test-playing twins.
Adnan Akmal: brother of Kamran and Umar Akmal.
Amar Singh, L.: brother of L. Ramji.
Azmat Rana: brother of Shafqat Rana.
Bazid Khan (Pakistan): son of Majid Khan (Pakistan) and grandson of M. Jahangir Khan (India).
Bravo, D. J. and D. M.: half-brothers.
Chappell, G. S., I. M. and T. M.: grandsons of V. Y. Richardson.
Collins, P. T.: half-brother of F. H. Edwards.
Cooper, W. H.: great-grandfather of A. P. Sheahan.
Edwards, F. H.: half-brother of P. T. Collins.
Hanif Mohammad: brother of Mushtaq, Sadiq and Wazir Mohammad; father of Shoaib Mohammad.
Headley, D. W (England): son of R. G. A. and grandson of G. A. Headley (both West Indies).
Hearne, F. (England and South Africa): father of G. A. L. Hearne (South Africa).
Jahangir Khan, M. (India): father of Majid Khan and grandfather of Bazid Khan (both Pakistan).
Kamran Akmal: brother of Adnan and Umar Akmal.
Khalid Wazir (Pakistan): son of S. Wazir Ali (India).
Kirsten, G. and P. N.: half-brothers.
Majid Khan (Pakistan): son of M. Jahangir Khan (India) and father of Bazid Khan (Pakistan).
Manzoor Elahi: brother of Salim and Zahoor Elahi.
Moin Khan: brother of Nadeem Khan.
Mudassar Nazar: son of Nazar Mohammad.
Murray, D. A.: son of E. D. Weekes.
Mushtaq Mohammad: brother of Hanif, Sadiq and Wazir Mohammad.
Nadeem Khan: brother of Moin Khan.
Nafis Iqbal: brother of Tamim Iqbal.
Nazar Mohammad: father of Mudassar Nazar.
Nazir Ali, S.: brother of S. Wazir Ali.
Pattinson, D. J. (England): brother of J. L. Pattinson (Australia).
Pervez Sajjad: brother of Waqar Hassan.
Ramiz Raja: brother of Wasim Raja.
Ramji, L.: brother of L. Amar Singh.
Richardson, V. Y.: grandfather of G. S., I. M. and T. M. Chappell.
Sadiq Mohammad: brother of Hanif, Mushtaq and Wazir Mohammad.
Saeed Ahmed: brother of Younis Ahmed.
Salim Elahi: brother of Manzoor and Zahoor Elahi.
Shafqat Rana: brother of Azmat Rana.
Sheahan, A. P.: great-grandson of W. H. Cooper.
Shoaib Mohammad: son of Hanif Mohammad.
Tamim Iqbal: brother of Nafis Iqbal.
Umar Akmal: brother of Adnan and Kamran Akmal.
Waqar Hassan: brother of Pervez Sajjad.
Wasim Raja: brother of Ramiz Raja.
Wazir Ali, S. (India): brother of S. Nazir Ali (India) and father of Khalid Wazir (Pakistan).
Wazir Mohammad: brother of Hanif, Mushtaq and Sadiq Mohammad.
Weekes, E. D.: father of D. A. Murray.
Yograj Singh: father of Yuvraj Singh.
Younis Ahmed: brother of Saeed Ahmed.
Yuvraj Singh: son of Yograj Singh.
Zahoor Elahi: brother of Manzoor and Salim Elahi.

Teams are listed only where relatives played for different sides.

PLAYERS APPEARING FOR MORE THAN ONE TEST TEAM

Fourteen cricketers have appeared for two countries in Test matches, namely:

Amir Elahi (India 1, Pakistan 5)
J. J. Ferris (Australia 8, England 1)
S. C. Guillen (West Indies 5, New Zealand 3)
Gul Mahomed (India 8, Pakistan 1)
F. Hearne (England 2, South Africa 4)
A. H. Kardar (India 3, Pakistan 23)
W. E. Midwinter (England 4, Australia 8)

F. Mitchell (England 2, South Africa 3)
W. L. Murdoch (Australia 18, England 1)
Nawab of Pataudi, sen. (England 3, India 3)
A. J. Traicos (South Africa 3, Zimbabwe 4)
A. E. Trott (Australia 3, England 2)
K. C. Wessels (Australia 24, South Africa 16)
S. M. J. Woods (Australia 3, England 3)

Wessels also played 54 one-day internationals for Australia and 55 for South Africa.

The following players appeared for the ICC World XI against Australia in the Super Series Test in 2005-06: M. V. Boucher, R. Dravid, A. Flintoff, S. J. Harmison, Inzamam-ul-Haq, J. H. Kallis, B. C. Lara, M. Muralitharan, V. Sehwag, G. C. Smith, D. L. Vettori.

In 1970, England played five first-class matches against the Rest of the World after the cancellation of South Africa's tour. Players were awarded England caps, but the matches are no longer considered to have Test status. Alan Jones (born 4.11.1938) made his only appearance for England in this series, scoring 5 and 0; he did not bowl and took no catches.

ONE-DAY AND TWENTY20 INTERNATIONAL CRICKETERS

The following players had appeared for Test-playing countries in one-day internationals or Twenty20 internationals by January 10, 2016, but had not represented their countries in Test matches by January 26, 2016. (Numbers in brackets signify number of one-day internationals for each player: where a second number appears, e.g. (5/1), it signifies the number of Twenty20 internationals for that player.)

By January 2016, N. L. McCullum was the most experienced international player never to have appeared in Test cricket, with 84 one-day internationals and 61 Twenty20 internationals. R. G. Sharma held the record for most international appearances before making his Test debut, with 108 one-day internationals and 36 Twenty20 internationals.

England

M. W. Alleyne (10), Z. S. Ansari (1), I. D. Austin (9), S. W. Billings (5/5), D. R. Briggs (1/7), A. D. Brown (16), D. R. Brown (9), G. Chapple (1), J. W. M. Dalrymple (27/3), S. M. Davies (8/5), J. L. Denly (9/5), J. W. Dernbach (24/34), M. V. Fleming (11), P. J. Franks (1), I. J. Gould (18), A. P. Grayson (1), H. F. Gurney (10/2), G. W. Humpage (3), T. E. Jesty (10), E. C. Joyce (17/2), C. Kieswetter (46/25), G. D. Lloyd (6), A. G. R. Loudon (1), J. D. Love (3), M. B. Loye (7), M. J. Lumb (3/27), M. A. Lynch (3), A. D. Mascarenhas (20/14), S. C. Meaker (2/2), P. Mustard (10/2), P. A. Nixon (19/1), S. D. Parry (2/5), J. J. Roy (15/6), M. J. Smith (5), N. M. K. Smith (7), J. N. Snape (10/1), V. S. Solanki (51/3), R. J. W. Topley (5/2), J. O. Troughton (6), J. M. Vince (1/3), C. M. Wells (2), V. J. Wells (9), A. G. Wharf (1), D. J. Willey (10/4), L. J. Wright (50/51), M. H. Yardy (28/14).

D. R. Brown also played 16 one-day internationals for Scotland, and E. C. Joyce 39 one-day internationals and 16 Twenty20 internationals for Ireland.

Australia

S. A. Abbott (1/3), T. R. Birt (0/4), G. A. Bishop (2), C. J. Boyce (0/5), R. J. Campbell (2), D. T. Christian (19/15), M. J. Cosgrove (3), N. M. Coulter-Nile (13/11), B. J. Cutting (4/4), M. J. Di Venuto (9), B. R. Dorey (4), B. R. Dunk (0/3), Fawad Ahmed (3/2), C. J. Ferguson (30/3), A. J. Finch (52/22), P. J. Forrest (15), B. Geeves (2), S. F. Graf (11), I. J. Harvey (73), S. M. Harwood (1/3), J. R. Hopes (84/12), D. J. Hussey (69/39), B. Laughlin (5/3), S. Lee (45), M. L. Lewis (7/2), C. A. Lynn (0/2), R. J. McCurdy (11), K. H. MacLeay (16), N. J. Maddinson (0/2), J. P. Maher (26), J. M. Muirhead (0/5), D. P. Nannes (1/15), A. A. Noffke (1/2), L. A. Pomersbach (0/1), G. D. Porter (2), N. J. Reardon (0/2), K. W. Richardson (8/2), B. J. Rohrer (0/1), G. S. Sandhu (2), J. D. Siddons (1), M. P. Stoinis (1/1), A. M. Stuart (3), G. S. Trimble (2), B. E. Young (6), A. K. Zesers (2).

D. P. Nannes also played two Twenty20 internationals for the Netherlands.

South Africa

Y. A. Abdulla (0/2), S. Abrahams (1), F. Behardien (36/23), D. M. Benkenstein (23), G. H. Bodi (2/1), L. E. Bosman (13/14), R. E. Bryson (7), D. J. Callaghan (29), D. N. Crookes (32), H. Davids (2/9), T. Henderson (0/1), B. E. Hendricks (0/5), R. R. Hendricks (0/5), C. A. Ingram (31/9), J. C. Kent (2), L. J. Koen (5), G. J-P. Kruger (3/1), H. G. Kuhn (0/5), E. Leie (0/2), R. E. Levi (0/13), J. Louw (3/2), D. A. Miller (82/37), P. V. Mpitsang (2), S. J. Palframan (7), A. M. Phangiso (16/9), N. Pothas (3/9), A. G. Puttick (1), C. E. B. Rice (3), M. J. R. Rindel (22), R. R. Rossouw (26/10), D. B. Rundle (2), T. G. Shaw (9), M. Shezi (1), E. O. Simons (23), E. L. R. Stewart (6), R. Telemachus (37/3), J. Theron (4/9), A. C. Thomas (0/1), T. Tshabalala (4), R. E. van der Merwe (13/13), J. J. van der Wath (10/8), V. B. van Jaarsveld (2/3), M. N. van Wyk (17/8), C. J. P. G. van Zyl (2), D. Wiese (3/12), H. S. Williams (7), M. Yachad (1).

R. E. van der Merwe also played five Twenty20 internationals for the Netherlands.

West Indies

H. A. G. Anthony (3), S. Badree (0/22), C. D. Barnwell (0/6), M. C. Bascombe (0/1), N. E. Bonner (0/2), D. Brown (3), B. St A. Browne (4), P. A. Browne (5), H. R. Bryan (15), D. C. Butler (5/1), J. L. Carter (13), J. Charles (35/23), D. O. Christian (0/2), R. T. Crandon (1), M. L. Cummins (1), R. R. Emrit (2), S. E. Findlay (9/2), A. D. S. Fletcher (18/24), R. S. Gabriel (11), R. C. Haynes (8), R. O. Hurley (9), D. P. Hyatt (9/5), K. C. B. Jeremy (6), A. Martin (9/1), G. E. Mathurin (0/3), J. N. Mohammed (2), A. R. Nurse (0/4), W. K. D. Perkins (0/1), K. A. Pollard (91/45), M. R. Pydanna (3), A. C. L. Richards (1/1), K. Santokie (0/12), K. F. Semple (7), D. C. Thomas (21/3), C. M. Tuckett (1), L. R. Williams (15).

New Zealand

G. W. Aldridge (2/1), M. D. Bailey (1), M. D. Bates (2/3), B. R. Blair (14), N. T. Broom (22/10), C. E. Bulfin (4), T. K. Canning (4), P. G. Coman (3), C. de Grandhomme (1/4), A. P. Devcich (10/4), B. J. Diamanti (1/1), M. W. Douglas (6), A. M. Ellis (15/5), B. G. Hadlee (2), L. J. Hamilton (2), R. T. Hart (1), R. L. Hayes (1), R. M. Hira (0/15), P. A. Hitchcock (14/1), L. G. Howell (12), M. J. McClenaghan (47/22), N. L. McCullum (84/61), P. D. McGlashan (4/11), B. J. McKechnie (14), E. B. McSweeney (16), A. W. Mathieson (1), J. P. Millmow (5), A. F. Milne (29/11), T. S. Nethula (5), C. J. Nevin (37), H. M. Nicholls (5), A. J. Penn (5), R. G. Petrie (12), R. B. Reid (9), S. J. Roberts (2), S. L. Stewart (4), L. W. Stott (1), G. P. Sulzberger (3), A. R. Tait (5), E. P. Thompson (1/1), M. D. J. Walker (3), R. J. Webb (3), B. M. Wheeler (6), J. W. Wilson (6), W. A. Wisneski (3), L. J. Woodcock (4/3), G. H. Worker (2/2).

India

S. Aravind (0/1), P. Awana (0/2), A. C. Bedade (13), A. Bhandari (2), Bhupinder Singh, sen. (2), G. Bose (1), V. B. Chandrasekhar (7), U. Chatterjee (3), N. A. David (4), P. Dharmani (1), A. B. Dinda (13/9), R. S. Gavaskar (11), R. S. Ghai (6), M. S. Gony (2), K. M. Jadhav (4/2), Joginder Sharma (4/4), A. V. Kale (1), S. C. Khanna (10), G. K. Khoda (2), A. R. Khurasiya (12), D. S. Kulkarni (8), T. Kumaran (8), J. J. Martin (10), D. Mongia (57/11), S. P. Mukherjee (3), A. M. Nayar (3), G. K. Pandey (2), M. K. Pandey (1/2), J. V. Paranjpe (4), Parvez Rasool (1), A. K. Patel (8), A. R. Patel (22/4), Y. K. Pathan (57/22), Randhir Singh (2), S. S. Raul (2), A. T. Rayudu (31/3), A. M. Salvi (4), S. V. Samson (0/1), M. Sharma (26/8), R. Sharma (4/2), S. Sharma (0/2), L. R. Shukla (3), R. P. Singh (2), R. S. Sodhi (18), S. Somasunder (2), S. Sriram (4), Sudhakar Rao (1), M. K. Tiwary (12/3), S. S. Tiwary (3), S. Tyagi (4/1), R. V. Uthappa (46/13), P. S. Vaidya (4), Y. Venugopal Rao (16), Jai P. Yadav (12).

Pakistan

Aamer Hameed (2), Aamer Hanif (5), Aamer Yasin (3/1), Akhtar Sarfraz (4), Anwar Ali (21/14), Arshad Pervez (2), Asad Ali (4/2), Asif Mahmood (2), Awais Zia (0/5), Babar Azam (7), Bilal Asif (3), Faisal Athar (1), Ghulam Ali (3), Haafiz Shahid (3), Hammad Azam (11/5), Haris Sohail (22/4), Hasan Jamil (6), Iftikhar Ahmed (2), Imad Wasim (5/5), Imran Abbas (2), Imran Khan, jun. (0/3), Iqbal Sikandar (1), Irfan Bhatti (1), Javed Qadir (1), Junaid Zia (4), Kamran Hussain (2), Kashif Raza (1), Khalid Latif (5/7), Mahmood Hamid (1), Mansoor Amjad (1/1), Mansoor Rana (2), Manzoor Akhtar (7), Maqsood Rana (1), Masood Iqbal (1), Mohammad Wasim (14/8), Moin-ul-Atiq (5), Mujahid Jamshed (4), Mukhtar Ahmed (0/6), Naeem Ahmed (1), Naeem Ashraf (2), Najaf Shah (1), Naseer Malik (1), Nauman Anwar (0/1), Naumanullah (1), Parvez Mir (3), Rafatullah Mohmand (0/3), Rameez Raja (0/2), Raza Hasan (1/10), Rizwan Ahmed (1), Saad Nasim (3/3), Saadat Ali (8), Saeed Azad (4), Sajid Ali (13), Sajjad Akbar (2), Salim Pervez (1), Samiullah Khan (2), Shahid Anwar (1), Shahzaib Hasan (3/10), Shakeel Ansar (0/2), Shakil Khan (1), Sharjeel Khan (11/3),

Shoaib Khan (0/1), Sohaib Maqsood (25/18), Sohail Fazal (2), Tanvir Mehdi (1), Usman Khan (0/2), Usman Salahuddin (2), Wasim Haider (3), Zafar Gohar (1), Zafar Iqbal (8), Zahid Ahmed (2).

Sri Lanka

J. W. H. D. Boteju (2), A. Dananjaya (1/5), D. L. S. de Silva (2), D. M. de Silva (0/2), G. N. de Silva (4), P. C. de Silva (6), L. H. D. Dilhara (9/2), B. Fernando (0/2), E. R. Fernando (3), T. L. Fernando (1), U. N. K. Fernando (2), J. C. Gamage (4), P. L. S. Gamage (5), W. C. A. Ganegama (4), F. R. M. Goonatilleke (1), P. W. Gunaratne (23), M. D. Gunathilleke (6/2), A. A. W. Gunawardene (1), P. D. Heyn (2), W. S. Jayantha (17), P. S. Jayaprakashdaran (1), C. U. Jayasinghe (0/5), S. A. Jayasinghe (2), D. S. N. F. G. Jayasuriya (3/5), S. H. T. Kandamby (39/5), S. H. U. Karnain (19), H. G. J. M. Kulatunga (0/2), B. M. A. J. Mendis (54/16), C. Mendis (1), A. M. N. Munasinghe (5), E. M. D. Y. Munaweera (0/4), H. G. D. Nayanakantha (3), A. R. M. Opatha (5), S. P. Pasqual (2), S. S. Pathirana (4), A. K. Perera (3/2), K. G. Perera (1), H. S. M. Pieris (3), S. M. A. Priyanjan (23), M. Pushpakumara (3/1), R. L. B. Rambukwella (0/1), S. K. Ranasinghe (4), N. Ranatunga (2), N. L. K. Ratnayake (2), R. J. M. G. M. Rupasinghe (0/2), M. D. Shanaka (0/1), A. P. B. Tennekoon (4), M. H. Tissera (3), I. Udana (2/7), M. L. Udawatte (9/5), J. D. F. Vandersay (3/4), D. M. Vonhagt (1), A. P. Weerakkody (1), S. Weerakoon (2), K. Weeraratne (15/5), S. R. de S. Wettimuny (3), R. P. A. H. Wickremaratne (3).

Zimbabwe

R. D. Brown (7), C. J. Chibhabha (93/27), M. T. Chinouya (2), T. S. Chisoro (8/5), K. M. Curran (11), S. G. Davies (4), K. G. Duers (6), E. A. Essop-Adam (1), D. A. G. Fletcher (6), T. N. Garwe (1), J. G. Heron (6), R. S. Higgins (11), V. R. Hogg (2), A. J. Ireland (26/1), L. M. Jongwe (22/6), R. Kaia (1), F. Kasteni (3), A. J. Mackay (3), N. Madziva (11/4), G. C. Martin (5), W. P. Masakadza (10/2), M. A. Meman (1), S. F. Mire (10), P. J. Moor (7/2), T. V. Mufambisi (6), C. T. Mutombodzi (11/3), T. Muzarabani (6/5), I. A. Nicolson (2), G. A. Paterson (10), G. E. Peckover (3), E. C. Rainsford (39/2), P. W. E. Rawson (10), H. P. Rinke (18), R. W. Sims (3), G. M. Strydom (12), C. Zhuwao (1/5).

Bangladesh

Ahmed Kamal (1), Alam Talukdar (2), Aminul Islam, jun. (1), Anisur Rahman (2), Arafat Sunny (16/6), Ather Ali Khan (19), Azhar Hussain (7), Dhiman Ghosh (14/1), Dolar Mahmud (7), Farhad Reza (34/13), Faruq Ahmed (7), Gazi Ashraf (7), Ghulam Faruq (5), Ghulam Nausher (9), Hafizur Rahman (2), Harunur Rashid (2), Jahangir Alam (3), Jahangir Badshah (5), Jamaluddin Ahmed (1), Mafizur Rahman (4), Mahbubur Rahman (1), Mazharul Haque (1), Minhazul Abedin (27), Mithun Ali (2/2), Moniruzzaman (2), Morshed Ali Khan (3), Mosharraf Hossain (3), Nadif Chowdhury (0/3), Nasir Ahmed (7), Nazmus Sadat (0/1), Neeyamur Rashid (2), Nurul Abedin (4), Rafiqul Alam (2), Raqibul Hasan, sen. (2), Rony Talukdar (0/1), Sabbir Rahman (23/10), Saiful Islam (7), Sajjad Ahmed (2), Samiur Rahman (2), Shafiuddin Ahmed (11), Shahidur Rahman (2), Shariful Haq (1), Sheikh Salahuddin (6), Taskin Ahmed (14/3), Wahidul Gani (1), Zahid Razzak (2), Zakir Hassan (2).

PLAYERS APPEARING FOR MORE THAN ONE ONE-DAY/TWENTY20 INTERNATIONAL TEAM

The following players have played one-day internationals for the **African XI** in addition to their national side:

N. Boje (2), L. E. Bosman (1), J. Botha (2), M. V. Boucher (5), E. Chigumbura (3), A. B. de Villiers (5), H. H. Dippenaar (6), J. H. Kallis (2), J. M. Kemp (6), J. A. Morkel (2), M. Morkel (3), T. M. Odoyo (5), P. J. Ongondo (1), J. L. Ontong (1), S. M. Pollock (5), A. G. Prince (3), J. A. Rudolph (2), V. Sibanda (2), G. C. Smith (5), D. W. Steyn (2), H. H. Streak (2), T. Taibu (1), S. O. Tikolo (4), M. Zondeki (2). (Odoyo, Ongondo and Tikolo played for Kenya, who does not have Test status.)

The following players have played one-day internationals for the **Asian Cricket Council XI** in addition to their national side:

Abdul Razzaq (4), M. S. Dhoni (3), R. Dravid (1), C. R. D. Fernando (1), S. C. Ganguly (3), Harbhajan Singh (2), Inzamam-ul-Haq (3), S. T. Jayasuriya (4), D. P. M. D. Jayawardene (5), A. Kumble (2), Mashrafe bin Mortaza (2), Mohammad Ashraful (2), Mohammad Asif (3), Mohammad Rafique (2), Mohammad Yousuf (7), M. Muralitharan (4), A. Nehra (3), K. C. Sangakkara (4),

V. Sehwag (7), Shahid Afridi (3), Shoaib Akhtar (3), W. U. Tharanga (1), W. P. U. J. C. Vaas (1), Yuvraj Singh (3), Zaheer Khan (6).

The following players have played one-day internationals for the **ICC World XI** in addition to their national side:

C. L. Cairns (1), R. Dravid (3), S. P. Fleming (1), A. Flintoff (3), C. H. Gayle (1), A. C. Gilchrist (1), D. Gough (1), M. L. Hayden (1), J. H. Kallis (3), B. C. Lara (4), G. D. McGrath (1), M. Muralitharan (3), M. Ntini (1), K. P. Pietersen (2), S. M. Pollock (3), R. T. Ponting (1), K. C. Sangakkara (3), V. Sehwag (3), Shahid Afridi (2), Shoaib Akhtar (3), D. L. Vettori (4), S. K. Warne (1).

K. C. Wessels appeared for both Australia and South Africa. D. R. Brown appeared for both England and Scotland. C. B. Lambert appeared for both West Indies and USA. E. C. Joyce, E. J. G. Morgan and W. B. Rankin appeared for both Ireland and England. A. C. Cummins appeared for both West Indies and Canada.

G. M. Hamilton played Test cricket for England and one-day internationals for Scotland. D. P. Nannes played one-day and Twenty20 internationals for Australia and Twenty20 internationals for the Netherlands. W. B. Rankin played one-day and Twenty20 internationals for Ireland and all three formats for England. L. Ronchi played one-day and Twenty20 internationals for Australia and all three formats for New Zealand. G. O. Jones played in all three formats for England and one-day internationals for Papua New Guinea. R. E. van der Merwe played one-day and Twenty20 internationals for South Africa and Twenty20 internationals for the Netherlands.

ELITE TEST UMPIRES

The following umpires were on the ICC's elite panel in February 2016. The figures for Tests, one-day internationals and Twenty20 internationals and the Test Career dates refer to matches in which they have officiated as on-field umpires (excluding abandoned games). The totals of Tests are complete up to January 26, 2016, the totals of one-day internationals and Twenty20 internationals up to January 10, 2016.

	Country	Born	Tests	Test Career	ODIs	T20Is
Aleem Dar	P	6.6.1968	101	*2003–2015*	178	35
Dharmasena Handunnettige Deepthi						
Priyantha <u>Kumar</u>	SL	24.4.1971	36	*2010–2015*	68	17
Erasmus Marais	SA	27.2.1964	35	*2009–2015*	62	20
Gaffaney Christopher Blair	NZ	30.11.1975	7	*2014–2015*	43	15
Gould Ian James	E	19.8.1957	49	*2008–2015*	109	29
Illingworth Richard Keith	E	23.8.1963	20*	*2012–2015*	44	11
Kettleborough Richard Allan	E	15.3.1973	33	*2010–2015*	57	17
Llong Nigel James	E	11.2.1969	35	*2007–2015*	98	27
Oxenford Bruce Nicholas James	A	5.3.1960	31	*2010–2015*	72	17
Ravi Sundaram	I	22.4.1966	10	*2013–2015*	25	12
Reiffel Paul Ronald	A	19.4.1966	22	*2012–2015*	41	13
Tucker Rodney James	A	28.8.1964	41	*2009–2015*	64	23

*   *Includes one Test where he took over mid-match.*

BIRTHS AND DEATHS

OTHER CRICKETING NOTABLES

The following list shows the births and deaths of cricketers, and people associated with cricket, who have *not* played in men's Test matches.

Criteria for inclusion All non-Test players who have either (1) scored 20,000 runs in first-class cricket, or (2) taken 1,500 first-class wickets, or (3) achieved 750 dismissals, or (4) reached both 15,000 runs and 750 wickets. Also included are (5) the leading players who flourished before the start of Test cricket, (6) *Wisden* Cricketers of the Year who did not play Test cricket, and (7) others of particular merit or interest.

Names Where players were normally known by a name other than their first, this is underlined.

Teams Where only one team is listed, this is normally the one for which the player made most first-class appearances. Additional teams are listed only if the player appeared for them in more than 20 first-class matches, or if they are especially relevant to their career. School and university teams are not given unless especially relevant (e.g. for the schoolboys chosen as wartime Cricketers of the Year in the 1918 and 1919 *Wisdens*).

	Teams	Born	Died
Adams Percy Webster	Cheltenham College; *CY 1919*	5.9.1900	28.9.1962
Aird Ronald MC	Hampshire; sec. MCC 1953–62, pres. MCC 1968–69	4.5.1902	16.8.1986
Aislabie Benjamin	Surrey, secretary of MCC 1822–42	14.1.1774	2.6.1842
Alcock Charles William	Secretary of Surrey 1872–1907	2.12.1842	26.2.1907
Editor, Cricket magazine, 1882–1907. Captain of Wanderers and England football teams.			
Alley William Edward	NSW, Somerset; Test umpire; *CY 1962*	3.2.1919	26.11.2004
Alleyne Mark Wayne	Gloucestershire; *CY 2001*	23.5.1968	
Altham Harry Surtees CBE	Surrey, Hants; historian; pres. MCC 1959–60	30.11.1888	11.3.1965
Arlott Leslie Thomas <u>John</u> OBE	Broadcaster and writer	25.2.1914	14.12.1991
Arthur John <u>Michael</u>	Griq. W, OFS; South Africa coach 2005–10; Australia coach 2011–13	17.5.1968	
Ashdown William Henry	Kent	27.12.1898	15.9.1979
The only player to appear in English first-class cricket before and after the two world wars.			
Ashley-Cooper Frederick Samuel	Historian	22.3.1877	31.1.1932
Ashton *Sir* Hubert KBE MC	Cam. U, Essex; pres. MCC 1960–61; *CY 1922*	13.2.1898	17.6.1979
Austin *Sir* Harold Bruce Gardiner	Barbados	15.7.1877	27.7.1943
Austin Ian David	Lancashire; *CY 1999*	30.5.1966	
Bailey Jack Arthur	Essex; secretary of MCC 1974–87	22.6.1930	
Bainbridge Philip	Gloucestershire, Durham; *CY 1986*	16.4.1958	
Bakewell Enid *née* Turton	England Women	16.12.1940	
Bannister John David	Warwickshire; writer and broadcaster	23.8.1930	23.1.2016
Barker Gordon	Essex	6.7.1931	10.2.2006
Bartlett Hugh Tryon	Sussex; *CY 1939*	7.10.1914	26.6.1988
Bates Suzannah Wilson	New Zealand Women	16.9.1987	
Bayliss Trevor Harley	NSW; SL coach 2007–11; Eng. coach 2015–	21.12.1962	
Beauclerk *Rev. Lord* Frederick	Middlesex, Surrey, MCC	8.5.1773	22.4.1850
Beldam George William	Middlesex; photographer	1.5.1868	23.11.1937
Beldham William ("Silver Billy")	Hambledon, Surrey	5.2.1766	26.2.1862
Beloff Michael Jacob QC	Head of ICC Code of Conduct Commission	18.4.1942	
Benkenstein Dale Martin	KwaZulu-Natal, Durham; *CY 2009*	9.6.1974	
Berry Anthony Scyld Ivens	Editor of *Wisden* 2008–11	28.4.1954	
Berry Leslie George	Leicestershire	28.4.1906	5.2.1985
Bird Harold Dennis ("Dickie") OBE	Yorkshire, Leics; umpire in 66 Tests	19.4.1933	
Blofeld Henry Calthorpe OBE	Cambridge Univ; broadcaster	23.9.1939	
Bond John David	Lancashire; *CY 1971*	6.5.1932	
Booth Roy	Yorkshire, Worcestershire	1.10.1926	
Bowley Frederick Lloyd	Worcestershire	9.11.1873	31.5.1943
Bradshaw Keith	Tasmania; secretary/chief executive MCC 2006–11	2.10.1963	
Brewer Derek Michael	Secretary/chief executive MCC 2012–	2.4.1958	
Briers Nigel Edwin	Leicestershire; *CY 1993*	15.1.1955	

	Teams	Born	Died
Brookes Wilfrid H.	Editor of *Wisden* 1936–39	5.12.1894	28.5.1955
Bryan John Lindsay	Kent; *CY* 1922	26.5.1896	23.4.1985
Bucknor Stephen Anthony	Umpire in a record 128 Tests	31.5.1946	
Bull Frederick George	Essex; *CY* 1898	2.4.1875	16.9.1910
Buller John Sydney MBE	Worcestershire; Test umpire	23.8.1909	7.8.1970
Burnup Cuthbert James	Kent; *CY* 1903	21.11.1875	5.4.1960
Caine Charles Stewart	Editor of *Wisden* 1926–33	28.10.1861	14.4.1933
Calder Harry Lawton	Cranleigh School; *CY* 1918	24.1.1901	15.9.1995
Cardus Sir John Frederick Neville	Writer	3.4.1888	27.2.1975
Chapple Glen	Lancashire; *CY* 2012	23.1.1974	
Chester Frank	Worcestershire; Test umpire	20.1.1895	8.4.1957
Stood in 48 Tests between 1924 and 1955, a record that lasted until 1992.			
Clark Belinda Jane	Australia Women	10.9.1970	
Clark David Graham	Kent; president MCC 1977–78	27.1.1919	8.10.2013
Clarke Charles Giles CBE	Chairman of ECB, 2007–15, pres. ECB, 2015–	29.5.1953	
Clarke William	Nottinghamshire	24.12.1798	25.8.1856
Founded the All-England XI, Trent Bridge ground.			
Collier David Gordon OBE	Chief executive of ECB, 2005–14	22.4.1955	
Collins Arthur Edward Jeune	Clifton College	18.8.1885	11.11.1914
Made 628* in a house match in 1899, the highest score in any cricket until 2016.			
Conan Doyle Dr Sir Arthur Ignatius	MCC	22.5.1859	7.7.1930
Creator of Sherlock Holmes; his only victim in first-class cricket was W. G. Grace.			
Connor Clare Joanne OBE	England Women; administrator	1.9.1976	
Constant David John	Kent, Leics; first-class umpire 1969–2006	9.11.1941	
Cook Thomas Edwin Reed	Sussex	5.1.1901	15.1.1950
Cox George, jun.	Sussex	23.8.1911	30.3.1985
Cox George, sen.	Sussex	29.11.1873	24.3.1949
Cozier Winston Anthony Lloyd	Broadcaster and writer	10.7.1940	
Dalmiya Jagmohan	Pres. BCCI 2001–04, 2015; Pres. ICC 1997–2000	30.5.1940	20.9.2015
Davies Emrys	Glamorgan; Test umpire	27.6.1904	10.11.1975
Davison Brian Fettes	Rhodesia, Leics, Tasmania, Gloucestershire	21.12.1946	
Dawkes George Owen	Leicestershire, Derbyshire	19.7.1920	10.8.2006
Day Arthur Percival	Kent; *CY* 1910	10.4.1885	22.1.1969
de Lisle Timothy John March Phillipps	Editor of *Wisden* 2003	25.6.1962	
Dennett Edward George	Gloucestershire	27.4.1880	14.9.1937
Dhanawade Pranav Prashant	K. C. Gandhi English School	13.5.2000	
Made the highest score in any cricket, 1,009*, in a school match in Mumbai in January 2016.			
Di Venuto Michael James	Tas., Derbys, Durham; Surrey coach 2016–	12.12.1973	
Domingo Russell Craig	South Africa coach 2013–	30.8.1974	
Eagar Edward Patrick	Photographer	9.3.1944	
Edwards Charlotte Marie CBE	England Women; *CY* 2014	17.12.1979	
Ehsan Mani	President of ICC 2003–06	23.3.1945	
Engel Matthew Lewis	Editor of *Wisden* 1993–2000, 2004–07	11.6.1951	
Farbrace Paul	Kent, Middx; SL coach 2014; Eng. asst coach 2014–	7.7.1967	
"Felix" (Nicholas Wanostrocht)	Kent, Surrey, All-England	4.10.1804	3.9.1876
Batsman, artist, author (Felix on the Bat) and inventor of the Catapulta bowling machine.			
Ferguson William Henry BEM	Scorer	6.6.1880	22.9.1957
Scorer and baggage-master for five Test teams on 43 tours over 52 years and "never lost a bag".			
Findlay William	Oxford U, Lancs; sec. MCC 1926–36	22.6.1880	19.6.1953
Firth John D'Ewes Evelyn	Winchester College; *CY* 1918	21.2.1900	21.9.1957
Fitzpatrick Cathryn Lorraine	Australia Women	4.3.1968	
Fletcher Duncan Andrew Gwynne OBE	Zimbabwe; England coach 1999–2007; India coach 2011–15	27.9.1948	
Ford Graham Xavier	Natal B; South Africa coach 1999–2002; Sri Lanka coach 2012–14, 2016–	16.11.1960	
Foster Henry Knollys	Worcestershire; *CY* 1911	30.10.1873	23.6.1950
Frindall William Howard MBE	Statistician	3.3.1939	30.1.2009
Frith David Edward John	Writer	16.3.1937	
Gibbons Harold Harry Ian Haywood	Worcestershire	8.10.1904	16.2.1973
Gibson Clement Herbert	Eton, Cam. U, Sussex, Argentina; *CY* 1918	23.8.1900	31.12.1976

	Teams	Born	Died
Gibson Norman <u>Alan</u> Stanley	Writer	28.5.1923	10.4.1997
Gore Adrian Clements	Eton College; *CY 1919*	14.5.1900	7.6.1990
Grace *Mrs* Martha	Mother and cricketing mentor of WG	18.7.1812	25.7.1884
Grace William Gilbert, jun.	Gloucestershire; son of WG	6.7.1874	2.3.1905
Graveney David Anthony	Gloucestershire, Somerset, Durham	2.1.1953	
Chairman of England selectors 1997–2008.			
Graves Colin James	Chairman of ECB, 2015–	22.1.1948	
Gray James Roy	Hampshire	19.5.1926	
Gray Malcolm Alexander	President of ICC 2000–03	30.5.1940	
Green David Michael	Lancashire, Gloucestershire; *CY 1969*	10.11.1939	
Grieves Kenneth James	New South Wales, Lancashire	27.8.1925	3.1.1992
Haigh Gideon Clifford Jeffrey Davidson	Writer	29.12.1965	
Hall Louis	Yorkshire; *CY 1890*	1.11.1852	19.11.1915
Hallam Albert William	Lancashire, Nottinghamshire; *CY 1908*	12.11.1869	24.7.1940
Hallam Maurice Raymond	Leicestershire	10.9.1931	1.1.2000
Hallows James	Lancashire; *CY 1905*	14.11.1873	20.5.1910
Harrison Tom William	Derbyshire; chief executive of ECB 2015–	11.12.1971	
Hartley Alfred	Lancashire; *CY 1911*	11.4.1879	9.10.1918
Harvey Ian Joseph	Victoria, Gloucestershire; *CY 2004*	10.4.1972	
Hedges Lionel Paget	Tonbridge School, Kent, Glos; *CY 1919*	13.7.1900	12.1.1933
Henderson Robert	Surrey; *CY 1890*	30.3.1865	28.1.1931
Hesson Michael James	New Zealand coach 2012–	30.10.1974	
Hewett Herbert Tremenheere	Somerset; *CY 1893*	25.5.1864	4.3.1921
Heyhoe Flint *Baroness* [Rachael] OBE	England Women	11.6.1939	
Horton Henry	Hampshire	18.4.1923	2.11.1998
Howard Cecil <u>Geoffrey</u>	Middlesex; administrator	14.2.1909	8.11.2002
Hughes David Paul	Lancashire; *CY 1988*	13.5.1947	
Huish Frederick Henry	Kent	15.11.1869	16.3.1957
Humpage Geoffrey William	Warwickshire; *CY 1985*	24.4.1954	
Hunter David	Yorkshire	23.2.1860	11.1.1927
Hutchinson James Metcalf	Derbyshire	29.11.1896	7.11.2000
Believed to be the longest-lived first-class cricketer, at 103 years 344 days.			
Ingleby-Mackenzie Alexander <u>Colin</u> David OBE	Hants; pres. MCC 1996–98	15.9.1933	9.3.2006
Iremonger James	Nottinghamshire; *CY 1903*	5.3.1876	25.3.1956
Isaac Alan Raymond	Chair NZC 2008–10; president ICC 2012–	20.1.1952	
Jackson Victor Edward	NSW, Leicestershire	25.10.1916	30.1.1965
James Cyril Lionel Robert ("Nello")	Writer	4.1.1901	31.5.1989
Jesty Trevor Edward Hants, Griq W., Surrey, Lancs; umpire; *CY 1983*		2.6.1948	
Johnson Paul	Nottinghamshire	24.4.1965	
Johnston Brian Alexander CBE MC	Broadcaster	24.6.1912	5.1.1994
Jones Alan MBE	Glamorgan; *CY 1978*	4.11.1938	
Played once for England v Rest of the World, 1970, regarded at the time as a Test match.			
Jurgensen Shane John W. Aus, Tas, Qld; Bangladesh coach 2013–14		28.4.1976	
Kilburn James Maurice	Writer	8.7.1909	28.8.1993
King John Barton	Philadelphia	19.10.1873	17.10.1965
"Beyond question the greatest all-round cricketer produced by America" – Wisden.			
Knight Roger David Verdon CBE	Surrey, Glos, Sussex; sec. MCC 1994–2005, pres. MCC 2015–16	6.9.1946	
Knight W. H.	Editor of *Wisden* 1864–79	29.11.1812	16.8.1879
Koertzen Rudolf Eric	Umpire in 108 Tests	26.3.1949	
Lacey *Sir* Francis Eden	Hants; secretary of MCC 1898–1926	19.10.1859	26.5.1946
Langridge John George MBE	Sussex; Test umpire; *CY 1950*	10.2.1910	27.6.1999
Lanning Meghann Moira	Australia Women	25.3.1992	
Lee Peter Granville	Northamptonshire, Lancashire; *CY 1976*	27.8.1945	
Lillywhite Frederick William	Sussex	13.6.1792	21.8.1854
Long Arnold	Surrey, Sussex	18.12.1940	
Lord Thomas	Middlesex; founder of Lord's	23.11.1755	13.1.1832
Lorgat Haroon	Chief executive of ICC 2008–12	26.5.1960	
Lyon Beverley Hamilton	Gloucestershire; *CY 1931*	19.1.1902	22.6.1970

	Teams	Born	Died
McEwan Kenneth Scott	Eastern Province, Essex; *CY 1978*	16.7.1952	
McGilvray Alan David MBE	NSW; broadcaster	6.12.1909	17.7.1996
MacLaurin *Lord* [Ian Charter]	Chairman of ECB 1997–2002	30.3.1937	
Manohar Shashank Vyankatesh	Pres. BCCI 2008–11, 2015–; ICC chairman 2015–	29.9.1957	
Marlar Robin Geoffrey	Sussex; writer; pres. MCC 2005–06	2.1.1931	
Marshal Alan	Surrey; *CY 1909*	12.6.1883	23.7.1915
Martin-Jenkins Christopher Dennis Alexander MBE	Writer; broadcaster; pres. MCC 2010–11	20.1.1945	1.1.2013
Mendis Gehan Dixon	Sussex, Lancashire	20.4.1955	
Mercer John	Sussex, Glamorgan; coach and scorer; *CY 1927*	22.4.1893	31.8.1987
Meyer Rollo John Oliver OBE	Somerset	15.3.1905	9.3.1991
Modi Lalit Kumar	Chairman, Indian Premier League 2008–10	29.11.1963	
Moles Andrew James	Warwickshire, NZ coach 2008–09	12.2.1961	
Moores Peter	Sussex; England coach 2007–09, 2014–15	18.12.1962	
Morgan Derek Clifton	Derbyshire	26.2.1929	
Morgan Frederick David OBE	Chair ECB 2003–07, pres. ICC 2008–10, pres. MCC 2014–15	6.10.1937	
Mynn Alfred	Kent, All-England	19.1.1807	1.11.1861
Neale Phillip Anthony	Worcestershire; England manager; *CY 1989*	5.6.1954	
Newman John Alfred	Hampshire	12.11.1884	21.12.1973
Newstead John Thomas	Yorkshire; *CY 1909*	8.9.1877	25.3.1952
Nicholas Mark Charles Jefford	Hampshire; broadcaster	29.9.1957	
Nicholls Ronald Bernard	Gloucestershire	4.12.1933	21.7.1994
Nixon Paul Andrew	Leicestershire, Kent	21.10.1970	
Nyren John	Hampshire	15.12.1764	28.6.1837
Author of The Young Cricketer's Tutor, *1833.*			
Nyren Richard	Hampshire	1734	25.4.1797
Proprietor Bat & Ball Inn, Broadhalfpenny Down.			
Ontong Rodney Craig	Border, Glamorgan, N. Transvaal	9.9.1955	
Ormrod Joseph Alan	Worcestershire, Lancashire	22.12.1942	
Pardon Charles Frederick	Editor of *Wisden* 1887–90	28.3.1850	18.4.1890
Pardon Sydney Herbert	Editor of *Wisden* 1891–1925	23.9.1855	20.11.1925
Parks Henry William	Sussex	18.7.1906	7.5.1984
Parr George	Nottinghamshire, All-England	22.5.1826	23.6.1891
Captain and manager of the All-England XI.			
Partridge Norman Ernest	Malvern College, Warwickshire; *CY 1919*	10.8.1900	10.3.1982
Pawar Sharadchandra Govindrao	Pres. BCCI 2005–08, ICC 2010–12	12.12.1940	
Payton Wilfred Richard Daniel	Nottinghamshire	13.2.1882	2.5.1943
Pearce Thomas Neill	Essex; administrator	3.11.1905	10.4.1994
Pearson Frederick	Worcestershire	23.9.1880	10.11.1963
Perrin Percival Albert ("Peter")	Essex; *CY 1905*	26.5.1876	20.11.1945
Pilch Fuller	Norfolk, Kent	17.3.1804	1.5.1870
"The best batsman that has ever yet appeared" – Arthur Haygarth, 1862.			
Preston Hubert	Editor of *Wisden* 1944–51	16.12.1868	6.8.1960
Preston Norman MBE	Editor of *Wisden* 1952–80	18.3.1903	6.3.1980
Rait Kerr *Col.* Rowan Scrope	Europeans; sec. MCC 1936–52	13.4.1891	2.4.1961
Raj Mithali	India Women	3.12.1982	
Reeves William	Essex; Test umpire	22.1.1875	22.3.1944
Rice Clive Edward Butler	Transvaal, Nottinghamshire; *CY 1981*	23.7.1949	28.7.2015
Richardson Alan	Warwicks, Middx, Worcs; *CY 2012*	6.5.1975	
Robertson-Glasgow Raymond Charles	Somerset; writer	15.7.1901	4.3.1965
Robins Derrick Harold	Warwickshire; tour promoter	27.6.1914	3.5.2004
Robinson Mark Andrew	Northants, Yorkshire, Sussex, coach	23.11.1966	
Robinson Raymond John	Writer	8.7.1905	6.7.1982
Roebuck Peter Michael	Somerset; writer; *CY 1988*	6.3.1956	12.11.2011
Rotherham Gerard Alexander	Rugby School, Warwickshire; *CY 1918*	28.5.1899	31.1.1985
Sainsbury Peter James	Hampshire; *CY 1974*	13.6.1934	12.7.2014
Scott Stanley Winckworth	Middlesex; *CY 1893*	24.3.1854	8.12.1933
Sellers Arthur Brian MBE	Yorkshire; *CY 1940*	5.3.1907	20.2.1981

	Teams	Born	Died
Seymour James	Kent	25.10.1879	30.9.1930
Shepherd David Robert MBE	Gloucestershire; umpire in 92 Tests	27.12.1940	27.10.2009
Shepherd Donald John	Glamorgan; *CY 1970*	12.8.1927	
Silk Dennis Raoul Whitehall CBE	Somerset; pres. MCC 1992–94, chair TCCB 1994–96	8.10.1931	
Simmons Jack MBE	Lancashire, Tasmania; *CY 1985*	28.3.1941	
Skelding Alexander	Leicestershire; umpire	5.9.1886	17.4.1960
First-class umpire 1931–58, when he was 72.			
Smith Sydney Gordon	Northamptonshire; *CY 1915*	15.1.1881	25.10.1963
Smith William Charles ("Razor")	Surrey; *CY 1911*	4.10.1877	15.7.1946
Southerton Sydney James	Editor of *Wisden* 1934–35	7.7.1874	12.3.1935
Speed Malcolm Walter	Chief executive of ICC 2001–08	14.9.1948	
Spencer Thomas William OBE	Kent; Test umpire	22.3.1914	1.11.1995
Srinivasan Narayanaswami	Pres. BCCI 2011–14; ICC chair 2014–15	3.1.1945	
Stephenson Franklyn Dacosta	Nottinghamshire, Sussex; *CY 1989*	8.4.1959	
Stephenson Harold William	Somerset	18.7.1920	23.4.2008
Stephenson Heathfield Harman	Surrey, All-England	3.5.1832	17.12.1896
Captained first English team to Australia, 1861-62; umpired first Test in England, 1880.			
Stephenson Lt.-Col. John Robin CBE	Secretary of MCC 1987–93	25.2.1931	2.6.2003
Studd *Sir* John Edward Kynaston	Middlesex	26.7.1858	14.1.1944
Lord Mayor of London 1928–29; president of MCC 1930.			
Surridge Walter Stuart	Surrey; *CY 1953*	3.9.1917	13.4.1992
Sutherland James Alexander	Victoria; CEO Cricket Australia 2001–	14.7.1965	
Suttle Kenneth George	Sussex	25.8.1928	25.3.2005
Swanton Ernest William ("Jim") CBE	Middlesex; writer	11.2.1907	22.1.2000
Tarrant Francis Alfred	Victoria, Middlesex; *CY 1908*	11.12.1880	29.1.1951
Taylor Brian	Essex; *CY 1972*	19.6.1932	
Taylor Samantha Claire MBE	England Women; *CY 2009*	25.9.1975	
Taylor Tom Launcelot	Yorkshire; *CY 1901*	25.5.1878	16.3.1960
Thornton Charles Inglis ("Buns")	Middlesex	20.3.1850	10.12.1929
Timms John Edward	Northamptonshire	3.11.1906	18.5.1980
Todd Leslie John	Kent	19.6.1907	20.8.1967
Tunnicliffe John	Yorkshire; *CY 1901*	26.8.1866	11.7.1948
Turner Francis Michael MBE	Leicestershire; administrator	8.8.1934	21.7.2015
Turner Robert Julian	Somerset	25.11.1967	
Ufton Derek Gilbert	Kent	31.5.1928	
van der Bijl Vintcent Adriaan Pieter	Natal, Middx, Transvaal; *CY 1981*	19.3.1948	
Virgin Roy Thomas	Somerset, Northamptonshire; *CY 1971*	26.8.1939	
Ward William	Hampshire	24.7.1787	30.6.1849
Scorer of the first recorded double-century: 278 for MCC v Norfolk, 1820.			
Wass Thomas George	Nottinghamshire; *CY 1908*	26.12.1873	27.10.1953
Watson Frank	Lancashire	17.9.1898	1.2.1976
Webber Roy	Statistician	23.7.1914	14.11.1962
Weigall Gerald John Villiers	Kent; coach	19.10.1870	17.5.1944
West George H.	Editor of *Wisden* 1880–86	1851	6.10.1896
Wheatley Oswald Stephen CBE	Warwickshire, Glamorgan; *CY 1969*	28.5.1935	
Whitaker Edgar Haddon OBE	Editor of *Wisden* 1940–43	30.8.1908	5.1.1982
Wight Peter Bernard	Somerset; umpire	25.6.1930	31.12.2015
Wilson Elizabeth Rebecca ("Betty")	Australia Women	21.11.1921	22.1.2010
Wilson John Victor	Yorkshire; *CY 1961*	17.1.1921	5.6.2008
Wisden John	Sussex	5.9.1826	5.4.1884
"The Little Wonder"; founder of Wisden Cricketers' Almanack, *1864.*			
Wood Cecil John Burditt	Leicestershire; *CY 1911*	21.11.1875	5.6.1960
Woodcock John Charles OBE	Writer; editor of *Wisden* 1981–86	7.8.1926	
Wooller Wilfred	Glamorgan	20.11.1912	10.3.1997
Wright Graeme Alexander	Editor of *Wisden* 1987–92, 2001–02	23.4.1943	
Wright Levi George	Derbyshire; *CY 1906*	15.1.1862	11.1.1953
Young Douglas Martin	Worcestershire, Gloucestershire	15.4.1924	18.6.1993

CRICKETERS OF THE YEAR, 1889–2016

1889   *Six Great Bowlers of the Year:* J. Briggs, J. J. Ferris, G. A. Lohmann, R. Peel, C. T. B. Turner, S. M. J. Woods.

1890   *Nine Great Batsmen of the Year:* R. Abel, W. Barnes, W. Gunn, L. Hall, R. Henderson, J. M. Read, A. Shrewsbury, F. H. Sugg, A. Ward.

1891   *Five Great Wicketkeepers:* J. McC. Blackham, G. MacGregor, R. Pilling, M. Sherwin, H. Wood.

1892   *Five Great Bowlers:* W. Attewell, J. T. Hearne, F. Martin, A. W. Mold, J. W. Sharpe.

1893   *Five Batsmen of the Year:* H. T. Hewett, L. C. H. Palairet, W. W. Read, S. W. Scott, A. E. Stoddart.

1894   *Five All-Round Cricketers:* G. Giffen, A. Hearne, F. S. Jackson, G. H. S. Trott, E. Wainwright.

1895   *Five Young Batsmen of the Season:* W. Brockwell, J. T. Brown, C. B. Fry, T. W. Hayward, A. C. MacLaren.

1896   W. G. Grace.

1897   *Five Cricketers of the Season:* S. E. Gregory, A. A. Lilley, K. S. Ranjitsinhji, T. Richardson, H. Trumble.

1898   *Five Cricketers of the Year:* F. G. Bull, W. R. Cuttell, N. F. Druce, G. L. Jessop, J. R. Mason.

1899   *Five Great Players of the Season:* W. H. Lockwood, W. Rhodes, W. Storer, C. L. Townsend, A. E. Trott.

1900   *Five Cricketers of the Season:* J. Darling, C. Hill, A. O. Jones, M. A. Noble, Major R. M. Poore.

1901   *Mr R. E. Foster and Four Yorkshiremen:* R. E. Foster, S. Haigh, G. H. Hirst, T. L. Taylor, J. Tunnicliffe.

1902   L. C. Braund, C. P. McGahey, F. Mitchell, W. G. Quaife, J. T. Tyldesley.

1903   W. W. Armstrong, C. J. Burnup, J. Iremonger, J. J. Kelly, V. T. Trumper.

1904   C. Blythe, J. Gunn, A. E. Knight, W. Mead, P. F. Warner.

1905   B. J. T. Bosanquet, E. A. Halliwell, J. Hallows, P. A. Perrin, R. H. Spooner.

1906   D. Denton, W. S. Lees, G. J. Thompson, J. Vine, L. G. Wright.

1907   J. N. Crawford, A. Fielder, E. G. Hayes, K. L. Hutchings, N. A. Knox.

1908   A. W. Hallam, R. O. Schwarz, F. A. Tarrant, A. E. E. Vogler, T. G. Wass.

1909   *Lord Hawke and Four Cricketers of the Year:* W. Brearley, Lord Hawke, J. B. Hobbs, A. Marshal, J. T. Newstead.

1910   W. Bardsley, S. F. Barnes, D. W. Carr, A. P. Day, V. S. Ransford.

1911   H. K. Foster, A. Hartley, C. B. Llewellyn, W. C. Smith, F. E. Woolley.

1912   *Five Members of MCC's team in Australia:* F. R. Foster, J. W. Hearne, S. P. Kinneir, C. P. Mead, H. Strudwick.

1913   *Special Portrait:* John Wisden.

1914   M. W. Booth, G. Gunn, J. W. Hitch, A. E. Relf, Hon. L. H. Tennyson.

1915   J. W. H. T. Douglas, P. G. H. Fender, H. T. W. Hardinge, D. J. Knight, S. G. Smith.

1916–17   No portraits appeared.

1918   *School Bowlers of the Year:* H. L. Calder, J. D. E. Firth, C. H. Gibson, G. A. Rotherham, G. T. S. Stevens.

1919   *Five Public School Cricketers of the Year:* P. W. Adams, A. P. F. Chapman, A. C. Gore, L. P. Hedges, N. E. Partridge.

1920   *Five Batsmen of the Year:* A. Ducat, E. H. Hendren, P. Holmes, H. Sutcliffe, E. Tyldesley.

1921   *Special Portrait:* P. F. Warner.

1922   H. Ashton, J. L. Bryan, J. M. Gregory, C. G. Macartney, E. A. McDonald.

1923   A. W. Carr, A. P. Freeman, C. W. L. Parker, A. C. Russell, A. Sandham.

1924   *Five Bowlers of the Year:* A. E. R. Gilligan, R. Kilner, G. G. Macaulay, C. H. Parkin, M. W. Tate.

1925   R. H. Catterall, J. C. W. MacBryan, H. W. Taylor, R. K. Tyldesley, W. W. Whysall.

1926   *Special Portrait:* J. B. Hobbs.

1927   G. Geary, H. Larwood, J. Mercer, W. A. Oldfield, W. M. Woodfull.

1928   R. C. Blunt, C. Hallows, W. R. Hammond, D. R. Jardine, V. W. C. Jupp.

1929   L. E. G. Ames, G. Duckworth, M. Leyland, S. J. Staples, J. C. White.

1930   E. H. Bowley, K. S. Duleepsinhji, H. G. Owen-Smith, R. W. V. Robins, R. E. S. Wyatt.

1931   D. G. Bradman, C. V. Grimmett, B. H. Lyon, I. A. R. Peebles, M. J. Turnbull.

1932	W. E. Bowes, C. S. Dempster, James Langridge, Nawab of Pataudi sen, H. Verity.
1933	W. E. Astill, F. R. Brown, A. S. Kennedy, C. K. Nayudu, W. Voce.
1934	A. H. Bakewell, G. A. Headley, M. S. Nichols, L. F. Townsend, C. F. Walters.
1935	S. J. McCabe, W. J. O'Reilly, G. A. E. Paine, W. H. Ponsford, C. I. J. Smith.
1936	H. B. Cameron, E. R. T. Holmes, B. Mitchell, D. Smith, A. W. Wellard.
1937	C. J. Barnett, W. H. Copson, A. R. Gover, V. M. Merchant, T. S. Worthington.
1938	T. W. J. Goddard, J. Hardstaff jun, L. Hutton, J. H. Parks, E. Paynter.
1939	H. T. Bartlett, W. A. Brown, D. C. S. Compton, K. Farnes, A. Wood.
1940	L. N. Constantine, W. J. Edrich, W. W. Keeton, A. B. Sellers, D. V. P. Wright.
1941–46	No portraits appeared.
1947	A. V. Bedser, L. B. Fishlock, V. (M. H.) Mankad, T. P. B. Smith, C. Washbrook.
1948	M. P. Donnelly, A. Melville, A. D. Nourse, J. D. Robertson, N. W. D. Yardley.
1949	A. L. Hassett, W. A. Johnston, R. R. Lindwall, A. R. Morris, D. Tallon.
1950	T. E. Bailey, R. O. Jenkins, John Langridge, R. T. Simpson, B. Sutcliffe.
1951	T. G. Evans, S. Ramadhin, A. L. Valentine, E. D. Weekes, F. M. M. Worrell.
1952	R. Appleyard, H. E. Dollery, J. C. Laker, P. B. H. May, E. A. B. Rowan.
1953	H. Gimblett, T. W. Graveney, D. S. Sheppard, W. S. Surridge, F. S. Trueman.
1954	R. N. Harvey, G. A. R. Lock, K. R. Miller, J. H. Wardle, W. Watson.
1955	B. Dooland, Fazal Mahmood, W. E. Hollies, J. B. Statham, G. E. Tribe.
1956	M. C. Cowdrey, D. J. Insole, D. J. McGlew, H. J. Tayfield, F. H. Tyson.
1957	D. Brookes, J. W. Burke, M. J. Hilton, G. R. A. Langley, P. E. Richardson.
1958	P. J. Loader, A. J. McIntyre, O. G. Smith, M. J. Stewart, C. L. Walcott.
1959	H. L. Jackson, R. E. Marshall, C. A. Milton, J. R. Reid, D. Shackleton.
1960	K. F. Barrington, D. B. Carr, R. Illingworth, G. Pullar, M. J. K. Smith.
1961	N. A. T. Adcock, E. R. Dexter, R. A. McLean, R. Subba Row, J. V. Wilson.
1962	W. E. Alley, R. Benaud, A. K. Davidson, W. M. Lawry, N. C. O'Neill.
1963	D. Kenyon, Mushtaq Mohammad, P. H. Parfitt, P. J. Sharpe, F. J. Titmus.
1964	D. B. Close, C. C. Griffith, C. C. Hunte, R. B. Kanhai, G. S. Sobers.
1965	G. Boycott, P. J. Burge, J. A. Flavell, G. D. McKenzie, R. B. Simpson.
1966	K. C. Bland, J. H. Edrich, R. C. Motz, P. M. Pollock, R. G. Pollock.
1967	R. W. Barber, B. L. D'Oliveira, C. Milburn, J. T. Murray, S. M. Nurse.
1968	Asif Iqbal, Hanif Mohammad, K. Higgs, J. M. Parks, Nawab of Pataudi jun.
1969	J. G. Binks, D. M. Green, B. A. Richards, D. L. Underwood, O. S. Wheatley.
1970	B. F. Butcher, A. P. E. Knott, Majid Khan, M. J. Procter, D. J. Shepherd.
1971	J. D. Bond, C. H. Lloyd, B. W. Luckhurst, G. M. Turner, R. T. Virgin.
1972	G. G. Arnold, B. S. Chandrasekhar, L. R. Gibbs, B. Taylor, Zaheer Abbas.
1973	G. S. Chappell, D. K. Lillee, R. A. L. Massie, J. A. Snow, K. R. Stackpole.
1974	K. D. Boyce, B. E. Congdon, K. W. R. Fletcher, R. C. Fredericks, P. J. Sainsbury.
1975	D. L. Amiss, M. H. Denness, N. Gifford, A. W. Greig, A. M. E. Roberts.
1976	I. M. Chappell, P. G. Lee, R. B. McCosker, D. S. Steele, R. A. Woolmer.
1977	J. M. Brearley, C. G. Greenidge, M. A. Holding, I. V. A. Richards, R. W. Taylor.
1978	I. T. Botham, M. Hendrick, A. Jones, K. S. McEwan, R. G. D. Willis.
1979	D. I. Gower, J. K. Lever, C. M. Old, C. T. Radley, J. N. Shepherd.
1980	J. Garner, S. M. Gavaskar, G. A. Gooch, D. W. Randall, B. C. Rose.
1981	K. J. Hughes, R. D. Jackman, A. J. Lamb, C. E. B. Rice, V. A. P. van der Bijl.
1982	T. M. Alderman, A. R. Border, R. J. Hadlee, Javed Miandad, R. W. Marsh.
1983	Imran Khan, T. E. Jesty, A. I. Kallicharran, Kapil Dev, M. D. Marshall.
1984	M. Amarnath, J. V. Coney, J. E. Emburey, M. W. Gatting, C. L. Smith.
1985	M. D. Crowe, H. A. Gomes, G. W. Humpage, J. Simmons, S. Wettimuny.
1986	P. Bainbridge, R. M. Ellison, C. J. McDermott, N. V. Radford, R. T. Robinson.
1987	J. H. Childs, G. A. Hick, D. B. Vengsarkar, C. A. Walsh, J. J. Whitaker.
1988	J. P. Agnew, N. A. Foster, D. P. Hughes, P. M. Roebuck, Salim Malik.
1989	K. J. Barnett, P. J. L. Dujon, P. A. Neale, F. D. Stephenson, S. R. Waugh.
1990	S. J. Cook, D. M. Jones, R. C. Russell, R. A. Smith, M. A. Taylor.
1991	M. A. Atherton, M. Azharuddin, A. R. Butcher, D. L. Haynes, M. E. Waugh.
1992	C. E. L. Ambrose, P. A. J. DeFreitas, A. A. Donald, R. B. Richardson, Waqar Younis.
1993	N. E. Briers, M. D. Moxon, I. D. K. Salisbury, A. J. Stewart, Wasim Akram.
1994	D. C. Boon, I. A. Healy, M. G. Hughes, S. K. Warne, S. L. Watkin.
1995	B. C. Lara, D. E. Malcolm, T. A. Munton, S. J. Rhodes, K. C. Wessels.
1996	D. G. Cork, P. A. de Silva, A. R. C. Fraser, A. Kumble, D. A. Reeve.
1997	S. T. Jayasuriya, Mushtaq Ahmed, Saeed Anwar, P. V. Simmons, S. R. Tendulkar.

1998	M. T. G. Elliott, S. G. Law, G. D. McGrath, M. P. Maynard, G. P. Thorpe.
1999	I. D. Austin, D. Gough, M. Muralitharan, A. Ranatunga, J. N. Rhodes.
2000	C. L. Cairns, R. Dravid, L. Klusener, T. M. Moody, Saqlain Mushtaq.
Cricketers of the Century	D. G. Bradman, G. S. Sobers, J. B. Hobbs, S. K. Warne, I. V. A. Richards.
2001	M. W. Alleyne, M. P. Bicknell, A. R. Caddick, J. L. Langer, D. S. Lehmann.
2002	A. Flower, A. C. Gilchrist, J. N. Gillespie, V. V. S. Laxman, D. R. Martyn.
2003	M. L. Hayden, A. J. Hollioake, N. Hussain, S. M. Pollock, M. P. Vaughan.
2004	C. J. Adams, A. Flintoff, I. J. Harvey, G. Kirsten, G. C. Smith.
2005	A. F. Giles, S. J. Harmison, R. W. T. Key, A. J. Strauss, M. E. Trescothick.
2006	M. J. Hoggard, S. P. Jones, B. Lee, K. P. Pietersen, R. T. Ponting.
2007	P. D. Collingwood, D. P. M. D. Jayawardene, Mohammad Yousuf, M. S. Panesar, M. R. Ramprakash.
2008	I. R. Bell, S. Chanderpaul, O. D. Gibson, R. J. Sidebottom, Zaheer Khan.
2009	J. M. Anderson, M. J. Benkenstein, M. V. Boucher, N. D. McKenzie, S. C. Taylor.
2010	S. C. J. Broad, M. J. Clarke, G. Onions, M. J. Prior, G. P. Swann.
2011	E. J. G. Morgan, C. M. W. Read, Tamim Iqbal, I. J. L. Trott.
2012	T. T. Bresnan, G. Chapple, A. N. Cook, A. Richardson, K. C. Sangakkara.
2013	H. M. Amla, N. R. D. Compton, J. H. Kallis, M. N. Samuels, D. W. Steyn.
2014	S. Dhawan, C. M. Edwards, R. J. Harris, C. J. L. Rogers, J. E. Root.
2015	M. M. Ali, G. S. Ballance, A. Lyth, A. D. Mathews, J. S. Patel.
2016	J. M. Bairstow, B. B. McCullum, S. P. D. Smith, B. A. Stokes, K. S. Williamson.

From 2001 to 2003 the award was made on the basis of all cricket round the world, not just the English season. This ended in 2004 with the start of Wisden's Leading Cricketer in the World award. Sanath Jayasuriya was chosen in 1997 for his influence on the English season, stemming from the 1996 World Cup. In 2011, only four were named after an ICC tribunal investigating the Lord's spot-fixing scandal made the selection of one of the five unsustainable.

CRICKETERS OF THE YEAR: AN ANALYSIS

The special portrait of John Wisden in 1913 marked the 50th anniversary of his retirement as a player – and the 50th edition of the Almanack. Wisden died in 1884. The special portraits of P. F. Warner in 1921 and J. B. Hobbs in 1926 were in addition to their earlier selection as a Cricketer of the Year in 1904 and 1909 respectively. These three special portraits and the Cricketers of the Century in 2000 are excluded from the following analysis.

The five players selected to be Cricketers of the Year for 2016 bring the number chosen since selection began in 1889 to 585. They have been chosen from 40 different teams as follows:

Derbyshire	13	Northants	14	Australians	73	Staffordshire	1
Durham	8	Nottinghamshire	29	South Africans	28	Cheltenham College	1
Essex	24	Somerset	19	West Indians	26	Cranleigh School	1
Glamorgan	12	Surrey	49	New Zealanders	10	Eton College	2
Gloucestershire	17	Sussex	21	Indians	15	Malvern College	1
Hampshire	16	Warwickshire	24	Pakistanis	12	Rugby School	1
Kent	26	Worcestershire	17	Sri Lankans	7	Tonbridge School	1
Lancashire	34	Yorkshire	47	Zimbabweans	1	Univ. Coll. School	1
Leicestershire	8	Oxford Univ.	7	Bangladeshis	1	Uppingham School	1
Middlesex	29	Cambridge Univ.	10	England Women	2	Winchester College	1

Schoolboys were chosen in 1918 and 1919 when first-class cricket was suspended due to war. The total of sides comes to 610 because 25 players played regularly for two teams (England excluded) in the year for which they were chosen.

Types of Players

Of the 585 Cricketers of the Year, 291 are best classified as batsmen, 160 as bowlers, 95 as all-rounders and 39 as wicketkeepers or wicketkeeper-batsmen.

Research: Robert Brooke

PART EIGHT

The Almanack

OFFICIAL BODIES

INTERNATIONAL CRICKET COUNCIL

The ICC are world cricket's governing body. They are responsible for managing the playing conditions and Code of Conduct for international fixtures, expanding the game and organising the major tournaments, including the World Cup and World Twenty20. Their mission statement says the ICC "will lead by providing a world-class environment for international cricket, delivering major events across three formats, providing targeted support to members and promoting the global game".

Ten national governing bodies are currently Full Members of the ICC; full membership qualifies a nation (or geographic area) to play official Test matches. A candidate for full membership must meet a number of playing and administrative criteria, after which elevation is decided by a vote among existing Full Members. There are also currently 38 Associate Members and 57 Affiliate Members.

The ICC were founded in 1909 as the Imperial Cricket Conference by three Foundation Members: England, Australia and South Africa. Other countries (or geographic areas) became Full Members and thus acquired Test status as follows: India, New Zealand and West Indies in 1926, Pakistan in 1952, Sri Lanka in 1981, Zimbabwe in 1992 and Bangladesh in 2000. South Africa ceased to be a member on leaving the Commonwealth in 1961, but were re-elected as a Full Member in 1991.

In 1965, "Imperial" was replaced by "International", and countries from outside the Commonwealth were elected for the first time. The first Associate Members were Ceylon (later Sri Lanka), Fiji and USA. Foundation Members retained a veto over all resolutions. In 1989, the renamed International Cricket Council (rather than "Conference") adopted revised rules, aimed at producing an organisation which could make a larger number of binding decisions, rather than simply make recommendations to national governing bodies. In 1993, the Council, previously administered by MCC, gained their own secretariat and chief executive. The category of Foundation Member was abolished.

In 1997, the Council became an incorporated body, with an executive board, and a president instead of a chairman. The ICC remained at Lord's, with a commercial base in Monaco, until August 2005, when after 96 years they moved to Dubai in the United Arab Emirates, which offered organisational and tax advantages.

In 2014 the ICC board approved a new structure, under which they were led by a chairman again. India, Australia and England took permanent places on both of two key committees, the Executive Committee and the Finance and Commercial Affairs Committee, with two other Full Member representatives also serving on each. But in 2016 steps were taken to dismantle these three's special privileges.

Officers

Chairman: S. V. Manohar. *President:* Zaheer Abbas. *Chief Executive:* D. J. Richardson.

Chairs of Committees – Chief Executives' Committee: D. J. Richardson. *Executive Committee:* D. A. Peever. *Finance and Commercial Affairs:* C. G. Clarke. *Cricket:* A. Kumble. *Audit:* A. Zaidi. *Governance Review:* Nazmul Hassan. *Human Resources and Remuneration:* C. Nenzani. *Development:* S. V. Manohar. *Code of Conduct Commission:* M. J. Beloff QC. *Women's Committee:* C. J. Connor. *Nominations Committee:* S. V. Manohar. *Disputes Resolution Committee:* M. J. Beloff QC. *Anti-Corruption Unit:* Sir Ronnie Flanagan. *ICC Ethics Officer:* P. Nicholson.

ICC Board: The president and chief executive sit on the board *ex officio*. They are joined by S. V. Manohar (India) (*chairman*), G. J. Barclay (New Zealand), W. O. Cameron (West Indies), C. G. Clarke (England), F. Erasmus (Namibia), I. Khwaja (Singapore), T. Mukuhlani (Zimbabwe), Nazmul Hassan (Bangladesh), C. Nenzani (South Africa), D. A. Peever (Australia), Shaharyar Khan (Pakistan), N. Speight (Bermuda). The Sri Lankan representative was to be confirmed.

Chief Executives' Committee: The chief executive, chairman and the chairs of the cricket committee and women's committee sit on this committee *ex officio*. They are joined by the chief executives of the ten Full Member boards and three Associate Member boards: G. D. Campbell (Papua New Guinea), J. A. Cribbin (Hong Kong), A. M. de Silva (Sri Lanka), W. Deutrom (Ireland), T. W. Harrison (England), H. Lorgat (South Africa), M. Muirhead (West Indies), W. Mukondiwa (Zimbabwe), Nizam Uddin Chowdhury (Bangladesh), Subhan Ahmad (Pakistan), J. A. Sutherland (Australia), A. S. Thakur (India), D. J. White (New Zealand).

Cricket Committee: The chief executive and chairman sit on the committee *ex officio*. They are joined by A. Kumble (*chairman*), C. J. Connor, S. J. Davis, D. S. Lehmann, R. S. Madugalle, K. J. O'Brien, K. C. Sangakkara, R. J. Shastri, L. Sivaramakrishnan, J. P. Stephenson, A. J. Strauss, M. A. Taylor, D. J. White.

General Manager – Cricket: G. J. Allardice. *General Manager – Commercial:* D. C. Jamieson. *General Manager – Anti-Corruption Unit:* Y. P. Singh. *Chief Financial Officer:* Faisal Hasnain. *Chief Operating Officer / General Counsel:* I. Higgins. *Head of Media / Communications:* Sami Ul Hasan. *Head of Global Development:* T. L. Anderson. *Head of Internal Audit:* Muhammad Ali.

Membership

Full Members (10): Australia, Bangladesh, England, India, New Zealand, Pakistan, South Africa, Sri Lanka, West Indies and Zimbabwe.

Associate Members* (38): Afghanistan (2001), Argentina (1974), Belgium (2005), Bermuda (1966), Botswana (2005), Canada (1968), Cayman Islands (2002), Denmark (1966), Fiji (1965), France (1998), Germany (1999), Gibraltar (1969), Guernsey (2005), Hong Kong (1969), Ireland (1993), Israel (1974), Italy (1995), Japan (2005), Jersey (2007), Kenya (1981), Kuwait (2005), Malaysia (1967), Namibia (1992), Nepal (1996), Netherlands (1966), Nigeria (2002), Oman (2000), Papua New Guinea (1973), Scotland (1994), Singapore (1974), Suriname (2002), Tanzania (2001), Thailand (2005), Uganda (1998), United Arab Emirates (1990), USA (1965), Vanuatu (1995), Zambia (2003).

Affiliate Members* (57): Austria (1992), Bahamas (1987), Bahrain (2001), Belize (1997), Bhutan (2001), Brazil (2002), Bulgaria (2008), Cameroon (2007), Chile (2002), China (2004), Cook Islands (2000), Costa Rica (2002), Croatia (2001), Cyprus (1999), Czech Republic (2000), Estonia (2008), Falkland Islands (2007), Finland (2000), Gambia (2002), Ghana (2002), Greece (1995), Hungary (2012), Indonesia (2001), Iran (2003), Isle of Man (2004), Lesotho (2001), Luxembourg (1998), Malawi (2003), Maldives (2001), Mali (2005), Malta (1998), Mexico (2004), Morocco (1999), Mozambique (2003), Myanmar (2006), Norway (2000), Panama (2002), Peru (2007), Philippines (2000), Portugal (1996), Qatar (1999), Romania (2013), Russia (2012), Rwanda (2003), St Helena (2001), Samoa (2000), Saudi Arabia (2003), Serbia (2015), Seychelles (2010), Sierra Leone (2002), Slovenia (2005), South Korea (2001), Spain (1992), Swaziland (2007), Sweden (1997), Turkey (2008), Turks & Caicos Islands (2002).

* Year of election shown in parentheses. Switzerland (1985) were removed in 2012 for failing to comply with the ICC's membership criteria; Cuba (2002) and Tonga (2000) in 2013 for failing to demonstrate a suitable administrative structure; and Brunei in 2014. USA, Morocco and Turkey were suspended in 2015.

Full Member The governing body for cricket of a country recognised by the ICC, or nations associated for cricket purposes, or a geographical area, from which representative teams are qualified to play official Test matches.

Associate Member The governing body for cricket of a country recognised by the ICC, or countries associated for cricket purposes, or a geographical area, which does not qualify as a Full Member, but where cricket is firmly established and organised.

Affiliate Member The governing body for cricket of a country recognised by ICC, or countries associated for cricket purposes, or a geographical area (which is not part of one of those already constituted as a Full Member or Associate Member) where the ICC recognises that cricket is played in accordance with the Laws of Cricket.

Addresses

ICC Street 69, Dubai Sports City, Sh Mohammed Bin Zayed Road, PO Box 500 070, Dubai, United Arab Emirates (+971 4382 8800; website www.icc-cricket.com; email enquiry@icc-cricket.com).

Australia Cricket Australia, 60 Jolimont Street, Jolimont, Victoria 3002 (+61 3 9653 9999; website www.cricket.com.au; email penquiries@cricket.com.au).

Bangladesh Bangladesh Cricket Board, Sher-e-Bangla National Cricket Stadium, Mirpur, Dhaka 1216 (+880 2 803 1001; website www.tigercricket.com; email office@bcb-cricket.com).

England England and Wales Cricket Board (see below).

India Board of Control for Cricket in India, Cricket Centre, 4th Floor, Wankhede Stadium, D Road, Churchgate, Mumbai 400 020 (+91 22 2289 8800; website www.bcci.tv; email bcci@vsnl.com).

New Zealand New Zealand Cricket, PO Box 8353, Level 3, 8 Nugent Street, Grafton, Auckland 1023 (+64 9 972 0605; website www.blackcaps.co.nz; email info@nzcricket.org.nz).

Pakistan Pakistan Cricket Board, Gaddafi Stadium, Ferozpur Road, Lahore 54600 (+92 42 3571 7231; website www.pcb.com.pk; email online@pcb.com.pk).

South Africa Cricket South Africa, Wanderers Club, PO Box 55009, 21 North Street, Illovo, Northlands 2116 (+27 11 880 2810; website www.cricket.co.za; email info@cricket.co.za).

Sri Lanka Sri Lanka Cricket, 35 Maitland Place, Colombo 07000 (+94 112 681 601; website www.srilankacricket.lk; email info@srilankacricket.lk).

West Indies West Indies Cricket Board, PO Box 616 W, Factory Road, St John's, Antigua (+1 268 481 2450; website www.windiescricket.com; email wicb@windiescricket.com).

Zimbabwe Zimbabwe Cricket, PO Box 2739, 28 Maiden Drive, Highlands, Harare (+263 4 788 090; website www.zimcricket.org; email info@zimcricket.com).

Associate and Affiliate Members' addresses may be found on the ICC website www.icc-cricket.com

ENGLAND AND WALES CRICKET BOARD

The England and Wales Cricket Board (ECB) became responsible for the administration of all cricket – professional and recreational – in England and Wales in 1997. They took over the functions of the Cricket Council, the Test and County Cricket Board and the National Cricket Association, which had run the game in England and Wales since 1968. In 2005, a new constitution streamlined and modernised the governance of English cricket. The Management Board of 18 directors were replaced by a Board of Directors numbering 12, with three appointed by the first-class counties and two by the county boards. In 2010, this expanded to 14, with the appointment of the ECB's first two women directors.

Officers

President: C. G. Clarke. *Chairman:* C. J. Graves. *Chief Executive Officer:* T. W. Harrison.

Board of Directors: C. G. Clarke, M. V. Fleming, C. J. Graves, T. W. Harrison, Baroness Heyhoe Flint, I. N. Lovett, A. J. Nash, Lord Patel of Bradford, J. B. Pickup, J. Stichbury, R. W. Thompson, J. Wood, P. G. Wright.

Committee Chairs – Executive Committee: T. W. Harrison. *Anti-Corruption Commission for Education, Standards and Security:* J. Stichbury. *Audit, Risk and Governance:* I. N. Lovett. *Commercial and Communications:* R. W. Thompson. *Cricket:* P. G. Wright. *Discipline:* G. Elias QC. *Recreational Assembly:* J. B. Pickup. *Remuneration:* C. J. Graves.

Director, England Cricket: A. J. Strauss. *Chief Operating Officer:* G. Hollins. *Director, Media and Communications:* C. Haynes. *Director, Events:* S. Elworthy. *Director, England Cricket Operations:* J. D. Carr. *Director, Participation:* M. Dwyer. *Commercial Director:* S. Patel. *People Director:* R. Ranganathan. *Director, England Women's Cricket:* C. J. Connor. *Head of Information Technology:* D. Smith. *Head of Corporate Communications:* A. J. Walpole. *Head of Operations (First-class cricket):* A. Fordham. *Cricket Operations Manager (Non-first-class cricket):* P. Bedford. *National Selector:* J. J. Whitaker. *Other Selectors:* A. R. C. Fraser and M. Newell.

ECB: Lord's Ground, London NW8 8QZ (020 7432 1200; website www.ecb.co.uk).

THE MARYLEBONE CRICKET CLUB

The Marylebone Cricket Club evolved out of the White Conduit Club in 1787, when Thomas Lord laid out his first ground in Dorset Square. Their members revised the Laws in 1788 and gradually took responsibility for cricket throughout the world. However, they relinquished control of the game in the UK in 1968, and the International Cricket Council finally established their own secretariat in 1993. MCC still own Lord's and remain the guardian of the Laws. They call themselves "a private club with a public function" and aim to support cricket everywhere, especially at grassroots level and in countries where the game is least developed.

Patron: HER MAJESTY THE QUEEN

Officers

President: 2015–16 – R. D. V. Knight. *Club Chairman:* G. M. N. Corbett. *Treasurer:* R. S. Leigh. *Trustees:* P. A. B. Beecroft, A. N. W. Beeson, M. G. Griffith. *Hon. Life Vice-Presidents:* Lord Bramall, E. R. Dexter, G. H. G. Doggart, D. J. Insole, A. R. Lewis, Sir Oliver Popplewell, D. R. W. Silk, M. O. C. Sturt, J. J. Warr, J. C. Woodcock.

Chief Executive and Secretary: D. M. Brewer. *Deputy Secretary:* C. Maynard. *Assistant Secretaries – Cricket:* J. P. Stephenson. *Estates:* R. J. Ebdon. *Finance:* A. D. Cameron. *Legal:* H. A-M. Roper-Curzon. *Commercial:* J. D. Robinson.

MCC Committee: A. J. Alt, I. S. Duncan, M. W. Gatting, V. K. Griffiths, C. M. Gupte, C. J. Guyver, S. P. Hughes, G. W. Jones, P. L. O. Leaver, G. T. E. Monkhouse, N. E. J. Pocock, G. J. Toogood. The president, club chairman, treasurer and committee chairmen are also on the committee.

Chairmen of Committees – Arts and Library: D. J. C. Faber. *Cricket:* M. V. Fleming. *Estates:* C. J. Maber. *Finance:* R. S. Leigh. *Membership and General Purposes:* N. M. Peters. *World Cricket:* J. M. Brearley.

MCC: The Chief Executive and Secretary, Lord's Ground, London NW8 8QN (020 7616 8500; email reception@mcc.org.uk; website www.lords.org. Tickets 020 7432 1000; email ticketing@mcc.org.uk).

PROFESSIONAL CRICKETERS' ASSOCIATION

The Professional Cricketers' Association were formed in 1967 (as the Cricketers' Association) to be the collective voice of first-class professional players, and enhance and protect their interests. During the 1970s, they succeeded in establishing pension schemes and a minimum wage. In recent years their strong commercial operations and greater funding from the ECB have increased their services to current and past players, including education, legal, financial and benevolent help. In 2011, these services were extended to England's women cricketers.

President: A. Flintoff. *Chairman:* M. A. Wallace. *President – Benevolent Fund:* D. A. Graveney. *Non-Executive Chairman:* M. B. H. Wheeler. *Non-Executive Director:* P. G. Read. *Chief Executive:* D. A. Leatherdale. *Assistant Chief Executive:* J. D. Ratcliffe. *Commercial Director:* J. M. Grave. *Financial Director:* P. Garrett. *Business Development Manager:* G. M. Hamilton. *Commercial Partnerships Manager:* A. Phipps. *Head of Events and Fundraising:* E. Lewis. *Head of Team England Commercial Partnerships:* E. M. Reid. *Ambassador Commercial Manager:* E. Caldwell. *Social Media Executive:* L. Reynolds. *Member Services Manager:* A. Prosser. *National Personal Development Manager:* I. J. Thomas.

PCA: *London Office* – The Laker Stand, The Oval, Kennington, London SE11 5SS (0207 449 4226; email 903club@thepca.co.uk; website www.thepca.co.uk). *Birmingham Office* – Box 108–9, R. E. S. Wyatt Stand, Warwickshire CCC, Edgbaston, Birmingham B5 7QU.

CRIME AND PUNISHMENT

ICC Code of Conduct – Breaches and Penalties in 2014-15 to 2015-16

D. A. Warner   Australia v India, one-day international at Melbourne.
Aggressive confrontation with batsman R. G. Sharma. Fined 50% of match fee by A. J. Pycroft.

D. J. G. Sammy   West Indies v Ireland, World Cup match at Nelson.
Obscene language while batting. Fined 30% of match fee by B. C. Broad.

J. F. Mooney   Ireland v West Indies, World Cup match at Nelson.
Obscene language when fielder failed to prevent a six. Fined 30% of match fee by B. C. Broad.

D. M. Bravo   West Indies v Pakistan, World Cup match at Christchurch.
Obscene language while batting. Warned and reprimanded by D. C. Boon.

T. L. Chatara   Zimbabwe v West Indies, World Cup match at Canberra.
Bowled consecutive high full tosses at C. H. Gayle. Warned and reprimanded by R. S. Mahanama.

K. J. O'Brien   Ireland v United Arab Emirates, World Cup match at Brisbane.
Demonstrative dissent when umpire called wide. Fined 30% of match fee by R. S. Madugalle.

R. A. S. Lakmal   Sri Lanka v England, World Cup match at Wellington.
Bowled two waist-high full tosses in the final over. Fined 30% of match fee by D. C. Boon.

S. R. Watson   Australia v Pakistan, World Cup quarter-final at Adelaide.
Verbally engaged bowler Wahab Riaz despite warning. Fined 15% of match fee by R. S. Madugalle.

Wahab Riaz   Pakistan v Australia, World Cup quarter-final at Adelaide.
Obscene language after being provoked by S. R. Watson. Fined 50% of match fee by R. S. Madugalle.

Wahab Riaz   Pakistan v Bangladesh, First Test at Khulna.
Halted play to confront batsman Shakib Al Hasan. Fined 30% of match fee by J. J. Crowe.

Shakib Al Hasan   Bangladesh v Pakistan, First Test at Khulna.
Halted play to confront bowler Wahab Riaz. Fined 30% of match fee by J. J. Crowe.

Imran Khan, sen.   Pakistan v Bangladesh, Second Test at Mirpur.
Aggressive send-off to batsman Tamim Iqbal. Warned and reprimanded by J. J. Crowe.

Mustafizur Rahman   Bangladesh v India, first one-day international at Mirpur.
Avoidable physical contact with batsman M. S. Dhoni. Fined 50% of match fee by A. J. Pycroft.

M. S. Dhoni   India v Bangladesh, first one-day international at Mirpur.
Inappropriate deliberate contact with Mustafizur Rahman. Fined 75% of match fee by A. J. Pycroft.

R. R. Rossouw   South Africa v Bangladesh, second one-day international at Mirpur.
Brushed shoulders with dismissed batsman Tamim Iqbal. Fined 50% of match fee by D. C. Boon.

Q. de Kock   South Africa v Bangladesh, First Test at Chittagong.
Brushed shoulders with Tamim Iqbal as they left the field. Fined 75% of match fee by B. C. Broad.

H. D. R. L. Thirimanne   Sri Lanka v India, Second Test at Colombo (PSO).
Stood ground shaking his head when given caught behind. Fined 30% of match fee by A. J. Pycroft.

I. Sharma   India v Sri Lanka, Second Test at Colombo (PSO).
Inappropriate language on dismissing Thirimanne. Fined 15% of match fee by A. J. Pycroft.

I. Sharma   India v Sri Lanka, Second Test at Colombo (PSO).
Yelled loudly at L. D. Chandimal after dismissing him. Fined 50% of match fee by A. J. Pycroft.

K. T. G. D. Prasad   Sri Lanka v India, Third Test at Colombo (SSC).
Refused to quit altercation; disrespectful to I. Sharma. Fined 50% of match fee by A. J. Pycroft.

H. D. R. L. Thirimanne   Sri Lanka v India, Third Test at Colombo (SSC).
Refused to quit altercation; disrespectful to I. Sharma. Fined 50% of match fee by A. J. Pycroft.

L. D. Chandimal   Sri Lanka v India, Third Test at Colombo (SSC).
Ran at I. Sharma and made deliberate physical contact. Suspended for one game by A. J. Pycroft.

I. Sharma   India v Sri Lanka, Third Test at Colombo (SSC).
Yelled at W. U. Tharanga on dismissing him. Third offence: suspended for one Test by A. J. Pycroft.

V. Phadke (team manager)   India v South Africa, first one-day international at Kanpur.
Criticised umpires' performance in this and in first T20I. Fined 40% of match fee by B. C. Broad.

F. du Plessis   South Africa v India, fourth one-day international at Chennai.
Obvious dissent when given out caught behind. Fined 15% of match fee by B. C. Broad.

Sikandar Raza   Zimbabwe v Bangladesh, first one-day international at Mirpur.
Delayed and shook his head when given out caught behind. Fined 15% of match fee by J. Srinath.

M. A. Starc   Australia v New Zealand, First Test at Brisbane.
Threw ball dangerously near batsman M. D. Craig. Fined 50% of match fee by R. S. Mahanama.

M. Vijay   India v South Africa, Fourth Test at Delhi.
Pointed at arm-guard when given out caught behind. Fined 30% of match fee by J. J. Crowe.

S. C. J. Broad   England v South Africa, Second Test at Cape Town.
Yelled at umpire after warning when he kicked pitch. Fined 30% of match fee by R. S. Madugalle.

Dawlat Zadran   Afghanistan v Zimbabwe, fourth one-day international at Sharjah.
Clear send-off to batsman A. G. Cremer. Fined 15% of match fee by D. T. Jukes.

Mohammad Shahzad   Afghanistan v Zimbabwe, first Twenty20 international at Sharjah.
Excessive celebration after dismissal of H. Masakadza. Fined 15% of match fee by D. T. Jukes.

R. J. W. Topley   England v South Africa, first Twenty20 international at Cape Town.
Smashed stumps after failing to prevent winning runs. Officially reprimanded by A. J. Pycroft.

*Details of these and six further breaches which took place in Associate Member or Under-19 matches
may be found on the ICC website (www.icc-cricket.com). There were also four breaches in women's
internationals in 2015.*

*Under ICC regulations on minor over-rate offences, players are fined 10% of their match fee for
every over their side fails to bowl in the allotted time, with the captain fined double that amount.
There were 12 such instances in this period, excluding one in the women's Ashes Test:*

G. J. Bailey/Australia v India, ODI at Melbourne, 20%/10%, A. J. Pycroft.
  Bailey suspended for one ODI as it was a second offence within 12 months.

A. B. de Villiers/South Africa v India, World Cup at Melbourne, 20%/10%, J. J. Crowe.

P. L. Mommsen/Scotland v Afghanistan, WC at Dunedin, 20%/10%, D. C. Boon.

Mashrafe bin Mortaza/Bangladesh v England, WC at Adelaide, 40%/20%, R. S. Madugalle.

Mashrafe bin Mortaza/Bangladesh v India, WC q-f at Melbourne, 40%/20%, R. S. Mahanama.
  Mortaza suspended for one ODI as it was his second offence in the tournament.

Misbah-ul-Haq/Pakistan v Bangladesh, 2nd Test at Mirpur, 40%/20%, J. J. Crowe.

E. Chigumbura/Zimbabwe v Pakistan, 1st ODI at Lahore, team fined 40%, R. S. Mahanama.
  *Chigumbura suspended for two ODIs as Zimbabwe were three overs short. The ICC did not send
officials for this series, so the referee was the PCB's Azhar Khan, but the disciplinary measures had
to be confirmed by Mahanama.*

A. D. Mathews/Sri Lanka v Pakistan, 2nd Test at Colombo (PSO), 40%/20%, B. C. Broad.

A. N. Cook/England v Australia, 5th Test at The Oval, 40%/20%, J. J. Crowe.

A. B. de Villiers/South Africa v India, 1st ODI at Kanpur, 40%/20%, B. C. Broad.

J. O. Holder/West Indies v Sri Lanka, 1st ODI at Colombo (RPS), 40%/20%, D. C. Boon.
  Holder suspended for one ODI as it was a second offence within 12 months.

J. O. Holder/West Indies v Australia at Hobart, 1st Test at Hobart, 60%/30%, B. C. Broad.

INTERNATIONAL UMPIRES' PANELS

In 1993, the ICC formed an international umpires' panel, containing at least two officials from each Full Member. A third-country umpire from this panel stood with a home umpire, not necessarily from the panel, in every Test from February 1994 onwards. In March 2002, an elite panel was appointed: two elite umpires – both independent – were to stand in all Tests from April 2002, and at least one in every one-day international, where one home umpire was allowed. A supporting panel of international umpires was created to provide cover at peak times in the Test schedule, and to provide a second umpire in one-day internationals. The ICC also appointed specialist third umpires to give rulings from TV replays. The panels are sponsored by Emirates Airlines.

At the start of 2016, the following umpires were on the elite panel: Aleem Dar (Pakistan), H. D. P. K. Dharmasena (Sri Lanka), M. Erasmus (South Africa), C. B. Gaffaney (New Zealand), I. J. Gould (England), R. K. Illingworth (England), R. A. Kettleborough (England), N. J. Llong (England), B. N. J. Oxenford (Australia), S. Ravi (India), P. R. Reiffel (Australia) and R. J. Tucker (Australia). Gaffaney and Ravi replaced B. F. Bowden (New Zealand) and J. S. Davis (Australia).

The international panel consisted of Ahsan Raza (Pakistan), R. J. Bailey (England), B. F. Bowden (New Zealand), J. D. Cloete (South Africa), Enamul Haque (Bangladesh), S. D. Fry (Australia), S. George (South Africa), M. A. Gough (England), V. A. Kulkarni (India), R. E. J. Martinesz (Sri Lanka), T. J. Matibiri (Zimbabwe), P. J. Nero (West Indies), R. S. A. Palliyaguruge (Sri Lanka), C. Shamshuddin (India), Sharfuddoula (Bangladesh), Shozab Raza (Pakistan), R. B. Tiffin (Zimbabwe), D. J. Walker (New Zealand), J. D. Ward (Australia) and J. S. Wilson (West Indies).

The third umpires were Ahmed Shahab (Pakistan), Anisur Rahman (Bangladesh), G. O. Brathwaite (West Indies), A. K. Chowdhury (India), N. Duguid (West Indies), A. T. Holdstock (South Africa), P. D. Jones (New Zealand), M. D. Martell (Australia), C. K. Nandan (India), R. T. Robinson (England), L. Rusere (Zimbabwe), P. Wilson (Australia) and R. R. Wimalasiri (Sri Lanka).

There is also an Associate and Affiliate international umpires' panel, consisting of S. N. Bandekar (USA), K. Cross (New Zealand), D. A. Haggo (Scotland), M. Hawthorne (Ireland), A. W. Louw (Namibia), N. Morrison (Vanuatu), D. Odhiambo (Kenya), B. B. Pradhan (Nepal), S. S. Prasad (Singapore), I. N. Ramage (Scotland) and C. Young (Cayman Islands).

ICC REFEREES' PANEL

In 1991, the ICC formed a panel of referees to enforce their Code of Conduct for Tests and one-day internationals, to impose penalties for slow over-rates, breaches of the Code and other ICC regulations, and to support the umpires in upholding the conduct of the game. In March 2002, the ICC launched an elite panel of referees, on full-time contracts, to act as their independent representatives in all international cricket. The panel is sponsored by Emirates Airlines.

At the start of 2016, the panel consisted of D. C. Boon (Australia), B. C. Broad (England), J. J. Crowe (New Zealand), R. S. Madugalle (Sri Lanka), A. J. Pycroft (Zimbabwe), R. B. Richardson (West Indies) and J. Srinath (India). Richardson had replaced R. S. Mahanama (Sri Lanka) at the start of the year.

A further panel of regional referees, covering East Asia–Pacific, Africa, Europe, Asia and the Americas, consisted of S. R. Bernard (Australia), D. Govindjee (South Africa), D. T. Jukes (England) and G. F. Labrooy (Sri Lanka).

ENGLISH UMPIRES FOR 2016

First-class: R. J. Bailey, N. L. Bainton, P. K. Baldwin, M. Burns, N. G. B. Cook, N. G. C. Cowley, J. H. Evans, R. Evans, S. C. Gale, S. A. Garratt, M. A. Gough, I. J. Gould, P. J. Hartley, R. K. Illingworth, R. A. Kettleborough, N. J. Llong, G. D. Lloyd, J. W. Lloyds, N. A. Mallender, D. J. Millns, S. J. O'Shaughnessy, R. T. Robinson, M. J. Saggers, B. V. Taylor, A. G. Wharf. *Reserves:* I. D. Blackwell, B. J. Debenham, T. Lungley, P. R. Pollard, R. J. Warren, C. M. Watts.

Minor Counties: R. G. B. Allen, J. Attridge, J. S. Beckwith, S. F. Bishopp, J. R. Burn, G. I. Callaway, K. Coburn, R. G. Eagleton, M. T. Ennis, A. H. Forward, D. J. Gower, S. Green, N. J. Hall, R. C. Hampshire, A. C. Harris, Hasan Adnan, I. L. Herbert, A. Hicks, N. Kent, I. P. Laurence, S. E. Lavis, S. J. Malone, P. W. Matten, R. P. Medland, J. D. Middlebrook, Naeem Ashraf, R. J. Newham, P. D. Nicholls, R. Parker, D. N. Pedley, N. Pratt, D. Price, M. Qureshi, S. J. Ross, J. R. Tomsett, D. M. Warburton, I. G. Warne, M. D. Watton, A. J. Wheeler, R. A. White.

THE DUCKWORTH/LEWIS/STERN METHOD

In 1997, the ECB's one-day competitions adopted a new method to revise targets in interrupted games, devised by Frank Duckworth of the Royal Statistical Society and Tony Lewis of the University of the West of England. The method was gradually taken up by other countries and, in 1999, the ICC decided to incorporate it into the standard playing conditions for one-day internationals.

The system aims to preserve any advantage that one team has established before the interruption. It uses the idea that teams have two resources from which they make runs – an allocated number of overs, and ten wickets. It also takes into account when the interruption occurs, because of the different scoring-rates typical of different stages of an innings. Traditional run-rate calculations relied only on the overs available, and ignored wickets lost.

It uses one table with 50 rows, covering matches of up to 50 overs, and ten columns, from nought to nine wickets down. Each figure gives the percentage of the total runs that would, on average, be scored with a certain number of overs left and wickets lost. If a match is shortened before it begins, to, say, 33 overs a side, the figure for 33 overs and ten wickets remaining would be the starting point.

If overs are lost, the table is used to calculate the percentage of runs the team would be expected to score in those missing overs. This is obtained by reading the figure for the number of overs left, and wickets down, when play stops, and subtracting the figure for the number of overs left when it resumes. If the delay occurs between innings, and the second team's allocation of overs is reduced, then their target is obtained by calculating the appropriate percentage for the reduced number of overs with all ten wickets standing. For instance, if the second team's innings halves from 50 overs to 25, the table shows that they still have 66.5% of their resources left, so have to beat two-thirds of the first team's total, rather than half. If the first innings is complete and the second innings interrupted or prematurely terminated, the score to beat is reduced by the percentage of the innings lost.

The version known as the "Professional Edition" was introduced into one-day internationals from 2003, and subsequently into most national one-day competitions. Using a more advanced mathematical formula (it is entirely computerised), it adjusts the tables to allow for the different scoring-rates that emerge in matches with above-average first-innings scores. In 2014, analysis by Steven Stern of the Queensland University of Technology, responsible for the method after Duckworth and Lewis retired, indicated further modification was needed. The Duckworth/Lewis/Stern method is now used in all one-day and Twenty20 internationals, as well as most national competitions. The original "Standard Edition" is used where computers are unavailable, and at lower levels of the game.

The system also covers first-innings interruptions, multiple interruptions and innings ended by rain. The tables are revised slightly every two years, taking account of changing scoring-rates; the average total in a 50-over international is now just under 249 (up from 225 in 1999).

In the World Cup semi-final between South Africa and New Zealand at Auckland in March 2015, South Africa were 216 for three from 38 overs when seven overs were lost to rain; after the innings resumed, they finished on 281. With three wickets down, they used only 85.15%. By contrast, New Zealand's 43-over chase constituted 90% of the resources of a full innings. Their revised target was determined by multiplying South Africa's total, 281, by 90% divided by 85.15% and adding one run: 281 x (90/85.15) + 1 = 298. New Zealand scored 299 for six in 42.5 overs to win, with a six off the penultimate delivery. Had South Africa been two down at the interruption, the lost overs would have constituted a higher percentage of their scoring resources; the revised target would have been 301 and New Zealand would have needed two more runs off the final ball.

A similar system, usually known as the VJD method, is used in some domestic matches in India. It was devised by V. Jayadevan, a civil engineer from Kerala.

POWERPLAYS

In one-day and Twenty20 internationals, two semi-circles of 30-yard (27.43 metres) radius are drawn on the field behind each set of stumps, joined by straight lines parallel to the pitch.

At the instant of delivery in the first ten overs of an uninterrupted one-day international innings (the first six overs in a Twenty20 international), only two fielders may be positioned outside this 30-yard area. During the next 30 overs (11–40), no more than four fielders may be stationed outside the 30-yard area; and in the final ten overs, no more than five. (In Twenty20 internationals, no more than five may be positioned outside the area for the last 14 overs.) In matches affected by the weather, the number of overs in each powerplay stage is reduced in proportion to the overall reduction of overs.

In July 2015, the one-day international requirement for two close fielders in the first ten overs, and the five-over batting powerplay, to be claimed between the 11th and 40th overs, was abolished.

MEETINGS AND DECISIONS IN 2015

ECB BROADCASTING DEAL

On January 8, the England and Wales Cricket Board and Sky Sports extended their current agreement, running from 2014 to 2017, for a further two years to 2019. This covered all England home games, some women's and England Lions matches, and at least 60 days of domestic cricket each summer.

ECB BOARD

On January 13, the ECB completed a structure and strategy meeting with representatives of the first-class counties and MCC. The new chief executive, Tom Harrison, also attended. Constitutional changes would be put to the 41 ECB members in writing; should they be approved, the meeting recommended the nomination of Giles Clarke, the current chairman, to the new role of ECB president, to serve from the AGM in May.

The following day, the ECB invited clubs to apply for the England and Wales Cricket Trust Small Grant Scheme (sponsored by Waitrose) through their local county board. This scheme, which topped up an existing fund, aimed to help clubs through grants of up to £4,000 to improve facilities. Waitrose had pledged £100 for every four or six scored by England, England Women, England Lions and England Under-19 in the summer of 2014 (Gary Ballance was the England team's biggest contributor).

ICC BOARD

The ICC Board met in Dubai on January 28, and finalised the 2015 World Cup's playing conditions. They reinstated the use of an eliminator over for a tied final, and ruled that captains should be suspended only for over-rate offences during the competition; prior offences would be carried on to the next bilateral series.

The board agreed Afghanistan and Ireland should join the ten Test sides in the qualification system for the 2019 World Cup. The top eight in the ODI rankings on September 30, 2017, would go straight through; the bottom four would play in a World Cup Qualifier to determine the last two teams. Afghanistan and Ireland withdrew from the one-day World Cricket League for leading Associates and Affiliates; in their place, Kenya and Nepal joined Hong Kong, Namibia, the Netherlands, Papua New Guinea, Scotland and the United Arab Emirates. Promotion and relegation would be determined by a play-off between the lowest-ranked Associate and the winners of the World Cricket League. Ireland and Afghanistan remained in the first-class Intercontinental Cup.

The board considered player safety after the death of Australia's Phillip Hughes, and were briefed on a new British Standard for helmets.

Dates and venues were approved for Under-19 World Cups in Bangladesh in 2016 and New Zealand in 2018, the World Twenty20 in India in 2016, the Champions Trophy and the Women's World Cup, both in England in 2017, the Women's World Twenty20 in the West Indies in 2018, and the next World Cup, in England in 2019.

It was explained that the Anti-Corruption Unit chairman Sir Ronnie Flanagan had allowed Mohammad Amir to return to domestic cricket before his five-year ban expired in September 2015, with the approval of the ICC and Pakistan Cricket Board. Flanagan was satisfied that Amir had fully disclosed his role in the spot-fixing affair, shown remorse, and continued to cooperate with the ACU's work.

ICC membership criteria were revised: a member need no longer be the sole governing body in their jurisdiction, but only one would be recognised in any territory. The USA Cricket Association would be questioned on their compliance with the ICC constitution and membership criteria.

The annual anti-doping report stated that, despite a 17% increase in drug testing in 2014, none of the 1,210 tests across domestic and international cricket revealed any violation (though there were two resulting from domestic tests in late 2013).

ECB BOARD

On February 24, the ECB announced that the board's 41 members had approved the constitutional changes proposed in January, and Yorkshire chairman Colin Graves had been elected unopposed as chairman to succeed Giles Clarke for a five-year term from the AGM in May, when Clarke became president.

ICC BOARD

The ICC Board met in Dubai on April 15–16, and congratulated Australia and New Zealand on their staging of the World Cup, which attracted more than a million spectators and was broadcast across 220 territories.

After the World Cup, on April 1, Mustafa Kamal had stood down as president "on personal grounds". This followed his criticism of an umpiring decision in a match between India and Bangladesh. In his resignation letter, he had offered his apologies to all associated with the ICC and said he had no complaints. The board accepted his resignation but ruled that no stand-in would be appointed, as his term expired in June.

The board were concerned that the Sri Lankan government had appointed an interim committee to run Sri Lanka Cricket, apparently breaching the ICC's requirement for free and fair elections within member boards, and sought an explanation from the sports minister. They were not satisfied that the USA Cricket Association complied with membership criteria, and appointed a task force led by chief executive David Richardson to visit the USA.

Procedures on suspect bowling actions were revised: the turnaround from a bowler being reported to the test results being announced was reduced from 35 to 24 days.

The board noted the achievements of the late Richie Benaud; approved a rankings system for women's cricket based on all three formats; provisionally approved Nepal to host the Under-19 World Cup Qualifier in 2015; ratified the appointment of former UN and International Criminal Court investigator Peter Nicholson as the ICC's independent ethics officer; received reports on anti-corruption and anti-doping; and approved the 2014 accounts.

MCC ANNUAL GENERAL MEETING

The 228th AGM of the Marylebone Cricket Club was held at Lord's on May 6, with president David Morgan in the chair. He announced that his successor, from October, would be Roger Knight, the former Surrey captain who served as MCC secretary and chief executive between 1994 and 2006. The meeting also approved the appointment of Gerald Corbett to succeed Oliver Stocken as chairman.

Members voted for the first phase of the redevelopment at Lord's. The demolition of the current Warner Stand would start after a one-day game between England and Australia in September, and the new stand should be completed by April 2017, with some seating available in 2016. It was agreed that the legroom in the new Tavern and Allen stands should be no less than 900mm, as for the Warner Stand. The committee were directed to commission a review of the development plans.

Membership on December 31, 2014, totalled 23,409, made up of 17,895 full members, 5,010 associate members, 337 honorary members, 72 senior members and 95 out-match members. There were 11,340 candidates awaiting election to full membership; 430 vacancies arose in 2014.

ENGLAND DIRECTOR AND COACH

On May 9, former England captain Andrew Strauss was appointed director of England cricket to succeed Paul Downton, sacked in April after a disappointing World Cup.

On the same day, the ECB confirmed that Peter Moores had left his role as England head coach; his second spell in the job had lasted just over a year. Assistant coach Paul Farbrace took charge of the team for their series with New Zealand in May and June.

On May 26, the ECB named New South Wales's Trevor Bayliss as Moores's successor, to take over ahead of the Ashes in July. Bayliss had coached Sri Lanka from 2007 to 2011, and Strauss emphasised his expertise in the game's shorter forms.

ICC CRICKET COMMITTEE

The ICC Cricket Committee met in Mumbai on May 15–16 to discuss issues and make recommendations to the annual conference in June.

After a report from MCC on the latest first-class day/night match with the county champions at Abu Dhabi, and an inspection of the pink balls used, the committee recommended that member countries should look at opportunities to extend Tests into the evening. They also discussed four-day Test cricket, though they continued to prefer five.

Amid concern that the balance between bat and ball had shifted too far towards batsmen, the committee agreed to provide data on the size of bats to MCC ahead of the redrafting of the Laws in 2017. They reiterated that boundaries at international venues should be set at the maximum for each ground, and agreed to consult with ball manufacturers on whether the size and durability of the white-ball seam could be altered.

Reviewing ODI playing conditions, the committee were encouraged by some of the attacking captaincy in the World Cup, but felt that, towards the end of an innings, bowlers and fielding captains had limited defensive options. They recommended dropping the requirement for two compulsory catchers in the first ten overs; abolishing the batting powerplay; and allowing five (rather than four) fielders outside the circle in the last ten overs. This would mean two fielders outside the 30-yard circle for the first ten, four for the next 30, and five for the last ten.

The committee also recommended that all no-balls in ODIs and T20Is, not just foot-fault no-balls, should result in a free hit. They asked the ICC to investigate quicker methods of reviewing wicket-taking deliveries as possible no-balls, to reduce delays.

The committee were concerned at an increase in send-offs when a batsman was out. They encouraged referees to use suspensions rather than fines for repeat offenders, and for more serious offences such as physical contact, and strongly supported suspending captains for over-rate breaches.

They discussed the performance of the Decision Review System and the use of technology in umpiring; the ICC had engaged engineers from the Field Intelligence Lab at the Massachusetts Institute of Technology to oversee testing of the technologies.

The committee were pleased by a reduction in the number of international bowlers with suspect actions. Dr Craig Ranson presented the results of testing over the past year: five ICC-accredited centres had examined 100 bowlers in nine months. He also addressed helmet safety and the new British Standard. The committee did not believe they should be mandatory at international level, but strongly recommended that all helmets worn by international players should meet this standard.

ICC ANNUAL CONFERENCE

The ICC annual conference took place in Bridgetown on June 22–26.

Former Pakistan captain Zaheer Abbas was appointed ICC president for 2015-16. It was Pakistan's turn to nominate, and their earlier candidate, journalist and former PCB president Najam Sethi, had withdrawn so the ICC could adopt a policy of keeping the now ceremonial role for "iconic former international cricketers".

The ICC approved Serbia as an Affiliate Member, but removed Brunei and suspended Morocco and Turkey from affiliate membership. They also suspended the associate membership of the USA Cricket Association because of "significant concerns about its governance, finance, reputation and cricketing activities". Though USACA would lose ICC funding, the USA would be allowed to play in the imminent World Twenty20 Qualifier in Ireland and Scotland, and an Americas Under-19 Championship in Bermuda. The ICC chief executive David Richardson would monitor their efforts to satisfy the reinstatement conditions.

The board noted amendments to the playing conditions, recommended by the Cricket Committee in May and approved by the Chief Executives' Committee earlier in the week. From July 5, there would be no compulsory catchers in the first ten overs of ODIs, five fielders were allowed outside the circle in the last ten, and the batting powerplay was abolished; in ODIs and T20Is, all no-balls (not just foot faults) would bring a free hit.

The board confirmed that the ICC's Anti-Corruption Unit should be the focal point in the battle against the global risks of corruption, and needed greater coordination with national anti-corruption bodies. All Full Members and Associates with ODI/T20I status were to adopt an anti-corruption code within six months, and members were urged to lobby for the criminalisation of match-fixing in their countries and form stronger relationships with law enforcement.

In international cricket, the board noted the emergence of elite umpires from a wider range of countries; good pitches and good behaviour, particularly in the recent England–New Zealand series; and strong home performances from Bangladesh, who had defeated Pakistan and India in one-day series. The PCB gave a presentation on Zimbabwe's recent tour of Pakistan. A new five-year strategy was designed to provide a world-class environment for cricket, protect the game's integrity, deliver successful major events and improve the quality and reach of international cricket.

MCC WORLD CRICKET COMMITTEE

The MCC World Cricket Committee met at Lord's on July 13–14, and discussed moves to make cricket an Olympic sport with ECB chairman Colin Graves and chief executive Tom Harrison. In addition to attracting new audiences and boosting developing cricket nations, inclusion could unlock investment in Associate and Affiliate countries, as government funding was often linked to a sport's Olympic status. With three ICC events in every four-year cycle, cricket could enter the Olympics without detracting from those tournaments.

The committee asked the ICC to reconsider their decision to limit the 2019 and 2023 World Cups to ten teams, a retrograde step damaging cricket's developing nations, and argued for a 12-team World Cup following a preliminary qualification round for lower-ranked Full Members and top Associates.

The committee heard about plans for an Australian domestic women's Twenty20 tournament, the Women's Big Bash League, and were pleased that MCC were interested in co-hosting a team with Middlesex in the English Women's Super League.

ICC chairman N. Srinivasan took questions on the ICC's new administrative and financial arrangements, declining Test attendances and the Decision Review System. The committee urged the ICC to investigate why people are not watching Tests in certain countries, and to consider subsidising tickets in these countries. They also asked Srinivasan, a DRS sceptic, to implement the system in all international cricket should the Massachusetts Institute of Technology's research confirm its accuracy.

The committee did not favour four-day Tests as an answer to falling attendance; a changed format (with longer hours) could not be applied universally, as conditions and hours of daylight vary greatly between Test nations, and there could be an extra strain on players' bodies. They felt day/night Test cricket was a better way to arrest the decline, and praised Australia and New Zealand, who would play the first pink-ball Test in November.

They called on the ICC to create a working group to consider the lack of context for international cricket away from iconic series such as the Ashes, and to debate the shape of the game after 2019; they believed this should include a World Test League, perhaps extending to ODIs and T20Is.

With regard to the balance between bat and ball, reasons for more sixes being hit in modern cricket included bigger bats, smaller boundaries, the use of two white balls in the one-day game, and today's cricketers generally being stronger athletes. There was no appetite for reducing bat sizes, though they should not increase further. The committee undertook to consult bat manufacturers, while MCC would work with the ICC on research into the size of the seam on cricket balls.

Chairman Mike Brearley thanked outgoing committee members Rahul Dravid and Steve Bucknor for their contributions.

ENGLAND PLAYER CONTRACTS

On September 23, the ECB awarded 11 England central contracts running for 12 months from October 1, 2015, one fewer than the previous year. They went to Moeen Ali, James Anderson, Ian Bell, Stuart Broad, Jos Buttler, Alastair Cook, Steven Finn, Eoin Morgan, Joe Root, Ben Stokes and Mark Wood. Compared with the previous list, Morgan and Wood had replaced Gary Ballance, Chris Jordan and Chris Woakes.

Incremental contracts were awarded to Jonny Bairstow, Ballance, Alex Hales, Jordan, Liam Plunkett, Adil Rashid, James Taylor and Woakes; Bairstow, Ballance, Jordan, Rashid, Taylor and Woakes replaced Morgan (central contract), Ravi Bopara and James Tredwell. Players on incremental contracts receive a one-off ECB payment on top of their county salary, whereas centrally contracted players are paid by the ECB rather than their county. Incremental contracts can be earned by amassing 20 appearance points between October and September (five for a Test, two for an ODI or T20I). Taylor had previously been awarded a contract on this basis in February, and Wood in June.

The selectors also named 18 players for the England Performance Programme in 2015-16. Directed by Andy Flower, the programme was to consist of training at the National Cricket Performance Centre in Loughborough, before a camp in Dubai for spin bowlers and batsmen, and another for fast bowlers in South Africa. The batsmen and spinners travelling to Dubai were Daniel Bell-Drummond, Danny Briggs, Joe Clarke, Ben Foakes, Lewis Gregory, Dawid Malan, Stephen Parry, James Vince, Tom Westley and Ross Whiteley. (Zafar Ansari, though selected, was not expected to travel to Dubai as he was still recovering from a severe thumb injury.) The fast bowlers going to South Africa were Jake Ball, Tom Curran, Craig Miles, Tymal Mills, Craig Overton, Jamie Overton and Olly Stone. On October 28, Liam Dawson was added to the spin group and Mark Footitt to the pace group, bringing the total to 20.

ICC BOARD

The ICC Board met in Dubai on October 12–13, and paid respects to former president Jagmohan Dalmiya, who had died in September.

They approved an increase in direct funding to Associates and Affiliates from $US125m in the previous eight-year cycle to $208m for 2016–23. There would be an immediate increase to the annual funding pool from $20m in 2015 to $26m in 2016.

Following the suspension of the USA Cricket Association in June, the board were pleased with an update on work to develop a strategy unifying all USA stakeholders.

Bangladesh was confirmed as host for the 2016 Under-19 World Cup. The Bangladesh Cricket Board and the government were developing a security plan to meet the ICC security advisor's requirements.

The board approved $65m in prize money – up 41% – for the top-ranked Test sides and for men's and women's tournaments from 2016 to 2023. The prize for the side topping the

Test Championship on April 1 would double from $500,000 to $1m. The board approved a five-fold increase in the prize money allocated to six women's events over the next eight years, to $4.4m, including $1m for the Women's World Cup 2017.

The format of the Women's World Cup, to be hosted by England, was revised: instead of two groups of four plus a Super Six and a final, the eight teams would play a round robin leading to semi-finals. The board decided to stage a second Women's Championship post-2017. To encourage attacking cricket, women should immediately adopt all July's changes to the men's playing conditions, except that the batting powerplay would remain and there would still be only four fielders outside the circle in the last ten overs.

A joint session of the board and the Chief Executives' Committee discussed ways to enhance the context and value of future bilateral cricket.

The board noted that the ICC had received several approaches from multi-sport organisations; ICC chief executive David Richardson was expected to meet the International Olympic Committee in November.

The ICC complimented umpires on a record figure of 95.2% of pre-DRS decisions being proved correct in all internationals since the World Cup earlier in the year, and congratulated Cricket Ireland and Cricket Scotland on their successful hosting of the World Twenty20 Qualifier in July.

ICC CHAIRMAN

On November 9, the AGM of the Board of Control for Cricket in India decided to replace N. Srinivasan as ICC chairman with BCCI president Shashank Manohar. (From June 2015 to June 2016, the chairman was India's nominee.) Srinivasan had been forced out as BCCI president in 2014, when India's Supreme Court ordered him to step down during investigations into IPL corruption, in which his son-in-law was implicated. Former president Jagmohan Dalmiya had resumed the role, but died in September 2015, and Manohar was elected for a second term as BCCI president in October. Within weeks of becoming ICC chairman, he criticised the constitutional reforms orchestrated by Srinivasan which gave the BCCI, the ECB and Cricket Australia control of the ICC, saying he didn't agree with the Big Three "bullying", and that offices should be filled by the best men for the job.

ENGLAND WOMEN'S COACH

On November 11, the ECB announced that Mark Robinson would take over as head coach of the England women's team, succeeding Paul Shaw, who had held a similar role from June 2013. Robinson had spent the previous ten years managing his old county, Sussex, and had also coached recent England Lions tours of Sri Lanka and South Africa.

On December 15, the ECB announced 19 women's central contracts, to run from February 1, 2016. They went to Tamsin Beaumont, Katherine Brunt, Kate Cross, Charlotte Edwards, Georgia Elwiss, Natasha Farrant, Lydia Greenway, Rebecca Grundy, Jenny Gunn, Danielle Hazell, Amy Jones, Heather Knight, Laura Marsh, Natalie Sciver, Anya Shrubsole, Sarah Taylor, Fran Wilson, Lauren Winfield and Danielle Wyatt. Wilson was the one addition to the original list of central contracts in 2014.

MCC WORLD CRICKET COMMITTEE

The MCC World Cricket Committee met in Adelaide on November 25–26, just before the Australia–New Zealand day/night Test. MCC had supported and funded the development of pink-ball cricket, and the committee believed it was an opportunity for other nations struggling to attract spectators to Tests. They welcomed the additional Test Match Fund money the ICC were allocating to the seven Full Members apart from Australia, England and India, but hoped the use of the money was properly monitored.

The committee welcomed the ICC's recent dialogue with the International Olympic Committee; Rodney Miles, president of the Hong Kong Cricket Association, explained how the game could grow in China if it became an Olympic sport.

Former international umpire Simon Taufel reported on technology enabling the third umpire to monitor front-foot no-balls. The committee were still waiting for the Massachusetts Institute of Technology's report on the accuracy of the Decision Review System, but hoped a favourable assessment would accelerate its universal use. They debated the umpire's call for lbws, and felt the fielding side should not lose a review if the ball was shown to be clipping the stumps in the umpire's-call zone.

There was concern about the fact that, in the past three years, home teams had won over 70% of Test victories. Shorter tours and a lack of adequate preparation in local conditions also contributed, but it appeared pitches were being prepared to suit home teams. The committee wanted ground authorities to be left alone to produce pitches reflecting local conditions, while encouraging a fair balance between bat and ball. They would monitor the ECB's 2016 experiment in the County Championship, whereby away teams would be offered the chance to bowl first, with no toss unless they declined that option.

England women's captain Charlotte Edwards reported on the introduction of the Women's Big Bash League in Australia and the Women's Super League in England. Only England, Australia and India now staged women's Tests; Edwards argued that more Test and multi-day cricket was needed for it to thrive. The committee liked the Ashes scoring system, with points for all three formats, and recommended it for all women's series.

James Sutherland, chief executive of Cricket Australia, and former CA chairman Wally Edwards addressed the committee on the need for greater context in international cricket, perhaps through a World Test League and through making most one-day internationals count towards World Cup qualification.

MEETINGS AND DECISIONS IN 2016

ICC BOARD

The ICC Board met in Dubai on February 4, 2016, under new chairman Shashank Manohar, and reconsidered the 2014 changes to the ICC constitution. They agreed to re-establish an independent chairman, to be elected in June 2016 by secret ballot. In future, chairmen should not hold any post with any member board while in office. They would serve two years but might be re-elected, for a maximum of three terms.

The board agreed to remove the right of India, Australia and England to permanent positions on the Finance and Commercial Affairs Committee and the Executive Committee; these would be open to all Full and Associate Members, the sole criteria being skill, competence and experience. The present composition of the committees would be reviewed. They also agreed to a complete review of the 2014 changes, with a view to establishing appropriate and effective governance, finance, corporate and cricketing structures. A steering group comprising Manohar and the chairmen of the Governance Review Committee, Executive Committee, Finance and Commercial Affairs Committee and Associate/Affiliate Member Group would work on changes to be voted on in June.

To improve governance and transparency among members, the board reinstated the requirement that Full Members must submit audited statements on an annual basis, like Associates and Affiliates. It was decided that three of the four annual meetings should take place outside the UAE: the 2016 annual conference would be in Edinburgh.

Manohar said: "We collectively want to improve the governance in a transparent manner, not only of the ICC but also the member boards. This, in turn, will enhance the image and quality of the sport. No member of the ICC is bigger than the other."

DATES IN CRICKET HISTORY

c. 1550	Evidence of cricket being played in Guildford, Surrey.
1610	Reference to "cricketing" between Weald & Upland and North Downs near Chevening, Kent.
1611	Randle Cotgrave's French–English dictionary translates the French word "crosse" as a cricket staff. Two youths fined for playing cricket at Sidlesham, Sussex.
1624	Jasper Vinall becomes first man known to be killed playing cricket: hit by a bat while trying to catch the ball – at Horsted Green, Sussex.
1676	First reference to cricket being played abroad, by British residents in Aleppo, Syria.
1694	Two shillings and sixpence paid for a "wagger" (wager) about a match at Lewes.
1697	First reference to "a great match" with 11 players a side for 50 guineas, in Sussex.
1700	Cricket match announced on Clapham Common.
1709	First recorded inter-county match: Kent v Surrey.
1710	First reference to cricket at Cambridge University.
1727	Articles of Agreement written governing the conduct of matches between the teams of the Duke of Richmond and Mr Brodrick of Peperharow, Surrey.
1729	Date of earliest surviving bat, belonging to John Chitty, now in the Oval pavilion.
1730	First recorded match at the Artillery Ground, off City Road, central London, still the cricketing home of the Honourable Artillery Company.
1744	Kent beat All-England by one wicket at the Artillery Ground. First known version of the Laws of Cricket, issued by the London Club, formalising the pitch as 22 yards long.
c. 1767	Foundation of the Hambledon Club in Hampshire, the leading club in England for the next 30 years.
1769	First recorded century, by John Minshull for Duke of Dorset's XI v Wrotham.
1771	Width of bat limited to 4$\frac{1}{4}$ inches, where it has remained ever since.
1774	Lbw law devised.
1776	Earliest known scorecards, at the Vine Club, Sevenoaks, Kent.
1780	The first six-seamed cricket ball, manufactured by Dukes of Penshurst, Kent.
1787	First match at Thomas Lord's first ground, Dorset Square, Marylebone – White Conduit Club v Middlesex. Formation of Marylebone Cricket Club by members of the White Conduit Club.
1788	First revision of the Laws of Cricket by MCC.
1794	First recorded inter-school match: Charterhouse v Westminster.
1795	First recorded case of a dismissal "leg before wicket".
1806	First Gentlemen v Players match at Lord's.
1807	First mention of "straight-armed" (i.e. roundarm) bowling: by John Willes of Kent.
1809	Thomas Lord's second ground opened, at North Bank, St John's Wood.
1811	First recorded women's county match: Surrey v Hampshire at Ball's Pond, London.
1814	Lord's third ground opened on its present site, also in St John's Wood.
1827	First Oxford v Cambridge match, at Lord's: a draw.
1828	MCC authorise the bowler to raise his hand level with the elbow.

1833	John Nyren publishes *Young Cricketer's Tutor* and *The Cricketers of My Time*.
1836	First North v South match, for years regarded as the principal fixture of the season.
c. **1836**	Batting pads invented.
1841	General Lord Hill, commander-in-chief of the British Army, orders that a cricket ground be made an adjunct of every military barracks.
1844	First official international match: Canada v United States.
1845	First match played at The Oval.
1846	The All-England XI, organised by William Clarke, begin playing matches, often against odds, throughout the country.
1849	First Yorkshire v Lancashire match.
c. **1850**	Wicketkeeping gloves first used.
1850	John Wisden bowls all ten batsmen in an innings for North v South.
1853	First mention of a champion county: Nottinghamshire.
1858	First recorded instance of a hat being awarded to a bowler taking wickets with three consecutive balls.
1859	First touring team to leave England, captained by George Parr, draws enthusiastic crowds in the US and Canada.
1864	"Overhand bowling" authorised by MCC. John Wisden's *The Cricketer's Almanack* first published.
1868	Team of Australian Aborigines tour England.
1873	W. G. Grace becomes the first player to record 1,000 runs and 100 wickets in a season. First regulations restricting county qualifications, regarded by some as the official start of the County Championship.
1877	First Test match: Australia beat England by 45 runs at Melbourne.
1880	First Test in England: a five-wicket win against Australia at The Oval.
1882	Following England's first defeat by Australia in England, an "obituary notice" to English cricket in the *Sporting Times* leads to the tradition of the Ashes.
1889	Work begins on present Lord's Pavilion. South Africa's first Test match. Declarations first authorised, but only on the third day, or in a one-day match.
1890	County Championship officially constituted.
1895	W. G. Grace scores 1,000 runs in May, and reaches his 100th hundred.
1899	A. E. J. Collins scores 628 not out in a junior house match at Clifton College, the highest recorded individual score in any game – until 2016. Selectors choose England team for home Tests, instead of host club issuing invitations.
1900	In England, six-ball over becomes the norm, instead of five.
1909	Imperial Cricket Conference (ICC – now the International Cricket Council) set up, with England, Australia and South Africa the original members.
1910	Six runs given for any hit over the boundary, instead of only for a hit out of the ground.
1912	First and only triangular Test series played in England, involving England, Australia and South Africa.
1915	W. G. Grace dies, aged 67.
1926	Victoria score 1,107 v New South Wales at Melbourne, still a first-class record.
1928	West Indies' first Test match. A. P. Freeman of Kent and England becomes the only player to take more than 300 first-class wickets in a season: 304.

1930	New Zealand's first Test match.
	Donald Bradman's first tour of England: he scores 974 runs in five Tests, still a record for any series.
1931	Stumps made higher (28 inches not 27) and wider (nine inches not eight – this was optional until 1947).
1932	India's first Test match.
	Hedley Verity of Yorkshire takes ten wickets for ten runs v Nottinghamshire, the best innings analysis in first-class cricket.
1932-33	The Bodyline tour of Australia in which England bowl at batsmen's bodies with a packed leg-side field to neutralise Bradman's scoring.
1934	Jack Hobbs retires, with 197 centuries and 61,237 runs, both records.
	First women's Test: Australia v England at Brisbane.
1935	MCC condemn and outlaw Bodyline.
1947	Denis Compton (Middlesex and England) hits a record 3,816 runs in an English season.
1948	First five-day Tests in England.
	Bradman concludes Test career with a second-ball duck at The Oval and an average of 99.94 – four runs would have made it 100.
1952	Pakistan's first Test match.
1953	England regain the Ashes after a 19-year gap, the longest ever.
1956	Jim Laker of England takes 19 wickets for 90 v Australia at Manchester, the best match analysis in first-class cricket.
1960	First tied Test: Australia v West Indies at Brisbane.
1963	Distinction between amateurs and professionals abolished in English cricket.
	The first major one-day tournament begins in England: the Gillette Cup.
1969	Limited-over Sunday league inaugurated for first-class counties.
1970	Proposed South African tour of England cancelled; South Africa excluded from international cricket because of their government's apartheid policies.
1971	First one-day international: Australia beat England at Melbourne by five wickets.
1973	First women's World Cup: England are the winners.
1975	First men's World Cup: West Indies beat Australia in final at Lord's.
1976	First women's match at Lord's: England beat Australia by eight wickets.
1977	Centenary Test at Melbourne, with identical result to the first match: Australia beat England by 45 runs.
	Australian media tycoon Kerry Packer signs 51 of the world's leading players in defiance of the cricketing authorities.
1978	Graham Yallop of Australia is the first batsman to wear a protective helmet in a Test.
1979	Packer and official cricket agree peace deal.
1981	England beat Australia in Leeds Test, after following on with bookmakers offering odds of 500-1 against them winning.
1982	Sri Lanka's first Test match.
1991	South Africa return, with a one-day international in India.
1992	Zimbabwe's first Test match.
	Durham become first county since Glamorgan in 1921 to attain first-class status.
1993	The ICC cease to be administered by MCC, becoming an independent organisation.
1994	Brian Lara becomes the first player to pass 500 in a first-class innings: 501 not out for Warwickshire v Durham.

2000	South Africa's captain Hansie Cronje banned from cricket for life after admitting receiving bribes from bookmakers in match-fixing scandal.
	Bangladesh's first Test match.
	County Championship split into two divisions, with promotion and relegation.
2001	Sir Donald Bradman dies, aged 92.
2003	First Twenty20 game played, in England.
2004	Lara is the first to score 400 in a Test innings, for West Indies v England in Antigua.
2005	England regain the Ashes after 16 years.
2006	Pakistan become first team to forfeit a Test, for refusing to resume at The Oval.
	England lose the Ashes after 462 days, the shortest tenure in history.
	Shane Warne becomes the first man to take 700 Test wickets.
2007	Australia complete 5–0 Ashes whitewash for the first time since 1920-21.
	Australia win the World Cup for the third time running.
	India beat Pakistan in the final of the inaugural World Twenty20 tournament.
2008	Indian Premier League of 20-over matches launched.
	Sachin Tendulkar becomes the leading scorer in Tests, passing Lara.
2009	Terrorists in Lahore attack buses containing Sri Lankan team and match officials.
2010	Tendulkar scores the first double-century in a one-day international, against South Africa; later in the year, he scores his 50th Test century.
	Muttiah Muralitharan retires from Test cricket, after taking his 800th wicket.
	Pakistan bowl three deliberate no-balls in Lord's Test against England; the ICC ban the three players responsible.
2011	India become the first team to win the World Cup on home soil.
	Salman Butt, Mohammad Asif and Mohammad Amir are given custodial sentences of between six and 30 months for their part in the Lord's spot-fix.
	Virender Sehwag makes a world-record 219 in a one-day international, for India against West Indies at Indore.
2012	Tendulkar scores his 100th international century, in a one-day game against Bangladesh at Mirpur.
	Hashim Amla makes 311 not out at The Oval, South Africa's first Test triple-century.
	England win 2–1 in India, their first Test series victory there since 1984-85.
2013	150th edition of *Wisden Cricketers' Almanack*.
	Tendulkar retires after his 200th Test match, with a record 15,921 runs.
2014	Australia complete only the third 5–0 Ashes whitewash.
	ICC agree far-reaching changes to their governance, pushed through by India, Australia and England.
	Brendon McCullum makes 302, New Zealand's first Test triple-century.
	India's Rohit Sharma hits 264 in one-day international against Sri Lanka at Kolkata.
	Australian batsman Phillip Hughes, 25, dies after being hit on the neck by a bouncer.
2015	Former Australian captain and TV commentator Richie Benaud dies aged 85.
	Australia win World Cup for fifth time, beating New Zealand in final at Melbourne.
	England win fourth successive home Ashes series.
2016	Pranav Dhanawade, 15, makes 1,009 not out – the highest recorded individual score in any match – in a school game in Mumbai.
	McCullum hits Test cricket's fastest hundred, from 54 balls, in his final match, against Australia at Christchurch.

ANNIVERSARIES IN 2016-17

Compiled by Steven Lynch

2016

April 29   Phil Tufnell (Middlesex) born, 1966.
Idiosyncratic spinner who claimed 121 Test wickets before moving into the media.

May 23   Graeme Hick (Worcestershire) born, 1966.
Prolific county batsman who hit a quadruple-century at Taunton in 1988.

June 3   Wasim Akram (Pakistan) born, 1966.
Lethal left-armer who took 916 international wickets; Man of Match in 1992 World Cup final.

June 16   Basil D'Oliveira (England) makes Test debut, 1966.
England's first South African-born Test player, "Dolly" started against West Indies at Lord's.

June 23   Len Hutton (Yorkshire) born, 1916.
One of England's greatest batsmen; as captain, won the Ashes in 1953 and 1954-55.

July 31   W. G. Grace (England) scores 224* against Surrey at The Oval, 1866.
This was WG's first senior double-century; he had turned 18 less than a fortnight earlier.

August 5   G. H. S. "Harry" Trott (Australia) born, 1866.
Captain in 1893 (when he scored 143 at Lord's) and 1894-95 Ashes.

August 20   Ken Higgs and John Snow (England) put on 128 for tenth wicket, 1966.
Their stand against West Indies at The Oval remains the highest by Nos 10 and 11 in a Test.

September 3   Kenneth Hutchings (Kent) killed in action in France, 1916.
One of the most graceful batsman of the "Golden Age", Hutchings was only 33 when he died.

October 20   Allan Donald (South Africa) born, 1966.
Fast bowler known as "White Lightning": 330 Test wickets.

November 28   A. F. A. "Dick" Lilley (Warwickshire) born, 1866.
England's first great wicketkeeper, in 35 Tests from 1896 to 1909.

December 9   Colin McCool (Australia) born, 1916.
Leg-spinner who was one of the 1948 Invincibles; later played for Somerset.

December 15   Carl Hooper (West Indies) born, 1966.
Graceful batsman who scored 5,762 runs in Tests – and 5,761 in one-day internationals.

December 19   Merv Wallace (Auckland) born, 1916.
One of New Zealand's finest batsmen; prominent on 1937 and 1949 tours of England.

2017

January 5   George Duckworth (Lancashire) dies, 1966.
Popular wicketkeeper in 24 Tests, later England's scorer; died aged 64.

January 25   Bill Storer (Surrey) born, 1867.
One of the first wicketkeepers to stand up to the stumps regularly; six Tests for England.

January 30   Bobby Abel (Surrey) carries bat at Sydney, 1892.
The first instance for England in a Test; the diminutive Abel scored 132 in a total of 307.*

February 22   Jack Robertson (Middlesex) born, 1917.
Stylish opener who paved the way for Denis Compton and Bill Edrich in 1947.

March 4   Daryll Cullinan (South Africa) born, 1967.
Precocious batsman who hit a first-class century aged 16, still a national record; 70 Tests.

April 12   M. H. "Vinoo" Mankad (India) born, 1917.
Tireless all-rounder who scored 72 and 184 – and bowled 97 overs – in 1952 Lord's Test.

April 13   S. M. J. "Sammy" Woods (Somerset) born, 1867.
Sporting all-rounder who played Tests for England and his native Australia.

ONE HUNDRED AND FIFTY YEARS AGO

from Wisden Cricketers' Almanack 1866

TO THE READER   John Wisden and Co. have again to thank the Cricketing Public for the encouragement given to the Almanack, and they beg respectfully to offer the third number for the perusal of their friends, trusting that it will be received with as much favour as its predecessors.

J. W. and Co. have this year published the matches of the three All England Elevens, feeling certain, from the great favour with which these celebrated Elevens are received in all parts of the country, their doings will be read with interest.

J. W. and Co. have carefully avoided making any remarks upon the play or players, as the purport of this little work is to record the scores of the matches published as a book of reference.

2, New Coventry Street, W.
January, 1866.

ONE HUNDRED YEARS AGO

from WISDEN CRICKETERS' ALMANACK 1917

PREFACE   The 54th edition of *Wisden's Almanack* is of necessity rather a mournful volume. Its chief feature is a record of the cricketers who have fallen in the war – the Roll of Honour, so far as the national game is concerned... Last year the wisdom of publishing *Wisden* in wartime seemed very doubtful, but the experiment was more than justified, a small edition being sold out in a few days... The outlook for the game is as dark as possible.

MCC IN 1916   In the Pavilion the MCC staff and one or two members and their friends have occupied their spare time in making, at the request of the War Office, hay nets for horses. About 18,000 nets have been completed and sent to Woolwich... At the request of the Canadian Contingent a baseball match was played at Lord's, in September, between Canadians and London Americans for the benefit of a fund raised for the widows and orphans of Canadians who fall in battle. HRH Princess Louise (Duchess of Argyll) graciously gave her patronage to the undertaking and watched the game from the Pavilion. The proceeds exceeded £100.

DEATHS IN THE WAR, 1916: PERCY JEEVES   Percy Jeeves (Royal Warwickshire Regiment) was killed on July 22, England losing a cricketer of whom very high hopes had been entertained... In 1913 he did brilliant work for Warwickshire, both as bowler and batsman, and firmly established his position. He took 106 wickets in first-class matches that season at a cost of 20.88 each, and scored 765 runs with an average of 20.13. In 1914... he was chosen for Players against Gentlemen at The Oval, and by his fine bowling helped the Players to win the match, sending down in the Gentlemen's second innings 15 overs for 44 runs and four wickets. Mr P. F. Warner was greatly impressed and predicated that Jeeves would be an England bowler in the near future. Within a month War had been declared. Jeeves was a right-handed bowler on the quick side of medium pace, and with an easy action came off the ground with plenty of spin. He was very popular among his brother players.

Jeeves was immortalised in the P. G. Wodehouse stories.

OTHER DEATHS IN 1916: ALFRED GRACE   The last of the famous brotherhood, who was born at Downend on May 17, 1840, died in a nursing home in Bristol on May 24, and was buried at Chipping Sodbury. He never appeared at Lord's, but was a very useful cricketer, his usual post in the field being long stop. As a player he at no time ranked with his brothers, but… he stood out as one of the finest horsemen in England, and for many years followed the Duke of Beaufort's hounds three or four times a week. He was known as The Hunting Doctor. For many years he practised as a surgeon at Chipping Sodbury, Gloucestershire. He never got over the tragic death of his son, Dr Gerald Grace, in South Africa.

DEATHS IN THE WAR, 1916: KENNETH HUTCHINGS   Lt K. L. Hutchings (King's Liverpool Regiment, attached to Welsh Regiment) was killed in action during the first week in September. He was struck by a shell, death being instantaneous. Of all the cricketers who have fallen in the War he may fairly be described as the most famous… at his best he was one of the most remarkable batsmen seen in this generation.

NOTTINGHAMSHIRE IN 1916   For over two years the pavilion at Trent Bridge has been used as a hospital, and more recently the ladies' pavilion has been converted into one. During the month of November a hundred wounded soldiers were in residence. The Trent Bridge ground has been thoroughly kept up, and the turf never looked better than in 1916.

DEATHS IN THE WAR, 1916: HENRY WEBBER   Lt. Henry Webber (South Lancashire Regiment), of Horley, Surrey, and a JP for the County, was killed in action on July 21, aged 68… He made his first hundred in 1863 and as recently as August 6, 1904, when 56 years of age, made 209 not out for Horley v. Lowfield Heath, at Horley, in three hours after a full round of golf in the morning. His pluck and patriotism in insisting on being given a commission at his advanced age were much admired.

Webber is the oldest-known battle casualty of the Great War.

OTHER DEATHS IN 1916: PERCY HARDY   Private Frederick Percy Hardy (County of London Yeomanry)… was found dead on the floor of a lavatory at King's Cross station (GNR) on March 9. His throat was cut and a blood-stained knife was by his side. He was on the Oval groundstaff in 1900 and 1901, and began to appear for Somerset in 1903.

Hardy, who played 99 first-class matches for Somerset, committed suicide for fear of returning to the trenches.

PUBLIC SCHOOL CRICKET IN 1916 by E. B. Noel   Next to military matches the chief interest in cricket last summer centred in the public schools. As in 1915 the schools adopted various procedures: some played their usual school matches, others played schools which they do not usually play in peace time, in order to make up for the lack of foreign matches… The amount of public school cricket played in the holidays was probably larger than ever before… [because] there is not much chance of there being half the amount of country house cricket… in which many schoolboys used to take part. In the heyday of country house cricket in the 1890s, a boy in the South of England could certainly have played cricket every weekend probably every day from August 1 to September 14. Those days are gone, perhaps never to return.

> **❝** It was as if the Folkestone film club had made movie shorts that outshone Hollywood blockbusters."
> The NatWest T20 Blast in 2015, page 719

FIFTY YEARS AGO

from WISDEN CRICKETERS' ALMANACK 1967

CRICKETER OF THE YEAR, B. L. D'OLIVEIRA   The story of Basil D'Oliveira is a fairytale come true; the story of a nonentity in the country of his birth who because of the colour of his skin was confined to cricket on crude mudheaps until he was 25, yet after only one season in the County Championship played for England. No Test player has had to overcome such tremendous disadvantages along the road to success as the Cape Coloured D'Oliveira. Admirable though his achievements were against West Indies in 1966, undoubtedly his triumph in ever attaining Test status was more commendable. That he did not fall by the wayside of the stony path he was compelled to tread is a tribute to the courage and skill of this player from the land of apartheid. To say that he never contemplated giving up the game before reaching the hour of glory was hardly the case. The hazards he encountered were very nearly too great even for the stout-hearted D'Oliveira. Suffice to say that, of the 25,000 South African coloured cricketers who would dearly love to make county grade over here, D'Oliveira is the first to have done so. Hundreds of others are doomed to spend their lives in a class of cricket far beneath their skill. They will stay because no one ever sees them in this unfashionable outpost of the game.

THE H. J. RHODES CONTROVERSY   At the request of Derbyshire, the special committee set up on March 1 [1966] to deal with suspect throwers met at Lord's on March 25 to consider the bowling action of H. J. Rhodes. They watched several films before Rhodes, in his full cricketing kit, went to the practice ground and bowled for 15 minutes with his full run of 20 yards at his fastest pace. He hit a single stump several times. Mr W. E. Tucker, the surgeon, gave evidence, including demonstrations with the help of a human skeleton, which showed that Rhodes's right arm naturally bent back from the straight. Afterwards, the committee issued this statement: "The committee unanimously considered his basic action to be fair, but were divided on the evidence before them as to whether or not his action was occasionally suspect."

NOTES BY THE EDITOR [Norman Preston]   For the past 20 years we have had one change after another, including the abolition of the distinction between amateur and professional, experiments on taking the new ball varying from 55 to 85 overs, declarations, limitation of the leg-side field, two years without the follow-on, boundaries limited to 75 yards, various pitch-covering rules, insistence on sightscreens on all grounds, numerous ways of reckoning the County Championship, including number of matches played and, the final abomination, the limit of 65 overs for the first innings in some matches in 1966. Also the controversies over throwing and the bowler's drag, polishing the ball, bowler's run-up limited to 20 yards and permission to captains to forfeit their second innings. Small wonder that the ordinary follower of the game has become so utterly confused… And what about the players? Surely this constant tampering with the rules has been of little benefit to them.

MCC TEAM IN AUSTRALIA AND NEW ZEALAND, 1965-66 by E .M. Wellings   For the first time the team flew by fast jet aircraft all the way to Australia – and in the cramping discomfort of economy class – and numerous players suffered stomach disorders and odd indispositions, which were grandly called virus diseases. Even the common cold was thus termed. The complaint was just the same but with a vital difference. Called a cold, it was too insignificant to keep a cricketer from playing. Described in highfalutin fashion as a virus infection, it became grand enough to keep him out of action. Subsequently two other touring sides from Britain transported at high speed and great height to Australia, the rugby union and rugby league teams, suffered in the same virulent way on arrival. It is a fair assumption that rapid transportation into different conditions is at least in part the cause of such maladies, which were not suffered when teams travelled more slowly by sea. In that time a further amendment to the tour travel arrangements seems necessary.

SOBERS – THE LION OF CRICKET by Sir Neville Cardus   Garfield St Aubrun Sobers... the most renowned name of any cricketer since Bradman's high noon. He is, in fact, even more famous than Bradman ever was; for he is accomplished in every department of the game, and has exhibited his genius in all climes and conditions. Test matches everywhere, West Indies, India, Pakistan, Australia, New Zealand, England; in Lancashire League and Sheffield Shield cricket. We can safely agree that no player has proven versatility of skill as convincingly as Sobers has done, effortlessly, and after the manner born. He is a stylish, prolific batsman; two bowlers in one, fastish left-arm, seaming the new ball, and slow-to-medium back-of-the-hand spinner with the old ball; a swift, accurate, slip fieldsman in the class of Hammond and Simpson, and generally an astute captain... He makes a stroke with moments to spare. His fastest ball – and it can be very fast – is bowled as though he could, with physical pressure, have bowled it a shade faster. He can, in the slips catch the lightning snick with the grace and nonchalance of Hammond himself. The sure sign of mastery, of genius.

LANCASHIRE v. YORKSHIRE, AT OLD TRAFFORD, July 30, August 1, 2 [1966] Yorkshire won by 12 runs. Cricket history was made in this match when, after play had been limited to 95 minutes on the first day and washed out completely on the second, Yorkshire became the first side to forfeit an innings. They did so after declaring at lunchtime on the third day and in answer to a Lancashire declaration immediately afterwards. To make the match even more memorable Yorkshire gained victory with the last ball of the match, when Greenhough was lbw to Illingworth.

OBITUARY – DUCKWORTH, GEORGE, who died on January 5, aged 64, was an outstanding character in first-class cricket in the period between the two World Wars, a time when the game possessed far more players of popular personality than at the present time. Small of stature, but big of heart and voice, Duckworth used an "Owzat" shout of such piercing quality and volume that his appeal alone would have made him a figure to be remembered. But Duckworth possessed many other qualities. He was one of the finest wicketkeepers the game has produced; as a batsman he could be relied upon to fight in a crisis; he ended his first-class career, perhaps prematurely, in 1938. He took up journalism, but hardly had time to establish himself before war broke out in 1939. Then he spent spells in hotel management and farming before his post-war career, which included journalism, broadcasting, and acting as baggage-master and scorer for MCC teams abroad, and for touring countries here... His jovial personality, wise counsel and experience were of benefit to many a team and individual cricketer. His radio and television commentaries, typically humorous and forthright, became well-known, both on cricket and on rugby league.

VICTORIA v QUEENSLAND, AT MELBOURNE, January 7, 8, 10, 11 [1966]   Victoria won by three wickets. Victoria ended the first innings 50 runs in arrears, after the pace bowler Peter Allan had taken all ten wickets (15.6–3–61–10). Allan's figures were four for 32 at the end of the first day, with Victoria 76 for four. Allan next day actually took six for 14, these runs including five overthrows.

THE COUNTY CHAMPIONSHIP IN 1966   For the first time in the history of the County Championship the first innings of 102 matches in a total of 238 were restricted to 65 overs. These were the first 12 matches played by each of the 17 counties on a home and away basis. Where counties met only once in the season normal conditions prevailed, as they did in the return matches. On the whole the experiment did not succeed, although in some matches it produced excellent cricket. For most of the summer Yorkshire led the way and they won the title for the 29th time.

Compiled by Christopher Lane

HONOURS AND AWARDS IN 2015-16

In 2015-16, the following were decorated for their services to cricket:

Queen's Birthday Honours, 2015: J. M. Anderson (Lancashire and England) OBE; C. Evans (Ashford CC; services to grassroots cricket) BEM; W. Miller (services to cricket and charity in Northern Ireland) MBE; R. Simpson (services to education, cricket and the community in Durham) MBE; M. Vaughan (Etwall CC; services to cricket in Derbyshire) BEM.

Queen's Birthday Honours (Australia), 2015: R. W. Cattrall (services to analytical chemistry and to cricket) AM; M. W. Speed (former chief executive of the ACB and ICC; services to cricket and legal education) AO; J. A. Turner (Queensland; services to community through public administration and to cricket) AM.

Queen's Birthday Honours (New Zealand), 2015: B. Andrews (former convenor of Canterbury selectors; services to the community and sport) QSM; M. J. Hesson (New Zealand coach; services to cricket) ONZM; B. B. McCullum (Otago, Canterbury and New Zealand; services to cricket) ONZM; J. G. Sutherland (administrator with Nelson and New Zealand Cricket; services to cricket) QSM; T. M. Walsh (head of New Zealand World Cup operations; services to sports administration) DNZM.

New Year's Honours, 2016: R. Harrison (Ireland; president of Irish Cricket Union; services to cricket in Northern Ireland) MBE; J. E. Hilsum (services to cricket and the community in the Isle of Wight) BEM.

New Year's Honours (New Zealand), 2016: S. L. Boock (Otago, Canterbury and New Zealand; NZC president; services to sport and the community) ONZM; W. P. Francis (broadcaster, former NZC director; services to broadcasting and cricket) ONZM; R. Smith (chair of Auckland CA; services to cricket) MNZM.

Australia Day Honours, 2016: M. J. Ball (services to the community through urban planning and heritage preservation, and to the history of cricket) AO; S. J. Pascoe (services to cricket as player and administrator in Ringwood, Victoria) OAM; G. N. Scannell (services to cricket as groundsman and chair of grounds committee in Geelong, Victoria) OAM.

ICC AWARDS

The International Cricket Council's 12th annual awards were announced in December 2015.

Cricketer of the Year (Sir Garfield Sobers Trophy)	**Steve Smith (A)**
Test Player of the Year	**Steve Smith (A)**
One-Day International Player of the Year	**A. B. de Villiers (SA)**
Women's One-Day International Cricketer of the Year	**Meg Lanning (A)**
Women's Twenty20 International Cricketer of the Year	**Stafanie Taylor (WI)**
Twenty20 International Performance of the Year	**Faf du Plessis (SA)**
Emerging Player of the Year	**Josh Hazlewood (A)**
Associate/Affiliate Player of the Year	**Khurram Khan (UAE)**
Spirit of Cricket Award	**Brendon McCullum (NZ)**
Umpire of the Year (David Shepherd Trophy)	**Richard Kettleborough (E)**

A panel of five also selected two World XIs from the previous 12 months:

	ICC World Test team		*ICC World one-day team*
1	David Warner (A)	1	Tillekeratne Dilshan (SL)
2	*Alastair Cook (E)	2	Hashim Amla (SA)
3	Kane Williamson (NZ)	3	†Kumar Sangakkara (SL)
4	Younis Khan (P)	4	*A. B. de Villiers (SA)
5	Steve Smith (A)	5	Steve Smith (A)
6	Joe Root (E)	6	Ross Taylor (NZ)
7	†Sarfraz Ahmed (P)	7	Trent Boult (NZ)
8	Stuart Broad (E)	8	Mohammed Shami (I)
9	Trent Boult (NZ)	9	Mitchell Starc (A)
10	Yasir Shah (P)	10	Mustafizur Rahman (B)
11	Josh Hazlewood (A)	11	Imran Tahir (SA)
12th	Ravichandran Ashwin (I)	12th	Joe Root (E)

Previous Cricketers of the Year were Rahul Dravid (2004), Andrew Flintoff and Jacques Kallis (jointly in 2005), Ricky Ponting (2006 and 2007), Shivnarine Chanderpaul (2008), Mitchell Johnson (2009 and 2014), Sachin Tendulkar (2010), Jonathan Trott (2011), Kumar Sangakkara (2012) and Michael Clarke (2013).

ICC CRICKET HALL OF FAME

The ICC Cricket Hall of Fame was launched in 2009 in association with the Federation of International Cricketers' Associations to recognise legends of the game. In the first year, 60 members were inducted: 55 from the earlier FICA Hall of Fame, plus five new players elected in October 2009 by a voting academy made up of the ICC president, 11 ICC member representatives, a FICA representative, a women's cricket representative, ten journalists, a statistician, and all living members of the Hall of Fame. New members have been elected every year since. Candidates must have retired from international cricket at least five years ago.

The members elected in 2015 were Anil Kumble (India), the late Betty Wilson (Australia), Martin Crowe (New Zealand) and Wes Hall (West Indies), who brought the total to 80.

ICC DEVELOPMENT PROGRAMME AWARDS

The International Cricket Council announced the global winners of their 2014 Development Programme Awards in April 2015.

Best Overall Cricket Development Programme	**Cricket Papua New Guinea**
Spirit of Cricket Award	**Cricket Thailand**
Photo of the Year	**Cricket Argentina**
Lifetime Service Award	**The late Keith Dennis (Jersey)**
Volunteer of the Year	**Ahmad Feisal Tajuddin (Malaysia)**
Women's Cricket Behind the Scenes Award	**Habib Mugalula (Uganda)**

ALLAN BORDER MEDAL

Steve Smith won the Allan Border Medal, for the best Australian international player of the past 12 months, in January 2015. Previous winners were Glenn McGrath, Steve Waugh, Matthew Hayden, Adam Gilchrist, Ricky Ponting (four times), Michael Clarke (four times), Brett Lee, Shane Watson (twice) and Mitchell Johnson. Smith received 243 votes from team-mates, umpires and journalists, 68 more than runner-up David Warner, and also took the awards for Test Cricketer of the Year and One-Day International Player of the Year. The only senior men's international award he missed was Twenty20 International Cricketer of the Year, which went to **Glenn Maxwell**. Australia Women's captain **Meg Lanning** retained the Belinda Clark Award for the Women's International Cricketer of the Year. **Jason Behrendorff** of Western Australia was named Domestic Cricketer of the Year, and **Sean Abbott** of New South Wales was Bradman Young Player of the Year.

SHEFFIELD SHIELD PLAYER OF THE YEAR

The Sheffield Shield Player of the Year Award for 2014-15 was won by Western Australian captain **Adam Voges**, who had led his team to their second successive Shield final. He had scored 1,215 at 101 in ten qualifying games, with five centuries, and added a sixth in the final. The award, instituted in 1975-76, is adjudicated by umpires over the season. The Toyota Futures League Player of the Year award was shared by **Ben Dunk** of Tasmania and **Ben Rohrer** of New South Wales. Queensland's **Jess Jonassen** won the Women's National Cricket League Player of the Year, and **Heather Knight**, Tasmania's English all-rounder, the Women's Twenty20 Player of the Year. Meanwhile 17-year-old **Ashleigh Gardner** became the first woman to be named the Lord's Taverners Indigenous Cricketer of the Year. **Simon Fry** retained his title as Umpire of the Year, while the Benaud Spirit of Cricket Awards for fair play throughout the season went to the men of **Queensland** and the women of **New South Wales**.

CRICKET SOUTH AFRICA AWARDS

For the second year running, **A. B. de Villiers** won four CSA player awards: in June 2015, he was named South African Cricketer of the Year, One-Day International Cricketer of the Year, Players' Player of the Year and Fans' Player of the Year (in 2014, he won the Test award but not the ODI one). The KFC "So Good!" award also went to de Villiers for his ODI record 31-ball century against West Indies in January. The Test Cricketer of the Year was **Hashim Amla**, and the Twenty20 International Cricketer of the Year **Morné van Wyk**. **Dale Steyn** retained the Delivery of the Year award. The Women's Cricketer of the Year was **Shabnim Ismail**. In the domestic awards, there were three awards for first-class champions Highveld Lions, whose captain **Stephen Cook** was Sunfoil Series Cricketer of the Season, while **Geoffrey Toyana** was Coach of the Year and **Kagiso Rabada** Domestic Newcomer of the Season. **Robin Peterson** of Cape Cobras was the Momentum One-Day Cup Cricketer, and his team-mate **Kieron Pollard** the Ram Slammer of the Season. **Dane Paterson** of Cape Cobras was the Domestic Players' Player again, and also the SA Cricket Association's Most Valuable Player. **Titans** won the CSA Fair Play award. **Johan Cloete** was Umpire of the Year for the third time running, and **Adrian Holdstock** the Umpires' Umpire. **Rudolph du Preez** of Centurion was best groundsman, and **Gauteng** were the best scorers' association for the eighth time running. The Khaya Majola Lifetime Achievement Award went to **Shepherd Ngcaba**, the driving force behind the Good Hope Cricket Club in King Williamstown, who also served on the Border Cricket Board.

ENGLAND PLAYERS OF THE YEAR

In May 2015, **Joe Root** won the title of the ECB Men's Cricketer of the Year, ahead of James Anderson, Moeen Ali and Gary Ballance. In the previous 12 months, he had scored 1,135 Test runs at 94, including four centuries, all unbeaten, plus three further hundreds in one-day internationals. **Charlotte Edwards** retained the award for the Women's Cricketer of the Year; she had averaged 76 as she led England to one-day series wins over India and New Zealand, and 59 as they beat South Africa and New Zealand in Twenty20 cricket. Edwards was also presented with a silver cap to commemorate her 200th match as England captain in February. Lancashire and England Under-19 seamer **Saqib Mahmood** was named the England Development Programme Cricketer of the Year; he had taken three for 12 to rout South Africa for 77 on his debut for England Under-19 in August 2014. The England Disability Cricketer of the Year award went to **Luke Sugg**, from the England Visually Impaired team, who scored 634 runs at 126, including four centuries, to help England reach the semi-finals of the 2014 Blind Cricket World Cup in South Africa.

PROFESSIONAL CRICKETERS' ASSOCIATION AWARDS

The following awards were announced at the PCA's annual dinner in September 2015.

Reg Hayter Cup (NatWest PCA Player of the Year)	**Chris Rushworth** (Durham)
John Arlott Cup (NatWest PCA Young Player of the Year)	**Tom Curran** (Surrey)
County MVP of the Summer	**Chris Rushworth** (Durham)
Investec Test Player of the Summer	**Stuart Broad**
Waitrose Women's Player of the Summer	**Anya Shrubsole**
NatWest T20 Blast Player of the Year	**Michael Klinger** (Gloucestershire)
Royal London One-Day Cup Player of the Year	**Michael Klinger** (Gloucestershire)
Sky Sports Sixes Award	**Ross Whiteley** (Worcestershire)
PCA England Masters MVP	**Usman Afzaal**
Harold Goldblatt Award (PCA Umpire of the Year)	**Michael Gough**
ECB Special Award	**Lord (Bill) Morris of Handsworth**
PCA Special Merit Award	**Jim Cumbes**

PCA Team of the Year **Alastair Cook, Alex Hales, Joe Root, Sam Northeast, Luke Wright, Ben Stokes, †Alex Davies, Stuart Broad, Matt Coles, Jeetan Patel, Chris Rushworth.*

CHRISTOPHER MARTIN-JENKINS SPIRIT OF CRICKET AWARDS

MCC and the BBC introduced the Spirit of Cricket awards in memory of Christopher Martin-Jenkins, the former MCC president and *Test Match Special* commentator, in 2013. In September 2015, the Pro Elite Award, for the professional cricketer making the biggest contribution to the Spirit of Cricket in the English season, went to New Zealand captain **Brendon McCullum** for "his leadership qualities and the culture of fair play his team displayed" on their tour of England. The Girls' Award winners were **Ballinger Waggoners Under-13**, who helped out opponents Chesham Girls when they were four players short, letting two pairs bat for eight overs each and one for four, to ensure they used up their 20 overs, then loaned them four fielders, one of whom ran out a team-mate. Chesham won and finished top of their league; Ballinger narrowly missed out on promotion. The Boys' Award was won by **Oliver Steward** of Burn CC Under-15 in North Yorkshire, for calling back a batsman given out off his bowling because he realised it was a bump ball; the reprieved batsman went on to win the game. The Ballinger girls and Steward attended the Royal London One-Day Cup final at Lord's and were interviewed on *TMS*. The Schools' Award went to **King Solomon Academy** in Marylebone, in one of London's poorest wards; they had introduced cricket to students from challenging backgrounds and set up a mixed Under-13 side, who won their first fixture. They planned to spend a joint donation of £2,000 from MCC and the BBC on hiring facilities for coaching sessions, adding nets to their sports hall and starting an Under-15 team.

WALTER LAWRENCE TROPHY

The Walter Lawrence Trophy for the fastest century in 2015 went to **David Willey**, who reached 100 in 40 balls for Northamptonshire in the NatWest Twenty20 Blast quarter-final against Sussex at Hove on August 12. He won £3,000, along with the trophy. Since 2008, the award has covered all senior cricket in England; traditionally, it was for the fastest first-class hundred against authentic bowling (in 2015, Steven Davies's 57-ball century for Surrey against Leicestershire at The Oval). **Lloyd Sabin** of Oxford MCCU won the award for the highest score by an MCCU batsman after scoring 216 in 258 balls against Cambridge MCCU, at Cambridge on May 12. The award for the highest score in women's cricket went to **Lilly Reynolds** of Essex, for her 170 in 154 balls against Worcestershire in the Royal London Women's One-Day Cup at Southend on July 19. Sabin and Reynolds each received a silver medallion and £500. The highest score by a school batsman against MCC was by **Oscar Gutierrez**, who hit 134 in 98 balls for Leighton Park School in Reading on June 17; he received a medallion and a Gray-Nicolls bat.

CRICKET WRITERS' CLUB AWARDS

For the second year running, Yorkshire won both of the Cricket Writers' Club awards for players, presented on September 28. **Jack Leaning**, who scored 922 Championship runs at 40, was the Young Cricketer of the Year. **Jonny Bairstow**, who made 1,108 at 92, despite missing seven matches when on England duty, became the fourth County Player of the Year – and the first to win both awards, as he was the Young Cricketer in 2011. The Peter Smith Memorial Award "for services to the presentation of cricket to the public" was made to the late Australian broadcaster and Test captain **Richie Benaud**. *Summer's Crown: The Story of Cricket's County Championship* by **Stephen Chalke** was the Cricket Book of the Year.

LV= COUNTY CHAMPIONSHIP BREAKTHROUGH PLAYER

Somerset opener **Tom Abell** was named the 2015 LV= County Championship Breakthrough Player in September, ahead of Yorkshire's Jack Leaning and Surrey's Tom Curran. Previous winners of the award, which is voted for by the public, were Joe Root, Rory Burns and Alex Lees.

SECOND XI PLAYER OF THE YEAR

The Association of Cricket Statisticians and Historians named Kent's South African-born batsman **Sean Dickson** as the Les Hatton Second XI Player of the Year for 2015. Dickson was the leading run-scorer in the Second XI Championship, with 797 at 61 in eight matches, with three centuries; he also scored 216 at 54 in the one-day Second XI Trophy, and 270 at 45 in the Twenty20 tournament, including a 51-ball 108 against MCC Young Cricketers.

GROUNDSMEN OF THE YEAR

In another triumph for Yorkshire, **Andy Fogarty** was named the ECB's Groundsman of the Year for his four-day pitches at Headingley. **Simon Lee** of Taunton was the runner-up, and also won the award for the best one-day pitches, where **Nigel Gray** of Southampton's Rose Bowl came second. There were commendations for Neil Godrich (Derby) and Simon Williamson (Canterbury) in the four-day category, and for Fogarty, Steve Birks (Trent Bridge) and Andy Mackay (Hove) in the one-day category. **Bill Clutterbuck** of Guildford won the award for the best outground, pushing **John Dodds** of Scarborough into second place after three successive wins, with Stuart Kerrison (Colchester) and David Summersell (Uxbridge) commended. **Paul Derrick** won the MCC Universities award for the Racecourse Ground in Durham, with **John Moden** (Cambridge) runner-up.

CRICKET SOCIETY AWARDS

Wetherell Award Leading First-class All-rounder	**Zafar Ansari** (Surrey)
Wetherell Award for Leading Schools All-rounder	**Lee Tyrell** (Aldenham School)
Most Promising Young Cricketer	**Jack Leaning** (Yorkshire)
Most Promising Young Woman Cricketer	**Sophie Luff** (Somerset)
Sir John Hobbs Silver Jubilee Memorial Prize	**George Lavelle**
(for Outstanding Under-16 Schoolboy)	(Merchant Taylors' School, Crosby)
A. A. Thomson Fielding Prize	**Andrew Bramley**
(for Best Schoolboy Fielder)	(The Leys, Cambridge)
Christopher Box-Grainger Memorial Trophy	**Woodfield School, Kingsbury**
(for schools promoting cricket to underprivileged children)	
Don Rowan Memorial Trophy	**Michael Tippett School, Lambeth**
(for schools promoting cricket for disabled children)	
Ian Jackson Award for Services to Cricket	**Dennis Amiss**
The Perry-Lewis/Kershaw Trophy	**Peter Hardy**
(for contribution to the Cricket Society XI)	

WOMBWELL CRICKET LOVERS' SOCIETY AWARDS

George Spofforth Cricketer of the Year	**Joe Root** (Yorkshire)
Brian Sellers County Captain of the Year	**Andrew Gale** (Yorkshire)
C. B. Fry Young Cricketer of the Year	**Jack Leaning** (Yorkshire)
Arthur Wood Wicketkeeper of the Year	**Niall O'Brien** (Leicestershire)
Learie Constantine Fielder of the Year	**Ollie Rayner** (Middlesex)
Denis Compton Memorial Award for Flair	**Jonny Bairstow** (Yorkshire)
Les Bailey Most Promising Young Yorkshire Player	**Matthew Fisher**
Ted Umbers Award – Services to Yorkshire Cricket	**James Greenfield***
J. M. Kilburn Cricket Writer of the Year	**Stephen Chalke**
Jack Fingleton Cricket Commentator of the Year	**David Lloyd**

* For services to Yorkshire CCC's website, yearbook and magazine.

SUNDAY TIMES/SKY SPORTS SPORTSWOMEN OF THE YEAR

In November 2015, **Enid Bakewell** won the Lifetime Achievement Award at *The Sunday Times* and Sky Sports Sportswomen of the Year Awards. Bakewell played for England Women from 1968 to 1982, scoring 1,078 runs at 59 and taking 50 wickets at 16 in her 12 Tests. She was the second woman cricketer to win the award, after Rachael Heyhoe Flint.

ECB COUNTY JOURNALISM AWARDS

The ECB announced the fifth County Cricket Journalism Awards for reporting the domestic game on December 3. **Tim Wigmore** (ESPNcricinfo/*Daily Telegraph*) was named the Christopher Martin-Jenkins Young Journalist of the Year, and **Clive Eakin** (BBC Radio Coventry & Warwickshire) was the Christopher Martin-Jenkins County Broadcaster of the Year. Each received £5,000. *The Times* was the National Newspaper of the Year, with *The Cricket Paper* also commended. The Regional

Newspaper of the Year award was shared by *The Journal* and the *Sunday Sun* for Stuart Rayner's coverage of Durham, with *The Sentinel* (Staffordshire) and *South London Press* (Surrey) commended. **ESPNcricinfo** was Online Publication of the Year for the fourth time in a row.

ECB BUSINESS OF CRICKET AWARDS

The ECB's awards for cricket marketing and PR were made on December 3. **Nottinghamshire** won the Digital Campaign Award and the Customer Match Day Experience Award. Other awards were as follows: Commercial Partnership – **Lancashire**; Marketing and Communications Category A – **Warwickshire**; Marketing and Communications Category B&C – **Sussex**; Business Change and Innovation – **Kent**; Community Engagement – **Glamorgan**; County Recognition – **Yorkshire**; ECB Special Award – **George Foster** (head of marketing, Surrey).

ECB OSCAs

The ECB presented the 2015 NatWest Outstanding Service to Cricket Awards to volunteers from recreational cricket in October. The winners were:

NatWest CricketForce Award   **Jim Yorath** (Middlesex)
Saved Turnham Green & Polytechnic CC by securing a long-term lease on their ground and organising the takeover of responsibility for running it, while involving the local community.

Get the Game On   **Graeme Smith** (Yorkshire)
Managed the North Yorks and South Durham Cricket League's campaign to boost participation through restructuring competitions, making presentations, social media publicity, etc.

Heartbeat of the Club   **Jock Spry** (Devon)
During 38 years at Thorverton CC he has led the First and Second XIs, been chairman of the youth section and youth coach/team manager, run softball teams and helped out on the ground.

Leagues and Boards Award   **Gary Stanley** (Sussex)
Chairman of the West Sussex Invitation Cricket League and Sussex Cricket Board who introduced fundamental changes in its format to adapt to the needs of players and increase participation.

Officiating – umpires and scorers   **John Golding** (Berkshire)
Training officer for Berkshire Cricket Officials Association who developed a pre-season programme for umpires and scorers, and runs workshops to help them understand each other better.

Coach of the Year   **Edwin Lee** (Leicestershire)
Set up coaching programmes at Ratby CC for age groups from Under-10 to Under-15, promoted them in local schools and secured funding to train coaches.

Young Coach of the Year   **Matt Earl** (Northamptonshire)
Junior development officer with Kettering and Corby District Youth League, lead coach of the league's Under-14 and junior section at Kettering Town CC.

Outstanding Contribution to Coaching   **Alan Hyatt** (Warwickshire)
Managed Kings Heath CC's youth cricket programme for more than ten years, then nurtured new coaches, giving Kings Heath one of the biggest coaching pools in the Midlands.

Young Volunteer Award (for Under-25s)   **Adam Nichol** (Northumberland)
Junior co-ordinator at Ashington CC, responsible for coaching more than 70 juniors, the Northumberland Cricket Board's Under-11 performance squad and local schoolchildren.

Lifetime Achiever   **John Gurney** (Bedfordshire)
Joined Sandy CC and has given his all to the club for 60 years.

Outstanding Contribution to Disability Cricket   **Graham Furber** (Shropshire)
Active in the Shropshire Disabled Cricket Association, Winter Indoor Disability League and Cricket Federation for People with Disabilities; coach of Shropshire's Disabled county teams.

Under-19 Twenty20 Club of the Year   **Uphill Castle CC** (Somerset)
Inaugural award for clubs involved in the new NatWest Under-19 T20 tournament, aimed at keeping young players in the game. Sadly, Ashley Doyle, one of the Uphill Castle members who attended the Lord's ceremony, was killed in a road accident on the way home, and six others were injured.

ACS STATISTICIAN OF THE YEAR

In March 2016, the Association of Cricket Statisticians and Historians awarded the Statistician of the Year trophy to **Stephen Chalke** for his history of the County Championship, *Summer's Crown*, published the previous year.

2016 FIXTURES

Inv Test	Investec Test match
RL ODI	Royal London one-day international
NW T20I	NatWest Twenty20 international
LV=CC D1/2	LV= County Championship Division 1/Division 2
RLODC	Royal London One-Day Cup
NW T20	NatWest T20 Blast
Univs	First-class university match
Univs (nfc)	Non-first-class university match
♀	Day/night or floodlit game

Only the first two of each MCCU's three fixtures carry first-class status.

Sun Mar 20–Wed 23	Friendly	MCC	v Yorkshire	Abu Dhabi
Thu Mar 31–Sat Apr 2	Univs	Cambridge MCCU	v Essex	Cambridge
		Gloucestershire	v Durham MCCU	Bristol
		Oxford MCCU	v Worcestershire	Oxford
		Surrey	v Loughboro MCCU	The Oval
		Warwickshire	v Leeds/Brad MCCU	Birmingham
Mon Apr 4–Wed 6	Univs	Hampshire	v Cardiff MCCU	Southampton
Tue Apr 5–Thu 7	Univs	Cambridge MCCU	v Nottinghamshire	Cambridge
		Durham	v Durham MCCU	Chester-le-St
		Kent	v Loughboro MCCU	Canterbury
		Oxford MCCU	v Northamptonshire	Oxford
		Sussex	v Leeds/Brad MCCU	Hove
Sun Apr 10–Wed 13	LV=CC D1	Durham	v Somerset	Chester-le-St
		Hampshire	v Warwickshire	Southampton
	LV=CC D2	Nottinghamshire	v Surrey	Nottingham
		Essex	v Gloucestershire	Chelmsford
		Northamptonshire	v Sussex	Northampton
		Worcestershire	v Kent	Worcester
Mon Apr 11–Wed 13	Univs	Glamorgan	v Cardiff MCCU	Cardiff
	Univs (nfc)	Cambridge MCCU	v Lancashire	Cambridge
		Derbyshire	v Durham MCCU	Derby
		Leicestershire	v Loughboro MCCU	Leicester
		Oxford MCCU	v Middlesex	Oxford
		Yorkshire	v Leeds/Brad MCCU	Leeds
Sun Apr 17–Wed 20	LV=CC D1	Lancashire	v Nottinghamshire	Manchester
		Middlesex	v Warwickshire	Lord's
		Yorkshire	v Hampshire	Leeds
	LV=CC D2	Glamorgan	v Leicestershire	Cardiff
		Gloucestershire	v Derbyshire	Bristol
		Sussex	v Essex	Hove
Sun Apr 17–Tue 19	Univs (nfc)	Somerset	v Cardiff MCCU	Taunton Vale
Sun Apr 24–Wed 27	LV=CC D1	Durham	v Middlesex	Chester-le-St
		Surrey	v Somerset	The Oval
		Warwickshire	v Yorkshire	Birmingham
	LV=CC D2	Derbyshire	v Glamorgan	Derby
		Essex	v Northamptonshire	Chelmsford
		Gloucestershire	v Worcestershire	Bristol
		Leicestershire	v Kent	Leicester

Sun May 1–Wed 4	LV=CC D1	Hampshire	v Middlesex	Southampton
		Nottinghamshire	v Yorkshire	Nottingham
		Somerset	v Lancashire	Taunton
		Surrey	v Durham	The Oval
	LV=CC D2	Kent	v Glamorgan	Canterbury
		Northamptonshire	v Derbyshire	Northampton
		Sussex	v Leicestershire	Hove
		Worcestershire	v Essex	Worcester
Sun May 8–Wed 11	LV=CC D1	Lancashire	v Hampshire	Manchester
		Middlesex	v Nottinghamshire	Lord's
		Warwickshire	v Somerset	Birmingham
		Yorkshire	v Surrey	Leeds
	LV=CC D2	Derbyshire	v Sussex	Derby
		Glamorgan	v Worcestershire	Cardiff
		Kent	v Gloucestershire	Canterbury
		Leicestershire	v Northamptonshire	Leicester
Sun May 8–Tue 10	Tour match	Essex	v Sri Lanka	Chelmsford
Fri May 13–Sun 15	Tour match	Leicestershire	v Sri Lanka	Leicester
Sun May 15–Wed 18	LV=CC D1	Durham	v Lancashire	Chester-le-St
		Nottinghamshire	v Warwickshire	Nottingham
		Somerset	v Yorkshire	Taunton
		Surrey	v Middlesex	The Oval
	LV=CC D2	Essex	v Derbyshire	Chelmsford
		Gloucestershire	v Glamorgan	Bristol
		Northamptonshire	v Kent	Northampton
		Worcestershire	v Sussex	Worcester
Thu May 19–Mon 23	1st Inv Test	**ENGLAND**	**v SRI LANKA**	**Leeds**
Fri May 20	NW T20	Essex	v Surrey	Chelmsford ♀
		Gloucestershire	v Sussex	Bristol ♀
		Kent	v Somerset	Canterbury ♀
		Leicestershire	v Northamptonshire	Leicester
		Nottinghamshire	v Warwickshire	Nottingham ♀
		Worcestershire	v Durham	Worcester
	Univs T20	Oxford U	v Cambridge U	Oxford
Sat May 21	NW T20	Lancashire	v Derbyshire	Manchester
Sun May 22–Wed 25	LV=CC D1	Hampshire	v Nottinghamshire	Southampton
		Lancashire	v Surrey	Manchester
		Middlesex	v Somerset	Lord's
		Warwickshire	v Durham	Birmingham
	LV=CC D2	Derbyshire	v Kent	Derby
		Glamorgan	v Essex	Cardiff
		Gloucestershire	v Northamptonshire	Bristol
		Leicestershire	v Worcestershire	Leicester
Thu May 26	NW T20	Surrey	v Glamorgan	The Oval ♀
Fri May 27	NW T20	Lancashire	v Durham	Manchester ♀
		Middlesex	v Hampshire	Uxbridge
		Northamptonshire	v Derbyshire	Northampton ♀
		Yorkshire	v Leicestershire	Leeds ♀
Fri May 27–Tue 31	2nd Inv Test	**ENGLAND**	**v SRI LANKA**	**Chester-le-St**
Fri May 27	NW T20	Warwickshire	v Worcestershire	Birmingham ♀
Sat May 28–Tue 31	LV=CC D1	Nottinghamshire	v Durham	Nottingham
		Somerset	v Surrey	Taunton
	LV=CC D2	Northamptonshire	v Essex	Northampton
		Sussex	v Derbyshire	Hove

Date	Comp	Match		Venue
Sun May 29–Wed 1 Jun	LV=CC D1	Middlesex	v Hampshire	Northwood
		Yorkshire	v Lancashire	Leeds
	LV=CC D2	Kent	v Leicestershire	Canterbury
		Worcestershire	v Gloucestershire	Worcester
Wed Jun 1	NW T20	Durham	v Nottinghamshire	Chester-le-St
		Glamorgan	v Essex	Cardiff
		Sussex	v Somerset	Hove
Thu Jun 2	NW T20	Hampshire	v Kent	Southampton
		Middlesex	v Gloucestershire	Northwood
		Worcestershire	v Yorkshire	Worcester
Fri Jun 3	NW T20	Derbyshire	v Leicestershire	Derby
		Glamorgan	v Hampshire	Cardiff
		Kent	v Gloucestershire	Beckenham
		Lancashire	v Yorkshire	Manchester
		Northamptonshire	v Worcestershire	Northampton
		Somerset	v Essex	Taunton
		Sussex	v Surrey	Hove
		Warwickshire	v Durham	Birmingham
Sat Jun 4	NW T20	Leicestershire	v Durham	Leicester
		Nottinghamshire	v Lancashire	Nottingham
Sun Jun 5	RLODC	Hampshire	v Essex	Southampton
		Kent	v Surrey	Beckenham
		Lancashire	v Warwickshire	Manchester
		Leicestershire	v Durham	Leicester
		Somerset	v Gloucestershire	Taunton
		Worcestershire	v Derbyshire	Worcester
Mon Jun 6	RLODC	Glamorgan	v Gloucestershire	Cardiff
		Nottinghamshire	v Northamptonshire	Nottingham
		Sussex	v Essex	Hove
Tue Jun 7	RLODC	Derbyshire	v Durham	Derby
		Middlesex	v Hampshire	Radlett
		Warwickshire	v Leicestershire	Birmingham
		Yorkshire	v Worcestershire	Leeds
Wed Jun 8	RLODC	Glamorgan	v Sussex	Cardiff
		Gloucestershire	v Middlesex	Bristol
		Northamptonshire	v Lancashire	Northampton
		Nottinghamshire	v Warwickshire	Nottingham
		Surrey	v Somerset	The Oval
	NW T20	Kent	v Hampshire	Canterbury
Thu Jun 9–Mon 13	3rd Inv Test	ENGLAND	v SRI LANKA	Lord's
Fri Jun 10	NW T20	Essex	v Middlesex	Chelmsford
		Gloucestershire	v Glamorgan	Bristol
		Lancashire	v Leicestershire	Manchester
		Nottinghamshire	v Derbyshire	Nottingham
		Somerset	v Surrey	Taunton
		Sussex	v Kent	Hove
		Warwickshire	v Yorkshire	Birmingham
		Worcestershire	v Northamptonshire	Worcester
Sun Jun 12	RLODC	Derbyshire	v Yorkshire	Derby
		Durham	v Worcestershire	Chester-le-St
		Essex	v Somerset	Chelmsford
		Kent	v Glamorgan	Canterbury
		Lancashire	v Nottinghamshire	Blackpool
		Northamptonshire	v Leicestershire	Northampton
		Sussex	v Middlesex	Hove

Date	Competition			Venue	
Tue Jun 14	RLODC	Glamorgan	v Middlesex	Cardiff	♀
		Gloucestershire	v Hampshire	Bristol	♀
		Kent	v Somerset	Canterbury	
		Surrey	v Sussex	Guildford	
		Yorkshire	v Northamptonshire	Scarborough	
Wed Jun 15	RLODC	Durham	v Nottinghamshire	Chester-le-St	♀
		Essex	v Kent	Chelmsford	
		Hampshire	v Surrey	Southampton	♀
		Lancashire	v Yorkshire	Manchester	♀
		Warwickshire	v Derbyshire	Birmingham	♀
		Worcestershire	v Leicestershire	Worcester	
	NW T20	Somerset	v Glamorgan	Taunton	
Thu Jun 16	ODI	**IRELAND**	**v SRI LANKA**	**Malahide**	
	NW T20	Essex	v Gloucestershire	Chelmsford	♀
		Lancashire	v Northamptonshire	Manchester	♀
		Middlesex	v Sussex	Lord's	♀
Fri Jun 17	NW T20	Derbyshire	v Warwickshire	Derby	♀
		Glamorgan	v Kent	Cardiff	♀
		Gloucestershire	v Somerset	Bristol	♀
		Hampshire	v Sussex	Southampton	♀
		Leicestershire	v Worcestershire	Leicester	
		Northamptonshire	v Durham	Northampton	♀
		Surrey	v Middlesex	The Oval	♀
		Yorkshire	v Nottinghamshire	Leeds	♀
Sat Jun 18	ODI	**IRELAND**	**v SRI LANKA**	**Malahide**	
	NW T20	Worcestershire	v Nottinghamshire	Worcester	
Sun Jun 19–Wed 22	LV=CC D1	Surrey	v Nottinghamshire	The Oval	
	LV=CC D2	Essex	v Leicestershire	Chelmsford	
		Glamorgan	v Kent	Cardiff	
Sun Jun 19	NW T20	Somerset	v Hampshire	Taunton	
		Warwickshire	v Lancashire	Birmingham	
		Yorkshire	v Derbyshire	Leeds	
Mon Jun 20	Women's ODI	**ENGLAND W**	**v PAKISTAN W**	**Leicester**	
Mon Jun 20–Thu 23	LV=CC D1	Durham	v Yorkshire	Chester-le-St	
		Lancashire	v Warwickshire	Manchester	
	LV=CC D2	Derbyshire	v Worcestershire	Derby	
Tue Jun 21	RL ODI	**ENGLAND**	**v SRI LANKA**	**Nottingham**	♀
Wed Jun 22	Women's ODI	**ENGLAND W**	**v PAKISTAN W**	**Worcester**	
Wed Jun 22–Sat 25	LV=CC D2	Sussex	v Northamptonshire	Arundel	
Thu Jun 23	NW T20	Middlesex	v Somerset	Lord's	♀
Fri Jun 24	RL ODI	**ENGLAND**	**v SRI LANKA**	**Birmingham**	♀
	NW T20	Derbyshire	v Nottinghamshire	Derby	♀
		Durham	v Yorkshire	Chester-le-St	♀
		Essex	v Hampshire	Chelmsford	♀
		Kent	v Middlesex	Canterbury	♀
		Glamorgan	v Surrey	Cardiff	♀
		Lancashire	v Worcestershire	Manchester	♀
		Leicestershire	v Warwickshire	Leicester	
Sat Jun 25	NW T20	Hampshire	v Gloucestershire	Southampton	
		Surrey	v Essex	The Oval	
Sun Jun 26	RL ODI	**ENGLAND**	**v SRI LANKA**	**Bristol**	

Sun Jun 26–Wed 29	LV=CC D1	Hampshire	v Somerset	Southampton
		Middlesex	v Lancashire	Lord's
		Warwickshire	v Nottinghamshire	Birmingham
	LV=CC D2	Kent	v Derbyshire	Canterbury
	Tour match	Durham	v Sri Lanka A	Chester-le-St
		Yorkshire	v Pakistan A	Leeds
Sun Jun 26	NW T20	Sussex	v Gloucestershire	Arundel
		Northamptonshire	v Leicestershire	Northampton
Mon Jun 27	Women's ODI	**ENGLAND W**	**v PAKISTAN W**	**Taunton**
Mon Jun 27–Thu 30	LV=CC D2	Leicestershire	v Gloucestershire	Leicester
Wed Jun 29	RL ODI	**ENGLAND**	**v SRI LANKA**	**The Oval** ♀
Thu Jun 30	NW T20	Durham	v Worcestershire	Chester-le-St ♀
		Kent	v Sussex	Canterbury ♀
Fri Jul 1	Univs (o-d)	Oxford U	v Cambridge U	Lord's
	NW T20	Essex	v Kent	Chelmsford ♀
		Nottinghamshire	v Durham	Nottingham ♀
		Somerset	v Gloucestershire	Taunton
		Surrey	v Hampshire	The Oval ♀
		Sussex	v Middlesex	Hove ♀
		Warwickshire	v Northamptonshire	Birmingham ♀
		Worcestershire	v Derbyshire	Worcester
		Yorkshire	v Lancashire	Leeds ♀
Sat Jul 2	RL ODI	**ENGLAND**	**v SRI LANKA**	**Cardiff**
Sat Jul 2–Tue 5	LV=CC D1	Surrey	v Warwickshire	Guildford
	LV=CC D2	Sussex	v Glamorgan	Hove
Sun Jul 3–Wed 6	LV=CC D1	Durham	v Hampshire	Chester-le-St
		Nottinghamshire	v Lancashire	Nottingham
		Yorkshire	v Middlesex	Scarborough
	LV=CC D2	Essex	v Kent	Chelmsford
		Worcestershire	v Leicestershire	Worcester
Sun Jul 3	NW T20	Derbyshire	v Northamptonshire	Chesterfield
	Women's T20I	**ENGLAND W**	**v PAKISTAN W**	**Bristol**
Sun Jul 3–Wed 6	Tour match	Pakistan A	v Sri Lanka A	Leicester
Sun Jul 3–Tue 5	Tour match	Somerset	v Pakistan	Taunton
Mon Jul 4–Thu 7	LV=CC D2	Derbyshire	v Northamptonshire	Chesterfield
Tue Jul 5	Women's T20I	**ENGLAND W**	**v PAKISTAN W**	**Southampton**
	NW T20	**ENGLAND**	**v SRI LANKA**	**Southampton** ♀
Tue Jul 5–Fri 8	Univs	Oxford U	v Cambridge U	Oxford
Wed Jul 6	NW T20	Gloucestershire	v Surrey	Bristol ♀
Thu Jul 7	Women's T20I	**ENGLAND W**	**v PAKISTAN W**	**Chelmsford** ♀
	NW T20	Glamorgan	v Sussex	Cardiff ♀
		Somerset	v Kent	Taunton
Fri Jul 8–Sun 10	Tour match	Sussex	v Pakistan	Hove
Fri Jul 8	NW T20	Gloucestershire	v Kent	Bristol ♀
		Hampshire	v Essex	Southampton ♀
		Leicestershire	v Derbyshire	Leicester
		Middlesex	v Glamorgan	Richmond
		Northamptonshire	v Nottinghamshire	Northampton ♀
		Surrey	v Somerset	The Oval ♀
		Worcestershire	v Lancashire	Worcester
		Yorkshire	v Warwickshire	Leeds ♀

Sat Jul 9	NW T20	Nottinghamshire	v Worcestershire	Nottingham	
Sun Jul 10–Wed 13	LV=CC D1	Somerset	v Middlesex	Taunton	
		Warwickshire	v Hampshire	Birmingham	
	LV=CC D2	Northamptonshire	v Worcestershire	Northampton	
	Tour match	Pakistan A	v Sri Lanka A	Worcester	
Sun Jul 10	NW T20	Derbyshire	v Yorkshire	Chesterfield	
		Glamorgan	v Gloucestershire	Cardiff	
		Durham	v Leicestershire	Chester-le-St	
Mon Jul 11–Thu 14	LV=CC D1	Surrey	v Yorkshire	The Oval	
Tue Jul 12	NW T20	Leicestershire	v Nottinghamshire	Leicester	
Wed Jul 13–Sat 16	LV=CC D2	Gloucestershire	v Essex	Cheltenham	
Wed Jul 13	NW T20	Derbyshire	v Lancashire	Derby	♀
Thu Jul 14–Mon 18	1st Inv Test	ENGLAND	v PAKISTAN	Lord's	
Thu Jul 14	NW T20	Hampshire	v Glamorgan	Southampton	♀
Fri Jul 15	Tour match (o-d)	Derbyshire	v Sri Lanka A	Derby	♀
		Glamorgan	v Pakistan A	Newport	
	NW T20	Durham	v Northamptonshire	Chester-le-St	♀
		Kent	v Surrey	Tunbridge Wells	
		Leicestershire	v Lancashire	Leicester	
		Nottinghamshire	v Yorkshire	Nottingham	♀
		Somerset	v Middlesex	Taunton	
		Sussex	v Hampshire	Hove	♀
		Worcestershire	v Warwickshire	Worcester	
Sat Jul 16–Tue 19	LV=CC D1	Lancashire	v Durham	Southport	
Sun Jul 17–Wed 20	LV=CC D1	Hampshire	v Surrey	Southampton	
		Nottinghamshire	v Somerset	Nottingham	
	LV=CC D2	Glamorgan	v Derbyshire	Colwyn Bay	
		Kent	v Sussex	Tunbridge Wells	
Sun Jul 17	NW T20	Gloucestershire	v Essex	Cheltenham	
		Warwickshire	v Leicestershire	Birmingham	
Mon Jul 18	Tour match (o-d)	Pakistan A	v Sri Lanka A	Cheltenham	
Tue Jul 19	NW T20	Northamptonshire	v Warwickshire	Northampton	♀
	Tour match (o-d)	England Lions	v Pakistan A	Cheltenham	
Wed Jul 20–Sat 23	LV=CC D2	Gloucestershire	v Leicestershire	Cheltenham	
Wed Jul 20	NW T20	Yorkshire	v Durham	Leeds	♀
Thu Jul 21	Tour match (o-d)	England Lions	v Sri Lanka A	Northampton	♀
	NW T20	Essex	v Sussex	Chelmsford	♀
		Middlesex	v Surrey	Lord's	♀
Fri Jul 22–Tue 26	2nd Inv Test	ENGLAND	v PAKISTAN	Manchester	
Fri Jul 22	Tour match (o-d)	Pakistan A	v Sri Lanka A	Northampton	♀
	NW T20	Derbyshire	v Worcestershire	Derby	♀
		Durham	v Lancashire	Chester-le-St	♀
		Hampshire	v Middlesex	Southampton	♀
		Glamorgan	v Somerset	Cardiff	♀
		Kent	v Essex	Canterbury	♀
		Surrey	v Sussex	The Oval	♀
		Warwickshire	v Nottinghamshire	Birmingham	♀
		Yorkshire	v Northamptonshire	Leeds	♀

Sun Jul 24	RLODC	Essex	v Surrey	Chelmsford	
		Gloucestershire	v Sussex	Cheltenham	
		Leicestershire	v Yorkshire	Leicester	
		Middlesex	v Kent	Lord's	
		Northamptonshire	v Durham	Northampton	
		Nottinghamshire	v Derbyshire	Sookholme	
		Somerset	v Glamorgan	Taunton	
		Warwickshire	v Worcestershire	Birmingham	
	Tour match (o-d)	England Lions	v Pakistan A	Canterbury	
Mon Jul 25	Tour match (o-d)	England Lions	v Sri Lanka A	Canterbury	
Tue Jul 26	RLODC	Essex	v Glamorgan	Chelmsford	
		Hampshire	v Kent	Southampton	🌂
		Leicestershire	v Lancashire	Leicester	
		Somerset	v Middlesex	Taunton	
		Warwickshire	v Northamptonshire	Birmingham	
Tue Jul 26–Fri 29	U19 Test	England U19	v Sri Lanka U19	Cambridge	
Wed Jul 27	RLODC	Derbyshire	v Lancashire	Derby	🌂
		Durham	v Warwickshire	Chester-le-St	🌂
		Surrey	v Gloucestershire	The Oval	🌂
		Sussex	v Hampshire	Hove	🌂
		Worcestershire	v Northamptonshire	Worcester	
		Yorkshire	v Nottinghamshire	Scarborough	
Thu Jul 28	NW T20	Middlesex	v Essex	Lord's	🌂
		Sussex	v Glamorgan	Hove	🌂
Fri Jul 29–Sat 30	Tour match	Worcestershire	v Pakistan	Worcester	
Fri Jul 29	NW T20	Durham	v Derbyshire	Chester-le-St	🌂
		Essex	v Glamorgan	Chelmsford	🌂
		Gloucestershire	v Middlesex	Bristol	🌂
		Hampshire	v Somerset	Southampton	🌂
		Lancashire	v Warwickshire	Manchester	🌂
		Northamptonshire	v Yorkshire	Northampton	🌂
		Nottinghamshire	v Leicestershire	Nottingham	🌂
		Surrey	v Kent	The Oval	🌂
Sat Jul 30	RLODC	Somerset	v Sussex	Taunton	
Sun Jul 31	RLODC	Durham	v Yorkshire	Chester-le-St	
		Glamorgan	v Hampshire	Swansea	
		Kent	v Gloucestershire	Canterbury	
		Leicestershire	v Nottinghamshire	Leicester	
		Middlesex	v Essex	Lord's	
		Northamptonshire	v Derbyshire	Northampton	
		Worcestershire	v Lancashire	Worcester	
Mon Aug 1	RLODC	Derbyshire	v Leicestershire	Derby	🌂
		Lancashire	v Durham	Manchester	🌂
		Nottinghamshire	v Worcestershire	Nottingham	🌂
		Surrey	v Glamorgan	The Oval	🌂
		Yorkshire	v Warwickshire	Leeds	🌂
Tue Aug 2	RLODC	Gloucestershire	v Essex	Bristol	🌂
		Hampshire	v Somerset	Southampton	🌂
		Middlesex	v Surrey	Lord's	🌂
		Sussex	v Kent	Hove	🌂
Wed Aug 3–Sun 7	3rd Inv Test	**ENGLAND**	**v PAKISTAN**	**Birmingham**	
Wed Aug 3–Sat 6	LV=CC D2	Glamorgan	v Northamptonshire	Swansea	
		Kent	v Worcestershire	Canterbury	
	U19 Test	England U19	v Sri Lanka U19	Northampton	

Thu Aug 4–Sun 7	LV=CC D1	Hampshire v Lancashire	Southampton
		Middlesex v Surrey	Lord's
		Somerset v Durham	Taunton
		Yorkshire v Warwickshire	Leeds
	LV=CC D2	Essex v Sussex	Colchester
		Leicestershire v Derbyshire	Leicester
Mon Aug 8	NW T20	**Quarter-final**	
Tue Aug 9	NW T20	**Quarter-final**	
Wed Aug 10	U19 ODI	England U19 v Sri Lanka U19	Wormsley
	NW T20	**Quarter-final**	
Thu Aug 11–Mon 15	4th Inv Test	**ENGLAND v PAKISTAN**	The Oval
Thu Aug 11	NW T20	**Quarter-final**	
Sat Aug 13–Tue 16	LV=CC D1	Lancashire v Yorkshire	Manchester
		Middlesex v Durham	Lord's
		Nottinghamshire v Hampshire	Nottingham
		Warwickshire v Surrey	Birmingham
	LV=CC D2	Derbyshire v Essex	Derby
		Sussex v Gloucestershire	Hove
		Worcestershire v Glamorgan	Worcester
		Northamptonshire v Leicestershire	Northampton
Sat Aug 13	U19 ODI	England U19 v Sri Lanka U19	Chelmsford
Tue Aug 16	U19 ODI	England U19 v Sri Lanka U19	Canterbury
Wed Aug 17	RLODC	**Quarter-finals**	
Thu Aug 18	ODI	**IRELAND v PAKISTAN**	Malahide
	RLODC	**Quarter-finals**	
Sat Aug 20	ODI	**IRELAND v PAKISTAN**	Malahide
	NW T20	**Semi-finals and final**	
Tue Aug 23–Fri 26	LV=CC D1	Durham v Warwickshire	Chester-le-St
		Somerset v Hampshire	Taunton
		Surrey v Lancashire	The Oval
		Yorkshire v Nottinghamshire	Scarborough
	LV=CC D2	Glamorgan v Sussex	Cardiff
		Gloucestershire v Kent	Bristol
		Leicestershire v Essex	Leicester
		Worcestershire v Northamptonshire	Worcester
Wed Aug 24	RL ODI	**ENGLAND v PAKISTAN**	Southampton ♀
Sat Aug 27	RL ODI	**ENGLAND v PAKISTAN**	Lord's
Sun Aug 28	RLODC	**Semi-final**	
Mon Aug 29	RLODC	**Semi-final**	
Tue Aug 30	RL ODI	**ENGLAND v PAKISTAN**	Nottingham ♀
Wed Aug 31–Sat Sep 3	LV=CC D1	Durham v Nottinghamshire	Chester-le-St
		Hampshire v Yorkshire	Southampton
		Lancashire v Somerset	Manchester
		Warwickshire v Middlesex	Birmingham
	LV=CC D2	Derbyshire v Gloucestershire	Derby
		Essex v Worcestershire	Chelmsford
		Northamptonshire v Glamorgan	Northampton
		Sussex v Kent	Hove
Thu Sep 1	RL ODI	**ENGLAND v PAKISTAN**	Leeds ♀

Sun Sep 4	RL ODI	**ENGLAND**	**v PAKISTAN**	**Cardiff**
	Village Cup	Final		Lord's
Tue Sep 6–Fri 9	LV=CC D1	Nottinghamshire	v Middlesex	Nottingham
		Somerset	v Warwickshire	Taunton
		Surrey	v Hampshire	The Oval
		Yorkshire	v Durham	Leeds
	LV=CC D2	Glamorgan	v Gloucestershire	Cardiff
		Kent	v Northamptonshire	Beckenham
		Leicestershire	v Sussex	Leicester
Wed Sep 7	NW T20I	**ENGLAND**	**v PAKISTAN**	**Manchester**
Mon Sep 12–Thu 15	LV=CC D1	Durham	v Surrey	Chester-le-St
		Lancashire	v Middlesex	Manchester
		Yorkshire	v Somerset	Leeds
	LV=CC D2	Derbyshire	v Leicestershire	Derby
		Essex	v Glamorgan	Chelmsford
		Northamptonshire	v Gloucestershire	Northampton
		Sussex	v Worcestershire	Hove
Sat Sep 17	RLODC	Final		Lord's
Tue Sep 20–Fri 23	LV=CC D1	Hampshire	v Durham	Southampton
		Middlesex	v Yorkshire	Lord's
		Somerset	v Nottinghamshire	Taunton
		Warwickshire	v Lancashire	Birmingham
	LV=CC D2	Gloucestershire	v Sussex	Bristol
		Kent	v Essex	Canterbury
		Leicestershire	v Glamorgan	Leicester
		Worcestershire	v Derbyshire	Worcester

ERRATA

Wisden 1989	Page 961	In the seventh one-day international between India and West Indies, Sanjeev Sharma bowled 6.5 overs not 7.5, and the innings lasted 42.5 overs rather than 43.5.
Wisden 2004	Page 1258	On the first day of Australia's First Test against Zimbabwe, they were 372-3, not 368-3.
Wisden 2014	Page 347	In England's second innings against Australia at Lord's, Joe Root had eight, not four, when he tickled a Watson seamer between Haddin and Clarke.
Wisden 2015	Page 108	Peter Hayter covered England's tour of the West Indies in the spring of 1994, not 1993.
	Page 328	In the caption, the Tied Test was in 1960-61, not 1950-51.
	Page 361	Tredwell had 57 maidens in all first-class cricket, not 58.
	Page 372	Hampshire played seven first-class matches on the Isle of Wight between 1956 and 1962.
	Page 421	In Essex's first innings against Kent, Tredwell bowled two maidens not three.
	Page 448	Chanderpaul's match-winning 52 was 30 days before his 40th birthday.
	Page 467	Tredwell had 22 maidens in the Championship, not 23.
	Page 780	M. G. Johnson conceded 1,093 runs, average 23.25, in the calendar year 2015.
	Page 843	M. G. Johnson conceded 461 runs, average 35.46; I. Sharma scored 2 runs, average 1.00.
	Page 847	In India's second innings at Adelaide, I. Sharma was out for 0; there were 16 extras (including 9 leg-byes); and Johnson's figures were 16-2-44-2.
	Pages 861-2	The play-off and final of the Ryobi Cup took place in October 2013, not 2014.
	Page 889	Australia, not England, were 0-3 on their way to 32-7 dec in the Brisbane Test of 1950-51.
	Page 936	Bangalore is the capital of Karnataka, not the captain.
	Page 947	Karun Nair and Amit Verma added 206* for Karnataka's sixth wicket, not the fifth.
	Page 1131	Stephen Katwaroo reached 91, his highest first-class score but not a maiden century, in Trinidad & Tobago's match against Leeward Islands on March 14–17.
	Page 1191	England's No. 3 in the Women's World Twenty20 final was Heather Knight, not Helen.
	Page 1207	K. M. Beams and Maham Tariq made their Twenty20 international debuts in the match between Australia's and Pakistan's women on September 3; B. M. Bezuidenhout made her Twenty20 international debut for South Africa's women against England on September 7.

CHARITIES IN 2015

ARUNDEL CASTLE CRICKET FOUNDATION – more than 300,000 disadvantaged youngsters, many with special needs and mainly from inner-city areas (London's boroughs in particular), have received instruction and encouragement at Arundel since 1986. In 2015, there were 99 days devoted to activities, and 5,000 young people benefited. Director of cricket: John Barclay, Arundel Park Sussex BN18 9LH. Tel: 01903 882602; website: www.arundelcastlecricketfoundation.co.uk.

THE BRIAN JOHNSTON MEMORIAL TRUST supports cricket for the blind, and aims to ease the financial worries of talented young cricketers through scholarships. The BJMT spin-bowling programme, in support of the ECB, was launched in 2010 to provide expert coaching to all the first-class county Academies and the MCCUs. Registered Charity No. 1045946. Trust administrator: Richard Anstey, 178 Manor Drive North, Worcester Park, Surrey KT4 7RU. Email: contact@lordstaverners.org; website: www.lordstaverners.org.

BRITISH ASSOCIATION FOR CRICKETERS WITH DISABILITIES was formed in 1991 to promote playing opportunities for cricketers with physical and learning difficulties. We work in close partnership with the ECB. President: Bill Higginson, 07455 219526, higgi.b1936@gmail.com Chairman: David Lloyd, 07739 146762, david53lloyd@googlemail.com.

BUNBURY CRICKET CLUB has raised more than £17m for national charities and worthwhile causes. This year is the club's 30th anniversary. Since 1987, a total of 1,680 boys have played in the Bunbury Festival; 684 have gone on to play first-class cricket, and 70 for England, including ten of the side which beat South Africa in 2015-16. Further information from Dr David English CBE, 1 Highwood Cottages, Nan Clark's Lane, London NW7 4HJ; website: www.bunburycricket.com.

CAPITAL KIDS CRICKET, formed in 1990, delivers cricket tuition to boys and girls in state schools throughout inner London, establishes and assists emerging clubs, organises competitions in local communities, and offers out-of-London residential festivals. Its British Land Kids Cricket League involves 2,500 primary schoolchildren. Contact John Challinor (chairman), 79 Gore Road, London E9 7HN or johnchallinor@hotmail.com; or Shahidul Alam Ratan (director of cricket), 07748 114811 or shahidul.alam@capitalkidscricket.co.uk. Website: www.capitalkidscricket.org.uk.

CHANCE TO SHINE is a national charity on a mission to spread the power of cricket throughout schools and communities. Since launching in 2005, Chance to Shine has reached almost 3m children across 11,000 state schools. Chief executive: Luke Swanson, Kia Oval, Kennington, London SE11 5SS. Tel: 020 7820 9379; website: www.chancetoshine.org.

CRICKET FOR CHANGE is now part of THE CHANGE FOUNDATION, and uses sport to change young lives. In partnership with Investec we use Street20 cricket for the Inner City World Cup in London, and also run the Refugee Cricket Project in partnership with the Refugee Council. Our disability sports programme Hit The Top continues to deliver many thriving clubs and projects. Overseas work has included initiatives in Europe (in partnership with ICC), Afghanistan, Israel and the West Bank, Brazil, Jamaica, Barbados, Rwanda, Uganda, Sri Lanka, India, Bangladesh, Hong Kong, Ghana and New York. Chief executive: Andy Sellins, The Cricket Centre, Plough Lane, Wallington, Surrey SM6 8JQ. Tel: 020 8669 2177; email: office@thechangefoundation.org.uk; website: thechangefoundation.org.uk.

THE CRICKET SOCIETY TRUST'S principal aim is to support schools and organisations to encourage enjoyment of the game and develop skills. Particular effort and concentration is given to children with special needs, through programmes arranged with the Arundel Castle Cricket Foundation and the Belvoir Castle Cricket Trust. Hon. secretary: Ken Merchant, 16 Louise Road, Rayleigh, Essex SS6 8LW. Tel: 01268 747414; website: www.cricketsocietytrust.org.uk.

THE DICKIE BIRD FOUNDATION, set up by the former umpire in 2004, helps financially disadvantaged youngsters to participate in the sport of their choice. Grants are made towards the cost of equipment and clothing. Trustee: Ted Cowley, 3 The Tower, Tower Drive, Arthington Lane, Otley, Yorkshire LS21 1NQ. Tel: 07503 641457; website: www.thedickiebirdfoundation.co.uk.

ENGLAND AND WALES CRICKET TRUST was established in 2005 to aid community participation, with a fund from which to make interest-free loans to amateur cricket clubs. In its latest financial year it incurred costs on charitable activities of £12.8m – primarily grants to cricket charities and amateur clubs, and to county boards. Contact: ECB, Lord's Cricket Ground, London NW8 8QZ. Tel: 020 7432 1200; email: info@ecb.co.uk.

THE EVELINA LONDON CHILDREN'S HOSPITAL is the official charity partner of Surrey CCC and The Kia Oval. Ten minutes from the ground, in Waterloo, Evelina is one of the country's leading children's hospitals, treating patients from all over the south-east of England. Partnership head: Jon Surtees, The Kia Oval, Kennington, London SE11 5SS. Tel: 020 7820 5780; website: www.kiaoval.com.

FIELDS IN TRUST is the only national charity protecting and improving outdoor space for sport, play and recreation for current and future generations to enjoy. We currently safeguard over 2,600 sites and more than 30,000 acres of land. Chief executive: Helen Griffiths, 36 Woodstock Grove, London W12 8LE. Tel: 020 7427 2110; website: www.fieldsintrust.org; Facebook: www. facebook.com/fieldsintrust; Twitter: @FieldsInTrust

THE HORNSBY PROFESSIONAL CRICKETERS' FUND supports former professional cricketers and their dependants, through regular financial help or one-off grants towards healthcare or similar essential needs. It was established in 1928 from a bequest from the estate of J. H. J. Hornsby (Middlesex, MCC and the Gentlemen), augmented more recently by a bequest from Sir Alec and Eric Bedser, and also by the Walter Hammond Memorial Fund merging with the Trust, which works closely with the PCA and, where appropriate, a player's former county. Secretary: The Rev. Prebendary Mike Vockins, OBE, Birchwood Lodge, Birchwood, Storridge, Malvern, Worcestershire WR13 5EZ. Tel: 01886 884366.

THE LEARNING FOR A BETTER WORLD (LBW) TRUST, established in 2006, provides tertiary education to disadvantaged students in the cricket-playing countries of the developing world. In 2015 it was assisting some 1,000 students in India, Pakistan, Nepal, Uganda, Afghanistan, Sri Lanka and South Africa, a commitment which will expand in 2016 to include Jamaica. Chairman: David Vaux, GPO Box 3029, Sydney, NSW 2000, Australia; website: www.lbwtrust.com.au.

THE LORD'S TAVERNERS is the official charity of recreational cricket, and the UK's leading youth cricket and disability sports charity, dedicated to giving disadvantaged and disabled young people a sporting chance. This year the charity will donate over £3m to help young people of all abilities and backgrounds to participate in cricket and other sporting activities. Registered Charity No. 306054. The Lord's Taverners, 90 Chancery Lane, London WC2A 1EU. Tel: 020 7025 0000; email: contact@lordstaverners.org; website: www.lordstaverners.org.

THE PCA BENEVOLENT FUND is part of the commitment of the Professional Cricketers' Association to aid current and former players and their dependants in times of hardship and upheaval, or to help them readjust to the world beyond the game. Assistant chief executive: Jason Ratcliffe, PCA, The Kia Oval, Kennington, London SE11 5SS. Tel: 07768 558050; website: www.thepca.co.uk.

THE PRIMARY CLUB provides sporting and recreational facilities for the blind and partially sighted. Membership is nominally restricted to those dismissed first ball in any form of cricket; almost 10,000 belong. In total, the club has raised £3m, helped by sales of its tie, popularised by *Test Match Special*. Andrew Strauss is president of the Primary Club Juniors. Hon. secretary: Chris Larlham, PO Box 12121, Saffron Walden, Essex CB10 2ZF. Tel: 01799 586507; website: www.primaryclub.org.

THE PRINCE'S TRUST helps disadvantaged young people get their lives on track. This year they are celebrating 40 years of supporting 13–30-year-olds who are unemployed, and those struggling at school and at risk of exclusion. The Trust's programmes use a variety of activities, including cricket and other sports, to engage young people and help them gain skills, confidence and qualifications. Prince's Trust House, 9 Eldon Street, London EC2M 7LS. Tel: 0800 842842. Website: www. princes-trust.org.uk.

THE TOM MAYNARD TRUST – formed in 2012 after Tom's tragic death – covers three main areas: helping aspiring young professionals with education projects, currently across four sports; running an academy in Spain for young county cricketers on the first rung of the career ladder; and providing grants for sportspeople to help with travel, kit, coaching, training and education. Contact: Mike Fatkin, 67a Radnor Road, Canton, Cardiff CF5 1RA; website: www.tommaynardtrust.com.

YOUTH TRUSTS – most of the first-class counties operate youth trusts through which donations, legacies and the proceeds of fundraising are channelled for the development of youth cricket and cricket in the community. Information may be obtained from the county chief executives.

CRICKET TRADE DIRECTORY

BOOKSELLERS

AARDVARK BOOKS, 10 Briardene Avenue, Scarborough, North Yorkshire YO12 6PL. Tel: 01723 374072; email: pete@aardvarkcricketbooks.co.uk or **pandlaardvark@btinternet.com.** Peter Taylor specialises in *Wisdens*, including rare hardbacks and early editions. *Wisdens* purchased. Restoration of hardbacks and softbacks, cleaning and gilding undertaken.

ACUMEN BOOKS, Pennyfields, New Road, Bignall End, Stoke-on-Trent ST7 8QF. Tel: 01782 720753; email: wca@acumenbooks.co.uk; website: www.acumenbooks.co.uk. Everything for umpires, scorers, officials, etc. MCC Lawbooks, open-learning manuals, Tom Smith and other textbooks, Duckworth/Lewis, scorebooks, equipment, over & run counters, gauges, heavy and Hi-Vis bails, etc; import/export.

BOUNDARY BOOKS, The Haven, West Street, Childrey OX12 9UL. Tel: 01235 751021; email: mike@boundarybooks.com; website: www.boundarybooks.com. Rare and second-hand books, autographs and memorabilia bought and sold. Catalogues issued. Large Oxfordshire showroom open by appointment. Unusual and scarce items always available.

CHRISTOPHER SAUNDERS, Kingston House, High Street, Newnham-on-Severn, Gloucestershire GL14 1BB. Tel: 01594 516030; email: chris@cricket-books.com; website: www.cricket-books.com. Office/bookroom open by appointment. Second-hand/antiquarian cricket books and memorabilia bought and sold. Regular catalogues issued containing selections from over 12,000 items in stock.

GRACE BOOKS AND CARDS (TED KIRWAN), Donkey Cart Cottage, Main Street, Bruntingthorpe, Lutterworth, Leics LE17 5QE. Tel: 0116 247 8417; email: ted@gracecricketana.co.uk. Second-hand and antiquarian cricket books, *Wisdens*, autographed material and cricket ephemera of all kinds. Now also modern postcards of current international cricketers.

JOHN JEFFERS, The Old Mill, Aylesbury Road, Wing, Leighton Buzzard LU7 0PG. Tel: 01296 688543; mobile: 07846 537692; e-mail: edgwarerover@live.co.uk. *Wisden* specialist. Immediate decision and top settlement for purchase of *Wisden* collections. Why wait for the next auction? Why pay the auctioneer's commission anyway?

J. W. McKENZIE, 12 Stoneleigh Park Road, Ewell, Epsom, Surrey KT19 0QT. Tel: 020 8393 7700; email: mckenziecricket@btconnect.com; website: www.mckenzie-cricket.co.uk. Specialist since 1971. Antiquarian and second-hand cricket books and memorabilia bought and sold. Regular catalogues issued. Large shop premises open regular business hours, 30 minutes from London Waterloo. Please phone before visiting.

KEN FAULKNER, 65 Brookside, Wokingham, Berkshire RG41 2ST. Tel: 0118 978 5255; email: kfaulkner@bowmore.demon.co.uk; website: www.bowmore.demon.co.uk. Bookroom open by appointment. My stall, with a strong *Wisden* content, will be operating at the Cheltenham Cricket Festival in July 2016. We purchase *Wisden* collections which include pre-1946 editions.

ROGER PAGE, 10 Ekari Court, Yallambie, Victoria 3085, Australia. Tel: (+61) 3 9435 6332; email: rpcricketbooks@unite.com.au; website: www.rpcricketbooks.com. Australia's only full-time dealer in new and second-hand cricket books. Distributor of overseas cricket annuals and magazines. Agent for Association of Cricket Statisticians and Cricket Memorabilia Society.

ST MARY'S BOOKS & PRINTS, 9 St Mary's Hill, Stamford, Lincolnshire PE9 2DP. Tel: 01780 763033; email: info@stmarysbooks.com; website: www.stmarysbooks.com. Dealers in *Wisdens* 1864–2015, second-hand, rare cricket books and *Vanity Fair* prints. Book-search service offered.

SPORTSPAGES, 7 Finns Business Park, Mill Lane, Farnham, Surrey GU10 5RX. Tel: 01252 851040; email: info@sportspages.com; website: www.sportspages.com. Large stock of *Wisdens*, fine sports books and memorabilia, including cricket, rugby, football and golf. Books and memorabilia also purchased, please offer. Visitors welcome to browse by appointment.

TIM BEDDOW, 66 Oak Road, Oldbury, West Midlands B68 0BD. Tel: 0121 421 7117; mobile: 07956 456112; email: wisden1864@hotmail.com. Wanted: cash paid for football, cricket, speedway, motorsport and rugby union memorabilia, badges, books, programmes (amateur and professional), autographed items, match tickets, yearbooks and photographs – anything considered.

WILLIAM H. ROBERTS, Long Low, 27 Gernhill Avenue, Fixby, Huddersfield, West Yorkshire HD2 2HR. Tel: 01484 654463; email: william.roberts2@virgin.net; website: www.williamroberts-cricket.com. Second-hand/antiquarian cricket books, *Wisdens*, autographs and memorabilia bought and sold. Many thanks for your continued support.

WILLOWS PUBLISHING, 17 The Willows, Stone, Staffordshire ST15 0DE. Tel: 01785 814700; email: jenkins.willows@ntlworld.com; website: www.willowsreprints.com. *Wisden* reprints 1864–1946.

WISDEN DIRECT, website: www.wisden.com. Various editions of *Wisden Cricketers' Almanack* since 2001 and other Wisden publications, all at discounted prices.

WISDENS.ORG, Tel: 07793 060706; email: wisdens@cridler.com; website: www.wisdens.org; Twitter: @Wisdens. The unofficial *Wisden* collectors' website. Valuations, guide, discussion forum, all free to use. *Wisden* prices updated constantly. We also buy and sell *Wisdens* for our members. Email us for free advice about absolutely anything to do with collecting *Wisdens*.

WISDENWORLD.COM, Tel: 01480 819272; email: bill.wisden@btinternet.com; website: www.wisdenworld.com. A unique and friendly service; quality *Wisdens* bought and sold at fair prices, along with free advice on the value of your collection. The UK's largest *Wisden*-only seller; licensed by Wisden.

AUCTIONEERS

CHRISTIE'S, 8 King Street, St. James's, London SW1Y 6QT. Tel: 0207 389 2674; email: rneelands@christies.com; website: www.christies.com. Christie's were MCC's auctioneer of choice in 1987 and again in 2010. Rare and valuable cricket books are the firm's speciality. For valuations of complete collections or single items, contact Rupert Neelands, a senior book specialist.

DOMINIC WINTER, Specialist Auctioneers & Valuers, Mallard House, Broadway Lane, South Cerney, Gloucestershire GL7 5UQ. Tel: 01285 860006; website: www.dominicwinter.co.uk. Check our website for forthcoming specialist sales.

GRAHAM BUDD AUCTIONS in association with Sotheby's, PO Box 47519, London N14 6XD. Tel: 020 8366 2525; website: www.grahambuddauctions.co.uk. Specialist auctioneer of sporting memorabilia.

KNIGHTS WISDEN, Norfolk. Tel: 01263 768488; email: tim@knights.co.uk; website: www.knightswisden.co.uk. Established and respected auctioneers. World-record *Wisden* prices achieved in 2007. Four major cricket/sporting memorabilia auctions per year including specialist *Wisden* sale in May. Entries invited.

WISDENAUCTION.COM. Tel: 07793 060706; email: wisdenauction@cridler.com; website: www.wisdenauction.com. A specially designed auction website for buying and selling *Wisdens*. List your spares today and bid live for that missing year. No sale, no fee. Many books ending daily. Built by collectors for collectors, with the best descriptions on the internet. See advert on page 168.

CRICKET DATABASES

CSW DATABASE FOR PCs. Contact Ric Finlay, email: ricf@netspace.net.au; website: www.tastats.com.au. Men's and women's international, IPL, Australian, NZ and English domestic. Full scorecards and over 2,000 records. Suitable for professionals and hobbyists alike.

WISDEN RECORDS: www.wisdenrecords.com. Up-to-date and in-depth cricket records from *Wisden*.

CRICKET COLLECTING, MEMORABILIA AND MUSEUMS

CRICKET MEMORABILIA SOCIETY. Honorary Secretary: Steve Cashmore, 4 Stoke Park Court, Stoke Road, Bishops Cleeve, Cheltenham, Gloucestershire GL52 8US. Email: cms87@btinternet.com; website: www.cricketmemorabilia.org. To promote and support the collection and appreciation of all cricket memorabilia. Four meetings annually at first-class grounds with two auctions. Meetings attended by former Test players. Regular members' magazine. Research and valuations undertaken.

LORD'S MUSEUM & TOURS, Lord's Cricket Ground, St John's Wood, London NW8 8QN. Tel: 020 7616 8595; email: tours@mcc.org.uk; website: www.lords.org/tours. A tour of Lord's provides a fascinating behind-the-scenes insight into the world's most famous cricket ground. See the original Ashes urn, plus an outstanding collection of art, cricketing memorabilia and much more.

SIR DONALD BRADMAN'S CHILDHOOD HOME, 52 Shepherd Street, Bowral, NSW 2576, Australia. Tel: (+61) 478 779 642; email: andrewleeming@mac.com; website: www.52shepherdstreet.com.au. The house where Don Bradman developed his phenomenal cricketing skills by throwing a golf ball against the base of a tank stand. Open for visits, accommodation, and special events.

SPORTS MEMORABILIA AUSTRALIA, PO Box 585, Lane Cove, NSW 2066, Australia. Tel: (+61) 2 9420 0558; email: michael@sportsmem.com.au; website: www.sportsmem.com.au. SMA auctioneer and valuer in Australia and NZ since 1993. Official valuer to National Sports, SCG & Bradman Museums. For valuations or consignment contact Michael Fahey, an approved Australian Governments Cultural Gifts programme valuer.

WILLOW STAMPS, 10 Mentmore Close, Harrow, Middlesex HA3 0EA. Tel: 020 8907 4200; email: willowstamps@tinyonline.co.uk. Standing order service for new cricket stamp issues, comprehensive back stocks of most earlier issues.

WISDEN COLLECTORS' CLUB: Tel: 01480 819272; email: bill.wisden@btinternet.com; website: www.wisdencollectorsclub.co.uk. Free and completely impartial advice on *Wisdens*. We also offer *Wisdens* and other cricket books to our members, usually at no charge except postage. Quarterly newsletter, discounts on publications and a great website. Licensed by Wisden.

CRICKET EQUIPMENT

ALL ROUNDER CRICKET, 39 St Michaels Lane, Headingley, Leeds LS6 3BR. Tel: 0113 203 3679; email: info@allroundercricket.com; website: www.allroundercricket.com. One of the UK's leading cricket retailers, stocking all the top brands, hand-picked by ex-professionals. Open every day, including our new megastore at the Penistone Road Trading Estate in Hillsborough, Sheffield. Also online with next day delivery available.

BOLA MANUFACTURING LTD, 6 Brookfield Road, Cotham, Bristol BS6 5PQ. Tel: 0117 924 3569; email: info@bola.co.uk; website: www.bola.co.uk. Manufacturer of bowling machines and ball-throwing machines for all sports. Machines for professional and all recreational levels for sale to the UK and overseas.

CHASE CRICKET, Dummer Down Farm, Basingstoke, Hampshire RG25 2AR. Tel: 01256 397499; email: info@chasecricket.co.uk; website: www.chasecricket.co.uk. Chase Cricket specialises in handmade bats and hi-tech soft goods. Established 1996. "Support British Manufacturing."

DUKE SPORTSWEAR, Unit 4, Magdalene Road, Torquay, Devon TQ1 4AF. Tel: 01803 292012; email: dukeknitwear@btconnect.com. Test-standard sweaters to order in your club colours, using the finest yarns.

FORDHAM SPORTS, 81/85 Robin Hood Way, Kingston Vale, London SW15 3PW. Tel: 020 8974 5654; email: fordham@fordhamsports.co.uk; website: fordhamsports.co.uk. Cricket, hockey and rugby equipment specialist with largest range of branded stock in London at discounted prices. Mail order available.

CRICKET SPEAKERS

LOOK WHO'S TALKING (Ian Holroyd), PO Box 3257, Ufton, Leamington Spa CV33 9YZ. Tel: 01926 614443; mobile: 07831 602131; email: ian@look-whos-talking.co.uk; website: www.look-whos-talking.co.uk. A company specialising in providing first-class public speakers for cricket and other sporting events. Contact us to discuss the event and type of speaker. All budgets catered for.

CRICKET TOUR OPERATORS

SMILE GROUP TRAVEL LTD, Gateway House, Stonehouse Lane, Purfleet, Essex RM19 1NS. Tel: 01708 893250; email: info@smilegrouptravel.com; website: www.smilegrouptravel.com. Smile are experts in tours for both participation and supporters. We work with many professional clubs, including Hampshire and Warwickshire, etc. Our tours are defined by their excellence and value for money.

WISDEN CRICKET TOURS by Pope&Sons Ltd, 48 Campriano Drive, Warwick CV34 4NZ. Tel: 01926 658797; email: cricket@wisdentours.com; website: www.wisdentours.com. Pope&Sons are delighted to be working in partnership with Wisden to provide exclusive Wisden Cricket Tours around the world and in the UK. We create unique, quality travel experiences with unparalleled levels of personal customer service.

PITCHES AND GROUND EQUIPMENT

CRICKET CARPETS DIRECT, Standards House, Meridian East, Meridian Business Park, Leicester LE19 1WZ. Tel: 08702 400 700; email: sales@cricketcarpetsdirect.co.uk; website: www.cricketcarpetsdirect.co.uk. Installation and refurbishment of artificial cricket pitches. Save money. Top-quality carpets supplied and installed direct from the manufacturer. Over 20 years' experience. Nationwide service.

HUCK NETS (UK) LTD, Gore Cross Business Park, Corbin Way, Bradpole, Bridport, Dorset DT6 3UX. Tel: 01308 425100; email: sales@huckcricket.co.uk; website: www.huckcricket.co.uk. Alongside manufacturing our unique knotless high-quality polypropylene cricket netting, we offer the complete portfolio of ground and club equipment necessary for cricket clubs of all levels.

NOTTS SPORT, Innovation House, Magna Park, Lutterworth LE17 4XH. Tel: 01455 883730; email: info@nottssport.com; website: www.nottssport.com. Celebrating over 30 years as a leading supplier of ECB-approved, non-turf cricket pitch systems for coaching, practice and matchplay. Also awarded the ECB NTP Code of Practice Accreditation in 2013.

PLUVIUS, King Henry VIII Farm, Myton Road, Warwick CV34 6SB. Tel: 01926 311324; email: pluviusltd@aol.com; website: www.pluvius.uk.com. Manufacturers of value-for-money pitch covers and sightscreens, currently used on Test, county, school and club grounds throughout the UK.

TILDENET LTD, Hartcliffe Way, Bristol BS3 5RJ. Tel: 0117 966 9684; email: enquiries@tildenet.co.uk; website: www.tildenet.co.uk. Extensive range of equipment – grass germination sheets, mobile practice nets, fixed nets and frames, portable practice nets, netting and fabric, layflat and mobile rain covers, ball-stop fencing, boundary ropes, and sightscreens.

TOTAL-PLAY LTD, Quinton Green Park, Quinton Green, Northampton NN7 2EG. Tel: 01604 864575; email: info@total-play.co.uk; website: www.total-play.co.uk. Natural & non-turf cricket pitch experts. Design & installation of ECB approved non-turf cricket systems and home to www.thecricketgroundshop.co.uk; outlet for the Climate Cover™ range.

TOTAL TURF SOLUTIONS LTD, Quinton Green Park, Quinton Green, Northampton NN7 2EG. Tel: 01604 862925; email: info@totalturfsolutions.co.uk; website: www.totalturfsolutions.co.uk. Total Turf Solutions is a Sport England consultancy services for natural grass pitches framework provider and is recognised by the ECB; offering consultancy and project management for natural and non-turf pitch projects.

CHRONICLE OF 2015

JANUARY

8 ECB extend TV deal for home internationals with Sky Sports until 2019. **10** India draw Fourth Test at Sydney, but Australia win series 2–0. **16** Kumar Sangakkara signs two-year deal with Surrey. Chris Cairns pleads not guilty to charges of perjury and perverting the course of justice, at Old Bailey; trial set for October. **18 A. B. de Villiers hits 149 in 44 balls in ODI against West Indies at Johannesburg, reaching 100 in just 31, a record. 29** Mohammad Amir cleared to return in Pakistan domestic cricket, after five-year ban for spot-fixing.

FEBRUARY

14 World Cup starts: New Zealand beat Sri Lanka, and Australia beat England. 16 Yuvraj Singh fetches a record \$US2.67m from Delhi Daredevils at IPL auction. Ireland chase down 304 to beat West Indies at Nelson. **20** Tim Southee takes seven for 33 as New Zealand demolish England at Wellington. **24** Chris Gayle hammers 215, the first World Cup double-century, against Zimbabwe at Canberra. **24** Yorkshire's Colin Graves elected chairman of the ECB; Giles Clarke to become their first president. **27** De Villiers hits 162 from 66 balls as South Africa overwhelm West Indies at Sydney.

MARCH

2 Jagmohan Dalmiya re-elected as BCCI president after 11 years. **9** England eliminated from World Cup, after losing to Bangladesh at Adelaide. **11** Sangakkara scores fourth successive century for Sri Lanka. Zimbabwe's Brendan Taylor, 29, announces international retirement; joins Nottinghamshire as Kolpak player. **16** David Saker quits role with England's fast bowlers to coach Melbourne Renegades Twenty20 team; Ottis Gibson later replaces him. **20** Ireland's coach Phil Simmons resigns, to take up similar role with West Indies. **21** New Zealand's Martin Guptill scores 237 not out against West Indies in World Cup quarter-final at Wellington. **24** Kevin Pietersen released from IPL deal, and rejoins Surrey in bid to win back England place. **29 Australia win World Cup for the fifth time, beating New Zealand in final at Melbourne. 30** Azhar Ali appointed Pakistan's one-day captain, after Misbah-ul-Haq's retirement from the format. **31** New Zealand's Daniel Vettori retires.

APRIL

1 Bangladesh's Mustafa Kamal resigns as ICC president, after being sidelined from World Cup presentation party. **8** Paul Downton sacked as managing director of England cricket after 15 months, following poor World Cup showing. **10 Richie Benaud dies, aged 85. 22** Bangladesh complete 3–0 whitewash of Pakistan in ODIs; they later win a Twenty20 international too, but lose Test series 1–0. **25** England win Second Test against West Indies in Grenada. **28** Essex's Daniel Lawrence becomes third-youngest Championship centurion at 17, against Surrey at The Oval. **29** John Bracewell appointed coach of Ireland.

MAY

3 West Indies square series with three-day victory over England in Barbados. **9 Andrew Strauss appointed England's new director of cricket; his first task is to sack coach Peter Moores. 11** Pietersen hits triple-century for Surrey v Leicestershire – but the same evening learns from Strauss he will not be considered for England selection because of "a lack of trust". **22** Zimbabwe are the first Full Member to tour Pakistan since the terrorist attack on the Sri Lankan team in March 2009; Pakistan win 50-over series in Lahore 2–0. **25** England win First Test against New Zealand at Lord's. **26** Australian Trevor Bayliss appointed as England's new coach. **30** Alastair Cook becomes England's leading Test run-scorer, passing Graham Gooch (8,900) on second day at Headingley. Shivnarine Chanderpaul dropped by West Indies after 164 Tests.

JUNE

2 New Zealand square Test series with 199-run victory at Headingley. **3** Leicestershire beat Essex at Chelmsford, their first Championship victory since September 2012. **4** Adam Voges, 35, scores century on Test debut against West Indies in Dominica; Australia win by nine wickets. **5** Former England wicketkeeper Craig Kieswetter forced to retire by eye injury. **9 England make 408 for nine, their record ODI total, against New Zealand at Birmingham. 11** Another England keeper, Matt Prior, forced to retire by leg injury. **12** New Zealand level one-day series after scoring 398 (the highest *against* England) at The Oval. **14** Australia win Second Test in Jamaica by 277 runs, to take series 2–0. Sussex's T20 Blast match at Arundel abandoned after Surrey fielders Rory Burns and Moises Henriques are taken to hospital following on-field collision. **17** England make 350 for three, their record ODI chase, to win at Nottingham. **20** England prevail at Chester-le-Street to win one-day series against New Zealand 3–2. **21** Pakistan win First Test against Sri Lanka at Galle. Bangladesh win home ODI series against India. **25** Former Pakistan batsman Zaheer Abbas named president of ICC. **29** Sri Lanka win Second Test in Colombo, to square series with Pakistan. **30** Peter Moores joins Nottinghamshire as consultant.

JULY

3 Brendon McCullum hits 158 not out for Warwickshire v Derbyshire in T20 Blast. **4** Chronic knee injury forces Australia's Ryan Harris to retire ahead of Ashes. **10** South African fast bowler Kagiso Rabada takes a hat-trick against Bangladesh in figures of six for 16, the best by an ODI debutant. **11** England win First Ashes Test at Cardiff by 169 runs. **14 Indian judicial inquiry into spot-fixing suspends IPL teams Chennai Super Kings and Rajasthan Royals for two years, and bans two officials for life. 15** Champions League T20 competition discontinued owing to lack of interest. **19** Australia level Ashes with 405-run win at Lord's, with Steve Smith making 215. **20** Alviro Petersen and Ashwell Prince complete Lancashire-record stand of 501 against Glamorgan at Colwyn Bay. **26** Scotland, Netherlands, Ireland, Hong Kong, Afghanistan and Oman all qualify for 2016 World Twenty20 in India. **28** Former South African captain Clive Rice dies, aged 66. **31** England take 2–1 Ashes lead after winning Third Test at Birmingham inside three days.

AUGUST

2 Glamorgan's Royal London One-Day Cup game against Hampshire is abandoned because of dangerous pitch at Cardiff. **3** Bangladesh and South Africa share Test series after second rain-affected draw. **6** Stuart Broad takes eight for 15 as Australia are bowled out for 60 on first morning of Fourth Test at Nottingham. **8 England complete innings victory in 10.2 overs on third day, and regain Ashes; Michael Clarke says he will retire after the series. 14** Australia's women win one-off Test against England at Canterbury. **15** Rangana Herath takes seven for 49 as India, set 176 to win First Test at Galle, are skittled for 112. **22** Arthur Morris, one of Australia's 1948 Invincibles, dies aged 93. **23** Australia win Fifth Test at The Oval by an innings, but lose Ashes 3–2. **24** India win in Colombo, Sangakkara's 134th and final Test. **28** Australia clinch women's Ashes with victory in second Twenty20 international at Hove. **29** Lancashire win their first domestic T20 title, beating Northamptonshire in the Birmingham final.

SEPTEMBER

1 India, for whom Cheteshwar Pujara carries his bat for 145, win Third Test in Colombo to take series 2–1. **4** Jason Holder replaces Denesh Ramdin as West Indies Test captain for tour of Sri Lanka. **5** Ben Stokes out obstructing the field in ODI against Australia against Lord's. **6** Shane Watson announces Test retirement; Brad Haddin follows suit three day later. **9 Yorkshire retain County Championship. 13** Australia win final ODI at Manchester and take series 3–2. **13** Former England captain Brian Close dies aged 84. **20** Jagmohan Dalmiya dies at 73. **25** Surrey clinch Championship second division title. **27** Former England fast bowler Frank Tyson, star of the 1954-55 Ashes, dies aged 85.

OCTOBER

1 Australia postpone two-Test tour of Bangladesh over security worries. **5** Chris Cairns trial begins in London. **13** Younis Khan becomes Pakistan's leading run-scorer during First Test against England in Abu Dhabi. **15** Indian fast bowler Zaheer Khan announces retirement. **16 Alastair Cook scores 263 in 836 minutes – the third-longest Test innings – in First Test. 17** Bad light thwarts England's last-gasp bid for victory in Abu Dhabi. Sri Lanka beat West Indies by an innings in First Test at Galle. **24** Afghanistan win final ODI in Zimbabwe to take series 3–2; they later win both Twenty20 games. **26** Pakistan clinch victory in Second Test against England in Dubai with 6.3 overs remaining. Sri Lanka win Second Test, in Colombo, to beat West Indies 2–0. **31** Victoria opener Travis Dean becomes the first to score two unbeaten centuries on first-class debut, against Queensland at Melbourne.

NOVEMBER

3 Former England batsman Tom Graveney dies, aged 88. **5** Pakistan win Third Test in Sharjah to complete 2–0 series win over England. Caribbean government committee suggests immediate replacement of "antiquated and obsolete" West Indian board by new authority. **7** India win First Test against South Africa inside three days on turning track at Mohali. **9** Australia beat New Zealand in First Test at Brisbane, with David Warner scoring twin centuries. New BCCI president Shashank Manohar replaces N. Srinivasan as ICC chairman. **11** Sussex head coach Mark Robinson to take charge of England women's team. **14** De Villiers wins his 100th Test cap, at Bangalore; rain prevents any play after the first day. **16** Ross Taylor scores 290, the highest by a visiting batsman in Australia, in Second Test at Perth. **17** Australian fast bowler Mitchell Johnson announces immediate retirement from international cricket, during drawn Perth Test. **20** Jos Buttler hits a 46-ball century, England's fastest in one-day internationals, to clinch 50-over series against Pakistan 3–1. **25** ECB announce plan to offer visiting teams in Championship matches the chance to bowl first. **27 First day/night Test, using a pink ball, starts in Adelaide; Australia beat New Zealand to take series 2–0.** India beat South Africa inside three days – and clinch series – on controversial pitch at Nagpur which is later censured by ICC. **29** West Indian spinner Sunil Narine – the top-ranked bowler in one-day and Twenty20 internationals – is banned from bowling. **30** Cairns found not guilty at Southwark Crown Court. England complete 3–0 Twenty20 victory over Pakistan, following their first super over.

DECEMBER

7 India beat South Africa 3–0 with victory in Fourth Test at Delhi. Sri Lanka wicketkeeper Kusal Perera sent home from New Zealand tour after failing drug test. **8** Pune and Rajkot named as new IPL franchise locations. **12** Australia crush West Indies by an innings and 212 runs in First Test at Hobart. **14** New Zealand win First Test against Sri Lanka at Dunedin. **21 Brendon McCullum announces imminent retirement from international cricket. 27** Pakistan leg-spinner Yasir Shah suspended after testing positive for banned substance. **28** New Zealand reach target of 118 in 8.2 overs to beat Sri Lanka in one-day international at Christchurch. **29** Australia beat West Indies at Melbourne to clinch series 2–0. Pakistan board refuse to accept Azhar Ali's resignation as one-day captain after Mohammad Amir was included in a training camp; both were later named to tour New Zealand. **30** England win First Test at Durban by 241 runs.

The following items were also reported during 2015:

MAIL ON SUNDAY   January 3
Government officials have blocked an attempt by home secretary Theresa May to award Geoff Boycott a knighthood. The Cabinet Office cited Boycott's 1996 conviction in France for assaulting his then lover. The campaign was led by Conservative backbench MPs, but Mrs May lent her name to it. She couldn't get past the civil servants, though. One of the MPs, Nigel Adams, said: "It sounds as if some jobsworth numpty who doesn't understand Geoffrey's contribution to sport has let his pen get carried away."

THE TIMES   January 7/8
MCC's ticket service now offers 52 possible titles for people to use when applying in the public ballot. These range alphabetically from Baron to Wing Commander, and also include Begum, Brother, Count, Don, Monsieur, Sheikh and, most improbably, Queen. However, the Royal Opera House boast 129 options, including Viscondessa. MCC later reverted to six, excluding even Sir.

THE GUARDIAN   January 9
The former Pakistan captain Imran Khan married Reham Khan, a one-time BBC weather presenter and divorced mother of three, in a low-key ceremony at his home near Islamabad. It was boycotted by some disapproving relatives. Reham Khan was also abused on social media, where pictures circulated of her on TV wearing a skirt and other clothes considered unacceptable by conservative Muslims. Imran was previously married to the socialite Jemima Goldsmith. (See also October 30.)

AGENCE FRANCE-PRESSE   January 13
A lethal batch of home-made liquor sold at a cricket match has killed at least
31 people near Lucknow, with more than 100 others ill in hospital, according
to police and medical officials. A suspect has been arrested. Such incidents are
not uncommon in India: in 2011, 170 people died in West Bengal from
drinking moonshine.

CYCLING WEEKLY   January 21
Former Australian Test player Bronwyn Calver, 45, needed eight stitches after
being knocked off her bike in Canberra by a kangaroo. Her assailant came off
worse, however. Having hopped off down the road, it was knocked down by a
motorist and killed. Calver played three women's Tests and 45 one-day
internationals.

AGENCE FRANCE-PRESSE   January 27
Pakistani all-rounder Haris Sohail was awoken in the night at his hotel in New
Zealand, convinced of a ghost in the room. Team manager Naveed Akram
Cheema said Sohail had called a member of the coaching staff, who arrived to
find him "visibly shaken". He spent the rest of the night in the coach's room
before being given a new one. Cheema thought fever was responsible, but
added: "The player still believes his bed was shaken by something, and it was
a supernatural something."

SUNDAY HERALD SUN, MELBOURNE   February 8
Bowling seam-up, Jackson Warne, 14, took four wickets in five balls, including
a hat-trick, for the Year 10 team at Brighton Grammar School. His better-
known father, Shane, was watching: "Jackson did it!!!!" he tweeted. Jackson
had previously preferred football to cricket.

IS THERE INTELLIGENT LIFE OUT THERE — AND IF SO, COULD IT EXPLAIN THE DUCKWORTH/LEWIS METHOD?

DAILY EXPRESS
February 13

Scientists trying to discover if there is intelligent life in space are planning to use the Laws of Cricket to test the aliens' ability to grasp difficult concepts. Members of the California-based SETI Institute (Search for Extra-Terrestrial Intelligence) want to use "Active Seti" – beaming material from the internet into the cosmos in the hope of a response – instead of just listening. SETI's senior astronomer Seth Shostak said: "If they look up cricket, there are descriptions, pictures, diagrams showing a pitch, and footage. They'll cross-correlate all this and put it together, and if they are clever at all, they will figure out something about cricket. Do they want to hear what the structure of the hydrogen atom is? No, they know that."

THE GUARDIAN
February 17

In his role as general manager of the new One Pro cycling team, former Test wicketkeeper Matt Prior said he wanted his cyclists to emulate the England cricket team from around 2010, and not the "closed-off" group they became as they lost the 2013-14 Ashes. "I saw the negative effect that had on our fan base, and the public perception towards us," said Prior. "I want the riders to go out and show off their character and personalities. I don't want to see media-trained robots."

AGENCE FRANCE-PRESSE
February 23

Swiss tennis star Roger Federer had to apologise for causing outrage in Pakistan after being pictured admiring an Indian shirt on the eve of the India–Pakistan World Cup showdown in Adelaide. "It was more of a Nike thing, to be quite honest," he said later. "The idea wasn't to spark any fire, and I'm sorry if it did that."

BELFAST TELEGRAPH
February 23

Martin McGuinness, the Republican leader who is now Northern Ireland's Deputy First Minister, dressed up as W. G. Grace in a fund-raising stunt for a children's hospice. McGuinness, an ardent cricket fan, said: "I always admired the ability of a man to stand at a crease and take on all comers."

BBC
March 5

Prisoners on remand in the Indian city of Guwahati have successfully petitioned a judge for the right to watch World Cup cricket. Justice Arup Kumar Goswami agreed that watching TV counted as a constitutional right, and added: "Prisoners need recreation for a healthy mind." They were already allowed to watch India matches, shown on the state channel Doordarshan, but not the other games, which were on cable.

THE GUARDIAN
March 5/July 31

Several English cricketers, including members of the 2005 Ashes-winning team, are facing "very substantial" tax bills through their involvement in film investment. Revenue inspectors have sent demands to investors in partnerships set up by the company Ingenious Media, claiming these constituted tax-avoidance schemes. An attempt by the investors to get the demands quashed on human rights grounds was rejected in July. A senior official from HM Revenue and Customs described arrangements such as these as "schemes for scumbags". However, David Gower, one of those involved, said: "As a sportsman you earn the most money you will ever earn in your life by the age of 32, so planning is about trying to provide the best you can for the future."

DAILY TELEGRAPH   March 14

Club cricketer Nadeem Alam, who reached the peak of his career playing for Huddersfield, posed as the former Pakistan Test player Nadeem Abbasi to give "expert" opinion on a succession of BBC radio programmes. The BBC announced an investigation. Alam said he had now given up his career as an Abbasi impersonator, but added: "I like to think I have been talking good cricket." The real Abbasi said: "If I ever find Nadeem Alam, I will punch him in the face for damaging the country's reputation."

BBC   March 15

Andrew Flintoff ate rat's tails and was covered in elephant dung to win the Australian TV version of *I'm A Celebrity… Get Me Out of Here!* It was set in the South African bush.

DAILY MIRROR, COLOMBO   March 22

Seven students were injured in a clash between supporters after the match between rival colleges, D. S. Senanayake and Mahanama, at the SSC Stadium in Colombo.

TIMES OF INDIA   March 28

A policeman in Lucknow has sent 1,000 rupees (about £10) to Indian captain M. S. Dhoni to thank him for leading the team to defeat in the World Cup semi-final. Amitabh Thakur, an inspector-general of civil defence, was grateful that Indians would not waste yet more working time watching the tournament. In an accompanying letter he told Dhoni: "It is your societal duty to not allow people to suspend government, financial and personal work in order to watch cricket matches."

DAILY MIRROR   April 3
Yorkshire president Dickie Bird, 81, has paid £135,000 for a new players' balcony at Headingley.

SOUTH WALES EVENING POST   April 18
Two long-established Swansea cricket leagues have collapsed inside a month. Following the demise of the Swansea Central League (founded 1933), the midweek Swansea Industrial Welfare League (founded 1946) has also been forced to give up. Both once had four divisions, but were left with three teams each. The Welfare League secretary, Dave Williams said: "It's a sign of the times. The backbones of teams are getting older by the season, and no youngsters are coming through. We are all devastated."

BBC   April 28
Kevin Pietersen had to be picked up by his wife after getting lost on a train following Surrey's Championship fixture with Essex. After leaving The Oval he boarded a train at Waterloo and excitedly tweeted: "Ferrari can't fly, so this is the quickest way to get home and beat London traffic". But the tweets grew increasingly desperate, and he eventually found himself in Wraysbury, eight miles from his home in Wentworth. "Never heard of the joint before – now I do!" he insisted on telling his almost three million followers.

TIMES OF INDIA   April 28

Police in the Indian city of Surat have banned street cricket in an attempt to prevent inter-communal clashes.

THE TIMES   May 6

Natalie Bennett, the former journalist who leads the British Green Party, received an email two days before the general election asking about her availability for *The Times* cricket team's fixture the following Saturday. Bennett kept wicket for the team when she worked for the paper. Despite the timing, she replied within 20 minutes, giving apologies "due to the possibility of being in a non-smoke-filled room", thrashing out a coalition deal. (In the event the Conservatives won an overall majority, and the Greens just one seat, so she could have played.)

DAILY POST, WALES   May 7

Gareth Davies, 19, took all ten Buckley wickets bowling for Mold in a Second XI match in the North Wales League. His figures were 12–7–11–10. He claimed the final wicket with an lbw decision from a clubmate-umpire off the final ball of his allotted 12. "It was dead in line," Davies insisted. "I had gone up for five or six lbws and, to be fair to him, he didn't just give them."

THE TIMES   May 11

Scientists from the Australian National University in Canberra are studying what makes English willow the best bat-making material, in the hope of developing a cheaper alternative. Mohammad Saadatfar, from the university's research school of physics and engineering, said the best bats were made from the female of one particular species of English willow. "It's too expensive, and it's just one small part of the world that is producing it," he said. "You want to diversify: the price is going up every year because it's just so limited, and there's no reason why every kid in the world should not play with a top-quality cricket bat."

THE TIMES   May 20

Bryn Darbyshire, playing for Lymington Second XI against South Wiltshire, was given out handled the ball after he threw it back to the bowler; no-ball had been called and he had hit it only a few inches. The dismissal led to a Lymington collapse and a 58-run defeat. Darbyshire admitted the umpire was probably right, but accused the opposition of bad sportsmanship for appealing: "I had hit the same bowler for six off my second ball and was taking him apart. They probably wanted to see the back of me."

PORTSMOUTH NEWS   May 22

Australian cricketer Andrew Webb was detained for 30 hours at Heathrow, then deported after he arrived to play his third season for Portchester in the Hampshire League. "Unfortunately he lacked the required paperwork," said club captain Paul Hungerford.

TIMES OF INDIA   May 24
Ten-year-old left-arm spinner Musheer Khan, who had just been overlooked
for the selection trial for Mumbai's Under-14 team, replied by taking nine for
nine for Dadar Union Matunga against Virar Centre. His 17-year-old brother
Sarfaraz had been playing in the IPL.

TIMES OF INDIA   May 27
The organisers of a corporate cricket tournament held on the Air India grounds
near Mumbai Airport were arrested for releasing party balloons to mark the
start of the semi-finals. "By releasing balloons that entered the airport's
airspace, they obstructed the take-off and landing of flights, and endangered
passengers' lives," said an airport police inspector.

THE STOKE SENTINEL   May 28
The Pakistani all-rounder Iftikhar Anjum, who played a Test and 62 one-day
internationals, found life in Stoke-on-Trent a comedown after he signed to
play for Porthill Park CC. When he applied for a wheelie bin, he was told to
pile up his rubbish in his back garden – because there was a 12-week wait.
"Having a bin is a basic right," he said. "Unbelievably, the waste-disposal
service in Stoke-on-Trent is worse than in Pakistan. Over there you ask them
for a bin and they give you two because they want you to do your bit and keep
the place tidy."

THE TIMES   June 5
One of Scotland's leading independent schools, Morrison's Academy in Crieff,
has decided to stop playing cricket. Their director of sport, Scott Weston, cited
the exam timetable, a short summer term, the technical demands of cricket,
and the Scottish climate. Pupils will instead be offered individual activities,
such as canoeing, climbing and mountain biking.

MID-DAY, MUMBAI   June 6
A teenage boy died in Madurai after reportedly being attacked with a bat by an
opponent. They had quarrelled over which team should bat first.

INDIAN EXPRESS   June 8
Anil Pandey, 30, described as a gangster, was killed by a mob who allegedly
burst into his Mumbai house armed with swords, knives and stumps. This was
apparently a revenge attack following an incident in nearby woods the previous
day when Pandey was walking his pet Doberman, Kiwi, near a cricket match.
Inspector Siddheshwar Gove said: "When their cricket ball strayed near Kiwi
she grabbed it in her mouth and damaged it, and also bit the hand of one man
who tried to pull it out of her mouth."

SYDNEY MORNING HERALD   June 8
ESPNcricinfo correspondent Daniel Brettig, covering Australia's tour of the
Caribbean, was mugged at knifepoint in the Dominican capital, Roseau, after
withdrawing money from a cash machine. He was beaten up and had his wallet
and phones stolen. Dominica is considered one of the safer countries in the
West Indies.

BBC   June 9

Former England all-rounder Chris Lewis, 47, has been released from prison after serving just under half a 13-year sentence for drug smuggling. He said worries about money had led to his attempt to import £140,000 worth of dissolved cocaine into the UK. "I became afraid of what the future held, and at that point the thinking went awry," he said in an interview with the Professional Cricketers' Association. "I made choices. They were the wrong choices, and I say sorry for them."

SYDNEY MORNING HERALD   June 15

Brendon Julian, the former Australian Test player who was leading the Ten Sports coverage of Australia's tour of the West Indies, ended the Test series by announcing the presentation of the Sir Wank Forrell Trophy.

CRICLIFE.COM   June 18

The game between Bohemian CC and Prague CC Second XI in the Czech Pro40 League included 13 ducks in the two innings: four in the Bohemians' 126; nine in Prague's 54. One Bohemian batsman, Amit Shinde, was given out hit the ball twice, but he had scored five.

DAILY MAIL   June 19

Kevin Pietersen apologised on Twitter after making a joke about the fate of two suspected stowaways from Johannesburg who fell from a plane as it approached Heathrow. He sent a link to the story with the comment "Captain and opening bowler in England's WC cricket team in 2019 right there…" One of the two was killed, and the other critically injured. "Oh no…" began his next tweet.

THE NEWS, PAKISTAN   June 26

Hockey experts complained that the Indian TV channel showing the World Hockey League fixture in Antwerp between India and Pakistan were using cricketers rather than hockey stars as commentators.

DAILY TELEGRAPH   June 26

A village cricket match in Wiltshire was abandoned after a fight broke out on the pitch. Andrew Footner, the 51-year-old secretary of Beanacre & Melksham CC, was knocked out. It happened in the match against Swindon Civil Service and was described by an onlooker as "a general handbags situation and a disagreement that got out of hand". Footner tweeted a picture of his facial injuries, saying: "First time I have ever seen a person punched on a cricket pitch in 40 years playing and it had to be me."

RACING POST   June 28

Jack Hobbs, trained by John Gosden, won the Irish Derby by five lengths, having finished runner-up in the Epsom Derby. Racing historian John Randall said the colt joined a list of successful horses named after cricketers. These included: Don Bradman, who won two races over the Grand National fences

in 1936 (though not the National itself); Intikhab, officially rated the best horse in Europe in 1998 after romping home in the Queen Anne Stakes at Royal Ascot; Tendulkar, third in the 2001 Dewhurst Stakes at Newmarket; Flintoff, who was jointly owned by the eponymous Andrew when runner-up in the 2009 Midlands Grand National; Warne, winner of the 2014 Fox Hunters' Chase at Aintree; and Bishan Bedi, a son of Intikhab, who has been winning races at Dundalk for trainer Aidan O'Brien. Randall understandably overlooked the fate of another Irish-bred son of Intikhab, Wisden. He ran once at Wolverhampton in 2015, came eighth out of ten, was gelded and sold to run in Bahrain. "Such a disappointment with all his issues," said a spokeswoman for trainer Sir Michael Stoute.

THE OLDIE   July

Five players from a London-based nomadic club, The Weekenders, crossed the Channel, armed with donated kit and a length of coconut matting, to play a team of Afghan refugees at the migrant encampment in Calais. Fortified by four extra players picked up in the breakfast queue on the ferry, and two more donated by the Afghans, they managed to play an 11-a-side Twenty20 match. "The odd thing was that once the game started it felt like any other weekend friendly," wrote Weekenders secretary Christopher Douglas. "The unusual local conditions, such as the menacing presence of the riot police truck glimpsed through the trees and an earth-shaking sound system rigged up by the Eritreans, seemed no more threatening than an overhanging Buckinghamshire beech bough. We simply became absorbed in the game."

THE SPIN   July 7

The Redruth Fourth XI, playing Grampound Road in the Cornish League Division 6 West, included club president Mark Richards, 47, plus his son, wife and two daughters. There was no case of c Richards b Richards but, said Mark, "We did have a dropped father, bowled daughter, which I've got nothing but stick for ever since."

KENT ONLINE July 10

Paul Belsey, 34, hit six sixes in an over for High Halstow off Blackheath Wanderers bowler Mayank Patel. Belsey made an unbeaten 41 from eight balls, and later dismissed Patel for 17.

THE GUARDIAN July 14

Sachin Tendulkar sparked a Pietersenesque social-media frenzy when he had dinner in an Oxfordshire village after watching Andy Murray at Wimbledon. He posted pictures of himself by a bus stop with the words "In Great Haseley, Oxfordshire. Missed the last bus, can anyone give me a lift?" He was bombarded with messages from adoring fans either offering to help or apologising that they couldn't – mainly because they were in India. One claimed to have arrived to look for him. Tendulkar was indeed in Great Haseley, but had travelled by car. Two days later, he reposted the same pictures, overwritten with the words: "Not the bus. But some seem to have missed the joke." One respondent said: "God-level sarcasm is obviously difficult to understand for humans."

WESTERN MORNING NEWS July 14

A firm of Devon estate agents, Helmores, arranged for a five-metre-high bat to stand sentinel by the boundary at Shobrooke Park CC in Crediton. It was carved from a Scots pine badly damaged in a storm in 2012, and any batsman hitting it will be awarded a bottle of whisky.

GLOUCESTERSHIRE ECHO July 15

Left-hander Aaron Brown hit 356 not out for Cheltenham club St Stephens against Hatherley & Reddings Third XI in the Gloucestershire Third Division. The scoreboard read 12 for three before Brown got going. He hit 24 fours and 36 sixes. The team scored 456 for six in their 40 overs and won by 282 runs.

Henley Standard   July 23/September 20

The wicket at Henley CC in Oxfordshire turned brown after the groundsman, Tony King, used an unsuitable weedkiller. Chairman Brian Kenworthy said it was an innocent mistake caused by picking up the wrong container. Two months later Kenworthy announced King would not be continuing as groundsman. "I think sacked is too strong a term," he said. "We have agreed to go our separate ways."

Peterborough Telegraph   July 25

Peterborough Town fast bowler Joe Dawborn, 21, took ten for 22, the best figures in the history of the Northants Premier Division, against Brixworth.

The Island, Colombo/Wikipedia   July 29

An Indian development firm is planning to construct Sri Lanka's tallest building, the 96-storey '96 Iconic Tower, dedicated to the Sri Lankan team who won the 1996 World Cup. It will be designed as four cricket-bat-shaped structures with a ball balanced between the handles.

Sunday Independent   August 2

Mick Massey, 82, took five for 38 for the Hatherleigh CC midweek team against the Englefield Green touring side. This increased his determination to continue for another season. His captain, David Manning, said: "I'm 68, but I can't even think of packing up when Mick's doing so well."

Lancashire Telegraph   August 3

Clitheroe's Sri Lankan pro Janaka Gunaratne became the first player in the 122-year history of the Ribblesdale League to hit six sixes in an over, and lost four balls in the process. But furious Ribblesdale Wanderers players believed he should have been out for a duck. Ian Britcliffe, who conceded the sixes, said Gunaratne had actually been bowled second ball, but the square-leg umpire believed it had bounced back off the keeper.

The Guardian   August 5

The former Pakistan captain Wasim Akram has said he escaped a gun attack in Karachi. He was on his way to hold a bowling camp at the National Stadium when another driver rammed his car and opened fire before fleeing. Wasim said his assailant looked like an official: "If he can do this to me, what will he do to the common man?" Senior police officer Munir Shaikh said he believed the incident was road rage rather than a premeditated assassination attempt.

Sydney Morning Herald   August 15

Alexander Campbell, the Australian-born First Soloist of the Royal Ballet, has been working for the ECB for the past five years as part of a programme of getting people from different disciplines to talk to aspiring coaches about

PREPARE FOR THE NUTCRACKER

training. Campbell, a cricket fan whose father Alan was a talent-spotter for Cricket New South Wales, said batting and ballet had much in common: "It's all co-ordination and timing."

FREE PRESS JOURNAL, MUMBAI   August 20
Indian captain M. S. Dhoni successfully completed his first parachute jump as a "special" officer of the Indian territorial army's elite para regiment. However, some army officers have expressed disquiet at his involvement. "Army is spending money on Dhoni to train him as parachute," said one. "However, his knowledge and expertise are not going to be of any use to the Army or the nation."

DERBY TELEGRAPH   August 21
The Derby County Ground received one star out of a possible five from food-hygiene inspectors. Derbyshire chief executive Simon Storey said the club had taken various steps to remedy the situation, including the appointment of a new catering manager.

THE GUARDIAN   August 27
Andrew Flintoff's "immensely likeable" one-man show was among the 3,300 productions on the 2015 Edinburgh Festival fringe. "Nothing will douse his natural ebullience," wrote critic Lyn Gardner. "He hits the audience for six in a show that is full of laughter, cricketing anecdotes, self-deprecating good humour and indiscretions."

NOTTINGHAM POST   August 28
Businessman Michael Whitaker left his car unlocked overnight, and found a man sleeping in it next morning. A police officer was called and woke the intruder, who turned out to be Nottinghamshire's Zimbabwean batsman,

Brendan Taylor. "Neither myself, the police, nor Brendan knew what to do," said Whitaker. "I don't think he knew where he was, but he was very apologetic, and it quickly became clear that it was very innocent." A spokesman for Nottinghamshire Police said: "We attended the scene but concluded that no offence had been committed."

AYCLIFFE TODAY   August 29

Swing bowler Jack Slatcher, 20, had figures of 5.3–3–4–10 for Newton Aycliffe Second XI when he bowled out Yarm Second XI for 33 in the North Yorkshire and South Durham League. Slatcher took up the game in 2014.

SHROPSHIRE STAR   September 1

Nick Ball of Prees CC was banned for ten weeks by the Shropshire Cricket League for assaulting an opponent. The opposition, Church Stretton, suffered a ten-point deduction "for making the incident public".

WORCESTER NEWS   September 3

Stourport captain Allan Moss marked his 38th birthday by scoring his maiden Worcestershire League century – and went on to make an unbeaten 302 in a Third XI match against Enville, who failed to take a wicket. Moss put on 459 with opening partner Mark Gleeson before declaring; Stourport won by 306 runs. It was the final match of a season in which Moss had totalled only 167 runs: he had batted at No. 9 the previous week but promoted himself because the regular opener was unavailable.

SOUTHERN DAILY ECHO   September 4

Old Bournemouthians' openers got into a fight with each other after a dispute over a run in a Hampshire League game. Malick Kudmany and Peter Kritzinger received multiple match bans after Kudmany used racist abuse, and Kritzinger hit him in response.

THE HINDU   October 1

The 1,895 residents of a remote village in Andhra Pradesh have had their lives transformed since they were "adopted" by Sachin Tendulkar a year ago under a national scheme whereby MPs and VIPs help a poor village. The Ministry of Rural Development named the village, Puttamrajuvari Kandriga, among the top three villages of the 300 involved as an example of what can be done. The villagers have gained paved roads, footpaths, drainage, power, drinking water, sanitation, a hall, a school and a sports ground.

SHEPTON MALLET JOURNAL   October 15

Roy Thorne, the last surviving founder member of Dinder and Croscombe CC, Somerset, has retired as the club's honorary secretary after 50 years. Thorne, 83, has held almost every other post in the club since it began in 1948. Though he often opened the batting, his highest score was 26. "I'm more gifted in organising things," he said.

WESTERN DAILY PRESS   October 17

Yorkley Star CC, on the edge of the Forest of Dean in Gloucestershire, is to close after more than 130 years because the pitch, at Cut and Fry Green, is being destroyed by wild boar. In 2014, Yorkley were top of their league until the ground was churned up by the boar and their season had to be abandoned. The club paid for the ground to be relaid, but the beasts struck again. Trustee Alec Kear, 80, said: "The forest is overrun with these things. The ground is like a war zone. It's unbelievable. Nothing has stopped play before. We were going all the way through the war, but we just can't cope with this."

NEWS.COM.AU   October 21

Thomas Wrigglesworth, aged ten, took five for nine with his "looping leggies" in a Victorian senior fourth-grade match for Sale against Stratford. It was his second senior appearance, but the first time he had attempted leg-spin in a match. "He was a wicketkeeper last year," said his father Ian, who played for Victoria in the 1990s. "And he's just decided the leggies were worth a try, and pestered everyone enough to the point where he was given a bowl." He refused to be drawn about the chances of his son following him into first-class cricket: "We were more inclined to talk about the duck he made in the morning. We're not going to pump him up."

THE TIMES   October 21

New research has revealed how British intelligence officers helped some of the most daring escapes by wartime POWs. Maps were concealed in gifts sent out to prisoners, such as hollowed-out chess sets, Christmas crackers – and the handles of cricket bats.

THE GUARDIAN   October 30

Imran Khan announced that he and his second wife, Reham, were divorcing after ten months of marriage. He said it was a painful time for them both.

FOX SPORTS   November 2

Devlin Malone, a 17-year-old leg-spinner, took ten for 115 for Sutherland against Sydney University in a second-grade game, giving him 16 for 138 in the match. In 2014-15, he took three wickets in his opening over in first grade.

DECCAN CHRONICLE   November 7

The prison authorities in Pune rejected a request from the BCCI to provide two iron bars to create the Freedom Trophy for Tests between India and South Africa. The trophy honours Mahatma Gandhi and Nelson Mandela, and the bars were to come from the cells where they were held. However, prison official B. K. Upadhyay said: "The cell where Gandhi was kept is declared as 'heritage', and the rods of the heritage cannot be removed."

DAILY MAIL   November 10

Steven Finn, England's 6ft 7in opening bowler, gashed his head on a street sign while trying to walk and text simultaneously.

BBC   November 13

After Sachin Tendulkar complained to British Airways about poor service and what he called a "don't care" attitude from staff, the airline responded by apologising – and asking for his full name and address. This enraged Tendulkar's fan army, who declared social-media war on the airline for not recognising him. Some called for the Indian prime minister to cancel his visit to the UK. Other posts included: "How dare you ask his full name, you swines" and, more subtly, "Try Sachin Ramesh Tendulkar, India. I'm sure this is enough."

THE TIMES   November 16

Street cricket has become the latest battleground for a growing women's rights movement in Pakistan. Women and girls are posting photos of themselves taking part in traditionally male pursuits such as cricket, hanging out at the beach, climbing trees and eating in roadside cafes known as *dhabas*. "Most of us could narrate instances of childhood where we were either told by the boys playing street cricket that we can't play with them or were discouraged or not allowed by parents," said Sadia Khatri, one of the movement's founders. "Cricket on the streets is something girls aren't supposed to do, so it seemed like a natural next step to take."

DAILY TELEGRAPH   November 27

In-demand teachers are being offered extra days off to attend events such as cricket during school hours in a bid to lure them into jobs, according to Ben Thompson, the head of Trinity Academy in south London, an area where it has been difficult to recruit. Maths, English and physics teachers are currently hard to find, particularly in inner cities.

FINANCIAL TIMES   November 28

The Treasury have announced plans to "simplify" the tax situation regarding sports stars' benefits and testimonials. This means cricketers in Britain will lose most of a long-standing tax perk.

HINDUSTAN TIMES   December 7

Three years after he was first nominated to the Rajya Sabha, India's upper house, Sachin Tendulkar asked his first question: about the zoning system used on suburban railways in India's four main cities.

9NEWS   December 7

An angry cabbie stopped play in the match between Macgregor and Griffith University in Brisbane. A six smashed the cab's windscreen, and the driver avenged himself by driving on to the middle of the pitch. Police persuaded him to move after eight overs had been lost.

THE SPIN   December 15

Cricket South Africa had to apologise to users of their Facebook page after it was hacked. Unexpected posts included "Best sex positions couples should try" and "Meet the World's Sexiest Mexican Instagram Model".

ABC NEWS   December 16

One of the purest gold nuggets ever found, the Maitland Bar, has been unwittingly used for years by New South Wales Treasury officials as a wicket. The bar, NSW Premier Mike Baird explained, had been entrusted to the Treasury some years ago: "Someone studiously decided they'd place it in a box. The problem was they forgot to tell anyone, and that box became used for hallway cricket." The bar has a gold content of 8.87kg. "My good friends in Treasury – I love them dearly, but that was not their finest moment," Mr Baird sighed.

BBC   December 22

Angela Reakes, who plays for the ACT Meteors in the Australian Women's League, has been given a two-year suspended ban for placing five bets, totalling nine dollars, on the match award for the men's World Cup final. The chief of Cricket Australia's integrity unit said: "All elite cricketers are reminded regularly that betting on any form of cricket is strictly prohibited."

INDIAN EXPRESS   December 25

The improbable but evidently much-coveted record for the longest individual net session (see previous *Wisdens*) was broken again when Virga Mare of Pune batted for 50 hours, five minutes and 51 seconds, beating the previous best of 48 hours. He faced 14,682 balls.

DNA INDIA   December 31

A Harris Shield match between two Mumbai schools turned to farce after 14-year-old left-arm spinner Daksh Agarwal of Vibgyor High took the first nine wickets against St Joseph's Secondary. With the last pair still 71 short, Agarwal's team-mates devoted themselves to ensuring he got all ten. Their efforts included the wicketkeeper standing with the ball by the stumps as the batsmen ran nine, and intentionally bad bowling from the other end. Finally, Agarwal ended the nonsense by effecting a run-out off his own bowling for a 51-run win. "I am not disappointed," he said. "I have an all-ten. My team won. So what if my tenth wicket is a run-out? I am proud."

We are always grateful for contributions from readers, especially stories from local or non-UK media. Items from club and school websites are also welcome. Please send newspaper cuttings to Matthew Engel at Fair Oak, Bacton, Herefordshire HR2 0AT (always including the paper's name and date) and weblinks to almanack@wisden.com.

INDEX OF UNUSUAL OCCURRENCES

INDEX OF ADVERTISEMENTS

PART TITLES